McGREGOR'S

WHO OWNS WHOM

Mc GREGOR'S

WHO OWNS WHOM

13TH EDITION
1993

by
Robin McGregor

Graham & Trotman
A member of Wolters Kluwer Academic Publishers
LONDON/DORDRECHT/BOSTON

First Published 1980
Thirteenth Edition 1993

Co-Published outside southern Africa by
Graham & Trotman Ltd
66 Wilton Road, London SW1V 1DE, United Kingdom

PO Box 14373, Kenwyn 7790

Assistant Editors
Simon McGregor and Andrew McGregor

Researchers
Anne McGregor, Lindy Ndzeku and Betsie Bezuidenhout

Consultant
Guy McGregor

Database Development
McGregors Online Information (Pty) Ltd
Glenda Whitelaw

PO Box 651302, Benmore 2010
Tel: (011) 884-3301. Fax· (011) 883-8266

Where individuals or directors are shown as 'ultimate controlling shareholder' this could represent direct, indirect, direct partial, indirect partial, beneficial or non-beneficial interests

Whilst every care has been taken in compiling this book, the publishers or author do not give any warranty as to the completeness or accuracy of its contents nor of any supplementary information, explanation or opinion

ISBN 1 85333 908 3

CONTENTS

PART ONE

WHO OWNS WHOM MAIN SECTION

The Investors' Handbook

PART TWO

INDEXES

PART THREE

SCHEDULES

FINANCIAL RATIOS GIVEN IN THIS BOOK

WHAT THEY MEASURE

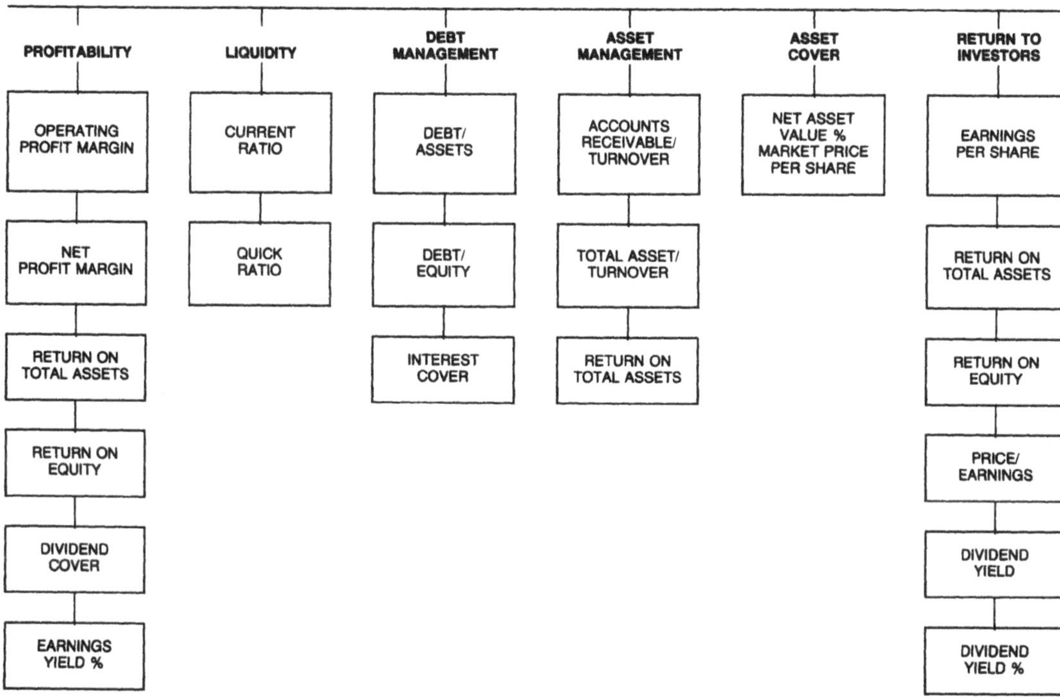

NOTES

Financial information has been extracted from the published Accounts as reported. Apart from the following:

- Tax as shown in the financial statistics is current South African and foreign tax paid for the period under review, excluding deferred tax etc.
- Foreign exchange losses/(gains) have been deducted/(added) to operating profit/(loss).
- Outside shareholders and preference shareholders have been included in long term loans.

See back of book for foldout giving definitions, methods of calculation and significance of these ratios.

PART ONE

McGREGOR'S

WHO OWNS WHOM

MAIN SECTION

The net asset values in this section have *not* been adjusted to market values.

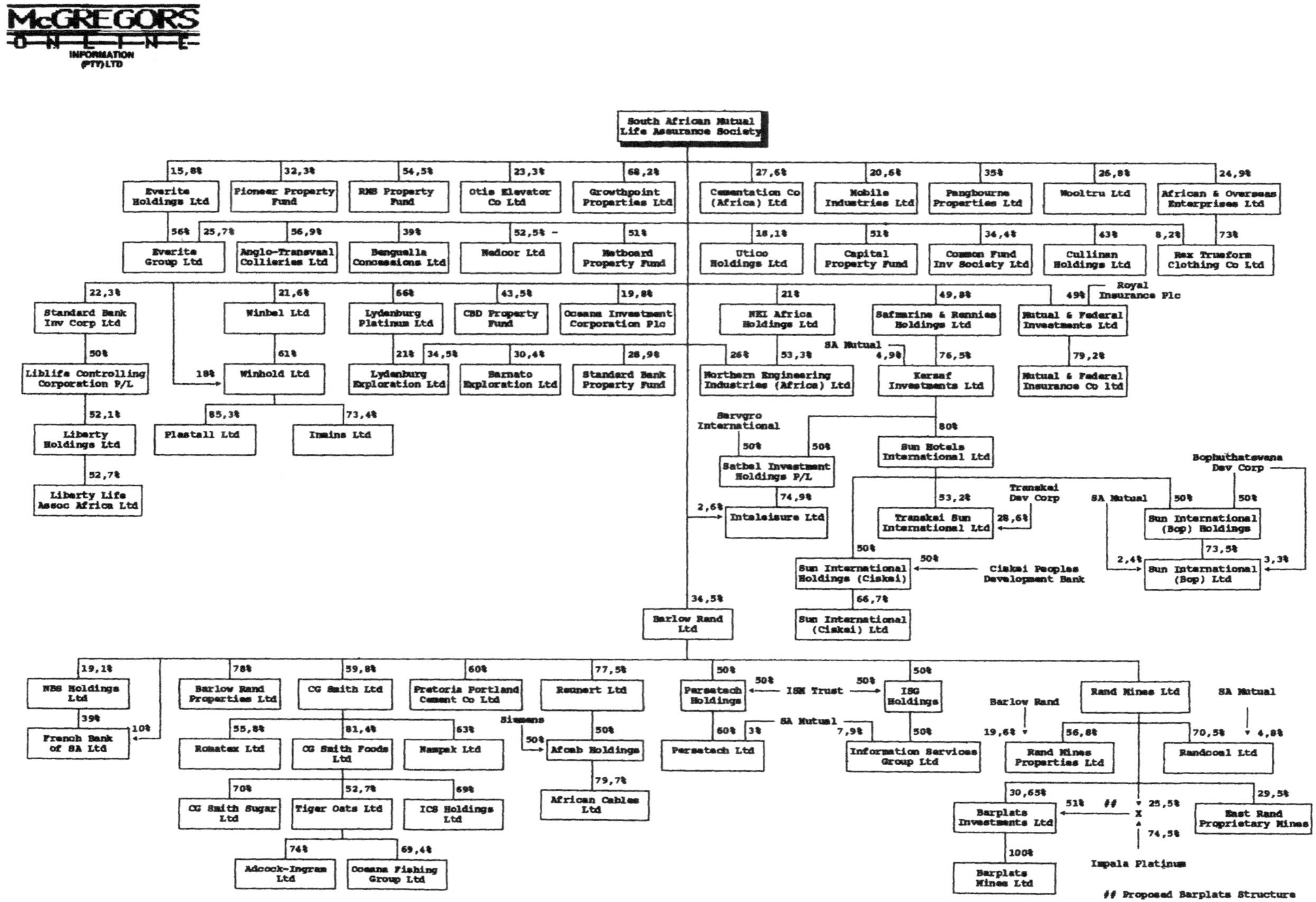
McGREGORS ONLINE INFORMATION (PTY) LTD
South African Mutual Life Assurance Society
15,8%
Everite Holdings Ltd
32,3%
Pioneer Property Fund
54,5%
RMB Property Fund
23,3%
Otis Elevator Co Ltd
68,2%
Growthpoint Properties Ltd
27,6%
Cementation Co (Africa) Ltd
20,6%
Mobile Industries Ltd
35%
Pangbourne Properties Ltd
26,8%
Wooltru Ltd
24,9%
African & Overseas Enterprises Ltd
56%
25,7%
Everite Group Ltd
56,9%
Anglo-Transvaal Collieries Ltd
39%
Benguella Concessions Ltd
52,5%
Nedcor Ltd
51%
Metboard Property Fund
18,1%
Utico Holdings Ltd
51%
Capital Property Fund
34,4%
Common Fund Inv Society Ltd
43%
Cullinan Holdings Ltd
8,2%
73%
Rex Trueform Clothing Co Ltd
22,3%
Standard Bank Inv Corp Ltd
50%
Liblife Controlling Corporation P/L
52,1%
Liberty Holdings Ltd
52,7%
Liberty Life Assoc Africa Ltd
18%
21,6%
Winbel Ltd
61%
Winhold Ltd
85,3%
Plastall Ltd
73,4%
Inmins Ltd
66%
Lydenburg Platinum Ltd
21%
Lydenburg Exploration Ltd
34,5%
43,5%
CBD Property Fund
30,4%
Barnato Exploration Ltd
19,8%
Oceana Investment Corporation Plc
28,9%
Standard Bank Property Fund
21%
NEI Africa Holdings Ltd
26%
53,3%
Northern Engineering Industries (Africa) Ltd
SA Mutual
49,8%
Safmarine & Rennies Holdings Ltd
4,9%
76,5%
Kersaf Investments Ltd
49%
Royal Insurance Plc
Mutual & Federal Investments Ltd
79,2%
Mutual & Federal Insurance Co Ltd
Sarvgro International
50%
50%
Satbel Investment Holdings P/L
74,9%
2,6%
Intaleisure Ltd
80%
Sun Hotels International Ltd
53,2%
Transkei Sun International Ltd
Transkei Dev Corp
28,6%
Bophuthatswana Dev Corp
SA Mutual
50%
50%
Sun International (Bop) Holdings
73,5%
2,4%
3,3%
Sun International (Bop) Ltd
50%
50%
Sun International Holdings (Ciskei)
Ciskei Peoples Development Bank
66,7%
Sun International (Ciskei) Ltd
34,5%
Barlow Rand Ltd
19,1%
NBS Holdings Ltd
39%
French Bank of SA Ltd
10%
78%
Barlow Rand Properties Ltd
59,8%
CG Smith Ltd
55,8%
Romatex Ltd
81,4%
CG Smith Foods Ltd
63%
Nampak Ltd
70%
CG Smith Sugar Ltd
52,7%
Tiger Oats Ltd
69%
ICS Holdings Ltd
74%
Adcock-Ingram Ltd
69,4%
Oceana Fishing Group Ltd
60%
Pretoria Portland Cement Co Ltd
Siemens
50%
77,5%
Reunert Ltd
50%
Afcab Holdings
79,7%
African Cables Ltd
50%
Persetech Holdings
50%
ISM Trust
50%
60%
3%
Persetech Ltd
SA Mutual
7,9%
50%
ISG Holdings
50%
Information Services Group Ltd
Rand Mines Ltd
Barlow Rand
19,6%
56,8%
Rand Mines Properties Ltd
SA Mutual
70,5%
4,8%
Randcoal Ltd
30,65%
Barplats Investments Ltd
51%
##
25,5%
X
74,5%
Impala Platinum
100%
Barplats Mines Ltd
29,5%
East Rand Proprietary Mines
Proposed Barplats Structure

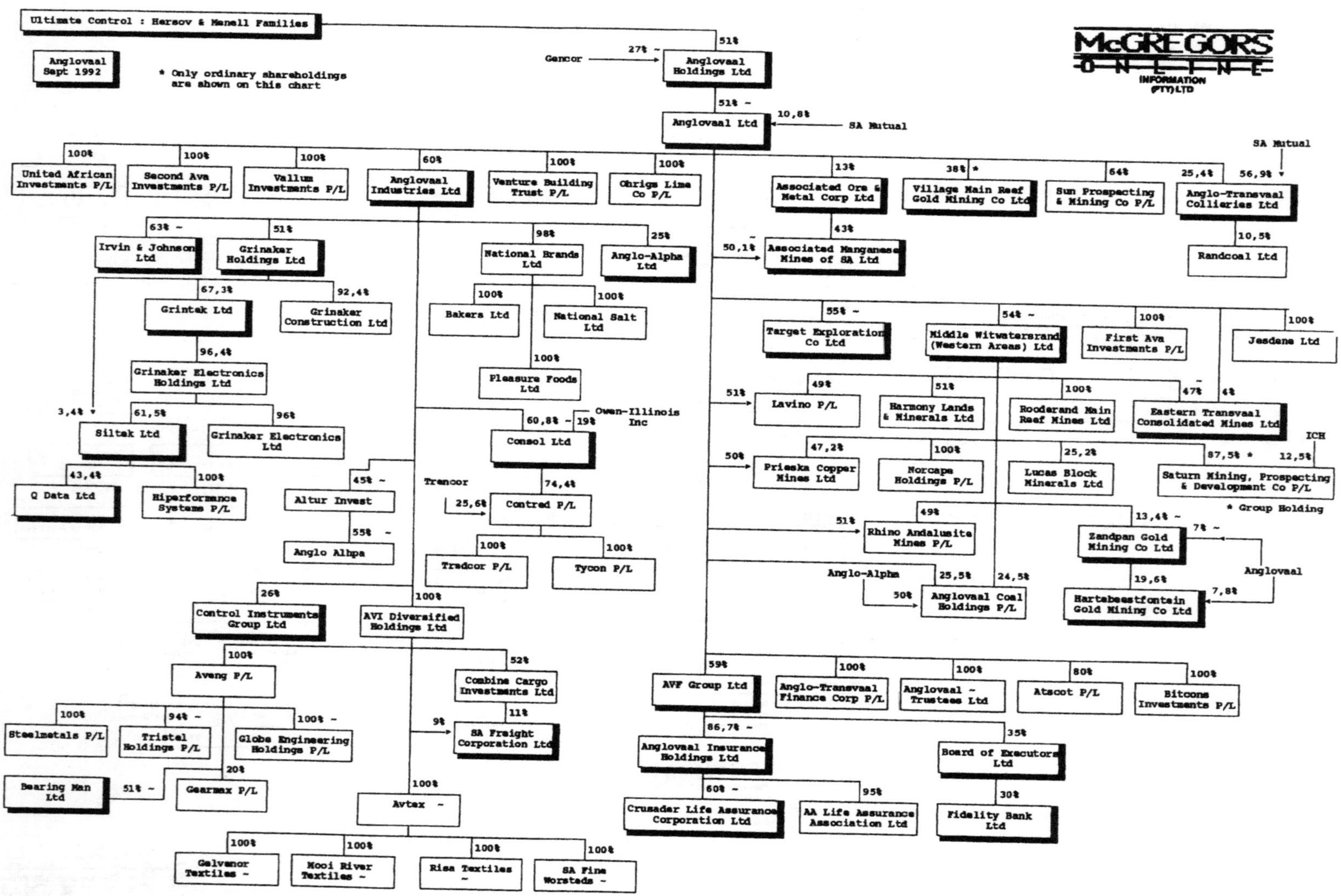

Ultimate Control : Hersov & Menell Families
Anglovaal
Sept 1992
* Only ordinary shareholdings are shown on this chart
McGREGORS ONLINE INFORMATION (PTY) LTD
51%
Gencor
27% ~
Anglovaal Holdings Ltd
51% ~
Anglovaal Ltd
10,8%
SA Mutual
100%
United African Investments P/L
100%
Second Ava Investments P/L
100%
Vallum Investments P/L
60%
Anglovaal Industries Ltd
100%
Venture Building Trust P/L
100%
Ohrigs Lime Co P/L
13%
Associated Ore & Metal Corp Ltd
38% *
Village Main Reef Gold Mining Co Ltd
64%
Sun Prospecting & Mining Co P/L
25,4%
SA Mutual
56,9%
Anglo-Transvaal Collieries Ltd
10,5%
Randcoal Ltd
43%
50,1%
Associated Manganese Mines of SA Ltd
63% ~
Irvin & Johnson Ltd
51%
Grinaker Holdings Ltd
98%
National Brands Ltd
25%
Anglo-Alpha Ltd
67,3%
Grintek Ltd
92,4%
Grinaker Construction Ltd
100%
Bakers Ltd
100%
National Salt Ltd
100%
Pleasure Foods Ltd
96,4%
Grinaker Electronics Holdings Ltd
3,4%
61,5%
Siltek Ltd
96%
Grinaker Electronics Ltd
43,4%
Q Data Ltd
100%
Hiperformance Systems P/L
60,8% ~
19%
Owen-Illinois Inc
Consol Ltd
74,4%
Trencor
25,6%
Contred P/L
100%
Tredcor P/L
100%
Tycon P/L
45% ~
Altur Invest
55% ~
Anglo Alhpa
26%
Control Instruments Group Ltd
100%
AVI Diversified Holdings Ltd
100%
Aveng P/L
52%
Combine Cargo Investments Ltd
11%
9%
SA Freight Corporation Ltd
100%
Steelmetals P/L
94% ~
Tristel Holdings P/L
100% ~
Globe Engineering Holdings P/L
20%
Bearing Man Ltd
51% ~
Gearmax P/L
100%
Avtex ~
100%
Galvenor Textiles ~
100%
Mooi River Textiles ~
100%
Risa Textiles ~
100%
SA Fine Worsteds ~
55% ~
Target Exploration Co Ltd
54% ~
Middle Witwatersrand (Western Areas) Ltd
100%
First Ava Investments P/L
100%
Jesdene Ltd
51%
49%
Lavino P/L
51%
Harmony Lands & Minerals Ltd
100%
Rooderand Main Reef Mines Ltd
47%
4%
Eastern Transvaal Consolidated Mines Ltd
ICH
50%
47,2%
Prieska Copper Mines Ltd
100%
Norcape Holdings P/L
25,2%
Lucas Block Minerals Ltd
87,5% *
12,5%
Saturn Mining, Prospecting & Development Co P/L
* Group Holding
51%
49%
Rhino Andalusite Mines P/L
13,4% ~
7% ~
Zandpan Gold Mining Co Ltd
Anglovaal
19,6%
7,8%
Hartebeestfontein Gold Mining Co Ltd
Anglo-Alpha
50%
25,5%
24,5%
Anglovaal Coal Holdings P/L
59%
AVF Group Ltd
100%
Anglo-Transvaal Finance Corp P/L
100%
Anglovaal ~ Trustees Ltd
80%
Atscot P/L
100%
Bitcons Investments P/L
86,7% ~
Anglovaal Insurance Holdings Ltd
35%
Board of Executors Ltd
60% ~
Crusader Life Assurance Corporation Ltd
95%
AA Life Assurance Association Ltd
30%
Fidelity Bank Ltd

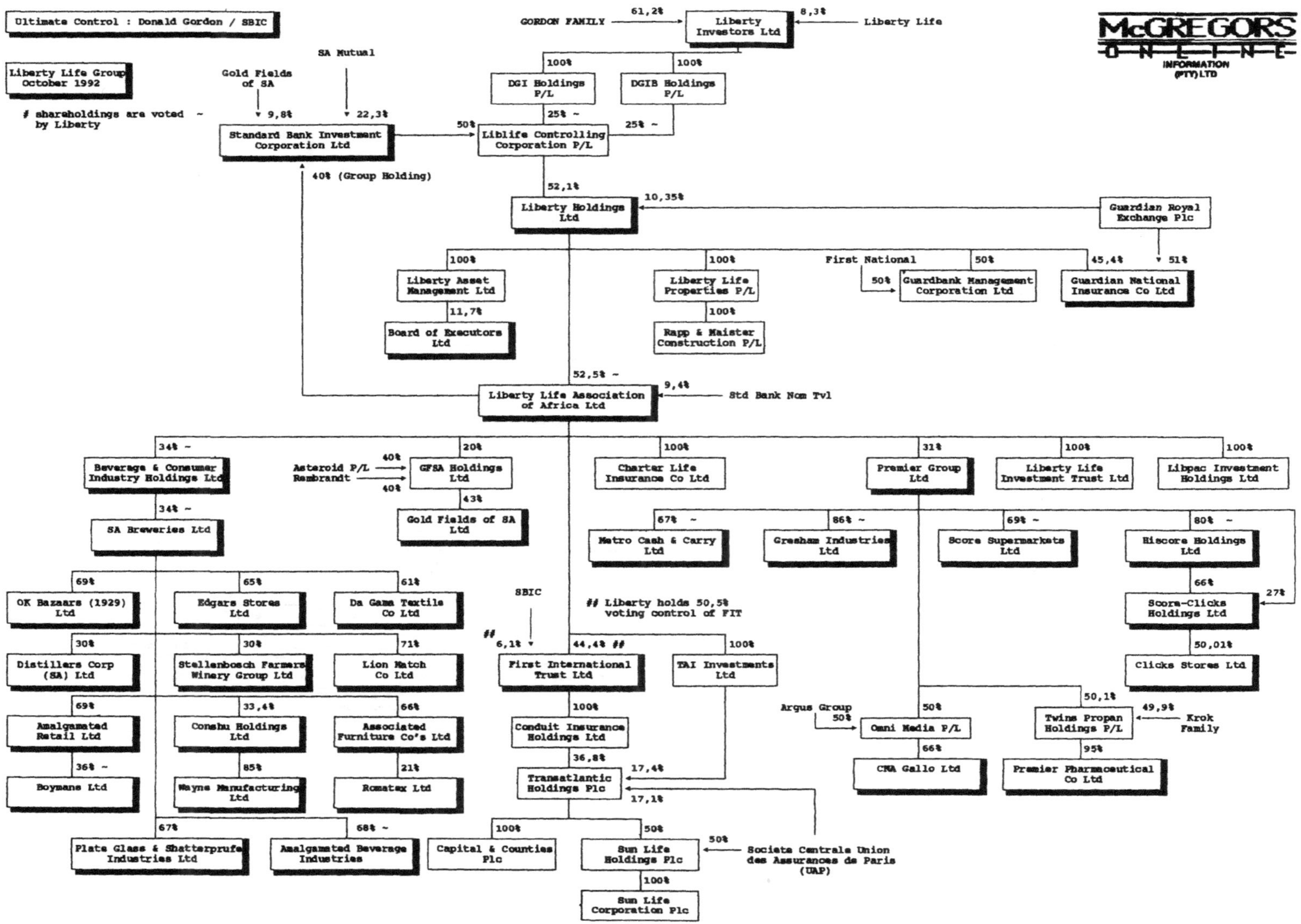

Ultimate Control : Donald Gordon / SBIC
Liberty Life Group
October 1992
shareholdings are voted ~ by Liberty
McGREGORS ONLINE INFORMATION (PTY) LTD
GORDON FAMILY
61,2%
Liberty Investors Ltd
8,3%
Liberty Life
100%
DGI Holdings P/L
100%
DGIB Holdings P/L
SA Mutual
Gold Fields of SA
9,8%
22,3%
Standard Bank Investment Corporation Ltd
50%
25% ~
25% ~
Liblife Controlling Corporation P/L
40% (Group Holding)
52,1%
Liberty Holdings Ltd
10,35%
Guardian Royal Exchange Plc
100%
Liberty Asset Management Ltd
11,7%
Board of Executors Ltd
100%
Liberty Life Properties P/L
100%
Rapp & Maister Construction P/L
First National
50%
50%
Guardbank Management Corporation Ltd
45,4%
51%
Guardian National Insurance Co Ltd
52,5% ~
9,4%
Liberty Life Association of Africa Ltd
Std Bank Nom Tvl
34% ~
Beverage & Consumer Industry Holdings Ltd
34% ~
SA Breweries Ltd
Asteroid P/L
Rembrandt
40%
40%
20%
GFSA Holdings Ltd
43%
Gold Fields of SA Ltd
100%
Charter Life Insurance Co Ltd
31%
Premier Group Ltd
100%
Liberty Life Investment Trust Ltd
100%
Libpac Investment Holdings Ltd
67% ~
Metro Cash & Carry Ltd
86% ~
Gresham Industries Ltd
69% ~
Score Supermarkets Ltd
80% ~
Hiscore Holdings Ltd
66%
27%
Score-Clicks Holdings Ltd
50,01%
Clicks Stores Ltd
69%
OK Bazaars (1929) Ltd
65%
Edgars Stores Ltd
61%
Da Gama Textile Co Ltd
30%
Distillers Corp (SA) Ltd
30%
Stellenbosch Farmers Winery Group Ltd
71%
Lion Match Co Ltd
69%
Amalgamated Retail Ltd
33,4%
Conshu Holdings Ltd
66%
Associated Furniture Co's Ltd
36% ~
Boymans Ltd
85%
Wayne Manufacturing Ltd
21%
Romatex Ltd
67%
Plate Glass & Shatterprufe Industries Ltd
68% ~
Amalgamated Beverage Industries
SBIC
##
6,1%
44,4% ##
Liberty holds 50,5% voting control of FIT
First International Trust Ltd
100%
TAI Investments Ltd
100%
Conduit Insurance Holdings Ltd
36,8%
17,4%
Transatlantic Holdings Plc
17,1%
100%
Capital & Counties Plc
50%
Sun Life Holdings Plc
50%
Societe Centrale Union des Assurances de Paris (UAP)
100%
Sun Life Corporation Plc
Argus Group
50%
50%
Omni Media P/L
66%
CNA Gallo Ltd
50,1%
Twins Propan Holdings P/L
49,9%
Krok Family
95%
Premier Pharmaceutical Co Ltd

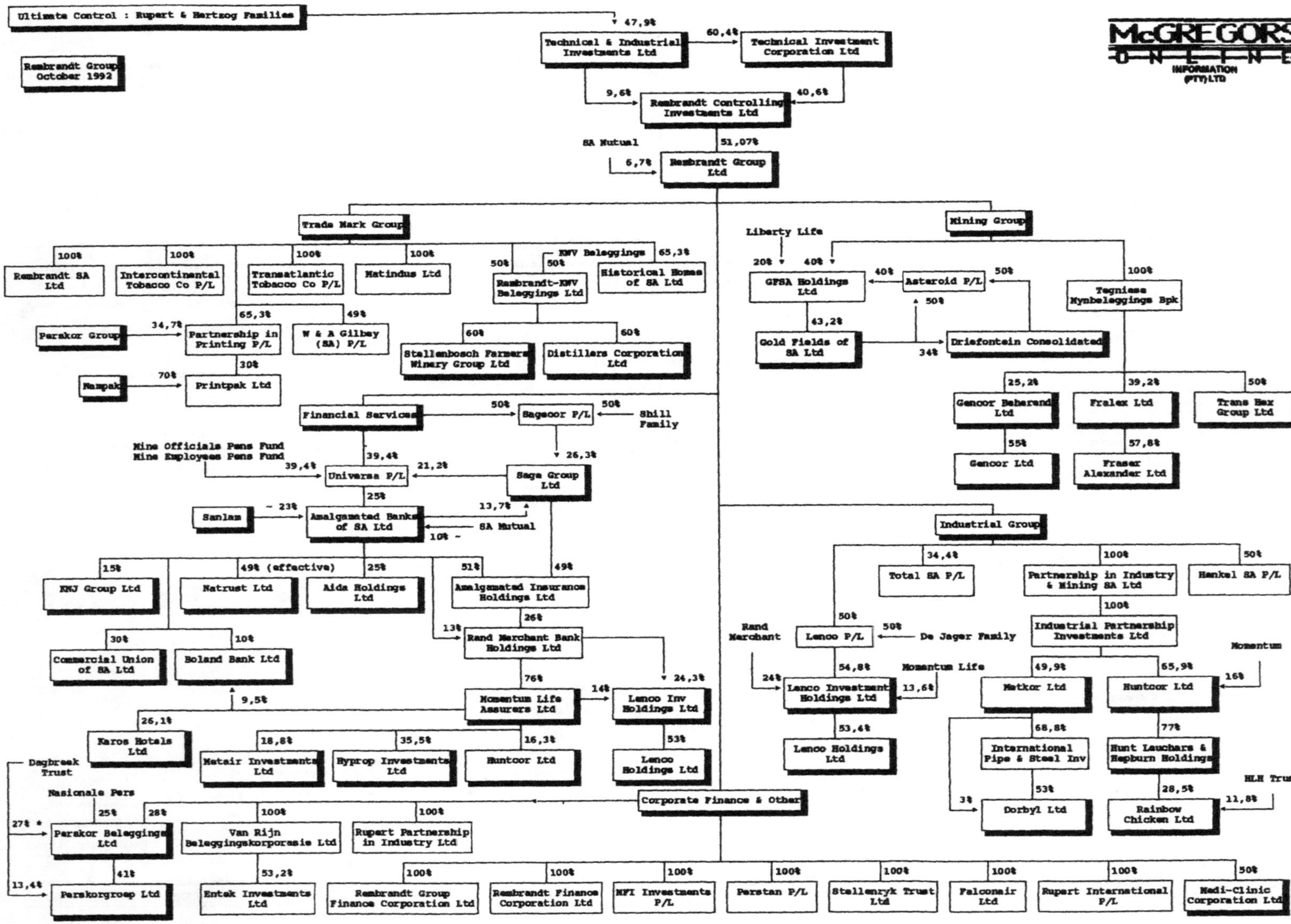
Ultimate Control : Rupert & Hertzog Families
Rembrandt Group October 1992
McGREGORS ONLINE INFORMATION (PTY) LTD
47,9%
Technical & Industrial Investments Ltd
60,4%
Technical Investment Corporation Ltd
9,6%
40,6%
Rembrandt Controlling Investments Ltd
SA Mutual
6,7%
51,07%
Rembrandt Group Ltd
Trade Mark Group
100%
Rembrandt SA Ltd
100%
Intercontinental Tobacco Co P/L
100%
Transatlantic Tobacco Co P/L
100%
Matindus Ltd
50%
KWV Beleggings
50%
Rembrandt-KWV Beleggings Ltd
65,3%
Historical Homes of SA Ltd
Parakor Group
34,7%
65,3%
Partnership in Printing P/L
49%
W & A Gilbey (SA) P/L
60%
Stellenbosch Farmers Winery Group Ltd
60%
Distillers Corporation Ltd
Nampak
70%
30%
Printpak Ltd
Mining Group
Liberty Life
20%
40%
GFSA Holdings Ltd
40%
Asteroid P/L
50%
50%
100%
Tegniese Mynbeleggings Bpk
43,2%
Gold Fields of SA Ltd
34%
Driefontein Consolidated
25,2%
Gencor Beherend Ltd
39,2%
Fralex Ltd
50%
Trans Hex Group Ltd
55%
Gencor Ltd
57,8%
Fraser Alexander Ltd
Financial Services
50%
Sagecor P/L
50%
Shill Family
Mine Officials Pens Fund
Mine Employees Pens Fund
39,4%
39,4%
Universa P/L
21,2%
26,3%
Saga Group Ltd
25%
Sanlam
~ 23%
Amalgamated Banks of SA Ltd
13,7%
SA Mutual
10% ~
15%
KNJ Group Ltd
49% (effective)
Natrust Ltd
25%
Aida Holdings Ltd
51%
49%
Amalgamated Insurance Holdings Ltd
26%
13%
Rand Merchant Bank Holdings Ltd
24,3%
30%
Commercial Union of SA Ltd
10%
Boland Bank Ltd
9,5%
76%
Momentum Life Assurers Ltd
14%
Lenco Inv Holdings Ltd
53%
Lenco Holdings Ltd
26,1%
Karos Hotels Ltd
18,8%
Metair Investments Ltd
35,5%
Hyprop Investments Ltd
16,3%
Huntcor Ltd
Industrial Group
34,4%
Total SA P/L
100%
Partnership in Industry & Mining SA Ltd
50%
Henkel SA P/L
100%
Industrial Partnership Investments Ltd
Rand Merchant
50%
Lenco P/L
50%
De Jager Family
24%
54,8%
Lenco Investment Holdings Ltd
Momentum Life
13,6%
53,4%
Lenco Holdings Ltd
49,9%
Metkor Ltd
65,9%
Huntcor Ltd
Momentum
16%
68,8%
International Pipe & Steel Inv
77%
Hunt Leuchars & Hepburn Holdings
3%
53%
Dorbyl Ltd
28,5%
Rainbow Chicken Ltd
HLH Trust
11,8%
Corporate Finance & Other
Dagbreek Trust
Nasionale Pers
27% *
25%
28%
Parakor Beleggings Ltd
100%
Van Rijn Beleggingskorporasie Ltd
100%
Rupert Partnership in Industry Ltd
13,4%
41%
Perskorgroep Ltd
53,2%
Entek Investments Ltd
100%
Rembrandt Group Finance Corporation Ltd
100%
Rembrandt Finance Corporation Ltd
100%
MFI Investments P/L
100%
Perstan P/L
100%
Stellenryk Trust Ltd
100%
Falconair Ltd
100%
Rupert International P/L
50%
Medi-Clinic Corporation Ltd

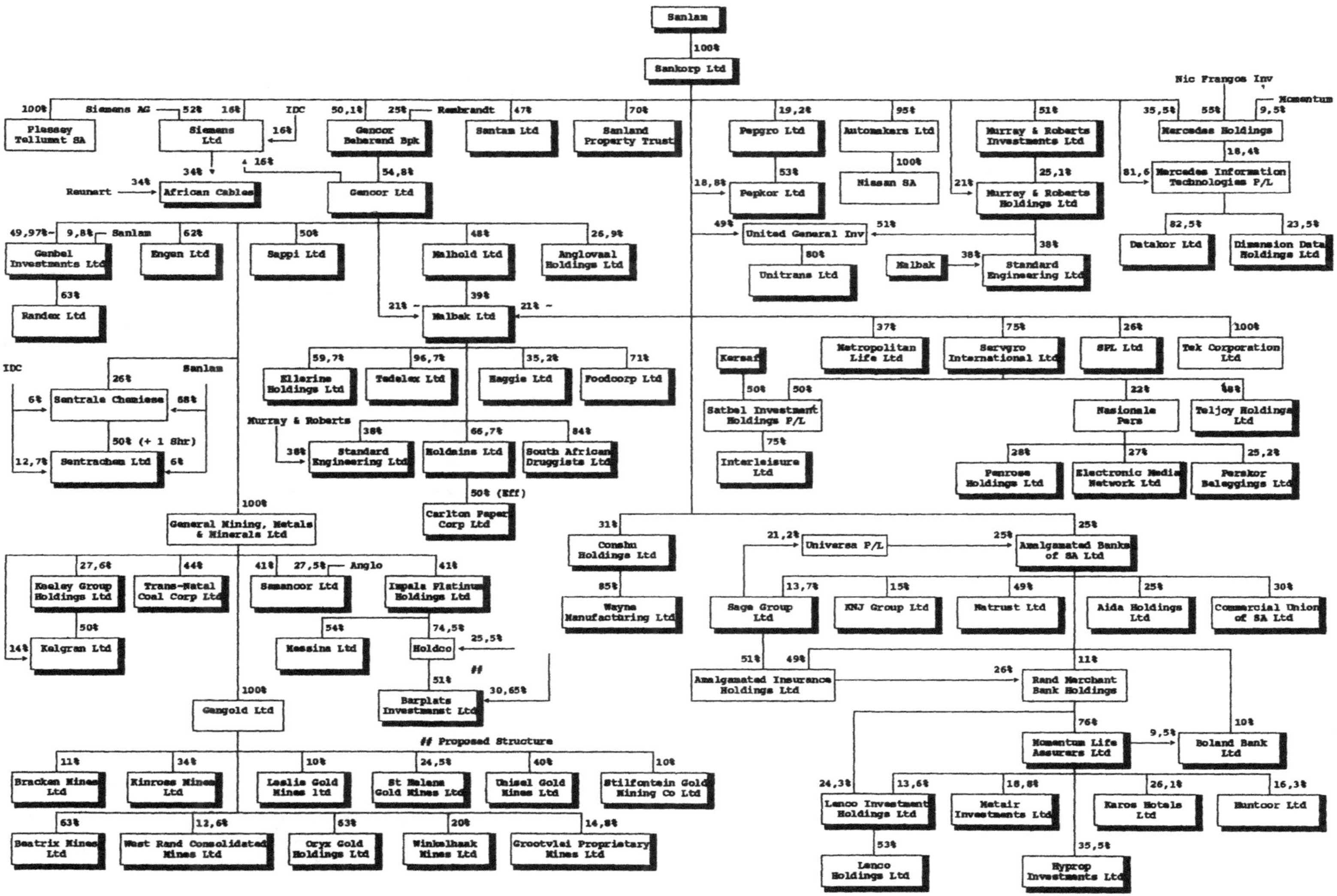
Sanlam
Sankorp Ltd
Nic Frangos Inv
Momentum
Siemens AG
IDC
Rembrandt
Plessey Tellumat SA
Siemens Ltd
Gencor Beherend Bpk
Santam Ltd
Sanlamd Property Trust
Pepgro Ltd
Automakers Ltd
Murray & Roberts Investments Ltd
Mercedes Holdings
Reunert
African Cables
Gencor Ltd
Pepkor Ltd
Nissan SA
Murray & Roberts Holdings Ltd
Mercedes Information Technologies P/L
Sanlam
Genbel Investments Ltd
Engen Ltd
Sappi Ltd
Malhold Ltd
Anglovaal Holdings Ltd
United General Inv
Unitrans Ltd
Malbak
Standard Engineering Ltd
Datakor Ltd
Dimension Data Holdings Ltd
Randex Ltd
Malbak Ltd
Metropolitan Life Ltd
Servgro International Ltd
SPL Ltd
Tek Corporation Ltd
IDC
Sanlam
Sentrale Chemiese
Ellerine Holdings Ltd
Tedelex Ltd
Haggie Ltd
Foodcorp Ltd
Kersaf
Satbel Investment Holdings P/L
Nasionale Pers
Teljoy Holdings Ltd
Murray & Roberts
Sentrachem Ltd
Standard Engineering Ltd
Holdains Ltd
South African Druggists Ltd
Interleisure Ltd
Penrose Holdings Ltd
Electronic Media Network Ltd
Perskor Beleggings Ltd
General Mining, Metals & Minerals Ltd
Carlton Paper Corp Ltd
Consbu Holdings Ltd
Universa P/L
Amalgamated Banks of SA Ltd
Anglo
Keeley Group Holdings Ltd
Trans-Natal Coal Corp Ltd
Samancor Ltd
Impala Platinum Holdings Ltd
Wayne Manufacturing Ltd
Sage Group Ltd
KNJ Group Ltd
Natrust Ltd
Aida Holdings Ltd
Commercial Union of SA Ltd
Kelgran Ltd
Messina Ltd
Holdco
##
Amalgamated Insurance Holdings Ltd
Rand Merchant Bank Holdings
Gengold Ltd
Barplats Investment Ltd
Proposed Structure
Momentum Life Assurers Ltd
Boland Bank Ltd
Bracken Mines Ltd
Kinross Mines Ltd
Leslie Gold Mines ltd
St Helena Gold Mines Ltd
Unisel Gold Mines Ltd
Stilfontein Gold Mining Co Ltd
Lenco Investment Holdings Ltd
Metair Investments Ltd
Karos Hotels Ltd
Buntoor Ltd
Beatrix Mines Ltd
West Rand Consolidated Mines Ltd
Oryx Gold Holdings Ltd
Winkelhaak Mines Ltd
Grootvlei Proprietary Mines Ltd
Lenco Holdings Ltd
Hyprop Investments Ltd

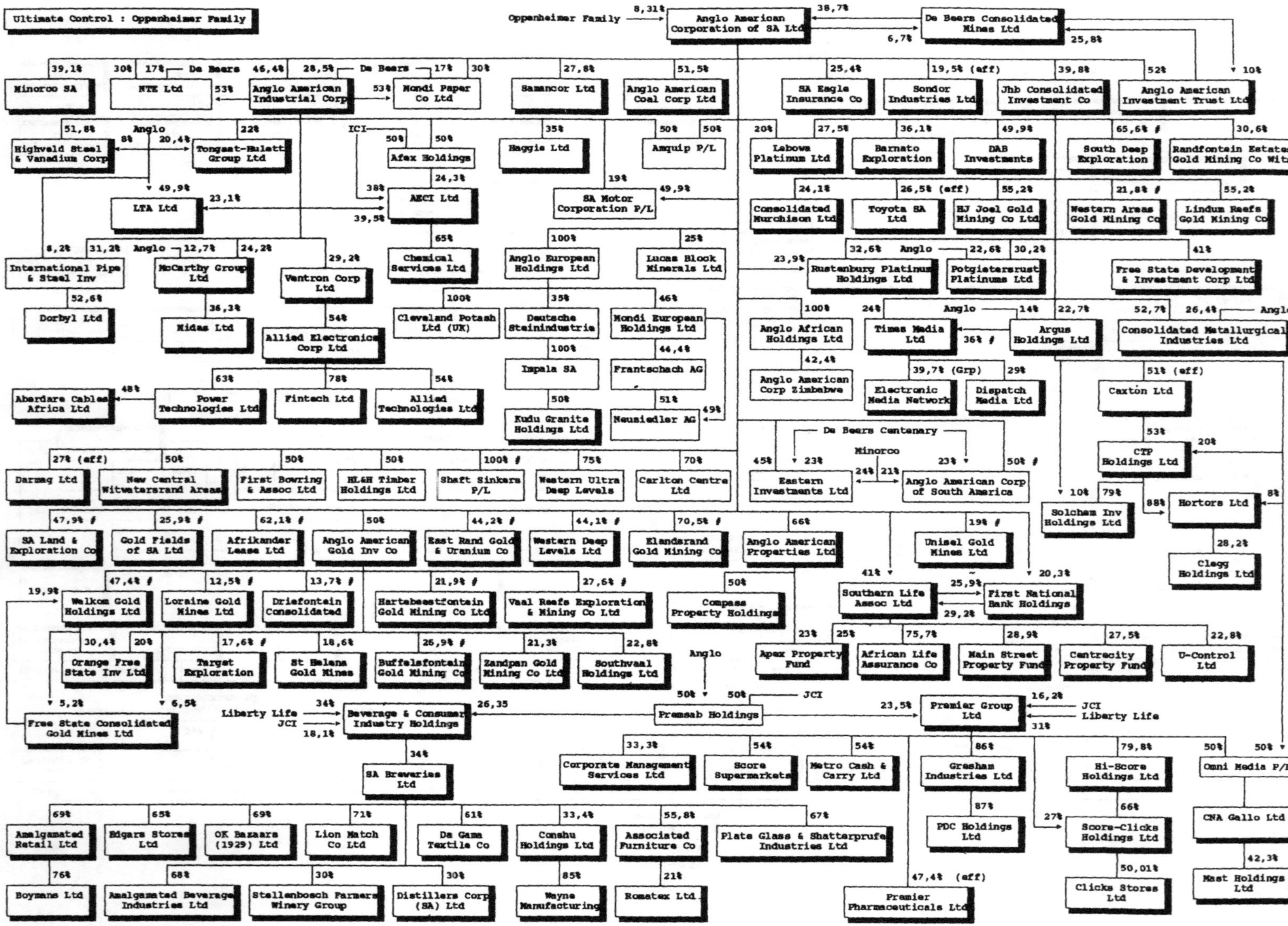
Ultimate Control : Oppenheimer Family
Oppenheimer Family
Anglo American Corporation of SA Ltd
De Beers Consolidated Mines Ltd
Minorco SA
NTE Ltd
Anglo American Industrial Corp
Mondi Paper Co Ltd
Samancor Ltd
Anglo American Coal Corp Ltd
SA Eagle Insurance Co
Sondor Industries Ltd
Jhb Consolidated Investment Co
Anglo American Investment Trust Ltd
Highveld Steel & Vanadium Corp
Tongaat-Hulett Group Ltd
Afex Holdings
Haggie Ltd
Amquip P/L
Lebowa Platinum Ltd
Barnato Exploration
DAB Investments
South Deep Exploration
Randfontein Estates Gold Mining Co Wits
LTA Ltd
AECI Ltd
SA Motor Corporation P/L
Consolidated Murchison Ltd
Toyota SA Ltd
HJ Joel Gold Mining Co Ltd
Western Areas Gold Mining Co
Lindum Reefs Gold Mining Co
International Pipe & Steel Inv
McCarthy Group Ltd
Ventron Corp Ltd
Chemical Services Ltd
Anglo European Holdings Ltd
Lucas Block Minerals Ltd
Rustenburg Platinum Holdings Ltd
Potgietersrust Platinums Ltd
Free State Development & Investment Corp Ltd
Dorbyl Ltd
Midas Ltd
Allied Electronics Corp Ltd
Cleveland Potash Ltd (UK)
Deutsche Steinindustrie
Mondi European Holdings Ltd
Anglo African Holdings Ltd
Times Media Ltd
Argus Holdings Ltd
Consolidated Metallurgical Industries Ltd
Impala SA
Frantschach AG
Anglo American Corp Zimbabwe
Electronic Media Network
Dispatch Media Ltd
Caxton Ltd
Aberdare Cables Africa Ltd
Power Technologies Ltd
Fintech Ltd
Allied Technologies Ltd
Kudu Granite Holdings Ltd
Neusiedler AG
De Beers Centenary
Minorco
CTP Holdings Ltd
Darmag Ltd
New Central Witwatersrand Areas
First Bowring & Assoc Ltd
HL&H Timber Holdings Ltd
Shaft Sinkers P/L
Western Ultra Deep Levels
Carlton Centre Ltd
Eastern Investments Ltd
Anglo American Corp of South America
Solchem Inv Holdings Ltd
Hortors Ltd
SA Land & Exploration Co
Gold Fields of SA Ltd
Afrikander Lease Ltd
Anglo American Gold Inv Co
East Rand Gold & Uranium Co
Western Deep Levels Ltd
Elandsrand Gold Mining Co
Anglo American Properties Ltd
Unisel Gold Mines Ltd
Clegg Holdings Ltd
Welkom Gold Holdings Ltd
Loraine Gold Mines Ltd
Driefontein Consolidated
Hartebeestfontein Gold Mining Co Ltd
Vaal Reefs Exploration & Mining Co Ltd
Compass Property Holdings
Southern Life Assoc Ltd
First National Bank Holdings
Orange Free State Inv Ltd
Target Exploration
St Helena Gold Mines
Buffelsfontein Gold Mining Co
Zandpan Gold Mining Co Ltd
Southvaal Holdings Ltd
Apex Property Fund
African Life Assurance Co
Main Street Property Fund
Centrecity Property Fund
U-Control Ltd
Anglo
JCI
Liberty Life
Free State Consolidated Gold Mines Ltd
Beverage & Consumer Industry Holdings
Premsab Holdings
Premier Group Ltd
SA Breweries Ltd
Corporate Management Services Ltd
Score Supermarkets
Metro Cash & Carry Ltd
Gresham Industries Ltd
Hi-Score Holdings Ltd
Omni Media P/L
PDC Holdings Ltd
Score-Clicks Holdings Ltd
CNA Gallo Ltd
Amalgamated Retail Ltd
Edgars Stores Ltd
OK Bazaars (1929) Ltd
Lion Match Co Ltd
Da Gama Textile Co
Conshu Holdings Ltd
Associated Furniture Co
Plate Glass & Shatterprufe Industries Ltd
Boymans Ltd
Amalgamated Beverage Industries Ltd
Stellenbosch Farmers Winery Group
Distillers Corp (SA) Ltd
Wayne Manufacturing
Romatex Ltd
Premier Pharmaceuticals Ltd
Clicks Stores Ltd
Mast Holdings Ltd

IDENTIFICATION OF NOMINEE, HOLDING AND INVESTMENT COMPANIES

NOMINEE	ASSOCIATED WITH
ABERCORN ESTATES P/L	MOWSZOWSKI FAMILY
ABERDARE INV P/L	POWERTECH & PHILIPS
ADBREST P/L	B C BENFIELD
AFEX HOLDINGS P/L	AMIC & ICI
AFRICAN & EUROPEAN INV CO LTD	ANGLO AMERICAN
AFRICAN METALS LTD	GENCOR
ALTENA MEWS P/L	SANLAM
ALTUR INV LTD	HOLDERBANK FINANCIERE
AMOSITE NOM LTD	BARLOW RAND
ANCHUSA LTD	SANLAM
ANGLO AFRICAN SHIPPING CO 1936 P/L	RAND MERCHANT BANK
ASHTREE INV P/L	SA MUTUAL
AVENG P/L	ANGLOVAAL IND
BANK OF NEW YORK NOM LTD	AMERICAN SHAREHOLDERS
BANNER NOM P/L	STANDARD MERCHANT BANK
BARCLAYS NAT NOM P/L GATR DEPOT	AMERICAN SHAREHOLDERS
BARMONT NOM P/L	BERNSTEIN B P
BARNATO HLDGS LTD	JCI
BAROB INV P/L	BARLOWS
BASSER P/L	PREMIER GROUP
BENREN NOM P/L	VAN RENSBURG B J
BERTIE H P/L	UNIDEV
BEVLIT INV HOLDINGS LTD	LIBERTY
BILVEN P/L	ALTECH
BP CENTRE NOM P/L	BP SOUTHERN AFRICA P/L
BP THIBAULT NOM P/L	BP SOUTHERN AFRICA P/L
BRIHEPWELL INV LTD	ASSOCIATED ENGINEERING (PTY) LTD
BRIVIK BROS P/L	CLINIC HOLDINGS
BURG NOM P/L	SANLAM
CALINA INV HOLDINGS LTD	ANGLO AMERICAN
CAPITAL NOM P/L	GUARDIAN LIBERTY
CAPITAL SECURITIES LTD	SA MUTUAL
CARLEO ENTERPRISES P/L	CARLEO FAMILY
CENTRAL MINING FINANCE LTD	CHARTER
CHALKTON NOM CO P/L	DAVIS BORKUM HARE
CINOA HOLDINGS LTD	TOLLGATE GROUP
CITIBANK NOM P/L	AMERICAN SHAREHOLDERS
CMB NOM P/L	BANKORP
CONSOLIDATED CABLE INV P/L	POWERTECH & PHILIPS
CONSOLIDATED NOM P/L	GENCOR
CONSOLIDATED STEEL INV P/L	MACSTEEL
CONSTEIN INV P/L	COOPERS THERON DU TOIT
CORGROUP MERCURY INV LTD	RAND MINES
CORNER HOUSE INV CO LTD	BARLOW RAND
CORPORATE ASSET MANAGEMENT P/L	FIRSTCORP
CYLIL INV P/L	KIMET
DA GAMA HOLDING CO P/L	SA BREWERIES
DALGLAND NOM P/L	J D ANDERSON
DANECH P/L	N G PARRY
DARGARVEL P/L	LIBERTY LIFE ASSOC
DE BEERS IND CORP LTD	AMIC
DELAUNAY LTD	ANGLO AMERICAN

NOMINEE	ASSOCIATED WITH
DELAUNAY TWO LTD	ANGLO AMERICAN
DEMOCRAT NOM P/L	PREMIER GROUP
DEPOSITARY NOM INC	AMERICAN SHAREHOLDERS
DIAGONAL NOM P/L	GEORGE HUYSAMER & CO
DIAMOND CORP P/L	DE BEERS
DIDO NOM LTD	ANGLO AMERICAN
DUNLOP NOM SA P/L	BTR PLC
EDIMED P/L	SANLAM
EIGHTY ONE MAIN STREET NOM LTD	NEDCOR
ERONIA INV P/L	DE BEERS
FALTIG INV P/L	FRASERS CONSOLIDATED LTD
FEBRIS LTD	ANGLO AMERICAN
FEDERALE SELEKSIES BPK	FED VOLKS
FERBROS NOM P/L	FERGUSSON BROS
FERMAIN NOM LTD	ANGLO AMERICAN
FINANCIAL SECURITIES LTD	REMBRANDT
FIRST NAT NOM P/L GATR DEPOT	AMERICAN SHAREHOLDERS
FMB INV BPK	SANLAM
FNP PENS FUND	NESTLE
FOX STREET NOM P/L	HERSOV & MENELL
FOXGLEN INV LTD	JCI
FOXVALLEY INV P/L	JCI
FRANTIG INV LTD	TIGER OATS
FRENCH CAPE NOM P/L	AMERICAN SHAREHOLDERS
FRENCHCITY NOM P/L	AMERICAN SHAREHOLDERS
FULIT P/L	LIBERTY LIFE
FURNCOL LTD	AFCOL
GALATES INV HLDGS LTD	ANGLO AMERICAN
GEMLIB INV P/L	BEVCON
GEMZO NOM P/L	ISCOR RETIREMENT FUND
GENEX INV P/L	MURRAY & ROBERTS
GEOC NOM LTD	NEDBANK
GRAYSTON NOM P/L	MOMENTUM LIFE
GREENMARKET SQUARE NOM P/L	LIBERTY LIFE
GRESHAM TRADING CO P/L	JAFFE FAMILY
GUARDIAN NOM P/L	GUARDBANK MANAGEMENT
HARVEST SECURITIES LTD	SIMPSON MCKIE
HASHAY NOM P/L	HAYES J P
HERBEST NOM P/L	HAB HERBST
HIGHWICK PROPERTY P/L	ROY FAMILY
HLDGS NOM P/L	UNION CORP
HOLDEM P/L	A C DEMMERS
HOLDINGS NOM P/L	GENBEL INVESTMENTS
HOLLARD NOM P/L	EAST RAND CONS
HOLLARDSTRAAT SES INV BPK	GENCOR BEHEREND
IND & MINING INV LTD	REMBRANDT
INDO-CHINA NOM P/L	FRENCH BANK OF SA
INSTITUTIONAL INV LTD	ANGLO AMERICAN
ISLEV INV P/L	KIMET LTD
JOCELYN LTD	FRASERS CONSOLIDATED LTD
JR NOM P/L	IVOR JONES & CO
JUSPOINT NOM P/L	SP REID & MACKEURTON
KONOIL P/L	IDC
LAGAN INV HLDGS LTD	ANGLO AMERICAN
LEON TRAUB INV P/L	KIMET
LEWTOP P/L	LEWER & CO
LIBIC INV HOLDINGS P/L	STANDARD BANK
LIMIN INV P/L	KIMET

IDENTIFICATION OF NOMINEE, HOLDING AND INVESTMENT COMPANIES

NOMINEE	ASSOCIATED WITH
LODESTONE HLDGS LTD	ANGLO AMERICAN
LOISEL NOM P/L	LURIE JOHNSTON
M F I INV P/L	REMBRANDT
MACVEN NOM P/L	SIMPSON MCKIE
MAESTRO SECURITIES P/L	MARTINDALE STACEY TROLLIP
MALARUS P/L	TRADE & IND
MANBOS NOM P/L	J BOSMAN & CO
MARJORAM HOLDINGS LTD	ANGLO AMERICAN
MARLED NOM P/L	IRISH MENELL ROSENBERG
MAUDSLEY HOLDINGS LTD	ANGLO AMERICAN
MAXERIC NOM P/L	MAX POLLAK & FREEMANTLE
MEK INV P/L	M E KING
MENBLACK NOM P/L	IRISH MENELL ROSENBERG
METGROUPHOLD LTD	PREMIER GROUP
MFI INV P/L	REMBRANDT
MINU NOM LTD	GOLD FIELDS
MONTRIQUE P/L	SHILL FAMILY
MORGANFREN NOM P/L	AMERICAN SHAREHOLDERS
MOYANA NOM P/L	HANCOCK FAMILY
MUFREN NOM P/L	STANDARD MERCHANT BANK
MUST NOM P/L	MURRAY & ROBERTS
NAT BRANDS LTD	ANGLOVAAL
NAT CITY NOM LTD	FIRSTCORP
NAT FISHERIES OF NAMIBIA LTD	P C KUTTEL
NEVA INV P/L	SAND CONS INV
NEW ERA CONSOLIDATED LTD	ANGLO AMERICAN
NINETEEN SYNDICATE P/L	TUCKER FAMILY
NOOIENSFONTEIN INV P/L	NABABEEP MINING EXPL CO
NUMITOR INV HLDGS	ANGLO AMERICAN
NYWERBEL BPK	FEDERALE VOLKS
ORANGE FREE STATE INV TRUST LTD	ANGLO AMERICAN
ORIOLE INV LTD	ANGLO AMERICAN
OUSAKOR BPK	SANLAM
OVERSEAS NOM CO INC	AMERICAN SHAREHOLDERS
PAG HOLDINGS P/L	SE CATTON
PALMERS TRUST NOM P/L	NEDBANK
PETARD NOM LTD	ANGLO AMERICAN
PHIMAX P/L	AIKEN & PEAT
PINTAIL INV LTD	ANGLO AMERICAN
PIONEER NOM LTD	ISSUES & INV LTD
PLASTALL INV P/L	DANGLO LTD
PREMSAB HOLDINGS LTD	ANGLO & JCI
RAL NOM (PVT) LTD	ANGLO AMERICAN
RAND AMERICAN INV P/L	ANGLO AMERICAN
RAND SELECTION CORP LTD	ANGLO AMERICAN
RANDSEL INV LTD	ANGLO AMERICAN
RESIDENT NOM LTD	ANGLO AMERICAN
RHODES INV LTD	ANGLO AMERICAN
RINRIC NOM P/L	RICE & RINALDI
ROBROY BELANGE P/L	MULLER S L
ROCK PENS FUND	EVERITE GROUP
ROHIRRIM INV P/L	A DRUSINSKY
RUNCORN HLDGS LTD	ANGLO AMERICAN
SA MINES SELECTION LTD	ANGLO AMERICAN
SA TOWNSHIPS MINING & FINANCE CORP LTD	ANGLO AMERICAN
SAGECOR P/L	REMBRANDT / SHILL FAMILY
SANFORD NOM P/L	SAUNDERS & TAYLOR
SANKERN E/B	SANLAM
SANKORP BPK	SANLAM
SANKORP SPEC E/B	SANLAM
SANTHOLD INV LTD	ROMATEX
SECURITY NOM LTD	ANGLO AMERICAN
SERPOLLET HOLDINGS LTD	ANGLO AMERICAN
SFSS NOM P/L	SIMPSON MCKIE
SGM INV P/L	SILVERMAN FAMILY

NOMINEE	ASSOCIATED WITH
SHAPE INV P/L	PREMIER GROUP
SHARESTOCK NOM P/L	MARTIN & CO INC
SHELF NOM NINE P/L	IMPALA PLATINUM
SIXTY SIX MARSHALL STREET NOM P/L	UAL MERCHANT BANK
SLAM NOM P/L	SOUTHERN LIFE
SLAMAN P/L	SANLAM
SLAWAL NOM P/L	UNISEC
SMK NOM P/L	SENEKAL MOUTON & KITSHOF
SOCIETE GENERALE SA LTD	SOCIETE GENERALE (FRANCE)
SOUTHERN LIFE SPECIAL INV P/L	SOUTHERN LIFE
SQUARE DEAL INV P/L	DOS SANTOS, KRAMER, McLEAN, ROSENBERG &
SSI SECURITIES P/L	SAGE GROUP
STATUS BELEGGINGS E/B	SANLAM
STATUS INV P/L	SANLAM
STOCKSHARE NOM P/L	FRANKEL KRUGER
SYFRETS NOM LTD	NEDBANK
TARL INV LTD	ANGLO AMERICAN
TAURUS NOM LTD	ANGLO AMERICAN
THATON LTD	ANGLO AMERICAN
THOMASCUS NOM P/L	SIMPSON MCKIE
TORINO INV P/L	HALSEY BUTTON & PERRY (DBN)
TOTTIES INV P/L	PREMIER MILLING
TOWNSTATE NOM P/L	ANGLOVAAL
TRAMID INV P/L	ANGLOVAAL
TRIPLEBEE NOM P/L	BOLAND BANK
TURNBERRY HLDGS LTD	AMIC
UAL NOM P/L	NEDBANK
UNISECURE NOM P/L	UNISEC
UNITED AFRICAN INV LTD	ANGLOVAAL
UNITED FINANCE CORP OF SA LTD	MH FINGER
UNITED OCEANA HOLDINGS LTD	TIGER OATS
URD INV P/L	SANLAM
UTAS INV P/L	EUREVEST
VAN RIJN INV CORP LTD	REMBRANDT
VERSPREIDE INV P/L	BREMER FAMILY
VIRGINIA MERRIESPRUIT INV LTD	RAND MINES
VIZOMA P/L	AROMOVSKY FAMILY
VKP NOM P/L	COOPER THERON DU TOIT
VMB NOM P/L	VOLKSKAS
WALE STREET NOM LTD	BOARD OF EXECUTORS
WESTERN HLDGS LTD	ANGLO AMERICAN
WPH INV LTD	LONRHO
YORKFREN NOM P/L	AMERICAN SHAREHOLDERS
ZIMCO HOLDINGS P/L	ANGLO AMERICAN
ZIMCO INDUSTRIES P/L	ANGLO AMERICAN
ZYLVOS P/L	COOPERS THERON DU TOIT

STOCK BROKING FIRMS & ADDRESSES

BENONI

FRANKEL, MAX POLLAK, VINDERINE INC
BOX 285
BENONI
1500
8451159(Tel No.)
8451159(Fax No.)

BLOEMFONTEIN

ED HERN, RUDOLPH INC
BOX 2915
BLOEMFONTEIN
9300
051-476304(Tel No.)
051-477028(Fax No.)

HERBST H A B INC
BOX 6747
BLOEMFONTEIN
9300
051-470819(Tel No.)
051-470796(Fax No.)

CAPE TOWN

BALDERSON E W INC
BOX 189
CAPE TOWN
8000
021-4197217(Tel No.)
021-214695(Fax No.)

DAVIS, BORKUM, HARE & CO INC
BOX 2269
CAPE TOWN
8000
021-231440(Tel No.)
021-238600(Fax No.)

ED HERN, RUDOLPH INC
BOX 2836
CAPE TOWN
8000
021-237266(Tel No.)
021-242582(Fax No.)

FERGUSSON BROS, HALL, STEWART & CO INC
BOX 4059
CAPE TOWN
8000
021-4196610(Tel No.)
021-4197344(Fax No.)

FRANKEL, MAX POLLAK, VINDERINE INC
BOX 5333
CAPE TOWN
8000
021-253871(Tel No.)
021-4194821(Fax No.)

GEORGE HUYSAMER & PARTNERS INC
BOX 165
CAPE TOWN
8000
021-248020(Tel No.)
021-230691(Fax No.)

IVOR JONES, ROY & CO INC
BOX 601
CAPE TOWN
8000
021-4194235(Tel No.)
021-4195935(Fax No.)

KAPLAN & STEWART INC
BOX 3454
CAPE TOWN
8000
021-215100(Tel No.)
021-214937(Fax No.)

LOWENTHAL & CO
BOX 607
CAPE TOWN
8000
021-262370(Tel No.)
021-232034(Fax No.)

MARTIN & CO INC
BOX 3996
CAPE TOWN
8000
021-245316(Tel No.)
021-262423(Fax No.)

MATHISON & HOLLIDGE INC
BOX 213
CAPE TOWN
8000
021-4621270(Tel No.)
021-4612244(Fax No.)

SENEKAL, MOUTON & KITSHOFF INC
BOX 1054
CAPE TOWN
8000
021-4190011(Tel No.)
021-252120(Fax No.)

SIMPSON, MCKIE INC
BOX 4805
CAPE TOWN
8000
021-4616320(Tel No.)
021-4613904(Fax No.)

DURBAN

DAVIS, BORKUM, HARE & CO INC
BOX 553
DURBAN
4000
031-3056231(Tel No.)
031-3051347(Fax No.)

FERGUSSON BROS, HALL, STEWART & CO INC
BOX 553
DURBAN
4000
031-3041567(Tel No.)
031-3042882(Fax No.)

FRANKEL, MAX POLLAK, VINDERINE INC
BOX 1558
DURBAN
4000
031-3019724(Tel No.)
031-3010566(Fax No.)

MATHISON & HOLLIDGE INC
BOX 2216
DURBAN
4000
031-3040431(Tel No.)
031-3040698(Fax No.)

EAST LONDON

FRANKEL, MAX POLLAK, VINDERINE INC
BOX 290
EAST LONDON
5200
0431-26725(Tel No.)
0431-434862(Fax No.)

GEORGE

GEORGE HUYSAMER & PARTNERS INC
BOX 894
GEORGE
6530
0441-742616(Tel No.)
0441-746848(Fax No.)

JOHANNESBURG

ANDERSON J D & CO INC
BOX 61028
MARSHALLTOWN
2107
8362601/9(Tel No.)
8342772(Fax No.)

ANDERSON, WILSON & PARTNERS INC
BOX 61309
MARSHALLTOWN
2107
8363281(Tel No.)
8383798(Fax No.)

BALDERSON E W INC
BOX 61037
MARSHALLTOWN
2107
4921333(Tel No.)
8345619(Fax No.)

BERNSTEIN B P
BOX 61339
MARSHALLTOWN
2107
8331560/6(Tel No.)
8360392(Fax No.)

BONER & FREEMANTLE INC
BOX 62042
MARSHALLTOWN
2107
8383781(Tel No.)
8348465(Fax No.)

DAVIES B C & CO
BOX 61655
MARSHALLTOWN
2107
8332537/9(Tel No.)
8347526(Fax No.)

DAVIS, BORKUM, HARE & CO INC
BOX 5591
JOHANNESBURG
2000
8322711(Tel No.)
8331967/8(Fax No.)

DE WITT, MORGAN & CO
BOX 61459
MARSHALLTOWN
2107
8321266(Tel No.)
8366173(Fax No.)

DIAMOND C
BOX 2240
JOHANNESBURG
2000
8343448/9(Tel No.)

ED HERN, RUDOLPH INC
BOX 1007
JOHANNESBURG
2000
8365211(Tel No.)
8383488(Fax No.)

EDEY, ROGERS & CO INC
BOX 61320
MARSHALLTOWN
2107
8335530(Tel No.)
8387653(Fax No.)

FERGUSSON BROS, HALL, STEWART & CO INC
BOX 691
JOHANNESBURG
2000
8335740(Tel No.)
8342877(Fax No.)

FRANKEL, MAX POLLAK, VINDERINE INC
BOX 299
JOHANNESBURG
2000
011-8336911(Tel No.)
011-8360402(Fax No.)

FRIEDLANDER L R
BOX 2921
JOHANNESBURG
2000
8321370(Tel No.)
8321378(Fax No.)

GEORGE HUYSAMER & PARTNERS INC
BOX 11461
JOHANNESBURG
2000
8367871(Tel No.)
8365811(Fax No.)

GOLDING & CO

BOX 2514
JOHANNESBURG
2000
8367151(Tel No.)
8364502(Fax No.)

HAYES, CUTTEN & CO INC
BOX 62009
MARSHALLTOWN
2107
8322761(Tel No.)
8346908(Fax No.)

HERBST H A B INC
BOX 25107
FERREIRASDORP
2048
8366521(Tel No.)
8387916(Fax No.)

HUMAN M P
BOX 61295
MARSHALLTOWN
2107
8360236(Tel No.)
8360237(Fax No.)

IRISH, MENELL & ROSENBERG INC
BOX 183
NEWTOWN
2113
8368141(Tel No.)
8384202(Fax No.)

IVOR JONES, ROY & CO INC
BOX 61043
MARSHALLTOWN
2107
4922000(Tel No.)
8367271(Fax No.)

KAPLAN & STEWART INC
BOX 6799
JOHANNESBURG
2000
8337777(Tel No.)
8360794(Fax No.)

KRUGER & CO
BOX 61834
MARSHALLTOWN
2107
8360527(Tel No.)
8332497(Fax No.)

LEWER & CO
BOX 61345
MARSHALLTOWN
2107
8336550(Tel No.)
8347154(Fax No.)

LOWENTHAL & CO
BOX 62143
MARSHALLTOWN
2107
8367431(Tel No.)
8387232(Fax No.)

LURIE, JOHNSTON & CO INC
BOX 61046
MARSHALLTOWN
2107
8332123(Tel No.)
8366294(Fax No.)

MARTIN & CO INC
BOX 934
JOHANNESBURG
2000
8321891(Tel No.)
8382344(Fax No.)

MARTINDALE, STACEY, TROLLIP INC
BOX 61059
MARSHALLTOWN
2107
8382131(Tel No.)
8381433(Fax No.)

MATHISON & HOLLIDGE INC
BOX 693
JOHANNESBURG
2000
8336331(Tel No.)
8368911(Fax No.)

MEADES DE KLERK INC
BOX 61750
MARSHALLTOWN
2107
8386160/4(Tel No.)
8346195(Fax No.)

O'FLAHERTY G & CO
BOX 155
NEWTOWN
2113
8368367(Tel No.)
8345639(Fax No.)

PRICE E & CO
BOX 61068
MARSHALLTOWN
2107
011-8331975(Tel No.)
011-8346801(Fax No.)

REID S P & MACKEURTAN INC
BOX 969
JOHANNESBURG
2000
8342161(Tel No.)
8383544(Fax No.)

RICE, RINALDI & CO
BOX 61757
MARSHALLTOWN
2107
8362440(Tel No.)
8382919(Fax No.)

ROYDEN ROCHE & CO
BOX 61717
MARSHALLTOWN
2107
8364786(Tel No.)
8369614(Fax No.)

SENEKAL, MOUTON & KITSHOFF INC
BOX 61346
MARSHALLTOWN
2107
8338110(Tel No.)
8369118(Fax No.)

SHAPIRO B INC
BOX 4295
JOHANNESBURG
2000
8331430(Tel No.)
8365911(Fax No.)

SILVIS, BARNARD, JACOBS, MELLET & CO INC
BOX 62200
MARSHALLTOWN
2107
8362510(Tel No.)
8341085(Fax No.)

SIMMONS V H & CO INC
239 THE STOCK EXCHANGE
17 DIAGONAL STREET
JOHANNESBURG
2001
8323121(Tel No.)
8348485(Fax No.)

SIMPSON, MCKIE INC
BOX 2055
JOHANNESBURG
2000
8367415(Tel No.)
8344068(Fax No.)

SOLMS J & CO
BOX 61940
MARSHALLTOWN
2107
8322171(Tel No.)
8368856(Fax No.)

THERON & CO
BOX 61632
MARSHALLTOWN
2107
8342811(Tel No.)
8342690(Fax No.)

TURNER G O
BOX 896
JOHANNESBURG
2000
8386731(Tel No.)
8346351(Fax No.)

TURNER PATERSON FAURE INC
BOX 61759
MARSHALLTOWN
2107
8321586(Tel No.)
8385648(Fax No.)

VAN RENSBURG P L J & PARTNERS INC
BOX 61465
MARSHALLTOWN
2107
8360381(Tel No.)
8369924(Fax No.)

PIETERMARITZBURG

ED HERN, RUDOLPH INC
BOX 502
PIETERMARITZBURG
3200
0331-946757(Tel No.)
0331-949535(Fax No.)

MARTIN & CO INC
BOX 594
PIETERMARITZBURG
3200
0331-429168(Tel No.)
0331-421561(Fax No.)

PORT ELIZABETH

FERGUSSON BROS, HALL, STEWART & CO INC
BOX 623
PORT ELIZABETH
6000
041-521087(Tel No.)
041-554314(Fax No.)

KAPLAN & STEWART INC
BOX 714
PORT ELIZABETH
6000
041-563434(Tel No.)
041-560294(Fax No.)

PRETORIA

DAVIS, BORKUM, HARE & CO INC
BOX 606
PRETORIA
0001
012-218141(Tel No.)
012-218161(Fax No.)

ED HERN, RUDOLPH INC
BOX 6287
PRETORIA
0001
012-3227583(Tel No.)
012-3226332(Fax No.)

FRANKEL, MAX POLLAK, VINDERINE INC
BOX 142
PRETORIA
0001
012-3203070(Tel No.)
012-3204000(Fax No.)

GEORGE HUYSAMER & PARTNERS INC
BOX 40738
ARCADIA
0007
012-3417851(Tel No.)
012-3417859(Fax No.)

RONDEBOSCH

SIMPSON, MCKIE INC
BOX 4805
CAPE TOWN
8000
021-6857990(Tel No.)
021-6852031(Fax No.)

SANDTON

FRANKEL, MAX POLLAK, VINDERINE INC
BOX 781403
SANDTON
2199
011-8832337(Tel No.)
011-8832337(Fax No.)

SWITZERLAND

EDEY, ROGERS & CO INC
P O BOX CASEPOSTLE 3521211
GENEVA
SWITZERLAND
0941-22-467969(Tel No.)
0941-22-476395(Fax No.)

UNITED KINGDOM

MACINTOSH, MARTIN
42 NEW BROAD STREET
LONDON
EC2MIJD
UNITED KINGDOM
0944-71-4573835(Tel No.)
0944-71-3744815(Fax No.)

WINDHOEK

GEORGE HUYSAMER & PARTNERS INC
BOX 196
WINDHOEK
9000
061-37477(Tel No.)
061-227321(Fax No.)

STOCK BROKING FIRMS & PARTNERS

BENONI

FRANKEL, MAX POLLAK, VINDERINE INC :
G NESTADT

BLOEMFONTEIN

ED HERN, RUDOLPH INC :
D J RICHTER

HERBST H A B INC :
M J VERMEULEN

CAPE TOWN

BALDERSON E W INC :
G M VAN BESOUW

DAVIS, BORKUM, HARE & CO INC :
R J PYOTT, P R M LOMBERG

ED HERN, RUDOLPH INC :
J MAARTINS, J L VAN ZYL

FERGUSSON BROS, HALL, STEWART & CO INC :
E K C HALL

FRANKEL, MAX POLLAK, VINDERINE INC :
G J STEENKAMP, P J JOSLIN

GEORGE HUYSAMER & PARTNERS INC :
J A BAARD, B ROBERTS

IVOR JONES, ROY & CO INC :
D E CLELAND

KAPLAN & STEWART INC :
M K FLORENCE

LOWENTHAL & CO :
G N ROSSITER

MARTIN & CO INC :
S A BIRD

MATHISON & HOLLIDGE INC :
P E BARTHOLOMEW, J MATHER, K A WHITE

SENEKAL, MOUTON & KITSHOFF INC :
H J TERREBLANCHE

SIMPSON, MCKIE INC :
K J M FRATER, D R STRONG, J R CRAVEN
J O MELROSE, J R A SIMPSON
P TRENGROVE JONES, G ROSSITER

DURBAN

DAVIS, BORKUM, HARE & CO INC :
R R FIRTH, C A MASSEY

FERGUSSON BROS, HALL, STEWART & CO INC :
J B CRADOCK, C N CROWHURST
G J COLLINGWOOD

FRANKEL, MAX POLLAK, VINDERINE INC :
D S CAIRNS, D R BENNETT

MATHISON & HOLLIDGE INC :
A J DEAKIN, I G J JOUBERT

EAST LONDON

FRANKEL, MAX POLLAK, VINDERINE INC :
B A RUSSELL

GEORGE

GEORGE HUYSAMER & PARTNERS INC :
S F VAN DEVENTER

JOHANNESBURG

ANDERSON JD & CO INC :
M R BASFORD, P L MCIVER, A R CARTER
H M BOONZAAIER, C N BOOTH, D DU TOIT
C FREEMANTLE, W LAWSON-TURNBULL
MRS S H STRUMPHER, P C IUEL
B WILLIAMSON, P A FIELDGATE

ANDERSON, WILSON & PARTNERS INC :
W ROUX, M St J WYCHE, C W McCABE
M L SIMS, R J HASKINS, M A B BLACK
F J RAHN, B B BLACK, D J ELLISH
R HOCHREITER

BALDERSON E W INC :
J E BALDERSON, C J BALDERSON
T H BRAMWELL-JONES, B K BROWN-BROWN
A D THOMPSON, N GOODWIN, J B M WEEPLE
G R GOODWIN

BEN JANSE VAN RENSBURG :
B B T JANSE VAN RENSBURG
H JANSE VAN RENSBURG

BERNSTEIN B P :
G de JAGER, MRS A STURINO
DR J B E JACOBSON

BONER & FREEMANTLE INC :
N BONER, L R FREEMANTLE

DAVIES B C & CO :
B C DAVIES

DAVIS, BORKUM, HARE & CO INC :
M M BORKUM, H A HARE, J A BISHOP
J D K EYLES, H J BORKUM, G R JOUBERT
P A GREYVENSTYN, N W BAKER, M S REBE
J S MORRIS, D C FELL, G A P MONTANO
A C FIGGE, A HARE, G S CHAPMAN
A C FARINHA, P A EYLES, A G J HARRISON
MISS N G WADDINGTON, DR E C POHL
F WILENSKY, G A WAKFER

DE WITT, MORGAN & CO :

P P M DE WITT, W J MORGAN

DIAMOND C :
C DIAMOND

ED HERN, RUDOLPH INC :
E A HERN, M A BOLUS, J BLERSCH
A E MCCONNOCHIE, A G MUNCHA
A J VAN VELDEN

EDEY, ROGERS & CO INC :
M B EDEY, P B J ALLEN, F R BUSETTI
J A ROGERS, M SHAM

FERGUSSON BROS, HALL, STEWART & CO INC :
P R A FERGUSON, P L B CLUCAS
M F FERGUSON, W H BOWLER, P D JARDINE
I O DAVIDSON, D C RITCHIE
S M RUBENSTEIN, A A VAN HEERDEN
J SCOTT

FRANKEL, MAX POLLAK, VINDERINE INC :
L F G FRANKEL, S L FRANKEL
G ROTHSCHILD, A VINDERINE
MISS H COOPER, D H SHAPIRO, T AMOILS
A DERMEDGOGLOU, S A EBRAHIM
M J FISHER, M FRANKS, G FRANTZESKOU
G J POULTNEY, R STOPPELMAN, D EVANS
S L BACHER, R W GARDY, K G KARTUN
J L LOUBSER, P NICOLATOS, S G H OLIVER
J C RAYNER, L D ROSENBERG
R E WAKELING, J SHAPIRO

FRIEDLANDER L R :
L R FRIEDLANDER

G O'FLAHERTY :
G A O'FLAHERTY

GEORGE HUYSAMER & PARTNERS INC :
G G HUYSAMER, N C COOPER, W STALS
L M LOUBSER, W STALTS, T C VERMAAK
G G HUYSAMER (JNR)

GOLDING & CO :
B R GOLDING, T E SCHLEBUSCH

HAYES, CUTTEN & CO :
J A CUTTEN, P F SUTTON

HERBST H A B INC :
H A B HERBST, H J LE ROES

HUMAN M P :
M P HUMAN

IRISH, MENELL & ROSENBERG INC :
M C IRISH, R A LEDERLE, W ROSENBERG
G L ROSENBERG

IVOR JONES, ROY & CO INC :
I R JONES, R S ROY, I K ANDERSON
D L BROOKING, E M WOODS, B L WALKER
B C SMITHER, C H WOOD, J G GREENER
P C ENSLIN, P J MCALLISTER, C A WILDE
G D BELL

KAPLAN & STEWART INC :
M STEWART, J REID, S M LORGE
B L MONTGOMERY, W EDWARDS

KRUGER & CO :
F J T KRUGER

LEWER & CO :
D O C LEWER, R D LEWER, M ARONOWITZ
P R LEWER, C C WOTHERSPOON
D OBERHOLZER

LOWENTHAL & CO :
N D LOWENTHAL, M F LOWENTHAL
T D PARISI, A HURWITZ

LURIE, JOHNSTON & CO INC :
R LURIE, M R JOHNSTON, E V SAMMONS
R D PROUDFOOT, W J FENTON

MARTIN & CO INC :
W T FLOQUET, J F TOLKEN, R I K JESSE
R G L STUART, L C PENGILLY
B D PHILLIPS, D C S GLYN
N FREDERICKSZ, M L HOFFMANN, J K MILLS
J G BORRAGEIRO, C E MAYNARD
M L M BARNS, A G WIGGILL
B E VON GLEHN, P A J TISON, J O'REGAN
C VAN HOLDT

MARTINDALE, STACEY, TROLLIP INC :
J D MARTINDALE, M E STACEY
A G TROLLIP, C H A DU TOIT, C VOUNNOU

MATHISON & HOLLIDGE INC :
C L HOLLIDGE, W G BATY, T C DEVEREUX
C G HOLLIDGE, N N C LOUW
H O MULHOLLAND, M J R O'FARRELL
P G REDMAN

MEADES DE KLERK INC :
D J MEADES, G M DE KLERK, J KRITZINGER

O'FLAHERTY G & CO :
G O'FLAHERTY

PRICE E & CO :
MISS E PRICE

REID S P & MACKEURTAN INC :
G G MACKEURTAN, MRS A C H MACKEURTAN
N R BURNETT

RICE, RINALDI & CO :
V RICE, R C RINALDI, R W FIELDGATE
C M VAN ZYL

ROYDEN ROCHE & CO :
R W ROCHE

SENEKAL, MOUTON & KITSHOFF INC :
J F MOUTON, J MACRIDES, D P BRINK
J H SCHOEMAN, H B L KLOPPER
L GELDENHUYS, W F VAN NIEKERK
J H ASHTON, J A GROBBELAAR
C J SLABBERT, J DU TOIT
J M BREDENKAMP, A O PIETERSE
J DU PLESSIS

SHAPIRO B INC :
G D CAHN

SILVIS, BARNARD, JACOBS, MELLET & CO INC :
J SILVIS, P A BARNARD, K G JACOBS
S M MELLET, J E VAN DER HOVEN, N OU
DR P J VAN SCHAIK, MRS R Y KEARNEY

SIMMONS V H & CO INC :
B MICHEL, J FISHER, T S PLANT

D W SHAW, MRS C BRAUN, A B WILLIAMS

SIMPSON, MCKIE INC :
N R O BROWN, D J COBBETT
I J FRASER JONES, I D MACLARTY
T P MURPHY, L G WILLIAMS, R S YALDWYN
W S YEOWART, M C SOEKOE, C C NIEHAUS
H E BLUMENTHAL, K I BASSETT, F GRAY
MISS H VOLLMER

SOLMS J & CO :
R V TODD, J G SOLMS

THERON & CO :
J P THERON, F J M POTGIETER

TURNER G O :
J H TURNER, R D EARL

TURNER PATERSON FAURE INC :
J F TURNER, A A PATERSON, K P FAURE

VAN RENSBURG P L J & PARTNERS INC :
P L J VAN RENSBURG, L VAN RENSBURG
D J VAN DEN BERG, T J GOUS, G LAMPEN
P VAN RENSBURG

PIETERMARITZBURG

ED HERN, RUDOLPH INC :
D FRANKISH

MARTIN & CO INC :
G C CROOKES, A M SMYTHE

PORT ELIZABETH

FERGUSSON BROS, HALL, STEWART & CO INC :
C MURRAY, A G VOGEL

KAPLAN & STEWART INC :
H J MARKS

PRETORIA

DAVIS, BORKUM, HARE & CO INC :
O A DAVIS

ED HERN, RUDOLPH INC :
A O LAAS

GEORGE HUYSAMER & PARTNERS INC :
G JANSE VAN VUUREN, L M LOUBSER

RONDEBOSCH

SIMPSON, MCKIE INC :
B H L MACDONALD

SANDTON

FRANKEL, MAX POLLAK, VINDERINE INC :
R M LACHMAN

SWITZERLAND

EDEY, ROGERS & CO INC :
T A BLENCH

UNITED KINGDOM

MACINTOSH, MARTIN :
A GARNETT

WINDHOEK

GEORGE HUYSAMER & PARTNERS INC :
L A HANEKOM

TRANSFER SECRETARIES

Anglovaal Ltd
P O Box 62379
Marshalltown
2107
011-634 9111

Argus Holdings Ltd
P O Box 1014
Johannesburg
2000
011-633 2994

CIH Trading & Finance (Pvt) Ltd
P O Box 1342
Bulawayo
Zimbabwe
092634-70636

Capri Group Ltd
P O Box 690
Harare
Zimbabwe
092634-737005

Cementation Co (Africa) Ltd
P O Box 2371
Southdale
2135
011-639 9111

Central Registrars Ltd
P O Box 4844
Johannesburg
2000
011-331 0051

Consolidated Share Registrars Ltd
P O Box 61051
Marshalltown
2107
011-492 1620

Coopers & Lybrand Services (Pty) Ltd
P O Box 702
Harare
Zimbabwe
0926 34 702771

Dalys Ltd
P O Box 1177
Durban
4000
031-29 4371

Ernst & Young
P O Box 1857
Windhoek
9000
061-38 260

Finpak Registrars (Pty) Ltd
2100 Cartwrights Corner House
Adderley Street
Cape Town
8000
021-418 5040

First Transfer Secretaries (Pvt) Ltd
P O Box 437
Bulawayo
Zimbabwe
092634 - 702905

Fraser Street Registrars (Pty) Ltd
P O Box 61178
Marshalltown
2107
011-491 0911

Gold Equity Registrars (Pty) Ltd
P O Box 62185
Marshalltown
2107
011-834 5623

Gold Fields of SA Ltd
P O Box 1167
Johannesburg
2000
011-639 9111

Investment Registrars (Pty) Ltd
P O Box 9167
Johannesburg
2000
011-725 6004

Johannesburg Consolidated Inv Co Ltd
P O Box 590
Johannesburg
2000
011-373 9111

KPMG Aiken & Peat
P O Box 7400
Johannesburg
2000
011-332 7111

KPMG Peat Marwick
P O Box 702
Harare
Zimbabwe
09263 962831

Kilgetty Trust (Pty) Ltd
P O Box 4033
Cape Town
8000
021-21 1860

Lonrho Zimbabwe Management Serv (Pvt)Ltd
P O Box 1480
Harare
Zimbabwe
706661

Mercantile Registrars Ltd
P O Box 1053
Johannesburg
2000
011-333 8181

Natal Registrars (Pty) Ltd
P O Box 548
Durban
4000
031-305 2781

Natal Securities Trust (Pty) Ltd
P O Box 225
Durban
4000
031-304 9851

National Tyre Services Ltd
P O Box 3018
Harare
Zimbabwe
092634-3018

Ovbel Registrars Ltd
Tannery Park
23 Belmont Road
Rondebosch
7700
021-685 4032

PW Business Services (Pty) Ltd
P O Box 1453
Gaberone
Botswana
09267-351081

Picardi Investments Ltd
P O Box 1134
Cape Town
8000
021-419 2220

Piyushkant Virendrakumar Desai
P O Box 867
Gaberone
Botswana
09267-353077

R D Hugo
9 Hopkins Rd
Salt River
7925
021-55 2975

Rand Merchant Bank Ltd
P O Box 786273
Sandton
2146
011-883 3650

Rand Registrars Ltd
P O Box 82549
Southdale
2135
011-835 1016

Retail Share Registrars (Pty) Ltd
P O Box 23087
Claremont
7735
021-683 2140

SARB
P O Box 427
Pretoria
0001
012-313 3911

Sagit Transfer Secretaries (Pvt) ltd
P O Box 11
Harare
Zimbabwe
092634-738814

Sagit Trust Ltd
P O Box 11
Harare
Zimbabwe
092634-738 814

Stability Services (Pty) Ltd
6th Floor
112 Kerk Street
Johannesburg
2001
011-337 4030

T A Trading Corporation (Pvt) Ltd
P O Box 3546
Harare
Zimbabwe
702905

Technical & Industrial Investments Ltd
P O Box 106
Stellenbosch
7600
02231-3801

The Dagbreek Trust
P O Box 8161
Johannesburg
011-776 9111

Tuffias Shapiro Braude
P O Box 87009
Houghton
2041
011-486 1460

Union Provident Trust (Botswana) Ltd
P O Box 41015
Gaberone
Botswana
09267-41015

Union Provident Trust SA Ltd
P O Box 2322
Johannesburg
2000
011-833 6700

Zimbabwe Banking Corporation Ltd
P O Box 3198
Harare
Zimbabwe
092634-735011

ABACUS INDUSTRIAL HOLDINGS LTD

ABBREVIATION : ABACUS

JSE SHORT CODE : ABA

SECTOR : Industrial-Electronics, Electrical & Bat

SHAREHOLDERS

Who Owns Whom's Assessment of the Identity of the Ultimate Controlling Shareholder:
HOSKENS VIA IGI

SHAREHOLDER	PERCENTAGE 1992	1991
SAFEGRO NOM P/L	80 0	61 0
ABSA NOM P/L	5 9	---
SLOFAM NOM P/L	---	1 1
FIRST NAT NOM P/L	---	2 5
VOLKSKAS NOM P/L	---	9 1
IGI BOTSWANA LTD	---	7 6
TOTAL	85 9	81 1

DIRECTORS :
CAPPER TM (Financial Director)
COULSON TG (Chairman),DAVIDSON KM ,IRISH MC
LEWIS IMA ,MOXON JRT NATHAN L ,NOSSEL H

REGISTRATION NUMBER : 05/23582/06

REGISTERED OFFICE
162 Anderson St, Johannesburg
2001
TEL: 011-335 1911
FAX 011-29 0491

TRANSFER SECRETARY
Mercantile Registrars Ltd
P O Box 1053, Johannesburg
2000
TEL 011-333 8181

COMPANY SECRETARY
WT Green

NATURE OF BUSINESS
The activities of the group consist primarily of the manufacture and distribution of doors and audio equipment, as well as property ownership

BANKERS :
First National Bank of SA Ltd
Nedcor Bank Ltd

AUDITORS :
BDO Spencer Steward

FAMILIAR BRAND NAMES
BERGSUN DOORS,BRUPLY,CAPE DOORS & BOARDS
DOORCOR,DOORS & DEURE,LTN,MARILYN,ROBECOR
SUPERSONIC,TEMPEST,ZADCO

CONTRIBUTION BY ACTIVITY
N/A

YEAR END : March

DIVIDEND : (Ldr)23/06/89 (Pay)30/06/89

NUMBER OF EMPLOYEES : 4474

CAPITAL STRUCTURE

	AUTHORISED	ISSUED
Ords 1c	200000000	87762730
18% Sec Conv Red Debentures 25c	24682198	24682198

FINANCIAL STATISTICS (AT FINANCIAL YEAR END)

(Amts in R'000)	1992 Mar	1991 Feb	1990 Feb	1989 Feb	1988 Feb
Ord S/H Int	29493	28813	29555	164436	132887
Long Trm Loans	14679	31496	67830	59252	9925
Iss Ord Share	87763	162256	162256	162256	152798
Total Liab	77756	122044	161515	129997	30831
Current Liab	63077	90548	93685	70745	20906
Total Assets	107249	150506	182571	294433	163718
Intang Assets	*	351	8499	*	*
Current Assets	68831	94219	109856	110011	66215
Debtors	33217	47912	47634	47449	23336
Inventory	35614	42895	43023	50386	15217
Turnover	199688	204576	225388	188103	95364
Oper Profit	-19137	-890	-6376	22067	16869
Interest Paid	10210	9745	18053	-	1351
Tax Paid	-243	44	4	18	1
Prf af Int&Tax	-28999	-9550	-17625	22049	15517
Prf att Ord Sh	-22502	-6643	-15743	21294	14346
Btm Line Earn	-32028	-1207	-126013	24538	14412
Dividend Paid	-	-	-	11845	9168
Mkt Prce(c) YE	25	35	48	75	100
Depreciation	3262	2249	6365	7246	4190

PER SHARE STATISTICS (CENTS)

	1992	1991	1990	1989	1988
Net Asst Val	33 61	17 54	12 98	101 34	86 97
Net Earnings	-32 60	-4 09	-9 70	13 23	9 98
Dividends	-	-	-	7 30	6 00
Cash Flow	-25 73	-2 71	-5 78	17 73	12 90

RATIOS AND OTHER INFORMATION

	1992	1991	1990	1989	1988
Mrk Cap(R000)	21941	56790	77883	121692	152798
Current Ratio	1 09	1 04	1 17	1 56	3 17
Quik/Acid Tst	0 53	0 57	0 71	0 84	2 44
A/C Rec T/ovr	5 55	4 27	4 73	3 96	4 09
Tot Ass T/ovr	1 72	1 36	1 23	0 64	0 58
Debt/Ass Rat	0 73	0 65	0 88	0 41	0 13
L T L Tot Ass	0 14	0 05	0 37	0 17	0 01
Debt to Eqity	2 64	3 42	5 43	0 74	0 17
Interest Cover	-1 87	-0 09	-0 24	-	12 49
Oper Prof Mrg	-9 58	-0 44	-2 83	11 73	17 69
Net Prof Marg%	-11 27	-3 25	-6 98	11 32	15 04
Ret on Assets	-16 38	0 16	0 24	7 49	10 30
Ret on Equity%	-70 43	-23 06	-53 27	12 95	10 80
Price/Earnings	-0 77	-8 56	-4 95	5 67	10 02
Divid Cover	-	-	-	1 81	1 66
Divid Yield	-	-	-	9 73	6 00
Earning Yield%	-130 40	-11 69	-20 21	17 64	9 98
NAV % Mrk Pr	134 42	50 12	27 04	135 12	86 97
Effec Tax Rate	0 83	-0 46	-0 02	0 08	0 01
Def Interval	-2 56	-14 48	13 15	2 97	0 31
Sus Grth Rate	-76 30	-23 06	-53 27	5 75	3 90

SUBSIDIARY & ASSOCIATED COMPANIES

ABACUS ASSETS (PTY) LTD
AMS MANAGEMENT SERVICES (PTY) LTD
BRUPLY DOORS (PTY) LTD
CALCULATED INVESTMENTS (PTY) LTD
EXPRESS FURNITURE MANUFACTURERS (PTY) LT
FINE TUNE INVESTMENTS (PTY) LTD

FIRST PRIZE INVESTMENTS (PTY) LTD
HOMECO (PTY) LTD
INTERBOARD SWAZILAND (PTY) LTD
KEYBOARD PROJECTS (PTY) LTD
MELBOARD (PTY) LIMITED
TEMPEST ELECTRONICS (PTY) LTD
TEMPEST HOLDINGS LTD
TEMPEST INTERNATIONAL (PTY) LTD
TEMPEST PROPERTIES (PTY) LTD
TEMPEST RADIO & HI-FI (PTY) LTD

INVESTMENTS

None

ABBEY HOLDINGS LTD

ABBREVIATION : ABBEY

JSE SHORT CODE : ABY

SECTOR : Financial-Property

SHAREHOLDERS

Who Owns Whom's Assessment of the Identity of the Ultimate Controlling Shareholder: DIRECTORS

SHAREHOLDER	PERCENTAGE 1992	1991
ABBEY CONTROLLING INTEREST P/L	33 1	2 0
NAT BRICK HOLDINGS P/L	20 0	17 4
QUARTET INV LTD	16 9	---
RABFAM SECURITIES P/L	6 3	---
GREEK R N TRUSTEES DORFMAN CHILDREN	6 1	6 1
DORFMAN D	4 2	4 2
LUCK A	1 8	1 8
PCSA HOLDINGS P/L	--	48 0
NAT PROPERTIES & INDUSTRIES P/L	- -	6 3
TOTAL	88 4	85 9

DIRECTORS :
CHAPMAN DE ,EDELSTEIN WH ,RABIN J
RABINOWITZ BP (Chairman),SAREMBOCK ML
SCHAFFER JE

REGISTRATION NUMBER : 83/08037/06

REGISTERED OFFICE
1002 NBS Waldorf, 80 St Georges Mall
Cape Town
8001
TEL 021-22 2424
FAX 021-22 2626

TRANSFER SECRETARY
Mercantile Registrars Ltd
P O Box 1053, Johannesburg
2000
TEL 011-333 8181

COMPANY SECRETARY
C Penny

NATURE OF BUSINESS
An investment holding company with controlling interests in quoted Property Corporation, Fenix Industries, and Debonair Group The activities consists of textile manufacturing, property holding , development and trading and share trading.

BANKERS :
First National Bank of SA Ltd, Bankorp Ltd
Nedcor Bank Ltd

AUDITORS :
Coopers Theron Du Toit

FAMILIAR BRAND NAMES
N/A

CONTRIBUTION BY ACTIVITY
N/A

YEAR END : December

DIVIDEND : Ords no par value

Special No 10	(Ldr)05/01/90	(Pay)17/01/90	Amt(c)40
Interim No 11	(Ldr)23/03/90	(Pay)05/04/90	Amt(c)5 5
Special No 12	(Ldr)23/03/90	(Pay)05/04/90	Amt(c)82 5
Special No 13	(Ldr)13/07/90	(Pay)27/07/90	Amt(c)40
Final No 14	(Ldr)14/09/90	(Pay)28/09/90	Amt(c)12

NUMBER OF EMPLOYEES : 863

CAPITAL STRUCTURE

	AUTHORISED	ISSUED
Ords no par value	30000000	17750000

FINANCIAL STATISTICS (AT FINANCIAL YEAR END)

(Amts in R'000)	1991 Dec	1990 Jun	1989 Jun	1988 Jun	1987 Jun
Ord S/H Int	34604	44111	66110	63893	57683
Long Trm Loans	34062	15835	29644	229912	34452
Iss Ord Share	17750	17750	17750	17750	16000
Total Liab	68568	42844	60739	296556	47267
Current Liab	34506	27009	31095	66644	12815
Total Assets	103172	81176	120790	360449	104950
Intang Assets	*	5779	6059	*	*
Current Assets	54999	64598	56264	117729	6351
Debtors	17307	14497	11043	13185	3150
Inventory	3854	2871	22224	965	-
Oper Profit	-13480	-43	4151	20084	8067
Interest Paid	9997	2228	5990	13428	2886
Tax Paid	-269	408	2229	1785	1087
Prf af Int&Tax	-18100	3495	5557	4871	4094
Prf att Ord Sh	-15233	2553	6935	5942	2715
Btm Line Earn	-22356	8595	5276	4495	2490
Dividend Paid	-	31950	2928	2397	1050
Mkt Prce(c) YE	100	160	150	150	450
Depreciation	1700	563	351	315	64

PER SHARE STATISTICS (CENTS)

Net Asst Val	194 95	215 95	338 32	359 96	360 52
Net Earnings	-85 80	14 38	39 10	33 50	22 20
Dividends	-	180 00	16 50	13 50	7 00
Cash Flow	51 95	16 37	16 96	13 34	17 37

RATIOS AND OTHER INFORMATION

Mrk Cap(R000)	17750	28400	26625	26625	72000
Current Ratio	1 59	2 39	1 81	1 77	0 50
Quik/Acid Tst	1 48	2 29	1 09	1 75	0 50
Debt/Ass Rat	0 51	0 34	0 28	0 75	0 24

L T L Tot Ass	0 17	0 00	0 02	0 57	0 12
Debt to Eqity	1 51	0 62	0 50	4 24	0 44
Interest Cover	-1 34	0 71	1 16	1 50	2 80
Ret on Assets	-5 41	7 83	15 08	6 64	7 69
Ret on Equity%	-29 35	5 79	10 49	9 30	4 71
Price/Earnings	-1 17	11 13	3 84	4 48	20 27
Divid Cover	-	0 08	2 37	2 48	3 17
Divid Yield	-	112 50	11 00	9 00	1 56
Earning Yield%	-85 80	8 99	26 07	22 33	4 93
NAV % Mrk Pr	194 95	134 97	225 54	239 97	80 12
Effec Tax Rate	-	17 23	38 17	12 36	-
Def Interval	-1 85	2 92	3 54	100 54	6 85
Sus Grth Rate	-44 02	-66 64	6 06	5 55	2 89

SUBSIDIARY & ASSOCIATED COMPANIES

ABBEY (FNX) HOLDINGS LTD
ABBEY (PROPCOR) HOLDINGS LTD
ABBEY MANAGEMENT SERVICES LTD
ABBEY TRADING LTD
FENIX INDUSTRIES LTD
LANSDOWNE TEXTILE INDUSTRIES (PTY) LTD
PROPERTY CORPORATION OF SA LTD
PROPGROUP (RETPROP) HOLDINGS LTD
PROPGROUP MANAGEMENT SERVICES LTD

INVESTMENTS

COMPASS PROPERTY HOLDINGS LTD (UNSEC VAR (136830 SH)
QUALITATIVE CONSULTANCY (PTY) LTD (17%)

ABCON PROPERTIES LTD

ABBREVIATION : ABCON

JSE SHORT CODE : ABN

SECTOR : Financial-Property Loan Stock

SHAREHOLDERS

Who Owns Whom's Assessment of the Identity of the Ultimate Controlling Shareholder:
DIRECTORS

SHAREHOLDER	PERCENTAGE 1992	1991
MOMENTUM LIFE ASSURE LTD	27 0	---
EIGHTY ONE MAIN STREET NOM LTD	22 8	---
SIXTY SIX MARSHALL STREET NOM P/L	7 4	---
STD BANK NOM TVL P/L	4 1	---
KNOESEN H	3 3	---
SA PROPERTY INV P/L	3 3	---
BRICK M	3 1	---
BRICK E M	2 9	---
METAL IND GROUP PENS FUND	2 9	---
BRICK M F	2 8	---
ENGINEERING INDUSTRIES PENS FUND	2 0	---
NESER M S B	1 8	---
SEVEN SIXTY TWO PARKWOOD LTD	1 8	---
NESER MSB, JM, LC & LEONARD M	1 5	---
DESBAR INV P/L	1 2	---
KROOK S B	1 1	---
KROOK R D	1 1	---
TOTAL	90 0	---

DIRECTORS :
BOLLEURS AA ,CONRADIE DCU DR (Chairman)
CRONJE GS ,GEYER DA ,KREINER L ,VAN DEN BERG MP
VONTAS NG (Managing Director

REGISTRATION NUMBER : 91/04879/06

REGISTERED OFFICE
Abcon House, 45 Wierda Road West
Wierda Valley, Sandton
2146
TEL 011-884 6666
FAX 011-883 5765

TRANSFER SECRETARY
Consolidated Share Registrars Ltd
P O Box 61051, Marshalltown
2107
TEL 011-492 1620

COMPANY SECRETARY
Abreal Property Management Services (Pty) Ltd

NATURE OF BUSINESS
Abcon holds a portfolio of 29 office & industrial buildings situated in the PWV area The company is managed by Abcon Property Management Services

BANKERS :
Nedcor Bank Ltd

AUDITORS :
Kessel Feinstein

FAMILIAR BRAND NAMES
N/A

CONTRIBUTION BY ACTIVITY
Offices (Property Type Spread) (59 0%)
High Tech / Industrial (22 0%)
Motorcity One & Two (19 0%)

YEAR END : February

DIVIDEND : Units

Final	(Ldr)24/04/92	(Pay)30/04/92	Amt(c)14 169
Interim	(Ldr)23/10/92	(Pay)30/10/92	Amt(c)27 925

NUMBER OF EMPLOYEES : 5

CAPITAL STRUCTURE

	AUTHORISED	ISSUED
Ords 1c (1 Ord 1 Deb)	45000000	41840713
Unsec Var Rate Debs 493c	41840713	41840713

FINANCIAL STATISTICS (AT FINANCIAL YEAR END)

(Amts in R'000)	1992 Feb	1991 Nov
Ord S/H Int	418	418
Long Trm Loans	206652	206590
Iss Ord Share	41841	41841
Total Liab	212942	206590
Current Liab	6290	-
Total Assets	213360	207008
Current Assets	40537	25000
Debtors	4074	-
Turnover	5100	-
Oper Profit	3981	-
Tax Paid	6	-
Prf af Int&Tax	5928	-
Prf att Ord Sh	6	-
Btm Line Earn	6	-

Dividend Paid	6	-
Mkt Prce(c) YE	500	-

PER SHARE STATISTICS (CENTS)

Net Asst Val	1 00	1 00
Net Earnings	57 00	-
Dividends	57 00	-
Cash Flow	56 98	-

RATIOS AND OTHER INFORMATION

Mrk Cap(R000)	209205	-
Current Ratio	6 44	-
Quik/Acid Tst	6 44	-
A/C Rec T/ovr	1 25	-
Tot Ass T/ovr	0 02	-
Debt/Ass Rat	1 00	-
L T L Tot Ass	0 97	-
Debt to Eqity	509 42	-
Oper Prof Mrg	78 06	-
Net Prof Marg%	0 12	-
Ret on Assets	2 78	-
Ret on Equity%	1 44	-
Price/Earnings	8 77	-
Divid Cover	1 00	-
Divid Yield	11 40	-
Earning Yield%	11 40	-
NAV % Mrk Pr	0 20	-
Sus Grth Rate	0 00	-

SUBSIDIARY & ASSOCIATED COMPANIES

BOLIVER PROPERTIES (PTY) LTD
CLIDET NO 32 (PTY) LTD
CLIDET NO 27 (PTY) LTD
CLIDET NO 35 (PTY) LTD
CONWES SHARE BLOCK (PTY) LTD
ERF 766 WOODMEAD EXT 22 (PTY) LTD
HILCAR INVESTMENTS (PTY) LTD
LENCHEN PROPERTY DEVELOPMENTS (PTY) LTD
LYNN HOLD PROPERTY (PTY) LTD
MOTORCITY CENTRE (INDUSTRIA) (PTY) LTD
PORTION 1 ERF 59 VERWOERDBURG (PTY) LTD
PORTION 2 OF LOT 694 FERNDALE (PTY) LTD
PORTION 3 ERF 59 VERWOERDBURG (PTY) LTD
PORTION 4 ERF 59 VERWOEDBURG (PTY) LTD
PROBATE INVESTMENTS (PTY) LTD
RIVWES PROPERTY MANAGERS (PTY) LTD
SANDHAVON OFFICE PARK PORTION 3 (PTY) LT
SANDTON SQUARE (PTY) LTD
STRYDOM PARK EXT 22 (PTY) LTD
WIERDA VALLEY PLACE (PTY) LTD

INVESTMENTS

None

ABERDARE CABLES AFRICA LTD

ABBREVIATION : ABERDARE

JSE SHORT CODE : ABR

SECTOR : Industrial-Electronics, Electrical & Bat

SHAREHOLDERS

Who Owns Whom's Assessment of the Identity of the Ultimate Controlling Shareholder: W VENTER VIA POWERTECH

SHAREHOLDER	PERCENTAGE 1992	1991
ABERDARE INV P/L	34 3	34 4
CONSOLIDATED CABLE INV P/L	34 3	34 4
POWERTECH INV HOLDINGS P/L	12 8	12 8
POWERTECH PROPERTIES & INV LTD	7 4	7 4
CMB NOM P/L	1 5	---
STD BANK NOM TVL P/L	1 2	1 2
FORDOUN INV CO P/L	-	1 2
SANLAM	---	1 5
TOTAL	91 6	92 9

DIRECTORS :
BARNES ID ,IRWIN JB ,MCKENZIE DB
MEIRING CJ (Commercial Director)
SEYMOUR RA (Manufacturing Director),SNEDDEN DC
VENTER WP DR,WATT PA (Executive Chairman)
WILSON PB (Managing Director)
WOOLARD CC (Financial Director

REGISTRATION NUMBER : 05/22805/06

REGISTERED OFFICE
Main Road, Eastleigh
Edenvale
1610
TEL 011-609 4020
FAX 011-452 6237

TRANSFER SECRETARY
Mercantile Registrars Ltd
P O Box 1053, Johannesburg
2000
TEL 011 333 8181

COMPANY SECRETARY
P C Desai

NATURE OF BUSINESS
The group is a manufacturer & supplier of power, telecommunications & instrumentation cable in copper, aluminium & optical fibre The company has a joint venture arrangement with the Berzack group for the manufacture of cable drums & cable accessories, & specialised materials for cable manufacture

BANKERS :
Standard Bank of SA Ltd

AUDITORS :
KPMG Aiken & Peat

FAMILIAR BRAND NAMES
ABERDARE,AGRIDAC,AIRDAC,DURACAST

CONTRIBUTION BY ACTIVITY
N/A

YEAR END : December

DIVIDEND : Ords 50c

Interim No 62	(Ldr)31/08/90	(Pay)14/09/90	Amt(c)58
Final No 63	(Ldr)28/03/91	(Pay)26/04/91	Amt(c)92
Interim No 64	(Ldr)11/10/91	(Pay)18/10/91	Amt(c)55
Final No 65	(Ldr)13/04/92	(Pay)27/04/92	Amt(c)77

Interim No 66 (Ldr)09/10/92 (Pay)16/10/92 Amt(c)56 5

NUMBER OF EMPLOYEES : 1910

CAPITAL STRUCTURE

	AUTHORISED	ISSUED
5,5% Cum Prefs R2	100000	100000
Ords 50c	17000000	14577079

FINANCIAL STATISTICS (AT FINANCIAL YEAR END)

(Amts in R'000)	1991 Dec	1990 Dec	1989 Dec	1988 Dec	1987 Dec
Ord S/H Int	191388	171622	143691	124568	120662
Long Trm Loans	2063	523	1902	4183	6592
Iss Ord Share	14577	14559	14523	14516	14516
Total Liab	89633	96840	106789	79358	40503
Current Liab	87570	96317	104887	75175	33911
Total Assets	281021	268462	250480	203926	161165
Current Assets	182311	193841	188213	146141	98473
Debtors	52735	51820	55818	47589	40772
Inventory	66751	70800	65679	61921	37498
Turnover	376617	432409	434799	321128	256042
Oper Profit	57886	73455	68910	36954	23380
Interest Paid	-	-	101	150	127
Tax Paid	33064	40818	36878	19220	10303
Prf af Int&Tax	37285	42965	38103	20610	12950
Prf att Ord Sh	38302	43667	38092	20599	12950
Btm Line Earn	38878	43667	38092	20599	12950
Dividend Paid	19242	21850	19023	16693	6543
Mkt Prce(c) YE	2800	1750	1475	1000	875
Depreciation	7653	7154	6522	6873	7191

PER SHARE STATISTICS (CENTS)

Net Asst Val	1312 95	1178 80	989 40	858 14	831 23
Net Earnings	263 00	300 00	262 00	142 00	89 00
Dividends	132 00	150 00	131 00	115 00	45 00
Cash Flow	315 52	338 11	293 18	168 03	138 52

RATIOS AND OTHER INFORMATION

Mrk Cap(R000)	408156	254783	214214	145160	127015
Current Ratio	2 08	2 01	1 79	1 94	2 90
Quik/Acid Tst	1 32	1 28	1 17	1 12	1 80
A/C Rec T/ovr	7 14	8 34	7 79	6 75	6 28
Tot Ass T/ovr	1 34	1 61	1 74	1 57	1 59
Debt/Ass Rat	0 31	0 36	0 42	0 37	0 21
Debt to Eqity	0 46	0 56	0 73	0 60	0 28
Interest Cover	-	-	689 21	254 95	184 09
Oper Prof Mrg	15 37	16 99	15 85	11 51	9 13
Net Prof Marg%	10 17	10 10	8 76	6 41	5 06
Ret on Assets	25 03	31 21	29 98	19 61	14 51
Ret on Equity%	20 01	25 44	26 51	16 54	10 73
Price/Earnings	10 65	5 83	5 63	7 04	9 83
Divid Cover	1 99	2 00	2 00	1 23	1 98
Divid Yield	4 71	8 57	8 88	11 50	5 14
Earning Yield%	9 39	17 14	17 76	14 20	10 17
NAV % Mrk Pr	46 89	67 36	67 08	85 81	95 00
Effec Tax Rate	45 78	49 98	52 05	57 28	43 98
Def Interval	0 00	0 00	0 00	0 01	0 01
Sus Grth Rate	9 96	12 71	13 27	3 14	5 31

SUBSIDIARY & ASSOCIATED COMPANIES

ABERDARE MANAGEMENT SERVICES (PTY) LTD
ABERDARE MARKETING (PTY) LTD
AIB INVESTMENTS (PTY) LTD (50%)
AUBOT PROPERTIES (PTY) LTD
EDENVALE PLASTIC PRODUCTS (PTY) LTD
EPI (PTY) LTD (20%)
IPA LIEBENBERG (PTY) LTD
RICHARDS BAY CABLE DISTRIBUTORS (PTY) LT
SCOTTISH CABLES (NAMIBIA) (PTY) LTD
SCOTTISH CABLES (PTY) LTD

INVESTMENTS

ALUSTANG (PTY) LTD (15%)
EPI (PTY) LTD (20%)

ABS HOLDINGS LTD

ABBREVIATION : ABS

JSE SHORT CODE : ABS

SECTOR : Industrial-Electronics, Electrical & Bat

SHAREHOLDERS

Who Owns Whom's Assessment of the Identity of the Ultimate Controlling Shareholder: DIRECTORS

SHAREHOLDER	PERCENTAGE 1992	1991
ABS MANAGEMENT P/L	41 6	41 6
HARVEST SECURITIES LTD	4 1	2 5
LSP INV N04 P/L	3 6	---
LE GRANGE J P	3 2	3 2
CMB NOM P/L	3 1	---
STOCKSHARE NOM P/L	2 9	2 9
ELLERINE BROS P/L	2 5	2 5
JOHANNESBURG MUNICIPAL PENS FUND	2 5	---
MENBLACK NOM P/L	2 1	2 2
ABS COMPUTER (NATAL) CC	2 1	---
RAWLINS G K	2 0	2 0
LEVENSTEIN E B	1 9	1 9
LLP INV P/L	1 9	---
M INV P/L	1 9	---
RSP INV P/L	1 9	---
SMITH A M	1 4	1 4
SFSS NOM P/L	1 4	-
COLES D F	1 3	1 3
BRIGHT J D	1 3	1 3
SHARESTOCK NOM P/L	1 3	1 3
STD BANK NOM T/L P/L	1 2	---
GOODMAN D R	1 1	1 1
GROUP INV P/L	---	2 5
MAXERIC NOM P/L	---	1 0
RINRIC NOM P/L	---	1 6
SANLAM	---	6 4
SMYTHE M G	- -	2 1
THOMPSON A A	---	1 2
BERTIE H P/L	- -	4 3
TOTAL	86 1	84 1

DIRECTORS :
BRIGHT JD ,FITZGERALD JD (Executive Chairman)
LE GRANGE JP ,LEAL CR ,PHELPS LS ,RODGERS MW
STEYTLER WB ,TILLETT RJ

REGISTRATION NUMBER : 82/03828/06

REGISTERED OFFICE
ABS Centre, Dartfield Road
Eastgate Ext 13, Sandton
2192

TEL 011-444 2450
FAX 011 444 2481

TRANSFER SECRETARY
Stabılıty Services (Pty) Ltd
6th Floor, 112 Kerk Street
Johannesburg
2001
TEL 011-337 4030

COMPANY SECRETARY
R J Tıllett

NATURE OF BUSINESS
The company ıs a holdıng company wıth subsıdıarıes operatıng ın a number of computer related areas These ınclude the operatıon of a large scale computer bureau, the supply of software packages, the ınstallatıons of networkıng systems as well as a range of credıt card products

BANKERS :
Fırst Natıonal Bank of SA Ltd

AUDITORS :
Prıce Waterhouse Meyernel

FAMILIAR BRAND NAMES
CHAMELEON,HAPAS,IBS,MILLENNIUM,PACE,SITE SOLUTION 6,UNIPENSION,UNIPERSONNEL UNIPRODUCTS,VERIFONE

CONTRIBUTION BY ACTIVITY
N/A

YEAR END : September

DIVIDEND :Ords 1c

Dıvıdend	(Ldr)06/12/91	(Pay)27/12/91	Amt(c)4 5
Dıvıdend	(Ldr)07/12/92	(Pay)28/12/92	Amt(c)5 2
Specıal	(Ldr)07/12/92	(Pay)28/12/92	Amt(c)2 5

NUMBER OF EMPLOYEES : 200

CAPITAL STRUCTURE

	AUTHORISED	ISSUED
Ords 1c	50000000	24292900

FINANCIAL STATISTICS (AT FINANCIAL YEAR END)

(Amts ın R'000)	1991 Sep	1990 Sep	1989 Sep	1988 Sep	1987 Sep
Ord S/H Int	7346	6586	4721	12029	6315
Long Trm Loans	3506	4441	3621	2462	3043
Iss Ord Share	24293	24293	24293	24293	21864
Total Lıab	18451	15161	16892	11682	12318
Current Lıab	14945	10720	13271	9220	9275
Total Assets	25460	21316	21156	19371	18633
Intang Assets	337	431	457	4340	*
Current Assets	15990	10147	13454	13943	13289
Debtors	8743	7528	9049	8965	10318
Inventory	887	2400	4263	4050	2902
Turnover	45425	42372	37805	32211	22348
Oper Profıt	6270	4988	-132	3702	2599
Interest Paıd	1571	2403	1271	73	498
Tax Paıd	2231	720	172	671	-
Prf af Int&Tax	2468	1865	-1575	2958	2101
Prf att Ord Sh	2468	1865	-1575	2958	2101
Btm Lıne Earn	1853	1865	-1575	2885	2931
Dıvıdend Paıd	1093	-	-	1458	437
Mkt Prce(c) YE	40	20	25	50	140
Deprecıatıon	4618	3429	1172	1053	746

PER SHARE STATISTICS (CENTS)

Net Asst Val	28 85	25 34	17 55	31 65	28 88
Net Earnıngs	10 20	7 70	-6 50	12 20	11 20
Dıvıdends	4 50	-	-	6 00	2 00
Cash Flow	27 64	23 73	-2 56	17 04	15 16

RATIOS AND OTHER INFORMATION

Mrk Cap(R000)	9717	4859	6073	12147	30610
Current Ratıo	1 07	0 95	1 01	1 51	1 43
Quık/Acıd Tst	1 01	0 72	0 69	1 07	1 12
A/C Rec T/ovr	5 20	5 63	4 18	3 59	2 17
Tot Ass T/ovr	1 78	1 99	1 79	1 66	1 20
Debt/Ass Rat	0 72	0 69	0 80	0 59	0 65
L T L Tot Ass	0 13	0 19	0 17	0 11	0 15
Debt to Eqıty	2 50	2 23	3 58	0 94	1 90
Interest Cover	3 99	2 08	-0 10	50 71	5 22
Oper Prof Mrg	13 80	11 77	-0 35	11 49	11 63
Net Prof Marg%	5 43	4 40	-4 17	9 18	9 40
Ret on Assets	24 63	23 40	-0 62	19 11	13 95
Ret on Equıty%	33 60	28 32	-33 36	24 59	33 27
Prıce/Earnıngs	3 92	2 60	-3 85	4 10	12 50
Dıvıd Cover	2 27	-	-	2 03	5 60
Dıvıd Yıeld	11 25	-	-	12 00	1 43
Earnıng Yıeld%	25 50	38 50	-26 00	24 40	8 00
NAV % Mrk Pr	72 13	126 68	70 21	63 30	20 63
Effec Tax Rate	55 25	9 63	-6 34	6 09	-
Def Interval	1 07	1 47	-11 35	0 89	1 42
Sus Grth Rate	18 72	28 32	-33 36	12 47	26 35

SUBSIDIARY & ASSOCIATED COMPANIES

ABS COMPUTERS (PTY) LTD
ABS PRINTING SYSTEMS (PTY) LTD
AUTOMATED BUSINESS SYSTEMS (PTY) LTD
INTRODEL (PTY) LTD
PETERBOROUGH SOFTWARE SA (PTY) LTD
TELEPLAN COMPUTER SERVICES (PTY) LTD
UNIVERSAL COMPUTER SERVICES (PTY) LTD

INVESTMENTS

None

ACREM HOLDINGS LTD

ABBREVIATION : ACREM

JSE SHORT CODE : ACM

SECTOR : Industrıal-Retaılers & Wholesalers

SHAREHOLDERS

Who Owns Whom's Assessment of the Identıty of the Ultımate Controllıng Shareholder: COLUMBIA CONSULTANTS

SHAREHOLDER	PERCENTAGE 1992	1991
COLUMBIA CONSULTANTS LTD	86 1	86 1
HERBERT & TRAKMAN NOM P/L	7 6	8 8
CMB NOM P/L	3 9	---
SANLAM	---	3 9
TOTAL	97 6	98 7

DIRECTORS :
HERBERT BB ,HIRSHOWITZ AG (Chief Executive)
POLOVIN GA ,TUNSTALL PA (Financial Director

REGISTRATION NUMBER : 86/01616/06

REGISTERED OFFICE
1st Floor, Dunkeld Cresc West, Albury Road
Dunkeld West
2196
TEL 011-442 9290
FAX 011-442 9299

TRANSFER SECRETARY
Mercantile Registrars Ltd
P O Box 1053, Johannesburg
2000
TEL 011-333 8181

COMPANY SECRETARY
Columbia Management (Pty) Ltd

NATURE OF BUSINESS
An investment holding company with subsidiaries engaged in general retailing Acme Stores operates on the basis of granting credit to the customer base for the purchase of a diversified range of merchandise, including consumer electronics, arms and ammunition, sporting equipment, jewellery, white goods and furniture

BANKERS :
Standard Bank of SA Ltd

AUDITORS :
Glass Arenson

FAMILIAR BRAND NAMES
ACME STORES

CONTRIBUTION BY ACTIVITY
N/A

YEAR END : March

DIVIDEND :Ords 1c

Interim	(Ldr)11/01/91	(Pay)25/01/91	Amt(c)2
Final	(Ldr)22/02/91	(Pay)28/06/91	Amt(c)4
Special	(Ldr)18/09/92	(Pay)25/09/92	Amt(c)9

NUMBER OF EMPLOYEES : 330

CAPITAL STRUCTURE

	AUTHORISED	ISSUED
Ords 1c	100000000	77551020

FINANCIAL STATISTICS (AT FINANCIAL YEAR END)

(Amts in R'000)	1992 Mar	1991 Mar	1990 Mar	1989 Feb
Ord S/H Int	40193	39904	22555	11530
Long Trm Loans	10719	14851	21273	375
Iss Ord Share	77551	77551	38776	25000
Total Liab	21485	29421	34905	24319
Current Liab	10766	14570	13632	23944
Total Assets	58280	62719	50554	31128
Intang Assets	3398	6606	6906	4721
Current Assets	44882	51810	45742	27765
Debtors	40912	42695	35386	11752
Inventory	2882	8114	6980	15510
Turnover	36830	56427	53710	42900
Oper Profit	5432	9724	10260	2211
Interest Paid	3798	3843	2955	869
Tax Paid	1886		1392	-
Prf af Int&Tax	289	6616	6066	1823
Prf att Ord Sh	289	6616	6066	1823
Btm Line Earn	289	6616	6214	1823
Dividend Paid	-	4653	1939	-
Mkt Prce(c) YE	30	60	50	40
Depreciation	207	296	209	337

PER SHARE STATISTICS (CENTS)

Net Asst Val	47 45	42 94	40 36	27 24
Net Earnings	0 40	8 50	15 60	11 60
Dividends	-	6 00	5 00	-
Cash Flow	0 64	8 91	18 54	8 64

RATIOS AND OTHER INFORMATION

Mrk Cap(R000)	23265	46531	19388	10000
Current Ratio	4 17	3 56	3 36	1 16
Quik/Acid Tst	3 90	3 00	2 84	0 51
A/C Rec T/ovr	0 90	1 32	1 52	3 65
Tot Ass T/ovr	0 63	0 90	1 06	1 38
Debt/Ass Rat	0 37	0 47	0 67	0 78
L T L Tot Ass	0 18	0 24	0 40	0 01
Debt to Eqity	0 53	0 74	1 51	2 11
Interest Cover	1 43	2 53	3 47	2 54
Oper Prof Mrg	14 75	17 23	19 10	5 15
Net Prof Marg%	0 78	11 72	11 29	4 25
Ret on Assets	10 25	16 68	20 60	8 65
Ret on Equity%	0 72	16 58	26 89	15 81
Price/Earnings	75 00	7 06	3 21	3 45
Divid Cover		1 42	3 12	-
Divid Yield	-	10 00	10 00	-
Earning Yield%	1 33	14 17	31 20	29 00
NAV % Mrk Pr	158 15	71 56	80 71	68 09
Effec Tax Rate	97 09		6 40	-
Def Interval	37 64	3 22	3 66	4 85
Sus Grth Rate	0 72	4 92	18 30	15 81

SUBSIDIARY & ASSOCIATED COMPANIES

ACME FURNITURE ENTERPRISES (PTY) LTD
ACME STORES (PTY) LTD
ACREM HOLDING CO (PTY) LTD
ASHMOD HOLDINGS (PTY) LTD
DAN KITCHENS 2000 (PTY) LTD
DECOR FURNISHERS (PTY) LTD
GYPSEY INVESTMENTS (PTY) LTD
TITAN TOOL & HARDWARE (PTY) LTD

INVESTMENTS

COASTAL CLOTHING MANUFACTURERS LTD

ADCOCK INGRAM LTD

ABBREVIATION : ADCOCK

JSE SHORT CODE : ADC

SECTOR : Industrial Pharmaceutical & Medical

SHAREHOLDERS

Who Owns Whom's Assessment of the Identity of the Ultimate Controlling Shareholder:
SA MUTUAL VIA BARLOWS & TIGER OATS

SHAREHOLDER	PERCENTAGE 1992	1991
TIGER OATS LTD	74 1	74 1
LIBERTY LIFE ASSOC OF AFRICA LTD	8 3	8 6
CMB NOM P/L	2 9	---
MOMENTUM LIFE ASSURE LTD	2 2	2 2
GUARDIAN NOM P/L	1 6	3 5
ADCOCK-INGRAM SHARE TRUST	---	2 2
TOTAL	89 3	90 6

DIRECTORS :
ADAM BH ,BERNSTEIN HL
BODLEY DC (Chief Executive),CLEWLOW WAM
HOLMES WRC (Financial Director),MACROBERT DL
MOTLANA NH DR,NORRIS MC ,NOSSEL NW
STRAUSS SA PROF,WILLIAMS RA (Chairman),WOLPERT C

REGISTRATION NUMBER : 05/34385/06

REGISTERED OFFICE
209 15th Road, Randjespark
Midrand
1685
TEL 011-315 2384
FAX 011-315 2410

TRANSFER SECRETARY
Rand Registrars Ltd
P O Box 82549, Southdale
2135
TEL 011-835 1016

COMPANY SECRETARY
W R C Holmes

NATURE OF BUSINESS
The group is engaged in development, manufacture & marketing of healthcare, toiletry and retail self medication products, Wholesale & distribution of pharmaceutical products, Manufacture & distrib of critical care products

BANKERS :
First National Bank of SA Ltd

AUDITORS :
Arthur Andersen & Co

FAMILIAR BRAND NAMES
ACTOPHLEM,ADCO DICLOPHENAC
ADCO PHARMACEUTICA,ADCO-AMOXYCILLIN
ADCO-ERYTHROMYCIN,ADCO-INDOMETHACIN,ADFEN
BETADINE,BURINEX K,CAMPHOR,CEFADROX,COLCAPS
CYCLOKAPRON,DOMAMINE-SABAX
DREWS SPARKLING SALTS,EASY WAVES,EPIGEN
EXPIGEN,FUCIDIN,FUCITHALMIC,GENOTROPIN,GILL
INGRAMS,IOHEXOL,JE T'AIME,KABIKINASE
KEATINGS,LEO MEDICAL,LEUCOSTOP,LOSEC
MAINTELYTE,MINI-BAG,MOCAINE,MYPRODOL,PADAX
PANADOC,PHISAC,PONDOCILLIN,PULMICORT,PYNSTOP
RHINOCORT,RIO ETHICALS,ROXY,RUBRAGEL,SABAX
SALAZOPYRIN,SAPHAR-MED,SOLPHYLLEX,SOLPHYLLIN
SOMATONORM,SOSENOL,STEARNS PINE TAR & HONEY
STERI-NAPPI,SYLVASUN,SYNTHAMIN,THEODUR
VIAFLEX,XYLOTOX

CONTRIBUTION BY ACTIVITY
Pharmaceuticals (16 5%)
Critical care products (22 1%)
Self-medication products (11 6%)
Consumer products (8 6%)
Generic products (1 9%)
Wholesale and retail (39 3%)

YEAR END : September

DIVIDEND :Ords 50c

Interim No 82	(Ldr)11/05/90	(Pay)03/07/90	Amt(c)21 5
Final No 83	(Ldr)09/11/90	(Pay)03/01/91	Amt(c)46 5
Interim No 84	(Ldr)10/05/91	(Pay)02/07/91	Amt(c)28
Final No 85	(Ldr)08/11/91	(Pay)03/01/92	Amt(c)60
Final No 85	(Ldr)03/11/91	(Pay)02/01/92	Amt(c)60
Interim No 86	(Ldr)08/05/92	(Pay)03/07/92	Amt(c)33
Final No 87	(Ldr)13/11/92	(Pay)06/01/93	Amt(c)72

NUMBER OF EMPLOYEES : 2889

CAPITAL STRUCTURE

	AUTHORISED	ISSUED
Ords 50c	40000000	27384450

FINANCIAL STATISTICS (AT FINANCIAL YEAR END)

(Amts in R'000)	1992 Sep	1991 Sep	1990 Sep	1989 Sep	1988 Sep
Ord S/H Int	274798	211352	171087	138901	112530
Long Trm Loans	16772	13302	15032	15080	15121
Iss Ord Share	27384	27384	27174	26999	26636
Total Liab	227007	203104	178580	140441	109259
Current Liab	210235	189802	163548	125361	94138
Total Assets	501805	414456	349667	279342	221789
Current Assets	302501	232362	193697	150185	123826
Debtors	152869	129089	103585	74683	60276
Inventory	111329	102913	89847	74695	63237
Turnover	914997	773630	615730	471235	334640
Oper Profit	140860	118408	94299	67501	49941
Interest Paid	5754	6022	6509	5842	4812
Tax Paid	63347	51476	41724	24967	19337
Prf af Int&Tax	75901	63974	48955	37867	25792
Prf att Ord Sh	76493	64226	49376	38285	26209
Btm Line Earn	92200	62024	49376	38285	-18466
Dividend Paid	28754	24093	18459	14268	11211
Mkt Prce(c) YE	6350	5700	3425	2550	1100
Depreciation	19788	17093	15215	12031	8436

PER SHARE STATISTICS (CENTS)

Net Asst Val	1003 50	771 81	629 60	514 47	422 47
Net Earnings	279 00	235 00	182 00	143 00	118 00
Dividends	105 00	88 00	68 00	53 00	44 00
Cash Flow	362 62	296 44	236 58	186 17	147 32

RATIOS AND OTHER INFORMATION

Mrk Cap(R000)	1738884	1560888	930710	688475	292996
Current Ratio	1 44	1 22	1 18	1 20	1 32
Quik/Acid Tst	0 91	0 68	0 63	0 60	0 64
A/C Rec T/ovr	5 99	5 99	5 94	6 31	5 55
Tot Ass T/ovr	1 82	1 87	1 76	1 69	1 51
Debt/Ass Rat	0 42	0 46	0 47	0 45	0 42
Debt to Eqity	0 77	0 90	0 96	0 90	0 84
Interest Cover	24 68	19 88	14 65	11 61	10 38
Oper Prof Mrg	15 39	15 31	15 31	14 32	14 92
Net Prof Marg%	8 36	8 30	8 02	8 12	7 83
Ret on Assets	29 02	29 37	27 92	24 74	22 72
Ret on Equity%	27 84	30 39	28 86	27 56	23 29
Price/Earnings	22 76	24 26	18 82	17 83	9 32
Divid Cover	2 66	2 67	2 68	2 70	2 68
Divid Yield	1 65	1 54	1 99	2 08	4 00
Earning Yield%	4 39	4 12	5 31	5 61	10 73
NAV % Mrk Pr	15 80	13 54	18 38	20 18	38 41
Effec Tax Rate	43 24	45 08	46 65	40 26	46 40
Def Interval	-	0 15	0 33	0 53	0 55

Sus Grth Rate	17 37	18 99	18 07	17 29	13 33

SUBSIDIARY & ASSOCIATED COMPANIES

ADCO DRUG COMPANY (PTY) LTD
ADCOCK INGRAM CONSUMER PRODUCTS (PTY) LT
ADCOCK INGRAM CRITICAL CARE LTD
ADCOCK INGRAM PHARMACEUTICALS LTD
ADCOCK INGRAM SELF MEDICATIONAL (PTY) LT
ADCOCK INGRAM WHOLESALE LTD
ADCOCK INGRAM LABORATORIES LTD
ADCOCK INGRAM MANAGEMENT SERVICES (PTY)
ADCOKEN (PTY) LTD (50%)
DEEJAY APTEEK (EDMS) BPK (50%)
EJA CHEMISTS LTD (50%)
EVANDER PHARMACY (PTY) LTD (50%)
METAMORPHOSA (PTY) LTD (50%)
PROP ROBIN (PTY) LTD (50%)
RANDGATE PHARMACY (PTY) LTD (50%)
REED & CHAMPION LTD
ROBINSON HOSPITAL (PTY) LTD (50%)
TRANSWEST WHOLESALE CHEMISTS (PTY) LTD
VENDING PROPERTIES (PTY) LTD
WELSTATE WHOLESALE CHEMISTS (PTY) LTD
WESTONARIA PHARMACY (PTY) LTD (45%)

INVESTMENTS

MINERALS AND RESOURCES CORPORATION LTD (164 SH)
NORISTAN HOLDINGS LTD (12750 SH)
S A DRUGGISTS LTD (583 SH)

ADCORP HOLDINGS LTD

ABBREVIATION : ADCORP

JSE SHORT CODE : ADR

SECTOR . Financial Banks & Financial Services

SHAREHOLDERS

Who Owns Whom's Assessment of the Identity of the Ultimate Controlling Shareholder·
DIRECTORS

SHAREHOLDER	PERCENTAGE 1992	1991
BARRY J K P	46 2	46 2
GANTRY HOLDINGS P/L	17 2	17 2
RAMNIT P/L	7 2	7 2
RHODES FAMILY TRUST	5 2	5 2
ADCORP SHARE TRUST	4 4	4 3
ANDERSON B N	3 1	3 1
BRADLEY D V	2 3	2 3
SFSS NOM P/L	2 2	2 3
DAWSON H I	1 6	1 6
CONFOR INV P/L	1 6	1 6
PUBLICITY CONSULTANTS INC	1 2	1 2
BAKER V C	1 1	1 1
TOTAL	93 3	93 3

DIRECTORS :
BARRY JKP (Executive Chairman) DU TOIT E
JACOBSZ FP DR MACKENZIE JLP
RHODES K (Managing Director),WAGNER R
WORTHINGTON AJ (Financial Director

REGISTRATION NUMBER : 74/01804/06

REGISTERED OFFICE
Miller Weedon House, 44 Twist Street
Joubert Park
2001
TEL 011-725 1310
FAX 011-725 1435

TRANSFER SECRETARY
Central Registrars Ltd
P O Box 4844, Johannesburg
2000
TEL 011-331 0051

COMPANY SECRETARY
L Smith

NATURE OF BUSINESS
Is an investment holding company whose subsidiaries and associates carry on the business in the manpower,communications and research sectors of the services industries in South Africa & Namibia

BANKERS :
First National Bank of SA Ltd
Nedperm Bank Ltd, Senbank

AUDITORS :
P Kamstra

FAMILIAR BRAND NAMES
ADMARK RECRUITMENT,ADPLAN INTERNATIONAL
ALTOLEVEL RECRUITMENT,EFFECTIVE RECRUITMENT
JSA DESIGN,OMNICHECK QUALITATIVE CONSULTANT
RESEARCH SURVEYS,TWS COMMUNICATIONS

CONTRIBUTION BY ACTIVITY
N/A

YEAR END : December

DIVIDEND : Ords 2,5c

Final	(Ldr)02/03/90	(Pay)23/03/90	Amt(c)9
Dividend	(Ldr)22/02/91	(Pay)30/04/91	Amt(c)7
Dividend	(Ldr)24/04/92	(Pay)29/05/92	Amt(c)4

NUMBER OF EMPLOYEES : 286

CAPITAL STRUCTURE

	AUTHORISED	ISSUED
Ords 2,5c	15000000	7700000
Auto Conv Unsec Var Rate Sub Debs	1386000	1386000

FINANCIAL STATISTICS (AT FINANCIAL YEAR END)

(Amts in R 000)	1991 Dec	1990 Dec	1989 Dec	1988 Dec	1987 Dec
Ord S/H Int	5777	4995	3281	889	412
Long Trm Loans	3908	4301	2619	69	100
Iss Ord Share	7700	7700	6740	6300	6300
Total Liab	14613	13633	10361	3714	3504
Current Liab	10705	9332	7742	3645	3404
Total Assets	13629	12269	10572	4603	3916
Intang Assets	6761	6359	3070	*	*
Current Assets	9236	8198	8608	4388	3751
Debtors	8647	7393	5604	3410	2738
Turnover	44634	44592	31747	23300	16224
Oper Profit	2660	2562	2542	1927	1253
Interest Paid	1426	362	86		

Tax Paid	321	777	1304	1005	577
Prf af Int&Tax	1444	1543	1304	922	676
Prf att Ord Sh	1090	1389	1304	922	676
Btm Line Earn	1090	1389	1304	922	676
Dividend Paid	308	539	606	441	378
Mkt Prce(c) YE	100	120	100	90	100
Depreciation	804	776	266	49	21

PER SHARE STATISTICS (CENTS)

Net Asst Val	-12 78	-17 71	3 13	14 11	6 54
Net Earnings	14 20	18 00	20 00	14 60	10 70
Dividends	4 00	7 00	9 00	7 00	6 00
Cash Flow	24 60	28 12	24 08	15 41	11 06

RATIOS AND OTHER INFORMATION

Mrk Cap(R000)	7700	9240	6740	5670	6300
Current Ratio	0 86	0 88	1 11	1 20	1 10
Quik/Acid Tst	0 86	0 88	1 11	1 20	1 10
A/C Rec T/ovr	5 16	6 03	5 67	6 83	5 93
Tot Ass T/ovr	3 27	3 63	3 00	5 06	4 14
Debt/Ass Rat	0 92	0 97	0 94	0 81	0 89
L T L Tot Ass	0 14	0 21	0 20	0 01	0 03
Debt to Eqity	2 18	2 38	3 02	4 18	8 50
Interest Cover	1 87	7 08	29 56	-	-
Oper Prof Mrg	5 96	5 75	8 01	8 27	7 72
Net Prof Marg%	2 44	3 11	4 11	3 96	4 17
Ret on Assets	23 41	21 86	25 48	41 86	32 00
Ret on Equity%	18 87	27 81	39 74	103 71	164 08
Price/Earnings	7 04	6 67	5 00	6 16	9 35
Divid Cover	3 55	2 57	2 22	2 09	1 78
Divid Yield	4 00	5 83	9 00	7 78	6 00
Earning Yield%	14 20	15 00	20 00	16 22	10 70
NAV % Mrk Pr	-12 78	-14 76	3 13	15 68	6 54
Effec Tax Rate	18 19	33 49	50 00	52 15	46 05
Def Interval	1 83	2 09	1 38	-	
Sus Grth Rate	13 54	17 02	21 27	54 11	72 33

SUBSIDIARY & ASSOCIATED COMPANIES

ADMARK (PTY) LTD
ADMARK RECRUITMENT (CAPE) (PTY) LTD
ADMARK RECRUITMENT (NATAL) (PTY) LTD
ADMARK RECRUITMENT (SWA/NAMIBIA) (PTY) L
ADMARK RECRUITMENT ADVERTISING (PTY) LTD
ADPLAN INTERNATIONAL (SA) (PTY) LTD
ALTOLEVEL RECRUITMENT ADVERTISING (PTY)
CORPCOM LTD
DESIGN INTERNATIONAL (PTY) LTD
EFFECTIVE RECRUITMENT ADVERTISING (PTY)
EQUITY MARKET COMMUNICATIONS (PTY) LTD
INTERIOR DESIGN & EXHIBITION ASSOCIATES
JSA DESIGN INTERNATIONAL (PTY) LTD
PREPRESS REPRODUCTION (PTY) LTD
QUALITATIVE CONSULTANCY (PTY) LTD, THE
RESEARCH SURVEYS (PTY) LTD (50%)
THE COMPANY GROUP (PTY) LTD
TWS COMMUNICATIONS LTD
TWS INTERNATIONAL (PTY) LTD

INVESTMENTS

TRIAD SPONSORSHIP MARKETING (PTY) LTD (15%)

ADONIS KNITWEAR HOLDINGS LTD

ABBREVIATION : ADONIS

JSE SHORT CODE : ADO

SECTOR : Industrial Clothing, Footwear & Textiles

SHAREHOLDERS

Who Owns Whom's Assessment of the Identity of the Ultimate Controlling Shareholder·
BENCEN FAMILY

SHAREHOLDER	PERCENTAGE 1992	1991
BENCEN K	45 5	45 5
BENCEN J	24 4	24 4
ADONIS KNITWEAR SHARE TRUST	5 6	5 6
FIRST NAT NOM P/L	2 9	2 5
JOFFE C	2 0	2 0
LAVANREN NOM P/L	1 5	1 5
NUSSBAUM R A W	1 0	--
TOTAL	83 0	81 6

DIRECTORS :
BENCEN J (Chairman & Chief Exec),BENCEN K MRS
CHAITEL SL (Financial Director)
JOFFE C (Manufacturing Director

REGISTRATION NUMBER : 69/02908/06

REGISTERED OFFICE
3rd Floor, Cedar Grove, Grove City
196 Louis Botha Ave, Houghton Estate
2198
TEL 011-833 7100
FAX 011-836 5507

TRANSFER SECRETARY
Central Registrars Ltd
P O Box 4844, Johannesburg
2000
TEL 011-331 0051

COMPANY SECRETARY
S L Chaitel

NATURE OF BUSINESS
The company manufactures and markets mens and childrens knitwear

BANKERS :
Nedperm Bank Ltd

AUDITORS :
Leveton Boner

FAMILIAR BRAND NAMES
ADONIS,DINO MILANO,HENRY BALLANTYNE
LYLE & SCOTT,PAUL D'ORSAY

CONTRIBUTION BY ACTIVITY
N/A

YEAR END : September

DIVIDEND : Ords 50c

Final No 31	(Ldr)04/01/91	(Pay)08/02/91	Amt(c)14
Interim No 32	(Ldr)22/02/91	(Pay)28/03/91	Amt(c)20

NUMBER OF EMPLOYEES : 350

CAPITAL STRUCTURE

	AUTHORISED	ISSUED
Ords 50c	4000000	3545000

FINANCIAL STATISTICS (AT FINANCIAL YEAR END)

(Amts in R'000)	1991 Sep	1990 Sep	1989 Sep	1988 Sep	1987 Sep
Ord S/H Int	8081	7596	5963	5184	3713
Long Trm Loans	430	705	983	1054	1144
Iss Ord Share	3545	3545	3520	3520	3345
Total Liab	2544	3207	4777	3116	3778
Current Liab	2114	2502	3794	2062	2634
Total Assets	10625	10803	10740	8300	7491
Current Assets	8076	7625	7281	6237	5718
Debtors	1010	3098	2945	2268	1871
Inventory	3072	3232	4012	2521	2721
Oper Profit	2442	2553	3643	1978	1775
Interest Paid	189	265	204	249	106
Tax Paid	1059	-146	1740	60	853
Prf af Int&Tax	1194	2434	1699	1669	816
Prf att Ord Sh	1194	2434	1699	1669	816
Btm Line Earn	1194	2434	1699	1669	816
Dividend Paid	709	851	849	634	401
Mkt Prce(c) YE	190	230	200	125	130
Depreciation	568	683	788	442	742

PER SHARE STATISTICS (CENTS)

Net Asst Val	227 95	214 27	169 40	147 27	111 00
Net Earnings	33 70	68 70	46 70	50 25	24 40
Dividends	20 00	24 00	24 00	18 00	12 00
Cash Flow	51 28	83 81	79 46	60 35	46 58

RATIOS AND OTHER INFORMATION

Mrk Cap(R000)	6736	8154	7040	4400	4349
Current Ratio	3 82	3 05	1 92	3 02	2 17
Quik/Acid Tst	2 37	1 76	0 86	1 80	1 14
Debt/Ass Rat	0 20	0 26	0 40	0 35	0 50
L T L Tot Ass	0 00	0 03	0 04	0 10	0 15
Debt to Eqity	0 26	0 37	0 72	0 56	1 02
Interest Cover	12 92	9 63	17 86	7 94	16 75
Ret on Assets	22 98	23 63	33 92	23 83	23 70
Ret on Equity%	14 78	32 04	28 49	32 20	21 98
Price/Earnings	5 64	3 35	4 28	2 49	5 33
Divid Cover	1 69	2 86	1 95	2 79	2 03
Divid Yield	10 53	10 43	12 00	14 40	9 23
Earning Yield%	17 74	29 87	23 35	40 20	18 77
NAV % Mrk Pr	119 98	93 16	84 70	117 82	85 39
Effec Tax Rate	44 52	-	41 58	6 30	51 11
Def Interval		0 21	0 24	0 42	0 82
Sus Grth Rate	6 00	20 84	14 25	19 97	11 18

SUBSIDIARY & ASSOCIATED COMPANIES

CREATEX KNITWEAR (PTY) LTD
IVY S TEXTILES (PTY) LTD

INVESTMENTS

None

ADVANCED TECHNICAL SYSTEMS LTD

ABBREVIATION : ADVTECH

JSE SHORT CODE : ADT

SECTOR : Industrial Electronics, Electrical & Bat

SHAREHOLDERS

Who Owns Whom's Assessment of the Identity of the Ultimate Controlling Shareholder: DIRECTORS

SHAREHOLDER	PERCENTAGE 1992	1991
BUCKHAM B D	54 4	54 2
AUERBACH N W	20 2	20 0
AUERBACH FAMILY TRUST	4 3	4 3
RIVERBANK LTD	3 6	3 6
STD BANK NOM TVL P/L	2 1	1 9
SPURR R T	1 8	1 8
SAGE LIFE LTD	-	3 0
TOTAL	86 5	88 8

DIRECTORS :
AUERBACH NW ,BORKUM HJ
BUCKHAM BD (Chairman & Managing Dir),LEVIN HR
PLIT RD (Financial Director

REGISTRATION NUMBER : 87/04735/06

REGISTERED OFFICE
6th Floor, Saambou National Building
130 Commissioner Street, Johannesburg
2001
TEL 011-886 5100
FAX 011-886 7302

TRANSFER SECRETARY
Fraser Street Registrars (Pty) Ltd
P O Box 61178, Marshalltown
2107
TEL 011-491 0911

COMPANY SECRETARY
R D Plit

NATURE OF BUSINESS
The company is an investment holding company and its subsidiaries carry on the business of training services in the technological human resources development, industrial and manufacturing fields, the supply of educational material in the school technikon, corporate and broadcast areas, the sale of training equipment and computer systems including hardware, software and LANS

BANKERS :
Standard Bank of SA Ltd

AUDITORS :
Goldberg Jaffe

FAMILIAR BRAND NAMES
N/A

CONTRIBUTION BY ACTIVITY
N/A

YEAR END : February

DIVIDEND : Ords 1c

Dividend	(Ldr)14/06/91	(Pay)15/07/91	Amt(c)1 5
Dividend	(Ldr)19/06/92	(Pay)16/07/92	Amt(c)2 5

NUMBER OF EMPLOYEES : 120

CAPITAL STRUCTURE

	AUTHORISED	ISSUED
Ords 1c	30000000	20375000

FINANCIAL STATISTICS (AT FINANCIAL YEAR END)

(Amts in R'000)	1992 Feb	1991 Feb	1990 Feb	1989 Feb	1988 Feb
Ord S/H Int	17555	16885	16246	14346	12440
Long Trm Loans	6619	6784	13558	9489	5835
Iss Ord Share	20375	20375	20375	20375	20000
Total Liab	18287	19693	27547	22432	10479
Current Liab	11668	12909	13989	12943	4644
Total Assets	27971	28740	35955	28940	15436
Intang Assets	7871	7838	7838	7838	7483
Current Assets	15219	15551	14958	14648	6775
Debtors	13657	14398	13688	12331	5449
Inventory	1125	1147	1264	1118	328
Turnover	23082	23941	27008	16945	9128
Oper Profit	2305	2316	4093	2807	1650
Interest Paid	367	784	872	351	86
Tax Paid	759	587	346	40	14
Prf af Int&Tax	1179	945	2875	2416	1550
Prf att Ord Sh	1179	945	2875	2416	1550
Btm Line Earn	1179	945	2714	2416	1550
Dividend Paid	509	306	815	714	-
Mkt Prce(c) YE	30	65	85	75	45
Depreciation	1523	1843	1637	706	405

PER SHARE STATISTICS (CENTS)

Net Asst Val	47 53	44 40	41 27	31 94	24 79
Net Earnings	5 80	4 64	14 11	11 85	9 02
Dividends	2 50	1 50	4 00	3 50	-
Cash Flow	13 26	13 68	22 14	15 32	11 39

RATIOS AND OTHER INFORMATION

Mrk Cap(R000)	6113	13244	17319	15281	9000
Current Ratio	1 30	1 20	1 07	1 13	1 46
Quik/Acid Tst	1 21	1 12	0 98	1 05	1 39
A/C Rec T/ovr	1 69	1 66	1 97	1 37	1 68
Tot Ass T/ovr	0 83	0 83	0 75	0 59	0 59
Debt/Ass Rat	0 42	0 47	0 53	0 56	0 42
L T L Tot Ass	0 01	0 02	0 14	0 11	0 12
Debt to Eqity	0 67	0 80	1 18	1 12	0 52
Interest Cover	6 28	2 95	4 69	8 00	19 19
Oper Prof Mrg	9 99	9 67	15 15	16 57	18 08
Net Prof Marg%	5 11	3 95	10 64	14 26	16 98
Ret on Assets	8 24	8 06	11 38	9 70	10 69
Ret on Equity%	6 72	5 60	17 70	16 84	12 46
Price/Earnings	5 17	14 01	6 02	6 33	4 99
Divid Cover	2 32	3 09	3 53	3 39	-
Divid Yield	8 33	2 31	4 71	4 67	
Earning Yield%	19 33	7 14	16 60	15 80	20 04
NAV % Mrk Pr	158 43	68 31	48 55	42 59	55 08
Effec Tax Rate	39 16	36 62	10 74	1 63	0 90
Def Interval	0 07	0 35	0 56	0 72	0 03
Sus Grth Rate	3 82	3 78	12 68	11 86	12 46

SUBSIDIARY & ASSOCIATED COMPANIES

ADVANCED TRAINING SYSTEMS (PTY) LTD
APPLED LEARNING (PTY) LTD
APPLIED LEARNING CENTRE (PTY) LTD
LAZFIN FINANCE (PTY) LTD (50%)
LEARNTRON (PTY) LTD
VIEWCOM (PTY) LTD

INVESTMENTS

None

AECI LTD

ABBREVIATION : AECI

JSE SHORT CODE : AFE

SECTOR : Industrial-Chemicals & Oils

SHAREHOLDERS

Who Owns Whom's Assessment of the Identity of the Ultimate Controlling Shareholder: ANGLO AMERICAN VIA AMIC

SHAREHOLDER	PERCENTAGE 1992	1991
AFEX HOLDINGS P/L	24 3	24 3
ICI SA LTD	20 4	20 4
DE BEERS IND CORP LTD	15 6	15 6
ANGLO AMERICAN IND CORP LTD	11 8	11 8
SA MUTUAL	6 0	5 8
ICI THETA BV	5 8	5 8
CMB NOM P/L	1 8	
STD BANK NOM TVL P/L	1 5	1 4
ENGINEERING INDUSTRIES PENS FUND	1 3	1 2
RESIDENT NOM LTD	1 1	1 1
PETARD NOM LTD	1 1	1 1
METAL IND GROUP PENS FUND	1 1	-
SANLAM	--	1 8
TOTAL	91 7	90 3

DIRECTORS :
AXELSON NC (Financial Director),BOUSTRED WG
BOYD L ,DAUBENEY PEG ,HARRISON JT
OGILVIE THOMPSON J ,OPPENHEIMER NF
RELLY GWH (Chairman)
SANDER MA (Managing Director),SMITH MP
VAN LEEUWEN JP ,WHITELEY F (Chief Executive

REGISTRATION NUMBER : 04/02590/06

REGISTERED OFFICE
16th Floor, Office Tower, Carlton Centre
Johannesburg
2001
TEL 011-223 9111
FAX 011-331 6358

TRANSFER SECRETARY
Consolidated Share Registrars Ltd
P O Box 61051, Marshalltown
2107
TEL 011-492 1620

COMPANY SECRETARY
M J F Potgieter

NATURE OF BUSINESS
The holding company of a group engaged in the manufacture and supply of commercial explosives, polyvinyl chloride, synthetic fibres, low density polyethylene, industrial and specialty chemicals and fertilizers, and paints The group also has interests in the plastics conversion industry

BANKERS :
First National Bank of SA Ltd
Nedperm Bank Ltd, Standard Bank of SA Ltd
UAL Merchant Bank Ltd

AUDITORS :
KPMG Aiken & Peat, Deloitte Pim Goldby

FAMILIAR BRAND NAMES
AECI,AMERON,ANFO,AUTOPLASTIC,BERGERMASTER DPI,DULUX,ELVOLAC,FASHIONTEX,KANSAI,KYNOCH LEISURE-LAZE,MAGNADET,MELINAR,PENTHOUSE PERSPEX,PET,POLYCON,POLYFOS,POLYVINYL POWERGEL,PVC,RENOLIT,ROCKGRIP,SANS,SIGMA STOPEFUSE,STOPELINE,SUPER-S,TENSOL,THORAN VENT X,VYMURA,VYNIDE,WOODGARD

CONTRIBUTION BY ACTIVITY
AECI Chlor-Alkali & Plastics Ltd (27 6%)
Explosives/Chemicals/Agricultural Prdts (34 1%)
Speciality Products & Services (38 3%)

YEAR END : December

DIVIDEND :Ords R1

Final No 111	(Ldr)23/03/90	(Pay)20/04/90	Amt(c)57
Interim No 112	(Ldr)24/08/90	(Pay)21/09/90	Amt(c)30
Final No 113	(Ldr)22/03/91	(Pay)18/04/91	Amt(c)57
Interim No 114	(Ldr)23/08/91	(Pay)20/09/91	Amt(c)18
Final No 115	(Ldr)20/03/92	(Pay)21/04/92	Amt(c)40
Interim No 116	(Ldr)28/08/92	(Pay)18/09/92	Amt(c)18

NUMBER OF EMPLOYEES : 24100

CAPITAL STRUCTURE

	AUTHORISED	ISSUED
5,5% Cum Prefs R2	3000000	3000000
Ords R1	180000000	154666813

FINANCIAL STATISTICS (AT FINANCIAL YEAR END)

(Amts in R'000)	1991 Dec	1990 Dec	1989 Dec	1988 Dec	1987 Dec
Ord S/H Int	1941000	1331000	1311000	1133800	1006800
Long Trm Loans	742000	578000	495000	482000	484000
Iss Ord Share	154667	154667	154667	154667	154667
Total Liab	2087000	1904000	1792000	1701400	1311400
Current Liab	1345000	1326000	1297000	1219400	827400
Total Assets	4028000	3235000	3103000	2835200	2318200
Current Assets	1987000	1819000	1804000	1654400	1249000
Debtors	988000	852000	799000	782400	565000
Inventory	997000	965000	948000	865000	671000
Turnover	5280000	5031000	4757000	4083000	3276000
Oper Profit	405000	502000	604000	473000	379000
Interest Paid	175000	149000	122000	82800	76000
Tax Paid	72000	146000	210300	163000	111000
Prf af Int&Tax	191000	245000	308400	254000	219000
Prf att Ord Sh	187000	238000	313800	255500	213000
Btm Line Earn	187000	238000	313800	255500	213000
Dividend Paid	90000	135000	135000	116000	102000
Mkt Prce(c) YE	900	1325	1650	1450	1100
Depreciation	193000	171300	152600	156700	143900

PER SHARE STATISTICS (CENTS)

Net Asst Val	1254 95	860 56	847 63	733 06	650 95
Net Earnings	121 00	154 00	203 00	165 00	138 00
Dividends	58 00	87 00	87 00	75 00	66 00
Cash Flow	250 86	280 15	290 43	261 01	230 75

RATIOS AND OTHER INFORMATION

Mrk Cap(R000)	1392003	2049338	2552006	2242672	1701337
Current Ratio	1 48	1 37	1 39	1 36	1 51
Quik/Acid Tst	0 74	0 64	0 66	0 65	0 70
A/C Rec T/ovr	5 34	5 90	5 95	5 22	5 80
Tot Ass T/ovr	1 31	1 56	1 53	1 44	1 41
Debt/Ass Rat	0 45	0 51	0 53	0 55	0 51
L T L Tot Ass	0 12	0 10	0 11	0 12	0 15
Debt to Eqity	0 94	1 24	1 24	1 37	1 17
Interest Cover	2 43	3 52	5 15	5 94	5 34
Oper Prof Mrg	7 67	9 98	12 70	11 58	11 57
Net Prof Marg%	3 54	4 73	6 60	6 26	6 50
Ret on Assets	11 07	16 79	21 08	17 96	17 51
Ret on Equity%	9 63	17 88	23 94	22 53	21 16
Price/Earnings	7 44	8 60	8 13	8 79	7 97
Divid Cover	2 09	1 77	2 33	2 20	2 09
Divid Yield	6 44	6 57	5 27	5 17	6 00
Earning Yield%	13 44	11 62	12 30	11 38	12 55
NAV % Mrk Pr	139 44	64 95	51 37	50 56	59 18
Effec Tax Rate	28 40	36 31	45 33	43 43	40 26
Def Interval	2 46	1 84	1 40	1 68	1 49
Sus Grth Rate	5 00	7 74	13 64	12 30	11 03

SUBSIDIARY & ASSOCIATED COMPANIES

ACRYLIC PRODUCTS (PTY) LTD
AEC ELECTRONICS (PTY) LTD
AECI (BOPHUTHATSWANA) (PTY) LTD
AECI (PHARMACEUTICALS) (PTY) LTD
AECI CHLOR ALKALI & PLASTICS LTD
AECI ELECTRONICS (PTY) LTD
AECI ENGINEERING CAPE (PTY) LTD
AECI EXPLOSIVES & CHEMICALS LTD
AECI INDUSTRIAL CHEMICAL (PTY) LTD
AECI INFORMATION SERVICES (PTY) LTD
AECI MODDERFONTEIN PROPERTIES (PTY) LTD
AECI NETWORKING SERVICES (PTY) LTD
ALLIANCE PEROXIDE PROPERTIES (PTY) LTD (50%)
ALUMINIUM CHEMICALS (PTY) LTD (40%)
ANIKEM (PTY) LTD (50%)
AUTOPLASTIC (PTY) LTD
AZON CONTROLS (PTY) LTD
BERG AGRI SOLUTIONS (PTY) LTD (50%)
BLASTING & EXCAVATING (PTY) LTD (50%)
CAPE CHEMICAL STORAGE (PTY) LTD
CAPEX (PTY) LTD
CHEMICAL RESOURCES (PTY) LTD
CHEMICAL SERVICES LTD
CHEMIESE NYWERHEDE VAN SA (EDMS) BPK (50%)
CHEMRISK SERVICES (PTY) LTD
CLIVE TEUBES (PTY) LTD (50%)
CONSOLIDATED SALT (PTY) LTD
CREST CHEMICALS (PTY) LTD (50%)
CURNOW M&G LTD (35%)
DPI HOLDINGS (PTY) LTD
DPI PLASTICS (PTY) LTD (50%)
DUCO FRANCHISING (PTY) LTD (50%)
DULUX (PTY) LTD
DULUX PAINT N PAPER (PTY) LTD
EXACTUM (PTY) LTD
EXPERT EXPLOSIVES (PTY) LTD
EXPLO CARRIERS (PTY) LTD
FEDMIS PHALABORWA (PTY) LTD
GOLDCHEM (PTY) LTD (50%)

ICI-KYNOCH AGROCHEMICALS (PTY) LTD (40%)
INDUSTRIAL URETHANES (PTY) LTD
JAMES SYDNEY & CO (PTY) LTD
KYNOCH AGROCHEMICAL HOLDINGS (PTY) LTD
KYNOCH CHEMICALS (PTY) LTD
KYNOCH FEEDS (PTY) LTD
KYNOCH FERTILIZER LTD
MOCOM PLASTIC MANUFACTURERS (PTY) LTD
MOCOM PLASTICS MANUFACTURING (PTY) LTD
NETHERLANDS FERTILIZER (EDMS) BPK
PALCASE (EDMS) BPK (50%)
PD TERMINALS (PTY) LTD (24%)
PEROXIDE CHEMICALS (PTY) LTD
PLASTAMID (PTY) LTD (50%)
POLYFOS (PTY) LTD (50%)
POLYOL CHEMICALS (PTY) LTD
POTEC SHIPPING (EDMS) BPK (50%)
PVC COMPOUNDERS (PTY) LTD
RECYCLING PLASTIC (PTY) LTD
RESINKEM (PTY) LTD (50%)
RICHARDS BAY BULK STORAGE (PTY) LTD (25%)
RICHARDS BAY FERTILIZER (PTY) LTD (50%)
ROLFES (ORGANIC COLOURS) (PTY) LTD (50%)
SAARCHEM (PTY) LTD
SALDANHA BAY ALUMINIUM CO. (PTY) LTD
SANS TEXTILES LTD
SIDI PARANI (PTY) LTD
SILTECH SERVICES (PTY) LTD
SILTECH SERVICES (PTY) LTD
SOUTH AFRICAN NYLON SPINNERS (PTY) LTD
SPECTRUM CHEMICALS (PTY) LTD
SWIMLINE (PTY) LTD
SWIMLINE HOLDINGS LTD
TIOXIDE SOUTHERN AFRICA (PTY) LTD (40%)
VAALWES LANDBOU DIENSTE (EDMS) BPK (50%)
VACUUM METALLISING (PTY) LTD
VYNIDE (PTY) LTD
WTS MINERALS (PTY) LTD

INVESTMENTS

SMALL BUSINESS DEV. CORP. LTD (1500000 SH)

AFCOM GROUP LTD

ABBREVIATION : AFRICOM

JSE SHORT CODE : AFM

SECTOR : Industrial-Paper & Packaging

SHAREHOLDERS

Who Owns Whom's Assessment of the Identity of the Ultimate Controlling Shareholder: BIDCORP VIA BIDVEST

SHAREHOLDER	PERCENTAGE 1992	1991
BIDVEST LTD	80.0	80.1
BIDVEST GROUP LTD	6.8	2.5
LIBERTY LIFE ASSOC OF AFRICA LTD	3.8	3.8
SA MUTUAL	1.6	---
STD BANK NOM TVL P/L	1.3	1.4
ANGLO AMERICAN GROUP PENS FUND	---	2.9
INVESTEC NOM P/L	---	3.3
SAGE LIFE LTD	---	1.4
TOTAL	93.5	95.4

DIRECTORS :
BERSON BL MR (Financial Director),CHIPKIN M MR
DEMETRIADES G MR,HARRISBERG RA MR
JOFFE B MR (Executive Chairman),PAMENSKY JL MR
RALPHS L MR,SALOMON AC MR (Managing Director)
VAN RYSSEN JLC MR (Technical Director

REGISTRATION NUMBER : 85/01287/06

REGISTERED OFFICE
Afcom House, 3 Fortune Road, Old Mutual Industrial Park
City Deep, Johannesburg
2001
TEL: 011-613 7421
FAX: 011-613 7441

TRANSFER SECRETARY
Mercantile Registrars Ltd
P O Box 1053, Johannesburg
2000
TEL: 011-333 8181

COMPANY SECRETARY
B G Kerkhoff

NATURE OF BUSINESS
Company is a manufacturer, convertor and distributor of fastening, packaging, strapping, adhesive tape and stationery products to a broad cross-section of commerce and industry,mining and agriculture.

BANKERS :
Nedcor Bank Ltd

AUDITORS :
KPMG Aiken & Peat

FAMILIAR BRAND NAMES
ADENAX,AFTAK,BUFFSTIK,CELLUX,HARTCO,INSEAL
ITIPACK,JONROD,KWIKSTIK,MARKWELL,PASLODE
RAPID,ROTOR,SELLOTAPE,SENCO,SIAT,SIGNODE
SOFRAGRAF,STRAPACK,STRAPEX,TESA,TI-STRAP

CONTRIBUTION BY ACTIVITY
N/A

YEAR END : June

DIVIDEND : Ords 1c

Final	(Ldr)31/08/90	(Pay)18/09/90	Amt(c)5
Interim	(Ldr)22/02/91	(Pay)28/02/91	Amt(c)3.25
Final	(Ldr)06/09/91	(Pay)16/09/91	Amt(c)3.75
Interim	(Ldr)21/02/92	(Pay)28/02/92	Amt(c)4.25
Final	(Ldr)28/08/92	(Pay)18/09/92	Amt(c)4.45

NUMBER OF EMPLOYEES : 860

CAPITAL STRUCTURE

	AUTHORISED	ISSUED
Ords 1c	60000000	34277668
Unsec Comp Conv Debs 150c	4000000	4000000
Unsec Comp Conv Debs 105c	8917032	8917032

FINANCIAL STATISTICS (AT FINANCIAL YEAR END)

(Amts in R'000)	1992 Jun	1991 Jun	1990 Jun	1989 Feb	1988 Feb

Ord S/H Int	25438	21441	20064	15898	14316
Long Trm Loans	17910	22510	23606	16220	6905
Iss Ord Share	34278	34278	29710	27460	23860
Total Liab	36152	35801	42311	38587	21741
Current Liab	18242	13291	18705	22367	14836
Total Assets	56240	51892	57025	49069	36057
Intang Assets	5350	5350	5350	5416	*
Current Assets	49728	45646	49755	43825	26249
Debtors	21745	19828	22326	17306	12736
Inventory	27970	25807	27263	26328	13277
Turnover	120007	107101	151278	94479	53143
Oper Profit	15620	10864	20508	16722	8641
Interest Paid	3590	3432	4095	1839	859
Tax Paid	4580	2995	7680	7013	3316
Prf af Int&Tax	7450	5818	8733	7870	4466
Prf att Ord Sh	7450	5818	6054	5455	4466
Btm Line Earn	7450	5818	5246	5378	2606
Dividend Paid	2982	2399	2377	2362	1670
Mkt Prce(c) YE	180	110	95	165	110
Depreciation	949	1480	1897	1022	903

PER SHARE STATISTICS (CENTS)

Net Asst Val	58 60	46 94	49 53	38 17	60 00
Net Earnings	21 70	17 60	20 80	24 50	18 70
Dividends	8 70	7 00	5 60	13 50	7 00
Cash Flow	25 08	22 73	20 57	23 48	23 51

RATIOS AND OTHER INFORMATION

Mrk Cap(R000)	61700	37706	28225	45309	26246
Current Ratio	2 73	3 43	2 66	1 96	1 77
Quik/Acid Tst	1 19	1 49	1 20	0 78	0 87
A/C Rec T/ovr	5 52	5 40	5 08	5 46	4 17
Tot Ass T/ovr	2 13	2 06	1 99	1 93	1 47
Debt/Ass Rat	0 63	0 68	0 57	0 63	0 59
L T L Tot Ass	0 30	0 42	0 25	0 17	0 18
Debt to Eqity	1 38	1 64	1 63	1 94	1 49
Interest Cover	4 35	3 57	5 01	9 09	10 06
Oper Prof Mrg	13 02	10 14	13 56	17 70	16 26
Net Prof Marg%	6 21	5 43	4 00	5 77	8 40
Ret on Assets	27 77	23 60	26 97	34 08	23 96
Ret on Equity%	29 29	27 13	22 63	34 31	31 20
Price/Earnings	8 29	6 25	4 57	6 73	5 88
Divid Cover	2 49	2 51	3 71	1 81	2 67
Divid Yield	4 83	6 36	5 89	8 18	6 36
Earning Yield%	12 06	16 00	21 89	14 85	17 00
NAV % Mrk Pr	32 56	42 68	52 13	23 13	54 55
Effec Tax Rate	36 43	37 15	46 52	47 32	39 53
Def Interval	0 19	0 85	0 76	1 11	0 64
Sus Grth Rate	17 56	15 95	18 33	19 46	19 53

SUBSIDIARY & ASSOCIATED COMPANIES

AFRICAN COMMERCE DEVELOPING CO (PTY) LTD
BIDPAC LTD
BUFFALO TAPES (PTY) LTD
JONROD MANUFACTURING (PTY) LTD
MARKWELL (AFRICA) (PTY) LTD
TI STRAP (PTY) LTD

INVESTMENTS

None

AFEX CORPORATION SOCIETE ANONYME

ABBREVIATION : AFEX SA

JSE SHORT CODE : AXR

SECTOR : Industrial-Industrial Holding

SHAREHOLDERS

Who Owns Whom's Assessment of the Identity of the Ultimate Controlling Shareholder: CONSOLIDATED AFEX CORP

SHAREHOLDER	PERCENTAGE 1992	1991
LONDON CONTROL ACCOUNT	95 0	95 1
SAREMBOCK L A	1 5	1 9
TOTAL	96 5	96 9

DIRECTORS :
KERR RC ,LATILLA CAMPBELL CP ,LATILLA-CAMPBELL P
MARSHALL DC (Chairman),ROBOTHAM JM ,WIGLEY FL

REGISTRATION NUMBER : B19600 (Lux)

REGISTERED OFFICE
68-70 Boulevard de la Petrusse, L-2320, Luxembourg
SA 11 Floor, Field Street, Durban
4001
TEL 031-305 6521
FAX 031-301 9791

TRANSFER SECRETARY
Central Registrars Ltd
P O Box 4844, Johannesburg
2000
TEL 011-331 0051

COMPANY SECRETARY
City Group Ltd

NATURE OF BUSINESS
The corporation acts as an authentic Luxembourg holding company divided into three divisions
a In Luxembourg it deals in currencies and listed investments predominantly in the USA.
b In Zimbabwe it owns rent producing properties and farms tobacco, maize and livestock and also has investments in gold producers, brick producers, potteries and wire products
c In SA it owns properties,farms and a portfolio of gold and industrial holdings

BANKERS :
Credit Suisse

AUDITORS :
Deloitte Pim Goldby

FAMILIAR BRAND NAMES
N/A

CONTRIBUTION BY ACTIVITY
South Africa (% turnover) (66 6%)
South Africa (% Trading Profit) (35 8%)
Zimbabwe (% turnover) (24 6%)
Australia and others (% turnover) (8 8%)

Zimbabwe (% Trading Profit) (55 5%)
Australia and others (% Trading Profit) (8 7%)

YEAR END : September

DIVIDEND : Ords US$1 50

Dividend (Ldr)08/03/91 (Pay)19/04/91 Amt(c)10

CAPITAL STRUCTURE

	AUTHORISED	ISSUED
Ords US$1 50	7500000	6536543

FINANCIAL STATISTICS (AT FINANCIAL YEAR END)

(Amts in $)	1991 Sep	1990 Sep	1989 Sep	1988 Sep	1987
Ord S/H Int	21068	15701	14667	10346	18132
Long Trm Loans	10177	8994	6450	6643	14037
Iss Ord Share	6114	3819	3691	3517	3561
Total Liab	18577	16284	10431	11325	19253
Current Liab	8400	7290	3981	4682	5216
Total Assets	39645	31985	25098	21671	40991
Current Assets	13895	10104	6591	4734	8822
Debtors	5053	4637	3197	2319	-
Inventory	5270	4483	2276	1725	8822
Turnover	43978	32403	20680	18754	12427
Oper Profit	2596	2795	3003	2423	1926
Interest Paid	1618	1350	908	851	639
Tax Paid	662	438	729	979	930
Prf af Int&Tax	1385	2139	2374	1568	1287
Prf att Ord Sh	-576	2	383	84	994
Btm Line Earn	-1151	845	3444	1793	994
Dividend Paid	611	382	332	317	285
Mkt Prce(c) YE	575	750	675	625	350
Depreciation	1135	407	417	377	-

PER SHARE STATISTICS (CENTS)

Net Asst Val	344 59	411 13	397 37	294 17	509 18
Net Earnings	6 60	42 90	49 60	27 30	-
Dividends	10 00	10 00	9 00	9 00	-
Cash Flow	33 73	50 04	62 14	38 37	36 14

RATIOS AND OTHER INFORMATION

Mrk Cap(R000)	35156	28643	24914	21981	12464
Current Ratio	1 65	1 39	1 66	1 01	1 69
Quik/Acid Tst	1 03	0 77	1 08	0 64	-
A/C Rec T/ovr	8 70	6 99	6 47	8 09	-
Tot Ass T/ovr	1 11	1 01	0 82	0 87	0 30
Debt/Ass Rat	0 40	0 43	0 38	0 48	0 47
L T L Tot Ass	0 19	0 20	0 22	0 26	0 34
Debt to Eqity	0 75	0 88	0 66	1 00	1 06
Interest Cover	2 22	2 88	4 09	3 89	4 47
Oper Prof Mrg	5 90	8 63	14 52	12 92	15 50
Net Prof Marg%	-1 31	0 01	1 85	0 45	8 00
Ret on Assets	9 00	12 28	15 98	15 68	6 97
Ret on Equity%	-2 73	0 01	2 61	0 81	5 48
Price/Earnings	87 12	17 48	13 61	22 89	
Divid Cover	0 66	4 29	5 51	3 03	
Divid Yield	1 74	1 33	1 33	1 44	-
Earning Yield%	1 15	5 72	7 35	4 37	-
NAV % Mrk Pr	59 93	54 82	58 87	47 07	145 48
Effec Tax Rate	52 42	28 64	30 03	57 25	72 26
Def Interval	5 56	4 47	2 56		10 91
Sus Grth Rate	-5 63	-2 42	0 35	-2 25	3 91

SUBSIDIARY & ASSOCIATED COMPANIES

287 MARSHALL STREET (PTY) LTD (50%)
AFEX INTERNATIONAL FINANCE LTD
BULAWAYO BOARD OF EXECUTORS AND TRUST CO (37 4%)
CALAFEX INC
CALAFEX INC USA
CERAMIC INDUSTRIES (BOTSWANA) (PTY) LTD
DELMAS KUIKEN (PTY) LTD
FALCON MINES PLC (26%)
FINAFEX HOLDINGS A G
GVL INDUSTRIES (PTY) LTD (25%)
INDUSTRIAL CHEMICALS (PTY) LTD
L & G TOOL & MACHINERY DISTRIBUTORS LTD (50 1%)
MASTER TOOL & MACHINERY LTD (ENGLAND)
MASTER TOOL AND MACHINERY LTD (50 1%)
OLYMPUS GOLD MINES LTD (50 1%)
OLYMPUS GOLD MINES LTD (ZIMBABWE) (20%)
PLAZAFAX INC
PLAZAFEX INC USA
QUEENSLAND TOOL AND MACHINERY DISTRIBUTI (50 1%)
SOUTHERN CERAMICS (PTY) LTD (40%)
SUBAFEX INVESTMENTS LTD
SUSSEX INVESTMENTS (PTY) LTD
SUSSEX PROPERTIES (PTY) LTD
SUSSEX SECURITIES LTD
SUSSEX TRADING HOLDINGS (PTY) LTD
TOOL & ELECTRICAL DISTRIBUTORS (PTY) LTD (50 1%)
WILLSGROVE BRICK AND POTTERIES LTD (34 5%)
ZIMCOR LTD
ZIMCOR LTD (ZIMBABWE)

INVESTMENTS

None

AFMIN HOLDINGS LTD

ABBREVIATION : AFMIN

JSE SHORT CODE : AFN

SECTOR : Mining Financial-Mining Holding

SHAREHOLDERS

Who Owns Whom's Assessment of the Identity of the Ultimate Controlling Shareholder: DIRECTORS/FOREIGN INSTITUTIONS

SHAREHOLDER	PERCENTAGE 1992	1991
CMH INV P/L	53 3	53 3
FIRST NAT NOM P/L	9 8	9 8
AURORA CACEY SA	6 7	6 7
STD BANK NOM TVL P/L	6 6	5 8
INDO CHINA NOM P/L	6 0	---
MARCH NOM SOC ANONYME	1 5	1 5
VAN DEN HEEVER P J	1 4	1 8
INDO CHINA NOM SA P/L	---	5 9
TOTAL	85 3	84 9

DIRECTORS :
BERRY MK ,HEEVER C (Chairman),ROBINSON WL
TUCKER PE ,VORSTER MD

REGISTRATION NUMBER : 85/03339/06

REGISTERED OFFICE
3rd Floor, 165 Smit Street
Braamfontein
2001

TEL 011-403 2930
FAX 011-339 3694

TRANSFER SECRETARY
Central Registrars Ltd
P O Box 4844, Johannesburg
2000
TEL 011-331 0051

COMPANY SECRETARY
African Exploration Company Ltd

NATURE OF BUSINESS
An investment holding company with interests in base metals,dimension stone,gold mining & mining supplies

BANKERS :
First National Bank of SA Ltd

AUDITORS :
RA Hellman & Co

FAMILIAR BRAND NAMES
N/A

CONTRIBUTION BY ACTIVITY
N/A

YEAR END : December

DIVIDEND :Ords no par value

Interim No 1	(Ldr)09/03/90	(Pay)23/04/90	Amt(c)0 5
Final No 2	(Ldr)10/05/91	(Pay)24/05/91	Amt(c)3

NUMBER OF EMPLOYEES : 407

CAPITAL STRUCTURE

	AUTHORISED	ISSUED
Ords no par value	123204000	23606372
'A Deferred Ords no par value	33544000	166660

FINANCIAL STATISTICS (AT FINANCIAL YEAR END)

(Amts in R 000)	1991 Dec	1990 Dec	1989 Jun	1988 Jun	1987
Ord S/H Int	24105	41762	14327	14080	13413
Long Trm Loans	42084	32453	52	145	1297
Iss Ord Share	23606	22909	24000	24000	24000
Total Liab	58632	51285	1866	1670	2594
Current Liab	16548	18832	1814	1525	1297
Total Assets	67291	77598	16193	15750	23752
Intang Assets	15446	15449	*	*	*
Current Assets	35064	39675	1282	2436	9042
Debtors	9963	10141	354	767	-
Inventory	9585	4857	408	225	9042
Turnover	36978	35767	8484	4656	-
Oper Profit	4524	6734	192	789	39
Interest Paid	3258	1308	50	-	15
Tax Paid	573	761	90	121	17
Prf af Int&Tax	2978	6003	247	668	7
Prf att Ord Sh	-657	3523	247	668	7
Btm Line Earn	657	3523	247	668	7
Dividend Paid	772	1992			-
Mkt Prce(c) YE	20	45	27	60	110
Depreciation	1292	3056		-	-

PER SHARE STATISTICS (CENTS)

Net Asst Val	36 68	114 86	59 70	58 67	55 89
Net Earnings	12 62	44 16	-	-	-
Dividends	3 30	3 50			
Cash Flow	2 78	19 15	1 03	2 78	0 03

RATIOS AND OTHER INFORMATION

Mrk Cap(R000)	4721	10309	6480	14400	26400
Current Ratio	2 12	2 11	0 71	1 60	6 97
Quik/Acid Tst	1 54	1 85	0 48	1 45	-
A/C Rec T/ovr	3 71	2 35	23 97	6 07	-
Tot Ass T/ovr	0 55	0 31	0 52	0 30	
Debt/Ass Rat	0 43	0 33	0 12	0 11	0 11
L T L Tot Ass	0 19	0 08	0 00	0 01	0 05
Debt to Eqity	1 21	0 61	0 13	0 12	0 19
Interest Cover	1 39	5 15	3 84	-	2 60
Oper Prof Mrg	12 23	18 83	2 26	16 95	
Net Prof Marg%	-1 78	9 85	2 91	14 35	-
Ret on Assets	10 12	6 93	2 39	5 01	0 16
Ret on Equity%	2 73	5 62	1 72	4 74	0 05
Price/Earnings	1 58	1 02	-	-	
Divid Cover	3 82	12 62	-	-	-
Divid Yield	16 50	7 78	-	-	-
Earning Yield%	63 10	98 13	-	-	-
NAV % Mrk Pr	183 41	255 24	221 10	97 78	50 81
Effec Tax Rate	6 51	10 54	26 71	14 07	70 83
Def Interval	17 41	0 57	1 26	0 25	185 29
Sus Grth Rate	-5 93	3 67	1 72	4 74	0 05

SUBSIDIARY & ASSOCIATED COMPANIES

AFRICAN EXPLORATION CO LTD
MINACO GRANITE & MARBLE LTD (31 6%)
MINERAL COMMODITY MARKETING LTD
NAMIB LEAD MINES (PTY) LTD
NAMIBIA LITHIUM MINES (PTY) LTD
ROODEPOORT GOLD MINE (PTY) LTD

INVESTMENTS

None

AFRICAN & OVERSEAS ENTERPRISES LTD

ABBREVIATION : AF-&-OVER

JSE SHORT CODE : AOO

SECTOR : Industrial Clothing, Footwear & Textiles

SHAREHOLDERS

Who Owns Whom's Assessment of the Identity of the Ultimate Controlling Shareholder: DIRECTORS

SHAREHOLDER	PERCENTAGE 1992	1991
BERNMOND P/L	51 8	51 8
SA MUTUAL	24 9	24 9
STD BANK NOM TVL P/L	5 7	5 7
SCOTT W J D	5 2	---
MOORE P H	2 2	2 2
FERBROS NOM P/L	1 1	-
EIGHTY ONE MAIN STREET NOM LTD	- -	1 3
FIRST NAT NOM P/L	---	4 9
TOTAL	90 8	90 8

DIRECTORS :
AXELSON NC ,DIBOWITZ PJ ,SHUB CM
SHUB SC (Chairman),SINCLAIRE CJ ,THOMAS GM

REGISTRATION NUMBER : 05/27461/06

REGISTERED OFFICE
263 Victoria Road, Salt River
Cape Town
7925
TEL 021 448 4660
FAX 021-448 1552

TRANSFER SECRETARY
Mercantile Registrars Ltd
P O Box 1053, Johannesburg
2000
TEL 011-333 8181

COMPANY SECRETARY
A A Hodgkinson

NATURE OF BUSINESS
An investment holding company with a controlling interest in quoted Rex Trueform Group activities include manufacturing & marketing of clothing

BANKERS .
Standard Bank of SA Ltd
UAL Merchant Bank Ltd

AUDITORS :
Ernst & Young

FAMILIAR BRAND NAMES
DAKS OF LONDON,JOHN STEPHEN OF LON
LANVIN OF PARIS

CONTRIBUTION BY ACTIVITY
N/A

YEAR END : June

DIVIDEND : Ords 50c

Final No 38	(Ldr)23/11/90	(Pay)07/12/90	Amt(c)80
Final No 40	(Ldr)20/11/92	(Pay)04/12/92	Amt(c)72

CAPITAL STRUCTURE

	AUTHORISED	ISSUED
6% Partic Cum Prefs R2	275000	275000
Ords 50c	1250000	1250000
A Ords (Non Voting) 50c	1250000	1250000

FINANCIAL STATISTICS (AT FINANCIAL YEAR END)

(Amts in R 000)	1992 Jun	1991 Jun	1990 Jun	1989 Jun	1988 Jun
Ord S/H Int	49012	46960	44310	39839	31932
Long Trm Loans	43165	42583	47142	50498	46413
Iss Ord Share	1250	1250	1250	1250	1250
Total Liab	66457	66085	68278	66904	60784
Current Liab	23292	23502	21136	16406	14371
Total Assets	115469	113045	112588	106743	92716
Current Assets	100132	99332	100227	95719	83327
Debtors	30393	30799	36127	34219	32516
Inventory	66377	58577	46785	41394	34925
Oper Profit	6722	7574	15900	16312	11314
Interest Paid	1819	1583	619	784	
Tax Paid	412	2064	7354	422	343
Prf af Int&Tax	6421	7860	12069	18175	12808
Prf att Ord Sh	3674	4594	6346	9502	6544
Btm Line Earn	3674	4594	6346	9502	5988
Dividend Paid	1800	2000	2000	2000	1500
Mkt Prce(c) YE	700	1025	1150	1200	850
Depreciation	2428	2461	2176	1630	1373

PER SHARE STATISTICS (CENTS)

Net Asst Val	3920 96	3756 80	3544 80	3187 12	2554 56
Net Earnings	147 00	183 80	253 80	380 10	261 80
Dividends	72 00	80 00	80 00	80 00	60 00
Cash Flow	228 40	293 76	323 44	418 68	297 92

RATIOS AND OTHER INFORMATION

Mrk Cap(R000)	8750	12813	14375	15000	10625
Current Ratio	4 30	4 23	4 74	5 83	5 80
Quik/Acid Tst	1 45	1 73	2 53	3 31	3 37
Debt/Ass Rat	0 22	0 23	0 27	0 20	0 22
L T L Tot Ass	0 02	0 03	0 09	0 04	0 07
Debt to Eqity	0 52	0 56	0 70	0 53	0 64
Interest Cover	3 93	5 15	25 69	20 81	-
Ret on Assets	7 55	10 21	18 19	18 78	14 69
Ret on Equity%	7 50	9 78	14 32	23 85	20 49
Price/Earnings	4 76	5 58	4 53	3 16	3 25
Divid Cover	2 04	2 30	3 17	4 75	4 36
Divid Yield	10 29	7 80	6 96	6 67	7 06
Earning Yield%	21 00	17 93	22 07	31 68	30 80
NAV % Mrk Pr	560 14	366 52	308 24	265 59	300 54
Effec Tax Rate	10 29	18 25	37 73	2 27	2 91
Def Interval	1 85	1 41	1 38	0 66	1 12
Sus Grth Rate	3 82	5 52	9 81	18 83	15 80

SUBSIDIARY & ASSOCIATED COMPANIES

EVEREST MARKETING CORPORATION LTD (50%)
JUDGE PROPERTY INVESTMENTS (PTY) LTD (50%)
L'UOMO ATLANTIS (PTY) LTD
REX TRUEFORM CLOTHING CO LTD
TWEEDSMUIR INVESTMENTS (PTY) LTD
VELCO INVESTMENTS (PTY) LTD
VELLA SPORTSWEAR LTD

INVESTMENTS

SA FRANCHISING (PTY) LTD (2 SH)
SMALL BUSINESS DEV CORP (104800 SH)
SOUTHERN LIFE ASSOCIATION LTD (900 SH)
TWEEDSPROP INVESTMENTS (PTY) LTD (150 SH)

AFRICAN CABLES LTD

ABBREVIATION : AF-CABLE

JSE SHORT CODE : ACA

SECTOR : Industrial Electronics, Electrical & Bat

SHAREHOLDERS

Who Owns Whom's Assessment of the Identity of the Ultimate Controlling Shareholder.
SA MUTUAL VIA BARLOWS

SHAREHOLDER	PERCENTAGE 1992	1991
AFCAB HOLDINGS P/L	79 7	-
ASSOCIATED ELECTRICAL IND LTD	9 6	15 9

STD BANK NOM TVL P/L	7 5	15 6
DE BEERS PENS FUND	1 4	2 2
ANGLO AMERICAN CORP PENS FUND	1 2	1 8
CULLINAN HOLDINGS LTD	- -	50 9
FIRST NAT NOM P/L	---	2 3
SANLAM	---	7 3
TOTAL	99 4	96 0

DIRECTORS :
ELLINGFORD AJ ,GOSMANN GRD ,JOHNSON OS
MULLER PJ (Managing Director)
PARKER CC (Chairman),PFEDERKAEMPER WE
SANNE RJF ,TAYLOR WJ ,VAUX CFH

REGISTRATION NUMBER : 05/07491/06

REGISTERED OFFICE
Steel Road, Peacehaven
Vereeniging
1939
TEL 016-4 5821
FAX 016-4 5425

TRANSFER SECRETARY
Consolidated Share Registrars Ltd
P O Box 61051, Marshalltown
2107
TEL 011-492 1620

COMPANY SECRETARY
D J de Jager

NATURE OF BUSINESS
Manufacture & sale of electric power cables, low tension PVC cable, medium tension XLPE cable, telecommunication cable & house wiring The group also installs supertension cable

BANKERS :
Standard Bank of SA Ltd, Nedperm Bank Ltd

AUDITORS :
Deloitte Pim Goldby

FAMILIAR BRAND NAMES
ZEROTOX

CONTRIBUTION BY ACTIVITY
N/A

YEAR END : September

DIVIDEND : Ords 25c

Interim No 64	(Ldr)23/03/90	(Pay)02/05/90	Amt(c)11
Final No 65	(Ldr)05/10/90	(Pay)31/10/90	Amt(c)22
Interim No 66	(Ldr)22/03/91	(Pay)02/05/91	Amt(c)11
Final No 67	(Ldr)04/10/91	(Pay)31/10/91	Amt(c)11
Interim No 68	(Ldr)22/05/92	(Pay)26/06/92	Amt(c)12
Final No 69	(Ldr)20/11/92	(Pay)31/12/92	Amt(c)15

NUMBER OF EMPLOYEES : 1044

CAPITAL STRUCTURE

	AUTHORISED	ISSUED
Ords 25c	39930000	39544391

FINANCIAL STATISTICS (AT FINANCIAL YEAR END)

(Amts in R'000)	1992 Sep	1991 Jun	1990 Jun	1989 Jun	1988 Jun
Ord S/H Int	108304	92450	85982	75327	60504
Long Trm Loans	1569	-	-	62	5253
Iss Ord Share	39544	23800	23800	23800	23800
Total Liab	52989	44860	42942	42942	40190
Current Liab	51420	44860	42942	42880	34937
Total Assets	161293	137310	128924	118269	100694
Current Assets	111550	82355	81717	95259	78162
Debtors	32347	36249	29726	4080	29023
Inventory	50086	46087	45699	44945	27786
Turnover	310062	171682	187160	156305	109577
Oper Profit	36408	18571	34391	28644	17635
Interest Paid	3881	3673	2898	1721	-
Tax Paid	15649	5963	15608	11975	9064
Prf af Int&Tax	20524	11380	18383	16992	10095
Prf att Ord Sh	20650	11188	18509	17061	10095
Btm Line Earn	17662	11188	18509	17061	10095
Dividend Paid	10735	5236	7854	7378	6664
Mkt Prce(c) YE	320	650	400	375	260
Depreciation	7836	2626	2341	2194	2377

PER SHARE STATISTICS (CENTS)

Net Asst Val	273 88	388 45	361 27	316 50	254 22
Net Earnings	56 80	47 00	77 80	71 70	42 40
Dividends	27 00	22 00	33 00	31 00	28 00
Cash Flow	63 28	58 85	87 08	80 61	52 92

RATIOS AND OTHER INFORMATION

Mrk Cap(R000)	126541	154700	95200	89250	61880
Current Ratio	2 17	1 84	1 90	2 22	2 24
Quik/Acid Tst	1 20	0 81	0 84	1 17	1 44
A/C Rec T/ovr	7 67	4 74	6 30	3 83	4 12
Tot Ass T/ovr	1 54	1 25	1 45	1 32	1 19
Debt/Ass Rat	0 32	0 33	0 33	0 36	0 35
L T L Tot Ass	0 00	-	-	0 00	0 00
Debt to Eqity	0 48	0 49	0 50	0 57	0 58
Interest Cover	10 06	5 65	12 55	17 58	-
Oper Prof Mrg	11 74	10 82	18 38	18 33	16 09
Net Prof Marg%	6 66	6 52	9 89	10 92	9 21
Ret on Assets	19 93	15 17	28 71	26 01	20 76
Ret on Equity%	15 25	12 10	21 53	22 65	18 20
Price/Earnings	5 63	13 83	5 14	5 23	6 13
Divid Cover	2 10	2 14	2 36	2 31	1 51
Divid Yield	8 44	3 38	8 25	8 27	10 77
Earning Yield%	17 75	7 23	19 45	19 12	16 31
NAV % Mrk Pr	85 59	59 76	90 32	84 40	97 78
Effec Tax Rate	45 40	36 63	48 75	43 76	56 55
Def Interval	0 13	1 18	0 14	0 00	0 01
Sus Grth Rate	9 15	6 44	12 39	12 85	5 67

SUBSIDIARY & ASSOCIATED COMPANIES

ELECTRIC PRODUCTS INTERNATIONAL (PTY) LT (20%)
POWER TRANSMISSION CONSULTING (PTY) LTD
SIEMENS CABLES (PTY) LTD

INVESTMENTS

None

AFRICAN DISTILLERS LTD

ABBREVIATION : AFDISTIL

SECTOR : Zimbabwe Stock Exchange

SHAREHOLDERS

Who Owns Whom's Assessment of the Identity of the Ultimate Controlling Shareholder:
AFDIS HOLDINGS (PVT) LTD

SHAREHOLDER	PERCENTAGE 1992	1991
AFDIS HOLDINGS PVT LTD	58 4	---
SECURITY NOM LTD	4 3	---
FIRST NOM PVT LTD	3 9	---
OLD MUTUAL INV CORP (PVT) LTD	2 9	---
FIDELITY LIFE ASSURE OF ZIM PVT LTD	2 7	---
TEXTURED YARNS PVT LTD	1 8	---
GODDEN I D F	1 7	---
ZIMBABWE ASSETS INV CO LTD	1 2	---
TURNER R	1 0	- -
TOTAL	78 0	--

DIRECTORS :
ALLSOP RJ ,BARNARD R ,BRANDON PT ,CHIURA ED
GODDEN ID (Managing Director)
GUNN KD (Chairman),NYANDORO GB ,PATRICK J
STROEBEL FH

REGISTERED OFFICE
St Marnocks, Stapleford
Harare, Zimbabwe

TEL 32901
FAX 33909

TRANSFER SECRETARY
Sagit Transfer Secretaries (Pvt) ltd
P O Box 11, Harare
Zimbabwe

TEL 092634-738814

COMPANY SECRETARY
N H Higginbottom

NATURE OF BUSINESS
The main business of the group,all of whose subsidiaries are incorporated in Zimbabwe, consists of the manufacture, importation and wholesale distribution of wines and spirits, crushes and cordials

BANKERS :
Barclays Bank of Zimbabwe Ltd
Standard Chartered Bank Zimbabwe Ltd

AUDITORS :
Deloitte & Touche

FAMILIAR BRAND NAMES
N/A

CONTRIBUTION BY ACTIVITY
N/A

YEAR END : March

DIVIDEND : Ords Z$1

Dividend	(Ldr)18/11/91	(Pay)28/11/91	Amt(c)4
Dividend	(Ldr)29/05/92	(Pay)12/06/92	Amt(c)6

CAPITAL STRUCTURE

	AUTHORISED	ISSUED
Ords Z$1	44000000	40339620
6% Cum Prefs Z$2	75000	63100

FINANCIAL STATISTICS (AT FINANCIAL YEAR END)

(Amts in Z$)	1992 Mar	1991 Mar
Ord S/H Int	68496	60725
Long Trm Loans	7432	5023
Iss Ord Share	40340	20170
Total Liab	56802	34159
Current Liab	49370	29136
Total Assets	124713	94299
Intang Assets	585	585
Current Assets	41833	27418
Debtors	8332	6927
Inventory	33313	20394
Turnover	105833	83370
Oper Profit	24518	11177
Interest Paid	3064	1238
Tax Paid	9530	4127
Prf af Int&Tax	11944	5843
Prf att Ord Sh	11944	5983
Btm Line Earn	11944	5983
Dividend Paid	4042	2630
Depreciation	6279	3126

PER SHARE STATISTICS (CENTS)

Net Asst Val	168 35	298 17
Net Earnings	29 60	14 50
Dividends	10 00	6 50
Cash Flow	45 17	44 47

RATIOS AND OTHER INFORMATION

Current Ratio	0 85	0 94
Quik/Acid Tst	0 17	0 24
A/C Rec T/ovr	12 70	12 04
Tot Ass T/ovr	0 85	0 88
Debt/Ass Rat	0 40	0 31
Debt to Eqity	0 72	0 48
Interest Cover	8 00	9 03
Oper Prof Mrg	23 17	13 41
Net Prof Marg%	11 29	7 18
Ret on Assets	19 68	11 89
Ret on Equity%	17 44	9 85
Divid Cover	2 96	2 23
Effec Tax Rate	44 38	41 39
Def Interval	1 60	1 65
Sus Grth Rate	11 54	5 52

SUBSIDIARY & ASSOCIATED COMPANIES

GREEN VALLEY VINEYARDS (1982) (PVT) LTD
NATIONAL INDUSTRIAL CHEMICALS (PVT) LTD
WORRINGHAM VINEYARDS (PVT) LTD

INVESTMENTS

None

AFRICAN LIFE ASSURANCE CO LTD

ABBREVIATION : AFLIFE

JSE SHORT CODE : AFI

SECTOR : Financial-Insurance

SHAREHOLDERS

Who Owns Whom's Assessment of the Identity of the Ultimate Controlling Shareholder:
ANGLO VIA SOUTHERN LIFE

SHAREHOLDER	PERCENTAGE 1992	1991
SOUTHERN LIFE ASSOC LTD	75 7	78 2
CHALKTON NOM CO P/L	2 4	---
AFRICAN LIFE PENS FUND	2 4	2 5
SHARESTOCK NOM P/L	1 6	1 3
JACK W A	1 6	1 7
ROBERTS H B	---	1 1
TOTAL	83 8	84 9

DIRECTORS :
ARNOTT AH (Chairman),BODASING PR ,BRADFORD DG
JACK WA (Managing Director),MAPONYA MN MS
STAFFORD AH

REGISTRATION NUMBER : 01/03818/06

REGISTERED OFFICE
African Life Centre, 111 Commissioner Street
Johannesburg
2001
TEL 011-333 7553
FAX 011-29 3613

TRANSFER SECRETARY
Consolidated Share Registrars Ltd
P O Box 61051, Marshalltown
2107
TEL 011-492 1620

COMPANY SECRETARY
S Selamolela

NATURE OF BUSINESS
The company underwrites life assurance and invests the funds derived therefrom The activities of the company's subsidiaries consists of investment in property,the marketing of housing,providing leasing finance,the provision of added value to policyholders and training

BANKERS :
Standard Bank of SA Ltd

AUDITORS :
Ernst & Young

FAMILIAR BRAND NAMES
N/A

CONTRIBUTION BY ACTIVITY
N/A

YEAR END : March

DIVIDEND : Ords 10c

Final No 5	(Ldr)17/05/91	(Pay)12/06/91	Amt(c)5 8
Final No 7	(Ldr)08/05/92	(Pay)29/05/92	Amt(c)2 8
Interim No 8	(Ldr)13/11/92	(Pay)10/12/92	Amt(c)6

NUMBER OF EMPLOYEES : 800

CAPITAL STRUCTURE

	AUTHORISED	ISSUED
Ords 10c	100000000	61484307

FINANCIAL STATISTICS (AT FINANCIAL YEAR END)

(Amts in R'000)	1991 Mar	1990 Mar
Ord S/H Int	55129	47908
Long Trm Loans	129515	124095
Iss Ord Share	56835	53374
Total Liab	154191	140429
Current Liab	24676	16334
Total Assets	209320	188337
Current Assets	33962	25855
Debtors	30025	25705
Turnover	66241	49916
Oper Profit	25202	13783
Tax Paid	1186	-1651
Prf af Int&Tax	24016	15434
Prf att Ord Sh	24016	15434
Btm Line Earn	23641	15434
Dividend Paid	1228	1569
Mkt Prce(c) YE	205	-

PER SHARE STATISTICS (CENTS)

Net Asst Val	97 00	89 76
Net Earnings	15 30	12 30
Dividends	9 80	7 90
Cash Flow	42 26	28 92

RATIOS AND OTHER INFORMATION

Mrk Cap(R000)	116512	-
Current Ratio	1 38	1 58
Quik/Acid Tst	1 38	1 58
A/C Rec T/ovr	2 21	1 94
Tot Ass T/ovr	0 32	0 27
Debt/Ass Rat	0 12	0 09
Debt to Eqity	0 45	0 34
Oper Prof Mrg	38 05	27 61
Net Prof Marg%	36 26	30 92
Ret on Assets	12 04	7 32
Ret on Equity%	43 56	32 22
Price/Earnings	13 40	-
Divid Cover	1 56	1 56
Divid Yield	4 78	-
Earning Yield%	7 46	-
NAV % Mrk Pr	47 32	-
Effec Tax Rate	4 71	11 98
Sus Grth Rate	41 34	28 94

SUBSIDIARY & ASSOCIATED COMPANIES

AFRICAN LIFE BETTER LIFE MEMBER PROGRAMM
AFRICAN LIFE HOMES (PTY) LTD
AFRICAN LIFE LEASING & FINANCE (PTY) LTD
AFRICAN LIFE PROPERTY HOLDINGS (PTY) LTD
GUARANTEE LIFE PROPERTIES (SOUTHDALE) (P
IVY SKILLS (PTY) LTD
MALYORK ESTATES (PTY) LTD

INVESTMENTS

None

AFRICAN OXYGEN LTD

ABBREVIATION : AFROX

JSE SHORT CODE : AFX

SECTOR : Industrial Engineering

SHAREHOLDERS

Who Owns Whom's Assessment of the Identity of the Ultimate Controlling Shareholder:
BOC GROUP PLC

SHAREHOLDER	PERCENTAGE 1992	1991
BOC HOLDINGS	57 7	57 7
AFRICAN OXYGEN UNIT TRUST	7 6	7 4
SA MUTUAL	6 1	6 0
STD BANK NOM TVL P/L	3 0	2 7
CMB NOM P/L	1 5	
COMMERCIAL UNION LIFE ASSURE CO SA LTD	1 4	---
AECI PENS FUND	1 2	1 2
NEDBANK NOM LTD	1 1	1 3
FIRST NAT NOM P/L	1 1	1 1
METAL IND GROUP PENS FUND	--	1 5
ENGINEERING INDUSTRIES PENS FUND	-	1 5
COMMERCIAL UNION ASSURE CO SA LTD	---	1 7
SANLAM	---	1 3
TOTAL	80 7	83 3

DIRECTORS :
CLUBB IM ,DE VILLIERS HP ,DYER AP
JOUBERT PG (Chairman & Managing Dir)
MACNAIR LA ,O'GRADY MT ,O'GRADY S DE C ,RILEY DB

REGISTRATION NUMBER : 05/00089/06

REGISTERED OFFICE
Afrox House, 23 Webber Street
Selby, Johannesburg
2001
TEL 011-493 3900
FAX 011-493 8828

TRANSFER SECRETARY
Mercantile Registrars Ltd
P O Box 1053, Johannesburg
2000
TEL 011-333 8181

COMPANY SECRETARY
P J Bordiss

NATURE OF BUSINESS
Afrox manufactures & markets welding products, gases, fluid-handling systems and a range of specialised industrial products such as valves, process equipment, pressure vessels, cryogenic equipment and heat exchangers The group also operates & has interests in private hospitals

BANKERS :
First National Bank of SA Ltd
Standard Bank of SA Ltd

AUDITORS :
Coopers Theron Du Toit

FAMILIAR BRAND NAMES
AFROX,BENONI DAY CLINIC,BRENTHURST HOSPITAL
DOWSON & DOBSON,EMPANGENI CLINIC
ENTABENI HOSPITAL,EUGENE MARAIS
FLORENCE HOSPITAL,GLYNNWOOD HOSPITAL
HANDIGAS,HARRIS WELDING,HOME & HOSPITAL,IPV
LADY DUDLEY HOSPITAL,NICOWELD,NORYL
PRINCESS HOSPITAL,SAFFIRE GAS
ST DOMINICS HOSPITAL,ST GEORGE'S HOSPITAL
TRANSARC,VACUREG

CONTRIBUTION BY ACTIVITY
Gases / Welding (% Operating Profit) (71 1%)
Healthcare (16 2%)
Other (12 7%)

YEAR END : September

DIVIDEND : Ords 50c

Interim No 128	(Ldr)15/06/90	(Pay)31/07/90	Amt(c)50
Final No 129	(Ldr)16/11/90	(Pay)31/01/91	Amt(c)85
Interim No 130	(Ldr)14/06/91	(Pay)31/07/91	Amt(c)63
Final No 131	(Ldr)15/11/91	(Pay)31/01/92	Amt(c)107
Interim No 132	(Ldr)12/06/92	(Pay)31/07/92	Amt(c)71

NUMBER OF EMPLOYEES : 7059

CAPITAL STRUCTURE

	AUTHORISED	ISSUED
Ords 50c	35000000	29956529

FINANCIAL STATISTICS (AT FINANCIAL YEAR END)

(Amts in R'000)	1992 Sep	1991 Sep	1990 Sep	1989 Sep	1988 Sep
Ord S/H Int	685975	615974	558856	441470	390556
Long Trm Loans	236600	311659	231286	187817	117910
Iss Ord Share	29957	29957	29957	29957	29957
Total Liab	623270	559721	509293	434606	298176
Current Liab	386670	248062	278007	246789	180266
Total Assets	1309245	1175695	1068149	876076	688732
Current Assets	321477	299127	270445	242958	179299
Debtors	221741	204071	162754	142954	109907
Inventory	93997	87499	93574	90633	65266
Turnover	1113248	1044427	903878	728030	566659
Oper Profit	225121	215737	180004	147252	112134
Interest Paid	37610	37986	39216	20241	7692
Tax Paid	84659	88003	75307	64373	51180
Prf af Int&Tax	114276	104484	78395	66164	57878
Prf att Ord Sh	93228	83413	64816	51066	43954
Btm Line Earn	94338	84464	66753	51678	43974
Dividend Paid	56917	50927	40441	29958	22467
Mkt Prce(c) YE	9600	6900	3600	2500	1775
Depreciation	59410	44906	41162	52126	40282

PER SHARE STATISTICS (CENTS)

Net Asst Val	2289 87	2056 19	1865 53	1473 68	1303 72
Net Earnings	311 00	278 00	216 00	170 46	146 72
Dividends	190 00	170 00	135 00	100 00	75 00
Cash Flow	549 37	558 66	403 26	423 82	325 18

RATIOS AND OTHER INFORMATION

Mrk Cap(R000)	2875872	2067033	1078452	748925	531737
Current Ratio	0 83	1 21	0 97	0 98	0 99
Quik/Acid Tst	0 59	0 85	0 64	0 62	0 63
A/C Rec T/ovr	5 02	5 12	5 55	5 09	5 16
Tot Ass T/ovr	0 85	0 89	0 85	0 83	0 82
Debt/Ass Rat	0 40	0 39	0 40	0 42	0 35
L T L Tot Ass	0 11	0 18	0 14	0 14	0 09
Debt to Eqity	0 77	0 74	0 77	0 83	0 62
Interest Cover	6 22	5 89	4 70	7 27	14 58

Oper Prof Mrg	20.22	20.66	19.91	20.23	19.79
Net Prof Marg%	8.37	7.99	7.17	7.01	7.76
Ret on Assets	18.02	19.55	18.32	17.44	17.14
Ret on Equity%	13.59	13.54	11.60	11.57	11.25
Price/Earnings	30.87	24.82	16.67	14.67	12.10
Divid Cover	1.64	1.64	1.60	1.70	1.96
Divid Yield	1.98	2.46	3.75	4.00	4.23
Earning Yield%	3.24	4.03	6.00	6.82	8.27
NAV % Mrk Pr	23.85	29.80	51.82	58.95	73.45
Effec Tax Rate	30.72	22.93	31.31	26.61	23.35
Def Interval	1.45	1.21	1.70	1.38	0.89
Sus Grth Rate	5.29	5.27	4.36	4.78	5.50

SUBSIDIARY & ASSOCIATED COMPANIES

AFROX FINANCE LTD
AFROX LTD
AFROX PROPERTIES (PTY) LTD
AMALGAMATED MEDICAL SERVICES LTD
ARNOX PLANT FINANCING (PTY) LTD (24%)
CYLINDER LEASING (PTY) LTD
DOWSON & DOBSON LTD
EMPANGENI CLINIC (PTY) LTD
ENTABENI HOSPITAL LTD
GAS & WELDING PRODUCTS NAMIBIA (PTY) LTD
GLYNNWOOD NURSING HOME (PTY) LTD
GREEN MEADOW PARK (PTY) LTD (33%)
HARRIS CALORIFIC SOUTH AFRICA (PTY) LTD
HIWAY MEDICAL CENTRE (PTY) LTD (33%)
HIWAY MEDICAL HOLDINGS (PTY) LTD (42%)
HOME & HOSPITAL DISPENSARIES (PTY) LTD
HUMAN PERFORMANCE SYSTEMS (PTY) LTD (40%)
IGL (PTY) LTD
IGL PROPERTIES (PTY) LTD
INDUSTRIAL & PETROLEUM VALVES (INTERNATI
INDUSTRIAL & PETROLEUM VALVES HOLDINGS (
INDUSTRIAL GASES LTD (MALAWI)
INDUSTRIAL RESEARCH & DEVELOPMENT (PTY)
MEDIMO LTD (33%)
NEW MERCANTILE HOSPITAL (PTY) LTD (23%)
NICOWELD (PTY) LTD
SPRINGS NURSING HOME HOLDINGS (PTY) LTD (35%)
ST GEORGES' HOSPITAL (PTY) LTD
SWAZI OXYGEN (PTY) LTD

INVESTMENTS

LESEDI CLINIC (PTY) LTD (10%)

AFRIKANDER LEASE LTD

ABBREVIATION : AFR-LEASE

JSE SHORT CODE : AFL

SECTOR : Gold-Klerksdorp

SHAREHOLDERS

Who Owns Whom's Assessment of the Identity of the Ultimate Controlling Shareholder: ANGLO AMERICAN

SHAREHOLDER	PERCENTAGE 1992	1991
RESIDENT NOM LTD	23.5	23.5
INDO-CHINA NOM P/L	16.0	---
PETARD NOM LTD	9.7	9.7
TAURUS NOM LTD	9.7	9.7
FERMAIN NOM LTD	9.6	9.6
NEDBANK NOM LTD	7.5	---
EPF OLD MUTUAL NOM P/L	3.0	5.1
FIRST CORP NOM P/L	2.3	2.3
DIDO NOM LTD	2.2	9.7
AECI PENS FUND	1.5	1.5
EDWIN W BALDERSON NOM P/L	1.4	2.2
FIRST NAT NOM P/L	1.1	1.2
INDO-CHINA NOM SA P/L	---	16.1
TOTAL	87.3	90.5

DIRECTORS :
EUSTACE PJ ,HEWITT L (Chairman),HOLFORD GM
HOSKING KM ,SUNTER CL ,VAN DER COLF SW
WOODWARD GW

REGISTRATION NUMBER : 01/06955/06

REGISTERED OFFICE
44 Main Street, Johannesburg
2001
TEL: 011-638 9111
FAX: 011-638 5281

TRANSFER SECRETARY
Consolidated Share Registrars Ltd
P O Box 61051, Marshalltown
2107
TEL: 011-492 1620

COMPANY SECRETARY
Anglo American Corp. of SA Ltd

NATURE OF BUSINESS
Holds certain mineral rights in the Klerksdorp district.Since April 1979 VAAL REEFS has leased its main block and the arrangements providing for the mining of the uranium reserves and treatment but, because of the unfavourable condition of the uranium market,mining operations were suspended. AF LEASE is still entitled to a mimimum royalty of R50 000 a year.Gold bearing ore from the old AFRIKANDER MINE is treated by VAAL REEFS who pay AF LEASE a royalty of 25% of revenue from it.

BANKERS :
First National Bank of SA Ltd

AUDITORS :
Ernst & Young

FAMILIAR BRAND NAMES
N/A

CONTRIBUTION BY ACTIVITY
Royalty Received - Gold (98.0%)
Royalty Received - Uranium (2.0%)

YEAR END : December

DIVIDEND : Ords 2c

Final No 85	(Ldr)08/02/91	(Pay)15/03/91	Amt(c)2
Final No 86	(Ldr)07/02/92	(Pay)13/03/92	Amt(c)12

CAPITAL STRUCTURE

	AUTHORISED	ISSUED
Ords 2c	8000000	6727500

FINANCIAL STATISTICS (AT FINANCIAL YEAR END)

(Amts in R'000)	1991 Dec	1990 Dec	1989 Dec	1988	1987
Ord S/H Int	1395	889	994	1207	1500
Long Trm Loans	-	-	-	750	563
Iss Ord Share	6727	6727	6727	6727	6727
Total Liab	2280	159	362	1500	1126
Current Liab	2280	159	362	750	563
Total Assets	3675	1048	1356	3502	3594
Current Assets	3113	486	794	1485	1531
Debtors	265	-	-	-	-
Inventory	-	-	-	1485	1531
Oper Profit	2474	-20	-17	880	603
Tax Paid	1214	32	64	440	302
Prf af Int&Tax	1313	30	63	440	307
Prf att Ord Sh	1313	30	63	440	301
Btm Line Earn	1313	30	63	440	301
Dividend Paid	807	135	336	673	538
Mkt Prce(c) YE	70	85	175	180	300

PER SHARE STATISTICS (CENTS)

Net Asst Val	20 74	13 22	14 78	17 94	22 30
Net Earnings	19 50	0 50	0 90	-	-
Dividends	12 00	2 00	5 00	-	-
Cash Flow	19 52	0 45	0 94	6 54	4 56

RATIOS AND OTHER INFORMATION

Mrk Cap(R000)	4709	5718	11772	12109	20181
Current Ratio	1 37	3 06	2 19	1 98	2 72
Quik/Acid Tst	1 37	3 06	2 19	-	-
Debt/Ass Rat	0 62	0 15	0 27	0 43	0 31
L T L Tot Ass	-	-	-	0 21	0 16
Debt to Eqity	1 63	0 18	0 36	1 24	0 75
Ret on Assets	68 76	5 92	9 37	25 13	16 94
Ret on Equity%	94 12	3 37	6 34	36 45	20 07
Price/Earnings	3 59	170 00	194 44	-	-
Divid Cover	1 63	0 25	0 18	-	-
Divid Yield	17 14	2 35	2 86	-	-
Earning Yield%	27 86	0 59	0 51	-	-
NAV % Mrk Pr	29 62	15 55	8 44	9 97	7 43
Effec Tax Rate	48 04	51 61	50 39	50 00	50 08
Def Interval		-	-	1 70	1 83
Sus Grth Rate	36 27	-11 81	-27 46	-19 30	-15 80

SUBSIDIARY & ASSOCIATED COMPANIES

None

INVESTMENTS

None

AGRICOR LTD

ABBREVIATION : AGRICOR

SECTOR : Zimbabwe Stock Exchange

SHAREHOLDERS

Who Owns Whom's Assessment of the Identity of the Ultimate Controlling Shareholder:
TSL LTD

SHAREHOLDER	PERCENTAGE 1992	1991
TSL LTD	35 9	---
BONKEM INC	32 5	---
OLD MUTUAL INV CORP (PVT) LTD	16 5	---
SOUTHERN LIFE ASSOC LTD	4 2	--
CORNER PROPERTIES PVT LTD	3 9	---
TOTAL	93 0	---

DIRECTORS :
BRINK AJ ,BUTLER ME ,ELLMAN-BROWN DA
GUNN CA (Financial Director)
KELLY JAW (Executive Director),LOUW GN
MANSFIELD RJ ,NICHOLSON JS
PHEAR SC (Managing Director),TAWENGWA SC
TRACEY CG (Chairman)
WILSON KJ (Executive Director

REGISTERED OFFICE
62 Birmingham Road, Industrial Sites
Harare, Zimbabwe

TEL 67511/2
FAX 68770

TRANSFER SECRETARY
First Transfer Secretaries (Pvt) Ltd
P O Box 437, Bulawayo
Zimbabwe

TEL 092634 - 702905

COMPANY SECRETARY
P D Ward

NATURE OF BUSINESS
AGRICOR has holding interests in a varied agricultural-based group of companies which manufacture and distribute agricultural chemicals,maize products and stockfeeds It has also diversified into the production of refined salt and other con sumer products

BANKERS :
N/A

AUDITORS :
Ernst & Young

FAMILIAR BRAND NAMES
GUARD PRECOOKED MEAL

CONTRIBUTION BY ACTIVITY
N/A

YEAR END : June

DIVIDEND :Ords Z$0,25c

Dividend	(Ldr)11/01/91	(Pay)25/10/91	Amt(c)10 5
Dividend	(Ldr)07/02/92	(Pay)21/02/92	Amt(c)5

CAPITAL STRUCTURE

	AUTHORISED	ISSUED
Ords Z$0,25	20000000	13223308

SUBSIDIARY & ASSOCIATED COMPANIES

AGRICOR DEVELOPMENT (PVT) LTD
AGRICOR INTERNATIONAL LTD
AGRICURA (PVT) LTD

AGRICURA PEST CONTROL SERVICES LTD
AUCKLAND ROAD INVESTMENTS (PVT) LTD
FERNDALE LTD
PREMIER MILLING CO (PVT) LTD
PREMIER MILLING LTD
R.F.S. (PVT) LTD
RUMEVITE (PVT) LTD
SIEMSSEN MAUNDER (PVT) LTD
SPECIALITY ANIMAL FEED CO LTD (40%)
WALLACE LABORATORIES LTD

INVESTMENTS

None

AIDA HOLDINGS LTD

ABBREVIATION : AIDA

JSE SHORT CODE : ADA

SECTOR : Development Capital Market

SHAREHOLDERS

Who Owns Whom's Assessment of the Identity of the Ultimate Controlling Shareholder: GEFFEN A

SHAREHOLDER	PERCENTAGE 1992	1991
AIDA FAMILY TRUST	51.1	51.1
UBS HOLDINGS LTD	25.3	25.3
GEFFEN A	12.4	12.4
STD BANK NOM TVL P/L	2.2	1.9
BARNARD W	1.3	1.3
LURIE S	---	1.1
TOTAL	92.3	93.0

DIRECTORS :
ANDREWS GS ,BOOYSEN SR ,GALASKO PE
GEFFEN A MS (Chairman & Managing Dir.),LEA CC MS
LEIBMAN RE (Commercial Director),MOSKOVITZ I
PORTER D (Financial Director)
RICHTER J MS (Sales Director

REGISTRATION NUMBER : 87/00111/06

REGISTERED OFFICE
FHS House, 15 Girton Road, Parktown
Johannesburg
2193
TEL: 011-788 2035
FAX: 011-880 4757

TRANSFER SECRETARY
Central Registrars Ltd
P O Box 4844, Johannesburg
2000
TEL: 011-331 0051

COMPANY SECRETARY
D Porter

NATURE OF BUSINESS
The company operates as an estate agent and national real estate franchisor.

BANKERS :
Standard Bank of SA Ltd

AUDITORS :
Fisher Hoffman Stride

FAMILIAR BRAND NAMES
N/A

CONTRIBUTION BY ACTIVITY
N/A

YEAR END : February

DIVIDEND : Ords 1c

Final No 2	(Ldr)03/08/89	(Pay)18/08/89	Amt(c)2.6
Interim No 3	(Ldr)10/08/90	(Pay)27/08/90	Amt(c)1.5
Final No 4	(Ldr)22/02/91	(Pay)28/03/91	Amt(c)1.5
Final No 5	(Ldr)31/07/92	(Pay)07/08/92	Amt(c)1

NUMBER OF EMPLOYEES : 800

CAPITAL STRUCTURE

	AUTHORISED	ISSUED
Ords 1c	20000000	14280000

FINANCIAL STATISTICS (AT FINANCIAL YEAR END)

(Amts in R'000)	1992 Feb	1991 Feb	1990 Feb	1989 Feb	1988 Feb
Ord S/H Int	6567	6125	5334	5033	4593
Long Trm Loans	210	150	188	30	-
Iss Ord Share	14280	14280	12000	12000	12000
Total Liab	5773	6628	6595	5368	4833
Current Liab	5563	6478	6407	5338	4833
Total Assets	8354	8767	7943	6415	5440
Intang Assets	3986	3986	3986	3986	3986
Current Assets	7122	7481	7270	6075	5323
Debtors	4151	4167	4043	3381	3306
Inventory	65	72	48	60	-
Turnover	11141	10023	7674	7854	7010
Oper Profit	399	592	781	1364	1395
Interest Paid	47	26	47	50	34
Tax Paid	-78	674	334	562	652
Prf af Int&Tax	585	103	516	752	709
Prf att Ord Sh	585	103	516	752	709
Btm Line Earn	585	103	516	752	709
Dividend Paid	143	214	214	312	156
Mkt Prce(c) YE	25	25	40	30	35
Depreciation	184	127	75	28	9

PER SHARE STATISTICS (CENTS)

Net Asst Val	18.07	14.98	11.23	8.73	5.06
Net Earnings	4.10	0.70	4.30	6.20	5.90
Dividends	1.00	1.50	1.50	2.60	1.30
Cash Flow	6.15	3.51	4.93	6.50	5.98

RATIOS AND OTHER INFORMATION

Mrk Cap(R000)	3570	3570	4800	3600	4200
Current Ratio	1.28	1.15	1.13	1.14	1.10
Quik/Acid Tst	1.27	1.14	1.13	1.13	1.10
A/C Rec T/ovr	2.68	2.41	1.90	2.32	2.12
Tot Ass T/ovr	1.33	1.14	0.97	1.22	1.29
Debt/Ass Rat	0.68	0.76	0.83	0.84	0.89
L T L Tot Ass	0.01	0.02	0.02	0.00	-
Debt to Eqity	0.86	1.08	1.24	1.07	1.05
Interest Cover	8.49	22.77	16.62	27.28	41.03

Oper Prof Mrg	3 58	5 91	10 18	17 37	19 90
Net Prof Marg%	5 25	1 03	6 72	9 57	10 11
Ret on Assets	6 63	9 16	11 29	21 26	25 64
Ret on Equity%	8 91	1 68	9 67	14 94	15 44
Price/Earnings	6 10	35 71	9 30	4 84	5 93
Divid Cover	4 10	0 47	2 87	2 38	4 54
Divid Yield	4 00	6 00	3 75	8 67	3 71
Earning Yield%	16 40	2 80	10 75	20 67	16 86
NAV % Mrk Pr	72 30	59 92	28 08	29 08	14 45
Effec Tax Rate	31 36	51 87	39 29	42 77	47 91
Def Interval	0 12	0 30	0 32	0 04	-
Sus Grth Rate	6 73	-1 81	5 66	8 74	12 04

SUBSIDIARY & ASSOCIATED COMPANIES

AIDA NATIONAL FRANCHISES (PTY) LTD
AIDA REAL ESTATE (PTY) LTD
DAMMI NOMINEES (PTY) LTD (25%)

INVESTMENTS

None

AIMARK HOLDINGS LTD

ABBREVIATION : AIMARK

JSE SHORT CODE : ARK

SECTOR : Development Capital Market

SHAREHOLDERS

Who Owns Whom's Assessment of the Identity of the Ultimate Controlling Shareholder: DIRECTORS

SHAREHOLDER	PERCENTAGE 1992	1991
KLEIN M S	30 0	30 0
COHEN I	23 0	22 9
IVAN COHEN FAMILY TRUST	8 8	8 8
COURTENAY A G	3 7	3 7
COURTENAY AG & P,KOURIE MA,WISE JARVIS L	3 1	3 1
CAVENDISH SECURITIES LTD	3 1	---
KLEIN W J	1 9	1 9
NEDBANK NOM LTD	1 8	1 9
STD BANK NOM TVL P/L	1 7	1 7
AIM TRUST CHIDRAWI	1 6	1 6
COHEN H	1 4	1 4
STOCKSHARE NOM P/L	1 3	-
HAWKINS C A TRUST	1 3	1 3
MBS FINANCE P/L	1 3	---
F & A ESKAKOV NOM	1 2	1 2
BORUCH & ZELICK NOM	1 1	1 1
C ORDIT NOM	1 1	1 1
MAXERIC NOM P/L	-	1 2
SAGE LIFE LTD	---	2 5
STONEHAGE INTERNATIONAL LTD	--	3 1
TOTAL	87 2	88 4

DIRECTORS :
CHIDRAWI PA (Financial Director)
COHEN I (Executive Chairman)
COURTENAY AG (Sales Director)
HAWKINS CA (Sales Director)
KLEIN MS (Managing Director),KLEIN RM

REGISTRATION NUMBER : 87/04338/06

REGISTERED OFFICE
Serenade Road, Elandsfontein
1406
TEL 011-392 1257
FAX 011-828 0596

TRANSFER SECRETARY
Central Registrars Ltd
P O Box 4844, Johannesburg
2000
TEL 011-331 0051

COMPANY SECRETARY
E M van der Walt

NATURE OF BUSINESS
Aimark supplies consumer durables to the retail sector Merchandise is sourced from international groups, & include small electrical & electronic appliances, TV, VCR, microwave ovens, microwave cookware, audio products, video and audio tapes, electronic calculators and non-stick cookware Some products are also locally sourced

BANKERS :
Nedperm Bank Ltd

AUDITORS :
Ernst & Young

FAMILIAR BRAND NAMES
AIM,AURORA,DAEWOO,NORDICWARE,SAISHO,SKC TEFAL,WIK

CONTRIBUTION BY ACTIVITY
N/A

YEAR END : December

DIVIDEND : Ords 1c
Final (Ldr)20/03/92 (Pay)03/04/92 Amt(c)1

NUMBER OF EMPLOYEES : 45

CAPITAL STRUCTURE

	AUTHORISED	ISSUED
Ords 1c	24000000	15950000

FINANCIAL STATISTICS (AT FINANCIAL YEAR END)

(Amts in R 000)	1991 Dec	1990 Dec	1989 Jun	1988 Jun	1987
Ord S/H Int	3767	3229	2862	2141	340
Long Trm Loans	205	222	600	642	2429
Iss Ord Share	15950	15750	15500	15500	-
Total Liab	25425	15711	7388	2991	4720
Current Liab	25220	15489	6788	2349	2291
Total Assets	29180	18928	10237	5132	5434
Intang Assets	12	12	13	*	*
Current Assets	28539	18442	9734	4869	2665
Debtors	13635	9281	4051	2613	
Inventory	14885	9158	5657	2238	2665
Oper Profit	2692	2137	2215	1742	956
Interest Paid	1332	1493	399	21	113
Tax Paid	703	324	899	617	412
Prf af Int&Tax	657	323	930	1104	431
Prf att Ord Sh	657	323	930	1104	431
Btm Line Earn	657	323	930	1104	431
Dividend Paid	159	-	186	450	-

Mkt Prce(c) YE	15	20	38	35	-
Depreciation	101	145	74	27	-

PER SHARE STATISTICS (CENTS)

Net Asst Val	23 54	20 43	18 38	13 81	-
Net Earnings	4 14	2 07	6 00	7 12	-
Dividends	1 00		1 20	2 90	-
Cash Flow	4 58	0 56	6 08	11 15	-

RATIOS AND OTHER INFORMATION

Mrk Cap(R000)	2393	3150	5890	5425	-
Current Ratio	1 13	1 19	1 43	2 07	1 16
Quik/Acid Tst	0 54	0 60	0 60	1 12	-
Debt/Ass Rat	0 86	0 82	0 66	0 46	0 87
L T L Tot Ass	-	-	-	-	0 45
Debt to Eqity	6 69	4 80	2 37	1 10	13 88
Interest Cover	2 02	1 43	5 55	82 95	8 46
Ret on Assets	9 23	7 54	21 76	33 94	13 19
Ret on Equity%	17 44	6 67	32 49	51 56	95 07
Price/Earnings	3 62	9 66	6 33	4 92	-
Divid Cover	4 14	-	5 00	2 46	-
Divid Yield	6 67	-	3 16	8 29	-
Earning Yield%	27 60	10 35	15 79	20 34	-
NAV % Mrk Pr	156 95	102 13	48 37	39 47	-
Effec Tax Rate	53 90	102 16	52 54	1 16	48 87
Def Interval	9 68	24 55	2 55	0 27	4 23
Sus Grth Rate	13 22	10 00	26 00	30 55	126 76

SUBSIDIARY & ASSOCIATED COMPANIES

2CK IMPORTERS (PTY) LTD
AIM MARKETING (PTY) LTD
AMICO DISTRIBUTORS (PTY) LTD

INVESTMENTS

None

ALEX WHITE HOLDINGS LTD

ABBREVIATION : ALEXWYT

JSE SHORT CODE : ALX

SECTOR : Industrial Paper & Packaging

SHAREHOLDERS

Who Owns Whom's Assessment of the Identity of the Ultimate Controlling Shareholder: DIRECTORS

SHAREHOLDER	PERCENTAGE 1992	1991
KANE T P	11 9	12 0
KAY P D	10 5	10 6
KANE P J	8 9	9 0
KAY K	7 2	7 3
KANE R	7 0	7 1
KANE S A	7 0	7 1
OSTROWIAK T J	7 0	7 1
DAVIES B T	6 2	6 2
DORITOS HOLDINGS LTD	6 2	6 2
OSTROWIAK D M FAMILY TRUST	5 4	5 5
BV SECURITIES P/L	1 6	1 5
HAYWARD G E	1 5	1 6
DAWSON A R	1 4	1 4
TOTAL	81 8	82 4

DIRECTORS :
BORTZ JM ,CUTTEN JA
DAVIES BT (Executive Director)
KANE PJ (Financial Director)
KANE TP (Chairman & Managing Dir)
KAY K (Executive Director),KAY PD ,OSTROWIAK DM
OSTROWIAK TJ

REGISTRATION NUMBER : 05/35016/06

REGISTERED OFFICE
22 Yaron Ave, Lea Glen
Roodepoort
1709
TEL 011-674 1227

TRANSFER SECRETARY
Central Registrars Ltd
P O Box 4844, Johannesburg
2000
TEL 011 331 0051

COMPANY SECRETARY
Mercantile Secretaries (Pty) Ltd

NATURE OF BUSINESS
A holding company which, through its subsidiaries operates in three main areas packaging, printing and property

BANKERS :
First National Bank of SA Ltd
Allied Bank Ltd

AUDITORS :
Leveton Boner

FAMILIAR BRAND NAMES
N/A

CONTRIBUTION BY ACTIVITY
Packaging (% Turnover) (69 6%)
Printing (30 1%)
Property & Investments (0 3%)

YEAR END : June

DIVIDEND : Ords 10c

Dividend	(Ldr)13/09/91	(Pay)11/10/91	Amt(c)2 5
Dividend	(Ldr)31/07/92	(Pay)07/08/92	Amt(c)6

NUMBER OF EMPLOYEES : 322

CAPITAL STRUCTURE

	AUTHORISED	ISSUED
Ords 10c	25000000	16237614

FINANCIAL STATISTICS (AT FINANCIAL YEAR END)

(Amts in R'000)	1992 Jun	1991 Jun	1990 Jun	1989 Jun	1988 Jun
Ord S/H Int	20784	17343	17049	17544	16303
Long Trm Loans	7590	7214	8627	3344	688
Iss Ord Share	16238	16100	16100	15600	15600
Total Liab	26810	24012	26689	18459	7919
Current Liab	19220	16798	18062	15115	7231

Total Assets	47402	41355	43542	35851	24222
Intang Assets	192	*	196	152	*
Current Assets	24356	20617	21309	18969	12050
Debtors	14449	11446	11780	10525	6679
Inventory	9423	8996	8917	7896	4768
Turnover	67255	57241	46335	40102	28295
Oper Profit	6456	4661	2422	2844	3629
Interest Paid	2441	3131	2815	1035	529
Tax Paid	1795	754	-19	881	1304
Prf af Int&Tax	2308	905	-258	1042	1930
Prf att Ord Sh	2308	905	-258	1042	1930
Btm Line Earn	2308	905	-258	1891	1930
Dividend Paid	1012	410	640	650	-
Mkt Prce(c) YE	50	40	40	70	80
Depreciation	2297	2005	1716	759	492

PER SHARE STATISTICS (CENTS)

Net Asst Val	126 81	107 72	104 68	111 49	104 51
Net Earnings	14 30	5 60	-1 60	6 70	12 40
Dividends	6 00	2 50	-	4 10	-
Cash Flow	38 46	20 60	8 20	15 83	18 72

RATIOS AND OTHER INFORMATION

Mrk Cap(R000)	8119	6440	6440	10920	12480
Current Ratio	1 27	1 23	1 18	1 25	1 67
Quik/Acid Tst	0 78	0 69	0 69	0 73	1 01
A/C Rec T/ovr	4 65	5 00	3 93	3 81	4 24
Tot Ass T/ovr	1 42	1 38	1 06	1 12	1 17
Debt/Ass Rat	0 50	0 54	0 59	0 48	0 31
L T L Tot Ass	0 09	0 14	0 17	0 06	0 01
Debt to Eqity	1 14	1 29	1 49	0 99	0 46
Interest Cover	2 64	1 49	0 86	2 75	6 86
Oper Prof Mrg	9 60	8 14	5 23	7 09	12 83
Net Prof Marg%	3 43	1 58	0 56	2 60	6 82
Ret on Assets	13 81	11 58	5 83	8 25	15 54
Ret on Equity%	11 10	5 22	-1 51	5 94	11 84
Price/Earnings	3 50	7 14	-25 00	10 45	6 45
Divid Cover	2 38	2 24		1 63	-
Divid Yield	12 00	6 25	-	5 86	-
Earning Yield%	28 60	14 00	-4 00	9 57	15 50
NAV % Mrk Pr	253 63	269 30	261 69	159 27	130 63
Effec Tax Rate	4 75	20 92	44 04	11 02	32 62
Def Interval	1 92	4 65	14 62	4 50	0 78
Sus Grth Rate	6 24	2 85	5 27	2 23	11 84

SUBSIDIARY & ASSOCIATED COMPANIES

ALEX WHITE & CO (PTY) LTD
BOOKS & GAMES (PTY) LTD
CAPE WRAPPERS (PTY) LTD
FORM MATE (PTY) LTD
FRUIT WRAPPERS (SA) (PTY) LTD
HORTIPRINT MARKETING SERVICES (PTY) LTD
INDUSTRIAL PUBLISHING CORP (PTY) LTD
LITHOCRAFT (1974) (PTY) LTD
MULTITAPE LABELS (PTY) LTD
NAMIBIA PACKAGING (PTY) LTD
NELSPRUIT PRINTERS (PTY) LTD
RAND DATA FORMS (PTY) LTD
SYSTEMFORMS (PTY) LTD
WHITE INVESTMENTS (PTY) LTD
WHITEHOUSE PROPERTIES (GLENLEA) (PTY) LT
WHITEHOUSE PROPERTIES (NATAL) (PTY) LTD
WHITEHOUSE PROPERTIES (NELSPRUIT) (PTY)
WHITEHOUSE PROPERTIES (PAARL) (PTY) LTD

INVESTMENTS

None

ALLIED ELECTRONICS CORP. LTD

ABBREVIATION : ALTRON

JSE SHORT CODE : ATN

SECTOR : Industrial-Electronics, Electrical & Bat

SHAREHOLDERS

Who Owns Whom's Assessment of the Identity of the Ultimate Controlling Shareholder:
W VENTER VIA VENTRON

SHAREHOLDER	PERCENTAGE 1992	1991
VENTECH P/L	40 5	40 6
VENTRON CORP LTD	13 0	13 1
SA MUTUAL	10 7	10 9
CMB NOM P/L	6 3	
RESIDENT NOM LTD	4 2	4 2
ANGLO AMERICAN CORP OF SA LTD	4 2	4 2
ANGLO AMERICAN IND CORP LTD	3 6	3 6
LIBERTY LIFE ASSOC OF AFRICA LTD	2 2	2 1
ESCOM PENS & PROV FUND	1 6	1 3
BILTRON P/L	1 3	1 3
EIGHTY ONE MAIN STREET NOM LTD	1 3	1 4
VENTER L TRUST	1 2	1 2
SANLAM	---	5 7
TOTAL	90 2	89 5

DIRECTORS :
BOUSTRED WG ,BOYD L ,HAWTON DA ,JACOBSON DH DR
REDSHAW PD ,SAYERS JWC (Financial Director)
SNEDDEN DC ,STEGMANN JA DR
STRIDE CA (Deputy Chairman)
VENTER WP DR (Executive Chairman),WATT PA

REGISTRATION NUMBER : 05/24583/06

REGISTERED OFFICE
Cnr Brakpan & Van Dyk Roads, Boksburg East
1459
TEL 011-899 6111
FAX 011-914 3984

TRANSFER SECRETARY
Central Registrars Ltd
P O Box 4844, Johannesburg
2000
TEL 011-331 0051

COMPANY SECRETARY
Altron Man Services (Pty) Ltd - PA Armstrong

NATURE OF BUSINESS
An investment holding company whose principal listed subsidiaries, Altech, Powtech & Fintech are invested in the telecommunications, power electrical, information technology & electronics industries

BANKERS :
Standard Bank of SA Ltd
First National Bank of SA Ltd
Absa Bank Ltd, Nedcor Bank Ltd

AUDITORS :
KPMG Aiken & Peat, Fisher Hoffman Stride

FAMILIAR BRAND NAMES
N/A

CONTRIBUTION BY ACTIVITY
Altech (% Turnover) (35 0%)
Powtech (44 0%)
Fintech (21 0%)

YEAR END : February

DIVIDEND : Ords 10c

Dividend No 42	(Ldr)25/05/90	(Pay)11/06/90	Amt(c)123
Dividena No 43	(Ldr)24/05/91	(Pay)10/06/91	Amt(c)142
Dividend No 44	(Ldr)29/05/92	(Pay)08/06/92	Amt(c)159

NUMBER OF EMPLOYEES : 14500

CAPITAL STRUCTURE

	AUTHORISED	ISSUED
Ords 10c	21000000	18989383

FINANCIAL STATISTICS (AT FINANCIAL YEAR END)

(Amts in R 000)	1992 Feb	1991 Feb	1990 Feb	1989 Feb	1988 Feb
Ord S/H Int	499406	438783	390246	330354	280997
Long Trm Loans	565807	523318	400005	358753	299403
Iss Ord Share	18989	18927	18913	17893	17893
Total Liab	1238036	1166107	1155888	1071667	780756
Current Liab	672229	642789	755883	712914	481353
Total Assets	1607711	1478668	1420547	1334315	1007939
Intang Assets	129731	126222	125587	67706	53814
Current Assets	1186538	1025550	1001988	993710	716655
Debtors	431335	425591	432128	464768	359389
Inventory	446183	413718	482641	472321	293413
Turnover	2645461	2655030	2630696	2153776	1565469
Oper Profit	274776	286093	251663	231410	211385
Interest Paid	7007	66975	66449	42686	17994
Tax Paid	119207	116173	81429	83267	75222
Prf af Int&Tax	192736	173069	139766	146867	118169
Prf att Ord Sh	92682	77664	55824	72575	58004
Btm Line Earn	86645	74815	34204	71365	58004
Dividend Paid	30220	26876	23263	22008	17535
Mkt Prce(c) YE	5600	5000	3500	4900	4000
Depreciation	61567	55464	55641	39439	35039

PER SHARE STATISTICS (CENTS)

Net Asst Val	1946 78	1651 40	1399 35	1467 88	1269 68
Net Earnings	488 90	410 50	302 70	405 60	324 20
Dividends	159 00	142 00	123 00	123 00	98 00
Cash Flow	744 28	690 89	595 32	612 57	530 77

RATIOS AND OTHER INFORMATION

Mrk Cap(R000)	1063384	946350	661955	876757	715720
Current Ratio	1 77	1 60	1 33	1 39	1 49
Quik/Acid Tst	1 10	0 95	0 69	0 73	0 88
A/C Rec T/ovr	6 13	6 24	6 09	4 63	4 36
Tot Ass T/ovr	1 65	1 80	1 85	1 61	1 55
Debt/Ass Rat	0 43	0 45	0 54	0 54	0 49
L T L Tot Ass	0 02	0 02	0 01	0 01	0 01
Debt to Eqity	1 40	1 53	1 97	2 20	1 76
Interest Cover	42 03	4 49	3 83	5 70	11 75
Oper Prof Mrg	10 39	10 78	9 57	10 74	13 50
Net Prof Marg%	3 50	2 93	2 12	3 37	3 71
Ret on Assets	19 93	24 17	20 33	20 53	20 97
Ret on Equity%	18 56	17 70	14 30	21 97	20 64
Price/Earnings	11 45	12 18	11 56	12 08	12 34
Divid Cover	3 07	2 89	2 46	3 30	3 31
Divid Yield	2 84	2 84	3 51	2 51	2 45
Earning Yield%	8 73	8 21	8 65	8 28	8 11
NAV % Mrk Pr	34 76	33 03	39 98	29 96	31 74
Effec Tax Rate	43 45	39 53	41 56	39 19	37 65
Def Interval	0 21	0 27	1 39	1 27	0 48
Sus Grth Rate	12 51	11 57	8 34	15 31	14 40

SUBSIDIARY & ASSOCIATED COMPANIES

140 DAISY STREET (PTY) LTD
AEROMARITIME INTERNATIONAL MANAGEMENT SE (50%)
ALLIED TECHNOLOGIES LTD
ALTRON FINANCE (PTY) LTD
ALTRON INFORMATION SYSTEMS (PTY) LTD
ALTRON INVESTMENT HOLDINGS (PTY) LTD
ALTRON MANAGEMENT SERVICES (PTY) LTD
ALTRON PROPERTIES (PTY) LTD
ALTRON PROPERTY HOLDINGS (PTY) LTD
BILVEN (PTY) LTD
CONCURRENT TECHNOLOGY SYSTEMS (PTY) LTD (25%)
FINTECH LTD
GORDON R HAIN (PTY) LTD
HEALTH TECH (PTY) LTD
INTERNATIONAL RISK CONSULTANTS (PTY) LTD
NET INDUSTRIES (PTY) LTD
POWER TECHNOLOGIES LTD
REPUBLIC ACCEPTANCES (PTY) LTD
SECO (PTY) LTD
SEVENTEEEN FORTY MAFIKENG (PTY) LTD
TECHNOLOGIES ACCEPTANCES (PTY) LTD
TECHNOLOGIES ACCEPTANCES FINANCE (PTY) L

INVESTMENTS

AIB INVESTMENTS (PTY) LTD (17%)
ALUSTANG (PTY) LTD (5%)
SOUTH AFRICAN MICRO ELECTRONIC SYSTEMS ((4%)
TELEMETRIX PLC (7,2%)

ALLIED TECHNOLOGIES LTD

ABBREVIATION : ALTECH

JSE SHORT CODE . ALT

SECTOR : Industrial Electronics, Electrical & Bat

SHAREHOLDERS

Who Owns Whom's Assessment of the Identity of the Ultimate Controlling Shareholder:
W VENTER VIA VENTRON & ALTRON

SHAREHOLDER	PERCENTAGE 1992	1991
BILVEN P/L	36 6	36 8
ALLIED ELECTRONICS CORP LTD	14 9	15 2
CMB NOM P/L	10 7	- -
SA MUTUAL	8 4	9 3
FULMEN TELECOMMUNICATIONS P/L	5 9	5 9
STD BANK NOM TVL P/L	4 1	3 2
EIGHTY ONE MAIN STREET NOM LTD	2 7	3 1
RESIDENT NOM LTD	2 5	2 5
ALTRON INV HOLDINGS P/L	1 7	1 1
MOMENTUM LIFE ASSURE LTD	1 6	2 0

METAL IND GROUP PENS FUND	1 5	1 8
ALTRON GROUP PENS FUND	1 3	---
ENGINEERING INDUSTRIES PENS FUND	1 3	1 5
SANLAM	---	10 4
TOTAL	93 1	92 8

DIRECTORS :
BOUSTRED WG ,BOYD DJ (Financial Director)
BOYD L ,GARBERS CF DR,GUICHET P
SNEDDEN DC (Executive Chairman),STEYN JL DR
STRIDE CA ,VENTER WP D

REGISTRATION NUMBER : 05/20415/06

REGISTERED OFFICE
Cnr Brakpan & Van Dyk Rds, Boksburg
1460
TEL 011-899 6111
FAX 011-901 3910

TRANSFER SECRETARY
Central Registrars Ltd
P O Box 4844, Johannesburg
2000
TEL 011-331 0051

COMPANY SECRETARY
Altech Management Services (Pty) Ltd

NATURE OF BUSINESS
The group is active in the following sectors Electronic systems, industrial electronics, and electronic distribution Group operations include· Design, manufacture, supply, installation and maintenance of hardware & software solutions for telecommunications & electronic systems, Sourcing, marketing, distribution & sale of electrical and electronic components, products & systems, Design, manufacture & supply of electronic components and products and hybrid circuits

BANKERS :
Nedperm Bank Ltd

AUDITORS :
Fisher Hoffman Stride

FAMILIAR BRAND NAMES
AFRICAN CAPACITORS,ALCOM SYSTEMS
ALLIED ELECTRONIC COMPONENTS,ALTECH DATA
ALTECH INDUSTRIAL ELECTRONICS
ALTECH INSTRUMENTS,ALTECH PUBLIC NETWORKS
ALTECH SPACE TECHNOLOGIES
AUTOMOTIVE ELECTRONIC TECH,AUTOPAGE
CONCURRENT TECHNOLOGY SYSTEMS
CONTELEC COMPONENTS,CYPRESS SEMICONDUCTOR
ELECTRONIC BUILDING ELEMENTS
FAIRMONT ELECTRONICS
ISIS INFORMATION SYSTEMS
KENWOOD LAND & MARINE PRODUCTS
KENWOOD RADIO COMMS PRODUCTS,LAN DESIGN
MESSINA ELECTRONICS,MICRO PRESS TOOL
MSN PRODUCTS,MULTIKOMPONENT,PACE ELECTRONICS
SCD PERIPHERALS,STAR MICRONICS
STC COMPONENTS DISTRIBUTION,STC DATA SYSTEMS
STC FREQUENCY TECHNOLOGIES
SUPRACORP ELECTRONICS,SYNOPTICS,TEK LOGIC
TELETTRA,TELSAF,TELSIS,TRANS RSA
UEC PROJECTS,WISE DECISIONS

CONTRIBUTION BY ACTIVITY
N/A

YEAR END : February

DIVIDEND : Ords 5c

Dividend No 47	(Ldr)25/05/90	(Pay)11/06/90	Amt(c)268
Dividend No 48	(Ldr)24/05/91	(Pay)10/06/91	Amt(c)268
Dividend No 49	(Ldr)29/05/92	(Pay)08/06/92	Amt(c)297

NUMBER OF EMPLOYEES : 4514

CAPITAL STRUCTURE

	AUTHORISED	ISSUED
Ords 5c	104182060	10483261

FINANCIAL STATISTICS (AT FINANCIAL YEAR END)

(Amts in R'000)	1992 Feb	1991 Feb	1990 Feb	1989 Feb	1988 Feb
Ord S/H Int	479967	416095	317030	356231	296506
Long Trm Loans	14835	19562	41673	28888	24012
Iss Ord Share	10483	10439	9815	9811	9811
Total Liab	248709	236981	239419	255604	242898
Current Liab	233874	217419	197746	226716	218886
Total Assets	671987	596535	519176	596907	533438
Intang Assets	56689	56541	37273	14928	*
Current Assets	535965	446193	364342	355314	325986
Debtors	122504	137059	120955	139619	127840
Inventory	168700	137270	175720	140489	76339
Turnover	929997	925484	793200	754070	708850
Oper Profit	105910	115419	134259	134765	133203
Interest Paid	-	-	22200	11482	-
Tax Paid	57785	52896	43742	55749	55567
Prf af Int&Tax	94775	88202	89574	88654	77636
Prf att Ord Sh	92077	83199	81847	86752	74722
Btm Line Earn	92077	83199	-13163	86036	89267
Dividend Paid	31164	27975	26305	26294	22565
Mkt Prce(c) YE	11000	9000	7300	9700	9100
Depreciation	33563	28795	29846	20666	15557

PER SHARE STATISTICS (CENTS)

Net Asst Val	4037 76	3444 33	2850 30	3478 78	3022 18
Net Earnings	880 10	821 60	834 00	884 20	761 60
Dividends	297 00	268 00	268 00	268 00	230 00
Cash Flow	1157 87	1061 27	1209 07	1060 97	909 43

RATIOS AND OTHER INFORMATION

Mrk Cap(R000)	1153130	939510	716495	951667	892801
Current Ratio	2 29	2 05	1 84	1 57	1 49
Quik/Acid Tst	1 57	1 42	0 95	0 95	1 14
A/C Rec T/ovr	7 59	6 75	6 56	5 40	5 54
Tot Ass T/ovr	1 38	1 55	1 53	1 26	1 33
Debt/Ass Rat	0 35	0 37	0 38	0 38	0 41
L T L Tot Ass	0 00	0 00	0 00	0 00	0 00
Debt to Eqity	0 49	0 52	0 63	0 64	0 74
Interest Cover	-	-	6 05	12 04	-
Oper Prof Mrg	11 39	12 47	16 93	17 87	18 79
Net Prof Marg%	9 90	8 99	10 32	11 50	10 54
Ret on Assets	22 69	23 67	29 89	27 01	25 50
Ret on Equity%	19 18	20 00	25 82	24 35	25 20
Price/Earnings	12 50	10 95	8 75	10 97	11 95
Divid Cover	2 96	3 07	3 11	3 30	3 31
Divid Yield	2 70	2 98	3 67	2 76	2 53
Earning Yield%	8 00	9 13	11 42	9 12	8 37
NAV % Mrk Pr	36 71	38 27	39 05	35 86	33 21
Effec Tax Rate	44 65	42 03	35 99	39 40	40 10
Def Interval	0 01	0 00	0 00	0 01	0 03
Sus Grth Rate	12 69	13 27	17 52	16 97	17 59

SUBSIDIARY & ASSOCIATED COMPANIES

AFRICAN CAPACITORS (PTY) LTD
ALCOM SYSTEMS (PTY) LTD
ALLIED ELECTRONIC COMPONENTS (PTY) LTD
ALTECH COMPONENT INDUSTRIES (PTY) LTD
ALTECH DATA (PTY) LTD
ALTECH ELECTRONIC DISTRIBUTION (PTY) LTD
ALTECH ELECTRONIC SYSTEMS (PTY) LTD
ALTECH INDUSTRIAL ELECTRONICS (PTY) LTD
ALTECH INSTRUMENTS (PTY) LTD
ALTECH INVESTMENT HOLDINGS (PTY) LTD
ALTECH MANAGEMENT SERVICES (PTY) LTD
ALTECH SPACE TECHNOLOGIES (PTY) LTD
AMALGAMATED RADIO (PTY) LTD
AUTOMOTIVE ELECTRONIC TECHNOLOGIES (PTY)
AUTOPAGE HOLDINGS LTD
CONCURRENT TECHNOLOGY SYSTEMS (PTY) LTD (47%)
CONTELEC COMPONENTS (PTY) LTD
ELECTRONIC BUILDING ELEMENTS (PTY) LTD
FAIRMONT ELECTRONICS (PTY) LTD
ISIS (PTY) LTD
MESSINA ELECTRONICS (PTY) LTD
MSN PRODUCTS (PTY) LTD
MULTIKOMPONENT (PTY) LTD
PACE ELECTRONIC COMPONENTS (PTY) LTD
SOCROSS INVESTMENT HOLDINGS (PTY) LTD
SOUTH CONTINENTAL DEVICES (PTY) LTD
STANDARD TELEPHONES & CABLES (SA) (PTY)
STC COMPONENTS (PTY) LTD
SUPRACORP ELECTRONICS (PTY) LTD
TEK LOGIC (PTY) LTD
TELSAF (PTY) LTD
TELSAF DATA (PTY) LTD (46%)
TELSIS (PTY) LTD
TRANS RSA (PTY) LTD
UEC PROJECTS (PTY) LTD
UNITED ELECTRONICS HOLDINGS (PTY) LTD

INVESTMENTS

SA MICRO-ELECTRONIC SYSTEMS (PTY) LTD (8,33%)

ALLWEAR GROUP LTD

ABBREVIATION : ALLGRP

JSE SHORT CODE : AGR

SECTOR : Industrial-Clothing, Footwear & Textiles

SHAREHOLDERS

Who Owns Whom's Assessment of the Identity of the Ultimate Controlling Shareholder:
HICOR LTD

SHAREHOLDER	PERCENTAGE 1992	1991
HICOR P/L	88 6	87 2
GOSSYN E G	1 2	1 2
TOTAL	89 9	88 4

DIRECTORS :
MOUTON JF ,NEL JD ,VAN DER MERWE WA
VAN ROOYEN R (Chairman

REGISTRATION NUMBER : 87/05287/06

REGISTERED OFFICE
Old Mutual Industrial Park, Building no 4, Section 2
2 Fortune Street, City Deep
2001
TEL: 011-613 8865
FAX 011-613 4131

TRANSFER SECRETARY
Mercantile Registrars Ltd
P O Box 1053, Johannesburg
2000
TEL: 011-333 8181

COMPANY SECRETARY
W A van der Merwe

NATURE OF BUSINESS
An investment holding company with a controlling interest in quoted Allwear Ltd Group activities comprise the manufacture of clothing

BANKERS :
First National Bank of SA Ltd

AUDITORS :
Coopers Theron Du Toit

FAMILIAR BRAND NAMES
DEES

CONTRIBUTION BY ACTIVITY
N/A

YEAR END : February

DIVIDEND : Ords no par value

Final No 2	(Ldr)29/06/90	(Pay)06/07/90	Amt(c)16
Final No 3	(Ldr)22/02/91	(Pay)10/05/91	Amt(c)16

NUMBER OF EMPLOYEES : 2

CAPITAL STRUCTURE

	AUTHORISED	ISSUED
Ords no par value	15000000	8298988

FINANCIAL STATISTICS (AT FINANCIAL YEAR END)

(Amts in R'000)	1992 Feb	1991 Feb	1990 Feb	1989 Feb	1988 Feb
Ord S/H Int	11540	11587	8683	2704	242
Long Trm Loans	-	-	-	-	3070
Iss Ord Share	8299	8299	4611	10000	10000
Total Liab	25	1336	864	350	5436
Current Liab	25	1336	864	350	2366
Total Assets	11565	12923	9547	3054	5678
Current Assets	4	1436	738	320	4261
Debtors	-	-	-	-	1986
Inventory	-	-	-	-	2274
Turnover	-	-	-	-	1260
Oper Profit	-45	-21	2	321	210
Interest Paid	2	3	2	1	60
Prf af Int&Tax	-47	1327	738	320	150
Prf att Ord Sh	-47	1327	738	320	150
Btm Line Earn	-47	1327	2002	320	150
Dividend Paid		1328	738	320	-
Mkt Prce(c) YE	60	85	125	32	-
Depreciation	-	-	-	-	6

PER SHARE STATISTICS (CENTS)

Net Asst Val	139 05	139 62	188 31	27 04	2 42
Net Earnings	-	16 00	16 00	16 00	-
Dividends	-	16 00	16 00	16 00	-
Cash Flow	-0 57	15 99	16 01	16 00	1 56

RATIOS AND OTHER INFORMATION

Mrk Cap(R000)	4979	7054	5764	3200	-
Current Ratio	0 16	1 07	0 85	0 91	1 80
Quik/Acid Tst	0 16	1 07	0 85	0 91	0 84
A/C Rec T/ovr	-	-	-	-	0 63
Tot Ass T/ovr	-	-	-	-	0 22
Debt/Ass Rat	0 00	0 10	0 09	0 11	0 96
L T L Tot Ass	-	-	-	-	0 54
Debt to Eqity	0 00	0 12	0 10	0 13	22 46
Interest Cover	-22 50	435 67	370 00	321 00	3 50
Oper Prof Mrg	-		-	-	16 67
Net Prof Marg%	-	-	-	-	11 90
Ret on Assets	-0 39	10 29	7 75	10 51	3 70
Ret on Equity%	-0 41	11 45	8 50	11 83	61 98
Price/Earnings	-	5 31	7 81	2 00	-
Divid Cover	-	1 00	1 00	1 00	-
Divid Yield	-	18 82	12 80	50 00	-
Earning Yield%	-	18 82	12 80	50 00	-
NAV % Mrk Pr	231 75	164 26	150 65	84 50	-
Def Interval	-	0 00	0 00	0 01	31 80
Sus Grth Rate	-0 41	-0 01	0 00	0 00	61 98

SUBSIDIARY & ASSOCIATED COMPANIES

ALLWEAR LTD

INVESTMENTS

None

ALLWEAR LTD

ABBREVIATION : ALLWEAR

JSE SHORT CODE : AWR

SECTOR : Industrial-Clothing, Footwear & Textiles

SHAREHOLDERS

Who Owns Whom's Assessment of the Identity of the Ultimate Controlling Shareholder: ALLWEAR GROUP

SHAREHOLDER	PERCENTAGE 1992	1991
ALLWEAR GROUP LTD	59 0	--
HICOR P/L	24 7	88 0
OOSTHUIZEN A J H	1 3	- -
GOSSYN E G		1 2
TOTAL	84 9	89 2

DIRECTORS :

JORDAAN JH (Deputy Chairman),NEL AG ,NEL NN
VAN ROOYEN R (Chairman),WOOF AD

REGISTRATION NUMBER : 05/13394/06

REGISTERED OFFICE

Old Mutual Industrial Park, Building no 4, Section 2
2 Fortune Street, City Deep
2001
TEL 011-613 8865
FAX 011-613 4131

TRANSFER SECRETARY

Mercantile Registrars Ltd
P O Box 1053, Johannesburg
2000
TEL 011-333 8181

COMPANY SECRETARY

W A van der Merwe

NATURE OF BUSINESS

Group activities comprise clothing manufacture esp schoolwear, menswear, babywear, toddlerswear and childrens wear

BANKERS :

Volkskas Ltd

AUDITORS :

Coopers Theron Du Toit

FAMILIAR BRAND NAMES

ALLWEAR,DEE,GIOVANNI NERO,PREFECT PLUS PRIMARIUS,SHERLEYS,TURF

CONTRIBUTION BY ACTIVITY

N/A

YEAR END : February

DIVIDEND : Ords no par value

Dividend No 81	(Ldr)27/04/90	(Pay)11/05/90	Amt(c)16
Dividend No 82	(Ldr)22/02/91	(Pay)10/05/91	Amt(c)16

NUMBER OF EMPLOYEES : 1753

CAPITAL STRUCTURE

	AUTHORISED	ISSUED
Ords no par value	20000000	14094000
6,5% Cum Prefs R2	175000	175000

FINANCIAL STATISTICS (AT FINANCIAL YEAR END)

(Amts in R'000)	1992 Feb	1991 Feb	1990 Feb	1988 Dec	1987 Dec
Ord S/H Int	24344	23330	17688	11301	8238
Long Trm Loans	5231	5771	5646	3327	2898
Iss Ord Share	14094	14094	7830	5773	5773
Total Liab	31033	27251	30163	22341	19758
Current Liab	25802	21480	24517	19014	16860
Total Assets	55377	50581	47589	33642	27996
Intang Assets	*	*	262	*	*
Current Assets	42313	37344	34913	25024	20609
Debtors	22275	17481	16749	14728	11170
Inventory	20031	19859	18161	10292	9436
Turnover	66319	60348	62277	37480	25807
Oper Profit	5345	8132	8690	5196	3462
Interest Paid	4180	4892	4785	2148	1355
Prf af Int&Tax	1176	3264	3941	3072	2107
Prf att Ord Sh	1153	3241	3918	3049	2027
Btm Line Earn	1012	2979	3918	3049	2027
Dividend Paid	-	2255	1253		577
Mkt Prce(c) YE	57	60	130	33	36
Depreciation	876	713	712	427	181

PER SHARE STATISTICS (CENTS)

Net Asst Val	172 73	165 53	222 55	195 76	142 70
Net Earnings	8 20	38 80	52 00	10 70	7 20
Dividends	-	16 00	16 00	-	2 00
Cash Flow	14 40	47 34	61 50	60 21	38 25

RATIOS AND OTHER INFORMATION

Mrk Cap(R000)	8034	8456	10179	1905	2078
Current Ratio	1 64	1 74	1 42	1 32	1 22
Quik/Acid Tst	0 86	0 81	0 68	0 77	0 66
A/C Rec T/ovr	2 98	3 45	3 72	2 54	2 31
Tot Ass T/ovr	1 20	1 19	1 31	1 11	0 92
Debt/Ass Rat	0 55	0 53	0 63	0 65	0 69
L T L Tot Ass	0 09	0 11	0 11	0 09	0 09
Debt to Eqity	1 26	1 15	1 69	1 95	2 36
Interest Cover	1 28	1 67	1 82	2 43	2 55
Oper Prof Mrg	8 06	13 48	13 95	13 86	13 41
Net Prof Marg%	1 74	5 37	6 29	8 14	7 85
Ret on Assets	9 67	16 12	18 34	15 52	12 37
Ret on Equity%	4 74	13 89	22 15	26 98	24 61
Price/Earnings	6 95	1 55	2 50	3 08	5 00
Divid Cover	-	2 43	3 25	-	3 60
Divid Yield	-	26 67	12 31	-	5 56
Earning Yield%	14 39	64 67	40 00	32 42	20 00
NAV % Mrk Pr	303 03	275 89	171 20	593 20	396 39
Def Interval	10 80	4 59	4 51	5 07	6 12
Sus Grth Rate	4 74	4 23	15 07	26 98	17 60

SUBSIDIARY & ASSOCIATED COMPANIES

364 VICTORIAWEG (PTY) LTD
JUVENILE CLOTHING CO (PTY) LTD
KLEINHANDEL ONTWIKKELINGSKORPORASIE (PTY
M BERTISH & CO LTD (UK)
SHERLEY'S PRODUCTS (1975) (PTY) LTD
VEKA FASHION GROUP (PTY) LTD
VEKA NYWERHEDE (NEWCASTLE) (PTY) LTD
VEKA WERKSKLERE (PTY) LTD

INVESTMENTS

None

AMALGAMATED BANKS OF SA LTD

ABBREVIATION : ABSA

JSE SHORT CODE : ASA

SECTOR : Financial-Banks & Financial Services

SHAREHOLDERS

Who Owns Whom's Assessment of the Identity of the Ultimate Controlling Shareholder:
REMBRANDT GROUP / INSTITUTIONS

SHAREHOLDER	PERCENTAGE 1992	1991
CMB NOM P/L	24 2	---
UNIVERSA P/L	16 0	19 9
EIGHTY ONE MAIN STREET NOM LTD	5 1	4 5
SA MUTUAL	4 6	4 9
FINANCIAL SECURITIES LTD	4 3	5 3
STD BANK NOM TVL P/L	2 5	2 7
MINE OFFICIALS PENS FUND	2 4	2 9
MINE EMPLOYEES PENS FUND	2 0	2 4
MOMENTUM LIFE ASSURE LTD	1 8	2 3
FIRST NAT NOM P/L	1 4	3 0
ABSA NOM P/L	1 3	---
METAL IND GROUP PENS FUND	1 2	---
NEDBANK NOM LTD	1 1	1 4
ENGINEERING INDUSTRIES PENS FUND	1 1	---
SANLAM	---	4 1
SOUTHERN LIFE ASSOC LTD	---	2 3
SYFRETS NOM LTD	---	1 2
TOTAL	69 0	56 8

DIRECTORS :
ALDWORTH ARM ,BADENHORST PJ (Chief Executive)
BOTES AJ ,BOUSTRED WG (Vice Chairman),BOYD L
BRINK DC ,CRONJE DC (Deputy Chief Executive)
DALING MH ,DE BLANCHE EM ,DICKASON GB
DU PLESSIS AS ,HEFER HV (Chairman)
LIEBENBERG PJ (Dep Chief Exec & Vice Cha)
PAMENSKY JL ,ROUX MJ ,SCHOLTZ AP DR
SHILL HL (Vice Chairman)
STEGMANN JA (Deputy Chairman),STEYN P
THOMAS GS ,VAN DER MERWE SW ,VAN WYK T

REGISTRATION NUMBER : 86/03934/06

REGISTERED OFFICE
27th Floor, ABSA Towers, 160 Main Street
Johannesburg
2001
TEL 011-335 4000
FAX 011-335 4900

TRANSFER SECRETARY
Central Registrars Ltd
P O Box 4844, Johannesburg
2000
TEL 011-331 0051

COMPANY SECRETARY
I C Pretorius

NATURE OF BUSINESS
The holding company of deposit taking institutions registered in RSA. The group is active in the full spectrum of national and international banking and financial services to both the retail & corporate markets, and in long and short term insurance and property services

BANKERS :
N/A

AUDITORS :
KPMG Aiken & Peat, Ernst & Young

FAMILIAR BRAND NAMES
ALLIED BANK,ALLIED BUILDING SOC
BANK OF TRANSKEI (50%),BANK WINDHOEK (19%)
BANKORP,MLS BANK,RAND MERCHANT BANK
SAGE LIFE (49%),TRUSTBANK,UNITED BANK
UNITED BUILDING SOC,VOLKSKAS BANK

CONTRIBUTION BY ACTIVITY
Banking (% attributable income) (63 9%)
Insurance (26 3%)
Other (9 8%)

YEAR END : March

DIVIDEND :Ords R2

Interim No 8	(Ldr)14/12/90	(Pay)31/12/90	Amt(c)14
Final No 9	(Ldr)14/06/91	(Pay)30/06/91	Amt(c)22
Interim No 10	(Ldr)13/12/91	(Pay)31/12/91	Amt(c)15 5
Final No 11	(Ldr)12/06/92	(Pay)30/06/92	Amt(c)24
Interim No 12	(Ldr)18/12/92	(Pay)31/12/92	Amt(c)17

NUMBER OF EMPLOYEES : 26583

CAPITAL STRUCTURE

	AUTHORISED	ISSUED
Ords R2	700000000	565838966

FINANCIAL STATISTICS (AT FINANCIAL YEAR END)

(Amts in R'000)	1992 Mar	1991 Mar	1990 Mar	1989 Mar	1988 Mar
Ord S/H Int	3173800	2841300	1453700	1300000	1153200
Long Trm Loans	455900	396900	494700	11688800	5797000
Iss Ord Share	456666	456666	241001	238946	238846
Total Liab	53046400	48986600	14390700	11917100	10092600
Current Liab	52590500	48589700	13896000	228300	4295600
Total Assets	56220200	51827900	15844400	13217100	11245800
Current Assets	5701000	5887200	793200	199200	201800
Debtors	877800	928500	15000	58500	44600
Inventory	-	-	23000	33700	25300
Oper Profit	661700	417800	251400	1294300	189000
Interest Paid	-	-	-	1267400	-
Tax Paid	191900	120600	85100	92200	87800
Prf af Int&Tax	469800	297200	166300	122900	101200
Prf att Ord Sh	491400	321300	196900	150700	125700
Btm Line Earn	491400	321300	197500	150700	125700
Dividend Paid	180400	134200	77200	64500	57200
Mkt Prce(c) YE	1005	725	620	435	330
Depreciation	147300	88300	44300	34200	25300

PER SHARE STATISTICS (CENTS)

Net Asst Val	694 99	622 18	603 19	544 06	482 82
Net Earnings	107 60	93 40	82 10	63 10	51 30
Dividends	39 50	36 00	32 00	27 00	24 00
Cash Flow	147 96	131 87	93 13	61 79	53 13

RATIOS AND OTHER INFORMATION

Mrk Cap(R000)	4589493	3310829	1494206	1039415	788192
Current Ratio	0 11	0 12	0 06	0 87	0 05
Quik/Acid Tst	0 11	0 12	0 06	0 72	0 04
Debt/Ass Rat	0 94	0 94	0 89	0 03	0 89
L T L Tot Ass	-	-	0 02	0 01	0 50
Debt to Eqity	16 57	17 10	9 73	0 28	8 63
Interest Cover	-	-	-	1 17	-
Ret on Assets	1 22	0 85	1 79	11 42	1 90
Ret on Equity%	15 48	11 31	13 54	11 59	10 90
Price/Earnings	9 34	7 76	7 55	6 89	6 43
Divid Cover	2 72	2 59	2 57	2 34	2 14
Divid Yield	3 93	4 97	5 16	6 21	7 27
Earning Yield%	10 71	12 88	13 24	14 51	15 55
NAV % Mrk Pr	69 15	85 82	97 29	125 07	146 31
Effec Tax Rate	13 66	12 16	28 04	365 43	46 40
Def Interval	75 86	105 02	61 98	0 90	77 00
Sus Grth Rate	9 80	6 59	8 23	6 63	5 94

SUBSIDIARY & ASSOCIATED COMPANIES

ABSA BANK LTD
ABSA CONSULTANTS & ACTUARIES (PTY) LTD
ABSA FINANCIAL SERVICES LTD
ABSA FUND MANAGERS (PTY) LTD
ABSA INSURANCE BROKERS (PTY) LTD
ABSA LIFE LTD
ABSA MERCHANT BANK LTD
AIDA HOLDINGS LTD (25%)
ALLIED DEVELOPMENT CO (PTY) LTD
ALLIED INSURANCE COMPANY LTD
AMALGAMATED INSURANCE HOLDINGS LTD (49%)
BANK OF TRANSKEI LTD (50%)
BANK WINDHOEK LTD (38%)
BANKFIL LTD
BANKORP HOLDINGS LTD
BANKORP INVESTMENTS LTD
BANKORP PROPERTY (PTY) LTD
CENTRAL REGISTRARS LTD
COMMERCIAL UNION OF SA LTD (30%)
HANS HUIZEMAN (PTY) LTD (25%)
J H ISAACS GROUP HOLDINGS LTD (29%)
MLS BANK LTD
MOMENTUM LIFE ASSURERS LTD (30%)
NATRUST LTD (23%)
PRICE FORBES GROUP HOLDINGS (PTY) LTD (25%)
REAL ESTATE MULTI - SERVICES SA LTD
SEEFF PROPERTY HOLDINGS (PTY) LTD (25%)
UBS INSURANCE COMPANY LTD
UNITED DEVELOPMENT CORP (PTY) LTD
VOLKSKAS INVESTMENTS LTD
VOLKSKAS PROPERTY SERVICES LTD - ALL PRO
WAKEFIELD GROUP (PTY) LTD (25%)

INVESTMENTS

AEGIS INSURANCE CO LTD (7,4%)
BANK WINDHOEK LTD (19%)
BOLAND BANK LTD (10%)
HH ROBERTSON AFRICA (PTY) LTD (11,8%)
KNJ GROUP LTD (13%)
SAAMBOU HOLDINGS LTD (9%)
TOTAL SA (PTY) LTD (13,1%)

AMALGAMATED BEVERAGE INDUSTRIES LTD

ABBREVIATION : ABI

JSE SHORT CODE : ABI

SECTOR : Industrial Beverages & Hotels

SHAREHOLDERS

Who Owns Whom's Assessment of the Identity of the Ultimate Controlling Shareholder: ANGLO AMERICAN VIA SA BREWERIES

SHAREHOLDER	PERCENTAGE 1992	1991
SA BREWERIES LTD	67 6	67 6
CADBURY SCHWEPPES SA LTD	19 0	19 0
SA BOTTLING CO P/L	1 9	1 9
CMB NOM P/L	1 3	
T J C TRADING P/L	-	1 3
TOTAL	89 7	89 7

DIRECTORS :
BESTER PM ,BIND MS
BUSSCHAU JM (Financial Director)
COMRIE GW (Technical Director),KAHN JM
LLOYD RL (Chairman),MACFARLANE WS
ODGERS ET (Operations Director)

REID HA (Managing Director)
ROBBERTSE GC (Dir Human Resources),WYMAN MI

REGISTRATION NUMBER : 70/06820/06

REGISTERED OFFICE
ABI House, 14 Pongola Crescent, Eastgate Ext 17
Sandton
2199
TEL 011-444 8444
FAX 011-444 8315

TRANSFER SECRETARY
Mercantile Registrars Ltd
P O Box 1053, Johannesburg
2000
TEL 011-333 8181

COMPANY SECRETARY
J M Busshau

NATURE OF BUSINESS
Bottling and distribution of soft drinks under franchise licence Brands include Appletiser, Fanta, Krest, Schweppes, Sparletta, & Coca-Cola

BANKERS :
First National Bank of SA Ltd

AUDITORS :
Ernst & Young

FAMILIAR BRAND NAMES
N/A

CONTRIBUTION BY ACTIVITY
N/A

YEAR END : March

DIVIDEND .Ords 1c

Interim	(Ldr)14/12/90	(Pay)31/12/90	Amt(c)6
Final	(Ldr)14/06/91	(Pay)01/07/91	Amt(c)20
Interim	(Ldr)13/12/91	(Pay)31/12/91	Amt(c)7
Final	(Ldr)12/06/92	(Pay)01/07/92	Amt(c)24 5
Interim	(Ldr)11/12/92	(Pay)31/12/92	Amt(c)8

NUMBER OF EMPLOYEES : 4782

CAPITAL STRUCTURE

	AUTHORISED	ISSUED
Ords 1c	125000000	106000000

FINANCIAL STATISTICS (AT FINANCIAL YEAR END)

(Amts in R 000)	1992 Mar	1991 Mar	1990 Mar
Ord S/H Int	309508	266725	224704
Long Trm Loans	69712	47131	49918
Iss Ord Share	106000	106000	106000
Total Liab	249068	220791	171425
Current Liab	179356	173660	121507
Total Assets	558576	487516	396129
Current Assets	176034	174121	144957
Debtors	110550	114579	104460
Inventory	65484	59542	40497
Turnover	1045400	884253	739625
Oper Profit	124554	109637	87900
Interest Paid	8869	7588	7722
Tax Paid	55718	52238	40905
Prf af Int&Tax	66078	56505	44029
Prf att Ord Sh	68383	56939	45382
Btm Line Earn	69628	56939	45382
Dividend Paid	33390	27560	22260
Mkt Prce(c) YE	1475	1350	715
Depreciation	35205	34287	29450

PER SHARE STATISTICS (CENTS)

Net Asst Val	291 99	251 63	211 98
Net Earnings	64 50	53 70	42 80
Dividends	31 50	26 00	21 00
Cash Flow	98 49	86 39	77 36

RATIOS AND OTHER INFORMATION

Mrk Cap(R000)	1563500	1431000	757900
Current Ratio	0 98	1 00	1 19
Quik/Acid Tst	0 62	0 66	0 86
A/C Rec T/ovr	9 46	7 72	7 08
Tot Ass T/ovr	1 87	1 81	1 87
Debt/Ass Rat	0 36	0 36	0 33
L T L Tot Ass	0 04	0 01	0 02
Debt to Eqity	0 65	0 67	0 58
Interest Cover	14 52	15 01	11 74
Oper Prof Mrg	11 91	12 40	11 88
Net Prof Marg%	6 54	6 44	6 14
Ret on Assets	24 20	24 34	24 11
Ret on Equity%	22 09	21 35	20 20
Price/Earnings	22 87	25 14	16 71
Divid Cover	2 05	2 07	2 04
Divid Yield	2 14	1 93	2 94
Earning Yield%	4 37	3 98	5 99
NAV % Mrk Pr	19 80	18 64	29 65
Effec Tax Rate	43 27	48 78	39 35
Def Interval	0 28	0 41	0 10
Sus Grth Rate	11 31	11 01	10 29

SUBSIDIARY & ASSOCIATED COMPANIES

AMALGAMATED BEVERAGE CANNERS (PTY) LTD (24%)
AMALGAMATED BEVERAGE INDUSTRIES (BOP) (P
AMALGAMATED BEVERAGE INDUSTRIES (NATAL)
AMALGAMATED BEVERAGE INDUSTRIES (PRETORI
AMALGAMATED BEVERAGE PROPERTIES (PTY) LT
DASUS INVESTMENTS (PTY) LTD
JOBACS (PTY) LTD
LENGALE (PTY) LTD

INVESTMENTS

None

AMALGAMATED RETAIL LTD

ABBREVIATION : AMREL

JSE SHORT CODE : AMR

SECTOR : Industrial Furniture & Household

SHAREHOLDERS

Who Owns Whom's Assessment of the Identity of the Ultimate Controlling Shareholder.
ANGLO AMERICAN VIA SA BREWS

SHAREHOLDER	PERCENTAGE 1992	1991

SA BREWERIES LTD	68 7	68 7
CMB NOM P/L	12 4	---
SA MUTUAL	6 5	6 3
ABSA NOM P/L	1 8	---
EIGHTY ONE MAIN STREET NOM LTD	1 2	1 5
SIXTY SIX MARSHALL STREET NOM P/L	1 0	1 0
STD BANK NOM TVL P/L	---	1 0
SANLAM	---	12 4
VOLKSKAS NOM P/L	---	1 1
TOTAL	91 6	91 9

DIRECTORS :
BERGER SJ (Chief Executive & M D)
BRODIE NM (Commercial Director),BUSSCHAU MJ
HART JHR ,JOHNSTON KR ,KAHN JM (Chairman)
KANARECK WS ,LOGAN A ,LOGAN RL ,MACFARLANE WS
SINCLAIR RBG (Financial Director),WOLPERT D

REGISTRATION NUMBER : 05/10108/06

REGISTERED OFFICE
1st Floor, Uhde House, 3 St David's Place
Parktown
2193
TEL 011 643 4891
FAX 011-643 4187

TRANSFER SECRETARY
Consolidated Share Registrars Ltd
P O Box 61051, Marshalltown
2107
TEL 011-492 1620

COMPANY SECRETARY
N M Brodie

NATURE OF BUSINESS
The group is engaged in the retail of furniture & footwear, provision of TV & video maintenance services, printing services and footwear repair services via 1138 outlets

BANKERS :
Standard Bank of SA Ltd, Nedperm Bank Ltd
First National Bank of SA Ltd

AUDITORS :
Deloitte Pim Goldby

FAMILIAR BRAND NAMES
ABC/BARNES,AMCOM,BLAIKIES/FAIRDEAL
CROWN FURNISHERS,LUBNERS/MELODYS,MCNAMEE
PRONTAPRINT (FRANCHISE,ROCK BOTTOM
TIP TOP FURNISHERS,TRIANGLE FURNISHERS

CONTRIBUTION BY ACTIVITY
Furniture (% Turnover) (64 8%)
Footwear & apparel (29 7%)
Services (5 5%)

YEAR END : March

DIVIDEND : Ords 25c

Interim No 26	(Ldr)24/11/89	(Pay)29/12/89	Amt(c)27
Final No 27	(Ldr)25/05/90	(Pay)02/07/90	Amt(c)55
Interim No 28	(Ldr)23/11/90	(Pay)31/12/90	Amt(c)28
Interim No 30	(Ldr)29/11/91	(Pay)31/12/91	Amt(c)19
FinAL No 31	(Ldr)22/05/92	(Pay)01/07/92	Amt(c)38
Final No 29	(Ldr)24/05/91	(Pay)01/07/91	Amt(c)59

NUMBER OF EMPLOYEES : 9076

CAPITAL STRUCTURE

	AUTHORISED	ISSUED
Ords 25c	14000000	9211464
8% Cum Red Prefs 87c	1704000	0

FINANCIAL STATISTICS (AT FINANCIAL YEAR END)

(Amts in R'000)	1992 Mar	1991 Mar	1990 Mar	1989 Mar	1988 Mar
Ord S/H Int	146697	145037	129057	118125	109219
Long Trm Loans	209504	213371	184027	181181	182854
Iss Ord Share	9211	9211	9211	9211	9211
Total Liab	345507	331293	281537	282165	272814
Current Liab	136003	117922	97510	100984	89960
Total Assets	492204	476330	410594	400290	382033
Current Assets	230267	210616	193317	147502	127372
Debtors	87160	77722	76851	38675	35431
Inventory	142245	131800	115022	107828	90793
Turnover	1003124	1030736	849057	759735	694322
Oper Profit	33720	59231	46944	52869	52805
Interest Paid	25562	18042	8416	16061	15866
Tax Paid	-6136	18189	19175	17294	18063
Prf af Int&Tax	15764	24178	21188	20246	18876
Prf att Ord Sh	15686	23993	22566	22176	21218
Btm Line Earn	6910	23993	22589	22176	19300
Dividend Paid	5250	8013	7553	7461	7093
Mkt Prce(c) YE	825	1350	825	865	1250
Depreciation	20785	19125	14766	12578	10676

PER SHARE STATISTICS (CENTS)

Net Asst Val	1592 63	1574 61	1401 12	1282 43	1185 75
Net Earnings	170 00	260 00	245 00	241 00	231 00
Dividends	57 00	87 00	82 00	81 00	77 00
Cash Flow	407 44	442 43	739 11	451 02	345 13

RATIOS AND OTHER INFORMATION

Mrk Cap(R000)	75991	124349	75991	79675	115138
Current Ratio	1 69	1 79	1 98	1 46	1 42
Quik/Acid Tst	0 65	0 67	0 80	0 39	0 41
A/C Rec T/ovr	11 51	13 26	11 05	19 64	19 60
Tot Ass T/ovr	2 04	2 16	2 07	1 90	1 82
Debt/Ass Rat	0 52	0 48	0 47	0 56	0 58
L T L Tot Ass	0 25	0 24	0 23	0 30	0 35
Debt to Eqity	1 75	1 59	1 49	1 88	2 04
Interest Cover	1 32	3 28	5 63	3 34	3 33
Oper Prof Mrg	3 36	5 75	5 53	6 96	7 61
Net Prof Marg%	1 56	2 33	2 66	2 92	3 06
Ret on Assets	7 20	12 87	12 22	13 87	14 44
Ret on Equity%	10 69	16 54	17 49	18 77	19 43
Price/Earnings	4 85	5 19	3 37	3 59	5 41
Divid Cover	2 98	2 99	2 99	2 98	3 00
Divid Yield	6 91	6 44	9 94	9 36	6 16
Earning Yield%	20 61	19 26	29 70	27 86	18 48
NAV % Mrk Pr	193 05	116 64	169 83	148 26	94 86
Effec Tax Rate	71 01	17 08	11 18	26 63	8 35
Def Interval	3 40	2 79	1 40	3 09	4 37
Sus Grth Rate	7 11	11 02	11 63	12 46	12 93

SUBSIDIARY & ASSOCIATED COMPANIES

ABC SHOE (PTY) LTD
ABC SHOE CORPORATION LTD
ALL MANAGEMENT CO (PTY) LTD
AMALGAMATED FURNISHERS (BOPHUTHATSWANA) (50%)
AMREL LOAN FINANCE (PTY) LTD
AMRETFIN (PTY) LTD (50%)
AMSTERDAM FURNITURE HOLDINGS LTD
BEO MANAGEMENT SERVICES (PTY) LTD
BOYMANS LTD
BPM MANAGEMENT CO (PTY) LTD
CH MANAGEMENT SERVICES (PTY) LTD

CROWN FURNISHERS EASTERN CAPE (PTY) LTD
CUTHBERTS (BOPHUTHATSWANA) (PTY) LTD
EARLY BIRD SERVICES LTD
FOOTPRINTS (PTY) LTD
GEEN & RICHARDS (SWAZILAND) (PTY) LTD
GEEN & RICHARDS (SWAZILAND) (PTY) LTD
HPD COMPANY LTD
IDUTYWA FASHION BOUTIQUE (PTY) LTD
KING DRAGON (PTY) LTD (50%)
KREMS INVESTMENTS (PTY) LTD
LTR MANAGEMENT CO (PTY) LTD
LUBNER'S FURNISHERS (PTY) LTD
LUBNERS STORES LTD
MCNAMEE & CO LTD
MELODY'S HOLDINGS LTD
MICHAELS CASH STORE (PTY) LTD
MILLANA LTD
MJL MANAGEMENT CO (PTY) LTD
MJP MANAGEMENT CO (PTY) LTD
MODA BELLE (PTY) LTD
MTM TRADING CO (PTY) LTD
MULTISERV (PTY) LTD
MULTISERV BOPHUTHATSWANA (PTY) LTD
MVOL STORES (PTY) LTD
PENINSULA FURNISHERS (PTY) LTD (50%)
PENINSULA SHOES LTD (50%)
PRONTAPRINT FRANCHISE OUTLETS
QUEEN'S FURNISHING CO. (PTY) LTD
REGENCY CENTRE (PTY) LTD (50%)
SBM TRADING CO (PTY) LTD
SCOTTS (SWAZILAND) (PTY) LTD
SCOTTS MANAGEMENT (PTY) LTD
SCOTTS RETAIL (BOP) (PTY) LTD (50%)
SCOTTS RETAIL (BOTSHABELO) (PTY) LTD (50%)
SCOTTS RETAIL (CISKEI) (PTY) LTD
SCOTTS RETAIL (PTY) LTD
SCOTTS STORE (LESOTHO) (PTY) LTD
SELECT-A-SHOE (PTY) LTD
SELECT-A-SHOE KWAZULU LTD (50%)
SHOECORP SHOE STORE (CISKEI) (PTY) LTD (50%)
SHOECORP SHOE STORE (QWA-QWA) (PTY) LTD (50%)
SHOECORP SHOE STORE (VENDA) (PTY) LTD
SHOECORP SHOE STORES (BOPHUTHATSWANA) (P (50%)
SHOECORP SHOE STORES (LESOTHO) (PTY) LTD
SHOECORP SHOE STORES (PTY) LTD
SHOECORP SHOE STORES (SWAZILAND) (PTY) L
TIP TOP FURNISHERS (PTY) LTD
TRIANGLE FURNISHERS (PTY) LTD
TRIANGLE FURNISHERS (VENDA) (PTY) LTD
VIOLET'S TRADING CO (PTY) LTD
WM CUTHBERT & CO LTD
ZEBLON TRADING CO (PTY) LTD

INVESTMENTS

None

AMALGAMATED SHOES LTD

ABBREVIATION : AMSHOE

JSE SHORT CODE : AMS

SECTOR : Industrial-Clothing, Footwear & Textiles

SHAREHOLDERS

Who Owns Whom's Assessment of the Identity of the Ultimate Controlling Shareholder:
LENCO HOLDINGS

SHAREHOLDER	PERCENTAGE 1992	1991
LENCO HOLDINGS LTD	55.0	53.8
FLASHSPORTS P/L	34.9	35.2
CMB NOM P/L	5.9	---
SANLAM	---	5.9
TOTAL	95.8	94.9

DIRECTORS :
DE JAGER GD (Chairman)
ECKSTEIN RS (Chief Executive),SPAIN HS
STUBBS SFW ,WARD JP (Financial Director)
WIESE CH AD

REGISTRATION NUMBER : 84/007782/06

REGISTERED OFFICE
37 Willowton Road, Pietermaritzburg
3201
TEL: 0331-71 455
FAX: 0331-71 428

TRANSFER SECRETARY
Central Registrars Ltd
P O Box 4844, Johannesburg
2000
TEL: 011-331 0051

COMPANY SECRETARY
J P Ward

NATURE OF BUSINESS
An investment holding company with subsidiaries engaged in the manufacture and distribution of footwear, footwear components and EVA products, & the distribution of sports & leisure clothing.

BANKERS :
Nedcor Bank Ltd

AUDITORS :
KPMG Aiken & Peat

FAMILIAR BRAND NAMES
BERBI,DELTA,MUSTANG,REEVA,REYNOLDS
STEVEN CHARLES,STUDIO

CONTRIBUTION BY ACTIVITY
N/A

YEAR END : February

DIVIDEND : Ords 1c

Dividend No 3	(Ldr)01/06/90	(Pay)18/06/90	Amt(c)9
Dividend No 4	(Ldr)22/02/91	(Pay)28/02/91	Amt(c)9
Dividend No 5	(Ldr)28/02/92	(Pay)09/04/92	Amt(c)9

NUMBER OF EMPLOYEES : 4750

CAPITAL STRUCTURE

	AUTHORISED	ISSUED
Ords 1c	100000000	58568612

FINANCIAL STATISTICS (AT FINANCIAL YEAR END)

(Amts in R'000)	1992	1991	1990	1989	1987

	Feb	Feb	Feb	Feb	Dec
Ord S/H Int	86006	74256	63811	49509	15806
Long Trm Loans	8785	8576	8790	9548	589
Iss Ord Share	58569	58138	57687	57466	42027
Total Liab	44838	52394	39356	38266	9247
Current Liab	36053	43818	30566	28718	8658
Total Assets	110215	106021	81969	58903	25053
Intang Assets	20629	20629	21198	28872	*
Current Assets	87469	85665	62132	49969	22233
Debtors	41630	39366	28563	24214	13345
Inventory	45355	42719	32776	25247	8856
Turnover	233451	219113	207534	157310	56172
Oper Profit	27997	27367	31846	21969	6857
Interest Paid	6637	5507	4879	1572	739
Tax Paid	4926	6060	7790	5199	320
Prf af Int&Tax	16730	15949	19343	15472	5798
Prf att Ord Sh	16698	15949	19343	15472	5798
Btm Line Earn	16698	15949	19343	15472	5798
Dividend Paid	5271	5273	5207	4936	-
Mkt Prce(c) YE	130	130	150	110	-
Depreciation	3764	2923	2207	2090	534

PER SHARE STATISTICS (CENTS)

Net Asst Val	111 62	92 24	73 87	35 91	37 61
Net Earnings	28 50	27 40	33 50	27 90	-
Dividends	9 00	9 00	9 00	7 00	-
Cash Flow	36 06	33 74	37 96	27 59	17 03

RATIOS AND OTHER INFORMATION

Mrk Cap(R000)	76140	75579	86531	63213	-
Current Ratio	2 43	1 96	2 03	1 74	2 57
Quik/Acid Tst	1 17	0 98	0 96	0 86	1 55
A/C Rec T/ovr	5 61	5 57	7 27	5 57	4 21
Tot Ass T/ovr	2 12	2 07	2 53	2 29	2 24
Debt/Ass Rat	0 38	0 47	0 46	0 63	0 37
L T L Tot Ass	0 06	0 06	0 09	0 15	0 02
Debt to Eqity	0 49	0 68	0 60	0 75	0 58
Interest Cover	4 22	4 97	6 53	13 98	9 28
Oper Prof Mrg	11 99	12 49	15 34	13 97	12 21
Net Prof Marg%	7 15	7 28	9 32	9 84	10 32
Ret on Assets	25 64	25 95	39 05	32 37	27 37
Ret on Equity%	19 41	21 48	30 31	26 79	36 68
Price/Earnings	4 56	4 74	4 48	3 94	-
Divid Cover	3 17	3 04	3 72	3 99	-
Divid Yield	6 92	6 92	6 00	6 36	-
Earning Yield%	21 92	21 08	22 33	25 36	-
NAV % Mrk Pr	85 86	70 95	49 25	32 65	-
Effec Tax Rate	20 38	24 25	17 27	10 13	5 23
Def Interval	0 65	1 01	0 41	0 64	0 09
Sus Grth Rate	13 29	14 38	22 15	21 28	36 68

SUBSIDIARY & ASSOCIATED COMPANIES

BOOGIE HOLDINGS NV
BUDGET SHOES (1989) (PTY) LTD
EMA SHOES (PTY) LTD
JAGUAR SHOES (PTY) LTD
JAGUAR SHOES FINANCE (PTY) LTD
LESOTHO COMPONENT PRODUCTS (PTY) LTD
LESOTHO SHOES (PTY) LTD
MUSTANG SHOE COMPANY (PTY) LTD
TEMPO SHOE COMPANY (PTY) LTD

INVESTMENTS

None

ANBEECO INVESTMENT HOLDINGS LTD

ABBREVIATION : ANBEECO

JSE SHORT CODE : AEC

SECTOR : Industrial-Electronics, Electrical & Bat

SHAREHOLDERS

Who Owns Whom's Assessment of the Identity of the Ultimate Controlling Shareholder: DIRECTORS

SHAREHOLDER	PERCENTAGE 1992	1991
ANB HOLDINGS P/L	27 9	29 9
MANUFACTURERS INV CO P/L	21 8	21 8
MENBLACK NOM P/L	13 7	1 5
CMB NOM P/L	10 9	---
IRVROB INV P/L	10 7	10 7
SANTAMGROEI NOM P/L	2 1	---
CHAPPEL M H	1 5	1 5
ANGLO AMERICAN CORP PENS FUND	---	2 2
ANGLO AMERICAN GROUP PENS FUND	---	1 1
BENN A	---	1 5
CYRIL COHEN FAMILY HOLDINGS CC	---	6 4
IVAN COHEN FAMILY TRUST	---	6 4
SANLAM	---	1 6
TOTAL	88 5	84 6

DIRECTORS :
BROOKSTONE AN (Chairman & Managing Dir)
BROOKSTONE IL ,COHEN C ,JACOBSON SI ,JANKELOW W
PHILLIPS BR (Financial Director),ROSENBERG GL
SHATENSTEIN SI (Commercial Director

REGISTRATION NUMBER : 84/02788/06

REGISTERED OFFICE
Anbeeco House, 50 Mimetes Road
Denver
2094
TEL 011-622 2000
FAX 011-622 1364

TRANSFER SECRETARY
Central Registrars Ltd
P O Box 4844, Johannesburg
2000
TEL 011-331 0051

COMPANY SECRETARY
BR Phillips

NATURE OF BUSINESS
A holding company with subsidiaries engaged in the importing, marketing & servicing of watches, clocks, audio equipment & television sets

BANKERS :
FirstCorp Merchant Bank Ltd

AUDITORS :
Litvin Hack

FAMILIAR BRAND NAMES
LASSALE,LORUS,PULSAR,SABA (TV SETS),SEIKO

CONTRIBUTION BY ACTIVITY
Audio/TV & Allied Products (% Turnover) (57 7%)
Watches & Allied Products (42 3%)
Audio/TV (% Earnings per Share) (36 6%)
Watches Etc (63 4%)

YEAR END : April

DIVIDEND :Ords 1c

Final No 6	(Ldr)16/03/90	(Pay)20/04/90	Amt(c)6
Interim No 7	(Ldr)01/02/91	(Pay)15/02/91	Amt(c)6
Final No 8	(Ldr)19/07/91	(Pay)16/08/91	Amt(c)6
Interim no 9	(Ldr)07/02/92	(Pay)21/02/92	Amt(c)6
Final No 10	(Ldr)17/07/92	(Pay)14/08/92	Amt(c)4

NUMBER OF EMPLOYEES : 100

CAPITAL STRUCTURE

	AUTHORISED	ISSUED
Ords 1c	25000000	14978039

FINANCIAL STATISTICS (AT FINANCIAL YEAR END)

(Amts in R'000)	1992 Apr	1991 Apr	1990 Apr	1988 Dec	1987 Dec
Ord S/H Int	18743	16800	13514	11314	8431
Long Trm Loans	5598	5732	4843	4134	2706
Iss Ord Share	14978	14978	14978	14978	14978
Total Liab	24162	32775	21925	18679	18808
Current Liab	18564	27043	17082	14545	16102
Total Assets	42548	49218	35082	29636	27239
Intang Assets	357	357	357	357	*
Current Assets	40470	46646	33184	28559	25813
Debtors	18558	20599	17242	13575	17259
Inventory	15657	18100	10733	10766	8550
Turnover	102059	114063	95538	72777	52384
Oper Profit	9626	15771	10460	9814	7015
Interest Paid	897	1008	414	778	374
Tax Paid	4149	6933	5173	4456	3197
Prf af Int&Tax	4580	7830	4873	4580	3444
Prf att Ord Sh	3441	5123	3399	3038	2582
Btm Line Earn	3441	5123	3399	3658	2582
Dividend Paid	1498	1797	1198	1198	1008
Mkt Prce(c) YE	100	130	60	57	115
Depreciation	473	481	404	251	137

PER SHARE STATISTICS (CENTS)

Net Asst Val	122 75	109 78	87 84	73 15	56 29
Net Earnings	23 00	34 20	22 70	20 30	20 10
Dividends	10 00	12 00	8 00	8 00	7 00
Cash Flow	26 13	37 41	18 93	22 03	21 01

RATIOS AND OTHER INFORMATION

Mrk Cap(R000)	14978	19471	8987	8537	17225
Current Ratio	2 18	1 72	1 94	1 96	1 60
Quik/Acid Tst	1 34	1 06	1 31	1 22	1 07
A/C Rec T/ovr	5 50	5 54	4 16	5 36	3 04
Tot Ass T/ovr	2 40	2 32	2 04	2 46	1 92
Debt/Ass Rat	0 45	0 56	0 51	0 50	0 60
L T L Tot Ass	0 01	0 01	0 02	0 01	0 01
Debt to Eqity	1 01	1 65	1 31	1 31	1 94
Interest Cover	10 73	15 65	25 27	12 61	18 76
Oper Prof Mrg	9 43	13 83	10 95	13 49	13 39
Net Prof Marg%	3 37	4 49	3 56	4 17	4 93
Ret on Assets	22 62	32 04	22 36	33 12	25 75
Ret on Equity%	18 36	30 49	18 86	26 85	30 63
Price/Earnings	4 35	3 80	2 64	2 81	5 72
Divid Cover	2 30	2 85	2 84	2 54	2 87
Divid Yield	10 00	9 23	13 33	14 04	6 09
Earning Yield%	23 00	26 31	37 83	35 61	17 48
NAV % Mrk Pr	122 75	84 45	146 40	128 34	48 95
Effec Tax Rate	47 76	46 75	51 23	49 20	48 43
Def Interval	0 10	0 13	0 13	0 09	0 81
Sus Grth Rate	10 37	19 80	16 29	16 26	18 67

SUBSIDIARY & ASSOCIATED COMPANIES

A N BROOKSTONE AND COMPANY (PTY) LTD
ANBEECO (PTY) LTD
SOUTH AFRICAN WATCH COMPANY (PTY) LTD
SUPALEK HOLDINGS LTD

INVESTMENTS

None

ANGLO ALPHA LTD

ABBREVIATION : ANG-ALPHA

JSE SHORT CODE : AAL

SECTOR : Industrial Building & Construction

SHAREHOLDERS

Who Owns Whom's Assessment of the Identity of the Ultimate Controlling Shareholder: HOLDERBANK FINANCIERE GLARIS LTD

SHAREHOLDER	PERCENTAGE 1992	1991
ALTUR INV LTD	54 8	12 3
SA MUTUAL	5 3	5 0
STD BANK NOM TVL P/L	4 1	4 2
METAL IND GROUP PENS FUND	2 7	2 5
LIBERTY LIFE ASSOC OF AFRICA LTD	2 6	2 5
ENGINEERING INDUSTRIES PENS FUND	2 5	2 2
ABSA NOM P/L	2 5	---
SOCIETE SUISSE DE CIMENT PORTLAND	2 3	2 3
CMB NOM P/L	2 1	---
YSKOR PENS FUND	1 5	1 5
EIGHTY ONE MAIN STREET NOM LTD	1 3	1 5
FOX STREET NOM P/L	1 2	8 4
ANGLOVAAL LTD	---	1 1
HOLDERBANK FINANCIERE GLARIS LTD	- -	33 5
SANLAM	---	1 7
VOLKSKAS NOM P/L	-	2 3
TOTAL	82 8	81 1

DIRECTORS :
BAKER DR ,BURGESS MB (Dir Human Resources)
BYLAND P (Chairman),GRINDROD WM ,HALL CA
HERSOV BE (Deputy Chairman),MENELL CS
PRETORIUS JG (Managing Director),RIDSDALE FJ
ROBBERTZE JC ,SCHMIDHEINY TM ,SCHRAFL AE
SEARLE RFC (Deputy Managing Director)
STRASZACKER RL

REGISTRATION NUMBER : 05/05750/06

REGISTERED OFFICE
94 Rivonia Road, Sandton
2199

TEL 011-783 5143
FAX 011-783 8950

TRANSFER SECRETARY
Anglovaal Ltd
P O Box 62379, Marshalltown
2107
TEL 011-634 9111

COMPANY SECRETARY
P D Buchner

NATURE OF BUSINESS
The holding company of a group engaged in the production of cement, stone aggregates, building sand, paper sacks, industrial minerals, lime and limestone products & ready-mixed concrete Group products include portland & masonry cement, silica fume, crushed stone, sand & agricultural limestone stone for gold extraction, burnt lime & limestone, calcite, dolomite, silica, feldspar, masterbatch, calcium carbonate, magnetite, multiwall paper sack The group has joint coal interests with Anglovaal

BANKERS :
First National Bank of SA Ltd

AUDITORS :
KPMG Aiken & Peat

FAMILIAR BRAND NAMES
N/A

CONTRIBUTION BY ACTIVITY
Cement (% turnover) (51 3%)
Stone (16 3%)
Industrial (30 4%)
Other (incl investments) (2 0%)

YEAR END : December

DIVIDEND :Ords no par value

Interim No 80	(Ldr)24/08/90	(Pay)14/09/90	Amt(c)43
Final No 81	(Ldr)22/02/91	(Pay)15/03/91	Amt(c)89
Interim No 82	(Ldr)23/08/91	(Pay)13/09/91	Amt(c)46
Final No 83	(Ldr)21/02/92	(Pay)13/03/92	Amt(c)106
Interim No 84	(Ldr)21/08/92	(Pay)11/09/92	Amt(c)46

NUMBER OF EMPLOYEES : 3829

CAPITAL STRUCTURE

	AUTHORISED	ISSUED
Cum Red Prefs R1	1000	256
Ords no par value	36000000	30076848

FINANCIAL STATISTICS (AT FINANCIAL YEAR END)

(Amts in R'000)	1991 Dec	1990 Dec	1989 Dec	1988 Dec	1987 Dec
Ord S/H Int	1580301	1497178	1329666	1175242	821001
Long Trm Loans	145106	92578	82019	88652	338991
Iss Ord Share	30077	30077	30077	30077	30077
Total Liab	320541	280247	275622	263821	481038
Current Liab	175435	187669	193603	175169	142047
Total Assets	1900842	1777425	1605288	1439063	1302039
Current Assets	305568	267041	248905	201946	151771
Debtors	147126	132433	137960	105956	82880
Inventory	137134	127193	109957	93020	67654
Turnover	728226	697277	624664	530574	417983
Oper Profit	135651	167769	169198	149530	74005
Interest Paid	20980	13587	17482	18986	23325
Tax Paid	24439	58635	55020	41103	24622
Prf af Int&Tax	103312	105067	110633	98220	29775
Prf att Ord Sh	63329	65424	77694	65210	28901
Btm Line Earn	63329	60379	76454	65210	28901
Dividend Paid	45717	39701	34588	28573	21054
Mkt Prce(c) YE	3925	2250	1950	1575	1350
Depreciation	126377	115432	40118	37332	34225

PER SHARE STATISTICS (CENTS)

Net Asst Val	5254 18	4977 82	4420 87	3907 44	2729 66
Net Earnings	343 00	349 80	367 20	257 40	185 50
Dividends	152 00	132 00	115 00	95 00	70 00
Cash Flow	760 95	734 09	500 20	450 34	209 97

RATIOS AND OTHER INFORMATION

Mrk Cap(R000)	1180522	676733	586502	473713	406040
Current Ratio	1 74	1 42	1 29	1 15	1 07
Quik/Acid Tst	0 96	0 75	0 72	0 62	0 59
A/C Rec T/ovr	4 95	5 27	4 53	5 01	5 04
Tot Ass T/ovr	0 38	0 39	0 39	0 37	0 32
Debt/Ass Rat	0 16	0 15	0 17	0 18	0 22
L T L Tot Ass	0 07	0 05	0 05	0 06	0 12
Debt to Eqity	0 20	0 18	0 20	0 22	0 36
Interest Cover	6 96	12 89	10 39	8 34	3 33
Oper Prof Mrg	18 63	24 06	27 09	28 18	17 71
Net Prof Marg%	8 70	9 38	12 44	12 29	6 91
Ret on Assets	8 10	10 27	11 86	11 00	5 97
Ret on Equity%	4 01	4 37	5 84	5 55	3 52
Price/Earnings	11 44	6 43	5 31	6 12	7 28
Divid Cover	2 26	2 65	3 19	2 71	2 65
Divid Yield	3 87	5 87	5 90	6 03	5 19
Earning Yield%	8 74	15 55	18 83	16 34	13 74
NAV % Mrk Pr	133 86	221 24	226 71	248 09	202 20
Effec Tax Rate	21 52	37 41	35 93	31 14	0 50
Def Interval	0 81	0 46	0 80	1 01	3 57
Sus Grth Rate	1 11	1 72	3 24	3 12	0 96

SUBSIDIARY & ASSOCIATED COMPANIES

ABCP FINANCE COMPANY (PTY) LTD (33%)
ANGALP AIR (PTY) LTD
ANGLO ALPHA (BOPHUTHATSWANA) (PTY) LTD
ANGLO ALPHA COAL (PTY) LTD
ANGLO ALPHA FINANCE (PTY) LTD
ANGLO ALPHA INDUSTRIAL MINERALS LTD
ANGLO ALPHA STONE LTD
ANGLO ALPHA TECHNICAL SERVICES LTD
ANGLOVAAL COAL HOLDINGS (PTY) LTD (50%)
ASH RESOURCES (PTY) LTD (25%)
BENONI CRUSHERS (PTY) LTD
BLESKOP STONE CRUSHERS (PTY) LTD
BON ACCORD QUARRIES (PTY) LTD
BRAKPAN CRUSHERS (PTY) LTD
CANNON QUARRIES (PTY) LTD
CANONBY QUARRIES (PTY) LTD
CAPPA SACKS (PTY) LTD
CEMENT DISTRIBUTORS SA (PTY) LTD (33%)
CERAMIC MINERALS (PTY) LTD
CLEVELAND CRUSHERS (1934) (PTY) LTD
CONCRETE ADDITIVES (PTY) LTD
CONSTONE (REEF) (PTY) LTD
CONSTONE LTD
CORONDALE PROSPECTING & MINING CO (PTY) (50%)
CRANKSHAW QUARRIES (PTY) LTD
CROWN CRUSHERS (PTY) LTD
E R PROPERTIES (PTY) LTD
EAST RAND COAL HOLDINGS (PTY) LTD (50%)
EFFINGHAM QUARRIES (PTY) LTD
ELAND QUARRIES (PTY) LTD
FALCON INVESTMENTS LTD
FERRO CRUSHERS (1959) (PTY) LTD
HIGHLANDS ENTERPRISES (PTY) LTD
HILLCREST QUARRIES (PTY) LTD
HILLSIDE MOBILE CRUSHERS (PTY) LTD

HILTON QUARRIES HOLDINGS (PTY) LTD
HIPCON CRUSHER HOLDINGS (PTY) LTD
HIPPO CRUSHER HOLDINGS (PTY) LTD
HIPPO QUARIES (LESOTHO) (PTY) LTD
HIPPO QUARRIES (NATAL) (PTY) LTD
HIPPO QUARRIES (PTY) LTD
HIPPO QUARRIES (TRANSVAAL) (PTY) LTD
HIPPO QUARRIES GRANITE (PTY) LTD
INDUSTRIAL SEALANTS (PTY) LTD
KLIPBRUG QUARRIES (PTY) LTD
KLIPSTONE TRANSPORT (PTY) LTD
KORHAAN INVESTMENTS LTD
LEACH & BROWN HOLDINGS (PTY) LTD
LEWIS & EVERITT (PTY) LTD
LIBANON TRANSPORT (PTY) LTD
LUIPAARDSVLEI CRUSHERS (PTY) LTD
MACDONALD & VOLCK (PTY) LTD
MESSINA DOLOMITE (PTY) LTD
METAL RECOVERY BUYING CO (PTY) LTD
MIDDELBURG KLIPBREKERY (EDMS) BPK
NAMIBIA PORTLAND CEMENT LTD
NATAL CRUSHERS (PTY) LTD
NATAL PORTLAND CEMENT COMPANY (PTY) LTD (33%)
NATIONAL PORTLAND CEMENT CO. LTD
NEW CAPITAL GRANITE QUARRIES (PTY) LTD
NEW KUSASA MINING (PTY) LTD
NGAGANE QUARRYING COMPANY (PTY) LTD
NORTHERN CAPE MILLING CO LTD
OLIFANTSFONTEIN QUARRIES (PTY) LTD
OMNIA HOLDINGS LTD (26%)
ORIBI LIME WORKS (PTY) LTD
PAREM ENTERPRISES (PTY) LTD (50%)
PENINSULA QUARRIES (PTY) LTD
PHILIPPI INDUSTRIAL TOWNSHIPS (PTY) LTD
PIONEER CRUSHERS (PTY) LTD
PLASTOCARB (PTY) LTD
POORT CRUSHERS (PTY) LTD
POWER CRUSHERS TRANSVAAL (PTY) LTD
PRETORIA AMALGAMATED CRUSHERS (PTY) LTD
R SNOW ENTERPRISES (PTY) LTD
RANDFONTEIN CRUSHED STONE DISTRIBUTORS (
REEF QUARRIES (PTY) LTD
RHEEBOK QUARRIES (PTY) LTD
ROOZEBOOM BRICKWORKS (PTY) LTD (50%)
SLAGMENT (PTY) LTD (33%)
SPECIALISED CONCRETE PRODUCTS (PTY) LTD
SPILO (PTY) LTD (25%)
SPRINGS CRUSHERS (PTY) LTD
STEYNS SAND (PTY) LTD
STOMPNEUS GIPS (EDMS) BPK
TRANS ATLAS LTD
TRANSVAAL GRAPHITE & MINERAL CO. (PTY) L
TRANSVAAL MAGNETITE (PTY) LTD
UNIFIED STONE CRUSHERS (PTY) LTD
UNION LIME COMPANY LTD
VENTERSPOST CRUSHERS (PTY) LTD
VERULAM QUARRIES (PTY) LTD
WEST CRUSHERS (PTY) LTD
WINDMILL QUARRIES (PTY) LTD
WMG ESTATES (PTY) LTD
ZEEKOEWATER CRUSHERS (PTY) LTD

INVESTMENTS

CIMENTS DE BOURBON S.A (7%)
SOUTH AFRICAN LAND & EXPLORATION CO LTD, (2%)

ANGLO AMERICAN PROPERTIES LTD

ABBREVIATION : AMAPROP

JSE SHORT CODE : ARO

SECTOR : Financial-Property Loan Stock

SHAREHOLDERS

Who Owns Whom's Assessment of the Identity of the Ultimate Controlling Shareholder: ANGLO AMERICAN

SHAREHOLDER	PERCENTAGE 1992	1991
RESIDENT NOM LTD	56.8	56.8
PETARD NOM LTD	5.9	5.9
DIDO NOM LTD	4.7	4.7
FERMAIN NOM LTD	4.5	4.5
TAURUS NOM LTD	4.5	4.5
STD BANK NOM TVL P/L	3.3	3.3
RUNCORN HLDGS LTD	3.0	3.0
EIGHTY ONE MAIN STREET NOM LTD	2.3	2.3
AECI PENS FUND	1.9	1.9
NEDBANK NOM LTD	1.7	1.6
TOTAL	88.6	88.5

DIRECTORS :
BAUM PM ,BIHL JF ,BRAGG WFE ,GARDINER GP
GULLAN AG ,HENRY MJ ,KING MW
LEISSNER GGL (Chairman),LINDOP G
OPPENHEIMER NF ,SUNTER CL ,WHITFIELD AC

REGISTRATION NUMBER : 62/04693/06

REGISTERED OFFICE
1st Floor, First National House
11 Diagonal Street, Johannesburg
2001
TEL: 011-4919111
FAX: 011-838 5136

TRANSFER SECRETARY
Consolidated Share Registrars Ltd
P O Box 61051, Marshalltown
2107
TEL: 011-492 1620

COMPANY SECRETARY
Anglo American Property Services (Pty) Ltd

NATURE OF BUSINESS
A property investment company with a portfolio of commercial property developments, suburban shopping complexes, hotels & parking garages. In addition it has interests in residential and industrial townships and development schemes within those townships.

BANKERS :
First National Bank of SA Ltd

AUDITORS :
Coopers Theron Du Toit

FAMILIAR BRAND NAMES

N/A

CONTRIBUTION BY ACTIVITY

Investment Properties (% net income) (99.0%)
Township Land Sales (3.0%)
Hotel Operations (Loss) (-2.0%)

YEAR END : March

DIVIDEND :Ords R2

Final No 21	(Ldr)25/05/90	(Pay)22/06/90	Amt(c)42
Interim No 22	(Ldr)23/11/90	(Pay)21/12/90	Amt(c)15
Final No 24	(Ldr)28/03/91	(Pay)22/06/91	Amt(c)32
Final No 26	(Ldr)29/05/92	(Pay)25/06/92	Amt(c)35
Interim No 27	(Ldr)27/11/92	(Pay)21/12/92	Amt(c)15

CAPITAL STRUCTURE

	AUTHORISED	ISSUED
Ords R2	57865000	44979050
1st Cum Partic Prefs 1c	9444000	0

FINANCIAL STATISTICS (AT FINANCIAL YEAR END)

(Amts in R'000)	1991 Mar	1990 Mar	1989 Mar	1988 Mar	1987
Ord S/H Int	582040	442524	413058	388839	370265
Long Trm Loans	327910	311606	322108	317616	366132
Iss Ord Share	44979	44979	44979	42926	42926
Total Liab	431001	382139	391983	365856	418667
Current Liab	103091	70533	69875	48240	52535
Total Assets	1013041	824663	805041	754695	786672
Current Assets	32968	55012	33166	30383	50275
Debtors	29931	35268	32380	30247	-
Inventory	2919	1474	-	-	50275
Turnover	200128	209201	161819	125481	103150
Oper Profit	68559	71248	64916	53765	49208
Interest Paid	24941	27499	26231	24320	23128
Tax Paid	10208	8034	9222	5908	4644
Prf af Int&Tax	36996	35715	29463	23537	20740
Prf att Ord Sh	32827	30322	24664	19885	17345
Btm Line Earn	36703	40687	28698	20580	17345
Dividend Paid	21140	18891	15743	12878	12448
Mkt Prce(c) YE	800	670	610	530	540
Depreciation	1586	1880	1391	993	-

PER SHARE STATISTICS (CENTS)

Net Asst Val	1294.03	983.85	918.34	905.84	862.57
Net Earnings	72.98	67.41	54.84	46.32	-
Dividends	47.00	42.00	35.00	30.00	-
Cash Flow	79.11	78.27	63.14	47.76	48.32

RATIOS AND OTHER INFORMATION

Mrk Cap(R000)	359832	301359	274372	227508	231800
Current Ratio	0.32	0.78	0.47	0.63	0.96
Quik/Acid Tst	0.29	0.76	0.47	0.63	-
A/C Rec T/ovr	6.69	5.93	5.00	4.15	-
Tot Ass T/ovr	0.20	0.25	0.20	0.17	0.13
Debt/Ass Rat	0.31	0.35	0.36	0.37	0.53
L T L Tot Ass	0.21	0.26	0.28	0.30	0.47
Debt to Eqity	0.54	0.65	0.71	0.71	1.13
Interest Cover	2.89	2.59	2.47	2.21	2.10
Oper Prof Mrg	34.26	34.06	40.12	42.85	47.71
Net Prof Marg%	16.40	14.49	15.24	15.85	16.82
Ret on Assets	7.13	8.64	8.06	7.12	6.17
Ret on Equity%	5.64	6.85	5.97	5.11	4.68
Price/Earnings	10.96	9.94	11.12	11.44	-
Divid Cover	1.55	1.61	1.57	1.54	-
Divid Yield	5.88	6.27	5.74	5.66	-
Earning Yield%	9.12	10.06	8.99	8.74	-
NAV % Mrk Pr	161.75	146.84	150.55	170.91	159.73
Effec Tax Rate	20.50	11.50	17.78	21.34	17.81
Def Interval	6.38	6.27	8.19	11.33	17.65
Sus Grth Rate	2.01	2.58	2.16	1.80	1.32

SUBSIDIARY & ASSOCIATED COMPANIES

ABERFELDY DEVELOPMENTS (PTY) LTD
ADREC PROPERTIES (PTY) LTD
AMAPROP TOWNSHIPS LTD
ARJAY (PTY) LTD
AUBAR PROPERTIES (PTY) LTD
BICCARD STREET PROPERTIES (PTY) LTD
C.D.L. PROPERTIES (DURBAN) (PTY) LTD
CARLTON CENTRE LTD
CARLTON HOTELS LTD
COMPASS PROPERTY HOLDINGS LTD (50%)
EAST CITY CENTRE (PTY) LTD
EDURA PROPERTIES (PTY) LTD
EMBASSY HOUSE (PTY) LTD
GARPAND INVESTMENTS (PTY) LTD (50%)
GOWER PROPERTIES (PTY) LTD
HEDGE INVESTMENTS (PTY) LTD
IVANEL PROPERTIES (PTY) LTD
KANSTEEN INVESTMENTS (PTY) LTD
KILLARNEY CENTRE (PTY) LTD
KILLARNEY DEVELOPMENTS (EAST) (PTY) LTD
LEA BUILDINGS (PTY) LTD
LISHEEN ESTATES (PTY) LTD
MONTE SOLE HEIGHTS (PTY) LTD
SCYLLA INVESTMENTS (PTY) LTD
SOREC LTD
SOREC PROPERTIES BRAAMFONTEIN LTD
SOREC PROPERTIES GARDENS LTD
SOREC PROPERTIES HILLBROW (PTY) LTD
SOREC PROPERTIES SUNNYSIDE (PTY) LTD
TREVESEN PROPERTIES (PTY) LTD

INVESTMENTS

APEX PROPERTY FUND (13,2%)
MAIN STREET PROPERTY FUND (2,75%)

ANGLO AMERICAN COAL CORP LTD

ABBREVIATION : AMCOAL

JSE SHORT CODE : AMC

SECTOR : Mining-Coal

SHAREHOLDERS

Who Owns Whom's Assessment of the Identity of the Ultimate Controlling Shareholder:
ANGLO AMERICAN

SHAREHOLDER	PERCENTAGE 1992	1991
AFRICAN & EUROPEAN INV CO LTD	19.5	19.5
SA MUTUAL	12.8	12.2
FERMAIN NOM LTD	8.1	8.1
STD BANK NOM TVL P/L	6.4	5.7
RESIDENT NOM LTD	6.2	6.3
DIDO NOM LTD	6.1	6.1
PETARD NOM LTD	5.4	5.4

LIBERTY LIFE ASSOC OF AFRICA LTD	4 6	4 7
TAURUS NOM LTD	3 6	3 7
CMB NOM P/L	2 7	---
ANGLO AMERICAN CORP OF SA LTD	2 4	2 3
EIGHTY ONE MAIN STREET NOM LTD	1 7	1 4
SOUTHERN LIFE ASSOC LTD	1 6	2 1
OVERSEAS NOM CO INC	1 4	2 2
ENGINEERING INDUSTRIES PENS FUND	1 1	1 1
FIRST NAT NOM P/L	---	1 0
SANLAM	---	2 4
TOTAL	83 5	84 0

DIRECTORS :
BOUSTRED WG ,BOYD L
CAMPBELL JW DR (Managing Director),COHEN RL
KING MW ,KRUGER LW ,LAYBOURNE RA
LESLIE JS (Financial Director)
OGILVIE THOMPSON J ,OPPENHEIMER NF ,PRETORIUS TL
RANKIN D (Chairman),REID HR ,RITSON DJ
ST JOHN BA ,STACEY HB ,SUNTER CL ,SUTHERLAND C
WIGGILL DB (Dir Human Resources

REGISTRATION NUMBER : 01/01469/06

REGISTERED OFFICE
44 Main Street, Johannesburg
2001
TEL 011-638 9111
FAX 011-638 5428

TRANSFER SECRETARY
Consolidated Share Registrars Ltd
P O Box 61051, Marshalltown
2107
TEL 011-492 1620

COMPANY SECRETARY
Anglo American Corp of SA Ltd

NATURE OF BUSINESS
The group is engaged in the mining of anthracite and coal for the domestic and export markets, and its industrial operations manufacture a range of refractory materials, ceramic tiles, concrete roof tiles and clay sewer pipes and fittings The group also mines andalusite, chrome ore, building clays, fireclays, silica, and owns property and mineral and coal rights in the Tvl, Natal and the OFS The group also conducts coal exploration activities

BANKERS :
First National Bank of SA Ltd

AUDITORS :
Ernst & Young

FAMILIAR BRAND NAMES
ARNOT COLLIERY,BANK COLLIERY,COVERLAND
GOEDEHOOP COLLIERY,KLEINKOPJE COLLIERY
KRIEL COLLIERY,LANDAU COLLIERY
NATAL ANTHRACITE COLL,NEW DENMARK COLLIERY
NEW VAAL COLLIERY,SPRINGFIELD COLLIERY,VITRO
VRYHEID CORONATION COL

CONTRIBUTION BY ACTIVITY
Domestic - Eskom (% Sales) (70 5%)
Domestic - Industrial (1 9%)
Domestic - Metallurgical (2 5%)
Domestic - Coke (0 7%)
Domestic - Anthracite (0 1%)
Export - Metallurgical (5 1%)
Export - Steam Coal (18 5%)
Export - Coke (0 2%)
Export - Anthracite (0 5%)

YEAR END : March

DIVIDEND : Ords 50c

Final No 134	(Ldr)01/06/90	(Pay)22/06/90	Amt(c)260
Interim No 135	(Ldr)23/11/90	(Pay)28/12/90	Amt(c)138
Final No 136	(Ldr)30/05/91	(Pay)21/06/91	Amt(c)287
Interim No 137	(Ldr)22/11/91	(Pay)24/12/91	Amt(c)150
Final No 138	(Ldr)29/05/92	(Pay)26/06/92	Amt(c)315
Interim No 139	(Ldr)20/11/92	(Pay)24/12/92	Amt(c)150

NUMBER OF EMPLOYEES : 16621

CAPITAL STRUCTURE

	AUTHORISED	ISSUED
Ords 50c	30000000	25191750

FINANCIAL STATISTICS (AT FINANCIAL YEAR END)

(Amts in R'000)	1992 Mar	1991 Mar	1990 Mar	1989 Mar	1988 Mar
Ord S/H Int	1423140	1213444	1027201	921600	811466
Long Trm Loans	915593	791315	722913	653685	639680
Iss Ord Share	25192	25147	24990	24899	24440
Total Liab	1541097	1293169	1414557	1145225	1136656
Current Liab	625504	501854	691644	491540	496976
Total Assets	2964237	2506613	2441758	2066825	1948122
Current Assets	987072	909133	1094226	765986	735566
Debtors	290703	222452	187782	166436	149816
Inventory	151048	140238	130707	113277	97244
Turnover	1859646	1818779	1752594	1445716	1144141
Oper Profit	419095	412425	459374	311206	221653
Interest Paid	816	1266	1119	1692	2042
Tax Paid	189423	261292	305774	193675	118244
Prf af Int&Tax	321110	275539	257886	170536	111613
Prf att Ord Sh	321110	275539	196727	165612	104941
Btm Line Earn	321110	275539	196727	165612	104941
Dividend Paid	117074	106801	96564	74973	58834
Mkt Prce(c) YE	12600	9850	8050	6000	3300
Depreciation	70567	63102	69044	50236	43838

PER SHARE STATISTICS (CENTS)

Net Asst Val	5649 17	4825 40	4110 45	3701 35	3320 24
Net Earnings	1274 70	1095 70	1025 30	665 10	429 40
Dividends	465 00	425 00	385 00	300 00	240 00
Cash Flow	2253 18	1795 80	1335 49	1043 04	941 38

RATIOS AND OTHER INFORMATION

Mrk Cap(R000)	3174192	2476980	2011695	1493940	806520
Current Ratio	1 58	1 81	1 58	1 56	1 48
Quik/Acid Tst	1 34	1 53	1 39	1 33	1 28
A/C Rec T/ovr	6 40	8 18	9 33	8 69	7 64
Tot Ass T/ovr	0 63	0 73	0 72	0 70	0 59
Debt/Ass Rat	0 21	0 20	0 28	0 24	0 26
L T L Tot Ass	-	-	0 00	0 00	0 01
Debt to Eqity	0 44	0 41	0 68	0 54	0 63
Interest Cover	515 56	326 75	410 68	190 59	113 56
Oper Prof Mrg	22 54	22 68	26 21	21 53	19 37
Net Prof Marg%	17 27	15 15	11 22	11 46	9 17
Ret on Assets	17 25	21 47	23 13	17 70	11 90
Ret on Equity%	22 56	22 71	19 15	17 97	12 93
Price/Earnings	9 88	8 99	7 85	9 02	7 69
Divid Cover	2 74	2 58	2 66	2 22	1 79
Divid Yield	3 69	4 31	4 78	5 00	7 27
Earning Yield%	10 12	11 12	12 74	11 09	13 01
NAV % Mrk Pr	44 83	48 99	51 06	61 69	100 61
Effec Tax Rate	12 80	31 13	51 91	42 44	16 58
Def Interval	0 18	0 15	0 22	0 48	1 01
Sus Grth Rate	14 34	13 91	9 75	9 83	5 68

SUBSIDIARY & ASSOCIATED COMPANIES

ACRO (HANISE) (PTY) LTD
ACRO (HANISE) (TRANSKEI) (PTY) LTD
AFRICAN HAWK EAGLE HOLDINGS LTD (20%)
AMALGAMATED COLLIERIES OF S.A. LTD
AMCOAL COLLIERIES LTD
AMCOAL COLLIERIES RECRUITING ORG. (LESOT
AMCOAL COLLIERIES RECRUITING ORG. (PTY)
AMCOAL COLLIERY & INDUSTRIAL OPERATIONS
AMCOAL EXPLORATION & FINANCE LTD
AMCOAL EXPORT SERVICES LTD
ANGLO POWER COLLIERIES (PTY) LTD
BALGRAY COLLIERIES (PTY) LTD
BLESBOK COLLIERY LTD
BOOTED EAGLE HOLDINGS LTD (20%)
BOPHUTHATSWANA CHROME CO. (PTY) LTD (50%)
CALAMAR (PTY) LTD
CARNARVON ANTHRACITE COAL MINES (PTY) LT
CEZA HOLDINGS LTD (20%)
CORONATION COLLIERIES LTD, THE
COVERLAND ROOF TILES (PTY) LTD
COVERLAND TILES (NATAL) (PTY) LTD
COVERTILE HOLDINGS (PTY) LTD
CROWNED EAGLE HOLDINGS LTD (20%)
ELGIN REFRACTORIES LTD
ENYATI COLLIERY LTD
FERROBAR HOLDINGS LTD (20%)
HAVEN COURT (PTY) LTD
HAVERCROFT MINERLAS (PTY) LTD
IMPATI ANTHRACITE LTD
INDUMENI COAL MINES LTD
INGAGANE COLLIERY (PTY) LTD (25%)
MARICO CHROME CORP. (PTY) LTD (50%)
MARTIAL EAGLE HOLDINGS LTD (20%)
MORUPULE COLLIERY LTD (20%)
NATAL ANTHRACITE COLLIERY LTD
NATAL COAL SYNDICATE (PTY) LTD (25%)
NEW LARGO COLLIERY LTD
ROY POINT-BRAAKFONTEIN COLLIERY LTD (22,5%)
S & G CHAMBERS (PTY) LTD
SLADOX LTD
SPRINGBOK COLLIERY LTD
SPRINGFIELD COLLIERIES LTD
STEPPE EAGLE HOLDINGS LTD (20%)
SUMMIT SAND (PTY) LTD
TAWNY EAGLE HOLDINGS LTD (20%)
TAYBARD HOLDINGS LTD (20%)
TRANSVAAL COAL CORPORATION LTD
VEREENIGING REFRACTORIES LTD
VERREF HOUSING INVESTMENTS (PTY) LTD
VERREF MINERALS (PTY) LTD
VITRO CLAY PIPES LTD
VRYHEID COKE LTD
VRYHEID CORONATION LTD
WITBANK COAL HOLDINGS LTD

INVESTMENTS

9,5% VEREENIGING MUNICIPAL STOCKS (200000SH)
BARBROOK MINES LTD (406 SH)
BARLOW RAND LTD (8130 SH)
CALLIOPE HOLDINGS LTD (7.8%)
LANSAN INVESTMENT HOLDINGS LTD (11%)

ANGLO AMERICAN GOLD INVEST CO LTD

ABBREVIATION : AMGOLD

JSE SHORT CODE : AMG

SECTOR : Mining Financial-Mining Holding

SHAREHOLDERS

Who Owns Whom's Assessment of the Identity of the Ultimate Controlling Shareholder:
ANGLO AMERICAN

SHAREHOLDER	PERCENTAGE 1992	1991
ANGLO AMERICAN CORP OF SA LTD	13.3	13.3
RESIDENT NOM LTD	7.8	7.8
UNION BANK OF SWITZERLAND	7.7	6.7
SA TOWNSHIPS MINING & FINANCE CORP LTD	7.6	7.6
RAND SELECTION CORP LTD	7.4	7.4
CREDIT SUISSE	6.1	---
FERMAIN NOM LTD	5.7	5.7
SOCIETE DE BANQUE SUISSE	5.6	5.3
PETARD NOM LTD	5.0	5.0
STD BANK NOM TVL P/L	4.3	3.9
INDO-CHINA NOM P/L	3.3	2.4
TAURUS NOM LTD	3.0	3.0
FIRST NAT NOM P/L	2.4	2.3
SA MUTUAL	2.3	2.3
SOUTHERN LIFE ASSOC LTD	2.2	2.6
LONDON CONTROL ACCOUNT	2.0	3.3
EIGHTY ONE MAIN STREET NOM LTD	1.6	1.2
CMB NOM P/L	1.3	---
DEPOSITARY NOM INC	1.3	3.2
CREDIT SUISSE LONDON NOM LTD	---	4.7
INDO-CHINA NOM SA P/L	---	2.4
SANLAM	---	1.3
TOTAL	89.7	91.1

DIRECTORS :
DESMIDT JMP ,DICKMAN AB ,GODSELL RM ,GUSH EP
HERSOV BE ,HEWITT L ,KING MW ,OGILVIE THOMPSON J
OPPENHEIMER NF (Chairman),PRETORIUS TL
SUNTER CL ,WILLIAMS KH

REGISTRATION NUMBER : 05/09084/06

REGISTERED OFFICE
44 Main Street, Johannesburg
2001
TEL: 011-638 9111
FAX: 011-638 3221

TRANSFER SECRETARY
Consolidated Share Registrars Ltd
P O Box 61051, Marshalltown
2107
TEL: 011-492 1620

COMPANY SECRETARY
Anglo American Corp of SA Ltd

NATURE OF BUSINESS
An investment company with substantial interests in gold and uranium mines in SA and interests in South America, Australia and the Far East.
The company also participates in gold-uranium

prospecting in Southern Africa and other parts of the world

BANKERS :
First National Bank of SA Ltd

AUDITORS :
Deloitte Pim Goldby

FAMILIAR BRAND NAMES
N/A

CONTRIBUTION BY ACTIVITY
N/A

YEAR END : March

DIVIDEND : Ords R1

Final No 84	(Ldr)23/03/90	(Pay)03/05/90	Amt(c)600
Interim No 85	(Ldr)21/09/90	(Pay)02/11/90	Amt(c)400
Final No 86	(Ldr)26/04/91	(Pay)04/06/91	Amt(c)375
Interim No 87	(Ldr)25/10/91	(Pay)03/12/91	Amt(c)475
Final No 88	(Ldr)24/04/92	(Pay)02/06/92	Amt(c)500
Interim No 89	(Ldr)30/10/92	(Pay)01/12/92	Amt(c)525

CAPITAL STRUCTURE

	AUTHORISED	ISSUED
Ords R1	28200000	24147213

FINANCIAL STATISTICS (AT FINANCIAL YEAR END)

(Amts in R'000)	1992 Mar	1991 Mar	1990 Feb	1989 Feb	1988
Ord S/H Int	952400	952300	452900	418800	384800
Long Trm Loans	-	-	-	-	161300
Iss Ord Share	24147	24147	21952	21952	21952
Total Liab	127700	92100	174600	160100	322600
Current Liab	127700	92100	174600	160100	161300
Total Assets	1048900	1014400	602500	558800	733000
Intang Assets	31200	30000	25000	20100	*
Current Assets	457400	414400	70800	182300	186900
Debtors	2600	1100	70500	77000	-
Inventory	-	-	-	-	186900
Turnover	-	-	-	-	369500
Oper Profit	-51900	-73600	-41700	-35400	341800
Interest Paid	-	13600	5000	-	-
Tax Paid	-	-	-	-	500
Prf af Int&Tax	235500	178200	308500	330300	341300
Prf att Ord Sh	235500	178200	308500	330300	341300
Btm Line Earn	235500	178200	308500	330300	341300
Dividend Paid	235400	178300	274400	296300	312800
Mkt Prce(c) YE	20700	18950	36000	27800	22700

PER SHARE STATISTICS (CENTS)

Net Asst Val	3814 97	3819 52	1949 25	1816 24	1752 92
Net Earnings	975 00	788 00	1405 00	1505 00	-
Dividends	975 00	775 00	1250 00	1350 00	-
Cash Flow	975 28	726 97	1405 34	1504 65	1554 76

RATIOS AND OTHER INFORMATION

Mrk Cap(R000)	4998429	4575857	7902720	6102656	4983104
Current Ratio	3 58	4 50	0 41	1 14	1 16
Quik/Acid Tst	3 58	4 50	0 41	1 14	-
Tot Ass T/ovr	-	-	-	-	0 50
Debt/Ass Rat	0 12	0 09	0 29	0 29	0 44
L T L Tot Ass			-	-	0 22
Debt to Eqity	0 13	0 10	0 39	0 38	0 84
Interest Cover		12 29	59 64	-	-
Oper Prof Mrg	-	-	-		92 50
Net Prof Marg%			-		92 37
Ret on Assets	22 45	17 45	52 03	59 11	46 63
Ret on Equity%	24 73	17 27	68 12	78 87	88 70
Price/Earnings	21 23	24 05	25 62	18 47	-
Divid Cover	1 00	1 02	1 12	1 11	-
Divid Yield	4 71	4 09	3 47	4 86	-
Earning Yield%	4 71	4 16	3 90	5 41	-
NAV % Mrk Pr	18 43	20 16	5 41	6 53	7 72
Effec Tax Rate	-	-	-	-	0 15
Def Interval	-	-	0 13	0 01	0 47
Sus Grth Rate	0 01	-0 01	7 53	8 12	7 41

SUBSIDIARY & ASSOCIATED COMPANIES

AURORA HOLDINGS LTD
BUFFELSFONTEIN GOLD MINING CO LTD (20 2%)
ELANDSRAND GOLD MINING CO LTD (23 3%)
JEANETTE GOLD MINES LTD (25 1%)
ORANGE FREE STATE INV TRUST LTD
WELKOM GOLD HOLDINGS LTD (30 7%)
WESTERN ULTRA DEEP LEVELS LTD (29 0%)

INVESTMENTS

AFRIKANDER LEASE LTD, THE (17,5%)
BARBROOK MINES LTD (8%)
BEATRIX MINES LTD (2,5%)
BLYVOORUITZICHT GOLD MINING CO LTD (6,8%)
CAPE VERDE (PTY) LTD (10%)
DEELKRAAL GOLD MINING CO LTD (8,6%)
DOORNFONTEIN GOLD MINING CO LTD (7%)
DRIEFONTEIN CONSOLIDATED LTD (11 5%)
EAST RAND GOLD & URANIUM CO (18 5%)
EASTERN GOLD HOLDINGS LTD (9,5%)
ELSBURG GOLD MINING CO LTD (4,5%)
FREE STATE CONSOLIDATED GOLD MINES LTD (6 5%)
GOLD FIELDS OF S A LTD (10,8%)
GOLDRIDGE GOLD MINING CO (PTY) LTD (13,6%)
H J JOEL GOLD MINING CO LTD (2,6%)
HARMONY GOLD MINING CO LTD (2,7%)
HARMONY GOLD MINING COMPANY LTD (2 74%)
HARTEBEESFONTEIN GOLD MINING CO LTD (15 5%)
KINROSS MINES LTD
KLOOF GOLD MINING CO LTD (8%)
KLOOF GOLD MINING COMPANY LTD (FINANCIA (7 98%)
LORAINE GOLD MINES LTD (12 2%)
NEW WITS LTD (0 5%)
ORANGE FREE STATE INVESTMENTS LTD (15%)
ORYX GOLD HOLDINGS LTD
SOUTH AFRICAN LAND & EXPLORATION CO LTD, (17,7%)
SOUTH AMERICAN INVESTMENTS LTD (11%)
SOUTH DEEP EXPLORATION CO LTD (5 7%)
SOUTH SEA INVESTMENTS LTD S A (11%)
SOUTHVAAL HOLDINGS LTD (13 3%)
ST HELENA GOLD MINES LTD (18 6%)
TARGET EXPLORATION CO LTD (10 8%)
UNISEL GOLD MINES LTD (6 7%)
VAAL REEFS EXPLORATION & MINING CO LTD (16 8%)
WESTERN AREAS GOLD MINING CO LTD (2,5%)
WESTERN DEEP LEVELS LTD (13 9%)
ZANDPAN GOLD MINING CO LTD (13.2%)

ANGLO AMERICAN INDUSTRIAL CORP LTD

ABBREVIATION : AMIC

JSE SHORT CODE : AMI

SECTOR : Industrial Industrial Holding

SHAREHOLDERS

Who Owns Whom's Assessment of the Identity of the Ultimate Controlling Shareholder:
ANGLO AMERICAN

SHAREHOLDER	PERCENTAGE 1992	1991
RESIDENT NOM LTD	22 7	20 7
DE BEERS CONSOLIDATED MINES LTD	12 2	12 5
DIDO NOM LTD	7 3	7 5
DE BEERS HOLDINGS P/L	7 3	7 5
SA MUTUAL	5 8	5 4
TAURUS NOM LTD	5 2	5 3
FERMAIN NOM LTD	3 9	4 1
ANGLO AMERICAN CORP OF SA LTD	3 4	3 4
STD BANK NOM TVL P/L	3 1	2 3
FEBRIS LTD	2 8	2 9
SOUTHERN LIFE ASSOC LTD	2 1	3 2
AFRICAN & EUROPEAN INV CO LTD	2 0	2 0
MARJORAM HOLDINGS LTD	2 0	2 0
EIGHTY ONE MAIN STREET NOM LTD	1 7	1 2
CMB NOM P/L	1 6	- -
CALINA INV HOLDINGS LTD	1 5	1 6
MAUDSLEY HOLDINGS LTD	1 1	1 2
LODESTONE HLDGS LTD	1 1	1 1
METAL IND GROUP PENS FUND	1 0	---
SANLAM	---	1 5
TOTAL	87 7	85 2

DIRECTORS :
BOUSTRED RA ,BOUSTRED WG ,BOYD L (Chairman)
BULLETT BE ,DAVIES HK (Deputy Chairman),GUSH EP
HARRIS A ,HULL CJ ,JONES TE ,KING MW ,LINCOLN LA
MACGILLIVRAY DM ,MCCARTHY BC ,OGILVIE THOMPSON J
OPPENHEIMER NF ,RELLY GWH ,SANDER MA
SAUNDERS CJ ,STERLING SL ,SUNTER CL
TRAHAR AJ (Deputy Chairman),VENTER WP D

REGISTRATION NUMBER : 63/05282/06

REGISTERED OFFICE
44 Main Street, Johannesburg
2001
TEL 011-638 9111
FAX 011-638 3221

TRANSFER SECRETARY
Consolidated Share Registrars Ltd
P O Box 61051, Marshalltown
2107
TEL 011-492 1620

COMPANY SECRETARY
Anglo American Corporation of SA Ltd

NATURE OF BUSINESS
Holding company of a group with diverse industrial interests Areas of operations include Industrial explosives & chemicals, iron, steel & engineering, pulp, paper, forestry & timber products, building & construction, freight & travel, motor assembly, components & distribution, electronic & electrical engineering, sugar & food, mining & construction equipment, tools & contracting services The group holds controlling interests in quoted Haggie, AECI Tongaat-Hulett, LTA, Highveld Steel & McCarthy Grp

BANKERS :
N/A

AUDITORS :
KPMG Aiken & Peat

FAMILIAR BRAND NAMES
N/A

CONTRIBUTION BY ACTIVITY
Textiles (% group equity earnings) (3 8%)
Steel/Vanadium/Ferro-Alloys/Aluminium (40 4%)
Pulp/Paper/Forestry/Timber/Bldg Products (13 7%)
Mining & Constr equip/Tools/Contracting (11 6%)
Industrial Explosives & Chemicals (16 1%)
Sugar & Food (4 2%)
Motor Assembly & Distribution (1 9%)
Electronics & Electrical Engineering (4 7%)
Freight & Travel (3 6%)

YEAR END : December

DIVIDEND :Ords R1

Interim No 53	(Ldr)14/09/90	(Pay)19/10/90	Amt(c)110
Final No 54	(Ldr)28/03/91	(Pay)26/04/91	Amt(c)240
Interim No 55	(Ldr)06/09/91	(Pay)18/10/91	Amt(c)110
Final No 56	(Ldr)27/03/92	(Pay)24/04/92	Amt(c)240
Interim No 57	(Ldr)04/09/92	(Pay)16/10/92	Amt(c)110

NUMBER OF EMPLOYEES : 176938

CAPITAL STRUCTURE

	AUTHORISED	ISSUED
Ords R1	64000000	56762350
5,625% First Cum Prefs R2	1000000	1000000
12,375% Second Cum Red Prefs R1	6000000	1505362

FINANCIAL STATISTICS (AT FINANCIAL YEAR END)

(Amts in R'000)	1991 Dec	1990 Dec	1989 Dec	1988 Dec	1987 Dec
Ord S/H Int	4195000	3718000	3155000	2721000	2288000
Long Trm Loans	3548000	3015000	2201000	1565000	1613000
Iss Ord Share	56762	54043	53940	53860	53600
Total Liab	5462000	4701000	3969000	3026000	2563000
Current Liab	1914000	1686000	1768000	1461000	950000
Total Assets	9657000	8419000	7124000	5747000	4851000
Current Assets	3161000	2497000	2414000	1785000	1291000
Debtors	1351000	1054000	951000	798000	591000
Inventory	1164000	1005000	988000	735000	554000
Turnover	6460000	6123000	5777000	4728000	3546000
Oper Profit	434000	570000	1128000	989000	564000
Interest Paid	113000	121000	127000	37000	40000
Tax Paid	50000	152000	444000	337000	119000
Prf af Int&Tax	450000	491000	751000	690000	474000
Prf att Ord Sh	401000	451000	636000	517000	352000
Btm Line Earn	417000	448000	622000	515000	345000
Dividend Paid	196000	190000	189000	156000	121000
Mkt Prce(c) YE	7350	8000	9800	6100	4300
Depreciation	284000	246000	215000	193000	164000

PER SHARE STATISTICS (CENTS)

Net Asst Val	7390 51	6879 71	5849 09	5051 99	4268 66
Net Earnings	731 00	836 00	1211 00	963 00	663 00
Dividends	350 00	350 00	350 00	290 00	225 00
Cash Flow	1038 18	1183 27	1636 15	1771 69	1105 66

RATIOS AND OTHER INFORMATION

Mrk Cap(R000)	4172007	4323440	5286120	3285460	2304800
Current Ratio	1 65	1 48	1 37	1 22	1 36
Quik/Acid Tst	1 04	0 88	0 81	0 72	0 78

A/C Rec T/ovr	4.78	5.81	6.07	5.92	6.00
Tot Ass T/ovr	0.67	0.73	0.81	0.82	0.73
Debt/Ass Rat	0.25	0.23	0.31	0.27	0.27
L T L Tot Ass	0.05	0.03	0.06	0.02	0.07
Debt to Eqity	0.58	0.53	0.70	0.58	0.57
Interest Cover	4.75	5.64	9.74	28.76	15.83
Oper Prof Mrg	6.72	9.31	19.53	20.92	15.91
Net Prof Marg%	6.21	7.37	11.01	10.93	9.93
Ret on Assets	7.45	10.45	20.59	18.51	13.05
Ret on Equity%	9.56	12.13	20.16	19.00	15.38
Price/Earnings	10.05	9.57	8.09	6.33	6.49
Divid Cover	2.09	2.39	3.46	3.32	2.95
Divid Yield	4.76	4.38	3.57	4.75	5.23
Earning Yield%	9.95	10.45	12.36	15.79	15.42
NAV % Mrk Pr	100.55	86.00	59.68	82.82	99.27
Effec Tax Rate	14.86	13.58	24.68	9.98	11.07
Def Interval	2.58	1.68	1.31	1.02	1.95
Sus Grth Rate	4.89	7.02	14.17	13.27	10.10

SUBSIDIARY & ASSOCIATED COMPANIES

AECI LTD (39,5%)
AFEX HOLDINGS (PTY) LTD (50%)
ALLIED ELECTRONIC CORPORATION LTD (22,3%)
AMHOLD INDUSTRIAL CO LTD
AMITRON LTD
AMQUIP (PTY) LTD (50%)
ANESTRUS INVESTMENT HOLDINGS LIMITED (50%)
ANGLO AMERICAN INDUSTRIAL INVESTMENTS LT
ANTHEUS INVESTMENT HOLDINGS LTD
AUTOMATIC OVERSEAS INVESTMENTS (PTY) LTD
BOART EXPLORATION SERVICES (PTY) LTD
BOART HARDMETALS (PTY) LTD
BOART INTERNATIONAL LTD
BOART MSA (PTY) LTD
CALAR INVESTMENT HOLDINGS LTD (50%)
CARDIUM HOLDINGS LTD
CONTROL LOGIC (PTY) LTD
DRILLS STEELS (PTY) LTD (42,0%)
FERROVELD (PTY) LTD (50%)
FLOCCOTAN (PTY) LTD (50%)
HAGGIE LTD (35,3%)
HIGHVELD STEEL & VANADIUM CORP LTD
INTERNATIONAL PIPE & STEEL INVESTMENTS ((31,2%)
KOLBENCO (PTY) LTD
LANSAN INVESTMENT HOLDINGS LTD (29,7%)
LENCA FERROUS PROCESSORS (PTY) LTD (50%)
LTA LTD (22,5%)
MAINSTRAAT BELEGGINGS (1965) LTD (40%)
MCCARTHY GROUP LTD (24,4%)
MCCARTHY-MAIN HOLDINGS LTD (25%)
MONDI PAPER CO LTD
NTE LTD
OSBORN MMD ENGINEERING (PTY) LTD
PG BISON (PTY) LTD (23,9%)
POWER TECHNOLOGIES LTD (20%)
REDBURY HOLDINGS LTD (50%)
RHEEM SOUTH AFRICA (PTY) LTD
S & T INVESTMENTS LTD
SCAW METALS LTD
SEAMAN'S TRAVEL SERVICES S A (PTY) LTD (50%)
STANLEY MOTORS LIMITED (50%)
STEEL ENGINEERING CO LTD
TONGAAT-HULETT GROUP LTD (22,9%)
TURNBERRY HOLDINGS LTD
TURNSTONE TWO LTD (50%)
UNION CARRIAGE & WAGON COMPANY (PTY) LTD (28,5%)
VENTRON CORPORATION LTD (29,2%)
VIERFONTEIN COAL HOLDINGS LTD (33,3%)
VIERFONTEIN COLLIERY LTD (33,3%)

INVESTMENTS

ANGLO AMERICAN CORPORATION OF SOUTH AFRI (0.5%)
DORBYL LTD (16,4%)
HALL LONGMORE & CO (PTY) LTD (2.9%)
INDUSTRIAL GRIT DISTRIBUTORS (SHANNON) L (16%)
S A MOTOR CORPORATION (PTY) LTD (19%)
UNION CARRIAGE & WAGON COMPANY (PTY) LTD (1.9%)

ANGLO AMERICAN INVESTMENT TRUST LTD

ABBREVIATION : ANAMINT

JSE SHORT CODE : AIT

SECTOR : Mining-Diamonds

SHAREHOLDERS

Who Owns Whom's Assessment of the Identity of the Ultimate Controlling Shareholder:
ANGLO AMERICAN

SHAREHOLDER	PERCENTAGE 1992	1991
ANGLO AMERICAN CORP OF SA LTD	32.8	32.8
SA MUTUAL	13.1	13.2
DE BEERS CONSOLIDATED MINES LTD	10.0	10.0
RAND SELECTION CORP LTD	7.5	7.5
RESIDENT NOM LTD	6.1	6.1
STD BANK NOM TVL P/L	4.2	3.1
CMB NOM P/L	2.9	---
FERMAIN NOM LTD	2.7	2.7
NEW ERA CONSOLIDATED LTD	2.0	2.0
LIBERTY LIFE ASSOC OF AFRICA LTD	1.4	1.4
FIRST NAT NOM P/L	1.2	1.3
SIXTY SIX MARSHALL STREET NOM P/L	1.0	1.0
SOUTHERN LIFE ASSOC LTD	---	1.1
SANKERN E/B	---	1.0
TOTAL	85.0	83.3

DIRECTORS :
CRAWFORD RM ,GUSH EP ,KING MW ,LINCOLN LA
OGILVIE THOMPSON J (Chairman),OPPENHEIMER AE
OPPENHEIMER NF ,OPPENHEIMER SIR PHILIP ,RELLY GWH

REGISTRATION NUMBER : 05/08081/06

REGISTERED OFFICE
44 Main Street, Johannesburg
2001
TEL: 011-638 9111
FAX: 011-638 2455

TRANSFER SECRETARY
Consolidated Share Registrars Ltd
P O Box 61051, Marshalltown
2107
TEL: 011-492 1620

COMPANY SECRETARY
Anglo American Corp. of SA Ltd

NATURE OF BUSINESS

An investment holding company, the major assets being investments of 23,38% in De Beers Centenary, & 25,83% in De Beers Consolidated. These interests arise from a holding of 98,2m De Beers/Centenary linked units, tradeable only as linked units.

BANKERS :

N/A

AUDITORS :

Deloitte & Touche

FAMILIAR BRAND NAMES

N/A

CONTRIBUTION BY ACTIVITY

N/A

YEAR END : March

DIVIDEND : Ords 50c

Final No 100	(Ldr)27/04/90	(Pay)08/06/90	Amt(c)3050
Interim No 101	(Ldr)19/10/90	(Pay)04/12/90	Amt(c)72
Final No 102	(Ldr)26/04/91	(Pay)04/06/91	Amt(c)308

DIVIDEND : Ords 5c

Interim No 103	(Ldr)25/10/91	(Pay)03/12/91	Amt(c)72
Final No 104	(Ldr)24/04/92	(Pay)02/06/92	Amt(c)310
Interim No 105	(Ldr)30/10/92	(Pay)01/12/92	Amt(c)72

CAPITAL STRUCTURE

	AUTHORISED	ISSUED
6% Cum Pref R2	2500000	2500000
Ords 5c	100000000	100000000

FINANCIAL STATISTICS (AT FINANCIAL YEAR END)

(Amts in R'000)	1992 Mar	1991 Mar	1990 Mar	1989	1988
Ord S/H Int	3910100	3513100	2781900	2095400	1449000
Long Trm Loans	5000	5000	5000	238600	128600
Iss Ord Share	100000	100000	100000	10000	10000
Total Liab	320700	314400	310700	477200	257200
Current Liab	315700	309400	305700	238600	128600
Total Assets	4230800	3827500	3092600	2577000	1708200
Current Assets	321800	314100	309900	243000	130600
Debtors	313600	309500	295600	-	-
Inventory	-	-	-	243000	130600
Oper Profit	-11700	-4800	-4100	293500	160800
Tax Paid	900	3800	500	800	500
Prf af Int&Tax	383700	380800	377100	292700	160300
Prf att Ord Sh	856800	999000	1128600	861400	440100
Btm Line Earn	779400	1111600	1126400	861400	440100
Dividend Paid	382000	380000	377000	290000	160000
Mkt Prce(c) YE	10500	9000	11250	72000	34000

PER SHARE STATISTICS (CENTS)

Net Asst Val	3910.10	3513.10	2781.90	20954.00	14490.00
Net Earnings	383.00	381.00	377.00	-	-
Dividends	382.00	380.00	377.00	-	-
Cash Flow	383.40	380.50	376.80	2927.00	1603.00

RATIOS AND OTHER INFORMATION

Mrk Cap(R000)	10500000	9000000	11250000	7200000	3400000
Current Ratio	1.02	1.02	1.01	1.02	1.02
Quik/Acid Tst	1.02	1.02	1.01	-	-
Debt/Ass Rat	0.07	0.08	0.10	0.19	0.15
L T L Tot Ass	-	-	-	0.09	0.08
Debt to Eqity	0.08	0.09	0.11	0.23	0.18
Ret on Assets	20.28	26.21	36.52	11.39	9.41
Ret on Equity%	21.91	28.44	40.57	41.11	30.37
Price/Earnings	27.42	23.62	29.84	-	-
Divid Cover	1.00	1.00	1.00	-	-
Divid Yield	3.64	4.22	3.35	-	-
Earning Yield%	3.65	4.23	3.35	-	-
NAV % Mrk Pr	37.24	39.03	24.73	29.10	42.62
Effec Tax Rate	-9.18	-1266.67	500.00	0.27	0.31
Def Interval	0.01	0.01	0.01	0.82	0.80
Sus Grth Rate	12.14	17.62	27.02	27.27	19.33

SUBSIDIARY & ASSOCIATED COMPANIES

DE BEERS CENTENARY AG (23,38%)
DE BEERS CONSOLIDATED MINES LTD (25,84%)

INVESTMENTS

ABRASIVE GRIT SALES LTD (A SHARES) (12.0%)
CYMBERLINE (PTY) LTD (10%)
CYMBERLINE (PTY) LTD (VAR RATE CUM PREFS (100%)
INDUSTRIAL DISTRIBUTORS (1946) (PTY) LTD (13,2%)
INDUSTRIAL DISTRIBUTORS (1946) P/L (5% C (30%)
INDUSTRIAL GRIT DISTRIBUTORS (SHANNON) L (15,6%)
INDUSTRIAL GRIT DISTRIBUTORS (SHANNON) L (16%)
THE DIAMOND PURCHASING AND TRADING CO (P (18.5%)
THE DIAMOND TRADING COMPANY (PTY) LTD (18.5%)

ANGLO AMERICAN CORPORATION OF SA LTD

ABBREVIATION : ANGLO-S

JSE SHORT CODE : AAC

SECTOR : Mining Financial-Mining Houses

SHAREHOLDERS

Who Owns Whom's Assessment of the Identity of the Ultimate Controlling Shareholder:
OPPENHEIMER FAMILY

SHAREHOLDER	PERCENTAGE 1992	1991
RESIDENT NOM LTD	11.7	11.7
FERMAIN NOM LTD	8.5	8.5
SA MUTUAL	7.6	7.6
DE BEERS HOLDINGS P/L	6.5	6.5
PETARD NOM LTD	5.6	5.6
STD BANK NOM TVL P/L	4.7	4.1
CMB NOM P/L	4.1	---
TAURUS NOM LTD	3.4	3.4
DIAMOND CORP P/L	3.2	3.2
DIDO NOM LTD	2.9	2.9
EIGHTY ONE MAIN STREET NOM LTD	2.5	1.7
LONDON CONTROL ACCOUNT	2.4	2.8
SOUTHERN LIFE ASSOC LTD	2.2	2.4
LIBERTY LIFE ASSOC OF AFRICA LTD	2.2	2.3
CAPRICORN TRUSTEES LTD	2.0	2.0
DE BEERS CONSOLIDATED MINES LTD	1.7	1.7
CAPITAL SECURITIES LTD	1.6	1.6
FIRST NAT NOM P/L	1.4	1.4
SANLAM	---	1.5
SANKERN E/B	---	1.8
TOTAL	74.3	72.9

DIRECTORS :
BOUSTRED WG (Deputy Chairman)
BOYD L (Deputy Chairman),CHAPMAN TN
FERREIRA EMAF DR (Executive Director)
GODSELL RM (Executive Director)
GUSH EP (Deputy Chairman),HAMBRO RN
HEWITT L (Executive Director)
HOLMES JA (Executive Director)
KING MW (Executive Director)
LANDER RP (Executive Director),LEYDEN PJR
MCKERRON AB (Executive Director),NICHOLSON DG
O'DOWD MC (Executive Director)
OGILVIE THOMPSON J (Chairman),OPPENHEIMER AE
OPPENHEIMER NF (Deputy Chairman)
PRETORIUS TL (Executive Director),RAMPHELE MA DR
RANKIN D (Executive Director)
RELLY GWH (Executive Director),RETIEF PF
SAUNDERS CJ ,SLACK HR ,STEYN JH THE HON
SUNTER CL (Executive Director)
TRAHAR AJ (Executive Director),VILAKAZI AL DR
YOUNG GS (Executive Director

REGISTRATION NUMBER : 01/05309/06

REGISTERED OFFICE
44 Main Street, Johannesburg
2001
TEL 011-638 9111
FAX 011-638 2455

TRANSFER SECRETARY
Consolidated Share Registrars Ltd
P O Box 61051, Marshalltown
2107
TEL 011-492 1620

COMPANY SECRETARY
C L Maltby

NATURE OF BUSINESS
A mining holding group with extensive interests in precious metal mining & coal, uranium, diamond, base metal, platinum & other minerals mining, Industry & commerce, Finance & investment & property The company provides technical & administrative services to its investments
The group is also involved in prospecting

BANKERS :
First National Bank of SA Ltd

AUDITORS :
KPMG Aiken & Peat, Deloitte & Touche

FAMILIAR BRAND NAMES
N/A

CONTRIBUTION BY ACTIVITY
Diamonds (% equity accounted earnings) (24 5%)
Mining Finance (21 6%)
Gold/Uranium (9 4%)
Industry/Commerce (14 3%)
Platinum/Base Metals & Other Mining (9 0%)
Banking/Insurance/Property (8 5%)
Coal (6 4%)
Other (12 7%)
Prospecting (Loss) (-6 4%)

YEAR END : March

DIVIDEND : Ords 10c

Interim No 107	(Ldr)22/12/89	(Pay)19/01/90	Amt(c)85
Final No 108	(Ldr)22/06/90	(Pay)03/08/90	Amt(c)240
Interim No 109	(Ldr)07/12/90	(Pay)18/01/91	Amt(c)85
Final No 110	(Ldr)28/06/91	(Pay)02/08/91	Amt(c)240
Interim No 111	(Ldr)13/12/91	(Pay)17/01/92	Amt(c)90
Final No 112	(Ldr)26/06/92	(Pay)04/08/92	Amt(c)255
Interim No 113	(Ldr)11/12/92	(Pay)15/01/93	Amt(c)90

NUMBER OF EMPLOYEES : 2500

CAPITAL STRUCTURE

	AUTHORISED	ISSUED
Ords 10c	300000000	232024815

FINANCIAL STATISTICS (AT FINANCIAL YEAR END)

(Amts in R'000)	1992 Mar	1991 Mar	1990 Mar	1989 Mar	1988 Mar
Ord S/H Int	17144000	15171000	13221000	10145000	7950000
Long Trm Loans	4080000	4093000	2965000	3284000	3157000
Iss Ord Share	232025	228546	228546	228546	228546
Total Liab	5706000	5649000	4551000	4546000	4122000
Current Liab	1626000	1556000	1586000	1262000	965000
Total Assets	22645000	20618000	17610000	14691000	12072000
Intang Assets	205000	202000	162000	*	*
Current Assets	3560000	3022000	2816000	3187000	2618000
Debtors	1239000	1172000	1026000	853000	623000
Inventory	300000	282000	245000	239000	185000
Oper Profit	1081000	820000	1004000	798000	395191
Interest Paid	283000	211000	280000	282000	191
Tax Paid	254000	313000	389000	274000	206000
Prf af Int&Tax	2198000	1822000	1865000	1524000	1204000
Prf att Ord Sh	2607000	2591000	3117000	2645000	1809000
Btm Line Earn	2662000	2464000	3803000	2669000	2258000
Dividend Paid	801000	754000	752000	622000	516000
Mkt Prce(c) YE	11975	9750	13350	8750	5200
Depreciation	108000	109000	89000	74000	61000

PER SHARE STATISTICS (CENTS)

Net Asst Val	7300 51	6549 67	5713 95	4438 93	3478 51
Net Earnings	724 00	604 00	1352 00	1148 00	790 00
Dividends	345 00	325 00	325 00	270 00	225 00
Cash Flow	828 79	705 33	707 52	602 50	516 31

RATIOS AND OTHER INFORMATION

Mrk Cap(R000)	27784994	22283235	30510891	19997775	11884392
Current Ratio	2 19	1 94	1 78	2 53	2 71
Quik/Acid Tst	2 00	1 76	1 62	2 34	2 52
Debt/Ass Rat	0 14	0 16	0 17	0 22	0 25
L T L Tot Ass	0 07	0 08	0 08	0 14	0 17
Debt to Eqity	0 18	0 21	0 23	0 32	0 38
Interest Cover	9 66	11 12	9 05	7 38	7383 20
Ret on Assets	16 17	17 15	23 53	23 63	18 08
Ret on Equity%	15 21	17 08	23 58	26 07	22 75
Price/Earnings	16 54	16 14	9 87	7 62	6 58
Divid Cover	2 10	1 86	4 16	4 25	3 51
Divid Yield	2 88	3 33	2 43	3 09	4 33
Earning Yield%	6 05	6 19	10 13	13 12	15 19
NAV % Mrk Pr	60 96	67 18	42 80	50 73	66 89
Effec Tax Rate	14 54	34 32	50 28	43 60	31 39
Def Interval	0 81	0 14	0 13	0 16	0 19
Sus Grth Rate	10 53	12 11	17 89	19 94	16 26

SUBSIDIARY & ASSOCIATED COMPANIES

ABALYN INVESTMENT HOLDINGS LTD
AEH LTD
AFRICAN AND EUROPEAN INVESTMENT CO LTD
AFRICAN GOLD MINING LTD (50%)
AFRIKANDER LEASE LTD (44,6%)
AMQUIP (PTY) LTD (50%)
ANGLO AMERICAN COAL CORPORATION LTD
ANGLO AMERICAN FARMS LTD (50%)
ANGLO AMERICAN GOLD INVESTMENT CO LTD (48,6%)

ANGLO AMERICAN INDUSTRIAL CORP. LTD (45%)
ANGLO AMERICAN INVESTMENT TRUST LTD
ANGLO AMERICAN PROPERTIES LTD
ANGLO AMERICAN PROPERTY SERVICES (PTY) L
ANMERCOSA LAND AND ESTATES LTD
BAILEYS FURNITURE MANUFACTURERS (PTY) LT (25%)
BARBROOK MINES LTD (44%)
CALINA INVESTMENT HOLDINGS LTD
CARDIUM HOLDINGS LTD (30%)
CARLTON CENTRE LTD
CENTESIS INVESTMENT HOLDINGS LTD
CENTRAL RESERVES (PTY) LTD (50%)
CLEVELAND POTASH LTD (50%)
CONSOLIDATED METALLURGICAL INDUSTRIES LT (26,4%)
CONSOLIDATED SHARE REGISTRARS LTD (50%)
CREATIVE HOMES LTD (28,7%)
DARMAG LTD (50,6%)
DELAUNAY LTD
DELAUNAY THREE LTD
DELAUNAY TWO LIMITED
DEUTSCHE STEININDUSTRIE AG (35%)
EAST RAND GOLD & URANIUM CO (43,5%)
EASTERN GOLD HOLDINGS LTD (49.8%)
EASTERN INVESTMENTS LTD (45%)
EASTERN TRANSVAAL TIMBER CO. (PTY) LTD (50%)
ELANDSRAND GOLD MINING CO. LTD
EPOCH INVESTMENTS LTD (50%)
ERONGO MINING & EXPLORATION CO LTD (50%)
FEBRIS LTD
FIRST BOWRING & ASSOCIATE HOLDINGS LTD (50%)
FIRST NATIONAL BANK HOLDINGS LTD (20.3%)
GAMSBERG ZINC CORP. LTD (33,3%)
GOEIEHOOP FARMING LTD
GOLD FIELDS OF SA LTD (20%)
H L & H TIMBER HOLDINGS LTD (50%)
IMPALA GRANITE SA
ISATIN INVESTMENT HOLDINGS (PTY) LTD (50%)
IXION INVESTMENT HOLDINGS LTD
JOHANNESBURG CONSOLIDATED INVESTMENT COM (45,2%)
LABOUR INTENSIVE INDUSTRIES TRUST LTD (50%)
LAGAN INVESTMENT HOLDINGS LTD
LITET LTD (50%)
LODESTONE HOLDINGS LTD
LTA LTD (28,4%)
LUCAS BLOCK MINERALS LTD (25%)
MAIN PLACE HOLDINGS LTD (27,9%)
MAIN STREET PROPERTY FUND MANAGERS LTD (40%)
MAINSTRAAT BELEGGINGS (1965) BPK (30%)
MARJORAM HOLDINGS LTD
MAUDSLEY HOLDINGS LTD
MEDGENIX GROUP (31.1%)
MIDWAY INVESTMENT LTD (50%)
MINORCO SOCIETE ANONYME (39,1%)
MONDI PAPER COMPANY LTD (30%)
MOOIHOEK COLLIERY LTD (20%)
MORUPULE COLLIERY (PTY) LTD (BOTSWANA)
NEW CENTRAL WITWATERSRAND AREAS LTD (49,8%)
NEW ERA CONSOLIDATED LTD
NTE LTD (30%)
NUMITOR INVESTMENT HOLDINGS LTD
ORANGE FREE STATE INVESTMENTS LTD (21%)
PINTAIL INVESTMENTS LTD
PREMSAB HOLDINGS LTD (50%)
RAND AMERICAN INVESTMENTS LTD
RAND SELECTION CORPORATION LTD
RANDSEL INVESTMENTS LTD
RUNCORN HOLDINGS LTD
RUSTENBURG PLATINUM HOLDINGS LTD (23,9%)
SA SMELTING WORKS (PTY) LTD (50%)
SAMANCOR LTD (24,9%)
SHAFT SINKERS (PTY) LTD (50%)
SMADE HOLDINGS (PTY) LTD (50%)
SONDOR INDUSTRIES LTD (37,3%)
SOUTH AFRICAN EAGLE INSURANCE CO. LTD (25,7%)
SOUTH AFRICAN LAND & EXPLORATION CO LTD (47.9%)
SOUTH AFRICAN MINES SELECTION LTD
SOUTH AFRICAN MOTOR CORPORATION (PTY) LT (49,9%)
SOUTH AFRICAN TOWNSHIPS MINING & FINANCE
SOUTH AMERICAN INVESTMENTS LTD (40%)
SOUTHERN LIFE ASSOCIATION LTD (40.6%)
ST LUCIA SUGAR FARMS LTD (50%)
STANLEY MOTORS LTD (50%)
SWAZILAND COLLIERIES LTD (48,3%)
TARL INVESTMENTS LTD (50%)
THE TYREQUIP COMPANY (PTY) LTD (50%)
TINANA HOLDINGS LTD (50%)
TONGAAT-HULETT GROUP LTD (20%)
TURNSTONE TWO LTD (50%)
VEREENIGING REFRACTORIES LTD
WANKIE COLLIERY CO LTD
WESTERN DEEP LEVELS LTD (44,1%)
WESTERN ULTRA DEEP LEVELS LTD
ZAAIPLAATS MINING LTD
ZIMCO HOLDINGS (PTY) LTD
ZIMRO LTD
ZINCHEM (PTY) LTD - DORMANT

INVESTMENTS

ABRASIVE GRIT SALES LTD (21600 SH)
AECI LTD (962087 SH)
ALLIED ELECTRONICS CORP. LTD (5,7%)
ALLIED TECHNOLOGIES LTD (264000 SH)
ANGLO AMERICAN (OFS) HOUSING CO. LTD (637500 SH)
APEX PROPERTY FUND (14084800 S)
ARGUS HOLDINGS LTD (196551 SH)
BARLOW RAND LTD (2523335 SH)
BEATRIX MINES LTD (3238500 SH)
BEISA MINES LTD (380952 SH)
BEISA ORYX (PTY) LTD (380952 SH)
BEVERAGE & CONSUMER INDUSTRY HOLDINGS LT (655003 SH)
BOTSWANA RST LTD (2166171 SH)
BRACKEN MINES LTD (24012 SH)
BUFFELSFONTEIN GOLD MINING CO. LTD (956067 SH)
CNA GALLO LTD (399865 SH)
CULLINAN HOLDINGS LTD (2450557 SH)
CYMBERLINE (PTY) LTD (100 SH)
DE BEERS CONSOLIDATED MINES LTD (6,85%)
DEELKRAAL GOLD MINING CO. LTD (1014186 SH)
DENVER BELEGGINGS BPK (492000 SH)
DIAMOND PURCHASING & TRADING CO (PTY) LT (461756 SH)
DIAMOND TRADING CO (PTY) LTD (185000 SH)
DISCOUNT HOUSE GROUP LTD (140000 SH)
DORBYL LTD (156017 SH)
DRIEFONTEIN CONSOLIDATED LTD (5046878 SH)
EDESA SOCIETE ANONYME (4800 SH)
ELSBURG GOLD MINING CO. LTD (1843160 SH)
FREE STATE CONSOLIDATED GOLD MINES LTD (3743801 SH)
GENCOR LTD (55973050 S)
GOLD FIELDS OF SA LTD (8489267 SH)
H J JOEL GOLD MINING CO LTD (7533688 SH)
HALL LONGMORE AND CO. (PTY) LTD (147 SH)
HARTEBEESTFONTEIN GOLD MINING CO. LTD (8577880 SH)
INDUSTRIAL DISTRIBUTORS (1946) (PTY) LTD (330000 SH)
INDUSTRIAL GRIT DISTRIBUTORS (SHANNON) L (28000 SH)
INTERNATIONAL PIPE & STEEL INVEST. S.A. (4119197 SH)
ISCOR LTD (12644616 S)
KINROSS MINES LTD (161790 SH)
LEBOWA PLATINUM MINES LTD (17216334 S)
LIBERTY LIFE ASSOCIATION OF AFRICA LTD (34650 SH)
LYDENBURG PLATINUM LTD (342000 SH)
MCCARTHY GROUP LTD (11027720 S)
MCCARTHY MAIN HOLDINGS LTD (730 SH)
MESSINA LTD (556850 SH)
ORANGE FREE STATE INVESTMENTS LTD (1377992 SH)
ORYX GOLD HOLDINGS LTD (4658031 SH)
PALABORA MINING CO LTD (19.1%)
POTGIETERSRUST PLATINUMS LTD

RANDCOAL LTD (33000 SH)
RANDFONTEIN ESTATES GOLD MINING CO WITS (487000 SH)
SASOL LTD (1005296 SH)
SMALL BUSINESS DEVELOPMENT CORP LTD (3718304 SH)
SODA ASH BOTSWANA (PTY) LTD (12,75%)
SOUTH AFRICAN BREWERIES LTD (623817 SH)
SOUTHVAAL HOLDINGS LTD (2453984 SH)
THE PREMIER GROUP LTD (655003 SH)
UNION CARRIAGE & WAGON COMPANY (PTY) LTD (454776 SH)
UNISEL GOLD MINES LTD (2320000 SH)
VAAL REEFS EXPLORATION & MINING CO LTD (1995623 SH)
VIERFONTEIN COLLIERY LTD (305604 SH)
WELKOM GOLD HOLDINGS LTD (6525379 SH)
WESTERN AREAS GOLD MINING CO. LTD (896334 SH)
WINKELHAAK MINES LTD (983800 SH)
ZAMBIA COPPER INVESTMENTS LTD (755402 SH)
ZANDPAN GOLD MINING CO. LTD (11718250 S)

ANGLO-TRANSVAAL COLLIERIES LTD

ABBREVIATION : A-T-COLL

JSE SHORT CODE : AVC

SECTOR : Mining-Coal

SHAREHOLDERS

Who Owns Whom's Assessment of the Identity of the Ultimate Controlling Shareholder:
SA MUTUAL/ANGLOVAAL

SHAREHOLDER	PERCENTAGE 1992	1991
SA MUTUAL	56.9	56.3
FOX STREET NOM P/L	25.7	25.2
MALGAS P/L	1.3	1.3
RUTHVAN P/L	1.1	1.3
PROTEA ASSURE CO LTD	---	1.0
TOTAL	84.9	85.1

DIRECTORS :
BENFIELD IL ,CROWE DJ ,DU TOIT RL
VAN TICHELEN AH ,WILSON RAD (Chairman

REGISTRATION NUMBER : 05/08294/06

REGISTERED OFFICE
Anglovaal House, 56 Main Street
Johannesburg
2001
TEL: 011-634 9111
FAX: 011-634 0038

TRANSFER SECRETARY
Anglovaal Ltd
P O Box 62379, Marshalltown
2107
TEL: 011-634 9111

COMPANY SECRETARY
Anglovaal Ltd

NATURE OF BUSINESS
The company holds 10,52% of quoted Witbank Colliery as its only investment.

BANKERS :
Standard Bank of SA Ltd

AUDITORS :
Coopers Theron Du Toit

FAMILIAR BRAND NAMES
N/A

CONTRIBUTION BY ACTIVITY
N/A

YEAR END : September

DIVIDEND : Ords 50c

Interim No 101	(Ldr)02/11/90	(Pay)23/11/90	Amt(c)242
Final No 102	(Ldr)10/05/91	(Pay)30/05/91	Amt(c)133
Interim No 103	(Ldr)08/11/91	(Pay)29/11/91	Amt(c)245
Final No 104	(Ldr)15/05/92	(Pay)04/06/92	Amt(c)142
Interim No 105	(Ldr)06/11/92	(Pay)27/11/92	Amt(c)231

CAPITAL STRUCTURE

	AUTHORISED	ISSUED
6% Partic Cum Prefs 50c	1000000	1000000
Ords 50c	1600000	1600000

FINANCIAL STATISTICS (AT FINANCIAL YEAR END)

(Amts in R'000)	1991 Sep	1990 Sep	1989 Sep	1988 Sep	1987
Ord S/H Int	3047	3031	3033	2970	2953
Long Trm Loans	500	500	500	500	580
Iss Ord Share	1600	1600	1600	1600	1600
Total Liab	528	513	514	590	660
Current Liab	28	13	14	90	80
Total Assets	3575	3544	3547	3560	3730
Current Assets	190	159	162	224	197
Debtors	2	2	2	3	-
Inventory	-	-	-	-	197
Turnover	6508	6344	4415	4121	4920
Oper Profit	-141	-132	4311	4027	4831
Tax Paid	20	19	18	15	10
Prf af Int&Tax	6347	6193	4293	4012	4821
Prf att Ord Sh	6016	5870	4063	3793	4563
Btm Line Earn	6016	5870	4063	3793	4563
Dividend Paid	6000	5872	4000	3776	4560
Mkt Prce(c) YE	7500	5750	4100	3400	2300

PER SHARE STATISTICS (CENTS)

Net Asst Val	190.44	189.44	189.56	185.63	184.56
Net Earnings	376.00	367.00	254.00	236.00	-
Dividends	375.00	367.00	250.00	236.00	-
Cash Flow	376.00	366.88	253.94	237.06	301.31

RATIOS AND OTHER INFORMATION

Mrk Cap(R000)	120000	92000	65600	54400	36800
Current Ratio	6.79	12.23	11.57	2.49	2.46
Quik/Acid Tst	6.79	12.23	11.57	2.49	-
A/C Rec T/ovr	3254.00	3172.00	2207.50	1373.67	-
Tot Ass T/ovr	1.82	1.79	1.24	1.16	1.32
Debt/Ass Rat	0.01	0.00	0.00	0.03	0.18
L T L Tot Ass	-	-	-	-	0.16
Debt to Eqity	0.01	0.00	0.00	0.03	0.22
Oper Prof Mrg	-2.17	-2.08	97.64	97.72	98.19
Net Prof Marg%	92.44	92.53	92.03	92.04	92.74
Ret on Assets	178.10	175.28	121.54	113.12	129.52
Ret on Equity%	197.44	193.67	133.96	127.71	154.52

Price/Earnings	19 95	15 67	16 14	14 41	-
Divid Cover	1 00	1 00	1 02	1 00	-
Divid Yield	5 00	6 38	6 10	6 94	-
Earning Yield%	5 01	6 38	6 20	6 94	-
NAV % Mrk Pr	2 54	3 29	4 62	5 46	8 02
Effec Tax Rate	-20 20	-20 43	0 42	0 37	0 21
Def Interval	0 08	0 09	0 12	0 13	0 12
Sus Grth Rate	0 53	-0 07	2 08	0 57	0 10

SUBSIDIARY & ASSOCIATED COMPANIES

None

INVESTMENTS

RANDCOAL LTD (10,5%)

ANGLOVAAL HOLDINGS LTD

ABBREVIATION : A-V-HOLD

JSE SHORT CODE : ATO

SECTOR : Mining Financial-Mining Houses

SHAREHOLDERS

Who Owns Whom's Assessment of the Identity of the Ultimate Controlling Shareholder: ANGLOVAAL-HERSOV & MENELL FAMILIES

SHAREHOLDER	PERCENTAGE 1992	1991
FOX STREET NOM P/L	51 0	51 0
CONSOLIDATED NOM P/L	26 9	21 8
STD BANK NOM TVL P/L	3 8	2 6
SA MUTUAL	3 1	3 1
FOXCLAUDE P/L	2 3	1 7
MAXERIC NOM P/L	2 1	2 1
LEON TRUSTEES P/L	1 3	1 4
ANGLOVAAL PENS FUND	---	1 9
VOLKSKAS NOM P/L	---	5 1
TOTAL	90 5	90 6

DIRECTORS :
BERNSTEIN BL ,HERSOV BE (Deputy Chairman)
HERSOV RL ,MENELL CS (Chairman),MENELL RP

REGISTRATION NUMBER : 68/09249/06

REGISTERED OFFICE
Anglovaal House, 56 Main Street
Johannesburg
2001
TEL 011-634 9111
FAX 011 634 0038

TRANSFER SECRETARY
Anglovaal Ltd
P O Box 62379, Marshalltown
2107
TEL 011-634 9111

COMPANY SECRETARY
E G D Gordon

NATURE OF BUSINESS
Holding and investments company The company is the holding company of the Anglovaal Group and together with its wholly owned subsidiaries holds 50% of the issued shares of Anglovaal Ltd

BANKERS :
First National Bank of SA Ltd

AUDITORS :
KPMG Aiken & Peat

FAMILIAR BRAND NAMES
N/A

CONTRIBUTION BY ACTIVITY
N/A

YEAR END : June

DIVIDEND : Ords 10c

Interim No 45	(Ldr)21/12/90	(Pay)25/01/91	Amt(c)2 36
Final No 46	(Ldr)28/06/91	(Pay)02/08/91	Amt(c)4 96
Interim No 47	(Ldr)20/03/92	(Pay)16/04/92	Amt(c)2 64
Final No 48	(Ldr)16/10/92	(Pay)13/11/92	Amt(c)5 36

CAPITAL STRUCTURE

	AUTHORISED	ISSUED
Ords 10c	46000000	45765645
Partic Prefs 0,2c	46000000	45765645

FINANCIAL STATISTICS (AT FINANCIAL YEAR END)

(Amts in R'000)	1992 Jun	1991 Jun	1990 Jun	1989 Jun	1988 Jun
Ord S/H Int	12601	11930	12134	11904	11853
Long Trm Loans	92	92	-	-	-
Iss Ord Share	45766	45766	9153	9153	9153
Total Liab	6263	5796	5700	4692	3957
Current Liab	6171	5704	5700	4692	3957
Total Assets	18864	17726	17834	16596	15810
Current Assets	6717	5724	5832	4707	4013
Debtors	6306	5590	5649	4604	3884
Oper Profit	71	-148	45	-120	5979
Tax Paid	20	16	17	10	5
Prf af Int&Tax	9824	8451	8605	6962	5974
Prf att Ord Sh	9824	8451	8605	6962	5974
Btm Line Earn	9824	8451	8605	6962	5974
Dividend Paid	9153	8375	8375	6911	5904
Mkt Prce(c) YE	875	575	1000	1000	600

PER SHARE STATISTICS (CENTS)

Net Asst Val	27 53	26 07	132 57	130 06	129 50
Net Earnings	37 60	38 10	42 20	33 50	26 70
Dividends	8 00	7 32	7 32	6 04	5 16
Cash Flow	21 47	18 47	94 01	76 06	65 27

RATIOS AND OTHER INFORMATION

Mrk Cap(R000)	400453	263155	91530	91530	54918
Current Ratio	1 09	1 00	1 02	1 00	1 01
Quik/Acid Tst	1 09	1 00	1 02	1 00	1 01
Debt/Ass Rat	0 33	0 32	0 32	0 28	0 25
Debt to Eqity	0 49	0 48	0 47	0 39	0 33
Ret on Assets	52 18	47 77	48 35	42 01	37 82
Ret on Equity%	77 96	70 84	70 92	58 48	50 40
Price/Earnings	23 27	15 09	23 70	29 85	22 47
Divid Cover	4 70	5 20	5 77	5 55	5 17
Divid Yield	0 91	1 27	0 73	0 60	0 86
Earning Yield%	4 30	6 63	4 22	3 35	4 45
NAV % Mrk Pr	3 15	4 53	13 26	13 01	21 58
Effec Tax Rate	15 75	-14 16	21 25	-10 10	0 08

Def Interval	0 01	0 01	-	-	-
Sus Grth Rate	5 32	0 64	1 90	0 43	0 59

SUBSIDIARY & ASSOCIATED COMPANIES

ANGLOVAAL LTD
AT INVESTMENTS (PTY) LTD
DAMMI NOMINEES (PTY) LTD (25%)
HOLDAV (PTY) LTD
M & H TRUST (PTY) LTD

INVESTMENTS

None

ANGLOVAAL INDUSTRIES LTD

ABBREVIATION : A-V-I

JSE SHORT CODE : AVI

SECTOR : Industrial-Industrial Holding

SHAREHOLDERS

Who Owns Whom's Assessment of the Identity of the Ultimate Controlling Shareholder: HERSOV & MENELL FAMILIES VIA AVHOLD

SHAREHOLDER	PERCENTAGE 1992	1991
FOX STREET NOM P/L	52 7	57 5
SA MUTUAL	10 1	11 2
ANGLOVAAL LTD	6 3	2 9
STD BANK NOM TVL P/L	5 2	4 9
CMB NOM P/L	3 6	---
SOUTHERN LIFE ASSOC LTD	2 5	---
EIGHTY ONE MAIN STREET NOM LTD	2 3	1 4
FIRST NAT NOM P/L	2 3	2 6
MUTUAL & FEDERAL INSURANCE CO LTD	1 2	1 3
LIBERTY LIFE ASSOC OF AFRICA LTD	1 0	1 6
SANLAM	---	2 4
TOTAL	87 0	85 7

DIRECTORS :
BERNSTEIN BL ,BRYANT J ,HERSOV BE (Chairman)
MENELL CS ,NEETHLING PJ
ROBBERTZE JC (Managing Director),ROYSTON D
SAULEZ AN ,SAVAGE RB ,WILLIAMS JJ

REGISTRATION NUMBER : 05/17201/06

REGISTERED OFFICE
Anglovaal House, 56 Main Street
Johannesburg
2001
TEL 011-634 9111
FAX 011-634 0038

TRANSFER SECRETARY
Anglovaal Ltd
P O Box 62379, Marshalltown
2107
TEL 011-634 9111

COMPANY SECRETARY
Anglovaal Ltd

NATURE OF BUSINESS
AVI is an industrial, investment and management company whose subsidiaries are involved in food, packaging, construction, electronics, textile and engineering related sectors

BANKERS :
First National Bank of SA Ltd

AUDITORS :
Ernst & Young

FAMILIAR BRAND NAMES
BAKERS,BAUMANS,BECKETTS,BROMOR,CEREBOS
FIVE ROSES,GELVENOR,IDENTILITE,JUICY LUICY
KING-PAC,OUTDOOR,PAKCO,PRONUTRO,PUMA PALETTE
PYOTTS,TRIDENT STEEL,YARDLEY

CONTRIBUTION BY ACTIVITY
AVI Divers Holdings (% of Turnover) (13 0%)
Consol Ltd (26 0%)
Grinaker Holdings Ltd (27 0%)
Irvin & Johnson Ltd (21 0%)
National Brands Ltd (13 0%)

YEAR END : June

DIVIDEND :5,5% Cum PrefS R2
Interim No 92 (Ldr)01/06/90 (Pay)30/06/90 Amt(c)5 5
DIVIDEND :8% Red Cum Prefs R1
Interim No 36 (Ldr)01/06/90 (Pay)30/06/90 Amt(c)4
DIVIDEND : Ords 50c
Final No 45 (Ldr)28/09/90 (Pay)19/10/90 Amt(c)135
Final No 46 (Ldr)27/09/91 (Pay)18/10/91 Amt(c)150
Final No 47 (Ldr)25/09/92 (Pay)16/10/92 Amt(c)165

NUMBER OF EMPLOYEES : 42000

CAPITAL STRUCTURE

	AUTHORISED	ISSUED
Red Cum Pref 8% R1	2952000	1363019
Cum Pref 5 5% R2	1000000	1000000
Ords 50c	78500000	31737045
5% Unsec Auto Conv Sub Debs R97	4001839	4001839

FINANCIAL STATISTICS (AT FINANCIAL YEAR END)

(Amts in R'000)	1992 Jun	1991 Jun	1990 Jun	1989 Jun	1988 Jun
Ord S/H Int	1929700	1247200	1056400	886800	629200
Long Trm Loans	1432900	1068100	1042200	694900	600400
Iss Ord Share	31737	28585	28347	27709	24903
Total Liab	3198100	2565600	2480200	1911700	1433600
Current Liab	1765200	1497500	1438000	1216800	833200
Total Assets	4731200	3547000	3284300	2674100	2010300
Intang Assets	396600	265800	252300	124400	52500
Current Assets	3385100	2512500	2322900	1830200	1388300
Debtors	1337400	1172900	1046600	751600	564500
Inventory	1221800	1132600	1067000	739900	607900
Turnover	7957700	7386400	6485900	4575000	3712200
Oper Profit	652100	722700	631400	476900	392200
Interest Paid	95900	88800	100200	44800	23900
Tax Paid	290500	299800	248500	212600	167800
Prf af Int&Tax	390300	388700	338700	268300	222000
Prf att Ord Sh	270600	234100	207800	164600	140100
Btm Line Earn	331300	209200	190800	163300	139200
Dividend Paid	52400	42900	38300	33300	24900
Mkt Prce(c) YE	14500	10700	5950	4700	3225
Depreciation	159600	146400	132000	92200	81300

PER SHARE STATISTICS (CENTS)

Net Asst Val	4830 64	3433 27	2836 63	2751 45	2315 79
Net Earnings	907 00	825 00	733 00	657 00	563 00
Dividends	165 00	150 00	135 00	120 00	100 00
Cash Flow	1294 16	1310 23	1249 16	1031 98	894 67

RATIOS AND OTHER INFORMATION

Mrk Cap(R000)	4601865	3058595	1686647	1302323	803122
Current Ratio	1 92	1 68	1 62	1 50	1 67
Quik/Acid Tst	1 23	0 92	0 87	0 90	0 94
A/C Rec T/ovr	5 95	6 30	6 20	6 09	6 58
Tot Ass T/ovr	1 68	2 08	1 97	1 71	1 85
Debt/Ass Rat	0 48	0 50	0 53	0 54	0 46
L T L Tot Ass	0 10	0 08	0 09	0 08	0 05
Debt to Eqity	1 17	1 42	1 65	1 63	1 48
Interest Cover	6 88	8 24	6 34	11 73	17 31
Oper Prof Mrg	8 19	9 78	9 73	10 42	10 57
Net Prof Marg%	3 40	3 17	3 20	3 60	3 77
Ret on Assets	16 73	22 05	21 12	20 13	20 86
Ret on Equity%	14 02	18 77	19 67	18 56	22 27
Price/Earnings	15 99	12 97	8 12	7 15	5 73
Divid Cover	5 50	5 50	5 43	5 48	5 63
Divid Yield	1 14	1 40	2 27	2 55	3 10
Earning Yield%	6 26	7 71	12 32	13 98	17 46
NAV % Mrk Pr	33 31	32 09	47 67	58 54	71 81
Effec Tax Rate	39 32	38 69	32 94	42 07	40 59
Def Interval	0 93	1 30	1 45	1 89	0 98
Sus Grth Rate	11 31	15 33	16 05	14 81	18 31

SUBSIDIARY & ASSOCIATED COMPANIES

ANGLO ALPHA LTD (25%)
AVENG (PTY) LTD
AVGRIN HOLDINGS LTD
AVTEX HOLDINGS LTD
AVTEX HOLDINGS LTD
AVTEX LTD (MOOI RIV)
BEARING MAN LTD
COMBINE CARGO INVESTMENTS LTD
CONSOL LTD
GLOBE ENGINEERING HOLDINGS (PTY) LTD
GLOBE ENGINEERING WORKS LTD
GRINAKER HOLDINGS LTD
IRVIN & JOHNSON LTD
NATIONAL BRANDS LTD
NATIONAL BRANDS LTD
NATIONAL SALT LTD
NATIONAL SALT LTD
PLEASURE FOODS LTD
SOUTH AFRICAN FREIGHT CORPORATION LTD (20%)
STEELMETALS (PTY) LTD
TRISTEL HOLDINGS (PTY) LTD

INVESTMENTS

None

ANGLOVAAL INSURANCE HOLDINGS LTD

ABBREVIATION : AVINS

JSE SHORT CODE : AVN

SECTOR : Financial-Insurance

SHAREHOLDERS

Who Owns Whom's Assessment of the Identity of the Ultimate Controlling Shareholder:
ANGLOVAAL VIA AVF GROUP

SHAREHOLDER	PERCENTAGE 1992	1991
AVF GROUP LTD	86 7	86 3
ROTHSEY INV CO P/L	2 9	3 9
STD BANK NOM TVL P/L	1 6	---
JESDENE LTD	1 0	---
UAL NOM P/L	1 0	2 7
SIXTY SIX MARSHALL STREET NOM P/L	---	1 1
TOTAL	93 3	93 9

DIRECTORS :
BARBER DD ,BROWN JJ
DE BEER DD (Managing Director),ELLIOTT PJ
GORDON EGD ,KING ME ,MENELL CS (Chairman)
ROWAND AR (Deputy Chairman),ROWAND R DE V
VLOK DJJ

REGISTRATION NUMBER : 87/04233/06

REGISTERED OFFICE
Crusader House, 6 Anderson Street
Johannesburg
2001
TEL 011-492 2330
FAX 011-838 1817

TRANSFER SECRETARY
Anglovaal Ltd
P O Box 62379, Marshalltown
2107
TEL 011-634 9111

COMPANY SECRETARY
B V Moore

NATURE OF BUSINESS
An investment holding company with a controlling interest in JSE-quoted life assurer Crusader Life Assurance

BANKERS :
First National Bank of SA Ltd
Nedperm Bank Ltd, Standard Bank of SA Ltd
Trust Bank of Africa Ltd

AUDITORS :
Coopers Theron Du Toit

FAMILIAR BRAND NAMES
AA LIFE

CONTRIBUTION BY ACTIVITY
N/A

YEAR END : June

DIVIDEND : Ords 1c
Interim No 4 (Ldr)15/02/91 (Pay)27/03/91 Amt(c)5 5

NUMBER OF EMPLOYEES : 303

ANGLOVAAL LTD

ABBREVIATION : ANGLOVAAL

JSE SHORT CODE : ATO

SECTOR : Mining Financial-Mining Houses

SHAREHOLDERS

Who Owns Whom's Assessment of the Identity of the Ultimate Controlling Shareholder: HERSOV & MENELL FAMILIES VIA AVHOLD

SHAREHOLDER	PERCENTAGE 1992	1991
ANGLOVAAL HOLDINGS LTD	49 4	49 8
SA MUTUAL	10 8	10 9
STD BANK NOM TVL P/L	5 9	4 7
FOX STREET NOM P/L	4 8	3 7
LIBERTY LIFE ASSOC OF AFRICA LTD	2 9	3 3
ESCOM PENS & PROV FUND	2 6	2 7
CMB NOM P/L	1 7	---
SIXTY SIX MARSHALL STREET NOM P/L	1 5	1 8
LEON TRUSTEES P/L	1 1	1 1
ANGLOVAAL PENS FUND	---	1 0
SANLAM	- -	1 1
TOTAL	80 6	80 1

DIRECTORS :
BERNSTEIN BL ,DHLOMO OD DR,FOX EH ,GELDENHUYS JJ
GORDON EGD ,HERSOV BE (Chairman & Managing Dir)
MABUZA EJ ,MENELL CS (Deputy Chairman)
ROBBERTZE JC ,SWEMMER RT ,WILSON RAD

REGISTRATION NUMBER : 05/04580/06

REGISTERED OFFICE
Anglovaal House, 56 Main Street
Johannesburg
2001
TEL 011-634 9111
FAX 011-634 0038

TRANSFER SECRETARY
Anglovaal Ltd
P O Box 62379, Marshalltown
2107
TEL 011-634 9111

COMPANY SECRETARY
E G D Gordon

NATURE OF BUSINESS
Financial investment and holding company with widespread interests in mining, finance and industry

BANKERS :
First National Bank of SA Ltd

AUDITORS :
KPMG Aiken & Peat, Ernst & Young

FAMILIAR BRAND NAMES
N/A

CAPITAL STRUCTURE

	AUTHORISED	ISSUED
Ords 1c	306000000	241002034

FINANCIAL STATISTICS (AT FINANCIAL YEAR END)

(Amts in R'000)	1992 Jun	1991 Jun	1989 Dec	1988 Dec	1987 Dec
Ord S/H Int	-33598	14217	13387	12614	12771
Long Trm Loans	665115	412275	61387	65453	43348
Iss Ord Share	241002	147854	23970	23969	23969
Total Liab	719716	478194	84167	92002	56671
Current Liab	54601	65919	22780	26549	13323
Total Assets	686118	492411	97554	104616	69442
Current Assets	182516	111081	35258	51094	34284
Debtors	63216	68541	20387	41226	30290
Turnover	302963	246375	57002	-	-
Oper Profit	-89763	-31485	4261	2911	34
Interest Paid	779	231	400	3	-
Tax Paid	-	-2	-245	633	-
Prf af Int&Tax	-90542	-31714	4106	2275	34
Prf att Ord Sh	-93699	-35695	1678	1348	20
Btm Line Earn	-93699	-35695	1678	1348	20
Dividend Paid	-	8132	1678	1347	-
Mkt Prce(c) YE	45	115	100	80	65
Depreciation	6892	6674	1867	-	-

PER SHARE STATISTICS (CENTS)

Net Asst Val	-13 94	9 62	55 85	52 63	53 28
Net Earnings	-52 40	-	7 00	5 60	6 80
Dividends	-	7 60	7 00	5 60	-
Cash Flow	-36 02	-13 09	14 79	5 62	0 25

RATIOS AND OTHER INFORMATION

Mrk Cap(R000)	108451	170032	23970	19175	15580
Current Ratio	3 34	1 69	1 55	1 92	2 57
Quik/Acid Tst	3 34	1 69	1 55	1 92	2 57
A/C Rec T/ovr	4 79	2 40	2 80	-	-
Tot Ass T/ovr	0 44	0 33	0 58	-	-
Debt/Ass Rat	0 10	0 15	0 23	0 25	0 22
L T L Tot Ass	0 02	0 02	-	0 00	0 03
Debt to Eqity	-1 99	5 34	1 70	2 11	1 22
Interest Cover	-115 23	-136 30	10 65	970 33	
Oper Prof Mrg	29 63	-12 78	7 48	-	-
Net Prof Marg%	-30 93	-14 49	2 94	-	-
Ret on Assets	-13 08	-4 26	4 37	2 78	0 15
Ret on Equity%	278 88	-167 38	12 53	10 69	0 47
Price/Earnings	-0 86	-	14 29	14 29	9 56
Divid Cover	-	-	1 00	1 00	-
Divid Yield	-	6 61	7 00	7 00	-
Earning Yield%	-116 44	-	7 00	7 00	10 46
NAV % Mrk Pr	-30 98	8 36	55 85	65 78	81 97
Effec Tax Rate	-	0 01	-6 35	21 77	-
Def Interval	-0 14	-0 23	0 67	1 79	333 45
Sus Grth Rate	278 88	-308 27	0 00	0 01	0 16

SUBSIDIARY & ASSOCIATED COMPANIES

AA LIFE ASSURANCE ASSOCIATION LTD
ANGLOVAAL INSURANCE INTERNATIONAL HOLDIN
AVINS ASSET MANAGEMENT (PTY) LTD
AVINS BUSINESS SYSTEMS (PTY) LTD
AVINS PROJECT FINANCE (PTY) LTD
CRUSADER LIFE ASSURANCE CORP LTD

INVESTMENTS

None

CONTRIBUTION BY ACTIVITY

Engineering & Textiles (13.0%)
Construction & Electronics (1.0%)
Base metals & minerals (20.0%)
Branded fast moving consumer goods (13.0%)
Packaging & Rubber (20.0%)
Fishing & Frozen Food (12.0%)
Interest & other (21.0%)

YEAR END : June

DIVIDEND :Ords 5c

Interim No 90	(Ldr)21/12/90	(Pay)25/01/91	Amt(c)30
Final No 91	(Ldr)28/06/91	(Pay)02/08/91	Amt(c)62
Interim No 92	(Ldr)20/03/92	(Pay)16/04/92	Amt(c)33
Final No 93	(Ldr)16/10/92	(Pay)13/11/92	Amt(c)67

NUMBER OF EMPLOYEES : 76000

CAPITAL STRUCTURE

	AUTHORISED	ISSUED
Ords 5c	18000000	18000000
"N" Ords 0,01c	60000000	43125650

FINANCIAL STATISTICS (AT FINANCIAL YEAR END)

(Amts in R'000)	1992 Jun	1991 Jun	1990 Jun	1989 Jun	1988 Jun
Ord S/H Int	2328900	1974300	1811100	838800	677800
Long Trm Loans	2659500	2224200	2069900	1458900	1114800
Iss Ord Share	18000	17832	17832	17832	17832
Total Liab	4690200	4099200	3961700	3257700	2513700
Current Liab	2030700	1875000	1891800	1798800	1398900
Total Assets	6679200	5787700	5517900	3972100	3191500
Intang Assets	339900	285800	254900	124400	*
Current Assets	4053600	3694200	3789700	2489500	2221000
Debtors	1406300	1231300	1116800	763000	602600
Inventory	1221800	1132800	1067600	741000	608000
Turnover	8205800	7735700	6719700	4802800	3913100
Oper Profit	860000	932500	710800	539600	404000
Interest Paid	112200	116900	123000	64200	-
Tax Paid	331500	375700	261600	218400	180900
Prf af Int&Tax	501400	510000	374200	322500	280400
Prf att Ord Sh	277700	285100	238200	182600	145300
Btm Line Earn	262300	239000	209700	178000	144300
Dividend Paid	60200	54900	39400	26600	22800
Mkt Prce(c) YE	8200	6500	4850	4750	2800
Depreciation	164300	148300	137100	96400	84300

PER SHARE STATISTICS (CENTS)

Net Asst Val	11050.00	9468.93	8727.01	4006.28	3801.03
Net Earnings	464.00	478.00	530.00	427.00	340.00
Dividends	100.00	92.00	92.00	76.00	65.00
Cash Flow	620.39	649.26	653.69	565.80	522.44

RATIOS AND OTHER INFORMATION

Mrk Cap(R000)	1476000	1159080	864852	847020	499296
Current Ratio	2.00	1.97	2.00	1.38	1.59
Quik/Acid Tst	1.39	1.37	1.44	0.97	1.15
A/C Rec T/ovr	5.84	6.28	6.02	6.29	6.49
Tot Ass T/ovr	1.23	1.34	1.22	1.21	1.23
Debt/Ass Rat	0.36	0.42	0.44	0.59	0.54
L T L Tot Ass	0.06	0.09	0.10	0.13	0.10
Debt to Eqity	1.03	1.22	1.36	2.77	2.54
Interest Cover	8.42	8.58	6.17	9.43	-
Oper Prof Mrg	10.48	12.05	10.58	11.24	10.32
Net Prof Marg%	3.38	3.69	3.54	3.80	3.71
Ret on Assets	14.75	18.22	15.63	16.39	14.90
Ret on Equity%	11.92	14.44	13.15	21.77	21.44
Price/Earnings	17.67	13.60	9.15	11.12	8.24
Divid Cover	4.64	5.20	5.76	5.62	5.23
Divid Yield	1.22	1.42	1.90	1.60	2.32
Earning Yield%	5.66	7.35	10.93	8.99	12.14
NAV % Mrk Pr	134.76	145.68	179.94	84.34	135.75
Effec Tax Rate	41.11	40.29	34.79	40.30	39.31
Def Interval	1.15	1.37	1.96	2.36	1.05
Sus Grth Rate	9.34	11.66	10.98	18.60	18.07

SUBSIDIARY & ASSOCIATED COMPANIES

ALTUR INVESTMENTS (PTY) LTD (46%)
ANGLO PACIFIC RESOURCES PLC (29.9%)
ANGLO-TRANSVAAL COLLIERIES LTD (26%)
ANGLOVAAL COAL HILDINGS (PTY) LTD (25.5%)
ANGLOVAAL INDUSTRIES LTD
ANGLOVAAL TRANSVAAL FINANCE CORP (PTY) L
ANGLOVAAL TRUSTEES LTD
ASSOCIATED MANGANESE MINES OF SA LTD (47%)
ATSCOT (PTY) LTD
AVF GROUP LTD
BITCONS INVESTMENTS (PTY) LTD
BOARD OF EXECUTORS LTD (35%)
CONTROL INSTRUMENTS GROUP LTD (26%)
EASTERN TRANSVAAL CONSOLIDATED MINES LTD (26%)
FIRST AVA INVESTMENTS (PTY) LTD
GEARMAX (PTY) LTD (20%)
JESDENE LTD
LAVINO (PTY) LTD
MIDDLE WITWATERSRAND (WESTERN AREAS) LTD
OHRIGS LIME COMPANY (PTY) LTD
PRIESKA COPPER MINES LTD
PRIESKA COPPER MINES LTD
RHINO ANDASITE MINES (PTY) LTD
SECOND AVA INVESTMENTS (PTY) LTD
SOUTH AFRICAN FREIGHT CORPORATION LTD (20%)
SOUTH AFRICAN FREIGHT CORPORATION LTD (20%)
SUN PROSPECTING AND MINING CO. (PTY) LTD (46%)
TARGET EXPLORATION COMPANY LTD
UNITED AFRICAN INVESTMENTS (PTY) LTD
VALLUM INVESTMENTS (PTY) LTD
VENTURE BUILDING TRUST (PTY) LTD
VILLAGE MAIN REEF GOLD MINING COMPANY (1 (38%)

INVESTMENTS

ANGLO ALPHA LTD (2444500 SH)
ANGLO AMERICAN GOLD INVESTMENT CO. LTD (7000 SH)
ASSOCIATED ORE & METAL CORP. LTD (181400 SH)
CONSOLIDATED MURCHISON LTD (497500 SH)
DAB INVESTMENTS LTD (125374 SH)
DOORNFONTEIN GOLD MINING CO. LTD (771600 SH)
DRIEFONTEIN CONSOLIDATED LTD (756310 SH)
FINSCH DIAMONDS (PTY) LTD (180 SH)
FREE STATE CONSOLIDATED GOLD MINES LTD (483939 SH)
FREE STATE DEVELOPMENT AND INVESTMENT CO (501500 SH)
HARTEBEESTFONTEIN GOLD MINING CO. LTD (8839000 SH)
KLOOF GOLD MINING CO LTD (34000 SH)
LORAINE GOLD MINES LTD (1336957 SH)
ORANGE FREE STATE INVESTMENT LTD (74182 SH)
PALABORA MINING CO LTD (146600 SH)
RANDFONTEIN ESTATES GOLD MINE CO.WITWATE (1007320 SH)
SOUTH DEEP EXPLORATION CO LTD (945960 SH)
SOUTHVAAL HOLDINGS LTD (72600 SH)
UAL MINING & RESOURCES UNIT TRUST (9925500 SH)
VAAL REEF EXPLORATION AND MINING CO. LTD (179560 SH)
WESTERN DEEP LEVELS LTD (213250 SH)
ZANDPAN GOLD MINING CO. LTD (26336700 S)

APEX PROPERTY FUND

ABBREVIATION : APEX

JSE SHORT CODE : APX

SECTOR : Financial-Property Trust

SHAREHOLDERS

Who Owns Whom's Assessment of the Identity of the Ultimate Controlling Shareholder: ANGLO AMERICAN

SHAREHOLDER	PERCENTAGE 1992	1991
SOUTHERN LIFE ASSOC LTD	25 1	25 5
SIXTY SIX MARSHALL STREET NOM P/L	18 4	17 7
ANGLO AMERICAN PROPERTIES LTD	13 2	13 2
DE BEERS PENS FUND	7 5	5 1
ANGLO AMERICAN CORP PENS FUND	5 5	3 8
CMB NOM P/L	3 4	---
ANGLO AMERICAN GROUP PENS FUND	3 4	3 3
UAL NOM P/L	2 2	2 6
I & J PENS FUND	1 3	---
NEDBANK NOM LTD	1 3	1 3
MOMENTUM LIFE ASSURE LTD	-	2 4
SANLAM	- -	5 2
TOTAL	81 3	80 2

DIRECTORS :
BAUM PM ,BRADFORD DG ,BRAGG WFE ,HASLETT FN
JOHNSON JGW ,LEISSNER GGL (Chairman)
MCDONALD SA ,SUNTER CL ,WHITFIELD AC

REGISTRATION NUMBER : 57/02743/06

REGISTERED OFFICE
1st Floor, First National House
11 Diagonal Street, Johannesburg
2001
TEL 011-491 9111
FAX 011-836 5136

TRANSFER SECRETARY
Consolidated Share Registrars Ltd
P O Box 61051, Marshalltown
2107
TEL 011-492 1620

COMPANY SECRETARY
Anglo American Property Services (Pty) Ltd

NATURE OF BUSINESS
A property unit trust fund, managed by Anglo American Property Fund Managers

BANKERS :
First National Bank of SA Ltd

AUDITORS :
Coopers Theron Du Toit

FAMILIAR BRAND NAMES
N/A

CONTRIBUTION BY ACTIVITY
N/A

YEAR END : March

DIVIDEND : Units

Interim No 2	(Ldr)16/11/90	(Pay)29/11/90	Amt(c)14 4
Final No 3	(Ldr)10/05/91	(Pay)30/05/91	Amt(c)13 76
Interim No 6	(Ldr)13/11/92	(Pay)27/11/92	Amt(c)15 6

CAPITAL STRUCTURE

	AUTHORISED	ISSUED
Units	82356000	82356000

FINANCIAL STATISTICS (AT FINANCIAL YEAR END)

(Amts in R'000)	1991 Mar
Ord S/H Int	202135
Iss Ord Share	82356
Total Liab	11532
Current Liab	11532
Total Assets	213667
Current Assets	26351
Debtors	2272
Oper Profit	-1619
Prf af Int&Tax	33375
Prf att Ord Sh	33375
Btm Line Earn	33375
Dividend Paid	33370
Mkt Prce(c) YE	280

PER SHARE STATISTICS (CENTS)

Net Asst Val	245 44
Net Earnings	40 53
Dividends	40 53
Cash Flow	40 53

RATIOS AND OTHER INFORMATION

Mrk Cap(R000)	230597
Current Ratio	2 29
Quik/Acid Tst	2 29
Debt/Ass Rat	0 05
Debt to Eqity	0 06
Ret on Assets	15 62
Ret on Equity%	16 51
Price/Earnings	6 91
Divid Cover	1 00
Divid Yield	14 48
Earning Yield%	14 48
NAV % Mrk Pr	87 66
Sus Grth Rate	0 00

SUBSIDIARY & ASSOCIATED COMPANIES

30 SIMMONDS STREET (PTY) LTD
ANGLO PENSION NOMINEES NO 2 (PTY) LTD
BRYANSTON HOBART (PTY) LTD
CONTRACTORS PROPERTIES (ROSEBANK) (PTY)
KENILWORTH CENTRE (PTY) LTD
LANARIA PROPERTIES (PTY) LTD
NINTH STAGE INVESTMENTS (PTY) LTD
NINTH STAGE PROPERTIES (JHB) (PTY) LTD
NORTHMEAD CENTRE (PTY) LTD
RAYRICH (PTY) LTD
SABEL DEVELOPMENTS (PTY) LTD
SANSO PROPERTIES JOUBERT STREET (PTY) LT
SOREC PROPERTIES KRUGERSDORP (PTY) LTD
STIEMOND PROPERTIES (PTY) LTD
TRANSVAAL HOUSE INVESTMENT (PTY) LTD

INVESTMENTS

None

ARGUS HOLDINGS LTD

ABBREVIATION : ARGUS

JSE SHORT CODE : ARG

SECTOR : Industrial-Printing & Publishing

SHAREHOLDERS

Who Owns Whom's Assessment of the Identity of the Ultimate Controlling Shareholder: ANGLO AMERICAN VIA JOHNIES

SHAREHOLDER	PERCENTAGE 1992	1991
STD BANK NOM TVL P/L	37.0	37.2
ARGUS PENS FUND	9.9	10.0
RESIDENT NOM LTD	9.3	9.3
EIGHTY ONE MAIN STREET NOM LTD	7.0	7.4
SA MUTUAL	5.9	5.9
DE BEERS PENS FUND	3.7	3.7
ANGLO AMERICAN CORP PENS FUND	3.5	3.5
HILLFAM INV P/L	2.7	3.3
FIRST NAT NOM P/L	2.5	2.5
ANGLO AMERICAN GROUP PENS FUND	1.7	1.7
BAILEYS NOM P/L	1.1	1.1
TOTAL	84.1	85.6

DIRECTORS :
BAND DDB (Deputy Chairman), BRAY VG
FEATHERSTONE JG, HOFMEYER MB (Chairman)
MCLEAN PW, MOOLMAN TD, TYSON HW, WILSON R

REGISTRATION NUMBER : 01/00352/06

REGISTERED OFFICE
47 Sauer Street, Johannesburg
2001
TEL: 011-633 2994
FAX: 011-834 6059

TRANSFER SECRETARY
Argus Holdings Ltd
P O Box 1014, Johannesburg
2000
TEL: 011-633 2994

COMPANY SECRETARY
J Sturgeon

NATURE OF BUSINESS
An investment holding company with subsidiaries involved in the printing and publishing of newspapers in the major metropolitan areas of SA; manufacture and distribution of gramophone records, tapes, video cassettes, music publishing and the provision of video production; manufacture and sale of greeting cards, stationery products and shop fittings and magazine distribution, and freight forwarding & clearing. The company also has an interest in the M-Net television service.

BANKERS :
Standard Bank of SA Ltd

AUDITORS :
Ernst & Young

FAMILIAR BRAND NAMES
DIAMOND FIELDS ADVERTISER,INFO,M-NET
MAISTER DIRECTORIES,POST NATAL
SOWETAN DAILY MIRROR,SUNDAY TRIBUNE
THE ARGUS,THE DAILY NEWS,THE NATAL MERCURY
THE PRETORIA NEWS,THE STAR,THE SUNDAY STAR
WEEKEND ARGUS

CONTRIBUTION BY ACTIVITY
Metropolitan Newspapers (% Earnings) (51.8%)
Community Newspapers/Commercial Printing (20.7%)
Entertainment/Retail/Other (27.5%)

YEAR END : March

DIVIDEND : Ords R2

Interim No 166	(Ldr)08/12/89	(Pay)18/12/89	Amt(c)275
Final No 167	(Ldr)29/06/90	(Pay)06/07/90	Amt(c)600

DIVIDEND : Ords 10c

Final No 169	(Ldr)28/06/91	(Pay)12/07/91	Amt(c)36.25
Interim No 170	(Ldr)13/12/91	(Pay)31/12/91	Amt(c)15
Final No 171	(Ldr)17/07/92	(Pay)31/07/92	Amt(c)40

NUMBER OF EMPLOYEES : 15257

CAPITAL STRUCTURE

	AUTHORISED	ISSUED
Ords 10c	60000000	42365980

FINANCIAL STATISTICS (AT FINANCIAL YEAR END)

(Amts in R'000)	1992 Mar	1991 Mar	1990 Mar	1989 Mar	1988 Mar
Ord S/H Int	385641	318032	261245	220931	179661
Long Trm Loans	338750	282393	251416	206890	167566
Iss Ord Share	42366	41846	41056	2019	2019
Total Liab	787746	693232	574273	527511	416700
Current Liab	448996	410839	322857	320621	249134
Total Assets	1157804	996290	822387	739751	587130
Intang Assets	15583	14974	13131	8691	9231
Current Assets	545865	515391	421957	406800	299849
Debtors	276919	246600	211416	193045	137193
Inventory	213726	214905	182084	174472	117278
Turnover	2011539	1806212	1582131	1344883	1041382
Oper Profit	202790	175518	143133	117832	89605
Interest Paid	27654	25800	23415	13686	8957
Tax Paid	85440	76760	59642	47728	40889
Prf af Int&Tax	118180	106047	82726	71958	51108
Prf att Ord Sh	89670	72994	56548	51467	40510
Btm Line Earn	87091	73352	55813	59269	42905
Dividend Paid	23348	20896	18079	15139	12112
Mkt Prce(c) YE	2800	1400	850	600	8000
Depreciation	45532	42284	36137	33404	30031

PER SHARE STATISTICS (CENTS)

Net Asst Val	873.48	724.22	604.33	10512.13	8441.31
Net Earnings	213.00	177.00	138.00	2550.00	2029.00
Dividends	55.00	50.00	43.75	750.00	600.00
Cash Flow	260.06	242.97	227.41	3704.80	3207.82

RATIOS AND OTHER INFORMATION

Mrk Cap(R000)	1186248	585844	348976	12114	161520
Current Ratio	1.22	1.25	1.31	1.27	1.20
Quik/Acid Tst	0.74	0.73	0.74	0.72	0.73

A/C Rec T/ovr	7.26	7.32	7.48	6.97	7.59
Tot Ass T/ovr	1.74	1.81	1.92	1.82	1.77
Debt/Ass Rat	0.43	0.45	0.44	0.49	0.48
L T L Tot Ass	0.05	0.04	0.05	0.05	0.05
Debt to Eqity	1.30	1.42	1.38	1.63	1.56
Interest Cover	7.98	7.67	6.65	9.23	10.88
Oper Prof Mrg	10.08	9.72	9.05	8.76	8.60
Net Prof Marg%	4.46	4.04	3.57	3.83	3.89
Ret on Assets	22.17	22.54	21.59	19.83	19.35
Ret on Equity%	23.25	22.95	21.65	23.30	22.55
Price/Earnings	13.15	7.91	6.16	0.24	3.94
Divid Cover	3.87	3.54	3.15	3.40	3.38
Divid Yield	1.96	3.57	5.15	125.00	7.50
Earning Yield%	7.61	12.64	16.24	425.00	25.36
NAV % Mrk Pr	31.20	51.73	71.10	1752.02	105.52
Effec Tax Rate	45.95	47.16	35.89	39.72	39.66
Def Interval	0.79	0.50	0.66	1.35	1.10
Sus Grth Rate	17.20	16.38	14.73	16.44	15.81

SUBSIDIARY & ASSOCIATED COMPANIES

AFMED (PTY) LTD (50%)
ALLIED PUBLISHING LTD
ARGUS NEWSPAPERS LTD
CAPITAL MEDIA (PTY) LTD (25%)
CAXTON LTD
CNA GALLO LTD (32.6%)
CTP HOLDINGS LTD (47.5%)
CTP LTD (47.5%)
ELECTRONIC MEDIA NETWORK HOLDINGS (PTY) (23%)
GALLO (AFRICA) LTD (33%)
MAISTER DIRECTORIES (1981) (PTY) LTD (25%)
NATAL NEWSPAPERS (PTY) LTD
OMNI MEDIA (PTY) LTD (50%)
PRETORIA NEWS (PTY) LTD
TIMES MEDIA LTD (36.7%)

INVESTMENTS

AUDIT BUREAU OF CIRCULATIONS OF SA (PTY) (21 SH)
HISTORICAL HOMES OF SA LTD (10000 SH)
LLG GROUP INVESTMENT (PTY) LTD
SMALL BUSINESS DEVELOPMENT CORP LTD (148732 SH)
TRANS SA BOOK DISTRIBUTORS (PTY) LTD (16,1%)

ARIES PACKAGING LTD

ABBREVIATION : ARIES

JSE SHORT CODE : ARE

SECTOR : Industrial-Paper & Packaging

SHAREHOLDERS

Who Owns Whom's Assessment of the Identity of the Ultimate Controlling Shareholder:
DIRECTORS CONTROL 71,4%

SHAREHOLDER	PERCENTAGE 1992	1991
ERIC KOHLER TRUST	31.8	31.8
GLASBY G H	19.9	19.9
NECKEL D	19.7	19.7
STD BANK NOM TVL P/L	11.0	---
SFSS NOM P/L	3.1	---
FRATER K J M	1.8	---
WALE STREET NOM LTD	1.8	---
NORTH & OSBORNE P/L	1.5	1.5
BOARD OF EXECUTORS NOM P/L	---	5.7
JOHN ORR HOLDINGS LTD PENS FUND	---	3.0
SANAFCO PENS FUND	---	1.6
SOUTHERN LIFE ASSOC LTD	---	9.1
TOTAL	90.6	92.3

DIRECTORS :
GLASBY GH ,KOHLER GE (Chairman)
NECKEL D (Managing Director),PETYT PJ ,WOLFSON JP

REGISTRATION NUMBER : 81/03665/06

REGISTERED OFFICE
C/O Deloitte Pim Goldby, 1st Floor, Sanclare
21 Dreyer Str, Claremont
7700
TEL: 0226-73095
FAX: 0226-71753

TRANSFER SECRETARY
Mercantile Registrars Ltd
P O Box 1053, Johannesburg
2000
TEL: 011-333 8181

COMPANY SECRETARY
J D Faller

NATURE OF BUSINESS
The company is a corrugated-carton manufacturer specialising in E-flute board.

BANKERS :
Standard Bank of SA Ltd

AUDITORS :
Deloitte Pim Goldby

FAMILIAR BRAND NAMES
N/A

CONTRIBUTION BY ACTIVITY
N/A

YEAR END : December

DIVIDEND :Ords no par value

Interim	(Ldr)18/08/89	(Pay)15/09/89	Amt(c)2
Final	(Ldr)09/03/90	(Pay)30/03/90	Amt(c)3
Interim	(Ldr)22/02/91	(Pay)15/03/91	Amt(c)2.5
Interim	(Ldr)30/08/91	(Pay)27/09/91	Amt(c)1
Final	(Ldr)28/02/92	(Pay)20/03/92	Amt(c)2.5
Final	(Ldr)22/02/91	(Pay)15/03/91	Amt(c)2.5
Interim	(Ldr)21/08/92	(Pay)18/09/92	Amt(c)1

NUMBER OF EMPLOYEES : 247

CAPITAL STRUCTURE

	AUTHORISED	ISSUED
Ords no par value	15000000	11000000

FINANCIAL STATISTICS (AT FINANCIAL YEAR END)

(Amts in R'000)	1991 Dec	1990 Dec	1989 Dec	1988 Dec	1987 Dec
Ord S/H Int	7327	6562	6312	5170	2892
Long Trm Loans	2622	888	750	92	157
Iss Ord Share	11000	11000	11000	11000	11000

Total Liab	6335	4334	2894	1387	1786
Current Liab	3713	3446	2144	1295	1629
Total Assets	13662	10896	8928	5453	4678
Intang Assets	*	*	278	1104	*
Current Assets	8471	6018	5853	4225	3445
Debtors	5605	4122	3551	2286	2013
Inventory	2863	1796	1487	678	591
Turnover	26342	21700	17931	16213	11803
Oper Profit	2630	1701	3085	2341	2050
Interest Paid	532	200	10	1	56
Tax Paid	967	813	1524	725	691
Prf af Int&Tax	1150	803	1692	1669	1303
Prf att Ord Sh	1150	803	1692	1669	1303
Btm Line Earn	1150	803	1692	1669	1303
Dividend Paid	385	275	550	495	385
Mkt Prce(c) YE	65	70	55	85	80
Depreciation	1057	800	512	385	306

PER SHARE STATISTICS (CENTS)

Net Asst Val	66 61	59 65	54 85	36 96	26 29
Net Earnings	10 50	7 30	15 40	15 20	11 80
Dividends	3 50	2 50	5 00	4 50	3 50
Cash Flow	21 55	15 40	23 54	17 96	15 75

RATIOS AND OTHER INFORMATION

Mrk Cap(R000)	7150	7700	6050	9350	8800
Current Ratio	2 28	1 75	2 73	3 26	2 11
Quik/Acid Tst	1 51	1 23	2 04	2 74	1 75
A/C Rec T/ovr	4 70	5 26	5 05	7 09	5 86
Tot Ass T/ovr	1 93	1 99	2 01	2 97	2 52
Debt/Ass Rat	0 41	0 35	0 27	0 24	0 36
L T L Tot Ass	0 14	0 03	0 03	-	0 01
Debt to Eqity	0 77	0 57	0 38	0 25	0 58
Interest Cover	4 94	8 51	308 50	2341 00	36 61
Oper Prof Mrg	9 98	7 84	17 20	14 44	17 37
Net Prof Marg%	4 37	3 70	9 44	10 29	11 04
Ret on Assets	19 39	16 67	36 13	43 92	43 82
Ret on Equity%	15 70	12 24	26 81	32 28	45 06
Price/Earnings	6 19	9 59	3 57	5 59	6 78
Divid Cover	3 00	2 92	3 08	3 38	3 37
Divid Yield	5 38	3 57	9 09	5 29	4 38
Earning Yield%	16 15	10 43	28 00	17 88	14 75
NAV % Mrk Pr	102 48	85 22	99 74	43 49	32 86
Effec Tax Rate	39 06	44 68	36 04	27 28	28 03
Def Interval	1 44	0 52	0 31	-	0 06
Sus Grth Rate	10 44	8 05	18 09	22 71	31 74

SUBSIDIARY & ASSOCIATED COMPANIES

ARIES SCREENPRINT (PTY) LTD
BOXPAK (PTY) LTD
GRAPHIC DISPLAY SCREENPRINT (PTY) LTD

INVESTMENTS

None

AROMA LIQUOR HOLDINGS LTD

ABBREVIATION : AROMA

JSE SHORT CODE : ARM

SECTOR : Industrial-Retailers & Wholesalers

SHAREHOLDERS

Who Owns Whom's Assessment of the Identity of the Ultimate Controlling Shareholder: KOVENSKY FAMILY

SHAREHOLDER	PERCENTAGE 1992	1991
AROMA WINE & BRANDY CO P/L	34 1	24 2
KOVENSKY FAMILY TRUST	25 8	25 8
KOVENSKY M L	25 3	25 3
SMIT J	1 0	1 0
STD BANK NOM TVL P/L	---	9 9
TOTAL	86 1	86 1

DIRECTORS :
KOVENSKY ML MR (Chairman & Managing Dir)
SCHNEIDER CL MS (Personnel Director)
SCHNEIDER SM MR (Operations Director),SMITH MM MR
WIESE BF M

REGISTRATION NUMBER : 87/01960/06

REGISTERED OFFICE
3rd Floor, First National Bank Building
Pier Place, Heerengracht, Cape Town
8001
TEL 021-981 4510
FAX 021-981 5411

TRANSFER SECRETARY
Central Registrars Ltd
P O Box 4844, Johannesburg
2000
TEL 011-331 0051

COMPANY SECRETARY
J Smit

NATURE OF BUSINESS
Subsidiaries carry on business as retail liquor outlets, provide management services to the general liquor industry and conduct a hotel operation

BANKERS :
First National Bank of SA Ltd

AUDITORS :
Rosenberg Shoolman & Gordon

FAMILIAR BRAND NAMES
AROMA,CAPE RENDEZVOUS

CONTRIBUTION BY ACTIVITY
N/A

YEAR END : February

DIVIDEND :Ords 1c

Final No 2	(Ldr)09/06/89	(Pay)29/06/89	Amt(c)2 5
Final No 3	(Ldr)15/06/90	(Pay)06/07/90	Amt(c)2 5
Final No 4	(Ldr)14/06/91	(Pay)05/07/91	Amt(c)2
Final No 5	(Ldr)12/06/92	(Pay)03/07/92	Amt(c)1

NUMBER OF EMPLOYEES : 215

CAPITAL STRUCTURE

	AUTHORISED	ISSUED
Ord 1c	20000000	16095320

FINANCIAL STATISTICS (AT FINANCIAL YEAR END)

(Amts in R'000)	1992 Feb	1991 Feb	1990 Feb	1989 Feb	1988 Feb
Ord S/H Int	11949	11617	11505	10945	10277
Long Trm Loans	475	759	980	139	387
Iss Ord Share	16095	16095	16095	16095	16095
Total Liab	8020	7854	7907	4782	2530
Current Liab	7545	7095	6927	4643	2143
Total Assets	13821	13555	12770	15727	12807
Intang Assets	6148	5916	6642	*	*
Current Assets	5777	5621	5335	4489	3258
Debtors	2483	2354	1237	1137	588
Inventory	3270	3246	4073	3313	1170
Oper Profit	1034	1108	1736	2083	1124
Interest Paid	356	381	324	371	86
Tax Paid	180	263	461	792	322
Prf af Int&Tax	510	597	962	1070	716
Prf att Ord Sh	492	597	962	1070	716
Btm Line Earn	492	434	962	1070	716
Dividend Paid	160	322	402	402	362
Mkt Prce(c) YE	20	15	30	43	50
Depreciation	488	449	459	244	97

PER SHARE STATISTICS (CENTS)

Net Asst Val	36 04	35 42	30 21	68 00	63 85
Net Earnings	3 10	3 70	6 00	6 70	6 80
Dividends	1 00	2 00	2 50	2 50	2 25
Cash Flow	6 20	6 50	8 83	8 16	7 76

RATIOS AND OTHER INFORMATION

Mrk Cap(R000)	3219	2414	4829	6921	8048
Current Ratio	0 77	0 79	0 77	0 97	1 52
Quik/Acid Tst	0 33	0 33	0 18	0 25	0 97
Debt/Ass Rat	0 58	0 58	0 62	0 30	0 20
L T L Tot Ass	0 03	0 06	0 08	0 01	0 03
Debt to Eqity	0 67	0 68	0 69	0 44	0 25
Interest Cover	2 90	2 91	5 36	5 61	13 07
Ret on Assets	7 44	9 16	13 68	14 20	8 78
Ret on Equity%	4 12	5 14	8 36	9 78	6 97
Price/Earnings	6 45	4 05	5 00	6 42	7 35
Divid Cover	3 10	1 85	2 40	2 68	3 02
Divid Yield	5 00	13 33	8 33	5 81	4 50
Earning Yield%	15 50	24 67	20 00	15 58	13 60
NAV % Mrk Pr	180 21	236 14	100 71	158 15	127 70
Effec Tax Rate	26 09	30 58	32 40	42 53	31 02
Def Interval	4 51	3 74	2 31	0 78	1 06
Sus Grth Rate	2 78	2 37	4 87	6 10	3 44

SUBSIDIARY & ASSOCIATED COMPANIES

A1 BOTTLE STORE (PTY) LTD
AROMA INN (PTY) LTD
AROMA LIQUORS (WELTEVREDEN) (PTY) LTD
AROMA MANAGEMENT SERVICES (PTY) LTD
AROMA SANDS (PTY) LTD
EERSTE RIVER LIQUORS (PTY) LTD
REDHILL INVESTMENTS (PTY) LTD

INVESTMENTS

None

ART CORPORATION LTD

ABBREVIATION : ART

SECTOR : Zimbabwe Stock Exchange

SHAREHOLDERS

Who Owns Whom's Assessment of the Identity of the Ultimate Controlling Shareholder: NEDLAW INV & TRUST CORP / OLD MUTUAL INV

SHAREHOLDER	PERCENTAGE 1992	1991
NEDLAW INV & TRUST CORP LTD	46 0	---
OLD MUTUAL INV CORP (PVT) LTD	21 2	---
ART GROUP EMPLYEES TRUST PVT LTD	11 8	---
IPCORN LTD	2 9	---
FIDELITY LIFE ASSURE OF ZIM PVT LTD	1 7	---
DENBI STATIONERY PVT LTD	1 7	---
NAT RAILWAYS OF ZIM CONTR PENS FUND	1 6	---
STD CHART MERCHANT BANK ZIM NOM PVT LTD	1 6	---
SECURITY NOM LTD	1 3	---
SOUTHAMPTON ASSURE CO ZIM LTD	1 1	---
TOTAL	90 8	---

DIRECTORS :
BION DP ,DICKIE AC ,EASTWOOD ANH ,MHLANGA L DR
NYANDORO GB (Chairman),WAKELING JB

REGISTERED OFFICE
Nedlaw House, 202 Seke Road
Graniteside

TEL 738011
FAX 738036

TRANSFER SECRETARY
First Transfer Secretaries (Pvt) Ltd
P O Box 437, Bulawayo
Zimbabwe

TEL 092634 - 702905

COMPANY SECRETARY
Art Corporation Management Services

NATURE OF BUSINESS
ART CORPORATION's principal acitvities are the manufacture of stationery,products for scholars, wire, tube and sheet metal products,rigid and flex ible plastic packaging and the distribution of a wide range of goods to the industrial and consumer markets

BANKERS :
ANZ Grindlays Bank Plc
Standard Chartered Bank Zimbabwe Ltd

AUDITORS :
Ernst & Young

FAMILIAR BRAND NAMES
N/A

CONTRIBUTION BY ACTIVITY
N/A

YEAR END : December

DIVIDEND Ords Z$1

Dividend	(Ldr)06/09/91	(Pay)27/09/91	Amt(c)2 22
Dividend	(Ldr)20/03/92	(Pay)03/04/92	Amt(c)4 0

CAPITAL STRUCTURE

	AUTHORISED	ISSUED
Ords Z$1	280000000	251651436

FINANCIAL STATISTICS (AT FINANCIAL YEAR END)

(Amts in Z$)	1991 Dec	1990 Dec
Ord S/H Int	307998	223021
Long Trm Loans	152626	139117
Iss Ord Share	251700	118900
Total Liab	233846	168647
Current Liab	81220	29530
Total Assets	541844	391668
Current Assets	118828	76177
Debtors	39814	28326
Inventory	76999	40048
Turnover	220143	177711
Oper Profit	52544	45140
Interest Paid	6535	8517
Prf af Int&Tax	46009	36623
Prf att Ord Sh	39832	32857
Btm Line Earn	39832	32857
Dividend Paid	49503	11892
Depreciation	8638	6114

PER SHARE STATISTICS (CENTS)

Net Asst Val	122 37	187 57
Net Earnings	16 70	15 40
Dividends	6 20	4 70
Cash Flow	19 38	32 78

RATIOS AND OTHER INFORMATION

Current Ratio	1 46	2 58
Quik/Acid Tst	0 52	1 22
A/C Rec T/ovr	5 53	6 27
Tot Ass T/ovr	0 41	0 45
Debt/Ass Rat	0 35	0 37
L T L Tot Ass	0 20	0 30
Debt to Eqity	0 62	0 66
Interest Cover	8 04	5 30
Oper Prof Mrg	23 87	25 40
Net Prof Marg%	18 09	18 49
Ret on Assets	9 70	11 53
Ret on Equity%	12 93	14 73
Divid Cover	2 69	3 28
Def Interval	2 81	3 10
Sus Grth Rate	-3 14	9 40

SUBSIDIARY & ASSOCIATED COMPANIES

ART PROPERTIES (PVT) LTD
KADOMA CONSOLIDATED INDUSTRIES LTD (50,61%)
KADOMA CONSOLIDATED PROPERTIES (PVT) LTD (50 61%)
SOFTEX TISSUE PRODUCTS (PVT) LTD
ZIMTIES (PVT) LTD

INVESTMENTS

None

ARTHUR KAPLAN JEWELLERY HOLDINGS LTD

ABBREVIATION : AKJ

JSE SHORT CODE : AKJ

SECTOR : Industrial-Retailers & Wholesalers

SHAREHOLDERS

Who Owns Whom's Assessment of the Identity of the Ultimate Controlling Shareholder: DIRECTORS

SHAREHOLDER	PERCENTAGE 1992	1991
KAPLAN A N INV CC	69 3	69 3
EMDON A L	7 7	7 7
JOUBERT L T	5 2	5 2
GERBRI FINANCE INV HOLDINGS CC	4 7	4 7
FIRST NAT NOM P/L	3 4	3 4
KAPLAN A N	1 7	1 5
ARTHUR KAPLAN JEWELLERS SHARE INC TRUST	1 4	1 4
TOTAL	93 4	93 1

DIRECTORS :
EMDON AL ,JOUBERT LT
KAPLAN AN (Chairman & Managing Dir),LOWENTHAL ND

REGISTRATION NUMBER : 86/01385/06

REGISTERED OFFICE
3rd floor "Die Meent" Building, Andries Street
Pretoria
0002
TEL 012 324 1800
FAX 012-324 1800

TRANSFER SECRETARY
Central Registrars Ltd
P O Box 4844, Johannesburg
2000
TEL 011-331 0051

COMPANY SECRETARY
P Linnevelt

NATURE OF BUSINESS
An investment holding company Subsidiaries carry on the business of jewellery retail from 19 stores A subsidiary also manufactures jewellery

BANKERS :
First National Bank of SA Ltd

AUDITORS :
Kessel Feinstein

FAMILIAR BRAND NAMES
ARTHUR KAPLAN

CONTRIBUTION BY ACTIVITY
N/A

YEAR END : February

DIVIDEND : Ords 1c
Final No 2 (Ldr)16/06/89 (Pay)14/07/89 Amt(c)4

Final No 3	(Ldr)29/06/90	(Pay)20/07/90	Amt(c)4 5
Final No 4	(Ldr)28/06/91	(Pay)26/07/91	Amt(c)5
Final No 5	(Ldr)03/07/92	(Pay)17/08/92	Amt(c)2

NUMBER OF EMPLOYEES : 140

CAPITAL STRUCTURE

	AUTHORISED	ISSUED
Ords 1c	20000000	15000000

FINANCIAL STATISTICS (AT FINANCIAL YEAR END)

(Amts in R'000)	1992 Feb	1991 Feb	1990 Feb	1989 Feb	1988 Feb
Ord S/H Int	10325	9617	8249	7179	6324
Long Trm Loans	3904	2922	2880	3213	825
Iss Ord Share	15000	15000	14500	14500	14500
Total Liab	10228	8970	5798	7070	3607
Current Liab	6324	6048	2918	3857	2782
Total Assets	20553	18587	14047	14249	9931
Current Assets	17642	15910	12074	12633	8814
Debtors	6195	4861	3707	3770	3271
Inventory	11434	10958	8257	8708	5174
Oper Profit	2808	4212	4005	3025	2794
Interest Paid	1384	942	837	350	161
Tax Paid	826	1577	1565	1353	1315
Prf af Int&Tax	1008	1918	1723	1432	1318
Prf att Ord Sh	1008	1918	1723	1435	1321
Btm Line Earn	1008	1918	1723	1435	1339
Dividend Paid	300	750	653	580	254
Mkt Prce(c) YE	35	45	43	50	55
Depreciation	329	297	240	190	85

PER SHARE STATISTICS (CENTS)

Net Asst Val	68 83	64 11	56 89	49 51	43 61
Net Earnings	6 70	12 80	11 90	9 90	9 10
Dividends	2 00	5 00	4 50	4 00	1 75
Cash Flow	7 89	14 31	11 19	11 32	9 91

RATIOS AND OTHER INFORMATION

Mrk Cap(R000)	5250	6750	6235	7250	7975
Current Ratio	2 79	2 63	4 14	3 28	3 17
Quik/Acid Tst	0 98	0 82	1 31	1 02	1 31
Debt/Ass Rat	0 49	0 46	0 40	0 46	0 32
L T L Tot Ass	0 18	0 14	0 19	0 19	0 04
Debt to Eqity	0 97	0 89	0 68	0 92	0 50
Interest Cover	2 03	4 47	4 78	8 64	17 35
Ret on Assets	15 66	23 87	29 37	22 02	28 16
Ret on Equity%	9 76	19 94	20 89	19 99	20 89
Price/Earnings	5 22	3 52	3 61	5 05	6 04
Divid Cover	3 35	2 56	2 64	2 48	5 20
Divid Yield	5 71	11 11	10 47	8 00	3 18
Earning Yield%	19 14	28 44	27 67	19 80	16 55
NAV % Mrk Pr	196 67	142 47	132 30	99 02	79 30
Effec Tax Rate	53 11	47 10	57 94	47 86	49 34
Def Interval	6 44	3 02	2 11	2 98	0 63
Sus Grth Rate	6 86	12 15	12 97	11 91	16 87

SUBSIDIARY & ASSOCIATED COMPANIES

A K J MANUFACTURING JEWELLERS (PTY) LTD
AKJ MANUFACTURING JEWELLERS (PTY) LTD
ARTHUR KAPLAN JEWELLERS (BOP) (PTY) LTD
FESTIVAL JEWELLERY SALES (PTY) LTD
HOMES FABULOUS (PTY) LTD

INVESTMENTS

None

ASSOCIATED FURNITURE COMPANIES LTD

ABBREVIATION : AFCOL

JSE SHORT CODE : AFC

SECTOR : Industrial Furniture & Household

SHAREHOLDERS

Who Owns Whom's Assessment of the Identity of the Ultimate Controlling Shareholder: ANGLO AMERICAN VIA BEVCON & SA BREWS

SHAREHOLDER	PERCENTAGE 1992	1991
SA BREWERIES LTD	55 9	55 9
FURNCOL LTD	14 8	14 8
SA MUTUAL	6 8	6 5
CMB NOM P/L	5 8	- -
STD BANK NOM TVL P/L	5 6	5 6
LIBERTY LIFE ASSOC OF AFRICA LTD	3 7	4 0
EIGHTY ONE MAIN STREET NOM LTD	1 7	1 9
AFCOL SHARE TRUST	1 3	1 3
SANLAM	---	5 8
TOTAL	95 7	95 8

DIRECTORS :

BREYTENBACH P ,COX RH ,DIKE CW
ECCLES ATO (Joint Managing Director),KAHN JM
KINMONT GA (Dir Human Resources),MCFARLANE WS
ROGER LUND CKD (Joint Managing Director)
SHERRARD AC ,VAN DER WATT L (Chairman)
WILMOT NN (Financial Director),WYMAN MI

REGISTRATION NUMBER : 64/02648/06

REGISTERED OFFICE

5th Floor, Ogilvy Centre, Cnr Fifth Str & Fredman Dr
Sandton
2199
TEL 011-883 7500
FAX 011-883 7555

TRANSFER SECRETARY

Consolidated Share Registrars Ltd
P O Box 61051, Marshalltown
2107
TEL 011-492 1620

COMPANY SECRETARY

P R Barrable

NATURE OF BUSINESS

The investment holding company of a group which is active in furniture & small appliance manufacture Manufacturing operations are supported by a series of subsidiaries which produce raw material such as foam, textiles, spring components and thin board, for supply to Afcol & the general furniture, motor & building industries Afcol also has a minority investment in quoted Romatex Ltd

BANKERS :

Standard Bank of SA Ltd

AUDITORS :
KPMG Aiken & Peat

FAMILIAR BRAND NAMES
BASSETT FURNITURE,CASTELLI,COMFORTO,EDBLO
EKCO APPLIANCES,FINE SEAT,FUJIKA
GRAFTON EVEREST,GREAVES & THOMAS,MAUSER
PARKER KNOLL,PEACH HATTON,PLANMOBEL,RUF
SEALY,SLUMBERLAND,THER A PEDIC,ULTRABORD
WILKHAHN

CONTRIBUTION BY ACTIVITY
Furniture Manufacture (% Attrib Earning) (11 7%)
Raw Materials Producing (51 5%)
Strategic Investments (36 8%)

YEAR END : March

DIVIDEND .Ords 50c

Interim No 47	(Ldr)10/11/89	(Pay)29/12/89	Amt(c)52 5
Final No 48	(Ldr)25/05/90	(Pay)02/07/90	Amt(c)42 5
Interim No 49	(Ldr)09/11/90	(Pay)31/12/90	Amt(c)47 5
Final No 50	(Ldr)25/05/91	(Pay)01/07/91	Amt(c)34
Interim No 51	(Ldr)29/11/91	(Pay)31/12/91	Amt(c)25 5
Final No 52	(Ldr)22/05/92	(Pay)01/07/92	Amt(c)27 5
Interim No 53	(Ldr)20/11/92	(Pay)31/12/92	Amt(c)26

NUMBER OF EMPLOYEES : 7991

CAPITAL STRUCTURE

	AUTHORISED	ISSUED
Ords 50c	29506000	24539931
Ords (Non Voting auth d incl ab	0	4273316
6% Cum Prefs R1	550000	550000

FINANCIAL STATISTICS (AT FINANCIAL YEAR END)

(Amts in R 000)	1992 Mar	1991 Mar	1990 Mar	1989 Mar	1988 Mar
Ord S/H Int	258091	249897	237371	211991	192014
Long Trm Loans	120279	108839	116476	105236	67153
Iss Ord Share	24540	24540	24540	24438	24184
Total Liab	272603	245012	248522	212169	168821
Current Liab	152324	136173	132046	106933	101668
Total Assets	530694	494909	485893	424160	360835
Current Assets	288488	249433	254595	221178	211866
Debtors	198915	157577	177096	150676	136791
Inventory	89573	91856	77499	70222	74588
Turnover	785638	772311	690941	571690	510177
Oper Profit	44270	64165	58440	48179	43064
Interest Paid	23144	25487	19781	12748	6169
Tax Paid	5506	16776	16977	15749	17969
Prf af Int&Tax	21470	29684	32106	27754	25438
Prf att Ord Sh	26040	40013	46691	41555	35025
Btm Line Earn	15888	34475	55260	39310	34721
Dividend Paid	13006	20000	23260	20875	17533
Mkt Prce(c) YE	1175	1400	1350	1075	975
Depreciation	11822	11068	9967	8332	7594

PER SHARE STATISTICS (CENTS)

Net Asst Val	1051 72	1018 33	967 28	867 46	793 97
Net Earnings	106 10	163 10	190 30	170 00	144 80
Dividends	53 00	81 50	95 00	85 00	72 50
Cash Flow	128 22	158 57	181 81	141 10	140 51

RATIOS AND OTHER INFORMATION

Mrk Cap(R000)	288345	343560	331290	262709	235794
Current Ratio	1 89	1 83	1 93	2 07	2 08
Quik/Acid Tst	1 31	1 16	1 34	1 41	1 35
A/C Rec T/ovr	3 95	4 90	3 90	3 79	3 73
Tot Ass T/ovr	1 48	1 56	1 42	1 35	1 41
Debt/Ass Rat	0 49	0 46	0 47	0 47	0 43
L T L Tot Ass	0 20	0 19	0 20	0 22	0 15
Debt to Eqity	1 01	0 92	0 96	0 94	0 81
Interest Cover	2 15	2 82	3 47	4 41	8 04
Oper Prof Mrg	5 63	8 31	8 46	8 43	8 44
Net Prof Marg%	3 31	5 18	6 76	7 27	6 87
Ret on Assets	10 49	16 86	17 41	16 75	16 68
Ret on Equity%	10 09	16 01	19 67	19 60	18 24
Price/Earnings	11 07	8 58	7 09	6 32	6 73
Divid Cover	2 00	2 00	2 00	2 00	2 00
Divid Yield	4 51	5 82	7 04	7 91	7 44
Earning Yield%	9 03	11 65	14 10	15 81	14 85
NAV % Mrk Pr	89 51	72 74	71 65	80 69	81 43
Effec Tax Rate	33 14	45 88	34 27	46 09	43 09
Def Interval	3 51	2 46	2 24	2 77	1 64
Sus Grth Rate	5 05	8 01	9 87	9 76	9 11

SUBSIDIARY & ASSOCIATED COMPANIES

AFCHAIR (PTY) LTD
AFCOL (E P) (PTY) LTD
AFCOL CAPE (PTY) LTD
AFCOL CONTRACTS (NATAL) (PTY) LTD
AFCOL FINANCE CO (PTY) LTD
AFCOL INVESTMENTS (PTY) LTD
AFCOL MANUFACTURING (NATAL) LTD
AFCOL MANUFACTURING LTD
AFCOL PROPERTIES (PTY) LTD
AFCOL REAL ESTATE HOLDINGS (PTY) LTD
AFCOL SERVICES (PTY) LTD
AFCOL STAFF LOAN & BENEVOLENT CO (PTY) L
AFMAN BEDDING (NATAL) (PTY) LTD
AFMAN BEDDING CAPE (PTY) LTD
AFMAN SHIPPING CO (PTY) LTD
AFMAN TIMBER AGENCIES (PTY) LTD
AFU FINANCE CO (PTY) LTD
AFU PROPERTIES (PTY) LTD
ALPINE UPHOLSTERY (PTY) LTD
ANGLO AMERICAN DISTRIBUTORS (PTY) LTD
ANGLO DUTCH (PTY) LTD (50%)
ANGLO DUTCH CHAIR MANUFACTURING CO (PTY
ANGLO DUTCH EQUIPMENT CO (CAPE) (PTY) L
ANGLO DUTCH EQUIPMENT CO (JOHANNESBURG)
ANGLO DUTCH EQUIPMENT CO (PRETORIA) (PT
ANGLO DUTCH EQUIPMENT CO (PTY) LTD
ANGLO DUTCH INDUSTRIES (PTY) LTD
ANGLO DUTCH METAL PRODUCTS (PTY) LTD
ANGLO DUTCH PROPERTIES (PTY) LTD
ASM HOLDINGS (PTY) LTD
BAYNE INVESTMENTS (PTY) LTD
BISON CHEMICALS (PTY) LTD
BISON LAMINATES (PTY) LTD
BISONBORD PROPERTIES LTD
BORDER BEDDING & FURNITURE (PTY) LTD
BRIGHTON FURNISHERS (PTY) LTD
BRIMART INVESTMENT HOLDINGS (PTY) LTD (25,5%)
BROOD (PTY) LTD, THE
BROWN & NEETHLING (PTY) LTD (50%)
BROWN & NEETHLING (TVL) (PTY) LTD (50%)
BROWN & NEETHLING CONTROLLING (PTY) LTD (50%)
BROWN & NEETHLING MANAGEMENT CO (PTY) LT (50%)
CASUARINA SAWMILLS (PTY) LTD (50%)
CB ESTATES LTD
CD & S ENGINEERING (PTY) LTD
CENTRE SYNDICATE (THE) (PTY) LTD
CICS MARKETING (PTY) LTD
CICS PROGRAMMING (PTY) LTD
COMMERCIAL & INDUSTRIAL COMPUTER SERVICE
CONTRACT FURNITURE SERVICES (PTY) LTD
CROWNFLEX S A (PTY) LTD
D & O FRYE STARCK & CO (PTY) LTD
DASHING OFFICE FURNITURE (PTY) LTD (50%)
DESK CRAFT (PTY) LTD
DREAMLAND PRODUCTS (PTY) LTD

DUNCAN BAYNE (PTY) LTD
DUNCAN BAYNE (SWAZILAND) (PTY) LTD
EAGLE DESIGNS (PTY) LTD
EASTERN CAPE BEDDING & FURNITURE (PTY) L
EDBLO (AFRICA) LTD
EDBLO (CAPE) LTD
EDBLO (NATAL) LTD
EDBLO TRANSVAAL LTD
EIAN INVESTMENTS (PTY) LTD
EMBASSY DESIGNS (PTY) LTD
ETABLISSEMENT ZAMBELO
EXCELSIOR METAL PRODUCTS (PTY) LTD
FINESEAT MANUFACTURERS (PTY) LTD (25,5%)
FRIKKIE NEETHLING BELEGGINGS (PTY) LTD (50%)
FRYSTARK (E.P.) (PTY) LTD
FRYSTARK S.A. (PTY) LTD
FURNCOL LTD
FURNCOL PROPERTIES (PTY) LTD
FURNITURE CONTRACTS (CAPE) (PTY) LTD
G CONSANI (PTY) LTD
GLENDOWNIE INVESTMENTS (PTY) LTD
GLITTERING INVESTMENTS (PTY) LTD
GLOBE NUFURN (NATAL) (PTY) LTD
GRAFTON EVEREST (TRANSVAAL) (PTY) LTD
GRAFTON FURNITURE MNFRS. (PTY) LTD
GREAVES & THOMAS (SA) LTD
HARDY STREET INVESTMENTS (PTY) LTD
HARMIL PROPERTIES (PTY) LTD
HIGH POINT FURNITURE INDUSTRIES (PTY) LT
I LUBNER (PTY) LTD
IMPALA FURNISHERS (PTY) LTD
IMPALA TEXTILES (PTY) LTD
IMPULSE DESIGNS (PTY) LTD
INDUSTRIA TRANSPORT SERVICES (PTY) LTD
INTERFORM (PTY) LTD
JATEX (KWANDEBELA) (PTY) LTD
JATEX (SA) (PTY) LTD
JUBELA PROPERTIES (PTY) LTD
KAIGOR MANUFACTURING COMPANY (PTY) LTD
KAISTAR HOLDINGS LTD
KALLENBACH-HENDLER (PTY) LTD (50%)
LURAND INVESTMENTS (PTY) LTD
LUXAIRE MATTRESS & BEDDING CORP. (PTY) L
MADISON UPHOLSTERERS (PTY) LTD
MATTEX (PTY) LTD
MODERN FRAMEMAKERS (PTY) LTD
MORPHEUS BEDDING COMPANY (PTY) LTD
NAPLY PROPERTIES LTD
NEWFIELDS SUPPLIES (PTY) LTD
NOORDENSTRAAT BESITTINGS (EDMS) BPK
NUCHROME ELECTROPLATING (PTY) LTD
NUFURN (CAPE) (PTY) LTD
NUFURN (NATAL) (PTY) LTD
NUFURN INDUSTRIES (PTY) LTD
NUTUBE (PTY) LTD
OFFEX OFFICE FURNITURE (PTY) LTD (50%)
OMNI STRUCTURAL PRODUCTS (PTY) LTD
PAULGAR INVESTMENTS (PTY) LTD
PEACH & HATTON HERITAGE (PTY) LTD
PG BISON LTD (23,9%)
PG ENVIRONMENTAL SYSTEMS (PTY) LTD
PLANNED SPACE (PTY) LTD
PLANOMATIC (PTY) LTD
POWERCRAFT HOLDINGS (PTY) LTD
POWERCRAFT UPHOLSTERY PRODUCTS (PTY) LTD
PREMIER SPRING INDUSTRIES (PTY) LTD
RAL HOLDINGS (PTY) LTD
RAND UPHOLSTERERS (PTY) LTD
RANDLEIGH SALES (PTY) LTD
RELIABLE FURNITURE MANUFACTURING CO. (PT
RESIN PRODUCTS (PTY) LTD - SWAZILAND
RESINKEM (PTY) LTD (50%)
RK FACTORS & FINANCE CO (PTY) LTD
ROMATEX LTD (21%)
RUF INTERNATIONAL S.A. (PTY) LTD
RUF INTERNATIONAL SA (PTY) LTD
SA FLOCK (PTY) LTD
SAMLYTE (PTY) LTD
SAMSTAR HOLDINGS (PTY) LTD
SAMSTAR SERVICES (PTY) LTD
SARMA MEUBELVERVAARDIGERS (EDMS) BPK
SEALY (CAPE) (PTY) LTD
SEALY OF SOUTH AFRICA (PTY) LTD
SOFTEX MATTRESS (PTY) LTD
SPANKOR LTD (50%)
SPRINGBOK KITCHEN & BEDDING (PTY) LTD
SPRINGBOK MANUFACTURING CO. (PTY) LTD
STAPLE INVESTMENTS (PTY) LTD
STAR FURNITURE MANUFACTURERS (PTY) LTD
STEELCRAFT MANUFACTURING CO. (PTY) LTD
STEELEX WIRE PRODUCTS (PTY) LTD (25,5%)
STEELFURN (CENTRAL) (PTY) LTD
STEELFURN (CISKEI) (PTY) LTD
STEELFURN (NATAL) (PTY) LTD
STEELFURN (NORTH) (PTY) LTD
STEELFURN (SOUTH) (PTY) LTD
THER-A-PEDIC (SOUTH AFRICA) (PTY) LTD
TOOLPLAST HOLDINGS (PTY) LTD
TRANSVAAL MATTRESS & FURNISHING CO. LTD
ULTRABORD (PTY) LTD
UNITA PLANNED FURNITURE (PTY) LTD
VITAFOAM (SA) (PTY) LTD
W SAMUEL FURNITURE MANUFACTURERS (PTY) L
WOODMET (PTY) LTD (50%)
WOODSTUFF (PTY) LTD

INVESTMENTS

None

ASSOCIATED MANGANESE MINES OF SA LTD

ABBREVIATION : ASS-MANG

JSE SHORT CODE : AMN

SECTOR : Metals & Minerals-Manganese

SHAREHOLDERS

Who Owns Whom's Assessment of the Identity of the Ultimate Controlling Shareholder:
ASSOCIATED ORE & METAL CORP / ANGLOVAAL

SHAREHOLDER	PERCENTAGE 1992	1991
ASSOCIATED ORE & METAL CORP LTD	43.0	42.9
FOX STREET NOM P/L	41.6	36.6
ANGLOVAAL LTD	5.1	5.1
STD BANK NOM TVL P/L	4.2	4.1
FIRST NAT NOM P/L	1.7	1.8
UAL NOM P/L	1.4	1.4
OHRIGGS LIME CO P/L	---	1.4
UNITED AFRICAN INV LTD	---	3.1
TOTAL	97.1	96.5

DIRECTORS :
CARPENTER RJ ,CROWE DJ ,HERSOV BE (Chairman)
MENELL CS ,MILLING JW
SACCO DG (Deputy Chairman)
SACCO G (Technical Director),WILSON RAD

REGISTRATION NUMBER : 05/07343/06

REGISTERED OFFICE
Anglovaal House, 56 Main Street
Johannesburg
2001
TEL 011-634 9111

TRANSFER SECRETARY
Anglovaal Ltd
P O Box 62379, Marshalltown
2107
TEL 011 634 9111

COMPANY SECRETARY
Anglovaal Ltd

NATURE OF BUSINESS
The company mines manganese and iron ores in the Northern Cape Subsidiaries produce chrome alloys and ferro-manganese, and own and receive rentals from land and improvements in the Cato Ridge area

BANKERS :
Standard Bank of SA Ltd

AUDITORS :
Ernst & Young

FAMILIAR BRAND NAMES
N/A

CONTRIBUTION BY ACTIVITY
Mining (% profit after tax) (100 0%)

YEAR END : December

DIVIDEND .Ords 50c

Interim No 102	(Ldr)14/09/90	(Pay)05/10/90	Amt(c)500
Final No 103	(Ldr)28/03/91	(Pay)19/04/91	Amt(c)250
Interim No 104	(Ldr)13/09/91	(Pay)04/10/91	Amt(c)250
Final No 105	(Ldr)27/03/92	(Pay)16/04/92	Amt(c)500
Interim No 106	(Ldr)18/09/92	(Pay)09/10/92	Amt(c)250

NUMBER OF EMPLOYEES : 1981

CAPITAL STRUCTURE

	AUTHORISED	ISSUED
Ords 50c	3636260	3548206
Unclassified 50c	63740	0

FINANCIAL STATISTICS (AT FINANCIAL YEAR END)

(Amts in R 000)	1991 Dec	1990 Dec	1989 Dec	1988	1987
Ord S/H Int	403027	324299	251589	214383	202583
Long Trm Loans	12241	25112	15385	119719	99719
Iss Ord Share	3548	3548	3548	3548	3548
Total Liab	132636	219756	140473	196442	163782
Current Liab	120395	194644	125088	76723	64063
Total Assets	535663	544055	392062	540939	483190
Current Assets	332756	339871	245697	206837	180888
Debtors	64612	111690	72607		
Inventory	267642	228145	163567	206837	180888
Turnover	575231	613881	717639	445321	247162
Oper Profit	204353	201675	287680	102371	24286
Interest Paid	12583	14864	11912	7107	5675
Tax Paid	92402	81109	131550	26696	1471
Prf af Int&Tax	105340	108069	156306	68928	16952
Prf att Ord Sh	105340	108069	156306	57039	15334
Btm Line Earn	105340	108069	156306	57039	15334
Dividend Paid	26612	26612	85156	45239	8870
Mkt Prce(c) YE	32750	29500	28000	19500	15000
Depreciation	6086	4140	2839	-	-

PER SHARE STATISTICS (CENTS)

Net Asst Val	11359 27	9140 33	7091 01	6042 36	5709 78
Net Earnings	2922 00	2695 00	4191 00	-	-
Dividends	750 00	750 00	2400 00	-	-
Cash Flow	2839 35	3190 22	4642 59	1942 73	477 79

RATIOS AND OTHER INFORMATION

Mrk Cap(R000)	1161970	1046660	993440	691860	532200
Current Ratio	2 76	1 75	1 96	2 70	2 82
Quik/Acid Tst	0 54	0 57	0 66	-	-
A/C Rec T/ovr	8 90	5 50	9 88	-	-
Tot Ass T/ovr	1 07	1 13	1 83	0 82	0 51
Debt/Ass Rat	0 22	0 36	0 32	0 36	0 34
L T L Tot Ass	-	-	-	0 22	0 21
Debt to Eqity	0 30	0 60	0 50	0 92	0 81
Interest Cover	16 24	13 57	24 15	14 45	4 25
Oper Prof Mrg	35 53	32 85	40 09	22 99	9 83
Net Prof Marg%	18 31	17 60	21 78	12 81	6 20
Ret on Assets	39 26	37 50	76 46	18 99	4 99
Ret on Equity%	26 14	33 32	62 13	26 61	7 57
Price/Earnings	11 21	10 95	6 68	-	-
Divid Cover	3 90	3 59	1 75		
Divid Yield	2 29	2 54	8 57	-	-
Earning Yield%	8 92	9 14	14 97	-	
NAV % Mrk Pr	34 68	30 98	25 33	30 99	38 07
Effec Tax Rate	43 13	34 09	39 17	28 02	7 90
Def Interval	0 49	1 04	0 04	1 74	5 88
Sus Grth Rate	19 53	25 12	28 28	5 50	3 19

SUBSIDIARY & ASSOCIATED COMPANIES

CATO RIDGE DEVELOPMENT CO LTD
FERALLOYS LTD

INVESTMENTS

RAND MUTUAL ASSURANCE LTD (24 SH)
ZEERUST CHROME MINES LTD (8%)

ASSOCIATED ORE AND METAL CORP LTD

ABBREVIATION : ASSORE

JSE SHORT CODE : AOM

SECTOR : Mining Financial Mining Holding

SHAREHOLDERS

Who Owns Whom's Assessment of the Identity of the Ultimate Controlling Shareholder·
SACCO FAMILY

SHAREHOLDER	PERCENTAGE 1992	1991
ORESTEEL INV P/L	52 0	52 1
SA MUTUAL	14 7	---
FOX STREET NOM P/L	12 4	12 4
STD BANK NOM TVL P/L	8 2	8 4
EIGHTY ONE MAIN STREET NOM LTD	2 3	1 5
BP THIBAULT NOM P/L	1 1	1 1
RAESLIP CORP P/L	- -	1 2
SOUTHERN LIFE ASSOC LTD	---	14 5
TOTAL	90 7	91 2

DIRECTORS :
CARPENTER RJ ,CHUTE RA ,CORY CJ ,ENGLISH G
MILLING JW ,SACCO D (Chairman & Managing Dir)
SACCO G (President),VAN DER HORST JC D

REGISTRATION NUMBER : 05/37394/06

REGISTERED OFFICE
Assore House, 6 St Andrews Road
Parktown
2193
TEL 011-725 4810
FAX 011-484 2754

TRANSFER SECRETARY
Union Provident Trust SA Ltd
P O Box 2322, Johannesburg
2000
TEL 011-833 6700

COMPANY SECRETARY
G English

NATURE OF BUSINESS
A mining holding company with a controlling interest in quoted Associated Manganese Mines The group is principally interested in base minerals & metals, including manganese, iron ore, ferromanganese, chrome ore & wonderstone The Group also manufactures grinding wheels, cordum tiles & abrasive materials for resale, & develops & sells township property

BANKERS :
Standard Bank of SA Ltd

AUDITORS :
Ernst & Young

FAMILIAR BRAND NAMES
N/A

CONTRIBUTION BY ACTIVITY
Investments (% Income after tax) (78 0%)
Technical admin & Shipping (17 0%)
Mining (1 0%)
Township Property (3 0%)
Manufacturing (1 0%)

YEAR END : June

DIVIDEND :Ords 50c

Interim No 66	(Ldr)30/03/90	(Pay)25/04/90	Amt(c)500
Final No 67	(Ldr)05/10/90	(Pay)25/10/90	Amt(c)500
Interim No 68	(Ldr)12/04/91	(Pay)25/04/91	Amt(c)200
Final No 69	(Ldr)11/10/91	(Pay)24/10/91	Amt(c)350
Interim No 70	(Ldr)15/04/92	(Pay)29/04/92	Amt(c)300
Final No 71	(Ldr)09/10/92	(Pay)22/10/92	Amt(c)250

NUMBER OF EMPLOYEES : 650

CAPITAL STRUCTURE

	AUTHORISED	ISSUED
Ords 50c	2000000	1400000

FINANCIAL STATISTICS (AT FINANCIAL YEAR END)

(Amts in R'000)	1992 Jun	1991 Jun	1990 Jun	1989 Jun	1988 Jun
Ord S/H Int	542289	539804	492218	429836	350590
Long Trm Loans	-	-	-	1899	303
Iss Ord Share	1400	1400	1400	1400	1400
Total Liab	35817	33788	32473	54114	21522
Current Liab	35817	33788	32473	52215	21219
Total Assets	578106	573592	524691	483950	372112
Current Assets	50292	43840	36827	38192	23395
Debtors	12431	17065	10872	13648	11680
Inventory	6611	5696	5254	4573	3879
Oper Profit	6328	13277	17333	9433	6792
Interest Paid	30	26	887	432	-
Tax Paid	3012	5280	5126	5417	2888
Prf af Int&Tax	15277	15944	38451	35842	3904
Prf att Ord Sh	15277	15944	38451	36170	4533
Btm Line Earn	15277	15944	38451	36170	4533
Dividend Paid	7700	7700	14000	9800	4200
Mkt Prce(c) YE	22000	20000	21000	17500	8700
Depreciation	1169	1070	943	831	471

PER SHARE STATISTICS (CENTS)

Net Asst Val	38734 93	38557 43	35158 43	30702 57	25042 14
Net Earnings	953 00	991 00	2747 00	1573 00	324 00
Dividends	550 00	550 00	1000 00	700 00	300 00
Cash Flow	1174 71	1215 29	2811 57	2709 93	357 93

RATIOS AND OTHER INFORMATION

Mrk Cap(R000)	308000	280000	294000	245000	121800
Current Ratio	1 40	1 30	1 13	0 73	1 10
Quik/Acid Tst	1 22	1 13	0 97	0 64	0 92
Debt/Ass Rat	0 06	0 06	0 06	0 11	0 06
Debt to Eqity	0 07	0 06	0 07	0 12	0 06
Interest Cover	610 63	817 31	50 13	96 51	-
Ret on Assets	3 17	3 70	8 47	8 61	1 83
Ret on Equity%	2 82	2 95	7 81	8 41	1 29
Price/Earnings	23 08	20 18	7 64	11 13	26 85
Divid Cover	1 73	1 80	2 75	2 25	1 08
Divid Yield	2 50	2 75	4 76	4 00	3 45
Earning Yield%	4 33	4 96	13 08	8 99	3 72
NAV % Mrk Pr	176 07	192 79	167 42	175 44	287 84
Effec Tax Rate	46 74	40 18	31 28	49 28	34 53
Def Interval	-		-	0 32	-
Sus Grth Rate	1 40	1 53	4 97	6 13	0 09

SUBSIDIARY & ASSOCIATED COMPANIES

A M T INVESTMENTS (PTY) LTD
AFRICAN GRANITE CO (PTY) LTD (1992 ONLY)
AFRICAN MINING AND TRUST COMPANY LTD
ASSOCIATED ASBESTOS LTD
ASSOCIATED MANAGANESE MINES OF SA LTD (44,9%)
GENERAL NOMINEES (PTY) LTD
KRANTZBERG MINES LTD (NAMIBIA)
LAGERDRAAI ASBESTOS LTD
ORE & METAL COMPANY LTD
RUSTENBURG MINERALS DEVELOPMENT CO (PTY
SOUTH AFRICAN CORUNDUM CO LTD
TRANSVAAL CORUNDUM CO LTD
WONDERSTONE 1937 LTD
ZEERUST CHROME MINES LTD

INVESTMENTS

AFRICAN GRANITE (PTY) LTD (50000 SH)
ANGLOVAAL LTD (10000 SH)
SMALL BUSINESS DEV CORP LTD (108000 SH)
USKO LTD (600000 SH)

AUDIODEK HOLDINGS LTD

ABBREVIATION : AUTODEK

JSE SHORT CODE : ADK

SECTOR : Industrial-Electronics, Electrical & Bat

SHAREHOLDERS

Who Owns Whom's Assessment of the Identity of the Ultimate Controlling Shareholder: DIRECTORS

SHAREHOLDER	PERCENTAGE 1992	1991
FIRST NAT NOM P/L	73 2	73 2
AUDIODEK SHARE INCENTIVE TRUST	1 8	1 2
LOWENCO NOM P/L	1 4	1 3
TOTAL	76 3	75 7

DIRECTORS :
FLAXMAN JL (Technical Director)
FLOWERS HM (Sales Director)
SAITOWITZ J (Financial Director)
TOLKIN MM (Chairman & Managing Dir),VALKIN AB

REGISTRATION NUMBER : 87/00896/06

REGISTERED OFFICE
166 Main Reef Road, Selby Extension 19
Johannesburg
2001
TEL 011-836 4011
FAX 011-836 0434

TRANSFER SECRETARY
Central Registrars Ltd
P O Box 4844, Johannesburg
2000
TEL 011-331 0051

COMPANY SECRETARY
J Saitowitz

NATURE OF BUSINESS
The company is a holding company and its subsidiaries carry on the business of importers and exclusive distributors of the Autodek,Fairmate,Proline & Alpine ranges of audio equipment and allied products

BANKERS :
First National Bank of SA Ltd

AUDITORS :
Fisher Hoffman Stride

FAMILIAR BRAND NAMES
,ALPINE,AUTODEK,FAIRMATE,PROLINE

CONTRIBUTION BY ACTIVITY
N/A

YEAR END : December

DIVIDEND : Ords 1c

Special No 4	(Ldr)22/02/91	(Pay)28/02/91	Amt(c)2 5
Final No 5	(Ldr)21/06/91	(Pay)19/07/91	Amt(c)1 5
Final No 6	(Ldr)16/04/92	(Pay)30/04/92	Amt(c)3

NUMBER OF EMPLOYEES : 120

CAPITAL STRUCTURE

	AUTHORISED	ISSUED
Ords 1c	40000000	19865000

FINANCIAL STATISTICS (AT FINANCIAL YEAR END)

(Amts in R'000)	1991 Mar	1991 Dec	1990 Mar	1989 Mar	1988 Mar
Ord S/H Int	7370	8024	6418	5780	4828
Long Trm Loans	485	795	575	227	280
Iss Ord Share	19865	19865	19400	19400	19400
Total Liab	11188	15186	11385	10284	7754
Current Liab	10703	14391	10810	10057	7474
Total Assets	18558	23210	17803	16064	12582
Current Assets	14988	20183	14893	14362	11151
Debtors	11278	15921	8892	8520	6300
Inventory	3710	4245	6001	5838	4847
Turnover	60676	50274	47278	42012	30596
Oper Profit	4796	3463	3660	3801	3259
Interest Paid	1398	1079	1167	624	231
Tax Paid	1753	1185	1337	1594	1505
Prf af Int&Tax	1672	1251	1172	1583	1523
Prf att Ord Sh	1672	1251	1172	1583	1523
Btm Line Earn	1672	1251	1172	1583	1523
Dividend Paid	795	596	534	631	631
Mkt Prce(c) YE	23	25	20	40	37
Depreciation	755	587	650	435	286

PER SHARE STATISTICS (CENTS)

Net Asst Val	37 10	40 39	33 08	29 79	24 89
Net Earnings	8 50	6 30	6 00	8 10	7 80
Dividends	4 00	3 00	2 75	3 25	3 25
Cash Flow	12 05	12 87	10 25	10 66	9 78

RATIOS AND OTHER INFORMATION

Mrk Cap(R000)	4569	4966	3880	7760	7178
Current Ratio	1 40	1 40	1 38	1 43	1 49
Quik/Acid Tst	1 05	1 11	0 82	0 85	0 84
A/C Rec T/ovr	5 38	4 21	5 32	4 93	4 86
Tot Ass T/ovr	3 27	2 89	2 66	2 62	2 43
Debt/Ass Rat	0 59	0 64	0 62	0 63	0 61
L T L Tot Ass	0 02	0 02	0 01	0 01	0 02
Debt to Eqity	1 49	1 86	1 73	1 75	1 59
Interest Cover	3 43	3 21	3 14	6 09	14 11
Oper Prof Mrg	7 90	6 89	7 74	9 05	10 65
Net Prof Marg%	2 76	2 49	2 48	3 77	4 98
Ret on Assets	25 99	20 19	20 65	23 66	25 90
Ret on Equity%	22 69	20 79	18 26	27 39	31 55
Price/Earnings	2 71	3 97	3 33	4 94	4 74
Divid Cover	2 13	2 10	2 18	2 49	2 40
Divid Yield	17 39	12 00	13 75	8 13	8 78
Earning Yield%	36 96	25 20	30 00	20 25	21 08
NAV % Mrk Pr	161 31	161 57	165 41	74 48	67 26

Effec Tax Rate	51 04	45 36	45 56	48 60	46 76
Def Interval	2 09	4 82	2 74	2 74	0 54
Sus Grth Rate	11 90	8 16	9 94	16 47	18 48

SUBSIDIARY & ASSOCIATED COMPANIES

AETV ELECTRONIC DEVELOPMENT CORPORATION
AUDIODEK (ALPINE DIVISION) SA (PTY) LTD
AUDIODEK (PTY) LTD
AUDIODEK CAPE (PTY) LTD
AUDIODEK ENTERPRISES (PTY) LTD

INVESTMENTS

None

AUTOPAGE HOLDINGS LTD

ABBREVIATION : AUTOPGE

JSE SHORT CODE : APG

SECTOR : Industrial-Electronics, Electrical & Bat

SHAREHOLDERS

Who Owns Whom's Assessment of the Identity of the Ultimate Controlling Shareholder: VENTRON VIA ALTECH

SHAREHOLDER	PERCENTAGE 1992	1991
ALLIED TECHNOLOGIES LTD	70 8	70 8
STD BANK NOM TVL P/L	16 5	14 6
JR NOM P/L	2 3	
HARVEST SECURITIES LTD	2 2	---
BOE NOM P/L	1 7	2 2
GABY M F		1 1
CLAYTON L A		1 4
VERLAINE Y L B	- -	1 0
NEL S, M E & NOSWORTHY R E T TRUST		2 3
TOTAL	93 5	93 4

DIRECTORS :
BERRY LT (Operations Director),CARSTENS JEW
HANNA GB (Financial Director)
MOON WNL (Managing Director)
NEL P (Operations Director)
SNEDDEN DC (Chairman),TROLLOPE GJ
WYLDE IBT (Technical Director

REGISTRATION NUMBER . 87/01071/06

REGISTERED OFFICE
Cnr Brakpan & Van Dyk Roads, Boksburg
1459
TEL 011-899 9111
FAX 011-914 4032

TRANSFER SECRETARY
Mercantile Registrars Ltd
P O Box 1053, Johannesburg
2000
TEL 011-333 8181

COMPANY SECRETARY
Altech Management Services (Pty) Ltd

NATURE OF BUSINESS
Autopage is an investment holding company whose subsidiaries are engaged in radio paging, surveillance equipment, and financial information systems

BANKERS :
Nedperm Bank Ltd

AUDITORS :
Fisher Hoffman Stride

FAMILIAR BRAND NAMES
4-WARN,AUTOPAGE,BELLBOY
BUSINESS PEOPLES PAGING,MULTICALL,TELERATE

CONTRIBUTION BY ACTIVITY
N/A

YEAR END : February

DIVIDEND :Ords no par value

Dividend No 3	(Ldr)25/05/90	(Pay)20/06/90	Amt(c)8
Dividend No 4	(Ldr)24/05/91	(Pay)10/06/91	Amt(c)8
Dividend No 5	(Ldr)29/05/92	(Pay)08/06/92	Amt(c)8

NUMBER OF EMPLOYEES : 151

CAPITAL STRUCTURE

	AUTHORISED	ISSUED
Ords no par value	50000000	27911985

FINANCIAL STATISTICS (AT FINANCIAL YEAR END)

(Amts in R 000)	1992 Feb	1991 Feb	1990 Feb	1989 Feb	1988 Feb
Ord S/H Int	23528	20052	16867	6322	1504
Long Trm Loans	2152	2579	2901	118	36
Iss Ord Share	27912	27912	26975	19250	12050
Total Liab	15909	14719	13045	6352	875
Current Liab	13757	12140	10144	6234	839
Total Assets	25621	21308	15669	7444	2379
Intang Assets	13816	13463	14243	5230	*
Current Assets	7968	4180	1596	687	218
Debtors	3155	1205	1435	534	205
Inventory	200	41	140	141	
Turnover	36671	30108	26043	9935	4101
Oper Profit	10180	9500	8110	3213	1098
Interest Paid	382	486	882	-	-
Tax Paid	4730	4270	2841	1236	423
Prf af Int&Tax	5774	4779	4410	1977	675
Prf att Ord Sh	5774	4779	4410	1977	675
Btm Line Earn	5709	3925	4410	1977	675
Dividend Paid	2233	2233	2158	1636	301
Mkt Prce(c) YE	135	90	140	125	-
Depreciation	5379	4702	3705	1582	572

PER SHARE STATISTICS (CENTS)

Net Asst Val	34 80	23 61	9 73	5 67	12 48
Net Earnings	20 70	17 30	16 40	12 00	6 30
Dividends	8 00	8 00	8 00	8 50	2 50
Cash Flow	39 93	34 41	31 44	21 41	11 98

RATIOS AND OTHER INFORMATION

Mrk Cap(R000)	37681	25121	37765	24063	-
Current Ratio	0 58	0 34	0 16	0 11	0 26
Quik/Acid Tst	0 56	0 34	0 14	0 09	0 26
A/C Rec T/ovr	11 62	24 99	18 15	18 60	20 00

Tot Ass T/ovr	1 43	1 41	1 66	1 33	1 72
Debt/Ass Rat	0 60	0 67	0 81	0 85	0 35
L T L Tot Ass	0 07	0 10	0 16	0 02	-
Debt to Eqity	0 66	0 71	0 75	1 00	0 56
Interest Cover	26 65	19 55	9 20	-	-
Oper Prof Mrg	27 76	31 55	31 14	32 34	26 77
Net Prof Marg%	15 75	15 87	16 93	19 90	16 46
Ret on Assets	42 49	44 75	51 91	43 16	46 15
Ret on Equity%	24 54	23 83	26 15	31 27	44 88
Price/Earnings	6 52	5 20	8 54	10 42	-
Divid Cover	2 59	2 16	2 05	1 41	2 52
Divid Yield	5 93	8 89	5 71	6 80	-
Earning Yield%	15 33	19 22	11 71	9 60	-
NAV % Mrk Pr	25 77	26 23	6 95	4 54	-
Effec Tax Rate	46 06	46 98	34 74	0 44	5 28
Def Interval	0 12	0 18	0 39	0 94	-
Sus Grth Rate	15 05	12 70	13 35	5 39	24 87

SUBSIDIARY & ASSOCIATED COMPANIES

AUTOPAGE (CAPE) (PTY) LTD
AUTOPAGE (NATAL) (PTY) LTD
AUTOPAGE (PTY) LTD
BUSINESS PEOPLES RADIO PAGING (PTY) LTD
INTERFINET (PTY) LTD
MULTICALL PAGING (PTY) LTD

INVESTMENTS

None

AUTOQUIP GROUP LTD

ABBREVIATION : AUTOQIP

JSE SHORT CODE : ATQ

SECTOR : Industrial-Retailers & Wholesalers

SHAREHOLDERS

Who Owns Whom's Assessment of the Identity of the Ultimate Controlling Shareholder: DIRECTORS CONTROL 57,4% (JUNE 1991)

SHAREHOLDER	PERCENTAGE 1992	1991
NEDBANK NOM LTD	26 5	57 8
MERHOLD SECURITIES P/L	20 3	20 0
CARELSE R M E/L BUCKERFIELD G H (EXORS)	2 1	---
SMITH T I	2 0	2 0
SHARESTOCK NOM P/L	1 6	1 9
JAFFE FAMILY TRUST	1 0	1 0
CARELSE R M	-	2 1
TOTAL	53 6	84 8

DIRECTORS :
COOMBES GR
COQUELLE BD (Chairman & Managing Dir)
FLEISCH JI (Financial Director), SEABROOKE CS

REGISTRATION NUMBER : 87/02838/06

REGISTERED OFFICE
7th floor, Saambou National Building
130 Commissioner Street, Johannesburg
2001
TEL 011-334 0340
FAX 011-334 4862

TRANSFER SECRETARY
Fraser Street Registrars (Pty) Ltd
P O Box 61178, Marshalltown
2107
TEL 011-491 0911

COMPANY SECRETARY
J I Fleisch

NATURE OF BUSINESS
An investment holding company with subsidiaries engaged in wholesale distribution of automotive accessories, auto replacement parts, tyres and industrial bearings and allied products

BANKERS :
Nedperm Bank Ltd

AUDITORS :
Goldberg Jaffe Joselowsky & Partners

FAMILIAR BRAND NAMES
AUTO SHIELD,BRIDGESTONE,BULLBAR,CARISMA
COMPOMOTIVE,DIGITEK,KONI,MANGELS,MOMO,MSW
OMP RACEWEAR,PARTCO,PARTQUIP,PERANA,RECARO
ROS FENDER TRIM,RUOTE O Z ,SPARCO,ZENDER

CONTRIBUTION BY ACTIVITY
N/A

YEAR END : June

DIVIDEND : Ords no par value

Interim	(Ldr)12/04/90	(Pay)23/04/90	Amt(c)3
Final	(Ldr)28/09/90	(Pay)12/10/90	Amt(c)2
Interim	(Ldr)28/03/91	(Pay)12/04/91	Amt(c)2 5
Final	(Ldr)26/09/91	(Pay)11/10/91	Amt(c)2 5
Interim	(Ldr)10/04/92	(Pay)21/04/92	Amt(c)2 5

NUMBER OF EMPLOYEES : 221

CAPITAL STRUCTURE

	AUTHORISED	ISSUED
Ords no par value	24000000	16000000

FINANCIAL STATISTICS (AT FINANCIAL YEAR END)

(Amts in R'000)	1991 Jun	1990 Jun	1989 Jun	1988 Jun
Ord S/H Int	10925	9930	8658	7210
Long Trm Loans	257	386	353	146
Iss Ord Share	16000	16000	16000	16000
Total Liab	15995	14387	13465	7491
Current Liab	15738	14001	13112	7345
Total Assets	25596	22993	20799	13377
Intang Assets	1324	1324	1324	1324
Current Assets	23811	21158	19648	12177
Debtors	8236	6854	5657	3941
Inventory	15548	14086	13945	7886
Turnover	50010	44516	35546	22163
Oper Profit	5031	5242	5205	2588
Interest Paid	1614	1222	583	175
Tax Paid	1639	1915	2161	904
Prf af Int&Tax	1778	2105	2461	1509
Prf att Ord Sh	1778	2104	2511	1509
Btm Line Earn	1795	2072	2511	1509
Dividend Paid	800	800	1040	480
Mkt Prce(c) YE	37	60	70	45
Depreciation	489	331	218	134

PER SHARE STATISTICS (CENTS)

Net Asst Val	60 01	53 79	45 84	36 79
Net Earnings	11 10	13 10	15 70	10 50
Dividends	5 00	5 00	6 50	3 00
Cash Flow	14 17	15 14	16 73	11 41

RATIOS AND OTHER INFORMATION

Mrk Cap(R000)	5920	9600	11200	7200
Current Ratio	1 51	1 51	1 50	1 66
Quik/Acid Tst	0 53	0 51	0 43	0 58
A/C Rec T/ovr	6 07	6 49	6 28	5 62
Tot Ass T/ovr	1 95	1 94	1 71	1 66
Debt/Ass Rat	0 62	0 62	0 65	0 56
L T L Tot Ass	0 01	0 02	0 02	0 01
Debt to Eqity	1 46	1 45	1 55	1 04
Interest Cover	3 12	4 29	8 93	14 79
Oper Prof Mrg	10 06	11 78	14 64	11 68
Net Prof Marg%	3 56	4 73	7 06	6 81
Ret on Assets	19 66	22 85	25 28	19 35
Ret on Equity%	16 27	21 19	29 00	20 93
Price/Earnings	3 33	4 58	4 46	4 29
Divid Cover	2 22	2 62	2 42	3 50
Divid Yield	13 51	8 33	9 29	6 67
Earning Yield%	30 00	21 83	22 43	23 33
NAV % Mrk Pr	162 18	89 65	65 48	81 75
Effec Tax Rate	48 00	47 64	46 75	37 46
Def Interval	1 93	1 98	1 55	0 09
Sus Grth Rate	8 95	13 13	16 99	14 27

SUBSIDIARY & ASSOCIATED COMPANIES

AUTOQUIP (CAPE) (PTY) LTD
AUTOQUIP (NATAL) (PTY) LTD
AUTOQUIP (PTY) LTD
AUTOQUIP (VAAL) (PTY) LTD
PART CONCEPTS (PTY) LTD
PARTQUIP (PTY) LTD
TECHNIQUIP (PTY) LTD

INVESTMENTS

None

AVF GROUP LTD

ABBREVIATION : AVF GRP

JSE SHORT CODE : AVF

SECTOR : Financial-Insurance

SHAREHOLDERS

Who Owns Whom's Assessment of the Identity of the Ultimate Controlling Shareholder: ANGLOVAAL LTD

SHAREHOLDER	PERCENTAGE 1992	1991
ANGLOVAAL LTD	57 5	57 0
VMB NOM P/L	14 0	13 2
UAL NOM P/L	5 5	
UBS INSURANCE CO LTD	5 2	7 1
STD BANK NOM TVL P/L	4 8	---
FOX STREET NOM P/L	1 9	2 5
SA MUTUAL	1 8	---
EIGHTY ONE MAIN STREET NOM LTD	1 5	---
AUTOMOBILE ASSOC OF SA	---	8 1
MEK INV P/L	---	2 2
BOARD OF EXECUTORS NOM P/L	---	1 1
ADBREST P/L	---	4 1
TOTAL	92 3	95 2

DIRECTORS :
BARBER DD ,BROWN JJ ,DE BEER DD ,ELLIOTT PJ
GORDON EGD ,KING ME ,MENELL CS (Chairman)
VLOK DJJ

REGISTRATION NUMBER : 01/01705/06

REGISTERED OFFICE
Anglovaal House, 56 Main Street
Johannesburg
2001
TEL 011-634 9111
FAX 011-634 0038

TRANSFER SECRETARY
Anglovaal Ltd
P O Box 62379, Marshalltown
2107
TEL 011-634 9111

COMPANY SECRETARY
Anglovaal Limited

NATURE OF BUSINESS
An investment holding company Subsidiaries transact life assurance & pensions business Other activities include funds investment, finance, leasing, property investment, and portfolio management AVF has a controlling interest in quoted Anglovaal Insurance Holdings

BANKERS :
Volkskas Ltd

AUDITORS :
Coopers Theron Du Toit

FAMILIAR BRAND NAMES
N/A

CONTRIBUTION BY ACTIVITY
N/A

YEAR END : June

DIVIDEND :15/01/92 and 15/07/91

NUMBER OF EMPLOYEES : 689

CAPITAL STRUCTURE

	AUTHORISED	ISSUED
Ords 0,01c	160000000	129293589

FINANCIAL STATISTICS (AT FINANCIAL YEAR END)

(Amts in R'000)	1992 Jun	1991 Jun	1990 Apr
Ord S/H Int	33583	71695	59368
Long Trm Loans	665115	411068	234956
Iss Ord Share	129294	98697	71866
Total Liab	720106	481396	259521

Current Liab	54991	70328	24565
Total Assets	753689	553091	318889
Current Assets	186549	112005	65702
Debtors	63359	68555	25783
Oper Profit	-89603	-32998	6654
Interest Paid	779	415	-
Tax Paid	546	170	185
Prf af Int&Tax	-90928	-33583	6469
Prf att Ord Sh	-80433	-30488	6155
Btm Line Earn	-80433	-16909	18632
Dividend Paid	-	7043	18530
Mkt Prce(c) YE	135	208	240
Depreciation	6892	6674	530

PER SHARE STATISTICS (CENTS)

Net Asst Val	25 97	72 64	82 61
Net Earnings	-74 10	-	8 60
Dividends	-	9 80	365 90
Cash Flow	-72 69	-25 00	8 59

RATIOS AND OTHER INFORMATION

Mrk Cap(R000)	174547	205290	172478
Current Ratio	3 39	1 59	2 67
Quik/Acid Tst	3 39	1 59	2 67
Debt/Ass Rat	0 09	0 15	0 08
L T L Tot Ass	0 02	0 02	-
Debt to Eqity	2 00	1 12	0 41
Interest Cover	-115 02	-79 51	-
Ret on Assets	-11 17	-4 78	1 93
Ret on Equity%	-239 51	-36 45	9 57
Price/Earnings	-1 82	-	27 91
Divid Cover	-	-	0 02
Divid Yield	-	4 71	152 46
Earning Yield%	-54 89		3 58
NAV % Mrk Pr	19 24	34 92	34 42
Effec Tax Rate	-0 60	-0 51	2 78
Def Interval	-0 16	0 33	-
Sus Grth Rate	-239 51	-52 35	20 84

SUBSIDIARY & ASSOCIATED COMPANIES

AA LIFE ASSURANCE ASSOCIATION LTD
ANGLOVAAL INSURANCE HOLDINGS LTD
CRUSADER LIFE ASSURANCE CORP LTD

INVESTMENTS

None

B.A.T. ZIMBABWE LTD

ABBREVIATION : BAT

SECTOR : Zimbabwe Stock Exchange

SHAREHOLDERS

Who Owns Whom's Assessment of the Identity of the Ultimate Controlling Shareholder:
BRITISH AMERICAN TOBACCO CO

DIRECTORS :
BELL IA (Financial Director)
BENNISON RE (Dir Public Affairs),HARTLEY RS
MSWAKA TE ,NDHLUKULA AR (Personnel Director)
NYEREYEGONA C ,SADZA AW ,VAN HEERDEN JJ (Chairman)

REGISTERED OFFICE
4 - 12 Paisley Road, Southerton
Harare, Zimbabwe

TEL 735883
FAX 702516

TRANSFER SECRETARY
N/A

COMPANY SECRETARY
R B Marsh

NATURE OF BUSINESS
Zimbabwean-incorporated company involved in the manufacture and distribution of tobacco products

BANKERS :
N/A

AUDITORS :
Deloitte & Touche

FAMILIAR BRAND NAMES
N/A

CONTRIBUTION BY ACTIVITY
N/A

YEAR END : December

DIVIDEND : Ords Z$0,50

Dividend	(Ldr)13/03/92	(Pay)01/04/92	Amt(c)11 43
Dividend	(Ldr)14/08/92	(Pay)01/09/92	Amt(c)18 23

CAPITAL STRUCTURE

	AUTHORISED	ISSUED
Ords Z$0,50	16200000	16200000

FINANCIAL STATISTICS (AT FINANCIAL YEAR END)

(Amts in Z$)	1991 Dec	1990 Dec
Ord S/H Int	92806	33982
Long Trm Loans	-	305
Iss Ord Share	16200	15000
Total Liab	19053	10238
Current Liab	19053	9933
Total Assets	111859	44220
Current Assets	37367	23870
Debtors	7089	4594
Inventory	16456	14126
Turnover	83991	62135
Oper Profit	14147	6143
Interest Paid	44	18
Tax Paid	6236	1975
Prf af Int&Tax	8396	4520
Prf att Ord Sh	8396	4520
Btm Line Earn	8396	4978
Dividend Paid	2557	1040
Depreciation	1014	824

PER SHARE STATISTICS (CENTS)

Net Asst Val	572 88	226 55
Net Earnings	51 83	27 90
Dividends	16 13	6 93
Cash Flow	56 20	37 66

RATIOS AND OTHER INFORMATION

Current Ratio	1 96	2 40
Quik/Acid Tst	1 10	0 98

A/C Rec T/ovr	11 85	13 53
Tot Ass T/ovr	0 75	1 41
Debt/Ass Rat	0 17	0 22
Debt to Eqity	0 21	0 29
Interest Cover	321 52	341 28
Oper Prof Mrg	16 84	9 89
Net Prof Marg%	10 00	7 27
Ret on Assets	13 12	14 73
Ret on Equity%	9 05	13 30
Divid Cover	3 21	4 03
Effec Tax Rate	44 70	24 96
Def Interval	0 01	0 08
Sus Grth Rate	6 29	10 24

SUBSIDIARY & ASSOCIATED COMPANIES

None

INVESTMENTS

None

BARCLAYS BANK OF ZIMBABWE LTD

ABBREVIATION : BBZIM

SECTOR : Zimbabwe Stock Exchange

SHAREHOLDERS

Who Owns Whom's Assessment of the Identity of the Ultimate Controlling Shareholder:
BARCLAYS BANK PLC

DIRECTORS :
CARTER JD (Chairman),CHAMBATI AM ,ESCOTT RAG
KIRKMAN KD (Deputy Chairman),KOHLER PH
LANDER RP ,LEWIS DJ ,MUPAWOSE RM Dr
TAKAWIRA IG (Managing Director),WHICKER JHC
ZAMCHIYA DM

REGISTERED OFFICE
Barclay House, Corner First Street
Jason Moyo Avenue, Harare

TEL 729811
FAX 707293

TRANSFER SECRETARY
N/A

COMPANY SECRETARY
M Jones

NATURE OF BUSINESS
The overall holding company of BARCLAYS BANK OF ZIMBABWE is BARCLAYS PLC BARCLAYS BANK OF ZIMBABWE carries out commercial and merchant banking activities through its branches at main centres in Zimbabwe

BANKERS :
Barclays Bank of Zimbabwe Ltd

AUDITORS :
Deloitte & Touche

FAMILIAR BRAND NAMES
N/A

CONTRIBUTION BY ACTIVITY
N/A

YEAR END : December

DIVIDEND : Ords Z$0,50

Dividend	(Ldr)02/03/92	(Pay)27/03/92	Amt(c)10
Dividend	(Ldr)14/08/92	(Pay)27/08/92	Amt(c)5

CAPITAL STRUCTURE

	AUTHORISED	ISSUED
Ords Z$0,50	200000000	131127144

FINANCIAL STATISTICS (AT FINANCIAL YEAR END)

(Amts in Z$)	1991 Dec	1990 Dec
Ord S/H Int	164359	101336
Iss Ord Share	130356	130356
Total Liab	1733923	1233420
Current Liab	1733923	1233420
Total Assets	1898282	1334756
Current Assets	1849872	1291719
Debtors	1305825	685813
Oper Profit	49497	30402
Tax Paid	22664	13526
Prf af Int&Tax	26833	16876
Prf att Ord Sh	26833	16876
Btm Line Earn	26833	16876
Dividend Paid	13113	4134
Depreciation	4557	2301

PER SHARE STATISTICS (CENTS)

Net Asst Val	126 08	77 74
Net Earnings	23 90	18 30
Dividends	10 10	3 20
Cash Flow	24 08	14 71

RATIOS AND OTHER INFORMATION

Current Ratio	1 07	1 05
Quik/Acid Tst	1 07	1 05
Debt/Ass Rat	0 91	0 92
Debt to Eqity	10 55	12 17
Ret on Assets	2 61	2 28
Ret on Equity%	16 33	16 65
Divid Cover	2 37	5 72
Effec Tax Rate	45 79	44 49
Def Interval	54 10	63 41
Sus Grth Rate	8 35	12 57

SUBSIDIARY & ASSOCIATED COMPANIES

None

INVESTMENTS

None

BARCLAYS BANK OF BOTSWANA LTD

ABBREVIATION : BB BOT

SECTOR : Botswana Stock Exchange

SHAREHOLDERS

Who Owns Whom's Assessment of the Identity of the Ultimate Controlling Shareholder:
BARCLAYS BANK ENGLAND

SHAREHOLDER	PERCENTAGE 1992	1991
BARCLAYS BANK PLC	74 9	---
DEBSWANA PENS FUND	3 2	- -
IGI BOTSWANA LIFE ASSURE LTD	1 3	---
TOTAL	79 3	---

DIRECTORS :
BRINK PF ,CAMPBELL AC
CLARK E (Chairman & Managing Dir)
MANNATHOKO RN ,MATENGE GW ,TEBAPE JJ
TEVERSHAM MS (Deputy Managing Director

REGISTERED OFFICE
Barclays House, Khama Crescent
Gabarone, Botswana

TEL 354021
FAX 313672

TRANSFER SECRETARY
N/A

COMPANY SECRETARY
Deloitte Pim Goldby Management Services

NATURE OF BUSINESS
The group provides all sorts of banking services

BANKERS :
Barclays Bank of Botswana Ltd

AUDITORS :
Deloitte Pim Goldby

FAMILIAR BRAND NAMES
N/A

CONTRIBUTION BY ACTIVITY
N/A

YEAR END : December

CAPITAL STRUCTURE

	AUTHORISED	ISSUED
Ords P0,25	80000000	34086450

FINANCIAL STATISTICS (AT FINANCIAL YEAR END)

(Amts in P)	1991 Dec	1990 Dec
Ord S/H Int	82342	51818
Iss Ord Share	34086	32800
Total Liab	843439	664261
Current Liab	843439	664261
Total Assets	925781	716079
Current Assets	838943	644940
Oper Profit	32862	19941
Tax Paid	13126	7400
Prf af Int&Tax	19736	12541
Prf att Ord Sh	19736	12541
Btm Line Earn	19736	12541
Dividend Paid	8380	5576
Depreciation	3529	2219

PER SHARE STATISTICS (CENTS)

Net Asst Val	241 57	157 98
Net Earnings	59 97	38 20
Dividends	25 00	17 00
Cash Flow	68 25	45 00

RATIOS AND OTHER INFORMATION

Current Ratio	0 99	0 97
Quik/Acid Tst	0 99	0 97
Debt/Ass Rat	0 91	0 93
Debt to Eqity	10 24	12 82
Ret on Assets	3 55	2 78
Ret on Equity%	23 97	24 20
Divid Cover	2 40	2 25
Effec Tax Rate	39 94	38 11
Def Interval	0 57	0 89
Sus Grth Rate	13 79	13 44

SUBSIDIARY & ASSOCIATED COMPANIES

INSURANCE BROKERS BOTSWANA (PTY) LTD (22,5%)

INVESTMENTS

None

BARLOW RAND LTD

ABBREVIATION : BARLOWS

JSE SHORT CODE : BAR

SECTOR : Industrial-Industrial Holding

SHAREHOLDERS

Who Owns Whom's Assessment of the Identity of the Ultimate Controlling Shareholder:
SA MUTUAL

SHAREHOLDER	PERCENTAGE 1992	1991
SA MUTUAL	22 2	22 3
CAPITAL SECURITIES LTD	10 4	10 3
CMB NOM P/L	8 3	--
STD BANK NOM TVL P/L	8 3	8 2
SOUTHERN LIFE ASSOC LTD	3 6	4 3
EIGHTY ONE MAIN STREET NOM LTD	3 1	2 3
LIBERTY LIFE ASSOC OF AFRICA LTD	2 4	2 4
FIRST NAT NOM P/L	2 0	2 3
ASHTREE INV P/L	1 9	1 9
MOMENTUM LIFE ASSURE LTD	1 9	1 8

ENGINEERING INDUSTRIES PENS FUND	1 9	1 6
METAL IND GROUP PENS FUND	1 7	1 5
UK BRANCH REGISTER CONTROL ACCOUNT	1 2	1 4
FERMAIN NOM LTD	1 2	1 2
SIXTY SIX MARSHALL STREET NOM P/L	1 1	-
ESCOM PENS & PROV FUND	1 1	1 1
SANLAM	---	2 2
SANKERN E/B	---	4 9
TOTAL	72 3	69 5

DIRECTORS :
BULTERMAN GH (Deputy Chairman)
CHAMBERS RKJ (Dir Human Resources)
CLEWLOW WAM (Chairman)
CONNELLAN BP (Dir Packaging & Textile)
COOPER DE (Vice Chairman & M D),CURTIS T
GOMERSALL JE (Dir Cement & Lime),GOSS RJ
GROENEWEG EM (Financial Director)
HALL JC (Dir Mining & Mining Benef),LEVETT MJ
MANSELL-JONES RM (Dir J Bibby (UK)),MAREE JB DR
MOTSUENYANE SM DR,PARKER CC (Dir Industry)
SEALEY AA (Dir Mining),STEYN JH HON,TAGER L PROF
WILLIAMS RA (Dir Food & Pharmaceutical)
WOLPERT C (Dir Food

REGISTRATION NUMBER : 02/00095/06

REGISTERED OFFICE
Barlow Park, Katherine Street
Sandton
2146
TEL 011-801 9111
FAX 011-444 3643

TRANSFER SECRETARY
Rand Registrars Ltd
P O Box 82549, Southdale
2135
TEL 011-835 1016

COMPANY SECRETARY
K A Bagg

NATURE OF BUSINESS
An industrial holding company with controlling interests in quoted Reunert, Pretoria Portland Cement,Barlow Rand Properties,CG Smith & Rand Mines The group has interest in mining,mineral beneficiation, manufacturing, distribution, food, pharmaceuticals & property Operations are both national & international

BANKERS :
Standard Bank of SA Ltd

AUDITORS :
Deloitte Pim Goldby

FAMILIAR BRAND NAMES
ADVANCE,AEROLAK,AGA PIPES,AGRIGRADER
AIROMATIC,ALMEX TRADING
ALRODE COMPONENT MANUFACTURERS
ARMSTRONG FORD,AUTO ATLANTIC,BAR REACH
BARAIR,BARCEP,BARKRANE
BARLAND INDUSTRIAL EQUIPMENT,BARLOADER
BARLOW HANDLING,BARMOT SUPPORT SERVICES
BARMOT TRUCK HIRE,BARONS,BARTON,BARTONS
BLAIKIE-JOHNSTONE,BLOEMFONTEIN BEARING WORKS
BP JONES,BRL FLEET & RENTAL,BRL LEASING
BROLLO AFRICA,BROSEC,BROWELD,CATERPILLAR
CIRCLE FREIGHT INTERNATIONAL
CITY ABRASIVE & PAINT,CLARK COMPONENTS
CLUB MOTORS,COPON,CROWN (PAINT),DELTA CITY
ELECTROCOL,ELECTROLUX,ELECTROSTAR,EROICA
EXTRAM AFRICA,EXTRAM EUROPE,EXTRAM HONG KONG
EXTRAM INTERNATIONAL,EXTRAM KOREA
EXTRAM PACIFIC,EXTRAM SINGAPORE
EXTRAM TAIWAN,EXTRAM THAILAND
FEDERATED-BLAIKIE,FLYMO,FRIGIDAIRE,FROMM
FT BUILDING SUPPLIES,FT PLUMBING SUPPLIES
FUCHSWARE,G E HUDSON,GARDEN CITY MOTORS
GEAR RATIO ENGINEERING,GOLDSTAR,GRADEMASTER
GRATE,HARDWARE DISTRIBUTORS
HITACHI(NAIL EQUIPMENT),HOTZ-HER,HYSTER
ISANDO TIMBERS,JIA-IN,JOHN PALMER STEEL
JOHN WILLIAMS MOTORS,KELVINATOR,KNIGHT
LAMEAKER PLUMBING SUPPLIES,LEONARD
LIFESTYLE 2000,LIFESTYLE INTERNATIONAL
MABSTRONG TRADING,MALUTI EQUIPMENT,MANITOU
MARAMA,MARSH,MARTEX INVESTMENTS
MCA COMMUNITA,MEIWA,MICATEX,MODU OPT
MONOLOCK,MONOPIPE,MOTAPARTZ,NAMTRAC
NARROW AISLE,NASHUA,NASHUA
NATAL MOTOR INDUSTRIES,NATIONAL
NATIONAL PANASONIC,NEWTEC,NORDSEN
ORGAPAK BORBE WANNER,PANASONIC
PANASONIC BUSINESS SYSTEMS
PARTHENON PAINTS (LESOTHO),PETERS PAPERS
PILOT,PLASCON,PLASCON INKS,PLASCON PAINTS
PLUMBING DISTRIBUTORS SA,POLYCELL
POLYCELL PRODUCTS SOUTH AFRICA,POLYFILLA
PRECAST CONCRETE INDUSTRIES,QUADRISECTION
RAND REGISTRARS,RICOH,RIH INTERNATIONAL
ROBOR COASTAL,ROBOR INDUSTRIAL,ROBOR METALS
RODERICK NISSAN,ROLLAX,SANDTON TOYOTA,SAUVEN
SCOTSMAN,SHERWOOD,SONNEX - DULUX PAINTS
SONNEX - SCHUSTERS,SONNEX - SESCO
SONNEX APPLIANCES,SONNEX INVESTMENTS,SPICERS
SPIES HECKER,STANDOX,STRAPEX,STRONG ARM
SUPRA TOYOTA,TECHNICS,TEXAS INSTRUMENTS
THESENS,TITAN UMREIFUNGSTECHNIK,UNIGRADER
UNIPLY,UNIVERSAL (GRADER),VESTEL
W F JOHNSTONE,WALL AND ALL,WARDKISS HOMECARE
WESTERN PROVINCE HARDWARE,WHOLESALE PLUMBING
WOODLYTE,WRIGHT,WRIGHTECH

CONTRIBUTION BY ACTIVITY
Industry (29 0%)
Packaging & Textiles (15 0%)
Food & Pharmaceuticals (35 0%)
International (9 0%)
Fin Services,Property & Group Admin (1 0%)
Mining & Mineral Beneficiation (% Sales) (11 0%)

YEAR END : September

DIVIDEND : Ords 10c

Interim No 121	(Ldr)21/05/90	(Pay)13/07/90	Amt(c)51
Final No 122	(Ldr)07/12/90	(Pay)11/01/91	Amt(c)119
Interim No 123	(Ldr)07/06/91	(Pay)15/07/91	Amt(c)51
Final No 124	(Ldr)06/11/91	(Pay)13/01/92	Amt(c)119
Interim No 125	(Ldr)05/06/92	(Pay)13/07/92	Amt(c)54
Final No 126	(Ldr)27/11/92	(Pay)11/01/93	Amt(c)119

NUMBER OF EMPLOYEES : 186745

CAPITAL STRUCTURE

	AUTHORISED	ISSUED
Ords 10c	212500000	195401157
6% Cum Prefs R2	500000	375000

FINANCIAL STATISTICS (AT FINANCIAL YEAR END)

(Amts in R'000)	1991 Sep	1990 Sep	1989 Sep	1988 Sep	1987 Sep
Ord S/H Int	4107000	3873000	3413000	2777600	2319300

Long Trm Loans	7201000	7589000	6251000	5503000	4826300
Iss Ord Share	190160	185465	184699	183413	181446
Total Liab	14943000	14281000	12560000	10814900	8573500
Current Liab	7742000	6692000	6309000	5311900	3747200
Total Assets	19050000	18154000	15973000	13592500	10892800
Current Assets	10697000	8960000	8337000	7523500	5774900
Debtors	5538000	3994000	3592000	3181500	2432500
Inventory	4317000	4257000	4047000	3241100	2346100
Turnover	31994000	29119000	26432000	21178800	16530400
Oper Profit	2569000	2471000	2703000	2022600	1418400
Interest Paid	674000	586000	452000	302800	241300
Tax Paid	643000	666000	837000	640100	420800
Prf af Int&Tax	1549000	1529000	1714000	1300600	926400
Prf att Ord Sh	806000	855000	1001000	742100	535400
Btm Line Earn	373000	740000	916000	603700	504800
Dividend Paid	322000	316000	314000	237700	181500
Mkt Prce(c) YE	4825	3000	4250	2300	2825
Depreciation	787000	672000	548400	472300	399100

PER SHARE STATISTICS (CENTS)

Net Asst Val	2159 76	2088 26	1847 87	1514 40	1278 23
Net Earnings	430 90	462 40	543 80	408 20	297 30
Dividends	170 00	170 00	170 00	130 00	100 00
Cash Flow	828 49	817 44	847 33	668 63	510 69

RATIOS AND OTHER INFORMATION

Mrk Cap(R000)	9175220	5563950	7849708	4218499	5125850
Current Ratio	1 38	1 34	1 32	1 42	1 54
Quik/Acid Tst	0 82	0 70	0 68	0 81	0 92
A/C Rec T/ovr	5 78	7 29	7 36	6 66	6 80
Tot Ass T/ovr	1 68	1 60	1 65	1 56	1 52
Debt/Ass Rat	0 53	0 52	0 52	0 53	0 50
L T L Tot Ass	0 12	0 15	0 13	0 14	0 15
Debt to Eqity	2 46	2 42	2 45	2 59	2 34
Interest Cover	3 91	4 35	6 25	7 01	6 26
Oper Prof Mrg	8 03	8 49	10 23	9 55	8 58
Net Prof Marg%	2 52	2 94	3 79	3 50	3 24
Ret on Assets	15 34	15 55	18 86	16 68	14 81
Ret on Equity%	19 63	22 08	29 33	26 72	23 08
Price/Earnings	11 20	6 49	7 82	5 63	9 50
Divid Cover	2 53	2 72	3 20	3 14	2 97
Divid Yield	3 52	5 67	4 00	5 65	3 54
Earning Yield%	8 93	15 41	12 80	17 75	10 52
NAV % Mrk Pr	44 76	69 61	43 48	65 84	45 25
Effec Tax Rate	29 98	30 23	33 50	33 27	32 46
Def Interval	2 82	2 75	2 19	2 45	2 62
Sus Grth Rate	11 78	13 92	20 13	18 16	15 26

SUBSIDIARY & ASSOCIATED COMPANIES

A BLAIKIE & CO LTD
A BLAIKIE & CO LTD
AEI HENLEY AFRICA (PTY) LTD
AFCAB HOLDINGS (PTY) LTD (39%)
AFRICAN CABLES LTD (26%)
ALUMINIUM EXTRUSION CO (PTY) LTD
ASERMA MANUFACTURING (PTY) LTD
ATC (PTY) LTD (22%)
B & D EDUCATION SYSTEMS (PTY) LTD
BARCOM ELECTRONICS (PTY) LTD
BARLOW HANDLING (PTY) LTD
BARLOW MOTOR INVESTMENTS LTD
BARLOW MOTOR INVESTMENTS LTD
BARLOW RAND COMPUTER SERVICES (PTY) LTD
BARLOW RAND PROPERTIES LTD
BARLOWS (CAPE) LTD
BARLOWS (OFS) LTD
BARLOWS CENTRAL FINANCE CORPORATION LTD
BARLOWS ENGINE CO (PTY) LTD
BARLOWS MANUFACTURING CO LTD
BARLOWS MINING HOLDINGS & ESTATES LTD
BARLOWS SHIPPING SERVICES (PTY) LTD
BARLOWS TRACTOR CO (PTY) LTD
BELON INDUSTRIES (PTY) LTD
BERG RIVER TEXTILES (PTY) LTD (36%)
BLAJOHN (PTY) LTD
CG SMITH LTD
CIRCLE FREIGHT INTERNATIONAL SA (PTY) LT
CIRCUIT BREAKER INDUSTRIES LTD
CONSOLIDATED CITRUS CONTAINERS (PTY) LTD (38%)
COOPER & DE BEER (PTY) LTD
CORNER HOUSE INVESTMENT CO LTD, THE
DUVHA OPENCAST SERVICES (PTY) LTD
ERMETEK (PTY) LTD
ESD (PTY) LTD
FEDERATED TIMBERS (PIETERMARITZBURG) (PT
FEDERATED TIMBERS LTD
FEDERATED BLAIKIE LTD
FELT INDUSTRIES (PTY) LTD (36%)
FELTEX LTD (36%)
FILTAFLO (PTY) LTD (36%)
FIRSTPIPE (PTY) LTD
FIRSTSTEEL (PTY) LTD
FIRSTTUBE (PTY) LTD
FUCHS ELECTRONICS (PTY) LTD
GE HUDSON (PTY) LTD
GEC ALSTHOM SOUTH AFRICA (PTY) LTD (39%)
GEC SOUTH AFRICA (PTY) LTD (39%)
GOLDEN LAY FARMS LTD (26%)
HEINEMANN HOLDINGS LTD
INFORMATION SERVICES GROUP LTD (30%)
INFORMATION SYSTEM MANAGEMENT (PTY) LTD (30%)
J BIBBY & SONS PLC (UK)
KHULANI BUILDING SUPPLIES (PTY) LTD
KING FOOD CORPORATION (PTY) LTD (26%)
KOHLER SACKS LTD (33%)
LOGISTICS & SYSTEMS SUPPORT CO (PTY) LT
LOGOS PHARMACEUTICALS (PTY) LTD (26%)
MABSTRONG TRADING (PTY) LTD
MARICO FLUORSPAR (PTY) LTD
MEADOW FEED MILLS LTD (26%)
METAL BOX (SOUTH AFRICA) LIMITED (38%)
MIDDELBURG STEEL & ALLOYS HOLDINGS (PTY)
MILLSEL CHROME MINES (PTY) LTD
NAMPAK LTD (38%)
NAMPAK PAPER LTD (38%)
NAMPAK PRODUCTS LTD (38%)
NASHUA LTD
OMC ENGINEERING (PTY) LTD
PAK PROJECTS (PTY) LTD (38%)
PERSETEL (PTY) LTD (30%)
PERSEUS COMPUTER SYSTEMS (PTY) LTD (30%)
PLASCON (PTY) LTD
PLASCON INKS & PACKAGING COATINGS (PTY)
POLYCELL PRODUCTS SOUTH AFRICA (PTY) LTD
PPC LIME LTD
PRETORIA PORTLAND CEMENT CO LTD
PRETORIA PORTLAND CEMENT CO LTD
PRINTPAK LTD (27%)
RADUE WEIR HOLDINGS LTD (26%)
RAND MINES (MINING & SERVICES) LTD
RAND MINES LTD
RAND MINES MILLING & MINING CO LTD
RAND MINES PROPERTIES LTD
RAND REGISTRARS LTD
RCP GROUP (PTY) LTD (30%)
REUNERT LTD
REUNERT TECHNOLOGY SYSTEMS (PTY) LTD
ROBOR INDUSTRIAL HOLDINGS LTD
ROMATEX LTD (36%)
S A SUGAR DISTRIBUTORS (PTY) LTD (31%)
SACO SYSTEMS (PTY) LTD
SANDOCK AUSTRAL LTD
SANTHOLD INVESTMENTS LTD (36%)
SONNEX INVESTMENTS (PTY) LTD
STAR FOODS (PTY) LTD (26%)

TASTIC RICE CORP LTD (26%)
TECHNOLOGY SYSTEMS DISTRIBUTION (PTY) LT (30%)
TECHNOLOGY SYSTEMS MANUFACTURING (PTY) L (30%)
TECHNOLOGY SYSTEMS SOFTWARE (PTY) LTD (30%)
TELEPHONE MANUFACTURERS OF SOUTH AFRICA
TELKOR (PTY) LTD
TELKOR BUSINESS SYSTEMS (PTY) LTD
THESEN & CO. (PTY) LTD
THOS BARLOW & SONS (NATAL) LTD
TIGER FOODS LTD (26%)
TIGER MILLING & FEEDS LTD (26%)
TIGER OATS LTD (26%)
TRANSVAAL GOLD MINING ESTATES LTD
TS HOLDINGS (PTY) LTD (50%)
UNIPLY (PTY) LTD
VANSA VANADIUM SA LTD (37%)
VELDSPUN (PTY) LTD (36%)
W.G. BROWN INVESTMENTS LTD (26%)
WF JOHNSTONE & CO LTD
WINTERVELD CHROME MINES LTD (37%)
WITBANK COLLIERY LTD
WRIGHTECH (PTY) LTD

INVESTMENTS

ADCOCK INGRAM LTD (19%)
ADCOCK INGRAM PHARMACEUTICALS LTD (19%)
ALLIED LYONS PLC (272266S)
ASH RESOURCES (PTY) LTD (50S)
BARBROOK MINES LTD (59993648S)
BARPLATS MINES LTD (93784388)
BARPLATS MINES LTD CON DEBS (5705552SH)
BETRAM (PTY) LTD (4900S)
BLUE CONTINENT PRODUCTS (PTY) LTD (18%)
BLYVOORUITZICHT GOLD MINING CO LTD (1172228S)
BROWN DAVIS & MCCORQUODALE (PTY) LTD (19%)
BROWN DAVIS & MCCORQUODALE SECURIT PRINT (19%)
CACTUS (PTY) LTD (PREFS) (1774290S)
CALGENE INC (142825S)
CAPE INVESTMENT BANK LTD (504900S)
DURBAN CONFECTIONERY WORKS (PTY) LTD (19%)
DURBAN ROODEPOORT DEEP LTD (351923S)
E.J. ADCOCK LTD (19%)
EAST RAND GOLD & URANIUM CO (80000S)
EAST RAND PROPRIETARY MINES LTD (4907680S)
EAST RAND PROPRIETARY MINES LTD (PREFS) (350000S)
FRENCH BANK OF SOUTHERN AFRICA LTD (10%)
FURMANITE INTERNATIONAL LTD (6% PREFS) (937500S)
HARMONY GOLD MINING CO LTD (3736151S)
IMPALA PLATINUM HOLDINGS LTD (267800S)
INTERNATIONAL PAINT SA (PTY) LTD (9800S)
KINROSS GOLD MINING CO LTD (500S)
LANGEBERG HOLDINGS LTD (13%)
MEMIX (PTY) LTD (19%)
MICA PLUS LTD (65000S)
MULTI SECURITY TECHNOLOGY (PTY) LTD (19%)
NASIONALE VISSERYE (EDMS) BPK (42S)
NATAL PORTLAND CEMENT CO (PTY) LTD (10000000S)
NATIONAL FOOD HOLDINGS LTD (9406260S)
NBS HOLDINGS LTD (18,7%)
NILE INVESTMENTS (PTY) LTD (PREFS) (300000S)
OCEANA FISHING GROUP LTD (18%)
ORANJERIVIER VISSERYE BPK (3200S)
PAREM ENTERPRISES (PTY) LTD (2000000S)
PESCANOVA SA (675000S)
PREMIER GROUP LTD (131507S)
PRESTRESSED PRECAST BETON (SA) (PTY) LTD (5000000S)
RUSTENBURG PLATINUM HOLDINGS LTD (224800S)
SABAX LTD (19%)
SAPHAR-MED (PTY) LTD (19%)
SCHENECTADY CHEMICALS (SA) (PTY) LTD (17640S)
SLAGMENT LTD (3866667S)
SMALL BUSINESS DEVELOPMENT CORP LTD (2378252S)
SMART CENTRE HOLDINGS LTD (1129523S)
STANDARD ENGINEERING LTD (450000S)
VAAL REEFS EXPLORATION & MINING CO LTD (500S)
WESTERN DEEP LEVELS LTD (500S)
WINKELHAAK MINES LTD (500SH)
ZANDPAN GOLD MINING CO LTD (100000S)

BARLOW RAND PROPERTIES LTD

ABBREVIATION : BARPROP

JSE SHORT CODE : BPR

SECTOR : Financial-Property Loan Stock

SHAREHOLDERS

Who Owns Whom's Assessment of the Identity of the Ultimate Controlling Shareholder: SA MUTUAL VIA BARLOW RAND

SHAREHOLDER	PERCENTAGE 1992	1991
BARLOW RAND LTD	62.2	62.2
BAROB INV P/L	15.9	15.9
MUTUAL & FEDERAL INSURANCE CO LTD	11.2	11.2
BAILEYS NOM P/L	2.2	2.4
STD BANK NOM TVL P/L	1.0	1.1
TOTAL	92.4	92.8

DIRECTORS :
BULTERMAN GH ,BUSS AM
CHAPLIN RE (Technical Director),CLEWLOW WAM
COMBRINK AD ,GROENEWEG EM (Chairman)
MOSES EPM (Managing Director),WATT IDR

REGISTRATION NUMBER : 05/09815/06

REGISTERED OFFICE
Barprop Centre, 8 Gemsbok Lane
Rivonia
2128
TEL: 011-803 7575
FAX: 011-803 7676

TRANSFER SECRETARY
Rand Registrars Ltd
P O Box 82549, Southdale
2135
TEL: 011-835 1016

COMPANY SECRETARY
R G Selbst

NATURE OF BUSINESS
A property holding company with investments in prime industrial and commercial properties. It is actively engaged in the acquisition and development of investment properties in both centralised and decentralised areas, the maintenance of existing developed properties and the leasing of accomodation to financially sound tenants.

BANKERS :
Nedperm Bank Ltd

AUDITORS :
Deloitte Pim Goldby

FAMILIAR BRAND NAMES
N/A

CONTRIBUTION BY ACTIVITY
Industrial (% of total rental income) (50 0%)
Motor Dealerships (20 0%)
Building Material Facilities (14 0%)
Offices & Parking (10 0%)
Distribution (6 0%)

YEAR END : September

DIVIDEND : Ords 10c

Final 72	(Ldr)09/11/90	(Pay)27/11/90	Amt(c)60 194
Interim No 73	(Ldr)10/05/91	(Pay)30/05/91	Amt(c)64 78333
Final No 74	(Ldr)08/11/91	(Pay)29/11/91	Amt(c)65 121
Interim No 75	(Ldr)08/05/92	(Pay)29/05/92	Amt(c)68 839
Final No 76	(Ldr)06/11/92	(Pay)30/11/92	Amt(c)68 952

NUMBER OF EMPLOYEES : 29

CAPITAL STRUCTURE

	AUTHORISED	ISSUED
First Cum Partic Prefs 1c	30000000	0
Def Ord 10c	8925519	8925519
Ords 10c	82960481	76960481

FINANCIAL STATISTICS (AT FINANCIAL YEAR END)

(Amts in R'000)	1992 Sep	1991 Sep	1990 Sep	1989 Sep	1988 Sep
Ord S/H Int	104250	99041	94599	87550	86140
Long Trm Loans	214608	215179	216235	215241	214314
Iss Ord Share	76960	76960	76750	74587	74587
Total Liab	245878	245761	242150	239505	233898
Current Liab	31270	30582	25915	24264	19584
Total Assets	350128	344802	336749	327055	320038
Current Assets	52905	65689	64149	33035	41670
Debtors	791	1785	2863	829	331
Turnover	53590	48882	48531	43998	39191
Oper Profit	47226	42979	43796	39490	35151
Interest Paid	37668	35512	32987	29722	26950
Tax Paid	7304	7940	9558	6799	5560
Prf af Int&Tax	11329	10891	9754	8591	7679
Prf att Ord Sh	11329	10891	9754	8591	7679
Btm Line Earn	14621	13303	15153	8607	7718
Dividend Paid	9412	8861	8104	7197	6526
Mkt Prce(c) YE	150	135	140	115	100
Depreciation	354	285	284	207	133

PER SHARE STATISTICS (CENTS)

Net Asst Val	135 46	128 69	123 26	117 38	115 49
Net Earnings	14 72	14 18	12 96	11 52	10 32
Dividends	12 23	11 53	10 71	9 65	8 75
Cash Flow	14 44	13 31	14 65	13 04	12 48

RATIOS AND OTHER INFORMATION

Mrk Cap(R000)	115440	103896	107450	85775	74587
Current Ratio	1 69	2 15	2 48	1 36	2 13
Quik/Acid Tst	1 69	2 15	2 48	1 36	2 13
A/C Rec T/ovr	67 75	27 38	16 95	53 07	118 40
Tot Ass T/ovr	0 15	0 14	0 14	0 13	0 12
Debt/Ass Rat	0 69	0 70	0 70	0 72	0 72
L T L Tot Ass	0 60	0 61	0 62	0 64	0 66
Debt to Eqity	2 31	2 43	2 49	2 68	2 67
Interest Cover	1 29	1 22	1 33	1 52	1 49
Oper Prof Mrg	88 12	87 92	90 24	89 75	89 69
Net Prof Marg%	21 14	22 28	20 10	19 53	19 59
Ret on Assets	16 08	15 76	15 53	13 79	12 56
Ret on Equity%	10 87	11 00	10 31	9 81	8 91
Price/Earnings	10 19	9 52	10 80	9 98	9 69
Divid Cover	1 20	1 23	1 21	1 19	1 18
Divid Yield	8 15	8 54	7 65	8 39	8 75
Earning Yield%	9 81	10 50	9 26	10 02	10 32
NAV % Mrk Pr	90 31	95 33	88 04	102 07	115 49
Effec Tax Rate	45 54	48 18	44 35	60 32	49 93
Def Interval	20 59	22 28	20 53	21 59	22 63
Sus Grth Rate	1 84	2 05	1 74	1 59	1 34

SUBSIDIARY & ASSOCIATED COMPANIES

BARPROP MANAGEMENT SERVICES (PTY) LTD
ERF 203 RIVONIA (PTY) LTD

INVESTMENTS

None

BARNATO EXPLORATION LTD

ABBREVIATION : BARNEX

JSE SHORT CODE : BNX

SECTOR : Mining Exploration

SHAREHOLDERS

Who Owns Whom's Assessment of the Identity of the Ultimate Controlling Shareholder·
ANGLO VIA JCI

SHAREHOLDER	PERCENTAGE 1992	1991
STD BANK NOM TVL P/L	38 4	39 0
SA MUTUAL	30 4	30 4
ABSA NOM P/L	16 3	
CMB NOM P/L	3 4	
SANDTON NOM LTD	2 7	2 7
LONDON REGISTER ACCOUNT	1 8	1 9
SANLAM		3 4
VOLKSKAS NOM P/L		15 8
TOTAL	93 0	93 0

DIRECTORS :
BRAY VG ,DE VILLIERS JS DR,MAXWELL KW (Chairman)
MCKENNA P ,NAIRN WA ,SCOTT RUSSELL H D

REGISTRATION NUMBER . 88/03756/06

REGISTERED OFFICE
Consolidated Building, Cnr Fox & Harrison Streets
Johannesburg
2001
TEL 011 373 9111
FAX 011 836 6130

TRANSFER SECRETARY
Consolidated Share Registrars Ltd
P O Box 61051, Marshalltown
2107
TEL 011-492 1620

COMPANY SECRETARY
Johannesburg Consolidated Inv Co Ltd

NATURE OF BUSINESS
The funding of the mining exploration activities of Randfontein Estates Gold Mining Co Wits Ltd Barnex is entitled to 80% of the benefits arising from Randfonteins participations

BANKERS :
N/A

AUDITORS :
Deloitte Pim Goldby

FAMILIAR BRAND NAMES
N/A

CONTRIBUTION BY ACTIVITY
N/A

YEAR END : June

DIVIDEND : Ords 1c
Special (Ldr)08/12/89 (Pay)29/12/89 Amt(c)4 15

CAPITAL STRUCTURE

	AUTHORISED	ISSUED
Ords 1c	25000000	24454212

FINANCIAL STATISTICS (AT FINANCIAL YEAR END)

(Amts in R 000)	1992 Jun	1991 Jun	1990 Jun	1989 Jun
Ord S/H Int	79978	80900	78924	77161
Iss Ord Share	24454	24454	24454	24454
Total Liab	288	202	11	21
Current Liab	288	202	11	21
Total Assets	80266	81102	78935	77182
Current Assets	55719	57266	59515	73110
Debtors	10110	6603	3815	4884
Oper Profit	-5959	-3610	-1560	2098
Tax Paid	478	194	-	-
Prf af Int&Tax	-922	1976	2778	2098
Prf att Ord Sh	-922	1976	2778	2098
Btm Line Earn	-922	1976	2778	2098
Dividend Paid	-	-	1015	-
Mkt Prce(c) YE	65	85	325	445

PER SHARE STATISTICS (CENTS)

Net Asst Val	327 05	330 83	322 74	315 54
Net Earnings	-3 80	8 10	11 40	8 60
Dividends	-	-	4 15	-
Cash Flow	-3 77	8 08	11 36	8 58

RATIOS AND OTHER INFORMATION

Mrk Cap(R000)	15895	20786	79476	108820
Current Ratio	193 47	283 50	5410 45	3481 43
Quik/Acid Tst	193 47	283 50	5410 45	3481 43
Debt/Ass Rat	0 00	0 00	0 00	0 00
Debt to Eqity	0 00	0 00	0 00	0 00
Ret on Assets	-0 55	2 68	3 52	2 72
Ret on Equity%	-1 15	2 44	3 52	2 72
Price/Earnings	17 11	10 49	28 51	51 74
Divid Cover		-	2 75	-
Divid Yield	-	-	1 28	-
Earning Yield%	-5 85	9 53	3 51	1 93
NAV % Mrk Pr	503 16	389 21	99 31	70 91
Effec Tax Rate	-9 73	-6 55	-	-
Sus Grth Rate	-1 15	2 44	2 23	2 72

SUBSIDIARY & ASSOCIATED COMPANIES

None

INVESTMENTS

None

BARNETTS GROUP LTD

ABBREVIATION : BARNETS

JSE SHORT CODE : BRT

SECTOR : Industrial-Furniture & Household

SHAREHOLDERS

Who Owns Whom's Assessment of the Identity of the Ultimate Controlling Shareholder: DIRECTORS

SHAREHOLDER	PERCENTAGE 1992	1991
MJBC INV P/L	52 4	52 4
INVESTEC SHARE NOM P/L	17 6	17 6
INVESTEC MERCHANT BANK LTD	10 5	10 5
NEDPERM BANK LTD	7 1	7 1
PILLAY B	1 6	---
BEARE A		1 5
TOTAL	89 2	89 1

DIRECTORS :
LEWKOWSKI MM (Chairman & Managing Dir)
PILLAY B (Deputy Managing Director)
RAUTENBACH GJ ,VAN ZYL D

REGISTRATION NUMBER : 05/06107/06

REGISTERED OFFICE
42 Plein Street, Johannesburg
2001
TEL 011-23 9191
FAX 011 29 8591

TRANSFER SECRETARY
Mercantile Registrars Ltd
P O Box 1053, Johannesburg
2000
TEL 011-333 8181

COMPANY SECRETARY
C Poznanovich

NATURE OF BUSINESS
The main business of the group is the retailing of household furniture, and the financing of consumer credit The group also manufactures and retails synthetic marble products

BANKERS :
Nedperm Bank Ltd

AUDITORS :
Ernst & Young

FAMILIAR BRAND NAMES
ABC FURNISHERS,BARNETTS FURNISHERS

CONTRIBUTION BY ACTIVITY
N/A

YEAR END : June

DIVIDEND : Ords 10c

Final No 5	(Ldr)11/10/91	(Pay)01/11/91	Amt(c)2 5
Final No 6	(Ldr)30/10/92	(Pay)09/11/92	Amt(c)3 5

NUMBER OF EMPLOYEES : 600

CAPITAL STRUCTURE

	AUTHORISED	ISSUED
Ords 10c	18000000	13823560

FINANCIAL STATISTICS (AT FINANCIAL YEAR END)

(Amts in R 000)	1992 Jun	1991 Jun	1990 Jun	1989 Jun	1988 Jun
Ord S/H Int	18664	17337	16465	15212	14121
Long Trm Loans	11923	11293	10092	12578	8502
Iss Ord Share	13824	13524	13524	13000	13000
Total Liab	28258	26334	26373	27089	19646
Current Liab	16335	15041	16281	14511	11144
Total Assets	46922	43671	42838	42301	33767
Current Assets	44491	42059	42232	41220	33179
Debtors	38332	35927	38050	35848	29460
Inventory	5764	3830	4179	5371	3713
Turnover	63587	52174	50038	44533	35134
Oper Profit	3499	4694	5661	4416	5559
Interest Paid	1146	1948	3113	1153	401
Tax Paid	620	873	1487	1684	2542
Prf af Int&Tax	1733	1873	1061	1579	2616
Prf att Ord Sh	1733	1873	1061	1579	2616
Btm Line Earn	1733	1232	1061	1579	1189
Dividend Paid	484	338		488	780
Mkt Prce(c) YE	40	25	30	40	65
Depreciation	620	133	266	298	186

PER SHARE STATISTICS (CENTS)

Net Asst Val	135 01	128 19	121 75	117 02	108 62
Net Earnings	12 50	13 90	9 90	10 10	20 12
Dividends	3 50	2 50		3 75	6 00
Cash Flow	21 39	23 74	17 56	27 39	41 11

RATIOS AND OTHER INFORMATION

Mrk Cap(R000)	5530	3381	4057	5200	8450
Current Ratio	2 72	2 80	2 59	2 84	2 98
Quik/Acid Tst	2 37	2 54	2 34	2 47	2 64
A/C Rec T/ovr	1 66	1 45	1 32	1 24	1 19
Tot Ass T/ovr	1 36	1 19	1 17	1 05	1 04
Debt/Ass Rat	0 39	0 38	0 41	0 47	0 42
L T L Tot Ass	0 04	0 04	0 03	0 13	0 09
Debt to Eqity	0 97	0 97	1 07	1 31	1 00
Interest Cover	3 05	2 41	1 82	3 83	13 86
Oper Prof Mrg	5 50	9 00	11 31	9 92	15 82
Net Prof Marg%	2 73	3 59	2 12	3 55	7 45
Ret on Assets	7 46	10 75	13 21	10 44	16 46
Ret on Equity%	9 29	10 80	6 44	10 38	18 53
Price/Earnings	3 20	1 80	3 03	3 96	3 23
Divid Cover	3 57	5 56		2 69	3 35
Divid Yield	8 75	10 00		9 38	9 23
Earning Yield%	31 25	55 60	33 00	25 25	30 95
NAV % Mrk Pr	337 53	512 78	405 82	292 54	167 11
Effec Tax Rate	0 68	-	-	-	-
Def Interval	1 72	2 20	4 00	2 36	0 70
Sus Grth Rate	6 69	8 85	6 44	7 17	13 00

SUBSIDIARY & ASSOCIATED COMPANIES

ABC FURNISHERS (PTY) LTD
ABC FURNISHERS BOPHUTHATSWANA (PTY) LTD
AJAX FURNISHING (PTY) LTD
BARFIN (PTY) LTD
BARNETT'S (BOTSWANA) (PTY) LTD
BARNETT'S (NATAL) (PTY) LTD
BARNETT'S (PTY) LTD
BARNETT'S (RUSTENBURG) (PTY) LTD
BARNETT'S (SWAZILAND) (PTY) LTD
BARNETT'S (WEST RAND) (PTY) LTD
BARNETT'S FURNITURE HOLDINGS (CAPE) (PTY
BARNETT'S MAFEKING (PTY) LTD
BARNETT'S MIDDELBURG (PTY) LTD
BARNETT'S THE FURNITURE CENTRE (ALBERTON
BARNETT'S THE FURNITURE CENTRE (GERMISTO
BARNETT'S THE FURNITURE CENTRE (LICHTENB
BARNETT'S THE FURNITURE CENTRE (MAITLAND
BARNETT'S THE FURNITURE CENTRE (MALVERN)
BARNETT'S THE FURNITURE CENTRE (PAROW) (
BARNETT'S THE FURNITURE CENTRE (SALT RIV
BARNETT'S THE FURNITURE CENTRE (VILJOENS
BARNETT'S THE FURNITURE CENTRE (VIRGINIA
BARNETT'S THE FURNITURE CENTRE (WELKOM)
BARNETT'S THE FURNITURE CENTRE (WHOLESAL
BARNETT'S THE FURNITURE CENTRE (ZEERUST)
BARNETT'S WITBANK (PTY) LTD
BARTNETT'S (VENDA) (PTY) LTD
BROOKLYN HOUSE FURNISHERS (PTY) LTD
CURRIES EQUIPMENT SALES (PTY) LTD
HACKS GENERAL SERVICES (PTY) LTD
JOUBERTON FURNISHERS (PTY) LTD
NEW ROADWAY FURNISHERS (PTY) LTD
NORMAN KOPELOWITZ (PTY) LTD
STONE ART INDUSTRIES (PTY) LTD
WOODLEY'S FURNISHERS (RUSTENBURG) (PTY)

INVESTMENTS

None

BARPLATS INVESTMENTS LTD

ABBREVIATION : BARPLAT

JSE SHORT CODE : BPL

SECTOR : Metals & Minerals Platinum

SHAREHOLDERS

Who Owns Whom's Assessment of the Identity of the Ultimate Controlling Shareholder·
SANLAM VIA IMPALA PLATINUM/SA MUTUAL VIA

SHAREHOLDER	PERCENTAGE 1992	1991
BARPLATS HOLDINGS P/L	59 8	

RAND MINES LTD	12 2	64 7
LONFIN INV P/L	4 0	---
LOWENCO NOM P/L	3 7	---
STD BANK NOM TVL P/L	2 2	3 0
HANNA R	1 5	---
FIRST NAT NOM P/L	1 1	---
MARSHALL METALLIC CORP SA LTD	---	3 2
VANSA VANADIUM SA LTD	---	14 5
TOTAL	84 5	85 4

DIRECTORS :
KEARNEY SV
MCMAHON JM (Chairman & Managing Dir)
MENNELL MV MS,O'KEEFFE HJ ,STEVENS IG ,TURNER JPS

REGISTRATION NUMBER : 87/04830/06

REGISTERED OFFICE
3rd Floor, Unicorn House
70 Marshall Street, Johannesburg
2001
TEL 011-376 2800
FAX 011-836 5954

TRANSFER SECRETARY
Central Registrars Ltd
P O Box 4844, Johannesburg
2000
TEL 011-331 0051

COMPANY SECRETARY
AM Snashall (Implats Consult & Man Serv (Pty) Ltd)

NATURE OF BUSINESS
Barplats operates as a financial and investment holding company The company's major asset is its controlling interest in Barplats Mines Ltd

BANKERS :
First National Bank of SA Ltd
Standard Bank of SA Ltd

AUDITORS :
Coopers Theron Du Toit

FAMILIAR BRAND NAMES
N/A

CONTRIBUTION BY ACTIVITY
N/A

YEAR END : June

NUMBER OF EMPLOYEES : 30

CAPITAL STRUCTURE

	AUTHORISED	ISSUED
Ords 1c	900000000	48361736
8% Comp Conv Debs R20	9296000	9296000

FINANCIAL STATISTICS (AT FINANCIAL YEAR END)

(Amts in R'000)	1992 Jun	1991 Sep	1990 Sep	1989 Sep	1988 Sep
Ord S/H Int	460724	461706	459887	229891	234992
Long Trm Loans	788763	811647	577730	468761	185920
Iss Ord Share	48362	48362	48362	29142	29142
Total Liab	815399	863812	656885	557436	220155
Current Liab	26636	52165	79155	88675	34235
Total Assets	1276123	1325518	1116772	787327	455147
Current Assets	15313	20521	23342	14564	300428
Debtors	6662	5543	7761	3662	18621
Inventory	7938	10304	15328	8519	-
Oper Profit	-1078	-1675	-449	7075	20173
Interest Paid	-	38	-	-	-
Tax Paid	1	2271	8123	1047	5718
Prf af Int&Tax	-982	1502	7980	6028	14455
Prf att Ord Sh	-982	1482	7153	5707	14455
Btm Line Earn	-982	1482	4483	-5101	14455
Mkt Prce(c) YE	55	105	660	1700	1020

PER SHARE STATISTICS (CENTS)

Net Asst Val	952 66	954 69	950 93	788 86	806 37
Net Earnings	-0 02	3 10	16 00	20 00	49 60
Cash Flow	-2 71	3 06	15 97	19 58	49 60

RATIOS AND OTHER INFORMATION

Mrk Cap(R000)	26599	50780	319189	495414	297248
Current Ratio	0 57	0 39	0 29	0 16	8 78
Quik/Acid Tst	0 28	0 20	0 10	0 07	8 78
Debt/Ass Rat	0 44	0 46	0 37	0 50	0 48
L T L Tot Ass	0 42	0 43	0 30	0 39	0 41
Debt to Eqity	1 23	1 33	0 90	1 73	0 94
Interest Cover	-	100 29	-	-	
Ret on Assets	-0 10	0 29	1 44	0 90	4 43
Ret on Equity%	-0 16	0 18	1 56	2 48	6 15
Price/Earnings	-2750 00	33 87	41 25	85 00	20 56
Earning Yield%	-0 04	2 95	2 42	1 18	4 86
NAV % Mrk Pr	1732 10	909 23	144 08	46 40	79 06
Effec Tax Rate	-0 09	-132 57	-1793 10	14 80	28 34
Def Interval	-487 23	258 27	23 30	24 33	0 06
Sus Grth Rate	0 21	0 32	1 56	2 48	6 15

SUBSIDIARY & ASSOCIATED COMPANIES

BARPLATS MINES LTD

INVESTMENTS

None

BARPLATS MINES LTD

ABBREVIATION : BARMINE

JSE SHORT CODE : BAM

SECTOR : Metals & Minerals-Platinum

SHAREHOLDERS

Who Owns Whom's Assessment of the Identity of the Ultimate Controlling Shareholder: SANLAM / SA MUTUAL VIA BARPLATS INV

SHAREHOLDER	PERCENTAGE 1992	1991
BARPLATS INV LTD	66 0	66 0
SA MUTUAL	12 5	12 6
CMB NOM P/L	5 6	-
STD BANK NOM TVL P/L	1 9	1 9
SOUTHERN LIFE ASSOC LTD	- -	1 4
SANLAM	---	5 5
TOTAL	86 0	87 5

DIRECTORS :

KEARNEY SV
MCMAHON JM (Chairman & Managing Dir)
MENNELL MV MS,O'KEEFFE HJ ,STEVENS IG ,TURNER JPS

REGISTRATION NUMBER : 86/05057/06

REGISTERED OFFICE

3rd Floor, Unicorn House
70 Marshall Street, Johannesburg
2001
TEL 011-376 2800
FAX 011 836 5954

TRANSFER SECRETARY

Central Registrars Ltd
P O Box 4844, Johannesburg
2000
TEL 011 331 0051

COMPANY SECRETARY

AM Snashall (Implats Consult & Man Serv (Pty) Ltd)

NATURE OF BUSINESS

The company is establishing two platinum mines, the Crocodile River Mine near Brits, and the Kennedy's Vale Mine near Steelport, and operates precious and base metals refineries at Brakpan

BANKERS :

Standard Bank of SA Ltd

AUDITORS :

Coopers Theron Du Toit

FAMILIAR BRAND NAMES

N/A

CONTRIBUTION BY ACTIVITY

N/A

YEAR END : June

DIVIDEND :15/00/91

NUMBER OF EMPLOYEES : 30

CAPITAL STRUCTURE

	AUTHORISED	ISSUED
Ords no par value	500000000	169646259
8% Comp Conv Debs 490c	37959184	37959184

FINANCIAL STATISTICS (AT FINANCIAL YEAR END)

(Amts in R'000)	1992 Jun	1991 Sep	1990 Sep	1989 Sep	1988 Sep
Ord S/H Int	707358	707357	702472	397935	217831
Long Trm Loans	575240	599058	334335	308683	1080
Iss Ord Share	169646	169646	168646	99778	60000
Total Liab	601156	648110	443814	421708	83615
Current Liab	25916	49052	109479	113025	82535
Total Assets	1308514	1355467	1146286	819643	301446
Current Assets	14704	17470	19856	13880	89549
Debtors	6053	5528	4291	2978	786
Inventory	7938	10304	15328	8519	
Oper Profit	-1	-3	-		
Tax Paid	1	65	3017	1560	5515
Prf af Int&Tax	1	69	3018	2748	6904
Prf att Ord Sh	1	69	3018	2748	6904
Btm Line Earn	1	69	3018	2748	6904
Mkt Prce(c) YE	23	40	300	700	460

PER SHARE STATISTICS (CENTS)

Net Asst Val	416 96	416 96	416 54	398 82	363 05
Net Earnings	-	-	2 00	3 00	12 00
Cash Flow	0 00	0 04	2 01	2 99	11 97

RATIOS AND OTHER INFORMATION

Mrk Cap(R000)	39019	67858	505938	698446	276000
Current Ratio	0 57	0 36	0 18	0 12	1 08
Quik/Acid Tst	0 26	0 15	0 04	0 05	1 08
Debt/Ass Rat	0 46	0 48	0 39	0 51	0 28
L T L Tot Ass	0 44	0 44	0 29	0 38	0 00
Debt to Eqity	0 85	0 92	0 63	1 06	0 38
Ret on Assets	0 00	0 01	0 53	0 53	4 12
Ret on Equity%	0 00	0 01	0 43	0 69	3 17
Price/Earnings	-	-	150 00	233 33	38 33
Earning Yield%	-	-	0 67	0 43	2 61
NAV % Mrk Pr	1812 87	1042 40	138 85	56 97	78 92
Effec Tax Rate	-100 00	-2166 67	-	50 00	50 00
Def Interval	524197 33	6081 25	68 05	49 39	4 16
Sus Grth Rate	0 00	0 01	0 43	0 69	3 17

SUBSIDIARY & ASSOCIATED COMPANIES

BARPLATS MINES (BOPHUTHATSWANA) LTD
BARPLATS REFINERIES (PTY) LTD
RHODIUM REEFS LTD

INVESTMENTS

None

BASIL READ HOLDINGS LTD

ABBREVIATION : BASREAD

JSE SHORT CODE : BSR

SECTOR : Industrial-Building & Construction

SHAREHOLDERS

Who Owns Whom's Assessment of the Identity of the Ultimate Controlling Shareholder:
DIRECTORS / SA MUTUAL

SHAREHOLDER	PERCENTAGE 1992	1991
NEDBANK NOM LTD	25 9	---
ABSA NOM P/L	6 5	---
BASIL READ HOLDINGS SHARE TRUST	6 1	3 0
ILSE F G INV P/L	3 9	---
WASSUNG D C L	2 5	2 5
DALY A N S	2 2	2 2
MCMILLAN A N	2 2	2 1
SHARESTOCK NOM P/L	2 2	-
JARVIS C C	1 9	1 8
SALZWEDEL H B	1 8	1 7
JOHANSSON B E G	1 6	1 5
JARDINE E E	1 5	1 5
CULLIGAN FAMILY TRUST	1 4	1 7
FIRST NAT NOM P/L	1 1	- -
DORBYL PENS FUND	-	3 4
EIGHTY ONE MAIN STREET NOM LTD		11 8
SA MUTUAL	-	16 5

SANLAM	---	1 5
VOLKSKAS NOM P/L	---	6 3
TOTAL	60 6	57 5

DIRECTORS :
DISON L (Chairman),GERHARD IR
JARVIS CC (Managing Director),LAWRENCE DLJ
WASSUNG DCL ,WHYTE KC

REGISTRATION NUMBER : 84/07758/06

REGISTERED OFFICE
388 Gild Road, Lilianton
Boksburg
1460
TEL 011-826 6631
FAX 011-826 4716

TRANSFER SECRETARY
Central Registrars Ltd
P O Box 4844, Johannesburg
2000
TEL 011-331 0051

COMPANY SECRETARY
S F Verster

NATURE OF BUSINESS
An investment holding company which controls companies active in civil engineering, road and rail construction, building, mining, housing and property development

BANKERS :
Standard Bank of SA Ltd, Absa Bank Ltd

AUDITORS :
Coopers Theron Du Toit

FAMILIAR BRAND NAMES
N/A

CONTRIBUTION BY ACTIVITY
Mining (% of Turnover) (14 9%)
Civil Engineering (47 2%)
Housing (5 9%)
Building (31 4%)
Waste Recycling (0 6%)

YEAR END : June

DIVIDEND :Ords no par value

Interim No 11	(Ldr)16/03/90	(Pay)30/03/90	Amt(c)10
Final No 12	(Ldr)14/09/90	(Pay)26/10/90	Amt(c)20
Interim No 13	(Ldr)22/02/91	(Pay)28/03/91	Amt(c)10

NUMBER OF EMPLOYEES : 6250

CAPITAL STRUCTURE

	AUTHORISED	ISSUED
Ords no par value	20000000	14301090

FINANCIAL STATISTICS (AT FINANCIAL YEAR END)

(Amts in R'000)	1992 Jun	1991 Jun	1990 Jun	1989 Jun	1988 Jun
Ord S/H Int	42922	52429	49410	43391	38686
Long Trm Loans	19388	18702	32847	26160	11757
Iss Ord Share	14301	14301	14301	14301	13500
Total Liab	198704	170278	138052	101595	87876
Current Liab	179316	151576	105205	75435	76119
Total Assets	239924	221161	187462	144986	126562
Intang Assets	1702	1546	*	*	*
Current Assets	163389	132651	140824	95358	83821
Debtors	27838	34595	79785	63185	25050
Inventory	133553	91711	35627	32036	58515
Turnover	460152	508409	413714	329144	290797
Oper Profit	645	12716	26278	18610	13776
Interest Paid	17033	8446	8457	7298	3321
Tax Paid	-1275	1644	6919	1666	-453
Prf af Int&Tax	-8866	6014	13744	12401	10908
Prf att Ord Sh	-9075	6000	13744	12401	10908
Btm Line Earn	-9507	6021	10252	12300	10908
Dividend Paid	-	1339	4102	3157	670
Mkt Prce(c) YE	60	265	230	270	215
Depreciation	9602	10413	8337	7904	7217

PER SHARE STATISTICS (CENTS)

Net Asst Val	288 23	355 80	345 50	303 41	286 56
Net Earnings	-63 50	42 00	96 10	86 70	80 80
Dividends	-	10 00	30 00	25 00	5 00
Cash Flow	3 69	114 77	193 90	153 47	127 30

RATIOS AND OTHER INFORMATION

Mrk Cap(R000)	8581	37898	32892	38613	29025
Current Ratio	0 91	0 88	1 34	1 26	1 10
Quik/Acid Tst	0 17	0 27	1 00	0 84	0 33
A/C Rec T/ovr	16 53	14 70	5 19	5 21	11 61
Tot Ass T/ovr	1 92	2 30	2 21	2 27	2 30
Debt/Ass Rat	0 78	0 71	0 66	0 64	0 69
L T L Tot Ass	0 03	0 02	0 10	0 12	0 09
Debt to Eqity	4 33	2 99	2 51	2 15	2 26
Interest Cover	0 29	1 70	3 11	2 55	4 15
Oper Prof Mrg	0 14	2 50	6 35	5 65	4 74
Net Prof Marg%	-1 97	1 18	3 32	3 77	3 75
Ret on Assets	2 87	7 28	15 53	14 74	10 88
Ret on Equity%	-21 14	11 44	27 82	28 58	28 20
Price/Earnings	-0 94	6 31	2 39	3 11	2 66
Divid Cover	-	4 20	3 20	3 47	16 16
Divid Yield	-	3 77	13 04	9 26	2 33
Earning Yield%	105 83	15 85	41 78	32 11	37 58
NAV % Mrk Pr	480 39	134 26	150 22	112 37	133 29
Effec Tax Rate	14 95	39 84	6 08	0 16	4 66
Def Interval	164 21	3 51	1 18	1 44	2 66
Sus Grth Rate	-21 14	8 89	19 51	21 30	26 46

SUBSIDIARY & ASSOCIATED COMPANIES

BASIL READ (BOPHUTHATSWANA) (PTY) LTD
BASIL READ (PTY) LTD
BASIL READ BOTSWANA (PTY) LTD
BASIL READ CIVIL ENGINEERING (PTY) LTD
BASIL READ FINANCE (PTY) LTD (50%)
BASIL READ HOMES (PTY) LTD
BASIL READ MINING (PTY) LTD
BASIL READ NAMIBIA (PTY) LTD
BASIL READ PROPERTIES (PTY) LTD
BASIL READ SUN HOMES (PTY) LTD
BASIL READ ROCAM TUBULAR TRACK (PTY) LTD
BASRECO PLANT HIRE (PTY) LTD
BELVIDERE ESTATES (PTY) LTD (33 3%)
BORCHARDS PROPERTIES (PTY) LTD
BR SURVEY (PTY) LTD
CLIFFORD HARRIS (BUILDINGS) (PTY) LTD
CLIFFORD HARRIS (PTY) LTD
CLIFFORD HARRIS EAST CAPE (PTY) LTD
CLIFFORD HARRIS PROPERTIES (PTY) LTD
CLIFFORD HARRIS TRANSKEI (PTY) LTD
CLIFFORD HARRIS WEST CAPE (PTY) LTD
D REYNOLDS PLANT SALES (PTY) LTD
GCSC CONSTRUCTION (PTY) LTD
HILMORE INVESTMENTS (PTY) LTD
LESOTHO DEVELOPMENT CONTRACTORS (PTY) LT
REEF RAIL (PTY) LTD

REINFORCED EARTH MINING SERVICES (PTY) L (33,3%)
SIR LOWRY'S PASS DEVELOPMENTS (PTY) LTD
WASTE FLOW (PTY) LTD

INVESTMENTS

ANGLO AMERICAN CORPORATION ZIMBABWE LTD (18%)
FEDSURE HOLDINGS LTD (8200 SH)
GARDEN ROUTE INVESTMENTS (PTY) LTD (2 SH)
INVESTEC LTD (1250 SH)
LIBERTAS CONSOLIDATED HOLDINGS (PTY) LTD (17500 SH)
ROBBERG NOMINEES (PTY) LTD (2 SH)

BASIL STARKE GROUP LTD

ABBREVIATION : BSG

JSE SHORT CODE : BSG

SECTOR : Industrial Building & Construction

SHAREHOLDERS

Who Owns Whom's Assessment of the Identity of the Ultimate Controlling Shareholder:
B E STARKE VIA BSI

SHAREHOLDER	PERCENTAGE 1992	1991
BASIL STARKE INV LTD	86 8	86 8
SHAPIRO C S	1 3	1 3
BAILEY A G	1 1	1 1
STARKE R L	1 1	1 1
TOTAL	90 3	90 3

DIRECTORS :
BRAND JG ,DAVIN FJ ,DUMARESQ DWF
LOMBAARD K (Joint Managing Director)
PHILLIPS M (Managing Director)
REID DFM (Joint Managing Director)
STARKE BE (Executive Chairman

REGISTRATION NUMBER : 06/01829/06

REGISTERED OFFICE
12th Floor, 2 Long Street
Cape Town
8001
TEL 021-419 4330
FAX 021-949 0089

TRANSFER SECRETARY
Fraser Street Registrars (Pty) Ltd
P O Box 61178, Marshalltown
2107
TEL 011-491 0911

COMPANY SECRETARY
R W H Garschagen

NATURE OF BUSINESS
The company operates in two areas Construction-civil engineering, building, shot-blasting, plant hire, & plumbing, Manufacturing - manufacture of automotive parts, general engineering & shop fittings, cement bricks, blocks and allied products

BANKERS :
Standard Bank of SA Ltd
Trust Bank of Africa Ltd
First National Bank of SA Ltd

AUDITORS :
Deloitte Pim Goldby, Valentine Sargeant

FAMILIAR BRAND NAMES
N/A

CONTRIBUTION BY ACTIVITY
Construction (% turnover) (76 1%)
Manufacturing (23 9%)

YEAR END : December

DIVIDEND :15/05/91 and 15/11/91

NUMBER OF EMPLOYEES : 1408

CAPITAL STRUCTURE

	AUTHORISED	ISSUED
Ords no par value	12500000	8792521
10% Cum Red Prefs 1c	5000000	3500000
Var Rate Red Cum Prefs 1c	2500000	0

FINANCIAL STATISTICS (AT FINANCIAL YEAR END)

(Amts in R'000)	1991 Dec	1990 Dec	1989 Dec	1988 Dec	1987 Dec
Ord S/H Int	11950	11928	6686	3830	7704
Long Trm Loans	12126	11702	11974	17448	10640
Iss Ord Share	8793	8793	8793	8793	8793
Total Liab	35409	45597	41131	37374	23562
Current Liab	23283	33895	29157	19926	12922
Total Assets	47359	57525	47817	41204	31266
Current Assets	18713	30530	25755	22839	19538
Debtors	12768	24831	20226	19266	16024
Inventory	5945	5699	5529	3573	3514
Turnover	143907	171199	148351	134707	77146
Oper Profit	4626	7974	7063	-132	3550
Interest Paid	4254	4739	4331	2343	845
Tax Paid	-	-	-573	-	-
Prf af Int&Tax	372	3235	3305	-2474	2706
Prf att Ord Sh	22	2885	2856	-2703	2206
Btm Line Earn	22	2841	2856	-2916	5730
Dividend Paid	-	-	-	352	704
Mkt Prce(c) YE	30	32	40	70	-
Depreciation	4188	4052	3625	2109	1076

PER SHARE STATISTICS (CENTS)

Net Asst Val	135 90	135 65	76 04	43 56	87 62
Net Earnings	0 30	32 80	32 50	-30 70	25 10
Cash Flow	47 88	78 89	73 71	-6 76	37 33

RATIOS AND OTHER INFORMATION

Mrk Cap(R000)	2638	2814	3517	6155	-
Current Ratio	0 80	0 90	0 88	1 15	1 51
Quik/Acid Tst	0 55	0 73	0 69	0 97	1 24
A/C Rec T/ovr	11 27	6 89	7 33	6 99	4 81
Tot Ass T/ovr	3 04	2 98	3 10	3 27	2 47
Debt/Ass Rat	0 67	0 73	0 79	0 78	0 54
L T L Tot Ass	0 18	0 14	0 18	0 29	0 13
Debt to Eqity	2 67	3 53	5 63	8 35	2 21
Interest Cover	1 09	1 68	1 63	-0 06	4 20
Oper Prof Mrg	3 21	4 66	4 76	-0 10	4 60
Net Prof Marg%	0 02	1 69	1 93	-2 01	2 86
Ret on Assets	9 77	13 86	14 77	-0 32	11 36

Ret on Equity%	0 18	24 19	42 72	-70 57	28 63
Price/Earnings	100 00	0 98	1 23	-2 28	-
Earning Yield%	1 00	102 50	81 25	-43 86	-
NAV % Mrk Pr	453 01	423 92	190 09	62 22	-
Effec Tax Rate	-	-	-20 97		
Def Interval	5 48	3 15	3 54	-41 40	4 45
Sus Grth Rate	0 18	24 19	42 72	79 77	19 50

SUBSIDIARY & ASSOCIATED COMPANIES

BASIL STARKE HOLDINGS (PTY) LTD
BASIL STARKE PREMIER MARKETING (PTY) LTD
BASIL STARKE SOMERSET PARK (PTY) LTD
IVYDENE INVESTMENTS (PTY) LTD
PRIME BRICK (PTY) LTD

INVESTMENTS

None

BASIL STARKE INVESTMENTS LTD

ABBREVIATION : BSI

JSE SHORT CODE : BSI

SECTOR : Industrial Building & Construction

SHAREHOLDERS

Who Owns Whom's Assessment of the Identity of the Ultimate Controlling Shareholder:
BASIL STARKE FAMILY HOLDINGS

SHAREHOLDER	PERCENTAGE 1992	1991
BASIL STARKE FAMILY HOLDINGS P/L	56 6	56 6
GLEN C P	5 5	5 5
REID D F M	4 5	4 4
FRADAV TRUST	3 3	3 3
DUMARESQ D W	3 1	
TABLE MOUNTAIN TRUST NOM P/L	2 4	2 4
STARKE B E	2 0	2 0
PATERNOSTER NOM P/L	1 8	1 8
MARSH N	1 8	1 8
BASIL STARKE STAFF SHARE TRUST	1 7	1 7
TOTAL	82 9	79 6

DIRECTORS :
BRAND JG ,DAVIN FJ
PHILLIPS M (Managing Director)
STARKE BE (Chairman

REGISTRATION NUMBER . 06/00650/06

REGISTERED OFFICE
12th Floor, 2 Long Street
Cape Town
8001
TEL 021-419 4330
FAX 021-418 2330

TRANSFER SECRETARY
Fraser Street Registrars (Pty) Ltd
P O Box 61178, Marshalltown
2107
TEL 011-491 0911

COMPANY SECRETARY
R W H Garschagen

NATURE OF BUSINESS
The holding company of JSE-quoted Basil Starke Group Ltd The group is active in construction, building & manufacturing (steel & alloy parts for the motor & general engineering industries, cement bricks & blocks & allied products)

BANKERS :
Standard Bank of SA Ltd
Trust Bank of Africa Ltd
First National Bank of SA Ltd

AUDITORS :
Deloitte Pim Goldby, Valentine Sargeant

FAMILIAR BRAND NAMES
N/A

CONTRIBUTION BY ACTIVITY
Construction (% of turnover) (76 2%)
Manufacturing (23 9%)

YEAR END : December

DIVIDEND :15/05/91 and 15/11/91

NUMBER OF EMPLOYEES : 1408

CAPITAL STRUCTURE

	AUTHORISED	ISSUED
Ords no par value	24464060	17448555
8% Red Cum Prefs R1	965934	0
8,5% Red Cum Prefs R1	2351800	0
8,5% Partly Conv Red Cum Prefs R1	2556598	0
10% Red Cum Prefs R1	2125000	0
11% Red Cum Prefs R1	4732119	0

FINANCIAL STATISTICS (AT FINANCIAL YEAR END)

(Amts in R 000)	1991 Dec	1990 Dec	1989 Dec	1988 Dec	1987 Dec
Ord S/H Int	13387	13283	9084	6630	1747
Long Trm Loans	8718	9062	10238	9020	15676
Iss Ord Share	17449	17449	17449	17449	3171
Total Liab	34166	44899	43973	37353	33288
Current Liab	25448	35837	33735	28333	17612
Total Assets	47553	58182	53057	43983	35035
Current Assets	18788	31078	29511	25429	22917
Debtors	12843	25379	21765	19623	16872
Inventory	5945	5699	7746	5795	5745
Turnover	143999	171300	151656	136863	77298
Oper Profit	4630	7894	7664	393	3662
Interest Paid	4523	5043	5009	2736	958
Tax Paid			573		
Prf af Int&Tax	107	2852	3229	3126	2705
Prf att Ord Sh	104	2430	2704	3803	1484
Btm Line Earn	104	2566	2454	4389	3802
Dividend Paid					309
Mkt Prce(c) YE	25	22	25	40	
Depreciation	4219	4068	7764	2156	1116

PER SHARE STATISTICS (CENTS)

Net Asst Val	76 72	76 12	52 06	38 00	55 09

Net Earnings	0 60	13 90	15 50	-36 96	24 00
Cash Flow	24 78	37 24	59 99	-15 98	56 18

RATIOS AND OTHER INFORMATION

Mrk Cap(R000)	4362	3839	4362	6980	-
Current Ratio	0 74	0 87	0 87	0 90	1 30
Quik/Acid Tst	0 50	0 71	0 65	0 69	0 98
A/C Rec T/ovr	11 21	6 75	6 97	6 97	6 11
Tot Ass T/ovr	3 03	2 94	2 86	3 11	2 94
Debt/Ass Rat	0 69	0 74	0 81	0 79	0 58
L T L Tot Ass	0 15	0 13	0 18	0 15	0 07
Debt to Eqity	2 43	3 26	4 74	5 27	11 57
Interest Cover	1 02	1 57	1 53	-0 14	3 82
Oper Prof Mrg	3 22	4 61	5 05	-0 29	4 74
Net Prof Marg%	0 07	1 42	1 78	-2 78	1 92
Ret on Assets	9 74	13 57	14 45	-0 89	13 94
Ret on Equity%	0 78	18 29	29 77	-57 36	113 26
Price/Earnings	41 67	1 58	1 61	-1 08	-
Earning Yield%	2 40	63 18	62 00	-92 40	-
NAV % Mrk Pr	306 88	346 02	208 24	94 99	-
Effec Tax Rate	-	-	-21 58	-	-
Def Interval	4 65	2 99	2 31	-15 50	10 19
Sus Grth Rate	0 78	18 29	29 77	-57 36	67 26

SUBSIDIARY & ASSOCIATED COMPANIES

BASIL STARKE GROUP LTD

INVESTMENTS

FILATI LTD (100000 SH)

BEARING MAN LTD

ABBREVIATION : BEARMAN

JSE SHORT CODE : BRM

SECTOR : Industrial-Retailers & Wholesalers

SHAREHOLDERS

Who Owns Whom's Assessment of the Identity of the Ultimate Controlling Shareholder: ANGLOVAAL VIA STEELMETALS

SHAREHOLDER	PERCENTAGE 1992	1991
AVENG P/L	51 0	---
SMK NOM P/L	20 0	45 9
L M TRUST	12 0	22 4
SHERRELL R E	8 1	8 1
ABSA NOM P/L	1 6	--
TILL G	1 5	2 9
TILL G J		1 3
FIRST NAT NOM P/L	-	1 1
NEWVEST INV P/L	- -	2 0
VOLKSKAS NOM P/L	- -	3 0
TOTAL	94 2	86 6

DIRECTORS :
BEKKER A ,DEAN T
FORDHAM WEA (Financial Director),GARETY CF
JOHNSTON GD ,KADAR IM ,MOSELEY BL ,READ KL
ROBBERTZE JC ,ROYSTON D (Chairman),SHERRELL RE
TENNANT MJJ ,TILL GJ (Managing Director),TILL LM

REGISTRATION NUMBER : 55/02109/06

REGISTERED OFFICE
Bearing Man House, 105 West Street
Durban
4001
TEL 031-368 3492
FAX 031-328 300

TRANSFER SECRETARY
Central Registrars Ltd
P O Box 4844, Johannesburg
2000
TEL 011-331 0051

COMPANY SECRETARY
M J J Tennant

NATURE OF BUSINESS
The group's principal trading activity is the distribution of a comprehensive range of ball & roller bearings, power transmission products, seals and related products through 28 branches situated in the major industrial areas of SA.
The company services the industrial and mining replacement market, as well as being a supplier to selected original equipment manufacturer

BANKERS :
First National Bank of SA Ltd, Senbank
Trust Bank of Africa Ltd

AUDITORS :
Price Waterhouse Meyernel

FAMILIAR BRAND NAMES
IKO,NACHI,NSK

CONTRIBUTION BY ACTIVITY
N/A

YEAR END : June

DIVIDEND : Ords no par value

Final No 4	(Ldr)20/04/90	(Pay)04/05/90	Amt(c)25
Interim No 5	(Ldr)12/10/90	(Pay)26/10/90	Amt(c)15
Final No 6	(Ldr)12/04/91	(Pay)26/04/91	Amt(c)15
Interim No 7	(Ldr)04/10/91	(Pay)18/10/91	Amt(c)15
Final No 8	(Ldr)14/08/92	(Pay)28/08/92	Amt(c)15

NUMBER OF EMPLOYEES : 458

CAPITAL STRUCTURE

	AUTHORISED	ISSUED
Ords no par value	78620394	9361366

FINANCIAL STATISTICS (AT FINANCIAL YEAR END)

(Amts in R'000)	1992 Jun	1991 Feb	1990 Feb	1989 Feb	1988 Feb
Ord S/H Int	42855	21735	18891	14051	10427
Long Trm Loans	13941	6462	3975	1693	4400
Iss Ord Share	9361	4912	4912	4912	4712
Total Liab	55933	41505	44341	25661	18541
Current Liab	41992	35043	40366	23968	14141
Total Assets	98788	63240	63232	39712	28968
Current Assets	84060	48553	49943	33140	25101
Debtors	28434	15779	17230	12641	10050
Inventory	55626	32774	32713	20499	14988
Turnover	158160	95981	86438	51957	41742
Oper Profit	18479	16178	16430	9110	7406

Interest Paid	6140	6753	3273	1451	1169
Tax Paid	5578	4764	6483	3715	61
Prf af Int&Tax	6761	4661	6674	3944	6176
Prf att Ord Sh	6761	4661	6496	3855	6176
Btm Line Earn	5051	4318	6048	3855	5599
Dividend Paid	3808	1474	1965	982	-
Mkt Prce(c) YE	450	300	460	280	45
Depreciation	3627	2630	1701	724	477

PER SHARE STATISTICS (CENTS)

Net Asst Val	457 80	442 49	384 59	286 05	221 29
Net Earnings	91 00	95 00	132 00	80 00	131 00
Dividends	63 00	30 00	40 00	20 00	-
Cash Flow	100 58	153 52	170 87	94 95	141 19

RATIOS AND OTHER INFORMATION

Mrk Cap(R000)	42125	14736	22595	13754	2120
Current Ratio	2 00	1 39	1 24	1 38	1 78
Quik/Acid Tst	0 68	0 45	0 43	0 53	0 72
A/C Rec T/ovr	4 17	6 08	5 02	4 11	4 15
Tot Ass T/ovr	1 20	1 52	1 37	1 31	1 44
Debt/Ass Rat	0 57	0 65	0 70	0 65	0 64
L T L Tot Ass	0 14	0 10	0 06	0 04	0 15
Debt to Eqity	1 31	1 89	2 34	1 83	1 78
Interest Cover	3 01	2 40	5 02	6 28	6 34
Oper Prof Mrg	11 68	16 86	19 01	17 53	17 74
Net Prof Marg%	4 27	4 86	7 52	7 42	14 80
Ret on Assets	14 03	25 58	25 98	22 94	25 57
Ret on Equity%	11 83	21 44	34 39	27 44	59 23
Price/Earnings	4 95	3 16	3 48	3 50	0 34
Divid Cover	1 44	3 17	3 30	4 00	-
Divid Yield	14 00	10 00	8 70	7 14	-
Earning Yield%	20 22	31 67	28 70	28 57	291 11
NAV % Mrk Pr	101 73	147 50	83 61	102 16	491 75
Effec Tax Rate	47 92	47 09	46 73	48 64	0 98
Def Interval	1 61	3 53	3 18	2 40	1 65
Sus Grth Rate	6 89	14 66	23 98	20 45	59 23

SUBSIDIARY & ASSOCIATED COMPANIES

AFRICA BEARING CENTRE (PTY) LTD
AUTOMOTIVE BEARING SUPPLIES (PTY) LTD
BEARING MAN (SWAZILAND) (PTY) LTD
BEARING MAN (TRANSKEI) (PTY) LTD
BEARING MAN HOUSE (PTY) LTD
BRODERICK HALLITE (PTY) LTD
CENTRAL BEARINGS (PTY) LTD
DORR TRADING COMPANY (PTY) LTD
H SOLARSH & CO (PTY) LTD
IKO NEEDLE ROLLER BEARINGS (PTY) LTD
IRLES (PTY) LTD
SEALCO (PTY) LTD
TRANS WORLD BEARINGS (PTY) LTD

INVESTMENTS

None

BEATRIX MINES LTD

ABBREVIATION : BEATRIX

JSE SHORT CODE : BET

SECTOR : Gold-OFS

SHAREHOLDERS

Who Owns Whom's Assessment of the Identity of the Ultimate Controlling Shareholder:
GENCOR

SHAREHOLDER	PERCENTAGE 1992	1991
CONSOLIDATED NOM P/L	63 3	63 3
CMB NOM P/L	9 0	---
ABSA NOM P/L	5 1	---
STD BANK NOM TVL P/L	4 4	4 2
FIRST NAT NOM P/L	1 8	1 9
INDO-CHINA NOM P/L	1 7	1 3
NEDBANK NOM LTD	1 6	1 6
FERMAIN NOM LTD	1 5	1 5
RESIDENT NOM LTD	1 5	1 5
SA MUTUAL	1 4	1 6
DIDO NOM LTD	1 3	1 3
SANLAM	---	8 4
VOLKSKAS NOM P/L	---	5 0
TOTAL	92 5	91 4

DIRECTORS :
BOTHA AD ,ELLIS SP ,EUSTACE PJ
MAUDE G (Chairman),OLIVIER JE ,RADEMEYER P DE V
ROBINSON PDK

REGISTRATION NUMBER : 77/02138/06

REGISTERED OFFICE
General Mining Building, 6 Hollard Street
Johannesburg
2001
TEL 011-376 9111
FAX 011-836 6130

TRANSFER SECRETARY
Central Registrars Ltd
P O Box 4844, Johannesburg
2000
TEL 011-331 0051

COMPANY SECRETARY
General Mining Metals & Minerals Ltd

NATURE OF BUSINESS
The company owns all the cum pref shares issued by Buffelsfontein GM Co Ltd as part consideration for Buffels' acquisition of the Beatrix mine The pref shr's entitle the company, as holder, to dividends equal to 84% of the annual distributable profits derived by Buffels from certain operations at the Beatrix mine, after certain expenses In addition the company owns the mineral rights to the Beatrix mine's mining lease area and receives royalties from the exploitation thereof

BANKERS :
Nedperm Bank Ltd

AUDITORS :
Price Waterhouse Meyernel

FAMILIAR BRAND NAMES
N/A

CONTRIBUTION BY ACTIVITY
Royalties (% Turnover) (66 4%)
Dividends (27 8%)
Interest (5 8%)

YEAR END : August

DIVIDEND : Ords no par value

Interim No 9	(Ldr)16/03/90	(Pay)27/04/90	Amt(c)50
Final No 10	(Ldr)14/09/90	(Pay)12/10/90	Amt(c)48
Interim No 11	(Ldr)15/03/91	(Pay)26/04/91	Amt(c)39
Final No 12	(Ldr)13/09/91	(Pay)25/10/91	Amt(c)31
Interim No 13	(Ldr)13/03/92	(Pay)24/04/92	Amt(c)35
Final No 14	(Ldr)11/09/92	(Pay)23/10/92	Amt(c)35

NUMBER OF EMPLOYEES : 8339

CAPITAL STRUCTURE

	AUTHORISED	ISSUED
Ords no par value	150000000	85000000

FINANCIAL STATISTICS (AT FINANCIAL YEAR END)

(Amts in R'000)	1991 Aug	1990 Aug	1989 Aug	1988 Aug	1987
Ord S/H Int	132981	132895	133851	142181	136390
Long Trm Loans	-	-	-	24571	113257
Iss Ord Share	85000	85000	85000	85000	85000
Total Liab	26991	45198	57918	58442	178137
Current Liab	26991	45198	57918	33871	64880
Total Assets	159972	178093	191769	200623	353641
Current Assets	29132	47264	62001	55071	103994
Debtors	10005	10465	13375	11987	-
Inventory	-	-	-	-	103994
Turnover	91678	118382	111824	64702	99851
Oper Profit	60237	62887	60313	58839	98935
Interest Paid	1	83	-	-	12051
Tax Paid	31479	35302	32952	21598	28143
Prf af Int&Tax	59586	82344	76670	37241	58723
Prf att Ord Sh	59586	82344	76670	37241	58723
Btm Line Earn	59586	82344	76670	37241	58723
Dividend Paid	59500	83300	85000	31450	57800
Mkt Prce(c) YE	1700	2300	1875	1250	2500

PER SHARE STATISTICS (CENTS)

Net Asst Val	156 45	156 35	157 47	167 27	160 46
Net Earnings	70 00	97 00	90 00	44 00	
Dividends	70 00	98 00	100 00	37 00	-
Cash Flow	70 10	96 88	90 20	43 81	69 09

RATIOS AND OTHER INFORMATION

Mrk Cap(R000)	1445000	1955000	1593750	1062500	2125000
Current Ratio	1 08	1 05	1 07	1 63	1 60
Quik/Acid Tst	1 08	1 05	1 07	1 63	-
A/C Rec T/ovr	9 16	11 31	8 36	5 40	-
Tot Ass T/ovr	0 57	0 66	0 58	0 32	0 28
Debt/Ass Rat	0 17	0 25	0 30	0 29	0 50
L T L Tot Ass	-	-	-	0 12	0 32
Debt to Eqity	0 20	0 34	0 43	0 41	1 31
Interest Cover	85737 00	1323 94	-		8 21
Oper Prof Mrg	65 70	53 12	53 94	90 94	99 08
Net Prof Marg%	64 99	69 56	68 56	57 56	58 81
Ret on Assets	56 93	66 11	57 16	29 33	27 97
Ret on Equity%	44 81	61 96	57 28	26 19	43 06
Price/Earnings	24 29	23 71	20 83	28 41	-
Divid Cover	1 00	0 99	0 90	1 19	
Divid Yield	4 12	4 26	5 33	2 96	-
Earning Yield%	4 12	4 22	4 80	3 52	-
NAV % Mrk Pr	9 20	6 80	8 40	13 38	6 42
Effec Tax Rate	48 01	49 97	50 70	36 71	32 39
Def Interval		-	-	1 54	1 93
Sus Grth Rate	0 06	-0 72	-6 22	4 07	0 68

SUBSIDIARY & ASSOCIATED COMPANIES

None

INVESTMENTS

BUFFELSFONTEIN GOLD MINING CO LTD (CUM P (12400158 S)

BENGUELA CONCESSIONS LTD

ABBREVIATION : BENCO

JSE SHORT CODE : BNC

SECTOR : Mining-Exploration

SHAREHOLDERS

Who Owns Whom's Assessment of the Identity of the Ultimate Controlling Shareholder:
SA MUTUAL

SHAREHOLDER	PERCENTAGE 1992	1991
SA MUTUAL	39 1	39 1
LYDENBURG PLATINUM LTD	5 6	5 6
METROPOLITAN LIFE LTD	4 8	-
STD BANK NOM TVL P/L	4 3	3 1
MINERALE DIENSTE BELEGGINGS E/B	3 9	3 9
LYDENBURG EXPLORATION LTD	3 3	3 3
TBA NOM P/L	2 1	2 1
ROBRIAN INV P/L	2 0	2 0
ALLEN R N	1 3	1 3
LEVIN J	1 1	1 1
CMB NOM P/L		4 9
RANDEX LTD	-	3 3
TOTAL	67 4	69 7

DIRECTORS :
BIEBER EPH DR,GURNEY JJ DR (Executive Chairman)
HEYNS G ,LOWENTHAL ND
PHARO AJ (Managing Director)
SMITH HS DR (Managing Director)
WILSON JR (Chief Executive

REGISTRATION NUMBER : 88/03608/06

REGISTERED OFFICE
1st Floor Block A, Technosqaure
42 Morningside, Ndabeni
7405
TEL 021-531 7900
FAX 021-531 0256

TRANSFER SECRETARY
Mercantile Registrars Ltd
P O Box 1053, Johannesburg
2000
TEL 011-333 8181

COMPANY SECRETARY
V L Pregnolato

NATURE OF BUSINESS
A marine diamond exploration company which was incorporated to acquire, explore, develop and exploit sea diamond concessions off the West coast of Southern Africa

BANKERS :
First National Bank of SA Ltd

AUDITORS :
Baker Musikanth

FAMILIAR BRAND NAMES
N/A

CONTRIBUTION BY ACTIVITY
N/A

YEAR END : June

NUMBER OF EMPLOYEES : 230

CAPITAL STRUCTURE

	AUTHORISED	ISSUED
Ords 1c (Linked to Options - 100	70000000	44849000

FINANCIAL STATISTICS (AT FINANCIAL YEAR END)

(Amts in R'000)	1992 Jun	1991 Jun	1990 Jun
Ord S/H Int	42031	45699	41902
Long Trm Loans	7215	3308	1205
Iss Ord Share	44849	44849	15000
Total Liab	10397	6220	3263
Current Liab	3182	2912	2058
Total Assets	14640	18929	16168
Intang Assets	37788	32990	28997
Current Assets	1429	5634	8541
Debtors	785	665	983
Inventory	419	448	347
Turnover	16223	19231	8141
Oper Profit	-2977	6	-690
Interest Paid	583	763	152
Tax Paid	269	78	200
Prf af Int&Tax	-3668	59	1186
Prf att Ord Sh	-3668	59	1186
Btm Line Earn	-3668	59	1186
Mkt Prce(c) YE	32	44	100
Depreciation	1212	694	331

PER SHARE STATISTICS (CENTS)

Net Asst Val	9 46	28 34	86 03
Net Earnings	-8 18	0 10	6 50
Cash Flow	-5 48	1 73	6 19

RATIOS AND OTHER INFORMATION

Mrk Cap(R000)	14352	19734	15000
Current Ratio	0 45	1 93	4 15
Quik/Acid Tst	0 32	1 78	3 98
A/C Rec T/ovr	20 67	28 92	6 21
Tot Ass T/ovr	1 11	1 02	0 38
Debt/Ass Rat	0 71	0 33	0 20
L T L Tot Ass	0 49	0 17	0 07
Debt to Eqity	0 25	0 14	0 08
Interest Cover	-5 11	0 01	2 14
Oper Prof Mrg	-18 35	0 03	-8 48
Net Prof Marg%	-22 61	0 31	14 57
Ret on Assets	19 23	4 75	7 13
Ret on Equity%	-8 73	0 13	2 12
Price/Earnings	-3 91	440 00	15 38
Earning Yield%	-25 56	0 23	6 50
NAV % Mrk Pr	29 56	64 40	86 03
Effec Tax Rate	-	13 87	53 91
Def Interval	-3 31	5 19	0 77
Sus Grth Rate	-8 73	0 13	2 83

SUBSIDIARY & ASSOCIATED COMPANIES

BENGUELA EXPLORATION (PTY) LTD (49%)
BENGUELA MINING CO (PTY) LTD
BENGUELA NAMIBIA (PTY) LTD
CLIFFS DIAMOND VENTURES (PTY) LTD
DAWN DIAMOND CO LTD
DESOL MARINE (PTY) LTD
KRIHAL CHARTERING (PTY) LTD
LIBRAGEM HOLDINGS (PTY) LTD
LIBRAGEM MINING (PTY) LTD
LUDERITZ OCEAN DIAMONDS (PTY) LTD
MARINE WEST (PTY) LTD
MARINE WEST DIAMOND CONCESSION HOLDERS (
SEE-DIAMANTKONSESSIE 2B (EDMS) BPK (49%)
SIX FOURTEEN SEA MINES (PTY) LTD
TERNCOR (PTY) LTD
UFM (PTY) LTD

INVESTMENTS

None

BENONI GOLD HOLDINGS LTD

ABBREVIATION : BENONI

JSE SHORT CODE : BNI

SECTOR : Gold-Rand & others

SHAREHOLDERS

Who Owns Whom's Assessment of the Identity of the Ultimate Controlling Shareholder: CONSOLIDATED MINING VIA SOUTHGO

SHAREHOLDER	PERCENTAGE 1992	1991
SOUTH EAST RAND GOLD HLDGS LTD	63 3	63 3
CONS MINING MANAGEMENT SERVICES LTD	18 1	15 9
EIGHTY ONE MAIN STREET NOM LTD	10 6	4 9
POTCHEFSTROOM GOLD AREAS LTD	---	2 2
SYFRETS NOM LTD	---	4 6
UNIVERSITY OF NATAL	---	1 1
TOTAL	91 9	92 1

DIRECTORS :
BUITENDAG HC (Financial Director),DONALD JC FLOWERDAY RA ,LEE RA (Chairman),LOWENTHAL ND LOWENTHAL RY ,RUBENSTEIN GB ,SCHECHTER M SUDDENS BD ,THOMPSON MW ,TURNER CF

REGISTRATION NUMBER : 77/02304/06

REGISTERED OFFICE
39th Floor, Carlton Centre, Commissioner Street
Johannesburg
2001
TEL 011-331 9181

FAX 011-331 6189

TRANSFER SECRETARY
Mercantile Registrars Ltd
P O Box 1053, Johannesburg
2000
TEL 011-333 8181

COMPANY SECRETARY
Consolidated Mining Management Services Ltd

NATURE OF BUSINESS
Benoni recovers gold & other minerals from sands & slimes dumps in the Benoni area of the East Rand

BANKERS :
Standard Bank of SA Ltd
First National Bank of SA Ltd

AUDITORS :
Charles Orbach & Co

FAMILIAR BRAND NAMES
N/A

CONTRIBUTION BY ACTIVITY
N/A

YEAR END : March

DIVIDEND .Ords 1c
Final No 1 (Ldr)22/05/92 (Pay)29/05/92 Amt(c)1

CAPITAL STRUCTURE

	AUTHORISED	ISSUED
Ords 1c	240000000	179450000

FINANCIAL STATISTICS (AT FINANCIAL YEAR END)

(Amts in R'000)	1992 Mar	1991 Mar	1989 Feb	1989 Dec	1988 Dec
Ord S/H Int	67626	44001	2069	42113	1675
Long Trm Loans	920	1380	1113	-	498
Iss Ord Share	179450	104000	11831	-	11335
Total Liab	9342	27168	9272	405	5944
Current Liab	8422	25788	8159	405	5446
Total Assets	76968	71169	11061	42518	7537
Intang Assets	*	*	280	*	82
Current Assets	3944	3347	9860	16386	7094
Debtors	1981	2856	5183	55	2594
Inventory	631	443	4648	-	4155
Turnover	43975	14399	21950	-	12007
Oper Profit	8023	3269	1208	-	419
Interest Paid	1603	1025	502	-	205
Tax Paid	90	690	332	-	306
Prf af Int&Tax	6457	2009	374	-	92
Prf att Ord Sh	6457	2009	245	-	53
Btm Line Earn	6457	2099	245	-	53
Dividend Paid	1794	-	-	-	-
Mkt Prce(c) YE	15	80	30	-	45
Depreciation	-	-	206	-	81

PER SHARE STATISTICS (CENTS)

Net Asst Val	37 69	42 31	15 12	-	14 05
Net Earnings	4 40	1 90	2 60	-	0 50
Dividends	1 00	-	-	-	-
Cash Flow	4 44	1 55	4 34	-	1 18

RATIOS AND OTHER INFORMATION

Mrk Cap(R000)	26918	83200	3549	-	5101
Current Ratio	0 47	0 13	1 21	40 46	1 30
Quik/Acid Tst	0 39	0 11	0 64	40 46	0 54
A/C Rec T/ovr	22 20	4 03	4 23	-	4 63
Tot Ass T/ovr	0 57	0 16	1 98	-	1 59
Debt/Ass Rat	0 12	0 38	0 79	0 01	0 74
L T L Tot Ass	0 01	0 02	0 05	-	0 02
Debt to Eqity	0 14	0 62	4 20	0 01	3 33
Interest Cover	5 00	3 19	2 41	-	2 04
Oper Prof Mrg	18 24	22 70	5 50	-	3 49
Net Prof Marg%	14 68	13 95	1 12	-	0 44
Ret on Assets	10 59	4 19	10 92	-	5 56
Ret on Equity%	9 55	3 65	11 84	-	3 16
Price/Earnings	3 41	42 11	11 54	-	90 00
Divid Cover	4 40	-	-	-	-
Divid Yield	6 67	-	-	-	-
Earning Yield%	29 33	2 38	8 67	-	1 11
NAV % Mrk Pr	251 23	52 89	50 40	-	31 23
Effec Tax Rate	5 71	25 57	47 03	-	20 56
Def Interval	0 07	3 97	5 47	-	7 06
Sus Grth Rate	6 90	4 57	11 84	-	3 16

SUBSIDIARY & ASSOCIATED COMPANIES

BENONI GOLD MINING CO LTD
TERIKIM LANDGOED (EDMS) BPK

INVESTMENTS

None

BERGERS GROUP LTD

ABBREVIATION : BERGERS

JSE SHORT CODE : BGR

SECTOR : Industrial-Retailers & Wholesalers

SHAREHOLDERS

Who Owns Whom's Assessment of the Identity of the Ultimate Controlling Shareholder: DIRECTORS

SHAREHOLDER	PERCENTAGE 1992	1991
BERGERS HOLDINGS LTD	44 1	43 9
DEVITT R	10 7	10 7
ANGLO AMERICAN GROUP PENS FUND	7 2	7 1
METROPOLITAN LIFE LTD	5 2	5 2
RAYOCT P/L	3 7	3 7
MAUERBERGER H	3 6	3 6
STD BANK NOM TVL P/L	2 5	2 5
LIBERTY LIFE ASSOC OF AFRICA LTD	2 5	2 5
FERBROS NOM P/L	1 8	1 9
JACOBSON MERVYN	1 6	1 6
DERMAN A J	1 5	1 5
TOTAL	84 4	84 1

DIRECTORS :
DEVITT RB ,JACOBSON M (Managing Director)
JOHNSTONE JD ,MAUERBERGER HV (Chairman)
MILLER LN

REGISTRATION NUMBER : 86/04649/06

REGISTERED OFFICE
101 Harrington House, 37 Barrack Street
Cape Town
8001
TEL 021-46 1020
FAX 021-45 4693

TRANSFER SECRETARY
Central Registrars Ltd
P O Box 4844, Johannesburg
2000
TEL 011-331 0051

COMPANY SECRETARY
J G von Molendorff

NATURE OF BUSINESS
The company holds a controlling interest in quoted Bergers Trading Holdings The group is engaged in the ratailing of clothing through 271 outlets

BANKERS :
Nedbank Ltd

AUDITORS :
Ernst & Young

FAMILIAR BRAND NAMES
SEE BERTRAD

CONTRIBUTION BY ACTIVITY
N/A

YEAR END : December

DIVIDEND :Ords 1c

Dividend No 3	(Ldr)20/04/90	(Pay)15/05/90	Amt(c)13
Dividend No 4	(Ldr)10/05/91	(Pay)14/06/91	Amt(c)14 75
Dividend No 5	(Ldr)24/04/92	(Pay)05/06/92	Amt(c)6

NUMBER OF EMPLOYEES : 1400

CAPITAL STRUCTURE

	AUTHORISED	ISSUED
Ords 1c	40000000	20190000

FINANCIAL STATISTICS (AT FINANCIAL YEAR END)

(Amts in R'000)	1991 Dec	1990 Dec	1989 Dec	1988 Dec	1987 Dec
Ord S/H Int	12696	12624	12872	9405	7182
Long Trm Loans	-	-	1401	736	541
Iss Ord Share	20190	20190	20190	20190	20190
Total Liab	4291	3080	30625	19233	15692
Current Liab	4291	3080	29224	18497	15151
Total Assets	16987	15704	43234	28375	22611
Intang Assets	*	*	263	263	263
Current Assets	-	-	34197	22183	19208
Debtors	-	-	3626	2214	1506
Inventory	-	-	24172	12330	11144
Turnover	-	-	83547	62823	44999
Oper Profit	335	-	9693	6845	4329
Interest Paid	-	-	666	430	97
Tax Paid		-	3026	2411	1601
Prf af Int&Tax	1283	2993	6166	4200	2631
Prf att Ord Sh	1283	2993	6092	4141	2609
Btm Line Earn	1283	2993	6092	4141	2609
Dividend Paid	1211	2978	2625	1918	1262
Mkt Prce(c) YE	300	200	135	130	120
Depreciation	4398	3405	1927	1186	843

PER SHARE STATISTICS (CENTS)

Net Asst Val	62 88	62 53	62 45	45 28	34 27
Net Earnings	24 70	34 30	30 20	20 50	12 90
Dividends	6 00	14 75	13 00	9 50	6 25
Cash Flow	28 14	31 69	41 54	26 67	17 46

RATIOS AND OTHER INFORMATION

Mrk Cap(R000)	60570	40380	27257	26247	24228
Current Ratio	-	-	1 17	1 20	1 27
Quik/Acid Tst		-	0 34	0 53	0 53
A/C Rec T/ovr	-	-	23 04	28 38	29 88
Tot Ass T/ovr	-	-	1 93	2 21	1 99
Debt/Ass Rat	0 25	0 20	0 69	0 66	0 68
L T L Tot Ass	-	-	0 01	0 01	0 01
Debt to Eqity	0 34	0 24	2 31	2 00	2 14
Interest Cover	-		14 55	15 92	44 63
Oper Prof Mrg	-	-	11 60	10 90	9 62
Net Prof Marg%	-	-	7 29	6 59	5 80
Ret on Assets	7 55	19 06	22 80	24 81	19 15
Ret on Equity%	10 11	23 71	47 33	44 03	36 33
Price/Earnings	12 15	5 83	4 47	6 34	9 30
Divid Cover	4 12	2 33	2 32	2 16	2 06
Divid Yield	2 00	7 38	9 63	7 31	5 21
Earning Yield%	8 23	17 15	22 37	15 77	10 75
NAV % Mrk Pr	20 96	31 26	46 26	34 83	28 56
Effec Tax Rate	-	-	26 19	35 53	35 80
Def Interval	0 53	0 01	0 55	0 20	0 28
Sus Grth Rate	0 57	0 12	26 93	23 64	18 76

SUBSIDIARY & ASSOCIATED COMPANIES

BERGERS STORE (CISKEI) (PTY) LTD
BERGERS TRADING HOLDINGS LTD

INVESTMENTS

None

BERGERS TRADING HOLDINGS LTD

ABBREVIATION : BERTRAD

JSE SHORT CODE : BTD

SECTOR : Industrial-Retailers & Wholesalers

SHAREHOLDERS

Who Owns Whom's Assessment of the Identity of the Ultimate Controlling Shareholder:
BERGERS GROUP LTD

SHAREHOLDER	PERCENTAGE 1992	1991
BERGERS GROUP LTD	93 3	93 3
STERNBERG F	1 8	1 8
METROPOLITAN LIFE LTD	1 5	1 5
PENNYSHINE FOUNDATION	1 0	1 0
TOTAL	97 5	97 5

DIRECTORS :
DEVITT RB JACOBSON M (Managing Director)
JOHNSTONE JD ,MAUERBERGER HV (Chairman)
STERNBERG F ,WISEMAN TB

REGISTRATION NUMBER : 87/04218/06

REGISTERED OFFICE
101 Harrington House, 37 Barrack Street
Cape Town
8001
TEL 021-461 1020
FAX 021-45 4693

TRANSFER SECRETARY
Central Registrars Ltd
P O Box 4844, Johannesburg
2000
TEL 011-331 0051

COMPANY SECRETARY
J G von Molendorff

NATURE OF BUSINESS
An investment holding company with subsidiaries engaged in the retailing of family and fashion clothing to the B and C income group The group operates out of 271 retail outlets

BANKERS :
Nedbank Ltd

AUDITORS :
Ernst & Young

FAMILIAR BRAND NAMES
BERGERS,BUIRSKIS,CAPRI,DRESSKING,GLAMOUR
HILTON WEINER,JANINES,JONES,LADY J,SPLENDOR
VALMONT

CONTRIBUTION BY ACTIVITY
N/A

YEAR END : December

DIVIDEND .Ords 1c

Dividend No 3	(Ldr)10/05/91	(Pay)14/06/91	Amt(c)3 7
Dividend No 4	(Ldr)24/04/92	(Pay)05/06/92	Amt(c)2

NUMBER OF EMPLOYEES : 1400

CAPITAL STRUCTURE

	AUTHORISED	ISSUED
Ords 1c	100000000	86000000

FINANCIAL STATISTICS (AT FINANCIAL YEAR END)

(Amts in R'000)	1991 Dec	1990 Feb	1990 Dec	1989 Feb	1988
Ord S/H Int	26555	7546	23443	5388	1157
Long Trm Loans	4503	2731	4427	478	3019
Iss Ord Share	86000	9616	86000	7911	6018
Total Liab	68247	11384	53841	5174	5557
Current Liab	63744	8653	49414	4696	2538
Total Assets	86798	12446	69170	6428	7300
Intang Assets	8004	6484	8114	4134	*
Current Assets	68029	11064	53182	5542	3124
Debtors	19827	5675	15099	3186	-
Inventory	45730	5339	35231	2352	3124
Turnover	165128	27584	134261	13443	7612
Oper Profit	11748	1979	13877	1722	695
Interest Paid	5130	762	3345	236	67
Tax Paid	1284	258	3109	611	250
Prf af Int&Tax	5397	992	7505	900	378
Prf att Ord Sh	5307	992	7361	900	378
Btm Line Earn	4832	992	7361	801	378
Dividend Paid	1720	-	3182	277	-
Mkt Prce(c) YE	80	90	40	68	-
Depreciation	4398	133	3405	63	-

PER SHARE STATISTICS (CENTS)

Net Asst Val	21 57	11 04	17 82	15 85	19 23
Net Earnings	6 40	11 00	8 60	11 40	-
Dividends	2 00	-	3 70	3 50	-
Cash Flow	10 63	12 28	14 82	12 23	6 28

RATIOS AND OTHER INFORMATION

Mrk Cap(R000)	68800	8654	34400	5379	-
Current Ratio	1 07	1 28	1 08	1 18	1 23
Quik/Acid Tst	0 35	0 66	0 36	0 68	-
A/C Rec T/ovr	8 33	4 86	10 67	4 22	-
Tot Ass T/ovr	1 90	2 22	2 33	2 09	1 04
Debt/Ass Rat	0 78	0 91	0 76	0 78	0 76
L T L Tot Ass	0 05	0 21	0 05	0 05	0 41
Debt to Eqity	2 55	1 49	2 25	0 94	4 80
Interest Cover	2 30	2 64	4 16	7 40	10 37
Oper Prof Mrg	7 11	7 17	10 33	12 81	9 13
Net Prof Marg%	3 21	3 60	5 48	6 69	4 97
Ret on Assets	13 75	16 17	24 30	27 18	9 52
Ret on Equity%	19 98	13 15	37 68	16 70	32 67
Price/Earnings	12 50	8 18	4 65	5 96	-
Divid Cover	3 20	-	2 32	3 26	-
Divid Yield	2 50	-	9 25	5 15	-
Earning Yield%	8 00	12 22	21 50	16 76	-
NAV % Mrk Pr	26 96	12 27	44 56	23 31	-
Effec Tax Rate	21 79	22 43	29 85	20 93	39 81
Def Interval	2 54	4 92	1 59	2 16	7 99
Sus Grth Rate	13 51	13 15	17 83	11 56	32 67

SUBSIDIARY & ASSOCIATED COMPANIES

BERGERS (BOPHUTHATSWANA) (PTY) LTD
BERGERS (BOTSHABELO) (PTY) LTD (50%)
BERGERS (BOTSWANA) (PTY) LTD
BERGERS (CAPE) (PTY) LTD
BERGERS (LEBOWA) (PTY) LTD (50%)
BERGERS (LESOTHO) (PTY) LTD
BERGERS (NAMIBIA) (PTY) LTD
BERGERS (NQUTU) LTD (49%)
BERGERS (PAARL) (PTY) LTD
BERGERS (QWAQWA) (PTY) LTD (50%)
BERGERS (STERKSPRUIT) (PTY) LTD (50%)
BERGERS (SWAZILAND) (PTY) LTD
BERGERS (UMTATA) (PTY) LTD
BERGERS MANAGEMENT SERVICES (PTY) LTD (T
BERGERS STORES (CISKEI) (PTY) LTD
BERGERS STORES LTD
BERGERS TRADING LTD (MALAWI) (49%)
BUIRSKI'S SHOWROOM (PTY) LTD
CAPITAL RADIO & ELECTRICAL (PTY) LTD
DRESSKING (PTY) LTD
FIRST SA REJECTS (PTY) LTD
HILTON WEINER (CAPE TOWN) (PTY) LTD
HILTON WEINER (CLAREMONT) (PTY) LTD
HILTON WEINER (NATAL) (PTY) LTD
HILTON WEINER (TVL) (PTY) LTD
ITS STORES (BIZANA) (PTY) LTD
ITS STORES (BUTTERWORTH) (PTY) LTD
ITS STORES (ENGCOBO) (PTY) LTD
ITS STORES (IDUTYWA) (PTY) LTD
ITS STORES (LUSIKISIKI) (PTY) LTD
ITS STORES (MOUNT FRERE) (PTY) LTD
ITS STORES (STERKSPRUIT) (PTY) LTD
ITS STORES (UMTATA) (PTY) LTD
ITS STORES (UMZIMKULU) (PTY) LTD
JONES PURCHASING (PTY) LTD
LONGPARK INVESTMENTS LTD (JERSEY)
NURSERY FAYRE (PTY) LTD
STEWART & WALLETT (PTY) LTD

INVESTMENTS

None

BERZACK BROTHERS (HOLDINGS) LTD

ABBREVIATION : BERZACK

JSE SHORT CODE : BZK

SECTOR : Industrial-Engineering

SHAREHOLDERS

Who Owns Whom's Assessment of the Identity of the Ultimate Controlling Shareholder: BERZACK-ILLMAN INV CORP (BIVEC)

SHAREHOLDER	PERCENTAGE 1992	1991
BERZACK ILLMAN INV CORP LTD	50 3	50 3
EIGHTY ONE MAIN STREET NOM LTD	17 9	4 8
STD BANK NOM TVL P/L	10 7	11 9
H BERZACK FAMILY HOLDINGS P/L	2 6	2 7
INVESTEC INV TRUST LTD	1 3	---
FIRST NAT NOM P/L	1 3	---
BERZACK M C	1 2	1 2
BERZACK A	1 2	1 2
HARRYL P/L	1 2	1 2
BERZACK R M	1 1	1 1
INVESTEC NOM P/L	---	1 3
SYFRETS NOM LTD	---	10 1
TOTAL	88 6	85 6

DIRECTORS :
BERZACK A ,BERZACK E ,BERZACK H ,BERZACK HL
BERZACK M ,BERZACK MC (Joint Managing Director)
BERZACK RM ,BERZACK Z ,BORTZ JM
ILLMAN B (Chairman)
ILLMAN SH (Joint Managing Director),MAGID PB

REGISTRATION NUMBER : 51/00020/06

REGISTERED OFFICE
Bivec House, 2 Nugget Street
Johannesburg
2001
TEL 011-337 4130
FAX 011-337 8579

TRANSFER SECRETARY
Mercantile Registrars Ltd
P O Box 1053, Johannesburg
2000
TEL 011-333 8181

COMPANY SECRETARY
P B Magid

NATURE OF BUSINESS
An investment holding company with subsidiaries engaged in the following activities Distribution of machinery, equipment & supplies to the clothing industry, Distribution of labelling equipment and supplies, Confirming & finance, Property ownership Manufacture and distribution of trimmings to the clothing industry, Wholesale & retail distribution of household products The company holds 40% of quoted Voltex

BANKERS :
Nedcor Bank Ltd

AUDITORS :
Papilsky Hurwitz

FAMILIAR BRAND NAMES
HARRISON,SNIER

CONTRIBUTION BY ACTIVITY
N/A

YEAR END : June

DIVIDEND : Ords 2,5c

Final No 79	(Ldr)23/11/90	(Pay)12/12/90	Amt(c)37
Interim No 80	(Ldr)19/04/91	(Pay)03/05/91	Amt(c)18
Final No 81	(Ldr)15/11/91	(Pay)29/11/91	Amt(c)37

DIVIDEND : Ords 5,2c

Interim No 78	(Ldr)29/06/90	(Pay)27/07/90	Amt(c)15

DIVIDEND : Ords 2,5c

Interim No 82	(Ldr)08/05/92	(Pay)22/05/92	Amt(c)15
Final No 83	(Ldr)30/10/92	(Pay)16/11/92	Amt(c)25

CAPITAL STRUCTURE

	AUTHORISED	ISSUED
Ords 2,5c	50000000	26544372

FINANCIAL STATISTICS (AT FINANCIAL YEAR END)

(Amts in R'000)	1992 Jun	1991 Jun	1990 Jun	1989 Jun	1988 Jun
Ord S/H Int	334694	343183	327974	109979	80477
Long Trm Loans	240028	20665	24710	22054	31396
Iss Ord Share	26544	26544	26544	25710	1216
Total Liab	287725	71127	73814	120990	119419
Current Liab	47697	50462	49104	98936	88023
Total Assets	605003	414310	401788	229929	198765
Intang Assets	17416	*	*	1040	1131
Current Assets	110153	79088	72822	172842	146430
Debtors	52504	35142	36623	100746	89933
Inventory	41046	38980	33855	64617	50254
Turnover	108673	100309	108129	470430	344191
Oper Profit	14009	10685	14718	58658	32782
Interest Paid	9684	1479	6347	8098	3925
Tax Paid	3637	4770	2716	18779	11979
Prf af Int&Tax	13799	19692	5655	31781	16878
Prf att Ord Sh	28559	36820	44179	30586	15704
Btm Line Earn	984	29953	230582	30586	15704
Dividend Paid	10618	14599	13331	1614	1889
Mkt Prce(c) YE	700	1025	875	650	5500
Depreciation	1161	971	757	7055	6205

PER SHARE STATISTICS (CENTS)

Net Asst Val	1195 29	1292 88	1235 59	423 72	6525 16
Net Earnings	107 60	138 70	166 40	119 00	1291 30
Dividends	40 00	55 00	52 00	31 50	335 00
Cash Flow	48 34	79 00	24 40	151 09	1860 44

RATIOS AND OTHER INFORMATION

Mrk Cap(R000)	185808	272076	232260	167115	66880
Current Ratio	2 31	1 57	1 48	1 75	1 66
Quik/Acid Tst	1 45	0 79	0 79	1 09	1 09
A/C Rec T/ovr	2 07	2 85	2 95	4 67	3 83

Tot Ass T/ovr	0 18	0 24	0 27	2 05	1 73
Debt/Ass Rat	0 17	0 14	0 15	0 45	0 52
L T L Tot Ass	0 09	0 02	0 03	0 02	0 08
Debt to Eqity	0 31	0 17	0 18	0 93	1 29
Interest Cover	2 02	15 54	2 32	7 24	8 35
Oper Prof Mrg	12 89	10 65	13 61	12 47	9 52
Net Prof Marg%	26 28	36 71	40 86	6 50	4 56
Ret on Assets	7 88	10 24	13 21	25 51	16 49
Ret on Equity%	8 53	10 73	13 47	27 81	19 51
Price/Earnings	6 51	7 39	5 26	5 46	4 26
Divid Cover	2 69	2 52	3 20	3 78	3 85
Divid Yield	5 71	5 37	5 94	4 85	6 09
Earning Yield%	15 37	13 53	19 02	18 31	23 48
NAV % Mrk Pr	170 76	126 13	141 21	65 19	118 64
Effec Tax Rate	28 78	45 54	30 04	16 35	35 81
Def Interval	5 55	1 35	3 16	0 70	1 64
Sus Grth Rate	5 36	6 47	9 41	26 34	17 17

SUBSIDIARY & ASSOCIATED COMPANIES

ALLIED BIAS BINDING MANUFACTURERS & SUPP
ALLIED WOOLLENS (PTY) LTD
BERBRO (PTY) LTD
BERZACK BROTHERS (CAPE) (PTY) LTD
BERZACK BROTHERS (DURBAN) (PTY) LTD
BERZACK BROTHERS (P E) (PTY) LTD
BERZACK BROTHERS (PTY) LTD
BERZACK ILLMAN INVESTMENTS CORPORATION L (50,3%)
BIVEC CONFIRMING (PTY) LTD
BIVEC CONFIRMING (U K.) LTD
BIVEC CONFIRMING (U S A) INC
BLOCH & LEVITAN (PTY) LTD
EASTMAN EXPORT LTD (U K) (50%)
EASTMAN FINANCE LTD (U K.) (50%)
EASTMAN MACHINE CO LTD (U K) (50%)
ELCENTRE GROUP HOLDINGS LTD
MARATHON BUILDING CO HOLDINGS (PTY) LTD
MARSAT PRINTING ENTERPRISES (PTY) LTD
OUTSPAN PROPERTIES (PTY) LTD
PURCHASE CONFIRMING (JERSEY) LTD (50%)
PURCHASE CONFIRMING LTD (U K) (50%)
RADRIS FABRICS (CAPE) (PTY) LTD
RADRIS INVESTMENTS (PTY) LTD
SANLIC HARDWARE HOLDINGS LTD
SATO LABELLING SYSTEMS (PTY) LTD
SEWING MACHINES & HOME APPLIANCES (PTY)
SEWMAC (PTY) LTD (50%)
SKIRTWEAR (PTY) LTD
THORNTREND LTD (50%)
VEVO PLASTICS (PTY) LTD
VOLTEX HOLDINGS LTD (39,8%)

INVESTMENTS

None

BERZACK-ILLMAN INVESTMENT CORPORATION LTD

ABBREVIATION : BIVEC

JSE SHORT CODE : BIV

SECTOR : Industrial-Engineering

SHAREHOLDERS

Who Owns Whom's Assessment of the Identity of the Ultimate Controlling Shareholder:
BERZACK & ILLMAN FAMILIES

SHAREHOLDER	PERCENTAGE 1992	1991
ILLMAN S H	17 6	17 6
BERZACK A	7 8	5 7
STD BANK NOM TVL P/L	6 7	6 7
BERZACK M C	5 6	5 5
BERZACK R M	5 0	4 9
HARRYL P/L	4 9	4 9
SYFRETS NOM LTD	4 8	4 8
ILLMAN B	4 6	4 2
H BERZACK FAMILY HOLDINGS P/L	3 7	3 7
BERZACK M	3 7	3 7
ZACKILL INV P/L	3 4	3 4
STEPHILL P/L	2 2	2 2
ABBOTT D W	2 1	2 1
MARGILLA P/L	2 0	2 0
MAGID M	1 9	1 9
ABSA NOM P/L	1 7	--
BERZACK H	1 4	1 4
AIB NOM LTD	1 4	1 4
BERZACK L	1 3	1 3
BERZACK L TRUST	1 1	1 1
MEINERT J	1 1	-
BERZACK E	1 1	1 1
MEINERT J C	--	1 1
VOLKSKAS NOM P/L	-	1 7
TOTAL	85 1	82 4

DIRECTORS :
BERZACK A ,BERZACK E ,BERZACK H ,BERZACK HL
BERZACK M ,BERZACK MC (Joint Managing Director)
BERZACK RM ,BORTZ JM ,ILLMAN B (Chairman)
ILLMAN SH (Joint Managing Director),MAGID PB

REGISTRATION NUMBER : 69/01167/06

REGISTERED OFFICE
Bivec House, 2 Nugget Street
Johannesburg
2001
TEL 011-337 4130
FAX 011-337 8579

TRANSFER SECRETARY
Mercantile Registrars Ltd
P O Box 1053, Johannesburg
2000
TEL 011-333 8181

COMPANY SECRETARY
P B Magid

NATURE OF BUSINESS
An investment holding company with a controlling interest in quoted Berzack Brothers (Holdings)

BANKERS :
Nedperm Bank Ltd

AUDITORS :
Papilsky Hurwitz

FAMILIAR BRAND NAMES
SINGER

CONTRIBUTION BY ACTIVITY
N/A

YEAR END : June

DIVIDEND : Ords 10c

Interim No 40	(Ldr)29/06/90	(Pay)27/07/90	Amt(c)11
Final No 41	(Ldr)23/11/90	(Pay)12/12/90	Amt(c)26
Interim No 42	(Ldr)19/04/91	(Pay)03/05/91	Amt(c)13
Final No 43	(Ldr)15/11/91	(Pay)29/11/91	Amt(c)26
Interim No 44	(Ldr)08/05/92	(Pay)22/05/92	Amt(c)11
Final No 45	(Ldr)30/10/92	(Pay)16/11/92	Amt(c)17

CAPITAL STRUCTURE

	AUTHORISED	ISSUED
Ords 10c	25000000	19213591

FINANCIAL STATISTICS (AT FINANCIAL YEAR END)

(Amts in R'000)	1992 Jun	1991 Jun	1990 Jun	1989 Jun	1988 Jun
Ord S/H Int	175473	179485	170869	61387	46366
Long Trm Loans	398606	181855	177169	76428	71215
Iss Ord Share	19214	19214	19214	18639	3567
Total Liab	449854	237719	233815	176652	160422
Current Liab	51248	55864	56646	100224	89207
Total Assets	607911	417204	404684	235292	203974
Intang Assets	17416	*	*	2747	2814
Current Assets	110194	79107	72841	172869	146481
Debtors	52537	35160	36641	100773	89962
Inventory	41045	38980	33855	64617	50254
Turnover	108786	100570	108423	470707	344439
Oper Profit	13745	10213	14301	58985	33211
Interest Paid	8800	810	5060	8007	3993
Tax Paid	3963	5160	3172	18973	12157
Prf af Int&Tax	14093	19990	6069	32005	17061
Prf att Ord Sh	14659	18818	22503	15517	8035
Btm Line Earn	-201	16182	116131	15517	8035
Dividend Paid	5380	7493	7021	772	1139
Mkt Prce(c) YE	475	650	630	450	1275
Depreciation	1161	971	757	7056	6206

PER SHARE STATISTICS (CENTS)

Net Asst Val	822 61	934 14	889 29	314 61	1220 97
Net Earnings	76 30	97 90	37 00	171 70	225 30
Dividends	28 00	55 00	37 00	22 00	56 00
Cash Flow	-5 56	15 45	79 10	127 57	419 26

RATIOS AND OTHER INFORMATION

Mrk Cap(R000)	91267	124891	121048	83876	45479
Current Ratio	2 15	1 42	1 29	1 72	1 64
Quik/Acid Tst	1 35	0 72	0 69	1 08	1 08
A/C Rec T/ovr	2 07	2 86	2 96	4 67	3 83
Tot Ass T/ovr	0 18	0 24	0 27	2 00	1 69
Debt/Ass Rat	0 16	0 13	0 14	0 44	0 51
L T L Tot Ass	0 08	0 00	0 00	0 01	0 08
Debt to Eqity	0 57	0 31	0 33	1 69	2 26
Interest Cover	2 19	27 79	2 83	7 37	8 32
Oper Prof Mrg	12 63	10 16	13 19	12 53	9 64
Net Prof Marg%	13 48	18 71	20 75	3 30	2 33
Ret on Assets	7 80	10 17	13 01	25 07	16 28
Ret on Equity%	8 35	10 48	13 17	25 28	17 33
Price/Earnings	6 23	6 64	17 03	2 62	5 66
Divid Cover	2 73	1 78	1 00	7 80	4 02
Divid Yield	5 89	8 46	5 87	4 89	4 39
Earning Yield%	16 06	15 06	5 87	38 16	17 67
NAV % Mrk Pr	173 18	143 71	141 16	69 91	95 76
Effec Tax Rate	29 96	46 14	32 15	16 60	35 98
Def Interval	-59 38	6 38	-0 60	1 13	2 47
Sus Grth Rate	5 29	6 31	9 06	24 02	14 87

SUBSIDIARY & ASSOCIATED COMPANIES

ALLIED PROPERTIES (PTY) LTD
BERDUR PROPERTIES (PTY) LTD
BERZACK BROTHERS (HOLDINGS) LTD (50%)

INVESTMENTS

None

BESTER INVESTMENTS LTD

ABBREVIATION : BESTER

JSE SHORT CODE : BST

SECTOR : Financial-Property

SHAREHOLDERS

Who Owns Whom's Assessment of the Identity of the Ultimate Controlling Shareholder:
BESTER FAMILY

SHAREHOLDER	PERCENTAGE 1992	1991
GRONDKOR P/L	50 0	50 0
BESTER T	20 0	20 0
SESBES P/L	5 0	5 0
GELDKOR P/L	4 6	4 6
BASSON J A	4 2	---
OUDOU P/L	3 4	3 4
BESTER J J	2 6	2 6
VERSPREIDE INV P/L	---	3 6
TOTAL	89 8	89 1

DIRECTORS :
BESTER T (Executive Chairman),EVENWEL JK
LOUWRENS MJ ,VILJOEN AA

REGISTRATION NUMBER : 69/00683/06

REGISTERED OFFICE
530 Moreleta Street, Silverton
0184
TEL 012-86 8111
FAX 012-86 5446

TRANSFER SECRETARY
Central Registrars Ltd
P O Box 4844, Johannesburg
2000
TEL 011-331 0051

COMPANY SECRETARY
Bester Administrative Services (Pty) Ltd

NATURE OF BUSINESS
A controlling investment company whose subsidiaries are active in the following areas the erection of residential, industrial, institutional and commercial buildings, township and sectional title developments, the supply of materials and services to the building industry, the supply of housing to retired persons in terms of the life rights concept

BANKERS :
First National Bank of SA Ltd
Boland Bank Ltd, Standard Bank of SA Ltd
Absa Bank Ltd

AUDITORS :
Ernst & Young, Den Boer & Van Der Laan
Coopers Theron Du Toit

FAMILIAR BRAND NAMES
N/A

CONTRIBUTION BY ACTIVITY
Construction (% of turnover) (81 6%)
Properties (% of turnover) (13 1%)
Industrial (% of turnover) (5 2%)

YEAR END : February

DIVIDEND :15/08/91 and 15/02/91

NUMBER OF EMPLOYEES : 2750

CAPITAL STRUCTURE

	AUTHORISED	ISSUED
Ords 50c	15000000	12000000

FINANCIAL STATISTICS (AT FINANCIAL YEAR END)

(Amts in R'000)	1992 Feb	1991 Feb	1990 Feb	1989 Feb	1988 Feb
Ord S/H Int	8630	43929	54190	55072	53538
Long Trm Loans	2225	5141	32033	49438	60430
Iss Ord Share	12000	12000	12000	12000	12000
Total Liab	168791	201492	235368	223439	249289
Current Liab	166566	196351	203335	174001	188859
Total Assets	177421	245171	289308	278511	302827
Intang Assets	*	250	250	*	*
Current Assets	144667	205824	242182	225353	250023
Debtors	22217	51550	58784	49786	79034
Inventory	119688	151158	181830	174282	169690
Turnover	182030	249775	260556	-	-
Oper Profit	9827	10596	8539	-4137	26812
Interest Paid	26562	28204	-	-	21003
Tax Paid	-	-4778	6882	-2893	-2072
Prf af Int&Tax	35114	-10724	-1314	-1244	7881
Prf att Ord Sh	-35114	-10724	-1314	-1128	8038
Btm Line Earn	35364	-10448	438	2167	8374
Dividend Paid	-	-	-	-	1920
Mkt Prce(c) YE	50	70	180	250	210
Depreciation	2636	3462	4399	3986	3610

PER SHARE STATISTICS (CENTS)

Net Asst Val	71 92	363 99	449 50	458 93	446 15
Net Earnings	-297 40	87 10	-11 00	-9 40	67 00
Dividends		-	-		16 00
Cash Flow	270 65	60 52	25 71	-4 06	111 43

RATIOS AND OTHER INFORMATION

Mrk Cap(R000)	6000	8400	21600	30000	25200
Current Ratio	0 87	1 05	1 19	1 30	1 32
Quik/Acid Tst	0 15	0 28	0 30	0 29	0 43
A/C Rec T/ovr	8 19	4 85	4 43		
Tot Ass T/ovr	1 03	1 02	0 90		
Debt/Ass Rat	0 95	0 82	0 80	0 77	0 78
L T L Tot Ass	0 01	0 02	0 09	0 14	0 16
Debt to Eqity	19 56	4 59	4 26	3 88	4 41
Interest Cover	-0 37	0 38		-	1 28
Oper Prof Mrg	-5 40	4 24	3 28	-	
Net Prof Marg%	19 29	4 29	0 50		
Ret on Assets	-4 82	5 18	-2 83	-1 44	8 91
Ret on Equity%	-406 88	-24 41	-2 42	2 05	15 01
Price/Earnings	-0 17	-0 80	-16 36	26 60	3 13
Divid Cover	-	-	-	-	4 19
Divid Yield	-	-	-	-	7 62
Earning Yield%	-594 80	-124 43	-6 11	-3 76	31 90
NAV % Mrk Pr	143 83	519 99	249 72	183 57	212 45
Effec Tax Rate	-	30 32	81 99	-7 69	3 67
Def Interval	-4 15	-20 15	52 14	-353 25	13 82
Sus Grth Rate	-406 88	-24 41	-2 42	-2 05	11 43

SUBSIDIARY & ASSOCIATED COMPANIES

BESTBEL (EDMS) BPK
BESTBRICK (EDMS) BPK
BESTCONSTRUCTO (EDMS) BPK
BESTER ADMINISTRATIEWE DIENSTE (EDMS) BP
BESTER EIENDOMME (EDMS) BPK
BESTER EIENDOMSONTWIKKELINGSMAATSKAPPY (
BESTER FINANCE (EDMS) BPK (50%)
BESTER HOMES BOPHUTHATSWANA (EDMS) BPK
BESTER VERVOERDIENSTE (EDMS) BPK
BESTER WONINGS (EDMS) BPK
BESTERECTA (EDMS) BPK
BESTERS IVYDALE BELEGGINGS (EDMS) BPK
BESTFAB (EDMS) BPK
BESTFIN (EDMS) BPK
BESTINDUSTRA (EDMS) BPK
BRUMMERIA RENAISSANCE (EDMS) BPK
CONREE PRODUCTS (EDMS) BPK
FERTILIS BELEGGINGS (EDMS) BPK
FRIDAY INVESTMENTS (EDMS) BPK
GLEN VISTA RANAISSANCE (EDMS) BPK
INTYD BELEGGINGS (EDMS) BPK
LOT 5189 JOHANNESBURG (EDMS) BPK
LUTOPI STAALWERKE (EDMS) BPK
MASTER COATINGS (EDMS) BPK
MAZISTALITE (EDMS) BPK
MITCHELLS PLAIN HOUSING SALES (EDMS) BPK
MONTANA RENAISSANCE (EDMS) BPK
PALMS RENAISSANCE (PTY) LTD
PROTOKOL KONSTRUKSIE (EDMS) BPK
RANDPOORT RENAISSANCE (PTY) LTD
SHAWU BELEGGINGS (EDMS) BPK
SILVERTON BUILDERS SUPPLIES (EDMS) BPK
WARMBAD RENAISSANCE (EDMS) BPK
WATWOU BELEGGINGS (EDMS) BPK
WESCULES (EDMS) BPK

INVESTMENTS

None

BEVERAGE & CONSUMER INDUSTRY HOLDINGS LTD

ABBREVIATION : BEVCON

JSE SHORT CODE : BVC

SECTOR : Industrial Beverages & Hotels

SHAREHOLDERS

Who Owns Whom's Assessment of the Identity of the Ultimate Controlling Shareholder:
ANGLO AMERICAN / LIBERTY LIFE

SHAREHOLDER	PERCENTAGE 1992	1991
BEVLIT INV HOLDINGS LTD	27 3	27 3
PREMSAB HOLDINGS LTD	26 3	26 3
STD BANK NOM TVL P/L	20 1	19 9
LIBERTY LIFE ASSOC OF AFRICA LTD	6 8	6 8
DE BEERS HOLDINGS P/L	2 9	2 9
CMB NOM P/L	2 4	---
SOUTHERN LIFE ASSOC LTD	2 3	2 0
EIGHTY ONE MAIN STREET NOM LTD	1 4	---
FIRST NAT NOM P/L	1 4	1 4
SANLAM	---	2 3
TOTAL	90 6	88 7

DIRECTORS :
BRAY VG ,DE VILLIERS HP ,GORDON D ,KAHN JM
MAXWELL KW ,MCALPINE JR ,RETIEF PF (Chairman)
SHER FB ,SUNTER CL

REGISTRATION NUMBER : 63/02648/06

REGISTERED OFFICE
Consolidated Building, Cnr Fox & Harrison Streets
Johannesburg
2001
TEL 011-373 9111
FAX 011-836 6130

TRANSFER SECRETARY
Consolidated Share Registrars Ltd
P O Box 61051, Marshalltown
2107
TEL 011-492 1620

COMPANY SECRETARY
Johannesburg Consolidated Inv Co Ltd

NATURE OF BUSINESS
An investment holding company with a substantial minority interest in JSE-quoted SA Breweries Ltd

BANKERS :
N/A

AUDITORS :
Price Waterhouse Meyernel

FAMILIAR BRAND NAMES
N/A

CONTRIBUTION BY ACTIVITY
N/A

YEAR END : March

DIVIDEND : Ords 1c

Interim No 1	(Ldr)01/12/89	(Pay)29/12/89	Amt(c)32 9
Final No 2	(Ldr)08/06/90	(Pay)06/07/90	Amt(c)100 24
Interim No 3	(Ldr)30/11/90	(Pay)31/12/90	Amt(c)39 54
Final No 4	(Ldr)07/06/91	(Pay)01/07/91	Amt(c)116
Interim No 5	(Ldr)06/12/91	(Pay)31/12/91	Amt(c)43 5
Final No 6	(Ldr)29/05/92	(Pay)02/07/92	Amt(c)127 87
Interim No 7	(Ldr)04/12/92	(Pay)31/12/92	Amt(c)46

CAPITAL STRUCTURE

	AUTHORISED	ISSUED
Ords 1c	100000000	70980284
Var Rate Red Cum Prefs 1c	50000000	0

FINANCIAL STATISTICS (AT FINANCIAL YEAR END)

(Amts in R'000)	1992 Mar	1991 Mar	1990 Mar
Ord S/H Int	1960700	1753400	1562600
Iss Ord Share	70980	70980	70980
Total Liab	90800	82300	71100
Current Liab	90800	82300	71100
Total Assets	2051500	1835700	1633700
Current Assets	90800	82300	71100
Prf af Int&Tax	121600	110400	94500
Prf att Ord Sh	266900	243600	207000
Btm Line Earn	263100	240300	209600
Dividend Paid	121600	110400	94500
Mkt Prce(c) YE	7100	6000	4300

PER SHARE STATISTICS (CENTS)

Net Asst Val	2762 33	2470 27	2201 47
Net Earnings	376 02	343 24	291 60
Dividends	171 37	155 54	133 14
Cash Flow	171 32	155 54	133 14

RATIOS AND OTHER INFORMATION

Mrk Cap(R000)	5039580	4258800	3052140
Current Ratio	1 00	1 00	1 00
Quik/Acid Tst	1 00	1 00	1 00
Debt/Ass Rat	0 04	0 04	0 04
Debt to Eqity	0 05	0 05	0 05
Ret on Assets	13 01	13 27	12 67
Ret on Equity%	13 61	13 89	13 25
Price/Earnings	18 88	17 48	14 75
Divid Cover	2 19	2 21	2 19
Divid Yield	2 41	2 59	3 10
Earning Yield%	5 30	5 72	6 78
NAV % Mrk Pr	38 91	41 17	51 20
Sus Grth Rate	7 41	7 60	7 20

SUBSIDIARY & ASSOCIATED COMPANIES

GEMLIB INVESTMENTS LTD
SOUTH AFRICAN BREWERIES LTD (30 82%)

INVESTMENTS

None

BID CORPORATION LTD

ABBREVIATION : BIDCORP

JSE SHORT CODE : BCR

SECTOR : Industrial-Industrial Holding

SHAREHOLDERS

Who Owns Whom's Assessment of the Identity of the Ultimate Controlling Shareholder: DIRECTORS / MINORITIES

SHAREHOLDER	PERCENTAGE 1992	1991
INVESTEC NOM P/L	20 4	20 4

JOFFE B	17 1	16 9
CHIPKIN M, B R, I A & SHIRES H & LEVENBE	11 0	---
CMB NOM P/L	10 8	---
ELLERINE BROS P/L	6 1	6 1
CHALKTON NOM CO P/L	5 1	5 1
LEONMED INV P/L	4 2	4 2
STD BANK NOM TVL P/L	2 6	---
EIGHTY ONE MAIN STREET NOM LTD	1 8	---
BERMAN A TRUST	1 4	1 4
BERMAN M TRUST	1 4	1 4
SAFEGRO NOM P/L	1 0	1 1
FIRST NAT NOM P/L	- -	1 2
NEDBANK NOM LTD	---	1 1
SAGE LIFE LTD	---	1 5
SANLAM	---	10 8
CHIPKIN M TRUST	---	11 0
TOTAL	82 7	82 0

DIRECTORS :
BEHRMANN AJ MR,BRODIE MH MR
CHIPKIN M MR (Deputy Chairman),DEMETRIADES G MR
ELLERINE E MR,JOFFE B MR (Executive Chairman)
KOSEFF S MR,PAMENSKY JL M

REGISTRATION NUMBER : 65/08182/06

REGISTERED OFFICE
Cnr Kelvin & Bunsen Streets, Industria
Johannesburg
2092
TEL 011-474 1640
FAX 011-474 8413

TRANSFER SECRETARY
Mercantile Registrars Ltd
P O Box 1053, Johannesburg
2000
TEL 011-333 8181

COMPANY SECRETARY
M Goldin

NATURE OF BUSINESS
An investment holding company with a controlling interest in quoted Bidvest Group Group activities include distribution of food & allied products to the catering industry, manufacture & distribution of packaging, stapling, fastening & adhesive tape to the packaging industry, an investment in the formulation, manufacture & marketing of women's skin care products, cosmetics & toiletries

BANKERS :
Nedperm Bank Ltd, Standard Bank of SA Ltd
First National Bank of SA Ltd

AUDITORS :
KPMG Aiken & Peat

FAMILIAR BRAND NAMES
JUSTINE (50%)

CONTRIBUTION BY ACTIVITY
N/A

YEAR END : June

DIVIDEND :Ords 50c

Interim	(Ldr)09/03/90	(Pay)29/03/90	Amt(c)15
Final	(Ldr)07/09/90	(Pay)18/09/90	Amt(c)35
Interim	(Ldr)22/02/91	(Pay)28/02/91	Amt(c)25
Final	(Ldr)06/09/91	(Pay)18/09/91	Amt(c)35
Interim	(Ldr)21/02/92	(Pay)28/02/92	Amt(c)40
Final	(Ldr)28/08/92	(Pay)18/09/92	Amt(c)44

NUMBER OF EMPLOYEES : 2500

CAPITAL STRUCTURE

	AUTHORISED	ISSUED
Ords 50c	15000000	9819824

FINANCIAL STATISTICS (AT FINANCIAL YEAR END)

(Amts in R'000)	1992 Jun	1991 Jun	1990 Jun	1989 Jun
Ord S/H Int	65008	52303	43662	36024
Long Trm Loans	201919	127352	54436	24497
Iss Ord Share	9820	9820	9790	9710
Total Liab	313111	270672	117200	61459
Current Liab	111192	143320	62764	36962
Total Assets	361955	309971	141310	92347
Intang Assets	16164	13004	19552	5136
Current Assets	287697	241459	126171	73414
Debtors	110606	89118	64400	28350
Inventory	126842	102174	58816	22806
Turnover	595994	411694	363296	120434
Oper Profit	59584	35190	41680	9220
Interest Paid	27490	16048	14549	1129
Tax Paid	11229	7999	13925	5213
Prf af Int&Tax	28439	19005	17809	5857
Prf att Ord Sh	21079	14269	12278	5375
Btm Line Earn	21079	14099	11958	5375
Dividend Paid	8248	5884	4886	2142
Mkt Prce(c) YE	2350	1400	850	715
Depreciation	7592	3720	2570	979

PER SHARE STATISTICS (CENTS)

Net Asst Val	497 39	400 19	246 27	318 11
Net Earnings	214 70	145 50	126 00	92 00
Dividends	84 00	60 00	50 00	22 00
Cash Flow	353 96	210 31	218 56	127 11

RATIOS AND OTHER INFORMATION

Mrk Cap(R000)	230770	137480	83215	69427
Current Ratio	2 59	1 68	2 01	1 99
Quik/Acid Tst	1 45	0 97	1 07	1 37
A/C Rec T/ovr	5 39	4 62	5 64	4 25
Tot Ass T/ovr	1 65	1 33	2 57	1 30
Debt/Ass Rat	0 57	0 59	0 52	0 47
L T L Tot Ass	0 27	0 13	0 07	0 07
Debt to Eqity	3 19	3 51	1 67	1 19
Interest Cover	2 18	2 20	2 89	8 29
Oper Prof Mrg	10 00	8 55	11 47	7 66
Net Prof Marg%	3 54	3 47	3 38	4 46
Ret on Assets	18 61	13 89	33 03	13 21
Ret on Equity%	32 43	27 28	28 12	14 92
Price/Earnings	10 95	9 62	6 75	7 77
Divid Cover	2 56	2 43	2 52	4 18
Divid Yield	3 57	4 29	5 88	3 08
Earning Yield%	9 14	10 39	14 82	12 87
NAV % Mrk Pr	21 17	28 59	28 97	44 49
Effec Tax Rate	12 30	21 94	22 59	37 96
Def Interval	2 77	1 96	0 17	-
Sus Grth Rate	19 74	16 03	16 93	8 97

SUBSIDIARY & ASSOCIATED COMPANIES

BIDSUB (PTY) LTD
BIDVEST LTD

INVESTMENTS

None

BIDVEST GROUP LTD

ABBREVIATION : BIDVEST

JSE SHORT CODE : BVT

SECTOR : Industrial-Industrial Holding

SHAREHOLDERS

Who Owns Whom's Assessment of the Identity of the Ultimate Controlling Shareholder:
BIDCORP

SHAREHOLDER	PERCENTAGE 1992	1991
BID CORP LTD	77.5	23.0
CMB NOM P/L	5.6	---
INVESTEC INV TRUST LTD	4.6	---
STD BANK NOM TVL P/L	3.5	---
ELMES B	2.4	2.4
MCEVEDY B F	1.2	1.2
INVESTEC NOM P/L	---	3.9
SAGE LIFE LTD	---	1.5
SANLAM	---	5.6
VOLKSKAS NOM P/L	---	1.5
BB INV CO P/L	---	2.4
BIDSUB P/L	---	53.8
TOTAL	94.8	95.3

DIRECTORS :
BERMAN IA MR,CHIPKIN BR MR
CHIPKIN M MR (Deputy Chairman),DEMETRIADES G MR
GOLDIN M MR,JOFFE B MR (Executive Chairman)
KRETZMAN CH ,MASSON D ,MCEVEDY BF MR,NYMAN P MR
PAMENSKY JL MR,RALPHS L ,ROSEVEAR DK
SALOMON AC MR,WAINER R MR,WATT CE M

REGISTRATION NUMBER : 05/21180/06

REGISTERED OFFICE
Milner Place, Sunnyside Office Park
4 Carse O'Gowrie, Parktown
2193
TEL: 011-474 1640
FAX: 011-474 8413

TRANSFER SECRETARY
Mercantile Registrars Ltd
P O Box 1053, Johannesburg
2000
TEL: 011-333 8181

COMPANY SECRETARY
M Viljoen

NATURE OF BUSINESS
An investment holding company with controlling interests in quoted Afcom & Crown Food. Activities of the group include distribution of food & allied products to the catering industry; Manufacture & distribution of packaging, stapling, fastening & adhesive tapes; An investment in the formulation, manufacture & marketing of cosmetics, toiletries & skin care products. The group also supplies towel cabinets, soap dispensers, garment & linen rentals, sanitary disposal & industrial laundering

BANKERS :
Nedperm Bank Ltd, Standard Bank of SA Ltd
First National Bank of SA Ltd

AUDITORS :
KPMG Aiken & Peat

FAMILIAR BRAND NAMES
BARILLA PASTA,BEL CHEESE,CATERPLUS,CHIPKINS
GOLD CREST,ISRAELI GHERKINS,PATLEYS,SEAWORLD

CONTRIBUTION BY ACTIVITY
N/A

YEAR END : June

DIVIDEND : Ords 50c

Interim	(Ldr)09/03/90	(Pay)29/03/90	Amt(c)45
Final	(Ldr)31/08/90	(Pay)18/09/90	Amt(c)51
Interim	(Ldr)22/02/91	(Pay)28/02/91	Amt(c)50
Final	(Ldr)06/09/91	(Pay)18/09/91	Amt(c)65
Interim	(Ldr)21/02/92	(Pay)28/02/92	Amt(c)80
Final	(Ldr)28/08/92	(Pay)18/09/92	Amt(c)84

NUMBER OF EMPLOYEES : 2500

CAPITAL STRUCTURE

	AUTHORISED	ISSUED
Ords 50c	11000000	6566141
6% Cum Prefs R2	100000	50000
Var Rate Unsec Conv Debs 1800c	3289039	3289039

FINANCIAL STATISTICS (AT FINANCIAL YEAR END)

(Amts in R'000)	1992 Jun	1991 Jun	1990 Jun	1989 Jun
Ord S/H Int	163418	143248	45380	41971
Long Trm Loans	197806	129245	28217	1631
Iss Ord Share	6566	6566	2346	2346
Total Liab	313967	273931	47473	7497
Current Liab	116161	144686	19256	5866
Total Assets	362325	311070	75591	49468
Intang Assets	115060	106109	17262	*
Current Assets	287215	241708	68604	34604
Debtors	110136	89381	22635	609
Inventory	126830	102160	26816	-
Turnover	595994	411694	115129	85880
Oper Profit	59587	35279	17558	11539
Interest Paid	27490	15952	5164	232
Tax Paid	11167	8219	8338	5346
Prf af Int&Tax	28380	18737	9323	6287
Prf att Ord Sh	27053	17589	5661	6281
Btm Line Earn	27053	17375	5661	15664
Dividend Paid	10769	7176	2252	2346
Mkt Prce(c) YE	4000	2800	2150	-
Depreciation	7592	3720	1422	934

PER SHARE STATISTICS (CENTS)

Net Asst Val	736 49	565.63	1198.55	1789.05
Net Earnings	412.00	352 00	241.00	-
Dividends	164.00	115.00	96.00	-
Cash Flow	620.36	484.82	336 10	372 21

RATIOS AND OTHER INFORMATION

Mrk Cap(R000)	262640	183848	50439	-
Current Ratio	2.47	1.67	3.56	5.90
Quik/Acid Tst	1.38	0.96	2.17	5.90
A/C Rec T/ovr	5 41	4.61	5 09	141.02
Tot Ass T/ovr	1.64	1.32	1.52	1.74

Debt/Ass Rat	0.75	0.77	0.30	0.12
L T L Tot Ass	0.43	0.31	0.05	-
Debt to Eqity	1.66	1.68	0.51	0.14
Interest Cover	2.18	2.22	3.44	51.14
Oper Prof Mrg	10.00	8.57	15.25	13.44
Net Prof Marg%	4.54	4.27	4 92	7 31
Ret on Assets	18.56	13.79	30 20	23 99
Ret on Equity%	16.55	12.28	12.47	14.97
Price/Earnings	9.71	7.95	8.92	-
Divid Cover	2.51	3.06	2.51	-
Divid Yield	4.10	4.11	4.47	-
Earning Yield%	10.30	12.57	11.21	-
NAV % Mrk Pr	18.41	20 20	55.75	-
Effec Tax Rate	12.19	21.01	43.14	33.37
Def Interval	2.37	1.67	0.48	0.01
Sus Grth Rate	9.96	7.27	7.51	9 38

SUBSIDIARY & ASSOCIATED COMPANIES

AFCOM GROUP LTD
AUTOMATIC TOWEL SERVICES (PTY) LTD
BB INVESTMENT CO (PTY) LTD
BID CORPORATE SERVICES (PTY) LTD
BIDVEST CISKEI (PTY) LTD
CATER PLUS (PTY) LTD
COINPACK (PTY) LTD
CROWN FOOD HOLDINGS LTD
CUISINE HOLDINGS INCOPORATED
CYRIL HURVITZ SEAFOODS (PTY) LTD
D & R LOWE (PTY) LTD
DENIS LOWEN (PTY) LTD
ERLE & STEPHENS (PTY) LTD
EXECUTIVE HOT DRINK MACHINES (PTY) LTD
GIANT WORKWEAR (PTY) LTD
GOLD CREST FOODS (PTY) LTD
JUSTINE (PTY) LTD (50%)
LUSITANIA SEA PRODUCTS O F.S. (PTY) LTD
MA PRODUCTS (PTY) LTD
METROPOLITAN LAUNDRY (PROPERTY) SHARE BL
NATIONAL SPICE (NATAL) (PTY) LTD
NATIONAL SPICE CASINGS (PTY) LTD
NATIONAL SPICE WORKS (PTY) LTD
PATLEYS (PTY) LTD
PRESTIGE OVERALL HIRE (PTY) LTD
SADA TEXTILE MANUFACTURING (PTY) LTD
SANITARY HYGIENE EQUIPMENT (PTY) LTD
STEINER CATERING & INDUSTRIAL SUPPLIES
STEINER SERVICES (PTY) LTD
STEINER SERVICES CISKEI (PTY) LTD
TOWEL CRAFT (PTY) LTD
TOWELMASTER SERVICES (PTY) LTD
W A CHIPKIN (EASTERN PROVINCE) (PTY) LTD
WALTER A CHIPKIN (NAMIBIA) (PTY) LTD
WALTER A CHIPKIN (NATAL) (PTY) LTD
WALTER A CHIPKIN (PTY) LTD

INVESTMENTS

None

BINDURA NICKEL CORPORATION LTD

ABBREVIATION : BINDURA

SECTOR : Zimbabwe Stock Exchange

SHAREHOLDERS

Who Owns Whom's Assessment of the Identity of the Ultimate Controlling Shareholder: ANGLO AMERICAN

SHAREHOLDER	PERCENTAGE 1992	1991
SECURITY NOM LTD	64 5	---
PROSPECTS OF ZIMBABWE PVT LTD	8.7	---
FIRST NOM PVT LTD	1.3	---
TEXTURED YARNS PVT LTD	1.3	---
TRUST NOM (PVT) LTD	1.3	---
CAPRICORN TRUSTEES LTD	1.2	---
JURVEST HOLDINGS PVT LTD	1 2	---
TOTAL	79 5	---

DIRECTORS :
CLAVER AH ,KUDENGA N ,LANDER RP (Chairman)
MANCAMA BV ,MASUNDA MA
NGUGAMA EG (Managing Director),NICHOLSON DG
PIENAAR SP ,RAMSAY AG
SMART WK (Deputy Chairman),TAYLOR JR ,WISHART AB

REGISTERED OFFICE
70 Samora Machel Avenue, Harare C4
Zimbabwe

TEL: 6231/6 6001/3

TRANSFER SECRETARY
N/A

COMPANY SECRETARY
Anglo American Corporation Services

NATURE OF BUSINESS
The company and its subsidiaries are incorporated in Zimbabwe with the main activities consisting of mining operations, and the smelting and refining of nickel, copper and cobalt.

BANKERS :
N/A

AUDITORS :
Deloitte & Touche

FAMILIAR BRAND NAMES
N/A

CONTRIBUTION BY ACTIVITY
N/A

YEAR END : December

DIVIDEND :Ords Z$1

Dividend	(Ldr)30/03/92	(Pay)23/04/92	Amt(c)25
Dividend	(Ldr)25/08/92	(Pay)24/09/92	Amt(c)17

CAPITAL STRUCTURE

	AUTHORISED	ISSUED
Ords Z$1	120000000	116808384

FINANCIAL STATISTICS (AT FINANCIAL YEAR END)

(Amts in Z$)	1991 Dec	1990 Dec
Ord S/H Int	363377	283663
Iss Ord Share	116808	116808
Total Liab	153118	118874

Current Liab	153118	118874
Total Assets	516495	402537
Current Assets	313096	215737
Debtors	95741	49430
Inventory	113738	73986
Turnover	372957	287089
Oper Profit	184499	115967
Tax Paid	71138	50029
Prf af Int&Tax	120597	70644
Prf att Ord Sh	120597	70644
Btm Line Earn	120597	70644
Dividend Paid	40883	29202

PER SHARE STATISTICS (CENTS)

Net Asst Val	311 09	242 85
Net Earnings	103 20	60 50
Dividends	35 00	25 00
Cash Flow	103 24	60 48

RATIOS AND OTHER INFORMATION

Current Ratio	2 04	1 81
Quik/Acid Tst	1 30	1 19
A/C Rec T/ovr	3 90	5 81
Tot Ass T/ovr	0 72	0 71
Debt/Ass Rat	0 30	0 30
Debt to Eqity	0 42	0 42
Oper Prof Mrg	49 47	40 39
Net Prof Marg%	32 34	24 61
Ret on Assets	37 12	29 98
Ret on Equity%	33 19	24 90
Divid Cover	2 95	2 42
Effec Tax Rate	37 05	41 45
Sus Grth Rate	21 94	14 61

SUBSIDIARY & ASSOCIATED COMPANIES

BSR LIMITED
TROJAN NICKEL MINE LIMITED

INVESTMENTS

None

BLOCH LTD

ABBREVIATION : BLOCHS

JSE SHORT CODE : BLC

SECTOR : Development Capital Market

SHAREHOLDERS

Who Owns Whom's Assessment of the Identity of the Ultimate Controlling Shareholder: RABINOWITZ FAMILY

SHAREHOLDER	PERCENTAGE 1992	1991
BLOCH HOLDINGS CHANNEL ISLANDS LTD	25 0	25 0
FIRST NAT NOM P/L	16 0	16 0
RABINOWITZ D (NOMINEE)	10 6	---
RABINOWITZ B (NOMINEE)	10 6	---
BLOCH HOLDINGS P/L	10 0	10 0
CMB NOM P/L	6 3	---
WILSEN D A B	5 4	5 4
BLOCH SUPERMARKETS PENS FUND	3 6	3 6
GAUSS W	1 3	1 3
RABINOWITZ D	---	9 9
RABINOWITZ B	---	10 0
SANLAM	---	6 3
TOTAL	88 9	87 6

DIRECTORS :
DOWER JMR ,RABINOWITZ B (Chairman)
RABINOWITZ D (Managing Director)
WILSEN DAB (Financial Director

REGISTRATION NUMBER : 87/001115

REGISTERED OFFICE
20 Amatola Business Village, Bisho
Ciskei

TEL 0401-91841
FAX 0401-91841

TRANSFER SECRETARY
Central Registrars Ltd
P O Box 4844, Johannesburg
2000
TEL 011-331 0051

COMPANY SECRETARY
D A B Wilsen

NATURE OF BUSINESS
Blochs owns certain trade marks, and derives most of its income from royalties paid for the use of the trade marks by trading companies in the Bloch Supermarket group, which at present operate in the Southern, Western and Eastern Cape

BANKERS :
First National Bank of SA Ltd

AUDITORS :
N/A

FAMILIAR BRAND NAMES
BLOCH,BLOCHBUSTER,BLOCHKOR,BLOCHMART

CONTRIBUTION BY ACTIVITY
N/A

YEAR END : June

DIVIDEND : Ords no par value

Dividend No 7	(Ldr)22/02/91	(Pay)08/03/91	Amt(c)1 9
Dividend No 8	(Ldr)23/08/91	(Pay)06/09/91	Amt(c)2 6
Dividend No 9	(Ldr)21/02/92	(Pay)06/03/92	Amt(c)2 2
Dividend No 10	(Ldr)04/09/92	(Pay)18/09/92	Amt(c)3 9

CAPITAL STRUCTURE

	AUTHORISED	ISSUED
Ords no par value	25000000	18700000

FINANCIAL STATISTICS (AT FINANCIAL YEAR END)

(Amts in R'000)	1992 Jun	1991 Jun	1990 Jun	1989 Jun	1988 Jun
Ord S/H Int	3029	3194	3180	3164	3146
Iss Ord Share	18700	18700	18700	18700	18700
Total Liab	796	516	477	399	259
Current Liab	796	516	477	399	259

Total Assets	819	704	651	3563	3405
Intang Assets	3006	3006	3006	*	*
Current Assets	816	700	647	554	398
Debtors	235	91	91	77	56
Oper Profit	1049	903	854	733	660
Tax Paid	162	145	137	117	99
Prf af Int&Tax	976	855	801	672	561
Prf att Ord Sh	976	855	801	672	561
Btm Line Earn	976	855	801	672	561
Dividend Paid	1141	842	786	655	430
Mkt Prce(c) YE	40	30	16	22	35
Depreciation	1	1	1	-	-

PER SHARE STATISTICS (CENTS)

Net Asst Val	0 12	1 01	0 93	16 92	16 82
Net Earnings	5 20	4 60	4 30	3 60	3 00
Dividends	6 10	4 50	4 20	3 50	2 30
Cash Flow	5 22	4 58	4 29	3 59	2 25

RATIOS AND OTHER INFORMATION

Mrk Cap(R000)	7480	5610	2992	4114	6545
Current Ratio	1 03	1 36	1 36	1 39	1 54
Quik/Acid Tst	1 03	1 36	1 36	1 39	1 54
Debt/Ass Rat	0 97	0 73	0 73	0 11	0 08
Debt to Eqity	0 26	0 16	0 15	0 13	0 08
Ret on Assets	138 95	142 05	144 09	22 14	14 54
Ret on Equity%	32 22	26 77	25 19	21 24	13 37
Price/Earnings	7 69	6 52	3 72	6 11	11 67
Divid Cover	0 85	1 02	1 02	1 03	1 30
Divid Yield	15 25	15 00	26 25	15 91	6 57
Earning Yield%	13 00	15 33	26 88	16 36	8 57
NAV % Mrk Pr	0 31	3 35	5 82	76 91	48 07
Effec Tax Rate	14 24	14 50	14 61	14 83	15 00
Sus Grth Rate	-5 45	0 41	0 47	0 54	4 16

SUBSIDIARY & ASSOCIATED COMPANIES

None

INVESTMENTS

None

BLYVOORUITZICHT GOLD MINING CO LTD

ABBREVIATION : BLYVOOR

JSE SHORT CODE : BLY

SECTOR : Gold West Witwatersrand

SHAREHOLDERS

Who Owns Whom's Assessment of the Identity of the Ultimate Controlling Shareholder:
MANAGED BY RAND MINES

SHAREHOLDER	PERCENTAGE 1992	1991
STD BANK NOM TVL P/L	49 9	47 9
INDO CHINA NOM P/L	17 2	
ANGLO AMERICAN GOLD INV CO LTD	6 7	6 7
FIRST NAT NOM P/L GATR DEPOT	6 5	7 9
UK BRANCH REGISTER CONTROL ACCOUNT	5 1	5 5
RAND MINES LTD	4 9	4 9
NAT CITY NOM LTD	4 5	4 4
DEPOSITARY NOM INC	1 5	9 9
BANK OF NEW YORK NOM LTD	1 1	1 1
INDO CHINA NOM SA P/L	---	8 9
TOTAL	97 2	97 1

DIRECTORS :
CLEWLOW WAM ,CROCKER EB (Managing Director)
EICK KFW ,EUSTACE PJ ,HALL JC ,HEYNS MR
SEALEY AA ,STEVENS IG ,TURNER JPS (Chairman)
VOS P

REGISTRATION NUMBER : 05/09743/06

REGISTERED OFFICE
15th Floor, The Corner House
63 Fox Street, Johannesburg
2001
TEL 011-491 2911
FAX 011-834 3850

TRANSFER SECRETARY
Rand Registrars Ltd
P O Box 82549, Southdale
2135
TEL 011-835 1016

COMPANY SECRETARY
Rand Mines (Mining & Services) Ltd

NATURE OF BUSINESS
The company conducts gold mining operations on the far West Witwatersrand Silver is recovered as a by-product

BANKERS :
First National Bank of SA Ltd

AUDITORS :
Deloitte & Touche

FAMILIAR BRAND NAMES
N/A

CONTRIBUTION BY ACTIVITY
N/A

YEAR END : June

DIVIDEND : Ords 25c

Interim No 87	(Ldr)29/12/89	(Pay)26/01/90	Amt(c)5
Final No 88	(Ldr)06/07/90	(Pay)27/07/90	Amt(c)30
Interim No 89	(Ldr)08/02/91	(Pay)01/03/91	Amt(c)15
Final No 90	(Ldr)09/08/91	(Pay)30/08/91	Amt(c)15
Interim No 91	(Ldr)07/02/92	(Pay)28/02/92	Amt(c)15

NUMBER OF EMPLOYEES : 9311

CAPITAL STRUCTURE

	AUTHORISED	ISSUED
Ords 25c	26400000	24000000

FINANCIAL STATISTICS (AT FINANCIAL YEAR END)

(Amts in R 000)	1992 Jun	1991 Jun	1990 Jun	1989 Jun	1988 Jun
Ord S/H Int	355716	344057	329942	310868	287666
Iss Ord Share	24000	24000	24000	24000	24000

Total Liab	31034	40430	42719	34838	67328
Current Liab	31034	40430	42719	34838	67328
Total Assets	386750	384487	372661	345706	354994
Current Assets	73684	75585	66317	45613	73116
Debtors	6158	3734	5710	3228	4272
Inventory	4883	6131	6390	3931	2771
Turnover	290608	303673	308689	316193	344486
Oper Profit	9331	17219	18668	34930	92883
Tax Paid	5360	5131	4474	3328	38483
Prf af Int&Tax	15259	21315	22275	31602	54400
Prf att Ord Sh	15259	21315	22275	31602	54400
Btm Line Earn	15259	21315	22275	31602	54400
Dividend Paid	3600	7200	8400	8400	36000
Mkt Prce(c) YE	375	725	1050	1125	1550

PER SHARE STATISTICS (CENTS)

Net Asst Val	1482 15	1433 57	1374 76	1295 28	1198 61
Net Earnings	51 00	79 00	78 00	51 00	143 00
Dividends	15 00	30 00	35 00	35 00	150 00
Cash Flow	63 58	88 81	108 23	131 68	226 67

RATIOS AND OTHER INFORMATION

Mrk Cap(R000)	90000	174000	252000	270000	372000
Current Ratio	2 37	1 87	1 55	1 31	1 09
Quik/Acid Tst	2 22	1 72	1 40	1 20	1 04
A/C Rec T/ovr	47 19	81 33	54 06	97 95	80 64
Tot Ass T/ovr	0 75	0 79	0 83	0 91	0 97
Debt/Ass Rat	0 08	0 11	0 11	0 10	0 19
Debt to Eqity	0 09	0 12	0 13	0 11	0 23
Oper Prof Mrg	3 21	5 67	6 05	11 05	26 96
Net Prof Marg%	5 25	7 02	7 22	9 99	15 79
Ret on Assets	5 33	6 88	7 18	10 10	26 16
Ret on Equity%	4 29	6 20	6 75	10 17	18 91
Price/Earnings	7 35	9 18	13 46	22 06	10 84
Divid Cover	3 40	2 63	2 23	1 46	0 95
Divid Yield	4 00	4 14	3 33	3 11	9 68
Earning Yield%	13 60	10 90	7 43	4 53	9 23
NAV % Mrk Pr	395 24	197 73	130 93	115 14	77 33
Effec Tax Rate	27 85	19 27	2 94		-
Sus Grth Rate	3 28	4 10	4 21	7 46	6 40

SUBSIDIARY & ASSOCIATED COMPANIES

None

INVESTMENTS

None

BOARD OF EXECUTORS LTD

ABBREVIATION : BOE

JSE SHORT CODE : BOE

SECTOR : Financial-Banks & Financial Services

SHAREHOLDERS

Who Owns Whom's Assessment of the Identity of the Ultimate Controlling Shareholder: DIRECTORS / ANGLOVAAL VIA AVF GROUP

SHAREHOLDER	PERCENTAGE 1992	1991
AVF GROUP LTD	39 8	31 9
LIBERTY ASSET MANAGEMENT LTD	11 7	16 3
REALLY NOBLE INV LTD	8 6	11 9
BOARD OF EXECUTORS NOM P/L	6 3	5 8
FOX STREET NOM P/L	1 9	---
MENTEITH INV LTD	1 5	2 1
FOLIO INV CO P/L	1 2	1 5
SFSS NOM P/L	1 2	---
TOTAL	72 1	69 5

DIRECTORS :
BARBER DD ,BIDEN PN (Deputy Managing Director)
BOARDMAN TA ,CHAPMAN HG ,DICKSON AJL
DUNNINGHAM GW ,GORDON EGD
MCADAM WJ (Managing Director),MCALPINE JR
MCGREGOR JAC (Financial Director),MENELL CS
OVENSTONE ADP ,SWAIN WJ ,THOMPSON MA
WILSON PW (Chairman

REGISTRATION NUMBER : 87/03281/06

REGISTERED OFFICE
4 Wale Street, Cape Town
8001
TEL 021-24 1100
FAX 021-23 2946

TRANSFER SECRETARY
Mercantile Registrars Ltd
P O Box 1053, Johannesburg
2000
TEL 011 333 8181

COMPANY SECRETARY
J Kevitt

NATURE OF BUSINESS
An investment house which operates as a financial services company in the fields of investment management, money market operations, participation mortgage scheme administration, corporate finance, administration of estates, financial planning, tax consultancy and appliance, property broking and syndication, and insolvencies

BANKERS :
First National Bank of SA Ltd
Standard Bank of SA Ltd

AUDITORS :
Deloitte Pim Goldby

FAMILIAR BRAND NAMES
N/A

CONTRIBUTION BY ACTIVITY
N/A

YEAR END . September

DIVIDEND . Ords 10c

Interim No 6	(Ldr)25/05/90	(Pay)13/06/90	Amt(c)10
Final No 7	(Ldr)23/11/90	(Pay)12/12/90	Amt(c)22
Interim No 8	(Ldr)24/05/91	(Pay)12/06/91	Amt(c)13
Final No 9	(Ldr)22/11/91	(Pay)11/12/91	Amt(c)25
Interim No 10	(Ldr)22/05/92	(Pay)10/06/92	Amt(c)14
Final No 11	(Ldr)27/11/92	(Pay)09/12/92	Amt(c)26

NUMBER OF EMPLOYEES : 331

CAPITAL STRUCTURE

	AUTHORISED	ISSUED
Ords 10c	20000000	12776617
Unsec Comp Conv Partic Loan Stock	5600000	1741764

FINANCIAL STATISTICS (AT FINANCIAL YEAR END)

(Amts in R'000)	1992 Sep	1991 Sep	1990 Sep	1989 Sep	1988 Sep
Ord S/H Int	86388	69004	54627	41115	32682
Long Trm Loans	4354	13288	13723	-	-
Iss Ord Share	12777	9203	9029	5600	5600
Total Liab	1488341	565270	62803	19154	28025
Current Liab	1483987	551982	49080	19154	28025
Total Assets	1574729	634274	117430	60269	57107
Intang Assets	*	*	*	*	3600
Current Assets	1450677	553180	40989	35421	44072
Debtors	33188	28461	30666	15631	7707
Oper Profit	3525	4406	2773	-	-
Interest Paid	3566	3545	3845	2800	2100
Tax Paid	2552	3068	1400	1705	406
Prf af Int&Tax	12558	12461	9381	3106	2100
Prf att Ord Sh	13487	11816	9206	4500	2100
Btm Line Earn	13561	17622	12702	13433	7020
Dividend Paid	5111	3497	2889	1400	1050
Mkt Prce(c) YE	825	1425	475	540	280
Depreciation	1909	1819	1424	1196	1020

PER SHARE STATISTICS (CENTS)

Net Asst Val	676 12	749 80	605 02	734 20	519 32
Net Earnings	97 00	93 00	102 00	80 40	37 50
Dividends	40 00	38 00	32 00	25 00	18 75
Cash Flow	113 23	155 17	119 67	76 82	55 71

RATIOS AND OTHER INFORMATION

Mrk Cap(R000)	105410	131143	42888	30240	15680
Current Ratio	0 98	1 00	0 84	1 85	1 57
Quik/Acid Tst	0 98	1 00	0 84	1 85	1 57
Debt/Ass Rat	0 95	0 89	0 53	0 32	0 49
L T L Tot Ass	0 00	0 02	0 12	-	-
Debt to Eqity	17 23	8 19	1 15	0 47	0 86
Interest Cover	3 49	3 13	2 17	2 72	2 19
Ret on Assets	1 31	3 43	15 23	14 94	8 07
Ret on Equity%	15 61	17 12	16 85	10 94	6 43
Price/Earnings	8 51	15 32	4 66	6 72	7 47
Divid Cover	2 43	2 45	3 19	3 22	2 00
Divid Yield	4 85	2 67	6 74	4 63	6 70
Earning Yield%	11 76	6 53	21 47	14 89	13 39
NAV % Mrk Pr	81 95	52 62	127 37	135 96	185 47
Effec Tax Rate	2 69	17 35	20 96	-	-19 24
Def Interval	0 23	0 09	0 18	0 08	4 32
Sus Grth Rate	9 70	12 06	11 56	7 54	3 21

SUBSIDIARY & ASSOCIATED COMPANIES

BOARD OF EXECUTORS (PTY) LTD
BOARD OF EXECUTORS INTERNATIONAL LTD
BOARDPROP MANAGEMENT COMPANY (PTY) LTD
BOE MERCHANT BANK LTD
BOE NATAL LTD
BOE PROPERTIES (PTY) LTD
BOE UNIT TRUST MANAGEMENT COMPANY (PTY)
CAPE TOWN PROPERTIES (PTY) LTD
DONROD PROPERTIES SHARE BLOCK (PTY) LTD
MERCURY SECURITES (PTY) LTD

INVESTMENTS

BOE GROWTH FUND COMMERCIAL FINANCE CO LT (1976766 SH)
CAPITAL SECURITIES LTD (PREFS) (2500000 SH)
COMMERCIAL FINANCE CO LTD (89600 SH)
CONGELLA FEDERATION LTD (500 SH)
ELECTRA INVESTMENT (SA) LTD (PREFS) (15000000 S)
FIDELITY BANK LTD (2450000 SH)
GOLDEN ARROW BUS SERVICES LTD DEBS (2540000SH)
IMMOBILIA PROPERTY INVESTMENT CO LTD (10%)
MOOIKELDER INVESTMENTS (PTY) LTD (PREFS) (60000 SH)
PHOTRACOMP (PTY) LTD (1400SH)
REALLY NOBLE INVESTMENTS LTD (300 SH)
THE ADDERLEY DEVELOPMENT SYNDICATION LTD (1350SH)
URD BELEGGINGS (PTY) LTD (RED CUM PREFS) (6000000SH)
YELLOWWOOD PROPERTY FUND MANAGERS LTD (260000SH)

BOARDPROP LTD

ABBREVIATION : BOEPROP

JSE SHORT CODE : BOR

SECTOR : Financial-Property Loan Stock

SHAREHOLDERS

Who Owns Whom's Assessment of the Identity of the Ultimate Controlling Shareholder:
INSTITUTIONAL INVESTORS

SHAREHOLDER	PERCENTAGE 1992	1991
EIGHTY ONE MAIN STREET NOM LTD	39 7	38 7
STD BANK NOM TVL P/L	15 9	---
NEDBANK NOM LTD	4 9	4 9
SOUTHERN LIFE ASSOC LTD	4 8	4 8
FIRST NAT NOM P/L	4 4	4 3
DURBAN MUNICIPAL PENS FUND	4 1	4 1
METAL IND GROUP PENS FUND	3 6	2 9
SMBL NOM P/L	3 1	2 4
ENGINEERING INDUSTRIES PENS FUND	2 9	2 9
DURBAN CORP SUPERANNUATION FUND	1 6	1 6
SAFEGRO NOM P/L	1 5	3 8
NAMPAK PENS FUND	1 4	1 4
SA MUTUAL	1 3	- -
BOARD OF EXECUTORS NOM P/L	---	11 8
MOMENTUM LIFE ASSURE LTD	---	1 1
BOE NOM P/L	---	1 9
TOTAL	89 1	86 6

DIRECTORS :
BARNETSON AU ,DICKSON AJL ,DUNNINGHAM GW
GEYER DA ,HASLETT FN ,KREINER L
MCADAM WJ (Chairman

REGISTRATION NUMBER : 88/00742/06

REGISTERED OFFICE
4 Wale Street, Cape Town
8001
TEL 021-24 1100
FAX 021-23 2946

TRANSFER SECRETARY
Mercantile Registrars Ltd
P O Box 1053, Johannesburg
2000
TEL: 011-333 8181

COMPANY SECRETARY
The Board of Executors

NATURE OF BUSINESS
An investment holding company involved in the investment, development & management of retail, commercial & industrial properties located in the metropolitan areas of SA.

BANKERS :
First National Bank of SA Ltd

AUDITORS :
Deloitte Pim Goldby

FAMILIAR BRAND NAMES
N/A

CONTRIBUTION BY ACTIVITY
Industrial (% net rental income) (7.0%)
Office (83.0%)
Retail (10.0%)

YEAR END : September

DIVIDEND :Ords 5c

Interim No 4	(Ldr)25/05/90	(Pay)13/06/90	Amt(c)29 24
Final No 5	(Ldr)23/11/90	(Pay)19/12/90	Amt(c)28.71
Interim No 6	(Ldr)24/05/91	(Pay)12/06/91	Amt(c)31.28
Final No 7	(Ldr)22/11/91	(Pay)11/12/91	Amt(c)29.93
Interim No 8	(Ldr)22/05/92	(Pay)10/06/92	Amt(c)25 90
Final No 9	(Ldr)27/11/92	(Pay)09/12/92	Amt(c)27.91

CAPITAL STRUCTURE

	AUTHORISED	ISSUED
Ords 5c (1 Debenture linked to 1	20000000	19674029
Var Rate Partic Prefs 1c	1000	0
Unsec Var Rate Sub Debs 495c	19674029	19674029

FINANCIAL STATISTICS (AT FINANCIAL YEAR END)

(Amts in R'000)	1991 Sep	1990 Sep	1989 Sep	1988 Sep
Ord S/H Int	5581	5068	53679	537
Long Trm Loans	97386	96870	-	53142
Iss Ord Share	19674	19570	10736	10736
Total Liab	103987	103220	3674	55919
Current Liab	6601	6350	3674	2777
Total Assets	109568	108288	57353	56456
Current Assets	16435	23151	5521	8791
Debtors	1171	761	246	432
Turnover	15386	11767	8207	2877
Oper Profit	9239	6947	4869	1498
Interest Paid	11997	9153	5875	2232
Tax Paid	73	47	30	11
Prf af Int&Tax	48	47	30	11
Prf att Ord Sh	48	47	30	11
Btm Line Earn	556	93	30	11
Dividend Paid	49	46	30	11
Mkt Prce(c) YE	500	525	525	500
Depreciation	121	56	45	9

PER SHARE STATISTICS (CENTS)

Net Asst Val	28.37	25.90	499 99	5 00
Net Earnings	0 25	0 29	-	-
Dividends	0 25	0 29	0 28	0.10
Cash Flow	0.86	0.53	0.70	0.56

RATIOS AND OTHER INFORMATION

Mrk Cap(R000)	98370	102743	56364	53680
Current Ratio	2.49	3.65	1.50	3.17
Quik/Acid Tst	2 49	3.65	1.50	3.17
A/C Rec T/ovr	13 14	15.46	33.36	19.98
Tot Ass T/ovr	0.14	0.11	0.14	0 15
Debt/Ass Rat	0 95	0.95	0 06	0 99
L T L Tot Ass	0 89	0 89	-	0 94
Debt to Eqity	18.63	20 37	0.07	104.13
Interest Cover	0.77	0.76	1.01	1.01
Oper Prof Mrg	60 05	59.04	59 33	52.07
Net Prof Marg%	0.31	0.40	0 37	0.38
Ret on Assets	11.06	8.54	10 35	11.98
Ret on Equity%	0.86	0.93	0.06	6.15
Price/Earnings	2000.00	1810.34	-	-
Divid Cover	1 00	1.00	-	-
Divid Yield	0 05	0.06	0.05	0.02
Earning Yield%	0 05	0.06	-	-
NAV % Mrk Pr	5.67	4.93	95 24	1.00
Effec Tax Rate	60.33	50.00	-2 98	-1.50
Def Interval	610.97	994.77	-	8304.30
Sus Grth Rate	-0.02	0 02	0.00	0.00

SUBSIDIARY & ASSOCIATED COMPANIES

91 PHOENIX PARK SHARE BLOCK (PTY) LTD
ABERFELD HOUSE SHARE BLOCK (PTY) LTD
ARNOLD ROAD SHARE BLOCK (PTY) LTD
CONLOT 28 INVESTMENTS SHARE BLOCK (PTY)
DONROD PROPERTIES SHARE BLOCK (PTY) LTD
ERF 61 KRAMERVILLE SHARE BLOCK (PTY) LTD
ERF 965 FERNDALE SHARE BLOCK (PTY) LTD
FERRISTER SHARE BLOCK (PTY) LTD
MIDPOINT SHARE BLOCK (PTY) LTD
ORMONDE EXT 5 SHARE BLOCK (PTY) LTD
POLLIACKS BUILDING SHARE BLOCK (PTY) LTD
PORTION 3 FERNDALE (PTY) LTD
SADDLE DRIVE PROPERTIES SHARE BLOCK (PTY
SEVENTEEN BAKER STREET SHARE BLOCK (PTY)
STAND 10 BRYANSTON WEST (PTY) LTD
STAND 20 WIERDA VALLEY SHARE BLOCK (PTY)
STAND 696 FERNDALE SHARE BLOCK (PTY) LTD
WIERDA ROAD SHARE BLOCK (PTY) LTD

INVESTMENTS

None

BOLAND BANK LTD

ABBREVIATION : BOLAND

JSE SHORT CODE : BOL

SECTOR : Financial-Banks & Financial Services

SHAREHOLDERS

Who Owns Whom's Assessment of the Identity of the Ultimate Controlling Shareholder:
REMBRANDT GROUP

SHAREHOLDER	PERCENTAGE 1992	1991
SANLAM	11 3	10 8
FINANCIAL SECURITIES LTD	9 9	9 9
AMALGAMATED BANKS OF SA LTD	9 7	9 7
MOMENTUM LIFE ASSURE LTD	9 3	9 3
TITAN NOM P/L	5 2	5 2
BOLAND BANK PENS FUND	4 8	4 8
NOOIENSFONTEIN INV P/L	3 7	3 7
MINE OFFICIALS PENS FUND	2 6	2 6
BB SHARE PURCHASE SCHEME	1 6	1 6
GUARDIAN NAT INSURANCE CO LTD	1 5	1 5
MINE EMPLOYEES PENS FUND	1 4	1 4
EIGHTY ONE MAIN STREET NOM LTD	1 2	1 2
SANTAM BPK	1 1	---
SECURITIES EQUITIES P/L	1 1	---
METROPOLITAN LIFE LTD	1 0	1 0
HERBEST NOM P/L	---	1 7
TOTAL	65 2	64 2

DIRECTORS :
BURGER AJH ,CONRADIE DCU DR,DE VRIES AJM PROF
DE VRIES MJ PROF,DU PLESSIS CJ ,DU PREEZ IP
HUGO PBB (Chairman),LE ROUX JG
LIEBENBERG GZ (Vice Chairman & M D),MORKEL CT DR
SCHOEMAN HSJ ,SWIEGERS GJ ,VAN DER SPUY MT
VAN WYK AH PRO

REGISTRATION NUMBER : 04/00312/06

REGISTERED OFFICE
333 Main Street, Paarl
7646
TEL 02211-7 2911
FAX 02211-7 2811

TRANSFER SECRETARY
Central Registrars Ltd
P O Box 4844, Johannesburg
2000
TEL 011-331 0051

COMPANY SECRETARY
P R Botha

NATURE OF BUSINESS
A registered deposit-taking institution, with subsidiaries providing banking and commission services, estate and trust services, property and auctioneering services, long and short - term insurance and pension broking services

BANKERS :
Boland Bank Ltd

AUDITORS :
Price Waterhouse Meyernel
Coopers Theron Du Toit

FAMILIAR BRAND NAMES
BANK WINDHOEK (25%),BOLAND BANK
DISTRICT BANK (30%)

CONTRIBUTION BY ACTIVITY
N/A

YEAR END : March

DIVIDEND : Ords 25c

Interim No 109	(Ldr)23/11/90	(Pay)11/01/91	Amt(c)21
Final No 110	(Ldr)24/05/91	(Pay)02/07/91	Amt(c)27
Interim No 111	(Ldr)22/11/91	(Pay)10/01/92	Amt(c)23
Final No 112	(Ldr)22/05/92	(Pay)03/07/92	Amt(c)29
Interim No 113	(Ldr)20/11/92	(Pay)06/01/93	Amt(c)23

NUMBER OF EMPLOYEES : 2200

CAPITAL STRUCTURE

	AUTHORISED	ISSUED
Ords 25c	20000000	13451320

FINANCIAL STATISTICS (AT FINANCIAL YEAR END)

(Amts in R'000)	1992 Mar	1991 Mar	1990 Mar	1989 Mar	1988 Mar
Ord S/H Int	136921	133885	123352	114051	106604
Long Trm Loans	-	-	-	71650	42360
Iss Ord Share	13451	13451	13451	13451	13451
Total Liab	3359513	3159565	3081749	2309437	1663328
Current Liab	3359513	3159565	3081749	2237787	1620968
Total Assets	3496434	3293450	3205101	2423488	1769932
Current Assets	543709	627998	566430	228696	115185
Debtors	-	-	-	-	115185
Oper Profit	19000	17000	14900	13635	11650
Prf af Int&Tax	19000	17000	14900	13635	11650
Prf att Ord Sh	19000	17000	14900	13635	11650
Btm Line Earn	19000	17000	14900	13635	11650
Dividend Paid	6995	6456	6188	6188	5650
Mkt Prce(c) YE	1060	725	440	490	470

PER SHARE STATISTICS (CENTS)

Net Asst Val	1017 92	995 35	917 05	847 90	792 54
Net Earnings	141 30	126 40	110 80	101 40	87 00
Dividends	52 00	48 00	46 00	46 00	42 00
Cash Flow	141 25	126 38	110 77	101 37	86 61

RATIOS AND OTHER INFORMATION

Mrk Cap(R000)	142581	97520	59184	65910	63220
Current Ratio	0 16	0 20	0 18	0 10	0 07
Quik/Acid Tst	0 16	0 20	0 18	0 10	0 07
Debt/Ass Rat	0 96	0 96	0 96	0 92	0 92
Debt to Eqity	24 54	23 60	24 98	19 62	15 21
Ret on Assets	0 54	0 52	0 46	0 56	0 66
Ret on Equity%	13 88	12 70	12 08	11 96	10 93
Price/Earnings	7 50	5 74	3 97	4 83	5 40
Divid Cover	2 72	2 63	2 41	2 20	2 07
Divid Yield	4 91	6 62	10 45	9 39	8 94
Earning Yield%	13 33	17 43	25 18	20 69	18 51
NAV % Mrk Pr	96 03	137 29	208 42	173 04	168 62
Def Interval	171 35	179 89	203 07	158 85	133 74
Sus Grth Rate	8 77	7 88	7 06	6 53	5 63

SUBSIDIARY & ASSOCIATED COMPANIES

AFRICAN MUTUAL TRUST CO LTD
ALLEGRO NOMINEES (PTY) LTD
BBWG PROPERTIES (PTY) LTD
BOLAND BANK INSURANCE SERVICES LTD
BOLAND BANK INVESTMENT NOMINEES (PTY) LT
BOLAND BANK INVESTMENT SERVICES LTD
BOLAND BANK PROPERTY SERVICES AND AUCTIO
BOLAND BOARD OF EXECUTORS (EAST CAPE) LT
BOLAND BOARD OF EXECUTORS (MALMESBURY) L
BOLAND BOARD OF EXECUTORS (MIDLANDS) LTD
BOLAND BOARD OF EXECUTORS (MONTAGU) LTD
BOLAND BOARD OF EXECUTORS (PAARL) LTD
BOLAND BOARD OF EXECUTORS (STELLENBOSCH)
BOLAND BOARD OF EXECUTORS (WORCESTER) LT
BOLAND DEVELOPMENT CORP (PTY) LTD
CLANWILLIAM BOARD OF EXECUTORS LTD
DISTRICT SECURITIES BANK LTD (30%)

EAST LONDON ESTATES (PTY) LTD
EAST LONDON ESTATES NOMINEES (PTY) LTD
GABBEMA INVESTMENTS (PTY) LTD
HARTEBEESPOORT GEDEELTE 22 (PTY) LTD
HOME 695 INVESTMENTS (PTY) LTD
KROONSTAD BOARD NOMINEES (PTY) LTD
KROONSTAD BOARD OF EXECUTORS & TRUST CO
KROONSTAD ESTATES AND FINANCE CORP. (PTY
LPWK INVESTMENTS (PTY) LTD
MAXPROP HOLDINGS (PTY) LTD (30%)
NEW SILVERTON ESTATES (PTY) LTD
PAARL AFRICAN TRUST (PTY) LTD
PRO MARK NETWORK (PTY) LTD
SANTAM GROW NOMINEES (PTY) LTD
SUTCO MINING NOMINEES (PTY) LTD
SUTCO SHARE NOMINEES (PTY) LTD
T N M FINANCE COMPANY (PTY) LTD
TARKA BOARD OF EXECUTORS AND TRUST CO. L
TBA NOMINEES (PTY) LTD
TRITON PROPERTIES (PTY) LTD
VAN DER STEL MOTORS FINANCE CO. (PTY) LT
VOOGDY TRUST LTD
WESTERN CAPE AUCTIONEERS (PTY) LTD
ZENTANHOF (PTY) LTD

INVESTMENTS

None

BOLTON FOOTWEAR LTD

ABBREVIATION : BOLWEAR

JSE SHORT CODE : BWR

SECTOR : Industrial-Clothing, Footwear & Textiles

SHAREHOLDERS

Who Owns Whom's Assessment of the Identity of the Ultimate Controlling Shareholder: BOLTON FAMILY

SHAREHOLDER	PERCENTAGE 1992	1991
BOLTONS INDUSTRIAL HOLDINGS LTD	74.1	74.1
SA MUTUAL	7.3	10.8
BOLTON FOOTWEAR INC TRUST	2.7	2.7
SMBL NOM P/L	2.7	---
RIDGE NOM P/L	1.9	1.9
DARGARVEL P/L	1.1	---
TOTAL	89.8	89.5

DIRECTORS :
BOLTON GD ,BOLTON MJ ,CHILVERS SG
FINLAYSON SRB (Managing Director)
LOUW MJ (Financial Director),NICHOLSON RG
NOVIS CM ,STEIN GH (Chairman),STRYDOM DJ

REGISTRATION NUMBER : 05/35036/06

REGISTERED OFFICE
Charles Street, Great Brak River
6525
TEL: 04442-2111
FAX: 04442-2378

TRANSFER SECRETARY
Fraser Street Registrars (Pty) Ltd
P O Box 61178, Marshalltown
2107
TEL: 011-491 0911

COMPANY SECRETARY
H A Fleetwood

NATURE OF BUSINESS
Group business includes manufacture, distribution & retail of footwear, distribution of sportswear, hardware retail, building & construction interests & the operation of Mercedes-Benz, Toyota & Honda dealerships.

BANKERS :
First National Bank of SA Ltd
Standard Bank of SA Ltd

AUDITORS :
Ernst & Young

FAMILIAR BRAND NAMES
A & D SPITZ,BAGSHAW FOOTWEAR,BANCHETTI
BOLTON SPORTSWEAR,COASTAL TOYOTA
ELGIN CONSTRUCTION,ELGIN TIMBERS
GRASSHOPPERS,HONDA (DEALER),KLINIK
MERCEDES BENZ (DEALER),MITRE
OUDTSHOORN FOOTWEAR,PAOLO FALCONE
PATRICK SPORTSWEAR,SEARLES HOMES,SHOERAMA
STANMAR MOTORS,TOYOTA (DEALER),WATSON

CONTRIBUTION BY ACTIVITY
Footwear Manufacturing (% turnover) (48.0%)
Footwear Retailing & Wholesaling (32.0%)
Building & Construction (7.0%)
Motor Dealerships (13.0%)

YEAR END : February

DIVIDEND : Ords 1c

Interim No 4	(Ldr)01/12/89	(Pay)29/12/89	Amt(c)4
Final No 5	(Ldr)25/05/90	(Pay)29/06/90	Amt(c)7
Interim No 6	(Ldr)07/12/90	(Pay)28/12/90	Amt(c)3.0
Final No 7	(Ldr)24/05/91	(Pay)28/06/91	Amt(c)5.4
Interim No 8	(Ldr)06/12/91	(Pay)27/12/91	Amt(c)3
Final No 9	(Ldr)22/05/92	(Pay)26/06/92	Amt(c)5
Interim No 10	(Ldr)07/12/92	(Pay)28/12/92	Amt(c)2

NUMBER OF EMPLOYEES : 2300

CAPITAL STRUCTURE

	AUTHORISED	ISSUED
Ords 1c	25000000	20000000

FINANCIAL STATISTICS (AT FINANCIAL YEAR END)

(Amts in R'000)	1992 Feb	1991 Feb	1990 Feb	1989 Feb	1988 Feb
Ord S/H Int	48343	45605	42435	38470	34324
Long Trm Loans	11122	10391	9475	1009	740
Iss Ord Share	20000	20000	20000	20000	20000
Total Liab	54940	50364	52032	22473	14427
Current Liab	43818	39973	42557	21464	13687
Total Assets	103283	95969	94467	60943	48751
Current Assets	77558	71723	71529	42708	34366
Debtors	33196	31252	29071	20212	16897
Inventory	43941	40471	42458	22496	17469
Turnover	198946	191480	188049	115684	94968
Oper Profit	13786	17250	20003	11474	9024
Interest Paid	4060	4537	4320	873	398

Tax Paid	4508	6396	7780	4547	4070
Prf af Int&Tax	5218	6379	7934	6054	4556
Prf att Ord Sh	4338	5049	6672	6054	4246
Btm Line Earn	4338	5049	6672	6054	4246
Dividend Paid	1600	1680	2200	1920	1000
Mkt Prce(c) YE	100	158	140	135	105
Depreciation	2533	1781	1513	771	733

PER SHARE STATISTICS (CENTS)

Net Asst Val	241 72	228 03	212 18	192 35	171 62
Net Earnings	21 70	25 20	33 40	30 30	22 78
Dividends	8 00	8 40	11 00	9 60	5 00
Cash Flow	34 36	34 15	40 93	34 13	26 45

RATIOS AND OTHER INFORMATION

Mrk Cap(R000)	20000	31600	28000	27000	21000
Current Ratio	1 77	1 79	1 68	1 99	2 51
Quik/Acid Tst	0 77	0 78	0 68	0 94	1 23
A/C Rec T/ovr	5 99	6 13	6 47	5 72	5 62
Tot Ass T/ovr	1 93	2 00	1 99	1 90	1 95
Debt/Ass Rat	0 44	0 43	0 46	0 36	0 30
L T L Tot Ass	0 02	0 01	0 01	0 01	0 02
Debt to Eqity	0 94	0 90	1 02	0 58	0 42
Interest Cover	3 40	3 82	4 64	13 14	22 67
Oper Prof Mrg	6 93	9 01	10 64	9 92	9 50
Net Prof Marg%	2 18	2 64	3 55	5 23	4 47
Ret on Assets	13 35	18 04	21 21	18 83	18 51
Ret on Equity%	8 97	11 07	15 72	15 74	12 37
Price/Earnings	4 61	6 27	4 19	4 46	4 61
Divid Cover	2 71	3 00	3 04	3 16	4 56
Divid Yield	8 00	5 32	7 86	7 11	4 76
Earning Yield%	21 70	15 95	23 86	22 44	21 70
NAV % Mrk Pr	241 72	144 32	151 55	142 48	163 45
Effec Tax Rate	46 43	50 43	49 66	47 60	46 99
Def Interval	3 65	3 15	2 67	1 01	0 49
Sus Grth Rate	5 66	7 39	10 54	10 75	9 46

SUBSIDIARY & ASSOCIATED COMPANIES

ATHSHOE CO (PTY) LTD
ELGIN TIMBER BUILDINGS (PTY) LTD
ELGIN TIMBERS (PTY) LTD
FIBAFABS (PTY) LTD
OUDTSHOORN FOOTWEAR (PTY) LTD
PALS BUILDING (PTY) LTD
PATRICK SPORTSWEAR (PTY) LTD
PRESTIGE SHOE INVESTMENTS (PTY) LTD (50%)
SA FRANCHISING (PTY) LTD (50%)
SHOERAMA (PTY) LTD
STANMAR MOTORS (PTY) LTD
T & C SALES CORPORATION (PTY) LTD
WATSON SHOES (PTY) LTD
WOB PROPERTIES (PTY) LTD

INVESTMENTS

None

BOLTON INDUSTRIAL HOLDINGS LTD

ABBREVIATION : BOLTONS

JSE SHORT CODE : BLT

SECTOR : Industrial-Industrial Holding

SHAREHOLDERS

Who Owns Whom's Assessment of the Identity of the Ultimate Controlling Shareholder: BOLTON FAMILY

SHAREHOLDER	PERCENTAGE 1992	1991
CARGO CARRIERS HOLDINGS P/L	63 8	63 8
SA MUTUAL	8 7	8 7
CAPE CLOTHING INDUSTRY PROV FUND	1 9	1 9
LONRHO GROUP PENS FUND	1 9	2 1
RIDGE NOM P/L	1 7	1 7
NOMINEES ONLY P/L	1 5	1 3
GEMEENSKAPLIKE MUNISIPALE OFS PENS FUND	1 5	1 5
SFSS NOM P/L	1 4	1 8
SECURITIES EQUITIES P/L	1 2	---
RITOS AKTIENGESELLSCHAFT	1 2	1 2
FOSKOR PENS FUND	1 2	1 2
STEINMULLER SA PENS FUND	1 2	1 2
BOARD OF EXECUTORS NOM P/L	---	1 1
TOTAL	87 1	87 5

DIRECTORS :
BOLTON GD ,BOLTON MJ ,BOLTON S
CHILVERS SG (Managing Director)
STEIN GH (Chairman

REGISTRATION NUMBER : 05/24557/06

REGISTERED OFFICE
Cnr Barbara & North Reef Roads, Elandsfontein
1406
TEL 011-974 6311
FAX 011-944 2375

TRANSFER SECRETARY
Fraser Street Registrars (Pty) Ltd
P O Box 61178, Marshalltown
2107
TEL 011-491 0911

COMPANY SECRETARY
Cargo Carriers Management Services (Pty) Ltd

NATURE OF BUSINESS
An investment holding company with its principle interests in bulk transport services, and footwear manufacturing and merchandising industries
The company holds controlling interests in JSE-quoted Bolton Footwear and Cargo Carriers

BANKERS :
Standard Bank of SA Ltd

AUDITORS :
Ernst & Young

FAMILIAR BRAND NAMES
PATRICK SHOES,SWANEES,WATSON SHOES

CONTRIBUTION BY ACTIVITY
N/A

YEAR END : February

DIVIDEND : Ords R1

Interim No 41	(Ldr)01/12/89	(Pay)29/12/89	Amt(c)18
Final No 42	(Ldr)25/05/90	(Pay)29/06/90	Amt(c)28
Interim No 43	(Ldr)07/12/90	(Pay)28/12/90	Amt(c)12

Final No 44	(Ldr)24/05/91	(Pay)28/06/91	Amt(c)14
Final No 46	(Ldr)22/05/92	(Pay)26/06/92	Amt(c)14
Interim No 45	(Ldr)06/12/91	(Pay)27/12/91	Amt(c)7 5

NUMBER OF EMPLOYEES : 4400

CAPITAL STRUCTURE

	AUTHORISED	ISSUED
Ords R1	6600000	5173750
5,5% Prefs R2	200000	175000

FINANCIAL STATISTICS (AT FINANCIAL YEAR END)

(Amts in R'000)	1992 Feb	1991 Feb	1990 Feb	1989 Feb	1988 Feb
Ord S/H Int	56693	54754	53490	49002	44824
Long Trm Loans	72086	76091	82664	72624	53863
Iss Ord Share	5174	5174	5174	5174	5174
Total Liab	156955	162377	168045	121946	86823
Current Liab	84869	86286	85381	49322	32960
Total Assets	213648	217131	221535	170948	131647
Current Assets	111387	103261	104473	70798	69514
Debtors	62195	56450	56513	41209	35253
Inventory	48540	45705	47940	29414	22360
Turnover	380837	370179	362607	258202	215987
Oper Profit	14718	25341	36921	21646	27354
Interest Paid	11454	12702	9074	1944	1119
Tax Paid	1209	6335	12384	8480	12654
Prf af Int&Tax	2055	6304	15463	11222	13581
Prf att Ord Sh	2074	3667	7449	6239	6556
Btm Line Earn	1926	3333	6558	6248	12019
Dividend Paid	1112	2069	2070	2070	310
Mkt Prce(c) YE	400	475	820	650	800
Depreciation	23856	24414	21702	16556	11411

PER SHARE STATISTICS (CENTS)

Net Asst Val	1095 73	1058 25	1033 82	947 08	866 33
Net Earnings	40 10	70 90	144 00	120 60	126 70
Dividends	21 50	26 00	46 00	38 00	24 00
Cash Flow	411 19	528 91	619 98	499 52	358 74

RATIOS AND OTHER INFORMATION

Mrk Cap(R000)	20696	24577	42427	33631	41392
Current Ratio	1 31	1 20	1 22	1 44	2 11
Quik/Acid Tst	0 74	0 67	0 66	0 84	1 43
A/C Rec T/ovr	6 12	6 56	6 42	6 27	6 13
Tot Ass T/ovr	1 78	1 70	1 64	1 51	1 64
Debt/Ass Rat	0 44	0 44	0 44	0 38	0 28
L T L Tot Ass	0 04	0 04	0 05	0 09	0 03
Debt to Eqity	1 65	1 73	1 81	1 33	0 81
Interest Cover	1 28	2 00	4 07	11 13	24 45
Oper Prof Mrg	3 86	6 85	10 18	8 38	12 66
Net Prof Marg%	0 54	0 99	2 05	2 42	3 04
Ret on Assets	6 89	11 67	16 67	12 66	20 78
Ret on Equity%	3 66	6 70	13 93	12 73	14 63
Price/Earnings	9 98	6 70	5 69	5 39	6 31
Divid Cover	1 87	2 73	3 13	3 17	5 28
Divid Yield	5 38	5 47	5 61	5 85	3 00
Earning Yield%	10 03	14 93	17 56	18 55	15 84
NAV % Mrk Pr	273 93	222 79	126 08	145 70	108 29
Effec Tax Rate	176 04	53 58	34 03	29 99	42 44
Def Interval	2 53	2 11	1 53	0 69	0 42
Sus Grth Rate	1 70	2 92	10 06	8 51	13 93

SUBSIDIARY & ASSOCIATED COMPANIES

BOLTON FOOTWEAR LTD
CARGO CARRIERS LTD
CC INVESTMENTS (PTY) LTD (50,1%)

INVESTMENTS

None

BOLTON PROPERTIES LTD

ABBREVIATION : BOLPRO

JSE SHORT CODE : BLR

SECTOR : Financial-Property

SHAREHOLDERS

Who Owns Whom's Assessment of the Identity of the Ultimate Controlling Shareholder: BOLTON FAMILY

SHAREHOLDER	PERCENTAGE 1992	1991
CARGO CARRIERS HOLDINGS P/L	63 8	63 8
SA SPECIAL RISKS INSURANCE ASSOC LTD	8 5	8 5
PHEZULU INV CC	3 5	--
HARDING D C	3 1	3 1
LEWTOP P/L	1 8	---
RIDGE NOM P/L	1 7	1 7
VAN DYK G	1 7	1 7
RITOS AKTIENGESELLSCHAFT	1 2	1 2
STD BANK NOM TVL P/L	---	1 0
BOARD OF EXECUTORS NOM P/L	---	1 5
TOTAL	85 1	82 4

DIRECTORS :
CHILVERS SG (Managing Director),FINLAYSON SRB LOUW MJ ,PUCHERT BF ,STEIN GH (Chairman

REGISTRATION NUMBER : 71/03132/06

REGISTERED OFFICE
Cnr Barbara & North Reef Roads, Elandsfontein
Germiston
1406
TEL 011-828 0570
FAX 011-828 0346

TRANSFER SECRETARY
Fraser Street Registrars (Pty) Ltd
P O Box 61178, Marshalltown
2107
TEL 011-491 0911

COMPANY SECRETARY
Cargo Carriers Management Services (Pty) Ltd

NATURE OF BUSINESS
The main activity of the group is holding fixed property for investment purposes It also owns pine plantations, purifies and supplies water to Great Brak River and surrounding areas and generates electricity to supplement the needs of BOLTON FOOTWEAR

BANKERS :
Standard Bank of SA Ltd

AUDITORS :
Ernst & Young

FAMILIAR BRAND NAMES
N/A

CONTRIBUTION BY ACTIVITY
Property Rentals (% Turnover) (100.0%)

YEAR END : February

DIVIDEND : Ords 1c

Interim No 4	(Ldr)01/12/89	(Pay)29/12/89	Amt(c)4
Final No 5	(Ldr)25/05/90	(Pay)29/06/90	Amt(c)15
Interim No 6	(Ldr)07/12/90	(Pay)28/12/90	Amt(c)9.0
Special No 7	(Ldr)15/02/91	(Pay)25/02/91	Amt(c)72
Final No 8	(Ldr)24/05/91	(Pay)28/06/91	Amt(c)6
Special No 9	(Ldr)28/06/91	(Pay)05/07/91	Amt(c)40
Final No 10	(Ldr)22/05/92	(Pay)26/06/92	Amt(c)5

CAPITAL STRUCTURE

	AUTHORISED	ISSUED
Ords 1c	6000000	5173750

FINANCIAL STATISTICS (AT FINANCIAL YEAR END)

(Amts in R'000)	1992 Feb	1991 Feb	1990 Feb	1989 Aug	1989 Feb
Ord S/H Int	10585	12606	15692	16051	25163
Long Trm Loans	34	35	81	-	371
Iss Ord Share	5174	5174	5174	5174	5174
Total Liab	424	695	14969	1489	980
Current Liab	390	660	14888	1489	609
Total Assets	11009	13301	30661	17540	26143
Current Assets	870	2538	14240	1215	3382
Debtors	222	228	274	250	247
Inventory	48	48	49	52	632
Turnover	369	1187	5396	-	2547
Oper Profit	538	1230	4262	-	1733
Interest Paid	-	-	6	-	8
Tax Paid	263	623	2235	-	852
Prf af Int&Tax	275	607	2021	-	873
Prf att Ord Sh	275	607	2021	-	873
Btm Line Earn	306	1415	3411	-	878
Dividend Paid	259	4501	983	-	626
Mkt Prce(c) YE	100	150	400	235	175
Depreciation	-	-	6	-	7

PER SHARE STATISTICS (CENTS)

Net Asst Val	204.58	243.64	303.29	310.22	486.34
Net Earnings	5.30	11.70	39.10	-	16.90
Dividends	5.00	87.00	19.00	-	12.10
Cash Flow	5.32	11.62	33.82	-	16.18

RATIOS AND OTHER INFORMATION

Mrk Cap(R000)	5174	7761	20696	12159	9055
Current Ratio	2.23	3.85	0.96	0.82	5.55
Quik/Acid Tst	2.11	3.77	0.95	0.78	4.52
A/C Rec T/ovr	1.66	5.21	19.69	-	10.31
Tot Ass T/ovr	0.03	0.09	0.18	-	0.10
Debt/Ass Rat	0.04	0.05	0.49	0.08	0.03
L T L Tot Ass	-	-	0.00	-	0.00
Debt to Eqity	0.04	0.05	0.95	0.09	0.03
Interest Cover	-	-	710.33	-	216.63
Oper Prof Mrg	145.80	103.62	78.98	-	68.04
Net Prof Marg%	74.53	51.14	37.45	-	34.28
Ret on Assets	4.89	9.25	13.90	-	6.63
Ret on Equity%	2.60	4.82	12.85	-	3.46
Price/Earnings	18.87	12.82	10.23	-	10.36
Divid Cover	1.06	0.13	2.06	-	1.40
Divid Yield	5.00	58.00	4.75	-	6.91
Earning Yield%	5.30	7.80	9.78	-	9.66
NAV % Mrk Pr	204.58	162.43	75.82	132.01	277.91
Effec Tax Rate	49.07	51.14	58.32	-	51.36
Def Interval	-	0.22	0.02	-	0.10
Sus Grth Rate	0.15	-30.89	6.61	-	0.98

SUBSIDIARY & ASSOCIATED COMPANIES

CARRICK PROPERTIES (NEWCASTLE) (PTY) LTD
GBR PROPERTIES LTD
HERPA PROPERTIES (PTY) LTD
HERSHAM BEACH REALISATION CO (PTY) LTD
PALS BUILDING (PTY) LTD

INVESTMENTS

None

BORDER TIMBERS LTD

ABBREVIATION : BORDER

SECTOR : Zimbabwe Stock Exchange

SHAREHOLDERS

Who Owns Whom's Assessment of the Identity of the Ultimate Controlling Shareholder:
ANGLO AMERICAN

SHAREHOLDER	PERCENTAGE 1992	1991
SECURITY NOM LTD	54.2	---
TANKS INV ZIMBABWE LTD	25.0	---
NAT RAILWAYS OF ZIM CONTR PENS FUND	2.0	---
FIRST MUTUAL LIFE ASSURE SOC OF ZIM	1.1	---
TOTAL	82.3	---

DIRECTORS :
BRUCE LR ,DENNETT DE ,FRY DJ ,MANCAMA BV
MARGESSON MV (Chairman

REGISTERED OFFICE
70 Samora Machel Avenue, Harare
Zimbabwe

TEL: 704461
FAX: TELEX:70734

TRANSFER SECRETARY
N/A

COMPANY SECRETARY
Anglo American Corporation Services Ltd

NATURE OF BUSINESS
Incorporated in Zimbabwe and engages in the growing a processing of hardwood and softwood timbers.

BANKERS :
N/A

AUDITORS :
Deloitte & Touche

FAMILIAR BRAND NAMES
N/A

CONTRIBUTION BY ACTIVITY
N/A

YEAR END : September

DIVIDEND :Ords Z$2

Dividend	(Ldr)12/12/91	(Pay)14/01/92	Amt(c)13
Dividend	(Ldr)22/05/92	(Pay)22/06/92	Amt(c)5

CAPITAL STRUCTURE

	AUTHORISED	ISSUED
Ords Z$2	31000000	30528719

FINANCIAL STATISTICS (AT FINANCIAL YEAR END)

(Amts in Z$)	1991 Sep	1990 Sep
Ord S/H Int	182355	83745
Long Trm Loans	6711	1750
Iss Ord Share	30529	30529
Total Liab	34812	17476
Current Liab	28101	15726
Total Assets	217167	101221
Current Assets	37168	23341
Debtors	17611	11385
Inventory	14169	11847
Turnover	97927	62924
Oper Profit	28279	12904
Interest Paid	373	876
Tax Paid	10964	2780
Prf af Int&Tax	17055	9324
Prf att Ord Sh	17055	9324
Btm Line Earn	17055	9324
Dividend Paid	5801	2748
Depreciation	6165	3436

PER SHARE STATISTICS (CENTS)

Net Asst Val	597.32	274.31
Net Earnings	55.86	30.54
Dividends	19.00	9.00
Cash Flow	76.06	41.80

RATIOS AND OTHER INFORMATION

Current Ratio	1.32	1.48
Quik/Acid Tst	0.82	0.73
A/C Rec T/ovr	5.56	5.53
Tot Ass T/ovr	0.45	0.62
Debt/Ass Rat	0.16	0.17
L T L Tot Ass	0.03	0.02
Debt to Eqity	0.19	0.21
Interest Cover	75.82	14.73
Oper Prof Mrg	28.88	20.51
Net Prof Marg%	17.42	14.82
Ret on Assets	13.07	12.82
Ret on Equity%	9.35	11.13
Divid Cover	2.94	3.39
Effec Tax Rate	39.13	22.97
Def Interval	0.31	0.33
Sus Grth Rate	6.17	7.85

SUBSIDIARY & ASSOCIATED COMPANIES

None

INVESTMENTS

None

BOTSWANA INSURANCE HOLDINGS LTD

ABBREVIATION : BOTINS

SECTOR : Botswana Stock Exchange

SHAREHOLDERS

Who Owns Whom's Assessment of the Identity of the Ultimate Controlling Shareholder:
ST PAUL UK LTD / BOTSWANA DEVELOPMENT CO

SHAREHOLDER	PERCENTAGE 1992	1991
ST PAUL (UK) LTD	30.9	---
BOTSWANA DEVELOPMENT CORPORATION	17.9	---
SECHABA INV TRUST CO LTD	16.2	---
SOUTHERN LIFE ASSOC LTD	10.0	---
IGI BOTSWANA LIFE ASSURE LTD	1.7	---
BOTSWANA LIFE INSURANCE LTD	1.4	---
DEBSWANA PENS FUND	1.4	---
TOTAL	79.4	---

DIRECTORS :
AYRES G ,HOPKINS ME ,JANSEN GD ,LARWOOD DR
MOLEFANE MO (Chairman)
PARTON JG (Managing Director)
SMALL WD (Technical Director)
SWINDELL TA (Financial Director)
TSIANE B (Personnel Director),VAN DER ZWAN AJJ

REGISTRATION NUMBER : 90/1818

REGISTERED OFFICE
BIC House, Lot 12583
Nyerere Drive, Gaberone

TEL: 351791
FAX: 313290

TRANSFER SECRETARY
Coopers & Lybrand Services (Pty) Ltd
P O Box 702, Harare
Zimbabwe

TEL: 0926 34 702771

COMPANY SECRETARY
N/A

NATURE OF BUSINESS
The group underwrites all classes of general insurance and long term insurance.It also underwrites deposit administration schemes and manages investments of Life and Pension funds.

BANKERS :
Barclays Bank of Botswana Ltd
Standard Chartered Bank Zimbabwe Ltd

AUDITORS :
Deloitte Pim Goldby

FAMILIAR BRAND NAMES
N/A

CONTRIBUTION BY ACTIVITY
N/A

YEAR END : December

CAPITAL STRUCTURE

	AUTHORISED	ISSUED
Ords P0,50	60000000	11851900

FINANCIAL STATISTICS (AT FINANCIAL YEAR END)

(Amts in P)	1991 Dec
Ord S/H Int	14450
Long Trm Loans	107779
Iss Ord Share	11852
Total Liab	115472
Current Liab	7693
Total Assets	129922
Current Assets	24660
Debtors	7594
Oper Profit	4964
Tax Paid	1271
Prf af Int&Tax	3693
Prf att Ord Sh	3693
Btm Line Earn	3693
Dividend Paid	1422
Depreciation	193

PER SHARE STATISTICS (CENTS)

Net Asst Val	121 92
Net Earnings	35 60
Dividends	12 00
Cash Flow	32 79

RATIOS AND OTHER INFORMATION

Current Ratio	3 21
Quik/Acid Tst	3 21
Debt/Ass Rat	0 06
Debt to Eqity	0 53
Ret on Assets	3 82
Ret on Equity%	25 56
Divid Cover	2 97
Effec Tax Rate	29 90
Sus Grth Rate	15 72

SUBSIDIARY & ASSOCIATED COMPANIES

BOTSWANA GENERAL INSURANCE LTD
BOTSWANA LIFE INSURANCE LTD
ST PAUL UK LTD (30,9%)

INVESTMENTS

BOTSWANA DEVELOPMENT CORPORATION LTD (17,8%)
SECHABA INVESTMENT TRUST CO LTD (16,20%)
SOUTHERN LIFE ASSOCIATION LTD (BOTSWANA) (10,01%)

BOTSWANA RST LTD

ABBREVIATION : BOTREST

JSE SHORT CODE : BRS

SECTOR : Metals & Minerals-Copper

SHAREHOLDERS

Who Owns Whom's Assessment of the Identity of the Ultimate Controlling Shareholder: ANGLO AMERICAN / AMAX INC (USA)

SHAREHOLDER	PERCENTAGE 1992	1991
LONDON CONTROL ACCOUNT	55 4	---
SECURITY NOM LTD	12 1	12 1
DOMINO LTD	11 8	11 8
SOGES FIDUCEM SOC ANONYME	8 0	7 7
RESIDENT NOM LTD	4 5	4 5
STD BANK NOM TVL P/L	2 8	2 7
TOTAL	94 5	38 8

DIRECTORS :
BLANCO JL ,FOREMAN MA (Managing Director)
JOHNSON SM (Chairman),KABELO MC ,KEYS NJ
KING MW ,LEKAUKAU CM ,MCKERRON AB ,MOKGETHI DN
NCHINDO LG ,NEALON RT
RALLS JL (Financial Director

REGISTERED OFFICE
Administration Block, BCL Mine Site
Selebi Phikwe, Botswana

TEL 09267-810211
FAX 09267-81041

TRANSFER SECRETARY
Consolidated Share Registrars Ltd
P O Box 61051, Marshalltown
2107
TEL 011-492 1620

COMPANY SECRETARY
J B Galeforolwe

NATURE OF BUSINESS
An investment holding company whose only active subsidiary operates underground mines, and an ore treatment and flash smelting facility at Selebi-Phikwe in Botswana Nickel, copper and cobalt are produced

BANKERS :
Barclays Bank of Botswana Ltd
Barclays Bank Plc

AUDITORS :
Deloitte Pim Goldby

FAMILIAR BRAND NAMES
N/A

CONTRIBUTION BY ACTIVITY
N/A

YEAR END : December

DIVIDEND :15/00/91

NUMBER OF EMPLOYEES : 4737

CAPITAL STRUCTURE

	AUTHORISED	ISSUED
Ords Pula 2	40000000	17979282

FINANCIAL STATISTICS (AT FINANCIAL YEAR END)

(Amts in P)	1991 Dec	1990 Dec	1989 Dec	1988 Dec	1987 Dec
Ord S/H Int	-1737839	-1366425	-1217702	-1310490	-1128225
Long Trm Loans	2173857	1769908	1582519	1633092	1287103
Iss Ord Share	17979	17979	17979	17979	17979
Total Liab	2253676	1846417	1656584	1724427	1484795
Current Liab	79819	76509	74065	91335	197692
Total Assets	515837	479992	438882	413937	356570
Current Assets	145592	133295	119662	125848	75078
Debtors	28767	31372	41130	61846	16827
Inventory	74570	69949	35879	37177	42525
Turnover	250703	255917	431989	420938	128711
Oper Profit	34386	68663	139816	-163977	29808
Interest Paid	4856	34180	47028	18288	5024
Prf af Int&Tax	32223	38313	92788	-182265	24784
Prf att Ord Sh	-371414	-148723	92788	-182265	24784
Btm Line Earn	371414	-148723	92788	-182265	24784
Mkt Prce(c) YE	50	200	175	305	366

PER SHARE STATISTICS (CENTS)

Net Asst Val	9665 94	-7600 12	-6772 91	-7289 00	-6275 24
Cash Flow	179 23	213 10	516 09	-1013 77	137 85

RATIOS AND OTHER INFORMATION

Mrk Cap(R000)	8990	35958	31463	54836	65803
Current Ratio	1 82	1 74	1 62	1 38	0 38
Quik/Acid Tst	0 89	0 83	1 13	0 97	0 16
A/C Rec T/ovr	8 71	8 16	10 50	6 81	7 65
Tot Ass T/ovr	0 49	0 53	0 98	1 02	0 36
Debt/Ass Rat	4 37	3 85	3 77	4 17	4 16
L T L Tot Ass	4 21	3 69	3 61	3 95	3 61
Debt to Eqity	-1 30	-1 35	-1 36	-1 32	-1 32
Interest Cover	7 08	2 01	2 97	-8 97	5 93
Oper Prof Mrg	13 72	26 83	32 37	-38 96	23 16
Net Prof Marg%	-148 15	-58 11	21 48	-43 30	19 26
Ret on Assets	7 19	15 10	31 86	-39 61	8 36
Ret on Equity%	-224 16	-80 66	58 84	6280 67	-16 44
NAV % Mrk Pr	-19331 88	-3800 06	-3870 24	2389 84	-1714 55
Def Interval	67 46	46 20	17 10	-8 98	55 19
Sus Grth Rate	21 37	10 88	-7 62	13 91	-2 20

SUBSIDIARY & ASSOCIATED COMPANIES

BCL LTD
PHIKWE MINE
SELEBI MINE
SELEBI NORTH MINE

INVESTMENTS

None

BOUMAT LTD

ABBREVIATION : BOUMAT

JSE SHORT CODE : BOU

SECTOR : Industrial-Building & Construction

SHAREHOLDERS

Who Owns Whom's Assessment of the Identity of the Ultimate Controlling Shareholder: SAKERS VIA SAFICON

SHAREHOLDER	PERCENTAGE 1992	1991
SAKERS IND HOLDINGS LTD	51 0	38 0
STD BANK NOM TVL P/L	7 4	2 2
SANLAM	3 6	13 7
FIRST NAT NOM P/L	3 4	2 0
CMB NOM P/L	3 2	---
ANGLO AMERICAN GROUP PENS FUND	2 4	2 4
METAL IND GROUP PENS FUND	2 2	3 3
SAFICON BOUMAT PENS FUND	2 2	3 4
SA MUTUAL	2 1	6 1
ENGINEERING INDUSTRIES PENS FUND	2 1	2 9
ALTRON GROUP PENS FUND	2 0	---
NGK SINODALE TVL PENS FUND	1 5	1 2
SAGE LIFE LTD	1 3	1 5
W & I BRITTAN INV CC	---	1 5
CRONJE P J P	---	1 3
BUCHEL O C	---	1 1
GEVISSER D	---	1 1
BOARD OF EXECUTORS NOM P/L	---	2 3
TONGAAT HULETT PENS FUND	---	1 4
TOTAL	84 3	85 4

DIRECTORS :
ALBERTS LM ,BORSOOK S (Chairman),BRITTAN ID
EVERED RHH ,GEVISSER DJ (Chief Executive)
GLENDINING PR ,HIPPER KJ
KLEIN A (Chief Executive),KOLBE AL ,TRUSLER RT
VENTER GA

REGISTRATION NUMBER : 04/01284/06

REGISTERED OFFICE
86 Grayston Drive, Sandown
Sandton
2196
TEL 011-884 1355
FAX 011-884 2401

TRANSFER SECRETARY
Central Registrars Ltd
P O Box 4844, Johannesburg
2000
TEL 011-331 0051

COMPANY SECRETARY
P R Marais

NATURE OF BUSINESS
An investment holding company with subsidiaries active in the following fields Distribution of products to the building sector sanitaryware, bathroom fittings, plumbing materials, builders' hardware, tiles, architectural ironmongery & tools To the civil engineering sector non-ferrous, plastic & steel tube & fittings, valves, portable power plants, watermeters & engineering tools The Manufacture of Electric water heaters, stainless steel sanitaryware & holloware & acrylic

BANKERS :
Standard Bank of SA Ltd

AUDITORS :
KPMG Aiken & Peat

FAMILIAR BRAND NAMES
BERLESELL,BLAIKIE,BORDER PLUMBING
BREDELL TILES,BREDELLS,BRENNER & BUCHANAN
BUCHEL HARDWARE,BUILDERS MARKET
CAPE SHEET METAL,COASTAL HARDWARE,CONWAY
DAISHIN PORTABLE PUMPS,DESIGN HARDWARE
DURATILE,INCLEDON,JACK HOBSON,JUST TILES
KONBILD,KWIKOT,LE ROY SOMER,MILLERS
NATAL IRONMONGERS,SAFFER,SAMKOR PLUMBING
SANITARY CITY GROUP,SANITAS
SEABOARD CERAMICA,TUB TAP & TILE
UNION TRADING,V&R LOODGIETERWARE
VRYHEID HARDWARE,WAUD & BLACKMAN,YANMAR

CONTRIBUTION BY ACTIVITY
N/A

YEAR END : March

DIVIDEND : Ords 50c

Interim No 66	(Ldr)22/12/89	(Pay)26/01/90	Amt(c)22.5
Interim No 68	(Ldr)21/12/90	(Pay)25/01/91	Amt(c)24
Final No 69	(Ldr)21/06/91	(Pay)26/07/91	Amt(c)24
Final No 71	(Ldr)10/07/92	(Pay)31/07/92	Amt(c)6
Interim No 70	(Ldr)10/01/92	(Pay)31/01/92	Amt(c)4

NUMBER OF EMPLOYEES : 4103

CAPITAL STRUCTURE

	AUTHORISED	ISSUED
Ords 50c	35500000	31054163

FINANCIAL STATISTICS (AT FINANCIAL YEAR END)

(Amts in R'000)	1992 Mar	1991 Mar	1990 Mar	1989 Mar	1988 Mar
Ord S/H Int	136029	105919	114309	97645	75593
Long Trm Loans	20878	58469	59167	52182	40680
Iss Ord Share	31054	25398	23778	21745	19872
Total Liab	361080	377263	335269	301273	231919
Current Liab	340202	318794	276102	249091	191239
Total Assets	497109	483182	449578	398918	307512
Current Assets	450865	435058	406441	363286	290235
Debtors	187999	170307	165538	146410	120242
Inventory	181040	200603	193521	169413	128873
Turnover	1163235	1091214	1002180	842710	617754
Oper Profit	39268	28961	57852	57236	36926
Interest Paid	23415	25307	19461	10386	7080
Tax Paid	10545	3538	19321	23547	14886
Prf af Int&Tax	11326	2212	19070	23303	14960
Prf att Ord Sh	11502	1828	18532	22747	14204
Btm Line Earn	10443	-3170	18234	22246	22070
Dividend Paid	3336	5805	1078	811	350
Mkt Prce(c) YE	400	400	450	690	550
Depreciation	12478	13432	10294	3742	2825

PER SHARE STATISTICS (CENTS)

Net Asst Val	438.04	417.04	480.73	449.05	380.40
Net Earnings	43.00	7.00	82.00	110.00	75.20
Dividends	10.00	48.00	45.00	38.00	29.00
Cash Flow	91.16	59.41	134.71	123.95	94.68

RATIOS AND OTHER INFORMATION

Mrk Cap(R000)	124216	101592	107001	150041	109296
Current Ratio	1.33	1.36	1.47	1.46	1.52
Quik/Acid Tst	0.79	0.74	0.77	0.78	0.84
A/C Rec T/ovr	6.19	6.41	6.05	5.76	5.14
Tot Ass T/ovr	2.34	2.26	2.23	2.11	2.01
Debt/Ass Rat	0.72	0.77	0.74	0.75	0.74
L T L Tot Ass	0.04	0.11	0.12	0.12	0.12
Debt to Eqity	2.64	3.53	2.90	3.06	3.01
Interest Cover	1.68	1.14	2.97	5.51	5.22
Oper Prof Mrg	3.38	2.65	5.77	6.79	5.98
Net Prof Marg%	0.99	0.17	1.85	2.70	2.30
Ret on Assets	9.11	6.43	12.87	14.35	12.01
Ret on Equity%	8.46	1.73	16.21	23.30	18.79
Price/Earnings	9.30	57.14	5.49	6.27	7.31
Divid Cover	4.30	0.15	1.82	2.89	2.59
Divid Yield	2.50	12.00	10.00	5.51	5.27
Earning Yield%	10.75	1.75	18.22	15.94	13.67
NAV % Mrk Pr	109.51	104.26	106.83	65.08	69.16
Effec Tax Rate	47.26	75.06	45.99	51.60	47.34
Def Interval	3.75	7.44	2.88	1.75	1.98
Sus Grth Rate	6.00	-3.75	15.27	22.47	18.33

SUBSIDIARY & ASSOCIATED COMPANIES

A BLAIKIE (RAND) (PTY) LTD
AUBREY BREDELL (PTY) LTD
AW BLEKTON & CO (PTY) LTD
BATHROOM & TILE CENTRE (PTY) LTD
BERLESELL (PTY) LTD
BILDWARE (PTY) LTD
BORDER PLUMBING SUPPLIES (PTY) LTD
BOUMAT CREDIT MANAGEMENT (PTY) LTD
BOUMAT INFORMATION SYSTEMS (PTY) LTD
BOUMAT PROPERTIES (PTY) LTD (50%)
BREDELL TILES (PTY) LTD
BREDELLS NORTHERN CAPE (PTY) LTD
BRENNER & BUCHMAN (PTY) LTD
BRITTAN BOUSTRED (CONTRACTS) (PTY) LTD
BRITTAN BOUSTRED (EAST RAND) (PTY) LTD
BRITTAN BOUSTRED (IRONMONGERS) (PTY) LTD
BRITTAN BOUSTRED LTD
BUCHEL (PTY) LTD
BUCHEL HARDWARE (PTY) LTD
BUCHEL TOOL CENTRE (PTY) LTD
BUILDERS MARKET (PIETERSBURG) (PTY) LTD
BUILDERS MARKET CAPE TOWN (PTY) LTD
CAPE TIMBER BOARDS (PTY) LTD
CENTRAL AGENCIES & IMPORT COMPANY (PTY)
CITIWARE STAINLESS STEEL PRODUCTS (PTY)
CITY METAL PRODUCTS (PTY) LTD
COASTAL HARDWARE (PTY) LTD
COASTAL HARDWARE (SOUTH COAST) (PTY) LTD
COASTAL HARDWARE (ZULULAND) (PTY) LTD
COLOURTILE (PTY) LTD
DESIGN HARDWARE (PTY) LTD
DURATILE (EP) (PTY) LTD
DURATILE (PTY) LTD
DURITY ALPHA (PTY) LTD
DURITY CERAMICS (PTY) LTD
DURITY ENGINEERING SERVICES (PTY) LTD
DURITY MINING & INDUSTRIAL TRADING (PTY)
DURITY NATAL (PTY) LTD
DURITY OMEGA (PTY) LTD
DURITY POWER PRODUCTS (PTY) LTD
DURITY TILE WHOLESALERS (PTY) LTD
DURITY TILEWARE (PTY) LTD
DURITY TRANSVAAL (PTY) LTD
EDDIE NEL (PTY) LTD
EVANDER PLUMBING & MINING SUPPLIES (PTY)
G.P. BUILDING & HARDWARE SUPPLIES (PTY)
GAGE PLUMBING SUPPLIES (PTY) LTD
GENERAL PLUMBING SUPPLIES (PTY) LTD
HIRAN INVESTMENTS (PTY) LTD
HOME BUILD SUPPLIERS (PTY) LTD
IL BAGNO (PTY) LTD
INCLEDON (BORDER) (PTY) LTD

INCLEDON (GEORGE) (PTY) LTD
INCLEDON (PMB) (PTY) LTD
INCLEDON (WELKOM) (PTY) LTD
INCLEDON BLOEMFONTEIN (PTY) LTD
INCLEDON CAPE TOWN (PTY) LTD
INCLEDON DURBAN (PTY) LTD
INCLEDON EAST CAPE ENGINEERING EQUIPMENT
INCLEDON ENGINEERING (NATAL) (PTY) LTD
INCLEDON ENGINEERING (WESTERN CAPE) (PTY
INCLEDON ERMELO (PTY) LTD
INCLEDON EVANDER (PTY) LTD
INCLEDON JOHANNESBURG (PTY) LTD
INCLEDON KLERKSDORP (PTY) LTD
INCLEDON KOMATI (PTY) LTD
INCLEDON LADYSMITH (PTY) LTD
INCLEDON LOWVELD (PTY) LTD
INCLEDON NELSPRUIT (PTY) LTD
INCLEDON PINETOWN (PTY) LTD
INCLEDON PRETORIA (PTY) LTD
INCLEDON TILES (PTY) LTD
INCLEDON VAAL (PTY) LTD
JACK HOBSON (PTY) LTD
JUST TILES (PTY) LTD
KONBILD (PTY) LTD
KONBILD WEST (PTY) LTD
KOOP-EN-BOU (EDMS) BPK
KWIKOT (CAPE) LTD
KWIKOT (EAST CAPE) LTD
KWIKOT (NATAL) LTD
KWIKOT INDUSTRIAL LTD
KWIKOT LTD
LEON SWARTZBERG & CO. (PTY) LTD
LN CONWAY & CO (PTY) LTD
LOWVELD TILES (PTY) LTD
MBS WHOLESALERS (PTY) LTD
MIDLAND PIPE & PLUMBING SUPPLIES (PTY) L
NATAL IRONMONGERS (PTY) LTD
PINEAPPLE BUSINESS DEVELOPMENT (PTY) LTD
PLETT PAINT & HARDWARE (PTY) LTD
PLUMBWARE EASTERN TRANSVAAL (PTY) LTD
PLUMBWARE INVESTMENTS (NATAL) (PTY) LTD
PLUMBWARE INVESTMENTS (OFS) (PTY) LTD
PLUMBWARE INVESTMENTS (PTY) LTD
PLUMBWARE INVESTMENTS (PWV) (PTY) LTD
PLUMBWARE INVESTMENTS EASTERN CAPE (PTY)
PLUMBWARE NATAL (PTY) LTD
PLUMBWARE NORTHERN NATAL (PTY) LTD
POWER INDUSTRIAL CENTRE (PTY) LTD
PRESTIGE PIPE & POWER (PTY) LTD
SAFFER & CO (NAMIBIA) (PTY) LTD
SAFFER & CO (OFS) (PTY) LTD
SAFFER & CO. (CAPE) (PTY) LTD
SAFFER & CO. (EAST CAPE) (PTY) LTD
SAFFER & CO. (JOHANNESBURG) (PTY) LTD
SAFFER & CO. (LOWVELD) (PTY) LTD
SAFFER & CO. (NATAL) (PTY) LTD
SAFFER & CO. (NORTH) (PTY) LTD
SAFFER & CO. (PTY) LTD
SALES INTERNATIONAL (PTY) LTD
SAMKOR PLUMBING & BUILDING CENTRE (PTY)
SANITARY CITY (BOKSBURG) (PTY) LTD
SANITARY CITY (BOKSBURG) (PTY) LTD
SANITARY CITY (JOHANNESBURG) (PTY) LTD
SANITARY CITY (JOHANNESBURG) (PTY) LTD
SANITARY CITY (PRETORIA) (PTY) LTD
SANITARY CITY (PRETORIA) (PTY) LTD
SANITARY CITY (SANDTON) (PTY) LTD
SANITARY CITY GROUP (PTY) LTD
SANITAS (GEORGE) (PTY) LTD
SANITAS (PLETT) (PTY) LTD
SEABOARD INDUSTRIAL PRODUCTS (PTY) LTD
STELLENBOSCH BOUHANDEL (PTY) LTD
TILE-IT (PTY) LTD
TUB TAP & TILE (TRANSVAAL) (PTY) LTD
V & R LOODGIETERWARE (EDMS) BPK
VRYHEID HARDWARE (PTY) LTD
W & B HARDWARE (PTY) LTD
W MILLER (PTY) LTD
WAUD & BLACKMAN (PTY) LTD
WB CAMERON (PTY) LTD

INVESTMENTS

None

BOWLER METCALF LTD

ABBREVIATION : BOWCALF

JSE SHORT CODE : BCF

SECTOR : Industrial-Paper & Packaging

SHAREHOLDERS

Who Owns Whom's Assessment of the Identity of the Ultimate Controlling Shareholder: DIRECTORS

SHAREHOLDER	PERCENTAGE 1992	1991
BOWCALF INV HOLDINGS P/L	80.5	80.0
JENKINS P L	2.2	1.7
BRAIN M	2.1	2.1
SASS H W	2.0	2.0
TINDALE E G	---	1.4
FERBROS NOM P/L	---	1.1
TOTAL	86.7	88.2

DIRECTORS :
BRAIN M ,DOYLE BW ,OLDS MA
SASS HW (Managing Director)
SPALDING GF (Chairman),TINDALE EG

REGISTRATION NUMBER : 72/05921/06

REGISTERED OFFICE
Myhof Road, Claremont
Cape
7700
TEL: 021-61 3050
FAX: 021-61 6219

TRANSFER SECRETARY
Gold Equity Registrars (Pty) Ltd
P O Box 62185, Marshalltown
2107
TEL: 011-834 5623

COMPANY SECRETARY
M Brain

NATURE OF BUSINESS
Manufacture of plastic mouldings and moulds.

BANKERS :
First National Bank of SA Ltd

AUDITORS :
Baker Musikanth

FAMILIAR BRAND NAMES
N/A

CONTRIBUTION BY ACTIVITY
N/A

YEAR END : December

DIVIDEND : Ords no par value

Interim No 5	(Ldr)17/08/90	(Pay)23/08/90	Amt(c)1.25
Final No 6	(Ldr)22/02/91	(Pay)05/04/91	Amt(c)1.5
Interim No 7	(Ldr)16/08/91	(Pay)21/08/91	Amt(c)1.5
Final No 8	(Ldr)24/04/92	(Pay)29/04/92	Amt(c)2
Interim No 9	(Ldr)04/09/92	(Pay)10/09/92	Amt(c)2

NUMBER OF EMPLOYEES : 143

CAPITAL STRUCTURE

	AUTHORISED	ISSUED
Ords no par value	40000000	25000000

FINANCIAL STATISTICS (AT FINANCIAL YEAR END)

(Amts in R'000)	1991 Dec	1990 Dec	1989 Dec	1988 Dec	1987
Ord S/H Int	4321	3369	4667	3828	3226
Long Trm Loans	3016	3713	1592	606	3069
Iss Ord Share	25000	25000	25000	25000	25000
Total Liab	7250	7843	4209	2949	5440
Current Liab	4234	4130	2617	2343	2371
Total Assets	11423	11064	8728	6777	9618
Intang Assets	148	148	148	*	*
Current Assets	4213	3751	2656	2940	3323
Debtors	2629	2292	1654	1666	-
Inventory	1354	1449	993	1262	3323
Turnover	17510	14521	12323	10670	7220
Oper Profit	3874	2860	1962	1471	1205
Interest Paid	542	548	563	416	165
Tax Paid	1524	1133	-	-	-
Prf af Int&Tax	1827	1184	1401	1102	1040
Prf att Ord Sh	1827	1184	1401	1102	1040
Btm Line Earn	1827	1084	1401	1102	1040
Dividend Paid	875	687	563	500	-
Mkt Prce(c) YE	48	30	25	25	30
Depreciation	1052	923	679	780	-

PER SHARE STATISTICS (CENTS)

Net Asst Val	16.69	12.88	18.08	15.31	12.90
Net Earnings	7.30	4.70	5.60	4.40	-
Dividends	3.50	2.75	2.25	2.00	-
Cash Flow	12.69	10.51	8.32	7.53	4.16

RATIOS AND OTHER INFORMATION

Mrk Cap(R000)	12000	7500	6250	6250	7500
Current Ratio	1.00	0.91	1.01	1.25	1.40
Quik/Acid Tst	0.68	0.56	0.64	0.72	-
A/C Rec T/ovr	6.66	6.34	7.45	6.40	-
Tot Ass T/ovr	1.53	1.31	1.41	1.57	0.75
Debt/Ass Rat	0.42	0.51	0.48	0.44	0.57
L T L Tot Ass	0.04	0.14	0.18	0.09	0.32
Debt to Eqity	1.10	1.67	0.90	0.77	1.69
Interest Cover	7.15	5.22	3.48	3.54	7.30
Oper Prof Mrg	22.12	19.70	15.92	13.79	16.69
Net Prof Marg%	10.43	8.15	11.37	10.33	14.40
Ret on Assets	34.08	25.89	22.50	22.40	12.53
Ret on Equity%	42.28	35.14	30.02	28.79	32.24
Price/Earnings	6.58	6.38	4.46	5.68	-
Divid Cover	2.09	1.71	2.49	2.20	-
Divid Yield	7.29	9.17	9.00	8.00	-
Earning Yield%	15.21	15.67	22.40	17.60	-
NAV % Mrk Pr	34.78	42.95	72.30	61.25	43.01
Effec Tax Rate	36.71	26.41	-	-	-
Def Interval	0.33	0.91	1.02	0.65	2.95
Sus Grth Rate	22.03	14.75	17.96	15.73	32.24

SUBSIDIARY & ASSOCIATED COMPANIES

CALL TECH (PTY) LTD

INVESTMENTS

THE BOWLER METCALF SHARE TRUST (63000 SH)

BOYMANS LTD

ABBREVIATION : BOYMANS

JSE SHORT CODE : BOY

SECTOR : Industrial-Retailers & Wholesalers

SHAREHOLDERS

Who Owns Whom's Assessment of the Identity of the Ultimate Controlling Shareholder:
DIRECTORS / AMREL

SHAREHOLDER	PERCENTAGE 1992	1991
AMALGAMATED RETAIL LTD	75.7	36.0
ELLERINE BROS P/L	5.7	15.2
BRODKIN A	2.9	7.5
BRODKIN A H	2.9	7.5
REGENBAUM H	2.4	6.3
STD BANK NOM TVL P/L	2.2	5.9
HOGG G B	1.5	4.0
SHEVITZ C	1.4	3.8
BOYMANS SHARE OPTION SCHEME	1.4	3.6
FIRST NAT NOM P/L	1.2	3.1
ERIC ELLERINE TRUST P/L	---	1.4
TOTAL	97.2	94.3

DIRECTORS :
BERGER SJ ,BRODKIN A (Joint Managing Director)
BRODKIN AH ,CONNAWAY JF (Financial Director)
ELLERINE E (Chairman),ELLERINE S ,LOGAN RL
REGENBAUM H (Joint Managing Director),SHEIN MA

REGISTRATION NUMBER : 05/00067/06

REGISTERED OFFICE
2nd Floor, Access City, 5 Beacon Road
New Doornfontein
2094
TEL: 011-402 2637
FAX: 011-402 6926

TRANSFER SECRETARY
Central Registrars Ltd
P O Box 4844, Johannesburg
2000
TEL: 011-331 0051

COMPANY SECRETARY
J F Connaway

NATURE OF BUSINESS
An investment holding company with subsidiaries engaged in clothing retail through 51 outlets.

BANKERS :
Standard Bank of SA Ltd

AUDITORS :
Schneider Katz & Levy

FAMILIAR BRAND NAMES
BOYMANS,CULHANE,CYRILS,DEANS,GABACCI,JAS JOHN ORRS,JOHN SCOTT,LACOSTE,LEVISONS WOOLFSONS

CONTRIBUTION BY ACTIVITY
N/A

YEAR END : February

DIVIDEND : Ords 50c
Interim (Ldr)18/08/89 (Pay)01/09/89 Amt(c)6.5

NUMBER OF EMPLOYEES : 1381

CAPITAL STRUCTURE

	AUTHORISED	ISSUED
Ords 50c	32500000	28382207
6% Cum Prefs R2	100000	100000

FINANCIAL STATISTICS (AT FINANCIAL YEAR END)

(Amts in R'000)	1992 Feb	1991 Feb	1990 Feb	1989	1988 Dec
Ord S/H Int	28414	27627	26937	26953	25170
Long Trm Loans	38781	30871	33088	71213	21887
Iss Ord Share	10751	10751	10751	-	10751
Total Liab	83177	81703	74479	110579	61695
Current Liab	44396	50832	41391	39366	39808
Total Assets	111591	109330	100826	181423	86275
Intang Assets	*	*	590	*	590
Current Assets	97068	93209	83257	83257	72745
Debtors	60108	55260	41841	-	36531
Inventory	36704	37561	41176	83257	35247
Turnover	189763	189898	188200	188200	132123
Oper Profit	11325	14203	12827	12380	10662
Interest Paid	9340	9304	8102	7527	3548
Tax Paid	1293	2436	2461	2357	3087
Prf af Int&Tax	799	2535	2459	2496	4138
Prf att Ord Sh	787	2523	2445	2482	4126
Btm Line Earn	787	2523	2445	2482	4126
Dividend Paid	-	-	699	699	1398
Mkt Prce(c) YE	125	130	160	180	190
Depreciation	3390	3285	3044	-	2279

PER SHARE STATISTICS (CENTS)

Net Asst Val	264.29	256.97	245.07	-	228.63
Net Earnings	7.30	23.50	22.70	-	38.40
Dividends	-	-	6.50	-	13.00
Cash Flow	39.70	54.70	44.03	-	59.58

RATIOS AND OTHER INFORMATION

Mrk Cap(R000)	13439	13976	17202	-	20427
Current Ratio	2.19	1.83	2.01	2.11	1.83
Quik/Acid Tst	1.36	1.09	1.02	-	0.94
A/C Rec T/ovr	3.16	3.44	3.86	-	3.62
Tot Ass T/ovr	1.70	1.74	1.60	1.04	1.53
Debt/Ass Rat	0.73	0.73	0.74	0.61	0.71
L T L Tot Ass	0.33	0.27	0.33	0.39	0.25
Debt to Eqity	2.87	2.90	2.76	4.10	2.44
Interest Cover	1.21	1.53	1.58	1.64	3.01
Oper Prof Mrg	5.97	7.48	6.82	6.58	8.07
Net Prof Marg%	0.41	1.33	1.30	1.32	3.12
Ret on Assets	10.24	13.06	11.07	6.82	12.49
Ret on Equity%	2.77	9.13	7.78	9.21	16.39
Price/Earnings	17.12	5.53	7.05	-	4.95
Divid Cover	-	-	3.49	-	2.95
Divid Yield	-	-	4.06	-	6.84
Earning Yield%	5.84	18.08	14.19	-	20.21
NAV % Mrk Pr	211.43	197.67	153.17	-	120.33
Effec Tax Rate	52.77	45.64	45.87	48.57	43.18
Def Interval	10.75	7.77	6.28	28.53	3.52
Sus Grth Rate	2.77	9.13	6.48	6.62	10.84

SUBSIDIARY & ASSOCIATED COMPANIES

BOYMANS CLOTHIERS (PTY) LTD
DEBONAIR (PTY) LTD
ESQUIRE (PTY) LTD
GABICCI (PTY) LTD
LANSAL (PTY) LTD
LEVISONS STORES (PTY) LTD
PRESTIGE STORES (PTY) LTD

INVESTMENTS

None

BRACKEN MINES LTD

ABBREVIATION : BRACKEN

JSE SHORT CODE : BRA

SECTOR : Gold-Evander

SHAREHOLDERS

Who Owns Whom's Assessment of the Identity of the Ultimate Controlling Shareholder: SANLAM VIA GENCOR

SHAREHOLDER	PERCENTAGE 1992	1991
INDO-CHINA NOM P/L	24.7	---
CONSOLIDATED NOM P/L	10.7	10.7
LONDON CONTROL ACCOUNT	10.5	10.2
FIRST CORP NOM P/L	10.2	10.2
SEPON LTD	9.8	9.6
FIRST NAT NOM P/L GATR DEPOT	6.7	6.4
FIRST NAT NOM P/L	4.3	5.4
STD BANK NOM TVL P/L	3.8	3.7
NAT CITY NOM LTD	2.9	2.9
DEPOSITARY NOM INC	2.5	2.1
ABSA NOM P/L	1.4	---
KAYEMESS NOM P/L	1.0	1.0
INDO-CHINA NOM SA P/L	---	22.9
VOLKSKAS NOM P/L	---	1.7
TOTAL	88.5	86.7

DIRECTORS :
BURKE JHJ (Financial Director),EICK KFW ,LEE GS
MAUDE G (Managing Director)
OLIVIER JE (Chairman),RADEMEYER P DE V

STEENKAMP TI

REGISTRATION NUMBER : 59/01126/06

REGISTERED OFFICE
General Mining Building, 6 Hollard Street
Johannesburg
2001
TEL 011-376 9111

TRANSFER SECRETARY
Central Registrars Ltd
P O Box 4844, Johannesburg
2000
TEL 011-331 0051

COMPANY SECRETARY
General Mining Metals & Minerals Ltd

NATURE OF BUSINESS
The company operates a gold mine in the Evander area, Eastern Transvaal Silver & osmiridium are recovered as by-products of gold

BANKERS :
First National Bank of SA Ltd

AUDITORS :
Deloitte Pim Goldby

FAMILIAR BRAND NAMES
N/A

CONTRIBUTION BY ACTIVITY
Gold (% of Turnover) (98 8%)
Silver (0 1%)
Osmiridium (0 1%)

YEAR END : September

DIVIDEND : Ords 90c

Interim No 55	(Ldr)14/05/90	(Pay)15/06/90	Amt(c)30
Final No 56	(Ldr)02/11/90	(Pay)14/12/90	Amt(c)25
Interim No 57	(Ldr)01/05/91	(Pay)18/06/91	Amt(c)10
Final No 58	(Ldr)01/11/91	(Pay)13/12/91	Amt(c)15

NUMBER OF EMPLOYEES : 1379

CAPITAL STRUCTURE

	AUTHORISED	ISSUED
Ords 90c	14000000	14000000

FINANCIAL STATISTICS (AT FINANCIAL YEAR END)

(Amts in R'000)	1991 Sep	1990 Sep	1989 Sep	1988 Sep	1987
Ord S/H Int	41269	38730	38466	37074	34505
Long Trm Loans	49	75	-	-	21669
Iss Ord Share	14000	14000	14000	14000	14000
Total Liab	15030	16725	16211	13919	43298
Current Liab	14981	16650	16211	13919	21629
Total Assets	56299	55455	54677	50993	85523
Current Assets	27055	26225	24718	22546	29349
Debtors	1288	1561	1553	1420	
Inventory	3092	4470	4640	4782	29349
Turnover	62340	71324	73896	78550	79604
Oper Profit	10123	10658	7224	10444	21967
Interest Paid	10	16	-		
Tax Paid	4746	3821	1314	1771	10901
Prf af Int&Tax	6054	7973	6992	8874	11054
Prf att Ord Sh	6039	7964	6992	8869	8900
Btm Line Earn	6039	7964	6992	8869	8900
Dividend Paid	3500	7700	5600	6300	9100

Mkt Prce(c) YE	120	305	250	300	760

PER SHARE STATISTICS (CENTS)

Net Asst Val	294 78	276 64	274 76	264 81	246 46
Net Earnings	43 00	63 00	40 00	52 00	-
Dividends	25 00	55 00	40 00	45 00	-
Cash Flow	43 24	56 95	49 94	63 10	78 96

RATIOS AND OTHER INFORMATION

Mrk Cap(R000)	16800	42700	35000	42000	106400
Current Ratio	1 81	1 58	1 52	1 62	1 36
Quik/Acid Tst	1 60	1 31	1 24	1 28	-
A/C Rec T/ovr	48 40	45 69	47 58	55 32	-
Tot Ass T/ovr	1 11	1 29	1 35	1 54	0 93
Debt/Ass Rat	0 27	0 30	0 30	0 27	0 51
L T L Tot Ass	0 00	0 00	-	-	0 25
Debt to Eqity	0 36	0 43	0 42	0 38	1 25
Interest Cover	1081 00	738 13	-	-	-
Oper Prof Mrg	16 24	14 94	9 78	13 30	27 60
Net Prof Marg%	9 69	11 17	9 46	11 29	11 18
Ret on Assets	19 20	21 30	15 19	20 88	25 67
Ret on Equity%	14 63	20 56	18 18	23 92	25 79
Price/Earnings	2 79	4 84	6 25	5 77	-
Divid Cover	1 72	1 15	1 00	1 16	-
Divid Yield	20 83	18 03	16 00	15 00	-
Earning Yield%	35 83	20 66	16 00	17 33	-
NAV % Mrk Pr	245 65	90 70	109 90	88 27	32 43
Effec Tax Rate	46 93	35 90	18 19	17 34	49 62
Def Interval	0 01	0 01	-	-	1 96
Sus Grth Rate	6 15	0 68	3 62	6 93	0 58

SUBSIDIARY & ASSOCIATED COMPANIES

EVANDER TOWNSHIP LTD (25%)

INVESTMENTS

None

BRENNER MILLS LTD

ABBREVIATION : BRENMIL

JSE SHORT CODE : BRL

SECTOR : Industrial-Food

SHAREHOLDERS

Who Owns Whom's Assessment of the Identity of the Ultimate Controlling Shareholder:
BRENNER FAMILY

SHAREHOLDER	PERCENTAGE 1992	1991
SAMBREN P/L	43 3	43 2
CMB NOM P/L	5 1	-
GABI BRENNER INV P/L	4 5	4 5
HAYLEY BRENNER INV P/L	4 5	4 5
BRENNER M	3 2	3 0
GAYLE BRENNER INV P/L	3 0	3 0
SALLY ANN BRENNER INV P/L	3 0	3 0
STEVEN BRENNER INV P/L	3 0	3 0

BRENNER A	3 0	3 0
BRENNER Z	3 0	3 0
FRAN BRENNER INV P/L	1 8	1 8
JOSS BRENNER INV P/L	1 8	1 8
LARRY EARL BRENNER INV P/L	1 8	1 8
SHELLEY BRENNER INV P/L	1 8	1 8
TRACY BRENNER INV P/L	1 8	1 8
SANLAM	---	5 0
TOTAL	84 7	84 4

DIRECTORS :
BRENNER A (Chairman & Joint MD),BRENNER K
BRENNER M (Joint Managing Director)
BRENNER S (Joint Managing Director),MANSELL B

REGISTRATION NUMBER : 87/01547/06

REGISTERED OFFICE
12th Floor, Penmor Tower, 1 Rissik Str
Johannesburg
2001
TEL 015331-3997
FAX 015331-4406

TRANSFER SECRETARY
Central Registrars Ltd
P O Box 4844, Johannesburg
2000
TEL 011-331 0051

COMPANY SECRETARY
Rudman Roome & Company

NATURE OF BUSINESS
The group operates as a maize miller in the N Tvl Products are distributed via wholesalers and retailers throughout N Tvl and the neighbouring states Malt for sorghum beer and animal feeds are also manufactured

BANKERS :
Standard Bank of SA Ltd

AUDITORS :
Kessel Feinstein

FAMILIAR BRAND NAMES
BRENNCO FEEDS,CUP FINAL
LOUIS TRICHARDT ROLLER,SHAYA
TSWANA FEEDS & PACK,TSWANA MILLING & TRAD
WARMBATHS MILLING,ZOUTPANSBERG MILLING

CONTRIBUTION BY ACTIVITY
N/A

YEAR END : February

DIVIDEND : Ords 10c

Interim No 5	(Ldr)15/12/89	(Pay)29/12/89	Amt(c)3
Final No 6	(Ldr)15/06/90	(Pay)29/06/90	Amt(c)2
Interim No 7	(Ldr)28/12/90	(Pay)11/01/91	Amt(c)2 75
Final No 8	(Ldr)14/06/91	(Pay)28/06/91	Amt(c)1
Interim No 9	(Ldr)27/12/91	(Pay)10/01/92	Amt(c)2 75
Final No 10	(Ldr)12/06/92	(Pay)26/06/92	Amt(c)5 25
Interim No 11	(Ldr)04/12/92	(Pay)18/12/92	Amt(c)8

CAPITAL STRUCTURE

	AUTHORISED	ISSUED
Ords 10c	30000000	23300000

FINANCIAL STATISTICS (AT FINANCIAL YEAR END)

(Amts in R 000)	1992	1991	1990	1989	1988
	Feb	Feb	Feb	Feb	Feb
Ord S/H Int	27437	25478	39480	24036	22463
Long Trm Loans	764	848	762	211	169
Iss Ord Share	23300	23300	23300	23300	23300
Total Liab	11327	12481	9901	7351	5238
Current Liab	10563	11633	9139	7140	5069
Total Assets	38764	37959	34771	31387	27701
Intang Assets	*	*	14610	*	*
Current Assets	25707	23868	20773	20146	17341
Debtors	12458	17779	12966	11671	8098
Inventory	7034	6081	6685	7326	6419
Oper Profit	7454	3977	4886	3317	5969
Interest Paid	753	1129	525	140	10
Tax Paid	3350	1534	2048	1606	3708
Prf af Int&Tax	3823	1687	2313	2738	3766
Prf att Ord Sh	3823	1687	2313	2738	3766
Btm Line Earn	3823	1687	2313	2738	3766
Dividend Paid	1864	874	1165	1165	1515
Mkt Prce(c) YE	60	60	60	75	135
Depreciation	1719	1879	1384	1269	1028

PER SHARE STATISTICS (CENTS)

Net Asst Val	117 76	109 35	106 74	103 16	96 41
Net Earnings	16 40	7 20	9 90	11 80	16 20
Dividends	8 00	3 75	5 00	5 00	6 50
Cash Flow	23 57	14 79	16 87	17 38	21 10

RATIOS AND OTHER INFORMATION

Mrk Cap(R000)	13980	13980	13980	17475	31455
Current Ratio	2 43	2 05	2 27	2 82	3 42
Quik/Acid Tst	1 77	1 53	1 54	1 80	2 15
Debt/Ass Rat	0 27	0 31	0 26	0 23	0 18
Debt to Eqity	0 38	0 46	0 23	0 30	0 23
Interest Cover	9 90	3 52	9 31	32 03	748 40
Ret on Assets	20 45	11 46	14 05	14 29	29 47
Ret on Equity%	13 93	6 62	5 86	11 39	18 29
Price/Earnings	3 66	8 33	6 06	6 36	8 33
Divid Cover	2 05	1 92	1 98	2 36	2 49
Divid Yield	13 33	6 25	8 33	6 67	4 81
Earning Yield%	27 33	12 00	16 50	15 73	12 00
NAV % Mrk Pr	196 26	182 25	177 90	137 55	71 41
Effec Tax Rate	47 87	51 32	41 41	49 23	64 14
Def Interval	-	1 20	0 43		
Sus Grth Rate	7 14	3 19	2 91	6 54	10 02

SUBSIDIARY & ASSOCIATED COMPANIES

LOUIS TRICHARDT ROLLER MILLS (PTY) LTD
TSWANA FEEDS & PACKAGING (PTY) LTD
TSWANA MILLING & TRADING (PTY) LTD
WARMBATHS MILLING CO (PTY) LTD, THE
ZOUTPANSBERG MILLING COMPANY (PTY) LTD

INVESTMENTS

None

BRIAN PORTER HOLDINGS LTD

ABBREVIATION · PORT

JSE SHORT CODE · POT

SECTOR · Industrial Motor

SHAREHOLDERS

Who Owns Whom's Assessment of the Identity of the Ultimate Controlling Shareholder:
DIRECTORS

SHAREHOLDER	PERCENTAGE 1992	1991
SYFRETS NOM LTD	30 2	30 2
PORTER B J L	22 2	22 1
BRIAN PORTER HLDGS P/L	10 6	10 6
SYFRETS TRUST LTD	8 7	8 8
MARAIS INV TRUST P/L	5 9	5 9
BUTLER F H	4 1	4 1
NEDBANK NOM LTD	2 0	1 9
PORTER A M	1 4	1 4
CARTER E	1 1	1 1
EIGHTY ONE MAIN STREET NOM LTD	1 1	--
TOTAL	87 2	86 0

DIRECTORS :
BAUDERT K (Executive Director),LAZARUS R
MARAIS CL ,PORTER AM (Managing Director)
RAMSBOTTOM R (Financial Director)
ROBINSON BB (Chairman),SIMPSON JD

REGISTRATION NUMBER : 05/19667/06

REGISTERED OFFICE
Porter House, Belmont Road
Rondebosch
7700
TEL 021-689 4711
FAX 021-689 1576

TRANSFER SECRETARY
Fraser Street Registrars (Pty) Ltd
P O Box 61178, Marshalltown
2107
TEL 011-491 0911

COMPANY SECRETARY
B W Irving

NATURE OF BUSINESS
The company is a holding company which has motor trading & property owning subsidiaries The group derives income from the sale of new & used vehicles, service, parts, car airconditioning, panelshop, petrol, & Action Display boards The properties are used for retail motor trading purposes

BANKERS :
Standard Bank of SA Ltd
First National Bank of SA Ltd
Trust Bank of Africa Ltd, Nedcor Bank Ltd

AUDITORS :
Ernst & Young

FAMILIAR BRAND NAMES
BENTLEY,BMW,COSMOS AIRWAVES,DELTA\ISUZU FRIENDLY FORD,GERMISTON MOTORS MMI JAGUAR\DAIMLER,LAND ROVER\RANGE ROVER MAZDA\MITSUBISHI,NISSAN\UNO,NOVA FORD PORT DELTA,PORTER BMW,PORTER MMI PORTER NISSAN,PRESTIGE CARS,RANDBURG MMI REEF MMI,ROLLS ROYCE,SOMERSET TOYOTA,URGIES

CONTRIBUTION BY ACTIVITY
N/A

YEAR END : June

DIVIDEND :Ords 50c

Interim No 84	(Ldr)30/03/90	(Pay)12/04/90	Amt(c)12
Final No 85	(Ldr)21/09/90	(Pay)12/10/90	Amt(c)13
Interim No 86	(Ldr)05/04/91	(Pay)19/04/91	Amt(c)8
Final No 87	(Ldr)20/09/91	(Pay)11/10/91	Amt(c)13
Interim No 88	(Ldr)03/04/92	(Pay)21/04/92	Amt(c)10
Final No 89	(Ldr)02/10/92	(Pay)16/10/92	Amt(c)8

NUMBER OF EMPLOYEES : 1338

CAPITAL STRUCTURE

	AUTHORISED	ISSUED
5,5% Cum Prefs R2	225000	162500
Ords 50c	3000000	2830000

FINANCIAL STATISTICS (AT FINANCIAL YEAR END)

(Amts in R'000)	1992 Jun	1991 Jun	1990 Jun	1989 Jun	1988 Jun
Ord S/H Int	24184	22899	21279	19401	17086
Long Trm Loans	4375	4419	4386	4224	4302
Iss Ord Share	2830	2830	2830	2830	2830
Total Liab	51353	41829	37543	33690	28081
Current Liab	46978	37410	33157	29466	23779
Total Assets	75537	64728	58822	53091	45167
Current Assets	61919	53448	47721	43150	36377
Debtors	12877	10663	9092	8386	6910
Inventory	49009	42757	38583	34718	29433
Turnover	340821	307177	286578	244544	208100
Oper Profit	7601	7418	7878	7853	5250
Interest Paid	4213	3214	3212	2194	946
Tax Paid	1984	2136	2043	2462	1452
Prf af Int&Tax	1867	2296	2663	3215	2852
Prf att Ord Sh	1794	2214	2586	3164	2814
Btm Line Earn	1794	2214	2586	3164	2600
Dividend Paid	509	594	708	849	708
Mkt Prce(c) YE	490	425	440	350	350
Depreciation	1593	1131	1033	818	561

PER SHARE STATISTICS (CENTS)

Net Asst Val	854 56	809 15	751 91	685 55	603 75
Net Earnings	63 40	78 20	91 40	111 80	100 00
Dividends	18 00	21 00	25 00	30 00	25 00
Cash Flow	120 25	118 59	128 09	139 08	119 58

RATIOS AND OTHER INFORMATION

Mrk Cap(R000)	13867	12028	12452	9905	9905
Current Ratio	1 32	1 43	1 44	1 46	1 53
Quik/Acid Tst	0 27	0 29	0 28	0 29	0 29
A/C Rec T/ovr	26 47	28 81	31 52	29 16	30 12
Tot Ass T/ovr	4 51	4 75	4 87	4 61	4 61
Debt/Ass Rat	0 67	0 64	0 63	0 62	0 61
L T L Tot Ass	0 05	0 06	0 07	0 07	0 08
Debt to Eqity	2 10	1 80	1 74	1 71	1 61
Interest Cover	1 80	2 31	2 45	3 58	5 55
Oper Prof Mrg	2 23	2 41	2 75	3 21	2 52
Net Prof Marg%	0 53	0 72	0 90	1 29	1 35
Ret on Assets	10 68	11 81	13 46	14 83	11 62
Ret on Equity%	7 42	9 67	12 15	16 31	16 47
Price/Earnings	7 73	5 43	4 81	3 13	3 50
Divid Cover	3 52	3 72	3 66	3 73	4 00
Divid Yield	3 67	4 94	5 68	8 57	7 14
Earning Yield%	12 94	18 40	20 77	31 94	28 57
NAV % Mrk Pr	174 40	190 39	170 89	195 87	172 50
Effec Tax Rate	49 26	52 12	43 29	45 08	39 94
Def Interval	5 26	3 92	3 07	3 00	2 39

Sus Grth Rate	5.31	7.07	8.83	11.93	12.33

SUBSIDIARY & ASSOCIATED COMPANIES

ACTIVE DISPLAYS (PTY) LTD
APHRODITE HOLDINGS (PTY) LTD
BRIAN PORTER MOTORS LTD
CHRIS VLOK MOTORS (1991) (PTY) LTD
CORNER MOTOR PROPERTIES (PTY) LTD
FROSTAIR (PTY) LTD
GERMISTON MOTORS (PTY) LTD
HENIM (PTY) LTD
JAYBER (PTY) LTD
LANGMOT INVESTMENTS (PTY) LTD
LEON DEACON MOTORS (PTY) LTD
MARINE GARAGE (PTY) LTD
NEWPORT MOTORS (ALBERTON) (PTY) LTD
NEWPORT MOTORS (PTY) LTD
NOORDHOEK MOTORS (PTY) LTD
NOORDHOF MOTORS (PTY) LTD
PARKER'S INVESTMENTS SHAREBLOCK (PTY) LT
PHF INVESTMENTS (PTY) LTD
PORTER ROBBS MOTORS PROPERTIES (KUILS RI
RAYMOND DUNCAN MOTOR SPARES (PTY) LTD
ROBB MOTORS (BOLAND) LTD
ROBB MOTORS (S.W.D.) LTD
ROBB MOTORS PROPERTIES LTD
SA LEASING SERVICES (PTY) LTD
SM RETREADS (CAPE TOWN) (PTY) LTD
SOUTH EAST RAND INVESTMENTS (PTY) LTD
URGENT DISCOUNT MOTOR SPARES (PTY) LTD
VICTORIA STREET HOLDINGS (PTY) LTD
WIGANDIA (PTY) LTD
WIZARD DEVELOPMENTS (PTY) LTD

INVESTMENTS

None

BRISTOL INDUSTRIAL CORP LTD

ABBREVIATION : BRISTOL-I

JSE SHORT CODE : BRI

SECTOR : Financial-Property

SHAREHOLDERS

Who Owns Whom's Assessment of the Identity of the Ultimate Controlling Shareholder: DIRECTORS

SHAREHOLDER	PERCENTAGE 1992	1991
TEXTILE & GENERAL HOLDINGS LTD	55.9	55.9
PROPCOR (BRISTOL) HOLDINGS LTD	21.4	20.3
STD BANK NOM TVL P/L	4.2	4.2
SOLPHIL INV P/L	2.7	2.7
DOMINION IND TRUST P/L	1.6	1.6
MAURO INV P/L	1.2	1.2
TOTAL	86.9	85.9

DIRECTORS :
LENTIN A ,LEVY IS ,POKROY EL
SHER AI (Managing Director

REGISTRATION NUMBER : 05/23123/06

REGISTERED OFFICE
4th Floor, Aloe Grove, 196 Louis Botha Ave
Johannesburg
2198
TEL: 011-403 3675
FAX: 011-339 7821

TRANSFER SECRETARY
Stability Services (Pty) Ltd
6th Floor, 112 Kerk Street
Johannesburg
2001
TEL: 011-337 4030

COMPANY SECRETARY
A Lentin

NATURE OF BUSINESS
The principal acitvities of the group remain the holding of properties as investments, and, through various subsidiaries, trading in property.

BANKERS :
Standard Bank of SA Ltd, Nedcor Bank Ltd

AUDITORS :
Levitt Kirson

FAMILIAR BRAND NAMES
N/A

CONTRIBUTION BY ACTIVITY
N/A

YEAR END : February

DIVIDEND : Ords 12,5c

Final No 38	(Ldr)31/08/90	(Pay)24/09/90	Amt(c)3
Final No 39	(Ldr)30/08/91	(Pay)23/09/91	Amt(c)3
Final No 40	(Ldr)28/08/92	(Pay)21/09/92	Amt(c)4

NUMBER OF EMPLOYEES : 7

CAPITAL STRUCTURE

	AUTHORISED	ISSUED
Ords 12,5c	12800000	10250000

FINANCIAL STATISTICS (AT FINANCIAL YEAR END)

(Amts in R'000)	1992 Feb	1991 Feb	1990 Feb	1989 Feb	1988 Feb
Ord S/H Int	16319	13098	12086	11274	9429
Long Trm Loans	460	460	460	460	-
Iss Ord Share	10250	10250	10250	10250	10250
Total Liab	1551	1743	1597	1791	331
Current Liab	1091	1283	1137	1331	331
Total Assets	17870	14841	13683	13065	9760
Current Assets	6503	7083	6210	6456	1454
Debtors	2042	1427	1467	947	233
Inventory	366	488	741	832	472
Turnover	5784	4844	3503	2555	1302
Oper Profit	-451	189	109	140	32
Interest Paid	-	-	-	7	3
Tax Paid	683	1008	726	484	253
Prf af Int&Tax	1281	970	775	510	279
Prf att Ord Sh	1624	1320	1120	656	434
Btm Line Earn	1624	1320	1120	2050	850

Dividend Paid	410	308	308	205	102
Mkt Prce(c) YE	115	110	110	85	51
Depreciation	25	27	20	20	20

PER SHARE STATISTICS (CENTS)

Net Asst Val	159.21	127.79	117.91	109.99	91.99
Net Earnings	15.84	12.87	10.93	6.41	4.23
Dividends	4.00	3.00	3.00	2.00	1.00
Cash Flow	12.74	9.73	7.76	5.17	2.92

RATIOS AND OTHER INFORMATION

Mrk Cap(R000)	11788	11275	11275	8713	5228
Current Ratio	5.96	5.52	5.46	4.85	4.39
Quik/Acid Tst	5.63	5.14	4.81	4.23	2.97
A/C Rec T/ovr	2.83	3.39	2.39	2.70	5.59
Tot Ass T/ovr	0.32	0.33	0.26	0.20	0.13
Debt/Ass Rat	0.09	0.12	0.12	0.14	0.03
L T L Tot Ass	0.03	0.03	0.03	0.04	-
Debt to Eqity	0.10	0.13	0.13	0.16	0.04
Interest Cover	-	-	-	66.57	125.33
Oper Prof Mrg	-7.80	3.90	3.11	5.48	2.46
Net Prof Marg%	28.08	27.25	31.97	25.68	33.33
Ret on Assets	12.91	15.69	13.49	8.78	7.07
Ret on Equity%	9.95	10.08	9.27	5.82	4.60
Price/Earnings	7.26	8.55	10.06	13.26	12.06
Divid Cover	3.96	4.29	3.64	3.21	4.23
Divid Yield	3.48	2.73	2.73	2.35	1.96
Earning Yield%	13.77	11.70	9.94	7.54	8.29
NAV % Mrk Pr	138.44	116.17	107.19	129.40	180.37
Effec Tax Rate	102.09	70.64	70.97	72.46	134.57
Def Interval	-	-	-	0.87	-
Sus Grth Rate	7.44	7.73	6.72	4.00	3.52

SUBSIDIARY & ASSOCIATED COMPANIES

ALLIED ESTATES LTD
BARNEY MILLER LTD
BEZUIDENHOUT STREET INVESTMENTS (PTY) LT
CELAH PROPERTIES (PTY) LTD
COMBERGEN PROPERTIES (PTY) LTD
INLAND PLANT HIRE (PTY) LTD
INLAND PROPERTY DEVELOPMENT CORP. (PTY)
JIGS & DIES LTD
LAMICH PROPERTIES (PTY) LTD
NATMAL PROPERTIES (PTY) LTD
OTANI INVESTMENT CO. (PTY) LTD
QUEEN ELIZABETH HOUSE (PTY) LTD
SA REAL ESTATE HOLDINGS (PTY) LTD
SAVEKOR (EDMS) BPK
SIEMARK INVESTMENTS (PTY) LTD
TASHKENT PROPERTIES (PTY) LTD
VAUDE PROPERTIES (PTY) LTD

INVESTMENTS

AMALGAMATED BANK OF SA LIMITED (8191 SH)
BARLOW RAND LTD (500 SH)
C.G. SMITH SUGAR LTD (250 SH)
CG SMITH FOODS LTD (500 SH)
CHARTER CONSOLIDATED PLC (10000 SH)
DE BEERS CENTENARY AG (SWITZERLAND) (500 SH)
ENGEN LTD (1000 SH)
FIRST INTERNATIONAL TRUST LIMITED (1420 SH)
GRINAKER HOLDINGS LTD (500 SH)
HARTEBEESFONTEIN GOLD MINING CO LTD (1000 SH)
ISCOR LTD (103000 SH)
KLOOF GOLD MINING COMPANY LTD (1000 SH)
LIBERTY HOLDINGS LTD (1000 SH)
MCCARTHY RETAIL LTD (6000 SH)
METBOARD PROPERTY FUND (90000 SH)
METROPOLITAN LIFE LTD (9600 SH)
PRETORIA PORTLAND CEMENT COMPANY LTD (500 SH)
RICHEMONT SECURITIES AG (1000 SH)
SANLAM INDEX TRUST (1838 SH)
SASOL LTD (1000 SH)
STANDARD BANK INVESTMENT CORPORATION LTD (500 SH)
TONGAAT HULETT GROUP LTD SUPERVISION FOO (1000 SH)
VLAKFONTEIN GOLD MINING CO LTD (10000 SH)

BROADACRES INVESTMENTS LTD

ABBREVIATION : BROADACRE

JSE SHORT CODE : BIL

SECTOR : Mining-Diamonds

SHAREHOLDERS

Who Owns Whom's Assessment of the Identity of the Ultimate Controlling Shareholder: DIRECTORS

SHAREHOLDER	PERCENTAGE 1992	1991
SHUI LUNG INVESTMENT CO LTD	70.6	70.6
LEVY C L	4.9	4.9
GREYLING J H	4.2	1.1
JR NOM P/L	2.4	2.4
HILL R S	1.1	---
NEDBANK NOM LTD	---	1.2
DIAGONAL NOM P/L	---	3.1
TOTAL	83.1	83.2

DIRECTORS :
HSU MC ,K'UNG LK DR
SLABBERT G (Managing Director)
TCHENG J (Chairman

REGISTRATION NUMBER : 05/21193/06

REGISTERED OFFICE
6th Floor, Van Der Stel Place
20 Melle Street, Braamfontein
2001
TEL: 02725-71157
FAX: 02725-71500

TRANSFER SECRETARY
Central Registrars Ltd
P O Box 4844, Johannesburg
2000
TEL: 011-331 0051

COMPANY SECRETARY
G Slabbert

NATURE OF BUSINESS
Diamond mining on the West Coast.

BANKERS :
First National Bank of SA Ltd, Volkskas Ltd

AUDITORS :
Charles Orbach & Co

FAMILIAR BRAND NAMES
N/A

CONTRIBUTION BY ACTIVITY
N/A

YEAR END : June

DIVIDEND : Ords 25c

Interim	(Ldr)12/05/89	(Pay)19/05/89	Amt(c)5
Final	(Ldr)10/11/89	(Pay)30/11/89	Amt(c)5
Interim	(Ldr)13/04/90	(Pay)30/04/90	Amt(c)6
Final	(Ldr)09/11/90	(Pay)23/11/90	Amt(c)4
Interim	(Ldr)12/04/91	(Pay)30/04/91	Amt(c)2

CAPITAL STRUCTURE

	AUTHORISED	ISSUED
Ords 25c	6000000	3409394

FINANCIAL STATISTICS (AT FINANCIAL YEAR END)

(Amts in R'000)	1992 Jun	1991 Jun	1990 Jun	1989 Jun	1988 Jun
Ord S/H Int	2939	3414	3321	2992	2778
Iss Ord Share	3409	3409	3409	3409	3409
Total Liab	416	770	1152	1491	603
Current Liab	416	770	1152	1491	603
Total Assets	3267	4096	4385	4483	3381
Intang Assets	88	88	88	*	*
Current Assets	702	1571	2362	2430	1561
Debtors	413	798	653	1057	912
Inventory	33	22	-	-	-
Oper Profit	-250	403	1494	1566	745
Interest Paid	16	2	23	-	-
Tax Paid	287	557	1199	1004	480
Prf af Int&Tax	-475	161	582	562	265
Prf att Ord Sh	-475	161	582	562	265
Btm Line Earn	-475	161	582	562	237
Dividend Paid	-	68	341	341	-
Mkt Prce(c) YE	30	50	85	80	70
Depreciation	291	244	223	185	139

PER SHARE STATISTICS (CENTS)

Net Asst Val	83.63	97.57	94.84	87.77	81.49
Net Earnings	-13.90	4.70	17.10	16.30	7.80
Dividends	-	2.00	10.00	10.00	5.00
Cash Flow	-5.40	11.88	23.61	21.91	11.85

RATIOS AND OTHER INFORMATION

Mrk Cap(R000)	1023	1705	2898	2727	2386
Current Ratio	1.69	2.04	2.05	1.63	2.59
Quik/Acid Tst	1.61	2.01	2.05	1.63	2.59
Debt/Ass Rat	0.13	0.19	0.26	0.33	0.18
Debt to Eqity	0.14	0.23	0.35	0.50	0.22
Interest Cover	-15.63	201.50	64.96	-	-
Ret on Assets	-5.26	17.58	41.14	34.93	22.03
Ret on Equity%	-16.16	4.72	17.52	18.78	9.54
Price/Earnings	-2.16	10.64	4.97	4.91	8.97
Divid Cover	-	2.35	1.71	1.63	1.56
Divid Yield	-	4.00	11.76	12.50	7.14
Earning Yield%	-46.33	9.40	20.12	20.38	11.14
NAV % Mrk Pr	278.77	195.13	111.57	109.71	116.41
Effec Tax Rate	-78.19	50.28	67.32	64.11	64.43
Def Interval	-	0.11	0.01	-	-
Sus Grth Rate	-16.16	2.72	7.26	7.39	9.54

SUBSIDIARY & ASSOCIATED COMPANIES

BROADACRES DIAMONDS (PTY) LTD
DE PUNT PLASE (EDMS) BPK
DE PUNT PLASE DIAMANT MAATSKAPPY (EDMS)
NAMIROS (EDMS) BPK
ROBPELSE BEMARKING (EDMS) BPK
STRANDFONTEIN MINERALE (EDMS) BPK
STRYKLOOF DIAMANTE (EDMS) BPK
STRYKPUNT BELEGGINGS BPK

INVESTMENTS

None

BTR DUNLOP LTD

ABBREVIATION : BTRDUN

JSE SHORT CODE : BDN

SECTOR : Industrial-Industrial Holding

SHAREHOLDERS

Who Owns Whom's Assessment of the Identity of the Ultimate Controlling Shareholder:
BTR PLC

SHAREHOLDER	PERCENTAGE 1992	1991
DUNLOP NOM SA P/L	37.9	38.3
BTR PLC	11.8	11.9
STD BANK NOM TVL P/L	7.9	7.3
EIGHTY ONE MAIN STREET NOM LTD	6.8	6.0
METAL IND GROUP PENS FUND	5.2	5.1
ENGINEERING INDUSTRIES PENS FUND	5.2	4.8
LIBERTY LIFE ASSOC OF AFRICA LTD	3.8	3.7
BP THIBAULT NOM P/L	2.9	3.0
BTR INTERNATIONAL LTD	2.4	1.7
FIRST NAT NOM P/L	2.4	3.0
COMMERCIAL UNION LIFE ASSURE CO SA LTD	2.3	---
BTR DUNLOP LTD EXECUTIVE SHARE	1.2	---
COMMERCIAL UNION ASSURE CO SA LTD	---	3.3
TOTAL	89.9	88.1

DIRECTORS :
FILMER ARH ,GNODDE AMD (Chairman)
HOOPER CR (Managing Director),KEMP GP ,LOWE JE

REGISTRATION NUMBER : 05/12141/06

REGISTERED OFFICE
265 Sydney Road, Durban
4001
TEL: 031-25 1411
FAX: 031-25 4180

TRANSFER SECRETARY
Mercantile Registrars Ltd
P O Box 1053, Johannesburg
2000
TEL: 011-333 8181

COMPANY SECRETARY
D M Goodhead

NATURE OF BUSINESS
BTR Dunlop is a holding company which also conducts part of the groups manufacturing and trading. The business of the BTR Dunlop group is

manufacturing and marketing Industrial and Engineering, Automotive and consumer products in which competitive efficiency requires a capital intensive manufacturing approach

BANKERS :
Standard Bank of SA Ltd, Nedperm Bank Ltd
First National Bank of SA Ltd

AUDITORS :
Deloitte Pim Goldby

FAMILIAR BRAND NAMES
BTR,DDH,DUNLOP,DUNLOP SLAZENGER,DUNLOPILLO GATES,LAURSENS,POWER,POWER PRODUCTS,SARMCOL SHELLAGH,SLAZENGER,SP33,SP55

CONTRIBUTION BY ACTIVITY
Motor (% Turnover) (40 0%)
Motor (% Trading Profit) (40 0%)
Engineering & Industrial (% Turnover) (49 0%)
Consumer (% Turnover) (11 0%)
Engineering & Industr (% Trading Profit) (48 0%)
Consumer (% Trading Profit) (12 0%)

YEAR END : December

DIVIDEND : Ords 50c

Interim No 78	(Ldr)31/08/90	(Pay)28/09/90	Amt(c)60
Final No 79	(Ldr)08/03/91	(Pay)25/04/91	Amt(c)105
Interim No 80	(Ldr)06/09/91	(Pay)24/10/91	Amt(c)60
Final No 81	(Ldr)13/03/92	(Pay)24/04/92	Amt(c)105
Interim No 82	(Ldr)04/09/92	(Pay)26/10/92	Amt(c)60

NUMBER OF EMPLOYEES : 5604

CAPITAL STRUCTURE

	AUTHORISED	ISSUED
Ords 50c	30000000	23601660
6% Cum Prefs R2	1000000	750000

FINANCIAL STATISTICS (AT FINANCIAL YEAR END)

(Amts in R 000)	1991 Dec	1990 Dec	1989 Dec	1988 Dec	1987 Dec
Ord S/H Int	259424	241928	265743	202973	162842
Long Trm Loans	79901	75546	2042	1837	21333
Iss Ord Share	23602	23554	23396	23324	22971
Total Liab	202703	222561	143902	124240	118367
Current Liab	122802	147015	141860	122403	97034
Total Assets	462127	464489	409645	327213	281209
Current Assets	274309	283844	244884	202426	162001
Debtors	122535	124580	113040	100735	78296
Inventory	151774	149694	128429	101691	83705
Turnover	671980	700803	631790	529270	411343
Oper Profit	101239	134267	110888	74056	48117
Interest Paid	12916	12784	6536	3724	4440
Tax Paid	33118	57997	34358	32168	19103
Prf af Int&Tax	56560	67439	72511	38164	24574
Prf att Ord Sh	56470	67349	72421	38074	24484
Btm Line Earn	56470	67349	72421	38074	24484
Dividend Paid	38945	38925	32748	24470	19525
Mkt Prce(c) YE	2000	2400	1500	950	900
Depreciation	15680	18357	14277	14613	14114

PER SHARE STATISTICS (CENTS)

Net Asst Val	1099 16	1027 12	1135 85	870 23	708 90
Net Earnings	239 00	287 00	310 00	157 00	106 60
Dividends	165 00	165 00	140 00	105 00	85 00
Cash Flow	337 84	450 06	370 93	227 82	178 99

RATIOS AND OTHER INFORMATION

Mrk Cap(R000)	472040	565296	350940	221578	206739
Current Ratio	2 23	1 93	1 73	1 65	1 67
Quik/Acid Tst	1 00	0 91	0 82	0 82	0 81
A/C Rec T/ovr	5 48	5 63	5 59	5 25	5 25
Tot Ass T/ovr	1 45	1 51	1 54	1 62	1 46
Debt/Ass Rat	0 27	0 32	0 35	0 38	0 35
L T L Tot Ass	0 00	0 00	0 00	0 00	0 00
Debt to Eqity	0 47	0 61	0 54	0 60	0 60
Interest Cover	7 84	10 50	16 97	19 89	10 84
Oper Prof Mrg	15 07	19 16	17 55	13 99	11 70
Net Prof Marg%	8 40	9 61	11 46	7 19	5 95
Ret on Assets	22 20	29 76	27 68	22 63	17 11
Ret on Equity%	21 77	27 84	27 25	18 76	15 04
Price/Earnings	8 37	8 36	4 84	6 05	8 44
Divid Cover	1 45	1 74	2 21	1 50	1 25
Divid Yield	8 25	6 88	9 33	11 05	9 44
Earning Yield%	11 95	11 96	20 67	16 53	11 84
NAV % Mrk Pr	54 96	42 80	75 72	91 60	78 77
Effec Tax Rate	32 44	29 63	32 15	45 74	37 97
Def Interval	0 07	0 05	0 06	0 29	0 50
Sus Grth Rate	6 76	11 75	14 93	6 70	3 05

SUBSIDIARY & ASSOCIATED COMPANIES

BTR INDUSTRIAL S A (PTY) LTD
BTR PROPERTY (SELBY) (PTY) LTD
BTR SA LTD
BTR SARMCOL (PTY) LTD
BTRD PROPERTY (KIMBERLEY) (PTY) LTD
BTRD PROPERTY (ROSEBANK GARDEN) (PTY) LT
BTRD PROPERTY (WILSONIA) (PTY) LTD
BTRD PROPERTY KRUGERSDORP (PTY) LTD
DUNLOP OZITE (PTY) LTD
DUNLOP PROPERTIES (BENONI) (PTY) LTD
DUNLOP PROPERTIES (BOOYSENS) (PTY) LTD
DUNLOP PROPERTIES (DENVER) (PTY) LTD
DUNLOP PROPERTIES (EAST LONDON) (PTY) LT
DUNLOP PROPERTIES (LADYSMITH) (PTY) LTD
DUNLOP PROPERTIES (LINCOLN ROAD) (PTY) L
DUNLOP PROPERTIES (MOBENI) (PTY) LTD
DUNLOP PROPERTIES (PORT ELIZABETH) (PTY)
DUNLOP TYRES (PTY) LTD
INDIA TYRES SOUTH AFRICA (PTY) LTD
LAURSEN BROTHERS (PTY) LTD DORM
LAURSEN BROTHERS PROPERTY (PTY) LTD
RESILIENCY HOLDINGS (PTY) LTD
RUBBER INSURANCE AGENCIES SA (PTY) LTD
SLAZENGERS (PTY) LTD

INVESTMENTS

None

BUFFALO CORPORATION LTD

ABBREVIATION : BUFFCOR

JSE SHORT CODE : BFF

SECTOR : Industrial Engineering

SHAREHOLDERS

Who Owns Whom's Assessment of the Identity of the Ultimate Controlling Shareholder:
DIRECTORS CONTROL 53% (JUNE 1991)

SHAREHOLDER	PERCENTAGE 1992	1991
B P S E INV P/L	36 8	36 8
LOWENCO NOM P/L	18 8	19 3
JENAPR INV P/L	12 5	12 5
MENASHE I	11 0	11 0
STD BANK NOM TVL P/L	2 9	2 2
STOCKSHARE NOM P/L	2 1	---
OSCHINSKY P	1 7	2 3
CHAGAN N P	1 6	1 6
MERCABANK BPK	1 5	1 5
DORET INV CC	---	1 2
TOTAL	88 7	88 3

DIRECTORS :
FERREIRA CG DR (Chairman),FLUXMAN MJ
LIPWORTH JP ,MENASHE I (Chief Executive)
OFSOWITZ H

REGISTRATION NUMBER : 05/25532/06

REGISTERED OFFICE
76 Maraisburg Road, Industria
Johannesburg
2092
TEL 011-474 1341
FAX 011-474 9428

TRANSFER SECRETARY
Central Registrars Ltd
P O Box 4844, Johannesburg
2000
TEL 011-331 0051

COMPANY SECRETARY
Buffalo Secretarial Services (Pty) Ltd

NATURE OF BUSINESS
An investment holding company which, together with its subsidiaries, is engaged in the manufacture & distribution of reflective & non-reflective number plates and safety signs Group companies are also engaged in the distribution of silkscreen products as well as property ownership and letting A major subsidiary is a franchise supplier & manufacturer of number plate blanks and accessories

BANKERS :
Standard Bank of SA Ltd

AUDITORS :
Fisher Hoffman Stride

FAMILIAR BRAND NAMES
N/A

CONTRIBUTION BY ACTIVITY
Investment/Leasing/Finance (% turnover) (12 0%)
No Plate Blanks/Safety Signs (84 4%)
Textile Converting/Silkscreen Printing (0 6%)
Property Ownership/Letting (3 0%)

YEAR END : June

DIVIDEND : Ords 50c

Final No 9	(Ldr)28/12/90	(Pay)15/01/91	Amt(c)2 5
Final No 10	(Ldr)08/11/91	(Pay)09/12/91	Amt(c)10
Dividend No 11	(Ldr)11/12/92	(Pay)18/12/92	Amt(c)50
Dividend No 12	(Ldr)11/12/92	(Pay)18/12/92	Amt(c)35

NUMBER OF EMPLOYEES : 350

CAPITAL STRUCTURE

	AUTHORISED	ISSUED
Ords 50c	7000000	6399500

FINANCIAL STATISTICS (AT FINANCIAL YEAR END)

(Amts in R'000)	1991 Jun	1990 Jun	1989 Jun	1988 Jun	1987 Jun
Ord S/H Int	12288	10860	7011	3697	3261
Long Trm Loans	3548	5229	4894	6429	5893
Iss Ord Share	6400	6400	5800	5000	4762
Total Liab	10721	9759	9685	11064	15379
Current Liab	7173	4530	4791	4635	9486
Total Assets	22361	20480	16554	14610	18640
Intang Assets	648	139	142	151	*
Current Assets	13107	11142	10955	8785	12498
Debtors	4921	5267	4689	3625	3407
Inventory	5558	5237	5755	4174	2281
Turnover	26130	20044	18736	16137	30345
Oper Profit	7016	3741	3831	3986	4016
Interest Paid	1432	1575	1421	1195	2675
Tax Paid	2401	597	160	634	1446
Prf af Int&Tax	3394	1620	2250	2157	-105
Prf att Ord Sh	3291	1555	2270	2165	-414
Btm Line Earn	1547	1438	2585	1197	-83
Dividend Paid	640	160	-	-	-
Mkt Prce(c) YE	105	77	62	55	125
Depreciation	387	399	403	437	829

PER SHARE STATISTICS (CENTS)

Net Asst Val	181 88	167 52	118 43	70 92	68 48
Net Earnings	51 40	24 40	37 00	40 80	-11 40
Dividends	10 00	2 50	-	-	-
Cash Flow	57 09	31 93	45 72	51 28	8 46

RATIOS AND OTHER INFORMATION

Mrk Cap(R000)	6720	4928	3596	2750	5953
Current Ratio	1 83	2 46	2 29	1 90	1 32
Quik/Acid Tst	1 05	1 30	1 09	0 99	1 08
A/C Rec T/ovr	5 31	3 81	4 00	4 45	8 91
Tot Ass T/ovr	1 17	0 98	1 13	1 10	1 63
Debt/Ass Rat	0 47	0 46	0 57	0 74	0 80
L T L Tot Ass	0 15	0 24	0 28	0 42	0 29
Debt to Eqity	0 85	0 87	1 34	2 91	4 56
Interest Cover	4 92	2 38	2 70	3 34	1 50
Oper Prof Mrg	26 85	18 66	20 45	24 70	13 23
Net Prof Marg%	12 59	7 76	12 12	13 42	-1 36
Ret on Assets	32 43	18 51	23 25	27 34	21 28
Ret on Equity%	26 78	14 32	32 38	58 56	-12 70
Price/Earnings	2 04	3 16	1 68	1 35	-10 96
Divid Cover	5 14	9 76	-	-	-
Divid Yield	9 52	3 25	-	-	-
Earning Yield%	48 95	31 69	59 68	74 18	-9 12
NAV % Mrk Pr	173 21	217 55	191 02	128 95	54 78
Effec Tax Rate	40 78	24 99	10 17	23 79	104 33
Def Interval	1 30	3 83	2 25	3 06	26 55
Sus Grth Rate	21 57	12 85	32 38	58 56	12 70

SUBSIDIARY & ASSOCIATED COMPANIES

BINDCHEM (PTY) LTD
BUFFALO PROPERTIES LTD
BUFFALO RETAIL HOLDINGS (PTY) LTD
BUFFALO SECRETARIAL SERVICES (PTY) LTD
BUFFCHEM (PTY) LTD
BUFFCOR PROPERTIES LTD
C A NUMBER PLATES AND SIGNS (PTY) LTD
COMPACT MARKETING (PTY) LTD (50%)
DP PLATES (PTY) LTD

EMPI AUTO PLATES & SIGNS (PTY) LTD (50%)
GRAPHTEX (PTY) LTD
IMPACT PACKINGS (PTY) LTD
IMPACT TRADING (PTY) LTD
JOHANNESBURG NUMBER PLATE CENTRE (PTY) L
MADTAR INVESTMENTS (PTY) LTD
MILNER DISCOUNT NUMBER PLATES (PTY) LTD
MINIT TEKENS (PTY) LTD
MR SIGN (PTY) LTD
P C B SILKSCREENERS (PTY) LTD
R J HICKSON-MAHONY (PTY) LTD (50%)
RETROPLATE ENGINEERING (PTY) LTD
RICKSEY INVESTMENTS (PTY) LTD
TREK PLATES (PTY) LTD (50%)
UNITED REFLECTIVE CONVERTERS (PTY) LTD

INVESTMENTS

None

BUFFELSFONTEIN GOLD MINING CO LTD

ABBREVIATION : BUFFELS

JSE SHORT CODE : BUF

SECTOR : Gold-Klerksdorp

SHAREHOLDERS

Who Owns Whom's Assessment of the Identity of the Ultimate Controlling Shareholder:
SANLAM / ANGLO AMERICAN

SHAREHOLDER	PERCENTAGE 1992	1991
INDO-CHINA NOM P/L	22 3	---
LONDON CONTROL ACCOUNT	16 6	16 3
FERMAIN NOM LTD	9 3	9 3
PETARD NOM LTD	8 8	8 8
CONSOLIDATED NOM P/L	8 6	8 0
DEPOSITARY NOM INC	5 6	1 1
FIRST NAT NOM P/L	5 1	5 4
SOCIETE INTERPROF POUR LA COMPENSATION	4 3	3 3
NEDBANK NOM LTD	4 0	---
RESIDENT NOM LTD	3 9	9 8
SEPON LTD J ACCOUNT	2 0	1 6
STD BANK NOM TVL P/L	1 8	1 8
FIRST NAT NOM P/L GATR DEPOT	1 4	1 7
ABSA NOM P/L	1 3	---
RAND SELECTION CORP LTD	1 0	1 0
BANK OF NEW YORK NOM LTD	---	4 5
INDO-CHINA NOM SA P/L	- -	21 7
VOLKSKAS NOM P/L	- -	1 1
TOTAL	96 1	95 4

DIRECTORS :
ELLIS SP ,EUSTACE PJ ,FEWELL PT ,FIELD AJ
GELDENHUYS JJ ,MAUDE G ,RADEMEYER P DE V
STEENKAMP TI (Chairman),SUNTER CL ,VAN NIEKERK JE

REGISTRATION NUMBER : 05/33934/06

REGISTERED OFFICE
General Mining Building, 6 Hollard Street
Johannesburg
2001
TEL 011-376 9111
FAX 011-838 4716

TRANSFER SECRETARY
Central Registrars Ltd
P O Box 4844, Johannesburg
2000
TEL 011-331 0051

COMPANY SECRETARY
General Mining Metals & Minerals Ltd

NATURE OF BUSINESS
The company operates the BUFFELSFONTEIN gold mine in the Klerksdorp area, Transvaal Uranium, pyrite and silver are recovered as by-products and sulphuric acid is produced from the pyrite The company also operates the BEATRIX gold mine in the Theunissen area, Orange free State, where silver is recovered as a by-product

BANKERS :
First National Bank of SA Ltd
Standard Bank of SA Ltd

AUDITORS :
KPMG Aiken & Peat

FAMILIAR BRAND NAMES
N/A

CONTRIBUTION BY ACTIVITY
Gold & By-products (% Working Income) (120 9%)
Uranium (-20 9%)

YEAR END : June

DIVIDEND : Ords R1

Interim No 65	(Ldr)02/02/90	(Pay)16/03/90	Amt(c)300
Final No 66	(Ldr)03/08/90	(Pay)14/09/90	Amt(c)340
Interim No 67	(Ldr)01/02/91	(Pay)15/03/91	Amt(c)180
Final No 68	(Ldr)02/08/91	(Pay)13/09/91	Amt(c)30
Interim No 69	(Ldr)31/01/92	(Pay)13/03/92	Amt(c)90
Final No 70	(Ldr)31/07/92	(Pay)11/09/92	Amt(c)100

NUMBER OF EMPLOYEES : 8082

CAPITAL STRUCTURE

	AUTHORISED	ISSUED
Cum Pref R1	20000000	15289000
Ords R1	11000000	11000000

FINANCIAL STATISTICS (AT FINANCIAL YEAR END)

(Amts in R'000)	1992 Jun	1991 Jun	1990 Jun	1989 Jun	1988 Jun
Ord S/H Int	1351353	1333231	1258619	1238256	1186026
Long Trm Loans	541	805	62558	61511	67709
Iss Ord Share	*11000*	*11000*	*11000*	*11000*	*11000*
Total Liab	92023	110771	311181	242524	243631
Current Liab	91482	109966	248623	181013	175922
Total Assets	1443376	1444002	1569800	1480780	1429657
Current Assets	140336	154799	276625	212698	209459
Debtors	25612	10827	10635	9133	7379
Inventory	18717	29812	8515	5358	2284
Turnover	806752	820058	917138	922891	889002
Oper Profit	105646	102012	239983	233294	260879

Interest Paid	-	-	80	3	-
Tax Paid	37776	36077	104641	68233	110848
Prf af Int&Tax	67870	65935	135262	166549	150031
Prf att Ord Sh	41870	40435	88262	122820	118063
Btm Line Earn	41870	40435	88262	122820	118063
Dividend Paid	20900	23100	70400	59950	64350
Mkt Prce(c) YE	2350	4100	5875	4950	5100

PER SHARE STATISTICS (CENTS)

Net Asst Val	12285.03	12120.28	11441.99	11256.87	10782.05
Net Earnings	380.00	368.00	627.00	541.00	619.00
Dividends	190.00	210.00	210.00	60.00	64.40
Cash Flow	380.64	367.59	802.38	1116.55	1065.93

RATIOS AND OTHER INFORMATION

Mrk Cap(R000)	258500	451000	646250	544500	561000
Current Ratio	1.53	1.41	1.11	1.18	1.19
Quik/Acid Tst	1.33	1.14	1.08	1.15	1.18
A/C Rec T/ovr	31.50	75.74	86.24	101.05	120.48
Tot Ass T/ovr	0.56	0.57	0.58	0.62	0.62
Debt/Ass Rat	0.06	0.08	0.19	0.16	0.17
L T L Tot Ass	0.00	0.00	0.03	0.03	0.05
Debt to Eqity	0.07	0.08	0.24	0.19	0.21
Interest Cover	-	-	2999.79	78261.67	-
Oper Prof Mrg	13.10	12.44	26.17	25.28	29.35
Net Prof Marg%	5.19	4.93	9.62	13.31	13.28
Ret on Assets	7.32	7.06	15.29	15.86	18.25
Ret on Equity%	3.10	3.03	7.01	9.92	9.95
Price/Earnings	6.18	11.14	9.37	9.15	8.24
Divid Cover	2.00	1.75	2.99	9.02	9.61
Divid Yield	8.09	5.12	3.57	1.21	1.26
Earning Yield%	16.17	8.98	10.67	10.93	12.14
NAV % Mrk Pr	522.77	295.62	194.76	227.41	211.41
Effec Tax Rate	35.76	35.37	43.62	29.25	42.80
Def Interval	0.01	0.02	0.71	0.50	0.58
Sus Grth Rate	1.55	1.30	1.42	5.08	4.53

SUBSIDIARY & ASSOCIATED COMPANIES

None

INVESTMENTS

None

BURLINGTON INDUSTRIES LTD

ABBREVIATION : BURLINGTN

JSE SHORT CODE : BUR

SECTOR : Industrial-Clothing, Footwear & Textiles

SHAREHOLDERS

Who Owns Whom's Assessment of the Identity of the Ultimate Controlling Shareholder:
KAWITZKY FAMILY

SHAREHOLDER	PERCENTAGE 1992	1991
BERMAN C	---	4.4
DOMIRO P/L	---	16.7
FILBEL HOLDINGS P/L	---	46.0
KAWITZKY P	---	3.6
NUSSBAUM R S A W	---	2.0
PATRIVIA INV P/L	---	2.4
PHR SECURITIES P/L	---	15.2
RESNICK L	---	4.4
TOTAL	---	94.7

DIRECTORS :
KAWITZKY ANTHONY ,KAWITZKY ISRAEL
KAWITZKY PERRY ,KAWITZKY PHILIP (Chairman

REGISTRATION NUMBER : 05/21549/06

REGISTERED OFFICE
9 Hopkins Street, Salt River
Cape Town
7925
TEL: 021-593 8826
FAX: 021-448 4264

TRANSFER SECRETARY
R D Hugo
9 Hopkins Rd, Salt River
7925
TEL: 021-55 2975

COMPANY SECRETARY
R D Hugo

NATURE OF BUSINESS
An investment holding company with subsidiaries engaged in the manufacture of mens, womens and childrens clothing.

BANKERS :
Standard Bank of SA Ltd

AUDITORS :
Kessel Feinstein

FAMILIAR BRAND NAMES
ANTON PARIS,BIJOU,BROOKS OF LONDON,ELSI-JO
GINO CASTEL,HOOKWAY CLASSICS,ICEBERG
JENNY JONES,MANZETTI DI MILANO,MARLBORO
ROYAL PALM

CONTRIBUTION BY ACTIVITY
N/A

YEAR END : December

DIVIDEND : Ords 50c
Dividend (Ldr)20/06/92 (Pay)10/07/92 Amt(c)10

CAPITAL STRUCTURE

	AUTHORISED	ISSUED
6% Cum Prefs R2	50000	50000
Ords 50c	800000	600000

FINANCIAL STATISTICS (AT FINANCIAL YEAR END)

(Amts in R'000)	1991 Dec	1990 Dec	1989 Dec	1988 Dec	1987
Ord S/H Int	5463	5159	4734	3873	3623
Long Trm Loans	2527	2476	2552	3002	5724
Iss Ord Share	600	600	600	600	600
Total Liab	5682	4988	5720	6410	8764
Current Liab	3155	2512	3168	3408	3040
Total Assets	10258	9260	9567	9480	15524
Intang Assets	887	887	887	803	*
Current Assets	8618	7504	7865	7675	6176

Debtors	3147	3164	2634	2056	-
Inventory	5315	4324	5206	5588	6176
Oper Profit	1181	1413	1324	1008	774
Interest Paid	661	801	791	654	506
Tax Paid	15	68	61	63	-
Prf af Int&Tax	505	544	472	291	245
Prf att Ord Sh	499	538	466	285	239
Btm Line Earn	379	538	940	285	239
Dividend Paid	75	75	60	36	36
Mkt Prce(c) YE	330	320	235	220	180
Depreciation	116	117	125	85	-

PER SHARE STATISTICS (CENTS)

Net Asst Val	762 67	712 00	641 17	511 67	603 83
Net Earnings	63 20	89 60	77 60	47 40	-
Dividends	10 00	12 50	10 00	7 50	-
Cash Flow	98 83	105 67	108 00	69 83	40 83

RATIOS AND OTHER INFORMATION

Mrk Cap(R000)	1980	1920	1410	1320	1080
Current Ratio	2 73	2 99	2 48	2 25	2 03
Quik/Acid Tst	1 05	1 27	0 84	0 61	-
Debt/Ass Rat	0 53	0 52	0 57	0 66	0 56
L T L Tot Ass	0 23	0 24	0 24	0 30	0 37
Debt to Eqity	1 00	0 92	1 16	1 61	2 42
Interest Cover	1 79	1 76	1 67	1 54	1 48
Ret on Assets	11 51	15 26	13 84	10 63	4 84
Ret on Equity%	9 13	10 43	9 84	7 36	6 60
Price/Earnings	5 22	3 57	3 03	4 64	-
Divid Cover	6 32	7 17	7 76	6 32	-
Divid Yield	3 03	3 91	4 26	3 41	-
Earning Yield%	19 15	28 00	33 02	21 55	-
NAV % Mrk Pr	231 11	222 50	272 84	232 58	335 46
Effec Tax Rate	7 12	14 54	-	3 95	-
Def Interval	5 34	5 14	5 31	10 94	23 36
Sus Grth Rate	7 76	8 97	8 58	6 43	5 60

SUBSIDIARY & ASSOCIATED COMPANIES

A FRASER & CO (LONDON) LTD
A FRASER & CO LTD
BERNTEX CASUAL (PTY) LTD
BERNTEX MANUFACTURING (PTY) LTD
BLACK IVY (PTY) LTD
CORONET INDUSTRIES (PTY) LTD
CORONET SPORTSWEAR (PTY) LTD
CRISTA (PTY) LTD
FE GORDON HOLDINGS (PTY) LTD
GOLDKNIT (PTY) LTD
HARRIS AND KAY LTD
HIGHFIELD CLOTHING CO LTD
ICEBERG CLOTHING CO (PTY) LTD
JENNY JONES (PTY) LTD
MARLBORO SHIRT COMPANY S A LTD
PREMIER SHIRT & CLOTHING FACTORY LTD
PROVIDENT SUPPLIERS LTD
RAND UNIVERSAL (PTY) LTD
WELDON PAJAMAS S A LTD

INVESTMENTS

None

CADBURY SCHWEPPES SA LTD

ABBREVIATION : CADSWEP

JSE SHORT CODE : CAS

SECTOR : Industrial-Food

SHAREHOLDERS

Who Owns Whom's Assessment of the Identity of the Ultimate Controlling Shareholder: CADBURY SCHWEPPES PLC (UK)

SHAREHOLDER	PERCENTAGE 1992	1991
CADBURY SCHWEPPES HLDGS P/L	53 0	53 4
TEMPORA INV LTD	21 5	5 7
STD BANK NOM TVL P/L	4 8	4 6
CMB NOM P/L	3 0	---
ESCOM PENS & PROV FUND	2 3	2 2
DE BEERS PENS FUND	1 1	1 1
EIGHTY ONE MAIN STREET NOM LTD	---	1 5
COMMERCIAL UNION ASSURE CO SA LTD	---	1 1
NAT BRANDS LTD	---	16 0
SANLAM	---	2 4
TOTAL	85 7	87 9

DIRECTORS :
ADCOCK CS ,BESTER PM (Chief Executive)
BEYERS PE ,BUCHANAN JF (Financial Director)
CADBURY ND ,CLARK AJL (Chairman),FLEMING PJ
WELLINGS DG

REGISTRATION NUMBER : 04/00415/06

REGISTERED OFFICE
Astron Road, Denver Ext 6
Johannesburg
2094
TEL 011-616 1920
FAX 011-616 2642

TRANSFER SECRETARY
Mercantile Registrars Ltd
P O Box 1053, Johannesburg
2000
TEL 011-333 8181

COMPANY SECRETARY
A R Holt

NATURE OF BUSINESS
The company and its subsidiaries are engaged in the manufacture and distribution of the following products Chocolate and sugar confectionery, cocoa and beverages, concentrates for the carbonated soft drink industry, squashes, cordials, bases and syrups for in-home carbonating, jellies, packaged desserts, baking aids, jams and marmalades, glace cherries and spices

BANKERS .
Standard Bank of SA Ltd
UAL Merchant Bank Ltd

AUDITORS :
Coopers Theron Du Toit

FAMILIAR BRAND NAMES
BROOKES,CADBURYS,CHAKLAS,CHAPELAT-HUMPHRIES
CHAPPIES,ESTO,MIXADRINK,MOIR'S,OROS,ROSES
SHAH CURRY POWDER,SODASTREAM,SPRINGER
SUPER SEVEN,SWEETO

CONTRIBUTION BY ACTIVITY
Soft Drinks (% operating profit) (25.7%)
Confectionery/Cocoa/Beverages/Foods (74.3%)

YEAR END : December

DIVIDEND :Ords 10c

Interim No 39	(Ldr)15/09/89	(Pay)06/10/89	Amt(c)8
Final No 40	(Ldr)16/03/90	(Pay)09/04/90	Amt(c)28
Interim No 41	(Ldr)14/09/90	(Pay)05/10/90	Amt(c)9.5
Final No 42	(Ldr)22/03/91	(Pay)08/04/91	Amt(c)31.5
Interim No 43	(Ldr)13/09/91	(Pay)04/10/91	Amt(c)12
Final No 44	(Ldr)20/03/92	(Pay)07/04/92	Amt(c)42
Interim No 45	(Ldr)11/09/92	(Pay)02/10/92	Amt(c)15

NUMBER OF EMPLOYEES : 4336

CAPITAL STRUCTURE

	AUTHORISED	ISSUED
Ords 10c	41375000	35118260

FINANCIAL STATISTICS (AT FINANCIAL YEAR END)

(Amts in R'000)	1991 Dec	1990 Dec	1989 Dec	1988 Dec	1987 Dec
Ord S/H Int	175983	163968	138949	105058	82021
Long Trm Loans	50766	34734	45729	16413	34121
Iss Ord Share	35118	34964	34776	6560	6325
Total Liab	203295	152596	142640	80190	81856
Current Liab	152529	117862	96911	63777	47735
Total Assets	379278	316564	281589	185248	163877
Current Assets	186541	165199	145826	101672	87170
Debtors	110980	98207	82131	56980	49841
Inventory	62729	59352	50782	38157	36846
Turnover	609992	537725	440184	326487	271179
Oper Profit	60567	47098	41943	33042	24722
Interest Paid	13135	11795	7313	3787	2969
Tax Paid	12951	10657	13132	11567	9185
Prf af Int&Tax	40524	30700	23294	17688	12568
Prf att Ord Sh	46836	35095	30704	22844	16069
Btm Line Earn	46836	35095	30704	22844	16069
Dividend Paid	18959	14335	12513	9836	6957
Mkt Prce(c) YE	3150	2200	1425	3800	1800
Depreciation	11368	9267	7612	5627	5485

PER SHARE STATISTICS (CENTS)

Net Asst Val	501.12	468.96	399.55	1601.49	1296.77
Net Earnings	133.60	100.50	88.40	348.60	254.10
Dividends	54.00	41.00	36.00	150.00	110.00
Cash Flow	150.59	111.37	89.54	381.24	335.49

RATIOS AND OTHER INFORMATION

Mrk Cap(R000)	1106217	769208	495558	249280	113850
Current Ratio	1.22	1.40	1.50	1.59	1.83
Quik/Acid Tst	0.81	0.90	0.98	1.00	1.05
A/C Rec T/ovr	5.50	5.48	5.36	5.73	5.44
Tot Ass T/ovr	1.61	1.70	1.56	1.76	1.65
Debt/Ass Rat	0.53	0.46	0.48	0.42	0.45
L T L Tot Ass	0.12	0.09	0.14	0.08	0.16
Debt to Eqity	1.13	0.89	0.97	0.74	0.90
Interest Cover	5.03	4.37	5.74	8.73	8.33
Oper Prof Mrg	9.93	8.76	9.53	10.12	9.12
Net Prof Marg%	7.68	6.53	6.98	7.00	5.93
Ret on Assets	19.23	18.57	18.30	20.86	17.66
Ret on Equity%	26.61	21.40	22.10	21.74	19.59
Price/Earnings	23.58	21.89	16.12	10.90	7.08
Divid Cover	2.47	2.45	2.46	2.32	2.31
Divid Yield	1.71	1.86	2.53	3.95	6.11
Earning Yield%	4.24	4.57	6.20	9.17	14.12
NAV % Mrk Pr	15.91	21.32	28.04	42.14	72.04
Effec Tax Rate	25.05	29.24	34.48	34.84	28.22
Def Interval	1.29	1.61	1.80	0.59	1.07
Sus Grth Rate	15.84	12.66	13.09	12.38	11.11

SUBSIDIARY & ASSOCIATED COMPANIES

BROMOR FOODS (PTY) LTD
CADBURY (PTY) LTD
CHAPELAT-HUMPHRIES INV (PTY) LTD
SPRINGER INVESTMENTS (PTY) LTD (49%)

INVESTMENTS

AMALGAMATED BEVERAGE INDUSTRIES LTD (19,1%)

CAIRNS HOLDINGS LTD

ABBREVIATION : CAIRNS

SECTOR : Zimbabwe Stock Exchange

SHAREHOLDERS

Who Owns Whom's Assessment of the Identity of the Ultimate Controlling Shareholder:
Astra Foods (Pvt) Ltd

SHAREHOLDER	PERCENTAGE 1992	1991
ASTRA FOODS PVT LTD	55.3	---
OLD MUTUAL INV CORP (PVT) LTD	10.5	---
CAIRNS B TRUST	3.5	---
CAIRNS J H	3.5	---
FIDELITY LIFE ASSURE OF ZIM PVT LTD	3.0	---
CAIRNS H E	1.7	---
FIRST MUTUAL LIFE ASSURE SOC OF ZIM	1.4	---
COMPUTER PRODUCTS & MINI COMPUTERS PVT L	1.3	---
OSBORN W G	1.2	---
TOTAL	81.4	---

DIRECTORS :
CAIRNS JH ,COOK LH ,FOURIE TC
JACKSON MJM (Chairman)
JOHNSON TM (Managing Director),KNIGHT AH
MSIPA CG ,MUPANEMUNDA SD ,SPRAGUE WI ,TIPLER RB

REGISTERED OFFICE
11th Floor, Livingstone House
48 Samora Machel Avenue, Harare

TEL: 727460
FAX: 727460

TRANSFER SECRETARY
First Transfer Secretaries (Pvt) Ltd
P O Box 437, Bulawayo
Zimbabwe

TEL: 092634 - 702905

COMPANY SECRETARY
Cairns Holdings Management Services (Private)

NATURE OF BUSINESS
Incorporated in Zimbabwe, the company produces a wide range of wines and foodstuffs, including chips and snacks,grocery and fish products, canned goods, coffee and pet foods.It also manufactures and distributes chemicals.

BANKERS :
N/A

AUDITORS :
Price Waterhouse Meyernel

FAMILIAR BRAND NAMES
BORDER STREAMS,FRESH NET FISH,NYANGA TROUT
PRONUTRO,TOMANGO,WILLARDS

CONTRIBUTION BY ACTIVITY
Food, Liquor & Agricultural (% Turnover) (75.8%)
Industrial Spirit & Chemical Products (23.3%)
Dividend & Inv Income (0.9%)

YEAR END : August

DIVIDEND : Ords Z$1

Dividend	(Ldr)01/11/91	(Pay)13/12/91	Amt(c)12
Dividend	(Ldr)24/04/92	(Pay)22/05/92	Amt(c)10

CAPITAL STRUCTURE

	AUTHORISED	ISSUED
Ords Z$1	20000000	15173219

FINANCIAL STATISTICS (AT FINANCIAL YEAR END)

(Amts in Z$)	1991 Aug	1990 Aug
Ord S/H Int	62136	58452
Long Trm Loans	3596	7132
Iss Ord Share	15173	15173
Total Liab	37682	32412
Current Liab	34086	25280
Total Assets	99818	90864
Current Assets	39822	35753
Debtors	15238	12380
Inventory	23871	20133
Turnover	107645	88874
Oper Profit	14394	7651
Interest Paid	1606	1946
Tax Paid	6553	2103
Prf af Int&Tax	7060	4240
Prf att Ord Sh	6695	4532
Btm Line Earn	6695	5364
Dividend Paid	3035	2427
Depreciation	3628	2425

PER SHARE STATISTICS (CENTS)

Net Asst Val	409.52	385.24
Net Earnings	44.10	35.40
Dividends	20.00	16.00
Cash Flow	68.04	42.10

RATIOS AND OTHER INFORMATION

Current Ratio	1.17	1.41
Quik/Acid Tst	0.47	0.62
A/C Rec T/ovr	7.06	7.18
Tot Ass T/ovr	1.08	0.98
Debt/Ass Rat	0.35	0.33
L T L Tot Ass	0.01	0.05
Debt to Eqity	0.56	0.51
Interest Cover	9.48	4.26
Oper Prof Mrg	13.37	8.61
Net Prof Marg%	6.22	5.10
Ret on Assets	15.25	9.75
Ret on Equity%	10.77	7.75
Divid Cover	2.21	2.21
Effec Tax Rate	51.24	36.86
Def Interval	1.35	2.64
Sus Grth Rate	5.89	3.60

SUBSIDIARY & ASSOCIATED COMPANIES

BORDER STREAMS PRODUCTS (PRIVATE) LTD
CAIRNS CHEMICALS (PRIVATE) LTD
CAIRNS HOLDINGS MANAGEMENT SREVICES (PRI
CAIRNS INDUSTRIES (PTY) LTD
FRESH NET FISHERIES (PRIVATE) LTD
MATEPPE ESTATE (PRIVATE) LTD
UNIVERSAL MACARONI FACTORY (PRIVATE) LTD
WILLARDS FOOD CORPORATION (PRIVATE) LTD
WILLARDS MARKETING LIMITED

INVESTMENTS

T A HOLDINGS LTD - ZIMBABWE (3750000S)

CANADIAN OVERSEAS PACKAGING INDUSTRIES LTD

ABBREVIATION : COPI

JSE SHORT CODE : CAN

SECTOR : Industrial-Paper & Packaging

SHAREHOLDERS

Who Owns Whom's Assessment of the Identity of the Ultimate Controlling Shareholder:
KALMANSON FAMILY - CANADA

SHAREHOLDER	PERCENTAGE 1992	1991
MONTREAL CONTROL A/C CANADA	79.3	---
STD BANK NOM TVL P/L	8.9	---
EIGHTY ONE MAIN STREET NOM LTD	2.2	---
FIRST NAT NOM P/L	1.7	---
PRESS H	1.1	---
SAGE LIFE LTD	1.1	---
TOTAL	94.3	---

DIRECTORS :
BERLIS DA ,CORRIGAN H
FRYLAND S (Deputy Chairman),HOARE JAC
JOHNSTON MC ,KALMANSON JM (Chairman)
KALMANSON M ,LAMPARD MR ,PAINE PB
SAMUEL DJ THE HON,STEVENSON BB (Chief Executive

REGISTERED OFFICE
Suite 1212, 1 Brunswick Square, Germain Str, Saint John
New Brunswick, Canada E2L 4V1

TEL: 091514-8457211

TRANSFER SECRETARY
Consolidated Share Registrars Ltd
P O Box 61051, Marshalltown
2107
TEL: 011-492 1620

COMPANY SECRETARY
M C Johnston

NATURE OF BUSINESS
The manufacture and distribution of packaging materials and allied products.

BANKERS :
N/A

AUDITORS :
Doane Raymond Pannell Associates

FAMILIAR BRAND NAMES
N/A

CONTRIBUTION BY ACTIVITY
N/A

YEAR END : June

DIVIDEND :Ords no par value

Dividend No 32	(Ldr)23/11/90	(Pay)14/12/90	Amt(c)45
Dividend No 33	(Ldr)22/11/91	(Pay)13/12/91	Amt(c)50
Dividend No 34	(Ldr)20/11/92	(Pay)11/12/92	Amt(c)55

CAPITAL STRUCTURE

	AUTHORISED	ISSUED
Ords no par value	17578125	17578125

FINANCIAL STATISTICS (AT FINANCIAL YEAR END)

(Amts in $)	1992 Jun	1991 Jun	1990 Jun	1989 Jun	1988 Jun
Ord S/H Int	215286	201063	192850	188226	182167
Long Trm Loans	3707	3238	4406	4985	5731
Iss Ord Share	17578	17578	17578	17578	17578
Total Liab	43104	33802	35770	36491	35098
Current Liab	39397	30564	31364	31506	29367
Total Assets	258390	234865	228620	224717	217265
Current Assets	143818	118528	118269	118229	115296
Debtors	24450	21457	20414	22049	22033
Inventory	13461	10654	12796	17665	13995
Turnover	103956	106604	93122	99950	102889
Oper Profit	22068	22367	18091	5591	21334
Interest Paid	1766	2254	1702	1203	1105
Tax Paid	4145	3242	2154	4041	4457
Prf af Int&Tax	16157	16871	14235	12384	15772
Prf att Ord Sh	23361	21237	15594	11500	15772
Btm Line Earn	23361	21237	15594	11500	15772
Dividend Paid	9668	8789	7910	7734	7734
Mkt Prce(c) YE	3125	2500	3050	2500	1900
Depreciation	2775	2872	2721	2786	2736

PER SHARE STATISTICS (CENTS)

Net Asst Val	1224.75	1143.83	1097.11	1070.80	1036.34
Net Earnings	133.00	121.00	89.00	65.00	90.00
Dividends	55.00	50.00	45.00	44.00	44.00
Cash Flow	104.22	108.40	91.22	85.17	107.52

RATIOS AND OTHER INFORMATION

Mrk Cap(R000)	549313	439450	536129	439450	333982
Current Ratio	3.65	3.88	3.77	3.75	3.93
Quik/Acid Tst	3.31	3.53	3.36	3.19	3.45
A/C Rec T/ovr	4.25	4.97	4.56	4.53	4.67
Tot Ass T/ovr	0.40	0.45	0.41	0.44	0.47
Debt/Ass Rat	0.15	0.13	0.14	0.14	0.14
Debt to Eqity	0.18	0.15	0.16	0.17	0.16
Interest Cover	12.50	9.92	10.63	14.65	19.31
Oper Prof Mrg	21.23	20.98	19.43	5.59	20.73
Net Prof Marg%	22.47	19.92	16.75	11.51	15.33
Ret on Assets	8.54	9.52	7.91	7.84	9.82
Ret on Equity%	10.85	10.56	8.09	6.11	8.66
Price/Earnings	23.50	20.66	34.27	38.46	21.11
Divid Cover	2.42	2.42	1.98	1.48	2.05
Divid Yield	1.76	2.00	1.48	1.76	2.32
Earning Yield%	4.26	4.84	2.92	2.60	4.74
NAV % Mrk Pr	39.19	45.75	35.97	42.83	54.54
Effec Tax Rate	21.07	17.89	16.94	90.50	20.09
Def Interval	0.52	0.30	0.51	0.46	0.42
Sus Grth Rate	6.36	6.19	3.98	2.00	4.41

SUBSIDIARY & ASSOCIATED COMPANIES

BARBADOS PACKAGING INDUSTRIES LTD
CROWN CORRUGATED (SCOTLAND) LTD (49%)
EAST AFRICAN PACKAGING INDUSTRIES LTD
ENCASE HOLDINGS LTD

INVESTMENTS

None

CAPITAL PROPERTY FUND

ABBREVIATION : CAPITAL

JSE SHORT CODE : CPL

SECTOR : Financial-Property Trust

SHAREHOLDERS

Who Owns Whom's Assessment of the Identity of the Ultimate Controlling Shareholder:
SA MUTUAL

SHAREHOLDER	PERCENTAGE 1992	1991
SA MUTUAL	51.4	51.9
SOUTHERN LIFE ASSOC LTD	8.0	8.2
CMB NOM P/L	6.4	---
METAL IND GROUP PENS FUND	4.3	4.3
AECI PENS FUND	4.2	4.2
CITY COUNCIL OF DURBAN	4.0	4.0
ENGINEERING INDUSTRIES PENS FUND	2.5	2.5
BP THIBAULT NOM P/L	2.0	2.0
DURBAN MUNICIPAL PENS FUND	1.4	1.4
SIXTY SIX MARSHALL STREET NOM P/L	1.3	1.3
DURBAN CORP SUPERANNUATION FUND	1.3	1.3
SANLAM	---	6.2
TOTAL	86.8	87.4

DIRECTORS :
JOHNSON JGW (Chairman),KRUGER HG ,LEWIS K
MCCLELLAND C MCK ,PRICE PD ,THOMAS GM

REGISTERED OFFICE
2nd Floor, JHI House, 11 Craddock Avenue
Rosebank
2196

TEL: 011-333 0123
FAX: 011-23 3256

TRANSFER SECRETARY
Central Registrars Ltd
P O Box 4844, Johannesburg
2000
TEL: 011-331 0051

COMPANY SECRETARY
J H Isaacs Group Ltd

NATURE OF BUSINESS
A property unit trust.

BANKERS :
Nedperm Bank Ltd

AUDITORS :
KPMG Aiken & Peat

FAMILIAR BRAND NAMES
N/A

CONTRIBUTION BY ACTIVITY
Industrial (% income) (38.0%)
Warehouse/Showroom (17.2%)
Offices (11.1%)
Retail (4.9%)
Interest (26.4%)
Parking (2.4%)

YEAR END : December

DIVIDEND : Units

Interim No 13	(Ldr)10/08/90	(Pay)31/08/90	Amt(c)13.94
Final No 14	(Ldr)22/02/91	(Pay)28/02/91	Amt(c)16.05
Final No 17	(Ldr)21/02/92	(Pay)28/02/92	Amt(c)16.70
Special No 15	(Ldr)10/05/91	(Pay)31/08/91	Amt(c)13.37
Interim No 16	(Ldr)16/08/91	(Pay)30/08/91	Amt(c)2.04
Interim No 18	(Ldr)21/08/92	(Pay)31/08/92	Amt(c)15.93

NUMBER OF EMPLOYEES : 3

CAPITAL STRUCTURE

	AUTHORISED	ISSUED
Units	129285184	129285184

FINANCIAL STATISTICS (AT FINANCIAL YEAR END)

(Amts in R'000)	1991 Dec	1990 Dec	1989 Dec	1988	1987
Ord S/H Int	266046	177121	183431	183483	148737
Long Trm Loans	-	-	-	12343	8073
Iss Ord Share	129285	92347	92347	92347	75079
Total Liab	21850	15130	13639	24686	16146
Current Liab	21850	15130	13639	12343	8073
Total Assets	287896	192251	197070	231563	171401
Current Assets	75678	27825	37470	35737	14591
Debtors	1193	294	755	-	-
Inventory	-	-	-	35737	14591
Turnover	-	-	-	19070	-
Oper Profit	-1551	-1181	-1138	20402	15536
Prf af Int&Tax	36575	27699	24865	20402	15536
Prf att Ord Sh	36575	27699	24865	20402	15536
Btm Line Earn	36575	27699	24865	20402	15536
Dividend Paid	36575	27695	24869	20404	15536
Mkt Prce(c) YE	310	260	285	190	225

PER SHARE STATISTICS (CENTS)

Net Asst Val	205.78	191.80	198.63	198.69	198.11
Net Earnings	32.11	29.99	26.93	-	-
Dividends	32.11	29.99	26.93	-	-
Cash Flow	28.29	29.99	26.93	22.09	20.69

RATIOS AND OTHER INFORMATION

Mrk Cap(R000)	400784	240102	263189	175459	168928
Current Ratio	3.46	1.84	2.75	2.90	1.81
Quik/Acid Tst	3.46	1.84	2.75	-	-
Tot Ass T/ovr	-	-	-	0.08	-
Debt/Ass Rat	0.08	0.08	0.07	0.11	0.09
L T L Tot Ass	-	-	-	0.05	0.05
Debt to Eqity	0.08	0.09	0.07	0.13	0.11
Oper Prof Mrg	-	-	-	106.98	-
Net Prof Marg%	-	-	-	106.98	-
Ret on Assets	12.70	14.41	12.62	8.81	9.06
Ret on Equity%	13.75	15.64	13.56	11.12	10.45
Price/Earnings	9.65	8.67	10.58	-	-
Divid Cover	1.00	1.00	1.00	-	-
Divid Yield	10.36	11.53	9.45	-	-
Earning Yield%	10.36	11.53	9.45	-	-
NAV % Mrk Pr	66.38	73.77	69.70	104.57	88.05
Def Interval	-	-	-	0.60	0.52
Sus Grth Rate	0.00	0.00	0.00	0.00	0.00

SUBSIDIARY & ASSOCIATED COMPANIES

ALFEO (PTY) LTD
ALFESKOR EIENDOMME (PTY) LTD
ALPEARCO PROPERTIES (PTY) LTD
APR PROPERTY CO. (PTY) LTD
ARLU INVESTMENTS (PTY) LTD
ATLANTIS PROPERTY CO (PTY) LTD
BANDS PROPERTIES (PTY) LTD
BOCO INVESTMENTS (PTY) LTD
COLLEGE AND MAYBAKER HOUSES (PTY) LTD
CONMENT PROPERTIES (PTY) LTD
CRESTON INVESTMENTS (PTY) LTD
CURLEW PROPERTIES (PTY) LTD
DEEFOR INVESTMENTS (PTY) LTD
DGL INVESTMENTS (PTY) LTD
DIESEL RD PROPERTIES (PTY) LTD
DISTRO DEE (PTY) LTD
DURTON INVESTMENTS (PTY) LTD
ELECTRON AVENUE 48 PROPERTY HOLDINGS (PT
ERF 107/1, KYA SAND (PTY) LTD
ERF 107/2 KYA SAND (PTY) LTD
ERF 109219 NOURSE AVE (PTY) LTD
ERF 117 ROGGEBAAI (PTY) LTD
ERF 210 ISANDO (PTY) LTD
ERF 478 WYNBERG EXT 4 (PTY) LTD
ERF 73 KYA SAND (PTY) LTD
ERF 75 HERMANSTAD (PTY) LTD
ERIKAY PROPERTY COMPANY (PTY) LTD
FIDELITY CENTRE (PTY) LTD
GARMAN INVESTMENTS (PTY) LTD
GEMDENE (PTY) LTD
GLOBAL HOLDINGS (PTY) LTD
GOLDCHIP INVESTMENT HOLDINGS (PTY) LTD
HONEYPARK PROPERTY CO (PTY) LTD
HUMCOR (PTY) LTD
J & M INVESTMENTS (PTY) LTD
JUST INVESTMENTS (PTY) LTD
KARIMA PROPERTY CO (PTY) LTD
KEMPTON VIEW PROPERTIES (PTY) LTD
KEMSTON AVE (PTY) LTD
LEONARD BRUSHWARE PROPERTIES (PTY) LTD
LOT 11 PINESIDE (PTY) LTD
M & R PROPERTIES PROJECT 32 (PTY) LTD
MANROY INVESTMENTS (PTY) LTD
MANSYN FOUR (PTY) LTD
MARKET STREET NOMINEES SEVEN (PTY) LTD
MENTIS CORNER (SPARTAN) (PTY) LTD
MIKETOM PROPERTY CO (PTY) LTD
NELSPRUIT CORNER (PTY) LTD

NORTRUSCO PINETOWN (PTY) LTD
NOURSEPACK PROPERTY CO (PTY) LTD
OMLAP (PTY) LTD
OMNEL (PTY) LTD
PACTOLE INVESTMENTS (PTY) LTD
PALM CENTRE (PTY) LTD
PEGASUS PROPERTIES (PTY) LTD
RADIANT INVESTMENTS (PTY) LTD
RANDJES PARK EXT 13 (PTY) LTD
ROMAF (PTY) LTD
SAMJAY HOLDINGS (PTY) LTD
SATG PROPERTIES (PTY) LTD
SEIDWOLP PROPERTY INVESTMENTS (PTY) LTD
SHAGAR PROPERTIES (PTY) LTD
SIXWAY PROPERTIES (PTY) LTD
STAND 179 EASTGATE EXT 12 (PTY) LTD
STAND 2290 ROODEKOP (PTY) LTD
STAND 48 STORMILL (PTY) LTD
STAND 640 SOUTH GERMISTON EXT. 4 (PTY) L
STRYDOM PARK GARDEN INVESTMENTS (PTY) LT
SUB 550 SHORTYS RETREAT (PTY) LTD
TALAS PROPERTIES PRIMROSE (PTY) LTD
TURNROSE INVESTMENTS (PTY) LTD
TWO NINE NOUGHT HALFWAY HOUSE (PTY) LTD
TYMOL INVESTMENTS (PTY) LTD
VENTURON PROPERTY CO PTY LTD
WEINBERG BROTHERS PROPERTY CO (PTY) LTD
WELRO PROPERTIES (PTY) LTD
WYNBERG 26 (PTY) LTD
XACTINVEST (PTY) LTD

INVESTMENTS

None

CAPRI GROUP LTD

ABBREVIATION : CAPRI

SECTOR : Zimbabwe Stock Exchange

SHAREHOLDERS

Who Owns Whom's Assessment of the Identity of the Ultimate Controlling Shareholder:
SCMBZ / SHIMDOR (PVT) LTD

DIRECTORS :
GIBSON AL ,KRETZMANN MS ,MACINTYRE DM
MCGREGOR I ,MORGAN DLL (Vice Chairman)
MORLEY JW ,SCHWARTZ C (Chairman

REGISTERED OFFICE
176 Seke Road, Harare
Zimbabwe

TEL: 737005
FAX: 737004

TRANSFER SECRETARY
Capri Group Ltd
P O Box 690, Harare
Zimbabwe

TEL: 092634-737005

COMPANY SECRETARY
A L Gibson

NATURE OF BUSINESS
CAPRI GROUP,whose principal business is the making of illuminated signs,is now also one of the largest manufacturers of domestic refrigerators and freezers in Zimbabwe, as also the servicing and repair of a wide range of domestic appliances.It also produces steel furniture and is involved in general engineering, particularly for the motor trade.It also produces automotive components,including grease nipples and special synchro-mesh gear assemblies for heavy vehicles.It has a 22%

BANKERS :
Barclays Bank of Zimbabwe Ltd

AUDITORS :
KPMG Peat Marwick

FAMILIAR BRAND NAMES
N/A

CONTRIBUTION BY ACTIVITY
N/A

YEAR END : June

DIVIDEND : Ords Z$1

Dividend	(Ldr)11/10/91	(Pay)22/10/91	Amt(c)14
Dividend	(Ldr)20/03/92	(Pay)26/03/92	Amt(c)9

CAPITAL STRUCTURE

	AUTHORISED	ISSUED
Ords Z$1	7500000	5159912

FINANCIAL STATISTICS (AT FINANCIAL YEAR END)

(Amts in Z$)	1991 Jun	1990 Jun
Ord S/H Int	20960	11571
Long Trm Loans	130	174
Iss Ord Share	5160	5160
Total Liab	7012	6468
Current Liab	6882	6294
Total Assets	27972	18039
Current Assets	10026	9624
Debtors	2119	2023
Inventory	3694	3136
Turnover	19232	14813
Oper Profit	2813	1927
Interest Paid	237	117
Tax Paid	1227	832
Prf af Int&Tax	2336	1745
Prf att Ord Sh	2558	1878
Btm Line Earn	2558	3893
Dividend Paid	1032	774
Depreciation	702	521

PER SHARE STATISTICS (CENTS)

Net Asst Val	406.20	224.24
Net Earnings	49.60	36.40
Dividends	20.00	15.00
Cash Flow	58.88	43.91

RATIOS AND OTHER INFORMATION

Current Ratio	1.46	1.53
Quik/Acid Tst	0.92	1.03
A/C Rec T/ovr	9.08	7.32
Tot Ass T/ovr	0.69	0.82
Debt/Ass Rat	0.25	0.35
Debt to Eqity	0.33	0.54
Interest Cover	11.87	16.47

Oper Prof Mrg	14.63	13.01
Net Prof Marg%	13.30	12.68
Ret on Assets	14.38	15.67
Ret on Equity%	12.20	16.23
Divid Cover	2.48	2.43
Effec Tax Rate	21.92	18.32
Def Interval	0.40	0.73
Sus Grth Rate	7.28	9.54

SUBSIDIARY & ASSOCIATED COMPANIES

CAPRI CORPORATION LIMITED
CAPRI ELECTRICAL HOLDINGS (PTY) LTD
CAPRI ENGINEERING (PVT) LTD
CAPRI SIGNS (PVT) LTD
CAPRI WIRE PRODUCTS (PVT) LTD
ELECTROLUX (PVT) LTD
WORLD RADIO SYSTEMS (PVT) LTD (22%)

INVESTMENTS

None

CAPS HOLDINGS LTD

ABBREVIATION : CAPS

SECTOR : Zimbabwe Stock Exchange

SHAREHOLDERS

Who Owns Whom's Assessment of the Identity of the Ultimate Controlling Shareholder: ZIMBABWE GOVERMENT / OLD MUTUAL INV CORP

SHAREHOLDER	PERCENTAGE 1992	1991
ZIMBABWE GOVERNMENT	42.8	---
OLD MUTUAL INV CORP (PVT) LTD	11.5	---
SECURITY NOM LTD	9.2	---
IPCORN LTD	3.7	---
FIDELITY LIFE ASSURE OF ZIM PVT LTD	3.0	---
NAT RAILWAYS OF ZIM CONTR PENS FUND	2.9	---
FIRST MUTUAL LIFE ASSURE SOC OF ZIM	2.6	---
E S C STAFF PENS FUND	1.7	---
K E THOMSON PVT LTD	1.7	---
TOBACCO HAIL INSURANCE PVT LTD	1.1	---
R M INSURANCE CO PVT LTD	1.1	---
TRUST NOM (PVT) LTD	1.0	---
TOTAL	82.2	---

DIRECTORS :
CHADWICK RH ,GRIFFITH RA (Chairman)
HOVE MJ (Chief Executive),MASHANYARE A MRS
NHAMBO LRM ,PARROT JH (Deputy Chief Executive)
RUZIVE L

REGISTERED OFFICE
Manchester Road, Southerton
Harare, Zimbabwe

TEL: 63581
FAX: 61228

TRANSFER SECRETARY
N/A

COMPANY SECRETARY
CAPS Management Services (Private) Ltd.

NATURE OF BUSINESS
CAPS is involved in the manufacture,import and export and distribution of pharmaceutical products as well as medical and educational equipment for the medical,veterinary and dental sectors.It also involved in freight, glass blown products for industrial laboratories and specialised market requirements.

BANKERS :
N/A

AUDITORS :
Ernst & Young

FAMILIAR BRAND NAMES
N/A

CONTRIBUTION BY ACTIVITY
N/A

YEAR END : March

DIVIDEND : Ords Z$0,50

Dividend	(Ldr)16/08/91	(Pay)30/08/91	Amt(c)14
Dividend	(Ldr)20/12/91	(Pay)06/01/92	Amt(c)10.5

CAPITAL STRUCTURE

	AUTHORISED	ISSUED
Ords Z$0,50	10000000	8961018

FINANCIAL STATISTICS (AT FINANCIAL YEAR END)

(Amts in Z$)	1991 Mar	1990 Mar
Ord S/H Int	47140	41972
Long Trm Loans	1914	2029
Iss Ord Share	8961	8961
Total Liab	56595	43248
Current Liab	54681	41219
Total Assets	103735	85220
Current Assets	78507	60636
Debtors	29137	18145
Inventory	46437	38766
Turnover	119476	92637
Oper Profit	16329	14197
Interest Paid	2570	2696
Tax Paid	6675	5611
Prf af Int&Tax	7084	5890
Prf att Ord Sh	7140	6018
Btm Line Earn	7140	6018
Dividend Paid	1972	1747
Depreciation	2427	2156

PER SHARE STATISTICS (CENTS)

Net Asst Val	526.06	468.39
Net Earnings	79.67	67.15
Dividends	22.00	19.50
Cash Flow	105.83	89.50

RATIOS AND OTHER INFORMATION

Current Ratio	1.44	1.47
Quik/Acid Tst	0.59	0.53
A/C Rec T/ovr	4.10	5.11
Tot Ass T/ovr	1.15	1.09

Debt/Ass Rat	0 55	0 51
L T L Tot Ass	0 02	0 02
Debt to Eqity	1 20	1 03
Interest Cover	6 35	5 27
Oper Prof Mrg	13 67	15 33
Net Prof Marg%	5 98	6 50
Ret on Assets	15 82	16 84
Ret on Equity%	15 15	14 34
Dvid Cover	3 62	3 44
Effec Tax Rate	48 51	48 79
Def Interval	3 09	2 96
Sus Grth Rate	10 96	10 18

SUBSIDIARY & ASSOCIATED COMPANIES

None

INVESTMENTS

None

CARGO CARRIERS LTD

ABBREVIATION : CARGO

JSE SHORT CODE : CRG

SECTOR : Industrial-Transportation

SHAREHOLDERS

Who Owns Whom's Assessment of the Identity of the Ultimate Controlling Shareholder:
BOLTON FAMILY

SHAREHOLDER	PERCENTAGE 1992	1991
C C INV P/L	69 1	69 1
CARGO CARRIERS HOLDINGS P/L	5 0	5 0
MOMENTUM LIFE ASSURE LTD	2 7	2 7
METAL IND GROUP PENS FUND	2 3	2 3
ENGINEERING INDUSTRIES PENS FUND	2 3	2 3
RIDGE NOM P/L	2 2	2 2
EIGHTY ONE MAIN STREET NOM LTD	2 0	3 9
SMBL NOM P/L	1 9	- -
CARGO CARRIERS INCENTIVE TRUST	1 7	1 7
STD BANK NOM TVL P/L	- -	1 1
TOTAL	89 3	90 4

DIRECTORS :
ANGREWS GS DR,BOLTON GD ,BOLTON MJ ,CHILVERS SG
MURRAY PE (Managing Director),STEIN GH (Chairman

REGISTRATION NUMBER : 59/03254/06

REGISTERED OFFICE
Cnr Barbara & North Reef Roads, Elandsfontein
1406
TEL 011-974 6311
FAX 011-974 2375

TRANSFER SECRETARY
Fraser Street Registrars (Pty) Ltd
P O Box 61178, Marshalltown
2107
TEL 011-491 0911

COMPANY SECRETARY
Cargo Carriers Management Services (Pty) Ltd

NATURE OF BUSINESS
The group operates a road transportation business throughout the Republic and neighbouring states

BANKERS :
Standard Bank of SA Ltd

AUDITORS :
Ernst & Young

FAMILIAR BRAND NAMES
CARGO CARRIERS

CONTRIBUTION BY ACTIVITY
N/A

YEAR END : February

DIVIDEND : Ords 1c

Interim No 4	(Ldr)01/12/89	(Pay)29/12/89	Amt(c)6
Final No 5	(Ldr)25/05/90	(Pay)29/06/90	Amt(c)7
Interim No 6	(Ldr)07/12/90	(Pay)28/12/90	Amt(c)3 5

NUMBER OF EMPLOYEES : 2600

CAPITAL STRUCTURE

	AUTHORISED	ISSUED
Ords 1c	25000000	20000000

FINANCIAL STATISTICS (AT FINANCIAL YEAR END)

(Amts in R'000)	1992 Feb	1991 Feb	1990 Feb	1989 Feb	1988 Feb
Ord S/H Int	56757	56584	58151	55011	51612
Long Trm Loans	10751	16038	22867	24632	9653
Iss Ord Share	20000	20000	20000	20000	20000
Total Liab	53152	62750	68834	54252	30138
Current Liab	42401	46712	45967	29620	20485
Total Assets	109909	119334	126985	109263	81750
Current Assets	33617	30497	32939	27863	34522
Debtors	28999	25235	27447	20935	18148
Inventory	4599	5234	5482	6918	4891
Turnover	181891	180341	174559	142518	121019
Oper Profit	960	8135	16949	10219	18105
Interest Paid	7393	8213	4753	1071	688
Tax Paid	-3328	-93	4606	3949	8501
Prf af Int&Tax	-3105	15	7590	5199	8916
Prf att Ord Sh	-3075	98	7460	5199	8916
Btm Line Earn	-3499	-867	5740	5199	8952
Dividend Paid		700	2600	1800	1460
Mkt Prce(c) YE	170	180	200	215	230
Depreciation	21322	22633	20254	15785	10678

PER SHARE STATISTICS (CENTS)

Net Asst Val	283 79	282 92	290 76	275 06	258 06
Net Earnings	-15 40	0 50	37 30	26 00	44 58
Dividends	-	3 50	13 00	9 00	7 30
Cash Flow	68 46	105 98	150 11	118 58	101 60

RATIOS AND OTHER INFORMATION

Mrk Cap(R000)	34000	36000	40000	43000	46000
Current Ratio	0 79	0 65	0 72	0 94	1 69
Quik/Acid Tst	0 68	0 54	0 60	0 71	1 45
A/C Rec T/ovr	6 27	7 15	6 36	6 81	6 67
Tot Ass T/ovr	1 65	1 51	1 37	1 30	1 48
Debt/Ass Rat	0 45	0 45	0 45	0 41	0 28
L T L Tot Ass	0 07	0 06	0 09	0 14	0 03

Debt to Eqity	0.87	0.96	0.98	0.81	0.45
Interest Cover	0.13	0.99	3.57	9.54	26.32
Oper Prof Mrg	0.53	4.51	9.71	7.17	14.96
Net Prof Marg%	-1.69	0.05	4.27	3.65	7.37
Ret on Assets	0.87	6.82	13.35	9.35	22.15
Ret on Equity%	-5.42	0.17	12.83	9.45	17.28
Price/Earnings	-11.04	360.00	5.36	8 27	5.16
Divid Cover	-	0.14	2.87	2.89	6.11
Divid Yield	-	1.94	6.50	4.19	3.17
Earning Yield%	-9.06	0.28	18 65	12.09	19.38
NAV % Mrk Pr	166.93	157.18	145.38	127.93	112.20
Effec Tax Rate	-17.16	-1455.13	18.92	12.76	39.32
Def Interval	2.04	1.66	0 93	0.91	0.12
Sus Grth Rate	-5.42	-1.06	8.36	6.18	14.45

SUBSIDIARY & ASSOCIATED COMPANIES

CARGO CARRIERS (TRANSVAAL) (PTY) LTD
CARGO CARRIERS ALRODE PROPERTIES (PTY) L
CARGO CARRIERS MANAGEMENT SERVICES (PTY)
CARGO CARRIERS WORKSHOP PROPERTY (PTY) L
CARGOTRAIN (PTY) LTD
DESMOND BOLTON HOLDING CO (PTY) LTD
EXECUTIVE AIR (PTY) LTD
STANGRAY PROPERTIES (PTY) LTD
SWANEE'S CARTAGE (PTY) LTD

INVESTMENTS

None

CARLTON PAPER CORP LTD

ABBREVIATION : CARLCOR

JSE SHORT CODE : CLM

SECTOR : Industrial-Paper & Packaging

SHAREHOLDERS

Who Owns Whom's Assessment of the Identity of the Ultimate Controlling Shareholder:
SANLAM VIA MALBAK

SHAREHOLDER	PERCENTAGE 1992	1991
KCSA HOLDINGS P/L	52 0	52.0
MALBAK INV (CARLCOR) P/L	15.8	15.8
KIMBERLEY-CLARK CORP	12.7	12.7
HOLDAINS INV (CARLCOR) P/L	8 2	8 2
CMB NOM P/L	8 2	---
SANLAM	---	6.8
TOTAL	96.9	95.5

DIRECTORS :
DONEHOWER JW ,MACMAHON JA ,MICHAEL MH
PARTRIDGE KJ (Chief Executive & M.D.),PRICE DNJ
WILLIS OI (Chairman

REGISTRATION NUMBER : 69/02685/06

REGISTERED OFFICE
3rd Floor, Bedford Centre, Smith Street
Bedfordview
2008
TEL: 011-616 1890
FAX: 011-615 8910

TRANSFER SECRETARY
Central Registrars Ltd
P O Box 4844, Johannesburg
2000
TEL: 011-331 0051

COMPANY SECRETARY
I D Parker

NATURE OF BUSINESS
CARLTON PAPER CORPORATION is the holding company of a group which manufactures, sells and distributes creped tissue paper, toilet and facial tissue, roll towels, serviettes, feminine hygiene products,diapers, and non-woven fabric and other disposable products in the consumer and commercial markets. Certain of the subsidiaries own properties which house the group's manufacturing facilities.

BANKERS :
Nedperm Bank Ltd

AUDITORS :
Deloitte Pim Goldby

FAMILIAR BRAND NAMES
BABY SOFT,BASIC,EEZY,GARY PLAYER,JOB SQUAD
KIMBIES,KIMTEX,KIMWIPES,KOTEX,MAXI DRI
PURITY,SERV-PAK,SPENCO,SPUNGUARD
THICK'N THIRSTY

CONTRIBUTION BY ACTIVITY
N/A

YEAR END : August

DIVIDEND : Ords 50c

Interim No 43	(Ldr)24/08/90	(Pay)21/09/90	Amt(c)31
Final No 44	(Ldr)25/03/91	(Pay)15/04/91	Amt(c)44
Final No 45	(Ldr)22/11/91	(Pay)17/12/91	Amt(c)75
Interim No 46	(Ldr)10/04/92	(Pay)08/05/92	Amt(c)42
Final No 47	(Ldr)20/11/92	(Pay)15/12/92	Amt(c)33

NUMBER OF EMPLOYEES : 1755

CAPITAL STRUCTURE

	AUTHORISED	ISSUED
Ords 50c	25000000	15798444

FINANCIAL STATISTICS (AT FINANCIAL YEAR END)

(Amts in R'000)	1991 Aug	1990 Dec	1989 Dec	1988 Dec	1987 Dec
Ord S/H Int	124100	106376	89075	74638	49762
Long Trm Loans	16477	7835	19895	12912	35271
Iss Ord Share	15798	15798	15798	15798	15789
Total Liab	107509	98700	93533	73321	82838
Current Liab	91032	90865	73638	60409	47567
Total Assets	231609	205076	182608	147959	132600
Current Assets	130602	119007	112164	86608	70120
Debtors	70723	57498	59294	46620	39118
Inventory	40653	40289	42548	37508	27932
Turnover	302776	393975	317327	258237	221683
Oper Profit	47695	50266	37602	32133	18268
Interest Paid	1794	3803	5459	3207	3455
Tax Paid	16325	17309	11468	13902	7683
Prf af Int&Tax	29576	29154	20675	15024	7130
Prf att Ord Sh	29576	29154	20675	15024	7130
Btm Line Earn	29576	29154	23916	15024	8729

Dividend Paid	11852	11853	9479	8215	3950
Mkt Prce(c) YE	3600	1550	750	750	600
Depreciation	5128	7125	5636	5862	5688

PER SHARE STATISTICS (CENTS)

Net Asst Val	785.54	673.35	563.84	472.45	315.17
Net Earnings	187.20	184.50	130.90	95.10	45.10
Dividends	75.00	75.00	60.00	52.00	25.00
Cash Flow	329.51	229.64	166.55	129.81	84.12

RATIOS AND OTHER INFORMATION

Mrk Cap(R000)	568728	244869	118485	118485	94734
Current Ratio	1.43	1.31	1.52	1.43	1.47
Quik/Acid Tst	0.99	0.87	0.95	0.81	0.89
A/C Rec T/ovr	6.42	6.85	5.35	5.54	5.67
Tot Ass T/ovr	1.96	1.92	1.74	1.75	1.67
Debt/Ass Rat	0.46	0.48	0.51	0.50	0.49
L T L Tot Ass	0.07	0.04	0.11	0.09	0.13
Debt to Eqity	0.87	0.93	1.05	0.98	1.29
Interest Cover	26.59	13.22	6.89	10.02	5.29
Oper Prof Mrg	15.75	12.76	11.85	12.44	8.24
Net Prof Marg%	9.77	7.40	6.52	5.82	3.22
Ret on Assets	30.89	24.51	20.59	21.72	13.78
Ret on Equity%	35.75	27.41	23.21	20.13	14.33
Price/Earnings	19.23	8.40	5.73	7.89	13.30
Divid Cover	2.50	2.46	2.18	1.83	1.80
Divid Yield	2.08	4.84	8.00	6.93	4.17
Earning Yield%	5.20	11.90	17.45	12.68	7.52
NAV % Mrk Pr	21.82	43.44	75.18	62.99	52.53
Effec Tax Rate	35.23	37.30	35.68	49.37	48.74
Def Interval	0.90	0.43	1.12	0.81	2.18
Sus Grth Rate	14.28	16.26	12.57	9.12	6.39

SUBSIDIARY & ASSOCIATED COMPANIES

CARLKIM (PTY) LTD
CARLTON PAPER OF SOUTH AFRICA (PTY) LTD
CARLTON PAPER PRODUCTS (PTY) LTD
CITY LAND CORPORATION (PTY) LTD
KIMBERLY-CLARK OF S.A. (PTY) LTD
LARRYLIND LAND CORPORATION (PTY) LTD
LESLIE D. FRENKEL (PTY) LTD
MANLAK INVESTMENTS (PTY) LTD
S.A. PAPER PROCESSING (1956) (PTY) LTD

INVESTMENTS

None

CARRIG DIAMONDS LTD

ABBREVIATION : CARRIGS

JSE SHORT CODE : CAR

SECTOR : Mining-Diamonds

SHAREHOLDERS

Who Owns Whom's Assessment of the Identity of the Ultimate Controlling Shareholder: CONSOLIDATED MINING VIA EGOLI

SHAREHOLDER	PERCENTAGE 1992	1991
EGOLI CONSOLIDATED MINES LTD	76.6	76.6
LOWENCO NOM P/L	7.1	6.9
CORPORATE MANAGEMENT & INV P/L	1.5	1.5
STD BANK NOM TVL P/L	---	1.0
TOTAL	85.2	86.0

DIRECTORS :
BUITENDAG HC ,FLOWERDAY RA ,LEE RA
LOWENTHAL ND (Chairman),LOWENTHAL RY
RUBENSTEIN GB ,SCHECHTER M ,SUDDENS BD
THOMPSON MW ,TURNER CF

REGISTRATION NUMBER : 01/08797/06

REGISTERED OFFICE
39th Floor, Carlton Centre
Johannesburg
2001
TEL: 011-331 9181
FAX: 011-331 6189

TRANSFER SECRETARY
Mercantile Registrars Ltd
P O Box 1053, Johannesburg
2000
TEL: 011-333 8181

COMPANY SECRETARY
Consolidated Mining Management Services Ltd

NATURE OF BUSINESS
The company is engaged in exploration for & the production of diamonds. It owns properties & mineral rights over areas having diamond-bearing potential.

BANKERS :
Bank of Lisbon International Ltd
First National Bank of SA Ltd

AUDITORS :
Charles Orbach & Co

FAMILIAR BRAND NAMES
N/A

CONTRIBUTION BY ACTIVITY
N/A

YEAR END : March

DIVIDEND : Ords 10c
Final No 18 (Ldr)02/05/90 (Pay)15/06/90 Amt(c)2

CAPITAL STRUCTURE

	AUTHORISED	ISSUED
Ords 10c	30000000	20085000

FINANCIAL STATISTICS (AT FINANCIAL YEAR END)

(Amts in R'000)	1992 Mar	1991 Mar	1990 Mar	1989 Mar	1988 Mar
Ord S/H Int	9751	9116	10463	9515	14443
Long Trm Loans	2	2	101	434	17
Iss Ord Share	20085	20085	19085	18000	18000
Total Liab	5239	6684	1983	1091	1370
Current Liab	5237	6682	1882	657	1353

Total Assets	14990	15800	12446	10606	15813
Current Assets	1132	1472	1688	2032	3306
Debtors	167	124	55	1125	79
Inventory	934	1288	1156	347	137
Turnover	7283	8687	6831	5142	3067
Oper Profit	-1539	-1438	854	-138	-545
Interest Paid	629	567	5	161	-
Tax Paid	-	47	24	25	137
Prf af Int&Tax	-2161	-2050	1012	-324	-682
Prf att Ord Sh	-2161	-1951	1012	-294	-682
Btm Line Earn	635	-1946	1012	-4928	-682
Dividend Paid	-	-	382	-	-
Mkt Prce(c) YE	13	35	80	45	50

PER SHARE STATISTICS (CENTS)

Net Asst Val	48.55	45.39	54.82	52.86	80.24
Net Earnings	-10.80	-10.20	5.50	-1.60	-5.35
Dividends	-	-	2.00	-	-
Cash Flow	-10.76	-10.19	5.46	-1.63	-5.35

RATIOS AND OTHER INFORMATION

Mrk Cap(R000)	2611	7030	15268	8100	9000
Current Ratio	0.22	0.22	0.90	3.09	2.44
Quik/Acid Tst	0.04	0.03	0.28	2.56	2.34
A/C Rec T/ovr	43.61	70.06	124.20	4.57	38.82
Tot Ass T/ovr	0.49	0.55	0.55	0.48	0.19
Debt/Ass Rat	0.35	0.42	0.15	0.07	0.09
L T L Tot Ass	0.00	0.00	0.00	0.01	0.00
Debt to Eqity	0.54	0.73	0.18	0.08	0.09
Interest Cover	-2.45	-2.54	170.80	-0.86	-
Oper Prof Mrg	-21.13	-16.55	12.50	-2.68	-17.77
Net Prof Marg%	-29.67	-22.46	14.81	-5.72	-22.24
Ret on Assets	-10.22	-9.09	8.36	-1.30	-3.45
Ret on Equity%	-22.16	-21.40	9.67	-3.09	-4.72
Price/Earnings	-1.20	-3.43	14.55	-28.13	-9.35
Divid Cover	-	-	2.75	-	-
Divid Yield	-	-	2.50	-	-
Earning Yield%	-83.08	-29.14	6.88	-3.56	-10.70
NAV % Mrk Pr	373.45	129.68	68.53	117.47	160.48
Effec Tax Rate	-	-	2.61	-8.36	-8.62
Def Interval	-0.07	-0.01	0.02	-0.56	-1.35
Sus Grth Rate	-22.16	-21.40	6.02	-3.09	-4.72

SUBSIDIARY & ASSOCIATED COMPANIES

BONTE KOE MYNBOU ONDERNEMINGS (EDMS) BPK
CARBON LEADER LTD
LOXTON EXPLORATION (PTY) LTD
SOUTHERN FISSURES LTD
WOLFBERG MYNBOU (EDMS) BPK

INVESTMENTS

None

CASHBUILD LTD

ABBREVIATION : CASHBIL

JSE SHORT CODE : CSB

SECTOR : Industrial-Retailers & Wholesalers

SHAREHOLDERS

Who Owns Whom's Assessment of the Identity of the Ultimate Controlling Shareholder:
PEPGRO VIA PEPKOR

SHAREHOLDER	PERCENTAGE 1992	1991
CASH-HOLD LTD	55.0	13.9
SA MUTUAL	7.3	9.3
STD BANK NOM TVL P/L	4.8	5.7
FIRST NAT NOM P/L	4.3	2.5
METROPOLITAN LIFE LTD	3.5	3.5
FIRST NAT BANK LTD	3.1	3.1
CMB NOM P/L	1.5	---
DE BEERS PENS FUND	1.1	1.1
ANGLO AMERICAN CORP PENS FUND	1.1	1.1
SHARESTOCK NOM P/L	---	1.1
YSKOR PENS FUND	---	2.3
EIGHTY ONE MAIN STREET NOM LTD	---	1.1
SANKORP BPK	---	5.5
SANLAM	---	12.5
STATUS INV P/L	---	13.5
TOTAL	81.5	76.2

DIRECTORS :
HAUMANT GRS (Chief Executive),LOUW JA ,LYON RD
MASSON D ,STASSEN C ,WIESE CH (Chairman

REGISTRATION NUMBER : 86/01503/06

REGISTERED OFFICE
Cnr Aerodrome & Aeroton Rd's, Aeroton
Johannesburg
2001
TEL: 011-494 4330
FAX: 011-494 1225

TRANSFER SECRETARY
Central Registrars Ltd
P O Box 4844, Johannesburg
2000
TEL: 011-331 0051

COMPANY SECRETARY
E J Ryan

NATURE OF BUSINESS
The group carries on business as a wholesale & retail builders' materials distributor.

BANKERS :
Standard Bank of SA Ltd

AUDITORS :
Fisher Hoffman Stride

FAMILIAR BRAND NAMES
BUY'N BUILD

CONTRIBUTION BY ACTIVITY
N/A

YEAR END : June

DIVIDEND : Ords 1c

Final	(Ldr)14/09/90	(Pay)03/10/90	Amt(c)9
Interim	(Ldr)09/03/90	(Pay)02/04/90	Amt(c)4
Interim	(Ldr)08/03/91	(Pay)02/04/91	Amt(c)5
Final	(Ldr)13/09/91	(Pay)13/10/91	Amt(c)10
Interim	(Ldr)06/03/92	(Pay)01/04/92	Amt(c)5
Final	(Ldr)04/09/92	(Pay)25/09/92	Amt(c)8.5

NUMBER OF EMPLOYEES : 1194

CAPITAL STRUCTURE

	AUTHORISED	ISSUED
Ords 1c	25000000	21400000

FINANCIAL STATISTICS (AT FINANCIAL YEAR END)

(Amts in R'000)	1991 Jun	1990 Jun	1989 Jun	1988 Jun	1987 Jun
Ord S/H Int	28264	23592	19840	15641	11026
Long Trm Loans	6463	4929	4862	1294	1238
Iss Ord Share	21400	21400	21400	21400	20000
Total Liab	77294	71497	53205	40813	19000
Current Liab	70831	66568	48343	39519	17762
Total Assets	105519	95056	73026	56454	30026
Intang Assets	39	33	19	*	*
Current Assets	82409	75754	59661	48981	26827
Debtors	12894	8116	6685	4174	1708
Inventory	58783	50948	38078	23989	14920
Turnover	387011	321061	242065	192098	117231
Oper Profit	17712	13578	10448	7794	5244
Interest Paid	2377	1206	1253	-	-
Tax Paid	7930	6246	4638	3710	2350
Prf af Int&Tax	9572	7826	5796	4084	2894
Prf att Ord Sh	7882	6534	4842	3344	2364
Btm Line Earn	7882	6534	4842	3344	2364
Dividend Paid	3210	2782	2140	1445	1050
Mkt Prce(c) YE	425	175	210	210	370
Depreciation	2546	2272	1450	998	601

PER SHARE STATISTICS (CENTS)

Net Asst Val	131.89	110.09	92.62	73.09	55.13
Net Earnings	36.80	30.50	22.60	15.60	11.80
Dividends	15.00	13.00	10.00	6.75	5.25
Cash Flow	48.73	41.15	29.40	20.29	14.83

RATIOS AND OTHER INFORMATION

Mrk Cap(R000)	90950	37450	44940	44940	74000
Current Ratio	1.16	1.14	1.23	1.24	1.51
Quik/Acid Tst	0.33	0.37	0.45	0.63	0.67
A/C Rec T/ovr	30.01	39.56	36.21	46.02	68.64
Tot Ass T/ovr	3.67	3.38	3.31	3.40	3.90
Debt/Ass Rat	0.68	0.71	0.69	0.72	0.63
L T L Tot Ass	0.01	0.01	0.03	0.02	0.04
Debt to Eqity	2.55	2.87	2.55	2.61	1.72
Interest Cover	7.45	11.26	8.34	-	-
Oper Prof Mrg	4.58	4.23	4.32	4.06	4.47
Net Prof Marg%	2.04	2.04	2.00	1.74	2.02
Ret on Assets	18.84	16.07	16.00	13.81	17.46
Ret on Equity%	27.89	27.70	24.41	21.38	21.44
Price/Earnings	11.55	5.74	9.29	13.46	31.36
Divid Cover	2.45	2.35	2.26	2.31	2.25
Divid Yield	3.53	7.43	4.76	3.21	1.42
Earning Yield%	8.66	17.43	10.76	7.43	3.19
NAV % Mrk Pr	31.03	62.91	44.11	34.80	14.90
Effec Tax Rate	45.55	13.99	37.26	47.60	44.81
Def Interval	0.11	0.14	0.64	0.30	0.42
Sus Grth Rate	16.53	15.90	13.62	12.14	11.92

SUBSIDIARY & ASSOCIATED COMPANIES

ASN DEVELOPERS (PTY) LTD (50%)
BUY & BUILD (BOPHUTHATSWANA) (PTY) LTD
BUY & BUILD (MAFETENG) (PTY) LTD
BUY & BUILD (MOHALESHOEK) (PTY) LTD
BUY & BUILD (QWAQWA) (PTY) LTD (50%)
CASHBUILD (BOPHUTHATSWANA) (PTY) LTD (50%)
CASHBUILD (BOTSWANA) (PTY) LTD
CASHBUILD (CISKEI) (PTY) LTD
CASHBUILD (COFIMVABA) LTD
CASHBUILD (GAZANKULU) LTD (50%)
CASHBUILD (KANGWANE) (PTY) LTD
CASHBUILD (KANYE) (PTY) LTD
CASHBUILD (KWANDEBELE) (PTY) LTD (50%)
CASHBUILD (LEBOWA) LTD (50%)
CASHBUILD (LESOTHO) (PTY) LTD (50%)
CASHBUILD (NAMIBIA) (PTY) LTD]
CASHBUILD (QWAQWA) LTD (50%)
CASHBUILD (RSA) (PTY) LTD
CASHBUILD (SWAZILAND) (PTY) LTD (50%)
CASHBUILD (TRANSKEI) (PTY) LTD (50%)
CASHBUILD (VENDA) LTD (50%)
CASHBUILD MANAGEMENT SERVICES (PTY) LTD
FRASERS MANUFACTURING (LESOTHO) LTD
TRADEBUILD (PTY) LTD
U-BUILD (JABULANI) (PTY) LTD (50%)
U-BUILD (PTY) LTD
U-BUILD (SOSHANGUVE) (PY) LTD (50%)

INVESTMENTS

KHAYELIHLE HOMEMAKERS (PTY) LTD (10%)
MABULA TIMESHARING SHARE BLOCK LTD (4 SH)

CAXTON LTD

ABBREVIATION : CAXTON

JSE SHORT CODE : CXN

SECTOR : Industrial-Printing & Publishing

SHAREHOLDERS

Who Owns Whom's Assessment of the Identity of the Ultimate Controlling Shareholder:
MOOLMAN & COBURN / ARGUS BOARD

SHAREHOLDER	PERCENTAGE 1992	1991
AFMED P/L	74.5	74.5
ARGUS HOLDINGS LTD	13.8	13.8
COBURN N M	4.3	4.3
MOOLMAN T D	4.3	4.3
TOTAL	97.0	97.0

DIRECTORS :
BAND DDB ,COBURN NM (Joint Managing Director)
JANKELOWITZ EM ,MCLEAN PW
MOOLMAN TD (Joint Managing Director),PAULSEN BG
SHORT MDW (Chairman),SMUTS JHL

REGISTRATION NUMBER : 05/00183/06

REGISTERED OFFICE
1 Blumberg Street, Industria West
Johannesburg
2092
TEL: 011-474 0460
FAX: 011-474 8229

TRANSFER SECRETARY
Central Registrars Ltd
P O Box 4844, Johannesburg
2000
TEL 011-331 0051

COMPANY SECRETARY
K J Bownass

NATURE OF BUSINESS
The holding company of a group involved in newspaper & magazine printing & publishing, packaging, and ink manufacturing & marketing The company has a controlling interest in JSE quoted CTP Holdings

BANKERS :
First National Bank of SA Ltd

AUDITORS :
Ernst & Young

FAMILIAR BRAND NAMES
SA JOURNAL OF EPIDIOMOLOGY
SECRETARY'S HANDBOOK

CONTRIBUTION BY ACTIVITY
N/A

YEAR END : March

DIVIDEND Ords 50c

Interim No 35	(Ldr)21/12/90	(Pay)11/01/91	Amt(c)113
Final No 36	(Ldr)21/06/91	(Pay)12/07/91	Amt(c)190
Interim No 37	(Ldr)20/12/91	(Pay)10/01/92	Amt(c)124

DIVIDEND :Ords 2c

Final	(Ldr)03/07/92	(Pay)24/07/92	Amt(c)7 85
Interim	(Ldr)18/12/92	(Pay)12/01/93	Amt(c)4

NUMBER OF EMPLOYEES : 3011

CAPITAL STRUCTURE

	AUTHORISED	ISSUED
Ords 2c	75000000	25113400

FINANCIAL STATISTICS (AT FINANCIAL YEAR END)

(Amts in R'000)	1992 Mar	1991 Mar	1990 Mar	1989 Mar	1988 Mar
Ord S/H Int	79379	62153	52872	45215	36748
Long Trm Loans	133548	102123	104039	90514	73281
Iss Ord Share	718	718	718	718	718
Total Liab	258463	207264	179798	197754	142485
Current Liab	124915	105141	75759	107240	69204
Total Assets	336214	268192	232670	242969	179233
Intang Assets	1628	1225	*	*	*
Current Assets	189629	152658	134128	145992	86210
Debtors	108675	87114	75520	77150	48926
Inventory	58100	57748	56473	65513	33954
Turnover	562846	482141	453831	415894	289555
Oper Profit	67360	45500	38324	35790	29378
Interest Paid	8212	5559	7878	7788	4079
Tax Paid	28127	20353	16075	12965	12055
Prf af Int&Tax	37487	22990	17207	18263	15099
Prf att Ord Sh	19842	13046	10419	10950	9628
Btm Line Earn	18023	11455	9372	10060	8031
Dividend Paid	2863	2174	1765	1593	1434
Mkt Prce(c) YE	14000	14000	10000	10000	8000
Depreciation	16863	14780	14713	14063	12593

PER SHARE STATISTICS (CENTS)

Net Asst Val	10828 83	8485 79	7363 79	6297 35	5118 11
Net Earnings	2765 00	1818 00	1452 00	1526 00	1343 00
Dividends	399 00	303 00	246 00	222 00	200 00
Cash Flow	4994 29	3690 39	3959 19	3630 92	3392 62

RATIOS AND OTHER INFORMATION

Mrk Cap(R000)	100520	100520	71800	71800	57440
Current Ratio	1 52	1 45	1 77	1 36	1 25
Quik/Acid Tst	1 05	0 90	1 03	0 75	0 76
A/C Rec T/ovr	5 18	5 53	6 01	5 39	5 92
Tot Ass T/ovr	1 67	1 80	1 95	1 71	1 62
Debt/Ass Rat	0 43	0 41	0 37	0 49	0 45
L T L Tot Ass	0 06	0 02	0 04	0 05	0 06
Debt to Eqity	1 83	1 78	1 63	2 64	2 18
Interest Cover	8 71	8 59	4 96	4 79	7 50
Oper Prof Mrg	11 97	9 44	8 44	8 61	10 15
Net Prof Marg%	3 53	2 71	2 30	2 63	3 33
Ret on Assets	22 78	18 65	18 75	16 92	18 21
Ret on Equity%	25 00	20 99	19 71	24 22	26 20
Price/Earnings	5 06	7 70	6 89	6 55	5 96
Divid Cover	6 93	6 00	5 90	6 87	6 72
Divid Yield	2 85	2 16	2 46	2 22	2 50
Earning Yield%	19 75	12 99	14 52	15 26	16 79
NAV % Mrk Pr	77 35	60 61	73 64	62 97	63 98
Effec Tax Rate	43 94	49 78	31 68	32 53	32 55
Def Interval	1 04	1 00	1 15	1 93	1 17
Sus Grth Rate	21 39	17 49	16 37	20 69	22 30

SUBSIDIARY & ASSOCIATED COMPANIES

CTP HOLDINGS LTD

INVESTMENTS

COATES BROTHERS LTD (14800SH)
REDGWOODS LTD (89681 SH)

CBD PROPERTY FUND

ABBREVIATION : CBD FUND

JSE SHORT CODE : CBD

SECTOR : Financial Property Trust

SHAREHOLDERS

Who Owns Whom's Assessment of the Identity of the Ultimate Controlling Shareholder:
SA MUTUAL

SHAREHOLDER	PERCENTAGE 1992	1991
SA MUTUAL	42 9	42 0
SAGE LIFE LTD	16 1	15 3
NEDBANK NOM LTD	6 6	1 2
EIGHTY ONE MAIN STREET NOM LTD	4 0	2 4
CITY COUNCIL OF DURBAN	3 9	3 9
NESTLE PENS FUND	2 2	
BP THIBAULT NOM P/L	2 0	2 0
STD BANK NOM TVL P/L	1 7	5 7
AECI PENS FUND	1 6	1 6
BARLOWS PENS FUND	1 6	1 6
CMB NOM P/L	1 5	
ENGINEERING INDUSTRIES PENS FUND	1 4	1 4

METAL IND GROUP PENS FUND	1 3	1 3
DURBAN CORP SUPERANNUATION FUND	---	2 7
DURBAN MUNICIPAL PENS FUND	---	1 2
FNP PENS FUND	---	1 6
SANLAM	---	1 4
TOTAL	86 9	85 2

DIRECTORS :
BLAKE FG ,DE VILLIERS NA
MILLS ANB (Managing Director),NACKAN B
SHILL HL (Chairman

REGISTRATION NUMBER : 75/00613/06

REGISTERED OFFICE
11th Floor, Sage Centre, 10 Fraser Street
Johannesburg
2001
TEL 011 491 0911
FAX 011-834 2107

TRANSFER SECRETARY
Fraser Street Registrars (Pty) Ltd
P O Box 61178, Marshalltown
2107
TEL 011-491 0911

COMPANY SECRETARY
C S Cant

NATURE OF BUSINESS
A property unit trust investing primarily in retail & office properties

BANKERS :
Nedbank Ltd

AUDITORS :
Kessel Feinstein, KPMG Aiken & Peat

FAMILIAR BRAND NAMES
N/A

CONTRIBUTION BY ACTIVITY
Offices (% rental income) (50 2%)
Retail (36 4%)
Parking (9 6%)
Residential (3 8%)

YEAR END : March

DIVIDEND Units

Interim No 15	(Ldr)18/08/89	(Pay)31/08/89	Amt(c)13 72
Final No 16	(Ldr)16/02/90	(Pay)28/02/90	Amt(c)17 79
Interim No 17	(Ldr)24/08/90	(Pay)31/08/90	Amt(c)13 75
Final No 18	(Ldr)28/12/90	(Pay)28/02/91	Amt(c)16 96
Special No 19	(Ldr)24/05/91	(Pay)31/05/91	Amt(c)7 64
Interim No 20	(Ldr)22/11/91	(Pay)29/11/91	Amt(c)14 03
Final No 21	(Ldr)22/05/92	(Pay)29/05/92	Amt(c)17
Interim No 22	(Ldr)20/11/92	(Pay)30/11/92	Amt(c)14 75

CAPITAL STRUCTURE

	AUTHORISED	ISSUED
Units	122137500	122137500

FINANCIAL STATISTICS (AT FINANCIAL YEAR END)

(Amts in R'000)	1992 Mar	1991 Mar	1989 Dec	1988	1987
Ord S/H Int	236204	184488	166020	62510	61030
Long Trm Loans	2091	30281		10216	9171
Iss Ord Share	122138	122138	122138	61500	61500
Total Liab	23735	40318	22586	20432	18342
Current Liab	21644	10037	22586	10216	9171
Total Assets	259939	224806	188606	91582	82763
Current Assets	64039	38123	24062	18856	12562
Debtors	20073	18585	3200	-	-
Inventory	-	-	-	18856	12562
Oper Profit	4044	5592	3281	17810	16667
Prf af Int&Tax	37898	47804	39266	17810	16667
Prf att Ord Sh	37898	47804	39266	17810	16667
Btm Line Earn	37898	47804	39266	17810	16667
Dividend Paid	37899	47802	39266	17810	16667
Mkt Prce(c) YE	250	280	320	240	315

PER SHARE STATISTICS (CENTS)

Net Asst Val	193 39	151 05	135 93	101 64	99 24
Net Earnings	31 03	39 14	32 14	-	-
Dividends	31 03	39 14	32 14	-	-
Cash Flow	31 03	31 31	32 15	28 96	27 10

RATIOS AND OTHER INFORMATION

Mrk Cap(R000)	305345	341986	390842	147600	193725
Current Ratio	2 96	3 80	1 07	1 85	1 37
Quik/Acid Tst	2 96	3 80	1 07	-	
Debt/Ass Rat	0 09	0 18	0 12	0 22	0 22
L T L Tot Ass	0 01	0 13	-	0 11	0 11
Debt to Eqity	0 10	0 22	0 14	0 33	0 30
Ret on Assets	14 58	17 01	20 82	19 45	20 14
Ret on Equity%	16 04	20 73	23 65	28 49	27 31
Price/Earnings	8 06	7 15	9 96	-	
Divid Cover	1 00	1 00	1 00	-	
Divid Yield	12 41	13 98	10 04	-	-
Earning Yield%	12 41	13 98	10 04	-	-
NAV % Mrk Pr	77 36	53 95	42 48	42 35	31 50
Def Interval	0 08	0 52	0 01	0 57	0 55
Sus Grth Rate	0 00	0 00	0 00	0 00	0 00

SUBSIDIARY & ASSOCIATED COMPANIES

AFRICAN CITY PROPERTIES TRUST (1952) (PT
BEAUMONDES (PTY) LTD
CATIME (PTY) LTD
CBD (KERK STREET) (PTY) LTD
CBD ANNUITY HOUSE (PTY) LTD
CBD JUTA STREET (PTY) LTD
CBD PAROW (PTY) LTD
CBD PRESIDENT PLACE (PTY) LTD
CBD RAND CENTRAL (PTY) LTD
DELVERS DEVELOPMENT (PTY) LTD
DONNA PROPERTY & INVESTMENT CO (PTY) LTD
ELKAM (PTY) LTD
FEDERATED PROPERTIES BENONI (PTY) LTD
FEDERATED PROPERTIES BOKSBURG (PTY) LTD
FEDERATED PROPERTIES BORDER (PTY) LTD
FEDERATED PROPERTIES CLAREMONT (PTY) LTD
FEDERATED PROPERTIES CONMIL (PTY) LTD
FEDERATED PROPERTIES EAST LONDON (PTY) L
FEDERATED PROPERTIES EDENVALE (PTY) LTD
FEDERATED PROPERTIES KERK STREET (PTY) L
FEDERATED PROPERTIES PORT ELIZABETH (PTY
FEDERATED PROPERTIES ROODEPOORT (PTY) LT
FEDERATED PROPERTIES SALT RIVER (PTY) LT
FEDERATED PROPERTIES SMAL STREET (PTY) L
FEDERATED PROPERTIES TVL (PTY) LTD
FEDERATED PROPERTIES VON BRANDIS (PTY) L
FEDERATED PROPERTIES WYNBERG (PTY) LTD
FEDERATED PROPERTIES WYNBERG CAPE (PTY)
HALLMARK PROPERTIES (PTY) LTD
HORTA PROPERTY INVESTMENTS (PTY) LTD
KELHOF (PTY) LTD
KING GEORGE STREET PROPERTIES (PTY) LTD
KRUIS STREET PROPERTIES (PTY) LTD
LA ROCHELLE INVESTMENTS (PTY) LTD

MARKHALL PROPERTIES (PTY) LTD
NOSWAL HALL (PTY) LTD
SALAMANDER INVESTMENTS (PTY) LTD
STEYNS CENTRAL BUILDING (PTY) LTD
TEMPLE COURT (PTY) LTD
TOWER CENTRAL HOLDINGS (PTY) LTD
VAN DER MERWE STREET PROPERTIES (PTY) LT
ZANZA BELEGGINGS (EDMS) BPK

INVESTMENTS

None

CEMENTATION CO (AFRICA) LTD

ABBREVIATION : CEMENCO

JSE SHORT CODE : CMT

SECTOR : Industrial-Engineering

SHAREHOLDERS

Who Owns Whom's Assessment of the Identity of the Ultimate Controlling Shareholder:
TRAFALGAR HOUSE PLC / SA MUTUAL / GFSA

SHAREHOLDER	PERCENTAGE 1992	1991
TRAFALGAR HSE O/SEAS CONSTR HLDGS LTD	37 3	37 3
SA MUTUAL	27 2	27 6
MINU NOM LTD	24 0	24 0
FIRST NAT NOM P/L	1 5	1 5
CEMENTATION CO PROVIDENT FUND	1 5	1 3
TOTAL	91 5	91 6

DIRECTORS :
DOUGLAS AAB ,FORSTER ABA ,FULLER-GOOD MR
KNOLL LB DR,LOTTER GB (Managing Director)
MYERS B ,NISBET GY ,SHAW RT (Chairman)
THOMSON WW ,WATSON AJ (Financial Director)
WRIGHT AJ

REGISTRATION NUMBER : 01/08840/06

REGISTERED OFFICE
50 Booysens Road, Selby, Johannesburg
2001
TEL 011-493 3400
FAX 011-493 8283

TRANSFER SECRETARY
Cementation Co (Africa) Ltd
P O Box 2371, Southdale
2135
TEL 011-639 9111

COMPANY SECRETARY
J A Roussouw

NATURE OF BUSINESS
A holding company with subsidiaries engaged in general engineering and contracting operations, principally for the infrastructure and services to the mining industry, such as deep level shaft sinking, tunnelling, mine development, control of underground water, raise boring, support of mine workings, surface drilling programmes, manufacture of diamond drilling crowns & ancillary equipment

BANKERS :
Standard Bank of SA Ltd

AUDITORS :
Ernst & Young

FAMILIAR BRAND NAMES
CEMENCO,CEMTEC-FENZY,GFC,MOIR'S RAILWAY SIDING CONSTRUCTION,WILLIAM BAIN

CONTRIBUTION BY ACTIVITY
N/A

YEAR END : September

DIVIDEND : Ords 50c

Interim No 78	(Ldr)30/06/89	(Pay)28/07/89	Amt(c)35
Final No 79	(Ldr)29/12/89	(Pay)31/01/90	Amt(c)40
Interim No 80	(Ldr)29/06/90	(Pay)27/07/90	Amt(c)35
Final No 81	(Ldr)28/12/90	(Pay)30/01/91	Amt(c)15

NUMBER OF EMPLOYEES : 4550

CAPITAL STRUCTURE

	AUTHORISED	ISSUED
6% Cum Pref R2	150000	150000
Ords 50c	12000000	8952000
Non-Red Comp Conv Cum Prefs 50c	10300000	0

FINANCIAL STATISTICS (AT FINANCIAL YEAR END)

(Amts in R'000)	1991 Sep	1990 Sep	1989 Sep	1988 Sep	1987 Sep
Ord S/H Int	59426	69705	56265	50690	45494
Long Trm Loans	12639	23806	24533	29510	30870
Iss Ord Share	8952	8952	6892	6875	6875
Total Liab	113696	150383	150874	134102	129110
Current Liab	101057	126577	126341	104592	98240
Total Assets	173122	220088	207139	184792	174604
Current Assets	108070	146254	143175	119390	102629
Debtors	57597	80461	78324	60104	47366
Inventory	35281	62757	54068	41297	41411
Turnover	325209	356105	334703	314211	273289
Oper Profit	-4088	25183	24985	20603	13979
Interest Paid	11061	10824	9602	5998	5554
Tax Paid	-6814	6778	4564	5656	3955
Prf af Int&Tax	-6967	8875	12243	9588	4470
Prf att Ord Sh	-6985	9009	10679	8282	3146
Btm Line Earn	-10508	6809	10679	8774	2677
Dividend Paid	-	4476	5169	2887	1509
Mkt Prce(c) YE	300	575	850	325	620
Depreciation	11441	9856	14063	12909	13182

PER SHARE STATISTICS (CENTS)

Net Asst Val	663 83	778 65	816 38	737 31	661 73
Net Earnings	-78 00	100 60	155 00	86 00	46 04
Dividends	-	50 00	75 00	42 00	22 00
Cash Flow	-41 29	275 92	325 37	390 50	291 58

RATIOS AND OTHER INFORMATION

Mrk Cap(R000)	26856	51474	58582	22344	42625
Current Ratio	1 07	1 16	1 13	1 14	1 04
Quik/Acid Tst	0 72	0 66	0 71	0 75	0 62
A/C Rec T/ovr	5 65	4 43	4 27	5 23	5 77
Tot Ass T/ovr	1 88	1 62	1 62	1 70	1 57
Debt/Ass Rat	0 62	0 62	0 66	0 64	0 68
L T L Tot Ass	0 04	0 04	0 05	0 07	0 12

Debt to Eqity	1.81	1.95	2.44	2.33	2.60
Interest Cover	-0.37	2.33	2.60	3.43	2.52
Oper Prof Mrg	-1.26	7.07	7.46	6.56	5.12
Net Prof Marg%	-2.15	2.53	3.19	2.64	1.15
Ret on Assets	-1.57	12.03	12.75	11.50	8.01
Ret on Equity%	-11.75	12.92	18.98	16.34	6.92
Price/Earnings	-3.85	5.72	5.48	3.78	13.47
Divid Cover	-	2.01	2.07	2.05	2.09
Divid Yield	-	8.70	8.82	12.92	3.55
Earning Yield%	-26.00	17.50	18.24	26.46	7.43
NAV % Mrk Pr	221.28	135.42	96.04	226.86	106.73
Effec Tax Rate	-7.10	3.61	41.08	-	2.43
Def Interval	-11.37	2.04	1.86	1.34	2.01
Sus Grth Rate	-11.75	6.50	9.79	10.64	3.60

SUBSIDIARY & ASSOCIATED COMPANIES

BARRACUDA GRANITE TILE (PTY) LTD (50%)
CEMENCO FOUNDRY (PTY) LTD
CEMENTATION (AFRICA CONTRACTS) (PTY) LTD
CEMENTATION (BOTSWANA) (PTY) LTD
CEMENTATION ENGINEERING (PTY) LTD
FANTECNIC (PTY) LTD
GF DIAMOND DRILLING & DEVELOPMENT CO (PT
GOLD FIELDS CEMENTATION MINING CO (NAMIB
GOLDFIELDS CEMENTATION MINING CO LTD
IES ENGINEERING CO (PTY) LTD
JH RITCHIE & CO (PTY) LTD
MOIR'S RAILWAY ENGINEERING WORKS (PTY) L
P & E EUSTICE STAMPINGS (PTY) LTD
PANMILL (PTY) LTD
REVALVE SERVICES (PTY) LTD
SIDING CONSTRUCTION & MAINTENANCE CO. (P
UNILEC (BOTSWANA) (PTY) LTD
UNIVEST (PTY) LTD
WD WIGGILL PROPERTY HOLDINGS (PTY) LTD
WILLIAM BAIN & CO (SA) (PTY) LTD

INVESTMENTS

None

CENMAG HOLDINGS LTD

ABBREVIATION : CENMAG

JSE SHORT CODE : CMG

SECTOR : Development Capital Market

SHAREHOLDERS

Who Owns Whom's Assessment of the Identity of the Ultimate Controlling Shareholder: DIRECTORS

SHAREHOLDER	PERCENTAGE 1992	1991
FARKAS V	25.0	24.9
GREENBLATT B	25.0	24.9
BARLOW A W	18.3	18.1
LANE FAMILY INV P/L	10.3	10.5
BLAF INV CC	4.4	4.9
SPENCER BARLOW TRUST	3.3	3.3
WARREN BARLOW TRUST	3.3	3.3
LANE C J E	3.0	2.8
CENMAG SHARE INC SCHEME	2.1	2.2
BATTISS J L	1.0	1.1
TOTAL	95.7	96.0

DIRECTORS :
BARLOW AW ,FARKAS V (Financial Director)
GREENBLATT B ,LANE CJE

REGISTRATION NUMBER : 87/04821/06

REGISTERED OFFICE
Hertz Drive, Meadowdale
Ext 3, Route 24

TEL: 011-622 2600

TRANSFER SECRETARY
Central Registrars Ltd
P O Box 4844, Johannesburg
2000
TEL: 011-331 0051

COMPANY SECRETARY
V Farkas

NATURE OF BUSINESS
An investment holding company. The group is active in the following: Distribution of electrical and related equipment; Distribution of tubing, fitting & valves; Motor rewinding; Manufacture & servicing of electromagnets.

BANKERS :
Standard Bank of SA Ltd

AUDITORS :
Henry Ginsberg Lieberthal & Abrahams
Karlin Taback Pelkowitz

FAMILIAR BRAND NAMES
N/A

CONTRIBUTION BY ACTIVITY
N/A

YEAR END : February

DIVIDEND : Ords 1c
Dividend No 5 (Ldr)25/10/91 (Pay)29/11/91 Amt(c)7

CAPITAL STRUCTURE

	AUTHORISED	ISSUED
Ords 1c	20000000	9600000

FINANCIAL STATISTICS (AT FINANCIAL YEAR END)

(Amts in R'000)	1992 Feb	1991 Feb	1990 Feb	1989 Feb	1988 Feb
Ord S/H Int	11694	10537	9596	8514	7682
Long Trm Loans	2447	3032	3336	2791	1837
Iss Ord Share	9600	9000	9000	9000	9000
Total Liab	14285	15127	12449	10460	7875
Current Liab	11838	12095	9113	7669	6038
Total Assets	20378	20316	16680	13579	10143
Intang Assets	5601	5348	5365	5395	5414
Current Assets	16857	17301	14064	11416	9185
Debtors	9697	7405	9388	6667	4880
Inventory	5233	5170	3333	3549	2716
Turnover	50036	46119	52015	40684	13956
Oper Profit	2028	2723	3519	2557	627
Interest Paid	2166	1675	1160	409	94

Tax Paid	326	713	1313	932	290
Prf af Int&Tax	907	1654	1766	1356	311
Prf att Ord Sh	857	1571	1622	1287	300
Btm Line Earn	857	1571	1622	1287	300
Dividend Paid	-	630	540	450	-
Mkt Prce(c) YE	64	60	75	75	95
Depreciation	436	192	201	160	51

PER SHARE STATISTICS (CENTS)

Net Asst Val	63 47	57 66	47 01	34 66	25 20
Net Earnings	8 93	16 36	18 02	14 30	10 20
Dividends	-	7 00	6 00	5 00	-
Cash Flow	14 34	25 41	31 47	24 61	11 87

RATIOS AND OTHER INFORMATION

Mrk Cap(R000)	6144	5400	6750	6750	8550
Current Ratio	1 42	1 43	1 54	1 49	1 52
Quik/Acid Tst	0 98	1 00	1 18	1 03	1 07
A/C Rec T/ovr	5 16	6 23	5 54	6 10	2 86
Tot Ass T/ovr	2 46	2 27	3 12	3 00	1 38
Debt/Ass Rat	0 67	0 68	0 66	0 69	0 75
L T L Tot Ass	0 09	0 08	0 11	0 12	0 15
Debt to Eqity	1 16	1 31	1 14	1 10	0 99
Interest Cover	0 96	1 72	3 03	6 25	6 67
Oper Prof Mrg	4 05	5 90	6 77	6 29	4 49
Net Prof Marg%	1 71	3 41	3 12	3 16	2 15
Ret on Assets	16 68	19 90	25 41	19 86	6 85
Ret on Equity%	7 33	14 91	16 90	15 12	3 91
Price/Earnings	7 17	3 67	4 16	5 24	9 31
Divid Cover	-	2 34	3 00	2 86	-
Divid Yield	-	11 67	8 00	6 67	-
Earning Yield%	13 95	27 27	24 03	19 07	10 74
NAV % Mrk Pr	99 17	96 09	62 68	46 21	26 53
Effec Tax Rate	20 34	8 53	9 87	7 17	48 59
Def Interval	5 25	3 03	1 07	0 87	4 86
Sus Grth Rate	7 33	8 93	11 28	9 83	3 91

SUBSIDIARY & ASSOCIATED COMPANIES

AFRICAN MAGNETS (PTY) LTD
CASTLE ENGINEERING SUPPLIERS (EVANDER) (
CASTLE ENGINEERING SUPPLIERS (PTY) LTD
CASTLE ENGINEERING SUPPLIERS (VAAL) (PTY
CASTLE ENGINEERING SUPPLIERS (WITBANK) (
CENTURY ELECTRICAL WHOLESALERS (EVANDER)
CENTURY ELECTRICAL WHOLESALERS (JHB) (PT
CENTURY ELECTRICAL WHOLESALERS (NEWCASTL
CENTURY ELECTRICAL WHOLESALERS (WITBANK)
ELECTRO MAGNET CO (PTY) LTD
MAGNETIC TECHNOLOGY CONSULTANTS (PTY) LT
MECHANI MAG (PTY) LTD

INVESTMENTS

COLFIN INVESTMENTS LTD (13,6%)

CENTRAL AFRICAN CABLES LTD

ABBREVIATION : CAFCA

JSE SHORT CODE : CAF

SECTOR : Industrial-Electronics, Electrical & Bat

SHAREHOLDERS

Who Owns Whom's Assessment of the Identity of the Ultimate Controlling Shareholder:
BICC PLC

SHAREHOLDER	PERCENTAGE 1992	1991
WILSON K R	16 8	16 9
ABSA NOM P/L	6 9	---
BARTEL H O E/L	6 3	---
FIRST NAT NOM P/L	4 9	3 0
ESTERHUYSEN J P	4 0	4 1
GAGGINS C	3 6	3 6
PONSFORD F	2 6	2 6
RONOEL PROPERTIES P/L	1 7	1 7
SMEDLEY V	1 7	1 7
BOTTING S M	1 5	1 5
MAHOMMEDY H	1 5	1 5
GROVE M C	1 4	1 4
HUGHES I W	1 3	1 3
BISSET E/L J J	1 2	1 2
GRUNSHAW D	1 2	1 2
JOPAIR P/L	1 2	1 2
DE VOS C D	1 1	1 1
WHITE J N	1 1	1 1
BARTEL H O	---	6 5
VOLKSKAS NOM P/L	---	6 9
TOTAL	59 9	58 5

DIRECTORS :
BIBBY P ,BOTSH AA
GALBRAITH WR (Chief Executive & M D),GRUBB BP
MAGOWAN JM (Chairman),MAWEMA NT ,MKUSHI HP

REGISTERED OFFICE
Lytton Road, Workington
Harare, Zimbabwe

TEL 68601
FAX 68606

TRANSFER SECRETARY
Mercantile Registrars Ltd
P O Box 1053, Johannesburg
2000
TEL 011-333 8181

COMPANY SECRETARY
A J Macfarlane

NATURE OF BUSINESS
The manufacture of copper electric cables up to 3 3kV, and overhead aluminium conductors, and the marketing and distribution of electric cables, high voltage equipment and cable related products

BANKERS :
Barclays Bank of Zimbabwe Ltd
Grindlays Bank Plc
Standard Chartered Merchant Bank Zim Ltd

AUDITORS :
Price Waterhouse Meyernel

FAMILIAR BRAND NAMES
N/A

CONTRIBUTION BY ACTIVITY
Copper Products (% turnover) (92 0%)
Aluminium Products (8 0%)

YEAR END : December

DIVIDEND :Ords Z$1

Interim No 51	(Ldr)24/08/90	(Pay)30/09/90	Amt(c)30
Final No 52	(Ldr)08/03/91	(Pay)01/04/91	Amt(c)34

DIVIDEND :Ords Z$0,50

Interim No 53	(Ldr)16/08/91	(Pay)01/10/91	Amt(c)7
Final No 54	(Ldr)06/03/92	(Pay)03/04/92	Amt(c)8.7
Interim No 55	(Ldr)21/08/92	(Pay)04/09/92	Amt(c)7

NUMBER OF EMPLOYEES : 343

CAPITAL STRUCTURE

	AUTHORISED	ISSUED
Ords Z$0,50	50000000	30600000
5,5% Cum Prefs Z$2	100000	0

FINANCIAL STATISTICS (AT FINANCIAL YEAR END)

(Amts in Zim$)	1991 Dec	1990 Dec	1989 Dec	1988 Jun	1987 Jun
Ord S/H Int	54693	40260	30358	19609	16243
Long Trm Loans	777	-	-	-	-
Iss Ord Share	30600	30600	30600	30600	30600
Total Liab	34311	25841	16387	13399	7260
Current Liab	33534	25841	16387	13399	7260
Total Assets	89004	66101	46745	33008	23503
Current Assets	56185	45922	28204	20210	10791
Debtors	24661	23804	16341	12584	4926
Inventory	22769	17752	10223	7471	5414
Turnover	121384	93042	68901	54613	22226
Oper Profit	30041	23960	15963	6779	4240
Interest Paid	6	6	489	1253	-
Tax Paid	11276	11055	7993	1139	1180
Prf af Int&Tax	19275	13166	7610	4437	3060
Prf att Ord Sh	19275	13166	7610	4437	3060
Btm Line Earn	19275	13166	7610	4437	3060
Dividend Paid	4804	3264	1887	1071	765
Mkt Prce(c) YE	490	250	140	180	270
Depreciation	1428	1366	955	1304	771

PER SHARE STATISTICS (CENTS)

Net Asst Val	178.74	131.57	99.21	64.08	53.08
Net Earnings	63.00	43.00	149.00	87.00	60.00
Dividends	15.70	10.70	37.00	21.00	15.00
Cash Flow	67.66	47.49	27.99	12.92	11.91

RATIOS AND OTHER INFORMATION

Mrk Cap(R000)	149940	76500	42840	55080	82620
Current Ratio	1.68	1.78	1.72	1.51	1.49
Quik/Acid Tst	1.00	1.09	1.10	0.95	0.74
A/C Rec T/ovr	4.92	3.91	4.22	2.89	4.51
Tot Ass T/ovr	1.36	1.41	1.47	1.10	0.95
Debt/Ass Rat	0.39	0.39	0.35	0.41	0.31
L T L Tot Ass	0.01	-	-	-	-
Debt to Eqity	0.63	0.64	0.54	0.68	0.45
Interest Cover	5006.83	3993.33	32.64	5.41	-
Oper Prof Mrg	24.75	25.75	23.17	12.41	19.08
Net Prof Marg%	15.88	14.15	11.04	8.12	13.77
Ret on Assets	34.33	36.65	34.43	13.79	18.04
Ret on Equity%	35.24	32.70	25.07	15.08	18.84
Price/Earnings	7.78	5.81	0.94	2.07	4.50
Divid Cover	4.01	4.02	4.03	4.14	4.00
Divid Yield	3.20	4.28	26.43	11.67	5.56
Earning Yield%	12.86	17.20	106.43	48.33	22.22
NAV % Mrk Pr	36.48	52.63	70.86	35.60	19.66
Effec Tax Rate	36.80	45.56	51.19	16.88	31.65
Def Interval	0.04	-	-	0.55	0.48
Sus Grth Rate	26.46	24.60	18.85	17.17	14.13

SUBSIDIARY & ASSOCIATED COMPANIES

BICC (CENTRAL AFRICA) (PVT) LTD

INVESTMENTS

None

CENTRECITY PROPERTY FUND

ABBREVIATION : CENPROP

JSE SHORT CODE : CEN

SECTOR : Financial-Property Trust

SHAREHOLDERS

Who Owns Whom's Assessment of the Identity of the Ultimate Controlling Shareholder: SOUTHERN LIFE / VARIOUS INSTITUTIONS

SHAREHOLDER	PERCENTAGE 1992	1991
SOUTHERN LIFE ASSOC LTD	27.5	28.1
CMB NOM P/L	21.0	---
SIXTY SIX MARSHALL STREET NOM P/L	6.9	5.3
SA MUTUAL	6.7	6.9
GREENMARKET SQUARE NOM P/L	5.7	6.1
AECI PENS FUND	5.4	5.4
EIGHTY ONE MAIN STREET NOM LTD	3.8	3.7
PROFESSIONAL PROV SOC OF SA	2.6	2.6
METAL IND GROUP PENS FUND	1.6	1.6
ENGINEERING INDUSTRIES PENS FUND	1.5	1.5
FIRST NAT NOM P/L	1.4	1.5
BARLOWS PENS FUND	1.1	---
BP THIBAULT NOM P/L	---	1.8
CITY COUNCIL OF DURBAN	---	4.9
SANLAM	---	12.8
TOTAL	85.2	82.2

DIRECTORS :
JOHNSON JGW (Chairman),KRUGER HG ,LEWIS K
MCCLELLAND C MCK ,PRICE PD ,THOMAS GM

REGISTERED OFFICE
2nd Floor, JHI House
11 Craddock Avenue, Rosebank
2001
TEL: 011-333 0123
FAX: 011-23 3256

TRANSFER SECRETARY
Central Registrars Ltd
P O Box 4844, Johannesburg
2000
TEL: 011-331 0051

COMPANY SECRETARY
J H Isaacs Group Ltd

NATURE OF BUSINESS
A property unit trust.

BANKERS :
Nedperm Bank Ltd

AUDITORS :
KPMG Aiken & Peat

FAMILIAR BRAND NAMES
N/A

CONTRIBUTION BY ACTIVITY
Retail (% rental income by sector) (34.8%)
Offices (31.7%)
Parking (3.6%)
Interest (29.9%)

YEAR END : December

DIVIDEND : Units

Interim No 20	(Ldr)11/08/89	(Pay)31/08/89	Amt(c)9.61
Final No 21	(Ldr)16/02/90	(Pay)28/02/90	Amt(c)10.91
Interim No 22	(Ldr)10/08/90	(Pay)31/08/90	Amt(c)3.8
Final No 23	(Ldr)22/02/91	(Pay)28/02/91	Amt(c)13.52
Interim No 24	(Ldr)16/08/91	(Pay)30/08/91	Amt(c)12.88
Final No 25	(Ldr)21/02/92	(Pay)28/02/92	Amt(c)12.5
Interim No 26	(Ldr)21/08/92	(Pay)31/08/92	Amt(c)12.89

NUMBER OF EMPLOYEES : 3

CAPITAL STRUCTURE

	AUTHORISED	ISSUED
Units	163490707	163490707

FINANCIAL STATISTICS (AT FINANCIAL YEAR END)

(Amts in R'000)	1991 Dec	1990 Dec	1989 Dec	1988 Dec	1987
Ord S/H Int	239794	239789	160264	160267	100825
Long Trm Loans	-	-	-	-	7962
Iss Ord Share	163491	163491	136242	136242	97316
Total Liab	22056	22546	15160	12113	15924
Current Liab	22056	22546	15160	12113	7962
Total Assets	261850	262335	175424	172380	127566
Current Assets	47008	89171	31413	53512	18779
Debtors	1788	3525	-	610	-
Inventory	-	-	-	-	18779
Oper Profit	-2351	-1910	-1486	-992	14804
Prf af Int&Tax	41499	39976	27954	21190	14804
Prf att Ord Sh	41499	39976	27954	21192	14804
Btm Line Earn	41499	39976	27954	21192	14804
Dividend Paid	41494	39979	27957	21184	14802
Mkt Prce(c) YE	310	250	260	155	170

PER SHARE STATISTICS (CENTS)

Net Asst Val	146.67	146.67	117.63	117.63	103.61
Net Earnings	25.38	25.88	20.52	16.66	-
Dividends	25.38	25.88	20.52	16.66	-
Cash Flow	25.38	24.45	20.52	15.55	15.21

RATIOS AND OTHER INFORMATION

Mrk Cap(R000)	506822	408728	354229	211175	165437
Current Ratio	2.13	3.96	2.07	4.42	2.36
Quik/Acid Tst	2.13	3.96	2.07	4.42	-
Debt/Ass Rat	0.08	0.09	0.09	0.07	0.12
L T L Tot Ass	-	-	-	-	0.06
Debt to Eqity	0.09	0.09	0.09	0.08	0.16
Ret on Assets	15.85	15.24	15.94	12.29	11.60
Ret on Equity%	17.31	16.67	17.44	13.22	14.68
Price/Earnings	12.21	9.66	12.67	9.30	-
Divid Cover	1.00	1.00	1.00	1.00	-
Divid Yield	8.19	10.35	7.89	10.75	-
Earning Yield%	8.19	10.35	7.89	10.75	-
NAV % Mrk Pr	47.31	58.67	45.24	75.89	60.94
Def Interval	-	-	-	-	0.54
Sus Grth Rate	0.00	0.00	0.00	0.00	0.00

SUBSIDIARY & ASSOCIATED COMPANIES

BELMARK PROPERTIES (PTY) LTD
DOWNBRAM HOLDINGS (PTY) LTD
DOWNKEW (PTY) LTD
GARFORRES INVESTMENTS (PTY) LTD
MARKELL HOLDINGS (PTY) LTD
MIDTOWN INVESTMENTS (PTY) LTD
NEW CORPORATION BUILDINGS (PTY) LTD
PLANDIT (PTY) LTD
ROSEBANK MALL (PTY) LTD
SEADOONE MALL (PTY) LTD
STAND NINE SEVEN SEVEN FERNDALE (PTY) LT
SUMMIT ROAD PROPERTIES (PTY) LTD
TEMPLE INN INVESTMENTS (PTY) LTD
TITREN ROAD PROPERTIES (PTY) LTD

INVESTMENTS

None

CERAMIC INDUSTRIES LTD

ABBREVIATION : CERAMIC

JSE SHORT CODE : CRM

SECTOR : Industrial-Building & Construction

SHAREHOLDERS

Who Owns Whom's Assessment of the Identity of the Ultimate Controlling Shareholder: ITALTILE LTD

SHAREHOLDER	PERCENTAGE 1992	1991
INTERBOARD HOLDINGS BV	---	1.5
SAFEGRO NOM P/L	---	36.9
ABACUS INDUSTRIAL HOLDINGS LTD	---	59.5
TOTAL	---	97.9

DIRECTORS :
CAPPER TM (Financial Director)
COULSEN TG (C E & Vice Chairman),DAVIDSON KM
LEWIS IMA ,MOXON JRT ,SUSSMAN P

REGISTRATION NUMBER : 82/08520/06

REGISTERED OFFICE
Cnr Manchester &, Bezuidenhout Roads
Wadeville
1407
TEL: 011-886 4764
FAX: 011-789 1387

TRANSFER SECRETARY
Mercantile Registrars Ltd
P O Box 1053, Johannesburg
2000
TEL: 011-333 8181

COMPANY SECRETARY
T M Capper

NATURE OF BUSINESS
An investment holding company with subsidiaries & operating divisions engaged in the manufacture, marketing & distribution of portable doors, hi-fi units, doors, components for kitchen units and building materials.

BANKERS :
Nedperm Bank Ltd

AUDITORS :
Ernst & Young

FAMILIAR BRAND NAMES
N/A

CONTRIBUTION BY ACTIVITY
N/A

YEAR END : February

DIVIDEND : Ords no par value
Final No 5 (Ldr)15/05/92 (Pay)05/06/92 Amt(c)7

NUMBER OF EMPLOYEES : 1195

CAPITAL STRUCTURE

	AUTHORISED	ISSUED
Ords no par value	100000000	73765809

FINANCIAL STATISTICS (AT FINANCIAL YEAR END)

(Amts in R'000)	1992 Feb	1991 Feb	1990 Feb	1989 Feb	1988 Feb
Ord S/H Int	62938	59881	5267	44461	43591
Long Trm Loans	22287	4673	6161	5653	1578
Iss Ord Share	17964	73766	122891	122891	122239
Total Liab	42154	64540	34177	24663	8437
Current Liab	19867	59867	28016	19010	6859
Total Assets	105092	124421	39403	55198	38156
Intang Assets	*	*	41	13926	13872
Current Assets	43864	84528	30128	29178	17271
Debtors	24057	41269	12795	12177	8581
Inventory	11133	41668	15402	16778	8234
Turnover	-	-	68935	59303	44386
Oper Profit	-3111	2367	-6236	5148	6348
Interest Paid	5499	8809	3088	1173	257
Tax Paid	1171	-	-	-	-
Prf af Int&Tax	-8359	-6442	-9041	4104	6091
Prf att Ord Sh	-8799	-6442	-9041	4104	6091
Btm Line Earn	-8799	-6863	-39194	4104	6347
Dividend Paid	1257	-	-	3502	3025
Mkt Prce(c) YE	400	80	15	28	40
Depreciation	5916	2072	2691	1830	1656

PER SHARE STATISTICS (CENTS)

Net Asst Val	350.36	81.18	4.25	24.85	24.31
Net Earnings	34.10	-5.60	-73.57	3.27	6.00
Dividends	7.00	-	-	2.85	2.85
Cash Flow	-5.22	-6.90	-5.17	4.84	7.63

RATIOS AND OTHER INFORMATION

Mrk Cap(R000)	71856	59013	18434	34409	48896
Current Ratio	2.21	1.41	1.08	1.53	2.52
Quik/Acid Tst	1.65	0.72	0.53	0.65	1.32
A/C Rec T/ovr	-	-	5.39	4.87	5.17
Tot Ass T/ovr	-	-	1.75	1.07	1.16
Debt/Ass Rat	0.32	0.52	0.87	0.45	0.22
L T L Tot Ass	0.14	0.04	0.16	0.10	0.04
Debt to Eqity	0.54	1.08	6.49	0.55	0.19
Interest Cover	-0.57	0.27	-2.02	4.39	24.70
Oper Prof Mrg	-	-	-9.05	8.68	14.30
Net Prof Marg%	-	-	-13.12	6.92	13.72
Ret on Assets	-1.61	1.90	-15.11	9.56	16.64
Ret on Equity%	-13.98	-10.76	-171.65	9.23	13.97
Price/Earnings	11.73	-14.29	-0.20	8.56	6.67
Divid Cover	4.87	-	-	1.15	2.11
Divid Yield	1.75	-	-	10.18	7.13
Earning Yield%	8.53	-7.00	-490.47	11.68	15.00
NAV % Mrk Pr	87.59	101.47	28.35	88.74	60.78
Effec Tax Rate	-3.48	-	-	-	-
Def Interval	-15.18	-9.05	-3.90	1.59	0.08
Sus Grth Rate	-15.98	-10.76	-171.65	1.35	7.03

SUBSIDIARY & ASSOCIATED COMPANIES

AUDIOCOR (PTY) LTD
LESOTHO DOORS AND JOINERY (PTY) LTD
TEMPEST INTERNATIONAL (PTY) LTD
TILECOR (PTY) LTD

INVESTMENTS

None

CG SMITH FOODS LTD

ABBREVIATION : CGS-FOOD

JSE SHORT CODE : CSF

SECTOR : Industrial-Food

SHAREHOLDERS

Who Owns Whom's Assessment of the Identity of the Ultimate Controlling Shareholder:
SA MUTUAL VIA BARLOWS

SHAREHOLDER	PERCENTAGE 1992	1991
C G SMITH LTD	81.4	81.4
CMB NOM P/L	2.8	—
STD BANK NOM TVL P/L	2.4	2.2
SA MUTUAL	2.2	2.2
COMMON FUND INV SOC LTD	1.1	1.1
SOUTHERN LIFE ASSOC LTD	1.0	1.1
SANLAM	—	2.5
TOTAL	90.9	90.4

DIRECTORS :
BODLEY DC ,CHAMBERS RKJ ,CLEWLOW WAM ,COOPER DE
DENNIS N ,LEWIS WA ,NOYCE MJ ,SEALEY AA
SMITH HA ,STEELE BP (Financial Director)
TAYLOR G ,WILLIAMS RA (Chairman),WOLPERT C
ZULMAN AN

REGISTRATION NUMBER : 70/10062/06

REGISTERED OFFICE
Barlow Park, Katherine Street
Sandton
2199
TEL: 011-801 9143

FAX 011-444 5579

TRANSFER SECRETARY
Rand Registrars Ltd
P O Box 82549, Southdale
2135
TEL 011-835 1016

COMPANY SECRETARY
DA Austin

NATURE OF BUSINESS
An investment holding company with subsidiaries engaged in sugar milling, refining and syrup manufacture, cane agriculture, sugar warehousing and distribution The company holds controlling interests in quoted Tiger Oats & Imperial Cold Storage

BANKERS :
Standard Bank of SA Ltd

AUDITORS :
Deloitte Pim Goldby

FAMILIAR BRAND NAMES
N/A

CONTRIBUTION BY ACTIVITY
Foods (% Turnover) (78 0%)
Sugar & related activities (11 0%)
Fishing (3 0%)
Pharmaceuticals (8 0%)

YEAR END : September

DIVIDEND : Ords 25c

Interim No 19	(Ldr)01/06/90	(Pay)12/07/90	Amt(c)34
Final No 20	(Ldr)30/11/90	(Pay)09/01/91	Amt(c)53
Interim No 21	(Ldr)07/06/91	(Pay)12/07/91	Amt(c)37
Final No 22	(Ldr)29/11/91	(Pay)13/01/92	Amt(c)62
Interim No 23	(Ldr)29/05/92	(Pay)13/07/92	Amt(c)39
Final No 24	(Ldr)27/11/92	(Pay)11/01/93	Amt(c)66

NUMBER OF EMPLOYEES : 53649

CAPITAL STRUCTURE

	AUTHORISED	ISSUED
Ords 25c	120000000	94491738

FINANCIAL STATISTICS (AT FINANCIAL YEAR END)

(Amts in R'000)	1991 Sep	1990 Sep	1989 Sep	1988 Sep	1987 Sep
Ord S/H Int	1469400	1286400	1129000	980900	875400
Long Trm Loans	1493600	1351600	1159900	1105400	888200
Iss Ord Share	94492	94492	94492	94336	94336
Total Liab	3976200	3632300	3100800	2778300	2132700
Current Liab	2482600	2280700	1940900	1672900	1244500
Total Assets	5445600	4918700	4229800	3759200	3008100
Current Assets	2983600	2684800	2338300	2159300	1664300
Debtors	1551800	1364500	1200700	998900	778500
Inventory	1303300	1187000	1029600	880400	579500
Turnover	11334400	9925800	8586100	6863500	5612600
Oper Profit	797100	671400	630500	534000	387600
Interest Paid	177700	143100	109500	67000	58600
Tax Paid	216200	195600	209100	165500	110400
Prf af Int&Tax	472600	404700	388300	301500	218600
Prf att Ord Sh	284300	249000	221900	181700	129900
Btm Line Earn	267900	244800	210100	149400	110500
Dividend Paid	93500	82200	73700	60400	48100
Mkt Prce(c) YE	4100	2650	2750	1650	1725
Depreciation	236600	213100	158600	126100	113600

PER SHARE STATISTICS (CENTS)

Net Asst Val	1555 05	1361 39	1194 81	1039 79	927 96
Net Earnings	300 80	263 60	235 10	192 60	124 40
Dividends	99 00	87 00	78 00	64 00	51 00
Cash Flow	545 23	500 57	395 84	320 45	248 79

RATIOS AND OTHER INFORMATION

Mrk Cap(R000)	3874172	2504038	2598530	1556544	1627296
Current Ratio	1 20	1 18	1 20	1 29	1 34
Quik/Acid Tst	0 68	0 66	0 67	0 76	0 87
A/C Rec T/ovr	7 30	7 27	7 15	6 87	7 21
Tot Ass T/ovr	2 08	2 02	2 03	1 83	1 87
Debt/Ass Rat	0 53	0 54	0 54	0 53	0 50
L T L Tot Ass	0 07	0 07	0 08	0 09	0 08
Debt to Eqity	1 95	2 05	2 01	2 04	1 71
Interest Cover	4 60	4 89	6 04	7 97	6 61
Oper Prof Mrg	7 03	6 76	7 34	7 78	6 91
Net Prof Marg%	2 51	2 51	2 58	2 65	2 31
Ret on Assets	16 49	15 46	16 98	14 50	13 31
Ret on Equity%	19 35	19 36	19 65	18 52	14 84
Price/Earnings	13 63	10 05	11 70	8 57	13 87
Divid Cover	3 04	3 03	3 01	3 01	2 44
Divid Yield	2 41	3 28	2 84	3 88	2 96
Earning Yield%	7 34	9 95	8 55	11 67	7 21
NAV % Mrk Pr	37 93	51 37	43 45	63 02	53 79
Effec Tax Rate	28 91	30 30	37 75	34 09	32 64
Def Interval	2 03	2 14	2 13	2 72	2 58
Sus Grth Rate	12 98	12 97	13 13	12 37	9 34

SUBSIDIARY & ASSOCIATED COMPANIES

BULL BRAND HOLDINGS (PTY) LTD (50%)
CG SMITH CHEMICAL HOLDINGS LTD
CG SMITH SUGAR AGENCIES (PTY) LTD
CG SMITH SUGAR LTD
CG SMITH SUGAR LTD DIVISION
CG SMITH WAREHOUSES (PTY) LTD
FEDICS (PTY) LTD (45,9%)
GLEDHOW SUGAR CO LTD
ICS HOLDINGS LTD
ILLOVO SUGAR (PTY) LTD
INKANYEZI LTD
JORGENSEN DISTRIBUTORS (SWAZILAND) LTD
LESOTHO MILLING COMPANY (PTY) LTD (50%)
MEREPARK PROPERTIES (PTY) LTD
MPUMALANGA LTD
NOODSBERG SUGAR CO LTD
OKK FOODS LTD (50%)
PESCANOVO SA (20,7%)
PETZ PRODUCTS (PTY) LTD (50%)
PEZ KWOMKHONO LTD
PINETOWN INDUSTRIAL LABORATORIES (PTY) L
PONGOLA SUGAR MILLING CO LTD
REYNOLDS BROTHERS LTD
ROELKOR VLEIS (PTY) LTD (50%)
S A SUGAR DISTRIBUTORS (PTY) LTD
SEA HARVEST CORPORATION (PTY) LTD (50%)
SMITHCHEM (PTY) LTD
SUGAR TRANSPORT SERVICES (PTY) LTD (49%)
THE BEAUMONT WATTLE CO LTD
THE FOOD YEAST CO (PTY) LTD
THE NATAL CANE BY PRODUCTS LTD
TIGER OATS LTD
UMTWALUME VALLEY ESTATES LTD
UMZIMKULU SUGAR CO LTD

INVESTMENTS

ALLIED LYONS PLC (278597 SH)

CG SMITH LTD

ABBREVIATION : CGSMITH

JSE SHORT CODE : CGS

SECTOR : Industrial-Industrial Holding

SHAREHOLDERS

Who Owns Whom's Assessment of the Identity of the Ultimate Controlling Shareholder:
SA MUTUAL VIA BARLOW RAND

SHAREHOLDER	PERCENTAGE 1992	1991
BARLOW RAND LTD	38.2	38.2
CORNER HOUSE INV CO LTD	21.6	21.6
CMB NOM P/L	4.7	---
INDUSTRIAL SELECTIONS LTD	4.2	4.2
METAL IND GROUP PENS FUND	2.7	2.7
ENGINEERING INDUSTRIES PENS FUND	2.7	2.7
NAT SELECTIONS LTD	2.6	2.6
LIBERTY LIFE ASSOC OF AFRICA LTD	2.2	2.2
STD BANK NOM TVL P/L	2.0	1.6
INDUSTRIAL FINANCE CORP OF SA LTD	1.7	1.7
ESCOM PENS & PROV FUND	1.0	1.0
SANLAM	---	1.6
SANKERN E/B	---	3.0
TOTAL	83.5	82.9

DIRECTORS :
CLEWLOW WAM ,CONNELLAN BP ,COOPER DE
CRUTCHLEY AL ,MCCARTHY BC ,SMITH HA
STEELE BP (Financial Director),TAYLOR G
VAN DER HORST JC DR,WARD JH
WILLIAMS RA (Chairman

REGISTRATION NUMBER : 02/01185/06

REGISTERED OFFICE
Barlow Park, Katherine Street
Sandton
2199
TEL: 011-801 9143
FAX: 011-444 5579

TRANSFER SECRETARY
Rand Registrars Ltd
P O Box 82549, Southdale
2135
TEL: 011-835 1016

COMPANY SECRETARY
DA Austin

NATURE OF BUSINESS
An investment holding company with controlling interests in quoted Nampak, Romatex & CG Smith. The Company through its subsidiaries, has substantial interest in the food,suger and related activities,fishing,packaging,paper,carpets,textile and pharmaceutical industries.

BANKERS :
Standard Bank of SA Ltd

AUDITORS :
Deloitte Pim Goldby

FAMILIAR BRAND NAMES
N/A

CONTRIBUTION BY ACTIVITY
CG Smith Foods Group (% Turnover) (70.5%)
Nampak (24.9%)
Romatex (4.6%)

YEAR END : September

DIVIDEND : Ords R1

Interim No 19	(Ldr)01/06/90	(Pay)12/07/90	Amt(c)105
Final No 20	(Ldr)30/11/90	(Pay)09/01/91	Amt(c)158
Interim No 21	(Ldr)07/06/91	(Pay)12/07/91	Amt(c)111
Final No 22	(Ldr)29/11/91	(Pay)13/01/92	Amt(c)175
Interim No 23	(Ldr)29/05/92	(Pay)13/07/92	Amt(c)117
Final No 24	(Ldr)27/11/92	(Pay)11/01/93	Amt(c)191

NUMBER OF EMPLOYEES : 86000

CAPITAL STRUCTURE

	AUTHORISED	ISSUED
Ords R1	51400000	47012403

FINANCIAL STATISTICS (AT FINANCIAL YEAR END)

(Amts in R'000)	1991 Sep	1990 Sep	1989 Sep	1988 Sep	1987 Sep
Ord S/H Int	1999700	1766100	1538300	1305800	1157600
Long Trm Loans	2667000	2401800	2088200	1894300	1649900
Iss Ord Share	47012	46944	46901	46858	46854
Total Liab	6236800	5611900	4948600	4364500	3464400
Current Liab	3569800	3210100	2860400	2470200	1814500
Total Assets	8236500	7378000	6486900	5670300	4622000
Current Assets	4546700	4076500	3672300	3293000	2609800
Debtors	2235300	1952400	1764800	1481500	1158300
Inventory	2124500	1955400	1745000	1493500	1066000
Turnover	16068900	14158000	12424000	10064200	8231200
Oper Profit	1278100	1148200	1111200	942000	696000
Interest Paid	254400	223300	178100	92000	80600
Tax Paid	381700	360900	354700	308200	218400
Prf af Int&Tax	726200	650200	666500	541800	397000
Prf att Ord Sh	384700	352400	349800	287100	205300
Btm Line Earn	360600	356000	349200	228500	190200
Dividend Paid	134500	123400	122000	99600	76400
Mkt Prce(c) YE	11000	6650	6675	3975	4850
Depreciation	391700	342800	267700	220100	198400

PER SHARE STATISTICS (CENTS)

Net Asst Val	4253.59	3762.14	3279.89	2786.72	2470.65
Net Earnings	818.60	751.00	746.10	612.70	390.40
Dividends	286.00	263.00	260.00	212.50	163.00
Cash Flow	1663.40	1512.02	1306.79	1063.00	833.65

RATIOS AND OTHER INFORMATION

Mrk Cap(R000)	5171320	3121776	3130642	1862606	2272419
Current Ratio	1.27	1.27	1.28	1.33	1.44
Quik/Acid Tst	0.68	0.66	0.67	0.73	0.85
A/C Rec T/ovr	7.19	7.25	7.04	6.79	7.11
Tot Ass T/ovr	1.95	1.92	1.92	1.77	1.78
Debt/Ass Rat	0.51	0.51	0.52	0.52	0.47
L T L Tot Ass	0.08	0.08	0.08	0.09	0.07
Debt to Eqity	2.11	2.15	2.20	2.27	1.86
Interest Cover	5.14	5.31	6.45	10.24	8.64
Oper Prof Mrg	7.95	8.11	8.94	9.36	8.46
Net Prof Marg%	2.39	2.49	2.82	2.85	2.49
Ret on Assets	16.91	16.97	18.67	16.82	15.35
Ret on Equity%	19.24	19.95	22.74	21.99	17.73

Price/Earnings	13.44	8.85	8.95	6.49	12.42
Divid Cover	2.86	2.86	2.87	2.88	2.40
Divid Yield	2.60	3.95	3.90	5.35	3.36
Earning Yield%	7.44	11.29	11.18	15.41	8.05
NAV % Mrk Pr	38.67	56.57	49.14	70.11	50.94
Effec Tax Rate	32.85	34.74	36.84	35.51	34.95
Def Interval	2.06	2.05	1.94	2.17	1.88
Sus Grth Rate	12.51	12.97	14.81	14.36	11.14

SUBSIDIARY & ASSOCIATED COMPANIES

CG SMITH FOODS LTD
NAMPAK LTD
ROMATEX LTD

INVESTMENTS

None

CG SMITH SUGAR LTD

ABBREVIATION : CG SUGAR

JSE SHORT CODE : CSS

SECTOR : Industrial-Sugar

SHAREHOLDERS

Who Owns Whom's Assessment of the Identity of the Ultimate Controlling Shareholder:
BARLOWS VIA CG SMITH

SHAREHOLDER	PERCENTAGE 1992	1991
C G SMITH FOODS LTD	70.0	---
CMB NOM P/L	7.5	---
CRYOLITE NOM LTD	7.2	---
EIGHTY ONE MAIN STREET NOM LTD	5.6	---
SA MUTUAL	2.9	---
SOUTHERN LIFE ASSOC LTD	2.0	---
TOTAL	95.3	---

DIRECTORS :
CHRISTIE AG (Commercial Director),CLEWLOW WAM
COOPER DE ,CROOKES DV (Operations Director)
HAMILTON RD ,HORLOCK WB (Personnel Director)
MACLEOD DG (Managing Director),NOYCE MJ
RAVNO AB ,TAYLOR G (Executive Chairman),WARD JH
WILLIAMS RA ,ZULMAN AN

REGISTRATION NUMBER : 02/00622/06

REGISTERED OFFICE
10th Floor, Eagle Building
359 West Street, Durban
4001
TEL: 031-305 1511
FAX: 031-304 4322

TRANSFER SECRETARY
Rand Registrars Ltd
P O Box 82549, Southdale
2135
TEL: 011-835 1016

COMPANY SECRETARY
G D Knox

NATURE OF BUSINESS
The company operates three business divisions - Sugar, Chemicals and Warehousing & Distribution. Sugar - Interest ranging from cane growing to milling,refining and packaging.Syrup is also manufactured.Chemicals - The production of furfural,furfuryl alcohol,diacetyl and solvent from bagasse,ethyl alcohol,diethyl ether,carbon dioxide,vinegar,food yeast and hydrogen peroxide. The Warehousing & Distribution division handles and stores the bagged sugar production.

BANKERS :
Standard Bank of SA Ltd
First National Bank of SA Ltd
Standard Merchant Bank Ltd

AUDITORS :
Deloitte Pim Goldby

FAMILIAR BRAND NAMES
N/A

CONTRIBUTION BY ACTIVITY
Sugar (% of Operating Profit) (72.0%)
Chemicals (16.0%)
Warehousing & Distribution (12.0%)

YEAR END : September

DIVIDEND : Ords 4c

Interim No 1	(Ldr)15/05/92	(Pay)13/07/92	Amt(c)9
Final No 2	(Ldr)27/11/92	(Pay)11/01/93	Amt(c)14

NUMBER OF EMPLOYEES : 7000

CAPITAL STRUCTURE

	AUTHORISED	ISSUED
Ords 4c	900000000	157692308

FINANCIAL STATISTICS (AT FINANCIAL YEAR END)

(Amts in R'000)	1991 Sep
Ord S/H Int	417688
Long Trm Loans	190863
Iss Ord Share	6000
Total Liab	587957
Current Liab	397094
Total Assets	1005645
Current Assets	474371
Debtors	302573
Inventory	170881
Turnover	991384
Oper Profit	135059
Interest Paid	30809
Tax Paid	29794
Prf af Int&Tax	81936
Prf att Ord Sh	80383
Btm Line Earn	78798
Dividend Paid	31680
Depreciation	40756

PER SHARE STATISTICS (CENTS)

Net Asst Val	6961.47
Net Earnings	1340.00
Dividends	528.00
Cash Flow	2331.37

RATIOS AND OTHER INFORMATION

Current Ratio	1.19
Quik/Acid Tst	0.76
A/C Rec T/ovr	3.28
Tot Ass T/ovr	0.99
Debt/Ass Rat	0.50
L T L Tot Ass	0.11
Debt to Eqity	1.21
Interest Cover	4.38
Oper Prof Mrg	13.62
Net Prof Marg%	8.11
Ret on Assets	14.17
Ret on Equity%	19.24
Divid Cover	2.54
Effec Tax Rate	9.89
Def Interval	1.52
Sus Grth Rate	11.66

SUBSIDIARY & ASSOCIATED COMPANIES

CG SMITH CHEMICAL HOLDINGS LTD
CG SMITH SUGAR AGENCIES (PTY) LTD
CGS WAREHOUSE (PTY) LTD
GLEDHOW SUGAR CO. LTD
ILLOVO SUGAR (PTY) LTD
INKANYEZI LTD
JORGENSEN DISTRIBUTORS (SWAZILAND) LTD
MEREPARK PROPERTIES (PTY) LTD
MPUMALANGA LTD
NOODSBERG SUGAR CO. LTD
S A SUGAR DISTRIBUTORS (PTY) LTD

INVESTMENTS

None

CHARTER CONSOLIDATED PLC

ABBREVIATION : CHARTER

JSE SHORT CODE : CHC

SECTOR : Mining Financial-Mining Houses

SHAREHOLDERS

Who Owns Whom's Assessment of the Identity of the Ultimate Controlling Shareholder: ANGLO AMERICAN VIA MINORCO

SHAREHOLDER	PERCENTAGE 1992	1991
LONDON CONTROL ACCOUNT	85.5	89.1
CMB NOM P/L	5.0	---
LIBERTY LIFE ASSOC OF AFRICA LTD	1.5	1.6
GUARDIAN NOM P/L	1.1	1.1
SANLAM	---	1.5
SANKERN E/B	---	3.7
TOTAL	93.1	97.1

DIRECTORS :
BURNELL PCD ,COOK DE ,EDWARDES M SIR (Chairman)
HERBERT JW (Chief Executive),KESWICK JCL
LEA AW ,PARKER CH (Commercial Director)
RELLY GWH ,ROBSON NE

REGISTRATION NUMBER : 65/00007/10

REGISTERED OFFICE
7 Hobart Place, London SW1W 0HH
London

TEL: 094471-8387000
FAX: 094471-2595112

TRANSFER SECRETARY
Consolidated Share Registrars Ltd
P O Box 61051, Marshalltown
2107
TEL: 011-492 1620

COMPANY SECRETARY
P M Thwaite

NATURE OF BUSINESS
An industrial holding company with significant international interests in mining equipment, building products & services, rail track equipment & quarrying. The group is also active in the marketing, refining & fabrication of precious metals & the manufacture of catalytic systems.

BANKERS :
N/A

AUDITORS :
Coopers & Lybrand

FAMILIAR BRAND NAMES
N/A

CONTRIBUTION BY ACTIVITY
N/A

YEAR END : March

DIVIDEND : Ords 2p
Final No 55 (Ldr)24/07/92 (Pay)18/08/92 Amt(c)21.5

NUMBER OF EMPLOYEES : 9500

CAPITAL STRUCTURE

	AUTHORISED	ISSUED
Ords 2p	135000000	105832024

FINANCIAL STATISTICS (AT FINANCIAL YEAR END)

(Amts in PS)	1992 Mar	1991 Mar	1990 Mar	1989 Mar	1988 Mar
Ord S/H Int	394100	379700	374500	388400	366176
Long Trm Loans	146700	141100	124400	116200	115300
Iss Ord Share	105832	105754	105690	105496	105430
Total Liab	309700	297000	292800	251400	261873
Current Liab	163000	155900	168400	135200	146573
Total Assets	703800	676700	667300	639800	628049
Current Assets	421400	405600	395400	385000	396988
Debtors	131300	121100	119100	97500	104834
Inventory	76100	72000	84000	79000	83495
Turnover	1128800	1114600	1033100	1009600	948269
Oper Profit	29700	28000	26700	53000	55828
Interest Paid	8700	11500	11200	8200	-
Tax Paid	24100	24800	23700	17400	14812
Prf af Int&Tax	23800	26300	32700	50300	41016
Prf att Ord Sh	45000	47200	46100	78700	37718
Btm Line Earn	59800	48700	51800	79600	50304
Dividend Paid	22800	22200	20600	18200	15287
Mkt Prce(c) YE	2950	2900	2850	3425	1650
Depreciation	800	800	17200	15800	17523

PER SHARE STATISTICS (CENTS)

Net Asst Val	372 38	359 04	354 34	368 17	347 32
Net Earnings	42 50	44 60	43 60	43 10	35 80
Dividends	21 50	21 00	19 50	17 25	14 50
Cash Flow	22 21	20 80	41 25	55 36	48 73

RATIOS AND OTHER INFORMATION

Mrk Cap(R000)	3122044	3066866	3012165	3613238	1739595
Current Ratio	2 59	2 60	2 35	2 85	2 71
Quik/Acid Tst	2 12	2 14	1 85	2 26	2 14
A/C Rec T/ovr	8 60	9 20	8 67	10 35	9 05
Tot Ass T/ovr	1 60	1 65	1 55	1 58	1 51
Debt/Ass Rat	0 40	0 39	0 38	0 35	0 38
L T L Tot Ass	0 16	0 16	0 13	0 14	0 15
Debt to Eqity	0 71	0 70	0 68	0 58	0 65
Interest Cover	3 83	2 77	3 54	6 46	-
Oper Prof Mrg	2 63	2 51	2 58	5 25	5 89
Net Prof Marg%	3 99	4 23	4 46	7 80	3 98
Ret on Assets	11 72	13 15	13 04	11 86	8 89
Ret on Equity%	11 42	12 43	12 31	20 26	10 30
Price/Earnings	69 41	65 02	65 37	79 47	46 09
Divid Cover	1 98	2 12	2 24	2 50	2 47
Divid Yield	0 73	0 72	0 68	0 50	0 88
Earning Yield%	1 44	1 54	1 53	1 26	2 17
NAV % Mrk Pr	12 62	12 38	12 43	10 75	21 05
Effec Tax Rate	31 60	36 02	41 61	26 59	25 81
Def Interval	3 83	3 39	2 18	1 17	1 43
Sus Grth Rate	5 63	6 58	6 81	15 58	6 13

SUBSIDIARY & ASSOCIATED COMPANIES

ANDERSON GROUP LTD
ANGLO AMERICAN CORP ZIMBABWE LTD (33 5%)
CAPE PLC
CECIL HOLDINGS LTD
CENTRAL MINING FINANCE LTD
CHARTER CONSOLIDATED FINANCE LTD
CHARTER CONSOLIDATED FINANCIAL SERVICES
CHARTER CONSOLIDATED INVESTMENTS LTD
CHARTER CONSOLIDATED SERVICES LTD (ENGLA
COVENANT INDUSTRIES LTD (ENGLAND) (50%)
HARGREAVES QUARRIES LIMITED (ENGLAND)
JOHNSON MATTHEY (38 5%)
JOHNSON MATTHEY PLC (38 5%)
PANDROL INTERNATIONAL LTD
SHAND MINING INC

INVESTMENTS

BOTSWANA RST LTD (4,5%)

CHEMICAL SERVICES LTD

ABBREVIATION : CHEMSERVE

JSE SHORT CODE : CHE

SECTOR : Industrial-Chemicals & Oils

SHAREHOLDERS

Who Owns Whom's Assessment of the Identity of the Ultimate Controlling Shareholder:
ANGLO AMERICAN VIA AECI

SHAREHOLDER	PERCENTAGE 1992	1991
AECI LTD	64 6	64 6
LIBERTY LIFE ASSOC OF AFRICA LTD	3 1	2 8
EIGHTY ONE MAIN STREET NOM LTD	3 0	3 0
STD BANK NOM TVL P/L	2 8	2 1
FIRST NAT NOM P/L	2 5	2 8
SHARESTOCK NOM P/L	2 5	1 9
SA MUTUAL	1 4	3 2
AFRICAN OXYGEN LTD PENS FUND	1 1	---
TOTAL	81 0	80 4

DIRECTORS :
ENGELBRECHT S ,FRANCOIS PT (Managing Director)
PETERS JD ,PLANTING DS ,SANDER MA (Chairman)
STREET TA ,VAN VUGHT LC ,WOOLLEY TK

REGISTRATION NUMBER : 67/03338/06

REGISTERED OFFICE
Chemserve House, 16 Riepen Avenue
Riepen Park, Sandton
2199
TEL 011-881 1000
FAX 011-783 2125

TRANSFER SECRETARY
Central Registrars Ltd
P O Box 4844, Johannesburg
2000
TEL 011-331 0051

COMPANY SECRETARY
K J MacCallum

NATURE OF BUSINESS
An investment holding company with subsidiaries engaged in the manufacture, supply and marketing of industrial, commercial and specialty chemicals, and chemical raw materials

BANKERS :
First National Bank of SA Ltd

AUDITORS :
Coopers Theron Du Toit

FAMILIAR BRAND NAMES
N/A

CONTRIBUTION BY ACTIVITY
Formulated Chemicals (% Turnover) (29 0%)
Process Chemicals (41 0%)
Agency/Distribution (30 0%)

YEAR END : December

DIVIDEND : Ords R1

Final No 46	(Ldr)02/03/90	(Pay)02/04/90	Amt(c)62
Interim No 47	(Ldr)03/08/90	(Pay)27/08/90	Amt(c)45 5
Final No 48	(Ldr)22/02/91	(Pay)28/03/91	Amt(c)74 5
Interim No 49	(Ldr)02/08/91	(Pay)26/08/91	Amt(c)53
Final No 50	(Ldr)06/03/92	(Pay)30/03/92	Amt(c)87

NUMBER OF EMPLOYEES : 1270

CAPITAL STRUCTURE

	AUTHORISED	ISSUED
Ords R1	12000000	6221090
10,9% Unsec Debs R1	1000500	1000500

FINANCIAL STATISTICS (AT FINANCIAL YEAR END)

(Amts in R'000)	1991 Dec	1990 Dec	1989 Dec	1988 Dec	1987 Dec
Ord S/H Int	98088	84952	82003	67398	56932
Long Trm Loans	19763	17285	13231	11826	10590
Iss Ord Share	6221	6221	6221	6221	6221
Total Liab	139119	141534	96089	90365	67153
Current Liab	119356	124249	82858	78539	56563
Total Assets	237207	226486	178092	157763	124085
Current Assets	173814	161871	120839	108764	78397
Debtors	81684	63259	47297	45514	31406
Inventory	88372	93063	65606	58701	37915
Turnover	477925	445768	335672	283428	202403
Oper Profit	59794	53871	36850	34333	26126
Interest Paid	10382	10140	6905	3832	2225
Tax Paid	22468	22163	13514	14472	12193
Prf af Int&Tax	27463	23565	18382	18815	11708
Prf att Ord Sh	26726	22827	18969	18703	14281
Btm Line Earn	26726	22827	18969	20720	14169
Dividend Paid	8710	7465	6221	6221	4977
Mkt Prce(c) YE	4000	1975	1825	2025	1450
Depreciation	7633	6356	3758	3130	2001

PER SHARE STATISTICS (CENTS)

Net Asst Val	1576.72	1365.57	1318.16	1083.39	915.16
Net Earnings	429.60	366.90	305.00	300.60	229.60
Dividends	140.00	120.00	100.00	100.00	80.00
Cash Flow	555.31	492.19	328.32	348.79	225.62

RATIOS AND OTHER INFORMATION

Mrk Cap(R000)	248840	122865	113533	125975	90205
Current Ratio	1.46	1.30	1.46	1.38	1.39
Quik/Acid Tst	0.72	0.55	0.67	0.64	0.72
A/C Rec T/ovr	5.85	7.05	7.10	6.23	6.44
Tot Ass T/ovr	2.01	1.97	1.88	1.80	1.63
Debt/Ass Rat	0.57	0.61	0.53	0.57	0.53
L T L Tot Ass	0.07	0.06	0.06	0.07	0.08
Debt to Eqity	1.38	1.62	1.14	1.32	1.16
Interest Cover	5.78	5.36	5.50	9.54	11.74
Oper Prof Mrg	12.51	12.08	10.98	12.11	12.91
Net Prof Marg%	5.59	5.12	5.65	6.60	7.06
Ret on Assets	25.28	24.49	22.49	23.77	23.16
Ret on Equity%	27.25	26.87	23.13	27.75	25.08
Price/Earnings	9.31	5.38	5.98	6.74	6.32
Divid Cover	3.07	3.06	3.05	3.01	2.87
Divid Yield	3.50	6.08	5.48	4.94	5.52
Earning Yield%	10.74	18.58	16.71	14.84	15.83
NAV % Mrk Pr	39.42	69.14	72.23	53.50	63.11
Effec Tax Rate	45.12	46.64	48.22	45.58	49.39
Def Interval	1.19	1.66	1.68	0.94	0.31
Sus Grth Rate	18.37	18.08	15.55	18.52	16.34

SUBSIDIARY & ASSOCIATED COMPANIES

ACSAP INVESTMENTS (PTY) LTD
AKULU-MARCHON (PTY) LTD
APPLIED TECHNICAL PRODUCTS (PTY) LTD (50%)
ATP HOLDINGS LTD
CERNOL CHEMICALS (NAMIBIA) (PTY) LTD
CHEMAX HOLDINGS (PTY) LTD
CHEMHOLD INVESTMENTS (PTY) LTD
CHEMOLEO (PTY) LTD (50%)
CHEMOLEO HOLDINGS (PTY) LTD
CHEMREX (PTY) LTD
CHEMSERVE COLLOIDS (PTY) LTD
CHEMSERVE MANUFACTURING (PTY) LTD
CHEMSERVE METAL SCIENCES (PTY) LTD (50%)
CHEMSERVE PERLITE (PTY) LTD
CHEMSERVE POLYMER SCIENCES (PTY) LTD
CHEMSERVE STEINHALL (PTY) LTD
CHEMSERVE SYSTEMS (PTY) LTD
CHEMSERVE TECHNICAL PRODUCTS (PTY) LTD
CHEMSERVE TRIO (PTY) LTD
CREST CHEMICALS (PTY) LTD (50%)
CREST CHEMICALS LTD
DUSSEK BROTHERS (SA) (PTY) LTD (49%)
INDUSTRIAL OLEOCHEMICAL PRODUCTS (PTY) L
IOP INVESTMENTS (PTY) LTD
J&N CHEMICALS (PTY) LTD
PERMAQUIM SA (30%)
PINECHEM (PTY) LTD (50%)
SA PAPER CHEMICALS (PTY) LTD
SILPRO (PTY) LTD
SUACHEM (PTY) LTD
TROHALL (PTY) LTD (50%)
UPAG HOLDING AG (49%)

INVESTMENTS

None

CHOICE HOLDINGS LTD

ABBREVIATION : CHOICE

JSE SHORT CODE : COI

SECTOR : Development Capital Market

SHAREHOLDERS

Who Owns Whom's Assessment of the Identity of the Ultimate Controlling Shareholder:
I LIMBEROPOULOS

SHAREHOLDER	PERCENTAGE 1992	1991
LIMBEROPOULOS I	49.3	49.3
DURBAN DEEP	14.9	14.9
STD BANK NOM TVL P/L	12.7	12.7
BARRADAS FAMILY TRUST	5.2	5.2
LIMBEROPOULOS P	5.0	5.0
LINBEROPLOS J	2.7	2.7
MARLED NOM P/L	2.2	2.2
WYNBERG HYPERMEAT CC	1.6	1.4
ANAGNOSTAPOULOS J	1.2	1.2
SIERRA HOLDINGS LTD	1.2	1.2
TOTAL	95.8	95.7

DIRECTORS :
LIMBEROPOULOS I (Chairman),PACHIS D
SCALCO CR MS,WIGGILL JM

REGISTRATION NUMBER : 87/04241/06

REGISTERED OFFICE
Suite 4604, 46th Floor, Carlton Centre
Johannesburg
2001
TEL: 011-331 7871
FAX: 011-331 7805

TRANSFER SECRETARY
Central Registrars Ltd
P O Box 4844, Johannesburg
2000
TEL 011-331 0051

COMPANY SECRETARY
C R Scalco

NATURE OF BUSINESS
An investment holding company which, through its subsidiaries, is engaged in the meat processing, distribution and retailing industries

BANKERS :
Volkskas Ltd

AUDITORS :
Levitt Kirson

FAMILIAR BRAND NAMES
N/A

CONTRIBUTION BY ACTIVITY
N/A

YEAR END : February

DIVIDEND :15/05/91

NUMBER OF EMPLOYEES : 63

CAPITAL STRUCTURE

	AUTHORISED	ISSUED
Ords 15c	20000000	10087913

FINANCIAL STATISTICS (AT FINANCIAL YEAR END)

(Amts in R'000)	1992 Feb	1991 Feb	1990 Feb
Ord S/H Int	139	475	2282
Long Trm Loans	3926	3275	1616
Iss Ord Share	10088	10088	10088
Total Liab	9989	8923	6757
Current Liab	6063	5648	5141
Total Assets	8411	7435	6831
Intang Assets	1717	1963	2208
Current Assets	4996	4353	3747
Debtors	3472	3127	3062
Inventory	1522	869	684
Oper Profit	864	-756	-1298
Interest Paid	774	560	253
Tax Paid	114	-	-
Prf af Int&Tax	-24	-1316	-1551
Prf att Ord Sh	-73	-1513	-1551
Btm Line Earn	-291	-1780	-1521
Mkt Prce(c) YE	30	15	25
Depreciation	728	628	569

PER SHARE STATISTICS (CENTS)

Net Asst Val	-15 64	-14 75	0 73
Net Earnings	-0 72	-15 00	-15 37
Cash Flow	7 55	-8 77	-9 73

RATIOS AND OTHER INFORMATION

Mrk Cap(R000)	3026	1513	2522
Current Ratio	0 82	0 77	0 73
Quik/Acid Tst	0 57	0 62	0 60
Debt/Ass Rat	1 11	1 13	0 99
L T L Tot Ass	0 39	0 37	0 24
Debt to Eqity	67 09	17 70	2 96
Interest Cover	1 12	-1 35	-5 13
Ret on Assets	10 27	-10 17	-19 00
Ret on Equity%	-51 41	-299 01	-63 85
Price/Earnings	-41 67	-1 00	-1 63
Earning Yield%	-2 40	-100 00	-61 48
NAV % Mrk Pr	-52 14	-98 33	2 93
Def Interval	3 52	-2 99	-2 26
Sus Grth Rate	-52 52	-318 53	-67 97

SUBSIDIARY & ASSOCIATED COMPANIES

CATERCHOICE (PTY) LTD
MOGALE MMABATHO BUTCHERIES (PTY) LTD (50%)

INVESTMENTS

None

CHUBB HOLDINGS LTD

ABBREVIATION : CHUBB

JSE SHORT CODE : CHU

SECTOR : Industrial-Engineering

SHAREHOLDERS

Who Owns Whom's Assessment of the Identity of the Ultimate Controlling Shareholder:
RACAL ELECTRONICS PLC (UK)

SHAREHOLDER	PERCENTAGE 1992	1991
CHUBB INTERNATIONAL LTD	67 8	67 8
SAGE LIFE LTD	7 0	7 1
EIGHTY ONE MAIN STREET NOM LTD	4 0	7 0
SA MUTUAL	2 7	2 5
CHUBB EXECUTIVE EMPLOYEE TRUST	2 4	2 5
ABSA NOM P/L	1 9	---
ELLERINE BROS P/L	1 8	---
WORKMENS COMPENS COMMISSIONER IN TRUST	1 8	---
STD BANK NOM TVL P/L	-	3 4
TOTAL	89 4	90 2

DIRECTORS :
ACKERMAN DE (Chairman & Chief Exec),BILES JA
DICKERSON RI
FRIEDERICKSEN GR (Financial Director)
LANGLEY DF ,SHAW RT ,VAN DER WALT PJJ

REGISTRATION NUMBER : 05/30757/06

REGISTERED OFFICE
26 Wellington Road, Parktown
Johannesburg
2000
TEL 011-643 8351
FAX 011-643 1730

TRANSFER SECRETARY
Mercantile Registrars Ltd
P O Box 1053, Johannesburg
2000
TEL 011-333 8181

COMPANY SECRETARY
A J Williamson

O

NATURE OF BUSINESS
The manufacture, distribution & installation & service of safes, strongroom doors & demountable strongrooms, fire-resistant equipment & custom-engineered structures; Manufacture of locks & associated door furniture & builders hardware; Manufacture, installation & service of electronic alarms & protection systems; Manufacture, distribution, installation & service of portable & fixed fire-fighting appliances, apparatus, chemicals & powders.

BANKERS :
First National Bank of SA Ltd
Nedperm Bank Ltd, Standard Bank of SA Ltd
Trust Bank of Africa Ltd, Volkskas Ltd

AUDITORS :
Coopers Theron Du Toit

FAMILIAR BRAND NAMES
CHUBB,UNION,WEISER

CONTRIBUTION BY ACTIVITY
Physical Security (% turnover) (36.7%)
Physical Security (% trading profit) (10.5%)
Electronics Security (% turnover) (41.3%)
Fire Security (% turnover) (22.0%)
Electronics Security (% trading profit) (71.8%)
Fire Security (% trading profit) (17.7%)

YEAR END : March

DIVIDEND : Ords 50c

Interim No 32	(Ldr)15/12/89	(Pay)26/01/90	Amt(c)11
Final No 33	(Ldr)20/07/90	(Pay)14/08/90	Amt(c)14
Interim No 34	(Ldr)28/12/90	(Pay)25/01/91	Amt(c)11
Final No 35	(Ldr)19/07/91	(Pay)14/08/91	Amt(c)17
Interim No 36	(Ldr)27/12/91	(Pay)24/01/92	Amt(c)9
Final No 37	(Ldr)17/07/92	(Pay)12/08/92	Amt(c)16
Interim No 38	(Ldr)24/12/92	(Pay)22/01/93	Amt(c)14

NUMBER OF EMPLOYEES : 1811

CAPITAL STRUCTURE

	AUTHORISED	ISSUED
Ords 50c	6000000	5528125

FINANCIAL STATISTICS (AT FINANCIAL YEAR END)

(Amts in R'000)	1992 Mar	1991 Mar	1990 Mar	1989 Mar	1988 Mar
Ord S/H Int	42795	38108	32669	26440	20946
Long Trm Loans	4442	7357	9384	4296	2311
Iss Ord Share	5528	5528	5528	5428	5428
Total Liab	46706	50857	57589	41942	35843
Current Liab	42264	43500	48205	37646	33532
Total Assets	89501	88965	90258	68382	56789
Current Assets	59899	58401	56711	48531	41197
Debtors	29296	29957	29099	20792	18228
Inventory	24142	25245	23544	21874	15776
Turnover	167187	172827	143579	121559	98555
Oper Profit	13885	16929	13667	15451	10815
Interest Paid	5187	5734	4450	1446	938
Tax Paid	2837	4033	4466	6405	4749
Prf af Int&Tax	6906	7625	5410	7896	5288
Prf att Ord Sh	6906	7625	5410	7896	5288
Btm Line Earn	6906	7625	5410	7896	5288
Dividend Paid	1382	1548	1382	2280	2063
Mkt Prce(c) YE	470	750	825	1000	600
Depreciation	5700	5301	3680	3061	2078

PER SHARE STATISTICS (CENTS)

Net Asst Val	774.15	689.36	590.97	487.10	385.89
Net Earnings	124.90	137.90	98.60	145.50	97.20
Dividends	25.00	28.00	25.00	42.00	38.00
Cash Flow	212.10	242.26	167.49	200.35	140.05

RATIOS AND OTHER INFORMATION

Mrk Cap(R000)	25982	41460	45606	54280	32568
Current Ratio	1.42	1.34	1.18	1.29	1.23
Quik/Acid Tst	0.85	0.76	0.69	0.71	0.76
A/C Rec T/ovr	5.71	5.77	4.93	5.85	5.41
Tot Ass T/ovr	1.87	1.94	1.59	1.78	1.74
Debt/Ass Rat	0.52	0.56	0.63	0.60	0.62
L T L Tot Ass	0.05	0.07	0.09	0.05	0.03
Debt to Eqity	1.08	1.30	1.74	1.55	1.68
Interest Cover	2.72	2.99	3.18	10.78	11.70
Oper Prof Mrg	8.31	9.80	9.52	12.71	10.97
Net Prof Marg%	4.13	4.41	3.77	6.50	5.37
Ret on Assets	16.68	19.55	15.87	23.03	19.33
Ret on Equity%	16.14	20.01	16.56	29.86	25.25
Price/Earnings	3.76	5.44	8.37	6.87	6.17
Divid Cover	5.00	4.93	3.94	3.46	2.56
Divid Yield	5.32	3.73	3.03	4.20	6.33
Earning Yield%	26.57	18.39	11.95	14.55	16.20
NAV % Mrk Pr	164.71	91.92	71.63	48.71	64.31
Effec Tax Rate	40.48	30.96	48.88	48.95	45.86
Def Interval	1.65	1.62	2.55	1.09	1.21
Sus Grth Rate	12.91	15.95	12.33	21.24	15.40

SUBSIDIARY & ASSOCIATED COMPANIES

ALERS HANKEY FIRE PROTECTION (PTY) LTD
ANDREWS ALARMS (PTY) LTD
AUTOMATIC BURGLAR ALARMS (PTY) LTD
AUTOSONIC ALARMS (PTY) LTD
CHATWOOD-MILNER (PTY) LTD
CHUBB ALARMS (PTY) LTD
CHUBB ELECTRONICS (PTY) LTD
CHUBB FIRE SECURITY (PTY) LTD
CHUBB GROUP SERVICES (PTY) LTD
CHUBB LOCK & SAFE CO. (PTY) LTD
CHUBB SECURITY (PTY) LTD
CHUBB SECURITY INSTALLATIONS (PTY) LTD
CHUBB SECURITY PROJECTS (PTY) LTD
CHUBB SYSTEMS (PTY) LTD
FLASH ALARMS (PTY) LTD
JOSIAH PARKES & SONS (S.A.) LTD
JP INDUSTRIES (PTY) LTD
MINIMAX (S.A.) LTD
PYRENE CO (PTY) LTD
RENNIES ELECTRONIC SECURITY (CAPE) (PTY)
RENNIES ELECTRONIC SECURITY (NATAL) (PTY
RENNIES ELECTRONIC SECURITY (PTY) LTD
RES SECURITY SYSTEMS (PTY) LTD
TRATHFIX PROPERTIES (PTY) LTD

INVESTMENTS

None

CIRCLE CEMENT LTD

ABBREVIATION : CIRCLE

SECTOR : Zimbabwe Stock Exchange

SHAREHOLDERS

Who Owns Whom's Assessment of the Identity of the Ultimate Controlling Shareholder: ASSOCIATED INTERNATIONAL CEMENT LTD

SHAREHOLDER	PERCENTAGE 1992	1991
ASSOCIATED INTERNATIONAL CEMENT LTD	76.5	---
K E THOMSON PVT LTD	3.2	---
TONLY INV PVT LTD	1.5	---
FIRST NOM PVT LTD	1.4	---
TOTAL	82.5	---

DIRECTORS :
BEEVOR HG ,COULTER I ,FIELD MH
GEORGE GI (Managing Director),GEORGE KW
MORLEY JW (Chairman),OVERMENT PR
TAWENGWA SC (Deputy Chairman),WAKATAMA JB

REGISTERED OFFICE
Manresa Works, Arcturus Road
Harare, Zimbabwe

TEL: 48151
FAX: 48553

TRANSFER SECRETARY
N/A

COMPANY SECRETARY
J Hopgood

NATURE OF BUSINESS
CIRCLE CEMENT is incorporated in Zimbabwe and,together with its subsidiary,CIRCLE TRUCKING, is engaged in the manufacture and distribution of cement and allied products.

BANKERS :
First Merchant Bank of Zimbabwe Ltd
Standard Chartered Bank Zimbabwe Ltd

AUDITORS :
Coopers & Lybrand

FAMILIAR BRAND NAMES
N/A

CONTRIBUTION BY ACTIVITY
N/A

YEAR END : November

CAPITAL STRUCTURE

	AUTHORISED	ISSUED
Ords Z$1,50	5000000	5000000

FINANCIAL STATISTICS (AT FINANCIAL YEAR END)

(Amts in Z$)	1991 Nov	1990 Nov
Ord S/H Int	45687	37527
Long Trm Loans	6932	4906
Iss Ord Share	5000	5000
Total Liab	39083	26703
Current Liab	32151	21797
Total Assets	84770	64230
Current Assets	37467	21766
Debtors	10025	4778
Inventory	26986	16532
Turnover	79727	48493
Oper Profit	10179	-927
Interest Paid	1983	1023
Tax Paid	36	-
Prf af Int&Tax	8160	-1950
Prf att Ord Sh	8160	-1950
Btm Line Earn	8160	-1950
Depreciation	2413	1780

PER SHARE STATISTICS (CENTS)

Net Asst Val	913.74	750.54
Net Earnings	163.20	-39.00
Cash Flow	211.46	-3.40

RATIOS AND OTHER INFORMATION

Current Ratio	1.17	1.00
Quik/Acid Tst	0.33	0.24
A/C Rec T/ovr	7.95	10.15
Tot Ass T/ovr	0.94	0.75
Debt/Ass Rat	0.46	0.42
L T L Tot Ass	0.08	0.08
Debt to Eqity	0.86	0.71
Interest Cover	5.13	-0.91
Oper Prof Mrg	12.77	-1.91
Net Prof Marg%	10.23	-4.02
Ret on Assets	12.01	-1.44
Ret on Equity%	17.86	-5.20
Effec Tax Rate	0.44	-
Def Interval	1.57	-67.41
Sus Grth Rate	17.86	-5.20

SUBSIDIARY & ASSOCIATED COMPANIES

BINDURA ESTATES (PVT) LIMITED
CIRCLE TRUCKING LIMITED

INVESTMENTS

BEIRA CORRIDOR GROUP LTD (200 DEFS)
MEDICAL INVESTMENTS LIMITED (20000 SH)

CITY INVESTMENT HOLDINGS LTD

ABBREVIATION : CITYHLD

JSE SHORT CODE : CTY

SECTOR : Development Capital Market

SHAREHOLDERS

Who Owns Whom's Assessment of the Identity of the Ultimate Controlling Shareholder: DIRECTORS CONTROL 66,8%

SHAREHOLDER	PERCENTAGE 1992	1991
DIENSVENNOTE P/L	50.3	50.3
BARNARD P A	16.0	16.0
DIENSVENNOTE CC	13.8	13.8

JAN SILVIS NOM P/L	7 0	6 9
ELOFF F	3 6	3 6
SLABBER J	2 5	2 5
DU PREEZ K	1 3	1 3
TOTAL	94 4	94 3

DIRECTORS :
BARNARD FJ ,BREYTENBACH FS
ELOFF FC PROF (Managing Director),SLABBER JP

REGISTRATION NUMBER : 84/08265/06

REGISTERED OFFICE
9 Colenso Street, Powerville
Vereeniging
1930
TEL 016-211 443
FAX 016-223 526

TRANSFER SECRETARY
Central Registrars Ltd
P O Box 4844, Johannesburg
2000
TEL 011-331 0051

COMPANY SECRETARY
City Corporate Management Services (Pty) Ltd

NATURE OF BUSINESS
An investment holding company with subsidiaries engaged in the following activities Manufacture of copper,electroplated,stainless steel and resistence wire & the manufacture of copper,brass & aluminium extruded profiles,Manufacturers of specialised electrical and electronic cables Financial and management services

BANKERS :
Standard Bank of SA Ltd

AUDITORS :
Du Plessis Smith & Co

FAMILIAR BRAND NAMES
N/A

CONTRIBUTION BY ACTIVITY
N/A

YEAR END : September

DIVIDEND :Ords 1c

Final No 2	(Ldr)12/01/90	(Pay)26/01/90	Amt(c)0 5
Final No 3	(Ldr)13/02/92	(Pay)02/03/92	Amt(c)5

NUMBER OF EMPLOYEES : 110

CAPITAL STRUCTURE

	AUTHORISED	ISSUED
Ords 1c	16000000	8000000

FINANCIAL STATISTICS (AT FINANCIAL YEAR END)

(Amts in R 000)	1991 Sep	1990 Sep	1989 Aug	1988	1987
Ord S/H Int	3505	1837	2522	2519	287
Long Trm Loans	-	5674	4027	5013	2213
Iss Ord Share	8000	8000	8000	8000	400
Total Liab	623	8894	6944	7492	3212
Current Liab	623	3220	2917	2479	999
Total Assets	4128	10731	9466	9140	3741
Current Assets	320	3872	2419	1608	1241
Debtors	257	2335	1335	-	-
Inventory	-	1067	1043	1608	1241
Turnover	-	17734	12651	8108	5734
Oper Profit	769	134	904	1049	444
Interest Paid	12	994	559	191	161
Tax Paid	-249	38	302	170	-
Prf af Int&Tax	1006	-898	43	540	351
Prf att Ord Sh	1006	-898	43	540	351
Btm Line Earn	1006	-898	43	540	351
Dividend Paid	400	-	40	240	-
Mkt Prce(c) YE	60	50	55	65	
Depreciation	5	608	566	-	-

PER SHARE STATISTICS (CENTS)

Net Asst Val	43 81	22 96	31 53	31 49	71 75
Net Earnings	12 57	-11 22	54 00	-	-
Dividends	5 00	-	0 50	-	-
Cash Flow	9 53	-4 37	9 99	6 75	87 75

RATIOS AND OTHER INFORMATION

Mrk Cap(R000)	4800	4000	4400	5200	-
Current Ratio	0 51	1 20	0 83	0 65	1 24
Quik/Acid Tst	0 51	0 87	0 47	-	-
A/C Rec T/ovr	-	7 01	9 48	-	-
Tot Ass T/ovr	-	1 53	1 34	0 89	1 53
Debt/Ass Rat	0 15	0 51	0 68	0 82	0 86
L T L Tot Ass	-	0 21	0 37	0 55	0 59
Debt to Eqity	0 18	2 97	2 55	2 97	11 19
Interest Cover	64 08	0 13	1 62	4 72	3 18
Oper Prof Mrg	-	0 76	7 15	12 94	7 74
Net Prof Marg%	-	-5 06	0 34	6 66	6 12
Ret on Assets	18 63	1 15	9 55	9 86	13 69
Ret on Equity%	28 70	-29 47	1 14	21 44	122 30
Price/Earnings	4 77	-4 46	1 02	-	-
Divid Cover	2 51	-	108 00	-	-
Divid Yield	8 33	-	0 91	-	-
Earning Yield%	20 95	-22 44	98 18	-	-
NAV % Mrk Pr	73 02	45 93	57 32	48 44	-
Effec Tax Rate	-	-14 77	32 46	19 81	-
Def Interval	0 22	-7 92	5 72	9 28	6 30
Sus Grth Rate	17 29	-48 88	0 12	11 91	122 30

SUBSIDIARY & ASSOCIATED COMPANIES

ALMAR WIRES (PTY) LTD
CITY CORPORATE MANAGEMENT SERVICES (PTY) (50%)
CITY INDUSTRIAL HOLDINGS (PTY) LTD
CITY WIRES (PTY) LTD

INVESTMENTS

None

CITY LODGE HOTELS LTD

ABBREVIATION : CITYLDG

JSE SHORT CODE : CRH

SECTOR : Industrial-Beverages & Hotels

SHAREHOLDERS

Who Owns Whom's Assessment of the Identity of the Ultimate Controlling Shareholder:
ENDERLE & ASS

DIRECTORS :
BOTES AJ ,CULLABINE MJ ,DICKASON GB (Chairman)
DICKSON WM (Financial Director)
ENDERLE HR (Managing Director),MATTHEWS IN
ROSS C

REGISTRATION NUMBER : 86/02864/06

REGISTERED OFFICE
1st Floor, 2 Pybus Rd
Wierda Valley, Sandown
2196
TEL: 011-884 5327
FAX: 011-883 3640

TRANSFER SECRETARY
Central Registrars Ltd
P O Box 4844, Johannesburg
2000
TEL: 011-331 0051

COMPANY SECRETARY
WM Dickson

NATURE OF BUSINESS
A Hotel operator with its prime business to offer affordable, quality accomodation to travellers.

BANKERS :
Standard Bank of SA Ltd

AUDITORS :
KPMG Aiken & Peat

FAMILIAR BRAND NAMES
CITY LODGE

CONTRIBUTION BY ACTIVITY
N/A

YEAR END : July

CAPITAL STRUCTURE

	AUTHORISED	ISSUED
Ords 10c	50000000	24821917
11% Unsec Comp Conv Sub Debs	13636364	13636364

FINANCIAL STATISTICS (AT FINANCIAL YEAR END)

(Amts in R'000)	1992 Jul
Ord S/H Int	12885
Long Trm Loans	90545
Iss Ord Share	24822
Total Liab	99575
Current Liab	9030
Total Assets	112460
Current Assets	16224
Debtors	3248
Inventory	266
Turnover	46519
Oper Profit	23300
Interest Paid	8218
Tax Paid	6477
Prf af Int&Tax	8605
Prf att Ord Sh	8605
Btm Line Earn	8605
Dividend Paid	6093

PER SHARE STATISTICS (CENTS)

Net Asst Val	51.91
Net Earnings	34.70
Cash Flow	34.67

RATIOS AND OTHER INFORMATION

Current Ratio	1.80
Quik/Acid Tst	1.77
A/C Rec T/ovr	14.32
Tot Ass T/ovr	0.41
Debt/Ass Rat	0.86
L T L Tot Ass	0.78
Debt to Eqity	7.52
Interest Cover	2.84
Oper Prof Mrg	50.09
Net Prof Marg%	18.50
Ret on Assets	20.72
Ret on Equity%	66.78
Effec Tax Rate	42.95
Def Interval	1.50
Sus Grth Rate	19.50

SUBSIDIARY & ASSOCIATED COMPANIES

CITY LODGE (AIRPORT PROPERTY) (PTY) LTD
CITY LODGE (RANDBURG) (PTY) LTD
CITY LODGE HOLDINGS (SHARE BLOCK) (PTY)
PROPERTY LODGING INVESTMENTS (PTY) LTD
TWENTY THIRD FLOOR INVESTMENTS SEVENTEEN

INVESTMENTS

None

CLAW INVESTMENT HOLDINGS LTD

ABBREVIATION : CLAW

JSE SHORT CODE : CLW

SECTOR : Industrial-Retailers & Wholesalers

SHAREHOLDERS

Who Owns Whom's Assessment of the Identity of the Ultimate Controlling Shareholder: DIRECTORS

SHAREHOLDER	PERCENTAGE 1992	1991
GOUDSTAD NOM P/L	93.0	93.0
JOFAMILY INV P/L	4.6	4.6
TOTAL	97.6	97.6

DIRECTORS :
COERTSE HL ,ENGELBRECHT P ,HAMILTON DT
KLEBE EHK ,KNEEN JR ,MACLEOD RH ,NISBET VC

REGISTRATION NUMBER : 87/00997/06

REGISTERED OFFICE
91 Concordia Road, Silverton
0184
TEL: 012-804 2130
FAX: 012-804 1123

TRANSFER SECRETARY
Central Registrars Ltd
P O Box 4844, Johannesburg
2000
TEL: 011-331 0051

COMPANY SECRETARY
N/A

NATURE OF BUSINESS
The company has a controlling interest in Vadek Paints, a company quoted on the JSE. Vadek is a manufacturer, wholesaler, distributor & retailer of paints to the industrial & decorative markets.

BANKERS :
Nedperm Bank Ltd
First National Bank of SA Ltd
International Bank of Johannesburg Ltd

AUDITORS :
Herbert & Trakman

FAMILIAR BRAND NAMES
N/A

CONTRIBUTION BY ACTIVITY
N/A

YEAR END : February

DIVIDEND :15/12/91 and 15/06/91

CAPITAL STRUCTURE

	AUTHORISED	ISSUED
Ords 1c	40000000	18200000

FINANCIAL STATISTICS (AT FINANCIAL YEAR END)

(Amts in R'000)	1989 Mar
Ord S/H Int	9676
Long Trm Loans	15494
Iss Ord Share	18200
Total Liab	26906
Current Liab	11412
Total Assets	30812
Intang Assets	5770
Current Assets	19228
Debtors	11406
Inventory	7114

PER SHARE STATISTICS (CENTS)

Net Asst Val	21.46

RATIOS AND OTHER INFORMATION

Current Ratio	1.68
Quik/Acid Tst	1.06
Debt/Ass Rat	0.83
L T L Tot Ass	0.46
Debt to Eqity	2.63

SUBSIDIARY & ASSOCIATED COMPANIES

CLAW MANAGEMENT SERVICES (PTY) LTD
VADEK HOLDINGS (PTY) LTD
VADEK PAINTS LTD

INVESTMENTS

None

CLEGG HOLDINGS LTD

ABBREVIATION : CLEGG

JSE SHORT CODE : CLG

SECTOR : Industrial-Paper & Packaging

SHAREHOLDERS

Who Owns Whom's Assessment of the Identity of the Ultimate Controlling Shareholder:
CONSORTIUM OF HORTORS / A SHARP

SHAREHOLDER	PERCENTAGE 1992	1991
HORTORS LTD	28.2	---
INDO-CHINA NOM P/L	18.4	---
EGGER G A	16.8	21.2
CLEGG W	15.7	19.9
MACOSA AGENCIES P/L	5.7	2.6
EPSIDON TECHNOLOGY P/L	3.5	---
E KAHN TEXTILES P/L	2.6	---
COLOUR TIME P/L	1.5	1.9
CTP HOLDINGS LTD	1.0	---
CLEGG H R	---	22.3
SIMMONSCO NOM P/L	---	24.7
TOTAL	93.3	92.5

DIRECTORS :
CORMACK S ,EGGER GA (Managing Director)
JANKELOWITZ E ,SHARP A (Chairman

REGISTRATION NUMBER : 87/04376/06

REGISTERED OFFICE
19 Daniel Road, Benrose
Johannesburg
2094
TEL: 011-614 2381
FAX: 011-614 3881

TRANSFER SECRETARY
Central Registrars Ltd
P O Box 4844, Johannesburg
2000
TEL: 011-331 0051

COMPANY SECRETARY
A Sharp

NATURE OF BUSINESS
An investment holding company with subsidiaries engaged in lithographic & flexographic printing, packaging & silkscreen and label manufacturing.

BANKERS :
Standard Bank of SA Ltd

AUDITORS :
Fisher Hoffman Stride

FAMILIAR BRAND NAMES
N/A

CONTRIBUTION BY ACTIVITY
N/A

YEAR END : June

CAPITAL STRUCTURE

	AUTHORISED	ISSUED
Ords 1c	50000000	38083000

FINANCIAL STATISTICS (AT FINANCIAL YEAR END)

(Amts in R'000)	1992 Jun	1991 Jun	1990 Jun	1989 Jun	1988 Jun
Ord S/H Int	9463	7826	8806	8330	7309
Long Trm Loans	3167	3871	4686	4961	5556
Iss Ord Share	38083	30083	30083	30083	30083
Total Liab	9962	9594	12531	10862	10363
Current Liab	6795	5723	7845	5901	4807
Total Assets	19291	17253	21170	19025	17505
Intang Assets	134	167	167	167	167
Current Assets	9848	8058	11313	9472	8380
Debtors	4905	4220	5657	6274	4950
Inventory	4925	3750	5587	3150	2804
Turnover	24724	23548	22792	20595	16602
Oper Profit	1554	512	2019	2409	1650
Interest Paid	1083	1492	1551	1387	512
Tax Paid	1	-	-8	1	8
Prf af Int&Tax	470	-980	476	1021	1130
Prf att Ord Sh	470	-980	476	1021	1130
Btm Line Earn	437	-980	476	1021	1003
Dividend Paid	-	-	-	-	301
Mkt Prce(c) YE	30	25	40	25	52
Depreciation	1182	1177	1070	938	502

PER SHARE STATISTICS (CENTS)

Net Asst Val	24 50	25 46	28 72	27 13	23 74
Net Earnings	1 35	-3 26	1 58	3 40	2 50
Dividends	-	-	-	-	1 00
Cash Flow	4 34	0 65	5 14	6 51	5 98

RATIOS AND OTHER INFORMATION

Mrk Cap(R000)	11425	7521	12033	7521	15643
Current Ratio	1 45	1 41	1 44	1 61	1 74
Quik/Acid Tst	0 72	0 75	0 73	1 07	1 16
A/C Rec T/ovr	5 04	5 58	4 03	3 28	3 35
Tot Ass T/ovr	1 28	1 36	1 08	1 08	0 95
Debt/Ass Rat	0 52	0 56	0 59	0 57	0 59
L T L Tot Ass	0 16	0 22	0 22	0 26	0 32
Debt to Eqity	1 05	1 23	1 42	1 30	1 42
Interest Cover	1 43	0 34	1 30	1 74	3 22
Oper Prof Mrg	6 29	2 17	8 86	11 70	9 94
Net Prof Marg%	1 90	-4 16	2 09	4 96	6 81
Ret on Assets	8 06	2 97	9 54	12 66	9 43
Ret on Equity%	4 97	-12 52	5 41	12 26	15 46
Price/Earnings	22 22	-7 67	25 32	7 35	20 80
Divid Cover	-	-	-	-	2 50
Divid Yield	-	-	-	-	1 92
Earning Yield%	4 50	-13 04	3 95	13 60	4 81
NAV % Mrk Pr	81 65	101 84	71 79	108 54	45 66
Effec Tax Rate	-	-	-	0 10	0 70
Def Interval	3 06	35 01	5 34	4 20	4 20
Sus Grth Rate	4 97	-12 52	5 41	12 26	11 34

SUBSIDIARY & ASSOCIATED COMPANIES

CLEGGPAK (PTY) LTD
CRAIGLEA (PTY) LTD
HR CLEGG & CO (PTY) LTD
HR CLEGG INVESTMENTS (PTY) LTD
HR CLEGG LABELS (PTY) LTD
HR CLEGG LITHO (PTY) LTD
HR CLEGG SILKSCREEN (TVL) (PTY) LTD
ISABLUM PROPERTIES (PTY) LTD

INVESTMENTS

None

CLICKS STORES LTD

ABBREVIATION : CLICKS

JSE SHORT CODE : CLK

SECTOR : Industrial-Retailers & Wholesalers

SHAREHOLDERS

Who Owns Whom's Assessment of the Identity of the Ultimate Controlling Shareholder:
HI-SCORE VIA SCORE-CLICKS

SHAREHOLDER	PERCENTAGE 1992	1991
SCORE-CLICKS HOLDINGS LTD	50 1	---
STD BANK NOM TVL P/L	12 8	12 7
CMB NOM P/L	11 4	- -
DE BEERS PENS FUND	5 2	5 2
AECI PENS FUND	2 0	2 0
ANGLO AMERICAN CORP PENS FUND	1 5	1 5
COMMERCIAL UNION LIFE ASSURE CO SA LTD	1 3	---
METAL IND GROUP PENS FUND	1 3	1 3
ENGINEERING INDUSTRIES PENS FUND	1 1	1 1
SANLAM	---	11 4
SCORECLICKS	---	50 0
TOTAL	86 5	85 1

DIRECTORS :
DANZIGER DJ ,DOS SANTOS CS ,GODFREY RB
GREEN PWG (Financial Director)
HONNEYSETT TC (Chief Executive & M D),OSRIN E
SPENGLER RP (Dir Human Resources),TAUROG RD
UTIAN GM (Chairman

REGISTRATION NUMBER : 79/01598/06

REGISTERED OFFICE
18 Searle Street, Cape Town
8001
TEL 021-461 7505
FAX 021-461 8221

TRANSFER SECRETARY
Central Registrars Ltd
P O Box 4844, Johannesburg
2000
TEL 011-331 0051

COMPANY SECRETARY
W J Gouws

NATURE OF BUSINESS
An investment holding company with subsidiaries engaged in the discount retailing of cosmetics, toiletries, small appliances & other household merchandise via 130 Clicks stores, & 73 Diskom outlets The company also owns properties

BANKERS :
Standard Bank of SA Ltd
First National Bank of SA Ltd

AUDITORS :
Arthur Andersen & Co

FAMILIAR BRAND NAMES
MUSICA

CONTRIBUTION BY ACTIVITY
N/A

YEAR END : April

DIVIDEND .Ords no par value

Interim No 20	(Ldr)10/11/89	(Pay)17/11/89	Amt(c)12
Final No 21	(Ldr)25/05/90	(Pay)08/06/90	Amt(c)22
Interim No 22	(Ldr)26/10/90	(Pay)09/11/90	Amt(c)15
Final No 23	(Ldr)30/05/91	(Pay)14/06/91	Amt(c)28
Interim No 24	(Ldr)03/01/92	(Pay)16/01/92	Amt(c)22
Final No 25	(Ldr)17/07/92	(Pay)29/07/92	Amt(c)26
Interim No 26	(Ldr)31/12/92	(Pay)08/01/93	Amt(c)19

NUMBER OF EMPLOYEES : 3777

CAPITAL STRUCTURE

	AUTHORISED	ISSUED
Ords no par value	25000000	22600000

FINANCIAL STATISTICS (AT FINANCIAL YEAR END)

(Amts in R'000)	1992 Apr	1991 Apr	1990 Feb	1989 Feb	1988 Jun
Ord S/H Int	130871	65902	53702	47226	40547
Long Trm Loans	8697	7649	7125	3468	3003
Iss Ord Share	22600	20000	20000	20000	20000
Total Liab	135747	128671	85825	65077	59182
Current Liab	127050	121022	78700	61609	56179
Total Assets	266618	194573	139527	112303	99729
Current Assets	218569	152131	105481	82740	75962
Debtors	14988	10190	8339	6635	6251
Inventory	160151	134196	86021	73072	58648
Turnover	836818	551906	426175	246431	282235
Oper Profit	52865	41351	32677	20030	22240
Interest Paid	5645	1792	1051	698	231
Tax Paid	23341	20165	16030	9740	10763
Prf af Int&Tax	24822	20530	16397	9900	11246
Prf att Ord Sh	24752	20457	16364	9815	11195
Btm Line Earn	24752	20457	16289	7275	11195
Dividend Paid	10276	8600	6800	4200	5400
Mkt Prce(c) YE	2550	1400	975	600	650
Depreciation	7658	4955	3328	1732	1915

PER SHARE STATISTICS (CENTS)

Net Asst Val	579 08	329 51	268 51	236 13	202 74
Net Earnings	122 62	102 29	81 82	49 08	55 98
Dividends	48 00	43 00	34 00	21 00	27 00
Cash Flow	148 18	129 48	102 24	89 55	69 56

RATIOS AND OTHER INFORMATION

Mrk Cap(R000)	576300	280000	195000	120000	130000
Current Ratio	1 72	1 26	1 34	1 34	1 35
Quik/Acid Tst	0 46	0 15	0 25	0 16	0 31
A/C Rec T/ovr	55 83	54 16	51 11	55 71	45 15
Tot Ass T/ovr	3 14	2 84	3 05	3 29	2 83
Debt/Ass Rat	0 48	0 62	0 56	0 55	0 56
Debt to Eqity	0 97	1 84	1 47	1 30	1 39
Interest Cover	9 36	23 08	31 09	28 70	96 28
Oper Prof Mrg	6 32	7 49	7 67	8 13	7 88
Net Prof Marg%	2 96	3 71	3 84	3 98	3 97
Ret on Assets	20 18	21 84	23 99	27 16	22 30
Ret on Equity%	18 91	31 04	30 47	31 17	27 61
Price/Earnings	20 80	13 69	11 92	12 22	11 61
Divid Cover	2 55	2 38	2 41	2 34	2 07
Divid Yield	1 88	3 07	3 49	3 50	4 15
Earning Yield%	4 81	7 31	8 39	8 18	8 61
NAV % Mrk Pr	22 71	23 54	27 54	39 36	31 19
Effec Tax Rate	46 22	48 12	46 99	47 57	45 45
Sus Grth Rate	11 06	17 99	17 81	11 89	14 29

SUBSIDIARY & ASSOCIATED COMPANIES

ARUNDEL DISTRIBUTORS (PTY) LTD
AURORA RUFFOLO INTERNATIONAL (PTY) LTD
CLICKS STORES (NATAL) PROPERTIES (PTY) L
CLICKS STORES (TRANSVAAL) PROPERTIES (PT
CLICKS STORES (WAREHOUSES) (PTY) LTD
CLICKS STORES (WESTERN CAPE) (PTY) LTD
CLICKS STORES HOLDINGS (PTY) LTD
DISKOM (CAPE) (PTY) LTD
DISKOM (PENINSULA) (PTY) LTD
DISKOM (WESTERN CAPE) (PTY) LTD
DISKOM ENTERPRISES (PTY) LTD
H GOLDIN & CO (PTY) LTD
OKELFED LTD

INVESTMENTS

None

CLINIC HOLDINGS LTD

ABBREVIATION : CLINICS

JSE SHORT CODE : CLC

SECTOR : Industrial-Pharmaceutical & Medical

SHAREHOLDERS

Who Owns Whom's Assessment of the Identity of the Ultimate Controlling Shareholder: DIRECTORS

SHAREHOLDER	PERCENTAGE 1992	1991
BERCO TRUST	27 0	27 0
HURWITZ B	23 4	23 4
STD BANK NOM TVL P/L	6 8	3 8
EIGHTY ONE MAIN STREET NOM LTD	5 6	1 1
SMILG J H & CO INV P/L	5 1	5 1
FEDERATED INDUSTRIAL & FINANCE CORP P/L	4 2	4 2
SOUTHERN LIFE ASSOC LTD	3 7	7 6
SMILG J H	2 9	2 9
FIRST NAT NOM P/L	2 8	2 6

HURWITZ J L	2 4	2 4
KRUGER AJ &SHARP A ADMIN E/LC DUT KRUGER	1 6	1 6
SHARP A	1 2	1 2
BERGER S M	1 1	1 1
SINGER E M	1 0	1 0
LIBERTY LIFE ASSOC OF AFRICA LTD	---	2 6
MOMENTUM LIFE ASSURE LTD	---	1 4
TOTAL	88 8	89 0

DIRECTORS :
ANDERSON GR ,BERGER SM (Financial Director)
BLOCH IS ,BLOU A ,DE LOOR DR JH ,FEINBLUM SG
GELDENHUYS DR FG ,HUPKES PROF GJ
HURWITZ B (Executive Chairman)
HURWITZ JL (Managing Director),JACOBSZ DR FP
MILLER LH ,PENCHARZ P ,SHARP A ,SINGER EM
SMILG JH ,WIEHAHN PROF NE

REGISTRATION NUMBER : 87/04106/06

REGISTERED OFFICE
7th Floor, JHS Executive Centre
112 Kerk Street, Johannesburg
2001
TEL 011-29 1951
FAX 011-23 6698

TRANSFER SECRETARY
Stability Services (Pty) Ltd
6th Floor, 112 Kerk Street
Johannesburg
2001
TEL 011-337 4030

COMPANY SECRETARY
S G Feinblum

NATURE OF BUSINESS
The holding company of a group providing surgical and medical private hospital facilities

BANKERS :
Trust Bank of Africa Ltd
Standard Bank of SA Ltd, Nedperm Bank Ltd
First National Bank of SA Ltd

AUDITORS :
Kessel Feinstein

FAMILIAR BRAND NAMES
CITY PARK HOSPITAL,GARDEN CITY CLINIC
JAKARANDA HOSPITAAL,KINGSWAY HOSPITAL
MILPARK HOSPITAL,NEDPARK CLINIC
PARK LANE CLINIC,PARKLANDS HOSPITAL
RAND CLINIC,ROSEBANK CLINIC
ST AUGUSTINES HOSPITAL,UNION HOSPITAL

CONTRIBUTION BY ACTIVITY
N/A

YEAR END : September

DIVIDEND : Ords 1c

Interim No 5	(Ldr)25/05/90	(Pay)21/06/90	Amt(c)4 5
Final No 6	(Ldr)14/12/90	(Pay)20/12/90	Amt(c)7
Interim No 7	(Ldr)14/06/91	(Pay)25/06/91	Amt(c)5 25
Final No 8	(Ldr)03/01/92	(Pay)13/01/92	Amt(c)8 25
Interim No 9	(Ldr)24/07/92	(Pay)31/07/92	Amt(c)6

NUMBER OF EMPLOYEES : 7000

CAPITAL STRUCTURE

	AUTHORISED	ISSUED
Ords 1c	500000000	99000000

FINANCIAL STATISTICS (AT FINANCIAL YEAR END)

(Amts in R'000)	1991 Sep	1990 Sep	1989 Sep	1988 Sep	1987
Ord S/H Int	80503	64347	52053	41927	1009
Long Trm Loans	49884	41420	36730	2739	46376
Iss Ord Share	99000	99000	99000	99000	99000
Total Liab	135743	116296	97876	51205	52389
Current Liab	85859	74876	61146	48466	6013
Total Assets	216246	180643	149929	93132	40683
Current Assets	161909	131526	103601	57933	11254
Debtors	127657	102054	80497	35712	-
Inventory	29410	24189	18744	15486	11254
Oper Profit	57816	48237	39381	36108	24034
Interest Paid	4681	2077	27	19	1238
Tax Paid	26372	2392?	20080	15124	11398
Prf af Int&Tax	29521	23679	20026	21256	11398
Prf att Ord Sh	29521	23679	20026	21256	11398
Btm Line Earn	29521	23679	20026	21256	11398
Dividend Paid	13365	11385	9900	8910	-
Mkt Prce(c) YE	250	170	135	240	200
Depreciation	16541	13320	9572	7520	-

PER SHARE STATISTICS (CENTS)

Net Asst Val	81 32	65 00	52 58	42 35	1 02
Net Earnings	29 80	23 90	20 20	21 50	-
Dividends	13 50	11 50	10 00	9 00	-
Cash Flow	55 74	39 08	42 01	31 83	11 51

RATIOS AND OTHER INFORMATION

Mrk Cap(R000)	247500	168300	133650	237600	198000
Current Ratio	1 89	1 76	1 69	1 20	1 87
Quik/Acid Tst	1 54	1 43	1 39	0 88	-
Debt/Ass Rat	0 51	0 55	0 55	0 52	1 29
L T L Tot Ass	0 12	0 14	0 15	-	1 14
Debt to Eqity	1 38	1 55	1 60	1 16	51 92
Interest Cover	12 35	23 22	1458 56	1900 42	19 41
Ret on Assets	28 01	27 50	26 77	39 08	59 08
Ret on Equity%	36 67	36 80	38 47	50 70	1129 63
Price/Earnings	8 39	7 11	6 68	11 16	-
Divid Cover	2 21	2 08	2 02	2 39	-
Divid Yield	5 40	6 76	7 41	3 75	-
Earning Yield%	11 92	14 06	14 96	8 96	-
NAV % Mrk Pr	32 53	38 23	38 95	17 65	0 51
Effec Tax Rate	32 04	46 70	20 17	34 04	50 00
Def Interval	0 72	0 65	0 53	-	4 07
Sus Grth Rate	20 07	19 11	19 45	29 45	1129 63

SUBSIDIARY & ASSOCIATED COMPANIES

BARNEY HURWITZ & ASSOCIATES (PTY) LTD
CLINIC GROUP OF HOSPITALS (PTY) LTD
ROSEBANK CLINIC (PTY) LTD

INVESTMENTS

None

CLUFF RESOURCES ZIMBABWE LTD

ABBREVIATION : CLUFF ZIM

SECTOR : Zimbabwe Stock Exchange

SHAREHOLDERS

Who Owns Whom's Assessment of the Identity of the Ultimate Controlling Shareholder:
CLUFF MINERAL EXPLORATION LTD

SHAREHOLDER	PERCENTAGE 1992	1991
CLUFF MINERAL EXPLORATION LTD	82.4	---
CLUFF RESOURCES ZIMBABWE EMPL TRUST	3.1	---
ZIMBABWE DEVELOPMENT CORP LTD	1.3	---
SYFRETS NOM (PVT) LTD	1.1	---
PFI GROUP PENS FUND	1.1	---
TOTAL	88.9	---

DIRECTORS :
ADAMSON RG ,ARMSTRONG RH ,ASHLEY MJ
CLUFF JG (Chairman),DE LA RUE A ,GOMWE GG
JACOBS CA ,KRAAN M ,LONG DEB (Deputy Chairman)
PITCHFORD RA (Managing Director),TRACEY CG

REGISTERED OFFICE
16th Floor, Karigamombe Centre
53 Samora Machel Avenue, Harare

TRANSFER SECRETARY
Zimbabwe Banking Corporation Ltd
P O Box 3198, Harare
Zimbabwe

TEL: 092634-735011

COMPANY SECRETARY
S E Dunne

NATURE OF BUSINESS
The primary business of the company is the exporation and production of gold,which is produced from the group's two open pit mines:the FREDA/ REBECCA mine and the ROYAL FAMILY mine.CLUFF also pursues an active programme of exploration through out Zimbabwe for other metals and minerals.

BANKERS :
Standard Chartered Merchant Bank Zim Ltd

AUDITORS :
N/A

FAMILIAR BRAND NAMES
N/A

CONTRIBUTION BY ACTIVITY
N/A

YEAR END : December

DIVIDEND : Ords Z$0,25

Dividend	(Ldr)13/03/92	(Pay)27/03/92	Amt(c)5.55
Dividend	(Ldr)28/08/92	(Pay)15/09/92	Amt(c)5.99

CAPITAL STRUCTURE

	AUTHORISED	ISSUED
Ords Z$0,25	300000000	238544324

FINANCIAL STATISTICS (AT FINANCIAL YEAR END)

(Amts in Z$)	1991 Dec	1990 Dec
Ord S/H Int	461111	323139
Long Trm Loans	3472	-
Iss Ord Share	238544	231242
Total Liab	50866	16821
Current Liab	47394	16821
Total Assets	511977	339960
Current Assets	26917	29646
Debtors	10755	4636
Inventory	16156	11666
Turnover	90756	70317
Oper Profit	42162	32752
Prf af Int&Tax	42523	33216
Prf att Ord Sh	42523	33216
Btm Line Earn	42523	33216
Dividend Paid	21254	16590
Depreciation	1089	700

PER SHARE STATISTICS (CENTS)

Net Asst Val	193.30	139.74
Net Earnings	18.14	17.68
Dividends	8.91	8.16
Cash Flow	18.28	14.67

RATIOS AND OTHER INFORMATION

Current Ratio	0.57	1.76
Quik/Acid Tst	0.23	1.07
A/C Rec T/ovr	8.44	15.17
Tot Ass T/ovr	0.18	0.21
Debt/Ass Rat	0.10	0.05
L T L Tot Ass	0.01	-
Debt to Eqity	0.11	0.05
Oper Prof Mrg	46.46	46.58
Net Prof Marg%	46.85	47.24
Ret on Assets	8.31	9.77
Ret on Equity%	9.22	10.28
Divid Cover	2.04	2.17
Def Interval	0.52	-
Sus Grth Rate	4.61	5.15

SUBSIDIARY & ASSOCIATED COMPANIES

BINDURA ESTATES (PVT) LIMITED

INVESTMENTS

None

CLYDE INDUSTRIAL CORPORATION LTD

ABBREVIATION : CLYDE

JSE SHORT CODE : CLY

SECTOR : Industrial-Engineering

SHAREHOLDERS

Who Owns Whom's Assessment of the Identity of the Ultimate Controlling Shareholder:
WILSON FAMILY

SHAREHOLDER	PERCENTAGE 1992	1991
GORDON WILSON FAMILY TRUST	40.8	40.7
DOCWIL TRUST NO 1	38.8	38.8
UAL MERCHANT BANK LTD	3.7	3.8
WILSON G D FAMILY TRUST	2.8	2.8
NUSSBAUM R S A W	1.4	1.3
TOTAL	87.5	87.4

DIRECTORS :
DE KLERK AM (Financial Director),ROOS SJ
SCOTT-DAWKINS EM
WILSON GD (Chairman & Managing Dir.

REGISTRATION NUMBER : 01/05977/06

REGISTERED OFFICE
4 Boniface Road, Selection Park
Springs
1559
TEL: 011-56 4118
FAX: 011-815 3720

TRANSFER SECRETARY
Central Registrars Ltd
P O Box 4844, Johannesburg
2000
TEL: 011-331 0051

COMPANY SECRETARY
A M de Klerk

NATURE OF BUSINESS
The group manufactures and distributes secondary steel products to the mining & industrial markets. Products include general purpose & seamless piping pipe fittings, industrial steel strip & strapping, reconditioned rail, rail fittings, pipe insulation cut-to-length steel and steel flanges.

BANKERS :
First National Bank of SA Ltd, Bankfin

AUDITORS :
Campbell Bode Brown

FAMILIAR BRAND NAMES
BENBREW STEEL,CLYDE STEEL,RAILCOR,SUDOR
ZAK STEEL

CONTRIBUTION BY ACTIVITY
N/A

YEAR END : February

DIVIDEND :Ords 2c

Interim No 4	(Ldr)21/11/89	(Pay)28/12/89	Amt(c)0.75
Final No 5	(Ldr)18/05/90	(Pay)28/06/90	Amt(c)1.25
Interim No 6	(Ldr)23/11/90	(Pay)21/12/90	Amt(c)1.25
Final No 7	(Ldr)24/05/91	(Pay)28/06/91	Amt(c)2
Interim No 8	(Ldr)22/11/91	(Pay)20/12/91	Amt(c)1.25
Final No 9	(Ldr)22/05/92	(Pay)26/06/92	Amt(c)2.0
Interim No 10	(Ldr)20/11/92	(Pay)18/12/92	Amt(c)1.25

NUMBER OF EMPLOYEES : 347

CAPITAL STRUCTURE

	AUTHORISED	ISSUED
Ords 2c	27000000	17600000

FINANCIAL STATISTICS (AT FINANCIAL YEAR END)

(Amts in R'000)	1992 Feb	1991 Feb	1990 Feb	1989 Feb	1988 Feb
Ord S/H Int	14161	12901	11629	10692	9685
Long Trm Loans	2364	1786	1863	1970	700
Iss Ord Share	17600	17600	17600	17600	17600
Total Liab	23438	19030	15312	15854	11932
Current Liab	21074	17244	13449	13884	11232
Total Assets	37201	31469	26415	25956	21617
Intang Assets	398	462	526	590	*
Current Assets	29633	24544	19410	18502	16177
Debtors	15281	11047	12461	10183	7929
Inventory	14309	13490	6942	8313	7635
Turnover	82657	68747	67161	62034	51849
Oper Profit	4541	4239	3733	3341	5638
Interest Paid	1062	388	1200	833	649
Tax Paid	1583	1943	1180	1004	662
Prf af Int&Tax	1896	1908	1353	1504	4327
Prf att Ord Sh	1896	1908	1353	1504	4327
Btm Line Earn	1832	1844	1289	1465	4315
Dividend Paid	572	572	352	458	458
Mkt Prce(c) YE	28	25	30	38	65
Depreciation	922	759	712	510	468

PER SHARE STATISTICS (CENTS)

Net Asst Val	78.20	70.68	63.09	57.40	55.03
Net Earnings	10.80	10.80	7.70	8.50	12.30
Dividends	3.25	3.25	2.00	2.60	5.00
Cash Flow	16.10	16.41	12.95	14.70	23.41

RATIOS AND OTHER INFORMATION

Mrk Cap(R000)	4928	4400	5280	6688	11440
Current Ratio	1.41	1.42	1.44	1.33	1.44
Quik/Acid Tst	0.73	0.64	0.93	0.73	0.76
A/C Rec T/ovr	5.41	6.22	5.39	6.09	4.62
Tot Ass T/ovr	2.22	2.18	2.54	2.39	1.69
Debt/Ass Rat	0.60	0.57	0.55	0.59	0.55
L T L Tot Ass	0.04	0.02	0.04	0.05	0.03
Debt to Eqity	1.58	1.40	1.25	1.43	1.23
Interest Cover	4.28	10.93	3.11	4.01	8.69
Oper Prof Mrg	5.49	6.17	5.56	5.39	10.87
Net Prof Marg%	2.29	2.78	2.01	2.42	8.35
Ret on Assets	12.21	13.47	14.13	12.87	18.41
Ret on Equity%	13.39	14.79	11.63	14.07	31.54
Price/Earnings	2.59	2.31	3.90	4.47	5.28
Divid Cover	3.32	3.32	3.85	3.27	2.46
Divid Yield	11.61	13.00	6.67	6.84	7.69
Earning Yield%	38.57	43.20	25.67	22.37	18.92
NAV % Mrk Pr	279.28	282.70	210.28	151.05	84.66
Effec Tax Rate	45.04	44.90	39.32	20.61	13.59
Def Interval	2.26	2.33	0.88	2.44	0.28
Sus Grth Rate	9.35	10.36	8.61	9.78	39.95

SUBSIDIARY & ASSOCIATED COMPANIES

HEAVY ENGINEERING IND INVEST (PTY) LTD
KALAHARI STEEL ROLLING MILLS (PTY) LTD
RAILCOR INVESTMENT HOLDINGS (PTY) LTD

INVESTMENTS

None

CNA GALLO LTD

ABBREVIATION : CNAGALO

JSE SHORT CODE : CNG

SECTOR : Industrial-Retailers & Wholesalers

SHAREHOLDERS

Who Owns Whom's Assessment of the Identity of the Ultimate Controlling Shareholder:
ANGLO VIA PREMIER GROUP/ARGUS HOLDINGS

SHAREHOLDER	PERCENTAGE 1992	1991
OMNI MEDIA P/L	65 2	65 3
JOAN ST LEDGER LINDBURGH NOM CO P/L	6 0	6 0
STD BANK NOM TVL P/L	4 4	4 5
EIGHTY ONE MAIN STREET NOM LTD	2 3	1 8
SAGE LIFE LTD	1 8	1 8
FIRST NAT NOM P/L	1 4	1 8
SHARESTOCK NOM P/L	1 3	1 3
NEDBANK NOM LTD	1 3	1 1
RESIDENT NOM LTD	1 2	1 2
TOTAL	84 9	84 7

DIRECTORS :
BAND DDB (Chairman), BRAY VG
CHERRY AR (Financial Director)
CUZEN ADL (Managing Director), GALLO EGP
INGLIS JG, JAMES MCH, MACKNESS JA, MCLEAN PW
OUTRAM IL, ROBINSON BB, SMITH AA, UTIAN GM
WRIGHTON PGA

REGISTRATION NUMBER : 05/08061/06

REGISTERED OFFICE
10th Floor The Atrium, 41 Stanley Avenue
Milpark, Johannesburg
2092
TEL 011-482 2600
FAX 011-726 1374

TRANSFER SECRETARY
Fraser Street Registrars (Pty) Ltd
P O Box 61178, Marshalltown
2107
TEL 011-491 0911

COMPANY SECRETARY
A R Cherry

NATURE OF BUSINESS
The Group's main business the CNA & Literary Group of retail stores (325 outlets), the manufacture & distribution of gramophone records, music & video cassettes, music publishing & the provision of video production & post-production facilities, the manufacture & sale of greeting cards & stationery products, general book publishing, freight forwarding & clearing & corporate training & education

BANKERS :
First National Bank of SA Ltd

AUDITORS :
Deloitte Pim Goldby

FAMILIAR BRAND NAMES
BOOKWORM, CAMPUS BOOKSHOP
CENTAUR PUBLICATIONS, DISNEY, EXCLUSIVE BOOKS
GALLO AFRICA, GALLO HOME VIDEOS
HALLMARK CARDS, LITERARY GROUP
LOGANS UNIV BOOKSHOPS, NU METRO CINEMAS (50%)
PANACHE, PILGRIMS BOOKSHOPS
PREMIER FREIGHT (50%), RPM STUDIOS, SHOE BOX
SILVERAY STATIONERY (50%), STRUIK GROUP (50%)
SUBSCRIPTIONS, TEAL TRUTONE, TOP 40 VIDEOS
TOUCHSTONE, UMKHONTO RECORDS, UNIVERSITAS
WARNER, WESTDENE SERVICES, YOUNG READING

CONTRIBUTION BY ACTIVITY
Entertainment Division (22 1%)
Support Division (17 2%)
Retail Division (% of Pretax profit) (60 7%)

YEAR END : March

DIVIDEND : Ords 10c

Interim No 106	(Ldr)24/11/89	(Pay)19/12/89	Amt(c)11
Final No 107	(Ldr)08/06/90	(Pay)11/07/90	Amt(c)44
Interin No 108	(Ldr)23/11/90	(Pay)19/12/90	Amt(c)13 0
Final No 109	(Ldr)07/06/91	(Pay)11/07/91	Amt(c)54
Interim No 110	(Ldr)22/11/91	(Pay)19/12/91	Amt(c)13
Final No 111	(Ldr)05/06/92	(Pay)11/07/92	Amt(c)54
Interim No 112	(Ldr)27/11/92	(Pay)19/12/92	Amt(c)13

NUMBER OF EMPLOYEES : 5249

CAPITAL STRUCTURE

	AUTHORISED	ISSUED
Ords 10c	39561520	33166985
"B" Share Purchase Prefs 10c	2304180	1151380
6,5% Cum Prefs R2	150000	150000
5% Cum Prefs R2	500000	500000
"A" Share Purchase Prefs 10c	71820	23010

FINANCIAL STATISTICS (AT FINANCIAL YEAR END)

(Amts in R'000)	1992 Mar	1991 Mar	1990 Mar	1989 Mar	1988 Mar
Ord S/H Int	216604	185495	147212	122566	93470
Long Trm Loans	33966	33479	32497	16690	15019
Iss Ord Share	33167	32789	32299	31858	31680
Total Liab	212884	258594	194899	147013	116413
Current Liab	178918	225115	162402	130323	101394
Total Assets	409122	423723	326031	261365	209883
Intang Assets	20366	20366	16080	8214	*
Current Assets	198369	235512	173672	166003	139266
Debtors	51751	66757	50845	45704	35603
Inventory	141885	141851	110457	89195	68643
Turnover	840359	798356	679947	549763	429849
Oper Profit	84660	92058	73683	52817	37929
Interest Paid	17567	17149	11629	1195	1169
Tax Paid	33419	37205	29103	24401	18475
Prf af Int&Tax	42749	51877	38680	30518	20618
Prf att Ord Sh	53152	55249	45784	35953	23328
Btm Line Earn	53292	57648	42356	36487	29122
Dividend Paid	22221	22012	17754	14328	9185
Mkt Prce(c) YE	2725	2425	1225	800	575
Depreciation	13245	13168	10583	8808	6993

PER SHARE STATISTICS (CENTS)

Net Asst Val	591 67	503 61	405 99	358 94	295 04
Net Earnings	160 30	168 50	141 80	112 90	73 60
Dividends	67 00	67 00	55 00	45 00	29 00
Cash Flow	159 40	184 71	146 51	118 70	83 72

RATIOS AND OTHER INFORMATION

Mrk Cap(R000)	903801	795133	395663	254864	182160
Current Ratio	1.11	1.05	1.07	1.27	1.37
Quik/Acid Tst	0.32	0.42	0.39	0.59	0.70
A/C Rec T/ovr	16.24	11.96	13.37	12.03	12.07
Tot Ass T/ovr	2.05	1.88	2.09	2.10	2.05
Debt/Ass Rat	0.46	0.55	0.51	0.51	0.51
L T L Tot Ass	0.02	0.02	0.02	0.02	0.02
Debt to Eqity	0.86	1.26	1.14	1.10	1.13
Interest Cover	5.21	6.06	6.72	44.25	34.44
Oper Prof Mrg	10.07	11.53	10.84	9.61	8.82
Net Prof Marg%	6.32	6.92	6.73	6.54	5.43
Ret on Assets	25.87	26.40	27.18	24.18	21.10
Ret on Equity%	24.54	29.78	31.10	29.33	24.96
Price/Earnings	17.00	14.39	8.64	7.09	7.81
Divid Cover	2.39	2.51	2.58	2.51	2.54
Divid Yield	2.46	2.76	4.49	5.63	5.04
Earning Yield%	5.88	6.95	11.58	14.11	12.80
NAV % Mrk Pr	21.71	20.77	33.14	44.87	51.31
Effec Tax Rate	49.54	51.24	46.60	45.95	48.23
Def Interval	0.45	0.35	0.34	0.33	0.41
Sus Grth Rate	14.28	17.92	19.04	17.64	15.13

SUBSIDIARY & ASSOCIATED COMPANIES

CENTRAL NEWS AGENCY (BOPHUTHATSWANA) (PT
CENTRAL NEWS AGENCY (LESOTHO) (PTY) LTD
CENTRAL NEWS AGENCY LTD
CNA GALLO MANAGEMENT & FINANCE (PTY) LTD
CNA OPERATIONS (PTY) LTD
CNA PROPERTIES (BARAGWANATH) (PTY) LTD
CNA PROPERTIES (CITY DEEP) (PTY) LTD
CNA PROPERTIES (ELANDSFONTEIN) (PTY) LTD
CNA PROPERTIES (EPPING) (PTY) LTD
CNA PROPERTIES (ROSSBURGH) (PTY) LTD
CNA PROPERTIES (TURFFONTEIN) (PTY) LTD
CNA PROPERTIES LTD
COMMISSIONER INSURANCE BROKERS (PTY) LTD
CONSTANTIA GREETINGS (PTY) LTD
DOWNTOWN RECORDING STUDIOS (PTY) LTD
GALLO (AFRICA) LTD
GALLO DISTRIBUTION CENTRE (PTY) LTD
GALLO MANAGEMENT SERVICES (PTY) LTD
GALLO PROPERTIES (PTY) LTD
GALLO RECORD CO (PTY) LTD
INTECH (PTY) LTD
LITERARY GROUP (PTY) LTD, THE
PIRIE APPLETON & CO. AFRICA (PTY) LTD (50%)
PORT SHEPSTONE NEWS AGENCY (PTY) LTD
RPM RECORD COMPANY (PTY) LTD
SILVERAY STATIONERY (TRANSVAAL) (PTY) LT (50%)
SWAZILAND NEWS AGENCY (PTY) LTD
SYMMETRICAL INVESTMENTS (PTY) LTD (50,01%)
VIDEO LAB HOLDINGS LTD

INVESTMENTS

CTP HOLDINGS (PTY) LTD (492287SH)
DIE AFRIKAANSE PERS (1962) BPK (500SH)
MULTIPRO HOLDINGS LTD (11%)
PELIKAN PRODUCTS (PTY) LTD (200000SH)
SOLCHEM INVESTMENT HOLDINGS LTD (100000SH)
VIDEO LAB HOLDINGS LTD (18200SH)
WALTONS CONSOLIDATED INVESTMENT HOLDINGS (19,9%)
WALTONS STATIONERY CO LTD (1,4%)

COASTAL CLOTHING MANUFACTURERS LTD

ABBREVIATION : COASTAL

JSE SHORT CODE : CTL

SECTOR : Industrial-Clothing, Footwear & Textiles

SHAREHOLDERS

Who Owns Whom's Assessment of the Identity of the Ultimate Controlling Shareholder: DIRECTORS

SHAREHOLDER	PERCENTAGE 1992	1991
NEALE-MAY G	32.3	32.3
GRACELANDS FAMILY TRUST	23.8	23.8
MORFORD R A	17.1	17.1
COLUMBIA CONSULTANTS LTD	7.8	7.8
COASTAL SHARE TRUST	3.0	3.0
WOOLFSON H L	1.4	1.4
JUSCO NOM P/L	1.3	1.3
TOTAL	86.7	86.7

DIRECTORS :
MARTIN CB (Financial Director)
NEALE-MAY G (Chairman & Managing Dir.)
REYNOLDS JC ,SANDBERG BG

REGISTRATION NUMBER : 05/20661/06

REGISTERED OFFICE
1139 South Coast Road, Mobeni
4092
TEL: 031-42 6124
FAX: 031-42 9345

TRANSFER SECRETARY
Central Registrars Ltd
P O Box 4844, Johannesburg
2000
TEL: 011-331 0051

COMPANY SECRETARY
C B Martin

NATURE OF BUSINESS
The company is engaged in clothing manufacture.

BANKERS :
First National Bank of SA Ltd

AUDITORS :
David Strachan & Tayler

FAMILIAR BRAND NAMES
CARBON COPY,HUGGERS,LIMACO MODES,VAN HEUSEN
WAIKIKI

CONTRIBUTION BY ACTIVITY
N/A

YEAR END : February

DIVIDEND : (Ldr)30/06/89 (Pay)04/08/89

NUMBER OF EMPLOYEES : 290

CAPITAL STRUCTURE

	AUTHORISED	ISSUED
Ords no par value	20000000	11182626
9% Cum Red Prefs R1	5	0

FINANCIAL STATISTICS (AT FINANCIAL YEAR END)

(Amts in R'000)	1992 Feb	1991 Feb	1990 Feb	1989 Feb	1988 Feb
Ord S/H Int	3813	3483	3392	3599	2793
Long Trm Loans	899	530	384	165	-
Iss Ord Share	11183	11183	11183	10415	10000
Total Liab	3602	2758	2549	2223	1746
Current Liab	2703	2228	2165	2058	1746
Total Assets	7415	6241	5941	5822	4539
Current Assets	5518	5122	4559	4730	3475
Debtors	2006	2409	886	2276	1207
Inventory	3269	2538	3581	2369	2202
Turnover	20014	14101	14265	-	-
Oper Profit	1087	1182	49	1651	1566
Interest Paid	743	523	373	143	90
Tax Paid	197	305	-103	578	220
Prf af Int&Tax	166	368	-283	930	1256
Prf att Ord Sh	166	368	-283	930	1234
Btm Line Earn	166	203	-213	864	1234
Dividend Paid	-	112	-14	43	60
Mkt Prce(c) YE	18	20	25	45	50
Depreciation	177	118	128	138	94

PER SHARE STATISTICS (CENTS)

Net Asst Val	34 10	31 15	30 33	34 56	27 93
Net Earnings	1 49	3 29	-2 61	9 08	12 71
Dividends	-	1 00	-	2 50	2 50
Cash Flow	3 68	5 68	-1 80	10 82	13 68

RATIOS AND OTHER INFORMATION

Mrk Cap(R000)	2013	2237	2796	4687	5000
Current Ratio	2 04	2 30	2 11	2 30	1 99
Quik/Acid Tst	0 83	1 16	0 45	1 15	0 73
A/C Rec T/ovr	9 98	5 85	16 10	-	-
Tot Ass T/ovr	2 70	2 26	2 40	-	-
Debt/Ass Rat	0 46	0 42	0 43	0 37	0 38
L T L Tot Ass	0 09	0 06	0 06	0 02	
Debt to Eqity	0 89	0 75	0 75	0 61	0 63
Interest Cover	1 46	2 26	-0 13	11 55	17 40
Oper Prof Mrg	5 43	8 38	-0 34	-	-
Net Prof Marg%	0 83	2 61	-1 98	-	-
Ret on Assets	14 92	19 16	-0 22	28 36	34 50
Ret on Equity%	4 35	10 57	-8 34	25 84	44 18
Price/Earnings	12 08	6 08	-9 58	4 96	3 93
Divid Cover	-	3 29	-	3 63	5 08
Divid Yield	-	5 00	-	5 56	5 00
Earning Yield%	8 28	16 45	-10 44	20 18	25 42
NAV % Mrk Pr	189 42	155 73	121 33	76 79	55 86
Effec Tax Rate	35 26	23 18	16 32	35 68	14 91
Def Interval	1 65	0 60	-2 14	0 14	0 05
Sus Grth Rate	4 35	7 35	-7 93	24 65	42 03

SUBSIDIARY & ASSOCIATED COMPANIES

JON AL FASHIONS (PTY) LTD

INVESTMENTS

None

COATES BROTHERS SA LTD

ABBREVIATION : COATES

JSE SHORT CODE : COT

SECTOR : Industrial-Paper & Packaging

SHAREHOLDERS

Who Owns Whom's Assessment of the Identity of the Ultimate Controlling Shareholder:
TOTAL CFP (FRANCE) VIA COATES BROS PLC

SHAREHOLDER	PERCENTAGE 1992	1991
COATES BROS PLC	68 4	68 4
SA MUTUAL	11 4	11 4
BENNETT J D	5 2	5 2
FAIRHEADS NOM P/L	1 6	---
COATES P	1 2	1 2
COATES V E	1 2	1 2
G J COATES INV P/L	1 0	1 0
TOTAL	90 0	88 5

DIRECTORS :
AITCHISON RA MR,DE LA HARPE BECK WF MR (Chairman)
GEISSELER G MR,KING DF MR,PATON-ASH C MR
ROGOW SM MR,ROSE BS MR
WILLIAMS EF MR (Managing Director),YOUNGMAN DJ M

REGISTRATION NUMBER : 05/07944/06

REGISTERED OFFICE
7, 18th Avenue, Maitland
Cape Town
7405
TEL 021-593 1140
FAX 021-593 0604

TRANSFER SECRETARY
Fraser Street Registrars (Pty) Ltd
P O Box 61178, Marshalltown
2107
TEL 011-491 0911

COMPANY SECRETARY
S M Rogow

NATURE OF BUSINESS
The company is engaged in the manufacture & sale of printing inks, synthetic resins & industrial surface coatings It is an importer & distributor of products for the printing & graphic arts industries The company is also involved, via its subsidiary, in the manufacture & sale of sealing compounds for the closure & can industries

BANKERS :
Standard Bank of SA Ltd

AUDITORS :
Deloitte Pim Goldby

FAMILIAR BRAND NAMES
COATES,LORILLEUX CRAY,VALLEY PRODUCTS (CVP)

CONTRIBUTION BY ACTIVITY
N/A

YEAR END : December

DIVIDEND :Ords 50c

Interim No 76	(Ldr)14/09/90	(Pay)15/10/90	Amt(c)16
Final No 77	(Ldr)15/03/91	(Pay)15/05/91	Amt(c)45
Interim No 78	(Ldr)13/09/91	(Pay)15/10/91	Amt(c)19
Final No 79	(Ldr)20/03/92	(Pay)15/05/92	Amt(c)53
Interim No 80	(Ldr)11/09/92	(Pay)15/10/92	Amt(c)21

NUMBER OF EMPLOYEES : 493

CAPITAL STRUCTURE

	AUTHORISED	ISSUED
Ords 50c	6000000	3400000

FINANCIAL STATISTICS (AT FINANCIAL YEAR END)

(Amts in R 000)	1991 Dec	1990 Dec	1989 Dec	1988 Dec	1987 Dec
Ord S/H Int	46836	39882	24807	20663	17061
Long Trm Loans	1951	981	2115	2599	2404
Iss Ord Share	3400	3400	3400	3400	3400
Total Liab	28009	30238	25931	28716	22641
Current Liab	26058	29257	23816	26117	20237
Total Assets	74845	70120	50738	49379	39702
Current Assets	52715	52095	42809	41718	33602
Debtors	21836	21899	18405	13558	11301
Inventory	30638	28808	24389	27964	18168
Turnover	158503	145089	121970	94266	73521
Oper Profit	17741	15469	12127	10090	7425
Interest Paid	466	260	1044	312	209
Tax Paid	8196	7700	5367	5001	3518
Prf af Int&Tax	9442	7928	5791	5007	3714
Prf att Ord Sh	9402	7909	5810	5030	3714
Btm Line Earn	9402	7909	5810	5030	3714
Dividend Paid	2448	2074	1666	1428	1156
Mkt Prce(c) YE	2200	920	650	510	400
Depreciation	2060	1734	1614	1353	1133

PER SHARE STATISTICS (CENTS)

Net Asst Val	1377 53	1173 00	729 62	607 74	501 79
Net Earnings	276 50	232 60	170 90	147 90	109 20
Dividends	72 00	61 00	49 00	42 00	34 00
Cash Flow	370 59	253 85	212 68	190 24	145 79

RATIOS AND OTHER INFORMATION

Mrk Cap(R000)	74800	31280	22100	17340	13600
Current Ratio	2 02	1 78	1 80	1 60	1 66
Quik/Acid Tst	0 85	0 80	0 77	0 53	0 76
A/C Rec T/ovr	7 26	6 63	6 63	6 95	6 51
Tot Ass T/ovr	2 12	2 07	2 40	1 91	1 85
Debt/Ass Rat	0 35	0 42	0 48	0 55	0 54
L T L Tot Ass	0 00	0 01	0 01	0 02	0 03
Debt to Eqity	0 56	0 75	0 99	1 31	1 26
Interest Cover	38 07	59 50	11 62	32 63	35 60
Oper Prof Mrg	11 19	10 66	9 94	10 70	10 10
Net Prof Marg%	5 93	5 45	4 76	5 34	5 05
Ret on Assets	24 19	22 66	24 05	20 90	18 74
Ret on Equity%	20 07	19 83	23 42	24 34	21 77
Price/Earnings	7 96	3 96	3 80	3 45	3 66
Divid Cover	3 84	3 81	3 49	3 52	3 21
Divid Yield	3 27	6 63	7 54	8 24	8 50
Earning Yield%	12 57	25 28	26 29	29 00	27 30
NAV % Mrk Pr	62 61	127 50	112 25	119 16	125 45
Effec Tax Rate	40 02	55 77	49 97	49 47	48 05
Def Interval	0 30	0 09	0 31	0 65	0 36
Sus Grth Rate	14 85	14 63	16 70	17 43	14 99

SUBSIDIARY & ASSOCIATED COMPANIES

COATES BROTHERS PLC (UK)
COATES CHEMIE COMPOUNDS (PTY) LTD

INVESTMENTS

None

COMBINED MOTOR HOLDINGS LTD

ABBREVIATION : CMH

JSE SHORT CODE : CMH

SECTOR : Industrial Motor

SHAREHOLDERS

Who Owns Whom's Assessment of the Identity of the Ultimate Controlling Shareholder
DIRECTORS

SHAREHOLDER	PERCENTAGE 1992	1991
MALDWYN ZIMMERMAN INV HLDGS CO P/L	38 7	38 7
JEBB MCINTOSH INV HLDGS CO P/L	17 3	17 3
CMH TRUST	5 1	5 2
FIRST NAT NOM P/L	4 8	4 8
CMB NOM P/L	3 8	
SA MUTUAL	3 6	3 6
SKJ FAMILY HOLDINGS P/L	3 4	3 1
MCINTOSH J	3 1	3 1
ZIMMERMAN M	2 9	3 1
ZIMMERMAN A L	2 6	2 6
STD BANK NOM TVL P/L	1 9	
HALL G W	1 5	
EMZED CC	1 3	
AA MUTUAL LIFE ASSURE ASSOC LTD		1 8
SANLAM		5 5
TOTAL	89 9	88 8

DIRECTORS .
JACKSON SK ,MCINTOSH JD ,SCHAFFER AL
ZIMMERMAN M (Chairman & Managing Dir

REGISTRATION NUMBER 65/00270/06

REGISTERED OFFICE
1st Floor, CMH Building, 206 West Street
Durban
4001
TEL 031-37 8281
FAX 031-37 4411

TRANSFER SECRETARY
Central Registrars Ltd
P O Box 4844, Johannesburg
2000
TEL 011 331 0051

COMPANY SECRETARY
S K Jackson

NATURE OF BUSINESS
An investment holding company with subsidiaries operating in the retail motor trade The group holds franchises for the sale of Ford, Toyota, Nissan/Uno, MMI, Delta & Mercedes Benz/Honda products

BANKERS :
First National Bank of SA Ltd

AUDITORS :
N/A

FAMILIAR BRAND NAMES
DATCENTRE NISSAN, KEMPSTER FORD
MERCRON MOTORS, METRO MMI
MMI (MAZDA/MITSUBISHI), ROODEPOORT DELTA
STEYNS FORD, WHITEHOUSE TOYOTA, ZULULAND DELTA

CONTRIBUTION BY ACTIVITY
New Vehicles (% operating income) (31 0%)
Used Vehicles (22 0%)
Parts (34 0%)
Service (11 0%)
Investment/Other (2 0%)
Ford (% Income from Franchise) (42 0%)
Nissan/Uno (27 0%)
MMI (10 0%)
Delta (9 0%)
Mercedes/Honda (7 0%)
Toyota (5 0%)

YEAR END : February

DIVIDEND : Ords no par value

Interim No 5	(Ldr)01/12/89	(Pay)22/12/89	Amt(c)4
Final No 6	(Ldr)11/05/90	(Pay)15/06/90	Amt(c)6 7
Interim No 7	(Ldr)30/11/90	(Pay)21/12/90	Amt(c)3
Final No 8	(Ldr)10/05/91	(Pay)14/06/91	Amt(c)7 7
Interim No 9	(Ldr)29/11/91	(Pay)20/12/91	Amt(c)2 1
Final No 10	(Ldr)08/05/92	(Pay)12/06/92	Amt(c)7 2

NUMBER OF EMPLOYEES : 1032

CAPITAL STRUCTURE

	AUTHORISED	ISSUED
Ords no par value	58748400	19000000
7,5% 'C Red Cum Prefs R1	1032400	516200

FINANCIAL STATISTICS (AT FINANCIAL YEAR END)

(Amts in R 000)	1992 Feb	1991 Feb	1990 Feb	1989 Feb	1988 Feb
Ord S/H Int	29805	28393	26423	24960	20120
Long Trm Loans	1504	1737	2584	1417	1585
Iss Ord Share	19000	19000	19000	19000	19000
Total Liab	51143	40588	41190	39436	27717
Current Liab	49639	38851	38606	38019	26132
Total Assets	79396	66944	66953	64396	47837
Intang Assets	1552	2037	660	*	*
Current Assets	73625	60603	62149	60919	44685
Debtors	16743	13548	14076	14471	8461
Inventory	52611	41543	44761	43221	29911
Turnover	416300	367077	370323	314784	221858
Oper Profit	9119	10902	14043	14503	10019
Interest Paid	3756	4925	5350	2326	1252
Tax Paid	2291	4100	5240	5824	4287
Prf af Int&Tax	3721	4265	5368	6353	4480
Prf att Ord Sh	3678	4234	5324	6299	4418
Btm Line Earn	3166	4003	3496	6873	3997
Dividend Paid	1767	2033	2033	2033	1482
Mkt Prce(c) YE	60	90	135	140	170
Depreciation	1411	981	650	530	347

PER SHARE STATISTICS (CENTS)

Net Asst Val	148 70	138 72	135 59	131 37	105 89
Net Earnings	19 40	22 30	28 00	33 20	23 60
Dividends	9 30	10 70	10 70	10 70	7 80
Cash Flow	26 76	28 91	31 32	35 73	22 74

RATIOS AND OTHER INFORMATION

Mrk Cap(R000)	11400	17100	25650	26600	32300
Current Ratio	1 48	1 56	1 61	1 60	1 71
Quik/Acid Tst	0 42	0 49	0 45	0 47	0 57
A/C Rec T/ovr	24 86	27 09	26 31	21 75	26 22
Tot Ass T/ovr	5 24	5 48	5 53	4 89	4 64
Debt/Ass Rat	0 63	0 58	0 58	0 59	0 55
L T L Tot Ass	-		-	0 00	0 00
Debt to Eqity	1 67	1 37	1 46	1 52	1 31
Interest Cover	2 43	2 21	2 62	6 24	8 00
Oper Prof Mrg	2 19	2 97	3 79	4 61	4 52
Net Prof Marg%	0 88	1 15	1 44	2 00	1 99
Ret on Assets	12 30	19 89	23 87	22 56	20 98
Ret on Equity%	12 34	14 91	20 15	25 24	21 96
Price/Earnings	3 09	4 04	4 82	4 22	7 20
Divid Cover	2 09	2 08	2 62	3 10	3 03
Divid Yield	15 50	11 89	7 93	7 64	4 59
Earning Yield%	32 33	24 78	20 74	23 71	13 88
NAV % Mrk Pr	247 83	154 13	100 44	93 83	62 29
Effec Tax Rate	38 17	45 18	49 40	45 26	54 55
Def Interval	1 54	0 55	1 49	1 31	1 18
Sus Grth Rate	6 41	7 75	12 46	17 09	14 59

SUBSIDIARY & ASSOCIATED COMPANIES

AUTO RENOVATORS (PTY) LTD
COMBINED MOTOR FINANCE (PTY) LTD (50%)
COMCAR MOTORS (PTY) LTD
DATCENTRE MOTORS (PTY) LTD
KEMPSTER SEDGWICK (PTY) LTD
LEASECOR AFRICA (PTY) LTD
MERCRON AFRICA (PTY) LTD
SIGMA FINANCE CORPORATION (PTY) LTD
WHITEHOUSE MOTORS (PTY) LTD

INVESTMENTS

None

COMMERCIAL & INDUSTRIAL HOLDINGS LTD (ZIMBABWE)

ABBREVIATION : CIH

SECTOR : Zimbabwe Stock Exchange

SHAREHOLDERS

Who Owns Whom's Assessment of the Identity of the Ultimate Controlling Shareholder:
ANGLO AMERICAN

SHAREHOLDER	PERCENTAGE 1992	1991
SECURITY TECHNOLOGY HOLDINGS LTD	30 7	

NRZ CONTRIBUTORY PENS FUND	25 6	---
FIRST NOM PVT LTD	9 5	---
CARSAN INV CO (PVT) LTD	6 2	- -
OLD MUTUAL INV CORP (PVT) LTD	4 0	---
MINING INDUSTRY PENS FUND	2 6	---
FIDELITY LIFE ASSURE OF ZIM PVT LTD	2 5	---
FRANCIS MINELECT PROPERTIES PVT LTD	1 5	---
FINANCIAL SERVICES (PVT) LTD	1 2	---
TOTAL	83 8	---

DIRECTORS :
CHITRIN RH ,KING RD ,MACDONALD NJ ,MCCLELLAND AH
NICHOLSON R ,PERATT RH (Managing Director)
THOMPSON AC (Chairman),WALSH F ,WISHART AB

REGISTERED OFFICE
First Floor, 104 George Silundika Street
Bulawayo, Zimbabwe

TEL 70636

TRANSFER SECRETARY
CIH Trading & Finance (Pvt) Ltd
P O Box 1342, Bulawayo
Zimbabwe

TEL 092634-70636

COMPANY SECRETARY
K J Scott

NATURE OF BUSINESS
COMMERCIAL & INDUSTRIAL HOLDINGS is the parent of a group operating in Zimbabwe in the clothing,textile, button, furniture and printing industries, the motor, wholesale trade and fencing sector

BANKERS :
N/A

AUDITORS :
Coopers & Lybrand

FAMILIAR BRAND NAMES
N/A

CONTRIBUTION BY ACTIVITY
N/A

YEAR END : December

DIVIDEND :Ords Z$0,25

Dividend	(Ldr)20/03/92	(Pay)27/04/92	Amt(c)3 10
Dividend	(Ldr)07/09/92	(Pay)09/10/92	Amt(c)1 60

CAPITAL STRUCTURE

	AUTHORISED	ISSUED
Ords Z$0,25	80000000	68000000

FINANCIAL STATISTICS (AT FINANCIAL YEAR END)

(Amts in Z$)	1991 Dec	1990 Dec
Ord S/H Int	41249	21255
Long Trm Loans	14392	15969
Iss Ord Share	68000	17000
Total Liab	45347	40133
Current Liab	30955	24164
Total Assets	86596	61388
Current Assets	54648	33702
Debtors	22169	15767
Inventory	25169	17057
Turnover	103367	69713
Oper Profit	15328	11030
Interest Paid	3356	1689
Tax Paid	4962	3910
Prf af Int&Tax	7194	5478
Prf att Ord Sh	7178	5468
Btm Line Earn	7178	5168
Dividend Paid	2924	1790
Depreciation	1850	1413

PER SHARE STATISTICS (CENTS)

Net Asst Val	60 66	125 03
Net Earnings	13 60	11 60
Dividends	4 70	3 70
Cash Flow	14 49	58 29

RATIOS AND OTHER INFORMATION

Current Ratio	1 77	1 39
Quik/Acid Tst	0 95	0 69
A/C Rec T/ovr	4 66	4 42
Tot Ass T/ovr	1 19	1 14
Debt/Ass Rat	0 43	0 53
L T L Tot Ass	0 07	0 13
Debt to Eqity	0 90	1 52
Interest Cover	4 57	6 53
Oper Prof Mrg	14 83	15 82
Net Prof Marg%	6 94	7 84
Ret on Assets	17 91	18 04
Ret on Equity%	17 40	25 73
Divid Cover	2 89	3 14
Effec Tax Rate	37 14	12 77
Def Interval	1 98	2 05
Sus Grth Rate	10 31	17 30

SUBSIDIARY & ASSOCIATED COMPANIES

BULAWAYO CLOTHING (PTY) LTD
C I H TRADING & FINANCE (PTY) LTD
HART INVESTMENTS (PTY) LTD
INGWE PROPERTY (PTY) LTD
MASTERBUILD (PTY) LTD
REGENT INVICTA (PTY) LTD (ZIMBABWE)
VERO GARMENTS (PTY) LTD

INVESTMENTS

None

COMMERCIAL FINANCE CO LTD

ABBREVIATION : CFC

JSE SHORT CODE : CFC

SECTOR : Development Capital Market

SHAREHOLDERS

Who Owns Whom's Assessment of the Identity of the Ultimate Controlling Shareholder:
DIRECTORS & ASSOCIATES

DIRECTORS :
BIDEN PN ,DAUGHERTY DE ,MCADAM WJ ,SWAIN WJ
VAN DER POL C DR (Chairman

REGISTRATION NUMBER : 02/00264/06

REGISTERED OFFICE
1100 Mansion House, 12 Field Street
Durban
4001
TEL: 031-304 3481
FAX: 031-304 2670

TRANSFER SECRETARY
Natal Registrars (Pty) Ltd
P O Box 548, Durban
4000
TEL: 031-305 2781

COMPANY SECRETARY
Natal Registrars (Pty) ltd

NATURE OF BUSINESS
An investment holding company. The company's major assets are investments in subsidiaries with shares in listed and unlisted companies and property, a 72% interest in quoted Congella Federation, and a 53% interest in Communication Engineering group, which is engaged in civil engineering, electrical & telecommunication contracting & manufacture & sale of related products, sandwinning & a foundry.

BANKERS :
First National Bank of SA Ltd

AUDITORS :
Price Waterhouse Meyernel

FAMILIAR BRAND NAMES
N/A

CONTRIBUTION BY ACTIVITY
Investments (% Income after Tax) (87.0%)
Property (Rentals) (54.0%)
Operations (Sales & Services) (-41.0%)

YEAR END : December

DIVIDEND :Ords 2,5c

Interim No 140	(Ldr)11/10/91	(Pay)25/10/91	Amt(c)8
Final No 141	(Ldr)16/04/92	(Pay)29/04/92	Amt(c)14
Interim No 142	(Ldr)16/10/92	(Pay)30/10/92	Amt(c)8

CAPITAL STRUCTURE

	AUTHORISED	ISSUED
Ords 2,5c	11000000	9920400
6% Cum Prefs R2	75000	50000
7% Cum Prefs R2	50000	30272

FINANCIAL STATISTICS (AT FINANCIAL YEAR END)

(Amts in R'000)	1991 Dec	1990 Dec	1989 Dec	1988 Dec	1987 Dec
Ord S/H Int	48555	47164	41694	33461	32524
Long Trm Loans	10172	8008	7272	5858	4135
Iss Ord Share	9920	9920	9920	9920	9920
Total Liab	21806	14481	15076	12200	7649
Current Liab	11634	6473	7804	6342	3514
Total Assets	68361	61645	56770	45661	40173
Intang Assets	2000	*	*	*	*
Current Assets	8780	6519	9324	9150	7569
Debtors	5296	3397	6058	3683	1925
Inventory	1693	1289	2023	4758	4085
Oper Profit	3179	2585	4064	2470	2001
Interest Paid	1447	860	648	294	21
Tax Paid	2719	1805	1556	1640	1069
Prf af Int&Tax	2530	3773	4509	3345	2396
Prf att Ord Sh	3497	4095	4059	2584	2354
Btm Line Earn	3497	4095	4059	2584	2354
Dividend Paid	2182	2182	2084	1697	1498
Mkt Prce(c) YE	740	500	600	400	400
Depreciation	1505	1409	874	723	548

PER SHARE STATISTICS (CENTS)

Net Asst Val	469.30	475.44	420.30	337.31	327.86
Net Earnings	35.30	41.30	40.90	25.90	23.60
Dividends	22.00	22.00	21.00	17.00	15.00
Cash Flow	52.33	54.45	50.26	40.56	29.81

RATIOS AND OTHER INFORMATION

Mrk Cap(R000)	73408	49600	59520	39680	39680
Current Ratio	0.75	1.01	1.19	1.44	2.15
Quik/Acid Tst	0.61	0.81	0.94	0.69	0.99
Debt/Ass Rat	0.25	0.14	0.16	0.16	0.09
L T L Tot Ass	0.08	0.04	0.02	0.03	-
Debt to Eqity	0.36	0.19	0.22	0.22	0.11
Interest Cover	4.63	7.49	10.36	17.96	166.00
Ret on Assets	9.70	10.77	11.82	10.62	8.54
Ret on Equity%	7.20	8.68	9.74	7.72	7.24
Price/Earnings	20.96	12.11	14.67	15.44	16.95
Divid Cover	1.60	1.88	1.95	1.52	1.57
Divid Yield	2.97	4.40	3.50	4.25	3.75
Earning Yield%	4.77	8.26	6.82	6.48	5.90
NAV % Mrk Pr	63.42	95.09	70.05	84.33	81.97
Effec Tax Rate	143.76	98.78	44.00	62.18	53.99
Def Interval	1.69	0.59	0.89	0.52	0.23
Sus Grth Rate	2.71	4.06	4.74	2.65	2.63

SUBSIDIARY & ASSOCIATED COMPANIES

ALBATROSS INVESTMENT LTD
AUBERO (PTY) LTD
BAYSIDE LTD
BDP PROPERTIES NO. 1 (PTY) LTD
BRITISH MOTORS FINANCE CORP. (PTY) LTD
CARRONADE INVESTMENTS LTD
CFC INVESTMENT TRUST CO LTD
CFC OPERATIONS LTD
CFC PROPERTY HOLDINGS LTD
CHEMICON NATURAL PRODUCTS (PTY) LTD (27.20%)
COMM. ENGINEERING (SWAZILAND) (PTY) LTD
COMMUNICATION ENGINEERING LTD
CONGELLA FEDERATION LTD
CONGELLA STORES LTD
CONMEAD (PTY) LTD
CONTRAIL (PTY) LTD
CONWEST (PTY) LTD
DEBEN LTD
ELEK TEL (PTY) LTD
HARBANK INVESTMENTS LTD
LOUWARDS ENGINEERING CO. (PTY) LTD
MARITZBURG MOTOR CO. (PTY) LTD
MAZAL INVESTMENTS LTD
MENTEITH INVESTMENTS LTD
NORTH & OSBORNE (PTY) LTD
NORTHCOTE INVESTMENTS LTD
OXFORD AUTO SERVICES (PTY) LTD
UNIPLAN (PTY) LTD
XMECO FOUNDRY (PTY) LTD (27,2%)

INVESTMENTS

ANGLO AMERICAN CORPORATION OF SA LTD (73700 SH)
ANGLO AMERICAN INVESTMENT TRUST LTD (28000 SH)
BARLOW RAND LTD (28585 SH)
BOARD OF EXECUTORS (190802 SH)
BTR DUNLOP LTD (2580 SH)
CG SMITH FOODS LTD (6759 SH)
CG SMITH LTD (22532 SH)

COATES BROTHERS (SA) (20600 SH)
DE BEERS CENTENARY LINKED UNITS (12000 SH)
DRIEFONTEIN CONSOLIDATED (7710 SH)
EAST RAND GOLD & URANIUM CO (12500 SH)
EDWARD L BATEMAN (18400 SH)
FIRST NATIONAL BANK HOLDINGS LTD (2931 SH)
GENBEL INVESTMENTS (353000 SH)
GENCOR LTD (136890 SH)
GOLDFIELDS COAL LTD (3300 SH)
H J JOEL GOLD MINING CO LTD (14800 SH)
HIGHVELD STEEL & VANADIUM CORP LTD (10000 SH)
IMPALA PLATINUM HOLDINGS LTD (10000 SH)
INDUSTRIAL & COMMERCIAL HOLDINGS GROUP (338790 SH)
JOHANNESBURG CONSOLIDATED INVESTMENT COM (100000 SH)
KINROSS MINES LTD (5000 SH)
KLOOF GOLD MINING COMPANY LTD (FINANCIA (7000 SH)
MCCARTHY GROUP LTD (595000 SH)
MURRAY & ROBERTS INVESTMENTS LTD (14700 SH)
NBS HOLDINGS LTD (45000 SH)
NEDCOR LTD (47000 SH)
OVBEL HOLDINGS LTD (2129000 SH)
RUSTENBURG PLATINUM HOLDINGS (12754 SH)
SAPPI LTD (31875 SH)
SASOL LTD (40000 SH)
SOUTHVAAL HOLDINGS LTD (8848 SH)
SPECIALITY STORE CO LTD, THE (587178 SH)
STANDARD BANK INVESTMENT CORP (3081 SH)
STORECO LTD (599963 SH)
SUN PACKAGING INVESTMENTS LTD (182000 SH)
TONGAAT-HULETT GROUP LTD (1122679 SH)
VAAL REEFS EXPLORATION & MINING CO LTD (2108 SH)
WESTERN DEEP LEVELS LTD (2200 SH)

COMMERCIAL UNION OF SA LTD

ABBREVIATION : CUSAF

JSE SHORT CODE : CUA

SECTOR : Financial-Insurance

SHAREHOLDERS

Who Owns Whom's Assessment of the Identity of the Ultimate Controlling Shareholder: COMMERCIAL UNION ASSURE PLC / ABSA

SHAREHOLDER	PERCENTAGE 1992	1991
COMMERCIAL UNION ASSURE CO PLC	36 0	---
AMALGAMATED BANKS OF SA LTD	30 0	---
MINU NOM LTD	24 1	24 1
DRURY A M	2 7	---
COMMERCIAL UNION SA STAFF PENS FUND	1 1	1 1
COMMERCIAL UNION ASSURE CO SA LTD	---	36 0
MOMENTUM LIFE ASSURE LTD	-	1 5
UBS HOLDINGS LTD	---	30 0
TOTAL	93 9	92 6

DIRECTORS :
BADENHORST PJ ,BREND AL ,DE BLANCHE EM
DE WET CPC THE HON,FULLER-GOOD MR
GNODDE AMD (Chairman)
KINVIG JA (Managing Director),RATTRAY JS
RUTHERFORD WA ,WRIGHT AJ

REGISTRATION NUMBER : 64/06856/06

REGISTERED OFFICE
Commercial Union House, 26 Loveday Street
Johannesburg
2001
TEL 011-491 1911
FAX 011-838 2600

TRANSFER SECRETARY
Gold Fields of SA Ltd
P O Box 1167, Johannesburg
2000
TEL 011-639 9111

COMPANY SECRETARY
R R McL Wanless

NATURE OF BUSINESS
The group transacts all classes of short- & long-term insurance and pension business Revenue is also derived from the investment of funds

BANKERS :
N/A

AUDITORS :
Coopers Theron Du Toit

FAMILIAR BRAND NAMES
N/A

CONTRIBUTION BY ACTIVITY
Life & Pensions (% premiums written) (50 9%)
Fire, Accident & Marine (49 1%)

YEAR END : December

DIVIDEND : Ords 50c

Interim No 35	(Ldr)18/08/89	(Pay)22/09/89	Amt(c)30
Final No 36	(Ldr)09/03/90	(Pay)11/04/90	Amt(c)65
Interim No 37	(Ldr)17/08/90	(Pay)21/09/90	Amt(c)35
Final No 38	(Ldr)15/03/91	(Pay)17/04/91	Amt(c)70
Interim No 39	(Ldr)16/08/91	(Pay)20/09/91	Amt(c)42
Final No 40	(Ldr)13/03/92	(Pay)15/04/92	Amt(c)100
Interim No 41	(Ldr)21/08/92	(Pay)25/09/92	Amt(c)50

NUMBER OF EMPLOYEES : 1350

CAPITAL STRUCTURE

	AUTHORISED	ISSUED
Ords 50c	10000000	10000000

FINANCIAL STATISTICS (AT FINANCIAL YEAR END)

(Amts in R'000)	1991 Dec	1990 Dec	1989 Dec	1988 Dec	1987 Dec
Ord S/H Int	365063	280529	233492	162958	87176
Long Trm Loans	230263	186474	200449	142936	118717
Iss Ord Share	10000	10000	10000	10000	8000
Total Liab	606082	443623	338924	269657	217791
Current Liab	375819	257149	138475	126721	99074
Total Assets	971145	724152	572416	432615	304967
Current Assets	339595	209147	48937	57467	50917
Debtors	249133	131251	32793	30271	30098
Oper Profit	58876	27258	50508	31244	14967
Tax Paid	9555	-1887	11777	-	-
Prf af Int&Tax	49321	29145	38731	31244	14967
Prf att Ord Sh	48842	29138	38731	31244	14967
Btm Line Earn	48842	29138	38731	31244	14967
Dividend Paid	14200	10500	9500	7500	4560
Mkt Prce(c) YE	3100	2325	1600	1250	1900

PER SHARE STATISTICS (CENTS)

Net Asst Val	3650.63	2805.29	2334.92	1629.58	1089.70
Net Earnings	488.40	291.40	387.30	312.40	187.10
Dividends	142.00	105.00	95.00	75.00	57.00
Cash Flow	488.42	291.38	387.31	312.44	187.09

RATIOS AND OTHER INFORMATION

Mrk Cap(R000)	310000	232500	160000	125000	152000
Current Ratio	0.90	0.81	0.35	0.45	0.51
Quik/Acid Tst	0.90	0.81	0.35	0.45	0.51
Debt/Ass Rat	0.39	0.36	0.24	0.29	0.32
Debt to Eqity	1.03	0.92	0.59	0.78	1.14
Ret on Assets	6.06	3.76	8.82	7.22	4.91
Ret on Equity%	13.38	10.39	16.59	19.17	17.17
Price/Earnings	6.35	7.98	4.13	4.00	10.15
Divid Cover	3.44	2.78	4.08	4.17	3.28
Divid Yield	4.58	4.52	5.94	6.00	3.00
Earning Yield%	15.75	12.53	24.21	24.99	9.85
NAV % Mrk Pr	117.76	120.66	145.93	130.37	57.35
Effec Tax Rate	16.23	-7.15	23.32	-	-
Def Interval	5.41	6.51	-	-	-
Sus Grth Rate	9.49	6.64	12.52	14.57	11.94

SUBSIDIARY & ASSOCIATED COMPANIES

COMMERCIAL UNION INVESTMENTS SA LTD
COMMERCIAL UNION TRADE FINANCE (PTY) LTD
COMMERCIAL UNION UNIT TRUST MANAGEMENT C
KELVIN PLANE MOTORHAWE (EINDOMS) BEPERK
PORTION 8 OF LOT 30 SANDOWN (PTY) LTD
TERAMA (PTY) LTD

INVESTMENTS

None

COMMON FUND INVESTMENT SOCIETY LTD

ABBREVIATION : COM-FUND

JSE SHORT CODE : CFI

SECTOR : Financial-Investment Trusts

SHAREHOLDERS

Who Owns Whom's Assessment of the Identity of the Ultimate Controlling Shareholder: SA MUTUAL / DIRECTORS

SHAREHOLDER	PERCENTAGE 1992	1991
SA MUTUAL	34.8	34.7
HAYREES P/L	20.9	18.9
DOREG INV P/L	13.4	15.0
MUTUAL & FEDERAL INSURANCE CO LTD	6.9	6.5
KOMMETJE ESTATES LTD	3.9	3.9
FAIRHEADS NOM P/L	1.7	1.4
STD BANK NOM TVL P/L	1.7	---
VAN DER HORST J G	1.6	1.6
BOARD OF EXECUTORS NOM P/L	---	1.5
TOTAL	84.8	83.5

DIRECTORS :
GODLEY GH ,PARKER RDM (Deputy Chairman)
VAN DER HORST JC DR,VAN DER HORST JG DR (Chairman

REGISTRATION NUMBER : 05/06353/06

REGISTERED OFFICE
1505 Pleinpark, Plein Street
Cape Town
8001
TEL: 021-461 1060
FAX: 021-462 2256

TRANSFER SECRETARY
Fraser Street Registrars (Pty) Ltd
P O Box 61178, Marshalltown
2107
TEL: 011-491 0911

COMPANY SECRETARY
M D Emmett

NATURE OF BUSINESS
Investment company, with various interests mainly in companies whose shares are listed on the Stock Exchange.

BANKERS :
Standard Bank of SA Ltd

AUDITORS :
Coopers Theron Du Toit

FAMILIAR BRAND NAMES
N/A

CONTRIBUTION BY ACTIVITY
Dividends (% Total Income) (92.9%)
Interest (7.1%)

YEAR END : March

DIVIDEND : Ords 10c

Interim No 76	(Ldr)05/01/90	(Pay)02/02/90	Amt(c)45
Final No 77	(Ldr)26/06/90	(Pay)25/07/90	Amt(c)72
Interim No 78	(Ldr)04/01/91	(Pay)01/02/91	Amt(c)66
Final No 79	(Ldr)22/02/91	(Pay)28/02/91	Amt(c)130
Interim No 80	(Ldr)06/09/91	(Pay)23/09/91	Amt(c)66
Final No 81	(Ldr)14/02/92	(Pay)28/02/92	Amt(c)130
Interim No 82	(Ldr)04/09/92	(Pay)09/10/92	Amt(c)66

CAPITAL STRUCTURE

	AUTHORISED	ISSUED
Ords 10c	10000000	7392236
11% Red Cum Prefs R1	10000000	10000000

FINANCIAL STATISTICS (AT FINANCIAL YEAR END)

(Amts in R'000)	1992 Mar	1991 Mar	1990 Mar	1989 Mar	1988 Mar
Ord S/H Int	642117	484883	472975	338667	206697
Long Trm Loans	10000	10000	10000	10000	-
Iss Ord Share	7321	7321	7321	7321	7321
Total Liab	10558	10896	15868	14899	3475
Current Liab	558	896	5868	4899	3475
Total Assets	652675	495779	488843	353566	210172
Current Assets	3446	6422	7728	9296	8443
Debtors	399	151	1404	1682	138
Oper Profit	-396	-347	-306	-	11086
Tax Paid	685	996	678	570	541
Prf af Int&Tax	19373	18852	18086	14085	10545
Prf att Ord Sh	18273	17752	16986	12985	9445

Btm Line Earn	18273	17752	16986	12985	9445
Dividend Paid	14348	14345	8565	6515	4758
Mkt Prce(c) YE	6250	4400	4100	2700	1500

PER SHARE STATISTICS (CENTS)

Net Asst Val	8770 89	6623 18	6460 52	4625 97	2823 34
Net Earnings	249 60	242 50	232 00	117 40	129 00
Dividends	196 00	196 00	117 00	89 00	65 00
Cash Flow	249 60	242 48	232 02	177 37	129 01

RATIOS AND OTHER INFORMATION

Mrk Cap(R000)	457563	322124	300161	197667	109815
Current Ratio	6 18	7 17	1 32	1 90	2 43
Quik/Acid Tst	6 18	7 17	1 32	1 90	2 43
Debt/Ass Rat	0 00	0 00	0 01	0 01	0 02
Debt to Eqity	0 00	0 00	0 01	0 01	0 02
Ret on Assets	3 07	4 00	3 84	4 14	5 27
Ret on Equity%	2 85	3 66	3 59	3 83	4 57
Price/Earnings	25 04	18 14	17 67	23 00	11 63
Divid Cover	1 27	1 24	1 98	1 32	1 98
Divid Yield	3 14	4 45	2 85	3 30	4 33
Earning Yield%	3 99	5 51	5 66	4 35	8 60
NAV % Mrk Pr	140 33	150 53	157 57	171 33	188 22
Effec Tax Rate	64 68	59 89	63 31	49 35	4 88
Def Interval	0 55	0 56	0 59	0 77	-
Sus Grth Rate	0 61	0 70	1 78	1 91	2 27

SUBSIDIARY & ASSOCIATED COMPANIES

None

INVESTMENTS

ADCOCK INGRAM (45980 SH)
AECI (15000 SH)
AMALGAMATED BANK OF SA LIMITED (200000SH)
ANGLO AMERICAN COAL CORP LTD (150000 SH)
ANGLO AMERICAN CORP OF SA (165200 SH)
ANGLO AMERICAN GOLD INVESTMENT (25000 SH)
ANGLO AMERICAN INDUSTRIAL CORP LTD (10000 SH)
ANGLO AMERICAN INVESTMENT TRUST LTD (80000 SH)
ANGLO ALPHA (205008 SH)
BARLOW RAND (1656481 SH)
BARLOW RAND PROPERTIES (500000 SH)
BLUE CIRCLE (9562 SH)
C G SMITH SUGAR LTD (200000 SH)
CG SMITH FOODS (1000000 SH)
DE BEERS/CENTENARY LINKED UNITS (301000 SH)
DORBYL (34500 SH)
DRIEFONTEIN CONSOLIDATED (254814 SH)
EAST RAND GOLD & URANIUM CO (200000 SH)
EVERITE GROUP (30000 SH)
EVERITE HOLDINGS (30000 SH)
FIRST NATIONAL BANK HOLDINGS LTD (200000 SH)
GENBEL INVESTMENT (345000 SH)
GENCOR LTD (274170 SH)
GOLDFIELDS OF SOUTH AFRICA (110919 SH)
IMPALA PLATINUM HOLDINGS LTD FI (200000 SH)
KERSAF INVESTMENTS (100000 SH)
LEBOWA PLATINUM MINES (32244 SH)
LONGMILE (500000 SH)
METROPOLITAN LIFE LTD (0 3%)
MURRAY & ROBERTS HOLDINGS LTD - F (34768 SH)
NAMPAK (14786 SH)
NEDCOR (750000 SH)
PALABORA MINING CO LTD (150000 SH)
POTGIETERSRUST PLATINUM (50124 SH)
PRETORIA PORTLAND CEMENT (300000 SH)
PRIMROSE GOLD MINES (14,99%)
REMBRANDT GROUP (962200 SH)
RICHEMONT SECURITIES AG (962200 SH)
RUSTENBURG PLATINUM HOLDINGS (58625 SH)
SAFMARINE & RENNIES HOLDINGS LTD (610713 SH)
SAMANCOR LTD (1800000 SH)
SAPPI (45750 SH)
SASOL (600000 SH)
SOUTH AFRICAN BREWERIES (583550 SH)
SOUTHVAAL HOLDINGS (31500 SH)
STANDARD BANK INVESTMENT CORPORATION (587492 SH)
TIGER OATS (230000 SH)
VAAL REEFS EXPLORATION & MINING CO LTD (5000 SH)
WESTERN DEEP LEVELS (30000 SH)
WOOLTRU LTD ("A" ORDS) (500000 SH)

COMPASS PROPERTY HOLDINGS LTD

ABBREVIATION : COMPASS

JSE SHORT CODE : CPS

SECTOR : Financial-Property Loan Stock

SHAREHOLDERS

Who Owns Whom's Assessment of the Identity of the Ultimate Controlling Shareholder: ANGLO AMERICAN VIA AMAPROP

SHAREHOLDER	PERCENTAGE 1992	1991
ANGLO AMERICAN PROPERTIES LTD	50 0	50 0
FIRST NAT NOM P/L	10 6	11 4
SAVATKO INV CC	10 3	---
STD BANK NOM TVL P/L	8 3	8 3
VATKO P/L	5 0	4 9
TITAN NOM P/L	4 7	4 7
RUBENSTEIN L	2 8	2 8
FOORD & MEINTJES GROUP PROV FUND	1 1	---
WHITFIELD A C	1 1	---
BRODOVCKY FIXED HOLDINGS C C	---	3 4
BROSIM RETPROP STAFF SHARES C C	---	2 3
CHACHA FIXED HOLDINGS CC	---	3 2
WRAGGE J M	---	1 7
GRUFFIN FIXED INV CC	---	3 4
TOTAL	93 9	96 0

DIRECTORS :
BAUM PM ,BIHL JF ,BRAGG WFE ,GARDINER GP
GULLAN AG ,HENREY MJ ,KING MW
LEISSNER GGL (Chairman),LINDOP G
OPPENHEIMER NF ,SUNTER CL ,WHITFIELD AC M

REGISTRATION NUMBER : 87/03591/06

REGISTERED OFFICE
1st Floor, First National Hse, 11 Diagonal Str
Johannesburg
2001
TEL 011-491 9111
FAX 011-838 5136

TRANSFER SECRETARY
Consolidated Share Registrars Ltd
P O Box 61051, Marshalltown
2107
TEL 011-492 1620

COMPANY SECRETARY
Anglo American Property Services (Pty) Ltd

NATURE OF BUSINESS
Compass is a property holding company, owning and letting retail and office accommodation & parking garages.

BANKERS :
First National Bank of SA Ltd
Allied Bank Ltd, Finansbank Ltd
Trust Bank of Africa Ltd

AUDITORS :
Coopers Theron Du Toit

FAMILIAR BRAND NAMES
N/A

CONTRIBUTION BY ACTIVITY
Pretoria (% Geographical Spread) (38 3%)
Cape Town (8 5%)
Randburg/Roodepoort (13 7%)
Durban (13 5%)
Bloemfontein (10 8%)
Johannesburg (9 6%)
Potchefstroom (5 6%)

YEAR END : March

DIVIDEND : Ords 1c

Interim No 4	(Ldr)02/03/90	(Pay)30/03/90	Amt(c)33
Final No 5	(Ldr)21/09/90	(Pay)15/10/90	Amt(c)32 5
Interim No 6	(Ldr)15/03/91	(Pay)28/03/91	Amt(c)27
Final No 7	(Ldr)07/06/91	(Pay)25/06/91	Amt(c)17 75
Final No 9	(Ldr)05/06/92	(Pay)25/06/92	Amt(c)31
Interim No 8	(Ldr)22/11/91	(Pay)12/12/91	Amt(c)26 2
Interim No 10	(Ldr)27/11/92	(Pay)21/12/92	Amt(c)29

CAPITAL STRUCTURE

	AUTHORISED	ISSUED
Ords 1c	15000000	8800070
Var Rate Partic Prefs 1c	500000000	0
Conv Def Prefs 1c	50000000	0
Unsec Var Rate Sub Debs R5	53400755	53400755

FINANCIAL STATISTICS (AT FINANCIAL YEAR END)

(Amts in R'000)	1992 Mar	1991 Mar	1990 Jun	1989 Jun	1988 Jun
Ord S/H Int	56555	33879	33773	33580	652
Long Trm Loans	275411	236895	263945	211078	207821
Iss Ord Share	8800	8800	8800	8800	8800
Total Liab	302937	277212	301093	223838	219411
Current Liab	27526	40317	37148	12760	11590
Total Assets	359492	311091	334866	257418	220063
Current Assets	34897	25512	49033	23136	32506
Debtors	6855	15625	27420	10772	18045
Turnover	44345	29624	36728	-	-
Oper Profit	27356	20029	24873	19987	12535
Interest Paid	4743	5895	6369	4195	12381
Tax Paid	-	-	-	-	5
Prf af Int&Tax	25690	18100	22539	19312	149
Prf att Ord Sh	533	467	402	315	149
Btm Line Earn	1622	215	592	315	149
Dividend Paid	484	352	396	308	132
Mkt Prce(c) YE	60	35	45	30	48

PER SHARE STATISTICS (CENTS)

Net Asst Val	642 67	384 99	383 78	381 59	7 41
Net Earnings	6 06	5 31	4 50	3 50	1 50
Dividends	5 50	4 00	4 50	3 50	1 50
Cash Flow	291 93	274 24	256 13	219 45	1 85

RATIOS AND OTHER INFORMATION

Mrk Cap(R000)	5280	3080	3960	2640	4224
Current Ratio	1 27	0 63	1 32	1 81	2 80
Quik/Acid Tst	1 27	0 63	1 32	1 81	2 80
A/C Rec T/ovr	6 47	2 53	1 34	-	-
Tot Ass T/ovr	0 12	0 13	0 11	-	-
Debt/Ass Rat	0 84	0 89	0 90	0 87	1 00
L T L Tot Ass	0 77	0 76	0 79	0 82	0 94
Debt to Eqity	5 36	8 18	8 92	6 67	336 52
Interest Cover	5 77	3 40	3 91	4 76	1 01
Oper Prof Mrg	61 69	67 61	67 72	-	-
Net Prof Marg%	1 20	1 58	1 09	-	-
Ret on Assets	8 47	10 28	8 63	9 13	6 21
Ret on Equity%	0 94	1 84	1 19	0 94	24 93
Price/Earnings	9 90	6 59	10 00	8 57	32 00
Divid Cover	1 10	1 33	1 00	1 00	1 00
Divid Yield	9 17	11 43	10 00	11 67	3 13
Earning Yield%	10 10	15 17	10 00	11 67	3 13
NAV % Mrk Pr	1071 12	1099 97	852 85	1271 97	15 44
Effec Tax Rate	-	-	-	-	3 25
Def Interval	0 34	2 72	2 74	1 96	252 90
Sus Grth Rate	0 09	0 34	0 02	0 02	2 61

SUBSIDIARY & ASSOCIATED COMPANIES

35 WALE STREET PARKING GARAGE SHARE BLOC
COMPASS (MIDDESTAD) SHARE BLOCK (PTY) LT
COMPASS (MONEX) SHARE BLOCK (PTY) LTD
COMPASS (MORKELS) SHARE BLOCK (PTY) LTD
COMPASS (NEWSPAPER HOUSE) SHARE BLOCK (P
COMPASS (POTCHEFSTROOM) SHARE BLOCK (PTY
COMPASS (POYNTONS) SHARE BLOCK (PTY) LTD
COMPASS (ROODEPOORT PLAZA) SHARE BI OCK (
COMPASS (SALMON GROVE) LTD
COMPASS (THOMSON HOUSE) SHARE BLOCK (PTY
COMPASS (THOMSON PARKING) SHARE BLOCK (P
COMPASS (UNIPARK) SHARE BLOCK (PTY) LTD
COMPASS (WALE STREET) SHARE BLOCK (PTY)
COMPASS (WITPOORTJIE) SHARE BLOCK (PTY)
COMPASS FIXED INVESTMENTS LTD
COMPASS FIXED INVESTMENTS NO 3 LTD
COMPASS FIXED INVESTMENTS NO 4 LTD
COMPASS FIXED INVESTMENTS NO 5 LTD
DURBAN STATION SHARE BLOCK LTD
ROBSTOCKS PARKING GARAGE SHARE BLOCK (PT (50%)

INVESTMENTS

None

COMPUTERMATIC HOLDINGS LTD

ABBREVIATION : C-MATIC

JSE SHORT CODE : CTC

SECTOR : Industrial-Electronics, Electrical & Bat

SHAREHOLDERS

Who Owns Whom's Assessment of the Identity of the Ultimate Controlling Shareholder:
EUREKA INDUSTRIAL

SHAREHOLDER	PERCENTAGE 1992	1991
EUREKA INDUSTRIES LTD	56 3	56 3
GROUP INV P/L	31 3	31 3
LLP INV P/L	2 0	2 0
M INV P/L	2 0	2 0
RSP INV P/L	2 0	2 0
TOTAL	93 5	93 5

DIRECTORS :
CRUTCHLEY SW ,GOMER S ,HILLS CS
PRICE RS (Executive Chairman

REGISTRATION NUMBER : 86/02065/06

REGISTERED OFFICE
92 Marlborough Road, Springfield
Johannesburg
2197
TEL 011-683 9323
FAX 683 9662

TRANSFER SECRETARY
Central Registrars Ltd
P O Box 4844, Johannesburg
2000
TEL 011-331 0051

COMPANY SECRETARY
S Gomer

NATURE OF BUSINESS
The group carries on computer operations which are comprised of On line, real-time processing of instalment credit and stock transactions, Distribution & support of packaged software systems for the motor industry, Laser printing for personalised mail shots
The company is currently (March 1992) a cash shell

BANKERS :
Standard Bank of SA Ltd

AUDITORS :
Kessel Feinstein

FAMILIAR BRAND NAMES
C-MATIC SYSTEMS,COMPUTER BUREAU
LASER PRINTING BUREAU

CONTRIBUTION BY ACTIVITY
N/A

YEAR END : February

DIVIDEND : Ords 1c

Final No 8	(Ldr)01/06/90	(Pay)11/06/90	Amt(c)6
Special No 9	(Ldr)01/06/90	(Pay)11/06/90	Amt(c)20

CAPITAL STRUCTURE

	AUTHORISED	ISSUED
Ords 1c	30000000	20475000

FINANCIAL STATISTICS (AT FINANCIAL YEAR END)

(Amts in R'000)	1991 Feb	1990 Feb	1989 Feb	1988 Feb	1987
Ord S/H Int	4950	5483	22550	32332	8799
Long Trm Loans	2629	3334	1831	2354	24611
Iss Ord Share	20475	20475	20475	20475	20475
Total Liab	6716	8817	19745	14769	37006
Current Liab	4087	5483	17914	12415	12395
Total Assets	11666	14300	42295	44181	54999
Intang Assets	*	*	*	2920	*
Current Assets	4570	5544	29717	32660	21589
Debtors	2134	2787	14897	11198	-
Inventory	350	1625	14759	12926	21589
Turnover	17270	19457	55051	55823	53392
Oper Profit	1854	3231	6815	8224	5861
Interest Paid	1473	1138	1106	1382	1253
Tax Paid	-	218	1608	1450	1
Prf af Int&Tax	520	2006	4101	5392	4598
Prf att Ord Sh	520	2006	4101	5392	4598
Btm Line Earn	3562	1291	810	25849	4598
Dividend Paid	4095	2047	6143	2457	2044
Mkt Prce(c) YE	24	75	95	225	720
Depreciation	2656	2622	2759	1810	-

PER SHARE STATISTICS (CENTS)

Net Asst Val	24 18	26 78	110 13	143 65	42 97
Net Earnings	2 50	9 80	20 00	26 30	-
Dividends	20 00	10 00	30 00	12 00	-
Cash Flow	15 51	22 60	34 89	35 17	22 46

RATIOS AND OTHER INFORMATION

Mrk Cap(R000)	4914	15356	19451	46069	147420
Current Ratio	1 12	1 01	1 66	2 63	1 74
Quik/Acid Tst	1 03	0 71	0 83	1 59	-
A/C Rec T/ovr	8 09	6 98	3 70	4 99	-
Tot Ass T/ovr	1 48	1 36	1 30	1 26	0 97
Debt/Ass Rat	0 58	0 62	0 46	0 33	0 67
L T L Tot Ass	0 23	0 23	0 04	0 05	0 45
Debt to Eqity	1 36	1 61	0 86	0 46	4 21
Interest Cover	1 35	2 95	6 16	5 95	4 67
Oper Prof Mrg	10 74	16 61	12 38	14 73	10 98
Net Prof Marg%	3 01	10 31	7 45	9 66	8 61
Ret on Assets	17 08	23 51	16 11	18 61	10 64
Ret on Equity%	10 51	36 59	18 19	16 68	52 26
Price/Earnings	9 60	7 65	4 75	8 56	-
Divid Cover	0 13	0 98	0 67	2 19	-
Divid Yield	83 33	13 33	31 58	5 33	-
Earning Yield%	10 42	13 07	21 05	11 69	-
NAV % Mrk Pr	100 73	35 71	115 93	63 84	5 97
Effec Tax Rate	-	10 42	21 00	20 70	0 02
Def Interval	1 31	1 02	1 11	0 81	5 35
Sus Grth Rate	-72 22	-0 75	9 06	9 08	29 03

SUBSIDIARY & ASSOCIATED COMPANIES

C MATIC COMMUNICATIONS HOLDINGS (PTY) LT
C-MATIC SYSTEMS (PTY) LTD
COMPUTERMATIC (PTY) LTD
COMPUTERMATIC (TRAINING) (PTY) LTD
COMPUTERMATIC BUREAU (PTY) LTD
COMPUTERMATIC PC (CAPE) (PTY) LTD
COMPUTERMATIC PC (PTY) LTD
DION BUSINESS SYSTEMS (PTY) LTD
H LE ROUX & ASSOCIATES (PTY) LTD
H LE ROUX & ASSOCIATES INFORMATION SYSTE
H LE ROUX HOLDINGS (PTY) LTD
IQ 2000 (JOHANNESBURG) (PTY) LTD
IQ 2000 (PRETORIA) (PTY) LTD
IQ 2000 (SOUTH AFRICA) (PTY) LTD
LASER PRINTING BUREAU (PTY) LTD
MICROPHOTO (PTY) LTD
ODYSSEY COMPUTER SERVICES (PTY) LTD
ODYSSEY DATA (PTY) LTD
ODYSSEY FARM COMPUTERS (PTY) LTD
ODYSSEY MICRO SYSTEMS (PTY) LTD
REYNOLDS & REYNOLDS S A LTD
ROGERS & WHITEHOUSE (PTY) LTD

SOUTHERN STATIONERY (PTY) LTD
TRANSVAAL SLATE & TILE COMPANY (PTY) LTD
TRANSVAAL SLATE & TILE SALES (PTY) LTD

INVESTMENTS

EUREKA INDUSTRIAL LTD VAR RATE RED CUM (1000000 SH)

CONCOR LTD

ABBREVIATION : CONCOR

JSE SHORT CODE : CNC

SECTOR : Industrial Building & Construction

SHAREHOLDERS

Who Owns Whom's Assessment of the Identity of the Ultimate Controlling Shareholder:
HOCHTIEF AG GERMANY

SHAREHOLDER	PERCENTAGE 1992	1991
EURAFRICA GNBH	34 8	34 8
STD BANK NOM TVL P/L	11 0	9 9
ROCCON HLDGS A G	10 8	10 4
R H TRUST	7 3	7 7
ATAG ASSET MANAGEMENT LTD	4 6	---
ILSE F G INV P/L	3 8	3 1
MULTITECH P/L	2 9	2 9
KAMACON P/L	2 1	2 1
MASEGRE P/L	1 5	1 5
SERENVEST P/L	1 5	---
FRITIN P/L	1 3	2 4
HASHAY NOM P/L	1 2	7 9
SCHILBACH K G D	1 1	1 1
TOTAL	83 7	83 8

DIRECTORS :
AAB FAW ,FERGUSON PRA ,MURPHY BW (Chairman)
PICCININI F DR,SCHULTZ JJC ,VOCKE EF D

REGISTRATION NUMBER : 69/03076/06

REGISTERED OFFICE
13 Church Street Ext, Crown Industria
Johannesburg
2092
TEL 011-839 2500
FAX 011-837 2255

TRANSFER SECRETARY
Mercantile Registrars Ltd
P O Box 1053, Johannesburg
2000
TEL 011-333 8181

COMPANY SECRETARY
G L Mullany

NATURE OF BUSINESS
An investment holding company with subsidiaries active in the fields of civil, mechanical, mining & electrical engineering, building, earthworks, roads, property development, concrete products, data processing, toll management services and hardware supplies

BANKERS :
Standard Bank of SA Ltd

AUDITORS :
KPMG Aiken & Peat

FAMILIAR BRAND NAMES
N/A

CONTRIBUTION BY ACTIVITY
Concor Construction (% Turnover) (55 0%)
Concor Roads (15 0%)
Concor Engineering (8 0%)
Concor Technicrete (20 0%)
Concor Investments (2 0%)

YEAR END : June

DIVIDEND : Ords 25c

Dividend No 22	(Ldr)29/09/89	(Pay)31/10/89	Amt(c)8
Dividend No 23	(Ldr)28/09/90	(Pay)31/10/90	Amt(c)20
Dividend No 24	(Ldr)15/03/91	(Pay)30/03/91	Amt(c)10
Dividend No 25	(Ldr)27/09/91	(Pay)31/10/91	Amt(c)20
Dividend No 26	(Ldr)13/03/92	(Pay)27/03/92	Amt(c)10

DIVIDEND : Ords 50c

Final No 27	(Ldr)25/09/92	(Pay)30/10/92	Amt(c)20

NUMBER OF EMPLOYEES : 6000

CAPITAL STRUCTURE

	AUTHORISED	ISSUED
Ords 50c	12000000	11408200

FINANCIAL STATISTICS (AT FINANCIAL YEAR END)

(Amts in R'000)	1992 Jun	1991 Jun	1990 Jun	1989 Jun	1988 Jun
Ord S/H Int	51127	44592	35848	26751	22453
Long Trm Loans	11767	10862	9846	4762	5588
Iss Ord Share	11408	11408	11408	11408	11408
Total Liab	162675	138739	122718	121696	104951
Current Liab	150908	127877	112872	116934	99363
Total Assets	213802	183331	158566	148447	127404
Current Assets	184079	154052	131197	121939	101703
Debtors	53341	29699	20641	20922	22635
Inventory	85893	75989	85637	89236	66286
Oper Profit	10937	11636	14065	6076	4026
Interest Paid	2302	1868	1668	1313	-
Tax Paid	8070	6072	4979	-25	613
Prf af Int&Tax	10167	12645	10262	5789	3413
Prf att Ord Sh	10241	12794	10594	5399	2999
Btm Line Earn	9957	12166	11379	5211	2784
Dividend Paid	3422	3422	2282	913	456
Mkt Prce(c) YE	350	180	80	65	75
Depreciation	6568	6258	6761	7137	5640

PER SHARE STATISTICS (CENTS)

Net Asst Val	448 17	390 88	314 24	234 49	196 82
Net Earnings	89 80	112 10	92 90	47 30	28 30
Dividends	30 00	30 00	20 00	8 00	4 00
Cash Flow	154 41	189 17	192 96	104 15	40 87

RATIOS AND OTHER INFORMATION

Mrk Cap(R000)	39928	20534	9126	7415	8556
Current Ratio	1 22	1 20	1 16	1 04	1 02
Quik/Acid Tst	0 65	0 61	0 40	0 28	0 36
Debt/Ass Rat	0 72	0 71	0 74	0 82	0 80
L T L Tot Ass	0 01	0 02	0 03	0 03	0 02

Debt to Eqity	3 01	2 93	3 28	4 54	4 54
Interest Cover	4 95	6 23	8 58	4 63	-
Ret on Assets	9 65	11 32	10 87	4 87	3 26
Ret on Equity%	20 03	28 69	29 55	20 18	13 36
Price/Earnings	3 90	1 61	0 86	1 37	2 65
Divid Cover	2 99	3 74	4 65	5 91	7 08
Divid Yield	8 57	16 67	25 00	12 31	5 33
Earning Yield%	25 66	62 28	116 13	72 77	37 73
NAV % Mrk Pr	128 05	217 16	392 79	360 76	262 42
Effec Tax Rate	40 39	16 79	-0 05	8 24	11 60
Def Interval	0 26	0 24	0 40	0 77	1 02
Sus Grth Rate	13 34	21 02	23 19	16 77	11 33

SUBSIDIARY & ASSOCIATED COMPANIES

AMALGAM ONE THREE NINE (PTY) LTD
ANCOR INDUSTRIES (PTY) LTD
CARWIL (PTY) LTD
CCL SA (PTY) LTD (27%)
COLTOI INVESTMENTS (PTY) LTD (25%)
CONCOR (WESTERN CAPE) (PTY) LTD
CONCOR BOTSWANA (PTY) LTD
CONCOR BUILDING (PTY) LTD
CONCOR CISKEI (PTY) LTD
CONCOR CONSTRUCTION (BOPHUTHATSWANA) (PT
CONCOR CONSTRUCTION (NATAL) (PTY) LTD
CONCOR CONSTRUCTION (SWAZILAND) (PTY) LT
CONCOR CONSTRUCTION (WEST) (PTY) LTD
CONCOR CONSTRUCTION ZIMBABWE (PVT) LTD
CONCOR HOLDINGS (PTY) LTD
CONCOR HOMES (PTY) LTD (50%)
CONCOR INDUSTRIAL (PTY) LTD
CONCOR INVESTMENTS (PTY) LTD
CONCOR IRONCRETE (PTY) LTD
CONCOR LESOTHO (PTY) LTD
CONCOR MINING SUPPLIES (PTY) LTD
CONCOR NAMIBIA (PTY) LTD
CONCOR PAVING PRODUCTS (PTY) LTD
CONCOR PRECAST (PTY) LTD
CONCOR ROADS (PTY) LTD
CONCOR ROADS (TRANSVAAL) (PTY) LTD
CONCOR SA (PTY) LTD
CONCOR SLIDING (PTY) LTD
CONCOR TECHNICRETE (NORTH) (PTY) LTD
CONCOR TECHNICRETE (PTY) LTD
CONCOR TECHNICRETE (PWV) (PTY) LTD
CONCOR TECHNICRETE (QWA QWA) (PTY) LTD
CONCOR TECHNIHIRE (W TVL) (PTY) LTD
CONCOR TECNICRETE (E TVL) (PTY) LTD
CONCOR TRANSKEI (PTY) LTD
DATAPLAN (PTY) LTD
DUNAMEN ENGINEERING (PTY) LTD
ECON PROPERTIES (PTY) LTD
ELECTRO NETWORK (PTY) LTD
EPWING ENGINEERING TRADING (PTY) LTD (27%)
ERF 936 FOCHVILLE (PTY) LTD
EXECON CONSTRUCTION PROJECTS (PTY) LTD
EXEPLANT HIRE (PTY) LTD
FOUR FACTORIA STREET (PTY) LTD
FOUR NINE EIGHT SECUNDA (PTY) LTD
GEORGE AND ERIK INVESTMENTS (PTY) LTD
GILLWAL INVESTMENTS (PTY) LTD
GREY IMPACT (PTY) LTD (33%)
H T CONSTRUCTION (PTY) LTD
INTERNATIONAL PROJECT SERVICES (PTY) LTD
MAN DIRK (PTY) LTD (30%)
MECHANIPLAN (PTY) LTD
MEMEC (PTY) LTD
MINE LINE (PTY) LTD (30%)
NEW THIRD INVESTMENTS (PTY) LTD (20%)
NOCOR (PTY) LTD
NOROC PROPERTIES (PTY) LTD
PIETERSBURG CONCRETE PRODUCTS (PTY) LTD
PROCEMENT (PTY) LTD
SKILLCRAFT AGENCIES (PTY) LTD (27%)
SUPERTOOL DISTRIBUTORS (PTY) LTD (30%)
TEKNIPLAN (PTY) LTD
TOLL HIGHWAY DEVELOPMENT CO (PTY) LTD (20%)
TRAUMAN (PTY) LTD
TWIN SPRINGS (PTY) LTD
UCC HOUSING (PTY) LTD

INVESTMENTS

None

CONCORDE TRAVEL HOLDINGS LTD

ABBREVIATION : CONTRAV

JSE SHORT CODE : CTV

SECTOR : Industrial-Retailers & Wholesalers

SHAREHOLDERS

Who Owns Whom's Assessment of the Identity of the Ultimate Controlling Shareholder:
MARVOL HOLDINGS SA

SHAREHOLDER	PERCENTAGE 1992	1991
MARVOL HOLDINGS SA	51 0	---
ROGOFF A	14 4	24 1
STEINGOLD N J	7 0	12 8
FIRST NAT NOM P/L	6 1	12 5
WEINSTEIN J	5 2	10 8
BEARE J H	3 2	2 0
SYFRETS NOM LTD	2 4	2 5
FAYJUL LTD	1 7	1 7
BORSUK M	---	1 3
BEARE A & ROGOFF A BEARE FOUNDATION	---	2 2
BEARE A	- -	24 1
TOTAL	91 0	94 2

DIRECTORS :
ALTBEKER L MRS,BEARE JH MR,DURHAM LW MR
LEVIN HR MR,LUNZ AD MR (Managing Director)
ROGOFF A MR (Joint Deputy Chairman)
SCHARFSCHWERDT A MR,SCHUMACHER L MR
STEINGOLD NJ MR (Financial Director)
VOLOSHIN M DR (Chairman),WEINSTEIN J MR
WEISS MF MR,WOLF L MR (Joint Deputy Chairman

REGISTRATION NUMBER : 87/02975/06

REGISTERED OFFICE
3rd Floor, Killarney Mall
Riviera Road, Killarney
2193
TEL 011-486 1850
FAX 011-486 1876

TRANSFER SECRETARY
Mercantile Registrars Ltd
P O Box 1053, Johannesburg
2000
TEL 011-333 8181

COMPANY SECRETARY
D A McCartney

NATURE OF BUSINESS
An investment holding company Subsidiaries are engaged in providing travel services mainly to corporations,business people and professionals, incentive and special interest groups,covering a spectrum of airline ticketing,land arrangements and travel insurance The group operates through 22 travel outlets

BANKERS :
Standard Bank of SA Ltd, Bankorp Ltd

AUDITORS :
Arthur Andersen & Co

FAMILIAR BRAND NAMES
COLUMBIA TRAVEL,CONCORDE
MILLER WEEDON TRAVEL,PELTOURS,SUMMIT TRAVEL

CONTRIBUTION BY ACTIVITY
N/A

YEAR END : March

DIVIDEND : Ords 1c

Final No 3	(Ldr)13/07/90	(Pay)25/07/90	Amt(c)3 75
Final No 4	(Ldr)05/07/91	(Pay)17/07/91	Amt(c)2 75
Final No 5	(Ldr)03/07/92	(Pay)15/07/92	Amt(c)2 5

NUMBER OF EMPLOYEES : 200

CAPITAL STRUCTURE

	AUTHORISED	ISSUED
Ords 1c	30000000	16000000

FINANCIAL STATISTICS (AT FINANCIAL YEAR END)

(Amts in R 000)	1992 Mar	1991 Mar	1990 Mar	1989 Mar	1988 Mar
Ord S/H Int	10727	10228	9552	9130	8132
Iss Ord Share	16000	16000	16000	16000	16000
Total Liab	7007	9412	9580	6991	4401
Current Liab	7007	9412	9580	6991	4401
Total Assets	10036	11917	12413	12410	8870
Intang Assets	7698	7723	6719	3711	3663
Current Assets	9222	11018	11531	7714	8613
Debtors	7621	8537	10149	5958	4581
Oper Profit	1131	1763	2272	1150	1512
Interest Paid	458	439	418	144	27
Tax Paid	251	481	378	427	606
Prf af Int&Tax	899	1116	1656	855	1005
Prf att Ord Sh	899	1116	1656	1558	1005
Btm Line Earn	899	1116	1022	1558	1005
Dividend Paid	400	440	600	560	320
Mkt Prce(c) YE	30	30	50	40	50
Depreciation	195	140	148	72	31

PER SHARE STATISTICS (CENTS)

Net Asst Val	18 93	15 66	17 71	33 87	27 93
Net Earnings	5 60	7 00	10 40	9 70	8 40
Dividends	2 50	2 75	3 75	3 50	2 00
Cash Flow	6 83	7 91	11 34	5 79	8 63

RATIOS AND OTHER INFORMATION

Mrk Cap(R000)	4800	4800	8000	6400	8000
Current Ratio	1 32	1 17	1 20	1 10	1 96
Quik/Acid Tst	1 32	1 17	1 20	1 10	1 96
Debt/Ass Rat	0 70	0 79	0 77	0 56	0 50
Debt to Eqity	0 65	0 92	1 00	0 77	0 54
Interest Cover	2 47	4 02	5 44	9 90	60 67
Ret on Assets	16 02	17 08	19 75	17 16	18 47
Ret on Equity%	8 38	10 91	17 34	17 06	12 36
Price/Earnings	5 36	4 29	4 81	4 12	5 95
Divid Cover	2 24	2 55	2 77	2 77	4 20
Divid Yield	8 33	9 17	7 50	8 75	4 00
Earning Yield%	18 67	23 33	20 80	24 25	16 80
NAV % Mrk Pr	63 10	52 19	35 41	84 67	55 86
Effec Tax Rate	21 91	29 49	18 04	41 35	41 08
Def Interval			0 35	-	
Sus Grth Rate	4 65	6 61	11 06	10 93	8 42

SUBSIDIARY & ASSOCIATED COMPANIES

BYBELLAND TOERE (EIENDOMS) BPK
COLUMBIA TRAVEL (PTY) LTD
CONCORDE INCENTIVE TRAVEL (PTY) LTD
CONCORDE TRAVEL (PTY) LTD
MILLER WEEDON TRAVEL (BRAAMFONTEIN) (PTY
MILLER WEEDON TRAVEL (JHB) (PTY) LTD
MILLER WEEDON TRAVEL (NATAL) (PTY) LTD
MILLER WEEDON TRAVEL (RANDBURG) (PTY) LT
ON IMPULSE TRAVEL (PTY) LTD
PELTOURS (NATAL) (PTY) LTD
PELTOURS (SOUTH AFRICA) (PTY) LTD
SUMMIT TRAVEL (PTY) LTD
TRADE & INDUSTRY TRAVEL (PTY) LTD

INVESTMENTS

None

CONGELLA FEDERATION LTD

ABBREVIATION : CONFED

JSE SHORT CODE CNF

SECTOR : Financial Property

SHAREHOLDERS

Who Owns Whom's Assessment of the Identity of the Ultimate Controlling Shareholder
COMMERCIAL FINANCE CO (CFC)

SHAREHOLDER	PERCENTAGE 1992	1991
BYRD A G	1 2	
CAPSTONE INV LTD	1 1	
KOEGELENBERG J H D	1 0	
SHARESTOCK NOM P/L	1 2	
THOMAS F	1 2	
TOWY TRUST P/L	6 3	
BYRD A G & SWAIN W J	4 7	
CFC PROPERTY HOLDINGS LTD	70 5	
TOTAL	87 3	

DIRECTORS .
BYRD AG ,DAUGHERTY DE ,KEMP AR
SWAIN WJ (Chairman

REGISTRATION NUMBER : 05/25767/06

REGISTERED OFFICE
1100 Mansion House, 12 Field Street
Durban
4001
TEL: 031-305 2781

TRANSFER SECRETARY
Natal Registrars (Pty) Ltd
P O Box 548, Durban
4000
TEL: 031-305 2781

COMPANY SECRETARY
Natal Registrars (Pty) Ltd

NATURE OF BUSINESS
An investment holding company with subsidiaries with investments in property and listed shares. Income consists of rents, dividends and interest.

BANKERS :
First National Bank of SA Ltd

AUDITORS :
KPMG Aiken & Peat

FAMILIAR BRAND NAMES
N/A

CONTRIBUTION BY ACTIVITY
N/A

YEAR END : December

DIVIDEND : Ords 50c

Interim No 70	(Ldr)27/10/89	(Pay)10/11/89	Amt(c)14
Final No 71	(Ldr)20/04/90	(Pay)12/05/90	Amt(c)35
Interim No 72	(Ldr)26/10/90	(Pay)09/11/90	Amt(c)15
Final No 73	(Ldr)19/04/91	(Pay)11/05/91	Amt(c)42
Final No 75	(Ldr)18/04/92	(Pay)09/05/92	Amt(c)49
Interim No 74	(Ldr)25/10/91	(Pay)08/11/91	Amt(c)16
Interim No 76	(Ldr)23/10/92	(Pay)06/11/92	Amt(c)18

CAPITAL STRUCTURE

	AUTHORISED	ISSUED
Ords 50c	2500000	846986

FINANCIAL STATISTICS (AT FINANCIAL YEAR END)

(Amts in R'000)	1991 Dec	1990 Dec	1989 Dec	1988	1987
Ord S/H Int	9292	8089	7353	6290	5648
Long Trm Loans	110	110	110	2000	974
Iss Ord Share	847	847	847	847	847
Total Liab	1016	1043	1236	4000	1948
Current Liab	906	933	1126	2000	974
Total Assets	10308	9132	8589	8394	6671
Current Assets	265	262	395	104	49
Debtors	168	146	64	-	-
Inventory	-	-	-	104	49
Oper Profit	2488	2063	1953	1958	1673
Interest Paid	-	1	110	151	6
Tax Paid	1214	1185	927	788	733
Prf af Int&Tax	1733	1264	1214	1019	934
Prf att Ord Sh	1726	1257	1207	1013	927
Btm Line Earn	1753	1217	1588	1013	927
Dividend Paid	551	483	415	373	339
Mkt Prce(c) YE	2300	1450	1100	950	900
Depreciation	44	24	33	-	-

PER SHARE STATISTICS (CENTS)

Net Asst Val	1097.05	955.02	868.12	742.62	666.82
Net Earnings	203.70	148.50	142.50	-	-
Dividends	65.00	57.00	49.00	-	-
Cash Flow	208.97	151.24	146.40	120.31	110.27

RATIOS AND OTHER INFORMATION

Mrk Cap(R000)	19481	12282	9317	8047	7623
Current Ratio	0.29	0.28	0.35	0.05	0.05
Quik/Acid Tst	0.29	0.28	0.35	-	-
Debt/Ass Rat	0.09	0.10	0.13	0.48	0.29
L T L Tot Ass	-	-	-	0.24	0.15
Debt to Eqity	0.10	0.12	0.15	0.64	0.34
Interest Cover	-	2371.00	20.37	12.97	278.83
Ret on Assets	28.59	26.83	26.21	23.33	25.08
Ret on Equity%	18.58	15.54	16.42	16.10	16.41
Price/Earnings	11.29	9.76	7.72	-	-
Divid Cover	3.13	2.61	2.91	-	-
Divid Yield	2.83	3.93	4.45	-	-
Earning Yield%	8.86	10.24	12.95	-	-
NAV % Mrk Pr	47.70	65.86	78.92	78.17	74.09
Effec Tax Rate	46.00	55.35	50.03	43.61	43.97
Def Interval	0.06	0.09	0.43	1.96	1.04
Sus Grth Rate	12.65	9.57	10.77	10.17	10.41

SUBSIDIARY & ASSOCIATED COMPANIES

AUBERO (PTY) LTD
CONGELLA STORES LTD
CONMEAD (PTY) LTD
CONTRAIL (PTY) LTD
CONWEST (PTY) LTD

INVESTMENTS

ANGLO AMERICAN CORP OF SA LTD (19000 SH)
ANGLO AMERICAN INVESTMENT TRUST LTD (16000 SH)
BARLOW RAND LTD (20698 SH)
GENBEL INVESTMENTS LTD (92000 SH)
GENCOR LTD (7290 SH)
GOLD FIELDS COAL LTD (3300 SH)
HIGHVELD STEEL & VANADIUM CORP LTD (10000 SH)
NEDCOR LTD (42000 SH)
SAPPI LTD (22500 SH)
TONGAAT-HULETT GROUP LTD (51581 SH)

CONSHU HOLDINGS LTD

ABBREVIATION : CONSHU

JSE SHORT CODE : CNS

SECTOR : Industrial-Clothing, Footwear & Textiles

SHAREHOLDERS

Who Owns Whom's Assessment of the Identity of the Ultimate Controlling Shareholder:
SA BREWERIES / SANLAM

SHAREHOLDER	PERCENTAGE 1992	1991
CMB NOM P/L	36.7	---
SA BREWERIES LTD	33.1	33.2

STD BANK NOM TVL P/L	10 9	11 1
METROPOLITAN LIFE LTD	3 7	3 3
LIBERTY LIFE ASSOC OF AFRICA LTD	3 5	2 8
EIGHTY ONE MAIN STREET NOM LTD	3 4	3 9
SA MUTUAL	1 1	1 1
SANKORP BPK	- -	30 4
SANLAM	---	5 2
TOTAL	92 3	91 1

DIRECTORS :
DU PLESSIS AS ,FEINBLUM RM (Chief Executive)
MCGINLEY JP ,PAIZES D ,RADFORD RD ,RAPP CEL
SANTRUCEK RJ ,VAN DEN BERG JL
VAN DER WATT L (Chairman),WYMAN MI

REGISTRATION NUMBER : 68/06778/06

REGISTERED OFFICE
4th Floor, Hyde Park Corner, Jan Smuts Avenue
Hyde Park, Sandton
2196
TEL 011-788 7250
FAX 011-880 2395

TRANSFER SECRETARY
Central Registrars Ltd
P O Box 4844, Johannesburg
2000
TEL 011-331 0051

COMPANY SECRETARY
J H Granger

NATURE OF BUSINESS
Manufacture & distribution of footwear & rubber mouldings The company has a controlling interest in JSE-quoted Wayne Manufacturing

BANKERS :
Standard Bank of SA Ltd
Trust Bank of Africa Ltd

AUDITORS :
Deloitte Pim Goldby

FAMILIAR BRAND NAMES
ADIDAS,AMAZON,BALDUCCI,BARKER,BISHOP,BLUCHER
BOSTONIAN,CROCKETT & JONES,DICK WHITTINGTON
DINGOES,EDDELS,EUROPA,FIRENZE,FRAMS
GINO PAOLI,GINO RIATTI,GISELLE,HUSH PUPPIES
HUSKIES,JACK & JILL,JACQUES MARTELL,JARMAN
JOHN DRAKE,JOHNSTON & MURPHY,JORDAN
JUST-IN-TIME,KRONIES,MILLANA,OLYMPIC,PANTHER
PHOENIX RUBBER,PUPPETS,RICCARDO,RICHLEIGH
SPORTSHOE,STARMERS,SYLVIA,TIMES SQUARE
TOP STAR,UNIFRAM,UNIVERSE

CONTRIBUTION BY ACTIVITY
General Footwear (% Turnover) (81 0%)
Rubber & Plastic Products (19 0%)

YEAR END : June

DIVIDEND : Ords 5c

Interim No 6	(Ldr)09/03/90	(Pay)30/03/90	Amt(c)10 5
Final No 7	(Ldr)07/09/90	(Pay)28/09/90	Amt(c)14
Interim No 8	(Ldr)08/03/91	(Pay)29/03/91	Amt(c)11 5
Final No 9	(Ldr)06/09/91	(Pay)27/09/91	Amt(c)16 5
Interim No 10	(Ldr)06/03/92	(Pay)27/03/92	Amt(c)11 5
Final No 11	(Ldr)04/09/92	(Pay)25/09/92	Amt(c)13

NUMBER OF EMPLOYEES : 9786

CAPITAL STRUCTURE

	AUTHORISED	ISSUED
Ords 5c	50000000	46506000

FINANCIAL STATISTICS (AT FINANCIAL YEAR END)

(Amts in R'000)	1992 Jun	1991 Jun	1990 Jun	1989 Jun	1988 Jun
Ord S/H Int	147318	132740	114876	83217	65570
Long Trm Loans	35277	66209	46401	26991	8952
Iss Ord Share	46506	46290	46290	41700	40500
Total Liab	191607	174338	146608	109239	68200
Current Liab	156330	108129	100207	82248	59248
Total Assets	333325	300632	254179	192290	133770
Intang Assets	5600	6446	7305	166	*
Current Assets	247060	221344	188440	155952	111272
Debtors	145017	131075	109914	89745	68725
Inventory	101130	89841	78271	61666	40673
Turnover	620826	621562	531938	420264	329271
Oper Profit	55141	71560	61514	49683	38124
Interest Paid	18860	14462	11419	5035	2279
Tax Paid	14167	24955	22086	20973	18106
Prf af Int&Tax	26282	32810	28388	23707	17739
Prf att Ord Sh	24678	30828	27108	23703	17739
Btm Line Earn	24868	30828	27108	23703	17739
Dividend Paid	11369	12961	11341	9630	7207
Mkt Prce(c) YE	400	500	445	420	290
Depreciation	15799	10037	9342	5756	4265

PER SHARE STATISTICS (CENTS)

	1992	1991	1990	1989	1988
Net Asst Val	304 73	272 83	232 38	199 16	161 90
Net Earnings	53 10	66 60	58 60	56 80	43 80
Dividends	24 50	28 00	24 50	22 50	17 50
Cash Flow	87 92	98 11	83 45	74 93	57 09

RATIOS AND OTHER INFORMATION

	1992	1991	1990	1989	1988
Mrk Cap(R000)	186024	231450	205991	175140	117450
Current Ratio	1 58	2 05	1 88	1 90	1 88
Quik/Acid Tst	0 93	1 22	1 10	1 15	1 19
A/C Rec T/ovr	4 28	4 74	4 84	4 68	4 79
Tot Ass T/ovr	1 86	2 07	2 09	2 19	2 46
Debt/Ass Rat	0 51	0 48	0 48	0 50	0 44
L T L Tot Ass	0 04	0 12	0 08	0 08	0 00
Debt to Eqity	1 15	1 08	1 06	1 17	0 90
Interest Cover	2 92	4 95	5 39	9 87	16 73
Oper Prof Mrg	8 88	11 51	11 56	11 82	11 58
Net Prof Marg%	3 98	4 96	5 10	5 64	5 39
Ret on Assets	17 79	24 03	24 35	25 85	28 50
Ret on Equity%	16 75	23 22	23 60	28 48	27 05
Price/Earnings	7 53	7 51	7 59	7 39	6 62
Divid Cover	2 17	2 38	2 39	2 52	2 50
Divid Yield	6 13	5 60	5 51	5 36	6 03
Earning Yield%	13 28	13 32	13 17	13 52	15 10
NAV % Mrk Pr	76 18	54 57	52 22	47 42	55 83
Effec Tax Rate	36 85	35 49	39 17	42 82	47 33
Def Interval	1 55	0 87	0 83	0 59	0 00
Sus Grth Rate	9 03	13 46	13 73	16 91	16 06

SUBSIDIARY & ASSOCIATED COMPANIES

BARKER FOOTWEAR LTD
BCL FOOTWEAR LTD
BIKRON HOLDINGS (PTY) LTD
CALAN LTD
CALANA RETREAD SERVICES (PTY) LTD
CONSHU LTD
DICK WHITTINGTON SHOES (PTY) LTD
EDDELS (SA) (PTY) LTD
FIFTH SHOECORP PROPERTIES LTD
FOURTH SHOECORP PROPERTIES LTD
H W INJECTION MOULDERS LTD

J & J CANVAS (PTY) LTD
JACK AND JILL FOOTWEAR (PTY) LTD
JORDAN & CO (PTY) LTD
OLYMPIC FOOTWEAR (PTY) LTD (50%)
OLYMPIC SPORTS (PTY) LTD
PERSALTUM (PTY) LTD
PHOENIX RUBBER (PTY) LTD
RAINY DAY INVESTMENTS (PTY) LTD
RICHLEIGH CONTRACTING (PTY) LTD
RICHLEIGH SHOES (PTY) LTD
SECOND SHOECORP PROPERTIES LTD
SHOE CORPORATION OF AFRICA LTD
SHOECORP PROPERTIES LTD
SHOETOWN (PTY) LTD
SPORTSHOE (PTY) LTD
STERLING & HUNT LTD
THIRD SHOECORP PROPERTIES LTD
UNITED-FRAM (BOP) (PTY) LTD
UNITED-FRAM FOOTWEAR MANUFACTURERS (PTY)
WAYNE MANAGEMENT (PTY) LTD
WAYNE MANUFACTURING LTD
WAYNE PLASTICS (PTY) LTD
WAYNE RESIN (PTY) LTD
WAYNE RUBBER CO (PTY) LTD
WAYNE RUBBER WESTERN CAPE (PTY) LTD

INVESTMENTS

None

CONSOL LTD

ABBREVIATION : CONSOL

JSE SHORT CODE : CGW

SECTOR : Industrial-Paper & Packaging

SHAREHOLDERS

Who Owns Whom's Assessment of the Identity of the Ultimate Controlling Shareholder: ANGLOVAAL VIA ANGLOVAAL INDUSTRIES

SHAREHOLDER	PERCENTAGE 1992	1991
ANGLOVAAL IND LTD	55 9	51 8
OWENS ILLINOIS INC	19 3	19 3
LIBERTY LIFE ASSOC OF AFRICA LTD	4 6	5 3
FOX STREET NOM P/L	3 9	6 8
CMB NOM P/L	2 1	---
NESTLE PENS FUND	1 6	---
FIRST NAT NOM P/L	1 1	1 1
FNP PENS FUND	---	1 2
SANLAM	---	1 1
TOTAL	88 4	86 6

DIRECTORS :
BERNSTEIN BL ,BOTHA AF ,BOTHA FB ,DU TOIT GJ
FORGAN KH (Financial Director),HERSOV BE
MACNAMARA MC ,MENELL CS (Chairman)
NEETHLING PJ (Managing Director),ROBBERTZE JC
ROOS HA ,SAVAGE RB ,SPINDLER DCB ,WUNSH B

REGISTRATION NUMBER : 05/21828/06

REGISTERED OFFICE
Osborn Road, Wadeville
Germiston
1407
TEL 011-827 4311
FAX 011-824 3897

TRANSFER SECRETARY
Anglovaal Ltd
P O Box 62379, Marshalltown
2107
TEL 011-634 9111

COMPANY SECRETARY
R T Golding

NATURE OF BUSINESS
An industrial holding company Group activities are divided into two sectors - packaging & rubber The packaging sector manufactures & markets glass, plastics & paper packaging, glass tableware and processes industrial silica sand The rubber sector manufactures, markets and distributes new & retreaded tyres, and industrial rubber products

BANKERS :
First National Bank of SA Ltd
Standard Bank of SA Ltd, Nedcor Bank Ltd

AUDITORS :
KPMG Aiken & Peat, Deloitte & Touche

FAMILIAR BRAND NAMES
CONSOL,GOODYEAR TYRES,KELLY TYRES

CONTRIBUTION BY ACTIVITY
Packaging & Related (% Turnover) (43 5%)
Rubber & Related (56 5%)

YEAR END : June

DIVIDEND .Ords 5c

Final No 39	(Ldr)07/09/90	(Pay)12/10/90	Amt(c)45
Final No 40	(Ldr)13/09/91	(Pay)11/10/91	Amt(c)55
Final No 41	(Ldr)11/09/92	(Pay)09/10/92	Amt(c)62

NUMBER OF EMPLOYEES : 12423

CAPITAL STRUCTURE

	AUTHORISED	ISSUED
Ords 5c	73500000	64348500
Red Cum Prefs 1c	50000000	50000000
5% Unsec Auto Conv Sub Debs R36	8376550	8376550

FINANCIAL STATISTICS (AT FINANCIAL YEAR END)

(Amts in R'000)	1992 Jun	1991 Jun	1990 Jun	1989 Jun	1988 Jun
Ord S/H Int	484495	376352	285941	222422	177570
Long Trm Loans	616607	384361	369565	172570	78750
Iss Ord Share	64348	64196	64036	63999	6348
Total Liab	1018757	733247	683434	364837	237829
Current Liab	402150	348886	313869	192267	159079
Total Assets	1370176	1023487	884710	587259	415399
Intang Assets	133076	86112	84665	*	*
Current Assets	1044912	704956	597316	430385	274626
Debtors	367881	340882	291256	124925	109486
Inventory	372181	363653	291828	133295	109884
Turnover	2097600	2071500	1555900	737700	636900
Oper Profit	290923	319421	214771	120801	96247
Interest Paid	26411	34308	33162	5375	3909

Tax Paid	124590	132516	69393	56897	44412
Prf af Int&Tax	165775	155811	117931	68347	51704
Prf att Ord Sh	139166	124513	100968	68347	51704
Btm Line Earn	149442	125119	92081	69364	52123
Dividend Paid	39896	35308	28816	21130	17279
Mkt Prce(c) YE	3350	3700	1875	1350	508
Depreciation	51295	44836	37020	22025	22419

PER SHARE STATISTICS (CENTS)

Net Asst Val	546.12	452.12	314.32	347.54	2797.26
Net Earnings	216.70	194.30	157.70	102.30	815.00
Dividends	62.00	55.00	45.00	33.00	270.00
Cash Flow	307.60	276.14	214.92	141.14	1033.35

RATIOS AND OTHER INFORMATION

Mrk Cap(R000)	2155658	2375252	1200675	863987	32248
Current Ratio	2.60	2.02	1.90	2.24	1.73
Quik/Acid Tst	1.67	0.98	0.97	1.55	1.04
A/C Rec T/ovr	5.70	6.08	5.34	5.91	5.82
Tot Ass T/ovr	1.53	2.02	1.76	1.26	1.53
Debt/Ass Rat	0.56	0.47	0.52	0.44	0.50
L T L Tot Ass	0.26	0.13	0.16	0.11	0.12
Debt to Eqity	1.58	1.29	1.60	1.15	1.17
Interest Cover	11.02	9.31	6.48	22.96	24.87
Oper Prof Mrg	13.87	15.42	13.80	16.38	15.11
Net Prof Marg%	6.63	6.01	6.49	9.26	8.12
Ret on Assets	23.12	31.52	24.92	22.24	24.08
Ret on Equity%	28.72	33.08	35.31	30.73	29.12
Price/Earnings	15.46	19.04	11.89	13.20	0.62
Divid Cover	3.50	3.53	3.50	3.10	3.02
Divid Yield	1.85	1.49	2.40	2.44	53.15
Earning Yield%	6.47	5.25	8.41	7.58	160.43
NAV % Mrk Pr	16.30	12.22	16.76	25.74	550.64
Effec Tax Rate	31.60	33.69	20.95	39.72	50.28
Def Interval	0.71	1.18	1.57	1.12	0.33
Sus Grth Rate	20.49	23.70	25.23	21.23	19.39

SUBSIDIARY & ASSOCIATED COMPANIES

ARMOUR TYRE CO (PTY) LTD (38%)
CAPE GLASS WORKS LTD
CONSOL PAPER PACKAGING (PTY) LTD
CONSOL PLASTICS (ATLANTIS) (PTY) LTD
CONSOL PLASTICS (CISKEI) (PTY) LTD
CONSOL PLASTICS (KWAZULU) (PTY) LTD
CONTRED (PTY) LTD
CORRO-PACK (PTY) LTD
DEERING INVESTMENTS (PTY) LTD
FABRIEK STREET (PTY) LTD
GUNDLE PLASTICS (PTY) LTD
HI-HO VULCANIZING WORKS (SWAZILAND) (PTY
HUNSLET ROAD (PTY) LTD
HYPERTREADS (CAPE) (PTY) LTD
HYPERTREADS (PTY) LTD
INDUSTRIAL SAND AND ENGINEERING CO. LTD
JR FIELD SERVICES (PTY) LTD
KILLIAN WOONSTELLE (PTY) LTD
KOPERBERG MOTORS (PTY) LTD
KOPERBERG MOTORS PROPERTIES (NATAL) (PTY
MANAGEMENT SERVICES (PTY) LTD
MASTERTREADS (BOPHUTHATSWANA) (PTY) LTD
MASTERTREADS (CAPE) (PTY) LTD
MASTERTREADS (KIMBERLEY) (PTY) LTD
MASTERTREADS (LESOTHO) (PTY) LTD
MASTERTREADS (NAMIBIA) (PTY) LTD
MASTERTREADS (NATAL) (PTY) LTD
MASTERTREADS (PWV) (PTY) LTD
MASTERTREADS (TVL) (PTY) LTD
MKM ENGINEERING (PTY) LTD
MONARCH TYRE REPAIRS (PTY) LTD
NATAL TYRE SERVICES (PTY) LTD
NOVA TYRE (NAMIBIA) (PTY) LTD
NOVA TYRE (PTY) LTD
OFF-THE-ROAD TYRES (PTY) LTD
POTGIETER STREET 257 (PTY) LTD
PRETORIA ERF NO. 114 (PTY) LTD
RUBBER & ASSOCIATED MANUFACTURERS (PTY)
SAN MARCO (PTY) LTD
SAN PORTO (PTY) LTD
SPEEDBOX (PTY) LTD
STATION INVESTMENTS (PTY) LTD
TRENTYRE (CAPE TOWN) (PTY) LTD
TRENTYRE (EASTERN CAPE) (PTY) LTD
TRENTYRE (LESOTHO) (PTY) LTD
TRENTYRE (NAMIBIA) (PTY) LTD
TRENTYRE (NATAL) (PTY) LTD
TRENTYRE (OFS) (PTY) LTD
TRENTYRE (TVL) (PTY) LTD
TRENTYRE-BANDAG (PTY) LTD
TYCON (PTY) LTD (PREVIOUSLY GOODYEAR TYR
TYRE-TRADE (PTY) LTD
UNION GLASS LTD
VULCAN TYRE & RUBBER CO (PTY) LTD
WADEVILLE EXTENSION 2BC (PTY) LTD

INVESTMENTS

None

CONSOLIDATED AFEX CORPORATION SA

ABBREVIATION : CONAFEX

JSE SHORT CODE : CFX

SECTOR : Industrial-Industrial Holding

SHAREHOLDERS

Who Owns Whom's Assessment of the Identity of the Ultimate Controlling Shareholder: MARSHALL FAMILY

SHAREHOLDER	PERCENTAGE 1992	1991
LONDON CONTROL ACCOUNT	61.5	61.1
LUXDURBAN INV HOLDINGS P/L	25.6	25.3
STD BANK NOM TVL P/L	3.2	3.3
EEN MARGARET	1.0	---
KIGHTLEY K M	---	1.1
TOTAL	91.3	90.8

DIRECTORS :
KERR RC ,LATILLA-CAMPBELL P ,MARKHAM AH
MARSHALL DC (Chairman),ROBOTHAM JM

REGISTRATION NUMBER : B17789 (Luxe

REGISTERED OFFICE
68-70 Boulevard de la Petrusse, L-2320 Luxembourg
SA: 11th floor, Field Street, Durban
4001
TEL: 031-305 6521
FAX: 031-305 9791

TRANSFER SECRETARY
Central Registrars Ltd
P O Box 4844, Johannesburg
2000
TEL 011-331 0051

COMPANY SECRETARY
City Group Ltd

NATURE OF BUSINESS
The Corporation is a Luxembourg holding Company with a general portfolio of listed investments, concentrated on the New York Stock Exchange The Corporation holds 52% of Afex Corporation SA (Afex) The Corporation's shares are listed on the Luxembourg and Johannesburg Stock Exchanges

BANKERS :
Credit Suisse

AUDITORS :
Deloitte Pim Goldby

FAMILIAR BRAND NAMES
N/A

CONTRIBUTION BY ACTIVITY
South Africa (% turnover - geographic) (66 6%)
South Africa (% Trading Profit) (35 8%)
Zimbabwe (% turnover) (24 6%)
Australia and others (% turnover) (8 8%)
Zimbabwe (% Trading Profit) (55 5%)
Australia and others (% Trading Profit) (8 7%)

YEAR END : September

DIVIDEND :Ords no par value

Dividend (Ldr)08/03/91 (Pay)19/04/91 Amt(c)5 5

CAPITAL STRUCTURE

	AUTHORISED	ISSUED
Ords no par value	65000000	3219780

FINANCIAL STATISTICS (AT FINANCIAL YEAR END)

(Amts in $)	1991 Sep	1990 Sep	1989 Sep	1988 Sep	1987 Sep
Ord S/H Int	11564	10292	9770	7414	11606
Long Trm Loans	20056	16468	13717	12012	18626
Iss Ord Share	3003	3003	4699	4699	2435
Total Liab	28373	23589	17367	16687	24975
Current Liab	8317	7121	3650	4675	6349
Total Assets	39937	33881	27137	24101	36581
Current Assets	14173	11721	6725	5393	9747
Debtors	5053	4639	3186	2307	3683
Inventory	5270	4483	2308	1752	4998
Turnover	43978	35322	24414	22767	15602
Oper Profit	2405	3506	3940	3886	3386
Interest Paid	1619	1357	904	822	613
Tax Paid	670	820	1084	1154	1421
Prf af Int&Tax	1276	2536	2881	2574	2230
Prf att Ord Sh	-417	-49	147	-30	974
Btm Line Earn	-709	280	1864	1166	1510
Dividend Paid	170	165	146	141	134
Mkt Prce(c) YE	450	270	400	425	750
Depreciation	1135	992	543	633	483

PER SHARE STATISTICS (CENTS)

Net Asst Val	385 08	342 72	207 92	157 78	476 63
Net Earnings	2 00	30 70	34 30	28 00	38 80
Dividends	5 50	5 50	3 00	3 00	5 50
Cash Flow	45 93	59 69	31 97	28 94	59 96

RATIOS AND OTHER INFORMATION

Mrk Cap(R000)	13514	8108	18796	19971	18263
Current Ratio	1 70	1 65	1 84	1 15	1 54
Quik/Acid Tst	1 07	1 02	1 21	0 78	0 75
A/C Rec T/ovr	8 70	7 61	7 66	9 87	4 24
Tot Ass T/ovr	1 10	1 04	0 90	0 94	0 43
Debt/Ass Rat	0 40	0 40	0 34	0 43	0 35
L T L Tot Ass	0 19	0 19	0 20	0 23	0 17
Debt to Eqity	1 37	1 32	0 94	1 38	1 09
Interest Cover	2 11	3 41	5 00	5 54	6 96
Oper Prof Mrg	5 47	9 93	16 14	17 07	21 70
Net Prof Marg%	-0 95	-0 14	0 60	-0 13	6 24
Ret on Assets	8 69	13 91	17 94	18 88	11 66
Ret on Equity%	-3 61	-0 48	1 50	-0 40	8 39
Price/Earnings	225 00	8 79	11 66	15 18	19 33
Divid Cover	0 36	5 58	11 43	9 33	7 05
Divid Yield	1 22	2 04	0 75	0 71	0 73
Earning Yield%	0 44	11 37	8 57	6 59	5 17
NAV % Mrk Pr	85 57	126 93	51 98	37 12	63 55
Effec Tax Rate	59 87	34 23	27 58	29 34	44 14
Def Interval	1 24	1 08	0 40	-	-
Sus Grth Rate	-5 08	-2 08	0 01	2 31	7 24

SUBSIDIARY & ASSOCIATED COMPANIES

AFEX CORPORATION SOCIETE ANONYME
BULAWAYO BOARD OF EXECUTORS & TRUST CO L (37,4%)
CONAFEX INTERNATIONAL FINANCE LTD
FALCON MINES PLC (26%)
SOUTHERN CERAMICS (PTY) LTD (40%)
WILLSGROVE BRICK & POTTERIES LTD (34,5%)

INVESTMENTS

AMERICAN BRANDS INC (400 SH)
BANK LEU FS 100 (BONS DE PART) (84 SH)
BOEING CO INC (1000 SH)
COLGATE PALMOLIVE CO INC (1000 SH)
COLT INDUSTRIES INC (300 SH)
CONSOLIDATED FREIGHTWAYS INC (640 SH)
COORS (ADOLPH) COMPANY 'B' (3000 SH)
CREDIT SUISSE FS500/BON P CS HOLD (ACT) (20 SH)
CSX CORPORATION INC (1600 SH)
DIGITAL EQUIPMENT INC (400 SH)
EMERSON ELECTRIC INC (400 SH)
EXXON CORP INC (500 SH)
FEDERATED DEPT STORES INC (600 SH)
FMC CORP INC (300 SH)
GRAND MAGASINS GLOBUS (BONS DE PART) (90 SH)
GRAND PASSAGE S A FS 100 (ACT) (80 SH)
H J HEINZ CO INC (450 SH)
HARSCO CORP INC (600 SH)
HILTON HOTELS CORP INC (500 SH)
INTERNATIONAL BUSINESS MACHINES INC (500 SH)
INTERNATIONAL PAPER CO INC (600 SH)
KANSAS CITY SOUTHERN INDUSTRIES INC (1000 SH)
LEAR SIEGLER INC (300 SH)
LILLY (ELI) & COMPANY (400 SH)
MACY (R H) & CO INC (1050 SH)
MAY DEPT STORES INC (750 SH)
MERCK & CO INC (500 SH)
MINNESOTA MINING & MANUFACTURING INC (300 SH)
MOEVENPICK HOLDING AG ZH FS 500 (ACT) (13 SH)
MONSANTO CO INC (800 SH)
MOTT'S SUPERMARKET INC (1000 SH)
NATIONAL CONVENIENCE STORES INC (3000 SH)
NESTLE S A FS 100 INCL UNILAC $12 (ACT (11 SH)
NORTON CO INC (850 SH)
OLYMPUS CONSOLIDATED MINES LIMITED (88000 SH)
PACIFIC LUMBER INC (1500 SH)
PAY 'PAK STORES INC (2100 SH)
PORTLATCH CORPORATION (1000 SH)

PROCTER & GAMBLE CO. INC.F (400 SH)
QUAKER OATS CO. INC. (400 SH)
SCHERING PLOUGH CORP. INC. (500 SH)
TRAVELERS CORPORATION INC. (600 SH)
UNION DES BANQUES SUISSES (BS DE PART.) (400 SH)
UNIVERSAL LEAF TOBACCO INC. (920 SH)
UPJOHN CO. INC. (500 SH)
VULCAN MATERIALS INC. (200 SH)

CONSOLIDATED DIAMOND CORPORATION LTD

ABBREVIATION : CDC

JSE SHORT CODE : CDC

SECTOR : Mining-Diamonds

SHAREHOLDERS

Who Owns Whom's Assessment of the Identity of the Ultimate Controlling Shareholder:
SPERIAM SECURITIES INC (PANAMA)

SHAREHOLDER	PERCENTAGE 1992	1991
SPERIAM SECURITIES INC	98.4	98.4
TOTAL	98.4	98.4

DIRECTORS :
IMRIE WNB (Financial Director),KATZ A
MUMBY CC (Chairman),TORRINGTON VISCOUNT

REGISTRATION NUMBER : 86/04840/06

REGISTERED OFFICE
5th Floor, Southern Life Gardens
3 Gwen Lane, Sandton
2146
TEL: 011-883 6646
FAX: 011-884 5552

TRANSFER SECRETARY
Mercantile Registrars Ltd
P O Box 1053, Johannesburg
2000
TEL: 011-333 8181

COMPANY SECRETARY
Process & Mining Consultants (Pty) Ltd

NATURE OF BUSINESS
The company operates the Samada diamond mine in the district of Ventersburg, OFS.

BANKERS :
First National Bank of SA Ltd

AUDITORS :
Kessel Feinstein

FAMILIAR BRAND NAMES
N/A

CONTRIBUTION BY ACTIVITY
N/A

YEAR END : June

DIVIDEND :15/11/91 and 15/05/91

NUMBER OF EMPLOYEES : 160

CAPITAL STRUCTURE

	AUTHORISED	ISSUED
Ords 1c	90000000	75000000

FINANCIAL STATISTICS (AT FINANCIAL YEAR END)

(Amts in R'000)	1990 Feb	1989 Feb	1988 Feb
Ord S/H Int	8969	15880	23000
Long Trm Loans	100	100	-
Iss Ord Share	23680	14800	14800
Total Liab	1828	2302	1484
Current Liab	1728	2202	1484
Total Assets	10797	18182	24484
Current Assets	866	825	2573
Debtors	591	532	1199
Inventory	273	292	457
Turnover	4702	5765	4069
Oper Profit	-1156	-1111	461
Interest Paid	251	113	233
Tax Paid	-	-	8
Prf af Int&Tax	-1407	-1224	220
Prf att Ord Sh	-1407	-1224	220
Btm Line Earn	-9019	-1224	220
Mkt Prce(c) YE	26	35	145

PER SHARE STATISTICS (CENTS)

Net Asst Val	37.88	107.30	155.41
Cash Flow	-5.94	-8.27	1.49

RATIOS AND OTHER INFORMATION

Mrk Cap(R000)	6157	5180	21460
Current Ratio	0.50	0.37	1.73
Quik/Acid Tst	0.34	0.24	1.43
A/C Rec T/ovr	7.96	10.84	3.39
Tot Ass T/ovr	0.44	0.32	0.17
Debt/Ass Rat	0.17	0.13	0.06
L T L Tot Ass	0.01	0.01	-
Debt to Eqity	0.20	0.14	0.06
Interest Cover	-4.61	-9.83	1.98
Oper Prof Mrg	-24.59	-19.27	11.33
Net Prof Marg%	-29.92	-21.23	5.41
Ret on Assets	-10.71	-6.11	1.88
Ret on Equity%	-15.69	-7.71	0.96
NAV % Mrk Pr	145.68	306.56	107.18
Effec Tax Rate	-	-	3.51
Def Interval	-0.71	-0.99	0.98
Sus Grth Rate	-15.69	-7.71	0.96

SUBSIDIARY & ASSOCIATED COMPANIES

SAMADA DIAMONDS (1987) (PTY) LTD
SAMADA DIAMONDS (PTY) LTD

INVESTMENTS

None

CONSOLIDATED FRAME TEXTILES LTD

ABBREVIATION : CONFRAM

JSE SHORT CODE : CFM

SECTOR : Industrial-Clothing, Footwear & Textiles

SHAREHOLDERS

Who Owns Whom's Assessment of the Identity of the Ultimate Controlling Shareholder:
SEARDEL INV CORP / SABLE FAMILY VIA FRAM

SHAREHOLDER	PERCENTAGE 1992	1991
FRAME GROUP HOLDINGS LTD	67 3	68 9
PHIMAX P/L	5 8	6 0
EIGHTY ONE MAIN STREET NOM LTD	4 2	4 1
SOUTHERN LIFE ASSOC LTD	3 6	3 7
NATAL IND SUPPLIERS P/L	3 1	3 2
FRAME POLYPROPYLENE MILLS P/L	2 7	2 7
CONFRAME SHARE INC SCHEME ACCOUNT NOM	2 4	---
STD BANK NOM TVL P/L	1 2	1 3
TOTAL	90 2	89 8

DIRECTORS :
BORKUM MM ,DE VILLIERS HP
KING ME (Executive Chairman),SABLE R
SANDERS BF ,SEARLL A DR
SIMEONI W (Executive Director),STEIN GH
WHITEFORD RJ (Financial Director

REGISTRATION NUMBER : 05/05005/06

REGISTERED OFFICE
Blase Road, New Germany
3610
TEL 031-705 1370
FAX 031-705 1370

TRANSFER SECRETARY
Mercantile Registrars Ltd
P O Box 1053, Johannesburg
2000
TEL 011-333 8181

COMPANY SECRETARY
JH Acutt

NATURE OF BUSINESS
A holding and investment company whose subsidiaries are involved in producing woollen, cotton and synthetic products

BANKERS :
First National Bank of SA Ltd
Standard Bank of SA Ltd, Absa Bank Ltd
Nedcor Bank Ltd, Rand Merchant Bank Ltd

AUDITORS :
Arthur Andersen & Co, KPMG Aiken & Peat

FAMILIAR BRAND NAMES
CARAVEL,COTTON CO ,DUET,FOLKLORE,GALA
JACQUARD,SLEEPLINE,SYMPHONY,VISION,WAVERLEY

CONTRIBUTION BY ACTIVITY
N/A

YEAR END : June

DIVIDEND : (Ldr)03/03/89 (Pay)17/03/89
DIVIDEND : (Ldr)08/09/89 (Pay)22/09/89

NUMBER OF EMPLOYEES : 18596

CAPITAL STRUCTURE

	AUTHORISED	ISSUED
Ords 5c	57000000	56245960
5,5% Cum Prefs R2	400000	400000

FINANCIAL STATISTICS (AT FINANCIAL YEAR END)

(Amts in R'000)	1992 Jun	1991 Jun	1990 Jun	1989 Jun	1988 Jun
Ord S/H Int	566344	680922	983492	974935	946390
Long Trm Loans	23986	66475	118792	115556	113527
Iss Ord Share	56246	56246	56246	56088	56088
Total Liab	318358	526586	464138	344315	210606
Current Liab	294372	460111	345346	228759	97079
Total Assets	884702	1206358	1446289	1319250	1156996
Intang Assets	*	1150	1341	*	*
Current Assets	439258	624496	768503	667451	542805
Debtors	209670	305682	344470	315601	222766
Inventory	226058	308092	400869	314799	275667
Turnover	652170	789093	984258	869652	700873
Oper Profit	-38180	-123292	68745	80918	41611
Interest Paid	46674	44704	31292	13122	-
Tax Paid	329	923	6008	24613	17956
Prf af Int&Tax	-73871	-163588	41316	52549	30808
Prf att Ord Sh	-73915	-163632	41272	51908	30376
Btm Line Earn	-130033	-366284	27444	51908	31471
Dividend Paid	-	-	19686	20753	19070
Mkt Prce(c) YE	115	270	480	750	530
Depreciation	42341	54999	49065	47418	41498

PER SHARE STATISTICS (CENTS)

Net Asst Val	1006 91	1208 57	1746 17	1738 22	1687 33
Net Earnings	-131 40	-290 90	73 40	92 50	54 80
Dividends	-	-	35 00	37 00	34 00
Cash Flow	-56 14	-193 65	161 36	177 11	126 14

RATIOS AND OTHER INFORMATION

Mrk Cap(R000)	64683	151864	269981	420660	297266
Current Ratio	1 49	1 36	2 23	2 92	5 59
Quik/Acid Tst	0 72	0 69	1 06	1 54	2 75
A/C Rec T/ovr	3 11	2 58	2 86	2 76	3 15
Tot Ass T/ovr	0 74	0 65	0 68	0 66	0 61
Debt/Ass Rat	0 36	0 39	0 24	0 18	0 08
L T L Tot Ass	0 03	0 01	0 01	0 00	
Debt to Eqity	0 56	0 70	0 36	0 24	0 10
Interest Cover	-0 78	-2 73	2 31	6 46	-
Oper Prof Mrg	-5 85	-15 62	6 98	9 30	5 94
Net Prof Marg%	-11 33	-20 74	4 19	5 97	4 33
Ret on Assets	-3 04	-9 78	5 44	6 84	4 21
Ret on Equity%	-13 05	-24 03	4 20	5 32	3 21
Price/Earnings	-0 88	-0 93	6 54	8 11	9 67
Divid Cover	-	-	2 10	2 50	1 61
Divid Yield	-	-	7 29	4 93	6 42
Earning Yield%	-114 26	107 74	15 29	12 33	10 34
NAV % Mrk Pr	875 57	447 62	363 79	231 76	318 36
Effec Tax Rate	-0 37	0 73	12 74	33 54	42 28
Def Interval	-5 75	-2 10	1 80	0 75	0 08
Sus Grth Rate	-13 05	-24 03	2 19	3 20	1 19

SUBSIDIARY & ASSOCIATED COMPANIES

BAKER, KING (HOLDINGS) LTD
CONFRAM CAPE TOWN PROPERTIES (PTY) LTD
CONFRAM CISKEI PROPERTIES (PTY) LTD
CONFRAM EAST LONDON PROPERTIES (PTY) LTD
CONFRAM FRAMETEX PROPERTIES (PTY) LTD
CONFRAM HARRISMITH PROPERTIES LTD
CONFRAM LADYSMITH PROPERTIES LTD
CONFRAM LAWLEY PROPERTIES (PTY) LTD
CONFRAM PINETEX II PROPERTIES LTD
CONFRAM PINETEX PROPERTIES LTD
CONFRAM PINETOWN PROPERTIES LTD
CONFRAM PROPERTY HOLDINGS LTD
CONFRAM TEXFIN PROPERTIES LTD
CONSOLIDATED TEXTILES (PTY) LTD
CONSOLIDATED WOVEN PACKAGING (PTY) LTD
F
FRAME FACTORY SHOPS LTD
FRAME FIBRES (PTY LTD
FRAME KNITTING MANUFACTURERS LTD
FRAME POLYESTER FIBRE CORPORATION (PTY)
FRAME TEXTILE CORPORATION LTD
MULTITEXTILES TRADING LTD
MULTITEXTILES TRADING LTD (REGISTERED IN
NATAL INDENTING & EXPORTING AGENCIES (PT
NATAL INSURANCE AGENCY LTD
NATAL RUBBER INDUSTRIAL COMPONENTS (PTY)
REBRI INVESTMENTS (PTY) LTD

INVESTMENTS

GLODINA HOLDINGS LTD (420000 SH)
SMALL BUSINESS DEVELOPMENT CORP LTD
UNISPIN HOLDINGS LTD (CUM RED CONV PREFS (30000000 S)

CONSOLIDATED METALLURGICAL INDUSTRIES LTD

ABBREVIATION : CMI

JSE SHORT CODE : CMI

SECTOR : Industrial-Steel & Allied

SHAREHOLDERS

Who Owns Whom's Assessment of the Identity of the Ultimate Controlling Shareholder:
ANGLO AMERICAN VIA JCI

SHAREHOLDER	PERCENTAGE 1992	1991
JOHANNESBURG CONSOLIDATED INV CO LTD	35.4	35.4
RESIDENT NOM LTD	13.6	13.6
STD BANK NOM TVL P/L	10.8	10.5
FOXVALLEY INV P/L	6.5	6.5
FOXGLEN INV LTD	4.9	4.9
SA MUTUAL	3.8	3.4
BARNATO HLDGS LTD	3.1	3.1
DIDO NOM LTD	3.0	3.0
FERMAIN NOM LTD	3.0	3.0
PETARD NOM LTD	3.0	3.0
TAURUS NOM LTD	3.0	3.0
SANDVELT INV P/L	2.4	---
VOLKSKAS INTERGROEI INV P/L	1.2	1.2
JUBILEE PROSPECTORS LTD	---	2.4
TOTAL	93.6	92.9

DIRECTORS :
DAVISON BE (Chairman),HAWARDEN MW ,JONES TE
KING MW ,KUHNERT AW ,TAYELOR CJ
VAN DER WALT Z (Managing Director)
VAN JAARSVELD RJ (Financial Director)
WOOD AI (Dep. Chair. & Chief Exec.

REGISTRATION NUMBER : 75/00230/06

REGISTERED OFFICE
Consolidated Building, Cnr Fox & Harrison Streets
Johannesburg
2001
TEL: 011-373 9111
FAX: 011-836 6130

TRANSFER SECRETARY
Consolidated Share Registrars Ltd
P O Box 61051, Marshalltown
2107
TEL: 011-492 1620

COMPANY SECRETARY
Johannesburg Consolidated Inv Co Ltd

NATURE OF BUSINESS
Producers of ferrochrome and other chemical and metallurgical products. The company is predominantly export-orientated.

BANKERS :
Standard Bank of SA Ltd

AUDITORS :
Deloitte & Touche

FAMILIAR BRAND NAMES
N/A

CONTRIBUTION BY ACTIVITY
N/A

YEAR END : June

DIVIDEND : Ords 105c

Interim No 10	(Ldr)12/01/90	(Pay)19/02/90	Amt(c)35
Final No 11	(Ldr)17/08/90	(Pay)15/09/90	Amt(c)80

NUMBER OF EMPLOYEES : 1074

CAPITAL STRUCTURE

	AUTHORISED	ISSUED
Ords 105c	52033716	42533716
10% Cum Conv Prefs 105c	29966284	17124284

FINANCIAL STATISTICS (AT FINANCIAL YEAR END)

(Amts in R'000)	1992 Jun	1991 Jun	1990 Jun	1989 Jun	1988 Jun
Ord S/H Int	230962	151674	176379	154146	102468
Long Trm Loans	150529	124579	791	929	1108
Iss Ord Share	42531	42500	42500	42500	42500
Total Liab	223253	284718	100282	134178	63347
Current Liab	72724	160139	99491	133249	62239
Total Assets	454215	436392	276661	288324	165815
Current Assets	211758	185082	190934	245057	133666
Debtors	100563	83104	42805	93099	41265

Inventory	93851	85024	53613	30871	30097
Turnover	306358	274605	215399	324339	158430
Oper Profit	14851	-6400	68950	171157	56490
Interest Paid	12335	22345	160	154	151
Tax Paid	115	665	15146	79475	18437
Prf af Int&Tax	4169	-24705	70994	100553	37902
Prf att Ord Sh	-5263	-24705	70994	100553	37902
Btm Line Earn	-5263	-24705	70994	100553	37902
Dividend Paid	-	-	48875	48875	27625
Mkt Prce(c) YE	1000	875	1325	1875	875
Depreciation	18369	20753	7695	4362	4086

PER SHARE STATISTICS (CENTS)

Net Asst Val	543 04	356 88	415 01	362 70	241 10
Net Earnings	-12 00	-58 00	167 00	237 00	89 00
Dividends	-	-	115 00	115 00	65 00
Cash Flow	30 82	-9 30	185 15	246 86	98 80

RATIOS AND OTHER INFORMATION

Mrk Cap(R000)	425310	371875	563125	796875	371875
Current Ratio	2 91	1 16	1 92	1 84	2 15
Quik/Acid Tst	1 62	0 62	1 38	1 61	1 66
A/C Rec T/ovr	3 05	3 30	5 03	3 48	3 84
Tot Ass T/ovr	0 67	0 63	0 78	1 12	0 96
Debt/Ass Rat	0 45	0 65	0 36	0 47	0 38
L T L Tot Ass	0 29	0 29	0 00	0 00	0 01
Debt to Eqity	0 89	1 88	0 57	0 87	0 62
Interest Cover	1 21	-0 21	469 41	1136 63	374 11
Oper Prof Mrg	4 85	-2 33	32 01	52 77	35 66
Net Prof Marg%	-1 72	-9 00	32 96	31 00	23 92
Ret on Assets	3 66	-0 39	31 19	62 49	34 07
Ret on Equity%	-2 28	-16 29	40 25	65 23	36 99
Price/Earnings	83 33	-15 09	7 93	7 91	9 83
Divid Cover	-	-	1 45	2 06	1 37
Divid Yield	-	-	8 68	6 13	7 43
Earning Yield%	-1 20	-6 63	12 60	12 64	10 17
NAV % Mrk Pr	54 30	40 79	31 32	19 34	27 55
Effec Tax Rate	-	-	18 94	45 12	32 73
Def Interval	10 13	-54 70	0 01	0 01	0 03
Sus Grth Rate	-2 28	-16 29	12 54	33 53	10 03

SUBSIDIARY & ASSOCIATED COMPANIES

PURITY CHROME (PTY) LTD

INVESTMENTS

None

CONSOLIDATED MINING CORPORATION LTD

ABBREVIATION : CONSMNG

JSE SHORT CODE : CSM

SECTOR : Mining Financial-Mining Houses

SHAREHOLDERS

Who Owns Whom's Assessment of the Identity of the Ultimate Controlling Shareholder:
DIRECTORS

SHAREHOLDER	PERCENTAGE 1992	1991
BOARD OF EXECUTORS NOM P/L	---	1 1
EGOLI CONSOLIDATED MINES LTD	---	1 8
EIGHTY ONE MAIN STREET NOM LTD	---	3 9
KRUGER INTERNAT INV CO LTD	---	1 2
LAING G J S	---	2 5
LOWENCO NOM P/L	---	31 6
SA MUTUAL	- -	5 6
SOLID G NOM P/L	---	3 5
STD BANK NOM TVL P/L	---	33 3
SYFRETS TRUST LTD	---	3 2
TOTAL	---	87 6

DIRECTORS :
BUITENDAH HC ,FLOWERDAY RA
LEE RA (Deputy Chairman),LOWENTHAL ND
LOWENTHAL RY ,RUBENSTEIN GB (Chairman)
SCHECHTER M ,SUDDENS BD ,THOMPSON MW ,TURNER CF

REGISTRATION NUMBER : 81/11639/06

REGISTERED OFFICE
39th Floor, Carlton Centre
Johannesburg
2001
TEL 011-331 9181
FAX 011-331 6189

TRANSFER SECRETARY
Mercantile Registrars Ltd
P O Box 1053, Johannesburg
2000
TEL 011-333 8181

COMPANY SECRETARY
Consolidated Mining Management Services Ltd

NATURE OF BUSINESS
A Mining House with a controlling interest in JSE-quoted Egoli Consolidated Mines The group has interests in gold & diamond mining, exploration & management & finance

BANKERS :
First National Bank of SA Ltd

AUDITORS :
Charles Orbach & Co

FAMILIAR BRAND NAMES
N/A

CONTRIBUTION BY ACTIVITY
N/A

YEAR END : March

DIVIDEND : Pref Ords 10c
Final No 1 (Ldr)27/07/90 (Pay)24/08/90 Amt(c)0 9

NUMBER OF EMPLOYEES : 5000

CAPITAL STRUCTURE

	AUTHORISED	ISSUED
Sec Comp Conv Debs	21637176	21637176
Ords 1c	500000000	354888000
Pref ords 1c	55000000	55000000

FINANCIAL STATISTICS (AT FINANCIAL YEAR END)

(Amts in R'000)	1992 Mar	1991 Mar	1990 Mar	1989 Mar	1988 Mar
Ord S/H Int	66335	88756	92111	1062	232193
Long Trm Loans	93456	171389	167155	97664	138811
Iss Ord Share	354887	354887	354887	136640	125000
Total Liab	127371	227178	202537	147686	177419
Current Liab	33915	55789	35382	50022	38608
Total Assets	193706	315934	294648	148748	409612
Current Assets	25980	26283	59727	34580	49887
Debtors	6854	14390	9547	19056	4976
Inventory	7819	8699	13734	12940	24169
Turnover	139822	139494	149478	108363	65378
Oper Profit	14713	9745	23321	4944	19275
Interest Paid	2793	4836	7435	9689	-
Tax Paid	547	894	213	596	1156
Prf af Int&Tax	12501	8396	20381	-5280	18119
Prf att Ord Sh	4269	4605	6361	-4705	14018
Btm Line Earn	-41558	-1322	20058	-248889	14018
Dividend Paid	990	990	495	-	516
Mkt Prce(c) YE	4	10	40	19	60
Depreciation	86	127	171	347	145

PER SHARE STATISTICS (CENTS)

Net Asst Val	18.69	25.01	25.96	0.78	185.75
Net Earnings	1.10	1.20	2.20	-3.60	11.20
Dividends	1.80	1.80	-	-	6.00
Cash Flow	1.01	1.10	1.84	-5.39	9.98

RATIOS AND OTHER INFORMATION

Mrk Cap(R000)	14195	35489	141955	25962	75000
Current Ratio	0.77	0.47	1.69	0.69	1.29
Quik/Acid Tst	0.54	0.32	1.30	0.43	0.67
A/C Rec T/ovr	20.40	9.69	15.66	5.69	13.14
Tot Ass T/ovr	0.72	0.44	0.51	0.73	0.16
Debt/Ass Rat	0.23	0.22	0.16	0.54	0.15
L T L Tot Ass	0.05	0.05	0.04	0.20	0.06
Debt to Eqity	0.66	0.79	0.53	75.46	0.27
Interest Cover	5.27	2.22	3.28	0.52	-
Oper Prof Mrg	10.52	6.99	15.60	4.56	29.48
Net Prof Marg%	3.05	3.30	4.26	-4.34	21.44
Ret on Assets	8.18	4.47	9.51	5.22	5.14
Ret on Equity%	6.44	5.19	6.91	-443.03	6.04
Price/Earnings	3.64	8.33	18.18	-5.28	5.36
Divid Cover	0.61	0.67	-	-	1.87
Divid Yield	45.00	18.00	-	-	10.00
Earning Yield%	27.50	12.00	5.50	-18.95	18.67
NAV % Mrk Pr	467.30	250.10	64.89	4.09	309.59
Effec Tax Rate	5.35	8.87	0.62	-8.47	5.58
Def Interval	2.91	7.12	2.95	-8.35	3.56
Sus Grth Rate	4.94	4.07	6.37	-443.03	5.81

SUBSIDIARY & ASSOCIATED COMPANIES

BENONI GOLD HOLDINGS LTD (32%)
BENONI GOLD MINES (PTY) LTD
BENONI GOLD MINING CO LTD (34%)
BONTE KOE MYNBOU ONDERNEMINGS (EDMS) BPK (48%)
BRAKPAN VAN DYK EXTENSIONS LTD
BRAKPAN VAN DYK MINES LTD
CARBON LEADER LTD
CARRIG DIAMONDS LTD
CERTAURSA (PTY) LTD
CMC MINERASS (PTY) LTD
CONSOLIDATED MINING MANAGEMENT SERVICES
CONSOLIDATED RESOURCES & EXPLORATION LTD
EAST CHAMP D'Or GOLD MINE LTD
EGOLI CONSOLIDATED MINES LTD
ELANDSLAAGTE GOLD MINING COMPANY (PTY) L
HVL ASBESTOS (SWAZILAND) LTD (34%)
INCORPORATED MANAGEMENT AND FINANCE LTD
INVESTMENTS AND TECHNICAL MANAGEMENT LTD
JOHANNESBURG INDUSTRIAL & COMMERCIAL INV
JOHANNESBURG MINING INVESTMENTS LTD
KLERKSDORP GOLD HOLDINGS (PTY) LTD
LIBRA ASSAY LABORATORY (PTY) LTD (50%)
LOXTON EXPLORATION (PTY) LTD
MÁNTECH SERVICES (PTY) LTD
NIGEL GOLD MINING COMPANY (PTY) LTD (30%)
NIGEL GOLD MINING HOLDINGS LTD (30%)
NIPROP PROPERTY INVESTMENTS (PTY) LTD (30%)
SOUTH EAST RAND GOLD HOLDINGS LTD
SOUTHERN FISSURES LTD
TANKS OIL AND PLATINUM HOLDINGS LTD
TERIKIM LANDGOED (EDMS) BPK (32%)
WEST WITWATERSRAND GOLD HOLDINGS LTD (32%)
WEST WITWATERSRAND GOLD MINES LTD (32%)
WITWATERSRAND NIGEL LTD (37%)
WOLFBERG MYNBOU (EDMS) BPK

INVESTMENTS

FRIGATE GROUP LTD (1493660 SH)

CONSOLIDATED MODDERFONTEIN MINES LTD

ABBREVIATION : MODDER

JSE SHORT CODE : MDR

SECTOR : Gold-Rand & others

SHAREHOLDERS

Who Owns Whom's Assessment of the Identity of the Ultimate Controlling Shareholder: DIRECTORS CONTROL 27,85% (JUNE 1991)

SHAREHOLDER	PERCENTAGE 1992	1991
INDO-CHINA NOM P/L	24.9	---
SALENE MINING P/L	20.9	24.3
FIRST NAT NOM P/L	8.5	8.8
STD BANK NOM TVL P/L	4.8	6.2
POUROULIS L C	2.7	2.7
FIRST NAT NOM P/L GATR DEPOT	2.3	1.2
LEVY C L	1.0	---
INDO-CHINA NOM SA P/L	---	25.1
SA MUTUAL	---	4.2
TOTAL	65.2	72.5

DIRECTORS :
COOMBES ED ,CROSS TA ,DANIEL RJ
GIBBS TL (Chairman)
POUROULIS LC (Managing Director

REGISTRATION NUMBER : 01/03323/06

REGISTERED OFFICE
4th Floor, Burlington House
22 Rissik Str, Johannesburg
2001
TEL: 011-463 2020
FAX: 011-463 2066

TRANSFER SECRETARY
Gold Equity Registrars (Pty) Ltd
P O Box 62185, Marshalltown
2107
TEL 011-834 5623

COMPANY SECRETARY
Gold Equity Registrars (Pty) Ltd

NATURE OF BUSINESS
The group conducts gold mining operations in the Benoni, Brakpan & Springs areas of the Transvaal

BANKERS :
Volkskas Ltd

AUDITORS :
Coopers Theron Du Toit

FAMILIAR BRAND NAMES
N/A

CONTRIBUTION BY ACTIVITY
N/A

YEAR END : June

DIVIDEND :15/02/91 and 15/08/91

NUMBER OF EMPLOYEES : 1481

CAPITAL STRUCTURE

	AUTHORISED	ISSUED
Ords 5c	49695547	49695547

FINANCIAL STATISTICS (AT FINANCIAL YEAR END)

(Amts in R'000)	1991 Jun	1990 Jun	1989 Jun	1988 Jun	1987
Ord S/H Int	306325	302754	142158	138616	138108
Long Trm Loans	722	1626	11391	1927	34233
Iss Ord Share	49696	49696	34752	34752	21440
Total Liab	26725	34293	61448	65843	67546
Current Liab	26003	32667	50057	63916	33313
Total Assets	202466	206463	203606	204459	185755
Intang Assets	130584	130584	*	*	*
Current Assets	4323	7547	4556	6111	13414
Debtors	3019	6375	3131	3825	-
Inventory	949	1130	1385	2260	13414
Turnover	60864	78748	69639	80513	74144
Oper Profit	-950	9390	3770	5115	34609
Interest Paid	2613	8907	7864	4570	894
Tax Paid	3	73	-113	37	718
Prf af Int&Tax	-3486	540	-3918	508	33174
Prf att Ord Sh	-3486	540	-3918	508	33174
Btm Line Earn	3571	540	3542	508	33174
Dividend Paid	-	-	-	-	19296
Mkt Prce(c) YE	130	185	175	300	1225

PER SHARE STATISTICS (CENTS)

Net Asst Val	353 63	346 45	409 06	398 87	644 16
Net Earnings	-7 01	1 55	-11 30	1 50	-
Cash Flow	-7 01	1 55	11 27	1 46	154 73

RATIOS AND OTHER INFORMATION

Mrk Cap(R000)	64605	91938	60816	104256	262640
Current Ratio	0 17	0 23	0 09	0 10	0 40
Quik/Acid Tst	0 13	0 20	0 06	0 06	-
A/C Rec T/ovr	20 16	12 35	22 24	21 05	-
Tot Ass T/ovr	0 30	0 38	0 34	0 39	0 40
Debt/Ass Rat	0 13	0 17	0 30	0 32	0 36
L T L Tot Ass	0 00	0 01	0 06	0 01	0 18
Debt to Eqity	0 09	0 11	0 43	0 48	0 49
Interest Cover	-0 36	1 06	0 49	1 12	38 91
Oper Prof Mrg	-1 56	11 92	5 41	6 35	46 68
Net Prof Marg%	-5 73	0 69	-5 63	0 63	44 74
Ret on Assets	-0 43	4 61	1 88	2 50	18 73
Ret on Equity%	-1 14	0 18	-2 76	0 37	24 02
Price/Earnings	-18 54	119 35	-15 49	200 00	-
Earning Yield%	-5 39	0 84	-6 46	0 50	-
NAV % Mrk Pr	272 02	187 27	233 75	132 96	52 58
Effec Tax Rate	-0 09	13 80	-0 71	6 79	2 13
Def Interval	-2 19	22 12	-9 98	79 45	1 03
Sus Grth Rate	-1 14	0 18	-2 76	0 37	10 05

SUBSIDIARY & ASSOCIATED COMPANIES

AURUM TRANSPORT SERVICES (PTY) LTD
CONSOLIDATED MODDERFONTEIN MINES 1979 LT
MACHINERY TRADING CO (PTY) LTD
MODDERFONTEIN SEVENTY-FOUR (PTY) LTD
NORTHSIDE ENGINEERING (PTY) LTD
SPRINGS DAGGA GOLD MINES LTD

INVESTMENTS

GEDEX (PTY) LTD (CUM RED PREFS) (950000 SH)

CONSOLIDATED MURCHISON LTD

ABBREVIATION : CON-MURCH

JSE SHORT CODE : CMU

SECTOR : Metals & Minerals-Other

SHAREHOLDERS

Who Owns Whom's Assessment of the Identity of the Ultimate Controlling Shareholder:
ANGLO AMERICAN VIA JCI

SHAREHOLDER	PERCENTAGE 1992	1991
STD BANK NOM TVL P/L	33 8	20 8
LONDON CONTROL ACCOUNT	22 8	18 2
FOX STREET NOM P/L	7 3	4 9
FIRST NAT NOM P/L	5 5	4 1
VOLKSKAS NOM P/L	3 9	2 8
INDO CHINA NOM P/L	1 7	---
LOCARNO EXPLORATION CO P/L	1 5	1 0
ISIDOR BALTSTEIN TRUST NOM P/L	1 3	- -
BALTSTEIN I	1 2	---
SUTTNER H	1 1	---
INDO CHINA NOM SA P/L	---	1 3
TOTAL	79 9	53 0

DIRECTORS :
DUMPLETON MJ ,FAUCONNIER CJ DR
HAWARDEN MW (Chairman),JONKER GJ ,MCKENNA P

REGISTRATION NUMBER : 05/05478/06

REGISTERED OFFICE
Consolidated Building, Corner Fox & Harrison Streets
Johannesburg
2001

TEL: 011-373 9111
FAX: 011-836 6130

TRANSFER SECRETARY
Consolidated Share Registrars Ltd
P O Box 61051, Marshalltown
2107
TEL: 011-492 1620

COMPANY SECRETARY
Johannesburg Consolidated Inv Co Ltd

NATURE OF BUSINESS
The company mines and processes antimony ore in the Letaba district.Gold is recovered as a by-product.

BANKERS :
Standard Bank of SA Ltd

AUDITORS :
Ernst & Young

FAMILIAR BRAND NAMES
N/A

CONTRIBUTION BY ACTIVITY
Antimony revenue (% of turnover) (29.2%)
Gold revenue (% of turnover) (70.3%)
Sundry (0.5%)

YEAR END : June

DIVIDEND :Ords 10c
Final No 82 (Ldr)07/08/92 (Pay)11/09/92 Amt(c)15

NUMBER OF EMPLOYEES : 1189

CAPITAL STRUCTURE

	AUTHORISED	ISSUED
Ords 10c	9000000	6240000

FINANCIAL STATISTICS (AT FINANCIAL YEAR END)

(Amts in R'000)	1992 Jun	1991 Jun	1990 Jun	1989 Jun	1988 Jun
Ord S/H Int	90360	87998	88178	94605	86257
Iss Ord Share	6240	6240	6240	6240	6240
Total Liab	8652	7728	8777	7963	7011
Current Liab	8652	7728	8777	7963	7011
Total Assets	99012	95726	96955	102568	93268
Current Assets	14710	11309	12507	22423	18690
Debtors	4983	4325	5231	11400	9216
Inventory	5654	6817	6539	3712	5293
Turnover	48346	39169	34263	54570	43011
Oper Profit	2750	128	-6807	9794	6026
Interest Paid	184	528	618	-	-
Tax Paid	-	-	-	927	1236
Prf af Int&Tax	3298	-180	-6427	10220	4790
Prf att Ord Sh	3298	-180	-6427	10220	4790
Btm Line Earn	3298	-180	-6427	10220	4790
Dividend Paid	936	-	-	1872	1872
Mkt Prce(c) YE	140	275	260	760	810

PER SHARE STATISTICS (CENTS)

Net Asst Val	1448.08	1410.22	1413.11	1516.11	1382.32
Net Earnings	55.00	-2.00	-170.00	75.00	-82.00
Dividends	15.00	-	-	30.00	30.00
Cash Flow	52.85	-2.88	-103.00	163.78	76.76

RATIOS AND OTHER INFORMATION

Mrk Cap(R000)	8736	17160	16224	47424	50544
Current Ratio	1.70	1.46	1.42	2.82	2.67
Quik/Acid Tst	1.05	0.58	0.68	2.35	1.91
A/C Rec T/ovr	9.70	9.06	6.55	4.79	4.67
Tot Ass T/ovr	0.49	0.41	0.35	0.53	0.46
Debt/Ass Rat	0.09	0.08	0.09	0.08	0.08
Debt to Eqity	0.10	0.09	0.10	0.08	0.08
Interest Cover	15.16	0.29	-10.66	-	-
Oper Prof Mrg	5.69	0.33	-19.87	17.95	14.01
Net Prof Marg%	6.82	-0.46	-18.76	18.73	11.14
Ret on Assets	3.52	0.36	-5.99	10.87	6.46
Ret on Equity%	3.65	-0.20	-7.29	10.80	5.55
Price/Earnings	2.55	-137.50	-1.53	10.13	-9.88
Divid Cover	3.67	-	-	2.50	-2.73
Divid Yield	10.71	-	-	3.95	3.70
Earning Yield%	39.29	-0.73	-65.38	9.87	-10.12
NAV % Mrk Pr	1034.34	512.81	543.50	199.49	170.66
Effec Tax Rate	-	-	-	8.36	20.51
Def Interval	-	-	-0.35	-	0.01
Sus Grth Rate	2.61	-0.20	-7.29	8.82	3.38

SUBSIDIARY & ASSOCIATED COMPANIES

ANTIMONY PRODUCTS (PTY) LTD (25%)

INVESTMENTS

RAND MUTUAL ASSURANCE CO LTD (45 SH)

CONSOLIDATED PROPERTY & FINANCE LTD

ABBREVIATION : PROPFIN

JSE SHORT CODE : PFN

SECTOR : Financial-Property

SHAREHOLDERS

Who Owns Whom's Assessment of the Identity of the Ultimate Controlling Shareholder:
TARRY FAMILY

SHAREHOLDER	PERCENTAGE 1992	1991
TARRY F J	42.8	46.1
TARRY M A	12.6	12.6
HASHAY NOM P/L	8.9	8.9
TARRY ANN	7.8	7.8
TARRY V	7.8	7.8
ST ANTONIO INV INC	3.6	---
FORD V	2.2	2.2
RETAN NOM P/L	1.7	1.7
PETER A	1.7	1.7
COLFIN LTD	1.4	---
TARRY J	1.4	1.4
HORNE F	1.0	1.0
TOTAL	93.0	91.3

DIRECTORS :
BURGER J ,COETZEE PH ,MARCUS P
TARRY FJ (Chairman & Managing Dir.)
TARRY MA (Systems Director

REGISTRATION NUMBER : 89/06570/06

REGISTERED OFFICE
4th Floor, 52 Joubert Str
Johannesburg
2001
TEL: 011-337 5210

TRANSFER SECRETARY
Consolidated Share Registrars Ltd
P O Box 61051, Marshalltown
2107
TEL: 011-492 1620

COMPANY SECRETARY
Prorsum Registrars (Pty) Ltd

NATURE OF BUSINESS
The company's principal business is the holding of long-term investments in companies which are engaged in the following activities: Property investment; Property development and Construction.

BANKERS :
Trust Bank of Africa Ltd

AUDITORS :
Levitt Kirson

FAMILIAR BRAND NAMES
N/A

CONTRIBUTION BY ACTIVITY
N/A

YEAR END : February

DIVIDEND :15/06/91

CAPITAL STRUCTURE

	AUTHORISED	ISSUED
Ords 1c	100000000	18000000

FINANCIAL STATISTICS (AT FINANCIAL YEAR END)

(Amts in R'000)	1990 Feb
Ord S/H Int	25352
Iss Ord Share	18000
Total Liab	330
Current Liab	330
Total Assets	25682
Current Assets	18945
Inventory	18945
Turnover	16000
Oper Profit	5500
Prf af Int&Tax	5500
Prf att Ord Sh	5500
Btm Line Earn	5500

PER SHARE STATISTICS (CENTS)

Net Asst Val	140.84
Cash Flow	30.56

RATIOS AND OTHER INFORMATION

Current Ratio	57.41
Tot Ass T/ovr	0.62
Debt/Ass Rat	0.01
Debt to Eqity	0.01
Oper Prof Mrg	34.38
Net Prof Marg%	34.38
Ret on Assets	21.42
Ret on Equity%	21.69
Def Interval	0.06
Sus Grth Rate	21.69

SUBSIDIARY & ASSOCIATED COMPANIES

COTTON TAIL HOMES (PTY) LTD
HOLIDAY TIME MARKETING (PTY) LTD
KNIGHTSBRIDGE INVESTMENT (PTY) LTD
LOT 6234 MARIONHILL (PTY) LTD
MIDNORTH FINANCE (PTY) LTD (50%)
NORTH OF JUDE (PTY) LTD
ROLBREN ENTERPRISES (PTY) LTD
SOLID GOLD CONSTRUCTION LTD
STENOTYPE HOUSE (PTY) LTD

INVESTMENTS

None

CONTROL INSTRUMENTS GROUP LTD

ABBREVIATION : CONTROL

JSE SHORT CODE : CNL

SECTOR : Industrial-Electronics, Electrical & Bat

SHAREHOLDERS

Who Owns Whom's Assessment of the Identity of the Ultimate Controlling Shareholder:
DIRECTORS / ANGLOVAAL

SHAREHOLDER	PERCENTAGE 1992	1991
MATELECT NOM P/L	29.6	29.6
ANGLOVAAL IND LTD	26.2	26.2
FIRST NAT MERCHANT BANK LTD	6.0	6.0
BURROW W T	5.5	5.5
BECK G J	3.6	---
GILLETT A C	3.4	3.4
HERSOV B	3.0	3.0
M-C NOM P/L	1.8	1.8
STD MERCHANT BANK LTD	1.8	1.8
FOX STREET NOM P/L	1.4	1.4
AFC INV LTD	1.3	1.3
MANTRAK NOM P/L	1.2	1.2
CHALKTON NOM CO P/L	1.0	1.3
FRIEDMAN C	---	3.6
TOTAL	85.5	85.8

DIRECTORS :
BURROW WT ,BUZER TE (Executive Director)
FRIEDMAN C (Vice Chairman)
FRIEDMAN R (Managing Director)
HEFER HV (Chairman),ROBBERTZE JC ,SAVAGE RB

REGISTRATION NUMBER : 64/03987/06

REGISTERED OFFICE
8th Floor JHI House, 11 Cradock Ave
Rosebank, Johannesburg

2196
TEL: 011-880 7335
FAX: 011-880 7366

TRANSFER SECRETARY
Union Provident Trust SA Ltd
P O Box 2322, Johannesburg
2000
TEL: 011-833 6700

COMPANY SECRETARY
P J Visser

NATURE OF BUSINESS
The company is an investment company with interests in private companies which design, manufacture, sell and service products which provide its customers with advanced electronic and electromechanical products and systems. Subsidiaries also manufacture & sell products in the industrial instrumentation field.

BANKERS :
First National Bank of SA Ltd

AUDITORS :
Ernst & Young

FAMILIAR BRAND NAMES
AMANO,KIENZLE,VDO

CONTRIBUTION BY ACTIVITY
N/A

YEAR END : June

DIVIDEND : (Ldr)03/03/89 (Pay)17/03/89
DIVIDEND : (Ldr)25/08/89 (Pay)22/09/89

NUMBER OF EMPLOYEES : 460

CAPITAL STRUCTURE

	AUTHORISED	ISSUED
Ords 5c	100000000	67693850

FINANCIAL STATISTICS (AT FINANCIAL YEAR END)

(Amts in R'000)	1992 Jun	1991 Jun	1990 Jun	1989 Jun	1988 Jun
Ord S/H Int	24379	24091	24086	37220	34166
Long Trm Loans	2712	3035	1626	1430	1276
Iss Ord Share	67694	67694	67694	69600	69600
Total Liab	24354	25836	27924	28162	17950
Current Liab	21642	22801	26298	26732	16674
Total Assets	48733	49927	52010	65382	52116
Current Assets	39230	39884	42343	51544	39841
Debtors	12549	11120	14991	20070	14321
Inventory	19043	22443	21269	23038	14582
Turnover	66348	65144	67555	73000	50868
Oper Profit	1991	2412	-154	5054	6790
Interest Paid	3166	3673	4445	1164	755
Prf af Int&Tax	288	5	-4599	4502	6035
Prf att Ord Sh	288	5	-4599	4502	6048
Btm Line Earn	288	5	-9513	4585	6048
Dividend Paid	-	-	-	1531	1531
Mkt Prce(c) YE	25	23	27	50	60
Depreciation	2281	2195	2052	1771	1224

PER SHARE STATISTICS (CENTS)

Net Asst Val	36.01	35.59	35.58	53.48	49.09
Net Earnings	0.40	-	-6.70	6.50	9.30
Dividends	-	-	-	2.20	2.20
Cash Flow	3.80	3.25	-3.71	9.01	11.18

RATIOS AND OTHER INFORMATION

Mrk Cap(R000)	16924	15570	18277	34800	41760
Current Ratio	1.81	1.75	1.61	1.93	2.39
Quik/Acid Tst	0.93	0.76	0.80	1.07	1.51
A/C Rec T/ovr	5.29	5.86	4.51	3.64	3.55
Tot Ass T/ovr	1.36	1.30	1.30	1.12	0.98
Debt/Ass Rat	0.50	0.52	0.54	0.43	0.34
L T L Tot Ass	0.06	0.06	0.03	0.02	0.02
Debt to Eqity	1.00	1.07	1.16	0.76	0.53
Interest Cover	0.63	0.66	-0.03	4.34	8.99
Oper Prof Mrg	3.00	3.70	-0.23	6.92	13.35
Net Prof Marg%	0.43	0.01	-6.81	6.17	11.89
Ret on Assets	7.09	7.37	-0.30	8.67	13.05
Ret on Equity%	1.18	0.02	-19.09	12.10	17.70
Price/Earnings	62.50	-	-4.03	7.69	6.45
Divid Cover	-	-	-	2.95	4.23
Divid Yield	-	-	-	4.40	3.67
Earning Yield%	1.60	-	-24.81	13.00	15.50
NAV % Mrk Pr	144.05	154.73	131.78	106.95	81.82
Def Interval	5.33	7.94	-7.24	2.47	0.93
Sus Grth Rate	1.18	0.02	-19.09	7.98	13.22

SUBSIDIARY & ASSOCIATED COMPANIES

CONTROL INSTRUMENTS MANAGEMENT SERVICES
CONTROL INSTRUMENTS NOMINEES (PTY) LTD
ELECTROMATIC (PTY) LTD
ERF 399 WYNBERG (PTY) LTD

INVESTMENTS

None

CORONATION SYNDICATE LTD

ABBREVIATION : COR-SYND

JSE SHORT CODE : COS

SECTOR : Mining Financial-Mining Holding

SHAREHOLDERS

Who Owns Whom's Assessment of the Identity of the Ultimate Controlling Shareholder: DL BARNES/GMC RYAN/UAL MERCHANT BANK

SHAREHOLDER	PERCENTAGE 1992	1991
TWEEFONTEIN UNITED COLLIERIES LTD	62.2	62.2
UK CONTROL ACCOUNT	20.5	22.2
HARVEST SECURITIES LTD	4.3	3.3
FIRST NAT NOM P/L	1.7	1.4
STD BANK NOM TVL P/L	1.5	---
NORTHCHART INV LTD	1.0	1.0
INDO-CHINA NOM SA P/L	---	1.3
TOTAL	91.2	91.4

DIRECTORS :
ADAMS T ,DE VILLIERS JTM DR,HOSSY IM
SCHEEPERS KF ,WILKINSON KP
WILKINSON TA (Chairman & Managing Dir.

REGISTRATION NUMBER : 01/01739/06

REGISTERED OFFICE
First Floor, 19 Girton Road
Parktown
2193
TEL 011-642 7691
FAX 011-642 9717

TRANSFER SECRETARY
Mercantile Registrars Ltd
P O Box 1053, Johannesburg
2000
TEL 011-333 8181

COMPANY SECRETARY
Lonrho Management Services (Pty) Ltd

NATURE OF BUSINESS
An investment holding company with a portfolio of JSE-quoted shares, the principal investment being Duiker Exploration Ltd

BANKERS :
First National Bank of SA Ltd

AUDITORS :
KPMG Aiken & Peat

FAMILIAR BRAND NAMES
N/A

CONTRIBUTION BY ACTIVITY
N/A

YEAR END : September

DIVIDEND :Ords 25c

Interim No 64	(Ldr)30/03/90	(Pay)25/04/90	Amt(c)15
Final No 65	(Ldr)28/09/90	(Pay)24/10/90	Amt(c)2
Interim No 66	(Ldr)28/03/91	(Pay)24/04/91	Amt(c)14
Final No 67	(Ldr)27/09/91	(Pay)23/10/91	Amt(c)2
Interim No 68	(Ldr)27/03/92	(Pay)23/04/92	Amt(c)5
Final No 69	(Ldr)25/09/92	(Pay)21/10/92	Amt(c)3

CAPITAL STRUCTURE

	AUTHORISED	ISSUED
Ords 25c	19000000	6000000
Red Pref 25c	1000000	0

FINANCIAL STATISTICS (AT FINANCIAL YEAR END)

(Amts in R'000)	1992 Sep	1991 Sep	1990 Sep	1989 Sep	1988 Sep
Ord S/H Int	3486	3263	3210	3186	3110
Iss Ord Share	6000	6000	6000	6000	6000
Total Liab	271	246	242	418	548
Current Liab	271	246	242	418	548
Total Assets	3757	3509	3452	3604	3658
Current Assets	282	379	293	445	751
Debtors	214	123	103	139	108
Oper Profit	235	560	681	1257	1165
Tax Paid	-	-	-	-139	50
Prf af Int&Tax	678	964	1044	1396	1115
Prf att Ord Sh	678	964	1044	1396	1115
Btm Line Earn	703	1013	1044	1396	1178
Dividend Paid	480	960	1020	1320	2700
Mkt Prce(c) YE	150	70	100	130	145

PER SHARE STATISTICS (CENTS)

Net Asst Val	58 10	54 38	53 50	53 10	51 83
Net Earnings	11 30	16 10	17 40	23 30	18 60
Dividends	8 00	16 00	17 00	22 00	45 00
Cash Flow	11 30	16 07	17 40	23 27	18 58

RATIOS AND OTHER INFORMATION

Mrk Cap(R000)	9000	4200	6000	7800	8700
Current Ratio	1 04	1 54	1 21	1 06	1 37
Quik/Acid Tst	1 04	1 54	1 21	1 06	1 37
Debt/Ass Rat	0 07	0 07	0 07	0 12	0 15
Debt to Eqity	0 08	0 08	0 08	0 13	0 18
Ret on Assets	18 05	27 47	30 24	34 88	31 85
Ret on Equity%	19 45	29 54	32 52	43 82	35 85
Price/Earnings	13 27	4 35	5 75	5 58	7 80
Divid Cover	1 41	1 01	1 02	1 06	0 41
Divid Yield	5 33	22 86	17 00	16 92	31 03
Earning Yield%	7 53	23 00	17 40	17 92	12 83
NAV % Mrk Pr	38 73	77 69	53 50	40 85	35 75
Effec Tax Rate	-	-	-	-	4 29
Sus Grth Rate	5 68	0 12	0 75	2 39	50 96

SUBSIDIARY & ASSOCIATED COMPANIES

None

INVESTMENTS

DUIKER EXPLORATION LTD (567030 SH)
GENCOR BEHEREND BEPERK (139287 SH)
GENCOR LTD (105861SH)
NEW WITS LTD (64600 SH)

CORPORATE MANAGEMENT SERVICES LTD

ABBREVIATION : CMS

JSE SHORT CODE · CMS

SECTOR : Industrial Electronics, Electrical & Bat

SHAREHOLDERS

Who Owns Whom's Assessment of the Identity of the Ultimate Controlling Shareholder: DIRECTORS / PREMIER GROUP

SHAREHOLDER	PERCENTAGE 1992	1991
PREMIER GROUP HLDGS LTD	33 3	33 3
BAXTER A J	27 3	27 4
FIRST NAT NOM P/L	11 0	11 0
PRYCE-WILLIAMS K	7 0	7 4
STD BANK NOM TVL P/L	5 3	7 8
NPL NOM P/L	3 5	---
CMS SHARE TRUSTEES	3 1	1 4
TOTAL	90 5	88 2

DIRECTORS :
BAXTER AJ (Chairman & Chief Exec),DAVIES AJ
GREEN CR (Financial Director)
MCMAHON DJ (Deputy Managing Director)
PRYCE WILLIAMS K ,UTIAN GM ,WAPENAAR JJ

REGISTRATION NUMBER : 68/10017/06

REGISTERED OFFICE
CMS House, Hurlingham Park
William Nicol Drive, Sandton
2196
TEL. 011-789 2505
FAX 011-886 2843

TRANSFER SECRETARY
Mercantile Registrars Ltd
P O Box 1053, Johannesburg
2000
TEL 011-333 8181

COMPANY SECRETARY
JL Harvey (Ms)

NATURE OF BUSINESS
Selling & maintenance of mainframe computer hardware and information storage products, and performance software

BANKERS :
First National Bank of SA Ltd
Standard Bank of SA Ltd

AUDITORS :
Price Waterhouse Meyernel

FAMILIAR BRAND NAMES
ALB,CINCOM,FIXIT,MANTIS,MSA,NEARLINE
NETMASTER,STORAGETEK,SUPRA,SYBERCACHE

CONTRIBUTION BY ACTIVITY
Mainframe Hardware/Info Storage (%Sales) (75 3%)
Systems & Packaged Application Software (7 0%)
Independent Maintenance Services (17 7%)

YEAR END : April

DIVIDEND : Ords 1c

Final No 3	(Ldr)01/06/90	(Pay)15/06/90	Amt(c)3
Final No 5	(Ldr)03/07/92	(Pay)20/07/92	Amt(c)3
Final No 4	(Ldr)30/05/91	(Pay)17/06/91	Amt(c)3 5

NUMBER OF EMPLOYEES : 80

CAPITAL STRUCTURE

	AUTHORISED	ISSUED
Ords 1c	40000000	29847500

FINANCIAL STATISTICS (AT FINANCIAL YEAR END)

(Amts in R'000)	1992 Apr	1991 Mar	1990 Mar	1989 Mar	1988 Mar
Ord S/H Int	10719	10090	13356	15708	7048
Long Trm Loans	3612	3830	3172	670	-
Iss Ord Share	29848	29848	29848	29680	18550
Total Liab	13903	20248	15808	13056	15992
Current Liab	10291	16418	12636	12386	15992
Total Assets	24622	30338	24672	24272	19615
Intang Assets	*	*	4492	4492	3425
Current Assets	22625	27145	20719	19663	16105
Debtors	3655	14893	11787	9205	11198
Inventory	15217	12250	8929	9846	4882
Turnover	44651	58101	40702	32249	25826
Oper Profit	4585	4911	3139	2379	2400
Interest Paid	802	746	1024	156	6
Tax Paid	1736	1620	-	-1	960
Prf af Int&Tax	2182	2578	2260	2339	1434
Prf att Ord Sh	2182	2578	2260	2339	1434
Btm Line Earn	2182	-1080	-499	2339	1434
Dividend Paid	895	1045	895	1039	603
Mkt Prce(c) YE	35	35	30	48	65
Depreciation	661	381	271	128	62

PER SHARE STATISTICS (CENTS)

Net Asst Val	35 91	33 80	29 70	37 79	19 53
Net Earnings	7 30	8 60	7 60	8 20	8 30
Dividends	3 00	3 50	3 00	3 50	3 25
Cash Flow	8 19	13 04	8 51	8 62	8 02

RATIOS AND OTHER INFORMATION

Mrk Cap(R000)	10447	10447	8954	14246	12058
Current Ratio	2 20	1 65	1 64	1 59	1 01
Quik/Acid Tst	0 72	0 91	0 93	0 79	0 70
A/C Rec T/ovr	11 28	3 90	3 45	3 50	2 13
Tot Ass T/ovr	1 67	1 92	1 65	1 33	1 22
Debt/Ass Rat	0 42	0 55	0 51	0 51	0 82
L T L Tot Ass	0 00	0 00	-	-	-
Debt to Eqity	0 97	1 64	0 95	0 79	2 27
Interest Cover	5 72	6 58	3 07	15 25	400 00
Oper Prof Mrg	10 27	8 45	7 71	7 38	9 29
Net Prof Marg%	4 89	4 44	5 55	7 25	5 55
Ret on Assets	17 70	16 30	13 31	10 28	11 29
Ret on Equity%	18 79	25 55	16 92	14 89	18 78
Price/Earnings	4 79	4 07	3 95	5 85	7 83
Divid Cover	2 43	2 46	2 53	2 34	2 55
Divid Yield	8 57	10 00	10 00	7 29	5 00
Earning Yield%	20 86	24 57	25 33	17 08	12 77
NAV % Mrk Pr	102 61	96 58	98 99	78 73	30 05
Effec Tax Rate	49 26	16 36	-	0 13	40 10
Def Interval	0 26	0 50	0 63	0 00	1 96
Sus Grth Rate	12 01	15 19	10 22	8 28	11 79

SUBSIDIARY & ASSOCIATED COMPANIES

CMS SUPPORT SERVICES (PTY) LTD
I T INTEGRATED TECHNOLOGIES (PTY) LTD
SOURCE SQUARED (PTY) LTD

INVESTMENTS

None

CORWIL INVESTMENTS LTD

ABBREVIATION : CORWIL

JSE SHORT CODE : CRW

SECTOR : Financial-Investment Trusts

SHAREHOLDERS

Who Owns Whom's Assessment of the Identity of the Ultimate Controlling Shareholder:
MANN FAMILY / INSTITUTIONS

SHAREHOLDER	PERCENTAGE 1992	1991
STD BANK NOM TVL P/L	34 3	33 8
MANN E/L MAX	23 1	23 1
MESSINA INV LTD	11 3	11 3
FIRST NAT NOM P/L	11 2	11 7
TOTAL	79 9	79 9

DIRECTORS :
LEE RA (Chairman),MANN J ,NEL MM ,ROUX W
WILKINSON KP

REGISTRATION NUMBER : 87/00732/06

REGISTERED OFFICE
19 Girton Road, Parktown
Johannesburg
2193
TEL 011-642 7691
FAX 011-642 9717

TRANSFER SECRETARY
Mercantile Registrars Ltd
P O Box 1053, Johannesburg
2000
TEL 011-333 8181

COMPANY SECRETARY
Lonrho Management Services (Pty) Ltd

NATURE OF BUSINESS
An investment holding company Its sole investment is a 15,3% interest in the ordinary stock, & 25,4% interest in the preferred stock of Willoughby's Consolidatd Plc, quoted on the International Stock Xchange, London Willoughby's has mining, ranching & investmnt interests in Zimbabwe, where the major part of its assets is held & where it conducts its principal trading activities

BANKERS :
First National Bank of SA Ltd

AUDITORS :
KPMG Aiken & Peat

FAMILIAR BRAND NAMES
N/A

CONTRIBUTION BY ACTIVITY
N/A

YEAR END . March

DIVIDEND Ords 1c

Interim No 4	(Ldr)28/07/89	(Pay)16/08/89	Amt(c)16
Final No 5	(Ldr)20/04/90	(Pay)03/05/90	Amt(c)17
Interim No 6	(Ldr)10/08/90	(Pay)21/08/90	Amt(c)5
Final No 7	(Ldr)26/04/91	(Pay)13/05/91	Amt(c)5
Interim No 8	(Ldr)16/08/91	(Pay)28/08/91	Amt(c)5
Final No 9	(Ldr)24/04/92	(Pay)12/02/92	Amt(c)6
Interim No 10	(Ldr)14/08/92	(Pay)25/08/92	Amt(c)6

CAPITAL STRUCTURE

	AUTHORISED	ISSUED
Ords 1c	4000000	1858689

FINANCIAL STATISTICS (AT FINANCIAL YEAR END)

(Amts in R 000)	1992 Mar	1991 Mar	1990 Mar	1989 Mar	1988 Mar
Ord S/H Int	4861	4849	4825	4795	4784
Iss Ord Share	1859	1859	1859	1859	1859
Total Liab	131	112	327	353	185
Current Liab	131	112	327	353	185
Total Assets	4992	4961	5152	5148	4969
Current Assets	215	184	375	371	192
Oper Profit	45	42	37	628	174
Tax Paid	6	5	6	3	
Prf af Int&Tax	216	210	643	625	174
Prf att Ord Sh	216	210	643	625	174
Btm Line Earn	216	210	643	625	174
Dividend Paid	204	186	613	614	167
Mkt Prce(c) YE	250	250	450	380	190

PER SHARE STATISTICS (CENTS)

Net Asst Val	261 48	260 84	259 55	257 93	257 34
Net Earnings	11 60	11 30	34 60	33 60	9 40
Dividends	11 00	10 00	33 00	33 00	9 00
Cash Flow	11 62	11 30	34 59	33 62	18 72

RATIOS AND OTHER INFORMATION

Mrk Cap(R000)	4648	4648	8366	7064	3532
Current Ratio	1 64	1 64	1 15	1 05	1 04
Quik/Acid Tst	1 64	1 64	1 15	1 05	1 04
Debt/Ass Rat	0 03	0 02	0 06	0 07	0 04
Debt to Eqity	0 03	0 02	0 07	0 07	0 04
Ret on Assets	4 45	4 33	12 60	12 20	7 00
Ret on Equity%	4 44	4 33	13 33	13 03	7 27
Price/Earnings	21 55	22 12	13 01	11 31	20 21
Divid Cover	1 05	1 13	1 05	1 02	1 04
Divid Yield	4 40	4 00	7 33	8 68	4 74
Earning Yield%	4 64	4 52	7 69	8 84	4 95
NAV % Mrk Pr	104 59	104 34	57 68	67 88	135 44
Effec Tax Rate	19 35	17 24	24 00	0 48	
Sus Grth Rate	0 25	0 49	0 62	0 23	0 15

SUBSIDIARY & ASSOCIATED COMPANIES

ESTATE LATE M MANN (23 51%)
STANDARD BANK NOMINEES (TVL) (PTY) LTD (34 51%)

INVESTMENTS

FIRST NATIONAL NOMINEES (PTY) LTD (11 72%)
MESSINA INVESTMENTS LTD (11 29%)
WILLOUGHBY'S CONSOLIDATED PLC (15,3%)
WILLOUGHBYS CONSOLIDATED PLC (PREFERRED (25,4%)

CRENDELL INVESTMENT CORPORATION LTD

ABBREVIATION · CRENDEL

JSE SHORT CODE · CRL

SECTOR : Financial Investment Trusts

SHAREHOLDERS

Who Owns Whom's Assessment of the Identity of the Ultimate Controlling Shareholder:
HOSKEN CONSOLIDATED INVESTMENTS

SHAREHOLDER	PERCENTAGE 1992	1991
HOSKEN CONSOLIDATED INV LTD	73 1	
SAFEGRO NOM P/L	26 4	93 9
TRUST BANK NOM P/L		3 4
TOTAL	99 5	97 3

DIRECTORS :
CUSHWAY PM ,DENNISS PS ,LEWIS IMA (Chairman

REGISTRATION NUMBER : 55/00259/06

REGISTERED OFFICE
IGI House, 162 Anderson Street
Johannesburg
2001
TEL: 011-335 1911
FAX: 011-29 0491

TRANSFER SECRETARY
Mercantile Registrars Ltd
P O Box 1053, Johannesburg
2000
TEL: 011-333 8181

COMPANY SECRETARY
W T Green

NATURE OF BUSINESS
An investment holding company, with investments of approx 24,2% in quoted Safrican Life & approx 4,2% in quoted Hosken Consolidated Investments.

BANKERS :
N/A

AUDITORS :
BDO Spencer Steward

FAMILIAR BRAND NAMES
N/A

CONTRIBUTION BY ACTIVITY
N/A

YEAR END : March

DIVIDEND : Ords no par value

Dividend No 3	(Ldr)29/11/91	(Pay)20/12/91	Amt(c)8
Dividend No 4	(Ldr)31/07/92	(Pay)21/08/92	Amt(c)8
Specie No 5	(Ldr)31/07/92	(Pay)21/08/92	Amt(c)41.4
Dividend No 6	(Ldr)04/12/92	(Pay)14/12/92	Amt(c)5

CAPITAL STRUCTURE

	AUTHORISED	ISSUED
Ords no par value	121679794	23131886
Var Rate Red Prefs NPV	1500000	0

FINANCIAL STATISTICS (AT FINANCIAL YEAR END)

(Amts in R'000)	1992 Mar	1990 Dec	1989 Dec	1988 Dec	1987 Dec
Ord S/H Int	45845	44304	33307	19589	13219
Long Trm Loans	-	-	50246	7069	2787
Iss Ord Share	23132	23132	23132	18093	16979
Total Liab	2123	25	81791	45626	16572
Current Liab	2123	25	31545	38557	13785
Total Assets	47968	44329	102388	65215	29791
Intang Assets	*	*	12710	*	*
Current Assets	11520	9194	69134	42834	18666
Debtors	1568	89	31661	20372	8062
Inventory	-	-	36029	18419	10198
Oper Profit	344	608	5617	10287	5818
Interest Paid	-	-	7864	2804	967
Tax Paid	260	-	570	514	18
Prf af Int&Tax	3929	1588	-2817	6969	4833
Prf att Ord Sh	5242	2304	-2817	6960	4833
Btm Line Earn	5242	16485	-3303	7290	3915
Dividend Paid	3701	-	-	1809	1196
Mkt Prce(c) YE	250	200	330	290	285
Depreciation	-	-	2757	1343	795

PER SHARE STATISTICS (CENTS)

Net Asst Val	198.19	191.53	89.04	108.27	77.85
Net Earnings	22.70	10.00	-2.60	36.50	28.50
Dividends	16.00	-	-	8.30	7.00
Cash Flow	13.59	6.86	-2.63	46.06	33.15

RATIOS AND OTHER INFORMATION

Mrk Cap(R000)	57830	46264	76336	52470	48390
Current Ratio	5.43	367.76	2.19	1.11	1.35
Quik/Acid Tst	5.43	367.76	1.05	0.63	0.61
Debt/Ass Rat	0.04	0.00	0.80	0.68	0.56
L T L Tot Ass	-	-	0.49	0.09	0.09
Debt to Eqity	0.05	0.00	2.46	2.26	1.25
Interest Cover	-	-	0.71	3.67	6.02
Ret on Assets	9.18	5.20	5.49	15.77	19.53
Ret on Equity%	9.15	5.20	-8.46	35.53	36.56
Price/Earnings	11.01	20.00	-126.92	7.95	10.00
Divid Cover	1.42	-	-	4.40	4.07
Divid Yield	6.40	-	-	2.86	2.46
Earning Yield%	9.08	5.00	-0.79	12.59	10.00
NAV % Mrk Pr	79.28	95.76	26.98	37.33	27.32
Effec Tax Rate	75.58	-	-49.71	0.75	0.37
Def Interval	-	-	-93.51	2.32	1.05
Sus Grth Rate	3.36	5.20	-8.46	26.30	27.51

SUBSIDIARY & ASSOCIATED COMPANIES

SAFRICAN LIFE INVESTMENT HOLDINGS LTD (24,2%)

INVESTMENTS

HOSKEN CONSOLIDATED INVESTMENTS LTD (4,2%)

CROOKES BROTHERS LTD

ABBREVIATION : CROOKES

JSE SHORT CODE : CKS

SECTOR : Industrial-Sugar

SHAREHOLDERS

Who Owns Whom's Assessment of the Identity of the Ultimate Controlling Shareholder:
CROOKES FAMILY

SHAREHOLDER	PERCENTAGE 1992	1991
CROOKES P J M	8.2	8.2
MISYB TRUST	7.7	7.7
ELLINGHAM ESTATE P/L	7.0	7.0
CARBINE NOM P/L	6.6	6.6
CROOKES T C B	6.5	6.5
FIRST NAT NOM P/L	6.5	6.6
STD BANK NOM TVL P/L	5.1	7.7
CHANCE E K	2.7	2.7
EIGHTY ONE MAIN STREET NOM LTD	2.7	---
TONGAAT-HULETT PENS FUND	2.7	2.6
LORNWOOD P/L	2.1	2.1
CROOKES C L (ESTATE LATE)	2.0	2.0

EDGCUMBE A A	1 5	1 5
CROOKES C INV P/L	1 4	1 4
ELIJEAN INV P/L	1 2	1 2
BIGGS C R M	1 2	1 2
CROOKES J J (DAUGHTER'S TRUST)	1 2	1 2
COOK I B	1 2	1 2
GILLATT I H WILL TRUST	1 2	1 2
JENNIRO INV P/L	1 1	1 1
GILLATT I F G	1 0	1 1
MOULTRIE I A	1 0	1 0
TOTAL	71 7	71 6

DIRECTORS :
CAMPBELL PL ,CROOKES AC
CROOKES DJ (Managing Director),CROOKES DV
GILLATT IFG (Chairman),PALMER JFC

REGISTRATION NUMBER : 02/00290/06

REGISTERED OFFICE
Renishaw, Natal
4181
TEL 0323 21210
FAX 0323-21423

TRANSFER SECRETARY
Natal Securities Trust (Pty) Ltd
P O Box 225, Durban
4000
TEL 031-304 9851

COMPANY SECRETARY
B Darbyshire-Roberts

NATURE OF BUSINESS
An agricultural and investment holding company engaged in cane, citrus, cattle, grain, sheep and crocodile farming

BANKERS :
First National Bank of SA Ltd

AUDITORS :
Deloitte Pim Goldby

FAMILIAR BRAND NAMES
N/A

CONTRIBUTION BY ACTIVITY
N/A

YEAR END : March

DIVIDEND : Ords 25c

Interim	(Ldr)21/12/90	(Pay)15/01/91	Amt(c)7 5
Final	(Ldr)28/06/91	(Pay)15/07/91	Amt(c)11 5
Interim	(Ldr)20/12/91	(Pay)15/01/92	Amt(c)7 5
Final	(Ldr)26/06/92	(Pay)15/07/92	Amt(c)13 5
Interim	(Ldr)18/12/92	(Pay)15/01/93	Amt(c)7 5

CAPITAL STRUCTURE

	AUTHORISED	ISSUED
Ords 25c	16000000	12000000

FINANCIAL STATISTICS (AT FINANCIAL YEAR END)

(Amts in R'000)	1992 Mar	1991 Mar	1990 Mar	1989 Mar	1988 Mar
Ord S/H Int	90080	77457	75778	73073	70336
Long Trm Loans	2092	2241	1350	1314	773
Iss Ord Share	12000	12000	3000	3000	3000
Total Liab	8632	6750	15101	6362	4389
Current Liab	6540	4509	13751	5048	3616
Total Assets	98712	84207	90879	79435	74725
Current Assets	4971	2925	2594	3742	3735
Debtors	2149	824	896	277	541
Inventory	2761	2038	1665	1050	836
Turnover	44012	35427	35105	29834	24002
Oper Profit	6913	4915	4035	4484	5080
Interest Paid	770	974	494	167	221
Tax Paid	812	-65	-39	1754	660
Prf af Int&Tax	7198	6238	7302	6167	4199
Prf att Ord Sh	15143	13172	6455	6037	4199
Btm Line Earn	15143	13172	6455	6037	10192
Dividend Paid	2520	13270	3750	3300	2610
Mkt Prce(c) YE	575	475	3650	2350	2000
Depreciation	2802	2485	2249	1815	1610

PER SHARE STATISTICS (CENTS)

Net Asst Val	750 67	645 48	2525 93	2435 77	2344 53
Net Earnings	60 00	52 00	60 80	51 50	35 00
Dividends	21 00	19 00	31 25	27 50	21 75
Cash Flow	86 26	71 78	318 37	284 10	211 40

RATIOS AND OTHER INFORMATION

Mrk Cap(R000)	69000	57000	109500	70500	60000
Current Ratio	0 76	0 65	0 19	0 74	1 03
Quik/Acid Tst	0 34	0 20	0 07	0 53	0 80
A/C Rec T/ovr	20 48	42 99	39 18	107 70	44 37
Tot Ass T/ovr	0 45	0 42	0 39	0 38	0 32
Debt/Ass Rat	0 07	0 07	0 15	0 06	0 05
L T L Tot Ass	0 01	0 01	-	-	
Debt to Eqity	0 08	0 07	0 18	0 07	0 05
Interest Cover	10 09	6 93	15 09	44 65	22 99
Oper Prof Mrg	15 71	13 87	11 49	15 03	21 16
Net Prof Marg%	34 41	37 18	18 39	20 24	17 49
Ret on Assets	8 89	8 49	8 54	10 18	6 80
Ret on Equity%	16 81	17 01	8 52	8 26	5 97
Price/Earnings	9 58	9 13	60 03	45 63	57 14
Divid Cover	2 86	2 74	1 95	1 87	1 61
Divid Yield	3 65	4 00	0 86	1 17	1 09
Earning Yield%	10 43	10 95	1 67	2 19	1 75
NAV % Mrk Pr	130 55	135 89	69 20	103 65	117 23
Effec Tax Rate	6 45	1 08	2 16	24 54	2 92
Def Interval	0 20	0 27	0 93	0 06	0 06
Sus Grth Rate	14 01	0 13	3 57	3 75	2 26

SUBSIDIARY & ASSOCIATED COMPANIES

BAR J LTD (SWAZILAND)
CROOKES PLANTATIONS LTD (SWAZILAND)
ETTEN SUGAR & CITRUS ESTATES (PTY) LTD

INVESTMENTS

C G SMITH LTD (300000 SH)
NKWA LINI PROCESSORS (PTY) LTD (71 SH)
PRIESKA COPPER MINES (PTY) LTD (50000 SH)
VALLEY PACKERS CO-OP LTD (1180000SH)

CROWN FOOD HOLDINGS LTD

ABBREVIATION · CROWN

JSE SHORT CODE : CRN

SECTOR . Industrial Food

SHAREHOLDERS

Who Owns Whom's Assessment of the Identity of the Ultimate Controlling Shareholder: BIDCORP VIA BIDVEST

SHAREHOLDER	PERCENTAGE 1992	1991
BIDVEST GROUP LTD	71 2	- -
SMBL NOM P/L	9 0	---
SA MUTUAL	4 1	---
METAL IND GROUP PENS FUND	1 7	2 9
ELLERINE BROS P/L	1 6	---
ENGINEERING INDUSTRIES PENS FUND	1 3	2 2
M & R INDUSTRIAL LTD	---	77 9
MECHIEL DU TOIT NOM P/L	---	1 1
TOTAL	88 8	84 2

DIRECTORS :
CHIPKIN M ,DEMETRIADES G ,DU PLESSIS RJ
JOFFE B (Chairman),JOFFE J ,KRAMER J ,MASSON D
PAMENSKY JL ,ROSE LE ,ROSEVEAR DK ,SINGER CE

REGISTRATION NUMBER : 66/11512/06

REGISTERED OFFICE
Milner Place, Sunnyside Office Park
4 Carse O'Gowrie, Parktown
2193
TEL 011-838 5201
FAX 011-834 7961

TRANSFER SECRETARY
Central Registrars Ltd
P O Box 4844, Johannesburg
2000
TEL 011-331 0051

COMPANY SECRETARY
M Viljoen

NATURE OF BUSINESS
Supplier of ingredients and light meat processing equipment to butchers and the meat industry and of equipment, sauces and dressings to the catering industry

BANKERS :
Nedcor Bank Ltd, Standard Bank of SA Ltd

AUDITORS :
Deloitte Pim Goldby

FAMILIAR BRAND NAMES
ALOE CATERING,VULCAN FOOD SERVICE

CONTRIBUTION BY ACTIVITY
N/A

YEAR END : June

DIVIDEND :Ords 1c

Interim No 5	(Ldr)16/03/90	(Pay)23/03/90	Amt(c)1 5
Final No 6	(Ldr)21/09/90	(Pay)28/09/90	Amt(c)1 5
Interim No 7	(Ldr)22/02/91	(Pay)01/03/91	Amt(c)1 5
Final No 8	(Ldr)30/08/91	(Pay)09/09/91	Amt(c)2 0

NUMBER OF EMPLOYEES : 1037

CAPITAL STRUCTURE

	AUTHORISED	ISSUED
Ords 1c	120000000	60986640

FINANCIAL STATISTICS (AT FINANCIAL YEAR END)

(Amts in R'000)	1992 Jun	1991 Jun	1990 Jun	1989 Jun	1988 Jun
Ord S/H Int	22034	28522	26234	24624	21854
Long Trm Loans	12242	9511	16449	13288	12559
Iss Ord Share	56329	34773	34773	34773	34773
Total Liab	46030	34066	34125	32922	33046
Current Liab	33788	24555	17676	19634	20487
Total Assets	63545	62588	60359	57546	54900
Intang Assets	4519	*	*	*	*
Current Assets	57173	57936	56040	52772	49758
Debtors	24819	24226	21514	22304	18098
Inventory	31036	31120	34500	29270	30909
Turnover	136834	121438	112491	115250	90581
Oper Profit	-13781	9750	8927	12124	8311
Interest Paid	3192	3732	3922	3574	1267
Tax Paid	-841	2513	2352	4215	3359
Prf af Int&Tax	-16132	3505	2653	4335	3685
Prf att Ord Sh	-16132	3505	2653	4335	3685
Btm Line Earn	-16132	3505	2653	4335	3685
Dividend Paid	-	1217	1043	1565	1391
Mkt Prce(c) YE	105	43	35	60	52
Depreciation	1476	1171	1242	1579	1846

PER SHARE STATISTICS (CENTS)

Net Asst Val	31 09	82 02	75 44	70 81	62 85
Net Earnings	38 40	10 10	7 60	12 50	10 60
Dividends	-	3 50	3 00	4 50	4 00
Cash Flow	-36 93	13 44	12 00	16 97	17 57

RATIOS AND OTHER INFORMATION

Mrk Cap(R000)	59145	14952	12171	20864	18082
Current Ratio	1 69	2 36	3 17	2 69	2 43
Quik/Acid Tst	0 77	1 09	1 22	1 20	0 92
A/C Rec T/ovr	5 51	5 01	5 23	5 17	5 01
Tot Ass T/ovr	2 15	1 94	1 86	2 00	1 65
Debt/Ass Rat	0 72	0 53	0 55	0 56	0 59
L T L Tot Ass	0 19	0 14	0 26	0 22	0 22
Debt to Eqity	2 09	1 16	1 27	1 31	1 49
Interest Cover	-4 32	2 61	2 28	3 39	6 56
Oper Prof Mrg	-10 07	8 03	7 94	10 52	9 18
Net Prof Marg%	11 79	2 89	2 36	3 76	4 07
Ret on Assets	-21 69	15 58	14 79	21 07	15 14
Ret on Equity%	-73 21	12 29	10 11	17 60	16 86
Price/Earnings	-2 73	4 26	4 61	4 80	4 91
Divid Cover	-	2 89	2 53	2 78	2 65
Divid Yield	-	8 14	8 57	7 50	7 69
Earning Yield%	-36 57	23 49	21 71	20 83	20 38
NAV % Mrk Pr	29 61	190 75	215 55	118 02	120 86
Effec Tax Rate	-	41 29	38 94	49 46	39 48
Def Interval	-1 55	3 53	4 43	2 41	2 13
Sus Grth Rate	73 21	8 02	6 14	11 25	10 50

SUBSIDIARY & ASSOCIATED COMPANIES

CROWN FOODS (PTY) LTD
CROWN MILLS (CISKEI) (PTY) LTD
CROWN NATIONAL (PTY) LTD
CRWON MILLS (NAMIBIA) (PTY) LTD
FOOD SERVICES CONCEPTS (PTY) LTD
OKTO PRODUCTS (PTY) LTD
VULCAN FOOD SERVICE EQUIPMENT (PTY) LTD

INVESTMENTS

None

CRUSADER LIFE ASSURANCE CORP LTD

ABBREVIATION : CRULIFE

JSE SHORT CODE : CLF

SECTOR : Financial-Insurance

SHAREHOLDERS

Who Owns Whom's Assessment of the Identity of the Ultimate Controlling Shareholder: ANGLOVAAL VIA ANGLOVAAL INS HOLDINGS

SHAREHOLDER	PERCENTAGE 1992	1991
ANGLOVAAL INSURANCE HOLDINGS LTD	60.0	---
UAL NOM P/L	4.3	4 4
ROTHSEY INV CO P/L	3 8	5 9
NEDBANK NOM LTD	3.1	---
FERBROS NOM P/L	2 4	2 5
CRUSADER LIFE EXEC SHARE SCHEME TRUST	2 0	2.0
PROTEA ASSURE CO PENS FUND	1.5	---
SHARESTOCK NOM P/L	1.5	1.2
SYFRETS NOM LTD	1.4	---
SFSS NOM P/L	1.4	---
STD BANK NOM TVL P/L	1 2	2.3
MURRAY & ROBERTS STAFF PENS FUND	1.1	1.6
ANGLO AMERICAN GROUP PENS FUND	---	1 4
CRULIFE ASSURE CORP EXEC SHR PURCH SCH	---	1 7
CRUSADER LIFE HOLDINGS LTD	---	59 5
TOTAL	83 5	82 7

DIRECTORS :
BARBER DD ,BARNARD MS DR,BROWN DM ,DE BEER DD
HERBERT BB ,JACK BH
PETERS BA (Executive Director)
PRINSLOO LJ (Executive Director),REUNERT JM
ROWAND AR (Executive Chairman)
ROWAND R DE V (Managing Director),SINGER RN

REGISTRATION NUMBER : 73/16606/06

REGISTERED OFFICE
Crusader House, 6 Anderson Street
Johannesburg
2001
TEL: 011-492 2330
FAX: 011-838 1817

TRANSFER SECRETARY
Anglovaal Ltd
P O Box 62379, Marshalltown
2107
TEL: 011-634 9111

COMPANY SECRETARY
C McAleenan (Ms)

NATURE OF BUSINESS
CRUSADER LIFE is a life assurer. Activities comprise individual life policies including single premiums; credit life including mortgage protection;underwriting of group life and disability assurance; provident and pension fund business and the investment of funds derived from those acitvities.

BANKERS :
First National Bank of SA Ltd
Standard Bank of SA Ltd, Nedcor Bank Ltd

AUDITORS :
Coopers Theron Du Toit

FAMILIAR BRAND NAMES
N/A

CONTRIBUTION BY ACTIVITY
Premium Income (% Total income) (94.0%)
Investment (6 0%)

YEAR END : June

DIVIDEND : Ords 15c

Interim No 22	(Ldr)15/02/91	(Pay)27/03/91	Amt(c)17.25
Final	(Ldr)13/11/92	(Pay)18/12/92	Amt(c)20

NUMBER OF EMPLOYEES : 303

CAPITAL STRUCTURE

	AUTHORISED	ISSUED
Ords 15c	40000000	30190105
Var Rate Red Cum Prefs R1 (Not Li	10	10
Cum Red Prefs R1	30	10

FINANCIAL STATISTICS (AT FINANCIAL YEAR END)

(Amts in R'000)	1992 Jun	1991 Jun	1989 Dec	1988 Dec	1987 Dec
Ord S/H Int	48668	23704	22475	21178	21178
Long Trm Loans	216141	99078	52293	56884	34779
Iss Ord Share	30190	19710	19710	19710	19710
Total Liab	230579	112170	75076	80998	47988
Current Liab	14438	13092	22783	24114	13209
Total Assets	279247	135874	97551	102176	69166
Current Assets	112139	47788	34483	48577	33884
Debtors	41646	34262	20203	9297	30290
Turnover	160694	118615	57002	46213	-
Oper Profit	114058	66094	26659	19089	2150
Tax Paid	-	-72	-251	621	-
Prf af Int&Tax	124920	75965	33634	18468	2150
Prf att Ord Sh	96703	40939	13095	18468	2150
Btm Line Earn	96703	40939	13095	18468	2150
Dividend Paid	2264	4824	2833	2267	1658
Mkt Prce(c) YE	230	250	190	180	170
Depreciation	3078	4059	1867	-	-

PER SHARE STATISTICS (CENTS)

Net Asst Val	161.21	120.26	114.03	107.45	107.45
Net Earnings	24.00	26.75	14 38	11.50	14.00
Dividends	20.00	26.75	14.38	11 50	9.60
Cash Flow	423 97	270 67	180 12	93.70	10 91

RATIOS AND OTHER INFORMATION

Mrk Cap(R000)	69437	49275	37449	35478	33507
Current Ratio	7.77	3.65	1.51	2 01	2.57
Quik/Acid Tst	7.77	3.65	1.51	2.01	2.57
A/C Rec T/ovr	3.86	2.31	2.82	4.97	-
Tot Ass T/ovr	0.58	0 58	0.58	0.45	-

Debt/Ass Rat	0 05	0 10	0 23	0 24	0 22
L T L Tot Ass	-	-	-	0 00	0 03
Debt to Eqity	0 30	0 55	1 01	1 14	0 73
Oper Prof Mrg	70 98	55 72	46 77	41 31	-
Net Prof Marg%	60 18	34 51	22 97	39 96	-
Ret on Assets	44 73	37 24	34 22	18 68	3 11
Ret on Equity%	198 70	115 14	58 26	87 20	10 15
Price/Earnings	9 58	9 35	13 21	15 65	12 14
Divid Cover	1 20	1 00	1 00	1 00	1 46
Divid Yield	8 70	10 70	7 57	6 39	5 65
Earning Yield%	10 43	10 70	7 57	6 39	8 24
NAV % Mrk Pr	70 09	48 11	60 01	59 69	63 20
Effec Tax Rate	-	-	-	3 25	-
Def Interval	0 16	0 09	-	0 01	1 03
Sus Grth Rate	194 05	152 38	45 66	76 50	2 32

SUBSIDIARY & ASSOCIATED COMPANIES

10 ANDERSON STREET (PTY) LTD (50%)
CRULIFE INVESTMENTS (PTY) LTD
CRULIFE PROPERTY ADMINISTRATORS (PTY) LT
JTG REINSURANCE BROKERS (SA) (PTY) LTD
LANFRANC PROPERTY HOLDINGS LTD (24,9%)
LANFRANC PROPERTY HOLDINGS LTD (LANFRANC (38,9%)
MAST PROPERTIES (PTY) LTD
RESIDE PROPERTIES (PTY) LTD (50%)

INVESTMENTS

None

CTP HOLDINGS LTD

ABBREVIATION : CTP

JSE SHORT CODE : CTP

SECTOR : Industrial Paper & Packaging

SHAREHOLDERS

Who Owns Whom's Assessment of the Identity of the Ultimate Controlling Shareholder:
ANGLO VIA ARGUS

SHAREHOLDER	PERCENTAGE 1992	1991
CAXTON LTD	52 7	52 7
ARGUS HOLDINGS LTD	19 9	19 9
EIGHTY ONE MAIN STREET NOM LTD	4 2	4 5
STD BANK NOM TVL P/L	4 1	3 9
GALLO AFRICA LTD	2 2	2 2
ANGLO AMERICAN CORP PENS FUND	1 9	1 9
DE BEERS PENS FUND	1 9	1 9
ANGLO AMERICAN GROUP PENS FUND	1 3	1 3
MOOLMAN T D & COBURN N M	1 2	--
TOTAL	89 3	88 2

DIRECTORS :
BAND DDB (Chairman),BURGER APJ ,COBURN NM
FEATHERSTONE JG
JANKELOWITZ EM (Managing Director),MCLEAN PW
MOOLMAN TD (Chief Operations Officer)
PAULSEN BG ,SHORT MDW ,WOODBURN JM
WOULIDGE RM (Deputy Managing Director

REGISTRATION NUMBER : 05/26616/06

REGISTERED OFFICE
1 Blumberg Street, Industria West
Johannesburg
2092
TEL 011-474 0460
FAX 011-474 8229

TRANSFER SECRETARY
Mercantile Registrars Ltd
P O Box 1053, Johannesburg
2000
TEL 011-333 8181

COMPANY SECRETARY
K J Bownass

NATURE OF BUSINESS
An investment holding company with controlling interests in JSE-quoted Solchem & Hortors The group is engaged in the production of printing inks, printing and packaging, and newspaper and magazine publishing

BANKERS :
First National Bank of SA Ltd

AUDITORS :
Ernst & Young

FAMILIAR BRAND NAMES
APOLLO DISTRIBUTION,AVERY LABELS
KNL WEB PRINTERS,PLASTICWRAP,RUSTICA PRESS
S A LITHO

CONTRIBUTION BY ACTIVITY
N/A

YEAR END : March

DIVIDEND : Ords 25c

Interim No 53	(Ldr)22/12/89	(Pay)12/01/90	Amt(c)6 5
Final No 54	(Ldr)29/06/90	(Pay)20/07/90	Amt(c)9
Interim No 55	(Ldr)21/12/90	(Pay)11/01/91	Amt(c)7
Final No 56	(Ldr)21/06/91	(Pay)12/07/91	Amt(c)12
Interim No 57	(Ldr)20/12/91	(Pay)10/01/92	Amt(c)8
Final No 58	(Ldr)03/07/92	(Pay)24/07/92	Amt(c)14
Interim No 59	(Ldr)18/12/92	(Pay)12/01/93	Amt(c)6 7

NUMBER OF EMPLOYEES : 3011

CAPITAL STRUCTURE

	AUTHORISED	ISSUED
Ords 25c	40000000	29488533
6% Cum Partic Prefs R2	100000	50000

FINANCIAL STATISTICS (AT FINANCIAL YEAR END)

(Amts in R 000)	1992 Mar	1991 Mar	1990 Mar	1989 Mar	1988 Mar
Ord S/H Int	177351	146011	130238	118254	99287
Long Trm Loans	36543	19759	26521	23641	22600
Iss Ord Share	22683	22683	22479	22291	20744
Total Liab	161496	125110	104650	132293	93182
Current Liab	124953	105351	78129	108652	70582
Total Assets	338847	271121	234888	250547	192469
Current Assets	189630	152648	134070	145935	86363
Debtors	108676	87105	75520	77151	48926
Inventory	58100	57748	56473	65513	33954
Turnover	562846	482141	453831	415894	286342
Oper Profit	66884	44975	33036	30102	24315
Interest Paid	6224	4962	7897	7786	4079

Tax Paid	28075	19873	12829	9778	9548
Prf af Int&Tax	37062	22944	15146	15764	12530
Prf att Ord Sh	36860	22538	16420	16427	12874
Btm Line Earn	33406	19382	14589	12055	10259
Dividend Paid	5943	4310	3472	3121	2647
Mkt Prce(c) YE	890	600	550	520	600
Depreciation	17563	15350	19570	19511	17128

PER SHARE STATISTICS (CENTS)

Net Asst Val	781.87	643.70	579.38	530.50	478.63
Net Earnings	162.50	99.40	73.50	76.30	65.00
Dividends	26.20	19.00	15.50	14.00	13.00
Cash Flow	233.66	159.06	161.55	151.67	150.42

RATIOS AND OTHER INFORMATION

Mrk Cap(R000)	201879	136098	123635	115913	124464
Current Ratio	1.52	1.45	1.72	1.34	1.22
Quik/Acid Tst	1.05	0.90	0.99	0.74	0.74
A/C Rec T/ovr	5.18	5.54	6.01	5.39	5.85
Tot Ass T/ovr	1.66	1.78	1.93	1.66	1.49
Debt/Ass Rat	0.43	0.41	0.38	0.48	0.42
L T L Tot Ass	0.06	0.02	0.04	0.05	0.06
Debt to Eqity	0.82	0.76	0.68	1.02	0.82
Interest Cover	11.10	9.40	4.28	4.06	6.26
Oper Prof Mrg	11.88	9.33	7.28	7.24	8.49
Net Prof Marg%	6.55	4.67	3.62	3.95	4.50
Ret on Assets	21.88	18.03	16.32	14.14	14.34
Ret on Equity%	20.78	15.44	12.61	13.89	12.97
Price/Earnings	5.48	6.04	7.48	6.82	9.23
Divid Cover	6.20	5.23	4.74	5.45	5.00
Divid Yield	2.94	3.17	2.82	2.69	2.17
Earning Yield%	18.26	16.57	13.36	14.67	10.83
NAV % Mrk Pr	87.85	107.28	105.34	102.02	79.77
Effec Tax Rate	42.88	49.71	37.29	40.23	39.47
Def Interval	0.70	0.74	0.84	1.53	1.02
Sus Grth Rate	17.43	12.48	9.94	11.25	10.30

SUBSIDIARY & ASSOCIATED COMPANIES

ADVERTISING MARKETING SERVICES (PTY) LTD
AMALGAMATED PRESS (PTY) LTD
AMANZIMTOTI PRINTING & PUBLISHING (PTY
APALMA (PTY) LTD
AVERY LABEL SYSTEMS S.A. (PTY) LTD
BRITS POS (PTY) LTD
BUCKLEY MAP PRODUCTIONS (PTY) LTD
CAPE & TRANSVAAL PRINTERS (PTY) LTD
CAPITAL MEDIA (PTY) LTD (25%)
COMBINED PUBLISHERS (PTY) LTD
CTP BOOK PRINTERS (PTY) LTD
CTP BUSINESS FORMS (PTY) LTD
CTP EXPORTS (PTY) LTD
CTP LTD
CTP WEB PRINTERS (PTY) LTD
DARWAIN INVESTMENTS (PTY) LTD
DISCORN LTD
DISTRIBUTION ENTERPRISES (PTY) LTD
DM PUBLICATIONS (PTY) LTD
DROCNIF (PTY) LTD
DUAL DATA STORAGE SYSTEMS (PTY) LTD
EDENVALE NEWS (PTY) LTD
EDSON-CLYDE HOLDINGS (PTY) LTD (50%)
EXPRESS DEVELOPMENT CO. (PTY) LTD
FELSTAR PUBLISHERS (PTY) LTD
FINNO-RAND PRODUCTIONS (PTY) LTD
FS DIARY PUBLICATIONS (PTY) LTD
GRAPHIC PACKAGING (PTY) LTD
HAN EYBERS DRUKKERS (EDMS) BPK
HIGHWAY MAIL (PTY) LTD
HORTORS & CTP (CAPE) (PTY) LTD
HORTORS LTD
INVESTING TODAY PUBLICATIONS & MARKETING
JUBILEE PROSPECTUS (PTY) LTD (50%)
KEMPTON FORUM (PTY) LTD
KEMPTON MEDICAL CENTRE (PTY) LTD
KNL PRINTING (PTY) LTD
LASM INVESTMENTS (PTY) LTD
LEO OFFICE FURNITURE (PTY) LTD (30%)
LITHOCORP (PTY) LTD
MARKETING OPPORTUNITIES (PTY) LTD
MEDIA PROMOTION AFRICA (PTY) LTD
NATAL MONITOR (PTY) LTD
NATAL REGIONAL NEWSPAPERS (PTY) LTD
NEWCASTLE ADVERTISER (PTY) LTD
NORTHERN ISSUE (PTY) LTD
PLASTICWRAP (PTY) LTD
PREMIER PRINTING WORKS (PTY) LTD
PROFESSIONAL PAMPHLETS (PTY) LTD
RACING DIGEST (PTY) LTD
RACING NETWORK (PTY) LTD (50%)
RALPH R BOFFARD ASSOCIATES (PTY) LTD
RETAIL ADVERTISING BUREAU (PTY) LTD
RIDGE TIMES (PTY) LTD (50%)
RUSTENBURG KOERANTE (PTY) LTD
RUSTICA PRESS (PTY) LTD
SA LITHO CO LTD
SETRONIC (PTY) LTD
SIMONDIUM PUBLISHERS CO (PTY) LTD
SOEKLIG BEMARKING (EDMS) BPK
SOLCHEM INVESTMENT HOLDINGS LTD
TAMBUTI ENTERPRISES (PTY) LTD (50%)
TAMBUTI UPINGTON (PTY) LTD (50%)
TAMBUTI VRYBURG (PTY) LTD (50%)
TRIO-RAND ENTERPRISES (PTY) LTD
VAALDRIEHOEK UITGEWERS (EDMS) BPK (50%)
WESECHOR UITGEWERS (PTY) LTD
WORLD PRINTING & PUBLISHING (PTY) LTD
ZULULAND OBSERVER (PTY) LTD (38%)

INVESTMENTS

COATES LTD (14800 SH)
ELECTRA INVESTMENTS (SA) LTD (RED CUM PR (15000000 S)
REDGWOODS LTD (89681 SH)

CULLINAN HOLDINGS LTD

ABBREVIATION : CULLINAN

JSE SHORT CODE : CUL

SECTOR : Industrial-Industrial Holding

SHAREHOLDERS

Who Owns Whom's Assessment of the Identity of the Ultimate Controlling Shareholder: SA MUTUAL

SHAREHOLDER	PERCENTAGE 1992	1991
SA MUTUAL	43.1	42.5
FERMAIN NOM LTD	8.0	8.0
PETARD NOM LTD	7.6	7.6
CULLINAN HOLDINGS LTD SHARE PURC TRUST	6.1	---
METAL IND GROUP PENS FUND	5.7	5.7
ENGINEERING INDUSTRIES PENS FUND	5.4	5.4

STD BANK NOM TVL P/L	3 3	2 4
FIRST NAT NOM P/L	1 7	1 8
ANGLO AMERICAN CORP PENS FUND	1 5	1 5
CULLINAN N M TRUST	1 3	2 0
SOLOMON P (W HERRICK TRUST)	1 1	1 1
DE BEERS PENS FUND	---	1 5
TYLER R R TRUST	---	1 0
TOTAL	84 8	80 4

DIRECTORS :
ADCOCK CS ,BECKLEY BC ,BIEBER EPH ,CLARK AJL
CLARK AJL (Chairman),CULINNAN NM ,GOSS RJ
HARBUZ E (Managing Director)
HILLARY DW (Financial Director),JOUBERT PG
STEWART RW ,STEYN E

REGISTRATION NUMBER : 01/01808/06

REGISTERED OFFICE
Cullinan Building, Premier Street
Olifantsfontein, Midrand
1665
TEL 011-316 3636
FAX 011-316 4226

TRANSFER SECRETARY
Central Registrars Ltd
P O Box 4844, Johannesburg
2000
TEL 011-331 0051

COMPANY SECRETARY
A M Craddock

NATURE OF BUSINESS
The group is active in three areas Electrical, Ceramics & Property Activities include Heavy electrical contracting & installation, electrical cables, electrical distribution, measurement and control products, electrical consulting & design services, refractories, porcelain products, bricks industrial & ceramic minerals, materials handling products, engineering, industrial & commercial real estate

BANKERS :
Standard Bank of SA Ltd
Rand Merchant Bank Ltd
First National Corp & Investment Bank

AUDITORS :
KPMG Aiken & Peat

FAMILIAR BRAND NAMES
N/A

CONTRIBUTION BY ACTIVITY
Property (2 2%)
Ceramics (29 2%)
Electrical (% Turnover) (68 6%)

YEAR END : June

DIVIDEND : Ords 50c

Interim No 119	(Ldr)20/04/90	(Pay)25/05/90	Amt(c)17
Final No 120	(Ldr)26/10/90	(Pay)23/11/90	Amt(c)36
Interim No 121	(Ldr)19/04/91	(Pay)24/05/91	Amt(c)17
Final No 122	(Ldr)25/10/91	(Pay)22/11/91	Amt(c)17

NUMBER OF EMPLOYEES : 4303

CAPITAL STRUCTURE

	AUTHORISED	ISSUED
5,5% Cum Prefs R2	500000	500000
Ords 50c	20000000	14533169

FINANCIAL STATISTICS (AT FINANCIAL YEAR END)

(Amts in R'000)	1992 Jun	1991 Jun	1990 Jun	1989 Jun	1988 Jun
Ord S/H Int	146764	174433	180749	163876	126322
Long Trm Loans	74910	159512	114203	81148	78786
Iss Ord Share	14533	14533	14533	13973	13883
Total Liab	186442	321019	326434	261499	200109
Current Liab	111532	161507	212231	180351	121323
Total Assets	324734	478780	490487	408698	311064
Intang Assets	8472	16672	16696	16677	15367
Current Assets	159182	308270	282249	252731	179116
Debtors	83175	88623	117220	120209	88772
Inventory	68864	83660	137875	116373	87129
Turnover	509564	666441	667754	553879	414975
Oper Profit	-13154	9600	54132	58760	43196
Interest Paid	21933	23056	18977	10150	4685
Tax Paid	52	-6940	7308	15426	16521
Prf af Int&Tax	-35139	-6230	28115	33184	21990
Prf att Ord Sh	-33479	-322	19110	24742	17343
Btm Line Earn	-26884	424	12303	24742	17097
Dividend Paid	-	4941	7703	7406	6247
Mkt Prce(c) YE	330	720	700	760	775
Depreciation	12041	9652	12958	11836	9568

PER SHARE STATISTICS (CENTS)

Net Asst Val	951 57	1085 54	1128 83	1053 45	799 21
Net Earnings	-230 40	-2 20	135 00	146 20	127 60
Dividends	-	34 00	53 00	53 00	45 00
Cash Flow	-159 35	-24 83	157 27	262 41	211 33

RATIOS AND OTHER INFORMATION

Mrk Cap(R000)	47959	104638	101731	106195	107593
Current Ratio	1 43	1 91	1 33	1 40	1 48
Quik/Acid Tst	0 81	1 39	0 68	0 76	0 76
A/C Rec T/ovr	6 13	7 52	5 70	4 61	4 67
Tot Ass T/ovr	1 57	1 39	1 36	1 36	1 33
Debt/Ass Rat	0 57	0 56	0 56	0 53	0 45
L T L Tot Ass	0 23	0 22	0 13	0 09	0 06
Debt to Eqity	1 26	1 54	1 53	1 32	1 11
Interest Cover	-0 60	0 43	2 87	5 79	9 22
Oper Prof Mrg	-2 58	1 44	8 11	10 61	10 41
Net Prof Marg%	6 57	-0 05	2 86	4 47	4 18
Ret on Assets	-4 05	2 06	11 12	14 39	14 01
Ret on Equity%	-22 81	-0 18	10 57	15 10	13 73
Price/Earnings	-1 43	-327 27	5 19	5 20	6 07
Divid Cover	-	0 06	2 55	2 76	2 84
Divid Yield	-	4 72	7 57	6 97	5 81
Earning Yield%	-69 82	-0 31	19 29	19 24	16 46
NAV % Mrk Pr	288 36	150 77	161 26	138 61	103 12
Effec Tax Rate	-0 73	-19 25	49 59	32 44	38 59
Def Interval	-4 17	-49 65	6 07	2 50	1 18
Sus Grth Rate	-22 81	-3 02	6 31	10 58	8 78

SUBSIDIARY & ASSOCIATED COMPANIES

BOKSBURG BRICK AND FIRECLAY CO LTD
CULLINAN DEVELOPMENTS (PTY) LTD (50%)
CULLINAN GROUP HOUSING (PTY) LTD
CULLINAN POWER PROJECTS (PTY) LTD
CULLINAN PROPERTIES LTD
CULLINAN REFRACTORIES (50%)
DANSE KRAAL INVESTMENTS (PTY) LTD
DENGE POWER PROJECTS LTD
ILLOVO INVESTMENTS (PTY) LTD
RACEC IN BRONKHORSTSPRUIT (PTY) LTD (50%)

REPUBLIC POWER AND COMMUNICATION CO (PTY (30%)
SAG CERAMICS (PTY) LTD
TRANSMISSION & DISTRIBUTION INTERNATIONA

INVESTMENTS

None

CURNOW M&G LTD

ABBREVIATION : CURNOW

JSE SHORT CODE : CNW

SECTOR : Industrial-Retailers & Wholesalers

SHAREHOLDERS

Who Owns Whom's Assessment of the Identity of the Ultimate Controlling Shareholder:
FSI CORP / AECI

SHAREHOLDER	PERCENTAGE 1992	1991
AECI LTD	35 9	35 9
TARRY GROUP P/L	35 8	---
FERBROS NOM P/L	2 2	---
CMB NOM P/L	1 8	---
MOTOR & GENERAL SUPPLIES P/L	1 5	37 3
POWELL O	1 3	---
NUSSBAUM R A W	1 3	-
SANLAM	- -	5 5
TOTAL	79 7	78 7

DIRECTORS :
BLOOM ML (Managing Director),HART HG ,MUNDAY TS
RALPHS LP ,SCHLESINGER AM (Chairman)
VAN NIEKERK MD (Financial Director

REGISTRATION NUMBER : 05/27737/06

REGISTERED OFFICE
6th Floor, FSI Centre, 35 Siemert Road
Doornfontein
2094
TEL 011-402 3200
FAX 011-402 7508

TRANSFER SECRETARY
Mercantile Registrars Ltd
P O Box 1053, Johannesburg
2000
TEL 011-333 8181

COMPANY SECRETARY
B E Liebesman

NATURE OF BUSINESS
The company distributes automotive paints, body fillers, thinners, abrasives, panelbeating and spray painting equipment and tools and related automotive refinishing products via 14 branches

BANKERS :
Standard Bank of SA Ltd

AUDITORS :
KPMG Aiken & Peat

FAMILIAR BRAND NAMES
3M,DAGRAM,SYKES

CONTRIBUTION BY ACTIVITY
N/A

YEAR END : December

DIVIDEND : Ords no par value

Interim	(Ldr)08/09/89	(Pay)29/09/89	Amt(c)1
Final	(Ldr)16/03/90	(Pay)09/04/90	Amt(c)0 75
Interim	(Ldr)14/09/90	(Pay)05/10/90	Amt(c)1
Final	(Ldr)15/03/91	(Pay)08/04/91	Amt(c)1 25
Interim	(Ldr)04/10/91	(Pay)25/10/91	Amt(c)1
Final	(Ldr)10/04/92	(Pay)04/05/92	Amt(c)1
Interim	(Ldr)11/09/92	(Pay)02/10/92	Amt(c)1

NUMBER OF EMPLOYEES : 203

CAPITAL STRUCTURE

	AUTHORISED	ISSUED
Ords no par value	30000000	22150555

FINANCIAL STATISTICS (AT FINANCIAL YEAR END)

(Amts in R'000)	1991 Dec	1990 Dec	1989 Dec	1988 Dec	1987 Dec
Ord S/H Int	7040	6537	5677	5136	4379
Iss Ord Share	22151	22151	21621	21621	21621
Total Liab	9713	8737	7843	6084	4819
Current Liab	9713	8737	7843	6084	4819
Total Assets	15401	13922	12168	9868	7846
Intang Assets	1352	1352	1352	1352	1352
Current Assets	14630	13140	11264	9355	7492
Debtors	8834	7250	6135	4267	3124
Inventory	5777	5874	5114	4452	2953
Turnover	44597	39098	33916	27507	22247
Oper Profit	2790	3111	2152	2771	2532
Interest Paid	891	699	358	5	53
Tax Paid	922	1214	876	1360	1222
Prf af Int&Tax	1017	1236	919	1406	1257
Prf att Ord Sh	1017	1236	919	1406	1257
Btm Line Earn	946	1236	919	1406	1257
Dividend Paid	443	498	378	649	649
Mkt Prce(c) YE	20	22	28	35	52
Depreciation	222	213	198	151	142

PER SHARE STATISTICS (CENTS)

Net Asst Val	25 68	23 41	20 00	17 50	14 00
Net Earnings	4 60	5 60	4 30	6 50	6 40
Dividends	2 00	2 25	1 75	3 00	3 00
Cash Flow	5 59	6 58	5 17	7 20	7 11

RATIOS AND OTHER INFORMATION

Mrk Cap(R000)	4430	4873	6054	7567	11243
Current Ratio	1 51	1 50	1 44	1 54	1 55
Quik/Acid Tst	0 91	0 83	0 78	0 81	0 94
A/C Rec T/ovr	5 05	5 39	5 53	6 45	7 12
Tot Ass T/ovr	2 90	2 81	2 79	2 79	2 84
Debt/Ass Rat	0 63	0 63	0 64	0 62	0 61
Debt to Eqity	1 38	1 34	1 38	1 18	1 10
Interest Cover	3 13	4 45	6 01	554 20	47 77
Oper Prof Mrg	6 26	7 96	6 35	10 07	11 38
Net Prof Marg%	2 28	3 16	2 71	5 11	5 65
Ret on Assets	18 38	22 62	17 69	28 08	32 27

Ret on Equity%	14.45	18.91	16.19	27.38	28.71
Price/Earnings	4.35	3.93	6.51	5.38	8.13
Divid Cover	2.30	2.49	2.46	2.17	2.13
Divid Yield	10.00	10.23	6.25	8.57	5.77
Earning Yield%	23.00	25.45	15.36	18.57	12.31
NAV % Mrk Pr	128.39	106.40	71.44	50.00	26.92
Effec Tax Rate	44.20	49.55	48.80	49.17	49.29
Def Interval	3.32	2.04	2.70	-	-
Sus Grth Rate	8.15	11.29	9.53	14.74	13.88

SUBSIDIARY & ASSOCIATED COMPANIES

AUTOLEC (TRANSVAAL) (PTY) LTD
DAVE'S AUTOMOTIVE PAINTS (PTY) LTD
HARVEYS EQUIPMENT CO (PORT ELIZABETH) (P
R MACKENZIE PAINTS (PTY) LTD

INVESTMENTS

None

CURRIE FINANCE CORP LTD

ABBREVIATION : CURFIN

JSE SHORT CODE : CFN

SECTOR : Industrial-Industrial Holding

SHAREHOLDERS

Who Owns Whom's Assessment of the Identity of the Ultimate Controlling Shareholder:
JAFFE FAMILY

SHAREHOLDER	PERCENTAGE 1992	1991
GRESHAM TRADING CO P/L	31.8	31.8
EIGHTY ONE MAIN STREET NOM LTD	11.4	---
A JAFFE INDUSTRIAL HOLDINGS P/L	7.1	7.1
STD BANK NOM TVL P/L	6.1	7.1
SHARESTOCK NOM P/L	4.3	4.1
A JAFFE COMMERCIAL HOLDINGS P/L	4.3	4.3
CMB NOM P/L	3.9	---
JOHANNESBURG MUNICIPAL PENS FUND	1.6	1.2
SFSS NOM P/L	1.6	1.5
HARVEST SECURITIES LTD	1.4	1.4
GOLDBERG H M	1.4	1.4
ABSA NOM P/L	1.4	---
JACOBS M F	1.0	1.0
BP CENTRE NOM P/L	---	2.2
MOMENTUM LIFE ASSURE LTD	---	8.2
SANLAM	---	3.9
VOLKSKAS NOM P/L	---	1.6
TOTAL	77.3	76.7

DIRECTORS :
BRODIE MH (Executive Chairman),DESILLA JP
MCCORMICK H ,THOMPSON NB

REGISTRATION NUMBER : 68/12133/06

REGISTERED OFFICE
80 Grant Avenue, Norwood
Johannesburg
2192
TEL: 011-483 2150
FAX: 011-483 2045

TRANSFER SECRETARY
Mercantile Registrars Ltd
P O Box 1053, Johannesburg
2000
TEL: 011-333 8181

COMPANY SECRETARY
H McCormick

NATURE OF BUSINESS
A finance & investment company which controls subsidiaries engaged in freight operations and related activities, credit finance and leasing and hire purchase transactions; administration of fixed properties and township development. The company has a controlling interest in quoted SA Freight Corp.

BANKERS :
First National Bank of SA Ltd
Standard Bank of SA Ltd

AUDITORS :
Ernst & Young

FAMILIAR BRAND NAMES
SAFCON FREIGHT

CONTRIBUTION BY ACTIVITY
Leasing/Finance/Property/Township Dev'nt (0.7%)
Clearing & Freight (% of Turnover) (99.3%)

YEAR END : June

DIVIDEND : Ords 1c

Interim No 44	(Ldr)02/03/90	(Pay)16/03/90	Amt(c)15
Final No 45	(Ldr)14/09/90	(Pay)21/09/90	Amt(c)23
Interim No 46	(Ldr)01/03/91	(Pay)15/03/91	Amt(c)16
Final No 47	(Ldr)30/08/91	(Pay)20/09/91	Amt(c)27
Interim No 48	(Ldr)28/02/92	(Pay)16/03/92	Amt(c)17
Final No 49	(Ldr)18/09/92	(Pay)29/09/92	Amt(c)33

NUMBER OF EMPLOYEES : 1578

CAPITAL STRUCTURE

	AUTHORISED	ISSUED
Ords 1c	14900000	14030274
"A" Red Prefs 50c	100000	0

FINANCIAL STATISTICS (AT FINANCIAL YEAR END)

(Amts in R'000)	1992 Jun	1991 Jun	1990 Jun	1989 Jun	1988 Jun
Ord S/H Int	67592	56229	51031	46236	41749
Long Trm Loans	32354	27131	24155	20520	33915
Iss Ord Share	14030	14030	14030	14030	14030
Total Liab	106012	113352	116983	112489	117151
Current Liab	73658	86221	92828	91969	83236
Total Assets	173604	169581	168014	158725	158900
Current Assets	123648	124161	117609	125701	112310
Debtors	102671	78096	78576	88046	75252
Inventory	630	298	1414	2871	14465
Turnover	1210323	926184	968990	913016	703455
Oper Profit	39525	36258	31439	34326	25290
Interest Paid	297	1638	1309	2038	317
Tax Paid	18468	16208	14504	17312	12977
Prf af Int&Tax	20914	18797	15935	15475	11996
Prf att Ord Sh	11519	10843	9636	8157	6652
Btm Line Earn	12192	11245	10167	11681	5230
Dividend Paid	7015	6033	5332	4770	4209

Mkt Prce(c) YE	710	575	305	325	380
Depreciation	4837	5319	5599	4731	4067

PER SHARE STATISTICS (CENTS)

Net Asst Val	481 77	400 78	363 73	329 55	297 57
Net Earnings	82 10	77 30	68 70	58 10	47 40
Dividends	50 00	43 00	38 00	34 00	30 00
Cash Flow	118 52	111 07	105 11	87 70	74 59

RATIOS AND OTHER INFORMATION

Mrk Cap(R000)	99613	80673	42792	45598	53314
Current Ratio	1 68	1 44	1 27	1 37	1 35
Quik/Acid Tst	1 67	1 44	1 25	1 34	1 18
A/C Rec T/ovr	11 79	11 86	12 33	10 37	9 35
Tot Ass T/ovr	6 97	5 46	5 77	5 75	4 43
Debt/Ass Rat	0 42	0 51	0 56	0 59	0 53
L T L Tot Ass	-	-	0 01	0 02	0 01
Debt to Eqity	1 09	1 53	1 86	2 04	2 02
Interest Cover	133 60	22 37	24 25	17 09	79 78
Oper Prof Mrg	3 27	3 91	3 24	3 76	3 60
Net Prof Marg%	0 95	1 17	0 99	0 89	0 95
Ret on Assets	22 86	21 76	19 18	22 28	16 19
Ret on Equity%	17 04	19 28	18 88	17 64	15 93
Price/Earnings	8 65	7 44	4 44	5 59	8 02
Divid Cover	1 64	1 80	1 81	1 71	1 58
Divid Yield	7 04	7 48	12 46	10 46	7 89
Earning Yield%	11 56	13 44	22 52	17 88	12 47
NAV % Mrk Pr	67 85	69 70	119 25	101 40	78 31
Effec Tax Rate	47 81	47 70	48 15	51 36	50 84
Def Interval	-	0 28	0 27	0 20	0 11
Sus Grth Rate	6 66	8 55	8 43	7 33	5 85

SUBSIDIARY & ASSOCIATED COMPANIES

AIRCARGO PROPERTIES (PTY) LTD
APPROVED PROPERTIES LTD
AUTO REPLACEMENTS (PTY) LTD
CURFIN (PINETOWN) PROPERTIES (PTY) LTD
CURFIN GERMISTON PROPERTIES (PTY) LTD
CURFIN HERIOTDALE PROPERTIES (EAST) (PTY
CURFIN HERIOTDALE PROPERTIES (PTY) LTD
CURFUNE INVESTMENTS (PTY) LTD
CURRIE MOTORS (PTY) LTD
CURRIE MOTORS (WELKOM) (PTY) LTD
CURRIE MOTORS KEMPTON PROPERTIES (PTY) L
CURRIE MOTORS PROPERTY INVESTMENTS (PTY)
F & A SILVA'S INVESTMENTS (PTY) LTD
FINCOR LEASING (PTY) LTD
GOLDIES MOTOR PROPERTIES (JOHANNESBURG)
GOLDIES MOTOR PROPERTIES (SPRINGS) (PTY)
MARO INVESTMENTS (PTY) LTD
NORTHRIDGE COUNTRY CLUB (PTY) LTD
ORIAC INVESTMENTS (PTY) LTD
ORIBI MOTORS LTD
PATROJAN (PTY) LTD
PLYMOUTH PROPERTIES (PTY) LTD
PROESAND PROPERTIES (PTY) LTD
RAND NISSAN (PTY) LTD
SOUTH AFRICAN FREIGHT CORP LTD (50,02%)

INVESTMENTS

ANDPROES (PTY) LTD (420 SH)
BENVOORT PROPERTIES (PTY) LTD (420 SH)
EXETER HALL SHARE BLOCK LTD (3038 SH)
H CANARD & COMPANY (PTY) LTD (50 SH)

CUTRITE INVESTMENTS LTD

ABBREVIATION : CUTRITE

JSE SHORT CODE : CTR

SECTOR : Industrial-Clothing, Footwear & Textiles

SHAREHOLDERS

Who Owns Whom's Assessment of the Identity of the Ultimate Controlling Shareholder: DIRECTORS

SHAREHOLDER	PERCENTAGE 1992	1991
NEDBANK NOM LTD	22 6	23 8
SAGE LIFE LTD	18 5	18 4
HYMAN A J	12 6	12 6
SYDNEY COPE FAMILY TRUST	9 9	9 9
COPE G B	7 8	7 8
COPE E	7 2	7 2
EDEL P R	5 7	4 5
SPARKS N D	1 5	1 5
STD BANK NOM TVL P/L	1 3	1 3
JR NOM P/L	1 3	1 3
TOTAL	88 2	88 1

DIRECTORS :
COPE E ,COPE S (Chairman)
EDEL PR (Managing Director)
FEINBERG H (Financial Director),HYMAN AJ
KUNSTLER JK

REGISTRATION NUMBER : 87/03019/06

REGISTERED OFFICE
Gladiator House, Kimberley Road
Nancefield
1812
TEL 011-945 1051
FAX 011-342 1074

TRANSFER SECRETARY
Fraser Street Registrars (Pty) Ltd
P O Box 61178, Marshalltown
2107
TEL 011-491 0911

COMPANY SECRETARY
H Feinberg

NATURE OF BUSINESS
The company acts as an investment holding company and through its subsidiaries carries on business as manufacturers & distributors of clothing

BANKERS :
Nedperm Bank Ltd

AUDITORS :
Arthur Andersen & Co

FAMILIAR BRAND NAMES
AVIATION,CUTRICELLI,CUTRITE,CUTWOOD,DIJON
LA FINESSE,PURE NEW WOOL,SPORTY SHORTS

Def Interval	1.28	1.81	2.12	1.79	1.54
Sus Grth Rate	8.50	9.53	9.32	8.53	22.07

CONTRIBUTION BY ACTIVITY
N/A

YEAR END : February

DIVIDEND :Ords 1c

Interim No 4	(Ldr)27/10/89	(Pay)15/11/89	Amt(c)3
Final No 5	(Ldr)25/05/90	(Pay)10/06/90	Amt(c)3.5
Interim No 6	(Ldr)26/10/90	(Pay)15/11/90	Amt(c)3
Final No 7	(Ldr)30/05/91	(Pay)14/06/91	Amt(c)4
Interim No 8	(Ldr)25/10/91	(Pay)15/11/91	Amt(c)3
Final No 9	(Ldr)29/05/92	(Pay)12/06/92	Amt(c)4
Interim No 10	(Ldr)30/10/92	(Pay)13/11/92	Amt(c)3

NUMBER OF EMPLOYEES : 650

CAPITAL STRUCTURE

	AUTHORISED	ISSUED
Ords 1c	25000000	16525000

FINANCIAL STATISTICS (AT FINANCIAL YEAR END)

(Amts in R'000)	1992 Feb	1991 Feb	1990 Feb	1989 Feb	1988 Feb
Ord S/H Int	21549	19717	17838	16175	6453
Long Trm Loans	1317	1784	2302	929	768
Iss Ord Share	16525	16525	16525	16525	16525
Total Liab	8130	10319	11009	7811	6308
Current Liab	6813	8535	8707	6882	5540
Total Assets	21336	21693	20504	15643	12761
Intang Assets	8343	8343	8343	8343	*
Current Assets	19815	20079	18578	14643	11751
Debtors	12476	12504	11327	9251	7875
Inventory	6896	7235	7178	5340	3842
Turnover	47213	44918	39159	32177	26390
Oper Profit	6646	7009	6285	5125	4068
Interest Paid	957	1084	856	635	362
Tax Paid	2771	3037	2746	2233	1869
Prf af Int&Tax	2989	3036	2737	2288	1837
Prf att Ord Sh	2989	3036	2737	2288	1837
Btm Line Earn	2989	3036	2737	2288	1837
Dividend Paid	1157	1157	1074	909	413
Mkt Prce(c) YE	70	60	85	60	75
Depreciation	285	330	363	172	145

PER SHARE STATISTICS (CENTS)

Net Asst Val	79.92	68.83	57.46	47.39	39.05
Net Earnings	18.10	18.40	16.60	13.80	12.80
Dividends	7.00	7.00	6.50	5.50	2.50
Cash Flow	19.60	19.92	18.82	14.62	14.34

RATIOS AND OTHER INFORMATION

Mrk Cap(R000)	11568	9915	14046	9915	12394
Current Ratio	2.91	2.35	2.13	2.13	2.12
Quik/Acid Tst	1.90	1.50	1.31	1.35	1.43
A/C Rec T/ovr	3.78	3.59	3.46	3.48	3.35
Tot Ass T/ovr	2.21	2.07	1.91	2.06	2.07
Debt/Ass Rat	0.38	0.47	0.53	0.49	0.48
L T L Tot Ass	0.06	0.08	0.10	0.05	0.04
Debt to Eqity	0.37	0.52	0.61	0.47	0.94
Interest Cover	6.94	6.47	7.34	8.07	11.24
Oper Prof Mrg	14.08	15.60	16.05	15.93	15.41
Net Prof Marg%	6.33	6.76	6.99	7.11	6.96
Ret on Assets	31.48	32.99	30.92	32.96	31.88
Ret on Equity%	13.87	15.40	15.34	14.15	28.47
Price/Earnings	3.87	3.26	5.12	4.35	5.86
Divid Cover	2.59	2.63	2.55	2.51	5.12
Divid Yield	10.00	11.67	7.65	9.17	3.33
Earning Yield%	25.86	30.67	19.53	23.00	17.07
NAV % Mrk Pr	114.16	114.72	67.60	78.99	52.07
Effec Tax Rate	48.72	51.23	49.90	50.36	48.54

SUBSIDIARY & ASSOCIATED COMPANIES

CUTRITE APPAREL MANUFACTURERS (PTY) LTD
DIVA FASHIONS (PTY) LTD

INVESTMENTS

None

DA GAMA TEXTILE CO LTD

ABBREVIATION : DA-GAMA

JSE SHORT CODE : DAG

SECTOR : Industrial-Clothing, Footwear & Textiles

SHAREHOLDERS

Who Owns Whom's Assessment of the Identity of the Ultimate Controlling Shareholder: ANGLO AMERICAN VIA SA BREWS

SHAREHOLDER	PERCENTAGE 1992	1991
DA GAMA HOLDING CO P/L	49.0	49.0
SA BREWERIES LTD	11.7	11.7
EIGHTY ONE MAIN STREET NOM LTD	8.7	7.9
SA MUTUAL	7.0	6.1
SOUTHERN LIFE ASSOC LTD	5.0	6.8
CMB NOM P/L	4.4	---
STD BANK NOM TVL P/L	1.6	---
FIRST NAT NOM P/L	1.3	---
YSKOR PENS FUND	1.2	---
SANLAM	---	4.3
TOTAL	89.9	85.8

DIRECTORS :
CUNNINGHAM VJ ,HARRISON JA ,KAHN JM
MACFARLANE WS ,MADDOX RA
PEARCE TH (Chief Executive)
PIETERSMA NJ (Financial Director),SCHROEDER GE
STONESTREET SJ (Sales Director)
VAN DER WATT L (Chairman),WOLFAARDT C ,WYMAN MI

REGISTRATION NUMBER : 68/15435/06

REGISTERED OFFICE
Da Gama House, Old KWT National Road
Arnoldton, East London
5201
TEL: 0431-45 1124
FAX: 0431-45 1410

TRANSFER SECRETARY
Mercantile Registrars Ltd
P O Box 1053, Johannesburg
2000
TEL: 011-333 8181

COMPANY SECRETARY
A E Swift

NATURE OF BUSINESS

The business of the company & its subsidiaries is the manufacture & make-up of cotton & synthetic fibre textile goods. This includes the blending & spinning of the fibres, weaving, bleaching, dyeing printing & finishing of fabrics, & the sewing of made-up articles.

BANKERS :

First National Bank of SA Ltd
Nedperm Bank Ltd, Standard Bank of SA Ltd

AUDITORS :

N/A

FAMILIAR BRAND NAMES

3 LEOPARDS,COTTAGE LOOK,DAYDAWN,DAYMIST DREAMTEX,EDENROSE,FASCO,FINE FEATHERS FIRSTLINE,GLENDALENE,ROSELEA,SPRINGMOON SUNGLEAM,TOTO,UNITEX

CONTRIBUTION BY ACTIVITY

N/A

YEAR END : March

DIVIDEND : Ords 2c

Interim No 6	(Ldr)01/09/89	(Pay)06/10/89	Amt(c)17.5
Final No 7	(Ldr)25/05/90	(Pay)02/07/90	Amt(c)47
Interim No 8	(Ldr)23/11/90	(Pay)31/12/90	Amt(c)16
Final No 9	(Ldr)24/05/91	(Pay)01/07/91	Amt(c)20
Interim No 10	(Ldr)22/11/91	(Pay)31/12/91	Amt(c)10
Final No 11	(Ldr)22/05/92	(Pay)01/07/92	Amt(c)15.5
Interim No 12	(Ldr)27/11/92	(Pay)31/12/92	Amt(c)6.5

NUMBER OF EMPLOYEES : 4300

CAPITAL STRUCTURE

	AUTHORISED	ISSUED
Ords 2c	70000000	51007500
"A" Red Partic Prefs R1	3004000	0
"B" Red Partic Prefs 1c	17337707	0
"C" Red Partic Prefs 1c	15000000	0

FINANCIAL STATISTICS (AT FINANCIAL YEAR END)

(Amts in R'000)	1992 Mar	1991 Mar	1990 Mar	1988 Dec	1987 Dec
Ord S/H Int	214022	197000	172874	127681	96748
Long Trm Loans	11260	7074	5674	3993	4226
Iss Ord Share	51008	51008	50975	50200	50200
Total Liab	61135	59271	73737	60909	43609
Current Liab	49875	52197	68063	56916	39383
Total Assets	275157	256271	246611	188590	140357
Current Assets	183804	165221	166235	141691	103178
Debtors	52598	47536	46508	37005	31498
Inventory	116766	97135	91495	72928	64570
Turnover	259032	260690	344935	248233	209561
Oper Profit	37418	50335	87464	62467	44947
Interest Paid	2583	840	350	201	284
Tax Paid	6543	9850	16398	11919	7806
Prf af Int&Tax	30029	42410	75635	53501	36857
Prf att Ord Sh	30029	42410	75635	53501	36697
Btm Line Earn	30029	42410	75987	54025	36697
Dividend Paid	13007	18370	32831	23092	15813
Mkt Prce(c) YE	430	700	1020	950	670
Depreciation	14237	12176	10697	6514	4792

PER SHARE STATISTICS (CENTS)

Net Asst Val	419.59	386.21	339.13	254.34	192.73
Net Earnings	58.90	83.20	149.50	106.60	73.10
Dividends	25.50	36.00	64.50	46.00	31.50
Cash Flow	87.16	108.03	174.33	119.38	84.86

RATIOS AND OTHER INFORMATION

Mrk Cap(R000)	219334	357056	519945	476900	336340
Current Ratio	3.69	3.17	2.44	2.49	2.62
Quik/Acid Tst	1.34	1.30	1.10	1.21	0.98
A/C Rec T/ovr	4.92	5.48	7.42	6.71	6.65
Tot Ass T/ovr	0.94	1.02	1.40	1.32	1.49
Debt/Ass Rat	0.20	0.21	0.28	0.31	0.29
L T L Tot Ass	0.02	0.01	0.00	0.00	0.01
Debt to Eqity	0.26	0.27	0.40	0.45	0.41
Interest Cover	14.49	59.93	249.91	310.81	158.26
Oper Prof Mrg	14.45	19.31	25.36	25.16	21.45
Net Prof Marg%	11.59	16.27	21.93	21.55	17.51
Ret on Assets	14.23	20.72	37.46	34.80	32.02
Ret on Equity%	14.03	21.53	43.75	41.90	37.93
Price/Earnings	7.30	8.41	6.82	8.91	9.17
Divid Cover	2.31	2.31	2.32	2.32	2.32
Divid Yield	5.93	5.14	6.32	4.84	4.70
Earning Yield%	13.70	11.89	14.66	11.22	10.91
NAV % Mrk Pr	97.58	55.17	33.25	26.77	28.76
Effec Tax Rate	12.39	14.75	15.79	17.98	14.99
Def Interval	0.26	0.03	0.01	0.01	0.02
Sus Grth Rate	7.95	12.20	24.76	23.82	21.59

SUBSIDIARY & ASSOCIATED COMPANIES

CYRIL LORD (SA) (PTY) LTD
CYRIL LORD PROPERTIES (PTY) LTD
DA GAMA DISTRIBUTORS (PTY) LTD
DA GAMA FACTORY PROPERTIES (PTY) LTD
DA GAMA HOME FASHIONS (PTY) LTD
DA GAMA PROPERTY DEVELOPERS (PTY) LTD
GOOD HOPE TEXTILE CORPORATION (PTY) LTD
RAGS & FABRICS (NAMIBIA) (PTY) LTD
RAGS & FABRICS (SA) (PTY) LTD
RAGS & FABRICS (TRANSKEI) (PTY) LTD
UMDANZANI ESTATES (PTY) LTD

INVESTMENTS

None

DAB INVESTMENTS LTD

ABBREVIATION : DABI

JSE SHORT CODE : DAB

SECTOR : Mining Financial-Mining Holding

SHAREHOLDERS

Who Owns Whom's Assessment of the Identity of the Ultimate Controlling Shareholder: ANGLO AMERICAN VIA JOHNNIES

SHAREHOLDER	PERCENTAGE 1992	1991
STD BANK NOM TVL P/L	59.3	57.6
SA SPECIAL RISKS INSURANCE ASSOC LTD	5.1	2.9
INDO-CHINA NOM P/L	3.5	---
ROODERAND MAIN REEF MINES LTD	2.6	---
FIRST NAT NOM P/L	2.5	3.1

DALGLAND NOM P/L	2.4	---
LONDON REGISTER ACCOUNT	1.6	1.8
HORTORS GROUP PENS FUND	1.1	---
NGK SINODALE TVL PENS FUND	---	2.2
ROODENRAND MAIN REEF MINES LTD	---	2.6
TOTAL	77.9	70.2

DIRECTORS :
BARBER DD ,BRAY VG ,CROSS GMW (Chairman)
DRAUDSING AJE ,EARLE PS ,KOVARSKY DC

REGISTRATION NUMBER : 85/05440/06

REGISTERED OFFICE
Consolidated Building, Fox & Harrison Streets
Johannesburg
2001
TEL: 011-373 9111
FAX: 011-836 6130

TRANSFER SECRETARY
Consolidated Share Registrars Ltd
P O Box 61051, Marshalltown
2107
TEL: 011-492 1620

COMPANY SECRETARY
Johannesburg Consolidated Inv Co Ltd

NATURE OF BUSINESS
An investment holding company managing a portfolio of predominantly mining shares.
The company is in the process of liquidating the investment portfolio.

BANKERS :
Standard Bank of SA Ltd

AUDITORS :
Deloitte Pim Goldby

FAMILIAR BRAND NAMES
N/A

CONTRIBUTION BY ACTIVITY
N/A

YEAR END : June

DIVIDEND : Ords 1c

Interim No 8	(Ldr)12/01/90	(Pay)06/02/90	Amt(c)47
Final No 9	(Ldr)25/06/90	(Pay)13/08/90	Amt(c)32
Interim No 10	(Ldr)11/01/91	(Pay)04/02/91	Amt(c)60
Final No 11	(Ldr)12/07/91	(Pay)05/08/91	Amt(c)34
Interim No 12	(Ldr)07/02/92	(Pay)24/02/92	Amt(c)23
Final No 13	(Ldr)14/08/92	(Pay)28/09/92	Amt(c)17

CAPITAL STRUCTURE

	AUTHORISED	ISSUED
Ords 1c	6000000	4537500

FINANCIAL STATISTICS (AT FINANCIAL YEAR END)

(Amts in R'000)	1992 Jun	1991 Jun	1990 Jun	1989 Jun	1988 Jun
Ord S/H Int	11575	10229	11041	11125	10602
Long Trm Loans	-	1070	1400	1439	1072
Iss Ord Share	4538	4538	4538	4538	4538
Total Liab	1173	2827	3044	4636	4206
Current Liab	1173	1757	1644	3197	3134
Total Assets	12748	13056	14085	15761	14808
Current Assets	234	1048	1599	3220	1869
Debtors	215	214	176	1800	1145
Oper Profit	2119	3474	3278	5790	6746
Interest Paid	65	76	31	-	-
Tax Paid	-1070	99	-39	367	1072
Prf af Int&Tax	3161	3453	3501	5423	5674
Prf att Ord Sh	3161	3453	3501	5423	5674
Btm Line Earn	3161	3453	3501	5423	5674
Dividend Paid	1815	4265	3585	4900	4537
Mkt Prce(c) YE	1200	1350	1600	1850	1200

PER SHARE STATISTICS (CENTS)

Net Asst Val	255.07	225.41	243.30	245.15	233.63
Net Earnings	69.70	76.10	77.20	119.50	99.80
Dividends	40.00	94.00	79.00	108.00	100.00
Cash Flow	46.08	70.05	76.29	127.59	148.66

RATIOS AND OTHER INFORMATION

Mrk Cap(R000)	54456	61263	72608	83953	54456
Current Ratio	0.20	0.60	0.97	1.01	0.60
Quik/Acid Tst	0.20	0.60	0.97	1.01	0.60
Debt/Ass Rat	0.09	0.13	0.12	0.20	0.21
Debt to Eqity	0.10	0.17	0.15	0.29	0.30
Interest Cover	32.60	45.71	105.74	-	-
Ret on Assets	16.91	27.79	24.80	36.74	45.56
Ret on Equity%	27.31	33.76	31.71	48.75	53.52
Price/Earnings	17.22	17.74	20.73	15.48	12.02
Divid Cover	1.74	0.81	0.98	1.11	1.00
Divid Yield	3.33	6.96	4.94	5.84	8.33
Earning Yield%	5.81	5.64	4.83	6.46	8.32
NAV % Mrk Pr	21.26	16.70	15.21	13.25	19.47
Sus Grth Rate	11.63	-7.94	-0.76	4.70	10.72

SUBSIDIARY & ASSOCIATED COMPANIES

CONSOLIDATED METALLURGICAL INDUSTRIES LT (23.1%)
RUSTENBURG PLATINUM HOLDINGS LTD (33.8%)

INVESTMENTS

DE BEERS CONSOLIDATED MINES LTD (CENTENA (100000 SH)
DRIEFONTEIN CONSOLIDATED LTD (200000 SH)
HJ JOEL GOLD MINING CO LTD (50000 SH)
JOHANNESBURG CONSOLIDATED INVESTMENT COM (40000 SH)
LEBOWA PLATINUM MINES LTD (264000 SH)
LIBANON G.M. CO. LTD (75000 SH)
PALABORA MINING COMPANY LTD (26500 SH)
POTGIETERSRUST PLATINUMS LTD (2.3%)
RANDFONTEIN ESTATES GOLD MINING CO WITS (21000 SH)
SOUTH DEEP EXPLORATION CO LTD (92000 SH)
SOUTHVAAL HOLDINGS LTD (100000 SH)
UNISEL G.M. LTD (450200 SH)
WESTERN AREAS G.M. CO. LTD (100000 SH)
WINKELHAAK MINES LTD (35100 SH)

DALYS LTD

ABBREVIATION : DALYS

JSE SHORT CODE : DLS

SECTOR : Industrial-Beverages & Hotels

SHAREHOLDERS

Who Owns Whom's Assessment of the Identity of the Ultimate Controlling Shareholder:
HAMILTON FAMILY

SHAREHOLDER	PERCENTAGE 1992	1991
RONHAM INV P/L	25 8	25 8
HAMILTON MANAGEMENT CONSULTANTS P/L	25 4	25 4
TEMPORA INV LTD	20 6	20 6
CMB NOM P/L	6 7	---
HAMILTON R D	4 4	4 4
STD BANK NOM TVL P/L	3 6	3 1
EIGHTY ONE MAIN STREET NOM LTD	1 6	1 6
VOLKSKAS OPEN TRUST INV P/L	1 6	1 6
COMMERCIAL UNION LIFE ASSURE CO SA LTD	1 4	---
COMMERCIAL UNION ASSURE CO SA LTD	---	1 4
SANLAM	---	6 1
TOTAL	91 0	90 1

DIRECTORS :
COOK DB ,EVANS IJS ,HAMILTON JW
HAMILTON RD (Chairman

REGISTRATION NUMBER : 02/00299/06

REGISTERED OFFICE
491 Ridge Road, Durban
4001
TEL 031-29 4371
FAX 031-29 9125

TRANSFER SECRETARY
Dalys Ltd
P O Box 1177, Durban
4000
TEL 031-29 4371

COMPANY SECRETARY
J Reekie

NATURE OF BUSINESS
An investment holding company with a controlling interest in quoted Suncrush Ltd The group manufactures & markets soft drinks

BANKERS :
Standard Bank of SA Ltd

AUDITORS :
Deloitte Pim Goldby

FAMILIAR BRAND NAMES
N/A

CONTRIBUTION BY ACTIVITY
N/A

YEAR END : June

DIVIDEND : Ords 1c

Interim No 131	(Ldr)16/03/90	(Pay)30/03/90	Amt(c)8
Final No 132	(Ldr)12/10/90	(Pay)02/11/90	Amt(c)25
Interim No 133	(Ldr)15/03/91	(Pay)26/03/91	Amt(c)12
Final No 134	(Ldr)11/10/91	(Pay)01/11/91	Amt(c)32
Interim No 135	(Ldr)13/03/92	(Pay)27/03/92	Amt(c)14 5
Final No 136	(Ldr)09/10/92	(Pay)30/10/92	Amt(c)37 5

CAPITAL STRUCTURE

	AUTHORISED	ISSUED
Ords 1c	20000000	14000000

FINANCIAL STATISTICS (AT FINANCIAL YEAR END)

(Amts in R'000)	1992 Jun	1991 Jun	1990 Jun	1989 Jun	1988 Jun
Ord S/H Int	3677	3593	3462	3333	2877
Iss Ord Share	14000	14000	14000	14000	14000
Total Liab	5343	4610	3632	2131	1610
Current Liab	5343	4610	3632	2131	1610
Total Assets	9020	8203	7094	5464	4487
Current Assets	5366	4575	3524	2391	1973
Debtors	-	-	-	-	1967
Oper Profit	-103	-92	-91	-68	35
Tax Paid	103	104	70	60	9
Prf af Int&Tax	7364	6291	4749	3396	2777
Prf att Ord Sh	7364	6291	4749	3396	2777
Btm Line Earn	7364	6291	4749	3396	2777
Dividend Paid	7280	6160	4620	2940	2240
Mkt Prce(c) YE	4450	3950	1600	1000	590

PER SHARE STATISTICS (CENTS)

Net Asst Val	26 26	25 66	24 73	23 81	20 55
Net Earnings	52 60	44 90	34 00	24 00	20 00
Dividends	52 00	44 00	33 00	21 00	16 00
Cash Flow	52 60	44 94	33 92	24 26	19 84

RATIOS AND OTHER INFORMATION

Mrk Cap(R000)	623000	553000	224000	140000	82600
Current Ratio	1 00	0 99	0 97	1 12	1 23
Quik/Acid Tst	1 00	0 99	0 97	1 12	1 23
Debt/Ass Rat	0 59	0 56	0 51	0 39	0 36
Debt to Eqty	1 45	1 28	1 05	0 64	0 56
Ret on Assets	82 78	77 96	67 93	63 25	62 09
Ret on Equity%	200 27	175 09	137 18	101 89	96 52
Price/Earnings	84 60	87 97	47 06	41 67	29 50
Divid Cover	1 01	1 02	1 03	1 14	1 25
Divid Yield	1 17	1 11	2 06	2 10	2 71
Earning Yield%	1 18	1 14	2 13	2 40	3 39
NAV % Mrk Pr	0 59	0 65	1 55	2 38	3 48
Effec Tax Rate	93 64	81 25	137 25	115 38	180 00
Sus Grth Rate	2 28	3 65	3 73	13 68	18 67

SUBSIDIARY & ASSOCIATED COMPANIES

SUNCRUSH LTD (50,22%)

INVESTMENTS

None

DARMAG LTD

ABBREVIATION : DARMAG

JSE SHORT CODE : DMG

SECTOR : Industrial-Electronics, Electrical & Bat

SHAREHOLDERS

Who Owns Whom's Assessment of the Identity of the Ultimate Controlling Shareholder:
ANGLO AMERICAN

SHAREHOLDER	PERCENTAGE 1992	1991

ZIMCO INDUSTRIES P/L	53 2	23 7
LORD HENDRY TRUST	22 2	22 2
DERSLEY R M	6 2	6 2
ALBERT P	3 4	3 4
CMB NOM P/L	2 2	---
BUCHANAN D A	1 7	1 5
SANLAM	---	4 7
ZIMCO HOLDINGS P/L	---	26 9
TOTAL	88 9	88 6

DIRECTORS :
ALBERT P ,BEZUIDENHOUDT JJM
BUCHANAN DA (Chairman),DERSLEY RM ,DREW NE
HAUGLAND NPJ ,KINNEAR BH

REGISTRATION NUMBER : 80/02577/06

REGISTERED OFFICE
5th Floor, Sandton City, Cnr Rivonia Rd & 5th Str
Sandton
2199
TEL: 011-783 7023
FAX 011-783 0732

TRANSFER SECRETARY
Central Registrars Ltd
P O Box 4844, Johannesburg
2000
TEL 011-331 0051

COMPANY SECRETARY
Zimco Industries (Pty) Ltd

NATURE OF BUSINESS
Business is conducted by the company and its subsidiaries through three divisions-plastics, rubber & separators The group's products are plastic and rubber battery components

BANKERS :
First National Bank of SA Ltd

AUDITORS :
Coopers Theron Du Toit

FAMILIAR BRAND NAMES
N/A

CONTRIBUTION BY ACTIVITY
N/A

YEAR END : March

DIVIDEND : Ords no par value

Final	(Ldr)19/07/91	(Pay)09/08/91	Amt(c)2 0
Final	(Ldr)17/07/92	(Pay)07/08/92	Amt(c)2 25

NUMBER OF EMPLOYEES : 340

CAPITAL STRUCTURE

	AUTHORISED	ISSUED
Ords no par value	58484000	22150000
14% Cum Prefs 1c	750000	750000

FINANCIAL STATISTICS (AT FINANCIAL YEAR END)

(Amts in R'000)	1992 Mar	1991 Mar	1990 Mar	1989 Feb	1988 Feb
Ord S/H Int	12221	10909	9397	8669	6582
Long Trm Loans	1206	1766	2775	2708	3717
Iss Ord Share	22150	22150	22150	22150	22000
Total Liab	5895	7232	10749	9665	8968
Current Liab	4689	5466	7974	6957	5251
Total Assets	18116	18141	20146	18334	15550
Current Assets	8154	9260	10621	10204	8911
Debtors	4057	5807	5715	4305	3627
Inventory	1986	3346	4608	5829	4176
Turnover	24703	26221	26383	23841	18893
Oper Profit	2684	3155	1480	3995	3127
Interest Paid	535	1012	1900	657	468
Tax Paid	123	220	-409	491	364
Prf af Int&Tax	2271	1955	728	2930	2369
Prf att Ord Sh	2271	1955	728	2930	2248
Btm Line Earn	1810	1955	728	3625	2248
Dividend Paid	498	443	-	1174	440
Mkt Prce(c) YE	30	30	33	105	90
Depreciation	1172	1061	1010	815	625

PER SHARE STATISTICS (CENTS)

Net Asst Val	55 17	49 25	42 42	39 14	29 92
Net Earnings	10 20	8 80	3 30	13 20	11 00
Dividends	2 25	2 00	-	5 30	2 00
Cash Flow	15 58	13 64	5 89	16 85	14 11

RATIOS AND OTHER INFORMATION

Mrk Cap(R000)	6645	6645	7310	23258	19800
Current Ratio	1 74	1 69	1 33	1 47	1 70
Quik/Acid Tst	1 32	1 08	0 75	0 63	0 90
A/C Rec T/ovr	6 09	4 52	4 26	5 54	5 21
Tot Ass T/ovr	1 36	1 45	1 21	1 30	1 21
Debt/Ass Rat	0 32	0 39	0 53	0 51	0 49
L T L Tot Ass	0 06	0 09	0 13	0 13	0 15
Debt to Eqity	0 48	0 66	1 14	1 07	1 16
Interest Cover	5 02	3 12	0 78	6 08	6 68
Oper Prof Mrg	10 87	12 03	5 61	16 76	16 55
Net Prof Marg%	9 19	7 46	2 76	12 29	11 90
Ret on Assets	16 17	17 57	10 17	22 24	20 59
Ret on Equity%	18 58	17 92	7 15	33 80	34 15
Price/Earnings	2 94	3 41	10 00	7 95	8 18
Divid Cover	4 53	4 40	-	2 49	5 50
Divid Yield	7 50	6 67	-	5 05	2 22
Earning Yield%	34 00	29 33	10 00	12 57	12 22
NAV % Mrk Pr	183 91	164 17	128 56	37 27	33 24
Effec Tax Rate	0 42	1 29	-26 33	14 85	14 05
Def Interval	0 33	0 95	4 25	0 79	0 88
Sus Grth Rate	14 51	13 86	7 75	20 26	27 47

SUBSIDIARY & ASSOCIATED COMPANIES

DARMAG INDUSTRIES (PTY) LTD
DARMAG PROPERTIES (PTY) LTD
DARMAG SEPARATORS (PTY) LTD
MASTERBATCHERS (PTY) LTD
SOLID TYRES (PTY) LTD

INVESTMENTS

None

DATAKOR LTD

ABBREVIATION DATAKOR

JSE SHORT CODE : DTR

SECTOR : Industrial Electronics, Electrical & Bat

SHAREHOLDERS

Who Owns Whom's Assessment of the Identity of the Ultimate Controlling Shareholder:
SANLAM VIA SANKORP

SHAREHOLDER	PERCENTAGE 1992	1991
MERCEDES INFORMATION TECHNOLOGIES P/L	82.5	82.5
DATAKOR LTD SHARE TRUST	3.3	---
CMB NOM P/L	2.7	---
FIRST NAT NOM P/L	2.1	2.1
SA MUTUAL	1.9	1.9
SANLAM	---	2.7
MERCEDES DATAKOR LTD SHARE TRUST	---	3.5
TOTAL	92.5	92.7

DIRECTORS :
BOSHOFF WH ,BRUNETTE CN ,DE VILLIERS LM
FRANGOS NJ (Chairman & Chief Exec.)
HUNT-DAVIS DNA ,JANSEN VAN VUUREN C ,MCEVOY M
MOFFETT PJ ,ROUTLEDGE AA (Financial Director)
WASON NDR

REGISTRATION NUMBER : 77/00915/06

REGISTERED OFFICE
Unidata Park, 4 Keyes Avenue
Rosebank, Johannesburg
2196
TEL: 011-441 4111
FAX: 011-441 4601

TRANSFER SECRETARY
Consolidated Share Registrars Ltd
P O Box 61051, Marshalltown
2107
TEL: 011-492 1620

COMPANY SECRETARY
M Harvey

NATURE OF BUSINESS
Datakor is an information technology business providing a comprehensive range of data processing, office automation and communication products and services through subsidiary companies and divisions on a nation-wide basis.

BANKERS :
Nedperm Bank Ltd

AUDITORS :
Coopers Theron Du Toit

FAMILIAR BRAND NAMES
AVANT GARDE,BANYAN VINES LAN,COMPUSON
CONVEX (MINI-COMPUTER),LINC,MAPPER
MICRODATA INTERNATIONAL,REFLECTIONS,SEPCO
UNIDATA,UNISYS

CONTRIBUTION BY ACTIVITY
N/A

YEAR END : March

DIVIDEND :Ords no par value

Interim	(Ldr)08/12/89	(Pay)31/12/89	Amt(c)2.5
Final	(Ldr)22/06/90	(Pay)02/07/90	Amt(c)4.5
Interim	(Ldr)07/12/90	(Pay)28/12/90	Amt(c)3
Final	(Ldr)28/06/91	(Pay)02/07/91	Amt(c)5.5
Interim	(Ldr)15/11/91	(Pay)29/11/91	Amt(c)4
Final	(Ldr)22/05/92	(Pay)05/06/92	Amt(c)7
Interim	(Ldr)13/11/92	(Pay)27/11/92	Amt(c)4.6
Special	(Ldr)13/11/92	(Pay)27/11/92	Amt(c)14

NUMBER OF EMPLOYEES : 1414

CAPITAL STRUCTURE

	AUTHORISED	ISSUED
Ords no par value	170000000	140350850

FINANCIAL STATISTICS (AT FINANCIAL YEAR END)

(Amts in R'000)	1992 Mar	1991 Mar	1990 Mar	1989 Mar	1988 Mar
Ord S/H Int	136646	111908	101861	98814	32827
Long Trm Loans	43244	46024	48319	49603	18307
Iss Ord Share	140351	140351	140351	135983	50696
Total Liab	198912	147518	141164	197596	49270
Current Liab	155668	101494	92845	147993	30963
Total Assets	335558	257400	236326	285868	75600
Intang Assets	*	2026	6699	10542	6497
Current Assets	293666	210526	190019	228015	47109
Debtors	89408	68886	84101	90761	26050
Inventory	87203	95084	105918	125657	16558
Turnover	554746	498595	448873	362637	105198
Oper Profit	61993	45389	51494	40031	12324
Interest Paid	10405	14211	20499	8644	193
Tax Paid	31976	9199	18067	14537	5876
Prf af Int&Tax	35400	27717	20687	17682	8114
Prf att Ord Sh	35617	28071	21877	20019	8502
Btm Line Earn	40177	24944	8723	20019	8502
Dividend Paid	15439	11931	9825	7519	2664
Mkt Prce(c) YE	155	110	85	110	185
Depreciation	13313	9999	9083	5853	556

PER SHARE STATISTICS (CENTS)

	1992	1991	1990	1989	1988
Net Asst Val	97.36	78.29	67.80	64.91	51.94
Net Earnings	25.40	20.00	15.90	17.30	15.40
Dividends	11.00	8.50	7.00	7.00	4.00
Cash Flow	34.37	27.12	30.84	31.14	19.70

RATIOS AND OTHER INFORMATION

	1992	1991	1990	1989	1988
Mrk Cap(R000)	217544	154386	119298	149581	93788
Current Ratio	1.89	2.07	2.05	1.54	1.52
Quik/Acid Tst	1.33	1.14	0.91	0.69	0.99
A/C Rec T/ovr	6.20	7.24	5.34	4.00	4.04
Tot Ass T/ovr	1.65	1.94	1.90	1.27	1.39
Debt/Ass Rat	0.49	0.46	0.47	0.62	0.61
L T L Tot Ass	0.03	0.06	0.07	0.10	0.20
Debt to Eqity	1.21	1.05	1.08	1.78	1.39
Interest Cover	5.98	3.23	2.51	4.63	63.85
Oper Prof Mrg	11.18	9.10	11.47	11.04	11.72
Net Prof Marg%	6.42	5.63	4.87	5.52	8.08
Ret on Assets	23.24	20.00	25.58	15.11	19.27
Ret on Equity%	26.07	25.08	21.48	20.26	25.90
Price/Earnings	6.10	5.50	5.35	6.36	12.01
Divid Cover	2.31	2.35	2.27	2.47	3.85
Divid Yield	7.10	7.73	8.24	6.36	2.16
Earning Yield%	16.39	18.18	18.71	15.73	8.32
NAV % Mrk Pr	62.81	71.17	79.77	59.01	28.07
Effec Tax Rate	47.77	26.22	13.77	6.07	33.66
Def Interval	0.35	0.55	1.13	1.90	0.80
Sus Grth Rate	14.77	14.42	11.83	12.65	17.78

SUBSIDIARY & ASSOCIATED COMPANIES

COMPUSONS (PTY) LTD
DATAKOR ENGINEERING (PTY) LTD
DATAKOR HOLDINGS (PTY) LTD
SEP COMPUTERS (PTY) LTD
VOICE COMMUNICATIONS SYSTEMS (PTY) LTD

INVESTMENTS

TIMEPLEX INC (16,3%)

DAVID WHITEHEAD TEXTILES LTD (ZIMBABWE)

ABBREVIATION : DW TEX

SECTOR : Zimbabwe Stock Exchange

SHAREHOLDERS

Who Owns Whom's Assessment of the Identity of the Ultimate Controlling Shareholder:
TEXTILE INVESTMENT CO

DIRECTORS :
CAMBITZIS N ,CULLEN TP (Managing Director)
GWAKU OM ,JONES SC ,MUNANGATIRE HMD
PARVIN ACL (Chairman),ROBINSON TJ ,ROWLAND RW
TIGERE G ,WOOLLEY R (Dep Chair & Chief Exec

REGISTERED OFFICE
Stand 351, Heavy Industrial Sites
Chegutu, Zimbabwe

TEL 730744
FAX 728120

TRANSFER SECRETARY
Lonrho Zimbabwe Management Serv (Pvt)Ltd
P O Box 1480, Harare
Zimbabwe

TEL 706661

COMPANY SECRETARY
C B Roberts

NATURE OF BUSINESS
Manufacturer of textiles, including spinning, weaving, dyeing, finishing and hosiery knitting
Exporters of yarn and loomstate fabric

BANKERS :
First Merchant Bank of Zimbabwe Ltd
Merchant Bank of Central Africa

AUDITORS :
Deloitte & Touche

FAMILIAR BRAND NAMES
N/A

CONTRIBUTION BY ACTIVITY
N/A

YEAR END : September

DIVIDEND : Ords Z$0,50

Dividend	(Ldr)24/11/91	(Pay)06/12/91	Amt(c)5 5
Dividend	(Ldr)14/07/92	(Pay)21/07/92	Amt(c)2 5

CAPITAL STRUCTURE

	AUTHORISED	ISSUED
Ords Z$0,50	199800000	138986295
5% Non Cum Prefs Z$2	50000	50000

FINANCIAL STATISTICS (AT FINANCIAL YEAR END)

(Amts in Z$)	1991 Sep	1990 Sep
Ord S/H Int	152412	77292
Long Trm Loans	9827	800
Iss Ord Share	138986	46329
Total Liab	85767	51964
Current Liab	75940	51164
Total Assets	238179	129256
Current Assets	95046	74672
Debtors	23341	18789
Inventory	71669	55787
Turnover	203496	147909
Oper Profit	37797	27339
Interest Paid	3482	1535
Tax Paid	12205	5999
Prf af Int&Tax	24318	20524
Prf att Ord Sh	24318	20524
Btm Line Earn	24318	20524
Dividend Paid	11124	8344
Depreciation	7597	5665

PER SHARE STATISTICS (CENTS)

Net Asst Val	109 66	166 83
Net Earnings	17 50	14 80
Dividends	8 00	6 00
Cash Flow	22 96	56 53

RATIOS AND OTHER INFORMATION

Current Ratio	1 25	1 46
Quik/Acid Tst	0 31	0 37
A/C Rec T/ovr	8 72	7 87
Tot Ass T/ovr	0 85	1 14
Debt/Ass Rat	0 36	0 40
L T L Tot Ass	0 04	0 01
Debt to Eqity	0 56	0 67
Interest Cover	10 85	17 81
Oper Prof Mrg	18 57	18 48
Net Prof Marg%	11 95	13 88
Ret on Assets	16 80	21 71
Ret on Equity%	15 96	26 55
Divid Cover	2 19	2 47
Effec Tax Rate	33 42	22 49
Def Interval	0 33	0 04
Sus Grth Rate	8 66	15 76

SUBSIDIARY & ASSOCIATED COMPANIES

None

INVESTMENTS

None

DE BEERS CENTENARY AG

ABBREVIATION : DEB CENT

SECTOR : Mining-Diamonds

SHAREHOLDERS

Who Owns Whom's Assessment of the Identity of the Ultimate Controlling Shareholder:
N/A

DIRECTORS :
BARBOUR JA ,CAPON TWH ,CRAWFORD RM
DE ROTHSCHILD BARON E ,DE ROTHSCHILD E SIR
DYER HB DR,FLETCHER GC ,HODGSON FM ,LEKAUKAU CM
LEYDEN PJR ,LINCOLN LA
OGILVIE THOMPSON J (Chairman),OPPENHEIMER AE
OPPENHEIMER HF ,OPPENHEIMER NF (Deputy Chairman)
OPPENHEIMER PHILIP SIR,RALFE GM ,RELLY GWH
STONEHAM GJ

REGISTERED OFFICE
Langensandstrasse 27, CH-6000 Lucerne 14
Switzerland

TRANSFER SECRETARY
Consolidated Share Registrars Ltd
P O Box 61051, Marshalltown
2107
TEL: 011-492 1620

COMPANY SECRETARY
N/A

NATURE OF BUSINESS
Holds the foreign interests of De Beers.

BANKERS :
N/A

AUDITORS :
Deloitte Pim Goldby

FAMILIAR BRAND NAMES
N/A

CONTRIBUTION BY ACTIVITY
N/A

DIVIDEND :Ords SFr 200
Interim No 5 (Ldr)18/09/92 (Pay)04/11/92 Amt(c)15
DIVIDEND :Ords Sfr 200
Dividend No 5 (Ldr)21/09/92 (Pay)03/11/92 Amt(c)42 71

NUMBER OF EMPLOYEES : 10970

CAPITAL STRUCTURE

	AUTHORISED	ISSUED
Ords SFr 200	4200000	4200000

FINANCIAL STATISTICS (AT FINANCIAL YEAR END)

(Amts in $)	1991 Dec	1990 Dec
Ord S/H Int	4130000	3929000
Long Trm Loans	1345000	1155000
Iss Ord Share	4200	4200
Total Liab	2286000	2238000
Current Liab	941000	1083000
Total Assets	6416000	6167000
Current Assets	4180000	3992000
Debtors	571000	727000
Inventory	3048000	2698000
Oper Profit	708000	842000
Interest Paid	63000	27000
Tax Paid	178000	151000
Prf af Int&Tax	599000	798000
Prf att Ord Sh	618000	817000
Btm Line Earn	546000	827000
Dividend Paid	338000	356000
Mkt Prce(c) YE	9100	-

PER SHARE STATISTICS (CENTS)

Net Asst Val	98333 33	93547.62
Net Earnings	147.00	195.00
Dividends	80.40	84.80
Cash Flow	13904.76	18285.71

RATIOS AND OTHER INFORMATION

Mrk Cap(R000)	382200	-
Current Ratio	4 44	3.69
Quik/Acid Tst	1.20	1.19
Debt/Ass Rat	0.34	0.35
L T L Tot Ass	0.19	0.17
Debt to Eqity	0 53	0 54
Interest Cover	11.67	32.37
Ret on Assets	13.62	16.62
Ret on Equity%	14.96	20.79
Price/Earnings	61.90	-
Divid Cover	1.83	2 30
Divid Yield	0.88	-
Earning Yield%	1.62	-
NAV % Mrk Pr	1080.59	-
Effec Tax Rate	23.73	16 47
Def Interval	2 15	1.39
Sus Grth Rate	6.78	11.73

SUBSIDIARY & ASSOCIATED COMPANIES

CDM (PTY) LTD (NAMIBIA)
CDM PROPERTIES (PTY) LTD (NAMIBIA)
CDM PROSPECTING (PTY) LTD (NAMIBIA)
CENTENARY HOLDINGS (LUXENBOURG)
DCS CORPORATION AG (SWITZERLAND)
DE BEERS BOTSWANA MINING CO. (PTY) LTD (50%)
DE BEERS INDUSTRIAL DIAMOND DIVISION (PT
DE BEERS INDUSTRIAL DIAMONDS (IRELAND) (
DE BEERS INDUSTRIAL DIAMONDS (JAPAN) LIM
DEBID (PTY) LTD (AUSTRALIA)
EASTERN INVESTMENTS LTD (26%)
EXCLUSIVE PROPERTIES (PTY) LTD (NAMIBIA)
INTERNATIONAL DIAMOND PRODUCTS (IRELAND) (50%)
JUMART LIMITED (23%)
MINORCO SOCIETE ANONYME (21 1%)
NAMIB FINANCE CORPORATION (PTY) LTD (NAM
SCANDIAMANT AB (SWEDEN) (50%)
SOUTH AMERICAN INVESTMENTS LTD (23%)
THE DIAMOND CORPORATION BOTSWANA (PTY) L
ULTRA HIGH PRESSURE SYSTEM (PTY) LTD (IR (50%)
ULTRA HIGH PRESSURE UNITS (IRELAND) LTD (50%)

INVESTMENTS

ANTWERPSE DIAMANTBANK N.V. (986218 SH)
CONSOLIDATED RESERVES LTD (500 SH)
INDUSTRIAL GRIT DISTRIBUTORS (SHANNON) L (6400 SH)
LEXAN TRADING INC. (49 SH)
NORTH SEA INVESTMENTS LIMITED (9500 SH)
SIBEKA SOCIETE D'ENTERPRISE ET D'INVESTI (206889 SH)

DE BEERS CONSOLIDATED MINES LTD

ABBREVIATION : DE BEERS

JSE SHORT CODE : DBR

SECTOR : Mining-Diamonds

SHAREHOLDERS

Who Owns Whom's Assessment of the Identity of the Ultimate Controlling Shareholder:
ANGLO AMERICAN

SHAREHOLDER	PERCENTAGE 1992	1991
ANGLO AMERICAN INV TRUST LTD	23 7	23 7
SA MUTUAL	12 0	11 7
LONDON CONTROL ACCOUNT	7 3	8 2
CMB NOM P/L	6 2	---
DEBSWANA DIAMOND CO P/L	5 3	---
STD BANK NOM TVL P/L	5 0	4 9
RESIDENT NOM LTD	2 9	2 8
EIGHTY ONE MAIN STREET NOM LTD	2 8	2 1
NUMITOR INV HLDGS	2 4	2 4
SOUTHERN LIFE ASSOC LTD	2 2	2 5
INDO-CHINA NOM P/L	1 8	2 0
FIRST NAT NOM P/L GATR DEPOT	1 6	1 9
FIRST NAT NOM P/L	1 6	1 7
LIBERTY LIFE ASSOC OF AFRICA LTD	1 3	1 4
ABSA NOM P/L	1 1	---
DE BEERS BOTSWANA MINING CO P/L	---	5 3
SANLAM	---	2 6
SANKERN E/B	---	1 8
TOTAL	77 2	74 8

DIRECTORS :
BARBOUR JA ,CAPON TWH ,CRAWFORD RM
DE ROTHSCHILD BARON E ,DE ROTHSCHILD E SIR
DYER HB DR,FLETCHER GC ,GUSH EP ,LEKAUKAU CM
LEYDEN PJR ,LINCOLN LA
OGILVIE THOMPSON J (Chairman),OPPENHEIMER AE
OPPENHEIMER HF ,OPPENHEIMER PHILIP SIR
OPPENHIEMER NF (Deputy Chairman),PUDNEY JP
RALFE GM ,RELLY GWH ,STONEHAM GJ

REGISTRATION NUMBER : 11/00007/06

REGISTERED OFFICE
36 Stockdale Street, Kimberley
8301
TEL 0531-2 2171
FAX 0531-24611

TRANSFER SECRETARY
Consolidated Share Registrars Ltd
P O Box 61051, Marshalltown
2107
TEL 011-492 1620

COMPANY SECRETARY
R W Ketley

NATURE OF BUSINESS
The principal activities of the DE BEERS group are i the mining of gem and industrial diamonds ii the marketing through the CENTRAL SELLING ORGAN ISATION of diamonds produced by the group and other producers iii the manufacture and marketing of synthetic diamond and related hard materials for use in the industry iv The management of a portfolio of inter national investments in mining, industrial and companies

BANKERS :
N/A

AUDITORS :
Deloitte & Touche

FAMILIAR BRAND NAMES
N/A

CONTRIBUTION BY ACTIVITY
Diamond Account (% total income) (27 0%)
Investment Income (47 0%)
Other (Interest & Loans recovered) (26 0%)
Gold (% invest income excl diamond a/c) (19 0%)
Industrial (32 0%)
Finance (14 0%)
Diamonds (9 0%)
Platinum (10 0%)
Property (2 0%)
Coal (4 0%)
Copper (1 0%)
Other Minerals (9 0%)

YEAR END : December

DIVIDEND : Ords Def 5c

Interim No 141	(Ldr)21/09/90	(Pay)07/11/90	Amt(c)26
Final No 142	(Ldr)28/03/91	(Pay)29/05/91	Amt(c)42
Interim No 143	(Ldr)27/09/91	(Pay)06/11/91	Amt(c)28
Final No 144	(Ldr)27/03/92	(Pay)27/05/92	Amt(c)59
Interim No 145	(Ldr)18/09/92	(Pay)04/11/92	Amt(c)28

NUMBER OF EMPLOYEES : 13600

CAPITAL STRUCTURE

	AUTHORISED	ISSUED
40% Cum Prefs R5	800000	800000
Ords Def 5c (Linked to Centenary	420000000	380141140
8% 2nd Cum Prefs R1	2866929	2866929

FINANCIAL STATISTICS (AT FINANCIAL YEAR END)

(Amts in R'000)	1991 Dec	1990 Dec	1989 Dec	1988 Dec	1987 Dec
Ord S/H Int	11065000	10417000	16630000	13244000	9677000
Long Trm Loans	107000	86000	892000	679000	623000
Iss Ord Share	380141	380054	359789	359789	359789
Total Liab	1060000	1015000	3679000	2688000	1937000
Current Liab	953000	929000	2787000	2009000	1314000
Total Assets	12125000	11432000	20309000	15932000	11614000
Current Assets	2139000	2603000	5109000	4069000	1797000
Debtors	1289000	933000	828000	639000	720000
Inventory	135000	141000	-	-	-
Oper Profit	7000	-112000	2662000	2225000	1570000
Interest Paid	10000	22000	85000	59000	36000
Tax Paid	209000	265000	807000	573000	374000
Prf af Int&Tax	580000	561000	3036000	2299000	1160000
Prf att Ord Sh	1414000	1476000	4088000	2961000	1501000
Btm Line Earn	1302000	1887000	4077000	3251000	1510000
Dividend Paid	331000	259000	1064000	760000	418000
Mkt Prce(c) YE	9100	6660	6160	4175	2965

PER SHARE STATISTICS (CENTS)

Net Asst Val	2910 76	2740 93	4622 15	3681 05	2689 63
Net Earnings	372 00	388 00	432 00	780 00	410 00

Dividends	87.00	68.00	280.00	200.00	110.00
Cash Flow	151.52	145.77	796.30	550.21	282.51

RATIOS AND OTHER INFORMATION

Mrk Cap(R000)	34592831	25311596	22163002	15021191	10667744
Current Ratio	2.24	2.80	1.83	2.03	1.37
Quik/Acid Tst	2.10	2.65	1.83	2.03	1.37
Debt/Ass Rat	0.08	0.08	0.17	0.16	0.15
L T L Tot Ass	0.00	0.00	0.03	0.03	0.04
Debt to Eqity	0.09	0.09	0.20	0.19	0.19
Interest Cover	51.40	17.59	37.41	43.92	43.61
Ret on Assets	13.50	15.48	25.36	23.86	17.53
Ret on Equity%	12.78	14.17	24.58	22.36	15.51
Price/Earnings	24.46	17.16	14.26	5.35	7.23
Divid Cover	4.28	5.71	1.54	3.90	3.73
Divid Yield	0.96	1.02	4.55	4.79	3.71
Earning Yield%	4.09	5.83	7.01	18.68	13.83
NAV % Mrk Pr	31.99	41.16	75.03	88.17	90.71
Effec Tax Rate	74.11	81.04	24.27	22.87	24.38
Def Interval	0.23	0.18	0.27	0.27	0.50
Sus Grth Rate	9.79	11.68	18.18	16.62	11.19

SUBSIDIARY & ASSOCIATED COMPANIES

ANGLO AMERICAN CORPORATION OF SA LTD (38.7%)
ANGLO AMERICAN FARMS LTD (38.2%)
ANGLO AMERICAN INDUSTRIAL CORP LTD (28.5%)
CENTRAL RESERVES (PTY) LTD (50%)
CONSOLIDATED COMPANY BULTFONTEIN MINE LT
DE BEERS HOLDINGS (PTY) LTD
DE BEERS INDUSTRIAL DIAMOND DIVISION (PT
DE BEERS INDUSTRIAL DIAMONDS (S.A.) (PTY
DE BEERS MARINE (PTY) LTD
DE BEERS PROSPECTING BOTSWANA (PTY) LTD
DE BEERS SERVICES (PTY) LTD (NAMIBIA)
DEBEX (PTY) LTD
DELAUNAY LTD - B & E SHARES
DIAMOND CORPORATION (PTY) LTD
DIAMOND PURCHASING AND TRADING CO (PTY) (50%)
EPOCH INVESTMENTS LTD (50%)
FINSCH DIAMONDS (PTY) LTD
GRIQUALAND WEST DIAMOND MINING CO DUTOIT
MARINE DIAMOND CORPORATION (PTY) LTD (NA
MARINE GROUP INVESTMENTS (PTY) LTD (NAMI
OLIVIA PROPERTIES (PTY) LTD
ORAMA HOLDINGS (PTY) LTD
PREMIER (TVL) DIAMOND MINING CO. (PTY) L
SEA DIAMOND CORPORATION (PTY) LTD
THETA PROPERTIES NORTH (PTY) LTD
THETA PROPERTIES SOUTH (PTY) LTD
ULTRA HIGH PRESSURE UNITS (PTY) LTD (50%)

INVESTMENTS

ABRASIVE GRIT SALES LTD (A SHARES) (26100 SH)
AECI LTD (4432242)
ANGLO AMERICAN COAL CORP. LTD (50960 UN)
ANGLO AMERICAN CORP OF SA LTD (89653087U)
ANGLO AMERICAN CORP. ZIMBABWE LTD (226608 SH)
ANGLO AMERICAN GOLD INVESTMENT CO. LTD (123499UN)
ANGLO AMERICAN INDUSTRIAL CORPORATION LT (15606033U)
ANGLO AMERICAN INVESTMENT TRUST LTD (10000000U)
ANGLO AMERICAN PROPERTIES LTD (3252561UN)
ANGLOVAAL LTD (501055 UN)
BARBROOK MINES LTD (4177748UN)
BARLOW RAND LIMITED (608843 UN)
BCL LIMITED PREF (7250061SH)
BEVERAGE & CONSUMER INDUSTRY HOLDINGS LT (2025754U)
BOTSWANA RST LTD (162464UN)
CACTUS INVESTMENTS (PTY) LTD (60000 SH)
CACTUS INVESTMENTS (PTY) LTD (PREFS) (60000 UN)
CARAT INVESTMENTS LIMITED (500000SH)
CARLTON CENTRE LTD (1504229)
CENTRAL RESERVES (PTY) LTD (50 UNITS)
CREATIVE HOMES LTD (388539 SH)
DE BEERS CENTENARY AG (9.5%)
DELAUNAY FOUR LTD PREF (100000 SH)
DEPFIN INVESTMENTS (PTY) LTD (RED CUM PR (40000000S)
DISCOUNT HOUSE GROUP LTD (140000UN)
EAST RAND GOLD & URANIUM CO LTD (5317346UN)
ELANDSRAND GOLD MINING CO LTD (530051 UN)
EPOCH INVESTMENTS LTD (250000UN)
FIRST NATIONAL BANK OF SA LTD (4647676)
FIRST NATIONAL BANK OF SOUTHERN AFRICA L (4718471U)
GAMSBERG ZINC CORP. LTD (999999 SH)
GOLD FIELDS OF SOUTH AFRICA LTD (1260773UN)
HIGHVELD STEEL & VANADIUM CORPORATION LT (2719112U)
HISTORICAL HOMES OF S.A. LTD (20000 SH)
INDUSTRIAL GRIT DISTRIBUTORS (SHANNON) L (18500)
INTERNATIONAL PIPE & STEEL INVEST. S.A. (410077 SH)
ISCOR LTD (63403884U)
JOHANNESBURG CONSOLIDATED INVESTMENT CO (12384580U)
MAIN PLACE HOLDINGS LTD (215 SH)
MONDI PAPER COMPANY LTD (17%)
MORUPULE COLLIERY (PTY) LTD (400 SH)
PALABORA HOLDINGS LTD (612569)
PREMIER GROUP LTD (2025754U)
SASOL LTD (3274300U)
SHAFT SINKERS (PTY) LTD (478500 SH)
SMALL BUSINESS DEVELOPMENT CORP LTD (4606589SH)
SOUTH DEEP EXPLORATION LIMITED (3677848UN)
STANDARD BANK INVESTMENT COPRORATION LTD (1096197U)
THE PREMIER GROUP LTD (1825797)
UNISEL GOLD MINES LTD (1160000UN)
WEST CITY INVESTMENTS (PTY) LTD (50000 SH)
WEST END PROPERTY CO (PTY) LTD (2500)
WESTERN DEEP LEVELS LTD (706370UN)
ZAMBIA COPPER INVESTMENTS LTD (253401 UN)

DEBONAIR GROUP LTD

ABBREVIATION : DEBNAIR

JSE SHORT CODE : DNR

SECTOR : Industrial-Clothing, Footwear & Textiles

SHAREHOLDERS

Who Owns Whom's Assessment of the Identity of the Ultimate Controlling Shareholder: ABBEY HOLDINGS

SHAREHOLDER	PERCENTAGE 1992	1991
ABBEY TRADING LTD	65.9	---
FOSTER I & SCHWINGES C INV P/L	12.8	12.8
NAT BRICK HOLDINGS P/L	5.3	---
DEBONAIR GROUP SHARE INC SCHEME	1.9	1.9
GREEK R N TRUSTEES DORFMAN CHILDREN	1.8	---
FIRST NAT NOM P/L	1.1	1.1
FOSTER I	---	4.8
SCHWINGES C-H H M	---	3.2
FNX (DEBONAIR) HOLDINGS LTD	---	65.8
TOTAL	88.8	89.5

DIRECTORS :
CALITZ I (Managing Director),CHAPMAN DE
PENNY C ,RABINOWITZ BP ,RABINOWITZ BP
SAREMBOCK ML ,SCHAEFER JE (Chairman)
SCHWINGES CHHM (Operations Director),WALTON CL
WALTON CL

REGISTRATION NUMBER : 83/05882/06

REGISTERED OFFICE
80 St Georges Mall, Cape Town
8001
TEL: 021-54 7515
FAX: 021-54 7517

TRANSFER SECRETARY
Mercantile Registrars Ltd
P O Box 1053, Johannesburg
2000
TEL: 011-333 8181

COMPANY SECRETARY
H Calitz

NATURE OF BUSINESS
The group manufactures, distributes & markets bed linen, & manufactures curtains, pelmet covers, drapes & blinds. Company currently in liquidation.

BANKERS :
First National Bank of SA Ltd

AUDITORS :
Kessel Feinstein

FAMILIAR BRAND NAMES
DEBONAIR,DUVET-LIN,POLYBOND,WITTLES INTERIORS

CONTRIBUTION BY ACTIVITY
N/A

YEAR END : June

DIVIDEND : (Ldr)26/05/89 (Pay)30/06/89

NUMBER OF EMPLOYEES : 250

CAPITAL STRUCTURE

	AUTHORISED	ISSUED
Ords no par value	20000000	10035278
7% Red Prefs R1	300000	300000

FINANCIAL STATISTICS (AT FINANCIAL YEAR END)

(Amts in R'000)	1990 Feb	1989 Feb	1988 Feb	1987	1986
Ord S/H Int	11408	9125	5863	365	105
Long Trm Loans	2612	998	546	2653	2033
Iss Ord Share	20071	17038	14190	10	10
Total Liab	14632	13556	4873	4510	3322
Current Liab	12020	12558	4327	1857	1289
Total Assets	20418	19731	8117	5190	3726
Intang Assets	5622	2950	2619	*	*
Current Assets	16806	17270	7046	2172	1588
Debtors	6541	7889	2985	-	-
Inventory	10261	9365	4020	2172	1588
Turnover	-	-	15175	5795	4245
Oper Profit	1830	3581	2010	411	295
Interest Paid	1748	775	51	78	52
Tax Paid	-15	804	816	72	40
Prf af Int&Tax	97	2002	1143	260	203
Prf att Ord Sh	76	1981	1143	260	203
Btm Line Earn	76	1981	1143	260	203
Dividend Paid	716	497	21	-	-
Mkt Prce(c) YE	38	60	45	-	-
Depreciation	311	378	127	-	-

PER SHARE STATISTICS (CENTS)

Net Asst Val	28.83	36.24	22.86	3650.00	1050.00
Net Earnings	0.60	12.70	8.60	-	-
Dividends	-	4.20	3.50	-	-
Cash Flow	2.23	15.89	10.24	2600.00	2030.00

RATIOS AND OTHER INFORMATION

Mrk Cap(R000)	7627	10223	6386	-	-
Current Ratio	1.40	1.38	1.63	1.17	1.23
Quik/Acid Tst	0.54	0.63	0.70	-	-
A/C Rec T/ovr	-	-	5.08	-	-
Tot Ass T/ovr	-	-	1.87	1.12	1.14
Debt/Ass Rat	0.70	0.66	0.54	0.87	0.89
L T L Tot Ass	0.11	0.02	0.01	0.51	0.55
Debt to Eqity	1.26	1.42	0.75	12.36	31.64
Interest Cover	1.05	4.62	39.41	5.26	5.67
Oper Prof Mrg	-	-	13.25	7.09	6.95
Net Prof Marg%	-	-	7.53	4.49	4.78
Ret on Assets	8.96	18.15	24.76	7.90	7.92
Ret on Equity%	0.67	21.71	19.50	71.23	193.33
Price/Earnings	63.33	4.72	5.23	-	-
Divid Cover	-	3.02	2.46	-	-
Divid Yield	-	7.00	7.78	-	-
Earning Yield%	1.58	21.17	19.11	-	-
NAV % Mrk Pr	75.86	60.40	50.80	-	-
Effec Tax Rate	-	-	4.85	21.62	16.46
Def Interval	21.61	2.27	1.35	10.20	10.01
Sus Grth Rate	-5.61	16.26	19.14	71.23	193.33

SUBSIDIARY & ASSOCIATED COMPANIES

CAPE DOWN & FEATHER CO (PTY) LTD
DREYER & STATHAM (PTY) LTD
DUVET-LIN (PTY) LTD
POLYBOND (PTY) LTD
POLYDOWN QUILTING CORP (PTY) LTD
QUILTEX (PTY) LTD
RAND CARPET & SOFT FURNISHINGS (PTY) LTD

INVESTMENTS

None

DECOR INVESTMENT HOLDINGS LTD

ABBREVIATION : DECHOLD

JSE SHORT CODE : DCL

SECTOR : Industrial-Retailers & Wholesalers

SHAREHOLDERS

Who Owns Whom's Assessment of the Identity of the Ultimate Controlling Shareholder: DIRECTORS CONTROL 73,26% (JUNE 1991)

SHAREHOLDER	PERCENTAGE 1992	1991
GRAHAM C	60 3	60 3
BURLAND B	12 3	12 3
FIRST NAT NOM P/L	8 4	8 7
LANDSDOWN SECURITIES LTD	7 6	7 6
CHARLES G FAMILY TRUST	3 7	3 7
DECOR SHARE INCENTIVE TRUST	2 7	2 7
TOTAL	95 2	95 4

DIRECTORS :
COPELOWITZ S ,DAVIES GSJ ,GRAHAM A
GRAHAM C (Chairman & Managing Dir

REGISTRATION NUMBER : 64/01296/06

REGISTERED OFFICE
Decor House, 203 President Street
Johannesburg
2001
TEL 011-402 1960
FAX 011-402 7674

TRANSFER SECRETARY
Central Registrars Ltd
P O Box 4844, Johannesburg
2000
TEL 011-331 0051

COMPANY SECRETARY
A I Fakir

NATURE OF BUSINESS
The group is engaged in the importation and distribution of wallpaper, the supply of locally manufactured wall coverings, the distribution of decorative wall items, the manufacture and distribution of a pipe repair clamp, the manufacture and export of pine furniture and louvre doors The group also provides a wallpaper hanging and wall cladding service

BANKERS :
Standard Bank of SA Ltd

AUDITORS :
Tuffias Shapiro Braude

FAMILIAR BRAND NAMES
CASCADE,DECOR,DREAMCOAT,HARDYLAST

CONTRIBUTION BY ACTIVITY
N/A

YEAR END : June

DIVIDEND : (Ldr)22/09/89 (Pay)18/10/89

NUMBER OF EMPLOYEES : 650

CAPITAL STRUCTURE

	AUTHORISED	ISSUED
Ords 1c	40000000	17446818

FINANCIAL STATISTICS (AT FINANCIAL YEAR END)

(Amts in R'000)	1991 Jun	1990 Jun	1988 Dec	1987 Dec
Ord S/H Int	5634	6464	6993	3840
Long Trm Loans	674	405	178	456
Iss Ord Share	17447	17447	16500	14050
Total Liab	5448	4092	2285	4286
Current Liab	4774	3687	2107	3830
Total Assets	11082	8824	7433	6382
Intang Assets	*	1732	1845	1744
Current Assets	8817	6717	5091	4529
Debtors	3305	3195	2394	2666
Inventory	5478	3427	2556	1845
Turnover	21917	27492	20362	14924
Oper Profit	1160	1643	2775	1608
Interest Paid	226	860	188	154
Tax Paid	31	61	523	488
Prf af Int&Tax	903	722	2064	966
Prf att Ord Sh	903	729	2064	802
Btm Line Earn	-829	-496	2064	802
Dividend Paid	-	495	-	-
Mkt Prce(c) YE	15	35	53	-
Depreciation	462	851	406	276

PER SHARE STATISTICS (CENTS)

Net Asst Val	32 29	27 12	31 20	14 92
Net Earnings	5 17	2 87	14 23	-
Dividends	-	3 00	-	-
Cash Flow	7 90	6 14	16 96	7 44

RATIOS AND OTHER INFORMATION

Mrk Cap(R000)	2617	6106	8745	-
Current Ratio	1 85	1 82	2 42	1 18
Quik/Acid Tst	0 70	0 89	1 20	0 70
A/C Rec T/ovr	6 63	5 74	8 51	5 60
Tot Ass T/ovr	1 98	2 08	2 74	2 34
Debt/Ass Rat	0 49	0 46	0 30	0 64
L T L Tot Ass	0 06	0 05	0 02	0 04
Debt to Eqity	0 96	0 63	0 32	1 07
Interest Cover	5 13	1 91	14 76	10 44
Oper Prof Mrg	5 29	5 98	13 63	10 77
Net Prof Marg%	4 12	2 65	10 14	5 37
Ret on Assets	10 47	12 41	37 33	25 20
Ret on Equity%	16 03	7 52	29 52	20 89
Price/Earnings	2 90	12 20	3 72	-
Divid Cover	-	0 96	-	-
Divid Yield	-	8 57	-	-
Earning Yield%	34 47	8 20	26 85	-
NAV % Mrk Pr	215 28	77 49	58 87	-
Effec Tax Rate	3 64	10 47	20 60	35 83
Def Interval	1 86	0 56	0 15	1 98
Sus Grth Rate	16 03	3 62	29 52	20 89

SUBSIDIARY & ASSOCIATED COMPANIES

DECOR INTERIOR CONTRACTS (PTY) LTD
DECOR PAINTING & DECORATING CONTRACTORS
DECOR WALLPAPER CO (NATAL) (PTY) LTD
DREAMCOAT WALLPAPERS (PTY) LTD
GABLE HOUSE PRODUCTS (PTY) LTD
HARDYLAST COATING SYSTEMS (PTY) LTD
ONUS LOUVRES (EDMS) BPK
PINE CONVERTERS (AFRICA) (PTY) LTD
TEX DECOR (PTY) LTD

INVESTMENTS

None

DECOVO INVESTMENTS LTD

ABBREVIATION : DECOVO

JSE SHORT CODE : DCV

SECTOR : Industrial-Furniture & Household

SHAREHOLDERS

Who Owns Whom's Assessment of the Identity of the Ultimate Controlling Shareholder: DIRECTORS

SHAREHOLDER	PERCENTAGE 1992	1991
MAYFAIR SPECULATORS P/L	53 6	58 2
MICHAEL DELPORT INV P/L	34 9	---
BM NOM CC	6 8	---
DECAGON INV P/L	---	37 9
TOTAL	95 4	96 1

DIRECTORS :
DELPORT MM MR (Chairman),HARLOW GD MR
JOOSTE MJ MR (Managing Director),STEYGER R MR
WILLEMSE PJ M

REGISTRATION NUMBER : 87/01511/06

REGISTERED OFFICE
2201 Trust Bank Centre, Heerengracht
Cape Town
8001
TEL 01461-31181
FAX 01461-31188

TRANSFER SECRETARY
Central Registrars Ltd
P O Box 4844, Johannesburg
2000
TEL 011-331 0051

COMPANY SECRETARY
F J Nel

NATURE OF BUSINESS
An investment holding company Subsidiaries manufacture upholstered and show-wood lounge furniture, beds and accessories which they distribute nationwide to the retail and export trade The company has a minority stake in a cement manufacturer in Namibia

BANKERS :
Trust Bank of Africa Ltd

AUDITORS :
Greenwoods

FAMILIAR BRAND NAMES
GOMMAGOMMA,LA-Z-BOY (UNDER LICENCE),STEELBRO

CONTRIBUTION BY ACTIVITY
N/A

YEAR END : December

NUMBER OF EMPLOYEES : 900

CAPITAL STRUCTURE

	AUTHORISED	ISSUED
Ords 5c	20000000	12680000

FINANCIAL STATISTICS (AT FINANCIAL YEAR END)

(Amts in R'000)	1991 Dec	1990 Dec	1989 Mar	1989 Dec	1988 Mar
Ord S/H Int	18110	6520	5506	7895	9327
Long Trm Loans	38525	34140	1143	6765	721
Iss Ord Share	12680	15700	15700	15700	15700
Total Liab	60695	58736	13043	29943	8119
Current Liab	22170	24596	11900	23178	7398
Total Assets	78805	65256	18549	37838	17446
Current Assets	38735	37738	13505	25470	14161
Debtors	21566	17245	6787	15469	7152
Inventory	17147	15295	6718	9805	6446
Turnover	55600	40401	34744	34041	34916
Oper Profit	-6134	1357	-1536	2251	79
Interest Paid	4468	2752	1367	2506	403
Tax Paid	-	-	-	-	7
Prf af Int&Tax	-8488	-1130	-2903	-255	-331
Prf att Ord Sh	-7239	-1130	-2903	-255	-331
Btm Line Earn	-9365	-1375	-4155	125	-331
Mkt Prce(c) YE	280	225	155	275	210
Depreciation	1992	1537	679	1096	518

PER SHARE STATISTICS (CENTS)

Net Asst Val	142 82	41 53	35 07	50 29	59 41
Net Earnings	-77 00	36 00	-18 50	-1 60	-2 30
Cash Flow	-41 38	2 59	-14 17	7 14	1 32

RATIOS AND OTHER INFORMATION

Mrk Cap(R000)	35504	35325	24335	43175	32970
Current Ratio	1 75	1 53	1 13	1 10	1 91
Quik/Acid Tst	0 97	0 91	0 57	0 68	1 04
A/C Rec T/ovr	2 58	2 34	5 12	2 93	4 88
Tot Ass T/ovr	0 71	0 62	1 87	1 20	2 00
Debt/Ass Rat	0 41	0 90	0 70	0 79	0 47
L T L Tot Ass	0 12	0 52	0 06	0 18	0 04
Debt to Eqity	1 77	9 01	2 37	3 79	0 87
Interest Cover	-1 37	0 49	-1 12	0 90	0 20
Oper Prof Mrg	-11 03	3 36	-4 42	6 61	0 23
Net Prof Marg%	-13 02	-2 80	-8 36	-0 75	-0 95
Ret on Assets	-5 10	2 49	-8 28	7 93	0 45
Ret on Equity%	-39 97	17 33	-52 72	-4 31	-3 55
Price/Earnings	-3 64	-6 25	-8 38	-171 88	91 30
Earning Yield%	27 50	-16 00	-11 94	-0 58	-1 10
NAV % Mrk Pr	51 01	18 46	22 63	18 29	28 29
Def Interval	-4 75	122 70	-4 28	39 91	23 87
Sus Grth Rate	-39 97	-17 33	-52 72	-3 23	3 55

SUBSIDIARY & ASSOCIATED COMPANIES

BAKKER & STEYGER (PTY) LTD
FURNITURE PRODUCERS (BOPHUTHATSWANA) (PT
GOMMAGOMMA (BOPHUTHATSWANA) (PTY) LTD
GOMMAGOMMA HOLDINGS (PTY) LTD
GOMMAGOMMA PROPERTIES (PTY) LTD
GOMMAGOMMA UPHOLSTERY (PTY) LTD
STEEL BROS (PTY) LTD

INVESTMENTS

PREFCOR HOLDINGS LTD DEBS & ORDS SHARES (4200SH)

DEELKRAAL GOLD MINING CO LTD

ABBREVIATION : DEELKRL

JSE SHORT CODE : DLK

SECTOR : Gold-West Witwatersrand

SHAREHOLDERS

Who Owns Whom's Assessment of the Identity of the Ultimate Controlling Shareholder:
GFSA

DIRECTORS :
ADAN MJ ,FENTON CT ,FULLER-GOOD MR ,HEWITT L
HOSKING KM ,HOUGHTON AB
MUNRO AH (Chairman & Managing Dir.),TAGG MJ
WOLFE-COOTE CA ,WRIGHT AJ

REGISTRATION NUMBER : 74/00160/06

REGISTERED OFFICE
75 Fox Street, Johannesburg
2001
TEL: 011-639 9111
FAX: 011-639 2101/2

TRANSFER SECRETARY
Gold Fields of SA Ltd
P O Box 1167, Johannesburg
2000
TEL: 011-639 9111

COMPANY SECRETARY
Gold Fields of South Africa Limited

NATURE OF BUSINESS
The company carries on gold mining operations on the farms Deelkraal 142 IQ and Kleinfontein 141 IQ.

BANKERS :
Standard Bank of SA Ltd

AUDITORS :
Ernst & Young

FAMILIAR BRAND NAMES
N/A

CONTRIBUTION BY ACTIVITY
N/A

YEAR END : June

DIVIDEND : Ords 20c

Interim No 16	(Ldr)28/12/90	(Pay)06/02/91	Amt(c)10
Final No 17	(Ldr)28/06/91	(Pay)07/08/91	Amt(c)10
Interim No 18	(Ldr)27/12/91	(Pay)05/02/92	Amt(c)15
Final No 19	(Ldr)26/06/92	(Pay)05/08/92	Amt(c)15

NUMBER OF EMPLOYEES : 6928

CAPITAL STRUCTURE

	AUTHORISED	ISSUED
Ords 20c	100000000	99540000

FINANCIAL STATISTICS (AT FINANCIAL YEAR END)

(Amts in R'000)	1992 Jun	1991 Jun	1990 Jun	1989 Jun	1988 Jun
Ord S/H Int	630971	571174	531968	470050	384506
Iss Ord Share	99540	99540	99540	99540	99540
Total Liab	55377	40495	68399	80858	71425
Current Liab	55377	40495	68399	80858	71425
Total Assets	686348	611669	600367	550908	455931
Current Assets	80989	65341	119758	144533	120488
Debtors	12271	6909	7259	4183	3035
Inventory	11834	11242	9022	8840	8582
Turnover	317750	289103	312158	328969	270748
Oper Profit	83430	52456	112592	180539	143427
Tax Paid	5807	5874	10636	15652	5063
Prf af Int&Tax	90506	58735	121748	164887	138364
Prf att Ord Sh	90506	58735	121748	164887	138364
Btm Line Earn	90506	58735	121748	164887	138364
Dividend Paid	29862	19908	59724	79632	69678
Mkt Prce(c) YE	530	760	1290	1300	1025

PER SHARE STATISTICS (CENTS)

Net Asst Val	633.89	573.81	534.43	472.22	386.28
Net Earnings	90.00	19.00	60.00	-	-
Dividends	30.00	20.00	60.00	80.00	70.00
Cash Flow	90.92	59.01	122.31	165.65	139.00

RATIOS AND OTHER INFORMATION

Mrk Cap(R000)	527562	756504	1284066	1294020	1020285
Current Ratio	1.46	1.61	1.75	1.79	1.69
Quik/Acid Tst	1.25	1.34	1.62	1.68	1.57
A/C Rec T/ovr	25.89	41.84	43.00	78.64	89.21
Tot Ass T/ovr	0.46	0.47	0.52	0.60	0.59
Debt/Ass Rat	0.08	0.07	0.11	0.15	0.16
Debt to Eqity	0.09	0.07	0.13	0.17	0.19
Oper Prof Mrg	26.26	18.14	36.07	54.88	52.97
Net Prof Marg%	28.48	20.32	39.00	50.12	51.10
Ret on Assets	14.03	10.56	22.05	32.77	31.46
Ret on Equity%	14.34	10.28	22.89	35.08	35.98
Price/Earnings	5.89	40.00	21.50	-	-
Divid Cover	3.00	0.95	1.00	-	-
Divid Yield	5.66	2.63	4.65	6.15	6.83
Earning Yield%	16.98	2.50	4.65	-	-
NAV % Mrk Pr	119.60	75.50	41.43	36.32	37.69
Effec Tax Rate	6.03	9.09	6.88	4.30	3.53
Sus Grth Rate	9.61	6.80	11.66	18.14	17.86

SUBSIDIARY & ASSOCIATED COMPANIES

None

INVESTMENTS

None

DELSWA LTD

ABBREVIATION : DELSWA

JSE SHORT CODE : DWA

SECTOR : Industrial-Clothing, Footwear & Textiles

SHAREHOLDERS

Who Owns Whom's Assessment of the Identity of the Ultimate Controlling Shareholder:
JAFF-DELSWA

SHAREHOLDER	PERCENTAGE 1992	1991
JAFF DELSWA INV LTD	46 6	46 5
MONITOR INV P/L	11 1	11 1
FERBROS NOM P/L	5 1	5 1
JAFF S L	3 9	3 9
R-V INV NOM CC	3 6	3 6
STD BANK NOM TVL P/L	3 0	2 7
SHARESTOCK NOM P/L	1 9	-
DELSWA LTD SHARE PARTICIPATION FUND	1 9	1 9
GORDON H	1 4	1 4
STEINER M	1 4	1 4
JAFF P H	1 4	1 4
ARONSOHN M	1 1	---
NEDBANK NOM LTD	-	1 9
TOTAL	82 4	80 9

DIRECTORS :
JAFF F ,JAFF NR ,JAFF P
JAFF PH (Financial Director)
JAFF SH (Managing Director)
JAFF SL (Executive Chairman),LAIRD SMITH A
MURRAY C ,PECHEY NR

REGISTRATION NUMBER : 05/27685/06

REGISTERED OFFICE
104 President Street, Johannesburg
2001
TEL 011-337 3131
FAX 011-333 3336

TRANSFER SECRETARY
Mercantile Registrars Ltd
P O Box 1053, Johannesburg
2000
TEL 011-333 8181

COMPANY SECRETARY
N R Pechey

NATURE OF BUSINESS
An investment holding company with core activity being the manufacture and sale of children's and women's outerwear and sportswear to retailers

BANKERS :
Standard Bank of SA Ltd

AUDITORS :
KPMG Aiken & Peat

FAMILIAR BRAND NAMES
DELSWA,DELTON,JADE,JAY ZEE,MARCHESA
SCHOOL MAID,TOMORROWS SET,WHOOT

CONTRIBUTION BY ACTIVITY
N/A

YEAR END : April

DIVIDEND :Ords 5c

Interim No 81	(Ldr)02/02/90	(Pay)20/02/90	Amt(c)3 5
Final No 82	(Ldr)20/07/90	(Pay)17/08/90	Amt(c)5 5
Interim No 83	(Ldr)01/02/91	(Pay)22/02/91	Amt(c)3 5
Final No 84	(Ldr)19/07/91	(Pay)16/08/91	Amt(c)6 5
Interim No 85	(Ldr)07/02/92	(Pay)21/02/92	Amt(c)3 5
Final No 86	(Ldr)24/07/92	(Pay)21/08/92	Amt(c)5 5

NUMBER OF EMPLOYEES : 1879

CAPITAL STRUCTURE

	AUTHORISED	ISSUED
5,5% Cum Prefs R2	120000	100000
Ords 5c	7200000	6963000

FINANCIAL STATISTICS (AT FINANCIAL YEAR END)

(Amts in R'000)	1992 Apr	1991 Apr	1990 Apr	1989 Apr	1988 Apr
Ord S/H Int	25951	23549	20435	14081	11600
Long Trm Loans	4717	3698	4698	2734	2795
Iss Ord Share	6963	6963	6963	696	696
Total Liab	19454	18898	23009	19395	14530
Current Liab	14737	15200	18311	16661	11735
Total Assets	45405	42447	43444	33476	26130
Current Assets	35760	32830	34011	29317	22216
Debtors	24100	21802	22945	20471	14152
Inventory	11130	10928	10918	8826	7792
Oper Profit	7012	9273	8057	8489	5507
Interest Paid	2197	2613	2746	1608	872
Tax Paid	2219	2948	2656	3246	2171
Prf af Int&Tax	2838	3814	2727	3666	2502
Prf att Ord Sh	3029	3810	2043	3121	2463
Btm Line Earn	3029	3810	2043	3351	1927
Dividend Paid	629	696	627	870	731
Mkt Prce(c) YE	115	125	170	1625	1250
Depreciation	1261	1065	813	621	576

PER SHARE STATISTICS (CENTS)

Net Asst Val	372 70	338 20	293 48	2023 13	1666 67
Net Earnings	40 60	54 40	39 60	52 30	35 70
Dividends	9 00	10 00	9 00	12 50	10 50
Cash Flow	58 98	71 31	53 20	622 56	442 53

RATIOS AND OTHER INFORMATION

Mrk Cap(R000)	8007	8704	11837	11310	8700
Current Ratio	2 43	2 16	1 86	1 76	1 89
Quik/Acid Tst	1 67	1 44	1 26	1 23	1 23
Debt/Ass Rat	0 41	0 43	0 52	0 57	0 54
L T L Tot Ass	0 09	0 07	0 10	0 07	0 09
Debt to Eqity	0 72	0 77	1 10	1 34	1 22
Interest Cover	3 19	3 55	2 93	5 28	6 32
Ret on Assets	15 98	22 09	18 71	25 45	21 22
Ret on Equity%	11 67	16 18	10 00	22 16	21 23
Price/Earnings	2 83	2 30	4 29	31 07	35 01
Divid Cover	4 51	5 44	4 40	4 18	3 40
Divid Yield	7 83	8 00	5 29	0 77	0 84
Earning Yield%	35 30	43 52	23 29	3 22	2 86
NAV % Mrk Pr	324 09	270 56	172 64	124 50	133 33
Effec Tax Rate	44 12	40 92	46 16	46 76	46 14
Def Interval	3 02	2 34	4 39	2 86	3 13
Sus Grth Rate	9 25	13 22	6 93	15 99	14 93

SUBSIDIARY & ASSOCIATED COMPANIES

DELSWA PROPERTIES (PTY) LTD
DELTON KNITWEAR (PTY) LTD
JAFF & CO LTD
MARKSTAN (PTY) LTD
MSG HOLDINGS (PTY) LTD
YOUNGSET ORIGINALS (PTY) LTD

INVESTMENTS

None

DELTA CORPORATION LTD (ZIMBABWE)

ABBREVIATION : DELTA ZIM

SECTOR : Zimbabwe Stock Exchange

SHAREHOLDERS

Who Owns Whom's Assessment of the Identity of the Ultimate Controlling Shareholder:
ZIMBABWE DEVELOPMENT CORP / OLD MUTUAL I

SHAREHOLDER	PERCENTAGE 1992	1991
ZIMBABWE DEVELOPMENT CORP LTD	38 4	---
OLD MUTUAL INV CORP (PVT) LTD	16.6	---
RAINIER INC	14.6	---
TIGATEL BV	8 2	---
DELTA EMPL PART TRUST CO PVT LTD	2.9	---
FIRST MUTUAL LIFE ASSURE SOC OF ZIM	2.1	---
NAT RAILWAYS OF ZIM CONTR PENS FUND	1.7	---
BROWNING INV NV	1.7	---
TOTAL	86.0	---

DIRECTORS :
CARTER JD ,CHIURA ED (Chairman),MUNDAWARARA SC
NYAMATORE AS ,ROONEY JP (Managing Director)
SANSOLE EW ,TURPIN WH ,USHEWOKUNZE CM ,WILLIAMS KR

REGISTERED OFFICE
Northridge Close, Borrowdale
Harare, Zimbabwe

TEL: 739822
FAX: 739820

TRANSFER SECRETARY
First Transfer Secretaries (Pvt) Ltd
P O Box 437, Bulawayo
Zimbabwe

TEL: 092634 - 702905

COMPANY SECRETARY
Gaitskell H D

NATURE OF BUSINESS
DELTA CORPORATION,which is incorporated in Zimbab we,is principally involved in brewing(domestic and export) and the distribution of clear and traditio nal beers, barley malting and the production of soft drinks through its transport division,DELTA DISTRIBUTION.It has interests in the hotel trade through ZIMBABWE SUN HOTELS.It retails food and clothing through OK BAZAARS & BON MARCHE, and also wholesales a wide range of goods through PAX CASH & CARRY DELTA manufactures and retails furniture

BANKERS :
N/A

AUDITORS :
Deloitte & Touche

FAMILIAR BRAND NAMES
N/A

CONTRIBUTION BY ACTIVITY
Beverages (% of Turnover) (49 2%)
Retail (31.2%)
Hotels (11.7%)
Transport (5.0%)
Agro-Industrial (2.5%)
Other (0.4%)

YEAR END : March

DIVIDEND : Ords Z$1,50

Dividend	(Ldr)29/11/91	(Pay)23/12/91	Amt(c)65.5
Dividned	(Ldr)29/05/92	(Pay)19/06/92	Amt(c)169.5

CAPITAL STRUCTURE

	AUTHORISED	ISSUED
Ords Z$1,50	30000000	24129689

FINANCIAL STATISTICS (AT FINANCIAL YEAR END)

(Amts in Z$)	1992 Mar	1991 Mar
Ord S/H Int	837619	649468
Long Trm Loans	438105	203784
Iss Ord Share	24130	24130
Total Liab	803921	435153
Current Liab	365816	231369
Total Assets	1624280	1074237
Intang Assets	17260	10384
Current Assets	434378	286416
Debtors	202057	132008
Inventory	211135	138507
Turnover	1681369	1242655
Oper Profit	235326	129892
Interest Paid	19253	7592
Tax Paid	65525	23136
Prf af Int&Tax	153167	100470
Prf att Ord Sh	136472	91133
Btm Line Earn	113514	84957
Dividend Paid	56705	42468
Depreciation	31418	20796

PER SHARE STATISTICS (CENTS)

Net Asst Val	3399.75	2648 50
Net Earnings	565.60	381.20
Dividends	235.00	176.00
Cash Flow	683.40	453.76

RATIOS AND OTHER INFORMATION

Current Ratio	1.19	1.24
Quik/Acid Tst	0.61	0.64
A/C Rec T/ovr	8.32	9.41
Tot Ass T/ovr	1.04	1.16
Debt/Ass Rat	0.40	0.30
L T L Tot Ass	0.17	0 09
Debt to Eqity	0.78	0 50
Interest Cover	12.22	17.11
Oper Prof Mrg	14 00	10.45
Net Prof Marg%	8.12	7.33
Ret on Assets	14.83	12 44
Ret on Equity%	16.29	14 03
Divid Cover	2.41	2 17
Effec Tax Rate	29.96	18.72
Def Interval	2.10	1.12
Sus Grth Rate	9.52	7.49

SUBSIDIARY & ASSOCIATED COMPANIES

None

INVESTMENTS

AFRICAN DISTILLERS LTD (15%)

DELTA ELECTRICAL INDUSTRIES LTD

ABBREVIATION : DELTA

JSE SHORT CODE : DEL

SECTOR : Industrial Electronics, Electrical & Bat

SHAREHOLDERS

Who Owns Whom's Assessment of the Identity of the Ultimate Controlling Shareholder:
DELTA PLC

SHAREHOLDER	PERCENTAGE 1992	1991
DELTA SA P/L	49 6	49 9
STD BANK NOM TVL P/L	13 9	14 1
SA MUTUAL	10 3	10 4
EIGHTY ONE MAIN STREET NOM LTD	9 6	---
FIRST NAT NOM P/L	3 2	3 2
SYFRETS NOM LTD	-	7 4
TOTAL	86 6	85 0

DIRECTORS :
BURY NA (Chairman),CHARLES AL ,DAVIES DC
EASTON RA DR,GEACH CH ,GLEESON DJ ,LOS RP
SALTER GE ,TEMPLE WR
VAN ZYL EW (Managing Director)
WRIGHT BR (Commercial Director

REGISTRATION NUMBER : 01/06020/06

REGISTERED OFFICE
2nd Floor, Sandton City Office Tower
Sandown
2196
TEL 011-783 4500
FAX 011-884 5398

TRANSFER SECRETARY
Central Registrars Ltd
P O Box 4844, Johannesburg
2000
TEL 011-331 0051

COMPANY SECRETARY
S G Sheppard

NATURE OF BUSINESS
The company provides electrical and mechanical services and consumable products to the broad spectrum of South African industry and where feasible the export of these services & products

BANKERS :
First National Bank of SA Ltd
Nedperm Bank Ltd, Standard Bank of SA Ltd

AUDITORS :
Deloitte Pim Goldby

FAMILIAR BRAND NAMES
AVILEC,DELTA CABLES,DELTA EMD,ESP,KEVAL
LH MARTHINUSEN,METALPLUS,MIPROD,TRANSWIRE

CONTRIBUTION BY ACTIVITY
Industrial Products (% attrib income) (19 0%)
Electrical Repair Engineering (28 0%)
Insulations,Conductors,Cables & Acces (26 0%)
Electrolytic Manganese dioxide (29 0%)
Finance (-2 0%)

YEAR END : December

DIVIDEND :Ords 9c

Interim No 37	(Ldr)31/08/90	(Pay)21/09/90	Amt(c)8
Final No 38	(Ldr)01/03/91	(Pay)28/03/91	Amt(c)16 5
Interim No 39	(Ldr)30/08/91	(Pay)20/09/91	Amt(c)9 5
Final No 40	(Ldr)28/02/92	(Pay)27/03/92	Amt(c)18
Interim No 41	(Ldr)04/09/92	(Pay)18/09/92	Amt(c)9 5

NUMBER OF EMPLOYEES : 1890

CAPITAL STRUCTURE

	AUTHORISED	ISSUED
Ords 9c	50000000	41095295

FINANCIAL STATISTICS (AT FINANCIAL YEAR END)

(Amts in R'000)	1991 Dec	1990 Dec	1989 Dec	1988 Dec	1987 Dec
Ord S/H Int	71707	62228	52853	44421	37384
Long Trm Loans	22031	21167	19328	7935	7098
Iss Ord Share	41095	41095	41095	35606	35606
Total Liab	96709	83378	75752	45225	35248
Current Liab	74678	62211	56424	37290	28150
Total Assets	168416	145606	128605	89646	72632
Current Assets	106349	87206	81834	67114	51399
Debtors	57502	46094	43354	31716	26397
Inventory	48806	41080	38449	29290	22879
Oper Profit	47586	47985	37173	22530	18348
Interest Paid	1733	2282	1787	316	379
Tax Paid	18397	21061	16927	11681	8960
Prf af Int&Tax	28241	25491	19090	11819	9009
Prf att Ord Sh	25794	22691	17573	11488	8829
Btm Line Earn	20780	19443	16129	11488	5866
Dividend Paid	11301	10068	12507	4451	3553
Mkt Prce(c) YE	910	540	428	360	200
Depreciation	8944	7673	5783	3272	2778

PER SHARE STATISTICS (CENTS)

Net Asst Val	174 49	151 42	128 61	124 76	104 99
Net Earnings	62 80	55 20	42 90	32 30	24 90
Dividends	27 50	24 50	44 00	12 50	10 00
Cash Flow	74 06	68 37	57 76	40 61	32 05

RATIOS AND OTHER INFORMATION

Mrk Cap(R000)	373965	221913	175887	128182	71212
Current Ratio	1 42	1 40	1 45	1 80	1 83
Quik/Acid Tst	0 77	0 74	0 77	1 01	1 01
Debt/Ass Rat	0 44	0 43	0 44	0 42	0 39
Debt to Eqity	1 04	1 00	1 07	0 84	0 75
Interest Cover	27 46	21 03	20 80	71 30	48 41
Ret on Assets	30 38	34 67	30 51	27 02	25 83
Ret on Equity%	35 97	36 46	33 25	25 86	23 62
Price/Earnings	14 49	9 78	9 98	11 15	8 03
Divid Cover	2 28	2 25	0 98	2 58	2 49
Divid Yield	3 02	4 54	10 28	3 47	5 00
Earning Yield%	6 90	10 22	10 02	8 97	12 45

NAV % Mrk Pr	19.17	28.04	30.05	34.65	52.50
Effec Tax Rate	43.43	46.59	42.33	50.11	49.10
Def Interval	0.39	0.14	0.29	0.01	0.01
Sus Grth Rate	20.21	20.29	9.59	15.84	14.11

SUBSIDIARY & ASSOCIATED COMPANIES

AVILEC (PTY) LTD
DEI SERVICES (PTY) LTD
DELTA (EMD) (PTY) LTD
DELTA CABLES (PTY) LTD
ELECTRICAL REPAIR ENGINEERING (PTY) LTD
EQUIPMENT SPARE PARTS AFRICA (PTY) LTD
JASCO ELECTRONICS HOLDINGS LTD (20,7%)
KEVAL (PTY) LTD
METALPLUS (PTY) LTD
MIPROD INSULATIONS (PTY) LTD
TEMSO (PTY) LTD
TRANSWIRE (PTY) LTD
VALHOLD LTD (21,1%)
WIRE ELECTRIC (TVL) (PTY) LTD

INVESTMENTS

None

DIAL-A-MOVIE LTD

ABBREVIATION : DIALMOV

JSE SHORT CODE : DLM

SECTOR : Industrial-Retailers & Wholesalers

SHAREHOLDERS

Who Owns Whom's Assessment of the Identity of the Ultimate Controlling Shareholder:
CUNNINGHAM FAMILY

SHAREHOLDER	PERCENTAGE 1992	1991
TOP CORP P/L	31.8	31.8
DIAL-A-MOVIE MENLYN P/L	11.3	11.3
CUNNINGHAM B A	11.1	1.0
SFSS NOM P/L	7.3	7.0
JANSZ A L	4.9	4.9
MITCHELL J I	4.9	4.9
OLIVIER C J	4.9	4.9
PEDLAR D S	4.9	4.9
WALE STREET NOM LTD	3.1	2.8
ALLSOP M J	1.9	1.7
MACVEN NOM P/L	1.1	1.2
CUNNINGHAM B J G	---	9.8
TOTAL	87.3	86.2

DIRECTORS :
CLAVEN DF
CUNNINGHAM BA (Chairman & Managing Dir.)
MERRIFIELD PW ,MITCHELL JI
NEL GF (Financial Director),PEDLAR AGW ,PEDLAR DS

REGISTRATION NUMBER : 77/03591/06

REGISTERED OFFICE
Tuinhof, 265 West Avenue
Verwoerdburgstad
0157
TEL: 012-663 4562
FAX: 012-663 4591

TRANSFER SECRETARY
Consolidated Share Registrars Ltd
P O Box 61051, Marshalltown
2107
TEL: 011-492 1620

COMPANY SECRETARY
G F Nel

NATURE OF BUSINESS
The group operates and franchises video rental and compact discs outlets.

BANKERS :
Nedperm Bank Ltd, Trust Bank of Africa Ltd

AUDITORS :
Ernst & Young

FAMILIAR BRAND NAMES
DIAL-A-MOVIE,TOP CD

CONTRIBUTION BY ACTIVITY
N/A

YEAR END : June

DIVIDEND : Ords no par value
Dividend (Ldr)30/09/92 (Pay)29/10/92 Amt(c)4

CAPITAL STRUCTURE

	AUTHORISED	ISSUED
Ords no par value	20000000	9111897

FINANCIAL STATISTICS (AT FINANCIAL YEAR END)

(Amts in R'000)	1992 Jun	1991 Jun	1990 Jun	1989 Jun	1988 Jun
Ord S/H Int	3412	2295	3687	4577	4329
Long Trm Loans	1104	1576	927	951	373
Iss Ord Share	9112	8828	8828	8828	8828
Total Liab	7111	4252	3960	4193	2014
Current Liab	6007	2676	3033	3242	1641
Total Assets	9994	5896	6873	7873	5496
Intang Assets	529	651	774	897	847
Current Assets	8620	4297	5207	5363	3996
Debtors	8024	3766	2842	1682	1378
Inventory	339	376	2273	3608	1492
Turnover	20450	13848	15019	12737	4613
Oper Profit	1487	-328	-13	1367	1698
Interest Paid	442	335	374	168	31
Tax Paid	-137	-88	424	564	870
Prf af Int&Tax	1182	-575	-811	635	797
Prf att Ord Sh	1182	-575	-811	635	797
Btm Line Earn	1454	-1392	-916	513	675
Dividend Paid	365	-	-	265	247
Mkt Prce(c) YE	11	10	22	25	36
Depreciation	374	540	696	721	526

PER SHARE STATISTICS (CENTS)

Net Asst Val	31.64	18.62	33.00	41.69	39.44
Net Earnings	13.00	-7.00	-9.00	7.00	10.10
Dividends	4.00	-	-	3.00	2.80
Cash Flow	15.23	-1.99	-1.06	15.16	18.61

RATIOS AND OTHER INFORMATION

Mrk Cap(R000)	1002	883	1942	2207	3178
Current Ratio	1.43	1.61	1.72	1.65	2.44
Quik/Acid Tst	1.38	1.47	0.97	0.54	1.53
A/C Rec T/ovr	2.55	3.68	5.28	7.57	3.35
Tot Ass T/ovr	2.05	2.35	2.19	1.62	0.84
Debt/Ass Rat	0.70	0.68	0.52	0.49	0.30
L T L Tot Ass	0.10	0.23	0.08	0.08	-
Debt to Eqity	2.06	1.75	0.97	0.84	0.38
Interest Cover	3.36	-0.98	-0.03	8.14	54.77
Oper Prof Mrg	7.27	-2.37	-0.09	10.73	36.81
Net Prof Marg%	5.78	-4.15	-5.40	4.99	17.28
Ret on Assets	14.88	-5.56	-0.19	17.36	30.90
Ret on Equity%	34.64	-25.05	-22.00	13.87	18.41
Price/Earnings	0.85	-1.43	-2.44	3.57	3.56
Divid Cover	3.25	-	-	2.33	3.61
Divid Yield	36.36	-	-	12.00	7.78
Earning Yield%	118.18	-70.00	-40.91	28.00	28.06
NAV % Mrk Pr	287.63	186.23	149.99	166.74	109.56
Effec Tax Rate	1.15	-7.99	-104.13	48.54	43.61
Def Interval	1.24	-12.03	-15.11	1.43	0.20
Sus Grth Rate	23.94	-25.05	-22.00	8.08	12.71

SUBSIDIARY & ASSOCIATED COMPANIES

DIAL-A-MOVIE (FRANCHISE) (PTY) LTD
DIAL-A-MOVIE (RETAIL) (PTY) LTD
EXPRESS FOTO (SOUTH AFRICA) (PTY) LTD
TOP CD SA (PTY) LTD
TOP RENT (PTY) LTD

INVESTMENTS

SOUTHERN LIFE ASSOCIATION LTD (200 SH)
TELJOY HOLDINGS LTD (100 SH)

DIGOCO MINING LTD

ABBREVIATION : DIGOCO

JSE SHORT CODE : DGC

SECTOR : Mining-Exploration

SHAREHOLDERS

Who Owns Whom's Assessment of the Identity of the Ultimate Controlling Shareholder:
J A NEL

SHAREHOLDER	PERCENTAGE 1992	1991
EXPLOMARK MINING P/L	35.7	---
KIRKNESS INV P/L	7.0	7.0
HAASBROEK G A	5.6	3.4
SMIT M E	1.9	2.1
VAN LANDSBERG J P H E/L	1.7	---
KHAN R	1.2	---
BADENHORST L J	1.2	1.2
NEL P J & BROERS BOUKONTRAKTEURS P/L	---	34.8
VON LANDSBERG J P H	---	1.7
COETZEE G	---	2.0
LIEDENBERG H A	---	2.0
TOTAL	54.4	54.1

DIRECTORS :
HUDSON PDR ,NEL JA (Chairman),NEL JJS
SMIT ME (Financial Director),THORNHILL MA

REGISTRATION NUMBER : 87/01112/06

REGISTERED OFFICE
2nd Floor, 270 Struben Street
Pretoria
0002
TEL: 012-663 4520

TRANSFER SECRETARY
Consolidated Share Registrars Ltd
P O Box 61051, Marshalltown
2107
TEL: 011-492 1620

COMPANY SECRETARY
M E Smit

NATURE OF BUSINESS
The company is involved in mineral and metal exploration.

BANKERS :
First National Bank of SA Ltd

AUDITORS :
HB van Schalkwyk

FAMILIAR BRAND NAMES
N/A

CONTRIBUTION BY ACTIVITY
N/A

YEAR END : February

NUMBER OF EMPLOYEES : 163

CAPITAL STRUCTURE

	AUTHORISED	ISSUED
Ords 10c	50000000	5000000
Comp Conv Prefs 10c	50000000	50000000

FINANCIAL STATISTICS (AT FINANCIAL YEAR END)

(Amts in R'000)	1991 Feb	1990 Feb
Ord S/H Int	42461	39022
Long Trm Loans	5688	5802
Iss Ord Share	5000	50000
Total Liab	6328	7177
Current Liab	640	1375
Total Assets	29475	27186
Intang Assets	19314	19013
Current Assets	581	199
Debtors	567	199
Inventory	14	-
Turnover	698	991
Oper Profit	-497	-84
Interest Paid	847	545
Prf af Int&Tax	-1339	-629
Prf att Ord Sh	-1339	-629
Btm Line Earn	-1339	-629
Mkt Prce(c) YE	27	-
Depreciation	59	46

PER SHARE STATISTICS (CENTS)

Net Asst Val	462.94	40.02

Net Earnings	-2.43	-1.26
Cash Flow	-25.60	-1.17

RATIOS AND OTHER INFORMATION

Mrk Cap(R000)	1350	-
Current Ratio	0.91	0.14
Quik/Acid Tst	0.89	0.14
A/C Rec T/ovr	1.23	4.98
Tot Ass T/ovr	0.02	0.04
Debt/Ass Rat	0.21	0.26
L T L Tot Ass	0.19	0.21
Debt to Eqity	0.15	0.18
Interest Cover	-0.59	-0.15
Oper Prof Mrg	-71.20	-8.48
Net Prof Marg%	-191.83	-63.47
Ret on Assets	-1.67	-0.31
Ret on Equity%	-3.15	-1.61
Price/Earnings	-11.11	-
Earning Yield%	-9.00	-
NAV % Mrk Pr	1714.59	-
Def Interval	-4.53	-8.94
Sus Grth Rate	-3.15	-1.61

SUBSIDIARY & ASSOCIATED COMPANIES

ENDLESS PIT DIAMONDS & MINERALS (PTY) LT
MARNITE MINING LTD (30%)

INVESTMENTS

None

DIMENSION DATA HOLDINGS LTD

ABBREVIATION : DIDATA

JSE SHORT CODE : DDT

SECTOR : Industrial-Electronics, Electrical & Bat

SHAREHOLDERS

Who Owns Whom's Assessment of the Identity of the Ultimate Controlling Shareholder:
DIRECTORS

SHAREHOLDER	PERCENTAGE 1992	1991
MERCEDES INFORMATION TECHNOLOGIES P/L	23.5	24.5
DIMENSION DATA INV P/L	20.3	22.1
NEDBANK NOM LTD	8.1	6.8
ELOFF STREET NOM P/L	5.4	6.7
STD BANK NOM TVL P/L	5.3	2.5
FIRST NAT NOM P/L	4.5	4.4
METROPOLITAN LIFE LTD	4.2	2.4
SOUTHERN LIFE ASSOC LTD	3.9	1.0
SUTCO AANDELE NOM P/L	3.2	---
SIXTY SIX MARSHALL STREET NOM P/L	1.2	3.2
SHARESTOCK NOM P/L	1.2	1.3
CMB NOM P/L	1.0	---
FORBES J A	1.0	---
EIGHTY ONE MAIN STREET NOM LTD	---	1.2
JR NOM P/L	---	1.1
MCLACHLAN K T	---	3.0
SA MUTUAL	---	2.5
SANLAM	---	1.0
TOTAL	82.9	83.8

DIRECTORS :
BUTCHER NP ,CAME RDS ,FORBES JA ,HIRD PGT
LABUSCHAGNE MF ,MCLACHLAN KT ,ORD JJ (Chairman)
PHILLIPS FD ,REECE WM (Sales Director)
SCOTT RM (Financial Director),WATSON B

REGISTRATION NUMBER : 87/01527/06

REGISTERED OFFICE
272 Kent Avenue, Ferndale
Randburg
2194
TEL: 011-789 2123
FAX: 011-789 3858

TRANSFER SECRETARY
Central Registrars Ltd
P O Box 4844, Johannesburg
2000
TEL: 011-331 0051

COMPANY SECRETARY
R M Scott

NATURE OF BUSINESS
The group is active in the design, supply and implementation of communications networks. Group operations include the manufacture of data comms equipment and the writing of systems software iro such equipment, and the provision of educational and training services in the fields of wide and local area networks, communications and end user applications. The group provides cabling solutions incl coaxial cable, twisted pair & optical fibre, and markets networking products.

BANKERS :
First National Bank of SA Ltd

AUDITORS :
Meyer Wilson & Marsh

FAMILIAR BRAND NAMES
ACT,AMNET,BANYAN,CAUSEWAY,COMDESIGN,DCIS,DSD
HAYES,INFOTRON,LATTICE,MICROCOM,NETLINK
PENTRONIX,PICTURETEL,THE LOCAL DATA,VINES
WANS

CONTRIBUTION BY ACTIVITY
Wide-area Networks (% turnover) (41.0%)
Local-area Networks (30.0%)
Engineering (11.0%)
Local Production (12.0%)
Cabling (6.0%)

YEAR END : December

DIVIDEND : Ords 1c

Final	(Ldr)22/02/91	(Pay)15/03/91	Amt(c)13.5
Final	(Ldr)28/02/92	(Pay)13/03/92	Amt(c)17.5

NUMBER OF EMPLOYEES : 240

CAPITAL STRUCTURE

	AUTHORISED	ISSUED
Ords 1c	40000000	21905719

FINANCIAL STATISTICS (AT FINANCIAL YEAR END)

(Amts in R'000)	1991 Dec	1990 Dec	1989 Dec	1988 Dec	1987 Dec
Ord S/H Int	25654	20310	16005	12947	10489
Long Trm Loans	1503	1583	1295	376	97
Iss Ord Share	21906	20642	20328	20328	20045
Total Liab	25765	19723	16880	7825	4726
Current Liab	24262	18140	15585	7449	4629
Total Assets	51419	40033	32738	20628	15215
Intang Assets	*	*	147	144	*
Current Assets	46837	36353	30412	19027	14507
Debtors	26933	22792	15743	9078	4698
Inventory	14008	9521	6628	5414	3539
Oper Profit	16789	12726	9696	5959	4463
Interest Paid	191	41	27	18	34
Tax Paid	8159	6379	4743	3034	2129
Prf af Int&Tax	8856	7048	5597	3544	2300
Prf att Ord Sh	8663	6701	5438	3472	2322
Btm Line Earn	8663	6701	5438	3472	2322
Dividend Paid	3896	2810	2236	1427	481
Mkt Prce(c) YE	430	240	200	120	
Depreciation	734	535	314	156	133

PER SHARE STATISTICS (CENTS)

Net Asst Val	117 11	98 39	78 01	62 98	52 33
Net Earnings	40 70	32 90	26 70	17 10	13 40
Dividends	17 50	13 50	11 00	7 00	2 40
Cash Flow	44 33	35 72	31 95	18 43	14 45

RATIOS AND OTHER INFORMATION

Mrk Cap(R000)	94196	49541	40656	24394	-
Current Ratio	1 93	2 00	1 95	2 55	3 13
Quik/Acid Tst	1 35	1 48	1 53	1 83	2 37
Debt/Ass Rat	0 47	0 45	0 48	0 36	0 30
Debt to Eqity	0 95	0 89	0 97	0 58	0 44
Interest Cover	87 90	310 39	359 11	331 06	131 26
Ret on Assets	33 46	33 64	31 67	31 98	29 51
Ret on Equity%	33 77	32 99	33 98	26 82	22 14
Price/Earnings	10 57	7 29	7 49	7 02	-
Divid Cover	2 33	2 44	2 43	2 44	5 58
Divid Yield	4 07	5 63	5 50	5 83	-
Earning Yield%	9 47	13 71	13 35	14 25	-
NAV % Mrk Pr	27 23	41 00	39 01	52 49	-
Effec Tax Rate	47 66	47 06	34 97	44 56	46 35
Def Interval	-	-	-	0 16	0 59
Sus Grth Rate	18 58	19 16	20 01	15 80	17 55

SUBSIDIARY & ASSOCIATED COMPANIES

ACCUNET (PTY) LTD
ADVANCED CABLING (CAPE) (PTY) LTD
ADVANCED CABLING (NATAL) (PTY) LTD
ADVANCED CABLING (PTY) LTD
ADVANCED CABLING (TVL) (PTY) LTD
CAUSEWAY COMMUNICATIONS (CAPE) (PTY) LTD
CAUSEWAY COMMUNICATIONS (NATAL) (PTY) LT
CAUSEWAY COMMUNICATIONS (PTY) LTD
CAUSEWAY COMMUNICATIONS (TVL) (PTY) LTD
CIM SOFTWARE APPLICATIONS (PTY) LTD
DATA COMMUNICATION INFORMATION SERVICES
DATA SYSTEMS DESIGN (PTY) LTD
DIMENSION DATA (CAPE) (PTY) LTD
DIMENSION DATA (EASTERN CAPE) (PTY) LTD
DIMENSION DATA (NATAL) (PTY) LTD
DIMENSION DATA (NTHN TVL) (PTY) LTD
DIMENSION DATA (OFS) (PTY) LTD
DIMENSION DATA (PTY) LTD
DIMENSION DATA (TVL) (PTY) LTD
DSD SOFTWARE DEVELOPMENT (PTY) LTD
LATTICE TECHNOLOGIES (CAPE) (PTY) LTD
LATTICE TECHNOLOGIES (PTY) LTD
LATTICE TECHNOLOGIES (TVL) (PTY) LTD

INVESTMENTS

None

DINETTE INDUSTRIES LTD

ABBREVIATION : DINETTE

JSE SHORT CODE : DIN

SECTOR : Venture Capital Market

SHAREHOLDERS

Who Owns Whom's Assessment of the Identity of the Ultimate Controlling Shareholder: DIRECTORS

SHAREHOLDER	PERCENTAGE 1992	1991
NAPIER HOLDINGS INC	17 0	17 0
SIMCHOWITZ M	13 3	13 3
VAN NIEKERK J J	10 0	10 0
LUBNER D M	9 6	10 0
SHARESTOCK NOM P/L	7 3	7 8
LUBNER J	5 5	5 5
CHASKELSON J	4 7	4 7
STOCKSHARE NOM P/L	3 4	3 4
ELLERINE BROS P/L	3 3	3 3
GROLMAN E	3 3	3 3
JANKELOWITZ I	3 3	3 3
TORF R	3 3	3 3
MANKOWITZ L	1 7	1 7
VAN FLYMEN B	1 7	1 7
LIPSCHITZ G	1 5	1 5
ENERSAVE P/L	-	1 1
TOTAL	89 0	91 0

DIRECTORS :
CHASKELSON J (Chairman),JANKELOWITZ I
LUBNER DM ,MANKOWITZ D (Chairman),MANKOWITZ L
SHAPIRO M ,TORF R
VAN NIEKERK JJ (Managing Director

REGISTRATION NUMBER : 91/02413/06

REGISTERED OFFICE
FHS House, 15 Girton Road
Parktown
2193

TRANSFER SECRETARY
Consolidated Share Registrars Ltd
P O Box 61051, Marshalltown
2107
TEL 011-492 1620

COMPANY SECRETARY
J J van Niekerk

NATURE OF BUSINESS
The main business of the company will be the manufacture of low to medium price chrome and brass table and chair sets

BANKERS :
Standard Bank of SA Ltd

AUDITORS :
Fisher Hoffman Stride

FAMILIAR BRAND NAMES
N/A

CONTRIBUTION BY ACTIVITY
N/A

YEAR END : June

DIVIDEND :15/10/91

NUMBER OF EMPLOYEES : 128

CAPITAL STRUCTURE

	AUTHORISED	ISSUED
Ords 1c	6000000	2999990

SUBSIDIARY & ASSOCIATED COMPANIES

None

INVESTMENTS

None

DISA DEVELOPMENT CORPORATION LTD

ABBREVIATION : DISA

JSE SHORT CODE : DSA

SECTOR : Financial-Property

SHAREHOLDERS

Who Owns Whom's Assessment of the Identity of the Ultimate Controlling Shareholder: T STERGIANOS

SHAREHOLDER	PERCENTAGE 1992	1991
STERVIS INV P/L	40 0	40 0
ALMONTE INV P/L	39 3	39 3
CMB NOM P/L	10 0	---
SANLAM	---	9 8
TOTAL	89 3	89 1

DIRECTORS :
BUYS DF ,FERGUSON DB ,JANSSEN CD ,MICHAEKS EJ
STANFORD DMH
STERGIANOS T (Chairman & Managing Dir)
VISSER JF ,WEERTS AM

REGISTRATION NUMBER : 87/04269/06

REGISTERED OFFICE
400 Theresa Court, 37 Durban Road
Bellville
7530
TEL: 021-948 8381
FAX: 021-948 5956

TRANSFER SECRETARY
Central Registrars Ltd
P O Box 4844, Johannesburg
2000
TEL. 011-331 0051

COMPANY SECRETARY
D B Ferguson

NATURE OF BUSINESS
Provides project management and financial services to customers commited to acquiring residential homes as well as commercial buildings. The group also finances and installs services in housing housing developments.

BANKERS :
First National Bank of SA Ltd

AUDITORS :
N/A

FAMILIAR BRAND NAMES
N/A

CONTRIBUTION BY ACTIVITY
N/A

YEAR END : August

CAPITAL STRUCTURE

	AUTHORISED	ISSUED
Ords no par value	40000000	30000000

FINANCIAL STATISTICS (AT FINANCIAL YEAR END)

(Amts in R'000)	1991 Aug	1990 Aug	1989 Aug	1988 Aug	1987
Ord S/H Int	7679	11143	9371	7773	240
Long Trm Loans	900	900	1500	926	4508
Iss Ord Share	30000	30000	30000	30000	24000
Total Liab	11278	7203	7963	5602	5516
Current Liab	10378	6303	6463	4676	1008
Total Assets	16423	15812	17334	13375	4748
Intang Assets	2534	2534	*	*	*
Current Assets	16276	14351	14330	10331	-
Debtors	6537	7742	8555	4888	-
Inventory	9286	6294	5740	-	-
Oper Profit	-2866	1125	4693	5138	-
Interest Paid	598	-	-	-	-
Tax Paid	-	-315	245	1241	861
Prf af Int&Tax	-3464	1772	4448	3897	850
Prf att Ord Sh	-3464	1772	4448	3897	850
Btm Line Earn	-3464	1772	4448	3897	850
Dividend Paid	-	-	2850	1200	-
Mkt Prce(c) YE	20	20	50	47	-
Depreciation	68	190	222	182	-

PER SHARE STATISTICS (CENTS)

Net Asst Val	17 15	28 70	31 24	25 91	1 00
Net Earnings	-11 50	5 90	14 80	13 40	-
Dividends	-	2 00	4 50	4 00	-
Cash Flow	-11 32	6 54	12 48	17 26	3 54

RATIOS AND OTHER INFORMATION

Mrk Cap(R000)	6000	6000	15000	14100	-
Current Ratio	1 57	2 28	2 22	2 21	-

Quik/Acid Tst	0.67	1.28	1.33	2.21	-
Debt/Ass Rat	0.69	0.46	0.46	0.35	1.16
L T L Tot Ass	0.05	0.06	0.09	-	0.95
Debt to Eqity	1.47	0.65	0.85	0.60	22.98
Interest Cover	-4.79	-	-	-	-
Ret on Assets	-17.45	9.21	27.07	38.41	36.04
Ret on Equity%	-40.38	14.71	40.92	50.14	354.17
Price/Earnings	-1.74	3.39	3.38	3.51	-
Divid Cover	-	2.95	3.29	3.35	-
Divid Yield	-	10.00	9.00	8.51	-
Earning Yield%	-57.50	29.50	29.60	28.51	-
NAV % Mrk Pr	85.75	143.48	62.47	55.13	-
Effec Tax Rate	-	-	24.95	6.13	-
Def Interval	-2.47	1.36	0.49	0.21	5.30
Sus Grth Rate	-45.11	15.90	17.05	34.70	354.17

SUBSIDIARY & ASSOCIATED COMPANIES

DISA HOMES (EASTERN CAPE) (PTY) LTD
DISA HOMES (WESTERN CAPE) (PTY) LTD
GREEN PASTURES (PTY) LTD
OCEAN MARKETING LTD (GILBRATOR)

INVESTMENTS

None

DISPATCH MEDIA LTD

ABBREVIATION : DISPTCH

JSE SHORT CODE : DCH

SECTOR : Industrial-Printing & Publishing

SHAREHOLDERS

Who Owns Whom's Assessment of the Identity of the Ultimate Controlling Shareholder:
DIRECTORS / TIMES MEDIA

SHAREHOLDER	PERCENTAGE 1992	1991
TIMES MEDIA LTD	28.7	28.8
FARR G A INV P/L	18.1	17.6
A BEAUMONT INV P/L	16.4	16.5
BRICELAND D INV P/L	15.9	16.0
BEACOM L E	1.9	---
STOCKSHARE NOM P/L	1.4	1.6
BEACON L E	---	1.9
TOTAL	82.5	82.4

DIRECTORS :
BEACOM LE (Technical Director)
BEAUMONT EA (Financial Director)
BELCHERS M (Chairman)
BRICELAND D (Managing Director),MULHOLLAND S

REGISTRATION NUMBER : 82/01863/06

REGISTERED OFFICE
35 Caxton Street, East London
5201
TEL: 0431-43 0010
FAX: 0431-43 4630

TRANSFER SECRETARY
Central Registrars Ltd
P O Box 4844, Johannesburg
2000
TEL: 011-331 0051

COMPANY SECRETARY
V B L Martin

NATURE OF BUSINESS
The company owns a number of newspapers which it prints & distributes throughout the Border, E Cape Transkei & Ciskei. In addition the company prints newspapers for other companies & distributes both newspapers & magazines within the circulation area on behalf of other publishing groups. The company also has an interest in a local travel agency.

BANKERS :
Standard Bank of SA Ltd

AUDITORS :
KPMG Aiken & Peat

FAMILIAR BRAND NAMES
EAST LONDON MIRROR,INDABA,THE REPRESENTATIVE
WILSON COLLINS TRAVEL

CONTRIBUTION BY ACTIVITY
N/A

YEAR END : June

DIVIDEND : Ords 1c

Dividend	(Ldr)22/09/89	(Pay)23/10/89	Amt(c)7
Dividend	(Ldr)12/10/90	(Pay)05/11/90	Amt(c)8.5
Dividend	(Ldr)27/09/91	(Pay)21/10/91	Amt(c)9
Dividend	(Ldr)25/09/92	(Pay)19/10/92	Amt(c)10

NUMBER OF EMPLOYEES : 357

CAPITAL STRUCTURE

	AUTHORISED	ISSUED
Ords 1c	25000000	14634000

FINANCIAL STATISTICS (AT FINANCIAL YEAR END)

(Amts in R'000)	1992 Jun	1991 Jun	1990 Jun	1989 Jun	1988 Jun
Ord S/H Int	14582	13414	12365	11349	10407
Long Trm Loans	362	426	690	951	-
Iss Ord Share	14634	14564	14506	14500	14500
Total Liab	4999	4686	4709	4842	4140
Current Liab	4637	4260	4019	3891	4140
Total Assets	16512	14417	12777	11281	9023
Intang Assets	3069	3683	4297	4910	5524
Current Assets	5263	8024	7610	6808	5853
Debtors	4353	4446	4353	3425	2818
Inventory	561	709	589	451	475
Turnover	25069	22520	20200	17709	14933
Oper Profit	4156	3545	3558	3400	2555
Interest Paid	157	124	186	-	-
Tax Paid	2113	1926	1949	1839	1326
Prf af Int&Tax	2598	2332	2246	1957	1368
Prf att Ord Sh	2598	2332	2246	1957	1368
Btm Line Earn	2598	2332	2246	1957	1368
Dividend Paid	1466	1313	1233	1015	798
Mkt Prce(c) YE	190	160	75	72	50
Depreciation	1124	709	616	455	309

PER SHARE STATISTICS (CENTS)

Net Asst Val	78.67	66.82	55.62	44.41	33.68

Net Earnings	17 80	16 00	15 50	13 50	9 40
Dividends	10 00	9 00	8 50	7 00	5 50
Cash Flow	25 22	21 22	20 47	17 95	11 57

RATIOS AND OTHER INFORMATION

Mrk Cap(R000)	27805	23302	10880	10440	7250
Current Ratio	1 14	1 88	1 89	1 75	1 41
Quik/Acid Tst	1 01	1 72	1 75	1 63	1 30
A/C Rec T/ovr	5 76	5 07	4 64	5 17	5 30
Tot Ass T/ovr	1 52	1 56	1 58	1 57	1 65
Debt/Ass Rat	0 28	0 30	0 35	0 41	0 46
L T L Tot Ass	0 00	0 01	0 03	0 07	-
Debt to Eqity	0 32	0 32	0 36	0 41	0 40
Interest Cover	28 20	30 28	20 39	-	-
Oper Prof Mrg	16 58	15 74	17 61	19 20	17 11
Net Prof Marg%	10 36	10 36	11 12	11 05	9 16
Ret on Assets	29 48	30 39	34 29	33 65	29 86
Ret on Equity%	17 82	17 38	18 16	17 24	13 14
Price/Earnings	10 67	10 00	4 84	5 33	5 32
Divid Cover	1 78	1 78	1 82	1 93	1 71
Divid Yield	5 26	5 63	11 33	9 72	11 00
Earning Yield%	9 37	10 00	20 67	18 75	18 80
NAV % Mrk Pr	41 41	41 76	74 16	61 68	67 35
Effec Tax Rate	48 31	44 66	46 49	43 41	49 22
Def Interval	0 02	0 13	0 27	0 54	0 02
Sus Grth Rate	7 76	7 60	8 19	8 30	5 48

SUBSIDIARY & ASSOCIATED COMPANIES

DAVMAX (PTY) LTD (49,9%)

INVESTMENTS

ELECTRONIC MEDIA NETWORK HOLDINGS (PTY) (2 5%)
ELECTRONIC MEDIA NETWORK LTD

DISTILLERS CORPORATION (SA) LTD

ABBREVIATION : DISTIL

JSE SHORT CODE : DSL

SECTOR : Industrial-Beverages & Hotels

SHAREHOLDERS

Who Owns Whom's Assessment of the Identity of the Ultimate Controlling Shareholder: REMBRANDT/KWV

SHAREHOLDER	PERCENTAGE 1992	1991
REMBRANDT-KWV INV LTD	60 0	60 0
SA BREWERIES LTD	30 0	30 0
LIBERTY LIFE ASSOC OF AFRICA LTD	3 7	3 7
CMB NOM P/L	1 6	--
SANLAM		1 6
TOTAL	95 3	95 3

DIRECTORS :
DU PRE' LE ROUX MS (Managing Director)
GROVE' EL DR,HUGO PBB ,MACFARLANE WS ,SENEKAL JC
SWARTZ PEI ,VAN NIEKERK J
VAN WYK AH PROF (Chairman),VAN ZYL JJM
VENTER PJ D

REGISTRATION NUMBER : 88/05808/06

REGISTERED OFFICE
Aan-De-Wagenweg, Stellenbosch
7600
TEL 02231-73480
FAX 02231-4611

TRANSFER SECRETARY
Central Registrars Ltd
P O Box 4844, Johannesburg
2000
TEL 011-331 0051

COMPANY SECRETARY
C J Cronje

NATURE OF BUSINESS
An investment holding company with subsidiaries engaged in the production of spirits & wines, and their wholesale distribution The group also has a financial interest in the retail marketing of alcoholic beverages

BANKERS :
Volkskas Ltd, Standard Bank of SA Ltd

AUDITORS :
Coopers Theron Du Toit

FAMILIAR BRAND NAMES
BACARDI,BEEFEATER,CASTELO,CELLAR CASK
COUNT PUSHKIN,DROSTDY HOF,FLEUR DU CAP
FLIGHT OF THE FISH EAGLE,GORDONS
GREAT WESTERN COOLER,GRUNBERGER
HERE XVII SOUVEREIN,JOHNNIE WALKER,KLIPDRIFT
MACLEANS,OUDE MEESTER,PAARL PERLE,PAARL ROCK
RICHELIEU,ROYAL OAK,SEVEN SEAS,WHITE HORSE
WITZENBERG

CONTRIBUTION BY ACTIVITY
N/A

YEAR END : June

DIVIDEND : Ords no par value

Interim No 3	(Ldr)23/03/90	(Pay)12/04/90	Amt(c)10
Final No 4	(Ldr)21/09/90	(Pay)22/10/90	Amt(c)20
Interim No 5	(Ldr)22/02/91	(Pay)28/02/91	Amt(c)11
Final No 6	(Ldr)20/09/91	(Pay)23/10/91	Amt(c)24
Interim No 7	(Ldr)21/02/92	(Pay)28/02/92	Amt(c)12
Final No 8	(Ldr)25/09/92	(Pay)23/10/92	Amt(c)27

NUMBER OF EMPLOYEES : 3300

CAPITAL STRUCTURE

	AUTHORISED	ISSUED
Ords no par value	160000000	140000000

FINANCIAL STATISTICS (AT FINANCIAL YEAR END)

(Amts in R'000)	1992 Jun	1991 Jun	1990 Jun	1989 Jun	1988 Jun
Ord S/H Int	599589	538226	473567	440958	360437
Long Trm Loans	36626	34092	29933	12397	7686
Iss Ord Share	140000	140000	140000	140000	140000
Total Liab	236682	230382	213683	157321	146204
Current Liab	200056	196290	183750	144924	138518
Total Assets	836271	768608	687250	598279	506641
Current Assets	504866	462456	398324	338013	296173

Debtors	86833	89874	80375	70810	55165
Inventory	372150	368286	317859	262640	221781
Oper Profit	176849	176080	155746	142680	109553
Interest Paid	836	7616	5860	606	2362
Tax Paid	79534	79958	75603	72052	52017
Prf af Int&Tax	106775	99484	84748	78249	58477
Prf att Ord Sh	93853	88803	78093	71384	55822
Btm Line Earn	93853	88803	78093	71384	55822
Dividend Paid	54600	49000	42000	35000	24000
Mkt Prce(c) YE	735	570	375	200	-
Depreciation	20458	15966	15686	9093	-

PER SHARE STATISTICS (CENTS)

Net Asst Val	428.28	384.45	338.26	314.97	257.46
Net Earnings	67.00	63.40	62.80	58.80	43.80
Dividends	39.00	35.00	30.00	25.00	17.10
Cash Flow	93.28	84.26	70.53	66.38	41.36

RATIOS AND OTHER INFORMATION

Mrk Cap(R000)	1029000	798000	525000	280000	-
Current Ratio	2.52	2.36	2.17	2.33	2.14
Quik/Acid Tst	0.66	0.48	0.44	0.52	0.54
Debt/Ass Rat	0.26	0.28	0.30	0.24	0.27
L T L Tot Ass	0.02	0.02	0.03	0.00	0.00
Debt to Eqity	0.36	0.40	0.43	0.33	0.39
Interest Cover	213.83	23.41	26.69	235.49	46.38
Ret on Assets	22.46	24.63	24.64	25.91	22.86
Ret on Equity%	15.65	16.50	16.49	16.19	15.49
Price/Earnings	10.97	8.99	5.97	3.40	-
Divid Cover	1.72	1.81	2.09	2.35	2.56
Divid Yield	5.31	6.14	8.00	12.50	-
Earning Yield%	9.12	11.12	16.75	29.40	-
NAV % Mrk Pr	58.27	67.45	90.20	157.49	-
Effec Tax Rate	43.22	44.29	48.40	44.23	47.46
Def Interval	0.10	0.18	0.36	0.12	0.04
Sus Grth Rate	6.55	7.40	7.62	8.25	8.83

SUBSIDIARY & ASSOCIATED COMPANIES

ALTO WYNLANDGOED (EDMS) BPK
BRANWIN (PTY) LTD
CASTLE WINE AND E K GREEN LTD
DIE BERGKELDER BPK
DISTILLERS & CASTLE WINE (CISKEI) LTD
DISTILLERS & CASTLE WINE (TRANSKEI) LTD
DISTILLERS CORPORATION (NAMIBIA) LTD
DISTILLERS CORPORATION (NAMIBIA) LTD
EXPO LIQUOR (BOPHUTHATSWANA) LTD
EXPO LIQUOR LTD
HENRY C COLLISON & SONS LTD = MARKETING
HENRY C COLLISON & SONS LTD, LONDON
KAAPSCHE WIJN EN BRANDEWIJN MAATSCHAPPIJ
LE BONHEUR WYNLANDGOED (EDMS) BPK
SOUTH AFRICAN DISTILLERIES & WINES (SA)
UITKYK FARM ESTATES (PTY) LTD

INVESTMENTS

CACTUS INVESTMENTS (PTY) LTD
SMALL BUSINESS DEVELOPMENT CORP LTD

DOORNFONTEIN GOLD MINING CO LTD

ABBREVIATION : DOORNS

JSE SHORT CODE : DOR

SECTOR : Gold-West Witwatersrand

SHAREHOLDERS

Who Owns Whom's Assessment of the Identity of the Ultimate Controlling Shareholder:
GFSA

SHAREHOLDER	PERCENTAGE 1992	1991
AECI PENS FUND	---	3.7
ANGLO AMERICAN GOLD INV CO LTD	---	4.4
BANK OF NEW YORK NOM LTD	---	1.1
DEPOSITARY NOM INC	---	5.9
FERMAIN NOM LTD	---	1.4
FIRST NAT NOM P/L	---	4.1
FIRST NAT NOM P/L GATR DEPOT	---	1.1
FOX STREET NOM P/L	---	2.0
INDO-CHINA NOM SA P/L	---	18.7
MINU NOM LTD	---	35.5
RESIDENT NOM LTD	---	1.6
SANLAM	---	1.8
SOUTHERN LIFE ASSOC LTD	---	1.5
STD BANK NOM TVL P/L	---	3.5
VOLKSKAS NOM P/L	---	1.6
TOTAL	---	87.8

DIRECTORS :
DAY BA ,EUSTACE PJ ,FENTON CT ,FULLER-GOOD MR
JANISCH PR ,KAHLE H ,MOOLMAN A ,MUNRO AH
TAGG MJ (Chairman & Managing Dir.)
VAN DER COLF SW

REGISTRATION NUMBER : 05/24709/06

REGISTERED OFFICE
75 Fox Street, Johannesburg
2001
TEL: 011-639 9111
FAX: 011-639 2101

TRANSFER SECRETARY
Gold Fields of SA Ltd
P O Box 1167, Johannesburg
2000
TEL: 011-639 9111

COMPANY SECRETARY
Gold Fields of SA Ltd

NATURE OF BUSINESS
The company carries on gold mining operations in the Carletonville area of the West Witwatersrand.

BANKERS :
Standard Bank of SA Ltd

AUDITORS :
Ernst & Young

FAMILIAR BRAND NAMES
N/A

CONTRIBUTION BY ACTIVITY
N/A

YEAR END : June

DIVIDEND :Ords 25c

Interim No 64	(Ldr)30/12/88	(Pay)08/02/89	Amt(c)10
Final No 65	(Ldr)30/06/89	(Pay)09/08/89	Amt(c)5

NUMBER OF EMPLOYEES : 6350

CAPITAL STRUCTURE

	AUTHORISED	ISSUED
Ords 25c	45000000	40000000

FINANCIAL STATISTICS (AT FINANCIAL YEAR END)

(Amts in R'000)	1992 Jun	1991 Jun	1990 Jun	1989 Jun	1988 Jun
Ord S/H Int	441514	456569	456329	442306	426067
Iss Ord Share	40000	40000	40000	40000	40000
Total Liab	47949	35789	36449	33048	42391
Current Liab	47949	35789	36449	33048	42391
Total Assets	489463	492358	492778	475354	468458
Current Assets	17754	22055	35137	52874	77365
Debtors	6326	4808	4898	2981	2919
Inventory	7139	7988	14343	11427	9425
Turnover	188635	235817	263450	245450	237432
Oper Profit	-17846	2388	10701	25928	38241
Tax Paid	-184	5346	2822	3941	1621
Prf af Int&Tax	-13729	-613	14330	21987	36620
Prf att Ord Sh	-13729	-613	14330	21987	36620
Btm Line Earn	-13729	-613	14330	21987	36620
Dividend Paid	-	-	-	6000	18000
Mkt Prce(c) YE	115	350	505	425	550

PER SHARE STATISTICS (CENTS)

Net Asst Val	1103.79	1141.42	1140.82	1105.77	1065.17
Net Earnings	-34.32	-7.00	-2.00	15.00	47.00
Dividends	-	-	-	15.00	45.00
Cash Flow	-34.32	-1.53	35.83	54.97	91.55

RATIOS AND OTHER INFORMATION

Mrk Cap(R000)	46000	140000	202000	170000	220000
Current Ratio	0.37	0.62	0.96	1.60	1.83
Quik/Acid Tst	0.22	0.39	0.57	1.25	1.60
A/C Rec T/ovr	29.82	49.05	53.79	82.34	81.34
Tot Ass T/ovr	0.39	0.48	0.53	0.52	0.51
Debt/Ass Rat	0.10	0.07	0.07	0.07	0.09
Debt to Eqity	0.11	0.08	0.08	0.07	0.10
Oper Prof Mrg	-9.46	1.01	4.06	10.56	16.11
Net Prof Marg%	-7.28	-0.26	5.44	8.96	15.42
Ret on Assets	-2.84	0.96	3.48	5.45	8.16
Ret on Equity%	-3.11	-0.13	3.14	4.97	8.59
Price/Earnings	-3.35	-50.00	-252.50	28.33	11.70
Divid Cover	-	-	-	1.00	1.04
Divid Yield	-	-	-	3.53	8.18
Earning Yield%	-29.84	-2.00	-0.40	3.53	8.55
NAV % Mrk Pr	959.81	326.12	225.91	260.18	193.67
Effec Tax Rate	-	112.95	16.45	15.20	4.50
Def Interval	-1.59	-	-	-	-
Sus Grth Rate	-3.11	-0.13	3.14	3.61	4.37

SUBSIDIARY & ASSOCIATED COMPANIES

None

INVESTMENTS

None

DORBYL LTD

ABBREVIATION : DORBYL

JSE SHORT CODE : DLV

SECTOR : Industrial-Engineering

SHAREHOLDERS

Who Owns Whom's Assessment of the Identity of the Ultimate Controlling Shareholder:
REMBRANDT VIA METKOR

SHAREHOLDER	PERCENTAGE 1992	1991
INTERNAT PIPE & STEEL INV SA P/L	52.0	52.6
IND PARTNERSHIP INV LTD	9.9	10.0
CMB NOM P/L	8.3	---
STD BANK NOM TVL P/L	6.7	6.6
EIGHTY ONE MAIN STREET NOM LTD	4.1	3.6
METKOR GROUP LTD	3.0	3.0
FIRST NAT NOM P/L	2.5	3.0
ENGINEERING INDUSTRIES PENS FUND	2.5	2.5
METAL IND GROUP PENS FUND	2.2	2.2
AFRICAN TUBES & PIPES P/L	1.6	1.6
SANLAM	---	6.3
TOTAL	92.8	91.4

DIRECTORS :
BOUSTRED WG ,BOYD L ,BULLETT BE ,KING MW
KOTZEE FP (Chairman)
MOSTERT DB (Chief Executive),O'CONNOR BP
OLIVIER PA ,ROUX MJ ,SMITHYMAN MJ ,TALJAARD LCJ
VAN WYK T ,VAN WYK W
WELTON AR (Financial Director

REGISTRATION NUMBER : 02/01510/06

REGISTERED OFFICE
4th Floor, Dorbyl Park, Skeen Boulevard
Bedfordview
2008
TEL: 011-607 0111
FAX: 011-607 2066

TRANSFER SECRETARY
Consolidated Share Registrars Ltd
P O Box 61051, Marshalltown
2107
TEL: 011-492 1620

COMPANY SECRETARY
D Orwin

NATURE OF BUSINESS
An industrial holding company. Group activities include the following : Manufacture of roll formed steel products, automotive & engineering component Heavy & light engineering; Manufacture & import of industrial products incl windmills, pumps, coal mining machinery, air conditioning & refrigeration

equipment; Shipbuilding & repair; Manufacture of railway rolling stock & commercial vehicle body work, structural steel & platework & steel tubing; Distribution of tube, pipe & fittings; Property.

BANKERS :
First National Bank of SA Ltd

AUDITORS :
KPMG Aiken & Peat

FAMILIAR BRAND NAMES
N/A

CONTRIBUTION BY ACTIVITY
N/A

YEAR END : September

DIVIDEND : Ords no par value

Interim No 81	(Ldr)01/12/89	(Pay)05/01/90	Amt(c)28
Final No 82	(Ldr)30/11/90	(Pay)04/01/91	Amt(c)75
Interim No 83	(Ldr)30/05/91	(Pay)24/06/91	Amt(c)28
Final No 84	(Ldr)06/12/91	(Pay)03/01/92	Amt(c)80
Interim No 85	(Ldr)05/06/92	(Pay)26/06/92	Amt(c)28
Final No 86	(Ldr)08/01/93	(Pay)04/12/92	Amt(c)80

NUMBER OF EMPLOYEES : 17502

CAPITAL STRUCTURE

	AUTHORISED	ISSUED
Ords no par value	40000000	32258946
5% Cum Prefs R2	750000	740025
5,75% Red Cum Prefs R2	2000000	0
5,5% Cum Prefs R2	1250000	1250000

FINANCIAL STATISTICS (AT FINANCIAL YEAR END)

(Amts in R'000)	1992 Sep	1991 Sep	1990 Sep	1989 Sep	1988 Sep
Ord S/H Int	844326	789907	738059	704587	623167
Long Trm Loans	199388	177544	243671	162682	193562
Iss Ord Share	32259	31906	31897	31888	31888
Total Liab	808300	686274	767533	677722	604767
Current Liab	608912	508730	523862	515040	411205
Total Assets	1652626	1476181	1505592	1382309	1227934
Current Assets	934279	842636	890266	874293	751308
Debtors	456114	466301	472383	427564	362858
Inventory	451859	371298	417883	446729	388450
Turnover	2977051	2896025	2843558	2504767	2076790
Oper Profit	141096	173229	183465	185709	129023
Interest Paid	44415	41791	47539	36252	23174
Tax Paid	11843	21944	33728	39756	20817
Prf af Int&Tax	92058	118221	113653	116386	85032
Prf att Ord Sh	92305	116531	110108	112065	80192
Btm Line Earn	81530	114531	96694	113608	85687
Dividend Paid	34836	34457	32851	31888	24554
Mkt Prce(c) YE	1700	1950	1575	2200	1025
Depreciation	69177	60937	53699	43652	39773

PER SHARE STATISTICS (CENTS)

Net Asst Val	2617.33	2475.73	2313.88	2209.57	1954.24
Net Earnings	287.60	365.20	345.20	351.40	245.50
Dividends	108.00	108.00	103.00	100.00	77.00
Cash Flow	502.97	555.54	514.63	488.24	375.93

RATIOS AND OTHER INFORMATION

Mrk Cap(R000)	548403	622167	502378	701536	326852
Current Ratio	1.53	1.66	1.70	1.70	1.83
Quik/Acid Tst	0.79	0.93	0.90	0.83	0.88
A/C Rec T/ovr	6.53	6.21	6.02	5.86	5.72
Tot Ass T/ovr	1.80	1.96	1.89	1.81	1.69
Debt/Ass Rat	0.46	0.43	0.47	0.47	0.47
L T L Tot Ass	0.09	0.09	0.12	0.10	0.13
Debt to Eqity	0.90	0.81	0.96	0.93	0.92
Interest Cover	3.18	4.15	3.87	5.13	5.57
Oper Prof Mrg	4.74	5.98	6.45	7.41	6.21
Net Prof Marg%	3.10	4.02	3.87	4.47	3.86
Ret on Assets	8.97	12.33	12.95	13.92	10.51
Ret on Equity%	10.93	14.75	14.92	15.91	12.87
Price/Earnings	5.91	5.34	4.56	6.26	4.18
Divid Cover	2.66	3.38	3.35	3.51	3.19
Divid Yield	6.35	5.54	6.54	4.55	7.51
Earning Yield%	16.92	18.73	21.92	15.97	23.95
NAV % Mrk Pr	153.96	126.96	146.91	100.43	190.66
Effec Tax Rate	11.47	15.72	22.62	25.51	19.67
Def Interval	1.61	0.99	1.15	0.92	1.39
Sus Grth Rate	6.81	10.39	10.47	11.38	8.93

SUBSIDIARY & ASSOCIATED COMPANIES

AFRICAN ENGINEERING PROJECTS (PTY) LTD
AFRICAN MALLEABLE HOLDINGS (PTY) LTD
ALPHEUS WILLIAMS & DOWSE (PTY) LTD
AUTOMATIC PRESSINGS AND DIE MANUFACTURER
AUTOMOTIVE STEERING WHEELS (PTY) LTD
BALATON INVESTMENTS (PTY) LTD
BALDWINS (PTY) LTD
BALDWINS MANUFACTURING (PTY) LTD
BALDWINS STEEL (PTY) LTD
BALDWINS STEEL SERVICES (PTY) LTD
BARLOW PNEUMATICS (PTY) LTD
BENJAMIN HOLDINGS (PTY) LTD
BERNLEA PROPERTIES SIX (PTY) LTD
BIRO PROPERTIES (PTY) LTD
BREARLEY STREET HOLDINGS (PTY) LTD
BRODERICK ENGINEERING WORKS (PTY) LTD
BRODERICK INVESTMENTS (PTY) LTD
BRODERICK PROPERTIES (PTY) LTD
BROWNBUILT INVESTMENTS (PTY) LTD
BUNDY TUBING CO OF SA LTD
BUSAF BAUER (PTY) LTD
BUSAF ENGINEERING (PTY) LTD
BUSCRAFT PROPERTIES (PTY) LTD
BUTABA PROPERTIES (PTY) LTD
CAR-PART INDUSTRIES (PTY) LTD
CARENA COURT (PTY) LTD
CENTURATOR AIR CONDITIONING (PTY) LTD
CENTURATOR PRODUCTS (PTY) LTD
CLARK SANDERSON (PTY) LTD
CLIMAX WINDMILLS (PTY) LTD
CONSIDERED INVESTMENTS (PTY) LTD
COSMO ENGINEERING (PTY) LTD
DAP (ELANDSFONTEIN) (PTY) LTD
DAVIES CRESCENT FLATS (PTY) LTD
DHE HOLDINGS (BENONI) (PTY) LTD
DLSH STOCK COMPANY (PTY) LTD
DORBYL (ALTON) PROPERTIES (PTY) LTD
DORBYL (EASTERN CAPE) (PTY) LTD
DORBYL AIR (PTY) LTD
DORBYL AUTOMOTIVE PRODUCTS (PTY) LTD
DORBYL BABELEGI (PTY) LTD
DORBYL COASTAL ENGINEERING (PTY) LTD
DORBYL GROUP HOUSING ORGANISATION (PTY)
DORBYL HEAVY ENGINEERING (PTY) LTD - DOR
DORBYL HOUSING CO. (PTY) LTD
DORBYL LIGHT & GENERAL ENGINEERING (PTY)
DORBYL MARINE (PTY) LTD
DORBYL METAL PRESSING (PTY) LTD
DORBYL PROJECTS AND CONSTRUCTION (PTY) L
DORBYL PROPERTIES (PTY) LTD
DORBYL PROPERTIES TRUST (PTY) LTD
DORBYL RAILWAY COMPONENTS (PTY) LTD
DORBYL STEEL HOLDINGS LTD
DORBYL STRUCTURAL ENGINEERING (PTY) LTD

DORBYL TRANSPORT PRODUCTS (PTY) LTD
DORMAN LONG SWAN HUNTER (PTY) LTD
DORPROP (ELANDSFONTEIN) (PTY) LTD
DORPROP (HEIDELBURG) (PTY) LTD
DORPROP (LABORIA) (PTY) LTD
DORPROP (PIETERSBURG) (PTY) LTD
DORPROP (VANDERBIJL) (PTY) LTD
DORPROP (VOORBAAI) (PTY) LTD
DORPROP ALGOA BAY (PTY) LTD
DORPROP BOKSBURG (PTY) LTD
DORPROP CLAREMONT (PTY) LTD
DORPROP EAST LONDON (PTY) LTD
DORPROP EPPING (PTY) LTD
DORPROP GEORGE (PTY) LTD
DORPROP GERMISTON (PTY) LTD
DORPROP RANDBURG (PTY) LTD
DORPROP RICHARDS BAY (PTY) LTD
DORPROP THREE RIVERS (PTY) LTD
DORPROP VEREENIGING (PTY) LTD
EAGLE TUBE CO (PTY) LTD
ECC PROPERTIES (PTY) LTD
FELDRO HOLDINGS (PTY) LTD
GLOBE NAUTILUS HOLDINGS (PTY) LTD (50%)
GUESTRO ALLOY WHEELS (PTY) LTD
GUESTRO AUTOMOTIVE WHEELS (PTY) LTD
GUESTRO UITENHAGE PROPERTIES (PTY) LTD
HILLMAN DEVELOPMENTS (PTY) LTD
HOLLOSEC (PTY) LTD
HOLLOSEC HOLDINGS (PTY) LTD
HOLLOSEC SALES (PTY) LTD
IRVINE CHAPMAN HOLDINGS (PTY) LTD
J & C MALLEABLE (PTY) LTD
J & C MALLEABLE PROPERTIES (PTY) LTD
JA BRODERICK FACTORY LTD
JANMARK PROPERTIES (PTY) LTD
JH VIVIAN & CO (PTY) LTD
JH VIVIAN INVESTMENTS (PTY) LTD
JK FULTON (PTY) LTD
JL CLARK & CO LTD
JL CLARK DURBAN PROPERTIES (PTY) LTD
JL CLARK ENGINEERING (PTY) LTD
KGALAGADI ENGINEERING CO. (PTY) LTD
KOOLMASTER MANUFACTURING (PTY) LTD
KUTALO PROPERTIES (PTY) LTD
MARITZBURG STEEL AND WIRE (PTY) LTD
MARTEK (PTY) LTD
METEK (PTY) LTD
PETTER DIESELS (PTY) LTD
PIPE COUPLINGS (PTY) LTD
PLUTUS HOLDINGS (PTY) LTD
PULLMAFLEX SOUTHERN AFRICA (PTY) LTD
REFAIRCON SWA (PTY) LTD
REFRIGERATION AGENCIES (PTY) LTD
S & L PROPERTIES (WINDHOEK) (PTY) LTD
S E SES EIENDOMME (PTY) LTD
SA INSTRUMENTATION (PTY) LTD
SA TUBES & FITTINGS CO (PTY) LTD
SALCAST (PTY) LTD
SALCHAIN (PTY) LTD
SALISTER DIESELS (PTY) LTD
SALMAC STAINLESS TUBE (PTY) LTD
SALPUMP PROPERTIES (PTY) LTD
SALTRADING HOLDINGS (PTY) LTD
SALTRONICS (PTY) LTD
SALVALVE (PTY) LTD
SALWEIR (PTY) LTD
SAMAL INVESTMENTS (PTY) LTD
SCOTTISH TUBE COMPANY (PTY) LTD
SEASPRAY MAINTENANCE (PTY) LTD
SINTERED METAL COMPONENTS (PTY) LTD
STANDSAL PROPERTY HOLDINGS (PTY) LTD
STEEL PIPE INDUSTRIES (PTY) LTD
STEEL WHEEL & AXLE SA (PTY) LTD
STEWART & LLOYDS OF SA (PTY) LTD
STEWARTS & LLOYDS OF NAMIBIA (PTY) LTD
STEWARTS & LLOYDS TRADING (PTY) LTD
SWASAP PROPERTIES (PTY) LTD
TASGUMAR (PTY) LTD
TEBSA PROJECTS (PTY) LTD
TOSA IRRIGATION COMPANY (PTY) LTD
TOSA LTD
TUBE & PIPE INDUSTRIES (PTY) LTD
TUBEMAKERS OF SOUTH AFRICA PROPERTIES (P
TUBEWRIGHT PROPERTIES (PTY) LTD
TURBINE MANUFACTURERS SA (PTY) LTD
UNIVEL TRANSMISSIONS (PTY) LTD
VANDERBIJL ENGINEERING CORP. (PTY) LTD
VANMAR ENGINEERING (PTY) LTD
VECOR (NEWCASTLE) ENGINEERING CO. (PTY)
VHE PROPERTIES (PTY) LTD
VOSA PROPERTIES (PTY) LTD
WESTBRIDGE INVESTMENTS (PTY) LTD
WIELE KORPORASIE (PTY) LTD
WILLOWS FOUR (PTY) LTD
WOLCUT PROPERTIES (PTY) LTD
WOLHUNTER STEEL NATAL PROPERTIES (PTY) L
WOLHUTER EXPORT (PTY) LTD
WOLHUTER STEEL (NATAL) (PTY) LTD
WOLHUTER STEEL (PTY) LTD
WOLHUTER WATTLES ROODEKOP (PTY) LTD
WOLTUBE PROPERTIES (PTY) LTD
WRIGHT ANDERSON (S.A.) (PTY) LTD

INVESTMENTS

None

DPF INVESTMENTS LTD

ABBREVIATION : DPF-INV

JSE SHORT CODE : DPF

SECTOR : Financial-Property

SHAREHOLDERS

Who Owns Whom's Assessment of the Identity of the Ultimate Controlling Shareholder: DELANEY FAMILY

SHAREHOLDER	PERCENTAGE 1992	1991
DELMAT INV P/L	---	67.9
PRIMA BANK LTD	---	13.3
PEER A C	---	1.9
HEAVEN INV P/L	---	3.1
TOTAL	---	86.0

DIRECTORS :
BAKER PJH (Systems Director)
DELANEY PP (Managing Director)
MATHIR MR (Financial Director),MCCOWAN SJM
ORATOR RW (Systems Director

REGISTRATION NUMBER : 87/02932/06

REGISTERED OFFICE
402 Salisbury House, 332 Smith Street
Durban

4001
TEL. 031-266 8460

TRANSFER SECRETARY
Mercantile Registrars Ltd
P O Box 1053, Johannesburg
2000
TEL 011-333 8181

COMPANY SECRETARY
M R Mathir

NATURE OF BUSINESS
An investment company involved in property development The activities of subsidiaries consist of property investments & developments & the provision of management services to group companies & third parties

BANKERS :
Standard Bank of SA Ltd

AUDITORS :
Coopers Theron Du Toit

FAMILIAR BRAND NAMES
N/A

CONTRIBUTION BY ACTIVITY
N/A

YEAR END : June

DIVIDEND : Ords no par value
Final No 1 (Ldr)16/11/90 (Pay)21/12/90 Amt(c)9

CAPITAL STRUCTURE

	AUTHORISED	ISSUED
Ords no par value	50000000	15897900
Var Rate Red Prefs 1c	20000000	1480800
Var Rate Sec Red Debs 100c	20000000	1480800

FINANCIAL STATISTICS (AT FINANCIAL YEAR END)

(Amts in R'000)	1990 Jun	1989 Jun
Ord S/H Int	2610	2366
Long Trm Loans	285	2830
Iss Ord Share	5053	20210
Total Liab	24844	6650
Current Liab	24559	3820
Total Assets	26721	9016
Intang Assets	733	*
Current Assets	25542	7535
Debtors	1881	2986
Turnover	6082	2660
Oper Profit	1611	962
Interest Paid	530	86
Tax Paid	-16	317
Prf af Int&Tax	1106	563
Prf att Ord Sh	1108	541
Btm Line Earn	979	948
Dividend Paid	455	86
Mkt Prce(c) YE	115	90
Depreciation	126	30

PER SHARE STATISTICS (CENTS)

Net Asst Val	37 15	11 71
Net Earnings	21 90	10 70
Dividends	9 00	0 50
Cash Flow	24 08	2 90

RATIOS AND OTHER INFORMATION

Mrk Cap(R000)	5811	18189
Current Ratio	1 04	1 97
Quik/Acid Tst	1 04	1 97
A/C Rec T/ovr	3 23	0 89
Tot Ass T/ovr	0 23	0 30
Debt/Ass Rat	0 93	0 73
L T L Tot Ass	0 01	0 31
Debt to Eqity	9 50	2 78
Interest Cover	3 04	11 19
Oper Prof Mrg	26 49	36 17
Net Prof Marg%	18 22	20 34
Ret on Assets	6 06	10 71
Ret on Equity%	42 45	22 87
Price/Earnings	5 25	8 41
Divid Cover	2 43	21 40
Divid Yield	7 83	0 56
Earning Yield%	19 04	11 89
NAV % Mrk Pr	32 30	13 01
Effec Tax Rate	0 09	34 20
Def Interval	2 12	5 64
Sus Grth Rate	25 02	19 23

SUBSIDIARY & ASSOCIATED COMPANIES

ARMSTRONG CURRIE & CO (PTY) LTD
ARMSTRONG CURRIE PROPERTIES HOLDINGS (PT
CATTERAL, EDWARDS & GOUDRE' (PTY) LTD
DPF HOUSING LTD
DPF MANAGEMENT SERVICES (PTY) LTD
DPF MENSTONE (PTY) LTD
DPF PROPERTIES (PTY) LTD
DPF PROPFIN HOLDINGS LTD
DPF THE BRIDGE (PTY) LTD
DPF TWIN (PTY) LTD
DPF WESTVILLE (PTY) LTD
HEAVEN INVESTMENTS (PTY) LTD
LARWARD HOLDINGS (PTY) LTD
SILBURNE INVESTMENTS (PTY) LTD
UMHLANGA PROPERTY & LEASING ADMINISTRATI
WESTDALE GARDENS (PTY) LTD

INVESTMENTS

None

DRIEFONTEIN CONSOLIDATED LTD

ABBREVIATION : DRIES

JSE SHORT CODE : DRE

SECTOR : Gold-West Witwatersrand

SHAREHOLDERS

Who Owns Whom's Assessment of the Identity of the Ultimate Controlling Shareholder:
GFSA

SHAREHOLDER	PERCENTAGE 1992	1991
MINU NOM LTD	35 0	34 2
INDO CHINA NOM P/L	6 3	7 1

ANGLO AMERICAN GOLD INV CO LTD	5 1	5 1
CMB NOM P/L	4 7	---
FIRST NAT NOM P/L GATR DEPOT	4 4	4 3
STD BANK NOM TVL P/L	4 0	3 5
SA MUTUAL	3 6	3 7
OVERSEAS NOM CO INC	3 1	3 1
PETARD NOM LTD	3 0	3 0
TAURUS NOM LTD	2 8	2 8
NAT CITY NOM LTD	1 6	1 5
FERMAIN NOM LTD	1 4	1 4
FIRST NAT NOM P/L	1 2	1 2
FIRST CORP NOM P/L	1 1	1 4
SANLAM	-	4 3
TOTAL	77 4	76 4

DIRECTORS :
FENTON CT (Chairman),FULLERGOOD MR ,GNODDE AMD HEWITT L ,HOPWOOD JG ,JANISCH PR ,MUNRO AH PLUMBRIDGE RA ,SUNTER CL ,TAGG MJ ,VAN ROOYEN BR WRIGHT AJ

REGISTRATION NUMBER : 68/04880/06

REGISTERED OFFICE
75 Fox Street, Johannesburg
2001
TEL 011-639 9111
FAX 011-639 2101

TRANSFER SECRETARY
Gold Fields of SA Ltd
P O Box 1167, Johannesburg
2000
TEL 011-639 9111

COMPANY SECRETARY
Gold Fields of SA Ltd

NATURE OF BUSINESS
The company carries on gold mining operations at East Driefontein & West Driefontein, and owns mineral rights in the Oberholzer & Potchefstroom districts

BANKERS :
Standard Bank of SA Ltd

AUDITORS :
Ernst & Young

FAMILIAR BRAND NAMES
N/A

CONTRIBUTION BY ACTIVITY
N/A

YEAR END : June

DIVIDEND : Ords 50c

Interim No 33	(Ldr)29/12/89	(Pay)07/02/90	Amt(c)65
Final No 34	(Ldr)29/06/90	(Pay)08/08/90	Amt(c)80
Interim No 35	(Ldr)28/12/90	(Pay)06/02/91	Amt(c)60
Final No 36	(Ldr)28/06/91	(Pay)07/08/91	Amt(c)95
Interim No 37	(Ldr)27/12/91	(Pay)05/02/92	Amt(c)65
Final No 38	(Ldr)26/06/92	(Pay)05/08/92	Amt(c)100

NUMBER OF EMPLOYEES : 29338

CAPITAL STRUCTURE

	AUTHORISED	ISSUED
Ords 50c	220000000	204000000

FINANCIAL STATISTICS (AT FINANCIAL YEAR END)

(Amts in R'000)	1992 Jun	1991 Jun	1990 Jun	1989 Jun	1988 Jun
Ord S/H Int	2409450	2202593	2012980	1816551	1627142
Iss Ord Share	204000	204000	204000	204000	204000
Total Liab	409485	540165	482760	680269	750502
Current Liab	409485	540165	482760	680269	750502
Total Assets	2818935	2742758	2495740	2496820	2377644
Current Assets	393263	512654	432062	830285	922442
Debtors	46460	35043	32403	26020	15697
Inventory	45823	52346	54846	58502	56695
Turnover	1861122	1774561	1695474	1895726	1997313
Oper Profit	851001	829337	824877	1263396	1431374
Tax Paid	387303	403674	403143	664876	819396
Prf af Int&Tax	550995	502454	490657	598520	611978
Prf att Ord Sh	550995	502454	490657	598520	611978
Btm Line Earn	550995	502454	490657	598520	611978
Dividend Paid	336600	316200	295800	408000	408000
Mkt Prce(c) YE	4125	4150	4400	4200	3400

PER SHARE STATISTICS (CENTS)

Net Asst Val	1181 10	1079 70	986 75	890 47	797 62
Net Earnings	270 00	261 00	143 00	200 00	201 00
Dividends	165 00	155 00	145 00	200 00	200 00
Cash Flow	270 10	246 30	240 52	293 39	299 99

RATIOS AND OTHER INFORMATION

Mrk Cap(R000)	8415000	8466000	8976000	8568000	6936000
Current Ratio	0 96	0 95	0 89	1 22	1 23
Quik/Acid Tst	0 85	0 85	0 78	1 13	1 15
A/C Rec T/ovr	40 06	50 64	52 32	72 86	127 24
Tot Ass T/ovr	0 66	0 65	0 68	0 76	0 84
Debt/Ass Rat	0 15	0 20	0 19	0 27	0 32
Debt to Eqity	0 17	0 25	0 24	0 37	0 46
Oper Prof Mrg	45 73	46 73	48 65	66 64	71 66
Net Prof Marg%	29 61	28 31	28 94	31 57	30 64
Ret on Assets	33 29	33 04	35 81	50 60	60 20
Ret on Equity%	22 87	22 81	24 37	32 95	37 61
Price/Earnings	15 28	15 90	30 77	21 00	16 92
Divid Cover	1 64	1 68	0 99	1 00	1 01
Divid Yield	4 00	3 73	3 30	4 76	5 88
Earning Yield%	6 55	6 29	3 25	4 76	5 91
NAV % Mrk Pr	28 63	26 02	22 43	21 20	23 46
Effec Tax Rate	42 38	45 74	37 42	43 31	47 07
Sus Grth Rate	8 90	8 46	9 68	10 49	12 54

SUBSIDIARY & ASSOCIATED COMPANIES

ASTEROID LTD (50%)
GFSA HOLDINGS LTD (ASTEROID P/L HOLDS 40 (20%)
WEST DRIEFONTEIN GOLD MINING CO LTD

INVESTMENTS

None

DUIKER EXPLORATION LTD

ABBREVIATION : DUIKERS

JSE SHORT CODE : DUK

SECTOR : Mining Financial-Mining Holding

SHAREHOLDERS

Who Owns Whom's Assessment of the Identity of the Ultimate Controlling Shareholder: LONRHO PLC

SHAREHOLDER	PERCENTAGE 1992	1991
WPH INV LTD	51 6	51 6
TWEEFONTEIN UNITED COLLIERIES LTD	22 2	22 2
CORONATION SYNDICATE LTD	3 9	3 9
EIGHTY ONE MAIN STREET NOM LTD	3 9	4 3
STD BANK NOM TVL P/L	2 8	3 8
LONRHO GROUP PENS FUND	2 2	2 2
DUIKER EXPL LTD SHR INC SCHEME TRUST	1 7	1 7
MANN E/L MAX	1 6	1 6
TOTAL	89 9	91 3

DIRECTORS :
DAVIES CJ (Technical Director)
DE VILLIERS JTM DR,DU PREEZ RI ,HARRIS DC
HOSSY IM ,LEE RA ,NEL MM ,REEVES DC ,ROUX W
WAGNER RJ ,WILKINSON KP
WILKINSON TA (Chairman & Managing Dir

REGISTRATION NUMBER : 05/22288/06

REGISTERED OFFICE
1st Floor, 19 Girton Road
Parktown
2193
TEL 011-642 7691
FAX 011-642 9717

TRANSFER SECRETARY
Mercantile Registrars Ltd
P O Box 1053, Johannesburg
2000
TEL 011-333 8181

COMPANY SECRETARY
Lonrho Management Services (Pty) Ltd

NATURE OF BUSINESS
The company operates bituminous and anthracite collieries and a gold mine and has a 36% holding in Eastern Gold Holdings Ltd which has an effective 85% interest in Erfdeel, a section of Free State Consolidated Gold Mines Ltd (Freegold) it also has a 25,8% interest in a venture with Freegold and Anglo American Corporation of SA Ltd for the possible exploitation of an area contiguous to Freegolds Northern Division The company retains asbestos interest in the NW Cape

BANKERS :
First National Bank of SA Ltd

AUDITORS :
KPMG Aiken & Peat

FAMILIAR BRAND NAMES
N/A

CONTRIBUTION BY ACTIVITY
N/A

YEAR END : September

DIVIDEND :Ords 35c

Interim No 41	(Ldr)30/03/90	(Pay)25/04/90	Amt(c)15
Final No 42	(Ldr)28/09/90	(Pay)24/10/90	Amt(c)15
Interim No 43	(Ldr)28/03/91	(Pay)24/04/91	Amt(c)15
Final No 44	(Ldr)27/09/91	(Pay)23/10/91	Amt(c)20
Interim No 45	(Ldr)27/03/92	(Pay)23/04/92	Amt(c)18
Final No 46	(Ldr)25/09/92	(Pay)21/10/92	Amt(c)32

NUMBER OF EMPLOYEES : 2770

CAPITAL STRUCTURE

	AUTHORISED	ISSUED
Ords 35c	17000000	14390086

FINANCIAL STATISTICS (AT FINANCIAL YEAR END)

(Amts in R'000)	1991 Sep	1990 Sep	1989 Sep	1988 Sep	1987
Ord S/H Int	145373	134694	128026	113702	104034
Long Trm Loans	32315	34223	45009	19303	67948
Iss Ord Share	14390	14390	14390	14390	14155
Total Liab	102210	103127	118055	77161	114850
Current Liab	69895	68904	73046	57858	46902
Total Assets	247583	237821	246081	190863	212625
Current Assets	85802	75237	75957	46703	40643
Debtors	62695	53425	60114	15723	-
Inventory	14165	19686	13717	28854	40643
Turnover	161460	140619	138496	97652	88807
Oper Profit	29021	22960	37031	8374	4644
Interest Paid	3295	8839	7139	-	1212
Tax Paid	15461	7098	12657	794	4769
Prf af Int&Tax	15715	10985	17922	7580	4335
Prf att Ord Sh	15715	10985	17922	9633	4335
Btm Line Earn	15715	10985	17922	9633	4335
Dividend Paid	5036	4317	3598	2159	4246
Mkt Prce(c) YE	645	790	950	1155	3050
Depreciation	4821	4800	4719	5159	-

PER SHARE STATISTICS (CENTS)

Net Asst Val	1010 24	936 03	889 69	790 15	734 96
Net Earnings	109 20	76 30	124 50	53 30	-
Dividends	35 00	30 00	25 00	15 00	-
Cash Flow	146 67	102 70	185 59	62 75	30 63

RATIOS AND OTHER INFORMATION

Mrk Cap(R000)	92816	113681	136705	166205	431728
Current Ratio	1 23	1 09	1 04	0 81	0 87
Quik/Acid Tst	1 02	0 81	0 85	0 31	-
A/C Rec T/ovr	2 58	2 63	2 30	6 21	-
Tot Ass T/ovr	0 65	0 59	0 56	0 51	0 42
Debt/Ass Rat	0 33	0 33	0 38	0 32	0 54
L T L Tot Ass	0 04	0 04	0 09	0 02	0 32
Debt to Eqity	0 56	0 59	0 74	0 54	1 10
Interest Cover	8 90	2 60	5 19	-	8 51
Oper Prof Mrg	17 97	16 33	26 74	8 58	5 23
Net Prof Marg%	9 73	7 81	12 94	9 86	4 88
Ret on Assets	13 92	11 32	15 33	5 46	4 85
Ret on Equity%	10 81	8 16	14 00	8 47	4 17
Price/Earnings	5 91	10 35	7 63	21 67	-
Divid Cover	3 12	2 54	4 98	3 55	-
Divid Yield	5 43	3 80	2 63	1 30	-
Earning Yield%	16 93	9 66	13 11	4 61	-
NAV % Mrk Pr	156 63	118 48	93 65	68 41	24 10
Effec Tax Rate	52 25	44 82	29 40	47 58	138 96
Def Interval	0 51	1 83	1 72	3 18	15 67
Sus Grth Rate	7 35	4 95	11 19	6 57	0 09

SUBSIDIARY & ASSOCIATED COMPANIES

BOSVELD MINES (PTY) LTD
EASTERN GOLD HOLDINGS LTD (36%)
EMMARENTIA ASBESTOS (PTY) LTD
RAND COLLIERIES & FUEL LTD
WANDRAG ASBESTOS (PTY) LTD

INVESTMENTS

DURBAN COAL TERMINAL CO LTD (131574 SH)
NATAL COAL PROSPECTING & MINING CO (PTY) (500SH)
NNAB PROMOTIONS (PTY) LTD (25SH)
RHO-GRIQUA MINING (PTY) LTD (400SH)
RICHARDS BAY COAL TERMINAL CO LTD (3,118%)
SOUTH MOLOPO EXPLORATION CO (PTY) LTD (15833SH)

DUNLOP ZIMBABWE LTD

ABBREVIATION : DUN ZIM

SECTOR : Zimbabwe Stock Exchange

SHAREHOLDERS

Who Owns Whom's Assessment of the Identity of the Ultimate Controlling Shareholder: DUNLOP HOLDINGS

DIRECTORS :
ANDREWS JD ,BUYSSE P ,DAVIDSON P ,GONDO JBA
JOHNSTON JBA ,LEWIS DJ (Chairman),NDLOVU NK
NGANGIRA AB ,NYASHANU HG
SELLWOOD DJ (Managing Director

REGISTERED OFFICE
Dunlop/Plumtree Roads, Bulawayo
Zimbabwe

TEL: 725751
FAX: 725256

TRANSFER SECRETARY
KPMG Peat Marwick
P O Box 702, Harare
Zimbabwe

TEL: 09263 962831

COMPANY SECRETARY
J D Andrews

BANKERS :
Barclays Bank of Zimbabwe Ltd
Merchant Bank of Central Africa
Standard Chartered Bank Zimbabwe Ltd

AUDITORS :
Deloitte & Touche

FAMILIAR BRAND NAMES
N/A

CONTRIBUTION BY ACTIVITY
N/A

YEAR END : December

DIVIDEND : Ords Z$0,50

Dividend	(Ldr)06/04/92	(Pay)05/04/92	Amt(c)20 7
Dividend	(Ldr)01/09/92	(Pay)02/10/92	Amt(c)11.7

CAPITAL STRUCTURE

	AUTHORISED	ISSUED
Ords Z$0,50	39999976	23999976
"A" Ords Z$0,50	24	24

FINANCIAL STATISTICS (AT FINANCIAL YEAR END)

(Amts in Z$)	1991 Dec	1990 Dec
Ord S/H Int	94567	82995
Iss Ord Share	24000	24000
Total Liab	69633	41642
Current Liab	69633	41642
Total Assets	161884	121934
Intang Assets	2316	2703
Current Assets	101859	69771
Debtors	48333	20419
Inventory	52709	39858
Turnover	215756	154765
Oper Profit	29522	22601
Interest Paid	781	322
Tax Paid	13675	7509
Prf af Int&Tax	15728	15317
Prf att Ord Sh	18460	17158
Btm Line Earn	18460	17158
Dividend Paid	6888	5256
Depreciation	3275	3310

PER SHARE STATISTICS (CENTS)

Net Asst Val	384.38	334.55
Net Earnings	76.90	71.50
Dividends	28.70	21.90
Cash Flow	79.18	77.61

RATIOS AND OTHER INFORMATION

Current Ratio	1.46	1.68
Quik/Acid Tst	0.71	0.72
A/C Rec T/ovr	4.46	7.58
Tot Ass T/ovr	1.33	1.27
Debt/Ass Rat	0.43	0.34
Debt to Eqity	0.74	0.50
Interest Cover	37.85	70.53
Oper Prof Mrg	13.68	14.60
Net Prof Marg%	8.56	11.09
Ret on Assets	20.33	20 49
Ret on Equity%	19.52	20 67
Divid Cover	2.68	3 26
Effec Tax Rate	46.77	33.04
Sus Grth Rate	12.24	14.34

SUBSIDIARY & ASSOCIATED COMPANIES

COBRA TYRES (PVT) LTD (25%)
DANUM PROPERTIES (PVT) LTD
DATABASE (PVT) LTD (33%)
FASHION INDUSTRIAL HOLDINGS (PVT) LTD (34%)
FLUID SEALS (PVT) LTD
INDIA TYRES ZIMBABWE (PVT) LTD
WALLABY INVESTMENTS (PVT) LTD

INVESTMENTS

GENERAL BELTINGS (PVT) LTD (ZIMBABWE) (18%)
UNITED TYRE SERVICES (PVT) LTD (10%)

DURBAN ROODEPOORT DEEP LTD

ABBREVIATION : DBN-DEEP

JSE SHORT CODE : DUR

SECTOR : Gold-Rand & others

SHAREHOLDERS

Who Owns Whom's Assessment of the Identity of the Ultimate Controlling Shareholder:
SA MUTUAL VIA BARLOWS

SHAREHOLDER	PERCENTAGE 1992	1991
INDO-CHINA NOM P/L	26.2	24.7
UK BRANCH REGISTER CONTROL ACCOUNT	17.9	17.1
RAND MINES LTD	15.0	15.0
FIRST NAT NOM P/L	13.8	12.1
NAT CITY NOM LTD	5.0	5.0
STD BANK NOM TVL P/L	4.6	4.4
FIRST NAT NOM P/L GATR DEPOT	3.1	2.9
RINRIC NOM P/L	1.0	---
LOWENCO NOM P/L	---	1.5
ZINGEL H W	---	2.2
TOTAL	86.6	84.8

DIRECTORS :
BRADSHAW GL ,CROCKER EB ,EICK KFW ,HEYNS MR MURTON VM ,STEVENS IG ,TURNER JPS (Chairman) VOS P (Managing Director),WATERSON CH

REGISTRATION NUMBER : 01/00926/06

REGISTERED OFFICE
15th Floor, The Corner House
63 Fox Street, Johannesburg
2001
TEL: 011-491 2911
FAX: 011-838 1430

TRANSFER SECRETARY
Rand Registrars Ltd
P O Box 82549, Southdale
2135
TEL: 011-835 1016

COMPANY SECRETARY
Rand Mines (Mining & Services) Ltd

NATURE OF BUSINESS
Operation of a gold mine at Roodepoort, Tvl.

BANKERS :
Standard Bank of SA Ltd

AUDITORS :
Deloitte Pim Goldby

FAMILIAR BRAND NAMES
N/A

CONTRIBUTION BY ACTIVITY
N/A

YEAR END : December

DIVIDEND :15/01/92 and 15/07/91

NUMBER OF EMPLOYEES : 4103

CAPITAL STRUCTURE

	AUTHORISED	ISSUED
Ords R1	2400000	2325000

FINANCIAL STATISTICS (AT FINANCIAL YEAR END)

(Amts in R'000)	1991 Dec	1990 Dec	1989 Dec	1988	1987
Ord S/H Int	195890	180727	150779	164862	171088
Long Trm Loans	80	365	-	29762	29279
Iss Ord Share	2325	2325	2325	2325	2325
Total Liab	27766	18364	43517	59524	58558
Current Liab	27686	17999	43517	29762	29279
Total Assets	223656	199091	194296	207551	231485
Current Assets	29092	9048	12448	12927	31118
Debtors	4454	3439	3803	-	-
Inventory	-	-	6989	12927	31118
Turnover	157784	132008	164922	225675	211309
Oper Profit	14142	11778	-17278	-5765	-1284
Interest Paid	98	1331	2610	71	-
Tax Paid	1149	-	-	388	-
Prf af Int&Tax	15163	11220	-19394	-6226	12245
Prf att Ord Sh	15163	11220	-19394	-6226	-15958
Btm Line Earn	15163	29948	-18296	-6226	-15958
Mkt Prce(c) YE	1915	1700	3300	1175	2750

PER SHARE STATISTICS (CENTS)

Net Asst Val	8425.38	7773.20	6485.12	7090.84	7358.62
Net Earnings	60.00	-11.00	-856.00	-	-
Cash Flow	652.17	482.58	-834.15	-267.78	526.67

RATIOS AND OTHER INFORMATION

Mrk Cap(R000)	44524	39525	76725	27319	63938
Current Ratio	1.05	0.50	0.29	0.43	1.06
Quik/Acid Tst	1.05	0.50	0.13	-	-
A/C Rec T/ovr	35.43	38.39	43.37	-	-
Tot Ass T/ovr	0.71	0.66	0.85	1.09	0.91
Debt/Ass Rat	0.12	0.09	0.22	0.29	0.25
L T L Tot Ass	0.00	0.00	-	0.14	0.13
Debt to Eqity	0.14	0.10	0.29	0.36	0.34
Interest Cover	144.86	9.00	-6.61	-81.23	-
Oper Prof Mrg	8.96	8.92	-10.48	-2.55	-0.61
Net Prof Marg%	9.61	8.50	-11.76	-2.76	-7.55
Ret on Assets	7.34	6.30	-8.64	-2.78	5.29
Ret on Equity%	7.74	6.21	-12.86	-3.78	-9.33
Price/Earnings	31.92	-154.55	-3.86	-	-
Earning Yield%	3.13	-0.65	-25.94	-	-
NAV % Mrk Pr	439.97	457.25	196.52	603.48	267.59
Effec Tax Rate	7.07	-	-	-6.65	-
Def Interval	0.02	0.05	-1.38	-4.78	2.39
Sus Grth Rate	7.74	6.21	-12.86	-3.78	-9.33

SUBSIDIARY & ASSOCIATED COMPANIES

None

INVESTMENTS

None

EAST DAGGAFONTEIN MINES LTD

ABBREVIATION : E-DAGGA

JSE SHORT CODE : EDG

SECTOR : Mining Financial-Mining Holding

SHAREHOLDERS

Who Owns Whom's Assessment of the Identity of the Ultimate Controlling Shareholder: INSTITUTIONS

SHAREHOLDER	PERCENTAGE 1992	1991
STD BANK NOM TVL P/L	18.9	13.8
INDO-CHINA NOM P/L	14.2	---
SA MUTUAL	13.3	18.9
CMB NOM P/L	10.4	---
FIRST NAT NOM P/L	5.1	9.3
MINU NOM LTD	5.0	---
MOMENTUM LIFE ASSURE LTD	3.8	5.1
FIRST NAT NOM P/L GATR DEPOT	3.3	1.7
UK CONTROL ACCOUNT	2.8	2.9
EIGHTY ONE MAIN STREET NOM LTD	2.3	3.1
PREMIER GROUP PENS FUND	2.3	1.7
DEPOSITARY NOM INC	1.4	1.4
SAGE LIFE LTD	1.4	---
BANK OF NEW YORK NOM LTD	1.2	1.2
BARCLAYS NAT NOM P/L GATR DEPOT	1.1	---
INDO-CHINA NOM SA P/L	---	7.2
BARCLAYS NAT NOM P/L	---	2.6
SANDTON NOM LTD	---	3.0
SANLAM	---	10.4
GOLD FIELDS PROPERTY CO LTD	---	5.0
TOTAL	86.4	87.1

DIRECTORS :
BIEBER EPH (Chairman),BRIGGS CP ,FERGUSON PRA
SHEAD RB ,VON CHRISTIERSON CI ,WHYTE KC

REGISTRATION NUMBER : 05/04237/06

REGISTERED OFFICE
7th Floor, Marshall Place
66 Marshall Street, Johannesburg
2001
TEL: 011-834 4211
FAX: 011-834 6343

TRANSFER SECRETARY
Mercantile Registrars Ltd
P O Box 1053, Johannesburg
2000
TEL: 011-333 8181

COMPANY SECRETARY
R B Shead

NATURE OF BUSINESS
An investment holding company. Its wholly owned subsidiary, Dumpco, holds the rights to a number of gold & uranium bearing slimes dams on the far East Rand, which are currently being treated by Ergo. The company also holds minor investments in JSE-quoted Lydenburg Exploration & Randex.

BANKERS :
Standard Bank of SA Ltd

AUDITORS :
Coopers Theron Du Toit

FAMILIAR BRAND NAMES
N/A

CONTRIBUTION BY ACTIVITY
N/A

YEAR END : March

DIVIDEND : Ords R1

Final No 79	(Ldr)25/05/90	(Pay)08/06/90	Amt(c)58
Interim No 80	(Ldr)16/11/90	(Pay)07/12/90	Amt(c)55
Final No 81	(Ldr)24/05/91	(Pay)07/06/91	Amt(c)45
Final No 83	(Ldr)29/05/92	(Pay)12/06/92	Amt(c)25
Interim No 82	(Ldr)22/11/91	(Pay)06/12/91	Amt(c)31
Interim No 84	(Ldr)27/11/92	(Pay)11/12/92	Amt(c)25

CAPITAL STRUCTURE

	AUTHORISED	ISSUED
Ords R1	17000000	15123087

FINANCIAL STATISTICS (AT FINANCIAL YEAR END)

(Amts in R'000)	1992 Mar	1991 Mar	1990 Mar	1989 Mar	1988 Mar
Ord S/H Int	61420	64731	43848	46627	42182
Long Trm Loans	-	12686	-	10135	10977
Iss Ord Share	15123	14274	14274	14274	13510
Total Liab	4872	27010	15883	30497	34410
Current Liab	4872	14324	15883	20362	23433
Total Assets	66292	91741	59731	77124	76592
Current Assets	10480	17432	23413	36506	41239
Debtors	3918	5990	9932	10336	11574
Oper Profit	14924	24991	30440	28743	17996
Interest Paid	43	10	279	-	-
Tax Paid	8134	14929	17109	17698	10915
Prf af Int&Tax	8974	14823	16857	15383	7081
Prf att Ord Sh	8974	14823	16857	16226	8784
Btm Line Earn	-7199	35539	20663	16226	8864
Dividend Paid	8469	14656	16844	17130	10538
Mkt Prce(c) YE	900	1225	2350	1950	2050
Depreciation	-	-	-	79	69

PER SHARE STATISTICS (CENTS)

Net Asst Val	406.14	453.49	307.19	326.66	312.23
Net Earnings	61.00	104.00	118.00	116.00	65.00
Dividends	56.00	100.00	118.00	120.00	78.00
Cash Flow	59.34	103.85	118.10	116.84	65.67

RATIOS AND OTHER INFORMATION

Mrk Cap(R000)	136107	174857	335439	278343	276955
Current Ratio	2.15	1.22	1.47	1.79	1.76
Quik/Acid Tst	2.15	1.22	1.47	1.79	1.76
Debt/Ass Rat	0.07	0.29	0.27	0.26	0.31
L T L Tot Ass	-	0.14	-	-	-
Debt to Eqity	0.08	0.42	0.36	0.44	0.56
Interest Cover	357.07	2499.10	109.10	-	-
Ret on Assets	25.87	32.44	57.33	42.89	23.50
Ret on Equity%	14.61	22.90	38.44	34.80	20.82
Price/Earnings	14.75	11.78	19.92	16.81	31.54
Divid Cover	1.09	1.04	1.00	0.97	0.83
Divid Yield	6.22	8.16	5.02	6.15	3.80
Earning Yield%	6.78	8.49	5.02	5.95	3.17
NAV % Mrk Pr	45.13	37.02	13.07	16.75	15.23
Effec Tax Rate	48.77	50.18	50.37	53.50	60.65
Sus Grth Rate	0.82	0.26	0.03	-1.94	-4.16

SUBSIDIARY & ASSOCIATED COMPANIES

DUMPCO LTD
EAST DAGGAFONTEIN HOLDINGS (PTY) LTD
JOHANNESBURG EXPLORATION & MINING CORP.
JOINT VENTURE (PTY) LTD (50%)

INVESTMENTS

CMB NOMINEES (EDMS) BPK (10.43%)
FIRST NATIONAL NOMINEES (PTY) LTD (11.82%)
INDO-CHINA NOMINEES (PTY) LIMITED (6.25%)
MINU NOMINEES LIMITED (5.03%)
MOMENTUM LIFE ASSURERS LTD (5.05%)
SOUTH AFRICAN MUTUAL LIFE ASSURANCE SOCI (17.82%)
STANDARD BANK NOMINEES (TVL) (PTY) LTD (14.26%)

EAST RAND GOLD AND URANIUM CO LTD

ABBREVIATION : ERGO

JSE SHORT CODE : ERG

SECTOR : Gold-Rand & others

SHAREHOLDERS

Who Owns Whom's Assessment of the Identity of the Ultimate Controlling Shareholder: ANGLO AMERICAN

SHAREHOLDER	PERCENTAGE 1992	1991
RESIDENT NOM LTD	11.1	4.7
STD BANK NOM TVL P/L	9.1	3.0
SA MUTUAL	8.2	5.4
INDO-CHINA NOM P/L	6.0	---
ANGLO AMERICAN GOLD INV CO LTD	5.0	10.2
AFRICAN & EUROPEAN INV CO LTD	4.7	5.1
MARJORAM HOLDINGS LTD	4.7	5.1
SA MINES SELECTION LTD	4.7	5.1
THATON LTD	3.7	4.0
ANGLO AMERICAN CORP OF SA LTD	3.2	3.2
FIRST NAT NOM P/L	2.6	1.5
RAND SELECTION CORP LTD	2.4	2.7
SA TOWNSHIPS MINING & FINANCE CORP LTD	2.4	2.7
LODESTONE HLDGS LTD	2.3	2.6
RAND AMERICAN INV P/L	2.3	2.6
RANDSEL INV LTD	2.3	2.6
MINU NOM LTD	2.1	---
CMB NOM P/L	2.0	---
EIGHTY ONE MAIN STREET NOM LTD	1.7	---
ORIOLE INV LTD	1.5	1.7
DEPOSITARY NOM INC	1.4	3.3
LONDON CONTROL ACCOUNT	1.3	5.6
DE BEERS HOLDINGS P/L	1.3	1.4
VOLKSKAS NOM P/L	---	1.7
INDO-CHINA NOM SA P/L	---	3.6
SANLAM	---	2.2
TOTAL	86.0	79.9

DIRECTORS :
EUSTACE PJ ,HENREY MJ
HEWITT L (Managing Director),HOLFORD GM
HOSKING KM (Financial Director),KING MW
MOSTERT PJ ,SCHMID E
SUNTER CL (Chairman & Chief Exec.)
VAN DER COLF SW (Dir Human Resources),WILLIAMS KH

REGISTRATION NUMBER : 71/07001/06

REGISTERED OFFICE
44 Main Street, Johannesburg
2001
TEL: 011-638 9111
FAX: 011-638 5281

TRANSFER SECRETARY
Consolidated Share Registrars Ltd
P O Box 61051, Marshalltown
2107
TEL: 011-492 1620

COMPANY SECRETARY
Anglo American Corp of SA Ltd

NATURE OF BUSINESS
The company treats slimes dams & sand dumps on the Central, East & Far East Rand to recover gold & to produce sulphuric acid.

BANKERS :
First National Bank of SA Ltd

AUDITORS :
KPMG Aiken & Peat

FAMILIAR BRAND NAMES
N/A

CONTRIBUTION BY ACTIVITY
N/A

YEAR END : March

DIVIDEND : Ords 50c

Dividend No 24	(Ldr)02/11/90	(Pay)14/12/90	Amt(c)35
Dividend No 25	(Ldr)18/04/91	(Pay)14/06/91	Amt(c)35
Dividend No 26	(Ldr)08/05/92	(Pay)12/06/92	Amt(c)30
Dividend No 27	(Ldr)08/05/92	(Pay)12/06/92	Amt(c)30
Dividend No 28	(Ldr)13/11/92	(Pay)18/12/92	Amt(c)20

NUMBER OF EMPLOYEES : 1992

CAPITAL STRUCTURE

	AUTHORISED	ISSUED
Ords 50c	60000000	50080515

FINANCIAL STATISTICS (AT FINANCIAL YEAR END)

(Amts in R'000)	1992 Mar	1991 Mar	1990 Mar	1989 Mar	1988 Mar
Ord S/H Int	736849	655459	613678	576847	501970
Long Trm Loans	-	1681	13836	15983	48236
Iss Ord Share	50081	42079	42079	42079	42079
Total Liab	59564	82050	97362	113375	138271
Current Liab	59564	80369	83526	97392	90035
Total Assets	796413	737509	711040	690222	640241
Current Assets	56167	70329	86007	106441	95375
Debtors	26749	23582	21993	29771	20192
Inventory	5671	9859	8161	3939	4601
Turnover	410429	411403	430728	451729	373395
Oper Profit	73424	51523	90609	147534	115613
Interest Paid	316	633	875	2174	6124
Tax Paid	2901	5180	17877	41387	16748
Prf af Int&Tax	76279	55876	83729	103973	92741
Prf att Ord Sh	25085	34557	48067	69074	49639
Btm Line Earn	25085	34557	48067	69074	49639
Dividend Paid	25040	33321	47823	61439	48526
Mkt Prce(c) YE	515	675	1675	1600	1525

PER SHARE STATISTICS (CENTS)

Net Asst Val	1471.31	1557.69	1458.39	1370.87	1192.92
Net Earnings	50.00	73.00	105.00	144.00	118.00
Dividends	50.00	70.00	105.00	135.00	115.00
Cash Flow	152.31	132.79	198.98	247.09	220.40

RATIOS AND OTHER INFORMATION

Mrk Cap(R000)	257917	284033	704823	673264	641705
Current Ratio	0.94	0.88	1.03	1.09	1.06
Quik/Acid Tst	0.85	0.75	0.93	1.05	1.01
A/C Rec T/ovr	15.34	17.45	19.58	15.17	18.49
Tot Ass T/ovr	0.52	0.56	0.61	0.65	0.58
Debt/Ass Rat	0.07	0.11	0.14	0.16	0.22
L T L Tot Ass	-	0.00	0.02	0.02	0.08
Debt to Eqity	0.08	0.13	0.16	0.20	0.28
Interest Cover	235.03	82.83	104.29	67.86	18.88
Oper Prof Mrg	17.89	12.52	21.04	32.66	30.96
Net Prof Marg%	6.11	8.40	11.16	15.29	13.29
Ret on Assets	9.98	8.36	14.41	21.37	18.06
Ret on Equity%	3.40	5.27	7.83	11.97	9.89
Price/Earnings	10.30	9.25	15.95	11.11	12.92
Divid Cover	1.00	1.04	1.00	1.07	1.03
Divid Yield	9.71	10.37	6.27	8.44	7.54
Earning Yield%	9.71	10.81	6.27	9.00	7.74
NAV % Mrk Pr	285.69	230.77	87.07	85.68	78.22
Effec Tax Rate	3.70	8.61	17.71	28.47	15.30
Def Interval	-	0.03	0.06	0.06	0.42
Sus Grth Rate	0.01	0.19	0.04	1.32	0.22

SUBSIDIARY & ASSOCIATED COMPANIES

DAGGA NUMBER ONE (PTY) LTD
DAGGA NUMBER TWO (PTY) LTD
GARBIN HOLDINGS LTD

INVESTMENTS

CACTUS INVESTMENTS (PTY) LTD (RED CUM PR (1306 SH)
GOLDCO LTD (1 SH)
INTER-MINE SERVICES OFS (PTY) LTD (560 SH)
LANSAN INVESTMENT HOLDINGS LTD (509 SH)
NUCLEAR FUELS CORPORATION OF SA (PTY) LT (36543 SH)
THE RAND MUTUAL ASSURANCE CO. LTD (85 SH)

EAST RAND PROPRIETARY MINES LTD

ABBREVIATION : E-R-P-M

JSE SHORT CODE : ERA

SECTOR : Gold-Rand & others

SHAREHOLDERS

Who Owns Whom's Assessment of the Identity of the Ultimate Controlling Shareholder: SIVOCAM (FRANCE) / RAND MINES

SHAREHOLDER	PERCENTAGE 1992	1991
UK BRANCH REGISTER CONTROL ACCOUNT	62.6	63.2
RAND MINES LTD	28.3	28.3
INDO-CHINA NOM P/L	2.6	1.9
AMOSITE NOM LTD	1.2	1.2
STD BANK NOM TVL P/L	1.0	---
TOTAL	95.8	94.5

DIRECTORS :
BRADSHAW RL ,CLEWLOW WAM
EICK KFW (Managing Director),STEVENS IG
TURNER JPS (Chairman),VOS P ,WATERSON CH ,WATT DT

REGISTRATION NUMBER : 01/00773/06

REGISTERED OFFICE
15th Floor, The Corner House
63 Fox Street, Johannesburg
2001
TEL: 011-491 2911
FAX: 011-834 5936

TRANSFER SECRETARY
Rand Registrars Ltd
P O Box 82549, Southdale
2135
TEL: 011-835 1016

COMPANY SECRETARY
Rand Mines (Mining & Services) Ltd

NATURE OF BUSINESS
The company operates a gold mine at Boksburg on the East Witwatersrand.

BANKERS :
First National Bank of SA Ltd

AUDITORS :
Deloitte Pim Goldby

FAMILIAR BRAND NAMES
N/A

CONTRIBUTION BY ACTIVITY
N/A

YEAR END : December

NUMBER OF EMPLOYEES : 5541

CAPITAL STRUCTURE

	AUTHORISED	ISSUED
Ords R1	35000000	16632000
"A" Var Rate Cum Red Prefs 1c	1000000	0
"B" Var Rate Cum Red Prefs 1c	500000	350000

FINANCIAL STATISTICS (AT FINANCIAL YEAR END)

(Amts in R'000)	1991 Dec	1990 Dec	1989 Dec	1988	1987
Ord S/H Int	217394	244541	285501	53667	27632
Long Trm Loans	435034	402006	305848	351671	266257
Iss Ord Share	16632	16632	16632	16632	11088
Total Liab	457941	422666	360947	503342	332514
Current Liab	22907	20660	55099	151671	66257
Total Assets	675335	667207	646448	431209	316444
Current Assets	65871	44217	32015	25871	22555
Debtors	9756	7122	16866	-	-
Inventory	4713	3662	4792	25871	22555
Turnover	227017	181854	250613	296716	260093
Oper Profit	20078	-5913	-37202	-54077	-63933
Interest Paid	52873	37818	17138	7758	3272
Prf af Int&Tax	-27147	-40960	-54200	-61835	-67205

Prf att Ord Sh	-27147	-40960	-54200	-61835	-67205
Btm Line Earn	-27147	-40960	-54200	-61835	-67205
Mkt Prce(c) YE	900	1500	1900	1625	2900

PER SHARE STATISTICS (CENTS)

Net Asst Val	1307 08	1470 30	1716 58	322 67	249 21
Cash Flow	-163 22	-246 27	-325 88	-371 78	-606 11

RATIOS AND OTHER INFORMATION

Mrk Cap(R000)	149688	249480	316008	270270	321552
Current Ratio	2 88	2 14	0 58	0 17	0 34
Quik/Acid Tst	2 67	1 96	0 49	-	-
A/C Rec T/ovr	23 27	25 53	14 86	-	-
Tot Ass T/ovr	0 34	0 27	0 39	0 69	0 82
Debt/Ass Rat	0 68	0 63	0 56	1 17	1 05
L T L Tot Ass	0 64	0 60	0 47	0 82	0 84
Debt to Eqity	2 11	1 73	1 26	9 38	12 03
Interest Cover	0 38	-0 15	-2 17	-6 97	-19 54
Oper Prof Mrg	8 84	-3 25	-14 84	-18 23	-24 58
Net Prof Marg%	-11 96	-22 52	-21 63	-20 84	-25 84
Ret on Assets	3 81	-0 47	-5 73	-12 54	-20 20
Ret on Equity%	-12 49	-16 75	-18 98	-115 22	-243 21
NAV % Mrk Pr	145 23	98 02	90 35	19 86	8 59
Def Interval	-15 29	-9 47	-5 78	-5 69	-3 96
Sus Grth Rate	-12 49	-16 75	-18 98	-115 22	-243 21

SUBSIDIARY & ASSOCIATED COMPANIES

None

INVESTMENTS

None

EASTERN TRANSVAAL CONSOLIDATED MINES LTD

ABBREVIATION : E-T-CONS

JSE SHORT CODE : ETC

SECTOR : Gold-Rand & others

SHAREHOLDERS

Who Owns Whom's Assessment of the Identity of the Ultimate Controlling Shareholder: ANGLOVAAL

SHAREHOLDER	PERCENTAGE 1992	1991
FOX STREET NOM P/L	51 6	---
INDO-CHINA NOM P/L	6 7	---
FIRST NAT NOM P/L	5 9	---
STD BANK NOM TVL P/L	2 0	--
VOLKSKAS INTERGROEI INV P/L	1 9	---
CMB NOM P/L	1 8	---
STOCKSHARE NOM P/L	1 6	---
MENBLACK NOM P/L	1 2	---
TOTAL	72 7	---

DIRECTORS :
GELDENHUYS JJ ,HERSOV BE ,MENELL CS
ROBBERTZE GJ ,SPINDLER TV ,VAN NIEKERK JE
WILSON RAD (Chairman

REGISTRATION NUMBER : 01/08442/06

REGISTERED OFFICE
Anglovaal House, 56 Main Street
Johannesburg
2001
TEL 011-634 9111
FAX 011-634 0038

TRANSFER SECRETARY
Anglovaal Ltd
P O Box 62379, Marshalltown
2107
TEL 011-634 9111

COMPANY SECRETARY
Anglovaal Ltd

NATURE OF BUSINESS
As its main business the company conducts gold mining operations in the Barberton district of the Transvaal It also owns farming property in Barberton as well as operating the New Consort, Agnes and Sheba mines

BANKERS :
Standard Bank of SA Ltd

AUDITORS :
Ernst & Young

FAMILIAR BRAND NAMES
N/A

CONTRIBUTION BY ACTIVITY
N/A

YEAR END : June

DIVIDEND : Ords 2,5c

Interim No 81	(Ldr)21/12/90	(Pay)25/01/91	Amt(c)7
Final No 82	(Ldr)21/06/91	(Pay)26/07/91	Amt(c)7
Final No 84	(Ldr)19/06/92	(Pay)24/07/92	Amt(c)7
Interim No 83	(Ldr)20/12/91	(Pay)24/01/92	Amt(c)7
Interim No 85	(Ldr)11/12/92	(Pay)15/01/93	Amt(c)5

NUMBER OF EMPLOYEES : 2000

CAPITAL STRUCTURE

	AUTHORISED	ISSUED
Ords 2,5c	120000000	86333560

FINANCIAL STATISTICS (AT FINANCIAL YEAR END)

(Amts in R 000)	1992 Jun	1991 Jun	1990 Jun	1989 Jun	1988 Jun
Ord S/H Int	225588	218594	212131	194621	164807
Iss Ord Share	86334	86334	4317	4317	4317
Total Liab	21108	22088	28514	30382	26548
Current Liab	21108	22088	28514	30382	26548
Total Assets	246696	240682	240645	225003	191355
Current Assets	30943	31673	36430	40692	36617
Debtors	3873	2755	1924	3170	999
Inventory	11489	11018	13160	8843	9502
Turnover	116846	107624	117944	116182	108895
Oper Profit	24555	24182	52122	65370	64274
Tax Paid	7871	8766	20066	17644	14752
Prf af Int&Tax	19081	18550	35851	47726	49522

Prf att Ord Sh	19081	18550	35851	47726	49522
Btm Line Earn	19081	18550	35851	47726	49522
Dividend Paid	12087	12087	17266	17914	13382
Mkt Prce(c) YE	235	415	10500	7100	6000

PER SHARE STATISTICS (CENTS)

Net Asst Val	261 30	253 20	4913 85	4508 25	3817 63
Net Earnings	14 30	15 90	19 90	421 00	321 00
Dividends	14 00	14 00	20 00	415 00	310 00
Cash Flow	22 10	21 49	830 46	1105 54	1147 14

RATIOS AND OTHER INFORMATION

Mrk Cap(R000)	202885	358286	453285	306507	259020
Current Ratio	1 47	1 43	1 28	1 34	1 38
Quik/Acid Tst	0 92	0 94	0 82	1 05	1 02
A/C Rec T/ovr	30 17	39 06	61 30	36 65	109 00
Tot Ass T/ovr	0 47	0 45	0 49	0 52	0 57
Debt/Ass Rat	0 09	0 09	0 12	0 14	0 14
Debt to Eqity	0 09	0 10	0 13	0 16	0 16
Oper Prof Mrg	21 01	22 47	44 19	56 27	59 02
Net Prof Marg%	16 33	17 24	30 40	41 08	45 48
Ret on Assets	10 93	11 35	23 24	29 05	33 59
Ret on Equity%	8 46	8 49	16 90	24 52	30 05
Price/Earnings	16 43	26 10	527 64	16 86	18 69
Divid Cover	1 02	1 14	0 99	1 01	1 04
Divid Yield	5 96	3 37	0 19	5 85	5 17
Earning Yield%	6 09	3 83	0 19	5 93	5 35
NAV % Mrk Pr	111 19	61 01	46 80	63 50	63 63
Effec Tax Rate	29 20	32 09	35 89	26 99	22 95
Sus Grth Rate	3 10	2 96	8 76	15 32	21 93

SUBSIDIARY & ASSOCIATED COMPANIES

None

INVESTMENTS

None

EDDIES STORES LTD

ABBREVIATION EDDIES

JSE SHORT CODE . EIS

SECTOR Industrial Retailers & Wholesalers

SHAREHOLDERS

Who Owns Whom's Assessment of the Identity of the Ultimate Controlling Shareholder
FSI VIA VEKTRA

SHAREHOLDER	PERCENTAGE 1992	1991
EDSPARE INV HOLDINGS LTD	65 2	65 2
GOUDSTAD NOM P/L	24 9	26 1
MENBLACK NOM P/L	4 9	2 4
EDDIE KARP MOTORS CC		1 6
TOTAL	95 0	95 3

DIRECTORS :
BROZIN LZ ,BROZIN MS ,COCKCROFT KS ,COHEN S
SLOTOW L (Managing Director

REGISTRATION NUMBER : 87/01319/06

REGISTERED OFFICE
10 Prinsloo Street, Pretoria
0002
TEL 012 326 5376
FAX 012-21 5875

TRANSFER SECRETARY
Mercantile Registrars Ltd
P O Box 1053, Johannesburg
2000
TEL 011-333 8181

COMPANY SECRETARY
GJ Schoeman

NATURE OF BUSINESS
Eddies retails motor spares & accessories

BANKERS :
Trust Bank of Africa Ltd

AUDITORS :
Kessel Feinstein

FAMILIAR BRAND NAMES
N/A

CONTRIBUTION BY ACTIVITY
N/A

YEAR END February

DIVIDEND Ords 1c
Interim (Ldr)27/11/92 (Pay)09/12/92 Amt(c)1 5

NUMBER OF EMPLOYEES 82

CAPITAL STRUCTURE

	AUTHORISED	ISSUED
Ords 1c	40000000	27858667

FINANCIAL STATISTICS (AT FINANCIAL YEAR END)

(Amts In R 000)	1992 Feb	1991 Feb	1990 Jun	1989 Jun	1988 Jun
Ord S/H Int	3807	1589	830	25094	19790
Long Trm Loans	81	120	29	283	1158
Iss Ord Share	27859	27859	27859	25019	22300
Total Liab	2729	3296	5538	10761	9976
Current Liab	2648	3176	5509	10478	8818
Total Assets	6536	4885	6368	16202	13314
Intang Assets	*	*	*	19653	16452
Current Assets	6034	4158	5677	13612	10721
Debtors	299	279	1040	944	773
Inventory	4749	3874	3996	12644	9027
Turnover	18851	12078	30657	37922	
Oper Profit	2376	1695	3607	5555	4875
Interest Paid	19	327	1196	840	94
Tax Paid				281	488
Prf af Int&Tax	2439	1425	2484	4434	4293
Prf att Ord Sh	2439	1425	2484	4434	4293
Btm Line Earn	2217	760	24265	4141	4143
Dividend Paid				1126	1895
Mkt Prce(c) YE	25	20	30	75	95
Depreciation	287	175	412	326	215

PER SHARE STATISTICS (CENTS)

Net Asst Val	13.67	5.70	2.98	21.75	14.97
Net Earnings	8.80	5.10	8.90	15.90	17.50
Dividends	-	-	-	4.50	8.50
Cash Flow	9.78	8.61	10.40	17.09	16.74

RATIOS AND OTHER INFORMATION

Mrk Cap(R000)	6965	5572	8358	18764	21185
Current Ratio	2.28	1.31	1.03	1.30	1.22
Quik/Acid Tst	0.49	0.09	0.31	0.09	0.19
A/C Rec T/ovr	63.05	64.94	29.48	40.17	-
Tot Ass T/ovr	2.88	3.71	4.81	2.34	-
Debt/Ass Rat	0.42	0.67	0.87	0.66	0.75
L T L Tot Ass	0.01	0.02	0.00	0.02	0.09
Debt to Eqity	0.72	2.07	6.67	0.43	0.50
Interest Cover	125.05	5.18	3.02	6.61	51.86
Oper Prof Mrg	12.60	14.03	11.77	14.65	-
Net Prof Marg%	12.94	11.80	8.10	11.69	-
Ret on Assets	37.61	53.80	57.79	34.29	36.62
Ret on Equity%	64.07	134.52	299.28	17.67	21.69
Price/Earnings	2.84	3.92	3.37	4.72	5.43
Divid Cover	-	-	-	3.53	2.06
Divid Yield	-	-	-	6.00	8.95
Earning Yield%	35.20	25.50	29.67	21.20	18.42
NAV % Mrk Pr	54.66	28.52	9.93	29.00	15.76
Effec Tax Rate	-	-	-	5.96	10.21
Def Interval	0.05	0.77	1.24	1.57	1.26
Sus Grth Rate	64.07	89.68	299.28	13.18	12.12

SUBSIDIARY & ASSOCIATED COMPANIES

NATIONWIDE MOTORS SPARES (PTY) LTD

INVESTMENTS

None

EDGARS STORES LTD

ABBREVIATION : EDGARS

JSE SHORT CODE : EDS

SECTOR : Industrial-Retailers & Wholesalers

SHAREHOLDERS

Who Owns Whom's Assessment of the Identity of the Ultimate Controlling Shareholder:
ANGLO AMERICAN VIA PREMIER VIA SA BREWS

SHAREHOLDER	PERCENTAGE 1992	1991
EDGARS CONSOLIDATED INV LTD	51.3	51.3
SA BREWERIES LTD	11.2	11.2
LIBERTY LIFE ASSOC OF AFRICA LTD	8.1	8.1
STD BANK NOM TVL P/L	6.4	6.3
SPIKE INV NOM P/L	2.4	2.4
ANGLO AMERICAN CORP PENS FUND	2.2	2.2
CMB NOM P/L	1.9	---
DE BEERS PENS FUND	1.9	1.9
FIRST NAT NOM P/L	1.7	1.7
COMMERCIAL UNION LIFE ASSURE CO SA LTD	1.4	---
COMMERCIAL UNION ASSURE CO SA LTD	---	1.6
SANLAM	---	1.7
TOTAL	88.3	88.4

DIRECTORS :
AARON AJ ,BECK DE LA H WF
BEETON GH (Chief Executive & M.D.),BELLIS J
BOWER MR (Financial Director),COUSINS DN
ETHERIDGE DW ,HAUPT FJ ,KAHN JM (Chairman)
MACFARLANE WS

REGISTRATION NUMBER : 05/22751/06

REGISTERED OFFICE
Edgardale, Press Avenue, Crown Mines
Johannesburg
2025
TEL: 011-495 6000
FAX: 011-837 5019

TRANSFER SECRETARY
Central Registrars Ltd
P O Box 4844, Johannesburg
2000
TEL: 011-331 0051

COMPANY SECRETARY
I K Ellis

NATURE OF BUSINESS
The groups business is the retailing of clothing, footwear, accessories & home textiles through its 385 stores in SA. In its four factories the group manufactures a range of family clothing for sale through its own outlets and to the outside market.

BANKERS :
First National Bank of SA Ltd

AUDITORS :
Ernst & Young

FAMILIAR BRAND NAMES
CELIO,CHARTER CLUB,DECISIONS MAIL ORDER
GOOSE BAY,MULTIPLES,PENNY C
PRIVATE COLLECTION,SIGNATURE E,STREETGEAR
VICTORIA'S SECRET

CONTRIBUTION BY ACTIVITY
Edgars (% Sales) (70.0%)
Sales House/Express (17.1%)
Jet (10.9%)
Other (2.0%)

YEAR END : March

DIVIDEND : Ords 10c

Final No 87	(Ldr)25/05/90	(Pay)02/07/90	Amt(c)66
Interim No 88	(Ldr)23/11/90	(Pay)31/12/90	Amt(c)33
Final No 89	(Ldr)24/05/91	(Pay)01/07/91	Amt(c)80
Interim No 90	(Ldr)22/11/91	(Pay)31/12/91	Amt(c)36
Final No 91	(Ldr)22/05/92	(Pay)01/07/92	Amt(c)83
Interim No 92	(Ldr)20/11/92	(Pay)31/12/92	Amt(c)38

NUMBER OF EMPLOYEES : 13644

CAPITAL STRUCTURE

	AUTHORISED	ISSUED
6% Prefs R2	150000	150000
Ords 10c	61500000	50833640

FINANCIAL STATISTICS (AT FINANCIAL YEAR END)

(Amts in R'000)	1992	1991	1990	1989	1988

	Mar	Mar	Mar	Mar	Mar
Ord S/H Int	570300	472400	378900	271900	208600
Long Trm Loans	404100	285000	237700	172600	113900
Iss Ord Share	50818	50803	50803	43049	43049
Total Liab	993900	883800	726400	570300	435900
Current Liab	589800	598800	488700	397700	322000
Total Assets	1564200	1356200	1105300	842200	644500
Current Assets	1324600	1133400	909600	683200	521500
Debtors	860400	745500	591100	436000	323500
Inventory	456300	375400	310800	236500	193400
Turnover	2748500	2475800	1981500	1579600	1177700
Oper Profit	373200	353000	287800	211900	138700
Interest Paid	73100	59000	45700	20300	18363
Tax Paid	143100	144000	119600	92052	57200
Prf af Int&Tax	157500	150400	123500	100248	63137
Prf att Ord Sh	157500	150400	123500	95248	59800
Btm Line Earn	157500	150400	123500	95248	59900
Dividend Paid	60500	57400	47300	32300	23000
Mkt Prce(c) YE	5100	5250	3625	1850	1850
Depreciation	52294	47909	38845	30000	22503

PER SHARE STATISTICS (CENTS)

Net Asst Val	1122 24	929 87	745 82	631 61	484 56
Net Earnings	310 00	296 00	243 00	221 00	141 70
Dividends	119 00	113 00	93 00	75 00	53 50
Cash Flow	425 43	367 91	340 62	302 56	196 91

RATIOS AND OTHER INFORMATION

Mrk Cap(R000)	2591718	2667158	1841609	796407	796407
Current Ratio	2 25	1 89	1 86	1 72	1 62
Quik/Acid Tst	1 47	1 27	1 23	1 12	1 02
A/C Rec T/ovr	3 19	3 32	3 35	3 62	3 64
Tot Ass T/ovr	1 76	1 83	1 79	1 88	1 83
Debt/Ass Rat	0 62	0 63	0 62	0 68	0 68
L T L Tot Ass	0 24	0 19	0 18	0 20	0 18
Debt to Eqity	1 70	1 82	1 82	2 10	2 09
Interest Cover	5 11	5 98	6 30	10 44	7 55
Oper Prof Mrg	13 58	14 26	14 52	13 41	11 78
Net Prof Marg%	5 73	6 07	6 23	6 03	5 08
Ret on Assets	23 89	26 06	26 13	25 24	21 78
Ret on Equity%	27 62	31 84	32 59	35 03	28 67
Price/Earnings	16 45	17 74	14 92	8 37	13 06
Divid Cover	2 61	2 62	2 61	2 95	2 65
Divid Yield	2 33	2 15	2 57	4 05	2 89
Earning Yield%	6 08	5 64	6 70	11 95	7 66
NAV % Mrk Pr	22 00	17 71	20 57	34 14	26 19
Effec Tax Rate	45 21	52 68	44 47	45 36	45 58
Def Interval	1 84	1 50	1 40	1 11	1 09
Sus Grth Rate	17 01	19 69	20 11	23 15	17 64

SUBSIDIARY & ASSOCIATED COMPANIES

CANNON CLOTHING (PTY) LTD
CELROSE LTD
DECISIONS HOME SHOPPING LTD
EDGARS FINANCE (PTY) LTD
EDGARS INVESTMENT HOLDING CO LTD
EDGARS LOAN FINANCE (PTY) LTD
EDGARS RETAIL TRADING (PTY) LTD
EDGARS STORES (MANAGEMENT) LTD
EDGARS STORES LESOTHO (PTY) LTD
EDGARS STORES SWAZILAND LTD
GOOSE BAY TRADING (PTY) LTD
H D LEE COMPANY (PTY) LTD
JET STORES (PTY) LTD
JET SUPERMARKETS BOTSWANA (PTY) LTD
JET SUPERMARKETS LESOTHO (PTY) LTD
JET SUPERMARKETS SWAZILAND (PTY) LTD
NATIONAL SECURITY CORP LTD
PEOPLES STORES (BOPHUTHATSWANA) (PTY) LT
PEOPLES STORES (CISKEI) (PTY) LTD
PEOPLES STORES (LEBOWA) (PTY) LTD
PEOPLES STORES (MANAGEMENT) (TRANSKEI) (
PEOPLES STORES (NAMIBIA) (PTY) LTD
PEOPLES STORES (TRANSKEI) (PTY) LTD
PEOPLES STORES (VENDA) (PTY) LTD
PEOPLES STORES (WALVIS BAY) (PTY) LTD
R22 PROPERTIES (PTY) LTD
SALES HOUSE (LESOTHO) (PTY) LTD
SALES HOUSE (PTY) LTD
UNITED PURCHASING CO LTD
UPC RETAIL SERVICES (PTY) LTD
VOC INVESTMENT HOLDING CO (PTY) LTD

INVESTMENTS

None

EDGARS STORES ZIMBABWE LTD

ABBREVIATION : ED ZIM

SECTOR : Zimbabwe Stock Exchange

SHAREHOLDERS

Who Owns Whom's Assessment of the Identity of the Ultimate Controlling Shareholder:
BELLFIELD LTD

DIRECTORS :
BOWER MR ,ETHERIDGE DW
FERGUSON HD (Managing Director),GUEST SD
MABADOKO NJ ,MAKOVAH E ,MASTERSON L ,MKUSHI JP
SMITH DC (Chairman),ZAMCHIYA DM

REGISTERED OFFICE
Cnr Ninth Avenue, Herbert Chitepo Street
Bulawayo, Zimbabwe

TEL 75085
FAX 76450

TRANSFER SECRETARY
KPMG Peat Marwick
P O Box 702, Harare
Zimbabwe

TEL 09263 962831

COMPANY SECRETARY
G J Geddes

NATURE OF BUSINESS
EDGARS STORES are retailers of clothing,footwear and household textiles through approximately fifty outlets in Zimbabwe Retail chains EDGARS and SALES HOUSE offer credit facilities EXPRESS STORES is the group's only cash outlet The group operates a clothing factory,CAROUSEL,which supplies its retail and export market

BANKERS :
N/A

AUDITORS :
Ernst & Young

FAMILIAR BRAND NAMES
N/A

CONTRIBUTION BY ACTIVITY
N/A

YEAR END : July

DIVIDEND : Ords Z$0,60

Dividend	(Ldr)20/09/91	(Pay)11/10/91	Amt(c)14
Dividend	(Ldr)13/03/92	(Pay)10/04/92	Amt(c)13

CAPITAL STRUCTURE

	AUTHORISED	ISSUED
Ords Z$0,60	45000000	36000000

FINANCIAL STATISTICS (AT FINANCIAL YEAR END)

(Amts in Z$)	1992 Jul	1991 Jul	1990 Jul
Ord S/H Int	80401	42323	33350
Long Trm Loans	-	7250	5250
Iss Ord Share	36000	31500	4500
Total Liab	49069	54451	35455
Current Liab	49069	47201	30205
Total Assets	129470	96774	68805
Current Assets	101872	76970	52589
Debtors	57541	49532	31064
Inventory	42294	27090	21186
Turnover	188046	156517	111080
Oper Profit	30479	24540	16792
Interest Paid	1059	1435	885
Tax Paid	11353	8149	5278
Prf af Int&Tax	20385	15376	10907
Prf att Ord Sh	20385	15376	10907
Btm Line Earn	20385	15376	10907
Dividend Paid	7442	7647	5450
Depreciation	3573	2799	1831

PER SHARE STATISTICS (CENTS)

Net Asst Val	223.34	134.36	741.11
Net Earnings	57.40	44.80	34.60
Dividends	23.00	22.40	17.30
Cash Flow	67.42	57.70	283.07

RATIOS AND OTHER INFORMATION

Current Ratio	2.08	1.63	1.74
Quik/Acid Tst	1.21	1.06	1.04
A/C Rec T/ovr	3.27	3.16	3.58
Tot Ass T/ovr	1.45	1.62	1.61
Debt/Ass Rat	0.38	0.56	0.52
L T L Tot Ass	-	0.07	0.08
Debt to Eqity	0.61	1.29	1.06
Interest Cover	28.78	17.10	18.97
Oper Prof Mrg	16.21	15.68	15.12
Net Prof Marg%	10.84	9.82	9.82
Ret on Assets	25.33	25.79	24.81
Ret on Equity%	25.35	36.33	32.70
Divid Cover	2.50	2.00	2.00
Effec Tax Rate	37.68	34.64	32.61
Def Interval	0.06	0.62	0.45
Sus Grth Rate	16.10	18.26	16.36

SUBSIDIARY & ASSOCIATED COMPANIES

ASSOCIATED MERCHANDISING CORPORATION (19
CAROUSEL (PVT) LTD
CONSUMER CREDIT SECURITY (PVT) LTD

INVESTMENTS

None

EDWARD L BATEMAN LTD

ABBREVIATION : ED-L-BATE

JSE SHORT CODE : ELB

SECTOR : Industrial-Engineering

SHAREHOLDERS

Who Owns Whom's Assessment of the Identity of the Ultimate Controlling Shareholder: DIRECTORS

SHAREHOLDER	PERCENTAGE 1992	1991
ED L BATE STAFF HOLDINGS P/L	24.8	24.8
VIRROXSAM INV P/L	9.9	9.9
WILSON S J	8.4	8.4
BATEMAN W G L & CLARKE D R	6.8	6.8
EIGHTY ONE MAIN STREET NOM LTD	6.2	3.6
BATEMAN C L	5.9	5.9
EDWARD L BATEMAN EXEC SHARE INC TRUST	3.5	3.5
SOFMORE CONSTRUCTION P/L	2.0	2.0
FIRST NAT NOM P/L	1.8	1.8
YSKOR PENS FUND	1.5	---
STD BANK NOM TVL P/L	1.4	3.5
CMB NOM P/L	1.2	---
CAPE CLOTHING INDUSTRY PROV FUND	1.1	1.1
LONRHO GROUP PENS FUND	1.1	1.4
ALTENA MEWS P/L	---	1.2
ED L BATE LTD EXEC SHARE INC SCHEME	---	2.0
TOTAL	75.7	75.8

DIRECTORS :
ALBERTS L DR,BATEMAN WGL (Chairman)
BRERETON HPN (Managing Director),FALLS RER
FLETCHER AG ,HERSELMAN JP DR (Managing Director)
HOOPER JB (Financial Director),LANGTON G
LEROY AJ ,MCILROY JL ,STAGG-MACEY I ,THERON PJJ
VEY RM

REGISTRATION NUMBER : 05/02553/06

REGISTERED OFFICE
Founders Building, Bartlett Road
Boksburg North
1459
TEL: 011-899 9111
FAX: 011-892 3258

TRANSFER SECRETARY
Central Registrars Ltd
P O Box 4844, Johannesburg
2000
TEL: 011-331 0051

COMPANY SECRETARY
W B van de Laar

NATURE OF BUSINESS
The group is engaged in the design, manufacture & marketing of engineered products and related services to the mining, process and construction industries, and engineering contracting & project management services.

BANKERS :
First National Bank of SA Ltd

AUDITORS :
KPMG Aiken & Peat

FAMILIAR BRAND NAMES
DITCH WITCH,FURUKAWA,SUMITOMO,TORO

CONTRIBUTION BY ACTIVITY
Engineering/Contracting (% attrb.profit) (42.0%)
Equipment Supply (58.0%)

YEAR END : June

DIVIDEND : Ords 4c

Interim No 88	(Ldr)21/02/92	(Pay)28/02/92	Amt(c)8.25
Interim No 84	(Ldr)05/04/90	(Pay)30/04/90	Amt(c)5.7
Final No 85	(Ldr)12/10/90	(Pay)09/11/90	Amt(c)15.9
Interim No 86	(Ldr)22/02/91	(Pay)02/04/91	Amt(c)7.2
Final No 87	(Ldr)04/10/91	(Pay)18/10/91	Amt(c)19.3
Final No 89	(Ldr)02/10/92	(Pay)16/10/92	Amt(c)22.25

NUMBER OF EMPLOYEES : 1653

CAPITAL STRUCTURE

	AUTHORISED	ISSUED
6% Fxd Cum Red Prefs R2	150000	7300
Ords 4c	50000000	27363220

FINANCIAL STATISTICS (AT FINANCIAL YEAR END)

(Amts in R'000)	1992 Jun	1991 Jun	1990 Jun	1989 Jun	1988 Jun
Ord S/H Int	104240	91772	80627	71290	61906
Long Trm Loans	27381	22510	19526	10922	5967
Iss Ord Share	27363	27323	27323	2697	2646
Total Liab	321549	319783	262864	220067	196632
Current Liab	294168	297273	243338	209145	190665
Total Assets	425789	411555	343491	291357	258538
Current Assets	362242	372224	307226	257260	223339
Debtors	149324	99507	113558	114249	105482
Inventory	84343	70448	85286	61471	59366
Turnover	633899	786107	588978	844143	735557
Oper Profit	36931	36190	29122	18533	12711
Interest Paid	5115	2372	2848	2170	2133
Tax Paid	1257	6301	4943	809	1363
Prf af Int&Tax	30559	27517	21331	15554	9215
Prf att Ord Sh	24085	21929	18307	14132	8421
Btm Line Earn	20749	20575	18041	15695	7324
Dividend Paid	8362	7241	5901	4622	3440
Mkt Prce(c) YE	680	520	340	230	180
Depreciation	8421	7732	6706	6343	6612

PER SHARE STATISTICS (CENTS)

Net Asst Val	380.95	335.88	295.09	2643.31	2339.61
Net Earnings	88.10	80.30	67.20	53.10	31.80
Dividends	30.50	26.50	21.60	17.00	13.00
Cash Flow	118.61	112.09	106.34	769.52	568.59

RATIOS AND OTHER INFORMATION

Mrk Cap(R000)	186068	142080	92898	6203	4763
Current Ratio	1.23	1.25	1.26	1.23	1.17
Quik/Acid Tst	0.94	1.02	0.91	0.94	0.86
A/C Rec T/ovr	4.25	7.90	5.19	7.39	6.97
Tot Ass T/ovr	1.49	1.91	1.71	2.90	2.85
Debt/Ass Rat	0.70	0.74	0.73	0.73	0.76
L T L Tot Ass	0.01	0.01	0.02	0.01	0.02
Debt to Eqity	2.88	3.31	3.10	2.97	3.15
Interest Cover	7.22	15.26	10.23	8.54	5.96
Oper Prof Mrg	5.83	4.60	4.94	2.20	1.73
Net Prof Marg%	3.80	2.79	3.11	1.67	1.14
Ret on Assets	8.67	8.79	8.48	6.36	4.92
Ret on Equity%	23.11	23.90	22.71	19.82	13.60
Price/Earnings	7.72	6.48	5.06	4.33	5.66
Divid Cover	2.89	3.03	3.11	3.12	2.45
Divid Yield	4.49	5.10	6.35	7.39	7.22
Earning Yield%	12.96	15.44	19.76	23.09	17.67
NAV % Mrk Pr	56.02	64.59	86.79	1149.26	1299.78
Effec Tax Rate	8.46	15.65	1.42	4.60	13.48
Def Interval	0.62	0.79	0.56	0.57	0.60
Sus Grth Rate	15.08	16.00	15.39	13.34	8.05

SUBSIDIARY & ASSOCIATED COMPANIES

AIRFILPAT HOLDINGS (PTY) LTD
AL ABBOTT LABORATORY SERVICES (PTY) LTD
AQUAFUND (PTY) LTD
ARMINCO (PTY) LTD (47%)
ASFA SERVICES (PTY) LTD (50%)
BATEMAN DAVY ENGINEERING (PTY) LTD (50%)
BATEMAN EARTHMOVING EQUIPMENT (PTY) LTD
BATEMAN ENGINEERING (INTERNATIONAL) LTD
BATEMAN ENGINEERING (INTERNATIONAL) LTD
BATEMAN ENGINEERING LTD
BATEMAN ENGINEERING LTD
BATEMAN ENGINEERING PROJECTS LTD
BATEMAN EQUIPMENT LTD
BATEMAN EQUIPMENT LTD
BATEMAN HYDRO SYSTEMS (PTY) LTD
BATEMAN INDUSTRIAL HOLDINGS LTD
BATEMAN INDUSTRIAL HOLDINGS LTD
BATEMAN INDUSTRIAL PROJECTS LTD
BATEMAN INDUSTRIAL PROJECTS LTD
BATEMAN MATERIALS HANDLING LTD
BATEMAN MATERIALS HANDLING LTD
BATEMAN MINING (PTY) LTD
BATEMAN MINING (PTY) LTD (SWA)
BATEMAN MINING EQUIPMENT (PTY) LTD
BATEMAN PROCESS INSTRUMENTATION LTD
BATEMAN PROJECT HOLDINGS LTD
BATEMAN WATER TREATMENT (PTY) LTD
BATEMAN WATER TREATMENT (PTY) LTD
BATESERV LTD
BATETECH LTD
BEP (PTY) LTD
COMPUTER ALLIANCE (PTY) LTD (40%)
CRYOGENIC ENGINEERING LTD
DW OSBORNE & CO (PTY) LTD
EDWARD L BATEMAN (PTY) LTD (SWA)
EDWARD L. BATEMAN (NATAL) LTD
ELB FLYING SERVICES LTD
ELB-BRANDT CONTRACTING (PTY) LTD
ELBENG HOLDINGS LTD
ELBENG HOLDINGS LTD
ELBEX (PTY) LTD
ELBQUIP HOLDINGS (PTY) LTD
ELBQUIP HOLDINGS LTD
ELBROC MINING PRODUCTS LTD
ERE FOUNDRY (PTY) LTD
GASAL MANAGEMENT SYSTEMS (PTY) LTD
INDUSTRIAL & PETROCHEMICAL CONSULTANTS (
INDUSTRIAL & PETROCHEMICAL CONSULTANTS (
INTEGRATED WASTE MANAGEMENT (PTY) LTD
INTEGRATED WASTE MANAGEMENT (PTY) LTD
IRON & STEEL TECHNOLOGY (PTY) LTD (47%)
LURGI SOUTH AFRICA (PTY) LTD (47%)
MAGNAFLUX PIPELINE SERVICES (PTY) LTD

MAGNAFLUX PIPELINE SERVICES (PTY) LTD
MEM BELEGGINGS (PTY) LTD
ORE SORTERS (AFRICA) (PTY) LTD
ORE SORTERS (SA) (PTY) LTD
RAINBOW DEVELOPMENT CORPORATION (PTY) LT
RESOURCE RECYCLING (PTY) LTD
ROCOR RAND (PTY) LTD
SUGAR CONSULTANTS INTERNATIONAL (PTY) LT
TECHNICAL TRAINING SERVICES (PTY) LTD
TECHPAC (PTY) LTD
TURNSTEEL MANUFACTURING (PTY) LTD
TURNSTEEL PRECISION ENGINEERING (PTY) LT
VAN ECK & LURIE (PTY) LTD
WESTERN CHEMICALS CORP LTD

INVESTMENTS

None

EERSTELING GOLD MINING CO LTD

ABBREVIATION : EERSLNG

JSE SHORT CODE : ESL

SECTOR : Gold-Rand & others

SHAREHOLDERS

Who Owns Whom's Assessment of the Identity of the Ultimate Controlling Shareholder:
ESOR ESTABLISHMENT SA (SWISS)

SHAREHOLDER	PERCENTAGE 1992	1991
SMBL NOM P/L	27.6	---
STD BANK NOM TVL P/L	9.4	9.4
SA MUTUAL	4.1	4.2
CMB NOM P/L	3.7	---
NEDBANK NOM LTD	3.5	---
SEVERIN F V	2.6	2.6
MUNRO T L R	1.6	1.6
DORBYL PENS FUND	1.1	1.2
ELECTRA SHARE VENTURES P/L	---	2.0
INDO-CHINA NOM SA P/L	---	2.7
SANLAM	---	1.7
SEVERIN-SOUTHERN SPHERE MINING	---	3.6
SEVERIN MINING & DEVELOPMENT CO P/L	---	23.3
TOTAL	53.6	52.1

DIRECTORS :
CARROLL LM ,CRONIN PH ,NISBET GY ,SEVERIN FV
SEVERIN S (Chairman

REGISTRATION NUMBER : 87/01814/06

REGISTERED OFFICE
Rand Leases Property, Main Reef Road
Florida, Roodepoort
1724
TEL: 011-803 6200
FAX: 011-674 3307

TRANSFER SECRETARY
Mercantile Registrars Ltd
P O Box 1053, Johannesburg
2000
TEL: 011-333 8181

COMPANY SECRETARY
Severin-Southern Sphere Mining (Pty) Ltd

NATURE OF BUSINESS
The company conducts gold mining operations in the Pietersburg district, Tvl.Company currently in liquidation.

BANKERS :
Standard Bank of SA Ltd

AUDITORS :
Arthur Andersen & Co

FAMILIAR BRAND NAMES
N/A

CONTRIBUTION BY ACTIVITY
N/A

YEAR END : June

NUMBER OF EMPLOYEES : 600

CAPITAL STRUCTURE

	AUTHORISED	ISSUED
Ords 1c	120000000	80000000

FINANCIAL STATISTICS (AT FINANCIAL YEAR END)

(Amts in R'000)	1990 Jun	1989 Jun	1988 Jun
Ord S/H Int	54544	25234	25234
Long Trm Loans	1282	12000	4445
Iss Ord Share	80000	40000	40000
Total Liab	5638	31748	13062
Current Liab	4356	19748	8617
Total Assets	60182	56982	38296
Current Assets	1278	1331	831
Debtors	82	199	140
Inventory	789	1132	662
Turnover	-	-	4134
Oper Profit	-560	-	-
Interest Paid	1414	-	195
Prf af Int&Tax	-1974	-	-195
Prf att Ord Sh	-1974	-	-195
Btm Line Earn	-1974	-	-195
Mkt Prce(c) YE	57	118	185

PER SHARE STATISTICS (CENTS)

Net Asst Val	68.18	63.09	63.09
Net Earnings	-3.20	-	1.30
Cash Flow	-3.15	-	-0.55

RATIOS AND OTHER INFORMATION

Mrk Cap(R000)	45600	47200	74000
Current Ratio	0.29	0.07	0.10
Quik/Acid Tst	0.11	0.01	0.02
A/C Rec T/ovr	-	-	29.53
Tot Ass T/ovr	-	-	0.11
Debt/Ass Rat	0.09	0.56	0.34
L T L Tot Ass	0.02	0.21	0.12
Debt to Eqity	0.10	1.26	0.52
Interest Cover	-0.40	-	-

Net Prof Marg%	-	-	-4.72
Ret on Assets	-0.93	-	-
Ret on Equity%	-3.62	-	-0.77
Price/Earnings	-17.81	-	142.31
Earning Yield%	-5.61	-	0.70
NAV % Mrk Pr	119.61	53.46	34.10
Def Interval	-0.65	-	-22.79
Sus Grth Rate	-3.62	-	-0.77

SUBSIDIARY & ASSOCIATED COMPANIES

None

INVESTMENTS

None

EGOLI CONSOLIDATED MINES LTD

ABBREVIATION : EGOLI

JSE SHORT CODE : EGL

SECTOR : Mining Financial-Mining Holding

SHAREHOLDERS

Who Owns Whom's Assessment of the Identity of the Ultimate Controlling Shareholder:
CONSOLIDATED MINING CORP

SHAREHOLDER	PERCENTAGE 1992	1991
CONSOLIDATED MINING CORP LTD	74.5	70.4
ABSA NOM P/L	2.2	---
SHARLAND J N	1.6	2.0
LOWENCO NOM P/L	1.4	1.4
STD BANK NOM TVL P/L	---	1.2
SOLID G NOM P/L	---	1.1
VOLKSKAS NOM P/L	---	2.2
TOTAL	79.7	78.3

DIRECTORS :
BUITENDAG HC ,FLOWERDAY RA ,LEE RA
LOWENTHAL ND (Chairman),LOWENTHAL RY
RUBENSTEIN GB ,SCHECHTER M ,SUDDENS BD
THOMPSON MW ,TURNER CF

REGISTRATION NUMBER : 68/15717/06

REGISTERED OFFICE
39th Floor, Carlton Centre
Commissioner Street, Johannesburg
2001
TEL: 011-331 9181
FAX: 011-331 6189

TRANSFER SECRETARY
Mercantile Registrars Ltd
P O Box 1053, Johannesburg
2000
TEL: 011-333 8181

COMPANY SECRETARY
Consolidated Mining Management Services Ltd

NATURE OF BUSINESS
Investment and mining holding company. The company is engaged in the recovery of gold and by-products from gold mining and the retreatment of surface dumps. These operations are conducted by subsidiary and associated companies on the East and West Rand.

BANKERS :
First National Bank of SA Ltd

AUDITORS :
Charles Orbach & Co

FAMILIAR BRAND NAMES
N/A

CONTRIBUTION BY ACTIVITY
N/A

YEAR END : March

DIVIDEND : Ords no par value

Final No 16	(Ldr)27/07/90	(Pay)24/08/90	Amt(c)6
Interim No 17	(Ldr)12/06/92	(Pay)03/07/92	Amt(c)3

CAPITAL STRUCTURE

	AUTHORISED	ISSUED
Ords no par value	100000000	52936000

FINANCIAL STATISTICS (AT FINANCIAL YEAR END)

(Amts in R'000)	1992 Mar	1991 Mar	1990 Mar	1989 Mar	1988 Mar
Ord S/H Int	49780	96020	99067	51602	96099
Long Trm Loans	90276	134147	129020	41645	49979
Iss Ord Share	42348	42348	42348	26000	26000
Total Liab	131286	203168	165572	61931	68329
Current Liab	41010	69021	36552	20286	18350
Total Assets	181066	299188	264639	113533	164428
Current Assets	17427	14304	33414	19879	15070
Debtors	6227	9581	9158	12517	4243
Inventory	2823	3949	3195	1994	3153
Turnover	136969	135991	143893	89012	76280
Oper Profit	16198	8457	21889	4157	8545
Interest Paid	3198	5340	4611	1939	-
Tax Paid	468	783	97	326	707
Prf af Int&Tax	12891	4631	19411	2977	7838
Prf att Ord Sh	4675	1198	7645	1543	5857
Btm Line Earn	-27324	777	17826	-44497	17469
Dividend Paid	1270	-	2541	-	3900
Mkt Prce(c) YE	30	70	250	95	280

PER SHARE STATISTICS (CENTS)

Net Asst Val	117.55	226.74	233.94	198.47	369.61
Net Earnings	11.00	2.80	18.10	5.90	67.20
Dividends	3.00	-	6.00	-	15.00
Cash Flow	11.04	2.83	18.05	5.93	18.33

RATIOS AND OTHER INFORMATION

Mrk Cap(R000)	12704	29644	105870	24700	72800
Current Ratio	0.42	0.21	0.91	0.98	0.82
Quik/Acid Tst	0.36	0.15	0.83	0.88	0.65
A/C Rec T/ovr	22.00	14.19	15.71	7.11	17.98
Tot Ass T/ovr	0.76	0.45	0.54	0.78	0.46
Debt/Ass Rat	0.23	0.25	0.15	0.22	0.14
L T L Tot Ass	0.01	0.02	0.02	0.04	0.03
Debt to Eqity	0.84	0.78	0.41	0.48	0.24
Interest Cover	5.07	1.77	4.98	2.14	-
Oper Prof Mrg	11.83	6.22	15.21	4.67	11.20
Net Prof Marg%	3.41	0.88	5.31	1.73	7.68

Ret on Assets	9.14	3.59	9.11	4.62	5.86
Ret on Equity%	9.39	1.25	7.72	2.99	6.09
Price/Earnings	2.73	25.00	13.81	16.10	4.17
Divid Cover	3.67	-	3.02	-	4.48
Divid Yield	10.00	-	2.40	-	5.36
Earning Yield%	36.67	4.00	7.24	6.21	24.00
NAV % Mrk Pr	391.83	323.91	93.57	208.91	132.00
Effec Tax Rate	4.65	16.54	0.66	8.84	7.01
Def Interval	3.50	35.78	1.89	7.07	1.99
Sus Grth Rate	6.84	1.25	5.15	2.99	2.04

SUBSIDIARY & ASSOCIATED COMPANIES

AMBERMIN INVESTMENTS LTD (50%)
BENONI GOLD HOLDINGS LTD (48,3%)
BENONI GOLD MINES (PTY) LTD
BENONI GOLD MINING CO LTD (45.2%)
BONTE KOE MYNBOU ONDERNEMINGS (EDMS) BPK
BRAKPAN VAN DYK EXTENSIONS LTD
BRAKPAN VAN DYK MINES LTD
CARBON LEADER LTD
CARRIG DIAMONDS LTD
CONSOLIDATED RESOURCES AND EXPLORATION L (30,8%)
ENERGY RESOURCES AND MINING CORPORATION (50%)
GOLD RECOVERY RESIDUES (PTY) LTD (42,3%)
JOHANNESBURG MINING INVESTMENTS LTD
KLEINFONTEIN SAND AND STONE LTD (45.2%)
KRUGERSDORP STONE CRUSHERS (PTY) LTD
LOXTON EXPLORATION (PTY) LTD
MANTECH SERVICES (PTY) LTD
NIGEL GOLD MINING COMPANY (PTY) LTD (42.3%)
NIGEL GOLD MINING HOLDINGS LTD (42.3%)
NIPROP PROPERTY INVESTMENTS (PTY) LTD (42.3%)
NUGO MINING CORPORATION LTD (45.2%)
SOUTH EAST RAND GOLD HOLDINGS LTD
SOUTHERN FISSURES LTD
TANKS OIL AND PLATINUM HOLDINGS LTD
TERIKIM LANDGOED (EDMS) BPK (48.3%)
WEST SPAARWATER LTD
WEST WITWATERSRAND GOLD HOLDINGS LTD (45,3%)
WEST WITWATERSRAND GOLD MINES LTD (45,8%)
WEST WITWATERSRAND MINERAL & MINING CORP
WITWATERSRAND NIGEL LTD
WOLFBERG MYNBOU (EDMS) BPK

INVESTMENTS

CONSOLIDATED MINING CORPORATION LTD (1,8%)

ELANDSRAND GOLD MINING CO LTD

ABBREVIATION : ELANDS

JSE SHORT CODE : ELA

SECTOR : Gold-West Witwatersrand

SHAREHOLDERS

Who Owns Whom's Assessment of the Identity of the Ultimate Controlling Shareholder: ANGLO AMERICAN

SHAREHOLDER	PERCENTAGE 1992	1991
ANGLO AMERICAN GOLD INV CO LTD	19.6	19.6
ANGLO AMERICAN CORP OF SA LTD	19.0	18.6
TAURUS NOM LTD	9.5	9.5
PETARD NOM LTD	6.4	6.4
INDO-CHINA NOM P/L	5.5	6.0
MINU NOM LTD	5.0	5.0
RESIDENT NOM LTD	3.9	3.9
FERMAIN NOM LTD	3.8	3.8
AFRICAN & EUROPEAN INV CO LTD	3.2	3.2
RAND SELECTION CORP LTD	2.8	2.8
SA TOWNSHIPS MINING & FINANCE CORP LTD	2.7	2.7
SA MUTUAL	2.6	2.6
STD BANK NOM TVL P/L	2.1	2.8
FIRST NAT NOM P/L	1.5	1.8
INDO-CHINA NOM SA P/L	---	6.0
TOTAL	87.6	94.6

DIRECTORS :
GODSELL RM ,MCLUSKIE J ,MUNRO AH ,SCHMID E
VAN DER POST WZ ,WRIGHT AJ

REGISTRATION NUMBER : 74/01477/06

REGISTERED OFFICE
44 Main Street, Johannesburg
2001
TEL: 011-638 9111
FAX: 011-638 5281

TRANSFER SECRETARY
Consolidated Share Registrars Ltd
P O Box 61051, Marshalltown
2107
TEL: 011-492 1620

COMPANY SECRETARY
Anglo American Corp. of SA Ltd

NATURE OF BUSINESS
The company, a subsidiary of Anglo American Corporation of South Africa, was incorporated in 1974 and conducts gold-mining operations in the Oberholzer and Potchefstroom districts, Transvaal.

BANKERS :
First National Bank of SA Ltd

AUDITORS :
KPMG Aiken & Peat

FAMILIAR BRAND NAMES
N/A

CONTRIBUTION BY ACTIVITY
N/A

YEAR END : December

DIVIDEND : Ords 20c

Interim No 16	(Ldr)03/08/90	(Pay)14/09/90	Amt(c)15
Final No 17	(Ldr)08/02/91	(Pay)15/03/91	Amt(c)15
Interim No 18	(Ldr)09/08/91	(Pay)12/09/91	Amt(c)15
Final No 19	(Ldr)07/02/92	(Pay)13/03/92	Amt(c)20

NUMBER OF EMPLOYEES : 10079

CAPITAL STRUCTURE

	AUTHORISED	ISSUED
Ords 20c	105000000	96976186

FINANCIAL STATISTICS (AT FINANCIAL YEAR END)

(Amts in R'000)	1991 Dec	1990 Dec	1989 Dec	1988	1987
Ord S/H Int	1061815	957758	842245	754443	673911
Long Trm Loans	-	-	-	68666	71204
Iss Ord Share	96976	96620	96620	96620	96620
Total Liab	86860	70887	65566	137332	142408
Current Liab	86860	70887	65566	68666	71204
Total Assets	1148675	1028645	907811	879779	828303
Current Assets	45670	32487	27498	56670	83188
Debtors	27557	22990	8542	-	
Inventory	-	-	-	56670	83188
Turnover	492805	453656	420329	385260	319313
Oper Profit	140190	144158	161399	170129	153393
Interest Paid	3919	4725	-	-	-
Tax Paid	1616	1728	2804	3889	3280
Prf af Int&Tax	137739	139987	162952	166240	150113
Prf att Ord Sh	137739	139987	162952	88496	87644
Btm Line Earn	33850	27279	77398	88496	87644
Dividend Paid	33941	29138	77500	87035	91789
Mkt Prce(c) YE	2375	2275	3225	1785	2650

PER SHARE STATISTICS (CENTS)

Net Asst Val	1094 93	991 26	871 71	780 84	697 49
Net Earnings	142 00	144 00	168 00	-	-
Dividends	35 00	30 00	80 00	-	-
Cash Flow	142 03	144 88	168 65	172 06	155 36

RATIOS AND OTHER INFORMATION

Mrk Cap(R000)	2303180	2198105	3115995	1724667	2560430
Current Ratio	0 53	0 46	0 42	0 83	1 17
Quik/Acid Tst	0 53	0 46	0 42	-	-
A/C Rec T/ovr	17 88	19 73	49 21	-	-
Tot Ass T/ovr	0 43	0 44	0 46	0 44	0 39
Debt/Ass Rat	0 08	0 07	0 07	0 16	0 17
L T L Tot Ass	-	-	-	0 08	0 09
Debt to Eqity	0 08	0 07	0 08	0 18	0 21
Interest Cover	35 85	30 57	-	-	-
Oper Prof Mrg	28 45	31 78	38 40	44 16	48 04
Net Prof Marg%	27 95	30 86	38 77	22 97	27 45
Ret on Assets	12 47	14 24	18 26	19 34	18 52
Ret on Equity%	12 97	14 62	19 35	11 73	13 01
Price/Earnings	16 73	15 80	19 20	-	
Divid Cover	4 06	4 80	2 10		
Divid Yield	1 47	1 32	2 48	-	-
Earning Yield%	5 98	6 33	5 21	-	-
NAV % Mrk Pr	46 10	43 57	27 03	43 74	26 32
Effec Tax Rate	1 16	1 22	-	2 29	2 14
Def Interval	0 18	0 22	-	0 41	0 47
Sus Grth Rate	9 78	11 57	10 15	0 19	-0 62

SUBSIDIARY & ASSOCIATED COMPANIES

None

INVESTMENTS

None

ELCENTRE CORPORATION LTD

ABBREVIATION : ELCENTR

JSE SHORT CODE : ELC

SECTOR : Industrial-Electronics, Electrical & Bat

SHAREHOLDERS

Who Owns Whom's Assessment of the Identity of the Ultimate Controlling Shareholder:
ELGRO

SHAREHOLDER	PERCENTAGE 1992	1991
ELCENTRE GROUP HOLDINGS LTD	54 1	54 1
STD BANK NOM TVL P/L	12 0	2 5
FSI CORP PENS FUND	10 1	---
FS DISTRIBUTORS LTD	5 5	- -
KAYEMESS NOM P/L	1 3	---
ANGLO AMERICAN GROUP PENS FUND	---	2 5
ELCENTRE SHARE INC TRUST	--	1 5
FS-TEAM DISTRIBUTORS LTD	---	25 1
TOTAL	83 0	85 5

DIRECTORS :
AGINSKY PC ,LEVIN HR ,LIEBESMAN JM
MOWSZOWSKI CA (Sales Director)
MOWSZOWSKI NP (Financial Director)
MOWSZOWSKI RL (Chairman & Managing Dir),ROLFE TW

REGISTRATION NUMBER : 68/11488/06

REGISTERED OFFICE
Voltex House, 3 River Road
Bedfordview
2008
TEL 011-402 1600

TRANSFER SECRETARY
Mercantile Registrars Ltd
P O Box 1053, Johannesburg
2000
TEL 011-333 8181

COMPANY SECRETARY
Elcentre Holdings (Pty) Ltd

NATURE OF BUSINESS
An investment holding company with controlling interests in quoted Sanlic and Voltex (together with Berzack) Group activities include the manufacture of low voltage cables, electrical wires, mouldings, rigid & soft extrusions and the distribution of cable, wire, industrial & commercial electrical, electronic and lighting requisites, locks & security related products, & products for DIY electrical & hardware markets

BANKERS :
Standard Bank of SA Ltd
Trust Bank of Africa Ltd, Nedperm Bank Ltd
First National Bank of SA Ltd

AUDITORS :
KPMG Aiken & Peat

FAMILIAR BRAND NAMES
BOKKIELITE,BOKKIEPAL,KEENS,SUPERSALES

CONTRIBUTION BY ACTIVITY
N/A

YEAR END : June

DIVIDEND :Ords 1c

Interim No 11	(Ldr)26/05/89	(Pay)07/06/89	Amt(c)19
Interim No 12	(Ldr)15/12/89	(Pay)17/01/90	Amt(c)21
Final No 13	(Ldr)14/12/90	(Pay)10/01/91	Amt(c)8
Interim No 14	(Ldr)26/04/91	(Pay) / /	Amt(c)15
Final No 15	(Ldr)18/10/91	(Pay)31/10/91	Amt(c)21
Interim No 16	(Ldr)08/05/92	(Pay)22/05/92	Amt(c)10
Final No 17	(Ldr)30/10/92	(Pay)16/11/92	Amt(c)15 5

NUMBER OF EMPLOYEES : 2000

CAPITAL STRUCTURE

	AUTHORISED	ISSUED
Ords 1c	100000000	63515755

FINANCIAL STATISTICS (AT FINANCIAL YEAR END)

(Amts in R'000)	1992 Jun	1991 Jun	1990 Jun	1989 Feb	1988 Feb
Ord S/H Int	360026	387182	452771	175023	151152
Long Trm Loans	51846	18229	182516	98352	20345
Iss Ord Share	63516	63516	63516	59255	59255
Total Liab	63692	41566	208236	253691	89251
Current Liab	11846	23337	25720	155339	68906
Total Assets	423718	428748	661007	324389	141535
Intang Assets	*	*	*	104325	98868
Current Assets	26504	22916	46932	182707	122179
Debtors	12444	15358	46563	97304	65841
Inventory	-		369	85348	56283
Turnover	-	-	112309	517787	338200
Oper Profit	-981	12111	27260	60539	32808
Interest Paid	4957	18044	38260	12468	2375
Tax Paid	2443	1735	66	4481	122
Prf af Int&Tax	12561	19130	27716	48876	30311
Prf att Ord Sh	27033	38531	73983	48876	30311
Btm Line Earn	-13263	703	292324	43421	26260
Dividend Paid	16197	22866	19241	19554	11280
Mkt Prce(c) YE	230	425	470	400	300
Depreciation	-	-	-	1561	1236

PER SHARE STATISTICS (CENTS)

Net Asst Val	566 83	609 58	712 85	119 31	88 24
Net Earnings	42 60	60 70	120 30	82 50	58 60
Dividends	25 50	36 00	48 00	33 00	23 00
Cash Flow	25 70	30 12	33 79	85 12	61 03

RATIOS AND OTHER INFORMATION

Mrk Cap(R000)	146087	269943	298525	237020	177765
Current Ratio	2 24	0 98	1 82	1 18	1 77
Quik/Acid Tst	2 24	0 98	1 81	0 63	0 96
A/C Rec T/ovr	-	-	1 81	5 32	5 14
Tot Ass T/ovr		-	0 13	1 60	2 39
Debt/Ass Rat	0 14	0 10	0 32	0 78	0 62
L T L Tot Ass	0 11	0 04	0 28	0 30	0 13
Debt to Eqity	0 17	0 11	0 46	1 44	0 58
Interest Cover	1 36	1 26	1 14	5 28	13 81
Oper Prof Mrg	-	-	24 27	11 69	9 70
Net Prof Marg%	-	-	65 87	9 44	8 96
Ret on Assets	8 13	13 60	12 74	20 29	23 18
Ret on Equity%	7 51	9 95	12 26	27 93	20 05
Price/Earnings	5 40	7 00	3 91	4 85	5 12
Divid Cover	1 67	1 69	2 51	2 50	2 55
Divid Yield	11 09	8 47	10 21	8 25	7 67
Earning Yield%	18 52	14 28	25 60	20 63	19 53
NAV % Mrk Pr	246 45	143 43	151 67	29 83	29 41
Effec Tax Rate	14 20	-	0 58	9 16	0 40
Def Interval	2 95	1 09	5 05	3 13	0 67
Sus Grth Rate	3 01	4 05	12 09	16 75	12 59

SUBSIDIARY & ASSOCIATED COMPANIES

ACCESS PROPERTIES (PTY) LTD
ACCESS SECURITIES (PTY) LTD
ACCESS TRAVEL (PTY) LTD
ALGOA ENGINEERING SUPPLY CO (PTY) LTD
ALL THE WAY INVESTMENTS (PTY) LTD
ANNE BOTHMA CAMERAS (PTY) LTD
ASSOCIATION CABLES (PTY) LTD
ATLAS CABLE SUPPLIES (PTY) LTD
AUDINO ELECTRICAL (PTY) LTD
AUTO SOUND AGENCIES (PTY) LTD
BONANZA ELECTRICAL WHOLESALERS (PTY) LTD
BOSE CORPORATION (PTY) LTD
CENTRELITE (PTY) LTD
CITY BAY ELECTRICAL WHOLESALERS (PTY) LT
CLUB ELECRICAL DISTRIBUTORS (PTY) LTD
ELCENTRE (BLOEMFONTEIN) (PTY) LTD
ELCENTRE (CAPE) (PTY) LTD
ELCENTRE (EAST RAND) (PTY) LTD
ELCENTRE (JOHANNESBURG) (PTY) LTD
ELCENTRE (NATAL) (PTY) LTD
ELCENTRE (NELSPRUIT) (PTY) LTD
ELCENTRE (NORTH) (PTY) LTD
ELCENTRE (PAARL) (PTY) LTD
ELCENTRE (PINETOWN) (PTY) LTD
ELCENTRE (PRETORIA) (PTY) LTD
ELCENTRE (PTY) LTD
ELCENTRE (ROSSLYN) (PTY) LTD
ELCENTRE (WEST RAND) (PTY) LTD
ELCENTRE (WORCESTER) (PTY) LTD
ELCENTRE ADMINISTRATION (PTY) LTD
ELCENTRE COMPUTER DEVELOPMENT (PTY) LTD
ELCENTRE COMPUTER SALES (PTY) LTD
ELCENTRE COMPUTER SERVICES (PTY) LTD
ELCENTRE CONTROL SYSTEMS (PTY) LTD
ELCENTRE ELECTRONICS (PTY) LTD
ELCENTRE HOLDINGS (PTY) LTD
ELCENTRE INVESTMENTS (PTY) LTD
ELCENTRE LEASING & FINANCE (PTY) LTD
ELCENTRE MARKETING (PTY) LTD
ELCENTRE SUPPLIES (PTY) LTD
ELECTRONIC TECHNOLOGY (PTY) LTD
EXECUTIVE ELECTRONIX (PTY) LTD
FOTOWILE DISTRIBUTORS (PTY) LTD
FREIGHTCO (PTY) LTD
GLOBE ELECTRIC (PTY) LTD
GLOBE ELECTRICAL (EAST RAND) PROPERTIES
GLOBE ELECTRICAL (TVL) (PTY) LTD
GLOLEC LTD
H&T ELECTRICAL WHOLESALERS (PTY) LTD
H&T ELECTRICAL WHOLESALERS (STRAND) (PTY
JLB INVESTMENTS (PTY) LTD
LERAMEL COMPANY (PTY) LTD
MAYFAIR COMMUNICATIONS (PTY) LTD
MAYFAIR HOLDINGS IN-SOUND (PTY) LTD
MULTILECTRONIC (CAPE) (PTY) LTD
MULTILECTRONIC (NATAL) (PTY) LTD
MULTILECTRONIC (PTY) LTD
MULTITECH ELECTRICAL DISTRIBUTORS (PTY)
NATAL CABLES & LIGHTING (PTY) LTD
NATIONAL COLLEGE OF PHOTOGRAPHY (PTY) LT
OREZ (BOPHUTHATSWANA) (PTY) LTD
OREZ (ERMELO) (PTY) LTD
OREZ (MIDDELBURG) (PTY) LTD
OREZ (PORT SHEPSTONE) (PTY) LTD
OREZ (PTY) LTD
OTLEY JARDINE (PTY) LTD

PACE CONSUMER HOLDINGS (PTY) LTD
PACE CONSUMER PRODUCTS (PTY) LTD
PECRON DISTRIBUTORS (PTY) LTD
POWERGROOVE (PTY) LTD
RASKIN HOLDINGS (PTY) LTD
RYALL (PTY) LTD
S.A. AUTO RADIO & T.V. (PTY) LTD
S.A. PHOTO PROCESSORS (PTY) LTD
SANLIC HARDWARE HOLDINGS LTD
SPRINGBOK ELECTRIC (PTY) LTD
STERN & PECK (PTY) LTD
TEAC CORPORATION (PTY) LTD
TEK SWAZILAND LTD
TON FINANSIERINGS (EDMS) BPK
VOLTEX HOLDINGS LTD
YELCO DISTRIBUTORS (PTY) LTD

INVESTMENTS

ELKORETTE ENGINEERING (PTY) LTD (VAR RAT (2500000 SH)
SANLIC HARDWARE HOLDINGS LTD (COMP CONV (42800000 D)
URD BELEGGINGS (PTY) LTD (VAR RATE RED C (120000000)
VOLTEX HOLDINGS LTD (COMP CONV DEBS) (101831184)

ELECTRONIC MEDIA NETWORK LTD

ABBREVIATION : M-NET

JSE SHORT CODE : MNE

SECTOR : Industrial-Beverages & Hotels

SHAREHOLDERS

Who Owns Whom's Assessment of the Identity of the Ultimate Controlling Shareholder:
ARGUS/DISPATCH/PERSKOR/NASPERS/NTL WITNS

SHAREHOLDER	PERCENTAGE 1992	1991
ELECTRONIC MEDIA NETWORK HOLDINGS P/L	60.9	78.8
NAT PERS BPK	6.3	---
ARGUS HOLDINGS LTD	4.1	---
TIMES MEDIA LTD	4.1	---
PERSKORPORASIE VAN SA BPK	2.9	---
CMB NOM P/L	1.9	---
VKP NOM P/L	1.8	2.2
ELECTRONIC MEDIA NETWORK SHARE TRUST	---	1.2
CHALKTON NOM CO P/L	---	1.1
TOTAL	81.8	83.3

DIRECTORS :
BAND DDB ,BEKKER JP (Managing Director)
BUITENDAG JM ,CONRADIE HF ,CRAIB DM ,KOVARSKY D
SIBIYA KB ,VOSLOO T (Chairman

REGISTRATION NUMBER : 85/02853/06

REGISTERED OFFICE
11 Grove Street, Randburg
2194
TEL: 011-889 1911
FAX: 011-889 1115

TRANSFER SECRETARY
Central Registrars Ltd
P O Box 4844, Johannesburg
2000
TEL: 011-331 0051

COMPANY SECRETARY
S Pacak

NATURE OF BUSINESS
M-Net conducts the business of a subscription television service in the entertainment and leisure industry, and markets information for credit purposes in the retail and commercial sectors of the business community. The company currently has 695000 home subscribers.

BANKERS :
Absa Bank Ltd

AUDITORS :
Coopers Theron Du Toit

FAMILIAR BRAND NAMES
ITC,KENYA TELEVISION NETWORK (50%)

CONTRIBUTION BY ACTIVITY
N/A

YEAR END : March

DIVIDEND : Ords 2c
Dividend (Ldr)28/02/92 (Pay)30/03/92 Amt(c)7

NUMBER OF EMPLOYEES : 1640

CAPITAL STRUCTURE

	AUTHORISED	ISSUED
Ords 2c	250000000	196725000

FINANCIAL STATISTICS (AT FINANCIAL YEAR END)

(Amts in R'000)	1992 Mar	1991 Mar	1990 Mar
Ord S/H Int	322801	52085	20326
Long Trm Loans	83945	50646	39588
Iss Ord Share	196725	152000	132000
Total Liab	292435	253066	209164
Current Liab	208490	202420	169576
Total Assets	615236	305151	229490
Current Assets	199389	202218	147354
Debtors	71595	52287	40278
Inventory	38672	29313	28750
Turnover	640673	426371	324207
Oper Profit	70003	51072	29056
Interest Paid	12967	9897	9969
Tax Paid	30134	13606	-
Prf af Int&Tax	32683	32455	19776
Prf att Ord Sh	27830	32455	14781
Btm Line Earn	27830	23485	14781
Dividend Paid	13771	10640	5060
Mkt Prce(c) YE	700	260	-
Depreciation	10963	8758	10846

PER SHARE STATISTICS (CENTS)

Net Asst Val	164.09	34.27	15.40
Net Earnings	17.40	22.30	11.20
Dividends	7.00	7.00	3.80
Cash Flow	46.26	34.07	19.41

RATIOS AND OTHER INFORMATION

Mrk Cap(R000)	1377075	395200	-
Current Ratio	0.96	1.00	0.87
Quik/Acid Tst	0.77	0.85	0.70
A/C Rec T/ovr	8.95	8.15	8.05
Tot Ass T/ovr	1.04	1.40	1.41
Debt/Ass Rat	0.42	0.81	0.91
L T L Tot Ass	0.08	0.15	0.17
Debt to Eqity	0.80	4.76	10.29
Interest Cover	5.40	5.16	2.91
Oper Prof Mrg	10.93	11.98	8.96
Net Prof Marg%	4.34	7.61	4.56
Ret on Assets	11.53	18.34	12.96
Ret on Equity%	8.62	62.31	72.72
Price/Earnings	40.23	11.66	-
Divid Cover	2.49	3.19	2.95
Divid Yield	1.00	2.69	-
Earning Yield%	2.49	8.58	-
NAV % Mrk Pr	23.44	13.18	-
Def Interval	0.66	0.88	1.54
Sus Grth Rate	4.36	41.88	47.83

SUBSIDIARY & ASSOCIATED COMPANIES

BCCB (PTY) LTD
CAMPBELLS CONSUMER ENQUIRY (PTY) LTD (30%)
CREDIT MANAGEMENT LEARNING SYSTEM (PTY) (50%)
DELPHIN SECURITIES (PTY) LTD
EAST VAAL CREDIT BUREAU (PTY) LTD (30%)
ELECTRONIC MEDIA NETWORK SALES (PTY) LTD
ELECTRONIC MEDIA NETWORK SUPPLIES (PTY) (50%)
ERNII (PTY) LTD (33,33%)
GREYLINGS CREDIT CONTROL (PTY) LTD (30%)
ITC BOTSWANA (PTY) LTD (50%)
ITC NAMIBIA (PTY) LTD
ITC-VISION (PTY) LTD (33,3%)
LESOTHO BROADCASTING (PTY) LTD
M-NET NAMIBIA (PTY) LTD (50%)
M-NET TELEVISION (PTY) LTD
M-NET TRANSKEI (PTY) LTD (50%)
NETWORK HOLDINGS SA (50%)
SAGE LAND HOLDINGS (PTY) LTD
VERI-CHEQUE (PTY) LTD

INVESTMENTS

None

ELLERINE HOLDINGS LTD

ABBREVIATION : ELLERINE

JSE SHORT CODE : ELH

SECTOR : Industrial-Furniture & Household

SHAREHOLDERS

Who Owns Whom's Assessment of the Identity of the Ultimate Controlling Shareholder:
SANLAM VIA GENCOR AND MALBAK

SHAREHOLDER	PERCENTAGE 1992	1991
MALBAK INV (ELLERINES) LTD	59.7	59.5
CMB NOM P/L	9.9	---
ERIC ELLERINE TRUST P/L	3.9	3.9
ELLERINE BROS P/L	3.2	3.2
SIDNEY ELLERINE TRUST P/L	2.6	2.6
METAL IND GROUP PENS FUND	2.0	2.0
ENGINEERING INDUSTRIES PENS FUND	1.4	1.4
YSKOR PENS FUND	1.2	---
BUSKIN J K	1.1	1.1
ELLERINE D T	1.1	1.1
ELLERINE N P	1.1	1.1
IMERMAN I L	1.1	1.1
STD BANK NOM TVL P/L	---	1.3
SANLAM	---	9.9
TOTAL	88.4	88.1

DIRECTORS :
CHALMERS TJ ,DRITZ J (Administration Director)
ELLERINE E (Chairman & Managing Dir.)
ELLERINE S ,FINKEL GF (Financial Director)
KENNEALY DP ,MCGLASHAN DS

REGISTRATION NUMBER : 68/13402/06

REGISTERED OFFICE
Ellerine Centre, 236 Victoria Road
Germiston
1401
TEL: 011-825 1000
FAX: 011-873 8180

TRANSFER SECRETARY
Central Registrars Ltd
P O Box 4844, Johannesburg
2000
TEL: 011-331 0051

COMPANY SECRETARY
J Dritz

NATURE OF BUSINESS
The group retails furniture & household appliances through 354 outlets situated in rural & urban SA.

BANKERS :
Nedperm Bank Ltd

AUDITORS :
Kessel Feinstein, Deloitte Pim Goldby

FAMILIAR BRAND NAMES
ELLEGOLD,EUROPA COLLECTION,FURNCITY
JAKO FURNISHERS,OXFORD FURNISHERS
RHEINGOLD FURNISHERS,ROYAL FURNISHERS
SLUMBER KING,SMART BUY,TOWN TALK
VOLKS HOME FURNISHERS

CONTRIBUTION BY ACTIVITY
Furniture (% profit after tax) (97.3%)
Property (2.7%)

YEAR END : August

DIVIDEND : Ords 50c

Interim No 42	(Ldr)27/04/90	(Pay)11/05/90	Amt(c)109
Final No 43	(Ldr)02/11/90	(Pay)30/11/90	Amt(c)112
Interim No 44	(Ldr)26/04/91	(Pay)10/05/91	Amt(c)125
Final No 45	(Ldr)01/11/91	(Pay)29/11/91	Amt(c)132
Interim No 46	(Ldr)24/04/92	(Pay)11/05/92	Amt(c)85
Final No 47	(Ldr)30/10/92	(Pay)27/11/92	Amt(c)148

NUMBER OF EMPLOYEES : 7000

CAPITAL STRUCTURE

	AUTHORISED	ISSUED
Ords 50c	10000000	7179800

FINANCIAL STATISTICS (AT FINANCIAL YEAR END)

(Amts in R'000)	1992 Aug	1991 Aug	1990 Aug	1989 Aug	1988 Aug
Ord S/H Int	258180	224617	185484	150473	135508
Long Trm Loans	85087	71631	60134	45561	46117
Iss Ord Share	7180	7180	7180	6900	6900
Total Liab	224970	200697	155462	130490	138783
Current Liab	139883	129066	95328	84929	92666
Total Assets	483150	425314	340946	280963	274291
Current Assets	414873	365453	293996	240964	235817
Debtors	368531	321400	257924	210670	210881
Inventory	45987	43957	35944	28178	24438
Turnover	588232	592360	483221	389453	205940
Oper Profit	97803	104768	87095	58926	26086
Interest Paid	2552	3584	1325	540	1372
Tax Paid	44895	49782	43176	29236	10678
Prf af Int&Tax	50736	55743	47694	30877	14036
Prf att Ord Sh	50369	57551	47675	30872	14036
Btm Line Earn	50369	57551	47675	30872	14036
Dividend Paid	16732	18452	15867	11798	3450
Mkt Prce(c) YE	4600	6200	2900	1250	750
Depreciation	10082	8339	7185	7203	4771

PER SHARE STATISTICS (CENTS)

Net Asst Val	3595.82	3128.37	2583.34	2180.77	1963.88
Net Earnings	702.00	774.00	669.00	447.00	203.00
Dividends	233.00	257.00	221.00	166.00	50.00
Cash Flow	1025.32	1073.59	918.55	553.06	397.87

RATIOS AND OTHER INFORMATION

Mrk Cap(R000)	330280	445160	208220	86250	51750
Current Ratio	2.97	2.83	3.08	2.84	2.54
Quik/Acid Tst	2.64	2.49	2.71	2.51	2.28
A/C Rec T/ovr	1.60	1.84	1.87	1.85	1.46
Tot Ass T/ovr	1.22	1.39	1.42	1.39	1.13
Debt/Ass Rat	0.29	0.30	0.28	0.30	0.34
Debt to Eqity	0.54	0.57	0.51	0.56	0.68
Interest Cover	38.32	29.23	65.73	109.12	19.01
Oper Prof Mrg	16.63	17.69	18.02	15.13	12.67
Net Prof Marg%	8.56	9.72	9.87	7.93	6.82
Ret on Assets	20.32	25.65	27.04	21.59	14.27
Ret on Equity%	19.51	25.62	25.70	20.52	15.54
Price/Earnings	6.55	8.01	4.33	2.80	3.69
Divid Cover	3.01	3.01	3.03	2.69	4.06
Divid Yield	5.07	4.15	7.62	13.28	6.67
Earning Yield%	15.26	12.48	23.07	35.76	27.07
NAV % Mrk Pr	78.17	50.46	89.08	174.46	261.85
Effec Tax Rate	31.49	32.09	23.13	38.43	43.13
Def Interval	0.59	0.30	-	-	1.93
Sus Grth Rate	13.03	17.41	17.15	12.68	7.81

SUBSIDIARY & ASSOCIATED COMPANIES

ALLIED RE-INSURANCE CO (PTY) LTD
ALLIED TRADING (PTY) LTD
BENONI FURNISHERS (PTY) LTD
COHEN BROTHERS FURNITURE (PTY) LTD
DENNIS STORES (BUTTERWORTH) (PTY) LTD
E.L. FURNISHERS (TRANSKEI) HOLDINGS LTD
ELLERINE ESTATES (SWAZILAND) (PTY) LTD
ELLERINE FURNISHERS (BOPHUTHATSWANA) (PT
ELLERINE FURNISHERS (BOTSWANA) (PTY) LTD
ELLERINE FURNISHERS (KWAZULU) (PTY) LTD
ELLERINE FURNISHERS (LEBOWA) (PTY) LTD (50%)
ELLERINE FURNISHERS (NAMIBIA) (PTY) LTD
ELLERINE FURNISHERS (PTY) LTD
ELLERINE FURNISHERS MAFIKENG HOLDINGS (P
ELLERINE FURNITURE (STERKSPRUIT) (PTY) L
ELLERINE JOINT VENTURE (BOPHUTHATSWANA) (50%)
ELLERINE PROPERTIES (BOTSWANA) (PTY) LTD
ELLERINE PROPERTIES (FLAGSTAFF) (PTY) LT
ELLERINE PROPERTIES (GIYANI) (PTY) LTD
ELLERINE PROPERTIES (IDUTYWA) (PTY) LTD
ELLERINE PROPERTIES (PTY) LTD
ELLERINE PROPERTIES (VENDA) (PTY) LTD
ELLERINES DEVELOPMENT (ENGCOBO) (PTY) LT
ELLERINES DEVELOPMENT (UMTATA) (PTY) LTD
ELLERINES FURNISHERS (BIZANA) (PTY) LTD
ELLERINES FURNISHERS (BUTTERWORH) (PTY)
ELLERINES FURNISHERS (CISKEI) (PTY) LTD
ELLERINES FURNISHERS (ENGCOBO) (PTY) LTD
ELLERINES FURNISHERS (LESOTHO) (PTY) LTD
ELLERINES FURNISHERS (SWAZI) (PTY) LTD
ELLERINES FURNISHERS (TABANKULU) (PTY) L
ELLERINES FURNISHERS (TRANSKEI) (PTY) LT
ELLERINES FURNISHERS (UMTATA) (PTY) LTD
ELLERINES FURNISHERS (VENDA) (PTY) LTD
ERF 151 UMTATA (PTY) LTD
FURNCITY (PTY) LTD
JAKO FURNISHERS (PTY) LTD
OXFORD FURNISHERS (LESOTHO) (PTY) LTD
RHEINGOLD FURNISHERS (PTY) LTD
ROYAL FURNISHERS (PTY) LTD
TOWN TALK (IDUTYWA) (PTY) LTD
TOWN TALK FURNISHERS (BUSHBUCKRIDGE) (PT (50%)
TOWN TALK FURNISHERS (LESOTHO) (PTY) LTD
TOWN TALK FURNISHERS (PTY) LTD
VOLKS FURNITURE STORES (PTY) LTD

INVESTMENTS

None

ENGEN BOTSWANA LTD

ABBREVIATION : ENBOT

SECTOR : Botswana Stock Exchange

SHAREHOLDERS

Who Owns Whom's Assessment of the Identity of the Ultimate Controlling Shareholder: ENGEN LTD SA

SHAREHOLDER	PERCENTAGE 1992	1991
PETROLEUM INV HOLDING CO LTD	70.0	---
DEBSWANA PENS FUND	6.2	---
P B INV & HOLDINGS P/L	3.9	---
BOTSWANA MOTOR VEHICLE INSURANCE FUND	3.5	---
BOTSWANA INSURANCE CO P/L	2.5	---
MADA TRUST P/L (BOUSFIELD S J)	2.0	---
HILL A R C	1.6	---
HILL P N	1.6	---
BECKER P	1.6	---
DESAI P	1.6	---
TOTAL	94.4	---

DIRECTORS :
BECKER PM (Managing Director),CAMPBELL AC
DESAI PV ,HILL ARC ,MAKGEKGENENE L
MATENGE GW (Chairman),MOFFETT MJ ,PARTON JG
STONEHAM GJ

REGISTRATION NUMBER : 335

REGISTERED OFFICE
Plot 252, Light Industrial Sites
Francistown, Botswana

TEL: 353077
FAX: 353070

TRANSFER SECRETARY
Piyushkant Virendrakumar Desai
P O Box 867, Gaberone
Botswana

TEL: 09267-353077

COMPANY SECRETARY
P V Desai

NATURE OF BUSINESS
The ENGEN group operates as an integrated refiner and distributor of petroleum products in southern Africa and, more recently,in wider international markets.In Botswana the products of ENGEN are marketed through OIL BOTSWANA,which is in nature a marketing and distribution company.

BANKERS :
N/A

AUDITORS :
Coopers & Lybrand

FAMILIAR BRAND NAMES
N/A

CONTRIBUTION BY ACTIVITY
N/A

YEAR END : August

CAPITAL STRUCTURE

	AUTHORISED	ISSUED
Ords P0,20	20000000	15972222

FINANCIAL STATISTICS (AT FINANCIAL YEAR END)

(Amts in P)	1991 Dec
Ord S/H Int	14431
Long Trm Loans	911
Iss Ord Share	5250
Total Liab	19744
Current Liab	18833
Total Assets	34175
Current Assets	22693
Debtors	15015
Inventory	3820
Oper Profit	4001
Tax Paid	1763
Prf af Int&Tax	2238
Prf att Ord Sh	2238
Btm Line Earn	1886

PER SHARE STATISTICS (CENTS)

Net Asst Val	274.88
Cash Flow	42.63

RATIOS AND OTHER INFORMATION

Current Ratio	1.20
Quik/Acid Tst	1.00
Debt/Ass Rat	0.58
L T L Tot Ass	0.03
Debt to Eqity	1.37
Ret on Assets	11.71
Ret on Equity%	15.51
Effec Tax Rate	44.06
Def Interval	1.55
Sus Grth Rate	15.51

SUBSIDIARY & ASSOCIATED COMPANIES

BGI AGENCIES (PTY) LTD
BGI MAHALAPYE (PTY) LTD
BGI MANUFACTURING (PTY) LTD
BGI MAUN (PTY) LTD
BGI PALAPYE (PTY) LTD
BGI PROPERTIES LTD
CAVALLO ENGINEERING & CONSTRUCTION (PTY)
D G PROPERTIES GABORONE (PTY) LTD
DROVE PROPERTIES (PTY) LTD
GAMESKIN MANUFACTURERS (PTY) LTD
GEDNEY PROPERTIES (PTY) LTD
IVORY PROPERTIES (PTY) LTD
OIL BOTSWANA (PTY) LTD
PHOENIX PROPERTIES (PTY) LTD
ROCKYHILL PROPERTIES (PTY) LTD

INVESTMENTS

None

ENGEN LTD

ABBREVIATION : ENGEN

JSE SHORT CODE : EGN

SECTOR : Industrial-Chemicals & Oils

SHAREHOLDERS

Who Owns Whom's Assessment of the Identity of the Ultimate Controlling Shareholder:
SANLAM VIA GENCOR

SHAREHOLDER	PERCENTAGE 1992	1991
CONSOLIDATED NOM P/L	61.7	61.9
STD BANK NOM TVL P/L	8.8	8.6
ABSA NOM P/L	6.4	---
CMB NOM P/L	4.8	---
SA MUTUAL	2.1	1.7
EIGHTY ONE MAIN STREET NOM LTD	1.8	---
ESCOM PENS & PROV FUND	---	1.0
SANLAM	---	4.6
VOLKSKAS NOM P/L	---	6.3
TOTAL	85.6	84.0

DIRECTORS :
ANGEL RJ (Chief Executive & M.D.),DE BEER TL
DEUDNEY NA ,GILBERTSON BP ,HUNT-DAVIS DNA
HURT BL ,KENNELLY ND ,MARTIN WE ,ROBERTS JV
SMITH BA (Chairman),STEENKAMP TI ,STEYN SJ
VAN DER PAS T

REGISTRATION NUMBER : 68/02086/06

REGISTERED OFFICE
Mobil Court, Thibault Square
Cape Town
8001
TEL: 021-403 4911
FAX: 021-403 4067

TRANSFER SECRETARY
Central Registrars Ltd
P O Box 4844, Johannesburg
2000
TEL: 011-331 0051

COMPANY SECRETARY
D E Curtis

NATURE OF BUSINESS
The group comprises three major activities; Marketing of fuels, lubricants and other petroleum products; Production by way of petroleum refining, the ability to produce various chemical feedstocks and a 30% interest in Mossgas; Exploration interests through contractual arrangements with Soekor.

BANKERS :
Trust Bank of Africa Ltd
Standard Bank of SA Ltd
First National Bank of SA Ltd

AUDITORS :
Coopers Theron Du Toit, Ernst & Young

FAMILIAR BRAND NAMES
GENREF,HOMEGAS,LAUREL,LUBRO
MOBIL (UNTIL 30/06/94),SONAP,TREK,WHITE ROSE

CONTRIBUTION BY ACTIVITY
Chemicals (2.2%)
Marketing (% of Turnover) (94.0%)
Logistics (3.8%)

YEAR END : August

DIVIDEND : Ords 50c

Final No 43	(Ldr)09/11/90	(Pay)05/12/90	Amt(c)62
Interim No 44	(Ldr)12/04/91	(Pay)27/04/91	Amt(c)42
Final No 45	(Ldr)08/11/91	(Pay)05/12/91	Amt(c)74
Interim No 46	(Ldr)16/04/92	(Pay)30/04/92	Amt(c)50
Final No 47	(Ldr)06/11/92	(Pay)04/12/92	Amt(c)87.5

NUMBER OF EMPLOYEES : 3693

CAPITAL STRUCTURE

	AUTHORISED	ISSUED
Ords 50c	221000000	154423020

FINANCIAL STATISTICS (AT FINANCIAL YEAR END)

(Amts in R'000)	1992 Aug	1991 Aug	1990 Aug	1989 Aug	1988 Aug
Ord S/H Int	2656000	2411000	1103704	154059	134049
Long Trm Loans	626000	256000	266686	4159	5882
Iss Ord Share	154423	154057	110041	20252	20252
Total Liab	1967000	1375000	1354999	177041	122562
Current Liab	1341000	1119000	1088313	172882	116680
Total Assets	4623000	3786000	2458703	331100	256611
Current Assets	2187000	2247000	1418233	254423	188296
Debtors	698000	581000	566711	88632	72207
Inventory	588000	556000	433191	44309	38278
Turnover	6560000	6098000	3168000	1018129	509733
Oper Profit	349000	463000	206170	36986	32259
Interest Paid	60000	39000	54045	965	488
Tax Paid	50000	118000	-10111	25238	13582
Prf af Int&Tax	439000	387000	209146	35996	18189
Prf att Ord Sh	437000	386000	208792	36818	18367
Btm Line Earn	442000	386000	242549	36818	18367
Dividend Paid	212000	160000	75313	16808	10531
Mkt Prce(c) YE	4250	3700	2750	1475	870
Depreciation	60000	56000	25788	7181	4234

PER SHARE STATISTICS (CENTS)

Net Asst Val	1719.95	1565.01	1002.99	760.71	661.90
Net Earnings	283.00	314.00	321.00	181.80	90.20
Dividends	137.50	116.00	97.00	83.00	52.00
Cash Flow	327.61	354.17	354.46	211.66	156.34

RATIOS AND OTHER INFORMATION

Mrk Cap(R000)	6562978	5700109	3026128	298717	176192
Current Ratio	1.63	2.01	1.30	1.47	1.61
Quik/Acid Tst	1.19	1.51	0.91	1.22	1.29
A/C Rec T/ovr	9.40	10.50	5.59	11.49	10.59
Tot Ass T/ovr	1.42	1.61	1.29	3.07	2.98
Debt/Ass Rat	0.42	0.36	0.55	0.52	0.45
L T L Tot Ass	0.13	0.07	0.11	-	-
Debt to Eqity	0.74	0.57	1.23	1.12	0.87
Interest Cover	6.87	11.92	3.90	52.43	66.10
Oper Prof Mrg	5.32	7.59	6.51	3.63	6.33
Net Prof Marg%	6.66	6.33	6.59	3.62	3.60
Ret on Assets	11.88	14.37	10.30	18.84	19.07
Ret on Equity%	16.45	16.01	18.92	23.90	20.55
Price/Earnings	15.02	11.78	8.57	8.11	9.65
Divid Cover	2.06	2.71	3.31	2.19	1.73
Divid Yield	3.24	3.14	3.53	5.63	5.98
Earning Yield%	6.66	8.49	11.67	12.33	10.37
NAV % Mrk Pr	40.47	42.30	36.47	51.57	76.08
Effec Tax Rate	9.86	24.85	-3.46	55.22	46.37
Def Interval	1.42	0.69	2.41	0.07	0.30
Sus Grth Rate	8.47	9.37	12.09	12.99	5.85

SUBSIDIARY & ASSOCIATED COMPANIES

CHEMICO (PTY) LTD
ENGEN MANAGEMENT SERVICES (PTY) LTD
GENREF LTD
SOUTHERN AFRICA ENERGY CO LTD
SOUTHERN AFRICA ENERGY HOLDING CO (PTY)
TREK PETROLEUM (PTY) LTD

INVESTMENTS

BRANDT HOLDINGS LTD RED CUM PREF (15 SH)
CACTUS INVESTMENTS (PTY) LTD RED CUM PRE (300000000)
CRICKETGROUND INVESTMENTS (PTY) LTD RED (1 SH)
DURRELL INVESTMENTS (PTY) LTD RED CUM PR (5000000SH)
ELECTRA INVESTMENTS (SA) LTD (RED CUM PR (250000SH)
HELAM MINING (PTY) LTD RED CUM PREF (10 SH)
INVICTA BEARINGS (PTY) LTD RED CUM PREF (25000SH)
KWAZULU FINANCE & INVESTMENTS CORP LTD R (15000000S)
MOSSGAS (PTY) LTD (300SH)
NILE INVESTMENTS (PTY) LTD RED CUM PREF (200000SH)
PRIMA BANK NOMINEES (PTY) LTD (20000000S)
SAFOR (PTY) LTD (2162000SH)
SENTRAKOOP HANDELAARS BPK RED CUM PREF (10000SH)

ENSIGN CLOTHING LTD

ABBREVIATION : ENSIGN

JSE SHORT CODE : ENS

SECTOR : Industrial-Clothing, Footwear & Textiles

SHAREHOLDERS

Who Owns Whom's Assessment of the Identity of the Ultimate Controlling Shareholder:
ROY FAMILY

SHAREHOLDER	PERCENTAGE 1992	1991
HIGHWICK PROPERTY P/L	41 5	41 5
SA EQUITIES LTD	24 1	24 6
ROY D	6 5	6 5
ROY R	4 9	4 9
BARTEL H O	2 2	2 2
ZIEGELSTEIN B	2 2	2 2
KATZ J	2 1	1 1
ROY L E	1 9	1 9
ROYTOWSKI R	1 6	1 6
NUSSBAUM R S A W	1 4	1 4
ZIEGELSTEIN L	1 1	1 1
TOTAL	89 4	88 8

DIRECTORS :
REELER CG ,ROY D (Deputy Managing Director)
ROY R (Chairman & Managing Dir),ROY S ,ROY SP
ROY Z

REGISTRATION NUMBER : 05/08786/06

REGISTERED OFFICE
Hyde Street, Cape Town
8001
TEL 021-45 5685
FAX 021-461 6874

TRANSFER SECRETARY
Finpak Registrars (Pty) Ltd
2100 Cartwrights Corner House, Adderley Street
Cape Town
8000
TEL 021-418 5040

COMPANY SECRETARY
A M Bissett

NATURE OF BUSINESS
Ensign are manufacturers of workwear, protective clothing, uniforms, leisurewear and PVC fabric

BANKERS :
First National Bank of SA Ltd

AUDITORS :
Deloitte Pim Goldby

FAMILIAR BRAND NAMES
ENSIGN,MACBEAN,SALVAGE,SAMSON
SAMSON INTERNATIONAL,SAMSON SUPREME

CONTRIBUTION BY ACTIVITY
N/A

YEAR END : December

DIVIDEND : Ords 50c

Final	(Ldr)29/05/92	(Pay)12/06/92	Amt(c)25
Interim	(Ldr)30/10/92	(Pay)13/11/92	Amt(c)15

NUMBER OF EMPLOYEES : 1310

CAPITAL STRUCTURE

	AUTHORISED	ISSUED
Ords 50c	1000000	660000
6% Cum Prefs R2	250000	185000

FINANCIAL STATISTICS (AT FINANCIAL YEAR END)

(Amts in R'000)	1991 Dec	1990 Dec	1989 Dec	1988 Dec	1987 Dec
Ord S/H Int	8279	7896	7187	6642	6078
Long Trm Loans	838	901	801	845	851
Iss Ord Share	660	660	660	660	660
Total Liab	11459	8291	5292	4851	3993
Current Liab	10621	7390	4491	4006	3142
Total Assets	19738	16187	12479	11493	10071
Current Assets	17994	14278	10728	9807	8361
Debtors	9858	7564	4993	4140	3532
Inventory	7932	6714	5700	5667	4829
Oper Profit	2721	2349	1692	1625	1511
Interest Paid	534	423	364	189	112
Tax Paid	940	931	529	620	586
Prf af Int&Tax	1247	995	799	816	813
Prf att Ord Sh	1225	973	777	794	791
Btm Line Earn	647	973	777	794	791
Dividend Paid	264	264	231	231	231
Mkt Prce(c) YE	600	500	625	625	610
Depreciation	250	258	232	269	242

PER SHARE STATISTICS (CENTS)

Net Asst Val	1254 39	1196 36	1088 94	1006 36	920 91
Net Earnings	186 00	147 00	118 00	120 00	120 00
Dividends	40 00	40 00	35 00	35 00	35 00
Cash Flow	189 09	186 52	152 88	161 06	156 52

RATIOS AND OTHER INFORMATION

Mrk Cap(R000)	3960	3300	4125	4125	4026
Current Ratio	1 69	1 93	2 39	2 45	2 66
Quik/Acid Tst	0 95	1 02	1 12	1 03	1 12
Debt/Ass Rat	0 56	0 49	0 39	0 39	0 36
L T L Tot Ass	0 02	0 03	0 03	0 04	0 05
Debt to Eqity	1 33	1 00	0 68	0 67	0 60
Interest Cover	5 10	5 55	4 65	8 60	13 49
Ret on Assets	13 79	14 51	13 56	14 14	15 00
Ret on Equity%	14 80	12 32	10 81	11 95	13 01
Price/Earnings	3 23	3 40	5 30	5 21	5 08
Divid Cover	4 65	3 68	3 37	3 43	3 43
Divid Yield	6 67	8 00	5 60	5 60	5 74
Earning Yield%	31 00	29 40	18 88	19 20	19 67
NAV % Mrk Pr	209 07	239 27	174 23	161 02	150 97
Effec Tax Rate	58 39	47 35	39 83	43 45	40 60
Def Interval	3 81	3 04	3 11	2 37	1 46
Sus Grth Rate	11 61	8 98	7 60	8 48	9 21

SUBSIDIARY & ASSOCIATED COMPANIES

ATHOL AMERICAN SHIRT COMPANY (PTY) LTD
BENMOR CLOTHING MANUFACTURERS (PTY) LTD
MACBEAN AFRICAN OILSKINS (PTY) LTD
PW HALL (AFRICA) (PTY) LTD

INVESTMENTS

None

ENVIRONMENTAL RESOURCES LTD

ABBREVIATION : ENROL

JSE SHORT CODE : ERL

SECTOR : Development Capital Market

SHAREHOLDERS

Who Owns Whom's Assessment of the Identity of the Ultimate Controlling Shareholder:
VENTAL HOLDINGS SA

SHAREHOLDER	PERCENTAGE 1992	1991
VENTAL HOLDINGS SA	88.0	87.1
METALMIL P/L	3.5	---
ENVIRONMENTAL RESOURCES SA	2.8	---
WILDMAN N	2.0	2.3
METAL RECOUP INC	1.4	---
TOUBOUL A	---	1.5
UPGRADE PROPERTY HOLDINGS P/L	---	3.2
WOLF INDUSTRIES P/L	---	3.2
TOTAL	97.6	97.2

DIRECTORS :
FRESEN AC MS,JACOBS S
JULLIENNE JRJ (Joint Managing Director)
MAROUN WA MS,WILDMAN N ,WOLF E
WOLF GC (Joint Managing Director

REGISTRATION NUMBER : 89/07464/06

REGISTERED OFFICE
21 Jellicoe Ave, Rosebank
Johannesburg
2196
TEL: 011-880 5386/7
FAX: 011-788 4880

TRANSFER SECRETARY
Mercantile Registrars Ltd
P O Box 1053, Johannesburg
2000
TEL: 011-333 8181

COMPANY SECRETARY
W A Maroun

NATURE OF BUSINESS
The company carries on the business of the reclamation of metal from slag arising in the production of steel.

BANKERS :
First National Bank of SA Ltd
Nedperm Bank Ltd

AUDITORS :
AD Starfield & Co
Goldberg Jaffe Joselowsky & Partners

FAMILIAR BRAND NAMES
N/A

CONTRIBUTION BY ACTIVITY
N/A

YEAR END : October

DIVIDEND :15/01/92

CAPITAL STRUCTURE

	AUTHORISED	ISSUED
Ords 1c	100000000	13527270

FINANCIAL STATISTICS (AT FINANCIAL YEAR END)

(Amts in R'000)	1992 Oct	1990 Oct	1989 Oct	1988 Oct
Ord S/H Int	6371	6311	1485	-
Long Trm Loans	277	221	-	-
Iss Ord Share	13527	13527	3300	-
Total Liab	336	1803	-	-
Current Liab	59	1582	-	-
Total Assets	6253	7660	1485	-
Intang Assets	454	454	*	*
Current Assets	108	2210	-	-
Debtors	59	102	-	-
Turnover	617	1041	881	734
Oper Profit	118	434	421	312
Tax Paid	56	221	210	156
Prf af Int&Tax	62	213	211	156
Prf att Ord Sh	62	213	211	156
Btm Line Earn	62	213	211	156
Mkt Prce(c) YE	60	45	-	-
Depreciation	63	156	-	-

PER SHARE STATISTICS (CENTS)

Net Asst Val	43.74	43.30	45.00	-
Net Earnings	0.50	4.60	-	-
Cash Flow	1.40	12.64	6.39	-

RATIOS AND OTHER INFORMATION

Mrk Cap(R000)	8116	6087	-	-
Current Ratio	1.83	1.40	-	-
Quik/Acid Tst	1.83	1.40	-	-
A/C Rec T/ovr	10.46	10.21	-	-
Tot Ass T/ovr	0.10	0.14	0.59	-
Debt/Ass Rat	0.01	0.21	-	-
Debt to Eqity	0.01	0.25	-	-
Oper Prof Mrg	19.12	41.69	47.79	42.51
Net Prof Marg%	10.05	20.46	23.95	21.25
Ret on Assets	1.89	5.67	28.35	-
Ret on Equity%	0.97	3.38	14.21	-
Price/Earnings	120.00	9.78	-	-
Earning Yield%	0.83	10.22	-	-
NAV % Mrk Pr	72.90	96.22	-	-
Effec Tax Rate	-	-	49.88	50.00
Sus Grth Rate	0.97	3.38	14.21	-

SUBSIDIARY & ASSOCIATED COMPANIES

MATERIAL RECYCLING TECHNOLOGY (PTY) LTD

INVESTMENTS

None

EQUIKOR HOLDINGS LTD

ABBREVIATION : EQUIKOR

JSE SHORT CODE : EQR

SECTOR : Financial-Property

SHAREHOLDERS

Who Owns Whom's Assessment of the Identity of the Ultimate Controlling Shareholder: DIRECTORS

SHAREHOLDER	PERCENTAGE 1992	1991
ANGLO RAND INV P/L	25.2	23.2
SAFEGRO NOM P/L	20.1	20.0
CMB NOM P/L	17.4	---
GRYLLS G P	5.8	5.8
ANGLO RAND INV HOLDINGS P/L	5.8	5.8
UNIDEV LTD	5.2	5.4
FIRST NAT NOM P/L	4.0	2.5
WILLMORE L H	2.9	4.6
LEVIN H	2.4	2.4
HIRSCHSON I T	1.1	---
PHELPS L S	1.1	---
COATES J J	---	1.7
SANLAM	---	17.3
TOTAL	91.1	88.7

DIRECTORS :
COATES JJ ,HIRSCHSON IT (Managing Director)
LEVIN J ,LEWIS IMA ,PHELPS LS
VORSTER HV (Chairman

REGISTRATION NUMBER : 68/04109/06

REGISTERED OFFICE
15th Floor, The Terraces, 34 Bree Street
Cape Town
8001
TEL: 021-214 014
FAX: 021-216 444

TRANSFER SECRETARY
Mercantile Registrars Ltd
P O Box 1053, Johannesburg
2000
TEL: 011-333 8181

COMPANY SECRETARY
J J Coates

NATURE OF BUSINESS
The group has subsidiary companies engaged in property development, property trading and property owning activities.

BANKERS :
Senbank, First National Bank of SA Ltd

AUDITORS :
Coopers Theron Du Toit, Braude Gordon & Co

FAMILIAR BRAND NAMES
N/A

CONTRIBUTION BY ACTIVITY
N/A

YEAR END : December

DIVIDEND : Ords 1c
Dividend (Ldr)03/08/92 (Pay)17/08/92 Amt(c)0.5

NUMBER OF EMPLOYEES : 32

CAPITAL STRUCTURE

	AUTHORISED	ISSUED
Ords 1c	1822080353	276230503

FINANCIAL STATISTICS (AT FINANCIAL YEAR END)

(Amts in R'000)	1991 Dec	1990 Dec	1989 Dec
Ord S/H Int	24619	21433	17526
Long Trm Loans	580	1847	9915
Iss Ord Share	276231	277156	180855
Total Liab	14361	10437	11961
Current Liab	13781	8590	2046
Total Assets	26980	19870	17487
Intang Assets	12000	12000	12000
Current Assets	25270	17871	13482
Debtors	2574	3006	5971
Inventory	22225	10896	451
Turnover	36376	37785	29600
Oper Profit	7370	4218	3680
Interest Paid	2803	207	73
Prf af Int&Tax	4567	4011	3607
Prf att Ord Sh	4567	4011	3664
Btm Line Earn	4567	4011	3664
Dividend Paid	1381	-	-
Mkt Prce(c) YE	10	10	10
Depreciation	136	90	63

PER SHARE STATISTICS (CENTS)

Net Asst Val	4.57	3.40	3.06
Net Earnings	1.70	1.40	1.30
Dividends	0.01	-	-
Cash Flow	1.70	1.48	1.33

RATIOS AND OTHER INFORMATION

Mrk Cap(R000)	27623	27716	18086
Current Ratio	1.83	2.08	6.59
Quik/Acid Tst	0.22	0.81	6.37
A/C Rec T/ovr	14.13	12.57	4.96
Tot Ass T/ovr	1.35	1.90	1.69
Debt/Ass Rat	0.53	0.53	0.68
L T L Tot Ass	0.02	0.09	0.57
Debt to Eqity	0.58	0.49	0.68
Interest Cover	2.63	20.38	50.41
Oper Prof Mrg	20.26	11.16	12.43
Net Prof Marg%	12.55	10.62	12.38
Ret on Assets	27.32	21.23	21.37
Ret on Equity%	18.55	18.71	20.91
Price/Earnings	5.88	7.14	7.69
Divid Cover	170.00	-	-
Divid Yield	0.10	-	-
Earning Yield%	17.00	14.00	13.00
NAV % Mrk Pr	45.68	34.03	30.55
Def Interval	2.28	1.90	0.25
Sus Grth Rate	12.94	18.71	20.91

SUBSIDIARY & ASSOCIATED COMPANIES

AIR KAROO (PTY) LTD
AQUANAUT INVESTMENTS (PTY) LTD (20%)
CAVENDISH CLOSE (PTY) LTD
DERMANS PLANT HIRE LTD
EQUIKOR LTD
EQUIKOR MANAGEMENT CO (PTY) LTD
GUNYALA PLASE (PTY) LTD
KERNGROEP ONTWIKKELAARS (PTY) LTD
LOMBARD FINANS (PTY) LTD
NATPROP MANAGEMENT SERVICES LTD
NATPROP TRADING INVESTMENTS LTD
PLOT 69 BOEKENHOUT (PTY) LTD
PRETORIA TOWN & TOWNLANDS PROJECT ONE (P
UITSKOT (PTY) LTD
VAN RIEBEECKSTAD DEVELOPMENT CO LTD

INVESTMENTS

None

EUREKA INDUSTRIAL LTD

ABBREVIATION : EUREKA

JSE SHORT CODE : EUR

SECTOR : Industrial-Industrial Holding

SHAREHOLDERS

Who Owns Whom's Assessment of the Identity of the Ultimate Controlling Shareholder:
PRICE FAMILY

SHAREHOLDER	PERCENTAGE 1992	1991
PRICE RONALD SYDNEY	34 5	33 5
STOCKSHARE NOM P/L	13 5	-
CAVERSHAM TRUSTEES LTD	11 0	11 0
LLP INV P/L	5 8	5 4
M INV P/L	5 8	5 4
RSP INV P/L	5 8	5 4
PRICE L	3 2	3 2
PRICE M R	3 2	3 2
PRICE RYAN SEAN	3 2	3 2
ELLERINE BROS P/L	1 7	1 7
MAXERIC NOM P/L	-	13 8
TOTAL	87 6	85 8

DIRECTORS :

ARTHUR DR ,GOMER S
HILLS CS (Financial Director)
PRICE RS (Executive Chairman),ROSENTHAL MD
TAYLOR GS

REGISTRATION NUMBER : 05/10958/06

REGISTERED OFFICE

92 Marlborough Road, Springfield
Johannesburg
2197
TEL 011-683 9323
FAX 011-683 9662

TRANSFER SECRETARY

Central Registrars Ltd
P O Box 4844, Johannesburg
2000
TEL 011-331 0051

COMPANY SECRETARY

S Gomer

NATURE OF BUSINESS

The group is active in the computer services electrical, wiring accessories, document management, audiovisual, leisure furniture and machine tool sectors

BANKERS :

Standard Bank of SA Ltd
First National Bank of SA Ltd
Absa Bank Ltd

AUDITORS :

Kessel Feinstein

FAMILIAR BRAND NAMES

DEFY,GENERAL ELECTRIC,HOTPOINT,KITCHENAIR
LUMEX,LUXOR,LX,MAGNALEC,MK,OAK,PIONEER
POWERPOINT,SNAPPER,TELEFUNKEN,ZANNUSSI

CONTRIBUTION BY ACTIVITY

N/A

YEAR END : February

DIVIDEND : Ords 0,25c

Final No 94	(Ldr)23/06/89	(Pay)24/07/89	Amt(c)2
Final No 95	(Ldr)13/07/90	(Pay)30/07/90	Amt(c)2
Final No 96	(Ldr)12/06/92	(Pay)29/06/92	Amt(c)1
Final No 97	(Ldr)27/11/92	(Pay)14/12/92	Amt(c)1

NUMBER OF EMPLOYEES : 1065

CAPITAL STRUCTURE

	AUTHORISED	ISSUED
15% Prefs 1c	20000000	10000000
Ords 0,25c	100000000	60000000
Var Rate Red Cum Prefs 0,25c	20000000	0

FINANCIAL STATISTICS (AT FINANCIAL YEAR END)

(Amts in R'000)	1992 Feb	1991 Feb	1990 Feb	1989 Feb	1988 Feb
Ord S/H Int	28023	36570	31268	32955	34502
Long Trm Loans	13207	36134	40048	40132	21100
Iss Ord Share	60000	60000	60000	60000	60000
Total Liab	58318	72355	91812	91507	22878
Current Liab	45111	36221	51764	51375	1778
Total Assets	86341	101749	115375	113182	44468
Intang Assets	*	7176	7705	11280	12912
Current Assets	61287	70309	79876	74178	397
Debtors	32712	34879	38367	33589	397
Inventory	26092	35162	40494	39252	
Turnover	108629	135729	141979	134042	108981
Oper Profit	10156	12778	15499	12960	207
Interest Paid	7315	8812	8215	4189	1143
Tax Paid	604	1308	1590	1944	1213
Prf af Int&Tax	3130	2775	5982	7302	2149
Prf att Ord Sh	1286	735	3121	2779	3956
Btm Line Earn	7947	3500	487	275	13875
Dividend Paid	600		1200	1200	1800
Mkt Prce(c) YE	19	26	23	43	45
Depreciation	4071	5382	5609	4699	

PER SHARE STATISTICS (CENTS)

Net Asst Val	46.71	48.99	39.27	36.13	35.98
Net Earnings	2.10	1.20	5.20	4.60	6.60
Dividends	1.00	-	2.00	2.00	3.00
Cash Flow	9.27	10.95	14.86	12.88	-4.74

RATIOS AND OTHER INFORMATION

Mrk Cap(R000)	11400	15600	13800	25800	27000
Current Ratio	1.36	1.94	1.54	1.44	0.22
Quik/Acid Tst	0.78	0.97	0.76	0.68	0.22
A/C Rec T/ovr	3.32	3.89	3.70	3.99	274.51
Tot Ass T/ovr	1.26	1.33	1.23	1.18	2.45
Debt/Ass Rat	0.65	0.48	0.56	0.55	0.11
L T L Tot Ass	0.12	0.12	0.12	0.10	0.07
Debt to Eqity	1.99	1.33	2.08	1.89	0.14
Interest Cover	1.39	1.46	1.92	3.21	0.18
Oper Prof Mrg	9.35	9.41	10.92	9.67	0.19
Net Prof Marg%	1.18	0.54	2.20	2.07	3.63
Ret on Assets	12.80	12.38	13.68	11.87	15.76
Ret on Equity%	4.59	2.01	9.98	8.43	11.47
Price/Earnings	9.05	21.67	4.42	9.35	6.82
Divid Cover	2.10	-	2.60	2.30	2.20
Divid Yield	5.26	-	8.70	4.65	6.67
Earning Yield%	11.05	4.62	22.61	10.70	14.67
NAV % Mrk Pr	245.82	188.42	170.75	84.01	79.96
Effec Tax Rate	9.88	27.89	19.32	17.87	-129.59
Def Interval	7.10	6.23	5.98	5.31	-7.53
Sus Grth Rate	2.45	2.01	6.14	4.79	6.25

SUBSIDIARY & ASSOCIATED COMPANIES

ATLAS-UTAS (PTY) LTD
C-MATIC SYSTEMS (PTY) LTD
EUREFIN (PTY) LTD
EUREKA HOUSE (PTY) LTD
EURELEC (PTY) LTD
EUREVEST LTD
H & J WIRE INDUSTRIES (PTY) LTD
KOZYHEAT (PTY) LTD
LUMEX (PTY) LTD
LUMEX PROPERTIES (BRITS) (PTY) LTD
MAGNALEC (PTY) LTD (50%)
METMAK INVESTMENTS (PTY) LTD
MICROGRAPHEY (PTY) LTD
MOULDED PLUGS & WIRING SYSTEMS (PTY) LTD
OTTERMIL (PTY) LTD
PLASCOR (PTY) LTD
POWERPOINT (PTY) LTD
S & M ENGINEERING WORKS (PTY) LTD
TEK PROPERTIES (INDUSTRIA) (PTY) LTD
THE TOKEN METER CO (PTY) LTD

INVESTMENTS

COLUMBIA CONSULTANTS LTD (15900 SH)
GLODINA HOLDINGS LTD (1000000 SH)
INTERLEISURE HOLDINGS LTD (70000 SH)
REICHMANS LTD (50000 SH)

EVERITE GROUP LTD

ABBREVIATION : EVERITE

JSE SHORT CODE : EVT

SECTOR : Industrial-Building & Construction

SHAREHOLDERS

Who Owns Whom's Assessment of the Identity of the Ultimate Controlling Shareholder: EVERITE HOLDINGS

SHAREHOLDER	PERCENTAGE 1992	1991
EVERITE HOLDINGS LTD	56.0	56.0
SA MUTUAL	25.7	25.7
AECI PENS FUND	3.9	---
EIGHTY ONE MAIN STREET NOM LTD	3.6	---
CMB NOM P/L	2.3	---
UAL MERCHANT BANK LTD	2.3	---
LIBERTY LIFE ASSOC OF AFRICA LTD	1.4	1.4
EVERITE EXEC SHARE PARTICIPATION SCHEME	1.1	---
STD BANK NOM TVL P/L	---	1.1
PANAC INC	---	2.3
SANLAM	---	2.3
NUEVA HOLDINGS AG	---	6.9
TOTAL	96.3	95.6

DIRECTORS :
BATH DW (Managing Director),CLAASEN EB
CLOGG PK ,HESEDING GB ,JORDAAN G
KOTZEE TJ (Executive Chairman),LURIE RC
PATMORE RB ,STOHR RV

REGISTRATION NUMBER : 05/14582/06

REGISTERED OFFICE
Everite House, 20 De Korte Street
Braamfontein
2001
TEL: 011-339 5411
FAX: 011-403 2390

TRANSFER SECRETARY
Mercantile Registrars Ltd
P O Box 1053, Johannesburg
2000
TEL: 011-333 8181

COMPANY SECRETARY
N/A

NATURE OF BUSINESS
Manufacture & marketing of products for the building & construction industries. These consist mainly of fibre-cement & nutec-cement, plastics, pitch-fibre & ceramic products.

BANKERS :
First National Bank of SA Ltd
Standard Bank of SA Ltd

AUDITORS :
Deloitte & Touche

FAMILIAR BRAND NAMES
AGRIPLAS,TIGER TILES

CONTRIBUTION BY ACTIVITY
N/A

YEAR END : June

DIVIDEND : Ords R1

Interim No 84	(Ldr)02/03/90	(Pay)28/03/90	Amt(c)7.5
Final No 85	(Ldr)24/08/90	(Pay)19/09/90	Amt(c)5.5
Interim No 86	(Ldr)15/03/91	(Pay)28/03/91	Amt(c)4
Final No 87	(Ldr)13/09/91	(Pay)30/09/91	Amt(c)2.5

Interim No 88	(Ldr)21/02/92	(Pay)25/03/92	Amt(c)5
Final No 89	(Ldr)16/10/92	(Pay)06/11/92	Amt(c)1.5

NUMBER OF EMPLOYEES : 3979

CAPITAL STRUCTURE

	AUTHORISED	ISSUED
Ords R1	100000000	88927200

FINANCIAL STATISTICS (AT FINANCIAL YEAR END)

(Amts in R'000)	1992 Jun	1991 Jun	1990 Jun	1989 Jun	1988 Jun
Ord S/H Int	304946	280895	316407	292865	267280
Long Trm Loans	29491	29833	10039	17606	16355
Iss Ord Share	88927	88927	88927	88927	88527
Total Liab	230792	120807	111328	98496	88482
Current Liab	201301	90974	101289	80890	72127
Total Assets	535738	401702	427735	391361	355762
Current Assets	215922	145766	163229	153300	140888
Debtors	109681	66704	73189	76354	66864
Inventory	94011	78055	78611	68809	67784
Turnover	392760	334191	351929	373233	326302
Oper Profit	24872	24452	35938	40472	26854
Interest Paid	7506	4303	4126	2326	-
Tax Paid	8241	9528	17652	21936	10019
Prf af Int&Tax	13986	14617	16246	19512	18983
Prf att Ord Sh	17087	16827	19166	23085	18617
Btm Line Earn	13661	13939	18427	23675	19645
Dividend Paid	5780	5780	11561	11561	9738
Mkt Prce(c) YE	300	260	270	315	260
Depreciation	15680	9302	21150	20166	19460

PER SHARE STATISTICS (CENTS)

Net Asst Val	342.92	315.87	355.81	329.33	301.92
Net Earnings	19.10	18.90	21.60	26.00	21.00
Dividends	6.50	6.50	13.00	13.00	11.00
Cash Flow	40.96	31.83	44.22	45.16	43.43

RATIOS AND OTHER INFORMATION

Mrk Cap(R000)	266781	231210	240103	280120	230170
Current Ratio	1.07	1.60	1.61	1.90	1.95
Quik/Acid Tst	0.61	0.74	0.84	1.04	1.01
A/C Rec T/ovr	3.58	5.01	4.81	4.89	4.88
Tot Ass T/ovr	0.73	0.83	0.82	0.95	0.92
Debt/Ass Rat	0.38	0.23	0.24	0.24	0.24
L T L Tot Ass	0.01	0.01	0.01	0.03	0.03
Debt to Eqlty	0.67	0.33	0.33	0.32	0.31
Interest Cover	3.96	6.61	9.22	17.62	-
Oper Prof Mrg	6.33	7.32	10.21	10.84	8.23
Net Prof Marg%	4.35	5.04	5.45	6.19	5.71
Ret on Assets	6.13	7.63	9.57	12.10	8.05
Ret on Equity%	5.60	5.99	6.06	7.88	6.97
Price/Earnings	15.71	13.76	12.50	12.12	12.38
Divid Cover	2.94	2.91	1.66	2.00	1.91
Divid Yield	2.17	2.50	4.81	4.13	4.23
Earning Yield%	6.37	7.27	8.00	8.25	8.08
NAV % Mrk Pr	114.31	121.49	131.78	104.55	116.12
Effec Tax Rate	8.52	25.50	49.43	52.40	4.79
Def Interval	2.80	0.64	0.66	0.41	0.58
Sus Grth Rate	3.71	3.93	2.40	3.93	3.32

SUBSIDIARY & ASSOCIATED COMPANIES

AGRIFIM IRRIGATION SA (PTY) LTD
AGRIPLAS (PTY) LTD
AGRIPLAS WRIGHTRAIN (PTY) LTD
AMALGAMATED REINFORCING (PTY) LTD (49%)
AQUA-GOLD SERVICES (PTY) LTD
AQUA-GOLD SERVICES BOPHUTHATSWANA (PTY)
AWR VERVAARDIGERS (PTY) LTD
BLANKBOU EIENDOMME (PTY) LTD
CAPE HAULIERS (PTY) LTD
CLADDING SPECIALISTS (PTY) LTD
COASTAL INDUSTRIAL CORPORATION (PTY) LTD
DELTA ROOFING (PTY) LTD
DRIPIN S A (PTY) LTD
DURO BRICK COMPANY (PTY) LTD
EVERITE (BOPHUTHATSWANA) (PTY) LTD
EVERITE (JACOBS) (PTY) LTD
EVERITE (JACOBS) PROPERTIES (PTY) LTD
EVERITE (TRANSKEI) (PTY) LTD
EVERITE PROPERTY INVEST (PTY) LTD
FALKIRK PROPERTIES NO 2 (PTY) LTD
FASCO (PTY) LTD
FIBRE CEMENT & ENGINEERING (PTY) LTD
FIBRE-CEMENT SALES (PTY) LTD
FIBRECEM (BOTSWANA) (PTY) LTD
FIBRECEM CORPORATION (USA)
GROUP FIVE INDUSTRIAL INVESTMENTS (PTY)
HIER'S ONS (PTY) LTD
KLIPWATER ESTATES (PTY) LTD
MIDWEST PROPERTIES 186 (PTY) LTD
MIDWEST PROPERTIES 187 (PTY) LTD
MINE SUPPORT PROPERTY HOLDINGS (PTY) LTD
N'TABA INVESTMENT HOLDINGS (PTY) LTD
NATURAL STONE QUARRIES (PTY) LTD
PAXIT PIPEKOR (PTY) LTD
PROLITH (PTY) LTD
RUSTENBURG GRANIETWERKE (EDMS) BPK
SA READYMIX CONCRETE (PTY) LTD
SANTAR PIPES (PTY) LTD
SAURON INVESTMENTS (PTY) LTD
SFM HOLDINGS (PTY) LTD
SFM MANUFACTURING (PTY) LTD
SFM SALES & HIRE (NATAL) (PTY) LTD
SFM SCAFFOLDING & FORMWORK (PTY) LTD
SOUTH WEST ASBEST CEMENT COMPANY (PTY) L
STERRENBERG BELEGGINGS (PTY) LTD
TERRAKWA MANUFACTURING (PTY) LTD
THOR STEEL (PTY) LTD
TIGER TILES (PTY) LTD
TUGELA REINFORCING (PTY) LTD
UNIPIPE (PTY) LTD (48%)
UNITED CEMENT INDUSTRIES (PTY) LTD
UPINGTON KOELKAMERS (PTY) LTD
VAAL POTTERIES (PTY) LTD
VON WIELLIGH STREET INVESTMENTS (PTY) LT
W Z PROPERTIES (PTY) LTD

INVESTMENTS

SMALL BUSINESS DEVELOPMENT CORP LTD

EVERITE HOLDINGS LTD

ABBREVIATION : EVHOLD

JSE SHORT CODE : EVH

SECTOR : Industrial-Building & Construction

SHAREHOLDERS

Who Owns Whom's Assessment of the Identity of the Ultimate Controlling Shareholder:
GROUP FIVE / FEDSURE

SHAREHOLDER	PERCENTAGE 1992	1991
STD BANK NOM TVL P/L	30.0	5.2
GROUP FIVE LTD	29.1	---
SA MUTUAL	15.8	15.9
MOMENTUM LIFE ASSURE LTD	9.9	---
ROCK PENS FUND	4.2	3.8
GRAYSTON NOM P/L	3.7	---
SIXTY SIX MARSHALL STREET NOM P/L	2.3	---
EVERITE EXEC SHARE PARTICIPATION SCHEME	1.9	2.3
SAGE LIFE LTD	1.7	1.7
ANGLO AMERICAN CORP PENS FUND	---	1.4
DE BEERS PENS FUND	---	1.1
LIBERTY LIFE ASSOC OF AFRICA LTD	---	7.8
PANAC INC	---	11.8
WESTERN IND CORP	---	1.9
YSKOR PENS FUND	---	3.2
NUEVA HOLDINGS AG	---	36.1
TOTAL	98.5	92.2

DIRECTORS :
BATH DW ,CLOGG PK (Chairman),DE LOOR JH
GOLDSTEIN SM ,GOSS RJ ,JACKSON TN
KOTZEE TJ (Managing Director),LOUBSER JGH
RIDLEY MT ,THOMAS GM (Deputy Chairman),THULA GJ
VAN DER MERWE SW

REGISTRATION NUMBER : 87/01785/06

REGISTERED OFFICE
Everite House, 20 De Korte Street
Braamfontein
2001
TEL: 011-339 5411
FAX: 011-403 2390

TRANSFER SECRETARY
Mercantile Registrars Ltd
P O Box 1053, Johannesburg
2000
TEL: 011-333 8181

COMPANY SECRETARY
T L Scholtz

NATURE OF BUSINESS
An investment holding company with a controlling interest in quoted Everite Ltd.

BANKERS :
First National Bank of SA Ltd
Standard Bank of SA Ltd

AUDITORS :
Deloitte Pim Goldby

FAMILIAR BRAND NAMES
PAXIT,SANTAR,VAAL

CONTRIBUTION BY ACTIVITY
N/A

YEAR END : June

DIVIDEND : Ords R1

Interim No 6	(Ldr)02/03/90	(Pay)28/03/90	Amt(c)21
Final No 7	(Ldr)24/08/90	(Pay)19/09/90	Amt(c)16
Interim No 8	(Ldr)15/03/91	(Pay)28/03/91	Amt(c)11.5
Final No 9	(Ldr)13/09/91	(Pay)30/09/91	Amt(c)7
Interim No 10	(Ldr)21/02/92	(Pay)25/03/92	Amt(c)14
Final No 11	(Ldr)16/10/92	(Pay)06/11/92	Amt(c)4.5

NUMBER OF EMPLOYEES : 3979

CAPITAL STRUCTURE

	AUTHORISED	ISSUED
Ords R1	20000000	17063800

FINANCIAL STATISTICS (AT FINANCIAL YEAR END)

(Amts in R'000)	1992 Jun	1991 Jun	1990 Jun	1989 Jun	1988 Jun
Ord S/H Int	173632	160084	180026	166829	150336
Long Trm Loans	164255	154405	151411	148619	135808
Iss Ord Share	17064	17064	17064	17064	16664
Total Liab	365005	244422	250546	227184	205432
Current Liab	200750	90017	99135	78565	69624
Total Assets	538637	404506	430572	394013	355768
Current Assets	216021	145770	163266	153152	140894
Debtors	109684	66708	73197	76358	66869
Inventory	94011	78055	78611	68809	67784
Turnover	392760	334191	351929	373233	326302
Oper Profit	24874	24316	35790	40345	31232
Interest Paid	7506	4303	4126	2326	2193
Tax Paid	8241	9528	17652	21936	10019
Prf af Int&Tax	13988	14481	16098	19385	19020
Prf att Ord Sh	9516	9287	10585	12800	10509
Btm Line Earn	7598	7670	10172	13432	8869
Dividend Paid	3157	3157	6313	6313	5499
Mkt Prce(c) YE	870	600	645	920	640
Depreciation	15680	9302	21150	20166	19460

PER SHARE STATISTICS (CENTS)

Net Asst Val	1017.53	938.14	1055.00	977.67	902.16
Net Earnings	55.80	54.40	62.00	75.00	63.10
Dividends	18.50	18.50	37.00	37.00	33.00
Cash Flow	169.11	121.71	180.16	175.06	156.03

RATIOS AND OTHER INFORMATION

Mrk Cap(R000)	148457	102384	110063	156989	106650
Current Ratio	1.08	1.62	1.65	1.95	2.02
Quik/Acid Tst	0.61	0.75	0.85	1.07	1.05
A/C Rec T/ovr	3.58	5.01	4.81	4.89	4.18
Tot Ass T/ovr	0.73	0.83	0.82	0.95	0.79
Debt/Ass Rat	0.38	0.23	0.24	0.23	0.23
L T L Tot Ass	0.01	0.01	0.01	0.03	0.03
Debt to Eqity	1.18	0.58	0.56	0.54	0.54
Interest Cover	3.96	6.58	9.18	17.56	14.24
Oper Prof Mrg	6.33	7.28	10.17	10.81	9.57
Net Prof Marg%	2.42	2.78	3.01	3.43	3.22
Ret on Assets	6.10	7.55	9.47	11.98	7.44
Ret on Equity%	5.48	5.80	5.88	7.67	5.99
Price/Earnings	15.59	11.03	10.40	12.27	10.14
Divid Cover	3.02	2.94	1.68	2.03	1.91
Divid Yield	2.13	3.08	5.74	4.02	5.16
Earning Yield%	6.41	9.07	9.61	8.15	9.86
NAV % Mrk Pr	116.96	156.36	163.57	106.27	140.96
Effec Tax Rate	8.52	25.67	49.66	52.56	4.43
Def Interval	3.54	0.88	0.84	0.55	0.64
Sus Grth Rate	3.66	3.83	2.37	3.89	3.33

SUBSIDIARY & ASSOCIATED COMPANIES

EVERITE GROUP LTD

INVESTMENTS

SMALL BUSINESS DEV. CORP. LTD (113000 SH)

FAIRCAPE HOMES LTD

ABBREVIATION : FAIRCAP

JSE SHORT CODE : FAR

SECTOR : Financial-Property

SHAREHOLDERS

Who Owns Whom's Assessment of the Identity of the Ultimate Controlling Shareholder: DIRECTORS CONTROL 54% (DEC 1990)

SHAREHOLDER	PERCENTAGE 1992	1991
FNX NOM LTD	27.1	---
NAT BRICK HOLDINGS P/L	24.9	---
VIETRI M J	11.3	11.3
STOCKSHARE NOM P/L	5.7	---
CHARISMA HOLDINGS P/L	5.6	---
EDWIN W BALDERSON NOM P/L	3.3	3.4
MOSER J E	3.3	19.7
KAYEMESS NOM P/L	2.6	2.6
CRISON P/L	2.4	2.4
TALBOT B	1.4	---
DIAGONAL NOM P/L	1.4	1.5
MAXERIC NOM P/L	---	6.4
PREMCON (FAIRCAPE) HLDGS LTD	---	22.0
SANLAM	---	6.2
SCHOONWINKEL A M	---	1.4
STD BANK NOM TVL P/L	---	3.0
VAN DER HOVEN N P J	---	6.7
TOTAL	89.0	86.4

DIRECTORS :
CHAPMAN DE ,MOSER JE (Joint Managing Director)
RABIE J ,VAN DER HOVEN NPJ ,VIETRI CD
VIETRI MJ (Joint Managing Director),WALTON CL

REGISTRATION NUMBER : 87/00770/06

REGISTERED OFFICE
4th Floor, 31 Riebeeck Street
Cape Town
8001
TEL: 021-461 0570
FAX: 021-45 2282

TRANSFER SECRETARY
Central Registrars Ltd
P O Box 4844, Johannesburg
2000
TEL: 011-331 0051

COMPANY SECRETARY
C D Vietri

NATURE OF BUSINESS
The company is a property development company.

BANKERS :
First National Bank of SA Ltd
Standard Bank of SA Ltd

AUDITORS :
Kessel Feinstein

FAMILIAR BRAND NAMES
N/A

CONTRIBUTION BY ACTIVITY
N/A

YEAR END : June

DIVIDEND : Ords no par value
Final No 3 (Ldr)30/03/90 (Pay)25/05/90 Amt(c)12

CAPITAL STRUCTURE

	AUTHORISED	ISSUED
Ords no par value	12000000	9092000

FINANCIAL STATISTICS (AT FINANCIAL YEAR END)

(Amts in R'000)	1990 Dec	1989 Dec	1988 Dec	1987 Dec
Ord S/H Int	5766	11662	6648	3809
Long Trm Loans	5256	7878	6426	1239
Iss Ord Share	9092	9092	8775	8775
Total Liab	29957	25241	29874	14737
Current Liab	24701	17363	23448	13498
Total Assets	35723	36903	36522	18546
Current Assets	33449	29782	32783	17532
Debtors	14886	19160	16540	8316
Inventory	18563	10622	-	-
Turnover	34973	45332	32969	19542
Oper Profit	-2981	6016	7582	3091
Interest Paid	4925	4391	2303	790
Tax Paid	-977	-678	2476	1142
Prf af Int&Tax	-6929	2303	2803	1159
Prf att Ord Sh	-6684	2934	2658	1159
Btm Line Earn	-5896	5804	2658	1159
Dividend Paid	-	1091	878	439
Mkt Prce(c) YE	60	100	100	160
Depreciation	345	184	106	71

PER SHARE STATISTICS (CENTS)

Net Asst Val	63.42	128.27	75.76	43.41
Net Earnings	-73.50	33.30	30.30	16.88
Dividends	-	12.00	10.00	5.00
Cash Flow	-83.11	19.23	55.84	33.33

RATIOS AND OTHER INFORMATION

Mrk Cap(R000)	5455	9092	8775	14040
Current Ratio	1.35	1.72	1.40	1.30
Quik/Acid Tst	0.60	1.10	1.40	1.30
A/C Rec T/ovr	2.35	2.37	1.99	2.35
Tot Ass T/ovr	0.98	1.23	0.90	1.05
Debt/Ass Rat	0.82	0.64	0.75	0.73
L T L Tot Ass	0.13	0.17	0.11	0.00
Debt to Eqity	5.09	2.03	4.14	3.57
Interest Cover	-0.61	1.37	3.29	3.91
Oper Prof Mrg	-8.52	13.27	23.00	15.82
Net Prof Marg%	-19.11	6.47	8.06	5.93
Ret on Assets	-7.66	18.01	20.76	16.67
Ret on Equity%	-115.92	25.16	39.98	30.43
Price/Earnings	-0.82	3.00	3.30	9.48
Divid Cover	-	2.78	3.03	3.38
Divid Yield	-	12.00	10.00	3.13
Earning Yield%	-122.50	33.30	30.30	10.55
NAV % Mrk Pr	105.70	128.27	75.76	27.13
Effec Tax Rate	-	7.14	6.44	3.61
Def Interval	-2.95	10.48	4.31	4.41
Sus Grth Rate	-115.92	15.80	26.77	18.90

SUBSIDIARY & ASSOCIATED COMPANIES

CLIFTON PROPERTY INVESTMENT TRUST
CONTENDO (PTY) LTD
HAZRA 20 (PTY) LTD
JFK AGRIPLASE NR 4 (PTY) LTD
RUGAY INVESTMENTS (PTY) LTD (49%)
SAMPROP CONSTRUCTION (PTY) LTD
SEA VISTA TRUST
VILLA LORENZO (PTY) LTD

INVESTMENTS

None

FALCON GOLD ZIMBABWE LTD

ABBREVIATION : FALGOLD

SECTOR : Zimbabwe Stock Exchange

SHAREHOLDERS

Who Owns Whom's Assessment of the Identity of the Ultimate Controlling Shareholder: ANGLO AMERICAN

SHAREHOLDER	PERCENTAGE 1992	1991
FALCON MINES PLC	71.7	---
SECURITY NOM LTD	6.2	---
UNITED FACTORS PVT LTD	2.0	---
NAT RAILWAYS OF ZIM CONTR PENS FUND	1.6	---
MINING INDUSTRY PENS FUND	1.1	---
TOTAL	82.7	---

DIRECTORS :
BEATTIE AD (Managing Director),JOUSSE CP
LATILLA-CAMPBELL P ,PALMGREN AM ,SMART WK
STEPHENS RG (Chairman

REGISTERED OFFICE
2nd Floor, Halyet House
9th Avenuer, Bulawayo

TEL: 70741
FAX: 64017

TRANSFER SECRETARY
Zimbabwe Banking Corporation Ltd
P O Box 3198, Harare
Zimbabwe

TEL: 092634-735011

COMPANY SECRETARY
N/A

NATURE OF BUSINESS
FALCON GOLD is a major Zimbawean gold producer.It has two operating mines, DALNY and VENICE and also owns a number of potentially valuable precious metal claims,including those which comprise the GOLDEN QUARRY MINE.

BANKERS :
Zimbabwe Banking Corporation Ltd

AUDITORS :
Deloitte & Touche

FAMILIAR BRAND NAMES
N/A

CONTRIBUTION BY ACTIVITY
N/A

YEAR END : March

DIVIDEND : Ords Z$1

Dividend	(Ldr)15/11/91	(Pay)13/12/91	Amt(c)7
Dividend	(Ldr)12/06/92	(Pay)26/06/92	Amt(c)8

CAPITAL STRUCTURE

	AUTHORISED	ISSUED
Ords Z$1	90000000	79060600

FINANCIAL STATISTICS (AT FINANCIAL YEAR END)

(Amts in Z$)	1992 Mar	1991 Mar
Ord S/H Int	113083	74337
Long Trm Loans	5620	17808
Iss Ord Share	79061	500
Total Liab	24652	30699
Current Liab	19032	12891
Total Assets	137735	105036
Current Assets	27654	12384
Debtors	3746	774
Inventory	13796	8454
Turnover	80000	55187
Oper Profit	23591	11365
Interest Paid	979	2037
Prf af Int&Tax	23914	9331
Prf att Ord Sh	23914	9331
Btm Line Earn	23914	9331
Dividend Paid	11928	3200

PER SHARE STATISTICS (CENTS)

Net Asst Val	143.03	14867.40
Net Earnings	38.50	-
Dividends	15.10	640.00
Cash Flow	30.25	1866.20

RATIOS AND OTHER INFORMATION

Current Ratio	1.45	0.96
Quik/Acid Tst	0.73	0.30
A/C Rec T/ovr	21.36	71.30
Tot Ass T/ovr	0.58	0.53
Debt/Ass Rat	0.18	0.29
L T L Tot Ass	0.04	0.17
Debt to Eqity	0.22	0.41
Interest Cover	24.10	5.58
Oper Prof Mrg	29.49	20.59
Net Prof Marg%	29.89	16.91
Ret on Assets	18.07	10.82
Ret on Equity%	21.15	12.55
Divid Cover	2.55	-
Def Interval	0.33	2.32
Sus Grth Rate	10.60	8.25

SUBSIDIARY & ASSOCIATED COMPANIES

None

INVESTMENTS

None

FALCON MINES PLC

ABBREVIATION : FALCON

JSE SHORT CODE : FAL

SECTOR : Gold-Rand & others

SHAREHOLDERS

Who Owns Whom's Assessment of the Identity of the Ultimate Controlling Shareholder:
MARSHALL FAMILY VIA AFEX CORP

SHAREHOLDER	PERCENTAGE 1992	1991
ZIMBABWE CONTROL ACCOUNT	50 4	50 4
LONDON CONTROL ACCOUNT	46 7	46 6
TOTAL	97 1	97 0

DIRECTORS :
BEATTIE AD ,JOUSSE CP ,PALMGREN AM
STEPHENS RG (Chairman & Managing Dir

REGISTRATION NUMBER : 107779 (Engl

REGISTERED OFFICE
25-35 City Road, London EC1Y 1BQ
England

TEL 092639-70741
FAX 092639-64017

TRANSFER SECRETARY
Central Registrars Ltd
P O Box 4844, Johannesburg
2000
TEL 011-331 0051

COMPANY SECRETARY
Bulawayo Board of Executors and Trust Company Ltd

NATURE OF BUSINESS
The company conducts gold mining operations in Zimbabwe

BANKERS :
N/A

AUDITORS :
Deloitte Pim Goldby

FAMILIAR BRAND NAMES
N/A

CONTRIBUTION BY ACTIVITY
N/A

YEAR END : March

DIVIDEND :Ords 50c FAL

Final No 68	(Ldr)12/07/91	(Pay)16/08/91	Amt(c)15
Interim No 69	(Ldr)15/11/91	(Pay)13/12/91	Amt(c)18

CAPITAL STRUCTURE

	AUTHORISED	ISSUED
Ord 50c FAL	24000000	19971720

FINANCIAL STATISTICS (AT FINANCIAL YEAR END)

(Amts in Z$)	1992 Mar	1991 Mar	1990 Mar	1989 Mar	1988 Mar
Ord S/H Int	92259	89715	16915	43289	46336
Long Trm Loans	32353	5833	10883	5200	-
Iss Ord Share	19972	19972	19972	1997	1997
Total Liab	51241	19385	19670	15374	6736
Current Liab	18888	13552	8787	10174	6736
Total Assets	143500	109100	36585	58663	53072
Current Assets	28877	12745	8221	7100	9640
Debtors	3998	966	724	915	1002
Inventory	13796	8454	7387	5892	5954
Turnover	80000	55187	42083	38847	47612
Oper Profit	23289	11237	1747	-3327	5201
Interest Paid	581	1554	1732	-	-
Tax Paid	2488	1013	305	256	256
Prf af Int&Tax	22362	9077	346	-3583	4945
Prf att Ord Sh	17326	9750	778	-2521	6076
Btm Line Earn	17326	9750	778	-2521	6076
Dividend Paid	7589	2996	-	-	999
Mkt Prce(c) YE	150	140	65	160	1300

PER SHARE STATISTICS (CENTS)

Net Asst Val	461 94	449 20	84 69	2167 70	2320 28
Net Earnings	86 80	48 80	3 90	-12 60	304 00
Dividends	38 00	15 00	-	-	50 00
Cash Flow	79 36	45 45	1 73	-179 42	247 62

RATIOS AND OTHER INFORMATION

Mrk Cap(R000)	29958	27961	12982	3195	25961
Current Ratio	1 53	0 94	0 94	0 70	1 43
Quik/Acid Tst	0 80	0 32	0 09	0 12	0 55
A/C Rec T/ovr	20 01	57 13	58 13	42 46	47 52
Tot Ass T/ovr	0 56	0 51	1 15	0 66	0 90
Debt/Ass Rat	0 13	0 18	0 54	0 26	0 13
L T L Tot Ass	-	0 05	0 30	0 09	-
Debt to Eqity	0 20	0 22	1 16	0 36	0 15
Interest Cover	41 12	7 49	1 36	-	-
Oper Prof Mrg	29 11	20 36	4 15	-8 56	10 92
Net Prof Marg%	21 66	17 67	1 85	-6 49	12 76
Ret on Assets	18 75	11 29	7 69	-3 86	11 93
Ret on Equity%	18 78	10 87	4 60	-5 82	13 11
Price/Earnings	1 73	2 87	16 67	-12 70	4 28
Divid Cover	2 28	3 25	-	-	6 08
Divid Yield	25 33	10 71	-	-	3 85
Earning Yield%	57 87	34 86	6 00	-7 88	23 38
NAV % Mrk Pr	307 96	320 86	130 30	1354 81	178 48
Effec Tax Rate	-	-	-	-5 59	3 00
Def Interval	0 15	1 06	37 49	-2 41	-
Sus Grth Rate	10 55	7 53	4 60	-5 82	10 96

SUBSIDIARY & ASSOCIATED COMPANIES

FALCON GOLD ZIMBABWE LTD
OLYMPUS GOLD MINES LTD (40%)

INVESTMENTS

None

FARM-AG LTD

ABBREVIATION : FARM-AG

JSE SHORT CODE : FAG

SECTOR : Industrial-Industrial Holding

SHAREHOLDERS

Who Owns Whom's Assessment of the Identity of the Ultimate Controlling Shareholder: RALE HOLDINGS

SHAREHOLDER	PERCENTAGE 1992	1991
RALE HOLDINGS LTD	65.1	65.0
CMB NOM P/L	6.9	---
ABSA NOM P/L	6.1	---
NATURAL SILK CO LTD	5.6	---
FIRST NAT NOM P/L	2.5	2.5
SMK NOM P/L	1.8	2.3
ELLERINE BROS P/L	1.7	1.7
SANLAM	---	6.6
VOLKSKAS NOM P/L	---	4.7
TOTAL	89.5	82.8

DIRECTORS :
MAINGARD LMJP ,MAINGARD LMJR (Managing Director)
SHERRELL RE (Chairman),VAN ROOYEN D

REGISTRATION NUMBER : 05/26632/06

REGISTERED OFFICE
Old Mill Site, Canelands
Natal
4341
TEL: 0322-33 4061
FAX: 0322-33 6293

TRANSFER SECRETARY
Central Registrars Ltd
P O Box 4844, Johannesburg
2000
TEL: 011-331 0051

COMPANY SECRETARY
B G D de Groot

NATURE OF BUSINESS
The manufacture, formulation and wholesale distribution and export of agricultural chemicals. The manufacture and distribution of hosiery and air-textured yarns; manufacture and distribution of patent medicines, toiletries & toiletry-related products. The company has a controlling interest in quoted Staalchem Ltd, and an investment in quoted Bearing Man Ltd.

BANKERS :
Bankorp Ltd

AUDITORS :
KPMG Aiken & Peat

FAMILIAR BRAND NAMES
GRUNDFOS

CONTRIBUTION BY ACTIVITY
N/A

YEAR END : August

DIVIDEND : (Ldr)07/07/89 (Pay)21/07/89
DIVIDEND : (Ldr)02/12/88 (Pay)19/12/88

NUMBER OF EMPLOYEES : 96

CAPITAL STRUCTURE

	AUTHORISED	ISSUED
5,5% Cum Prefs R2	100000	100000
Ords 50c	20000000	14348000
Red Prefs 1c	750000	0

FINANCIAL STATISTICS (AT FINANCIAL YEAR END)

(Amts in R'000)	1991 Feb	1990 Feb	1989 Feb	1988 Feb	1987
Ord S/H Int	29497	33198	45520	43606	19880
Long Trm Loans	917	6073	10658	16196	37757
Iss Ord Share	14348	14348	13548	12798	9468
Total Liab	67203	140333	99694	84906	74904
Current Liab	66286	134260	89036	68710	37147
Total Assets	96400	172463	143192	128512	99977
Intang Assets	300	1068	2022	*	*
Current Assets	43905	120727	94895	82150	42340
Debtors	27221	72419	53454	45670	-
Inventory	5899	13829	36589	34194	42340
Turnover	73127	205813	153589	128848	78868
Oper Profit	7284	9331	18479	17412	10033
Interest Paid	20115	24613	10087	4380	2916
Tax Paid	-	28	199	1396	-
Prf af Int&Tax	-5826	-10978	8193	11636	7107
Prf att Ord Sh	63	-7714	20791	13650	7096
Btm Line Earn	-3701	-8039	16896	4599	7096
Dividend Paid	-	-	6096	5759	3598
Mkt Prce(c) YE	215	230	400	470	700
Depreciation	962	4709	3500	2273	-

PER SHARE STATISTICS (CENTS)

Net Asst Val	203.49	223.93	321.07	340.73	209.97
Net Earnings	0.50	-56.90	82.70	110.40	-
Dividends	-	-	45.00	45.00	-
Cash Flow	-31.51	-47.97	87.08	114.64	75.06

RATIOS AND OTHER INFORMATION

Mrk Cap(R000)	30848	33000	54192	60151	66276
Current Ratio	0.66	0.90	1.07	1.20	1.14
Quik/Acid Tst	0.57	0.80	0.65	0.70	-
A/C Rec T/ovr	2.69	2.84	2.87	2.82	-
Tot Ass T/ovr	0.76	1.19	1.07	1.00	0.79
Debt/Ass Rat	0.69	0.79	0.69	0.63	0.75
L T L Tot Ass	0.01	0.01	0.07	0.10	0.38
Debt to Eqity	2.27	4.10	2.17	1.87	3.77
Interest Cover	0.36	0.38	1.83	3.98	3.44
Oper Prof Mrg	9.96	4.53	12.03	13.51	12.72
Net Prof Marg%	0.09	-3.75	13.54	10.59	9.00
Ret on Assets	20.58	9.96	14.94	15.52	10.03
Ret on Equity%	0.21	-23.24	45.67	31.30	35.69
Price/Earnings	430.00	-4.04	4.84	4.26	-
Divid Cover	-	-	1.84	2.45	-
Divid Yield	-	-	11.25	9.57	-
Earning Yield%	0.23	-24.74	20.68	23.49	-
NAV % Mrk Pr	94.65	97.36	80.27	72.49	30.00
Effec Tax Rate	-	-0.06	2.01	10.57	-
Def Interval	-13.02	-15.45	5.69	4.12	5.31
Sus Grth Rate	0.21	-23.24	32.28	18.10	17.60

SUBSIDIARY & ASSOCIATED COMPANIES

AGROGARD MARKETING (PTY) LTD
BIRMINGHAM INVESTMENTS (PTY) LTD
CHEMNET (PTY) LTD
CROP-SURE (PTY) LTD
ENEKO AGRICULTURAL INVESTMENT CHEMICALS
EXPONENT (PTY) LTD
FARM-AG CHEMICAL DISTRIBUTORS (PTY) LTD
FARM-AG ENGINEERING COMPONENTS (PTY) LTD
FARM AG EXPORT (PTY) LTD
FARM AG IMPORT (PTY) LTD
FARM-AG PACKAGING HOLDINGS (PTY) LTD
FARM-AG TEXTILE HOLDINGS (PTY) LTD
FARMNET (PTY) LTD
GULF SALES (PTY) LTD
GULF TOILETRIES (PTY) LTD
HACKS HOLDINGS (PTY) LTD (40%)
HARCHEM HOLDINGS (PTY) LTD
HARVEST CHEMICALS (PTY) LTD
HOEVELD VERSPREIDERS (EDMS) BPK
KEMPTON PRODUCE SUPPLY (PTY) LTD
MIRACLE MANUFACTURING CO (PTY) LTD
MOLLANT EXPORT ENTERPRISES (PTY) LTD
NU-CARE MARKETING & SALES (PTY) LTD
PESKOR (PTY) LTD
PORT NATAL HOLDINGS (PTY) LTD
POTTER & MOORE INTERNATIONAL SA (PTY) LT
PRO MO (PTY) LTD
SAFSAN AGRICULTURAL CHEMICALS (PTY) LTD
SANACHEM (PTY) LTD (50%)
STAALCHEM LTD
STILETTO MOWERS (PTY) LTD
UNION DRUG (PTY) LTD (50%)

INVESTMENTS

None

FEDSURE HOLDINGS LTD

ABBREVIATION : FEDSURE

JSE SHORT CODE : FDS

SECTOR : Financial-Insurance

SHAREHOLDERS

Who Owns Whom's Assessment of the Identity of the Ultimate Controlling Shareholder:
DIRECTORS / INVESTEC

SHAREHOLDER	PERCENTAGE 1992	1991
INVESTEC NOM P/L	26 1	4 4
FEDERATED EMPLOYERS MUTUAL ASSURE CO LTD	12 0	14 7
JONEL INV P/L	9 8	12 4
FIRST NAT NOM P/L	4 8	4 6
JAMMINE APH, SACKS MI & VAN STADEN EW (T	2 6	1 7
INVESTEC INV TRUST LTD	2 4	---
BUILDING INDUSTRIES FEDERATION SA	1 7	2 2
SMBL NOM P/L	1 6	---
BASSERABIE A I	1 3	1 8
MITCHELL B C	1 3	1 6
LOBBAN J H H	1 3	1 6
TVL EMERALD MINING CO P/L	1 2	1 6
SHARESTOCK NOM P/L	1 2	1 7
SMYTHE JM & MFJ, & EP NICALAIDES (TRUSTE	1 2	1 6
MITCHELL D H	1 1	1 7
NATAL MASTER BUILDERS & ALLIED IND ASSOC	1 1	1 4
NBS PENS FUND	---	1 2
CORPORATE ASSET MANAGEMENT P/L	---	1 4
FSI CORP PENS FUND	---	2 4
VMB NOM P/L	---	9 6
TOTAL	70 7	67 3

DIRECTORS :
BARROW DG ,BARROW JA (Chairman)
BASSERABIE AI (Chief Executive),JAMMINE APH DR
KARDOL B ,KOSEFF S ,MCCARTHY H
MITCHELL DH (Deputy Chairman),SACKS MI
STEIN GH ,VAN STADEN EW

REGISTRATION NUMBER : 69/12384/06

REGISTERED OFFICE
Fedlife House, 1 de Villiers Street
Johannesburg
2001
TEL 011-332 6000
FAX 011-492 1102

TRANSFER SECRETARY
Mercantile Registrars Ltd
P O Box 1053, Johannesburg
2000
TEL 011-333 8181

COMPANY SECRETARY
R A Krabbenhoft

NATURE OF BUSINESS
Investment holding company deriving income from subsidiaries in long term life assurance and short term insurance

BANKERS :
Standard Bank of SA Ltd
First National Bank of SA Ltd

AUDITORS :
Coopers Theron Du Toit

FAMILIAR BRAND NAMES
N/A

CONTRIBUTION BY ACTIVITY
N/A

YEAR END : December

DIVIDEND : Ords 2c

Interim No 4	(Ldr)01/09/89	(Pay)22/09/89	Amt(c)8 25
Final No 5	(Ldr)23/03/90	(Pay)20/04/90	Amt(c)12
Interim No 6	(Ldr)31/08/90	(Pay)21/09/90	Amt(c)10
Final No 7	(Ldr)22/02/91	(Pay)28/03/91	Amt(c)15
Interim No 8	(Ldr)30/08/91	(Pay)20/09/91	Amt(c)12 5
Final No 9	(Ldr)20/03/92	(Pay)24/04/92	Amt(c)18
Interim no 10	(Ldr)28/08/92	(Pay)18/09/92	Amt(c)15 25

NUMBER OF EMPLOYEES : 1821

CAPITAL STRUCTURE

	AUTHORISED	ISSUED
Ords 2c	360000000	85250000
13,5% Cum Auto Conv Prefs 2c	40000000	8140000

FINANCIAL STATISTICS (AT FINANCIAL YEAR END)

(Amts in R'000)	1991 Dec	1990 Dec	1989 Dec	1988	1987
Ord S/H Int	110800	99300	88555	82974	78606
Long Trm Loans	4776300	3783400	3141099	2680482	2406742
Iss Ord Share	67250	67250	67000	67000	67000
Total Liab	4984200	3983700	3274819	2787906	2578915
Current Liab	207900	200300	133720	107424	172173
Total Assets	5095000	4083000	3363374	3343251	2806167
Current Assets	993600	732700	686272	579795	320819
Debtors	378800	342500	285147	-	-
Inventory	-	-	-	579795	320819
Oper Profit	28600	23700	19278	15543	10190
Tax Paid	300	300	129	120	216
Prf af Int&Tax	28800	23600	19149	15423	9974
Prf att Ord Sh	28800	23600	19149	15423	9974
Btm Line Earn	28800	23600	19149	15423	9974
Dividend Paid	20500	16800	13568	11055	5230
Mkt Prce(c) YE	785	380	400	260	230
Depreciation	9200	7100	5959	-	

PER SHARE STATISTICS (CENTS)

Net Asst Val	164 76	147 66	132 17	123 84	117 32
Net Earnings	42 80	35 10	28 60	-	-
Dividends	30 50	25 00	20 25	-	-
Cash Flow	56 51	45 71	37 47	23 02	14 89

RATIOS AND OTHER INFORMATION

Mrk Cap(R000)	527913	255550	268000	174200	154100
Current Ratio	4 78	3 66	5 13	5 40	1 86
Quik/Acid Tst	4 78	3 66	5 13	-	-
Debt/Ass Rat	0 04	0 05	0 04	0 83	0 92
L T L Tot Ass	0 00	0 00	0 00	0 80	0 86
Debt to Eqity	1 91	2 03	1 53	33 60	32 81
Ret on Assets	0 57	0 59	0 57	0 46	0 36
Ret on Equity%	25 99	23 77	21 62	18 59	12 69
Price/Earnings	18 34	10 83	13 99	-	-
Divid Cover	1 40	1 40	1 41	-	-
Divid Yield	3 89	6 58	5 06	-	-
Earning Yield%	5 45	9 24	7 15	-	-
NAV % Mrk Pr	20 99	38 86	33 04	47 63	51 01
Effec Tax Rate	1 03	1 26	0 61	0 77	2 12
Def Interval	0 33	0 25	2 34	173 80	241 30
Sus Grth Rate	7 49	6 85	6 30	5 26	6 04

SUBSIDIARY & ASSOCIATED COMPANIES

FEDBEL LTD
FEDERATED EMPLOYERS' TRUST LTD, THE
FEDGEN INSURANCE LTD
FEDGROWTH MANAGEMENT CO LTD
FEDLIFE ASSURANCE LTD
FEDLIFE MORTGAGE PARTICIPATION BOND MANA
INVESTEC HOLDINGS LTD (35%)
SAAMBOU HOLDINGS LTD (31,45%)

INVESTMENTS

None

FEMCO TECHNOLOGY HOLDINGS LTD

ABBREVIATION : FMCOTEC

JSE SHORT CODE : FMT

SECTOR : Industrial Electronics, Electrical & Bat

SHAREHOLDERS

Who Owns Whom's Assessment of the Identity of the Ultimate Controlling Shareholder:
DIRECTORS CONTROL 63% (DEC 1990)

SHAREHOLDER	PERCENTAGE 1992	1991
MECHIEL DU TOIT NOM P/L	57 3	57 3
SA MUTUAL	17 2	17 2
STD BANK NOM TVL P/L	3 9	3 9
MOMENTUM LIFE ASSURE LTD	3 4	3 4
YSKOR PENS FUND	3 3	3 9
GINOCO P/L	2 4	2 4
EPF OLD MUTUAL NOM P/L	2 0	2 0
METROPOLITAN LIFE LTD	1 6	1 6
GREIG J E	1 2	1 2
TOTAL	92 4	92 9

DIRECTORS :
KEARNEY JP DR (Chairman),KENT BH ,SPINAZZE LC
VAN ZYL NL (Joint Chief Executive)
ZAMMIT G (Joint Chief Executive

REGISTRATION NUMBER : 87/04942/06

REGISTERED OFFICE
2nd Floor, Corporate Place, 23 Fredman Drive
Sandton
2199
TEL 011-883 4933
FAX 011-883 4995

TRANSFER SECRETARY
Central Registrars Ltd
P O Box 4844, Johannesburg
2000
TEL 011-331 0051

COMPANY SECRETARY
J D Vittle

NATURE OF BUSINESS
An investment holding company whose principal subsidiaries operate in the electric motor sector and in the manufacture & supply of electrical wiring to automobile manufacturers The group is also involved in the manufacture and sale of plastic products, and of tools and dies

BANKERS :
Nedperm Bank Ltd

AUDITORS :
N/A

FAMILIAR BRAND NAMES
N/A

CONTRIBUTION BY ACTIVITY
N/A

YEAR END : April

DIVIDEND : Ords no par value

Final	(Ldr)08/06/90	(Pay)18/06/90	Amt(c)4
Interim	(Ldr)07/09/90	(Pay)21/09/90	Amt(c)5

CAPITAL STRUCTURE

	AUTHORISED	ISSUED
Ords no par value	40000000	24581978

FINANCIAL STATISTICS (AT FINANCIAL YEAR END)

(Amts in R'000)	1990 Dec	1989 Dec	1988 Dec	1987
Ord S/H Int	47646	37242	30444	23437
Long Trm Loans	12849	21050	8690	11934
Iss Ord Share	24582	24582	23400	14650
Total Liab	38766	41374	27758	20164
Current Liab	25917	20324	19068	8230
Total Assets	86412	78616	58202	57618
Current Assets	42367	40303	33663	22247
Debtors	16330	19294	12048	-
Inventory	26037	21009	19328	22247
Turnover	107245	110082	79237	61295
Oper Profit	9286	9896	16504	12824
Interest Paid	5774	4248	2341	340
Tax Paid	146	240	6414	4523
Prf af Int&Tax	4339	7116	8775	7961
Prf att Ord Sh	11633	7363	8775	7961
Btm Line Earn	11633	7363	8775	7961
Dividend Paid	1229	2950	3996	-
Mkt Prce(c) YE	200	285	210	-
Depreciation	3680	3682	1348	-

PER SHARE STATISTICS (CENTS)

Net Asst Val	193.82	151.50	130.10	159.98
Net Earnings	21.20	30.90	37.50	-
Dividends	5.00	12.00	17.00	-
Cash Flow	33.04	44.18	48.61	54.34

RATIOS AND OTHER INFORMATION

Mrk Cap(R000)	49164	70059	49140	-
Current Ratio	1.63	1.98	1.77	2.70
Quik/Acid Tst	0.63	0.95	0.75	-
A/C Rec T/ovr	6.57	5.71	6.58	-
Tot Ass T/ovr	1.24	1.40	1.36	1.06
Debt/Ass Rat	0.43	0.51	0.45	0.35
L T L Tot Ass	0.13	0.25	0.12	0.21
Debt to Eqity	0.78	1.07	0.86	0.86
Interest Cover	1.61	2.33	7.05	37.72
Oper Prof Mrg	8.66	8.99	20.83	20.92
Net Prof Marg%	10.85	6.69	11.07	12.99
Ret on Assets	12.87	15.07	30.12	22.26
Ret on Equity%	24.42	19.77	28.82	33.97
Price/Earnings	9.43	9.22	5.60	-
Divid Cover	4.24	2.58	2.21	-
Divid Yield	2.50	4.21	8.10	-
Earning Yield%	10.60	10.84	17.86	-
NAV % Mrk Pr	96.91	53.16	61.95	-
Effec Tax Rate	0.94	2.41	33.99	36.23
Def Interval	2.65	2.38	0.78	1.50
Sus Grth Rate	21.84	11.85	15.70	33.97

SUBSIDIARY & ASSOCIATED COMPANIES

ACJOHN PLASTICS (PTY) LTD
ARAMBRO INVESTMENTS (PTY) LTD
AUTO CABLE MANUFACTURING COMPANY (PTY) L
FEMCO PROPERTIES (BRITS) (PTY) LTD
FEMCOTEC FINANCE (PTY) LTD (50%)
FEMEG (PTY) LTD
FEMTECH (CISKEI) (PTY) LTD
FEMTECH (PTY) LTD
FEMTECH TOOL AND DIE (PTY) LTD (47,6%)
MEGA ELECTRICAL (PTY) LTD
PRIME TECHNOLOGY SA (PTY) LTD (47,6%)

INVESTMENTS

None

FENIX INDUSTRIES LTD

ABBREVIATION : FENIX

JSE SHORT CODE : FEI

SECTOR : Industrial-Clothing, Footwear & Textiles

SHAREHOLDERS

Who Owns Whom's Assessment of the Identity of the Ultimate Controlling Shareholder: ABBEY HOLDINGS

SHAREHOLDER	PERCENTAGE 1992	1991
ABBEY HOLDINGS LTD	66.7	68.2
ABBEY (FNX) HOLDINGS LTD	12.2	16.7
QUARTET INV LTD	7.9	---
ABBEY TRADING LTD	4.2	---
GREEK R N TRUSTEES DORFMAN CHILDREN	2.7	2.8
BRYAN M	2.2	---
NAT BRICK HOLDINGS P/L	---	6.3
TOTAL	96.0	93.9

DIRECTORS :
BRYAN MJT (Managing Director),CHAPMAN DE
CONRADIE DCU DR,EDELSTEIN WH ,EGLIN CW ,LEVY V
PENNY C ,RABINOWITZ BP ,SAREMBOCK ML
SCHAFFER JE ,VAN HEESCH AJA ,WALTON CL (Chairman

REGISTRATION NUMBER : 68/01976/06

REGISTERED OFFICE
1002 NBS Waldorf, 80 St Georges Mall
Cape Town
8001
TEL: 021-22 2424
FAX: 021-22 2626

TRANSFER SECRETARY
Mercantile Registrars Ltd
P O Box 1053, Johannesburg
2000
TEL: 011-333 8181

COMPANY SECRETARY
C Penny

NATURE OF BUSINESS
The industrial arm of the Abbey Group. Activities comprise manufacture of knitted cotton fabrics for supply to the garment manufacturing industry.

BANKERS :
First National Bank of SA Ltd
Standard Bank of SA Ltd

AUDITORS :
Coopers Theron Du Toit

FAMILIAR BRAND NAMES
N/A

CONTRIBUTION BY ACTIVITY
Textiles (% Operating Income) (-131.0%)
Investments (31.0%)

YEAR END : December

DIVIDEND : Ords no par value

Interim No 22	(Ldr)31/03/89	(Pay)10/04/89	Amt(c)2.5
Final No 23	(Ldr)22/09/89	(Pay)06/10/89	Amt(c)5
Special No 24	(Ldr)05/01/90	(Pay)17/01/90	Amt(c)22.5
Interim No 25	(Ldr)23/03/90	(Pay)09/04/90	Amt(c)2.5
Special No 26	(Ldr)23/03/90	(Pay)09/04/90	Amt(c)45

NUMBER OF EMPLOYEES : 821

CAPITAL STRUCTURE

	AUTHORISED	ISSUED
Ords no par value	27000000	11250000

FINANCIAL STATISTICS (AT FINANCIAL YEAR END)

(Amts in R'000)	1991 Dec	1990 Jun	1989 Jun	1988 Jun	1987
Ord S/H Int	21076	34839	86032	75181	79299
Long Trm Loans	8919	1185	5529	6597	25625
Iss Ord Share	11250	11000	44000	44000	40000
Total Liab	22814	7715	16711	52316	38423
Current Liab	13895	6530	11182	45719	12798
Total Assets	43890	36775	96686	127497	111249
Intang Assets	*	5779	6057	*	*
Current Assets	14988	26240	33088	82523	6325
Debtors	10577	7629	10176	13790	-
Inventory	3854	2871	2476	965	6325
Turnover	74482	24883	-	-	-
Oper Profit	-10732	-1822	2117	8578	8067
Interest Paid	2957	227	3833	4054	2886
Tax Paid	-275	152	2011	1552	-
Prf af Int&Tax	-10464	2666	5087	4719	4094
Prf att Ord Sh	-9033	2239	8890	8043	3620
Btm Line Earn	-17244	-5881	6609	6556	3620
Dividend Paid	-	30800	3300	2860	1400
Mkt Prce(c) YE	290	85	85	95	200
Depreciation	1343	474	317	310	-

PER SHARE STATISTICS (CENTS)

Net Asst Val	187.34	264.18	181.76	170.87	198.25
Net Earnings	-82.10	20.40	20.20	18.28	-
Dividends	-	70.00	7.50	6.50	-
Cash Flow	-72.64	22.75	11.21	10.15	10.24

RATIOS AND OTHER INFORMATION

Mrk Cap(R000)	32625	9350	37400	41800	80000
Current Ratio	1.08	4.02	2.96	1.81	0.49
Quik/Acid Tst	0.80	3.58	2.74	1.78	-
A/C Rec T/ovr	7.04	3.26	-	-	-
Tot Ass T/ovr	1.70	0.68	-	-	-
Debt/Ass Rat	0.52	0.18	0.12	0.37	0.35
L T L Tot Ass	0.20	0.01	0.00	0.02	0.23
Debt to Eqity	1.08	0.19	0.13	0.63	0.48
Interest Cover	-3.63	-2.96	1.22	2.55	2.42
Oper Prof Mrg	-14.41	-7.32	-	-	-
Net Prof Marg%	-12.13	9.00	-	-	-
Ret on Assets	-17.73	8.90	15.89	11.11	6.27
Ret on Equity%	-42.86	6.43	10.33	10.70	4.57
Price/Earnings	-3.53	4.17	4.21	5.20	-
Divid Cover	-	0.29	2.69	2.81	-
Divid Yield	-	82.35	8.82	6.84	-
Earning Yield%	-28.31	24.00	23.76	19.24	-
NAV % Mrk Pr	64.60	310.80	213.84	179.86	99.12
Effec Tax Rate	-	8.15	37.35	13.04	-
Def Interval	-1.73	0.94	0.32	7.33	6.26
Sus Grth Rate	-42.86	-81.98	6.50	6.89	2.80

SUBSIDIARY & ASSOCIATED COMPANIES

DEBHOLD (PTY) LTD
FNX (LANSDOWNE) PROPERTY HOLDINGS LTD
FNX MANAGEMENT SERVICES LTD
FNX NOMINEES LTD
IVITEX (PTY) LTD
LANSDOWNE TEXTILE INDUSTRIES (PTY) LTD
LTI HOLDINGS LTD
MODATEX (PTY) LTD
RETCO (FRASERS) HOLDINGS LTD
RETCO CAXTON LTD
RETCO FIXED INVESTMENTS LTD
RETCO FIXED INVESTMENTS NO 11 LTD
RETCO PROPERTY HOLDINGS LTD
RETCO TRADING HOLDINGS LTD

INVESTMENTS

DEBHOLD (PTY) LTD (UNSEC VAR RATE DEBS) (8000000 SH)
PRESIDENT MEDICAL INV LTD (12,5% CONV DE (400 SH)
PRESIDENT MEDICAL INV LTD (12900 SH)
UNIDEV LTD (100000 SH)

FENNER GROUP SA LTD

ABBREVIATION : FENNER

JSE SHORT CODE : FNR

SECTOR : Industrial-Engineering

SHAREHOLDERS

Who Owns Whom's Assessment of the Identity of the Ultimate Controlling Shareholder: FENNER PLC

SHAREHOLDER	PERCENTAGE 1992	1991
FENNER INTERNATIONAL AFRICA P/L	50.0	50.0
INVESTEC INV TRUST LTD	28.4	---
SA MUTUAL	5.7	3.3
ENGINEERING INDUSTRIES PENS FUND	3.7	3.0
METAL IND GROUP PENS FUND	3.2	3.2
STD BANK NOM TVL P/L	---	15.4
INVESTEC SHARE NOM P/L	---	12.7
TOTAL	90.9	87.6

DIRECTORS :
ARTHUR RA (Chairman),BARKER PW
BIEHLER JJ (Managing Director),BROWN THP
CLEGG AST (Deputy Chairman),NAUDE SP

POETSCHKE F ,SAVAGE RB
STEYN W (Financial Director

REGISTRATION NUMBER : 05/26452/06

REGISTERED OFFICE
17 Diesel Road, Isando
Transvaal
1600
TEL: 011-974 8411
FAX: 011-974 8425

TRANSFER SECRETARY
Mercantile Registrars Ltd
P O Box 1053, Johannesburg
2000
TEL: 011-333 8181

COMPANY SECRETARY
F Van Wyk

NATURE OF BUSINESS
Group activities include the following :
Manufacture & distribution of power transmission products, PVC conveyor belting, hydraulic gear pumps & valves, moulded rubber products, slurry submersible & centrifugal pumps, control valves & systems, grey iron & SG castings, rubber wear protection, screening & dust sealing products. The group also offers on-site machining, valve repair & leak sealing services.

BANKERS :
Standard Bank of SA Ltd, Nedperm Bank Ltd

AUDITORS :
KPMG Aiken & Peat

FAMILIAR BRAND NAMES
FENAPLAST,FENNER,FISHER VALVES,KSB,LINK BELT PRO VOX,UNIVOX,VEE-BALL VALVES

CONTRIBUTION BY ACTIVITY
N/A

YEAR END : August

DIVIDEND :Ords 10c

Interim No 6	(Ldr)20/04/90	(Pay)17/05/90	Amt(c)6.5
Final No 7	(Ldr)16/11/90	(Pay)14/12/90	Amt(c)13.5
Interim No 8	(Ldr)17/05/91	(Pay)30/05/91	Amt(c)7.5
Final No 9	(Ldr)22/11/91	(Pay)18/12/91	Amt(c)14.5
Interim No 10	(Ldr)29/05/92	(Pay)18/06/92	Amt(c)7.5
Final No 11	(Ldr)04/12/92	(Pay)21/12/92	Amt(c)15.5

NUMBER OF EMPLOYEES : 1350

CAPITAL STRUCTURE

	AUTHORISED	ISSUED
Ords 10c	30000000	15000000
Var Rate Red Cum Prefs 1c	3150000	0

FINANCIAL STATISTICS (AT FINANCIAL YEAR END)

(Amts in R'000)	1991 Aug	1990 Aug	1989 Aug	1988 Aug	1987 Aug
Ord S/H Int	48864	42373	32478	27265	23519
Long Trm Loans	11098	9955	10610	11149	8848
Iss Ord Share	15000	15000	15000	15000	15000
Total Liab	67720	81230	53419	42998	33921
Current Liab	56622	71275	42809	31849	25073
Total Assets	116584	123603	85897	70263	57440
Current Assets	88080	95054	64750	52658	42343
Debtors	38317	42663	32079	24864	19815
Inventory	41817	50059	30570	26988	21349
Turnover	245802	209284	175881	131673	104563
Oper Profit	27774	24714	20237	14725	10855
Interest Paid	4875	3805	2862	1162	678
Tax Paid	11219	10276	8661	6598	4719
Prf af Int&Tax	12398	10954	8976	6965	5458
Prf att Ord Sh	9967	9101	7605	5621	4478
Btm Line Earn	9967	9101	7244	5621	2965
Dividend Paid	3300	3000	2475	1875	1975
Mkt Prce(c) YE	330	260	210	160	245
Depreciation	3525	3503	3251	2677	2341

PER SHARE STATISTICS (CENTS)

Net Asst Val	325.76	282.49	216.52	181.77	156.79
Net Earnings	66.40	60.70	50.70	37.50	29.90
Dividends	22.00	20.00	16.50	12.50	6.50
Cash Flow	92.48	89.07	76.01	60.11	45.87

RATIOS AND OTHER INFORMATION

Mrk Cap(R000)	49500	39000	31500	24000	36750
Current Ratio	1.56	1.33	1.51	1.65	1.69
Quik/Acid Tst	0.82	0.63	0.80	0.81	0.84
A/C Rec T/ovr	6.41	4.91	5.48	5.30	5.28
Tot Ass T/ovr	2.11	1.69	2.05	1.87	1.82
Debt/Ass Rat	0.49	0.58	0.54	0.50	0.45
L T L Tot Ass	0.00	0.00	0.04	0.05	0.02
Debt to Eqity	1.17	1.69	1.42	1.28	1.10
Interest Cover	5.70	6.50	7.07	12.67	16.01
Oper Prof Mrg	11.30	11.81	11.51	11.18	10.38
Net Prof Marg%	4.05	4.35	4.32	4.27	4.28
Ret on Assets	24.44	20.25	23.86	20.96	18.90
Ret on Equity%	20.40	21.48	23.42	20.62	19.04
Price/Earnings	4.97	4.28	4.14	4.27	8.19
Divid Cover	3.02	3.04	3.07	3.00	4.60
Divid Yield	6.67	7.69	7.86	7.81	2.65
Earning Yield%	20.12	23.35	24.14	23.44	12.20
NAV % Mrk Pr	98.72	108.65	103.10	113.60	64.00
Effec Tax Rate	46.22	44.84	46.02	43.40	45.65
Def Interval	1.08	1.65	1.19	1.13	1.40
Sus Grth Rate	13.64	14.40	15.80	13.74	10.64

SUBSIDIARY & ASSOCIATED COMPANIES

CLIMAX INVESTMENTS (PTY) LTD
CONTROL SPECIALISTS (PTY) LTD
FENNER (SA) (PTY) LTD
FENNER AFRICA (PTY) LTD
FENNER FLUID POWER (PTY) LTD
FENNER NAMIBIA (PTY) LTD
FENNER SWAZILAND (PTY) LTD
FIDELIO PROPERTIES (PTY) LTD
FORTY FOUR ACTIVIA PARK (PTY) LTD (50%)
FURMANITE AFRICA (PTY) LTD
JAKARANDA PATTERNMAKERS (PTY) LTD
KSB PUMPS (BOTSWANA) (PTY) LTD (26%)
KSB PUMPS (SA) (PTY) LTD (50%)
TREK ENGINEERING (PTY) LTD
TRELLEX (PTY) LTD
TRELLEX SPRINGBOK (PTY) LTD
WSJ CONVEYOR EQUIPMENT (PTY) LTD

INVESTMENTS

None

FIDELITY BANK LTD

ABBREVIATION : FIDBANK

JSE SHORT CODE : FBK

SECTOR : Financial-Banks & Financial Services

SHAREHOLDERS

Who Owns Whom's Assessment of the Identity of the Ultimate Controlling Shareholder: FEDSURE / BOARD OF EXECUTORS

SHAREHOLDER	PERCENTAGE 1992	1991
FEDLIFE ASSURE LTD	46 2	46 2
BOE SELECTIONS LTD	33 1	---
GUARDIAN NAT INSURANCE CO LTD	5 2	5 2
FERBROS NOM P/L	4 5	1 5
FIFTH NOM P/L	---	2 9
MERCURY TRUST LTD	---	33 1
TOTAL	89 0	88 9

DIRECTORS :
ANTONCICH M MR,BIDEN PN MR,FRASER ICP MR
FUCHS HO MR
LANGENBERG JEA MR (Chief Executive & M D)
LIPPSTREU RE MR (Chairman)
MURRAY C MR (Deputy Chairman),PHILIP RFD MR
THOMPSON MA MR,WOMERSLEY EHR M

REGISTRATION NUMBER : 04/02902/06

REGISTERED OFFICE
14th Floor Fidelity House, 190 Main Street
Port Elizabeth
6001
TEL 041-52 2141
FAX 041-55 4783

TRANSFER SECRETARY
Mercantile Registrars Ltd
P O Box 1053, Johannesburg
2000
TEL 011-333 8181

COMPANY SECRETARY
M W Newton

NATURE OF BUSINESS
A registered bank providing general banking, insurance broking, property sales, trustee and participation bond mortgage services throughout SA

BANKERS :
Standard Bank of SA Ltd

AUDITORS :
N/A

FAMILIAR BRAND NAMES
N/A

CONTRIBUTION BY ACTIVITY
N/A

YEAR END . September

DIVIDEND : Ords 100c

Interim	(Ldr)12/05/90	(Pay)06/06/90	Amt(c)6 4
Final	(Ldr)09/11/90	(Pay)05/12/90	Amt(c)13 6
Interim	(Ldr)10/05/91	(Pay)05/06/91	Amt(c)7 4
Final	(Ldr)25/10/91	(Pay)04/12/91	Amt(c)16 6

NUMBER OF EMPLOYEES : 130

CAPITAL STRUCTURE

	AUTHORISED	ISSUED
Ords 100c	21000000	11200000
Unsec Comp Conv Partic Loan Stock	7000000	7000000

FINANCIAL STATISTICS (AT FINANCIAL YEAR END)

(Amts in R'000)	1992 Sep	1991 Sep	1990 Sep	1989 Sep	1988 Sep
Ord S/H Int	44900	17755	14035	21935	20255
Long Trm Loans	535033	409408	361567	257345	191783
Iss Ord Share	11200	7000	7000	7000	7000
Total Liab	537228	410570	362519	258098	192273
Current Liab	2195	1162	952	753	490
Total Assets	582128	428325	376554	280033	212528
Current Assets	554427	423760	371993	277374	203060
Debtors	512996	400033	354768	267573	192342
Oper Profit	26272	20683	19312	3920	2801
Interest Paid	-	-	-	1120	700
Prf af Int&Tax	26272	20683	19494	2800	2101
Prf att Ord Sh	26272	20683	16869	2800	2101
Btm Line Earn	26272	20683	16869	2800	2101
Dividend Paid	3192	1680	1400	1120	840
Mkt Prce(c) YE	460	575	310	205	175

PER SHARE STATISTICS (CENTS)

Net Asst Val	400 89	253 64	200 50	313 36	289 36
Net Earnings	93 70	77 10	57 10	40 00	30 00
Dividends	28 50	24 00	20 00	16 00	12 00
Cash Flow	250 21	295 47	278 49	40 00	30 01

RATIOS AND OTHER INFORMATION

Mrk Cap(R000)	51520	40250	21700	14350	12250
Current Ratio	252 59	364 68	390 75	368 36	414 41
Quik/Acid Tst	252 59	364 68	390 75	368 36	414 41
Debt/Ass Rat	0 92	0 96	0 96	0 92	0 90
L T L Tot Ass	0 92	0 96	0 96	0 92	0 90
Debt to Eqity	11 96	23 12	25 83	11 77	9 49
Interest Cover	-	-	-	3 50	4 00
Ret on Assets	4 51	4 83	5 18	1 40	1 32
Ret on Equity%	58 51	116 49	120 19	12 76	10 37
Price/Earnings	4 91	7 46	5 43	5 13	5 83
Divid Cover	3 29	3 21	2 86	2 50	2 50
Divid Yield	6 20	4 17	6 45	7 80	6 86
Earning Yield%	20 37	13 41	18 42	19 51	17 14
NAV % Mrk Pr	87 15	44 11	64 68	152 86	165 35
Def Interval	19 97	19 29	18 01	91 91	91 28
Sus Grth Rate	51 40	107 03	110 22	7 66	6 23

SUBSIDIARY & ASSOCIATED COMPANIES

AEGIS INVESTMENT & TRUST CO LTD
AEGIS NOMINEES LTD
FIDELITY NOMINEES LTD
FIDELITY PROPERTY ADMINISTRATORS (PTY) L
FIDELITY PROPERTY BROKERS (PTY) LTD
FIDELITY TRUST CO LTD
GUARDIAN OF PE NOMINEES (PTY) LTD
THE INDEPENDENT LEASING CO (PTY) LTD

INVESTMENTS

None

FINANCIAL SERVICES CO OF BOTSWANA LTD

ABBREVIATION : FSC

SECTOR : Botswana Stock Exchange

SHAREHOLDERS

Who Owns Whom's Assessment of the Identity of the Ultimate Controlling Shareholder: NATIONAL DEVELOPMENT BANK /BOTSWANA DEV

SHAREHOLDER	PERCENTAGE 1992	1991
NAT DEVELOPMENT BANK	29.2	---
BOTSWANA DEVELOPMENT CORPORATION	28.0	---
DEBSWANA PENS FUND	10.1	---
IGI BOTSWANA LIFE ASSURE LTD	6.2	---
BOTSWANA LIFE INSURANCE LTD	3.3	---
BOTSWANA MOTOR VEHICLE INSURANCE FUND	3.2	---
BOTSWANA MEDICAL AID SOCIETY	2.8	---
STD CHARTERED BANK BOT LTD STAFF PENS FU	1.7	---
BARCLAYS BANK OF BOTSWANA STAFF PENS FUN	1.7	---
TOTAL	86.0	---

DIRECTORS :
HOPKINS ME (Chairman),JOHWA EW ,MOFFETT MJ MOONEY MB ,MUNAMATI KH ,MURPHY JP ,NAUDE SP PALIN D ,PAWSON RA (Managing Director) PHUMAPHI MP ,TOTHE BK

REGISTERED OFFICE
1st Floor, Botsalano House
The Mall, Gabarone

TEL: 351363
FAX: 357815

TRANSFER SECRETARY
Coopers & Lybrand Services (Pty) Ltd
P O Box 702, Harare
Zimbabwe

TEL: 0926 34 702771

COMPANY SECRETARY
Coopers & Lybrand Services

NATURE OF BUSINESS
FSC is the only citizen owned registered financial institution in Botswana, and is a leading provider of asset based financial facilities to a wide range of consumer and corporate customers. The company's principal activities continue to be in leasing, hire purchase, property mortgaging, factoring and invoice discounting.

BANKERS :
Bank of Botswana

AUDITORS :
Price Waterhouse Meyernel

FAMILIAR BRAND NAMES
N/A

CONTRIBUTION BY ACTIVITY
N/A

YEAR END : June

NUMBER OF EMPLOYEES : 100

CAPITAL STRUCTURE

	AUTHORISED	ISSUED
Ords P1	20000000	12000000

FINANCIAL STATISTICS (AT FINANCIAL YEAR END)

(Amts in P)	1992 Jun	1991 Jun
Ord S/H Int	24305	21418
Iss Ord Share	12000	12000
Total Liab	183183	114870
Current Liab	183183	114870
Total Assets	207488	136288
Current Assets	204105	133204
Debtors	1269	652
Oper Profit	7198	5018
Tax Paid	2391	2009
Prf af Int&Tax	4807	3009
Prf att Ord Sh	4807	3009
Btm Line Earn	4807	3009
Dividend Paid	1920	1500
Depreciation	285	219

PER SHARE STATISTICS (CENTS)

Net Asst Val	202.54	178.48
Net Earnings	40.10	30.60
Dividends	16.00	12.50
Cash Flow	51.19	29.54

RATIOS AND OTHER INFORMATION

Current Ratio	1.11	1.16
Quik/Acid Tst	1.11	1.16
Debt/Ass Rat	0.88	0.84
Debt to Eqity	7.54	5.36
Ret on Assets	3.47	3.68
Ret on Equity%	19.78	14.05
Divid Cover	2.51	2.45
Effec Tax Rate	21.26	33.72
Def Interval	27.98	30.36
Sus Grth Rate	11.88	7.05

SUBSIDIARY & ASSOCIATED COMPANIES

FB CORPORATE FINANCE BOTSWANA LTD (20%)
FINANCE HOUSE (PTY) LTD (48,8%)
FINANCIAL SERVICES PROPERTIES (PTY) LTD
PLOT FOUR NINE SEVEN TWO (PTY) LTD

INVESTMENTS

None

FINTECH LTD

ABBREVIATION : FINTECH

JSE SHORT CODE : FIN

SECTOR : Industrial-Electronics, Electrical & Bat

SHAREHOLDERS

Who Owns Whom's Assessment of the Identity of the Ultimate Controlling Shareholder:
W VENTER VIA VENTRON & ALTRON

SHAREHOLDER	PERCENTAGE 1992	1991
ALLIED ELECTRONICS CORP LTD	75 0	77 3
METAL IND GROUP PENS FUND	2 4	2 5
ENGINEERING INDUSTRIES PENS FUND	2 3	2 3
FIRST NAT NOM P/L	2 1	---
CMB NOM P/L	2 0	---
TITAN INSURANCE CO LTD	1 6	---
ALTRON INV HOLDINGS P/L	1 3	---
STOCKSHARE NOM P/L	---	1 7
FOLEY M P	---	1 9
SANLAM	---	2 1
TOTAL	86 7	87 7

DIRECTORS :
BORKUM HJ ,HOUSTON JR (Deputy Chairman)
JACOBSON DH DR,LAING BA (Financial Director)
REDSHAW PD (Executive Chairman),SEREBRO HA DR
STRIDE CA ,TRAHAR AJ ,VENTER WP D

REGISTRATION NUMBER : 69/10524/06

REGISTERED OFFICE
Momentum Business Park, Old Pretoria Road
Midrand
1685
TEL 011-313 1555
FAX 011-315 2691

TRANSFER SECRETARY
Central Registrars Ltd
P O Box 4844, Johannesburg
2000
TEL 011-331 0051

COMPANY SECRETARY
Fintech Management Services (Pty) Ltd

NATURE OF BUSINESS
The group is active in the information technology industry in the following areas Office automation & reprographics equipment, electronic telephone systems, computer technology - supplies, systems, peripherals & accessories, software development & distribution & hardware manufacture & distribution

BANKERS :
First National Bank of SA Ltd
Standard Bank of SA Ltd

AUDITORS :
Fisher Hoffman Stride

FAMILIAR BRAND NAMES
NATIONAL DATA SYSTEMS,NCR

CONTRIBUTION BY ACTIVITY
N/A

YEAR END : February

DIVIDEND : Ords 50c

Dividend No 26	(Ldr)24/05/91	(Pay)10/06/91	Amt(c)20
Dividend No 27	(Ldr)29/05/92	(Pay)08/06/92	Amt(c)40

NUMBER OF EMPLOYEES : 1975

CAPITAL STRUCTURE

	AUTHORISED	ISSUED
Ords 50c	20000000	11643118

FINANCIAL STATISTICS (AT FINANCIAL YEAR END)

(Amts in R'000)	1992 Feb	1991 Feb	1990 Feb	1989 Feb	1988 Feb
Ord S/H Int	63516	46295	40274	60659	55112
Long Trm Loans	74141	79680	14715	29403	12213
Iss Ord Share	11643	11139	11139	8232	8232
Total Liab	215988	212119	199588	203046	130613
Current Liab	141847	132439	184873	173643	118400
Total Assets	262873	241175	221499	263705	185725
Intang Assets	16631	17239	18363	*	*
Current Assets	232296	214707	194883	238080	166899
Debtors	100706	83784	97952	104065	79858
Inventory	97698	80250	96705	133925	86527
Turnover	561603	524024	674287	542250	256538
Oper Profit	30749	22759	-5892	33247	21093
Interest Paid	15152	5036	17702	18784	3323
Tax Paid	4535	2771	-1237	5750	2534
Prf af Int&Tax	24983	15320	-20001	14310	15236
Prf att Ord Sh	20019	9355	-20744	15149	12988
Btm Line Earn	16419	8249	-68363	9499	12988
Dividend Paid	4657	2228	-	3952	3952
Mkt Prce(c) YE	1475	700	450	2700	2600
Depreciation	7107	7070	8466	4239	5738

PER SHARE STATISTICS (CENTS)

	1992	1991	1990	1989	1988
Net Asst Val	402 69	260 85	196 71	736 87	669 48
Net Earnings	171 90	84 00	-183 20	184 00	201 20
Dividends	40 00	20 00	-	48 00	48 00
Cash Flow	266 04	170 09	-146 83	272 36	231 23

RATIOS AND OTHER INFORMATION

	1992	1991	1990	1989	1988
Mrk Cap(R000)	171734	77973	50126	222264	214032
Current Ratio	1 64	1 62	1 05	1 37	1 41
Quik/Acid Tst	0 95	1 02	0 53	0 60	0 68
A/C Rec T/ovr	5 58	6 25	6 88	5 21	3 21
Tot Ass T/ovr	2 14	2 17	3 04	2 06	1 38
Debt/Ass Rat	0 54	0 55	0 85	0 66	0 64
L T L Tot Ass	0 00	0 00	0 02	-	0 00
Debt to Eqity	2 23	2 87	4 67	2 86	2 16
Interest Cover	2 03	4 52	-0 33	1 77	6 35
Oper Prof Mrg	5 48	4 34	-0 87	6 13	8 22
Net Prof Marg%	3 56	1 79	-3 08	2 79	5 06
Ret on Assets	18 53	11 61	-1 05	14 83	11 63
Ret on Equity%	31 52	20 21	51 51	24 97	23 57
Price/Earnings	8 58	8 33	-2 46	14 67	12 92
Divid Cover	4 30	4 20	-	3 83	4 19
Divid Yield	2 71	2 86	-	1 78	1 85
Earning Yield%	11 65	12 00	-40 71	6 81	7 74
NAV % Mrk Pr	27 30	37 26	43 71	27 29	25 75
Effec Tax Rate	5 66		-8 27	12 37	9 59
Def Interval	0 05	0 21	-4 18	3 38	1 88
Sus Grth Rate	24 19	15 39	-51 51	18 46	16 40

SUBSIDIARY & ASSOCIATED COMPANIES

ADPROM HOLDINGS LTD (46%)
ADVANCE RIBBONS (PTY) LTD (46%)
ALTECH INFORMATICS (PTY) LTD
BLUE PETER COMPUTER MEDIA (PTY) LTD (46%)
COMPUTER WAREHOUSE (CISKEI) (PTY) LTD
COMPUTER WAREHOUSE (PTY) LTD (46%)
DISK IMPORTS (PTY) LTD (46%)
FINTECH (NAMIBIA) (PTY) LTD
FINTECH COMPUTER HOLDINGS (PTY) LTD
FINTECH INFORMATICS LTD
FINTECH INFORMATION TECHNOLOGIES (PTY) L
FINTECH MANAGEMENT SERVICES (PTY) LTD
FINTECH SHELF NO ONE (PTY) LTD
FINTECH SHELF NO THREE (PTY) LTD
FINTECH SHELF NO TWO (PTY) LTD
FLAGON MANAGEMENT & FINANCIAL SERVICES (
FUTUREWAVE TECHNOLOGIES LTD
HILLDALE INVESTMENTS (PTY) LTD
INTERTECH INFORMATION TECHNOLOGIES (BOP)
INTERTECH SYSTEMS (PTY) LTD
MICROBYTE (PTY) LTD
NATIONAL DATA SYSTEMS (PTY) LTD (50,1%)
NATIONAL DATA SYSTEMS (PTY) LTD (FORMERL
NDS SERVICES (PTY) LTD
NUMBER TWENTY-SIX (PTY) LTD (BOP)
PUNCH LINE (PTY) LTD
PUNCH LINE MANUFACTURING (PTY) LTD
RONEO AUTOMATION (PTY) LTD (46%)
RONEO AUTOMATION (PTY) LTD (46%)
STC BUSINESS COMMUNICATIONS (PTY) LTD
TECHNOLOGIES ACCEPTANCES (PTY) LTD
UNIQUE TECHNOLOGY (PTY) LTD
XERATECH (PTY) LTD

INVESTMENTS

FINTECH INFORMATICS LTD (10% CONV RED CU (99,69%)

FIRST INTERNATIONAL TRUST LTD

ABBREVIATION : FIT

JSE SHORT CODE : FIT

SECTOR : Financial-Investment Trusts

SHAREHOLDERS

Who Owns Whom's Assessment of the Identity of the Ultimate Controlling Shareholder:
LIBERTY LIFE HOLDS 40%+ (VOTING RIGHT =

SHAREHOLDER	PERCENTAGE 1992	1991
LIBERTY LIFE ASSOC OF AFRICA LTD	25 2	25 1
FULIT P/L	19 3	19 3
STD BANK NOM TVL P/L	8 5	7 6
LIBIC INV HOLDINGS P/L	6 1	6 1
SA MUTUAL	4 2	3 7
EIGHTY ONE MAIN STREET NOM LTD	2 8	2 0
GUARDIAN NOM P/L	2 1	2 1
GUARDIAN ASSURE CO LTD	1 3	1 3
GUARDIAN ASSURE CO SA LTD	1 2	1 2
GREENMARKET SQUARE NOM P/L	1 2	1 0
TOTAL	71 8	69 5

DIRECTORS :
CESMAN WE MR,DE VILLIERS HP MR (Deputy Chairman)
FISCHEL DA MR,GORDON D MR (Chairman),KAHN JM MR
MCALPINE JR MR,RAPP M MR,ROMANIS A MR,SHER FB MR
STRAUSS CB D

REGISTRATION NUMBER : 57/02956/06

REGISTERED OFFICE
Liberty Life Centre, 1 Ameshoff Street
Braamfontein
2001
TEL 011-408 3911
FAX 011-408 2109

TRANSFER SECRETARY
Central Registrars Ltd
P O Box 4844, Johannesburg
2000
TEL 011-331 0051

COMPANY SECRETARY
J Worwood

NATURE OF BUSINESS
An investment holding company with a controlling interest in Transatlantic Holdings Plc, which is quoted on the Luxembourg Stock Exchnge Activities include investment in the international insurance & real estate sectors, & in other fields related to the financial services industry

BANKERS :
Standard Bank of SA Ltd

AUDITORS :
Kessel Feinstein

FAMILIAR BRAND NAMES
N/A

CONTRIBUTION BY ACTIVITY
N/A

YEAR END : December

DIVIDEND .Ords 25c

Interim No 57	(Ldr)15/09/89	(Pay)06/10/89	Amt(c)6
Final No 58	(Ldr)30/03/90	(Pay)12/04/90	Amt(c)12
Interim No 59	(Ldr)14/09/90	(Pay)05/10/90	Amt(c)7
Final No 60	(Ldr)05/04/91	(Pay)19/04/91	Amt(c)13
Interim No 61	(Ldr)13/09/91	(Pay)11/10/91	Amt(c)7
Final No 62	(Ldr)27/03/92	(Pay)10/04/92	Amt(c)13
Interim No 63	(Ldr)04/09/92	(Pay)09/10/92	Amt(c)7

CAPITAL STRUCTURE

	AUTHORISED	ISSUED
Ords 25c	200000000	180286736
Cum Red Prefs 10c	20000000	0

FINANCIAL STATISTICS (AT FINANCIAL YEAR END)

(Amts in R'000)	1991 Dec	1990 Dec	1989 Dec	1988	1987
Ord S/H Int	1549500	1474600	1428066	1246479	601809
Long Trm Loans	282700	355700	399106	442865	14571

Iss Ord Share	180287	138682	138682	138682	79247
Total Liab	318000	419100	433571	455083	29142
Current Liab	35300	63400	34465	12218	14571
Total Assets	1867500	1893700	1861637	1741645	646180
Current Assets	85800	89900	73001	52301	29800
Debtors	51500	51300	50830	-	-
Inventory	-	-	-	52301	29800
Oper Profit	87700	87300	28500	54593	25308
Interest Paid	38600	40500	40638	8275	-
Tax Paid	11300	11700	18478	7417	194
Prf af Int&Tax	37800	35100	51684	38901	25114
Prf att Ord Sh	53700	66100	51684	38901	25114
Btm Line Earn	53700	66100	51684	38901	25114
Dividend Paid	33200	27700	24963	23774	20604
Mkt Prce(c) YE	1075	1260	1025	1165	740

PER SHARE STATISTICS (CENTS)

Net Asst Val	859.46	1063.30	1029.74	898.80	759.41
Net Earnings	36.30	47.70	37.30	-	-
Dividends	20.00	20.00	18.00	-	-
Cash Flow	20.97	25.31	37.27	28.05	31.69

RATIOS AND OTHER INFORMATION

Mrk Cap(R000)	1938085	1747393	1421491	1615645	586428
Current Ratio	2.43	1.42	2.12	4.28	2.05
Quik/Acid Tst	2.43	1.42	2.12	-	-
Debt/Ass Rat	0.17	0.22	0.23	0.26	0.05
L T L Tot Ass	0.15	0.19	0.21	0.25	0.02
Debt to Eqity	0.21	0.28	0.30	0.37	0.05
Interest Cover	2.27	2.16	2.66	6.60	-
Ret on Assets	5.55	6.25	5.95	3.13	3.92
Ret on Equity%	3.47	4.48	3.62	3.12	4.17
Price/Earnings	29.61	26.42	27.48	-	-
Divid Cover	1.82	2.39	2.07	-	-
Divid Yield	1.86	1.59	1.76	-	-
Earning Yield%	3.38	3.79	3.64	-	-
NAV % Mrk Pr	79.95	84.39	100.46	77.15	102.62
Effec Tax Rate	23.01	25.00	-14.74	16.01	0.77
Def Interval	7.48	10.84	7.72	11.38	0.58
Sus Grth Rate	1.32	2.60	1.87	1.21	0.75

SUBSIDIARY & ASSOCIATED COMPANIES

CAPITAL & COUNTIES PLC (40,2%)
CONDUIT INSURANCE HOLDINGS LTD
TRANSATLANTIC HOLDINGS PLC

INVESTMENTS

SUN LIFE ASSURANCE SOCIETY PLC (15,8%)

FIRST NATIONAL BANK HOLDINGS LTD

ABBREVIATION : FIRSTBK

JSE SHORT CODE : FSB

SECTOR : Financial-Banks & Financial Services

SHAREHOLDERS

Who Owns Whom's Assessment of the Identity of the Ultimate Controlling Shareholder: ANGLO AMERICAN

SHAREHOLDER	PERCENTAGE 1992	1991
SOUTHERN LIFE SPECIAL INV P/L	17.2	21.1
LAGAN INV HLDGS LTD	13.7	5.3
SOUTHERN LIFE ASSOC LTD	8.5	5.1
FIRST NAT NOM P/L	7.9	9.4
DE BEERS HOLDINGS P/L	6.5	6.8
STD BANK NOM TVL P/L	4.9	6.9
CMB NOM P/L	3.2	---
LIBERTY LIFE ASSOC OF AFRICA LTD	2.9	3.0
ENGINEERING INDUSTRIES PENS FUND	2.8	3.1
METAL IND GROUP PENS FUND	2.5	2.9
SA MUTUAL	2.4	3.1
RUNCORN HLDGS LTD	2.3	3.3
SIXTY SIX MARSHALL STREET NOM P/L	2.2	2.7
EIGHTY ONE MAIN STREET NOM LTD	2.2	2.1
MINE OFFICIALS PENS FUND	1.9	2.2
FEDLIFE ASSURE LTD	1.9	---
MINE EMPLOYEES PENS FUND	1.1	1.3
SANLAM	---	1.2
FEDERATED LIFE ASSURE CO LTD	---	1.3
RESIDENT NOM LTD	---	3.4
TOTAL	84.0	84.1

DIRECTORS :
BARROW JA ,CALITZ JR ,CHAPMAN TN (Vice Chairman)
DYER DW ,GRICE DC ,GUSH EP ,HERSOV BE (Chairman)
KING ME ,KING MW (Vice Chairman)
MOTSUENYANE SM DR,NAPIER RS ,NOYCE MJ ,SAVAGE RB
SEARLE PM ,STEYN JH
SWART BJ (Managing Director),VAHED AS
VAN ZYL LS ,WILLIAMS RA ,WRIGHTON PGA

REGISTRATION NUMBER : 71/09695/06

REGISTERED OFFICE
National Bank Building, 84 Market Street
Johannesburg
2001
TEL: 011-632 9111
FAX: 011-632 2201

TRANSFER SECRETARY
Consolidated Share Registrars Ltd
P O Box 61051, Marshalltown
2107
TEL: 011-492 1620

COMPANY SECRETARY
R B McElligott

NATURE OF BUSINESS
The group provides all forms of banking services.

BANKERS :
First National Bank of SA Ltd

AUDITORS :
Deloitte Pim Goldby, KPMG Aiken & Peat

FAMILIAR BRAND NAMES
BOB CARD,FUTUREBANK (50%)

CONTRIBUTION BY ACTIVITY
First National Bank (% Net Income) (51.3%)
Wesbank (31.2%)
Firstcorp (8.1%)
FirstNamib (5.5%)
Associates (2.3%)
Other (1.6%)

YEAR END : September

DIVIDEND :Ords R1

Interim No 40	(Ldr)11/05/90	(Pay)05/06/90	Amt(c)40
Final No 41	(Ldr)16/11/90	(Pay)11/12/90	Amt(c)110
Interim No 42	(Ldr)10/05/91	(Pay)04/06/91	Amt(c)45
Final No 43	(Ldr)15/11/91	(Pay)10/12/91	Amt(c)130
Interim No 44	(Ldr)15/05/92	(Pay)09/06/92	Amt(c)50
Final No 45	(Ldr)13/11/92	(Pay)08/12/92	Amt(c)150

NUMBER OF EMPLOYEES : 25226

CAPITAL STRUCTURE

	AUTHORISED	ISSUED
Ords R1	110000000	83666728

FINANCIAL STATISTICS (AT FINANCIAL YEAR END)

(Amts in R'000)	1991 Sep	1990 Sep	1989 Sep	1988 Sep	1987
Ord S/H Int	1690000	1430400	1206000	1018500	900000
Long Trm Loans	33213500	27535600	27777700	25864000	19703800
Iss Ord Share	72754	72754	72754	72754	58025
Total Liab	34906800	28848000	29141700	27131500	19703800
Current Liab	1693300	1312400	1364000	1267500	-
Total Assets	36596800	30278400	30347700	28150000	34587800
Current Assets	35107700	29090700	29218200	27150300	13984000
Debtors	1187100	887100	1114900	964200	-
Inventory	-	-	-	-	13984000
Oper Profit	-980000	-869100	-799900	306400	1645200
Interest Paid	4071000	3927600	3374100	-	1343300
Tax Paid	236700	218100	153100	128900	8500
Prf af Int&Tax	408900	320300	236900	177500	161400
Prf att Ord Sh	385100	329800	274300	206800	184600
Btm Line Earn	385100	329800	274300	206800	184600
Dividend Paid	127300	110200	98600	88300	87300
Mkt Prce(c) YE	4825	2750	1875	1325	2450
Depreciation	158900	145700	134000	97400	-

PER SHARE STATISTICS (CENTS)

Net Asst Val	2322.90	1966.08	1657.64	1399.92	1551.06
Net Earnings	529.30	453.30	377.00	284.50	-
Dividends	175.00	150.00	130.00	112.50	-
Cash Flow	969.16	709.10	632.13	534.54	278.16

RATIOS AND OTHER INFORMATION

Mrk Cap(R000)	3510381	2000735	1364138	963991	1421613
Current Ratio	20.73	22.17	21.42	21.42	-
Quik/Acid Tst	20.73	22.17	21.42	21.42	-
Debt/Ass Rat	0.05	0.05	0.05	0.05	0.57
L T L Tot Ass	0.01	0.01	0.01	0.01	0.57
Debt to Eqity	1.17	1.11	1.35	1.49	21.89
Interest Cover	-0.23	-0.21	-0.24	-	1.13
Ret on Assets	12.91	14.78	12.53	1.19	4.37
Ret on Equity%	22.79	23.06	22.74	20.30	20.51
Price/Earnings	9.12	6.07	4.97	4.66	-
Divid Cover	3.02	3.02	2.90	2.53	-
Divid Yield	3.63	5.45	6.93	8.49	-
Earning Yield%	10.97	16.48	20.11	21.47	-
NAV % Mrk Pr	48.14	71.49	88.41	105.65	63.31
Effec Tax Rate	12.51	28.53	5.04	5.87	2.82
Def Interval	0.41	0.53	0.58	0.66	122.08
Sus Grth Rate	15.25	15.35	14.57	11.63	10.81

SUBSIDIARY & ASSOCIATED COMPANIES

APEX MANAGERS FUND (25%)
AVFIN INDUSTRIAL FINANCE (PTY) LTD
BANK CITY BLOCK B (PTY) LTD
BANK CITY BLOCK C (PTY) LTD
BANK CITY BLOCK D (PTY) LTD
BANK CITY BLOCK E (PTY) LTD
BANK CITY STREETS (PTY) LTD
CASH PAYMASTER SERVICES (PTY) LTD (50%)
CBM FINANCIAL SERVICES LTD (MALAWI) (30%)
ERF SEVENTY NINE ST ANDREWS (PTY) LTD (50%)
ESSEXWOLD PROPERTIES (PTY) LTD
FINANCIAL INSTRUMENT CLEARING (PTY) LTD
FIRNAT TRAVELLER (PTY) LTD
FIRNESS INTERNATIONAL (PTY) LTD
FIRST BOND NOMINEES (PTY) LTD
FIRST BOWRING & ASSOCIATES HOLDINGS LTD (50%)
FIRST LAND DEVELOPMENTS LTD
FIRST NATIONAL ASSET MANAGEMENT AND TRUS
FIRST NATIONAL BANK OF BOTSWANA LTD
FIRST NATIONAL BANK OF NAMIBIA LTD
FIRST NATIONAL BANK OF SA LTD
FIRST NATIONAL CORPORATE & INVESTMENT BA
FIRST NATIONAL MERCHANT BANK LTD
FIRST NATIONAL MORTGAGES NOMINEES (PTY)
FIRST NATIONAL NOMINEES (PTY) LTD
FIRST NATIONAL SOUTH AFRICAN INVESTMENTS
FIRST NATIONAL WESTERN COMPANY LTD
FIRSTCORP NOMINEES (PTY) LTD
FIRSTCORP SERVICES (PTY) LTD
FIRSTNET (PTY) LTD
FORDOM FACTORING (PTY) LTD
GENERAL ACCIDENT INSURANCE CO SA LTD (26,4%)
GUARDBANK MANAGEMENT CORPORATION LTD (50%)
GUARDPLAN TRUST (PTY) LTD
KEMPWEST (PTY) LTD (50%)
MOBILE ACCEPTANCES (PTY) LTD (26%)
MOSSELBANK (PTY) LTD
NATAL LANDS LTD (50%)
NATIONAL BANK OF SOUTH AFRICA LTD
PAYMENT SOLUTIONS (PTY) LTD
ROGGEBAAI INVESTMENTS (PTY) LTD (33,3%)
RONALD SEWELL AND ASSOCIATES S.A. (PTY)
SHEPSTONE GARDENS (PTY) LTD
SOFTWARE BY FAX (PTY) LTD
SOUTH AFRICA BOARD REAL ESTATE (PTY) LTD
SOUTH AFRICAN BOARD OF EXECUTORS & TRUST
SOUTHERN LIFE ASSOCIATION LTD (29,2%)
SOUTHERN LIFE EQUIPMENT FINANCE (PTY) LT (27%)
TALAS PROPERTIES WINDHOEK (PTY) LTD
TANRAB PROPERTIES (PTY) LTD
VIGILANS PROPERTIES (PRETORIA) (PTY) LTD (50%)
WESCARE (PTY) LTD
WEST GARDINER DEVELOPMENT (PTY) LTD (50%)
ZEDA CAR LEASING (PTY) LTD (42%)

INVESTMENTS

AFRICAN BANK LTD (3,2%)
CORNERSTONE PROPERTY FUND MANAGERS LTD (12,1%)
CREDIT GUARANTEE INSURANCE CORP. OF AFRI (5,9%)
DISCOUNT HOUSE OF S.A. LTD (8,6%)
MAIN STREET PROPERTY FUND MANAGERS LTD (10%)
SMALL BUSINESS DEVELOPMENT CORP LTD (2,3%)
SYCOM PROPERTY FUND

FMB HOLDINGS LTD

ABBREVIATION : FMB

SECTOR : Zimbabwe Stock Exchange

SHAREHOLDERS

Who Owns Whom's Assessment of the Identity of the Ultimate Controlling Shareholder:
ANGLO AMERICAN

SHAREHOLDER	PERCENTAGE 1992	1991
SECURITY NOM LTD	43.1	---
OLD MUTUAL INV CORP (PVT) LTD	14.4	---
INTERNATIONAL FINANCE CORP LTD	10.0	---
FIRST MUTUAL LIFE ASSURE SOC OF ZIM	3.4	---
FMB HOLDINGS EMPL SHARE TRUST	2.5	---
FIRST SHELF CO PVT LTD	2.4	---
NAT RAILWAYS OF ZIM CONTR PENS FUND	2.3	---
STD BANK PENS FUND	1.7	---
BARD NOM (PVT) LTD	1.5	---
TRUST NOM (PVT) LTD	1.3	---
FIDELITY LIFE ASSURE OF ZIM PVT LTD	1.2	---
CATERING INDUSTRY PENS FUND	1.1	---
MINING INDUSTRY PENS FUND	1.0	---
TOTAL	85.8	---

DIRECTORS :
BARTH RM ,BLOCH EW ,CARTER JD ,CHIURA ED
DENNETT DE ,FELTOE R (Managing Director)
LANDER RP (Chairman),LEWIS DJ ,NICHOLSON DG
SMART WK ,WISHART AB ,YOUNG JRA

REGISTERED OFFICE
FMB House, 67 Samora Machel Avenue
Harare, Zimbabwe

TEL: 703071
FAX: 738810

TRANSFER SECRETARY
First Transfer Secretaries (Pvt) Ltd
P O Box 437, Bulawayo
Zimbabwe

TEL: 092634 - 702905

COMPANY SECRETARY
Musiwa C V

NATURE OF BUSINESS
FMB HOLDINGS is an investment holding company incorporated in Zimbabwe,whose subsidiaries oper ate in the merchant banking, property and trust fields.

BANKERS :
First Merchant Bank of Zimbabwe Ltd

AUDITORS :
Deloitte & Touche

FAMILIAR BRAND NAMES
N/A

CONTRIBUTION BY ACTIVITY
N/A

YEAR END : December

DIVIDEND :Ords Z$1

Dividend	(Ldr)23/08/91	(Pay)09/09/91	Amt(c)17.5
Dividend	(Ldr)06/02/92	(Pay)20/03/92	Amt(c)19.5

CAPITAL STRUCTURE

	AUTHORISED	ISSUED
Ords Z$1	18000000	15760117

FINANCIAL STATISTICS (AT FINANCIAL YEAR END)

(Amts in Z$)	1991 Dec	1990 Dec
Ord S/H Int	85143	57430
Long Trm Loans	56	14
Iss Ord Share	15760	13133
Total Liab	1150882	737797
Current Liab	1150826	737783
Total Assets	1236025	795227
Current Assets	1216222	745825
Debtors	693541	349436
Oper Profit	12946	8953
Prf af Int&Tax	12946	8953
Prf att Ord Sh	12894	8937
Btm Line Earn	13121	9399
Dividend Paid	5371	3947
Depreciation	2	7

PER SHARE STATISTICS (CENTS)

Net Asst Val	540.25	437.30
Net Earnings	94.70	76.20
Dividends	37.00	32.00
Cash Flow	81.83	68.10

RATIOS AND OTHER INFORMATION

Current Ratio	1.06	1.01
Quik/Acid Tst	1.06	1.01
Debt/Ass Rat	0.93	0.93
Debt to Eqity	13.52	12.85
Ret on Assets	1.05	1.13
Ret on Equity%	15.14	15.56
Divid Cover	2.56	2.38
Sus Grth Rate	8.84	8.69

SUBSIDIARY & ASSOCIATED COMPANIES

HARMONY PARTNERSHIP (33,33%)
KNIGHT FRANK & RUTLEY ZIMBABWE (34%)

INVESTMENTS

None

FOCUS HOLDINGS LTD

ABBREVIATION : FOCUS

JSE SHORT CODE : FCS

SECTOR : Industrial-Retailers & Wholesalers

SHAREHOLDERS

Who Owns Whom's Assessment of the Identity of the Ultimate Controlling Shareholder:
DIRECTORS CONTROL 65,6%

SHAREHOLDER	PERCENTAGE 1992	1991
BULLION INV P/L	73 1	66 3
STD BANK NOM TVL P/L	16 2	6 3
FIRST NAT NOM P/L	1 8	3 8
ANGLO AMERICAN GROUP PENS FUND	1 7	7 9
NTE PENS FUND	---	2 2
TOTAL	92 7	86 5

DIRECTORS :
COHEN MJ (Joint Managing Director)
DE KATZ G (Joint Managing Director)
SACKS I (Executive Chairman), VAN KATZ A

REGISTRATION NUMBER : 82/11813/06

REGISTERED OFFICE
Focus House, 86 Loveday Street
Johannesburg
2001
TEL 011-838 8900
FAX 011-834 8371

TRANSFER SECRETARY
Mercantile Registrars Ltd
P O Box 1053, Johannesburg
2000
TEL 011-333 8181

COMPANY SECRETARY
K H Wainer

NATURE OF BUSINESS
Retailing of clothing & bedding through a network of outlets

BANKERS :
Nedperm Bank Ltd

AUDITORS :
Fisher Hoffman Stride

FAMILIAR BRAND NAMES
ACA JOE, BACHELORS, BACKCARE COLLECTION
CASHWORTHS, EXTROVERT MAN, FORTY WINKS
GOOPHEES, GRANT MACKENZIES, HIP BED
M & H FACTORY SHOPS, SMILEY BLUE
SNOBS'N SLOBS, SPRACKLENS

CONTRIBUTION BY ACTIVITY
N/A

YEAR END : July

DIVIDEND : Ords 1c
Final No 6 (Ldr)07/12/90 (Pay)14/12/90 Amt(c)2

NUMBER OF EMPLOYEES : 152

CAPITAL STRUCTURE

	AUTHORISED	ISSUED
Ords 1c	149000000	78845302
12% Red Comp Conv 2nd Prefs 3c	1250000	198670

FINANCIAL STATISTICS (AT FINANCIAL YEAR END)

(Amts in R'000)	1991 Jul	1990 Jul	1989 Feb	1988 Feb	1987
Ord S/H Int	-4376	3087	3545	2600	587
Long Trm Loans	8662	11075	29	307	2739
Iss Ord Share	21871	20917	18917	18517	14400
Total Liab	34328	28140	8018	4963	5178
Current Liab	25666	17065	7989	4656	2439
Total Assets	29292	30567	11563	7563	6004
Intang Assets	660	660	*	*	*
Current Assets	25735	27435	10202	6460	2678
Debtors	10348	10774	4049	2335	-
Inventory	15387	16661	6153	3229	2678
Turnover	62985	76807	21295	10994	7653
Oper Profit	-5153	4379	2351	1496	823
Interest Paid	3997	3813	263	175	
Tax Paid	-	480	423	264	260
Prf af Int&Tax	-5878	2060	1665	1057	444
Prf att Ord Sh	-6984	2018	1598	1036	417
Btm Line Earn	-6984	-539	1295	1036	417
Dividend Paid	170	209	660	324	-
Mkt Prce(c) YE	21	30	50	35	-
Depreciation	349	306	112	77	-

PER SHARE STATISTICS (CENTS)

Net Asst Val	-23 03	11 60	18 74	14 04	4 08
Net Earnings	-14 40	9 93	8 49	6 30	-
Dividends	-	1 00	3 25	1 75	-
Cash Flow	-25 33	8 07	9 04	6 01	3 08

RATIOS AND OTHER INFORMATION

Mrk Cap(R000)	4593	6275	9459	6481	-
Current Ratio	1 00	1 61	1 28	1 39	1 10
Quik/Acid Tst	0 40	0 63	0 51	0 69	-
A/C Rec T/ovr	6 09	5 03	5 26	4 71	-
Tot Ass T/ovr	2 15	1 77	1 84	1 45	1 27
Debt/Ass Rat	1 17	0 90	0 69	0 62	0 86
L T L Tot Ass	0 29	0 35	-	-	0 46
Debt to Eqity	-7 80	8 95	2 25	1 79	8 82
Interest Cover	-1 29	1 15	8 94	8 55	-
Oper Prof Mrg	-8 18	5 70	11 04	13 61	10 75
Net Prof Marg%	-11 09	2 63	7 50	9 42	5 45
Ret on Assets	-6 42	14 67	20 33	19 78	11 73
Ret on Equity%	159 60	46 14	45 08	39 85	71 04
Price/Earnings	-1 46	3 02	5 89	5 56	
Divid Cover		9 93	2 61	3 60	-
Divid Yield	-	3 33	6 50	5 00	-
Earning Yield%	-68 57	33 10	16 98	18 00	-
NAV % Mrk Pr	-109 65	38 68	37 48	40 12	-
Effec Tax Rate	-	9 96	1 10	19 98	31 59
Def Interval	-2 03	2 21	0 60	0 27	6 17
Sus Grth Rate	163 48	58 60	26 46	27 38	71 04

SUBSIDIARY & ASSOCIATED COMPANIES

AMALGAMATED ADMINISTRATORS (PTY) LTD
BACHELORS HOLDINGS (PTY) LTD
BACKCARE COLLECTION (PTY) LTD
CASHWORTHS FASHIONS (1989) (PTY) LTD
CLOTHING FOCUS (PTY) LTD
DISTRIBUTION FOCUS (PTY) LTD
GRANT MACKENZIE & CO (PTY) LTD
HUMDINGER (PTY) LTD
JOSANN TRADING COMPANY (PTY) LTD
MANNIX GALTRUCCO (PTY) LTD
MANNIX L'UOMO HOLDINGS (PTY) LTD
MATTRESS WORLD FRANCHISE HOLDINGS (PTY)
MATTRESS WORLD HOLDINGS (PTY) LTD
PARISIAN MENSWEAR (PTY) LTD
RETAIL FOCUS (PTY) LTD
REVOLVER FASHION BOUTIQUES (PTY) LTD
SOMETHING BLUE MANUFACTURERS (PTY) LTD
THE BEDROOM SPECIALISTS (PTY) LTD
THE SLEEP GIANT (PTY) LTD

INVESTMENTS

None

FOODCORP LTD

ABBREVIATION : FOODCRP

JSE SHORT CODE : FDC

SECTOR : Industrial-Food

SHAREHOLDERS

Who Owns Whom's Assessment of the Identity of the Ultimate Controlling Shareholder: SANLAM VIA SANKORP VIA MALBAK

SHAREHOLDER	PERCENTAGE 1992	1991
MALBAK INV (FEDFOOD) P/L	71 2	---
CMB NOM P/L	7 5	---
EIGHTY ONE MAIN STREET NOM LTD	3 6	3 3
BP THIBAULT NOM P/L	2 1	2 1
ABSA NOM P/L	1 7	---
SMALL BUSNESS DEVELOPMENT CORP LTD	1 4	2 3
STD BANK NOM TVL P/L	1 4	1 5
METROPOLITAN LIFE LTD	1 1	1 8
SANLAM	---	8 0
FEDERALE VOLKS INV LTD	---	69 6
TOTAL	90 1	88 6

DIRECTORS :
DE BEER TL ,ISEMONGER NW
JACOBS DJ (Chief Executive),KILIAN C
SCHOEMAN HSJ ,SCHOONRAAD GP
THOMAS GS (Chairman),VAN DER WALT TJ

REGISTRATION NUMBER : 05/15583/06

REGISTERED OFFICE
Pellmeadow Park, 60 Civin Drive
Bedfordview
2008
TEL 011-453 1501
FAX 011-453 1638

TRANSFER SECRETARY
Central Registrars Ltd
P O Box 4844, Johannesburg
2000
TEL 011-331 0051

COMPANY SECRETARY
M S Viljoen

NATURE OF BUSINESS
An investment holding company Group activities include the processing of fish, wheat, maize, animal feeds, industrial oils, snacks and frozen foods, as well as wholesale operations & bakeries

BANKERS :
First National Bank of SA Ltd
Standard Bank of SA Ltd, Nedperm Bank Ltd
Volkskas Ltd, Central Merchant Bank Ltd

AUDITORS :
Coopers Theron Du Toit

FAMILIAR BRAND NAMES
A1 MAIZE MEAL,BELLISSIMA,BIG T,BOBTAIL
BOERSTRA,CAROUSEL,CATERCRAFT,CRESTA
CURRINASE,FRITOS,HARVESTIME,MAGEU NUMBER ONE
MANGO MAN,MARINE PRODUCTS,MARPRO,MNANTI,MOJO
MONATI,NIKNAKS,NOLA,O'GRADYS,PAPA JOE,PARK
PATOMA,PICK OF THE CROP,QUIX PACKAGING,REVO
RUFFLES,RUTO MILLS,SIMBA,SUN LOAF,SUN SLICE
SUN VALLEY,SUN WHEAT,SUNBAKE,TABLE TOP

CONTRIBUTION BY ACTIVITY
N/A

YEAR END : August

DIVIDEND : Ords 50c

Interim No 70	(Ldr)08/12/89	(Pay)05/01/90	Amt(c)17
Final No 71	(Ldr)08/06/90	(Pay)06/07/90	Amt(c)30
Interim No 72	(Ldr)07/12/90	(Pay)04/01/91	Amt(c)19
Final No 73	(Ldr)07/06/91	(Pay)05/07/91	Amt(c)34
Interim No 74	(Ldr)06/12/91	(Pay)03/01/92	Amt(c)19
Final No 75	(Ldr)12/06/92	(Pay)10/07/92	Amt(c)34
Interim No 76	(Ldr)20/11/92	(Pay)04/12/92	Amt(c)22

NUMBER OF EMPLOYEES : 13065

CAPITAL STRUCTURE

	AUTHORISED	ISSUED
Ords 50c	60000000	48083333
13% Unsec Sub Comp Conv Debs	6700000	6413838

FINANCIAL STATISTICS (AT FINANCIAL YEAR END)

(Amts in R'000)	1992 Aug	1991 Mar	1990 Mar	1989 Mar	1988 Mar
Ord S/H Int	575000	331000	295900	255800	251600
Long Trm Loans	86000	185000	99900	82000	44300
Iss Ord Share	48083	29750	29750	29485	28399
Total Liab	625000	521000	334100	310700	227400
Current Liab	539000	336000	234200	228700	183100
Total Assets	1200000	852000	626400	562900	479000
Intang Assets	*	*	3600	3600	*
Current Assets	643000	423000	322600	306100	262200
Debtors	361000	269000	178700	170600	141500
Inventory	282000	154000	143900	130000	120700
Turnover	2415000	1201000	1140300	1171300	1009955
Oper Profit	169000	109000	96600	100200	76000
Interest Paid	37000	25000	26900	19400	16600
Tax Paid	51000	33000	31500	35200	23700
Prf af Int&Tax	88000	56000	45200	48200	37200
Prf att Ord Sh	83000	58000	50900	49100	35500
Btm Line Earn	59000	51000	50100	49900	40300
Dividend Paid	27000	16000	14100	13400	10700
Mkt Prce(c) YE	2275	1400	890	850	835
Depreciation	75000	45000	35800	26400	20827

PER SHARE STATISTICS (CENTS)

Net Asst Val	1195 85	1112 61	982 52	855 35	885 95
Net Earnings	184 30	193 30	170 00	156 60	129 30
Dividends	56 00	53 00	47 00	45 00	38 00
Cash Flow	207 53	366 67	307 36	261 25	224 26

RATIOS AND OTHER INFORMATION

Mrk Cap(R000)	1093888	416500	264775	250623	237132
Current Ratio	1 19	1 26	1 38	1 34	1 43
Quik/Acid Tst	0 67	0 80	0 76	0 77	0 77
A/C Rec T/ovr	4 72	4 46	6 38	6 87	7 14

Tot Ass T/ovr	1 42	1 41	1 82	2 08	2 11
Debt/Ass Rat	0 50	0 56	0 46	0 50	0 42
L T L Tot Ass	0 05	0 16	0 09	0 09	0 04
Debt to Eqity	1 05	1 44	0 98	1 10	0 80
Interest Cover	4 76	4 56	3 75	5 21	4 67
Oper Prof Mrg	7 00	9 08	8 47	8 55	7 53
Net Prof Marg%	3 44	4 83	4 46	4 19	3 52
Ret on Assets	10 76	13 85	17 83	18 83	16 26
Ret on Equity%	10 19	17 52	17 20	19 19	14 11
Price/Earnings	12 34	7 24	5 24	5 43	6 46
Divid Cover	3 29	3 65	3 62	3 48	3 40
Divid Yield	2 46	3 79	5 28	5 29	4 55
Earning Yield%	8 10	13 81	19 10	18 42	15 49
NAV % Mrk Pr	52 56	79 47	110 40	100 63	106 10
Effec Tax Rate	43 18	15 48	27 66	38 98	30 47
Def Interval	1 31	2 41	1 09	0 31	0 40
Sus Grth Rate	9 74	12 69	12 44	13 96	9 86

SUBSIDIARY & ASSOCIATED COMPANIES

FOODCORP GROUP (PTY) LTD
FOODCORP OPERATION LTD
GANSBAAI MARINE (EDMS) BPK (50%)
MARCONFISH (PTY) LTD (50%)
MARINE PRODUCTS BPK
NOLKO (EDMS) BPK (40%)
PIETERSBURG ABATTOIR (PTY) LTD (50%)

INVESTMENTS

ATLANTIC CANNED FISH SALES (PTY) LTD (500 SH)
BALFOUR BAKERY (PTY) LTD (1673 SH)
BENONI MILLING CO (PTY) LTD (1 SH)
FEDERAL FISH PACKERS (PTY) LTD (2217 SH)
FEDERAL MARINE LTD (600 SH)
FISH MEAL MARKETING CO (WINDHOEK) (PTY) (2 SH)
FISH OIL MARKETING CO (WINDHOEK) (PTY) L (2 SH)
HERE XVII GEBOUE (PTY) LTD (22 SH)
HISTORICAL HOUSES OF SA LTD (5000 SH)
MAR LIMPIO LTD (3625 SH)
MINNIE ROOMS (PTY) LTD (60 SH)
SA FISH MEAL MARKETING CO (PTY) LTD (2 SH)
SA FISH MEAL PRODUCERS ASSOCIATION (PTY) (4 SH)
SA FISH OIL MARKETING CO (PTY) LTD (2 SH)
SA FISH OIL PRODUCERS ASSOCIATION (PTY) (4 SH)
SA FROZEN ROCK LOBSTER PACKERS (PTY) LTD (1 SH)

FORIM HOLDINGS LTD

ABBREVIATION : FORIM

JSE SHORT CODE : FOM

SECTOR : Financial-Property

SHAREHOLDERS

Who Owns Whom's Assessment of the Identity of the Ultimate Controlling Shareholder: FORMAN FAMILY

SHAREHOLDER	PERCENTAGE 1992	1991
FORMAN JOSEPH HOLDINGS P/L	18 2	20 4
BARNEY FORMAN HOLDINGS P/L	18 2	-
CHALKTON NOM CO P/L	12 8	14 3
FORMAN J	8 5	9 6
ARONSTAM B S	8 0	9 0
FORMAN J E	4 3	4 8
GELBART W F	4 3	4 8
BARNEY FORMAN WILL TRUST	4 3	---
FORMAN G	2 3	2 6
ODDES B S	1 4	1 6
FORMAN S	1 1	1 2
ISAACS B	1 0	1 1
KATZ A	- -	1 1
GAMSU E	---	1 1
FORMAN BARNEY HOLDINGS P/L	---	20 4
FORMAN BARNEY WILL TRUST	--	4 8
TOTAL	84 3	96 8

DIRECTORS :
FORMAN J (Chairman),FORMAN JE
GERLBART M (Managing Director),ISAACS BAB
LEVIN HR

REGISTRATION NUMBER : 86/04111/06

REGISTERED OFFICE
2nd Floor, Admin House, 245 Marshall Street
Johannesburg
2001
TEL 011-29 2041
FAX 011-23 1330

TRANSFER SECRETARY
Central Registrars Ltd
P O Box 4844, Johannesburg
2000
TEL 011 331 0051

COMPANY SECRETARY
Executive Secretarial Services CC

NATURE OF BUSINESS
An investment holding company deriving income from rentals received from property-owning subsidiaries

BANKERS :
Standard Bank of SA Ltd

AUDITORS :
Kessel Feinstein

FAMILIAR BRAND NAMES
N/A

CONTRIBUTION BY ACTIVITY
N/A

YEAR END : February

DIVIDEND .Ords 1c

Final	(Ldr)19/07/91	(Pay)26/07/91	Amt(c)1 5
Final	(Ldr)14/08/92	(Pay)19/08/92	Amt(c)2

NUMBER OF EMPLOYEES : 8

CAPITAL STRUCTURE

	AUTHORISED	ISSUED
Ords 1c	50000000	41904884

FINANCIAL STATISTICS (AT FINANCIAL YEAR END)

(Amts in R 000)	1991 Feb	1990 Feb	1989 Dec	1987	1986
Ord S/H Int	15317	4598	254	4472	1003

Long Trm Loans	5239	4762	-	4810	3423
Iss Ord Share	35550	17000	17000	17000	12000
Total Liab	5802	4982	183	9569	6750
Current Liab	563	220	183	4759	3327
Total Assets	21119	384	437	17864	8162
Current Assets	1470	265	437	8582	3736
Debtors	25	4	437	-	-
Inventory	-	-	-	8582	3736
Turnover	2410	-	-	-	-
Oper Profit	1505	-7	-	1306	1116
Interest Paid	88	-	-	561	432
Tax Paid	832	-	-	-	-
Prf af Int&Tax	878	-3	-	745	684
Prf att Ord Sh	878	-3	-	745	684
Btm Line Earn	902	-8568	-3713	745	684
Mkt Prce(c) YE	30	-	23	30	-
Depreciation	1	-	-	-	-

PER SHARE STATISTICS (CENTS)

Net Asst Val	43.09	-27.05	1.49	26.31	8.36
Net Earnings	2.50	-	-	-	-
Cash Flow	2.47	-0.02	-	4.38	5.70

RATIOS AND OTHER INFORMATION

Mrk Cap(R000)	10665	-	3910	5100	-
Current Ratio	2.61	1.20	2.39	1.80	1.12
Quik/Acid Tst	2.61	1.20	2.39	-	-
A/C Rec T/ovr	96.40	-	-	-	-
Tot Ass T/ovr	0.11	-	-	-	-
Debt/Ass Rat	0.27	12.97	0.42	0.54	0.83
L T L Tot Ass	0.25	12.40	-	0.27	0.42
Debt to Eqity	0.38	-1.08	0.72	2.14	6.73
Interest Cover	17.27	-	-	2.33	2.58
Oper Prof Mrg	62.45	-	-	-	-
Net Prof Marg%	36.43	-	-	-	-
Ret on Assets	8.51	-0.78	-	7.31	13.67
Ret on Equity%	5.73	0.07	-	16.66	68.20
Price/Earnings	12.00	-	-	-	-
Earning Yield%	8.33	-	-	-	-
NAV % Mrk Pr	143.62	-	6.50	87.69	-
Effec Tax Rate	49.09	-	-	-	-
Def Interval	5.99	-1587.33	-	6.46	5.00
Sus Grth Rate	5.73	0.07	-	16.66	68.20

SUBSIDIARY & ASSOCIATED COMPANIES

BERPHIL (PTY) LTD
BH PROPERTIES (PTY) LTD
FRANWYN (PTY) LTD
GJ & B INVESTMENTS (PTY) LTD
KEMTRADE DISTRIBUTORS SA (PTY) LTD
MAINDEL (PTY) LTD
MERROL (PTY) LTD
PERCY FORMAN HOLDINGS (PTY) LTD
SACADO (PTY) LTD
SHAVERLEY (PTY) LTD
TYRE IMPORT AGENCIES (PTY) LTD
VERDEL (PTY) LTD

INVESTMENTS

None

FOSCHINI LTD

ABBREVIATION : FOSCHINI

JSE SHORT CODE : FOS

SECTOR : Industrial-Retailers & Wholesalers

SHAREHOLDERS

Who Owns Whom's Assessment of the Identity of the Ultimate Controlling Shareholder:
LEWIS FOSCHINI

SHAREHOLDER	PERCENTAGE 1992	1991
LEWIS FOSCHINI INV P/L	50.0	50.0
SOUTHERN LIFE ASSOC LTD	8.2	8.2
SA MUTUAL	5.3	5.2
STD BANK NOM TVL P/L	3.9	3.2
CMB NOM P/L	2.8	---
EIGHTY ONE MAIN STREET NOM LTD	2.6	1.6
DE BEERS PENS FUND	1.9	1.9
METROPOLITAN LIFE LTD	1.7	1.4
MUTUAL & FEDERAL INSURANCE CO LTD	1.7	1.7
YSKOR PENS FUND	1.4	1.2
GEMEENSKAPLIKE MUNISIPALE TVL PENS FUND	1.3	1.3
ANGLO AMERICAN CORP PENS FUND	1.2	1.2
NEDBANK NOM LTD	1.1	1.4
SYFRETS NOM LTD	---	1.2
SANLAM	---	2.8
TOTAL	83.1	82.2

DIRECTORS :
BELCHER B ,DU PREEZ T (Systems Director)
GOODWIN NH ,GORVY HA
HIRSCHSOHN CLR (Managing Director),LEWIS M
LEWIS S (Chairman)
NORMAN RJ (Financial Director),NUREK DM
OSRIN E (Deputy Chairman)
PARK M (Dir Human Resources

REGISTRATION NUMBER : 05/09504/06

REGISTERED OFFICE
12th Floor, Shell House, 9 Riebeek Street
Cape Town
8001
TEL: 021-948 7340
FAX: 021-92 7063

TRANSFER SECRETARY
Mercantile Registrars Ltd
P O Box 1053, Johannesburg
2000
TEL: 011-333 8181

COMPANY SECRETARY
R J Norman

NATURE OF BUSINESS
The investment holding company of a group engaged in chainstore retailing of clothing and jewellery via 693 outlets.

BANKERS :
First National Bank of SA Ltd

AUDITORS :
Touche Ross & Co, Arthur Andersen & Co

FAMILIAR BRAND NAMES
AMERICAN SWISS,CIGNAL,FOSCHINI,MARKHAMS,PAGES

CONTRIBUTION BY ACTIVITY
N/A

YEAR END : March

DIVIDEND : Ords 5c

Interim No 96	(Ldr)29/09/89	(Pay)06/11/89	Amt(c)47 5
Final No 97	(Ldr)05/04/90	(Pay)04/05/90	Amt(c)194 5
Interim No 98	(Ldr)28/09/90	(Pay)05/11/90	Amt(c)86
Final No 99	(Ldr)05/04/91	(Pay)06/05/91	Amt(c)225

NUMBER OF EMPLOYEES : 5000

CAPITAL STRUCTURE

	AUTHORISED	ISSUED
6,5% Cum Prefs R2	200000	200000
Ords 5c	60000000	42938848

FINANCIAL STATISTICS (AT FINANCIAL YEAR END)

(Amts in R'000)	1992 Dec	1990 Dec	1989 Dec	1988 Dec	1987 Dec
Ord S/H Int	342577	250122	171347	145764	118180
Long Trm Loans	190773	81408	98064	56426	41125
Iss Ord Share	42939	10209	9701	9701	9701
Total Liab	423600	300885	267312	199299	152022
Current Liab	232827	219477	169248	142873	110897
Total Assets	766177	551007	438659	345063	270202
Current Assets	533834	457460	380137	311020	245602
Debtors	354929	320112	246977	205723	160615
Inventory	173621	134935	128137	102659	80338
Turnover	1153519	821990	661196	528476	406711
Oper Profit	210209	167854	127935	102903	69547
Interest Paid	44678	20113	17020	8985	4542
Tax Paid	78719	74057	55305	46574	32717
Prf af Int&Tax	90230	74827	55610	47344	32288
Prf att Ord Sh	92834	74801	55584	47318	32262
Btm Line Earn	92834	73337	55584	47568	31973
Dividend Paid	92776	71704	23476	19984	13717
Mkt Prce(c) YE	3750	7600	5700	4200	4000
Depreciation	30706	19278	18009	12502	7333

PER SHARE STATISTICS (CENTS)

Net Asst Val	797 82	2450 01	1766 28	1502 57	1218 22
Net Earnings	216 20	181 20	573 00	487 80	332 60
Dividends	-	311 00	242 00	206 00	141 40
Cash Flow	203 08	827 03	912 24	673 72	506 76

RATIOS AND OTHER INFORMATION

Mrk Cap(R000)	1610213	775884	552957	407442	388040
Current Ratio	2 29	2 08	2 25	2 18	2 21
Quik/Acid Tst	1 55	1 47	1 49	1 46	1 49
A/C Rec T/ovr	2 60	2 57	2 68	2 57	2 53
Tot Ass T/ovr	1 20	1 49	1 51	1 53	1 51
Debt/Ass Rat	0 54	0 50	0 52	0 53	0 52
L T L Tot Ass	0 23	0 10	0 14	0 12	0 11
Debt to Eqity	1 20	1 10	1 34	1 26	1 20
Interest Cover	4 78	8 40	7 52	11 45	15 31
Oper Prof Mrg	18 22	20 42	19 35	19 47	17 10
Net Prof Marg%	8 05	9 10	8 41	8 95	7 93
Ret on Assets	22 58	30 67	29 17	29 82	25 74
Ret on Equity%	21 68	29 91	32 44	32 46	27 30
Price/Earnings	17 35	41 94	9 95	8 61	12 03
Divid Cover		0 58	2 37	2 37	2 35
Divid Yield	-	4 09	4 25	4 90	3 54
Earning Yield%	5 77	2 38	10 05	11 61	8 32
NAV % Mrk Pr	21 28	32 24	30 99	35 78	30 46
Effec Tax Rate	31 49	40 97	14 24	14 38	2 36
Def Interval	1 40	0 88	0 85	0 66	0 91
Sus Grth Rate	0 02	1 24	18 74	18 75	15 69

SUBSIDIARY & ASSOCIATED COMPANIES

AMERICAN SWISS JEWELLERS (PTY) LTD
AMERICAN SWISS WATCH CO (ZIMBABWE) (PVT)
AMERICAN SWISS WATCH CO (BOTSWANA) (PTY
AMERICAN SWISS WATCH CO (LESOTHO) (PTY
AMERICAN SWISS WATCH CO (SWAZILAND) (PT
AMERICAN SWISS WATCH CO LTD
BRANSBY TRADING (PTY) LTD
BURNITA (PTY) LTD
CENTRAL COLLECTION BUREAU (PTY) LTD
FASHION RETAILERS (PTY) LTD
FOSCHINI (BOPHUTATSWANA) (PTY) LTD
FOSCHINI (BOTSWANA) (PTY) LTD
FOSCHINI (LESOTHO) (PTY) LTD
FOSCHINI (SWAZILAND) (PTY) LTD
FOSCHINI (ZIMBABWE) (PVT) LTD
FOSCHINI FINANCE (PTY) LTD
FOSCHINI GROUP (PTY) LTD
FOSCHINI PROPERTY ADDERLEY STREET LTD
FOSCHINI PROPERTY DUMINY STREET ONE LTD
FOSCHINI PROPERTY DUMINY STREET TWO (PTY
FOSCHINI PROPERTY ELOFF ONE LTD
FOSCHINI PROPERTY ELOFF THREE (PTY) LTD
FOSCHINI PROPERTY ELOFF TWO (PTY) LTD
FOSCHINI PROPERTY GOODWOOD (PTY) LTD
FOSCHINI PROPERTY HOLDINGS LTD
FOSCHINI PROPERTY HUGUENOT STREET (PTY)
FOSCHINI PROPERTY ISANDO (PTY) LTD
FOSCHINI SERVICES (PTY) LTD
FOSCHINI STORES (PTY) LTD
FOSCHINIDATA (PTY) LTD
IDUTYWA OUTFITTERS (PTY) LTD
MARKHAMS (PTY) LTD
MARKHAMS OUTFITTERS (BOTSWANA) (PTY) LT
MARKHAMS OUTFITTERS (CAPE) LTD
MARKHAMS OUTFITTERS (LESOTHO) (PTY) LTD
MARKHAMS OUTFITTERS (SWAZILAND) (PTY) LT
MARKHAMS OUTFITTERS (ZIMBABWE) (PVT) LTD
OCEANA INVESTMENT CORPORATION PLC (35,3%)
PAGES STORES (BOPHUTHATSWANA) (PTY) LTD
PAGES STORES (BOTSWANA) (PTY) LTD
PAGES STORES (GAZANKULU) (PTY) LTD
PAGES STORES (LESOTHO) (PTY) LTD
PAGES STORES (PTY) LTD
PAGES STORES (SWAZILAND) (PTY) LTD
PAGES STORES (TRANSKEI) (PTY) LTD
PAGES STORES (ZIMBABWE) (PVT) LTD
TROJAN ENTERPRISES (PTY) LTD
TRUSTFAM (PTY) LTD

INVESTMENTS

None

FOSTON LTD

ABBREVIATION : FOSTON

JSE SHORT CODE : FTN

SECTOR : Mining Exploration

SHAREHOLDERS

Who Owns Whom's Assessment of the Identity of the Ultimate Controlling Shareholder:
REVERE RESOURCES

SHAREHOLDER	PERCENTAGE 1992	1991
EDWIN W BALDERSON NOM P/L	75.5	---
ADRIANOPLE COLLIERY P/L	7.1	12.9
CORNWALL C	5.5	---
DU PREEZ F J	2.1	2.1
KEBBLE R B	1.4	---
VOLKSKAS NOM P/L	1.4	1.4
MULLER D S	---	35.6
PISTORIUS C W H	---	36.1
WESTACRES BEL POTCHEFSTROOM E/B	---	5.2
TOTAL	92.9	93.3

DIRECTORS :
CRAMER JA ,DE KLERK HJP
GLEASON ED (Managing Director)
LAING GJS (Chairman),MULLER DS

REGISTRATION NUMBER : 05/08939/06

REGISTERED OFFICE
15 Van der Bent Str, Potchefstroom
2520
TEL: 011-803 5752
FAX: 011-803 3959

TRANSFER SECRETARY
Central Registrars Ltd
P O Box 4844, Johannesburg
2000
TEL: 011-331 0051

COMPANY SECRETARY
J M Forsyth

NATURE OF BUSINESS
A coal exploration & mining group, activities include the acquisition, exploration, development and exploitation of coal concessions in the E Tvl and Northern Natal.

BANKERS :
Nedperm Bank Ltd, Cape Investment Bank Ltd

AUDITORS :
Coopers Theron Du Toit, JH Preller

FAMILIAR BRAND NAMES
N/A

CONTRIBUTION BY ACTIVITY
N/A

YEAR END : June

DIVIDEND :15/09/91

CAPITAL STRUCTURE

	AUTHORISED	ISSUED
Ords 50c	50000000	36480441
"A" Ords 20c	500000000	0

FINANCIAL STATISTICS (AT FINANCIAL YEAR END)

(Amts in R'000)	1990 Feb	1989 Jun	1988 Jun	1987 Jun	1986
Ord S/H Int	31081	8019	19407	7295	7243
Long Trm Loans	27	1499	588	2698	5143
Iss Ord Share	31780	9582	9582	4221	4221
Total Liab	122	32903	31665	3540	6022
Current Liab	95	31404	31077	842	879
Total Assets	5367	40922	51072	10835	17282
Intang Assets	25836	*	*	*	*
Current Assets	4360	33591	46920	9397	4896
Debtors	79	14880	26157	2623	-
Inventory	189	18704	4602	766	4896
Turnover	-	75741	90075	6411	8018
Oper Profit	-	-7021	4188	238	1040
Interest Paid	-	3060	1342	507	800
Tax Paid	-	-339	312	28	20
Prf af Int&Tax	-	-9742	2534	-297	220
Prf att Ord Sh	-	-9742	2534	-304	224
Btm Line Earn	-	-11145	3162	51	224
Dividend Paid	-	-	958	-	169
Mkt Prce(c) YE	-	80	140	200	85
Depreciation	-	445	373	83	-

PER SHARE STATISTICS (CENTS)

Net Asst Val	16.50	83.69	202.54	172.83	171.59
Net Earnings	-	-101.70	26.40	-7.20	-
Dividends	-	-	10.00	-	-
Cash Flow	-	-100.56	33.59	-5.40	5.21

RATIOS AND OTHER INFORMATION

Mrk Cap(R000)	-	7666	13415	8442	3588
Current Ratio	45.89	1.07	1.51	11.16	5.57
Quik/Acid Tst	43.91	0.47	1.36	10.25	-
A/C Rec T/ovr	-	5.09	3.44	2.44	-
Tot Ass T/ovr	-	1.85	1.76	0.59	0.46
Debt/Ass Rat	0.02	0.80	0.61	0.31	0.35
L T L Tot Ass	0.01	0.03	0.00	0.23	0.30
Debt to Eqity	0.00	4.09	1.61	0.46	0.83
Interest Cover	-	-2.29	3.12	0.47	1.30
Oper Prof Mrg	-	-9.27	4.65	3.71	12.97
Net Prof Marg%	-	-12.86	2.81	-4.74	2.79
Ret on Assets	-	-17.16	8.20	2.26	6.02
Ret on Equity%	-	-121.49	13.06	-4.17	3.09
Price/Earnings	-	-0.79	5.30	-27.78	-
Divid Cover	-	-	2.64	-	-
Divid Yield	-	-	7.14	-	-
Earning Yield%	-	-127.13	18.86	-3.60	-
NAV % Mrk Pr	-	104.61	144.67	86.41	201.88
Effec Tax Rate	-	-	-	-10.41	8.33
Def Interval	-	-1.10	3.60	-11.17	23.38
Sus Grth Rate	-	-121.49	8.12	-4.17	0.76

SUBSIDIARY & ASSOCIATED COMPANIES

DERDEHOEK ANTHRACITE MINE (PTY) LTD
MULTONLAND DEVELOPMENTS (PTY) LTD
RAPPFOS HOLDINGS (PTY) LTD
SINK-TON (PTY) LTD
VLAKVARKFONTEIN COLLIERY (PTY) LTD

INVESTMENTS

ALTERNATIVE STRATEGIES LTD (13%)
FEDSURE HOLDINGS LTD (10800 SH)

FP HOLDINGS LTD

ABBREVIATION : FP HOLD

SECTOR : Zimbabwe Stock Exchange

SHAREHOLDERS

Who Owns Whom's Assessment of the Identity of the Ultimate Controlling Shareholder:
SOUTHWIND INVESTMENTS (PVT) LTD

SHAREHOLDER	PERCENTAGE 1992	1991
SOUTHWIND INV PVT LTD	26.3	---
STD CHART MERCHANT BANK ZIM NOM PVT LTD	9.3	---
CHANCELESS INV PVT LTD	8.1	---
E T & M INV & FARMING PVT LTD	7.5	---
TINEYI INV PVT LTD	7.5	---
BREAKTHROUGH INV PVT LTD	6.8	---
CLAYTONS AGENCIES PVT LTD	6.0	---
LIFETIME INV PVT LTD	6.0	---
FARSIGHTED INV PVT LTD	5.3	---
SOUTHAMPTON ASSURE CO ZIM LTD	3.5	---
TOTAL	86.2	---

DIRECTORS :
FORD AW ,MUCHATUTA VT
MUHWATI FC (Chairman & Chief Exec.),RALSTON NC
RUSIKE ET ,WILKINS B

REGISTERED OFFICE
68 Birmingham Road, Southerton
Harare, Zimbabwe

TEL: 62731
FAX: 69145

TRANSFER SECRETARY
Zimbabwe Banking Corporation Ltd
P O Box 3198, Harare
Zimbabwe

TEL: 092634-735011

COMPANY SECRETARY
Flexible Packaging (Private) Ltd

NATURE OF BUSINESS
The Group's main operating subsidiary is Flexible Packaging (Pvt) Ltd whose divisions produce a wide range of products including packaging for the food processing, pharmaceutical and agricultural processing industries and the consumer market, paper sacks, stationery, industrial chemical products, detergents and cleansing materials, and a wide range of injection moulded plastic products.

BANKERS :
Merchant Bank of Central Africa
Standard Chartered Bank Zimbabwe Ltd
Standard Chartered Merchant Bank Zim Ltd

AUDITORS :
Price Waterhouse Meyernel

FAMILIAR BRAND NAMES
N/A

CONTRIBUTION BY ACTIVITY
N/A

YEAR END : August

CAPITAL STRUCTURE

	AUTHORISED	ISSUED
Ords Z$1	100000000	80000000

FINANCIAL STATISTICS (AT FINANCIAL YEAR END)

(Amts in Z$)	1991 Aug
Ord S/H Int	70422
Long Trm Loans	41741
Iss Ord Share	15000
Total Liab	72470
Current Liab	30729
Total Assets	141036
Intang Assets	1856
Current Assets	44250
Debtors	15778
Inventory	22998
Turnover	82309
Oper Profit	16959
Tax Paid	4620
Prf af Int&Tax	12339
Prf att Ord Sh	12339
Btm Line Earn	12339
Dividend Paid	5000

PER SHARE STATISTICS (CENTS)

Net Asst Val	457.11
Net Earnings	20.60
Dividends	8.30
Cash Flow	82.26

RATIOS AND OTHER INFORMATION

Current Ratio	1.44
Quik/Acid Tst	0.69
A/C Rec T/ovr	5.22
Tot Ass T/ovr	0.58
Debt/Ass Rat	0.49
L T L Tot Ass	0.28
Debt to Eqity	0.99
Oper Prof Mrg	20.60
Net Prof Marg%	14.99
Ret on Assets	12.02
Ret on Equity%	17.52
Divid Cover	2.48
Effec Tax Rate	27.24
Def Interval	4.53
Sus Grth Rate	10.42

SUBSIDIARY & ASSOCIATED COMPANIES

BULK PACKAGING (PVT) LTD
CENTRAL AFRICA PACKAGING CORPORATION (PV
CENTRAL MARKETING (PVT) LTD
FLEXIBLE MARKETING (PVT) LTD
FP CHEMICALS (PVT) LTD
FP PLASTICS (PVT) LTD
HOLDAIN BOXES (PVT) LTD
INDUSTRIAL CHEMICALS MANUFACTURING (PVT)
INTER-CITY TRANSPORT (PVT) LTD
N PRODUCTS (PVT) LTD
P&S PROCUREMENT AND SERVICES (PVT) LTD

REFLECTOR PRODUCTS (PVT) LTD
STATIONERY & SCHOLASTIC PRODUCTS (PVT) L
TALON INDUSTRIES (PVT) LTD
TISSUE & WADDING (PVT) LTD

INVESTMENTS

None

FRALEX LTD

ABBREVIATION : FRALEX

JSE SHORT CODE : FRX

SECTOR : Industrial-Engineering

SHAREHOLDERS

Who Owns Whom's Assessment of the Identity of the Ultimate Controlling Shareholder:
DIRECTORS / INSTITUTIONS

SHAREHOLDER	PERCENTAGE 1992	1991
TEGNIESE MYNBELEGGINGS BPK	39.2	---
DALY F W A	11.7	11.7
DALY M A & KOSEFF R	8.0	8.0
DALY D H	7.2	7.2
DALY M A	5.0	5.0
FRALEX SHARE TRUST	4.7	4.6
DALY S B	2.0	2.0
CAYANIS J	1.7	1.7
FRASER ALEXANDER PROV FUND	1.7	---
FLACK P H	1.6	1.6
STOKES F J	1.6	1.6
JONES R J	1.4	1.7
RAE G F	1.2	1.2
MCINTOSH D W	1.2	1.2
VISAGIE A J	---	1.1
IND PARTNERSHIP INV LTD	---	39.2
TOTAL	88.0	87.7

DIRECTORS :
CAYANIS J ,DALY PF ,DALY SB ,DIPPENAAR LL
FLACK PH (Deputy Chairman)
MAXWELL LA (Financial Director),RAE GF
RUPERT JP (Chairman),STOKES FJ ,VAN WYK T

REGISTRATION NUMBER : 05/06098/06

REGISTERED OFFICE
Marlin Road (off Kelly Rd), Jet Park
Boksburg
1460
TEL: 011-826 3481
FAX: 011-826 6918

TRANSFER SECRETARY
Mercantile Registrars Ltd
P O Box 1053, Johannesburg
2000
TEL: 011-333 8181

COMPANY SECRETARY
R W Smith

NATURE OF BUSINESS
An investment holding company with a controlling interest in quoted Fraser Alexander Ltd.

BANKERS :
N/A

AUDITORS :
Ernst & Young

FAMILIAR BRAND NAMES
N/A

CONTRIBUTION BY ACTIVITY
N/A

YEAR END : June

DIVIDEND : Ords 1c

Final	(Ldr)28/09/90	(Pay)15/10/90	Amt(c)18
Interim	(Ldr)01/03/91	(Pay)20/03/91	Amt(c)6.5
Final	(Ldr)27/09/91	(Pay)14/10/91	Amt(c)12
Interim	(Ldr)06/03/92	(Pay)18/03/92	Amt(c)7
Final	(Ldr)25/09/92	(Pay)12/10/92	Amt(c)15.5

NUMBER OF EMPLOYEES : 4169

CAPITAL STRUCTURE

	AUTHORISED	ISSUED
Ords 1c	20000000	16109972
10% Cum Redeemable Pref R1	800000	0

FINANCIAL STATISTICS (AT FINANCIAL YEAR END)

(Amts in R'000)	1992 Jun	1991 Jun	1990 Jun	1989 Jun
Ord S/H Int	70490	51646	48196	36470
Long Trm Loans	89743	51762	32496	26070
Iss Ord Share	16110	16110	16110	16110
Total Liab	181316	119728	90690	83000
Current Liab	91573	67966	58194	56930
Total Assets	236806	171374	136886	119470
Intang Assets	15000	*	*	*
Current Assets	110935	78574	62245	56141
Debtors	68910	52044	46979	40919
Inventory	28044	18836	13374	8829
Turnover	350315	233950	215140	176498
Oper Profit	37636	31547	34895	27552
Interest Paid	12910	9169	3030	2754
Tax Paid	8152	8868	13179	9151
Prf af Int&Tax	18242	15010	20305	16357
Prf att Ord Sh	10575	10807	14788	12115
Btm Line Earn	19667	8430	13470	11352
Dividend Paid	3625	2980	4189	3383
Mkt Prce(c) YE	575	700	850	290
Depreciation	21801	14991	14062	11211

PER SHARE STATISTICS (CENTS)

Net Asst Val	344.44	320.58	286.75	226.38
Net Earnings	65.60	67.10	91.80	75.20
Dividends	22.50	18.50	26.00	21.00
Cash Flow	161.54	168.09	194.03	158.67

RATIOS AND OTHER INFORMATION

Mrk Cap(R000)	92633	112770	136935	46719
Current Ratio	1.21	1.16	1.07	0.99
Quik/Acid Tst	0.91	0.88	0.84	0.83
A/C Rec T/ovr	5.08	4.50	4.58	4.31

Tot Ass T/ovr	1.48	1.37	1.57	1.48
Debt/Ass Rat	0.50	0.54	0.48	0.54
L T L Tot Ass	0.12	0.14	0.06	0.07
Debt to Eqity	1.69	1.79	1.42	1.78
Interest Cover	2.92	3.44	11.52	10.01
Oper Prof Mrg	10.74	13.48	16.22	15.61
Net Prof Marg%	3.02	4.62	6.87	6.86
Ret on Assets	16.60	19.28	26.67	23.66
Ret on Equity%	15.00	20.93	32.01	33.22
Price/Earnings	8.77	10.43	9.26	3.86
Divid Cover	2.92	3.63	3.53	3.58
Divid Yield	3.91	2.64	3.06	7.24
Earning Yield%	11.41	9.59	10.80	25.93
NAV % Mrk Pr	59.90	45.80	33.74	78.06
Effec Tax Rate	45.49	29.42	32.27	26.75
Def Interval	2.54	2.14	0.77	1.20
Sus Grth Rate	9.86	15.16	22.94	23.94

SUBSIDIARY & ASSOCIATED COMPANIES

FRASER ALEXANDER LTD

INVESTMENTS

None

FRAME GROUP HOLDINGS LTD

ABBREVIATION : FRAME

JSE SHORT CODE : FRM

SECTOR : Industrial-Clothing, Footwear & Textiles

SHAREHOLDERS

Who Owns Whom's Assessment of the Identity of the Ultimate Controlling Shareholder:
SEARDEL INV CORP / SABLE FAMILY

SHAREHOLDER	PERCENTAGE 1992	1991
SEARGREG INV P/L	32.2	---
CONSOLIDATED FRAME TEXTILES LTD	14.0	21.5
STD BANK NOM TVL P/L	13.0	14.3
EIGHTY ONE MAIN STREET NOM LTD	11.4	12.9
LIBERTY LIFE ASSOC OF AFRICA LTD	6.8	13.9
SOUTHERN LIFE ASSOC LTD	2.7	3.9
CONFRAME SHARE INC SCHEME ACCOUNT NOM	2.7	2.7
NAT PARKS BRD CURATORS STAFF PENS FUND	2.0	---
CMB NOM P/L	1.5	---
DE BEERS PENS FUND	1.3	1.8
ANGLO AMERICAN CORP PENS FUND	---	1.2
FIRST NAT NOM P/L	---	2.3
BOARD OF EXECUTORS NOM P/L	---	1.1
BP THIBAULT NOM P/L	---	2.1
GREENMARKET SQUARE NOM P/L	---	2.1
MOMENTUM LIFE ASSURE LTD	---	1.8
PREMIER GROUP PENS FUND	---	1.2
SANLAM	---	2.5
VOLKSKAS NOM P/L	---	1.0
TOTAL	87.5	86.2

DIRECTORS :
BORKUM MM ,DE VILLIERS HP
KING ME (Executive Chairman),SABLE R
SANDERS BF ,SEARLL A DR,SIMEONI W ,STEIN GH
WHITEFORD RJ

REGISTRATION NUMBER : 05/18543/06

REGISTERED OFFICE
Blase Road, New Germany
3610
TEL: 031-705 1370
FAX: 031-705 1370

TRANSFER SECRETARY
Mercantile Registrars Ltd
P O Box 1053, Johannesburg
2000
TEL: 011-333 8181

COMPANY SECRETARY
JH Acutt

NATURE OF BUSINESS
An investment holding company

BANKERS :
First National Bank of SA Ltd
Standard Bank of SA Ltd, Absa Bank Ltd
Nedcor Bank Ltd, Rand Merchant Bank Ltd

AUDITORS :
KPMG Aiken & Peat, Arthur Andersen & Co

FAMILIAR BRAND NAMES
N/A

CONTRIBUTION BY ACTIVITY
Frame Textile Corp (% Turnover) (97.0%)
Diversified Businesses (3.0%)

YEAR END : June

DIVIDEND : (Ldr)03/03/89 (Pay)17/03/89
DIVIDEND : (Ldr)08/09/89 (Pay)22/09/89
DIVIDEND : (Ldr)09/03/90 (Pay)30/03/90

NUMBER OF EMPLOYEES : 18596

CAPITAL STRUCTURE

	AUTHORISED	ISSUED
Ords 5c	27500000	24149550
5,5% cum pref of R2	250000	250000

FINANCIAL STATISTICS (AT FINANCIAL YEAR END)

(Amts in R'000)	1992 Jun	1991 Jun	1990 Jun	1989 Jun	1988 Jun
Ord S/H Int	379567	437336	622300	619303	601696
Long Trm Loans	229243	328194	495821	487810	474534
Iss Ord Share	24150	24150	24150	24150	24150
Total Liab	504470	769108	830287	709253	565994
Current Liab	275227	440914	334466	221443	91460
Total Assets	884037	1205294	1451246	1328556	1167690
Intang Assets	*	1150	1341	*	*
Current Assets	439263	624496	766948	665992	542901
Debtors	209670	305682	342915	314142	222767
Inventory	226058	308092	400869	314799	275667
Turnover	652170	789093	984258	869652	700873
Oper Profit	-38142	-123332	69459	81803	41594
Interest Paid	46674	44704	30555	13122	-
Tax Paid	389	990	6640	25112	18309
Prf af Int&Tax	-73893	-163692	39029	49840	27604

Prf att Ord Sh	-45640	-101108	24337	30602	17003
Btm Line Earn	-80289	-226231	15799	30602	17681
Dividend Paid	-	-	11378	11378	11378
Mkt Prce(c) YE	300	420	825	1250	1000
Depreciation	42341	54999	49065	47418	41498

PER SHARE STATISTICS (CENTS)

Net Asst Val	1571 71	1806 15	2571 26	2564 40	2491 49
Net Earnings	-238 80	-533 20	128 30	161 40	89 70
Dividends	-	-	60 00	60 00	60 00
Cash Flow	-13 66	-192 12	305 69	323 18	237 15

RATIOS AND OTHER INFORMATION

Mrk Cap(R000)	72450	101430	199238	301875	241500
Current Ratio	1 60	1 42	2 29	3 01	5 94
Quik/Acid Tst	0 77	0 72	1 09	1 59	2 92
A/C Rec T/ovr	3 11	2 58	2 87	2 77	3 15
Tot Ass T/ovr	0 74	0 65	0 68	0 65	0 60
Debt/Ass Rat	0 34	0 38	0 24	0 17	0 08
L T L Tot Ass	0 03	0 01	0 01	0 00	-
Debt to Eqity	0 79	1 04	0 55	0 37	0 15
Interest Cover	-0 78	-2 73	2 29	6 29	-
Oper Prof Mrg	-5 85	-15 63	7 06	9 41	5 93
Net Prof Marg%	-7 00	-12 81	2 47	3 52	2 43
Ret on Assets	-3 03	-9 79	5 25	6 63	3 93
Ret on Equity%	-12 02	-23 12	3 91	4 94	2 83
Price/Earnings	-1 26	-0 79	6 43	7 74	11 15
Divid Cover	-	-	2 14	2 69	1 50
Divid Yield	-	-	7 27	4 80	6 00
Earning Yield%	-79 60	-126 95	15 55	12 91	8 97
NAV % Mrk Pr	523 90	430 04	311 67	205 15	249 15
Effec Tax Rate	-0 45	-0 78	13 73	33 80	42 73
Def Interval	-54 90	-4 93	2 20	0 95	0 09
Sus Grth Rate	-12 02	-23 12	2 08	3 10	0 93

SUBSIDIARY & ASSOCIATED COMPANIES

CONSOLIDATED FRAME TEXTILES LTD

INVESTMENTS

None

FRASER ALEXANDER LTD

ABBREVIATION : ALEXNDR

JSE SHORT CODE : ALR

SECTOR : Industrial-Engineering

SHAREHOLDERS

Who Owns Whom's Assessment of the Identity of the Ultimate Controlling Shareholder:
REMBRANDT VIA FRALEX LTD

SHAREHOLDER	PERCENTAGE 1992	1991
FRALEX LTD	57 8	73 0
EIGHTY ONE MAIN STREET NOM LTD	13 6	1 1
STD BANK NOM TVL P/L	6 5	---
FRASER ALEXANDER SHARE TRUST	3 9	4 5
CMB NOM P/L	2 3	---
YSKOR PENS FUND	1 9	---
METROPOLITAN LIFE LTD	1 6	---
LIBERTY LIFE ASSOC OF AFRICA LTD	1 6	1 1
MERCANTILE & GEN REINSURANCE CO SA LTD	---	1 6
SA MUTUAL	---	4 2
MOMENTUM LIFE ASSURE LTD	---	5 8
TOTAL	89 0	91 2

DIRECTORS :
BROMFIELD KO ,CAYANIS J ,DALY SB
FLACK PH (Chairman),GOWAN MJ ,JONES RJ
MAXWELL LA (Financial Director),MCINTOSH DW
RAE GF (Deputy Chairman),SMITH RW ,SMITH RW
STOKES FJ ,VISAGIE AJ

REGISTRATION NUMBER : 64/00846/06

REGISTERED OFFICE
Marlin Road (off Kelly Rd), Jet Park
Boksburg
1460
TEL 011-826 3481
FAX 011-826 6918

TRANSFER SECRETARY
Mercantile Registrars Ltd
P O Box 1053, Johannesburg
2000
TEL 011-333 8181

COMPANY SECRETARY
R W Smith

NATURE OF BUSINESS
Group operations include coal mining and mining services, incl tailing services, installation of underground track, water and air systems, paving for trackless mining and wire mesh lacing, Ash-handling and stockpiling, Operation and management of landfill sites, Construction, Production of concrete bricks and blocks, Collection, handling treatment and disposal of domestic, medical and industrial waste

BANKERS :
Standard Bank of SA Ltd

AUDITORS :
Ernst & Young

FAMILIAR BRAND NAMES
WASTE-TECH

CONTRIBUTION BY ACTIVITY
N/A

YEAR END : June

DIVIDEND : Ords 50c

Final	(Ldr)28/09/90	(Pay)15/10/90	Amt(c)32
Interim	(Ldr)01/03/91	(Pay)20/03/91	Amt(c)11
Final	(Ldr)27/09/91	(Pay)14/10/91	Amt(c)28
Interim	(Ldr)06/03/92	(Pay)18/03/92	Amt(c)12
Final	(Ldr)25/09/92	(Pay)12/10/92	Amt(c)27

NUMBER OF EMPLOYEES : 4050

CAPITAL STRUCTURE

	AUTHORISED	ISSUED
Ords 50c	20000000	15730400
10c Red Cum Prefs 'A'	400000	0
10c Red Cum Prefs 'B'	1570000	0

10c Red Cum Prefs 'D'	800000	0

FINANCIAL STATISTICS (AT FINANCIAL YEAR END)

(Amts in R'000)	1992 Jun	1991 Jun	1990 Jun	1989 Jun	1988 Jun
Ord S/H Int	121524	70458	63017	48727	37924
Long Trm Loans	36653	31751	14359	12615	6997
Iss Ord Share	15730	12457	12457	12258	12258
Total Liab	129895	101202	73617	70350	52049
Current Liab	93242	69451	59258	57735	45052
Total Assets	236419	171660	136634	119077	89973
Intang Assets	15000	*	*	*	*
Current Assets	113571	80855	64234	56362	36599
Debtors	71546	54325	48968	41140	29813
Inventory	28044	18836	13374	8829	4242
Turnover	350315	233950	215140	176498	125958
Oper Profit	37518	32066	34863	27490	12652
Interest Paid	12908	9165	3026	2752	
Tax Paid	8152	8868	13179	9103	4492
Prf af Int&Tax	18155	15557	20401	16405	8160
Prf att Ord Sh	18155	15557	20401	16405	8160
Btm Line Earn	16345	12299	18870	15376	6945
Dividend Paid	6135	4858	5702	4658	3310
Mkt Prce(c) YE	1250	1000	1225	480	415
Depreciation	21801	14985	14062	11211	8330

PER SHARE STATISTICS (CENTS)

Net Asst Val	677 20	565 61	505 88	397 51	309 38
Net Earnings	115 40	124 90	165 50	133 80	66 60
Dividends	39 00	39 00	46 00	38 00	27 00
Cash Flow	213 63	255 47	295 99	243 53	137 80

RATIOS AND OTHER INFORMATION

Mrk Cap(R000)	196625	124570	152598	58838	50871
Current Ratio	1 22	1 16	1 08	0 98	0 81
Quik/Acid Tst	0 92	0 89	0 86	0 82	0 72
A/C Rec T/ovr	4 90	4 31	4 39	4 29	4 22
Tot Ass T/ovr	1 48	1 36	1 57	1 48	1 40
Debt/Ass Rat	0 51	0 55	0 49	0 55	0 56
L T L Tot Ass	0 12	0 14	0 06	0 07	0 06
Debt to Eqity	0 99	1 33	1 06	1 35	1 33
Interest Cover	2 91	3 50	11 52	9 99	
Oper Prof Mrg	10 71	13 71	16 20	15 58	10 04
Net Prof Marg%	5 18	6 65	9 48	9 29	6 48
Ret on Assets	16 59	19 57	26 79	23 73	14 06
Ret on Equity%	14 94	22 08	32 37	33 67	21 52
Price/Earnings	10 83	8 01	7 40	3 59	6 23
Divid Cover	2 96	3 20	3 60	3 52	2 47
Divid Yield	3 12	3 90	3 76	7 92	6 51
Earning Yield%	9 23	12 49	13 51	27 88	16 05
NAV % Mrk Pr	54 18	56 56	41 30	82 81	74 55
Effec Tax Rate	45 64	28 76	32 17	26 56	32 18
Def Interval	1 97	1 82	0 65	1 03	1 66
Sus Grth Rate	9 89	15 18	23 33	24 11	12 79

SUBSIDIARY & ASSOCIATED COMPANIES

BLOUKRANTZ ROAD PROPERTIES (PTY) LTD
DECCA COMMODITY TRADING (PTY) LTD
EROSION PROTECTION (PTY) LTD
FFA PROPERTIES (KLERKSDORP) (PTY) LTD
FRASER ALEXANDER BOPHUTHATSWANA (PTY) LT
FRASER ALEXANDER BULK MATERIALS HANDLING
FRASER ALEXANDER COAL (PTY) LTD
FRASER ALEXANDER CONSTRUCTION (PTY) LTD
FRASER ALEXANDER GROUP SERVICES (PTY) LT
FRASER ALEXANDER MINING SERVICES (PTY) L
FRASER ALEXANDER PLANT & EQUIPMENT SALES
FRASER ALEXANDER PLANT MANAGEMENT SERVIC
FRASER ALEXANDR WASTE (PTY) LTD
FRASER F ALEXANDER AND CO (PTY) LTD
FRASER FYFE (PTY) LTD
FRASER FYFE HOLDINGS (PTY) LTD
HYPERCOAL (PTY) LTD
M&L BRICKWORKS (PTY) LTD
MEDICAL WASTE SYSTEMS (PTY) LTD
MINE WASTE RECLAMATION (PTY) LTD
MURRAY TRANSPORT SERVICES (PTY) LTD
ORGANIC RECYCLING (PTY) LTD
PURLE INDUSTRIAL WASTE PROPERTIES (PTY)
RAILWAY AND CIVIL ENGINEERING CONSTRUCTI
STOFBERG MINING (PTY) LTD
TRANS ASH WASTE DISPOSAL SERVICES (PTY)
WASTE MANAGEMENT PROSPECTON PROPERTY (PT
WASTE-TECH (PTY) LTD
WASTE-TECH BOPHUTHATSWANA (PTY) LTD
WASTE-TECH TRANSVAAL (PTY) LTD

INVESTMENTS

ASFA SERVICES (PTY) LTD
ASFA SERVICES (PTY) LTD (6%)
BUFFELSBED SHARE BLOCK LTD (14%)
EAST RAND GOLD & URANIUM CO (200 SH)
INGWELALA SHARE BLOCK LTD (SHARE & LOAN) (80%)

FREE STATE CONSOLIDATED GOLD MINES LTD

ABBREVIATION : FREGOLD

JSE SHORT CODE : FRG

SECTOR : Gold-OFS

SHAREHOLDERS

Who Owns Whom's Assessment of the Identity of the Ultimate Controlling Shareholder:
ANGLO AMERICAN

SHAREHOLDER	PERCENTAGE 1992	1991
ORANGE FREE STATE INV LTD	49 9	50 6
STD BANK NOM TVL P/L	10 3	9 7
INDO CHINA NOM P/L	8 2	9 7
LONDON CONTROL ACCOUNT	5 3	5 9
WELKOM GOLD HOLDINGS LTD	5 2	5 3
FIRST NAT NOM P/L	2 8	2 0
ORANGE FREE STATE INV TRUST LTD	2 0	2 0
FERMAIN NOM LTD	1 9	1 9
FIRST NAT NOM P/L GATR DEPOT	1 8	1 9
AFRICAN & EUROPEAN INV CO LTD	1 7	1 7
ANGLO AMERICAN CORP OF SA LTD	1 4	
EIGHTY ONE MAIN STREET NOM LTD	1 2	
NEDBANK NOM LTD		1 2
INDO CHINA NOM SA P/L		9 7
TOTAL	91 6	****

DIRECTORS :

BERNING FS ,BOUSTRED WG ,CROWE DJ ,DICKS KV GODSELL RM ,HEWITT L (Managing Director) HOSKING KM ,LANGTON G ,OGILVIE THOMPSON J ROSSOUW JR ,SUNTER CL (Chairman),WILLIAMS KH

REGISTRATION NUMBER : 05/28210/06

REGISTERED OFFICE
44 Main Street, Johannesburg
2001
TEL 011-638 9111
FAX 011-638 5281

TRANSFER SECRETARY
Consolidated Share Registrars Ltd
P O Box 61051, Marshalltown
2107
TEL 011-492 1620

COMPANY SECRETARY
Anglo American Corp of SA Ltd

NATURE OF BUSINESS
The group conducts gold mining operations in the Odendaalsrus, Ventersburg and Welkom districts of the OFS The company also holds minor investments in JSE-quoted mining and mining finance companies

BANKERS :
First National Bank of SA Ltd

AUDITORS :
Deloitte Pim Goldby

FAMILIAR BRAND NAMES
N/A

CONTRIBUTION BY ACTIVITY
Gold,Silver & Osmiridium(% pre-tax prof) (86 0%)
Metallurgical Scheme (2 0%)
Other (12 0%)

YEAR END : March

DIVIDEND : Ords 50c

Interim No 71	(Ldr)18/10/90	(Pay)14/12/90	Amt(c)55
Final No 72	(Ldr)18/04/91	(Pay)14/06/91	Amt(c)85
Interim No 74	(Ldr)08/05/92	(Pay)12/05/92	Amt(c)130
Final No 75	(Ldr)13/11/92	(Pay)18/12/92	Amt(c)105

NUMBER OF EMPLOYEES : 103160

CAPITAL STRUCTURE

	AUTHORISED	ISSUED
Ords 50c	120000000	117753143

FINANCIAL STATISTICS (AT FINANCIAL YEAR END)

(Amts in R'000)	1992 Mar	1991 Mar	1990 Mar	1989 Mar	1987 Sep
Ord S/H Int	5379000	5126400	4854500	4467500	3690800
Long Trm Loans	218100	218100	208600	197000	150700
Iss Ord Share	117753	116179	116179	116179	116179
Total Liab	884400	726600	746900	734100	705300
Current Liab	666300	508500	538300	537100	554600
Total Assets	6263400	5853000	5601400	5201600	4396100
Current Assets	751500	567200	589400	616000	613800
Debtors	224800	200600	233300	228800	236800
Turnover	3848000	3763300	3737200	5190200	3044200
Oper Profit	558500	410600	664400	1427500	1090900
Interest Paid	26200	26000	29300	31500	16400
Tax Paid	114100	40800	64700	165200	230000
Prf af Int&Tax	531700	432900	697400	1269000	872300
Prf att Ord Sh	279500	167400	347000	520500	354900
Btm Line Earn	279500	167400	347000	520500	354900
Dividend Paid	276700	164800	346100	513200	360200
Mkt Prce(c) YE	2875	1825	4825	3500	5575

PER SHARE STATISTICS (CENTS)

Net Asst Val	4568 04	4412 50	4178 47	3845 36	3176 82
Net Earnings	237 00	142 00	295 00	445 00	305 00
Dividends	235 00	140 00	295 00	440 00	310 00
Cash Flow	448 82	372 61	600 28	728 19	750 82

RATIOS AND OTHER INFORMATION

Mrk Cap(R000)	3385399	2120267	5605637	4066265	6476979
Current Ratio	1 13	1 12	1 09	1 15	1 11
Quik/Acid Tst	1 13	1 12	1 09	1 15	1 11
A/C Rec T/ovr	17 12	18 76	16 02	15 12	12 86
Tot Ass T/ovr	0 61	0 64	0 67	0 67	0 69
Debt/Ass Rat	0 14	0 12	0 13	0 14	0 16
L T L Tot Ass	0 03	0 04	0 04	0 04	0 03
Debt to Eqity	0 16	0 14	0 15	0 16	0 19
Interest Cover	21 97	16 36	23 51	46 53	68 21
Oper Prof Mrg	14 51	10 91	17 78	27 50	35 84
Net Prof Marg%	7 26	4 45	9 29	10 03	11 66
Ret on Assets	10 73	8 54	14 13	18 79	25 45
Ret on Equity%	5 20	3 27	7 15	7 77	9 62
Price/Earnings	12 13	12 85	16 36	7 87	18 28
Divid Cover	1 01	1 01	1 00	1 01	0 98
Divid Yield	8 17	7 67	6 11	12 57	5 56
Earning Yield%	8 24	7 78	6 11	12 71	5 47
NAV % Mrk Pr	158 89	241 78	86 60	109 87	56 98
Effec Tax Rate	15 97	8 89	8 45	11 83	21 41
Def Interval	0 41	0 50	0 29	0 10	0 16
Sus Grth Rate	0 05	0 05	0 02	0 16	-0 14

SUBSIDIARY & ASSOCIATED COMPANIES

ANGLO AMERICAN (OFS) HOUSING CO LTD
FREE STATE CONSOLIDATED GOLD MINES (OPER

INVESTMENTS

ADVANCED MINING SOFTWARE LTD (18000 SH)
CACTUS INVESTMENTS (PTY) LTD (RED CUM PR (6811 SH)
CHAMBER OF MINES OF SOUTH AFRICA R (1 9%)
EASTERN GOLD HOLDINGS LTD (21 8%)
GOLDCO LTD (1 SH)
INTER MINE SERVICES OFS (PTY) LTD (560 SH)
INTERNATIONAL GOLD CORPORATION LTD (7129 SH)
JEANETTE GOLD MINES LTD (392588 SH)
LA RIVIERA (PTY) LTD (19 SH)
LAMPREY INVESTMENT HOLDINGS LIMITED (7886 SH)
LANSAN INVESTMENT HOLDINGS LTD (5730 SH)
MINE LABOUR ORGANISATIONS (N R C) LTD (67784 SH)
NUCLEAR FUELS CORPORATION OF SA (PTY) LT (0 1%)
RAND REFINERY LTD (1 3%)
SOUTHVAAL HOLDINGS LTD (887624 SH)
ST HELNA GOLD MINES LTD (315827 SH)
STONE & ALLIED INDUSTRIES (OFS) LTD (200000 SH)
THE EMPLOYMENT BUREAU OF AFRICA LTD (0 1%)
THE RAND MUTUAL ASSURANCE CO LTD (4362 SH)
WELKOM GOLD HOLDINGS LTD (7030000SH)
WELKOM GOLD INVESTMENTS LIMITED (1 8%)
WELTEVREDEN MINES LTD (120000 SH)

FREE STATE DEVELOPMENT & INVESTMENT CORP LTD

ABBREVIATION : FREDDEV

JSE SHORT CODE : FRE

SECTOR : Mining-Exploration

SHAREHOLDERS

Who Owns Whom's Assessment of the Identity of the Ultimate Controlling Shareholder: ANGLO AMERICAN VIA JOHNIES

SHAREHOLDER	PERCENTAGE 1992	1991
STD BANK NOM TVL P/L	44.9	---
CMB NOM P/L	5.5	---
INDO-CHINA NOM P/L	4.3	---
LONDON REGISTER ACCOUNT	3.5	---
ANDEX NOM P/L	2.4	---
DEMESNE INV P/L	2.2	---
ROODENRAND MAIN REEF MINES LTD	2.1	---
FIRST NAT NOM P/L	1.7	---
FIRST NAT NOM P/L GATR DEPOT	1.6	---
RINRIC NOM P/L	1.6	---
QUARTO NOM P/L	1.4	---
TOTAL	71.0	---

DIRECTORS :
BRAY VG (Chairman),DE VILLIERS JS DR,MCKENNA P VAN NIEKERK JE ,VON CHRISTIERSON CI ,WOOD BT

REGISTRATION NUMBER : 05/16931/06

REGISTERED OFFICE
Consolidated Building, cnr. Fox & Harrison Sts.
Johannesburg
2001
TEL: 011-373 9111
FAX: 011-836 6130

TRANSFER SECRETARY
Consolidated Share Registrars Ltd
P O Box 61051, Marshalltown
2107
TEL: 011-492 1620

COMPANY SECRETARY
Johannesburg Consolidated Inv Co Ltd

NATURE OF BUSINESS
The company holds mineral rights over 8804 ha in the OFS, & mineral participation interests in various gold, platinum, coal & other mineral prospects & mining operations in the OFS, Tvl, N Cape & N Natal.

BANKERS :
N/A

AUDITORS :
Deloitte & Touche

FAMILIAR BRAND NAMES
N/A

CONTRIBUTION BY ACTIVITY
N/A

YEAR END : June

CAPITAL STRUCTURE

	AUTHORISED	ISSUED
Ords 10c	29700000	22226597

FINANCIAL STATISTICS (AT FINANCIAL YEAR END)

(Amts in R'000)	1992 Jun	1991 Jun	1990 Jun	1989 Jun	1988 Jun
Ord S/H Int	16229	14662	15469	16420	17692
Long Trm Loans	-	19066	4677	835	-
Iss Ord Share	22227	21782	21782	21782	21782
Total Liab	146	19332	4776	1284	410
Current Liab	146	266	99	449	410
Total Assets	8639	27704	2780	2788	5580
Intang Assets	7736	6290	17465	14916	12522
Current Assets	5866	5336	84	92	5527
Debtors	39	8	25	45	126
Oper Profit	-768	-348	-450	-146	128
Interest Paid	-	785	495	64	-
Tax Paid	67	-	22	7	-4
Prf af Int&Tax	-125	-807	-951	-40	132
Prf att Ord Sh	-125	-807	-951	-40	132
Btm Line Earn	-125	-807	-951	-1272	132
Mkt Prce(c) YE	96	300	825	940	1150

PER SHARE STATISTICS (CENTS)

Net Asst Val	38.21	38.44	-9.16	6.90	23.74
Net Earnings	-0.50	-3.70	-4.40	-0.20	0.60
Cash Flow	-0.56	-3.70	-4.37	-0.18	0.61

RATIOS AND OTHER INFORMATION

Mrk Cap(R000)	21338	65346	179702	204751	250493
Current Ratio	40.18	20.06	0.85	0.20	13.48
Quik/Acid Tst	40.18	20.06	0.85	0.20	13.48
Debt/Ass Rat	0.02	0.01	1.72	0.46	0.07
L T L Tot Ass	-	-	1.68	0.30	-
Debt to Eqity	0.01	0.02	0.31	0.08	0.02
Interest Cover	-	-0.44	-0.91	-2.28	-
Ret on Assets	-0.67	-0.08	-15.61	1.11	2.29
Ret on Equity%	-0.77	-5.50	-6.15	-0.24	0.75
Price/Earnings	-192.00	-81.08	-187.50	-4700.00	1916.67
Earning Yield%	-0.52	-1.23	-0.53	-0.02	0.05
NAV % Mrk Pr	39.80	12.81	-1.11	0.73	2.06
Effec Tax Rate	-50.00	-	-2.37	-21.21	-3.13
Def Interval	-	-23.63	-4.92	-20.88	-
Sus Grth Rate	-0.77	-5.50	-6.15	-0.24	0.75

SUBSIDIARY & ASSOCIATED COMPANIES

PALMIETFONTEIN MINING VENTURES (PTY) LTD
SOUTHERN HOLDINGS LTD

INVESTMENTS

LYDENBURG EXPLORATION LTD (1472325 SH)
LYDENBURG EXPLORATION LTD (OPTIONS) (380133 SH)

FS GROUP LTD

ABBREVIATION : F-S-GROUP

JSE SHORT CODE : FSG

SECTOR : Industrial-Industrial Holding

SHAREHOLDERS

Who Owns Whom's Assessment of the Identity of the Ultimate Controlling Shareholder:
DIRECTORS

SHAREHOLDER	PERCENTAGE 1992	1991
CONFOR INV P/L	30.8	34.6
FORM-SCAFF INV P/L	18.1	18.1
CMB NOM P/L	17.8	---
KF INV HOLDINGS P/L	8.4	8.4
STD BANK NOM TVL P/L	4.5	4.5
BUILMA NOM P/L	4.3	---
REPUBLIC SHUTTERING P/L	2.3	2.3
ELLERINE BROS P/L	1.2	1.2
ELLERINE E	1.1	1.1
LIBSASRIA NOM P/L	1.1	1.1
SIXTY SIX MARSHALL STREET NOM P/L	---	2.9
ANGLO AMERICAN CORP PENS FUND	---	2.0
ANGLO AMERICAN GROUP PENS FUND	---	1.5
DE BEERS PENS FUND	---	2.0
SANLAM	---	9.0
TOTAL	89.6	88.7

DIRECTORS :
COHEN N (Financial Director),KAMINER B
LIEBESMAN JM (Chairman),ROLFE TW ,SLOM S
VAN DER MERWE HR

REGISTRATION NUMBER : 87/00432/06

REGISTERED OFFICE
6th Floor, FSI Centre
35 Siemert Road, Doornfontein
2001
TEL: 011-402 3200
FAX: 011-402 7508

TRANSFER SECRETARY
Mercantile Registrars Ltd
P O Box 1053, Johannesburg
2000
TEL: 011-333 8181

COMPANY SECRETARY
B E Liebesman

NATURE OF BUSINESS
An investment holding company which controls 64,5% of the share capital of FSI Corporation.

BANKERS :
Nedperm Bank Ltd

AUDITORS :
Kessel Feinstein

FAMILIAR BRAND NAMES
N/A

CONTRIBUTION BY ACTIVITY
N/A

YEAR END : December

DIVIDEND :Ords 1c

Interim No 5	(Ldr)06/10/89	(Pay)27/10/89	Amt(c)6
Final No 6	(Ldr)05/04/90	(Pay)27/04/90	Amt(c)11.5
Interim No 7	(Ldr)19/10/90	(Pay)09/11/90	Amt(c)6
Final No 8	(Ldr)26/04/91	(Pay)26/06/91	Amt(c)11.5
Interim No 9	(Ldr)04/10/91	(Pay)15/11/91	Amt(c)6
Final No 10	(Ldr)24/04/92	(Pay)13/05/92	Amt(c)11.5
Interim No 11	(Ldr)25/09/92	(Pay)06/11/92	Amt(c)4.25

CAPITAL STRUCTURE

	AUTHORISED	ISSUED
Ords 1c	80000000	54167770
Pref Ords 1c	12500000	8666843

FINANCIAL STATISTICS (AT FINANCIAL YEAR END)

(Amts in R'000)	1991 Dec	1990 Dec	1989 Dec	1988 Dec	1987 Jun
Ord S/H Int	196297	196297	196297	196297	170297
Iss Ord Share	54168	54168	54168	54168	54168
Total Liab	8120	8120	8120	6244	3581
Current Liab	8120	8120	8120	6244	3581
Total Assets	204417	204417	204417	202541	173878
Current Assets	7789	7789	7789	5913	3250
Prf af Int&Tax	12599	12599	12599	11329	3250
Prf att Ord Sh	12599	12599	12599	11329	3250
Btm Line Earn	12599	12599	12599	11329	3250
Dividend Paid	12599	12599	12599	11329	3250
Mkt Prce(c) YE	215	280	465	300	325

PER SHARE STATISTICS (CENTS)

Net Asst Val	362.39	362.39	362.39	362.39	314.39
Net Earnings	23.36	55.20	66.00	75.70	54.80
Dividends	17.50	17.50	17.50	20.00	6.00
Cash Flow	23.26	23.26	23.26	13.94	6.00

RATIOS AND OTHER INFORMATION

Mrk Cap(R000)	116461	151670	251881	162504	176046
Current Ratio	0.96	0.96	0.96	0.95	0.91
Quik/Acid Tst	0.96	0.96	0.96	0.95	0.91
Debt/Ass Rat	0.04	0.04	0.04	0.03	0.02
Debt to Eqity	0.04	0.04	0.04	0.03	0.02
Ret on Assets	6.16	6.16	6.16	3.73	1.87
Ret on Equity%	6.42	6.42	6.42	3.85	1.91
Price/Earnings	9.20	5.07	7.05	3.96	5.93
Divid Cover	1.33	3.15	3.77	3.79	9.13
Divid Yield	8.14	6.25	3.76	6.67	1.85
Earning Yield%	10.87	19.71	14.19	25.23	16.86
NAV % Mrk Pr	168.55	129.42	77.93	120.80	96.73
Def Interval	0.00	0.00	0.00	0.00	0.10
Sus Grth Rate	0.00	0.00	0.00	0.00	0.00

SUBSIDIARY & ASSOCIATED COMPANIES

FORM-SCAFF INDUSTRIES LTD
FSI CORPORATION LTD

INVESTMENTS

None

FSI CORPORATION LTD

ABBREVIATION : F-S-I

JSE SHORT CODE : FSI

SECTOR : Industrial-Industrial Holding

SHAREHOLDERS

Who Owns Whom's Assessment of the Identity of the Ultimate Controlling Shareholder:
FS GROUP

SHAREHOLDER	PERCENTAGE 1992	1991
FS GROUP LTD	64 5	64 5
CMB NOM P/L	10 2	---
FORM SCAFF TRUST SHARE INC	3 9	4 2
VMB NOM P/L	3 6	3 6
FIRST NAT NOM P/L	2 2	2 7
KF INV HOLDINGS P/L	2 1	2 1
STD BANK NOM TVL P/L	1 7	1 7
ROLFE T W	1 4	1 4
BUILMA NOM P/L	1 0	---
SANLAM	---	3 4
SIXTY SIX MARSHALL STREET NOM P/L	---	4 7
TOTAL	90 4	88 1

DIRECTORS :
COHEN N (Financial Director),KAMINER B ,KOCH EL
LIEBESMAN JM (Chairman),NOWITZ H
ROLFE TW (Deputy Chairman),SCHLESINGER AM
SLOM S ,SUSSMAN ID ,TUTTON CW
VAN DER MERWE HR (Deputy Chairman

REGISTRATION NUMBER : 01/06309/06

REGISTERED OFFICE
6th Floor, FSI Centre
35 Siemert Road, Doornfontein
2094
TEL 011-402 3200
FAX 011-402 7508

TRANSFER SECRETARY
Mercantile Registrars Ltd
P O Box 1053, Johannesburg
2000
TEL 011-333 8181

COMPANY SECRETARY
B E Liebesman

NATURE OF BUSINESS
An investment holding company with a controlling interest in JSE-quoted Walcor The group has significant interests in the manufacture & distribution of industrial & consumer products, corporate & financial services & property development

BANKERS :
First National Bank of SA Ltd
Nedperm Bank Ltd, Standard Bank of SA Ltd
Trust Bank of Africa Ltd, Bankorp Ltd

AUDITORS :
Kessel Feinstein

FAMILIAR BRAND NAMES
N/A

CONTRIBUTION BY ACTIVITY
N/A

YEAR END : December

DIVIDEND : Ords no par value

Interim No 63	(Ldr)06/10/89	(Pay)27/10/89	Amt(c)12
Final No 64	(Ldr)05/04/90	(Pay)27/04/90	Amt(c)23
Interim No 65	(Ldr)19/10/90	(Pay)09/11/90	Amt(c)12
Final No 66	(Ldr)26/04/91	(Pay)26/06/91	Amt(c)23
Interim No 67	(Ldr)04/10/91	(Pay)15/11/91	Amt(c)12
Final No 68	(Ldr)24/04/92	(Pay)13/05/92	Amt(c)23
Interim No 69	(Ldr)25/09/92	(Pay)06/11/92	Amt(c)8 5

CAPITAL STRUCTURE

	AUTHORISED	ISSUED
Ords no par value	51000000	42017591
6% Cum Prefs R2	125000	125000
Pref Ords 1c	9500000	6722815
Var Rate Red Cum Prefs 1c	100000000	17082000

FINANCIAL STATISTICS (AT FINANCIAL YEAR END)

(Amts in R'000)	1991 Dec	1990 Dec	1989 Dec	1988 Dec	1987 Jun
Ord S/H Int	269804	317980	271402	232153	86711
Long Trm Loans	2247211	2347311	1909782	1369081	159534
Iss Ord Share	42018	42018	42017	42017	40672
Total Liab	3114402	3135969	2625153	1734317	315671
Current Liab	867191	788658	715371	365236	156137
Total Assets	2955637	3054245	2582750	1866502	402382
Intang Assets	428569	399704	313805	99968	*
Current Assets	1417167	1682766	1432380	813301	215765
Debtors	785789	998063	814996	379896	100890
Inventory	556031	571276	479439	291258	108406
Turnover	3227630	3246507	2755574	2382096	284164
Oper Profit	349028	369000	377357	315855	41695
Interest Paid	225529	186029	122589	86843	11599
Tax Paid	3603	17700	70690	64459	4966
Prf af Int&Tax	122490	175991	190345	166383	25130
Prf att Ord Sh	23002	53787	64317	63621	17768
Btm Line Earn	1605	64191	60585	104084	15328
Dividend Paid	20542	20437	20240	17793	4881
Mkt Prce(c) YE	400	500	925	590	400
Depreciation	72227	57840	47338	46080	5124

PER SHARE STATISTICS (CENTS)

Net Asst Val	-377 85	-194 50	-100 92	314 60	213 20
Net Earnings	47 20	110 40	132 00	109 60	46 20
Dividends	35 00	35 00	35 00	30 00	12 00
Cash Flow	196 61	192 32	217 01	191 46	59 57

RATIOS AND OTHER INFORMATION

Mrk Cap(R000)	168072	210090	388657	247900	162688
Current Ratio	1 63	2 13	2 00	2 23	1 38
Quik/Acid Tst	0 99	1 41	1 33	1 43	0 69
A/C Rec T/ovr	4 11	3 25	3 38	4 18	2 82
Tot Ass T/ovr	1 09	1 06	1 07	0 85	0 71
Debt/Ass Rat	0 65	0 63	0 50	0 43	0 60
L T L Tot Ass	0 36	0 37	0 23	0 24	0 22
Debt to Eqity	7 15	6 02	4 79	3 46	2 81
Interest Cover	1 56	2 04	3 13	3 66	3 59
Oper Prof Mrg	10 81	11 37	13 69	13 26	14 67
Net Prof Marg%	0 71	1 66	2 33	2 67	6 25
Ret on Assets	11 91	12 60	15 23	11 35	10 36
Ret on Equity%	8 53	16 92	23 70	18 27	20 49
Price/Earnings	8 47	4 53	7 01	5 38	8 66
Divid Cover	1 35	3 15	3 77	3 65	3 85
Divid Yield	8 75	7 00	3 78	5 08	3 00
Earning Yield%	11 80	22 08	14 27	18 58	11 55
NAV % Mrk Pr	-94 46	-38 90	-10 91	53 32	53 30
Effec Tax Rate	7 73	12 43	23 86	22 79	16 43
Def Interval	14 89	14 85	8 52	2 88	3 82
Sus Grth Rate	0 91	10 49	16 24	19 74	14 86

SUBSIDIARY & ASSOCIATED COMPANIES

FORM-SCAFF (PTY) LTD
FSI CORPORATE SERVICES LTD
WAICOR LTD

INVESTMENTS

None

FSI HOLDINGS LTD (ZIMBABWE)

ABBREVIATION : FSI ZIM

SECTOR : Zimbabwe Stock Exchange

SHAREHOLDERS

Who Owns Whom's Assessment of the Identity of the Ultimate Controlling Shareholder: BURGASVEST SECURITIES (NETHERLANDS)

SHAREHOLDER	PERCENTAGE 1992	1991
FSI INV (PVT) LTD	42 1	---
OLD MUTUAL ZIMBABWE	21 9	---
NAT RAILWAYS OF ZIM CONTR PENS FUND	5 2	---
A W & J I INV (PVT) LTD	3 0	---
SYFRETS NOM (PVT) LTD	2 5	---
JOJILL (PVT) LTD	1 5	---
IPCORN SERVICES (PVT) LTD	1 0	---
TOTAL	77 3	---

DIRECTORS :
FRASER JL (Financial Director)
IRVINE AW (Chief Executive),PICHANICK ALA
ROLFE TW (Chairman),SPROULE GN ,THOMPSON AC
VAN DER MERWE HR

REGISTERED OFFICE
Cnr Newcastle/Austin Rds, Workington
Harare

TEL 723687
FAX 723687

TRANSFER SECRETARY
Zimbabwe Banking Corporation Ltd
P O Box 3198, Harare
Zimbabwe

TEL 092634 735011

COMPANY SECRETARY
FSI Management Services

NATURE OF BUSINESS
The FSI HOLDINGS group of companies is engaged in the manufacture and marketing of rubber products, tools and hardware for the mining and agriculture sectors With the assistance of FS GROUP in South Africa,the Zimbabwe operating companies have been upgrading their manufacturing capacities and quali ty of products so as to take advantage of Zimbabwe's ideal position for distribution of the group 's products throughout the PTA region,Southern and Central Africa.

BANKERS :
Standard Chartered Bank Zimbabwe Ltd

AUDITORS :
Price Waterhouse Meyernel

FAMILIAR BRAND NAMES
N/A

CONTRIBUTION BY ACTIVITY
N/A

YEAR END : December

CAPITAL STRUCTURE

	AUTHORISED	ISSUED
Ords Z$1	80000000	67300000

FINANCIAL STATISTICS (AT FINANCIAL YEAR END)

(Amts in Z$)	1991 Dec
Ord S/H Int	84470
Long Trm Loans	5924
Total Liab	35435
Current Liab	29511
Total Assets	119905
Current Assets	65992
Debtors	13672
Inventory	29027
Turnover	72959
Oper Profit	19457
Tax Paid	6229
Prf af Int&Tax	13228
Prf att Ord Sh	11721
Btm Line Earn	11721

PER SHARE STATISTICS (CENTS)

RATIOS AND OTHER INFORMATION

Current Ratio	2 24
Quik/Acid Tst	1 25
A/C Rec T/ovr	5 34
Tot Ass T/ovr	0 61
Debt/Ass Rat	0 25
Debt to Eqity	0 35
Oper Prof Mrg	26 67
Net Prof Marg%	16 07
Ret on Assets	16 23
Ret on Equity%	13 88
Effec Tax Rate	32 01
Def Interval	0 52
Sus Grth Rate	13 88

SUBSIDIARY & ASSOCIATED COMPANIES

E W TARRY (PVT) LTD
FSI TRADING (PVT) LTD
GENERAL BELTINGS (PVT) LTD (ZIMBABWE)
GENERAL TIRE & INDUSTRIAL PRODUCTS (PVT)
MUKWA PROPERTIES (PVT) LTD
PIGOTT MASKEW (PVT) LTD (ZIMBABWE)

INVESTMENTS

None

GAZANKULU GOLD HOLDINGS LTD

ABBREVIATION : GAZGOLD

JSE SHORT CODE : GAZ

SECTOR : Gold-Rand & others

SHAREHOLDERS

Who Owns Whom's Assessment of the Identity of the Ultimate Controlling Shareholder: NEWMAN FAMILY

SHAREHOLDER	PERCENTAGE 1992	1991
SAUDI INV SA P/L	31.2	31.6
CHOICEHOLD LTD	10.3	10.4
QUIBOY LTD	4.6	4.6
NEWMAN F H	4.1	4.1
VAN REIGERSBERG VERSLUYS M L H	3.6	2.9
DUROS LTD	3.3	3.4
SHARESTOCK NOM P/L	2.8	3.5
NEWMAN F H & A E TRUST	2.1	—
BETTY D R	2.1	2.1
MENBLACK NOM P/L	1.6	2.4
FIRST NAT NOM P/L	1.5	1.5
SACHSE E U H	1.4	1.4
MEGAFID INTERNATIONAL AG	1.3	1.3
O'DONNELL R	1.2	—
NEWMAN A E	1.1	—
MEDICAL SERVICES (EUROPE) LTD	1.0	1.2
BURTCOR CC	—	1.1
LOWENCO NOM P/L	—	1.3
SOLON NOM P/L	—	2.2
TOTAL	73.3	75.0

DIRECTORS :
ARTHUR PRN ,EATON RD (Financial Director)
FOWLER ARC (Chairman)
NEWMAN FH (Managing Director),O'DONNELL RP
RAHN FJ D

REGISTRATION NUMBER : 66/12397/06

REGISTERED OFFICE
Executive City, Cnr Cross & Charmaine Ave
Randburg
2194
TEL: 011-726 7255

TRANSFER SECRETARY
Union Provident Trust SA Ltd
P O Box 2322, Johannesburg
2000
TEL: 011-833 6700

COMPANY SECRETARY
Betty & Dickson

NATURE OF BUSINESS
The company operates gold mines in the Giyani area of Gazankulu, & has an interest in a gold prospect in the Pilansberg area.

BANKERS :
Standard Bank of SA Ltd

AUDITORS :
Ernst & Young

FAMILIAR BRAND NAMES
N/A

CONTRIBUTION BY ACTIVITY
N/A

YEAR END : March

DIVIDEND :15/00/91

NUMBER OF EMPLOYEES : 500

CAPITAL STRUCTURE

	AUTHORISED	ISSUED
Ords 1c	120000000	51235000
9% Cum Comp Conv Redeem Prefs 1c	60000000	51747350

FINANCIAL STATISTICS (AT FINANCIAL YEAR END)

(Amts in R'000)	1991 Feb	1990 Feb	1989 Feb	1988	1987
Ord S/H Int	43650	42099	39268	4725	1700
Long Trm Loans	3122	1699	679	5	40
Iss Ord Share	50625	50625	49200	2050	2050
Total Liab	13191	11198	8462	10	80
Current Liab	10069	9499	7783	5	40
Total Assets	56841	53297	47730	9460	3480
Current Assets	547	752	756	4730	1740
Debtors	153	292	235	-	-
Inventory	382	399	512	4730	1740
Turnover	9671	9001	3669	-	-
Oper Profit	3360	3712	1903	97	150
Interest Paid	1809	1451	-	98	81
Tax Paid	-	-	-	-	28
Prf af Int&Tax	1551	2261	1903	-1	40
Prf att Ord Sh	1551	2261	1903	-1	40
Btm Line Earn	1551	2261	1903	-1	40
Mkt Prce(c) YE	20	85	58	-	-

PER SHARE STATISTICS (CENTS)

	1991 Feb	1990 Feb	1989 Feb	1988	1987
Net Asst Val	86.22	83.16	79.81	230.49	82.93
Net Earnings	3.00	4.51	3.90	-	-
Cash Flow	3.06	4.47	3.87	-0.05	1.95

RATIOS AND OTHER INFORMATION

	1991 Feb	1990 Feb	1989 Feb	1988	1987
Mrk Cap(R000)	10125	43031	28536	-	-
Current Ratio	0.05	0.08	0.10	946.00	43.50
Quik/Acid Tst	0.02	0.04	0.03	-	-
A/C Rec T/ovr	63.21	30.83	15.61	-	-
Tot Ass T/ovr	0.17	0.17	0.08	-	-
Debt/Ass Rat	0.23	0.21	0.18	0.00	0.02
L T L Tot Ass	0.05	0.03	0.01	0.00	0.01
Debt to Eqity	0.30	0.27	0.22	0.00	0.05
Interest Cover	1.86	2.56	-	0.99	1.84
Oper Prof Mrg	34.74	41.24	51.87	-	-
Net Prof Marg%	16.04	25.12	51.87	-	-
Ret on Assets	5.91	6.96	3.99	1.03	4.28
Ret on Equity%	3.55	5.36	4.85	-0.02	2.35
Price/Earnings	6.67	18.85	14.87	-	-
Earning Yield%	15.00	5.31	6.72	-	-
NAV % Mrk Pr	431.11	97.83	137.61	-	-
Effec Tax Rate	-	-	-	-	40.58
Def Interval	7.63	4.27	3.73	-5.00	1.00
Sus Grth Rate	3.55	5.37	4.85	-0.02	2.35

SUBSIDIARY & ASSOCIATED COMPANIES

FAR NORTH RAND EXTENSIONS LTD
G&G GOLD MINING CO (PTY) LTD
GAZANKULU GOLD MINING COMPANY LTD
GEMSBOK GOLD MINING COMPANY LTD
MCP (PTY) LTD

INVESTMENTS

None

GDM FINANCE LTD

ABBREVIATION : GDM

JSE SHORT CODE : GDM

SECTOR : Financial-Banks & Financial Services

SHAREHOLDERS

Who Owns Whom's Assessment of the Identity of the Ultimate Controlling Shareholder: FM WARING VIA GOODE DURRANT PLC

SHAREHOLDER	PERCENTAGE 1992	1991
GOODE DURRANT FINANCE LTD	49.6	49.6
UAL MERCHANT BANK LTD	12.5	12.5
SA MUTUAL	11.2	11.2
COWPER J W G	5.3	5.3
STD BANK NOM TVL P/L	4.2	2.0
BERLIN C A	3.1	3.5
SHARESTOCK NOM P/L	2.8	2.0
FERBROS NOM P/L	1.9	---
KUPER R	1.3	1.5
FIRST NAT NOM P/L	---	3.9
TOTAL	91.7	91.5

DIRECTORS :
BAIKIE PJ ,BERLIN CA (Financial Director)
BURSCOUGH DC
COLLISON MJ (Operations Director)
COWPER JWG (Managing Director),DAVIDSON KM
KUPER R ,WARING FM (Chairman

REGISTRATION NUMBER : 52/00756/06

REGISTERED OFFICE
Medical Arts Building, 220 Jeppe Street
Johannesburg
2001
TEL: 011-29 4611
FAX: 011-337 6191

TRANSFER SECRETARY
Central Registrars Ltd
P O Box 4844, Johannesburg
2000
TEL: 011-331 0051

COMPANY SECRETARY
P J Baikie

NATURE OF BUSINESS
GDM and its subsidiaries provide trade finance, act as a confirming house & provide freight forwarding & clearing services.

BANKERS :
First National Bank of SA Ltd

AUDITORS :
Kessel Feinstein

FAMILIAR BRAND NAMES
N/A

CONTRIBUTION BY ACTIVITY
Clothing/Textiles (% Turnover by Sector) (26.0%)
Household/Consumer (21.0%)
Engineering Machinery/Light Industry (16.0%)
Computer Supplies/Consumer Electronics (9.0%)
Automotive & Transportation Products (5.0%)
Printing & Stationery Supplies (5.0%)
Steel/Chemicals/Plastics (8.0%)
Footwear (6.0%)
Construction/Hospital Supplies (3.0%)
Sundry (1.0%)

YEAR END : April

DIVIDEND : Ords 10c

Interim No 4	(Ldr)15/12/89	(Pay)12/01/90	Amt(c)4
Final No 5	(Ldr)21/07/90	(Pay)03/08/90	Amt(c)8
Interim No 6	(Ldr)21/12/90	(Pay)18/01/91	Amt(c)4.5
Final No 7	(Ldr)12/07/91	(Pay)26/07/91	Amt(c)9
Interim No 8	(Ldr)20/12/91	(Pay)17/01/92	Amt(c)5.25
Final No 9	(Ldr)10/07/92	(Pay)24/07/92	Amt(c)10.25
Interim No 10	(Ldr)18/12/92	(Pay)15/01/93	Amt(c)5.8

NUMBER OF EMPLOYEES : 136

CAPITAL STRUCTURE

	AUTHORISED	ISSUED
Ords 10c	35000000	25581000

FINANCIAL STATISTICS (AT FINANCIAL YEAR END)

(Amts in R'000)	1991 Apr	1990 Apr	1989 Apr	1988 Apr	1987
Ord S/H Int	30348	24783	20307	16923	4245
Long Trm Loans	4485	4613	319	-	31513
Iss Ord Share	25581	25581	25581	25581	375
Total Liab	116011	97009	75258	50383	59004
Current Liab	111526	92396	74939	50383	27491
Total Assets	143802	121792	95565	67306	71412
Intang Assets	2557	*	*	*	*
Current Assets	140291	117860	93712	65603	35654
Debtors	136138	116123	93301	64198	-
Inventory	-	-	-	-	35654
Oper Profit	11990	9840	8052	5045	1382
Interest Paid	14	38	-	-	-
Tax Paid	2442	2189	2602	1951	468
Prf af Int&Tax	9543	7624	5450	3094	854
Prf att Ord Sh	8630	7503	5450	3019	779
Btm Line Earn	8630	7503	5450	2730	779
Dividend Paid	3453	3069	2175	1495	520
Mkt Prce(c) YE	180	140	100	400	-
Depreciation	592	303	163	47	-

PER SHARE STATISTICS (CENTS)

Net Asst Val	108.64	96.88	79.38	66.15	1132.00
Net Earnings	33.70	29.30	21.30	13.80	-
Dividends	13.50	12.00	8.50	3.50	-
Cash Flow	36.93	30.31	23.19	11.75	455.47

RATIOS AND OTHER INFORMATION

Mrk Cap(R000)	46046	35813	25581	102324	-
Current Ratio	1 26	1 28	1 25	1 30	1 30
Quik/Acid Tst	1 26	1 28	1 25	1 30	-
Debt/Ass Rat	0 78	0 76	0 78	0 75	0 83
L T L Tot Ass	0 00	0 01	-		0 44
Debt to Eqity	3 69	3 75	3 69	2 98	13 90
Interest Cover	857 07	259 24	-	-	-
Ret on Assets	8 34	8 09	8 43	7 50	3 70
Ret on Equity%	28 44	30 27	26 84	17 84	36 70
Price/Earnings	5 34	4 78	4 69	28 99	-
Divid Cover	2 50	2 44	2 51	3 94	-
Divid Yield	7 50	8 57	8 50	0 88	-
Earning Yield%	18 72	20 93	21 30	3 45	-
NAV % Mrk Pr	60 36	69 20	79 38	16 54	-
Effec Tax Rate	13 81	16 84	19 13	39 86	33 86
Def Interval	10 86	10 96	12 06	15 63	73 80
Sus Grth Rate	17 06	17 89	16 13	9 01	6 10

SUBSIDIARY & ASSOCIATED COMPANIES

AFRICAN SHIPPING LTD
FOWLIE & WHYTOCK (PTY) LTD
GDM FINANCE (UK) LTD
GDM FINANCE INCORPORATED
GDM INTERNATIONAL (PTY) LTD
GDM LEASING LIMITED
KUPER CONFIRMING AND FINANCE (PTY) LTD
MACKINLAY AND COMPANY LONDON (SA) LTD
REPFIN HOLDINGS (PTY) LTD
REPFIN INVESTMENTS (PTY) LTD

INVESTMENTS

None

GENBEL INVESTMENTS LTD

ABBREVIATION : GENBEL

JSE SHORT CODE : GBL

SECTOR : Mining Financial-Mining Holding

SHAREHOLDERS

Who Owns Whom's Assessment of the Identity of the Ultimate Controlling Shareholder: SANLAM VIA GENCOR

SHAREHOLDER	PERCENTAGE 1992	1991
CONSOLIDATED NOM P/L	50 0	50 0
CMB NOM P/L	9 8	
STD BANK NOM TVL P/L	8 6	7 2
FIRST NAT NOM P/L	3 3	2 9
SA MUTUAL	3 2	2 1
ENGINEERING INDUSTRIES PENS FUND	1 9	1 5
METAL IND GROUP PENS FUND	1 4	1 2
METROPOLITAN LIFE LTD	1 3	1 3
LONDON CONTROL ACCOUNT	1 3	1 5
SOUTHERN LIFE ASSOC LTD	- -	2 8
ESCOM PENS & PROV FUND	--	1 2
SANLAM	---	9 5
TOTAL	80 8	81 2

DIRECTORS :
BARTLEET EK (Financial Director)
BOTHA AD (Managing Director),COOK PJ
CRONSHAW PJ (Executive Director),DALING MH
DE BEER TL (Chairman),FOUCHE JH ,GILBERTSON BP
MASSON R ,MAY RW (Executive Director),NKUHLU WL
SENEKAL JC ,SMITH HA ,WITKIN A ,WOOD CD

REGISTRATION NUMBER : 05/32379/06

REGISTERED OFFICE
General Mining Building, 6 Hollard Street
Johannesburg
2001
TEL 011-376 2440
FAX 011-834 3065

TRANSFER SECRETARY
Central Registrars Ltd
P O Box 4844, Johannesburg
2000
TEL 011-331 0051

COMPANY SECRETARY
H C De Wet

NATURE OF BUSINESS
The Genbel group is a long-term investor which holds a portfolio of investments predominantly in SA mining & resource industries Its principal investment activity is supported and facilitated by the control of significant mineral rights, as well as participation in local and offshore investment markets

BANKERS :
Trust Bank of Africa Ltd

AUDITORS :
N/A

FAMILIAR BRAND NAMES
N/A

CONTRIBUTION BY ACTIVITY
Gold (% of income) (5 0%)
Mining Finance (12 0%)
Energy & Industrial (11 0%)
Platinum (11 0%)
Diamonds (6 0%)
Finance/Insurance/property (43 0%)
Consumer Goods (1 0%)
Forestry/Paper Products (8 0%)
Mining - Metals/Minerals (3 0%)

YEAR END : June

DIVIDEND : Ords 10c

Interim No 54	(Ldr)16/02/90	(Pay)23/03/90	Amt(c)12
Final No 55	(Ldr)14/09/90	(Pay)12/10/90	Amt(c)15 5
Interim No 56	(Ldr)15/02/91	(Pay)22/03/91	Amt(c)13 5
Final No 57	(Ldr)13/09/91	(Pay)11/10/91	Amt(c)18 5
Interim No 58	(Ldr)14/02/92	(Pay)20/03/92	Amt(c)15
Final No 59	(Ldr)11/09/92	(Pay)16/10/92	Amt(c)19

NUMBER OF EMPLOYEES : 37

GENCOR BEHEREND BPK

ABBREVIATION : GENBEHEER

JSE SHORT CODE : GBR

SECTOR : Mining Financial-Mining Houses

SHAREHOLDERS

Who Owns Whom's Assessment of the Identity of the Ultimate Controlling Shareholder:
SANLAM

SHAREHOLDER	PERCENTAGE 1992	1991
CMB NOM P/L	54 0	---
TEGNIESE MYNBELEGGINGS BPK	25 2	25 2
ABSA NOM P/L	4 2	---
SA MUTUAL	3 5	3 5
EIGHTY ONE MAIN STREET NOM LTD	1 2	---
PUBLIC INV COMMISSIONERS	1 2	---
STD BANK NOM TVL P/L	1 2	1 1
SANKORP BPK	---	48 4
SANLAM	---	2 5
STATUS INV P/L	---	1 8
VOLKSKAS NOM P/L	---	6 3
TOTAL	90 5	88 8

DIRECTORS :
DALING MH (Chairman)
GILBERTSON BP (Managing Director)
HUNT-DAVIS DNA ,KATZ MM PROF,LOUBSER JGH DR
PRETORIUS WS ,STEINMETZ G ,VAN DEN BERG AJ DR
VAN WYK AJ ,VISSER MH

REGISTRATION NUMBER : 53/01008/06

REGISTERED OFFICE
6 Hollard Street, Johannesburg
2001
TEL 011-376 9111
FAX 011-836 8708

TRANSFER SECRETARY
Central Registrars Ltd
P O Box 4844, Johannesburg
2000
TEL 011-331 0051

COMPANY SECRETARY
L P Fourie

NATURE OF BUSINESS
An investment holding company with a controlling interest in JSE-quoted mining house Gencor

BANKERS :
Trust Bank of Africa Ltd

AUDITORS :
Coopers Theron Du Toit

FAMILIAR BRAND NAMES
N/A

CONTRIBUTION BY ACTIVITY
N/A

CAPITAL STRUCTURE

	AUTHORISED	ISSUED
Ords 10c	600000000	432230810

FINANCIAL STATISTICS (AT FINANCIAL YEAR END)

(Amts in R'000)	1992 Jun	1991 Jun	1990 Jun	1989 Jun	1988 Jun
Ord S/H Int	1300000	1114000	887000	539989	473327
Long Trm Loans	215000	192000	70000	-	-
Iss Ord Share	432231	432231	432231	37553	36180
Total Liab	317000	282000	383000	60038	70969
Current Liab	102000	90000	313000	60038	70969
Total Assets	1617000	1396000	1270000	600027	544296
Current Assets	461000	455000	131000	23954	85325
Debtors	15000	10000	8000	2683	13859
Oper Profit	-18000	-14000	1000	96905	90389
Interest Paid	-	9000	-	-	-
Tax Paid	16000	7000	4000	81	-427
Prf af Int&Tax	148000	138000	122000	96824	90816
Prf att Ord Sh	148000	138000	120000	100046	128462
Btm Line Earn	291000	415000	157000	100046	128462
Dividend Paid	147000	138000	119000	97637	90449
Mkt Prce(c) YE	580	635	650	5800	3900
Depreciation	-	-	5000	54	-

PER SHARE STATISTICS (CENTS)

Net Asst Val	300 77	257 73	205 21	1437 94	1308 26
Net Earnings	34 20	32 00	28 80	259 00	251 00
Dividends	34 00	32 00	27 50	260 00	250 00
Cash Flow	34 24	31 93	30 04	25 90	246 19

RATIOS AND OTHER INFORMATION

Mrk Cap(R000)	2506940	2744667	2809502	2178074	1411020
Current Ratio	4 52	5 06	0 42	0 40	1 20
Quik/Acid Tst	4 52	5 06	0 42	0 40	1 20
Debt/Ass Rat	0 06	0 06	0 25	0 10	0 13
Debt to Eqity	0 08	0 08	0 35	0 11	0 15
Interest Cover	-	13 11	-	-	-
Ret on Assets	10 14	11 03	9 92	16 15	16 73
Ret on Equity%	11 38	12 39	13 53	18 53	27 14
Price/Earnings	16 96	19 84	22 57	22 39	15 54
Divid Cover	1 01	1 00	1 05	1 00	1 00
Divid Yield	5 86	5 04	4 23	4 48	6 41
Earning Yield%	5 90	5 04	4 43	4 47	6 44
NAV % Mrk Pr	51 86	40 59	31 57	24 79	33 55
Effec Tax Rate	39 02	53 85	25 00	0 50	0 01
Def Interval	1 45	1 39	1 81	-	-
Sus Grth Rate	0 08	0 00	0 11	0 45	8 03

SUBSIDIARY & ASSOCIATED COMPANIES

GENBEL GOLD TRUST LTD
GENBEL GROWTH & RESOURCES LTD
GENBEL MANAGEMENT SERVICES LTD
GENBEL OFFSHORE INVESTMENTS LTD
UNISEN INVESTMENTS LTD

INVESTMENTS

GENCOR BEHEREND BPK (6,3%)
ORYX GOLD HOLDINGS LTD (14,5%)
SAPPI LTD (5,2%)

YEAR END : August

DIVIDEND : Ords 10c

Interim	(Ldr)11/05/90	(Pay)01/06/90	Amt(c)12 5
Final	(Ldr)09/11/90	(Pay)30/11/90	Amt(c)23
Interim	(Ldr)10/05/91	(Pay)30/05/91	Amt(c)13 3
Final	(Ldr)08/11/91	(Pay)29/11/91	Amt(c)24 7
Final	(Ldr)06/11/92	(Pay)26/11/92	Amt(c)25 7
Interim	(Ldr)31/01/92	(Pay)29/05/92	Amt(c)14 3

NUMBER OF EMPLOYEES : 230643

CAPITAL STRUCTURE

	AUTHORISED	ISSUED
Ords 10c	904000000	833840840
Red Cum Prefs 1c (Unlisted)	25000000	0

FINANCIAL STATISTICS (AT FINANCIAL YEAR END)

(Amts in R'000)	1991 Aug	1990 Aug	1989 Aug	1988 Aug	1987 Aug
Ord S/H Int	4561000	4030000	3256000	1798000	1499000
Long Trm Loans	50000	50000	271000	271000	271000
Iss Ord Share	706645	706645	610285	48286	48286
Total Liab	224000	215000	389000	367000	354000
Current Liab	174000	165000	118000	96000	83000
Total Assets	4785000	4245000	3645000	2165000	1853000
Current Assets	188000	181000	139000	103000	89000
Oper Profit	1000	4000	7000	109000	153000
Interest Paid	-	-	-	12000	18000
Tax Paid	1000	2000	4000	-	-
Prf af Int&Tax	277000	259000	185000	97000	135000
Prf att Ord Sh	764000	819000	571000	256000	352000
Btm Line Earn	775000	814000	691000	253000	352000
Dividend Paid	268000	251000	149000	96000	134000
Mkt Prce(c) YE	1100	910	8900	4800	6300

PER SHARE STATISTICS (CENTS)

Net Asst Val	645 44	570 30	533 52	3723 65	3104 42
Net Earnings	108 10	113 90	97 10	442 00	609 00
Dividends	38 00	35 50	30 80	162 00	225 00
Cash Flow	38 33	35 79	30 51	167 53	349 74

RATIOS AND OTHER INFORMATION

Mrk Cap(R000)	7773095	6430470	54315365	2317728	3042018
Current Ratio	1 08	1 10	1 18	1 07	1 07
Quik/Acid Tst	1 08	1 10	1 18	1 07	1 07
Debt/Ass Rat	0 04	0 04	0 07	0 11	0 12
L T L Tot Ass	-	-	0 04	0 07	0 08
Debt to Eqity	0 04	0 04	0 08	0 13	0 15
Interest Cover	-	-	-	9 08	8 50
Ret on Assets	16 11	19 15	15 97	12 38	29 95
Ret on Equity%	16 75	20 32	17 54	14 24	35 22
Price/Earnings	10 18	7 99	91 66	10 86	10 34
Divid Cover	2 84	3 21	3 15	2 73	2 71
Divid Yield	3 45	3 90	0 35	3 38	3 57
Earning Yield%	9 83	12 52	1 09	9 21	9 67
NAV % Mrk Pr	58 68	62 67	5 99	77 58	49 28
Effec Tax Rate	100 00	50 00	16 00		-
Def Interval	0 18	0 20	0 93	1 51	1 48
Sus Grth Rate	10 87	14 09	12 96	8 90	14 54

SUBSIDIARY & ASSOCIATED COMPANIES

FEDGEN REGTE UITGIFTE BPK
FEDMYNBOU BELEGGINGS BPK
GENCOR LTD
HOLLARDSTRAAT SES BELEGGINGS BPK

INVESTMENTS

None

GENCOR LTD

ABBREVIATION : GENCOR

JSE SHORT CODE : GMF

SECTOR : Mining Financial-Mining Houses

SHAREHOLDERS

Who Owns Whom's Assessment of the Identity of the Ultimate Controlling Shareholder:
SANLAM VIA GENCOR BEHEREND

SHAREHOLDER	PERCENTAGE 1992	1991
CONSOLIDATED NOM P/L	37 5	37 6
GENCOR BEHEREND LTD	10 9	10 8
SA MUTUAL	7 5	7 2
STD BANK NOM TVL P/L	6 1	5 6
HOLLARDSTRAAT SES INV BPK	5 0	5 0
CMB NOM P/L	3 4	1 1
SOUTHERN LIFE ASSOC LTD	2 6	2 9
LIBERTY LIFE ASSOC OF AFRICA LTD	2 3	2 5
FEDGEN REGTE-UITGIFTE LTD	2 0	2 0
EIGHTY ONE MAIN STREET NOM LTD	1 8	1 5
LONDON CONTROL ACCOUNT	1 4	1 7
ENGINEERING INDUSTRIES PENS FUND	1 0	- -
YSKOR PENS FUND	-	1 1
SANLAM	---	2 0
TOTAL	81 5	80 9

DIRECTORS :
DALING MH ,DE BEER TL ,FOUCHE JH
GILBERTSON BP (Executive Chairman)
HUNT-DAVIS DNA ,OFFICER NC ,SMITH BA
STEENKAMP TI ,THOMAS GS ,VAN AS E

REGISTRATION NUMBER : 01/01232/06

REGISTERED OFFICE
General Mining Building, 6 Hollard Street
Johannesburg
2001
TEL 011-376 9111
FAX 011-836 8708

TRANSFER SECRETARY
Central Registrars Ltd
P O Box 4844, Johannesburg
2000
TEL 011-331 0051

COMPANY SECRETARY
L P Fourie

NATURE OF BUSINESS
A Mining House with significant interests in gold, platinum, coal & mineral products, forestry, oil gas, ferroalloys, paper, packaging, engineering, food, construction supplies, international freight & trading, health care, chemicals & electronics

Gencor controls quoted Sappi, Trans-Natal Coal, Engen, Impala Platinum, Genbel & Malhold.

BANKERS :
Trust Bank of Africa Ltd, Volkskas Ltd

AUDITORS :
KPMG Aiken & Peat, Coopers Theron Du Toit

FAMILIAR BRAND NAMES
N/A

CONTRIBUTION BY ACTIVITY
Gengold (% of earnings) (8.0%)
Implats (8.0%)
Trans-Natal (7.0%)
Samancor (11.0%)
Minerals (5.0%)
International & other (1.0%)
Sappi (15.0%)
Malbak (10.0%)
Engen (20.0%)
Genbel & Investments (25.0%)
Exploration (Genmin) (-7.0%)
Corporate (Genmin) (-1.0%)
Corporate (Gencor) (-1.0%)

YEAR END : August

DIVIDEND : Ords 4c

Interim No 128	(Ldr)11/05/90	(Pay)01/06/90	Amt(c)14
Final No 129	(Ldr)09/11/90	(Pay)30/11/90	Amt(c)26
Interim No 130	(Ldr)10/05/91	(Pay)30/05/91	Amt(c)15
Final No 131	(Ldr)08/11/91	(Pay)29/11/91	Amt(c)28
Interim No 132	(Ldr)31/01/92	(Pay)29/05/92	Amt(c)16
Final No 133	(Ldr)06/11/92	(Pay)26/11/92	Amt(c)29

NUMBER OF EMPLOYEES : 230643

CAPITAL STRUCTURE

	AUTHORISED	ISSUED
6% Cum Prefs R2	250000	250000
Ords 4c	1500000000	1376125873

FINANCIAL STATISTICS (AT FINANCIAL YEAR END)

(Amts in R'000)	1992 Aug	1991 Aug	1990 Aug	1989 Aug	1988 Aug
Ord S/H Int	10985000	8389000	7423000	6004000	3366000
Long Trm Loans	602000	592000	486000	963000	752000
Iss Ord Share	1376126	1176176	1176176	102418	82455
Total Liab	1293000	1319000	968000	1519000	1278000
Current Liab	691000	727000	482000	556000	526000
Total Assets	12278000	9708000	8391000	7523000	4644000
Current Assets	2814000	2241000	2059000	1775000	604000
Debtors	470000	452000	511000	457000	216000
Inventory	343000	486000	520000	-	-
Oper Profit	21000	197000	80000	-99000	457000
Interest Paid	84000	88000	94000	76000	125000
Tax Paid	109000	240000	23000	8000	14000
Prf af Int&Tax	765000	766000	937000	601000	318000
Prf att Ord Sh	1261000	1405000	1504000	1048000	442000
Btm Line Earn	1251000	1425000	1494000	1267000	435000
Dividend Paid	587000	506000	470000	281000	149000
Mkt Prce(c) YE	1095	1230	1075	10200	5425
Depreciation	18000	21000	19000	14000	9000

PER SHARE STATISTICS (CENTS)

Net Asst Val	798.26	713.24	631.11	5862.25	4082.23
Net Earnings	98.80	119.50	125.80	105.50	485.00
Dividends	45.00	43.00	40.00	34.00	180.00
Cash Flow	63.95	73.55	81.12	62.15	594.87

RATIOS AND OTHER INFORMATION

Mrk Cap(R000)	15068580	14466965	12643892	10446636	4473184
Current Ratio	4.07	3.08	4.27	3.19	1.15
Quik/Acid Tst	3.58	2.41	3.19	3.19	1.15
Debt/Ass Rat	0.10	0.13	0.12	0.20	0.27
L T L Tot Ass	0.04	0.05	0.06	0.12	0.15
Debt to Eqity	0.11	0.15	0.13	0.24	0.37
Interest Cover	8.25	9.28	8.83	7.92	3.66
Ret on Assets	11.84	17.85	19.02	15.74	19.83
Ret on Equity%	11.48	16.75	20.26	17.46	19.70
Price/Earnings	11.08	10.29	8.55	96.68	11.19
Divid Cover	2.20	2.78	3.15	3.10	2.69
Divid Yield	4.11	3.50	3.72	0.33	3.32
Earning Yield%	9.02	9.72	11.70	1.03	8.94
NAV % Mrk Pr	72.90	57.99	58.71	57.47	75.25
Effec Tax Rate	38.12	31.09	11.90	-4.35	4.22
Def Interval	0.63	0.61	0.51	0.88	1.55
Sus Grth Rate	6.14	10.72	13.93	12.77	8.70

SUBSIDIARY & ASSOCIATED COMPANIES

ALUSAF (PTY) LTD (41%)
ANGLOVAAL HOLDINGS LTD (20%)
BEATRIX MINES LTD
BUSHBUCK VENTURES (PTY) LTD
ENGEN LTD
GENBEL INVESTMENTS LTD (50%)
IMPALA PLATINUM HOLDINGS LTD (42%)
KEELEY GROUP HOLDINGS LTD (27,6%)
KINROSS MINES LTD (34%)
MALBAK LIMITED (MALBAK) (21%)
MALHOLD LTD (48%)
ORYX GOLD HOLDINGS LTD
RICHBAY MINE HOLDINGS (PTY) LTD (50%)
RICHBAY SMELTER HOLDINGS (PTY) LTD (50%)
RUC MINING CONTRACTING CO (PTY) LTD (50%)
SAMANCOR LTD (41%)
SAPPI LTD (50%)
ST HELENA GOLD MINES LTD (24%)
TRANS NATAL COAL CORP LTD (45%)
TRANSVAAL MINING AND FINANCE CO. LTD
UNISEL GOLD MINES LTD (40%)
WINKELHAAK MINES LTD (40%)

INVESTMENTS

BRACKEN MINES LTD (11%)
BUFFELSFONTEIN GOLD MINING CO. LTD (9%)
GROOTVLEI PROPRIETARY MINES LTD (15%)
KELGRAN LTD (14,4%)
LESLIE GOLD MINES LTD (10%)
STILFONTEIN GOLD MINING CO LTD (10%)
WEST RAND CONSOLIDATED MINES LTD (13.2%)

GENERAL OPTICAL CO LTD

ABBREVIATION : GEN-OPTIC

JSE SHORT CODE : GOC

SECTOR : Industrial-Pharmaceutical & Medical

SHAREHOLDERS

Who Owns Whom's Assessment of the Identity of the Ultimate Controlling Shareholder:
DIRECTORS

SHAREHOLDER	PERCENTAGE 1992	1991
NEDBANK NOM LTD	21 0	21 0
ILLMAN B	10 7	10 7
DALGLAND NOM P/L	9 9	9 9
ANDERGAL NOM P/L	9 9	9 9
LIBRARY CHAMBERS NOM P/L	8 6	8 6
STD BANK NOM TVL P/L	7 8	7 8
FERLIM NOM LTD	5 2	5 2
LANDCO P/L	3 6	3 6
SONRIC P/L	3 0	3 0
FIRST NAT NOM P/L	2 4	2 4
ABRAHAMSON A E	2 1	2 0
EXMIL SA P/L	1 9	1 9
TOTAL	85 8	85 7

DIRECTORS :
ABRAHAMSON AE THE HON (Chairman),ABRAHAMSON LP
GERBER LL ,GODFREY ES ,JUGMANS GE
MANSELL VG (Deputy Chairman),SALOMON FS
SHEAR BE ,SMOLLAN SS

REGISTRATION NUMBER : 05/31268/06

REGISTERED OFFICE
Genop Centre, 2 Ove Street
New Doornfontein
2094
TEL 011-402 2325
FAX 011-402 9340

TRANSFER SECRETARY
Central Registrars Ltd
P O Box 4844, Johannesburg
2000
TEL 011-331 0051

COMPANY SECRETARY
E S Godfrey

NATURE OF BUSINESS
The company and its subsidiaries carry on the business of manufacturers, distributors, merchants & agents in respect of optical consumer & capital goods, pharmaceuticals & ancillary equipment, as well as the servicing, renting & leasing of such equipment

BANKERS :
Standard Bank of SA Ltd, Nedcor Bank Ltd

AUDITORS :
Ironsides Morrison Murray

FAMILIAR BRAND NAMES
AOSEPT,PROGRESSIVS

CONTRIBUTION BY ACTIVITY
N/A

YEAR END : June

DIVIDEND : Ords 20c

Interim No 51	(Ldr)20/04/90	(Pay)04/06/90	Amt(c)5
Final No 52	(Ldr)16/11/90	(Pay)03/12/90	Amt(c)11
Interim No 53	(Ldr)19/04/91	(Pay)03/06/91	Amt(c)5
Final No 54	(Ldr)15/11/91	(Pay)02/12/91	Amt(c)15
Interim No 55	(Ldr)10/04/92	(Pay)01/06/92	Amt(c)5
Final No 56	(Ldr)20/11/92	(Pay)07/12/92	Amt(c)15

NUMBER OF EMPLOYEES : 450

CAPITAL STRUCTURE

	AUTHORISED	ISSUED
Ords 20c	5000000	2755150

FINANCIAL STATISTICS (AT FINANCIAL YEAR END)

(Amts in R'000)	1992 Jun	1991 Jun	1990 Jun	1989 Jun	1988 Jun
Ord S/H Int	13017	11540	9904	8772	7598
Long Trm Loans	8978	7036	6889	6692	3690
Iss Ord Share	2755	2755	2733	2733	2733
Total Liab	32405	27154	24343	21678	13954
Current Liab	23427	20118	17454	14986	10264
Total Assets	45292	38564	34117	30310	21412
Intang Assets	130	130	130	140	140
Current Assets	34169	28796	23850	20681	15450
Debtors	18078	13872	11151	9583	8121
Inventory	16062	14896	12677	10842	7069
Oper Profit	7046	6699	5832	5148	3303
Interest Paid	3092	2823	2359	1961	757
Tax Paid	1927	1766	1549	1576	1287
Prf af Int&Tax	2027	2110	1924	1611	1259
Prf att Ord Sh	2027	2110	1569	1611	1259
Btm Line Earn	2027	2110	1569	1611	1259
Dividend Paid	551	550	437	437	383
Mkt Prce(c) YE	500	400	365	400	400
Depreciation	1745	1445	1194	942	677

PER SHARE STATISTICS (CENTS)

Net Asst Val	467 77	414 16	357 63	315 84	272 89
Net Earnings	73 60	76 57	57 40	58 95	46 10
Dividends	20 00	20 00	16 00	16 00	14 00
Cash Flow	134 81	134 37	121 30	111 34	79 91

RATIOS AND OTHER INFORMATION

Mrk Cap(R000)	13775	11020	9975	10932	10932
Current Ratio	1 46	1 43	1 37	1 38	1 51
Quik/Acid Tst	0 77	0 69	0 64	0 66	0 82
Debt/Ass Rat	0 69	0 67	0 68	0 68	0 63
L T L Tot Ass	0 17	0 15	0 17	0 19	0 15
Debt to Eqity	2 39	2 24	2 34	2 36	1 77
Interest Cover	2 28	2 37	2 47	2 63	4 36
Ret on Assets	15 56	17 37	17 09	16 98	15 43
Ret on Equity%	15 57	18 28	15 84	18 37	16 57
Price/Earnings	6 79	5 22	6 36	6 79	8 68
Divid Cover	3 68	3 83	3 59	3 68	3 29
Divid Yield	4 00	5 00	4 38	4 00	3 50
Earning Yield%	14 72	19 14	15 73	14 74	11 53
NAV % Mrk Pr	93 55	103 54	97 98	78 96	68 22
Effec Tax Rate	50 05	41 59	37 95	32 29	40 65
Def Interval	4 03	3 21	3 71	3 61	2 52
Sus Grth Rate	11 34	13 52	11 43	13 38	11 53

SUBSIDIARY & ASSOCIATED COMPANIES

AMPORT (PTY) LTD
ASSOCIATED MEDICAL PRODUCTS (PTY) LTD
AUDAN COURT (PTY) LTD
AURUM OPTICS (PTY) LTD
CENTRE CITY WHOLESALE OPTICIANS (PTY) LT
CONCEPT OPTICAL COMPANY (PTY) LTD
FISH OPTICAL COMPANY (S A) LTD
GENERAL OPTICAL CO (CAPE) (PTY) LTD
GENERAL OPTICAL CO (LESOTHO) (PTY) LTD
GENERAL OPTICAL CO (SWAZILAND) (PTY) LT
GENOP CENTRE (PTY) LTD
HAWKINS OPTICAL COMPANY LTD
NUTROSOL (PTY) LTD
OPTICAL INDUSTRIES LTD

PCL LABORATORIES (PTY) LTD
REPUBLIC OPTOMETRIC SUPPLIES (PTY) LTD
SHEAR OPTICAL (PTY) LTD
VACUUM COATING (PTY) LTD

INVESTMENTS

None

GENTYRE INDUSTRIES LTD

ABBREVIATION : GENTYRE-A

JSE SHORT CODE : GTA

SECTOR : Industrial-Motor

SHAREHOLDERS

Who Owns Whom's Assessment of the Identity of the Ultimate Controlling Shareholder:
FS GROUP VIA W & A

SHAREHOLDER	PERCENTAGE 1992	1991
HUNTS MANUFACTURING CO P/L	78 4	1 6
FIRST NAT NOM P/L	7 3	7 3
LIBERTY LIFE ASSOC OF AFRICA LTD	5 4	5 4
GENERAL TYRE SHARE INCENTIVE TRUST	1 6	1 8
GENTYRE INDUSTRIES SHARE INC TRUST	1 4	- -
STD BANK NOM TVL P/L	1 1	---
HUNTS LTD	---	76 7
TOTAL	95 2	92 8

DIRECTORS :
COHEN N ,LIEBESMAN JM ,NICHOLSON RG
PRETORIUS VTK ,ROLFE TW (Chairman)
SCHLESINGER AM ,SPROULE GN (Financial Director)
TUTTON CW (Chief Executive & M D

REGISTRATION NUMBER : 05/24337/06

REGISTERED OFFICE
6th Floor, FSI Centre, 35 Siemert Road
Doornfontein
2094
TEL 011-402 3200
FAX 011-402 7508

TRANSFER SECRETARY
Mercantile Registrars Ltd
P O Box 1053, Johannesburg
2000
TEL 011-333 8181

COMPANY SECRETARY
B E Liebesman

NATURE OF BUSINESS
The company is a manufacturer and distributor of natural and synthetic motor vehicle rubber products, including motor vehicle tyres and tubes, and of industrial rubber products of all kinds

BANKERS :
First National Bank of SA Ltd
Standard Bank of SA Ltd, Nedcor Bank Ltd

AUDITORS :
Deloitte Pim Goldby

FAMILIAR BRAND NAMES
GENERAL,HYDRAFLEX

CONTRIBUTION BY ACTIVITY
Tyre Division (% operating profit) (86 0%)
Industrial Rubber Products (14 0%)

YEAR END : December

DIVIDEND : Ords "A" 10c

Interim	(Ldr)28/09/90	(Pay)15/10/90	Amt(c)55
Final	(Ldr)05/04/91	(Pay)26/04/91	Amt(c)57
Interim	(Ldr)04/10/91	(Pay)21/10/91	Amt(c)55
Final	(Ldr)10/04/92	(Pay)29/04/92	Amt(c)57
Interim	(Ldr)25/09/92	(Pay)12/10/92	Amt(c)55

NUMBER OF EMPLOYEES : 3814

CAPITAL STRUCTURE

	AUTHORISED	ISSUED
Ords "A" 10c	19600000	10215250
Ords "B" 10c	5400000	5400000
5,5% Cum Prefs R2	400000	250000

FINANCIAL STATISTICS (AT FINANCIAL YEAR END)

(Amts in R'000)	1991 Dec	1990 Dec	1989 Dec	1988 Dec	1987 Dec
Ord S/H Int	284949	241226	194611	167208	142974
Long Trm Loans	6679	7842	5464	17964	12357
Iss Ord Share	250000	15615	15565	15565	15565
Total Liab	158803	82098	96625	80328	69370
Current Liab	152124	74256	91161	62364	57013
Total Assets	443752	323324	291236	247536	212344
Current Assets	309520	216202	212413	179712	112925
Debtors	88534	90146	95525	95050	54859
Inventory	85634	83693	73792	62403	56133
Turnover	484387	520001	452160	388531	330727
Oper Profit	53214	64794	64287	56791	39929
Interest Paid	1115	1366	1144	4138	2173
Tax Paid	-684	203	22961	22421	15704
Prf af Int&Tax	61302	68963	43611	31133	22052
Prf att Ord Sh	61212	68844	43583	31079	22013
Btm Line Earn	61212	63276	42564	34663	25135
Dividend Paid	17489	17461	14476	10429	7471
Mkt Prce(c) YE	2400	1725	1850	924	750
Depreciation	16968	15373	11685	11108	9161

PER SHARE STATISTICS (CENTS)

Net Asst Val	113 98	1544 84	1250 31	1074 26	918 56
Net Earnings	392 00	442 10	280 00	200 00	142 10
Dividends	112 00	112 00	93 00	67 00	48 00
Cash Flow	495 86	539 97	274 77	330 50	210 99

RATIOS AND OTHER INFORMATION

Mrk Cap(R000)	6000000	269359	287953	143821	116738
Current Ratio	2 03	2 91	2 33	2 88	1 98
Quik/Acid Tst	1 47	1 78	1 52	1 88	1 00
A/C Rec T/ovr	5 47	5 77	4 73	4 09	6 03
Tot Ass T/ovr	1 09	1 61	1 55	1 57	1 56
Debt/Ass Rat	0 34	0 23	0 31	0 25	0 29
L T L Tot Ass		-	-	-	0 02
Debt to Eqity	0 53	0 31	0 47	0 37	0 42
Interest Cover	48 34	47 95	56 32	13 94	18 38

Oper Prof Mrg	10.99	12.46	14.22	14.62	12.07
Net Prof Marg%	12.64	13.24	9.64	8.00	6.66
Ret on Assets	13.91	21.81	23.25	23.31	18.80
Ret on Equity%	21.48	28.54	22.39	18.59	15.40
Price/Earnings	6.12	3.90	6.61	4.62	5.28
Divid Cover	3.50	3.95	3.01	2.99	2.96
Divid Yield	4.67	6.49	5.03	7.25	6.40
Earning Yield%	16.33	25.63	15.14	21.65	18.95
NAV % Mrk Pr	4.75	89.56	67.58	116.26	122.47
Effec Tax Rate	0.56	1.09	52.50	23.98	37.56
Def Interval	1.01	0.07	0.11	0.01	0.13
Sus Grth Rate	15.34	21.30	14.96	12.35	10.17

SUBSIDIARY & ASSOCIATED COMPANIES

BERDSCAR LTD
BERDSCAR LTD (UNITED KINGDOM)
CORROSIVE RESISTANT COATINGS (PTY) LTD
FALMOUTH PROPERTIES LTD (ZAMBIA)
FARMEC (PTY) LTD
FERROPLASTIC & RUBBER INDUSTRIES (PTY) L
FLEXIBLE TUBE HOLDINGS LTD
FLEXIBLE TUBING AFRICA LTD
GENERAL BELTINGS (PVT) LTD (ZIMBABWE)
GENERAL BELTINGS (SA) (PTY) LTD
GENERAL TYRE & RUBBER CO LTD (ZAMBIA)
GENERAL TYRE & RUBBER CO SWAZILAND (PTY)
GENERAL TYRE & RUBBER COMPANY (SA) (PTY)
GENERAL TYRE AND INDUSTRIAL PRODUCTS (PV
GENERAL TYRE AND RUBBER CO (PVT) LTD (ZI
GENERAL TYRE INDUSTRIAL PRODUCTS LTD
GENTYRE PROPERTIES (BOKSBURG) (PTY) LTD
GENTYRE PROPERTIES (INDUSTRIA) (PTY) LTD
HIGH PRESSURE HOSE SERVICES (PTY) LTD
HYDRAFLEX (PTY) LTD
HYDRAULIC COMPONENT SUPPLIES (PTY) LTD
MINING AND INDUSTRIAL RUBBER CO. (PTY) L
MIRMADE INVESTMENTS (PTY) LTD
PARAGON RUBBER CO. (PTY) LTD
PIGOTT MASKEW & CO. LTD
PIGOTT MASKEW (PVT) LTD (ZIMBABWE)
PIGOTT MASKEW LTD (ZAMBIA)
POWERVILLE ENGINEERING WORKS (PTY) LTD
POWERVILLE SHARE BLOCK (PTY) LTD
RUBBER & PLASTIC INDUSTRIES (PTY) LTD
RUBBER CRUMBING (PTY) LTD
TRIPLE A RUBBER CO. (PTY) LTD
UNIROYAL TYRE AND RUBBER (SA) (PTY) LTD

INVESTMENTS

None

GLODINA HOLDINGS LTD

ABBREVIATION : GLODINA

JSE SHORT CODE : GDA

SECTOR : Industrial-Clothing, Footwear & Textiles

SHAREHOLDERS

Who Owns Whom's Assessment of the Identity of the Ultimate Controlling Shareholder:
BALLADON FAMILY

SHAREHOLDER	PERCENTAGE 1992	1991
B J BALLADON & SONS P/L	69.9	69.9
UTAS INV P/L	5.1	5.1
GLODINA EMPLOYEES SHARE TRUST	4.5	4.5
STD BANK NOM TVL P/L	3.7	3.7
CONSOLIDATED COTTON CORP	2.2	2.2
MOORE P H	1.5	1.0
FIRST NAT NOM P/L	1.3	1.3
BARTEL H O	1.2	---
TOTAL	89.3	87.7

DIRECTORS :
BALLADON AGS (Chairman),BALLADON JB ,HALL ME
LUIZ E ,MALLACH R

REGISTRATION NUMBER : 86/04150/06

REGISTERED OFFICE
1 Anderson Rd, Hammarsdale
Natal
3700
TEL: 0325-62 150
FAX: 0325-61 882

TRANSFER SECRETARY
Consolidated Share Registrars Ltd
P O Box 61051, Marshalltown
2107
TEL: 011-492 1620

COMPANY SECRETARY
M Balladon

NATURE OF BUSINESS
The group manufactures household textile products including baby napkins, towels & face cloths, and warp knitted fabrics for the garment industry.

BANKERS :
First National Bank of SA Ltd, Bankorp Ltd

AUDITORS :
Deloitte Pim Goldby

FAMILIAR BRAND NAMES
GLODINA,REGENT,WEAVIER

CONTRIBUTION BY ACTIVITY
Retail (% of Turnover) (75.8%)
Hotels (7.4%)
Goverment (5.2%)
Industrial (9.9%)
Exports (1.7%)

YEAR END : December

DIVIDEND : (Ldr)15/09/89 (Pay)06/10/89

NUMBER OF EMPLOYEES : 1585

CAPITAL STRUCTURE

	AUTHORISED	ISSUED
Ords 1c	40000000	19476305

FINANCIAL STATISTICS (AT FINANCIAL YEAR END)

(Amts in R'000)	1991 Dec	1990 Dec	1989 Dec	1988 Dec	1987 Dec

Ord S/H Int	35342	36262	37175	31953	28124
Long Trm Loans	5048	6125	4860	7327	3743
Iss Ord Share	19476	19476	19476	18750	18750
Total Liab	43496	41442	35779	38370	20755
Current Liab	38448	35317	30919	31043	17012
Total Assets	78838	77704	69560	66929	45485
Intang Assets	*	*	3394	3394	3394
Current Assets	46116	44441	38871	38776	26996
Debtors	23265	21544	15523	16547	13842
Inventory	22462	22263	22536	21915	13148
Turnover	94284	89504	75142	62709	50903
Oper Profit	8012	9225	9191	9168	9627
Interest Paid	5715	5636	4859	2029	1507
Tax Paid	-	-	11	170	3234
Prf af Int&Tax	2747	3859	6204	7508	5320
Prf att Ord Sh	2747	3859	6204	7508	5320
Btm Line Earn	-920	4602	6204	7488	5320
Dividend Paid	-	-	2435	3000	563
Mkt Prce(c) YE	50	80	170	190	190
Depreciation	2774	2498	2124	1856	1554

PER SHARE STATISTICS (CENTS)

Net Asst Val	181 46	186 19	173 45	152 31	131 89
Net Earnings	14 10	19 80	31 90	38 60	35 90
Dividends	-	-	12 50	16 00	14 40
Cash Flow	28 35	32 64	42 82	50 34	46 44

RATIOS AND OTHER INFORMATION

Mrk Cap(R000)	9738	15581	33109	35625	35625
Current Ratio	1 20	1 26	1 26	1 25	1 59
Quik/Acid Tst	0 62	0 63	0 53	0 54	0 81
A/C Rec T/ovr	4 05	4 15	4 84	3 79	3 68
Tot Ass T/ovr	1 20	1 15	1 08	0 94	1 12
Debt/Ass Rat	0 55	0 53	0 51	0 57	0 46
L T L Tot Ass	0 06	0 08	0 07	0 11	0 08
Debt to Eqity	1 23	1 14	0 96	1 20	0 74
Interest Cover	1 40	1 64	1 89	4 52	6 39
Oper Prof Mrg	8 50	10 31	12 23	14 62	18 91
Net Prof Marg%	2 91	4 31	8 26	11 97	10 45
Ret on Assets	10 73	12 22	15 92	14 50	22 12
Ret on Equity%	7 77	10 64	16 69	23 50	18 92
Price/Earnings	3 55	4 04	5 33	4 92	5 29
Divid Cover	-	-	2 55	2 41	2 49
Divid Yield	-	-	7 35	8 42	7 58
Earning Yield%	28 20	24 75	18 76	20 32	18 89
NAV % Mrk Pr	362 93	232 74	102 03	80 17	69 42
Effec Tax Rate	-	-	-	1 24	37 81
Def Interval	5 14	3 98	2 78	2 62	1 33
Sus Grth Rate	7 77	10 64	10 14	14 11	16 91

SUBSIDIARY & ASSOCIATED COMPANIES

CARLO DE FIRENZE (PTY) LTD
DANODUV INVESTMENTS (PTY) LTD
LANATEX WEAVING MANUFACTURERS (PTY) LTD
TEXTOWEL WEAVERS (PTY) LTD

INVESTMENTS

None

GOLD FIELDS COAL LTD

ABBREVIATION : G F-COAL

JSE SHORT CODE : GFC

SECTOR : Mining-Coal

SHAREHOLDERS

Who Owns Whom's Assessment of the Identity of the Ultimate Controlling Shareholder: GFSA

SHAREHOLDER	PERCENTAGE 1992	1991
MINU NOM LTD	79 2	79 2
STD BANK NOM TVL P/L	5 8	6 8
TOTAL	85 0	86 0

DIRECTORS :
ADAN MJ ,FENTON CT ,FULLER-GOOD MR
HOPWOOD JG (Chairman & Managing Dir)
HOUGHTON AB ,JANISCH PR ,KAHLE H ,ROBINSON RL

REGISTRATION NUMBER : 01/01124/06

REGISTERED OFFICE
75 Fox Street, Johannesburg
2001
TEL 011-639 9111
FAX 011-639 2101/2

TRANSFER SECRETARY
Gold Fields of SA Ltd
P O Box 1167, Johannesburg
2000
TEL 011-639 9111

COMPANY SECRETARY
Gold Fields of SA Ltd

NATURE OF BUSINESS
The company mines coal and operates the Greenside Colliery in the Witbank area of the Tvl It has a 50% interest in the Matla Joint Venture, and holds and leases mineral rights, freehold property and coal rights in the Heilbron and Sasolburg areas, OFS, and Bethal and Witbank districts of the Tvl

BANKERS :
Standard Bank of SA Ltd

AUDITORS :
Ernst & Young

FAMILIAR BRAND NAMES
N/A

CONTRIBUTION BY ACTIVITY
N/A

YEAR END : December

DIVIDEND : Ords 50c

Final No 153	(Ldr)29/12/89	(Pay)07/02/90	Amt(c)55
Interim No 154	(Ldr)29/06/90	(Pay)08/08/90	Amt(c)40
Final No 155	(Ldr)28/12/90	(Pay)06/02/91	Amt(c)50
Interim No 156	(Ldr)28/06/91	(Pay)07/08/91	Amt(c)40
Final No 157	(Ldr)27/12/91	(Pay)05/02/92	Amt(c)60
Interim No 158	(Ldr)26/06/92	(Pay)05/08/92	Amt(c)40

NUMBER OF EMPLOYEES : 2509

CAPITAL STRUCTURE

	AUTHORISED	ISSUED
Ords 50c	25000000	16862721

FINANCIAL STATISTICS (AT FINANCIAL YEAR END)

(Amts in R'000)	1991 Dec	1990 Dec	1989 Dec	1988	1987
Ord S/H Int	184967	174889	168936	170728	163119
Long Trm Loans	4459	5235	-	25742	24422
Iss Ord Share	16863	16863	16863	16863	16863
Total Liab	45987	48229	37190	51484	48844
Current Liab	41528	42994	37190	25742	24422
Total Assets	230954	223118	206126	242770	228502
Current Assets	70584	65438	60156	46300	40961
Debtors	33588	26030	23559	-	-
Inventory	20854	15286	7567	46300	40961
Turnover	271438	259239	232404	197972	174211
Oper Profit	44005	39010	39257	32309	31965
Interest Paid	-	-	-	-	10
Tax Paid	22041	20038	18712	11594	11753
Prf af Int&Tax	27887	27226	21182	20715	20212
Prf att Ord Sh	27887	27226	21182	13515	13512
Btm Line Earn	27887	22276	21182	13515	13512
Dividend Paid	16863	15176	16020	13490	13490
Mkt Prce(c) YE	825	850	900	600	525

PER SHARE STATISTICS (CENTS)

Net Asst Val	1096.88	1037.12	1001.81	1012.44	967.32
Net Earnings	165.00	120.00	96.00	-	-
Dividends	100.00	90.00	95.00	-	-
Cash Flow	165.37	161.45	125.61	122.84	119.86

RATIOS AND OTHER INFORMATION

Mrk Cap(R000)	139120	143336	151767	101178	88531
Current Ratio	1.70	1.52	1.62	1.80	1.68
Quik/Acid Tst	1.20	1.17	1.41	-	-
A/C Rec T/ovr	8.08	9.96	9.86	-	-
Tot Ass T/ovr	1.18	1.16	1.13	0.82	0.76
Debt/Ass Rat	0.18	0.19	0.18	0.21	0.21
L T L Tot Ass	-	-	-	0.11	0.11
Debt to Eqity	0.22	0.25	0.22	0.30	0.30
Interest Cover	-	-	-	-	3197.50
Oper Prof Mrg	16.21	15.05	16.89	16.32	18.35
Net Prof Marg%	10.27	10.50	9.11	6.83	7.76
Ret on Assets	21.62	21.18	19.35	13.31	13.99
Ret on Equity%	15.08	15.57	12.54	7.92	8.28
Price/Earnings	5.00	7.08	9.38	-	-
Divid Cover	1.65	1.33	1.01	-	-
Divid Yield	12.12	10.59	10.56	-	-
Earning Yield%	20.00	14.12	10.67	-	-
NAV % Mrk Pr	132.96	122.01	111.31	168.74	184.25
Effec Tax Rate	46.38	43.26	47.67	35.88	36.78
Def Interval	-	-	-	1.24	1.21
Sus Grth Rate	5.96	6.89	3.06	0.01	0.01

SUBSIDIARY & ASSOCIATED COMPANIES

APEX MINES LTD
MATLA JOINT VENTURE (50%)
MOOIPLAATS COAL HOLDINGS (PTY) LTD
VAALKRANS COAL, COKE AND FIRECLAY SYNDIC

INVESTMENTS

None

GOLD FIELDS NAMIBIA LTD

ABBREVIATION : GFNAMIB

JSE SHORT CODE : GNM

SECTOR : Mining Financial-Mining Holding

SHAREHOLDERS

Who Owns Whom's Assessment of the Identity of the Ultimate Controlling Shareholder: GFSA

SHAREHOLDER	PERCENTAGE 1992	1991
CONSOLIDATED NOM P/L	---	2.8
EIGHTY ONE MAIN STREET NOM LTD	---	13.5
MINU NOM LTD	---	8.0
SOUTHERN LIFE ASSOC LTD	---	4.9
STD BANK NOM TVL P/L	---	3.2
WAL HOLDINGS AG	---	61.1
TOTAL	---	93.4

DIRECTORS :
FENTON CT (Chairman),HOPWOOD JG ,JANISCH PR
ROBINSON RL ,VAN ROOYEN BR ,WRIGHT AJ

REGISTRATION NUMBER : 88/04951/10

REGISTERED OFFICE
4th Floor, Kenya House, cnr Leutwein & Koerner Streets
Windhoek
9000
TEL: 011-639 9111
FAX: 011-639 2101/2

TRANSFER SECRETARY
Gold Fields of SA Ltd
P O Box 1167, Johannesburg
2000
TEL: 011-639 9111

COMPANY SECRETARY
Gold Fields of SA Ltd

NATURE OF BUSINESS
A mining house operating in Namibia. Subsidiaries conduct mining operations, primarily for copper & lead. By-products from smelter operations include silver, gold, pyrite, sodium antimonite, cadmium & arsenic tri-oxide.

BANKERS :
Standard Bank of SA Ltd

AUDITORS :
Ernst & Young

FAMILIAR BRAND NAMES
N/A

CONTRIBUTION BY ACTIVITY
N/A

YEAR END : December

DIVIDEND : Ords R1

Final No 4	(Ldr)29/12/89	(Pay)07/02/90	Amt(c)60
Interim No 5	(Ldr)29/06/90	(Pay)08/08/90	Amt(c)10

Final No 6 (Ldr)28/12/90 (Pay)06/02/91 Amt(c)25

NUMBER OF EMPLOYEES : 3659

CAPITAL STRUCTURE

	AUTHORISED	ISSUED
Ords R1	20000000	16000000

FINANCIAL STATISTICS (AT FINANCIAL YEAR END)

(Amts in R'000)	1991 Dec	1990 Dec	1989 Dec
Ord S/H Int	228196	235302	234310
Long Trm Loans	14210	15410	16610
Iss Ord Share	16000	16000	16000
Total Liab	47172	63003	75655
Current Liab	32962	47593	59045
Total Assets	275368	298305	309965
Current Assets	113833	133856	144838
Debtors	46513	33725	43584
Inventory	59039	66090	50559
Turnover	290638	338268	391308
Oper Profit	-14326	825	47517
Interest Paid	-	619	1618
Tax Paid	139	2428	19013
Prf af Int&Tax	-7106	6592	40180
Prf att Ord Sh	-7106	6592	40180
Btm Line Earn	-7106	6592	31951
Dividend Paid	-	5600	19200
Mkt Prce(c) YE	450	725	1000

PER SHARE STATISTICS (CENTS)

Net Asst Val	1426 23	1470 64	1464 44
Net Earnings	-44 00	36 00	178 00
Dividends	-	35 00	120 00
Cash Flow	-44 41	41 20	251 13

RATIOS AND OTHER INFORMATION

Mrk Cap(R000)	72000	116000	160000
Current Ratio	3 45	2 81	2 45
Quik/Acid Tst	1 66	1 42	1 60
A/C Rec T/ovr	6 25	10 03	8 98
Tot Ass T/ovr	1 06	1 13	1 26
Debt/Ass Rat	0 17	0 21	0 24
L T L Tot Ass	0 05	0 05	0 05
Debt to Eqity	0 21	0 27	0 32
Interest Cover	-	1 33	29 37
Oper Prof Mrg	-4 93	0 24	12 14
Net Prof Marg%	-2 44	1 95	10 27
Ret on Assets	-2 53	3 23	19 62
Ret on Equity%	-3 11	2 80	17 15
Price/Earnings	10 23	20 14	5 62
Divid Cover	-	1 03	1 48
Divid Yield	-	4 83	12 00
Earning Yield%	-9 78	4 97	17 80
NAV % Mrk Pr	316 94	202 85	146 44
Effec Tax Rate	-2 00	26 92	32 12
Def Interval	-0 17	0 18	-
Sus Grth Rate	-3 11	0 42	8 95

SUBSIDIARY & ASSOCIATED COMPANIES

BERG AUKAS LTD
GF NAMIBIA MINING LTD
GOLD FIELDS PROSPECTING CO (PTY) LTD
NAMIB MINES LTD
TSUMEB CORPORATION LTD
TSUMEB EXPLORATION CO LTD
TSUMEB PHARMACY (PTY) LTD

INVESTMENTS

None

GOLD FIELDS OF SA LTD

ABBREVIATION : GFSA

JSE SHORT CODE : GFS

SECTOR : Mining Financial-Mining Houses

SHAREHOLDERS

Who Owns Whom's Assessment of the Identity of the Ultimate Controlling Shareholder:
REMBRANDT / LIBERTY / MANAGEMENT

SHAREHOLDER	PERCENTAGE 1992	1991
MINU NOM LTD	43 7	43 8
FERMAIN NOM LTD	9 1	9 1
ANGLO AMERICAN GOLD INV CO LTD	7 1	7 1
ASHTREE INV P/L	6 0	6 1
NEDBANK NOM LTD	5 2	5 3
RESIDENT NOM LTD	3 8	3 9
STD BANK NOM TVL P/L	3 8	3 5
SA MUTUAL	3 4	3 5
FIRST NAT NOM P/L GATR DEPOT	1 4	1 3
EIGHTY ONE MAIN STREET NOM LTD	1 0	---
TOTAL	84 7	83 5

DIRECTORS :
DE VILLIERS HP
FENTON CT (Deputy Chairman & M D),FLACK PH
HOPWOOD JG (Executive Director)
MUNRO AH (Executive Director)
PLUMBRIDGE RA (Chairman & Chief Exec)
STEGMANN JA DR,STRAUSS CB DR
VAN ROOYEN BR (Executive Director),VAN WYK T ADV
WRIGHT AJ (Executive Director

REGISTRATION NUMBER : 05/04181/06

REGISTERED OFFICE
75 Fox Street, Johannesburg
2001
TEL 011-639 9111
FAX 011-639 2101/2

TRANSFER SECRETARY
Gold Fields of SA Ltd
P O Box 1167, Johannesburg
2000
TEL 011-639 9111

COMPANY SECRETARY
D C Dykes

NATURE OF BUSINESS
A mining & finance house with ordinary shares listed on the JHB, London, Paris, Zurich, Basle & Geneva stock exchanges Group activities include investment in mining and the processing of metals & minerals, and exploration and development of new projects in these fields The principal asset and

major source of income of the Grp is its portfolio of investments, mainly in precious metal mining companies.

BANKERS :
Standard Bank of SA Ltd

AUDITORS :
Ernst & Young

FAMILIAR BRAND NAMES
N/A

CONTRIBUTION BY ACTIVITY
Gold & Platinum (% Group Income) (57.0%)
Other Minerals (5.0%)
Financial & Mining Finance (18.0%)
Cash (16.0%)
Industrial & Property (4.0%)

YEAR END : June

DIVIDEND : Ords 5c

Interim No 84	(Ldr)02/02/90	(Pay)07/03/90	Amt(c)70
Final No 85	(Ldr)07/09/90	(Pay)26/09/90	Amt(c)130
Interim No 86	(Ldr)01/02/91	(Pay)06/03/91	Amt(c)70
Final No 87	(Ldr)06/09/91	(Pay)25/09/91	Amt(c)130
Interim No 88	(Ldr)07/02/92	(Pay)11/03/92	Amt(c)70
Final No 89	(Ldr)04/09/92	(Pay)23/09/92	Amt(c)130

NUMBER OF EMPLOYEES : 94540

CAPITAL STRUCTURE

	AUTHORISED	ISSUED
Ords 5c	105000000	96294137
Conv Red Cum Prefs 5c	20000000	4395721

FINANCIAL STATISTICS (AT FINANCIAL YEAR END)

(Amts in R'000)	1992 Jun	1991 Jun	1990 Jun	1989 Jun	1988 Jun
Ord S/H Int	2927000	2810000	2682000	1384900	1193300
Long Trm Loans	73000	60000	43000	38600	38900
Iss Ord Share	96294	96141	95960	81925	81818
Total Liab	265000	282000	254000	179700	166500
Current Liab	192000	222000	211000	141100	127600
Total Assets	3192000	3092000	2936000	1564600	1359800
Current Assets	750000	708000	633000	235000	230100
Debtors	142000	144000	143000	191200	174900
Oper Profit	55000	60000	119000	366700	330100
Interest Paid	12000	10000	10000	-	-
Tax Paid	27000	31000	73000	18800	8100
Prf af Int&Tax	315000	327000	379000	347900	322000
Prf att Ord Sh	302000	314000	361000	329800	307900
Btm Line Earn	303000	316000	458000	352500	324400
Dividend Paid	192000	192000	192000	163800	155400
Mkt Prce(c) YE	7125	7900	7700	7800	5250
Depreciation	9000	9000	8000	8100	8200

PER SHARE STATISTICS (CENTS)

Net Asst Val	3039.65	2922.79	2794.91	1690.45	1458.48
Net Earnings	314.00	328.00	393.00	403.00	377.00
Dividends	200.00	200.00	200.00	200.00	190.00
Cash Flow	323.26	336.31	402.32	412.73	386.84

RATIOS AND OTHER INFORMATION

Mrk Cap(R000)	6860948	7595139	7388920	6390150	4295445
Current Ratio	3.91	3.19	3.00	1.67	1.80
Quik/Acid Tst	3.91	3.19	3.00	1.67	1.80
Debt/Ass Rat	0.08	0.09	0.09	0.11	0.12
L T L Tot Ass	0.02	0.02	0.01	0.02	0.03
Debt to Eqity	0.09	0.10	0.09	0.13	0.14
Interest Cover	29.50	36.80	46.20	-	-
Ret on Assets	11.09	11.90	15.74	23.44	24.28
Ret on Equity%	10.32	11.17	13.46	23.81	25.80
Price/Earnings	22.69	24.09	19.59	19.35	13.93
Divid Cover	1.57	1.64	1.97	2.02	1.98
Divid Yield	2.81	2.53	2.60	2.56	3.62
Earning Yield%	4.41	4.15	5.10	5.17	7.18
NAV % Mrk Pr	42.66	37.00	36.30	21.67	27.78
Effec Tax Rate	62.79	58.00	66.97	5.13	2.18
Def Interval	0.02	0.03	0.03	0.11	0.12
Sus Grth Rate	3.76	4.34	6.30	11.99	12.78

SUBSIDIARY & ASSOCIATED COMPANIES

ACTEON TRADERS LTD
APEX MINES LTD
ASTEROID LTD (50%)
BERG AUKAS LTD (NAMIBIA)
BETHAL COAL (PTY) LTD
BLACK MOUNTAIN MINERAL DEVELOPMENT CO (P
BOSKOP AREAS (WEST WITS) LTD
DWARSRIVIER FARMS LTD
EXPLORATION TRUST LTD
GAMSBERG ZINC CORP. LTD (27%)
GF INDUSTRIAL HOLDINGS CO LTD
GF NAMIBIA MINING LTD
GLENOVER PHOSPHATE LTD
GOLD FIELDS BOTSWANA (PTY) LTD
GOLD FIELDS COAL LTD
GOLD FIELDS CORPORATE SERVICES LTD (UK)
GOLD FIELDS ECUADER LTD (GUERNSEY)
GOLD FIELDS GUERNSEY LTD
GOLD FIELDS INTERNATIONAL LTD
GOLD FIELDS INVESTMENTS LTD
GOLD FIELDS LABORATORIES (PTY) LTD
GOLD FIELDS MINERAL SERVICES LTD (UK)
GOLD FIELDS MINING AND DEVELOPMENT LTD
GOLD FIELDS NAMIBIA LTD (NAMIBIA)
GOLD FIELDS PRINTING (PTY) LTD
GOLD FIELDS PROSPECTING CO. (PTY) LTD (N
GOLD FIELDS SECURITY LIMITED (33%)
GOLD FIELDS VENEZUELA LTD (GUERNSEY)
GROOTPAN COAL LTD
INTERNATIONAL COBALT & MOLYBDENUM (PTY)
MARIKANA PLATINUM (PTY) LTD
MINDEV AND ASSOCIATED LTD (GUERNSEY)
MOOIPLAATS COAL HOLDINGS (PTY) LTD
NAMIB MINES LTD (NAMIBIA)
NORTHAM PLATINUM LTD
NOSTRA INVESTMENTS (PTY) LTD
O'OKIEP COPPER CO. LTD (49%)
RED HILL MINES LTD
REGBELEG MINERALE BELEGGINGS (EDMS) BPK
SHEEPMOOR COAL (PTY) LTD
TREFKOR (EDMS) BPK
TSUMEB CORPORATION LTD (NAMIBIA)
TSUMEB EXPLORATION CO. LTD (NAMIBIA)
TSUMEB PHARMACY (PTY) LTD (NAMIBIA)
VAALKRANS COAL, COKE AND FIRECLAY SYNDIC
VELLEFONTEIN TIN MINING CO LTD
VICMARG FARMS (PTY) LTD
WAL HOLDING AG (SWITZERLAND)
WATERBERG COAL LTD
WATERVAL (RUSTENBURG) PLATINUM MINING CO
WITWATERSRAND DEEP INVESTMENTS LTD
WITWATERSRAND DEEP LIMITED
ZWARTKLOOF MINING LTD

INVESTMENTS

COMMERCIAL UNION ASSURANCE COMPANY OF SA (2007050SH)
DEELKRAAL GOLD MINING CO LTD (49000000S)
DOORNFONTEIN GOLD MINING CO LTD (13200000S)

DRIEFONTEIN CONSOLIDATED LTD (68142500S)
EAST RAND GOLD & URANIUM CO (893500SH)
ELANDSRAND GOLD MINING CO. LTD (4,77%)
GOLD FIELDS COAL LTD (10200000S)
GOLD FIELDS NAMIBIA LTD (NAMIBIA) (9767297SH)
GOLD FIELDS PROPERTY CO LTD (4467501SH)
KLOOF GOLD MINING CO LTD (41091386S)
LIBANON GOLD MINING CO LTD (12315000S)
LIBERTY LIFE ASSOCIATION OF AFRICA LTD (2.03%)
ROOIBERG TIN LTD (13%)
SASOL LTD (2,3%)
SMALL BUSINESS DEV. CORP. (10,3%)
SOUTH DEEP EXPLORATION CO LTD (8,6%)
STANDARD BANK INVESTMENT CORP. LTD (9,9%)
THE CEMENTATION CO (AFRICA) LTD (2040000S)
VENTERSPOST GOLD MINING CO LTD (20000000S)
VLAKSFONTEIN GOLD MINING CO LTD (2500000SH)
VOGELSTRUISBULT METAL HOLDINGS LTD (9000000SH)
WESTERN DEEP LEVELS LTD (3,36%)
WESTERN DEEP LEVELS LTD (915000 SH)
WESTERN ULTRA DEEP LEVELS LTD (10,15%)
ZINC CORPORATION OF S.A. LTD (18%)

GOLD FIELDS PROPERTY CO LTD

ABBREVIATION : GF-PROPS

JSE SHORT CODE : GFP

SECTOR : Financial-Property

SHAREHOLDERS

Who Owns Whom's Assessment of the Identity of the Ultimate Controlling Shareholder:
GFSA

SHAREHOLDER	PERCENTAGE 1992	1991
DORBYL PENS FUND	---	3.2
EIGHTY ONE MAIN STREET NOM LTD	---	4.4
FIRST NAT NOM P/L	---	1.4
INDO-CHINA NOM SA P/L	---	2.1
MINU NOM LTD	---	51.6
MOON M W W	---	2.3
STD BANK NOM TVL P/L	---	5.9
GRAYSTON NOM P/L	---	1.7
TOTAL	---	72.6

DIRECTORS :
ADAN MJ ,ALVEY GP ,DAY BA
FULLER-GOOD MR (Chairman),MOOLMAN A
WOLFE-COTTE CA ,WRIGHT AJ

REGISTRATION NUMBER : 01/01078/06

REGISTERED OFFICE
75 Fox Street, Johannesburg
2001
TEL: 011-639 9111
FAX: 011-639 2101/2

TRANSFER SECRETARY
Gold Fields of SA Ltd
P O Box 1167, Johannesburg
2000
TEL: 011-639 9111

COMPANY SECRETARY
Gold Fields of SA Ltd

NATURE OF BUSINESS
The company holds investments in companies engaged in property holding and development, holds listed & unlisted securities, and its operations include the financing of group subsidiaries.

BANKERS :
Standard Bank of SA Ltd

AUDITORS :
Deloitte Pim Goldby

FAMILIAR BRAND NAMES
N/A

CONTRIBUTION BY ACTIVITY
Property (% profit before tax) (38.7%)
Gold (3.7%)
Other Mining (51.9%)
Energy (0.5%)
Mining Finance (2.6%)
Industrial & Commercial (2.6%)

YEAR END : December

DIVIDEND : Ords 2,5c

Final No 134	(Ldr)26/01/90	(Pay)28/02/90	Amt(c)24
Interim No 135	(Ldr)31/08/90	(Pay)26/09/90	Amt(c)18
Final No 136	(Ldr)25/01/91	(Pay)26/02/91	Amt(c)32
Interim No 137	(Ldr)30/08/91	(Pay)24/09/91	Amt(c)18
Final No 138	(Ldr)31/01/92	(Pay)25/02/92	Amt(c)32
Interim No 139	(Ldr)28/08/92	(Pay)23/09/92	Amt(c)18

NUMBER OF EMPLOYEES : 13

CAPITAL STRUCTURE

	AUTHORISED	ISSUED
Ords 2,5c	12000000	10224350

FINANCIAL STATISTICS (AT FINANCIAL YEAR END)

(Amts in R'000)	1991 Dec	1990 Dec	1989 Dec	1988	1987
Ord S/H Int	72823	73345	48210	40378	37685
Long Trm Loans	879	1025	9475	16231	14760
Iss Ord Share	10224	10224	10224	10224	10224
Total Liab	7412	12062	15553	22684	20906
Current Liab	6533	11037	6078	6453	6146
Total Assets	80235	85407	63763	58214	56691
Current Assets	2140	7329	2730	1605	4246
Debtors	1795	2415	2207	-	-
Inventory	-	-	12	1605	4246
Oper Profit	16845	17634	15404	10177	16353
Interest Paid	11	426	16	52	29
Tax Paid	3520	6938	4467	3484	7599
Prf af Int&Tax	15406	12007	12126	6374	9176
Prf att Ord Sh	15406	12007	12126	6374	9176
Btm Line Earn	21256	30247	12126	6374	9176
Dividend Paid	21778	5112	4294	3681	4908
Mkt Prce(c) YE	700	425	480	395	395
Depreciation	37	43	105	-	-

PER SHARE STATISTICS (CENTS)

Net Asst Val	712.28	717.38	471.54	394.93	368.59
Net Earnings	151.00	117.00	119.00	-	-
Dividends	213.00	50.00	42.00	-	-
Cash Flow	149.62	118.67	120.57	62.34	59.83

RATIOS AND OTHER INFORMATION

Mrk Cap(R000)	71568	43452	49075	40385	40385
Current Ratio	0.33	0.66	0.45	0.25	0.69
Quik/Acid Tst	0.33	0.66	0.45	-	-
Debt/Ass Rat	0.08	0.13	0.10	0.39	0.37
L T L Tot Ass	-	-	-	0.28	0.26
Debt to Eqity	0.09	0.15	0.13	0.56	0.55
Interest Cover	1721.55	45.47	1038.06	190.58	579.45
Ret on Assets	23.60	22.68	26.05	17.02	19.76
Ret on Equity%	21.16	16.37	25.15	15.79	16.23
Price/Earnings	4.64	3.63	4.03	-	-
Divid Cover	0.71	2.34	2.83	-	-
Divid Yield	30.43	11.76	8.75	-	-
Earning Yield%	21.57	27.53	24.79	-	-
NAV % Mrk Pr	101.75	168.80	98.24	99.98	93.31
Effec Tax Rate	24.61	38.57	29.93	34.41	46.55
Def Interval	0.07	-	-	2.55	1.07
Sus Grth Rate	-8.75	9.40	16.25	6.67	11.33

SUBSIDIARY & ASSOCIATED COMPANIES

BOXWOOD (PTY) LTD
CARLETONVILLE ESTATES LTD
CHERRYFIELDS (PTY) LTD
EASTFIELDS (PTY) LTD
ELDERWOOD (PTY) LTD
FOURFIELDS (PTY) LTD
GATE TWELVE (PTY) LTD
GLENHARVIE HOUSE (PTY) LTD
GLENHARVIE SHOPPING CENTRE (PTY) LTD
GOLDMILL PROPERTIES (PTY) LTD
HORSEWOOD (PTY) LTD
JA CANN INVESTMENTS (PTY) LTD
LUIPAARDSVLEI ESTATE & G M CO LTD
MODERN TOWN PLANNING CO LTD, THE
NEW DURBAN GOLD AND INDUSTRIALS LTD
PALMWOOD (PTY) LTD
SAGEWOOD (PTY) LTD
SIVEBEECK HOUSE (PTY) LTD
SOUTH RIDGE PROPERTIES (PTY) LTD
STAND 55 STORMILL EXT 2 (PTY) LTD
WEST WITWATERSRAND AREAS LTD
WOODHAVEN LTD

INVESTMENTS

EAST RAND GOLD & URANIUM CO (2021053 SH)
GOLD FIELDS COAL LTD (72300 SH)
GOLD FIELDS OF S.A. LTD (145000 SH)
KLOOF GOLD MINING CO LTD (UNSECURED CONV (17440 DEBS)
KLOOF GOLD MINING COMPANY LTD (FINANCIA (54896 SH)
NEW WITS LTD (988000 SH)
SOUTH DEEP EXPLORATION CO LTD (114700 SH)
VENTERSPOST GOLD MINING CO LTD (DEF ORDS (99000 SH)
VLAKFONTEIN GOLD MINING CO LTD (100000 SH)

GOLDFIELDS INDUSTRIAL CORPORATION LTD

ABBREVIATION : G-I-C

JSE SHORT CODE : GIC

SECTOR : Industrial-Engineering

SHAREHOLDERS

Who Owns Whom's Assessment of the Identity of the Ultimate Controlling Shareholder: MANAGEMENT

SHAREHOLDER	PERCENTAGE 1992	1991
ELLIOTTONA INV P/L	61.9	61.9
LOWENCO NOM P/L	9.8	9.3
STD BANK NOM TVL P/L	6.5	6.5
WORKERS TRUST P/L	3.5	3.5
DALGLAND NOM P/L	1.7	1.2
TOTAL	83.3	82.4

DIRECTORS :
BROOKS TG (Deputy Chairman),COLEMAN JA
CRAWLEY AP (Managing Director)
FRYE MJE (Chairman),GILSON BN ,MONTHE RW
SMITH TJ

REGISTRATION NUMBER : 05/15235/06

REGISTERED OFFICE
4 Nywerheid Street, Manufacta
Roodepoort
1725
TEL: 011-763 4261
FAX: 011-766 4081

TRANSFER SECRETARY
Central Registrars Ltd
P O Box 4844, Johannesburg
2000
TEL: 011-331 0051

COMPANY SECRETARY
A P Crawley

NATURE OF BUSINESS
The company, through its subsidiary Strip Steel, supplies flat-rolled steel strip. Manufacturing processes used include slitting, cutting-to-length precision re-rolling, and annealing.

BANKERS :
Standard Bank of SA Ltd

AUDITORS :
N/A

FAMILIAR BRAND NAMES
STRIP STEEL

CONTRIBUTION BY ACTIVITY
N/A

YEAR END : March

DIVIDEND :Ords 50c

Final	(Ldr)24/08/90	(Pay)12/09/90	Amt(c)30
Interim	(Ldr)14/12/90	(Pay)16/01/91	Amt(c)20
Final	(Ldr)23/08/91	(Pay)11/09/91	Amt(c)30
Interim	(Ldr)10/01/92	(Pay)05/02/92	Amt(c)22
Final	(Ldr)05/06/92	(Pay)17/06/92	Amt(c)33

NUMBER OF EMPLOYEES : 344

GRESHAM INDUSTRIES LTD

ABBREVIATION : GRESHAM

JSE SHORT CODE : GRE

SECTOR : Industrial-Retailers & Wholesalers

SHAREHOLDERS

Who Owns Whom's Assessment of the Identity of the Ultimate Controlling Shareholder: ANGLO AMERICAN VIA PREMIER GROUP

SHAREHOLDER	PERCENTAGE 1992	1991
PRETORIA WHOLESALE DRUGGISTS	86.0	77.5
EIGHTY ONE MAIN STREET NOM LTD	3.6	4.8
PREMIER GROUP PENS FUND	1.2	1.2
BASSER P/L	---	1.5
NORLO TRUST CC	---	1.5
SA MUTUAL	---	1.0
SAFEGRO NOM P/L	---	1.5
TOTAL	90.7	89.1

DIRECTORS :
CESMAN WE ,ENGELBERG S ,GLICK E ,KEATING L
KOVARSKY DC ,MORRIS K ,UTIAN GM (Chairman)
WRIGHTON PGA

REGISTRATION NUMBER : 05/01420/06

REGISTERED OFFICE
Premier Group Centre, 1 Newtown Avenue
Killarney, Johannesburg
2193
TEL: 011-446 9111
FAX: 011-446 2239

TRANSFER SECRETARY
Mercantile Registrars Ltd
P O Box 1053, Johannesburg
2000
TEL: 011-333 8181

COMPANY SECRETARY
E V J Vermaak

NATURE OF BUSINESS
The group is engaged in the wholesale distribution of medical, surgical & pharmaceutical supplies & equipment; Wholesale & retail of tools, hardware & related products; Manufacture & distribution of belts; Wholesale & distribution of haberdashery, sewing accessories & babyware. The company holds a controlling interest in quoted pharmaceutical wholesaler PDC Holdings Ltd.

BANKERS :
First National Bank of SA Ltd
Standard Bank of SA Ltd, Nedperm Bank Ltd
Volkskas Ltd

AUDITORS :
Ernst & Young

FAMILIAR BRAND NAMES
ACTION DIY STORES,ATKINSONS DISTRIBUTORS
CAPE BELT,CRAFTOOL,INDUSTRIAL MEDICAL
JENSEN BELTS,MEDICLIN,MEDSURG

CAPITAL STRUCTURE

	AUTHORISED	ISSUED
Ords 50c	5000000	2574807

FINANCIAL STATISTICS (AT FINANCIAL YEAR END)

(Amts in R'000)	1992 Mar	1991 Mar	1990 Mar	1989 Mar	1988 Mar
Ord S/H Int	23640	21853	20237	18040	15641
Long Trm Loans	1556	2131	2673	1000	2352
Iss Ord Share	4081	4081	4081	3951	3951
Total Liab	28609	28178	25874	15076	20145
Current Liab	27053	26047	23201	14076	17793
Total Assets	52249	50031	46111	33116	35786
Current Assets	37934	34822	30654	19552	21477
Debtors	14045	11662	11998	10485	10100
Inventory	14481	14220	11392	8607	11377
Turnover	72289	74052	76174	67956	50216
Oper Profit	8334	7967	7679	6411	4480
Interest Paid	1131	1263	1244	1312	268
Tax Paid	3171	3047	2749	2346	1390
Prf af Int&Tax	4032	3657	3686	2753	2822
Prf att Ord Sh	4032	3657	3686	2753	2822
Btm Line Earn	4032	3657	3686	2628	2822
Dividend Paid	2245	2041	2041	1581	1581
Mkt Prce(c) YE	500	350	480	450	625
Depreciation	1967	1808	1598	1388	900

PER SHARE STATISTICS (CENTS)

Net Asst Val	579.27	535.48	495.88	456.59	395.87
Net Earnings	99.00	90.00	92.00	70.00	71.00
Dividends	55.00	50.00	50.00	40.00	40.00
Cash Flow	147.00	133.91	131.41	104.81	95.17

RATIOS AND OTHER INFORMATION

Mrk Cap(R000)	20405	14284	19589	17780	24694
Current Ratio	1.40	1.34	1.32	1.39	1.21
Quik/Acid Tst	0.87	0.79	0.83	0.78	0.57
A/C Rec T/ovr	5.15	6.35	6.35	6.48	4.97
Tot Ass T/ovr	1.38	1.48	1.65	2.05	1.40
Debt/Ass Rat	0.55	0.56	0.56	0.46	0.53
L T L Tot Ass	0.03	0.04	0.06	0.03	0.03
Debt to Eqity	1.21	1.29	1.28	0.84	1.20
Interest Cover	7.37	6.31	6.17	4.89	16.72
Oper Prof Mrg	11.53	10.76	10.08	9.43	8.92
Net Prof Marg%	5.58	4.94	4.84	4.05	5.62
Ret on Assets	15.95	15.92	16.65	19.36	12.52
Ret on Equity%	17.06	16.73	18.21	15.26	18.04
Price/Earnings	5.05	3.89	5.22	6.43	8.80
Divid Cover	1.80	1.80	1.84	1.75	1.78
Divid Yield	11.00	14.29	10.42	8.89	6.40
Earning Yield%	19.80	25.71	19.17	15.56	11.36
NAV % Mrk Pr	115.85	152.99	103.31	101.47	63.34
Effec Tax Rate	45.98	46.27	42.46	46.01	32.10
Def Interval	0.26	0.39	0.51	0.24	0.77
Sus Grth Rate	7.56	7.39	8.13	6.50	7.93

SUBSIDIARY & ASSOCIATED COMPANIES

STRIP STEEL (PTY) LTD
STRIP STEEL PROPERTIES (NO 2) LTD
STRIP STEEL PROPERTIES (PTY) LTD
VULCANIA STEELSTRIP PRODUCTS (PTY) LTD

INVESTMENTS

None

MEGA TOOL & HARDWARE,OCEANIC DISTRIBUTORS
PLUS CHEMISTS,RYOBI POWERTOOLS,SALTERS
SELWYN SHER,SWAN TRADING,TOOL WHOLESALE
UNION FIRST AID,UNOVEX

CONTRIBUTION BY ACTIVITY

Pharmaceutical (% of turnover) (87.4%)
Tool & Hardware (10.1%)
Other (2.5%)

YEAR END : April

DIVIDEND :Ords 25c

Interim No 53	(Ldr)24/11/89	(Pay)08/12/89	Amt(c)4
Final No 54	(Ldr)25/05/90	(Pay)08/06/90	Amt(c)2
Final No 55	(Ldr)14/06/91	(Pay)28/06/91	Amt(c)3
Interim No 56	(Ldr)20/12/91	(Pay)10/01/92	Amt(c)1.5

NUMBER OF EMPLOYEES : 1828

CAPITAL STRUCTURE

	AUTHORISED	ISSUED
6% Cum Prefs R2	200000	200000
Red Conv Cum Partic Prefs 25c	400000	81000
Ords 25c	80000000	52459469

FINANCIAL STATISTICS (AT FINANCIAL YEAR END)

(Amts in R'000)	1991 Mar	1990 Mar	1989 Mar	1988 Mar	1987
Ord S/H Int	51286	53013	48583	39573	32895
Long Trm Loans	120746	59448	51518	39814	37893
Iss Ord Share	52459	52459	52459	52459	50909
Total Liab	259180	191010	152480	87009	65708
Current Liab	138434	131562	100962	47195	27815
Total Assets	293466	226023	183063	126582	126932
Intang Assets	17000	18000	18000	*	*
Current Assets	275145	210995	176107	96363	56144
Debtors	141610	109088	86118	41732	-
Inventory	130389	100569	81376	53701	56144
Turnover	833132	625846	664962	280642	133539
Oper Profit	19155	18479	25807	20495	10567
Interest Paid	31277	18057	16705	4501	2568
Tax Paid	4027	6185	7721	4889	43
Prf af Int&Tax	4542	10156	11666	11105	5616
Prf att Ord Sh	3392	7577	9090	10553	5190
Btm Line Earn	-153	7577	13731	8482	5190
Dividend Paid	1574	3147	4721	4191	2546
Mkt Prce(c) YE	50	80	110	110	135
Depreciation	3433	2152	3082	1078	-

PER SHARE STATISTICS (CENTS)

Net Asst Val	65.36	66.74	58.30	75.44	64.62
Net Earnings	6.50	14.40	21.60	20.10	-
Dividends	3.00	6.00	9.00	8.00	-
Cash Flow	13.46	18.83	23.56	23.13	14.71

RATIOS AND OTHER INFORMATION

Mrk Cap(R000)	26230	41967	57705	57705	68727
Current Ratio	1.99	1.60	1.74	2.04	2.02
Quik/Acid Tst	1.05	0.84	0.94	0.90	-
A/C Rec T/ovr	5.88	5.74	7.72	6.72	-
Tot Ass T/ovr	2.84	2.77	3.63	2.22	1.40
Debt/Ass Rat	0.83	0.75	0.72	0.60	0.52
L T L Tot Ass	0.36	0.16	0.17	0.23	0.30
Debt to Eqity	4.77	3.18	2.72	1.93	2.00
Interest Cover	0.62	1.03	1.55	4.55	3.20
Oper Prof Mrg	2.30	2.95	3.88	7.30	7.91
Net Prof Marg%	0.41	1.21	1.37	3.76	3.89
Ret on Assets	13.58	15.22	19.72	16.19	8.64
Ret on Equity%	6.61	14.29	18.71	26.67	21.04
Price/Earnings	7.69	5.56	5.09	5.47	-
Divid Cover	2.17	2.40	2.40	2.51	-
Divid Yield	6.00	7.50	8.18	7.27	-
Earning Yield%	13.00	18.00	19.64	18.27	-
NAV % Mrk Pr	130.72	83.43	53.00	68.58	47.86
Effec Tax Rate	44.56	51.40	38.39	27.47	0.54
Def Interval	15.53	4.65	2.67	2.58	9.00
Sus Grth Rate	3.54	8.36	8.99	16.08	8.04

SUBSIDIARY & ASSOCIATED COMPANIES

ABRA HARDWARE (PTY) LTD
ACTION HARDWARE (PTY) LTD
AMALGAMATED CHEMISTS ASSOCIATION (PTY) L
ARROW HANDLES (PTY) LTD
B GUNDELFINGER & FRANSOFF (HOLDINGS) LTD
BIG TIME (PTY) LTD
BRIAN DA COSTA (PTY) LTD
CAPE BELT (PTY) LTD
FRANKEL & SEEHOFF (PTY) LTD
G & S CONSTRUCTION (PTY) LTD
GRESHAM MANAGEMENT SERVICES (PTY) LTD
GRESHAM WHOLESALERS (PTY) LTD
HERBERT JOHNS LTD
INDUSTRIAL MEDICAL SERVICES (PTY) LTD
J M ATKINSON (PTY) LTD
JENSEN BELTS PARTNERSHIP
KAYLAW (PTY) LTD
LESTAT HOLDINGS (PTY) LTD
LITTLE IMP (PTY) LTD
MEDICAL & SURGICAL DISTRIBUTORS (PTY) LT
MEGA TOOL & HARDWARE GROUP (PTY) LTD
OCEANIC DISTRIBUTORS (PTY) LTD
PDC HOLDINGS LTD
PLX INVESTMENT CO (PTY) LTD
SALTERS-FISHER MEDICAL HOLDINGS LTD
SELWYN SHER ELECTRO MEDICAL (PTY) LTD
SOUTH AFRICAN AGENCIES (PTY) LTD
TARGET TRADING CO (PTY) LTD
TOOL WHOLESALE (PTY) LTD
TRUE VALUE TOOL & HARDWARE CO (PTY) LTD
UNION FIRST AID & COMMERCIAL DISTRIBUTOR
UNOVEX (PTY) LTD

INVESTMENTS

BEACON ISLAND SHARE BLOCK (5500 SH)
SMALL BUSINESS DEVELOPMENT CORP LTD (25056 SH)
WILCO HOLDINGS (PTY) LTD (200000 (PR)

GRINAKER HOLDINGS LTD

ABBREVIATION : GRINAKER

JSE SHORT CODE : GRK

SECTOR : Industrial-Building & Construction

SHAREHOLDERS

Who Owns Whom's Assessment of the Identity of the Ultimate Controlling Shareholder: ANGLOVAAL VIA AVGRIN HOLDINGS LTD

SHAREHOLDER	PERCENTAGE 1992	1991

ANGLOVAAL IND LTD	51 0	51 0
CMB NOM P/L	10 9	---
SA MUTUAL	8 7	10 1
NEDBANK NOM LTD	4 8	---
OLAPEG INV P/L	2 6	3 6
STD BANK NOM TVL P/L	2 4	1 7
ELLIS I	2 3	2 3
GRINAKER EMPLOYEES SHARE PURC TRUST	2 0	2 2
EIGHTY ONE MAIN STREET NOM LTD	1 8	---
MOMENTUM LIFE ASSURE LTD	1 5	1 5
COMMERCIAL UNION ASSURE CO SA LTD	---	1 2
SANLAM	---	10 8
PEGGY GRINAKER TRUST	---	3 1
TOTAL	88 0	87 4

DIRECTORS :
BORNHEIMER O ,GOSS PM ,GRINAKER MI MRS
GROBBELAAR SA ,HERSOV BE ,LAIT PJ ,LUDIN HET
MCGRATH MJ ,MENELL CS ,MITCHELL AM
ROBBERTZE JC (Chairman),ROYSTON D
SAULEZ AN (Managing Director),SAVAGE RB

REGISTRATION NUMBER : 64/04561/06

REGISTERED OFFICE
Summit Park, 2 Summit Road
Dunkeld West
2196
TEL 011-880 4966
FAX 011-880 4955

TRANSFER SECRETARY
Anglovaal Ltd
P O Box 62379, Marshalltown
2107
TEL 011-634 9111

COMPANY SECRETARY
A M Mitchell

NATURE OF BUSINESS
An investment holding company with subsidiaries active in the field of construction & electronics The company has a controlling interest in quoted Grintek Ltd Group activities include project management, building, mining, civil, mechanical & electrical engineering contracting, housing and property development, manufacture & supply of crushed stone aggregates & steel reinforcement See also Grintek and Siltek nature of business

BANKERS :
Standard Bank of SA Ltd, Nedcor Bank Ltd

AUDITORS :
Ernst & Young

FAMILIAR BRAND NAMES
N/A

CONTRIBUTION BY ACTIVITY
N/A

YEAR END : June

DIVIDEND : Ords 10c

Interim No 50	(Ldr)16/03/90	(Pay)12/04/90	Amt(c)13
Final No 51	(Ldr)28/09/90	(Pay)19/10/90	Amt(c)25
Interim No 52	(Ldr)22/02/91	(Pay)12/04/91	Amt(c)10
Final No 53	(Ldr)27/09/91	(Pay)18/10/91	Amt(c)24
Interim No 54	(Ldr)13/03/92	(Pay)09/04/92	Amt(c)5

NUMBER OF EMPLOYEES : 9887

CAPITAL STRUCTURE

	AUTHORISED	ISSUED
Ords 10c	40000000	34948696
10% Cum Red Prefs 10c	3000000	0

FINANCIAL STATISTICS (AT FINANCIAL YEAR END)

(Amts in R'000)	1992 Jun	1991 Jun	1990 Jun	1989 Jun	1988 Jun
Ord S/H Int	151514	173693	181859	143398	127868
Long Trm Loans	143843	160040	167685	114619	92663
Iss Ord Share	34949	34949	34949	32340	32340
Total Liab	705472	654484	639559	448026	321105
Current Liab	561629	494444	471874	333407	228442
Total Assets	856986	828177	821418	591424	448973
Current Assets	670000	651586	658480	405450	348473
Debtors	321841	290757	271743	158105	110581
Inventory	322838	293884	331644	213195	189436
Turnover	2161181	2047026	1942694	1219291	886316
Oper Profit	40088	102529	126309	78336	72168
Interest Paid	15626	10289	20360	7180	4280
Tax Paid	25045	52694	49142	36144	31906
Prf af Int&Tax	21592	63448	83590	48160	35982
Prf att Ord Sh	-1169	37979	50281	34548	23046
Btm Line Earn	-20880	2870	24392	25090	24946
Dividend Paid	1747	11883	13280	9702	7115
Mkt Prce(c) YE	500	900	900	1165	660
Depreciation	29092	28804	31450	20906	19012

PER SHARE STATISTICS (CENTS)

Net Asst Val	433 53	496 99	520 36	443 41	395 39
Net Earnings	-3 30	108 70	143 90	106 80	71 40
Dividends	5 00	34 00	38 00	30 00	22 00
Cash Flow	18 02	189 89	194 34	165 78	145 44

RATIOS AND OTHER INFORMATION

Mrk Cap(R000)	174745	314541	314541	376761	213444
Current Ratio	1 19	1 32	1 40	1 22	1 53
Quik/Acid Tst	0 62	0 72	0 69	0 58	0 70
A/C Rec T/ovr	6 72	7 04	7 15	7 71	8 02
Tot Ass T/ovr	2 52	2 47	2 37	2 06	1 97
Debt/Ass Rat	0 67	0 62	0 60	0 60	0 52
L T L Tot Ass	0 01	0 02	0 03	0 03	0 01
Debt to Eqity	3 78	2 93	2 71	2 46	1 81
Interest Cover	2 82	10 27	6 28	11 50	16 86
Oper Prof Mrg	1 85	5 01	6 50	6 42	8 14
Net Prof Marg%	-0 05	1 86	2 59	2 83	2 60
Ret on Assets	7 64	15 53	18 89	16 28	16 12
Ret on Equity%	-0 77	21 87	27 65	24 09	18 02
Price/Earnings	-151 52	8 28	6 25	10 91	9 24
Divid Cover	-0 66	3 20	3 79	3 56	3 25
Divid Yield	1 00	3 78	4 22	2 58	3 33
Earning Yield%	-0 66	12 08	15 99	9 17	10 82
NAV % Mrk Pr	86 71	55 22	57 82	38 06	59 91
Effec Tax Rate	80 43	34 45	51 52	41 21	39 01
Def Interval	11 87	0 89	0 65	0 97	0 52
Sus Grth Rate	-1 92	15 02	20 35	17 33	12 46

SUBSIDIARY & ASSOCIATED COMPANIES

329 CURRIE ROAD (PTY) LTD (46%)
ALLIED GRINAKER PROPERTIES (PTY) LTD (36%)
AMALGAMATED REINFORCING (PTY) LTD (47%)
BAY STONE SALES (PTY) LTD (46%)
BILHARD HOMES (PTY) LTD
CONDECOR DEVELOPMENT (PTY) LTD
DURA BUILDING COMPANY (PTY) LTD
GOEDE & CO (PTY) LTD
GRINAKER (BOPHUTHATSWANA) (PTY) LTD

GRINAKER (BOTSWANA) (PTY) LTD
GRINAKER (CISKEI) (PTY) LTD
GRINAKER (NAMIBIA) (PTY) LTD
GRINAKER (SWAZILAND) (PTY) LTD
GRINAKER (TRANSKEI) (PTY) LTD
GRINAKER (VENDA) (PTY) LTD
GRINAKER COMPUTING SERVICES (PTY) LTD (46%)
GRINAKER CONSTRUCTION LTD
GRINAKER CONSTRUCTION LTD
GRINAKER ELECTRONICS HOLDINGS LTD
GRINAKER FINANCIAL SERVICES (PTY) LTD
GRINMARK (PTY) LTD
GRINTEK LTD
INLAND MARINE (PTY) LTD (47%)
J C PIETERSE & KIE (EDMS) BPK
KELVINCEE (PTY) LTD
LYNACRES PROJECTS (PTY) LTD (46%)
MACINTOSH PROPERTY HOLDING CO (PTY) LTD (46%)
MKM ENGINEERING (PTY) LTD (20%)
MOWCOP BOERDERY BELEGGINGS (EDMS) BPK
PEPPER STREET INVESTMENTS (PTY) LTD (28%)
REHM GRINAKER CONSTRUCTION CO LTD (37%)
SANDTON SQUARE PORTION 7 (PTY) LTD (46%)
SILTEK INVESTMENTS (PTY) LTD (47%)
SYDCOR ENGINEERING PROJECTS (PTY) LTD (46%)

INVESTMENTS

GRINAKER ELECTRONICS HOLDINGS LTD (4%)
NATIONAL SOCKET SCREWS (PTY) LTD (13%)
UMTATA REINFORCING (PTY) LTD (12%)

GRINDROD UNICORN GROUP LTD

ABBREVIATION . GRINCOR

JSE SHORT CODE : GNR

SECTOR . Industrial Industrial Holding

SHAREHOLDERS

Who Owns Whom's Assessment of the Identity of the Ultimate Controlling Shareholder
GRINDROD FAMILY

SHAREHOLDER	PERCENTAGE 1992	1991
GRINDROD HLDGS P/L	52 9	52 8
SCAC DELMAS V	6 9	
UAL NOM P/L	6 0	8 5
INVESTEC NOM P/L	5 6	7 9
EMOYENI MANAGEMENT & INV CO P/L	3 3	4 7
STD BANK NOM TVL P/L	2 8	3 9
CMB NOM P/L	2 4	
DCMR INV P/L	2 4	2 9
FIRST NAT NOM P/L	1 8	2 1
METAL IND GROUP PENS FUND	1 6	
ENGINEERING INDUSTRIES PENS FUND	1 6	
MOORE P H	1 4	1 4
NEDBANK NOM LTD		1 9
SANLAM		2 4
TOTAL	88 6	88 4

DIRECTORS :
GRINDROD WM (Chairman)
GROVES IM (Managing Director),MARTINEAU B
MEEHAN MG ,MORRISON A (Deputy Chairman)
RENAULT S ,WHITE DRD

REGISTRATION NUMBER : 66/09846/06

REGISTERED OFFICE
Quadrant House, 115 Victoria Embankment
Durban
4001
TEL 031-304 1451
FAX 031-305 2848

TRANSFER SECRETARY
Central Registrars Ltd
P O Box 4844, Johannesburg
2000
TEL 011-331 0051

COMPANY SECRETARY
H B Kenny

NATURE OF BUSINESS
An investment holding company with subsidiaries engaged in the transportation, storage & handling of goods by sea, air & on land Activities include ships agency, international freight, stevedoring, domestic distribution, road transport, container services, liner shipping services, international shipowning & operating, bulk trades, tankers, oil exploration services, marine services & container depots, warehousing & cargo services

BANKERS :
First National Bank of SA Ltd
Standard Bank of SA Ltd, Nedcor Bank Ltd

AUDITORS :
Morrison Murray

FAMILIAR BRAND NAMES
N/A

CONTRIBUTION BY ACTIVITY
Grindrod (% Operating Income) (7 0%)
Unicorn (93 0%)

YEAR END : December

DIVIDEND Ords 1c

Interim	(Ldr)07/09/90	(Pay)17/09/90	Amt(c)10
Final	(Ldr)15/02/91	(Pay)25/02/91	Amt(c)18
Interim	(Ldr)06/09/91	(Pay)16/09/91	Amt(c)10
Final	(Ldr)14/02/92	(Pay)24/02/92	Amt(c)20
Interim	(Ldr)18/09/92	(Pay)28/09/92	Amt(c)10

NUMBER OF EMPLOYEES . 3270

CAPITAL STRUCTURE

	AUTHORISED	ISSUED
Ords 1c	50000000	35640220

FINANCIAL STATISTICS (AT FINANCIAL YEAR END)

(Amts in R 000)	1991 Dec	1990 Dec	1989 Dec	1988 Dec	1987 Dec
Ord S/H Int	75313	68118	58289	49913	45172
Long Trm Loans	280254	197261	145581	142344	102092
Iss Ord Share	25417	25244	25244	25244	25244
Total Liab	444622	292494	243326	227426	165992
Current Liab	164368	95233	97745	85082	63900

Total Assets	510391	359154	300550	274601	208350
Intang Assets	9544	1458	1065	2738	2814
Current Assets	206152	145150	107751	92573	77538
Debtors	136760	71404	74646	79300	67890
Inventory	9513	11702	8500	7356	5546
Turnover	563900	497463	423965	345224	274626
Oper Profit	52239	50019	52168	33290	20864
Interest Paid	19250	23356	19326	13147	8232
Tax Paid	2527	10099	13243	6869	6476
Prf af Int&Tax	35978	31602	25824	17499	8159
Prf att Ord Sh	19993	18491	15735	10184	4640
Btm Line Earn	13214	18709	15200	9069	4598
Dividend Paid	7632	7068	5806	4544	3156
Mkt Prce(c) YE	500	350	310	180	235
Depreciation	19896	19031	16695	13734	11524

PER SHARE STATISTICS (CENTS)

Net Asst Val	258 76	264 06	226 68	186 88	167 79
Net Earnings	78 90	73 30	62 30	40 30	18 40
Dividends	30 00	28 00	23 00	18 00	12 50
Cash Flow	167 13	187 28	137 93	123 82	75 50

RATIOS AND OTHER INFORMATION

Mrk Cap(R000)	127085	88354	78256	45439	59323
Current Ratio	1 25	1 52	1 10	1 09	1 21
Quik/Acid Tst	1 20	1 40	1 02	1 00	1 13
A/C Rec T/ovr	4 12	6 97	5 68	4 35	4 05
Tot Ass T/ovr	1 10	1 39	1 41	1 26	1 32
Debt/Ass Rat	0 63	0 51	0 51	0 58	0 52
L T L Tot Ass	0 31	0 25	0 18	0 27	0 22
Debt to Eqity	4 30	2 70	2 61	3 17	2 42
Interest Cover	2 73	2 22	2 73	2 57	2 58
Oper Prof Mrg	9 26	10 05	12 30	9 64	7 60
Net Prof Marg%	3 55	3 72	3 71	2 95	1 69
Ret on Assets	11 30	18 15	19 43	13 72	10 99
Ret on Equity%	26 55	27 15	26 99	20 40	10 27
Price/Earnings	6 34	4 77	4 98	4 47	12 77
Divid Cover	2 63	2 62	2 71	2 24	1 47
Divid Yield	6 00	8 00	7 42	10 00	5 32
Earning Yield%	15 78	20 94	20 10	22 39	7 83
NAV % Mrk Pr	51 75	75 45	73 12	103 82	71 40
Effec Tax Rate	0 36	0 53	27 85	0 31	24 80
Def Interval	4 29	2 14	2 08	3 00	3 05
Sus Grth Rate	16 41	16 77	17 03	11 30	3 29

SUBSIDIARY & ASSOCIATED COMPANIES

A J KEELER & CO (PTY) LTD
AIROADEXPRESS (PTY) LTD
BIRCHGREY SA (INC IN PANAMA)
BOXRAINE SA (INC IN PANAMA)
BUSSICOTT SHIPPING SERVICES (PTY) LTD
CARGO MARINE & AIR (PTY) LTD
CARGO MARINE (PTY) LTD
CENTROMAR SHIPPING (PTY) LTD (25%)
COASTAL CONTAINER DEPOT (DURBAN) (PTY) L
DAIN PROPERTIES (PTY) LTD
DOM PEDRO PROPERTIES (PTY) LTD
DURBAN LINES (PTY) LTD
DURBAN MARINE CONTRACTORS (PTY) LTD
EPOCA MARITIMA SA (INC IN PANAMA)
ERF 439 WALVIS BAY (PTY) LTD
GATEWAY SHIPPING PANAMA SA (INC IN PANAM
GOLFLAND SA (INC IN PANAMA)
GRINCOR MANAGEMENTS SERVICES (PTY) LTD
GRINDROD & CO (PTY) LTD
GRINDROD (PTY) LTD
GRINDROD (SWD) (PTY) LTD
GRINDROD AIR FREIGHT (PTY) LTD
GRINDROD COTTS (WALVIS BAY) (PTY) LTD
GRINDROD COTTS STEVEDORING (PTY) LTD
GRINDROD INTRALINK (PTY) LTD
GRINDROD MARINE (PTY) LTD
GRINDROD PROPERTIES (SWA) (PTY) LTD
GRINDROD SHIPPING (NAMIBIA) (PTY) LTD
K H BRIEGEL INVESTMENTS (PTY) LTD
KEELER HOLDINGS (PTY) LTD
KING & SONS (PTY) LTD
KINGBAY (PTY) LTD
LAW & MILLER (PTY) LTD
LESOTHO FORWARDING (PTY) LTD
MARIMSTAD ARMADORA SA (INC IN PANAMA)
MITCHELL COTTS MARITIME (PTY) LTD
NCJ PROPERTIES (PTY) LTD
NEW BOUNDARY SHIPPING CO INC (INC IN PAN
NEW MAYDON SHIPPING CO INC (INC IN PANAM
NOURSE MINES SILICA BRICKS (PTY) LTD
PAK RENNIE SHIPPING CO (PTY) LTD
PARK A-TAINER (PTY) LTD
PHOSMARINE BRUSH KART (AFRICA) (PTY) LTD
PROROS BELEGGINGS (EDMS) BPK
RENMARINE CONTAINERS (PTY) LTD
RENNIES GRINDROD COTTS INVESTMENTS (PTY) (50%)
RICHBAY DEVELOPMENTS (PTY) LTD
SA STEVEDORES LTD (25%)
SDV (UK) LIMITED (25%)
SHELL CREEK (PTY) LTD
SKYRACER (SA) (PTY) LTD
SKYWAYS INTERNATIONAL (PTY) LTD
SMITH'S COASTERS (PTY) LTD
SOUTHERN GAS SHIPPING SA (INC IN PANAMA)
SPHERE SHIPPING LIMITED (INC IN PANAMA)
STABILO SHIPPING INC
STORM & CO (NATAL) (PTY) LTD
SUNGLADE PROPERTIES (PTY) LTD
SWAKOP LINES (PTY) LTD
THESEN'S STEAMSHIP CO (PTY) LTD
TRANSKEI CARGO SERVICES (PTY) LTD
UNICORN LINES (PTY) LTD
UNICORN OFFSHORE (PTY) LTD
UNICORN PROPERTIES METRO (PTY) LTD
UNICORN PROPERTIES MONTAGUE (PTY) LTD
UNICORN PROPERTIES RICHARDSBAY (PTY) LTD
UNICORN PROPERTY HOLDINGS LTD
UNICORN SHIPPING HOLDINGS LTD
WALON (PTY) LTD
ZA CARGO COMMUNITY SYSTEM (PTY) LTD

INVESTMENTS

CORNERSTONE PROPERTY FUND MANAGERS LTD (13%)

GRINTEK LTD

ABBREVIATION : GRINTEK

JSE SHORT CODE : GNK

SECTOR : Industrial-Electronics, Electrical & Bat

SHAREHOLDERS

Who Owns Whom's Assessment of the Identity of the Ultimate Controlling Shareholder:
ANGLOVAAL VIA GRINAKER

SHAREHOLDER	PERCENTAGE 1992	1991

GRINAKER FINANCIAL SERVICES P/L	60 8	60 9
SA MUTUAL	13 5	13 6
CMB NOM P/L	12 4	---
GRINAKER HOLDINGS LTD	6 7	6 8
MOMENTUM LIFE ASSURE LTD	1 4	- -
FIRST NAT NOM P/L	1 1	- -
SANLAM	- -	12 5
TOTAL	95 9	93 8

DIRECTORS :
GROBBELAAR SA ,LUDIN HET ,MASSON R ,MCGRATH MJ MITCHELL AM ,ROBBERTZE JC ,SAULEZ AN (Chairman

REGISTRATION NUMBER : 55/00013/06

REGISTERED OFFICE
1st Floor, North Wing, Summit Park, 2 Summit Road
Dunkeld West, Johannesburg
2196
TEL 011-880 4966
FAX 011-880 4955

TRANSFER SECRETARY
Anglovaal Ltd
P O Box 62379, Marshalltown
2107
TEL 011-634 9111

COMPANY SECRETARY
A M Mitchell

NATURE OF BUSINESS
An investment holding company with subsidiaries engaged in the following operations Design,manufacture,distribution and servicing of information technology equipment,manufacture and distribution of micro-computers, printers, software,computer peripheral products & services Design and development of voice and data radio communications and microwave sub systems, Analysis design and implementation of aircraft self-protection systems Design & supply of specialised

BANKERS :
Standard Bank of SA Ltd, Nedcor Bank Ltd

AUDITORS :
Ernst & Young

FAMILIAR BRAND NAMES
N/A

CONTRIBUTION BY ACTIVITY
N/A

YEAR END : June

DIVIDEND : Ords no par value

Interim No 49	(Ldr)22/02/91	(Pay)12/04/91	Amt(c)2 4
Final No 50	(Ldr)27/09/91	(Pay)18/10/91	Amt(c)3
Interim No 51	(Ldr)13/03/92	(Pay)09/04/92	Amt(c)1 7
Final No 52	(Ldr)11/09/92	(Pay)09/10/92	Amt(c)2

NUMBER OF EMPLOYEES : 3299

CAPITAL STRUCTURE

	AUTHORISED	ISSUED
Ords no par value	300000000	194251694

FINANCIAL STATISTICS (AT FINANCIAL YEAR END)

(Amts in R'000)	1992 Jun	1991 Jun	1990 Jun
Ord S/H Int	160636	153151	164753
Long Trm Loans	78996	66048	71479
Iss Ord Share	194252	193390	193170
Total Liab	401258	348085	373300
Current Liab	322262	282037	301821
Total Assets	540515	479857	516674
Intang Assets	21379	21379	21379
Current Assets	449226	400360	446488
Debtors	252072	207699	204859
Inventory	177499	154322	182707
Turnover	1235209	1075867	1030617
Oper Profit	74230	69773	100761
Interest Paid	6223	4688	11194
Tax Paid	36658	37804	37829
Prf af Int&Tax	44596	43144	71049
Prf att Ord Sh	26794	28740	50302
Btm Line Earn	13088	6600	96003
Dividend Paid	7173	10438	15093
Mkt Prce(c) YE	110	140	230
Depreciation	13979	13959	12171

PER SHARE STATISTICS (CENTS)

Net Asst Val	71 69	68 14	74 22
Net Earnings	13 80	14 90	35 90
Dividends	3 70	5 40	7 00
Cash Flow	20 57	21 42	18 04

RATIOS AND OTHER INFORMATION

Mrk Cap(R000)	213677	270746	444291
Current Ratio	1 39	1 42	1 48
Quik/Acid Tst	0 84	0 87	0 87
A/C Rec T/ovr	4 90	5 18	3 35
Tot Ass T/ovr	2 29	2 24	1 33
Debt/Ass Rat	0 60	0 59	0 59
L T L Tot Ass	0 01	0 00	0 00
Debt to Eqity	2 03	1 85	1 84
Interest Cover	12 16	15 22	9 03
Oper Prof Mrg	6 01	6 49	9 78
Net Prof Marg%	2 17	2 67	4 88
Ret on Assets	16 69	18 19	15 72
Ret on Equity%	16 68	18 77	20 35
Price/Earnings	7 97	9 40	6 41
Divid Cover	3 73	2 76	5 13
Divid Yield	3 36	3 86	3 04
Earning Yield%	12 55	10 64	15 61
NAV % Mrk Pr	65 17	48 67	32 27
Effec Tax Rate	43 00	48 20	57 76
Def Interval	0 49	0 37	0 08
Sus Grth Rate	12 21	11 95	21 37

SUBSIDIARY & ASSOCIATED COMPANIES

GRINAKER ELECTRONICS HOLDINGS LTD
GRINAKER ELECTRONICS LIMITED
GRINAKER ELECTRONICS LIMITED
SILTEK LIMITED

INVESTMENTS

None

GRIQUALAND EXPLORATION & FINANCE CO LTD

ABBREVIATION : GEFCO

JSE SHORT CODE : GEF

SECTOR : Metals & Minerals-Other

SHAREHOLDERS

Who Owns Whom's Assessment of the Identity of the Ultimate Controlling Shareholder:
DIRECTORS

SHAREHOLDER	PERCENTAGE 1992	1991
HANOVA MINING HOLDINGS P/L	48 4	48 4
SA MUTUAL	14 6	14 6
HERBEST NOM P/L	3 4	3 4
METALLIC INV P/L	2 8	1 7
LILLINGSTON M C	1 6	1 2
SHARESTOCK NOM P/L	1 6	- -
ISIDOR BALTSTEIN TRUST NOM P/L	1 1	1 1
INVESTEC MERCHANT BANK PENS FUND	---	1 2
RINRIC NOM P/L	---	1 4
METROPOLITAN BOARD NOM LTD	--	1 8
TOTAL	73 5	74 7

DIRECTORS :
HART HP (Executive Chairman),JOOSTE LK
KNOX FW (Technical Director),STRYDOM GL
VAN ZYL PA (Financial Director

REGISTRATION NUMBER : 70/11100/06

REGISTERED OFFICE
2nd Floor, Everite House
20 De Korte Street, Braamfontein
2001
TEL 011-339 5458
FAX 011-339 3722

TRANSFER SECRETARY
Central Registrars Ltd
P O Box 4844, Johannesburg
2000
TEL 011-331 0051

COMPANY SECRETARY
P P Buys

NATURE OF BUSINESS
The activities of the group comprise the exploitation of a number of crocidolite deposits in North-West Cape and Bophuthatswana and amosite deposits in the Eastern Transvaal The abestos fibre produced is sold internationally

BANKERS :
Volkskas Ltd, Central Merchant Bank Ltd

AUDITORS :
Coopers Theron Du Toit

FAMILIAR BRAND NAMES
N/A

CONTRIBUTION BY ACTIVITY
N/A

YEAR END : December

DIVIDEND : Ords 1c

Interim No 71	(Ldr)24/08/89	(Pay)29/09/89	Amt(c)7 5
Final No 72	(Ldr)16/03/90	(Pay)20/04/90	Amt(c)15
Interim No 73	(Ldr)24/08/90	(Pay)28/09/90	Amt(c)4
Final No 74	(Ldr)28/02/91	(Pay)22/03/91	Amt(c)4
Interim No 75	(Ldr)23/08/91	(Pay)27/09/91	Amt(c)2 5

CAPITAL STRUCTURE

	AUTHORISED	ISSUED
Ords 1c	179650000	35912500
Red Prefs 1c	350000	0

FINANCIAL STATISTICS (AT FINANCIAL YEAR END)

(Amts in R'000)	1991 Dec	1990 Dec	1989 Dec	1988	1987
Ord S/H Int	178861	176802	202285	186617	191595
Long Trm Loans	213	3	3	45973	41975
Iss Ord Share	35913	35913	35913	35913	35913
Total Liab	42000	44059	51895	91943	83933
Current Liab	41787	44056	51892	45970	41958
Total Assets	220861	220861	254180	329133	332772
Current Assets	94752	107012	125440	96543	99202
Debtors	49130	61918	56978	-	-
Inventory	38299	21091	19791	96543	99202
Turnover	92113	108123	98858	83817	64207
Oper Profit	862	895	22766	14822	2118
Interest Paid	846	672	459	848	2661
Tax Paid	243	500	7090	837	420
Prf af Int&Tax	2957	8749	23748	13138	5277
Prf att Ord Sh	2957	8749	23748	13138	-5277
Btm Line Earn	2957	8749	23748	13138	-5277
Dividend Paid	898	2873	8080	4489	
Mkt Prce(c) YE	68	95	245	105	58
Depreciation	5	5	12	-	

PER SHARE STATISTICS (CENTS)

Net Asst Val	498 04	492 31	563 26	519 64	533 50
Net Earnings	8 00	24 00	66 00	-	-
Dividends	2 50	8 00	22 50	-	-
Cash Flow	7 26	24 38	66 16	36 58	14 69

RATIOS AND OTHER INFORMATION

Mrk Cap(R000)	24421	34117	87987	37709	20830
Current Ratio	2 27	2 43	2 42	2 10	2 36
Quik/Acid Tst	1 35	1 95	2 04	-	-
A/C Rec T/ovr	1 87	1 75	1 74	-	-
Tot Ass T/ovr	0 42	0 49	0 39	0 25	0 19
Debt/Ass Rat	0 19	0 20	0 20	0 28	0 25
L T L Tot Ass	0 00	-	-	0 14	0 13
Debt to Eqity	0 23	0 25	0 26	0 49	0 44
Interest Cover	2 02	3 54	52 37	17 48	-0 83
Oper Prof Mrg	0 94	0 83	23 03	17 68	-3 30
Net Prof Marg%	3 21	8 09	24 02	15 67	-8 22
Ret on Assets	1 83	4 49	12 31	4 50	-0 66
Ret on Equity%	1 65	4 95	11 74	7 04	-2 75
Price/Earnings	8 50	3 96	3 71	-	
Divid Cover	3 20	3 00	2 93	-	-
Divid Yield	3 68	8 42	9 18	-	
Earning Yield%	11 76	25 26	26 94	-	
NAV % Mrk Pr	732 41	518 22	229 90	494 89	919 82
Effec Tax Rate	25 44	11 71	19 80	5 99	-8 79
Def Interval	1 81	0 14	2 18	3 50	-7 95
Sus Grth Rate	1 15	3 32	7 75	4 63	-2 75

SUBSIDIARY & ASSOCIATED COMPANIES

ANNANDALE COLLIERY (PTY) LTD
ASBESTOS REFINING CO (ZIMBABWE) (PVT) L
ASRECO FORWARDING AGENCY (S A) (PTY) LT
CAPE BLUE MINES LTD
CENBES SA (SWITZERLAND)
CENTRAL (CAC) (PTY) LTD
CENTRAL ASBESTOS (BOTSWANA) (PTY) LTD
CENTRAL ASBESTOS (S A) (PTY) LTD
CENTRAL ASBESTOS CO LTD (U K.)
CENTRAL MINERALS & TRADING LTD (U K.)
CENTRAL TRADIMPEX LTD (U K.)
COMMONWEALTH & OVERSEAS ASBESTOS CORP LT
CORETSI ASBESTOS (PTY) LTD
EGNEP LTD
ELCOR INVESTMENTS (PTY) LTD
MALOTILE PROPERTIES LTD
SENEKAL MINE LTD
SPRAYED INSULATIONS LTD (U K.)
SWEENEY ESTATES ASBESTOS LTD

INVESTMENTS

CONCORDE GLASS LTD (200000 SH)

GROOTVLEI PROPRIETARY MINES LTD

ABBREVIATION : GROOTVLEI

JSE SHORT CODE : GPM

SECTOR : Gold-Rand & others

SHAREHOLDERS

Who Owns Whom's Assessment of the Identity of the Ultimate Controlling Shareholder:
INSTITUTIONAL / MANAGED BY GENMIN

SHAREHOLDER	PERCENTAGE 1992	1991
INDO-CHINA NOM P/L	25 3	---
CONSOLIDATED NOM P/L	14 8	14 8
SEPON LTD J ACCOUNT	10 5	---
FIRST NAT NOM P/L GATR DEPOT	5 7	5 4
LONDON CONTROL & AMALGAMATED	3 9	4 7
FIRST NAT NOM P/L	3 7	5 1
STD BANK NOM TVL P/L	3 6	2 9
ABSA NOM P/L	2 7	---
ZORMAX PROPERTIES P/L	1 8	1 8
NAT CITY NOM LTD	1 5	1 5
FIRST CORP NOM P/L	1 4	1 4
INDO-CHINA NOM SA P/L	---	26 2
SEPON LTD	---	10 1
VOLKSKAS NOM P/L	---	1 6
TOTAL	74 7	75 4

DIRECTORS :
BOTHA AD ,DU PLESSIS AJ ,FEWELL PT
MAUDE G (Chairman & Managing Dir)
OBERHOLZER MR ,TALJAARD P

REGISTRATION NUMBER : 01/02088/06

REGISTERED OFFICE
General Mining Building, 6 Hollard Street
Johannesburg
2001
TEL 011-376 9111
FAX 011-836 8708

TRANSFER SECRETARY
Central Registrars Ltd
P O Box 4844, Johannesburg
2000
TEL 011-331 0051

COMPANY SECRETARY
General Mining Metals & Minerals Ltd

NATURE OF BUSINESS
The company operates a gold mine in the Springs area, Tvl Silver & osmiridium are recovered as by-products

BANKERS :
First National Bank of SA Ltd

AUDITORS :
Deloitte Pim Goldby

FAMILIAR BRAND NAMES
N/A

CONTRIBUTION BY ACTIVITY
Gold (% Turnover) (99 6%)
Silver (0 2%)
Osmiridium (0 2%)

YEAR END : December

DIVIDEND : Ords 25c

Interim No 101	(Ldr)04/08/89	(Pay)15/09/89	Amt(c)5
Final No 102	(Ldr)22/02/90	(Pay)16/03/90	Amt(c)30
Interim No 103	(Ldr)03/08/90	(Pay)14/09/90	Amt(c)25
Final No 104	(Ldr)01/02/91	(Pay)15/03/91	Amt(c)5
Final No 106	(Ldr)31/01/92	(Pay)13/03/92	Amt(c)25
Interim No 105	(Ldr)02/08/91	(Pay)13/09/91	Amt(c)30

NUMBER OF EMPLOYEES : 2144

CAPITAL STRUCTURE

	AUTHORISED	ISSUED
Ords 25c	11438816	11438816

FINANCIAL STATISTICS (AT FINANCIAL YEAR END)

(Amts in R'000)	1991 Dec	1990 Dec	1989 Dec	1988	1987
Ord S/H Int	80258	74115	75171	73544	70226
Long Trm Loans	-	-	-	27137	24601
Iss Ord Share	11439	11439	11439	11439	11439
Total Liab	13673	9748	17306	54274	49202
Current Liab	13673	9748	17306	27137	24601
Total Assets	93931	83863	92477	133898	123257
Current Assets	27066	22813	31347	33217	28430
Debtors	3108	1652	4940	-	-
Inventory	3192	3449	4335	33217	28430
Turnover	76602	77785	101319	136492	132551
Oper Profit	15308	3714	7805	15787	10979
Tax Paid	2874	1338	2257	4362	1136
Prf af Int&Tax	12434	2376	5631	11425	9843
Prf att Ord Sh	12434	2376	6110	10691	7667
Btm Line Earn	12434	2376	6110	10691	7667
Dividend Paid	6291	3432	4004	8007	8007

Mkt Prce(c) YE	475	375	1025	400	800

PER SHARE STATISTICS (CENTS)

Net Asst Val	701 62	647 92	657 15	642 92	613 92
Net Earnings	58 00	21 00	53 00	-	-
Dividends	55 00	30 00	35 00	-	-
Cash Flow	108 70	20 77	49 23	99 88	86 05

RATIOS AND OTHER INFORMATION

Mrk Cap(R000)	54335	42896	117250	45756	91512
Current Ratio	1 98	2 34	1 81	1 22	1 16
Quik/Acid Tst	1 75	1 99	1 56		
A/C Rec T/ovr	24 65	47 09	20 51	-	-
Tot Ass T/ovr	0 82	0 93	1 10	1 02	1 08
Debt/Ass Rat	0 15	0 12	0 19	0 41	0 40
L T L Tot Ass	-	-	-	0 20	0 20
Debt to Eqity	0 17	0 13	0 23	0 74	0 70
Oper Prof Mrg	19 98	4 77	7 70	11 57	8 28
Net Prof Marg%	16 23	3 05	6 03	7 83	5 78
Ret on Assets	16 30	4 43	8 53	11 79	8 91
Ret on Equity%	15 49	3 21	8 13	14 54	10 92
Price/Earnings	8 19	17 86	19 34	-	-
Divid Cover	1 05	0 70	1 51	-	
Divid Yield	11 58	8 00	3 41	-	-
Earning Yield%	12 21	5 60	5 17	-	-
NAV % Mrk Pr	147 71	172 78	64 11	160 73	76 74
Effec Tax Rate	16 53	35 30	27 47	27 63	10 35
Def Interval	-		-	2 38	2 50
Sus Grth Rate	7 65	-1 42	2 80	3 65	0 48

SUBSIDIARY & ASSOCIATED COMPANIES

None

INVESTMENTS

None

GROUP FIVE HOLDINGS LTD

ABBREVIATION : G5HOLD

JSE SHORT CODE : GRF

SECTOR : Industrial-Building & Construction

SHAREHOLDERS

Who Owns Whom's Assessment of the Identity of the Ultimate Controlling Shareholder: MANAGEMENT CONSORTIUM/S M GOLDSTEIN

SHAREHOLDER	PERCENTAGE 1992	1991
S M GOLDSTEIN LTD	45 4	45 4
MIV CONSTRUCTION HOLDINGS CO P/L	5 7	12 6
SA MUTUAL	5 5	1 1
ABSA NOM P/L	5 3	--
MOMENTUM LIFE ASSURE LTD	4 3	4 4
CMB NOM P/L	2 8	
CLOGG PETER INV P/L	2 2	2 4
HORTORS GROUP PENS FUND	2 2	
STD BANK NOM TVL P/L	2 0	--
NEDBANK NOM LTD	1 8	---
ELLERINE BROS P/L	1 4	1 4
JACKSON T N	1 1	1 1
NEDPERM BANK LTD	---	1 4
INDO-CHINA NOM SA P/L	---	1 1
SANLAM	--	2 8
VOLKSKAS NOM P/L	---	2 9
TOTAL	79 7	76 5

DIRECTORS :
CLOGG PK (Chief Executive),CUNNINGHAM RWW ENTHOVEN R ,GOLDSTEIN SM (Chairman),JACKSON TN KOTZEE TJ

REGISTRATION NUMBER : 88/00321/06

REGISTERED OFFICE
371 Rivonia Road, Rivonia
Sandton
2199
TEL 011-803 1155
FAX 011-803 5829

TRANSFER SECRETARY
Mercantile Registrars Ltd
P O Box 1053, Johannesburg
2000
TEL 011-333 8181

COMPANY SECRETARY
D Zuccolotto

NATURE OF BUSINESS
An investment holding company with a controlling interest in quoted Group Five Ltd

BANKERS :
Standard Bank of SA Ltd

AUDITORS :
Coopers Theron Du Toit

FAMILIAR BRAND NAMES
N/A

CONTRIBUTION BY ACTIVITY
N/A

YEAR END : June

DIVIDEND : Ords 5c

Interim No 4	(Ldr)02/03/90	(Pay)16/03/90	Amt(c)22
Final No 5	(Ldr)14/09/90	(Pay)29/09/90	Amt(c)31
Interim No 6	(Ldr)22/02/91	(Pay)15/03/91	Amt(c)26
Final No 7	(Ldr)20/09/91	(Pay)04/10/91	Amt(c)36
Interim No 8	(Ldr)20/03/92	(Pay)28/02/92	Amt(c)26
Final No 9	(Ldr)16/10/92	(Pay)06/11/92	Amt(c)6

NUMBER OF EMPLOYEES : 15515

CAPITAL STRUCTURE

	AUTHORISED	ISSUED
Ords 5c	15000000	9203018

FINANCIAL STATISTICS (AT FINANCIAL YEAR END)

(Amts in R'000)	1992 Jun	1991 Jun	1990 Jun	1989 Jun	1988 Jun
Ord S/H Int	49417	46996	35860	27530	21702
Long Trm Loans	361555	81013	65860	47052	30967
Iss Ord Share	9203	9203	9203	9203	9203
Total Liab	947284	491092	445230	378551	174423

Current Liab	585729	410079	379370	331499	143456
Total Assets	996701	538088	481090	406081	196125
Current Assets	604396	445433	379690	320722	155868
Debtors	344494	214365	225534	198091	88215
Inventory	215064	143663	94308	66916	37319
Turnover	1380296	1305322	1300243	1067063	105573
Oper Profit	18397	28909	23204	18192	3628
Interest Paid	22158	1232	1261	7515	-
Tax Paid	2879	13017	8049	3715	-19
Prf af Int&Tax	17411	28228	22503	20418	3647
Prf att Ord Sh	8871	17384	15272	12086	2003
Btm Line Earn	8253	18535	15272	11767	-3599
Dividend Paid	2945	5706	4878	4233	1748
Mkt Prce(c) YE	635	540	410	360	325
Depreciation	27085	27189	22981	14289	12914

PER SHARE STATISTICS (CENTS)

Net Asst Val	536 97	510 66	389 66	299 14	235 81
Net Earnings	96 00	189 00	166 00	131 00	21 80
Dividends	32 00	62 00	53 00	46 00	19 00
Cash Flow	306 65	457 56	424 81	287 17	322 42

RATIOS AND OTHER INFORMATION

Mrk Cap(R000)	58439	49696	37732	33131	29910
Current Ratio	1 03	1 09	1 00	0 97	1 09
Quik/Acid Tst	0 66	0 74	0 75	0 77	0 83
A/C Rec T/ovr	4 01	6 09	5 77	5 39	2 39
Tot Ass T/ovr	1 38	2 43	2 70	2 63	1 08
Debt/Ass Rat	0 59	0 76	0 79	0 82	0 78
L T L Tot Ass	0 00	-	-	0 01	0 05
Debt to Eqity	11 92	8 73	10 58	12 15	7 02
Interest Cover	1 11	28 14	22 33	2 98	
Oper Prof Mrg	1 33	2 21	1 78	1 70	3 44
Net Prof Marg%	0 64	1 33	1 17	1 13	1 90
Ret on Assets	4 63	8 71	7 82	8 24	3 78
Ret on Equity%	17 95	36 99	42 59	43 90	18 46
Price/Earnings	6 61	2 86	2 47	2 75	14 91
Divid Cover	3 00	3 05	3 13	2 85	1 15
Divid Yield	5 04	11 48	12 93	12 78	5 85
Earning Yield%	15 12	35 00	40 49	36 39	6 71
NAV % Mrk Pr	84 56	94 57	95 04	83 09	72 56
Effec Tax Rate	12 48	26 50	2 76	9 10	0 52
Def Interval	4 21	0 02	0 08	0 27	0 33
Sus Grth Rate	11 99	24 85	28 98	28 53	1 18

SUBSIDIARY & ASSOCIATED COMPANIES

GROUP FIVE LTD

INVESTMENTS

None

GROUP FIVE LTD

ABBREVIATION : GROUP-5

JSE SHORT CODE : GRF

SECTOR : Industrial-Building & Construction

SHAREHOLDERS

Who Owns Whom's Assessment of the Identity of the Ultimate Controlling Shareholder:
GROUP FIVE HOLDINGS

SHAREHOLDER	PERCENTAGE 1992	1991
GROUP FIVE HOLDINGS LTD	53 8	53 8
SA MUTUAL	19 7	18 1
MOMENTUM LIFE ASSURE LTD	8 8	8 6
CMB NOM P/L	6 1	---
ELLERINE BROS P/L	3 0	3 0
STD BANK NOM TVL P/L	1 6	1 5
SAAMBOU NBS LTD	---	1 5
SANLAM	---	6 1
TOTAL	93 1	92 6

DIRECTORS :
BATH DW ,CLOGG PK (Executive Chairman)
CUNINGHAM RWW ,ENTHOVEN R ,GOLDSTEIN SM
JACKSON TN ,KOTZEE TJ (Financial Director)
THULA GJ ,WILSON EF

REGISTRATION NUMBER : 69/00032/06

REGISTERED OFFICE
371 Rivonia Boulevard, Rivonia, Sandton
2128
TEL 011-803 1155
FAX 011-803 5829

TRANSFER SECRETARY
Mercantile Registrars Ltd
P O Box 1053, Johannesburg
2000
TEL 011-333 8181

COMPANY SECRETARY
D Zuccolotto

NATURE OF BUSINESS
The group is active in the following areas Building, road & structural construction, Property development & administration, Township development & housing, Operating sewerage & water treatment plants & maintenance of water reticulation, Cut, bend & fix steel reinforcing & provision of post-tension material & services, Manufacture for hire & sale of scaffolding & formwork, Quarry, cut, polish & marketing of dimensional granite stone, Project management, Control of quoted Everite

BANKERS :
Standard Bank of SA Ltd

AUDITORS :
Coopers Theron Du Toit

FAMILIAR BRAND NAMES
CMGM,COMBRINK CONSTRUCTION,GOLDSTEIN
GOUGH COOPER,GROUP FIVE BUILDING
HIGH STRUCTURES,R H MORRIS,SAVAGE & LOVEMORE
STEVENSON CONSTRUCTION

CONTRIBUTION BY ACTIVITY
Civils (19 8%)
Engineering (10 5%)
Roads (15 1%)
Homes (4 2%)
Industrial (21 2%)
Property (1 8%)

YEAR END · June

DIVIDEND Ords 50c

Interim No 27	(Ldr)02/03/90	(Pay)16/03/90	Amt(c)23
Final No 28	(Ldr)14/09/90	(Pay)29/09/90	Amt(c)32
Interim No 29	(Ldr)22/02/91	(Pay)15/03/91	Amt(c)27
Final No 30	(Ldr)20/09/91	(Pay)04/10/91	Amt(c)37
Interim No 31	(Ldr)28/02/92	(Pay)20/03/92	Amt(c)27
Final No 32	(Ldr)16/10/92	(Pay)06/11/92	Amt(c)6

NUMBER OF EMPLOYEES : 11557

CAPITAL STRUCTURE

	AUTHORISED	ISSUED
Ords 50c	20000000	16724975

FINANCIAL STATISTICS (AT FINANCIAL YEAR END)

(Amts in R'000)	1992 Jun	1991 Jun	1990 Jun	1989 Jun	1988 Jun
Ord S/H Int	91683	87152	66485	51064	40159
Long Trm Loans	319225	40775	35163	23476	12426
Iss Ord Share	16725	16725	16725	16725	16725
Total Liab	905018	450935	414605	355017	155966
Current Liab	585793	410160	379442	331541	143540
Total Assets	996701	538087	481090	406081	196125
Current Assets	604396	445432	379690	320722	155868
Debtors	344494	214364	225534	198091	88215
Inventory	215064	143663	94308	66916	37319
Turnover	1380296	1305322	1300243	1067063	765213
Oper Profit	21414	34716	28201	12064	23315
Interest Paid	22158	1232	1261	7515	3941
Tax Paid	2879	13017	8049	3715	-649
Prf af Int&Tax	17457	28273	22548	20458	20023
Prf att Ord Sh	16564	32377	28455	22254	20477
Btm Line Earn	15415	34515	28455	21935	20477
Dividend Paid	5519	10704	9199	7861	8026
Mkt Prce(c) YE	625	600	470	380	325
Depreciation	27085	27189	22981	14289	12914

PER SHARE STATISTICS (CENTS)

Net Asst Val	548.18	521.09	397.52	305.32	240.11
Net Earnings	99.00	194.00	170.00	133.00	-
Dividends	33.00	64.00	55.00	47.00	-
Cash Flow	214.73	341.42	312.57	218.81	128.05

RATIOS AND OTHER INFORMATION

Mrk Cap(R000)	104531	100350	78608	63555	54356
Current Ratio	1.03	1.09	1.00	0.97	1.09
Quik/Acid Tst	0.66	0.74	0.75	0.77	0.83
A/C Rec T/ovr	4.01	6.09	5.77	5.39	5.78
Tot Ass T/ovr	1.38	2.43	2.70	2.63	2.60
Debt/Ass Rat	0.59	0.76	0.79	0.82	0.78
L T L Tot Ass	0.00	-	-	0.01	0.05
Debt to Eqity	6.43	4.71	5.71	6.55	3.80
Interest Cover	1.11	28.18	22.36	2.99	5.92
Oper Prof Mrg	1.55	2.66	2.17	1.13	3.05
Net Prof Marg%	1.20	2.48	2.19	2.09	2.68
Ret on Assets	4.63	8.72	7.82	8.25	8.08
Ret on Equity%	18.07	37.15	42.80	43.58	33.99
Price/Earnings	6.31	3.09	2.76	2.86	-
Divid Cover	3.00	3.03	3.09	2.83	-
Divid Yield	5.28	10.67	11.70	12.37	-
Earning Yield%	15.84	32.33	36.17	35.00	-
NAV % Mrk Pr	87.71	86.85	84.58	80.35	73.88
Effec Tax Rate	10.28	22.77	2.31	13.14	1.01
Def Interval	3.31	0.01	0.06	0.19	0.05
Sus Grth Rate	12.05	24.87	28.96	28.19	31.00

SUBSIDIARY & ASSOCIATED COMPANIES

AIL (PTY) LTD (50%)
AMALGAMATED REINFORCING (PTY) LTD (49%)
CMGM (PTY) LTD
COMBRINK CONSTRUCTION SA (PTY) LTD
EVERITE HOLDINGS LTD (21,6%)
GLYBETON (EDMS) BPK
GOLDSTEIN BUILDING TRANSVAAL (PTY) LTD
GOLDSTEIN CIVIL TRANSVAAL (PTY) LTD
GOLDSTEIN COASTAL (PTY) LTD
GOLDSTEIN HOUSING (PTY) LTD
GOUGH COOPER HOMES (PTY) LTD
GROUP FIVE BUILDING (EAST CAPE) (PTY) LT
GROUP FIVE BUILDING (NATAL DISTRICTS) (P
GROUP FIVE BUILDING LTD
GROUP FIVE CONSTRUCTION (PTY) LTD
GROUP FIVE CORPORATE SERVICES (PTY) LTD
GROUP FIVE INDUSTRIAL HOLDINGS LTD
GROUP FIVE METS (PTY) LTD
GROUP FIVE PROJECTS (PTY) LTD
GROUP FIVE PROPERTIES (PTY) LTD
HIGH STRUCTURES (PTY) LTD (50%)
R H MORRIS (PTY) LTD
S M GOLDSTEIN & CO (PTY) LTD
SAVAGE & LOVEMORE (CAPE) (PTY) LTD
SAVAGE & LOVEMORE (EAST CAPE) (PTY) LTD
SAVAGE & LOVEMORE (NATAL) (PTY) LTD
SAVAGE & LOVEMORE (NORTH) (PTY) LTD
SAVAGE & LOVEMORE (WEST CAPE) (PTY) LTD
SM GOLDSTEIN LTD (45%)
STEVENSON CONSTRUCTION (PTY) LTD
TOLLROAD CONCESSIONARIES (PTY) LTD (36%)
WOODBURN HOSPITAL PROPERTIES (PTY) LTD

INVESTMENTS

None

GROVE PROPERTY FUND

ABBREVIATION : GROPROP

JSE SHORT CODE : GPR

SECTOR : Financial-Property Trust

SHAREHOLDERS

Who Owns Whom's Assessment of the Identity of the Ultimate Controlling Shareholder: INSTITUTIONAL CONTROL

SHAREHOLDER	PERCENTAGE 1992	1991
METROPOLITAN LIFE LTD	14.2	14.2
DURBAN CORP SUPERANNUATION FUND	13.6	5.6
SA MUTUAL	12.0	11.7
JOHANNESBURG MUNICIPAL PENS FUND	11.7	11.7
BARLOWS PENS FUND	7.9	7.5
EIGHTY ONE MAIN STREET NOM LTD	7.7	7.5
DURBAN MUNICIPAL PENS FUND	5.4	2.5
NAMPAK PENS FUND	3.8	3.8
CORNER HOUSE PENS FUND	2.6	2.6
METAL IND GROUP PENS FUND	2.0	2.0
ENGINEERING INDUSTRIES PENS FUND	1.5	1.5
SHARESTOCK NOM P/L	1.4	1.5
GROVE PROPERTY FUND MANAGERS LTD	1.3	1.3
PLEVANS PENS FUND	1.3	1.3
CITY COUNCIL OF DURBAN	---	11.3
TOTAL	86.1	85.8

DIRECTORS :
CARSTENS CJ ,GIBSON LJ ,HASLETT FN (Chairman)
MARTIN PT ,SCHLAPOBERSKY I ,TURRELL MF
VAN RENSBURG JJJ ,VEALE HT

REGISTRATION NUMBER : 84/11546/09

REGISTERED OFFICE
1st Floor, Fıeld House
25 Fıeld Street, Durban
4001
TEL 031-305 3336

TRANSFER SECRETARY
Central Regıstrars Ltd
P O Box 4844, Johannesburg
2000
TEL 011-331 0051

COMPANY SECRETARY
C J van Graan

NATURE OF BUSINESS
Groprop ıs a closed end property fund wıth sole ownershıp of a number of ındustrıal & commercıal propertıes

BANKERS :
Standard Bank of SA Ltd

AUDITORS :
Arthur Andersen & Co

FAMILIAR BRAND NAMES
N/A

CONTRIBUTION BY ACTIVITY
Industrıal (% net ıncome) (52 0%)
Retaıl/Commercıal (48 0%)

YEAR END : February

DIVIDEND : Unıts

Interım No 6	(Ldr)16/10/88	(Pay)28/10/88	Amt(c)13 40
Fınal No 7	(Ldr)14/04/89	(Pay)28/04/89	Amt(c)14 75
Interım No 8	(Ldr)13/10/89	(Pay)27/10/89	Amt(c)15 10
Fınal No 9	(Ldr)13/04/90	(Pay)27/04/90	Amt(c)16 40
Interım No 10	(Ldr)12/10/90	(Pay)26/10/90	Amt(c)16 60
Fınal No 11	(Ldr)12/04/91	(Pay)26/04/91	Amt(c)16 60
Interım No 12	(Ldr)11/10/91	(Pay)25/10/91	Amt(c)17 75
Fınal No 13	(Ldr)10/04/92	(Pay)24/04/92	Amt(c)19 10
Interım No 14	(Ldr)16/10/92	(Pay)30/10/92	Amt(c)19 10

NUMBER OF EMPLOYEES : 9

CAPITAL STRUCTURE

	AUTHORISED	ISSUED
Unıts	40000000	40000000

FINANCIAL STATISTICS (AT FINANCIAL YEAR END)

(Amts ın R'000)	1992 Feb	1991 Feb	1990 Feb	1989 Feb	1988
Ord S/H Int	82340	81456	80017	79166	78932
Long Trm Loans		-	-		5113
Iss Ord Share	40000	40000	40000	40000	40000
Total Lıab	7724	6710	6637	6731	10226
Current Lıab	7724	6710	6637	6731	5113
Total Assets	90064	88166	86654	85897	98714
Current Assets	11502	7798	12717	14108	14669
Debtors	127	90	88	119	-
Inventory	-	-	-	-	14669
Oper Profıt	-567	-552	-522	11266	9889
Prf af Int&Tax	14728	13277	12599	11266	9889
Prf att Ord Sh	14728	13277	12599	11266	9889
Btm Lıne Earn	14728	13277	12599	11266	9889
Dıvıdend Paıd	14740	13280	12600	11260	9880
Mkt Prce(c) YE	280	275	290	290	250

PER SHARE STATISTICS (CENTS)

Net Asst Val	205 85	203 64	200 04	197 92	197 33
Net Earnıngs	36 85	33 20	31 50	28 15	
Dıvıdends	36 85	33 20	31 50	28 15	
Cash Flow	36 82	33 19	31 50	28 17	24 72

RATIOS AND OTHER INFORMATION

Mrk Cap(R000)	112000	110000	116000	116000	100000
Current Ratıo	1 49	1 16	1 92	2 10	2 87
Quık/Acıd Tst	1 49	1 16	1 92	2 10	-
Debt/Ass Rat	0 09	0 08	0 08	0 08	0 10
L T L Tot Ass	-	-	-		0 05
Debt to Eqıty	0 09	0 08	0 08	0 09	0 13
Ret on Assets	16 35	15 06	14 54	13 12	10 02
Ret on Equıty%	17 89	16 30	15 75	14 23	12 53
Prıce/Earnıngs	7 60	8 28	9 21	10 30	
Dıvıd Cover	1 00	1 00	1 00	1 00	
Dıvıd Yıeld	13 16	12 07	10 86	9 71	-
Earnıng Yıeld%	13 16	12 07	10 86	9 71	-
NAV % Mrk Pr	73 52	74 05	68 98	68 25	78 93
Def Interval		-	-	-	0 52
Sus Grth Rate	-0 01	0 00	0 00	0 01	0 01

SUBSIDIARY & ASSOCIATED COMPANIES

190 PIETERMARITZ STREET (PTY) LTD
31 WRENCH ROAD (PTY) LTD
770 ANDRIES STREET WYNBERG (PTY) LTD
ALBERTA PROPERTIES (PTY) LTD
BEARTON PROPERTIES (PTY) LTD
BRONSBURY (PTY) LTD
CARLAJANE PROPERTIES (PTY) LTD
CLAIRMONT PROPERTIES (PTY) LTD
COTTAGE & HOME (PTY) LTD
DUOMO INVESTMENTS (PTY) LTD
ERF 17910 BEACONVALE (PTY) LTD
ERF 82 VANDERBIJLPARK (PTY) LTD
EXTENSION FIVE PROPERTIES (PTY) LTD
FIREBIRD INVESTMENTS (PTY) LTD
GULL STREET INVESTMENTS (PTY) LTD
HACK TWO (PTY) LTD
JONVID PROPERTIES (PTY) LTD
LANCEWILL (PTY) LTD
LOT THREE THREE FOUR EASTLEIGH (PTY) LTD
LOULET PROPERTIES (PTY) LTD
MAINPINE INVESTMENTS (PTY) LTD
MAWABY INVESTMENTS (PTY) LTD
MAXWELL PROPERTIES (PTY) LTD
MINI PARK (PTY) LTD
MIROPI PROPERTIES (PTY) LTD
SEVENTY SAGE ROAD (PTY) LTD
SHANELLY PROPERTIES (PTY) LTD
SUCOSA PROPERTIES (PTY) LTD
SUVLA (PTY) LTD
SYBLAKE (PTY) LTD
T R C PROPERTIES (PTY) LTD
THREE EDISON PLACE (PTY) LTD
TRUST SENTRUM (DURBAN) (PTY) LTD
UK PROPERTIES (PTY) LTD
VAN RIEBEECK UNDERTAKINGS (PTY) LTD
WEECO (PTY) LTD

INVESTMENTS

None

GROVEWALK HOLDINGS LTD

ABBREVIATION : GROWALK

JSE SHORT CODE : GRW

SECTOR : Financial-Property

SHAREHOLDERS

Who Owns Whom's Assessment of the Identity of the Ultimate Controlling Shareholder: DIRECTORS

SHAREHOLDER	PERCENTAGE 1992	1991
FIRST NAT NOM P/L	15 1	16 8
DPF INV LTD	11 2	11 2
GROVEWALK SHARE PURCHASE TRUST	8 3	8 3
SUSSEX INV P/L	4 8	---
LENCRES PROPERTIES P/L	3 7	1 8
STOCKSHARE NOM P/L	2 8	2 8
NAIAD INV LTD	2 7	2 7
D M C G INV C C	2 5	2 5
BEARE HOLDINGS P/L	2 1	2 1
MAROT J E M	1 9	1 9
SAAD P A	1 7	1 7
GROVEWALK LINKED UNIT PURCHASE SCHEME	1 5	1 5
ETGEN INV C C	1 3	1 3
EXODUS P/L	1 1	1 1
SUSSEX SECURITIES LTD	---	4 7
TOTAL	60 5	60 2

DIRECTORS :
DE RAUVILLE JPG (Chief Executive & M D)
MEYER SE ,NEL HW ,QUINN DG (Financial Director)
RIVALLAND JC ,ROGOFF A ,SAAD PA (Chairman)
SHERRELL RE

REGISTRATION NUMBER : 78/02272/06

REGISTERED OFFICE
4th Floor Grovewalk House, Old Well Court
Durban
4001
TEL 031-301 1302
FAX 031-305 6849

TRANSFER SECRETARY
Union Provident Trust SA Ltd
P O Box 2322, Johannesburg
2000
TEL 011-833 6700

COMPANY SECRETARY
H W Nel

NATURE OF BUSINESS
The group's activities include the following Property dealing & development, development & marketing of timeshare resorts, interior & exterior plantscaping, cleaning services, & the design & development of affordable housing

BANKERS :
Nedperm Bank Ltd
First National Bank of SA Ltd
Standard Bank of SA Ltd

AUDITORS :
Ernst & Young

FAMILIAR BRAND NAMES
AALSMEER,BERCO CLEANING,BRABANT,DEVCOR
PALACE HOTEL (DBN),PALM BAY
PARK LODGE GARDENS,PARKGROVE,SANTA BARBARA
SERVCOR,THE GABLES,THE PALACE

CONTRIBUTION BY ACTIVITY
N/A

YEAR END : June

DIVIDEND :15/09/91

NUMBER OF EMPLOYEES : 1200

CAPITAL STRUCTURE

	AUTHORISED	ISSUED
Ords 1c	50000000	13199750
Deferred Ords 1c	10000000	0
Partic Prefs 1c	20000000	0
Deferred Partic Prefs 1c	10000000	0

FINANCIAL STATISTICS (AT FINANCIAL YEAR END)

(Amts in R'000)	1991 Feb	1990 Feb	1989 Feb	1988	1987
Ord S/H Int	3113	9311	7535	8006	6285
Long Trm Loans	26817	23259	20485	24452	15032
Iss Ord Share	13200	12934	11934	10849	-
Total Liab	59800	42482	46645	32711	17480
Current Liab	33183	19223	26160	8259	2448
Total Assets	60330	47776	49326	37606	23765
Intang Assets	2583	4017	4854	3111	*
Current Assets	35668	19357	26607	16756	8616
Debtors	5766	4823	6435	2141	1186
Inventory	28849	12179	7612	112	125
Turnover	53255	64581	49492	24953	11097
Oper Profit	830	8537	6542	2178	1437
Interest Paid	6559	5589	4162	716	832
Tax Paid	-184	702	734	54	154
Prf af Int&Tax	-3450	3471	2020	1408	451
Prf att Ord Sh	-2534	1955	1815	1811	745
Btm Line Earn	-6063	1609	1300	1693	1032
Dividend Paid	-	194	293	209	984
Mkt Prce(c) YE	80	120	125	130	-
Depreciation	1076	893	611	552	446

PER SHARE STATISTICS (CENTS)

Net Asst Val	4 02	40 93	22 47	45 12	-
Net Earnings	-14 70	30 10	27 30	18 30	8 60
Dividends	-	16 00	15 00	11 30	11 30
Cash Flow	7 46	37 29	21 27	17 59	7 46

RATIOS AND OTHER INFORMATION

Mrk Cap(R000)	10560	15521	14918	14104	-
Current Ratio	1 07	1 01	1 02	2 03	3 52
Quik/Acid Tst	0 21	0 37	0 73	2 02	3 47
A/C Rec T/ovr	9 24	13 39	7 69	11 65	9 36
Tot Ass T/ovr	0 88	1 35	1 00	0 66	0 47
Debt/Ass Rat	0 96	0 79	0 86	0 77	0 57
L T L Tot Ass	0 41	0 38	0 33	0 55	0 47

Debt to Eqity	18.53	4.03	5.62	3.64	2.15
Interest Cover	0.16	1.56	1.57	3.04	1.73
Oper Prof Mrg	1.56	13.22	13.22	8.73	12.95
Net Prof Marg%	-4.76	3.03	3.67	7.26	6.71
Ret on Assets	4.85	20.43	14.02	7.36	6.69
Ret on Equity%	-15.53	8.79	9.32	22.62	11.85
Price/Earnings	-5.44	3.99	4.58	7.10	-
Divid Cover	-	1.88	1.82	1.62	0.76
Divid Yield	-	13.33	12.00	8.69	-
Earning Yield%	-18.38	25.08	21.84	14.08	-
NAV % Mrk Pr	5.02	34.11	17.97	34.71	-
Effec Tax Rate	-0.03	17.19	23.20	6.16	81.49
Def Interval	-37.11	6.75	11.88	3.34	-
Sus Grth Rate	-81.40	18.91	20.20	20.01	-3.80

SUBSIDIARY & ASSOCIATED COMPANIES

94 SPRINGFIELD RD (PTY) LTD
BENCORRUM HOLDINGS LTD
BERCO CLEANING SERVICES (PTY) LTD
BISAG (PTY) LTD
CANDOR CONSULTANTS (PTY) LTD
ESPIA INVESTMENTS (PTY) LTD
GABWILL INVESTMENTS LTD
GGR PROPERTIES (PTY) LTD
GLENWALK PARTNERSHIP (50%)
GROVESTOCKS (PTY) LTD
GROVEWALK NOMINEES (PTY) LTD
GROVEWALK PROJECTS (PTY) LTD
GROVEWALK PROPERTIES (PTY) LTD
GROVEWALK SERVICES (CAPE) (PTY) LTD
GROVEWALK SERVICES (PTY) LTD
H S BUILDING SYSTEMS (PTY) LTD (50%)
HIBBERDENE PLAZA LTD
LAUMAN INVESTMENTS (PTY) LTD
LIVSEY INVESTMENTS (PTY) LTD
LYNACRES PROJECTS (PTY) LTD (50%)
LYNGROVE DEVELOPMENTS (PTY) LTD (50%)
LYNGROVE SERVICES (PTY) LTD
LYNSTOCKS (PTY) LTD
LYNTON INVESTMENTS (PTY) LTD
MADONI PARK SHARE BLOCK LIMITED
MARINA GROVE (PTY) LTD
MILVERTON HOTELS (PTY) LTD
MILVERTON SHARE BLOCK LIMITED
NIGHTINGALE PROPERTY INVESTMENTS (PTY) L
NORHARD (EDMS) BPK
P M E DEVELOPMENTS (PTY) LTD (50%)
PAMAROSA (PTY) LTD
PARK LODGE HOLDINGS LTD
PLANTOPIA (PTY) LTD
PLANTPROP FARMS (PTY) LTD
R & S PROPERTIES (PTY) LTD
SERVCOR (PTY) LTD
STRATHMORE FARM (PTY) LTD
TREND DEVELOPMENTS (PTY) LTD
WELL BASED INVESTMENTS (PTY) LTD
WILLSBOROUGH PROPERTIES LTD

INVESTMENTS

HARROGATE VENTURE
IG VENDORS PARTNERSHIP
LAEVELD COOPERATIVE SOCIETY
MAPLETON TRUST

GROWTHPOINT PROPERTIES LTD

ABBREVIATION : GROWPNT

JSE SHORT CODE : GRT

SECTOR : Financial-Property Loan Stock

SHAREHOLDERS

Who Owns Whom's Assessment of the Identity of the Ultimate Controlling Shareholder:
SA MUTUAL

SHAREHOLDER	PERCENTAGE 1992	1991
SA MUTUAL	68.2	56.7
CMB NOM P/L	8.5	---
EIGHTY ONE MAIN STREET NOM LTD	3.4	3.5
NAMPAK PENS FUND	2.6	2.6
INVESTEC NOM P/L	2.6	10.4
HUGOHOF INV P/L	1.6	2.0
SAFEGRO NOM P/L	1.4	1.4
GARSFONTEIN PARK NOM CC	1.2	1.6
PILKINGTON GROUP PENS FUND	1.2	1.2
BP CENTRE NOM P/L	---	2.5
SANLAM	---	8.5
TOTAL	90.6	90.3

DIRECTORS :
FLANAGAN JPD ,GERARD PCM ,HACKNER S ,KANTOR B
KOSEFF S ,KUPER D ,RABINOWITZ J
VAN NIEKERK WP (Chairman),WAINER M

REGISTRATION NUMBER : 87/04988/06

REGISTERED OFFICE
2nd Floor, 55 Fox Street
Johannesburg
2001
TEL: 011-498 2399
FAX: 011-498 2388

TRANSFER SECRETARY
Mercantile Registrars Ltd
P O Box 1053, Johannesburg
2000
TEL: 011-333 8181

COMPANY SECRETARY
Metboard Ltd

NATURE OF BUSINESS
A property investment company which derives its main income from property rentals received.

BANKERS :
Trust Bank of Africa Ltd

AUDITORS :
Coopers Theron Du Toit

FAMILIAR BRAND NAMES
N/A

CONTRIBUTION BY ACTIVITY
Nelspruit (% rental income) (22.0%)
Pretoria (23.0%)
Cape Peninsula (14.0%)
George (13.0%)

Johannesburg (11.0%)
E Cape (7.0%)
Durban (2.0%)
Other (8.0%)

YEAR END : October

DIVIDEND : Units

Interim No 5	(Ldr)13/07/90	(Pay)23/07/90	Amt(c)31
Final No 6	(Ldr)04/01/91	(Pay)11/01/91	Amt(c)33
Interim No 7	(Ldr)28/06/91	(Pay)22/07/91	Amt(c)34
Final No 8	(Ldr)03/01/92	(Pay)17/01/92	Amt(c)34
Interim No 9	(Ldr)03/07/92	(Pay)24/07/92	Amt(c)32.5

CAPITAL STRUCTURE

	AUTHORISED	ISSUED
Units (1 Ord : 10 Debs)	34000000	25295808
Unsec Sub Var Rate Debs 50c	252958080	252958080

FINANCIAL STATISTICS (AT FINANCIAL YEAR END)

(Amts in R'000)	1991 Oct	1990 Oct	1989 Oct	1988 Oct
Ord S/H Int	682	665	110990	191
Long Trm Loans	147807	125148	-	93267
Iss Ord Share	25296	25296	22152	18200
Total Liab	159320	134215	9718	98954
Current Liab	11513	9067	9718	5687
Total Assets	160002	134880	120708	99145
Current Assets	6520	7350	7689	5703
Debtors	5481	2672	1747	411
Turnover	18528	17474	13735	11538
Oper Profit	16749	15757	11864	8815
Interest Paid	17459	16775	699	530
Tax Paid	-	16	12	19
Prf af Int&Tax	34	16	12327	9205
Prf att Ord Sh	34	16	12	18
Btm Line Earn	34	419	12	18
Dividend Paid	17	16	12	9
Mkt Prce(c) YE	575	500	550	460

PER SHARE STATISTICS (CENTS)

Net Asst Val	2.70	2.63	501.04	1.05
Net Earnings	68.00	64.00	61.00	50.53
Dividends	68.00	63.99	60.90	50.50
Cash Flow	0.13	0.06	61.10	50.58

RATIOS AND OTHER INFORMATION

Mrk Cap(R000)	145452	126480	121836	83720
Current Ratio	0.57	0.81	0.79	1.00
Quik/Acid Tst	0.57	0.81	0.79	1.00
A/C Rec T/ovr	3.38	6.54	7.86	28.07
Tot Ass T/ovr	0.12	0.13	0.11	0.12
Debt/Ass Rat	1.00	1.00	0.08	1.00
L T L Tot Ass	0.93	0.94	-	0.94
Debt to Eqity	235.56	203.83	0.09	518.08
Interest Cover	0.96	0.94	16.97	16.63
Oper Prof Mrg	90.40	90.17	86.38	76.40
Net Prof Marg%	0.18	0.09	0.09	0.16
Ret on Assets	10.93	12.46	10.80	9.84
Ret on Equity%	4.99	2.41	0.01	9.42
Price/Earnings	8.46	7.81	9.02	9.10
Divid Cover	1.00	1.00	1.00	1.00
Divid Yield	11.83	12.80	11.07	10.98
Earning Yield%	11.83	12.80	11.09	10.98
NAV % Mrk Pr	0.47	0.53	91.10	0.23
Effec Tax Rate	-	50.00	0.10	0.21
Def Interval	4386.41	7904.94	0.74	10.68
Sus Grth Rate	2.49	0.00	0.00	4.71

SUBSIDIARY & ASSOCIATED COMPANIES

CONSOLIDATED ERF 1252 TRANSVAAL INVESTME
DRAGON PROPERTIES SHARE BLOCK (PTY) LTD
ERF 3067 ELLISRAS SHARE BLOCK (PTY) LTD
ERF 53 VANDERBIJLPARK INVESTMENTS SHARE
ERF 67886 WYNBERG INVESTMENTS SHARE BLOC
ERF 7 PORT ELIZABETH INVESTMENTS SHARE B
ERF 758 KLERKSDORP INVESTMENTS SHARE BLO
ERVEN 1514 1512 & PORTION F/ERF 7 P E IN
ERVEN 22386 & 27457 GOODWOOD (PTY) LTD
GOLDENBAUM'S INVESTMENTS SHARE BLOCK (PT
L E T INVESTMENTS SHARE BLOCK (PTY) LTD
LOE GOLD PROPERTIES SHARE BLOCK (PTY) LT
LOT 2417 PINETOWN INVESTMENTS SHARE BLOC
LOT 519 BELLVILLE INVESTMENTS SHARE BLOC
LOT ABS BLOCK E EAST LONDON INVESTMENTS
LOUIS GOLDENBAUM PROPERTIES SHARE BLOCK
MARMOND SHARE BLOCK (PTY) LTD
METBOARD HOUSE SHARE BLOCK LTD
MORIMAR BUILDINGS SHARE BLOCK (PTY) LTD
NITELLA PROPERTIES SHARE BLOCK (PTY) LTD
PORTION 2 OF STAND 545 GERMISTON INVESTM
SANTA BARBARA PROPERTY INVESTMENTS SHARE
STAND 2158 NELSPRUIT SHARE BLOCK (PTY) L
SUNSET BOULEVARD INVESTMENTS (PTY) LTD
TRICOUNTY PROPERTY INVESTMENTS SHARE BLO

INVESTMENTS

None

GUARDIAN NATIONAL INSURANCE CO LTD

ABBREVIATION : GARDIAN

JSE SHORT CODE : GAR

SECTOR : Financial-Insurance

SHAREHOLDERS

Who Owns Whom's Assessment of the Identity of the Ultimate Controlling Shareholder:
GUARDIAN ROYAL EXCHANGE PLC / LIBERTY

SHAREHOLDER	PERCENTAGE 1992	1991
GRE SA HOLDINGS P/L	50.8	---
LIBERTY HOLDINGS LTD	45.4	45.6
BOLAND BANK PENS FUND	2.0	2.0
GUARDIAN ROYAL EXCHANGE ASSURE PLC	---	50.8
TOTAL	98.1	98.4

DIRECTORS :
COOPER DF ,DE VILLIERS HP ,GORDON D (Chairman)
HANDLER S ,HOPKINS SA
JACK AW (Operations Director),JONKER LN
KING JW ,LIEBENBERG GZ ,MCALPINE JR
MCDONOUGH JT ,NEWMAN MJS
NILSSON K (Managing Director),STRAUSS CB DR
WAKEHAM CMS (Financial Director

REGISTRATION NUMBER : 04/02086/06

REGISTERED OFFICE
11th Floor West, Libridge, 25 Ameshof Street
Braamfontein
2001
TEL 011-339 4511
FAX 011-339 7244

TRANSFER SECRETARY
Central Registrars Ltd
P O Box 4844, Johannesburg
2000
TEL 011-331 0051

COMPANY SECRETARY
J Worwood

NATURE OF BUSINESS
The company, a subsidiary of Guardian Royal Exchange Plc, conducts property, casualty, personal lines and marine insurance business in the RSA and neighbouring territories Liberty Holdings owns 45,6% of the company's equity

BANKERS :
Standard Bank of SA Ltd

AUDITORS :
Coopers Theron Du Toit

FAMILIAR BRAND NAMES
N/A

CONTRIBUTION BY ACTIVITY
N/A

YEAR END : December

DIVIDEND :Ords R1

Interim No 72	(Ldr)15/09/89	(Pay)06/10/89	Amt(c)45
Final No 73	(Ldr)30/03/90	(Pay)12/04/90	Amt(c)65
Interim No 74	(Ldr)14/09/90	(Pay)05/10/90	Amt(c)55
Final No 75	(Ldr)28/03/91	(Pay)12/04/91	Amt(c)75
Interim No 76	(Ldr)13/09/91	(Pay)04/10/91	Amt(c)65
Final No 77	(Ldr)03/04/92	(Pay)10/04/92	Amt(c)90
Interim No 78	(Ldr)11/09/92	(Pay)02/10/92	Amt(c)77 5

NUMBER OF EMPLOYEES : 700

CAPITAL STRUCTURE

	AUTHORISED	ISSUED
Ords R1	10200000	10047500

FINANCIAL STATISTICS (AT FINANCIAL YEAR END)

(Amts in R'000)	1991 Dec	1990 Dec	1989 Dec	1988	1987
Ord S/H Int	292949	215750	196223	141881	101406
Long Trm Loans	141489	123489	99152	269929	280094
Iss Ord Share	10048	10015	10000	10000	10000
Total Liab	425263	372986	322213	473494	501930
Current Liab	283774	249497	223061	203565	221836
Total Assets	718212	588736	518436	582888	586447
Current Assets	306664	286046	259098	171078	204947
Debtors	118856	88812	63472		-
Inventory	-	-	-	171078	204947
Turnover	600495	501398	423329	316107	292138
Oper Profit	50854	30834	9242	41393	28123
Tax Paid	11184	4165	15335	17217	10056
Prf af Int&Tax	39670	26669	30115	24963	16409
Prf att Ord Sh	39670	26669	30115	25159	16585
Btm Line Earn	39670	26669	23844	25159	16585
Dividend Paid	15572	13019	11000	9000	7000
Mkt Prce(c) YE	2400	1500	1700	1200	1350

PER SHARE STATISTICS (CENTS)

Net Asst Val	2915 50	2154 27	1962 23	1418 81	1014 06
Net Earnings	395 20	266 40	301 20		
Dividends	155 00	130 00	110 00	-	-
Cash Flow	484 99	251 51	300 27	249 63	164 09

RATIOS AND OTHER INFORMATION

Mrk Cap(R000)	241152	150225	170000	120000	135000
Current Ratio	1 08	1 15	1 16	0 84	0 92
Quik/Acid Tst	1 08	1 15	1 16	-	
A/C Rec T/ovr	5 05	5 65	6 67		
Tot Ass T/ovr	0 84	0 85	0 82	0 54	0 50
Debt/Ass Rat	0 40	0 42	0 43	0 81	0 86
L T L Tot Ass	-	-		0 46	0 48
Debt to Eqity	0 97	1 16	1 14	3 34	4 95
Oper Prof Mrg	8 47	6 15	2 18	13 09	9 63
Net Prof Marg%	6 61	5 32	7 11	7 96	5 68
Ret on Assets	7 08	5 24	8 77	7 24	4 51
Ret on Equity%	13 54	12 36	15 35	17 73	16 36
Price/Earnings	6 07	5 63	5 64	-	
Divid Cover	2 55	2 05	2 74	-	
Divid Yield	6 46	8 67	6 47		-
Earning Yield%	16 47	17 76	17 72	-	-
NAV % Mrk Pr	121 48	143 62	115 43	118 23	75 12
Effec Tax Rate	5 22	18 31	166 88	41 59	35 76
Def Interval	0 17	0 45	-	10 81	17 07
Sus Grth Rate	8 23	6 33	9 74	11 39	9 45

SUBSIDIARY & ASSOCIATED COMPANIES

GUARDIAN ASSURANCE PROPERTIES (PTY) LTD
UNSBIC LEASING CO (PTY) LTD

INVESTMENTS

None

GUBB AND INGGS LTD

ABBREVIATION : GUBINGS

JSE SHORT CODE : GUB

SECTOR : Industrial-Clothing, Footwear & Textiles

SHAREHOLDERS

Who Owns Whom's Assessment of the Identity of the Ultimate Controlling Shareholder:
STUCKEN FAMILY

SHAREHOLDER	PERCENTAGE 1992	1991
MERWOOL P/L	50 4	50 4
INDUSTRIAL SELECTIONS LTD	17 5	17 5
STUCKEN HLDGS P/L	11 6	11 6
MANN J, LEFTIN P M, KING D G T, MANN M	2 1	2 1
FIRST NAT NOM P/L	1 7	---
RELAG AG	1 4	1 4
ISENBECK O E W	---	3 5
TOTAL	84 7	86 5

DIRECTORS :
BONNER HN ,GOUWS GS ,ISENBECK OEW ,MACDONALD W
MIELKE KD ,STUCKEN JP (Chairman),STUCKEN RR
VAN DEEMTER DJ

REGISTRATION NUMBER : 04/01495/06

REGISTERED OFFICE
Hendrik van Eck Drive, Uitenhage
6230
TEL 0422-922 9113
FAX 0422-992 2162

TRANSFER SECRETARY
Consolidated Share Registrars Ltd
P O Box 61051, Marshalltown
2107
TEL 011-492 1620

COMPANY SECRETARY
D Forster

NATURE OF BUSINESS
Wool and mohair sorters, scourers and carbonizers, and combers and recoverers of woolgrease

BANKERS :
Standard Bank of SA Ltd

AUDITORS :
Fisher Hoffman Stride

FAMILIAR BRAND NAMES
N/A

CONTRIBUTION BY ACTIVITY
N/A

YEAR END : June

DIVIDEND : Ords 50c

Interim No 88	(Ldr)13/04/90	(Pay)11/05/90	Amt(c)15
Final No 89	(Ldr)16/11/90	(Pay)07/12/90	Amt(c)25
Final No 90	(Ldr)15/11/91	(Pay)06/12/91	Amt(c)40
Interim No 91	(Ldr)27/03/92	(Pay)29/04/92	Amt(c)20
Final No 92	(Ldr)13/11/92	(Pay)03/12/92	Amt(c)70

NUMBER OF EMPLOYEES : 1005

CAPITAL STRUCTURE

	AUTHORISED	ISSUED
Cum Red Prefs 10c	6000000	376725
Ords 50c	2100000	2031030

FINANCIAL STATISTICS (AT FINANCIAL YEAR END)

(Amts in R'000)	1992 Jun	1991 Jun	1990 Jun	1989 Jun	1988 Jun
Ord S/H Int	60016	50202	47218	47251	39600
Long Trm Loans	22218	22594	16522	19950	23971
Iss Ord Share	2031	2031	2031	2031	2031
Total Liab	104968	115663	101004	158446	162615
Current Liab	82750	93069	84482	138496	138644
Total Assets	164984	165865	148222	205697	202215
Current Assets	130023	129950	108236	161089	160944
Debtors	51059	59067	42685	59524	51915
Inventory	78601	69478	64660	100900	108784
Turnover	293858	261892	272337	402179	313981
Oper Profit	18834	12335	14044	25688	22876
Interest Paid	5025	7097	10551	17369	10184
Tax Paid	2	-333	272	2032	1751
Prf af Int&Tax	13814	5578	3820	10489	11026
Prf att Ord Sh	11698	3545	1799	8599	9707
Btm Line Earn	11698	3545	1799	8599	9707
Dividend Paid	1828	812	812	1320	1320
Mkt Prce(c) YE	870	750	810	1450	1450
Depreciation	3928	4081	4133	3364	2216

PER SHARE STATISTICS (CENTS)

Net Asst Val	2955 00	2471 79	2324 86	2326 49	1949 78
Net Earnings	576 00	174 50	88 60	423 40	477 90
Dividends	90 00	40 00	40 00	65 00	65 00
Cash Flow	740 97	383 60	294 78	470 61	659 38

RATIOS AND OTHER INFORMATION

Mrk Cap(R000)	17670	15233	16451	29450	29450
Current Ratio	1 57	1 40	1 28	1 16	1 16
Quik/Acid Tst	0 62	0 65	0 52	0 43	0 38
A/C Rec T/ovr	5 76	4 43	6 38	6 76	6 05
Tot Ass T/ovr	1 78	1 58	1 84	1 96	1 55
Debt/Ass Rat	0 51	0 57	0 58	0 68	0 69
L T L Tot Ass	0 01	0 01	0 01	0 01	0 01
Debt to Eqity	1 39	1 88	1 82	2 96	3 55
Interest Cover	3 75	1 74	1 33	1 49	2 25
Oper Prof Mrg	6 41	4 71	5 16	6 39	7 29
Net Prof Marg%	3 98	1 35	0 66	2 14	3 09
Ret on Assets	11 72	7 15	9 27	12 60	11 47
Ret on Equity%	19 49	7 06	3 81	18 20	24 51
Price/Earnings	1 51	4 30	9 14	3 42	3 03
Divid Cover	6 40	4 36	2 22	6 51	7 35
Divid Yield	10 34	5 33	4 94	4 48	4 48
Earning Yield%	66 21	23 27	10 94	29 20	32 96
NAV % Mrk Pr	339 65	329 57	287 02	160 45	134 47
Effec Tax Rate	0 64	1 09	-0 42	3 38	0 34
Def Interval	5 38	9 97	10 54	12 93	9 24
Sus Grth Rate	16 45	5 44	2 09	15 40	21 18

SUBSIDIARY & ASSOCIATED COMPANIES

BEWOOL EXPORT BROKERS (PTY) LTD
CAPMERINO WOOL & TRADING (PTY) LTD
GLOBAL FIBRES (PTY) LTD
HAROLD ELLA & SONS (PTY) LTD
LANAHAIR P E (PTY) LTD
LJ RACUSSEN & CO (PTY) LTD
OSB (WOOL) (PTY) LTD
OSB HAIR (PTY) LTD
OSB WASTE (PTY) LTD
PE WOOL EXPORTERS (PTY) LTD
RIVERSIDE UTILITY CO LTD (50%)
SCH KARSTAEDT & CO (PTY) LTD (50%)
SOUTHERN COMBING CO (PTY) LTD
SOUTHERN WOOL & MOHAIR (PTY) LTD
SPECIALITY FIBRES (PTY) LTD
STUCKEN & CO (WOOLS) (PTY) LTD
STUCKEN & CO (HAIR) (PTY) LTD
STUCKEN & CO (PTY) LTD
TOG COMBERS (PTY) LTD
TOPMAKERS (PTY) LTD
UNIVERSAL NATURAL FIBRES (PTY) LTD

INVESTMENTS

KWA NOBUHLE ELECTRICITY SUPPLY CO (PTY) (74000SH)

GULLIVER CONSOLIDATED LTD

ABBREVIATION : GULLIVER

SECTOR : Zimbabwe Stock Exchange

SHAREHOLDERS

Who Owns Whom's Assessment of the Identity of the Ultimate Controlling Shareholder: AMEC OVERSEAS INVESTMENTS

SHAREHOLDER	PERCENTAGE 1992	1991
AMEC OVERSEAS INV LTD	35 1	---
GULLIVER W J TRUST	19 7	---
SOUTHAMPTON ASSURE CO ZIM LTD	6 6	---
NAT RAILWAYS OF ZIM CONTR PENS FUND	5 2	---
FIDELITY LIFE ASSURE OF ZIM PVT LTD	2 8	---
BARD NOM (PVT) LTD	2 5	---
FIRST MUTUAL LIFE ASSURE SOC OF ZIM	1 8	---
LOGAN J	1 7	---
C U FIRE MARINE & GEN INSUR CO LIFE FUND	1 6	---
ZIMBABWE ASSETS INV CO LTD	1 4	---
FISONS INV HOLDINGS (ZIMBABWE)	1 3	---
NANGLE E J	1 0	---
TOTAL	80 7	---

DIRECTORS :
BIRSS CR ,GULLIVER WJ ,KISJES RJ
MAASDORP RAC (Chief Executive),MORLEY WM
NARRACOTT JB ,QUIGLEY PK ,STUMBLES RA (Chairman)
TURNER F

REGISTERED OFFICE
Stand 44, Tilbury Road
Willowvale, Harare

TEL 63611/6
FAX 63619

TRANSFER SECRETARY
First Transfer Secretaries (Pvt) Ltd
P O Box 437, Bulawayo
Zimbabwe

TEL 092634 - 702905

COMPANY SECRETARY
Gullivers Management Services

NATURE OF BUSINESS
GULLIVER CONSOLIDATED is incorporated in Zimbabwe Its principal activities are civil engineering,con struction of dams, roads and transport contracting It also sells spares and tyres,which are processed through TROJOAN TYRES It also maintains equipment through PLANT & EQUIPMENT SALES

BANKERS :
ANZ Grindlays Bank Plc

AUDITORS :
Coopers & Lybrand

FAMILIAR BRAND NAMES
N/A

CONTRIBUTION BY ACTIVITY
N/A

YEAR END : March

DIVIDEND : Ords Z$0,50

Dividend	(Ldr)13/12/91	(Pay)27/12/91	Amt(c)3 5
Dividend	(Ldr)07/08/92	(Pay)31/08/92	Amt(c)6 5

CAPITAL STRUCTURE

	AUTHORISED	ISSUED
Ords Z$0,50	15000000	9607253

FINANCIAL STATISTICS (AT FINANCIAL YEAR END)

(Amts in Z$)	1992 Mar	1991 Mar
Ord S/H Int	28306	20122
Long Trm Loans	10806	11032
Iss Ord Share	9607	6990
Total Liab	54888	43907
Current Liab	44082	32875
Total Assets	83194	64029
Current Assets	44165	33999
Debtors	31249	23654
Inventory	11530	6201
Turnover	159853	96177
Oper Profit	7232	5894
Interest Paid	833	609
Tax Paid	5502	1488
Prf af Int&Tax	2267	4086
Prf att Ord Sh	4122	5231
Btm Line Earn	4122	5231
Dividend Paid	959	454
Depreciation	8803	7108

PER SHARE STATISTICS (CENTS)

Net Asst Val	294 64	287 87
Net Earnings	47 00	68 90
Dividends	10 00	6 50
Cash Flow	165 60	164 69

RATIOS AND OTHER INFORMATION

Current Ratio	1 00	1 03
Quik/Acid Tst	0 74	0 85
A/C Rec T/ovr	5 12	4 07
Tot Ass T/ovr	1 92	1 50
Debt/Ass Rat	0 56	0 62
L T L Tot Ass	0 03	0 10
Debt to Eqity	1 66	1 96
Interest Cover	8 68	9 68
Oper Prof Mrg	4 52	6 13
Net Prof Marg%	2 58	5 44
Ret on Assets	12 57	11 44
Ret on Equity%	14 56	26 00
Divid Cover	4 70	10 60
Effec Tax Rate	26 54	3 27
Def Interval	0 28	0 52
Sus Grth Rate	11 17	23 74

SUBSIDIARY & ASSOCIATED COMPANIES

BALMORAL INVESTMENTS (PVT) LTD (47%)
E & M HOLDINGS (PRIVATE) LTD
G D HAULAGE (PVT) LTD (49%)
GULLIVER BOTSWANA (PTY) LTD
GULLIVER DEVELOPMENT PROPERTIES (PVT) LT
GULLIVERS MANAGEMENT SERVICES (PVT) LTD
HIGHWAY CONSTRUCTION COMPANY (PVT) LTD
PLANT & EQUIPMENT (SALES) (PVT) LTD (47%)
RESIDENTIAL SUBURBS (PVT) LTD (49%)

TOLLGATE PROPERTIES (PVT) LTD
TRANSPORT & CRANE HIRE (PVT) LTD
TREADMASTER (PVT) LTD (24%)
TROJAN TYRES (PVT) LTD (47%)
TYREQUIP (PVT) LTD (47%)
W.J & R L. GULLIVER (PVT) LTD

INVESTMENTS

None

GYPSUM INDUSTRIES LTD

ABBREVIATION : GYPSUM

JSE SHORT CODE : GPI

SECTOR : Industrial-Building & Construction

SHAREHOLDERS

Who Owns Whom's Assessment of the Identity of the Ultimate Controlling Shareholder:
BPB INDUSTRIES PLC

SHAREHOLDER	PERCENTAGE 1992	1991
BPB IND PLC	50 0	50 0
BLUE CIRCLE LTD	32 4	32 4
RUDOLF J A	2 1	---
NEDBANK NOM LTD	1 5	1 3
FIRST NAT NOM P/L	1 0	1 5
RUDOLF N S N	---	2 0
TOTAL	87 0	87 1

DIRECTORS :
CLAVEL JP ,COULSON TG ,DU PLESSIS SJP
FAIRBAIRN DA (Chairman),HARDY GD ,HERRING PL
HOLLOWAY JE ,SKILTON D
SNOWDEN SG (Managing Director),WRIGHT DR

REGISTRATION NUMBER : 05/10220/06

REGISTERED OFFICE
Rhino Hall, Bridle Close, Woodmead Park
Woodmead Ext 14, Sandton
2157
TEL 011-804 3334
FAX 011-804 3147

TRANSFER SECRETARY
Mercantile Registrars Ltd
P O Box 1053, Johannesburg
2000
TEL 011-333 8181

COMPANY SECRETARY
DR Wright

NATURE OF BUSINESS
The group's operating activities are the mining and selling of gypsum, the manufacture of Rhinoboard and cornice for domestic and commercial ceilings and walls, and the manufacture of plasters for both the building and industrial markets

BANKERS :
First National Bank of SA Ltd

AUDITORS :
KPMG Aiken & Peat

FAMILIAR BRAND NAMES
PARALINE, RHINOBOARD

CONTRIBUTION BY ACTIVITY
N/A

YEAR END : June

DIVIDEND : Ords 20c

Interim No 89	(Ldr)16/03/90	(Pay)31/03/90	Amt(c)20
Final No 90	(Ldr)21/09/90	(Pay)17/10/90	Amt(c)40
Interim No 91	(Ldr)22/03/91	(Pay)05/04/91	Amt(c)20
Final No 92	(Ldr)20/09/91	(Pay)17/10/91	Amt(c)40
Interim No 93	(Ldr)20/03/92	(Pay)03/04/92	Amt(c)20
Final No 94	(Ldr)10/07/92	(Pay)24/07/92	Amt(c)25
Interim No 95	(Ldr)11/12/92	(Pay)24/12/92	Amt(c)20

NUMBER OF EMPLOYEES : 986

CAPITAL STRUCTURE

	AUTHORISED	ISSUED
Ords 20c	10000000	8182500

FINANCIAL STATISTICS (AT FINANCIAL YEAR END)

(Amts in R'000)	1992 Mar	1991 Jun	1990 Jun	1989 Jun	1988 Jun
Ord S/H Int	74714	68539	58902	48504	39343
Long Trm Loans	45377	64114	12546	11022	11801
Iss Ord Share	8182	8182	8182	8182	8182
Total Liab	85923	97606	40623	31862	33046
Current Liab	40546	33492	28077	20840	21245
Total Assets	160637	166145	99525	80366	72389
Current Assets	63586	70077	47511	38965	33531
Debtors	30417	25383	22477	20519	17493
Inventory	24971	26729	24149	18388	15961
Turnover	-	-	166380	147248	116405
Oper Profit	24831	29947	30593	28793	21836
Interest Paid	6449	5819	920	577	496
Tax Paid	8549	12238	14582	13789	10447
Prf af Int&Tax	10757	17490	16587	14427	10893
Prf att Ord Sh	9857	15974	15307	13334	10048
Btm Line Earn	9857	14546	15307	13334	10048
Dividend Paid	3682	4909	4909	4173	3437
Mkt Prce(c) YE	950	775	700	675	
Depreciation	7051	6948	5837	4813	4705

PER SHARE STATISTICS (CENTS)

Net Asst Val	913 15	837 68	719 90	592 81	480 85
Net Earnings	120 50	195 20	187 10	163 00	122 80
Dividends	45 00	60 00	60 00	51 00	
Cash Flow	375 80	419 26	268 20	222 60	188 89

RATIOS AND OTHER INFORMATION

Mrk Cap(R000)	77729	63411	57274	55229	
Current Ratio	1 57	2 09	1 69	1 87	1 58
Quik/Acid Tst	0 95	1 29	0 83	0 99	0 83
A/C Rec T/ovr			7 40	7 18	6 65
Tot Ass T/ovr	-		1 67	1 83	1 61
Debt/Ass Rat	0 35	0 45	0 29	0 27	0 32
L T L Tot Ass	0 10	0 25	0 01	0 01	0 03
Debt to Eqity	0 75	1 09	0 49	0 45	0 60
Interest Cover	3 85	5 15	33 25	49 90	44 02
Oper Prof Mrg			18 39	19 55	18 76

Net Prof Marg%	-	-	9 20	9 06	8 63
Ret on Assets	21 38	21 40	32 24	35 83	30 16
Ret on Equity%	17 59	23 31	25 99	27 49	25 54
Price/Earnings	7 88	3 97	3 74	4 14	-
Divid Cover	2 68	3 25	3 12	3 20	-
Divid Yield	4 74	7 74	8 57	7 56	-
Earning Yield%	12 68	25 19	26 73	24 15	-
NAV % Mrk Pr	96 12	108 09	102 84	87 82	-
Effec Tax Rate	11 37	4 32	44 21	48 64	45 43
Def Interval	1 12	1 26	0 34	0 21	0 65
Sus Grth Rate	8 26	16 14	17 65	18 89	16 80

SUBSIDIARY & ASSOCIATED COMPANIES

B P B INDUSTRIES (PTY) LTD
DONN PRODUCTS (PTY) LTD
DONN SOUTH AFRICA (PTY) LTD
DONN TRADING LTD (GUERNSEY)
DONN ZIMBABWE (PVT) LTD (ZIMBABWE)
GI MINES (ZAMBIA) LTD
LISKEY (PTY) LTD

INVESTMENTS

SMALL BUSINESS DEVELOPMENT CORP LTD (175392 SH)

HADDON & SLY LTD

ABBREVIATION : H & S

SECTOR : Zimbabwe Stock Exchange

SHAREHOLDERS

Who Owns Whom's Assessment of the Identity of the Ultimate Controlling Shareholder:
MARARD INVESTMENTS (PVT) LTD

DIRECTORS :
CAUSTON GR ,SLY AG ,SLY JR (Chairman),SLY NJ
TASMER GV

REGISTERED OFFICE
Haddon & Sly Building, Fife Street
Bulawayo, Zimbabwe

TEL 733336

TRANSFER SECRETARY
N/A

COMPANY SECRETARY
G R Causton

NATURE OF BUSINESS
The main business of the group's companies,which are incorporated in Zimbabwe,is the retailing of a wide range of consumer products on a departmental store basis

BANKERS :
Standard Chartered Bank Zimbabwe Ltd

AUDITORS :
Deloitte & Touche

FAMILIAR BRAND NAMES
N/A

CONTRIBUTION BY ACTIVITY
N/A

YEAR END : February

DIVIDEND : Ords Z$1
Dividend (Ldr)10/07/92 (Pay)17/07/92 Amt(c)5

CAPITAL STRUCTURE

	AUTHORISED	ISSUED
Ords Z$1	6000000	4500000

FINANCIAL STATISTICS (AT FINANCIAL YEAR END)

(Amts in Z$)	1992 Feb	1991 Feb
Ord S/H Int	7482	6787
Long Trm Loans	316	296
Iss Ord Share	4500	1500
Total Liab	4603	3109
Current Liab	4287	2813
Total Assets	12085	9896
Current Assets	6728	4925
Debtors	1760	1305
Inventory	4770	3489
Turnover	26480	20476
Oper Profit	1345	1110
Interest Paid	16	50
Tax Paid	614	570
Prf af Int&Tax	966	640
Prf att Ord Sh	920	613
Btm Line Earn	920	613
Dividend Paid	225	150
Depreciation	211	129

PER SHARE STATISTICS (CENTS)

Net Asst Val	166 27	452 47
Net Earnings	20 44	13 64
Dividends	5 00	3 33
Cash Flow	24 98	53 47

RATIOS AND OTHER INFORMATION

Current Ratio	1 57	1 75
Quik/Acid Tst	0 46	0 51
A/C Rec T/ovr	15 05	15 69
Tot Ass T/ovr	2 19	2 07
Debt/Ass Rat	0 35	0 28
Debt to Eqty	0 57	0 41
Interest Cover	95 44	24 64
Oper Prof Mrg	5 08	5 42
Net Prof Marg%	3 47	2 99
Ret on Assets	13 21	12 73
Ret on Equity%	12 30	9 03
Divid Cover	4 09	4 10
Effec Tax Rate	44 78	47 24
Sus Grth Rate	9 29	6 82

SUBSIDIARY & ASSOCIATED COMPANIES

BARMORE INVESTMENTS (PVT) LTD
MAPLE INVESTMENTS (PVT) LTD
MCCULLAGH & BOTHWELL (BYO) (PVT) LTD
SEW RITE CENTRE (PVT) LTD
STANLEYS LTD
WOOL & HOME CRAFTS (PVT) LTD

INVESTMENTS

None

HAGGIE LTD

ABBREVIATION : HAGGIE

JSE SHORT CODE : HAG

SECTOR : Industrial-Engineering

SHAREHOLDERS

Who Owns Whom's Assessment of the Identity of the Ultimate Controlling Shareholder:
SANLAM / ANGLO AMERICAN

SHAREHOLDER	PERCENTAGE 1992	1991
RESIDENT NOM LTD	33 4	33 4
CONSOLIDATED NOM P/L	25 2	25 2
MALBAK INV (HAGGIE) LTD	10 0	10 0
LIBERTY LIFE ASSOC OF AFRICA LTD	5 9	5 9
SA MUTUAL	4 4	4 0
FIRST NAT NOM P/L	3 3	3 7
STD BANK NOM TVL P/L	3 2	3 0
HAGGIE LTD SHARE PURCHASE SCHEME	1 3	1 7
TOTAL	86 7	86 8

DIRECTORS :
BROWN HF ,BULLETT BE ,HAGGIE IS (President)
HARRIS A ,HARRISON WE ,MILBURN JM
MURRAY DCG (Managing Director)
SMART WD (Financial Director),SMITH BA
THOMAS GS (Chairman)

REGISTRATION NUMBER : 05/36946/06

REGISTERED OFFICE
Lower Germiston Road, Jupiter
Johannesburg
2094
TEL 011-629 1111
FAX 011-629 1001

TRANSFER SECRETARY
Mercantile Registrars Ltd
P O Box 1053, Johannesburg
2000
TEL 011-333 8181

COMPANY SECRETARY
C C McKie Thomson

NATURE OF BUSINESS
The group operates in 3 divisions steel rod conversion,copper-based products and engineering consumables Group products include steel wire strand & rope, high-carbon steel wire & strand, mild steel chain & wire, wire joining products, copper & brass extrusions, copper & alloy rolled products incl ingots, tube & castings, cutting tools, reamers, taps & dies, steel twist drills, saw blades, rivets & rivet tools The group also operates a waste disposal business

BANKERS :
First National Bank of SA Ltd

AUDITORS :
Ernst & Young, KPMG Aiken & Peat

FAMILIAR BRAND NAMES
BRITOOL TOOLS,BUNTEMETALE
CHICKS SCRAP METALS,DENVER METAL WORKS
ECLIPSE HAND TOOLS,ELLIOT LUCAS TOOLS,FASCOR
GRIPPLE,MAKSAL TUBES,MOORE & WRIGHT TOOLS
MOTTO,NEILL TOOLS,OSBORN,SARMCO,SOMTA TOOLS
VELDSPAN,WASTE SERVICES

CONTRIBUTION BY ACTIVITY
Steel, Wire and Rope (% Turnover) (54 0%)
Copper-based Products (% Turnover) (37 0%)
Engineering Consumables (% Turnover) (9 0%)

YEAR END : December

DIVIDEND : Ords 20c

Interim No 82	(Ldr)07/09/90	(Pay)05/10/90	Amt(c)47
Final No 83	(Ldr)01/03/91	(Pay)05/04/91	Amt(c)110
Interim No 84	(Ldr)06/09/91	(Pay)04/10/91	Amt(c)47
Final No 85	(Ldr)06/03/92	(Pay)03/04/92	Amt(c)110
Interim No 86	(Ldr)04/09/92	(Pay)02/10/92	Amt(c)47

NUMBER OF EMPLOYEES : 8891

CAPITAL STRUCTURE

	AUTHORISED	ISSUED
Ords 20c	25000000	19458487
Var Rate Red Cum Prefs R1	15000000	9000000

FINANCIAL STATISTICS (AT FINANCIAL YEAR END)

(Amts in R'000)	1991 Dec	1990 Dec	1989 Dec	1988 Dec	1987 Dec
Ord S/H Int	428573	402222	377066	324128	286430
Long Trm Loans	145981	113715	100958	81142	127107
Iss Ord Share	19458	19458	19320	19251	19249
Total Liab	398756	384415	336430	252368	232019
Current Liab	252775	270700	235472	171226	104912
Total Assets	827329	786637	713496	576496	518449
Current Assets	513805	497409	437084	346623	294116
Debtors	249298	250556	223815	162566	142694
Inventory	224069	225813	212980	179189	151368
Turnover	1181571	1254149	1179999	874675	794148
Oper Profit	105340	138188	149870	116774	115489
Interest Paid	29434	27628	16404	1958	244
Tax Paid	19341	36012	47870	40435	47160
Prf af Int&Tax	66680	81385	92256	74381	68085
Prf att Ord Sh	57508	70683	78476	61544	54943
Btm Line Earn	57494	65958	78952	61484	54768
Dividend Paid	30549	30549	30452	24641	21944
Mkt Prce(c) YE	2775	2300	2750	1900	1550
Depreciation	35994	33285	27764	20806	22472

PER SHARE STATISTICS (CENTS)

Net Asst Val	2202 55	2067 13	1951 69	1683 69	1488 03
Net Earnings	295 50	363 20	406 20	319 70	285 40
Dividends	157 00	157 00	157 00	128 00	114 00
Cash Flow	497 83	554 24	571 29	431 00	428 31

RATIOS AND OTHER INFORMATION

Mrk Cap(R000)	539960	447534	531300	365769	298360
Current Ratio	2 03	1 84	1 86	2 02	2 80
Quik/Acid Tst	1 15	1 00	0 95	0 98	1 36
A/C Rec T/ovr	4 74	5 01	5 27	5 38	5 57
Tot Ass T/ovr	1 43	1 59	1 65	1 52	1 53
Debt/Ass Rat	0 35	0 35	0 34	0 30	0 22
L T L Tot Ass	0 04	0 01	0 01	0 01	0 02
Debt to Eqity	0 67	0 68	0 64	0 54	0 40
Interest Cover	3 62	5 03	9 21	59 64	473 32
Oper Prof Mrg	8 92	11 02	12 70	13 35	14 54
Net Prof Marg%	4 87	5 64	6 65	7 04	6 92

Ret on Assets	13.96	18.44	21.94	20.26	22.28
Ret on Equity%	13.42	17.57	20.81	18.99	19.18
Price/Earnings	9.39	6.33	6.77	5.94	5.43
Divid Cover	1.88	2.31	2.59	2.50	2.50
Divid Yield	5.66	6.83	5.71	6.74	7.35
Earning Yield%	10.65	15.79	14.77	16.83	18.41
NAV % Mrk Pr	79.37	89.88	70.97	88.62	96.00
Effec Tax Rate	20.90	27.56	32.05	33.52	17.94
Def Interval	1.82	1.39	1.05	0.91	0.64
Sus Grth Rate	6.29	9.98	12.74	11.39	11.52

SUBSIDIARY & ASSOCIATED COMPANIES

AFRICAN WIRE ROPES (PTY) LTD
CONSOLIDATED WIRE INDUSTRIES LTD (50.1%)
COPALCOR MANUFACTURING (PTY) LTD
COPALCOR MANUFACTURING (PTY) LTD (50% + 1 SH)
DENVER METAL WORKS (PTY) LTD
FASCOR (PTY) LTD
GARDNER ENGINES SA (PTY) LTD
HAGGIE NEILL (PTY) LTD
HAGGIE RAND LTD
MACDEM (PTY) LTD
MAKSAL TUBES (PTY) LTD (50% + 1 SH)
MKONGE FARM (PTY) LTD
OSBORN INDUSTRIES (PTY) LTD
RECLAM (PTY) LTD
SARMCO (SOUTH AFRICA) (PTY) LTD
SENATOR PROPERTIES (PTY) LTD
SOMTA TOOLS (PTY) LTD

INVESTMENTS

None

HAIB COPPER MINING & EXPLORATION INVESTMENT CO.

ABBREVIATION : HAIB

JSE SHORT CODE : HAB

SECTOR : Mining-Exploration

SHAREHOLDERS

Who Owns Whom's Assessment of the Identity of the Ultimate Controlling Shareholder:
MEGA HOLDINGS SA

SHAREHOLDER	PERCENTAGE 1992	1991
REVERE RESOURCES SA LTD	79.9	---
SWANSON G E	6.3	---
PARKER G C	4.1	---
R M NOM P/L	3.9	---
SWANSON J D	1.1	---
MERCABANK NOM P/L	---	13.3
DIAGONAL NOM P/L	---	1.3
GOOD HOPE DIAMONDS & ESTATES P/L	---	1.2
INDO-CHINA NOM SA P/L	---	1.1
LEVIN J	---	2.0
PHILIP GUTKIN FAMILY TRUST P/L	---	2.0
ROBRIAN INV P/L	---	1.8
SA MUTUAL	---	14.7
SENBANK NOM P/L	---	8.3
STD BANK NOM TVL P/L	---	3.9
TBA NOM P/L	---	3.8
VAN DRIMMELEN W P	---	1.3
VOLKSKAS NOM P/L	---	1.1
WALSH J W	---	4.1
TOTAL	95.4	60.1

DIRECTORS :
HELLER MA ,LAING GJS (Chairman)
PARKER GC (Managing Director),VAN ZYL L

REGISTRATION NUMBER : 05/09010/06

REGISTERED OFFICE
Ground Floor, AMR Office Park
Building 2, Concorde Road East
2008
TEL: 011-884 4850

TRANSFER SECRETARY
Central Registrars Ltd
P O Box 4844, Johannesburg
2000
TEL: 011-331 0051

COMPANY SECRETARY
Revere Resources Management Services (Pty) Ltd

NATURE OF BUSINESS
Involved in the mining of copper.

BANKERS :
First National Bank of SA Ltd

AUDITORS :
Baker Musikanth

FAMILIAR BRAND NAMES
N/A

CONTRIBUTION BY ACTIVITY
N/A

YEAR END : December

DIVIDEND :15/00/91

CAPITAL STRUCTURE

	AUTHORISED	ISSUED
Ords no par value	79638800	59972800

FINANCIAL STATISTICS (AT FINANCIAL YEAR END)

(Amts in R'000)	1991 Dec	1990 Dec	1989 Dec	1988 Dec	1987 Dec
Ord S/H Int	12	12	11589	10884	9748
Long Trm Loans	-	-	1210	1658	1472
Iss Ord Share	59973	59973	59973	59973	59973
Total Liab	-	-	2780	2587	2289
Current Liab	-	-	1570	929	817
Total Assets	12	12	6964	6150	4716
Intang Assets	*	*	7405	7321	7321
Current Assets	-	-	1638	2470	1440
Debtors	-	-	873	1123	1067
Inventory	-	-	261	1176	373
Turnover	-	-	6749	5615	4729
Oper Profit	-	-	1478	1392	476
Interest Paid	-	-	173	253	189
Tax Paid	-	-	-	3	20
Prf af Int&Tax	-	-	1305	1136	267

Prf att Ord Sh	-	-	1305	1136	267
Btm Line Earn	-	-	1305	1136	267
Dividend Paid	-	-	600	-	-
Mkt Prce(c) YE	20	-	23	23	40
Depreciation	-	-	256	297	263

PER SHARE STATISTICS (CENTS)

Net Asst Val	0.02	0.02	6.98	5.94	4.05
Net Earnings	-	-	2.18	1.89	0.45
Dividends	-	-	1.00	-	-
Cash Flow	-	-	2.60	2.39	0.88

RATIOS AND OTHER INFORMATION

Mrk Cap(R000)	11995	-	13794	13794	23989
Current Ratio	-	-	1.04	2.66	1.76
Quik/Acid Tst	-	-	0.88	1.39	1.31
A/C Rec T/ovr	-	-	7.73	5.00	4.43
Tot Ass T/ovr	-	-	0.97	0.91	1.00
Debt/Ass Rat	-	-	0.40	0.42	0.49
L T L Tot Ass	-	-	0.17	0.27	0.31
Debt to Eqity	-	-	0.24	0.24	0.23
Interest Cover	-	-	8.54	5.50	2.52
Oper Prof Mrg	-	-	21.90	24.79	10.07
Net Prof Marg%	-	-	19.34	20.23	5.65
Ret on Assets	-	-	21.22	22.63	10.09
Ret on Equity%	-	-	11.26	10.44	2.74
Price/Earnings	-	-	10.55	12.17	88.89
Divid Cover	-	-	2.18	-	-
Divid Yield	-	-	4.35	-	-
Earning Yield%	-	-	9.48	8.22	1.13
NAV % Mrk Pr	0.10	-	30.33	25.83	10.12
Def Interval	-	-	0.98	1.21	3.80
Sus Grth Rate	-	-	6.08	10.44	2.74

SUBSIDIARY & ASSOCIATED COMPANIES

None

INVESTMENTS

None

HARMONY GOLD MINING CO LTD

ABBREVIATION : HARMONY

JSE SHORT CODE : HAR

SECTOR : Gold-OFS

SHAREHOLDERS

Who Owns Whom's Assessment of the Identity of the Ultimate Controlling Shareholder: SA MUTUAL VIA BARLOWS VIA RAND MINES

SHAREHOLDER	PERCENTAGE 1992	1991
STD BANK NOM TVL P/L	36.0	34.4
UK BRANCH REGISTER CONTROL ACCOUNT	30.8	29.1
RAND MINES LTD	12.3	12.3
INDO-CHINA NOM P/L	9.1	11.5
NEDBANK NOM LTD	2.5	---
DEPOSITARY NOM INC	1.6	1.4
VIRGINIA MERRIESPRUIT INV LTD	1.4	1.4
FIRST NAT NOM P/L	1.3	1.6
ABSA NOM P/L	1.2	---
FERMAIN NOM LTD	---	2.5
VOLKSKAS NOM P/L	---	1.2
TOTAL	96.1	95.3

DIRECTORS :
CROCKER EB ,EICK KFW (Managing Director)
EUSTACE PJ ,HALL JC ,HEYNS MR ,SEALEY AA
STEVENS IG ,TURNER JPS (Chairman),WILSON RAD

REGISTRATION NUMBER : 05/38232/06

REGISTERED OFFICE
15th Floor, 63 Fox Street
Johannesburg
2001
TEL: 011-491 2911
FAX: 011-834 3850

TRANSFER SECRETARY
Rand Registrars Ltd
P O Box 82549, Southdale
2135
TEL: 011-835 1016

COMPANY SECRETARY
Rand Mines (Mining & Services) Ltd

NATURE OF BUSINESS
The company conducts gold mining operations in the district of Virginia, OFS. Silver is recovered as a by-product of the gold extraction process.

BANKERS :
First National Bank of SA Ltd

AUDITORS :
Coopers Theron Du Toit

FAMILIAR BRAND NAMES
N/A

CONTRIBUTION BY ACTIVITY
N/A

YEAR END : June

DIVIDEND : Ords 50c

Final No 65	(Ldr)30/03/90	(Pay)04/05/90	Amt(c)50
Interim No 66	(Ldr)07/02/92	(Pay)28/02/92	Amt(c)20

NUMBER OF EMPLOYEES : 15108

CAPITAL STRUCTURE

	AUTHORISED	ISSUED
Ords 50c	27000000	26884650

FINANCIAL STATISTICS (AT FINANCIAL YEAR END)

(Amts in R'000)	1992 Jun	1991 Jun	1990 Jun	1989 Jun	1988
Ord S/H Int	911898	908634	941379	888880	50151
Long Trm Loans	-	-	-	-	121437
Iss Ord Share	26885	26885	26885	26885	26885
Total Liab	79933	75646	110287	113489	233940
Current Liab	79933	75646	110287	113489	112503
Total Assets	991831	984280	1051666	1002369	317551
Current Assets	94963	90819	164293	127705	145963
Debtors	19093	5393	10292	22046	-

Inventory	14960	15387	24139	-	145963
Turnover	809327	783189	965745	941357	856612
Oper Profit	-8333	-49026	37682	57453	72443
Interest Paid	40	12	-	9	-
Tax Paid	-	96	11201	7364	5146
Prf af Int&Tax	8641	-32745	49858	67065	67297
Prf att Ord Sh	8641	-32745	49858	16489	14734
Btm Line Earn	8641	-32745	49858	16489	14734
Dividend Paid	5377	-	13442	38982	30917
Mkt Prce(c) YE	1525	1925	2550	1900	2225

PER SHARE STATISTICS (CENTS)

Net Asst Val	3391 85	3379 71	3501 50	3306 23	186 54
Net Earnings	20 00	-111 00	108 00	61 00	-
Dividends	20 00	-	50 00	145 00	-
Cash Flow	32 14	-121 80	185 45	249 45	250 31

RATIOS AND OTHER INFORMATION

Mrk Cap(R000)	409996	517536	685568	510815	598191
Current Ratio	1 19	1 20	1 49	1 13	1 30
Quik/Acid Tst	1 00	1 00	1 27	1 13	-
A/C Rec T/ovr	42 39	145 22	93 83	42 70	-
Tot Ass T/ovr	0 82	0 80	0 92	0 94	2 70
Debt/Ass Rat	0 08	0 08	0 10	0 11	0 74
L T L Tot Ass	-	-	-	-	0 38
Debt to Eqity	0 09	0 08	0 12	0 13	4 66
Interest Cover	-185 18	-4061 00	-	6383 67	-
Oper Prof Mrg	-1 03	-6 26	3 90	6 10	8 46
Net Prof Marg%	1 07	-4 18	5 16	1 75	1 72
Ret on Assets	0 88	-3 32	5 81	7 43	22 81
Ret on Equity%	0 95	-3 60	5 30	1 86	29 38
Price/Earnings	76 25	-17 34	23 61	31 15	-
Divid Cover	1 00	-	2 16	0 42	-
Divid Yield	1 31	-	1 96	7 63	-
Earning Yield%	1 31	-5 77	4 24	3 21	-
NAV % Mrk Pr	222 42	175 57	137 31	174 01	8 38
Effec Tax Rate	-	-0 29	18 64	9 89	7 10
Def Interval	-	-	-	-	1 80
Sus Grth Rate	0 36	-3 60	3 87	-2 53	-32 27

SUBSIDIARY & ASSOCIATED COMPANIES

LA RIVIERA (PTY) LTD (33,33%)

INVESTMENTS

None

HARTEBEESTFONTEIN GOLD MINING CO LTD

ABBREVIATION : HARTIES

JSE SHORT CODE : HBN

SECTOR : Gold-Klerksdorp

SHAREHOLDERS

Who Owns Whom's Assessment of the Identity of the Ultimate Controlling Shareholder: ANGLOVAAL

SHAREHOLDER	PERCENTAGE 1992	1991
ZANDPAN GOLD MINING CO LTD	19 6	19 6
ANGLO AMERICAN GOLD INV CO LTD	15 2	15 2
INDO-CHINA NOM P/L	11 9	---
FOX STREET NOM P/L	7 8	7 9
CMB NOM P/L	6 4	---
FIRST NAT NOM P/L GATR DEPOT	5 6	5 5
STD BANK NOM TVL P/L	4 8	4 4
FIRST NAT NOM P/L	2 8	2 9
OVERSEAS NOM CO INC	2 2	2 2
SA MUTUAL	1 8	1 5
TAURUS NOM LTD	1 7	1 7
FIRST CORP NOM P/L	1 6	1 6
PETARD NOM LTD	1 5	1 5
NAT CITY NOM LTD	1 3	1 3
ABSA NOM P/L	1 1	---
FERMAIN NOM LTD	1 0	1 5
SOCIETE INTERPROF POUR LA COMPENSATION	---	1 1
INDO-CHINA NOM SA P/L	---	12 2
SANLAM	---	6 3
TOTAL	86 4	86 4

DIRECTORS :
BERNSTEIN BL ,GELDENHUYS JJ
HERSOV BE (Chairman),HEWITT L ,MENELL CS
SUNTER CL ,WILSON RAD

REGISTRATION NUMBER : 05/33926/06

REGISTERED OFFICE
Anglovaal House, 56 Main Street
Johannesburg
2001
TEL 011-634 9111
FAX 011-634 0038

TRANSFER SECRETARY
Anglovaal Ltd
P O Box 62379, Marshalltown
2107
TEL 011-634 9111

COMPANY SECRETARY
Anglovaal Ltd

NATURE OF BUSINESS
The company conducts, as its main business, gold mining operations in the Klerksdorp district of the Transvaal Uranium oxide, sulphuric acid, pyrite and silver are produced as by-products

BANKERS :
First National Bank of SA Ltd

AUDITORS :
KPMG Aiken & Peat

FAMILIAR BRAND NAMES
N/A

CONTRIBUTION BY ACTIVITY
N/A

YEAR END : June

DIVIDEND : Ords 10c

Interim No 70	(Ldr)21/12/90	(Pay)25/01/91	Amt(c)50
Final No 71	(Ldr)21/06/91	(Pay)26/07/91	Amt(c)50
Final No 73	(Ldr)19/06/92	(Pay)24/07/92	Amt(c)45

Interim No 72	(Ldr)20/12/91	(Pay)24/01/92	Amt(c)50
Interim No 74	(Ldr)11/12/92	(Pay)15/01/93	Amt(c)30

NUMBER OF EMPLOYEES : 18000

CAPITAL STRUCTURE

	AUTHORISED	ISSUED
Ords 10c	*112000000*	*112000000*

FINANCIAL STATISTICS (AT FINANCIAL YEAR END)

(Amts in R'000)	1992 Jun	1991 Jun	1990 Jun	1989 Jun	1988 Jun
Ord S/H Int	799719	766654	720365	698677	635604
Long Trm Loans	1190	3091	4823	6391	7550
Iss Ord Share	112000	112000	112000	112000	112000
Total Liab	210057	235205	333821	395687	430262
Current Liab	208867	232114	328998	389296	422712
Total Assets	1009776	1001859	1054186	1094364	1065866
Current Assets	274930	274970	356117	442555	474668
Debtors	30973	18846	21041	27415	21463
Inventory	81660	52344	41542	58057	30429
Turnover	950227	953920	1034753	1073945	1003741
Oper Profit	207886	246684	368636	588034	607458
Interest Paid	914	1168	1414	-	-
Tax Paid	90392	123478	243969	324381	372782
Prf af Int&Tax	141653	155907	172810	263653	234676
Prf att Ord Sh	141653	155907	172810	263653	234676
Btm Line Earn	141653	155907	172810	263653	234676
Dividend Paid	106400	112000	145600	201600	171360
Mkt Prce(c) YE	1335	2150	2175	2950	2115

PER SHARE STATISTICS (CENTS)

Net Asst Val	714.03	684.51	643.18	623.82	567.50
Net Earnings	*95.00*	*111.90*	*132.90*	*180.30*	*158.20*
Dividends	95.00	100.00	130.00	180.00	153.00
Cash Flow	126.48	139.20	154.29	235.40	209.53

RATIOS AND OTHER INFORMATION

Mrk Cap(R000)	1495200	2408000	2436000	3304000	2368800
Current Ratio	1.32	1.18	1.08	1.14	1.12
Quik/Acid Tst	0.93	0.96	0.96	0.99	1.05
A/C Rec T/ovr	30.68	50.62	49.18	39.17	46.77
Tot Ass T/ovr	0.94	0.95	0.98	0.98	0.94
Debt/Ass Rat	0.21	0.23	0.32	0.36	0.40
L T L Tot Ass	0.00	0.00	0.00	0.01	0.01
Debt to Eqity	0.26	0.31	0.46	0.57	0.68
Interest Cover	227.45	211.20	260.70	-	-
Oper Prof Mrg	21.88	25.86	35.63	54.75	60.52
Net Prof Marg%	14.91	16.34	16.70	24.55	23.38
Ret on Assets	23.07	28.00	39.67	53.73	56.99
Ret on Equity%	17.71	20.34	23.99	37.74	36.92
Price/Earnings	14.05	19.21	16.37	16.36	13.37
Divid Cover	1.00	1.12	1.02	1.00	1.03
Divid Yield	7.12	4.65	5.98	6.10	7.23
Earning Yield%	7.12	5.20	6.11	6.11	7.48
NAV % Mrk Pr	53.49	31.84	29.57	21.15	26.83
Effec Tax Rate	38.95	44.20	58.54	44.23	48.40
Def Interval	0.01	0.02	0.03	0.02	0.03
Sus Grth Rate	4.41	5.73	3.78	8.88	9.96

SUBSIDIARY & ASSOCIATED COMPANIES

None

INVESTMENTS

None

HARWILL INVESTMENTS LTD

ABBREVIATION : HARWILL

JSE SHORT CODE : HRL

SECTOR : Industrial-Paper & Packaging

SHAREHOLDERS

Who Owns Whom's Assessment of the Identity of the Ultimate Controlling Shareholder: DIRECTORS

SHAREHOLDER	PERCENTAGE 1992	1991
FIRST NAT NOM P/L	45.0	56.3
ABSA NOM P/L	15.8	---
INDO-CHINA NOM P/L	8.6	---
HOLMWOOD INV LTD	4.5	---
TITAN NOM P/L	2.8	1.0
ENGLAND A R	2.8	3.1
RENIER BEHERENDE E/B	2.0	3.6
BALL T	1.9	2.0
THIART S J J	1.3	1.4
STD BANK NOM TVL P/L	---	1.0
BARCLAYS TRUST LTD CHANNEL ISLANDS	---	8.4
VOLKSKAS NOM P/L	---	17.4
TOTAL	84.6	94.2

DIRECTORS :
BALL T (Managing Director), RADEMEYER JG
VAN ROOYEN J , VAN ROOYEN R (Chairman)
VAN ROOYEN R (JNR)

REGISTRATION NUMBER : 84/07492/06

REGISTERED OFFICE
2 Vygeboom Ave, Durbanville
7550
TEL: 021-96 8075
FAX: 021-96 7068

TRANSFER SECRETARY
Central Registrars Ltd
P O Box 4844, Johannesburg
2000
TEL: 011-331 0051

COMPANY SECRETARY
E S Esch

NATURE OF BUSINESS
Manufactures hard and soft plastic products as well as certain specific other applications.

BANKERS :
Senbank

AUDITORS :
Coopers Theron Du Toit

FAMILIAR BRAND NAMES
N/A

CONTRIBUTION BY ACTIVITY
N/A

YEAR END : June

DIVIDEND :Ords 10c

Final No 6	(Ldr)02/11/90	(Pay)16/11/90	Amt(c)5
Final No 7	(Ldr)01/11/91	(Pay)15/11/91	Amt(c)5
Final No 8	(Ldr)14/08/92	(Pay)18/09/92	Amt(c)7 5

NUMBER OF EMPLOYEES : 77

CAPITAL STRUCTURE

	AUTHORISED	ISSUED
Ords 10c	20000000	10750000

FINANCIAL STATISTICS (AT FINANCIAL YEAR END)

(Amts in R'000)	1992 Jun	1991 Jun	1990 Jun	1989 Jun	1988 Jun
Ord S/H Int	14918	13840	12356	10142	8547
Long Trm Loans	364	888	465	325	303
Iss Ord Share	9782	9782	9782	9782	9782
Total Liab	4132	4389	4127	2747	3952
Current Liab	3768	3501	3662	2422	3649
Total Assets	15530	15021	13074	9990	8828
Intang Assets	3520	3208	3409	2899	3671
Current Assets	11819	10780	7626	6097	5457
Debtors	3758	3615	3300	3172	3340
Inventory	2139	1315	739	1103	1276
Oper Profit	2697	3096	3398	2977	2241
Interest Paid	35	18	27	161	112
Tax Paid	1753	1957	1930	760	1012
Prf af Int&Tax	1806	2154	2076	2443	1117
Prf att Ord Sh	1806	1908	1890	2308	1021
Btm Line Earn	1812	1973	1419	1594	281
Dividend Paid	734	489	489	-	-
Mkt Prce(c) YE	210	295	200	200	200
Depreciation	732	643	312	200	251

PER SHARE STATISTICS (CENTS)

Net Asst Val	116 52	108 69	91 46	74 04	49 85
Net Earnings	18 40	19 50	19 32	23 60	10 43
Dividends	7 50	5 00	5 00	-	-
Cash Flow	27 22	29 75	24 21	21 69	13 46

RATIOS AND OTHER INFORMATION

Mrk Cap(R000)	20542	28857	19564	19564	19564
Current Ratio	3 14	3 08	2 08	2 52	1 50
Quik/Acid Tst	2 57	2 70	1 88	2 06	1 15
Debt/Ass Rat	0 24	0 23	0 28	0 24	0 41
L T L Tot Ass	-	-	-	-	0 00
Debt to Eqity	0 25	0 25	0 30	0 24	0 43
Interest Cover	77 49	172 06	129 04	19 07	20 01
Ret on Assets	23 14	27 49	30 85	33 67	25 39
Ret on Equity%	12 11	13 79	15 30	22 76	11 95
Price/Earnings	11 41	15 13	10 35	8 47	19 18
Divid Cover	2 45	3 90	3 86		
Divid Yield	3 57	1 69	2 50	-	
Earning Yield%	8 76	6 61	9 66	11 80	5 22
NAV % Mrk Pr	55 49	36 84	45 73	37 02	24 92
Effec Tax Rate	45 17	38 91	45 00	36 85	45 80
Def Interval		0 02		0 26	0 35
Sus Grth Rate	7 19	10 25	11 34	22 76	11 95

SUBSIDIARY & ASSOCIATED COMPANIES

DONAU METALCRAFT (PTY) LTD
HARWILL INDUSTRIES (PTY) LTD
HARWILL MANAGEMENT SERVICES (PTY) LTD
METPAK PLASTIKS (PTY) LTD

INVESTMENTS

None

HI-SCORE HOLDINGS LTD

ABBREVIATION : HISCORE

JSE SHORT CODE : HSC

SECTOR : Industrial-Retailers & Wholesalers

SHAREHOLDERS

Who Owns Whom's Assessment of the Identity of the Ultimate Controlling Shareholder:
PREMIER GROUP

SHAREHOLDER	PERCENTAGE 1992	1991
SCORE DISCOUNT FOOD HOLDINGS P/L	59 1	59 1
SHAPE INV P/L	20 7	8 7
CMB NOM P/L	7 1	-
NEDBANK NOM LTD	1 8	2 0
ENGINEERING INDUSTRIES PENS FUND	1 3	1 3
METAL IND GROUP PENS FUND	1 3	1 3
SHARESTOCK NOM P/L	---	1 8
STOCKSHARE NOM P/L	---	5 5
PREMIER GROUP PENS FUND	---	2 9
SANLAM	---	7 1
TOTAL	91 2	89 5

DIRECTORS :
BURGESS CJ ,DOS SANTOS CS ,RUBIN VD ,TAUROG RD
UTIAN GM (Chairman),WRIGHTON PGA

REGISTRATION NUMBER : 86/01584/06

REGISTERED OFFICE
Premier Group Centre, 1 Newtown Avenue
Killarney
2041
TEL 011-446 9111
FAX 011-446 2239

TRANSFER SECRETARY
Central Registrars Ltd
P O Box 4844, Johannesburg
2000
TEL 011-331 0051

COMPANY SECRETARY
S Gore

NATURE OF BUSINESS
An investment holding company with a controlling interest in Score-Clicks Holdings, which is quoted on the JSE Score-Clicks in turn controls quoted Clicks Stores Ltd

BANKERS :
First National Bank of SA Ltd
Standard Bank of SA Ltd
Trust Bank of Africa Ltd

AUDITORS :
Ernst & Young

FAMILIAR BRAND NAMES
N/A

CONTRIBUTION BY ACTIVITY
N/A

YEAR END : April

DIVIDEND :Ords 1c

Final No 12	(Ldr)10/07/92	(Pay)30/07/92	Amt(c)10
Interim No 11	(Ldr)06/01/92	(Pay)20/01/92	Amt(c)6

NUMBER OF EMPLOYEES : 8867

CAPITAL STRUCTURE

	AUTHORISED	ISSUED
Ords 1c	30000000	23372184

FINANCIAL STATISTICS (AT FINANCIAL YEAR END)

(Amts in R'000)	1992 Apr	1991 Feb	1990 Feb	1989 Feb	1988 Feb
Ord S/H Int	187861	149288	152913	146832	112382
Long Trm Loans	147061	122709	139702	115330	34636
Iss Ord Share	23372	20683	20683	20683	17867
Total Liab	270759	394125	424866	314379	148793
Current Liab	123698	271416	285164	199049	114157
Total Assets	458620	397786	427494	316291	169333
Intang Assets	*	145627	150285	144920	91842
Current Assets	221057	315467	340911	250298	137384
Debtors	15040	56000	45045	32294	25951
Inventory	160151	259467	255622	207390	108563
Turnover	1232710	1904207	1786451	1345701	923095
Oper Profit	55155	62846	75550	54545	29784
Interest Paid	9438	15845	19634	14559	2451
Tax Paid	22929	20120	26077	18319	11952
Prf af Int&Tax	22788	28996	31718	23550	15421
Prf att Ord Sh	7721	9810	11249	8984	8595
Btm Line Earn	2823	-110	11637	14185	8595
Dividend Paid	3578	3578	4592	4579	3305
Mkt Prce(c) YE	760	475	340	390	800
Depreciation	7658	10907	8657	5942	3993

PER SHARE STATISTICS (CENTS)

Net Asst Val	803 79	17 70	12 71	9 24	114 96
Net Earnings	37 00	47 43	54 38	43 44	48 11
Dividends	16 00	17 30	22 20	22 14	18 50
Cash Flow	67 29	94 05	105 48	75 99	70 45

RATIOS AND OTHER INFORMATION

Mrk Cap(R000)	177627	98244	70322	80664	142936
Current Ratio	1 79	1 16	1 20	1 26	1 20
Quik/Acid Tst	0 49	0 21	0 30	0 22	0 25
A/C Rec T/ovr	70 25	34 00	39 66	41 67	35 57
Tot Ass T/ovr	2 30	4 79	4 18	4 25	5 45
Debt/Ass Rat	0 27	0 71	0 70	0 66	0 72
L T L Tot Ass	-	0 03	0 04	0 03	0 04
Debt to Eqity	0 66	1 89	1 97	1 41	1 08
Interest Cover	5 84	3 97	3 85	3 77	12 17
Oper Prof Mrg	4 47	3 30	4 23	4 05	3 23
Net Prof Marg%	0 63	0 52	0 63	0 67	0 93
Ret on Assets	10 31	16 35	18 14	17 86	17 61
Ret on Equity%	3 52	6 57	7 36	6 12	7 65
Price/Earnings	20 54	10 01	6 25	8 98	16 63
Divid Cover	2 31	2 74	2 45	1 96	2 60
Divid Yield	2 11	3 64	6 53	5 68	2 31
Earning Yield%	4 87	9 99	15 99	11 14	6 01
NAV % Mrk Pr	105 76	3 73	3 74	2 37	14 37
Effec Tax Rate	47 94	40 67	36 68	39 51	36 83
Def Interval	-	2 07	2 74	2 34	0 57
Sus Grth Rate	2 21	4 17	4 35	3 00	4 71

SUBSIDIARY & ASSOCIATED COMPANIES

SCORE-CLICKS HOLDINGS LIMITED

INVESTMENTS

None

HICOR LTD

ABBREVIATION : HICORL

JSE SHORT CODE : HOR

SECTOR : Industrial-Retailers & Wholesalers

SHAREHOLDERS

Who Owns Whom's Assessment of the Identity of the Ultimate Controlling Shareholder: DIRECTORS

SHAREHOLDER	PERCENTAGE 1992	1991
RIWER NOM P/L	43 1	43 8
TRIDENT NOM LTD	13 3	13 3
INDO-CHINA NOM P/L	4 6	---
ZANDBERG D J A	2 8	2 2
NEL J D FAMILY TRUST	1 9	1 9
BM NOM CC	1 8	1 8
SMK NOM P/L	1 5	3 4
RETIEF M J TRUST	1 5	1 5
DAMORINA INV CC	1 5	1 5
CHENG TSIN KI	1 4	1 4
FIRST NAT NOM P/L	1 2	---
ANGLO AFRICAN SHIPPING CO 1936 P/L	1 1	1 5
VAN ROOYEN G J	1 1	1 1
VAN ROOYEN R	---	1 3
QUANTAM FINANCIAL SERVICES P/L	---	1 5
TOTAL	76 8	76 1

DIRECTORS :
BALL T ,DE BEER JW ,MOUTON JF ,RADEMEYER JG
VAN ROOYEN R (Chairman),VAN ROOYEN R (SNR)

REGISTRATION NUMBER : 81/11496/06

REGISTERED OFFICE
Cnr West & Fairbairn Sts , Parow East
7500
TEL 021-981 8614
FAX 021-981 1861

TRANSFER SECRETARY
Mercantile Registrars Ltd
P O Box 1053, Johannesburg
2000
TEL 011-333 8181

COMPANY SECRETARY
MI van der Merwe

NATURE OF BUSINESS
The holding company of a group invested in the retailing & manufacturing of clothing, footwear, blankets & household softs The company holds a controlling interest in quoted Allwear Group Ltd

BANKERS :
First National Bank of SA Ltd
Absa Bank Ltd

AUDITORS :
Coopers Theron Du Toit

FAMILIAR BRAND NAMES
N/A

CONTRIBUTION BY ACTIVITY
N/A

YEAR END : February

DIVIDEND : Ords 1c
Dividend (Ldr)05/07/91 (Pay)08/07/91 Amt(c)5

NUMBER OF EMPLOYEES : 1880

CAPITAL STRUCTURE

	AUTHORISED	ISSUED
Ords 1c	100000000	54000000

FINANCIAL STATISTICS (AT FINANCIAL YEAR END)

(Amts in R'000)	1992 Feb	1991 Feb	1990 Feb
Ord S/H Int	32293	31069	13733
Long Trm Loans	10711	12741	20902
Iss Ord Share	54000	54000	25301
Total Liab	42482	60321	71966
Current Liab	31771	47580	51064
Total Assets	74775	88911	84564
Intang Assets	*	2479	1135
Current Assets	44130	71272	67887
Debtors	23519	18146	17687
Inventory	20536	52249	49010
Turnover	79938	148072	128395
Oper Profit	3098	9557	11982
Interest Paid	5544	7830	6746
Tax Paid	-	50	204
Prf af Int&Tax	2435	1701	5068
Prf att Ord Sh	-2714	562	2307
Btm Line Earn	3979	562	2767
Dividend Paid	2700	-	380
Mkt Prce(c) YE	22	40	-
Depreciation	1194	2132	1852

PER SHARE STATISTICS (CENTS)

Net Asst Val	59 80	52 94	49 79
Net Earnings	-5 00	1 40	9 10
Dividends	5 00	-	1 50
Cash Flow	-2 81	6 49	16 83

RATIOS AND OTHER INFORMATION

Mrk Cap(R000)	11880	21600	-
Current Ratio	1 39	1 50	1 33
Quik/Acid Tst	0 74	0 40	0 37
A/C Rec T/ovr	3 40	8 16	7 26
Tot Ass T/ovr	1 07	1 67	1 52
Debt/Ass Rat	0 49	0 60	0 67
L T L Tot Ass	0 07	0 07	0 07
Debt to Eqity	1 13	1 73	4 15
Interest Cover	0 56	1 22	1 78
Oper Prof Mrg	3 88	6 45	9 33
Net Prof Marg%	-3 40	0 38	1 80
Ret on Assets	4 16	10 78	14 21
Ret on Equity%	-8 40	1 81	16 80
Price/Earnings	-4 40	28 57	-
Divid Cover	-1 00	-	6 07
Divid Yield	22 73	-	-
Earning Yield%	-22 73	3 50	-
NAV % Mrk Pr	271 83	132 36	-
Effec Tax Rate	-	2 90	2 02
Def Interval	-17 64	12 73	8 53
Sus Grth Rate	-16 77	1 81	14 03

SUBSIDIARY & ASSOCIATED COMPANIES

ALLWEAR GROUP LTD
ALLWEAR LTD (22 7%)
HICOR MANAGEMENT SERVICES
HICORL TRADING LTD

INVESTMENTS

None

HIGATE PROPERTY FUND

ABBREVIATION : HIGATE

JSE SHORT CODE : HGT

SECTOR : Financial-Property Trust

SHAREHOLDERS

Who Owns Whom's Assessment of the Identity of the Ultimate Controlling Shareholder:
INSTITUTIONAL OWNERSHIP

SHAREHOLDER	PERCENTAGE 1992	1991
SA MUTUAL	17 0	17 4
FIRST NAT NOM P/L	13 6	14 0
CMB NOM P/L	9 9	
ANGLO AMERICAN GROUP PENS FUND	6 2	4 1
EIGHTY ONE MAIN STREET NOM LTD	4 0	2 4
STD BANK NOM TVL P/L	2 7	2 8
CITY COUNCIL OF DURBAN	2 6	4 5
DURBAN CORP SUPERANNUATION FUND	2 5	2 5
ENGINEERING INDUSTRIES PENS FUND	2 2	2 2
METAL IND GROUP PENS FUND	2 2	2 2
BARLOWS PENS FUND	1 8	1 8
SIXTY SIX MARSHALL STREET NOM P/L	1 7	1 9
HIGHVELD STAFF PENS FUND	1 4	
AFRICAN OXYGEN LTD PENS FUND	1 4	1 4
SCAW METALS PENS FUND	1 4	-
JF KING LTD	1 3	1 3
EPF UAL NOM P/L	1 2	1 2
DURBAN MUNICIPAL PENS FUND	1 1	1 1
FAIRHEADS NOM P/L	1 0	
YSKOR PENS FUND	---	1 8
SOUTTER N M		1 3
SHARESTOCK NOM P/L	---	1 2
NEDBANK NOM LTD	--	1 1
SANLAM	---	5 4
SCOTT W J D	-	2 6
TOTAL	75 2	74 1

DIRECTORS :
ARDINGTON AJ (Chairman),FIELD TH ,GIBSON LJ
GROVES IM ,NOYCE MJ ,OVENSTONE ADP ,PARKHURST WR
SAVILLE D ,SQUIRE-HOWE RC ,TURRELL MF

REGISTRATION NUMBER : 87/00903/06

REGISTERED OFFICE
5th Floor, Protea Assurance Building
321 Smith Street, Durban
4001
TEL: 031-304 2731
FAX: 031-305 1521

TRANSFER SECRETARY
Mercantile Registrars Ltd
P O Box 1053, Johannesburg
2000
TEL: 011-333 8181

COMPANY SECRETARY
Russell Marriott & Boyd Trust (Pty) Ltd

NATURE OF BUSINESS
A property trust fund, with property investments in Industrial, Retail Hotel & Commercial sites.

BANKERS :
First National Bank of SA Ltd

AUDITORS :
Deloitte Pim Goldby

FAMILIAR BRAND NAMES
N/A

CONTRIBUTION BY ACTIVITY
Industrial (% portfolio by sector) (53.0%)
Retail (19.0%)
Office Blocks (22.0%)
Hotel (6.0%)

YEAR END : April

DIVIDEND : Units

Dividend No 2	(Ldr)14/12/90	(Pay)31/12/90	Amt(c)35
Dividend No 3	(Ldr)14/06/91	(Pay)28/06/91	Amt(c)36
Dividend No 4	(Ldr)13/12/91	(Pay)30/12/91	Amt(c)37.5
Dividend No 5	(Ldr)12/06/92	(Pay)30/06/92	Amt(c)39
Dividend No 6	(Ldr)18/12/92	(Pay)31/12/92	Amt(c)40

CAPITAL STRUCTURE

	AUTHORISED	ISSUED
Units	30893237	30893237

FINANCIAL STATISTICS (AT FINANCIAL YEAR END)

(Amts in R'000)	1992 Apr	1991 Apr	1990 Apr	1989	1988
Ord S/H Int	158193	156622	154788	124659	124316
Long Trm Loans	-	-	-	7814	5442
Iss Ord Share	30893	30893	30893	100	100
Total Liab	12180	11271	11535	15628	10884
Current Liab	12180	11271	11535	7814	5442
Total Assets	170373	167893	166323	148289	153398
Current Assets	25968	28824	32782	15816	23640
Debtors	286	582	1750	-	-
Inventory	-	-	-	15816	23640
Turnover	-	-	-	16442	5555
Oper Profit	487	493	-431	14347	4885
Tax Paid	-	-	-	119	39
Prf af Int&Tax	25204	23495	10198	14228	4846
Prf att Ord Sh	25204	23495	10198	14228	4846
Btm Line Earn	25204	23495	11222	14228	4846
Dividend Paid	23633	21935	10195	14115	4809
Mkt Prce(c) YE	725	635	630	420	490

PER SHARE STATISTICS (CENTS)

Net Asst Val	512.07	506.98	501.05	124659.00	124316.00
Net Earnings	76.50	71.00	33.00	-	-
Dividends	76.50	71.00	33.00	-	-
Cash Flow	81.58	76.05	69.63	14228.00	14538.00

RATIOS AND OTHER INFORMATION

Mrk Cap(R000)	223974	196171	194626	420	490
Current Ratio	2.13	2.56	2.84	2.02	4.34
Quik/Acid Tst	2.13	2.56	2.84	-	-
Tot Ass T/ovr	-	-	-	0.11	0.11
Debt/Ass Rat	0.07	0.07	0.07	0.11	0.07
L T L Tot Ass	-	-	-	0.05	0.04
Debt to Eqity	0.08	0.07	0.07	0.13	0.09
Oper Prof Mrg	-	-	-	87.26	87.94
Net Prof Marg%	-	-	-	86.53	87.24
Ret on Assets	14.79	13.99	12.26	9.68	9.55
Ret on Equity%	15.93	15.00	13.18	11.41	11.69
Price/Earnings	9.48	8.94	19.09	-	-
Divid Cover	1.00	1.00	1.00	-	-
Divid Yield	10.55	11.18	5.24	-	-
Earning Yield%	10.55	11.18	5.24	-	-
NAV % Mrk Pr	70.63	79.84	79.53	29680.71	25370.61
Effec Tax Rate	-	-	-	0.83	0.80
Def Interval	-	-	-	0.55	3.37
Sus Grth Rate	0.99	1.00	0.00	0.09	0.03

SUBSIDIARY & ASSOCIATED COMPANIES

117 OMR PINETOWN PROPERTIES (PTY) LTD
149 MARINE PARADE (PTY) LTD
AUK PROPERTIES (PTY) LTD
BANDED GOSHAWK INVESTMENTS (PTY) LTD
BAT HAWK (PTY) LTD
BAY TERRACE PROPERTIES (TWO) (PTY) LTD
BLACK SUNBIRD INVESTMENTS (PTY) LTD
BLUE HERON (PTY) LTD
BRONZE MANNIKIN INVESTMENTS (PTY) LTD
BUTTON QUAIL INVESTMENTS (PTY) LTD
CHATPROPS (PTY) LTD
CHELPROPS (TWO) (PTY) LTD
CHORISTER ROBIN INVESMENTS (PTY) LTD
CISTICOLA INVESTMENTS (PTY) LTD
CLOUDHILL INVESTMENTS (PTY) LTD
CRESTED BARBET INVESTMENTS (PTY) LTD
CROMBEC INVESTMENTS (PTY) LTD
CYGNET PROPERTIES (PTY) LTD
DELEGAR INVESTMENTS (PTY) LTD
DUNE LARK INVESTMENTS (PTY) LTD
FISCAL SHRIKE INVESTMENTS (PTY) LTD
FORKTAILED DRONGO INVESTMENTS (PTY) LTD
GABAR PROPERTIES (PTY) LTD
GENIPROPS (TWO) (PTY) LTD
GLOSSY IBIS INVESTMENTS (PTY) LTD
GOODWIT INVESTMENTS (PTY) LTD
GREENSHANK INVESTMENTS (PTY) LTD
GREY HERON INVESTMENTS (PTY) LTD
GRINDROD PROPERTIES (SPARTAN) (PTY) LTD
HONEYGUIDE (PROPERTIES) (PTY) LTD
HOUSE SPARROW INVESTMENTS (PTY) LTD
JENDI PROPERTIES (TWO) (PTY) LTD
LOERIE PROPERTIES (PTY) LTD
LONG CLAW INVESTMENTS (PTY) LTD
MARSH OWL INVESTMENTS (PTY) LTD
MILBARN PROPERTIES (TWO) (PTY) LTD
NATAL NIGHTJAR INVESTMENTS (PTY) LTD
NICATOR INVESTMENTS (PTY) LTD

PALMPINE PROPERTIES (TWO) (PTY) LTD
PETREL PROPERTIES (PTY) LTD
PIED KINGFISHER INVESTMENTS LTD
PIPPIT PROPERTIES (PTY) LTD
PORT NATAL PROPERTIES (PTY) LTD
PUFFINS INVESTMENTS (PTY) LTD
REDWING FRANCOLIN INVESTMENTS (PTY) LTD
RHEA PROPERTIES (PTY) LTD
ROCK KESTREL INVESTMENTS (PTY) LTD
ROCK MARTIN INVESTMENTS (PTY) LTD
SACCABULLA PROPERTIES (PTY) LTD
SANDMARTIN INVESTMENTS (PTY) LTD
SHELLEY'S FRANCOLIN INVESTMENTS (PTY) LT
SHIKRA INVESTMENTS (PTY) LTD
SNOW PETREL INVESTMENTS (PTY) LTD
SPURWING GOOSE INVESTMENTS (PTY) LTD
STAND 258 STRYDOM PARK EXT 9 (PTY) LTD
STAND 705 DENVER (PTY) LTD
STILTPROPS (TWO) (PTY) LTD
TCHAGRA INVESTMENTS (PTY) LTD
TURTLE DOVE INVESTMENTS (PTY) LTD
TWINSPOT INVESTMENTS (PTY) LTD
WHIMBREL INVESTMENTS (PTY) LTD
WHITE EYE INVESTMENTS (PTY) LTD
WIDAH BIRD INVESTMENTS (PTY) LTD
WOOD IBIS INVESTMENTS (PTY) LTD

INVESTMENTS

None

HIGHSTONE PROPERTY FUND

ABBREVIATION : HISTONE

JSE SHORT CODE : HST

SECTOR : Financial-Property Trust

SHAREHOLDERS

Who Owns Whom's Assessment of the Identity of the Ultimate Controlling Shareholder: INSTITUTIONAL INVESTORS

SHAREHOLDER	PERCENTAGE 1992	1991
STD BANK NOM TVL P/L	23.0	23.6
FIRST NAT NOM P/L	18.0	18.0
CMB NOM P/L	16.4	---
CITY COUNCIL OF DURBAN	12.3	12.3
BARLOWS PENS FUND	4.9	4.9
FECHTER P H	4.5	4.5
DURBAN CORP SUPERANNUATION FUND	4.1	4.1
ENGINEERING INDUSTRIES PENS FUND	3.3	3.3
PROTEA ASSURE CO PENS FUND	2.1	2.1
CORNER HOUSE PENS FUND	1.6	1.6
LION MATCH GROUP PENS FUND	1.6	1.6
EIGHTY ONE MAIN STREET NOM LTD	1.3	---
MERCANTILE & GEN REINSURANCE CO SA LTD	1.2	1.2
SA NAT MEDICAL FUND LTD	---	1.6
SANLAM	---	14.8
TOTAL	94.4	93.7

DIRECTORS :
ARDINGTON AJ (Chairman),FIRELD TH ,GIBSON LJ
GROVES IM ,NOYCE MJ ,OVENSTONE ADP ,PARKHURST WR
SAVILLE D ,SQUIRE-HOWE RC ,TURRELL MF

REGISTERED OFFICE
5th Floor, Protea Assurance Building
321 Smith Str, Durban
4001
TEL: 031-304 2731
FAX: 031-305 1521

TRANSFER SECRETARY
Mercantile Registrars Ltd
P O Box 1053, Johannesburg
2000
TEL: 011-333 8181

COMPANY SECRETARY
Russell Marriott & Boyd Trust (Pty) Ltd

NATURE OF BUSINESS
A property unit trust, invested in commercial properties, and managed by Cornerstone Property Fund Managers Ltd.

BANKERS :
First National Bank of SA Ltd

AUDITORS :
Deloitte Pim Goldby

FAMILIAR BRAND NAMES
N/A

CONTRIBUTION BY ACTIVITY
Suburban Offices (% Fund by Sector) (83.0%)
CBD Offices (13.0%)
Retail (4.0%)

YEAR END : April

DIVIDEND : Units

Dividend No 2	(Ldr)13/12/91	(Pay)30/12/91	Amt(c)10.5
Dividend No 3	(Ldr)12/06/92	(Pay)30/06/92	Amt(c)10.75
Dividend No 4	(Ldr)18/12/92	(Pay)31/12/92	Amt(c)10.9

CAPITAL STRUCTURE

	AUTHORISED	ISSUED
Units	61000000	61000000

FINANCIAL STATISTICS (AT FINANCIAL YEAR END)

(Amts in R'000)	1992 Apr	1991 Apr
Ord S/H Int	119403	119403
Iss Ord Share	61000	61000
Total Liab	6650	8692
Current Liab	6650	8692
Total Assets	126053	128095
Current Assets	10887	20843
Debtors	60	697
Oper Profit	-631	-379
Prf af Int&Tax	12963	8329
Prf att Ord Sh	12963	8329
Btm Line Earn	12963	8329
Dividend Paid	12963	8327
Mkt Prce(c) YE	200	200

PER SHARE STATISTICS (CENTS)

Net Asst Val	195.74	195.74
Net Earnings	21.25	13.65

Dividends	21.25	13.65
Cash Flow	21.25	13.65

RATIOS AND OTHER INFORMATION

Mrk Cap(R000)	122000	122000
Current Ratio	1.64	2.40
Quik/Acid Tst	1.64	2.40
Debt/Ass Rat	0.05	0.07
Debt to Eqity	0.06	0.07
Ret on Assets	10.28	6.50
Ret on Equity%	10.86	6.98
Price/Earnings	9.41	14.65
Divid Cover	1.00	1.00
Divid Yield	10.63	6.83
Earning Yield%	10.63	6.83
NAV % Mrk Pr	97.87	97.87
Sus Grth Rate	0.00	0.00

SUBSIDIARY & ASSOCIATED COMPANIES

AVALON (PTY) LTD
BARLOW SOUTH (PTY) LTD
BEE EATER INVESTMENTS (PTY) LTD
CHALKSTONE (PTY) LTD
DRAMATIC INVESTMENTS (PTY) LTD
ENTYPOR (PTY) LTD
ETON ROAD PROPERTIES (PTY) LTD
GOUDOES PROPERTIES (PTY) LTD
KENILWORTH PALACE INVESTMENTS (PTY) LTD
LMD INVESTMENTS (PTY) LTD
MARDOY INVESTMENTS (PTY) LTD
MOORHEN INVESTMENTS (PTY) LTD
NORTORIA INVESTMENTS (PTY) LTD
SHEMAR INVESTMENTS (PTY) LTD
STONEHAM (PTY) LTD
TAUNTON PROPERTIES (PTY) LTD

INVESTMENTS

None

HIGHVELD STEEL & VANADIUM CORP LTD

ABBREVIATION : HIVELD

JSE SHORT CODE : HVL

SECTOR : Industrial-Steel & Allied

SHAREHOLDERS

Who Owns Whom's Assessment of the Identity of the Ultimate Controlling Shareholder: ANGLO AMERICAN

SHAREHOLDER	PERCENTAGE 1992	1991
ANGLO AMERICAN IND CORP LTD	44.8	43.4
RESIDENT NOM LTD	9.9	---
TAURUS NOM LTD	7.8	9.7
SA MUTUAL	5.4	6.0
EIGHTY ONE MAIN STREET NOM LTD	5.4	6.7
STD BANK NOM TVL P/L	4.3	6.2
METAL IND GROUP PENS FUND	3.3	4.2
ENGINEERING INDUSTRIES PENS FUND	3.1	3.8
DEUTSCHER AKV	2.9	3.4
CONSOLIDATED NOM P/L	2.9	3.6
FIRST NAT NOM P/L	1.4	1.7
TOTAL	91.1	88.6

DIRECTORS :
BOSHOFF HF ,BOUSTRED WG ,BRAGG WFE ,BULLETT BE
CALLANAN RR ,CHEGWIDDEN JA ,DAVIES HK
ELLWOOD RR ,HALL J ,JONES TE (Managing Director)
KING MW ,LANGTON G ,NCUBE DMJ ,O'DOWD MC
OGILVIE THOMPSON J ,OPPENHEIMER NF ,PARK NS
PIENAAR AJ DR,TRAHAR AJ ,TURNBULL NC

REGISTRATION NUMBER : 60/01900/06

REGISTERED OFFICE
Ptn 29, Schoongezicht Farm, No 308 J S
District Witbank
1035
TEL: 0135-97011
FAX: 0135-97561

TRANSFER SECRETARY
Consolidated Share Registrars Ltd
P O Box 61051, Marshalltown
2107
TEL: 011-492 1620

COMPANY SECRETARY
H Cochius

NATURE OF BUSINESS
The company produces steel, vanadium products, ferro-alloys, carbonaceous products, and metal containers and closures. Ore for operations is obtained from the company's own mine.

BANKERS :
First National Bank of SA Ltd

AUDITORS :
Deloitte Pim Goldby

FAMILIAR BRAND NAMES
N/A

CONTRIBUTION BY ACTIVITY
N/A

YEAR END : December

DIVIDEND : Ords R1

Interim No 32	(Ldr)07/09/90	(Pay)19/10/90	Amt(c)30
Final No 33	(Ldr)15/03/91	(Pay)26/04/91	Amt(c)40
Interim No 34	(Ldr)06/09/91	(Pay)18/10/91	Amt(c)30
Final No 35	(Ldr)13/03/92	(Pay)24/04/92	Amt(c)40
Interim No 36	(Ldr)04/09/92	(Pay)16/10/92	Amt(c)20

NUMBER OF EMPLOYEES : 6577

CAPITAL STRUCTURE

	AUTHORISED	ISSUED
Ords R1	99990000	88337485
Var Rate Red Cum Prefs 1c	1000000	0

FINANCIAL STATISTICS (AT FINANCIAL YEAR END)

(Amts in R'000)	1991 Dec	1990 Dec	1989 Dec	1988 Sep	1987 Sep

Ord S/H Int	1064309	744313	640821	425968	345327
Long Trm Loans	408750	350916	324416	297511	404791
Iss Ord Share	88337	72171	71865	70954	70954
Total Liab	1007963	801711	894770	602266	604699
Current Liab	599213	450795	570354	304755	199908
Total Assets	2072272	1546024	1535591	1028234	950026
Current Assets	1032675	647373	691263	341715	238244
Debtors	304350	204882	142690	184982	93880
Inventory	280991	202530	223156	135819	120708
Turnover	1378434	1431711	1613967	1189389	849669
Oper Profit	72137	156624	534432	243117	106780
Interest Paid	7121	8561	7231	7171	15971
Tax Paid	13634	51112	243611	103054	17503
Prf af Int&Tax	95584	150189	322940	139989	73306
Prf att Ord Sh	95584	150189	322440	121469	56810
Btm Line Earn	91251	150074	321887	119518	56810
Dividend Paid	57031	50511	93362	40664	21296
Mkt Prce(c) YE	1450	1325	1350	830	460
Depreciation	54793	47885	43175	40992	33066

PER SHARE STATISTICS (CENTS)

Net Asst Val	1204 83	1031 32	891 70	600 34	486 69
Net Earnings	130 00	208 40	450 00	170 60	80 10
Dividends	70 00	70 00	130 00	57 00	30 00
Cash Flow	210 41	311 63	581 21	372 85	151 37

RATIOS AND OTHER INFORMATION

Mrk Cap(R000)	1280887	956266	970178	588918	326388
Current Ratio	1 72	1 44	1 21	1 12	1 19
Quik/Acid Tst	1 25	0 99	0 82	0 68	0 59
A/C Rec T/ovr	4 53	6 99	11 31	6 43	9 05
Tot Ass T/ovr	0 67	0 93	1 05	1 16	0 89
Debt/Ass Rat	0 32	0 29	0 37	0 30	0 21
L T L Tot Ass	0 03	-	-	-	-
Debt to Eqity	0 62	0 61	0 89	0 72	0 58
Interest Cover	10 13	18 30	73 99	33 94	6 69
Oper Prof Mrg	5 23	10 94	33 11	20 44	12 57
Net Prof Marg%	6 93	10 49	19 98	10 21	6 69
Ret on Assets	5 61	13 57	37 37	24 33	11 24
Ret on Equity%	8 98	20 18	50 32	28 52	16 45
Price/Earnings	11 15	6 36	3 00	4 87	5 74
Divid Cover	1 86	2 98	3 46	2 99	2 67
Divid Yield	4 83	5 28	9 63	6 87	6 52
Earning Yield%	8 97	15 73	33 33	20 55	17 41
NAV % Mrk Pr	83 09	77 84	66 05	72 33	105 80
Effec Tax Rate	8 50	12 23	34 07	0 02	0 00
Def Interval	1 42	0 20	0 01	0 28	2 44
Sus Grth Rate	3 62	13 39	35 75	18 97	10 28

SUBSIDIARY & ASSOCIATED COMPANIES

COLUMBUS JOINT VENTURE (50%)
FERROVELD (PTY) LTD (50%)
IRONSTONE MINERALS (PTY) LTD
MIDDELBURG STEEL & ALLOYS (PTY) LTD (25%)
RAND CARBIDE (PTY) LTD
RHEEM SOUTH AFRICA (PTY) LTD
STEEL BUS SERVICES (PTY) LTD
TRANSALLOYS (PTY) LTD
TRANSVAAL VANADIUM COMPANY (PTY) LTD
VANSTEEL ESTATES (PTY) LTD

INVESTMENTS

FERROUS SCRAP DISTRIBUTORS LTD (38034 SH)
LANSAN INVESTMENT HOLDINGS LTD (3568 SH)
SMALL BUSINESS DEVELOPMENT CORP LTD (550000 SH)

HIPPO VALLEY ESTATES LTD

ABBREVIATION : HIPPO

SECTOR : Zimbabwe Stock Exchange

SHAREHOLDERS

Who Owns Whom's Assessment of the Identity of the Ultimate Controlling Shareholder: ANGLO AMERICAN / OLD MUTUAL INV CORP

SHAREHOLDER	PERCENTAGE 1992	1991
SECURITY NOM LTD	43 4	---
OLD MUTUAL INV CORP (PVT) LTD	15 4	---
TATE & LYLE HOLDINGS LTD	8 3	---
FIRST NOM PVT LTD	3 5	--
MON CHOIX P/L	1 8	---
STD CHART MERCHANT BANK ZIM NOM PVT LTD	1 8	---
FIDELITY LIFE ASSURE OF ZIM PVT LTD	1 5	---
IPCORN LTD	1 2	---
TOTAL	76 9	---

DIRECTORS :
BAIN GT ,BRUCE LR (Deputy Managing Director)
BULLETT BE ,DENNETT DE (Managing Director)
DUMBUTSHENA E THE HON,GIFFORD S
LANDER RP (Chairman),MARGESSON MV
MUPAWOSE RM DR,NICHOLSON DG

REGISTERED OFFICE
70 Samora Machel Avenue, Harare
Zimbabwe

TEL 704461

TRANSFER SECRETARY
First Transfer Secretaries (Pvt) Ltd
P O Box 437, Bulawayo
Zimbabwe

TEL 092634 - 702905

COMPANY SECRETARY
Anglo American Corporation Services

NATURE OF BUSINESS
HIPPO VALLEY, incorporated in Zimbabwe,is mainly engaged in the growing and milling of sugar cane for the domestic, US and Botswana markets Ancillary activities include other farming operations and the conversion of molasses into alchohol

BANKERS :
N/A

AUDITORS :
Deloitte & Touche

FAMILIAR BRAND NAMES
N/A

CONTRIBUTION BY ACTIVITY
N/A

YEAR END : March

CAPITAL STRUCTURE

	AUTHORISED	ISSUED
Ords Z$1	200000000	192110814

FINANCIAL STATISTICS (AT FINANCIAL YEAR END)

(Amts in Z$)	1992 Mar	1991 Mar
Ord S/H Int	502261	482275
Long Trm Loans	2255	840
Iss Ord Share	192111	192111
Total Liab	56121	49900
Current Liab	53866	49060
Total Assets	558382	532175
Current Assets	104386	105787
Debtors	44087	41579
Inventory	39856	54549
Turnover	210465	197001
Oper Profit	12091	45983
Interest Paid	293	383
Tax Paid	12068	19968
Prf af Int&Tax	-270	25632
Prf att Ord Sh	-270	25632
Btm Line Earn	-270	25632
Dividend Paid	-	5763
Depreciation	18788	13646

PER SHARE STATISTICS (CENTS)

Net Asst Val	261.44	251.04
Net Earnings	-0.10	13.30
Dividends	-	3.00
Cash Flow	9.64	20.45

RATIOS AND OTHER INFORMATION

Current Ratio	1.94	2.16
Quik/Acid Tst	1.20	1.04
A/C Rec T/ovr	4.77	4.74
Tot Ass T/ovr	0.38	0.37
Debt/Ass Rat	0.10	0.09
L T L Tot Ass	0.00	0.00
Debt to Eqity	0.11	0.10
Interest Cover	41.27	120.06
Oper Prof Mrg	5.74	23.34
Net Prof Marg%	-0.13	13.01
Ret on Assets	2.17	8.64
Ret on Equity%	-0.05	5.31
Divid Cover	-	4.43
Effec Tax Rate	102.29	43.79
Def Interval	0.14	0.05
Sus Grth Rate	-0.05	4.12

SUBSIDIARY & ASSOCIATED COMPANIES

HOLDAIN PROPERTIES (PTY) LTD
TOKWANE BARRAGE & CANAL (ZIMBABWE)

INVESTMENTS

None

HJ JOEL GOLD MINING CO LTD

ABBREVIATION : JOEL

JSE SHORT CODE : JOE

SECTOR : Gold-OFS

SHAREHOLDERS

Who Owns Whom's Assessment of the Identity of the Ultimate Controlling Shareholder:
ANGLO AMERICAN VIA JOHNIES

SHAREHOLDER	PERCENTAGE 1992	1991
STD BANK NOM TVL P/L	54.8	53.8
RESIDENT NOM LTD	8.4	9.7
CMB NOM P/L	8.0	---
FIRST NAT NOM P/L	3.1	3.7
JOHANNESBURG CONSOLIDATED INV CO LTD	1.4	1.9
JUBILEE PROSPECTORS LTD	1.4	1.9
LONDON REGISTER ACCOUNT	1.1	1.0
ENGINEERING INDUSTRIES PENS FUND	---	1.1
SANLAM	---	10.1
TOTAL	78.1	83.2

DIRECTORS :
CONN WP ,CROSS GMW ,HENDERSON D DR,HEWITT L
KLINTWORTH RI ,MAXWELL KW (Chairman)
NAIRN WA (Managing Director),SCOTT-RUSSELL H DR
WANBLAD GP

REGISTRATION NUMBER : 85/01995/06

REGISTERED OFFICE
Consolidated Building, Fox and Harrison Streets
Johannesburg
2001
TEL: 011-373 9111
FAX: 011-834 5064

TRANSFER SECRETARY
Consolidated Share Registrars Ltd
P O Box 61051, Marshalltown
2107
TEL: 011-492 1620

COMPANY SECRETARY
Johannesburg Consolidated Inv Co Ltd

NATURE OF BUSINESS
The company operates a gold mine in the district of Theunissen, OFS.

BANKERS :
N/A

AUDITORS :
Deloitte & Touche

FAMILIAR BRAND NAMES
N/A

CONTRIBUTION BY ACTIVITY
N/A

YEAR END : June

NUMBER OF EMPLOYEES : 2710

CAPITAL STRUCTURE

	AUTHORISED	ISSUED
Ords 1c	200000000	97980267
Var Rate Red Prefs 1c	1000000	150

FINANCIAL STATISTICS (AT FINANCIAL YEAR END)

(Amts in R'000)	1992 Jun	1991 Jun	1990 Jun	1989 Jun	1988 Jun
Ord S/H Int	626214	612603	498966	559584	497747
Long Trm Loans	74516	72616	3213	3233	-
Iss Ord Share	97980	97980	97980	97980	70928
Total Liab	114174	111612	144767	30493	23161
Current Liab	39658	38996	141554	27260	23161
Total Assets	740388	724215	643733	590057	520908
Current Assets	54934	59192	12194	24444	72943
Debtors	6351	2599	552	744	1704
Inventory	16299	18213	11642	5654	3854
Turnover	197492	132504	56448	24833	-
Oper Profit	24156	-21918	-51029	-21284	-
Interest Paid	9769	14916	10898	439	-
Prf af Int&Tax	14416	-36822	-61876	-20947	-
Prf att Ord Sh	14416	-36822	-61876	-20947	-
Btm Line Earn	14416	-36822	-61876	-20947	-
Mkt Prce(c) YE	200	550	580	850	745

PER SHARE STATISTICS (CENTS)

Net Asst Val	639.12	625.23	509.25	571.10	701.76
Net Earnings	14.70	-37.60	-63.20	-23.00	-
Cash Flow	14.71	-37.58	-63.15	-21.38	-

RATIOS AND OTHER INFORMATION

Mrk Cap(R000)	195960	538890	568284	832830	528414
Current Ratio	1.39	1.52	0.09	0.90	3.15
Quik/Acid Tst	0.97	1.05	0.00	0.69	2.98
A/C Rec T/ovr	31.10	50.98	102.26	33.38	-
Tot Ass T/ovr	0.27	0.18	0.09	0.04	-
Debt/Ass Rat	0.15	0.15	0.22	0.05	0.04
L T L Tot Ass	0.10	0.10	0.00	0.01	-
Debt to Eqity	0.18	0.18	0.29	0.05	0.05
Interest Cover	2.48	-1.47	-4.68	-46.72	-
Oper Prof Mrg	12.23	-16.54	-90.40	-85.71	-
Net Prof Marg%	7.30	-27.79	-109.62	-84.35	-
Ret on Assets	3.27	-3.02	-7.92	-3.48	-
Ret on Equity%	2.30	-6.01	-12.40	-3.74	-
Price/Earnings	13.61	-14.63	-9.18	-36.96	-
Earning Yield%	7.35	-6.84	-10.90	-2.71	-
NAV % Mrk Pr	319.56	113.68	87.80	67.19	94.20
Def Interval	5.17	-1.97	-1.79	-0.15	-
Sus Grth Rate	2.30	-6.01	-12.40	-3.74	-

SUBSIDIARY & ASSOCIATED COMPANIES

None

INVESTMENTS

MINE LABOUR ORGANISATION (NRC) LTD (1070 SH)
RAND REFINERY LTD (3623 SH)
SANDVELT INVESTMENTS (PTY) LTD (17 SH)
SPANNE HOLDINGS AG (7 SH)
THE EMPLOYMENT BUREAU OF AFRICA LIMITED (7663 SH)
THE RAND MUTUAL ASSURANCE CO LTD (100 SH)

HOLDAINS LTD

ABBREVIATION : HOLDAIN

JSE SHORT CODE : HLN

SECTOR : Industrial-Paper & Packaging

SHAREHOLDERS

Who Owns Whom's Assessment of the Identity of the Ultimate Controlling Shareholder:
SANLAM VIA GENCOR VIA MALBAK

SHAREHOLDER	PERCENTAGE 1992	1991
MALBAK INV (HOLDAINS) LTD	67.4	66.3
CMB NOM P/L	9.8	---
METAL IND GROUP PENS FUND	2.5	3.0
ENGINEERING INDUSTRIES PENS FUND	2.3	2.6
NEDBANK NOM LTD	1.3	1.4
STD BANK NOM TVL P/L	1.3	2.1
BOARD OF EXECUTORS NOM P/L	---	1.1
SANLAM	---	7.9
TOTAL	84.5	84.4

DIRECTORS :

MCLEOD RN ,MINNIE ND ,NEWBURY JE ,PARTRIDGE KJ
PRICE DNJ (Financial Director),RILEY DB
SMITH DJ ,THOMAS GS (Chairman)
WILLIS I (Dep. Chair. & Chief Exec.

REGISTRATION NUMBER : 05/09845/06

REGISTERED OFFICE

Kohler House, 4 Pybus Road
Sandton
2199
TEL: 011-883 1901
FAX: 011-783 5708

TRANSFER SECRETARY

Central Registrars Ltd
P O Box 4844, Johannesburg
2000
TEL: 011-331 0051

COMPANY SECRETARY

P J Horrocks

NATURE OF BUSINESS

The group manufactures & markets paper, packaging and fibre products, and markets paper & printing equipment. The company controls quoted Carlton Paper Corp and Sun Packaging Investments.

BANKERS :

Standard Bank of SA Ltd, Nedperm Bank Ltd
First National Bank of SA Ltd

AUDITORS :

Deloitte Pim Goldby

FAMILIAR BRAND NAMES

ARJOMARIE,BABYSOFT,BAKKE,BE SURE,BIOPOLYMERS
BRABY'S,CAVERSHAM,DUPONT,FIRST PAPER HOUSE
FOMOPAK,FPCO,GRAPHTEC,HADDONS TRADING
HUGGIES,ICONOFIX,IDEM,INTRATEX,KIMCLOTH
KIMDRI,KLEENEX,KLIKLOCK,KOHLER,LABEC,LAWRIES
MAN ROLAND,MBO,MERRIMAKER,MILLER
MULLER MARTINI,NEW FREEDOM,OMNIPAK
OUTTASIGHT,PHOTRA-ALLGRAPHICS,SOFTIQUE
STAR PAPER,SUPERFOAM,SWAN PUBLISHERS,SYLKARD
SYLKO,WIGGINS TEAPE,ZANDERS

CONTRIBUTION BY ACTIVITY
Kohler Packaging (% Turnover) (57.0%)
Graphtec (31.0%)
Carlton (9.0%)
Sun Packaging Investments Ltd (3.0%)

YEAR END : August

DIVIDEND : Ords no par value

Interim No 67	(Ldr)11/05/90	(Pay)18/05/90	Amt(c)47
Final No 68	(Ldr)09/11/90	(Pay)07/12/90	Amt(c)63
Interim No 69	(Ldr)03/05/91	(Pay)17/05/91	Amt(c)51
Final No 70	(Ldr)08/11/91	(Pay)06/12/91	Amt(c)70
Interim No 71	(Ldr)24/04/92	(Pay)15/05/92	Amt(c)51
Final No 72	(Ldr)31/10/92	(Pay)07/12/92	Amt(c)70

NUMBER OF EMPLOYEES : 11159

CAPITAL STRUCTURE

	AUTHORISED	ISSUED
6,5% Non-Red Cum Prefs R2	225000	225000
Ords no par value	100000000	24285880

FINANCIAL STATISTICS (AT FINANCIAL YEAR END)

(Amts in R'000)	1991 Aug	1990 Aug	1989 Aug	1988 Aug	1987 Aug
Ord S/H Int	407323	356503	202184	143298	107955
Long Trm Loans	184920	54032	18238	93783	67932
Iss Ord Share	24286	22805	14797	14271	13013
Total Liab	712000	477601	291125	244260	174976
Current Liab	527080	423569	272887	150477	107044
Total Assets	1119323	834104	493309	387558	282931
Current Assets	720418	540600	297443	235159	171817
Debtors	360062	274996	154540	97465	71893
Inventory	323518	265127	142823	123993	89773
Turnover	1951836	1797833	982670	774606	385982
Oper Profit	170241	146604	81996	59710	24053
Interest Paid	42721	43219	21258	10223	5684
Tax Paid	39069	31446	10308	12383	1393
Prf af Int&Tax	91175	76467	57021	37104	16976
Prf att Ord Sh	82032	73343	47980	34954	15810
Btm Line Earn	30291	42361	46767	34666	11533
Dividend Paid	28792	25085	14769	12723	5263
Mkt Prce(c) YE	3700	1575	2000	1480	1650
Depreciation	28547	25137	22920	18433	12808

PER SHARE STATISTICS (CENTS)

Net Asst Val	1677.19	1563.27	1366.39	1004.12	829.59
Net Earnings	358.20	321.60	325.00	250.10	130.40
Dividends	121.00	110.00	100.00	90.00	40.00
Cash Flow	473.96	432.68	524.11	414.84	351.40

RATIOS AND OTHER INFORMATION

Mrk Cap(R000)	898582	359179	295940	211211	214715
Current Ratio	1.37	1.28	1.09	1.56	1.61
Quik/Acid Tst	0.75	0.65	0.57	0.74	0.77
A/C Rec T/ovr	5.42	6.54	6.36	7.95	8.05
Tot Ass T/ovr	1.74	2.16	1.99	2.00	2.05
Debt/Ass Rat	0.53	0.55	0.58	0.58	0.57
L T L Tot Ass	0.06	0.05	0.02	0.19	0.19
Debt to Eqity	1.46	1.29	1.41	1.56	1.49
Interest Cover	4.05	3.50	4.17	5.84	4.23
Oper Prof Mrg	8.72	8.15	8.34	7.71	6.23
Net Prof Marg%	4.20	4.08	4.88	4.51	4.10
Ret on Assets	15.45	18.12	17.96	15.41	12.75
Ret on Equity%	20.14	20.57	23.73	24.39	21.97
Price/Earnings	10.33	4.90	6.15	5.92	12.65
Divid Cover	2.96	2.92	3.25	2.78	3.26
Divid Yield	3.27	6.98	5.00	6.08	2.42
Earning Yield%	9.68	20.42	16.25	16.90	7.90
NAV % Mrk Pr	45.33	99.26	68.32	67.85	50.28
Effec Tax Rate	32.57	29.90	17.05	15.76	8.86
Def Interval	1.35	1.58	1.25	1.27	2.82
Sus Grth Rate	13.07	13.54	16.43	15.51	9.77

SUBSIDIARY & ASSOCIATED COMPANIES

ACME PRINT & PACK (PTY) LTD
AFRICAN CONTAINER CO. LTD
ALLGRAPHICS (PTY) LTD
BAKKE INDUSTRIES LTD
BAKKE PACKAGING (PTY) LTD
BEITH PROCESS (NATAL) (PTY) LTD
BRITISH FLEXIBLE PACKAGING (PTY) LTD
BUD PACKAGING CORPORATION (PTY) LTD
CARLTON PAPER CORP LTD (50,04%)
FIRST PAPER HOUSE LTD
GRAPHEX INDUSTRIES (PTY) LTD (50%)
GRAPHTEC LTD (50%)
HAYNE & GIBSON HOLDINGS LTD
HAYNE & GIBSON LTD
HOLDAIN BOXES (CAPE) (1968) (PTY) LTD
HOLDAIN PROPERTIES (PTY) LTD
INTRATEX PRINTING & PUBLISHING COMPANY (
KCSA HOLDINGS (PTY) LTD (50%)
KOHLER INVESTMENTS LTD
KOHLER PACKAGING LTD
KOHLER SACKS LTD (45%)
LOWVELD CONTAINER COMPANY (PTY) LTD
MALBAK INVESTMENTS (CARLCOR) (PTY) LTD
MWT PAPER PROCESSING LTD (MAURITIUS) (50%)
PHOTOFLEX PACKAGING & PRINTING (PTY) LTD
QUINPAK (PTY) LTD
REGMA SA (PTY) LTD (50%)
SMITHS DIRECTORY INVESTMENTS (PTY) LTD
SPINELLI CORPAK (PTY) LTD
SUN PACKAGING INVESTMENTS LTD
SYLKO PAPER CO LTD
TECSUFIN (PTY) LTD (50%)
TEXAC (PTY) LTD
THE WALVIS BAY CONTAINER CO. (PTY) LTD
TOOLPLAST HOLDINGS (PTY) LTD

INVESTMENTS

LENCO HOLDINGS LTD (2233 SH)
SMALL BUSINESS DEVELOPMENT CORP LTD

HORTORS LTD

ABBREVIATION : HORTORS

JSE SHORT CODE : HTR

SECTOR : Industrial-Paper & Packaging

SHAREHOLDERS

Who Owns Whom's Assessment of the Identity of the Ultimate Controlling Shareholder:
ANGLO VIA ARGUS VIA CTP HOLDINGS

SHAREHOLDER	PERCENTAGE 1992	1991
CTP HOLDINGS LTD	88.3	88.4

ARGUS HOLDINGS LTD	7.6	7.6
NEDBANK NOM LTD	2.9	2.9
TOTAL	98.8	99.0

DIRECTORS :
CORMACK SF (Managing Director),FEATHERSTONE JG
GOOSEN F (Financial Director)
JANKELOWITZ EM (Chairman),TODD AR

REGISTRATION NUMBER : 81/05794/06

REGISTERED OFFICE
1 Blumberg Road, Industria West
Johannesburg
2092
TEL: 011-474 8750
FAX: 011-474 8489

TRANSFER SECRETARY
Mercantile Registrars Ltd
P O Box 1053, Johannesburg
2000
TEL: 011-333 8181

COMPANY SECRETARY
F Goosen

NATURE OF BUSINESS
An investment holding company which, via its subsidiaries operates in the following fields:The manufacture and processing of cartons and labels for use in tobacco, pharmaceutical, food and cosmetic industries; the production of greeting cards and wrapping papers; the manufacture and processing of cigarette packaging and long run labels;packaging for records, pharmaceutical and cosmetic industries & the supply of printed matter to the music industry.

BANKERS :
First National Bank of SA Ltd

AUDITORS :
Ernst & Young

FAMILIAR BRAND NAMES
N/A

CONTRIBUTION BY ACTIVITY
N/A

YEAR END : March

DIVIDEND : Ords 1c

Final	(Ldr)29/06/90	(Pay)20/07/90	Amt(c)1.5
Final	(Ldr)21/06/91	(Pay)12/07/91	Amt(c)3
Final	(Ldr)03/07/92	(Pay)24/07/92	Amt(c)5

NUMBER OF EMPLOYEES : 434

CAPITAL STRUCTURE

	AUTHORISED	ISSUED
Ords 1c	100000000	51563346

FINANCIAL STATISTICS (AT FINANCIAL YEAR END)

(Amts in R'000)	1992 Mar	1991 Mar	1990 Mar	1989 Mar	1988 Mar
Ord S/H Int	42822	44162	41429	39476	7926
Long Trm Loans	5364	3528	2641	90	179
Iss Ord Share	51563	51563	51563	51563	6010
Total Liab	23377	14040	7136	9314	3629
Current Liab	18013	10512	4495	9224	3450
Total Assets	66199	58202	48565	48790	11555
Current Assets	38492	37951	26437	24795	3619
Debtors	14078	6490	6259	7244	2600
Inventory	8560	7530	7919	5829	822
Turnover	81812	48773	40891	40416	8381
Oper Profit	10347	5322	3437	3923	-1102
Interest Paid	93	26	132	313	256
Tax Paid	5153	4337	2588	43	-
Prf af Int&Tax	7843	4275	2769	4038	-802
Prf att Ord Sh	7343	4275	2769	4038	-802
Btm Line Earn	1238	4280	2727	7204	-644
Dividend Paid	2578	1547	774	1031	270
Mkt Prce(c) YE	80	60	45	65	160
Depreciation	4345	2106	2305	2127	379

PER SHARE STATISTICS (CENTS)

Net Asst Val	83.05	85.65	80.35	76.56	131.88
Net Earnings	14.20	8.30	5.40	7.80	-10.70
Dividends	5.00	3.00	1.50	2.00	4.50
Cash Flow	23.19	14.12	14.96	11.96	-7.04

RATIOS AND OTHER INFORMATION

Mrk Cap(R000)	41250	30938	23203	33516	9616
Current Ratio	2.14	3.61	5.88	2.69	1.05
Quik/Acid Tst	1.66	2.89	4.12	2.06	0.81
A/C Rec T/ovr	5.81	7.52	6.53	5.58	3.22
Tot Ass T/ovr	1.24	0.84	0.84	0.83	0.73
Debt/Ass Rat	0.29	0.18	0.09	0.19	0.31
L T L Tot Ass	0.02	0.00	0.00	0.00	0.02
Debt to Eqity	0.45	0.24	0.11	0.24	0.46
Interest Cover	111.27	204.69	26.06	12.81	-2.30
Oper Prof Mrg	12.65	10.91	8.41	9.71	-13.15
Net Prof Marg%	8.98	8.77	6.77	9.99	-9.57
Ret on Assets	19.80	14.84	11.30	9.01	-4.73
Ret on Equity%	17.15	9.68	6.68	10.23	-10.12
Price/Earnings	5.63	7.23	8.33	8.33	-14.95
Divid Cover	2.84	2.77	3.60	3.90	-2.38
Divid Yield	6.25	5.00	3.33	3.08	2.81
Earning Yield%	17.75	13.83	12.00	12.00	-6.69
NAV % Mrk Pr	103.81	142.74	178.55	117.78	82.43
Effec Tax Rate	40.50	39.91	-	1.48	-
Def Interval	0.11	0.03	0.06	0.41	-5.23
Sus Grth Rate	11.13	6.18	4.82	7.62	-13.53

SUBSIDIARY & ASSOCIATED COMPANIES

ACCOUNTING SYSTEMS BOTSWANA (PTY) LTD
ARTONE PRESS (PTY) LTD
COMPUQUIP (PTY) LTD
CTP-ARTONE (PTY) LTD
HORTORS PRINT (PTY) LTD
HORTORS TRADING (PTY) LTD

INVESTMENTS

REDGWOODS LTD (89681 SH)
SOLCHEM INVESTMENT HOLDINGS LTD (141208 SH)

HOSKEN CONSOLIDATED INVESTMENTS LTD

ABBREVIATION : HCI

JSE SHORT CODE : HCI

SECTOR : Financial-Insurance

SHAREHOLDERS

Who Owns Whom's Assessment of the Identity of the Ultimate Controlling Shareholder:
DIRECTORS / INSTITUTIONS

SHAREHOLDER	PERCENTAGE 1992	1991
NEDBANK NOM LTD	18.2	23.4
STD BANK NOM TVL P/L	14.4	---
LEWIS I M A	11.2	11.0
HOSKEN W TRUST	7.5	7.0
CRENDELL INV CORP LTD	4.0	4.0
HOSKEN HUBERT WILL TRUST	3.6	3.4
HOSKEN CONS INV SHARE INC TRUST	3.2	2.4
HOSKEN STAFF SHARE INC CONTROL ACC	2.4	3.0
NESTADT G	1.9	1.8
SAFEGRO NOM P/L	1.7	6.0
JNG FAMILY TRUST	1.6	1.5
WORKMENS COMPENS COMMISSIONER IN TRUST	1.5	---
CINOA HOLDINGS LTD	1.4	1.3
HOSKEN F W	1.4	1.3
JOHN ASBURY FAMILY HLDGS P/L	1.2	1.1
IRISH M C	---	1.3
EIGHTY ONE MAIN STREET NOM LTD	---	1.7
TRUCK & CAR CO P/L	---	7.5
TOTAL	75.1	77.8

DIRECTORS :
ANDREWS RC ,ASKIN JMC ,CUSHWAY PM ,DENNISS PS
HOSKEN JH ,HOSKEN W ,IRISH MC ,LEVIN J
LEVIN J (JNR) ,LEWIS IMAW (Executive Chairman)
MOXON JR ,NATHAN L ,NESTADT G

REGISTRATION NUMBER : 73/07111/06

REGISTERED OFFICE
IGI House, 162 Anderson Street
Johannesburg
2001
TEL: 011-335 1911
FAX: 011-29 0491

TRANSFER SECRETARY
Mercantile Registrars Ltd
P O Box 1053, Johannesburg
2000
TEL: 011-333 8181

COMPANY SECRETARY
W T Green

NATURE OF BUSINESS
An investment holding company for IGI. The prinpal activities of its subsidiary and associated companies are insurance underwriting, life and home services,assurance,insurance and re-insurance broking, property owning, administration, development and construction, manufacturing and other ancilliary services, including computer, printing and security services, project management and the assessing of insurance claims.

BANKERS :
First National Bank of SA Ltd
Nedperm Bank Ltd, Standard Bank of SA Ltd
Volkskas Ltd

AUDITORS :
BDO Spencer Steward

FAMILIAR BRAND NAMES
N/A

CONTRIBUTION BY ACTIVITY
Short-term Insurance (% Attrib.profit) (41.1%)
Life Assurance (30.9%)
Property & Other (28.0%)

YEAR END : March

DIVIDEND : Ords 25c

Interim No 30	(Ldr)01/12/89	(Pay)18/12/89	Amt(c)15
Final No 31	(Ldr)29/06/90	(Pay)09/07/90	Amt(c)21
Interim No 32	(Ldr)01/12/90	(Pay)18/12/90	Amt(c)15.0
Final No 33	(Ldr)21/06/91	(Pay)05/07/91	Amt(c)30
Interim No 34	(Ldr)29/11/91	(Pay)20/12/91	Amt(c)16
Final No 35	(Ldr)31/07/92	(Pay)21/08/92	Amt(c)32
Specie No 36	(Ldr)31/07/92	(Pay)21/08/92	Amt(c)55.1
Interim No 37	(Ldr)04/12/92	(Pay)14/12/92	Amt(c)18

NUMBER OF EMPLOYEES : 3204

CAPITAL STRUCTURE

	AUTHORISED	ISSUED
Ords 25c	17000000	14210052

FINANCIAL STATISTICS (AT FINANCIAL YEAR END)

(Amts in R'000)	1992 Mar	1991 Mar	1990 Mar	1989 Mar	1988 Mar
Ord S/H Int	112361	111087	68993	53279	35808
Long Trm Loans	1175422	893258	751208	531075	189907
Iss Ord Share	14210	14153	10829	10829	9828
Total Liab	1575095	1291067	975386	726152	357256
Current Liab	399673	397809	224178	195077	167349
Total Assets	1643034	1370606	1044379	779431	393064
Intang Assets	44422	31548	*	*	*
Current Assets	602683	526201	321495	296191	183308
Debtors	238949	181321	91640	79068	69238
Inventory	36219	1771	-	8089	14700
Turnover	-	-	-	-	490530
Oper Profit	-46678	-37776	-17494	27907	16741
Interest Paid	12439	6378	5125	5908	3813
Tax Paid	6904	8061	-1458	14973	4530
Prf af Int&Tax	40796	38864	33360	29818	21377
Prf att Ord Sh	20075	19727	17994	15444	13277
Btm Line Earn	3246	19648	21357	14501	13244
Dividend Paid	6821	5870	3898	3032	2260
Mkt Prce(c) YE	700	725	700	475	375
Depreciation	11412	5597	3850	3671	2267

PER SHARE STATISTICS (CENTS)

Net Asst Val	478.11	561.99	637.11	492.00	364.35
Net Earnings	141.30	166.60	166.20	148.70	135.10
Dividends	48.00	45.00	36.00	28.00	23.00
Cash Flow	239.82	205.20	155.57	157.09	138.21

RATIOS AND OTHER INFORMATION

Mrk Cap(R000)	99470	102609	75803	51438	36855
Current Ratio	1.51	1.32	1.43	1.52	1.10
Quik/Acid Tst	1.42	1.32	1.43	1.48	1.01
A/C Rec T/ovr	-	-	-	-	7.08
Tot Ass T/ovr	-	-	-	-	1.25
Debt/Ass Rat	0.26	0.29	0.21	0.25	0.43
L T L Tot Ass	0.02	0.00	0.00	0.00	0.01
Debt to Eqity	3.81	3.61	3.25	3.69	4.74
Interest Cover	4.83	8.36	7.22	8.58	7.79
Oper Prof Mrg	-	-	-	-	3.41

Net Prof Marg%	-	-	-	-	2.71
Ret on Assets	3.70	3.95	3.93	6.96	8.06
Ret on Equity%	17.87	17.76	26.08	28.99	37.08
Price/Earnings	4.95	4.35	4.21	3.19	2.78
Divid Cover	2.94	3.70	4.62	5.31	5.87
Divid Yield	6.86	6.21	5.14	5.89	6.13
Earning Yield%	20.19	22.98	23.74	31.31	36.03
NAV % Mrk Pr	68.30	77.52	91.02	103.58	97.16
Effec Tax Rate	-4.44	-10.30	-11.06	67.19	32.55
Def Interval	3.17	1.53	1.20	0.51	0.75
Sus Grth Rate	11.80	12.47	20.43	23.30	30.77

SUBSIDIARY & ASSOCIATED COMPANIES

AMITY INTERNATIONALE SA (LUXEMBOURG)
CRENDELL INVESTMENT CORPORATION LTD
HCI (UK) HOLDINGS LTD
HOSKEN CONSULTANTS (PTY) LTD
IGI INSURANCE CO LTD
WILLIAM HOSKEN & CO (PTY) LTD

INVESTMENTS

AFRICAN OXYGEN LTD (14600 SH)
ALLIED BANK LTD (25000 SH)
AMALGAMATED BANKS OF SA LTD (134000 SH)
ANGLO ALPHA LTD (36780 SH)
ANGLO AMERICAN CORP OF S.A. LTD (64500 SH)
ANGLO AMERICAN INDUSTRIAL CORP LTD (15000 SH)
ANGLO AMERICAN INVESTMENT TRUST LTD (25200 SH)
ANGLOVAAL LTD 'A' (87766 SH)
ANGLOVAAL LTD (N) (109266 SH)
BARLOW RAND LTD (67018 SH)
BERCON COMPONENTS CC = HEAVY DIESEL REPA (17376 SH)
BID CORP LTD (99700 SH)
BLUE CIRCLE LTD (34700 SH)
BOARD PROPERTIES LINK UNITS (225000 SH)
CADBURY SCHWEPPES SA LTD (14400 SH)
CG SMITH LTD (19660 SH)
COMBINED MOTOR HOLDINGS LTD (10700 SH)
CONSOL LTD (49700 SH)
DE BEERS CONSOLIDATED MINES LTD (126000 SH)
DELTA ELECTRICAL INDUSTRIES LTD (169500 SH)
DRIEFONTEIN CONSOLIDATED LTD (113000 SH)
EDGARS STORES LTD (62600 SH)
ELCENTRE CORPORATION LTD (214000 SH)
EQUIKOR LTD (34182300S)
GENBEL INVESTMENTS LTD (53000 SH)
GENCOR BEHEREND BPK (637649 SH)
GENCOR LTD (637649 SH)
GENERAL MINING UNION CORP LTD (12,5% DEB (134551 SH)
GROWTHPOINT PROPERTIES LTD (359500 SH)
HARTEBEESFONTEIN GOLD MINING CO LTD (84200 SH)
HOSKEN BROKERS (PTY) LTD (1530500SH)
HUNT LEUCHARS & HEPBURN HOLDINGS LTD (101126 SH)
IMPALA PLATINUM HOLDINGS LTD (2000 SH)
INVESTEC BANK LTD (1272100SH)
INVESTEC BANK LTD (PREF SHRS) (2000 SH)
INVESTEC HOLDINGS LTD (13,6% PREF SHRS) (500 SH)
INVESTEC HOLDINGS LTD (2559400SH)
ISCOR LTD (972000 SH)
ITALTILE LTD (3363083SH)
JOHANNESBURG CONSOLIDATED INVESTMENT CO (49000 SH)
KEELEY GROUP HOLDINGS LTD (10000 SH)
KELGRAN LTD (10000 SH)
KINROSS MINES LTD (45200 SH)
KLOOF GOLD MINING CO. LTD (108300 SH)
KLOOF GOLD MINING COMPANY LTD (FINANCIA (120900 SH)
LEBOWA PLATINUM MINES (54500 SH)
MALBAK LTD (174053 SH)
MAS HOLDINGS LTD (212700 SH)
MCCARTHY GROUP LTD (150000 SH)
MONEX SECURITIES LTD (PREF SHRS) (3000 SH)
MURRAY & ROBERTS HOLDINGS LTD (83000 SH)
ORYX GOLD HOLDINGS LTD (17400 SH)
PEPGRO LTD (19000 SH)
PICK 'N PAY HOLDINGS LTD (122800 SH)
POTGIETERSRUS PLATINUM (870 SH)
R MCCARTHY (OFS) LTD (PREF SHRS) (3000000SH)
R MCCARTHY (PTY) LTD (PREF SHRS) (1250000SH)
RABIE HOLDINGS LTD (100000 SH)
REMBRANDT BEHEREND BELEGGINGS (535000 SH)
REMBRANDT GROUP LTD (192400 SH)
RICHEMONT SECURITIES LTD (421000 SH)
ROYAL CORPORATION LTD (3088916 SH)
ROYAL FOODS LTD (562500 SH)
ROYAL GROUP HOLDINGS LTD (595000 SH)
RUSTENBURG PLATINUM HOLDINGS LTD (11500 SH)
SAFMARINE & RENNIES HOLDINGS LTD (28000 SH)
SAFRICAN LIFE INVESTMENT HOLDINGS LTD (10.65%)
SAPPI LTD (48060 SH)
SASOL LTD (308500 SH)
SECURITY 2000 LTD (A PREF SHRS) (500000 SH)
SECURITY 2000 LTD (B PREF SHRS) (1500000SH)
SILTEK LIMITED (10000 SH)
SMALL BUSINESS DEVELOPMENT CORP LTD (259686 SH)
SOUTH AFRICAN BREWERIES LTD (90300 SH)
SPARECO HOLDINGS LTD (14,25% PREF SHRS) (2000000SH)
SPARECO HOLDINGS LTD (2000000SH)
SUN INTERNATIONAL (BOP) LTD (44843 SH)
TIGER OATS LTD (107175 SH)
TIME HOLDINGS LTD (1314800SH)
TIME HOLDINGS LTD (14% PREF SHRS) (3175848SH)
TIME HOLDINGS LTD (6% PREF SHRS) (2656666S)
TIMES MEDIA LTD (135400 SH)
TOLLGATE HOLDINGS LTD (3843273SH)
TR SERVICES HOLDINGS LTD (98900 SH)
TRIM TRADE LTD (357125 SH)
TRIMTEX HOLDINGS LTD (1496375SH)
VAAL REEFS EXPLORATION & MINING CO LTD (300 SH)
VAALTRUCAR LTD (1157600SH)
WOOLTRU LTD (27400 SH)
YABENG INVESTMENT HOLDINGS CO LTD (401900 SH)

HUDACO INDUSTRIES LTD

ABBREVIATION : HUDACO

JSE SHORT CODE : HDC

SECTOR : Industrial-Engineering

SHAREHOLDERS

Who Owns Whom's Assessment of the Identity of the Ultimate Controlling Shareholder: INSTITUTIONS / DIRECTORS

SHAREHOLDER	PERCENTAGE 1992	1991
EIGHTY ONE MAIN STREET NOM LTD	15.7	2.6
SA MUTUAL	14.0	14.2
STD BANK NOM TVL P/L	11.3	10.4
CMB NOM P/L	7.1	---
LIBERTY LIFE ASSOC OF AFRICA LTD	6.2	7.9
FIRST NAT NOM P/L	5.0	6.2
SLAM NOM P/L	3.8	---
BURGESS T J F	2.6	4.1

METAL IND GROUP PENS FUND	2.6	2.3
ENGINEERING INDUSTRIES PENS FUND	2.6	1.5
MOMENTUM LIFE ASSURE LTD	2.1	2.7
SAGE LIFE LTD	1.8	1.9
MCINNES B G	1.8	2.9
AECI PENS FUND	1.7	---
WILLIAMS K R	1.7	2.8
UAL MERCHANT BANK LTD	1.4	---
LIBERTY PENS FUND	1.2	1.5
HIGHVELD STAFF PENS FUND	---	1.2
SCAW METALS PENS FUND	---	1.2
SOUTHERN LIFE ASSOC LTD	---	5.2
YSKOR PENS FUND	---	2.2
JOLLY M S	---	1.2
SYFRETS NOM LTD	---	7.3
SHARESTOCK NOM P/L	---	1.2
CLARKE K F	---	1.6
SANLAM	---	6.5
TOTAL	82.7	88.5

DIRECTORS :
BURGESS TJF ,CLARKE KF (Chief Executive)
CONNELLY SJ ,GARDINER GE ,MAKINS DR
MCCLELLAND CJD ,MCINNES BG DR,NASH SJ
POOLE PM (Financial Director),WILLIAMS KR

REGISTRATION NUMBER : 85/04617/06

REGISTERED OFFICE
Hudaco Park, 190 Barbara Road
Elandsfontein
1406
TEL: 011-974 8774
FAX: 011-392 1430

TRANSFER SECRETARY
Consolidated Share Registrars Ltd
P O Box 61051, Marshalltown
2107
TEL: 011-492 1620

COMPANY SECRETARY
M H Hodgson

NATURE OF BUSINESS
The principal activity of the HUDACO group is distribution. The group distributes diesel engines, hydraulic products, bearings, belting, abrasives, transmission components, oil and hydraulic seals and light construction equipment.

BANKERS :
First National Bank of SA Ltd
Nedperm Bank Ltd

AUDITORS :
Kessel Feinstein

FAMILIAR BRAND NAMES
ABCOR,AMMERAAL,ANGUS-HAWKEN,ARRO,BELTECH,BI
BOSWORTH,COOPER,CUMAR-ABRASIVES
DEUTZ DIESELPOWER,DEUTZ MWM,DOWTY,ELCO
ERNEST LOWE,EWART,FREUDENBERG,HABASIT
JEGKURT,KHD DEUTZ,KOYO,LOWARA,MARTONAIR
MATHER & PLATT,MERCURY,MINTEX DON,NORTON,PSI
REXNORD,RUTHERFORDS,SELFLEX,STRATOFLEX
SWIFTS,TIMKEN,TREKFLEX

CONTRIBUTION BY ACTIVITY
Manufacture (% of total sales) (23.0%)
Mining (30.0%)
Transport & Construction (14.0%)
Agriculture, Forestry & Fishing (15.0%)
Community Services & Gov't (9.0%)
Other (9.0%)

YEAR END : November

DIVIDEND : Ords 10c

Interim No 9	(Ldr)13/07/90	(Pay)02/08/90	Amt(c)21
Final No 10	(Ldr)22/02/91	(Pay)22/03/91	Amt(c)29
Interim No 11	(Ldr)05/07/91	(Pay)01/08/91	Amt(c)21
Final No 12	(Ldr)14/02/92	(Pay)20/03/92	Amt(c)30
Interim No 13	(Ldr)03/07/92	(Pay)30/07/92	Amt(c)23

NUMBER OF EMPLOYEES : 4884

CAPITAL STRUCTURE

	AUTHORISED	ISSUED
Ords 10c	40000000	28273189

FINANCIAL STATISTICS (AT FINANCIAL YEAR END)

(Amts in R'000)	1991 Nov	1990 Nov	1989 Nov	1988 Nov	1987 Nov
Ord S/H Int	99381	87921	77381	54206	30326
Long Trm Loans	17641	33381	31415	11727	17024
Iss Ord Share	22989	22767	22676	20629	20548
Total Liab	124332	146774	158752	96983	68874
Current Liab	106691	113393	127337	85256	51850
Total Assets	211708	217710	217971	136141	99200
Intang Assets	12005	16985	18162	15048	*
Current Assets	176972	180966	180340	122149	79344
Debtors	54439	62162	62853	43342	27956
Inventory	103585	112357	112199	60486	47164
Turnover	366753	403119	364664	252060	208399
Oper Profit	50891	54648	43840	27404	22631
Interest Paid	7156	10971	9377	2480	663
Tax Paid	16535	16592	11898	7012	8295
Prf af Int&Tax	29475	28874	24758	17912	13673
Prf att Ord Sh	25652	25091	23176	17610	12986
Btm Line Earn	25652	25091	23176	17610	11076
Dividend Paid	11707	11381	10480	7839	5685
Mkt Prce(c) YE	1200	900	800	530	420
Depreciation	6208	6493	5436	2459	2213

PER SHARE STATISTICS (CENTS)

Net Asst Val	380.08	311.57	261.15	189.82	147.59
Net Earnings	112.20	110.40	107.30	85.40	61.70
Dividends	51.00	50.00	48.00	38.00	28.00
Cash Flow	138.80	137.04	138.76	96.80	72.60

RATIOS AND OTHER INFORMATION

Mrk Cap(R000)	275868	204903	181408	109334	86302
Current Ratio	1.66	1.60	1.42	1.43	1.53
Quik/Acid Tst	0.69	0.61	0.54	0.72	0.62
A/C Rec T/ovr	6.74	6.48	5.80	5.82	7.45
Tot Ass T/ovr	1.73	1.85	1.67	1.85	2.10
Debt/Ass Rat	0.54	0.62	0.68	0.68	0.64
L T L Tot Ass	0.04	0.10	0.09	0.06	0.12
Debt to Eqity	1.16	1.53	1.90	1.72	2.09
Interest Cover	7.11	4.98	4.68	11.05	34.13
Oper Prof Mrg	13.88	13.56	12.02	10.87	10.86
Net Prof Marg%	6.99	6.22	6.36	6.99	6.23
Ret on Assets	25.11	25.92	21.12	20.13	22.81
Ret on Equity%	25.81	28.54	29.95	32.49	42.82
Price/Earnings	10.70	8.15	7.46	6.21	6.81
Divid Cover	2.20	2.21	2.24	2.25	2.20
Divid Yield	4.25	5.56	6.00	7.17	6.67
Earning Yield%	9.35	12.27	13.41	16.11	14.69
NAV % Mrk Pr	31.67	34.62	32.64	35.82	35.14
Effec Tax Rate	37.00	37.46	28.80	26.97	38.33
Def Interval	0.63	0.98	1.18	0.96	0.64
Sus Grth Rate	14.03	15.59	16.41	18.03	24.08

SUBSIDIARY & ASSOCIATED COMPANIES

ABES (PTY) LTD
ABES MARKETING (PTY) LTD
ABRASIVES CORPORATION (PTY) LTD (50%)
ABRASIVES SA (PTY) LTD (50%)
ANGUS HAWKEN (PTY) LTD
ANGUS HAWKEN MANUFACTURING (PTY) LTD
ARRO BEARING & COMPONENTS (PTY) LTD
AVEN ENGINE RECONDITIONERS (PTY) LTD (42%)
BARBARA ROAD INVESTMENTS (PTY) LTD
BBW PRODUCTS (PTY) LTD
BEARING INVESTMENTS (PTY) LTD
BEARINGS INTERNATIONAL (PTY) LTD
BELT SPLICING SERVICES (PTY) LTD
BELTECH (PTY) LTD
BELTING SUPPLY SERVICES (PTY) LTD
BRANDT CHAINS MARKETING (PTY) LTD
CAMPCO (PTY) LTD
CONSOLIDATED BEARING CO. (PTY) LTD
CONSUL PROPERTIES (PTY) LTD (50%)
CONVEYOR & TRANSMISSION SUPPLY (PTY) LTD
CONVEYOR & TRANSMISSION SUPPLY HOLDINGS
CUMAR ABRASIVES (PTY) LTD (50%)
CUMAR CAPE TOWN (PTY) LTD (50%)
CUMAR NEWCASTLE (PTY) LTD (50%)
CUMAR PE (PTY) LTD (50%)
CUMAR REEF (PTY) LTD (50%)
CUMAR RESISTANT MATERIALS (PTY) LTD (50%)
CUMAR SPRINGS (PTY) LTD (50%)
CUMAR SURFACE TECHNOLOGIES (PTY) LTD (50%)
CUMAR VEREENIGING (PTY) LTD (50%)
DD POWER (PTY) LTD
DD POWER (TVL) (PTY) LTD
DD POWER EASTERN PROVINCE (PTY) LTD
DD POWER ENGINES (PTY) LTD
DD POWER LC (PTY) LTD
DD POWER MANUFACTURING (PTY) LTD
DD POWER NATAL (PTY) LTD
DD POWER WESTERN PROVINCE (PTY) LTD
DUNEB HYDRAULICS (PTY) LTD
ERF 144 CASHAN EXT 2 (PTY) LTD
F E INVESTMENTS (PTY) LTD (50%)
FRENCORP (MANAGEMENT) (PTY) LTD
GLOBAL ABRASIVES HOLDINGS (PTY) LTD (50%)
HENAVEN ENGINE REBUILD CENTRES (PTY) LTD (42%)
HENLES ENGINEERING (PTY) LTD (42%)
HENTAL INVESTMENTS (PTY) LTD
HENVILLE SALARY BUREAU (PTY) LTD
HI TECH DIESEL & TURBO (PTY) LTD
HOSE DOCTOR (PTY) LTD
HUDACO GROUP FINANCIAL SERVICES (PTY) LT
HUDACO INDUSTRIAL HOLDINGS LTD
HUDACO PROPERTIES (PINETOWN) (PTY) LTD
HUDACO SEAL DISTRIBUTORS (PTY) LTD
HUDACO SEAL INVESTMENTS (PTY) LTD
HUDACO TRADING LTD
HUDACO TRANSMISSION INVESTMENTS (PTY) LT
INDUSTRIAL & MINING TRANSMISSION (PTY) L
KEYLINE AGENCIES (PTY) LTD (50%)
KHD (SA) (PTY) LTD
LONG STREET PROPERTIES (PTY) LTD
LUSNOC PROPERTIES LTD (50%)
MEDIA (PTY) LTD
METROPOLITAN BEARINGS (PTY) LTD
MINING ENGINE REPAIR CENTRE (PTY) LTD
MKONDENI PROPERTIES (PTY) LTD
NATAL BATTERY MANUFACTURERS (PTY) LTD
NATAL SEALS CO (PTY) LTD
NORTON ABRASIVES (PTY) LTD (50%)
NORTON CONSUMER PRODUCTS (PTY) LTD (50%)
OVERKAY PROPERTIES (PTY) LTD (50%)
POWER SYSTEMS INTERNATIONAL (PTY) LTD
PRIME COMPUTERS (PTY) LTD
PROVINCIAL BEARINGS (PTY) LTD
Q-PLUS TRADING (PTY) LTD
ROLLER CHAIN CO (PTY) LTD, THE
SEAL & CIRCLIP SERVICES (PTY) LTD
STRATOFLEX (PTY) LTD
SWIFT INDUSTRIAL SUPPLY CO (PTY) LTD, TH
TORQUE TRANSFER (PTY) LTD
VALARD LTD
VALHOLD LTD
WESTERN PROVINCE BEARINGS (PTY) LTD

INVESTMENTS

None

HUNT LEUCHARS & HEPBURN HOLDINGS LTD

ABBREVIATION : HLH

JSE SHORT CODE : HLH

SECTOR : Industrial-Industrial Holding

SHAREHOLDERS

Who Owns Whom's Assessment of the Identity of the Ultimate Controlling Shareholder:
REMBRANDT VIA HUNTCOR

SHAREHOLDER	PERCENTAGE 1992	1991
HUNTCOR LTD	76.6	76.6
CMB NOM P/L	6.9	---
STD BANK NOM TVL P/L	5.5	5.7
FIRST NAT NOM P/L	1.2	1.2
NEDBANK NOM LTD	1.1	1.2
SANLAM	---	4.7
TOTAL	91.4	89.6

DIRECTORS :
BEKKER WJS DR,BEZUIDENHOUT JLJ ,BROWNLEE MCC
COX RW (Dir Human Resources)
CROSSMAN GS (Financial Director),DHLOMO OD DR
DU TOIT PR ,GROVE EL DR,HANCOCK NJL ,HANCOCK RW
KATZ MM PROF,LOCH DAVIS DJ ,MARLOW DJ (Chairman)
MORRIS NJ (Chief Executive),O'HAUGHEY LJ
ROUX MJ ,VAN WYK T ,VILJOEN AFV

REGISTRATION NUMBER : 02/01164/06

REGISTERED OFFICE
4th Floor, First National Bank House
Cnr Fredman Dr & West Strs, Oxford Park, Sandown
2196
TEL: 011-883 4120
FAX: 011-884 2820

TRANSFER SECRETARY
Fraser Street Registrars (Pty) Ltd
P O Box 61178, Marshalltown
2107
TEL: 011-491 0911

COMPANY SECRETARY
J H Behrens

NATURE OF BUSINESS
Through its subsidiary and associate companies, the group is engaged in the food industry, manufacturing grocery and household products, sugar and tea and in the growing, processing and distribution of timber products for the mining, building, construction, paper, pulp and particle board industries.

BANKERS :
Standard Bank of SA Ltd
First National Bank of SA Ltd, Volkskas Ltd
Absa Bank Ltd, Nedbank Ltd

AUDITORS :
Deloitte Pim Goldby

FAMILIAR BRAND NAMES
AFRICAN MAID CORNFLOUR,AIROMA,AROMAT
BEECH-NUT,BLUE DEATH,BOVRIL,CASTORSNOW,DOOM
DYANT,DYROACH,FASTKILL,FLAMTARD,FLUSH CLEAN
HELLMANS,HERCULES,ICINGSNOW,KNORR,KNORROX
KOMATIDRAAI,MAIZENA,MARMITE,MOLATEK
MONATE ACHA,NAPOLINA PASTA
PACKSETTER (TIMBER),PEACEFUL SLEEP,PYAGRA
RAINBOW CHICKEN (25%),RAJAH CURRY,RATTEX
ROBERTSONS,SAM NEWMANS,SELATI,SENTEEKO,TSB

CONTRIBUTION BY ACTIVITY
N/A

YEAR END : March

DIVIDEND :Ords no par value

Final	(Ldr)25/05/90	(Pay)08/06/90	Amt(c)16.8
Interim	(Ldr)23/11/90	(Pay)07/12/90	Amt(c)13.5
Interim	(Ldr)22/11/91	(Pay)06/12/91	Amt(c)13.5
Final	(Ldr)22/05/92	(Pay)05/06/92	Amt(c)19
Interim	(Ldr)20/11/92	(Pay)04/12/92	Amt(c)13.5

NUMBER OF EMPLOYEES : 20000

CAPITAL STRUCTURE

	AUTHORISED	ISSUED
Ords no par value	180000000	149556488

FINANCIAL STATISTICS (AT FINANCIAL YEAR END)

(Amts in R'000)	1992 Mar	1991 Mar	1990 Mar	1989 Mar	1988 Mar
Ord S/H Int	1053153	764019	746953	498939	146233
Long Trm Loans	158319	144099	84041	58281	956
Iss Ord Share	149556	129930	129930	110870	48372
Total Liab	322650	285037	204492	145519	9834
Current Liab	164331	140938	120451	87238	8878
Total Assets	1279231	947583	843843	603575	156067
Intang Assets	96572	101473	107602	40883	*
Current Assets	222859	170705	141254	169177	66934
Debtors	143757	101681	82899	53656	1781
Inventory	74049	62839	51618	49338	-
Turnover	693724	587146	464207	371068	302100
Oper Profit	121886	117782	96313	79684	11786
Interest Paid	31890	24821	15333	5502	539
Tax Paid	24982	33023	35772	36238	198
Prf af Int&Tax	85684	83491	64465	37944	11049
Prf att Ord Sh	118551	117635	99954	61548	22493
Btm Line Earn	117551	117635	99954	61339	22493
Dividend Paid	48519	41973	37079	26207	8417
Mkt Prce(c) YE	1675	1325	1000	835	400
Depreciation	24754	20850	15769	11589	23

PER SHARE STATISTICS (CENTS)

Net Asst Val	639.61	509.93	492.07	413.15	302.31
Net Earnings	81.50	91.20	81.40	66.80	48.40
Dividends	32.50	32.50	28.80	24.00	18.00
Cash Flow	78.41	81.70	68.30	45.19	23.63

RATIOS AND OTHER INFORMATION

Mrk Cap(R000)	2505063	1721573	1299300	925765	193488
Current Ratio	1.36	1.21	1.17	1.94	7.54
Quik/Acid Tst	0.91	0.77	0.74	1.37	7.54
A/C Rec T/ovr	4.83	5.77	5.60	6.92	169.62
Tot Ass T/ovr	0.54	0.62	0.55	0.61	1.94
Debt/Ass Rat	0.24	0.28	0.22	0.22	0.06
L T L Tot Ass	0.11	0.14	0.08	0.08	0.01
Debt to Eqity	0.29	0.35	0.25	0.27	0.07
Interest Cover	4.47	5.69	7.54	14.48	21.87
Oper Prof Mrg	17.57	20.06	20.75	21.47	3.90
Net Prof Marg%	17.09	20.04	21.53	16.59	7.45
Ret on Assets	13.71	18.52	17.90	17.83	14.94
Ret on Equity%	11.26	15.40	13.38	12.34	15.38
Price/Earnings	20.55	14.53	12.29	12.50	8.26
Divid Cover	2.51	2.81	2.83	2.78	2.69
Divid Yield	1.94	2.45	2.88	2.87	4.50
Earning Yield%	4.87	6.88	8.14	8.00	12.10
NAV % Mrk Pr	38.19	38.48	49.21	49.48	75.58
Effec Tax Rate	24.36	35.54	40.23	43.39	5.32
Def Interval	1.03	0.96	0.61	1.18	0.01
Sus Grth Rate	6.65	9.90	8.42	7.08	9.63

SUBSIDIARY & ASSOCIATED COMPANIES

BONUSKOR LTD
CGP HOLDINGS (PTY) LTD
CGP INVESTMENTS (PTY) LTD
CONSOLIDATED GROCERY PRODUCTS (PTY) LTD
HL & H (TRUST COMPANY) (PTY) LTD
HL & H BUILDING SUPPLIES (PTY) LTD
HL & H ENGINEERING LTD
HL & H HOME CENTRE (TRANSVAAL) (PTY) LTD
HOLT WHITNEY (PTY) LTD
HUNT LEUCHARS & HEPBURN LTD
HUNTCON CONSTRUCTION (PTY) LTD
I PEREL (PTY) LTD
KAALRUG FARMS (EDMS) BPK
KOMATI DRAAI (PTY) LTD
KOMATI RIETVERWERKERS (EDMS) BPK
LAEVELDSE SUIKERMEULE BPK
MEDDENIN (PTY) LTD
MWETI (EDMS) BPK
NOORDELIKE BELEGGINGS -EN ONTWIKKELINGSK
PHILIP WULFSOHN & SONS (PTY) LTD
R G NUTTALL CONSTRUCTION (PTY) LTD
ROBERTSONS (PTY) LTD
ROBERTSONS PROPERTY HOLDINGS (PTY) LTD
SALISBURYKOP BOERDERY (EDMS) BPK
SAM NEWMAN (BELLVILLE) LTD
SAM NEWMAN (BOLAND) LTD
SAM NEWMAN (CLAREMONT) LTD

INVESTMENTS

None

HUNTCOR LTD

ABBREVIATION : HUNTCOR

JSE SHORT CODE : HNC

SECTOR : Industrial-Industrial Holding

SHAREHOLDERS

Who Owns Whom's Assessment of the Identity of the Ultimate Controlling Shareholder: REMBRANDT GROUP

SHAREHOLDER	PERCENTAGE 1992	1991
IND PARTNERSHIP INV LTD	65.9	65.9
MOMENTUM LIFE ASSURE LTD	16.2	16.3
CMB NOM P/L	6.6	---
EIGHTY ONE MAIN STREET NOM LTD	2.6	2.9
STD BANK NOM TVL P/L	---	1.4
GRAYSTON NOM P/L	---	1.1
SANLAM	---	4.8
TOTAL	91.3	92.4

DIRECTORS :
BEZUIDENHOUT JLJ ,DHLOMO OD DR,DU TOIT PR
GROVE EL DR,HANCOCK NJL ,HANCOCK RW ,KATZ MM PROF
LOCH DAVIS DJ ,MARLOW DJ (Chairman),MORRIS NJ
O'HAUGHEY LJ ,ROUX MJ ,VAN WYK T

REGISTRATION NUMBER : 84/02301/06

REGISTERED OFFICE
4th Floor, First National Bank House
Cnr Fredman Dr & West Str, Oxford Park, Sandown
2196
TEL: 011-883 4120
FAX: 011-884 2820

TRANSFER SECRETARY
Fraser Street Registrars (Pty) Ltd
P O Box 61178, Marshalltown
2107
TEL: 011-491 0911

COMPANY SECRETARY
J H Behrens

NATURE OF BUSINESS
An investment holding company with a controlling interest in JSE-quoted Hunt Leuchars & Hepburn.

BANKERS :
Nedperm Bank Ltd, Standard Bank of SA Ltd
First National Bank of SA Ltd, Volkskas Ltd

AUDITORS :
Deloitte Pim Goldby
Price Waterhouse Meyernel

FAMILIAR BRAND NAMES
N/A

CONTRIBUTION BY ACTIVITY
N/A

YEAR END : March

DIVIDEND : Ords no par value

Final	(Ldr)25/05/90	(Pay)08/06/90	Amt(c)33.87
Interim	(Ldr)23/11/90	(Pay)07/12/90	Amt(c)27.2
Interim	(Ldr)22/11/91	(Pay)06/12/91	Amt(c)27.2
Final	(Ldr)22/05/92	(Pay)05/06/92	Amt(c)38.3

NUMBER OF EMPLOYEES : 20000

CAPITAL STRUCTURE

	AUTHORISED	ISSUED
Ords no par value	84668950	57239884

FINANCIAL STATISTICS (AT FINANCIAL YEAR END)

(Amts in R'000)	1992 Mar	1991 Mar	1990 Mar	1989 Mar	1988 Mar
Ord S/H Int	806090	591183	625928	390876	93119
Long Trm Loans	403637	313060	238880	161595	54106
Iss Ord Share	57240	50210	50210	43313	15331
Total Liab	571705	457873	363516	253602	62968
Current Liab	168068	144813	124636	92007	8862
Total Assets	1281223	947583	843843	603595	156087
Intang Assets	96572	101473	145601	40883	*
Current Assets	222862	170705	141254	169197	66954
Debtors	143757	101681	82899	53656	1781
Inventory	74049	62839	51618	49338	-
Turnover	693724	587146	464207	371068	-
Oper Profit	121942	117782	96276	75873	11759
Interest Paid	31890	24821	15333	5502	539
Tax Paid	24982	33023	35777	36238	198
Prf af Int&Tax	85683	83491	64423	58191	11022
Prf att Ord Sh	90963	91324	77548	57002	14230
Btm Line Earn	95218	91324	77548	56838	14230
Dividend Paid	37274	32674	28945	20778	5466
Mkt Prce(c) YE	3300	2350	1850	1275	650

PER SHARE STATISTICS (CENTS)

Net Asst Val	1239.55	975.32	956.64	808.06	607.39
Net Earnings	163.60	183.10	162.20	132.70	95.40
Dividends	65.50	65.50	58.07	48.40	36.50
Cash Flow	107.73	115.98	95.65	97.82	46.37

RATIOS AND OTHER INFORMATION

Mrk Cap(R000)	1888920	1179935	928885	552241	99652
Current Ratio	1.33	1.18	1.13	1.84	7.56
Quik/Acid Tst	0.89	0.74	0.72	1.30	7.56
A/C Rec T/ovr	4.83	5.77	5.60	6.92	-
Tot Ass T/ovr	0.54	0.62	0.55	0.61	-
Debt/Ass Rat	0.24	0.28	0.22	0.22	0.06
L T L Tot Ass	0.11	0.13	0.08	0.07	-
Debt to Eqity	0.38	0.46	0.30	0.34	0.10
Interest Cover	4.47	5.69	7.53	18.16	21.82
Oper Prof Mrg	17.58	20.06	20.74	20.45	-
Net Prof Marg%	13.11	15.55	16.71	15.36	-
Ret on Assets	13.69	18.52	17.90	19.71	12.22
Ret on Equity%	11.28	15.45	12.39	14.58	15.28
Price/Earnings	20.17	12.83	11.41	9.61	6.81
Divid Cover	2.50	2.80	2.79	2.74	2.61
Divid Yield	1.98	2.79	3.14	3.80	5.62
Earning Yield%	4.96	7.79	8.77	10.41	14.68
NAV % Mrk Pr	37.56	41.50	51.71	63.38	93.44
Effec Tax Rate	24.35	35.54	40.25	45.74	5.33
Def Interval	1.90	1.74	1.12	1.38	0.01
Sus Grth Rate	6.66	9.92	7.76	9.27	9.41

SUBSIDIARY & ASSOCIATED COMPANIES

HUNT LEUCHARS & HEPBURN HOLDINGS LTD

INVESTMENTS

None

HUNYANI HOLDINGS LTD

ABBREVIATION : HUNYANI

SECTOR : Zimbabwe Stock Exchange

SHAREHOLDERS

Who Owns Whom's Assessment of the Identity of the Ultimate Controlling Shareholder:
ZIMBABWE MASS MEDIA TRUST / INDUSTRIAL D

SHAREHOLDER	PERCENTAGE 1992	1991
ZIMBABWE MASS MEDIA TRUST	26.0	---
IND DEVELOPMENT CORP OF ZIM LTD	23.9	---
OLD MUTUAL INV CORP (PVT) LTD	12.6	---
HUNYANI WORKERS TRUST	11.9	---
SYFRETS NOM (PVT) LTD	5.2	---
IPCORN LTD	3.8	---
GRINDLAYS NOM P/L	2.3	---
STD CHART MERCHANT BANK ZIM NOM PVT LTD	1.1	---
FIDELITY LIFE ASSURE OF ZIM PVT LTD	1.0	---
NAT RAILWAYS OF ZIM CONTR PENS FUND	1.0	---
NAT INSURANCE CO OF ZIM PVT LTD	1.0	---
TOTAL	89.7	---

DIRECTORS :
CHINYADZA W ,DZINOTYIWEYI HAM PROFESS
KADHANI XM (Chief Executive & M.D.),MIDZI DT
MUNYAWARARA L ,NDUBIWA MM ,PAZVAKAVAMBWA SC
ROWETT TS ,SADZA DM DR (Chairman),TEMPLER MH
WATERMEYER LM

REGISTERED OFFICE
8th Floor, Old Mutual Centre
Jason Moyo Avenue, Harare

TEL: 700141
FAX: 700147

TRANSFER SECRETARY
N/A

COMPANY SECRETARY
CJA Kimberley

BANKERS :
N/A

AUDITORS :
Price Waterhouse Meyernel

FAMILIAR BRAND NAMES
N/A

CONTRIBUTION BY ACTIVITY
N/A

YEAR END : September

DIVIDEND : Ords Z$0,70

Dividend	(Ldr)07/06/91	(Pay)20/06/91	Amt(c)1.88
Dividend	(Ldr)06/12/91	(Pay)20/12/91	Amt(c)3.375

NUMBER OF EMPLOYEES : 2903

CAPITAL STRUCTURE

	AUTHORISED	ISSUED
Ords Z$0,70	200000000	197443632

FINANCIAL STATISTICS (AT FINANCIAL YEAR END)

(Amts in Z$)	1991 Sep	1990 Sep
Ord S/H Int	224469	118970
Long Trm Loans	78895	24057
Iss Ord Share	197444	24680
Total Liab	186357	98848
Current Liab	107462	74791
Total Assets	410826	217818
Current Assets	108961	78745
Debtors	41147	31702
Inventory	58338	46033
Turnover	236448	165417
Oper Profit	34476	26320
Interest Paid	11381	5278
Tax Paid	1768	5534
Prf af Int&Tax	21725	15988
Prf att Ord Sh	23345	16572
Btm Line Earn	23345	16572
Dividend Paid	10366	8268
Depreciation	9655	6983

PER SHARE STATISTICS (CENTS)

Net Asst Val	113.69	482.05
Net Earnings	11.82	8.39
Dividends	5.25	4.19
Cash Flow	15.89	93.08

RATIOS AND OTHER INFORMATION

Current Ratio	1.01	1.05
Quik/Acid Tst	0.47	0.44
A/C Rec T/ovr	5.75	5.22
Tot Ass T/ovr	0.58	0.76
Debt/Ass Rat	0.45	0.45
L T L Tot Ass	0.19	0.11
Debt to Eqity	0.83	0.83
Interest Cover	3.03	4.99
Oper Prof Mrg	14.58	15.91
Net Prof Marg%	9.87	10.02
Ret on Assets	8.88	12.57
Ret on Equity%	10.40	13.93
Divid Cover	2.25	2.00
Effec Tax Rate	7.53	25.71
Def Interval	4.03	2.64
Sus Grth Rate	5.78	6.98

SUBSIDIARY & ASSOCIATED COMPANIES

HOLDAIN PROPERTIES (PTY) LTD
HUNYANI AGRI-FORESTRY LIMITED
HUNYANI HOLDINGS LTD
HUNYANI MANAGEMENT & SECRETARIAL SERVICE

INVESTMENTS

None

HYPERETTE STORES LTD

ABBREVIATION : HYPERET

JSE SHORT CODE : HYT

SECTOR : Development Capital Market

SHAREHOLDERS

Who Owns Whom's Assessment of the Identity of the Ultimate Controlling Shareholder: H EHLERS

SHAREHOLDER	PERCENTAGE 1992	1991
NILVOLARD P/L	41 8	41 8
UNIDEV STRATEGIC INV HOLDINGS P/L	25 8	27 3
BREAD BASKET P/L	9 6	9 6
HYPERETTE STORES SHARE INC SCHEME	5 9	5 9
UNIDEV RETAIL HOLDINGS LTD	5 5	4 0
ABRAMOWITZ M	4 3	4 3
MAROCK D	4 3	4 3
CLINTON NOM P/L	---	1 2
TOTAL	97 2	98 4

DIRECTORS :
BRETT JK ,CHONOWITZ AH ,EHLERS SH (Chairman)
KRECKLENBERG MA ,MOSS RM ,RUSHMERE CG

REGISTRATION NUMBER : 86/02517/06

REGISTERED OFFICE
Cnr Natal & Calcutta Str, Paarden Eiland
Cape Town
7405
TEL: 021-511 9156
FAX 021-510 4903

TRANSFER SECRETARY
Mercantile Registrars Ltd
P O Box 1053, Johannesburg
2000
TEL 011-333 8181

COMPANY SECRETARY
F Mantz

NATURE OF BUSINESS
The company operates a chain of stores which specialise in the retailing of processed and convenience foods, as well as the wholesaling and retailing of bakery products

BANKERS :
Nedperm Bank Ltd, Trust Bank of Africa Ltd
First National Bank of SA Ltd

AUDITORS :
Kessel Feinstein
Pharrel S Wener & Associates

FAMILIAR BRAND NAMES
BOTHASIG KWIKSAVE,BREAD BASKET,DELIS
FRESHBAKE,HOCTORS BUTCHERIES,HYPERETTE
KING SOLOMON,KWIKSHOP,METRO BAKERIES
MR CRUSTY,OVENBEST

CONTRIBUTION BY ACTIVITY
N/A

YEAR END : June

DIVIDEND :15/04/91 and 15/11/91

NUMBER OF EMPLOYEES : 475

CAPITAL STRUCTURE

	AUTHORISED	ISSUED
Ords no par value	148942000	136407000
"B" Prefs 1c	490000	490000
Var Rate Red Cum Prefs 1c	107000	10700

FINANCIAL STATISTICS (AT FINANCIAL YEAR END)

(Amts in R'000)	1990 Jul	1989 Jul	1988 Jun	1987 Jun	1986
Ord S/H Int	4208	-10584	-2279	810	1590
Long Trm Loans	13884	10842	2624	1344	302
Iss Ord Share	136407	6948	6948	6948	5380
Total Liab	23435	22056	6775	3889	604
Current Liab	9551	11214	4151	2545	302
Total Assets	16980	11300	4496	4699	2125
Intang Assets	10663	172	*	*	*
Current Assets	6718	640	827	559	233
Debtors	2356	426	480	142	-
Inventory	3958	208	307	407	233
Turnover	54959	7195	7816	5706	3030
Oper Profit	1775	-5928	-2855	-881	306
Interest Paid	479	-	125	47	-
Tax Paid	-	-73	-	98	142
Prf af Int&Tax	1356	-5855	-2980	-1026	164
Prf att Ord Sh	547	-5855	-2980	-1070	164
Btm Line Earn	547	-7356	-5606	-1070	164
Dividend Paid	-	-	-	135	-
Mkt Prce(c) YE	15	22	60	80	-
Depreciation	1327	453	403	118	-

PER SHARE STATISTICS (CENTS)

Net Asst Val	-4 73	-154 81	-32 80	11 66	29 55
Net Earnings	0 40	-84 27	-	-	-
Cash Flow	1 37	-71 77	-37 09	-17 70	3 05

RATIOS AND OTHER INFORMATION

Mrk Cap(R000)	20461	1529	4169	5558	-
Current Ratio	0 70	0 06	0 20	0 22	0 77
Quik/Acid Tst	0 29	0 04	0 13	0 06	-
A/C Rec T/ovr	23 33	15 59	16 28	40 18	-
Tot Ass T/ovr	3 24	0 59	1.74	1 21	1 43
Debt/Ass Rat	0 72	1 86	1 28	0 61	0 28
L T L Tot Ass	0 16	0 87	0 36	0 07	0 14
Debt to Eqity	2 91	-1 99	-2 53	3 54	0 38
Interest Cover	3 71	-	-22 84	-18 74	-
Oper Prof Mrg	3 23	-82 39	-36 53	-15 44	10 10
Net Prof Marg%	1 00	-81 38	-38 13	-18 75	5 41
Ret on Assets	10 81	-48 42	-63 50	-18 75	14 40
Ret on Equity%	13 00	51 06	130 76	-132 10	10 31
Price/Earnings	37 50	-0 26	-	-	-
Earning Yield%	2 67	-383 05	-	-	-
NAV % Mrk Pr	-31 55	-703 67	-54 67	14 57	-
Effec Tax Rate	-	-	-	-10 56	46 41
Def Interval	8 99	-3 35	-1 57	-2 20	1 84
Sus Grth Rate	13 00	55 32	130 76	-148 77	10 31

SUBSIDIARY & ASSOCIATED COMPANIES

DAVOS COFFEE BAR (PTY) LTD
FRESHBAKE FOODS (PTY) LTD
HOCTORS BUTCHERIES (PTY) LTD

HYPERETTE (PTY) LTD
I P M RENTALS (PTY) LTD
KWIKSHOP (PTY) LTD
MASTERCUTS (PTY) LTD
MAYS FRUIT & VEGETABLES DISTRIBUTORS (PT
METRO BAKERIES (PTY) LTD
MILLY'S CLAREMONT (PTY) LTD
MISTER CRUSTY CAPE (PTY) LTD
QUICK STOP (PTY) LTD

INVESTMENTS

None

HYPROP INVESTMENTS LTD

ABBREVIATION : HYPROP

JSE SHORT CODE : HYP

SECTOR : Financial-Property Loan Stock

SHAREHOLDERS

Who Owns Whom's Assessment of the Identity of the Ultimate Controlling Shareholder: BENTEL & BEHRMANN FAMILIES/LIFEGRO

SHAREHOLDER	PERCENTAGE 1992	1991
MOMENTUM LIFE ASSURE LTD	33.3	35.5
EIGHTY ONE MAIN STREET NOM LTD	15.1	8.9
CMB NOM P/L	7.6	---
GRAYSTON NOM P/L	6.5	---
SA MUTUAL	3.7	7.0
LIBERTY LIFE ASSOC OF AFRICA LTD	3.6	2.6
WORKMENS COMPENS COMMISSIONER IN TRUST	2.3	---
JR NOM P/L	2.2	---
ALTRON GROUP PENS FUND	1.7	1.4
MINES 1970 PENS FUND	1.5	---
BEHRMANN P J	1.5	2.4
METAL IND GROUP PENS FUND	1.5	1.5
PG GLASS PENS FUND	1.3	1.2
PG WOOD & PG BISON PENS FUND	1.2	1.2
PILKINGTON GROUP PENS FUND	1.2	1.2
ENGINEERING INDUSTRIES PENS FUND	1.2	1.2
HORTORS GROUP PENS FUND	1.2	---
USKO PENS FUND NOM P/L	1.1	---
BEHRMANN C G	---	1.4
SMBL NOM P/L	---	1.1
GALLO PENS FUND NOM P/L	---	1.1
PALABORA MINING PENS FUND	---	1.9
SANLAM	---	4.6
SYFRETS NOM LTD	---	3.2
TRUCK & CAR CO P/L	---	6.6
UNILEVER SA PENS FUND	---	1.7
TOTAL	87.6	85.6

DIRECTORS :
BEHRMANN PJ (Managing Director),BENTEL J
BENTEL LM ,DU TOIT PR (Chairman),LEVIN JA
SMITH JP

REGISTRATION NUMBER : 87/05284/06

REGISTERED OFFICE
1st Floor, North Block, Hyde Park Corner
Jan Smuts Avenue, Sandton
2196
TEL: 011-788 4750
FAX: 011-788 3866

TRANSFER SECRETARY
Rand Registrars Ltd
P O Box 82549, Southdale
2135
TEL: 011-835 1016

COMPANY SECRETARY
Mrs T Schultze

NATURE OF BUSINESS
A property loan stock company, with a portfolio of properties situated in Northen Jhb & East Rand.

BANKERS :
Standard Bank of SA Ltd
Standard Merchant Bank Ltd

AUDITORS :
Kessel Feinstein

FAMILIAR BRAND NAMES
N/A

CONTRIBUTION BY ACTIVITY
Retail (% Gross income by sector) (60.0%)
Offices (35.4%)
Parking (4.6%)

YEAR END : December

DIVIDEND : Units

Interim No 5	(Ldr)31/08/90	(Pay)10/09/90	Amt(c)30.72
Final No 6	(Ldr)22/03/91	(Pay)03/04/91	Amt(c)34.841
Interim No 7	(Ldr)30/08/91	(Pay)11/09/91	Amt(c)32.950
Final No 8	(Ldr)20/03/92	(Pay)01/04/92	Amt(c)37.98
Interim No 9	(Ldr)28/08/92	(Pay)08/09/92	Amt(c)32.95

NUMBER OF EMPLOYEES : 64

CAPITAL STRUCTURE

	AUTHORISED	ISSUED
Units (1 Ord : 1 Debenture)	100000000	30610298

FINANCIAL STATISTICS (AT FINANCIAL YEAR END)

(Amts in R'000)	1991 Dec	1990 Dec	1989 Dec	1988 Dec
Ord S/H Int	156096	156096	132403	110829
Long Trm Loans	57	-	-	-
Iss Ord Share	30610	30610	26783	22400
Total Liab	13155	11584	9875	7182
Current Liab	13098	11584	9875	7182
Total Assets	169251	167680	142278	118011
Current Assets	22809	34698	23845	23294
Debtors	1336	1203	1779	972
Turnover	23786	21642	16962	11102
Oper Profit	16313	13647	11334	7716
Interest Paid	21693	19668	25	10035
Tax Paid	-	65	43	20
Prf af Int&Tax	44	39	15199	20
Prf att Ord Sh	44	39	30	20
Btm Line Earn	44	39	30	20
Dividend Paid	44	39	30	20
Mkt Prce(c) YE	675	625	660	500

Depreciation	130	109	91	74

PER SHARE STATISTICS (CENTS)

Net Asst Val	509.95	509.95	494.35	494.77
Net Earnings	70.90	65.56	56.80	44.90
Dividends	70.93	65.56	56.80	44.90
Cash Flow	0.57	0.48	57.09	0.50

RATIOS AND OTHER INFORMATION

Mrk Cap(R000)	206618	191313	176768	112000
Current Ratio	1.74	3.00	2.41	3.24
Quik/Acid Tst	1.74	3.00	2.41	3.24
A/C Rec T/ovr	17.80	17.99	9.53	13.71
Tot Ass T/ovr	0.14	0.13	0.12	0.11
Debt/Ass Rat	0.08	0.07	0.07	0.06
L T L Tot Ass	0.00	-	-	-
Debt to Eqity	0.08	0.07	0.07	0.06
Interest Cover	0.75	0.69	453.36	0.77
Oper Prof Mrg	68.58	63.06	66.82	69.50
Net Prof Marg%	0.18	0.18	0.18	0.18
Ret on Assets	12.84	11.79	10.73	10.24
Ret on Equity%	0.03	0.02	0.02	0.02
Price/Earnings	9.52	9.53	11.62	11.14
Divid Cover	1.00	1.00	1.00	1.00
Divid Yield	10.51	10.49	8.61	8.98
Earning Yield%	10.50	10.49	8.61	8.98
NAV % Mrk Pr	75.55	81.59	74.90	98.95
Effec Tax Rate	-	62.50	0.28	50.00
Def Interval	0.33	-	-	-
Sus Grth Rate	0.00	0.00	0.00	0.00

SUBSIDIARY & ASSOCIATED COMPANIES

CYNKIRK PROPERTIES SHAREBLOCK (PTY) LTD
FIRECREST SHARE BLOCK (PTY) LTD
HILBOK PROPERTIES SHARE BLOCK (PTY) LTD
HYDE CLOSE PROPERTIES SHARE BLOCK (PTY)
HYDE PARK CORNER SHOPPING CENTRE (PTY) L
HYDE PARK INVESTMENTS SHARE BLOCK (PTY)
LIFEFIN SHARE BLOCK (PTY) LTD
MORNINGSIDE VIEWSITES SHARE BLOCK (PTY)

INVESTMENTS

None

IB JOFFE LTD

ABBREVIATION : IBJOFFE

JSE SHORT CODE : IBJ

SECTOR : Industrial-Retailers & Wholesalers

SHAREHOLDERS

Who Owns Whom's Assessment of the Identity of the Ultimate Controlling Shareholder: DIRECTORS

SHAREHOLDER	PERCENTAGE 1992	1991
B M JOFFE HOLDINGS P/L	78.0	78.0
REICHMANS IND INV P/L	8.4	8.4
CMB NOM P/L	4.5	---
ANDEX NOM P/L	3.2	3.2
STOCKSHARE NOM P/L	2.6	---
I B JOFFE SHARE TRUST	1.4	1.4
MAXERIC NOM P/L	---	2.6
SANLAM	---	4.5
TOTAL	98.2	98.2

DIRECTORS :
GOSS S ,JOFFE BM (Chairman),JOFFE FB
JOFFE PR (Managing Director

REGISTRATION NUMBER : 66/07844/06

REGISTERED OFFICE
201 Factor House, 12 Kruis Street
Johannesburg
2001
TEL: 011-764 2900
FAX: 011-764 4300

TRANSFER SECRETARY
Central Registrars Ltd
P O Box 4844, Johannesburg
2000
TEL: 011-331 0051

COMPANY SECRETARY
MR Diesel

NATURE OF BUSINESS
The group is engaged in the manufacture and distribution of leather and canvas goods and outdoor equipment and furniture. The main products produced are harnesses, saddlery, camping and back-packing products, as well as outdoor and kitchen furniture. Leasing facilities are also provided for the Group requirements as well as non-Group customers.

BANKERS :
Nedcor Bank Ltd

AUDITORS :
Beinash Klompas

FAMILIAR BRAND NAMES
GOLDEN HORSESHOE,KARRIMOR,LEISURE LAZE
SAGORIN BROS,SEA KING,SUNHOPPER,TELEK

CONTRIBUTION BY ACTIVITY
N/A

YEAR END : December

DIVIDEND : (Ldr)20/10/89 (Pay)31/10/89

NUMBER OF EMPLOYEES : 600

CAPITAL STRUCTURE

	AUTHORISED	ISSUED
Ords no par value	30000000	17769275

FINANCIAL STATISTICS (AT FINANCIAL YEAR END)

(Amts in R'000)	1991 Dec	1990 Dec	1989 Dec	1988 Dec	1987 Dec
Ord S/H Int	7991	13323	13274	10676	7309
Long Trm Loans	6690	8184	6142	6214	310
Iss Ord Share	17769	17769	15200	15200	15200
Total Liab	15269	16912	14007	13762	3256

Current Liab	8579	8728	7865	7548	2946
Total Assets	22601	29549	25641	24438	10565
Intang Assets	659	686	1640	*	*
Current Assets	17500	23002	19769	18275	8237
Debtors	8763	9661	7893	9672	4167
Inventory	8246	12739	10470	6698	3579
Turnover	30695	30549	28536	25929	14101
Oper Profit	-2928	1785	3941	3774	2640
Interest Paid	1703	1219	713	182	63
Tax Paid	239	157	910	1050	1163
Prf af Int&Tax	-4870	409	2318	2542	1414
Prf att Ord Sh	-4870	252	2170	2542	1414
Btm Line Earn	-5734	132	1889	1791	1414
Dividend Paid	-	-	912	760	-
Mkt Prce(c) YE	67	60	80	105	90
Depreciation	760	765	692	616	90

PER SHARE STATISTICS (CENTS)

Net Asst Val	41.26	71.12	76.54	70.24	48.09
Net Earnings	-27.40	1.50	14.30	16.70	9.30
Dividends	-	-	6.00	5.00	-
Cash Flow	-23.15	6.16	18.81	20.85	9.95

RATIOS AND OTHER INFORMATION

Mrk Cap(R000)	11905	10661	12160	15960	13680
Current Ratio	2.04	2.64	2.51	2.42	2.80
Quik/Acid Tst	1.08	1.18	1.18	1.53	1.58
A/C Rec T/ovr	3.50	3.16	3.62	2.68	3.38
Tot Ass T/ovr	1.36	1.03	1.11	1.06	1.33
Debt/Ass Rat	0.65	0.54	0.49	0.50	0.31
L T L Tot Ass	0.27	0.24	0.18	0.19	0.03
Debt to Eqity	1.84	1.19	0.94	1.15	0.44
Interest Cover	-1.72	1.46	5.53	20.74	41.90
Oper Prof Mrg	-9.54	5.84	13.81	14.56	18.72
Net Prof Marg%	-15.87	0.82	7.60	9.80	10.03
Ret on Assets	-12.96	6.04	15.37	15.44	24.99
Ret on Equity%	-60.94	1.89	16.35	23.81	19.35
Price/Earnings	-2.45	40.00	5.59	6.29	9.68
Divid Cover	-	-	2.38	3.34	-
Divid Yield	-	-	7.50	4.76	-
Earning Yield%	-40.90	2.50	17.88	15.90	10.33
NAV % Mrk Pr	61.59	118.53	95.67	66.89	53.43
Effec Tax Rate	-5.25	28.09	28.28	28.93	44.78
Def Interval	-2.15	12.42	2.42	1.92	0.73
Sus Grth Rate	-60.94	1.89	9.48	16.69	19.35

SUBSIDIARY & ASSOCIATED COMPANIES

BEMJAY LEASING (PTY) LTD
JOFFE SADDLERY (PTY) LTD
LEBOWA CANVAS WORKS (PTY) LTD
LEBOWA LEATHERWORKS (PTY) LTD
LEBOWA SADDLETREE (PTY) LTD
LEISURE LAZE (BOPHUTHATSWANA) (PTY) LTD
LLB MANUFACTURING (PTY) LTD
SAGORIN BROTHERS (PTY) LTD
SEA KING OILSKINS (PTY) LTD
SUNHOPPER PRODUCTS (PTY) LTD
TELEK MANUFACTURING CO (PTY) LTD
V S SIMPSON (1972) (PTY) LTD

INVESTMENTS

None

ICS HOLDINGS LTD

ABBREVIATION : I-C-S

JSE SHORT CODE : ICS

SECTOR : Industrial-Food

SHAREHOLDERS

Who Owns Whom's Assessment of the Identity of the Ultimate Controlling Shareholder: SA MUTUAL VIA BARLOWS VIA CG SMITH

SHAREHOLDER	PERCENTAGE 1992	1991
C G SMITH FOODS LTD	69.1	69.1
STD BANK NOM TVL P/L	7.2	7.3
EIGHTY ONE MAIN STREET NOM LTD	4.9	3.3
LIBERTY LIFE ASSOC OF AFRICA LTD	4.2	4.1
SA MUTUAL	3.2	3.2
FIRST NAT NOM P/L	1.8	2.2
TOTAL	90.4	89.3

DIRECTORS :
CHAMBERS RKJ ,CLEWLOW WAM
DENNIS N (Managing Director),HOWIE DS ,NEATE WH
PARKER RDM ,SAUNDERS CF ,SCHABORT CC ,SMITHER RV
WILLIAMS RA (Chairman

REGISTRATION NUMBER : 01/01674/06

REGISTERED OFFICE
West Wing, Northlands, 185 Katherine Street
Sandton
2146
TEL: 011-444 4700
FAX: 011-444 4062

TRANSFER SECRETARY
Rand Registrars Ltd
P O Box 82549, Southdale
2135
TEL: 011-835 1016

COMPANY SECRETARY
I W M Isdale

NATURE OF BUSINESS
An investment holding company with investments in subsidiaries & associates that are engaged in the production and/or distribution of perishable foods requiring controlled temperatures, incl red meat & meat products, poultry, fresh milk, butter, cheese milk powder, margarine, ice cream, fish & frozen vegetables. The group has interests in tanneries, commercial cold stores & feedlots.

BANKERS :
Standard Bank of SA Ltd

AUDITORS :
Ernst & Young

FAMILIAR BRAND NAMES
BULL BRAND,CHANDLING INTERNATNL,DAIRYBELLE
DAIRYMAID,FEDICS GROUP,FESTIVE,RENOWN
SEAHARVEST,SUN-SHINE D,THE COLD CHAIN

CONTRIBUTION BY ACTIVITY
N/A

YEAR END : September

DIVIDEND :5,5% Cum PrefS R2

Interim No 102	(Ldr)25/05/90	(Pay)30/06/90	Amt(c)5.5

DIVIDEND :Ords 25c

Interim No 110	(Ldr)08/06/90	(Pay)12/07/90	Amt(c)14
Final No 111	(Ldr)30/11/90	(Pay)09/01/90	Amt(c)18
Interim No 112	(Ldr)07/06/91	(Pay)12/07/91	Amt(c)14
Final No 113	(Ldr)29/11/91	(Pay)09/01/92	Amt(c)23
Interim No 114	(Ldr)05/06/92	(Pay)10/07/92	Amt(c)17
Final No 115	(Ldr)04/12/92	(Pay)11/01/93	Amt(c)28

NUMBER OF EMPLOYEES : 11496

CAPITAL STRUCTURE

	AUTHORISED	ISSUED
5,5% Cum Prefs R2	500000	500000
Ords 25c	42000000	38034038

FINANCIAL STATISTICS (AT FINANCIAL YEAR END)

(Amts in R'000)	1991 Sep	1990 Sep	1989 Sep	1988 Sep	1987 Sep
Ord S/H Int	410811	382119	360430	324663	287897
Long Trm Loans	81453	99882	85865	86196	87793
Iss Ord Share	38034	38034	38034	32327	26939
Total Liab	424650	449139	404910	347219	320970
Current Liab	343197	349257	319045	261023	233177
Total Assets	835461	831258	765340	671882	608867
Current Assets	370495	386527	366805	321225	279703
Debtors	233401	238101	219862	189619	172890
Inventory	123770	128168	129773	106671	89831
Turnover	2109259	2068257	1877568	1665759	1405042
Oper Profit	28101	25921	56007	49085	37225
Interest Paid	17847	19448	14201	11206	9638
Tax Paid	4619	6725	11008	8563	7635
Prf af Int&Tax	10026	7340	36274	29316	19952
Prf att Ord Sh	45513	36600	56061	45549	32620
Btm Line Earn	41751	40892	48447	48245	30768
Dividend Paid	14073	12171	18306	12931	9159
Mkt Prce(c) YE	1100	850	1425	850	1400
Depreciation	34717	31890	28676	26328	24864

PER SHARE STATISTICS (CENTS)

Net Asst Val	1080.12	1004.68	947.65	1004.31	1068.70
Net Earnings	119.70	96.20	147.40	141.00	121.00
Dividends	37.00	32.00	48.00	40.00	34.00
Cash Flow	109.53	94.29	160.39	162.94	157.33

RATIOS AND OTHER INFORMATION

Mrk Cap(R000)	418374	323289	541985	274780	377146
Current Ratio	1.08	1.11	1.15	1.23	1.20
Quik/Acid Tst	0.72	0.74	0.74	0.82	0.81
A/C Rec T/ovr	9.04	8.69	8.54	8.78	8.13
Tot Ass T/ovr	2.52	2.49	2.45	2.48	2.31
Debt/Ass Rat	0.49	0.52	0.51	0.49	0.50
L T L Tot Ass	0.08	0.10	0.09	0.10	0.12
Debt to Eqity	1.01	1.14	1.08	1.02	1.05
Interest Cover	1.65	1.43	4.03	4.38	3.86
Oper Prof Mrg	1.33	1.25	2.98	2.95	2.65
Net Prof Marg%	2.16	1.77	2.99	2.73	2.32
Ret on Assets	7.97	7.16	11.14	10.42	9.20
Ret on Equity%	11.08	9.58	15.55	14.03	11.33
Price/Earnings	9.19	8.84	9.67	6.03	11.57
Divid Cover	3.24	3.01	3.07	3.53	3.56
Divid Yield	3.36	3.76	3.37	4.71	2.43
Earning Yield%	10.88	11.32	10.34	16.59	8.64
NAV % Mrk Pr	98.19	118.20	66.50	118.15	76.34
Effec Tax Rate	40.17	54.98	25.63	22.22	23.49
Def Interval	2.43	3.80	1.87	1.70	2.39
Sus Grth Rate	7.65	6.39	10.47	10.05	8.15

SUBSIDIARY & ASSOCIATED COMPANIES

43 BERKLEY ROAD INVESTMENTS LTD
AFRICAN COLD STORAGE (PTY) LTD
BANDULA (PTY) LTD
BLOEMFONTEIN HIDES & SKINS (PTY) LTD
BLOEMFONTEIN VOEDSELMAATSKAPPY (EDMS) BP (50%)
BLUE RIBBON MEAT CORP (PTY) LTD (50%)
BROILER HOLDINGS (PTY) LTD
BULL BRAND HOLDINGS (PTY) LTD (50%)
CARR STREET PROPERTIES (PTY) LTD
CHANDLING INTERNATIONAL LTD (50%)
COLD CHAIN LTD, THE
COMMERCIAL COLD STORAGE LTD (40%)
CONCORD PIG PRODUCERS (PTY) LTD
COUNTRY GIRL BUTCHERIES (EASTERN CAPE) (
COUNTRY GIRL BUTCHERIES (EASTERN TRANSVA (30%)
COUNTRY GIRL BUTCHERIES (JEPPE STREET) ((40%)
COUNTRY GIRL BUTCHERIES (NATAL) (PTY) LT
COUNTRY GIRL BUTCHERIES (PRETORIA) (PTY)
COUNTRY GIRL BUTCHERIES (RENSA) (PTY) LT
COUNTRY GIRL BUTCHERIES (WEST COAST) (PT
COUNTRY GIRL BUTCHERIES (WESTERN CAPE) (
COUNTRY GIRL BUTCHERIES (WITWATERSRAND)
COUNTY GIRL BUTCHERIES (PTY) LTD (50%)
DAIRYMAID ICE CREAM CORPORATION (PTY) LT
DE BEER'S LEWENDEHAWE AGENTSKAP (EDMS) B
DEVKAP (PTY) LTD
ECONOMIC DAIRIES (PTY) LTD
FEDERATED HIDE & SKIN COMPANY (PTY) LTD
FEDICS FOOD SERVICES (PTY) LTD
FEDICS GROUP (PTY) LTD (45,9%)
FESTIVE FARMS (PTY) LTD
FRESH MEAT HOLDINGS (PTY) LTD
FRESH MEAT SUPPLY CO (PTY) LTD
HANS LE ROUX GROOTHANDEL (EDMS) BPK
HIDSKIN BROKERS (PTY) LTD
HIDSKIN INVESTMENTS (PTY) LTD
HIDSKIN PROCESSORS (PTY) LTD
HISCOCKS (1936) (PTY) LTD
ICS (DAIRY FACTORIES) LTD
ICS GROUP LTD
ICS GROUP PROPERTIES (ALIWAL NORTH) LTD
ICS GROUP PROPERTIES (BLOEMFONTEIN) (PTY
ICS GROUP PROPERTIES (CHELSEA) LTD
ICS GROUP PROPERTIES (PMB) (PTY) LTD
ICS GROUP PROPERTIES (SALT RIVER) (PTY)
ICS GROUP PROPERTIES (TRANSVAAL) LTD
ICS GROUP PROPERTIES (VRYBURG) LTD
ICS GROUP PROPERTIES (WARRENTON) (PTY) L
ICS PRODUCTS LTD
ICY FOODS LTD
IMPERIAL COLD STORAGE (SALES) LTD
IMPERIAL COLD STORAGE LTD
IMPERIAL FOODS LTD
IMPERIAL-IN-CLAYVILLE (PTY) LTD
JANEKS AGENCIES (PTY) LTD
JOHANNESBURG OFFAL POOL PROPERTIES (PTY)
KARBELKAR MEAT SUPPLY (PTY) LTD
LEADENHALL FRESH MEAT SUPPLY CO. (PTY) L
LOLATI PIGGERIES (PTY) LTD
MARKMAN TOWNSHIP PROPERTIES (PTY) LTD
MEYER & CROTS VERVOER (PTY) LTD
MICHELSENS LTD
MORIJA LIVESTOCK (PTY) LTD
NATIONAL LIVESTOCK AGENCY (TRANSVAAL) LT
NATIONAL POULTRY BREEDERS (PTY) LTD
NMS (PAROW) PROPERTIES LTD
NMS LTD
NORGEN VAAZ ICE CREAM (SA) (PTY) LTD

ODENDAALSRUS COLD STORAGE LTD
OKK FOODS LTD (50%)
OLAV PROPERTIES LTD
OOS-TRANSVAALSE VLEISVOORSIENERS (EDMS)
ORCHID FOODS (PTY) LTD
ORCHID HALAAL FOODS (PTY) LTD
PAARL MEAT SUPPLY (PTY) LTD
PE WHOLESALE MEAT SUPPLIERS (PTY) LTD
PEPLER & COMPANY LTD
PINETOWN PROCESSING (PTY) LTD
PJ DU PLESSIS (EDMS) BPK
PRETORIA MILK DISTRIBUTORS (PTY) LTD
PROTEM SUPPLIERS LTD
RAND OFFAL POOLS (PTY) LTD
RENOWN FOOD PRODUCTS CORP. (NATAL) (PTY)
RENOWN FOOD PRODUCTS CORPORATION (PTY) L
RENOWN FRESH MEAT CORPORATION (EASTERN C
RENOWN FRESH MEAT CORPORATION (NATAL) LT
RENOWN FRESH MEAT CORPORATION (RAND) LTD
RENOWN FRESH MEAT CORPORATION (TRANSVAAL
RENOWN FRESH MEAT CORPORATION (WESTERN C
RENOWN FRESH MEAT CORPORATION LTD
RENSA FRESH MEAT (PTY) LTD
ROELCOR SLAGTERYE (EDMS) BPK
ROELCOR VLEIS (EDMS) BPK (50%)
ROER'S MEAT PACKERS (PTY) LTD
ROYAL DAIRY LTD
SA MARGARINE CORP (PTY) LTD (50%)
SEA HARVEST CORP. OF NAMIBIA (PTY) LTD (50%)
SEA HARVEST CORPORATION (PTY) LTD (50%)
SERVUS BUTCHERIES (PTY) LTD
SOUTH WEST AFRICA COLD STORAGE & STOCK F
SUTHERLANDS TANNERY LTD
SWACS FOODS (PTY) LTD
TABLE TOP DISTRIBUTORS (PTY) LTD
TABLE TOP KOELKAMERS (PTY) LTD
TOM PARROCK & FRESH MEAT SUPPLY CO. (PTY
TRANSVAAL ASSOCIATED HOLDINGS (PTY) LTD
TRANSVAAL HIDE & SKIN PRODUCERS (PTY) LT
TSWANA FOODS (PTY) LTD
UNION HIDE & SKIN CO. (PTY) LTD
UNITED HIDE & SKIN EXPORT CO. (PTY) LTD
VEREENIGING ABATTOIR (PTY) LTD
WESTERN PROVINCE MILK PRODUCTS (PTY) LTD (50%)
WILLOW FARMING CO. (PTY) LTD
WL OCHSE HUIDE & VELLEMAKELAARS (EDMS) B
WOOLWORTHS BUTCHERIES (PTY) LTD
WORCESTER MEAT RETAILERS (PTY) LTD

INVESTMENTS

None

IGI BOTSWANA HOLDINGS LTD

ABBREVIATION : IGI BOT

SECTOR : Botswana Stock Exchange

SHAREHOLDERS

Who Owns Whom's Assessment of the Identity of the Ultimate Controlling Shareholder:
HCI VIA IGI INSURANCE SA

SHAREHOLDER	PERCENTAGE 1992	1991
IGI INSURANCE HOLDINGS LTD	74.3	---
DEBSWANA PENS FUND	2.0	---
LEWIS I M A	1.2	---
SECHABA INV TRUST CO LTD	1.1	---
MYNHARDT J T	1.1	---
TOTAL	79.6	---

DIRECTORS :
ANDREWS RC ,DENNISS PS ,FOURIE AJ ,HOSKEN JH
LETSUNYANE TJS ,LEWIS IMA (Chairman),NATHAN L
NCHINDO LG ,TIBONE MC
WALKIN JM (Managing Director

REGISTERED OFFICE
IGI House, The Mall
Gabarone, Botswana

TEL: 351521
FAX: 372867

TRANSFER SECRETARY
PW Business Services (Pty) Ltd
P O Box 1453, Gaberone
Botswana

TEL: 09267-351081

COMPANY SECRETARY
N/A

NATURE OF BUSINESS
The group writes all classes of short term insurance, life assurance and reinsurance business and manages pension and deposit administration funds in the Republic of Botswana. Subsidiary companies own residential property, offer services as a computer bureau and offer corporate consultancy services.

BANKERS :
Barclays Bank of Botswana Ltd
Standard Chartered Bank
Zimbank Botswana Ltd

AUDITORS :
Deloitte Pim Goldby

FAMILIAR BRAND NAMES
N/A

CONTRIBUTION BY ACTIVITY
N/A

YEAR END : March

CAPITAL STRUCTURE

	AUTHORISED	ISSUED
Ords P0,25	40000000	10146000

FINANCIAL STATISTICS (AT FINANCIAL YEAR END)

(Amts in P)	1992 Mar
Ord S/H Int	14310
Long Trm Loans	76162
Iss Ord Share	10146

Total Liab	86190
Current Liab	10028
Total Assets	100500
Current Assets	27779
Debtors	825
Turnover	59159
Oper Profit	5650
Interest Paid	80
Tax Paid	1957
Prf af Int&Tax	3613
Prf att Ord Sh	3613
Btm Line Earn	3613
Dividend Paid	1180
Depreciation	216

PER SHARE STATISTICS (CENTS)

Net Asst Val	141 04
Net Earnings	34 70
Dividends	12 00
Cash Flow	38 05

RATIOS AND OTHER INFORMATION

Current Ratio	2 77
Quik/Acid Tst	2 77
A/C Rec T/ovr	71 71
Tot Ass T/ovr	0 59
Debt/Ass Rat	0 11
L T L Tot Ass	0 01
Debt to Eqity	0 74
Interest Cover	70 63
Oper Prof Mrg	9 55
Net Prof Marg%	6 11
Ret on Assets	5 62
Ret on Equity%	25 25
Divid Cover	2 89
Effec Tax Rate	35 85
Def Interval	0 16
Sus Grth Rate	17 00

SUBSIDIARY & ASSOCIATED COMPANIES

BCS COMPUTER SERVICES (BOTSWANA) (PTY) L
BERYLANN PROPERTIES (PTY) LTD
DELLNO PROPERTIES (PTY) LTD
HOSKEN CORPORATE FINANCE (BOTSWANA) (PTY
IGI BOTSWANA HOLDINGS LTD (UK)
IGI BOTSWANA INSURANCE LTD
IGI BOTSWANA LIFE INSURANCE LTD
IGI HOUSE (PTY) LTD
IGI PARK (PTY) LTD (BOTSWANA)
IGI PROPERTIES (PTY) LTD (BOTSWANA)
INSURANCE TRAINING INSTITUTE (PTY) LTD
JEANETTE PROPERTIES (PTY) LTD (BOTSWANA)
KGAMA PROPERTIES (PTY) LTD (BOTSWANA)
KGOKONG PROPERTIES (PTY) LTD (BOTSWANA)
KUKAMA PROPERTIES (PTY) LTD (BOTSWANA)
M & K PROPERTIES (PTY) LTD (BOTSWANA)
PHOFU PROPERTIES (PTY) LTD (BOTSWANA)
PLOT 14391 (PTY) LTD (BOTSWANA)
SIXTY SIX NORTH RING ROAD (PTY) LTD
THOLO PROPERTIES (PTY) LTD
TSEPE PROPERTIES (PTY) LTD

INVESTMENTS

None

IGI INSURANCE CO LTD

ABBREVIATION : I-G-I

JSE SHORT CODE : IGI

SECTOR : Financial-Insurance

SHAREHOLDERS

Who Owns Whom's Assessment of the Identity of the Ultimate Controlling Shareholder: HOSKEN CONSOLIDATED INVESTMENTS

SHAREHOLDER	PERCENTAGE 1992	1991
HOSKEN CONSOLIDATED INV LTD	55 5	45 6
IGI INSURANCE CO LTD CONTROL ACC	9 9	11 6
STD BANK NOM TVL P/L	8 5	---
SAFEGRO NOM P/L	5 5	14 9
IGI SHARE INCENTIVE TRUST	1 6	---
VERSPREIDE INV P/L	1 3	1 3
TRUCK & CAR CO P/L	---	8 4
TOTAL	82 3	81 8

DIRECTORS :
ANDREWS RC (Deputy Managing Director),CARROL L
COCHRANE PD ,DENNISS PS (Managing Director)
HOSKEN JH ,LEWIS IMA (Executive Chairman)
NESTADT G ,WASSERFALL JK (Financial Director

REGISTRATION NUMBER : 54/02813/06

REGISTERED OFFICE
IGI House, 162 Anderson Street
Johannesburg
2001
TEL 011 335 1911
FAX 011-29 0491

TRANSFER SECRETARY
Mercantile Registrars Ltd
P O Box 1053, Johannesburg
2000
TEL 011-333 8181

COMPANY SECRETARY
W T Green

NATURE OF BUSINESS
I G I underwrites short-term insurance business in SA and SWA (Namibia), and specialised insurance business in the international market Life and home services assurance business is underwritten and pension funds administered in SA subsidiaries Other subsidiaries provide computer facilities, security services, own properties, conduct the business of printers and lithographers and act as short-term underwriting managers

BANKERS :
First National Bank of SA Ltd
Standard Bank of SA Ltd

AUDITORS :
BDO Spencer Steward

FAMILIAR BRAND NAMES
N/A

CONTRIBUTION BY ACTIVITY
- Marine (1.2%)
- Motor (54.6%)
- Personal Accident (0.5%)
- Guarantees (0.3%)
- Miscellaneous (17.2%)
- Life Assurance Annualised (17.2%)
- Life Assurance Single (4.2%)
- Fire (% Gross Income) (4.8%)

YEAR END : March

DIVIDEND :Ords 250c

Interim No 41	(Ldr)30/11/90	(Pay)17/12/90	Amt(c)17
Final No 42	(Ldr)21/06/91	(Pay)05/07/91	Amt(c)31
Interim No 43	(Ldr)29/11/91	(Pay)20/12/91	Amt(c)20
Final No 44	(Ldr)31/07/92	(Pay)21/08/92	Amt(c)35
Specle No 45	(Ldr)31/07/92	(Pay)21/08/92	Amt(c)8.6
Interim no 46	(Ldr)04/12/92	(Pay)14/12/92	Amt(c)21

NUMBER OF EMPLOYEES : 1333

CAPITAL STRUCTURE

	AUTHORISED	ISSUED
Ords 250c	19864132	15153868
12,5% Cum Red Prefs 100c	1000000	0
14,5% Cum Red Prefs 1c	2000000	0
10% Comp Conv Cum Prefs 1c	10000000	0

FINANCIAL STATISTICS (AT FINANCIAL YEAR END)

(Amts in R'000)	1992 Mar	1991 Mar	1990 Mar	1989 Mar	1988 Mar
Ord S/H Int	146728	148477	127275	99113	69053
Long Trm Loans	985584	823877	693725	484328	157318
Iss Ord Share	15127	15018	14991	12335	8783
Total Liab	1316854	1059719	908543	671392	294083
Current Liab	331270	235842	214818	187064	136765
Total Assets	1454799	1202967	1029920	770505	363136
Intang Assets	8783	5229	5898	*	*
Current Assets	521384	425563	318069	293292	158251
Debtors	175633	102941	80777	65101	37807
Inventory	36219	1611	1982	8060	3363
Oper Profit	36473	38179	-17070	30098	16131
Interest Paid	-	-	2975	3538	1607
Tax Paid	2152	4361	-1523	14966	4486
Prf af Int&Tax	34321	33818	34642	35243	23353
Prf att Ord Sh	26167	27019	30178	32585	21364
Btm Line Earn	-728	27019	31324	32184	21304
Dividend Paid	8320	7209	6296	4668	2635
Mkt Prce(c) YE	625	600	650	460	460
Depreciation	9320	5437	3824	2799	2086

PER SHARE STATISTICS (CENTS)

Net Asst Val	911.91	953.84	809.67	803.51	786.21
Net Earnings	173.00	179.00	201.80	274.50	246.00
Dividends	55.00	48.00	42.00	38.00	30.00
Cash Flow	224.29	202.41	209.37	275.38	256.75

RATIOS AND OTHER INFORMATION

Mrk Cap(R000)	94544	90108	97442	56741	40402
Current Ratio	1.57	1.80	1.48	1.57	1.16
Quik/Acid Tst	1.46	1.80	1.47	1.52	1.13
Debt/Ass Rat	0.25	0.20	0.21	0.24	0.38
L T L Tot Ass	0.02	0.00	0.00	0.00	0.00
Debt to Eqity	2.43	1.59	1.69	1.89	1.99
Interest Cover	-	-	12.13	15.19	18.32
Ret on Assets	2.61	3.33	3.67	7.16	8.19
Ret on Equity%	17.83	18.20	23.71	32.88	30.94
Price/Earnings	3.61	3.35	3.22	1.68	1.87
Divid Cover	3.15	3.73	4.80	7.22	8.20
Divid Yield	8.80	8.00	6.46	8.26	6.52
Earning Yield%	27.68	29.83	31.05	59.67	53.48
NAV % Mrk Pr	145.91	158.97	124.56	174.68	170.92
Effec Tax Rate	6.02	11.83	-15.20	58.54	33.07
Def Interval	3.26	2.04	4.19	1.01	1.50
Sus Grth Rate	12.16	13.34	18.76	28.17	27.12

SUBSIDIARY & ASSOCIATED COMPANIES

1301 TWIN TOWERS (PTY) LTD
249 PIONEERSPARK (PTY) LTD
45 IMBEZENA DRIVE (PTY) LTD
6 GALLOWAY ROAD (PTY) LTD (35%)
ABACUS FORESTRIES (PTY) LTD
ABACUS INDUSTRIAL HOLDINGS LTD
ALAN RICH & ASSOCIATES HOLDINGS LTD
BCS COMPUTER HOLDINGS LTD
BCS COMPUTER SERVICES (NAMIBIA) (PTY) LT
BCS COMPUTER SERVICES (PTY) LTD
BERJEFF (PTY) LTD
BIS INSURANCE SYSTEMS (PTY) LTD
BRABER INVESTMENTS (PTY) LTD
BUILDING CONSTRUCTION ADMINISTRATORS (PT
CIVCEN INVESTMENTS (PTY) LTD (41.4%)
CONTINENTAL HEATING (PTY) LTD
DALLA INVESTMENTS LTD
DRANNOCK HOLDINGS (PTY) LTD (41.4%)
ERF 349 KLERKSDORP (PTY) LTD
ERF 455 EINDOMME HARTSWATER (PTY) LTD
ERF 56 OLYMPIA (PTY) LTD
ERF 755 OLYMPIA (PTY) LTD
FENTON ROAD PROPERTIES (PTY) LTD
GARANKUWA PROPERTIES (PTY) LTD
GELPROP (PTY) LTD
GLEA PROPERTIES THREE (PTY) LTD
GLEA PROPERTIES TWO (PTY) LTD
GLOLIFE HOLDINGS LTD (41%)
HCI PRESS (PTY) LTD
IGI BOPHUTHATSWANA INSURANCE HOLDINGS LT
IGI BOPHUTHATSWANA LTD
IGI HOUSE (PTY) LTD
IGI NAMIBIA LTD
KIMBERLEY STAAL (PTY) LTD
LEYVAN (PTY) LTD
MACLYN HOUSE (PTY) LTD
MCCARTHY GLEN (PTY) LTD
OVERPARK (PTY) LTD
ROBECOR HOLDINGS (PTY) LTD
SAFRICAN LIFE INVESTMENT HOLDINGS LTD (41%)
SECONDARY SERVICES MARKETING (PTY) LTD
STAND TWO NOUGHT TWO ONE IMPI ROAD (PTY)
SURETY TECHNICAL SERVICES (PTY) LTD
TEMPEST PROPERTIES (PTY) LTD (41.4%)
TIMBER INVESTMENTS (PTY) LTD
UPLAND INVESTMENTS (PTY) LTD
VAALHARTS VERSPREIDERS (EDMS) BPK
VNB MEUBELFABRIEK (PTY) LTD
WH PRESS HOUSE LTD

INVESTMENTS

CERAMIC INDUSTRIES LTD (4,35%)
ITALTILE LTD (4,35%)

ILCO HOMES LTD

ABBREVIATION : ILCO

JSE SHORT CODE : ILC

SECTOR : Industrial-Building & Construction

SHAREHOLDERS

Who Owns Whom's Assessment of the Identity of the Ultimate Controlling Shareholder:
A C DEMMERS

SHAREHOLDER	PERCENTAGE 1992	1991
HOLDEM P/L	93.8	93.7
BOLAND BANK BPK	1.9	2.4
TOTAL	95.8	96.1

DIRECTORS :
DEMMERS AC (Chief Executive),ELS PS
KLOPPERS HB ,LOMBARD WA (Financial Director

REGISTRATION NUMBER : 68/10805/06

REGISTERED OFFICE
8th Floor, 75 Crompton Street
Pinetown
3600
TEL: 031-72 6223
FAX: 031-701 2955

TRANSFER SECRETARY
Consolidated Share Registrars Ltd
P O Box 61051, Marshalltown
2107
TEL: 011-492 1620

COMPANY SECRETARY
H Harrington (Mrs)

NATURE OF BUSINESS
The main business of Ilco is the construction & marketing of mass housing for the lower & middle income groups.

BANKERS :
Boland Bank Ltd

AUDITORS :
Ironsides Morrison Murray

FAMILIAR BRAND NAMES
N/A

CONTRIBUTION BY ACTIVITY
N/A

YEAR END : June

DIVIDEND : Ords no par value

Dividend No 4	(Ldr)06/09/91	(Pay)20/09/91	Amt(c)7.5
Dividend No 5	(Ldr)20/09/92	(Pay)30/09/92	Amt(c)7.5
Dividend No 5	(Ldr)18/09/92	(Pay)30/09/92	Amt(c)7.5

NUMBER OF EMPLOYEES : 224

CAPITAL STRUCTURE

	AUTHORISED	ISSUED
Ords no par value	100000000	30750000

FINANCIAL STATISTICS (AT FINANCIAL YEAR END)

(Amts in R'000)	1992 Jun	1991 Jun	1990 Jun	1989 Jun	1988 Jun
Ord S/H Int	44450	40539	37614	37310	30605
Long Trm Loans	7309	74	-	-	-
Iss Ord Share	30750	30750	30750	30750	30750
Total Liab	36309	32060	21566	18225	5252
Current Liab	29000	31986	21566	18225	5252
Total Assets	80759	72599	59180	55535	35857
Current Assets	72979	69687	55940	52904	17979
Debtors	4137	12231	1643	3362	3072
Inventory	66642	57450	51763	41793	14606
Oper Profit	11607	9259	4520	7213	7261
Interest Paid	6992	4860	3012	802	120
Prf af Int&Tax	6217	5231	2610	9011	8418
Prf att Ord Sh	6217	5231	2610	9011	8418
Btm Line Earn	6217	5231	2610	9011	8418
Dividend Paid	2306	2306	2306	2306	2153
Mkt Prce(c) YE	110	75	110	160	155
Depreciation	572	521	429	254	242

PER SHARE STATISTICS (CENTS)

Net Asst Val	144.55	131.83	122.32	121.33	99.53
Net Earnings	20.00	17.00	8.50	29.30	27.40
Dividends	7.50	7.50	7.50	7.50	7.00
Cash Flow	22.08	18.71	9.88	30.13	28.16

RATIOS AND OTHER INFORMATION

Mrk Cap(R000)	33825	23063	33825	49200	47663
Current Ratio	2.52	2.18	2.59	2.90	3.42
Quik/Acid Tst	0.22	0.38	0.19	0.61	0.84
Debt/Ass Rat	0.45	0.44	0.36	0.33	0.15
L T L Tot Ass	0.09	0.00	-	-	-
Debt to Eqity	0.82	0.79	0.57	0.49	0.17
Interest Cover	1.66	1.91	1.50	8.99	60.51
Ret on Assets	16.36	13.90	9.50	17.67	23.81
Ret on Equity%	13.99	12.90	6.94	24.15	27.51
Price/Earnings	5.50	4.41	12.94	5.46	5.66
Divid Cover	2.67	2.27	1.13	3.91	3.91
Divid Yield	6.82	10.00	6.82	4.69	4.52
Earning Yield%	18.18	22.67	7.73	18.31	17.68
NAV % Mrk Pr	131.41	175.78	111.20	75.83	64.21
Def Interval	4.76	2.67	5.85	1.46	0.03
Sus Grth Rate	8.80	7.22	0.81	17.97	20.47

SUBSIDIARY & ASSOCIATED COMPANIES

ILCO HOMES (CT) (PTY) LTD
ILCO HOMES (DBN) (PTY) LTD

INVESTMENTS

None

IMPALA PLATINUM HOLDINGS LTD

ABBREVIATION : IMPLATS

JSE SHORT CODE : IMP

SECTOR : Metals & Minerals-Platinum

SHAREHOLDERS

Who Owns Whom's Assessment of the Identity of the Ultimate Controlling Shareholder: SANLAM VIA GENCOR

SHAREHOLDER	PERCENTAGE 1992	1991
CONSOLIDATED NOM P/L	42.9	40.5
ABSA NOM P/L	11.4	---
CMB NOM P/L	7.6	---
INDO-CHINA NOM P/L	5.5	5.9
INDUSTRIAL SELECTIONS LTD	4.7	4.7
NAT SELECTIONS LTD	4.7	4.7
SA MUTUAL	3.6	3.6
STD BANK NOM TVL P/L	2.7	3.5
FIRST NAT NOM P/L	1.8	1.4
FIRST NAT NOM P/L GATR DEPOT	1.4	1.5
SOUTHERN LIFE ASSOC LTD	1.4	1.4
DEPOSITARY NOM INC	1.1	---
SANLAM	---	7.2
VOLKSKAS NOM P/L	---	11.4
TOTAL	88.7	86.0

DIRECTORS :
COOK PJ ,GILBERTSON BP (Chairman),KEARNEY SV
MCMAHON JM (Managing Director)
MENELL MV MS (Financial Director),NETSCHER TC
OFFICER NC ,SMITH BA ,VAN ROOY PJ ,WORTLEY CMG

REGISTRATION NUMBER : 57/01979/06

REGISTERED OFFICE
3rd Floor, Unicorn House, 70 Marshall Street
Johannesburg
2001
TEL: 011-376 2800
FAX: 011-836 5954

TRANSFER SECRETARY
Central Registrars Ltd
P O Box 4844, Johannesburg
2000
TEL: 011-331 0051

COMPANY SECRETARY
HJ Gaylard - Implats Cons & Man Serv (Pty) Ltd

NATURE OF BUSINESS
The group mines, processes, refines & markets platinum. The lease area is situated in the Bafokeng district of Bophuthatswana, and four mines are operated. In addition to platinum, Impala produces palladium, rhodium, ruthenium, iridium, gold, silver, nickel, copper & cobalt. Ammonium sulphate & sulphuric acid are produced as by-products of the metallurgical processes. The company holds a controlling interest in quoted Barplats Investments Ltd & Messina Ltd.

BANKERS :
N/A

AUDITORS :
Coopers Theron Du Toit

FAMILIAR BRAND NAMES
N/A

CONTRIBUTION BY ACTIVITY
N/A

YEAR END : June

DIVIDEND :Ords 20c

Interim	(Ldr)23/02/90	(Pay)22/03/90	Amt(c)80
Final	(Ldr)31/08/90	(Pay)04/10/90	Amt(c)170
Interim	(Ldr)22/02/91	(Pay)21/03/91	Amt(c)80
Final	(Ldr)13/09/91	(Pay)11/10/91	Amt(c)195
Interim	(Ldr)28/02/92	(Pay)26/03/92	Amt(c)55
Final	(Ldr)04/09/92	(Pay)01/10/92	Amt(c)115

NUMBER OF EMPLOYEES : 45000

CAPITAL STRUCTURE

	AUTHORISED	ISSUED
Ords 20c	77650000	62200000

FINANCIAL STATISTICS (AT FINANCIAL YEAR END)

(Amts in R'000)	1992 Jun	1991 Jun	1990 Jun	1989 Jun	1988 Jun
Ord S/H Int	2409000	2075300	1675200	1423315	1089664
Long Trm Loans	336100	137500	170400	49572	36679
Iss Ord Share	62200	62200	61162	57650	57650
Total Liab	1451000	1209100	1015400	1044224	763980
Current Liab	1114900	1071600	845000	994652	727301
Total Assets	3860000	3284400	2690600	2467539	1853644
Current Assets	1221700	1051200	775000	1165652	896956
Debtors	374000	248400	294700	375163	329229
Inventory	203500	307600	228000	473537	377956
Turnover	2263800	2269200	2089900	2091131	1588766
Oper Profit	470900	775500	590800	1119600	611500
Interest Paid	95100	62800	25500	24500	-
Tax Paid	277900	556600	392300	565065	311694
Prf af Int&Tax	233100	286700	255900	573935	299806
Prf att Ord Sh	260300	311800	250500	573935	299806
Btm Line Earn	260300	181600	266600	573935	299806
Dividend Paid	105700	168200	152900	144125	103770
Mkt Prce(c) YE	5350	6100	8325	5200	2775
Depreciation	5100	2700	2100	1245	890

PER SHARE STATISTICS (CENTS)

Net Asst Val	3872.99	3336.50	2738.96	2468.89	1890.14
Net Earnings	418.00	509.00	410.00	829.00	520.00
Dividends	170.00	275.00	250.00	250.00	180.00
Cash Flow	363.83	464.26	393.87	997.71	521.59

RATIOS AND OTHER INFORMATION

Mrk Cap(R000)	3327700	3794200	5091737	2997800	1599788
Current Ratio	1.10	0.98	0.92	1.17	1.23
Quik/Acid Tst	0.91	0.69	0.65	0.70	0.71
A/C Rec T/ovr	6.05	9.14	7.09	5.57	4.83
Tot Ass T/ovr	0.59	0.69	0.78	0.85	0.86
Debt/Ass Rat	0.35	0.33	0.33	0.42	0.41
L T L Tot Ass	0.06	0.01	0.02	0.02	0.02
Debt to Eqity	0.56	0.53	0.53	0.73	0.70
Interest Cover	4.95	12.35	23.17	45.70	-
Oper Prof Mrg	20.80	34.18	28.27	53.54	38.49
Net Prof Marg%	11.50	13.74	11.99	27.45	18.87
Ret on Assets	16.48	28.50	25.47	47.15	32.99
Ret on Equity%	10.81	15.02	14.95	40.32	27.51
Price/Earnings	12.80	11.98	20.30	6.27	5.34
Divid Cover	2.46	1.85	1.64	3.32	2.89
Divid Yield	3.18	4.51	3.00	4.81	6.49
Earning Yield%	7.81	8.34	4.92	15.94	18.74
NAV % Mrk Pr	72.39	54.70	32.90	47.48	68.11
Effec Tax Rate	19.43	37.33	60.34	49.61	50.97
Def Interval	3.15	1.47	1.02	0.40	0.57
Sus Grth Rate	6.42	6.92	5.83	30.20	17.99

SUBSIDIARY & ASSOCIATED COMPANIES

AYRTON LUXEMBOURG SA
AYRTON METALS LTD (UK)
BARPLATS INVESTMENTS LTD (38%)
EASTERN PLATINUM LTD (27%)
GAZELLE PLATINUM LTD
IMPALA PLATINUM INVESTMENTS (PTY) LTD
IMPALA PLATINUM LTD
IMPALA PLATINUM PROPERTIES (RUSTENBURG)
IMPALA PLATINUM PROPERTIES (SPRINGS) (PT
IMPLATS CONSULTANCY & MANAGEMENT SERVICE
MESSINA LTD
METALLURGICAL PROCESSES (PTY) LTD
PLATINUM SALES LTD
WESTERN PLATINUM LTD (SA) (27%)

INVESTMENTS

ENDOW PLATINUM LTD (6000 SH)
FERROUS SCRAP DISTRIBUTORS LTD (190 SH)
MAGALIESBURGSE GRAANKOOPERASIE BPK (283 SH)

IMPERIAL GROUP LTD

ABBREVIATION : IMPERIAL

JSE SHORT CODE : IML

SECTOR : Industrial-Industrial Holding

SHAREHOLDERS

Who Owns Whom's Assessment of the Identity of the Ultimate Controlling Shareholder:
DIRECTORS / MINORITIES

SHAREHOLDER	PERCENTAGE 1992	1991
VOLKSKAS NOM P/L	26.4	27.0
RAHAVANNIG INV P/L	16.2	---
SA MUTUAL	15.6	15.8
STD BANK NOM TVL P/L	8.5	2.9
METROPOLITAN LIFE LTD	6.2	6.3
BILL LYNCH FAMILY HOLDINGS P/L	4.9	5.0
LENWIL FAMILY HOLDINGS P/L	3.6	3.6
KAPLAN P	2.4	2.4
CMB NOM P/L	2.2	---
EIGHTY ONE MAIN STREET NOM LTD	1.9	1.7
SAAMBOU BANK LTD	1.7	1.7
BOARD OF EXECUTORS NOM P/L	---	5.4
PERCY ABELKOP FAMILY HOLDINGS P/L	---	16.4
SANLAM	---	2.0
TOTAL	89.4	90.1

DIRECTORS :
ABELKOP P (Chairman),ABELKOP SD ,FLUXMAN MJ
LYNCH WG (Managing Director)
WILDER L (Deputy Chairman

REGISTRATION NUMBER : 05/29723/06

REGISTERED OFFICE
First Floor, 157 Main Street
Johannesburg
2001
TEL: 011-334 5188
FAX: 011-29 8587

TRANSFER SECRETARY
Mercantile Registrars Ltd
P O Box 1053, Johannesburg
2000
TEL: 011-333 8181

COMPANY SECRETARY
A H Mahomed

NATURE OF BUSINESS
An investment holding company whose sole asset is an investment of 64,95% in its listed subsidiary Imphold Ltd.

BANKERS :
First National Bank of SA Ltd
Nedperm Bank Ltd

AUDITORS :
Levitt Kirson

FAMILIAR BRAND NAMES
N/A

CONTRIBUTION BY ACTIVITY
N/A

YEAR END : June

DIVIDEND : Ords 1c

Final No 7	(Ldr)14/09/90	(Pay)19/10/90	Amt(c)18.6
Interim No 8	(Ldr)22/03/91	(Pay)18/04/91	Amt(c)20.6
Final No 9	(Ldr)13/09/91	(Pay)18/10/91	Amt(c)23.6
Interim No 10	(Ldr)20/03/92	(Pay)14/04/92	Amt(c)25
Final No 11	(Ldr)18/09/92	(Pay)20/10/92	Amt(c)26

NUMBER OF EMPLOYEES : 2991

CAPITAL STRUCTURE

	AUTHORISED	ISSUED
Ords 1c	40000000	14379900

FINANCIAL STATISTICS (AT FINANCIAL YEAR END)

(Amts in R'000)	1992 Jun	1991 Jun	1990 Jun	1989 Jun	1988 Jun
Ord S/H Int	23433	23134	45013	38237	30541
Long Trm Loans	-	-	61354	50649	19380
Iss Ord Share	14380	14238	14094	14001	14001
Total Liab	3764	3370	176576	151401	76750
Current Liab	3764	3370	115222	100752	57370
Total Assets	27197	26504	221501	189550	107291
Intang Assets	*	*	88	88	*
Current Assets	-	-	176327	167216	93457
Debtors	-	-	32135	29971	21788
Inventory	-	-	39795	38156	25711
Turnover	-	-	544518	446471	321382
Oper Profit	-	-	50095	38816	18733
Interest Paid	-	-	7642	4975	2815
Tax Paid	-	-	21268	16893	4983
Prf af Int&Tax	7351	6300	21185	16948	10935
Prf att Ord Sh	7351	6300	12678	14030	8574
Btm Line Earn	7351	6300	11646	24415	8574
Dividend Paid	7351	6300	5061	4830	3500
Mkt Prce(c) YE	2050	1350	750	675	370
Depreciation	-	-	2723	1874	804

PER SHARE STATISTICS (CENTS)

Net Asst Val	162.96	162.48	318.75	272.47	218.13
Net Earnings	51.10	44.20	90.40	75.20	61.20
Dividends	51.00	44.20	35.85	30.00	25.00
Cash Flow	51.12	44.51	113.91	110.94	63.95

RATIOS AND OTHER INFORMATION

Mrk Cap(R000)	294790	192213	105705	94507	51804
Current Ratio	-	-	1.53	1.66	1.63
Quik/Acid Tst	-	-	1.18	1.28	1.18
A/C Rec T/ovr	-	-	16.94	14.90	14.75
Tot Ass T/ovr	-	-	2.46	2.36	3.00
Debt/Ass Rat	0.14	0.13	0.58	0.60	0.62
L T L Tot Ass	-	-	0.06	0.07	0.08
Debt to Eqity	0.16	0.15	2.83	2.99	2.17
Interest Cover	-	-	6.56	7.80	6.65
Oper Prof Mrg	-	-	9.20	8.69	5.83
Net Prof Marg%	-	-	2.33	3.14	2.67
Ret on Assets	27.03	23.77	22.72	20.66	17.59
Ret on Equity%	31.37	27.23	28.17	36.69	28.07
Price/Earnings	40.12	30.54	8.30	8.98	6.05
Divid Cover	1.00	1.00	2.52	2.51	2.45
Divid Yield	2.49	3.27	4.78	4.44	6.76
Earning Yield%	2.49	3.27	12.05	11.14	16.54
NAV % Mrk Pr	7.95	12.04	42.50	40.37	58.96
Effec Tax Rate	-	-	48.22	49.95	32.79
Def Interval	-	-	2.59	1.76	1.20
Sus Grth Rate	0.00	0.00	16.92	24.06	16.61

SUBSIDIARY & ASSOCIATED COMPANIES

IMPHOLD LTD

INVESTMENTS

None

IMPHOLD LTD

ABBREVIATION : IMPHOLD

JSE SHORT CODE : IMH

SECTOR : Industrial-Industrial Holding

SHAREHOLDERS

Who Owns Whom's Assessment of the Identity of the Ultimate Controlling Shareholder: IMPERIAL GROUP

SHAREHOLDER	PERCENTAGE 1992	1991
IMPERIAL GROUP LTD	60.4	70.0
VOLKSKAS NOM P/L	5.2	6.6
EIGHTY ONE MAIN STREET NOM LTD	4.1	---
SA MUTUAL	4.0	4.7
METAL IND GROUP PENS FUND	3.6	4.2
ENGINEERING INDUSTRIES PENS FUND	3.6	4.2
SCRIP NOM P/L	2.7	---
STD BANK NOM TVL P/L	2.5	---
CMB NOM P/L	2.1	---
FIRST NAT NOM P/L	1.9	---
EPF LIBAM NOM P/L	1.4	---
BOARD OF EXECUTORS NOM P/L	---	1.5
NOMINEES ONLY P/L	---	1.4
TOTAL	91.7	92.5

DIRECTORS :
ABELKOP P ,ABELKOP SD ,FLUXMAN MJ
LYNCH WG (Executive Chairman)
MAHOMED AH (Financial Director),RIECKHOFF ACJ
SCOTT CE MS,WILDER L

REGISTRATION NUMBER : 05/21048/06

REGISTERED OFFICE
First Floor, 157 Main Street
Johannesburg
2001
TEL: 011-334 5188
FAX: 011-29 8587

TRANSFER SECRETARY
Mercantile Registrars Ltd
P O Box 1053, Johannesburg
2000
TEL: 011-333 8181

COMPANY SECRETARY
A H Mahomed

NATURE OF BUSINESS
An industrial holding company involved in the following activities: car rental,truck hire, dedicated transport contracting,long-term car and truck rental,vehicle and heavy truck dealerships, used vehicle trading,commercial vehicle body-building,workshops,parts and accessories,property insurance and financial services.

BANKERS :
First National Bank of SA Ltd
Nedperm Bank Ltd

AUDITORS :
Levitt Kirson

FAMILIAR BRAND NAMES
AUTO PEDIGREE,IMPERIAL CAR RENTAL

CONTRIBUTION BY ACTIVITY
Car rental (% Turnover) (24.9%)
Motors (45.2%)
Truck Systems (22.7%)
Insurance Property (7.2%)

YEAR END : June

DIVIDEND : Ords 4c

Final No 3	(Ldr)14/09/90	(Pay)19/10/90	Amt(c)6.3
Interim No 4	(Ldr)22/03/91	(Pay)18/04/91	Amt(c)7
Final No 5	(Ldr)13/09/91	(Pay)18/10/91	Amt(c)8
Interim No 6	(Ldr)20/03/92	(Pay)14/04/92	Amt(c)8.5
Final No 7	(Ldr)18/09/92	(Pay)20/10/92	Amt(c)9

NUMBER OF EMPLOYEES : 2991

CAPITAL STRUCTURE

	AUTHORISED	ISSUED
Ords 4c	100000000	64672872

FINANCIAL STATISTICS (AT FINANCIAL YEAR END)

(Amts in R'000)	1992 Jun	1991 Jun	1990 Jun	1989 Jun	1988 Jun
Ord S/H Int	117454	75812	59857	50982	17514

Long Trm Loans	76861	69951	45680	37134	34300
Iss Ord Share	64673	56242	56097	56005	2
Total Liab	235706	180251	161805	138656	89773
Current Liab	158845	110300	116125	101522	55473
Total Assets	352232	255975	221574	189550	107287
Intang Assets	928	88	88	88	*
Current Assets	243545	190082	176327	167216	93453
Debtors	55961	38754	32135	29971	21788
Inventory	65614	47912	39795	38156	25711
Turnover	781253	597540	544518	446471	321382
Oper Profit	67599	53642	50095	38816	18618
Interest Paid	10318	6224	7642	4975	2700
Tax Paid	29990	24852	21268	16893	4983
Prf af Int&Tax	32280	25766	21185	16948	10935
Prf att Ord Sh	27661	21533	16904	14030	8574
Btm Line Earn	27278	21473	15573	39068	8574
Dividend Paid	11323	8439	6762	5600	3500
Mkt Prce(c) YE	710	450	245	-	-
Depreciation	4446	3245	2723	1874	1208

PER SHARE STATISTICS (CENTS)

Net Asst Val	180.18	134.64	106.55	90.87	875700.00
Net Earnings	45.70	38.30	30.20	25.00	15.30
Dividends	17.50	15.00	12.05	10.00	6.20
Cash Flow	57.12	45.14	35.93	27.74	16.71

RATIOS AND OTHER INFORMATION

Mrk Cap(R000)	459178	253089	137438	-	-
Current Ratio	1.53	1.72	1.52	1.65	1.68
Quik/Acid Tst	1.12	1.29	1.18	1.27	1.22
A/C Rec T/ovr	13.96	15.42	16.94	14.90	14.75
Tot Ass T/ovr	2.22	2.33	2.46	2.36	3.00
Debt/Ass Rat	0.51	0.53	0.58	0.61	0.74
L T L Tot Ass	0.06	0.09	0.06	0.07	0.22
Debt to Eqity	1.54	1.77	2.15	2.25	4.53
Interest Cover	6.65	8.76	6.56	7.80	6.90
Oper Prof Mrg	8.65	8.98	9.20	8.69	5.79
Net Prof Marg%	3.54	3.60	3.10	3.14	2.67
Ret on Assets	20.84	22.39	22.74	20.66	17.49
Ret on Equity%	23.55	28.40	28.24	27.52	48.96
Price/Earnings	15.54	11.75	8.11	-	-
Divid Cover	2.61	2.55	2.51	2.50	2.47
Divid Yield	2.46	3.33	4.92	-	-
Earning Yield%	6.44	8.51	12.33	-	-
NAV % Mrk Pr	25.38	29.92	43.49	-	-
Effec Tax Rate	42.97	45.83	48.22	49.95	32.79
Def Interval	1.74	1.50	2.06	1.76	1.15
Sus Grth Rate	13.91	17.27	16.94	16.54	28.97

SUBSIDIARY & ASSOCIATED COMPANIES

AFRICAN CAR HIRE (PTY) LTD
AFRICAN CAR HIRE (SWAZILAND) (PTY) LTD
ALMEYROSE INVESTMENTS (PTY) LTD
ANVIL FINANCIAL SERVICES (PTY) LTD
ANVIL INVESTMENTS (PTY) LTD
AUTO PEDIGREE (PTY) LTD
COMMISSIONER STREET PROPERTIES (PTY) LTD
COOPER INVESTMENTS (PTY) LTD (50%)
ERF FOUR NINE NINE SPARTAN (PTY) LTD
FALCON SPRING MANUFACTURERES (PTY) LTD
FARADAY INVESTMENTS (PTY) LTD
GMS PROPERTIES (PTY) LTD
GMS TRANSPORT (PTY) LTD
GODDARD & SERRANO (PTY) LTD - PROPERTY C
IMPERIAL CAR RENTAL (PTY) LTD
IMPERIAL CAR RENTAL FINANCE (NAMIBIA) P/ (30%)
IMPERIAL CAR RENTAL FINANCE (PTY) LTD (30%)
IMPERIAL CAR RENTAL FLEET (PTY) LTD
IMPERIAL CAR RENTAL NAMIBIA (PTY) LTD
IMPERIAL FINANCIAL SERVICES (PTY) LTD
IMPERIAL FLEXI-FLEET (PTY) LTD
IMPERIAL MANAGEMENT SERVICES (PTY) LTD
IMPERIAL MOTORS (JOHANNESBURG) (PTY) LTD
IMPERIAL MOTORS (PTY) LTD
IMPERIAL PANEL SHOPS (PTY) LTD
IMPERIAL TRANSPORT SERVICES (PTY) LTD
IMPERIAL TRUCK SYSTEMS (PTY) LTD
IMPERIAL TRUCK SYSTEMS HOLDINGS LTD
IMPERIAL TRUCK SYSTEMS RENTAL (PTY) LTD
IMPERIAL TRUCKS (PTY) LTD
LOADBODIES (PTY) LTD
MERCURIUS HOLDING (PTY) LTD
MERCURIUS MOTORS (PTY) LTD
MERCURIUS PROPERTIES (BOKSBURG) (PTY) LT
MERCURIUS PROPERTIES (KEMPTON PARK) (PTY
NATIONWIDE TRUCK HIRE (PTY) LTD
PRIME CAR LEASING (PTY) LTD (30%)
PROPERTIES OF IMPERIAL (PTY) LTD
QUATTRA CARRIERS (PTY) LTD
RAUDIERE INTERNATIONAL (USA) INC (CALIFO
RAUDIERE INVESTMENTS LTD (JERSEY)
REGENT INSURANCE COMPANY LTD
ROYALSTYLE MOTORS (PTY) LTD
SWIFT CAR HIRE (PTY) LTD
TEMPEST CAR HIRE (PTY) LTD
TIDE TRANSPORT (BOTSWANA) (PTY) LTD
TRANS AFRICA MOTORS (PTY) LTD
VAN ZYL'S SPRING WORKS (PTY) LTD
VAN ZYL'S SPRING WORKS (RANDBURG) (PTY)
WADEVILLE MOTORS PROPERTY (PTY) LTD

INVESTMENTS

None

INCO HOLDINGS LTD

ABBREVIATION : INCO

SECTOR : Botswana Stock Exchange

SHAREHOLDERS

Who Owns Whom's Assessment of the Identity of the Ultimate Controlling Shareholder: DIRECTORS

SHAREHOLDER	PERCENTAGE 1992	1991
BLEWETT B R	21.0	---
WARD M W	21.0	---
MPOTOKWANE L M	17.5	---
ISSADEEN A K	10.5	---
DEBSWANA PENS FUND	4.5	---
BOTSWANA MOTOR VEHICLE INSURANCE FUND	4.3	---
MYNHARDT J T	1.5	---
BOTSWANA MANAGED RETIREMENT FUND	1.2	---
IGI BOTSWANA LTD	1.2	---
TOTAL	82.6	---

DIRECTORS :
BLEWETT BR ,ISSADEEN AK
MPOTOKWANE LM (Chairman)
WARD MW (Managing Director

REGISTERED OFFICE
Fifth Floor, Barclays House
Khama Crescent, Gabarone

TEL: 312211
FAX: 314124

TRANSFER SECRETARY
N/A

COMPANY SECRETARY
P W Business Services

NATURE OF BUSINESS
INCO HOLDINGS owns equity in and provides management services to a diverse group of businesses, each of which trades under its own name.The present portfolio of businesses within the INCO group is detailed in the Annual Review.

BANKERS :
Standard Chartered Bank
Barclays Bank of Botswana Ltd
Zimbank Botswana Ltd

AUDITORS :
Deloitte Pim Goldby

FAMILIAR BRAND NAMES
N/A

CONTRIBUTION BY ACTIVITY
N/A

YEAR END : October

CAPITAL STRUCTURE

	AUTHORISED	ISSUED
Ords P0,10	20000000	8000000

FINANCIAL STATISTICS (AT FINANCIAL YEAR END)

(Amts in P)	1991 Oct	1990 Oct
Ord S/H Int	2249	704
Long Trm Loans	519	687
Iss Ord Share	8000	100
Total Liab	5681	4602
Current Liab	5162	3915
Total Assets	7423	4603
Intang Assets	507	703
Current Assets	5455	3438
Debtors	3406	1944
Inventory	1405	1293
Turnover	18470	13277
Oper Profit	893	989
Interest Paid	198	164
Tax Paid	196	361
Prf af Int&Tax	557	464
Prf att Ord Sh	557	464
Btm Line Earn	557	464
Dividend Paid	216	-
Depreciation	321	216

PER SHARE STATISTICS (CENTS)

Net Asst Val	21.78	1.00
Net Earnings	7.00	6.00
Dividends	2.70	-
Cash Flow	11.55	758.00

RATIOS AND OTHER INFORMATION

Current Ratio	1.06	0.88
Quik/Acid Tst	0.78	0.55
A/C Rec T/ovr	5.42	6.83
Tot Ass T/ovr	2.49	2.88
Debt/Ass Rat	0.74	0.97
L T L Tot Ass	0.04	0.12
Debt to Eqity	2.44	6.33
Interest Cover	4.51	6.03
Oper Prof Mrg	4.83	7.45
Net Prof Marg%	3.02	3.49
Ret on Assets	12.81	21.49
Ret on Equity%	24.77	59.18
Divid Cover	2.59	-
Effec Tax Rate	13.81	25.70
Def Interval	1.24	1.59
Sus Grth Rate	15.16	65.91

SUBSIDIARY & ASSOCIATED COMPANIES

AUTOMATED SECURITY (PTY) LTD
FIRE PROTECTION SERVICES (PTY) LTD
GENERAL INDUSTRIES (PTY) LTD
INCO FUEL CENTRES (PTY) LTD
INCO PROPERTIES (PTY) LTD
INSTALLEC (PTY) LTD
SECURITY EXPRESS (PTY) LTD
TYRE SERVICES (PTY) LTD (50%)

INVESTMENTS

None

INDUSTRIAL & COMMERCIAL HOLDINGS GROUP LTD

ABBREVIATION : ICH

JSE SHORT CODE : ICH

SECTOR : Mining-Diamonds

SHAREHOLDERS

Who Owns Whom's Assessment of the Identity of the Ultimate Controlling Shareholder:
CULLINAN/KOCH & HYLTON FAMILIES

SHAREHOLDER	PERCENTAGE 1992	1991
NOM INV & TRUST CO P/L	21.4	24.0
STD BANK NOM TVL P/L	11.4	1.2
EIGHTY ONE MAIN STREET NOM LTD	9.7	---
ANDEX NOM P/L	7.1	26.0
KOCH S TRUST	4.6	4.6
NEDBANK NOM LTD	4.3	5.0
SA MUTUAL	3.6	3.8
HYLTON V TRUST	2.6	2.6
MENTEITH INV LTD	2.5	2.5
HYLTON V E	2.3	2.3
JR NOM P/L	1.3	1.4
FERBROS NOM P/L	1.2	1.6
TOTAL	72.0	74.9

DIRECTORS :
AARON AJ ,CULLINAN NM ,GNODDE AMD (Chairman)
GURNEY JJ ,HYLTON VE MRS,KOCH JRR

REGISTRATION NUMBER : 01/07668/06

REGISTERED OFFICE
11 Floor, Ernst & Young House
4 Pritchard Street, Johannesburg
2001
TEL: 011-498 1000
FAX: 011-498 1238

TRANSFER SECRETARY
Union Provident Trust SA Ltd
P O Box 2322, Johannesburg
2000
TEL: 011-833 6700

COMPANY SECRETARY
Ernst & Young

NATURE OF BUSINESS
The company has a 12,5% interest in benefits from the exploitation by De Beers of diamond deposits and mineral rights on the farm Venetia (N Tvl).

BANKERS :
First National Bank of SA Ltd

AUDITORS :
KPMG Aiken & Peat, Ernst & Young

FAMILIAR BRAND NAMES
N/A

CONTRIBUTION BY ACTIVITY
N/A

YEAR END : June

DIVIDEND : Ords 15c

Dividend No 47	(Ldr)22/09/89	(Pay)11/10/89	Amt(c)110
Special No 48	(Ldr)08/06/90	(Pay)09/07/90	Amt(c)3750
Dividend No 49	(Ldr)02/10/92	(Pay)30/10/92	Amt(c)2

CAPITAL STRUCTURE

	AUTHORISED	ISSUED
Ords 15c	16585100	13830000
"B" Red Prefs 150c	34107	0
"C" Red Prefs 150c	7383	0

FINANCIAL STATISTICS (AT FINANCIAL YEAR END)

(Amts in R'000)	1992 Jun	1991 Jun	1990 Jun	1989 Jun	1988 Jun
Ord S/H Int	66606	62035	66518	56095	47563
Long Trm Loans	150	150	150	2001	1811
Iss Ord Share	13830	13830	13830	13830	13830
Total Liab	351	332	52018	48751	25748
Current Liab	201	182	51868	46750	23937
Total Assets	66957	62367	118536	104846	73311
Current Assets	283	41	51862	66152	37404
Debtors	3	41	51862	14651	10599
Inventory	-	-	-	50571	25847
Turnover	-	-	317499	250513	195527
Oper Profit	-221	-178	11015	13144	9410
Interest Paid	-	6	12138	2059	405
Tax Paid	6	-	421	4350	3051
Prf af Int&Tax	232	25	-1544	6735	5954
Prf att Ord Sh	222	15	-967	5769	5241
Btm Line Earn	4571	15	-5355	7062	5677
Dividend Paid	-	-	51862	2421	2005
Mkt Prce(c) YE	2800	1600	12500	5300	5000
Depreciation	-	-	1253	548	477

PER SHARE STATISTICS (CENTS)

Net Asst Val	481.61	448.55	480.97	405.60	343.91
Net Earnings	1.60	0.11	69.90	417.00	379.00
Dividends	-	-	3750.00	175.00	145.00
Cash Flow	1.61	0.11	-2.46	52.59	46.40

RATIOS AND OTHER INFORMATION

Mrk Cap(R000)	387240	221280	1728750	732990	691500
Current Ratio	1.41	0.23	1.00	1.42	1.56
Quik/Acid Tst	1.41	0.23	1.00	0.33	0.48
A/C Rec T/ovr	-	-	6.12	17.10	18.45
Tot Ass T/ovr	-	-	2.68	2.39	2.67
Debt/Ass Rat	0.00	0.00	0.44	0.45	0.33
L T L Tot Ass	-	-	-	-	0.00
Debt to Eqity	0.00	0.00	0.78	0.83	0.50
Interest Cover	-	-4.67	0.91	6.38	23.23
Oper Prof Mrg	-	-	3.47	5.25	4.81
Net Prof Marg%	-	-	-0.30	2.30	2.68
Ret on Assets	0.36	0.05	9.82	11.62	11.88
Ret on Equity%	0.33	0.02	-1.45	10.28	11.02
Price/Earnings	1750.00	14545.45	178.83	12.71	13.19
Divid Cover	-	-	0.02	2.38	2.61
Divid Yield	-	-	30.00	3.30	2.90
Earning Yield%	0.06	0.01	0.56	7.87	7.58
NAV % Mrk Pr	17.20	28.03	3.85	7.65	6.88
Effec Tax Rate	-3.06	-	-37.49	39.24	33.88
Def Interval	0.68	10.00	-0.44	2.53	0.60
Sus Grth Rate	0.33	0.02	-79.42	5.97	6.80

SUBSIDIARY & ASSOCIATED COMPANIES

FIXED PROPERTIES (SA) LTD

INVESTMENTS

SATURN MINING, PROSPECTING & DEVELOPMENT (12,5%)

INDUSTRIAL SELECTIONS LTD

ABBREVIATION : IND-SELE

JSE SHORT CODE : ISL

SECTOR : Financial-Investment Trusts

SHAREHOLDERS

Who Owns Whom's Assessment of the Identity of the Ultimate Controlling Shareholder: STATE VIA INDUSTRIAL DEVELOPMENT CORP.

SHAREHOLDER	PERCENTAGE 1992	1991
IND DEVELOPMENT CORP SA LTD	52.1	52.7
SA MUTUAL	18.5	16.6
CMB NOM P/L	7.4	---
STD BANK NOM TVL P/L	2.7	2.0
FIRST NAT NOM P/L	2.1	1.6
GEMEENSKAPLIKE MUNISIPALE TVL PENS FUND	1.5	1.5
SOUTHERN LIFE ASSOC LTD	1.3	2.1

EIGHTY ONE MAIN STREET NOM LTD	1.2	---
GREENMARKET SQUARE NOM P/L	---	1.1
SANLAM	---	5.1
TOTAL	86.6	82.6

DIRECTORS :
COOPER DE ,KAHN JM ,MCCRYSTAL LP DR,SCHOLTZ AP DR
TERREBLANCHE HJ ,VAN DER MERWE WC
VAN ROOY PJ (Chairman),VAN WYK CJ DR,WIESE CH AD

REGISTRATION NUMBER : 62/03461/06

REGISTERED OFFICE
19 Fredman Drive, Sandton
2199
TEL: 011-883 1600
FAX: 011-883 1655

TRANSFER SECRETARY
Consolidated Share Registrars Ltd
P O Box 61051, Marshalltown
2107
TEL: 011-492 1620

COMPANY SECRETARY
Industrial Development Corp. of SA Ltd

NATURE OF BUSINESS
A general investment company formed as a medium for investors to acquire an interest in a variety of companies engaged in the manufacturing and the beneficiation of minerals.Control is vested in the Industrial Development Corp, from whom almost all investments are acquired.

BANKERS :
Volkskas Ltd

AUDITORS :
Price Waterhouse Meyernel

FAMILIAR BRAND NAMES
N/A

CONTRIBUTION BY ACTIVITY
N/A

YEAR END : June

DIVIDEND : Ords no par value

Interim	(Ldr)09/03/90	(Pay)12/04/90	Amt(c)5.5
Final	(Ldr)14/09/90	(Pay)12/10/90	Amt(c)6
Interim	(Ldr)08/03/91	(Pay)12/04/91	Amt(c)5.5
Final	(Ldr)13/09/91	(Pay)11/10/91	Amt(c)6
Interim	(Ldr)06/03/92	(Pay)10/04/92	Amt(c)5.5
Final	(Ldr)11/09/92	(Pay)09/10/92	Amt(c)6.5

CAPITAL STRUCTURE

	AUTHORISED	ISSUED
Ords no par value	280000000	273800600

FINANCIAL STATISTICS (AT FINANCIAL YEAR END)

(Amts in R'000)	1992 Jun	1991 Jun	1990 Jun	1989 Jun	1988 Jun
Ord S/H Int	127945	116982	100971	89710	79241
Iss Ord Share	273801	273801	273801	273801	273801
Total Liab	18680	17362	18070	15940	12340
Current Liab	18680	17362	18070	15940	12340
Total Assets	146625	134344	119041	105650	91581
Current Assets	31697	37242	13285	18868	20021
Debtors	5607	6159	4184	2617	1960
Oper Profit	-682	-669	-698	37770	29905
Interest Paid	110	-	-	-	-
Tax Paid	671	1399	1593	843	786
Prf af Int&Tax	39312	38002	42748	36927	29119
Prf att Ord Sh	43819	47498	42748	37849	33606
Btm Line Earn	43819	47498	42748	37849	33606
Dividend Paid	32856	31487	31487	27380	21904
Mkt Prce(c) YE	270	280	260	280	170

PER SHARE STATISTICS (CENTS)

Net Asst Val	46.73	42.73	36.88	32.76	28.94
Net Earnings	14.36	13.88	15.61	13.50	10.64
Dividends	12.00	11.50	11.50	10.00	8.00
Cash Flow	14.36	13.88	15.61	13.49	10.64

RATIOS AND OTHER INFORMATION

Mrk Cap(R000)	739263	766643	711883	766643	465462
Current Ratio	1.70	2.15	0.74	1.18	1.62
Quik/Acid Tst	1.70	2.15	0.74	1.18	1.62
Debt/Ass Rat	0.13	0.13	0.15	0.15	0.13
Debt to Eqity	0.15	0.15	0.18	0.18	0.16
Interest Cover	351.07	-	-	-	-
Ret on Assets	27.34	29.33	37.25	35.75	32.65
Ret on Equity%	34.25	40.60	42.34	42.19	42.41
Price/Earnings	18.80	20.17	16.66	20.74	15.98
Divid Cover	1.20	1.21	1.36	1.35	1.33
Divid Yield	4.44	4.11	4.42	3.57	4.71
Earning Yield%	5.32	4.96	6.00	4.82	6.26
NAV % Mrk Pr	17.31	15.26	14.18	11.70	17.02
Effec Tax Rate	98.24	59.86	61.67	2.23	2.63
Sus Grth Rate	8.57	13.69	11.15	11.67	14.77

SUBSIDIARY & ASSOCIATED COMPANIES

INDUSTRIAL FINANCE CORP OF SA (PTY) LTD (50%)

INVESTMENTS

ADVANCED FOOD RESEARCH (PTY) LTD (1 SH)
ALGORAX (PTY) LTD (225000 SH)
ALUSAF (PTY) LTD (5250000 SH)
AUTOMOTIVE OVERSEAS INV (PTY) LTD (470 SH)
BANKORP HOLDINGS LTD (3520000 SH)
C G SMITH FOODS LTD (706499 SH)
C G SMITH LTD (1952812 SH)
C G SMITH LTD (HELD BY IND FIN CORP OF S (804375 SH)
DELFOS & ATLAS COPCO (PTY) LTD (25000 SH)
ERF SA (PTY) LTD (301372 SH)
GUBB & INGGS LTD (355840 SH)
IMPALA PLATINUM HOLDINGS LTD (2898512 SH)
L & C STEINMULLER (AFRICA) (PTY) LTD (753600 SH)
PALABORA MINING CO LTD (324500 SH)
RICHBAY MINE HOLDINGS (PTY) LTD (243 SH)
RICHBAY SMELTER HOLDINGS (PTY) LTD (243 SH)
SAPPI LTD (4793676 SH)
SAPPI MANAGEMENT SERVICES (PTY) LTD (RED (2510 SH)
SASOL LTD (1192500 SH)
SENTRACHEM LTD (HELD BY IND FIN CORP OF (1052860 SH)

INFORMATION SERVICES GROUP LTD

ABBREVIATION : ISG

JSE SHORT CODE : ISG

SECTOR : Industrial-Electronics, Electrical & Bat

SHAREHOLDERS

Who Owns Whom's Assessment of the Identity of the Ultimate Controlling Shareholder:
SA MUTUAL VIA BARLOWS

SHAREHOLDER	PERCENTAGE 1992	1991
ISG HOLDINGS P/L	60.4	---
SA MUTUAL	7.9	6.5
GUARDIAN NOM P/L	4.0	2.1
ISM TRUST	3.0	3.1
METAL IND GROUP PENS FUND	2.2	2.1
LIBERTY LIFE ASSOC OF AFRICA LTD	1.9	3.2
HG & S NOM P/L	1.8	5.3
ENGINEERING INDUSTRIES PENS FUND	1.8	1.8
CMB NOM P/L	1.8	---
EIGHTY ONE MAIN STREET NOM LTD	1.1	---
STD BANK NOM TVL P/L	---	1.9
SANLAM	---	1.8
TS HOLDINGS P/L	---	60.4
TOTAL	86.0	88.2

DIRECTORS :
BULTERMAN GH ,CLARKE JF ,COOPER DE (Chairman)
DE VILLIERS HP ,GEELING KLG ,GROENEWEG EM
KHOZA RJ ,MEHL BD (Chief Executive),TENNANT JS

REGISTRATION NUMBER : 87/00049/06

REGISTERED OFFICE
Third Floor,ISM Building, Cnr. Oxford & Baker Str
Rosebank
2196
TEL: 011-448 9111
FAX: 011-448 4100

TRANSFER SECRETARY
Rand Registrars Ltd
P O Box 82549, Southdale
2135
TEL: 011-835 1016

COMPANY SECRETARY
C G Graham

NATURE OF BUSINESS
Marketing and support of the full range of IBM and complementary products, incl hardware, software, telecommunications and networking products in the large, midrange and personal computer markets. The group also provides specialised services in the areas of software sales and development, education networking and tendering.

BANKERS :
Standard Bank of SA Ltd, Bankorp Ltd
Volkskas Ltd

AUDITORS :
Price Waterhouse Meyernel

FAMILIAR BRAND NAMES
DATA TECHNOLOGIES,IBM,INFOMET,ISM,POLYGON
TRADE NET (33%),TRAFEX (50%),TS EDUCATION

CONTRIBUTION BY ACTIVITY
N/A

YEAR END : September

DIVIDEND : Ords no par value

Interim No 5	(Ldr)25/05/90	(Pay)12/07/90	Amt(c)9
Final No 6	(Ldr)30/11/90	(Pay)10/01/91	Amt(c)15
Interim No 7	(Ldr)07/06/91	(Pay)12/07/91	Amt(c)10.5
Final No 8	(Ldr)06/12/91	(Pay)13/01/92	Amt(c)19.5
Interim No 9	(Ldr)05/06/92	(Pay)13/07/92	Amt(c)8.5
Final No 10	(Ldr)04/12/92	(Pay)11/01/93	Amt(c)13.5

NUMBER OF EMPLOYEES : 1600

CAPITAL STRUCTURE

	AUTHORISED	ISSUED
Ords no par value	200000000	148494044

FINANCIAL STATISTICS (AT FINANCIAL YEAR END)

(Amts in R'000)	1991 Sep	1990 Sep	1989 Sep	1988 Sep	1987
Ord S/H Int	132807	181800	171210	143534	102362
Long Trm Loans	30302	37642	38815	24716	196657
Iss Ord Share	148494	148494	148494	148494	148494
Total Liab	369359	307045	320950	320970	367390
Current Liab	339057	269403	282135	296254	170733
Total Assets	502166	488845	492160	464504	541678
Current Assets	410366	399834	404816	397550	242659
Debtors	156200	105328	155882	115323	-
Inventory	102361	126705	162357	193349	242659
Turnover	1049105	1184985	1351620	1086672	976534
Oper Profit	97413	100298	141697	138671	114349
Interest Paid	-	13200	7025	2210	-
Tax Paid	42773	54090	62460	61810	57175
Prf af Int&Tax	54640	65397	86739	74651	57174
Prf att Ord Sh	54455	65397	86739	74651	57174
Btm Line Earn	54455	46228	63314	74651	57174
Dividend Paid	-	35638	35638	29699	-
Mkt Prce(c) YE	580	375	700	560	-
Depreciation	-	20623	21578	16824	-

PER SHARE STATISTICS (CENTS)

Net Asst Val	89.44	122.43	115.30	96.66	68.93
Net Earnings	36.70	44.00	58.40	50.30	-
Dividends	20.70	24.00	24.00	20.00	-
Cash Flow	36.80	61.85	81.40	74.67	38.50

RATIOS AND OTHER INFORMATION

Mrk Cap(R000)	861265	556853	1039458	831566	-
Current Ratio	1.21	1.48	1.43	1.34	1.42
Quik/Acid Tst	0.91	1.01	0.86	0.69	-
A/C Rec T/ovr	6.72	11.25	8.67	9.42	-
Tot Ass T/ovr	2.09	2.42	2.75	2.34	1.80
Debt/Ass Rat	0.68	0.55	0.58	0.64	0:68
L T L Tot Ass	-	-	0.01	0.00	0.36
Debt to Eqity	2.55	1.48	1.67	2.08	3.59
Interest Cover	-	7.60	20.84	62.75	-
Oper Prof Mrg	9.29	8.46	10.48	12.76	11.71
Net Prof Marg%	5.19	5.52	6.42	6.87	5.85
Ret on Assets	19.36	27.14	31.74	29.85	21.11
Ret on Equity%	41.00	35.97	50.66	52.01	55.85
Price/Earnings	15.80	8.52	11.99	11.13	-
Divid Cover	1.77	1.83	2.43	2.52	-
Divid Yield	3.57	6.40	3.43	3.57	-
Earning Yield%	6.33	11.73	8.34	8.98	-
NAV % Mrk Pr	15.42	32.65	16.47	17.26	-
Effec Tax Rate	43.91	35.03	28.75	30.84	50.00
Def Interval	0.52	0.22	0.09	0.04	3.44
Sus Grth Rate	41.00	16.37	29.85	31.32	55.85

SUBSIDIARY & ASSOCIATED COMPANIES

BUSINESS FUTURES GROUP (PTY) LTD
DATA EXCHANGE INVESTMENT HOLDINGS (PTY) (50,05%)
DATA TECHNOLOGIES INFORMATION SYSTEMS (P
ERNII (PTY) LTD (33,33%)
INFOMET (PTY) LTD
INFOMET SYSTEM BUILDERS (PTY) LTD
INFORMATION SERVICES MANAGEMENT (PTY) LT
ISM PROPERTIES (PTY) LTD
POLYGON SYSTEMS (PTY) LTD
SAT-TRUCK SYSTEMS (PTY) LTD (50%)
TECHNOLOGY SYSTEMS EDUCATION (PTY) LTD
TECHNOLOGY SYSTEMS INDUSTRIES (PTY) LTD
TECHNOLOGY SYSTEMS SOFTWARE (PTY) LTD
TRADE INFORMATION SERVICES (PTY) LTD (33.33%)
TRAFEX (PTY) LTD (50,05%)

INVESTMENTS

None

INMINS LTD

ABBREVIATION : INMINS

JSE SHORT CODE : INM

SECTOR : Industrial-Engineering

SHAREHOLDERS

Who Owns Whom's Assessment of the Identity of the Ultimate Controlling Shareholder:
WINBEL VIA WINHOLD

SHAREHOLDER	PERCENTAGE 1992	1991
INMINS INV LTD	73.4	73.4
CMB NOM P/L	7.0	---
FERBROS NOM P/L	2.7	2.7
ALLSOP M J	2.3	2.3
NEDBANK NOM LTD	1.3	1.3
UAL NOM P/L	1.1	1.1
STD BANK NOM TVL P/L	---	2.3
SANLAM	---	7.0
TOTAL	87.7	90.0

DIRECTORS :
FOURIE JW ,HENDERSON JH (Chairman),NALSON SM
RAMSAY GD ,SIEBERT JJ
WENTELER WAR (Managing Director

REGISTRATION NUMBER : 69/04321/06

REGISTERED OFFICE
Linton Jones Street, Industries East
Germiston
1401
TEL: 011-873 3655
FAX: 011-873 4094

TRANSFER SECRETARY
Mercantile Registrars Ltd
P O Box 1053, Johannesburg
2000
TEL: 011-333 8181

COMPANY SECRETARY
Winhold Ltd

NATURE OF BUSINESS
The company is a holding company with interests in the mining and industrial supplies industry.

BANKERS :
Standard Bank of SA Ltd

AUDITORS :
Deloitte Pim Goldby

FAMILIAR BRAND NAMES
COMET-ZENITH,CONWAY JOHNSON,RANCE COLLY,VALIC

CONTRIBUTION BY ACTIVITY
N/A

YEAR END : September

DIVIDEND :15/06/91 and 15/01/92

NUMBER OF EMPLOYEES : 800

CAPITAL STRUCTURE

	AUTHORISED	ISSUED
Ords 60c	35000000	26539541
Var Rate Conv Cum Prefs R1	830000	0
Var Rate Conv Red Cum Prefs 10c	5000000	0
Unsec Auto Conv Debs 170c	6015873	6015873

FINANCIAL STATISTICS (AT FINANCIAL YEAR END)

(Amts in R'000)	1991 Sep	1990 Sep	1989 Sep	1987	1986
Ord S/H Int	-8455	-7736	6951	38497	18707
Long Trm Loans	18433	19074	17081	43428	16576
Iss Ord Share	26540	26540	26540	26540	17696
Total Liab	66731	72551	66243	70120	29981
Current Liab	48298	53477	49162	26692	13405
Total Assets	58276	64815	73194	135527	55916
Current Assets	47413	51411	57603	53602	20633
Debtors	26535	29727	32032	-	-
Inventory	19204	21684	25571	53602	20633
Turnover	168887	193220	204819	150580	73105
Oper Profit	7018	116	11248	6288	4115
Interest Paid	9115	9577	8308	1559	491
Tax Paid	59	5	74	462	20
Prf af Int&Tax	-1780	-9377	3572	4267	3603
Prf att Ord Sh	-1581	-10194	3355	4236	3603
Btm Line Earn	-719	-14687	-3330	4236	3603
Dividend Paid	-	-	-	2341	1532
Mkt Prce(c) YE	4	12	33	230	235
Depreciation	811	1580	1316	-	-

PER SHARE STATISTICS (CENTS)

Net Asst Val	-31.86	-29.15	26.19	145.05	105.71
Net Earnings	-5.90	-38.40	12.60	-	-
Cash Flow	-2.69	-32.46	17.50	16.08	20.36

RATIOS AND OTHER INFORMATION

Mrk Cap(R000)	1062	3185	8758	61042	41586
Current Ratio	0.98	0.96	1.17	2.01	1.54
Quik/Acid Tst	0.58	0.56	0.65	-	-

A/C Rec T/ovr	6.36	6.50	6.39	-	-
Tot Ass T/ovr	2.90	2.98	2.80	1.11	1.31
Debt/Ass Rat	1.15	1.12	0.91	0.52	0.54
L T L Tot Ass	0.32	0.29	0.23	0.32	0.30
Debt to Eqity	-7.89	-9.38	9.53	1.82	1.60
Interest Cover	0.77	0.01	1.35	4.03	8.38
Oper Prof Mrg	4.16	0.06	5.49	4.18	5.63
Net Prof Marg%	-0.94	-5.28	1.64	2.81	4.93
Ret on Assets	12.69	0.32	16.33	4.64	7.36
Ret on Equity%	18.70	131.77	48.27	11.00	19.26
Price/Earnings	-0.68	-0.31	2.62	-	-
Earning Yield%	-147.50	-320.00	38.18	-	-
NAV % Mrk Pr	-796.44	-242.90	79.37	63.07	44.98
Effec Tax Rate	-0.17	-0.05	2.74	9.77	0.55
Def Interval	-39.80	-3.34	5.34	10.18	4.60
Sus Grth Rate	18.70	131.77	48.27	4.92	11.07

SUBSIDIARY & ASSOCIATED COMPANIES

121 AND 167 URANIAVILLE, KLERKSDORP (PTY
1359 EVANDER, 1732 WITBANK, 37 PIETERMAR
1400 KLERKSDORP, 77 URANIAVILLE, 47/48 L
2084 & 2239 PHALABORWA & 2309 MIDDLEBURG
33 FERROBANK WITBANK (PTY) LTD
359 PIETERSBURG (PTY) LTD
963 VRYHEID (PTY) LTD
BELTING & SPROCKETS SA (PTY) LTD
BOLT & NUT SUPPLIES (PTY) LTD
BOLT ELECTRICAL WHOLESALERS (PTY) LTD
BOWCOR ENGINEERING (PTY) LTD
CHICK HENDERSON (PTY) LTD
CHICK HENDERSON NATAL (PTY) LTD
COMET ELECTRICAL WHOLESALERS (PTY) LTD
COMET-ZENITH ELECTRICAL (PTY) LTD
CONVEYOR HOSE HOLDINGS (PTY) LTD
ERF 8156 WELKOM (PTY) LTD
ERF 9088 WELKOM (PTY) LTD
ERVEN 2651, 2654 & 2655 KURUMAN (PTY) LT
HIGHVELD HOSE (PRETORIA) (PTY) LTD
HIGHVELD HOSE (PTY) LTD
HIGHVELD HOSE (VAAL) (PTY) LTD
INMINS SA (PTY) LTD
ISD ENGINEERING & MINING SUPPLIES (RUSTE
JOMY CONSTRUCTION (PTY) LTD
JOMY ENGINEERING (PTY) LTD
NORMAN CORNISH (EVANDER) (PTY) LTD
NORMAN CORNISH (PTY) LTD
PORTION 1, 1611 ROBERTSHAM (PTY) LTD
PORTION 5, 2540 BARBERTON (PTY) LTD
RANCE-COLLY (PTY) LTD
RUST INVESTMENTS (PTY) LTD
SUB 5, 160 VRYHEID (PTY) LTD
TURNCLIFF MINING GROUP (PTY) LTD T
VALIC (PTY) LTD
WELLBILT PRODUCTS (PTY) LTD
WINBEL MANAGEMENT SERVICES (PTY) LTD
YODALARM (PTY) LTD

INVESTMENTS

None

INTERLEISURE LTD

ABBREVIATION : INTELES

JSE SHORT CODE : ITL

SECTOR : Industrial-Beverages & Hotels

SHAREHOLDERS

Who Owns Whom's Assessment of the Identity of the Ultimate Controlling Shareholder: SA MUTUAL/SANLAM (VIA FED VOLK)

SHAREHOLDER	PERCENTAGE 1992	1991
SATBEL INV HOLDINGS P/L	74.9	75.5
ANGLO AMERICAN GROUP PENS FUND	3.7	3.7
CMB NOM P/L	3.3	---
EIGHTY ONE MAIN STREET NOM LTD	2.8	---
SERVGRO INTERNATIONAL BPK	2.6	---
MOMENTUM LIFE ASSURE LTD	1.8	1.3
SA SPECIAL RISKS INSURANCE ASSOC LTD	1.2	1.2
NEDBANK NOM LTD	1.1	---
STD BANK NOM TVL P/L	---	1.0
EPF OLD MUTUAL NOM P/L	---	1.6
SA MUTUAL	---	1.0
SANLAM	---	5.2
TOTAL	91.4	90.5

DIRECTORS :
BOHLMANN TRT ,BOLD EJ (Executive Director)
COMLEY MR (Executive Director)
EGAN MP (Managing Director)
HAWINKELS JHW (Executive Director)
HAWTON DA (Deputy Chairman)
MCDONALD PL (Executive Director)
SMITHYMAN RJ (Financial Director),VAN BILJON AF
VAN DER WALT PJJ (Chairman

REGISTRATION NUMBER : 86/03373/06

REGISTERED OFFICE
Interleisure House, 2 Johannesburg Road
Highlands North Ext 6
2192
TEL: 011-887 5480
FAX: 011-440 4114

TRANSFER SECRETARY
Fraser Street Registrars (Pty) Ltd
P O Box 61178, Marshalltown
2107
TEL: 011-491 0911

COMPANY SECRETARY
M Marnewick

NATURE OF BUSINESS
Interleisure is focused on the cinema, food, film production & sports sectors of the entertainment & leisure industry. Group activities include : Cinema exhibition & film distribution; Film & TV production; Operation of restaurants & fast foods outlets on both a company-owned & franchise basis; Sports wholesaling & retailing. Related activities include screen advertising, computerised advance booking service, video distribution, coin-operated amusement, film processing & bus shelter adverts.

BANKERS :
First National Bank of SA Ltd

AUDITORS :
Deloitte & Touche

FAMILIAR BRAND NAMES

ASICS TIGER,BEN HOGAN,BIMBO'S,CATTLEMAN
CINEMARK,COMPUTICKET,FOOTJOY,GAME
SET & MATCH,GOLF DISCOUNT CENTRE,HEAD,LYNX
MIKES KITCHEN,NEW BALANCE,PING,PORTERHOUSE
PRO KENNEX,PRO-SHOP,RJ'S,SPALDING,SQUIRES
STER-KINEKOR,TAYLOR MADE,TOMMY ARMOUR
TORON INTERNATIONAL,UNICORN DARTS

CONTRIBUTION BY ACTIVITY

Cinemas (% Operating Profit) (30.0%)
Services (20.0%)
Food (7.0%)
Film Production (13.0%)
Sport (30.0%)

YEAR END : June

DIVIDEND :Ords 1c

Interim	(Ldr)02/03/90	(Pay)21/03/90	Amt(c)4.25
Final	(Ldr)07/09/90	(Pay)24/09/90	Amt(c)5.5
Interim	(Ldr)01/03/91	(Pay)22/03/91	Amt(c)4.75
Final	(Ldr)06/09/91	(Pay)24/09/91	Amt(c)6.25
Interim	(Ldr)28/02/92	(Pay)23/03/92	Amt(c)5.25
Final	(Ldr)04/09/92	(Pay)21/09/92	Amt(c)5.75

NUMBER OF EMPLOYEES : 2574

CAPITAL STRUCTURE

	AUTHORISED	ISSUED
Ords 1c	200000000	189778401

FINANCIAL STATISTICS (AT FINANCIAL YEAR END)

(Amts in R'000)	1992 Jun	1991 Jun	1990 Jun	1989 Jun	1988 Jun
Ord S/H Int	110593	111643	91591	77136	165522
Long Trm Loans	24923	14143	12899	10735	12175
Iss Ord Share	189778	189778	186885	186755	172270
Total Liab	171095	126611	110763	115210	94284
Current Liab	146172	112468	97864	104475	82109
Total Assets	281688	238254	202266	192117	161586
Intang Assets	*	*	88	229	98220
Current Assets	125456	104625	93119	87467	68628
Debtors	64266	52493	54706	49281	38384
Inventory	60795	48570	31151	37286	24826
Turnover	400902	383129	386061	375034	263576
Oper Profit	65736	74328	61891	56734	38077
Interest Paid	5470	1657	6513	6335	1051
Tax Paid	22599	29229	17035	16622	12829
Prf af Int&Tax	39821	43797	38600	33777	24197
Prf att Ord Sh	38257	40704	35268	30856	22807
Btm Line Earn	34516	40677	32413	27372	25357
Dividend Paid	20876	20857	18216	16797	12570
Mkt Prce(c) YE	400	275	125	115	150
Depreciation	25412	18360	11675	10751	7201

PER SHARE STATISTICS (CENTS)

Net Asst Val	58.27	58.83	48.96	41.18	39.07
Net Earnings	20.20	21.70	18.90	17.00	13.50
Dividends	11.00	11.00	9.75	9.00	7.25
Cash Flow	35.25	32.75	25.40	23.22	17.48

RATIOS AND OTHER INFORMATION

Mrk Cap(R000)	759112	521890	233606	214768	258405
Current Ratio	0.86	0.93	0.95	0.84	0.84
Quik/Acid Tst	0.44	0.50	0.63	0.48	0.53
A/C Rec T/ovr	6.24	7.30	7.06	7.61	6.87
Tot Ass T/ovr	1.42	1.61	1.91	1.95	1.63
Debt/Ass Rat	0.52	0.47	0.49	0.55	0.54
L T L Tot Ass	-	-	0.00	0.00	0.03
Debt to Eqity	1.32	1.01	1.07	1.36	0.52
Interest Cover	12.02	44.87	9.50	8.96	36.23
Oper Prof Mrg	16.40	19.40	16.03	15.13	14.45
Net Prof Marg%	9.54	10.62	9.14	8.23	8.65
Ret on Assets	24.10	31.35	30.73	29.53	23.56
Ret on Equity%	34.59	36.46	38.51	40.00	13.78
Price/Earnings	19.80	12.67	6.61	6.76	11.11
Divid Cover	1.84	1.97	1.94	1.89	1.86
Divid Yield	2.75	4.00	7.80	7.83	4.83
Earning Yield%	5.05	7.89	15.12	14.78	9.00
NAV % Mrk Pr	14.57	21.39	39.17	35.81	26.05
Effec Tax Rate	29.37	32.94	4.61	8.78	15.21
Def Interval	0.59	0.05	0.47	0.80	1.06
Sus Grth Rate	15.72	17.78	18.62	18.23	6.18

SUBSIDIARY & ASSOCIATED COMPANIES

CHEMIX PRODUCTS (PTY) LTD
CINEMARK (PTY) LTD
COMPUTICKET (BOPHUTHATSWANA) (PTY) LTD
COMPUTICKET (PTY) LTD
GOLF DISTRIBUTORS (PTY) LTD
INDEPENDENT FILM CENTRE SA (PTY) LTD
INTERFARE (PTY) LTD
INTERFARE HOLDINGS (PTY) LTD
INTERLEISURE FINANCE (PTY) LTD
INTERLEISURE MANAGEMENT (PTY) LTD
INTERSPORT (PTY) LTD
IRENE FILM LABORATORIES (PTY) LTD
LONE HILL STUDIOS (PTY) LTD
OPAL SPORTSWEAR (PTY) LTD
PRO SHOP (PTY) LTD
RACQUETS OF SANDTON (PTY) LTD
RACQUETS OF SANDTON (PTY) LTD
ROHAN SUMMERS (PTY) LTD
SATBEL FILMS (PTY) LTD
STER-KINEKOR FILMS (PTY) LTD
STER-KINEKOR THEATRES (PTY) LTD
STER-KINEKOR VIDEO (PTY) LTD
SUN CITY FOODS (BOPHUTHATSWANA) (PTY) L
SWEAT SHOP (PTY) LTD
TORON INTERNATIONAL (PTY) LTD
TORON INTERNATIONAL (PTY) LTD
TORON STUDIOS (PTY) LTD
TREGER GOLF & SPORTS (PTY) LTD
VIDEO MAGIC (PTY) LTD (50%)
WILLOWS STER INRYTEATER (EDMS) BPK

INVESTMENTS

None

INTERNATIONAL HOLDINGS LTD

ABBREVIATION : INTERNAT

SECTOR : Zimbabwe Stock Exchange

SHAREHOLDERS

Who Owns Whom's Assessment of the Identity of the Ultimate Controlling Shareholder:
ELLERBY B.V.

SHAREHOLDER	PERCENTAGE 1992	1991

ELLERBY BV	71.5	---
SECURITY NOM LTD	5.1	---
MINING INDUSTRY PENS FUND	1.3	---
ZIMNAT LIFE ASSURE CO LTD	1.3	---
CATERING INDUSTRY PENS FUND	1.2	---
E S C STAFF PENS FUND	1.1	---
MERCANTILE & GEN REINSURANCE CO SA LTD	1.0	---
TOTAL	82.5	---

DIRECTORS :
BERK ER ,BUTTERFIELD KG ,DAY B (Chairman)
FRANCEY WA ,KADENHE DD ,MONK FJW ,ROULIER G
SINCLAIR JM (Deputy Chairman

REGISTERED OFFICE
Dale House, Cnr Watts & Leyland Roads
Arbennie Industrial Sites, Harare

TRANSFER SECRETARY
First Transfer Secretaries (Pvt) Ltd
P O Box 437, Bulawayo
Zimbabwe

TEL: 092634 - 702905

COMPANY SECRETARY
F J W Monk

NATURE OF BUSINESS
INTERNATIONAL HOLDINGS, incorporated in Zimbabwe, has investments in the construction, plastics, manufacturing and allied industries.

BANKERS :
Standard Chartered Bank Zimbabwe Ltd

AUDITORS :
Deloitte & Touche

FAMILIAR BRAND NAMES
N/A

CONTRIBUTION BY ACTIVITY
N/A

YEAR END : June

DIVIDEND : Ords Z$0,50

Dividend	(Ldr)19/07/91	(Pay)31/07/91	Amt(c)25
Dividend	(Ldr)14/02/92	(Pay)26/02/92	Amt(c)17.5

CAPITAL STRUCTURE

	AUTHORISED	ISSUED
Ords Z$0,50	7500000	6823374

FINANCIAL STATISTICS (AT FINANCIAL YEAR END)

(Amts in Z$)	1992 Jun	1991 Apr	1990 Apr
Ord S/H Int	40024	25958	14777
Long Trm Loans	9831	5825	3913
Iss Ord Share	6823	6823	6823
Total Liab	71693	38517	21882
Current Liab	61862	32692	17969
Total Assets	111085	63685	35711
Intang Assets	632	790	948
Current Assets	81527	45338	28260
Debtors	12746	9752	6773
Inventory	33354	17456	9786
Turnover	198341	89786	64601
Oper Profit	32491	14066	8719
Interest Paid	388	2	1
Tax Paid	12476	6284	4050
Prf af Int&Tax	21970	8276	5138
Prf att Ord Sh	18729	6928	4292
Btm Line Earn	18571	6770	4134
Dividend Paid	4503	2388	1911
Depreciation	3281	1816	964

PER SHARE STATISTICS (CENTS)

Net Asst Val	577.34	368.87	202.68
Net Earnings	274.48	101.54	62.90
Dividends	66.00	35.00	28.00
Cash Flow	276.50	128.15	77.03

RATIOS AND OTHER INFORMATION

Current Ratio	1.32	1.39	1.57
Quik/Acid Tst	0.78	0.85	1.03
A/C Rec T/ovr	13.34	9.21	9.54
Tot Ass T/ovr	1.53	1.41	1.81
Debt/Ass Rat	0.58	0.53	0.50
L T L Tot Ass	0.02	0.02	-
Debt to Eqity	1.61	1.30	1.22
Interest Cover	83.74	7033.00	8719.00
Oper Prof Mrg	16.38	15.67	13.50
Net Prof Marg%	9.44	7.72	6.64
Ret on Assets	26.88	22.87	25.73
Ret on Equity%	40.11	26.69	29.05
Divid Cover	4.16	2.90	2.25
Effec Tax Rate	36.22	43.16	44.08
Def Interval	0.10	0.12	-
Sus Grth Rate	35.54	17.49	16.11

SUBSIDIARY & ASSOCIATED COMPANIES

INDUSTRIAL INSULATOR INDUSTRIES (PVT) LT
INDUSTRIAL MOULDINGS (PRIVATE) LTD
INTERNATIONAL CONSTRUCTION PROPERTY DEVE
INTERNATIONAL CONSTRUCTION ZIMBABWE LTD
JARHEW ONE (PRIVATE) LIMITED
MULTI CONSTRUCTION (ROADS & EARTHWORKS)
PRODORITE (PRIVATE) LIMITED
PRODORITE HOLDINGS (PVT) LIMITED (50%)
PROMAT (PVT) LIMITED
UNITRANS ZIMBABWE (PVT) LTD

INVESTMENTS

None

INVESTEC BANK LTD

ABBREVIATION : INVSTEC

JSE SHORT CODE : INT

SECTOR : Financial-Banks & Financial Services

SHAREHOLDERS

Who Owns Whom's Assessment of the Identity of the Ultimate Controlling Shareholder:
INVESTEC HOLDINGS

SHAREHOLDER	PERCENTAGE 1992	1991
INVESTEC HOLDINGS LTD	48.0	75.7
FEDLIFE ASSURE LTD	15.6	---
CMB NOM P/L	5.8	---
SMBL NOM P/L	5.1	---
SAFEGRO NOM P/L	4.4	5.6
YSKOR PENS FUND	2.9	---
EIGHTY ONE MAIN STREET NOM LTD	2.4	---
STD BANK NOM TVL P/L	2.4	---
ENGINEERING INDUSTRIES PENS FUND	2.2	---
INDO-CHINA NOM P/L	2.0	---
INVESTEC NOM P/L	1.7	7.3
TOTAL	92.6	88.5

DIRECTORS :
DAVIN GH (Financial Director),HASLETT FN
JOHNSTON HW ,JOWELL DE
KANTOR B (Chief Executive),KANTOR IR
KARDOL B (Executive Chairman)
KOSEFF S (Managing Director),LEWIS IMAW
NESTADT G ,PIENAAR WD PROF,SENEKAL JC ,THOMAS PRS

REGISTRATION NUMBER : 04/02833/06

REGISTERED OFFICE
55 Fox Street, Johannesburg
2001
TEL: 011-498 2000
FAX: 011-498 2599

TRANSFER SECRETARY
Mercantile Registrars Ltd
P O Box 1053, Johannesburg
2000
TEL: 011-333 8181

COMPANY SECRETARY
E G Meredith

NATURE OF BUSINESS
A registered bank, providing banking, property & financial services. Activities include corporate, merchant & professional banking services, project finance, financial markets trading, treasury operations, property finance, trading & management & asset management.

BANKERS :
Standard Bank of SA Ltd
Trust Bank of Africa Ltd

AUDITORS :
Ernst & Young, BDO Spencer Steward

FAMILIAR BRAND NAMES
I KUPER & CO,INCITY REAL ESTATE,METBOARD

CONTRIBUTION BY ACTIVITY
Property (% Income Contribution) (22.9%)
Share Capital (26.3%)
Merchant Banking (13.6%)
Banking (12.0%)
Metboard (15.0%)
Branches & Subsidiaries (10.2%)

YEAR END : March

DIVIDEND :Ords 60c

Interim No 70	(Ldr)10/11/89	(Pay)27/11/89	Amt(c)16
Final No 71	(Ldr)01/06/90	(Pay)26/06/90	Amt(c)24
Final No 72	(Ldr)17/05/91	(Pay)14/06/91	Amt(c)36
Interim No 73	(Ldr)08/11/91	(Pay)29/11/91	Amt(c)28
Final No 74	(Ldr)15/05/92	(Pay)14/06/92	Amt(c)42
Interim No 75	(Ldr)06/11/92	(Pay)29/11/92	Amt(c)35

NUMBER OF EMPLOYEES : 704

CAPITAL STRUCTURE

	AUTHORISED	ISSUED
Ords 60c	25000000	20000000
Var Rate Red Cum Prefs 60c	50000	0
Cum Red Prefs 1c	5000	4470
Cum Red Prefs R1	4000000	0
12% Comp Conv Cum Prefs 60c	3000000	2500000

FINANCIAL STATISTICS (AT FINANCIAL YEAR END)

(Amts in R'000)	1991 Mar	1990 Mar	1989 Mar	1988 Mar
Ord S/H Int	131474	82649	66295	58882
Long Trm Loans	69500	-	887574	632323
Iss Ord Share	20000	20000	20000	20000
Total Liab	2750783	1179910	891574	635353
Current Liab	2681283	1179910	4000	3030
Total Assets	2859894	1255705	957869	694235
Intang Assets	22363	6854	*	*
Current Assets	843147	238669	287811	283638
Oper Profit	15673	17500	13994	11000
Prf af Int&Tax	24893	17500	13994	11000
Prf att Ord Sh	24000	17500	8308	11000
Btm Line Earn	24000	17500	8308	11016
Dividend Paid	11200	8000	3200	4800
Mkt Prce(c) YE	1400	675	420	375
Depreciation	7474	4831	-	-

PER SHARE STATISTICS (CENTS)

Net Asst Val	545.55	378.98	331.48	294.41
Net Earnings	120.00	87.50	70.00	55.00
Dividends	56.00	40.00	32.00	24.00
Cash Flow	141.97	111.66	41.54	55.00

RATIOS AND OTHER INFORMATION

Mrk Cap(R000)	280000	135000	84000	75000
Current Ratio	0.31	0.20	71.95	93.61
Quik/Acid Tst	0.31	0.20	71.95	93.61
Debt/Ass Rat	0.94	0.94	0.00	0.00
Debt to Eqity	20.39	14.28	0.06	0.05
Ret on Assets	0.98	1.39	1.46	1.58
Ret on Equity%	18.25	21.17	12.53	18.68
Price/Earnings	11.67	7.71	6.00	6.82
Divid Cover	2.14	2.19	2.19	2.29
Divid Yield	4.00	5.93	7.62	6.40
Earning Yield%	8.57	12.96	16.67	14.67
NAV % Mrk Pr	38.97	56.14	78.92	78.51
Def Interval	95.78	52.62	-	-
Sus Grth Rate	9.74	11.49	7.70	10.53

SUBSIDIARY & ASSOCIATED COMPANIES

AEROPAK CORPORATION (PTY) LTD
AUTOMATION CAR SALES (PTY) LTD
AUTOMATION LEASING (PTY) LTD
BIFCO (PTY) LTD
BKF PROJECTS (PTY) LTD
CHURCHILL DRIVE INVESTMENTS (PTY) LTD
COMDATA (PTY) LTD
CONSOLIDATED PRODUCE CORPORATION (PTY) L
CORBANK MANAGEMENT CO (PTY) LTD (50%)
CORPORATE PORTFOLIO MANAGERS (PTY) LTD
DASHNIMS INVESTMENTS (PTY) LTD

DUAL EQUITY LTD
ERF 1149 MARSHALLTOWN (PTY) LTD
GILMET INVESTMENTS (PTY) LTD
GROWTHPOINT MANAGEMENT CO (PTY) LTD
GRS OVERSEAS ESTABLISHMENT (LIECHTENSTEI
HYDEWOODS (PTY) LTD
I KUPER & CO (PTY) LTD
INCITY REAL ESTATE (PTY) LTD
INTRUST MANAGEMENT CO LTD
INVESTEC ASSET MANAGEMENT LTD
INVESTEC INSURANCE BROKERS LTD
INVESTEC INTERNATIONAL HOLDINGS (PTY) LT
INVESTEC INVESTMENT TRUST LTD
INVESTEC LTD
INVESTEC MANAGEMENT CO LTD
INVESTEC MERCHANT BANK LTD
INVESTEC PROPERTY GROUP LTD
INVESTFIN HOLDINGS (PTY) LTD
JACKSONS METALS (PTY) LTD (20%)
KINGSWOOD PARK (PTY) LTD
KUPER COMPUTER MANAGEMENT SYSTEMS (PTY)
LEASING ACCEPTANCES (PTY) LTD
LIONEL ISAACS LEASING (PTY) LTD
MANLEV LEASING (PTY) LTD
MARKETING DEVELOPMENT CO SOUTHERN AFRICA
MCCAUL ASSOCIATES (PTY) LTD
METBOARD (NATAL) LTD
METBOARD (PRETORIA) (PTY) LTD
METBOARD LTD
METBOARD PARTICIPATION NOMINEES (PTY) LT
METBOARD PROPERTIES LTD
METBOARD PROPERTY FUND MANAGERS LTD
METBOARD PROPERTY MANAGEMENT (PTY) LTD
METBOARD TRUST CO (PTY) LTD
METEQUITY LTD
METPROP (NATAL) ADMINISTRATORS (PTY) LTD
METROPOLITAN BOARD BOND PARTICIPATION NO
METROPOLITAN BOARD NOMINEES LTD
METRUST LTD
MY-BOX (PTY) LTD
NATAL MORTGAGES (PTY) LTD
NEW LEASING & FINANCE TRUST (PTY) LTD
NORTHERN TRANSVAAL DISCOUNT CORPORATION
P-E COMPUTER & TELECOMMUNICATIONS (PTY)
P-E CONSULTING GROUP SA (PTY) LTD
PARAMOUNT LEASING (PTY) LTD
PARTNERS IN EQUITY LTD
PEPPER STREET INVESTMENTS (PTY) LTD
PROJAT (PTY) LTD
PROJEK ADMINISTRASIE TEGNIEK (EDMS) BPK
PYRAMID FINANCE CORPORATION LTD
RADLEASE (PTY) LTD
REICHMAN CREDIT (PTY) LTD
REICHMANS (U.K) LTD
REICHMANS FACTORS (PTY) LTD
REICHMANS INDUSTRIAL INVESTMENTS (PTY) L
REICHMANS INTERNATIONAL SHIPPING INC.
REICHMANS INVESTMENTS SA (SWITZERLAND)
REICHMANS LTD
REICHMANS SA (SWITZERLAND)
S L LEASING LTD
SANDTON SALES (PTY) LTD
SEACAT INVESTMENTS (PTY) LTD
SECURITY EXECUTOR & TRUST CO LTD
SECURITY TRUST BOND NOMINEES CO (PTY) LT
SECURITY TRUST NOMINEES (PTY) LTD
SEVENTY-NINE ROSEBANK (PTY) LTD
SURGE HOLDINGS LTD
THE PROFESSIONAL CONSULTING GROUP (PTY)
THRUPUT LTD
TRADE POWER (PTY) LTD
VAN FLYMEN & ASSOCIATES (PTY) LTD (50.1%)

INVESTMENTS

None

INVESTEC HOLDINGS LTD

ABBREVIATION : INHOLD

JSE SHORT CODE : INH

SECTOR : Financial-Banks & Financial Services

SHAREHOLDERS

Who Owns Whom's Assessment of the Identity of the Ultimate Controlling Shareholder: DIRECTORATE / MANAGEMENT

SHAREHOLDER	PERCENTAGE 1992	1991
FEDLIFE ASSURE LTD	37.9	---
INVESTEC NOM P/L	8.8	2.3
PT INV CO P/L	7.0	7.0
FIRST NAT NOM P/L	6.2	34.2
KANTOR B INV HOLDINGS P/L	4.2	3.3
SA MUTUAL	3.0	3.0
KOSEFF S INV HOLDINGS P/L	2.5	2.5
MOGWAI INV HOLDINGS P/L	1.8	1.8
KARDOL B INV HOLDINGS P/L	1.6	1.6
BLUE CHIP INV P/L	1.4	1.4
THOMAS P R S	1.4	1.4
INVESTEC HOLDINGS-DES S3 FIVE CONTR ACC	1.1	---
INVESTEC HOLDINGS POOL ACCOUNT	1.1	1.1
BURGER G R INV HOLDINGS P/L	1.0	1.0
SAFEGRO NOM P/L	---	13.1
CHALKTON NOM CO P/L	---	2.7
TOTAL	79.0	76.4

DIRECTORS :
BASSERABIE AI ,DAVIN GH ,KANTOR B
KANTOR IR (Chairman),KARDOL B (Deputy Chairman)
KOSEFF S ,LEWIS IMAW ,MITCHELL DH ,THOMAS PRS

REGISTRATION NUMBER : 85/05574/06

REGISTERED OFFICE
55 Fox Street, Johannesburg
2001
TEL: 011-498 2000
FAX: 011-498 2599

TRANSFER SECRETARY
Mercantile Registrars Ltd
P O Box 1053, Johannesburg
2000
TEL: 011-333 8181

COMPANY SECRETARY
Dr Nick D Steen

NATURE OF BUSINESS
The controlling company of Deposit-Taking JSE-quoted Investec Bank Ltd.

BANKERS :
Standard Bank of SA Ltd
Trust Bank of Africa Ltd

AUDITORS :
BDO Spencer Steward, Ernst & Young

FAMILIAR BRAND NAMES
N/A

CONTRIBUTION BY ACTIVITY
N/A

YEAR END : March

DIVIDEND : Ords 10c

Final No 10	(Ldr)17/05/91	(Pay)14/06/91	Amt(c)18
Interim No 11	(Ldr)08/11/91	(Pay)29/11/91	Amt(c)14
Final No 12	(Ldr)15/05/92	(Pay)13/06/92	Amt(c)22
Interim No 13	(Ldr)06/11/92	(Pay)29/11/92	Amt(c)21

NUMBER OF EMPLOYEES : 807

CAPITAL STRUCTURE

	AUTHORISED	ISSUED
Ords 10c	50000000	20000000
Var Rate Red Cum Prefs 50c	25000	19800
Cum Conv Prefs 10c	7000000	2000000

FINANCIAL STATISTICS (AT FINANCIAL YEAR END)

(Amts in R'000)	1992 Mar	1991 Mar	1990 Mar	1989 Mar	1988 Mar
Ord S/H Int	161075	93763	57000	45222	78620
Long Trm Loans	291375	124143	40752	36770	530
Iss Ord Share	20000	20000	20000	20000	20000
Total Liab	3460376	2803151	1249699	879777	635427
Current Liab	3169001	2679008	1208947	843007	634897
Total Assets	3586013	2859896	1285256	924999	714047
Intang Assets	35438	37018	21443	*	*
Current Assets	3224429	2753726	1250464	891341	686369
Oper Profit	39124	24792	17328	13994	11000
Prf af Int&Tax	39124	24792	17328	13994	11000
Prf att Ord Sh	19879	15561	10688	2977	11000
Btm Line Earn	19879	15561	10688	2977	11016
Dividend Paid	7200	5600	4000	3200	4800
Mkt Prce(c) YE	1525	710	390	200	375

PER SHARE STATISTICS (CENTS)

Net Asst Val	628.19	283.73	177.79	226.11	393.10
Net Earnings	99.40	77.80	53.40	38.60	27.50
Dividends	36.00	28.00	20.00	16.00	12.00
Cash Flow	75.77	62.41	53.44	14.89	55.00

RATIOS AND OTHER INFORMATION

Mrk Cap(R000)	305000	142000	78000	40000	75000
Current Ratio	1.02	1.03	1.03	1.06	1.08
Quik/Acid Tst	1.02	1.03	1.03	1.06	1.08
Debt/Ass Rat	0.88	0.94	0.94	0.91	0.89
Debt to Eqity	19.67	28.57	21.21	18.64	8.08
Ret on Assets	1.27	0.97	1.35	1.51	1.54
Ret on Equity%	12.34	16.60	18.75	6.58	13.99
Price/Earnings	15.34	9.13	7.30	5.18	13.64
Divid Cover	2.76	2.78	2.67	2.41	2.29
Divid Yield	2.36	3.94	5.13	8.00	3.20
Earning Yield%	6.52	10.96	13.69	19.30	7.33
NAV % Mrk Pr	41.19	39.96	45.59	113.06	104.83
Def Interval	216.02	221.55	114.65	288.89	57.45
Sus Grth Rate	7.87	10.62	11.73	-0.49	7.89

SUBSIDIARY & ASSOCIATED COMPANIES

INVESTEC BANK LTD
INVESTEC GROUP DATA LIMITED

INVESTMENTS

None

INVESTEC INVESTMENT TRUST LTD

ABBREVIATION : INTRUST

JSE SHORT CODE : ITT

SECTOR : Financial-Investment Trusts

SHAREHOLDERS

Who Owns Whom's Assessment of the Identity of the Ultimate Controlling Shareholder:
INVESTEC LTD / FEDSURE

SHAREHOLDER	PERCENTAGE 1992	1991
INVESTEC INV LTD	47.8	70.5
STD BANK NOM TVL P/L	46.6	25.0
BROUZE D S	3.0	---
DALGLAND NOM P/L	---	1.6
TOTAL	97.3	97.0

DIRECTORS :
BASSERABIE AI ,KANTOR B ,KARDOL B (Chairman)
KOSEFF S ,WOOD C

REGISTRATION NUMBER : 05/24756/06

REGISTERED OFFICE
55 Fox Street, Johannesburg
2001
TEL: 011-498 2710
FAX: 011-498 2795

TRANSFER SECRETARY
Mercantile Registrars Ltd
P O Box 1053, Johannesburg
2000
TEL: 011-333 8181

COMPANY SECRETARY
Investec Merchant Bank Ltd

NATURE OF BUSINESS
An investment holding company holding a portfolio of shares in listed medium-sized companies.

BANKERS :
Trust Bank of Africa Ltd

AUDITORS :
N/A

FAMILIAR BRAND NAMES
N/A

CONTRIBUTION BY ACTIVITY
N/A

YEAR END : March

DIVIDEND :Ords 1c

Interim	(Ldr)30/03/91	(Pay)25/04/91	Amt(c)25
Final	(Ldr)19/07/91	(Pay)01/08/91	Amt(c)62
Interim	(Ldr)11/01/92	(Pay)01/02/92	Amt(c)36
Final	(Ldr)05/06/92	(Pay)19/06/92	Amt(c)45
Final	(Ldr)30/06/91	(Pay)01/08/91	Amt(c)62
Interim	(Ldr)27/11/92	(Pay)04/12/92	Amt(c)36

CAPITAL STRUCTURE

	AUTHORISED	ISSUED
Ords 1c	12000000	2089726

FINANCIAL STATISTICS (AT FINANCIAL YEAR END)

(Amts in R'000)	1992 Mar	1991 Mar	1989 Sep	1988 Sep	1987
Ord S/H Int	47545	22089	3797	3785	3790
Long Trm Loans	-	-	-	-	257
Iss Ord Share	2028	1226	920	920	920
Total Liab	1372	938	257	252	514
Current Liab	1372	938	257	252	257
Total Assets	48917	23027	4054	4037	4308
Current Assets	2706	2552	270	253	262
Debtors	360	150	253	253	-
Inventory	-	-	-	-	262
Turnover	-	-	-	255	-
Oper Profit	-340	-167	-43	216	480
Tax Paid	201	84	1	-	1
Prf af Int&Tax	1327	1044	380	216	479
Prf att Ord Sh	1327	1044	380	216	479
Btm Line Earn	1327	1044	380	216	479
Dividend Paid	1353	990	368	221	478
Mkt Prce(c) YE	2000	1700	1800	1850	3600

PER SHARE STATISTICS (CENTS)

Net Asst Val	2344 43	1801 71	412 72	411 41	411 96
Net Earnings	99 70	98 80	41 30	23 50	-
Dividends	81 00	87 00	40 00	24 00	-
Cash Flow	99 70	56 77	41 30	23 48	52 07

RATIOS AND OTHER INFORMATION

Mrk Cap(R000)	40560	20842	16560	17020	33120
Current Ratio	1 97	2 72	1 05	1 00	1 02
Quik/Acid Tst	1 97	2 72	1 05	1 00	-
A/C Rec T/ovr	-	-	-	1 01	-
Tot Ass T/ovr	-	-	-	0 06	-
Debt/Ass Rat	0 03	0 04	0 06	0 06	0 12
L T L Tot Ass	-	-	-	-	0 06
Debt to Eqity	0 03	0 04	0 07	0 07	0 14
Oper Prof Mrg	-	-	-	84 71	-
Net Prof Marg%	-	-	-	84 71	-
Ret on Assets	3 12	3 27	9 40	5 35	11 14
Ret on Equity%	2 79	3 15	10 01	5 71	12 64
Price/Earnings	20 06	17 21	43 58	78 72	-
Divid Cover	1 23	1 14	1 03	0 98	-
Divid Yield	4 05	5 12	2 22	1 30	-
Earning Yield%	4 98	5 81	2 29	1 27	-
NAV % Mrk Pr	117 22	105 98	22 93	22 24	11 44
Effec Tax Rate	318 75	67 74	-2 50	-	0 21
Def Interval	-	-	-	-	0 54
Sus Grth Rate	-0 05	0 24	0 32	-0 13	0 03

SUBSIDIARY & ASSOCIATED COMPANIES

FENNER GROUP SA LTD (28,4%)

INVESTMENTS

BERZACK BROTHERS HOLDINGS LTD (350006 SH)
FEDSURE HOLDINGS LTD (2000000SH)
THE BIDVEST GROUP LTD (CONV DEB SH) (353798SH)

INVICTA HOLDINGS LTD

ABBREVIATION : INVICTA

JSE SHORT CODE : IVT

SECTOR : Development Capital Market

SHAREHOLDERS

Who Owns Whom's Assessment of the Identity of the Ultimate Controlling Shareholder:
DL MCCKAY

SHAREHOLDER	PERCENTAGE 1992	1991
FIRST NAT NOM P/L	65 8	82 2
TITAN NOM P/L	9 4	---
ELLENMARY NOM P/L	8 6	---
CMB NOM P/L	3 1	---
STD BANK NOM TVL P/L	1 9	---
PROTEA ASSURE CO PENS FUND	1 5	4 1
ZANUSSI CO LTD	1 1	2 9
LYNARA HOLDINGS LTD	1 1	---
NORTH PENS FUND	1 1	- -
LEMON LANE NOM CC	---	1 2
DU PLESSIS M	---	2 0
TOTAL	93 4	92 4

DIRECTORS :
BREVAL BJ (Deputy Chairman),GOLDSTONE A
MCCAY DL (Chairman)
ROSE-INNES M (Chief Executive),WHITE DJA

REGISTRATION NUMBER : 66/02182/06

REGISTERED OFFICE
Nova Constantia, Nova Constantia Road
Constantia
7800
TEL 021-794 5141
FAX 021-794 2463

TRANSFER SECRETARY
Fraser Street Registrars (Pty) Ltd
P O Box 61178, Marshalltown
2107
TEL 011-491 0911

COMPANY SECRETARY
A Goldstone

NATURE OF BUSINESS
The business of the company is the marketing of bearings and transmission equipment, the manufacturing of rugby, cricket and hockey balls,

distributor of sports goods.

BANKERS :
Volkskas Ltd, Trust Bank of Africa Ltd
Standard Bank of SA Ltd

AUDITORS :
Kessel Feinstein

FAMILIAR BRAND NAMES
MITRE,SUPER SPRINGBOK

CONTRIBUTION BY ACTIVITY
Engineering (% Turnover) (59.2%)
Fabrics (13.5%)
Communications (20.8%)
Sports Goods (6.5%)

YEAR END : December

DIVIDEND :15/06/91

CAPITAL STRUCTURE

	AUTHORISED	ISSUED
Ords 5c	70000000	46988350
16% Unsec Conv Red Debs 100c	14068000	7034000
14% Comp Conv Prefs 5c	14000000	8500000

FINANCIAL STATISTICS (AT FINANCIAL YEAR END)

(Amts in R'000)	1991 Mar	1991 Dec	1990 Mar
Ord S/H Int	-5835	17636	4266
Long Trm Loans	44102	21370	20813
Iss Ord Share	4520	46988	22600
Total Liab	83103	50370	27371
Current Liab	39001	29000	6558
Total Assets	62635	54288	27232
Intang Assets	14633	13718	4405
Current Assets	42115	40781	8074
Debtors	12981	11149	4731
Inventory	29134	29632	2671
Turnover	-	-	11818
Oper Profit	1594	4101	1043
Interest Paid	3477	3562	1804
Prf af Int&Tax	-383	1339	-761
Prf att Ord Sh	-873	254	-761
Btm Line Earn	-11267	-6600	-1274
Mkt Prce(c) YE	120	60	20
Depreciation	655	1271	509

PER SHARE STATISTICS (CENTS)

Net Asst Val	-452.83	8.34	-0.62
Net Earnings	-19.30	1.80	2.80
Cash Flow	-4.82	4.33	-1.12

RATIOS AND OTHER INFORMATION

Mrk Cap(R000)	5424	28193	4520
Current Ratio	1.08	1.41	1.23
Quik/Acid Tst	0.33	0.38	0.82
A/C Rec T/ovr	-	-	2.50
Tot Ass T/ovr	-	-	0.43
Debt/Ass Rat	1.10	0.78	0.99
L T L Tot Ass	0.48	0.24	0.75
Debt to Eqity	-11.82	2.39	6.33
Interest Cover	0.89	1.38	0.58
Oper Prof Mrg	-	-	8.83
Net Prof Marg%	-	-	-6.44
Ret on Assets	4.94	12.04	3.83
Ret on Equity%	14.96	1.92	-15.31
Price/Earnings	-6.22	33.33	7.14
Earning Yield%	-16.08	3.00	14.00
NAV % Mrk Pr	-377.36	13.90	-3.08
Def Interval	-140.38	13.68	-39.19
Sus Grth Rate	14.96	1.44	-17.84

SUBSIDIARY & ASSOCIATED COMPANIES

ATLAS MARINE ENGINEERING (PTY) LTD - ATL
MANX MANUFACTURING (PTY) LTD
NTN BEARINGS SA (PTY) LTD
SUBNOVA (PTY) LTD
TABLE BAY ENGINEERING (PTY) LTD
TABLE BAY HOLDINGS (PTY) LTD
TSUBAKI SA (PTY) LTD

INVESTMENTS

INVICTA BEARINGS (PTY) LTD (CONV DEBS) (40%)

IRVIN & JOHNSON LTD

ABBREVIATION : I-&-J

JSE SHORT CODE : IRV

SECTOR : Industrial-Food

SHAREHOLDERS

Who Owns Whom's Assessment of the Identity of the Ultimate Controlling Shareholder: ANGLOVAAL

SHAREHOLDER	PERCENTAGE 1992	1991
ANGLOVAAL IND LTD	68.2	68.5
STD BANK NOM TVL P/L	5.6	4.7
CMB NOM P/L	3.4	---
I & J EMPLOYEE SHARE PURC TRUST LTD	2.4	2.1
SIXTY SIX MARSHALL STREET NOM P/L	2.1	2.1
EIGHTY ONE MAIN STREET NOM LTD	1.7	---
AECI PENS FUND	1.4	1.4
PROFESSIONAL PROV SOC OF SA	1.2	1.2
SHARESTOCK NOM P/L	1.1	1.1
SYFRETS NOM LTD	---	1.2
ANGLOVAAL PENS FUND	---	1.0
SANLAM	---	3.2
TOTAL	87.0	86.6

DIRECTORS :
ATKINS CA ,GORDON RC ,HERSOV BE ,MENELL CS
MORRISON JT ,ROBBERTZE JC (Chairman),SAVAGE RB
WILLIAMS JJ (Deputy Chairman

REGISTRATION NUMBER : 52/01693/06

REGISTERED OFFICE
20th Floor, Standard Bank Centre
Heerengracht, Cape Town
8001
TEL: 021-21 6400
FAX: 021-21 5993

TRANSFER SECRETARY
Anglovaal Ltd
P O Box 62379, Marshalltown
2107
TEL 011-634 9111

COMPANY SECRETARY
CA Schoeman

NATURE OF BUSINESS
Procuring, processing, marketing & distribution of especially frozen foodstuffs, including fish, vegetables, pastry products, pizza's, bottled pickles & condiments The group operates its own fleet of fishing trawlers & road distribution vehicles Vegetables are grown under contract

BANKERS :
Standard Bank of SA Ltd

AUDITORS :
Ernst & Young

FAMILIAR BRAND NAMES
CARMEL,I & J,OCEAN FRESH,RAINBOW CHICKENS
READ-Y DOE,RONDO,SARA LEE,YOUNG & TENDER

CONTRIBUTION BY ACTIVITY
N/A

YEAR END : June

DIVIDEND : Ords 50c

Dividend No 43	(Ldr)15/09/89	(Pay)13/10/89	Amt(c)70
Dividend No 44	(Ldr)14/09/90	(Pay)12/10/90	Amt(c)70
Dividend No 45	(Ldr)13/09/91	(Pay)11/10/91	Amt(c)78
Dividend No 46	(Ldr)11/09/92	(Pay)09/10/92	Amt(c)86

NUMBER OF EMPLOYEES : 7000

CAPITAL STRUCTURE

	AUTHORISED	ISSUED
Ords 50c	32300000	28733200
6% Unsec Auto Conv Sub Debs R34	2886900	2886900

FINANCIAL STATISTICS (AT FINANCIAL YEAR END)

(Amts In R 000)	1992 Jun	1991 Jun	1990 Jun	1989 Jun	1988 Jun
Ord S/H Int	351152	307895	252898	218445	167872
Long Trm Loans	160188	70762	80992	66419	64044
Iss Ord Share	28733	28557	28542	28281	28254
Total Liab	368601	277781	251769	238524	199383
Current Liab	208413	207019	170777	172105	135339
Total Assets	710692	575534	496157	456969	367255
Intang Assets	9061	10142	8510	*	*
Current Assets	479445	382214	323653	293917	235564
Debtors	208457	166499	140693	146797	110102
Inventory	155080	138899	120847	105915	74893
Turnover	1638490	1413889	1257274	1094045	889639
Oper Profit	107419	97195	89131	103120	85462
Interest Paid	10724	5533	6625	7635	5150
Tax Paid	34295	31203	32220	37411	29770
Prf af Int&Tax	73881	67217	57992	65409	50542
Prf att Ord Sh	74019	67177	58039	65589	50659
Btm Line Earn	74019	67177	56289	65589	50659
Dividend Paid	24711	22278	19983	19806	15540
Mkt Prce(c) YE	4400	3225	2100	2375	1435
Depreciation	31039	27305	23905	20383	15668

PER SHARE STATISTICS (CENTS)

Net Asst Val	1190 59	1042 66	856 24	772 41	594 15
Net Earnings	258 40	235 20	203 30	231 90	179 30
Dividends	86 00	78 00	70 00	70 00	55 00
Cash Flow	358 77	299 77	306 29	310 39	245 37

RATIOS AND OTHER INFORMATION

Mrk Cap(R000)	1264252	920963	599382	671674	405445
Current Ratio	2 30	1 85	1 90	1 71	1 74
Quik/Acid Tst	1 56	1 18	1 19	1 09	1 19
A/C Rec T/ovr	7 86	8 49	8 94	7 45	8 08
Tot Ass T/ovr	2 31	2 46	2 53	2 39	2 42
Debt/Ass Rat	0 45	0 40	0 41	0 46	0 47
L T L Tot Ass	0 16	0 04	0 07	0 08	0 10
Debt to Eqity	0 92	0 75	0 81	0 96	1 04
Interest Cover	10 02	17 58	13 47	13 54	16 59
Oper Prof Mrg	6 56	6 87	7 09	9 43	9 61
Net Prof Marg%	4 52	4 75	4 62	6 00	5 69
Ret on Assets	16 75	18 06	19 53	24 21	23 30
Ret on Equity%	21 08	21 82	22 95	30 03	30 18
Price/Earnings	17 03	13 71	10 33	10 24	8 00
Divid Cover	3 00	3 02	2 90	3 31	3 26
Divid Yield	1 95	2 42	3 33	2 95	3 83
Earning Yield%	5 87	7 29	9 68	9 76	12 49
NAV % Mrk Pr	27 06	32 33	40 77	32 52	41 40
Effec Tax Rate	32 88	40 19	29 70	34 55	32 30
Def Interval	0 24	0 52	0 53	0 67	0 77
Sus Grth Rate	14 04	14 56	15 05	20 96	20 92

SUBSIDIARY & ASSOCIATED COMPANIES

CAPENSIS FISHING COMPANY (PTY) LTD (50%)
CONCENTRA LTD
FRIEDMAN & RABINOWITZ (PTY) LTD
IRVIN & JOHNSON (MOSSEL BAY) LTD
IRVIN & JOHNSON (PORT ELIZABETH) LTD
IRVIN & JOHNSON (TRANSVAAL) LTD
IRVIN & JOHNSON (TRAWLERS) LTD
IRVIN & JOHNSON FINANCE CO (PTY) LTD
MOZAMBIQUE FISHING INVESTMENTS (PTY) LTD
OOSKUS VISSERYE (EDMS) BPK
SPRINGBOK SKYFIES & VOEDSELVERWERKERS (P
STERLING FISHERIES & COLD STORAGE (PTY)
STRUISBAAI FISHERIES (PTY) LTD
TRAWLER ENGINEERING CO LTD
TSS LTD
WALKER BAY CANNERS LTD

INVESTMENTS

NATAL OCEAN TRAWLING LTD (8,8%)
RAINBOW CHICKEN LTD (12,5% CUM PREFS) (100%)

ISCOR LTD

ABBREVIATION : ISCOR

JSE SHORT CODE : ISC

SECTOR : Industrial-Steel & Allied

SHAREHOLDERS

Who Owns Whom's Assessment of the Identity of the Ultimate Controlling Shareholder:
MINORITY HOLDERS

SHAREHOLDER	PERCENTAGE 1992	1991
IND DEVELOPMENT CORP SA LTD	16 1	16 1
STD BANK NOM TVL P/L	12 8	13 7
SA MUTUAL	10 1	10 0
CMB NOM P/L	9 8	---
EIGHTY ONE MAIN STREET NOM LTD	6 4	7 5
SOUTHERN LIFE ASSOC LTD	5 8	6 5
RESIDENT NOM LTD	3 1	3 1
METAL IND GROUP PENS FUND	3 0	2 9
ENGINEERING INDUSTRIES PENS FUND	2 2	2 1
YSKOR PENS FUND	2 0	2 0
SIXTY SIX MARSHALL STREET NOM P/L	1 6	1 5
STATE (ISCOR) SHARE TRUST	1 5	1 6
CONSOLIDATED NOM P/L	1 0	1 0
FIRST NAT NOM P/L	---	1 5
SANLAM	---	2 4
SANKERN E/B	---	3 2
TOTAL	75 4	74 9

DIRECTORS :
CLEWLOW WAM ,DE BEER TL ,DE WAAL MT DR (Chairman)
FENTON CT ,KAHN JM ,MORUM GP
OLIVIER PA (Deputy Managing Director)
VAN DEN BERG JL ,VAN WYK CJ DR
VAN WYK W (Managing Director

REGISTRATION NUMBER : 89/02164/06

REGISTERED OFFICE
Iscor Head Office Building, Roger Dyason Road
Pretoria West
0002
TEL 012-298 1111
FAX 012-326 2823

TRANSFER SECRETARY
Central Registrars Ltd
P O Box 4844, Johannesburg
2000
TEL 011-331 0051

COMPANY SECRETARY
A C Greyling

NATURE OF BUSINESS
Production and marketing of iron and steel products Certain mining operations are also undertaken as ancillary activities

BANKERS :
First National Bank of SA Ltd
Standard Bank of SA Ltd
Trust Bank of Africa Ltd, Volkskas Ltd
Nedcor Bank Ltd

AUDITORS :
KPMG Aiken & Peat

FAMILIAR BRAND NAMES
N/A

CONTRIBUTION BY ACTIVITY
National (% Steel Sales) (47 0%)
Export (53 0%)

YEAR END : June

DIVIDEND : Ords 100c

Interim No 1	(Ldr)16/03/90	(Pay)30/03/90	Amt(c)2
Final No 2	(Ldr)14/09/90	(Pay)19/10/90	Amt(c)12 2
Interim No 3	(Ldr)15/03/91	(Pay)02/04/91	Amt(c)4 5
Final No 4	(Ldr)13/09/91	(Pay)18/10/91	Amt(c)6 5
Interim No 5	(Ldr)13/03/92	(Pay)31/03/92	Amt(c)3
Final No 6	(Ldr)11/09/92	(Pay)16/10/92	Amt(c)3

NUMBER OF EMPLOYEES : 56500

CAPITAL STRUCTURE

	AUTHORISED	ISSUED
Ords 100c (000's)	5000000000	1868937500

FINANCIAL STATISTICS (AT FINANCIAL YEAR END)

(Amts in R'000)	1992 Jun	1991 Jun	1990 Jun	1989 Jun	1988
Ord S/H Int	6753600	6519800	6102500	5450700	4085471
Long Trm Loans	1713500	1122400	891600	796700	1816351
Iss Ord Share	1868937	1867588	1866407	1499600	-
Total Liab	3864100	3177500	2412300	2261400	2860220
Current Liab	2150600	2055100	1520700	1464700	1043869
Total Assets	10617700	9697300	8514800	7712100	7747494
Current Assets	3696300	3266600	2822600	2752500	1845672
Debtors	1039000	990500	824700	804600	-
Inventory	2187100	2172500	1829200	1361600	1845672
Turnover	8616100	7391900	6916100	5949700	4820249
Oper Profit	678300	796000	1128800	1182900	470465
Interest Paid	402600	233600	120800	134600	129598
Tax Paid	3300	32400	259100	327100	89398
Prf af Int&Tax	342200	608400	935400	807800	248574
Prf att Ord Sh	345900	623600	929200	811700	245585
Btm Line Earn	347400	605800	932200	826300	245585
Dividend Paid	112100	205400	327600	224900	64890
Mkt Prce(c) YE	137	212	198	-	-
Depreciation	380100	319600	269500	254500	

PER SHARE STATISTICS (CENTS)

Net Asst Val	361 36	349 10	326 97	363 48	-
Net Earnings	18 50	33 00	50 10	43 90	-
Dividends	6 00	11 00	17 60	12 20	-
Cash Flow	38 37	49 88	64 29	56 79	-

RATIOS AND OTHER INFORMATION

Mrk Cap(R000)	2560444	3959287	3695486	-	
Current Ratio	1 72	1 59	1 86	1 88	1 77
Quik/Acid Tst	0 70	0 53	0 65	0 95	
A/C Rec T/ovr	8 29	7 46	8 39	7 39	-
Tot Ass T/ovr	0 81	0 76	0 81	0 77	0 62
Debt/Ass Rat	0 36	0 33	0 28	0 29	0 37
L T L Tot Ass	0 16	0 11	0 10	0 10	0 23
Debt to Eqity	0 57	0 48	0 39	0 41	0 70
Interest Cover	1 75	3 44	9 57	8 92	3 61
Oper Prof Mrg	7 87	10 77	16 32	19 88	9 76
Net Prof Marg%	4 01	8 44	13 44	13 64	5 09
Ret on Assets	7 09	9 23	15 56	16 67	6 04
Ret on Equity%	5 12	9 56	15 23	14 89	6 01
Price/Earnings	7 41	6 42	3 95	-	-
Divid Cover	3 08	3 00	2 85	3 60	-
Divid Yield	4 38	5 19	8 89	-	-
Earning Yield%	13 50	15 57	25 30	-	
NAV % Mrk Pr	263 77	164 67	165 13	-	-
Effec Tax Rate	2 57	3 74	21 97	29 21	26 23
Def Interval	3 28	1 96	0 75	0 76	7 31
Sus Grth Rate	3 46	6 41	9 86	10 77	4 42

SUBSIDIARY & ASSOCIATED COMPANIES

BALATON HOLDINGS (PTY) LTD
CAPE TOWN IRON AND STEEL WORKS (PTY) LTD
COASTAL COAL (PTY) LTD
CONSOLIDATED WIRE INDUSTRIES LTD (50%)

CULLINAN REFRACTORIES (50%)
DALESTONE (PTY) LTD
DONKERHOEK QUARTZITE (PTY) LTD
DUNSWART IRON & STEEL WORKS LTD
DURBAN NAVIGATION COLLIERIES (PTY) LTD
FERROLAND GRONDTRUST (PTY) LTD
HECKETT SA (PTY) LTD (50%)
IMCOR TIN (PTY) LTD (NAMIBIA)
IMCOR ZINC (PTY) LTD (NAMIBIA)
ISCOR BERLIN (PTY) LTD
ISTORES (PTY) LTD THE
METKOR GROUP LTD (25.8%)
MINSA (PTY) LTD
NATIONAL METAL (PTY) LTD
PIETERSBURG IRON CO. (PTY) LTD (50%)
SAFORE (40%)
SAFORE (PTY) LTD (40%)
SISHEN SHIPPING (PTY) LTD (40%)
STEEL SALES CO. OF AFRICA (PTY) LTD
STEELFORCE (PTY) LTD
STEELREC (PTY) LTD
SUPRACHEM (PTY) LTD
TOSA SEAMLESS TUBES (TST) (40%)
TSHIKONDENI MINING CO. (PTY) LTD (VENDA)
USKO LTD (28,6%)
VANTIN (PTY) LTD
VRYHEID (NATAL) RAILWAY COAL & IRON CO.
YSKOR NEWCASTLE GRONDBESIT LTD
ZINC CORP. OF SA LTD (35%)

INVESTMENTS

None

ITALTILE LTD

ABBREVIATION : ITLTILE

JSE SHORT CODE : ITE

SECTOR : Industrial-Building & Construction

SHAREHOLDERS

Who Owns Whom's Assessment of the Identity of the Ultimate Controlling Shareholder: GAM RAVAZOTTI

SHAREHOLDER	PERCENTAGE 1992	1991
RALLEN P/L	57.6	60.2
ALTINI T G	7.8	8.1
GREENWAY R	5 3	5 5
RAKE INV P/L	5.0	5 2
SAFEGRO NOM P/L	4.5	---
DE GRANDIS G	3.9	4.1
MAESTRO SECURITIES P/L	3.1	1.2
SMK NOM P/L	2.3	2.4
ALTINI T	1.8	2.5
COUZIS J	---	1.1
RONSAND RANCH P/L	---	1 9
TOTAL	91.1	92.3

DIRECTORS :
ALTINI T ,COUZIS J ,GIATTAS G ,KEYSER M ,RABIN D
RAVAZZOTTI GAM (Chairman),SWATTON PD

REGISTRATION NUMBER : 55/00558/06

REGISTERED OFFICE
Italtile Centre, Cnr Burke & Hendrik Verwoerd
Randburg
2194
TEL: 011-886 4764
FAX: 011-789 1387

TRANSFER SECRETARY
Mercantile Registrars Ltd
P O Box 1053, Johannesburg
2000
TEL: 011-333 8181

COMPANY SECRETARY
P D Swatton

NATURE OF BUSINESS
The group retails ceramic wall and floor tiles, ceramic sanitaryware, brassware, extruded split tiles and bathroom accessories. Operations are conducted via 5 Italtile centres, and 14 Ceramic Tile Market (CTM) outlets. Five outlets operate as franchised CTM stores.

BANKERS :
Nedperm Bank Ltd

AUDITORS :
Ernst & Young

FAMILIAR BRAND NAMES
CTM,ITALTILE CENTRE

CONTRIBUTION BY ACTIVITY
N/A

YEAR END : June

DIVIDEND : Ords no par value

Final No 48	(Ldr)04/05/90	(Pay)15/06/90	Amt(c)12
Interim No 49	(Ldr)19/10/90	(Pay)16/11/90	Amt(c)6
Final No 50	(Ldr)26/04/91	(Pay)17/05/91	Amt(c)12
Interim No 51	(Ldr)01/11/91	(Pay)22/11/91	Amt(c)8
Final No 52	(Ldr)15/05/92	(Pay)05/06/92	Amt(c)6

NUMBER OF EMPLOYEES : 368

CAPITAL STRUCTURE

	AUTHORISED	ISSUED
Ords no par value	75000000	17950742

FINANCIAL STATISTICS (AT FINANCIAL YEAR END)

(Amts in R'000)	1992 Feb	1991 Feb	1990 Feb	1989 Feb	1988 Feb
Ord S/H Int	49439	93413	82836	62108	15425
Long Trm Loans	22476	37459	7293	2116	6032
Iss Ord Share	17951	17162	17021	16956	1930
Total Liab	64225	67360	41906	23022	13095
Current Liab	41749	29901	34613	20906	7063
Total Assets	113664	158773	122742	83130	28520
Intang Assets	*	2000	2000	2000	*
Current Assets	62093	52864	42279	40830	12198
Debtors	18174	14801	13874	11132	8903
Inventory	23336	26880	23564	16368	2906
Turnover	-	-	-	98300	54947
Oper Profit	16354	21630	23022	17086	2504

Interest Paid	3899	2242	265	233	639
Tax Paid	5197	8973	9652	5704	813
Prf af Int&Tax	11768	13033	15767	13151	1052
Prf att Ord Sh	11768	13033	15798	13076	841
Btm Line Earn	11768	13033	17493	5490	637
Dividend Paid	60474	3089	3081	2544	96
Mkt Prce(c) YE	350	375	420	370	385
Depreciation	6506	7538	6644	5093	577

PER SHARE STATISTICS (CENTS)

Net Asst Val	275 41	532 65	474 92	354 49	799 22
Net Earnings	67 00	76 10	92 90	79 00	75 70
Dividends	14 00	18 00	18 00	15 00	-
Cash Flow	96 38	171 69	144 97	121 04	99 48

RATIOS AND OTHER INFORMATION

Mrk Cap(R000)	62829	64358	71488	62737	7431
Current Ratio	1 49	1 76	1 22	1 95	1 73
Quik/Acid Tst	0 93	0 86	0 54	1 17	1 32
A/C Rec T/ovr	-	-	-	9 63	6 17
Tot Ass T/ovr	-	-	-	1 29	1 93
Debt/Ass Rat	0 53	0 35	0 32	0 26	0 42
L T L Tot Ass	0 16	0 16	0 04	0 01	0 17
Debt to Eqity	1 21	0 60	0 47	0 35	0 78
Interest Cover	4 69	9 94	96 92	81 92	3 92
Oper Prof Mrg	-	-		17 38	4 56
Net Prof Marg%	-	-	-	13 30	1 53
Ret on Assets	18 36	15 27	20 93	25 05	8 78
Ret on Equity%	23 80	13 95	19 07	22 97	5 45
Price/Earnings	5 22	4 93	4 52	4 68	5 09
Divid Cover	4 79	4 23	5 16	5 27	-
Divid Yield	4 00	4 80	4 29	4 05	-
Earning Yield%	19 14	20 29	22 12	21 35	19 66
NAV % Mrk Pr	78 69	142 04	113 08	95 81	207 59
Effec Tax Rate	45 38	0 53	35 26	29 26	7 13
Def Interval	1 07	0 87	0 18	0 05	2 57
Sus Grth Rate	-98 52	10 65	15 35	16 96	4 83

SUBSIDIARY & ASSOCIATED COMPANIES

ALMUSS PROPERTIES (PTY) LTD
CERAMIC TILE MARKET (EAST LONDON) (PTY)
CERAMIC TILE MARKET (EASTERN CAPE) (PTY)
CERAMIC TILE MARKET (GEORGE) (PTY) LTD
CERAMIC TILE MARKET (PTY) LTD
CTM PROPERTIES (RANDBURG) (PTY) LTD
F B ASHMAN (PTY) LTD
FRANJOH (PTY) LTD
ITALTILE CAPE (PTY) LTD
ITALTILE CERAMICS LTD
ITALTILE HOLDINGS (PTY) LTD
ITALTILE NATAL (PTY) LTD
ITALTILE PRETORIA (PTY) LTD
ITALTILE PRODUCTS (PTY) LTD
ITALTILE TWO (PTY) LTD
LSD PROPERTIES (PTY) LTD
NADJA INVESTMENTS (PTY) LTD
ROLROSE INVESTMENTS (PTY) LTD

INVESTMENTS

CONSPICUOUS INVESTMENTS (PTY) LTD
INVESTEC LTD
RUSFERN SECOND EXECUTIVE PARTICIPATION (

JAFF-DELSWA INVESTMENTS LTD

ABBREVIATION : JADE

JSE SHORT CODE : JAD

SECTOR : Industrial-Clothing, Footwear & Textiles

SHAREHOLDERS

Who Owns Whom's Assessment of the Identity of the Ultimate Controlling Shareholder:
JAFF FAMILY

SHAREHOLDER	PERCENTAGE 1992	1991
MONITOR INV P/L	56 0	56 0
JAFF P	9 3	9 3
FERBROS NOM P/L	6 5	7 5
JAFF S L	5 6	5 6
VOLKSKAS NOM P/L	3 1	3 1
JAFF S H	2 6	2 6
INBARR J G	2 6	2 6
COHEN J S	2 5	2 5
STD BANK NOM TVL P/L	2 2	1 1
TOTAL	90 4	90 3

DIRECTORS :
JAFF NR ,JAFF P ,JAFF PH (Financial Director)
JAFF SH (Managing Director)
JAFF SL (Executive Chairman),LAIRD SMITH A
MURRAY C ,PECHEY NR

REGISTRATION NUMBER : 68/04284/06

REGISTERED OFFICE
104 President Street, Johannesburg
2001
TEL 011-337 3131
FAX 011-333 3336

TRANSFER SECRETARY
Mercantile Registrars Ltd
P O Box 1053, Johannesburg
2000
TEL 011-333 8181

COMPANY SECRETARY
N R Pechey

NATURE OF BUSINESS
An investment holding company with a controlling interest in JSE-quoted Delswa Ltd

BANKERS :
Standard Bank of SA Ltd

AUDITORS :
KPMG Aiken & Peat

FAMILIAR BRAND NAMES
SEE DELSWA

CONTRIBUTION BY ACTIVITY
N/A

YEAR END : April

DIVIDEND : Ords 25c
Interim No 41 (Ldr)02/02/90 (Pay)20/02/90 Amt(c)3 75

Final No 42	(Ldr)02/07/90	(Pay)17/08/90	Amt(c)5 5
Interim No 43	(Ldr)01/02/91	(Pay)22/02/91	Amt(c)3 75
Final No 44	(Ldr)19/07/91	(Pay)16/08/91	Amt(c)6 75
Interim No 45	(Ldr)07/02/92	(Pay)21/02/92	Amt(c)3 75
Final No 46	(Ldr)24/07/92	(Pay)21/08/92	Amt(c)5 5

CAPITAL STRUCTURE

	AUTHORISED	ISSUED
Ords 25c	3200000	3198900

FINANCIAL STATISTICS (AT FINANCIAL YEAR END)

(Amts in R'000)	1992 Apr	1991 Apr	1990 Apr	1989 Apr	1988 Apr
Ord S/H Int	2553	2551	2551	2551	2551
Iss Ord Share	3199	3199	3199	1599	1599
Total Liab	198	233	190	309	262
Current Liab	198	233	190	309	262
Total Assets	2751	2784	2741	2860	2813
Current Assets	473	506	463	594	547
Oper Profit	-23	-19	-28	385	325
Tax Paid	24	25	27	22	16
Prf af Int&Tax	298	336	295	409	342
Prf att Ord Sh	298	336	295	409	342
Btm Line Earn	298	336	295	409	342
Dividend Paid	296	336	296	408	342
Mkt Prce(c) YE	105	135	160	360	225

PER SHARE STATISTICS (CENTS)

Net Asst Val	79 81	79 74	79 74	159 54	159 54
Net Earnings	9 33	10 49	9 23	12 75	10 70
Dividends	9 25	10 50	9 25	12 75	10 70
Cash Flow	9 32	10 50	9 22	25 58	21 39

RATIOS AND OTHER INFORMATION

Mrk Cap(R000)	3359	4319	5118	5756	3598
Current Ratio	2 39	2 17	2 44	1 92	2 09
Quik/Acid Tst	2 39	2 17	2 44	1 92	2 09
Debt/Ass Rat	0 07	0 08	0 07	0 11	0 09
Debt to Eqity	0 08	0 09	0 07	0 12	0 10
Ret on Assets	11 70	12 97	11 75	15 07	12 73
Ret on Equity%	11 67	13 17	11 56	16 03	13 41
Price/Earnings	11 25	12 87	17 33	28 24	21 03
Divid Cover	1 01	1 00	1 00	1 00	1 00
Divid Yield	8 81	7 78	5 78	3 54	4 76
Earning Yield%	8 89	7 77	5 77	3 54	4 76
NAV % Mrk Pr	76 01	59 07	49 84	44 32	70 91
Effec Tax Rate	80 00	67 57	90 00	5 10	4 47
Def Interval	0 05	0 02	-	0 00	0 04
Sus Grth Rate	0 08	0 00	-0 04	0 04	0 00

SUBSIDIARY & ASSOCIATED COMPANIES

DELSWA LTD (46,6%)

INVESTMENTS

None

JASCO ELECTRONICS HOLDINGS LTD

ABBREVIATION : JASCO

JSE SHORT CODE : JSC

SECTOR : Industrial-Electronics, Electrical & Bat

SHAREHOLDERS

Who Owns Whom's Assessment of the Identity of the Ultimate Controlling Shareholder: DIRECTORS

SHAREHOLDER	PERCENTAGE 1992	1991
DELTA ELECTRICAL INDUSTRIES LTD	20 7	20 7
SHERRY J A	20 4	20 4
FREDERICK EMARY INV TRUST CO P/L	9 7	9 7
JAMSEN INV P/L	9 6	9 6
FERBROS NOM P/L	4 0	3 5
A Y INV 280 P/L	3 1	3 1
DU PLESSIS E INV CO P/L	3 1	3 1
SA MUTUAL	3 1	3 1
RUSH P J	2 8	2 8
KOCH N R	2 6	2 6
CMB NOM P/L	2 4	- -
ROUSSOUW S A	2 1	2 1
DAVIES FAMILY TRUST	1 9	2 1
CHERAND INV C C	1 7	1 7
SHARESTOCK NOM P/L	1 1	1 0
SANLAM	---	4 0
TOTAL	88 2	89 5

DIRECTORS :
DAVIES MG ,DU PLESSIS G
EMARY FE (Deputy Chairman),GILLMAN RA
GILLVRAY S ,RUSH PJ (Managing Director)
SHERRY JA (Chairman),WEBB DM

REGISTRATION NUMBER : 87/03293/06

REGISTERED OFFICE
Centex Office Park, Katherine Str
Sandton
2199
TEL 011-444 3765
FAX 011-444 3771

TRANSFER SECRETARY
Central Registrars Ltd
P O Box 4844, Johannesburg
2000
TEL 011-331 0051

COMPANY SECRETARY
R A Gillman

NATURE OF BUSINESS
Holding company of suppliers of mechanical, electrical and electronic components and products used in the computer networking, two-way radio, domestic appliance,automotive and electromedical industries, Supply of cables & connectors for computers, telecommunications & industrial control applications, & power semi-conductors & heavy power couplers for the mining industry

BANKERS :
Nedperm Bank Ltd
First National Bank of SA Ltd
Standard Bank of SA Ltd

AUDITORS :
Ernst & Young

FAMILIAR BRAND NAMES
AMPHENOL,GALE,HIROSE,ILSA,JANED,JOUAN
PASCOM ELECTRONICS,PRECICONTACT
SA SCIENTIFIC GROUP,SHIMADZU,SKYPAGE,WESTCODE

CONTRIBUTION BY ACTIVITY
N/A

YEAR END : February

DIVIDEND :Ords 1c

Dividend No 3	(Ldr)01/06/90	(Pay)28/06/90	Amt(c)3.5
Dividend No 4	(Ldr)07/06/91	(Pay)28/06/91	Amt(c)4

NUMBER OF EMPLOYEES : 154

CAPITAL STRUCTURE

	AUTHORISED	ISSUED
Ords 1c	50000000	28908667

FINANCIAL STATISTICS (AT FINANCIAL YEAR END)

(Amts in R'000)	1992 Feb	1991 Feb	1990 Feb	1989 Feb	1988 Feb
Ord S/H Int	9862	10096	8334	8692	6999
Long Trm Loans	5747	5761	236	199	372
Iss Ord Share	28909	28909	25456	25000	25000
Total Liab	22829	20543	12817	8916	5846
Current Liab	17082	14782	12581	8717	5474
Total Assets	32691	30639	21151	17608	12845
Current Assets	29579	27446	19021	16067	11865
Debtors	15242	14475	10713	8181	4723
Inventory	14074	12904	7846	6809	4048
Turnover	72285	64188	54488	36263	24648
Oper Profit	3649	6989	5483	3378	2528
Interest Paid	2056	1095	1110	191	113
Tax Paid	289	1401	1200	988	1147
Prf af Int&Tax	1305	4497	3246	2416	1268
Prf att Ord Sh	1305	4497	3246	2412	1269
Btm Line Earn	-234	331	276	2212	263
Dividend Paid	-	1156	890	720	213
Mkt Prce(c) YE	40	60	42	53	50
Depreciation	817	731	492	325	176

PER SHARE STATISTICS (CENTS)

Net Asst Val	34.11	34.92	32.74	34.77	28.00
Net Earnings	4.50	16.40	12.80	9.70	5.74
Dividends	-	4.00	3.50	2.88	0.85
Cash Flow	7.33	19.04	14.96	10.95	6.52

RATIOS AND OTHER INFORMATION

Mrk Cap(R000)	11564	17345	10692	13250	12500
Current Ratio	1.73	1.86	1.51	1.84	2.17
Quik/Acid Tst	0.91	0.98	0.89	1.06	1.43
A/C Rec T/ovr	4.74	4.43	5.09	4.43	5.22
Tot Ass T/ovr	2.21	2.09	2.58	2.06	1.92
Debt/Ass Rat	0.70	0.67	0.61	0.51	0.46
L T L Tot Ass	0.18	0.19	0.01	0.01	0.03
Debt to Eqity	2.31	2.03	1.54	1.03	0.84
Interest Cover	1.77	6.38	4.94	17.69	22.37
Oper Prof Mrg	5.05	10.89	10.06	9.32	10.26
Net Prof Marg%	1.81	7.01	5.96	6.65	5.15
Ret on Assets	11.17	22.82	26.27	20.42	19.68
Ret on Equity%	13.23	44.54	38.95	27.75	18.13
Price/Earnings	8.89	3.66	3.28	5.46	8.71
Divid Cover	-	4.10	3.66	3.37	6.75
Divid Yield	-	6.67	8.33	5.43	1.70
Earning Yield%	11.25	27.33	30.48	18.30	11.48
NAV % Mrk Pr	85.28	58.21	77.95	65.60	55.99
Effec Tax Rate	17.88	15.77	2.65	1.88	56.11
Def Interval	4.80	1.18	0.80	1.40	0.41
Sus Grth Rate	13.23	33.09	28.27	19.47	15.09

SUBSIDIARY & ASSOCIATED COMPANIES

ANGIO SCIENTIFIC (PTY) LTD
EASYCALL (PTY) LTD
ILSA (PTY) LTD
JANED ELECTRONICS (PTY) LTD
JASCO INTERNATIONAL (PTY) LTD
PASCOM ELECTRONICS (PTY) LTD
SA SCIENTIFIC PHARMACEUTICALS (PTY) LTD
SA SCIENTIFIC PRODUCTS (PTY) LTD
SPECIAL CABLES (PTY) LTD
SPECIAL CABLES (PTY) LTD
WEBB INDUSTRIES (PTY) LTD

INVESTMENTS

None

JD GROUP LTD

ABBREVIATION : JDGROUP

JSE SHORT CODE : JDG

SECTOR : Industrial-Furniture & Household

SHAREHOLDERS

Who Owns Whom's Assessment of the Identity of the Ultimate Controlling Shareholder:
FS GROUP VIA HOMEMAKERS

SHAREHOLDER	PERCENTAGE 1992	1991
HOMEMAKERS GROUP LTD	50.1	---
SA MUTUAL	11.3	11.1
FIRST NAT NOM P/L	10.2	10.2
MOMENTUM LIFE ASSURE LTD	4.0	2.6
CMB NOM P/L	3.9	---
MAXERIC NOM P/L	3.7	4.6
STEIN C	3.5	3.9
ELLERINE BROS P/L	1.9	1.9
SUSSMAN D	1.8	3.9
NEDBANK NOM LTD	---	49.2
TOTAL	90.5	87.4

DIRECTORS :
BAIRD HJ ,BEHRENS BR ,COHEN N ,DU TOIT PR
FIELD DG ,GUTKIN M ,KOPMAN A ,LEIBOWITZ N
LIEBESMAN JM ,MANKOWITZ L ,NOWITZ H ,ROLFE TW
STEIN CM (Financial Director)
SUSSMAN ID (Chairman & Managing Dir.

REGISTRATION NUMBER : 81/09108/06

REGISTERED OFFICE
4th Floor, Nedbank Mall, 145 Commissioner Street
Johannesburg
2001
TEL: 011-331 4671
FAX: 011-331 3085

TRANSFER SECRETARY
Central Registrars Ltd
P O Box 4844, Johannesburg
2000
TEL 011-331 0051

COMPANY SECRETARY
C M Stein

NATURE OF BUSINESS
An investment holding company with subsidiaries involved in furniture retailing through direct trading with cash customers via 183 outlets
The group also manages the credit business of JD Sales (Pty) Ltd

BANKERS :
Volkskas Ltd

AUDITORS :
Ernst & Young

FAMILIAR BRAND NAMES
PRICE'N PRIDE

CONTRIBUTION BY ACTIVITY
N/A

YEAR END : December

DIVIDEND :Ords 5c

Interim No 12	(Ldr)08/09/89	(Pay)22/09/89	Amt(c)6
Final No 13	(Ldr)30/03/90	(Pay)17/04/90	Amt(c)11
Interim No 14	(Ldr)21/09/90	(Pay)12/10/90	Amt(c)8
Final No 15	(Ldr)28/03/91	(Pay)19/04/91	Amt(c)14
Interim No 16	(Ldr)11/10/91	(Pay)25/10/91	Amt(c)7
Final No 17	(Ldr)03/04/92	(Pay)24/04/92	Amt(c)15
Interim No 18	(Ldr)09/10/92	(Pay)23/10/92	Amt(c)4

NUMBER OF EMPLOYEES : 4875

CAPITAL STRUCTURE

	AUTHORISED	ISSUED
Ords 5c	70000000	35665000

FINANCIAL STATISTICS (AT FINANCIAL YEAR END)

(Amts in R'000)	1991 Dec	1990 Dec	1989 Dec	1988 Dec	1987 Jun
Ord S/H Int	237396	212827	165873	137038	31337
Long Trm Loans	-	115165	101562	104040	3673
Iss Ord Share	35665	35665	35665	35665	68830
Total Liab	200132	343118	260534	249009	57557
Current Liab	200132	227953	158972	144969	53884
Total Assets	436620	555339	407436	382380	88894
Intang Assets	908	606	18971	3667	*
Current Assets	230539	525793	381602	365389	86069
Debtors	75087	439070	322184	312775	69084
Inventory	96596	86843	59152	52175	16950
Turnover	542292	645664	471749	239213	119884
Oper Profit	60004	95056	75795	39911	9200
Interest Paid	33092	33347	25784	8831	1162
Tax Paid	-1956	10635	13417	8252	2126
Prf af Int&Tax	32415	51074	36594	22828	5912
Prf att Ord Sh	32415	51074	36594	22828	5912
Btm Line Earn	32415	51074	36038	21078	5912
Dividend Paid	7846	7846	6063	4993	1377
Mkt Prce(c) YE	400	535	325	200	275
Depreciation	3231	2332	1132	582	754

PER SHARE STATISTICS (CENTS)

Net Asst Val	663 08	595 04	411 89	373 95	45 53
Net Earnings	90 90	143 20	102 60	64 00	5 60
Dividends	22 00	22 00	17 00	14 00	2 00
Cash Flow	99 95	149 74	105 78	167 06	12 53

RATIOS AND OTHER INFORMATION

Mrk Cap(R000)	142660	190808	115911	71330	189283
Current Ratio	1 15	2 31	2 40	2 52	1 60
Quik/Acid Tst	0 67	1 93	2 03	2 16	1 28
A/C Rec T/ovr	7 22	1 47	1 46	1 53	1 74
Tot Ass T/ovr	1 24	1 16	1 16	1 25	1 35
Debt/Ass Rat	0 46	0 62	0 58	0 58	0 62
L T L Tot Ass	-	0 21	0 19	0 20	0 01
Debt to Eqity	0 84	1 61	1 44	1 62	1 76
Interest Cover	1 81	2 85	2 94	4 52	7 92
Oper Prof Mrg	11 06	14 72	16 07	16 68	7 67
Net Prof Marg%	5 98	7 91	7 76	9 54	4 93
Ret on Assets	14 56	17 12	18 60	20 88	10 35
Ret on Equity%	13 65	24 00	22 06	33 32	18 87
Price/Earnings	4 40	3 74	3 17	3 13	49 11
Divid Cover	4 13	6 51	6 04	4 57	2 80
Divid Yield	5 50	4 11	5 23	7 00	0 73
Earning Yield%	22 73	26 77	31 57	32 00	2 04
NAV % Mrk Pr	165 77	111 22	126 74	186 98	16 56
Effec Tax Rate	-6 64	15 14	26 83	4 82	2 05
Def Interval	0 01	2 16	2 11	5 21	1 60
Sus Grth Rate	10 35	20 31	18 41	13 01	14 47

SUBSIDIARY & ASSOCIATED COMPANIES

BRADLOWS STORES LTD
ELLIS & CO LTD
PRICE N PRIDE (MMABATHO) (PTY) LTD
PRICE N PRIDE (PTY) LTD
SCORE FURNISHERS (PTY) LTD
SUSTEIN (PTY) LTD
THE LOUNGE SUITE (PTY) LTD - DORMANT
WINNA FURNISHERS (SWAZILAND) (PTY) LTD
WORLD FURNISHERS (BOPHUTHATSWANA) (PTY)
WORLD FURNISHERS (VENDA) (PTY) LTD
WORLD FURNISHERS ADMINISTRATION (PTY) LT
WORLD FURNISHERS GROUP LTD

INVESTMENTS

JD SALES (PTY) LTD (VAR RATE RED PREF) (1 SH)

JOHANNESBURG CONSOLIDATED INVESTMENT CO LTD

ABBREVIATION : JOHNNIES

JSE SHORT CODE : JCI

SECTOR : Mining Financial-Mining Houses

SHAREHOLDERS

Who Owns Whom's Assessment of the Identity of the Ultimate Controlling Shareholder:
ANGLO AMERICAN

SHAREHOLDER	PERCENTAGE 1992	1991

RESIDENT NOM LTD	32.5	32.6
SA MUTUAL	10.7	10.5
STD BANK NOM TVL P/L	8.1	7.3
GALATES INV HLDGS LTD	7.5	7.5
ANGLO AMERICAN CORP OF SA LTD	5.1	5.2
LIBERTY LIFE ASSOC OF AFRICA LTD	2.6	2.8
LONDON CONTROL ACCOUNT	2.6	---
SOUTHERN LIFE ASSOC LTD	2.0	1.2
CMB NOM P/L	1.7	---
MOMENTUM LIFE ASSURE LTD	1.6	1.6
EIGHTY ONE MAIN STREET NOM LTD	1.5	1.2
FIRST NAT NOM P/L	1.4	1.3
FERMAIN NOM LTD	1.4	1.4
RUNCORN HLDGS LTD	1.1	1.1
LONDON REGISTER ACCOUNT	---	3.1
SANLAM	---	1.2
TOTAL	79.8	78.0

DIRECTORS :
BRAY VG ,DAVISON BE ,HAWARDEN MW ,KAHN JM
KING MW ,MAXWELL KW ,MCKERRON AB
NEL JJ (Dir Human Resources),PRETORIUS TL
RETIEF PF (Chairman),SCOTT-RUSSELL H DR
SUTHERLAND RB

REGISTRATION NUMBER : 01/00429/06

REGISTERED OFFICE
Consolidated Building, cnr Fox & Harrison
Johannesburg
2001
TEL: 011-373 9111
FAX: 011-836 6130

TRANSFER SECRETARY
Consolidated Share Registrars Ltd
P O Box 61051, Marshalltown
2107
TEL: 011-492 1620

COMPANY SECRETARY
M J Meyer

NATURE OF BUSINESS
A mining & financial holding company, with controlling interests in a number of quoted SA companies. The group has significant interests in platinum, gold, ferrochrome, coal, diamonds & secondary industries, incl food, beverages, property and industrial engineering.

BANKERS :
Standard Bank of SA Ltd

AUDITORS :
Deloitte Pim Goldby, KPMG Aiken & Peat

FAMILIAR BRAND NAMES
N/A

CONTRIBUTION BY ACTIVITY
Platinum (% Equity Earnings) (21.0%)
Industrial & Property (43.7%)
Gold (2.8%)
Diamonds (12.0%)
Ferrochrome/Base Metals/Mining & Other (9.6%)
Financial & Corporate Services (10.9%)

YEAR END : June

DIVIDEND :Ords 10c

Interim No 128	(Ldr)23/02/90	(Pay)19/03/90	Amt(c)42
Final No 129	(Ldr)21/09/90	(Pay)15/10/90	Amt(c)90
Interim No 130	(Ldr)22/02/91	(Pay)18/03/91	Amt(c)42
Final No 131	(Ldr)27/09/91	(Pay)28/10/91	Amt(c)90
Interim No 132	(Ldr)20/03/92	(Pay)13/04/92	Amt(c)42
Final No 133	(Ldr)25/09/92	(Pay)26/10/92	Amt(c)90

NUMBER OF EMPLOYEES : 1000

CAPITAL STRUCTURE

	AUTHORISED	ISSUED
Ords 10c	200000000	147698000
Var Rate Red Cum Prefs 10c	5500000	0
8,25% Cum Red Prefs R1	1300000	0
Fixed Rate Red Cum Prefs 10c	34500000	0
"A" Var Rate Red Cum Prefs 10c	40000000	0

FINANCIAL STATISTICS (AT FINANCIAL YEAR END)

(Amts in R'000)	1992 Jun	1991 Jun	1990 Jun	1989 Jun	1988 Jun
Ord S/H Int	2617200	2258100	1921200	1508600	1101000
Long Trm Loans	338600	223500	217700	176600	187000
Iss Ord Share	147698	147491	147466	147466	147466
Total Liab	2661700	2349000	2183800	1952400	1142400
Current Liab	2323100	2125500	1966100	1775800	955400
Total Assets	5278900	4607100	4101200	3369000	2243400
Intang Assets	*	*	3800	92000	*
Current Assets	1876700	1697200	1778100	1697600	943900
Debtors	430100	326800	525100	303300	210500
Inventory	43200	51200	145600	113300	90900
Oper Profit	85600	110200	437600	125400	322700
Interest Paid	256200	288700	594900	211100	-
Tax Paid	24200	26800	21700	42000	33800
Prf af Int&Tax	439600	418400	430300	363900	288900
Prf att Ord Sh	572100	576100	601600	569700	400700
Btm Line Earn	565200	533700	612900	570800	429900
Dividend Paid	195000	194600	194600	162200	129000
Mkt Prce(c) YE	6300	5100	5075	3725	2320
Depreciation	29100	29500	5000	31700	28100

PER SHARE STATISTICS (CENTS)

Net Asst Val	1771.99	1531.01	1300.23	960.63	746.61
Net Earnings	298.00	283.00	291.00	246.00	272.00
Dividends	132.00	132.00	132.00	110.00	88.00
Cash Flow	335.21	325.38	306.17	279.52	216.66

RATIOS AND OTHER INFORMATION

Mrk Cap(R000)	9304974	7522041	7483900	5493109	3421211
Current Ratio	0.81	0.80	0.90	0.96	0.99
Quik/Acid Tst	0.79	0.77	0.83	0.89	0.89
Debt/Ass Rat	0.47	0.48	0.50	0.55	0.47
L T L Tot Ass	0.03	0.02	0.02	0.02	0.04
Debt to Eqity	0.95	0.98	1.07	1.22	0.96
Interest Cover	1.78	1.60	1.35	1.99	-
Ret on Assets	16.15	19.36	29.72	24.44	19.45
Ret on Equity%	21.86	25.51	31.31	37.76	36.39
Price/Earnings	21.14	18.02	17.44	15.14	8.53
Divid Cover	2.26	2.14	2.20	2.24	3.09
Divid Yield	2.10	2.59	2.60	2.95	3.79
Earning Yield%	4.73	5.55	5.73	6.60	11.72
NAV % Mrk Pr	28.13	30.02	25.62	25.79	32.18
Effec Tax Rate	0.85	1.70	3.48	22.22	9.08
Def Interval	2.56	1.59	2.15	0.70	0.52
Sus Grth Rate	14.41	16.89	21.18	27.01	24.68

SUBSIDIARY & ASSOCIATED COMPANIES

AFP LTD
AFRICAN FENCING AND WIRE INDUSTRIES (PVT
AFRICAN STEEL FURNITURE MANUFACTURERS (P
AINSWORTH (PTY) LTD

AIV PROPERTIES (PTY) LTD
ALLIED ELECTRIC (1985) (PTY) LTD
ANDCOR (EAST CAPE) (PTY) LTD
ANDCOR HOLDINGS (PTY) LTD
ANDERMAIN INVESTMENTS (PTY) LTD
APEX BEHUISING (EDMS) BPK
APEX FOUNDRY (PTY) LTD
APEX IMPLEMENTE (EDMS) BPK
APEX INDUSTRIES LTD
APEX MAKELAARS (EDMS) BPK
APEX WEARPARTS (EDMS) BPK
ARGUS HOLDINGS LTD (20%)
ASSOCIATED INDUSTRIAL CHEMICALS (PTY) LT
ASTON BAY HOLIDAY RESORTS (PTY) LTD
B & D MITCHELL RAND (PTY) LTD
B & O MINERALS EXPLORATION CO (PTY) LTD
BARBERTON IRON AND STEEL LTD
BARNATO BROTHERS LTD (UK)
BARNATO EXPLORATION LTD (36%)
BARNATO HOLDINGS LTD
BENCO INDUSTRIES (PTY) LTD
BENONI ENGINEERING WORKS AND STEEL FOUND
BESAANS - DU PLESSIS (PRETORIA FOUNDRIES
BESAANS - DU PLESSIS ENGINEERING CO. (PT
BESAANS - DU PLESSIS FOUNDRIES (PTY) LTD
BESAANS - DU PLESSIS HOLDINGS (PTY) LTD
BESAANS - DU PLESSIS INVESTMENTS (PTY) L
BESDUTY PLANT HIRE (PTY) LTD
BISAND HOLDINGS (PTY) LTD
BM SHERMAN & CO (SA) (PTY) LTD
BOKEG INVESTMENTS (PTY) LTD
BOTHA-HARRIS LTD
BREYTEN COAL FARMS (PTY) LTD
BURGLEN (PTY) LTD
CENTFOX INVESTMENTS (PTY) LTD
CHARLMED INVESTMENTS LTD
CONCORDE FOUNDRY (VEREENIGING) (PTY) LTD
CONCORDE FOUNDRY LTD
CONSOLIDATED COLLIERIES LTD
CONSOLIDATED METALLURGICAL INDUSTRIES LT (49,9%)
CONSOLIDATED MURCHISON LTD (24,1%)
CREATIVE METALS (PTY) LTD
DAB INVESTMENTS LTD (49%)
DAB SECURITIES LTD
DAINFERN INVESTMENTS LTD
DARTRY COAL HOLDINGS (PTY) LTD
DEELGE INVESTMENTS (PTY) LTD
DELTIGHT INDUSTRIES (S.A.) (PTY) LTD
DOUGROM ENTERPRISES LTD
EC LENNING (PVT) LTD
EC LENNING BOTSWANA (PTY) LTD
EC LENNING LTD
EC LENNING PROPERTIES (PTY) LTD
ELECTRO METAL INDUSTRIES (PTY) LTD
ELSBURG GOLD MINING CO. LTD (26.2%)
ENVER INVESTMENTS (PTY) LTD
EXCHANGE ENGINEERING (PTY) LTD
FOXCAIRN INVESTMENTS LTD
FOXDALE INVESTMENTS LTD
FOXGLEN INVESTMENTS LTD
FOXHILL INVESTMENTS LTD
FOXVALLEY INVESTMENTS LTD
FOXWAY INVESTMENTS (PTY) LTD
FREE STATE DEVELOPMENT & INVESTMENT CORP (41,7%)
FREE STATE DEVELOPMENT & INVESTMENT CORP (41.1%)
GEORDIE INVESTMENTS LTD
GLENCAIRN HOLDINGS LTD
GLENNY BUCHNER INVESTMENT (PTY) LTD
GLENS ENGINEERING (PTY) LTD
GOBABIS MANGANESE (PTY) LTD
GOODMAN-LENNINGS (PTY) LTD
GOODMAN-LENNINGS RECONDITIONING RUSTENBU
GOROB MANAGEMENT AND MINING CO. (PTY) LT
GRANDIS TIMBER (PTY) LTD
HARMAIN INVESTMENTS (PTY) LTD
HJ JOEL GOLD MINING CO LTD
HODGES ENGINEERING AND METRICATION (PVT)
HUBERT STREET PROPERTIES (PTY) LTD
IC HARRISON (PTY) LTD
JACKS ENGINEERING (PTY) LTD
JAGGARD INVESTMENTS LTD
JCI (BOPHUTHATSWANA) (PTY) LTD
JCI GENERAL ENGINEERING LTD
JCI METAL HOLDINGS (PTY) LTD
JCI PROPERTY MANAGEMENT (PTY) LTD
JCI SERVICES (PTY) LTD
JENA INVESTMENTS (PTY) LTD
JESSAMIN INVESTMENTS LTD
JOHANNESBURG CENTRAL PROPERTIES (PTY) LT
JOHNNIES AIR SERVICES (PTY) LTD
JOHNNIES INDUSTRIALS LTD
JOHNNIES PROJECTS LTD
JONQUIL INVESTMENTS LTD
JUSTUS HOUSE (PTY) LTD
K KLING & CO (1963) (PTY) LTD
KNIGHTS ENGINEERING (1979) (PTY) LTD
KNIPPING (PTY) LTD
KNIPPING MANUFACTURING CO. (PTY) LTD
LEBOWA PLATINUM MINES LTD (20%)
LENNING (NAMIBIA) (PTY) LTD
LENNING BRANCHES (PTY) LTD
LENNING RUSTENBURG (PTY) LTD
LENNINGS ENGINEERING (PTY) LTD
LENNINGS EXPORTS (PTY) LTD
LENNINGS GROUP INTERNAL TRANSPORT (PTY)
LENNINGS LTD
LENNINGS MANGANESE (PTY) LTD (BOPHUTHATS
LENNINGS MANGANESE LTD
LENNINGS TRACKLESS MINING EQUIPMENT (PTY
LINDUM REEFS GOLD MINING CO LTD (48%)
LOUWS CREEK TIMBER (PTY) LTD
MAGAZINE CENTRE (PTY) LTD
MAIN PLACE HOLDINGS LTD
MAINWAY INVESTMENTS (PTY) LTD
MAINWEST INVESTMENTS (PTY) LTD
MIDDELBURG MINE JOINT VENTURE (40%)
MILPARK INVESTMENTS LTD
MINE STEEL PRODUCTS (PTY) LTD
MINORS STREET PROPERTIES (PTY) LTD
MODEL KITCHENS (1946) (PTY) LTD
MOSER INDUSTRIES (PTY) LTD (50%)
NEDBANK CENTRE (SCOTTSVILLE) LTD
NORTHLAND AGRICULTURAL LTD
NORTHLAND ENGINEERING LTD
OLDHILL MANUFACTURING CO. (PTY) LTD
PERMUS (1967) (PTY) LTD
PERMUS INVESTMENTS LTD
PHOENIX COLLIERY LTD
PLANET MANUFACTURING (PTY) LTD
POTGIETERSRUST PLATINUMS LTD
POWERVILLE INDUSTRIELE BELEGGINGS (EDMS)
PREMSAB HOLDINGS LTD (50%)
PRESIDENT ENGINEERING CO. (PTY) LTD
PRESIDENT STREET PROPERTIES LTD
PRETITAL (PTY) LTD
PRETORIA IRON AND STEEL AND BRASS FOUNDR
PRETORIA IRON AND STEEL INVESTMENTS (PTY
PUTSBERG EXPLORATION AND MINING CO. (PTY
RALTON INVESTMENTS (PTY) LTD
RAND TRANSMISSION CO. (PTY) LTD
RANDFONTEIN ESTATES GOLD MINING CO. (WIT (30,6%)
RC POWER (PTY) LTD
REDTHANE PLASTICS (PTY) LTD
RODLAND INVESTMENTS (PTY) LTD
ROGOW INVESTMENTS (PTY) LTD
RUSTENBURG ENGINEERS (PTY) LTD
RUSTENBURG FOUNDRY (PTY) LTD
RUSTENBURG PLATINUM HOLDINGS LTD (32,6%)

RUSTIVIA PROPERTIES (PTY) LTD
SA KITCHEN CREDIT CO (PTY) LTD
SANDVELDT INVESTMENTS (PTY) LTD
SARCOR PROPERTIES (PTY) LTD
SCHEDAR INVESTMENTS (PTY) LTD
SHAFT SINKERS (PTY) LTD (20%)
SHURA PAINTS (PTY) LTD
SMITH'S RTC (PTY) LTD
SMITH'S SADDLERY MINING AND ENGINEERING
SOMKELE PROSPECTING CO. (PTY) LTD
SOUTH AFRICAN ROLL CORP. (1971) (PTY) LT
SOUTH DEEP EXPLORATION CO LTD (41.1%)
SOUTH WITBANK COAL MINES LTD
SOUTHMAR INVESTMENTS (PTY) LTD
SPECTRAL (AFRICA) LTD
STAND 176 BLOCK CONGELLA (DURBAN) (PTY)
STANSA BALLAST MANUFACTURERS (PTY) LTD
STEPHENSON ROAD HOLDINGS (PTY) LTD
STERVYN ENGINEERING (PTY) LTD
STONESTREET & HANSEN (WELKOM) (PTY) LTD
STONESTREET & HANSEN INTERNATIONAL LTD
STONESTREET & HANSEN LEASING (PTY) LTD
STONESTREET & HANSEN LTD
STONESTREET OVERHEAD IRRIGATION (PTY) LT
STRATEGIC PLACEMENTS AND INVESTMENTS (PT
SUNSET PARK (PTY) LTD
TAVIS PROPERTIES (JOHANNESBURG) (PTY) LT
TAVISTOCK COLLIERIES LTD
TELROAD (PTY) LTD
TEMCO INVESTMENTS (PTY) LTD
TEMSO (PTY) LTD
TERRATEC AND ALLIED SERVICES LTD
TESNA PROPERTIES (PTY) LTD
THE PREMIER GROUP LTD (32.9%)
TILLEY DOORS (PTY) LTD
TILLEY MANUFACTURING (PTY) LTD
TILLEY-MACMILL (PTY) LTD
TIMES MEDIA LTD (24,1%)
TOYOTA SA LTD (21,4%)
VARIED INVESTMENTS (PTY) LTD
WATT ROAD PROPERTY INVESTMENTS (PTY) LTD
WELKOM ENGINEERING (PTY) LTD
WELKOM ENGINEERING HOLDINGS (PTY) LTD
WESTDALE INVESTMENTS LTD
WESTFOX INVESTMENTS (PTY) LTD
WESTMAR INVESTMENTS (PTY) LTD
WESTVAAL ENTERPRISES (PTY) LTD
WESTVAAL KITCHENS (PTY) LTD
WITBOERDERY (EDMS) BPK
WITWATERSRAND LTD (30%)
WJ LEITH & CO (PTY) LTD
ZELNEW PROPERTIES (PTY) LTD

INVESTMENTS

ABRASIVE GRIT SALES LTD - "A" (21600 SH)
CSO VALUATIONS (PTY) LTD (8650 SH)
DE BEERS CONSOLIDATED MINES LTD (3252000 SH)
DIAMOND PURCHASING & TRADING CO (PTY) LT (350940 SH)
DIAMOND TRADING CO (PTY) LTD (166107 SH)
FREE STATE DEVELOPMENT & INVESTMENT CORP
INDUSTRIAL DISTRIBUTORS (1946) (PTY) LTD (330000 SH)
INDUSTRIAL GRIT DISTRIBUTORS (SHANNON) L (28000 SH)
JUBILEE PROSPECTORS LTD (50 SH)
RICHARDS BAY COAL TERMINAL CO LTD (5,08%)
SA BREWERIES LTD (6043280 SH)
WESCO INVESTMENTS LTD (840200 SH)
WESTERN AREAS GOLD MINING CO. LTD (2622900 SH)

JOHNSON & FLETCHER LTD

ABBREVIATION : J & F

SECTOR : Zimbabwe Stock Exchange

SHAREHOLDERS

Who Owns Whom's Assessment of the Identity of the Ultimate Controlling Shareholder:
DONIAN PROPERTIES (PVT) LTD

SHAREHOLDER	PERCENTAGE 1992	1991
DONIAN PROPERTIES PVT LTD	44.5	---
MBCA NOM (PVT) LTD	5.6	---
SAPHIC HOLDINGS PVT LTD	4.3	---
OLD MUTUAL INV CORP (PVT) LTD	3.1	---
STOW C E J (NON RESIDENT)	3.0	---
FIRST MUTUAL LIFE ASSURE SOC OF ZIM	2.9	---
ABRY INV PVT LTD	2.7	---
COULMORE INV (PVT) LTD	2.3	---
NRZ CONTRIBUTORY PENS FUND	1.4	---
TOTAL	69.7	---

DIRECTORS :
CAMERON MV ,MILNE IF ,MOXON JRT (Chairman) ROUTLEDGE MHC (Managing Director),STEPHENS DE YOUNG JRA

REGISTERED OFFICE
21 Chinhoyi Street, Harare
Zimbabwe

TEL: 70541
FAX: 703163

TRANSFER SECRETARY
N/A

COMPANY SECRETARY
W K LUNT

NATURE OF BUSINESS
JOHNSON&FLETCHER is incorporated in Zimbabwe with a 92% locally owned capital base.The trading division sells building materials,particularly,timber tools,hardware and sanitaryware.Production division manufactures stock and purpose made joinery as well as specialising in hardwood doors.Gang-nail roof trusses are designed and fabricated at three strategically placed truss plants.

BANKERS :
Barclays Bank of Zimbabwe Ltd
Merchant Bank of Central Africa
Standard Chartered Bank Zimbabwe Ltd

AUDITORS :
Deloitte & Touche

FAMILIAR BRAND NAMES
N/A

CONTRIBUTION BY ACTIVITY
N/A

YEAR END : March

DIVIDEND : Ords Z$0,50

Dividend	(Ldr)13/12/91	(Pay)13/01/92	Amt(c)21
Dividend	(Ldr)26/06/92	(Pay)08/07/92	Amt(c)46

CAPITAL STRUCTURE

	AUTHORISED	ISSUED
Ords Z$0,50	9600000	8866897
7% Cum Prefs $2	100000	100000
"B" Prefs $1	500000	500000

FINANCIAL STATISTICS (AT FINANCIAL YEAR END)

(Amts in Z$)	1992 Mar	1991 Mar
Ord S/H Int	60864	41706
Long Trm Loans	1481	700
Iss Ord Share	8867	7882
Total Liab	30518	28449
Current Liab	29037	27749
Total Assets	91382	70155
Current Assets	50669	37896
Debtors	17068	11776
Inventory	33601	25662
Turnover	104716	75489
Oper Profit	19761	11435
Interest Paid	710	125
Tax Paid	8226	3417
Prf af Int&Tax	11776	8587
Prf att Ord Sh	11741	8556
Btm Line Earn	11741	8556
Dividend Paid	5941	4335
Depreciation	2201	1366

PER SHARE STATISTICS (CENTS)

Net Asst Val	686.41	529.13
Net Earnings	132.41	108.55
Dividends	67.00	55 00
Cash Flow	157.23	116 20

RATIOS AND OTHER INFORMATION

Current Ratio	1.74	1.37
Quik/Acid Tst	0.59	0.44
A/C Rec T/ovr	6.14	5 92
Tot Ass T/ovr	1.15	0 99
Debt/Ass Rat	0.33	0.40
L T L Tot Ass	0 01	-
Debt to Eqity	0.49	0 67
Interest Cover	28.19	94.02
Oper Prof Mrg	18.87	15.15
Net Prof Marg%	11 21	11.33
Ret on Assets	22 67	15.96
Ret on Equity%	19 29	18 94
Divid Cover	1.98	1.97
Effec Tax Rate	41.59	29.24
Def Interval	0.28	0.07
Sus Grth Rate	9.53	10.12

SUBSIDIARY & ASSOCIATED COMPANIES

GANG-NAIL ZIMBABWE (PVT) LTD

INVESTMENTS

ZECO LIMITED (11,33%)

KADOMA CONSOLIDATED INDUSTRIES LTD

ABBREVIATION : KADOMA

SECTOR : Zimbabwe Stock Exchange

SHAREHOLDERS

Who Owns Whom's Assessment of the Identity of the Ultimate Controlling Shareholder:
ART CORPORATION LTD

SHAREHOLDER	PERCENTAGE 1992	1991
ART CORP LTD	50.6	---
OLD MUTUAL INV CORP (PVT) LTD	16 1	---
ZIMBABWE REINSURANCE CORP LTD	4 1	---
SOUTHAMPTON ASSURE CO ZIM LTD	3.8	---
FIRST MUTUAL LIFE ASSURE SOC OF ZIM	2 3	---
FIDELITY LIFE ASSURE OF ZIM PVT LTD	1.5	---
TEXTURED YARNS PVT LTD	1.3	---
SOUTHERN LIFE ASSOC ZIM LTD	1.1	---
BARD NOM (PVT) LTD	1.0	---
TOTAL	81 8	---

DIRECTORS :
CANNON TN ,EASTWOOD ANH ,NYANDORO GB (Chairman)
RIDDLE DM ,TAZARURWA OM ,WAKELING JB

REGISTERED OFFICE
Nedlaw House, 202 Seke Road
Graniteside, Harare

FAX: (14) 735600

TRANSFER SECRETARY
Zimbabwe Banking Corporation Ltd
P O Box 3198, Harare
Zimbabwe

TEL: 092634-735011

COMPANY SECRETARY
Art Corporation Management Services

NATURE OF BUSINESS
The main business of the group is the production of tissue paper and the manufacture of polyol, a base material used in the manufacture of polyurethane.The group also provides motel services and facilities from its motel on the outskirts of Kadoma.

BANKERS :
Standard Chartered Merchant Bank Zim Ltd

AUDITORS :
Ernst & Young

FAMILIAR BRAND NAMES
N/A

CONTRIBUTION BY ACTIVITY
N/A

YEAR END : December

DIVIDEND : Ords Z$1

Dividend	(Ldr)17/05/91	(Pay)12/07/91	Amt(c)4
Dividend	(Ldr)02/03/92	(Pay)03/04/92	Amt(c)6.5

CAPITAL STRUCTURE

	AUTHORISED	ISSUED
Ords Z$1	60000000	57600000

FINANCIAL STATISTICS (AT FINANCIAL YEAR END)

(Amts in Z$)	1991 Dec	1990 Dec
Ord S/H Int	74911	49240
Long Trm Loans	1697	5041
Iss Ord Share	57600	45000
Total Liab	12820	10101
Current Liab	11123	5060
Total Assets	87731	59341
Current Assets	12811	5539
Debtors	1909	1880
Inventory	4960	3401
Turnover	26462	18007
Oper Profit	10781	7334
Interest Paid	492	442
Prf af Int&Tax	11213	6900
Prf att Ord Sh	11213	6900
Btm Line Earn	11213	6900
Dividend Paid	5544	3375
Depreciation	947	717

PER SHARE STATISTICS (CENTS)

Net Asst Val	130.05	109.42
Net Earnings	19.50	12.00
Dividends	10.50	5.90
Cash Flow	21.11	16.93

RATIOS AND OTHER INFORMATION

Current Ratio	1.15	1.09
Quik/Acid Tst	0.71	0.42
A/C Rec T/ovr	13.86	9.58
Tot Ass T/ovr	0.30	0.30
Debt/Ass Rat	0.15	0.17
L T L Tot Ass	0.02	0.08
Debt to Eqity	0.17	0.21
Interest Cover	21.91	16.59
Oper Prof Mrg	40.74	40.73
Net Prof Marg%	42.37	38.32
Ret on Assets	13.34	12.37
Ret on Equity%	14.97	14.01
Divid Cover	1.86	2.03
Def Interval	0.14	0.75
Sus Grth Rate	7.57	7.16

SUBSIDIARY & ASSOCIATED COMPANIES

EAGLE GRANITE (PTY) LTD
KADOMA CONSOLIDATED PROPERTIES (PVT) LTD

INVESTMENTS

None

KAROS HOTELS LTD

ABBREVIATION : KAROS

JSE SHORT CODE : KAR

SECTOR : Industrial-Beverages & Hotels

SHAREHOLDERS

Who Owns Whom's Assessment of the Identity of the Ultimate Controlling Shareholder:
DIRECTORS / MOMENTUM

SHAREHOLDER	PERCENTAGE 1992	1991
MOMENTUM LIFE ASSURE LTD	26.1	26.1
SIVE I B FAMILY HOLDINGS P/L	9.4	9.4
SBG HOLDINGS P/L	9.3	9.3
HURWITZ SELWIN FAMILY TRUST	7.5	7.6
STD BANK NOM TVL P/L	5.8	1.2
CMB NOM P/L	5.2	---
HOFFMANN J TRUST	3.7	3.7
HOTEL ADMINISTRATORS NATAL P/L	3.7	3.7
JOHNSON P M P	2.9	2.9
HOFFMAN S V	2.7	2.7
GOLDBERG J I	2.2	2.2
AUBREN HOLDINGS P/L	1.8	1.8
FEDERATED INDUSTRIAL & FINANCE CORP P/L	1.5	1.5
HALLMARK CONSOLIDATED CC	1.2	1.2
AA LIFE ASSURE ASSOC LTD	---	2.0
BOARD OF EXECUTORS NOM P/L	---	2.6
SANLAM	---	5.2
TOTAL	83.0	83.1

DIRECTORS :
DU TOIT PR MR,GOWER MP MR
HOFFMANN SV MR (Joint Managing Director)
HURWITZ S MR (Chairman & Joint MD),JOHNSON PMP MR
MARKOVITZ ME MR,MELAMET THE HON DA MR,SIVE IB M

REGISTRATION NUMBER : 57/03565/06

REGISTERED OFFICE
1st Floor, Park Terras, 33 Princess of Wales Terrace
Parktown, Johannesburg
2193
TEL: 011-643 8052
FAX: 011-643 4343

TRANSFER SECRETARY
Stability Services (Pty) Ltd
6th Floor, 112 Kerk Street
Johannesburg
2001
TEL: 011-337 4030

COMPANY SECRETARY
C N Welman

NATURE OF BUSINESS
Ownership, development and management of hotels, and timeshare development.

BANKERS :
First National Bank of SA Ltd
Nedperm Bank Ltd

AUDITORS :
Kessel Feinstein

FAMILIAR BRAND NAMES
EDWARD HOTEL (DBN),KAROS ARTHURS SEAT
KAROS BAYSHORE INN,KAROS CAPITAL TOWERS
KAROS INDABA,KAROS JOHANNESBURGER
KAROS LODGE (KRUGER),KAROS MANHATTAN

KAROS MONT AUX SOURCES,KAROS RICHARDS
KAROS SAFARI,KAROS TZANEEN,KAROS WILDERNESS
POLANA HOTEL (MAPUTO)

CONTRIBUTION BY ACTIVITY
N/A

YEAR END : March

DIVIDEND :Ords 40c

Interim No 33	(Ldr)04/01/91	(Pay)14/01/91	Amt(c)3
Final No 34	(Ldr)19/07/91	(Pay)29/07/91	Amt(c)3

CAPITAL STRUCTURE

	AUTHORISED	ISSUED
Ords 40c	40000000	28103852
12% Comp Conv Cum Prefs 40c	21000000	9836348

FINANCIAL STATISTICS (AT FINANCIAL YEAR END)

(Amts in R'000)	1992 Mar	1991 Mar	1990 Mar	1989 Mar
Ord S/H Int	94320	98283	94370	29908
Long Trm Loans	69220	58864	54603	-
Iss Ord Share	28104	28104	28104	15000
Total Liab	100292	83037	73182	380
Current Liab	31072	24173	18579	380
Total Assets	191439	181320	166243	30288
Intang Assets	3173	*	1309	*
Current Assets	12655	11685	11019	30269
Debtors	10261	9373	8135	37
Inventory	1436	1337	1032	-
Turnover	89003	70847	57769	-
Oper Profit	8894	11622	11240	3138
Interest Paid	10151	7076	4889	42
Tax Paid	56	48	80	312
Prf af Int&Tax	-856	5599	8931	2861
Prf att Ord Sh	-3894	4079	8524	2861
Btm Line Earn	-3894	-1112	8524	17658
Dividend Paid	-	1686	3372	1950
Mkt Prce(c) YE	140	155	250	-
Depreciation	4490	3034	2394	5

PER SHARE STATISTICS (CENTS)

Net Asst Val	324.32	349.71	331.13	199.39
Net Earnings	-13.90	14.50	30.60	19.10
Dividends	-	6.00	12.00	-
Cash Flow	-0.34	21.16	39.27	19.11

RATIOS AND OTHER INFORMATION

Mrk Cap(R000)	39346	43561	70260	-
Current Ratio	0.41	0.48	0.59	79.66
Quik/Acid Tst	0.36	0.43	0.54	79.66
A/C Rec T/ovr	8.67	7.56	7.10	-
Tot Ass T/ovr	0.46	0.39	0.35	-
Debt/Ass Rat	0.34	0.35	0.32	0.01
L T L Tot Ass	0.18	0.21	0.21	-
Debt to Eqity	0.70	0.64	0.56	0.01
Interest Cover	0.88	1.64	2.30	74.71
Oper Prof Mrg	9.99	16.40	19.46	-
Net Prof Marg%	-4.38	5.76	14.76	-
Ret on Assets	5.25	7.66	8.36	10.61
Ret on Equity%	-4.13	4.15	9.03	9.57
Price/Earnings	-10.07	10.69	8.17	-
Divid Cover	-	2.42	2.55	-
Divid Yield	-	3.87	4.80	-
Earning Yield%	-9.93	9.35	12.24	-
NAV % Mrk Pr	231.66	225.62	132.45	-
Effec Tax Rate	-7.00	0.85	0.89	9.01
Def Interval	-675.66	8.12	5.71	-
Sus Grth Rate	-4.13	2.43	5.46	3.05

SUBSIDIARY & ASSOCIATED COMPANIES

ABATEL HOLDINGS (PTY) LTD
ARTHUR'S SEAT HOTEL (PTY) LTD
ATHLONE MANSIONS (PTY) LTD
BREYTEN HOLDINGS (PTY) LTD
EASTERN TRANSVAAL BOTTLE STORES (PTY) LT
FOUR ACRES (PTY) LTD
FOURWAYS GARDEN HOTEL (PTY) LTD
HOFFTELS (PTY) LTD
KAROS (PTY) LTD
KAROS HOSPITALITY (PTY) LTD
KAROS HOTELS HOLDINGS (PTY) LTD
KAROS KRUGER SHAREBLOCK LTD
KAROS LEISURE (PTY) LTD
KAROS LODGE SHAREBLOCK LTD
KAROS MONT-AUX-SOURCES SHARE BLOCK LTD
KAROS WILDERNESS SHARE BLOCK LTD
NAMIB ETOSHA TOURISM GROUP (PTY) LTD (32%)
NEW BERNICA ELECTRONICS (PTY) LTD
NEW BERNICA INVESTMENTS (PTY) LTD
NEW BERNICA MANAGEMENT (PTY) LTD
NEW BERNICA SECURITIES (PTY) LTD
NORTHAM HOLDINGS (PTY) LTD
NORTHAM HOTEL & BOTTLE STORE (PTY) LTD
SAFARI HOTELS (PTY) LTD
SISHEN HOTEL (PTY) LTD
TZANEEN HOTEL INVESTMENTS (PTY) LTD

INVESTMENTS

None

KEELEY GROUP HOLDINGS LTD

ABBREVIATION : KEELEY

JSE SHORT CODE : KLY

SECTOR : Metals & Minerals-Other

SHAREHOLDERS

Who Owns Whom's Assessment of the Identity of the Ultimate Controlling Shareholder:
KEELEY FAMILY / GENCOR VIA GENMIN

SHAREHOLDER	PERCENTAGE 1992	1991
CONSOLIDATED NOM P/L	27.6	27.6
NOLENE KEELEY TRUST	7.2	7.2
CHANEL KEELEY TRUST	7.2	7.2
MALCOLM KEELEY TRUST	7.2	7.2
NERINA KEELEY TRUST	7.2	7.2
STD BANK NOM TVL P/L	5.7	3.2
CMB NOM P/L	4.5	---
SA MUTUAL	4.5	4.7
EIGHTY ONE MAIN STREET NOM LTD	3.4	---
FIRST NAT NOM P/L	2.3	2.3
ANGLO AMERICAN GROUP PENS FUND	2.3	2.3
SUTCO AANDELE NOM P/L	2.2	1.3
SANLAMTRUST NOM P/L	2.1	2.1
SYFRETS NOM LTD	2.0	5.6
NEDBANK NOM LTD	1.4	1.1

SMG RESOURCES P/L	1.1	---
ALTENA MEWS P/L	---	1.8
BANNER NOM P/L	---	4.3
SANLAM	---	1.6
TOTAL	87.8	86.6

DIRECTORS :

BROWN RFE (Administration Director)
BYL EH (Financial Director)
CANNATA LJ (Technical Director),DALE TG
KEELEY MF (Executive Chairman)
LOUW DJD (Operations Director)
OLDEWAGE LP (Operations Director)
RADEMEYER P DE V
RIEKERT MN (Deputy Chairman & M.D.),ROUX FJP DR
THURLOW JG (Administration Director

REGISTRATION NUMBER : 84/05947/06

REGISTERED OFFICE

4 Homestead Ave, Bryanston
Sandton
2199
TEL: 011-463 1910
FAX: 011-706 7823

TRANSFER SECRETARY

Central Registrars Ltd
P O Box 4844, Johannesburg
2000
TEL: 011-331 0051

COMPANY SECRETARY

R F E Brown

NATURE OF BUSINESS

A holding company whose subsidiaries & associates mine dimensional granite on group-owned & leased land. The granite is exported through group forwarding & stevedoring companies which also serve other exporters & importers. The company holds a controlling interest in quoted Kelgran Ltd, through which its operations are conducted.

BANKERS :

First National Bank of SA Ltd
Standard Bank of SA Ltd, Bankorp Ltd

AUDITORS :

Charles Orbach & Co

FAMILIAR BRAND NAMES

N/A

CONTRIBUTION BY ACTIVITY

N/A

YEAR END : February

DIVIDEND : Ords 1c

Interim No 4	(Ldr)10/11/89	(Pay)01/12/89	Amt(c)35
Final No 5	(Ldr)08/06/90	(Pay)29/06/90	Amt(c)40
Interim No 6	(Ldr)09/11/90	(Pay)30/11/90	Amt(c)40
Final No 7	(Ldr)22/02/91	(Pay)28/02/91	Amt(c)20
Interim No 8	(Ldr)13/12/91	(Pay)20/12/91	Amt(c)10
Final No 9	(Ldr)05/06/92	(Pay)26/06/92	Amt(c)10

NUMBER OF EMPLOYEES : 2400

CAPITAL STRUCTURE

	AUTHORISED	ISSUED
Ords 1c	50000000	35100000

FINANCIAL STATISTICS (AT FINANCIAL YEAR END)

(Amts in R'000)	1992 Feb	1991 Feb	1990 Feb	1989 Feb	1988 Feb
Ord S/H Int	41247	38119	63566	46780	33034
Long Trm Loans	43389	48095	18816	16305	5517
Iss Ord Share	35100	35100	35100	35100	35100
Total Liab	134944	99870	80130	55355	23308
Current Liab	91555	51775	61314	39050	17791
Total Assets	176191	137989	142711	101150	56342
Intang Assets	*	*	985	985	*
Current Assets	104735	70979	78055	56565	28821
Debtors	24903	27372	31199	11566	8146
Inventory	42242	26681	14001	4796	3561
Turnover	191383	200749	192287	144461	65578
Oper Profit	16902	47094	52566	36739	15799
Interest Paid	5015	5616	5907	1352	1083
Tax Paid	-3543	4259	8686	6137	1625
Prf af Int&Tax	18368	41303	43754	32373	13091
Prf att Ord Sh	9220	36273	43111	32271	13306
Btm Line Earn	10148	26235	43111	32472	13156
Dividend Paid	7020	51369	26325	19305	3861
Mkt Prce(c) YE	250	480	840	1110	410
Depreciation	12177	11920	9959	5999	3317

PER SHARE STATISTICS (CENTS)

Net Asst Val	117.51	108.60	178.29	130.47	94.11
Net Earnings	26.20	103.30	122.80	91.90	42.50
Dividends	20.00	60.00	75.00	55.00	11.00
Cash Flow	44.19	133.34	150.82	120.10	57.60

RATIOS AND OTHER INFORMATION

Mrk Cap(R000)	87750	168480	294840	389610	143910
Current Ratio	1.14	1.37	1.27	1.45	1.62
Quik/Acid Tst	0.68	0.86	1.04	1.33	1.42
A/C Rec T/ovr	7.69	7.33	6.16	12.49	8.05
Tot Ass T/ovr	1.09	1.45	1.35	1.43	1.16
Debt/Ass Rat	0.54	0.41	0.51	0.49	0.38
L T L Tot Ass	0.02	0.04	0.08	0.10	0.07
Debt to Eqity	2.30	1.49	1.15	1.06	0.66
Interest Cover	3.37	8.39	8.90	27.17	14.59
Oper Prof Mrg	8.83	23.46	27.34	25.43	24.09
Net Prof Marg%	4.82	18.07	22.42	22.34	20.29
Ret on Assets	11.60	37.81	41.31	39.64	28.42
Ret on Equity%	22.35	95.16	67.82	68.98	40.28
Price/Earnings	9.54	4.65	6.84	12.08	9.65
Divid Cover	1.31	1.72	1.64	1.67	3.86
Divid Yield	8.00	12.50	8.93	4.95	2.68
Earning Yield%	10.48	21.52	14.62	8.28	10.37
NAV % Mrk Pr	47.01	22.63	21.23	11.75	22.95
Effec Tax Rate	1.65	6.31	15.65	5.24	-
Def Interval	4.00	0.65	0.53	0.50	0.46
Sus Grth Rate	5.33	-39.60	26.41	27.72	28.59

SUBSIDIARY & ASSOCIATED COMPANIES

KELGRAN LTD (50%)

INVESTMENTS

None

KELGRAN LTD

ABBREVIATION : KELGRAN

JSE SHORT CODE : KLG

SECTOR : Metals & Minerals-Other

SHAREHOLDERS

Who Owns Whom's Assessment of the Identity of the Ultimate Controlling Shareholder:
KEELEY GROUP HOLDINGS

SHAREHOLDER	PERCENTAGE 1992	1991
KEELEY GROUP HOLDINGS LTD	50 0	50 0
CONSOLIDATED NOM P/L	14 4	14 4
STD BANK NOM TVL P/L	4 0	1 7
NOLENE KEELEY TRUST	3 5	3 5
CHANEL KEELEY TRUST	3 5	3 5
MALCOLM KEELEY TRUST	3 5	3 5
NERINA KEELEY TRUST	3 5	3 5
CMB NOM P/L	2 3	---
SA MUTUAL	2 2	2 3
EIGHTY ONE MAIN STREET NOM LTD	1 8	---
SOUTHERN LIFE ASSOC LTD	1 5	1 5
ANGLO AMERICAN GROUP PENS FUND	1 1	1 1
FIRST NAT NOM P/L	1 1	1 1
SANLAMTRUST NOM P/L	1 0	1 0
SYFRETS NOM LTD	1 0	2 8
BANNER NOM P/L	---	2 1
TOTAL	94 1	91 8

DIRECTORS :
BROWN RFE (Administration Director)
BYL EH (Financial Director)
CANNATA LJ (Operations Director),DALE TG
KEELEY MF (Executive Chairman),LOUW DJD
OLDEWAGE LP ,RADEMEYER P DE V
RIEKERT MN (Deputy Chairman & M D),ROUX FJP
THURLOW JG

REGISTRATION NUMBER : 75/04595/06

REGISTERED OFFICE
4 Homestead Ave, Bryanston
2021
TEL 011-463 1910
FAX 011-706 7823

TRANSFER SECRETARY
Central Registrars Ltd
P O Box 4844, Johannesburg
2000
TEL 011-331 0051

COMPANY SECRETARY
R F E Brown

NATURE OF BUSINESS
The group quarries & produces granite for national and export distribution Quarries are established in Brits, Belfast (SA), Zimbabwe, Bophuthatswana, Lebowa and Rustenburg, with a variety of colours being produced The group also conducts forwarding and stevedoring operations, & owns mineral rights to certain platinum deposits

BANKERS :
First National Bank of SA Ltd
Trust Bank of Africa Ltd
Standard Bank of SA Ltd, Bankorp Ltd

AUDITORS :
Charles Orbach & Co

FAMILIAR BRAND NAMES
N/A

CONTRIBUTION BY ACTIVITY
N/A

YEAR END : February

DIVIDEND : Ords 2c

Dividend No 1	(Ldr)22/02/91	(Pay)28/02/91	Amt(c)20
Dividend No 2	(Ldr)13/12/91	(Pay)20/12/91	Amt(c)10
Dividend No 3	(Ldr)05/06/92	(Pay)26/06/92	Amt(c)10

CAPITAL STRUCTURE

	AUTHORISED	ISSUED
Ords 2c	100000000	70200000

FINANCIAL STATISTICS (AT FINANCIAL YEAR END)

(Amts in R'000)	1992 Feb	1991 Feb	1990 Feb
Ord S/H Int	78567	72312	52548
Long Trm Loans	5641	12775	27871
Iss Ord Share	70200	70200	47900
Total Liab	97154	64533	89154
Current Liab	91513	51758	61283
Total Assets	175721	136845	140717
Intang Assets	*	*	985
Current Assets	104735	70972	78055
Debtors	24903	27372	31199
Inventory	42242	26681	14001
Turnover	191383	200749	192287
Oper Profit	16902	47173	52644
Interest Paid	5015	5616	5907
Tax Paid	-3543	4259	8686
Prf af Int&Tax	18368	41382	43832
Prf att Ord Sh	18439	41088	43189
Btm Line Earn	20295	39307	43189
Dividend Paid	14040	58469	26403
Mkt Prce(c) YE	225	480	-
Depreciation	12177	11920	9959

PER SHARE STATISTICS (CENTS)

Net Asst Val	111 92	103 01	107 65
Net Earnings	26 20	58 50	61 50
Dividends	20 00	92 66	55 12
Cash Flow	35 23	73 53	110 68

RATIOS AND OTHER INFORMATION

Mrk Cap(R000)	157950	336960	-
Current Ratio	1 14	1 37	1 27
Quik/Acid Tst	0 68	0 86	1 05
A/C Rec T/ovr	7 69	7 33	6 16
Tot Ass T/ovr	1 09	1 47	1 37
Debt/Ass Rat	0 55	0 42	0 58
L T L Tot Ass	0 03	0 04	0 15
Debt to Eqity	1 23	0 80	1 56
Interest Cover	3 37	8 40	8 91
Oper Prof Mrg	8 83	23 50	27 38
Net Prof Marg%	9 63	20 47	22 46
Ret on Assets	11 63	38 18	41 95
Ret on Equity%	23 47	56 82	82 19
Price/Earnings	8 59	8 21	

Divid Cover	1.31	0.63	1.12
Divid Yield	8.89	19.30	-
Earning Yield%	11.64	12.19	-
NAV % Mrk Pr	49.74	21.46	-
Effec Tax Rate	1.65	6.29	15.63
Def Interval	2.51	0.59	0.53
Sus Grth Rate	5.60	-24.04	31.94

SUBSIDIARY & ASSOCIATED COMPANIES

ASSOCIATED WHARF SERVICES (PTY) LTD
BAFOKENG GRANITE (PTY) LTD
BELFAST GRANITE QUARRIES (PTY) LTD
COMPUTER AFRICA (PTY) LTD
DANTIQUE INVESTMENTS (PTY) LTD
DICK BRASS STEVEDORING (PTY) LTD
DURBAN HARBOUR GRANITE TERMINALS (PTY) L
EAGLE GRANITE (PTY) LTD
GRANITE TILES (PTY) LTD
GULF MARINE SERVICES (PTY) LTD
INTERCONTINENTAL GRANITE EXPORT (PTY) LT
INTERSHIPPING OPERATIONS (PTY) LTD
KEELEY BULK STEVEDORING (PTY) LTD
KEELEY EXPLORATION INVESTMENTS (PTY) LTD
KEELEY GRANITE (PTY) LTD
KEELEY GRANITE LTD
KEELEY MAYDON WHARF PROPERTIES (PTY) LTD
KEELEY PROPERTIES (BRYANSTON) (PTY) LTD
KEELEY STEVEDORING (CAPE TOWN) (PTY) LTD
KEELEY STEVEDORING (EAST LONDON) (PTY) L
KEELEY STEVEDORING (PTY) LTD
KEELEY STEVEDORING (RICHARDS BAY) (PTY)
KEELEY STEVEDORING (WALVIS BAY) (PTY) LT
KEELEY UTILITIES (PTY) LTD
LEBOWA GRANITE (PTY) LTD
MARIKANA GRANITE QUARRIES (PTY) LTD
MFK GRANITE HOLDINGS (PTY) LTD
NAMIBIA GRANITE QUARRIES (PTY) LTD
NATAL GRANITE QUARRIES (PTY) LTD
NORITE GRANITE (PTY) LTD
PHOKENG GRANITE QUARRIES (PTY) LTD
PJ BEKKER (EDMS) BPK
PORT NATAL BULK STEVEDORING (PTY) LTD
SAFERT KEELEY SHIPPING (PTY) LTD (50%)
SEABULK STEVEDORING (PTY) LTD
SOUTHERN GRANITE (PTY) LTD
ZIMBABWE EXPORTS (PTY) LTD
ZIMBABWE GRANITE QUARRIES (PVT) LTD (50%)

INVESTMENTS

None

KERSAF INVESTMENTS LTD

ABBREVIATION : KERSAF

JSE SHORT CODE : KER

SECTOR : Industrial-Beverages & Hotels

SHAREHOLDERS

Who Owns Whom's Assessment of the Identity of the Ultimate Controlling Shareholder:
SA MUTUAL VIA SAFMARINE

SHAREHOLDER	PERCENTAGE 1992	1991
SAFMARINE & RENNIES HLDGS LTD	75.8	75.6
SA MUTUAL	4.5	4.6
CMB NOM P/L	3.6	---
STD BANK NOM TVL P/L	3.4	3.4
SOUTHERN LIFE ASSOC LTD	2.0	1.9
SUN INTERNAT EXECUTIVE INV LTD	2.0	2.0
EIGHTY ONE MAIN STREET NOM LTD	1.9	1.7
SANLAM	---	3.5
SYFRETS NOM LTD	---	1.1
TOTAL	93.2	93.7

DIRECTORS :
DE LA H BECK WF ,EGAN MP
HAWTON DA (Executive Chairman),MACMILLAN GA
ROSEVEAR KA ,VAN BILJON AF (Financial Director

REGISTRATION NUMBER : 67/07528/06

REGISTERED OFFICE
3 Sandown Valley Crescent, Sandown, Sandton
2199
FAX: 011-783 7446

TRANSFER SECRETARY
Fraser Street Registrars (Pty) Ltd
P O Box 61178, Marshalltown
2107
TEL: 011-491 0911

COMPANY SECRETARY
S A Bailes

NATURE OF BUSINESS
Kersaf has significant interests in the leisure & entertainment industry in SA and overseas. Group interests include casino resorts, hotels, cinemas, film & TV production and distribution, steakhouse & fast foods, sports goods wholesaling & specialist retailing, and liquor wholesaling and retailing.

BANKERS :
Nedperm Bank Ltd

AUDITORS :
N/A

FAMILIAR BRAND NAMES
BALLANTINES WHISKY,BELLINGHAM,COCKBURNS
COINTREAU,CONNOISSEUR BRANDY,CULEMBORG
DOUGLAS GREEN,KAHLUA,RED HEART RUM
REMY MARTIN,SCHOONSPRUIT MINERAL WATER
SEE SUN BOP,SEE TRANS SUN,TIA MARIA
VEUVE CLICQUOT

CONTRIBUTION BY ACTIVITY
Sun International (% Turnover) (72.0%)
Interleisure (20.0%)
Kersaf Liquor (8.0%)

YEAR END : June

DIVIDEND : Ords 8c

Interim	(Ldr)09/03/90	(Pay)30/03/90	Amt(c)50
Final	(Ldr)31/08/90	(Pay)28/09/90	Amt(c)66
Interim	(Ldr)08/03/91	(Pay)28/03/91	Amt(c)58
Final	(Ldr)06/09/91	(Pay)30/09/91	Amt(c)77
Interim	(Ldr)13/03/92	(Pay)16/04/92	Amt(c)66

Final (Ldr)04/09/92 (Pay)09/10/92 Amt(c)81

NUMBER OF EMPLOYEES : 18065

CAPITAL STRUCTURE

	AUTHORISED	ISSUED
Ords 8c	110000000	78299710

FINANCIAL STATISTICS (AT FINANCIAL YEAR END)

(Amts in R'000)	1992 Jun	1991 Jun	1990 Jun	1989 Jun	1988 Jun
Ord S/H Int	883162	696020	567095	491150	794591
Long Trm Loans	1413647	903826	795200	669410	584046
Iss Ord Share	76550	75176	74990	74990	74990
Total Liab	2344338	1711509	1513798	1307317	1010395
Current Liab	930691	807683	718598	637907	426349
Total Assets	3224424	2407470	2080805	1797443	1449171
Intang Assets	3076	59	88	1024	355815
Current Assets	472588	504022	624338	460284	408660
Debtors	189620	130001	201402	105227	98274
Inventory	106435	88602	60783	62679	43476
Turnover	2050216	1788596	1554249	1309102	948464
Oper Profit	451313	442004	373383	340862	261036
Interest Paid	28965	21071	39087	42435	7317
Tax Paid	111744	143059	128184	109911	68931
Prf af Int&Tax	405620	373475	297611	249367	184788
Prf att Ord Sh	181381	165287	140233	115367	82503
Btm Line Earn	203848	195218	136363	112307	109269
Dividend Paid	111640	101379	86988	71990	52493
Mkt Prce(c) YE	4400	3250	1950	1760	1375
Depreciation	87679	61852	47224	32221	24666

PER SHARE STATISTICS (CENTS)

Net Asst Val	1149.69	925.78	756.11	653.59	585.11
Net Earnings	240.30	220.40	187.00	153.80	110.00
Dividends	147.00	135.00	116.00	96.00	70.00
Cash Flow	328.81	280.78	209.89	175.58	142.23

RATIOS AND OTHER INFORMATION

Mrk Cap(R000)	3368200	2443220	1462305	1319824	1031113
Current Ratio	0.51	0.62	0.87	0.72	0.96
Quik/Acid Tst	0.39	0.51	0.78	0.62	0.86
A/C Rec T/ovr	10.81	13.76	7.72	12.44	9.65
Tot Ass T/ovr	0.64	0.74	0.75	0.73	0.65
Debt/Ass Rat	0.37	0.39	0.44	0.45	0.41
L T L Tot Ass	0.08	0.06	0.10	0.10	0.12
Debt to Eqity	1.34	1.36	1.62	1.66	0.75
Interest Cover	17.80	23.10	10.66	8.68	35.68
Oper Prof Mrg	22.01	24.71	24.02	26.04	27.52
Net Prof Marg%	8.85	9.24	9.02	8.81	8.70
Ret on Assets	17.67	23.22	23.89	23.27	18.01
Ret on Equity%	20.54	23.75	24.73	23.49	10.38
Price/Earnings	18.31	14.75	10.43	11.44	12.50
Divid Cover	1.63	1.63	1.61	1.60	1.57
Divid Yield	3.34	4.15	5.95	5.45	5.09
Earning Yield%	5.46	6.78	9.59	8.74	8.00
NAV % Mrk Pr	26.13	28.49	38.77	37.14	42.55
Effec Tax Rate	12.03	10.97	25.95	26.40	21.98
Def Interval	1.55	0.82	1.28	1.70	1.68
Sus Grth Rate	7.90	9.18	9.39	8.83	3.78

SUBSIDIARY & ASSOCIATED COMPANIES

CHEMIX PRODUCTS (PTY) LTD (28%)
CINEMARK (PTY) LTD (37%)
COMPUTICKET (PTY) LTD (32%)
DOUGLAS GREEN BELLINGHAM (50%)
INTERFARE HOLDINGS (PTY) LTD (37%)
INTERLEISURE FINANCE (PTY) LTD (37%)
INTERLEISURE LTD (37%)
INTERLEISURE MANAGEMENT (PTY) LTD (37%)
INTERSPORT (PTY) LTD (37%)
KERSAF LIQUOR HOLDINGS LTD
KERSAF LIQUOR HOLDINGS LTD (50%)
LESOTHO SUN (PTY) LTD (39%)
RIVIERA INTERNATIONAL (PTY) LTD
SANDS HOTELS HOLDINGS (NAMIBIA) (PTY) LT
SATBEL INVESTMENT HOLDINGS (PTY) LTD (40%)
STER-KINEKOR FILMS (PTY) LTD (37%)
STER-KINEKOR THEATRES (PTY) LTD (37%)
STER-KINEKOR VIDEO (PTY) LTD (37%)
SUN CITY FOODS (BOPHUTHATSWANA) (PTY) L (37%)
SUN HOTELS INTERNATIONAL LTD
SUN INTERNATIONAL (BOPHUTHATSWANA) LTD (32%)
SUN INTERNATIONAL (BOTSWANA) (PTY) LTD
SUN INTERNATIONAL (CISKEI) (PTY) LTD (27%)
SUN INTERNATIONAL OF LESOTHO (PTY) LTD (37%)
SWAZISPA HOLDINGS LTD (40%)
TORON INTERNATIONAL (PTY) LTD (37%)
TRANSGAMES (PTY) LTD (43%)
TRANSKEI SUN INTERNATIONAL LTD (43%)
VENDA SUN LTD (40%)
VIDEO MAGIC (PTY) LTD (37%)

INVESTMENTS

BOPHUTHATSWANA COMMERCIAL RADIO (PTY) LT (19%)

KINROSS MINES LTD

ABBREVIATION : KINROSS

JSE SHORT CODE : KRS

SECTOR : Gold-Evander

SHAREHOLDERS

Who Owns Whom's Assessment of the Identity of the Ultimate Controlling Shareholder: SANLAM VIA GENCOR

SHAREHOLDER	PERCENTAGE 1992	1991
CONSOLIDATED NOM P/L	33.7	33.7
ABSA NOM P/L	12.3	---
INDO-CHINA NOM P/L	11.0	---
STD BANK NOM TVL P/L	7.7	6.4
CMB NOM P/L	7.5	---
GUARDIAN NOM P/L	2.6	2.4
FIRST CORP NOM P/L	2.5	2.6
NEDBANK NOM LTD	2.5	2.3
FIRST NAT NOM P/L GATR DEPOT	2.4	1.4
DEPOSITARY NOM INC	1.8	---
SEPON LTD J ACCOUNT	1.4	1.3
LIBERTY LIFE ASSOC OF AFRICA LTD	1.4	1.4
FIRST NAT NOM P/L	1.2	2.8
SA MUTUAL	1.1	1.4
INDO-CHINA NOM SA P/L	---	12.0
SANDTON NOM LTD	---	1.0
SANLAM	---	6.5
VOLKSKAS NOM P/L	---	11.0
TOTAL	89.1	86.3

DIRECTORS :
BOTHA AD ,BURKE JHJ (Financial Director)
CROCKER EB ,ELLIS SP ,LEE GS
MAUDE G (Chairman & Managing Dir.),OLIVIER JE

REGISTRATION NUMBER : 63/06226/06

REGISTERED OFFICE
General Mining Building, 6 Hollard Street
Johannesburg
2001
TEL: 011-376 9111
FAX: 011-834 6025

TRANSFER SECRETARY
Central Registrars Ltd
P O Box 4844, Johannesburg
2000
TEL: 011-331 0051

COMPANY SECRETARY
General Mining Metals & Minerals Ltd

NATURE OF BUSINESS
The company operates a gold mine in the area of Evander, Eastern Transvaal. Silver & osmiridium are recovered as by-products of gold.

BANKERS :
Trust Bank of Africa Ltd

AUDITORS :
Coopers Theron Du Toit

FAMILIAR BRAND NAMES
N/A

CONTRIBUTION BY ACTIVITY
Gold (% of Turnover) (99.6%)
Silver (0.1%)
Osmiridium (0.3%)

YEAR END : September

DIVIDEND :Ords R1

Interim No 44	(Ldr)04/05/90	(Pay)15/06/90	Amt(c)160
Final No 45	(Ldr)02/11/90	(Pay)14/12/90	Amt(c)165
Interim No 46	(Ldr)03/05/91	(Pay)14/06/91	Amt(c)115
Final No 47	(Ldr)01/11/91	(Pay)13/12/91	Amt(c)120

NUMBER OF EMPLOYEES : 8208

CAPITAL STRUCTURE

	AUTHORISED	ISSUED
Ords R1	18000000	18000000

FINANCIAL STATISTICS (AT FINANCIAL YEAR END)

(Amts in R'000)	1991 Sep	1990 Sep	1989 Sep	1988	1987
Ord S/H Int	266069	233760	216245	186650	158816
Long Trm Loans	483	2990	3809	110858	127596
Iss Ord Share	18000	18000	18000	18000	18000
Total Liab	93489	112582	112025	217908	251287
Current Liab	93006	109592	108216	107050	123691
Total Assets	359558	346342	328270	408779	416056
Current Assets	102852	113818	101775	111271	129644
Debtors	4973	3695	5665	-	-
Inventory	6841	10154	-	111271	129644
Turnover	385448	399065	386148	372651	334822
Oper Profit	127542	171143	175043	172898	182489
Interest Paid	133	192	-	-	2
Tax Paid	53572	96173	93129	96464	110745
Prf af Int&Tax	74609	76015	83595	76434	71742
Prf att Ord Sh	74609	76015	83595	54407	56283
Btm Line Earn	74609	76015	83595	54407	56283
Dividend Paid	42300	58500	54000	48600	62100
Mkt Prce(c) YE	4300	6500	5550	3300	8200

PER SHARE STATISTICS (CENTS)

Net Asst Val	1478.16	1298.67	1201.36	1036.94	882.31
Net Earnings	266.00	322.00	299.00	-	-
Dividends	235.00	325.00	300.00	-	-
Cash Flow	414.49	422.31	464.42	424.63	398.57

RATIOS AND OTHER INFORMATION

Mrk Cap(R000)	774000	1170000	999000	594000	1476000
Current Ratio	1.11	1.04	0.94	1.04	1.05
Quik/Acid Tst	1.03	0.95	0.94	-	-
A/C Rec T/ovr	77.51	108.00	68.16	-	-
Tot Ass T/ovr	1.07	1.15	1.18	0.91	0.80
Debt/Ass Rat	0.26	0.33	0.34	0.53	0.60
L T L Tot Ass	0.00	0.01	0.01	0.27	0.31
Debt to Eqity	0.35	0.48	0.52	1.17	1.58
Interest Cover	964.77	897.81	-	-	91244.50
Oper Prof Mrg	33.09	42.89	45.33	46.40	54.50
Net Prof Marg%	19.36	19.05	21.65	14.60	16.81
Ret on Assets	35.69	49.77	53.83	42.30	43.86
Ret on Equity%	28.04	32.52	38.66	29.15	35.44
Price/Earnings	16.17	20.19	18.56	-	-
Divid Cover	1.13	0.99	1.00	-	-
Divid Yield	5.47	5.00	5.41	-	-
Earning Yield%	6.19	4.95	5.39	-	-
NAV % Mrk Pr	34.38	19.98	21.65	31.42	10.76
Effec Tax Rate	42.05	56.26	-	55.79	60.69
Def Interval	0.01	0.04	0.05	1.45	1.78
Sus Grth Rate	12.14	7.49	13.69	3.11	-3.66

SUBSIDIARY & ASSOCIATED COMPANIES

EVANDER TOWNSHIP LTD (25%)

INVESTMENTS

EVANDER STONE HOLDINGS (PTY) LTD (150 SH)
SALT HOLDINGS LTD (14950 SH)

KIRCHMANN-HURRY PROPERTIES LTD

ABBREVIATION : KH PROPS

JSE SHORT CODE : KHO

SECTOR : Financial-Property Loan Stock

SHAREHOLDERS

Who Owns Whom's Assessment of the Identity of the Ultimate Controlling Shareholder:
DIRECTORS / INSTITUTIONS

SHAREHOLDER	PERCENTAGE 1992	1991
SA MUTUAL	21.9	14.3

STD BANK NOM TVL P/L	17.6	17.2
SIXTY SIX MARSHALL STREET NOM P/L	11.5	1.8
EIGHTY ONE MAIN STREET NOM LTD	6.7	8.6
SMBL NOM P/L	4.0	---
AECI PENS FUND	3.7	4.8
ENGINEERING INDUSTRIES PENS FUND	2.9	3.8
KIRCHMANN P FAMILY HOLDINGS P/L	2.8	3.6
MOROSS H	2.5	3.0
RE-INVEST INV HOLDINGS P/L	2.2	5.8
HURRY R G FAMILY HOLDINGS P/L	2.0	2.6
MASON C H	2.0	2.0
GILLIS LEO FAMILY TRUST	2.0	2.0
WHEWELL P L	1.7	2.2
EPF UAL NOM P/L	1.5	---
KIRCHMANN P F	1.2	1.6
HURRY R G	---	1.2
DE OLIVEIRA J M M	---	1.0
PALABORA MINING PENS FUND	---	4.8
TOTAL	86.1	80.2

DIRECTORS :

HURRY RG ,KIRCHMANN PF
KIRCHMANN WM (Executive Chairman),MOROSS H
WHEWELL PL (Financial Director

REGISTRATION NUMBER : 90/04210/06

REGISTERED OFFICE

2 Albury Park, Magalieszicht Ave
Dunkeld West, Sandton
2196
TEL: 011-788 4943
FAX: 011-880 1577

TRANSFER SECRETARY

Rand Registrars Ltd
P O Box 82549, Southdale
2135
TEL: 011-835 1016

COMPANY SECRETARY

D N Martin

NATURE OF BUSINESS

A property loan stock company engaged in the acquisition and development of property.

BANKERS :

Standard Bank of SA Ltd

AUDITORS :

Meyer Wilson & Marsh

FAMILIAR BRAND NAMES

KIRCHMANN-HURRY

CONTRIBUTION BY ACTIVITY

N/A

YEAR END : December

DIVIDEND :Units

Dividend No 1	(Ldr)17/05/91	(Pay)04/06/91	Amt(c)27
Dividend No 2	(Ldr)22/11/91	(Pay)05/12/91	Amt(c)27
Dividend No 3	(Ldr)22/05/92	(Pay)05/06/92	Amt(c)27
Dividend No 4	(Ldr)20/11/92	(Pay)04/12/92	Amt(c)27

CAPITAL STRUCTURE

	AUTHORISED	ISSUED
Units (1 Ord : 1 Deb)	40000000	27353978

FINANCIAL STATISTICS (AT FINANCIAL YEAR END)

(Amts in R'000)	1992 Sep	1991 Sep	1990 Jul
Ord S/H Int	277	209	209
Long Trm Loans	134826	103292	102926
Iss Ord Share	27354	20947	-
Total Liab	143693	109475	102926
Current Liab	8867	6183	-
Total Assets	143970	109684	10000
Current Assets	24816	15940	10000
Debtors	1841	1088	-
Turnover	15810	13656	8369
Oper Profit	9750	8694	6891
Interest Paid	13029	11307	6685
Tax Paid	-4	10	-
Prf af Int&Tax	16	11	206
Prf att Ord Sh	16	11	206
Btm Line Earn	16	11	206
Dividend Paid	13	11	-
Mkt Prce(c) YE	475	500	-

PER SHARE STATISTICS (CENTS)

Net Asst Val	1.01	1.00	-
Net Earnings	55.96	54.03	-
Dividends	55.96	54.03	-
Cash Flow	0.04	0.10	-

RATIOS AND OTHER INFORMATION

Mrk Cap(R000)	129932	104735	-
Current Ratio	2.80	2.58	-
Quik/Acid Tst	2.80	2.58	-
A/C Rec T/ovr	8.59	12.55	-
Tot Ass T/ovr	0.11	0.12	1.67
Debt/Ass Rat	1.00	1.00	10.29
L T L Tot Ass	0.94	0.94	10.29
Debt to Eqity	518.72	523.76	492.47
Interest Cover	0.75	0.77	1.03
Oper Prof Mrg	61.67	63.66	82.34
Net Prof Marg%	0.10	0.08	2.46
Ret on Assets	9.06	10.33	137.82
Ret on Equity%	5.78	5.26	197.13
Price/Earnings	8.49	9.25	-
Divid Cover	1.00	1.00	-
Divid Yield	11.78	10.81	-
Earning Yield%	11.78	10.81	-
NAV % Mrk Pr	0.21	0.20	-
Def Interval	11234.92	4918.19	-
Sus Grth Rate	1.08	0.00	98.56

SUBSIDIARY & ASSOCIATED COMPANIES

ADOPT PROPERTY INVESTMENTS SHARE BLOCK (
ARBATH SHARE BLOCK (PTY) LTD
AUCKLAND GATE SHARE BLOCK (PTY) LTD
BOLTON GARDENS SHARE BLOCK (PTY) LTD
CHELSEA CLOSE SHARE BLOCK (PTY) LTD
DRAYCOTT PLACE SHARE BLOCK (PTY) LTD
GARPAND INVESTMENTS SHARE BLOCK (PTY) LT
HYDEWOOD PROPERTIES SHARE BLOCK (PTY) LT
JUNCTION PLACE SHARE BLOCK (PTY) LTD (50%)
KENVIEW SHARE BLOCK (PTY) LTD
MENTONE CENTRE SHARE BLOCK (PTY) LTD
NO 9 STURDEE HOLDINGS SHARE BLOCK (PTY)
NORTH CRESCENT (PTY) LTD
OXRIDGE (PTY) LTD
RICHMOND PLACE SHARE BLOCK (PTY) LTD
RISINGHILL PROPERTIES SHARE BLOCK (PTY)
RIVONIA CENTRE SHARE BLOCK (PTY) LTD
SANDTON PLACE SHARE BLOCK (PTY) LTD
STRY PARK SHARE BLOCK (PTY) LTD
SURGATE SHARE BLOCK (PTY) LTD
THE COLONY CENTRE (PTY) LTD

VICTORIA GATE SHARE BLOCK (PTY) LTD
WINDRIFTER SHARE BLOCK (PTY) LTD

INVESTMENTS

None

KLIPTON LTD

ABBREVIATION : KLIPTON

JSE SHORT CODE : KLN

SECTOR : Industrial-Industrial Holding

SHAREHOLDERS

Who Owns Whom's Assessment of the Identity of the Ultimate Controlling Shareholder: DIRECTORS / INSTITUTIONS

SHAREHOLDER	PERCENTAGE 1992	1991
STD BANK NOM TVL P/L	26.7	30.5
EIGHTY ONE MAIN STREET NOM LTD	12.8	13.5
SMBL NOM P/L	11.0	4.0
MOMENTUM LIFE ASSURE LTD	9.5	7.4
MATTHEWS R J L	6.4	1.1
LIBERTY LIFE ASSOC OF AFRICA LTD	5.3	6.5
MATTHEWS I N	3.0	3.7
AUSTEN N J	1.5	1.9
AUSTEN D C	1.4	2.1
NEDBANK NOM LTD	1.3	1.6
BUTLER P T	1.1	1.2
YORK H L	---	1.2
JEPHSON P G	---	1.6
PALABORA MINING PENS FUND	---	1.3
RAND MERCHANT BANK NOM P/L	---	7.6
TOTAL	80.1	85.2

DIRECTORS :
BUTLER PT (Financial Director),GOSS PM
JEPHSON PG ,MATTHEWS IN (Joint Chairman)
MATTHEWS RJL (Joint Chairman),YORK HL

REGISTRATION NUMBER : 01/01813/06

REGISTERED OFFICE
Ground Floor, 12 Baker Street
Rosebank, Johannesburg
2196
TEL: 011-788 5547
FAX: 011-880 4756

TRANSFER SECRETARY
Consolidated Share Registrars Ltd
P O Box 61051, Marshalltown
2107
TEL: 011-492 1620

COMPANY SECRETARY
P T Butler

NATURE OF BUSINESS
The group manufactures & distributes industrial products, including : Castors & wheels, aluminium ladders, scaffolding & towers, hand & pallet trucks, racking & shelving & roller conveyor systems, pneumatic tools, lifting equipment, welding equipment & consumables, physical security products & personal protective equipment and clothing.

BANKERS :
Standard Bank of SA Ltd, Nedperm Bank Ltd
Rand Merchant Bank Ltd, Absa Bank Ltd
First National Bank of SA Ltd

AUDITORS :
KPMG Aiken & Peat

FAMILIAR BRAND NAMES
ASHCROFT,AUSTEN SAFES,BANTAM,BISCHOFF
BLACK BEAR,BRANO,CAMBELLS,CASTOR & LADDER,CM
COMPACT,FORLEZER,GARDWELL,GIANT,JDN
PORTAVAULT,ROCKWELD,SANDTON SENTRY,SAPCO
SHIMANO,SUGINO,TOKU,URYU,WAG-N-BIETJIE

CONTRIBUTION BY ACTIVITY
N/A

YEAR END : June

DIVIDEND : Ords 1c

Final	(Ldr)07/09/90	(Pay)19/09/90	Amt(c)19
Final	(Ldr)13/09/91	(Pay)25/09/91	Amt(c)19
Final	(Ldr)11/09/92	(Pay)23/09/92	Amt(c)19

NUMBER OF EMPLOYEES : 989

CAPITAL STRUCTURE

	AUTHORISED	ISSUED
Ords 1c	20000000	14070250

FINANCIAL STATISTICS (AT FINANCIAL YEAR END)

(Amts in R'000)	1992 Jun	1991 Jun	1990 Jun	1989 Jun	1988 Jun
Ord S/H Int	23891	17885	13868	10994	9073
Long Trm Loans	10310	7449	5720	3012	2560
Iss Ord Share	14070	11500	9663	6320	6262
Total Liab	43584	38503	29405	17213	13117
Current Liab	33274	31054	23685	14201	10557
Total Assets	67475	56388	43273	28207	22190
Current Assets	53352	48016	37877	25203	19097
Debtors	20945	18639	16120	10267	7526
Inventory	29333	24439	18285	14456	11091
Turnover	122142	106776	88930	57009	40508
Oper Profit	8476	11746	9895	5455	2905
Interest Paid	2990	1863	1775	996	246
Tax Paid	753	3754	3677	1513	476
Prf af Int&Tax	4790	6482	5062	2975	2223
Prf att Ord Sh	4790	6323	5001	2945	2186
Btm Line Earn	4540	5469	4995	2945	1820
Dividend Paid	2673	2185	1836	963	751
Mkt Prce(c) YE	350	360	295	165	220
Depreciation	1946	1391	1012	571	535

PER SHARE STATISTICS (CENTS)

Net Asst Val	169.80	155.52	143.52	173.96	144.89
Net Earnings	39.00	59.00	58.60	46.70	37.60
Dividends	19.00	19.00	19.00	15.00	12.00
Cash Flow	49.00	71.85	71.80	58.94	45.64

RATIOS AND OTHER INFORMATION

Mrk Cap(R000)	49245	41400	28506	10428	13776
Current Ratio	1.60	1.55	1.60	1.77	1.81
Quik/Acid Tst	0.72	0.76	0.83	0.76	0.76
A/C Rec T/ovr	5.83	5.73	5.52	5.55	5.38
Tot Ass T/ovr	1.81	1.89	2.06	2.02	1.83
Debt/Ass Rat	0.65	0.66	0.66	0.60	0.59
L T L Tot Ass	0.15	0.11	0.12	0.09	0.11
Debt to Eqity	1.82	2.10	2.07	1.53	1.43
Interest Cover	2.83	6.30	5.57	5.48	11.81
Oper Prof Mrg	6.94	11.00	11.13	9.57	7.17
Net Prof Marg%	3.92	5.92	5.62	5.17	5.40
Ret on Assets	12.65	21.46	24.30	19.44	13.27
Ret on Equity%	20.05	35.35	36.06	26.79	24.09
Price/Earnings	8.97	6.10	5.03	3.53	5.85
Divid Cover	2.05	3.11	3.08	3.11	3.13
Divid Yield	5.43	5.28	6.44	9.09	5.45
Earning Yield%	11.14	16.39	19.86	28.30	17.09
NAV % Mrk Pr	48.51	43.20	48.65	105.43	65.86
Effec Tax Rate	26.41	36.94	39.20	30.97	20.12
Def Interval	2.88	1.41	1.36	1.24	1.47
Sus Grth Rate	8.86	23.14	22.82	18.03	15.82

SUBSIDIARY & ASSOCIATED COMPANIES

ACCESS & MOBILITY GROUP (PTY) LTD
AUSTEN HEERUM (PTY) LTD
AUSTEN SAFE CO (LESOTHO) (PTY) LTD
AUSTEN SAFE CO (PTY) LTD
CITADEL TRADING (PTY) LTD
DENTATECH (PTY) LTD
GARDWEL NATAL (PTY) LTD
J A CAMPBELL & SON (PTY) LTD
KLIPTON INDUSTRIAL HOLDINGS LTD
KLIPTON INDUSTRIAL PRODUCTS (PTY) LTD
KLIPTON INDUSTRIES LTD
KLIPTON PROPERTIES (PTY) LTD
KLIPTON SAFETY & SECURITY (PTY) LTD
KLIPTON SHARE VENTURES (PTY) LTD
SAFETY PRODUCTS CO (PTY) LTD
SANDTON SENTRY SECURITY (PTY) LTD

INVESTMENTS

None

KLOOF GOLD MINING CO LTD

ABBREVIATION : KLOOF

JSE SHORT CODE : KLO

SECTOR : Gold-West Witwatersrand

SHAREHOLDERS

Who Owns Whom's Assessment of the Identity of the Ultimate Controlling Shareholder:
GFSA

SHAREHOLDER	PERCENTAGE 1992	1991
MINU NOM LTD	34.3	34.3
INDO-CHINA NOM P/L	12.5	13.4
RESIDENT NOM LTD	8.0	8.0
CMB NOM P/L	7.9	---
FIRST NAT NOM P/L GATR DEPOT	5.1	5.2
OVERSEAS NOM CO INC	4.0	4.0
STD BANK NOM TVL P/L	3.3	2.6
FIRST NAT NOM P/L	2.5	2.9
ABSA NOM P/L	1.0	---
SANLAM	---	7.1
TOTAL	78.5	77.5

DIRECTORS :
FENTON CT ,HEWITT L ,HOPWOOD JG ,HOSKING KM
MAUDE G ,MUNRO AH (Chairman & Managing Dir.)
PLUMBRIDGE RA ,TAGG MJ ,VAN ROOYEN BR ,WRIGHT AJ

REGISTRATION NUMBER : 64/04462/06

REGISTERED OFFICE
75 Fox Street, Johannesburg
2001
TEL: 011-639 9111
FAX: 011-639 2101

TRANSFER SECRETARY
Gold Fields of SA Ltd
P O Box 1167, Johannesburg
2000
TEL: 011-639 9111

COMPANY SECRETARY
Gold Fields of SA Ltd

NATURE OF BUSINESS
The company carries on gold mining operations in the Western Witwatersrand area.

BANKERS :
Standard Bank of SA Ltd

AUDITORS :
Ernst & Young

FAMILIAR BRAND NAMES
N/A

CONTRIBUTION BY ACTIVITY
N/A

YEAR END : June

DIVIDEND : Ords 25c

Interim No 40	(Ldr)29/12/89	(Pay)07/02/90	Amt(c)60
Final No 41	(Ldr)29/06/90	(Pay)08/08/90	Amt(c)45
Interim No 42	(Ldr)28/12/90	(Pay)06/02/91	Amt(c)40
Final No 43	(Ldr)28/06/91	(Pay)07/08/91	Amt(c)50
Interim No 44	(Ldr)27/12/91	(Pay)05/02/92	Amt(c)40
Final No 45	(Ldr)26/06/92	(Pay)05/08/92	Amt(c)50

NUMBER OF EMPLOYEES : 21520

CAPITAL STRUCTURE

	AUTHORISED	ISSUED
Ords 25c	140000000	121100000
Unsec Conv Debs R44	2725000	2725000

FINANCIAL STATISTICS (AT FINANCIAL YEAR END)

(Amts in R'000)	1992 Jun	1991 Jun	1990 Jun	1989 Jun	1988 Jun
Ord S/H Int	2189777	1980896	1730736	1424074	1126061
Long Trm Loans	119900	119900	119900	84475	49050
Iss Ord Share	121100	121100	121100	121100	121100
Total Liab	331589	314560	260599	274056	303692

Current Liab	211689	194660	140699	189581	254642
Total Assets	2521366	2295456	1991335	1698130	1429753
Current Assets	59198	54609	128916	225263	286958
Debtors	26125	24629	17592	9755	7133
Inventory	28102	27344	25253	26057	19882
Turnover	1101384	915223	841262	883299	907673
Oper Profit	387912	371499	416075	541762	635823
Interest Paid	23863	12492	-	-	-
Tax Paid	49687	694	12517	92265	179889
Prf af Int&Tax	318173	360660	432959	449497	455934
Prf att Ord Sh	318173	360660	432959	449497	455934
Btm Line Earn	318173	360660	432959	449497	455934
Dividend Paid	108990	108990	127155	151375	169540
Mkt Prce(c) YE	2640	3300	3785	3500	3050

PER SHARE STATISTICS (CENTS)

Net Asst Val	1808.24	1635.75	1429.18	1175.95	929.86
Net Earnings	263.00	303.00	105.00	125.00	140.00
Dividends	90.00	90.00	105.00	125.00	140.00
Cash Flow	262.74	297.82	357.52	371.18	376.49

RATIOS AND OTHER INFORMATION

Mrk Cap(R000)	3197040	3996300	4583635	4238500	3693550
Current Ratio	0.28	0.28	0.92	1.19	1.13
Quik/Acid Tst	0.15	0.14	0.74	1.05	1.05
A/C Rec T/ovr	42.16	37.16	47.82	90.55	127.25
Tot Ass T/ovr	0.44	0.40	0.42	0.52	0.63
Debt/Ass Rat	0.13	0.14	0.13	0.16	0.21
L T L Tot Ass	0.05	0.05	0.06	0.05	0.03
Debt to Eqity	0.15	0.16	0.15	0.19	0.27
Interest Cover	16.26	29.74	-	-	-
Oper Prof Mrg	35.22	40.59	49.46	61.33	70.05
Net Prof Marg%	28.89	39.41	51.47	50.89	50.23
Ret on Assets	15.54	16.29	22.37	31.90	44.47
Ret on Equity%	14.53	18.21	25.02	31.56	40.49
Price/Earnings	10.04	10.89	36.05	28.00	21.79
Divid Cover	2.92	3.37	1.00	1.00	1.00
Divid Yield	3.41	2.73	2.77	3.57	4.59
Earning Yield%	9.96	9.18	2.77	3.57	4.59
NAV % Mrk Pr	68.49	49.57	37.76	33.60	30.49
Effec Tax Rate	13.51	0.19	2.81	13.89	23.10
Def Interval	0.04	0.16	-	-	-
Sus Grth Rate	9.55	12.70	17.67	20.93	25.43

SUBSIDIARY & ASSOCIATED COMPANIES

None

INVESTMENTS

None

KNIGHTS GOLD MINING COMPANY LTD

ABBREVIATION : KNIGHTS

JSE SHORT CODE : KNH

SECTOR : Gold-Rand & others

SHAREHOLDERS

Who Owns Whom's Assessment of the Identity of the Ultimate Controlling Shareholder:
MINORITIES / INSTITUTIONS

SHAREHOLDER	PERCENTAGE 1992	1991
DUNDEE CAPITAL CORP P/L	24.0	---
SOLID G NOM P/L	17.7	21.2
CMB NOM P/L	8.3	---
STD BANK NOM TVL P/L	6.1	5.6
NEDBANK NOM LTD	5.8	---
SA MUTUAL	2.4	6.0
CHALKTON NOM CO P/L	2.0	---
WITWATERSRAND GOLD MINING CO LTD	1.9	5.2
INDO-CHINA NOM P/L	1.8	---
ABSA NOM P/L	1.2	---
FIRST NAT NOM P/L	1.2	2.4
EMARJAY NOM P/L	---	11.9
NOMINEES ONLY P/L	---	2.3
MAGWIN INV P/L	---	1.1
RAHN F J	---	1.0
BOARD OF EXECUTORS NOM P/L	---	2.0
MINERAL & EXPLORATION CORP P/L	---	5.2
SANLAM	---	1.5
TOTAL	72.2	65.2

DIRECTORS :
BREALEY PG ,BUCHAN RM ,GOODMAN N ,IMRIE WNB
JOHNSTON MR ,KNOBBS C ,LEE RA (Chairman)
WASSUNG DCL

REGISTRATION NUMBER : 88/00139/06

REGISTERED OFFICE
S & J Land Holdings (Pty) Ltd, Simmer & Jack Mine
Main Reef Road, Germiston
1401
TEL: 011-873 0584/5
FAX: 011-825 6220

TRANSFER SECRETARY
Mercantile Registrars Ltd
P O Box 1053, Johannesburg
2000
TEL: 011-333 8181

COMPANY SECRETARY
R G Rainey

NATURE OF BUSINESS
The company has rights to treat sand & slimes dumps which have arisen from the mining operations of now defunct gold mines in the Germiston area.

BANKERS :
Standard Bank of SA Ltd

AUDITORS :
Kessel Feinstein

FAMILIAR BRAND NAMES
N/A

CONTRIBUTION BY ACTIVITY
N/A

YEAR END : June

DIVIDEND : Ords 1c

Final No 1	(Ldr)11/05/90	(Pay)15/06/90	Amt(c)6
Interim No 2	(Ldr)09/11/90	(Pay)07/12/90	Amt(c)3
Final No 3	(Ldr)10/05/91	(Pay)14/06/91	Amt(c)3

NUMBER OF EMPLOYEES : 121

CAPITAL STRUCTURE

	AUTHORISED	ISSUED
Ords 1c	100000000	96980000

FINANCIAL STATISTICS (AT FINANCIAL YEAR END)

(Amts In R'000)	1992 Mar	1991 Mar	1990 Mar	1988
Ord S/H Int	70887	56317	43879	35446
Long Trm Loans	3100	4200	300	8057
Iss Ord Share	96980	85480	76480	75750
Total Liab	12354	11361	10192	15714
Current Liab	9254	7161	9892	7657
Total Assets	83241	67678	54071	45476
Current Assets	4376	4809	3942	1973
Debtors	3371	2260	2302	-
Inventory	1005	932	735	1973
Turnover	46513	42293	47705	492
Oper Profit	7631	9598	12984	372
Interest Paid	476	69	814	32
Tax Paid	108	144	100	-
Prf af Int&Tax	7095	9621	12275	340
Prf att Ord Sh	7095	9621	12275	340
Btm Line Earn	7095	9621	12275	340
Dividend Paid	-	4723	4589	-
Mkt Prce(c) YE	44	84	170	100

PER SHARE STATISTICS (CENTS)

Net Asst Val	73 09	65 88	57 37	46 79
Net Earnings	7 90	12 60	12 80	-
Dividends	-	6 00	6 00	-
Cash Flow	7 94	12 58	12 89	0 45

RATIOS AND OTHER INFORMATION

Mrk Cap(R000)	42671	71803	130016	75750
Current Ratio	0 47	0 67	0 40	0 26
Quik/Acid Tst	0 36	0 54	0 32	
A/C Rec T/ovr	13 80	18 71	16 58	-
Tot Ass T/ovr	0 56	0 62	0 71	0 01
Debt/Ass Rat	0 15	0 17	0 19	0 35
L T L Tot Ass	0 04	0 06	0 01	0 18
Debt to Eqity	0 17	0 20	0 23	0 44
Interest Cover	16 03	139 10	15 95	11 63
Oper Prof Mrg	16 41	22 69	27 22	75 61
Net Prof Marg%	15 25	22 75	25 73	69 11
Ret on Assets	9 23	14 53	19 51	0 82
Ret on Equity%	10 01	17 08	22 38	0 96
Price/Earnings	5 57	6 67	13 28	-
Divid Cover	-	2 10	2 13	-
Divid Yield	-	7 14	3 53	-
Earning Yield%	17 95	15 00	7 53	-
NAV % Mrk Pr	166 12	78 43	33 75	46 79
Effec Tax Rate	1 50	1 47	0 81	-
Def Interval	0 63	0 12	0 10	23 70
Sus Grth Rate	10 01	8 70	17 52	0 96

SUBSIDIARY & ASSOCIATED COMPANIES

None

INVESTMENTS

None

KNJ GROUP LTD

ABBREVIATION : KNJ

JSE SHORT CODE : KNJ

SECTOR : Industrial-Industrial Holding

SHAREHOLDERS

Who Owns Whom's Assessment of the Identity of the Ultimate Controlling Shareholder:
ICHIKOWITZ FAMILY

SHAREHOLDER	PERCENTAGE 1992	1991
JENKINS K N	55 9	55 9
VOLKSKAS INV LTD	13 7	13 7
JAMIESON D B	6 5	6 5
REDMAN P G	4 8	4 8
VMB NOM P/L	3 6	- -
MACNAIR A D	3 3	3 3
MOMENTUM LIFE ASSURE LTD	2 6	2 6
SLUSHERS & FABRICATION INC (SWISS)	1 5	1 5
SHARESTOCK NOM P/L	1 5	1 6
ABSA NOM P/L	1 4	--
ALMONTE INV P/L	- -	3 3
VOLKSKAS NOM P/L		1 4
TOTAL	94 8	94 6

DIRECTORS :

BROWN JJ ,JAMIESON DB (Chief Executive)
JENKINS KN (Chairman),MACNAIR AD ,REDMAN PG
WEPENER JN

REGISTRATION NUMBER : 87/02927/06

REGISTERED OFFICE

Midmacor House, 60 Trump Street West
Selby Ext 4, Johannesburg
2001
TEL 011-493 3700
FAX 011-493 8823

TRANSFER SECRETARY

Central Registrars Ltd
P O Box 4844, Johannesburg
2000
TEL 011-331 0051

COMPANY SECRETARY

DA Braithwaite

NATURE OF BUSINESS

An investment holding company with subsidiaries engaged in the following operations Supply and merchanting of steel, Sales & service of mobile cranes & handling & construction equipment, Manufacture of trackless mining vehicles, machine tools & small tools, Installation of stainless steel systems for the food & beverage industries, Freight forwarding & clearing, Manufacture and marketing of "white goods" & electrical appliances Civil & mechanical engineering Control of Midmac

BANKERS :

Absa Bank Ltd, Nedcor Bank Ltd

AUDITORS :
KPMG Aiken & Peat

FAMILIAR BRAND NAMES
N/A

CONTRIBUTION BY ACTIVITY
N/A

YEAR END : June

DIVIDEND : Ords 2c

Dividend No 2	(Ldr)19/10/90	(Pay)02/11/90	Amt(c)6
Dividend No 3	(Ldr)15/11/91	(Pay)29/11/91	Amt(c)2

NUMBER OF EMPLOYEES : 2500

CAPITAL STRUCTURE

	AUTHORISED	ISSUED
Ords 2c	250000000	146313380
"A" Cum Red Prefs 1c	46000000	16000000

FINANCIAL STATISTICS (AT FINANCIAL YEAR END)

(Amts in R'000)	1992 Jun	1991 Jun	1990 Jun	1989 Jun	1988 Jun
Ord S/H Int	105043	126154	134213	112120	20590
Long Trm Loans	20621	20629	30804	35340	5372
Iss Ord Share	71313	71313	71313	71313	21500
Total Liab	85919	95100	113289	125998	20337
Current Liab	65298	74471	82485	90658	14965
Total Assets	190962	221254	247502	238118	40927
Current Assets	146368	167867	193465	184521	17550
Debtors	49343	56250	65972	70035	6665
Inventory	96081	111391	119038	109435	9800
Turnover	243962	289760	333887	338388	22422
Oper Profit	-2127	6615	27933	33651	255
Interest Paid	7600	7504	8001	5619	551
Tax Paid	313	2003	5100	696	-
Prf af Int&Tax	-10040	-2892	16392	27336	-296
Prf att Ord Sh	-11575	-2568	14810	26559	-296
Btm Line Earn	-21111	-4306	21519	26095	-1143
Dividend Paid	-	1426	4279	5705	-
Mkt Prce(c) YE	55	47	60	145	155
Depreciation	4981	6002	6758	8071	1009

PER SHARE STATISTICS (CENTS)

Net Asst Val	147.30	176.90	188.20	157.22	95.77
Net Earnings	-16.30	-3.60	20.80	37.20	-3.00
Dividends	-	2.00	6.00	8.00	-
Cash Flow	-9.18	2.41	30.39	48.56	7.99

RATIOS AND OTHER INFORMATION

Mrk Cap(R000)	39222	33517	42788	103404	33325
Current Ratio	2.24	2.25	2.35	2.04	1.17
Quik/Acid Tst	0.77	0.76	0.90	0.83	0.52
A/C Rec T/ovr	4.94	5.15	5.06	4.83	3.67
Tot Ass T/ovr	1.28	1.31	1.35	1.42	0.60
Debt/Ass Rat	0.36	0.35	0.35	0.42	0.50
L T L Tot Ass	0.01	0.01	0.01	0.04	0.13
Debt to Eqity	0.65	0.61	0.64	0.90	0.99
Interest Cover	-0.28	0.88	3.69	5.99	0.46
Oper Prof Mrg	-0.87	2.28	8.37	9.94	1.14
Net Prof Marg%	-4.74	-0.89	4.44	7.85	-1.32
Ret on Assets	-1.11	2.99	11.92	14.13	0.68
Ret on Equity%	-11.02	-2.04	11.03	23.69	-1.57
Price/Earnings	-3.37	-13.06	2.88	3.90	-51.67
Divid Cover	-	-1.80	3.47	4.65	-
Divid Yield	-	4.26	10.00	5.52	-
Earning Yield%	-29.64	-7.66	34.67	25.66	-1.94
NAV % Mrk Pr	267.82	376.39	313.67	108.43	61.79
Effec Tax Rate	-4.87	-243.08	24.19	2.01	-
Def Interval	-7.20	30.89	2.74	1.72	13.32
Sus Grth Rate	-11.02	-3.17	7.85	18.60	-1.44

SUBSIDIARY & ASSOCIATED COMPANIES

BONUSKOR STEEL (PTY) LTD
CAMEC (PTY) LTD
CME (PTY) LTD
CONSTRUCTION & MINING EQUIPMENT (PTY) LT
D & M PADAANLEG (TRANSVAAL) (PTY) LTD
DUNCANVILLE PROPS (PTY) LTD
ENTECH MINING EQUIPMENT (PTY) LTD
KNJ INDUSTRIAL HOLDINGS (PTY) LTD
LANGKAS BELEGGINGSMAATSKAPPY (EDMS) BPK
MACARL ENGINEERING (PTY) LTD
MIDMACOR INDUSTRIES LTD
MITCO TOOL CO (PTY) LTD
NJALA GEBOU (EDMS) BPK
PANAGIDES PROPERTIES (PTY) LTD
RAMBEN (PTY) LTD
REDMAN MACHINE TOOLS (PTY) LTD
REDMAN MACHINE TOOLS TRANSVAAL (PTY) LTD
STEELCUT HOLDINGS (PTY) LTD
SUBROC EQUIPMENT CO (PTY) LTD
SUBTERRANEAN SOUTH AFRICA (PTY) LTD
SWIFT PLANT HIRE (PTY) LTD
TMF (PTY) LTD
TRANSKIP (PTY) LTD
UNIVA HOLDINGS (PTY) LTD
WICKMAN MACHINE TOOLS (PTY) LTD (50%)

INVESTMENTS

None

KOPP ELECTRONICS LTD

ABBREVIATION : KOPP

JSE SHORT CODE : KOP

SECTOR : Industrial-Electronics, Electrical & Bat

SHAREHOLDERS

Who Owns Whom's Assessment of the Identity of the Ultimate Controlling Shareholder:
DIRECTORS CONTROL 67% (JUNE 1991)

SHAREHOLDER	PERCENTAGE 1992	1991
KOPP INV CC	52.6	52.6
CMB NOM P/L	8.7	---
STOCKSHARE NOM P/L	7.1	4.3
KOPP J	3.8	3.8
KRAINHOFNER W	3.4	3.3
SHARESTOCK NOM P/L	3.4	3.4
KOPP ELECTRONICS SHARE TRUST	3.0	3.1
NUSSBAUM R A W	2.9	---
KONG D	2.0	1.9
SANLAM	---	14.7
TOTAL	86.9	87.2

DIRECTORS :
BAKER K ,DIPPENAAR LL
GAINSFORD BK (Executive Director)
KONG D (Executive Director)
KOPP A (Executive Chairman)
KRAINHOEFNER W (Executive Director)
RADEMEYER FH (Executive Director)
WELLS MA MRS (Executive Director

REGISTRATION NUMBER : 69/06701/06

REGISTERED OFFICE
31 Commerce Crescent, Eastgate Ext 12
Kramerville, Sandton
2199
TEL 011-444 2333
FAX 011-444 1706

TRANSFER SECRETARY
Union Provident Trust SA Ltd
P O Box 2322, Johannesburg
2000
TEL 011-833 6700

COMPANY SECRETARY
M A Wells (Mrs)

NATURE OF BUSINESS
The company markets electronic components and equipment Subsidiaries are engaged in the manufacture and marketing of electronic components and equipment

BANKERS :
Standard Bank of SA Ltd
Rand Merchant Bank Ltd

AUDITORS :
Ernst & Young

FAMILIAR BRAND NAMES
N/A

CONTRIBUTION BY ACTIVITY
N/A

YEAR END : June

DIVIDEND :Ords no par value

Final	(Ldr)28/09/90	(Pay)12/10/90	Amt(c)2
Final	(Ldr)04/10/91	(Pay)11/10/91	Amt(c)2 5
Final	(Ldr)02/10/92	(Pay)16/10/92	Amt(c)2 5

NUMBER OF EMPLOYEES : 175

CAPITAL STRUCTURE

	AUTHORISED	ISSUED
Ords no par value	15000000	10511300

FINANCIAL STATISTICS (AT FINANCIAL YEAR END)

(Amts in R'000)	1992 Jun	1991 Jun	1990 Jun	1989 Jun	1988 Jun
Ord S/H Int	7273	6884	6322	7246	7164
Long Trm Loans	1227	996	907	844	1147
Iss Ord Share	10511	10511	10511	10511	10389
Total Liab	5346	5030	4549	4819	5098
Current Liab	4119	4034	3642	3975	3951
Total Assets	12619	11914	10871	10870	10769
Intang Assets	*	*	*	1195	1493
Current Assets	9656	9311	8476	8596	8791
Debtors	4867	4639	4084	4430	3888
Inventory	4724	4589	4270	4019	4757
Turnover	32439	27517	26888	27298	25486
Oper Profit	1802	1659	1705	1786	2809
Interest Paid	497	392	637	571	342
Tax Paid	653	442	456	903	1238
Prf af Int&Tax	652	825	675	312	1229
Prf att Ord Sh	652	825	675	312	1229
Btm Line Earn	652	825	-714	15	1229
Dividend Paid	263	263	210	-	364
Mkt Prce(c) YE	35	30	25	45	85
Depreciation	379	278	224	259	180

PER SHARE STATISTICS (CENTS)

Net Asst Val	69 19	65 49	60 15	57 57	54 59
Net Earnings	6 20	7 80	6 40	3 00	10 10
Dividends	2 50	2 50	2 00	-	2 60
Cash Flow	10 37	10 58	8 62	4 90	16 84

RATIOS AND OTHER INFORMATION

Mrk Cap(R000)	3679	3153	2628	4730	8831
Current Ratio	2 34	2 31	2 33	2 16	2 23
Quik/Acid Tst	1 20	1 17	1 15	1 15	1 02
A/C Rec T/ovr	6 67	5 93	6 58	6 16	6 56
Tot Ass T/ovr	2 57	2 31	2 47	2 51	2 37
Debt/Ass Rat	0 41	0 42	0 41	0 44	0 46
L T L Tot Ass	0 08	0 08	0 08	0 07	0 09
Debt to Eqity	0 71	0 72	0 71	0 65	0 69
Interest Cover	3 63	4 23	2 68	3 13	8 21
Oper Prof Mrg	5 56	6 03	6 34	6 54	11 02
Net Prof Marg%	2 01	3 00	2 51	1 14	4 82
Ret on Assets	14 28	13 92	16 26	16 43	26 08
Ret on Equity%	8 96	11 98	10 68	4 31	17 16
Price/Earnings	5 65	3 85	3 91	15 00	8 42
Divid Cover	2 48	3 12	3 20	-	3 88
Divid Yield	7 14	8 33	8 00	-	3 06
Earning Yield%	17 71	26 00	25 60	6 67	11 88
NAV % Mrk Pr	197 70	218 31	240 59	127 93	64 22
Effec Tax Rate	42 30	34 65	39 70	79 51	45 20
Def Interval	0 89	0 62	0 91	2 86	0 56
Sus Grth Rate	5 35	8 16	7 36	4 31	12 07

SUBSIDIARY & ASSOCIATED COMPANIES

ACTIVE TECHNOLOGY (PTY) LTD
ADVANCED SEMICONDUCTOR DEVICES (PTY) LTD
AUTOMATIC SYSTEMS MANUFACTURING (PTY) LT

INVESTMENTS

None

KUDU GRANITE HOLDINGS LTD

ABBREVIATION : KUDU

JSE SHORT CODE : KUD

SECTOR : Metals & Minerals-Other

SHAREHOLDERS

Who Owns Whom's Assessment of the Identity of the Ultimate Controlling Shareholder:
IMPALA SA

SHAREHOLDER	PERCENTAGE 1992	1991
DU TOIT P J TRUST	45.1	42.0
BALLY CASTLE INV P/L	18.2	7.9
EIGHTY ONE MAIN STREET NOM LTD	9.2	8.6
KUDU GRANITE HOLDINGS LTD	5.4	5.1
NEDBANK NOM LTD	4.2	4.1
HASHAY NOM P/L	2.0	2.6
SMIT H S TRUSTEES	1.1	1.0
FERBROS NOM P/L	---	4.2
RINRIC NOM P/L	---	2.8
SA MUTUAL	---	5.1
STD BANK NOM TVL P/L	---	2.9
TOTAL	85.1	86.2

DIRECTORS :
DU TOIT PJ (Managing Director),HALL CA ,KENT BH
SMIT HS (Operations Director)
VAN DER WESTHUIZEN PD (Administration Director

REGISTRATION NUMBER : 87/02083/07

REGISTERED OFFICE
Cnr Jonie & Anna Streets, Annlin
Pretoria
0082
TEL: 012-26 2065

TRANSFER SECRETARY
Central Registrars Ltd
P O Box 4844, Johannesburg
2000
TEL: 011-331 0051

COMPANY SECRETARY
N D van Coller

NATURE OF BUSINESS
The group is engaged in the production and export of dimensional granite from quarries in the Parys, Marikana, Potgietersrust & Belfast areas.

BANKERS :
Nedperm Bank Ltd, Bankorp Ltd

AUDITORS :
Price Waterhouse Meyernel

FAMILIAR BRAND NAMES
N/A

CONTRIBUTION BY ACTIVITY
N/A

YEAR END : June

DIVIDEND : Ords no par value

Interim	(Ldr)23/03/90	(Pay)12/04/90	Amt(c)4
Final	(Ldr)07/09/90	(Pay)28/09/90	Amt(c)12
Interim	(Ldr)28/02/92	(Pay)24/03/92	Amt(c)4
Interim	(Ldr)13/03/92	(Pay)24/03/92	Amt(c)4

NUMBER OF EMPLOYEES : 500

CAPITAL STRUCTURE

	AUTHORISED	ISSUED
Ords no par value	50000000	38927798

FINANCIAL STATISTICS (AT FINANCIAL YEAR END)

(Amts in R'000)	1991 Jun	1990 Jun	1989 Jun	1988 Jun
Ord S/H Int	31668	28731	19577	12859
Long Trm Loans	5276	10382	5875	4948
Iss Ord Share	19464	15750	15750	15000
Total Liab	28652	27990	14936	9088
Current Liab	23376	17608	9061	4140
Total Assets	60320	56721	34513	21947
Current Assets	19703	19045	8722	3333
Debtors	14449	15971	7857	3111
Inventory	5247	3014	831	189
Turnover	39071	35690	28161	10293
Oper Profit	3427	9789	8598	4009
Interest Paid	3381	1699	638	246
Tax Paid	-605	253	222	130
Prf af Int&Tax	651	7837	7738	3633
Prf att Ord Sh	622	7891	7738	3633
Btm Line Earn	-125	7891	7738	3633
Dividend Paid	-	2520	2520	1350
Mkt Prce(c) YE	120	190	430	195
Depreciation	3492	1949	1267	655

PER SHARE STATISTICS (CENTS)

Net Asst Val	162.70	182.42	124.30	85.73
Net Earnings	3.20	46.30	50.10	24.20
Dividends	-	16.00	16.00	9.00
Cash Flow	18.03	62.48	57.17	28.59

RATIOS AND OTHER INFORMATION

Mrk Cap(R000)	23357	29925	67725	29250
Current Ratio	0.84	1.08	0.96	0.81
Quik/Acid Tst	0.62	0.91	0.87	0.76
A/C Rec T/ovr	2.70	2.23	3.58	3.31
Tot Ass T/ovr	0.65	0.63	0.82	0.47
Debt/Ass Rat	0.48	0.42	0.42	0.41
L T L Tot Ass	0.09	0.11	0.16	0.22
Debt to Eqity	0.90	0.82	0.74	0.70
Interest Cover	1.01	5.76	13.48	16.30
Oper Prof Mrg	8.77	27.43	30.53	38.95
Net Prof Marg%	1.59	22.11	27.48	35.30
Ret on Assets	5.68	17.26	24.91	18.27
Ret on Equity%	1.96	27.47	39.53	28.25
Price/Earnings	37.50	4.10	8.58	8.06
Divid Cover	-	2.89	3.13	2.69
Divid Yield	-	8.42	3.72	4.62
Earning Yield%	2.67	24.37	11.65	12.41
NAV % Mrk Pr	135.58	96.01	28.91	43.96
Effec Tax Rate	-	-	-1.63	3.45
Def Interval	5.12	1.06	1.02	1.65
Sus Grth Rate	1.96	18.69	26.65	17.75

SUBSIDIARY & ASSOCIATED COMPANIES

AURORA GRANITE LTD
EXPORT FORWARDERS (PTY) LTD
GRANITE ENTERPRISES (VENDA) (PTY) LTD
KUDU GRANITE (MARIKANA) (PTY) LTD
KUDU GRANITE FINANCE COMPANY (PTY) LTD (50%)
KUDU GRANITE OPERATIONS (PTY) LTD
NOVA EXPLORATION (PTY) LTD

INVESTMENTS

None

KWV INVESTMENTS LTD

ABBREVIATION : KWV-BEL

JSE SHORT CODE : KWV

SECTOR : Industrial-Beverages & Hotels

SHAREHOLDERS

Who Owns Whom's Assessment of the Identity of the Ultimate Controlling Shareholder:
KWV

SHAREHOLDER	PERCENTAGE 1992	1991
WIJNGAARD INV P/L	60 7	60 7
SA MUTUAL	8 6	8 6
LIBERTY LIFE ASSOC OF AFRICA LTD	8 5	8 5
ENGINEERING INDUSTRIES PENS FUND	7 1	7 1
STD BANK NOM TVL P/L	2 3	1 9
GUARDIAN NAT INSURANCE CO LTD	1 9	1 9
CMB NOM P/L	1 2	---
SANLAM	---	1 2
TOTAL	90 2	89 8

DIRECTORS :
BRUWER EJ ,DE LA BAT RS ,HUGO PBB (Chairman)
JONKER LN ,MALHERBE GJ

REGISTRATION NUMBER : 79/07263/06

REGISTERED OFFICE
La Concorde, 57 Main Street
Suider-Paarl
7646
TEL 02211-631 001
FAX 02211-633 440

TRANSFER SECRETARY
Central Registrars Ltd
P O Box 4844, Johannesburg
2000
TEL 011-331 0051

COMPANY SECRETARY
S W Joubert

NATURE OF BUSINESS
The company has a 50% holding in Rembrandt-KWV Investments Ltd, which in turn holds 60% each of SFW and Distillers

BANKERS :
Boland Bank Ltd

AUDITORS :
Coopers Theron Du Toit

FAMILIAR BRAND NAMES
N/A

CONTRIBUTION BY ACTIVITY
N/A

YEAR END : June

DIVIDEND : Ords R1

Interim No 20	(Ldr)23/03/90	(Pay)12/04/90	Amt(c)14
Final No 21	(Ldr)28/09/90	(Pay)29/10/90	Amt(c)27 3
Interim No 22	(Ldr)22/02/91	(Pay)28/02/91	Amt(c)15
Final No 23	(Ldr)20/09/91	(Pay)23/10/91	Amt(c)31 3
Interim No 24	(Ldr)21/02/92	(Pay)28/02/92	Amt(c)16
Final No 25	(Ldr)25/09/92	(Pay)23/10/92	Amt(c)35

CAPITAL STRUCTURE

	AUTHORISED	ISSUED
Ords R1	56000000	42000000

FINANCIAL STATISTICS (AT FINANCIAL YEAR END)

(Amts in R'000)	1992 Jun	1991 Jun	1990 Jun	1989 Jun	1988 Jun
Ord S/H Int	357744	320992	288308	268203	221825
Iss Ord Share	42000	42000	42000	42000	42000
Total Liab	14880	13288	11592	11153	7152
Current Liab	14880	13288	11592	11153	7152
Total Assets	372624	334280	299900	279356	228977
Current Assets	14956	13348	11704	11286	7285
Debtors	2	2	-	-	-
Oper Profit	-215	-186	-161	-135	10013
Tax Paid	20	46	55	50	13
Prf af Int&Tax	21436	19394	17325	14826	10000
Prf att Ord Sh	40993	38254	36107	34611	28153
Btm Line Earn	40517	36888	36107	34611	28153
Dividend Paid	21420	19446	17346	14826	9996
Mkt Prce(c) YE	825	650	465	315	-

PER SHARE STATISTICS (CENTS)

Net Asst Val	851 77	764 27	686 45	638 58	528 15
Net Earnings	97 60	91 10	86 00	82 40	-
Dividends	51 00	46 30	41 30	35 30	-
Cash Flow	51 04	46 18	41 25	35 30	23 81

RATIOS AND OTHER INFORMATION

Mrk Cap(R000)	346500	273000	195300	132300	-
Current Ratio	1 01	1 00	1 01	1 01	1 02
Quik/Acid Tst	1 01	1 00	1 01	1 01	1 02
Debt/Ass Rat	0 04	0 04	0 04	0 04	0 03
Debt to Eqity	0 04	0 04	0 04	0 04	0 03
Ret on Assets	11 01	11 46	12 06	12 41	12 30
Ret on Equity%	11 46	11 92	12 52	12 90	12 69
Price/Earnings	8 45	7 14	5 41	3 82	-
Divid Cover	1 91	1 97	2 08	2 33	-
Divid Yield	6 18	7 12	8 88	11 21	-
Earning Yield%	11 83	14 02	18 49	26 16	-
NAV % Mrk Pr	103 25	117 58	147 62	202 72	-
Effec Tax Rate	-11 49	-51 11	-110 00	-147 06	0 13
Sus Grth Rate	5 47	5 86	6 51	7 38	8 19

SUBSIDIARY & ASSOCIATED COMPANIES

DISTILLERS CORPORATION (SA) LTD (30%)
REMBRANDT-KWV INVESTMENTS LTD (50%)
STELLENBOSCH FARMERS WINERY GROUP LTD (30%)

INVESTMENTS

None

LANCHEM LTD

ABBREVIATION : LANCHEM

JSE SHORT CODE : LCM

SECTOR : Development Capital Market

SHAREHOLDERS

Who Owns Whom's Assessment of the Identity of the Ultimate Controlling Shareholder: DIRECTORS

SHAREHOLDER	PERCENTAGE 1992	1991
ENGELBRECHT I Z	---	2.1
FIRST NAT NOM P/L	---	2.2
GREEN T R	---	1.7
HOUSE OF INV LTD	---	8.6
INVERSIONES MALDIVAS SA	---	6.6
IVELL D	---	1.6
NOMINEES ONLY P/L	---	5.0
SCHMET K	---	1.9
STD BANK NOM TVL P/L	---	3.7
TRUST BANK NOM P/L	---	3.6
CORPORACION ORIONO INTERNACIONAL SA	---	8.3
DE BRUYN D A	---	4.2
GLATANA HOLDINGS CC	---	4.8
O'CONNOR J J	---	2.0
RISTONE FINANCIAL HOLDINGS P/L	---	21.2
TOTAL	---	77.6

DIRECTORS :
DRYDEN G (Managing Director)
FERREIRA DR CG (Chairman),FLEMMER J
SCHROEDER HC ,TILLEY MRS ME

REGISTRATION NUMBER : 05/17084/06

REGISTERED OFFICE
1st Floor, Cradock Place, 5 Cradock Street
Rosebank, Johannesburg
2196
TEL: 011-880 6330

TRANSFER SECRETARY
Fraser Street Registrars (Pty) Ltd
P O Box 61178, Marshalltown
2107
TEL: 011-491 0911

COMPANY SECRETARY
M W A Gilbert

NATURE OF BUSINESS
Subsidiaries are involved in the following activities: The manufacture and supply of sliding door gear, industrial doors, vehicle doors and security equipment; manufacture and distribution of industrial and commercial sectional overhead insulated sliding doors, roller shutter doors, roller grills and purpose-made sliding and jack-knife doors; the manufacture of sliding-door gear mechanisms; The design, sale, finance and construction of garages and add-on rooms.

BANKERS :
Standard Bank of SA Ltd
First National Bank of SA Ltd

AUDITORS :
Price Waterhouse Meyernel

FAMILIAR BRAND NAMES
N/A

CONTRIBUTION BY ACTIVITY
N/A

YEAR END : June

CAPITAL STRUCTURE

	AUTHORISED	ISSUED
Ords 2,5c	64000000	25140000
Comp Conv Prefs 2,5c	20000000	20000000
Red Prefs 25c	31600000	0

FINANCIAL STATISTICS (AT FINANCIAL YEAR END)

(Amts in R'000)	1989
Ord S/H Int	1777
Long Trm Loans	2545
Iss Ord Share	25140
Total Liab	5090
Current Liab	2545
Total Assets	8408
Current Assets	4086
Inventory	4086
Turnover	14185
Oper Profit	1619
Interest Paid	76
Tax Paid	576
Prf af Int&Tax	967
Prf att Ord Sh	967
Btm Line Earn	967
Mkt Prce(c) YE	35

PER SHARE STATISTICS (CENTS)

Net Asst Val	7.07
Cash Flow	3.85

RATIOS AND OTHER INFORMATION

Mrk Cap(R000)	8799
Current Ratio	1.61
Tot Ass T/ovr	1.69
Debt/Ass Rat	0.61
L T L Tot Ass	0.30
Debt to Eqity	2.86
Interest Cover	21.30
Oper Prof Mrg	11.41
Net Prof Marg%	6.82
Ret on Assets	19.26
Ret on Equity%	54.42
NAV % Mrk Pr	20.20
Effec Tax Rate	37.33
Def Interval	2.63
Sus Grth Rate	54.42

SUBSIDIARY & ASSOCIATED COMPANIES

GARAGE DISTRIBUTORS (PTY) LTD
INDUSTRIAL INVESTMENT HOLDINGS LTD (26%)
MONUMENT HARDWARE & INDUSTRIAL SUPPLIES
P C HENDERSON (PTY) LTD
SUNSET GARAGES (PARTNERSHIP)
TANGENT ASSETS (PTY) LTD
TASK CEILINGS & PARTITIONS (PTY) LTD
WOT ROOMS (TVL) (PTY) LTD

INVESTMENTS

NORVIC MANUFACTURING CO LTD (16,7%)

LANGEBERG HOLDINGS LIMITED

ABBREVIATION : LANGBRG

JSE SHORT CODE : LGB

SECTOR : Industrial-Food

SHAREHOLDERS

Who Owns Whom's Assessment of the Identity of the Ultimate Controlling Shareholder:
BARLOWS VIA TIGER OATS

SHAREHOLDER	PERCENTAGE 1992	1991
TIGER OATS LTD	57 4	---
LANGEBERG CO-OPARATIVE LTD	30 0	---
FINANSBANK NOM P/L	1 6	---
SA MUTUAL	1 0	---
TOTAL	90 1	---

DIRECTORS :
APSEY CA ,BROWN RG (Managing Director)
JOUBERT JA ,LEWIS WA ,MALAN JF ,STEELE BP
VAN DER MERWE JH ,VAN VEIJEREN CG (Chairman)
WOLPERT C

REGISTRATION NUMBER : 05/02265/06

REGISTERED OFFICE
Parc du Cap, Willie van Schoor Ave
Belville
7530
TEL 021-946 3400
FAX 021-94 1902

TRANSFER SECRETARY
Rand Registrars Ltd
P O Box 82549, Southdale
2135
TEL 011-835 1016

COMPANY SECRETARY
A Human

NATURE OF BUSINESS
Langeberg comprises a major food processing and canning operation with nine factories spread across South Africa Products include canned vegetables,soups,jams & marmalade,juices,pickles & condiments,sauces,pulps & purees and also the processing, distribution and marketing of pineapples

BANKERS :
Volkskas Ltd, Finansbank Ltd

AUDITORS :
Coopers Theron Du Toit, Greenwoods

FAMILIAR BRAND NAMES
ALL GOLD,GOLD REEF,KOO

CONTRIBUTION BY ACTIVITY
N/A

YEAR END : September

DIVIDEND : Ords 1c
Final No 5 (Ldr)31/12/92 (Pay)11/01/93 Amt(c)11

CAPITAL STRUCTURE

	AUTHORISED	ISSUED
Ords 1c	168000000	160000000

FINANCIAL STATISTICS (AT FINANCIAL YEAR END)

(Amts in R'000)	1991 Sep
Ord S/H Int	243087
Long Trm Loans	50387
Total Liab	158265
Current Liab	107878
Total Assets	401352
Current Assets	281015
Debtors	101578
Inventory	179323
Turnover	645777
Oper Profit	79401
Interest Paid	17095
Tax Paid	8
Prf af Int&Tax	62298
Prf att Ord Sh	62298
Btm Line Earn	62298

PER SHARE STATISTICS (CENTS)

Net Earnings	38 90
Dividends	11 30

RATIOS AND OTHER INFORMATION

Current Ratio	2 60
Quik/Acid Tst	0 94
A/C Rec T/ovr	6 36
Tot Ass T/ovr	1 61
Debt/Ass Rat	0 39
L T L Tot Ass	0 13
Debt to Eqity	0 65
Interest Cover	4 64
Oper Prof Mrg	12 30
Net Prof Marg%	9 65
Ret on Assets	19 78
Ret on Equity%	25 63
Divid Cover	3 44
Effec Tax Rate	0 01
Def Interval	1 05
Sus Grth Rate	25 63

SUBSIDIARY & ASSOCIATED COMPANIES

ALL GOLD FOODS (PTY) LTD
CERES FRUIT CANNING COMPANY (PTY) LTD
KOO INTERNATIONAL LTD (UK)
LANGEBERG FOODS LTD

INVESTMENTS

None

LASER TRANSPORT HOLDINGS LTD

ABBREVIATION : LASER

JSE SHORT CODE : LSR

SECTOR : Industrial-Transportation

SHAREHOLDERS

Who Owns Whom's Assessment of the Identity of the Ultimate Controlling Shareholder:
DIRECTORS CONTROL 63,8%

SHAREHOLDER	PERCENTAGE 1992	1991
COMMERCIAL UNION ASSURE CO SA LTD	---	5.9
DENIS KAYE FAMILY TRUST	---	10.5
JAGINI TRUST	---	8.9
KAYE D	---	1.4
KAYE D H	---	25.8
KINALE TRUST	---	10.5
LASER TRANSPORT HOLDINGS PENS FUND	---	1.7
PETERBRIDGE TRUST	---	1.1
SANLAM	---	10.6
STD BANK NOM TVL P/L	---	2.5
LASER TRANSPORT HOLDINGS LTD	---	1.4
TOTAL	---	80.2

DIRECTORS :
PUCCINI E (Managing Director)
THOMAS PRS (Executive Chairman),VUKIC I

REGISTRATION NUMBER : 71/10431/06

REGISTERED OFFICE
4th Floor, Southern Life Place
21 Riebeek Street, Cape Town
8001
TEL: 021-54 7554
FAX: 021-54 1954

TRANSFER SECRETARY
Consolidated Share Registrars Ltd
P O Box 61051, Marshalltown
2107
TEL: 011-492 1620

COMPANY SECRETARY
E Puccini

NATURE OF BUSINESS
An investment holding company with subsidiaries engaged in the removal of furniture and household effects, machine moving and rigging, ancillary services, property investment and truck parts sales.

BANKERS :
First National Bank of SA Ltd
Standard Bank of SA Ltd

AUDITORS :
KPMG Aiken & Peat

FAMILIAR BRAND NAMES
ALPHA PACKAGING,FRASERS INTERNATIONAL
JACK WELLSTED,LASERTRANS,PICKFORDS
STUTTAFORDS VAN LINES
TRANSPLANT PLANT REMOVAL
VAN NIMWEGEN INTERNATIONAL

CONTRIBUTION BY ACTIVITY
Domestic Removals (% revenue) (71.0%)
Exports (14.0%)
Imports (5.0%)
Storage & Packaging (10.0%)

YEAR END : September

DIVIDEND : Ords 10c

Interim	(Ldr)24/08/90	(Pay)13/09/90	Amt(c)6
Final	(Ldr)01/03/91	(Pay)19/03/91	Amt(c)7
Interim	(Ldr)10/01/92	(Pay)05/02/92	Amt(c)5

NUMBER OF EMPLOYEES : 1477

CAPITAL STRUCTURE

	AUTHORISED	ISSUED
Ords 10c	12000000	10000000

FINANCIAL STATISTICS (AT FINANCIAL YEAR END)

(Amts in R'000)	1991 Dec	1990 Dec	1989 Dec	1988 Dec	1987 Dec
Ord S/H Int	26674	23801	21969	17442	13805
Long Trm Loans	22193	16362	11685	16039	11872
Iss Ord Share	10000	10000	10000	10000	10000
Total Liab	50084	37619	34786	35785	32209
Current Liab	27891	21257	23101	19746	20337
Total Assets	76758	61271	56148	52163	44492
Intang Assets	*	149	607	1064	1522
Current Assets	28220	20043	22062	16272	16256
Debtors	26523	18544	19860	14896	11417
Inventory	1181	1029	1799	1161	950
Turnover	87264	106488	106388	90051	80365
Oper Profit	6024	9327	14569	12401	8969
Interest Paid	2333	2741	3073	1862	870
Tax Paid	8664	3194	5309	3944	2895
Prf af Int&Tax	-4973	3392	6187	6595	5204
Prf att Ord Sh	-4973	3392	6187	6595	5204
Btm Line Earn	-4628	3436	5729	6137	4475
Dividend Paid	500	1300	2500	2500	2000
Mkt Prce(c) YE	115	145	250	275	350
Depreciation	2105	2762	2602	2061	1528

PER SHARE STATISTICS (CENTS)

Net Asst Val	266.74	236.52	213.62	163.78	122.83
Net Earnings	19.00	34.00	62.00	66.00	52.00
Dividends	5.00	13.00	25.00	25.00	20.00
Cash Flow	-29.21	70.99	99.50	91.42	66.20

RATIOS AND OTHER INFORMATION

Mrk Cap(R000)	11500	14500	25000	27500	35000
Current Ratio	1.01	0.94	0.96	0.82	0.80
Quik/Acid Tst	0.97	0.89	0.88	0.77	0.75
A/C Rec T/ovr	3.29	5.74	5.36	6.05	7.04
Tot Ass T/ovr	1.14	1.74	1.89	1.73	1.81
Debt/Ass Rat	0.62	0.57	0.58	0.66	0.71
L T L Tot Ass	0.25	0.22	0.17	0.29	0.25
Debt to Eqity	1.77	1.46	1.48	1.99	2.29
Interest Cover	2.58	3.40	4.74	6.66	10.31
Oper Prof Mrg	6.90	8.76	13.69	13.77	11.16
Net Prof Marg%	-5.70	3.19	5.82	7.32	6.48
Ret on Assets	7.85	15.22	25.95	23.77	20.16
Ret on Equity%	-18.64	14.25	28.16	37.81	37.70
Price/Earnings	6.05	4.26	4.03	4.17	6.73
Divid Cover	3.80	2.62	2.48	2.64	2.60
Divid Yield	4.35	8.97	10.00	9.09	5.71
Earning Yield%	16.52	23.45	24.80	24.00	14.86
NAV % Mrk Pr	231.95	163.12	85.45	59.56	35.09

Effec Tax Rate	50.31	33.46	31.11	10.72	8.06
Def Interval	-7.64	2.02	1.25	1.63	1.70
Sus Grth Rate	-20.52	8.79	16.78	23.48	23.21

SUBSIDIARY & ASSOCIATED COMPANIES

ALGOA TRANSPORT COMPANY (PTY) LTD
ALPHA PACKAGING SUPPLIES (PTY) LTD
DALY INTERNATIONAL (PTY) LTD
DE KOCK'S TRANSPORT (CAPE) (PTY) LTD
E J RORICH (PTY) LTD
FRASERS INTERNATIONAL (JHB) (PTY) LTD
FRASERS INTERNATIONAL (PTY) LTD
FRASERS INTERNATIONAL AIRCARGO (PTY) LTD
FRASERS INTERNATIONAL REMOVALS (PTY) LTD
GROUP FIVE CONSTRUCTION SA (PTY) LTD
JACK WELLSTED (PTY) LTD
JL VAN NIMWEGEN & CO (PTY) LTD
JOHAN NEL (PTY) LTD
LASER FREIGHT CARRIERS (PTY) LTD
LASER FREIGHT FORWARDERS (PTY) LTD
LASER INTERNATIONAL (PTY) LTD
LASER MANAGEMENT SERVICES (PTY) LTD
LASER PACKAGING & DISTRIBUTION (PTY) LTD
LASER PROPERTIES (GEORGE) (PTY) LTD
LASER PROPERTIES (GLEN AUSTIN) (PTY) LTD
LASER PROPERTIES (KIMBERLEY) (PTY) LTD
LASER PROPERTIES (KNYSNA) (PTY) LTD
LASER PROPERTIES (MARKMAN) (PTY) LTD
LASER PROPERTIES (MIDRAND) (PTY) LTD
LASER PROPERTIES (MONTAGUE GARDEN) (PTY)
LASER PROPERTIES (PHILIPPI) (PTY) LTD
LASER PROPERTIES (PORT ELIZABETH) (PTY)
LASER PROPERTIES (PROSPECTON) (PTY) LTD
LASER PROPERTIES (PTY) LTD
LASER PROPERTIES (SILVERTON) (PTY) LTD
LASER PROPERTIES (SOUTHERN CAPE) (PTY) L
LASER PROPERTIES (STORMILL) (PTY) LTD
LASER PROPERTIES (WINDHOEK) (PTY) LTD
LASER REMOVALS (PTY) LTD
LASER TRANSPLANT SERVICES (PTY) LTD
LASERTRANS (PTY) LTD
MORKELS TRANSPORT (PTY) LTD
PICKFORDS REMOVALS SOUTH AFRICA (PTY) LT
SALP PRODUCTS (PTY) LTD
STUTTAFORDS VAN LINES (PTY) LTD

INVESTMENTS

LASPROP (PTY) LTD (49 SH)

LEBOWA BAKERIES LTD

ABBREVIATION : LEBAKA

JSE SHORT CODE : LBA

SECTOR : Industrial-Food

SHAREHOLDERS

Who Owns Whom's Assessment of the Identity of the Ultimate Controlling Shareholder:
SASKO CO-OP

SHAREHOLDER	PERCENTAGE 1992	1991
SASKO BEHEREND E/B	74.2	71.2
MORENA J	4.0	4.0
LEBAKA EMPL SHARE INC TRUST	4.0	2.8
TOTAL	82.2	78.0

DIRECTORS :
BESTER PW ,LEDWABA MJ
LEHONG MT (Financial Director)
MANAKA SP PROF (Chairman)
MCKENNA JWB (Managing Director),PHASHA MJ
SWANEPOEL J PRO

REGISTRATION NUMBER : 75/04193/06

REGISTERED OFFICE
Stand 7985, Zone 7
Seshego
0742
TEL: 0156-35660
FAX: 01521-931165

TRANSFER SECRETARY
Mercantile Registrars Ltd
P O Box 1053, Johannesburg
2000
TEL: 011-333 8181

COMPANY SECRETARY
A W Schoeman

NATURE OF BUSINESS
The company and its subsidiaries carry on business as bakers & confectioner. The group has a fleet of 109 vehicles used for distribution.

BANKERS :
First National Bank of SA Ltd

AUDITORS :
Louw Futter & Partners, KPMG Aiken & Peat

FAMILIAR BRAND NAMES
BOCHUM BAKERY,BUSHBUCKRIDGE BAKERY
CAPITAL BAKERY,DINOKO BAKERY (75%)
G & D BAKERY,MOKOPANE BAKERY,PHOKWANE BAKERY
PRESIDENT BAKERY,SESHEGO BAKERY
TAFELKOP BAKERY (51%),TUBATSE BAKERY

CONTRIBUTION BY ACTIVITY
N/A

YEAR END : September

DIVIDEND : Ords 10c

Final No 6	(Ldr)15/06/90	(Pay)13/07/90	Amt(c)5
Interim No 5	(Ldr)23/11/90	(Pay)01/12/90	Amt(c)3
Final No 8	(Ldr)14/06/91	(Pay)12/07/91	Amt(c)6.25
Interim No 9	(Ldr)29/11/91	(Pay)13/12/91	Amt(c)3.5
Interim No 10	(Ldr)19/06/92	(Pay)17/07/92	Amt(c)7
Final No 11	(Ldr)11/12/92	(Pay)21/12/92	Amt(c)3.75

NUMBER OF EMPLOYEES : 1029

CAPITAL STRUCTURE

	AUTHORISED	ISSUED
Ords 10c	30000000	25000000

FINANCIAL STATISTICS (AT FINANCIAL YEAR END)

(Amts in R'000)	1991 Mar	1990 Mar	1989 Mar	1988 Mar	1987
Ord S/H Int	23994	20547	17259	14881	10456
Long Trm Loans	7439	7056	5076	2728	5711
Iss Ord Share	25000	25000	25000	25000	20000
Total Liab	16155	14743	11185	6128	11072
Current Liab	8716	7687	6109	3400	5361
Total Assets	39655	34739	27836	21009	26491
Intang Assets	494	551	608	*	*
Current Assets	18972	13744	13109	6693	10324
Debtors	2867	1301	2576	2331	-
Inventory	2102	1483	1086	1153	10324
Turnover	91143	73563	64384	38985	32022
Oper Profit	10339	8913	7714	5096	4881
Interest Paid	1006	1010	472	8	-
Tax Paid	5611	5104	3937	3082	2440
Prf af Int&Tax	6331	5487	4216	2817	2441
Prf att Ord Sh	5760	5225	3877	2685	2441
Btm Line Earn	5760	5225	3877	2550	2441
Dividend Paid	2313	1937	1500	1125	700
Mkt Prce(c) YE	70	53	50	-	-
Depreciation	3666	3098	2285	1380	-

PER SHARE STATISTICS (CENTS)

Net Asst Val	94 00	79 98	66 60	59 52	52 28
Net Earnings	23 00	20 90	15 50	11 10	-
Dividends	9 25	7 75	6 00	4 50	-
Cash Flow	41 61	35 62	25 12	18 71	12 21

RATIOS AND OTHER INFORMATION

Mrk Cap(R000)	17500	13250	12500	-	-
Current Ratio	2 18	1 79	2 15	1 97	1 93
Quik/Acid Tst	1 94	1 60	1 97	1 63	-
A/C Rec T/ovr	31 79	56 54	24 99	16 72	-
Tot Ass T/ovr	2 30	2 12	2 31	1 86	1 21
Debt/Ass Rat	0 30	0 34	0 34	0 23	0 42
L T L Tot Ass	0 08	0 12	0 12	0 07	0 22
Debt to Eqity	0 49	0 58	0 55	0 32	1 06
Interest Cover	10 28	9 24	16 76	637 00	-
Oper Prof Mrg	11 34	12 12	11 98	13 07	15 24
Net Prof Marg%	6 32	7 10	6 02	6 89	7 62
Ret on Assets	32 70	33 43	30 99	28 12	18 43
Ret on Equity%	24 01	25 43	22 46	18 04	23 35
Price/Earnings	3 04	2 54	3 23	-	-
Divid Cover	2 49	2 70	2 58	2 47	-
Divid Yield	13 21	14 62	12 00	-	-
Earning Yield%	32 86	39 43	31 00	-	-
NAV % Mrk Pr	134 29	150 91	133 21	-	-
Effec Tax Rate	39 11	44 44	47 98	43 43	49 99
Def Interval	0 35	0 48	0 53	-	2 34
Sus Grth Rate	14 37	16 00	13 77	10 48	16 65

SUBSIDIARY & ASSOCIATED COMPANIES

DINOKO BAKERY (PTY) LTD
KESTELL BAKKERYE (PTY) LTD (33,3%)
MOSHATE FOODS (PTY) LTD
NORTHERN BAKERY CONSORTIUM (PTY) LTD
TAFELKOP BAKERY (PTY) LTD

INVESTMENTS

None

LEBOWA PLATINUM MINES LTD

ABBREVIATION : LEPLAT

JSE SHORT CODE : LPT

SECTOR : Metals & Minerals-Platinum

SHAREHOLDERS

Who Owns Whom's Assessment of the Identity of the Ultimate Controlling Shareholder:
ANGLO AMERICAN VIA JOHNIES

SHAREHOLDER	PERCENTAGE 1992	1991
STD BANK NOM TVL P/L	35 8	26 5
LEBOWA DEVELOPMENT CORP LTD	8 4	8 4
RESIDENT NOM LTD	7 3	5 7
LYDENBURG PLATINUM LTD	7 3	5 5
DIDO NOM LTD	5 4	4 0
JOHANNESBURG CONSOLIDATED INV CO LTD	4 1	3 4
SA MUTUAL	3 6	6 2
FERMAIN NOM LTD	3 2	2 3
PETARD NOM LTD	2 2	1 6
CMB NOM P/L	2 0	---
EIGHTY ONE MAIN STREET NOM LTD	1 2	---
TAURUS NOM LTD	1 1	---
RUSTENBURG PLATINUM HLDGS LTD	---	21 5
SANLAM	---	1 4
TOTAL	81 5	86 5

DIRECTORS :
BRAY VG ,BRUCE JT ,DAVISON BE (Chairman)
KING MW ,LAMOLA MD
MACCONACHIE AW (Financial Director),MCKERRON AB
PRETORIUS JH DR,RETIEF PF ,SCOTT-RUSSELL H DR
STOTT CS ,SUTHERLAND RB

REGISTRATION NUMBER : 63/06144/06

REGISTERED OFFICE
Consolidated Building, Cnr Fox & Harrison Streets
Johannesburg
2001
TEL 011-373 9111
FAX 011-838 5537

TRANSFER SECRETARY
Consolidated Share Registrars Ltd
P O Box 61051, Marshalltown
2107
TEL 011-492 1620

COMPANY SECRETARY
Johannesburg Consolidated Inv Co Ltd

NATURE OF BUSINESS
The company operates the Atok mine, which exploits the platinum bearing ores of the Eastern Limb of the Bushveld Igneous Complex The primary product is platinum, palladium, rhodium, iridium, osmium, ruthenium, gold, silver, copper, nickel and cobalt sulphate are also recovered

BANKERS :
First National Bank of SA Ltd

AUDITORS :
Ernst & Young

FAMILIAR BRAND NAMES
N/A

CONTRIBUTION BY ACTIVITY
N/A

YEAR END : June

DIVIDEND : Ords 1c
Interim No 18 (Ldr)09/02/90 (Pay)09/03/90 Amt(c)2.5
Final No 19 (Ldr)17/08/90 (Pay)15/09/90 Amt(c)5

NUMBER OF EMPLOYEES : 1700

CAPITAL STRUCTURE

	AUTHORISED	ISSUED
Ords 1c	200000000	120000000
Red Prefs 50c	9568618	9568618

FINANCIAL STATISTICS (AT FINANCIAL YEAR END)

(Amts in R'000)	1992 Jun	1991 Jun	1990 Jun	1989 Jun	1988 Jun
Ord S/H Int	221319	250294	240090	230518	30926
Long Trm Loans	18642	11182	4784	4784	-
Iss Ord Share	120000	120000	120000	120000	86158
Total Liab	132499	41497	21709	38345	11048
Current Liab	113857	30315	16925	33561	11048
Total Assets	353818	291791	261799	239104	41974
Intang Assets	*	*	*	29759	*
Current Assets	17211	11122	32030	42461	23254
Debtors	13348	7907	5341	4535	7928
Inventory	3863	3215	13858	4681	5268
Turnover	112299	111934	77537	68505	52427
Oper Profit	-28810	9723	14787	16942	17813
Interest Paid	165	-	-	-	-
Tax Paid	-	319	1779	5047	2969
Prf af Int&Tax	-28975	10204	18572	23651	14844
Prf att Ord Sh	-28975	10204	18572	23651	14844
Btm Line Earn	-28975	10204	18572	23651	14844
Dividend Paid	-	-	9000	9000	5169
Mkt Prce(c) YE	125	410	860	835	550

PER SHARE STATISTICS (CENTS)

Net Asst Val	184.43	208.58	200.08	167.30	35.89
Net Earnings	-24.10	8.50	15.50	19.70	17.20
Dividends	-	-	7.50	7.50	6.00
Cash Flow	-24.15	8.50	15.48	19.71	17.23

RATIOS AND OTHER INFORMATION

Mrk Cap(R000)	150000	492000	1032000	1002000	473869
Current Ratio	0.15	0.37	1.89	1.27	2.10
Quik/Acid Tst	0.12	0.26	1.07	1.13	1.63
A/C Rec T/ovr	8.41	14.16	14.52	15.11	6.61
Tot Ass T/ovr	0.32	0.38	0.30	0.29	1.25
Debt/Ass Rat	0.36	0.13	0.06	0.14	0.26
L T L Tot Ass	0.04	0.02	-	-	-
Debt to Eqity	0.58	0.15	0.07	0.15	0.36
Interest Cover	-174.61	-	-	-	-
Oper Prof Mrg	-25.65	8.69	19.07	24.73	33.98
Net Prof Marg%	-25.80	9.12	23.95	34.52	28.31
Ret on Assets	-8.14	3.61	7.77	12.00	42.44
Ret on Equity%	-13.09	4.08	7.74	10.26	48.00
Price/Earnings	-5.19	48.24	55.48	42.39	31.98
Divid Cover	-	-	2.07	2.63	2.87
Divid Yield	-	-	0.87	0.90	1.09
Earning Yield%	-19.28	2.07	1.80	2.36	3.13
NAV % Mrk Pr	147.55	50.87	23.26	20.04	6.53
Effec Tax Rate	-	3.03	8.74	18.65	16.67
Def Interval	-2.22	0.94	0.26	0.20	-
Sus Grth Rate	-13.09	4.08	3.99	6.36	31.28

SUBSIDIARY & ASSOCIATED COMPANIES

POTGIETERSRUST PLATINUMS LTD

INVESTMENTS

POTGIETERSRUST PLATINUMS LTD (132312 SH)

LEEGALL CLOTHING CO LTD

ABBREVIATION : LEEGALL

JSE SHORT CODE : LGL

SECTOR : Industrial-Clothing, Footwear & Textiles

SHAREHOLDERS

Who Owns Whom's Assessment of the Identity of the Ultimate Controlling Shareholder: DIRECTORS 30% (MARCH 1991)

SHAREHOLDER	PERCENTAGE 1992	1991
QUARTO NOM P/L	---	43.3
SHELFORD P/L	---	15.7
SOLID G NOM P/L	---	30.4
STD BANK NOM TVL P/L	---	5.8
TOTAL	---	95.3

DIRECTORS :
FALOWITZ F (Managing Director),FALOWITZ L

REGISTRATION NUMBER : 05/34784/06

REGISTERED OFFICE
39/41 Joyner Road, Prospecton
Durban
4110
TEL: 031-902 6271
FAX: 031-902 3715

TRANSFER SECRETARY
Consolidated Share Registrars Ltd
P O Box 61051, Marshalltown
2107
TEL: 011-492 1620

COMPANY SECRETARY
F Falowitz

NATURE OF BUSINESS
The group manufactures mens, womens & childrens fashion garments, & distributes its products via the major chain stores & independents.

BANKERS :
Nedperm Bank Ltd

AUDITORS :
KPMG Aiken & Peat

FAMILIAR BRAND NAMES
CHIPIE,GALLANT,LEE (JEANS),MISS DEBUTANT
SHOUT

CONTRIBUTION BY ACTIVITY
(RSA) Lee (% Turnover) (45.6%)
(RSA) Gallant (49.6%)
Lesotho (4.8%)

YEAR END : March

DIVIDEND :15/12/91 and 15/06/91

CAPITAL STRUCTURE

	AUTHORISED	ISSUED
6% Red Cum Prefs R2	50000	50000
Ords 50c	10000000	7458000
Var Rate Red Cum Prefs 1c	7000000	7000000

FINANCIAL STATISTICS (AT FINANCIAL YEAR END)

(Amts in R'000)	1991 Mar	1990 Mar	1989 Jun	1988 Jun	1987 Jun
Ord S/H Int	6048	3031	8440	7393	7304
Long Trm Loans	1037	1807	1372	4068	4040
Iss Ord Share	7458	2260	2260	1550	1550
Total Liab	16050	26473	21546	14907	10488
Current Liab	15013	24666	20174	10839	6448
Total Assets	22098	29504	29986	22300	17792
Current Assets	17630	22177	22442	18400	14635
Debtors	8324	10402	7074	8635	5924
Inventory	9278	11453	14790	9463	7931
Turnover	52497	39722	53455	28398	-
Oper Profit	-2782	-2913	-2900	1380	886
Interest Paid	3383	2548	2426	1001	722
Tax Paid	-	19	14	198	466
Prf af Int&Tax	-6119	-5406	-5340	181	-302
Prf att Ord Sh	-6125	-5409	-5346	14	-460
Btm Line Earn	-6379	-5409	140	14	-835
Mkt Prce(c) YE	35	215	380	290	350
Depreciation	750	577	739	331	310

PER SHARE STATISTICS (CENTS)

Net Asst Val	81.09	134.12	373.45	476.97	471.23
Net Earnings	-149.40	-239.30	-236.50	0.90	-29.70
Cash Flow	-131.07	-213.81	-203.85	22.26	-6.45

RATIOS AND OTHER INFORMATION

Mrk Cap(R000)	2610	4859	8588	4495	5425
Current Ratio	1.17	0.90	1.11	1.70	2.27
Quik/Acid Tst	0.56	0.43	0.38	0.82	1.04
A/C Rec T/ovr	6.31	3.82	7.56	3.29	-
Tot Ass T/ovr	2.38	1.35	1.78	1.27	-
Debt/Ass Rat	0.72	0.89	0.72	0.62	0.54
L T L Tot Ass	0.04	0.06	0.04	0.14	0.18
Debt to Eqity	2.63	8.70	2.54	1.88	1.32
Interest Cover	-0.81	-1.11	-1.20	1.38	1.23
Oper Prof Mrg	-5.30	-7.33	-5.43	4.86	-
Net Prof Marg%	-11.67	-13.62	-10.00	0.05	-
Ret on Assets	-12.38	-9.62	-9.67	6.19	3.32
Ret on Equity%	-101.27	-178.46	-63.34	0.19	-4.20
Price/Earnings	-0.23	-0.90	-1.61	322.22	-11.78
Earning Yield%	-426.86	-111.30	-62.24	0.31	-8.49
NAV % Mrk Pr	231.70	62.38	98.28	164.47	134.64
Effec Tax Rate	-	-	-	52.24	284.15
Def Interval	-1.32	-3.94	-2.65	24.39	-29.20
Sus Grth Rate	-101.27	-178.46	-63.34	0.19	-6.30

SUBSIDIARY & ASSOCIATED COMPANIES

FRANCITAL (PTY) LTD
GALBERK CLOTHING MANUFACTURERS LESOTHO (
GALBERK MARKETING LESOTHO (PTY) LTD
GALLANT CLOTHING MANUFACTURERS (LESOTHO)
GALLANT CLOTHING MANUFACTURERS (PTY) LTD
HD LEE CO (SA) (PTY) LTD
SORANA (PTY) LTD

INVESTMENTS

None

LEISURE RESOURCES CORPORATION LTD

ABBREVIATION : DUKEL

JSE SHORT CODE : DKL

SECTOR : Industrial-Motor

SHAREHOLDERS

Who Owns Whom's Assessment of the Identity of the Ultimate Controlling Shareholder:
DIRECTORS CONTROL 76,5%

SHAREHOLDER	PERCENTAGE 1992	1991
LEON DU PLESSIS INV P/L	30.2	30.2
KELLY F H INV P/L	30.2	30.2
ALTER B M & OTHERS	21.8	---
DUNCAN VAN DER POEL INV P/L	7.3	7.3
OTTE K E	4.0	4.0
KERIAN INV CC	2.7	2.7
VAN DER POEL A D	1.3	1.3
STD BANK NOM TVL P/L	---	5.9
STOCKSHARE NOM P/L	---	1.8
TOTAL	97.5	83.4

DIRECTORS :
APTEKER D ,BUCHANAN I ,HARTMAN J
PEIRES S (Chairman),ROUP S ,SHONE C ,ZIETSMAN D

REGISTRATION NUMBER : 68/03527/06

REGISTERED OFFICE
4 Albury Park, Magalieszicht Avenue
Dunkeld West
2196
TEL: 011-880 2921
FAX: 011-880 3480

TRANSFER SECRETARY
Central Registrars Ltd
P O Box 4844, Johannesburg
2000
TEL: 011-331 0051

COMPANY SECRETARY
I Buchanan

NATURE OF BUSINESS
The group is involved in the provision, marketing & servicing of holiday accomodation, & leisure related activities Company is currently a Cash Shell

BANKERS :
First National Bank of SA Ltd
Standard Bank of SA Ltd

AUDITORS :
KPMG Aiken & Peat

FAMILIAR BRAND NAMES
N/A

CONTRIBUTION BY ACTIVITY
N/A

YEAR END : June

DIVIDEND :15/10/91

NUMBER OF EMPLOYEES : 160

CAPITAL STRUCTURE

	AUTHORISED	ISSUED
Ords 4c	25000000	15000000

FINANCIAL STATISTICS (AT FINANCIAL YEAR END)

(Amts in R'000)	1991 Jun	1990 Jun	1989 Jun	1988 Jun	1987
Ord S/H Int	7033	5988	5860	4446	3953
Long Trm Loans	-	-	172	192	3365
Iss Ord Share	15000	15000	15000	15000	15000
Total Liab	2131	5626	5672	3061	6450
Current Liab	2131	5626	5500	2869	3085
Total Assets	9164	11614	11532	7507	13719
Current Assets	8601	10935	10959	7170	6401
Debtors	2631	2071	2099	1432	
Inventory	5968	8433	8739	5730	6401
Turnover	70583	88935	71701	48776	48732
Oper Profit	2168	2185	3269	2096	2027
Interest Paid	959	1439	456	259	425
Tax Paid	231	279	1060	715	801
Prf af Int&Tax	1035	509	1805	1122	801
Prf att Ord Sh	1035	509	1805	1122	801
Btm Line Earn	1045	503	2089	967	801
Dividend Paid	-	375	675	480	-
Mkt Prce(c) YE	25	35	45	35	-
Depreciation	110	125	83	235	-

PER SHARE STATISTICS (CENTS)

Net Asst Val	46 89	39 92	39 07	29 64	26 35
Net Earnings	6 90	3 40	12 00	8 00	-
Dividends	-	2 50	4 50	3 20	
Cash Flow	7 63	3 08	12 45	9 06	3 56

RATIOS AND OTHER INFORMATION

Mrk Cap(R000)	3750	5250	6750	5250	-
Current Ratio	4 04	1 94	1 99	2 50	2 07
Quik/Acid Tst	1 24	0 44	0 40	0 50	-
A/C Rec T/ovr	26 83	42 94	34 16	34 06	
Tot Ass T/ovr	7 70	7 66	6 22	6 50	2 37
Debt/Ass Rat	0 23	0 48	0 48	0 38	0 47
L T L Tot Ass			-	-	0 25
Debt to Eqity	0 30	0 94	0 94	0 65	1 63
Interest Cover	2 26	1 52	7 17	8 09	4 77
Oper Prof Mrg	3 07	2 46	4 56	4 30	4 16
Net Prof Marg%	1 47	0 57	2 52	2 30	1 64
Ret on Assets	24 28	19 18	28 80	27 92	9 85
Ret on Equity%	14 72	8 50	30 80	25 24	13 51
Price/Earnings	3 62	10 29	3 75	4 38	-
Divid Cover	-	1 36	2 67	2 50	-
Divid Yield	-	7 14	10 00	9 14	-
Earning Yield%	27 60	9 71	26 67	22 86	-
NAV % Mrk Pr	187 55	114 06	86 81	84 69	-
Effec Tax Rate	18 25	57 23	37 70	43 71	50 00
Def Interval	0 30	6 35	0 78	-	2 80
Sus Grth Rate	14 72	2 24	19 28	14 44	20 26

SUBSIDIARY & ASSOCIATED COMPANIES

None

INVESTMENTS

None

LENCO HOLDINGS LTD

ABBREVIATION : LENCO

JSE SHORT CODE : LNC

SECTOR : Industrial-Clothing, Footwear & Textiles

SHAREHOLDERS

Who Owns Whom's Assessment of the Identity of the Ultimate Controlling Shareholder:
DE JAGER FAMILY / REMBRANDT GROUP

SHAREHOLDER	PERCENTAGE 1992	1991
LENCO INV HOLDINGS P/L	50 3	43 0
STD BANK NOM TVL P/L	12 0	---
EIGHTY ONE MAIN STREET NOM LTD	11 0	-
CMB NOM P/L	6 9	---
RAND MERCHANT BANK LTD	2 4	---
LENCO SHARE TRUST	1 9	---
SA MUTUAL	1 5	3 3
YSKOR PENS FUND	1 5	---
LENCO HOLDINGS LTD SHARE TRUST	1 5	---
EPF OLD MUTUAL NOM P/L	1 3	---
EPF SMB NOM P/L	1 3	---
GEMEENSKAPLIKE MUNISIPALE OFS PENS FUND	1 1	- -
LONRHO GROUP PENS FUND	1 1	---
SANLAM	- -	20 6
SYFRETS NOM LTD	---	5 6
TITAN NOM P/L	---	10 8
KOHLER PACKAGING LTD	---	3 7
RAKE INV P/L	---	1 7
DE JAGER FOUNDATION LTD	- -	2 1
TOTAL	93 5	90 7

DIRECTORS :
DE JAGER GD (Executive Chairman),DE JAGER GJ
ECKSTEIN RS ,FALCK DM ,FERREIRA GT ,KITSHOFF JJ
MALHERBE J ,SAREMBOCK JL
STUBBS SFW (Financial Director),WALBECK PA
WIESE CH AD

REGISTRATION NUMBER : 05/21962/06

REGISTERED OFFICE
364 Victoria Road, Salt River
7925
TEL: 021-54 2601
FAX: 021-54 8964

TRANSFER SECRETARY
Central Registrars Ltd
P O Box 4844, Johannesburg
2000
TEL: 011-331 0051

COMPANY SECRETARY
S F W Stubbs

NATURE OF BUSINESS
The group is engaged in manufacture of footwear, shoe components, clothing, rigid plastic packaging & property owning. The company holds a controlling interest in quoted Amalgamated Shoes.

BANKERS :
First National Bank of SA Ltd
Absa Bank Ltd, Rand Merchant Bank Ltd

AUDITORS :
Coopers Theron Du Toit

FAMILIAR BRAND NAMES
BLOKES,CONSULATE,EMBASSY,HARDY AMIES,MONATIC
PUMA,RICH RAGS,VIYELLA,XACTICS
YVES ST LAURENT

CONTRIBUTION BY ACTIVITY
N/A

YEAR END : February

DIVIDEND :Ords no par value

Dividend No 3	(Ldr)25/05/90	(Pay)12/06/90	Amt(c)9
Dividend No 4	(Ldr)22/02/91	(Pay)28/02/91	Amt(c)10
Dividend No 5	(Ldr)28/02/92	(Pay)09/04/92	Amt(c)11.5

NUMBER OF EMPLOYEES : 7215

CAPITAL STRUCTURE

	AUTHORISED	ISSUED
Ords no par value	100000000	68365729
Var Rate Red Cum Prefs 1c	50000000	0

FINANCIAL STATISTICS (AT FINANCIAL YEAR END)

(Amts in R'000)	1992 Feb	1991 Feb	1990 Feb	1989 Feb	1988 Feb
Ord S/H Int	122151	85340	58577	44071	32664
Long Trm Loans	63406	78204	59690	42886	13089
Iss Ord Share	61230	52394	39922	39922	39922
Total Liab	148193	174513	127251	97813	35740
Current Liab	84787	96309	67561	54927	22651
Total Assets	260592	255771	185828	136130	68404
Intang Assets	9752	4082	*	5754	*
Current Assets	186484	179705	113750	110557	51751
Debtors	90214	84981	52007	35512	27997
Inventory	86909	81576	56147	40220	18462
Turnover	455116	440766	283928	207461	119975
Oper Profit	58582	54358	42605	30123	12391
Interest Paid	17738	22577	14965	4778	4137
Tax Paid	5697	6062	7790	5403	-224
Prf af Int&Tax	37829	31834	27476	21484	8478
Prf att Ord Sh	30207	20858	18092	14202	8158
Btm Line Earn	26953	1395	18092	14202	7770
Dividend Paid	7041	5239	3593	2795	1996
Mkt Prce(c) YE	310	185	210	135	105
Depreciation	12629	14689	5127	4427	2420

PER SHARE STATISTICS (CENTS)

Net Asst Val	183.57	155.09	146.73	95.98	81.82
Net Earnings	49.30	43.20	45.30	35.60	21.20
Dividends	11.50	10.00	9.00	7.00	5.00
Cash Flow	72.22	72.71	58.13	49.01	26.82

RATIOS AND OTHER INFORMATION

Mrk Cap(R000)	189813	96929	83836	53895	41918
Current Ratio	2.20	1.87	1.68	2.01	2.28
Quik/Acid Tst	1.17	1.02	0.85	1.28	1.47
A/C Rec T/ovr	5.04	5.19	5.46	5.84	4.29
Tot Ass T/ovr	1.75	1.72	1.53	1.52	1.75
Debt/Ass Rat	0.43	0.51	0.54	0.56	0.49
L T L Tot Ass	0.11	0.13	0.18	0.16	0.16
Debt to Eqity	0.92	1.53	1.72	1.74	1.02
Interest Cover	3.34	2.41	2.85	6.33	3.00
Oper Prof Mrg	12.87	12.33	15.01	14.52	10.33
Net Prof Marg%	6.64	4.73	6.37	6.85	6.80
Ret on Assets	23.50	24.12	27.22	23.26	18.11
Ret on Equity%	24.73	24.44	30.89	32.23	24.98
Price/Earnings	6.29	4.28	4.64	3.79	4.95
Divid Cover	4.29	4.32	5.03	5.09	4.24
Divid Yield	3.71	5.41	4.29	5.19	4.76
Earning Yield%	15.90	23.35	21.57	26.37	20.19
NAV % Mrk Pr	59.22	83.83	69.87	71.10	77.92
Effec Tax Rate	10.29	14.10	13.32	8.97	0.52
Def Interval	1.04	2.05	1.72	2.24	1.73
Sus Grth Rate	18.97	18.30	24.75	25.88	18.86

SUBSIDIARY & ASSOCIATED COMPANIES

364 VICTORIA ROAD (PTY) LTD
AMALGAMATED SHOES LTD
COMBINED PACKAGING LTD
COMBINED PLASTIC PACKAGING KWAZULU (PTY)
COMBINED PLASTICS PACKAGING (PTY) LTD
ELVINCO PLASTICS (PTY) LTD
HOUSE OF MANUFACTURING (PTY) LTD
HOUSE OF MONATIC TRADING (PTY) LTD
LENCO PROPERTIES ATLANTIS (PTY) LTD
METKOR INDUSTRIES (PTY) LTD
PLASTO-FOAM HOLDINGS (PTY) LTD
RICH RAGS (PTY) LTD
ROSENWERTH COUTOURE (PTY) LTD (50%)
WEUSTHOFF (SOUTH AFRICA) LTD (50%)
YSEBRAND (1933) (PTY) LTD

INVESTMENTS

None

LENCO INVESTMENT HOLDINGS LIMITED

ABBREVIATION : LENVEST

JSE SHORT CODE : LVT

SECTOR : Industrial-Clothing, Footwear & Textiles

SHAREHOLDERS

Who Owns Whom's Assessment of the Identity of the Ultimate Controlling Shareholder:
DE JAGER FAMILY / RAND MERCHANT BANK

SHAREHOLDER	PERCENTAGE 1992	1991
LENCO P/L	39.8	---
RAND MERCHANT BANK LTD	17.3	---
CMB NOM P/L	12.8	---
MOMENTUM LIFE ASSURE LTD	12.7	---
SMK NOM P/L	5.2	---
STD BANK NOM TVL P/L	5.0	---
EIGHTY ONE MAIN STREET NOM LTD	5.0	---
ABSA NOM P/L	1.5	---
TOTAL	99.2	---

DIRECTORS :
DE JAGER GD (Executive Chairman),DE JAGER GJ
FALCK DM ,FERREIRA GT ,KITSHOFF JJ ,MALHERBE J
STUBBS SFW (Financial Director),WIESE CH

REGISTRATION NUMBER : 87/04875/06

REGISTERED OFFICE
364 Victoria Road, Salt River
7925
TEL: 021-54 2601
FAX: 021-54 8964

TRANSFER SECRETARY
Central Registrars Ltd
P O Box 4844, Johannesburg
2000
TEL: 011-331 0051

COMPANY SECRETARY
S F W Stubbs

NATURE OF BUSINESS
An investment holding company with a controlling shareholding in Lenco Holdings Ltd.

BANKERS :
Standard Bank of SA Ltd
First National Bank of SA Ltd
Rand Merchant Bank Ltd

AUDITORS :
Coopers Theron Du Toit

FAMILIAR BRAND NAMES
N/A

CONTRIBUTION BY ACTIVITY
N/A

YEAR END : February

CAPITAL STRUCTURE

	AUTHORISED	ISSUED
Ords 1c	60000000	51275563

FINANCIAL STATISTICS (AT FINANCIAL YEAR END)

(Amts in R'000)	1992 Feb	1991 Feb
Ord S/H Int	164168	134217
Long Trm Loans	30720	36456
Total Liab	102774	118611
Current Liab	72054	82155
Total Assets	251242	242986
Intang Assets	15700	9842
Current Assets	177134	166920
Inventory	177134	166920
Oper Profit	43403	37591
Tax Paid	5697	6087
Prf af Int&Tax	37706	31504
Prf att Ord Sh	37706	31504
Btm Line Earn	37706	31504

PER SHARE STATISTICS (CENTS)

Net Earnings	32.63	27.59
Dividends	7.60	6.50
Cash Flow	78.67	82.56

RATIOS AND OTHER INFORMATION

Current Ratio	2.46	2.03
Debt/Ass Rat	0.40	0.48
L T L Tot Ass	0.11	0.14
Debt to Eqity	0.61	0.87
Ret on Assets	17.28	15.47
Ret on Equity%	22.97	23.47
Divid Cover	4.29	4.24
Effec Tax Rate	13.13	16.19
Def Interval	0.73	1.09
Sus Grth Rate	22.97	23.47

SUBSIDIARY & ASSOCIATED COMPANIES

LENCO HOLDINGS LTD

INVESTMENTS

None

LEPPIN HOLDINGS LTD

ABBREVIATION : LEPPIN

JSE SHORT CODE : LPN

SECTOR : Development Capital Market

SHAREHOLDERS

Who Owns Whom's Assessment of the Identity of the Ultimate Controlling Shareholder:
DIRECTORS CONTROL 77% (JULY 1991)

SHAREHOLDER	PERCENTAGE 1992	1991
LEPPIN FAMILY HLD P/L	75.6	75.6
ROSENSTEIN M	7.0	---
SHER S	4.1	3.9
CHAFKIN M	2.3	2.3
GLICK E	1.1	1.1
SAGE LIFE LTD	---	7.0
TOTAL	90.0	89.9

DIRECTORS :
HANNEMANN N (Joint Managing Director)
HANNEMANN T (Joint Managing Director), HORN R
LEPPIN GW (Executive Chairman

REGISTRATION NUMBER : 87/03187/06

REGISTERED OFFICE
Merlin House, Von Wyk Street
Roodepoort
1724
TEL: 011-885 1862
FAX: 011-786 9520

TRANSFER SECRETARY
Mercantile Registrars Ltd
P O Box 1053, Johannesburg
2000
TEL: 011-333 8181

COMPANY SECRETARY
J Kirby (Ms)

NATURE OF BUSINESS
The holding company of subsidiary companies which import, manufacture, distribute and export vitamins, food supplements and foods to the retail & wholesale pharmaceutical trade.

BANKERS :
Standard Bank of SA Ltd

AUDITORS :
Fisher Hoffman Stride

FAMILIAR BRAND NAMES
LEPPIN

CONTRIBUTION BY ACTIVITY
N/A

YEAR END : July

DIVIDEND :15/12/91

NUMBER OF EMPLOYEES : 80

CAPITAL STRUCTURE

	AUTHORISED	ISSUED
Ords 1c	15000000	8600000

FINANCIAL STATISTICS (AT FINANCIAL YEAR END)

(Amts in R'000)	1991 Jul	1990 Jul	1989 Jul	1988 Jul	1987 Jul
Ord S/H Int	3421	3296	3098	3349	2536
Long Trm Loans	340	296	229	144	123
Iss Ord Share	8600	8600	8600	8600	-
Total Liab	3037	3484	2777	1663	1073
Current Liab	2697	3188	2548	1519	950
Total Assets	4384	4706	3817	2954	3609
Intang Assets	2074	2074	2058	2058	*
Current Assets	3314	3875	3040	2345	1226
Debtors	1478	1916	1144	1039	522
Inventory	1808	1910	1888	1299	704
Turnover	8352	8489	6103	4365	3719
Oper Profit	581	607	-82	302	356
Interest Paid	473	418	171	79	54
Tax Paid	-	-	-	-	91
Prf af Int&Tax	125	199	-252	223	211
Prf att Ord Sh	125	199	-252	223	211
Btm Line Earn	125	199	-252	223	211
Dividend Paid	-	-	-	86	-
Mkt Prce(c) YE	15	25	25	30	-
Depreciation	279	256	197	118	115

PER SHARE STATISTICS (CENTS)

Net Asst Val	15.66	14.21	12.09	15.01	-
Net Earnings	1.50	2.30	-2.90	2.70	-
Dividends	-	-	-	1.00	-
Cash Flow	4.70	5.29	-0.64	3.97	-

RATIOS AND OTHER INFORMATION

Mrk Cap(R000)	1290	2150	2150	2580	-
Current Ratio	1.23	1.22	1.19	1.54	1.29
Quik/Acid Tst	0.56	0.62	0.45	0.69	0.55
A/C Rec T/ovr	5.65	4.43	5.33	4.20	7.12
Tot Ass T/ovr	1.91	1.80	1.60	1.48	1.03
Debt/Ass Rat	0.69	0.74	0.73	0.56	0.30
L T L Tot Ass	0.08	0.06	0.06	0.05	0.03
Debt to Eqity	0.89	1.06	0.90	0.50	0.42
Interest Cover	1.23	1.45	-0.48	3.82	6.59
Oper Prof Mrg	6.96	7.15	-1.34	6.92	9.57
Net Prof Marg%	1.50	2.34	-4.13	5.11	5.67
Ret on Assets	13.64	13.11	-2.12	10.22	9.86
Ret on Equity%	3.65	6.04	-8.13	6.66	8.32
Price/Earnings	10.00	10.87	-8.62	11.11	-
Divid Cover	-	-	-	2.70	-
Divid Yield	-	-	-	3.33	-
Earning Yield%	10.00	9.20	-11.60	9.00	-
NAV % Mrk Pr	104.42	56.84	48.37	50.04	-
Effec Tax Rate	-	-	-	-	30.13
Def Interval	4.80	3.09	-17.05	1.27	0.83
Sus Grth Rate	3.65	6.04	-8.13	4.09	8.32

SUBSIDIARY & ASSOCIATED COMPANIES

GW LEPPIN (PTY) LTD
LEPPIN PRODUCTS (PTY) LTD

INVESTMENTS

None

LESLIE GOLD MINES LTD

ABBREVIATION : LESLIE

JSE SHORT CODE : LES

SECTOR : Gold-Evander

SHAREHOLDERS

Who Owns Whom's Assessment of the Identity of the Ultimate Controlling Shareholder:
SANLAM VIA GENCOR

SHAREHOLDER	PERCENTAGE 1992	1991
INDO-CHINA NOM P/L	14.0	---
SEPON LTD	13.3	13.4
CONSOLIDATED NOM P/L	10.0	10.0
LONDON CONTROL ACCOUNT	9.8	10.0
FIRST NAT NOM P/L	5.4	5.3
STD BANK NOM TVL P/L	5.2	5.0

NEDBANK NOM LTD	1 7	1 7
DEPOSITARY NOM INC	1 7	1 7
ABSA NOM P/L	1 5	---
ANDEX NOM P/L	1 2	1 2
FIRST CORP NOM P/L	1 1	1 2
SHARESTOCK NOM P/L	---	1 2
INDO-CHINA NOM SA P/L	--	14 3
VOLKSKAS NOM P/L	---	1 5
TOTAL	64 7	66 2

DIRECTORS :
BURKE JHJ ,CROCKER EB ,FEWELL PT ,LEE GS
MAUDE G ,OLIVIER JE (Chairman),RADEMEYER P DE V
STEENKAMP TI

REGISTRATION NUMBER : 59/01124/06

REGISTERED OFFICE
General Mining Building, 6 Hollard Street
Johannesburg
2001
TEL 011-376 9111

TRANSFER SECRETARY
Central Registrars Ltd
P O Box 4844, Johannesburg
2000
TEL 011-331 0051

COMPANY SECRETARY
General Mining Metals & Minerals Ltd

NATURE OF BUSINESS
The company operates a gold mine in the Evander area, E Tvl Silver & osmiridium are recovered as by-products of gold

BANKERS :
First National Bank of SA Ltd

AUDITORS :
N/A

FAMILIAR BRAND NAMES
N/A

CONTRIBUTION BY ACTIVITY
N/A

YEAR END : September

DIVIDEND : Ords 65c

Interim No 51	(Ldr)04/05/90	(Pay)15/06/90	Amt(c)40
Final No 52	(Ldr)02/11/90	(Pay)14/12/90	Amt(c)20
Interim No 53	(Ldr)03/05/91	(Pay)18/06/91	Amt(c)5
Final No 54	(Ldr)01/11/91	(Pay)13/12/91	Amt(c)15

NUMBER OF EMPLOYEES : 1914

CAPITAL STRUCTURE

	AUTHORISED	ISSUED
Ords 65c	16000000	16000000

FINANCIAL STATISTICS (AT FINANCIAL YEAR END)

(Amts in R'000)	1991 Sep	1990 Sep	1989 Sep	1988	1987
Ord S/H Int	55805	52641	50438	46827	42703
Long Trm Loans	63	95	-	13032	14053
Iss Ord Share	16000	16000	16000	16000	16000
Total Liab	10336	12576	16124	26064	28082
Current Liab	10273	12481	16124	13032	14029
Total Assets	66141	65217	66562	76209	74125
Current Assets	17657	17754	19674	16350	17369
Debtors	1552	2087	2368	-	-
Inventory	748	946	804	16350	17369
Turnover	69739	89510	96662	103271	98095
Oper Profit	7634	18529	14294	14797	21578
Tax Paid	1960	7889	3179	2673	9994
Prf af Int&Tax	6364	11803	12411	12124	11593
Prf att Ord Sh	6364	11803	12411	8106	9488
Btm Line Earn	6364	11803	12411	8106	9488
Dividend Paid	3200	9600	8800	8000	9600
Mkt Prce(c) YE	320	540	475	300	885

PER SHARE STATISTICS (CENTS)

Net Asst Val	348 78	329 01	315 24	292 67	266 89
Net Earnings	33 00	71 00	54 00	-	-
Dividends	20 00	60 00	-	-	
Cash Flow	39 78	73 77	77 57	75 78	72 46

RATIOS AND OTHER INFORMATION

Mrk Cap(R000)	51200	86400	76000	48000	141600
Current Ratio	1 72	1 42	1 22	1 25	1 24
Quik/Acid Tst	1 65	1 35	1 17	-	
A/C Rec T/ovr	44 93	42 89	40 82	-	-
Tot Ass T/ovr	1 05	1 37	1 45	1 36	1 32
Debt/Ass Rat	0 16	0 19	0 24	0 34	0 38
L T L Tot Ass	0 00	0 00	-	0 17	0 19
Debt to Eqity	0 19	0 24	0 32	0 56	0 66
Oper Prof Mrg	10 95	20 70	14 79	14 33	22 00
Net Prof Marg%	9 13	13 19	12 84	7 85	9 67
Ret on Assets	12 59	30 19	23 42	19 42	29 12
Ret on Equity%	11 40	22 42	24 61	17 31	22 22
Price/Earnings	9 70	7 61	8 80	-	
Divid Cover	1 65	1 18	-	-	
Divid Yield	6 25	11 11	-	-	
Earning Yield%	10 31	13 15	11 37	-	
NAV % Mrk Pr	108 99	60 93	66 37	97 56	30 16
Effec Tax Rate	25 67	42 58	22 24	18 06	46 32
Def Interval	0 01	0 01	-	1 07	1 21
Sus Grth Rate	5 67	4 18	7 16	0 23	0 26

SUBSIDIARY & ASSOCIATED COMPANIES

EVANDER TOWNSHIP LTD (25%)

INVESTMENTS

None

LEWIS FOSCHINI INVESTMENT CO LTD

ABBREVIATION : LEFIC

JSE SHORT CODE : LEF

SECTOR : Industrial-Retailers & Wholesalers

SHAREHOLDERS

Who Owns Whom's Assessment of the Identity of the Ultimate Controlling Shareholder:
LEWIS FAMILY

SHAREHOLDER	PERCENTAGE 1992	1991
STANLEY & ZEA LEWIS HOLDINGS LTD	20.3	---
SOUTHERN LIFE ASSOC LTD	15.6	15.5
SA MUTUAL	10.6	10.6
FOSCHINI LTD	10.0	10.0
LEWIS S	8.0	30.0
STD BANK NOM TVL P/L	3.3	4.6
PROTEA ASSURE CO LTD	2.2	2.6
CMB NOM P/L	2.1	---
DE BEERS PENS FUND	2.0	2.0
GREENMARKET SQUARE NOM P/L	1.9	1.9
CYNDRIAN INV P/L	1.9	1.9
LOUIS C M & S L TRUSTEES	1.9	---
EIGHTY ONE MAIN STREET NOM LTD	1.8	---
BARLOWS PENS FUND	1.4	1.4
SA MUTUAL PENS FUND	1.4	1.4
DAWN GLOW INV P/L	1.4	---
SANLAM	---	2.0
TOTAL	85.6	83.9

DIRECTORS :
BORKUM MM ,GORVY HA ,LEWIS M ,LEWIS S (Chairman)
OSRIN E

REGISTRATION NUMBER : 68/00204/06

REGISTERED OFFICE
12th Floor, Shell House, 9 Riebeek Street
Cape Town
8001
TEL: 021-948 7340
FAX: 021-92 7063

TRANSFER SECRETARY
Mercantile Registrars Ltd
P O Box 1053, Johannesburg
2000
TEL: 011-333 8181

COMPANY SECRETARY
R J Norman

NATURE OF BUSINESS
An investment holding company with a controlling interest in quoted Foschini Ltd. The group is engaged in chainstore retailing of jewellery, clothing & related items.

BANKERS :
First National Bank of SA Ltd

AUDITORS :
Touche Ross & Co

FAMILIAR BRAND NAMES
SEE FOSCHINI

CONTRIBUTION BY ACTIVITY
N/A

YEAR END : March

DIVIDEND : Ords 50c

Interim No 42	(Ldr)29/09/89	(Pay)06/11/89	Amt(c)23.75
Final No 43	(Ldr)05/04/90	(Pay)04/05/90	Amt(c)98.75
Interim No 44	(Ldr)28/09/90	(Pay)05/11/90	Amt(c)43
Final No 45	(Ldr)05/04/91	(Pay)06/05/91	Amt(c)114.25

CAPITAL STRUCTURE

	AUTHORISED	ISSUED
Ords 50c	60000000	42337444

FINANCIAL STATISTICS (AT FINANCIAL YEAR END)

(Amts in R'000)	1992 Mar	1990 Dec	1989 Dec	1988 Dec	1987
Ord S/H Int	176227	130083	8549	8548	8530
Long Trm Loans	-	-	-	-	5730
Iss Ord Share	42337	10047	9547	9547	9547
Total Liab	319	11528	9465	8191	11460
Current Liab	319	11528	9465	8191	5730
Total Assets	176546	141611	18014	16739	20014
Current Assets	123	11571	9508	8233	5754
Inventory	-	-	-	-	5754
Turnover	-	-	661196	528476	-
Oper Profit	41	15589	11717	9969	6835
Interest Paid	-	12	3	-	-
Tax Paid	-12	-6	18	-	-
Prf af Int&Tax	53	15583	11696	9970	6835
Prf att Ord Sh	46436	36595	27750	9970	6837
Btm Line Earn	46436	36595	27750	9970	6837
Dividend Paid	46323	36133	11695	9952	6826
Mkt Prce(c) YE	1800	3800	2850	2200	1950
Depreciation	-	-	18009	12502	-

PER SHARE STATISTICS (CENTS)

Net Asst Val	416.25	1294.74	89.55	89.54	89.35
Net Earnings	109.70	91.70	290.70	247.60	-
Dividends	-	157.25	122.50	104.25	-
Cash Flow	0.10	161.35	311.14	235.38	71.59

RATIOS AND OTHER INFORMATION

Mrk Cap(R000)	762066	381786	272090	210034	186167
Current Ratio	0.39	1.00	1.00	1.01	1.00
Quik/Acid Tst	0.39	1.00	1.00	1.01	-
Tot Ass T/ovr	-	-	36.70	31.57	-
Debt/Ass Rat	0.00	0.08	0.53	0.49	0.57
L T L Tot Ass	-	-	-	-	0.29
Debt to Eqity	0.00	0.09	1.11	0.96	1.34
Interest Cover	-	1299.08	3905.67	-	-
Oper Prof Mrg	-	-	1.77	1.89	-
Net Prof Marg%	-	-	4.20	1.89	-
Ret on Assets	21.04	25.85	154.16	59.56	34.15
Ret on Equity%	21.08	28.13	324.60	116.64	80.15
Price/Earnings	16.41	41.44	9.80	8.89	-
Divid Cover	-	0.58	2.37	2.38	-
Divid Yield	-	4.14	4.30	4.74	-
Earning Yield%	6.09	2.41	10.20	11.25	-
NAV % Mrk Pr	23.12	34.07	3.14	4.07	4.58
Effec Tax Rate	-	-	0.15	-	-
Def Interval	-	-	-	-	0.84
Sus Grth Rate	0.06	0.36	187.80	0.21	0.13

SUBSIDIARY & ASSOCIATED COMPANIES

FOSCHINI LTD (50%)
LEWIS FOSCHINI INVESTMENTS (PTY) LTD

INVESTMENTS

None

LIBANON GOLD MINING CO LTD

ABBREVIATION : LIBANON

JSE SHORT CODE : LIB

SECTOR : Gold-West Witwatersrand

SHAREHOLDERS

Who Owns Whom's Assessment of the Identity of the Ultimate Controlling Shareholder:
GFSA

SHAREHOLDER	PERCENTAGE 1992	1991
MINU NOM LTD	32 9	32 9
INDO-CHINA NOM P/L	24 5	---
FIRST NAT NOM P/L	4 2	4 3
CITIBANK NOM P/L	3 9	3 9
STD BANK NOM TVL P/L	3 3	3 2
NAT CITY NOM LTD	3 0	3 0
FIRST NAT NOM P/L GATR DEPOT	1 5	1 3
DEPOSITARY NOM INC	1 1	---
BANK OF NEW YORK NOM LTD	---	3 5
INDO-CHINA NOM SA P/L	---	20 5
VOLKSKAS NOM P/L	- -	1 3
TOTAL	74 3	73 7

DIRECTORS :
ADAN MJ ,DYKES DC ,FENTON CT ,FULLER-GOOD MR HOUGHTON AB ,JANISCH PR ,MUNRO AH ,ROBNSON RL ROSS CJ ,TAGG MJ (Chairman & Managing Dir

REGISTRATION NUMBER : 05/08381/06

REGISTERED OFFICE
75 Fox Street, Johannesburg
2001
TEL 011-639 9111
FAX 011-639 2101

TRANSFER SECRETARY
Gold Fields of SA Ltd
P O Box 1167, Johannesburg
2000
TEL 011-639 9111

COMPANY SECRETARY
Gold Fields of SA Ltd

NATURE OF BUSINESS
The company conducts gold mining operations in the Western Witwatersrand area.

BANKERS :
Standard Bank of SA Ltd

AUDITORS :
Ernst & Young

FAMILIAR BRAND NAMES
N/A

CONTRIBUTION BY ACTIVITY
N/A

YEAR END : June

DIVIDEND : Ords 20c

Final No 77	(Ldr)30/06/89	(Pay)09/08/89	Amt(c)20
Interim No 78	(Ldr)29/12/89	(Pay)07/02/90	Amt(c)10

NUMBER OF EMPLOYEES : 7468

CAPITAL STRUCTURE

	AUTHORISED	ISSUED
Ords 20c	45000000	40000000

FINANCIAL STATISTICS (AT FINANCIAL YEAR END)

(Amts in R'000)	1991 Jun	1990 Jun	1989 Jun	1988 Jun	1987
Ord S/H Int	365669	357112	353797	339273	311300
Long Trm Loans	-	-	-	-	64014
Iss Ord Share	40000	40000	40000	40000	8000
Total Liab	32492	37188	41733	48496	128028
Current Liab	32492	37188	41733	48496	64014
Total Assets	398161	394300	395530	387769	481342
Current Assets	31774	38410	63397	83672	106028
Debtors	5928	5902	3261	2956	
Inventory	9308	10793	11680	9748	106028
Turnover	256105	236720	-	242653	246177
Oper Profit	6585	5474	34217	69399	106974
Tax Paid	2316	5117	3824	6403	41540
Prf af Int&Tax	8528	6612	30393	62996	65434
Prf att Ord Sh	8528	6612	30393	62996	34434
Btm Line Earn	8528	6612	30393	62996	34434
Dividend Paid		4000	16000	34000	34000
Mkt Prce(c) YE	375	510	750	710	7700

PER SHARE STATISTICS (CENTS)

Net Asst Val	914 17	892 78	884 49	848 18	3891 25
Net Earnings	-1 00	7 00	38 00	85 00	
Dividends	-	10 00	40 00	85 00	-
Cash Flow	21 32	16 53	75 98	157 49	817 93

RATIOS AND OTHER INFORMATION

Mrk Cap(R000)	150000	204000	300000	284000	616000
Current Ratio	0 98	1 03	1 52	1 73	1 66
Quik/Acid Tst	0 69	0 74	1 24	1 52	-
A/C Rec T/ovr	43 20	40 11	-	82 09	-
Tot Ass T/ovr	0 64	0 60	-	0 63	0 51
Debt/Ass Rat	0 08	0 09	0 11	0 13	0 27
L T L Tot Ass	-	-	-	-	0 13
Debt to Eqity	0 09	0 10	0 12	0 14	0 41
Oper Prof Mrg	2 57	2 31	-	28 60	43 45
Net Prof Marg%	3 33	2 79	-	25 96	13 99
Ret on Assets	2 72	2 97	8 65	17 90	22 22
Ret on Equity%	2 33	1 85	8 59	18 57	11 06
Price/Earnings	375 00	72 86	19 74	8 35	-
Divid Cover	-	0 70	0 95	1 00	-
Divid Yield	-	1 96	5 33	11 97	-
Earning Yield%	-0 27	1 37	5 07	11 97	-
NAV % Mrk Pr	243 78	175 05	117 93	119 46	50 54
Effec Tax Rate	21 36	43 63	11 18	8 28	38 83
Def Interval	-	-	-	-	0 98
Sus Grth Rate	2 33	0 73	4 07	8 55	0 14

SUBSIDIARY & ASSOCIATED COMPANIES

None

INVESTMENTS

None

LIBERTY HOLDINGS LTD

ABBREVIATION : LIB HOLD

JSE SHORT CODE : LBH

SECTOR : Financial-Insurance

SHAREHOLDERS

Who Owns Whom's Assessment of the Identity of the Ultimate Controlling Shareholder:
STANDARD BANK/DONALD GORDON

SHAREHOLDER	PERCENTAGE 1992	1991
LIBLIFE CONTROLLING CORP P/L	52.0	52.1
GUARDIAN ASSURE CO LTD	7.4	10.3
STD BANK NOM TVL P/L	6.3	6.1
G R E NOM LTD	2.9	---
EIGHTY ONE MAIN STREET NOM LTD	2.3	1.6
CMB NOM P/L	1.9	---
FIRST NAT NOM P/L	1.7	1.7
GUARDIAN NOM P/L	1.5	1.5
ROHIRRIM INV P/L	1.1	1.1
DRUSINSKY A	1.0	1.0
SANLAM	---	1.9
TOTAL	78.2	77.3

DIRECTORS :
CESMAN WE ,DE VILLIERS HP (Deputy Chairman)
GEELING KLG ,GORDON D (Chairman),GORDON RM
HOPKINS SA ,INGLIS JG ,KAHN JM ,MCALPINE JR
NEUBURGER LJ ,NILSSON K ,RAPP M
SHER FB (Managing Director),STRAUSS DR CB
VOSLOO MH ,WRIGHTON PGA

REGISTRATION NUMBER : 68/02095/06

REGISTERED OFFICE
1 Ameshoff Street, Braamfontein
Johannesburg
2001
TEL: 011-408 3911
FAX: 011-408 2109

TRANSFER SECRETARY
Central Registrars Ltd
P O Box 4844, Johannesburg
2000
TEL: 011-331 0051

COMPANY SECRETARY
J Worwood

NATURE OF BUSINESS
An investment holding company controlling quoted Liberty Life Association. Group operations include transaction of life insurance & pension business, construction, development, management & ownership of fixed property, investment activities & mutual fund management. The company has a major interest in quoted Guardian National Insurance Co.

BANKERS :
Standard Bank of SA Ltd

AUDITORS :
Kessel Feinstein

FAMILIAR BRAND NAMES
N/A

CONTRIBUTION BY ACTIVITY
N/A

YEAR END : December

DIVIDEND : Ords 25c

Interim No 36	(Ldr)15/09/89	(Pay)06/10/89	Amt(c)58
Final No 37	(Ldr)30/03/90	(Pay)12/04/90	Amt(c)92
Interim No 38	(Ldr)14/09/90	(Pay)05/10/90	Amt(c)75
Special No 39	(Ldr)14/09/90	(Pay)05/10/90	Amt(c)120
Final No 40	(Ldr)22/02/91	(Pay)12/04/91	Amt(c)145
Special No 41	(Ldr)22/02/91	(Pay)19/04/91	Amt(c)522.9
Interim No 42	(Ldr)13/09/91	(Pay)04/10/91	Amt(c)110
Final No 43	(Ldr)28/02/92	(Pay)10/04/92	Amt(c)174
Interim No 44	(Ldr)04/09/92	(Pay)02/10/92	Amt(c)142
Special No 45	(Ldr)04/09/92	(Pay)02/10/92	Amt(c)300

CAPITAL STRUCTURE

	AUTHORISED	ISSUED
Ords 25c	60000000	45685422
11c Div Cum Prefs 10c	15000000	15000000
Var Rate Red Cum Prefs 10c	45000000	900000

FINANCIAL STATISTICS (AT FINANCIAL YEAR END)

(Amts in R'000)	1991 Dec	1990 Dec	1989 Dec	1988	1987
Ord S/H Int	2589100	1938900	1521500	1180100	898100
Long Trm Loans	29833000	25127300	17367400	13773100	10757600
Iss Ord Share	45685	45595	45595	45595	45591
Total Liab	32200300	26454900	17813400	14147500	11133800
Current Liab	2367300	1327600	446000	374400	376200
Total Assets	34789400	28393800	19334900	15516600	12257700
Current Assets	3289700	2753600	795300	566400	602000
Debtors	985100	899400	606500	-	-
Inventory	-	-	-	566400	602000
Oper Profit	473400	447600	368800	278000	211700
Interest Paid	-	-	34900	4100	11700
Tax Paid	156700	194200	119600	105700	55500
Prf af Int&Tax	316700	253400	214300	166100	142800
Prf att Ord Sh	180500	144200	119700	100500	84200
Btm Line Earn	180500	203100	134400	100500	84200
Dividend Paid	368000	155000	68300	60200	43700
Mkt Prce(c) YE	9500	6300	5200	3300	2350
Depreciation	5900	4400	1300	-	-

PER SHARE STATISTICS (CENTS)

Net Asst Val	5667.29	4252.44	3336.99	2588.22	1969.91
Net Earnings	395.70	316.30	262.80	-	-
Dividends	284.00	220.00	150.00	-	-
Cash Flow	413.70	333.59	271.08	364.29	313.22

RATIOS AND OTHER INFORMATION

Mrk Cap(R000)	4340075	2872485	2370940	1504635	1071389
Current Ratio	1.39	2.07	1.78	1.51	1.60
Quik/Acid Tst	1.39	2.07	1.78	-	-
Debt/Ass Rat	0.16	0.16	0.04	0.91	0.91
L T L Tot Ass	0.10	0.11	0.02	0.89	0.88
Debt to Eqity	2.22	2.35	0.56	11.99	12.40
Interest Cover	-	-	10.57	67.29	17.95
Ret on Assets	1.36	1.58	1.91	1.78	1.71
Ret on Equity%	6.97	7.44	7.87	8.52	9.38
Price/Earnings	24.01	19.92	19.79	-	-
Divid Cover	1.39	1.44	1.75	-	-
Divid Yield	2.99	3.49	2.88	-	-

Earning Yield%	4.17	5.02	5.05	-	-
NAV % Mrk Pr	59.66	67.50	64.17	78.43	83.83
Effec Tax Rate	32.55	42.61	35.04	38 59	27.75
Def Interval	19.29	23.05	3.25	82.92	75.33
Sus Grth Rate	-7.24	-0.56	3.38	3.41	4.51

SUBSIDIARY & ASSOCIATED COMPANIES

GUARDBANK MANAGEMENT CORPORATION LTD (50%)
GUARDIAN LIBERTY SERVICES (PTY) LTD
GUARDIAN NATIONAL INSURANCE CO LTD (45,5%)
LIBERTY LIFE ASSOCIATION OF AFRICA LTD
LIBERTY LIFE PROPERTIES (PTY) LTD

INVESTMENTS

BOARD OF EXECUTORS LTD (10,3%)

LIBERTY INVESTORS LTD

ABBREVIATION : LIBVEST

JSE SHORT CODE : LBV

SECTOR : Financial-Insurance

SHAREHOLDERS

Who Owns Whom's Assessment of the Identity of the Ultimate Controlling Shareholder:
DONALD GORDON

SHAREHOLDER	PERCENTAGE 1992	1991
CAPITAL NOM P/L 'A TO K' ACCOUNTS	57 2	58 2
LIBERTY LIFE ASSOC OF AFRICA LTD	9.6	7.8
REPUBLIC NOM P/L	7.3	7.3
VICTORY ENTERPRISES P/L	2.9	2.9
FIRST NAT NOM P/L	2 4	2.7
TOTAL	79.4	78.9

DIRECTORS :
APPELBAUM HI ,DE VILLIERS HP
GORDON D (Chairman),GORDON GJ ,GORDON P MRS
GORDON RM ,RAPP M ,SHER FB ,WUNSH B

REGISTRATION NUMBER : 71/04020/06

REGISTERED OFFICE
Liberty Life Centre, 1 Ameshoff Street
Braamfontein
2001
TEL: 011-408 3914
FAX: 011-408 2109

TRANSFER SECRETARY
Central Registrars Ltd
P O Box 4844, Johannesburg
2000
TEL: 011-331 0051

COMPANY SECRETARY
H E S Norman

NATURE OF BUSINESS
An investment holding company with investments predominantly in the institutional & financial fields. The company has an indirect, joint controlling interest in Liberty Holdings.

BANKERS :
Standard Bank of SA Ltd

AUDITORS :
Kessel Feinstein

FAMILIAR BRAND NAMES
N/A

CONTRIBUTION BY ACTIVITY
N/A

YEAR END : February

DIVIDEND : Ords 1c

Interim No 6	(Ldr)15/09/89	(Pay)06/10/89	Amt(c)4.8
Final No 7	(Ldr)30/03/90	(Pay)12/04/90	Amt(c)6
Interim No 8	(Ldr)14/09/90	(Pay)05/10/90	Amt(c)5.2
Special No 9	(Ldr)14/09/90	(Pay)05/10/90	Amt(c)6
Final No 10	(Ldr)22/02/91	(Pay)12/04/91	Amt(c)8.8
Special No 11	(Ldr)22/02/91	(Pay)19/04/91	Amt(c)31.125
Interim No 12	(Ldr)13/09/91	(Pay)11/10/91	Amt(c)6.2
Final No 13	(Ldr)28/02/92	(Pay)10/04/92	Amt(c)10.4
Interim No 14	(Ldr)18/09/92	(Pay)02/10/92	Amt(c)8
Special No 15	(Ldr)18/09/92	(Pay)02/10/92	Amt(c)17.5
Dividend No 16	(Ldr)27/11/92	(Pay)11/12/92	Amt(c)30

CAPITAL STRUCTURE

	AUTHORISED	ISSUED
Ords 1c	250000000	204853900

FINANCIAL STATISTICS (AT FINANCIAL YEAR END)

(Amts in R'000)	1992 Feb	1991 Feb	1990 Feb	1989 Feb	1988
Ord S/H Int	1341024	765496	577818	532523	297401
Long Trm Loans	-	-	72364	65592	52813
Iss Ord Share	204854	204854	186506	183406	180400
Total Liab	22061	85590	85869	77557	63132
Current Liab	22061	85590	13505	11965	10319
Total Assets	1363085	851086	663687	610080	357402
Current Assets	22120	83466	12538	19676	7188
Debtors	21572	80115	11370	8665	-
Inventory	-	-	-	-	7188
Oper Profit	15997	11790	12455	8460	25220
Interest Paid	45	-	-	-	-
Tax Paid	-	50	155	111	3
Prf af Int&Tax	50489	40327	34884	30249	25217
Prf att Ord Sh	50489	38615	31117	26573	21981
Btm Line Earn	50489	52047	31017	26589	21981
Dividend Paid	34006	102787	19994	18208	15875
Mkt Prce(c) YE	700	450	350	310	200

PER SHARE STATISTICS (CENTS)

Net Asst Val	654.62	373.68	309.81	290.35	164.86
Net Earnings	24.60	19.70	16.80	14.60	-
Dividends	16.60	14.00	10.80	10.00	-
Cash Flow	24.65	18.85	16 68	14.49	13 98

RATIOS AND OTHER INFORMATION

Mrk Cap(R000)	1433978	921843	652771	568559	360800
Current Ratio	1.00	0.98	0.93	1.64	0.70
Quik/Acid Tst	1.00	0.98	0.93	1.64	-
Debt/Ass Rat	0.02	0.10	0.02	0.02	0 18
L T L Tot Ass	-	-	-	-	0 15

Debt to Eqity	0 02	0 11	0 02	0 02	0 21
Interest Cover	1122 98	-	-	-	-
Ret on Assets	3 71	4 74	5 28	4 98	7 06
Ret on Equity%	3 76	5 04	5 39	4 99	7 39
Price/Earnings	28 46	22 84	20 83	21 23	-
Divid Cover	1 48	1 41	1 56	1 46	-
Divid Yield	2 37	3 11	3 09	3 23	-
Earning Yield%	3 51	4 38	4 80	4 71	-
NAV % Mrk Pr	93 52	83 04	88 52	93 66	82 43
Effec Tax Rate	-	0 42	1 21	1 28	0 01
Def Interval	-	-	-	-	2 09
Sus Grth Rate	1 23	-8 38	1 93	1 57	2 05

SUBSIDIARY & ASSOCIATED COMPANIES

DGI ASSOCIATES (PTY) LTD
DGI HOLDINGS (PTY) LTD
DGIB HOLDINGS (PTY) LTD
DONSHEL INVESTMENTS (PTY) LTD
LIBLIFE CONTROLLING CORP (PTY) LTD (50%)

INVESTMENTS

STANDARD BANK INVESTMENT CORP LTD (1%)

LIBERTY LIFE ASSOCIATION OF AFRICA LTD

ABBREVIATION : LIBERTY

JSE SHORT CODE : LLA

SECTOR : Financial-Insurance

SHAREHOLDERS

Who Owns Whom's Assessment of the Identity of the Ultimate Controlling Shareholder:
STANDARD BANK/DONALD GORDON VIA LIBHOLD

SHAREHOLDER	PERCENTAGE 1992	1991
LIBERTY HOLDINGS LTD	52 5	52 8
STD BANK NOM TVL P/L	9 5	9 0
LONDON REGISTER ACCOUNT	2 8	3 7
CMB NOM P/L	2 8	---
MINU NOM LTD	2 0	2 0
ESCOM PENS & PROV FUND	1 8	1 9
SA MUTUAL	1 8	---
EIGHTY ONE MAIN STREET NOM LTD	1 8	---
SOUTHERN LIFE ASSOC LTD	1 4	---
INDO-CHINA NOM P/L	---	1 2
SANLAM	---	2 6
TOTAL	76 3	73 3

DIRECTORS :
D'HALLUIN YGJ ,DE VILLIERS HP (Deputy Chairman)
FERGUSSON AJF ,GEELING KG ,GORDON D (Chairman)
HANDLER S ,HOPKINS SA ,KAHN JM ,NILSSON K
RAPP M ,ROMANIS A (Managing Director)
STRAUSS CB DR,VOSLOO M
WHARTON-HOOD PD (Vice Chairman)
WINTERTON M (Joint Managing Director)
WRIGHTON PGA

REGISTRATION NUMBER : 57/02788/06

REGISTERED OFFICE
Liberty Life Centre, 1 Ameshoff Street
Braamfontein
2001
TEL 011-408 3911
FAX 011-408 2109

TRANSFER SECRETARY
Central Registrars Ltd
P O Box 4844, Johannesburg
2000
TEL 011-331 0051

COMPANY SECRETARY
J Worwood

NATURE OF BUSINESS
The major activities of the Liberty Life group are the transaction of life insurance and pension fund business, Construction, development, management & ownership of fixed property, Investment activities & mutual fund management The company holds major investments in quoted SA Breweries, Premier Group, Placor Holdings, Standard Bank Investment Corp, & Beverage & Consumer Industry Holdings, & controls First International Trust, which holds the group's foreign (UK) investments

BANKERS :
Standard Bank of SA Ltd

AUDITORS :
Kessel Feinstein

FAMILIAR BRAND NAMES
N/A

CONTRIBUTION BY ACTIVITY
Net Investment Income (% total income) (41 5%)
Net Prem Income/Annuity Considerations (56 8%)
Sundry Income (1 7%)

YEAR END : December

DIVIDEND : Ords 10c

Interim No 43	(Ldr)15/09/89	(Pay)06/10/89	Amt(c)265
Final No 44	(Ldr)30/03/90	(Pay)12/04/90	Amt(c)378
Interim No 45	(Ldr)14/09/90	(Pay)05/10/90	Amt(c)32
Special No 46	(Ldr)14/09/90	(Pay)05/10/90	Amt(c)50
Final No 47	(Ldr)22/02/91	(Pay)12/04/91	Amt(c)54
Special No 48	(Ldr)22/02/91	(Pay)19/04/91	Amt(c)199 2
Interim No 49	(Ldr)13/09/91	(Pay)04/10/91	Amt(c)43
Final No 50	(Ldr)28/02/92	(Pay)10/04/92	Amt(c)65
Interim No 51	(Ldr)04/09/92	(Pay)02/10/92	Amt(c)54
Special No 52	(Ldr)04/09/92	(Pay)02/10/92	Amt(c)100

NUMBER OF EMPLOYEES : 3500

CAPITAL STRUCTURE

	AUTHORISED	ISSUED
Ords 10c	320000000	227756235
Conv Red Cum Prefs 10c	15000000	561250

FINANCIAL STATISTICS (AT FINANCIAL YEAR END)

(Amts in R'000)	1991 Dec	1990 Dec	1989 Dec	1988	1987
Ord S/H Int	4433400	3148900	2503800	1993700	1514500
Long Trm Loans	27781300	23771900	16294900	12803400	9871700
Iss Ord Share	227756	213942	188663	16205	15047
Total Liab	30089100	24987700	16698200	13139400	10108900

Current Liab	2307800	1215800	403300	336000	237200
Total Assets	34522500	28136600	19202000	15340500	11867400
Current Assets	3211100	2652600	803600	543400	481200
Debtors	912900	824800	526900	-	-
Inventory	-	-	-	543400	481200
Oper Profit	1945600	1687000	1580200	-	-
Tax Paid	140200	180300	107800	99400	50600
Prf af Int&Tax	1805400	1506700	1472400	1286000	1197800
Prf att Ord Sh	1805100	1506400	1438400	144000	123100
Btm Line Earn	1805100	1616400	1438400	144000	123100
Dividend Paid	666300	290600	118500	112200	96100
Mkt Prce(c) YE	3700	2600	2020	14000	9600

PER SHARE STATISTICS (CENTS)

Net Asst Val	1946.56	1471.85	1327.13	12302.99	10065.13
Net Earnings	127.00	102.10	84.70	-	-
Dividends	108.00	86.00	63.00	-	-
Cash Flow	792.56	705.33	689.86	7935.82	7960.39

RATIOS AND OTHER INFORMATION

Mrk Cap(R000)	8426972	5562492	3810993	2268700	1444512
Current Ratio	1.39	2.18	1.99	1.62	2.03
Quik/Acid Tst	1.39	2.18	1.99	-	-
Debt/Ass Rat	0.16	0.16	0.04	0.86	0.85
L T L Tot Ass	0.10	0.11	0.02	0.83	0.83
Debt to Eqity	1.28	1.41	0.32	6.59	6.67
Ret on Assets	5.64	6.00	8.23	9.03	10.52
Ret on Equity%	40.72	47.84	57.45	7.22	8.13
Price/Earnings	29.13	25.47	23.85	-	-
Divid Cover	1.18	1.19	1.34	-	-
Divid Yield	2.92	3.31	3.12	-	-
Earning Yield%	3.43	3.93	4.19	-	-
NAV % Mrk Pr	52.61	56.61	65.70	87.88	104.85
Effec Tax Rate	7.21	10.69	6.82	-	-
Def Interval	2.02	2.33	0.27	9.96	8.24
Sus Grth Rate	25.69	38.61	52.72	1.60	1.78

SUBSIDIARY & ASSOCIATED COMPANIES

ALABAMA INVESTMENTS (PTY) LTD
ALRODE INDUSTRIAL PROPERTIES (PTY) LTD
ALTIPIANO INVESTMENTS (PTY) LTD
BERON INVESTMENTS (PTY) LTD
BEVERAGE & CONSUMER INDUSTRY HOLDINGS LT (34%)
BIFON PROPERTIES (PTY) LTD
BRAAMRIDGE (PTY) LTD
BRONKS & RUDOLPH (PTY) LTD
BUTTERCUP HOLDINGS LTD
CARLYN INVESTMENTS (PTY) LTD
CHARTER LIFE INSURANCE CO. LTD
CLAIMSBURY INVESTMENTS (PTY) LTD
COLLEGE MANSIONS (PTY) LTD
COMO TRUST (PTY) LTD
CONNOCKS BUILDINGS (PTY) LTD
CORMORAN PROPERTIES (PTY) LTD
CUMBERLAND MANSIONS (PTY) LTD
DEJEUNE (PTY) LTD
EASTERN REGIONAL CENTRE (PTY) LTD
EASTGATE DEVELOPMENTS (PTY) LTD
EDWORKS PROPERTIES (PTY) LTD
ELFRED PROPERTIES (PTY) LTD
ELMAIN INVESTMENTS (PTY) LTD
EPPYARD PROPERTIES (PTY) LTD
FEARLESS INVESTMENTS (PTY) LTD
FEDERATED PROPERTIES (BELLVILLE) LTD
FEDERATED PROPERTIES (BLUFF) LTD
FEDERATED PROPERTIES (DURBAN NORTH) (PTY
FEDERATED PROPERTIES (FISH HOEK) LTD
FEDERATED PROPERTIES (KIMBERLEY) LTD
FEDERATED PROPERTIES (MALVERN) LTD
FEDERATED PROPERTIES (MONTCLAIR) LTD
FEDERATED PROPERTIES (NELSPRUIT) LTD
FEDERATED PROPERTIES (PIETERSBURG TRANSV
FEDERATED PROPERTIES (PIETERSBURG) LTD
FEDERATED PROPERTIES (PINETOWN) LTD
FEDERATED PROPERTIES (SASOL) LTD
FEDERATED PROPERTIES (STELLENBOSCH) LTD
FEDERATED PROPERTIES (WAVERLEY) LTD
FEDERATED PROPERTIES (WORCESTER) LTD
FIRST INTERNATIONAL TRUST LTD (40%)
FOGEL INVESTMENTS (PTY) LTD
FREDELLA INVESTMENTS LTD
FULIT (PTY) LTD
GFSA HOLDINGS LTD (20%)
GRAND NATIONAL BUILDINGS LTD
GUARDIAN LIBERTY PROPERTY ENTERPRISES (P
GUARDIAN REAL ESTATE CORPORATION LTD
HARRY MAGID INVESTMENTS (PTY) LTD
HEREWARD HOUSE (PTY) LTD
HILLMATE BUILDINGS (PTY) LTD
HURSTDOWN INVESTMENTS (PTY) LTD
IRALAINE PROPERTIES (PTY) LTD
JOUBERT STREET PROPERTIES (PTY) LTD
LANCET HALL (PTY) LTD
LANGERMAN DRIVE INVESTMENTS (PROPERTIES)
LANGERMAN DRIVE INVESTMENTS (PTY) LTD
LIBERTY LIFE ASS. OF AFRICA (WINDHOEK) (
LIBERTY LIFE INVESTMENT TRUST LTD
LIBERTY PROPERTIES (BEDFORDVIEW) (PTY) L
LIBERTY PROPERTIES (BRAAMFONTEIN) (PTY)
LIBERTY PROPERTIES (BRITS) (PTY) LTD
LIBERTY PROPERTIES (CITY CENTRE) (PTY) L
LIBERTY PROPERTIES (EASTERN PROVINCE) (P
LIBERTY PROPERTIES (INANDA) (PTY) LTD
LIBERTY PROPERTIES (LONG STREET) (PTY) L
LIBERTY PROPERTIES (MIDRAND) (PTY) LTD
LIBERTY PROPERTIES (OFS) (PTY) LTD
LIBERTY PROPERTIES (ORMONDE) (PTY) LTD
LIBERTY PROPERTIES (PORT ELIZABETH) (PTY
LIBERTY PROPERTIES (QUEENSTOWN) (PTY) LT
LIBERTY PROPERTIES (ROSEBANK) (PTY) LTD
LIBERTY PROPERTIES (SELBY) (PTY) LTD
LIBERTY PROPERTIES (SIMMONDS STREET) (PT
LIBERTY PROPERTY HOLDINGS LTD
LIBPAC INVESTMENT HOLDINGS LTD
LIFCO (PTY) LTD
LONGSBANK BUILDINGS (PTY) LTD
MANOR INVESTMENTS LTD
MARKGOLD (PTY) LTD
MURRAY & STEWART CENTRE (CAPE TOWN) (PTY
MUSTANG PROPERTIES (PTY) LTD
NORTH CITY BROKERS LTD
ONLANGER INVESTMENTS (PTY) LTD
PATARL PROPERTIES (PTY) LTD
PERIMETER PROPERTIES (PTY) LTD
PLACOR HOLDINGS LTD (29,9%)
PLETPROP (PTY) LTD
PLOVERS BARROWS (PTY) LTD
PREMIER GROUP LTD (33,3%)
PRESAUER DEVELOPMENTS (PTY) LTD
PRUDENTIAL PORTFOLIO MANAGERS LTD
RAPP & MAISTER (BENONI PROPERTIES) (PTY)
RAPP & MAISTER HOLDINGS LTD
SABLIT (PTY) LTD
SANDHURST RESIDENTIAL DEVELOPMENT (PTY)
SANDTON DEVELOPMENTS (PTY) LTD
SANDTON SUN (PTY) LTD
SCANTLEBURY BUILDINGS (PTY) LTD
STALIT (PTY) LTD
STANDARD BANK INVESTMENT CORP LTD (40%)
STANDARD PROPERTIES OF AFRICA (PTY) LTD
TAI INVESTMENTS LTD
TORCH INVESTMENTS (PTY) LTD
TOWER HILL (PTY) LTD
TWENTY BAKER STREET (PTY) LTD
UNION ESTATES (PTY) LTD

VALLEY GARDENS (PTY) LTD
VERDALE INVESTMENTS (PTY) LTD
VERSON INVESTMENTS (PTY) LTD
WESTALINE PROPERTIES (PTY) LTD
WHIZ PROPERTIES (PTY) LTD

INVESTMENTS

TRANSATLANTIC HOLDINGS PLC (12,1%)

LINDUM REEFS GOLD MINING CO LTD

ABBREVIATION : LINDUM

JSE SHORT CODE : LDM

SECTOR : Gold-Rand & others

SHAREHOLDERS

Who Owns Whom's Assessment of the Identity of the Ultimate Controlling Shareholder:
ANGLO VIA JOHNIES

SHAREHOLDER	PERCENTAGE 1992	1991
STD BANK NOM TVL P/L	77.0	77.3
LIBERTY LIFE ASSOC OF AFRICA LTD	4.4	4.4
GUARDIAN NOM P/L	3.3	3.3
LONDON CONTROL ACCOUNT	2.8	2.8
MAESTRO SECURITIES P/L	1.0	---
TOTAL	88.6	87.8

DIRECTORS :
HENDERSON D DR,TAVENDALE MJ ,TREGONING GW
VAN RENSBURG PWJ (Chairman

REGISTRATION NUMBER : 88/03804/06

REGISTERED OFFICE
SD 32 Shaft, Randfontein Road
Randfontein
1760
TEL: 011-692 4060
FAX: 011-692 4060

TRANSFER SECRETARY
Consolidated Share Registrars Ltd
P O Box 61051, Marshalltown
2107
TEL: 011-492 1620

COMPANY SECRETARY
N A Suttle

NATURE OF BUSINESS
The company carries on gold mining operations in the area known as the Old Randfontein Section, on the Western Witwatersrand.

BANKERS :
Standard Bank of SA Ltd

AUDITORS :
Deloitte Pim Goldby

FAMILIAR BRAND NAMES
N/A

CONTRIBUTION BY ACTIVITY
N/A

YEAR END : June

NUMBER OF EMPLOYEES : 101

CAPITAL STRUCTURE

	AUTHORISED	ISSUED
Ords 1c	20000000	18345659

FINANCIAL STATISTICS (AT FINANCIAL YEAR END)

(Amts in R'000)	1992 Jun	1991 Jun	1990 Jun	1989 Jun
Ord S/H Int	24087	21771	25790	29461
Iss Ord Share	18347	18347	18347	18341
Total Liab	2494	4172	2665	2494
Current Liab	2494	4172	2665	2494
Total Assets	26581	25943	28455	31955
Current Assets	740	234	2430	10996
Debtors	302	98	346	406
Inventory	259	135	-	-
Turnover	15551	14475	23699	2124
Oper Profit	1149	-3934	-4697	-1084
Interest Paid	289	112	-	-
Prf af Int&Tax	2316	-4019	-3680	-1084
Prf att Ord Sh	2316	-4019	-3680	-1084
Btm Line Earn	2316	-4019	-3680	-1084
Mkt Prce(c) YE	25	70	210	220

PER SHARE STATISTICS (CENTS)

Net Asst Val	131.29	118.66	140.57	160.63
Net Earnings	12.60	-21.90	-	-
Cash Flow	12.62	-21.91	-20.06	-5.91

RATIOS AND OTHER INFORMATION

Mrk Cap(R000)	4587	12843	38529	40350
Current Ratio	0.30	0.06	0.91	4.41
Quik/Acid Tst	0.19	0.02	0.91	4.41
A/C Rec T/ovr	51.49	147.70	68.49	5.23
Tot Ass T/ovr	0.59	0.56	0.83	0.07
Debt/Ass Rat	0.09	0.16	0.09	0.08
Debt to Eqity	0.10	0.19	0.10	0.08
Interest Cover	9.01	-34.88	-	-
Oper Prof Mrg	7.39	-27.18	-19.82	-51.04
Net Prof Marg%	14.89	-27.77	-15.53	-51.04
Ret on Assets	9.80	-15.06	-12.93	-3.39
Ret on Equity%	9.62	-18.46	-14.27	-3.68
Price/Earnings	1.98	-3.20	-	-
Earning Yield%	50.40	-31.29	-	-
NAV % Mrk Pr	525.14	169.52	66.94	73.01
Def Interval	-	-0.66	-	-
Sus Grth Rate	9.62	-18.46	-14.27	-3.68

SUBSIDIARY & ASSOCIATED COMPANIES

None

INVESTMENTS

None

LION MATCH CO LTD

ABBREVIATION : LIONMATCH

JSE SHORT CODE : LNM

SECTOR : Industrial-Tobacco & Match

SHAREHOLDERS

Who Owns Whom's Assessment of the Identity of the Ultimate Controlling Shareholder: ANGLO AMERICAN VIA SA BREWS

SHAREHOLDER	PERCENTAGE 1992	1991
SA BREWERIES LTD	70 6	70 6
FIRST NAT NOM P/L	9 3	9 0
METAL IND GROUP PENS FUND	4 8	4 8
ENGINEERING INDUSTRIES PENS FUND	4 1	4 1
FERDINAND PEWN & CO	1 1	1 1
SAGE LIFE LTD	1 1	1 1
TOTAL	90 9	90 6

DIRECTORS :
ALDERTON AJ ,HEALD JB ,KAHN JM ,MACFARLANE WS MOUNTFORD PW ,RUDSTON A ,TOD JOG ,TURNER EM TURNER TK ,VAN DER WATT L (Chairman),WYMAN MI

REGISTRATION NUMBER : 04/00663/06

REGISTERED OFFICE
892 Umgeni Road, Durban
4001
TEL 031-23 8251
FAX 031-23 9681

TRANSFER SECRETARY
KPMG Aiken & Peat
P O Box 7400, Johannesburg
2000
TEL 011-332 7111

COMPANY SECRETARY
G G Besson

NATURE OF BUSINESS
An investment holding company Subsidiaries are active in the following operations Manufacture and distribution of matches, bookmatches, match splints, small domestic electrical appliances, razors, razor blades, shaving accessories, garden tools, knives and disposable lighters The group also converts and prints board, paper and other substrates, operates processes in thermoforming of plastics and metallises & laminates substrates

BANKERS :
Standard Bank of SA Ltd, Nedcor Bank Ltd

AUDITORS :
KPMG Aiken & Peat

FAMILIAR BRAND NAMES
ALLUMETTES,AQUARIUS,BERDA,CONTACT II,CRICKET DURASHARP SCISSORS,GRUNDIG SHAVERS HANDY PRUNERS,KITCHEN DEVIL,LASER,LION MATCH LOVING TOUCH,NEW BLUE DISPOSABLE PERMASHARP KNIVES,PINEWARE,POPPEL LIGHTERS ROWENTA,SALTON,SUNBEAM,SUPER SWORD,SURELITE TULLEN CUTTERS,WKS KNIVES

CONTRIBUTION BY ACTIVITY
Packaging (34 2%)
Electrical Appliances (-3 3%)
Shaving, Home & Garden (9 2%)
Matches and Lighters (% Oper Profit) (59 9%)

YEAR END : March

DIVIDEND : Ords 20c

Interim	(Ldr)01/12/89	(Pay)29/12/89	Amt(c)6 5
Final	(Ldr)01/06/90	(Pay)02/07/90	Amt(c)6 5
Interim	(Ldr)30/11/90	(Pay)31/12/90	Amt(c)6 5
Final	(Ldr)31/05/91	(Pay)01/07/91	Amt(c)7 5
Interim	(Ldr)29/11/91	(Pay)31/12/91	Amt(c)4 5
Final	(Ldr)29/05/92	(Pay)01/07/92	Amt(c)7 0
Interim	(Ldr)27/11/92	(Pay)31/12/92	Amt(c)5 25

NUMBER OF EMPLOYEES : 2102

CAPITAL STRUCTURE

	AUTHORISED	ISSUED
Ords 20c	60000000	45378425

FINANCIAL STATISTICS (AT FINANCIAL YEAR END)

(Amts in R'000)	1992 Mar	1991 Mar	1990 Mar	1989 Feb	1988 Feb
Ord S/H Int	116254	109653	100612	79028	71093
Long Trm Loans	38340	63972	73908	52475	30478
Iss Ord Share	45378	45378	45378	45148	44048
Total Liab	111402	131028	120168	88523	61627
Current Liab	73062	67056	46260	36048	31149
Total Assets	226416	239259	219153	167101	132720
Intang Assets	1240	1422	1627	450	*
Current Assets	98548	114988	105020	88000	69438
Debtors	43407	51221	46473	32105	27151
Inventory	47926	63767	57867	55866	42287
Turnover	329563	331257	279983	230396	223197
Oper Profit	39233	40021	34255	25436	20311
Interest Paid	13322	12543	10617	5459	2758
Tax Paid	12288	12748	11378	9501	7899
Prf af Int&Tax	14420	15394	12823	10972	9654
Prf att Ord Sh	12560	15394	14019	12065	11197
Btm Line Earn	12560	15394	14019	12065	11533
Dividend Paid	5219	6353	5899	4966	15416
Mkt Prce(c) YE	275	270	220	235	200
Depreciation	9389	8089	6306	4661	4287

PER SHARE STATISTICS (CENTS)

Net Asst Val	253 46	238 51	218 13	174 05	161 40
Net Earnings	27 68	33 92	30 97	27 00	22 12
Dividends	11 50	14 00	13 00	11 00	35 00
Cash Flow	52 66	52 27	42 15	43 22	31 25

RATIOS AND OTHER INFORMATION

Mrk Cap(R000)	124790	122521	99832	106098	88096
Current Ratio	1 35	1 71	2 27	2 44	2 23
Quik/Acid Tst	0 69	0 76	1 02	0 89	0 87
A/C Rec T/ovr	7 59	6 47	6 02	7 18	6 58
Tot Ass T/ovr	1 46	1 38	1 28	1 38	1 35
Debt/Ass Rat	0 43	0 48	0 47	0 47	0 42
L T L Tot Ass	0 10	0 20	0 26	0 26	0 19
Debt to Eqity	0 83	1 06	1 03	1 00	0 79
Interest Cover	2 95	3 20	3 24	4 69	7 36
Oper Prof Mrg	11 90	12 08	12 23	11 04	9 10
Net Prof Marg%	3 81	4 65	5 01	5 24	5 02
Ret on Assets	16 86	17 00	16 43	16 17	13 17
Ret on Equity%	10 80	14 04	13 93	15 27	12 60
Price/Earnings	9 93	7 96	7 10	8 70	9 04

Divid Cover	2.41	2.42	2.38	2.45	0.63
Divid Yield	4.18	5.19	5.91	4.68	17.50
Earning Yield%	10.07	12.56	14.08	11.49	11.06
NAV % Mrk Pr	92.17	88.34	99.15	74.06	80.70
Effec Tax Rate	46.57	45.72	47.22	28.80	25.60
Def Interval	1.50	2.35	3.03	2.19	1.29
Sus Grth Rate	6.31	8.25	8.07	8.98	-5.93

SUBSIDIARY & ASSOCIATED COMPANIES

5 HAWTHORNE LANE (PTY) LTD
AMALGAMATED APPLIANCES (PTY) LTD (50%)
INTERPAK (CAPE) (PTY) LTD
INTERPAK (NATAL) (PTY) LTD
INTERPAK HOLDINGS (PTY) LTD
INTERPAK PROPERTIES (PTY) LTD
INTERPRINT (PTY) LTD
LION APPLIANCE ENTERPRISES (PTY) LTD
NATIONAL MATCH CO LTD
NATIONAL RAZOR BLADE MANUFACTURING CO. (
NATIONAL SHAVING PRODUCTS (PTY) LTD
RECORD PAC INCORPORATED (PTY) LTD
UMTOMBENI FARM (PTY) LTD
UNIVERSAL WOOD INDUSTRIES LTD
V-PAC (PTY) LTD

INVESTMENTS

UNION CO-OPERATIVE BARK & SUGAR CO LTD (2150 SH)

LITHOSAVER SYSTEMS LTD

ABBREVIATION : LITHO

JSE SHORT CODE : LTH

SECTOR : Industrial-Printing & Publishing

SHAREHOLDERS

Who Owns Whom's Assessment of the Identity of the Ultimate Controlling Shareholder:
DIRECTORS

SHAREHOLDER	PERCENTAGE 1992	1991
WALTONS STATIONERY CO LTD	29.8	29.8
PEPPER J D	15.8	14.2
DANNHEISSER M O	12.0	12.0
DANNHEISSER P S	12.0	12.0
DANNHEISSER H T	1.9	1.9
PEPPER SEAN MICHAEL	1.9	1.6
BIRCH D	1.6	1.6
PEPPER SHIRLEY MARGUARITE	1.6	1.6
BERGER M	1.2	---
BOILER TUBES AFRICA P/L	1.1	1.1
LITHOSAVER SHARE INC SCHEME	---	2.0
HASHAY NOM P/L	---	1.2
SANLAM	---	3.5
TOTAL	79.0	82.6

DIRECTORS :
BIRCH NW (Managing Director),CHIMES LI
DANNHEISSER MO (Deputy Chairman),DANNHEISSER PS
LONGE DW ,PEPPER JD (Executive Chairman)
ROBARTS FEA

REGISTRATION NUMBER : 69/15643/06

REGISTERED OFFICE
18 Richard Road, Industria North
Maraisburg
1709
TEL: 011-673 2180
FAX: 011-673 7039

TRANSFER SECRETARY
Fraser Street Registrars (Pty) Ltd
P O Box 61178, Marshalltown
2107
TEL: 011-491 0911

COMPANY SECRETARY
C R Adendorff

NATURE OF BUSINESS
Production & distribution of stock listing paper, Production of long, medium & short run business forms, cheques & self-adhesive labels, Production of credit card sets.

BANKERS :
Nedcor Bank Ltd

AUDITORS :
Deloitte Pim Goldby

FAMILIAR BRAND NAMES
N/A

CONTRIBUTION BY ACTIVITY
Transvaal (% Turnover) (70.7%)
Cape (29.3%)

YEAR END : February

DIVIDEND : Ords 1c

Interim No 5	(Ldr)25/10/91	(Pay)22/11/91	Amt(c)2
Final No 6	(Ldr)29/05/92	(Pay)26/06/92	Amt(c)4
Interim No 7	(Ldr)30/10/92	(Pay)20/11/92	Amt(c)4

NUMBER OF EMPLOYEES : 350

CAPITAL STRUCTURE

	AUTHORISED	ISSUED
Ords 1c	30000000	21538400

FINANCIAL STATISTICS (AT FINANCIAL YEAR END)

(Amts in R'000)	1992 Feb	1991 Feb	1990 Feb	1989 Feb	1988 Feb
Ord S/H Int	18290	15558	14669	15578	14183
Long Trm Loans	6318	6328	5435	5772	1481
Iss Ord Share	21538	21077	21077	21077	20662
Total Liab	17798	21432	24237	23852	8150
Current Liab	11480	15104	18802	18080	6669
Total Assets	36088	36990	38906	39430	22333
Current Assets	22515	21025	20938	19528	12755
Debtors	13008	14168	11954	11252	7360
Inventory	7498	6855	8898	8275	5393
Turnover	69865	58196	53316	46598	26933
Oper Profit	7875	3844	2125	3199	3953
Interest Paid	1374	2615	2987	1641	482
Tax Paid	2928	372	47	-38	147
Prf af Int&Tax	3831	889	-909	1730	3324
Prf att Ord Sh	3831	889	-909	1730	3324
Btm Line Earn	3831	889	-909	1730	3324
Dividend Paid	1283	-	-	626	1091
Mkt Prce(c) YE	50	25	35	80	80

Depreciation	2913	2033	2191	1458	764

PER SHARE STATISTICS (CENTS)

Net Asst Val	84.92	73.82	69.60	73.91	68.64
Net Earnings	18.10	4.20	-4.30	8.30	17.30
Dividends	6.00	-	-	3.00	5.50
Cash Flow	40.69	15.63	5.96	15.11	21.96

RATIOS AND OTHER INFORMATION

Mrk Cap(R000)	10769	5269	7377	16862	16530
Current Ratio	1.96	1.39	1.11	1.08	1.91
Quik/Acid Tst	1.31	0.94	0.64	0.62	1.10
A/C Rec T/ovr	5.37	4.11	4.46	4.14	3.66
Tot Ass T/ovr	1.94	1.57	1.37	1.18	1.21
Debt/Ass Rat	0.42	0.57	0.62	0.60	0.36
L T L Tot Ass	0.11	0.16	0.14	0.14	0.06
Debt to Eqity	0.84	1.35	1.64	1.52	0.56
Interest Cover	5.73	1.47	0.71	1.95	8.20
Oper Prof Mrg	11.27	6.61	3.99	6.87	14.68
Net Prof Marg%	5.48	1.53	-1.70	3.71	12.34
Ret on Assets	22.54	10.48	5.46	8.45	17.70
Ret on Equity%	20.95	5.71	-6.20	11.11	23.44
Price/Earnings	2.76	5.95	-8.14	9.64	4.62
Divid Cover	3.02	-	-	2.77	3.15
Divid Yield	12.00	-	-	3.75	6.88
Earning Yield%	36.20	16.80	-12.29	10.38	21.63
NAV % Mrk Pr	169.84	295.26	198.85	92.39	85.80
Effec Tax Rate	13.43	-	-8.35	-	0.78
Def Interval	0.69	3.30	13.42	5.47	1.18
Sus Grth Rate	13.93	5.71	-6.20	7.09	15.74

SUBSIDIARY & ASSOCIATED COMPANIES

BUSINESS FORMS PROPERTIES (PTY) LTD
LITHOSAVER WEST RAND (PTY) LTD
TRADEFORMS (PTY) LTD

INVESTMENTS

None

LOG-TEK HOLDINGS LTD

ABBREVIATION : LOGTEK

JSE SHORT CODE : LGT

SECTOR : Industrial-Electronics, Electrical & Bat

SHAREHOLDERS

Who Owns Whom's Assessment of the Identity of the Ultimate Controlling Shareholder: DIRECTORS

SHAREHOLDER	PERCENTAGE 1992	1991
SFSS NOM P/L	25.3	33.6
MERHOLD SECURITIES P/L	16.2	23.4
SA MUTUAL	9.0	13.4
MOSS M S	8.4	---
STD BANK NOM TVL P/L	4.7	2.1
MOSS J	2.0	---
REX J B	1.6	---
DANTWIN INV LTD	1.2	---
DE KOCK J B R	1.2	---
DAUPHIN F W	1.1	---
KROK R	1.0	---
MENBLACK NOM P/L	---	1.4
ONS DORP MEUBELEERDERS E/B	---	1.1
TOTAL	71.7	74.9

DIRECTORS :
BEHRMANN AJ (Chairman),BENBOW-HEBBERT SE MS
BRADLEY R ,ECKSTEIN RS
FRASER IH (Financial Director),KIRSH W
MOOLMAN MN ,PARUK YM ,SEABROOKE CS
SPAIN HS (Chief Executive

REGISTRATION NUMBER : 87/01807/06

REGISTERED OFFICE
24 - 15th Road, Randjespark
Midrand
1685
TEL: 011-314 2270
FAX: 011-314 1595

TRANSFER SECRETARY
Consolidated Share Registrars Ltd
P O Box 61051, Marshalltown
2107
TEL: 011-492 1620

COMPANY SECRETARY
I H Fraser

NATURE OF BUSINESS
An investment holding company. Subsidiaries are engaged in leasing & medium-term financing, and financial advertising; computer, management and business training; manufacture, installation and support of payroll, personnel and time management systems; provision of logistic support analysis.

BANKERS :
Nedperm Bank Ltd

AUDITORS :
Kessel Feinstein

FAMILIAR BRAND NAMES
N/A

CONTRIBUTION BY ACTIVITY
N/A

YEAR END : April

DIVIDEND : Ords 1c

Interim	(Ldr)31/01/92	(Pay)24/02/92	Amt(c)2
Final	(Ldr)28/08/92	(Pay)12/10/92	Amt(c)2

CAPITAL STRUCTURE

	AUTHORISED	ISSUED
Ords 5c	50000000	23180695

FINANCIAL STATISTICS (AT FINANCIAL YEAR END)

(Amts in R'000)	1992 Apr	1991 Apr	1990 Apr	1989 Apr
Ord S/H Int	11476	6892	5605	8957
Long Trm Loans	12454	16459	275	735
Iss Ord Share	23181	15000	15000	15000
Total Liab	18741	23327	8653	6144

Current Liab	6287	6868	8378	5409
Total Assets	26053	25980	9509	15101
Intang Assets	4164	4239	4749	*
Current Assets	11796	12449	5904	13071
Debtors	9806	10784	4320	10102
Inventory	1990	1359	609	2968
Turnover	45846	43815	18043	21014
Oper Profit	4971	6859	4027	-599
Interest Paid	2055	1278	555	680
Tax Paid	683	1743	1087	25
Prf af Int&Tax	2294	4205	2659	-1130
Prf att Ord Sh	2565	2966	2888	-1130
Btm Line Earn	1285	602	1479	780
Dividend Paid	927	750	900	-
Mkt Prce(c) YE	54	40	40	55
Depreciation	941	1254	291	438

PER SHARE STATISTICS (CENTS)

Net Asst Val	31.54	17.69	5.71	59.71
Net Earnings	11.10	19.80	19.30	-7.50
Dividends	4.00	5.00	6.00	-
Cash Flow	13.66	26.32	21.00	-4.61

RATIOS AND OTHER INFORMATION

Mrk Cap(R000)	12518	6000	6000	8250
Current Ratio	1.88	1.81	0.70	2.42
Quik/Acid Tst	1.56	1.61	0.63	1.87
A/C Rec T/ovr	4.68	4.06	4.18	2.08
Tot Ass T/ovr	1.76	1.69	1.90	1.39
Debt/Ass Rat	0.69	0.73	0.89	0.41
L T L Tot Ass	0.45	0.46	0.01	0.05
Debt to Eqity	1.57	2.73	1.51	0.69
Interest Cover	2.42	5.37	7.27	-0.88
Oper Prof Mrg	10.84	15.65	22.32	-2.85
Net Prof Marg%	5.59	6.77	16.01	-5.38
Ret on Assets	20.35	28.75	47.64	-2.81
Ret on Equity%	22.35	43.04	51.53	-12.62
Price/Earnings	4.86	2.02	2.07	-7.33
Divid Cover	2.78	3.96	3.22	-
Divid Yield	7.41	12.50	15.00	-
Earning Yield%	20.56	49.50	48.25	-13.64
NAV % Mrk Pr	58.41	44.22	14.27	108.57
Effec Tax Rate	25.26	0.17	23.72	-2.26
Def Interval	3.72	3.03	1.23	-6.40
Sus Grth Rate	14.27	32.15	35.47	-12.62

SUBSIDIARY & ASSOCIATED COMPANIES

ACADEMY OF LEARNING (PTY) LTD
ACCSYS (PTY) LTD
ACCSYS GROUP HOLDINGS (PTY) LTD
CHARTER TRAINING GROUP LTD
COLFIN ENTERTAINMENT FINANCE (PTY) LTD
COLFIN INVESTMENTS LTD
DON GRAY INDUSTRIAL RELATIONS SYSTEMS (P
FIFTH WHEEL BOUTIQUES (PTY) LTD
GOTSHY (PTY) LTD
IMPACT TRAINING (PTY) LTD
JACK LEVITT AND SONS (PTY) LTD
JAKES RETAIL PROPERTIES (PTY) LTD
JASMENEL (PTY) LTD
LOG-TEK (PTY) LTD
LOG-TEK MANAGEMENT SERVICES (PTY) LTD
LOGISTIC SUPPORT SERVICES (PTY) LTD
LOGISTIC TECHNOLOGIES (PTY) LTD
LOGSYSTEMS DEVELOPMENT (PTY) LTD
PUNCH LINE EDUCATION (PTY) LTD
Q-TECH SERVICES (PTY) LTD
TECHNICAL ILLUSTRATIONS (PTY) LTD
TECHNICAL PUBLICATIONS (PTY) LTD
TECHNIPRINT (PTY) LTD (50,01%)
WINGATE HOLDINGS LTD (20,3%)

INVESTMENTS

DECOR HOLDINGS LTD (30000 SH)

LONDON FINANCE AND INVESTMENT GROUP PLC

ABBREVIATION : LONFIN

JSE SHORT CODE : LNF

SECTOR : Mining Financial-Mining Holding

SHAREHOLDERS

Who Owns Whom's Assessment of the Identity of the Ultimate Controlling Shareholder:
MARSHALL FAMILY

SHAREHOLDER	PERCENTAGE 1992	1991
LONDON ACCOUNTS	66.1	65.7
LONDURBAN P/L	27.9	27.9
TOTAL	93.9	93.6

DIRECTORS :
LATILLA-CAMPBELL P ,MACMILLAN PD
MARSHALL DC (Chairman),ROBOTHAM JM

REGISTRATION NUMBER : 01/08765/10

REGISTERED OFFICE
25 City Road, London
EC1Y 1BQ, In SA: 11th Floor
4001
TEL: 031-305 6521
FAX: 031-301 9791

TRANSFER SECRETARY
Central Registrars Ltd
P O Box 4844, Johannesburg
2000
TEL: 011-331 0051

COMPANY SECRETARY
City Group Ltd

NATURE OF BUSINESS
An investment holding and finance company centred in London and operating through a group of listed associated companies in the United Kingdom and subsidiaries in SA. The company generates dividends, interest & dealing profits from its portfolio of listed investments.

BANKERS :
First National Bank of SA Ltd

AUDITORS :
Arthur Goddard & Co

FAMILIAR BRAND NAMES
N/A

CONTRIBUTION BY ACTIVITY
Dividends/Interest/Sundry (% Op Profit) (97.0%)
Profit from sale of Investments (3.0%)

YEAR END : December

DIVIDEND :Ords 5p
Dividend (Ldr)19/03/92 (Pay)10/04/92 Amt(c)0.75

NUMBER OF EMPLOYEES : 10

CAPITAL STRUCTURE

	AUTHORISED	ISSUED
Ords 5p	30000000	24966945

FINANCIAL STATISTICS (AT FINANCIAL YEAR END)

(Amts in PS)	1991 Dec	1990 Dec	1989 Dec	1988 Dec	1987 Dec
Ord S/H Int	5500	9073	17595	11731	6154
Long Trm Loans	115	-	-	14	41
Iss Ord Share	24967	24967	24967	24967	24967
Total Liab	631	736	972	1829	912
Current Liab	516	736	972	1815	871
Total Assets	6131	9809	18567	13560	7066
Current Assets	3170	3016	2096	4905	6886
Debtors	709	497	195	236	374
Oper Profit	-115	-36	-9	261	273
Interest Paid	1	1	63	131	47
Tax Paid	337	373	692	128	207
Prf af Int&Tax	444	597	324	344	343
Prf att Ord Sh	333	-55	713	344	343
Btm Line Earn	-3687	-7028	2125	10519	2876
Dividend Paid	187	187	325	300	275
Mkt Prce(c) YE	70	115	240	340	330
Depreciation	25	4	4	2	8

PER SHARE STATISTICS (CENTS)

Net Asst Val	22.03	36.34	70.47	46.99	24.65
Net Earnings	1.33	-0.22	3.19	1.38	2.20
Dividends	0.75	0.75	1.30	1.20	1.10
Cash Flow	1.88	2.41	1.31	1.39	1.41

RATIOS AND OTHER INFORMATION

Mrk Cap(R000)	17477	28712	59921	84888	82391
Current Ratio	6.14	4.10	2.16	2.70	7.91
Quik/Acid Tst	6.14	4.10	2.16	2.70	7.91
Debt/Ass Rat	0.08	0.08	0.05	0.13	0.13
L T L Tot Ass	-	-	-	0.00	0.01
Debt to Eqity	0.09	0.08	0.06	0.16	0.15
Interest Cover	57.00	118.00	2.59	4.60	12.70
Ret on Assets	10.93	3.25	7.91	4.45	8.45
Ret on Equity%	6.05	-0.61	4.05	2.93	5.57
Price/Earnings	52.63	-522.73	75.24	246.38	150.00
Divid Cover	1.77	-0.29	2.45	1.15	2.00
Divid Yield	1.07	0.65	0.54	0.35	0.33
Earning Yield%	1.90	-0.19	1.33	0.41	0.67
NAV % Mrk Pr	31.47	31.60	29.36	13.82	7.47
Effec Tax Rate	55.34	45.71	81.99	98.46	91.59
Def Interval	-	0.00	-	-	-
Sus Grth Rate	2.65	-2.67	2.21	0.38	1.10

SUBSIDIARY & ASSOCIATED COMPANIES

CITY GROUP LTD (ENGLAND)
CRESTON PLC (22%)
DURATUBE & WIRE LTD (UK) (46,09%)
LONFIN HOLDINGS AG
LONFIN INVESTMENTS LTD (ENGLAND)
MARSHALL METALLIC CORPORATION SA LTD
MARSHALL METALLIC HOLDINGS LTD
MARSHALL METALLIC TRADING LTD
MARSHALL METALS TRADING LTD
WESTERN SELECTION PLC (46,09%)

INVESTMENTS

ALUMINIUM & TIMBER SECURITIES LTD (18,8%)
BARPLATS INVESTMENTS LTD (4%)
BURLINGTON GROUP PLC (19.5%)
EX-LANDS PLC (3,2%)
NMC GROUP PLC (7,7%)
UNIVERSAL PACKAGING CORPORATION (USA) (7,7%)

LONGRAIL LTD

ABBREVIATION : LONGRAIL

JSE SHORT CODE : LNR

SECTOR : Industrial-Transportation

SHAREHOLDERS

Who Owns Whom's Assessment of the Identity of the Ultimate Controlling Shareholder: DIRECTORS

SHAREHOLDER	PERCENTAGE 1992	1991
MARIUS ELS INV P/L	58.7	58.7
KEEVY B	6.5	6.5
LUTHER A	6.5	6.5
WALKER P J	3.8	3.8
PRETORIUS A F	3.8	3.8
ELS M H O	2.7	2.4
LAURENS R C	1.2	1.2
TOTAL	83.2	82.9

DIRECTORS :
ELS MHO (Joint Managing Director)
KEEVY B (Joint Managing Director)
LAURENS RC DR (Chairman),LOOTS HA
LUTHER A (Operations Director)
PRETORIUS AF (Financial Director)
WALKER PJ (Operations Director

REGISTRATION NUMBER : 81/06368/06

REGISTERED OFFICE
30 Flamink Street, Alrode
1451
TEL: 011-864 5237
FAX: 011-864 7209

TRANSFER SECRETARY
Mercantile Registrars Ltd
P O Box 1053, Johannesburg
2000
TEL: 011-333 8181

COMPANY SECRETARY
A F Pretorius

NATURE OF BUSINESS

An investment holding company with subsidiaries engaged in the long-distance transportation of goods & equipment, both in container and break-bulk form, by road. The group also operates a short-haul service in the Pretoria, Witwatersrand and Vereeniging areas, engaged in the sale of new trucks, servicing and repairing heavy duty vehicles and retreading tires.

BANKERS :
Nedperm Bank Ltd

AUDITORS :
Coopers Theron Du Toit

FAMILIAR BRAND NAMES
LONG DISTANCE,SHORTHAULS

CONTRIBUTION BY ACTIVITY
N/A

YEAR END : February

DIVIDEND :Ords no par value

Interim No 5	(Ldr)09/11/90	(Pay)27/11/90	Amt(c)2.5
Final No 6	(Ldr)22/02/91	(Pay)22/04/91	Amt(c)2
Interim No 7	(Ldr)01/11/91	(Pay)15/11/91	Amt(c)1
Final No 8	(Ldr)03/04/92	(Pay)23/04/92	Amt(c)3
Interim No 9	(Ldr)13/11/92	(Pay)30/11/92	Amt(c)1

NUMBER OF EMPLOYEES : 800

CAPITAL STRUCTURE

	AUTHORISED	ISSUED
Ords no par value	46872800	30869900

FINANCIAL STATISTICS (AT FINANCIAL YEAR END)

(Amts in R'000)	1992 Feb	1991 Feb	1990 Feb	1989 Feb	1988 Feb
Ord S/H Int	12095	12614	20716	17799	13683
Long Trm Loans	14345	12568	17389	10945	7388
Iss Ord Share	30870	30870	60797	60797	60797
Total Liab	30058	25025	39193	27211	20231
Current Liab	15713	12457	21804	16266	12843
Total Assets	41001	34480	55152	40253	31536
Intang Assets	1152	3159	4757	4757	2378
Current Assets	15722	11676	17142	14224	10528
Debtors	9074	9142	13070	11383	8901
Inventory	1467	479	286	254	113
Oper Profit	6402	6405	14263	9724	9109
Interest Paid	2525	2650	8259	3119	1599
Tax Paid	1794	2436	3240	1077	3672
Prf af Int&Tax	2432	1599	3319	6064	3838
Prf att Ord Sh	2342	1599	3319	6064	3735
Btm Line Earn	716	-131	2917	5940	3735
Dividend Paid	1235	1389	-	1824	1524
Mkt Prce(c) YE	18	21	15	30	35
Depreciation	4574	4117	6114	4025	2571

PER SHARE STATISTICS (CENTS)

Net Asst Val	35.45	30.63	26.25	21.45	18.59
Net Earnings	7.60	5.20	5.50	10.00	7.40
Dividends	4.00	4.50	-	3.00	3.00
Cash Flow	24.42	23.78	17.76	17.56	13.09

RATIOS AND OTHER INFORMATION

Mrk Cap(R000)	5557	6483	9120	18239	21279
Current Ratio	1.00	0.94	0.79	0.87	0.82
Quik/Acid Tst	0.91	0.90	0.77	0.86	0.81
Debt/Ass Rat	0.61	0.60	0.66	0.65	0.62
L T L Tot Ass	0.23	0.24	0.27	0.25	0.22
Debt to Eqity	2.08	1.65	1.77	1.48	1.44
Interest Cover	2.54	2.42	1.73	3.12	5.70
Ret on Assets	16.47	19.39	26.87	25.49	28.88
Ret on Equity%	19.36	12.68	16.02	34.07	27.30
Price/Earnings	2.37	4.04	2.73	3.00	4.73
Divid Cover	1.90	1.16	-	3.33	2.47
Divid Yield	22.22	21.43	-	10.00	8.57
Earning Yield%	42.22	24.76	36.67	33.33	21.14
NAV % Mrk Pr	196.94	145.85	175.00	71.51	53.13
Effec Tax Rate	27.69	11.40	28.66	6.88	45.85
Def Interval	2.06	1.91	2.16	1.55	1.73
Sus Grth Rate	9.15	1.66	16.02	23.82	16.16

SUBSIDIARY & ASSOCIATED COMPANIES

BREYTRANS (PTY) LTD
CHRIBO PROPERTIES (PTY) LTD
DIESEL TRUCK SERVICES (PTY) LTD
ELS EN ELS (PTY) LTD
FREEM INVESTMENTS (PTY) LTD
LOADMASTERS (PTY) LTD
LONG DISTANCE (CAPE) (PTY) LTD
LONG DISTANCE RENTALS (PTY) LTD
LONG DISTANCE TRANSPORT (PTY) LTD
ROADLOADS (PTY) LTD
SHORTHAULS (PTY) LTD

INVESTMENTS

None

LONRHO PLC

ABBREVIATION : LONRHO

JSE SHORT CODE : LON

SECTOR : Industrial-Industrial Holding

SHAREHOLDERS

Who Owns Whom's Assessment of the Identity of the Ultimate Controlling Shareholder:
R W ROWLAND

SHAREHOLDER	PERCENTAGE 1992	1991
SA MUTUAL	2.8	3.8
EIGHTY ONE MAIN STREET NOM LTD	2.7	3.4
CMB NOM P/L	1.9	---
STD BANK NOM TVL P/L	1.1	1.3
SANLAM	---	1.9
TOTAL	8.3	10.3

DIRECTORS :
BADGER RG ,DUNLOP RF (Deputy Chairman)
LECLEZIO MJJR (Chairman),PLATTS-MILLS JL
ROWLAND RW (Chief Executive & M.D.)
SPICER PGB (Deputy Chairman),TARSH PM
WHITTEN RE ,YOUENS PW SI

REGISTRATION NUMBER : 69/00015/10

REGISTERED OFFICE
Cheapside House, 138 Cheapside
London, EC2V 6BL

TEL: 094471-6069898
FAX: 094471-6062285

TRANSFER SECRETARY
Mercantile Registrars Ltd
P O Box 1053, Johannesburg
2000
TEL: 011-333 8181

COMPANY SECRETARY
M J Pearce

NATURE OF BUSINESS
An international industrial & Agricultural group
Main activities embrace mining, agriculture, production & retailing of textiles, spirits, wines; engineering; printing and publishing; ownership & management of property, hotels, casinos; finance and general trading.

BANKERS :
Standard Chartered Bank, Barclays Bank Plc
Coutts & Co, Credit Suisse, Lloyds Bank Plc
National Westminster Bank Plc
Swiss Bank Corporation
Royal Bank of Scotland Plc

AUDITORS :
Peat Marwick McLintock

FAMILIAR BRAND NAMES
N/A

CONTRIBUTION BY ACTIVITY
Manufacturing (% profit before taxation) (17.9%)
Motor & Equipment Distribution (52.2%)
General Trade (6.6%)
Leisure, Wine & Spirits (6.6%)
Mineral Extraction & Refining (8.9%)
Agriculture (3.6%)
Financial Services (4.2%)

YEAR END : September

DIVIDEND :Ords 25p

Final No 112	(Ldr)09/02/90	(Pay)06/04/90	Amt(c)8
Interim No 113	(Ldr)09/02/90	(Pay)06/04/90	Amt(c)3
Interim No 114	(Ldr)03/08/90	(Pay)01/10/90	Amt(c)5
Final No 115	(Ldr)08/02/91	(Pay)08/04/91	Amt(c)8
Interim No 116	(Ldr)08/02/91	(Pay)08/04/91	Amt(c)3
Interim No 117	(Ldr)08/08/91	(Pay)01/10/91	Amt(c)5
Final No 118	(Ldr)07/02/92	(Pay)06/04/92	Amt(c)5

NUMBER OF EMPLOYEES : 151000

CAPITAL STRUCTURE

	AUTHORISED	ISSUED
Ords 25p	974000000	653405791

FINANCIAL STATISTICS (AT FINANCIAL YEAR END)

(Amts in PS)	1991 Sep	1990 Sep	1989 Sep	1988 Sep	1987 Sep
Ord S/H Int	1331000	1384000	1459500	1174200	923400
Long Trm Loans	1156000	1182000	958000	897200	779300
Iss Ord Share	653406	639620	566089	452104	375051
Total Liab	2340000	2341000	2135000	1830200	1621000
Current Liab	1184000	1159000	1177000	933000	841700
Total Assets	3540000	3596000	3393200	2880600	2544400
Intang Assets	131000	129000	201300	123800	*
Current Assets	1292000	1473000	1541400	1389900	1138500
Debtors	434000	426000	558900	389300	374900
Inventory	512000	573000	574400	506800	446700
Turnover	4846000	5476000	5107800	4215600	3616400
Oper Profit	264000	289000	298500	263800	253000
Interest Paid	138000	120000	102900	72400	91900
Tax Paid	63000	80000	91900	75900	83000
Prf af Int&Tax	92000	131000	145300	119000	80900
Prf att Ord Sh	92000	148000	164600	133100	104200
Btm Line Earn	74000	149000	230200	124600	147800
Dividend Paid	84000	100000	87700	58200	48000
Mkt Prce(c) YE	1363	1500	1740	345	286
Depreciation	60000	52000	47000	46300	45400

PER SHARE STATISTICS (CENTS)

Net Asst Val	183.65	196.21	222.26	232.34	246.21
Net Earnings	14.20	23.60	27.10	30.00	30.10
Dividends	13.00	16.00	16.00	13.00	13.00
Cash Flow	15.47	21.98	28.67	33.08	32.75

RATIOS AND OTHER INFORMATION

Mrk Cap(R000)	8905924	9594300	9849949	1559759	1072646
Current Ratio	1.09	1.27	1.31	1.49	1.35
Quik/Acid Tst	0.66	0.78	0.82	0.95	0.82
A/C Rec T/ovr	11.17	12.85	9.14	10.83	9.65
Tot Ass T/ovr	1.37	1.52	1.51	1.46	1.42
Debt/Ass Rat	0.59	0.59	0.60	0.60	0.60
L T L Tot Ass	0.26	0.26	0.25	0.28	0.26
Debt to Eqity	1.57	1.52	1.39	1.47	1.64
Interest Cover	1.93	2.48	2.97	3.69	2.78
Oper Prof Mrg	5.45	5.28	5.84	6.26	7.00
Net Prof Marg%	1.90	2.70	3.22	3.16	2.88
Ret on Assets	9.75	10.93	11.08	10.32	11.48
Ret on Equity%	6.91	10.69	11.28	11.34	11.28
Price/Earnings	95.99	63.56	64.21	11.50	9.50
Divid Cover	1.09	1.48	1.69	2.31	2.32
Divid Yield	0.95	1.07	0.92	3.77	4.55
Earning Yield%	1.04	1.57	1.56	8.70	10.52
NAV % Mrk Pr	13.47	13.08	12.77	67.34	86.09
Effec Tax Rate	15.13	-	41.46	35.74	53.63
Def Interval	13.79	9.59	7.78	8.14	8.81
Sus Grth Rate	0.60	3.47	5.27	6.38	6.09

SUBSIDIARY & ASSOCIATED COMPANIES

A/S INVESTA KG (GERMANY) (50%)
AFRICAN COMMERCIAL HOLDINGS LTD (ZAMBIA)
ASHANTI GOLDFIELDS CORP. LTD (UK)
BALFOUR WILLIAMSON AND CO LTD (UK)
BERNARD SUNLEY & SONS PLC (UK)
BLANTYRE NETTING CO LTD, THE (MALAWI)
CHARLES ROBERTS ENGINEERING LTD (UK)
CHARTER ESTATES LTD (ZIMBABWE)
CHIBUKU PRODUCTS LTD (MALAWI)
COMPANHIA AGRO-INDUSTRIAL LONRHO-MOCAMBI (50%)
COMPANHIA DO PIPELINE MOCAMBIQUE-ZIMBABW (50.10%)
CONSOLIDATED HOLDINGS LTD (KENYA)
CONSTRUCTION ASSOCIATES (PVT) LTD (ZIMBA
COPPERBELT BOTTLING CO LTD (ZAMBIA)
CORSYN CONSOLIDATED MINES LTD (ZIMBABWE)
CRITTAL-HOPE LTD (ZIMBABWE)
DAVID WHITEHEAD (TEXTILES) LTD (ZIMBABWE
DAVID WHITEHEAD AND SONS (MALAWI) LTD
DAVID WHITEHEAD AND SONS LTD (UK)
DELKINS LTD (ZAMBIA)
DOVERCOURT MOTOR CO LTD, THE (UK)
DUIKER EXPLORATION LTD (SA)
DUTTON-FORSHAW MOTOR GROUP LTD, THE (UK)
EASTERN PLATINUM LTD (BOPHUTHATSWANA)

EATEC LTD (KENYA)
F E WRIGHT GROUP LTD (UK)
FARMERS CHOICE LTD (KENYA)
FIRSTEEL COATED STRIP LTD (WALSALL)
FIRSTEEL COLD ROLLED PRODUCTS LTD (UK)
FIRSTEEL METAL PRODUCTS LTD (UK)
FIRSTEEL STRIP MILL PRODUCTS LTD (UK)
GEORGE OUTRAM & CO. LTD (UK)
GEWOG MBH (GERMANY) (50%)
GREENAWAY-HARRISON LTD (UK)
HARRISON AND SONS LTD (UK)
HEINRICHS SYNDICATE LTD (ZAMBIA)
HONDO OIL & GAS COMPANY (PTY) LTD (USA)
HOTEL INVESTMENTS (GHANA) LTD
I.A.M. AGRICULTURAL MACHINERY LTD (REPUB
INDEPENDENCE MINING (PVT) LTD (ZIMBABWE)
JACK BARCLAY LTD (UK)
JOHN HOLT AGRICULTURAL ENGINEERS LTD (NI
JOHN HOLT GROUP LTD (UK)
JOHN HOLT PLC (NIGERIA) (40%)
KALANGWA ESTATES LTD (ZAMBIA)
KRUPP LONRHO GMBH (GERMANY) (50%)
KUEHNE & NAGEL HOLDING INC (USA) (50%)
KUHNE & NAGEL INTERNATIONAL AG (SWITZERL (50%)
LONDON CITY AND INTERNATIONAL LTD (UK)
LONDON CITY AND WESTCLIFF PROPERTIES LTD
LONRHO (NAMIBIA) LTD
LONRHO AUTOMOTIVE & MACHINERY CO LTD (UK
LONRHO EXPORTS LTD (UK)
LONRHO FINANCE PLC (UK)
LONRHO INC (USA)
LONRHO MALAWI LTD
LONRHO PACIFIC LTD (JAPAN)
LONRHO SA LTD
LONRHO SUGAR CORPORATION LTD (SWAZILAND)
LONRHO ZAMBIA LTD
LONRHO ZIMBABWE LTD
LSA MOTORS LTD (SA)
LUSOLANDA S.A.R.L. (ANGOLA)
MAKANDI ESTATES LTD (UK)
MAN-VW TRUCK & BUS LTD (UK)
MASTERDRIVE LTD (LONDON)
MATERMACO SA (BELGIUM)
MERVILLE LTD (MAURITIUS)
METROPOLE HOTELS (HOLDINGS) LTD (UK)
MOTOR HOLDINGS (BOTSWANA) (PTY) LTD
MOTOR MART GROUP LTD (KENYA)
MOUNT KENYA SAFARI CLUB LTD (KENYA)
MUFINDI TEA CO LTD (TANZANIA)
MUMBWA COTTON GINNERY LTD (ZAMBIA)
NATIONAL AIRWAYS AND FINANCE CORP. (PTY)
NATIONAL BLANKET LTD (ZIMBABWE) (50%)
NATIONAL BREWERIES LTD (ZAMBIA) (49%)
NEWELL DUNFORD LTD (UK)
OBSERVER LTD, THE (UK)
OL PEJETA RANCHING LTD (KENYA)
P.S. MANDRIDES PLC (NIGERIA) (38%)
PAGE BROS (NORWICH) LTD (UK)
PETROZIM LINE (PVT) LTD (ZIMBABWE) (50%)
PHOENIX ELECTRICAL LTD (UK)
PLAND STAINLESS LTD (UK)
POWER EQUIPMENT LTD (ZAMBIA)
PRINCESS PROPERTIES INTERNATIONAL LTD (B
READY MIX CONRETE (BOTSWANA) (PTY) LTD
ROBERT HUDSON (MACHINERY SALES AND SERVI
ROVER ZAMBIA LTD
SAVILLE TRACTORS (BELFAST) LTD (UK)
SAVILLE TRACTORS LTD (UK)
SCOTTISH AND UNIVERSAL INVESTMENTS LTD (
SCOTTISH AND UNIVERSAL NEWSPAPER LTD (UK
SHEER PRIDE LTD (UK)
SOUTHERN WATCH AND CLOCK SUPPLIES LTD (U
SPORTWORKS LTD (UK)
STAINLESS STEEL PRODUCTS (MALTA) LTD
STAR COMMERCIAL LTD (ZAMBIA)
TEAL RECORD CO (ZAMBIA) LTD
THE NORFOLK LTD (KENYA)
TURNPAN ZIMBABWE LTD
V.A.G FINANCE LTD (EDINBURGH) (49%)
VAG (UNITED KINGDOM) LTD
VITRETEX PAINTS LTD (ZAMBIA)
W DAHMER AND CO (PVT) LTD (ZIMBABWE)
WANKEL INTERNATIONAL SA (LUXENBOURG)
WATTLE COMPANY LTD, THE (ZIMBABWE)
WESTERN MACHINERY AND EQUIPMENT CO LTD (
WESTERN PLATINUM LTD (SA) (50.44%)
WESTERN PLATINUM REFINERY LTD (SA)
WILLOUGHBY'S CONSOLIDATED PLC (UK)
ZAMBESI COACHWORKS LTD (ZIMBABWE)
ZIMOCO LTD (ZIMBABWE)

INVESTMENTS

CONTAINER SERVICES LTD (12.5%)
EXPRESS KENYA LTD (17.6%)
EXPRESS MANAGEMENT LTD (14.8%)
OCEANUS LTD (14.8%)

LONRHO SUGAR CORPORATION LTD

ABBREVIATION : LONSUGR

JSE SHORT CODE : LSU

SECTOR : Industrial-Sugar

SHAREHOLDERS

Who Owns Whom's Assessment of the Identity of the Ultimate Controlling Shareholder:
LONRHO PLC

SHAREHOLDER	PERCENTAGE 1992	1991
LONRHO INTERNATIONAL LTD	99.7	99.7
TOTAL	99.7	99.7

DIRECTORS :
DUNLOP RF ,GOSNELL JM DR
LECLEZIO MJJR (Chairman & Joint MD),ROBERTS KN
ROWLAND RW (Joint Managing Director),WHITE EPG

REGISTERED OFFICE
Ubombo Ranches, Big Bend
Swaziland

TEL: 09268-36511
FAX: 09268-36330

TRANSFER SECRETARY
Mercantile Registrars Ltd
P O Box 1053, Johannesburg
2000
TEL: 011-333 8181

COMPANY SECRETARY
DM le Roux

NATURE OF BUSINESS
The company, directly and via subsidiaries, grows sugar cane and produces sugar in Malawi, Swaziland SA and Mauritius.

BANKERS :
N/A

AUDITORS :
KPMG Aiken & Peat

FAMILIAR BRAND NAMES
N/A

CONTRIBUTION BY ACTIVITY
N/A

YEAR END : March

DIVIDEND : Ords E1

Interim No 54	(Ldr)05/01/90	(Pay)12/01/90	Amt(c)75
Final No 55	(Ldr)07/09/90	(Pay)14/09/90	Amt(c)100
Interim No 56	(Ldr)11/01/91	(Pay)25/01/91	Amt(c)100
Final No 57	(Ldr)20/09/91	(Pay)27/09/91	Amt(c)100
Interim No 58	(Ldr)17/01/92	(Pay)31/01/92	Amt(c)100
Final No 59	(Ldr)21/08/92	(Pay)28/08/92	Amt(c)120
Interim No 60	(Ldr)20/11/92	(Pay)01/12/92	Amt(c)110

NUMBER OF EMPLOYEES : 16458

CAPITAL STRUCTURE

	AUTHORISED	ISSUED
Ords E1 (Swaziland)	12000000	11278200

FINANCIAL STATISTICS (AT FINANCIAL YEAR END)

(Amts in E)	1992 Mar	1991 Mar	1990 Mar	1989 Mar	1988 Mar
Ord S/H Int	339884	307315	157848	131136	108452
Long Trm Loans	169749	139262	92919	75833	64519
Iss Ord Share	11278	11278	11278	11278	11278
Total Liab	237578	220794	167982	139011	116788
Current Liab	67829	81532	75063	63178	52269
Total Assets	577462	528109	325830	270147	225240
Current Assets	198360	194715	174165	142646	114341
Debtors	39123	38650	32931	28994	28931
Inventory	124983	116079	93005	78832	64985
Turnover	425317	382494	342982	281927	220786
Oper Profit	104255	103325	96486	61534	38049
Interest Paid	3008	3168	3283	3035	-
Tax Paid	24219	27837	26748	16232	10216
Prf af Int&Tax	79299	74482	67845	43136	27833
Prf att Ord Sh	57533	52877	46615	29711	19620
Btm Line Earn	57533	52877	46615	29533	20806
Dividend Paid	24812	22556	19737	11278	8459
Mkt Prce(c) YE	6000	2250	2001	2100	1600
Depreciation	15918	12902	10475	8985	7424

PER SHARE STATISTICS (CENTS)

Net Asst Val	3013.69	2724.91	1399.61	1162.76	961.62
Net Earnings	510.10	468.80	413.30	263.40	173.90
Dividends	220.00	200.00	175.00	100.00	75.00
Cash Flow	562.95	526.57	471.78	331.18	225.62

RATIOS AND OTHER INFORMATION

Mrk Cap(R000)	676680	253755	225673	236838	180448
Current Ratio	2.92	2.39	2.32	2.26	2.19
Quik/Acid Tst	1.08	0.96	1.08	1.01	0.94
A/C Rec T/ovr	10.87	9.90	10.42	9.72	7.63
Tot Ass T/ovr	0.74	0.72	1.05	1.04	0.98
Debt/Ass Rat	0.16	0.17	0.26	0.26	0.27
L T L Tot Ass	0.05	0.02	0.03	0.02	0.04
Debt to Eqity	0.28	0.30	0.53	0.53	0.57
Interest Cover	35.41	33.30	29.81	20.56	-
Oper Prof Mrg	24.51	27.01	28.13	21.83	17.23
Net Prof Marg%	13.53	13.82	13.59	10.54	8.89
Ret on Assets	20.17	21.18	31.23	23.60	17.60
Ret on Equity%	16.93	17.21	29.53	22.66	18.09
Price/Earnings	11.76	4.80	4.84	7.97	9.20
Divid Cover	2.32	2.34	2.36	2.63	2.32
Divid Yield	3.67	8.89	8.75	4.76	4.69
Earning Yield%	8.50	20.84	20.65	12.54	10.87
NAV % Mrk Pr	50.23	121.11	69.95	55.37	60.10
Effec Tax Rate	24.24	27.77	29.46	27.82	27.00
Def Interval	0.58	0.34	0.48	0.72	0.86
Sus Grth Rate	9.63	9.87	17.03	14.06	10.29

SUBSIDIARY & ASSOCIATED COMPANIES

BAR CIRCLE RANCH LTD
DWANGWA SUGAR CORPORATION LTD (26%)
GLENDALE DISTILLING CO (PTY) LTD (50%)
GLENDALE SUGAR MILLERS (PTY) LTD
MERVILLE BEACH HOTEL LTD (31,3%)
MON TRESOR AND MON DESERT LTD
SUGAR CORPORATION OF MALAWI LTD
UBOMBO RANCHES LTD

INVESTMENTS

None

LORAINE GOLD MINES LTD

ABBREVIATION : LORAINE

JSE SHORT CODE : LOR

SECTOR : Gold-OFS

SHAREHOLDERS

Who Owns Whom's Assessment of the Identity of the Ultimate Controlling Shareholder:
ANGLOVAAL (MANAGED BY)

SHAREHOLDER	PERCENTAGE 1992	1991
CITIBANK NOM P/L	---	2.5
FERMAIN NOM LTD	---	3.2
FIRST NAT NOM P/L	---	5.0
FIRST NAT NOM P/L GATR DEPOT	---	6.6
FOX STREET NOM P/L	---	7.6
MOMENTUM LIFE ASSURE LTD	---	3.5
NAT CITY NOM LTD	---	11.6
ORANGE FREE STATE INV TRUST LTD	---	1.2
PETARD NOM LTD	---	7.3
STD BANK NOM TVL P/L	---	2.9
STOCKSHARE NOM P/L	---	1.2
INDO-CHINA NOM P/L	---	12.6
TOTAL	---	65.1

DIRECTORS :
CROWE DJ (Chairman),EUSTACE PJ ,GELDENHUYS JJ HERSOV BE ,LAWRENSON BJ ,MAUDE G ,MENELL CS OLIVIER JE ,VAN DER COLF SW ,WILSON RAD

REGISTRATION NUMBER : 05/39138/06

REGISTERED OFFICE
Anglovaal House, 56 Main Street
Johannesburg
2001
TEL: 011-634 9111
FAX: 011-634 0038

TRANSFER SECRETARY
Anglovaal Ltd
P O Box 62379, Marshalltown
2107
TEL: 011-634 9111

COMPANY SECRETARY
Anglovaal Ltd

NATURE OF BUSINESS
The company operates a gold mine at Odendaalsrus, OFS. Silver & pyrite are recovered as by-products

BANKERS :
First National Bank of SA Ltd

AUDITORS :
Deloitte Pim Goldby

FAMILIAR BRAND NAMES
N/A

CONTRIBUTION BY ACTIVITY
N/A

YEAR END : September

DIVIDEND :15/12/91

NUMBER OF EMPLOYEES : 7722

CAPITAL STRUCTURE

	AUTHORISED	ISSUED
Ords R1	20000000	16366986

FINANCIAL STATISTICS (AT FINANCIAL YEAR END)

(Amts in R'000)	1991 Sep	1990 Sep	1989 Sep	1988 Sep	1987
Ord S/H Int	278562	286442	280673	263543	230804
Long Trm Loans	4074	4507	5041	5596	60515
Iss Ord Share	16367	16367	16367	16367	16367
Total Liab	35202	38217	53097	53533	115181
Current Liab	31128	33710	48056	47937	54666
Total Assets	313764	324659	333770	317076	392407
Current Assets	68327	83458	98798	97638	101088
Debtors	9177	7383	9080	10443	-
Inventory	6110	5924	5675	5589	101088
Turnover	236315	253408	258857	262218	241775
Oper Profit	-16919	-8511	28681	43434	66462
Interest Paid	971	1081	-	-	886
Tax Paid	-	662	12081	7726	17188
Prf af Int&Tax	-7607	6132	16600	35708	48388
Prf att Ord Sh	-7607	6132	16600	35708	26539
Btm Line Earn	-7607	6132	16600	35708	26539
Dividend Paid	-	-	-	4092	22095
Mkt Prce(c) YE	325	1085	1085	1010	3525

PER SHARE STATISTICS (CENTS)

Net Asst Val	1701.97	1750.12	1714.87	1610.21	1410.18
Net Earnings	-	-	7.00	43.00	-
Dividends	-	-	-	25.00	-
Cash Flow	-46.48	37.47	101.42	218.17	295.64

RATIOS AND OTHER INFORMATION

Mrk Cap(R000)	53193	177582	177582	165307	576937
Current Ratio	2.20	2.48	2.06	2.04	1.85
Quik/Acid Tst	2.00	2.30	1.94	1.92	-
A/C Rec T/ovr	25.75	34.32	28.51	25.11	-
Tot Ass T/ovr	0.75	0.78	0.78	0.83	0.62
Debt/Ass Rat	0.11	0.12	0.16	0.17	0.29
L T L Tot Ass	0.01	0.01	0.02	0.02	0.15
Debt to Eqity	0.13	0.13	0.19	0.20	0.50
Interest Cover	-17.42	-7.87	-	-	75.01
Oper Prof Mrg	-7.16	-3.36	11.08	16.56	27.49
Net Prof Marg%	-3.22	2.42	6.41	13.62	10.98
Ret on Assets	-2.11	2.43	8.59	13.70	16.94
Ret on Equity%	-2.73	2.14	5.91	13.55	11.50
Price/Earnings	-	-	155.00	23.49	-
Divid Cover	-	-	-	1.72	-
Divid Yield	-	-	-	2.48	-
Earning Yield%	-	-	0.65	4.26	-
NAV % Mrk Pr	523.68	161.30	158.05	159.43	40.01
Effec Tax Rate	-	9.74	41.88	15.96	26.21
Def Interval	-0.58	0.78	0.32	0.16	1.25
Sus Grth Rate	-2.73	2.14	5.91	12.00	1.93

SUBSIDIARY & ASSOCIATED COMPANIES

TARGET EXPLORATION CO LTD (25,1%)

INVESTMENTS

None

LTA LTD

ABBREVIATION : L-T-A

JSE SHORT CODE : LTA

SECTOR : Industrial-Building & Construction

SHAREHOLDERS

Who Owns Whom's Assessment of the Identity of the Ultimate Controlling Shareholder: ANGLO AMERICAN

SHAREHOLDER	PERCENTAGE 1992	1991
RESIDENT NOM LTD	41.6	42.4
BOART INTERNATIONAL LTD	22.8	22.5
EIGHTY ONE MAIN STREET NOM LTD	5.7	---
ANGLO AMERICAN CORP OF SA LTD	4.3	4.4
SA MUTUAL	4.0	9.7
NEDBANK NOM LTD	3.6	4.0
WOOLTRU GROUP RETIREMENT FUND	3.5	---
RAND SELECTION CORP LTD	2.9	3.0
STD BANK NOM TVL P/L	---	3.3
TOTAL	88.3	89.2

DIRECTORS :
BOYD L ,BULLETT BE
CAMPBELL CV (Deputy Managing Director)
CRAWFORD MP ,CROWLEY PF ,DAVIES HK (Chairman)
HALLIER PAC ,KOHLBERG KAH ,OOSTHUIZEN JD
PRETORIUS TL ,RATHBONE CJL ,THOMPSON DM

VALJEAUX RC ,WIEHAHN NE PROF
WOOD CJM (Managing Director),WOOD JH

REGISTRATION NUMBER : 05/03300/06

REGISTERED OFFICE
LTA Park, Jet Park Road
Jet Park
1459
TEL 011-826 9111
FAX 011-826 4650

TRANSFER SECRETARY
Union Provident Trust SA Ltd
P O Box 2322, Johannesburg
2000
TEL 011-833 6700

COMPANY SECRETARY
G J Baxter

NATURE OF BUSINESS
Group activities include Operations in all facets of the building industry, Earthmoving, roadmaking & plant operations, Civil & mechanical engineering Electrical contracting, instrumentation & process control, Property development & project management Structural steel, plant manufacture and founder & smith operations, Roofing, cladding & ventilation, Steel reinforcing, mesh & post tensioning, Process engineering, Industrial (factory manufactured) buildings, Construction & repair of railway track

BANKERS :
First National Bank of SA Ltd
Standard Bank of SA Ltd

AUDITORS :
Ernst & Young

FAMILIAR BRAND NAMES
LENNINGS RAIL SERVICES

CONTRIBUTION BY ACTIVITY
N/A

YEAR END . March

DIVIDEND :Ords R1

Dividend No 19	(Ldr)25/06/90	(Pay)27/07/90	Amt(c)20
Dividend No 20	(Ldr)12/07/91	(Pay)26/07/91	Amt(c)25
Dividend No 21	(Ldr)10/07/92	(Pay)24/07/92	Amt(c)32 5

NUMBER OF EMPLOYEES : 12000

CAPITAL STRUCTURE

	AUTHORISED	ISSUED
Ords R1	29686775	26919515
10% Auto Conv Cum Prefs R1	313025	14765

FINANCIAL STATISTICS (AT FINANCIAL YEAR END)

(Amts in R'000)	1992 Mar	1991 Mar	1990 Mar	1989 Mar	1988 Mar
Ord S/H Int	159110	108231	77558	69011	75941
Long Trm Loans	71463	37703	51430	75085	48695
Iss Ord Share	26598	26268	13288	13235	13235
Total Liab	595741	473927	479671	466912	335910
Current Liab	524278	436224	428241	391827	287215
Total Assets	754851	582158	557229	535923	411851
Current Assets	505280	438531	411703	402773	284725
Debtors	279014	238615	227856	211453	135520
Inventory	62086	92630	113077	137563	104281
Turnover	1876000	1870000	1832000	1662000	1241000
Oper Profit	49914	47781	41191	20600	10314
Interest Paid	8404	16378	22835	10258	2626
Tax Paid	19863	15625	8944	4321	3136
Prf af Int&Tax	34631	25982	15476	8900	6131
Prf att Ord Sh	30303	23201	11391	4700	5764
Btm Line Earn	29639	24186	11408	4045	8084
Dividend Paid	8644	6567	2658		2633
Mkt Prce(c) YE	360	300	210	215	185
Depreciation	33471	26997	26900	26078	21604

PER SHARE STATISTICS (CENTS)

Net Asst Val	598 20	412 03	583 67	521 43	573 79
Net Earnings	114 00	88 00	53 00	28 00	19 00
Dividends	32 50	25 00	20 00		
Cash Flow	217 85	222 14	303 70	253 38	209 39

RATIOS AND OTHER INFORMATION

Mrk Cap(R000)	95753	78804	27905	28455	24485
Current Ratio	0 96	1 01	0 96	1 03	0 99
Quik/Acid Tst	0 85	0 79	0 70	0 68	0 63
A/C Rec T/ovr	6 72	7 84	8 04	7 86	9 16
Tot Ass T/ovr	2 49	3 21	3 29	3 10	3 01
Debt/Ass Rat	0 74	0 76	0 79	0 77	0 72
L T L Tot Ass	0 04	0 01	0 02	0 03	0 03
Debt to Eqity	3 50	4 07	5 69	5 95	3 92
Interest Cover	5 94	2 92	1 80	2 01	4 53
Oper Prof Mrg	2 66	2 56	2 25	1 24	0 83
Net Prof Marg%	1 62	1 24	0 62	0 28	0 46
Ret on Assets	8 33	9 96	8 48	4 38	2 98
Ret on Equity%	19 05	21 44	14 69	6 81	7 59
Price/Earnings	3 16	3 41	3 96	7 68	9 74
Divid Cover	3 51	3 52	2 65		
Divid Yield	9 03	8 33	9 52		
Earning Yield%	31 67	29 33	25 24	13 02	10 27
NAV % Mrk Pr	166 17	137 34	277 94	242 52	310 16
Effec Tax Rate	38 26	16 41	24 23	8 45	30 33
Def Interval	0 81	0 26	1 03	1 83	1 23
Sus Grth Rate	13 61	15 37	11 26	6 81	4 12

SUBSIDIARY & ASSOCIATED COMPANIES

ACROW CPE
ADAMSON NIELSON CONSTRUCTION (PTY) LTD
ALPRET (PTY) LTD
COCHRANE STEEL PRODUCTS (PTY) LTD
CONALEC (PTY) LTD
CONSTRUCTION QUARRIES
CONSTRUCTORS PROPERTIES FINANCE (PTY) LT
CONTRACTORS PROPERTIES FINANCE (PTY) LTS
FASTFLOOR SYSTEMS
GROUND ENGINEERING AND PILING
INDUSTRIAL ELECTRICAL (LESOTHO) (PTY) LT
INDUSTRIAL ELECTRICAL COMPANY (PTY) LTD
JC GROENEWALDS CONSTRUCTION CO (PTY) LTD
KARRENA AFRICA (PTY) LTD (50%)
LENNINGS RAIL SERVICES
LESOTHO REINFORCING (PTY) LTD
LESOTHO STEEL (PTY) LTD
LTA BUILDING (CAPE)
LTA BUILDING (E CAPE)
LTA BUILDING (OFS & NORTH CAPE)
LTA CIVIL DESIGNS (PTY) LTD
LTA CIVIL ENGINEERING
LTA CONSTRACTING SERVICES LTD
LTA CONSTRUCTION (BOPHUTHATSWANA) LTD
LTA CONSTRUCTION (CISKEI) LTD
LTA CONSTRUCTION LTD
LTA EARTHWORKS (NORTH)
LTA EARTHWORKS (NORTH)
LTA EARTHWORKS (SOUTH)
LTA HOUSING DEVELOPMENT

LTA NATAL
LTA PLANT (NORTH)
LTA PLANT (SOUTH)
LTA PROCESS ENGINEERING LTD
LTA TRANSKEI LTD
LTA VENDA CONSTRUCTION LTD
MARITZBURG QUARRIES (PTY) LTD
MCCARTHY CONTRACTORS
MOOLMAN BROS. PLANT
MOOLMAN BROTHERS CONSTRUCTION CO
PENMAN & JOCHELSON (PTY) LTD
RAND ROAD-TECH (PTY) LTD (50%)
REINFORCING & ALLIED INDUSTRIES (OFS) (P
REINFORCING & ALLIED INDUSTRIES (PTY) LT
REINFORCING DESIGN & SUPPLY (PTY) LTD
REINFORCING DESIGN & SUPPLY (TRANSKEI) (
RIDGEWAY CONSTRUCTION (PTY) LTD
ROBERTSON-DEKEX (PTY) LTD
RPP DEVELOPMENTS (PTY) LTD
STEELDALE - FBE (EAST CAPE) (PTY) LTD
STEELDALE - FBE MANUFACTURING (PTY) LTD
STEELDALE FBE (NATAL)
STEELDALE SYSTEMS
STEELEDAG (PTY) LTD
STEELEDALE FBE (CAPE)
STEELEDALE MANUFACTURING CO. (PTY) LTD
STEELEDALE MESH (PTY) LTD
STEELEDALE REINFORCING & TRADING CO (CAP
STEELEDALE REINFORCING & TRADING CO (NAT
STEELEDALE REINFORCING AND ENGINEERING I
STEELEDALE REINFORCING AND TRADING CO. L
STEELFORM
TIMBERTEX
VENTCO ENGINEERING (PTY) LTD

INVESTMENTS

None

LYDENBERG EXPLORATION LTD

ABBREVIATION : LYDEX

JSE SHORT CODE : LDX

SECTOR : Mining-Exploration

SHAREHOLDERS

Who Owns Whom's Assessment of the Identity of the Ultimate Controlling Shareholder:
SA MUTUAL VIA LYDENBERG PLATINUM

SHAREHOLDER	PERCENTAGE 1992	1991
SA MUTUAL	34.5	34.5
LYDENBURG PLATINUM LTD	20.9	20.9
EAST DAGGAFONTEIN MINES LTD	12.4	12.4
STD BANK NOM TVL P/L	8.1	6.6
CMB NOM P/L	3.6	---
POTCHEFSTROOM GOLD AREAS LTD	2.8	2.8
RAND EXTENSIONS & EXPLORATION LTD	2.8	2.8
QUARTO NOM P/L	2.0	4.5
EMARJAY NOM P/L	1.9	1.7
SANLAM	---	3.5
TOTAL	89.0	89.8

DIRECTORS :
BIEBER EPH (Chairman),CHUTE RA ,FINNEMORE SH
HAMBRO RA ,SHEAD RB ,VAN CHRISTIERSIN CI ,WHYTE KC

REGISTRATION NUMBER : 88/01853/06

REGISTERED OFFICE
7th Floor, Marshall Place, 66 Marshall Street
Johannesburg
2001
TEL: 011-834 4211
FAX: 011-834 6343

TRANSFER SECRETARY
Mercantile Registrars Ltd
P O Box 1053, Johannesburg
2000
TEL: 011-333 8181

COMPANY SECRETARY
Southern Prospecting Management Services (Pty) Ltd

NATURE OF BUSINESS
The company's main object is the exploration and turning to account of its mineral interests which are located mainly in the Orange Free State. Lydex has mineral interest in eleven different areas in the Free State and in addition owns 6,7% of Benguela Concessions Ltd.

BANKERS :
Nedperm Bank Ltd

AUDITORS :
Coopers Theron Du Toit

FAMILIAR BRAND NAMES
N/A

CONTRIBUTION BY ACTIVITY
N/A

YEAR END : September

CAPITAL STRUCTURE

	AUTHORISED	ISSUED
Ords 30c	175000000	124270828

FINANCIAL STATISTICS (AT FINANCIAL YEAR END)

(Amts in R'000)	1991 Sep	1990 Sep	1989 Sep	1988 Sep
Ord S/H Int	92647	48410	37387	37800
Iss Ord Share	124271	69350	68323	68323
Total Liab	604	79	1540	401
Current Liab	604	79	1540	401
Total Assets	26852	31583	38927	38201
Intang Assets	66399	16906	*	*
Current Assets	18249	14377	20290	21667
Debtors	1595	221	-	-
Oper Profit	-10507	-5397	-353	-366
Prf af Int&Tax	-7429	-1896	-353	-366
Prf att Ord Sh	-7429	-1896	-353	-366
Btm Line Earn	-7429	-1896	-353	-366
Mkt Prce(c) YE	50	125	140	140

PER SHARE STATISTICS (CENTS)

Net Asst Val	21.12	45.43	54.72	55.33
Net Earnings	-0.70	-2.80	-0.50	-1.00
Cash Flow	-6.87	-2.76	-0.52	-1.02

RATIOS AND OTHER INFORMATION

Mrk Cap(R000)	62136	86688	95652	95652
Current Ratio	30 21	181 99	13 18	54 03
Quik/Acid Tst	30 21	181 99	13 18	54 03
Debt/Ass Rat	0 02	0 00	0 04	0 01
Debt to Eqity	0 01	0 00	0 04	0 01
Ret on Assets	-27 67	-6 00	-0 91	-0 96
Ret on Equity%	-8 02	-3 92	-0 94	-0 97
Price/Earnings	-71 43	-44 64	-280 00	-140 00
Earning Yield%	-1 40	-2 24	-0 36	-0 71
NAV % Mrk Pr	42 24	36 34	39 09	39 52
Sus Grth Rate	-8 02	-3 92	-0 94	-0 97

SUBSIDIARY & ASSOCIATED COMPANIES

PORTION 1 AND 3 WILDEBEESFONTEIN (PTY) L
POTCHEFSTROOM GOLD AREAS LTD
POTCHEFSTROOM GOLD HOLDINGS (PTY) LTD
PROJECT PLUTO JOINT VENTURE
RE AND PORTION 15 OF WILDEBEESFONTEIN (P
S P PARTNERSHIP (PTY) LTD
TRANSVAAL SANDS (PTY) LTD

INVESTMENTS

BENGUELA CONCESSIONS LTD (6,7%)
BENGUELA CONCESSIONS LTD (OPTIONS) (525000S)
TRODEX PLATINUM (PTY) LTD (4000S)
VYFHOEK EXPLORATION & MINING CO LTD (500000S)
WELTEVREDEN MINES LTD (380000S)

LYDENBURG PLATINUM LTD

ABBREVIATION : LYD-PLAT

JSE SHORT CODE : LYD

SECTOR : Metals & Minerals-Platinum

SHAREHOLDERS

Who Owns Whom's Assessment of the Identity of the Ultimate Controlling Shareholder:
SA MUTUAL

SHAREHOLDER	PERCENTAGE 1992	1991
SA MUTUAL	67 8	64 4
CMB NOM P/L	3 6	---
STD BANK NOM TVL P/L	3 1	1 8
NEDBANK NOM LTD	2 6	2 9
AECI PENS FUND	2 3	2 3
LONDON CONTROL ACCOUNT	1 4	1 8
EIGHTY ONE MAIN STREET NOM LTD	1 4	1 6
INDO-CHINA NOM P/L	1 3	---
FIRST NAT NOM P/L	---	2 7
INDO-CHINA NOM SA P/L	---	3 5
SANLAM	--	2 9
TOTAL	83 5	83 7

DIRECTORS :

CHUTE RA ,LANGFORD REJ ,LEVETT MJ (Chairman)
MOSTERT IB ,VAN DER HORST JC DR,VAN NIEKERK GS
WALKER DW

REGISTRATION NUMBER : 01/08063/06

REGISTERED OFFICE

Mutualpark, Jan Smuts Drive
Pinelands, Cape Town
7405
TEL 021-509 2412
FAX 021-509 4634

TRANSFER SECRETARY

Central Registrars Ltd
P O Box 4844, Johannesburg
2000
TEL 011-331 0051

COMPANY SECRETARY

South African Mutual Life Assurance Society

NATURE OF BUSINESS

Lydenburg Platinum is an investment company, its major investment being an 8,4% interest in quoted Rustenburg Platinum Holdings Its remaining assets comprise mainly listed investments in the platinum mining holdings and mining exploration sectors

BANKERS :

Standard Bank of SA Ltd

AUDITORS :

KPMG Aiken & Peat

FAMILIAR BRAND NAMES

N/A

CONTRIBUTION BY ACTIVITY

N/A

YEAR END : October

DIVIDEND ·Ords 12,5c

Interim No 72	(Ldr)16/02/90	(Pay)16/03/90	Amt(c)75
Final No 73	(Ldr)24/08/90	(Pay)21/09/90	Amt(c)110
Interim No 74	(Ldr)15/02/91	(Pay)15/03/91	Amt(c)75
Final No 75	(Ldr)11/10/91	(Pay)31/10/91	Amt(c)130
Interim No 76	(Ldr)21/02/92	(Pay)13/03/92	Amt(c)52
Final No 77	(Ldr)28/08/92	(Pay)02/10/92	Amt(c)83

CAPITAL STRUCTURE

	AUTHORISED	ISSUED
Ords 12,5c	14400000	14400000

FINANCIAL STATISTICS (AT FINANCIAL YEAR END)

(Amts In R'000)	1991 Oct	1990 Oct	1989 Oct	1988 Oct	1987
Ord S/H Int	848229	751085	843807	552498	381746
Long Trm Loans	-	-		-	217
Iss Ord Share	14400	14400	14400	14400	14400
Total Liab	8260	701	314	2527	434
Current Liab	8260	701	314	2527	217
Total Assets	856489	751786	844121	555025	382519
Current Assets	2539	522	654	61	556
Debtors	28	25	21	27	-
Inventory	-	-	-		556
Oper Profit	160	405	282	23633	22090
Interest Paid		7	8		
Tax Paid	131	96	3	9	58
Prf af Int&Tax	37136	33330	32559	23624	22032
Prf att Ord Sh	64501	33330	32559	32957	22032
Btm Line Earn	64501	33330	32559	32957	22032
Dividend Paid	29520	26640	25920	19440	21600
Mkt Prce(c) YE	4625	4500	5100	3800	3225

PER SHARE STATISTICS (CENTS)

Net Asst Val	5890.48	5215.87	5859.77	3836.79	2651.01
Net Earnings	258.00	231.00	226.00	164.00	-
Dividends	205.00	185.00	180.00	135.00	-
Cash Flow	257.89	231.46	226.10	164.06	153.00

RATIOS AND OTHER INFORMATION

Mrk Cap(R000)	666000	648000	734400	547200	464400
Current Ratio	0.31	0.74	2.08	0.02	2.56
Quik/Acid Tst	0.31	0.74	2.08	0.02	-
Debt/Ass Rat	0.01	0.00	0.00	0.00	0.00
L T L Tot Ass	-	-	-	-	0.00
Debt to Eqity	0.01	0.00	0.00	0.00	0.00
Interest Cover	-	4776.14	4071.25	-	-
Ret on Assets	4.35	4.45	3.86	4.26	5.77
Ret on Equity%	7.60	4.44	3.86	5.97	5.77
Price/Earnings	17.93	19.48	22.57	23.17	-
Divid Cover	1.26	1.25	1.26	1.21	-
Divid Yield	4.43	4.11	3.53	3.55	-
Earning Yield%	5.58	5.13	4.43	4.32	-
NAV % Mrk Pr	127.36	115.91	114.90	100.97	82.20
Effec Tax Rate	-81.88	-23.30	-1.03	0.01	0.26
Def Interval	-	-	-	0.09	0.01
Sus Grth Rate	4.12	0.89	0.79	2.45	0.11

SUBSIDIARY & ASSOCIATED COMPANIES

None

INVESTMENTS

BENGUELA CONCESSIONS LTD (2500000S)
BENGUELA CONCESSIONS LTD (OPTIONS) (525000S)
GENBEL INVESTMENT LTD (1569600S)
LEBOWA PLATINUM MINES LTD (8732000S)
LYDENBURG EXPLORATION LTD (26000000S)
LYDENBURG EXPLORATION LTD (OPTIONS) (7000000S)
POTGIETERSRUST PLATINUMS LTD (9434800S)
RUSTENBURG PLATINUM HOLDINGS LTD (10560000S)

MACADAMS BAKERY SUPPLIES HOLDINGS LTD

ABBREVIATION : MACADAM

JSE SHORT CODE : MDM

SECTOR : Industrial-Food

SHAREHOLDERS

Who Owns Whom's Assessment of the Identity of the Ultimate Controlling Shareholder: DIRECTORS

SHAREHOLDER	PERCENTAGE 1992	1991
POULIART R J	25.3	16.4
MCEVOY K J, C E & OTHER MCEVOY FAMILY	9.5	4.7
NEDBANK NOM LTD	8.1	7.1
REXHILL TRUST	6.0	6.5
SHARESTOCK NOM P/L	3.8	3.8
BOESCH A & P A & OTHERS FOR FAMILY TRUST	3.2	3.5
LLP INV P/L	3.1	3.1
M INV P/L	3.1	3.2
RSP INV P/L	3.1	3.2
DE VILLIERS J V	1.5	1.6
CLINTON NOM P/L	1.1	1.2
CAVERSHAM TRUSTEES LTD	1.0	1.1
MC EVOY K J	---	3.2
SCHUMANN W	---	6.2
GAUNT J P	---	1.6
ROBINSON B C	---	1.1
TOTAL	68.8	67.5

DIRECTORS :
ASHERSON JD ,HODGSON MJ (Sales Director)
MCEVOY KJ (Financial Director)
POULIART RJ (Chief Executive

REGISTRATION NUMBER : 79/04864/06

REGISTERED OFFICE
Range Road, Blackheath
7581
TEL: 021-905 3730
FAX: 021-905 1514

TRANSFER SECRETARY
Mercantile Registrars Ltd
P O Box 1053, Johannesburg
2000
TEL: 011-333 8181

COMPANY SECRETARY
K J McEvoy

NATURE OF BUSINESS
The group manufactures, sells, installs, services & reconditions equipment for the industrial baking catering and confectionery industries.

BANKERS :
Nedcor Bank Ltd

AUDITORS :
Bruk Rosenberg & Co

FAMILIAR BRAND NAMES
BENIER,CIMA,DEN BOER,DIOSNA,FALCON,JUNO
MAC-MIXER,MAC-MOULDER,MACBAKE,MAXOFLEX,OMEGA
REIMELT,STATUS,TOPLINE

CONTRIBUTION BY ACTIVITY
N/A

YEAR END : February

DIVIDEND : (Ldr)09/06/89 (Pay)30/06/89

NUMBER OF EMPLOYEES : 236

CAPITAL STRUCTURE

	AUTHORISED	ISSUED
Ords 1c	20000000	16625000

FINANCIAL STATISTICS (AT FINANCIAL YEAR END)

(Amts in R'000)	1992 Feb	1991 Feb	1990 Feb	1989 Feb	1988 Feb
Ord S/H Int	8183	6903	4449	7544	6996
Long Trm Loans	683	1037	3892	1852	536
Iss Ord Share	15985	15410	15410	15410	15410

Total Liab	11747	10393	19611	17651	12988
Current Liab	11064	9356	15719	15799	12452
Total Assets	19930	17296	24060	25195	19984
Current Assets	16994	14640	17258	22919	18811
Debtors	5725	5092	7990	9976	8082
Inventory	11238	9519	9253	12928	10712
Turnover	34200	28910	37661	41949	31037
Oper Profit	2533	2029	2443	2341	2097
Interest Paid	1311	1587	1492	1120	1004
Tax Paid	-	1	8	449	174
Prf af Int&Tax	1222	441	943	772	919
Prf att Ord Sh	1222	441	880	772	919
Btm Line Earn	1222	2453	-3095	810	919
Dividend Paid	-	-	-	262	370
Mkt Prce(c) YE	30	12	18	28	40
Depreciation	403	342	357	245	218

PER SHARE STATISTICS (CENTS)

Net Asst Val	51 19	44 80	28 87	48 96	45 40
Net Earnings	7 60	2 90	5 70	5 30	6 04
Dividends	-	-	-	1 70	2 40
Cash Flow	10 17	5 08	6 18	6 83	8 01

RATIOS AND OTHER INFORMATION

Mrk Cap(R000)	4796	1849	2774	4315	6164
Current Ratio	1 54	1 56	1 10	1 45	1 51
Quik/Acid Tst	0 52	0 55	0 51	0 63	0 65
A/C Rec T/ovr	5 97	5 68	4 71	4 20	3 84
Tot Ass T/ovr	1 72	1 67	1 57	1 66	1 55
Debt/Ass Rat	0 59	0 60	0 81	0 69	0 63
L T L Tot Ass	0 03	0 06	0 16	0 06	0 01
Debt to Eqity	1 43	1 50	4 41	2 29	1 81
Interest Cover	1 93	1 28	1 64	2 09	2 09
Oper Prof Mrg	7 41	7 02	6 49	5 58	6 76
Net Prof Marg%	3 57	1 53	2 34	1 84	2 96
Ret on Assets	12 71	11 73	10 15	9 29	10 49
Ret on Equity%	14 93	6 39	19 78	10 23	13 14
Price/Earnings	3 95	4 14	3 16	5 28	6 62
Divid Cover	-	-	-	3 12	2 52
Divid Yield		-	-	6 07	6 00
Earning Yield%	25 33	24 17	31 67	18 93	15 10
NAV % Mrk Pr	170 64	373 30	160 39	174 84	113 50
Effec Tax Rate	-	0 23	37 33	33 82	8 42
Def Interval	2 92	6 49	11 91	9 28	6 28
Sus Grth Rate	14 93	6 39	19 78	6 76	7 85

SUBSIDIARY & ASSOCIATED COMPANIES

ADW TRADING (PTY) LTD
BACKON SUPPLIERS (PTY) LTD
MACADAMS MANUFACTURING (PTY) LTD

INVESTMENTS

None

MACMED HEALTH CARE LTD

ABBREVIATION : MACMED

JSE SHORT CODE : MMD

SECTOR : Industrial-Pharmaceutical & Medical

SHAREHOLDERS

Who Owns Whom's Assessment of the Identity of the Ultimate Controlling Shareholder: DIRECTORS

SHAREHOLDER	PERCENTAGE 1992	1991
MACMED TRUST	58 3	66 0
NEARCO TRUSTEE CO JERSEY LTD	19 6	4 4
MACMED SHARE TRUST	9 2	2 7
GOTTGENS F T	1 5	1 7
H TIL TRUST	1 5	---
RETIEF J F	1 5	---
NORBERTON LTD	---	7 8
OSTEND INV CO LTD	---	9 4
TOTAL	91 6	92 0

DIRECTORS :
MCARTHUR DI (Chief Executive),REES TL
STRAGIER LGR ,TYFIELD MJL

REGISTRATION NUMBER : 73/06511/06

REGISTERED OFFICE
22 Fourth Street, Montague Gardens
Milnerton, Cape Town
7441
TEL 021-52 4844
FAX 021-52 4076

TRANSFER SECRETARY
Mercantile Registrars Ltd
P O Box 1053, Johannesburg
2000
TEL 011-333 8181

COMPANY SECRETARY
A S Hiscock

NATURE OF BUSINESS
Macmed manufactures & distributes medical products to private, provincial and state sectors of the market Products are also distributed to smaller institutions & doctor practices via dealer network

BANKERS :
Standard Bank of SA Ltd

AUDITORS :
Deloitte Pim Goldby

FAMILIAR BRAND NAMES
AQUA PAK,AQUA THERM,CONCHA PAK,CURITY
KENDALL,KENGUARD,MCGAW,POLYKEN,TELFLOW
WEBCOL,WEBLOCK,WEBRIL

CONTRIBUTION BY ACTIVITY
N/A

YEAR END : December

DIVIDEND : Ords 5c

Dividend No 1	(Ldr)18/11/88	(Pay)30/11/88	Amt(c)3 2
Special No 2	(Ldr)12/01/90	(Pay)07/02/90	Amt(c)20
Dividend No 3	(Ldr)13/09/91	(Pay)30/09/91	Amt(c)1
Dividend No 4	(Ldr)13/03/92	(Pay)31/03/92	Amt(c)0 5
Special No 5	(Ldr)13/03/92	(Pay)31/03/92	Amt(c)0 5
Dividend No 6	(Ldr)31/08/92	(Pay)14/08/92	Amt(c)0 75

MACPHAIL HOLDINGS LTD

ABBREVIATION : MCPHAIL

JSE SHORT CODE : MAC

SECTOR : Industrial-Industrial Holding

SHAREHOLDERS

Who Owns Whom's Assessment of the Identity of the Ultimate Controlling Shareholder:
FSI CORP VIA W&A

SHAREHOLDER	PERCENTAGE 1992	1991
W & A INV CORP LTD	62.9	63.2
WEINTROUB S	3.9	3.1
ELLERINE BROS P/L	3.4	3.4
SUZMAN D	2.2	2.2
ABSA NOM P/L	1.8	---
CALANJAM P/L	1.6	---
MACPHAIL EXECUTIVE SHARE PURCHASE SCHEME	1.5	3.4
LEVY C L	1.5	1.0
FOWLER A S	1.2	---
JOSSEL B	1.0	---
AIRIES B	---	1.0
CALAMJAM P/L	---	1.6
NGK SINODALE TVL PENS FUND	---	1.7
VOLKSKAS NOM P/L	---	1.8
TOTAL	81.0	82.3

DIRECTORS :
FOWLER AS (Operations Director),GAY DA
GEERTSHUIS JB (Financial Director),HORWITZ GJ
KETS ND (Managing Director),ROLFE TW (Chairman)
STOLOFF W ,SUZMAN D
WEINTROUB S (Dep. Chair. & Chief Exec.

REGISTRATION NUMBER : 62/04905/06

REGISTERED OFFICE
6th Floor, FSI Centre, 35 Siemert Rd
Doornfontein
2094
TEL: 011-402 3200
FAX: 011-402 7508

TRANSFER SECRETARY
Mercantile Registrars Ltd
P O Box 1053, Johannesburg
2000
TEL: 011-333 8181

COMPANY SECRETARY
B E Liebesman

NATURE OF BUSINESS
An investment holding company with subsidiaries engaged in the marketing & distribution of coal.

BANKERS :
Nedperm Bank Ltd

AUDITORS :
Kessel Feinstein

CAPITAL STRUCTURE

	AUTHORISED	ISSUED
Ords 5c	40000000	30474000
6% Cum Red Prefs 1c	10000	0

FINANCIAL STATISTICS (AT FINANCIAL YEAR END)

(Amts in R'000)	1991 Dec	1990 Jul	1989 Jul	1987
Ord S/H Int	4193	2898	4448	-
Long Trm Loans	272	222	293	2097
Iss Ord Share	30474	29474	19000	-
Total Liab	5431	3229	4439	2899
Current Liab	5159	3007	4146	802
Total Assets	9624	6127	8887	4147
Current Assets	8535	5347	8136	2050
Debtors	2931	2473	1836	-
Inventory	4500	2871	2351	2050
Turnover	-	9645	15371	4814
Oper Profit	2919	656	1465	1069
Interest Paid	306	435	292	41
Tax Paid	1157	-	-	514
Prf af Int&Tax	1504	500	1264	514
Prf att Ord Sh	1504	500	764	514
Btm Line Earn	1683	155	806	514
Dividend Paid	599	1705	-	-
Mkt Prce(c) YE	12	13	28	-
Depreciation	151	152	122	-

PER SHARE STATISTICS (CENTS)

Net Asst Val	13.76	9.83	23.41	-
Net Earnings	5.10	2.10	4.00	-
Dividends	2.00	20.00	-	-
Cash Flow	3.83	2.21	7.29	-

RATIOS AND OTHER INFORMATION

Mrk Cap(R000)	3657	3832	5320	-
Current Ratio	1.65	1.78	1.96	2.56
Quik/Acid Tst	0.78	0.82	1.40	-
A/C Rec T/ovr	-	3.90	8.37	-
Tot Ass T/ovr	-	1.57	1.73	1.16
Debt/Ass Rat	0.56	0.53	0.50	0.70
L T L Tot Ass	0.03	0.04	0.03	0.51
Debt to Eqity	1.30	1.11	1.00	-
Interest Cover	9.63	1.70	5.18	26.07
Oper Prof Mrg	-	6.80	9.53	22.21
Net Prof Marg%	-	5.18	4.97	10.68
Ret on Assets	21.76	15.26	17.51	25.78
Ret on Equity%	25.32	17.25	17.18	-
Price/Earnings	2.35	6.19	7.00	-
Divid Cover	2.55	0.11	-	-
Divid Yield	16.67	153.85	-	-
Earning Yield%	42.50	16.15	14.29	-
NAV % Mrk Pr	114.66	75.63	83.61	-
Effec Tax Rate	42.23	-	-	50.00
Def Interval	0.18	2.25	2.01	4.08
Sus Grth Rate	21.58	-41.58	17.18	-

SUBSIDIARY & ASSOCIATED COMPANIES

MACMED NAMIBIA (PTY) LTD
SUPPIES (PTY) LTD

INVESTMENTS

None

FAMILIAR BRAND NAMES
N/A

CONTRIBUTION BY ACTIVITY
N/A

YEAR END : December

DIVIDEND :Ords 50c

Interim No 5	(Ldr)15/09/89	(Pay)06/10/89	Amt(c)4
Final No 6	(Ldr)16/03/90	(Pay)09/04/90	Amt(c)12.5
Interim No 7	(Ldr)14/09/90	(Pay)05/10/90	Amt(c)5.5
Final No 8	(Ldr)05/04/91	(Pay)26/04/91	Amt(c)13.5
Interim No 9	(Ldr)13/09/91	(Pay)04/10/91	Amt(c)5.5
Final No 10	(Ldr)03/04/92	(Pay)24/04/92	Amt(c)13.5
Interim No 11	(Ldr)11/09/92	(Pay)02/10/92	Amt(c)5.5

CAPITAL STRUCTURE

	AUTHORISED	ISSUED
Ords 50c	20000000	14202852

FINANCIAL STATISTICS (AT FINANCIAL YEAR END)

(Amts in R'000)	1991 Dec	1990 Dec	1989 Dec	1988 Dec	1987 Dec
Ord S/H Int	25067	21113	17110	12924	12323
Long Trm Loans	1495	1395	967	1057	625
Iss Ord Share	14203	14203	14190	13214	10613
Total Liab	35270	34589	26188	17741	10753
Current Liab	33775	33194	25221	16684	10128
Total Assets	52354	49194	38080	26474	17365
Intang Assets	7983	6508	5218	4191	5711
Current Assets	47735	44635	33703	23116	15602
Debtors	29252	21915	18802	10709	6930
Inventory	5000	3269	2216	2603	546
Turnover	239903	211835	153391	100094	67467
Oper Profit	9916	10124	9247	5170	2810
Interest Paid	114	57	316	292	38
Tax Paid	4633	4584	4467	2212	1118
Prf af Int&Tax	7527	7309	5988	3599	1654
Prf att Ord Sh	7481	7171	5886	3504	1604
Btm Line Earn	6653	6679	5311	-1045	2405
Dividend Paid	2699	2699	2308	1401	743
Mkt Prce(c) YE	185	240	205	128	100
Depreciation	1017	919	664	829	459

PER SHARE STATISTICS (CENTS)

Net Asst Val	120.28	102.83	83.81	66.09	62.30
Net Earnings	52.70	50.50	41.50	26.40	3.90
Dividends	19.00	19.00	16.50	11.00	1.75
Cash Flow	59.30	59.11	45.22	32.32	20.21

RATIOS AND OTHER INFORMATION

Mrk Cap(R000)	26276	34087	29090	16914	10613
Current Ratio	1.41	1.34	1.34	1.39	1.54
Quik/Acid Tst	1.27	1.25	1.25	1.23	1.49
A/C Rec T/ovr	8.20	9.67	8.16	9.35	9.74
Tot Ass T/ovr	4.58	4.31	4.03	3.78	3.89
Debt/Ass Rat	0.66	0.69	0.67	0.64	0.60
L T L Tot Ass	0.02	0.01	0.01	0.01	0.01
Debt to Eqity	1.38	1.60	1.49	1.31	0.84
Interest Cover	86.98	177.61	29.26	17.74	73.95
Oper Prof Mrg	4.13	4.78	6.03	5.17	4.16
Net Prof Marg%	3.12	3.39	3.84	3.50	2.38
Ret on Assets	23.44	24.29	28.29	23.05	16.18
Ret on Equity%	29.84	33.96	34.40	27.11	13.02
Price/Earnings	3.51	4.75	4.94	4.85	25.64
Divid Cover	2.77	2.66	2.52	2.40	2.23
Divid Yield	10.27	7.92	8.05	8.59	1.75
Earning Yield%	28.49	21.04	20.24	20.63	3.90
NAV % Mrk Pr	65.02	42.85	40.88	51.63	62.30
Effec Tax Rate	38.72	35.98	44.00	39.21	40.33
Def Interval	0.06	0.02	0.02	0.17	0.16
Sus Grth Rate	19.08	21.18	20.91	16.27	6.99

SUBSIDIARY & ASSOCIATED COMPANIES

A J MODISE COAL CO. (PTY) LTD
B WOLPERT (PTY) LTD
BISHO COAL DISTRIBUTORS (PTY) LTD
BLOEMFONTEIN COAL DISTRIBUTORS (PTY) LTD
CARBON FUELS MARKETING LTD
EAST LONDON & BORDER COAL DISTRIBUTORS (
JENSAT COAL (PTY) LTD
KIMBERLEY COAL (PTY) LTD
LIBERTAS STEENKOOLVERSPREIDERS (PTY) LTD
MACPHAIL (PTY) LTD
MACPHAIL NAMIBIA (PTY) LTD
NATIONAL COAL HOLDINGS (PTY) LTD
OAKLEY INVESTMENTS (PTY) LTD
OMEGA COAL (PTY) LTD
PORT ELIZABETH COAL DISTRIBUTORS (PTY) L
REEF CARBON PRODUCTS (PTY) LTD
REEF COAL (BOPHUTHATSWANA) (PTY) LTD
REEF COAL (PTY) LTD
REEF COAL CAPE (PTY) LTD
RUSTENBURG COAL (PTY) LTD
SOUTHERN COAL TRADERS (PTY) LTD
SPRINGFIELD COAL AGENCY (PTY) LTD
SUPER COAL YARDS BOPHUTHATSWANA (PTY) LT
TEMBA COAL AGENCY (PTY) LTD

INVESTMENTS

DA GAMA TEXTILE CO LTD (15000 SH)
FREE STATE CONSOLIDATED GOLD MINES LTD
FREE STATE CONSOLIDATED MINES LTD (2000 SH)
GOLD FIRELDS COAL LTD
S.A. EAGLE INSURANCE CO LTD (100 SH)
TANSRANS NATAL COAL CORPORATION LTD
TRANS NATAL COAL CORPORATION LTD
TRANS-NATAL COAL CORPORATION LTD (10000 SH)
UNISPIN HOLDINGS LTD (10000 SH)

MAIN STREET PROPERTY FUND

ABBREVIATION : MAINPRO

JSE SHORT CODE : MNO

SECTOR : Financial-Property Trust

SHAREHOLDERS

Who Owns Whom's Assessment of the Identity of the Ultimate Controlling Shareholder: ANGLO AMERICAN

SHAREHOLDER	PERCENTAGE 1992	1991
STD BANK NOM TVL P/L	30.9	30.9
SOUTHERN LIFE ASSOC LTD	28.8	28.2
DE BEERS PENS FUND	6.4	6.3
ANGLO AMERICAN CORP PENS FUND	6.0	5.9
ENGINEERING INDUSTRIES PENS FUND	4.9	3.8
ANGLO AMERICAN GROUP PENS FUND	4.7	4.7

ANGLO AMERICAN PROPERTIES LTD	2.8	2.8
CMB NOM P/L	2.2	---
EIGHTY ONE MAIN STREET NOM LTD	1.7	4.4
WORKMENS COMPENS COMMISSIONER IN TRUST	1.7	---
FIRST NAT NOM P/L	1.3	---
AFRICAN LIFE ASSURE CO LTD	1.1	2.6
METAL IND GROUP PENS FUND	1.1	---
SA MUTUAL	1.1	---
CITY COUNCIL OF DURBAN	1.1	1.1
PHIMAX P/L	---	3.3
SANLAM	---	2.2
TOTAL	95.7	96.1

DIRECTORS :
BRADFORD DG ,BRAGG WFE ,DICKASON GB ,JOHNSON JGW
LEISSNER GGL ,LINDOP G ,MCDONALD SA ,STEWART MG
SUNTER CL ,WHITFIELD AC

REGISTERED OFFICE
First National House, 11 Diagonal Street
Johannesburg
2001
TEL: 011-491 9111
FAX: 011-838 5136

TRANSFER SECRETARY
Consolidated Share Registrars Ltd
P O Box 61051, Marshalltown
2107
TEL: 011-492 1620

COMPANY SECRETARY
Anglo American Property Services (Pty) Ltd

NATURE OF BUSINESS
A property unit trust, with a portfolio of commercial properties. The fund is managed by Main Street Property Fund Managers Ltd.

BANKERS :
First National Bank of SA Ltd

AUDITORS :
Coopers & Lybrand

FAMILIAR BRAND NAMES
N/A

CONTRIBUTION BY ACTIVITY
Offices (% Sectoral Spread) (59.3%)
Shops (30.0%)
Other (10.7%)

YEAR END : March

DIVIDEND : Units
Interim no 4 (Ldr)13/11/92 (Pay)27/11/92 Amt(c)27.99

CAPITAL STRUCTURE

	AUTHORISED	ISSUED
Units	91200000	91200000

FINANCIAL STATISTICS (AT FINANCIAL YEAR END)

(Amts in R'000)	1992 Mar
Ord S/H Int	446458
Iss Ord Share	91200
Total Liab	25449
Current Liab	25449
Total Assets	471907
Current Assets	38383
Debtors	812
Oper Profit	71058
Prf af Int&Tax	71058
Prf att Ord Sh	71058
Btm Line Earn	71308
Dividend Paid	71058
Mkt Prce(c) YE	550

PER SHARE STATISTICS (CENTS)

Net Asst Val	489.54
Net Earnings	77.90
Dividends	77.90
Cash Flow	55.00

RATIOS AND OTHER INFORMATION

Mrk Cap(R000)	501600
Current Ratio	1.51
Quik/Acid Tst	1.51
Debt/Ass Rat	0.05
Debt to Eqity	0.06
Ret on Assets	10.63
Ret on Equity%	11.23
Price/Earnings	7.06
Divid Cover	1.00
Divid Yield	14.16
Earning Yield%	14.16
NAV % Mrk Pr	89.01
Sus Grth Rate	0.00

SUBSIDIARY & ASSOCIATED COMPANIES

CAR FAIR PROPERTIES (PTY) LTD
DUNDRUM ESTATES (PTY) LTD
MAIN STREET PROPERTIES (PTY) LTD
MAIN STREET PROPERTIES CAPE TOWN (PTY) L
MCCARTHY PROPERTY INVESTMENTS LTD
OXBORNE (PTY) LTD
SANSO PROPERTIES PRETORIA (PTY) LTD
SHANAGOLDEN ESTATES (PTY) LTD
SOREC INVESTMENTS (PTY) LTD
TENTH PROPERTY CO (PTY) LTD
WANDERERS VIEW PROPERTY HOLDINGS (PTY) L
WHITEHALL COURT (PTY) LTD
ZEESTRAAT PROPERTIES (PTY) LTD

INVESTMENTS

None

MALBAK LTD

ABBREVIATION : MALBAK

JSE SHORT CODE : MLB

SECTOR : Industrial-Industrial Holding

SHAREHOLDERS

Who Owns Whom's Assessment of the Identity of the Ultimate Controlling Shareholder:
SANLAM VIA GENCOR & MALHOLD

SHAREHOLDER	PERCENTAGE 1992	1991
MALHOLD LTD	37.5	45.3
CONSOLIDATED NOM P/L	21.2	18.3
CMB NOM P/L	21.1	---
SA MUTUAL	3.6	3.0
EIGHTY ONE MAIN STREET NOM LTD	2.5	1.6
STD BANK NOM TVL P/L	1.8	1.1
SOUTHERN LIFE ASSOC LTD	1.5	1.6
RAND MERCHANT NOM P/L	---	1.1
SANKORP BPK	---	18.6
SANLAM	---	1.3
TOTAL	89.1	91.9

DIRECTORS :
BENINGFIELD PJJ ,BROWN HF ,CHALMERS TJ
JACOBS DJ ,KENNEALY DP (Financial Director)
MCGLASHAN DS ,STRUWIG M
THOMAS GS (Executive Chairman),WILLIS I

REGISTRATION NUMBER : 05/22234/06

REGISTERED OFFICE
Malbak House, Protea Place
off Fredman Drive, Sandton
2196
TEL: 011-783 4480
FAX: 011-783 0408

TRANSFER SECRETARY
Mercantile Registrars Ltd
P O Box 1053, Johannesburg
2000
TEL: 011-333 8181

COMPANY SECRETARY
Malbak Group Management Company (Pty) Ltd

NATURE OF BUSINESS
An industrial holding company with interests in packaging & paper, engineering & mining supplies, electronic consumer products, food, construction supplies, motor vehicle distribution, health care, chemicals, computer manufacture & distribution, paper & packaging, freight operations, automotive products, steel & timber. The company controls a number of quoted subsidiaries.

BANKERS :
Standard Bank of SA Ltd

AUDITORS :
Deloitte Pim Goldby, Ernst & Young
Coopers Theron Du Toit

FAMILIAR BRAND NAMES
AMERFORD INTERNATIONAL,EAGLE FREIGHT,ICL
MALBAK MOTOR HOLDINGS,MARKET MOTORS
PAT HINDE MOTORS,PROTEA CHEMICALS
PROTEA PHARMACEUTICALS,PROTEA TECHNOLOGY

CONTRIBUTION BY ACTIVITY
Packaging & Paper (% Turnover) (21.0%)
Branded Consumer Products (19.0%)
Food (22.0%)
International (9.0%)
Healthcare (18.0%)
Investments (11.0%)

YEAR END : August

DIVIDEND :Ords no par value

Interim	(Ldr)11/05/90	(Pay)25/05/90	Amt(c)12.5
Final	(Ldr)23/11/90	(Pay)13/12/90	Amt(c)18
Interim	(Ldr)10/05/91	(Pay)24/05/91	Amt(c)12.5
Final	(Ldr)22/11/91	(Pay)12/12/91	Amt(c)20
Interim	(Ldr)08/05/92	(Pay)22/05/92	Amt(c)12.5
Final	(Ldr)20/11/92	(Pay)11/12/92	Amt(c)21

NUMBER OF EMPLOYEES : 64000

CAPITAL STRUCTURE

	AUTHORISED	ISSUED
12,5c Div Cum Red Prefs 10c	5000000	0
Ords no par value	550000000	303282311
13% Comp Conv Debs 120c	9661976	9661976

FINANCIAL STATISTICS (AT FINANCIAL YEAR END)

(Amts in R'000)	1992 Aug	1991 Aug	1990 Aug	1989 Aug	1988 Aug
Ord S/H Int	2350000	1414000	1323000	1127000	956000
Long Trm Loans	953000	963000	733000	698000	587000
Iss Ord Share	303282	206638	197169	184555	178657
Total Liab	3431000	2842000	2672000	2398000	1760000
Current Liab	2478000	1879000	1939000	1700000	1173000
Total Assets	5781000	4256000	3995000	3525000	2716000
Current Assets	3818000	2726000	2612000	2327000	1851000
Debtors	1837000	1410000	1365000	1168000	877000
Inventory	1212000	1132000	1141000	1110000	824000
Turnover	10992000	8441000	8374000	7329000	5234000
Oper Profit	757000	686000	698000	639000	500000
Interest Paid	199000	176000	218000	171000	83000
Tax Paid	200000	163000	172000	154000	142000
Prf af Int&Tax	452000	381000	334000	358000	275000
Prf att Ord Sh	329000	256000	233000	251000	184000
Btm Line Earn	218000	141000	103000	176000	118000
Dividend Paid	102000	68000	61000	57000	43000
Mkt Prce(c) YE	1175	1065	600	875	650
Depreciation	187000	122000	113000	100000	71000

PER SHARE STATISTICS (CENTS)

Net Asst Val	774.86	684.29	671.00	610.66	535.10
Net Earnings	112.20	121.00	118.60	136.10	104.30
Dividends	33.50	32.50	30.50	30.50	25.00
Cash Flow	177.29	189.70	186.47	202.22	156.73

RATIOS AND OTHER INFORMATION

Mrk Cap(R000)	3563564	2200695	1183014	1614856	1161271
Current Ratio	1.54	1.45	1.35	1.37	1.58
Quik/Acid Tst	1.05	0.85	0.76	0.72	0.88
A/C Rec T/ovr	5.98	5.99	6.13	6.27	5.97
Tot Ass T/ovr	1.90	1.98	2.10	2.08	1.93
Debt/Ass Rat	0.46	0.49	0.54	0.55	0.52
L T L Tot Ass	0.03	0.05	0.05	0.07	0.09
Debt to Eqity	1.13	1.47	1.62	1.73	1.47
Interest Cover	3.80	3.90	3.20	3.74	6.02
Oper Prof Mrg	6.89	8.13	8.34	8.72	9.55
Net Prof Marg%	2.99	3.03	2.78	3.42	3.52
Ret on Assets	14.72	16.92	18.12	19.38	18.41
Ret on Equity%	14.00	18.10	17.61	22.27	19.25
Price/Earnings	10.47	8.80	5.06	6.43	6.23
Divid Cover	3.35	3.72	3.89	4.46	4.17
Divid Yield	2.85	3.05	5.08	3.49	3.85
Earning Yield%	9.55	11.36	19.77	15.55	16.05
NAV % Mrk Pr	65.95	64.25	111.83	69.79	82.32
Effec Tax Rate	28.83	26.47	28.26	25.98	29.74
Def Interval	1.70	1.89	2.25	2.02	1.73
Sus Grth Rate	9.66	13.30	13.00	17.21	14.75

SUBSIDIARY & ASSOCIATED COMPANIES

A F H DEVERS (PTY) LTD
A.W. FOYLE (PTY) LTD
ABERCOM GROUP LTD
ACE EAGLE HOLDINGS (PTY) LTD
ACME PRINT & PACK (PTY) LTD
AFRICAN FEATURERS (PTY) LTD
AKROMED PRODUCTS (PTY) LTD
AKURA MANUFACTURING ENGINEERING CO. (PTY
ALGOA ENGINEERING SUPPLY CO. (PTY) LTD
AMATOLA TYRES (PTY) LTD
ARBAN ENGINEERING (PTY) LTD
ARBAN GROUP HOLDINGS LTD (49,6%)
AROSON SALES (PTY) LTD
AVENUE INVESTMENTS (PTY) LTD
B. OWEN JONES LTD
BAKKE CHEMICALS (PTY) LTD
BAKKE FORMOST (PTY) LTD
BAKKE INDUSTRIES (NATAL) (PTY) LTD
BAKKE INDUSTRIES LTD
BAKKE INTERNATIONAL S A (REGISTERED IN L
BAKKE PACKAGING (PTY) LTD
BAKKE PACKAGING SYSTEMS (PTY) LTD
BAKKE PROPERTIES (PTY) LTD
BAKMAL PROPERTIES (PTY) LTD
BANDAG TYRES (TRANSKEI) (PTY) LTD
BERDEN GARMENT HIRE (PTY) LTD
BERDEN HOTEL SUPPLIES (PTY) LTD
BERDEN PROMOTIONS (PTY) LTD
BERDEN UNIFORMS (PTY) LTD
BERDEN WORKWEAR (NATAL) (PTY) LTD
BERNCO LABORATORY PROPERTIES (PTY) LTD
BINTECH (PTY) LTD
BONSTEEL PROPERTIES (PTY) LTD
BORDER RETREADING CO. (PTY) LTD
BORDER RUBBER PRODUCTS (PTY) LTD
BRITISH MEDICAL LABORATORIES S.A. (PTY)
BUFFALO ENGINEERING CO. (PTY) LTD
BURNOLITE (PTY) LTD
BUTTERWORTH PRODUCTIONS (PTY) LTD
C & W TOLLMAN (PTY) LTD
C.A. SIMPSON & WHITE (PTY) LTD
CAPITAL CARTAGE (PTY) LTD
CARNIVAL HOLDINGS (PTY) LTD
CAROL CARDS TRANSVAAL (PTY) LTD
CARTER HARRIS (PTY) LTD
CASTOR & LADDER HOLDINGS (PTY) LTD
CASTOR & LADDER PLASTICS (PTY) LTD
CASTOR & LADDER SALES (CAPE) (PTY) LTD
CASTOR & LADDER SALES (NATAL) (PTY) LTD
CASTOR & LADDER SALES (PTY) LTD
CHAKA MOTORS (PTY) LTD
CHARTER WRAPMASTER (PTY) LTD
CHEMPLAST EQUIPMENT (PTY) LTD
CHEMPLAST NATAL (PTY) LTD
CHEMPRO (PTY) LTD
CHEMTRA (PTY) LTD
CHEMTRA U.S.A. INC.
CIRCLE PUMPS DIVISION LTD
CLINIMED (PTY) LTD
COALEQUIP (PTY) LTD (49%)
COIRREROLL PROPERTIES (GS (PTY) LTD
CONCORD MOTORS (PTY) LTD
COURTEX PROPERTIES (PTY) LTD
COYS HIRE SERVICE LTD
COYS MOTORS LTD
COYS PROPERTIES LTD
CYCLOP-PHARMA (PTY) LTD
DAVE FREDRICKSON OVERALLS (PTY) LTD
DAVID & JONATHAN (PTY) LTD
DEEBAR ELECTRICAL (PTY) LTD
DON FRICTION (PTY) LTD
DON INTERNATIONAL (PTY) LTD
DURBAN OVERALL CO. (PTY) LTD
E.J. REED & ASSOCIATES (PTY) LTD
E.J. REED (PTY) LTD
EAGLE FREIGHT (PTY) LTD
EAGLE SHIPPING (PTY) LTD
ELECTRO-MEDICAL (PTY) LTD
ELITE CLOTHING MANUFACTURERS (PTY) LTD
ELLERINE HOLDINGS LTD
ELTERMAN SALES (PTY) LTD (76])
EMBEL DATA SYSTEMS (PTY) LTD
ENGINECRAFT (PTY) LTD
EQUIPMENT MANUFACTURING CO. OF S.A. (PTY
EVERLAST CLOTHING MANUFACTURERS (PTY) LT
FEMINA PRODUCTS (PTY) LTD
FILJO PUMPS (PTY) LTD
FINE INVESTMENTS (PTY) LTD
FIRST BADGE & TIE MANUFACTURERS (PTY) LT
FLEXIBLE WRAPPINGS (PTY) LTD
FLUKE INSTRUMENTS (SA) (PTY) LTD
FLUORO PLAST (PTY) LTD
FOODCORP LTD
FOXLAKE INVESTMENTS (PTY) LTD
FOXTOWN INVESTMENTS (PTY) LTD
FOXTREE (PTY) LTD
FOXWIN (PTY) LTD S.W.A.
FOXZAM INSTRUMENTATION LTD
FRANK BERGH (PTY) LTD
GENKEM CAPE (PTY) LTD
GIMA INVESTMENTS (PTY) LTD
GLOBE ELECTRICAL (TRANSVAAL) (PTY) LTD
GLOLEC LTD
GMD MARKETING SERVICES (PTY) LTD
GMD MORRISON (PTY) LTD
GMP PHARMACEUTICAL CO. (PTY) LTD
GRAPHIC ARTS EQUIPMENT DESIGNS (PTY) LTD
H. ALERS HANKEY LTD
H. ALERS HANKEY TRANSVAAL (PTY) LTD
H.T.J. MANUFACTURERS (PTY) LTD
HAGGIE LTD (35,3%)
HANDY PRINTING WORKS (PTY) LTD
HANKEY JARDINE HOLDINGS (PTY) LTD
HARRISON MOTORS LTD
HARVARD & CRAFT ENGINEERING (PTY) LTD
HOLDAINS LTD
HOMAG SHADES (PTY) LTD
HOSPITAL EQUIPMENT MANUFACTURERS (PTY) L
ICL TECHNOLOGY HOLDINGS (PTY) LTD (50%)
INDEPENDENT SOFTWARE SYSTEMS (PTY) LTD
INFONET
INTERPHARM (PTY) LTD
IRON & STEEL FOUNDRIES LTD
J.S.A. LEASING (PTY) LTD
K E K INVESTMENTS (TRANSKEI) (PTY) LTD
K.E.K. (PTY) LTD
KANHYM INVESTMENTS LTD
KAYDRILL SALES (PTY) LTD
KEMPURA REMEDIES (PTY) LTD
KENNET UNIFOAM (PTY) LTD
KLEIN WHOLESALE (PTY) LTD
KYMMENE (PTY) LTD
LABEQUIP (PTY) LTD
LABORATORY SERVICES (PTY) LTD
LADTOR LTD
LADTOR (PTY) LTD
LADTOR ENGINEERING (PTY) LTD
LADTOR HOLDINGS (PTY) LTD
LADTOR SALES (PTY) LTD
LAUDON LOCKS (PTY) LTD
LITECRAFT (PTY) LTD
M.M.H. MOTORS (PTY) LTD
MACCABEE INDUSTRIAL FINANCE LTD
MAIN INDUSTRIES (PTY) LTD (25%)
MAISEY MATRIX (PTY) LTD
MALBAK GROUP MANAGEMENT CO. (PTY) LTD

MALBAK GROUP SERVICES (PTY) LTD
MALBAK HOLDINGS LTD
MALBAK INDUSTRIAL HOLDINGS LTD
MALBAK INVESTMENTS LTD
MALBAK MOTOR HOLDINGS LTD
MALBAK MOTORS & TYRES (PTY) LTD
MALBAK TRADING LTD
MALCOM HYDRAULICS (PTY) LTD
MALCOMESS CREDIT CORP. (PTY) LTD
MALCOMESS LEASING CO. (PTY) LTD
MALCOMESS LTD
MALCOMESS MOTORS (PTY) LTD
MALCOMESS PROPERTIES (EAST LONDON SHOP)
MALCOMESS PROPERTIES (EAST LONDON) MOTOR
MALCOMESS PROPERTIES (ISANDO) (PTY) LTD
MALCOMESS PROPERTIES (PAROW TWO) (PTY) L
MALCOMESS PROPERTIES (PAROW) (PTY) LTD
MALCON INDUSTRIES (PTY) LTD
MALCON PRODUCTS (PTY) LTD
MANDATE CLOTHING DISTRIBUTORS (PTY) LTD
MANUPHARMA (PTY) LTD
MARBURG MANUFACTURERS (PTY) LTD
MARKET FINANCIAL SERVICES (PTY) LTD
MARKET MOTOR GROUP LTD
MARTCO ELECTRICAL (PTY) LTD
MARTIN RODGERS (PTY) LTD
MASTER OVERALL CO. (PTY) LTD
MATLEY MANUFACTURING CO. (PTY) LTD
MAXWELL CAMPBELL LTD
MAXWELL MOTOR (PTY) LTD
MCE (PTY) LTD
MEDICAL ENGINEERING CO. (PTY) LTD
MEDICAL EQUIPMENT (PTY) LTD
MERCURY TRANSPORT (PTY) LTD
MERRIMAKER INDUSTRIES (PTY) LTD
MILNERBERG PROPERTIES (PTY) LTD
MILTON SECURITIES LTD
MINLEIGH INVESTMENTS (PTY) LTD (50%)
MOBILITY ENGINEERING (PTY) LTD
MORGAN'S CHEMICALS LINENS CAPE (PTY) LTD
MORGAN'S WHOLESALE (PTY) LTD
MORGAN'S WHOLESALE LINENS (TRANSVAAL) (P
MOTOBRAKE (PTY) LTD
MOTOR & ALLIED HOLDINGS (PTY) LTD
MOTOR & ALLIED PRODUCTIONS (PTY) LTD
MY HOLDINGS PLC
N.T. SOLID (PTY) LTD
NATAL CABLES & LIGHTING (PTY) LTD
NATAL OVERALL MANUFACTURING CO. (PTY) LT
NATYRE BANDAG (NORTERN CAPE) (PTY) LTD
NATYRE BANDAG (OFS) (PTY) LTD
NATYRE BANDAG (TVL) (PTY) LTD
NOBLE'S MANCHESTER WAREHOUSE (PTY) LTD
NORCO (PTY) LTD
NOVOPAK (PTY) LTD
O. BAKKE & CO. (PTY) LTD
OCTOQUAT INVESTMENTS (PTY) LTD
OKIFAX (PTY) LTD
OSBORN MMD ENGINEERING (PTY) LTD (49%)
OUTAPACK (PTY) LTD
OVERVAAL MELKVERVOER (PTY) LTD
P C I PROJECTS (PTY) LTD
P C I PROPERTIES ONE (PTY) LTD
P C I PROPERTIES THREE (PTY) LTD
P C I PROPERTIES TWO (PTY) LTD
P V M DIE MAKER (PTY) LTD
P.V.M. DIEMAKERS (PTY) LTD
P.V.M. ENGINEERING (PTY) LTD (50%)
PACKAMAC SOUTH AFRICA (PTY) LTD
PARKO LTD
PEARL MOTORCOAT MANUFACTURING CO. (PTY)
PEDIATRIC LABORATORIES (PTY) LTD
PETROL & DIESEL ENGINE REBUILDERS (PTY)
PHOTRA (PTY) LTD
PHOTRA ELECTRONICS (PTY) LTD
PHOTRA HOLDINGS (PTY) LTD
PHOTRA INSTRUMENTS (PTY) LTD
PHOTRA INVESTMENTS (PTY) LTD
PHOTRA MANUFACTURING (PTY) LTD
PHOTRA U.K. LTD
PHOTRA U.S.A. INC.
PHOTRACOMP (PTY) LTD
PHOTRAFAX (PTY) LTD
PICKWICK PRODUCTS (PTY) LTD
PLASTAMID (PTY) LTD (50%)
PLASTELECT SERVICES (PTY) LTD
PLATRAND MILK TRANSPORT (PTY) LTD
PNI COMPUTERS (PTY) LTD
PNI ELECTRONICS (PTY) LTD
PNI SCIENTIFIC (PTY) LTD (50%)
POWER CLOTHING MANUFACTURERS (PTY) LTD
POWER TOILETRIES (PTY) LTD
PRAGWONINGS (EDMS) BPK
PROCESS CONTROL INSTRUMENTATION (PTY) LT
PROCESS CONTROL INSTRUMENTATION CONSOLID
PROMARDIS (CAPE) (PTY) LTD
PROMARDIS (PTY) LTD
PROMEX PLASTICS (PTY) LTD
PROTEA - VRN STEEL (50%)
PROTEA ALRODE PROPERTIES (PTY) LTD
PROTEA CHEMICALS LTD
PROTEA CLOTHING INDUSTRIES CISKEI (PTY)
PROTEA COMPONENTS (PTY) LTD
PROTEA CONSUMER PRODUCTS LTD
PROTEA ELECTRO-MEDICAL SERVICES (PTY) LT
PROTEA GRENSNYWERHEDE (EDMS) BPK
PROTEA HOLDINGS (PTY) LTD
PROTEA HOLDINGS CAPE (PTY) LTD
PROTEA HOLDINGS INSURANCE BROKERS (PTY)
PROTEA HOLDINGS LTD
PROTEA HOLDINGS MANAGEMENT CO (PTY) LTD
PROTEA HOLDINGS NATAL (PTY) LTD
PROTEA INDUSTRIAL CONTROLS (PTY) LTD
PROTEA INDUSTRIAL HOLDINGS LTD
PROTEA INTERNATIONAL (PTY) LTD
PROTEA LABORATORY SERVICES (PTY) LTD
PROTEA MEDICAL & LABORATORY LTD
PROTEA MEDICAL & LABORATY S.W.A. (PTY) L
PROTEA MEDICAL & LABORATY SUPPLIES (PTY)
PROTEA MEDICAL DISPOSABLES (PTY) LTD
PROTEA P.N.I. (PTY) LTD
PROTEA PHARMACEUTICALS (PTY) LTD
PROTEA SCIENTIFIC (BOTSWANA) (PTY) LTD
PROTEA SCIENTIFIC (SWAZILAND) (PTY) LTD
PROTEA SURGICAL (PTY) LTD
PROTEA TELECOMMUNICATION INDUSTRIES (PTY
PROTEA WORKWEAR (PTY) LTD
PROVON CHEMICALS (PTY) LTD (50%)
PTI COMMUNICATION (PTY) LTD
PVM ENGINEERING (PTY) LTD (50%)
QUEENS TYRE CO. (PTY) LTD
R T V RENTALS INVESTMENTS (PTY) LTD
R.I.P. (PTY) LTD
REGMA (SA) (PTY) LTD (50%)
RUFFYTEX (PTY) LTD
RUSHTON PROPERTIES LTD
S.A. WONDER IMPLEMENT CO. (PTY) LTD
SAMANTHA FASHIONS (PTY) LTD
SANDOWN MOTORS (PTY) LTD
SCREEN JOBBERS (PTY) LTD
SELQUIP (PTY) LTD
SEVERN MOTORS (PTY) LTD
SHIELD OVERALL MANUFACUTURERS (PTY) LTD
SIDMAL ENGINEERING (PTY) LTD
SIDMAL ENGINEERING WORKS (PTY) LTD
SOLIDUR PLASTICS (PTY) LTD
SOUTH AFRICAN DRUGGISTS LTD
SOUTH AFRICAN GRAPHIC ARTS & CHEMICAL IN

SOUTH AFRICAN LIQUID METERS (PTY) LTD
SPECIALISED BEARING APPLICATIONS (PTY) L
STANDARD ENGINEERING LTD (37%)
STEELDRILL WORKWEAR (PTY) LTD
STRATA CONTROL SYSTEMS (PTY) LTD (49%)
SUPER RICH (PTY) LTD
SYLKARD (PTY) LTD
SYLKO PAPER CO. (PTY) LTD
T. GIBSON & CO. (PTY) LTD
TARPON MOTORS (PTY) LTD
TEDELEX LTD
THE BERDEN GROUP LTD
THE STEELDRILL GROUP (PTY) LTD
THERAPION (PTY) LTD
THERMACOUST CAPE (PTY) LTD
TRANSKEI RETREADERS (PTY) LTD
TRANSPORTANDUS LTD
TRANSVAAL TRADING (PTY) LTD
TREK PETROLEUM (PTY) LTD
UITENHAGE ENGINE RECONDITIONERS (PTY) LT
ULTRA INSTRUMENTS (PTY) LTD
UNIFORMS 4 U (PTY) LTD
V-PRO (PTY) LTD
VELTOL COMPONENTS (PTY) LTD
VERSAPAK (PTY) LTD
VIVA COSMETICS (PTY) LTD
VREDEPLAAS (PTY) LTD
ZERUS (PTY) LTD
ZF OF SOUTH AFRICA (PTY) LTD (26%)

INVESTMENTS

LIQUID AIR (PTY) LTD (10.7%)

MALHOLD LTD

ABBREVIATION : MALHOLD

JSE SHORT CODE : MLH

SECTOR : Industrial-Industrial Holding

SHAREHOLDERS

Who Owns Whom's Assessment of the Identity of the Ultimate Controlling Shareholder:
SANLAM VIA GENCOR

SHAREHOLDER	PERCENTAGE 1992	1991
CONSOLIDATED NOM P/L	50.4	50.0
CMB NOM P/L	20.8	---
ABSA NOM P/L	5.6	---
SOUTHERN LIFE ASSOC LTD	4.7	4.4
METAL IND GROUP PENS FUND	2.0	1.9
ENGINEERING INDUSTRIES PENS FUND	1.8	1.5
FIRST NAT NOM P/L	1.7	1.4
YSKOR PENS FUND	1.2	1.1
METROPOLITAN LIFE LTD	1.2	1.2
CARGO INV P/L	1.2	1.2
EIGHTY ONE MAIN STREET NOM LTD	1.1	---
CLANOR PROPERTY & INV CO P/L	1.1	1.1
ESCOM PENS & PROV FUND	---	1.9
SANKORP BPK	---	15.2
SANLAM	---	5.0
VOLKSKAS NOM P/L	---	5.5
TOTAL	92.8	91.3

DIRECTORS :
DALING MH ,DE BEER TL ,HUNT-DAVIS DNA
JOUBERT PG ,RILEY DB ,SMITH BA
THOMAS GS (Chairman),VAN AS E ,WINBERG BSW

REGISTRATION NUMBER : 04/02682/06

REGISTERED OFFICE
Malbak House, Protea Place
off Fredman Drive, Sandton
2196
TEL: 011-783 4480
FAX: 011-783 0408

TRANSFER SECRETARY
Mercantile Registrars Ltd
P O Box 1053, Johannesburg
2000
TEL: 011-333 8181

COMPANY SECRETARY
Malbak Group Management Company (Pty) Ltd

NATURE OF BUSINESS
An industrial holding company with a controlling interest in quoted Malbak Ltd.

BANKERS :
N/A

AUDITORS :
Deloitte Pim Goldby

FAMILIAR BRAND NAMES
N/A

CONTRIBUTION BY ACTIVITY
N/A

YEAR END : August

DIVIDEND : Ords 50c

Interim	(Ldr)11/05/90	(Pay)25/05/90	Amt(c)33.5
Final	(Ldr)23/11/90	(Pay)13/12/90	Amt(c)52
Interim	(Ldr)10/05/91	(Pay)24/05/91	Amt(c)33.5
Final	(Ldr)22/11/91	(Pay)12/12/91	Amt(c)57.5
Interim	(Ldr)08/05/92	(Pay)22/05/92	Amt(c)35
Final	(Ldr)20/11/92	(Pay)11/12/92	Amt(c)58.5

NUMBER OF EMPLOYEES : 61000

CAPITAL STRUCTURE

	AUTHORISED	ISSUED
6% Cum Red Prefs R1	2000000	0
Var Rate Cum Red Prefs 1c	9000000	0
6,5% Cum Red Prefs R1	600000	0
Ords 50c	100000000	42008348

FINANCIAL STATISTICS (AT FINANCIAL YEAR END)

(Amts in R'000)	1992 Aug	1991 Aug	1990 Aug	1989 Aug	1988 Aug
Ord S/H Int	918000	795000	725000	660000	559000
Long Trm Loans	2385000	1582000	1329000	1164000	983000
Iss Ord Share	42008	41224	39576	39529	37731
Total Liab	4863000	3461000	3270000	2865000	2157000
Current Liab	2478000	1879000	1941000	1701000	1174000
Total Assets	5781000	4256000	3995000	3525000	2716000
Current Assets	3819000	2727000	2613000	2327000	1850000

Debtors	1837000	1410000	1366000	1168000	876000
Inventory	1212000	1132000	1141000	1110000	824000
Turnover	10992000	8441000	8374000	7329000	5234000
Oper Profit	757000	686000	698000	683000	500000
Interest Paid	199000	176000	217000	170000	83000
Tax Paid	200000	163000	173000	155000	142000
Prf af Int&Tax	452000	381000	334000	358000	275000
Prf att Ord Sh	135000	144000	127000	146000	111000
Btm Line Earn	97000	79000	57000	102000	71000
Dividend Paid	39000	37000	34000	34000	26000
Mkt Prce(c) YE	2850	2850	1575	2225	1760
Depreciation	187000	122000	113000	100000	71000

PER SHARE STATISTICS (CENTS)

Net Asst Val	2185.30	1928.49	1831.92	1669.66	1481.54
Net Earnings	316.80	341.70	321.70	369.00	288.20
Dividends	93.50	91.00	85.50	85.50	70.00
Cash Flow	761.76	679.22	659.49	677.98	522.12

RATIOS AND OTHER INFORMATION

Mrk Cap(R000)	1197228	1174884	623322	879520	664066
Current Ratio	1.54	1.45	1.35	1.37	1.58
Quik/Acid Tst	1.05	0.85	0.76	0.72	0.87
A/C Rec T/ovr	5.98	5.99	6.13	6.27	5.97
Tot Ass T/ovr	1.90	1.98	2.10	2.08	1.93
Debt/Ass Rat	0.46	0.49	0.54	0.55	0.52
L T L Tot Ass	0.03	0.05	0.05	0.07	0.08
Debt to Eqity	2.89	2.62	2.95	2.95	2.51
Interest Cover	3.80	3.90	3.22	4.02	6.02
Oper Prof Mrg	6.89	8.13	8.34	9.32	9.55
Net Prof Marg%	1.23	1.71	1.52	1.99	2.12
Ret on Assets	14.72	16.92	18.12	19.38	18.41
Ret on Equity%	14.71	18.11	17.52	22.12	19.86
Price/Earnings	9.00	8.34	4.90	6.03	6.11
Divid Cover	3.39	3.75	3.76	4.32	4.12
Divid Yield	3.28	3.19	5.43	3.84	3.98
Earning Yield%	11.12	11.99	20.43	16.58	16.38
NAV % Mrk Pr	76.68	67.67	116.31	75.04	84.18
Effec Tax Rate	28.83	26.47	28.40	26.12	30.46
Def Interval	2.73	2.64	3.17	2.82	2.37
Sus Grth Rate	10.46	13.46	12.83	16.97	15.21

SUBSIDIARY & ASSOCIATED COMPANIES

MALBAK LTD (39%)

INVESTMENTS

None

MANRO CHEMICAL HOLDINGS LTD

ABBREVIATION : MANRO

JSE SHORT CODE : MAN

SECTOR : Industrial-Chemicals & Oils

SHAREHOLDERS

Who Owns Whom's Assessment of the Identity of the Ultimate Controlling Shareholder:
HICKSON INTERNATIONAL PLC

SHAREHOLDER	PERCENTAGE 1992	1991
MANRO HOLDINGS P/L	66.1	66.5
NEDBANK NOM LTD	18.0	17.7
VMB NOM P/L	9.9	9.9
TOTAL	94.1	94.1

DIRECTORS :
ALLNATT MI ,JONES D (Financial Director)
KENT BH ,MURRAY BW (Managing Director),PARRY MH
RAYNER GG (Technical Director)
SCHOFIELD AI (Operations Director)
SCHOFIELD K (Chairman

REGISTRATION NUMBER : 87/03647/06

REGISTERED OFFICE
425 Cromarty Street, Wynberg
Sandton
2199
TEL: 011-887 0510
FAX: 011-887 7100

TRANSFER SECRETARY
Central Registrars Ltd
P O Box 4844, Johannesburg
2000
TEL: 011-331 0051

COMPANY SECRETARY
D Jones

NATURE OF BUSINESS
The group manufactures raw materials for use in the detergent & toiletry industries, as well as general chemical applications, which include : Supply of aromatic sulphonic acids; Supply of defoamers and dispersants to the pulp and paper manufacturing industries, processing chemicals for textile applications and emulsion polymers for carpet backing applications & surface coatings Manufacture of metallic driers, chemical salts, fire retardent & timber preservation chemicals.

BANKERS :
Standard Bank of SA Ltd, Volkskas Ltd

AUDITORS :
Price Waterhouse Meyernel

FAMILIAR BRAND NAMES
N/A

CONTRIBUTION BY ACTIVITY
South Africa (% Turnover by Market) (83.0%)
European Economic Community (7.0%)
Asia & Middle East (4.0%)
Australasia (2.0%)
The Americas (1.0%)
Rest of Africa (3.0%)

YEAR END : December

DIVIDEND :Ords 1c

Dividend No 5	(Ldr)15/03/91	(Pay)28/03/91	Amt(c)3.75
Interim No 6	(Ldr)30/09/91	(Pay)15/10/91	Amt(c)1.25
Final No 7	(Ldr)10/04/92	(Pay)24/04/92	Amt(c)2
Interim No 8	(Ldr)02/10/92	(Pay)16/10/92	Amt(c)1.25

NUMBER OF EMPLOYEES : 320

CAPITAL STRUCTURE

	AUTHORISED	ISSUED
Ords 1c	50000000	40816327

FINANCIAL STATISTICS (AT FINANCIAL YEAR END)

(Amts in R'000)	1991 Dec	1990 Dec	1989 Jun	1988 Jun
Ord S/H Int	27268	24499	4314	3653
Long Trm Loans	3810	4592	1585	916
Iss Ord Share	40816	40816	12000	12000
Total Liab	37010	33499	13889	8436
Current Liab	33200	28907	12304	7520
Total Assets	64278	57998	18203	12089
Current Assets	33974	29832	16579	11251
Debtors	21714	17395	9382	5509
Inventory	12211	12414	7197	4604
Turnover	89052	86315	60271	36183
Oper Profit	6886	9103	2795	1747
Interest Paid	3002	2068	392	87
Tax Paid	338	2722	1201	831
Prf af Int&Tax	3890	4744	1202	829
Prf att Ord Sh	3890	4744	1202	829
Btm Line Earn	3890	5786	1202	829
Dividend Paid	1327	1675	540	372
Mkt Prce(c) YE	40	55	40	40
Depreciation	2661	2100	357	147

PER SHARE STATISTICS (CENTS)

Net Asst Val	66.81	60.02	35.95	30.44
Net Earnings	9.53	11.62	10.00	6.91
Dividends	3.25	3.75	4.50	3.10
Cash Flow	15.72	12.88	16.14	11.27

RATIOS AND OTHER INFORMATION

Mrk Cap(R000)	16326	22449	4800	4800
Current Ratio	1.02	1.03	1.35	1.50
Quik/Acid Tst	0.66	0.60	0.76	0.88
A/C Rec T/ovr	4.10	3.31	6.42	6.57
Tot Ass T/ovr	1.39	0.99	3.31	2.99
Debt/Ass Rat	0.52	0.52	0.71	0.64
L T L Tot Ass	0.01	0.02	0.03	0.02
Debt to Eqity	1.23	1.22	2.98	2.13
Interest Cover	2.29	4.47	7.13	20.08
Oper Prof Mrg	7.73	10.55	4.64	4.83
Net Prof Marg%	4.37	5.50	1.99	2.29
Ret on Assets	11.25	10.96	15.35	14.45
Ret on Equity%	14.27	12.91	27.86	22.69
Price/Earnings	4.20	4.73	4.00	5.79
Divid Cover	2.93	3.10	2.22	2.23
Divid Yield	8.13	6.82	11.25	7.75
Earning Yield%	23.83	21.13	25.00	17.28
NAV % Mrk Pr	167.02	109.13	89.88	76.10
Effec Tax Rate	11.16	22.97	34.25	33.31
Def Interval	2.51	0.46	0.97	0.21
Sus Grth Rate	9.40	12.53	15.35	12.51

SUBSIDIARY & ASSOCIATED COMPANIES

BALLANTRAE INVESTMENTS (PTY) LTD
BEVALOID SA (PTY) LTD
ENTITY INVESTMENTS (PTY) LTD
GRAND VALLEY CHEMICAL CORP (PTY) LTD
HICKSON CHEMICAL CO (PTY) LTD
HICKSON MANAGEMENT SERVICES (PTY) LTD
HICKSON SWAZILAND (PTY) LTD
HICKSON TIMBER PRESERVATION (PTY) LTD
HICKSON TIMBER PRODUCTS (NATAL) (PTY) LT
MANRO CHEMICAL MARKETING CO (PTY) LTD
MANRO CHEMICALS (PTY) LTD
MANRO FINANCE (PTY) LTD
MANRO INDUSTRIES (PTY) LTD
MANRO PRODUCTS SA (PTY) LTD
MANRO SA (PTY) LTD
SA WOOD PRESERVING & FIRE RETARDANT CHEM

INVESTMENTS

None

MARLIN CORPORATION LTD

ABBREVIATION : MARLIN

JSE SHORT CODE : MLN

SECTOR : Metals & Minerals-Other

SHAREHOLDERS

Who Owns Whom's Assessment of the Identity of the Ultimate Controlling Shareholder:
PB GAIN VIA MARHOLD

SHAREHOLDER	PERCENTAGE 1992	1991
MARLIN HOLDINGS LTD	69.2	69.2
STD BANK NOM TVL P/L	6.8	3.4
CMB NOM P/L	4.0	---
USAT NOM P/L	3.2	4.7
METROPOLITAN LIFE LTD	3.1	3.1
MERCANTILE & GEN REINSURANCE CO SA LTD	1.4	1.4
COMMERCIAL UNION ASSURE CO SA LTD	---	1.9
BOARD OF EXECUTORS NOM P/L	---	1.5
SANLAM	---	4.0
TOTAL	87.6	89.1

DIRECTORS :
FROST SD (Administration Director)
GAIN PB (Executive Chairman),HART KP ,HUMAN JC
MACMILLAN IH (Financial Director),THOMAS NS
TREAGUS GR (Managing Director)

REGISTRATION NUMBER : 87/000717/06

REGISTERED OFFICE
7th Floor, 94 Main Street
Johannesburg
2001
TEL: 011-832 3221
FAX: 011-838 7611

TRANSFER SECRETARY
Mercantile Registrars Ltd
P O Box 1053, Johannesburg
2000
TEL: 011-333 8181

COMPANY SECRETARY
S D Frost

NATURE OF BUSINESS
The Marlin Group is engaged in the quarrying and international trading of dimensional stone, as well as the processing of dimensional stone

into finished granite products, including granite tiles. In addition, certain subsidiaries of the company undertake flooring and curtain wall cladding contracts.

BANKERS :
First National Bank of SA Ltd

AUDITORS :
KPMG Aiken & Peat

FAMILIAR BRAND NAMES
GRANITEX

CONTRIBUTION BY ACTIVITY
N/A

YEAR END : December

DIVIDEND :Ords 5c

Interim No 5	(Ldr)23/03/90	(Pay)25/05/90	Amt(c)7
Final No 6	(Ldr)28/09/90	(Pay)27/11/90	Amt(c)7
Interim No 7	(Ldr)22/03/91	(Pay)24/05/91	Amt(c)5

NUMBER OF EMPLOYEES : 600

CAPITAL STRUCTURE

	AUTHORISED	ISSUED
Ords 5c	60000000	46764100
9% Conv Red Cum Prefs 1c	17600000	71800

FINANCIAL STATISTICS (AT FINANCIAL YEAR END)

(Amts in R'000)	1991 Jun	1990 Jun	1989 Jun	1988 Jun
Ord S/H Int	156870	158007	112862	48955
Long Trm Loans	27199	24311	9108	54962
Iss Ord Share	46758	46353	34248	27200
Total Liab	81751	64391	45925	77505
Current Liab	54552	40080	36817	22543
Total Assets	204695	190502	130787	126460
Intang Assets	33926	31896	26000	*
Current Assets	85536	87683	43381	28689
Debtors	48009	41634	22122	18470
Inventory	28237	18689	6140	4700
Turnover	120673	91530	-	-
Oper Profit	18253	21947	30751	18328
Interest Paid	5397	3694	1557	124
Tax Paid	205	365	187	189
Prf af Int&Tax	12816	17888	29007	18015
Prf att Ord Sh	10630	14092	27311	15322
Btm Line Earn	10630	14092	27311	15322
Dividend Paid	2338	5733	10274	5440
Mkt Prce(c) YE	175	300	765	325
Depreciation	6902	6790	4807	2819

PER SHARE STATISTICS (CENTS)

Net Asst Val	262.94	272.07	247.79	179.98
Net Earnings	22.80	37.20	84.10	56.30
Dividends	5.00	14.00	30.00	20.00
Cash Flow	34.53	50.49	94.10	64.44

RATIOS AND OTHER INFORMATION

Mrk Cap(R000)	81827	139059	261997	88400
Current Ratio	1.57	2.19	1.18	1.27
Quik/Acid Tst	1.05	1.72	1.01	1.06
A/C Rec T/ovr	2.51	2.20	-	-
Tot Ass T/ovr	0.59	0.48	-	-
Debt/Ass Rat	0.32	0.25	0.34	0.21
L T L Tot Ass	0.05	0.04	0.06	0.03
Debt to Eqity	0.42	0.30	0.40	0.55
Interest Cover	3.41	5.94	19.75	147.81
Oper Prof Mrg	15.13	23.98	-	-
Net Prof Marg%	8.81	15.40	-	-
Ret on Assets	9.70	12.46	24.69	14.97
Ret on Equity%	6.78	8.92	24.20	31.30
Price/Earnings	7.68	8.06	9.10	5.77
Divid Cover	4.56	2.66	2.80	2.82
Divid Yield	2.86	4.67	3.92	6.15
Earning Yield%	13.03	12.40	10.99	17.32
NAV % Mrk Pr	150.25	90.69	32.39	55.38
Effec Tax Rate	1.55	1.66	0.62	1.08
Def Interval	2.35	1.09	0.52	2.10
Sus Grth Rate	5.29	5.29	15.10	20.19

SUBSIDIARY & ASSOCIATED COMPANIES

ABIQUA SLATE & SANDSTONE (PTY) LTD
BARRACUDA GRANITE TILE (PTY) LTD (50%)
BELBLOCK QUARRIES (PTY) LTD
BOKSAF QUARTZITE (PTY) LTD
BP GRANITE (PTY) LTD
CO-ORDINATED FINANCIAL SERVICES (PTY) LT
COLORADO GRANITE (PTY) LTD
DIMENSIONAL INVESTMENTS (PTY) LTD
ERF 419 SAXONWOLD (PTY) LTD
GABBRO GRANITE (PTY) LTD
GELUK MARKETING HOLDINGS (PTY) LTD
GOLDCREST FARMING (PTY) LTD
GRANITEX SALES (PTY) LTD
GRANITEX SALES (PTY) LTD (BOPHUTHATSWANA
MARBLE PENTELIC (PTY) LTD
MARLIN AIR (PTY) LTD
MARLIN GRANITE (PTY) LTD
MARLIN GRANITE (RUSTENBURG) (PTY) LTD
MARLIN QUARRY HOLDINGS (PTY) LTD
MARLIN VERDE (PTY) LTD
PARYS GRANITE (PTY) LTD
S VAN WYK BELEGGINGS (EDMS) BPK
TAMINAI PROPERTY DEVELOPMENT & FINANCE (
TRANSVAAL ROSSO (PTY) LTD

INVESTMENTS

None

MARLIN HOLDINGS LTD

ABBREVIATION : MLNHOLD

JSE SHORT CODE : MNH

SECTOR : Metals & Minerals-Other

SHAREHOLDERS

Who Owns Whom's Assessment of the Identity of the Ultimate Controlling Shareholder:
PB GAIN

SHAREHOLDER	PERCENTAGE 1992	1991
USAT NOM P/L	61.0	70.5
SA MUTUAL	11.1	11.9
STD BANK NOM TVL P/L	7.7	---
EIGHTY ONE MAIN STREET NOM LTD	3.3	3.6

PEDRETTI M	2.3	---
FIRST NAT NOM P/L	2.0	---
METROPOLITAN LIFE LTD	1.9	1.9
SEFALANA EMP BENEFITS ORG (SEBO)	1.6	---
YSKOR PENS FUND	1.2	1.2
EPF OLD MUTUAL NOM P/L	---	1.2
BOP GOVERNMENT SERV PENS FUND	---	1.1
TOTAL	92.2	91.5

DIRECTORS :
GAIN PB (Executive Chairman),HART KP
MACMILLAN IH (Financial Director)
TREAGUS GR (Managing Director

REGISTRATION NUMBER : 84/00634/06

REGISTERED OFFICE
7th Floor, 94 Main Street
Johannesburg
2001
TEL: 011-832 3221
FAX: 011-838 7611

TRANSFER SECRETARY
Mercantile Registrars Ltd
P O Box 1053, Johannesburg
2000
TEL: 011-333 8181

COMPANY SECRETARY
S D Frost

NATURE OF BUSINESS
The company holds a controlling interest in Marlin Corporation, which is also quoted on the JSE. Marlin Corporation quarries black, dark grey, pink green & yellow granite in the Belfast, Rustenburg, , Parys, Namaqualand and Walvis Bay areas. Most production is exported to Europe, N America & the Far East.

BANKERS :
First National Bank of SA Ltd

AUDITORS :
KPMG Aiken & Peat

FAMILIAR BRAND NAMES
N/A

CONTRIBUTION BY ACTIVITY
N/A

YEAR END : June

DIVIDEND : Ords 47c

Final	(Ldr)28/09/90	(Pay)27/11/90	Amt(c)5.6
Interim	(Ldr)22/03/91	(Pay)24/05/91	Amt(c)2.5

NUMBER OF EMPLOYEES : 764

CAPITAL STRUCTURE

	AUTHORISED	ISSUED
Ords 47c	64000000	61989600

FINANCIAL STATISTICS (AT FINANCIAL YEAR END)

(Amts in R'000)	1991 Jun	1990 Jun	1989 Jun
Ord S/H Int	118994	110960	36214
Long Trm Loans	85047	91270	-
Iss Ord Share	61990	61990	20950
Total Liab	139633	132617	-
Current Liab	54586	41347	-
Total Assets	203486	190468	36214
Intang Assets	55141	53109	*
Current Assets	85551	88746	-
Debtors	48024	41634	-
Inventory	28237	18689	-
Turnover	120673	22883	-
Oper Profit	18253	5531	-
Interest Paid	5397	946	-
Tax Paid	205	135	-
Prf af Int&Tax	12816	4450	-
Prf att Ord Sh	7325	3567	-
Btm Line Earn	7325	5062	-
Dividend Paid	1550	3471	-
Mkt Prce(c) YE	80	180	-
Depreciation	6902	1697	-

PER SHARE STATISTICS (CENTS)

Net Asst Val	103.01	93.32	172.86
Net Earnings	11.80	11.40	-
Dividends	3.00	5.60	-
Cash Flow	20.66	42.38	-

RATIOS AND OTHER INFORMATION

Mrk Cap(R000)	49592	111582	-
Current Ratio	1.57	2.15	-
Quik/Acid Tst	1.05	1.69	-
A/C Rec T/ovr	2.51	0.55	-
Tot Ass T/ovr	0.59	0.12	-
Debt/Ass Rat	0.32	0.26	-
L T L Tot Ass	0.05	0.04	-
Debt to Eqity	0.55	0.44	-
Interest Cover	3.41	5.85	-
Oper Prof Mrg	15.13	24.17	-
Net Prof Marg%	6.07	15.59	-
Ret on Assets	9.75	3.14	-
Ret on Equity%	6.16	3.21	-
Price/Earnings	6.78	15.79	-
Divid Cover	3.93	2.04	-
Divid Yield	3.75	3.11	-
Earning Yield%	14.75	6.33	-
NAV % Mrk Pr	128.76	51.85	-
Effec Tax Rate	1.55	2.62	-
Def Interval	2.95	4.28	-
Sus Grth Rate	4.85	0.09	-

SUBSIDIARY & ASSOCIATED COMPANIES

MARLIN CORPORATION LTD

INVESTMENTS

None

MARSHALLS CONTROLLING INVESTMENTS LTD

ABBREVIATION : MARCONS

JSE SHORT CODE : MCN

SECTOR : Financial-Property

SHAREHOLDERS

Who Owns Whom's Assessment of the Identity of the Ultimate Controlling Shareholder:
MARSHALL FAMILY

SHAREHOLDER	PERCENTAGE 1992	1991
MARSHALLS HOLDINGS CO P/L	55.1	55.1
NAIAD INV LTD	5.3	5.3
SUSSEX INV P/L	5.1	5.1
KATZ J	3.5	2.1
ZIEGELSTEIN B	2.2	2.2
ZIEGELSTEIN L	1.9	1.7
CELESTIAL P/L	1.6	1.6
DE RAUVILLE J P G TRUST	1.5	---
LONSDALE P N	1.4	1.4
MARSHALL D C	1.4	1.4
TULELE SUGAR ESTATES P/L	1.4	1.4
KATZ ADA	1.1	---
DE RAUVILLE P G	---	1.4
NEDBANK NOM LTD	---	2.0
TOTAL	81.6	80.7

DIRECTORS :
LONSDALE PN ,MAITRE JPA
MARSHALL DC (Chairman & Managing Dir.)
ROWSELL AJ ,VACY-LYLE DC

REGISTRATION NUMBER : 87/02656/06

REGISTERED OFFICE
11th Floor, 85 Field Street
Durban
4001
TEL: 031-305 6521
FAX: 031-301 9791

TRANSFER SECRETARY
Central Registrars Ltd
P O Box 4844, Johannesburg
2000
TEL: 011-331 0051

COMPANY SECRETARY
P N Lonsdale

NATURE OF BUSINESS
An investment holding company, with a controlling interest in quoted Marshalls Ltd.

BANKERS :
First National Bank of SA Ltd

AUDITORS :
Ernst & Young

FAMILIAR BRAND NAMES
N/A

CONTRIBUTION BY ACTIVITY
Dividends/Interest (13.0%)
Property/Parking Garage Rentals (65.3%)
Confirming Fees/Interest (25.0%)
Agricultural Equipment/Vehicles (Loss) (-3.3%)

YEAR END : December

DIVIDEND :Ords 1c

Interim	(Ldr)24/08/90	(Pay)07/09/90	Amt(c)4.25
Final	(Ldr)22/02/91	(Pay)28/02/91	Amt(c)4.75
Interim	(Ldr)16/08/91	(Pay)30/08/91	Amt(c)4.75
Final	(Ldr)21/02/92	(Pay)04/03/92	Amt(c)5
Interim	(Ldr)31/07/92	(Pay)10/08/92	Amt(c)5.75

CAPITAL STRUCTURE

	AUTHORISED	ISSUED
Ords 1c	20000000	12135000

FINANCIAL STATISTICS (AT FINANCIAL YEAR END)

(Amts In R'000)	1991 Dec	1990 Dec	1989 Dec	1988 Dec	1987 Dec
Ord S/H Int	48870	44576	36368	29402	22506
Long Trm Loans	29925	28122	22148	19059	15754
Iss Ord Share	12135	12135	12135	12135	12135
Total Liab	35335	32365	28759	24571	19930
Current Liab	5410	4243	6611	5512	4176
Total Assets	84205	76941	65127	53973	42436
Current Assets	15399	15336	11809	11630	5155
Debtors	6678	7425	2412	2380	1577
Inventory	1356	2099	4466	4612	3371
Turnover	22680	26096	33471	27724	10694
Oper Profit	6050	4397	2633	4468	1547
Interest Paid	1685	1521	204	943	371
Tax Paid	2335	1882	1944	1692	606
Prf af Int&Tax	2718	2114	1904	1833	570
Prf att Ord Sh	1847	1430	1288	1241	386
Btm Line Earn	1524	1373	2546	2088	386
Dividend Paid	1183	1092	971	849	334
Mkt Prce(c) YE	165	115	85	70	90
Depreciation	267	269	273	244	98

PER SHARE STATISTICS (CENTS)

Net Asst Val	402.72	367.33	299.70	242.29	185.46
Net Earnings	15.20	11.80	10.60	10.20	3.20
Dividends	9.80	9.00	8.00	7.00	2.75
Cash Flow	17.49	13.18	13.88	12.26	8.90

RATIOS AND OTHER INFORMATION

Mrk Cap(R000)	20023	13955	10315	8495	10922
Current Ratio	2.85	3.61	1.79	2.11	1.23
Quik/Acid Tst	2.60	3.12	1.11	1.27	0.43
A/C Rec T/ovr	3.40	3.51	13.88	11.65	14.80
Tot Ass T/ovr	0.27	0.34	0.51	0.51	0.55
Debt/Ass Rat	0.15	0.15	0.18	0.21	0.23
L T L Tot Ass	0.09	0.10	0.08	0.10	0.13
Debt to Eqity	0.26	0.27	0.33	0.38	0.43
Interest Cover	3.59	2.90	12.95	4.74	4.17
Oper Prof Mrg	26.68	16.85	7.87	16.12	14.47
Net Prof Marg%	8.14	5.48	3.85	4.48	3.61
Ret on Assets	8.00	7.17	6.22	8.28	7.95
Ret on Equity%	3.78	3.21	3.54	4.22	3.74
Price/Earnings	10.86	9.75	8.02	6.86	28.13
Divid Cover	1.55	1.31	1.33	1.46	1.16
Divid Yield	5.94	7.83	9.41	10.00	3.06
Earning Yield%	9.21	10.26	12.47	14.57	3.56
NAV % Mrk Pr	244.07	319.42	352.58	346.13	206.07
Effec Tax Rate	43.72	50.75	47.42	48.31	50.60
Def Interval	3.98	5.26	4.25	3.92	29.93
Sus Grth Rate	1.36	0.76	0.87	1.33	0.23

SUBSIDIARY & ASSOCIATED COMPANIES

MARSHALLS LTD

INVESTMENTS

None

MARSHALLS LTD

ABBREVIATION : MARSHAL

JSE SHORT CODE : MSH

SECTOR : Financial-Property

SHAREHOLDERS

Who Owns Whom's Assessment of the Identity of the Ultimate Controlling Shareholder: MARSHALLS CONTROLLING INVESTMENTS

SHAREHOLDER	PERCENTAGE 1992	1991
MARSHALLS CONTROLLING INV P/L	69.2	68.3
MARSHALLS HOLDINGS CO P/L	9.8	9.8
KATZ J	3.4	1.1
SUSSEX INV P/L	2.4	2.4
MARSHALL D C	1.2	---
ZIEGELSTEIN B	1.1	---
DE RAUVILLE J P G TRUST	---	2.4
MARSHALL D C TRUST	---	1.2
TOTAL	87.1	85.2

DIRECTORS :
LONSDALE PN ,MAITRE JPA
MARSHALL DC (Chairman & Managing Dir.)
ROWSELL AJ ,VACY-LYLE DC M

REGISTRATION NUMBER : 05/06398/06

REGISTERED OFFICE
11th Floor, 85 Field Street
Durban
4001
TEL: 031-305 6521
FAX: 031-301 9791

TRANSFER SECRETARY
Central Registrars Ltd
P O Box 4844, Johannesburg
2000
TEL: 011-331 0051

COMPANY SECRETARY
P N Lonsdale

NATURE OF BUSINESS
An investment holding company, receiving income in the form of dividends from its wholly owned subsidiary, which is the owner of rental income producing commercial and industrial properties, and parking garages, mainly in Durban, Pinetown and Cape Town. The subsidiary also operates a confirming & indent financing division, a motor & agricultural division consisting of the Massey-Ferguson & Nissan dealership in Estcourt.

BANKERS :
First National Bank of SA Ltd

AUDITORS :
Ernst & Young

FAMILIAR BRAND NAMES
JOHN DEERE (DEALER),MASSEY-FERGUSON
NISSAN (DEALER)

CONTRIBUTION BY ACTIVITY
Interest/Dividends (Pre-Tax Profit) (13.0%)
Property/Parking Garage Rentals (65.4%)
Confirming Fees/Interest (24.9%)
Agricultural/Vehicles (Loss) (-3.3%)

YEAR END : December

DIVIDEND : Ords no par value

Interim	(Ldr)24/08/90	(Pay)07/09/90	Amt(c)9
Final	(Ldr)22/02/91	(Pay)28/02/91	Amt(c)10
Interim	(Ldr)16/08/91	(Pay)30/08/91	Amt(c)10
Final	(Ldr)21/02/92	(Pay)04/03/92	Amt(c)11
Interim	(Ldr)31/07/92	(Pay)10/08/92	Amt(c)12

CAPITAL STRUCTURE

	AUTHORISED	ISSUED
2nd Cum Red Prefs 1c	1000000	0
Cum Red Prefs 1c	500000	0
6% Cum Red Prefs R2	250000	0
Ords no par value	17000000	8500000

FINANCIAL STATISTICS (AT FINANCIAL YEAR END)

(Amts in R'000)	1991 Dec	1990 Dec	1990 Dec	1989	1988 Dec
Ord S/H Int	70776	64528	64528	52512	42303
Long Trm Loans	7652	7797	7797	12189	5693
Iss Ord Share	8500	8500	8500	8500	8500
Total Liab	13089	12030	12030	18798	11205
Current Liab	5437	4233	4233	6609	5512
Total Assets	83865	76558	76558	76510	53508
Current Assets	15398	15335	15335	11809	11630
Debtors	6678	7424	7424	-	2380
Inventory	1356	2099	2099	11809	4612
Turnover	22680	26096	26096	33471	27724
Oper Profit	6059	4408	4408	4076	4491
Interest Paid	1685	1521	1521	204	943
Tax Paid	2334	1881	1882	1944	1691
Prf af Int&Tax	2728	2126	2125	1928	1857
Prf att Ord Sh	2718	2111	2110	1921	1852
Btm Line Earn	2245	2028	2027	1921	3092
Dividend Paid	1785	1615	1615	1445	1275
Mkt Prce(c) YE	320	225	225	190	140
Depreciation	267	269	269	-	244

PER SHARE STATISTICS (CENTS)

Net Asst Val	832.66	759.15	759.15	617.79	497.68
Net Earnings	32.00	24.80	-	-	21.80
Dividends	21.00	19.00	-	-	15.00
Cash Flow	35.20	26.82	26.81	22.68	24.69

RATIOS AND OTHER INFORMATION

Mrk Cap(R000)	27200	19125	19125	16150	11900
Current Ratio	2.83	3.62	3.62	1.79	2.11
Quik/Acid Tst	2.58	3.13	3.13	-	1.27
A/C Rec T/ovr	3.40	3.52	3.52	-	11.65
Tot Ass T/ovr	0.27	0.34	0.34	0.44	0.52
Debt/Ass Rat	0.15	0.16	0.16	0.25	0.21
L T L Tot Ass	0.09	0.10	0.10	0.16	0.11
Debt to Eqity	0.18	0.19	0.19	0.36	0.26
Interest Cover	3.60	2.90	2.90	19.98	4.76
Oper Prof Mrg	26.72	16.89	16.89	12.18	16.20
Net Prof Marg%	11.98	8.09	8.09	5.74	6.68
Ret on Assets	8.05	7.22	7.22	5.33	8.39
Ret on Equity%	3.84	3.27	3.27	3.66	4.38
Price/Earnings	10.00	9.07	-	-	6.42
Divid Cover	1.52	1.31	-	-	1.45
Divid Yield	6.56	8.44	-	-	10.71
Earning Yield%	10.00	11.02	-	-	15.57
NAV % Mrk Pr	260.21	337.40	337.40	325.15	355.49

Effec Tax Rate	45.97	49.56	50.61	50.21	47.58
Def Interval	2.88	3.74	3.75	6.32	2.78
Sus Grth Rate	1.32	0.77	0.77	0.91	1.36

SUBSIDIARY & ASSOCIATED COMPANIES

ALLER BLUFF PROPERTIES (PTY) LTD
ANGLO AFRICAN INDUSTRIES LTD
BELL STREET MOTORS (PTY) LTD
CITY AND COUNTRY PROPERTIES LTD
ESCOMBE MANUFACTURERS LTD
ESCOMBE WHOLESALERS LTD
F M S PROPERTIES LTD
INTERNAL RESERVES LTD
KERVILLEPORT (PTY) LTD
M I L CREDIT CO. LTD
MARSHALL INDUSTRIALS (NATAL) LTD
MARSHALL INDUSTRIALS (TVL) LTD
MARSHALL TIMBERS (PMB) LTD
MARSHALL TIMBERS LTD
MARSHALLS GROUP LTD
MURRAY SQUARE PROPERTIES (PTY) LTD
NICOL SQUARE GARAGE (PTY) LTD
NORMAN BEESON TRAVEL (PTY) LTD
PRINCE ALFRED INVESTMENTS LTD
SIX SEVEN PRINCE ALFRED STREET (PTY) LTD
SIXTY SIX RUSSELL STREET (PTY) LTD
STANGER INVESTMENTS (PTY) LTD
THREE EIGHTEEN GALE STREET LTD
THREE-SIX MILNE STREET (PTY) LTD
TWO-FOUR-FIVE CHAMBERLAIN ROAD (PTY) LTD
U F E HOLDINGS LTD
WESTGARD PROPERTIES (PTY) LTD
WINSTON ROAD PROPERTIES (PTY) LTD

INVESTMENTS

None

MARTIN JONKER HOLDINGS LTD

ABBREVIATION : MJM

JSE SHORT CODE : MJM

SECTOR : Industrial-Motor

SHAREHOLDERS

Who Owns Whom's Assessment of the Identity of the Ultimate Controlling Shareholder: DIRECTORS

SHAREHOLDER	PERCENTAGE 1992	1991
JONKER M TRUST	47.8	47.8
MICHAEL JORDAAN ENTERPRISES CC	15.9	5.7
INTERNATIONAL BUSINESS CORP LTD	15.9	9.9
MARTIN JONKER TRUST (BEHEREND)	5.9	5.9
VON RANTZAU L	3.2	3.2
VON RANTZAU E	3.1	3.1
VON RANTZAU H	3.1	3.1
VON RANTZAU LISELOTTE	2.9	2.9
MARMARE SHIPPING INC	---	7.5
XADEMU LUXEMBOURG SA	---	7.4
TOTAL	97.7	96.4

DIRECTORS :
DEKKER LW ,HUNTER RD ,JONKER M (Chairman)
JORDAAN M ,STRIEGEL F ,VAN DEVENTER J

REGISTRATION NUMBER : 68/11481/06

REGISTERED OFFICE
Martin Jonker Centre, 619 Voortrekkers Road
Gezina, Pretoria
0084
TEL: 012-761111
FAX: 012-761363

TRANSFER SECRETARY
Central Registrars Ltd
P O Box 4844, Johannesburg
2000
TEL: 011-331 0051

COMPANY SECRETARY
A Botes

NATURE OF BUSINESS
The company & its subsidiaries are engaged in the retailing of new and used passenger and light commercial vehicles, and the attendant sales of petrol, parts & service.

BANKERS :
Senbank

AUDITORS :
Venter & De Jager

FAMILIAR BRAND NAMES
N/A

CONTRIBUTION BY ACTIVITY
N/A

YEAR END : February

DIVIDEND : Ords no par value

Interim No 19	(Ldr)13/07/90	(Pay)27/07/90	Amt(c)2
Final No 20	(Ldr)22/02/91	(Pay)22/03/91	Amt(c)2

NUMBER OF EMPLOYEES : 376

CAPITAL STRUCTURE

	AUTHORISED	ISSUED
Ords no par value	40000000	39757444

FINANCIAL STATISTICS (AT FINANCIAL YEAR END)

(Amts in R'000)	1992 Feb	1991 Feb	1990 Feb	1989 Feb	1988 Feb
Ord S/H Int	8737	8556	8493	7376	1136
Long Trm Loans	292	394	525	628	780
Iss Ord Share	27998	27998	27998	27998	1856
Total Liab	26393	29206	26940	20713	10644
Current Liab	26101	28812	26415	20085	9864
Total Assets	31389	34021	31692	24348	11780
Intang Assets	3741	3741	3741	3741	*
Current Assets	29121	30340	28119	21415	10202
Debtors	10509	8326	9469	8452	2999
Inventory	18607	21992	18528	12753	6809
Turnover	151687	156819	136902	76702	60733
Oper Profit	3631	4579	4535	2458	1322
Interest Paid	3141	3510	2801	1100	1027
Tax Paid	284	446	1	12	-21
Prf af Int&Tax	206	623	1733	1346	316
Prf att Ord Sh	181	623	1733	1346	164

Btm Line Earn	181	623	1733	1346	89
Dividend Paid	-	560	560	494	-
Mkt Prce(c) YE	40	-	40	60	85
Depreciation	569	471	306	46	40

PER SHARE STATISTICS (CENTS)

Net Asst Val	17.84	17.20	16.97	12.98	61.21
Net Earnings	0.70	2.20	6.20	10.90	3.20
Dividends	-	2.00	2.00	4.00	-
Cash Flow	2.35	3.91	7.28	11.29	10.99

RATIOS AND OTHER INFORMATION

Mrk Cap(R000)	11199	-	11199	16799	1578
Current Ratio	1.12	1.05	1.06	1.07	1.03
Quik/Acid Tst	0.40	0.29	0.36	0.43	0.34
A/C Rec T/ovr	14.43	18.83	14.46	9.08	20.25
Tot Ass T/ovr	4.83	4.61	4.32	3.15	5.16
Debt/Ass Rat	0.84	0.86	0.85	0.85	0.90
L T L Tot Ass	0.01	0.01	0.02	0.03	0.07
Debt to Eqity	3.02	3.41	3.17	2.81	9.37
Interest Cover	1.16	1.30	1.62	2.23	1.29
Oper Prof Mrg	2.39	2.92	3.31	3.20	2.18
Net Prof Marg%	0.12	0.40	1.27	1.75	0.27
Ret on Assets	11.57	13.46	14.31	10.10	11.22
Ret on Equity%	2.07	7.28	20.41	18.25	14.44
Price/Earnings	57.14	-	6.45	5.50	26.56
Divid Cover	-	1.10	3.10	2.73	-
Divid Yield	-	-	5.00	6.67	-
Earning Yield%	1.75	-	15.50	18.17	3.76
NAV % Mrk Pr	44.61	-	42.43	21.64	72.01
Effec Tax Rate	76.33	38.35	0.06	0.88	-7.12
Def Interval	13.67	9.66	5.54	6.96	18.64
Sus Grth Rate	2.07	0.74	13.81	11.55	14.44

SUBSIDIARY & ASSOCIATED COMPANIES

CAPITIMUS (PTY) LTD
MARTIN JONKER MOTORS (PRETORIA) LTD
MARTIN JONKER MOTORS GEZINA LTD
MARTIN JONKER MOTORS LTD
SCHUS (CAPE) (PTY) LTD
SCHUS NISSAN (PTY) LTD

INVESTMENTS

None

MAS HOLDINGS LTD

ABBREVIATION : MASHOLD

JSE SHORT CODE : MHL

SECTOR : Industrial-Retailers & Wholesalers

SHAREHOLDERS

Who Owns Whom's Assessment of the Identity of the Ultimate Controlling Shareholder: MAS CONSOLIDATED INVESTMENT HOLDINGS

SHAREHOLDER	PERCENTAGE 1992	1991
MASHOLD CONSOLIDATED INV HOLDINGS LTD	57.9	62.6
SA MUTUAL	7.8	5.6
CMB NOM P/L	6.0	---
STD BANK NOM TVL P/L	5.6	4.6
AFRICAN LIFE ASSURE CO LTD	4.3	4.6
METROPOLITAN LIFE LTD	2.1	2.3
FIRST NAT NOM P/L	2.0	---
BROUZE D	1.8	---
SFSS NOM P/L	1.4	1.5
ANGLO AMERICAN GROUP PENS FUND	1.2	1.3
DAVJON TRUST	1.1	---
VAN EMBDEN S	---	1.1
SANLAM	---	6.5
TOTAL	91.1	90.0

DIRECTORS :
BIERMANN HH ADMIRAL,GETZ K
STEIN R (Vice Chairman),VAN EMBDEN H (Chairman)
VAN EMBDEN M (Managing Director

REGISTRATION NUMBER : 59/03905/06

REGISTERED OFFICE
African Wholesalers Centre, 33 Jack Craig Street
Foreshore, Cape Town
8001
TEL: 021-25 2690
FAX: 021-419 5780

TRANSFER SECRETARY
Mercantile Registrars Ltd
P O Box 1053, Johannesburg
2000
TEL: 011-333 8181

COMPANY SECRETARY
B L Taylor

NATURE OF BUSINESS
The group carries on the business of mail order retailing, general retailing, direct selling, mail insertion and advertising.

BANKERS :
First National Bank of SA Ltd, Volkskas Ltd
Standard Bank of SA Ltd, Senbank

AUDITORS :
Kessel Feinstein

FAMILIAR BRAND NAMES
CATALOGUE CORPORATION,GROLIER ENCYCLOPAEDIAS
MAGIC BY MAIL,NATIONAL GEOGRAPHIC
NEW BOOK OF KNOWLEDGE,NEW YOU BEAUTY CLUB
SONNY BOYS,TABLEKRAFT,TIME-LIFE BOOKS
WALT DISNEY BOOKS

CONTRIBUTION BY ACTIVITY
N/A

YEAR END : February

DIVIDEND : Ords no par value

Interim No 9	(Ldr)23/11/90	(Pay)13/12/90	Amt(c)7
Final No 10	(Ldr)22/02/91	(Pay)05/04/91	Amt(c)8
Dividend	(Ldr)05/07/91	(Pay)05/08/91	Amt(c)1
Interim No 11	(Ldr)06/12/91	(Pay)21/12/91	Amt(c)8
Final No 13	(Ldr)26/06/92	(Pay)05/08/92	Amt(c)8

NUMBER OF EMPLOYEES : 900

CAPITAL STRUCTURE

	AUTHORISED	ISSUED
Ords no par value	40714750	23402531

FINANCIAL STATISTICS (AT FINANCIAL YEAR END)

(Amts in R'000)	1992 Feb	1991 Feb	1990 Feb	1989 Feb	1988 Feb
Ord S/H Int	57319	42659	37443	28393	25024
Long Trm Loans	163	97	130	226	108
Iss Ord Share	23403	21647	19447	19447	18970
Total Liab	70888	53954	49867	28476	11659
Current Liab	70725	53857	49737	28250	11551
Total Assets	116870	90827	81804	52421	29810
Intang Assets	11337	5786	5506	4448	6873
Current Assets	99077	78709	70966	43375	21094
Debtors	51196	39455	33201	19242	7186
Inventory	47500	38463	37196	23536	12789
Oper Profit	16967	14740	12471	7401	4917
Interest Paid	7622	5405	4187	1225	269
Tax Paid	87	780	1810	1106	830
Prf af Int&Tax	9258	8555	6474	5070	3818
Prf att Ord Sh	9248	8547	6369	4933	3818
Btm Line Earn	8232	8547	6369	4739	3818
Dividend Paid	3610	3309	2819	2334	1897
Mkt Prce(c) YE	400	310	270	170	180
Depreciation	1014	697	495	441	262

PER SHARE STATISTICS (CENTS)

Net Asst Val	196.48	170.34	164.23	123.13	95.68
Net Earnings	41.88	41.60	32.75	25.56	20.13
Dividends	16.00	16.00	14.50	12.00	10.00
Cash Flow	46.47	44.99	34.76	27.94	21.96

RATIOS AND OTHER INFORMATION

Mrk Cap(R000)	93612	67106	52507	33060	34146
Current Ratio	1.40	1.46	1.43	1.54	1.83
Quik/Acid Tst	0.73	0.75	0.68	0.70	0.72
Debt/Ass Rat	0.61	0.59	0.61	0.54	0.39
L T L Tot Ass	-	-	-	0.00	0.00
Debt to Eqity	1.23	1.26	1.33	1.00	0.46
Interest Cover	2.23	2.73	2.98	6.04	18.28
Ret on Assets	14.52	16.23	15.24	14.12	16.49
Ret on Equity%	16.13	20.04	17.01	17.37	15.26
Price/Earnings	9.55	7.45	8.24	6.65	8.94
Divid Cover	2.62	2.60	2.26	2.13	2.01
Divid Yield	4.00	5.16	5.37	7.06	5.56
Earning Yield%	10.47	13.42	12.13	15.04	11.18
NAV % Mrk Pr	49.12	54.95	60.82	72.43	53.16
Effec Tax Rate	0.93	8.36	0.65	6.28	1.74
Def Interval	3.58	2.26	4.03	2.50	0.94
Sus Grth Rate	9.84	12.28	9.48	9.15	7.68

SUBSIDIARY & ASSOCIATED COMPANIES

AFRICAN WHOLESALERS (PTY) LTD
BOLDEN (PTY) LTD
CATALOGUE CORPORATION HOLDINGS (PTY) LTD
CHARLES VELKES MAIL ORDER (1973) (PTY) L
FAMILY SELECTIONS (PTY) LTD
GRO-TIME MAIL ORDER DISTRIBUTION (PTY) L
HEALTH HOLDINGS (PTY) LTD
KANSAS CITY MAIL ORDER (PTY) LTD
KNOBBS MATERIAL CENTRE (PTY) LTD
MAGIC BY MAIL (PTY) LTD
MAS FINANCE (PTY) LTD
MAS MANAGEMENT SERVICES (PTY) LTD
MAS MARKETING (PTY) LTD
PAN AMERICAN MAIL ORDER (PTY) LTD
SUMARD SERVICES (PTY) LTD
TABLEKRAFT (PTY) LTD
VINCENT SHANTALL (PTY) LTD

INVESTMENTS

SOUTHERN SUN PARTNERSHIP (8.98%)

MASHOLD CONSOLIDATED INV HOLDINGS LTD

ABBREVIATION : MASCON

JSE SHORT CODE : MSN

SECTOR : Industrial-Retailers & Wholesalers

SHAREHOLDERS

Who Owns Whom's Assessment of the Identity of the Ultimate Controlling Shareholder: VAN EMBDEN FAMILY TRUSTS

SHAREHOLDER	PERCENTAGE 1992	1991
MARCO VAN EMBDEN TRUST	24.4	24.6
VAN EMBDEN A TRUST	24.2	24.3
VAN EMBDEN S	22.9	22.9
ANGLO AMERICAN GROUP PENS FUND	9.6	9.6
CMB NOM P/L	8.9	---
STD BANK NOM TVL P/L	3.3	---
SA MUTUAL	1.4	1.4
BOARD OF EXECUTORS NOM P/L	---	3.1
SANLAM	---	8.9
TOTAL	94.6	94.9

DIRECTORS :
BIERMANN HH ADMIRAL,GETZ K ,GROSS S
STEIN R (Deputy Chairman)
VAN EMBDEN H (Chairman)
VAN EMBDEN M (Managing Director)

REGISTRATION NUMBER : 88/03352/06

REGISTERED OFFICE
African Wholesalers Centre, Jack Craig Street
Foreshore, Cape Town
8001
TEL: 021-25 2690
FAX: 021-419 5780

TRANSFER SECRETARY
Mercantile Registrars Ltd
P O Box 1053, Johannesburg
2000
TEL: 011-333 8181

COMPANY SECRETARY
B L Taylor

NATURE OF BUSINESS
An investment holding company with a controlling interest in JSE-quoted MAS Holdings. The group is involved in direct marketing & mail order.

BANKERS :
First National Bank of SA Ltd, Volkskas Ltd
Standard Bank of SA Ltd, Senbank

AUDITORS :
Kessel Feinstein

FAMILIAR BRAND NAMES
N/A

CONTRIBUTION BY ACTIVITY
N/A

YEAR END : February

DIVIDEND : Ords no par value

Interim No 5	(Ldr)23/11/90	(Pay)13/12/90	Amt(c)7
Final No 6	(Ldr)22/02/91	(Pay)05/04/91	Amt(c)8
Dividend No 7	(Ldr)05/07/91	(Pay)05/08/91	Amt(c)1
Final No 9	(Ldr)26/06/92	(Pay)05/08/92	Amt(c)8

NUMBER OF EMPLOYEES : 900

CAPITAL STRUCTURE

	AUTHORISED	ISSUED
Ords no par value	40000000	13541522

FINANCIAL STATISTICS (AT FINANCIAL YEAR END)

(Amts in R'000)	1992 Feb	1991 Feb	1990 Feb	1989 Feb	1988
Ord S/H Int	29782	29782	23649	23649	31428
Iss Ord Share	13542	13542	11042	11042	14285
Total Liab	-	-	-	1	-
Current Liab	-	-	-	1	-
Total Assets	29782	29782	23649	23650	31428
Prf af Int&Tax	2167	1991	1601	1325	-
Prf att Ord Sh	2167	1991	1601	1325	-
Btm Line Earn	2167	1991	1601	1325	-
Dividend Paid	2167	1991	1601	1325	-
Mkt Prce(c) YE	380	305	260	165	-

PER SHARE STATISTICS (CENTS)

Net Asst Val	219.92	219.92	214.17	214.17	220.01
Net Earnings	16.00	16.00	14.50	12.00	-
Dividends	16.00	16.00	14.50	12.00	-
Cash Flow	16.00	14.70	14.50	12.00	-

RATIOS AND OTHER INFORMATION

Mrk Cap(R000)	51460	41303	28709	18219	-
Debt/Ass Rat	-	-	-	0.00	-
Debt to Eqity	-	-	-	0.00	-
Ret on Assets	7.28	6.69	6.77	5.60	-
Ret on Equity%	7.28	6.69	6.77	5.60	-
Price/Earnings	23.75	19.06	17.93	13.75	-
Divid Cover	1.00	1.00	1.00	1.00	-
Divid Yield	4.21	5.25	5.58	7.27	-
Earning Yield%	4.21	5.25	5.58	7.27	-
NAV % Mrk Pr	57.87	72.11	82.37	129.80	-
Sus Grth Rate	0.00	0.00	0.00	0.00	-

SUBSIDIARY & ASSOCIATED COMPANIES

MAS HOLDINGS LTD

INVESTMENTS

None

MASHONALAND HOLDINGS LTD

ABBREVIATION : MASHONA

SECTOR : Zimbabwe Stock Exchange

SHAREHOLDERS

Who Owns Whom's Assessment of the Identity of the Ultimate Controlling Shareholder:
OLD MUTUAL INV CORP / INSTITUTIONS

SHAREHOLDER	PERCENTAGE 1992	1991
OLD MUTUAL INV CORP (PVT) LTD	20.9	—
FIRST NOM PVT LTD	19.3	—
SECURITY NOM LTD	5.1	—
ELECTRICAL SYSTEMS PVT LTD	4.4	—
NAT RAILWAYS OF ZIM CONTR PENS FUND	4.3	—
FIRST MUTUAL LIFE ASSURE SOC OF ZIM	4.0	—
FIDELITY LIFE ASSURE OF ZIM PVT LTD	3.2	—
MINING INDUSTRY PENS FUND	2.7	—
NORTHCHART INV LTD	1.9	—
TRUST NOM (PVT) LTD	1.9	—
ZIMBABWE REINSURANCE CORP LTD	1.7	—
SOUTHAMPTON ASSURE CO ZIM LTD	1.2	—
TOTAL	70.6	—

DIRECTORS :
BOTSH AA ,BREMNER MG ,BROOK JE ,CRAGG EA
DURLING JA ,HARDY TC (Chairman)
JOUGHIN MJ (Managing Director),JUMBE PA
MAHSUMBA WB ,NICHOLSON AK

REGISTERED OFFICE
Cnr Cripps/Kelvin Roads, Graniteside
Harare, Zimbabwe

TEL: 796261/6
FAX: 708019

TRANSFER SECRETARY
First Transfer Secretaries (Pvt) Ltd
P O Box 437, Bulawayo
Zimbabwe

TEL: 092634 - 702905

COMPANY SECRETARY
A K Nicholson

NATURE OF BUSINESS
MASHONALAND HOLDINGS, a holding company incorporated in Zimbabwe,whose subsidiaries and divisions operate in the engineering and electrical manufac turing sectors,including stainless steel castings, tools,wire products,electric motors,fans and mach inery for the agricultural industry and plastics recycling and production of plastic containers for the agro-chemical sector.Subsidiaries are also con cerned with the manufacture of circuit breakers. and contractors.Subsidiaries are also involved in

BANKERS :
N/A

AUDITORS :
Coopers & Lybrand

FAMILIAR BRAND NAMES
N/A

CONTRIBUTION BY ACTIVITY
N/A

YEAR END : March

DIVIDEND :Ords Z$0,50

Dividend	(Ldr)06/12/91	(Pay)13/12/91	Amt(c)6
Dividend	(Ldr)03/07/92	(Pay)17/07/92	Amt(c)8

CAPITAL STRUCTURE

	AUTHORISED	ISSUED
Ords Z$0,50	150000000	120509480

FINANCIAL STATISTICS (AT FINANCIAL YEAR END)

(Amts in Z$)	1992 Mar	1991 Mar
Ord S/H Int	223996	115545
Long Trm Loans	51976	38686
Iss Ord Share	120509	42007
Total Liab	148437	94387
Current Liab	96461	55701
Total Assets	372433	209932
Current Assets	166054	81583
Debtors	47578	29280
Inventory	98360	52264
Turnover	257855	163403
Oper Profit	51782	30208
Interest Paid	6377	4880
Tax Paid	6500	27
Prf af Int&Tax	38905	25301
Prf att Ord Sh	35858	24615
Btm Line Earn	35858	17865
Dividend Paid	16874	6726
Depreciation	16243	8841

PER SHARE STATISTICS (CENTS)

Net Asst Val	185.87	275.06
Net Earnings	34.00	29.90
Dividends	14.00	8.00
Cash Flow	49.43	79.64

RATIOS AND OTHER INFORMATION

Current Ratio	1.72	1.46
Quik/Acid Tst	0.70	0.53
A/C Rec T/ovr	5.42	5.58
Tot Ass T/ovr	0.69	0.78
Debt/Ass Rat	0.37	0.41
L T L Tot Ass	0.11	0.15
Debt to Eqity	0.62	0.75
Interest Cover	8.12	6.19
Oper Prof Mrg	20.08	18.49
Net Prof Marg%	13.91	15.06
Ret on Assets	13.90	14.39
Ret on Equity%	16.01	21.30
Divid Cover	2.43	3.74
Effec Tax Rate	14.32	0.11
Def Interval	1.48	1.15
Sus Grth Rate	8.48	15.48

SUBSIDIARY & ASSOCIATED COMPANIES

AIR TECHNICIANS (PVT) LTD (33%)
COMMAND SECURITY (PVT) LTD
ENGINEERING & ELECTRICAL HOLDINGS LTD
SHAW-CARTER COMPANY (PVT) LTD (49%)
SPRAY-TECH (PTY) LTD (BOTSWANA)
WILLDALE (PRIVATE) LTD
ZIMBABWE TIMBER PRODUCTS (PRIVATE) LTD

INVESTMENTS

None

MASONITE (AFRICA) LTD

ABBREVIATION : MASONITE

JSE SHORT CODE : MAS

SECTOR : Industrial-Building & Construction

SHAREHOLDERS

Who Owns Whom's Assessment of the Identity of the Ultimate Controlling Shareholder: INTERNATIONAL PAPER COMPANY (USA)

SHAREHOLDER	PERCENTAGE 1992	1991
MASONITE CORP	66.7	66.7
STD BANK NOM TVL P/L	7.2	---
WORKMENS COMPENS COMMISSIONER IN TRUST	4.2	---
AFRICAN OXYGEN LTD PENS FUND	3.6	---
MOORE P H	3.1	3.1
FIRST NAT NOM P/L	---	1.3
SA MUTUAL	---	4.1
PLATE GLASS & SHATTERPRUFE IND LTD	---	9.3
TOTAL	84.8	84.5

DIRECTORS :
COHEN LAH ,FARACI JV ,O'GRADY S DE C
RAUBENHEIMER FJ ,SPALT HA ,THOMAS WD
WILSON AH (Chairman & Managing Dir.

REGISTRATION NUMBER : 05/15502/06

REGISTERED OFFICE
14th Floor, Nedbank Centre, Durban Club Place
Durban
4001
TEL: 031-304 3231
FAX: 031-304 3826

TRANSFER SECRETARY
Central Registrars Ltd
P O Box 4844, Johannesburg
2000
TEL: 011-331 0051

COMPANY SECRETARY
D S Cooper

NATURE OF BUSINESS
The company manufactures hardboard, insulation board, cryogenic mineral wool, wood and mineral fibre ceiling panels & decorative wall panelling and owns and develops forests. Its subsidiary manufactures modular housing and shelter units.

BANKERS :
Nedperm Bank Ltd, Standard Bank of SA Ltd

AUDITORS :
Arthur Andersen & Co

FAMILIAR BRAND NAMES
COUNTRY WEST,CRATER,LEGACY,LUNAR,MASONITE
OAKTONE,ORBIT,ORLEANS,SOUNDSTOP,TIMBAPLANK

CONTRIBUTION BY ACTIVITY
N/A

YEAR END : December

DIVIDEND : Ords 50c

Interim No 38	(Ldr)07/09/90	(Pay)28/09/90	Amt(c)20
Final No 39	(Ldr)01/03/91	(Pay)22/03/91	Amt(c)23
Interim No 40	(Ldr)13/09/91	(Pay)04/10/91	Amt(c)25
Final No 41	(Ldr)28/02/92	(Pay)20/03/92	Amt(c)35

NUMBER OF EMPLOYEES : 1738

CAPITAL STRUCTURE

	AUTHORISED	ISSUED
Ords 50c	8000000	6817558
"A" 5,5% Cum Red Prefs R2	235000	0
"B" 6% Cum Red Prefs R2	115000	0

FINANCIAL STATISTICS (AT FINANCIAL YEAR END)

(Amts in R'000)	1991 Dec	1990 Dec	1989 Dec	1988 Dec	1987 Dec
Ord S/H Int	59778	48356	43893	38196	31472
Long Trm Loans	18006	25032	14140	8362	7464
Iss Ord Share	6818	6818	6818	6818	6750
Total Liab	42887	41358	30559	24172	20742
Current Liab	24881	16326	16419	15810	13278
Total Assets	101686	88690	73382	61253	52214
Intang Assets	979	1024	1070	1115	*
Current Assets	47967	39500	35898	32410	26020
Debtors	29928	21989	19959	14230	10416
Inventory	17965	17511	14591	11166	8215
Turnover	126488	113087	102010	90384	74314
Oper Profit	19605	12106	15358	16099	9998
Interest Paid	2210	2036	214	-	-
Tax Paid	5983	2675	5629	7024	3225
Prf af int&Tax	11412	7395	9515	9075	6773
Prf att Ord Sh	11412	7395	9515	9075	6773
Btm Line Earn	15512	7395	9515	9755	7630
Dividend Paid	4090	2932	3818	4568	4806
Mkt Prce(c) YE	950	700	1100	1425	700
Depreciation	5105	4180	3516	2982	2791

PER SHARE STATISTICS (CENTS)

Net Asst Val	862.41	694.22	628.09	543.87	466.25
Net Earnings	167.00	108.00	140.00	134.00	42.00
Dividends	60.00	43.00	56.00	67.00	72.00
Cash Flow	270.71	210.69	198.93	196.90	143.16

RATIOS AND OTHER INFORMATION

Mrk Cap(R000)	64771	47726	74998	97157	47250
Current Ratio	1.93	2.42	2.19	2.05	1.96
Quik/Acid Tst	1.21	1.35	1.30	1.34	1.34
A/C Rec T/ovr	4.23	5.14	5.11	6.35	7.13
Tot Ass T/ovr	1.24	1.28	1.39	1.48	1.42
Debt/Ass Rat	0.29	0.34	0.30	0.26	0.26
L T L Tot Ass	0.05	0.15	0.07	0.00	0.01
Debt to Eqity	0.50	0.62	0.50	0.42	0.43
Interest Cover	8.87	5.95	71.77	-	-
Oper Prof Mrg	15.50	10.71	15.06	17.81	13.45
Net Prof Marg%	9.02	6.54	9.33	10.04	9.11
Ret on Assets	19.28	13.65	20.93	26.28	19.15
Ret on Equity%	19.09	15.29	21.68	23.76	21.52
Price/Earnings	5.69	6.48	7.86	10.63	16.67
Divid Cover	2.78	2.51	2.50	2.00	0.58
Divid Yield	6.32	6.14	5.09	4.70	10.29
Earning Yield%	17.58	15.43	12.73	9.40	6.00
NAV % Mrk Pr	90.78	99.17	57.10	38.17	66.61
Effec Tax Rate	23.80	-0.19	34.45	36.51	33.60
Def Interval	0.49	1.11	0.61	0.00	0.03
Sus Grth Rate	12.25	9.23	12.98	11.80	6.25

SUBSIDIARY & ASSOCIATED COMPANIES

EZEBILT PRODUCTS (PTY) LTD

INVESTMENTS

None

MAST HOLDINGS LTD

ABBREVIATION : MAST

JSE SHORT CODE : MAT

SECTOR : Financial-Banks & Financial Services

SHAREHOLDERS

Who Owns Whom's Assessment of the Identity of the Ultimate Controlling Shareholder:
MANAGEMENT / CNA GALLO

SHAREHOLDER	PERCENTAGE 1992	1991
GALLO AFRICA LTD	30.9	30.9
SMBL NOM P/L	25.7	25.7
STD BANK NOM TVL P/L	15.3	22.5
TEAL RECORD CO LTD	7.0	7.0
GALLO INV HOLDINGS LTD	5.0	---
OLESEN H	1.9	---
CROSBY A G	1.6	---
NUPEN G R B	1.3	1.4
BIRD C D	1.3	---
DELOITTE HASKINS & SELLS	---	6.2
FIRST NAT NOM P/L	---	1.9
TOTAL	90.0	95.7

DIRECTORS :
CHERRY AR ,CUZEN ADL
DALLAMORE SWB (Executive Chairman),DYER DD
JOOSTE DJ ,MCBRIDE RW (Financial Director)
WALTERS HJ

REGISTRATION NUMBER : 81/07265/06

REGISTERED OFFICE
Deloitte Pim Goldby House, 2 Rissik Street
Johannesburg
2001
TEL: 011-880 3900
FAX: 011-880 3380

TRANSFER SECRETARY
Rand Registrars Ltd
P O Box 82549, Southdale
2135
TEL: 011-835 1016

COMPANY SECRETARY
R W McBride

NATURE OF BUSINESS
The group is active in management, motivational financial, computer and communication training, and supplies hardware for executive calender/planning systems.The group also handles recruitment of senior personnel,executive search, salary and benefit surveys.

BANKERS :
Standard Bank of SA Ltd, Nedbank Ltd

AUDITORS :
Deloitte Pim Goldby

FAMILIAR BRAND NAMES
N/A

CONTRIBUTION BY ACTIVITY
N/A

YEAR END : February

DIVIDEND : Ords 1c

Dividend No 3	(Ldr)11/05/90	(Pay)23/05/90	Amt(c)3.9
Dividend No 4	(Ldr)17/05/91	(Pay)04/06/91	Amt(c)3.9
Dividend No 5	(Ldr)22/05/92	(Pay)28/05/92	Amt(c)4.6

NUMBER OF EMPLOYEES : 100

CAPITAL STRUCTURE

	AUTHORISED	ISSUED
Ords 1c	25000000	21456118

FINANCIAL STATISTICS (AT FINANCIAL YEAR END)

(Amts in R'000)	1992 Feb	1991 Feb	1990 Feb	1989 Feb	1988
Ord S/H Int	4361	4183	3640	2750	3676
Long Trm Loans	1253	1379	1415	997	1016
Iss Ord Share	21456	21056	20566	17332	17332
Total Liab	7385	5775	4912	3299	2026
Current Liab	6132	4396	3497	2302	1010
Total Assets	11746	9359	7867	6049	7106
Intang Assets	*	599	685	*	*
Current Assets	9338	7075	6216	3419	2278
Debtors	4415	3402	3537	2370	-
Inventory	893	1122	894	512	2278
Turnover	23137	18378	15121	8419	4685
Oper Profit	2468	1865	2637	1581	1136
Interest Paid	22	49	70	-	63
Tax Paid	1227	691	1223	528	644
Prf af Int&Tax	1700	1365	1630	1102	629
Prf att Ord Sh	1700	1365	1630	1102	629
Btm Line Earn	1405	1448	1252	1102	629
Dividend Paid	987	837	833	520	416
Mkt Prce(c) YE	40	65	65	45	45
Depreciation	522	401	270	151	-

PER SHARE STATISTICS (CENTS)

Net Asst Val	20.33	17.02	14.37	15.87	21.21
Net Earnings	7.90	6.50	8.00	6.40	-
Dividends	4.60	3.90	3.90	3.00	-
Cash Flow	8.71	7.98	15.17	7.66	3.63

RATIOS AND OTHER INFORMATION

Mrk Cap(R000)	8582	13686	13368	7799	7799
Current Ratio	1.52	1.61	1.78	1.49	2.26
Quik/Acid Tst	1.38	1.35	1.52	1.26	-
A/C Rec T/ovr	5.24	5.40	4.28	3.55	-
Tot Ass T/ovr	1.97	1.96	1.92	1.39	0.66
Debt/Ass Rat	0.55	0.48	0.45	0.51	0.29
L T L Tot Ass	0.03	0.01	0.00	0.13	0.14
Debt to Eqity	1.47	1.07	0.97	1.12	0.55
Interest Cover	112.36	38.14	37.67	-	21.21
Oper Prof Mrg	10.67	10.15	17.44	18.78	24.25
Net Prof Marg%	7.35	7.43	10.78	13.09	13.43
Ret on Assets	25.11	22.49	37.16	26.95	18.80
Ret on Equity%	38.98	32.63	44.78	40.07	17.11
Price/Earnings	5.06	10.00	8.13	7.03	-
Divid Cover	1.72	1.67	2.05	2.13	-
Divid Yield	11.50	6.00	6.00	6.67	-
Earning Yield%	19.75	10.00	12.31	14.22	-
NAV % Mrk Pr	50.81	26.19	22.11	35.26	47.13
Effec Tax Rate	37.46	38.11	1.23	2.88	60.02
Def Interval	0.51	0.54	0.15	0.80	1.62
Sus Grth Rate	16.35	12.62	21.90	21.16	5.79

SUBSIDIARY & ASSOCIATED COMPANIES

BUSINESS LEARNING SYSTEM (PTY) LTD
LEXPRESS DATA (PTY) LTD
MAST COMMERCIAL OPERATIONS (PTY) LTD
TIME SYSTEM SA (PTY) LTD

INVESTMENTS

DE BEERS/CENTENARY (1400 SH)

MATHIESON & ASHLEY HOLDINGS LTD

ABBREVIATION : MATH-ASH

JSE SHORT CODE : MAH

SECTOR : Industrial-Furniture & Household

SHAREHOLDERS

Who Owns Whom's Assessment of the Identity of the Ultimate Controlling Shareholder:
RINGO FAMILY VIA VESTACOR LTD

SHAREHOLDER	PERCENTAGE 1992	1991
VESTACOR LTD	74.4	74.4
CMB NOM P/L	4.1	---
STD BANK NOM TVL P/L	2.8	2.8
MATHIESON & ASHLEY HLDGS SHARE TRUST	2.5	3.1
HELYAR D W H	2.0	1.5
SEDOW HOLDINGS P/L	1.6	1.6
STOCKSHARE NOM P/L	1.2	---
MENBLACK NOM P/L	---	1.1
MOMENTUM LIFE ASSURE LTD	---	1.8
SANLAM	---	4.1
TOTAL	88.7	90.3

DIRECTORS :
ANDREWS GS DR,DATNOW CS ,DAVIES NO
DE LA H BECK J (Managing Director)
GANT HM (Financial Director),HELYAR DWH
JANUTSCH MJ ,RINGO AL (Chairman

REGISTRATION NUMBER : 02/00093/06

REGISTERED OFFICE
25 Bath Avenue, Rosebank, Johannesburg
2196
TEL: 011-880 8080
FAX: 011-880 5858

TRANSFER SECRETARY
Central Registrars Ltd
P O Box 4844, Johannesburg
2000
TEL: 011-331 0051

COMPANY SECRETARY
Mathieson & Ashley Management Services (Pty) Ltd

NATURE OF BUSINESS
The company is an investment holding company and the main businesses through subsidiaries are the design, manufacture and distribution of office furniture.

BANKERS :
First National Bank of SA Ltd
Standard Bank of SA Ltd
Central Merchant Bank Ltd, Nedcor Bank Ltd

AUDITORS :
Ernst & Young

FAMILIAR BRAND NAMES
ADLINE,AIR SPACE,ANGLO DUTCH,BASYS
BROWN & NEETHLING,CITADEL,CONCEPT EXECUTIVE
DASHING,EBA,FINESEAT,FRANCOTYPE,FS,GIROFLEX
HALL-WELTER,KH,LAMINA,LISTA,MAFAX,MODEM,MS
OFFEX,OFFICEMART,OKAFOLD,OUTLINE,PFE,PLANAX
QUANTUM,SITLINE,SL,THEMA,TRIMODE,UNITY

CONTRIBUTION BY ACTIVITY
Office Furniture Operations (100.0%)

YEAR END : June

DIVIDEND :Ords 2,5c

Interim No 103	(Ldr)12/04/90	(Pay)27/04/90	Amt(c)8
Final No 104	(Ldr)26/10/90	(Pay)09/11/90	Amt(c)12

NUMBER OF EMPLOYEES : 1600

CAPITAL STRUCTURE

	AUTHORISED	ISSUED
Ords 2,5c	15200000	11460000
6% Cum Prefs R2	60000	60000

FINANCIAL STATISTICS (AT FINANCIAL YEAR END)

(Amts in R'000)	1992 Jun	1991 Jun	1990 Jun	1989 Jun	1988 Jun
Ord S/H Int	21988	23193	24483	22121	17862
Long Trm Loans	25649	31264	32667	22428	15052
Iss Ord Share	11460	11460	11460	2865	2865
Total Liab	57688	55495	57449	45110	33750
Current Liab	32039	24231	24782	22682	18698
Total Assets	79676	78688	81932	67231	51612
Current Assets	52194	50292	58208	54717	46158
Debtors	26006	23960	26927	24486	17730
Inventory	25861	24977	25137	18993	15328
Turnover	145681	125024	134822	99395	39019
Oper Profit	698	2359	11010	14881	7883
Interest Paid	5135	3542	2966	3061	214
Tax Paid	40	-374	391	219	3872
Prf af Int&Tax	-2829	27	9297	12189	3797
Prf att Ord Sh	-741	378	5748	7827	3790
Btm Line Earn	-2025	-1290	4854	6551	11876
Dividend Paid	-	-	2292	2292	1420
Mkt Prce(c) YE	225	250	1850	1375	1425
Depreciation	5050	3745	3945	1728	667

PER SHARE STATISTICS (CENTS)

Net Asst Val	191.87	202.38	213.64	772.11	623.46
Net Earnings	-6.50	3.30	50.20	68.30	135.20
Dividends	-	-	20.00	20.00	50.00
Cash Flow	37.71	31.50	86.01	83.52	156.72

RATIOS AND OTHER INFORMATION

Mrk Cap(R000)	25785	28650	212010	39394	40826
Current Ratio	1.63	2.08	2.35	2.41	2.47
Quik/Acid Tst	0.82	1.04	1.33	1.57	1.65
A/C Rec T/ovr	5.60	5.22	5.01	4.06	2.20
Tot Ass T/ovr	1.83	1.59	1.65	1.48	0.76
Debt/Ass Rat	0.52	0.47	0.45	0.47	0.43
L T L Tot Ass	0.12	0.16	0.15	0.13	0.07
Debt to Eqity	1.88	1.60	1.50	1.42	1.25
Interest Cover	0.14	0.67	3.71	4.86	36.84
Oper Prof Mrg	0.48	1.89	8.17	14.97	20.20
Net Prof Marg%	-0.51	0.30	4.26	7.87	9.71
Ret on Assets	2.94	4.06	15.44	23.01	15.27
Ret on Equity%	-3.37	1.63	23.48	35.38	21.22
Price/Earnings	-34.62	75.76	36.85	20.13	10.54
Divid Cover	-	-	2.51	3.42	2.70
Divid Yield	-	-	1.08	1.45	3.51
Earning Yield%	-2.89	1.32	2.71	4.97	9.49
NAV % Mrk Pr	85.27	80.95	11.55	56.15	43.75
Effec Tax Rate	-	-	2.34	0.75	51.58
Def Interval	3.36	3.72	1.22	0.93	0.79
Sus Grth Rate	-3.37	1.63	14.12	25.02	13.27

SUBSIDIARY & ASSOCIATED COMPANIES

ANGLO DUTCH (PTY) LTD (50%)
BRIMART INVESTMENTS HOLDINGS GROUP (50%)
BROWN & NEETHLING (PTY) LTD (50%)
BROWN & NEETHLING (TVL) (PTY) LTD (50%)
BROWN & NEETHLING CONTROLLING (PTY) LTD (50%)
BROWN & NEETHLING MANAGEMENT CO (PTY) LT (50%)
COMPE COMPUTER & COMPONENTS LTD (HK)
DASHING OFFICE FURNITURE (PTY) LTD (50%)
DOF FURNISHERS (PTY) LTD
DOF MANUFACTURING (PTY) LTD
EUROPLAN INVESTMENTS LIMITED (BVI)
EUROPLAN MANAGEMENT SERVICES LTD (UK)
FINESEAT MANUFACTURERS (PTY) LTD (50%)
FRIKKIE NEETHLING BELEGGINGS (PTY) LTD (50%)
GOVER DANDO & CO. (PTY) LTD
INDOPLAN TRADING LTD (UK)
INTERVISION TRADING CORPORATION (BVI)
KALLENBACH-HENDLER (PTY) LTD (50%)
MATHIESON & ASHLEY (PTY) LTD
OFFEX OFFICE FURNITURE (PTY) LTD (50%)
STEELEX WIRE PRODUCTS (PTY) LTD (50%)
WESTCHESTER TRUST (BVI)
WOODMET (PTY) LTD (50%)

INVESTMENTS

None

MAXMECH MECHANICAL SEALS LTD

ABBREVIATION : MAXMECH

JSE SHORT CODE : MXM

SECTOR : Development Capital Market

SHAREHOLDERS

Who Owns Whom's Assessment of the Identity of the Ultimate Controlling Shareholder: DIRECTORS

SHAREHOLDER	PERCENTAGE 1992	1991
DETTMANN I J	57.8	24.8
FRANKLE P M	10.6	10.6
LOI G	1.4	1.4
REED B S	1.2	1.2
REED W G	1.1	---
GROBLER D G	---	32.2
TOTAL	72.0	70.1

DIRECTORS :
DETTMANN IJ (Chairman & Managing Dir.),ETTER M
GROBLER DG ,WALTERS AC

REGISTRATION NUMBER : 80/00602/06

REGISTERED OFFICE
92 Butler Road, Nuffield
Springs
1559
TEL: 011-818 2136
FAX: 011-818 2280

TRANSFER SECRETARY
Rand Registrars Ltd
P O Box 82549, Southdale
2135
TEL: 011-835 1016

COMPANY SECRETARY
M J van der Merwe (Mrs)

NATURE OF BUSINESS
Manufacture, marketing, distribution & servicing of sealing systems used by process and related industries on rotating equipment.

BANKERS :
Standard Bank of SA Ltd

AUDITORS :
Auret Van Wyk

FAMILIAR BRAND NAMES
MAXMECH,SEALOL

CONTRIBUTION BY ACTIVITY
N/A

YEAR END : February

DIVIDEND :15/07/91

NUMBER OF EMPLOYEES : 60

CAPITAL STRUCTURE

	AUTHORISED	ISSUED
Ords no par value	6000000	5000000

FINANCIAL STATISTICS (AT FINANCIAL YEAR END)

(Amts in R'000)	1992 Feb	1991 Feb	1990 Feb	1989 Feb	1988 Feb
Ord S/H Int	721	681	1240	1195	1085
Long Trm Loans	263	371	449	641	577
Iss Ord Share	5000	5000	5000	5000	5000
Total Liab	1636	1252	1696	1757	1480
Current Liab	1373	881	1247	1116	903
Total Assets	2357	1933	2936	2945	2565
Intang Assets	*	*	*	7	*
Current Assets	1969	1491	2408	2152	1829
Debtors	754	714	1148	994	877
Inventory	1214	776	1242	1076	951
Turnover	4791	4495	5882	4612	4301
Oper Profit	228	-375	310	312	553
Interest Paid	198	198	224	171	107
Tax Paid	-10	-14	35	61	228
Prf af Int&Tax	40	-559	51	80	218
Prf att Ord Sh	40	-559	51	80	218
Btm Line Earn	40	-559	25	110	218
Mkt Prce(c) YE	8	10	14	21	90
Depreciation	147	156	203	241	230

PER SHARE STATISTICS (CENTS)

Net Asst Val	14.42	13.62	24.80	23.76	21.70
Net Earnings	0.80	-11.20	0.50	2.20	4.40
Cash Flow	3.38	-8.34	4.72	6.26	8.70

RATIOS AND OTHER INFORMATION

Mrk Cap(R000)	400	500	700	1050	4500
Current Ratio	1.43	1.69	1.93	1.93	2.03
Quik/Acid Tst	0.55	0.81	0.94	0.96	0.97
A/C Rec T/ovr	6.35	6.30	5.12	4.64	4.90
Tot Ass T/ovr	2.03	2.33	2.00	1.57	1.68
Debt/Ass Rat	0.67	0.61	0.55	0.57	0.56
L T L Tot Ass	0.09	0.16	0.13	0.19	0.20
Debt to Eqity	2.20	1.74	1.30	1.41	1.31
Interest Cover	1.15	-1.89	1.38	1.82	5.17
Oper Prof Mrg	4.76	-8.34	5.27	6.76	12.86
Net Prof Marg%	0.83	-12.44	0.87	1.73	5.07
Ret on Assets	9.67	-19.40	10.56	10.59	21.56
Ret on Equity%	4.39	-64.18	3.57	5.78	17.10
Price/Earnings	10.00	-0.89	28.00	9.55	20.45
Earning Yield%	10.00	-112.00	3.57	10.48	4.89
NAV % Mrk Pr	180.25	136.20	177.14	113.14	24.11
Effec Tax Rate	26.67	-	61.63	48.94	54.04
Def Interval	5.99	-1.77	4.39	4.35	2.20
Sus Grth Rate	5.55	-82.09	4.11	6.69	20.09

SUBSIDIARY & ASSOCIATED COMPANIES

MAXMECH ENGINEERING (PTY) LTD
MAXMECH MECHANICAL SEALS (NATAL) (PTY) L
MAXMECH MECHANICAL SEALS (VAAL) (PTY) LT
MAXMECH PACKING (PTY) LTD
MAXMECH PROPERTY INVESTMENTS (PTY) LTD

INVESTMENTS

None

MCCARTHY GROUP LTD

ABBREVIATION : MCCARTHY

JSE SHORT CODE : MCR

SECTOR : Industrial-Retailers & Wholesalers

SHAREHOLDERS

Who Owns Whom's Assessment of the Identity of the Ultimate Controlling Shareholder: ANGLO AMERICAN

SHAREHOLDER	PERCENTAGE 1992	1991
INNISFALLEN INV P/L	9.8	11.5
DIDO NOM LTD	8.6	10.2
RESIDENT NOM LTD	8.0	---
CMB NOM P/L	7.7	---
TAURUS NOM LTD	6.6	7.8
FYNBOS TRUST	5.9	---
ENGINEERING INDUSTRIES PENS FUND	5.0	5.9
FERMAIN NOM LTD	4.9	5.8
METAL IND GROUP PENS FUND	4.1	4.8
PETARD NOM LTD	3.2	3.8
SA MUTUAL	3.1	4.9
MAJORBEE INV P/L	2.8	---
STD BANK NOM TVL P/L	2.7	1.3
EIGHTY ONE MAIN STREET NOM LTD	2.5	1.3
ROSENBERG T	1.4	---
SIXTY SIX MARSHALL STREET NOM P/L	1.4	---
FIRST NAT NOM P/L	1.1	---
ABSA NOM P/L	1.1	---
I & J PENS FUND	1.0	1.2
KAMINER B	---	1.2
ANGLO AMERICAN IND CORP LTD	---	9.4
BOARD OF EXECUTORS NOM P/L	---	1.0
SANLAM	---	8.3
TOTAL	80.9	78.3

DIRECTORS :
BECK WF DE LA H ,BOYD L ,BULLETT BE ,HULL CJ
MCCARTHY BC (Chairman),MCCARTHY JR
PARKHURST WR (Executive Director),RILEY DB
ROSENBERG T ,SAVILLE D
SWART TJ (Managing Director),TRAHAR AJ

REGISTRATION NUMBER : 05/08191/06

REGISTERED OFFICE
McCarthy Centre, 203 North Ridge Road
Durban
4001
TEL: 031-29 0222
FAX: 031-29 0950

TRANSFER SECRETARY
Mercantile Registrars Ltd
P O Box 1053, Johannesburg
2000
TEL: 011-333 8181

COMPANY SECRETARY
B J Clouston

NATURE OF BUSINESS
A retail motor organisation. The Group retails particular new vehicle franchises & used vehicles, together with the attendant sales of accessories, parts & service, and imports & distributes motor cycles, industrial engines, generators, outboard motors, marine accessories & boats. Activities include truck and car rental, full maintenance leasing and auctioning of motor vehicles. The group also has extensive property interests, which are leased to its trading divisions.

BANKERS :
Standard Bank of SA Ltd
FirstCorp Merchant Bank Ltd

AUDITORS :
Deloitte & Touche

FAMILIAR BRAND NAMES
ATKINSONS TOYOTA,AUTOHAUS
BURCHMORES CAR AUCTION,CAR BAR
CITY MOTOR GROUP,DAN PERKINS,DAYTONA NISSAN
ENDURO,FLEETRENT,FORSDICKS,GERVIS TOYOTA
GROSVENOR FORD,MAZDA,OLYMPIC TOYOTA
PERKINS TRUCK HIRE,ROLLS-ROYCE
SUPREME TRUCK RENTAL,UNO

CONTRIBUTION BY ACTIVITY
New Passenger (% of total unit sales) (22.4%)
New Commercials (36.7%)
Used Vehicles (37.8%)
W/Sale Motor Cycles (3.1%)

YEAR END : June

DIVIDEND : Ords 10c

Interim No 98	(Ldr)24/02/90	(Pay)09/03/90	Amt(c)7.5
Final No 99	(Ldr)21/09/90	(Pay)12/10/90	Amt(c)13.5
Interim No 100	(Ldr)22/02/91	(Pay)28/02/91	Amt(c)10
Final No 101	(Ldr)20/09/91	(Pay)11/10/91	Amt(c)13.5
Interim No 102	(Ldr)28/02/92	(Pay)06/03/92	Amt(c)7.5
Final No 103	(Ldr)18/09/92	(Pay)09/10/92	Amt(c)13.5

NUMBER OF EMPLOYEES : 5832

CAPITAL STRUCTURE

	AUTHORISED	ISSUED
Ords 10c	172500000	110268200
5,5% Cum Prefs R2	150000	150000
14,5% Senior Conv Debs 500c	28053334	28053334
Junior Conv Debs 500c	34026666	34026666

FINANCIAL STATISTICS (AT FINANCIAL YEAR END)

(Amts in R'000)	1992 Jun	1991 Jun	1990 Jun	1989 Jun	1988 Jun
Ord S/H Int	261319	231503	197955	163321	133235
Long Trm Loans	28855	68699	67293	60392	36439
Iss Ord Share	86864	86504	85900	85332	85332
Total Liab	340698	332206	283921	277111	182226
Current Liab	311843	263507	216628	216719	145787
Total Assets	592822	561860	478479	434932	315461
Intang Assets	9195	1849	3397	5500	*
Current Assets	464700	466261	381754	336438	229375
Debtors	103072	84389	91326	77976	56969
Inventory	343813	310783	268828	249254	168976
Turnover	3072674	2893951	2738780	2385305	1769525
Oper Profit	118422	120880	126272	117815	62140
Interest Paid	32439	26417	39930	29844	5108
Tax Paid	44899	46258	39216	43349	27607
Prf af Int&Tax	42856	52926	49807	49461	29425
Prf att Ord Sh	44135	51445	50148	52645	30913
Btm Line Earn	23153	52954	49197	48006	33502
Dividend Paid	18238	20302	18027	17920	11093
Mkt Prce(c) YE	480	475	310	270	138
Depreciation	2592	2244	2468	1937	1318

PER SHARE STATISTICS (CENTS)

Net Asst Val	290.25	265.48	226.49	184.95	156.14
Net Earnings	50.90	59.80	58.60	61.70	181.10
Dividends	21.00	23.50	21.00	21.00	65.00
Cash Flow	-2.35	61.62	66.24	81.19	46.14

RATIOS AND OTHER INFORMATION

Mrk Cap(R000)	416947	410894	266290	230396	117758
Current Ratio	1.49	1.77	1.76	1.55	1.57
Quik/Acid Tst	0.39	0.59	0.52	0.40	0.41
A/C Rec T/ovr	29.81	34.29	29.99	30.59	31.06
Tot Ass T/ovr	5.18	5.15	5.72	5.48	5.61
Debt/Ass Rat	0.55	0.51	0.49	0.54	0.50
L T L Tot Ass	0.03	0.04	0.04	0.04	0.04
Debt to Eqity	1.26	1.23	1.18	1.43	1.19
Interest Cover	3.68	4.59	3.19	4.00	12.17
Oper Prof Mrg	3.85	4.18	4.61	4.94	3.51
Net Prof Marg%	1.44	1.78	1.83	2.21	1.75
Ret on Assets	20.65	22.47	27.31	28.97	20.20
Ret on Equity%	16.89	22.22	25.33	32.23	23.20
Price/Earnings	9.43	7.94	5.29	4.38	0.76
Divid Cover	2.42	2.54	2.79	2.94	2.79
Divid Yield	4.38	4.95	6.77	7.78	47.10
Earning Yield%	10.60	12.59	18.90	22.85	131.23
NAV % Mrk Pr	60.47	55.89	73.06	68.50	113.14
Effec Tax Rate	44.27	46.84	35.88	26.16	33.13
Def Interval	-47.64	0.44	0.73	0.55	0.61
Sus Grth Rate	9.91	13.45	16.23	21.26	14.88

SUBSIDIARY & ASSOCIATED COMPANIES

MCCARTHY CAR BAR (NATAL) (PTY) LTD
MCCARTHY MOTOR HOLDINGS LTD
MCCARTHY RETAIL LTD
OLYMPIC MOTORS LTD

INVESTMENTS

None

MCCARTHY RETAIL LTD

ABBREVIATION : MCRTAIL

JSE SHORT CODE : MRD

SECTOR : Industrial-Retailers & Wholesalers

SHAREHOLDERS

Who Owns Whom's Assessment of the Identity of the Ultimate Controlling Shareholder: MCCARTHY

SHAREHOLDER	PERCENTAGE 1992	1991
FYNBOS TRUST	25.7	25.7
INVESTEC NOM P/L	13.3	13.4
MAJORBEE INV P/L	12.0	12.0
FIRST NAT NOM P/L	10.5	---
ROSENBERG T	6.1	6.1
STD BANK NOM TVL P/L	5.4	4.2
ABSA NOM P/L	4.7	---
CMB NOM P/L	3.1	---
EIGHTY ONE MAIN STREET NOM LTD	2.6	1.5
NEDBANK NOM LTD	2.4	3.0
SIBUL H	1.8	1.8
ELLERINE BROS P/L	1.0	1.0
SAFEGRO NOM P/L	---	1.0
GENBEL INV LTD	---	5.1
SANLAM	---	3.1
SMBL NOM P/L	---	1.3
FIRST NAT BANK GROUP PENS FUND	---	2.6
NON-FERROUS METAL WORKS SA P/L	---	7.7
TOTAL	88.6	89.5

DIRECTORS :
GATTER B MR (Financial Director)
ROSENBERG T MR (Executive Chairman)
SIBUL H MR (Executive Deputy Chairman)
WEIL CN MR (Managing Director)

REGISTRATION NUMBER : 91/03245/06

REGISTERED OFFICE
Prefcor House, 396 West Street
Durban
4001
TEL: 031-307 6642
FAX: 031-302 8030

TRANSFER SECRETARY
Mercantile Registrars Ltd
P O Box 1053, Johannesburg
2000
TEL: 011-333 8181

COMPANY SECRETARY
B Gatter

NATURE OF BUSINESS
The group conducts the business of selling durable & semi-durable consumer goods via 304 outlets. The major product categories are furniture, household appliances, sound equipment, television, flooring, garden and outdoor leisure goods, and clothing.

BANKERS :
First National Bank of SA Ltd

AUDITORS :
Arthur Andersen & Co

FAMILIAR BRAND NAMES
BALLY,BEARES,BEE GEE,CARDUCCI,FURNITURE GAME GAME,LEE,PRICE,SAVELLS,VAN HEUSSEN

CONTRIBUTION BY ACTIVITY
Beare Group (% Turnover) (61.7%)
Game Division (29.0%)
Clobea Division (Bee Gee) (9.0%)

YEAR END : June

DIVIDEND : Ords no par value

Interim No 1	(Ldr)21/02/92	(Pay)04/03/92	Amt(c)15
Final No 2	(Ldr)25/09/92	(Pay)07/10/92	Amt(c)15

NUMBER OF EMPLOYEES : 8000

CAPITAL STRUCTURE

	AUTHORISED	ISSUED
Ords no par value	150000000	39007000
Senior Stepped Coupon Unsec Conv	35066667	35066667
Jnr Stpd Cpn Unsec Sub Comp Conv	42533333	42533333

18% Unsec Sub Red Debs R5 (unlist	6200000	6200000

FINANCIAL STATISTICS (AT FINANCIAL YEAR END)

(Amts in R'000)	1992 Jun
Ord S/H Int	217357
Long Trm Loans	430974
Iss Ord Share	39007
Total Liab	709402
Current Liab	278428
Total Assets	559837
Intang Assets	366922
Current Assets	278825
Debtors	131681
Inventory	75732
Turnover	1218698
Oper Profit	130392
Interest Paid	55072
Tax Paid	31089
Prf af Int&Tax	71354
Prf att Ord Sh	40143
Btm Line Earn	40143
Dividend Paid	11702
Mkt Prce(c) YE	330
Depreciation	18778

PER SHARE STATISTICS (CENTS)

Net Asst Val	-383.43
Net Earnings	102.90
Dividends	30.00
Cash Flow	305.16

RATIOS AND OTHER INFORMATION

Mrk Cap(R000)	128723
Current Ratio	1.00
Quik/Acid Tst	0.73
A/C Rec T/ovr	9.25
Tot Ass T/ovr	2.18
Debt/Ass Rat	1.26
L T L Tot Ass	0.76
Debt to Eqity	3.23
Interest Cover	2.37
Oper Prof Mrg	10.70
Net Prof Marg%	3.29
Ret on Assets	27.94
Ret on Equity%	18.47
Price/Earnings	3.21
Divid Cover	3.43
Divid Yield	9.09
Earning Yield%	31.18
NAV % Mrk Pr	-116.19
Effec Tax Rate	1.86
Def Interval	1.26
Sus Grth Rate	13.08

SUBSIDIARY & ASSOCIATED COMPANIES

BEARE GROUP (PTY) LTD
BEARES LTD
BEASTORES (PTY) LTD (VENDA)
CLOBEA (PTY) LTD
GAME DISCOUNT WORLD (PTY) LTD
HAPPY HOMES (PTY) LTD
PREF-CREDIT (PTY) LTD
PREF-INFO (PTY) LTD
PREF-STORES (BOPHUTHATSWANA) (PTY) LTD
PREF-STORES (CISKEI) (PTY) LTD
PREF-TECH (PTY) LTD
PREFCOR EXECUTIVE DEVELOPMENT (PTY) LTD
PREFCOR PROPERTY PROJECTS (PTY) LTD
PRICE FURNITURE & APPLIANCE DISCOUNTERS
SAVELLS (BOTSWANA) (PTY) LTD
SAVELLS KANGWANE (PTY) LTD
SAVELLS KWAZULU LTD
SAVELLS QWAQUA LTD
SAVELLS SWAZILAND (PTY) LTD

INVESTMENTS

None

ME STORES HOLDINGS LTD

ABBREVIATION : MESTORE

JSE SHORT CODE : MSR

SECTOR : Development Capital Market

SHAREHOLDERS

Who Owns Whom's Assessment of the Identity of the Ultimate Controlling Shareholder: WEC & BS STEVENS VIA DARIEN INV P/L

SHAREHOLDER	PERCENTAGE 1992	1991
DARIEN INV P/L	73.0	73.0
SMK NOM P/L	13.3	13.3
ABBOTT A D	6.4	6.4
TOTAL	92.7	92.7

DIRECTORS :
RICHARDSON RS ,STEVENS BS ,STEVENS WEC (Chairman

REGISTRATION NUMBER : 60/03746/06

REGISTERED OFFICE
2nd Floor, Business Forum
62 Juta Street, Braamfontein, Johannesburg
2107
TEL: 011-403 5410
FAX: 011-339 7572

TRANSFER SECRETARY
Central Registrars Ltd
P O Box 4844, Johannesburg
2000
TEL: 011-331 0051

COMPANY SECRETARY
R S Richardson

NATURE OF BUSINESS
Retailer of outdoor and leisure equipment including camping, back packing, mountaineering and angling equipment and arms and ammunition. The company is also involved in the powerboating, yachting & water sports business.

BANKERS :
N/A

AUDITORS :
Coopers Theron Du Toit

FAMILIAR BRAND NAMES
CAMP & CLIMB,M E OUTDOOR,THE QUARTERDECK

CONTRIBUTION BY ACTIVITY
N/A

YEAR END : April

DIVIDEND :15/08/91

CAPITAL STRUCTURE

	AUTHORISED	ISSUED
Ords no par value	20000000	7560000

FINANCIAL STATISTICS (AT FINANCIAL YEAR END)

(Amts in R'000)	1991 Apr	1990 Apr	1989 Apr	1988 Apr	1987 Apr
Ord S/H Int	2026	2118	2360	2276	583
Long Trm Loans	217	214	72	-	461
Iss Ord Share	7560	7560	7560	7560	5560
Total Liab	2948	1948	1247	1612	1370
Current Liab	2731	1734	1175	1612	909
Total Assets	4814	3906	3447	3888	1953
Intang Assets	160	160	160	*	*
Current Assets	4483	3505	3160	3756	1927
Debtors	231	413	363	423	245
Inventory	4147	2696	2610	2326	1679
Turnover	10046	10778	10843	9898	5980
Oper Profit	54	-194	-90	335	412
Interest Paid	151	89	73	14	7
Tax Paid	-	-	-	99	-
Prf af Int&Tax	-92	-243	-76	222	405
Prf att Ord Sh	-92	-243	-76	222	405
Btm Line Earn	-92	-243	-76	222	405
Dividend Paid	-	-	-	94	-
Mkt Prce(c) YE	28	28	13	20	-
Depreciation	179	136	53	35	36

PER SHARE STATISTICS (CENTS)

Net Asst Val	24.68	25.90	29.10	30.11	10.49
Net Earnings	-1.20	-3.20	-1.00	3.10	-
Dividends	-	-	-	1.25	-
Cash Flow	1.15	-1.42	-0.30	3.60	5.83

RATIOS AND OTHER INFORMATION

Mrk Cap(R000)	2117	2117	983	1512	-
Current Ratio	1.64	2.02	2.69	2.33	2.12
Quik/Acid Tst	0.12	0.47	0.47	0.89	0.27
A/C Rec T/ovr	43.49	26.10	29.87	23.40	24.41
Tot Ass T/ovr	2.09	2.76	3.15	2.55	3.06
Debt/Ass Rat	0.61	0.50	0.36	0.41	0.70
L T L Tot Ass	0.05	0.05	0.02	-	0.24
Debt to Eqity	1.46	0.92	0.53	0.71	2.35
Interest Cover	0.36	-2.18	-1.23	23.93	58.86
Oper Prof Mrg	0.54	-1.80	-0.83	3.38	6.89
Net Prof Marg%	-0.92	-2.25	-0.70	2.24	6.77
Ret on Assets	1.23	-3.94	-0.09	8.62	21.10
Ret on Equity%	-4.54	-11.47	-3.22	9.75	38.79
Price/Earnings	-23.33	-8.75	-13.00	6.45	-
Divid Cover	-	-	-	2.48	-
Divid Yield	-	-	-	6.25	-
Earning Yield%	-4.29	-11.43	-7.69	15.50	-
NAV % Mrk Pr	88.15	92.50	223.85	150.53	-
Effec Tax Rate	-	-	-	30.84	-
Def Interval	7.15	-2.00	-3.13	0.21	1.10
Sus Grth Rate	-4.54	-11.47	-3.22	5.62	69.47

SUBSIDIARY & ASSOCIATED COMPANIES

CAMPING SERVICES (PTY) LTD
M E CANVAS INDUSTRIES (PTY) LTD
M E STORES (PTY) LTD
UNION ARMY STORES (PTY) LTD

INVESTMENTS

None

MEDHOLD LTD

ABBREVIATION : MEDHOLD

JSE SHORT CODE : MRH

SECTOR : Industrial-Pharmaceutical & Medical

SHAREHOLDERS

Who Owns Whom's Assessment of the Identity of the Ultimate Controlling Shareholder: DIRECTORS

SHAREHOLDER	PERCENTAGE 1992	1991
INDO-CHINA NOM P/L	27.1	---
ABSA NOM P/L	15.6	---
CCGG INV HOLDINGS LTD	10.5	33.1
STRADLING C A	5.0	---
ELEMENT INV HOLDINGS P/L	3.6	4.0
SMBL NOM P/L	3.4	3.8
STOCKSHARE NOM P/L	1.4	1.1
BETTY & DICKSON CC	1.4	---
DACOMB R B	1.3	---
WEATHERED INV P/L	1.1	---
DIAGONAL NOM P/L	---	1.9
INDO-CHINA NOM SA P/L	---	30.4
KAYEMESS NOM P/L	---	1.9
VOLKSKAS NOM P/L	---	8.8
TOTAL	70.5	84.9

DIRECTORS :
BOTHA AJ ,DACOMB RB (Chairman),GULLACKSEN JP
MARCELINO JG (Managing Director)
SIMON RJ (Financial Director),STRADLING CA

REGISTRATION NUMBER : 85/02935/06

REGISTERED OFFICE
3rd Floor, Pentrob Building, 343 Surrey Ave Ferndale
Randburg
2194
TEL: 011-787 0535
FAX: 011-886 4488

TRANSFER SECRETARY
Central Registrars Ltd
P O Box 4844, Johannesburg
2000
TEL: 011-331 0051

COMPANY SECRETARY
R J Simon

NATURE OF BUSINESS
The group is engaged in the following activities: Wholesale & retail supply of medical disposable products,emergency care and life support electro-medical equipment. The manufacture of a limited range of medical products is undertaken.

BANKERS :
Standard Bank of SA Ltd

AUDITORS :
Coopers Theron Du Toit

FAMILIAR BRAND NAMES
CARDIO-TRACE,DIASURG,HYDROSONIC,NEO-TEMP
UMBICLAMP

CONTRIBUTION BY ACTIVITY
N/A

YEAR END : June

DIVIDEND :Ords 12,19c

Final	(Ldr)11/10/91	(Pay)25/10/91	Amt(c)3
Final	(Ldr)23/10/92	(Pay)06/11/92	Amt(c)3

NUMBER OF EMPLOYEES : 120

CAPITAL STRUCTURE

	AUTHORISED	ISSUED
Ords 12,19c	29490000	17250000

FINANCIAL STATISTICS (AT FINANCIAL YEAR END)

(Amts in R'000)	1991 Jun	1990 Jun	1989 Jun	1988 Jun	1987 Jun
Ord S/H Int	3448	1922	1847	1478	1224
Long Trm Loans	276	309	311	298	285
Iss Ord Share	15700	15700	10000	10000	10000
Total Liab	4671	955	757	764	1215
Current Liab	4395	646	446	466	930
Total Assets	7484	2696	2387	1988	2150
Intang Assets	635	181	217	254	289
Current Assets	6453	1622	2004	1748	2005
Debtors	3443	551	554	479	409
Inventory	2496	353	219	198	168
Oper Profit	1516	772	801	1012	965
Interest Paid	103	27	-	6	21
Tax Paid	579	355	286	474	461
Prf af Int&Tax	890	390	515	532	483
Prf att Ord Sh	854	390	501	518	469
Btm Line Earn	854	90	501	604	469
Dividend Paid	518	314	300	350	50
Mkt Prce(c) YE	18	28	42	45	62
Depreciation	261	39	46	28	20

PER SHARE STATISTICS (CENTS)

Net Asst Val	17.92	11.09	16.30	12.24	9.35
Net Earnings	5.40	3.70	5.00	5.20	5.20
Dividends	3.00	3.00	3.00	3.50	0.50
Cash Flow	7.12	2.80	5.60	5.73	5.62

RATIOS AND OTHER INFORMATION

Mrk Cap(R000)	2826	4396	4200	4500	6200
Current Ratio	1.47	2.51	4.49	3.75	2.16
Quik/Acid Tst	0.90	1.96	4.00	3.33	1.98
Debt/Ass Rat	0.60	0.29	0.19	0.23	0.43
L T L Tot Ass	0.01	0.05	-	-	-
Debt to Eqity	1.29	0.41	0.24	0.32	0.76
Interest Cover	14.72	28.59	-	168.67	45.95
Ret on Assets	21.00	28.64	33.56	50.91	44.88
Ret on Equity%	24.77	20.29	27.13	35.05	38.32
Price/Earnings	3.33	7.57	8.40	8.65	11.92
Divid Cover	1.80	1.23	1.67	1.49	10.40
Divid Yield	16.67	10.71	7.14	7.78	0.81
Earning Yield%	30.00	13.21	11.90	11.56	8.39
NAV % Mrk Pr	99.54	39.60	38.81	27.20	15.08
Effec Tax Rate	39.21	46.17	42.95	44.73	47.99
Def Interval	0.82	0.31	0.49	-	-
Sus Grth Rate	9.74	3.95	10.88	11.37	34.23

SUBSIDIARY & ASSOCIATED COMPANIES

FURNQUIP MANUFACTURING & WHOLESALE SUPPL
FURNQUIP MEDICAL (NATAL) (PTY) LTD
FURNQUIP MEDICAL BOPHUTHATSWANA (PTY) LT
IEM PRODUCTS (PTY) LTD
MEDEX ENTERPRISES (PTY) LTD
MEDSEARCH (PTY) LTD
SOUTH AFRICAN MEDICAL SUPPLIES (PTY) LTD
TRANSKEI MEDICAL INDUSTRIES (PTY) LTD

INVESTMENTS

None

MEDI-CLINIC CORPORATION LTD

ABBREVIATION : MEDCLIN

JSE SHORT CODE : MDC

SECTOR : Industrial-Pharmaceutical & Medical

SHAREHOLDERS

Who Owns Whom's Assessment of the Identity of the Ultimate Controlling Shareholder: REMBRANDT

SHAREHOLDER	PERCENTAGE 1992	1991
VAN RIJN INV CORP LTD	92.9	93.4
STD BANK NOM TVL P/L	2.0	2.0
TOTAL	94.9	95.4

DIRECTORS :
ALBERTS LJ (Managing Director),DE CLERK PB
DE VILLIERS JN (Chairman),DU T MARAIS J
HERTZOG E DE LA H (Executive Deputy Chairman)
VAN DER B VAN AS AC ,VAN WYK AL

REGISTRATION NUMBER : 83/10725/06

REGISTERED OFFICE
25 Du Toit Str, Stellenbosch
7600
TEL: 02231-7 6880
FAX: 02231-7 0908

TRANSFER SECRETARY
Central Registrars Ltd
P O Box 4844, Johannesburg
2000
TEL: 011-331 0051

COMPANY SECRETARY
J C Engelbrecht

NATURE OF BUSINESS
The group operates 8 private hospitals, providing medical practitioners, mainly specialists with consulting rooms, operating theatres and hospital beds. The company provides management services to the operating hospitals.

BANKERS :
Volkskas Ltd

AUDITORS :
Coopers Theron Du Toit

FAMILIAR BRAND NAMES
CONSTANTIABERG MEDI-C,LEEUWENDAL NURSING HM
LOUIS LEIPOLDT HOSP,MITCHELLS PLAIN HOSP
MORNINGSIDE CLINIC,PANORAMA MEDI-CLINIC
SANDTON CLINIC,STELLENBOSCH MEDI-CLINIC

CONTRIBUTION BY ACTIVITY
N/A

YEAR END : March

DIVIDEND :Ords 10c

Final No 1	(Ldr)29/06/90	(Pay)31/07/90	Amt(c)3
Interim No 2	(Ldr)07/12/90	(Pay)31/01/91	Amt(c)1.5
Final No 3	(Ldr)28/06/91	(Pay)31/07/91	Amt(c)2.5
Interim No 4	(Ldr)13/12/91	(Pay)31/01/92	Amt(c)2
Final No 5	(Ldr)26/06/92	(Pay)31/07/92	Amt(c)4

NUMBER OF EMPLOYEES : 2600

CAPITAL STRUCTURE

	AUTHORISED	ISSUED
Ords 10c	200000000	91461600
11% Unsec Sub Comp Conv Debs R1	78538400	78538400

FINANCIAL STATISTICS (AT FINANCIAL YEAR END)

(Amts in R'000)	1992 Mar	1991 Mar	1990 Mar	1989 Mar	1988 Mar
Ord S/H Int	94640	82438	72827	64262	60635
Long Trm Loans	85238	86517	79040	79040	88240
Iss Ord Share	91462	90983	90960	90960	90960
Total Liab	130159	122099	101862	104247	103571
Current Liab	44921	35582	22822	25207	15331
Total Assets	223007	202495	172397	168509	164206
Intang Assets	1792	2042	2292	*	*
Current Assets	71565	63963	50304	46787	37829
Debtors	43024	36063	29885	23994	18710
Inventory	7197	7392	5953	345	-
Oper Profit	33980	24739	16170	10734	7634
Interest Paid	1435	65	1549	1504	1359
Tax Paid	15946	7456	-	-	-
Prf af Int&Tax	24309	21722	19723	12321	6275
Prf att Ord Sh	15386	13228	11294	3627	-2419
Btm Line Earn	17222	13228	11294	3627	-2419
Dividend Paid	5499	3640	2729	-	-
Mkt Prce(c) YE	185	100	85	50	65
Depreciation	6746	7530	10182	8716	6273

PER SHARE STATISTICS (CENTS)

Net Asst Val	101.52	88.36	77.55	70.65	66.66
Net Earnings	14.10	12.90	11.80	7.20	-2.70
Dividends	6.00	4.00	3.00	-	-
Cash Flow	33.95	32.15	32.88	23.13	13.80

RATIOS AND OTHER INFORMATION

Mrk Cap(R000)	169205	90983	77316	45480	59124
Current Ratio	1.59	1.80	2.20	1.86	2.47
Quik/Acid Tst	1.43	1.59	1.94	1.84	2.47
Debt/Ass Rat	0.58	0.60	0.59	0.62	0.63
L T L Tot Ass	0.38	0.43	0.46	0.47	0.54
Debt to Eqity	1.38	1.48	1.40	1.62	1.71
Interest Cover	23.68	380.60	10.44	7.14	5.62
Ret on Assets	18.57	14.54	12.49	8.20	4.65
Ret on Equity%	16.26	16.05	15.51	5.64	-3.99
Price/Earnings	13.12	7.75	7.20	6.94	-24.07
Divid Cover	2.35	3.23	3.93	-	-
Divid Yield	3.24	4.00	3.53	-	-
Earning Yield%	7.62	12.90	13.88	14.40	-4.15
NAV % Mrk Pr	54.87	88.36	91.23	141.30	102.56
Effec Tax Rate	39.61	25.55	-	-	-
Def Interval	0.22	0.26	-	0.44	0.73
Sus Grth Rate	10.45	11.63	11.76	5.64	-3.99

SUBSIDIARY & ASSOCIATED COMPANIES

LEEUWENDAL NURSING HOME (PTY) LTD
LOUIS LEIPOLDT HOSPITAL (PTY) LTD
LYME PARK PROJECT (PTY) LTD
MEDI-CLINIC CAPE LTD
MEDI-CLINIC CONSTANTIABERG LTD
MEDI-CLINIC LTD
MEDI-CLINIC MITCHELLS PLAIN LTD (50%)
MEDI-CLINIC OCCUPATIONAL HEALTH SERVICES (50%)
MEDI-CLINIC PANORAMA LTD
MEDI-CLINIC TVL (PTY) LTD
MEDI-LAM MATERIAL MANAGEMENT SYSTEMS (PT
MEDICAL INNOVATIONS (PTY) LTD
MEDIMO LTD (50%)
MEDIPARK CLINIC (PTY) LTD
MORNINGSIDE CLINIC (PTY) LTD
NEWMED HOSPITAL SUPPLIES (PTY) LTD
SANDTON CLINIC (PTY) LTD
UNITED HOSPITAL SUPPLY CORPORATION (PTY) (50%)

INVESTMENTS

None

MERHOLD LTD

ABBREVIATION : MERHLD

JSE SHORT CODE : MRH

SECTOR : Financial-Banks & Financial Services

SHAREHOLDERS

Who Owns Whom's Assessment of the Identity of the Ultimate Controlling Shareholder:
SA BIAS HOLDINGS

SHAREHOLDER	PERCENTAGE 1992	1991
SA BIAS HOLDINGS LTD	79.8	77.8
ANGLO AMERICAN GROUP PENS FUND	4.6	4.6
MERHOLD GROUP SHARE TRUST	3.9	3.9
CMB NOM P/L	3.1	---
ELLERINE BROS P/L	1.9	1.9

AA MUTUAL LIFE ASSURE ASSOC LTD	—	3.2
SANLAM	—	3.0
TOTAL	93.2	94.5

DIRECTORS :
COUTTS-TROTTER P MR,HUGHES NSH MR
KLUGMAN KM MR (Deputy Chairman),PARUK YM MR
SEABROOKE CS MR (Chairman),TAYLOR RJR M

REGISTRATION NUMBER : 05/07962/06

REGISTERED OFFICE
SA Bias House, 72 Delvers Street
Johannesburg
2001
TEL: 011-337 5340
FAX: 011-337 6773

TRANSFER SECRETARY
Central Registrars Ltd
P O Box 4844, Johannesburg
2000
TEL: 011-331 0051

COMPANY SECRETARY
R Pleaner

NATURE OF BUSINESS
Merhold is a national & international finance group with activities in the following areas: Banking, Corporate investment & services, Export trading & Trade finance & factoring.

BANKERS :
First National Bank of SA Ltd
Nedcor Bank Ltd

AUDITORS :
Levitt Kirson

FAMILIAR BRAND NAMES
N/A

CONTRIBUTION BY ACTIVITY
Finance (Contr to Net Income) (68.8%)
Investment (13.2%)
Trading (18.0%)

YEAR END : December

DIVIDEND :Ords 50c

Interim No 4	(Ldr)01/09/89	(Pay)15/09/89	Amt(c)8
Final No 5	(Ldr)05/04/90	(Pay)14/04/90	Amt(c)9
Interim No 6	(Ldr)14/09/90	(Pay)28/09/90	Amt(c)8
Final No 7	(Ldr)22/02/91	(Pay)26/04/91	Amt(c)9
Interim No 8	(Ldr)30/08/91	(Pay)20/09/91	Amt(c)8
Final No 9	(Ldr)28/02/92	(Pay)10/04/92	Amt(c)9
Interim No 10	(Ldr)28/08/92	(Pay)25/09/92	Amt(c)9

NUMBER OF EMPLOYEES : 115

CAPITAL STRUCTURE

	AUTHORISED	ISSUED
Ords 50c	30000000	18273580
"A" 6% Cum Red Lim Partic Prefs R	35500	0
"B" 6% Cum Red Prefs R2	89500	0
"C" Conv Red Prefs 50c	2741037	2741037
Conv Sub Debs R2	5482074	5482074

FINANCIAL STATISTICS (AT FINANCIAL YEAR END)

(Amts in R'000)	1991 Dec	1990 Dec	1989 Dec	1988 Dec	1987 Dec
Ord S/H Int	51701	46075	41232	35565	28928
Long Trm Loans	18516	17733	17556	17152	1081
Iss Ord Share	18274	18274	18274	18274	18274
Total Liab	326425	313050	299384	232493	178407
Current Liab	307909	295317	281828	215341	177326
Total Assets	378126	359125	340616	268058	207335
Current Assets	352364	330644	318210	251146	200167
Debtors	317051	297278	18010	8683	6275
Oper Profit	12273	11652	10882	7472	5993
Tax Paid	-	24	20	33	119
Prf af Int&Tax	12273	11628	10862	7439	5874
Prf att Ord Sh	9049	8708	8472	6671	5152
Btm Line Earn	8400	8256	7922	6471	5152
Dividend Paid	3106	3106	3106	2558	1775
Mkt Prce(c) YE	160	250	220	160	200
Depreciation	742	891	762	618	538

PER SHARE STATISTICS (CENTS)

Net Asst Val	282.92	252.13	225.63	194.62	158.30
Net Earnings	49.50	51.60	54.40	47.10	46.60
Dividends	17.00	18.40	19.90	18.10	16.00
Cash Flow	59.43	59.74	55.54	41.42	35.26

RATIOS AND OTHER INFORMATION

Mrk Cap(R000)	29238	45685	40203	29238	36548
Current Ratio	1.14	1.12	1.13	1.17	1.13
Quik/Acid Tst	1.14	1.12	1.13	1.17	1.13
Debt/Ass Rat	0.85	0.85	0.86	0.84	0.86
L T L Tot Ass	0.04	0.03	0.03	0.04	-
Debt to Eqity	6.25	6.65	7.10	6.36	6.13
Ret on Assets	3.58	3.55	3.59	2.79	2.89
Ret on Equity%	17.50	18.90	20.55	18.76	17.81
Price/Earnings	3.23	4.84	4.04	3.40	4.29
Divid Cover	2.91	2.80	2.73	2.60	2.91
Divid Yield	10.63	7.36	9.05	11.31	8.00
Earning Yield%	30.94	20.64	24.73	29.44	23.30
NAV % Mrk Pr	176.83	100.85	102.56	121.64	79.15
Effec Tax Rate	-	0.21	0.18	0.44	1.99
Def Interval	25.49	24.36	24.95	26.19	28.34
Sus Grth Rate	11.49	12.16	13.01	11.56	11.67

SUBSIDIARY & ASSOCIATED COMPANIES

AC MORRISON (PTY) LTD
ACIERS TRANSAFRICA SA LTD
AFRICA COLOMBIA GREEN COFFEE (PTY) LTD
AKITA (PTY) LTD
AUTOQUIP GROUP LTD (20%)
BRITISH MINING SUPPLY CO. LTD
CGS INSTRUMENTATION (PARTNERSHIP) (50%)
CLIFF PRODUCTS (PTY) LTD
HOLLAND ASSOCIATES (PTY) LTD
INTERFREEZER (PTY) LTD
MASLEX (PTY) LTD
MASLEX TRADING (PTY) LTD
MERCHANT FACTORS (PTY) LTD
MERCHANT INTERNATIONAL CREDIT & GUARANTE
MERCHANT INTERNATIONAL HOLDINGS INC.
MERCHANT INTERNATIONAL TRADING INC.
MERCHANT INVESTMENTS (PTY) LTD
MERCHANT SHIPPERS (U.K.) LTD
MERCHANT SHIPPERS UK LTD
MERCHANT TRADE FINANCE (UK) LTD
MERCHANT TRADE FINANCE INC.
MERCHANT TRADE FINANCE LTD
MERHOLD CORPORATE LTD
MERHOLD FINANCIAL SERVICES (PTY) LTD
MERHOLD INVESTMENTS (PTY) LTD
MERHOLD KIRSCH CAPITAL (PTY) LTD (50%)
MERHOLD SECURITIES (PTY) LTD
MERHOLD SELECTIONS (PTY) LTD

MERHOLD STRATEGIC INVESTMENTS (PTY) LTD
MERSHIP FREIGHT FORWARDING (PTY) LTD
MERSHIP INT. TRADING (PTY) LTD
MERSHIP SECURITIES (PTY) LTD
MERSHIP TRADE HOLDINGS (PTY) LTD
MERSHIP TRADING (U.K.) LTD
MERTRADE (PTY) LTD
MESHCAPE INDUSTRIES (PARTNERSHIP) (40%)
NEW REPUBLIC BANK LTD (30%)
NUTRITIONAL FOODS (PTY) LTD (50%)
R & I FISHING (PTY) LTD
RAPHAELY INT. TRADING ZAIRE SPRL
REEDWAY INT. ZIMBABWE PVT. LTD
REEDWAY PVT. LTD
REYNOLDS (PTY) LTD
WOODROW HOLDINGS LTD (21%)

INVESTMENTS

DATATEC (PARTNERSHIP) (15%)
LOG-TEK HOLDINGS LTD (17.9%)
TRABILD GROUP HOLDING LTD (3%)

MERITEX HOLDINGS LTD

ABBREVIATION : MERITEX

JSE SHORT CODE : MRX

SECTOR : Industrial-Clothing, Footwear & Textiles

SHAREHOLDERS

Who Owns Whom's Assessment of the Identity of the Ultimate Controlling Shareholder: DIRECTORS

SHAREHOLDER	PERCENTAGE 1992	1991
STD BANK NOM TVL P/L	60.3	60.3
MOMENTUM LIFE ASSURE LTD	12.0	12.0
STD MERCHANT BANK LTD	11.5	11.5
CMB NOM P/L	6.1	---
MERITEX HOLDINGS LTD SIS ACC	3.7	3.7
EIGHTY ONE MAIN STREET NOM LTD	1.6	1.6
SHKUDSKY A	1.1	---
SANLAM	---	6.8
TOTAL	96.2	95.9

DIRECTORS :
FRATER KJM ,GORSON E (Chairman & Managing Dir.)
MORRIS JRP DR,O'DONOVAN DJP (Financial Director

REGISTRATION NUMBER : 51/04149/06

REGISTERED OFFICE
Jan Smuts Road, Beaconvale
Parowvallei
7500
TEL: 021-931 5111
FAX: 021-932 5247

TRANSFER SECRETARY
Mercantile Registrars Ltd
P O Box 1053, Johannesburg
2000
TEL: 011-333 8181

COMPANY SECRETARY
D J P O'Donovan

NATURE OF BUSINESS
The principal activities of the company and of its subsidiaries consist of the manufacture and distribution of underwear, leisurewear & weft-knitted fabrics, & commission textile printing.

BANKERS :
Standard Bank of SA Ltd

AUDITORS :
KPMG Aiken & Peat

FAMILIAR BRAND NAMES
ATTITUDE,G.A.S.,ITAL PRINT,MERITEX
NEW COLOURS CLOTHING,PAZAZ,TIDE FABRICS
TRIDENT

CONTRIBUTION BY ACTIVITY
N/A

YEAR END : January

DIVIDEND : (Ldr)08/05/89 (Pay)05/06/89

NUMBER OF EMPLOYEES : 1687

CAPITAL STRUCTURE

	AUTHORISED	ISSUED
Ords 10c	25000000	15711500
Red Cum Prefs R10	50000	0
6% Cum Prefs R2	100000	0
7% Red Cum Prefs R1	112500	0

FINANCIAL STATISTICS (AT FINANCIAL YEAR END)

(Amts in R'000)	1992 Jan	1991 Jan	1990 Jan	1989 Jan	1988 Jan
Ord S/H Int	12152	15736	15697	15555	10322
Long Trm Loans	3247	3087	3507	4015	5810
Iss Ord Share	15712	15712	15712	15687	15100
Total Liab	24652	22614	24550	16688	13054
Current Liab	21405	19527	21043	12673	7244
Total Assets	36804	38350	40247	32243	23376
Current Assets	29626	29877	29807	23426	18057
Debtors	10630	10312	9132	7365	5433
Inventory	18780	19273	20547	15975	9887
Oper Profit	-367	3617	3073	5802	2645
Interest Paid	2839	3247	2209	226	542
Tax Paid	187	127	437	1024	844
Prf af Int&Tax	-3393	243	427	4552	1259
Prf att Ord Sh	-3585	117	125	4458	1090
Btm Line Earn	-3585	39	125	4237	-2131
Dividend Paid	-	-	-	1098	453
Mkt Prce(c) YE	35	40	70	105	-
Depreciation	1828	1993	1937	1217	475

PER SHARE STATISTICS (CENTS)

Net Asst Val	77.34	100.15	99.90	99.16	68.36
Net Earnings	-23.00	1.00	1.00	27.00	19.00
Dividends	-	-	-	7.00	3.00
Cash Flow	-11.18	13.43	13.12	36.18	11.65

RATIOS AND OTHER INFORMATION

Mrk Cap(R000)	5499	6285	10998	16471	-
Current Ratio	1.38	1.53	1.42	1.85	2.49
Quik/Acid Tst	0.51	0.54	0.44	0.59	1.13
Debt/Ass Rat	0.65	0.57	0.59	0.50	0.46
L T L Tot Ass	0.07	0.07	0.07	0.11	0.15
Debt to Eqity	1.97	1.40	1.52	1.04	1.05
Interest Cover	-0.13	1.11	1.39	25.67	4.88
Ret on Assets	-1.00	9.43	7.64	17.99	11.32
Ret on Equity%	-29.50	0.74	0.80	28.66	10.56
Price/Earnings	-1.52	40.00	70.00	3.89	-
Divid Cover	-	-	-	3.86	6.33
Divid Yield	-	-	-	6.67	-
Earning Yield%	-65.71	2.50	1.43	25.71	-
NAV % Mrk Pr	220.98	250.38	142.72	94.44	-
Effec Tax Rate	-7.58	17.84	50.58	18.36	30.91
Def Interval	-7.02	5.60	6.46	0.99	2.85
Sus Grth Rate	-29.50	0.74	0.80	21.60	6.17

SUBSIDIARY & ASSOCIATED COMPANIES

ITAL PRINT (PTY) LTD
MERITEX (PTY) LTD
MERITEX INVESTMENTS (PTY) LTD
MERITEX OUTERWEAR HOLDINGS (PTY) LTD (50%)
MERITEX PROPERTY HOLDINGS (PTY) LTD (50%)

INVESTMENTS

None

MERLIN LTD

ABBREVIATION : MERLIN

SECTOR : Zimbabwe Stock Exchange

SHAREHOLDERS

Who Owns Whom's Assessment of the Identity of the Ultimate Controlling Shareholder:
ARELL HOLDINGS / OLD MUTUAL INV CORP

DIRECTORS :
BLOCH EW ,BROOMBERG CB (Managing Director)
BROOMBERG DJ (Chairman & Chief Exec.)
BROOMBERG RL ,GOODHEAD D ,MAPONDERA HE

REGISTERED OFFICE
Cnr Plumtree & Ironbridge Rds, Donnington
Bulawayo, Zimbabwe

TEL: 76541
FAX: 76540

TRANSFER SECRETARY
KPMG Peat Marwick
P O Box 702, Harare
Zimbabwe

TEL: 09263 962831

COMPANY SECRETARY
Merlin Management Services

NATURE OF BUSINESS
MERLIN,incorporated in Zimbawe, is involved in the manufacture and export of textiles, including towels and blankets.

BANKERS :
N/A

AUDITORS :
Price Waterhouse Meyernel

FAMILIAR BRAND NAMES
N/A

CONTRIBUTION BY ACTIVITY
Export (% of Turnover) (26.0%)
Local (74.0%)

YEAR END : December

DIVIDEND : Ords Z$0,40
Interim No 30 (Ldr)18/10/91 (Pay) / / Amt(c)8.5
Final No 31 (Ldr)29/05/92 (Pay) / / Amt(c)9

CAPITAL STRUCTURE

	AUTHORISED	ISSUED
Ords Z$0,40	30000000	19226997
Sec Unconv Red Debs Z$50 000	86	86

FINANCIAL STATISTICS (AT FINANCIAL YEAR END)

(Amts in Z$)	1991 Dec	1990 Dec
Ord S/H Int	123730	31285
Long Trm Loans	43814	27562
Iss Ord Share	19227	19227
Total Liab	80847	44314
Current Liab	37033	16752
Total Assets	204577	75599
Current Assets	43333	30067
Debtors	21979	9977
Inventory	20892	12061
Turnover	70762	51754
Oper Profit	19951	11506
Interest Paid	4561	2853
Tax Paid	370	2063
Prf af Int&Tax	15453	6820
Prf att Ord Sh	12389	6038
Btm Line Earn	12389	7187
Dividend Paid	3365	1923
Depreciation	3963	3525

PER SHARE STATISTICS (CENTS)

Net Asst Val	643.52	162.71
Net Earnings	64.40	37.40
Dividends	3.70	3.70
Cash Flow	85.05	49.74

RATIOS AND OTHER INFORMATION

Current Ratio	1.17	1.79
Quik/Acid Tst	0.61	1.07
A/C Rec T/ovr	3.22	5.19
Tot Ass T/ovr	0.35	0.68
Debt/Ass Rat	0.34	0.47
L T L Tot Ass	0.16	0.24
Debt to Eqity	0.57	1.12
Interest Cover	4.37	4.03
Oper Prof Mrg	28.19	22.23
Net Prof Marg%	17.51	11.67
Ret on Assets	9.96	15.52
Ret on Equity%	10.01	19.30
Divid Cover	17.41	10.11
Effec Tax Rate	1.99	23.22
Def Interval	3.51	2.61
Sus Grth Rate	7.29	13.15

SUBSIDIARY & ASSOCIATED COMPANIES

AUSTRAL INVESTMENTS (PRIVATE) LTD
E1 DACORO (BOTSWANA) (PTY) LTD
EDGE INVESTMENTS (PRIVATE) LTD
GARMENT LABELS (PRIVATE) LTD
MERLIN INVESTMENTS (PVT) LTD
MERLIN MANAGEMENT SERVICES (PRIVATE) LTD
MERLIN MARKETING (PRIVATE) LTD
MERSPIN LIMITED (40%)
PAGENT INVESTMENTS (PRIVATE) LTD

INVESTMENTS

None

MESSINA INVESTMENTS LTD

ABBREVIATION : MINVEST

JSE SHORT CODE : MVT

SECTOR : Mining Financial-Mining Holding

SHAREHOLDERS

Who Owns Whom's Assessment of the Identity of the Ultimate Controlling Shareholder: ADS BUCHAN AND DIRECTORS

SHAREHOLDER	PERCENTAGE 1992	1991
ANTHONY BUCHAN TRUST	39.2	39.2
STD BANK NOM TVL P/L	22.2	22.2
KIRSTEN D G	12.0	12.0
PARKER W B	6.0	6.0
SHARESTOCK NOM P/L	3.9	4.2
DICKS D W	2.8	2.8
ELLEN D M	2.4	2.4
LAW PETER FAMILY TRUST	2.4	2.4
SCHOEMAN W D O F	2.4	2.4
JAYFAM MINERALS P/L	2.0	2.0
TOTAL	95.3	95.6

DIRECTORS :
BUCHAN ADS (Executive Chairman),FREEMAN PC
KIRSTEN DG (Managing Director),SMIT WA

REGISTRATION NUMBER : 68/11414/06

REGISTERED OFFICE
Industrial Stand 380, Consolidated Main Reef
Mines Property, Maraisburg
1700
TEL: 011-674 1270
FAX: 011-672 8724

TRANSFER SECRETARY
Central Registrars Ltd
P O Box 4844, Johannesburg
2000
TEL: 011-331 0051

COMPANY SECRETARY
P C Freeman

NATURE OF BUSINESS
The group holds coal & anthracite mineral rights, & conducts diamond & copper mining operations. Copper operations will cease towards the end of 1993. The company conducts exploration for viable mining propositions.

BANKERS :
First National Bank of SA Ltd

AUDITORS :
KPMG Aiken & Peat

FAMILIAR BRAND NAMES
N/A

CONTRIBUTION BY ACTIVITY
Copper (% of net Income) (45.2%)
Diamonds (52.0%)
Other (2.8%)

YEAR END : June

DIVIDEND : Ords 1c
Dividend No 3 (Ldr)02/10/92 (Pay)16/10/92 Amt(c)9.75

NUMBER OF EMPLOYEES : 1650

CAPITAL STRUCTURE

	AUTHORISED	ISSUED
Ords 1c	25000000	12500000

FINANCIAL STATISTICS (AT FINANCIAL YEAR END)

(Amts in R'000)	1991 Jun
Ord S/H Int	26045
Long Trm Loans	1923
Iss Ord Share	12500
Total Liab	23245
Current Liab	21322
Total Assets	49290
Current Assets	27910
Debtors	4170
Inventory	10842
Turnover	47932
Oper Profit	13520
Interest Paid	93
Tax Paid	5112
Prf af Int&Tax	10033
Prf att Ord Sh	9807
Btm Line Earn	11371
Dividend Paid	2000

PER SHARE STATISTICS (CENTS)

Net Asst Val	208.36
Net Earnings	78.00
Dividends	16.00
Cash Flow	78.09

RATIOS AND OTHER INFORMATION

Current Ratio	1.31
Quik/Acid Tst	0.80
A/C Rec T/ovr	11.49
Tot Ass T/ovr	0.97
Debt/Ass Rat	0.43
Debt to Eqity	0.82
Interest Cover	145.38
Oper Prof Mrg	28.21
Net Prof Marg%	20.46
Ret on Assets	30.91

Ret on Equity%	37.65
Divid Cover	4.88
Effec Tax Rate	34.06
Def Interval	0.01
Sus Grth Rate	29.98

SUBSIDIARY & ASSOCIATED COMPANIES

HELPMEKAAR DIAMANTE (PTY) LTD
JOUMBIRA KOPERMYNE (PTY) LTD
MADELEINE ALLUVIAL DIAMONDS & MINERAL DE
MESSINA DIAMONDS (PTY) LTD
MESSINA REHABILITATION (PTY) LTD
MOUNT RUPERT DIAMOND MINING CO (PTY) LTD
PAARDEKRAAL PROPERTIES (PTY) LTD
VAN OUDTSHOORNSTROOM COAL (PTY) LTD

INVESTMENTS

None

MESSINA LTD

ABBREVIATION : MESSINA

JSE SHORT CODE : MES

SECTOR : Metals & Minerals-Platinum

SHAREHOLDERS

Who Owns Whom's Assessment of the Identity of the Ultimate Controlling Shareholder:
SANLAM VIA IMPLATS

SHAREHOLDER	PERCENTAGE 1992	1991
CONSOLIDATED NOM P/L	54.2	54.2
CMB NOM P/L	17.3	---
STD BANK NOM TVL P/L	12.0	1.9
ABSA NOM P/L	1.9	---
LOWENCO NOM P/L	1.0	---
MOMENTUM LIFE ASSURE LTD	---	1.6
SA MUTUAL	---	9.1
SANKORP BPK	---	9.2
STATUS INV P/L	---	7.2
VOLKSKAS NOM P/L	---	1.9
TOTAL	86.4	85.1

DIRECTORS :
KEARNEY SV MR,LAW PRB MR,MARKUS CE MS
MCMAHON JM MR (Chairman & Managing Dir.)
MENNELL MV MS,MURRAY WJ MR,O'KEEFFE HJ MR
SMITHIES JG M

REGISTRATION NUMBER : 05/35912/06

REGISTERED OFFICE
3rd Floor, Unicorn House, 70 Marshall Street
Johannesburg
2001
TEL: 011-376 2800
FAX: 011-836 5954

TRANSFER SECRETARY
Central Registrars Ltd
P O Box 4844, Johannesburg
2000
TEL: 011-331 0051

COMPANY SECRETARY
AM Snashall- Implats Consult & Man Serv (Pty) Ltd

NATURE OF BUSINESS
Principal activity is the development of the platinum rights held by Messina Platinum Mines Ltd.The company's other major operating interest is the Premier Equipment group which operates in the materials-handling and the construction equipment market.

BANKERS :
First National Bank of SA Ltd
Standard Bank of SA Ltd, Nedcor Bank Ltd

AUDITORS :
Coopers Theron Du Toit

FAMILIAR BRAND NAMES
CLARKE FORKLIFTS,EUCLID TRUCKS
HITACHI EXCAVATORS,MICHIGAN,VME

CONTRIBUTION BY ACTIVITY
N/A

YEAR END : June

DIVIDEND : Ords 50c

Interim	(Ldr)11/08/89	(Pay)21/08/89	Amt(c)32
Final	(Ldr)23/03/90	(Pay)30/03/90	Amt(c)50

CAPITAL STRUCTURE

	AUTHORISED	ISSUED
Conv Red Non-Cum Partic Prefs 50c	160716	0
Ords 50c	19839284	12964894
Cum Red Pref R1	2000000	0

FINANCIAL STATISTICS (AT FINANCIAL YEAR END)

(Amts in R'000)	1992 Jun	1991 Jun	1990 Jun	1989 Dec	1988 Dec
Ord S/H Int	184619	178787	183560	174472	105930
Long Trm Loans	4950	6181	4520	1913	4657
Iss Ord Share	12965	12965	12770	12770	11814
Total Liab	51976	36265	70293	59688	92024
Current Liab	47026	30084	65773	57775	87367
Total Assets	236595	215052	253853	234160	197954
Current Assets	112641	134205	191623	178852	154340
Debtors	16053	15544	19293	22839	45018
Inventory	44977	38515	50753	41728	56853
Turnover	-	-	100734	246392	400281
Oper Profit	3783	5697	12806	49912	46897
Interest Paid	1604	1610	1459	2372	2197
Tax Paid	5479	11128	10611	15015	6020
Prf af Int&Tax	5754	10526	11554	48838	43706
Prf att Ord Sh	5727	10466	11606	50232	45171
Btm Line Earn	5727	20201	9098	72870	72816
Dividend Paid	-	-	-	10259	8941
Mkt Prce(c) YE	180	850	2600	3500	1675
Depreciation	2092	696	281	695	896

PER SHARE STATISTICS (CENTS)

Net Asst Val	1423.98	1379.00	1437.43	1366.26	896.65
Net Earnings	44.00	80.70	90.90	398.00	362.00
Dividends	-	-	-	82.00	75.00
Cash Flow	59.51	83.99	186.17	383.14	359.90

RATIOS AND OTHER INFORMATION

Mrk Cap(R000)	23337	110203	332020	446950	197885
Current Ratio	2.40	4.46	2.91	3.10	1.77
Quik/Acid Tst	1.44	3.18	2.14	2.37	1.12
A/C Rec T/ovr	-	-	10.44	10.79	8.89
Tot Ass T/ovr	-	-	0.79	1.05	2.02
Debt/Ass Rat	0.21	0.16	0.26	0.25	0.44
L T L Tot Ass	0.01	0.02	0.00	0.00	0.00
Debt to Eqity	0.27	0.19	0.36	0.33	0.83
Interest Cover	2.36	3.54	8.78	21.04	21.35
Oper Prof Mrg	-	-	12.71	20.26	11.72
Net Prof Marg%	-	-	11.52	20.39	11.28
Ret on Assets	5.43	10.82	18.61	29.14	28.51
Ret on Equity%	3.10	5.85	12.65	28.79	42.64
Price/Earnings	4.09	10.53	28.60	8.79	4.63
Divid Cover	-	-	-	4.85	4.83
Divid Yield	-	-	-	2.34	4.48
Earning Yield%	24.44	9.49	3.50	11.37	21.61
NAV % Mrk Pr	791.10	162.23	55.29	39.04	53.53
Effec Tax Rate	49.70	52.72	46.59	23.47	10.16
Def Interval	0.90	1.08	3.05	0.04	0.21
Sus Grth Rate	3.10	5.85	6.32	22.91	34.20

SUBSIDIARY & ASSOCIATED COMPANIES

DAMMI NOMINEES (PTY) LTD (25%)
ERF ONE ONE THREE FOUR PHALABORWA (PTY)
ERF THREE NINE SEVEN SIX MIDDELBURG (PTY
EUCLID (SA) (PTY) LTD
MESSINA PLATINUM MINES LTD
ONE ONE THREE ONE INVESTMENTS (PTY) LTD
PREMIER EQUIPMENT CO (NAMIBIA) LTD
PREMIER EQUIPMENT CO. LTD
PREMIER EQUIPMENT HOLDINGS LTD
SIX THREE FIVE INVESTMENTS (PTY) LTD

INVESTMENTS

None

METAIR INVESTMENTS LTD

ABBREVIATION : METAIR

JSE SHORT CODE : MTA

SECTOR : Industrial-Motor

SHAREHOLDERS

Who Owns Whom's Assessment of the Identity of the Ultimate Controlling Shareholder:
WESCO INV / INSTITUTIONS

SHAREHOLDER	PERCENTAGE 1992	1991
JATI INV P/L	28.0	28.0
MOMENTUM LIFE ASSURE LTD	18.8	18.8
SA MUTUAL	15.9	17.1
WESCO INV LTD	13.0	13.0
STD BANK NOM TVL P/L	6.8	5.6
SA TRUST & FINANCE CO LTD	4.7	4.7
CONTAX INV P/L	2.8	2.8
NEDBANK NOM LTD	2.5	1.5
EIGHTY ONE MAIN STREET NOM LTD	1.0	1.0
TOTAL	93.4	92.5

DIRECTORS :
BRADLEY E LE R MS (Chairman)
PLUMMER AD (Managing Director),RAPP AR
STEWART DC
SWINFORD-MEYER BC (Manufacturing Director)
VAN DER MERWE CIJ (Financial Director

REGISTRATION NUMBER : 05/31013/06

REGISTERED OFFICE
3rd Floor, Albert Wessels Building
19 Girton Road, Parktown
2193
TEL: 011-643 4801
FAX: 011-484 3025

TRANSFER SECRETARY
Central Registrars Ltd
P O Box 4844, Johannesburg
2000
TEL: 011-331 0051

COMPANY SECRETARY
Metair Management Services (Pty) Ltd

NATURE OF BUSINESS
An investment holding company which, through its subsidiaries manufactures and distributes components for the motor,industrial, agricultural and other industries.

BANKERS :
Standard Bank of SA Ltd

AUDITORS :
Deloitte Pim Goldby

FAMILIAR BRAND NAMES
ARMSTRONG,FNB,MOTORUBBER
MRP II COMPUTER SYSTEM,SMITHS,SUPREME

CONTRIBUTION BY ACTIVITY
N/A

YEAR END : December

DIVIDEND : Ords 50c

Dividend No 41	(Ldr)07/06/91	(Pay)21/06/91	Amt(c)63
Dividend No 42	(Ldr)22/05/92	(Pay)05/06/92	Amt(c)74

NUMBER OF EMPLOYEES : 2645

CAPITAL STRUCTURE

	AUTHORISED	ISSUED
Ords 50c	7500000	5665000
6% Cum Prefs R2	25000	25000

FINANCIAL STATISTICS (AT FINANCIAL YEAR END)

(Amts in R'000)	1991 Dec	1990 Dec	1989 Dec	1988 Dec	1987 Dec
Ord S/H Int	138663	108821	109039	106729	71805
Long Trm Loans	47739	34499	15908	7396	1375
Iss Ord Share	5665	5665	5665	5665	5665
Total Liab	104930	73139	61421	39714	23787
Current Liab	57191	38640	45513	32318	22412
Total Assets	243593	181960	170460	146443	95592
Current Assets	105102	79780	76536	70295	60023

Debtors	33515	29991	27947	27509	19803
Inventory	50838	45614	46888	40747	27033
Turnover	389671	330389	309116	253219	175685
Oper Profit	35092	25030	31354	28894	14552
Interest Paid	8222	6372	4349	1554	537
Tax Paid	12796	10625	14085	12622	4165
Prf af Int&Tax	14274	8633	12920	14858	9850
Prf att Ord Sh	15577	8643	13873	13024	10131
Btm Line Earn	15577	5830	13397	13075	10131
Dividend Paid	4192	3569	3569	3002	2493
Mkt Prce(c) YE	1275	1125	1175	1125	950
Depreciation	6892	7256	11454	4468	3903

PER SHARE STATISTICS (CENTS)

Net Asst Val	2447.71	1920.94	1924.78	1884.01	1267.52
Net Earnings	275.00	153.00	245.00	223.00	179.00
Dividends	74.00	63.00	63.00	53.00	44.00
Cash Flow	409.64	351.47	466.53	371.53	246.35

RATIOS AND OTHER INFORMATION

Mrk Cap(R000)	72229	63731	66564	63731	53818
Current Ratio	1.84	2.06	1.68	2.18	2.68
Quik/Acid Tst	0.95	0.88	0.65	0.91	1.47
A/C Rec T/ovr	11.63	11.02	11.06	9.20	8.87
Tot Ass T/ovr	1.60	1.82	1.81	1.73	1.84
Debt/Ass Rat	0.38	0.36	0.31	0.24	0.24
L T L Tot Ass	0.15	0.14	0.05	0.01	0.01
Debt to Eqity	0.67	0.60	0.49	0.32	0.32
Interest Cover	4.29	4.02	7.21	18.68	27.10
Oper Prof Mrg	9.01	7.58	10.14	11.41	8.28
Net Prof Marg%	4.00	2.62	4.49	5.14	5.77
Ret on Assets	15.02	14.00	19.07	18.86	15.52
Ret on Equity%	11.23	7.94	12.72	12.20	14.11
Price/Earnings	4.64	7.35	4.80	5.04	5.31
Divid Cover	3.72	2.43	3.89	4.21	4.07
Divid Yield	5.80	5.60	5.36	4.71	4.63
Earning Yield%	21.57	13.60	20.85	19.82	18.84
NAV % Mrk Pr	191.98	170.75	163.81	167.47	133.42
Effec Tax Rate	34.01	41.33	47.07	6.87	28.74
Def Interval	1.87	1.40	0.34	0.07	0.07
Sus Grth Rate	8.21	4.66	9.45	9.39	10.64

SUBSIDIARY & ASSOCIATED COMPANIES

ARMSTRONG HOLDINGS (PTY) LTD
ARMSTRONG HYDRAULICS SOUTH AFRICA (PTY)
ARMSTRONG PROPERTIES (PTY) LTD
METAIR MANAGEMENT SERVICES (PTY) LTD
METLINK MANUFACTURING (PTY) LTD
MOTORUBBER CONSOLIDATED (PTY) LTD
MOTORUBBER INVESTMENTS (PTY) LTD
MOTORUBBER LTD
PITPROP INVESTMENTS (PTY) LTD
SMITHS CORPORATE SERVICES (PTY) LTD
SMITHS MANUFACTURING (SA) (PTY) LTD
SMSA PROPERTY (PTY) LTD
SUPREME SPRING SYSTEMS (PTY) LTD

INVESTMENTS

None

METBOARD PROPERTY FUND

ABBREVIATION : METPROP

JSE SHORT CODE : MPR

SECTOR : Financial-Property Trust

SHAREHOLDERS

Who Owns Whom's Assessment of the Identity of the Ultimate Controlling Shareholder:
SA MUTUAL

SHAREHOLDER	PERCENTAGE 1992	1991
SA MUTUAL	51.1	51.8
SIXTY SIX MARSHALL STREET NOM P/L	6.6	5.6
METAL IND GROUP PENS FUND	4.1	4.1
ENGINEERING INDUSTRIES PENS FUND	3.9	3.9
YSKOR PENS FUND	3.2	3.2
EIGHTY ONE MAIN STREET NOM LTD	2.5	2.4
STD BANK NOM TVL P/L	2.0	---
METBOARD PROP FUND MANAGERS LTD	1.9	1.6
EPF OLD MUTUAL NOM P/L	1.3	1.3
SHEIDAN INV P/L	1.1	1.1
HARSID INV P/L	---	1.2
TOTAL	77.5	76.1

DIRECTORS :
HACKNER S ,HASLETT FN ,KANTOR B (Chairman)
KOSEFF S ,KUPER D ,LIEBENBERG GZ ,QUINTON P
WOOLF R

REGISTRATION NUMBER : 86/00217/06

REGISTERED OFFICE
2nd Floor, 55 Fox Street
Johannesburg
2001
FAX: (011) 498-2388

TRANSFER SECRETARY
Mercantile Registrars Ltd
P O Box 1053, Johannesburg
2000
TEL: 011-333 8181

COMPANY SECRETARY
Metboard Ltd

NATURE OF BUSINESS
A closed-end property unit trust, invested in industrial, commercial and retail properties situated predominantly on the Witwatersrand.

BANKERS :
Standard Bank of SA Ltd, Boland Bank Ltd

AUDITORS :
Fisher Hoffman Stride

FAMILIAR BRAND NAMES
N/A

CONTRIBUTION BY ACTIVITY
Industrial (% Gross Income) (89.4%)
Retail (6.3%)
Commercial (4.3%)

YEAR END : March

DIVIDEND : Units

Final No 9	(Ldr)25/05/90	(Pay)11/06/90	Amt(c)15.5
Interim No 10	(Ldr)31/08/90	(Pay)03/12/90	Amt(c)16.8
Final No 11	(Ldr)07/06/91	(Pay)28/06/91	Amt(c)17

Interim No 12	(Ldr)22/11/91	(Pay)13/12/91	Amt(c)15.3
Final No 13	(Ldr)05/06/92	(Pay)26/06/92	Amt(c)15.3
Interim no 14	(Ldr)27/11/92	(Pay)14/12/92	Amt(c)15.3

CAPITAL STRUCTURE

	AUTHORISED	ISSUED
Units	58955325	58955325

FINANCIAL STATISTICS (AT FINANCIAL YEAR END)

(Amts in R'000)	1992 Mar	1991 Mar	1990 Mar	1989 Mar	1987 Dec
Ord S/H Int	132225	131302	71581	71148	70046
Iss Ord Share	58955	58955	35731	35731	35730
Total Liab	10155	10088	5599	2754	4889
Current Liab	10155	10088	5599	2754	4889
Total Assets	142380	141390	77180	73902	74935
Current Assets	30210	46005	5929	8701	7358
Debtors	-	789	134	174	521
Oper Profit	-805	-514	-411	11392	9087
Prf af Int&Tax	18040	16025	10898	12148	9288
Prf att Ord Sh	18040	16025	10898	12148	9288
Btm Line Earn	18040	16025	10898	12148	9288
Dividend Paid	18040	16025	10898	12148	9289
Mkt Prce(c) YE	230	285	285	210	245

PER SHARE STATISTICS (CENTS)

Net Asst Val	224.28	222.72	200.33	199.12	196.04
Net Earnings	30.60	33.80	30.50	34.00	26.00
Dividends	30.60	33.80	30.50	34.00	26.00
Cash Flow	30.60	27.18	30.50	34.00	20.80

RATIOS AND OTHER INFORMATION

Mrk Cap(R000)	135597	168022	101833	75035	87539
Current Ratio	2.97	4.56	1.06	3.16	1.51
Quik/Acid Tst	2.97	4.56	1.06	3.16	1.51
Debt/Ass Rat	0.07	0.07	0.07	0.04	0.07
Debt to Eqity	0.08	0.08	0.08	0.04	0.07
Ret on Assets	12.67	11.33	14.12	16.44	9.92
Ret on Equity%	13.64	12.20	15.22	17.07	10.61
Price/Earnings	7.52	8.43	9.34	6.18	9.42
Divid Cover	1.00	1.00	1.00	1.00	1.00
Divid Yield	13.30	11.86	10.70	16.19	10.61
Earning Yield%	13.30	11.86	10.70	16.19	10.61
NAV % Mrk Pr	97.51	78.15	70.29	94.82	80.02
Sus Grth Rate	0.00	0.00	0.00	0.00	0.00

SUBSIDIARY & ASSOCIATED COMPANIES

ALRODE TWEE VIER TWEE (EDMS) BPK
ASHWELL INVESTMENTS (PTY) LTD
CLETAL (PTY) LTD
CROWN 48 (PTY) LTD
CROWN 98 (PTY) LTD
EDENVALE BUILDINGS (PTY) LTD
ELVAN PROPERTY (PTY) LTD
ENDSTONE INVESTMENTS (PTY) LTD
ENZENHOFFER (PTY) LTD
EQUITABLE DEVELOPMENT CO (PTY) LTD
ERF 50 STAFFORD (PTY) LTD
FASTNER CENTRE (PTY) LTD
GUSMON INVESTMENTS (PTY) LTD
HEIDELBERG CENTRE (PTY) LTD
HEIDELBERG HOLDINGS (PTY) LTD
ILNOV INVESTMENTS (PTY) LTD
ISANDO 555 (PTY) LTD
ITALCRAFT PROPERTIES (PTY) LTD
JANHOPE (PTY) LTD
KARLA INVESTMENTS (PTY) LTD
KAROO EIENDOMME (EDMS) BPK
KATROLEA (PTY) LTD
KEISIL INVESTMENTS (PTY) LTD
KEISTER INVESTMENTS (PTY) LTD
KELBUN PROPERTIES (PTY) LTD
LOW COST MARKETING (PTY) LTD
MOLBER PROPERTY INVESTMENTS (PTY) LTD
MOOIWEN INVESTMENTS (PTY) LTD
PROCESSING MACHINE ENTERPRISES (PTY) LTD
PROUDFOOT PROPERTY INVESTMENTS (PTY) LTD
ROHAM (JBH) (EDMS) BPK
ROHAM JHB (EDMS) BPK
ROJOLEA (PTY) LTD
SALMART (PTY) LTD
SEBENZA 137 (PTY) LTD
SHAPAMRON (PTY) LTD
SHEIDAN PROPERTIES (PTY) LTD
ST GEORGES CENTRE (PTY) LTD
STORMILL 51 (PTY) LTD
STRIJDOM PARK 347 (PTY) LTD
TAMANAI (PTY) LTD
TASROY INVESTMENTS (PTY) LTD
TROJAN 1 (PTY) LTD
TROJAN 22 (PTY) LTD
TROJAN 39 (PTY) LTD
TROJAN 4 (PTY) LTD
TROJAN 40 (PTY) LTD
TROJAN 47 (PTY) LTD
TROJAN FOURTEEN (PTY) LTD
TROJAN TWENTY (PTY) LTD
TROYBELL INVESTMENTS (PTY) LTD
VEREENIGING 5 (PTY) LTD
VICJOEN (PTY) LTD
WYNTRUST INVESTMENTS (PTY) LTD

INVESTMENTS

None

METJE AND ZIEGLER LTD

ABBREVIATION : METJE-&-Z

JSE SHORT CODE : MZG

SECTOR : Industrial-Industrial Holding

SHAREHOLDERS

Who Owns Whom's Assessment of the Identity of the Ultimate Controlling Shareholder: DIRECTORS

SHAREHOLDER	PERCENTAGE 1992	1991
HERTA ERNST INV P/L	52.6	52.6
VAN DOORN C	27.8	27.8
SA MUTUAL	5.9	5.9
KARAX INV P/L	2.1	2.1
KATZ J	1.5	1.4
NEDBANK NOM LTD	1.3	1.3
ZIEGELSTEIN B	1.1	1.1
METJE I M	1.0	1.0
TOTAL	93.4	93.2

DIRECTORS :
BEHNSEN AM (Managing Director),BEHNSEN WEM
BIEBER EPH (Chairman),BOTTGER WA ,FRANCIS PA
MATHEWS D O'N ,ORAM D ,VAN DOORN CS MR

REGISTRATION NUMBER : 79/01570/10

REGISTERED OFFICE
Metje Behnsen Geb., Independence Ave
Windhoek, Namibia
9000
TEL: 061-227417
FAX: 061-222859

TRANSFER SECRETARY
Ernst & Young
P O Box 1857, Windhoek
9000
TEL: 061-38 260

COMPANY SECRETARY
KAHAS von der Pforte

NATURE OF BUSINESS
The group retails a range of products including timber, iron, steel, building materials, machine tools, hardware, petroleum products, electrical goods, paints, carpets, household & luxury goods, sports equipment & clothing. The group also holds the franchises for Mercedes-Benz, Honda, Audi and VW vehicles, & has property interests in Windhoek.

BANKERS :
Standard Bank Namibia Ltd

AUDITORS :
Ernst & Young

FAMILIAR BRAND NAMES
M & Z STORES

CONTRIBUTION BY ACTIVITY
General Merchandise (% of turnover) (31.0%)
Motor Business (66.0%)
Property (3.0%)

YEAR END : June

DIVIDEND :15/12/91

NUMBER OF EMPLOYEES : 512

CAPITAL STRUCTURE

	AUTHORISED	ISSUED
Ords R1	4800000	3466965
5,5% Cum Pref R2	100000	100000

FINANCIAL STATISTICS (AT FINANCIAL YEAR END)

(Amts in R'000)	1992 Jun	1991 Jun	1990 Jun	1989 Jun	1988 Jun
Ord S/H Int	28748	28285	29204	27984	24661
Long Trm Loans	1071	1122	1099	1265	1101
Iss Ord Share	3467	3467	3467	3467	3467
Total Liab	24214	23098	22051	20013	15710
Current Liab	23143	21976	20952	18748	14609
Total Assets	52962	51383	51255	47997	40371
Current Assets	40705	39893	40284	38363	31568
Debtors	12804	11908	13617	14179	11949
Inventory	27631	26959	25598	23903	18846
Oper Profit	2520	1770	4234	7856	5961
Interest Paid	1357	1863	784	444	-
Tax Paid	547	819	1774	3190	2461
Prf af Int&Tax	631	-905	1685	4251	3500
Prf att Ord Sh	636	-920	1567	4154	3454
Btm Line Earn	636	-920	1567	4154	3454
Dividend Paid	173	-	347	832	624
Mkt Prce(c) YE	300	330	360	350	350
Depreciation	893	817	581	504	338

PER SHARE STATISTICS (CENTS)

Net Asst Val	829.19	815.84	842.34	807.15	711.31
Net Earnings	18.40	-26.50	45.20	119.80	99.60
Dividends	5.00	-	10.00	24.00	18.00
Cash Flow	44.59	-2.08	55.75	136.26	108.83

RATIOS AND OTHER INFORMATION

Mrk Cap(R000)	10401	11441	12481	12135	12135
Current Ratio	1.76	1.82	1.92	2.05	2.16
Quik/Acid Tst	0.56	0.59	0.70	0.77	0.87
Debt/Ass Rat	0.44	0.43	0.41	0.40	0.37
L T L Tot Ass	0.00	0.00	0.00	0.00	0.01
Debt to Eqity	0.81	0.78	0.72	0.68	0.60
Interest Cover	1.87	0.95	5.41	17.75	-
Ret on Assets	4.85	3.49	8.30	16.52	14.88
Ret on Equity%	2.21	-3.25	5.37	14.84	14.01
Price/Earnings	16.30	-12.45	7.96	2.92	3.51
Divid Cover	3.68	-	4.52	4.99	5.53
Divid Yield	1.67	-	2.78	6.86	5.14
Earning Yield%	6.13	-8.03	12.56	34.23	28.46
NAV % Mrk Pr	276.40	247.22	233.98	230.62	203.23
Effec Tax Rate	43.85	-827.96	57.36	41.56	40.83
Def Interval	2.91	-129.53	5.56	1.14	0.74
Sus Grth Rate	1.61	-3.25	4.18	11.87	11.48

SUBSIDIARY & ASSOCIATED COMPANIES

AIR MEBECO (PTY) LTD
GUSTAV ROSENTHAL (PTY) LTD (50%)
LIONS MOTORS (PTY) LTD
M & Z MOTORS & ENGINEERING LTD
METJE & ZIEGLER (WALVIS BAY) (PTY) LTD
METROPOL (PTY) LTD
MIP MINING & INDUSTRIAL PROJECT CO (PTY)
SUDWEST AUTOHAUS (PTY) LTD
WEILBACHER & WEILBACHER (PTY) LTD (50%)

INVESTMENTS

None

METKOR GROUP LTD

ABBREVIATION : METKOR

JSE SHORT CODE : MTK

SECTOR : Industrial-Engineering

SHAREHOLDERS

Who Owns Whom's Assessment of the Identity of the Ultimate Controlling Shareholder:
REMBRANDT

SHAREHOLDER	PERCENTAGE 1992	1991

IND PARTNERSHIP INV LTD	50 0	50 0
SA IRON & STEEL INDUSTRIAL CORP LTD	25 8	25 6
EIGHTY ONE MAIN STREET NOM LTD	6 2	6 5
STD BANK NOM TVL P/L	2 1	3 8
FIRST NAT NOM P/L	1 7	1 5
CMB NOM P/L	1 6	---
MOMENTUM LIFE ASSURE LTD	1 5	1 6
GEMEENSKAPLIKE MUNISIPALE TVL PENS FUND	1 2	---
SANLAM	--	1 1
TOTAL	90 0	90 0

DIRECTORS :
KOTZEE FP (Chairman),MOSTERT DB ,OLIVIER PA
ROUX MJ ,VAN GRAAN WJJ ,VAN NIEKERK LL
VAN WYK T ,VAN WYK W

REGISTRATION NUMBER : 68/15448/06

REGISTERED OFFICE
2nd Floor, Dorbyl Park, 4 Skeen Boulevard
Bedfordview
2008
TEL 011-607 2500
FAX 011-607 2152

TRANSFER SECRETARY
Central Registrars Ltd
P O Box 4844, Johannesburg
2000
TEL 011-331 0051

COMPANY SECRETARY
R C Miller

NATURE OF BUSINESS
An investment holding company Group operations include metal & steel engineering, production & marketing of industrial gasses, manufacturing of housewares, machined ring forgings, aluminium & steel windows & doors, & composite brake blocks Metkor holds a controlling interest in quoted Dorbyl Ltd, and a substantial minority interest in quoted Usko Ltd

BANKERS :
Volkskas Ltd

AUDITORS :
N/A

FAMILIAR BRAND NAMES
AIR PRODUCTS,BALDWINS STEEL,DORBYL
HENDLER & HART,METPRO,POINTERWARE
RINGROLLERS,RW TOOLS,STEWARTS & LLOYDS,TITAN
TOSA,WISPECO

CONTRIBUTION BY ACTIVITY
N/A

YEAR END : September

DIVIDEND : Ords 50c

Final	(Ldr)07/12/90	(Pay)07/01/91	Amt(c)10 55
Interim	(Ldr)07/06/91	(Pay)24/06/91	Amt(c)4 71
Final	(Ldr)06/12/91	(Pay)06/01/92	Amt(c)10 97
Interim	(Ldr)05/06/92	(Pay)22/06/92	Amt(c)4 83
Final	(Ldr)04/12/92	(Pay)11/01/93	Amt(c)9 01

NUMBER OF EMPLOYEES : 21287

CAPITAL STRUCTURE

	AUTHORISED	ISSUED
Ords 50c	150000000	120484017
5% Red Cum Prefs 10c	20111800	0

FINANCIAL STATISTICS (AT FINANCIAL YEAR END)

(Amts in R'000)	1991 Sep	1990 Sep	1989 Sep	1988 Sep	1987 Sep
Ord S/H Int	380024	399152	410656	370812	331895
Long Trm Loans	712537	637123	569286	518603	506252
Iss Ord Share	108544	108544	108544	108544	108544
Total Liab	1345106	1401622	1294979	1178926	1053912
Current Liab	632569	764499	725693	660323	547660
Total Assets	1725130	1800774	1705635	1549738	1385807
Current Assets	972295	1048035	1049566	926766	791007
Debtors	531780	559276	518479	453652	379118
Inventory	435788	482153	529453	470788	411312
Turnover	3215524	3164239	2895089	2417137	1972910
Oper Profit	182447	191893	211633	141437	107038
Interest Paid	60821	69304	57989	43329	25204
Tax Paid	22186	33979	39916	21084	15827
Prf af Int&Tax	114034	105041	126399	88195	66007
Prf att Ord Sh	23346	32159	55743	36635	28811
Btm Line Earn	8294	15565	57067	39684	28409
Dividend Paid	17019	16064	17096	13568	10854
Mkt Prce(c) YE	230	210	385	165	210
Depreciation	71145	62361	53616	49235	47108

PER SHARE STATISTICS (CENTS)

Net Asst Val	350 11	367 73	378 33	341 62	305 77
Net Earnings	21 51	29 60	51 35	33 14	26 57
Dividends	15 68	14 80	15 75	12 50	10 00
Cash Flow	98 93	84 75	94 52	75 13	61 34

RATIOS AND OTHER INFORMATION

Mrk Cap(R000)	249651	227942	417894	179098	227942
Current Ratio	1 54	1 37	1 45	1 40	1 44
Quik/Acid Tst	0 85	0 74	0 72	0 69	0 69
A/C Rec T/ovr	6 05	5 66	5 58	5 33	5 20
Tot Ass T/ovr	1 86	1 76	1 70	1 56	1 42
Debt/Ass Rat	0 43	0 47	0 47	0 47	0 45
L T L Tot Ass	0 06	0 05	0 04	0 05	0 06
Debt to Eqity	1 96	2 13	1 95	1 98	1 89
Interest Cover	3 09	2 84	3 75	3 45	4 25
Oper Prof Mrg	5 67	6 06	7 31	5 85	5 43
Net Prof Marg%	0 73	1 02	1 93	1 52	1 46
Ret on Assets	10 66	11 71	13 55	10 21	8 10
Ret on Equity%	6 14	8 06	13 57	9 88	8 68
Price/Earnings	10 69	7 09	7 50	4 98	7 90
Divid Cover	1 37	2 00	3 26	2 65	2 66
Divid Yield	6 82	7 05	4 09	7 58	4 76
Earning Yield%	9 35	14 10	13 34	20 08	12 65
NAV % Mrk Pr	152 22	175 11	98 27	207 04	145 60
Effec Tax Rate	17 82	25 13	24 13	21 44	25 23
Def Interval	2 30	3 20	2 43	3 42	3 44
Sus Grth Rate	1 66	4 03	9 41	6 22	5 41

SUBSIDIARY & ASSOCIATED COMPANIES

AFGATE (BABELEGI) (PTY) LTD
AFGATE (PTY) LTD
AFRICAN GATE (PRETORIA) (PTY) LTD
AFRICAN GATE (V D BJL) (PTY) LTD
AFRICAN GATE PROPERTIES (PTY) LTD
AIR PRODUCTS S A (PTY) LTD
ALOE ENGINEERING IND (PTY) LTD
ALUSEC LTD
ANSO PRODUCTS (PTY) LTD
APSAP GAS (PTY) LTD (50%)
ARROW ALRODE (PTY) LTD

BALDWINS STEEL (PTY) LTD
BALDWINS STEEL SERVICES (PTY) LTD
BARLET (PTY) LTD
BRAND & MURRAY (PTY) LTD
BREEWEST (PTY) LTD
BUNDY TUBING COMPANY OF SA (PTY) LTD
CANNON CONTROL VALVES (PTY) LTD
CAR PART INDUSTRIES (PTY) LTD
CASTLETON (PTY) LTD
CENTURATOR PRODUCTS (PTY) LTD
CLIMAX WINDMILLS (PTY) LTD
COSMO ENGINEERING (PTY) LTD
CRITTAL-HOPE PROPERTIES LTD
CUISINEWARE LTD (UK)
D. MOREIRA (PTY) LTD
DHE HOLDINGS (BENONI) (PTY) LTD
DIALOY AFRICA (PTY) LTD
DORBYL LTD (34,6%)
DRAWBRIGHT STEELS (PTY) LTD
DUVENHAGE WISPECO (PTY) LTD
ERF 576 - BURMAN ROAD (PTY) LTD
FIESTA HOUSEWARES LTD
GRAVITY LADDERS (PTY) LTD
GREEN GLADE ETATES (PTY) LTD
GUESTRO ALLOY WHEELS (PTY) LTD
HART (PTY) LTD
HOLLOSEC (PTY) LTD
HOLLOSEC HOLDINGS (PTY) LTD
HOLLOSEC SALES (PTY) LTD
INTERNATIONAL PIPE & STEEL INVESTMENTS (
J. SEMPLE & SONS (PTY) LTD
JL CLARK AND COMPANY LTD
JL CLARK ENGINEERING (PTY) LTD
JOHN MULLER (PTY) LTD
KEMPTON PLUMBING (PTY) LTD
KOOLMASTER MANUFACTURING (PTY) LTD
KRAGGROND (PTY) LTD
LASHER PROPS (LADYSMITH) (PTY) LTD
LASHER TOOLS (PTY) LTD
LAZIMAN MANUFACTURING (PTY) LTD
LEGIS PROPERTIES (PTY) LTD
LOT 3090 LADYSMITH PROPS. (PTY) LTD
MAKOTI MANUFACTURING (PTY) LTD (SWAZILAN
MARITZBURG STEEL AND WIRE (PTY) LTD
METEK (PTY) LTD
METKOR INDUSTRIES (PTY) LTD
METKOR MANAGEMENT CO. (PTY) LTD
METKOR SALES (PTY) LTD
METPRO DEVELOPMENT CO. (PTY) LTD
METRO DEVELOPMENT CO (PTY) LTD
MEYERSTAN INVESTMENTS (PTY) LTD
PIPE COUPLINGS (PTY) LTD
PRESSPEED TOOLS (PTY) LTD
PROPTICOR INVESTMENTS (PTY) LTD
PULLMAFLEX SOUTHERN AFRICA (PTY) LTD
R.W. POWERVILLE LTD
RACEC (CIVIL ENGINEERING) (PTY) LTD
RACEC (MOOIFONTEIN) (PTY) LTD
RACEC (PTY) LTD
RACEC BOPHUTHATSWANA (PTY) LTD
RACEC EKANDUSTRIA (PTY) LTD
RACEC ELECTRIFICATION (PTY) LTD
RACEC FINANCING (PTY) LTD
RACEC HOLDINGS LTD
RACEC IN BRONKHORSTSPRUIT (PTY) LTD (50%)
RACEC MAINTENANCE (PTY) LTD
RACEC PROPERTIES (CAPE) (PTY) LTD
RACEC PROPERTIES (LADYSMITH) (PTY) LTD
RACEC PROPERTIES (NATAL) (PTY) LTD
RACEC PROPERTIES (PTY) LTD
RACEC PROPERTIES (SPARTAN) (PTY) LTD
RACEC PROPERTY HOLDINGS LTD
RACEC TRANSMISSION (PTY) LTD
RAILWAY & CIVIL ENGINEERING (PTY) LTD
RAILWAY CONSTRUCTION (CAPE) (PTY) LTD
RAILWAY CONSTRUCTION (NATAL) (PTY) LTD
RAILWAY TRACK SPECIALISTS (PTY) LTD
RAILWAY TRACK SUPPLIERS (PTY) LTD
RAVENSKLIP EXT FLATS (PTY) LTD
REFAIRCON (SWA) (PTY) LTD
REFRIGERATION AGENCIES (PTY) LTD
RENCO PROPERTIES (PTY) LTD
RHIWBINA PROPERTIES (PTY) LTD
RINGROLLERS OF S.A. (PTY) LTD
RIVER GATE & FENCE CO. (PTY) LTD
ROODIA BELEGGINGS (PTY) LTD
ROODIA BELEGGINGS BRITS (EDMS) BPK
S.A. LIGHT METAL WORKS LTD
SALCAST (PTY) LTD
SALCHAIN (PTY) LTD
SALISTER DIESEL (PTY) LTD
SALMAC STAINLESS TUBE (PTY) LTD
SALTRONICS (PTY) LTD
SALVALVE SAI (PTY) LTD
SALWEIR (PTY) LTD
SAMS ELECTRICAL CONTRACTORS (PTY) LTD
SINTERED METAL COMPONENTS (PTY) LTD
SOUTH AFRICAN LIGHT METAL WORKS LTD
SPIRAL PATENTS (PTY) LTD
SPRINGBOK TOOLS (PTY) LTD
STEEL PIPE INDUSTRIES (PTY) LTD
STEWARTS & LLOYDS OF SOUTH AFRICA LTD
STEWARTS & LLOYDS OF SWA LTD
STEWARTS & LLOYDS TRADING (PTY) LTD
TASGUMAR (PTY) LTD
TITAN INDUSTRIAL CORPORATION (PTY) LTD
TITAN TOWERS (PTY) LTD
TOSA LTD
TRANSVAAL PIPE MANUFACTURERS (PTY) LTD
TUBE AND PIPE INDUSTRIES (PTY) LTD
TURBINE MANUFACTURERS (PTY) LTD
TWINLAKE TOWERS (PTY) LTD
UMBILO PROPERTY INVESTMENTS (PTY) LTD
UNIVEL TRANSMISSIONS (PTY) LTD
USKO LTD (27%)
VANDERBIJL ENGINEERING CORP (PTY) LTD
VECOR (NEWCASTLE) ENGINEERING COMPANY (P
WESTERN STEEL INVESTMENTS (PTY) LTD
WIDNEY (ZIMBABWE) (PVT) LTD
WISCO (PTY) LTD
WISPECO (NAMIBIA) (PTY) LTD
WISPECO (PTY) LTD
WISPECO DU VENHAGE (PTY) LTD
WISPECO HOLDINGS (PTY) LTD
WISPECO HOUSING (PTY) LTD
WISPECO LTD
WISPECO PROPERTIES (PTY) LTD
WISPECO WESTLITE (PTY) LTD
WISPECO WIDNEY (PTY) LTD
WOLHUTER STEEL (PTY) LTD

INVESTMENTS

None

METRO CASH & CARRY LTD

ABBREVIATION : METCASH

JSE SHORT CODE : MTC

SECTOR : Industrial-Retailers & Wholesalers

SHAREHOLDERS

Who Owns Whom's Assessment of the Identity of the Ultimate Controlling Shareholder:
PREMIER GROUP LTD

SHAREHOLDER	PERCENTAGE 1992	1991
METGROUPHOLD LTD	29 2	29 3
STERKWIL INV P/L	24 5	---
SCORE-CLICKS HOLDINGS LTD	14 6	14 6
EIGHTY ONE MAIN STREET NOM LTD	6 4	6 4
STD BANK NOM TVL P/L	3 7	3 1
CMB NOM P/L	2 7	---
HI SCORE INV HOLDINGS P/L	1 8	---
PREMIER GROUP PENS FUND	1 7	---
LIBERTY LIFE ASSOC OF AFRICA LTD	1 6	1 6
SHAPE INV P/L	1 4	---
METROPOLITAN LIFE LTD	1 2	1 2
DEMOCRAT NOM P/L	---	1 2
SA MUTUAL	---	1 1
SANLAM	---	2 8
STATUS INV P/L	---	1 3
SUSPENCE ACCOUNT	---	27 5
TOTAL	88 8	90 0

DIRECTORS :
DOS SANTOS CS (Chief Executive),GRAINGER JL
JOSEPH B ,RUBIN VD ,RYKAART E ,TAUROG RD
UTIAN GM (Deputy Chairman)
WRIGHTON PGA (Chairman

REGISTRATION NUMBER : 05/21315/06

REGISTERED OFFICE
Cnr Crownwood & Amethyst Roads, Theta Township Ext 1
Johannesburg
2091
TEL 011-490 2000
FAX 011-496 1442

TRANSFER SECRETARY
Central Registrars Ltd
P O Box 4844, Johannesburg
2000
TEL 011-331 0051

COMPANY SECRETARY
A Ah Kun

NATURE OF BUSINESS
An investment holding company The subsidiaries & associates are engaged in the distribution of groceries and other related consumer goods on a cash and carry basis

BANKERS :
First National Bank of SA Ltd
Standard Bank of SA Ltd, Bankorp Ltd

AUDITORS :
Fisher Hoffman Stride, Ernst & Young

FAMILIAR BRAND NAMES
FAMILY FAVOURITE,METBUILD,METRO
STAX SUPERSTORES,TRADE CENTRE

CONTRIBUTION BY ACTIVITY
N/A

YEAR END : April

DIVIDEND :Ords no par value

Interim	(Ldr)09/03/90	(Pay)30/03/90	Amt(c)10 5
Final	(Ldr)12/10/90	(Pay)26/10/90	Amt(c)10 5
Final	(Ldr)17/07/92	(Pay)31/07/92	Amt(c)6
Interim	(Ldr)24/12/92	(Pay)15/01/93	Amt(c)6

NUMBER OF EMPLOYEES : 13702

CAPITAL STRUCTURE

	AUTHORISED	ISSUED
Ords no par value	200000000	164560662

FINANCIAL STATISTICS (AT FINANCIAL YEAR END)

(Amts in R'000)	1992 Apr	1991 Jun	1990 Jun	1989 Jun	1988 Jun
Ord S/H Int	269564	75064	319075	297111	279039
Long Trm Loans	54098	56179	17879	30128	22610
Iss Ord Share	164561	67023	67023	64922	64922
Total Liab	868815	827861	707273	617093	509699
Current Liab	814717	771682	689394	586965	487089
Total Assets	1021400	829579	910325	811348	687030
Intang Assets	116979	73346	116023	102856	101708
Current Assets	887095	658298	788636	702017	587323
Debtors	106176	139004	200798	158907	142722
Inventory	511351	511248	558310	476121	377547
Turnover	4074842	4064310	3491149	3143577	2718566
Oper Profit	47554	-17142	74162	82841	65975
Interest Paid	10495	34998	28499	23100	11065
Tax Paid	14889	7507	20486	25499	21541
Prf af Int&Tax	31832	-53966	29356	37918	33369
Prf att Ord Sh	28503	-53244	27462	34627	29861
Btm Line Earn	34089	-244011	25882	34627	29313
Dividend Paid	9874	-	14421	16555	13634
Mkt Prce(c) YE	290	325	475	475	500
Depreciation	14947	17950	16456	14001	13503

PER SHARE STATISTICS (CENTS)

Net Asst Val	92 72	2 56	302 96	299 21	273 14
Net Earnings	17 30	-79 40	41 30	53 30	46 00
Dividends	6 00	-	21 00	25 50	21 00
Cash Flow	37 67	-52 68	64 72	74 47	65 85

RATIOS AND OTHER INFORMATION

Mrk Cap(R000)	477227	217825	318359	308380	324610
Current Ratio	1 09	0 85	1 14	1 20	1 21
Quik/Acid Tst	0 46	0 19	0 33	0 38	0 43
A/C Rec T/ovr	46 05	29 24	17 39	19 78	19 05
Tot Ass T/ovr	4 79	4 90	3 84	3 87	3 96
Debt/Ass Rat	0 82	0 98	0 76	0 72	0 72
L T L Tot Ass	0 02	0 05	-	-	0 01
Debt to Eqity	3 11	10 81	2 16	1 98	1 77
Interest Cover	4 53	-0 39	2 63	3 59	5 96
Oper Prof Mrg	1 17	-0 42	2 12	2 64	2 43
Net Prof Marg%	0 70	-1 31	0 79	1 10	1 10
Ret on Assets	6 72	-1 38	8 61	10 66	9 62
Ret on Equity%	12 69	-70 93	8 61	11 65	10 70
Price/Earnings	16 76	-4 09	11 50	8 91	10 87
Divid Cover	2 88	-	1 97	2 09	2 19
Divid Yield	2 07		4 42	5 37	4 20
Earning Yield%	5 97	-24 43	8 69	11 22	9 20
NAV % Mrk Pr	31 97	0 79	63 78	62 99	54 63
Effec Tax Rate	14 30	-13 96	24 09	30 37	28 23
Def Interval	0 98	-5 11	1 55	1 61	0 84
Sus Grth Rate	6 91	-70 93	4 09	6 08	5 82

SUBSIDIARY & ASSOCIATED COMPANIES

AFRIMET LTD (49%)
ALMA E. PALACHE (PTY) LTD
ALMA E. PALACHE (PTY) LTD
ERF 4671 CHURCH STREET PROPERTY (PTY) LT (50%)
FB WHOLESALERS (PTY) LTD
FRASER-TIRISANO (PTY) LTD (50%)
FRASERS CASH & CARRY (MALUTI) LTD (50%)
FRASERS CASH & CARRY (VENDA) LTD (50%)
FRASERS FINANCE (PTY) LTD (50%)
FRASERS GAZANKULU (PTY) LTD (50%)
FRASERS NCEDISIZWE LTD
IAN FRASER LTD
JACK YUDELMAN LESOTHO WHOLESALERS (PTY)
K-AIR CHARTER (PTY) LTD (50%)
KAIR CHARTER (PTY) LTD (50%)
LONSDALE AVIATION (PTY) LTD
LOT 6417 JAN HOFMEYER ROAD PROPERTY (PTY (50%)
MAFETENG WHOLESALERS (PTY) LTD (50%)
METCASH TRADING LTD
METRO (SWA) (PTY) LTD
METRO BOTSHABELO LTD (50%)
METRO CASH & CARRY (BOPHUTHATSWANA) LTD (50%)
METRO CASH & CARRY (BOTSWANA) (PTY) LTD (50%)
METRO KANGWANE (PTY) LTD (50%)
METRO KWANDEBELE LTD (49%)
METRO LEBOWA LTD (50%)
METRO LESOTHO (PTY) LTD (50%)
METRO NOLIZWE LTD (50%)
METRO QWA QWA LTD (50%)
METRO SWAZILAND (PTY) LTD (50%)
METRO TRADE CENTRE (PTY) LTD
METRO VENDA LTD (50%)
METROTRACOC (PTY) LTD (50%)
MOSHAL GEVISSER (LESOTHO) LTD
NOLANS WHOLESALE LTD
PAN AFRICAN SALES (PTY) LTD (50%)
QUTHING CASH & CARRY (PTY) LTD
REMUS DISTRIBUTORS ZASTRON (PTY) LTD
SCORE FOOD HOLDINGS LTD
SCORE MANAGEMENT SERVICES (PTY) LTD
SW UNITED AGENCY (PTY) LTD (50%)
TF TRADING LTD (50%)
TRADOR CASH & CARRY (BOPHUTHATSWANA) (PT
TRADOR CASH & CARRY (TRANSKEI) (PTY) LTD
TRADOR DEVLAND (PTY) LTD
TRADOR HOLDINGS (PTY) LTD
TRADOR PROPERTIES (PTY) LTD

INVESTMENTS

SMALL BUSINESS DEVELOPMENT CORP LTD (263000 SH)
SOUTH AFRICAN NUMBERING ASSOCIATION (5000 SH)

METROPOLITAN LIFE LTD

ABBREVIATION : METPOL

JSE SHORT CODE : MET

SECTOR : Financial-Insurance

SHAREHOLDERS

Who Owns Whom's Assessment of the Identity of the Ultimate Controlling Shareholder:
SANLAM VIA SANKORP

SHAREHOLDER	PERCENTAGE 1992	1991
CMB NOM P/L	55.1	---
EIGHTY ONE MAIN STREET NOM LTD	4.7	2.1
YSKOR PENS FUND	4.6	4.8
SANLAMTRUST NOM P/L	2.8	2.8
STD BANK NOM TVL P/L	2.7	1.0
SIXTY SIX MARSHALL STREET NOM P/L	2.5	3.2
COMMERCIAL UNION LIFE ASSURE CO SA LTD	1.9	---
SHARESTOCK NOM P/L	1.8	1.6
FIRST NAT NOM P/L	1.6	1.8
ESCOM PENS & PROV FUND	1.5	1.4
ALTENA MEWS P/L	---	1.3
BANNER NOM P/L	---	2.1
COMMERCIAL UNION ASSURE CO SA LTD	---	1.8
SANKORP BPK	---	38.4
SANLAM	---	12.7
SYFRETS NOM LTD	---	2.0
TOTAL	79.1	76.9

DIRECTORS :
DU PLESSIS AS ,ESTERHUYSE WP PROF,MOKHOBO DNM MS
NKABINDE AC PROF,PETERS HA ,PICKARD JAJ
PRETORIUS WS (Chairman),SCHOLTZ PJF
SMITH ML (Managing Director),SONN FA
STEYN JC THE HON,SWART NJ PROF,WEBB RC
WIESE CH AD

REGISTRATION NUMBER : 05/32491/06

REGISTERED OFFICE
38 Wale Street, Cape Town
8001
TEL: 021-24 1134
FAX: 021-24 6972

TRANSFER SECRETARY
Central Registrars Ltd
P O Box 4844, Johannesburg
2000
TEL: 011-331 0051

COMPANY SECRETARY
P J Scannell

NATURE OF BUSINESS
Metropolitan Life is a registered life insurer that transacts individual life as well as long-term disability business. In other categories it transacts group life, disability, provident and pension scheme business, & home service insurance.

BANKERS :
Trust Bank of Africa Ltd, Volkskas Ltd
First National Bank of SA Ltd
Standard Bank of SA Ltd

AUDITORS :
Ernst & Young, Coopers Theron Du Toit

FAMILIAR BRAND NAMES
DYNAMIC LIFE

CONTRIBUTION BY ACTIVITY
Premium Income (% Income) (68.9%)
Investment Income (31.1%)

YEAR END : September

DIVIDEND : Ords no par value

Interim	(Ldr)07/06/91	(Pay)21/06/91	Amt(c)16 5
Special	(Ldr)02/08/91	(Pay)27/09/91	Amt(c)18
Prelim	(Ldr)20/12/91	(Pay)03/01/92	Amt(c)10 5
Interim	(Ldr)12/06/92	(Pay)26/06/92	Amt(c)20
Final	(Ldr)11/12/92	(Pay)30/12/92	Amt(c)35

NUMBER OF EMPLOYEES : 4616

CAPITAL STRUCTURE

	AUTHORISED	ISSUED
Ords no par value	75000000	67222160

FINANCIAL STATISTICS (AT FINANCIAL YEAR END)

(Amts in R'000)	1991 Sep	1990 Sep	1989 Sep	1988	1987
Ord S/H Int	298801	99258	80216	73161	67493
Long Trm Loans	2299186	1874510	1561923	1597504	1430937
Iss Ord Share	67222	44541	44541	44371	44209
Total Liab	2468637	2027325	1710520	1597504	1430937
Current Liab	169451	152815	148597	-	-
Total Assets	2767438	2126583	1790736	1670665	1498430
Current Assets	253015	191348	183732	-	-
Debtors	19619	9694	30419	-	-
Inventory	-	8628	13445	-	-
Turnover	702965	546280	437736	-	-
Oper Profit	776187	615956	46997	-	-
Tax Paid	27821	28379	27000	-	-
Prf af Int&Tax	748366	587577	19997	206772	170489
Prf att Ord Sh	457344	363022	19997	15991	12723
Btm Line Earn	457344	363022	19997	15991	12723
Dividend Paid	22978	16801	13572	10859	8662
Mkt Prce(c) YE	1150	600	500	370	470

PER SHARE STATISTICS (CENTS)

Net Asst Val	444 50	222 85	180 09	164 88	152 67
Net Earnings	70 00	56 50	45 00	-	-
Dividends	45 00	37 00	30 00	-	-
Cash Flow	1663 37	1371 75	46 72	466 01	385 64

RATIOS AND OTHER INFORMATION

Mrk Cap(R000)	773053	267246	222705	164173	207782
Current Ratio	1 49	1 25	1 24	-	
Quik/Acid Tst	1 49	1 20	1 15	-	-
A/C Rec T/ovr	35 83	56 35	14 39	-	-
Tot Ass T/ovr	0 25	0 26	0 24	-	-
Debt/Ass Rat	0 06	0 07	0 08	0 96	0 95
L T L Tot Ass	-	-	-	0 96	0 95
Debt to Eqity	0 57	1 54	1 85	21 84	21 20
Oper Prof Mrg	110 42	112 75	10 74	-	-
Net Prof Marg%	65 06	66 45	4 57	-	-
Ret on Assets	28 05	28 96	2 62	12 38	11 38
Ret on Equity%	153 06	365 74	24 93	21 86	18 85
Price/Earnings	16 43	10 62	11 11	-	-
Divid Cover	1 56	1 53	1 50	-	-
Divid Yield	3 91	6 17	6 00	-	-
Earning Yield%	6 09	9 42	9 00	-	-
NAV % Mrk Pr	38 65	37 14	36 02	44 56	32 48
Effec Tax Rate	3 58	4 61	57 45	-	-
Def Interval	-	-	0 07	7 73	8 39
Sus Grth Rate	145 37	348 81	8 01	7 01	6 02

SUBSIDIARY & ASSOCIATED COMPANIES

ALEXANDER BROS (PTY) LTD
BRIMAXDOR (PTY) LTD
CENTRAL CITY BUILDINGS (PTY) LTD
CITY TRUST HOUSE LTD
CONSOLIDATED CRAFTS (PTY) LTD
DESPATCH SAKESENTRUM (PTY) LTD
GAMAPHUTENG ENTERPRISES (PTY) LTD
HOMES TRUST (PTY) LTD
HOMES TRUST MOTOR FINANCE CO (PTY) LTD
HOMES TRUST-GEBOU JOHANNESBURG (PTY) LTD
KERKSTRAAT UITENHAGE BELEGGINS (PTY) LTD
KIRKNEY EXT 12 FIRST BLOCK (PTY) LTD
KIRKNEY EXT 12 FOURTH BLOCK (PTY) LTD
KIRKNEY EXT 12 SECOND BLOCK (PTY) LTD
KIRKNEY EXT 12 THIRD BLOCK (PTY) LTD
LA DAUPHINE PROPERTIES (CAPE) (PTY) LTD
LLOYDS BUILDINGS (CT) (PTY) LTD
LOT 3549 MARGATE SHARE BLOCK (PTY) LTD
LOUSTAN ASSOCIATES (PTY) LTD
MAYLOW PROPERTIES (PTY) LTD
METPOL INVESTMENT ENTERPRISES (PTY) LTD
METROPOLITAN BEREA (PTY) LTD
METROPOLITAN BUILDING FIELD STREET (PTY)
METROPOLITAN LEWENS EIENDOMME BPK
METROPOLITAN LIFE INVESTMENTS LTD
METROPOLITAN LIFE UNIT TRUST MANAGEMENT
METROPOLITAN-GEBOU PRETORIA (PTY) LTD
METRUST LTD
N B A (PTY) LTD
RAADZAALHOF (PTY) LTD
ROBRIAN INVESTMENTS (PTY) LTD
W H LE ROUX DELPORT (PTY) LTD

INVESTMENTS

None

MHANGURA COPPER MINES LTD

ABBREVIATION : M-C-M

JSE SHORT CODE : MCM

SECTOR : Metals & Minerals-Copper

SHAREHOLDERS

Who Owns Whom's Assessment of the Identity of the Ultimate Controlling Shareholder: ZIMBABWE MINING DEVELOPMENT CORP

SHAREHOLDER	PERCENTAGE 1992	1991
ZIMBABWE MINING DEVELOP CORP LTD	54 6	---
JOHANNESBURG REGISTER ACCOUNT	6 4	---
OLD MUTUAL INV CORP (PVT) LTD	6 3	---
LONDON REGISTER ACCOUNT	6 1	---
LONDON CONTROL ACCOUNT	---	8 7
ZIMBABWE CONTROL ACCOUNT	---	87 6
TOTAL	73 3	96 2

DIRECTORS :
ATKINSON JA ,CHIEZA G MS,HADDON MF ,MAPFUMO TJ
MASUNDA MA (Chairman),MATEMA ST ,PHIMISTER JG

REGISTERED OFFICE
Minerals Marketing Corp of Zim, Stand 107 Mutare Road
Msasa, Harare

TEL 01914-728331
FAX 01914-792974

TRANSFER SECRETARY
Central Registrars Ltd
P O Box 4844, Johannesburg
2000
TEL: 011-331 0051

COMPANY SECRETARY
ZMDC Management Services Ltd

NATURE OF BUSINESS
The company is incorporated in Zimbabwe. Principal activities are copper mining, smelting & refining.

BANKERS :
Barclays Bank of Zimbabwe Ltd
Bank of Credit & Commerce Zimbabwe Ltd
Standard Chartered Bank
First Merchant Bank of Zimbabwe Ltd

AUDITORS :
Ernst & Young

FAMILIAR BRAND NAMES
N/A

CONTRIBUTION BY ACTIVITY
N/A

YEAR END : June

DIVIDEND : Ords Z$1
Dividend No 44 (Ldr)14/02/92 (Pay)06/03/92 Amt(c)5

NUMBER OF EMPLOYEES : 2500

CAPITAL STRUCTURE

	AUTHORISED	ISSUED
Ords Z$1	20000000	20000000

FINANCIAL STATISTICS (AT FINANCIAL YEAR END)

(Amts in Zim$)	1992 Jun	1991 Jun	1990 Jun	1989 Jun	1988 Jun
Ord S/H Int	35189	32200	38920	36698	22883
Long Trm Loans	11800	13000	13000	13000	13000
Iss Ord Share	20000	20000	20000	20000	20000
Total Liab	100356	90259	69795	59573	58721
Current Liab	88556	77259	56795	46573	45721
Total Assets	135545	122459	108715	96271	81604
Current Assets	84249	70677	62236	52280	42233
Debtors	28537	15487	19000	14161	11670
Inventory	53074	38835	32864	23714	21572
Turnover	162939	109644	95257	105928	71166
Oper Profit	19402	-2342	6008	19031	6130
Interest Paid	11502	6288	5567	3637	3460
Tax Paid	4	7	-	2	2
Prf af Int&Tax	8549	-6720	2222	15392	2668
Prf att Ord Sh	8549	-6720	2222	15392	2668
Btm Line Earn	8549	-6720	2222	15392	2668
Dividend Paid	1000	-	-	-	-
Mkt Prce(c) YE	20	20	35	57	53

PER SHARE STATISTICS (CENTS)

Net Asst Val	175.95	161.00	194.60	183.49	114.42
Net Earnings	42.70	-33.60	11.10	69.10	13.30
Dividends	5.00	-	-	-	-
Cash Flow	42.75	-33.60	11.11	76.96	13.34

RATIOS AND OTHER INFORMATION

Mrk Cap(R000)	4000	4000	7000	11400	10600
Current Ratio	0.95	0.91	1.10	1.12	0.92
Quik/Acid Tst	0.35	0.41	0.52	0.61	0.45
A/C Rec T/ovr	5.71	7.08	5.01	7.48	6.10
Tot Ass T/ovr	1.20	0.90	0.88	1.10	0.87
Debt/Ass Rat	0.74	0.74	0.64	0.62	0.72
L T L Tot Ass	0.09	0.11	0.12	0.14	0.16
Debt to Eqity	2.85	2.80	1.79	1.62	2.57
Interest Cover	1.69	-0.37	1.08	5.23	1.77
Oper Prof Mrg	11.91	-2.14	6.31	17.97	8.61
Net Prof Marg%	5.25	-6.13	2.33	14.53	3.75
Ret on Assets	14.80	-0.35	7.16	19.77	7.51
Ret on Equity%	24.29	-20.87	5.71	41.94	11.66
Price/Earnings	0.47	-0.60	3.15	0.82	3.98
Divid Cover	8.54	-	-	-	-
Divid Yield	25.00	-	-	-	-
Earning Yield%	213.50	-168.00	31.71	121.23	25.09
NAV % Mrk Pr	879.73	805.00	556.00	321.91	215.88
Effec Tax Rate	0.05	-0.10	-	0.01	0.07
Def Interval	5.58	-8.78	21.15	2.18	14.73
Sus Grth Rate	21.45	-20.87	5.71	41.94	11.66

SUBSIDIARY & ASSOCIATED COMPANIES

MERITS LTD (25%)

INVESTMENTS

None

MICOR HOLDINGS LTD

ABBREVIATION : MICOR

JSE SHORT CODE : MIC

SECTOR : Industrial-Industrial Holding

SHAREHOLDERS

Who Owns Whom's Assessment of the Identity of the Ultimate Controlling Shareholder:
DIRECTORS

SHAREHOLDER	PERCENTAGE 1992	1991
CENTAUR MANAGERS P/L	30.2	30.2
STD BANK NOM TVL P/L	6.7	6.8
FIRST NAT NOM P/L	6.6	6.6
SECURITIES EQUITIES P/L	6.3	---
VOLKSKAS NOM P/L	4.1	5.6
TWENTY SIXTH STAGE INV P/L	3.6	3.6
EIGHTY ONE MAIN STREET NOM LTD	3.6	3.6
KAPLAN C B	3.2	3.2
CHAMPEL INC LTD	2.3	---
SAUNDERS P B	2.2	2.2
COSMOS NOM P/L	1.9	1.9
KAPLAN M J	1.8	1.8
SUSSEX INV P/L	1.7	1.5
BEEVERS M J	1.5	1.7
NEDBANK NOM LTD	1.5	1.0
ABSA NOM P/L	1.5	---
BARRADAS J	1.1	1.1
TELGAR HOLDINGS P/L	1.0	1.0
CARPA TRUST CO P/L	---	2.6
THOMAS INTERNATIONAL LTD	---	6.4
TOTAL	81.0	80.8

DIRECTORS :
BARRADAS J ,BEEVERS MJ ,DELAHUNT MJ
KAPLAN CB (Chairman)
KAPLAN MJ (Deputy Chairman),RUBENSTEIN GB

REGISTRATION NUMBER : 69/09561/06

REGISTERED OFFICE
9th Floor, New Plaza Centre, 150 Jeppe Street
Johannesburg
2001
TEL: 011-833 7020
FAX: 011-833 7037

TRANSFER SECRETARY
Fraser Street Registrars (Pty) Ltd
P O Box 61178, Marshalltown
2107
TEL: 011-491 0911

COMPANY SECRETARY
J Barradas

NATURE OF BUSINESS
A holding company whose subsidiaries are engaged in international and domestic freight, travel, finance, insurance broking, anti-corrosion services and sale of industrial equipment.
The company has a controlling interest in JSE-quoted Micor Industrial Corp Ltd.

BANKERS :
Nedcor Bank Ltd

AUDITORS :
Kessel Feinstein

FAMILIAR BRAND NAMES
N/A

CONTRIBUTION BY ACTIVITY
Transportation & Travel (% Turnover) (55.1%)
Insurance Broking & Finance (43.1%)
Industrial (1.8%)

YEAR END : June

DIVIDEND : Ords 10c

Dividend No 21	(Ldr)28/09/90	(Pay)19/10/90	Amt(c)12
Dividend No 22	(Ldr)04/10/91	(Pay)25/10/91	Amt(c)5
Dividend No 23	(Ldr)02/10/92	(Pay)23/10/92	Amt(c)6.5

CAPITAL STRUCTURE

	AUTHORISED	ISSUED
Ords 10c	25000000	16534500

FINANCIAL STATISTICS (AT FINANCIAL YEAR END)

(Amts in R'000)	1992 Jun	1991 Jun	1990 Jun	1989 Jun	1988 Jun
Ord S/H Int	33915	31038	28366	26141	19225
Long Trm Loans	6592	5396	5453	3584	4763
Iss Ord Share	16535	16535	16535	2947	2847
Total Liab	80847	63844	59369	54386	36487
Current Liab	74255	58448	53916	50802	31724
Total Assets	113939	94059	86912	79704	55712
Intang Assets	823	823	823	823	*
Current Assets	102194	77410	72182	68064	46599
Debtors	85532	67587	64106	60561	40363
Inventory	2291	2725	1831	1395	1535
Turnover	731181	526023	492284	425109	369515
Oper Profit	9816	10412	8886	8283	5813
Interest Paid	5865	7600	3654	3753	2858
Tax Paid	619	289	333	200	432
Prf af Int&Tax	3332	2523	4899	4330	2523
Prf att Ord Sh	3141	2512	4754	4510	2523
Btm Line Earn	2698	2512	3959	4287	2423
Dividend Paid	1075	827	1984	1444	810
Mkt Prce(c) YE	85	90	135	400	390
Depreciation	3414	3365	2964	2574	1675

PER SHARE STATISTICS (CENTS)

Net Asst Val	200.13	182.73	166.57	859.11	675.27
Net Earnings	19.00	15.20	29.10	29.60	86.00
Dividends	6.50	5.00	12.00	9.80	27.50
Cash Flow	39.98	35.54	47.21	46.42	149.02

RATIOS AND OTHER INFORMATION

Mrk Cap(R000)	14055	14882	22322	11788	11103
Current Ratio	1.38	1.32	1.34	1.34	1.47
Quik/Acid Tst	1.35	1.28	1.30	1.31	1.42
A/C Rec T/ovr	8.55	7.78	7.68	7.02	9.15
Tot Ass T/ovr	6.42	5.59	5.66	5.33	6.63
Debt/Ass Rat	0.68	0.65	0.65	0.67	0.62
L T L Tot Ass	0.03	0.03	0.03	0.03	0.05
Debt to Eqity	2.30	1.96	1.99	2.04	1.80
Interest Cover	1.67	1.37	2.43	2.21	2.03
Oper Prof Mrg	1.34	1.98	1.81	1.95	1.57
Net Prof Marg%	0.43	0.48	0.97	1.06	0.68
Ret on Assets	8.62	11.07	10.22	10.39	10.43
Ret on Equity%	9.26	8.09	16.76	17.25	13.12
Price/Earnings	4.47	5.92	4.64	13.51	4.53
Divid Cover	2.92	3.04	2.43	3.02	3.13
Divid Yield	7.65	5.56	8.89	2.45	7.05
Earning Yield%	22.35	16.89	21.56	7.40	22.05
NAV % Mrk Pr	235.45	203.04	123.39	214.78	173.15
Effec Tax Rate	14.25	10.28	7.11	4.42	14.62
Def Interval	3.56	6.17	2.99	2.94	3.61
Sus Grth Rate	6.09	5.43	9.77	11.73	8.91

SUBSIDIARY & ASSOCIATED COMPANIES

MEDKAP PROPERTIES (PTY) LTD
METROPOLITAN ENTERPRISES LTD
METROPOLITAN FACTORS LTD
METROPOLITAN INDUSTRIAL CORP. (PTY) LTD
MICOR EMPLOYEE BENEFITS (PTY) LTD
MICOR FINANCIAL PLANNING SERVICES (PTY)
MICOR INDUSTRIAL CORPORATION LTD
MICOR INSURANCE BROKERS (PTY) LTD
MICOR MANAGEMENT SERVICES (PTY) LTD
MICOR TRUST (PTY) LTD
RENTAL ACCEPTANCES (PTY) LTD
TSUNAMAI NO. 6 LTD

INVESTMENTS

None

MICOR INDUSTRIAL CORPORATION LTD

ABBREVIATION : MICIND

JSE SHORT CODE : MIN

SECTOR : Industrial-Industrial Holding

SHAREHOLDERS

Who Owns Whom's Assessment of the Identity of the Ultimate Controlling Shareholder: MICOR HOLDINGS

SHAREHOLDER	PERCENTAGE 1992	1991
MICOR HOLDINGS LTD	91.5	91.5
TOTAL	91.5	91.5

DIRECTORS :
BARRADAS J (Financial Director)
BEEVERS MJ (Deputy Managing Director)
CHEETHAM P ,COETZER GH ,DE JONG P ,DRUCKMAN DS
KAPLAN CB ,KAPLAN MJ (Chairman & Managing Dir.

REGISTRATION NUMBER : 87/01331/06

REGISTERED OFFICE
9th Floor, New Plaza Centre, 150 Jeppe Street
Johannesburg
2001
TEL: 011-833 7020
FAX: 011-836 3173

TRANSFER SECRETARY
Fraser Street Registrars (Pty) Ltd
P O Box 61178, Marshalltown
2107
TEL: 011-491 0911

COMPANY SECRETARY
J Barradas

NATURE OF BUSINESS
The company is a holding company with subsidiaries engaged in the business of international freight, travel and the sale of industrial equipment.

BANKERS :
Standard Bank of SA Ltd
First National Bank of SA Ltd
Central Merchant Bank Ltd, Volkskas Ltd
Nedcor Bank Ltd

AUDITORS :
Kessel Feinstein

FAMILIAR BRAND NAMES
N/A

CONTRIBUTION BY ACTIVITY
Transportation & Travel(% prof aft tax) (93.2%)
Industrial (6.8%)

YEAR END : June

DIVIDEND :Ords 1c

Dividend No 2	(Ldr)28/09/90	(Pay)19/10/90	Amt(c)5
Dividend No 3	(Ldr)04/10/91	(Pay)25/10/91	Amt(c)3
Dividend No 4	(Ldr)02/10/92	(Pay)23/10/92	Amt(c)2

CAPITAL STRUCTURE

	AUTHORISED	ISSUED
Ords 1c	40000000	23505658

FINANCIAL STATISTICS (AT FINANCIAL YEAR END)

(Amts in R'000)	1992 Jun	1991 Jun	1990 Jun	1989 Jun
Ord S/H Int	23253	23222	23202	10466
Long Trm Loans	7199	7234	7109	701
Iss Ord Share	23506	23506	23506	17208
Total Liab	63841	48436	42746	22852
Current Liab	56642	41202	35637	22151
Total Assets	77221	61785	56053	33318
Intang Assets	9873	9873	9895	*
Current Assets	66215	47167	41087	27208
Debtors	48647	36555	31637	11617
Inventory	1468	1744	1348	15286
Turnover	462351	356298	362123	-
Oper Profit	5724	5210	7216	3291
Interest Paid	5037	5828	4420	-
Tax Paid	34	48	217	1617
Prf af Int&Tax	991	736	3045	1674
Prf att Ord Sh	984	725	3010	1674
Btm Line Earn	501	725	8086	1674
Dividend Paid	470	705	1175	-
Mkt Prce(c) YE	35	35	70	88
Depreciation	1900	1970	1548	541

PER SHARE STATISTICS (CENTS)

Net Asst Val	56.92	56.79	56.81	60.82
Net Earnings	4.20	3.10	13.00	9.70
Dividends	2.00	3.00	5.00	-
Cash Flow	12.21	11.41	19.67	12.73

RATIOS AND OTHER INFORMATION

Mrk Cap(R000)	8227	8227	16454	15143
Current Ratio	1.17	1.14	1.15	1.23
Quik/Acid Tst	1.14	1.10	1.12	0.54
A/C Rec T/ovr	9.50	9.75	11.45	-
Tot Ass T/ovr	5.99	5.77	6.46	-
Debt/Ass Rat	0.83	0.78	0.76	0.69
L T L Tot Ass	0.09	0.12	0.13	0.02
Debt to Eqity	2.74	2.08	1.84	2.18
Interest Cover	1.14	0.89	1.63	-
Oper Prof Mrg	1.24	1.46	1.99	-
Net Prof Marg%	0.21	0.20	0.83	-
Ret on Assets	7.85	10.70	13.70	9.88
Ret on Equity%	4.23	3.12	12.97	15.99
Price/Earnings	8.33	11.29	5.38	9.07
Divid Cover	2.10	1.03	2.60	-
Divid Yield	5.71	8.57	7.14	-
Earning Yield%	12.00	8.86	18.57	11.02
NAV % Mrk Pr	162.63	162.26	80.87	69.11
Effec Tax Rate	4.68	7.91	6.47	49.86
Def Interval	5.72	10.10	4.82	1.09
Sus Grth Rate	2.21	0.09	7.91	15.99

SUBSIDIARY & ASSOCIATED COMPANIES

AFRICAN TRAVEL SERVICES (PTY) LTD
AIRLINE AGENTS (PTY) LTD
ASSOCIATED DIESEL CO (PTY) LTD
ASSOCIATED DIESEL INJECTION SERVICES (PT
ASSOCIATED DIESEL SERVICES (PRETORIA) (P
BANDSAWING SERVICES (PTY) LTD
CADRE MANAGEMENT SERVICES (PTY) LTD
KELLY'S CARTAGE (PTY) LTD
MIC KAPLAN (PTY) LTD
MICOR (PTY) LTD
MICOR MEADOWS AIRFREIGHT (PTY) LTD
MICOR SHIPPING (PTY) LTD
MICOR TOURS (PTY) LTD
PATSY DIESEL (PTY) LTD
SHIPPING SYSTEMS (PTY) LTD
TRAVAMARKT (PTY) LTD
TREK TOURS AFRICA (PTY) LTD
WILSON COLLINS & CO (PTY) LTD
WILSON COLLINS TRAVEL (PTY) LTD

INVESTMENTS

AFCOM GROUP LTD (17000 SH)
DAVMAX (PTY) LTD ("B" SHARES) (11025 SH)
MABULA TIME SHARING SHARE BLOCK LTD (10 SH)

MIDAS LTD

ABBREVIATION : MIDAS

JSE SHORT CODE : MDS

SECTOR : Industrial-Retailers & Wholesalers

SHAREHOLDERS

Who Owns Whom's Assessment of the Identity of the Ultimate Controlling Shareholder:
ANGLO VIA MCCARTHY GROUP

SHAREHOLDER	PERCENTAGE 1992	1991
MCCARTHY GROUP LTD	36.3	31.8
SA MUTUAL	11.8	12.1
CMB NOM P/L	11.7	---
STD BANK NOM TVL P/L	8.8	8.3
ANGLO AMERICAN CORP PENS FUND	2.8	2.8
ANGLO AMERICAN GROUP PENS FUND	2.1	2.1
METAL IND GROUP PENS FUND	1.6	---
ENGINEERING INDUSTRIES PENS FUND	1.6	---
RILEY D B	1.2	1.0
FIRST NAT NOM P/L	1.1	---
NORWITZ R	1.0	1.1
EIGHTY ONE MAIN STREET NOM LTD	---	1.2
FVB LTD	---	11.9
MOMENTUM LIFE ASSURE LTD	---	2.7
SANLAM	---	11.8
TOTAL	80.0	86.7

DIRECTORS :
AKAL WC ,ALISON AW (Financial Director)
BARNES AS ,BENZ WP ,DE VOS SJ ,GUDEGAST RD
MCCARTHY BC ,NORWITZ R
RICH JA (Managing Director),RILEY DB (Chairman)
SAVILLE D

REGISTRATION NUMBER : 68/02260/06

REGISTERED OFFICE
9 Old Main Pretoria Road, Halfway House
Midrand
1685
TEL: 011-315 0500
FAX: 011-315 1656

TRANSFER SECRETARY
Central Registrars Ltd
P O Box 4844, Johannesburg
2000
TEL: 011-331 0051

COMPANY SECRETARY
E E Pienaar

NATURE OF BUSINESS
The group markets automotive parts & accessories, as well as motorcycles, power products, selected hardware, sports equipment, tools, bicycles and bicycle parts and accessories.

BANKERS :
Standard Bank of SA Ltd
First National Bank of SA Ltd
Central Merchant Bank Ltd, Bankorp Ltd

AUDITORS :
Deloitte Pim Goldby

FAMILIAR BRAND NAMES
ACE ACCESSORIES,AKALS,ALFA ROMEO PARTS
ARMSTRONG,AUTOLUX,BEKA-MAX
BODA BUS BODY PARTS,BRIDGESTONE CYCLES
CHAMPION CHAIN STORE,DAIHATSU PARTS
DOGA BUS BODY PARTS,FISHINGQUIP
FRENZEL BUS PARTS,GELHARD RADIOS,GIOS FRAMES
HAPPICH BUS BODY PARTS,HELLA,HOMEQUIP
IRC TYRES,ISCASELLE SADDLES
KAWASAKI MOTORCYCLES,KAWASAKI POWER PRODUCT
KING ACESSORIES,KITAHARA,KKK DIESEL ENGINES
KL BUS BODY PARTS,MICROLITE
MIDAS PARTS CENTRE,MOTOLEK,MOTOQUIP,NEW-ERA
OMC DIESEL,OPTILUX,PARTS INC,PEUGEOT PARTS
QUAY BUFFALO,RENAULT PARTS,RESURGO DIESEL
S SILVERS MOTOR SPARES
SANJI SECURITY SYSTEMS,STANADYNE DIESEL
TELMA,WILSON,YANMAR DIESEL,ZEN
ZEXEL DIESEL ENGINES

CONTRIBUTION BY ACTIVITY
N/A

YEAR END : February

DIVIDEND : Ords 10c

Interim No 28	(Ldr)27/10/89	(Pay)10/11/89	Amt(c)14.5
Final No 29	(Ldr)18/05/90	(Pay)01/06/90	Amt(c)5.5
Interim No 30	(Ldr)09/11/90	(Pay)23/11/90	Amt(c)3
Final No 31	(Ldr)17/05/91	(Pay)30/05/91	Amt(c)5.5
Interim No 32	(Ldr)08/11/91	(Pay)22/11/91	Amt(c)6
Final No 33	(Ldr)22/05/92	(Pay)04/06/92	Amt(c)10

NUMBER OF EMPLOYEES : 950

CAPITAL STRUCTURE

	AUTHORISED	ISSUED
Ords 10c	25000000	14857078

FINANCIAL STATISTICS (AT FINANCIAL YEAR END)

(Amts in R'000)	1992 Feb	1991 Feb	1990 Feb	1989 Feb	1988 Feb
Ord S/H Int	62771	62338	63769	46914	33172
Long Trm Loans	671	493	1051	-	-
Iss Ord Share	14857	14781	14731	13155	12143
Total Liab	84194	64098	59690	47617	25405
Current Liab	83523	63605	58639	47617	25405
Total Assets	141672	116825	110018	83314	58577
Intang Assets	5293	9611	13441	11217	*
Current Assets	131981	104567	96095	71662	45243
Debtors	54754	45483	36737	23860	15642
Inventory	76579	58211	58201	47779	25670
Turnover	284439	241845	220791	175949	95420
Oper Profit	17883	12898	20963	21559	9763
Interest Paid	9580	8148	10866	3453	537
Tax Paid	225	301	1592	3336	2496
Prf af Int&Tax	8477	4508	8582	15262	6730
Prf att Ord Sh	9001	4640	8329	15632	7436

MC GREGOR'S
EDUCATION
ALTERNATIVES
EDUCATION ALTERNATIVES

Btm Line Earn	2593	-374	2744	12132	7207
Dividend Paid	2377	1256	2773	4604	2428
Mkt Prce(c) YE	365	325	550	1300	500
Depreciation	3431	2336	2197	693	384

PER SHARE STATISTICS (CENTS)

Net Asst Val	386.87	356.72	341.65	271.36	273.18
Net Earnings	60.70	31.50	60.30	118.80	61.20
Dividends	16.00	8.50	20.00	35.00	20.00
Cash Flow	79.46	47.95	78.00	121.28	58.59

RATIOS AND OTHER INFORMATION

Mrk Cap(R000)	54228	48038	81021	171015	60715
Current Ratio	1.58	1.64	1.64	1.50	1.78
Quik/Acid Tst	0.66	0.73	0.65	0.50	0.77
A/C Rec T/ovr	5.19	5.32	6.01	7.37	6.10
Tot Ass T/ovr	2.01	2.07	2.01	2.11	1.63
Debt/Ass Rat	0.59	0.54	0.53	0.57	0.43
Debt to Eqity	1.33	1.02	0.92	1.01	0.77
Interest Cover	1.87	1.58	1.93	6.24	18.18
Oper Prof Mrg	6.29	5.33	9.49	12.25	10.23
Net Prof Marg%	3.16	1.92	3.77	8.88	7.79
Ret on Assets	13.23	11.01	18.89	26.91	17.87
Ret on Equity%	14.34	7.44	13.06	33.32	22.42
Price/Earnings	6.01	10.32	9.12	10.94	8.17
Divid Cover	3.79	3.71	3.02	3.39	3.06
Divid Yield	4.38	2.62	3.64	2.69	4.00
Earning Yield%	16.63	9.69	10.96	9.14	12.24
NAV % Mrk Pr	105.99	109.76	62.12	20.87	54.64
Effec Tax Rate	4.67	6.26	15.65	18.25	27.05
Def Interval	2.57	3.45	2.84	1.23	0.58
Sus Grth Rate	10.55	5.43	8.71	23.51	15.10

SUBSIDIARY & ASSOCIATED COMPANIES

BUMPER-TO-BUMPER (PTY) LTD
DATA TIME HOLDINGS (PTY) LTD
E L B B INFORMATION SERVICES (PTY) LTD
GENUINE PARTS (PTY) LTD
HYPERQUIP WHOLESALE DISTRIBUTORS (PTY) L
KING MIDAS LTD
MONZA CASH & CARRY (PTY) LTD
MOTOLEK (SOUTH AFRICA) (PTY) LTD
MOTOLEK (ZIMBABWE) (PVT) LTD
MOTONET (PTY) LTD
NATIONAL AUTOMOBILE PARTS ASSOCIATION LT
PERCHILL INVESTMENTS (PTY) LTD
QUAY BUFFALO (PTY) LTD (45%)
S SILVERS MOTOR SPARES & ACCESSORIES (PT (41%)
WHEELS OF MAN (PTY) LTD

INVESTMENTS

None

MIDDLE WITWATERSRAND (WESTERN AREAS) LTD

ABBREVIATION : MID-WITS

JSE SHORT CODE : MWL

SECTOR : Mining Financial-Mining Holding

SHAREHOLDERS

Who Owns Whom's Assessment of the Identity of the Ultimate Controlling Shareholder:
ANGLOVAAL

SHAREHOLDER	PERCENTAGE 1992	1991
ANGLOVAAL LTD	31.1	31.1
FOX STREET NOM P/L	22.7	22.7
CMB NOM P/L	9.0	---
SA MUTUAL	7.0	7.1
STD BANK NOM TVL P/L	6.7	5.6
FIRST NAT NOM P/L	4.4	4.8
EIGHTY ONE MAIN STREET NOM LTD	3.1	1.3
BOARD OF EXECUTORS NOM P/L	---	1.1
SANLAM	---	5.7
VOLKSKAS NOM P/L	---	3.6
TOTAL	84.0	82.9

DIRECTORS :
BARBER DD ,BERNSTEIN BL ,HERSOV BE ,MANSELL VG
MENELL CS (Chairman),SWEMMER RT ,VAN NIEKERK JE
WILSON RAD

REGISTRATION NUMBER : 05/04469/06

REGISTERED OFFICE
Anglovaal House, 56 Main Street
Johannesburg
2001
TEL: 011-634 9111
FAX: 011-634 0038

TRANSFER SECRETARY
Anglovaal Ltd
P O Box 62379, Marshalltown
2107
TEL: 011-634 9111

COMPANY SECRETARY
Anglovaal Ltd

NATURE OF BUSINESS
The company and its subsidiaries hold investments in companies with interests in the mining industry and provide finance for and participate in mineral prospecting operations and mining development.

BANKERS :
First National Bank of SA Ltd

AUDITORS :
Ernst & Young

FAMILIAR BRAND NAMES
N/A

CONTRIBUTION BY ACTIVITY
N/A

YEAR END : June

DIVIDEND : Ords 1c

Interim No 75	(Ldr)05/01/90	(Pay)09/02/90	Amt(c)2
Final No 76	(Ldr)25/05/90	(Pay)03/08/90	Amt(c)4
Interim No 77	(Ldr)21/12/90	(Pay)25/01/91	Amt(c)2
Final No 78	(Ldr)28/06/91	(Pay)02/08/91	Amt(c)4
Final No 80	(Ldr)18/09/92	(Pay)16/10/92	Amt(c)5
Interim No 79	(Ldr)27/02/92	(Pay)06/04/92	Amt(c)2

CAPITAL STRUCTURE

	AUTHORISED	ISSUED
Ords 1c	350000000	321641747
Var Rate Red Cum Prefs 1c	50000000	50000000
Unclassified Shares R1	3592250	0

FINANCIAL STATISTICS (AT FINANCIAL YEAR END)

(Amts in R'000)	1992 Jun	1991 Jun	1990 Jun	1989 Jun	1988 Jun
Ord S/H Int	689043	657476	641042	146710	130421
Long Trm Loans	1234	1104	2329	50485	403
Iss Ord Share	321642	321642	321642	9673	9673
Total Liab	32421	42350	15840	63169	11547
Current Liab	31187	41246	13511	12684	11144
Total Assets	721348	699773	656831	209879	141968
Intang Assets	116	53	51	*	*
Current Assets	290349	382855	451845	23102	59087
Debtors	8890	5695	6679	9073	10617
Turnover	99571	104313	47430	46266	48331
Oper Profit	-1843	-14891	-9758	-12409	27355
Interest Paid	319	2807	-	1929	-
Tax Paid	27323	34876	460	-2654	1085
Prf af Int&Tax	53597	43862	20968	23406	26270
Prf att Ord Sh	54125	46631	26311	30788	31142
Btm Line Earn	54060	35897	26311	30788	31142
Dividend Paid	22515	19299	14510	14510	15477
Mkt Prce(c) YE	-	625	550	8325	6000

PER SHARE STATISTICS (CENTS)

Net Asst Val	214.19	204.40	199.29	1516.70	1348.30
Net Earnings	16.80	14.50	10.80	318.00	270.00
Dividends	7.00	6.00	6.00	150.00	160.00
Cash Flow	14.08	12.09	5.71	240.30	268.72

RATIOS AND OTHER INFORMATION

Mrk Cap(R000)	-	2010263	1769031	805277	580380
Current Ratio	9.31	9.28	33.44	1.82	5.30
Quik/Acid Tst	9.31	9.28	33.44	1.82	5.30
A/C Rec T/ovr	11.20	18.32	7.10	5.10	4.55
Tot Ass T/ovr	0.14	0.15	0.07	0.22	0.34
Debt/Ass Rat	0.04	0.06	0.02	0.06	0.08
Debt to Eqity	0.05	0.06	0.02	0.09	0.09
Interest Cover	81.72	1.07	-	8.67	-
Oper Prof Mrg	-1.85	-14.28	-20.57	-26.82	56.60
Net Prof Marg%	54.36	44.70	55.47	66.55	64.43
Ret on Assets	12.49	13.10	5.21	14.43	22.81
Ret on Equity%	7.86	7.09	4.10	20.99	23.88
Price/Earnings	-	43.10	50.93	26.18	22.22
Divid Cover	2.40	2.42	1.80	2.12	1.69
Divid Yield	-	0.96	1.09	1.80	2.67
Earning Yield%	-	2.32	1.96	3.82	4.50
NAV % Mrk Pr	-	32.70	36.23	18.22	22.47
Effec Tax Rate	52.12	53.48	-0.99	-0.41	4.39
Def Interval	0.01	0.01	0.13	2.15	-
Sus Grth Rate	4.59	4.16	1.84	11.10	12.01

SUBSIDIARY & ASSOCIATED COMPANIES

ALFA PROSPECTING & MINING CO (PTY) LTD
ANGLOVAAL COAL HOLDINGS (PTY) LTD (24,5%)
EAST RAND COAL HOLDINGS (PTY) LTD (24,5%)
EASTERN TRANSVAAL CONSOLIDATED MINES LTD (48%)
HARMONY LANDS AND MINERALS LTD
HIGHLAND GOLD MINING (PTY) LTD
KRANSBERG PROSPECTING & MINING CO (PTY)
LETABA COPPER & ZINC CORPORATION LTD
LUCAS BLOCK MINERALS LTD (25%)
NORCAPE HOLDINGS (PTY) LTD
PRIESKA COPPER MINES (PTY) LTD (47,2%)
RHINO ANDALUSITE MINES (PTY) LTD (49%)
ROODERAND MAIN REEF MINES LTD
SATURN MINING, PROSPECTING & DEVELOPMENT
SOUTH AFRICAN BASE MINERALS LTD
TRAMID INVESTMENTS LTD

INVESTMENTS

ANGLO AMERICAN COAL CORP. LTD (10000 SH)
ANGLO PACIFIC RESOURCES PLC (14,7%)
ANGLOVAAL INDUSTRIES LTD (48385 SH)
ANGLOVAAL LTD (519000 SH)
ANGLOVAAL LTD (N ORDS) (204275 SH)
ASSOCIATED MANGANESE MINES OF SA LTD (244797 SH)
ASSOCIATED ORE & METAL CORP LTD (128850 SH)
CONSOLIDATED MURCHISON LTD (346000 SH)
DAB INVESTMENTS LTD (124999 SH)
DOORNFONTEIN GOLD MINING CO. LTD (368000 SH)
DRIEFONTEIN CONSOLIDATED LTD (377340 SH)
EASTERN GOLD HOLDINGS LTD (15296 SH)
FINSCH DIAMONDS (PTY) LTD (60 SH)
FREE STATE CONSOLIDATED GOLD MINES LTD (382369 SH)
FREE STATE DEVELOPMENT & INVESTMENT CORP (500000 SH)
GOLD FIELDS COAL LTD (22500 SH)
HARTEBEESTFONTEIN GOLD MINING CO. LTD (3170000SH)
KLOOF GOLD MINING CO. LTD (13200 SH)
KLOOF GOLD MINING COMPANY LTD (FINANCIA (11200 SH)
LORAINE GOLD MINES LTD (570002 SH)
ORANGE FREE STATE INVESTMENTS LTD (54185 SH)
PALABORA MINING CO LTD (112700 SH)
RANDCOAL LTD (1030260SH)
RANDFONTEIN ESTATES GOLD MINING CO WITS (303450 SH)
SOUTHVAAL HOLDINGS LTD (46200 SH)
TRANS-NATAL COAL CORPORATION LTD (10000 SH)
UAL MINING & RESOURCES UNIT TRUST (9925500 SH)
VAAL REEFS EXPLORATION & MINING CO LTD (178000 SH)
WESTERN DEEP LEVELS LTD (64600 SH)
ZANDPAN GOLD MINING CO LTD (17450286)

MIDMACOR INDUSTRIES LTD

ABBREVIATION : MIDMAC

JSE SHORT CODE : MIM

SECTOR : Industrial-Motor

SHAREHOLDERS

Who Owns Whom's Assessment of the Identity of the Ultimate Controlling Shareholder: KNJ GROUP

SHAREHOLDER	PERCENTAGE 1992	1991
KNJ INDUSTRIAL HOLDINGS P/L	88.0	88.0
GRAHAM B D	2.9	2.9
MASON LTD	2.3	2.3
MEZ HLDGS P/L	2.0	2.0
TOTAL	95.2	95.2

DIRECTORS :
ADCOCK RJ ,JAMIESON DB ,JENKINS KN (Chairman)
MACNAIR AD ,WEBBER BW

REGISTRATION NUMBER : 87/03762/06

REGISTERED OFFICE
Midmacor House, 60 Trump Str West
Selby Ext 4, Johannesburg
2001
TEL: 011-493 3700
FAX: 011-493 8823

TRANSFER SECRETARY
Central Registrars Ltd
P O Box 4844, Johannesburg
2000
TEL: 011-331 0051

COMPANY SECRETARY
D A Braithwaite

NATURE OF BUSINESS
MIDMACOR is comprised of two main divisions: The industrial division comprises sole agency for HONDA products,franchise and agency for MILLER welding equipment,CEM welders, VM diesel engines DARI and Boge compressors.The leisure division holds the SA franchise for HONDA motorcycles and is a large distributor of motorcycle accessories.

BANKERS :
Nedperm Bank Ltd, Volkskas Ltd

AUDITORS :
KPMG Aiken & Peat

FAMILIAR BRAND NAMES
BIKETIQUE,CEM WELDERS
DARI & BOGE COMPRESSORS,FINESSE,HONDA CENTRE
HONDA LAWNMOWERS,HONDA MOTORCYCLES
HONDA POWER PRODUCTS,HONDA WYNBERG
LE TRICALORE,MILLER WELDING EQUIPMENT
VM DIESEL ENGINES

CONTRIBUTION BY ACTIVITY
N/A

YEAR END : June

DIVIDEND : Ords 1c
Final No 3 (Ldr)15/11/91 (Pay)29/11/91 Amt(c)2

CAPITAL STRUCTURE

	AUTHORISED	ISSUED
Ords 2c	11510750	7860000

FINANCIAL STATISTICS (AT FINANCIAL YEAR END)

(Amts in R'000)	1991 Jun	1990 Jun
Ord S/H Int	20481	20716
Long Trm Loans	5333	6079
Iss Ord Share	7860	7860
Total Liab	29836	26100
Current Liab	24503	20021
Total Assets	50317	46816
Current Assets	45056	42857
Debtors	15624	17253
Inventory	29279	25583
Turnover	78817	86835
Oper Profit	2890	7407
Interest Paid	2940	2682
Tax Paid	28	1867
Prf af Int&Tax	-78	2858
Prf att Ord Sh	-78	2858
Btm Line Earn	-78	2022
Dividend Paid	157	472
Mkt Prce(c) YE	35	10
Depreciation	1594	1321

PER SHARE STATISTICS (CENTS)

Net Asst Val	260.57	263.56
Net Earnings	-1.00	36.40
Dividends	2.00	6.00
Cash Flow	19.29	53.09

RATIOS AND OTHER INFORMATION

Mrk Cap(R000)	2751	786
Current Ratio	1.84	2.14
Quik/Acid Tst	0.64	0.86
A/C Rec T/ovr	5.04	5.03
Tot Ass T/ovr	1.57	1.85
Debt/Ass Rat	0.59	0.56
L T L Tot Ass	0.11	0.13
Debt to Eqity	1.46	1.26
Interest Cover	0.98	2.76
Oper Prof Mrg	3.67	8.53
Net Prof Marg%	-0.10	3.29
Ret on Assets	5.74	15.82
Ret on Equity%	-0.38	13.80
Price/Earnings	-35.00	0.27
Divid Cover	-0.50	6.07
Divid Yield	5.71	60.00
Earning Yield%	-2.86	364.00
NAV % Mrk Pr	744.49	2635.62
Effec Tax Rate	56.00	39.64
Def Interval	11.70	3.42
Sus Grth Rate	-1.15	11.52

SUBSIDIARY & ASSOCIATED COMPANIES

ENGINE FRANCHISES (PTY) LTD
GRABUR TRUCK & CAR (PTY) LTD
INDUSTRIAL FRANCHISE DISTRIBUTORS (PTY)
MIDMACOR (PTY) LTD
MIDMACOR HOLDINGS (PTY) LTD
MIDMACOR HONDA (NAMIBIA) (PTY) LTD
PDS DIESEL SERVICES (PTY) LTD
POWER PACK SERVICES (PTY) LTD
PROBASE PRODUCTS (PTY) LTD

INVESTMENTS

None

MILSTAN HOLDINGS LTD

ABBREVIATION : MILSTAN

JSE SHORT CODE : MLS

SECTOR : Industrial-Retailers & Wholesalers

SHAREHOLDERS

Who Owns Whom's Assessment of the Identity of the Ultimate Controlling Shareholder:
DIRECTORS CONTROL 50% (FEB 1991)

SHAREHOLDER	PERCENTAGE 1992	1991
NEDBANK NOM LTD	30.8	30.8
ETKIND S I	13.5	10.5
MILJAPP TRUST	11.5	11.5
DABSEC TRUST	9.0	9.0
ETKIND M B	8.2	7.8
ELLERINE BROS P/L	4.1	4.1
ETKIND L T	3.8	3.8
ELLERINE E	2.2	2.2
ELLERINE S	1.5	1.5
HARVEST SECURITIES LTD	1.4	1.1
SALDSMAN B D	1.0	1.0
SALDSMAN L B D	1.0	---
FIVE MAIDENS TRUST	---	3.0
MARLED NOM P/L	---	1.0
TOTAL	88.1	87.3

DIRECTORS :
DOS SANTOS M ,DU TOIT A
ETKIND LT (Financial Director)
ETKIND MB (Joint Managing Director),ETKIND R
ETKIND SI (Joint Managing Director),NOWITZ H

REGISTRATION NUMBER : 87/01408/06

REGISTERED OFFICE
6th Floor, FSI Centre, 35 Siemert Road
Doornfontein
2094
TEL: 011-402 3200
FAX: 011-402 7508

TRANSFER SECRETARY
Central Registrars Ltd
P O Box 4844, Johannesburg
2000
TEL: 011-331 0051

COMPANY SECRETARY
FSI Corporate Services (Pty) Ltd

NATURE OF BUSINESS
An investment holding company, which through its subsidiaries carries on the trade of retailer of photographic, electronic and consumer durable supplies via 31 outlets.

BANKERS :
Standard Bank of SA Ltd, Nedcor Bank Ltd

AUDITORS :
Glass-Arenson, S Taitz Kaplan & Co

FAMILIAR BRAND NAMES
AKAI,AR (51%),CANON,CLIVE'S
HI-FI SPECIALISTS,JVC,MARK'S,MILTONS
NAD (51%),NIKON,RADIO MANNIE,SOUTHERN SOUNDS
STAN'S BUSINESSWORLD,TEAC,TECHNICS,TELETEK

CONTRIBUTION BY ACTIVITY
N/A

YEAR END : February

DIVIDEND : Ords 1c

Final	(Ldr)29/06/90	(Pay)13/07/90	Amt(c)5.75
Interim	(Ldr)04/01/91	(Pay)01/02/91	Amt(c)2.25
Final	(Ldr)05/07/91	(Pay)26/07/91	Amt(c)2.25
Interim	(Ldr)03/01/92	(Pay)31/01/92	Amt(c)2
Final	(Ldr)03/07/92	(Pay)24/07/92	Amt(c)2

NUMBER OF EMPLOYEES : 265

CAPITAL STRUCTURE

	AUTHORISED	ISSUED
Ords 1c	30000000	27327867

FINANCIAL STATISTICS (AT FINANCIAL YEAR END)

(Amts in R'000)	1991 Feb	1990 Feb	1989 Feb	1988 Feb	1987
Ord S/H Int	20910	20180	17092	12252	6011
Long Trm Loans	2041	1278	324	395	12903
Iss Ord Share	27328	27328	27328	25000	-
Total Liab	54897	40900	39112	32521	25806
Current Liab	52856	39622	38788	32126	12903
Total Assets	75157	60430	56204	44773	33399
Intang Assets	650	650	*	*	*
Current Assets	66657	53220	49825	39306	14485
Debtors	17888	17483	12421	6982	-
Inventory	38347	28958	26249	21051	14485
Turnover	129720	109107	95745	70578	44144
Oper Profit	4338	8061	8555	6158	2666
Interest Paid	179	252	260	34	11
Tax Paid	1626	2702	3376	3509	1327
Prf af Int&Tax	2562	5479	6148	3500	1327
Prf att Ord Sh	2425	5274	6148	3500	1327
Btm Line Earn	2425	5274	6148	3500	1327
Dividend Paid	1230	2186	1913	1000	-
Mkt Prce(c) YE	70	70	100	80	-
Depreciation	704	612	589	380	-

PER SHARE STATISTICS (CENTS)

Net Asst Val	74.14	71.47	62.54	49.01	-
Net Earnings	8.90	19.30	22.60	14.76	-
Dividends	4.50	8.00	7.00	4.00	-
Cash Flow	11.45	21.54	24.69	15.52	-

RATIOS AND OTHER INFORMATION

Mrk Cap(R000)	19130	19130	27328	20000	-
Current Ratio	1.26	1.34	1.28	1.22	1.12
Quik/Acid Tst	0.54	0.61	0.61	0.57	-
A/C Rec T/ovr	7.25	6.24	7.71	10.11	-
Tot Ass T/ovr	1.73	1.81	1.70	1.58	1.32
Debt/Ass Rat	0.73	0.67	0.70	0.73	0.77
L T L Tot Ass	0.02	0.02	0.01	0.01	0.39
Debt to Eqity	2.62	2.02	2.29	2.65	4.29
Interest Cover	24.23	31.99	32.90	181.12	242.27
Oper Prof Mrg	3.34	7.39	8.94	8.73	6.04
Net Prof Marg%	1.87	4.83	6.42	4.96	3.01
Ret on Assets	5.81	13.95	17.41	15.73	7.98
Ret on Equity%	11.60	26.13	35.97	28.57	22.08
Price/Earnings	7.87	3.63	4.42	5.42	-
Divid Cover	1.98	2.41	3.23	3.69	-
Divid Yield	6.43	11.43	7.00	5.00	-
Earning Yield%	12.71	27.57	22.60	18.45	-
NAV % Mrk Pr	105.91	102.09	62.54	61.26	-
Effec Tax Rate	-	-	35.45	50.06	49.98
Def Interval	1.18	0.72	0.12	0.17	9.72
Sus Grth Rate	5.71	15.30	24.78	20.40	22.08

SUBSIDIARY & ASSOCIATED COMPANIES

CSL ELECTRONICS (PTY) LTD
ELEMES ELECTRONIC EQUIPMENT (PTY) LTD
HI-FI SPECIALISTS (PTY) LTD
MILTONS (1987) (PTY) LTD
RADIO MANNIE (PTY) LTD
STANS (1987) (PTY) LTD
STANS BUSINESS FLOOR (PTY) LTD

TELETEK ELECTRONIC EQUIPMENT (PTY) LTD

INVESTMENTS

None

MINACO GRANITE & MARBLE LTD

ABBREVIATION : MINGRAN

JSE SHORT CODE : MNG

SECTOR : Metals & Minerals-Other

SHAREHOLDERS

Who Owns Whom's Assessment of the Identity of the Ultimate Controlling Shareholder:
AFMIN / B SEIDLE

SHAREHOLDER	PERCENTAGE 1992	1991
MARCH NOM SOC ANONYME	19.7	19.7
AFRICAN EXPLORATION CO LTD	16.2	16.2
AFMIN HOLDINGS LTD	15.5	15.5
REA BROTHERS	11.6	11.6
LINKSFIELD INV P/L	7.8	7.8
STD BANK NOM TVL P/L	5.9	5.7
FIRST NAT NOM P/L	5.7	5.5
JAN SILVIS NOM P/L	3.4	---
INDO-CHINA NOM P/L	2.7	---
NEDBANK NOM LTD	2.1	2.1
SEIDLE BARNEY HOLDINGS P/L	1.9	1.9
JUSPOINT NOM P/L	1.7	1.8
INDO-CHINA NOM SA P/L	---	2.7
PORCARI A	---	3.4
TOTAL	94.1	93.9

DIRECTORS :
BELFIORE P MR,COETZEE FG MR (Chairman)
COETZEE GA MR,HEEVER C MR
ROBINSON WL MR (Managing Director),TUCKER PE MR
TURNER JS MR,VORSTER MD M

REGISTRATION NUMBER : 87/04368/06

REGISTERED OFFICE
165 Smit Str, Braamfontein
Johannesburg
2001
TEL: 011-403 2930
FAX: 330 3694

TRANSFER SECRETARY
Central Registrars Ltd
P O Box 4844, Johannesburg
2000
TEL: 011-331 0051

COMPANY SECRETARY
African Exploration Co Ltd

NATURE OF BUSINESS
The company is an investment holding company with interests in the quarrying,beneficiation, importing and exporting and the contracting divisions of the natural stone sevtor.

BANKERS :
First National Bank of SA Ltd
Nedcor Bank Ltd

AUDITORS :
RA Hellman & Co

FAMILIAR BRAND NAMES
N/A

CONTRIBUTION BY ACTIVITY
N/A

YEAR END : December

DIVIDEND : Ords 1c
Dividend No 1 (Ldr)10/05/91 (Pay)24/05/91 Amt(c)3.5

CAPITAL STRUCTURE

	AUTHORISED	ISSUED
Ords 1c	97425000	29482479
Conv Prefs 1c	8000000	8000000
"A" Conv Prefs 1c	575000	571429

FINANCIAL STATISTICS (AT FINANCIAL YEAR END)

(Amts in R'000)	1991 Dec	1990 Dec
Ord S/H Int	36319	31008
Long Trm Loans	15600	9564
Iss Ord Share	29482	29482
Total Liab	25793	22842
Current Liab	10193	13278
Total Assets	61069	52807
Intang Assets	1043	1043
Current Assets	34038	36116
Debtors	8765	7771
Inventory	9100	4492
Oper Profit	6497	5144
Interest Paid	2070	670
Tax Paid	253	220
Prf af Int&Tax	6088	5162
Prf att Ord Sh	6088	5162
Btm Line Earn	6088	5162
Dividend Paid	766	1032
Mkt Prce(c) YE	70	100
Depreciation	1196	2979

PER SHARE STATISTICS (CENTS)

Net Asst Val	119.65	101.64
Net Earnings	16.30	17.20
Dividends	2.60	3.50
Cash Flow	24.78	27.61

RATIOS AND OTHER INFORMATION

Mrk Cap(R000)	20637	29482
Current Ratio	3.34	2.72
Quik/Acid Tst	2.45	2.38
Debt/Ass Rat	0.34	0.34
L T L Tot Ass	0.17	0.08
Debt to Eqity	0.57	0.57
Interest Cover	3.14	7.68
Ret on Assets	13.77	11.46
Ret on Equity%	16.76	16.65
Price/Earnings	4.29	5.81
Divid Cover	6.27	4.91
Divid Yield	3.71	3.50
Earning Yield%	23.29	17.20
NAV % Mrk Pr	170.93	101.64

Effec Tax Rate	3.64	4.09
Def Interval	1.26	0.47
Sus Grth Rate	14.65	13.32

SUBSIDIARY & ASSOCIATED COMPANIES

ARANDIS GRANITE (PTY) LTD
EUROPEAN & PACIFIC DISTRIBUTORS LTD
MARBLE LIME & ASSOCIATED INDUSTRIES LTD
MINACO TRANSKEI (PTY) LTD
PRAIRIE GRANITE (PTY) LTD (35%)
SF GRANITE (PTY) LTD
TIVOLI GRANITE & MARBLE LTD
TIVOLI PROPERTIES (PTY) LTD
WORLDWIDE GRANITE SALES (PTY) LTD

INVESTMENTS

None

MINORCO SOCIETE ANONYME

ABBREVIATION : MINORCO

JSE SHORT CODE : MNR

SECTOR : Mining Financial-Mining Holding

SHAREHOLDERS

Who Owns Whom's Assessment of the Identity of the Ultimate Controlling Shareholder:
ANGLO AMERICAN

SHAREHOLDER	PERCENTAGE 1992	1991
LONDON CONTROL ACCOUNT	56.4	55.6
LUXEMBOURG GLOBAL ACCOUNT	24.5	24.5
STD BANK NOM TVL P/L	3.4	1.5
CMB NOM P/L	2.6	---
EIGHTY ONE MAIN STREET NOM LTD	2.1	1.7
SA MUTUAL	1.4	2.3
SOGES FIDUCEM SOC ANONYME	1.0	1.0
SOUTHERN LIFE ASSOC LTD	---	1.7
SANKERN E/B	---	2.0
TOTAL	91.4	90.2

DIRECTORS :
BOZANO JR DE A DR,CROCKER C DR,DAVIGNON E VISCOUN
EDWARDES M SIR,FISHER DE (Financial Director)
LEA AW (Joint Managing Director),LOOMIS WR
MUNERA GE
PHILLIMORE JRB (Joint Managing Director)
RICHARDS RF ,RITCHIE CE ,SCHREIBER HJ
SLACK HR (President)
WADESON TCA (Technical Director

REGISTRATION NUMBER : B12139 (Lux)

REGISTERED OFFICE
9 Rue Ste Zithe, L-2763, Luxembourg City
Luxembourg

TEL: 09352-4041101
FAX: 09352 404 11020

TRANSFER SECRETARY
Consolidated Share Registrars Ltd
P O Box 61051, Marshalltown
2107
TEL: 011-492 1620

COMPANY SECRETARY
N Jordan

NATURE OF BUSINESS
Minorco is a European-based natural resources group with its principal interests in mining and the processing of metals and industrial materials. The groups activities are concentrated in the USA.

BANKERS :
N/A

AUDITORS :
Deloitte & Touche

FAMILIAR BRAND NAMES
N/A

CONTRIBUTION BY ACTIVITY
Precious Metals (14.0%)
Base Metals (10.0%)
Agricultural (34.0%)
Construction Materials (17.0%)
Financials & Commercial (21.0%)
Energy (4.0%)

YEAR END : June

DIVIDEND :Ords US$1,40

Interim	(Ldr)05/04/91	(Pay)03/05/91	Amt(c)17

DIVIDEND :Ords US$ 1,40

Final	(Ldr)10/10/91	(Pay)19/11/91	Amt(c)34
Interim	(Ldr)10/04/92	(Pay)30/06/92	Amt(c)18
Final	(Ldr)09/10/92	(Pay)17/11/92	Amt(c)36

NUMBER OF EMPLOYEES : 711

CAPITAL STRUCTURE

	AUTHORISED	ISSUED
Ords US$ 1,40	189435674	170312074

FINANCIAL STATISTICS (AT FINANCIAL YEAR END)

(Amts in $)	1992 Jun	1991 Jun	1990 Jun	1989 Jun	1988 Jun
Ord S/H Int	2870000	2808700	2959000	2470600	2371800
Long Trm Loans	563000	516000	33400	21100	21100
Iss Ord Share	170312	170312	170312	170312	170312
Total Liab	1262100	1061400	78400	116600	69800
Current Liab	699100	545400	45000	95500	48700
Total Assets	4132100	3870100	3037400	2587200	2441600
Current Assets	2459100	2556600	1830000	889900	906900
Debtors	416000	409800	56400	19000	17200
Inventory	265500	257100	9600	-	-
Turnover	1666600	771000	28900	-	-
Oper Profit	21900	27900	13900	87900	43900
Interest Paid	32100	15700	1800	-	-
Tax Paid	37000	28800	27500	1100	1500
Prf af Int&Tax	121500	151300	160000	157300	103900
Prf att Ord Sh	206000	193500	229200	280000	262300
Btm Line Earn	216100	136700	784400	280100	774700
Dividend Paid	88000	83000	74500	71200	51100
Mkt Prce(c) YE	4865	4275	6375	6225	4700
Depreciation	-	-	8400	100	-

PER SHARE STATISTICS (CENTS)

Net Asst Val	1685.14	1649.15	1737.40	1450.63	1392.62
Net Earnings	1.22	1.14	1.35	1.64	4.55
Dividends	0.54	0.51	0.48	0.42	0.30
Cash Flow	65.06	75.91	97.28	91.66	60.30

RATIOS AND OTHER INFORMATION

Mrk Cap(R000)	8285679	7280838	10857390	10601922	8004664
Current Ratio	3.52	4.69	40.67	9.32	18.62
Quik/Acid Tst	3.14	4.22	40.45	9.32	18.62
A/C Rec T/ovr	4.01	1.88	0.51	-	-
Tot Ass T/ovr	0.40	0.20	0.01	-	-
Debt/Ass Rat	0.24	0.22	0.01	0.04	0.02
L T L Tot Ass	0.07	0.07	-	-	-
Debt to Eqity	0.34	0.30	0.02	0.04	0.02
Interest Cover	0.83	2.03	10.50	-	-
Oper Prof Mrg	1.31	3.62	48.10	-	-
Net Prof Marg%	12.36	25.10	793.08	-	-
Ret on Assets	6.91	6.71	8.63	10.92	10.85
Ret on Equity%	7.18	6.89	7.75	11.33	11.06
Price/Earnings	3987.70	3750.00	4722.22	3795.73	1032.97
Divid Cover	2.26	2.24	2.81	3.90	15.17
Divid Yield	0.01	0.01	0.01	0.01	0.01
Earning Yield%	0.03	0.03	0.02	0.03	0.10
NAV % Mrk Pr	34.64	38.58	27.25	23.30	29.63
Effec Tax Rate	3.70	2.61	1.81	1.25	3.42
Def Interval	4.11	2.55	0.11	0.01	0.03
Sus Grth Rate	4.11	3.93	5.23	8.45	8.90

SUBSIDIARY & ASSOCIATED COMPANIES

ANGLO AMERICAN CORPORATION OF SOUTH AMER (21%)
BERALT TIN & WOLFRAM (PORTUGAL) SA
BUXTON LIME INDUSTRIES LIMITED
CHARTER CONSOLIDATED PLC (36%)
EASTERN INVESTMENTS LTD (24%)
ELBEKIES GMBH MUHLBERG-PRETTIN
ENGELHARD CORPORATION (USA) (30%)
HUDSON BAY MINING & SMELTING CO. LTD (CA
INDEPENDENCE MINING CO INC (USA)
LAUSITZER GRAUWACKE GMBH INC.
MINORCO (USA) INC
MINORCO BETEILIGUNGSGESELLSCHAFT MBH
MONDI EUROPEAN HOLDINGS LIMITED (TORTOLA (21%)
NASH ROCKS LIMITED
TERRA INDUSTRIES INC. (USA)
WESTERN GOLD EXPLORATION & MINING COMPAN
ZAMBIA COPPER INVESTMENTS LTD (50%)

INVESTMENTS

JOHNSON MATTHEY (15,2%)
SALOMON INC U.S.A (14%)
SANTA FE ENERGY RESOURCES INC (USA) (10%)

MOBILE INDUSTRIES LTD

ABBREVIATION : MOBILE

JSE SHORT CODE : MOB

SECTOR : Industrial-Transportation

SHAREHOLDERS

Who Owns Whom's Assessment of the Identity of the Ultimate Controlling Shareholder:
DIRECTORS

SHAREHOLDER	PERCENTAGE 1992	1991
JOSEPH JOWELLS HLDGS P/L	39.8	51.8
SA MUTUAL	20.3	20.9
SOUTHERN LIFE ASSOC LTD	8.9	---
SIXTY SIX MARSHALL STREET NOM P/L	3.2	3.4
HASSON R R H	2.9	3.6
EIGHTY ONE MAIN STREET NOM LTD	2.4	---
SLAM NOM P/L	2.4	---
ANGLO AMERICAN GROUP PENS FUND	2.0	2.0
PRINTING INDUSTRY PENS FUND	1.5	---
PRESS H	1.3	1.3
STD BANK NOM TVL P/L	1.1	1.0
NAT IND COUNCIL PRINTING & NEWSPAPER SA	---	1.6
TOTAL	85.7	85.4

DIRECTORS :
GALOMBIK A ,GORVY HA ,HASSON RRH
JOWELL C (Chairman),JOWELL NI

REGISTRATION NUMBER : 65/14997/06

REGISTERED OFFICE
1313 Main Tower, Standard Bank Centre
Heerengracht, Cape Town
8001
TEL: 021-21 7310
FAX: 021-419 3692

TRANSFER SECRETARY
Consolidated Share Registrars Ltd
P O Box 61051, Marshalltown
2107
TEL: 011-492 1620

COMPANY SECRETARY
G W Norval

NATURE OF BUSINESS
The company controls a subsidiary which is engaged in the provision of instalment credit and truck financing facilities, & has a 48,25% interest in quoted Trencor Ltd.

BANKERS :
First National Bank of SA Ltd

AUDITORS :
Arthur Andersen & Co

FAMILIAR BRAND NAMES
N/A

CONTRIBUTION BY ACTIVITY
% of net income from Trencor Ltd (98.0%)
Finance Income (2.0%)

YEAR END : June

DIVIDEND :Ords 5c

Interim No 43	(Ldr)27/04/90	(Pay)18/05/90	Amt(c)7
Final No 44	(Ldr)26/10/90	(Pay)16/11/90	Amt(c)26
Interim No 45	(Ldr)22/02/91	(Pay)28/02/91	Amt(c)8.2
Final No 46	(Ldr)25/10/91	(Pay)15/11/91	Amt(c)32.4
Interim No 47	(Ldr)24/04/92	(Pay)15/05/92	Amt(c)10
Final No 48	(Ldr)11/09/92	(Pay)23/09/92	Amt(c)39.5

NUMBER OF EMPLOYEES : 3559

CAPITAL STRUCTURE

	AUTHORISED	ISSUED
Ords 5c	40000000	28363100
6% Unsec Auto Conv Sub Debs 2250c	5672620	5672620

FINANCIAL STATISTICS (AT FINANCIAL YEAR END)

(Amts in R'000)	1992 Jun	1991 Jun	1990 Jun	1989 Jun	1988 Jun
Ord S/H Int	199867	151823	113099	83065	60637
Long Trm Loans	155041	30753	19056	722	663
Iss Ord Share	28363	28363	28363	28363	28363
Total Liab	195668	68052	57522	54589	34514
Current Liab	40627	37299	38466	53867	33851
Total Assets	395535	219875	170621	137654	95151
Current Assets	41174	40648	39208	32985	33223
Debtors	17117	18484	17470	16466	22234
Oper Profit	4247	6062	6906	5204	7748
Interest Paid	14324	10592	9884	6680	3075
Tax Paid	1445	1436	1219	962	596
Prf af Int&Tax	15112	12204	10096	5484	4077
Prf att Ord Sh	62700	51291	40071	23809	17887
Btm Line Earn	63305	50773	39724	24643	18391
Dividend Paid	14039	11516	9359	5219	3900
Mkt Prce(c) YE	3500	2200	925	675	315
Depreciation	32	25	25	25	19

PER SHARE STATISTICS (CENTS)

Net Asst Val	704.68	535.29	398.76	292.86	213.79
Net Earnings	221.10	180.80	141.00	83.90	63.10
Dividends	49.50	40.60	33.00	18.40	13.75
Cash Flow	46.54	46.20	33.77	18.61	13.15

RATIOS AND OTHER INFORMATION

Mrk Cap(R000)	992705	623986	262358	191450	89343
Current Ratio	1.01	1.09	1.02	0.61	0.98
Quik/Acid Tst	1.01	1.09	1.02	0.61	0.98
Debt/Ass Rat	0.49	0.30	0.33	0.39	0.36
L T L Tot Ass	0.39	0.13	0.11	-	-
Debt to Eqity	0.97	0.44	0.50	0.65	0.56
Interest Cover	1.23	1.61	1.60	1.47	2.52
Ret on Assets	19.95	28.97	30.20	23.04	22.84
Ret on Equity%	31.37	33.78	35.43	28.66	29.50
Price/Earnings	15.83	12.17	6.56	8.05	4.99
Divid Cover	4.47	4.45	4.27	4.56	4.59
Divid Yield	1.41	1.85	3.57	2.73	4.37
Earning Yield%	6.32	8.22	15.24	12.43	20.03
NAV % Mrk Pr	20.13	24.33	43.11	43.39	67.87
Effec Tax Rate	4.89	6.93	3.93	13.43	2.40
Def Interval	3.83	4.21	4.88	8.94	7.51
Sus Grth Rate	24.35	26.20	27.15	22.38	23.07

SUBSIDIARY & ASSOCIATED COMPANIES

MOBILE ACCEPTANCES (PTY) LTD

INVESTMENTS

TRENCOR LTD (6% CONV DEBS) (1373078 DB)

MOLYSLIP LTD

ABBREVIATION : MOLYSLP

JSE SHORT CODE : MLY

SECTOR : Development Capital Market

SHAREHOLDERS

Who Owns Whom's Assessment of the Identity of the Ultimate Controlling Shareholder: DIRECTORS

SHAREHOLDER	PERCENTAGE 1992	1991
TYCOMET P/L	70.2	70.2
SPANJAARD R J W	7.3	7.0
SPANJAARD D	4.4	4.4
BOS K	4.2	4.2
SFSS NOM P/L	2.8	---
FIRST NAT NOM P/L	2.4	2.2
ZIMPANI INV CC	1.9	2.3
DE HAAS P	---	3.1
TOTAL	93.1	93.4

DIRECTORS :
BRAITHWAITE ER DR,DALEY SJ ,DE HAAS P ,GUEST RC
PETERSEN DH ,SPANJAARD RJW (Executive Chairman

REGISTRATION NUMBER : 60/04393/06

REGISTERED OFFICE
748-750 Fifth Street, Wynberg
Sandton
2090
TEL: 011-786 2210
FAX: 011-887 2962

TRANSFER SECRETARY
Central Registrars Ltd
P O Box 4844, Johannesburg
2000
TEL: 011-331 0051

COMPANY SECRETARY
R C Guest

NATURE OF BUSINESS
Manufacturer of specialised lubricants and allied chemical products for industrial and consumer applications.

BANKERS :
Standard Bank of SA Ltd

AUDITORS :
Coopers Theron Du Toit

FAMILIAR BRAND NAMES
COCKPIT,COMBAT,COPASLIP,MULTIGLIDE

CONTRIBUTION BY ACTIVITY
N/A

YEAR END : February

DIVIDEND : Ords 5c

Final No 2	(Ldr)06/07/90	(Pay)27/06/90	Amt(c)3
Interim No 3	(Ldr)12/06/92	(Pay)20/06/92	Amt(c)6

NUMBER OF EMPLOYEES : 60

MOMENTUM LIFE ASSURERS LTD

ABBREVIATION : MOMENTUM

JSE SHORT CODE : MOM

SECTOR : Financial-Insurance

SHAREHOLDERS

Who Owns Whom's Assessment of the Identity of the Ultimate Controlling Shareholder: RAND MERCHANT BANK HOLDINGS

SHAREHOLDER	PERCENTAGE 1992	1991
RAND MERCHANT BANK HOLDINGS LTD	43.2	---
VOLKSKAS INSURANCE INV LTD	17.1	30.0
FINANCIAL SECURITIES LTD	15.9	28.7
ENGINEERING INDUSTRIES PENS FUND	4.0	2.9
METAL IND GROUP PENS FUND	3.6	4.2
YSKOR PENS FUND	2.2	3.7
ABSA NOM P/L	2.0	---
SASOL PENS FUND	---	1.4
MOMENTUM LIFE SHARE PURCHASE SCHEME	---	1.5
GRAYSTON NOM P/L	---	1.6
SANLAM	---	2.5
STD BANK NOM TVL P/L	---	1.1
UBS GROUP PENS FUND	---	1.4
VOLKSKAS PENS FUND	---	1.7
TOTAL	88.0	80.6

DIRECTORS :
ADAMS BH ,DIPPENAAR L (Chairman),DU PREEZ DJ
DU TOIT PR ,FERREIRA GT
GOUWS RB (Executive Deputy Chairman),HARRIS PK
HUTCHINSON RJ ,KRIGE JD (Managing Director)
MALAN DJ

REGISTRATION NUMBER : 66/10753/06

REGISTERED OFFICE
Momentum Park, 267B West Avenue
Verwoerdburgstad
0157
TEL: 012-671 8911
FAX: 012-663 6336

TRANSFER SECRETARY
Central Registrars Ltd
P O Box 4844, Johannesburg
2000
TEL: 011-331 0051

COMPANY SECRETARY
F J C Truter

NATURE OF BUSINESS
Principal activities include all aspects of long term assurance, merchant banking and asset management which includes property management and unit trust management.

BANKERS :
Volkskas Ltd

AUDITORS :
N/A

CAPITAL STRUCTURE

	AUTHORISED	ISSUED
Ords 5c	15000000	5700000

FINANCIAL STATISTICS (AT FINANCIAL YEAR END)

(Amts in R'000)	1992 Feb	1991 Feb	1990 Feb	1988	1987
Ord S/H Int	3902	3542	2854	2047	991
Long Trm Loans	424	421	513	2040	1503
Iss Ord Share	5700	5700	5700	5700	-
Total Liab	4064	4481	2986	3623	2480
Current Liab	3640	4060	2473	1583	977
Total Assets	7966	8023	5677	6032	3549
Intang Assets	*	*	163	*	*
Current Assets	4971	5163	3403	1945	1055
Debtors	3736	3998	2375	-	-
Inventory	974	879	850	1945	1055
Turnover	14895	15725	13186	8253	5339
Oper Profit	1111	733	874	713	582
Interest Paid	409	470	372	251	200
Prf af Int&Tax	702	263	502	462	357
Prf att Ord Sh	702	263	502	556	357
Btm Line Earn	702	123	502	556	357
Dividend Paid	342	-	171	-	-
Mkt Prce(c) YE	80	80	95	65	-
Depreciation	193	183	129	-	-

PER SHARE STATISTICS (CENTS)

Net Asst Val	68.46	62.14	47.21	35.91	-
Net Earnings	12.30	4.60	8.80	-	-
Dividends	6.00	-	3.00	-	-
Cash Flow	15.70	7.82	11.07	8.11	-

RATIOS AND OTHER INFORMATION

Mrk Cap(R000)	4560	4560	5415	3705	-
Current Ratio	1.37	1.27	1.38	1.23	1.08
Quik/Acid Tst	1.10	1.06	1.03	-	-
A/C Rec T/ovr	3.99	3.93	5.55	-	-
Tot Ass T/ovr	1.87	1.96	2.32	1.37	1.50
Debt/Ass Rat	0.51	0.56	0.53	0.60	0.70
L T L Tot Ass	0.05	0.05	0.09	0.34	0.42
Debt to Eqity	1.04	1.27	1.05	1.77	2.50
Interest Cover	2.72	1.56	2.35	2.84	2.79
Oper Prof Mrg	7.46	4.66	6.63	8.64	10.90
Net Prof Marg%	4.71	1.67	3.81	6.74	6.69
Ret on Assets	13.95	9.14	15.40	11.82	15.69
Ret on Equity%	17.99	7.43	17.59	27.16	36.02
Price/Earnings	6.50	17.39	10.80	-	-
Divid Cover	2.05	-	2.93	-	-
Divid Yield	7.50	-	3.16	-	-
Earning Yield%	15.38	5.75	9.26	-	-
NAV % Mrk Pr	85.57	77.68	49.70	55.25	-
Def Interval	1.72	5.72	1.45	4.42	4.21
Sus Grth Rate	9.23	7.43	11.60	27.16	36.02

SUBSIDIARY & ASSOCIATED COMPANIES

TORPEDO INVESTMENTS (PTY) LTD
TWO ONE FOUR ERAND (PTY) LTD

INVESTMENTS

None

FAMILIAR BRAND NAMES
N/A

CONTRIBUTION BY ACTIVITY
Premiums (% Income) (60 4%)
Investments (39 6%)

YEAR END : March

DIVIDEND :Ords 10c

Interim	(Ldr)20/04/90	(Pay)16/05/90	Amt(c)6
Final	(Ldr)19/10/90	(Pay)14/11/90	Amt(c)7
Interim	(Ldr)19/04/91	(Pay)17/05/91	Amt(c)6 75
Final	(Ldr)01/11/91	(Pay)21/11/91	Amt(c)8 25
Interim	(Ldr)24/04/92	(Pay)22/05/92	Amt(c)7 5
Final	(Ldr)06/11/92	(Pay)26/11/92	Amt(c)9

NUMBER OF EMPLOYEES : 1259

CAPITAL STRUCTURE

	AUTHORISED	ISSUED
Ords 10c	150000000	70000000

FINANCIAL STATISTICS (AT FINANCIAL YEAR END)

(Amts in R'000)	1992 Jun	1991 Jun	1990 Jun	1989 Jun	1988 Jun
Ord S/H Int	119101	109651	102151	69838	19156
Long Trm Loans	7454478	6973415	5828826	4897404	470626
Iss Ord Share	70000	70000	70000	66993	2340
Total Liab	7572973	7023036	5914965	4991443	481371
Current Liab	118495	49621	86139	94039	10745
Total Assets	7692074	7132687	6017116	5061281	500527
Current Assets	127538	145533	110467	120337	16324
Debtors	41758	55355	36519	19044	4054
Oper Profit	1290178	1369846	540388	5250	1638
Tax Paid	39498	30757	35383	-	-
Prf af Int&Tax	1250680	1339089	505005	5250	1638
Prf att Ord Sh	63790	701226	505005	5250	1638
Btm Line Earn	63790	701226	505005	5250	1638
Dividend Paid	11550	10500	9100	3499	1638
Mkt Prce(c) YE	465	360	205	190	-

PER SHARE STATISTICS (CENTS)

Net Asst Val	170 14	156 64	145 93	104 25	818 63
Net Earnings	30 00	25 70	23 00	11 60	7 00
Dividends	16 50	15 00	13 00	7 50	7 00
Cash Flow	1786 69	1912 98	726 63	11 62	70 00

RATIOS AND OTHER INFORMATION

Mrk Cap(R000)	325500	252000	143500	127287	-
Current Ratio	1 08	2 93	1 28	1 28	1 52
Quik/Acid Tst	1 08	2 93	1 28	1 28	1 52
Debt/Ass Rat	0 02	0 01	0 01	0 02	0 02
Debt to Eqity	0 99	0 45	0 84	1 35	0 56
Ret on Assets	16 77	19 21	8 98	0 10	0 33
Ret on Equity%	53 56	639 51	494 37	7 52	8 55
Price/Earnings	15 50	14 01	8 91	16 38	-
Divid Cover	1 82	1 71	1 77	1 55	1 00
Divid Yield	3 55	4 17	6 34	3 95	-
Earning Yield%	6 45	7 14	11 22	6 11	-
NAV % Mrk Pr	36 59	43 51	71 19	54 87	-
Effec Tax Rate	2 59	2 19	6 55	-	-
Def Interval	-	-	-	1 44	1 35
Sus Grth Rate	43 86	629 93	485 46	2 51	0 00

SUBSIDIARY & ASSOCIATED COMPANIES

MOMENTUM ASSET TRUST LTD
MOMENTUM FUND MANAGERS LTD
MOMENTUM PROPERTY INVESTMENTS (PTY) LTD
RAND MERCHANT BANK LTD
SANDTON CENTRE POINT (PTY) LTD
WHEEL SHOPPING CENTRE (PTY) LTD, THE

INVESTMENTS

None

MORE WEAR INDUSTRIAL HOLDINGS LTD

ABBREVIATION : MWEAR

SECTOR : Zimbabwe Stock Exchange

SHAREHOLDERS

Who Owns Whom's Assessment of the Identity of the Ultimate Controlling Shareholder: APEX CORPORATION / INSTITUTIONS

SHAREHOLDER	PERCENTAGE 1992	1991
APEX CORP OF ZIMBABWE LTD	40 0	---
G A WARE HOLDINGS P/L	17 2	---
MBCA NOM (PVT) LTD	8 3	- -
ELHAR TRUST PVT LTD	2 0	---
WARE J M	1 8	---
WARE G C	1 7	-
WARE S G	1 7	--
ZIMBABWE INV CO PVT LTD	1 6	---
WARE J B	1 6	---
BARD NOM (PVT) LTD	1 2	---
G A WARE & ASSOCIATES PVT LTD	1 2	--
NAT RAILWAYS OF ZIM CONTR PENS FUND	1 0	---
B M KASS PVT LTD	1 0	--
TOTAL	80 2	---

DIRECTORS :
BOTSH AA (Chairman),CARTER JAL ,CHIMPHONDAH FJ
HOVE MJ ,KARNICKI ,MARTIN CA ,MILWID GF

REGISTERED OFFICE
53 Plymouth Road, Southerton
Harare, Zimbabwe

TEL 67802
FAX 67807

TRANSFER SECRETARY
First Transfer Secretaries (Pvt) Ltd
P O Box 437, Bulawayo
Zimbabwe

TEL 092634 - 702905

COMPANY SECRETARY
T B Ware

NATURE OF BUSINESS
MORE WEAR is a holding company incorporated in Zimbabwe, whose subsidiaries are engaged in engin eering, contracting, steel sales and hiring of equipment They are also manufacturers of rolling stock, heavy trailers, steel tanks, pressure ves

sels, large bore pipes,truck wheels,mining equipment,air receivers and heat exchangers They are also fabricators of steel work for buildings,bridges,cranes,air ducting,cyclones,aerials,lightning masts,mines,factories,conveyers and steel chimney

BANKERS :
N/A

AUDITORS :
Ernst & Young

FAMILIAR BRAND NAMES
N/A

CONTRIBUTION BY ACTIVITY
N/A

YEAR END : June

DIVIDEND : Ords Z$0,50

Dividend	(Ldr)20/12/91	(Pay)23/01/92	Amt(c)4
Dividend	(Ldr)13/03/92	(Pay)10/04/92	Amt(c)4

CAPITAL STRUCTURE

	AUTHORISED	ISSUED
Ords Z$0,50	20000000	19543458

FINANCIAL STATISTICS (AT FINANCIAL YEAR END)

(Amts in Z$)	1992 Jun	1991 Jun	1990 Jun
Ord S/H Int	54697	41365	37287
Long Trm Loans	7000	7206	8850
Iss Ord Share	19543	14658	7319
Total Liab	48062	31129	33385
Current Liab	41062	23923	24535
Total Assets	102759	72494	70672
Current Assets	54841	41639	43506
Debtors	18249	16099	16096
Inventory	35424	25540	27114
Turnover	87884	58475	52410
Oper Profit	9422	7922	5015
Interest Paid	3756	3005	1827
Tax Paid	595	488	3
Prf af Int&Tax	5071	4429	3185
Prf att Ord Sh	6513	5301	3398
Btm Line Earn	6513	5301	3398
Dividend Paid	1759	1222	657
Depreciation	2019	1255	946

PER SHARE STATISTICS (CENTS)

Net Asst Val	279 88	282 20	509 45
Net Earnings	33 00	36 00	27 00
Dividends	9 00	7 00	10 00
Cash Flow	36 54	38 70	56 13

RATIOS AND OTHER INFORMATION

Current Ratio	1 34	1 74	1 77
Quik/Acid Tst	0 47	0 67	0 67
A/C Rec T/ovr	4 82	3 63	3 26
Tot Ass T/ovr	0 86	0 81	0 74
Debt/Ass Rat	0 47	0 43	0 47
L T L Tot Ass	0 07	0 10	0 12
Debt to Eqity	0 88	0 75	0 89
Interest Cover	2 51	2 64	2 74
Oper Prof Mrg	10 72	13 55	9 57
Net Prof Marg%	7 41	9 07	6 48
Ret on Assets	10 58	12 15	7 43
Ret on Equity%	11 91	12 82	9 11
Divid Cover	3 67	5 14	2 70
Effec Tax Rate	10 50	9 92	0 09
Def Interval	3 39	3 47	4 58
Sus Grth Rate	8 69	9 86	7 35

SUBSIDIARY & ASSOCIATED COMPANIES

ALLIED ENGINEERING (PVT) LTD
ALLIED HOLDINGS (PVT) LTD
ALLIED PIPES (PVT) LTD
ALLIED STEEL (PVT) LTD
ALLIED STEEL LIMITED (MALAWI)
ASPINDALE INDUSTRIAL TOWNSHIP (PVT) LTD
F ISSELS & SON LIMITED (48%)
LYSAGHT & COMPANY (PVT) LTD
M W PROPERTIES (PVT) LTD
MOREWEAR CONSOLIDATED INDUSTRIES (PVT) L
MOREWEAR ENGINEERING (PVT) LTD
MOREWEAR INDUSTRIES (PVT) LTD
MOREWEAR INDUSTRIES BULAWAYO (PVT) LTD
MOREWEAR MANAGEMENT SERVICES (PVT) LTD
TRANSPORT & EQUIPMENT CO LTD (MALAWI)
WILLOWVALE ENGINEERING (PVT) LTD

INVESTMENTS

None

MORKELS LTD

ABBREVIATION : MORKELS

JSE SHORT CODE : MRK

SECTOR : Industrial-Retailers & Wholesalers

SHAREHOLDERS

Who Owns Whom's Assessment of the Identity of the Ultimate Controlling Shareholder:
DAUN ET CIE AG (WEST GERMANY)

SHAREHOLDER	PERCENTAGE 1992	1991
NEDBANK NOM LTD	75 3	78 8
SA MUTUAL	8 5	8 9
ATKINSON & JOSCELYNE P/L	4 3	---
CMB NOM P/L	4 1	---
SANLAM	---	4 2
TOTAL	92 2	91 8

DIRECTORS :
BRAND MD (Dir Human Resources),DAUN DE
HECKLINGER L MS,JANSEN CHM (Managing Director)
MELVILLE DR ,PAUW GR (Chairman)
ROHRS EHE (Commercial Director),SIMON TJ
SMITH RHL (Operations Director),SPERBER G
STUHLINGER JW

REGISTRATION NUMBER : 05/17149/06

REGISTERED OFFICE
201 Main Tower, Standard Bank Centre
Heerengracht, Cape Town
8001
TEL 021-21 4020
FAX 021-419 4803

TRANSFER SECRETARY
Central Registrars Ltd
P O Box 4844, Johannesburg
2000
TEL: 011-331 0051

COMPANY SECRETARY
J H van Heerden

NATURE OF BUSINESS
The group is engaged in speciality retailing of furniture, appliances, audio & video products, sporting goods & fashion sport apparel through a network of 113 outlets.

BANKERS :
First National Bank of SA Ltd

AUDITORS :
Coopers Theron Du Toit

FAMILIAR BRAND NAMES
AJAY SPORTS,MORKELS,TOTALSPORTS

CONTRIBUTION BY ACTIVITY
Furniture (% Sales) (79.7%)
Sporting Goods (16.6%)
Wholesale (3.7%)

YEAR END : March

DIVIDEND : Ords 4c

Interim	(Ldr)07/12/90	(Pay)28/12/90	Amt(c)3
Final	(Ldr)12/06/92	(Pay)03/07/92	Amt(c)4

NUMBER OF EMPLOYEES : 1357

CAPITAL STRUCTURE

	AUTHORISED	ISSUED
Ords 4c	50000000	41865000

FINANCIAL STATISTICS (AT FINANCIAL YEAR END)

(Amts in R'000)	1992 Mar	1991 Mar	1990 Mar	1989 Mar	1988 Mar
Ord S/H Int	65914	60350	52336	49400	42305
Long Trm Loans	37311	43972	34584	21776	16419
Iss Ord Share	41865	40065	40065	40065	40065
Total Liab	180799	160376	109429	97758	86186
Current Liab	143488	116404	74845	75982	69767
Total Assets	245963	220726	161765	147158	128491
Intang Assets	750	*	*	*	*
Current Assets	219373	199483	139249	134931	117511
Debtors	165037	144948	101026	104819	96325
Inventory	54336	54535	38223	30112	21186
Turnover	307577	268342	204562	199332	156550
Oper Profit	27776	33073	20477	23745	17225
Interest Paid	22305	13897	8847	4986	2138
Tax Paid	1257	9676	5924	9497	7546
Prf af Int&Tax	4214	9500	5800	9420	7541
Prf att Ord Sh	4214	9500	5800	9420	7541
Btm Line Earn	4214	12021	5800	9756	7927
Dividend Paid	1675	4007	2804	4007	3200
Mkt Prce(c) YE	55	120	80	80	90
Depreciation	7530	5890	4968	2608	2539

PER SHARE STATISTICS (CENTS)

Net Asst Val	155.65	150.63	130.63	123.30	105.59
Net Earnings	10.20	23.70	14.50	23.50	18.90
Dividends	4.00	10.00	7.00	10.00	8.00
Cash Flow	21.76	61.61	29.17	43.39	43.99

RATIOS AND OTHER INFORMATION

Mrk Cap(R000)	23026	48078	32052	32052	36059
Current Ratio	1.53	1.71	1.86	1.78	1.68
Quik/Acid Tst	1.15	1.25	1.35	1.38	1.38
A/C Rec T/ovr	1.86	1.85	2.02	1.90	1.63
Tot Ass T/ovr	1.25	1.22	1.26	1.35	1.22
Debt/Ass Rat	0.64	0.58	0.54	0.52	0.54
L T L Tot Ass	0.05	0.05	0.07	-	-
Debt to Eqity	2.37	2.13	1.66	1.54	1.65
Interest Cover	1.25	2.38	2.31	4.76	8.06
Oper Prof Mrg	9.03	12.32	10.01	11.91	11.00
Net Prof Marg%	1.37	3.54	2.84	4.73	4.82
Ret on Assets	11.29	14.98	12.72	16.24	13.41
Ret on Equity%	6.39	15.74	11.08	19.07	17.83
Price/Earnings	5.39	5.06	5.52	3.40	4.76
Divid Cover	2.55	2.37	2.07	2.35	2.36
Divid Yield	7.27	8.33	8.75	12.50	8.89
Earning Yield%	18.55	19.75	18.13	29.38	21.00
NAV % Mrk Pr	283.00	125.53	163.28	154.12	117.32
Effec Tax Rate	93.15	2.00	42.68	21.89	-
Def Interval	11.94	3.14	3.55	1.38	1.33
Sus Grth Rate	3.85	9.10	5.72	10.96	10.26

SUBSIDIARY & ASSOCIATED COMPANIES

AJAY SPORTS (PTY) LTD
COMMERCIAL CREDIT AND COLLECTION COMPANY
LITTLE BEAR INVESTMENTS (PTY) LTD
LIVINGSTONE FURNISHERS LIMITED
MORKEL PROPERTIES LIMITED
TOTAL SPORT (PTY) LTD

INVESTMENTS

None

MSAULI ASBES BPK

ABBREVIATION : MSAULI

JSE SHORT CODE : MSI

SECTOR : Metals & Minerals-Other

SHAREHOLDERS

Who Owns Whom's Assessment of the Identity of the Ultimate Controlling Shareholder: GEFCO

SHAREHOLDER	PERCENTAGE 1992	1991
GRIQUALAND EXPLORATION & FIN CO LTD	33.0	33.0
FIRST NAT NOM P/L	15.5	15.3
ISIDOR BALTSTEIN TRUST NOM P/L	7.7	7.7
RINRIC NOM P/L	3.1	---
HANOVA MINING HOLDINGS P/L	2.6	---
SHARESTOCK NOM P/L	1.8	---
LILLINGSTON M C	1.5	1.5
STRYDOM G L	1.4	---
ABSA NOM P/L	1.4	---
STD BANK NOM TVL P/L	1.3	1.3
STOCKSHARE NOM P/L	1.1	---

ALTENA MEWS P/L	---	1.9
SANTAMGROEI NOM P/L	---	2.5
TBA NOM P/L	---	1.0
VOLKSKAS NOM P/L	---	4.8
TOTAL	70.3	68.8

DIRECTORS :
HART HP (Executive Chairman),JOOSTE LK
KNOX FW (Technical Director),STRYDOM GL
VAN ZYL PA (Financial Director

REGISTRATION NUMBER : 51/01937/06

REGISTERED OFFICE
2nd Floor, Everite House
20 De Korte Street, Braamfontein
2001
TEL: 011-339 5458
FAX: 011-339 3722

TRANSFER SECRETARY
Central Registrars Ltd
P O Box 4844, Johannesburg
2000
TEL: 011-331 0051

COMPANY SECRETARY
P P Buys

NATURE OF BUSINESS
The company owns a chrysotile asbestos fibre mine situated in the KaNgwane homeland, and has a 50% interest in the Von Brandis gold prospect also in the KaNgwane homeland.

BANKERS :
Volkskas Ltd, Senbank

AUDITORS :
Coopers Theron Du Toit

FAMILIAR BRAND NAMES
N/A

CONTRIBUTION BY ACTIVITY
N/A

YEAR END : December

DIVIDEND : Ords 50c

Interim No 47	(Ldr)25/08/89	(Pay)29/09/89	Amt(c)25
Final No 48	(Ldr)16/03/90	(Pay)20/04/90	Amt(c)50
Interim No 49	(Ldr)27/08/90	(Pay)28/09/90	Amt(c)20
Final No 50	(Ldr)28/02/91	(Pay)22/03/91	Amt(c)30
Interim No 51	(Ldr)23/08/91	(Pay)27/09/91	Amt(c)10
Final No 52	(Ldr)20/03/92	(Pay)24/04/92	Amt(c)15
Interim No 53	(Ldr)28/08/92	(Pay)25/09/92	Amt(c)10

NUMBER OF EMPLOYEES : 1598

CAPITAL STRUCTURE

	AUTHORISED	ISSUED
Ords 50c	6500000	6451200

FINANCIAL STATISTICS (AT FINANCIAL YEAR END)

(Amts in R'000)	1991 Dec	1990 Dec	1989 Dec	1988	1987
Ord S/H Int	66264	60010	53368	40100	30926
Long Trm Loans	-	-	-	9891	6815
Iss Ord Share	6451	6451	6451	6451	6451
Total Liab	12343	12682	18513	19782	13630
Current Liab	12343	12682	18513	9891	6815
Total Assets	78607	72692	71881	67466	45482
Current Assets	23880	25888	36656	17475	7741
Debtors	19322	17785	12955	-	-
Inventory	3655	3973	-	17475	7741
Turnover	78005	70158	74092	57009	40417
Oper Profit	7360	9369	20359	11561	2384
Interest Paid	87	55	34	129	348
Tax Paid	569	2126	4277	-	-
Prf af Int&Tax	7867	9868	18106	11432	2036
Prf att Ord Sh	7867	9868	18106	11432	2036
Btm Line Earn	7867	9868	18106	11432	2036
Dividend Paid	1613	3226	4838	2258	-
Mkt Prce(c) YE	225	390	600	240	120

PER SHARE STATISTICS (CENTS)

Net Asst Val	1027.19	930.24	827.28	621.61	479.40
Net Earnings	121.90	153.00	280.70	-	-
Dividends	25.00	50.00	75.00	-	-
Cash Flow	121.95	152.97	280.67	177.21	31.56

RATIOS AND OTHER INFORMATION

Mrk Cap(R000)	14515	25159	38706	15482	7741
Current Ratio	1.93	2.04	1.98	1.77	1.14
Quik/Acid Tst	1.64	1.73	1.98	-	-
A/C Rec T/ovr	4.04	3.94	5.72	-	-
Tot Ass T/ovr	0.99	0.97	1.03	0.85	0.89
Debt/Ass Rat	0.16	0.17	0.26	0.29	0.30
L T L Tot Ass	-	-	-	0.15	0.15
Debt to Eqity	0.19	0.21	0.35	0.49	0.44
Interest Cover	84.60	170.35	598.79	89.62	6.85
Oper Prof Mrg	9.44	13.35	27.48	20.28	5.90
Net Prof Marg%	10.09	14.07	24.44	20.05	5.04
Ret on Assets	10.84	16.58	31.19	17.14	5.24
Ret on Equity%	11.87	16.44	33.93	28.51	6.58
Price/Earnings	1.85	2.55	2.14	-	-
Divid Cover	4.88	3.06	3.74	-	-
Divid Yield	11.11	12.82	12.50	-	-
Earning Yield%	54.18	39.23	46.78	-	-
NAV % Mrk Pr	456.53	238.52	137.88	259.00	399.50
Effec Tax Rate	6.74	17.73	19.11	-	-
Def Interval	0.19	0.11	0.03	0.87	3.35
Sus Grth Rate	9.44	11.07	24.86	22.88	6.58

SUBSIDIARY & ASSOCIATED COMPANIES

AFRICAN CHRYSOTILE ASBESTOS LTD

INVESTMENTS

None

MULTISOURCE HOLDINGS LTD

ABBREVIATION : MULTI

JSE SHORT CODE : MLT

SECTOR : Industrial-Electronics, Electrical & Bat

SHAREHOLDERS

Who Owns Whom's Assessment of the Identity of the Ultimate Controlling Shareholder:
DIRECTORS

SHAREHOLDER	PERCENTAGE 1992	1991
TPH HOLDINGS P/L	41.5	41.5
NANSEN INV LTD	27.4	27.4
TAVADAC P/L	7.1	7.1
SFSS NOM P/L	6.5	6.5
JARRARD C J	6.4	6.4
ELECTRONIC INV P/L	4.6	4.6
TOTAL	93.5	93.6

DIRECTORS :
HOLMES T (Managing Director),JARRARD CJ
JUDIN JM ,MOLE EW (Chairman)
PARK AN (Chief Executive

REGISTRATION NUMBER : 82/05758/06

REGISTERED OFFICE
Molloyd House, 639 Pretoria Main Road
Bramley, Johannesburg
2001
TEL: 011-786 2280
FAX: 011-440 3539

TRANSFER SECRETARY
Consolidated Share Registrars Ltd
P O Box 61051, Marshalltown
2107
TEL: 011-492 1620

COMPANY SECRETARY
T Holmes

NATURE OF BUSINESS
The supply, distribution and servicing of two-way radio equipment as well as the rendering of radio paging and radio telephone services.

BANKERS :
First National Bank of SA Ltd
Standard Bank of SA Ltd, Bankorp Ltd
Nedcor Bank Ltd

AUDITORS :
Kessel Feinstein

FAMILIAR BRAND NAMES
EXECUTIVE COMMS,ICOM,MULTISOURCE,QUICKVOICE
TECHTRON

CONTRIBUTION BY ACTIVITY
N/A

YEAR END : February

DIVIDEND : Ords 4c

Dividend	(Ldr)07/06/91	(Pay)28/06/91	Amt(c)8
Dividend	(Ldr)08/06/90	(Pay)29/06/90	Amt(c)5
Dividend	(Ldr)05/06/92	(Pay)26/06/92	Amt(c)12
Dividend	(Ldr)20/11/92	(Pay)11/12/92	Amt(c)12

NUMBER OF EMPLOYEES : 179

CAPITAL STRUCTURE

	AUTHORISED	ISSUED
Ords 4c	15000000	8575150

FINANCIAL STATISTICS (AT FINANCIAL YEAR END)

(Amts in R'000)	1992	1991	1990	1989
	Feb	Feb	Feb	Feb
Ord S/H Int	8409	7811	7372	11915
Long Trm Loans	491	501	518	-
Iss Ord Share	8575	8575	8575	34301
Total Liab	7721	6827	4230	93
Current Liab	7230	6326	3712	93
Total Assets	16130	14638	11441	12008
Intang Assets	*	*	161	*
Current Assets	8954	6424	4853	12008
Debtors	1925	2175	2342	11
Inventory	262	1047	1195	-
Turnover	19371	15797	14491	-
Oper Profit	2709	1806	1648	163
Interest Paid	45	48	58	-
Tax Paid	1780	955	3	82
Prf af Int&Tax	1624	1263	1781	81
Prf att Ord Sh	1627	1286	1796	81
Btm Line Earn	1627	1125	1798	5821
Dividend Paid	1029	686	600	-
Mkt Prce(c) YE	65	40	48	-
Depreciation	2331	1926	1357	-

PER SHARE STATISTICS (CENTS)

Net Asst Val	98.06	91.09	84.09	34.74
Net Earnings	18.90	15.00	20.90	18.00
Dividends	12.00	8.00	7.00	-
Cash Flow	46.16	37.46	36.77	0.24

RATIOS AND OTHER INFORMATION

Mrk Cap(R000)	5574	3430	4116	-
Current Ratio	1.24	1.02	1.31	129.12
Quik/Acid Tst	1.20	0.85	0.99	129.12
A/C Rec T/ovr	10.06	7.26	6.19	-
Tot Ass T/ovr	1.20	1.08	1.27	-
Debt/Ass Rat	0.45	0.44	0.33	0.01
L T L Tot Ass	0.00	0.01	0.01	-
Debt to Eqity	0.87	0.82	0.51	0.01
Interest Cover	60.20	37.63	28.41	-
Oper Prof Mrg	13.98	11.43	11.37	-
Net Prof Marg%	8.40	8.14	12.39	-
Ret on Assets	21.38	15.48	16.10	1.36
Ret on Equity%	19.35	16.46	24.36	0.68
Price/Earnings	3.44	2.67	2.30	-
Divid Cover	1.58	1.88	2.99	-
Divid Yield	18.46	20.00	14.58	-
Earning Yield%	29.08	37.50	43.54	-
NAV % Mrk Pr	150.87	227.73	175.19	-
Effec Tax Rate	52.29	41.61	0.17	50.31
Def Interval	0.07	0.23	0.03	-
Sus Grth Rate	7.11	7.68	16.22	0.68

SUBSIDIARY & ASSOCIATED COMPANIES

CONELECT (PTY) LTD
MOLLOYD INVESTMENTS (PTY) LTD (50%)
MULTISOURCE (PTY) LTD

INVESTMENTS

None

MURRAY & ROBERTS HOLDINGS LTD

ABBREVIATION : M&R-HLD

JSE SHORT CODE : MUR

SECTOR : Industrial-Industrial Holding

SHAREHOLDERS

Who Owns Whom's Assessment of the Identity of the Ultimate Controlling Shareholder: SANLAM VIA MURRAY & ROBERTS INVESTMENTS

SHAREHOLDER	PERCENTAGE 1992	1991
CMB NOM P/L	32.0	---
M & R INV LTD	25.1	35.0
STD BANK NOM TVL P/L	5.2	4.4
SOUTHERN LIFE ASSOC LTD	4.1	1.0
MURRAY & ROBERTS TRUST	3.9	5.4
EIGHTY ONE MAIN STREET NOM LTD	3.9	1.9
SA MUTUAL	2.2	---
NEDBANK NOM LTD	1.3	1.7
SIXTY SIX MARSHALL STREET NOM P/L	1.1	---
SYFRETS NOM LTD	---	1.4
SANLAM	---	3.6
COMMERCIAL UNION ASSURE CO SA LTD	---	1.5
SANKORP BPK	---	24.2
TOTAL	78.7	80.2

DIRECTORS :
BECK DE LA H WF ,BIRD LB (Financial Director)
BRINK DC (Chief Executive),CILLIERS C
COLEPEPER IG (Executive Director)
DALING MH (Chairman),DU PLESSIS AS
ESTERHUYSE WP ,FIELD ERM (Executive Director)
MALAN DJ ,RACTLIFFE GWJ (Executive Director)
VAN DER COLFF AM (Executive Director)
VAN DER MERWE CPJ (Executive Director

REGISTRATION NUMBER : 05/29826/06

REGISTERED OFFICE
Douglas Roberts Centre, Skeen Boulevard
Bedfordview
2008
TEL: 011-455 1410
FAX: 011-455 2222

TRANSFER SECRETARY
Central Registrars Ltd
P O Box 4844, Johannesburg
2000
TEL: 011-331 0051

COMPANY SECRETARY
L J Lindsay

NATURE OF BUSINESS
Industrial holding company with subsidiary and associated companies involved in construction, engineering, project management, manufacturing, service and food industries.

BANKERS :
Standard Bank of SA Ltd
First National Bank of SA Ltd
Nedcor Bank Ltd, Absa Bank Ltd

AUDITORS :
Deloitte & Touche

FAMILIAR BRAND NAMES
NORTON ABRASIVES

CONTRIBUTION BY ACTIVITY
Suppliers & Services (33.0%)
Properties (5.0%)
Engineering (30.0%)
Materials (% Operating Profit) (13.0%)
Construction (19.0%)

YEAR END : June

DIVIDEND : Ords 50c

Final No 83	(Ldr)21/09/90	(Pay)05/10/90	Amt(c)92
Interim No 84	(Ldr)15/03/91	(Pay)05/04/91	Amt(c)46
Final No 85	(Ldr)13/09/91	(Pay)04/10/91	Amt(c)110
Interim No 86	(Ldr)13/03/92	(Pay)03/04/92	Amt(c)53
Final No 87	(Ldr)18/09/92	(Pay)02/10/92	Amt(c)127

NUMBER OF EMPLOYEES : 50000

CAPITAL STRUCTURE

	AUTHORISED	ISSUED
Ords 50c	100000000	62749605

FINANCIAL STATISTICS (AT FINANCIAL YEAR END)

(Amts in R'000)	1992 Jun	1991 Jun	1990 Jun	1989 Jun	1988 Jun
Ord S/H Int	2150435	723690	502262	402594	289170
Long Trm Loans	900205	287955	281633	231318	234438
Iss Ord Share	62750	36135	28553	28103	27523
Total Liab	2170631	1177895	988787	774768	711211
Current Liab	1270426	889940	707154	543450	476773
Total Assets	3651632	1901498	1477303	1159045	992903
Intang Assets	669434	87	13746	18317	7478
Current Assets	1714199	1055080	822254	634245	538506
Debtors	631076	316130	271484	245537	238755
Inventory	822474	582226	383324	263237	269040
Turnover	5841876	4603960	4013720	3445019	3038857
Oper Profit	433677	242742	305683	225158	140506
Interest Paid	40027	28012	31832	29614	15898
Tax Paid	184872	109400	110134	72221	29806
Prf af Int&Tax	209291	105533	163790	126248	94802
Prf att Ord Sh	275481	192093	171177	132286	82055
Btm Line Earn	275481	192093	171177	163264	82055
Dividend Paid	106954	56279	37510	30810	22019
Mkt Prce(c) YE	5425	3625	2375	1900	1325
Depreciation	218575	117840	67943	52932	45963

PER SHARE STATISTICS (CENTS)

Net Asst Val	2360.16	2002.50	1710.91	1367.39	1023.48
Net Earnings	485.00	500.00	444.00	350.00	265.00
Dividends	180.00	156.00	132.00	110.00	80.00
Cash Flow	864.89	728.78	724.68	550.47	392.49

RATIOS AND OTHER INFORMATION

Mrk Cap(R000)	3404188	1309894	678134	533957	364680
Current Ratio	1.35	1.19	1.16	1.17	1.13
Quik/Acid Tst	0.70	0.53	0.62	0.68	0.57
A/C Rec T/ovr	9.26	14.56	14.78	14.03	12.73
Tot Ass T/ovr	1.60	2.42	2.72	2.97	3.06
Debt/Ass Rat	0.46	0.53	0.60	0.62	0.63

L T L Tot Ass	0.11	0.06	0.12	0.15	0.15
Debt to Eqity	0.78	1.40	1.76	1.77	2.17
Interest Cover	10.85	8.67	9.61	7.70	8.84
Oper Prof Mrg	7.42	5.27	7.62	6.54	4.62
Net Prof Marg%	4.72	4.17	4.26	3.84	2.70
Ret on Assets	14.15	17.84	21.88	20.87	14.15
Ret on Equity%	12.81	26.54	34.08	32.86	28.38
Price/Earnings	11.19	7.25	5.35	5.43	5.00
Divid Cover	2.69	3.21	3.36	3.18	3.31
Divid Yield	3.32	4.30	5.56	5.79	6.04
Earning Yield%	8.94	13.79	18.69	18.42	20.00
NAV % Mrk Pr	43.51	55.24	72.04	71.97	77.24
Effec Tax Rate	25.63	16.12	18.53	18.54	14.42
Def Interval	1.11	0.77	0.57	0.53	1.07
Sus Grth Rate	7.84	18.77	26.61	25.21	20.76

SUBSIDIARY & ASSOCIATED COMPANIES

ABECOL (PTY) LTD
ABRASIVES CORPORATION (PTY) LTD (50%)
AGRICULTURAL MANAGEMENT SERVICES (PTY) L
AMALGAMATED CONSTRUCTION CO (PTY) LTD
AMALGAMATED CONSTRUCTION COMPANY (PTY) L
ANCHUSA LTD
ARMCO SUPERLITE (PTY) LTD
BACKFILL PRODUCTS (PTY) LTD
BELLAMBIE MINING & INDUSTRIAL LTD
BRIDGE & STRUCTURES PROJECTS (PTY) LTD
C.I. - CARAVANS (PTY) LTD
CALSICA BRICKS (PTY) LTD
CARGO VAN (PTY) LTD
CONSANI ENGINEERING (PTY) LTD
CONSTRUCTION DEVELOPMENT HOLDINGS (PTY)
COURT AIR HOLDINGS (PTY) LTD (50%)
CV TRANSPORT HOLDINGS (PTY) LTD
D&A TIMBERS (PTY) LTD
DARLING & HODGSON LTD
DG MUST HOLDINGS (PTY) LTD
DRAGLINE CONSTRUCTION (PTY) LTD
DRILLS STEELS (PTY) LTD (22%)
ELGIN BROWN & HAMER (PTY) LTD
EMSO (PTY) LTD
ENGINEERING MANAGEMENT SERVICES (CAPE) (
ENGINEERING MANAGEMENT SERVICES LTD
FALCON ENGINEERING (PTY) LTD
FIRESTONE SA (PTY) LTD
FIRESTONE SOUTH AFRICA (PTY) LTD
GEMTEC (PTY) LTD
GENERAL ROLLING WORKS (PTY) LTD
GENREC (PTY) LTD
GENREC CONSTRUCTION (PTY) LTD
GENREC ENGINEERING (PTY) LTD
GENREC HOLDINGS LTD
GENREC MEI (PTY) LTD
GENREC MOSSEL BAY (PTY) LTD
GILLIS MASON CONSTRUCTION CO (PTY) LTD
HALL LONGMORE & CO (PTY) LTD (38%)
HARDWARE INDUSTRIES INVESTMENTS (PTY) LT
HIGH STRUCTURES (PTY) LTD (50%)
IMPROVAIR HOLDINGS (PTY) LTD
KLEP VALVES (PTY) LTD
KWIKSPACE HOLDINGS (PTY) LTD
LEEUWFONTEIN MYNE (EDMS) BPK
LONGDALE ENGINEERING EQUIPMENT (PTY) LTD
LONGDALE ENGINEERING EQUIPMENT (PTY) LTD
M & R (CAPE) (PTY) LTD
M & R (TRANSKEI) (PTY) LTD
M & R BUILDINGS (TVL) (PTY) LTD
M & R FOUNDRIES LTD
M & R PROPERTIES LTD
M & R STRUCTURES (PTY) LTD
M&R (BORDER) (PTY) LTD
M&R (EP) (PTY) LTD
M&R (NATAL) (PTY) LTD
M&R CIVILS (PTY) LTD
M&R FOUNDRY HOLDINGS (PTY) LTD
M&R LIGHT INDUSTRIES LTD
M&R PROPERTIES (N TVL) (PTY) LTD
M&R PROPERTIES (NATAL) (PTY) LTD
M&R PROPERTIES (TVL & OFS) (PTY) LTD
M&R PROPERTIES LTD
M&R SUPPLIERS & SERVICES LTD
MARTECH CONTROLS (PTY) LTD
MARTECH HOLDINGS LTD
MEI CONSTRUCTION (PTY) LTD
MUCH ASPHALT (PTY) LTD
MURJON INVEST HOLDING CO. (PTY) LTD (50%)
MURRAY & ROBERTS HOLDINGS LTD (43,6%)
MURRAY & ROBERTS HOUSING (TVL) (PTY) LTD
MURRAY & ROBERTS LTD
PACKPROP (PTY) LTD
PENTOW MARINE (PTY) LTD (50%)
PREMIER VALVES (PTY) LTD
PREMIER VALVES (PTY) LTD
PREMIER VALVES EAST CAPE (PTY) LTD
PROCESS INDUSTRY ENGINEERING (PTY) LTD
R U C MINING CONTRACTING CO (PTY) LTD (50%)
READY MIX MATERIALS (PTY) LTD
REINFORCING STEEL CONTRACTORS (PTY) LTD
RIBCO (PTY) LTD
RIBCO (PTY) LTD
SAFEX ENGINEERING CO. (PTY) LTD
SCREEN PRODUCTS (PTY) LTD
STANDARD ENGINEERING LTD (38%)
STONE STAMCOR TRADING (PTY) LTD
SUNFLOWER PROJECTS (PTY) LTD
TOLL ROAD CONCESSIONAIRES (PTY) LTD (36%)
TRANSPORTATION MOTOR SPARES (PTY) LTD
TRANSPORTATION MOTOR SPARES (PTY) LTD
TRICRETE (PTY) LTD
UNITRANS LTD
VSA MOTOR DISTRIBUTORS (PTY) LTD - DOR
WASTE MASTER SYSTEMS (PTY) LTD
WESTINGHOUSE BRAKE & EQUIPMENT (PTY) LTD
WOODLINE TIMBER INDUSTRIES (PTY) LTD (50%)

INVESTMENTS

ANCHUSA HOLDINGS LTD (15%)
FIDELITY GROUP LTD (0.7%)
HISTORICAL HOMES OF SA LTD (10000 SH)
HUDACO INDUSTRIES LTD (8,8%)
LEAGUE PROPERTIES (SHARE BLOCK) (PTY) LT (3.1%)
MICHELSENS LTD (4.5%)
SBDC (608000 SH)
VIGILANS PROPERTIES (PRETORIA) (PTY) LTD (7%)

MURRAY & ROBERTS INVESTMENTS LTD

ABBREVIATION : M&R-INV

JSE SHORT CODE : MRV

SECTOR : Industrial-Industrial Holding

SHAREHOLDERS

Who Owns Whom's Assessment of the Identity of the Ultimate Controlling Shareholder:
SANLAM VIA SANKORP

SHAREHOLDER	PERCENTAGE 1992	1991
CMB NOM P/L	60.7	---
EIGHTY ONE MAIN STREET NOM LTD	7.0	2.1
SA MUTUAL	5.3	5.3
DG MURRAY TRUST	4.7	4.7
STD BANK NOM TVL P/L	2.6	---
ROELOF LE ROUX VAN DER MERWE TRUST	2.3	2.3
SYFRETS NOM LTD	---	5.5
DOUGLAS MURRAY TRUST	---	1.2
SANKORP BPK	---	47.0
SANLAM	---	8.9
STATUS INV P/L	---	4.5
TOTAL	82.6	81.4

DIRECTORS :
BRINK DC ,CILLIERS C ,DALING MH (Chairman)
DE LA HARPE BECK WF ,DU PLESSIS AS
ESTERHUYSE WP PRO

REGISTRATION NUMBER : 01/03743/06

REGISTERED OFFICE
Douglas Roberts Centre, Skeen Boulevard
Bedfordview
2008
TEL: 011-455 1410
FAX: 011-455 2222

TRANSFER SECRETARY
Central Registrars Ltd
P O Box 4844, Johannesburg
2000
TEL: 011-331 0051

COMPANY SECRETARY
L J Lindsay

NATURE OF BUSINESS
The company holds a controlling interest in quoted Murray & Roberts Holdings Ltd.

BANKERS :
Standard Bank of SA Ltd

AUDITORS :
Deloitte Pim Goldby

FAMILIAR BRAND NAMES
N/A

CONTRIBUTION BY ACTIVITY
N/A

YEAR END : June

DIVIDEND : Ords 3c

Interim No 54	(Ldr)16/03/90	(Pay)04/04/90	Amt(c)33
Final No 55	(Ldr)21/09/90	(Pay)05/10/90	Amt(c)77
Interim No 56	(Ldr)15/03/91	(Pay)05/04/91	Amt(c)41
Final No 57	(Ldr)13/09/91	(Pay)04/10/91	Amt(c)98
Interim No 58	(Ldr)13/03/92	(Pay)03/04/92	Amt(c)47
Final No 59	(Ldr)18/09/92	(Pay)02/10/92	Amt(c)113

CAPITAL STRUCTURE

	AUTHORISED	ISSUED
Ords 3c	18300000	17656831

FINANCIAL STATISTICS (AT FINANCIAL YEAR END)

(Amts in R'000)	1992 Jun	1991 Jun	1990 Jun	1989 Jun	1988 Jun
Ord S/H Int	540886	316210	207747	164546	121036
Long Trm Loans	3749	4837	39764	40702	41639
Iss Ord Share	17657	17657	13794	13794	13794
Total Liab	25013	23362	53742	52531	49857
Current Liab	21264	18525	13978	11829	8218
Total Assets	565899	339572	261489	217077	170893
Current Assets	21241	18653	14316	17683	10718
Debtors	20025	17341	13704	11693	2222
Oper Profit	126216	123797	112586	86276	54161
Interest Paid	627	747	5092	5089	5090
Tax Paid	50421	45637	45193	32614	12679
Prf af Int&Tax	76259	78629	68227	53478	36392
Prf att Ord Sh	76257	78627	66100	51351	36288
Btm Line Earn	76392	78627	66100	65137	36530
Dividend Paid	28251	24543	15174	12139	8690
Mkt Prce(c) YE	4500	2900	1675	1575	1325
Depreciation	-	-	5	17	8

PER SHARE STATISTICS (CENTS)

Net Asst Val	3063.30	1790.85	1506.07	1192.88	877.45
Net Earnings	432.00	445.00	386.00	372.00	263.00
Dividends	160.00	139.00	110.00	88.00	63.00
Cash Flow	431.88	445.30	494.64	387.80	263.13

RATIOS AND OTHER INFORMATION

Mrk Cap(R000)	794565	512053	231050	217256	182771
Current Ratio	1.00	1.01	1.02	1.49	1.30
Quik/Acid Tst	1.00	1.01	1.02	1.49	1.30
Debt/Ass Rat	0.04	0.07	0.20	0.24	0.29
L T L Tot Ass	0.01	0.01	0.15	0.19	0.24
Debt to Eqity	0.05	0.07	0.26	0.32	0.41
Interest Cover	201.30	165.73	22.11	16.95	10.64
Ret on Assets	22.50	36.81	45.32	42.00	31.69
Ret on Equity%	14.10	24.87	31.82	31.21	29.98
Price/Earnings	10.42	6.52	4.34	4.23	5.04
Divid Cover	2.70	3.20	3.51	4.23	4.17
Divid Yield	3.56	4.79	6.57	5.59	4.75
Earning Yield%	9.60	15.34	23.04	23.62	19.85
NAV % Mrk Pr	68.07	61.75	89.91	75.74	66.22
Effec Tax Rate	39.80	36.73	39.85	37.88	25.84
Def Interval	0.06	0.07	0.10	0.14	0.21
Sus Grth Rate	8.88	17.10	24.51	23.83	22.80

SUBSIDIARY & ASSOCIATED COMPANIES

ANCHUSA LTD
DG MUST HOLDINGS (PTY) LTD
MURRAY & ROBERTS HOLDINGS LTD (43,6%)
PACKPROP (PTY) LTD

INVESTMENTS

None

MUTUAL & FEDERAL INSURANCE CO LTD

ABBREVIATION : M-&-F

JSE SHORT CODE : MAF

SECTOR : Financial-Insurance

SHAREHOLDERS

Who Owns Whom's Assessment of the Identity of the Ultimate Controlling Shareholder:
SA MUTUAL

SHAREHOLDER	PERCENTAGE 1992	1991
MUTUAL & FEDERAL INV LTD	79.1	79.3
EIGHTY ONE MAIN STREET NOM LTD	3.9	3.8
SA MUTUAL	3.2	2.8
BLUE CIRCLE PENS FUND	2.1	2.1
SIXTY SIX MARSHALL STREET NOM P/L	1.6	1.7
LIBERTY LIFE ASSOC OF AFRICA LTD	1.1	1.0
FIRST NAT NOM P/L	1.1	1.3
TOTAL	92.1	92.1

DIRECTORS :
ABRAHAMSE LG ,CILLIERS C ,DAVIN FJ
DUNNINGHAM GW ,ELMS RA ,GAMBLE RA ,HERSOV BE
LEVETT MJ (Deputy Chairman)
MACMILLAN GA (Chairman),MCCARTHY BC ,ROWLAND WR
RUSHTON IL ,SAGGERS KTM (Managing Director)
VAN RYNEVELD AJ ,VILJOEN AFV

REGISTRATION NUMBER : 70/06619/06

REGISTERED OFFICE
Mutual & Federal Centre, 69 President Street
Johannesburg
2001
TEL: 011-374 9111
FAX: 011-374 2665

TRANSFER SECRETARY
Central Registrars Ltd
P O Box 4844, Johannesburg
2000
TEL: 011-331 0051

COMPANY SECRETARY
K L Penwarden

NATURE OF BUSINESS
The company transacts all classes of short-term insurance business.

BANKERS :
First National Bank of SA Ltd
Standard Bank of SA Ltd, Nedcor Bank Ltd

AUDITORS :
KPMG Aiken & Peat

FAMILIAR BRAND NAMES
N/A

CONTRIBUTION BY ACTIVITY
N/A

YEAR END : June

DIVIDEND :Ords 50c

Interim No 40	(Ldr)05/04/90	(Pay)27/04/90	Amt(c)16
Final No 41	(Ldr)21/09/90	(Pay)22/10/90	Amt(c)24
Interim No 42	(Ldr)05/04/91	(Pay)26/04/91	Amt(c)20
Final No 43	(Ldr)20/09/91	(Pay)21/10/91	Amt(c)32
Interim No 44	(Ldr)03/04/92	(Pay)24/04/92	Amt(c)25
Final No 45	(Ldr)18/09/92	(Pay)19/10/92	Amt(c)43

NUMBER OF EMPLOYEES : 2230

CAPITAL STRUCTURE

	AUTHORISED	ISSUED
Ords 50c	50000000	46874500

FINANCIAL STATISTICS (AT FINANCIAL YEAR END)

(Amts in R'000)	1992 Jun	1991 Jun	1990 Jun	1989 Jun	1988 Jun
Ord S/H Int	1608116	1284388	1047353	783164	438472
Long Trm Loans	183130	179496	141303	172748	169185
Iss Ord Share	46875	46687	46527	46497	46497
Total Liab	954831	807017	716963	585623	460152
Current Liab	771701	627521	575660	412875	290967
Total Assets	2562947	2091405	1764316	1368787	898624
Current Assets	171805	140109	147672	115297	92465
Debtors	81782	52017	40029	34777	23529
Turnover	1291589	1202634	882911	826053	742612
Oper Profit	197758	145413	121288	143812	102601
Tax Paid	58194	37336	33030	53204	38271
Prf af Int&Tax	139564	108077	88258	90608	64330
Prf att Ord Sh	139564	108077	88258	90608	64330
Btm Line Earn	139564	108077	67665	90608	64330
Dividend Paid	31909	24292	18610	13949	10462
Mkt Prce(c) YE	3550	1750	1350	1000	600

PER SHARE STATISTICS (CENTS)

Net Asst Val	3430.65	2751.06	2251.06	1684.33	943.01
Net Earnings	298.00	232.00	190.00	194.90	138.40
Dividends	68.00	52.00	40.00	30.00	22.50
Cash Flow	199.76	276.04	217.49	174.21	196.47

RATIOS AND OTHER INFORMATION

Mrk Cap(R000)	1664063	817023	628115	464970	278982
Current Ratio	0.22	0.22	0.26	0.28	0.32
Quik/Acid Tst	0.22	0.22	0.26	0.28	0.32
A/C Rec T/ovr	15.79	23.12	22.06	23.75	31.56
Tot Ass T/ovr	0.50	0.58	0.50	0.60	0.83
Debt/Ass Rat	0.30	0.30	0.33	0.30	0.32
Debt to Eqity	0.48	0.49	0.55	0.53	0.66
Oper Prof Mrg	15.31	12.09	13.74	17.41	13.82
Net Prof Marg%	10.81	8.99	10.00	10.97	8.66
Ret on Assets	7.72	6.95	6.87	10.51	11.42
Ret on Equity%	8.68	8.41	8.43	11.57	14.67
Price/Earnings	11.91	7.54	7.11	5.13	4.34
Divid Cover	4.38	4.46	4.75	6.50	6.15
Divid Yield	1.92	2.97	2.96	3.00	3.75
Earning Yield%	8.39	13.26	14.07	19.49	23.07
NAV % Mrk Pr	96.64	157.20	166.75	168.43	157.17
Effec Tax Rate	52.11	11.52	16.67	43.59	10.96
Def Interval	0.21	0.15	0.19	0.25	0.23
Sus Grth Rate	6.69	6.52	6.65	9.79	12.29

SUBSIDIARY & ASSOCIATED COMPANIES

BRITISH ENGINE INSURANCE CO OF SA LTD
DAMMI NOMINEES (PTY) LTD (25%)
MUTUAL & FEDERAL INSURANCE CO OF NAMIBIA
NATIONAL EMPLOYERS GENERAL INSURANCE CO
ROYAL FIRE & GENERAL CO LTD
SA MUTUAL FIRE & GEN INSURANCE CO LTD

INVESTMENTS

JOHANNESBURG CONSOLIDATED INVESTMENT COM (526000 SH)
METAL BOX SA LTD (411200 SH)

NAMIBIAN FISHING INDUSTRIES LTD

ABBREVIATION : NAMFISH

JSE SHORT CODE : NFH

SECTOR : Industrial Fishing

SHAREHOLDERS

Who Owns Whom's Assessment of the Identity of the Ultimate Controlling Shareholder: NAMNOR AS (NORWAY) VIA NAMSEA

SHAREHOLDER	PERCENTAGE 1992	1991
NAMIBIAN SEA PRODUCTS LTD	26 4	26 4
SARUSAS DEVELOPMENT CORP P/L	11 8	11 8
SMALL BUSNESS DEVELOPMENT CORP LTD	11 1	11 1
STD BANK NOM WINDHOEK P/L	8 8	
SA MUTUAL	8 6	8 3
CITY DENTAL LABORATORIES P/L	8 6	---
STD BANK NOM TVL P/L	1 6	1 7
PROTEA ASSURE CO LTD	1 6	
SCHEBEN L H D	1 6	1 6
FIRST NAT NOM P/L	1 1	1 1
PHOENIX ASSURE SA LTD	---	1 6
NAT FISHERIES OF NAMIBIA LTD		16 5
TOTAL	81 2	80 2

DIRECTORS :
BARMEN A ,ELDOY LA (Chairman),GUHRING WEW KUTTEL PC ,PAETZOLD AT ,SCHWIEGER PA

REGISTRATION NUMBER : 342/1947 (Na

REGISTERED OFFICE
Ninth Floor, 154 Independence Avenue
Windhoek, Namibia
9000
TEL 061 22 8391
FAX 061 34 907

TRANSFER SECRETARY
Ernst & Young
P O Box 1857, Windhoek
9000
TEL 061-38 260

COMPANY SECRETARY
P A Schwieger

NATURE OF BUSINESS
The group participates in the Namibian inshore fishing industry Operations include catching & processing of rock lobster, & the catching & processing thereof into canned fish, fish meal & fish oil

BANKERS :
Bank Windhoek Ltd
Standard Bank Namibia Ltd

AUDITORS :
Ernst & Young

FAMILIAR BRAND NAMES
N/A

CONTRIBUTION BY ACTIVITY
Pelagic & Lobster (% income after tax) (66 0%)
Investments (34 0%)

YEAR END : December

DIVIDEND .Ords 50c

Interim	(Ldr)21/09/90	(Pay)22/10/90	Amt(c)20
Final	(Ldr)30/03/90	(Pay)08/05/90	Amt(c)60
Interim	(Ldr)20/09/91	(Pay)18/10/91	Amt(c)20
Final	(Ldr)24/04/92	(Pay)22/05/92	Amt(c)20
Interim	(Ldr)23/10/92	(Pay)27/11/92	Amt(c)20

NUMBER OF EMPLOYEES : 1700

CAPITAL STRUCTURE

	AUTHORISED	ISSUED
Ords 50c	3200000	3150450

FINANCIAL STATISTICS (AT FINANCIAL YEAR END)

(Amts in R'000)	1991 Dec	1990 Dec	1989 Dec	1988 Dec	1987 Dec
Ord S/H Int	26540	9060	7959	8064	19657
Long Trm Loans	2461	1262	1580	1346	5315
Iss Ord Share	3150	3150	3150	3150	3150
Total Liab	3340	2073	3758	15529	17249
Current Liab	879	811	2178	14183	11934
Total Assets	29880	11133	11717	23593	36906
Current Assets	12986	8279	8922	19705	30675
Debtors	3981	2997	3976	14950	8431
Inventory			-	-	311
Turnover	11600	11726	10764	20531	35894
Oper Profit	1750	2523	3024	7027	13639
Tax Paid	1315	1583	2073	4427	7600
Prf af Int&Tax	1903	2338	2979	5471	8362
Prf att Ord Sh	1955	2253	4088	8391	7278
Btm Line Earn	3054	1730	3833	17234	11629
Dividend Paid	1260	630	3938	28827	6301
Mkt Prce(c) YE	425	375	1175	1450	1525
Depreciation	42	53	63	362	458

PER SHARE STATISTICS (CENTS)

Net Asst Val	842 54	287 62	252 67	256 00	624 03
Net Earnings	62 00	72 00	130 00	266 00	231 00
Dividends	40 00	20 00	125 00	915 00	200 00
Cash Flow	102 70	65 46	103 43	154 48	243 11

RATIOS AND OTHER INFORMATION

Mrk Cap(R000)	13388	11813	37013	45675	48038
Current Ratio	14 77	10 21	4 10	1 39	2 57
Quik/Acid Tst	14 77	10 21	4 10	1 39	2 54
A/C Rec T/ovr	2 91	3 91	2 71	1 37	4 26
Tot Ass T/ovr	0 39	1 05	0 92	0 87	0 97
Debt/Ass Rat	0 04	0 11	0 23	0 62	0 37
L T L Tot Ass	0 01	0 03	0 04	0 02	0 04
Debt to Eqity	0 05	0 13	0 34	1 83	0 69
Oper Prof Mrg	15 09	21 52	28 09	34 23	38 00
Net Prof Marg%	16 85	19 21	37 98	40 87	20 28
Ret on Assets	10 94	34 46	52 58	57 86	43 51
Ret on Equity%	7 37	24 87	51 36	104 06	37 02
Price/Earnings	6 85	5 21	9 04	5 45	6 60
Divid Cover	1 55	3 60	1 04	0 29	1 16
Divid Yield	9 41	5 33	10 64	63 10	13 11
Earning Yield%	14 59	19 20	11 06	18 34	15 15
NAV % Mrk Pr	198 24	76 70	21 50	17 66	40 92
Effec Tax Rate	1 28	56 37	41 25	65 62	54 18
Def Interval					0 61

Sus Grth Rate	2.62	17.91	1.88	-253.42	4.97

SUBSIDIARY & ASSOCIATED COMPANIES

ATLANTIC HARVESTERS OF NAMIBIA (PTY) LTD (25%)
BREEMOND FISHING INDUSTRIES (PTY) LTD (25%)
CAPE LOBSTER CANNING CO. LTD
NORTHERN FISHING INDUSTRIES OF SWA (PTY)
SEAFLOWER INVESTMENTS LTD (35%)
SEAFLOWER LOBSTER CORP LTD (35%)
TABLE MOUNTAIN CANNING CO. LTD
UNITED FISHING ENTERPRISES (PTY) LTD (25%)
WALVIS BAY FISH PROCESSORS (PTY) LTD (25%)
WALVIS BAY TRAWLING CO. (PTY) LTD
WEST COAST FISHING INDUSTRIES LTD

INVESTMENTS

ATLANTIC CANNED FISH SALES (PTY) LTD (1000S)
FEDERAL MARINE LTD (600S)
FISH MEAL MARKETING CO (WINDHOEK) (PTY) (1S)
FISH OIL MARKETING CO (WINDHOEK) (PTY) L (1S)
GOLD FIELDS NAMIBIA LTD (5000S)
NAMIBIAN SEA PRODUCTS LTD (93083S)
S A FISHMEAL PRODUCERS ASSOCIATION (PTY) (1S)
UNITED FISHING ENTERPRISES (PTY) LTD (14,38%)

NAMIBIAN SEA PRODUCTS LTD

ABBREVIATION : NAMSEA

JSE SHORT CODE : NMS

SECTOR : Industrial-Fishing

SHAREHOLDERS

Who Owns Whom's Assessment of the Identity of the Ultimate Controlling Shareholder: NAMNOR AS (NORWAY) VIA ARUN HOLDINGS

SHAREHOLDER	PERCENTAGE 1992	1991
NAMNOR SA	22.4	---
STD BANK NOM WINDHOEK P/L	21.9	---
SA MUTUAL	8.3	12.0
SOUTHERN TUNA CO LTD	7.8	---
CMB NOM P/L	2.9	---
SHARESTOCK NOM P/L	1.7	---
INTERNATIONAL DIAMONDS P/L	1.6	---
ARUN HOLDINGS LTD	1.4	71.9
TIRAS P/L	1.1	---
FIRST NAT NOM P/L	1.0	3.0
S W A FISHING IND LTD	---	1.9
STD BANK NOM TVL P/L	---	2.0
TOTAL	70.0	90.7

DIRECTORS :
AKWENYE OS ,ASPARA F DR,BARMEN A
ELDOY LA (Chairman),GUHRING WEW ,KUTTEL PC
SCHWEIGER PA ,VOIGTS HD

REGISTRATION NUMBER : 709/1953 (Na

REGISTERED OFFICE
9th Floor, Sanlam Centre, 154 Independence Ave
Windhoek, Namibia
9000
TEL: 061-22 8391
FAX: 061-34 907

TRANSFER SECRETARY
Rand Registrars Ltd
P O Box 82549, Southdale
2135
TEL: 011-835 1016

COMPANY SECRETARY
P A Schwieger

NATURE OF BUSINESS
An investment holding company with investments in the inshore fishing industry off Namibia. Operations include pelagic fishing, and the production of canned fish, fish oil and fish meal, & the catching & processing of lobster,tuna & hake.

BANKERS :
Bank Windhoek Ltd
First National Bank of Namibia Ltd

AUDITORS :
Ernst & Young

FAMILIAR BRAND NAMES
N/A

CONTRIBUTION BY ACTIVITY
Investments (8.0%)
Pelagic Fish (% income after tax) (92.0%)

YEAR END : December

DIVIDEND : Ords 50c

Interim No 76	(Ldr)08/06/90	(Pay)06/07/90	Amt(c)15
Final No 77	(Ldr)24/04/92	(Pay)22/05/92	Amt(c)10
Interim No 78	(Ldr)23/10/92	(Pay)27/11/92	Amt(c)10

NUMBER OF EMPLOYEES : 1700

CAPITAL STRUCTURE

	AUTHORISED	ISSUED
Ords 50c	15000000	10878803
7% Red Cum Pref R2	250000	0
7% Non-Cum Pref 50c	2120000	2120000

FINANCIAL STATISTICS (AT FINANCIAL YEAR END)

(Amts in R'000)	1991 Dec	1990 Dec	1989 Sep	1988 Sep	1987 Sep
Ord S/H Int	63671	7893	6251	7165	13844
Long Trm Loans	8037	2175	3069	4921	4194
Iss Ord Share	10879	4200	4200	4200	4200
Total Liab	18404	3098	7199	13421	12136
Current Liab	10367	923	4130	8500	7942
Total Assets	82075	10991	13450	20586	25980
Current Assets	14069	5776	5975	9997	15214
Debtors	11460	2780	2420	3850	1191
Inventory	-	99	-	-	-
Turnover	39740	17126	8088	13826	19670
Oper Profit	3186	3518	2040	5388	7339
Interest Paid	543	1	25	-	-
Tax Paid	1954	2021	837	2705	3459
Prf af Int&Tax	2086	3216	9188	12124	7639
Prf att Ord Sh	2456	2816	6646	9657	7210
Btm Line Earn	2380	2272	8120	12221	10458
Dividend Paid	1088	630	8820	18900	6300
Mkt Prce(c) YE	350	540	675	900	1000

Depreciation	17	-	-	21	105

PER SHARE STATISTICS (CENTS)

Net Asst Val	585.27	187.93	148.83	170.60	329.62
Net Earnings	46.00	67.00	158.30	230.00	167.00
Dividends	10.00	15.00	210.00	200.00	150.00
Cash Flow	133.11	44.48	210.69	249.93	151.12

RATIOS AND OTHER INFORMATION

Mrk Cap(R000)	38077	22680	28350	37800	42000
Current Ratio	1.36	6.26	1.45	1.18	1.92
Quik/Acid Tst	1.36	6.15	1.45	1.18	1.92
A/C Rec T/ovr	3.47	4.93	3.34	3.59	16.52
Tot Ass T/ovr	0.48	1.25	0.60	0.67	0.76
Debt/Ass Rat	0.13	0.11	0.34	0.52	0.31
L T L Tot Ass	-	0.02	0.04	0.11	-
Debt to Eqity	0.16	0.15	0.74	1.51	0.57
Interest Cover	7.02	4568.00	355.84	-	-
Oper Prof Mrg	8.02	20.54	25.22	38.97	37.31
Net Prof Marg%	6.18	16.44	82.17	69.85	36.65
Ret on Assets	6.12	35.89	56.37	60.41	41.35
Ret on Equity%	3.86	28.54	106.32	134.78	52.08
Price/Earnings	7.61	8.06	4.26	3.91	5.99
Divid Cover	4.60	4.47	0.75	1.15	1.11
Divid Yield	2.86	2.78	31.11	22.22	15.00
Earning Yield%	13.14	12.41	23.45	25.56	16.70
NAV % Mrk Pr	167.22	34.80	22.05	18.96	32.96
Effec Tax Rate	-90.45	66.99	54.56	64.48	58.52
Def Interval	0.15	0.36	0.12	0.32	0.17
Sus Grth Rate	2.15	27.70	-34.78	-129.00	6.57

SUBSIDIARY & ASSOCIATED COMPANIES

AFRICAN CANNING CO (NAMIBIA) LTD
ATLANTIC HARVESTERS OF NAMIBIA (PTY) LTD
LUDERITZ BAY CANNERY LTD
LURIES CANNING FACTORY LTD
NAMIBIAN FISHING INDUSTRIES LTD (26.4%)
OCEANA FISHING CO. LTD
SARUSAS BELEGGINGS (EDMS) BPK
SARUSAS DEVELOPMENT CORPORATION LTD
SARUSAS VISSERYE (PTY) LTD
SEAFLOWER LOBSTER CORP LTD (35%)
UNITED FISHING ENTERPRISES (PTY) LTD (25%)

INVESTMENTS

ATLANTIC CANNED FISH SALES (PTY) LTD (2000)
DUINEVELD BELEGGINGSMAATSKAPPY BEPERK (75000)
FEDERAL MARINE LTD (600)
FISH MEAL MARKETING CO (WINDHOEK) (PTY) (2)
FISH OIL MARKETING CO (WINDHOEK) (PTY) L (2)
GOLD FIELDS NAMIBIA LTD (NAMIBIA) (5000)
NEW VELD VENTURES INV & DEVELOPMENT CO ((30000)
SOUTH AFRICAN FISHMEAL PRODUCERS ASSOC ((1)

NAMPAK LTD

ABBREVIATION : NAMPAK

JSE SHORT CODE : NPK

SECTOR : Industrial-Paper & Packaging

SHAREHOLDERS

Who Owns Whom's Assessment of the Identity of the Ultimate Controlling Shareholder: SA MUTUAL VIA BARLOWS & CG SMITH

SHAREHOLDER	PERCENTAGE 1992	1991
C G SMITH LTD	62.9	63.2
LIBERTY LIFE ASSOC OF AFRICA LTD	6.9	6.9
CMB NOM P/L	3.8	---
SOUTHERN LIFE ASSOC LTD	2.8	2.6
STD BANK NOM TVL P/L	2.7	2.6
METAL IND GROUP PENS FUND	1.7	1.7
FIRST NAT NOM P/L	1.7	1.7
ENGINEERING INDUSTRIES PENS FUND	1.5	1.5
SA MUTUAL	1.2	1.2
EIGHTY ONE MAIN STREET NOM LTD	1.1	---
GUARDIAN NOM P/L	1.0	---
ESCOM PENS & PROV FUND	---	1.0
SANLAM	---	3.8
TOTAL	87.1	86.1

DIRECTORS :
BORTOLAN GE ,BROWN D
CAMPBELL PL (Deputy Managing Director)
CLEWLOW WAM ,CONNELLAN BP (Chairman),COOPER DE
EVANS T ,HAWTON DA ,KATZ MM PROF,LANG AS
MARTHINUSEN AM ,MCCARTAN DB (Managing Director)
MCFADDEN DJ (Financial Director),SMIT AS
UPTON RAP ,WARD JH ,WHITE RC ,WILLIAMS RA

REGISTRATION NUMBER : 68/08070/06

REGISTERED OFFICE
Nampak Centre, 114 Dennis Road
Sandton
2196
TEL: 011-444 7418
FAX: 011-444 4794

TRANSFER SECRETARY
Rand Registrars Ltd
P O Box 82549, Southdale
2135
TEL: 011-835 1016

COMPANY SECRETARY
G V D Duffey

NATURE OF BUSINESS
An investment holding company with subsidiaries engaged in the manufacture of packaging based on metal, paper, paperboard, plastic & glass. The group is also engaged in the manufacture of brown and tissue papers, conversion and distribution of tissue wadding, paper merchanting and printing.

BANKERS :
Standard Bank of SA Ltd

AUDITORS :
Deloitte Pim Goldby

FAMILIAR BRAND NAMES
BARLAN FORMS,TWINSAVER

CONTRIBUTION BY ACTIVITY
N/A

YEAR END : September

DIVIDEND :Ords 50c

Interim No 43	(Ldr)17/11/89	(Pay)10/01/90	Amt(c)68
Final No 44	(Ldr)16/11/90	(Pay)09/01/91	Amt(c)98
Interim No 45	(Ldr)30/05/91	(Pay)15/07/91	Amt(c)75
Final No 46	(Ldr)15/11/91	(Pay)13/01/92	Amt(c)115
Interim No 47	(Ldr)29/05/92	(Pay)13/07/92	Amt(c)79
Final No 48	(Ldr)13/11/92	(Pay)11/01/93	Amt(c)126

NUMBER OF EMPLOYEES : 22309

CAPITAL STRUCTURE

	AUTHORISED	ISSUED
Ords 50c	60000000	48059647
6% Cum Prefs R2	400000	400000
6,5% Cum Prefs R2	100000	100000

FINANCIAL STATISTICS (AT FINANCIAL YEAR END)

(Amts in R'000)	1992 Sep	1991 Sep	1990 Sep	1989 Sep	1988 Sep
Ord S/H Int	1198500	1032500	891900	764400	614400
Long Trm Loans	305300	358700	313500	311600	300100
Iss Ord Share	48060	47592	47189	46996	46759
Total Liab	1308200	1310000	1132100	1090100	954500
Current Liab	1002900	951300	818600	778500	654400
Total Assets	2506700	2342500	2024000	1854500	1568900
Current Assets	1355200	1307200	1148100	1054900	881700
Debtors	571300	538800	467800	414900	361300
Inventory	723300	710000	634200	579600	489600
Turnover	4364200	3994000	3516400	3091600	2526300
Oper Profit	496600	443000	415000	398600	310900
Interest Paid	67200	71400	74200	66400	21300
Tax Paid	194700	153700	148200	120100	109500
Prf af Int&Tax	262600	241400	204500	222200	188800
Prf att Ord Sh	254500	232900	198700	214600	153300
Btm Line Earn	255200	224100	203000	225600	104700
Dividend Paid	98700	90400	78300	77900	59700
Mkt Prce(c) YE	8000	6400	3450	4050	2550
Depreciation	141300	123500	105300	87400	76200

PER SHARE STATISTICS (CENTS)

Net Asst Val	2493.76	2169.48	1890.06	1626.52	1313.97
Net Earnings	531.00	491.00	422.00	458.00	358.00
Dividends	205.00	190.00	166.00	166.00	133.00
Cash Flow	818.58	769.17	646.13	645.20	531.19

RATIOS AND OTHER INFORMATION

Mrk Cap(R000)	3844800	3045888	1628021	1903338	1192355
Current Ratio	1.35	1.37	1.40	1.36	1.35
Quik/Acid Tst	0.63	0.63	0.63	0.61	0.60
A/C Rec T/ovr	7.64	7.41	7.52	7.45	6.99
Tot Ass T/ovr	1.74	1.71	1.74	1.67	1.61
Debt/Ass Rat	0.46	0.49	0.49	0.51	0.52
L T L Tot Ass	0.06	0.09	0.08	0.09	0.10
Debt to Eqity	0.96	1.12	1.10	1.24	1.33
Interest Cover	7.58	6.34	5.72	6.11	15.00
Oper Prof Mrg	11.38	11.09	11.80	12.89	12.31
Net Prof Marg%	5.83	5.83	5.65	6.94	6.07
Ret on Assets	20.92	19.89	21.10	22.04	20.37
Ret on Equity%	21.23	22.56	22.28	28.07	24.95
Price/Earnings	15.07	13.03	8.18	8.84	7.12
Divid Cover	2.59	2.58	2.54	2.76	2.69
Divid Yield	2.56	2.97	4.81	4.10	5.22
Earning Yield%	6.64	7.67	12.23	11.31	14.04
NAV % Mrk Pr	31.17	33.90	54.78	40.16	51.53
Effec Tax Rate	44.60	38.51	43.09	36.21	38.81
Def Interval	0.88	1.29	1.19	1.16	1.10
Sus Grth Rate	13.00	13.80	13.50	17.88	15.23

SUBSIDIARY & ASSOCIATED COMPANIES

BDM PROPERTIES (RIVERSIDE DURBAN) (PTY)
BROWN DAVIS & MCCORQUODALE (PTY) LTD (50%)
BROWN DAVIS & MCCORQUODALE SECURITY PRIN (50%)
CISKEI BUYERS (PTY) LTD
CONSOLIDATED CITRUS CONTAINERS (PTY) LTD
MEMIX (PTY) LTD
METAL BOX BOTSWANA (PTY) LTD
METAL BOX SOUTH AFRICA LTD
MULTI SECURITY TECHNOLOGY (PTY) LTD
NAMPAK PAPER LTD
NAMPAK PRODUCTS LTD
NAMPAK PROPERTIES (PINETOWN) (PTY) LTD
NATIONAL CONTAINERS (PTY) LTD
NEOPAC (SWAZILAND) LTD
POLYAD (PTY) LTD
PRINTPAK (TRANSVAAL) LTD
PRINTPAK LTD
PROCHART (PTY) LTD

INVESTMENTS

INTER COMPANY SECURITY SERVICES (CAPE) ((460 SH)
RADIMED 1991 (PTY) LTD (50000 SH)
SMALL BUSINESS DEVELOPMENT CORP LTD (195666 SH)

NATAL OCEAN TRAWLING LTD

ABBREVIATION : NATRAWL

JSE SHORT CODE : NTR

SECTOR : Industrial-Fishing

SHAREHOLDERS

Who Owns Whom's Assessment of the Identity of the Ultimate Controlling Shareholder:
DIRECTORATE / INSTITUTIONAL

SHAREHOLDER	PERCENTAGE 1992	1991
LIBERTAS ADMIN & MANAGEMENT P/L	26.8	26.8
CMB NOM P/L	22.6	9.2
GALAXY INV LTD	13.5	13.4
IRVIN & JOHNSON LTD	8.9	8.8
WALSH J W	3.4	3.4
SHARLAND J N	3.0	2.9
DAJO INV P/L	2.5	2.4
BACON P N	2.3	2.3
WREFORD TRUST	1.4	1.4
NOYCE A G	1.2	1.3
STD BANK NOM TVL P/L	1.2	1.3
PHARO G H	1.2	1.4
PHOENIX ASSURE SA LTD	1.2	1.3
KAIYA INTERNATIONAL LTD	1.1	1.1
ALTENA MEWS P/L	---	7.8
SENBANK NOM P/L	---	5.5
TOTAL	90.2	90.3

DIRECTORS :

BACON N ,GROVE LM ,LOWENTHAL ND ,PHARO AJ
PHARO GH ,WALSH JW (Chairman

REGISTRATION NUMBER : 71/11294/06

REGISTERED OFFICE
9-15 Canal Road, Maydon Wharf
Durban
4001
TEL 092581-422750
FAX 092581-422070

TRANSFER SECRETARY
Central Registrars Ltd
P O Box 4844, Johannesburg
2000
TEL 011-331 0051

COMPANY SECRETARY
A F van Zyl

NATURE OF BUSINESS
A crustacean trawling enterprise presently operating of the Natal & Mozambique coasts

BANKERS :
First National Bank of SA Ltd

AUDITORS :
Baker Musikanth

FAMILIAR BRAND NAMES
N/A

CONTRIBUTION BY ACTIVITY
N/A

YEAR END : December

DIVIDEND : (Ldr)28/04/89 (Pay)26/05/89

NUMBER OF EMPLOYEES : 267

CAPITAL STRUCTURE

	AUTHORISED	ISSUED
Ords 1c	50000000	41630397

FINANCIAL STATISTICS (AT FINANCIAL YEAR END)

(Amts in R'000)	1991 Dec	1990 Dec	1989 Dec	1988 Dec	1987 Dec
Ord S/H Int	21268	14462	16096	8492	2095
Long Trm Loans	8147	9022	10875	12727	2448
Iss Ord Share	39590	19500	19500	14000	14000
Total Liab	11281	12671	16091	16733	3550
Current Liab	3134	3649	5216	4006	1102
Total Assets	27273	21857	27011	22183	5645
Intang Assets	5276	5276	5176	3042	*
Current Assets	5063	5717	5290	5048	1935
Debtors	1722	3519	1788	3096	340
Inventory	3333	2192	3496	1874	728
Turnover	11415	12370	15055	12990	4847
Oper Profit	1922	197	2063	2813	1444
Interest Paid	565	2456	1044	264	171
Tax Paid	-	-625	334	106	642
Prf af Int&Tax	1398	-1634	1358	2443	631
Prf att Ord Sh	1919	-1634	1358	2443	631
Btm Line Earn	1919	-1634	1082	2443	631
Dividend Paid	-			1170	420
Mkt Prce(c) YE	25	35	50	65	80
Depreciation	1021	1170	984	345	144

PER SHARE STATISTICS (CENTS)

Net Asst Val	40 39	47 11	56 00	38 93	14 96
Net Earnings	6 50	8 38	6 96	12 53	4 51
Dividends	2 00	-	-	6 00	3 00
Cash Flow	8 19	-5 58	10 30	14 84	10 12

RATIOS AND OTHER INFORMATION

Mrk Cap(R000)	9898	6825	9750	9100	11200
Current Ratio	1 62	1 57	1 01	1 26	1 76
Quik/Acid Tst	0 55	0 97	0 34	0 79	1 10
A/C Rec T/ovr	6 63	3 52	8 42	4 20	14 26
Tot Ass T/ovr	0 42	0 57	0 56	0 59	0 86
Debt/Ass Rat	0 37	0 52	0 53	0 66	0 41
L T L Tot Ass	0 25	0 36	0 33	0 48	0 21
Debt to Eqity	0 47	0 79	0 89	1 71	1 10
Interest Cover	3 40	0 08	1 98	10 66	8 44
Oper Prof Mrg	16 84	1 59	13 70	21 66	29 79
Net Prof Marg%	16 81	-13 21	9 02	18 81	13 02
Ret on Assets	9 11	0 90	7 66	12 68	25 58
Ret on Equity%	9 02	-11 30	8 44	28 77	30 12
Price/Earnings	3 85	-4 18	7 18	5 19	17 74
Divid Cover	3 25		-	2 09	1 50
Divid Yield	8 00	-	-	9 23	3 75
Earning Yield%	26 00	23 94	13 92	19 28	5 64
NAV % Mrk Pr	161 58	134 59	112 00	59 89	18 71
Def Interval	3 49	-8 33	5 52	3 25	0 94
Sus Grth Rate	9 02	-11 30	8 44	14 99	10 07

SUBSIDIARY & ASSOCIATED COMPANIES

MARINER TRAWLING (PTY) LTD
MECHAWELD ENGINEERING (PTY) LTD
MOULD FINANCE (PTY) LTD
NATAL INSHORE TRAWLERS (PTY) LTD
NATAL OCEAN TRAWLING MOZAMBIQUE (PTY) LT (40%)
OCEAN TRAWLING OF SOUTH AFRICA (PTY) LTD
P&F FISHING (PTY) LTD (32%)
RAUL QUINTAS INVESTMENTS (PTY) LTD
SILVER ADVENTURER (PTY) LTD
SULPESCA FISHING (PTY) LTD (CAPE TOWN) (20 4%)

INVESTMENTS

GAMBEIRA LDA (BEIRA) (12 8%)
PROPESCA LDA (MAPUTO) (12 8%)
SOCIEDADE DE PESCA DO SUL LDA (MAPUTO) ((16%)

NATIONAL FOODS HOLDINGS LTD

ABBREVIATION : NATFOOD

SECTOR : Zimbabwe Stock Exchange

SHAREHOLDERS

Who Owns Whom's Assessment of the Identity of the Ultimate Controlling Shareholder: ANGLO AMERICAN / ASTRA FOODS

SHAREHOLDER	PERCENTAGE 1992	1991
SECURITY NOM LTD	25 1	---
ASTRA FOODS PVT LTD	17 0	- -
OLD MUTUAL INV CORP (PVT) LTD	15 2	
NFH INV LTD	11 6	
NAT FOODS WORKERS TRUST PVT LTD	10 0	-
S M HARRIS PVT LTD	6 7	- -

FIRST NOM PVT LTD	1.5	---
FIRST MUTUAL LIFE ASSURE SOC OF ZIM	1.3	---
TOTAL	88.4	---

DIRECTORS :
JACKSON MJM ,LANDER RP (Chairman),MANCAMA BV
MARGESSON MV ,NYANDORO N ,ROBINSON CH ,TASKER ML
THOMSON JAL ,WATT CK ,WILLIAMS RA

REGISTERED OFFICE
Gloria House, 10 Stirling Road
Harare, Zimbabwe

TEL: 68720

TRANSFER SECRETARY
First Transfer Secretaries (Pvt) Ltd
P O Box 437, Bulawayo
Zimbabwe

TEL: 092634 - 702905

COMPANY SECRETARY
W Liddell

NATURE OF BUSINESS
NATIONAL FOODS,incorporated in Zimbabwe,operates throughout the country via a system of factories, depots and agencies.Merchandise is marketed Zim babwe mainly under the brand names of GLORIA, RED SEAL and NF STOCKFEEDS.Operating companies include NATPAK (PVT) LTD and NATPAK (Bulawayo) which manufacture polywoven bags.

BANKERS :
N/A

AUDITORS :
Coopers & Lybrand

FAMILIAR BRAND NAMES
GLORIA,N F STOCKFEEDS,RED SEAL

CONTRIBUTION BY ACTIVITY
N/A

YEAR END : March

DIVIDEND : Ords Z$0,80

Dividend	(Ldr)29/11/91	(Pay)19/12/91	Amt(c)10
Dividend	(Ldr)12/06/92	(Pay)07/07/92	Amt(c)14

CAPITAL STRUCTURE

	AUTHORISED	ISSUED
Ords Z$0,80	66000000	63802000

FINANCIAL STATISTICS (AT FINANCIAL YEAR END)

(Amts in Z$)	1992 Mar	1991 Mar
Ord S/H Int	296446	259037
Long Trm Loans	17287	6990
Iss Ord Share	63802	63689
Total Liab	155759	111053
Current Liab	138472	104063
Total Assets	452205	370090
Current Assets	164355	141165
Debtors	71962	56806
Inventory	90384	74079
Turnover	727183	513453
Oper Profit	82029	47873
Interest Paid	4245	1354
Tax Paid	26308	27004
Prf af Int&Tax	52418	20598
Prf att Ord Sh	52421	20601
Btm Line Earn	52421	30574
Dividend Paid	15310	11787
Depreciation	23785	16919

PER SHARE STATISTICS (CENTS)

Net Asst Val	464.63	406.72
Net Earnings	82.16	32.35
Dividends	24.00	18.50
Cash Flow	119.44	58.91

RATIOS AND OTHER INFORMATION

Current Ratio	1.19	1.36
Quik/Acid Tst	0.53	0.64
A/C Rec T/ovr	10.11	9.04
Tot Ass T/ovr	1.61	1.39
Debt/Ass Rat	0.34	0.30
L T L Tot Ass	0.04	0.02
Debt to Eqity	0.53	0.43
Interest Cover	19.32	35.36
Oper Prof Mrg	11.28	9.32
Net Prof Marg%	7.21	4.01
Ret on Assets	18.35	13.23
Ret on Equity%	17.68	7.95
Divid Cover	3.42	1.75
Effec Tax Rate	33.42	56.73
Def Interval	0.67	0.27
Sus Grth Rate	12.52	3.40

SUBSIDIARY & ASSOCIATED COMPANIES

BAKERY PRODUCTS (PRIVATE) LIMITED
HARRIS MAIZE MILLING & PRODUCE CO (PRIVA
J PALTE LIMITED
MEADOW MILLING COMPANY LIMITED
NATIONAL FOODS HOLDINGS LTD
NATIONAL FOODS LIMITED
NATPAK (BULAWAYO) (PRIVATE) LIMITED
NATPAK (PRIVATE) LIMITED
PALTE-HARRIS (PRIVATE) LIMITED
RICE MILLS (PRIVATE) LIMITED (50%)

INVESTMENTS

None

NATIONAL SELECTIONS LTD

ABBREVIATION : NATSEL

JSE SHORT CODE : NSE

SECTOR : Financial-Investment Trusts

SHAREHOLDERS

Who Owns Whom's Assessment of the Identity of the Ultimate Controlling Shareholder:
STATE VIA IDC

SHAREHOLDER	PERCENTAGE 1992	1991

IND DEVELOPMENT CORP SA LTD	50.8	50.8
SA MUTUAL	11.3	11.2
CMB NOM P/L	10.9	---
STD BANK NOM TVL P/L	4.2	2.6
EIGHTY ONE MAIN STREET NOM LTD	2.6	3.1
MUTUAL & FEDERAL INSURANCE CO LTD	2.0	2.0
SOUTHERN LIFE ASSOC LTD	1.4	3.6
FIRST NAT NOM P/L	1.3	1.3
LIBERTY LIFE ASSOC OF AFRICA LTD	1.2	1.8
SA SPECIAL RISKS INSURANCE ASSOC LTD	1.1	1.1
GEMEENSKAPLIKE MUNISIPALE TVL PENS FUND	---	1.1
SANLAM	---	7.7
TOTAL	86.8	86.2

DIRECTORS :
COOPER DE ,KAHN JM ,MCCRYSTAL LP DR,SCHOLTZ AP DR
TERREBLANCHE HJ ,VAN DER MERWE WC
VAN ROOY PJ (Chairman),VAN WYK CJ DR,WIESE CH AD

REGISTRATION NUMBER : 67/11900/06

REGISTERED OFFICE
19 Fredman Drive, Sandton
2199
TEL: 011-883 1600
FAX: 011-883 1655

TRANSFER SECRETARY
Central Registrars Ltd
P O Box 4844, Johannesburg
2000
TEL: 011-331 0051

COMPANY SECRETARY
Industrial Development Corp of SA Ltd

NATURE OF BUSINESS
A general investment company formed as a medium for investors to acquire an interest in a variety of companies engaged in manufacturing and the beneficiation of minerals.Control is vested in the IDC, from whom almost all share investments are acquired.

BANKERS :
Standard Bank of SA Ltd

AUDITORS :
Deloitte Pim Goldby

FAMILIAR BRAND NAMES
N/A

CONTRIBUTION BY ACTIVITY
N/A

YEAR END : June

DIVIDEND : Ords no par value

Interim	(Ldr)09/03/90	(Pay)12/04/90	Amt(c)6.5
Final	(Ldr)14/09/90	(Pay)12/10/90	Amt(c)7.5
Interim	(Ldr)08/03/91	(Pay)12/04/91	Amt(c)6.5
Final	(Ldr)13/09/91	(Pay)11/10/91	Amt(c)7.5
Interim	(Ldr)06/03/92	(Pay)10/04/92	Amt(c)6.5
Final	(Ldr)11/09/92	(Pay)09/10/92	Amt(c)8

CAPITAL STRUCTURE

	AUTHORISED	ISSUED
Ords no par value	240000000	230198480

FINANCIAL STATISTICS (AT FINANCIAL YEAR END)

(Amts in R'000)	1992	1991	1990	1989	1988
	Jun	Jun	Jun	Jun	Jun
Ord S/H Int	132228	102633	92476	81569	70807
Iss Ord Share	230198	230198	230198	230198	230198
Total Liab	19428	18205	19197	16243	11700
Current Liab	19428	18205	19197	16243	11700
Total Assets	151656	120838	111673	97812	82507
Current Assets	53947	30581	19373	24841	20769
Debtors	4696	5084	3187	1690	1226
Oper Profit	-691	-676	-719	38668	28270
Interest Paid	166	3	-	-	-
Tax Paid	600	1488	2216	1203	759
Prf af Int&Tax	39131	37904	43135	37465	27511
Prf att Ord Sh	62974	42385	43135	38386	32195
Btm Line Earn	62974	42385	43135	38386	32195
Dividend Paid	33379	32228	32228	27624	20718
Mkt Prce(c) YE	270	290	290	310	170

PER SHARE STATISTICS (CENTS)

Net Asst Val	57.44	44.58	40.17	35.43	30.76
Net Earnings	17.00	16.47	18.74	16.28	11.95
Dividends	14.50	14.00	14.00	12.00	9.00
Cash Flow	17.00	16.47	18.74	16.28	11.95

RATIOS AND OTHER INFORMATION

Mrk Cap(R000)	621535	667574	667574	713614	391337
Current Ratio	2.78	1.68	1.01	1.53	1.78
Quik/Acid Tst	2.78	1.68	1.01	1.53	1.78
Debt/Ass Rat	0.13	0.15	0.17	0.17	0.14
Debt to Eqity	0.15	0.18	0.21	0.20	0.17
Interest Cover	232.33	12065.67	-	-	-
Ret on Assets	26.31	32.60	40.61	39.53	34.26
Ret on Equity%	47.63	41.30	46.64	47.06	45.47
Price/Earnings	15.88	17.61	15.47	19.04	14.23
Divid Cover	1.17	1.18	1.34	1.36	1.33
Divid Yield	5.37	4.83	4.83	3.87	5.29
Earning Yield%	6.30	5.68	6.46	5.25	7.03
NAV % Mrk Pr	21.27	15.37	13.85	11.43	18.09
Effec Tax Rate	126.85	59.07	57.87	3.11	2.68
Sus Grth Rate	22.38	9.90	11.79	13.19	16.21

SUBSIDIARY & ASSOCIATED COMPANIES

ALUSAF (PTY) LTD (50%)
INDUSTRIAL FINANCE CORP OF SA (PTY) LTD (50%)

INVESTMENTS

ADVANCED FOOD RESEARCH (PTY) LTD (1 SH)
ALGORAX (PTY) LTD (225000 SH)
AUTOMOTIVE OVERSEAS INVESTMENTS (PTY) LT (360 SH)
C G SMITH LTD (50% ATTRIBUTABLE VIA IND (804375 SH)
CG SMITH FOODS LTD (488070 SH)
CG SMITH LTD (1224716 S)
ERF SA (PTY) LTD (301373 SH)
IMPALA PLATINUM HOLDINGS LTD (2898517 S)
L & C STEINMULLER (AFRICA) (PTY) LTD (825000 SH)
PALABORA MINING CO LTD (800000 SH)
RICHBAY MINE HOLDINGS (PTY) LTD (425 SH)
RICHBAY SMELTER HOLDINGS (PTY) LTD (425 SH)
SAICCOR (PTY) LTD (1 SH)
SAPPI LTD (3460113 SH)
SAPPI MANAGEMENT SERVICES (PTY) LTD (RED (1990 SH)
SASOL LTD (1192500 S)
SENTRACHEM LTD (50% ATTRIBUTABLE VIA IND (1052860 SH)

NATIONAL TYRE SERVICES LTD

ABBREVIATION : NAT TYRE

SECTOR : Zimbabwe Stock Exchange

SHAREHOLDERS

Who Owns Whom's Assessment of the Identity of the Ultimate Controlling Shareholder: INSTITUTIONS / WALTON BROTHERS (PVT) LTD

DIRECTORS :
BUTTERWORTH ME (Production Director)
EVANS BD (Technical Director)
O'ROURKE JP (Financial Director)
WALTON DP (Chairman & Managing Dir),WALTON EC

REGISTERED OFFICE
Stand 4608,Cnr Cripps/Seke Rds, Graniteside
Harare, Zimbabwe

TEL 739911
FAX 793223

TRANSFER SECRETARY
National Tyre Services Ltd
P O Box 3018, Harare
Zimbabwe

TEL 092634-3018

COMPANY SECRETARY
S N Mandimika

NATURE OF BUSINESS
Incorporated in Zimbabwe, NATIONAL TYRE SERVICES' main activities are the re-processing of tyres, manufacture of rubber products and the retailing of tyres, tubes and accessories

BANKERS :
Zimbabwe Banking Corporation Ltd
Standard Chartered Bank Zimbabwe Ltd
Merchant Bank of Central Africa

AUDITORS :
N/A

FAMILIAR BRAND NAMES
N/A

CONTRIBUTION BY ACTIVITY
N/A

YEAR END : June

DIVIDEND : Ords Z$0,50

Dividend	(Ldr)25/10/91	(Pay)29/11/91	Amt(c)4
Dividend	(Ldr)13/03/92	(Pay)16/04/92	Amt(c)5

CAPITAL STRUCTURE

	AUTHORISED	ISSUED
Ords Z$0,50	40000000	20821000

FINANCIAL STATISTICS (AT FINANCIAL YEAR END)

(Amts in Z$)	1992 Jun	1991 Jun
Ord S/H Int	33640	23429
Long Trm Loans	96	635
Iss Ord Share	20821	20821
Total Liab	26925	11242
Current Liab	26829	10607
Total Assets	60565	34671
Current Assets	37798	15255
Debtors	14413	6558
Inventory	23104	8416
Turnover	119395	62794
Oper Profit	23463	8575
Interest Paid	654	259
Tax Paid	9791	3464
Prf af Int&Tax	13126	4952
Prf att Ord Sh	13126	4952
Btm Line Earn	13126	4952
Dividend Paid	2915	1249
Depreciation	1299	1064

PER SHARE STATISTICS (CENTS)

Net Asst Val	161 57	112 53
Net Earnings	63 00	23 80
Dividends	14 00	6 00
Cash Flow	69 28	28 89

RATIOS AND OTHER INFORMATION

Current Ratio	1 41	1 44
Quik/Acid Tst	0 55	0 64
A/C Rec T/ovr	8 28	9 58
Tot Ass T/ovr	1 97	1 81
Debt/Ass Rat	0 44	0 32
L T L Tot Ass	0 00	0 02
Debt to Eqity	0 80	0 48
Interest Cover	35 88	33 11
Oper Prof Mrg	19 65	13 66
Net Prof Marg%	10 99	7 89
Ret on Assets	38 92	25 02
Ret on Equity%	39 02	21 14
Divid Cover	4 50	3 97
Effec Tax Rate	42 72	40 11
Def Interval	0 39	0 27
Sus Grth Rate	30 35	15 81

SUBSIDIARY & ASSOCIATED COMPANIES

AUTOWORLD (PVT) LTD
BUFFALO ENGINEERING (PVT) LTD
BUFFALO TREADS (CHEGUTU) (PVT) LTD
BUFFALO TREADS (HWANGE) (PVT) LTD
BUFFALO TREADS (PVT) LTD
DILMITIS MOTORS (PVT) LTD
FLEET TRANSPORT SERVICES (PVT) LTD
INDUSTRIAL RUBBER CO (PVT) LTD
MHANGURA MOTORS (1965) (PVT) LTD
NATIONAL RUBBER CO (PVT) LTD
NATIONAL TYRE SERVICES INVESTMENTS (PVT)
THERMOBOND (PVT) LTD
WALKER'S GARAGE (PVT) LTD

INVESTMENTS

None

NATRUST LTD

ABBREVIATION : NATRUST

JSE SHORT CODE · NTT

SECTOR : Financial Investment Trusts

SHAREHOLDERS

Who Owns Whom's Assessment of the Identity of the Ultimate Controlling Shareholder: SANLAM / ABSA

SHAREHOLDER	PERCENTAGE 1992	1991
CMB NOM P/L	26.6	---
SENTRALE AKSEPBANK BPK	26.0	26.5
ABSA NOM P/L	16.3	---
UBS INSURANCE CO LTD	6.0	---
SANLAM	---	25.9
VOLKSKAS INV LTD	---	22.4
TOTAL	74.9	74.8

DIRECTORS :
AUGUSTYN PJ MR,DU TOIT AB MR,MELROSE AB MR
WOOD RPA MR (Chairman

REGISTRATION NUMBER : 60/04801/06

REGISTERED OFFICE
31st Floor, Sanlamsentrum, 208/212 Jeppe Street
Johannesburg
2001
TEL: 011-330 3333
FAX: 011-333 9293

TRANSFER SECRETARY
Central Registrars Ltd
P O Box 4844, Johannesburg
2000
TEL: 011-331 0051

COMPANY SECRETARY
Bankorp Ltd

NATURE OF BUSINESS
An investment trust company, holding a portfolio of JSE-quoted shares.

BANKERS :
Trust Bank of Africa Ltd

AUDITORS :
Coopers Theron Du Toit

FAMILIAR BRAND NAMES
N/A

CONTRIBUTION BY ACTIVITY
N/A

YEAR END : December

DIVIDEND :Ords 10c
Dividend No 30 (Ldr)14/02/92 (Pay)28/02/92 Amt(c)6.7

CAPITAL STRUCTURE

	AUTHORISED	ISSUED
Ords 50c	8000000	5525220

FINANCIAL STATISTICS (AT FINANCIAL YEAR END)

(Amts in R'000)	1990 Dec	1989 Dec
Ord S/H Int	10481	9404
Iss Ord Share	5525	5525
Total Liab	1951	1706
Current Liab	1951	1706
Total Assets	12432	11110
Current Assets	3010	1917
Debtors	-	5
Oper Profit	-172	-133
Tax Paid	119	105
Prf af Int&Tax	2149	1757
Prf att Ord Sh	2149	1757
Btm Line Earn	2625	3668
Dividend Paid	1547	1271

PER SHARE STATISTICS (CENTS)

Net Asst Val	189.70	170.21
Net Earnings	38.90	31.80
Dividends	28.00	23.00
Cash Flow	38.90	31.80

RATIOS AND OTHER INFORMATION

Current Ratio	1.54	1.12
Quik/Acid Tst	1.54	1.12
Debt/Ass Rat	0.16	0.15
Debt to Eqity	0.19	0.18
Ret on Assets	18.24	16.76
Ret on Equity%	20.50	18.68
Divid Cover	1.39	1.38
Effec Tax Rate	150.63	125.00
Sus Grth Rate	5.74	5.17

SUBSIDIARY & ASSOCIATED COMPANIES

NATRUST EQUITIES (PTY) LTD

INVESTMENTS

ANGLO ALPHA LTD (50000 SH)
ANGLO AMERICAN CORP OF SA LTD (17856 SH)
ANGLOVAAL LTD ("N" SHARES) (94000 SH)
BARLOW RAND LTD (84400 SH)
BOUMAT LTD (165498 SH)
DE BEERS CONSOLIDATED MINES LTD (50000 SH)
GENCOR BEHEREND BPK (520940 SH)
GENCOR LTD (178320 SH)
GOLD FIELDS OF SA LTD (28000 SH)
ISCOR LTD (787900 SH)
MALBAK LTD (114000 SH)
METROPOLITAN LIFE LTD (53600 SH)
MURRAY & ROBERTS HOLDINGS LTD (64000 SH)
NAMPAK LTD (20296 SH)
NEDCOR LTD (66357 SH)
PALABORA MINING CO LTD (3000 SH)
PEPGRO LTD (83520 SH)
PEPKOR LTD (41760 SH)
REMBRANDT CONTROLLING INVESTMENTS LTD (370000 SH)
REMBRANDT GROUP LTD (500000 SH)
RICHEMONT SECURITIES AG (673985 SH)
SA BREWERIES LTD (100000 SH)
SAMANCOR LTD (50000 SH)
SANTAM INSURANCE LTD (50000 SH)
SASOL LTD (75000 SH)
TIGER OATS LTD (100000 SH)
TRANS NATAL COAL CORPORATION LTD (13,25% (3000 DEBS)

NBS HOLDINGS LTD

ABBREVIATION : NBSHOLD

JSE SHORT CODE : NBS

SECTOR : Financial-Banks & Financial Services

SHAREHOLDERS

Who Owns Whom's Assessment of the Identity of the Ultimate Controlling Shareholder:
NORWICH LIFE / MINORITIES

SHAREHOLDER	PERCENTAGE 1992	1991
NORWICH LIFE SA LTD	25 4	16 6
BAROB INV P/L	19 1	19 0
FIRST NAT NOM P/L	9 7	3 5
METAL IND GROUP PENS FUND	2 8	2 5
ENGINEERING INDUSTRIES PENS FUND	2 6	2 2
FEDERATED LIFE ASSURE CO LTD	1 7	--
COLEMAN PROPERTIES P/L	1 3	1 3
NEDBANK NOM LTD	- -	1 2
FIRST CORP NOM P/L	---	6 7
SLANY LTD	---	8 7
TOTAL	62 6	61 6

DIRECTORS :
BENNETT JS ,CHAMBERS RKJ ,DAVIES CP ,DUNN CJH
FARRER M (Executive Director)
GAFNEY JW (Managing Director),GROENEWEG EM
MCCARTHY BC (Chairman),MCCRYSTAL LP DR
NAPIER RS (Deputy Chairman),NOYCE MJ
SMALE JR (Executive Director),SWAIN WJ

REGISTRATION NUMBER : 87/00300/06

REGISTERED OFFICE
16th Floor, NBS Building, 300 Smith Street
Durban
4001
TEL 031-304 4271
FAX 031-304 2156

TRANSFER SECRETARY
Rand Registrars Ltd
P O Box 82549, Southdale
2135
TEL 011-835 1016

COMPANY SECRETARY
WJE Chapman (Mrs)

NATURE OF BUSINESS
The group's activities include the provision of mortgage finance & instalment lending together with a range of financial services by means of a national network of branches & agencies Housing development, short & long term insurance and fixed property investments also form part of the group's activities

BANKERS :
First National Bank of SA Ltd, Nedbank Ltd
Standard Bank of SA Ltd

AUDITORS :
KPMG Aiken & Peat, Deloitte & Touche

FAMILIAR BRAND NAMES
N/A

CONTRIBUTION BY ACTIVITY
Banking Activities (% attrib'le income) (67 1%)
Insurance (18 7%)
Township & Property Development (2 6%)
Other (11 6%)

YEAR END : March

DIVIDEND : Ords R2

Final No 6	(Ldr)25/05/90	(Pay)15/06/90	Amt(c)18
Interim No 7	(Ldr)09/11/90	(Pay)12/12/90	Amt(c)13
Final No 8	(Ldr)24/05/91	(Pay)14/06/91	Amt(c)21 5
Interim No 9	(Ldr)15/11/91	(Pay)11/12/91	Amt(c)15
Final No 10	(Ldr)22/05/92	(Pay)12/06/92	Amt(c)25
Interim No 11	(Ldr)06/11/92	(Pay)18/12/92	Amt(c)17

NUMBER OF EMPLOYEES : 2907

CAPITAL STRUCTURE

	AUTHORISED	ISSUED
Ords R2	100000000	66138125

FINANCIAL STATISTICS (AT FINANCIAL YEAR END)

(Amts in R'000)	1992 Mar	1991 Mar	1990 Mar	1989 Mar	1988 Mar
Ord S/H Int	483667	378598	308674	277601	258254
Long Trm Loans	94729	98273	106302	4055303	3029120
Iss Ord Share	66138	58785	58146	57773	57773
Total Liab	8591286	7086014	5451785	4237493	3146322
Current Liab	8496557	6987741	5345483	182190	117202
Total Assets	9074953	7464612	5760459	4515094	3404576
Current Assets	1088824	1104273	836705	709528	453484
Debtors	89443	57249	55305	42294	35280
Oper Profit	214549	-169128	-149044	41023	41275
Interest Paid	1149960	995775	676765	-	
Tax Paid	23572	29823	30926	17398	17429
Prf af Int&Tax	66356	53788	42277	31207	23846
Prf att Ord Sh	73295	56307	44556	31875	24239
Btm Line Earn	75417	59110	46419	32634	26398
Dividend Paid	26431	20259	16856	13287	10688
Mkt Prce(c) YE	1155	920	600	350	270
Depreciation	20369	18232	15900	12652	9192

PER SHARE STATISTICS (CENTS)

Net Asst Val	731 30	644 04	530 86	480 50	447 02
Net Earnings	115 60	96 60	76 60	55 20	42 00
Dividends	40 00	34 50	29 00	23 00	18 50
Cash Flow	135 21	123 30	103 86	78 16	57 68

RATIOS AND OTHER INFORMATION

Mrk Cap(R000)	763894	540822	348876	202206	155987
Current Ratio	0 13	0 16	0 16	3 89	3 87
Quik/Acid Tst	0 13	0 16	0 16	3 89	3 87
Debt/Ass Rat	0 94	0 94	0 94	0 04	0 04
L T L Tot Ass	0 00	0 00	0 01	0 00	0 00
Debt to Eqity	17 60	18 53	17 45	0 69	0 52
Interest Cover	-0 17	-0 15	-0 20	-	-
Ret on Assets	13 74	14 50	13 06	1 10	1 23
Ret on Equity%	15 15	14 87	14 43	11 48	9 39
Price/Earnings	9 99	9 52	7 83	6 34	6 43
Divid Cover	2 89	2 80	2 64	2 40	2 27
Divid Yield	3 46	3 75	4 83	6 57	6 85
Earning Yield%	10 01	10 50	12 77	15 77	15 56
NAV % Mrk Pr	63 32	70 00	88 48	137 29	165 56

Effec Tax Rate	21.40	37.54	41.27	24.96	40.20
Def Interval	98.03	96.25	87.91	0.40	0.54
Sus Grth Rate	9.69	9.52	8.97	6.70	5.25

SUBSIDIARY & ASSOCIATED COMPANIES

FRENCH BANK OF SOUTHERN AFRICA LTD (39%)
GERMISTON INVESTMENTS (PTY) LTD (50%)
LAGOON DEVELOPMENTS (PTY) LTD
MOSSGASS HOUSING FINANCE (PTY) LTD (50%)
NBS BANK (1987) LIMITED
NBS BANK LIMITED
NBS DEVELOPMENTS (PTY) LTD
NBS HALLMARK MANAGEMENT COMPANY LTD
NBS INSURANCE CO LTD
NBS INVESTMENTS (PTY) LTD
NBS MORTGAGE NOMINEES (PTY) LTD
NBS PARTICIPATION BOND MANAGERS (PTY) LT
NBS PROPERTIES (PTY) LTD
NBS RENTALS (PTY) LTD
NORWICH LIFE SA LTD (30%)

INVESTMENTS

None

NEDCOR LTD

ABBREVIATION : NEDCOR

JSE SHORT CODE : NED

SECTOR : Financial-Banks & Financial Services

SHAREHOLDERS

Who Owns Whom's Assessment of the Identity of the Ultimate Controlling Shareholder:
SA MUTUAL

SHAREHOLDER	PERCENTAGE 1992	1991
SA MUTUAL	51.1	51.1
EIGHTY ONE MAIN STREET NOM LTD	3.6	3.2
SIXTY SIX MARSHALL STREET NOM P/L	2.7	2.7
NEDBANK NOM LTD	2.7	2.7
SANLAM	2.2	2.3
STD BANK NOM TVL P/L	2.1	2.2
SOUTHERN LIFE ASSOC LTD	2.1	2.1
ENGINEERING INDUSTRIES PENS FUND	2.0	1.8
METAL IND GROUP PENS FUND	1.9	1.8
FIRST NAT NOM P/L	1.5	1.5
LIBERTY LIFE ASSOC OF AFRICA LTD	1.3	2.1
COMMERCIAL UNION LIFE ASSURE CO SA LTD	1.1	---
MINE OFFICIALS PENS FUND	1.0	1.0
FEDERATED LIFE ASSURE CO LTD	---	1.1
COMMERCIAL UNION ASSURE CO SA LTD	---	1.3
TOTAL	75.2	76.6

DIRECTORS :
ABRAHAMSE LG DR,ADCOCK CS ,DAVIN FJ
DE V GRAAFF J DR,GOSS RJ ,LAUBSCHER RCM
LEVETT MJ ,LIEBENBERG CF (Chief Executive)
MAREE JB DR (Chairman),PARKER CC ,PORTER LA DR
RICHARDSON G ,TUCKER RSK

REGISTRATION NUMBER : 66/10630/06

REGISTERED OFFICE
100 Main Street, Johannesburg
2001
TEL: 011-630 7111
FAX: 011-630 7558

TRANSFER SECRETARY
Rand Registrars Ltd
P O Box 82549, Southdale
2135
TEL: 011-835 1016

COMPANY SECRETARY
W J Kruger

NATURE OF BUSINESS
A Bank & Building Society controlling company.
The group provides banking, mortgage loan finance and general financial services.

BANKERS :
Nedperm Bank Ltd

AUDITORS :
Deloitte Pim Goldby, KPMG Aiken & Peat

FAMILIAR BRAND NAMES
CAPE OF GOOD HOPE,FINANSBANK,NEDBANK,NEDFIN
NEFIC,S A PERM,SYFRETS TRUST
UAL MERCHANT BANK

CONTRIBUTION BY ACTIVITY
N/A

YEAR END : September

DIVIDEND :Ords R1

Interim	(Ldr)11/05/90	(Pay)04/06/90	Amt(c)17
Final	(Ldr)30/11/90	(Pay)20/12/90	Amt(c)34
Interim	(Ldr)17/05/91	(Pay)10/06/91	Amt(c)19
Final	(Ldr)29/11/91	(Pay)10/01/92	Amt(c)38
Interim	(Ldr)22/05/92	(Pay)25/06/92	Amt(c)21
Final	(Ldr)04/12/92	(Pay)14/12/92	Amt(c)45

NUMBER OF EMPLOYEES : 16790

CAPITAL STRUCTURE

	AUTHORISED	ISSUED
Ords R1	203882937	192327030
"A" Ords R1 (Part of auth'd ords)	1117063	1076723

FINANCIAL STATISTICS (AT FINANCIAL YEAR END)

(Amts in R'000)	1991 Sep	1990 Sep	1989 Sep	1988 Sep	1987 Sep
Ord S/H Int	2177000	1894000	1343200	875700	726700
Long Trm Loans	39414000	33183000	26926200	15909500	13543600
Iss Ord Share	185962	185921	185921	156037	156037
Total Liab	39485000	33246000	26983800	15951600	13577900
Current Liab	71000	63000	57600	42100	34300
Total Assets	41605000	35080000	28327000	16827300	14304600
Intang Assets	57000	60000	*	*	*
Current Assets	5297000	4405000	2799400	2152800	1536900
Oper Profit	-819000	-647000	407300	250200	184700
Interest Paid	4531000	3951000	-	-	-
Tax Paid	182000	51000	19800	40500	43900
Prf af Int&Tax	375000	455000	387500	209700	140800
Prf att Ord Sh	344000	287000	387500	209700	140800
Btm Line Earn	344000	287000	387500	209200	142100
Dividend Paid	106000	95000	85500	62400	51500
Mkt Prce(c) YE	1325	1080	1050	590	765

Depreciation	112000	101000	85000	-	-

PER SHARE STATISTICS (CENTS)

Net Asst Val	1140.02	986.44	722.46	561.21	465.72
Net Earnings	185.00	154.00	138.50	111.30	85.10
Dividends	57.00	51.00	46.00	40.00	33.00
Cash Flow	327.96	306.45	253.82	148.85	103.72

RATIOS AND OTHER INFORMATION

Mrk Cap(R000)	2463997	2007947	1952171	920618	1193683
Current Ratio	74.61	69.92	48.60	51.14	44.81
Quik/Acid Tst	74.61	69.92	48.60	51.14	44.81
Debt/Ass Rat	0.00	0.00	0.00	0.00	0.00
Debt to Eqity	0.03	0.03	0.04	0.05	0.05
Interest Cover	-0.18	-0.16	-	-	-
Ret on Assets	12.23	12.71	1.44	1.49	1.29
Ret on Equity%	15.80	15.15	28.85	23.95	19.38
Price/Earnings	7.16	7.01	7.58	5.30	8.99
Divid Cover	3.25	3.02	3.01	2.78	2.58
Divid Yield	4.30	4.72	4.38	6.78	4.31
Earning Yield%	13.96	14.26	13.19	18.86	11.12
NAV % Mrk Pr	86.04	91.34	68.81	95.12	60.88
Effec Tax Rate	10.62	7.38	4.96	7.19	12.40
Sus Grth Rate	10.93	10.14	22.48	16.82	12.29

SUBSIDIARY & ASSOCIATED COMPANIES

AA FACTORS HOLDINGS (PTY) LTD
ADVANTAGE INVESTMENT CORP (PTY) LTD (50%)
AFRICAN DIAMOND CENTRE (PTY) LTD
ASSOCIATED AIR TRAVEL BUREAU (CAPE) (PTY
ASSOCIATED AIR TRAVEL BUREAU (EP) (PTY)
AYE COMPANY (PTY) LTD
BATH AVENUE PROPERTIES (PTY) LTD
BEDEVERE OVERSEAS FINANCE NV
BEEHIVE INVESTMENTS (PTY) LTD
BICCARD CORNER (PTY) LTD
BLEUWATER S.A.
BLEUWATER SA LTD
BLOEMBOARD HOLDINGS LTD
BRAAK INVESTMENTS LTD
BREWITT PARK ESTATES (PTY) LTD
BRIMARK (PTY) LTD
BULLION MERCHANTS OF S.A. LIMITED
CACTUS INVESTMENTS (PTY) LTD
CAPE OF GOOD HOPE BANK LTD
CAPTYRE (PTY) LTD
CATO QUEEN HOLDINGS (PTY) LTD
COC NOMINEES (PTY) LTD
COC TRUST CO LTD
COLONIAL ORPHAN CHAMBER & TRUST CO LTD
COURT HOLDINGS (PTY) LTD
COURT HOLDINGS LTD
CREDLEASE HOLDINGS LTD
DEPFIN INVESTMENTS (PTY) LTD
DRUTHTON PROPERTIES LTD
DUROS SA PROPERTIES (PTY) LTD
DYMAX RIVONIA (PTY) LTD
EIGHTY ONE MAIN STREET NOMINEES (PTY) LT
EQUIBOND (PTY) LTD
FINANSBANK LTD
FINANSCREDIT (PTY) LTD
FIRST CAPE DEVELOPMENT (PTY) LTDE
FIRST VENTURE (PTY) LTD
FRIGISTORE (PTY) LTD
FRIGISTORE INVESTMENTS (PTY) LTD
GENERAL ESTATE & ORPHAN CHAMBER
GENERAL LEASING CORP LTD
GEOC NOMINEES LTD
GREENMARKET ESTATES (PTY) LTD
GREVLER PROPERTIES (PTY) LTD
GW BOARD NOMINEES (PTY) LTD
HEP INVESTMENTS (PTY) LTD
HOF GENOMINEERDES BPK
HOFMANS PARKARAMA HOLDINGS (PTY) LTD
INTER-UNION FINANCE LTD
INTER-UNION PROPERTIES (PTY) LTD
INTERNATIONAL HARVESTER CREDIT CORP. (S.
JACARANDA INVESTMENT HOLDING CO (PTY) LT
JD SALES (PTY) LTD (22,5%)
JV THORNLEY INVESTMENTS (PTY) LTD
KG PARTNERSHIP (PTY) LTD
KG PROPERTIES (PTY) LTD
KLIPBULT (PORTION B) TOWNSHIP DEV (PTY)
KLIPBULT (PORTION C) TOWNSHIP DEV (PTY)
KLIPBULT (PORTION D) TOWNSHIP DEV (PTY)
KLIPBULT TOWNSHIP DEVELOPMENTS (PTY) LTD
KLIPPOORTJE PARK TOWNSHIPS (PTY) LTD
L & B ENTERPRISES (PTY) LTD
LANCELOT S.A.
LANCELOT SA LTD
LEASE PLAN INTERNATIONAL LTD
LIBERTAS BUILDING (PTY) LTD
LKH PROPERTIES LTD
MACRO LEASING INTERNATIONAL LTD
MAGALIESBERG UITSIG (EDMS) BPK
MAINBURG (PTY) LTD
MARSER NOMINEES (PTY) LTD
MELK HOUT PROPERTIES (PTY) LTD
METS (PTY) LTD
MIDLAND AGENCY TRUSTEE CO. (PTY) LTD
MILBEL (PTY) LTD
MORENED LTD
MURCHIES PROPERTY (PTY) LTD
NAL (PTY) LTD
NATIONAL BOARD (P.E.) LTD
NATIONAL BOARD DURBAN LTD
NATIONAL BOARD OF EXECUTORS (EAST LONDON
NATIONAL BOARD OF EXECUTORS LTD
NBSA NOMINEES LTD (UK)
NEBEX BOARD OF EXECUTORS AND TRUST CO. L
NEBICON LTD
NED FINANCE A.G. (SWITZERLAND)
NED FINANCE ASIA LTD (HONG KONG)
NEDBANK COMMERCIAL SERVICES LTD
NEDBANK FACTORS LTD
NEDBANK GROUP INVESTMENTS LTD
NEDBANK HOLDINGS LTD
NEDBANK NOMINEES LTD
NEDBEST INVESTMENTS (PTY) LTD
NEDCOR BANK LTD
NEDEUROPE AG
NEDFIN BANK LTD
NEDFINANCE AG
NEDFUND PROPERTIES (LINDEN) (PTY) LTD
NEDHOF LTD
NEDLEND LTD
NEDMORE LTD
NEDTRAVEL (PTY) LTD
NEDTRAVEL HOLIDAYS (PTY) LTD
NEW GERMANY DEVELOPMENTS (PTY) LTD
NHS PROPERTIES (PTY) LTD
NOMEZ HOLDINGS (PTY) LTD
NORFIN (PTY) LTD
NORTH CITY PROPERTIES LTD
OLD MUTUAL SYFRETS TRUST LTD
ONE HUNDRED MAIN STREET (PTY) LTD
OSSTOCK PROPERTIES (PTY) LTD
PALMERS TRUST INVESTMENT AND ESTATE ADMI
PALMERS TRUST NOMINEES (PTY) LTD
PERMANENT TRUST SYFRETS (PTY) LTD
PION INVESTMENTS (PTY) LTD
POINT CIRCLE (PTY) LTD
PORT ELIZABETH BOARD NOMINEES LTD
PRIME SECURITIES S.A. (LUXEMBOURG)
PRODUCT STREET PROPERTIES (PTY) LTD

PROFIT FROM PROPERTY (PTY) LTD
PROSPECT HILL PROPERTIES (PTY) LTD
PYRANED (PTY) LTD
QUEENSBRIDGE ESTATES (PTY) LTD
RANDBURG ENTERPRISES CO. (PTY) LTD
RMS SYFRETS TOWNHOUSES (PTY) LTD
ROODEKRAAL TOWNSHIP DEVELOPMENTS (PTY) L
ROSSLYN SHOPPING CENTRE (PTY) LTD
RUTH PROPERTIES (PTY) LTD
SA ASSOC FOR THE ADMIN & SETTLEMENT OF E
SA ASSOCIATION NOMINEES (PTY) LTD
SA PROFIN HOLDINGS LTD
SA PROPERTY INVESTMENTS LTD
SA PROSEC (PTY) LTD
SCARDO INVESTMENTS (PTY) LTD
SECUREBOND (PTY) LTD
SECURED COLLECTIONS (PTY) LTD
SECURED INVESTMENTS (PTY) LTD
SECURED INVESTMENTS NOMINEES (PTY) LTD
SECURITIES TRADING MANAGEMENT LTD
SECURITY HOUSE HOLDINGS LTD
SIDVALE PROPERTY LTD
SIXTY SIX MARSHALL STREET NOMINEES (PTY)
SMITH STREET WEST DEVELOPMENTS (PTY) LTD
SOUTH AFRICAN SCOTTISH FINANCE CORP. LTD
SRE HOLDINGS (PTY) LTD
STAND ONE THREE THREE SPARTAN (PTY) LTD
SURREY HOUSE PROPERTIES (PTY) LTD
SYFRETS BANK LTD
SYFRETS GROUP LTD
SYFRETS HOLDING NOMINEES LTD
SYFRETS HOLDINGS LTD
SYFRETS INCOME TRUST LTD
SYFRETS MANAGED ASSETS LTD
SYFRETS MORTGAGE NOMINEES LTD
SYFRETS NATAL NOMINEES LTD
SYFRETS NOMINEES LTD
SYFRETS PARTICIPATION BOND MANAGERS LTD
SYFRETS PROPERTY AGENCY HOLDINGS LTD
SYFRETS PROPERTY BROKERS, ADMINISTRATION
SYFRETS REAL ESTATE (CAPE MID.) (PTY) LT
SYFRETS REAL ESTATE (EASTERN CAPE) LTD
SYFRETS REAL ESTATE (PIETERMARITZBURG) L
SYFRETS REAL ESTATE (TRANSVAAL) LTD
SYFRETS SOUTH AFRICA NOMINEES (PTY) LTD
SYFRETS TRUST & EXECUTOR (CAPE MIDLANDS)
SYFRETS TRUST & EXECUTOR (EASTERN CAPE)
SYFRETS TRUST & EXECUTOR (NORTHERN CAPE)
SYFRETS TRUST & EXECUTOR (PRETORIA) LTD
SYFRETS TRUST & EXECUTOR CO. (GRAHAMSTOW
SYFRETS TRUST & EXECUTOR CO. NATAL LTD
SYFRETS TRUST & EXECUTOR CO. S.W.A. LTD
SYFRETS TRUST (JERSEY) LTD
SYFRETS TRUST LTD
TERM HOLDINGS LTD
TFC TRAVEL INTERNATIONAL (EP) (PTY) LTD
TFC TRAVEL INTERNATIONAL (NATAL) (PTY) L
TFC TRAVEL INTERNATIONAL (PRETORIA) (PTY
TFC TRAVEL INTERNATIONAL (PTY) LTD
THIBAULT TRUST CO. LTD
THIBAULT TRUST PENSION CONSULTANTS (PTY)
THIBAULT TRUST PROPERTIES (PTY) LTD
TIGCLOMA LTD
TRAFALGAR INVEST PARTNERS LTD
TRAFALGAR INVESTMENTS (PTY) LTD
TRAFALGAR PROPERTIES (PTY) LTD
UAL EXPORT FINANCE CO. (PTY) LTD
UAL FINANCE (PTY) LTD
UAL LEASING CORP. (PTY) LTD
UAL MANAGEMENT CO. LTD
UAL MERCHANT BANK LTD
UAL NOMINEES (PTY) LTD
UAL PROPERTY FUND MANAGERS LTD
ULVICK PROPERTIES (PTY) LTD
UNITY HOUSE INVESTMENTS (PTY) LTD
WAKEFIELD INVESTMENTS (PTY) LTD
WALE STREET NOMINEES LTD
WALMAN PROPERTIES (PTY) LTD
WILLOWBRAE INVESTMENTS (PTY) LTD
WORLD TRAVEL AGENCY (PTY) LTD

INVESTMENTS

None

NEI AFRICA HOLDINGS LTD

ABBREVIATION : NEIHOLD

JSE SHORT CODE : NEH

SECTOR : Industrial-Engineering

SHAREHOLDERS

Who Owns Whom's Assessment of the Identity of the Ultimate Controlling Shareholder: NORTHERN ENGINEERING INDUSTRIES PLC

SHAREHOLDER	PERCENTAGE 1992	1991
NEI OVERSEAS HOLDINGS LTD	56.7	54.3
SA MUTUAL	21.0	21.0
INDO-CHINA NOM P/L	4.8	---
MOMENTUM LIFE ASSURE LTD	3.7	3.7
METAL IND GROUP PENS FUND	3.6	3.6
ENGINEERING INDUSTRIES PENS FUND	3.6	3.6
FIRST NAT NOM P/L	3.2	3.9
SAGE LIFE LTD	---	1.7
MUFREN NOM P/L	---	3.9
TOTAL	96.6	95.5

DIRECTORS :
ABRAHAMSE LG (Chairman),ADCOCK CS ,BEAUMONT CW
HARRISON T ,HAWLEY R
HYSLOP LD (Managing Director),JOUBERT PG ,SIMS IJ

REGISTRATION NUMBER : 05/10167/06

REGISTERED OFFICE
2nd Floor, Ristone Office Park
15 Sherbourne Road, Parktown
2193
TEL: 011-482 1460
FAX: 011-726 8143

TRANSFER SECRETARY
Mercantile Registrars Ltd
P O Box 1053, Johannesburg
2000
TEL: 011-333 8181

COMPANY SECRETARY
J R Eaglesham

NATURE OF BUSINESS
An investment holding company with a controlling interest in quoted Northern Engineering Industries

BANKERS :
Nedperm Bank Ltd

AUDITORS :
KPMG Aiken & Peat

FAMILIAR BRAND NAMES
N/A

CONTRIBUTION BY ACTIVITY
N/A

YEAR END : December

DIVIDEND : Ords 5c

Interim No 8	(Ldr)28/09/90	(Pay)19/10/90	Amt(c)27.5
Final No 9	(Ldr)19/04/91	(Pay)10/05/91	Amt(c)55
Interim No 10	(Ldr)27/09/91	(Pay)18/10/91	Amt(c)3.5
Final No 11	(Ldr)15/05/92	(Pay)05/06/92	Amt(c)3.5

NUMBER OF EMPLOYEES : 20

CAPITAL STRUCTURE

	AUTHORISED	ISSUED
Ords 5c	10000000	6682720

FINANCIAL STATISTICS (AT FINANCIAL YEAR END)

(Amts in R'000)	1991 Dec	1990 Dec	1989 Dec	1988 Dec	1987 Dec
Ord S/H Int	77741	66952	90945	82822	135088
Long Trm Loans	79873	68342	93661	78434	8858
Iss Ord Share	6683	6683	6683	6683	6683
Total Liab	325831	323464	308758	251859	155279
Current Liab	245958	255122	215097	173425	146421
Total Assets	403572	390416	399703	334681	290367
Current Assets	304132	311200	326034	267884	224586
Debtors	174730	137510	134756	117805	87826
Inventory	114748	137292	129809	97991	85328
Turnover	797327	712191	587010	438742	391763
Oper Profit	36448	31001	69025	64213	48680
Interest Paid	39750	29536	9463	13715	8012
Tax Paid	7166	19455	27468	18974	13896
Prf af Int&Tax	177	-4082	32094	31524	26772
Prf att Ord Sh	-1001	-2278	17042	31524	26722
Btm Line Earn	-1001	-3461	15976	26410	26722
Dividend Paid	468	5513	7050	12608	10681
Mkt Prce(c) YE	650	900	1750	3500	-
Depreciation	7710	7527	6480	5784	5712

PER SHARE STATISTICS (CENTS)

Net Asst Val	1163.27	1001.83	1360.84	1239.29	2021.37
Net Earnings	-14.90	-34.10	255.00	261.40	225.30
Dividends	7.00	82.50	105.50	105.50	90.00
Cash Flow	215.41	-5.91	287.60	529.61	472.54

RATIOS AND OTHER INFORMATION

Mrk Cap(R000)	43440	60147	116953	233905	-
Current Ratio	1.24	1.22	1.52	1.54	1.53
Quik/Acid Tst	0.77	0.68	0.91	0.98	0.95
A/C Rec T/ovr	4.56	5.18	4.36	3.72	4.46
Tot Ass T/ovr	1.98	1.82	1.47	1.31	1.35
Debt/Ass Rat	0.62	0.66	0.55	0.53	0.52
L T L Tot Ass	0.01	0.01	0.01	0.02	0.02
Debt to Eqity	3.20	3.86	2.41	2.15	1.13
Interest Cover	0.92	1.05	7.29	4.68	6.08
Oper Prof Mrg	4.57	4.35	11.76	14.64	12.43
Net Prof Marg%	-0.13	-0.32	2.90	7.19	6.82
Ret on Assets	11.67	11.50	17.27	19.19	16.76
Ret on Equity%	-1.29	-3.40	18.74	38.06	19.78
Price/Earnings	-43.62	-26.39	6.86	13.39	-
Divid Cover	-2.13	-0.41	2.42	2.48	2.50
Divid Yield	1.08	9.17	6.03	3.01	-
Earning Yield%	-2.29	-3.79	14.57	7.47	-
NAV % Mrk Pr	178.96	111.31	77.76	35.41	-
Effec Tax Rate	29.58	162.52	53.34	41.36	36.27
Def Interval	12.23	-401.76	0.26	0.14	0.21
Sus Grth Rate	-1.89	-11.64	10.99	22.84	11.87

SUBSIDIARY & ASSOCIATED COMPANIES

NORTHERN ENGINEERING INDUSTRIES AFRICA L

INVESTMENTS

None

NEW CENTRAL WITWATERSRAND AREAS LTD

ABBREVIATION : NEW-CENT

JSE SHORT CODE : NCW

SECTOR : Mining Financial-Mining Holding

SHAREHOLDERS

Who Owns Whom's Assessment of the Identity of the Ultimate Controlling Shareholder:
ANGLO AMERICAN

SHAREHOLDER	PERCENTAGE 1992	1991
RESIDENT NOM LTD	34.5	34.5
WORKMENS COMPENS COMMISSIONER IN TRUST	7.4	---
LODESTONE HLDGS LTD	5.6	5.6
AFRICAN & EUROPEAN INV CO LTD	4.6	4.6
HORTORS GROUP PENS FUND	4.3	---
LONDON CONTROL ACCOUNT	4.0	---
PIONEER NOM LTD	3.5	5.1
DIDO NOM LTD	2.8	2.8
FERMAIN NOM LTD	2.8	2.8
YSKOR PENS FUND	2.3	2.3
ANDEX NOM P/L	2.3	---
EIGHTY ONE MAIN STREET NOM LTD	1.7	1.8
STD BANK NOM TVL P/L	1.4	8.8
PROTEA ASSURE CO PENS FUND	1.3	1.3
CMB NOM P/L	1.3	---
PROTEA ASSURE CO LTD	1.1	1.0
FIRST NAT NOM P/L	---	1.1
SA MUTUAL	---	1.9
SANLAM	---	1.3
TOTAL	81.0	74.9

DIRECTORS :
CULLINAN NM ,FISH DGK ,HOLFORD GM
KING MW (Chairman),O'DOWD MC ,PRETORIUS TL
YATES CWP

REGISTRATION NUMBER : 05/04747/06

REGISTERED OFFICE
44 Main Street, Johannesburg
2001
TEL: 011-638 9111

FAX: 011-638 3221

TRANSFER SECRETARY
Consolidated Share Registrars Ltd
P O Box 61051, Marshalltown
2107
TEL: 011-492 1620

COMPANY SECRETARY
Anglo American Corp of SA Ltd

NATURE OF BUSINESS
The company's principal businesses are the holding of mineral rights and prospecting for gold, and that of an investment holding company.

BANKERS :
Standard Bank of SA Ltd

AUDITORS :
Deloitte Pim Goldby

FAMILIAR BRAND NAMES
N/A

CONTRIBUTION BY ACTIVITY
N/A

YEAR END : March

DIVIDEND : Ords 50c

Interim No 49	(Ldr)27/04/90	(Pay)05/06/90	Amt(c)47
Final No 50	(Ldr)16/11/90	(Pay)14/12/90	Amt(c)104
Interim No 51	(Ldr)26/04/91	(Pay)04/06/91	Amt(c)39
Final No 52	(Ldr)08/11/91	(Pay)18/12/91	Amt(c)90
Interim No 53	(Ldr)08/05/92	(Pay)12/06/92	Amt(c)67
Final No 54	(Ldr)30/10/92	(Pay)02/12/92	Amt(c)72

CAPITAL STRUCTURE

	AUTHORISED	ISSUED
Ords 50c	2000000	1766396

FINANCIAL STATISTICS (AT FINANCIAL YEAR END)

(Amts in R'000)	1992 Mar	1990 Sep	1989 Jun	1988 Jun	1987
Ord S/H Int	6493	1879	1880	1877	1869
Long Trm Loans	-	-	-	-	1575
Iss Ord Share	1766	1766	1766	1766	1766
Total Liab	1516	2086	1825	1637	3150
Current Liab	1516	2086	1825	1637	1575
Total Assets	8009	3965	3705	3514	5148
Current Assets	3003	2225	1965	1774	1704
Debtors	545	491	963	813	-
Inventory	-	-	-	-	1704
Turnover	-	-	-	2540	2485
Oper Profit	3707	-335	-365	2277	2309
Tax Paid	-	-43	-	43	31
Prf af Int&Tax	8076	2666	2458	2234	2278
Prf att Ord Sh	8076	2666	2458	2234	2278
Btm Line Earn	8076	2666	2458	2234	2278
Dividend Paid	3462	2667	2455	2226	2261
Mkt Prce(c) YE	3500	3850	4500	3650	15500

PER SHARE STATISTICS (CENTS)

Net Asst Val	367.67	106.40	106.46	106.29	105.83
Net Earnings	196.50	151.00	139.20	126.40	-
Dividends	196.00	150.00	139.00	126.00	-
Cash Flow	304.87	150.96	139.18	126.50	128.99

RATIOS AND OTHER INFORMATION

Mrk Cap(R000)	61810	67991	79470	64459	273730
Current Ratio	1.98	1.07	1.08	1.08	1.08
Quik/Acid Tst	1.98	1.07	1.08	1.08	-
A/C Rec T/ovr	-	-	-	3.12	-
Tot Ass T/ovr	-	-	-	0.72	0.48
Debt/Ass Rat	0.19	0.53	0.49	0.47	0.61
L T L Tot Ass	-	-	-	-	0.31
Debt to Eqity	0.23	1.11	0.97	0.87	1.69
Oper Prof Mrg	-	-	-	89.65	92.92
Net Prof Marg%	-	-	-	87.95	91.67
Ret on Assets	67.22	66.15	66.34	64.80	44.85
Ret on Equity%	82.92	141.88	130.74	119.02	121.88
Price/Earnings	17.81	25.50	32.33	28.88	-
Divid Cover	1.00	1.01	1.00	1.00	-
Divid Yield	5.60	3.90	3.09	3.45	-
Earning Yield%	5.61	3.92	3.09	3.46	-
NAV % Mrk Pr	10.50	2.76	2.37	2.91	0.68
Effec Tax Rate	-	24.02	-	1.89	1.34
Def Interval	-	-	-	-	0.69
Sus Grth Rate	71.06	-0.05	0.16	0.43	0.91

SUBSIDIARY & ASSOCIATED COMPANIES

None

INVESTMENTS

ANGLO AMERICAN COAL CORP. LTD (115320S)
ANGLO AMERICAN CORP. OF S.A. LTD (84000S)
ANGLO AMERICAN GOLD INVESTMENT CO. LTD (65000S)
ANGLO AMERICAN INDUSTRIAL CORP. LTD (10800S)
BARLOW RAND LTD (28890S)
DE BEERS/CENTENARY LINKED UNITS (200000S)
DRIEFONTEIN CONSOLIDATED LTD (15000S)
JOHANNESBURG CONSOLIDATED INVESTMENT CO. (100000S)
JOHANNESBURG CONSOLIDATED INVESTMENT COM (100000 SH)
KINROSS MINES LTD (10000S)
LEBOWA PLATINUM MINES LTD (22935S)
MINORCO (40000S)
PALABORA MINING CO LTD (12600S)
POTGIETERSRUST PLATINUMS LTD (66511S)
RUSTENBURG PLATINUM HOLDINGS LTD (120000S)
SAMANCOR LTD (4600S)
VAAL REEFS EXPLORATION & MINING CO LTD (6800S)
WINKELHAAK MINES LTD (10000S)

NEW WITS LTD

ABBREVIATION : NEW-WITS

JSE SHORT CODE : NWT

SECTOR : Mining Financial-Mining Holding

SHAREHOLDERS

Who Owns Whom's Assessment of the Identity of the Ultimate Controlling Shareholder:
GFSA

SHAREHOLDER	PERCENTAGE 1992	1991
MINU NOM LTD	55.8	49.8
STD BANK NOM TVL P/L	6.9	2.7
FIRST NAT NOM P/L	6.4	6.7

CMB NOM P/L	4.7	---
SA MUTUAL	2.7	8.9
SA SPECIAL RISKS INSURANCE ASSOC LTD	1.3	---
SHARESTOCK NOM P/L	---	1.1
SANLAM	---	4.9
TOTAL	77.7	74.1

DIRECTORS :
DAY BA ,DYKES DC ,FULLER-GOOD MR ,JANISCH PR
ROSS CJ ,WOLFE-COOTE CA ,WRIGHT AJ (Chairman

REGISTRATION NUMBER : 05/04822/06

REGISTERED OFFICE
75 Fox Street, Johannesburg
2001
TEL: 011-639 9111
FAX: 011-639 2101/2

TRANSFER SECRETARY
Gold Fields of SA Ltd
P O Box 1167, Johannesburg
2000
TEL: 011-639 9111

COMPANY SECRETARY
Gold Fields of SA Ltd

NATURE OF BUSINESS
An investment,exploration and share-dealing company.The group's investments cover a number mining,financial,industrial & property shares. New Wits also has a portfolio of property and mineral,mining and participation rights and is involved in prospecting activities in certain of these areas.

BANKERS :
Standard Bank of SA Ltd

AUDITORS :
Deloitte Pim Goldby

FAMILIAR BRAND NAMES
N/A

CONTRIBUTION BY ACTIVITY
Gold (% Profit after tax) (36.7%)
Platinum (12.2%)
Energy (8.3%)
Base Minerals (11.9%)
Mining Finance (21.6%)
Industrial & Commercial (9.3%)

YEAR END : June

DIVIDEND : Ords 25c

Interim No 78	(Ldr)26/01/90	(Pay)28/02/90	Amt(c)17
Final No 79	(Ldr)31/08/90	(Pay)26/09/90	Amt(c)33
Interim No 80	(Ldr)25/01/91	(Pay)27/02/91	Amt(c)17
Final No 81	(Ldr)30/08/91	(Pay)25/09/91	Amt(c)35
Interim No 82	(Ldr)31/01/91	(Pay)26/02/92	Amt(c)17
Final No 83	(Ldr)28/08/92	(Pay)23/09/92	Amt(c)35

CAPITAL STRUCTURE

	AUTHORISED	ISSUED
Ords 25c	40000000	30635201

FINANCIAL STATISTICS (AT FINANCIAL YEAR END)

(Amts in R'000)	1992 Jun	1991 Jun	1990 Jun	1989 Jun	1988 Jun
Ord S/H Int	167785	166741	71430	63445	57552
Long Trm Loans	-	-	1086	1016	1095
Iss Ord Share	30635	30635	23104	23104	23104
Total Liab	16804	16678	29757	8455	8667
Current Liab	16804	16678	28671	7439	7572
Total Assets	184589	183419	101187	71900	66219
Current Assets	3545	3745	3951	8149	5561
Debtors	3542	3742	3837	3794	3482
Oper Profit	38	11741	2882	-715	17383
Interest Paid	1104	1409	296	410	-
Tax Paid	-	28	322	199	22
Prf af Int&Tax	17655	28592	19745	16474	17361
Prf att Ord Sh	17655	28592	19537	16290	17111
Btm Line Earn	17655	28592	19537	16290	17111
Dividend Paid	15930	15930	11552	10397	10397
Mkt Prce(c) YE	875	1200	1225	1425	1200

PER SHARE STATISTICS (CENTS)

Net Asst Val	547.69	544.28	309.17	274.61	249.10
Net Earnings	58.00	93.00	85.00	71.00	74.00
Dividends	52.00	52.00	50.00	45.00	45.00
Cash Flow	57.63	93.33	84.56	70.51	74.06

RATIOS AND OTHER INFORMATION

Mrk Cap(R000)	268056	367620	283024	329232	277248
Current Ratio	0.21	0.22	0.14	1.10	0.73
Quik/Acid Tst	0.21	0.22	0.14	1.10	0.73
Debt/Ass Rat	0.09	0.09	0.28	0.10	0.11
Debt to Eqity	0.10	0.10	0.40	0.12	0.13
Interest Cover	16.93	21.18	66.13	40.96	-
Ret on Assets	10.16	16.37	20.12	23.76	26.25
Ret on Equity%	10.52	17.15	27.35	25.68	29.73
Price/Earnings	15.09	12.90	14.41	20.07	16.22
Divid Cover	1.12	1.79	1.70	1.58	1.64
Divid Yield	5.94	4.33	4.08	3.16	3.75
Earning Yield%	6.63	7.75	6.94	4.98	6.17
NAV % Mrk Pr	62.59	45.36	25.24	19.27	20.76
Effec Tax Rate	-	0.03	7.50	-23.86	0.13
Def Interval	0.31	0.14	0.99	-	-
Sus Grth Rate	1.03	7.59	11.18	9.29	11.67

SUBSIDIARY & ASSOCIATED COMPANIES

LEO DISTRIBUTIONS LTD
NATIONAL TRUST OF AFRICA LTD
SELECTED MINING HOLDINGS LTD
WITWATERSRAND DEEP LTD

INVESTMENTS

ANGLO AMERICAN INVESTMENT TRUST LTD (120000 SH)
CEMENTATION CO (AFRICA) LTD (104300 SH)
COMMERCIAL UNION ASSURANCE CO. OF S.A. L (400000 SH)
DELFOS & ATLAS COPCO (PTY) LTD (40000 SH)
DOORNFONTEIN GOLD MINING CO. LTD (320000 SH)
DRIEFONTEIN CONSOLIDATED LTD (2369600SH)
EAST RAND GOLD & URANIUM CO (162000 SH)
ELANDSRAND GOLD MINING CO LTD (200000 SH)
GOLD FIELDS COAL LTD (740000 SH)
GOLD FIELDS OF SA LTD (946530 SH)
GOLD FIELDS PROPERTY CO. LTD (810000 SH)
GOLDFIELDS NAMIBIA LTD (660000 SH)
KINROSS MINES LTD (52300 SH)
KLOOF GOLD MINING COMPANY LTD (FINANCIA (416000 SH)
LIBANON GOLD MINING CO LTD (1147500 S)
NORTHAM PLATINUM LTD (1800000SH)
O'OKIEP COPPER CO LTD (200000 SH)
PALABORA MINING CO LTD (100000 SH)
RANDCOAL LTD (40000SH)
RANDFONTEIN ESTATES GOLD MINING CO WITS (888690 SH)
ROOIBERG TIN LTD (110000 SH)
RUSTENBURG PLATINUM HOLDINGS LTD (192126 SH)

SASOL LTD (1110000SH)
SOUTH DEEP EXPLORATION CO LTD (243000 SH)
VAAL REEFS EXPLORATION & MINING CO LTD (67003 SH)
VENTERSPOST GOLD MINING CO LTD (DEFERRED (1801600SH)
VENTERSPOST GOLD MINING CO LTD (OPTIONS) (337320)
VENTERSPOST GOLD MINING CO. LTD (447200SH)
VILLAGE MAIN REEF GOLD MINING CO (1934) (4200 SH)
VOGELSTRUISBULT METAL HOLDINGS LTD (3790000 S)
WESTERN DEEP LEVELS LTD (296600 SH)
WINKELHAAK MINES LTD (216600 SH)
ZINC CORPORATION OF S.A. LTD (513000 SH)

NICTUS FINANSIELE INSTELLING BPK

ABBREVIATION : NICTUS

JSE SHORT CODE : NCS

SECTOR : Industrial-Industrial Holding

SHAREHOLDERS

Who Owns Whom's Assessment of the Identity of the Ultimate Controlling Shareholder: DIRECTORS

SHAREHOLDER	PERCENTAGE 1992	1991
LANDSWYN INV BPK	29.7	29.7
VERITAS EKSEKUTEURSKAMER E/B	11.1	11.1
KOEKEMOER V	9.4	9.4
TROCOR P/L	9.0	9.0
LAVANREN NOM P/L	4.0	2.5
DIAGONAL NOM P/L	3.8	2.0
NEDBANK NOM LTD	3.7	3.7
KUHN W J	2.5	2.5
FILDRIAAN P/L	2.2	2.0
DOWNARD C R	2.1	2.1
NICTUS EKSEKUTEURSKAMER P/L	1.7	1.7
TOTAL	79.3	75.8

DIRECTORS :
DE KLERK IH ,DU PREEZ IG ,FICHARDT EA ,KUHN WJ
OLIVIER JL ,POTTAS JJ
TROMP NC (Managing Director)
TROMP PJdeW (Chairman

REGISTRATION NUMBER : 81/011858/06

REGISTERED OFFICE
Nictus Building, Cnr Pretoria Ave & Dover Str
Randburg
2125
TEL: 061-229 202
FAX: 061-228 552

TRANSFER SECRETARY
Fraser Street Registrars (Pty) Ltd
P O Box 61178, Marshalltown
2107
TEL: 011-491 0911

COMPANY SECRETARY
Veritas Eksekuteurskamer (Pty) Ltd

NATURE OF BUSINESS
A holding company whose subsidiaries are involved in furniture and motor retailing, property and carpet wholesale.

BANKERS :
First National Bank of SA Ltd

AUDITORS :
PJ Malherbe & Co, KPMG Aiken & Peat

FAMILIAR BRAND NAMES
N/A

CONTRIBUTION BY ACTIVITY
N/A

YEAR END : June

DIVIDEND :Ords 50c

Interim	(Ldr)28/04/89	(Pay)26/05/89	Amt(c)2
Interim	(Ldr)08/03/91	(Pay)05/04/91	Amt(c)2

NUMBER OF EMPLOYEES : 250

CAPITAL STRUCTURE

	AUTHORISED	ISSUED
Ords 50c	7500000	7124720

FINANCIAL STATISTICS (AT FINANCIAL YEAR END)

(Amts in R'000)	1992 Jun	1991 Jun	1990 Jun	1989 Jun	1988 Jun
Ord S/H Int	8634	8322	7978	8288	8900
Long Trm Loans	1748	1906	2226	2704	2800
Iss Ord Share	7125	7125	7125	7125	7125
Total Liab	11331	14188	12501	13995	13002
Current Liab	9583	12282	10275	11291	10202
Total Assets	19898	22443	20412	22216	21835
Intang Assets	67	67	67	67	67
Current Assets	14523	17678	15787	17390	16875
Debtors	8821	10594	9118	10726	10297
Inventory	5671	6915	6487	6425	6417
Oper Profit	2142	2207	1406	945	2452
Interest Paid	1637	1918	1833	1410	936
Tax Paid	63	-175	-34	61	239
Prf af Int&Tax	459	490	-349	-488	1277
Prf att Ord Sh	454	487	-360	-500	1253
Btm Line Earn	454	487	-311	-470	1319
Dividend Paid	142	142	-	142	285
Mkt Prce(c) YE	40	45	40	37	55
Depreciation	154	119	118	108	73

PER SHARE STATISTICS (CENTS)

Net Asst Val	120.24	115.86	111.03	115.38	123.97
Net Earnings	6.38	6.84	-5.04	-7.02	17.58
Dividends	2.00	2.00	-	2.00	4.00
Cash Flow	7.92	5.53	-4.86	-5.49	19.99

RATIOS AND OTHER INFORMATION

Mrk Cap(R000)	2850	3206	2850	2636	3919
Current Ratio	1.52	1.44	1.54	1.54	1.65
Quik/Acid Tst	0.92	0.88	0.91	0.97	1.03
Debt/Ass Rat	0.56	0.62	0.59	0.61	0.57
L T L Tot Ass	0.08	0.08	0.09	0.10	0.10
Debt to Eqity	1.29	1.68	1.51	1.63	1.40
Interest Cover	1.31	1.15	0.77	0.67	2.62
Ret on Assets	10.85	9.95	7.10	4.42	11.23

Ret on Equity%	5.26	5.85	-4.51	-6.03	14.08
Price/Earnings	6.27	6.58	-7.94	-5.27	3.13
Divid Cover	3.19	3.42	-	-3.51	4.40
Divid Yield	5.00	4.44	-	5.41	7.27
Earning Yield%	15.95	15.20	-12.60	-18.97	31.96
NAV % Mrk Pr	300.60	257.47	277.58	311.84	225.40
Effec Tax Rate	20.82	12.01	-17.95	-24.07	9.30
Def Interval	13.85	27.47	-26.34	-21.18	5.41
Sus Grth Rate	3.61	4.15	-4.51	-7.75	10.88

SUBSIDIARY & ASSOCIATED COMPANIES

AUAS MOTORS (PTY) LTD (NAMIBIA)
HOCHLAND 7191 (PTY) LTD
KRUBEN HOLDINGS (PTY) LTD
NICTUS (PTY) LTD
NICTUS EIENDOMME (PTY) LTD
NICTUS MEUBELS (EDMS) BPK
OREON PLACE (PTY) LTD
SWAFLOR LIMITED
TOCL INVESTMENTS (PTY) LTD
UNIFURN MEUBELS (PTY) LTD
WERDA WESKUSONTWIKKELING (PTY) LTD

INVESTMENTS

BANK WINDHOEK BEHEREND LTD (65000 SH)

NIGEL GOLD MINING HOLDINGS LTD

ABBREVIATION : NIGEL

JSE SHORT CODE : NGL

SECTOR : Gold-Rand & others

SHAREHOLDERS

Who Owns Whom's Assessment of the Identity of the Ultimate Controlling Shareholder:
CONSOLIDATED MINING VIA SOUTHGO

SHAREHOLDER	PERCENTAGE 1992	1991
SOUTH EAST RAND GOLD HLDGS LTD	57.6	57.6
MINU NOM LTD	23.1	23.1
STD BANK NOM TVL P/L	3.7	4.2
INDO-CHINA NOM P/L	2.3	---
LOWENCO NOM P/L	2.2	1.7
NIGEL GOLD MIN HLDGS SHARE INC TRUST	1.8	---
AA LIFE ASSURE ASSOC LTD	---	1.2
INDO-CHINA NOM SA P/L	---	1.7
LAING G J S NIGT ACC	---	1.4
TOTAL	90.6	90.8

DIRECTORS :
BUITENDAG HC ,DONALD JC ,FLOWERDAY RA
LEE RA (Chairman),LOWENTHAL ND ,LOWENTHAL RY
RUBENSTEIN GB ,SCHECHTER M ,SUDDENS BD
THOMPSON MW ,TURNER CF

REGISTRATION NUMBER : 80/02608/06

REGISTERED OFFICE
39th Floor, Carlton Centre, Commissioner Street
Johannesburg
2001
TEL: 011-331 9181
FAX: 011-331 6189

TRANSFER SECRETARY
Mercantile Registrars Ltd
P O Box 1053, Johannesburg
2000
TEL: 011-333 8181

COMPANY SECRETARY
Consolidated Mining Management Services Ltd

NATURE OF BUSINESS
A mining holding company.Its wholly-owned subsidiary,Nigel Gold Mining Company (Pty)Ltd, conducts gold mining and dump retreatment operations in the Transvaal district of Nigel.

BANKERS :
Nedperm Bank Ltd

AUDITORS :
Charles Orbach & Co

FAMILIAR BRAND NAMES
N/A

CONTRIBUTION BY ACTIVITY
N/A

YEAR END : March

DIVIDEND :15/08/91 and 15/02/91

NUMBER OF EMPLOYEES : 1005

CAPITAL STRUCTURE

	AUTHORISED	ISSUED
Ords 1c	150000000	148407221

FINANCIAL STATISTICS (AT FINANCIAL YEAR END)

(Amts in R'000)	1991 Mar	1990 Mar	1988 Dec	1987
Ord S/H Int	60449	61801	38413	2505
Long Trm Loans	16000	16000	3862	42694
Iss Ord Share	148407	148407	108611	250
Total Liab	27052	25739	22717	46994
Current Liab	11052	9739	18855	4300
Total Assets	87501	87540	61130	50868
Current Assets	2983	4892	2170	5669
Debtors	1993	2587	2060	-
Inventory	837	326	107	5669
Turnover	44704	53050	-	-
Oper Profit	434	9500	2947	1858
Interest Paid	653	1465	952	286
Tax Paid	-	73	-	48
Prf af Int&Tax	-219	7962	1995	1524
Prf att Ord Sh	-219	5	1995	1067
Btm Line Earn	-1352	5	4	1067
Dividend Paid	-	-	-	113
Mkt Prce(c) YE	15	70	60	-

PER SHARE STATISTICS (CENTS)

Net Asst Val	40.73	41.64	35.37	1002.00
Net Earnings	-0.10	6.30	1.90	-

Cash Flow	-0.15	5.00	1.87	609.60

RATIOS AND OTHER INFORMATION

Mrk Cap(R000)	22261	103885	65167	-
Current Ratio	0.27	0.50	0.12	1.32
Quik/Acid Tst	0.19	0.47	0.11	-
A/C Rec T/ovr	22.43	16.41	-	-
Tot Ass T/ovr	0.51	0.48	-	-
Debt/Ass Rat	0.31	0.29	0.37	0.92
L T L Tot Ass	0.18	0.18	0.06	0.84
Debt to Eqity	0.45	0.42	0.59	18.76
Interest Cover	0.66	6.48	3.10	6.50
Oper Prof Mrg	0.97	17.91	-	-
Net Prof Marg%	-0.49	0.01	-	-
Ret on Assets	0.50	8.68	4.82	3.65
Ret on Equity%	-0.36	0.01	5.19	42.59
Price/Earnings	-150.00	11.11	31.58	-
Earning Yield%	-0.67	9.00	3.17	-
NAV % Mrk Pr	271.55	59.49	58.95	-
Effec Tax Rate	-	0.91	-	3.05
Def Interval	-22.17	0.01	6.35	28.01
Sus Grth Rate	-0.36	0.01	5.19	38.08

SUBSIDIARY & ASSOCIATED COMPANIES

GOLD RECOVERY RESIDUES (PTY) LTD
NIGEL GOLD MINING COMPANY (PTY) LTD
NIPROP PROPERTY INVESTMENTS (PTY) LTD

INVESTMENTS

None

NINIAN & LESTER HOLDINGS LTD

ABBREVIATION : NINIAN

JSE SHORT CODE : NIN

SECTOR : Industrial-Clothing, Footwear & Textiles

SHAREHOLDERS

Who Owns Whom's Assessment of the Identity of the Ultimate Controlling Shareholder: DIRECTORS

SHAREHOLDER	PERCENTAGE 1992	1991
CONSOLIDATED JERSEY HLDGS LTD	19.4	19.4
ELFIN UNDIES P/L	9.7	9.7
SCHRODER D V	8.7	8.6
PELICAN LTD	8.2	8.2
PRIMSEC P/L	7.0	7.0
MCELLIGOTT M R A & SCHRODER D V	5.4	5.2
MCELLIGOTT M R A & SCHRODER J H	5.3	5.2
SCHRODER J H	4.2	4.2
CARBINE NOM P/L	4.1	---
DRYSDALE D M	2.9	2.9
SCHRODER J H & MCELLIGOTT M R A	2.9	2.7
SCHRODER D V & MCELLIGOTT M R A	2.7	2.7
SCOTT W J D I	2.2	---
CAMPBELL A F	2.1	2.1
PERLOV M	1.4	1.4
JANILL INV P/L	1.2	1.2
FIRST NAT NOM P/L	1.1	---
ZWI C	---	1.5
BARTEL H O	---	1.0
G C & M NOM NATAL P/L	---	2.5
MOORE P H	---	3.5
TOTAL	88.3	88.7

DIRECTORS :
DRYSDALE DM (Managing Director),FISHER RV
MCELLIGOTT MRA (Chairman),MCGREGOR DBH
RAHMER GW ,SCHRODER JH

REGISTRATION NUMBER : 69/02769/06

REGISTERED OFFICE
915 Umgeni Road, Durban
4001
TEL: 031-23 8301
FAX: 031-303 1745

TRANSFER SECRETARY
Fraser Street Registrars (Pty) Ltd
P O Box 61178, Marshalltown
2107
TEL: 011-491 0911

COMPANY SECRETARY
G W Rahmer

NATURE OF BUSINESS
An investment holding company with subsidiaries operating in the textile, clothing and hosiery industries. Products include knitted fabric for clothing, furnishing and industrial application, underwear and outerwear, socks and rugby jerseys.

BANKERS :
Standard Bank of SA Ltd, Nedbank Ltd

AUDITORS :
Deloitte Pim Goldby

FAMILIAR BRAND NAMES
BIOGUARD,BLACKBOARD,COMPUTER SOCK,CORDENE
DARE TO BE DIFFERENT,DIRECTION,ELMAR
FOOTFRESH,FREETIME,HILTON,JOCKEY
JOCKEY FOR HER,LEADING LADY,LUELYTE
MARK ANTONY,MARTILON,MAXLITE,MAXMORE,MONSOON
NINIAN,PJ,PRO,SKANTS,SLIM JAN,SORRENTO
SURRENDER,SWISNIT,TOP LADY,WOOLCRAFT

CONTRIBUTION BY ACTIVITY
N/A

YEAR END : December

DIVIDEND : Ords 50c

Final No 32	(Ldr)23/02/90	(Pay)14/03/90	Amt(c)55
Interim No 33	(Ldr)21/09/90	(Pay)08/10/90	Amt(c)6
Final No 34	(Ldr)22/02/91	(Pay)28/02/91	Amt(c)45
Interim No 35	(Ldr)20/09/91	(Pay)07/10/91	Amt(c)4
Final No 36	(Ldr)28/02/92	(Pay)09/03/92	Amt(c)27
Interim No 37	(Ldr)25/09/92	(Pay)12/10/92	Amt(c)4

NUMBER OF EMPLOYEES : 3500

CAPITAL STRUCTURE

	AUTHORISED	ISSUED
Ords 50c	5000000	3218725

FINANCIAL STATISTICS (AT FINANCIAL YEAR END)

(Amts in R'000)	1991 Dec	1990 Dec	1989 Dec	1988 Dec	1987 Dec
Ord S/H Int	49347	46448	39314	30712	23551
Long Trm Loans	18532	16944	4727	4578	4350
Iss Ord Share	3219	3219	3219	3219	3219
Total Liab	61234	55066	33059	27086	20892
Current Liab	42702	38122	28332	22508	16542
Total Assets	110581	101514	72373	57798	44443
Current Assets	88818	79461	56815	42383	33628
Debtors	48839	41723	29772	23092	17470
Inventory	39771	37599	27028	19260	16131
Oper Profit	14483	17442	14985	12640	7503
Interest Paid	5474	4888	4002	1926	1030
Tax Paid	3408	4657	4751	4577	1157
Prf af Int&Tax	5601	7897	6232	6137	5316
Prf att Ord Sh	3840	5869	8417	7622	5909
Btm Line Earn	3840	5869	10952	9249	6317
Dividend Paid	998	1641	2350	2092	1611
Mkt Prce(c) YE	600	650	800	575	550
Depreciation	6857	6467	4015	2501	2159

PER SHARE STATISTICS (CENTS)

Net Asst Val	1532.99	1442.93	1221.31	954.09	731.62
Net Earnings	119.00	182.00	261.00	237.00	184.00
Dividends	31.00	51.00	73.00	65.00	50.00
Cash Flow	325.91	409.13	320.66	273.56	232.87

RATIOS AND OTHER INFORMATION

Mrk Cap(R000)	19314	20924	25752	18509	17705
Current Ratio	2.08	2.08	2.01	1.88	2.03
Quik/Acid Tst	1.15	1.10	1.05	1.03	1.06
Debt/Ass Rat	0.43	0.42	0.45	0.46	0.46
L T L Tot Ass	0.04	0.04	0.06	0.07	0.09
Debt to Eqity	0.96	0.91	0.82	0.86	0.87
Interest Cover	2.65	3.57	3.74	6.56	7.28
Ret on Assets	13.10	17.18	23.82	24.53	18.29
Ret on Equity%	7.78	12.64	21.41	24.82	25.09
Price/Earnings	5.04	3.57	3.07	2.43	2.99
Divid Cover	3.84	3.57	3.58	3.65	3.68
Divid Yield	5.17	7.85	9.13	11.30	9.09
Earning Yield%	19.83	28.00	32.63	41.22	33.45
NAV % Mrk Pr	255.50	221.99	152.66	165.93	133.02
Effec Tax Rate	40.15	29.92	41.48	40.62	16.84
Def Interval	1.99	0.88	0.90	0.68	0.90
Sus Grth Rate	5.76	9.10	15.43	18.01	18.25

SUBSIDIARY & ASSOCIATED COMPANIES

GLENMORE TEXTILES (PTY) LTD
MAXMORE INVESTMENTS (PTY) LTD
MAXMORE KNITTING MILLS (PTY) LTD
NINIAN & LESTER (PTY) LTD
SWISNIT MANUFACTURING CO. (PTY) LTD

INVESTMENTS

None

NISWA LTD

ABBREVIATION : NISWA

JSE SHORT CODE : NSA

SECTOR : Development Capital Market

SHAREHOLDERS

Who Owns Whom's Assessment of the Identity of the Ultimate Controlling Shareholder: JA DU TOIT / ND SWART

SHAREHOLDER	PERCENTAGE 1992	1991
NAMIB CONSOLIDATED INV P/L	46.0	---
SWART N D	24.7	---
VAN DRIEL A	2.5	---
HANSEN J W	1.7	---
MOBICAST C C	1.7	---
KRIEL H	1.4	---
STORBECK G D J	1.2	---
JACOB I	1.2	---
ENGELBRECHT P	1.2	---
TOTAL	81.5	---

DIRECTORS :
DU TOIT JA ,DU TOIT JS
FRASER AJ (Financial Director)
SWART ND (Chairman),SWART NJ (Managing Director

REGISTRATION NUMBER : 05/26090/06

REGISTERED OFFICE
Gerling Global House, 15 Eton Road
Parktown
2193
TEL: 011-482 3780
FAX: 011-726 7518

TRANSFER SECRETARY
Central Registrars Ltd
P O Box 4844, Johannesburg
2000
TEL: 011-331 0051

COMPANY SECRETARY
A J Fraser

NATURE OF BUSINESS
A holding company, which through its subsidiary, operates a general-dealer store in the Gobabis district of Namibia. Besides the general-dealer store, Niswa Trading consists of a motor vehicle maintenance and repair business, a petrol and diesel filling-station and a bottle store.

BANKERS :
Standard Bank of SA Ltd

AUDITORS :
Deloitte Pim Goldby

FAMILIAR BRAND NAMES
N/A

CONTRIBUTION BY ACTIVITY
General dealer stores (% of Turnover) (54.0%)
Fuel & Workshop (41.0%)
Bottle Store (5.0%)

YEAR END : February

CAPITAL STRUCTURE

	AUTHORISED	ISSUED
Ords 0,05c	8500000	8100000

FINANCIAL STATISTICS (AT FINANCIAL YEAR END)

(Amts in R'000)	1992 Feb
Ord S/H Int	4516
Long Trm Loans	1157
Iss Ord Share	8100
Total Liab	1484
Current Liab	327
Total Assets	6000
Current Assets	1232
Debtors	431
Inventory	786
Oper Profit	260
Tax Paid	109
Prf af Int&Tax	151
Prf att Ord Sh	151
Btm Line Earn	151

PER SHARE STATISTICS (CENTS)

Net Asst Val	55.75
Cash Flow	1.86

RATIOS AND OTHER INFORMATION

Current Ratio	3.77
Quik/Acid Tst	1.36
Debt/Ass Rat	0.23
L T L Tot Ass	0.17
Debt to Eqity	0.30
Ret on Assets	4.33
Ret on Equity%	3.34
Effec Tax Rate	41.92
Def Interval	7.00
Sus Grth Rate	3.34

SUBSIDIARY & ASSOCIATED COMPANIES

NISWA TRADING (PTY) LTD

INVESTMENTS

AMALGAMATED BEEF INDUSTRIES LTD (3,8%)

NK PROPERTIES LTD

ABBREVIATION : N-KLEINS

JSE SHORT CODE : NKL

SECTOR : Financial-Property Loan Stock

SHAREHOLDERS

Who Owns Whom's Assessment of the Identity of the Ultimate Controlling Shareholder: AFRICAN FINANCE CORP (UK)

SHAREHOLDER	PERCENTAGE 1992	1991
AFC INV LTD	61.3	62.9
LONDON CONTROL ACCOUNT	14.3	15.0
HARVEST SECURITIES LTD	5.0	4.3
AFC GROUP PENS FUND	3.7	3.7
SFSS NOM P/L	1.8	1.3
MACVEN NOM P/L	1.5	1.6
CHALKTON NOM CO P/L	1.2	---
TOTAL	88.8	88.9

DIRECTORS :
DICKS JK ,FISCHER G (Managing Director)
MACKENZIE JW (Chairman),MACKENZIE JWG
MANSELL B ,VORSTER R

REGISTRATION NUMBER : 01/00854/06

REGISTERED OFFICE
AFC House, 25 Wellington Road
Parktown
2193
TEL: 011-484 3570
FAX: 011-642 0180

TRANSFER SECRETARY
Central Registrars Ltd
P O Box 4844, Johannesburg
2000
TEL: 011-331 0051

COMPANY SECRETARY
E R Hackland

NATURE OF BUSINESS
The company carries on the business of property development in the residential, industrial and commercial sectors.

BANKERS :
Standard Bank of SA Ltd

AUDITCRS :
Coopers Theron Du Toit

FAMILIAR BRAND NAMES
N/A

CONTRIBUTION BY ACTIVITY
N/A

YEAR END : June

DIVIDEND : Ords 25c

Final No 93	(Ldr)19/10/90	(Pay)07/11/90	Amt(c)34
Interim No 94	(Ldr)28/02/91	(Pay)26/03/91	Amt(c)16
Final No 95	(Ldr)09/10/91	(Pay)01/11/91	Amt(c)46
Interim No 96	(Ldr)06/03/92	(Pay)31/03/92	Amt(c)16
Final No 97	(Ldr)16/10/92	(Pay)06/11/92	Amt(c)46

NUMBER OF EMPLOYEES : 6

CAPITAL STRUCTURE

	AUTHORISED	ISSUED
Ords 25c	6940000	2010000

FINANCIAL STATISTICS (AT FINANCIAL YEAR END)

(Amts in R'000)	1992 Jun	1991 Jun	1990 Jun	1989 Jun	1988 Jun
Ord S/H Int	19510	20320	16859	14545	13287
Long Trm Loans	3171	4163	3321	2453	2071
Iss Ord Share	2010	2010	2010	2010	2010
Total Liab	8465	6614	11364	11475	2926

Current Liab	5294	2451	8043	9022	855
Total Assets	27975	26934	28223	26020	16213
Current Assets	6715	10428	5553	3016	4513
Debtors	5013	7404	5510	2942	2688
Turnover	7301	8779	8939	-	3791
Oper Profit	2900	4803	4654	2104	2167
Interest Paid	-	188	912	82	-
Tax Paid	1851	2311	2729	1671	800
Prf af Int&Tax	2285	3702	3319	1999	1367
Prf att Ord Sh	2308	3507	3319	2042	1376
Btm Line Earn	436	4707	3319	2042	1376
Dividend Paid	1246	1246	1005	784	563
Mkt Prce(c) YE	1025	750	675	450	385
Depreciation	10	8	7	8	1

PER SHARE STATISTICS (CENTS)

Net Asst Val	970.65	1010.95	838.76	723.63	661.04
Net Earnings	114.80	174.50	165.10	101.60	68.40
Dividends	62.00	62.00	50.00	39.00	28.00
Cash Flow	64.83	226.47	220.90	123.13	89.20

RATIOS AND OTHER INFORMATION

Mrk Cap(R000)	20603	15075	13568	9045	7739
Current Ratio	1.27	4.25	0.69	0.33	5.28
Quik/Acid Tst	1.27	4.25	0.69	0.33	5.28
A/C Rec T/ovr	1.46	1.19	1.62	-	1.41
Tot Ass T/ovr	0.26	0.33	0.32	-	0.23
Debt/Ass Rat	0.19	0.09	0.28	0.35	0.06
L T L Tot Ass	-	-	-	0.01	0.01
Debt to Eqity	0.27	0.12	0.48	0.63	0.08
Interest Cover	-	26.89	5.52	31.59	-
Oper Prof Mrg	39.72	54.71	52.06	-	57.16
Net Prof Marg%	31.61	39.95	37.13	-	36.30
Ret on Assets	14.87	22.30	24.66	14.42	13.37
Ret on Equity%	11.83	17.26	19.69	13.89	10.24
Price/Earnings	8.93	4.30	4.09	4.43	5.63
Divid Cover	1.85	2.81	3.30	2.61	2.44
Divid Yield	6.05	8.27	7.41	8.67	7.27
Earning Yield%	11.20	23.27	24.46	22.58	17.77
NAV % Mrk Pr	94.70	134.79	124.26	160.81	171.70
Effec Tax Rate	71.87	25.38	28.48	39.13	16.75
Def Interval	-	-	1.41	0.76	0.08
Sus Grth Rate	5.44	11.13	13.73	8.65	6.12

SUBSIDIARY & ASSOCIATED COMPANIES

BENONI MINI FACTORIES (PTY) LTD (50%)
ENKAY PROPERTIES LTD (UK)
LAND SECURITIES MANAGEMENT (PTY) LTD (50%)

INVESTMENTS

EAST RAND GOLD & URANIUM CO (360000 SH)

NORTHAM PLATINUM LTD

ABBREVIATION : NORTHAM

JSE SHORT CODE : NHM

SECTOR : Metals & Minerals-Platinum

SHAREHOLDERS

Who Owns Whom's Assessment of the Identity of the Ultimate Controlling Shareholder:
GFSA

SHAREHOLDER	PERCENTAGE 1992	1991
MINU NOM LTD	65.1	65.1
EIGHTY ONE MAIN STREET NOM LTD	9.2	9.9
STD BANK NOM TVL P/L	5.7	6.1
CMB NOM P/L	5.2	---
LIBERTY LIFE ASSOC OF AFRICA LTD	4.6	4.5
FIRST NAT NOM P/L	1.5	1.5
COMMERCIAL UNION LIFE ASSURE CO SA LTD	1.1	1.1
SANLAM	---	4.8
TOTAL	92.4	93.0

DIRECTORS :
DYKES DC ,FENTON CT ,FORSYTH MB ,HOPWOOD JG
PLUMBRIDGE RA ,ROBINSON RL
WRIGHT AJ (Chairman & Managing Dir.

REGISTRATION NUMBER : 77/03282/06

REGISTERED OFFICE
75 Fox Street, Johannesburg
2001
TEL: 011-639 9111
FAX: 011-639 2101/2

TRANSFER SECRETARY
Gold Fields of SA Ltd
P O Box 1167, Johannesburg
2000
TEL: 011-639 9111

COMPANY SECRETARY
Gold Fields of SA Ltd

NATURE OF BUSINESS
Northam owns a platinum mine near the town of Northam in the Transvaal. The Mine is being developed to recover platinum and other precious metals from the Merensky Reef.

BANKERS :
Standard Bank of SA Ltd

AUDITORS :
Ernst & Young

FAMILIAR BRAND NAMES
N/A

CONTRIBUTION BY ACTIVITY
N/A

YEAR END : June

NUMBER OF EMPLOYEES : 4614

CAPITAL STRUCTURE

	AUTHORISED	ISSUED
Ords 1c	60000000	57600000

FINANCIAL STATISTICS (AT FINANCIAL YEAR END)

(Amts in R'000)	1992 Jun	1991 Jun	1990 Jun	1989 Jun	1988 Jun
Ord S/H Int	1198073	1198073	1198073	572644	302026
Iss Ord Share	57600	57600	57600	28800	14400
Total Liab	63385	64925	36748	16086	11883
Current Liab	63385	64925	36748	16086	11883

Total Assets	1261458	1262998	1234821	588730	313909
Current Assets	28711	329711	619352	191987	44299
Debtors	12852	11600	9228	5681	3066
Inventory	15480	11901	5309	3520	2886
Mkt Prce(c) YE	2800	2450	2450	2300	2225

PER SHARE STATISTICS (CENTS)

Net Asst Val	2079.99	2079.99	2079.99	1988.35	2097.40

RATIOS AND OTHER INFORMATION

Mrk Cap(R000)	1612800	1411200	1411200	662400	320400
Current Ratio	0.45	5.08	16.85	11.94	3.73
Quik/Acid Tst	0.21	4.90	16.71	11.72	3.49
Debt/Ass Rat	0.05	0.05	0.03	0.03	0.04
Debt to Eqity	0.05	0.05	0.03	0.03	0.04
NAV % Mrk Pr	74.29	84.90	84.90	86.45	94.27

SUBSIDIARY & ASSOCIATED COMPANIES

None

INVESTMENTS

None

NORTHCHART INVESTMENTS LTD

ABBREVIATION : NORCHART

SECTOR : Zimbabwe Stock Exchange

SHAREHOLDERS

Who Owns Whom's Assessment of the Identity of the Ultimate Controlling Shareholder: WILLOUGHBYS CONSOLIDATED CO LTD

DIRECTORS :
JONES SC ,MUNANGATIRE HMD ,PARVIN ACL (Chairman)
RICHARDSON GA ,ROWLAND RW ,TILLET ER

REGISTERED OFFICE
Lonrho House, 96 Union Avenue
Harare, Zimbabwe

TEL: 706661
FAX: 730909

TRANSFER SECRETARY
Lonrho Zimbabwe Management Serv (Pvt)Ltd
P O Box 1480, Harare
Zimbabwe

TEL: 706661

COMPANY SECRETARY
LONRHO ZIMBABWE MANAGEMENT SERVICES

BANKERS :
Standard Chartered Bank Zimbabwe Ltd

AUDITORS :
Deloitte & Touche

FAMILIAR BRAND NAMES
N/A

CONTRIBUTION BY ACTIVITY
N/A

YEAR END : September

DIVIDEND : Ords Z$0,10

Dividend	(Ldr)20/12/91	(Pay)15/01/92	Amt(c)11
Dividend	(Ldr)12/06/92	(Pay)19/06/92	Amt(c)6

CAPITAL STRUCTURE

	AUTHORISED	ISSUED
Ords Z$0,10	15000000	9203544

FINANCIAL STATISTICS (AT FINANCIAL YEAR END)

(Amts in Z$)	1991 Sep	1990 Sep
Ord S/H Int	36643	22180
Long Trm Loans	9978	6598
Iss Ord Share	9204	9204
Total Liab	15419	11737
Current Liab	5441	5139
Total Assets	52062	33917
Current Assets	5995	4348
Debtors	1564	1721
Inventory	2025	2554
Turnover	11336	9350
Oper Profit	1054	845
Interest Paid	57	68
Tax Paid	517	504
Prf af Int&Tax	1946	1560
Prf att Ord Sh	1946	1562
Btm Line Earn	3287	1665
Dividend Paid	1381	828
Depreciation	135	95

PER SHARE STATISTICS (CENTS)

Net Asst Val	398.12	240.98
Net Earnings	21.00	17.00
Dividends	15.00	9.00
Cash Flow	22.61	17.98

RATIOS AND OTHER INFORMATION

Current Ratio	1.10	0.85
Quik/Acid Tst	0.73	0.35
A/C Rec T/ovr	7.25	5.43
Tot Ass T/ovr	0.22	0.28
Debt/Ass Rat	0.10	0.15
Debt to Eqity	0.15	0.23
Interest Cover	42.98	30.69
Oper Prof Mrg	9.30	9.04
Net Prof Marg%	17.17	16.71
Ret on Assets	4.84	6.29
Ret on Equity%	5.31	7.04
Divid Cover	1.40	1.89
Effec Tax Rate	1.78	2.19
Def Interval	0.01	0.00
Sus Grth Rate	1.54	3.31

SUBSIDIARY & ASSOCIATED COMPANIES

GREYSTONE DEVELOPMENT CO (PVT) LTD (50%)
KARIBA MINERALS LIMITED (20,4%)
NORTHERN MINERALS (ZAMBIA) LTD (30%)
SIMMS ELECTRICAL & DIESEL SERVICES (PVT)

INVESTMENTS

None

NORTHERN ENGINEERING INDUSTRIES AFRICA LTD

ABBREVIATION : NEI-AFR

JSE SHORT CODE : NEI

SECTOR : Industrial-Engineering

SHAREHOLDERS

Who Owns Whom's Assessment of the Identity of the Ultimate Controlling Shareholder:
NEI AFRICA HOLDINGS

SHAREHOLDER	PERCENTAGE 1992	1991
NEI AFRICA HLDGS P/L	53.3	53.4
SA MUTUAL	26.3	26.3
NEI OVERSEAS HOLDINGS LTD	3.0	1.1
METAL IND GROUP PENS FUND	2.7	2.7
ENGINEERING INDUSTRIES PENS FUND	2.7	2.7
FIRST NAT NOM P/L	2.0	2.4
NORTHERN ENG IND AFRICA EMPL S/P SCHEME	1.9	1.8
SAGE LIFE LTD	---	1.1
TOTAL	91.9	91.4

DIRECTORS :
ADCOCK CS ,BEAUMONT CW ,DUNLOP AL ,HARRISON T
HAWLEY R ,HYSLOP LD (Chief Executive & M.D.)
JOUBERT PG (Chairman),SIMS IJ

REGISTRATION NUMBER : 78/01240/06

REGISTERED OFFICE
2nd Floor, Ristone Office Park
15 Sherborne Road, Parktown
2193
TEL: 011-482 1460
FAX: 011-726 8143

TRANSFER SECRETARY
Mercantile Registrars Ltd
P O Box 1053, Johannesburg
2000
TEL: 011-333 8181

COMPANY SECRETARY
J R Eaglesham

NATURE OF BUSINESS
An engineering company, principally engaged in the manufacture, supply and maintenance of energy conversion & distribution equipment, and specific engineering products and services.

BANKERS :
Nedperm Bank Ltd

AUDITORS :
KPMG Aiken & Peat

FAMILIAR BRAND NAMES
ADE,AGW,APE,BELLISS & MORCOM,BYRON JACKSON
CHI,CROSSELY,CUMMINS,CUTLER HAMMER,EATON
FAIRBANKS MORSE,FLEETGUARD,FULLER,HOLEC
HOLSET,ICAL,ICAL-THORIC
INTERNATIONAL/NAVISTAR,JOHN THOMPSON,JTE
KILBER,LPG,MAHLE,MEISSNER,MITSUBISHI
MITSUBISHI DIESEL,MPS,NYK,PE,PERKINS
PIELSTIK,POWER ENGINEERS,POWERGUARD,PROBUILT
PROPOWER,REYROLLE,RITZ,ROBUSCHI,RSL,SANGUS
SHEARSTREAM,TIGERTOOTH,VALDISK,VALTEK
VALTEK VALVES

CONTRIBUTION BY ACTIVITY
N/A

YEAR END : December

DIVIDEND : Ords 50c

Interim No 24	(Ldr)31/08/90	(Pay)21/09/90	Amt(c)55
Final No 25	(Ldr)22/03/91	(Pay)12/04/91	Amt(c)110
Interim No 26	(Ldr)30/08/91	(Pay)20/09/91	Amt(c)7
Final No 27	(Ldr)16/04/92	(Pay)08/05/92	Amt(c)7

NUMBER OF EMPLOYEES : 4500

CAPITAL STRUCTURE

	AUTHORISED	ISSUED
Ords 50c	7500000	6264605
8,75% Conv Red Cum Prefs R1	810052	0

FINANCIAL STATISTICS (AT FINANCIAL YEAR END)

(Amts in R'000)	1991 Dec	1990 Dec	1989 Dec	1988 Dec	1987 Dec
Ord S/H Int	145796	125569	170557	149552	75462
Long Trm Loans	11637	6534	9514	7550	71949
Iss Ord Share	6265	6265	6265	6037	5975
Total Liab	257396	264809	229183	185096	214971
Current Liab	245759	258275	219669	177546	143022
Total Assets	403192	390378	399740	334648	290433
Current Assets	303752	311162	326071	267851	224652
Debtors	174553	137640	134961	117943	87826
Inventory	114748	137292	129809	97991	85328
Turnover	797327	712191	587010	438742	391763
Oper Profit	36448	31001	69095	57274	48629
Interest Paid	39750	29536	18304	6776	7947
Tax Paid	7166	19455	27468	18974	13902
Prf af Int&Tax	177	-4082	32164	31524	26780
Prf att Ord Sh	-1877	-4270	31957	31524	15053
Btm Line Earn	-1877	-6487	29957	26410	15053
Dividend Paid	878	10336	13093	12608	6014
Mkt Prce(c) YE	1300	1800	3400	3500	1475
Depreciation	7710	7527	6480	5784	-

PER SHARE STATISTICS (CENTS)

Net Asst Val	2327.15	2004.29	2722.38	2477.26	1262.96
Net Earnings	-29.90	-68.20	519.70	527.60	450.30
Dividends	14.00	165.00	211.00	211.00	180.00
Cash Flow	215.80	-38.10	555.04	592.37	239.28

RATIOS AND OTHER INFORMATION

Mrk Cap(R000)	81445	112770	213010	211295	88131
Current Ratio	1.24	1.20	1.48	1.51	1.57
Quik/Acid Tst	0.77	0.67	0.89	0.96	0.97
A/C Rec T/ovr	4.57	5.17	4.35	3.72	4.46
Tot Ass T/ovr	1.98	1.82	1.47	1.31	1.35
Debt/Ass Rat	0.62	0.67	0.56	0.55	0.51

L T L Tot Ass	0.01	0.01	0.01	0.02	0.02
Debt to Eqity	1.71	2.08	1.31	1.22	1.97
Interest Cover	0.92	1.05	3.77	8.45	6.12
Oper Prof Mrg	4.57	4.35	11.77	13.05	12.41
Net Prof Marg%	-0.24	-0.60	5.44	7.19	3.84
Ret on Assets	11.68	11.50	19.50	17.11	16.74
Ret on Equity%	-1.29	-3.40	18.74	21.08	19.95
Price/Earnings	-43.48	-26.39	6.54	6.63	3.28
Divid Cover	-2.14	-0.41	2.46	2.50	2.50
Divid Yield	1.08	9.17	6.21	6.03	12.20
Earning Yield%	-2.30	-3.79	15.29	15.07	30.53
NAV % Mrk Pr	179.01	111.35	80.07	70.78	85.62
Effec Tax Rate	29.58	162.52	53.28	41.36	36.27
Def Interval	13.03	-66.48	0.12	0.14	0.42
Sus Grth Rate	-1.89	-11.63	11.06	12.65	11.98

SUBSIDIARY & ASSOCIATED COMPANIES

A G WALKER (PTY) LTD
ALLEN-GWYNNES SA (PTY) LTD
ANODIZING INDUSTRIES (PTY) LTD
APE AFRICA (PTY) LTD
BELLISS & MORCOM SA (PTY) LTD
BUSHING CO (SA) (PTY) LTD, THE
C A PARSONS & CO (SA) (PTY) LTD
CHI CONTROL ANSTALT (PTY) LTD (LICHTENST
CHI CONTROL BABELEGI (PTY) LTD
CHI CONTROL LTD
CHI PROPERTIES (PTY) LTD
CHI PROPERTIES (PVT) LTD
COMBUSTION PROPERTIES (PTY) LTD
CUMMINS DIESEL (S.A.) (PTY) LTD
EDORAL PROPERTIES (PTY) LTD
FIVE ONE SEVEN PROP STREET (PTY) LTD
H G MEISSNER & CO (PTY) LTD
ICAL NAMIBIA (PTY) LTD
ICAL OFFSHORE (PTY) LTD
ICAL ONSHORE PROPERTIES (PTY) LTD
ICAL PETROCHEM (PTY) LTD (50%)
ICAL PROPERTIES (PTY) LTD
INTERNATIONAL COMBUSTION (BOTSWANA) (PTY
INTERNATIONAL COMBUSTION AFRICA LTD
INTERNATIONAL COMBUSTION ENGINEERING (PT
INTERNATIONAL CRANES AND ERECTION (PTY)
JOHN THOMPSON AFRICA (PTY) LTD
KENNICOTT (SA) (PTY) LTD
KILBER AUTOMOTIVE PRODUCTS (PTY) LTD
KILBER MARKETING (PTY) LTD
MASSLIFT AFRICA (PTY) LTD
NEI AFRICA OPERATIONS LTD
NEI AFRICA PROPERTIES (PTY) LTD
NEI INVESTMENTS (PVT) LTD
PARSONS PEEBLES (SA) (PTY) LTD
POWER ENGINEERS (PTY) LTD
POWERGUARD (1986) (PTY) LTD
PROBUILT DIESEL LTD
PROPOWER (NAMIBIA) (PTY) LTD
PROPOWER (PTY) LTD
PROPOWER DIESEL LTD
REYROLLE SWITCHGEAR LTD
SANGUS INDUSTRIAL DEVELOPMENT CO. (PTY)
SPECIALISED POWER SYSTEMS (1987) (PTY) L
STEAM & VALVE SPECIALISTS (PTY) LTD
TAYCUM PROPERTIES LTD
TURMEI INVESTMENTS (PTY) LTD

INVESTMENTS

None

NORVIC MANUFACTURING COMPANY LTD

ABBREVIATION : NORVIC

JSE SHORT CODE : NVC

SECTOR : Development Capital Market

SHAREHOLDERS

Who Owns Whom's Assessment of the Identity of the Ultimate Controlling Shareholder: A KREOUZIS

SHAREHOLDER	PERCENTAGE 1992	1991
MCGRATH M J	83.1	---
SHARESTOCK NOM P/L	11.4	67.9
WILSON J I M	---	1.8
STAN GLOBAL INV CC	---	2.0
TOTAL	94.5	71.6

DIRECTORS :
HUGH D ,KREOUZIS A (Chairman & Managing Dir.)
NEL G ,PRICE SA ,WILSON L

REGISTRATION NUMBER : 89/03862/06

REGISTERED OFFICE
Cnr Dan Jacobs & Arnold Sts, Alrode
Alberton
1450
TEL: 011-864 2866
FAX: 011-908 4827

TRANSFER SECRETARY
Gold Equity Registrars (Pty) Ltd
P O Box 62185, Marshalltown
2107
TEL: 011-834 5623

COMPANY SECRETARY
A Kreouzis

NATURE OF BUSINESS
The business of the company is the planning, design, manufacture and installation of retail shelving, cash-out counters, merchandising display units, turnstiles, shopping baskets, trolleys and pulpits.

BANKERS :
Standard Bank of SA Ltd, Nedperm Bank Ltd

AUDITORS :
Ernst & Young

FAMILIAR BRAND NAMES
N/A

CONTRIBUTION BY ACTIVITY
N/A

YEAR END : June

DIVIDEND :15/12/91

CAPITAL STRUCTURE

	AUTHORISED	ISSUED
Ords 0.1c	20000000	14223000

FINANCIAL STATISTICS (AT FINANCIAL YEAR END)

(Amts in R'000)	1991 Jun	1990 Jun
Ord S/H Int	519	4265
Long Trm Loans	199	269
Iss Ord Share	14223	14223
Total Liab	3791	2012
Current Liab	3592	1743
Total Assets	4310	6277
Current Assets	2512	3946
Debtors	330	1535
Inventory	2180	2393
Turnover	12546	11699
Oper Profit	-3197	-592
Interest Paid	199	99
Prf af Int&Tax	-3396	-590
Prf att Ord Sh	-3396	-590
Btm Line Earn	-3746	-288
Mkt Prce(c) YE	10	11
Depreciation	510	471

PER SHARE STATISTICS (CENTS)

Net Asst Val	3.65	29.99
Net Earnings	-23.90	-4.30
Cash Flow	-20.29	-0.95

RATIOS AND OTHER INFORMATION

Mrk Cap(R000)	1422	1565
Current Ratio	0.70	2.26
Quik/Acid Tst	0.09	0.89
A/C Rec T/ovr	38.02	8.31
Tot Ass T/ovr	2.91	2.03
Debt/Ass Rat	0.88	0.32
L T L Tot Ass	0.05	0.04
Debt to Eqity	7.30	0.47
Interest Cover	-16.07	-5.98
Oper Prof Mrg	-25.48	-5.06
Net Prof Marg%	-27.07	-5.04
Ret on Assets	-74.18	-8.53
Ret on Equity%	-654.34	-15.09
Price/Earnings	-0.42	-2.56
Earning Yield%	-239.00	-39.09
NAV % Mrk Pr	36.49	272.61
Def Interval	-0.57	-8.57
Sus Grth Rate	-654.34	-13.83

SUBSIDIARY & ASSOCIATED COMPANIES

None

INVESTMENTS

None

NU-WORLD HOLDINGS LTD

ABBREVIATION : NUWORLD

JSE SHORT CODE : NWL

SECTOR : Industrial-Electronics, Electrical & Bat

SHAREHOLDERS

Who Owns Whom's Assessment of the Identity of the Ultimate Controlling Shareholder: DIRECTORS

SHAREHOLDER	PERCENTAGE 1992	1991
GOLDBERG J A	29.8	29.8
GOLDBERG M S	29.8	29.8
HARRY GOLDBERG WILL TRUST	20.9	20.9
G VAN E DU PLESSIS INV P/L	10.8	---
SMK NOM P/L	3.0	7.0
SAGE LIFE LTD	---	6.5
TOTAL	94.3	93.9

DIRECTORS :
GOLDBERG JA ,GOLDBERG MS (Managing Director)
JUDIN JM ,TEMPLE JA DR (Chairman

REGISTRATION NUMBER : 68/02490/06

REGISTERED OFFICE
721 3rd Street, Wynberg
Sandton
2199
TEL: 011-786 2855

TRANSFER SECRETARY
Central Registrars Ltd
P O Box 4844, Johannesburg
2000
TEL: 011-331 0051

COMPANY SECRETARY
A H Lipchin

NATURE OF BUSINESS
The company manufactures small domestic electrical appliances and wiring accessories, and distributes a range of telephone extension cords.

BANKERS :
First National Bank of SA Ltd

AUDITORS :
Sandberg & Partners

FAMILIAR BRAND NAMES
IDEAL,NWI

CONTRIBUTION BY ACTIVITY
N/A

YEAR END : August

DIVIDEND : Ords 1c

Dividend No 3	(Ldr)30/11/90	(Pay)12/12/90	Amt(c)4.3
Dividend No 4	(Ldr)06/12/91	(Pay)12/12/91	Amt(c)2.6
Dividend No 5	(Ldr)11/12/92	(Pay)18/12/92	Amt(c)3

NUMBER OF EMPLOYEES : 800

CAPITAL STRUCTURE

	AUTHORISED	ISSUED
Ords 1c	20000000	12750000

FINANCIAL STATISTICS (AT FINANCIAL YEAR END)

(Amts in R'000)	1991	1990	1989	1988	1987

	Aug	Aug	Aug	Aug	
Ord S/H Int	7444	6300	6965	5391	2616
Long Trm Loans	5894	4091	1839	402	2511
Iss Ord Share	12750	12750	12750	12750	820
Total Liab	14373	12653	10397	4275	5022
Current Liab	8479	8562	8558	3873	2511
Total Assets	21817	18953	15474	7778	10054
Intang Assets	*	*	1888	1888	*
Current Assets	17783	16242	13251	7305	4927
Debtors	7395	8300	6544	3965	-
Inventory	8681	6500	6413	3050	4927
Turnover	40346	35098	25701	19006	12068
Oper Profit	3260	3169	3521	2943	1576
Interest Paid	1368	1017	598	138	18
Tax Paid	441	399	801	978	775
Prf af Int&Tax	1470	1771	2122	1827	783
Prf att Ord Sh	1470	1771	2122	1827	783
Btm Line Earn	1470	1771	2122	1827	783
Dividend Paid	326	548	548	548	-
Mkt Prce(c) YE	40	50	65	70	-
Depreciation	557	383	144	54	-

PER SHARE STATISTICS (CENTS)

Net Asst Val	58.38	49.41	39.82	27.47	319.02
Net Earnings	11.50	13.90	16.60	14.30	-
Dividends	2.60	4.30	4.30	4.30	-
Cash Flow	15.90	17.39	17.77	15.00	190.98

RATIOS AND OTHER INFORMATION

Mrk Cap(R000)	5100	6375	8288	8925	-
Current Ratio	2.10	1.90	1.55	1.89	1.96
Quik/Acid Tst	1.07	1.14	0.80	1.10	-
A/C Rec T/ovr	5.46	4.23	3.93	4.79	-
Tot Ass T/ovr	1.85	1.85	1.66	2.44	2.40
Debt/Ass Rat	0.65	0.66	0.67	0.55	0.50
L T L Tot Ass	0.27	0.21	0.12	0.05	0.25
Debt to Eqity	1.92	1.99	1.49	0.79	1.92
Interest Cover	2.38	3.12	5.89	21.33	87.56
Oper Prof Mrg	8.08	9.03	13.70	15.48	13.06
Net Prof Marg%	3.64	5.05	8.26	9.61	6.49
Ret on Assets	15.03	16.82	22.75	37.84	31.35
Ret on Equity%	19.75	28.11	30.47	33.89	59.86
Price/Earnings	3.48	3.60	3.92	4.90	-
Divid Cover	4.42	3.23	3.86	3.33	-
Divid Yield	6.50	8.60	6.62	6.14	-
Earning Yield%	28.75	27.80	25.54	20.43	-
NAV % Mrk Pr	145.96	98.82	61.26	39.25	-
Effec Tax Rate	23.08	15.48	0.03	11.48	49.74
Def Interval	4.10	2.59	2.13	0.45	6.41
Sus Grth Rate	15.37	19.41	22.60	23.72	29.93

SUBSIDIARY & ASSOCIATED COMPANIES

NU-WORLD INDUSTRIES (PTY) LTD

INVESTMENTS

None

OAKFIELDS THOROUGHBREDS LTD

ABBREVIATION : OAKFLDS

JSE SHORT CODE : OKF

SECTOR : Industrial-Beverages & Hotels

SHAREHOLDERS

Who Owns Whom's Assessment of the Identity of the Ultimate Controlling Shareholder:
SA MUTUAL VIA SYFRETS/UAL

SHAREHOLDER	PERCENTAGE 1992	1991
SYFRETS TRUST LTD	31.5	25.6
UAL MERCHANT BANK LTD	12.0	12.0
UAL NOM P/L	11.1	11.1
SYFRETS NOM LTD	9.5	3.6
BRIDGMAN J H M	5.9	—
GARDINER FAMILY HOLDINGS P/L	5.7	—
CMB NOM P/L	3.3	—
TOP DOG NOM P/L	2.9	8.8
LEVIN H R	2.1	—
NAT TURF INV LTD	1.7	—
FAIRLAWN P/L	1.5	—
SIMMONSCO NOM P/L	1.0	1.0
GIRD G C	—	13.5
NAL P/L	—	1.1
EDIMED P/L	—	2.6
NAUDE D F	—	5.2
TOTAL	88.2	84.5

DIRECTORS :
FARRUGIA JC (Financial Director),GARDINER AJF
LEVIN HR ,ROBINSON BB (Chairman

REGISTRATION NUMBER : 83/13789/06

REGISTERED OFFICE
3rd Floor, First National Bank Building
Heerengracht, Cape Town
8001
TEL: 021-217 238
FAX: 021-419 2814

TRANSFER SECRETARY
Union Provident Trust SA Ltd
P O Box 2322, Johannesburg
2000
TEL: 011-833 6700

COMPANY SECRETARY
J C Farrugia

NATURE OF BUSINESS
The breeding of thoroughbred horses for sale as yearlings and marketing of stallion shares and services.

BANKERS :
Standard Bank of SA Ltd

AUDITORS :
Ernst & Young

FAMILIAR BRAND NAMES
N/A

CONTRIBUTION BY ACTIVITY
N/A

YEAR END : July

DIVIDEND :15/01/92 and 15/07/91

OCEAN DIAMOND MINING HOLDINGS LTD

ABBREVIATION : ODMHOLD

JSE SHORT CODE : ODM

SECTOR : Mining-Exploration

SHAREHOLDERS

Who Owns Whom's Assessment of the Identity of the Ultimate Controlling Shareholder: MINORITIES

SHAREHOLDER	PERCENTAGE 1992	1991
MODUS CORP P/L	---	1 5
UNIDEV ELECTRONIC HOLDINGS LTD	---	23 5
CORTECH ELECTRONICS LTD	- -	66 9
TOTAL	---	91 9

DIRECTORS :
HOOGENHOUT DM ,KNOETZE FW
LOUW AC (Managing Director)
PRINSEP IRM (Chairman

REGISTRATION NUMBER : 79/03303/06

REGISTERED OFFICE
2nd Floor, 129 Beach Road
Mouille Point, Cape Town
8001
TEL 021-439 9635
FAX 021-439 9935

TRANSFER SECRETARY
Mercantile Registrars Ltd
P O Box 1053, Johannesburg
2000
TEL 011-333 8181

COMPANY SECRETARY
J W Consul

NATURE OF BUSINESS
The company's subsidiaries are engaged in the exploration for, and mining of, marine diamonds off the west coasts of South Africa and Namibia.

BANKERS :
First National Bank of SA Ltd
UAL Merchant Bank Ltd

AUDITORS :
Touche Ross & Co

FAMILIAR BRAND NAMES
N/A

CONTRIBUTION BY ACTIVITY
N/A

YEAR END : March

DIVIDEND :15/03/91

NUMBER OF EMPLOYEES : 140

CAPITAL STRUCTURE

	AUTHORISED	ISSUED
Ords 10c	45000000	17000000
9% Cum Red Prefs 10c	1500000	500000
12% Cum Red Prefs 10c	1000000	1000000

FINANCIAL STATISTICS (AT FINANCIAL YEAR END)

(Amts in R'000)	1991 Jul	1990 Jul	1989 Feb	1988
Ord S/H Int	7138	11541	10571	8683
Long Trm Loans	1594	2000	2500	400
Iss Ord Share	17000	17000	16000	10010
Total Liab	1822	2322	4370	800
Current Liab	228	322	1870	400
Total Assets	8960	13863	14941	11801
Current Assets	6398	4491	5269	2718
Debtors	5751	1959	2336	-
Inventory	218	1845	2136	2718
Turnover	12171	7006	5924	7164
Oper Profit	-3814	1340	3243	-
Interest Paid	362	66	-	201
Tax Paid	94	-	-	-
Prf af Int&Tax	-4188	1335	3362	-
Prf att Ord Sh	-4394	977	3308	2461
Btm Line Earn	-4394	977	3308	2461
Dividend Paid	-	-	800	-
Mkt Prce(c) YE	35	45	70	-

PER SHARE STATISTICS (CENTS)

Net Asst Val	41 99	67 89	66 07	86 74
Net Earnings	-25 90	5 80	-	-
Cash Flow	-25 29	4 06	20 68	-

RATIOS AND OTHER INFORMATION

Mrk Cap(R000)	5950	7650	11200	-
Current Ratio	28 06	13 95	2 82	6 80
Quik/Acid Tst	27 11	8 22	1 68	-
A/C Rec T/ovr	2 12	2 52	2 54	
Tot Ass T/ovr	1 36	0 36	0 40	0 61
Debt/Ass Rat	0 03	0 02	0 13	0 07
L T L Tot Ass	-	-	-	0 03
Debt to Eqity	0 03	0 03	0 18	0 09
Interest Cover	-10 52	20 48		1 00
Oper Prof Mrg	-31 34	19 13	54 74	-
Net Prof Marg%	-36 10	13 95	55 84	34 35
Ret on Assets	-41 65	7 13	22 50	1 70
Ret on Equity%	-61 56	5 98	31 29	28 34
Price/Earnings	-1 35	7 76	-	-
Earning Yield%	-74 00	12 89	-	-
NAV % Mrk Pr	119 97	150 86	94 38	-
Def Interval	-0 35	1 48	0 76	-
Sus Grth Rate	-61 56	8 47	23 73	28 34

SUBSIDIARY & ASSOCIATED COMPANIES

None

INVESTMENTS

None

CAPITAL STRUCTURE

	AUTHORISED	ISSUED
Ords 1c	40000000	20551830
6% Non Cum Conv Prefs 1c	4000000	3626794

FINANCIAL STATISTICS (AT FINANCIAL YEAR END)

(Amts in R'000)	1992 Mar	1990 Dec	1989 Dec	1988 Dec	1987 Dec
Ord S/H Int	5584	918	6769	8440	8459
Long Trm Loans	37	-	-	211	107
Iss Ord Share	20552	13450	13450	13450	13450
Total Liab	2359	4	2	9035	3796
Current Liab	2322	4	2	8824	3689
Total Assets	7943	922	6771	17475	12255
Current Assets	2752	-	10	14591	10385
Debtors	1667	-	10	7482	4055
Inventory	-	-	-	7102	4066
Turnover	739	-	-	27722	12377
Oper Profit	-19	-9	-15	35	1202
Interest Paid	45	-	-	47	47
Tax Paid	-	-	-	7	261
Prf af Int&Tax	-26	-9	-15	-19	894
Prf att Ord Sh	-26	-9	-15	-19	894
Btm Line Earn	5519	-5851	-796	-19	894
Mkt Prce(c) YE	200	4	18	50	100
Depreciation	116	-	388	388	107

PER SHARE STATISTICS (CENTS)

Net Asst Val	27.17	6.83	50.33	62.75	62.89
Net Earnings	-0.13	-	-24.90	-0.14	7.80
Cash Flow	0.35	-0.07	2.77	2.69	17.36

RATIOS AND OTHER INFORMATION

Mrk Cap(R000)	41104	538	2421	6725	13450
Current Ratio	1.19	-	5.00	1.65	2.82
Quik/Acid Tst	1.19	-	5.00	0.85	1.71
A/C Rec T/ovr	0.35	-	-	3.71	6.10
Tot Ass T/ovr	0.07	-	-	1.59	2.02
Debt/Ass Rat	0.29	0.00	0.00	0.52	0.31
L T L Tot Ass	0.00	-	-	0.01	0.01
Debt to Eqity	0.42	0.00	0.00	1.07	0.45
Interest Cover	-0.42	-	-	0.74	25.57
Oper Prof Mrg	-2.57	-	-	0.13	9.71
Net Prof Marg%	-3.52	-	-	-0.07	7.22
Ret on Assets	0.19	-0.98	-0.22	0.20	19.62
Ret on Equity%	-0.37	-0.98	-0.22	-0.23	21.14
Price/Earnings	-1538.46	-	-0.72	-357.14	12.82
Earning Yield%	-0.07	-	-138.33	-0.28	7.80
NAV % Mrk Pr	13.59	170.63	279.60	125.50	62.89
Effec Tax Rate	-	-	-	-58.33	-
Def Interval	15.25	-	-	3.91	0.21
Sus Grth Rate	-0.47	-0.98	-0.22	-0.23	10.57

SUBSIDIARY & ASSOCIATED COMPANIES

INSHORE DIAMOND MINING LTD
OCEAN DIAMOND MINING 14C (PTY) LTD
OCEAN DIAMOND MINING 6C (PTY) LTD
OCEAN DIAMOND MINING OF NAMIBIA (PTY) LT
OCEAN DIAMOND MINING SOUTHERN AFRICA LTD

INVESTMENTS

None

OCEANA FISHING GROUP LTD

ABBREVIATION : OCFISH

JSE SHORT CODE : OCF

SECTOR : Industrial-Fishing

SHAREHOLDERS

Who Owns Whom's Assessment of the Identity of the Ultimate Controlling Shareholder: SA MUTUAL VIA BARLOWS VIA TIG OATS

SHAREHOLDER	PERCENTAGE 1992	1991
TIGER OATS LTD	69.4	70.1
SMALL BUSNESS DEVELOPMENT CORP LTD	7.8	7.9
BLUE STAR HLDGS P/L	3.9	4.0
CMB NOM P/L	3.0	—
WORKMENS COMPENS COMMISSIONER IN TRUST	2.4	—
EIGHTY ONE MAIN STREET NOM LTD	—	2.4
SANLAM	—	3.0
TOTAL	86.5	87.4

DIRECTORS :
BEHRENS DF (Managing Director),BESSELING J
CLEWLOW WAM ,CONRADIE LH ,DYER DW ,KRAMER RM
LATSKY TE ,LEWIS WA (Executive Chairman)
NICOL RG ,PENTZ MJ ,PICK S ,POTGIETER MG
VAN DER MERWE PL ,VAN RENSBURG A ,VISAGIE AWS
WILLIAMS RA

REGISTRATION NUMBER : 04/01730/06

REGISTERED OFFICE
Oceana House, 20 Lower Burg Street
Cape Town
8001
TEL: 021-25 3180
FAX: 021-25 2413

TRANSFER SECRETARY
Rand Registrars Ltd
P O Box 82549, Southdale
2135
TEL: 011-835 1016

COMPANY SECRETARY
J D Cole

NATURE OF BUSINESS
The principal activities of the company and its subsidiaries are the catching and processing of pelagic fish into fish meal, fish oil, & canned fish; the catching & processing of rock lobster, provision of commercial cold storage facilities, trading in sundry fish products and provision of shipping, clearing and forwarding services. The group also carries on the business of investing funds surplus to its immediate requirements.

BANKERS :
Standard Bank of SA Ltd
First National Bank of SA Ltd

AUDITORS :
Deloitte Pim Goldby

FAMILIAR BRAND NAMES
BLUE CONTINENT,BRESSAY BANK RESTAURAN,DIVER
GOLD DEER,GOLD SHIP,HAPPY PET
LAUGHING LOBSTER,LIGHTHOUSE,SALDANHA
SNOEKIES FISH SHOP

CONTRIBUTION BY ACTIVITY
Fishing (% of Turnover) (40.7%)
Cold Storage (10.4%)
Trading & Shipping (48.9%)
Investment Income (14.0%)

YEAR END : September

DIVIDEND :Ords 1c

Interim No 93	(Ldr)08/06/90	(Pay)06/07/90	Amt(c)30
Final No 94	(Ldr)14/12/90	(Pay)04/01/91	Amt(c)60
Interim No 95	(Ldr)07/06/91	(Pay)05/07/91	Amt(c)25
Final No 96	(Ldr)13/12/91	(Pay)03/01/92	Amt(c)65
Interim No 97	(Ldr)05/06/92	(Pay)03/07/92	Amt(c)30
Final No 98	(Ldr)11/12/92	(Pay)05/01/92	Amt(c)90

NUMBER OF EMPLOYEES : 1400

CAPITAL STRUCTURE

	AUTHORISED	ISSUED
Ords 1c	12000000	9468090

FINANCIAL STATISTICS (AT FINANCIAL YEAR END)

(Amts in R'000)	1992 Sep	1991 Sep	1990 Sep	1989 Sep	1988 Sep
Ord S/H Int	94224	83736	72952	67775	57443
Long Trm Loans	16723	13799	2686	5094	5904
Iss Ord Share	9468	9392	9335	9276	9116
Total Liab	113319	85278	67095	79418	68629
Current Liab	96596	71479	64409	74324	62725
Total Assets	207543	169014	140047	147193	126072
Current Assets	143017	116207	93319	101154	89002
Debtors	47819	56164	50305	34899	31515
Inventory	50711	46945	32595	36074	29277
Turnover	375433	325889	309018	275004	226875
Oper Profit	36282	21172	22746	34704	48175
Interest Paid	849	1334	1706	332	-
Tax Paid	22607	10451	12230	18486	20717
Prf af Int&Tax	19464	14172	14277	30003	27458
Prf att Ord Sh	18186	13380	13315	24024	22758
Btm Line Earn	20842	14052	11766	24856	24370
Dividend Paid	11374	8476	8450	14914	20483
Mkt Prce(c) YE	1660	1400	1375	2525	1625
Depreciation	11597	10689	8726	6658	5009

PER SHARE STATISTICS (CENTS)

Net Asst Val	995.18	891.57	781.49	730.65	630.13
Net Earnings	192.80	142.80	142.90	260.70	250.20
Dividends	120.00	90.00	90.00	160.00	150.00
Cash Flow	306.66	243.53	229.60	354.30	284.89

RATIOS AND OTHER INFORMATION

Mrk Cap(R000)	157169	131488	128356	234219	148135
Current Ratio	1.48	1.63	1.45	1.36	1.42
Quik/Acid Tst	0.96	0.97	0.94	0.88	0.95
A/C Rec T/ovr	7.85	5.80	6.14	7.88	7.20
Tot Ass T/ovr	1.81	1.93	2.21	1.87	1.80
Debt/Ass Rat	0.51	0.46	0.46	0.51	0.50
L T L Tot Ass	0.05	0.04	0.00	0.00	0.01
Debt to Eqity	1.13	0.94	0.89	1.10	1.10
Interest Cover	43.55	16.73	14.17	132.53	-
Oper Prof Mrg	9.66	6.50	7.36	12.62	21.23
Net Prof Marg%	4.84	4.11	4.31	8.74	10.03
Ret on Assets	20.73	15.44	20.53	31.50	38.21
Ret on Equity%	19.30	15.98	18.25	35.45	39.62
Price/Earnings	8.61	9.80	9.62	9.69	6.49
Divid Cover	1.61	1.59	1.59	1.63	1.67
Divid Yield	7.23	6.43	6.55	6.34	9.23
Earning Yield%	11.61	10.20	10.39	10.32	15.40
NAV % Mrk Pr	59.95	63.68	56.84	28.94	38.78
Effec Tax Rate	57.21	52.32	49.96	51.70	48.12
Def Interval	-	0.00	0.03	0.04	0.03
Sus Grth Rate	7.23	5.86	6.67	13.44	3.96

SUBSIDIARY & ASSOCIATED COMPANIES

AFRICAN COLD STORAGE (PTY) LTD
AFRICAN FISH CANNING CO. LTD
ATLANTIC OCEAN HOLDINGS (PTY) LTD (25,5%)
BLUE CONTINENT COLD STORAGE CO. (PTY) LT
BLUE CONTINENT PRODUCTS (PTY) LTD
CALAMARI DISTRIBUTORS (PTY) LTD (50%)
COAST TRADING CO. (PTY) LTD
COMMERCIAL COLD STORAGE LTD
DUNCAN DOCK COLD STORAGE (PTY) LTD (42%)
EPPING COLD STORAGE (PTY) LTD
HICKSONS CANNING CO LTD
HOUT BAY SMOKERIES (PTY) LTD
LAMBERTS BAY CANNING CO. LTD
LM KNIGHT (PRETORIA) (PTY) LTD
MAYDON WHARF COLD STORAGE (PTY) LTD
NAMAQUA CANNING CO. LTD
OCEAN QUEEN (PTY) LTD
OCEANA FISHING DIVISION (PTY) LTD
SA SEA MERCHANTS (PTY) LTD
SA SEA PRODUCTS LTD
SALBURG (PTY) LTD
SANDY POINT CANNING CO. LTD
ST. HELENA BAY FISHING INDUSTRIES LTD
STEPHAN ROCK LOBSTER PACKERS LTD
THE NORTH BAY CANNING CO LTD
TRT SHIPPING SERVICES (PTY) LTD
TUNA MARINE (PTY) LTD

INVESTMENTS

ORANJERIVIER VISSERYE BPK (13,3%)

OCEANA INVESTMENT CORPORATION PLC

ABBREVIATION : OCEANA

JSE SHORT CODE : ODV

SECTOR : Industrial-Retailers & Wholesalers

SHAREHOLDERS

Who Owns Whom's Assessment of the Identity of the Ultimate Controlling Shareholder:
LEWIS FAMILY

SHAREHOLDER	PERCENTAGE 1992	1991
FOSCHINI LTD	41.8	40.2
SA MUTUAL	19.8	19.0
CMB NOM P/L	8.2	---

SOUTHERN LIFE ASSOC LTD	7.6	7.4
AECI PENS FUND	4.9	4.7
STANLEY & ZEA LEWIS HOLDINGS LTD	2.8	---
SLAM NOM P/L	2.6	2.5
TROY NOM P/L	2.0	1.9
PROTEA ASSURE CO LTD	1.3	---
UAL NOM P/L	1.0	---
UAL MERCHANT BANK LTD	---	1.2
ANGLO AMERICAN GROUP PENS FUND	---	1.6
DAWN GLOW INV P/L	---	2.0
SANLAM	---	7.9
TRAVPART INV P/L	---	4.3
TOTAL	92.0	92.7

DIRECTORS :
DAVIES RSP (Deputy Chairman),LEWIS M
LEWIS S (Chairman),LOCH DAVIS DJ

REGISTRATION NUMBER : 36515 (Engla

REGISTERED OFFICE
Park Lorne, 111 Park Road
London NW8 7JL

TEL: 094471-7237313
FAX: 094471-7230479

TRANSFER SECRETARY
Mercantile Registrars Ltd
P O Box 1053, Johannesburg
2000
TEL: 011-333 8181

COMPANY SECRETARY
D L Shore

NATURE OF BUSINESS
An investment holding co with investments in an international portfolio of shares and bonds. Mineral rights are held in the Heidelberg, Middelburg, Zoutpansberg, Schweizer-Reneke and Letaba districts.

BANKERS :
Bank of Scotland

AUDITORS :
Touche Ross & Co

FAMILIAR BRAND NAMES
HANDBAGS INTERNATIONAL

CONTRIBUTION BY ACTIVITY
N/A

YEAR END : March

DIVIDEND :Ords 25p

Final	(Ldr)02/08/90	(Pay)11/09/90	Amt(c)7.5
Interim	(Ldr)03/01/92	(Pay)17/01/92	Amt(c)1.5
Final	(Ldr)17/07/92	(Pay)01/10/92	Amt(c)9.5
Interim	(Ldr)11/12/92	(Pay)25/01/93	Amt(c)1.5

NUMBER OF EMPLOYEES : 5

CAPITAL STRUCTURE

	AUTHORISED	ISSUED
Ords 25p	28000000	20382028

FINANCIAL STATISTICS (AT FINANCIAL YEAR END)

(Amts in PS)	1992 Mar	1991 Mar	1990 Mar	1989 Mar	1988 Mar
Ord S/H Int	43197	14643	15794	13127	12931
Long Trm Loans	10	46	1	24	16
Iss Ord Share	20382	5995	5389	5273	5273
Total Liab	6579	2209	559	4081	347
Current Liab	6569	2163	558	4057	331
Total Assets	49776	16852	16353	17208	13278
Current Assets	17316	5425	6761	5240	3487
Debtors	1770	766	130	507	375
Oper Profit	-875	-384	501	-142	370
Interest Paid	454	465	274	59	36
Tax Paid	1747	365	403	162	100
Prf af Int&Tax	-1527	362	620	467	234
Prf att Ord Sh	3848	1097	620	467	234
Btm Line Earn	3848	1097	608	411	234
Dividend Paid	2242	659	439	290	116
Mkt Prce(c) YE	1750	1800	1700	1575	250
Depreciation	57	37	8	-	-

PER SHARE STATISTICS (CENTS)

Net Asst Val	211.94	244.25	293.08	248.95	245.23
Net Earnings	25.00	18.60	11.50	8.86	4.43
Dividends	11.00	11.00	7.50	5.50	2.20
Cash Flow	-10.53	9.75	9.58	8.84	5.48

RATIOS AND OTHER INFORMATION

Mrk Cap(R000)	356685	107910	91613	83050	13183
Current Ratio	2.64	2.51	12.12	1.29	10.53
Quik/Acid Tst	2.64	2.51	12.12	1.29	10.53
Debt/Ass Rat	0.13	0.13	0.03	0.24	0.02
Debt to Eqity	0.15	0.15	0.04	0.31	0.03
Interest Cover	-1.89	-0.70	2.40	-0.61	10.28
Ret on Assets	12.15	11.43	7.93	4.00	2.79
Ret on Equity%	8.91	7.49	3.93	3.56	1.81
Price/Earnings	70.00	96.77	147.83	177.77	56.43
Divid Cover	2.27	1.69	1.53	1.61	2.01
Divid Yield	0.63	0.61	0.44	0.35	0.88
Earning Yield%	1.43	1.03	0.68	0.56	1.77
NAV % Mrk Pr	12.11	13.57	17.24	15.81	98.09
Effec Tax Rate	82.76	-	30.45	26.96	13.47
Def Interval	-2.39	-	-	-	-
Sus Grth Rate	3.72	2.99	1.15	1.35	0.91

SUBSIDIARY & ASSOCIATED COMPANIES

ETAM PLC (UK) (34,4%)
GIOMA GROUP BV (HOLLAND) (50%)
HANDBAGS INTERNATIONAL (PTY) LTD (48.2%)

INVESTMENTS

TRANSATLANTIC HOLDINGS LTD (85000S)

OCTODEC INVESTMENTS LTD

ABBREVIATION : OCTODEC

JSE SHORT CODE : OCT

SECTOR : Financial-Property Loan Stock

SHAREHOLDERS

Who Owns Whom's Assessment of the Identity of the Ultimate Controlling Shareholder:
DIRECTORS

SHAREHOLDER	PERCENTAGE 1992	1991
ACCORD HOLDINGS P/L	---	3.6
ALTRON GROUP PENS FUND	---	2.1
EIGHTY ONE MAIN STREET NOM LTD	---	5.6
FIRST NAT NOM P/L	---	1.3
HEVANS HOLDINGS P/L	---	2.8
HEYNS J A J	---	1.8
LIBERTY LIFE ASSOC OF AFRICA LTD	---	9.9
NEDBANK NOM LTD	---	1.1
NEDPERM BANK LTD	---	8.5
STD BANK NOM TVL P/L	---	5.6
KRAMER SHARON FAMILY TRUST	---	6.3
OCTOGROWTH CC	---	1.1
OCTOGROWTH TWO CC	---	1.1
POLLACK MYRON INV CC	---	1.0
WAPNICK JEFFREY FAMILY TRUST	---	6.3
WAPNICK LISA FAMILY TRUST	---	6.3
POLLACK JOSEPH INV CC	---	2.4
SCHOEPAUL P/L	---	8.8
TOTAL	---	75.5

DIRECTORS :
HOLMES MJ ,POLLACK J ,VAN AARDT SM
VAN DER MERWE-VANCE A ,VAN DER WESTHUIZEN AL
WAPNICK A (Chairman & Managing Dir.

REGISTRATION NUMBER : 56/02868/06

REGISTERED OFFICE
City Property Administration, 373 Proes Street
Pretoria
0002
TEL: 012-326 8811
FAX: 012-325 5027

TRANSFER SECRETARY
Investment Registrars (Pty) Ltd
P O Box 9167, Johannesburg
2000
TEL: 011-725 6004

COMPANY SECRETARY
City Property Administration (Pty) Ltd

NATURE OF BUSINESS
A property loan stock company.

BANKERS :
Nedcor Bank Ltd

AUDITORS :
Deloitte Pim Goldby

FAMILIAR BRAND NAMES
N/A

CONTRIBUTION BY ACTIVITY
Industrial/Commercial (% Gross Income) (50.0%)
Retail (40.0%)
Offices (8.0%)
Residential (2.0%)

YEAR END : August

DIVIDEND : Ords 1c

Final No 2	(Ldr)04/10/91	(Pay)30/10/91	Amt(c)20.95
Interim No 3	(Ldr)16/04/92	(Pay)12/05/92	Amt(c)20.82
Final No 4	(Ldr)16/10/92	(Pay)04/11/92	Amt(c)20.82

CAPITAL STRUCTURE

	AUTHORISED	ISSUED
Ords 1c (1 Ord : 1 Deb)	100000000	47734097

FINANCIAL STATISTICS (AT FINANCIAL YEAR END)

(Amts in R'000)	1991 Aug
Ord S/H Int	6103
Long Trm Loans	141865
Iss Ord Share	47734
Total Liab	153987
Current Liab	12122
Total Assets	160090
Current Assets	12266
Debtors	835
Turnover	22951
Oper Profit	18091
Interest Paid	19172
Tax Paid	352
Prf af Int&Tax	387
Prf att Ord Sh	387
Btm Line Earn	387
Dividend Paid	868
Mkt Prce(c) YE	280

PER SHARE STATISTICS (CENTS)

Net Asst Val	12.79
Net Earnings	40.61
Cash Flow	0.89

RATIOS AND OTHER INFORMATION

Mrk Cap(R000)	133655
Current Ratio	1.01
Quik/Acid Tst	1.01
A/C Rec T/ovr	27.49
Tot Ass T/ovr	0.14
Debt/Ass Rat	0.96
L T L Tot Ass	0.89
Debt to Eqity	25.22
Interest Cover	0.94
Oper Prof Mrg	78.82
Net Prof Marg%	1.69
Ret on Assets	12.44
Ret on Equity%	6.34
Price/Earnings	6.89
Earning Yield%	14.50
NAV % Mrk Pr	4.57
Effec Tax Rate	42.22
Def Interval	355.10
Sus Grth Rate	-7.88

SUBSIDIARY & ASSOCIATED COMPANIES

AIROTERP INVESTMENTS SHAREBLOCK (PTY) LT
ALERT INVESTMENTS SHAREBLOCK (PTY) LTD
BRIANLEY PROPERTIES SHAREBLOCK (PTY) LTD
BRONKTRAM PROPERTIES SHAREBLOCK (PTY) LT
BROWBID INVESTMENTS SHAREBLOCK (PTY) LTD
COLD AIR INVESTMENTS SHAREBLOCK (PTY) LT
COOGERS SHAREBLOCK (PTY) LTD
CRADVOER INVESTMENTS SHAREBLOCK (PTY) LT
DAS PROPERTIES SHAREBLOCK (PTY) LTD
DIRK DU TOIT SHAREBLOCK (PTY) LTD
ERF AGT NUL NEGE SHAREBLOCK (PTY) LTD
ERF ONE EIGHT ONE HERMANSTAD SHAREBLOCK
ERF SIX FIVE ONE PRETORIA NORTH SHAREBLO
FAWN PROPERTIES SHAREBLOCK (PTY) LTD
FREDERIKASTRAAT BELEGGINGS SHAREBLOCK (P
FREDVOOR INVESTMENTS SHAREBLOCK (PTY) LT
GOLEDA PROPERTIES SHAREBLOCK (PTY) LTD

HANNYHOF SHAREBLOCK (PTY) LTD
HARDWOOD PROPERTIES SHAREBLOCK (PTY) LTD
HENWOODS (PRETORIA) DEVELOPMENT COMPANY
INDACOM PROPERTIES SHAREBLOCK (PTY) LTD
JANVOEL PROPERTIES SHAREBLOCK (PTY) LTD
KARKAP PROPERTIES SHAREBLOCK (PTY) LTD
LASMITCH SHAREBLOCK (PTY) LTD
LUTBRIDGE INVESTMENTS SHAREBLOCK (PTY) L
METROMITCH SHAREBLOCK (PTY) LTD
MIDDLEPIP SHAREBLOCK (PTY) LTD
MITCHPAP INVESTMENTS SHAREBLOCK (PTY) LT
MUNTSTREET PROPERTIES SHAREBLOCK (PTY) L
NEDWEST CENTRE SHAREBLOCK (PTY) LTD
NEXT DOOR INVESTMENTS SHAREBLOCK (PTY) L
NOTREVLIS SHAREBLOCK (PTY) LTD
PANAG INVESTMENTS SHAREBLOCK (PTY) LTD
PRETBOY SHAREBLOCK (PTY) LTD
PRETVIN INVESTMENTS SHAREBLOCK (PTY) LTD
PRETWADE SHAREBLOCK (PTY) LTD
PRINSBEN PROPERTIES SHAREBLOCK (PTY) LTD
PRINSTRUBEN INVESTMENTS SHAREBLOCK (PTY)
SKD BELEGGINGS SHAREBLOCK (PTY) LTD
STEYNSCOR SHAREBLOCK (PTY) LTD
STRUBGEL PROPERTIES SHAREBLOCK (PTY) LTD
SWEMVOOR INVESTMENTS SHAREBLOCK (PTY) LT
TALKAR PROPERTIES SHAREBLOCK (PTY) LTD
THOROBRED INVESTMENTS SHAREBLOCK (PTY) L
TOMHOFF INVESTMENTS SHAREBLOCK (PTY) LTD
TOMNICK INVESTMENTS SHAREBLOCK (PTY) LTD
TOMWEST INVESTMENTS SHAREBLOCK (PTY) LTD
TRONAP INVESTMENTS SHAREBLOCK (PTY) LTD
TUEL INVESTMENTS SHAREBLOCK (PTY) LTD
VAN RYNEVELD BELEGGINGS SHAREBLOCK (PTY)
VISKIN SHAREBLOCK (PTY) LTD
VOORHERTZ SHAREBLOCK (PTY) LTD

INVESTMENTS

None

OHIO GROUP LTD

ABBREVIATION : OHIO

JSE SHORT CODE : OHI

SECTOR : Industrial-Electronics, Electrical & Bat

SHAREHOLDERS

Who Owns Whom's Assessment of the Identity of the Ultimate Controlling Shareholder: DIRECTORS/UNIDEV VIA CORTECH

SHAREHOLDER	PERCENTAGE 1992	1991
VOSS P E	16.7	19.1
BROTHERS R	10.0	---
BROTHERS R H	6.1	6.1
SMITH W P M	5.9	---
VON VIVENOT C B	5.4	---
TOZER K G	4.8	1.4
MUKUNDE B	4.3	---
HASSON D	3.8	---
GRACEY J	3.7	---
LOW AH KAI	2.9	2.6
HIBBERD G	1.6	---
HINDS G	1.6	---
RICE K M	1.6	---
JR NOM P/L	1.3	---
OHIO SHARE INCENTIVE TRUST	1.1	---
MCCLUNG E	---	1.4
UAL NOM P/L	---	1.1
GRACEY J H	---	1.4
BRAUM M J	---	2.4
EDIMED P/L	---	8.7
FIRST NAT NOM P/L	---	12.4
HASSON D R	---	2.2
PATER N L	---	3.3
PATER V H	---	3.4
SANLAM	---	3.5
TOTAL	70.8	69.0

DIRECTORS :
BROTHERS RH (Executive Chairman)
HINDS GG (Financial Director),RICE KM
VOSS PE (Managing Director

REGISTRATION NUMBER : 86/04591/06

REGISTERED OFFICE
Ohio House, Cnr Dartfield & Commerce Cres.
Eastgate Ext 13, Sandton
2146
TEL: 011-444 4900
FAX: 011-444 5960

TRANSFER SECRETARY
Central Registrars Ltd
P O Box 4844, Johannesburg
2000
TEL: 011-331 0051

COMPANY SECRETARY
G G Hinds

NATURE OF BUSINESS
An investment holding company. The principal activities of subsidiaries are the developing & marketing of multi-user microcomputer systems & the sale & maintenance of optical recognition equipment.

BANKERS :
First National Bank of SA Ltd

AUDITORS :
Fisher Hoffman Stride

FAMILIAR BRAND NAMES
ALLOY,AST,BUSINESS SYSTEM,CITIZEN,CVCS
DYNAPLAN,LAWPLAN,MEDSTAT,MEDSTAT CLASSIC
OCTO-POS,PLEXUS (RECOGNITION),REDSTONE
TARTAN,TRACE

CONTRIBUTION BY ACTIVITY
PC Hardware (% Value Added) (25.0%)
Software (25.0%)
Services to user base (50.0%)

YEAR END : February

DIVIDEND : Ords 1c
Interim (Ldr)09/10/92 (Pay)23/10/92 Amt(c)1.8

NUMBER OF EMPLOYEES : 150

CAPITAL STRUCTURE

	AUTHORISED	ISSUED
Ords 1c	40000000	28411454
9% Unsec Red Debs 150c	694382	694382

FINANCIAL STATISTICS (AT FINANCIAL YEAR END)

(Amts in R'000)	1992 Feb	1991 Feb	1990 Feb	1989 Feb	1988 Feb
Ord S/H Int	801	-1932	-2518	3070	8607
Long Trm Loans	1389	2583	3583	5441	5393
Iss Ord Share	28411	28411	28411	21523	20400
Total Liab	4032	7079	8399	23564	12834
Current Liab	2643	4496	4816	18123	7441
Total Assets	4833	5147	5881	26242	14736
Intang Assets	*	*	*	392	6705
Current Assets	2247	3464	3834	23291	10793
Debtors	1217	2290	2328	9992	7109
Inventory	1030	1174	1454	13243	3684
Turnover	16607	14324	33767	60282	25576
Oper Profit	1947	1308	-3943	-3210	6496
Interest Paid	484	877	2492	2041	80
Tax Paid	-3	-2	-	-298	2810
Prf af Int&Tax	1466	433	-6435	-4953	3606
Prf att Ord Sh	1466	433	-6435	-4953	3606
Btm Line Earn	1699	586	-8131	-5844	3606
Dividend Paid	-	-	-	-117	306
Mkt Prce(c) YE	10	5	12	45	155
Depreciation	204	292	641	558	659

PER SHARE STATISTICS (CENTS)

Net Asst Val	2.82	-6.80	-8.86	12.44	9.32
Net Earnings	5.20	1.50	-22.60	-23.00	17.70
Dividends	-	-	-	-	7.50
Cash Flow	5.88	2.55	-20.39	-22.42	23.98

RATIOS AND OTHER INFORMATION

Mrk Cap(R000)	2841	1421	3409	9685	31620
Current Ratio	0.85	0.77	0.80	1.29	1.45
Quik/Acid Tst	0.46	0.51	0.49	0.55	0.96
A/C Rec T/ovr	13.65	6.26	14.50	6.03	3.60
Tot Ass T/ovr	3.44	2.78	5.74	2.30	1.74
Debt/Ass Rat	0.83	1.38	1.43	0.90	0.84
L T L Tot Ass	0.29	0.50	0.61	0.21	0.34
Debt to Eqity	5.03	-3.66	-3.34	7.68	1.44
Interest Cover	4.02	1.49	-1.58	-1.57	81.20
Oper Prof Mrg	11.72	9.13	-11.68	-5.32	25.40
Net Prof Marg%	8.83	3.02	-19.06	-8.22	14.10
Ret on Assets	40.29	25.41	-67.05	-12.23	44.08
Ret on Equity%	183.02	-22.41	255.56	-161.34	41.90
Price/Earnings	1.92	3.33	-0.53	-1.96	8.76
Divid Cover	-	-	-	-	2.36
Divid Yield	-	-	-	-	4.84
Earning Yield%	52.00	30.00	-188.33	-51.11	11.42
NAV % Mrk Pr	28.19	-136.00	-73.86	27.65	6.02
Effec Tax Rate	-	-	-	-0.30	37.09
Def Interval	1.33	6.28	-0.93	-1.39	0.56
Sus Grth Rate	183.02	-22.41	255.56	-157.52	38.34

SUBSIDIARY & ASSOCIATED COMPANIES

ELECTRONIC DESIGNS (PTY) LTD
OHIO COMPUTER SYSTEMS (PTY) LTD
OHIO POINT OF SALES SYSTEMS (PTY) LTD
SOFTWARE DESIGNS (PTY) LTD

INVESTMENTS

None

OK BAZAARS (1929) LTD

ABBREVIATION : O-K

JSE SHORT CODE : OKO

SECTOR : Industrial-Retailers & Wholesalers

SHAREHOLDERS

Who Owns Whom's Assessment of the Identity of the Ultimate Controlling Shareholder: ANGLO VIA SA BREWS

SHAREHOLDER	PERCENTAGE 1992	1991
SA BREWERIES LTD	69.0	69.0
STD BANK NOM TVL P/L	5.7	3.4
OK BAZAARS EXEC SHARE INC SCHEME	3.9	3.9
UK CONTROL ACCOUNT	3.2	2.7
CMB NOM P/L	2.5	---
EIGHTY ONE MAIN STREET NOM LTD	2.1	2.4
FIRST CORP NOM P/L	1.8	3.4
FIRST NAT NOM P/L	1.7	1.8
SAFICON-BOUMAT PENS FUND	1.0	1.0
MOMENTUM LIFE ASSURE LTD	---	2.9
SANLAM	---	2.4
TOTAL	90.8	92.9

DIRECTORS :
BLACKWELL RT (Systems Director)
BORCHERDS BV (Financial Director),COOMBES J
COPPIN AD ,HARTSHORNE KB (Personnel Director)
HEWSON DTR ,HOOD GW (Managing Director)
KAHN JM (Chairman),KRAITZICK M ,MACFARLANE WS
MANNE G ,MELVILLE PELS J ,NUNAN N ,SEREBRO HM
SNYMAN GJH ,SOLOMAN AD
VAN COLLER RJ (Dir Advertising/Public R.

REGISTRATION NUMBER : 05/01817/06

REGISTERED OFFICE
OK Building, 80 Eloff Street
Johannesburg
2001
TEL: 011-333 0910
FAX: 011-333 1471

TRANSFER SECRETARY
Mercantile Registrars Ltd
P O Box 1053, Johannesburg
2000
TEL: 011-333 8181

COMPANY SECRETARY
P E Kritzinger

NATURE OF BUSINESS
The group is a retailer of clothing, appliances, food and household goods through a network of 200 retail trading stores, comprising 154 conventional OK supermarkets, 22 free-standing OK furniture outlets, 12 Hyperamas, 5 service stations, and 7 House and Home units.

BANKERS :
Standard Bank of SA Ltd

AUDITORS :
KPMG Aiken & Peat

FAMILIAR BRAND NAMES
HOUSE & HOME,HYPERAMA,OK BAZAARS
OK PLAIN WRAP,POT O'GOLD,THE GAP

CONTRIBUTION BY ACTIVITY
N/A

YEAR END : March

DIVIDEND :Ords 50c

Final No 117	(Ldr)18/05/90	(Pay)02/07/90	Amt(c)53
Interim No 118	(Ldr)16/11/90	(Pay)28/12/90	Amt(c)37
Final No 119	(Ldr)17/05/91	(Pay)01/07/91	Amt(c)26
Interim No 120	(Ldr)22/11/91	(Pay)31/12/91	Amt(c)37
Interim No 121	(Ldr)20/11/92	(Pay)31/12/92	Amt(c)10

NUMBER OF EMPLOYEES : 24500

CAPITAL STRUCTURE

	AUTHORISED	ISSUED
Ords 50c	14000000	12422061
6% 1st Cum Prefs R2	300000	240000
6% 2nd Cum Prefs R2	500000	300000
5% 3rd Cum Prefs R2	500000	500000
6% 4th Red Cum Prefs R2	300000	0

FINANCIAL STATISTICS (AT FINANCIAL YEAR END)

(Amts in R'000)	1992 Mar	1991 Mar	1990 Mar	1989 Mar	1988 Mar
Ord S/H Int	347390	343372	344004	362760	351462
Long Trm Loans	114427	129292	143679	66086	67400
Iss Ord Share	12422	12422	12418	12268	12267
Total Liab	1113331	1041623	908908	693622	627782
Current Liab	998904	912331	765229	627536	560382
Total Assets	1460721	1384995	1252912	1056382	989244
Current Assets	991609	943809	867727	731228	657629
Debtors	203285	206664	173891	142503	117882
Inventory	781865	729402	688215	562781	527046
Turnover	5044793	4799769	4218898	3726491	3121774
Oper Profit	34701	53485	68426	67117	40492
Interest Paid	54966	41087	35756	25078	16452
Tax Paid	-13479	4364	14585	19334	11366
Prf af Int&Tax	3009	12535	21876	24954	14211
Prf att Ord Sh	9353	14942	20205	23923	19868
Btm Line Earn	8614	6144	20205	23923	18595
Dividend Paid	4596	7826	10791	12636	10918
Mkt Prce(c) YE	975	1400	1950	1550	1200
Depreciation	25164	19876	17989	16646	14925

PER SHARE STATISTICS (CENTS)

Net Asst Val	2796.57	2764.22	2770.20	2956.96	2865.10
Net Earnings	75.30	120.30	163.00	195.00	162.00
Dividends	37.00	63.00	86.00	103.00	89.00
Cash Flow	186.02	218.60	382.81	376.15	238.16

RATIOS AND OTHER INFORMATION

Mrk Cap(R000)	121115	173908	242151	190154	147204
Current Ratio	0.99	1.03	1.13	1.17	1.17
Quik/Acid Tst	0.21	0.24	0.23	0.27	0.23
A/C Rec T/ovr	24.82	23.22	24.26	26.15	26.48
Tot Ass T/ovr	3.45	3.47	3.37	3.53	3.16
Debt/Ass Rat	0.72	0.69	0.65	0.64	0.62
L T L Tot Ass	0.03	0.03	0.04	0.05	0.06
Debt to Eqity	3.01	2.77	2.36	1.88	1.75
Interest Cover	0.66	1.35	1.96	2.72	2.55
Oper Prof Mrg	0.69	1.11	1.62	1.80	1.30
Net Prof Marg%	0.19	0.31	0.48	0.64	0.64
Ret on Assets	3.52	4.50	5.76	6.57	4.99
Ret on Equity%	2.69	4.35	5.87	6.59	5.65
Price/Earnings	12.95	11.64	11.96	7.95	7.41
Divid Cover	2.04	1.91	1.90	1.89	1.82
Divid Yield	3.79	4.50	4.41	6.65	7.42
Earning Yield%	7.72	8.59	8.36	12.58	13.50
NAV % Mrk Pr	286.83	197.44	142.06	190.77	238.76
Effec Tax Rate	-26.62	36.60	17.84	31.46	41.64
Def Interval	17.78	9.64	5.10	3.90	6.61
Sus Grth Rate	1.37	2.07	2.74	3.11	2.55

SUBSIDIARY & ASSOCIATED COMPANIES

A ROSS & CO (PTY) LTD
ALGOA CLEARING & FORWARDING CO LTD
BLOEMFONTEIN HOLDINGS (PTY) LTD
BOPHUTHATSWANA OK BAZAARS LTD (50%)
CASH DISCO (PTY) LTD
CONGELLA WAREHOUSING (PTY) LTD
DE JONGH BROTHERS INVESTMENTS (PTY) LTD
EASTERN TRUST INVESTMENTS (PTY) LTD
FRESTA HOLDINGS LTD
HYPERAMA LTD
JCK INVESTMENTS (PTY) LTD (33,3%)
KENILWORTH PROPERTIES LTD
MENLYN INVESTMENTS (PTY) LTD
OK BAZAARS (ALBERTON) LTD
OK BAZAARS (ALPHA) (PTY) LTD
OK BAZAARS (ALRODE) LTD
OK BAZAARS (BETA) (PTY) LTD
OK BAZAARS (BLOEMFONTEIN) LTD
OK BAZAARS (BOTSWANA) (1976) (PTY) LTD
OK BAZAARS (CAMBRIDGE) LTD
OK BAZAARS (CAPE) LTD
OK BAZAARS (CISKEI) LTD (50%)
OK BAZAARS (DE AAR) LTD
OK BAZAARS (DURBAN) LTD
OK BAZAARS (EAST LONDON) LTD
OK BAZAARS (ETA) (PTY) LTD
OK BAZAARS (IOTA) (PTY) LTD
OK BAZAARS (KAPPA) (PTY) LTD
OK BAZAARS (KINGWILLIAMSTOWN) LTD
OK BAZAARS (KROONSTAD) LTD
OK BAZAARS (LESOTHO) (PTY) LTD (50%)
OK BAZAARS (LONDON)
OK BAZAARS (MAYFAIR) LTD
OK BAZAARS (MITCHELLS PLAIN) LTD (49,4%)
OK BAZAARS (NAMIBIA) LTD
OK BAZAARS (NATAL) LTD
OK BAZAARS (ORANGE GROVE) LTD
OK BAZAARS (PARK) LTD
OK BAZAARS (PRETORIA) LTD
OK BAZAARS (ROSEBANK) LTD
OK BAZAARS (RUSTENBURG) LTD
OK BAZAARS (SELCOURT) LTD
OK BAZAARS (STILFONTEIN) LTD
OK BAZAARS (SWAZILAND) (PTY) LTD
OK BAZAARS (UITENHAGE) LTD
OK BAZAARS (UPINGTON) LTD
OK BAZAARS (VALHALLA) LTD
OK BAZAARS (VENDA) LTD (50%)
OK BAZAARS (VILLAGE DEEP) LTD
OK BAZAARS (VIRGINIA) LTD
OK BAZAARS (VRYBURG) LTD
OK BAZAARS (WELKOM) LTD
OK BAZAARS (WOODSTOCK) LTD
OK BAZAARS (WORCESTOR) LTD
OK BAZAARS PROPERTIES (CAPE TOWN) LTD
OK EMPORIUM (PRETORIA) LTD
OK HYPERAMA LTD
OK HYPERMARKETS (PTY) LTD
OK KWAZULU LTD
OK MINIMART LTD
OK ORLANDO (PTY) LTD (50%)

OKFIN (PTY) LTD (50%)
PARAMOUNT BUILDINGS (PRETORIA) LTD
PELEG INVESTMENTS (PTY) LTD
PRETORIA EAST INVESTMENTS (PTY) LTD
RAINIER INC (CAY MAN ISLES)
RENPARK PROPERTIES LTD
ROYAL HOTEL (1906) LTD
SECOND PRIMROSE INVESTMENTS LTD
SNYBLOMME (EDMS) BPK
SOWDEN & STODDART LTD
STANLEN BUILDINGS (KLERKSDORP) LTD
STANLEN BUILDINGS (PARK) LTD
STANLEN BUILDINGS (VRYBURG) LTD
WORINAG AG (SWITZERLAND)
YEOVILLE ESTATES (PTY) LTD (33,3%)

INVESTMENTS

None

OMNIA HOLDINGS LTD

ABBREVIATION : OMNIA

JSE SHORT CODE : OMN

SECTOR : Industrial-Chemicals & Oils

SHAREHOLDERS

Who Owns Whom's Assessment of the Identity of the Ultimate Controlling Shareholder:
ANGLO ALPHA / DIRECTORS

SHAREHOLDER	PERCENTAGE 1992	1991
ANGLO ALPHA LTD	26.1	26.1
MARAIS W T TRUST P/L	12.2	12.2
WINKLER U M R	7.6	7.6
SOLID G NOM P/L	6.3	6.7
WINKLER O J	5.2	5.2
SA MUTUAL	4.6	4.6
NEDBANK NOM LTD	4.1	3.9
STD BANK NOM TVL P/L	2.7	2.0
MARAIS W T	2.3	2.3
OMNIA SHARE INCENTIVE SCHEME	2.3	2.1
FIRST NAT NOM P/L	2.2	2.1
CENTRAL HOLDINGS LTD	2.1	2.1
OMNIA EXEC SHARE PARTICIPATION SCHEME	1.9	3.6
CORTRUST AG	1.7	1.7
DIENST C W	1.2	1.2
TWINING INV P/L	1.1	1.1
PUTTER INV P/L	1.0	1.0
TOTAL	84.5	85.5

DIRECTORS :
BAKER DR ,CROSSE NJ (Managing Director)
FEARFIELD MA (Deputy Chairman),FLETCHER AG
MARAIS WT ,PRETORIUS JG ,SCHOEMAN HSJ
SPRINGETT PA ,VON ABO CL ,WHYTE KC
WINKLER OJ (Deputy Chairman)
WINKLER RKJ DR (Chairman

REGISTRATION NUMBER : 67/03680/06

REGISTERED OFFICE
1st Floor, Omnia House, 13 Sloane Street
Epsom Downs
2021
TEL: 011-463 2864
FAX: 011-463 3020

TRANSFER SECRETARY
Central Registrars Ltd
P O Box 4844, Johannesburg
2000
TEL: 011-331 0051

COMPANY SECRETARY
P R Janse van Rensburg

NATURE OF BUSINESS
An investment holding company with interests in fertilizer, farming, seed, explosives and trading subsidiaries.

BANKERS :
First National Bank of SA Ltd, Bankorp Ltd

AUDITORS :
Coopers Theron Du Toit

FAMILIAR BRAND NAMES
OMNIA

CONTRIBUTION BY ACTIVITY
N/A

YEAR END : December

DIVIDEND : Ords 50c

Interim	(Ldr)21/12/90	(Pay)08/01/91	Amt(c)8
Final	(Ldr)12/04/91	(Pay)22/04/91	Amt(c)22

DIVIDEND : Ords no par value

Interim	(Ldr)10/01/92	(Pay)22/01/92	Amt(c)12
Final	(Ldr)12/05/92	(Pay)24/04/92	Amt(c)23

NUMBER OF EMPLOYEES : 1500

CAPITAL STRUCTURE

	AUTHORISED	ISSUED
Ords no par value	41000000	38764975
15% Cum Red Prefs 1c	10000000	0

FINANCIAL STATISTICS (AT FINANCIAL YEAR END)

(Amts in R'000)	1991 Dec	1990 Dec	1989 Dec	1988 Dec	1987 Dec
Ord S/H Int	119630	101328	83641	66295	64487
Long Trm Loans	27518	31801	41129	52086	38576
Iss Ord Share	38765	38765	38765	36923	36923
Total Liab	217699	175823	166614	144217	114347
Current Liab	190181	144022	125485	92131	75771
Total Assets	337329	277151	250255	210512	178834
Current Assets	198905	155059	130703	100083	78070
Debtors	90009	76852	67518	57708	39799
Inventory	68598	73109	61815	41519	38261
Turnover	438435	380787	336200	242638	181093
Oper Profit	60475	49210	48054	29812	21107
Interest Paid	28026	22642	20003	13170	10206
Tax Paid	3247	-	4024	162	-
Prf af Int&Tax	31493	27934	25414	17038	10901
Prf att Ord Sh	31801	28385	25219	16086	7902
Btm Line Earn	31801	29030	25219	16086	8874
Dividend Paid	13568	11629	10079	5538	1846
Mkt Prce(c) YE	410	270	250	260	95

Depreciation	12494	11911	10478	7657	7013

PER SHARE STATISTICS (CENTS)

Net Asst Val	308 60	261 39	215 76	179 55	174 65
Net Earnings	82.04	73 22	66 64	43 57	25 46
Dividends	35 00	30 00	26 00	15 00	5 00
Cash Flow	113 47	102 79	103 33	62 82	40 39

RATIOS AND OTHER INFORMATION

Mrk Cap(R000)	158937	104666	96913	96000	35077
Current Ratio	1 05	1 08	1 04	1 09	1 03
Quik/Acid Tst	0 69	0 57	0 55	0 64	0 53
A/C Rec T/ovr	4 87	4 95	4 98	4 20	4 55
Tot Ass T/ovr	1 30	1 37	1 34	1 15	1 01
Debt/Ass Rat	0 63	0 62	0 65	0 64	0 63
L T L Tot Ass	0 07	0 10	0 15	0 20	0 21
Debt to Eqity	1 79	1 70	1 94	2 02	1 75
Interest Cover	2 17	2 17	2 40	2 26	2 07
Oper Prof Mrg	13 79	12 92	14 29	12 29	11 66
Net Prof Marg%	7 25	7 45	7 50	6 63	4 36
Ret on Assets	18 70	18 41	19 99	14 69	11 80
Ret on Equity%	26 58	28 01	30 15	24 26	12 25
Price/Earnings	5 00	3 69	3 75	5 97	3 73
Divid Cover	2 34	2 44	2 56	2 90	5 09
Divid Yield	8 54	11 11	10 40	5 77	5 26
Earning Yield%	20 01	27 12	26 66	16 76	26 80
NAV % Mrk Pr	75 27	96 81	86 31	69 06	183 84
Effec Tax Rate	9 56	-	0 08	0 94	-
Def Interval	1 53	1 72	2 13	3 27	4 81
Sus Grth Rate	15 24	16 54	18 10	15 91	9 39

SUBSIDIARY & ASSOCIATED COMPANIES

ALPHA KUNSMISDIENSTE (EDMS) BPK (26%)
BULK MINING EXPLOSIVES (PTY) LTD
CARNIA SEED (PTY) LTD
HIGHVELD EXPLORATION (PTY) LTD
NITROCHEM (PTY) LTD (26%)
OMNIA BOEREDIENSTE (EDMS) BPK
OMNIA CONSTRUCTION (PTY) LTD
OMNIA EIENDOMME (EDMS) BPK
OMNIA FARMING (PTY) LTD
OMNIA FERTILIZER LTD
OMNIA FINANS (EDMS) BPK
OMNIA HOUSING (PTY) LTD
OMNIA INDUSTRIAL CHEMICALS (PTY) LTD
OMNIA INDUSTRIAL PROPERTIES (PTY) LTD
OMNIA LANDBOU BPK
OMNIA LIQUIDS (PTY) LTD
OMNIA PHOSPHATES (PTY) LTD
OMNIA WITBANK PLASE (EDMS) BPK
RETRADCO (PTY) LTD
SCIENTIFIC AGRICULTURAL SERVICES S A (P
TELLUS INVESTMENTS (PTY) LTD

INVESTMENTS

None

ORANGE FREE STATE INVESTMENTS LTD

ABBREVIATION : OFSIL

JSE SHORT CODE : OSL

SECTOR : Gold-OFS

SHAREHOLDERS

Who Owns Whom's Assessment of the Identity of the Ultimate Controlling Shareholder:
ANGLO AMERICAN

SHAREHOLDER	PERCENTAGE 1992	1991
WELKOM GOLD MINING CO LTD	30 4	30 4
STD BANK NOM TVL P/L	11 7	10 4
INDO-CHINA NOM P/L	8 3	8 5
LONDON CONTROL ACCOUNT	5 7	6 3
FERMAIN NOM LTD	5 6	5 6
ORANGE FREE STATE INV TRUST LTD	5 1	5 1
SOUTHERN LIFE ASSOC LTD	4 5	5 5
DEPOSITARY NOM INC	3 0	---
SA MUTUAL	2 7	3 1
TAURUS NOM LTD	2 4	2 4
RESIDENT NOM LTD	2 3	2 3
FIRST NAT NOM P/L GATR DEPOT	2 2	2 1
AFRICAN & EUROPEAN INV CO LTD	1 7	1 7
EIGHTY ONE MAIN STREET NOM LTD	1 5	1 4
CMB NOM P/L	1 5	---
PETARD NOM LTD	1 4	1 4
FIRST NAT NOM P/L	1 4	1 4
BANK OF NEW YORK NOM LTD	---	2 3
INDO-CHINA NOM SA P/L	---	8 5
TOTAL	91 1	98 4

DIRECTORS :
HEWITT L (Managing Director),HOSKING KM
KING MW ,RICHARDSON JG ,SUNTER CL (Chairman)
VAN DER COLF SW ,WOODWARD GW

REGISTRATION NUMBER : 85/05715/06

REGISTERED OFFICE
44 Main Street, Johannesburg
2001
TEL 011-638 9111
FAX 011-638 5281

TRANSFER SECRETARY
Consolidated Share Registrars Ltd
P O Box 61051, Marshalltown
2107
TEL 011-492 1620

COMPANY SECRETARY
Anglo American Corporation of SA Ltd

NATURE OF BUSINESS
An investment holding company with a controlling interest in JSE-quoted Free State Consolidated Gold Mines

BANKERS :
N/A

AUDITORS :
Deloitte Pim Goldby

FAMILIAR BRAND NAMES
N/A

CONTRIBUTION BY ACTIVITY
N/A

YEAR END : March

DIVIDEND : Ords 1c

Interim No 10	(Ldr)18/10/90	(Pay)14/12/90	Amt(c)143
Final No 11	(Ldr)18/04/91	(Pay)14/06/91	Amt(c)220
Interim No 12	(Ldr)08/11/91	(Pay)13/12/91	Amt(c)272
Final No 13	(Ldr)08/05/92	(Pay)12/06/92	Amt(c)339
Interim No 14	(Ldr)13/11/92	(Pay)18/12/92	Amt(c)273

CAPITAL STRUCTURE

	AUTHORISED	ISSUED
Ords 1c	25000000	22514094

FINANCIAL STATISTICS (AT FINANCIAL YEAR END)

(Amts in R'000)	1992 Mar	1991 Mar	1990 Mar	1989 Mar	1987 Sep
Ord S/H Int	1356500	1356500	1356400	1356300	1868000
Long Trm Loans	-	-	-	-	2062500
Iss Ord Share	22514	22514	22514	22514	22514
Total Liab	76700	49900	85500	93900	2528900
Current Liab	76700	49900	85500	93900	466400
Total Assets	1433200	1406400	1441900	1450200	4396900
Current Assets	77100	50300	85800	94100	614600
Debtors	76400	50000	85200	94000	236800
Turnover	-	-	-	5190200	3044200
Oper Profit	137500	81700	172700	1464600	1118200
Interest Paid	-	-	-	31500	16500
Tax Paid	100	100	100	165200	230000
Prf af Int&Tax	137500	81800	173000	1267900	871700
Prf att Ord Sh	137500	81800	173000	260500	178800
Btm Line Earn	137500	81800	173000	260500	178800
Dividend Paid	137500	81700	172900	257700	181600
Mkt Prce(c) YE	6550	4475	11850	8600	13875

PER SHARE STATISTICS (CENTS)

Net Asst Val	6025.14	6025.14	6024.70	6024.25	8297.06
Net Earnings	611.00	363.00	768.00	1146.00	806.00
Dividends	611.00	363.00	768.00	1145.00	807.00
Cash Flow	610.73	363.33	768.41	2987.77	3092.30

RATIOS AND OTHER INFORMATION

Mrk Cap(R000)	1474667	1007502	2667909	1936204	3123818
Current Ratio	1.01	1.01	1.00	1.00	1.32
Quik/Acid Tst	1.01	1.01	1.00	1.00	1.32
A/C Rec T/ovr	-	-	-	36.81	12.86
Tot Ass T/ovr	-	-	-	2.39	0.69
Debt/Ass Rat	0.05	0.04	0.06	0.06	0.14
L T L Tot Ass	-	-	-	-	0.03
Debt to Eqity	0.06	0.04	0.06	0.07	0.33
Interest Cover	-	-	-	46.50	67.77
Oper Prof Mrg	-	-	-	28.22	36.73
Net Prof Marg%	-	-	-	5.02	5.87
Ret on Assets	9.60	5.82	12.00	67.33	25.43
Ret on Equity%	10.14	6.03	12.75	12.80	9.57
Price/Earnings	10.72	12.33	15.43	7.50	17.21
Divid Cover	1.00	1.00	1.00	1.00	1.00
Divid Yield	9.33	8.11	6.48	13.31	5.82
Earning Yield%	9.33	8.11	6.48	13.33	5.81
NAV % Mrk Pr	91.99	134.64	50.84	70.05	59.80
Effec Tax Rate	0.07	0.12	0.06	11.53	20.88
Def Interval	-	-	-	-	0.22
Sus Grth Rate	0.00	0.01	0.01	0.21	-0.15

SUBSIDIARY & ASSOCIATED COMPANIES

FREE STATE CONSOLIDATED GOLD MINES LTD (49,92%)
FREE STATE GEDULD MINES LTD
PRESIDENT BRAND GOLD MINING CO LTD

INVESTMENTS

ANGLO AMERICAN FARMS LTD (1000 SH)
DEPFIN INVESTMENTS (PTY) LTD (4600000 SH)
EASTERN GOLD HOLDINGS LTD (100000 SH)
GOLDCO LTD (1SH)
HIGHVELD STEEL (20 000 000)
INTERNATIONAL GOLD CORPORATION LTD (7129 SH)
JEANNETTE GOLD MINES LTD (392588 SH)
LA RIVIERA (PTY) LTD (19 SH)
LANSAN INVESTMENT HOLDINGS LTD (5730 SH)
MONDI PAPER CO LTD (8 000 000)
SOUTHVAAL HOLDINGS LTD (887624 SH)
ST HELENA GOLD MINES LTD (315827 SH)
WELKOM GOLD HOLDINGS LTD (7030000 SH)

ORYX GOLD HOLDINGS LTD

ABBREVIATION : ORYX

JSE SHORT CODE : ORX

SECTOR : Gold-OFS

SHAREHOLDERS

Who Owns Whom's Assessment of the Identity of the Ultimate Controlling Shareholder:
GENCOR

SHAREHOLDER	PERCENTAGE 1992	1991
CONSOLIDATED NOM P/L	62.7	62.7
CMB NOM P/L	17.0	---
ABSA NOM P/L	14.5	---
RESIDENT NOM LTD	3.0	3.0
STD BANK NOM TVL P/L	1.3	1.2
SANLAM	---	16.8
VOLKSKAS NOM P/L	---	14.5
TOTAL	98.4	98.1

DIRECTORS :
BOTHA AD ,BURKE JHJ ,HEWITT L ,LUND BNB
MAUDE G (Chairman),OLIVIER JE

REGISTRATION NUMBER : 69/01900/06

REGISTERED OFFICE
General Mining Building, 6 Hollard Street
Johannesburg
2001
TEL: 011-376 9111
FAX: 011-836 6130

TRANSFER SECRETARY
Central Registrars Ltd
P O Box 4844, Johannesburg
2000
TEL: 011-331 0051

COMPANY SECRETARY
General Mining Metals & Minerals Ltd

NATURE OF BUSINESS
The business of the company is directly linked with that of the Oryx Mine, which is a division of St Helena Gold Mines Ltd. The company provides Oryx Mine with funding. Once the Oryx Mine is in full operation, the company's primary source of income will be royalties based on the proceeds of gold mining at the Oryx Mine.

BANKERS :
Trust Bank of Africa Ltd
Standard Bank of SA Ltd, Nedperm Bank Ltd

AUDITORS :
Price Waterhouse Meyernel

FAMILIAR BRAND NAMES
N/A

CONTRIBUTION BY ACTIVITY
N/A

YEAR END : August

DIVIDEND : (Ldr)03/11/89 (Pay)15/12/89

NUMBER OF EMPLOYEES : 3619

CAPITAL STRUCTURE

	AUTHORISED	ISSUED
Ords no par value	587500100	165000200

FINANCIAL STATISTICS (AT FINANCIAL YEAR END)

(Amts in R'000)	1992 Aug	1991 Aug	1990 Aug	1989 Aug	1988 Aug
Ord S/H Int	634320	632927	632741	634049	624409
Long Trm Loans	980501	646940	309947	92823	57515
Iss Ord Share	165000	165000	165000	165000	165000
Total Liab	995683	652692	312272	95475	60479
Current Liab	15182	5752	2325	2652	2964
Total Assets	1628646	1284262	945013	729524	684888
Intang Assets	1357	1357	*	*	*
Current Assets	8291	13490	7529	1631	44088
Debtors	7851	13432	7078	1179	636
Turnover	95091	84316	39853	22868	8738
Oper Profit	-363	-419	-411	11058	4531
Interest Paid	94678	83588	39110	-	-
Tax Paid	-1343	123	1636	1383	1250
Prf af Int&Tax	1393	186	-1304	9675	3281
Prf att Ord Sh	1393	186	-1304	9675	3281
Btm Line Earn	1393	186	-1304	9675	3281
Mkt Prce(c) YE	425	775	825	800	790

PER SHARE STATISTICS (CENTS)

Net Asst Val	383.61	382.77	383.48	384.27	378.43
Net Earnings	0.80	0.10	-0.80	5.90	2.20
Cash Flow	0.87	0.22	0.20	6.06	3.53

RATIOS AND OTHER INFORMATION

Mrk Cap(R000)	701250	1278750	1361250	1320000	1303500
Current Ratio	0.55	2.35	3.24	0.62	14.87
Quik/Acid Tst	0.55	2.35	3.24	0.62	14.87
A/C Rec T/ovr	12.11	6.28	5.63	19.40	20.61
Tot Ass T/ovr	0.06	0.07	0.04	0.03	0.02
Debt/Ass Rat	0.61	0.51	0.33	0.13	0.09
L T L Tot Ass	0.60	0.50	0.33	0.13	0.08
Debt to Eqity	1.57	1.03	0.49	0.15	0.10
Interest Cover	0.00	-0.01	-0.01	-	-
Oper Prof Mrg	-0.38	-0.50	-1.03	48.36	51.85
Net Prof Marg%	1.46	0.22	-3.27	42.31	37.55
Ret on Assets	5.82	6.53	4.17	1.52	0.99
Ret on Equity%	0.13	0.03	-0.21	1.53	0.79
Price/Earnings	531.25	7750.00	-1031.25	135.59	359.09
Earning Yield%	0.19	0.01	-0.10	0.74	0.28
NAV % Mrk Pr	90.26	49.39	46.48	48.03	47.90
Effec Tax Rate	-	-	-	9.59	21.67
Def Interval	680.22	1799.47	931.20	9.23	24.20
Sus Grth Rate	0.22	0.03	-0.21	1.53	0.53

SUBSIDIARY & ASSOCIATED COMPANIES

None

INVESTMENTS

ST HELENA GOLD MINES LTD ("A" CUM PREFS) (3825035 SH)
ST HELENA GOLD MINES LTD ("B" CUM PREFS) (3825035 SH)

OSPREY GOLD MINE LTD

ABBREVIATION : OSPREY

JSE SHORT CODE : OPR

SECTOR : Gold-Rand & others

SHAREHOLDERS

Who Owns Whom's Assessment of the Identity of the Ultimate Controlling Shareholder:
GARDITEX INTERNATIONAL SA

SHAREHOLDER	PERCENTAGE 1992	1991
MAXERIC NOM P/L	---	7.0
NEDBANK NOM LTD	---	16.0
OSPREY SHARE INCETIVE	---	1.7
STD BANK NOM TVL P/L	---	5.1
FINANCIAL LTD	---	19.4
GUARDITEX INTERNATIONAL SA	---	7.2
MANAGEMENT SERVICES CORP LTD	---	15.6
TOTAL	---	72.0

DIRECTORS :
BOWRAN TM (Financial Director)
HODGEN RW (Managing Director)
JANSE VAN RENSBURG DR WC (Chairman)
KEARNS SCH (Operations Director),NIEMAN GH
WESSELS HJ

REGISTRATION NUMBER : 80/10081/06

REGISTERED OFFICE
Ristone Office Block, 1st Floor, North Block
Parktown
2193
TEL: 011-29 1311

TRANSFER SECRETARY
Investment Registrars (Pty) Ltd
P O Box 9167, Johannesburg
2000
TEL: 011-725 6004

COMPANY SECRETARY
E P J van Vuuren

NATURE OF BUSINESS
The company conducts gold mining on precious metal claims in the district of Malamulele, Gazankulu

BANKERS :
First National Bank of SA Ltd
Standard Bank of SA Ltd

AUDITORS :
Fisher Hoffman Stride

FAMILIAR BRAND NAMES
N/A

CONTRIBUTION BY ACTIVITY
N/A

YEAR END : June

DIVIDEND :15/00/91

NUMBER OF EMPLOYEES : 315

CAPITAL STRUCTURE

	AUTHORISED	ISSUED
Ords no par value	40000000	32000000

FINANCIAL STATISTICS (AT FINANCIAL YEAR END)

(Amts in R'000)	1990 Jun	1989 Jun	1988 Jun
Ord S/H Int	16113	16003	15091
Long Trm Loans	1766	1174	247
Iss Ord Share	32000	32000	32000
Total Liab	2744	2617	1970
Current Liab	978	1443	1723
Total Assets	18857	18620	17061
Current Assets	781	966	858
Debtors	[illegible]	259	104
Inventory	491	522	699
Turnover	5008	6392	5758
Oper Profit	999	947	449
Interest Paid	332		
Prf af Int&Tax	667	947	449
Prf att Ord Sh	667	947	449
Btm Line Earn	110	912	449
Mkt Prce(c) YE	40	53	110

PER SHARE STATISTICS (CENTS)

Net Asst Val	50 35	50 01	47 16
Net Earnings	2 10	2 90	0 30
Cash Flow	2 08	2 96	1 26

RATIOS AND OTHER INFORMATION

Mrk Cap(R000)	12800	16960	35200
Current Ratio	0 80	0 67	0 50
Quik/Acid Tst	0 30	0 31	0 09
A/C Rec T/ovr	77 05	24 68	44 29
Tot Ass T/ovr	0 27	0 34	0 27
Debt/Ass Rat	0 15	0 14	0 12
L T L Tot Ass	0 09	0 06	0 01
Debt to Eqity	0 17	0 16	0 13
Interest Cover	3 01		-
Oper Prof Mrg	19 95	14 82	7 80
Net Prof Marg%	13 32	14 82	7 80
Ret on Assets	5 30	5 09	2 11
Ret on Equity%	4 14	5 92	2 38
Price/Earnings	19 05	18 28	366 67
Earning Yield%	5 25	5 47	0 27
NAV % Mrk Pr	125 88	94 36	42 87
Def Interval	2 98	1 45	0 92
Sus Grth Rate	4 14	5 92	2 98

SUBSIDIARY & ASSOCIATED COMPANIES

None

INVESTMENTS

None

OTIS ELEVATOR CO LTD

ABBREVIATION : OTIS

JSE SHORT CODE : OTS

SECTOR : Industrial-Building & Construction

SHAREHOLDERS

Who Owns Whom's Assessment of the Identity of the Ultimate Controlling Shareholder:
UNITED TECH CORP (USA)

SHAREHOLDER	PERCENTAGE 1992	1991
OTIS ELEVATOR CO	42 5	51 0
SA MUTUAL	23 3	23 3
UNITED TECHNOLOGIES HOLDINGS PLC	9 0	-
FIRST NAT NOM P/L	1 6	1 1
HARVEST SECURITIES LTD	1 5	1 1
SFSS NOM P/L	1 4	
TOTAL	79 2	76 5

DIRECTORS :
FOUGERON PJ MR,GNODDE AMD MR (Chairman)
KRONE GN MR,KUNERT R MR,LIPHOSA M MR
MARKHAM RE MR (Managing Director),STAFFELBACH UJ M

REGISTRATION NUMBER : 05/30021/06

REGISTERED OFFICE
222 Marshall Street, Johannesburg
2001
TEL 011-334 5200
FAX 011-334 5936

TRANSFER SECRETARY
Mercantile Registrars Ltd
P O Box 1053, Johannesburg
2000
TEL 011-333 8181

COMPANY SECRETARY
W A Soulsby

NATURE OF BUSINESS
The company sells, manufactures, refurbishes, erects and services elevators and escalators It operates a factory in Wadeville, near Germiston, where its manufacturing operations are conducted

BANKERS :
Standard Bank of SA Ltd
First National Bank of SA Ltd

AUDITORS :
Price Waterhouse Meyernel

FAMILIAR BRAND NAMES
MELCORP,OTIS

CONTRIBUTION BY ACTIVITY
N/A

YEAR END : November

DIVIDEND :Ords 10c

Final	(Ldr)08/03/91	(Pay)28/03/91	Amt(c)4
Interim	(Ldr)26/07/91	(Pay)16/08/91	Amt(c)9
Final	(Ldr)24/01/92	(Pay)14/02/92	Amt(c)10
Interim	(Ldr)24/07/92	(Pay)14/08/92	Amt(c)12

NUMBER OF EMPLOYEES : 976

CAPITAL STRUCTURE

	AUTHORISED	ISSUED
Ords 10c	22000000	20400000

FINANCIAL STATISTICS (AT FINANCIAL YEAR END)

(Amts in R'000)	1991 Nov	1990 Nov	1989 Nov	1988 Nov	1987 Nov
Ord S/H Int	16449	13160	13167	12142	11250
Long Trm Loans	82	452	631	542	199
Iss Ord Share	17000	17000	17000	17000	17000
Total Liab	24822	17525	23876	20210	12302
Current Liab	24740	17073	23245	19668	12103
Total Assets	41271	30685	37043	32352	23552
Current Assets	25809	22176	29126	25454	17457
Debtors	19924	18979	19931	12232	10986
Inventory	307	2757	8176	10621	6240
Turnover	116955	98164	91814	72033	63384
Oper Profit	13070	6370	17201	16381	14657
Interest Paid	21	713	500	137	277
Tax Paid	7204	3835	8206	8422	7033
Prf af Int&Tax	6519	2033	8675	8032	7347
Prf att Ord Sh	6519	2033	8675	8032	7347
Btm Line Earn	6519	2033	8675	8032	7347
Dividend Paid	3230	2040	7650	7140	
Mkt Prce(c) YE	240	185	310	270	242
Depreciation	2315	1995	1743	1483	1290

PER SHARE STATISTICS (CENTS)

Net Asst Val	96 76	77 41	77 45	71 42	66 18
Net Earnings	38 30	12 00	51 00	47 20	43 20
Dividends	19 00	12 00	45 00	42 00	-
Cash Flow	49 82	22 65	61 75	58 09	7 06

RATIOS AND OTHER INFORMATION

Mrk Cap(R000)	40800	31450	52700	45900	41140
Current Ratio	1 04	1 30	1 25	1 29	1 44
Quik/Acid Tst	1 03	1 14	0 90	0 75	0 93
A/C Rec T/ovr	5 87	5 17	4 61	5 89	5 77
Tot Ass T/ovr	2 83	3 20	2 48	2 23	2 69
Debt/Ass Rat	0 60	0 56	0 63	0 61	0 52
L T L Tot Ass	0 00	0 00	0 00	0 00	0 00
Debt to Eqity	1 51	1 30	1 77	1 62	1 08
Interest Cover	622 38	8 93	34 40	119 57	52 91
Oper Prof Mrg	11 18	6 49	18 73	22 74	23 12
Net Prof Marg%	5 57	2 07	9 45	11 15	11 59
Ret on Assets	33 30	21 45	46 92	51 28	62 23
Ret on Equity%	39 63	15 45	65 88	66 15	65 31
Price/Earnings	6 27	15 42	6 08	5 72	5 60
Divid Cover	2 02	1 00	1 13	1 12	-
Divid Yield	7 92	6 49	14 52	15 56	-
Earning Yield%	15 96	6 49	16 45	17 48	17 85
NAV % Mrk Pr	40 32	41 84	24 98	26 45	27 35
Effec Tax Rate	55 16	68 39	48 14	48 99	100 63
Def Interval	0 01	0 47	0 35	0 01	0 18
Sus Grth Rate	20 00	-0 05	7 78	7 35	65 31

SUBSIDIARY & ASSOCIATED COMPANIES

CD CENTRE (EAST) (PTY) LTD
HARSTAN INVESTMENT CO (PTY) LTD
JEKANE INVESTMENTS (PTY) LTD
LESEC LIFT SYSTEMS (PTY) LTD
MELBLAKE PROPERTIES (PTY) LTD
MELCORP BOP (PTY) LTD
MELCORP SA (PTY) LTD
MELCORP SWAZILAND (PTY) LTD
OTIS ELEVATOR CO (BOTSWANA) (PTY) LTD

INVESTMENTS

None

OVBEL HOLDINGS LTD

ABBREVIATION : OVBEL

JSE SHORT CODE : OVB

SECTOR : Financial-Property

SHAREHOLDERS

Who Owns Whom's Assessment of the Identity of the Ultimate Controlling Shareholder:
OVENSTONE FAMILY

SHAREHOLDER	PERCENTAGE 1992	1991
BARNETSON A U	---	2 8
BARNETT HARRIS R C A	---	1 9
BOARD OF EXECUTORS NOM P/L	-	17 3
FERBROS NOM P/L	---	2 5
HOLLARD INSURANCE CO LTD	---	1 5
MENTEITH INV LTD	---	8 0
METROPOLITAN LIFE LTD	- -	2 5
STD BANK NOM TVL P/L	---	1 8
SYFRETS NOM LTD	---	1 2
TROGON P/L	-	1 8
CLARK J R S	---	2 1
JENKINGS F J	---	1 1
LEITH S J S	---	1 7
OVBEL R TRUST		9 5
OVENSTONE A D P	---	3 9
RUSSELL GROUP P/L	--	1 1
SELTEAM P/L	---	1 2
SENDER B M	--	1 0
SWISS SOUTH AFRICAN	--	3 0
TABLE MOUNTAIN SERVICES P/L	---	8 0
SEDGWICK E W & CO P/L	---	6 0
VILJOEN P DU T	---	3 0
TOTAL	---	82 5

DIRECTORS :
BARNETSON AU ,BARNETT-HARRIS RCA ,CLARK JRS
KAMINSKI JWS ,MILLAR JR (Financial Director)
OVENSTONE ADP (Chairman),OVENSTONE NM
RIVETT-CARNAC ES ,SENDER BM

REGISTRATION NUMBER : 05/19928/06

REGISTERED OFFICE
Tannery Park, 23 Belmont Road
Rondebosch, Cape Town
7700
TEL: 021-685 4032
FAX: 021-686 8920

TRANSFER SECRETARY

N/A

COMPANY SECRETARY
F J Jenkings

NATURE OF BUSINESS
An investment holding company with subsidiaries engaged in property development & property trading

BANKERS :
First National Bank of SA Ltd
Standard Bank of SA Ltd, Senbank
Nedbank Ltd

AUDITORS :
Deloitte Pim Goldby

FAMILIAR BRAND NAMES
BELLANDIA,OVCON,OVDECO,OVLAND,SANTAREME BAY
SUN TRAIL RESORTS

CONTRIBUTION BY ACTIVITY
N/A

YEAR END : March

DIVIDEND : Ords 1c

Interim No 7	(Ldr)13/12/91	(Pay)20/12/91	Amt(c)3
Interim No 5	(Ldr)07/12/89	(Pay)18/12/89	Amt(c)3.6
Final No 6	(Ldr)15/06/90	(Pay)29/06/90	Amt(c)4.9
Interim No 7	(Ldr)14/12/90	(Pay)21/12/90	Amt(c)3.6
Interim No 8	(Ldr)13/12/91	(Pay)20/12/91	Amt(c)3
Final No 9	(Ldr)19/06/92	(Pay)26/06/92	Amt(c)3.5

NUMBER OF EMPLOYEES : 120

CAPITAL STRUCTURE

	AUTHORISED	ISSUED
Ords 1c	40000000	29576200
Var Rate Red Cum Prefs 1c	4000000	0

FINANCIAL STATISTICS (AT FINANCIAL YEAR END)

(Amts in R'000)	1992 Mar	1991 Mar	1990 Mar	1989 Mar	1988 Mar
Ord S/H Int	33041	33136	36439	32503	33413
Long Trm Loans	33352	25692	33082	28480	18977
Iss Ord Share	29576	29420	29157	29000	29000
Total Liab	62463	47470	97223	88978	57418
Current Liab	29111	21778	64141	60498	38441
Total Assets	95504	80606	133662	121481	90831
Current Assets	77292	61443	110377	97477	61707
Debtors	16423	9880	69221	58809	29034
Inventory	32963	24050	37948	35507	26717
Turnover	53602	77833	322413	269383	166742
Oper Profit	19	5467	9346	13620	7449
Interest Paid	3544	6758	7549	6971	3095
Tax Paid	1902	2308	1875	1448	746
Prf af Int&Tax	2980	5515	7432	5932	3608
Prf att Ord Sh	2874	4485	6190	5183	3743
Btm Line Earn	2570	2640	6428	5223	3868
Dividend Paid	1919	6022	2548	2176	1914
Mkt Prce(c) YE	55	67	65	70	80
Depreciation	360	2437	2714	1693	772

PER SHARE STATISTICS (CENTS)

Net Asst Val	111.72	112.63	124.98	112.08	115.22
Net Earnings	9.80	15.30	21.00	17.40	12.30
Dividends	6.50	8.50	8.50	7.00	6.00
Cash Flow	7.63	23.03	30.48	25.62	13.86

RATIOS AND OTHER INFORMATION

Mrk Cap(R000)	16267	19711	18952	20300	23200
Current Ratio	2.66	2.82	1.72	1.61	1.61
Quik/Acid Tst	1.52	1.72	1.13	1.02	0.91
A/C Rec T/ovr	3.26	7.88	4.66	4.58	5.74
Tot Ass T/ovr	0.56	0.97	2.41	2.22	1.84
Debt/Ass Rat	0.49	0.40	0.58	0.57	0.52
L T L Tot Ass	0.18	0.13	0.10	0.07	0.10
Debt to Eqity	1.41	0.98	2.13	2.14	1.43
Interest Cover	0.23	0.83	1.28	1.95	2.41
Oper Prof Mrg	0.04	7.02	2.90	5.06	4.47
Net Prof Marg%	5.36	5.76	1.92	1.92	2.24
Ret on Assets	9.29	18.37	12.62	11.76	8.83
Ret on Equity%	8.70	13.54	16.99	15.95	11.20
Price/Earnings	5.61	4.38	3.10	4.02	6.50
Divid Cover	1.51	1.80	2.47	2.49	2.05
Divid Yield	11.82	12.69	13.08	10.00	7.50
Earning Yield%	17.82	22.84	32.31	24.86	15.38
NAV % Mrk Pr	203.12	168.11	192.27	160.11	144.02
Effec Tax Rate	60.79	25.27	20.85	13.12	13.28
Def Interval	12.80	2.31	2.76	2.04	4.59
Sus Grth Rate	2.89	-4.64	9.99	9.25	5.47

SUBSIDIARY & ASSOCIATED COMPANIES

ALADDIN PROPERTIES LTD (50%)
BELLANDIA LTD
BUSHMANS RIVER MOUTH TOWNSHIP EXTENSION (50%)
CALM ACRES (PTY) LTD (50%)
CAPE ST FRANCIS HOLDINGS (PTY) LTD
CLYDE SECURITIES (PTY) LTD
DAVIDIAN ESTATES (PTY) LTD
ERF 9298 MOSSEL BAY (PTY) LTD (50%)
HI-PLANT (PTY) LTD
MANSFIELD INVESTMENTS LTD (50%)
MENLO PARK 25 (PTY) LTD
OVBEL FINANCE LTD
OVBEL REGISTRARS (PTY) LTD
OVCON LTD (20%)
OVDECO HOLDINGS LTD
OVDECO LIMITED
OVDECO PROPERTIES LTD (50%)
OVENSTONE HOLDINGS (PTY) LTD
OVLAND CAPE DEVELOPMENTS (PTY) LTD
OVLAND GROUP LIMITED
OVLAND LEASING COMPANY LTD
OVLAND LTD
OVLAND MANAGEMENT (NATAL) (PTY) LTD
OVLAND REAL ESTATE AGENCY (PTY) LTD
OVLAND REAL ESTATE AGENCY (TRANSVAAL) (P
OVLAND TIMESHARING (PTY) LTD (50%)
SANTAREME BAY LTD
ST LEGER & VINEY (PTY) LTD (33%)
SUN TRAIL RESORTS LTD (50%)
UMSINDUSI RIVER SITE (PTY) LTD

INVESTMENTS

None

OVCON LTD

ABBREVIATION : OVCON

JSE SHORT CODE : OVC

SECTOR : Industrial-Building & Construction

SHAREHOLDERS

Who Owns Whom's Assessment of the Identity of the Ultimate Controlling Shareholder: DIRECTORS / OVBEL

SHAREHOLDER	PERCENTAGE 1992	1991
BOARD OF EXECUTORS NOM P/L	---	3.5
MENTEITH INV LTD	---	1.3
SOUTHERN LIFE ASSOC LTD	---	7.0
KAMINSKI J W S	---	7.6
OVBEL R TRUST	---	1.6
TABLE MOUNTAIN SERVICES P/L	---	1.3
CHARLES TRUSTEES	---	10.0
GAMBIE R	---	2.0
KNIGHT M D D	---	1.1
MACE D W	---	5.2
MOFFAT A A	---	1.1
OVBEL HOLDINGS LTD	---	20.0
PAUL I G	---	2.1
PECKETT R	---	1.6
SEEMAN E H J	---	1.5
SWISS SA REINSURANCE	---	1.9
THOMAS J M	---	7.5
VAN ALPHEN G T	---	1.1
VEEDEN M J	---	1.4
TOTAL	---	78.7

DIRECTORS :
GAMBLE R ,KAMINSKI JWS ,MACE DW ,MILLAR JR
OVENSTONE ADP (Chairman),PECKETT R ,SENDER BM
THOMAS JM ,WEEDEN MJ

REGISTRATION NUMBER : 82/11014/06

REGISTERED OFFICE
Ovcon House, Constantia Road
Constantia
7800
TEL: 021-794 1300
FAX: 021-794 1979

TRANSFER SECRETARY

N/A

COMPANY SECRETARY
A R Langham

NATURE OF BUSINESS
A holding company with subsidiaries engaged in building contracting and civil engineering in the Cape, Natal and Namibia.

BANKERS :
First National Bank of SA Ltd
Standard Bank of SA Ltd
Trust Bank of Africa Ltd

AUDITORS :
Coopers Theron Du Toit

FAMILIAR BRAND NAMES
N/A

CONTRIBUTION BY ACTIVITY
N/A

YEAR END : March

DIVIDEND : Ords 1c

Interim No 1	(Ldr)29/11/91	(Pay)13/12/91	Amt(c)4
Final No 2	(Ldr)29/05/92	(Pay)19/06/92	Amt(c)8.5
Interim No 3	(Ldr)27/11/92	(Pay)11/12/92	Amt(c)4

NUMBER OF EMPLOYEES : 300

CAPITAL STRUCTURE

	AUTHORISED	ISSUED
Ords 1c	15000000	9000000

FINANCIAL STATISTICS (AT FINANCIAL YEAR END)

(Amts in R'000)	1992 Mar	1991 Mar	1990 Mar
Ord S/H Int	11010	7920	7260
Long Trm Loans	3858	3541	2204
Iss Ord Share	9000	9000	9000
Total Liab	32256	36678	37018
Current Liab	28398	33137	34814
Total Assets	43266	44598	43166
Intang Assets	*	*	1112
Current Assets	31341	31637	28403
Debtors	1568	1524	5391
Inventory	11412	13177	18512
Turnover	133399	72728	151709
Oper Profit	1997	903	6222
Interest Paid	812	420	701
Tax Paid	-71	-	3215
Prf af Int&Tax	4215	1320	3216
Prf att Ord Sh	4215	1320	3216
Btm Line Earn	4215	1320	3216
Dividend Paid	1125	400	-
Mkt Prce(c) YE	115	60	-
Depreciation	2728	1345	-

PER SHARE STATISTICS (CENTS)

Net Asst Val	122.33	88.00	68.31
Net Earnings	46.80	14.70	-
Dividends	12.50	4.00	-
Cash Flow	75.67	59.22	35.73

RATIOS AND OTHER INFORMATION

Mrk Cap(R000)	10350	5400	-
Current Ratio	1.10	0.95	0.82
Quik/Acid Tst	0.70	0.56	0.28
A/C Rec T/ovr	85.08	95.44	28.14
Tot Ass T/ovr	3.08	3.26	3.51
Debt/Ass Rat	0.75	0.82	0.85
L T L Tot Ass	0.09	0.08	0.05
Debt to Eqity	2.93	4.61	5.08
Interest Cover	2.46	2.15	8.88
Oper Prof Mrg	1.50	1.24	4.10
Net Prof Marg%	3.16	1.81	2.12

Ret on Assets	11.45	7.80	16.52
Ret on Equity%	38 28	33.33	44 30
Price/Earnings	2.46	4.08	-
Divid Cover	3.74	3.68	-
Divid Yield	10 87	6.67	-
Earning Yield%	40.70	24.50	-
NAV % Mrk Pr	106.38	146.67	-
Effec Tax Rate	1.50	-	49 99
Def Interval	0.57	2.56	0.86
Sus Grth Rate	28 07	11.62	44 30

SUBSIDIARY & ASSOCIATED COMPANIES

JOD HOLDINGS (PTY) LTD
OVCON CONSTRUCTION (PTY) LTD
OVCON HOLDINGS (PTY) LTD
OVCON VENTURES (PTY) LTD

INVESTMENTS

None

OZZ LTD

ABBREVIATION : OZZ

JSE SHORT CODE : OZZ

SECTOR : Industrial-Industrial Holding

SHAREHOLDERS

Who Owns Whom's Assessment of the Identity of the Ultimate Controlling Shareholder: DIRECTORS

SHAREHOLDER	PERCENTAGE 1992	1991
FIRST NAT NOM P/L	26 3	26 4
CMB NOM P/L	19 7	---
STD BANK NOM TVL P/L	12.1	3 7
OZZ LTD SHARE TRUST CONTROL ACC	6.1	4 8
BECKER M	4 5	4 5
BECKER J P FAMILY HLDGS P/L	4 2	4 2
KAMINER L	3.8	---
JACK BECKER P/L	2.2	2 2
EDWARDS R	1.9	---
FIRST NAT MERCHANT BANK LTD	1 4	1 4
BURT B J R	1 3	2 7
STIRMSTOCK CC	1.1	1 3
STERN I H	1.1	---
EBURY HOLDINGS LTD	1 1	1.1
OZZ LTD SHARE TRUST	1.0	2.5
EDWARDS R A	---	1 9
FARM-AG PACKAGING HLDGS P/L	---	1.1
MENBLACK NOM P/L	---	6.0
SANLAM	---	21.2
TOTAL	87.7	85 1

DIRECTORS :
BECKER J ,BECKER M ,BURT BJR ,MAGID E JP
STERN IH (Financial Director)
ZULBERG G (Chairman),ZULBERG HA

REGISTRATION NUMBER : 05/24058/06

REGISTERED OFFICE
2nd Floor, Gerber Goldschmidt House
29 De Beer Street, Braamfontein
2001
TEL: 011-403 5170
FAX. 011-403 1606

TRANSFER SECRETARY
Mercantile Registrars Ltd
P O Box 1053, Johannesburg
2000
TEL: 011-333 8181

COMPANY SECRETARY
I Walker

NATURE OF BUSINESS
An investment holding company with operations in the following activities The manufacturing of foundry castings for the mining and industrial sectors;Manufacturing of air and water valve and fitting systems and specialized engineering components for the mining and industrial sectors; Manufacturing of foundry castings, pumps and filter presses; Property investment and finance; Property construction and development.

BANKERS :
First National Bank of SA Ltd

AUDITORS :
Kessel Feinstein, Fisher Hoffman Stride

FAMILIAR BRAND NAMES
N/A

CONTRIBUTION BY ACTIVITY
N/A

YEAR END : March

DIVIDEND : Ords no par value

Final	(Ldr)10/08/90	(Pay)31/08/90	Amt(c)13 6
Final	(Ldr)05/07/91	(Pay)22/07/91	Amt(c)17
Final	(Ldr)03/07/92	(Pay)22/07/92	Amt(c)21 5

NUMBER OF EMPLOYEES : 1519

CAPITAL STRUCTURE

	AUTHORISED	ISSUED
Ords no par value	40167961	13277346

FINANCIAL STATISTICS (AT FINANCIAL YEAR END)

(Amts in R'000)	1992 Mar	1991 Mar	1990 Mar	1989 Mar	1988 Mar
Ord S/H Int	55766	41987	36459	22149	17282
Long Trm Loans	30123	30927	32417	87	65
Iss Ord Share	13277	13277	12642	9157	9157
Total Liab	55847	50161	59739	5730	2749
Current Liab	25724	19234	27322	5643	2684
Total Assets	110785	91254	95237	27879	20031
Intang Assets	828	894	961	*	*
Current Assets	45019	33565	34706	4870	3084
Debtors	21896	15079	17189	2099	1801
Inventory	16436	18486	15711	1861	782
Turnover	124578	113999	85979	8655	9008
Oper Profit	18511	18021	9815	525	726
Interest Paid	2692	4807	1246	297	67
Tax Paid	7368	6203	4435	125	87
Prf af Int&Tax	8731	7270	5047	119	572

Prf att Ord Sh	7436	6122	4260	3014	3434
Btm Line Earn	7436	6832	6199	4994	4595
Dividend Paid	2855	2344	1719	915	732
Mkt Prce(c) YE	415	220	48	60	70
Depreciation	5041	4493	2671	284	168

PER SHARE STATISTICS (CENTS)

Net Asst Val	413.78	309.51	280.79	241.88	188.73
Net Earnings	56.00	46.10	38.10	32.80	37.60
Dividends	21.50	17.00	13.60	10.00	8.00
Cash Flow	137.36	124.72	100.24	4.65	8.16

RATIOS AND OTHER INFORMATION

Mrk Cap(R000)	55100	29209	6068	5494	6410
Current Ratio	1.75	1.75	1.27	0.86	1.15
Quik/Acid Tst	1.11	0.78	0.70	0.53	0.86
A/C Rec T/ovr	5.69	7.56	5.00	4.12	5.00
Tot Ass T/ovr	1.12	1.25	0.90	0.31	0.45
Debt/Ass Rat	0.30	0.40	0.55	0.20	0.14
L T L Tot Ass	0.07	0.19	0.27	0.00	0.00
Debt to Eqity	0.60	0.86	1.44	0.26	0.16
Interest Cover	6.88	3.75	7.88	1.77	10.84
Oper Prof Mrg	14.86	15.81	11.42	6.07	8.06
Net Prof Marg%	5.97	5.37	4.95	34.82	38.12
Ret on Assets	16.93	20.05	11.29	12.32	17.91
Ret on Equity%	13.33	14.58	11.68	13.61	19.87
Price/Earnings	7.41	4.77	1.26	1.83	1.86
Divid Cover	2.60	2.71	2.80	3.28	4.70
Divid Yield	5.18	7.73	28.33	16.67	11.43
Earning Yield%	13.49	20.95	79.38	54.67	53.71
NAV % Mrk Pr	99.71	140.68	584.99	403.13	269.61
Effec Tax Rate	10.24	1.81	1.35	41.80	13.20
Def Interval	0.41	1.04	2.59	8.45	1.07
Sus Grth Rate	8.21	9.00	6.97	9.48	15.63

SUBSIDIARY & ASSOCIATED COMPANIES

129 BRUMA (PTY) LTD
BRICK & CLAY HOLDINGS LTD
BRICK & CLAY TARLTON (PTY) LTD
BRUMA LAKE DEVELOPMENT TRUST (50%)
CAPEGAS LTD
CORADICK (PTY) LTD
DAYGLOW ENGINEERING PRODUCTS LTD
ECLIPSE MINING EQUIPMENT (PTY) LTD
FLORAMON PROPERTIES (PTY) LTD
GASU ENTERPRISES (PTY) LTD
KELSHER INVESTMENT HOLDINGS LTD
KIMBERLEY-ECLIPSE ENGINEERING (OFS) LTD
LUCEM ELECTRONICS (PTY) LTD
LUCEM HOLDINGS LTD
NATAL STEAM COAL COMPANY LTD
NIGEL BRICK & CLAY (PTY) LTD
ORIC (PTY) LTD
OZZ CONSTRUCTION (PTY) LTD
OZZ INDUSTRIAL LTD
OZZ MANAGEMENT SERVICES (PTY) LTD
STOCKWOOD ESTATES (PTY) LTD
TRADVEST INVESTMENTS (PTY) LTD
WEST RAND ENGINEERING WORKS (PTY) LTD
WIZDEAL INVESTMENTS (PTY) LTD
ZULGAR SHAREPROP INVESTMENTS (PTY) LTD

INVESTMENTS

None

P G INDUSTRIES (ZIMBABWE) LTD

ABBREVIATION : PGI

SECTOR : Zimbabwe Stock Exchange

SHAREHOLDERS

Who Owns Whom's Assessment of the Identity of the Ultimate Controlling Shareholder: PRESTIGE INVESTMENTS / OLD MUTUAL INV CO

SHAREHOLDER	PERCENTAGE 1992	1991
PRESTIGE INV PVT LTD	45.4	---
OLD MUTUAL INV CORP (PVT) LTD	32.2	---
FIRST MUTUAL LIFE ASSURE SOC OF ZIM	3.0	---
NAT RAILWAYS OF ZIM CONTR PENS FUND	2.4	---
SYFRETS NOM (PVT) LTD	1.3	---
MINING INDUSTRY PENS FUND	1.1	---
TOTAL	85.4	---

DIRECTORS :
BOSMAN EW ,BRADLEY JP ,CHIURA ED ,COHEN LAH
KIRKPATRICK CWM ,LUBNER B (Deputy Chairman)
MIDDLEMOST DE (Managing Director)
MORLEY JW (Chairman),MUJAJI GJ

REGISTERED OFFICE
Stand 14801, Seke Road
Harare, Zimbabwe

TEL: 796001/5
FAX: 791556

TRANSFER SECRETARY
First Transfer Secretaries (Pvt) Ltd
P O Box 437, Bulawayo
Zimbabwe

TEL: 092634 - 702905

COMPANY SECRETARY
G Winter

NATURE OF BUSINESS
P G INDUSTRIES is the holding company of a group with large, diversified operations throughout Zimbabwe.Part of an international group,it is involved in the procurement, manufacturing, processing and distribution of timber,glass and allied products to local and export markets.

BANKERS :
Barclays Bank of Zimbabwe Ltd

AUDITORS :
Coopers & Lybrand

FAMILIAR BRAND NAMES
N/A

CONTRIBUTION BY ACTIVITY
N/A

YEAR END : March

DIVIDEND : Ords Z$1

Dividend	(Ldr)21/11/91	(Pay)16/12/91	Amt(c)8.17
Dividend	(Ldr)29/05/92	(Pay)22/06/92	Amt(c)10.50

CAPITAL STRUCTURE

	AUTHORISED	ISSUED
Ords Z$1	100000000	91995586

FINANCIAL STATISTICS (AT FINANCIAL YEAR END)

(Amts in Z$)	1992 Mar	1991 Mar
Ord S/H Int	224464	109562
Long Trm Loans	1080	876
Iss Ord Share	91996	91676
Total Liab	97602	57009
Current Liab	96522	56133
Total Assets	322066	166571
Current Assets	187483	86360
Debtors	51611	35520
Inventory	84271	48975
Turnover	326789	223204
Oper Profit	53400	26985
Tax Paid	25156	10527
Prf af Int&Tax	34884	16640
Prf att Ord Sh	34884	16640
Btm Line Earn	35041	16640
Dividend Paid	17202	8263
Depreciation	4188	2565

PER SHARE STATISTICS (CENTS)

Net Asst Val	243.99	119.51
Net Earnings	37.92	18.15
Dividends	18.67	9.04
Cash Flow	42.47	20.95

RATIOS AND OTHER INFORMATION

Current Ratio	1.94	1.54
Quik/Acid Tst	1.07	0.67
A/C Rec T/ovr	6.33	6.28
Tot Ass T/ovr	1.01	1.34
Debt/Ass Rat	0.30	0.34
L T L Tot Ass	0.00	0.01
Debt to Eqity	0.43	0.52
Oper Prof Mrg	16.34	12.09
Net Prof Marg%	10.67	7.46
Ret on Assets	18.64	16.31
Ret on Equity%	15.54	15.19
Divid Cover	2.03	2.01
Effec Tax Rate	42.01	38.99
Def Interval	0.35	0.05
Sus Grth Rate	7.88	7.65

SUBSIDIARY & ASSOCIATED COMPANIES

AFRICAN LUMBER CO (PRIVATE) LTD
ALCO FOREST INDUSTRIES (PRIVATE) LTD
D S T (PRIVATE) LTD
GLUELAM PRODUCTS (PRIVATE) LIMITED
PG MANUFACTURING (PRIVATE) LTD
PG MERCHANDISING LIMITED
PG MUTARE (PRIVATE) LTD
ZIMBOARD PRODCUTS (PRIVATE) LTD

INVESTMENTS

None

PAG LTD

ABBREVIATION : PAG

JSE SHORT CODE : PAG

SECTOR : Financial-Banks & Financial Services

SHAREHOLDERS

Who Owns Whom's Assessment of the Identity of the Ultimate Controlling Shareholder:
SE CATTON

SHAREHOLDER	PERCENTAGE 1992	1991
PAG HOLDINGS P/L	49.6	51.8
PAG PERSONNEL LTD	24.3	26.6
STOCKSHARE NOM P/L	9.1	---
CATTON E A	4.6	4.6
PAG INCENTIVE TRUST	3.0	3.0
PAG NOM P/L	2.0	2.0
RAHELL NOM P/L	---	4.4
TOTAL	92.5	92.2

DIRECTORS :
CATTON SE (Executive Chairman)
FERROW P (Managing Director),OAKLEY DM
ROSSE RJ

REGISTRATION NUMBER : 70/08484/06

REGISTERED OFFICE
Endulini, 5a Jubilee Road
Parktown
2193
TEL: 011-643 8471
FAX: 011-642 3927

TRANSFER SECRETARY
Investment Registrars (Pty) Ltd
P O Box 9167, Johannesburg
2000
TEL: 011-725 6004

COMPANY SECRETARY
N/A

NATURE OF BUSINESS
A management & personnel consulting & contracting organisation engaged in employment, recruitment & placement of people.

BANKERS :
Nedcor Bank Ltd

AUDITORS :
RA Hellman & Co

FAMILIAR BRAND NAMES
COMPUTER ASSIGNMENTS,CONFIDENTIAL ASSIGN'S
EXECUTIVE TEMP,MARKETING ASSIGNMENTS
PERSONNEL ASSIGNMENTS,PROFESSIONAL ASSIGN'S

CONTRIBUTION BY ACTIVITY
N/A

YEAR END : February

DIVIDEND : Ords 1c

Interim	(Ldr)10/08/90	(Pay)16/08/90	Amt(c)24

NUMBER OF EMPLOYEES : 587

CAPITAL STRUCTURE

	AUTHORISED	ISSUED
Ords 1c	40000000	21818304

FINANCIAL STATISTICS (AT FINANCIAL YEAR END)

(Amts in R'000)	1992 Feb	1991 Feb	1990 Sep	1990 Apr	1989 Jun
Ord S/H Int	4969	4623	4100	5953	4108
Long Trm Loans	27	54	-	-	1813
Iss Ord Share	21818	21818	21818	14370	13910
Total Liab	2767	1873	2150	2506	8147
Current Liab	2740	1819	2150	2506	6334
Total Assets	4631	3391	3145	8459	12255
Intang Assets	3105	3105	3105	*	*
Current Assets	3802	2551	2541	6596	5108
Debtors	2310	2482	2026	-	3659
Inventory	-	-	-	-	1272
Turnover	24792	10656	-	-	18804
Oper Profit	861	-1720	-	-178	2551
Interest Paid	199	32	-	455	-
Tax Paid	276	240	-	-	1192
Prf af Int&Tax	596	705	-	-491	1359
Prf att Ord Sh	596	705	-	-491	1359
Btm Line Earn	596	735	-	3016	808
Dividend Paid	218	3449	-	-	417
Mkt Prce(c) YE	10	22	-	38	50
Depreciation	106	44	-	58	1239

PER SHARE STATISTICS (CENTS)

Net Asst Val	8.54	6.96	4.56	41.43	29.53
Net Earnings	2.70	3.20	-	-3.40	9.80
Dividends	1.00	0.16	-	-	3.00
Cash Flow	3.22	3.43	-	-3.62	19.85

RATIOS AND OTHER INFORMATION

Mrk Cap(R000)	2182	4800	-	5461	6955
Current Ratio	1.39	1.40	1.18	2.63	0.81
Quik/Acid Tst	1.39	1.40	1.18	2.63	0.61
A/C Rec T/ovr	10.73	4.29	-	-	5.14
Tot Ass T/ovr	5.35	3.14	-	-	1.53
Debt/Ass Rat	0.60	0.55	0.68	0.30	0.63
L T L Tot Ass	0.01	0.02	-	-	0.12
Debt to Eqity	0.56	0.41	0.52	0.42	1.89
Interest Cover	4.33	11.00	-	-0.39	-
Oper Prof Mrg	3.47	-16.14	-	-	13.57
Net Prof Marg%	2.40	6.62	-	-	7.23
Ret on Assets	23.13	28.81	-	-0.51	20.82
Ret on Equity%	11.99	15.25	-	-9.90	33.08
Price/Earnings	3.70	6.88	-	-11.18	5.10
Divid Cover	2.70	20.00	-	-	3.27
Divid Yield	10.00	0.73	-	-	6.00
Earning Yield%	27.00	14.55	-	-8.95	19.60
NAV % Mrk Pr	85.43	31.63	-	109.02	59.07
Effec Tax Rate	31.65	-21.30	-	-	40.06
Def Interval	0.80	0.15	-	-	0.96
Sus Grth Rate	7.61	-59.36	-	-8.25	22.93

SUBSIDIARY & ASSOCIATED COMPANIES

None

INVESTMENTS

None

PALABORA MINING CO LTD

ABBREVIATION : PALAMIN

JSE SHORT CODE : PAM

SECTOR : Metals & Minerals-Copper

SHAREHOLDERS

Who Owns Whom's Assessment of the Identity of the Ultimate Controlling Shareholder: RIO TINTO / ANGLO AMERICAN

SHAREHOLDER	PERCENTAGE 1992	1991
PALABORA HLDGS LTD	61.4	61.4
SA MUTUAL	7.5	6.6
STD BANK NOM TVL P/L	4.2	3.5
RIO TINTO SA LTD	3.5	3.5
NAT SELECTIONS LTD	2.8	2.8
RESIDENT NOM LTD	2.7	2.7
SIXTY SIX MARSHALL STREET NOM P/L	2.5	1.6
EIGHTY ONE MAIN STREET NOM LTD	2.0	1.3
INDUSTRIAL SELECTIONS LTD	1.2	1.2
SOUTHERN LIFE ASSOC LTD	---	1.1
TOTAL	87.7	85.6

DIRECTORS :
AITKEN BR MR, BAILEY DC MR, CHAPMAN TN MR, DAVIS LA
DEYZEL JG MR, FENWICK F MR (Managing Director)
KEYS NJ MR, LEROY AJ MR (Chairman)
LIGHTERNESS TJ MR, NTULI ZW, PRETORIUS TL MR
SHUTT NR MR (Commercial Director), VORSTER DR MR
WIEHAHN NE PRO

REGISTRATION NUMBER : 56/02134/06

REGISTERED OFFICE
4th Floor, Rio Tinto House, 122 Pybus Road
Sandton
2199
TEL: 011-883 3860
FAX: 011-883 2703

TRANSFER SECRETARY
Union Provident Trust SA Ltd
P O Box 2322, Johannesburg
2000
TEL: 011-833 6700

COMPANY SECRETARY
Rio Tinto Management Services SA (Pty) Ltd

NATURE OF BUSINESS
The main business of the group relates to the mining, extraction and sale of copper; process by-products include anode slimes, sulphuric acid, magnetite, uranium concentrates and zirconia. In a smaller business segment the company also exploits a vermiculite deposit adjacent to the copper operation.

BANKERS :
First National Bank of SA Ltd

AUDITORS :
Coopers Theron Du Toit

FAMILIAR BRAND NAMES
N/A

CONTRIBUTION BY ACTIVITY
Copper (% Turnover) (76 0%)
Vermiculite (12 0%)
Zirconia (8 0%)
Anode Slimes (3 0%)
Other (1 0%)

YEAR END : December

DIVIDEND : Ords R1

Interim No 92	(Ldr)08/06/90	(Pay)25/06/90	Amt(c)110
Final No 93	(Ldr)31/08/90	(Pay)28/09/90	Amt(c)180
Interim No 94	(Ldr)30/11/90	(Pay)09/01/91	Amt(c)250
Final No 95	(Ldr)01/03/91	(Pay)21/03/91	Amt(c)240
Interim No 96	(Ldr)07/06/91	(Pay)24/06/91	Amt(c)110
Interim No 97	(Ldr)30/08/91	(Pay)27/09/91	Amt(c)140
Interim No 98	(Ldr)13/12/91	(Pay)10/01/92	Amt(c)180
Final No 99	(Ldr)06/03/92	(Pay)26/03/92	Amt(c)350
Interim No 100	(Ldr)05/06/92	(Pay)26/06/92	Amt(c)110
Final No 102	(Ldr)11/12/92	(Pay)08/01/93	Amt(c)140

NUMBER OF EMPLOYEES : 3362

CAPITAL STRUCTURE

	AUTHORISED	ISSUED
Ords R1	28500000	28315500

FINANCIAL STATISTICS (AT FINANCIAL YEAR END)

(Amts in R'000)	1991 Dec	1990 Dec	1989 Dec	1988 Dec	1987 Dec
Ord S/H Int	344317	318521	274908	226403	206571
Long Trm Loans	354825	463925	335763	384748	335449
Iss Ord Share	28316	28316	28316	28316	28316
Total Liab	670763	712335	669518	640211	534753
Current Liab	315938	248410	333755	255463	199304
Total Assets	1015080	1030856	944426	866614	741324
Current Assets	416427	386953	340757	303547	264524
Debtors	177485	128832	124511	120168	75994
Inventory	178886	213316	130269	122731	90058
Turnover	1106081	1122458	1217657	921194	589356
Oper Profit	455935	513848	673643	422240	221773
Interest Paid	7094	10114	7705	8159	11328
Tax Paid	224879	287551	394411	246106	121052
Prf af Int&Tax	233590	228011	292341	174611	89393
Prf att Ord Sh	233590	228011	292341	174611	89393
Btm Line Earn	244459	231751	299734	174611	89393
Dividend Paid	220861	220861	247761	159983	83531
Mkt Prce(c) YE	7500	6400	5500	5000	3150
Depreciation	50882	45428	36277	27893	26399

PER SHARE STATISTICS (CENTS)

Net Asst Val	1215 98	1124 88	970 86	799 56	729 52
Net Earnings	825 00	805 00	1013 00	658 00	350 00
Dividends	780 00	780 00	875 00	565 00	295 00
Cash Flow	737 11	1284 46	1245 60	820 30	314 93

RATIOS AND OTHER INFORMATION

Mrk Cap(R000)	2123700	1812224	1557380	1415800	891954
Current Ratio	1 32	1 56	1 02	1 19	1 33
Quik/Acid Tst	0 75	0 70	0 63	0 71	0 88
A/C Rec T/ovr	6 23	8 71	9 78	7 67	7 76
Tot Ass T/ovr	1 09	1 09	1 29	1 06	0 80
Debt/Ass Rat	0 33	0 26	0 37	0 38	0 34
L T L Tot Ass	0 01	0 02	0 01	0 09	0 07
Debt to Eqity	0 96	0 85	1 25	1 46	1 23
Interest Cover	64 45	50 95	87 43	51 75	19 58
Oper Prof Mrg	41 22	45 78	55 32	45 84	37 63
Net Prof Marg%	21 12	20 31	24 01	18 95	15 17
Ret on Assets	45 86	50 99	73 53	49 49	29 92
Ret on Equity%	67 84	71 58	106 34	77 12	43 27
Price/Earnings	9 09	7 95	5 43	7 60	9 00
Divid Cover	1 06	1 03	1 16	1 16	1 19
Divid Yield	10 40	12 19	15 91	11 30	9 37
Earning Yield%	11 00	12 58	18 42	13 16	11 11
NAV % Mrk Pr	16 21	17 58	17 65	15 99	23 16
Effec Tax Rate	63 82	35 45	50 04	51 42	70 17
Def Interval	0 08	0 06	0 07	0 38	0 75
Sus Grth Rate	3 70	2 24	16 22	6 46	2 84

SUBSIDIARY & ASSOCIATED COMPANIES

AMERICAN VERMICULITE CORPORATION (U S A
MANDOVAL COATINGS LTD (U K)
MANDOVAL LTD (U K)
MANDOVAL VERMICULITE (PTY) LTD
MANDOVAL VERMICULITE PRODUCTS INC (USA)
TRANSVAAL COPPER ROD CO LTD (50%)
ZIRCONIA SALES (AMERICA) INC
ZIRCONIA SALES (JAPAN) KK
ZIRCONIA SALES (JERSEY) LTD
ZIRCONIA SALES (PTY) LTD
ZIRCONIA SALES (UK) LTD

INVESTMENTS

CACTUS INVESTMENTS (PTY) LTD (RED CUM PR (10500 SH)

PALS HOLDINGS LTD

ABBREVIATION : PALS

JSE SHORT CODE : PAL

SECTOR : Industrial-Clothing, Footwear & Textiles

SHAREHOLDERS

Who Owns Whom's Assessment of the Identity of the Ultimate Controlling Shareholder:
DIRECTORS

SHAREHOLDER	PERCENTAGE 1992	1991
KAGAN SECURITIES P/L	32 5	32 5
DETENTE NOM LTD	17 0	17 0
KAGAN G S TRUST	7 1	7 1
KAGAN H A TRUST	7 1	7 1
KAGAN S R	6 4	4 7
FINE N H	2 7	2 7
HERON R J	2 3	1 3
PARSONAGE S C	2 2	2 2
KAGAN J E	2 1	2 1
TOTAL	79 3	76 6

DIRECTORS :
FINE NH ,KAGAN JE
KAGAN SR (Chairman & Joint MD)
NOIK H (Joint Managing Director),PARSONAGE SC

REGISTRATION NUMBER : 87/02753/06

REGISTERED OFFICE
10th Floor, 2 Long Street

Cape Town
8001
TEL 021-47 0020
FAX 021-47 5473

TRANSFER SECRETARY
Central Registrars Ltd
P O Box 4844, Johannesburg
2000
TEL 011-331 0051

COMPANY SECRETARY
H Noik

NATURE OF BUSINESS
An investment holding company, with subsidiaries manufacturing menswear for local & export markets

BANKERS :
Standard Bank of SA Ltd

AUDITORS :
Baker Musikanth

FAMILIAR BRAND NAMES
BAY CITY,GERARD,PALS,PALUCCI

CONTRIBUTION BY ACTIVITY
N/A

YEAR END : June

DIVIDEND : Ords 1c

Interim	(Ldr)16/03/90	(Pay)30/03/90	Amt(c)1 4
Final	(Ldr)12/10/90	(Pay)30/10/90	Amt(c)1 6
Interim	(Ldr)22/02/91	(Pay)28/02/91	Amt(c)1 8
Final	(Ldr)18/10/91	(Pay)30/10/91	Amt(c)1 5
Interim	(Ldr)21/02/92	(Pay)28/02/92	Amt(c)2
Final	(Ldr)16/10/92	(Pay)02/11/92	Amt(c)1 3

NUMBER OF EMPLOYEES : 400

CAPITAL STRUCTURE

	AUTHORISED	ISSUED
Ords 1c	20000000	10000000

FINANCIAL STATISTICS (AT FINANCIAL YEAR END)

(Amts in R'000)	1992 Jun	1991 Jun	1990 Jun	1989 Jun	1988 Jun
Ord S/H Int	7871	8226	7846	7359	6862
Long Trm Loans	544	664	677	481	387
Iss Ord Share	10000	10000	10000	10000	10000
Total Liab	4860	5296	5331	3899	2449
Current Liab	4316	4632	4654	3418	2062
Total Assets	10217	10110	9643	7603	6421
Intang Assets	2514	3412	3534	3655	2890
Current Assets	8010	8441	8047	6206	4746
Debtors	4636	4266	4217	2799	2483
Inventory	3374	4174	3829	3406	2262
Oper Profit	1568	1703	1560	1275	1201
Interest Paid	557	662	619	267	87
Tax Paid	327	373	161	105	365
Prf af Int&Tax	752	710	787	918	749
Prf att Ord Sh	752	710	787	918	749
Btm Line Earn	-25	710	787	918	749
Dividend Paid	330	330	300	340	140
Mkt Prce(c) YE	22	25	30	37	36
Depreciation	444	456	426	319	216

PER SHARE STATISTICS (CENTS)

Net Asst Val	53 57	48 14	43 12	37 04	39 72
Net Earnings	7 50	7 10	7 90	9 20	8 20
Dividends	3 30	3 30	3 00	3 40	1 40
Cash Flow	11 59	11 80	12 42	12 81	11 16

RATIOS AND OTHER INFORMATION

Mrk Cap(R000)	2200	2500	3000	3700	3600
Current Ratio	1 86	1 82	1 73	1 82	2 30
Quik/Acid Tst	1 07	0 92	0 91	0 82	1 20
Debt/Ass Rat	0 46	0 51	0 54	0 50	0 37
L T L Tot Ass	0 04	0 05	0 05	0 05	0 05
Debt to Eqity	0 60	0 62	0 66	0 51	0 35
Interest Cover	2 82	2 57	2 52	4 83	13 80
Ret on Assets	16 01	17 26	16 25	16 97	18 70
Ret on Equity%	9 55	8 63	10 03	12 47	10 92
Price/Earnings	2 93	3 52	3 80	4 02	4 39
Divid Cover	2 27	2 15	2 63	2 71	5 86
Divid Yield	15 00	13 20	10 00	9 19	3 89
Earning Yield%	34 09	28 40	26 33	24 86	22 78
NAV % Mrk Pr	243 50	192 56	143 73	100 11	110 33
Effec Tax Rate	33 73	33 15	13 92	6 05	27 20
Def Interval	1 22	1 02	1 93	0 96	0 77
Sus Grth Rate	5 36	4 62	6 21	7 85	8 87

SUBSIDIARY & ASSOCIATED COMPANIES

FLORIETTE FASHIONS (PTY) LTD
FURILLO CLOTHING (PTY) LTD
HUGUENOT CLOTHING (PTY) LTD
MAGO FASHIONS (PTY) LTD
PALS CLOTHING (PTY) LTD

INVESTMENTS

None

PANGBOURNE PROPERTIES LTD

ABBREVIATION : PANPROP

JSE SHORT CODE : PAP

SECTOR : Financial-Property Loan Stock

SHAREHOLDERS

Who Owns Whom's Assessment of the Identity of the Ultimate Controlling Shareholder:
SA MUTUAL / INSTITUTIONS

SHAREHOLDER	PERCENTAGE 1992	1991
SA MUTUAL	35 0	33 8
EIGHTY ONE MAIN STREET NOM LTD	14 1	22 6
SOUTHERN LIFE ASSOC LTD	11 9	12 6
NEDBANK NOM LTD	5 4	4 0
STD BANK NOM TVL P/L	3 9	5 1
CMB NOM P/L	3 8	
ARC SECURITIES BVI LTD	2 8	---
FIRST NAT NOM P/L	1 8	2 7
LATEULERE SALES P/L	1 7	2 0
METAL IND GROUP PENS FUND	1 7	--
SA SPECIAL RISKS INSURANCE ASSOC LTD	1 3	1 5
CLARENCE B G	1 1	1 4
SANLAM	---	1 2
TOTAL	84 7	86 8

DIRECTORS :
CAMPBELL AMA ,CLARENCE BG ,KIMMEL HM
PAPENFUS EL ,WHITING JR (Chairman

REGISTRATION NUMBER : 87/02352/06

REGISTERED OFFICE
1st Floor, 112 Pybus Road
Sandton
2199
TEL: 011-884 5330
FAX: 011-783 0450

TRANSFER SECRETARY
Central Registrars Ltd
P O Box 4844, Johannesburg
2000
TEL: 011-331 0051

COMPANY SECRETARY
J C Dannhauser

NATURE OF BUSINESS
The group derives income from rentals received from its portfolio of properties, and from property transactions.

BANKERS :
Nedcor Bank Ltd

AUDITORS :
Deloitte Pim Goldby

FAMILIAR BRAND NAMES
N/A

CONTRIBUTION BY ACTIVITY
Offices (% Usage Spread) (35.0%)
Industrial (38.0%)
Shops (27.0%)

YEAR END : June

DIVIDEND : Units

Interim No 5	(Ldr)09/03/90	(Pay)02/04/90	Amt(c)33.66
Final No 6	(Ldr)14/09/90	(Pay)02/10/90	Amt(c)34.17
Interim No 7	(Ldr)15/03/91	(Pay)02/04/91	Amt(c)36.0009
Final No 8	(Ldr)13/09/91	(Pay)01/10/91	Amt(c)38.74
Interim No 9	(Ldr)13/03/92	(Pay)01/04/92	Amt(c)37.6176
Final No 10	(Ldr)18/09/92	(Pay)01/10/92	Amt(c)37.1178

NUMBER OF EMPLOYEES : 27

CAPITAL STRUCTURE

	AUTHORISED	ISSUED
Ords (1 Ord : 9 Var Rate Debs)	100000000	60373000
Var Rate Cum Partic Prefs 1c	100000000	0
Unsec Var Rate Sub Debs 50c	543357000	543357000
Def Ords 1c		507692

FINANCIAL STATISTICS (AT FINANCIAL YEAR END)

(Amts in R'000)	1992 Jun	1991 Jun	1990 Jun	1989 Jun	1988 Jun
Ord S/H Int	58974	43947	29334	14503	13522
Long Trm Loans	274963	237354	192646	139069	141918
Iss Ord Share	60373	41388	34675	28030	28030
Total Liab	299234	256439	207538	150299	152864
Current Liab	24271	19085	14892	11230	10946
Total Assets	358208	300386	236872	164802	166386
Current Assets	95424	95708	63212	14447	20376
Debtors	5202	3389	9671	3705	5273
Turnover	42170	32968	25869	23416	21194
Oper Profit	30158	25253	19215	17480	18105
Interest Paid	41599	30809	22469	2640	15089
Tax Paid	7	55	438	672	1508
Prf af Int&Tax	-397	659	1722	16648	1508
Prf att Ord Sh	-397	659	1722	1623	1508
Btm Line Earn	1653	2584	4020	2196	1801
Dividend Paid	832	606	419	1192	1031
Mkt Prce(c) YE	550	650	580	460	420

PER SHARE STATISTICS (CENTS)

Net Asst Val	97.68	106.18	84.60	51.74	48.24
Net Earnings	72.54	75.00	72.00	5.80	5.40
Dividends	74.74	74.73	67.83	4.23	3.69
Cash Flow	-0.70	1.59	5.47	59.07	5.41

RATIOS AND OTHER INFORMATION

Mrk Cap(R000)	332052	269022	201115	128938	117726
Current Ratio	3.93	5.01	4.24	1.29	1.86
Quik/Acid Tst	3.93	5.01	4.24	1.29	1.86
A/C Rec T/ovr	8.11	9.73	2.67	6.32	4.02
Tot Ass T/ovr	0.12	0.11	0.11	0.14	0.13
Debt/Ass Rat	0.84	0.85	0.86	0.91	0.92
L T L Tot Ass	0.77	0.79	0.80	0.84	0.85
Debt to Eqity	5.07	5.84	6.95	10.36	11.30
Interest Cover	0.72	0.82	0.86	6.62	1.20
Oper Prof Mrg	71.52	76.60	74.28	74.65	85.43
Net Prof Marg%	-0.94	2.00	6.66	6.93	7.12
Ret on Assets	11.50	10.49	10.40	12.11	10.88
Ret on Equity%	-0.67	1.50	5.87	11.19	11.15
Price/Earnings	7.58	8.67	8.06	79.31	77.78
Divid Cover	0.97	1.00	1.06	1.37	1.46
Divid Yield	13.59	11.50	11.69	0.92	0.88
Earning Yield%	13.19	11.54	12.41	1.26	1.29
NAV % Mrk Pr	17.76	16.34	14.59	11.25	11.49
Effec Tax Rate	-1.79	7.70	20.28	3.88	50.00
Def Interval	-690.08	362.14	109.82	0.79	94.26
Sus Grth Rate	-2.08	0.12	4.44	2.97	3.53

SUBSIDIARY & ASSOCIATED COMPANIES

385 SMITH STREET DURBAN SHARE BLOCK (PTY
5/4 WYNBERG X6 INVESTMENTS SHARE BLOCK (
ANMERITY INVESTMENTS SHARE BLOCK (PTY) L
BOBONE SHARE BLOCK (PTY) LTD
BROMHOF INDUSTRIAL ENTERPRISES SHARE BLO
CHIMES INVESTMENTS SHARE BLOCK (PTY) LTD
CORAL INVESTMENTS SHARE BLOCK (PTY) LTD
CRESTA DEVELOPMENTS (PTY) LTD
DEL PROPERTY HOLDINGS LTD
EIGHTEENTH STAGE INVESTMENTS SHARE BLOCK
ERF 1679 FERNDALE (PTY) LTD
ERF 17 ANCHORVILLE SHARE BLOCK (PTY) LTD
ERF 64 VERWOERDBURGSTAD (PTY) LTD
ERF 731 FERNDALE SHARE BLOCK (PTY) LTD
FLORIDA GLEN FOUR FIVE ONE (PTY) LTD
FLORIDA SENIORS SHARE BLOCK (PTY) LTD
GOLDLINE INVESTMENTS SHARE BLOCK (PTY) L
HORIZON VIEW SHOPPING CENTRE (PTY) LTD
HUME THABA'NCHU SHARE BLOCK (PTY) LTD
IMMU PROPERTIES SHARE BLOCK (PTY) LTD
INDUSTRY ROAD DEVELOPMENT (PTY) LTD
IOTA ESTATES SHARE BLOCK (PTY) LTD
JAGORY INVESTMENTS SHARE BLOCK (PTY) LTD
JAGORY PROPERTY INVESTMENTS (PTY) LTD
KYBO INVESTMENTS SHARE BLOCK (PTY) LTD
LIBHOF PROPERTY SHARE BLOCK (PTY) LTD
LYTTELTON TOWNSHIPS SHARE BLOCK (PTY) LT
MEET EN PEIL (PTY) LTD
MOROBEN INVESTMENTS SHARE BLOCK (PTY) LT
NIXMERCH (PTY) LTD
OAKLINK INVESTMENTS SHARE BLOCK (PTY) LT

PAB INVESTMENTS (PTY) LTD
PANGBOURNE PROPERTIES TRADING (PTY) LTD
PAPERTEX PROPERTIES SHARE BLOCK (PTY) LT
PORTION 31 RIETFONTEIN (PTY) LTD
PROCESS HOUSE SHARE BLOCK (PTY) LTD
PROPERTY & BUSINESS INVESTMENTS (SUNNYSI
PROPHECY INVESTMENTS SHARE BLOCK (PTY) L
RELIANCE PROPERTIES SHARE BLOCK (PTY) LT
RHO INVESTMENTS SHARE BLOCK (PTY) LTD
RICHARDS DRIVE PROPERTIES SHARE BLOCK (P
RODINIS INVESTMENTS SHARE BLOCK (PTY) LT
SAUNA MANUFACTURING COMPANY SHARE BLOCK
SERBIAN PROPERTIES SHARE BLOCK (PTY) LTD
SOUGHT OUT INVESTMENTS SHARE BLOCK (PTY)
STAND 1665 DAWN PARK SHARE BLOCK (PTY) L
STAND 1724 DAWN PARK (PTY) LTD
STAND 22 WILBART SHARE BLOCK (PTY) LTD
TEMPEST INVESTMENTS SHARE BLOCK (PTY) LT
TL KELLY INVESMENTS SHARE BLOCK (PTY) LT
TWENTY SECOND STAGE INVESTMENTS SHARE BL
TWENTY THIRD STAGE INVESTMENTS SHARE BLO
VERDI SHARE BLOCK (PTY) LTD
WYNPOL PROPERTIES SHARE BLOCK (PTY) LTD

INVESTMENTS

None

PDC HOLDINGS LTD

ABBREVIATION : PDC

JSE SHORT CODE : PDC

SECTOR : Industrial-Pharmaceutical & Medical

SHAREHOLDERS

Who Owns Whom's Assessment of the Identity of the Ultimate Controlling Shareholder:
ANGLO VIA GRESHAM

SHAREHOLDER	PERCENTAGE 1992	1991
GRESHAM IND LTD	87.1	85.9
TOTAL	87.1	85.9

DIRECTORS :
BLOOM JB MR,COETZEE CF MR,GLICK E MR
IZIKOWITZ SH MR,KATZ M MR
KEATING LA MR (Chief Executive),KLASS J MR
KOHN GM MR,MORRIS K MR (Commercial Director)
POGIR R MR,UTIAN GM MR (Chairman)
VAN ASWEGEN NJV M

REGISTRATION NUMBER : 56/02689/06

REGISTERED OFFICE
5 Laub Street, New Centre
Johannesburg
2000
TEL: 011-493 3600
FAX: 011-493 2324

TRANSFER SECRETARY
Mercantile Registrars Ltd
P O Box 1053, Johannesburg
2000
TEL: 011-333 8181

COMPANY SECRETARY
D S Wilson

NATURE OF BUSINESS
The group is engaged in the wholesale distribution of ethical products, patent medicines, toiletries, personal & health care products and photographic requirements. The group also provides financing to pharmacists, & controls Plus Promotions, a retail pharmacy franchise group.

BANKERS :
Volkskas Ltd

AUDITORS :
Ernst & Young

FAMILIAR BRAND NAMES
N/A

CONTRIBUTION BY ACTIVITY
N/A

YEAR END : April

DIVIDEND : Ords 1c

Interim No 1	(Ldr)30/11/90	(Pay)14/12/90	Amt(c)1.5
Final No 2	(Ldr)14/06/91	(Pay)28/06/91	Amt(c)1.5
Interim No 3	(Ldr)13/12/91	(Pay)03/01/92	Amt(c)1.5
Final No 4	(Ldr)10/07/92	(Pay)20/07/92	Amt(c)1.5

NUMBER OF EMPLOYEES : 1400

CAPITAL STRUCTURE

	AUTHORISED	ISSUED
Ords 1c	30000000	20935252

FINANCIAL STATISTICS (AT FINANCIAL YEAR END)

(Amts in R'000)	1991 Mar	1990 Mar
Ord S/H Int	57117	57447
Long Trm Loans	7430	587
Iss Ord Share	20935	20935
Total Liab	98231	104897
Current Liab	90801	104310
Total Assets	147348	152819
Intang Assets	8000	9525
Current Assets	140299	138886
Debtors	81103	80971
Inventory	57841	57013
Turnover	522313	511772
Oper Profit	1540	12007
Interest Paid	17156	15070
Tax Paid	2518	8274
Prf af Int&Tax	1823	8284
Prf att Ord Sh	1823	8284
Btm Line Earn	298	8284
Dividend Paid	628	-
Mkt Prce(c) YE	70	10
Depreciation	2005	1701

PER SHARE STATISTICS (CENTS)

Net Asst Val	234.62	228.91
Net Earnings	8.70	39.60
Dividends	3.00	-

Cash Flow	19.94	47.24

RATIOS AND OTHER INFORMATION

Mrk Cap(R000)	14655	2094
Current Ratio	1.55	1.33
Quik/Acid Tst	0.91	0.78
A/C Rec T/ovr	6.44	6.32
Tot Ass T/ovr	3.54	3.35
Debt/Ass Rat	0.66	0.68
L T L Tot Ass	0.04	-
Debt to Eqity	1.70	1.82
Interest Cover	0.09	0.80
Oper Prof Mrg	0.29	2.35
Net Prof Marg%	0.35	1.62
Ret on Assets	14.59	20.70
Ret on Equity%	3.19	14.42
Price/Earnings	8.05	0.25
Divid Cover	2.90	-
Divid Yield	4.29	-
Earning Yield%	12.43	396.00
NAV % Mrk Pr	335.17	2289.09
Effec Tax Rate	50.03	50.55
Def Interval	1.56	0.27
Sus Grth Rate	2.09	14.42

SUBSIDIARY & ASSOCIATED COMPANIES

PDC TRADING LTD
SAPDC (HEAD OFFICE BUILDINGS & WAREHOUSE
SAPDC (JOHANNESBURG BUILDING INVESTMENTS
UNITED PHOTOGRAPHIC LABORATORIES LTD

INVESTMENTS

None

PENROSE HOLDINGS LTD

ABBREVIATION : PENROSE

JSE SHORT CODE : PEN

SECTOR : Industrial-Printing & Publishing

SHAREHOLDERS

Who Owns Whom's Assessment of the Identity of the Ultimate Controlling Shareholder:
NASPERS/TOLLGATE/HOSKEN CONSOLIDATED

SHAREHOLDER	PERCENTAGE 1992	1991
NAT PERS BPK	29.1	---
SAFEGRO NOM P/L	20.1	16.1
CINOA HOLDINGS LTD	8.3	---
MEKLER J	7.4	20.6
MASON P J	5.5	15.4
JOUBERT G L	3.6	13.0
UAL MERCHANT BANK LTD	3.2	3.6
SAGE LIFE LTD	2.7	3.2
COLOUR TIME P/L	2.7	---
DALGLAND NOM P/L	2.1	1.1
DE KOCK M J	1.9	9.4
DEACON R	1.3	3.3
DELAHUNT-SMOLENIEC P B	---	1.3
LIBERTY LIFE ASSOC OF AFRICA LTD	---	2.8
TOTAL	87.7	89.6

DIRECTORS :
DE KOCK MJ
DELAHUNT SMOLENIEC PB (Financial Director)
JOUBERT GL (Sales Director),LEWIS IMA ,MASON PJ
MEKLER J (Chairman)
THOMPSON J (Managing Director),WIESE FJ
WILMOT-SITWELL AS

REGISTRATION NUMBER : 67/09848/06

REGISTERED OFFICE
Penrose House, 21 School Street
Johannesburg
2001
TEL: 011-334 1950
FAX: 011-334 1746

TRANSFER SECRETARY
Central Registrars Ltd
P O Box 4844, Johannesburg
2000
TEL: 011-331 0051

COMPANY SECRETARY
P J Mason

NATURE OF BUSINESS
The group is involved in the printing, binding & publishing industry, specialising in financial print, financial advertising, bookwork, magazines & diaries.

BANKERS :
First National Bank of SA Ltd

AUDITORS :
KPMG Aiken & Peat

FAMILIAR BRAND NAMES
CAREER SECRETARY,CAREER SUCCESS,COVER
HOTEL & CONFERENCE CENTRE
STATE DEPARTMENTS OF SA

CONTRIBUTION BY ACTIVITY
N/A

YEAR END : June

DIVIDEND :15/02/91 and 15/08/91

NUMBER OF EMPLOYEES : 200

CAPITAL STRUCTURE

	AUTHORISED	ISSUED
Ords 2c	30000000	21718200

FINANCIAL STATISTICS (AT FINANCIAL YEAR END)

(Amts in R'000)	1991 Jun	1990 Jun	1989 Jun	1988 Jun	1987 Jun
Ord S/H Int	9071	7970	7061	7525	3481
Long Trm Loans	2567	2136	2387	542	1487
Iss Ord Share	14860	14860	14860	14860	6100
Total Liab	8204	7603	7048	3968	5813
Current Liab	5637	5467	4661	3426	4326
Total Assets	17275	15573	14109	11493	9294
Current Assets	9704	6910	6069	6437	5213
Debtors	4992	5332	4838	4755	4146

Inventory	1506	1498	1127	899	707
Turnover	29590	26705	25920	26185	-
Oper Profit	2210	1906	180	3247	1917
Interest Paid	633	702	644	251	78
Tax Paid	476	295	-	1497	929
Prf af Int&Tax	1101	909	-464	1499	910
Prf att Ord Sh	1101	909	-464	1499	900
Btm Line Earn	1101	909	-464	1968	900
Dividend Paid	-	-	-	600	291
Mkt Prce(c) YE	20	30	40	90	-
Depreciation	1195	1117	847	566	239

PER SHARE STATISTICS (CENTS)

Net Asst Val	61.04	53.63	47.52	50.64	57.07
Net Earnings	7.40	6.10	-3.10	10.90	-
Dividends	-	-	-	4.00	-
Cash Flow	15.45	13.63	2.58	15.63	9.98

RATIOS AND OTHER INFORMATION

Mrk Cap(R000)	2972	4458	5944	13374	-
Current Ratio	1.72	1.26	1.30	1.88	1.21
Quik/Acid Tst	1.45	0.99	1.06	1.62	1.04
A/C Rec T/ovr	5.93	5.01	5.36	5.51	-
Tot Ass T/ovr	1.71	1.71	1.84	2.28	-
Debt/Ass Rat	0.42	0.46	0.49	0.34	0.62
L T L Tot Ass	0.10	0.11	0.16	0.04	0.15
Debt to Eqity	0.81	0.90	0.98	0.51	1.66
Interest Cover	3.49	2.72	0.28	12.94	24.58
Oper Prof Mrg	7.47	7.14	0.69	12.40	-
Net Prof Marg%	3.72	3.40	-1.79	5.72	-
Ret on Assets	12.79	12.24	1.28	28.25	20.63
Ret on Equity%	12.14	11.41	-6.57	19.92	25.85
Price/Earnings	2.70	4.92	-12.90	8.26	-
Divid Cover	-	-	-	2.73	-
Divid Yield	-	-	-	4.44	-
Earning Yield%	37.00	20.33	-7.75	12.11	-
NAV % Mrk Pr	305.22	178.78	118.79	56.27	-
Effec Tax Rate	31.39	25.42	-	47.20	48.99
Def Interval	1.08	1.80	11.67	0.30	1.72
Sus Grth Rate	12.14	11.41	-6.57	11.95	17.49

SUBSIDIARY & ASSOCIATED COMPANIES

MERCURY PRINTING WORKS (PTY) LTD
OPTIMUS COMPUTER SYSTEMS (PTY) LTD
PENROSE PRESS (PTY) LTD
PENROSET (PTY) LTD
RS-TM FINANCIAL ADVERTISING (PTY) LTD
TACTICS PROMOTIONAL AND INCENTIVE MARKET

INVESTMENTS

None

PEP BOTSWANA HOLDINGS LTD

ABBREVIATION : PEP BOT

SECTOR : Botswana Stock Exchange

SHAREHOLDERS

Who Owns Whom's Assessment of the Identity of the Ultimate Controlling Shareholder:
PEP LTD VIA TENDRIL LTD

SHAREHOLDER	PERCENTAGE 1992	1991
TENDRIL LTD	70.0	---
DEBSWANA PENS FUND	4.8	---
IGI BOTSWANA LIFE ASSURE LTD	2.6	---
BRANDON LTD	2.0	---
GENESIS EMERGING MARKETS FUND	1.9	---
BOTSWANA MOTOR VEHICLE INSURANCE FUND	1.8	---
BETA GLOBAL EMERGING MARKETS TRUST LTD	1.4	---
TOTAL	84.4	---

DIRECTORS :
DAMBE CS (Chief Executive),HAUGHTON TA ,LOUW JA
LYONS RA ,MOFFETT MJ ,ROELOFSE H ,TIBONE MC
WIESE CH (Chairman

REGISTRATION NUMBER : 1151/72

REGISTERED OFFICE
First Floor, Barclays House
Khama Crescent, Gabarone

TEL: 313830
FAX: 313598

TRANSFER SECRETARY
Union Provident Trust (Botswana) Ltd
P O Box 41015, Gaberone
Botswana

TEL: 09267-41015

COMPANY SECRETARY
N/A

NATURE OF BUSINESS
PEP is the holding company of PEP STORES and ACKER MANS.These companies are both committed to the pro vision of quality clothing, footwear and household textiles to all family members at affordable prices.

BANKERS :
Barclays Bank of Botswana Ltd
Standard Chartered Bank

AUDITORS :
Coopers & Lybrand

FAMILIAR BRAND NAMES
N/A

CONTRIBUTION BY ACTIVITY
N/A

YEAR END : February

CAPITAL STRUCTURE

	AUTHORISED	ISSUED
Ords P0,01	40000000	27000000

FINANCIAL STATISTICS (AT FINANCIAL YEAR END)

(Amts in P)	1992 Feb
Ord S/H Int	7135
Long Trm Loans	102
Iss Ord Share	24000

Total Liab	26129
Current Liab	26027
Total Assets	33264
Current Assets	32362
Debtors	131
Inventory	6150
Turnover	35911
Oper Profit	11115
Interest Paid	45
Tax Paid	3555
Prf af Int&Tax	7515
Prf att Ord Sh	7515
Btm Line Earn	7515

PER SHARE STATISTICS (CENTS)

Net Asst Val	29.73
Net Earnings	31.30
Cash Flow	31.31

RATIOS AND OTHER INFORMATION

Current Ratio	1.24
Quik/Acid Tst	1.01
A/C Rec T/ovr	274.13
Tot Ass T/ovr	1.08
Debt/Ass Rat	0.78
Debt to Eqity	3.65
Interest Cover	247.00
Oper Prof Mrg	30.95
Net Prof Marg%	20.93
Ret on Assets	33.41
Ret on Equity%	105.33
Effec Tax Rate	32.11
Def Interval	1.50
Sus Grth Rate	105.33

SUBSIDIARY & ASSOCIATED COMPANIES

ACKERMANS (BOTSWANA) (PTY) LTD
PEP STORES (PTY) LTD (BOTSWANA)

INVESTMENTS

None

PEP LTD

ABBREVIATION : PEP

JSE SHORT CODE : PEI

SECTOR : Industrial-Retailers & Wholesalers

SHAREHOLDERS

Who Owns Whom's Assessment of the Identity of the Ultimate Controlling Shareholder:
PEPGRO VIA PEPKOR

SHAREHOLDER	PERCENTAGE 1992	1991
PEPKOR BPK	78.6	71.9
MEYERSOHN WILFRED & CO P/L	5.4	5.2
STD BANK NOM TVL P/L	4.4	4.5
SA MUTUAL	3.8	3.8
CMB NOM P/L	1.3	7.3
SANLAM	—	1.3
TOTAL	93.4	93.9

DIRECTORS :
BASSON JW ,BRAND PJ (Dir Human Resources)
HAUGHTON TA (Managing Director),HERMAN HD PROF
HLONGWANE TR ,HOLTZHAUSEN JCF ,LOUBSER MJ
LOUW JA (Vice Chairman)
ROELOFSE H (Financial Director),SCHUTTE FG PROF
STEYN CJ ,VISSER JJ ,WEYERS BR
WIESE CH ADV (Chairman

REGISTRATION NUMBER : 05/18945/06

REGISTERED OFFICE
Radnor Road, Parow Industria
Cape Town
7490
TEL: 021-931 3151
FAX: 021-932 6189

TRANSFER SECRETARY
Central Registrars Ltd
P O Box 4844, Johannesburg
2000
TEL: 011-331 0051

COMPANY SECRETARY
R Stadler

NATURE OF BUSINESS
The group retails clothing, footwear and home textiles through 1154 retail outlets within RSA, and neighbouring states. The group manufactures clothing and blankets in 10 factories, and exports clothing, footwear & related products to the UK, Africa and the Continent. Commercial and general printing operations are conducted via Printkor.

BANKERS :
Trust Bank of Africa Ltd
First National Bank of SA Ltd
FirstCorp Merchant Bank Ltd

AUDITORS :
Coopers Theron Du Toit

FAMILIAR BRAND NAMES
N/A

CONTRIBUTION BY ACTIVITY
Manufacturing (13.5%)
Other (1.9%)
Retail (% Turnover) (84.6%)

YEAR END : February

DIVIDEND : Ords no par value

Final No 8	(Ldr)18/05/90	(Pay)01/06/90	Amt(c)42
Interim No 9	(Ldr)16/11/90	(Pay)30/11/90	Amt(c)30
Final No 10	(Ldr)24/05/91	(Pay)07/06/91	Amt(c)48
Interim No 11	(Ldr)15/11/91	(Pay)29/11/91	Amt(c)34
Final No 12	(Ldr)22/05/92	(Pay)05/06/92	Amt(c)55.5
Interim No 13	(Ldr)13/11/92	(Pay)27/11/92	Amt(c)7.5

NUMBER OF EMPLOYEES : 13223

CAPITAL STRUCTURE

	AUTHORISED	ISSUED
Ords no par value	265880740	230108910

FINANCIAL STATISTICS (AT FINANCIAL YEAR END)

(Amts in R'000)	1992 Feb	1991 Feb	1990 Feb	1989 Feb	1988 Feb
Ord S/H Int	344934	292718	239936	201317	154461
Long Trm Loans	49290	32739	29213	26230	10000
Iss Ord Share	46022	45644	45644	45644	45644
Total Liab	444721	328190	266769	208467	163288
Current Liab	395431	295451	237556	182237	153288
Total Assets	789655	620908	506705	409784	317749
Current Assets	618644	512717	420992	346814	269455
Debtors	38657	32454	32879	18020	14950
Inventory	494070	335274	326233	265979	206659
Turnover	1467621	1225258	988015	804819	648532
Oper Profit	145349	140763	117969	105696	70262
Interest Paid	13666	8508	11075	4642	2275
Tax Paid	54893	60412	37697	28572	9042
Prf af Int&Tax	96972	86670	78147	72482	58945
Prf att Ord Sh	98447	88484	79416	73329	58867
Btm Line Earn	80637	88484	79416	73329	58867
Dividend Paid	41061	35602	31038	26473	21909
Mkt Prce(c) YE	3600	3000	1600	1300	1500
Depreciation	21278	15168	10964	8443	7414

PER SHARE STATISTICS (CENTS)

Net Asst Val	749.50	641.31	525.67	441.06	338.40
Net Earnings	215.20	193.86	174.00	161.00	129.00
Dividends	89.50	78.00	68.00	58.00	48.00
Cash Flow	262.77	231.73	182.86	204.68	150.89

RATIOS AND OTHER INFORMATION

Mrk Cap(R000)	1656792	1369320	730304	593372	684660
Current Ratio	1.56	1.74	1.77	1.90	1.76
Quik/Acid Tst	0.32	0.60	0.40	0.44	0.41
A/C Rec T/ovr	37.97	37.75	30.05	44.66	43.38
Tot Ass T/ovr	1.86	1.97	1.95	1.96	2.04
Debt/Ass Rat	0.53	0.48	0.48	0.46	0.48
L T L Tot Ass	0.03	0.01	0.01	0.02	-
Debt to Eqity	1.20	1.03	1.01	0.94	0.99
Interest Cover	11.30	17.18	10.69	22.77	30.88
Oper Prof Mrg	9.90	11.49	11.94	13.13	10.83
Net Prof Marg%	6.71	7.22	8.04	9.11	9.08
Ret on Assets	21.15	25.35	25.31	26.17	22.42
Ret on Equity%	28.54	30.23	33.10	36.42	38.11
Price/Earnings	16.73	15.48	9.20	8.07	11.63
Divid Cover	2.40	2.49	2.56	2.78	2.69
Divid Yield	2.49	2.60	4.25	4.46	3.20
Earning Yield%	5.98	6.46	10.88	12.38	8.60
NAV % Mrk Pr	20.82	21.38	32.85	33.93	22.56
Effec Tax Rate	35.16	37.10	34.55	5.51	2.91
Def Interval	0.45	0.12	0.08	-	-
Sus Grth Rate	16.64	18.07	20.16	23.27	23.93

SUBSIDIARY & ASSOCIATED COMPANIES

ACKERMANS (BOPHUTHATSWANA) (PTY) LTD
ACKERMANS (BOTSWANA) (PTY) LTD
ACKERMANS (NAMIBIA) (PTY) LTD
ACKERMANS (TRANSKEI) (PTY) LTD
ACKERMANS (TRANSVAAL) LTD
ACKERMANS LESOTHO (PTY) LTD
ACKERMANS LTD
EDVIC (PTY) LTD (BOPHUTHATSWANA)
GAP STORES (PTY) LTD
HALF PRICE STORES (SA) (PTY) LTD
HARTIES MANAGEMENT SERVICES (TRANSKEI) (
HARTIES STORES (BOTSWANA) (PTY) LTD
HARTIES STORES (CISKEI) (PTY) LTD
HARTIES STORES (GAZANKULU) (PTY) LTD
HARTIES STORES (KWAZULU) (PTY) LTD
HARTIES STORES (LEBOWA) (PTY) LTD
HARTIES STORES (LESOTHO) (PTY) LTD
HARTIES STORES (NAMIBIA) (PTY) LTD
HARTIES STORES (SWAZILAND) (PTY) LTD
HARTIES STORES (VENDA) (PTY) LTD
JOHN TAYLOR (PTY) LTD
KULANI TRADING COMPANY (PTY) LTD (TRANSK
LEGAN INTERNATIONAL (PTY) LTD
M M RETAIL (PTY) LTD
PEP BOTSWANA HOLDINGS LTD
PEP GAZANKULU (PTY) LTD
PEP INTERNATIONAL (PTY) LTD
PEP INVESTMENTS (PTY) LTD
PEP MANUFACTURING (PTY) LTD
PEP PROP MITCHELL'S PLAIN (PTY) LTD (49%)
PEP REEF PROPERTIES (PTY) LTD
PEP RETAIL (PTY) LTD
PEP STORES (CISKEI) (PTY) LTD
PEP STORES (KWAZULU) LTD (50%)
PEP STORES (LEBOWA) (PTY) LTD (50%)
PEP STORES (LESOTHO) (PTY) LTD
PEP STORES (PRIVATE) LTD (ZIMBABWE)
PEP STORES (PTY) LTD
PEP STORES (PTY) LTD (SWAZILAND)
PEP STORES (REEF) LTD (49%)
PEP STORES (TRANSKEI) HOLDINGS (PTY) LTD
PEP STORES BOPHUTHATSWANA LTD
PEP STORES BOTSHABELO (PTY) LTD (50%)
PEP STORES BOTSWANA (PTY) LTD
PEP STORES BUSHBUCKRIDGE (PTY) LTD (50%)
PEP STORES NAMIBIA (PTY) LTD
PEP STORES PENINSULA (PTY) LTD
PEP STORES PENINSULA HOLDINGS LTD
PEP STORES QWA QWA (PTY) LTD (50%)
PEP STORES RETAIL (PTY) LTD (NAMIBIA) (50%)
PEP STORES TRANSKEI (PTY) LTD
PEP STORES VENDA LTD (50%)
PEP TEXTILE INDUSTRIES (PTY) LTD
PEP TRANSKEI MANAGEMENT & CONSULTANCY SE
PEPCLO LTD
PEPFIN (PTY) LTD
PRECIOUS STORES (PTY) LTD (TRANSKEI)
PRINTKOR (PTY) LTD
RITEPRICE (PTY) LTD
SELECT 'N SAVE (PTY) LTD
TANGO HOSIERY (PTY) LTD
TOTS 'N TEENS CLOTHING (PTY) LTD
TYATHANGA STORES (PTY) LTD
VANS STORES SWAZILAND (PTY) LTD

INVESTMENTS

CCJ DEVELOPMENTS (PTY) LTD (VAR RATE RED (3000000 SH)
URD BELEGGINGS (PTY) LTD (RED CUM PREFS) (35000000 S)

PEPGRO LTD

ABBREVIATION : PEPGRO

JSE SHORT CODE : PEG

SECTOR : Industrial-Retailers & Wholesalers

SHAREHOLDERS

Who Owns Whom's Assessment of the Identity of the Ultimate Controlling Shareholder: DIRECTORS

SHAREHOLDER	PERCENTAGE 1992	1991
CMB NOM P/L	19 2	---
TITAN NOM P/L	15 9	13 9
ABSA NOM P/L	9 8	---
MONEX INTERNATIONAL P/L	9 1	9 1
ROCAP INV P/L	7 9	7 9
MONEX SECURITIES P/L	7 4	7 4
ROTRUST P/L	4 3	4 3
PEPGRO LTD SHARE INC SCHEME	3 7	3 7
DEMELER INV P/L	2 8	2 8
METROPOLITAN LIFE LTD	1 7	1 7
GRANADINO INV P/L	1 7	1 7
LACIS INV P/L	1 5	1 5
MONEX INV P/L	1 3	1 3
ZYLTRUST NOM P/L	1 1	1 1
INDO-CHINA NOM P/L	1 1	---
SANLAM	---	18 4
VOLKSKAS NOM P/L	---	10 1
TOTAL	88 3	84 8

DIRECTORS :
BALL T ,PRETORIUS EF ,VAN ROOYEN R
WIESE CH ADV (Chairman

REGISTRATION NUMBER : 83/01066/06

REGISTERED OFFICE
36 Stellenberg Road, Parow Industria
7500
TEL 021-932 9911
FAX 021-931 0848

TRANSFER SECRETARY
Central Registrars Ltd
P O Box 4844, Johannesburg
2000
TEL 011-331 0051

COMPANY SECRETARY
J F Pienaar

NATURE OF BUSINESS
An investment holding company with a controlling interest in JSE quoted Pepkor Ltd Pepkor in turn controls quoted Shoprite Holdings, Smart Centre, Pep Ltd,Tradehold & Cashbuild Ltd

BANKERS :
First National Bank of SA Ltd, Senbank

AUDITORS :
Coopers Theron Du Toit

FAMILIAR BRAND NAMES
CASHBUILD

CONTRIBUTION BY ACTIVITY
N/A

YEAR END : February

DIVIDEND :Ords 10c

Interim	(Ldr)17/11/89	(Pay)01/12/89	Amt(c)25
Final	(Ldr)25/05/90	(Pay)08/06/90	Amt(c)61
Interim	(Ldr)16/11/90	(Pay)30/11/90	Amt(c)28 5
Final	(Ldr)24/05/91	(Pay)07/06/91	Amt(c)86 5
Interim	(Ldr)15/11/91	(Pay)29/11/91	Amt(c)32 5
Final	(Ldr)22/05/92	(Pay)05/06/92	Amt(c)100

DIVIDEND :Ords 2c

Interim	(Ldr)13/11/92	(Pay)27/11/92	Amt(c)7 5

CAPITAL STRUCTURE

	AUTHORISED	ISSUED
7% Partic Comp Conv Cum Prefs 10c	3360000	0
Ords 2c	150000000	75264640
6% Unsec Sub Auto Conv Debs R12	11289696	11289696

FINANCIAL STATISTICS (AT FINANCIAL YEAR END)

(Amts in R'000)	1992 Feb	1991 Feb	1990 Feb	1989 Feb	1988 Feb
Ord S/H Int	124192	67033	65118	65113	65111
Long Trm Loans	-	29568	48575	48737	34068
Iss Ord Share	15053	11693	11693	11693	11693
Total Liab	15117	60695	59699	57554	45879
Current Liab	15117	31127	11124	8817	11811
Total Assets	139309	127698	124817	122667	110990
Current Assets	19462	13904	9757	8823	8170
Debtors	14756	10850	9757	8823	8168
Oper Profit	-98	-34	-91	4500	13034
Interest Paid	429	4943	4892	5201	4803
Prf af Int&Tax	20402	11863	10125	9420	8231
Prf att Ord Sh	20402	11782	10061	9356	8186
Btm Line Earn	47566	15332	10061	9356	8186
Dividend Paid	19945	13447	10056	9354	8068
Mkt Prce(c) YE	5800	3000	1620	2000	1500

PER SHARE STATISTICS (CENTS)

Net Asst Val	825 03	573 02	556 90	556 85	556 84
Net Earnings	135 50	372 30	315 30	271 30	77 30
Dividends	132 50	115 00	86 00	80 00	69 00
Cash Flow	135 53	100 76	86 04	80 01	77 26

RATIOS AND OTHER INFORMATION

Mrk Cap(R000)	873074	350790	189427	233860	175395
Current Ratio	1 29	0 45	0 88	1 00	0 69
Quik/Acid Tst	1 29	0 45	0 88	1 00	0 69
Debt/Ass Rat	0 11	0 47	0 47	0 46	0 41
L T L Tot Ass	-	0 23	0 38	0 39	0 30
Debt to Eqity	0 12	0 90	0 91	0 87	0 69
Interest Cover	46 06	2 48	2 17	2 81	2 71
Ret on Assets	14 95	13 16	12 03	11 92	11 74
Ret on Equity%	16 43	17 58	15 45	14 37	12 57
Price/Earnings	42 80	8 06	5 14	7 37	19 40
Divid Cover	1 02	3 24	3 67	3 39	1 12
Divid Yield	2 28	3 83	5 31	4 00	4 60
Earning Yield%	2 34	12 41	19 46	13 57	5 15
NAV % Mrk Pr	14 22	19 10	34 38	27 84	37 12
Def Interval	-	0 38	2 07	2 05	1 02
Sus Grth Rate	0 37	-2 48	0 01	0 00	0 18

SUBSIDIARY & ASSOCIATED COMPANIES

PEPGROFIN (PTY) LTD (50%)
PEPKOR LTD

INVESTMENTS

None

PEPKOR LTD

ABBREVIATION : PEPKOR

JSE SHORT CODE : PEP

SECTOR : Industrial-Retailers & Wholesalers

SHAREHOLDERS

Who Owns Whom's Assessment of the Identity of the Ultimate Controlling Shareholder:
PEPGRO

SHAREHOLDER	PERCENTAGE 1992	1991
PEPGRO LTD	53.1	56.2
CMB NOM P/L	18.8	---
MOMENTUM LIFE ASSURE LTD	3.7	1.9
YSKOR PENS FUND	3.5	3.7
PUBLIC INV COMMISSIONERS	3.1	---
PEPKOR LTD SHR PURCHASE SCHEME - EXECUTI	1.5	2.6
ABSA NOM P/L	1.4	---
ESCOM PENS & PROV FUND	1.1	1.2
TITAN NOM P/L	---	1.3
SANLAM	---	14.8
VOLKSKAS NOM P/L	---	3.2
TOTAL	86.1	84.7

DIRECTORS :
ANDERSON DH ,BALL T ,BASSON JW ,FOUCHE JJ
HAUGHTON TA ,LOUBSER MG
LOUW JA (Deputy Chairman)
MOORE C (Financial Director),PRETORIUS EF
ROGUT B ,STASSEN C ,VAN ROOYEN R ,WEYERS BR
WIESE CH ADV (Chairman)

REGISTRATION NUMBER : 65/07765/06

REGISTERED OFFICE
36 Stellenberg Road, Parow Industria
7500
TEL: 021-932 9911
FAX: 021-931 0848

TRANSFER SECRETARY
Central Registrars Ltd
P O Box 4844, Johannesburg
2000
TEL: 011-331 0051

COMPANY SECRETARY
J F Pienaar

NATURE OF BUSINESS
An investment holding company with controlling interests in quoted Shoprite Holdings, Pep Ltd, Smart Centre, Tradehold & Cashbuild Ltd. Group operations include cash retailing of clothing, footwear, blankets, household softs/hardware, food, consumer durables & the wholesale & retail of builders' materials.

BANKERS :
First National Bank of SA Ltd, Senbank
Nedcor Bank Ltd

AUDITORS :
Coopers Theron Du Toit

FAMILIAR BRAND NAMES
ACKERMANS,BUY-N-BUILD,CASHBUILD
FRASERS MINE STORES,HARTIES
KHAYELIHLE HOMEMAKERS,PEP STORES
STUDENT PRINCE,U-BUILD

CONTRIBUTION BY ACTIVITY
Clothing (% Turnover) (40.0%)
Food (56.0%)
Building materials (4.0%)

YEAR END : February

DIVIDEND : Ords 50c

Interim	(Ldr)17/11/89	(Pay)01/12/89	Amt(c)54
Final	(Ldr)25/05/90	(Pay)08/06/90	Amt(c)131
Interim	(Ldr)16/11/90	(Pay)30/11/90	Amt(c)62
Final	(Ldr)24/05/91	(Pay)07/06/91	Amt(c)150
Interim	(Ldr)15/11/91	(Pay)29/11/91	Amt(c)71
Final	(Ldr)22/05/92	(Pay)05/06/92	Amt(c)173

DIVIDEND : Ords 5c

Interim	(Ldr)13/11/92	(Pay)27/11/92	Amt(c)8

NUMBER OF EMPLOYEES : 39605

CAPITAL STRUCTURE

	AUTHORISED	ISSUED
Ords 5c	300000000	159002950
6% Unsec Sub Auto Conv Debs R11	23850443	23850443

FINANCIAL STATISTICS (AT FINANCIAL YEAR END)

(Amts in R'000)	1992 Feb	1991 Feb	1990 Feb	1989 Feb	1988 Feb
Ord S/H Int	428029	217035	189735	148784	121300
Long Trm Loans	362210	162985	130303	126881	115310
Iss Ord Share	15900	11693	11693	11693	11693
Total Liab	1715023	631099	476499	405694	340894
Current Liab	1352813	468114	346196	278813	225584
Total Assets	2143052	848134	666234	554478	462194
Current Assets	1681921	705226	561181	467790	387478
Debtors	238379	51554	48559	35846	37577
Inventory	1066298	460256	413085	331081	249675
Turnover	4265818	1957364	1481213	1192532	939160
Oper Profit	196214	155311	129069	105519	71771
Interest Paid	42942	15250	15487	8346	7813
Tax Paid	76598	64381	42724	32555	12288
Prf af Int&Tax	115164	97434	86299	78773	51670
Prf att Ord Sh	93839	79352	67791	58091	39188
Btm Line Earn	169155	78258	72382	61738	69217
Dividend Paid	38195	24789	21632	18475	15201
Mkt Prce(c) YE	11100	7000	4700	3800	2750
Depreciation	48855	18858	13641	10362	9087

PER SHARE STATISTICS (CENTS)

Net Asst Val	2692.01	1856.11	1622.64	1272.42	1037.37
Net Earnings	612.30	558.00	579.80	496.80	369.90
Dividends	244.00	212.00	185.00	158.00	130.00
Cash Flow	915.42	699.12	749.16	745.49	516.33

RATIOS AND OTHER INFORMATION

Mrk Cap(R000)	1764900	818510	549571	444334	321558
Current Ratio	1.24	1.51	1.62	1.68	1.72
Quik/Acid Tst	0.46	0.52	0.43	0.49	0.61
A/C Rec T/ovr	17.90	37.97	30.50	33.27	24.99
Tot Ass T/ovr	1.99	2.31	2.22	2.15	2.03
Debt/Ass Rat	0.68	0.68	0.61	0.61	0.63
L T L Tot Ass	0.05	0.12	0.09	0.11	0.14
Debt to Eqity	3.41	2.64	2.14	2.28	2.39
Interest Cover	4.76	10.46	8.35	12.66	9.19
Oper Prof Mrg	4.60	7.93	8.71	8.85	7.64
Net Prof Marg%	2.20	4.05	4.58	4.87	4.17
Ret on Assets	11.25	20.88	21.82	21.86	16.44
Ret on Equity%	21.92	36.56	35.73	39.04	32.31
Price/Earnings	18.13	12.54	8.11	7.65	7.43
Divid Cover	2.51	2.63	3.13	3.14	2.85
Divid Yield	2.20	3.03	3.94	4.16	4.73

Earning Yield%	5.52	7.97	12.34	13.07	13.45
NAV % Mrk Pr	24.25	26.52	34.52	33.48	37.72
Effec Tax Rate	37.30	28.88	22.90	9.06	4.51
Def Interval	1.70	0.73	0.32	0.37	0.76
Sus Grth Rate	13.00	25.14	24.33	26.63	19.77

SUBSIDIARY & ASSOCIATED COMPANIES

CASHBUILD LTD (45,4%)
FISCO RETAIL HOLDINGS (PTY) LTD
JOFANDER (PTY) LTD (50%)
JOFINCO (PTY) LTD (50%)
JOFINCO DRIE (PTY) LTD (50%)
PEP LTD
PEPKOR CLOTHING INDUSTRIES LTD
PEPKOR PROPERTY HOLDINGS (PTY) LTD
PEPKOR TEXTILE INDUSTRIES (PTY) LTD
PEPKORFIN LTD
PEPLAND (PTY) LTD (50%)
SHOPRITE HOLDINGS LTD
SMART CENTRE HOLDINGS LTD
TRADEHOLD LTD
WILFRED MEYERSOHN & CO (PTY) LTD
WILFRED MEYERSOHN TWEE (PTY) LTD (50%)

INVESTMENTS

SMALL BUSINESS DEVELOPMENT CORPORATION ((222086 SH)

PERSETECH LTD

ABBREVIATION : PERSTEC

JSE SHORT CODE : PRC

SECTOR : Industrial-Electronics, Electrical & Bat

SHAREHOLDERS

Who Owns Whom's Assessment of the Identity of the Ultimate Controlling Shareholder:
SA MUTUAL VIA BARLOWS

SHAREHOLDER	PERCENTAGE 1992	1991
PERSETECH HOLDINGS P/L	58.0	---
STD BANK NOM TVL P/L	5.8	---
LIBERTY LIFE ASSOC OF AFRICA LTD	5.0	---
HG & S NOM P/L	5.0	---
ISM TRUST	3.0	---
METAL IND GROUP PENS FUND	2.1	---
ENGINEERING INDUSTRIES PENS FUND	1.8	---
CMB NOM P/L	1.7	---
WORKMENS COMPENS COMMISSIONER IN TRUST	1.3	---
SA SPECIAL RISKS INSURANCE ASSOC LTD	1.2	---
WOOLTRU GROUP RETIREMENT FUND	1.1	---
GREENMARKET SQUARE NOM P/L	1.0	---
EIGHTY ONE MAIN STREET NOM LTD	1.0	---
TOTAL	87.9	---

DIRECTORS :
CILLIERS PJH ,ERASMUS DH
EVANS KRM (Financial Director),FERRIMAN EA
IBBOTSON PJ (Chief Executive)
MARNITZ RJ (Chairman),PARKER CC ,SLOET HA
SMIT J ,SPRUYT WF

REGISTRATION NUMBER : 69/06371/06

REGISTERED OFFICE
No 1 Charles Crescent, Eastgate Ext 4
Sandton
2199
TEL: 011-444 2511
FAX: 011-444 1667

TRANSFER SECRETARY
Rand Registrars Ltd
P O Box 82549, Southdale
2135
TEL: 011-835 1016

COMPANY SECRETARY
K R M Evans

NATURE OF BUSINESS
The company through divisions & subsidiaries, has three main businesses which are engaged in the marketing and support of mainframe equipment and networks; the marketing and servicing of mid-range open computer systems and integrated solutions and the distribution of micro computers, printers and peripheral devices.

BANKERS :
Standard Merchant Bank Ltd

AUDITORS :
Deloitte Pim Goldby

FAMILIAR BRAND NAMES
ACER,C ITOH (PRINTERS),COMTEN,DATA GENERAL
DOWTY CASE,HITACHI,HYUNDAI,PERSETEL,PERSEUS
SAPEC,TSD,TSM

CONTRIBUTION BY ACTIVITY
N/A

YEAR END : September

DIVIDEND : Ords 1c

Interim No 1	(Ldr)05/06/92	(Pay)13/07/92	Amt(c)4.5
Final No 2	(Ldr)04/12/92	(Pay)11/01/93	Amt(c)6.5
Dividend	(Ldr)04/12/92	(Pay)11/01/93	Amt(c)10

CAPITAL STRUCTURE

	AUTHORISED	ISSUED
Ords 1c	200000000	154646044

FINANCIAL STATISTICS (AT FINANCIAL YEAR END)

(Amts in R'000)	1992 Sep	1991 Sep	1990 Sep
Ord S/H Int	91524	83775	70187
Long Trm Loans	18764	13051	9023
Iss Ord Share	154646	100	100
Total Liab	178280	149878	99649
Current Liab	159516	136827	90626
Total Assets	269668	233585	169604
Intang Assets	136	68	232
Current Assets	212653	213758	154339
Debtors	41378	39256	41964
Inventory	70867	89635	50690
Turnover	503992	397588	303155
Oper Profit	38991	24342	28606
Interest Paid	1333	1710	-
Tax Paid	26021	16969	11702
Prf af Int&Tax	32360	24560	16904
Prf att Ord Sh	32313	24560	16904

Btm Line Earn	32313	25438	16904
Dividend Paid	32869	11850	-
Mkt Prce(c) YE	160	-	-
Depreciation	4159	3439	4621

PER SHARE STATISTICS (CENTS)

Net Asst Val	59.09	83707.00	69955.00
Net Earnings	21.70	16.50	-
Dividends	21.00	8.00	-
Cash Flow	27.25	32403.00	18484.00

RATIOS AND OTHER INFORMATION

Mrk Cap(R000)	247434	-	-
Current Ratio	1.33	1.56	1.70
Quik/Acid Tst	0.89	0.91	1.14
A/C Rec T/ovr	12.18	10.13	7.22
Tot Ass T/ovr	1.87	1.70	1.79
Debt/Ass Rat	0.59	0.59	0.53
Debt to Eqity	1.74	1.63	1.29
Interest Cover	29.25	14.24	-
Oper Prof Mrg	7.74	6.12	9.44
Net Prof Marg%	6.41	6.18	5.58
Ret on Assets	22.14	18.51	16.87
Ret on Equity%	35.31	29.32	24.08
Price/Earnings	7.37	-	-
Divid Cover	1.03	2.06	-
Divid Yield	13.13	-	-
Earning Yield%	13.56	-	-
NAV % Mrk Pr	36.93	-	-
Effec Tax Rate	34.57	31.14	51.32
Def Interval	-	0.23	0.50
Sus Grth Rate	-0.61	15.17	24.08

SUBSIDIARY & ASSOCIATED COMPANIES

ENTERPRISE NETWORKING SYSTEMS (PTY) LTD
NAMIBIAN COMPUTER DISTRIBUTORS (PTY) LTD (50%)
NAMIBIAN COMPUTER SERVICES (PTY) LTD (50%)
OUTSOURCE (PTY) LTD
PERMATECH (PTY) LTD
PERSETEL (PTY) LTD
PERSEUS COMPUTER SYSTEMS (PTY) LTD
REUNERT MAINFRAME SYSTEMS (PTY) LTD
SOUTH AFRICAN PERIPHERAL EQUIPMENT COMPA
SUPPORTED SOFTWARE (PTY) LTD
TECHNOLOGY SYSTEMS DISTRIBUTION (PTY) LT
TECHNOLOGY SYSTEMS MANUFACTURING (PTY) L
TSD SOFTWARE (PTY) LTD

INVESTMENTS

None

PERSKOR BELEGGINGS BPK

ABBREVIATION : PERSBEL

JSE SHORT CODE : PRB

SECTOR : Industrial-Printing & Publishing

SHAREHOLDERS

Who Owns Whom's Assessment of the Identity of the Ultimate Controlling Shareholder: DAGBREEK TRUST / REMBRANDT / NASPERS

SHAREHOLDER	PERCENTAGE 1992	1991
VAN RIJN INV CORP LTD	28.4	28.4
NAT PERS BPK	25.2	25.2
AFRIKAANSE PERS FONDS	7.5	7.5
CMB NOM P/L	5.0	—
MOMENTUM LIFE ASSURE LTD	4.5	4.5
STD BANK NOM TVL P/L	2.1	8.9
CAMPOBELLO HOLDINGS P/L	2.0	—
SAAMBOU PENS FUND	1.8	1.8
FIRST NAT NOM P/L	1.6	1.5
STOCKSHARE NOM P/L	1.4	—
TORINO INV P/L	1.4	1.4
NEDBANK NOM LTD	1.2	—
NGK SINODALE TVL PENS FUND	—	1.4
PULP & PAPER ENGINEERING CO P/L	—	2.0
TOTAL	82.0	82.5

DIRECTORS :
BUITENDAG JM (Executive Chairman),CROUSE CF PROF
DU PREEZ DJ ,HOWELL J DR
JOUBERT DM PROF (Vice Chairman),KORSTEN LP
MAREE HO PROF,MEYER H PROF,SLOET HA
VAN ASWEGEN MJ ,VAN DER MERWE DS
VAN RENSBURG SJJ DR,VILJOEN JH ,WILKENS J

REGISTRATION NUMBER : 05/07139/06

REGISTERED OFFICE
28 Height Street, Doornfontein
Johannesburg
2001
TEL: 011-776 9111
FAX: 011-402 7648

TRANSFER SECRETARY
The Dagbreek Trust
P O Box 8161, Johannesburg

TEL: 011-776 9111

COMPANY SECRETARY
The Dagbreek Trust

NATURE OF BUSINESS
An investment holding company whose principal source of income derives from a 42% holding in quoted Perskorgroep Ltd.

BANKERS :
Volkskas Ltd

AUDITORS :
N/A

FAMILIAR BRAND NAMES
N/A

CONTRIBUTION BY ACTIVITY
N/A

YEAR END : June

DIVIDEND : Ords 50c

Final	(Ldr)15/11/91	(Pay)30/01/92	Amt(c)8.5
Interim	(Ldr)16/04/92	(Pay)01/07/92	Amt(c)5
Final	(Ldr)27/11/92	(Pay)31/01/93	Amt(c)9.5

NUMBER OF EMPLOYEES : 1

CAPITAL STRUCTURE

	AUTHORISED	ISSUED
Extraordinary R2	33000	33000
Ords 50c	12500000	11114999

FINANCIAL STATISTICS (AT FINANCIAL YEAR END)

(Amts in R'000)	1992 Jun	1991 Jun	1990 Jun	1989 Jun	1988 Jun
Ord S/H Int	75767	61061	40287	5190	4317
Long Trm Loans	1318	1298	823	826	-
Iss Ord Share	11115	11115	8318	8318	7703
Total Liab	3251	2729	1706	1622	601
Current Liab	1933	1431	883	796	601
Total Assets	79018	63790	41993	6812	4918
Current Assets	1637	1454	964	857	650
Debtors	-	-	59	59	65
Oper Profit	-12	-	866	-	-
Prf af Int&Tax	1625	1390	866	823	582
Prf att Ord Sh	12396	9974	5995	823	582
Btm Line Earn	16338	10609	6312	823	582
Dividend Paid	1631	1390	845	805	568
Mkt Prce(c) YE	895	600	220	240	150

PER SHARE STATISTICS (CENTS)

Net Asst Val	681.66	549.36	484.34	62.39	56.04
Net Earnings	110.21	100.10	70.86	63.04	52.99
Dividends	72.50	67.50	50.00	45.00	7.25
Cash Flow	14.62	13.95	10.41	9.89	7.56

RATIOS AND OTHER INFORMATION

Mrk Cap(R000)	99479	66690	18300	19963	11555
Current Ratio	0.85	1.02	1.09	1.08	1.08
Quik/Acid Tst	0.85	1.02	1.09	1.08	1.08
Debt/Ass Rat	0.04	0.04	0.04	0.24	0.12
L T L Tot Ass	0.02	0.02	0.02	0.12	-
Debt to Eqity	0.04	0.04	0.04	0.31	0.14
Ret on Assets	15.69	15.64	14.28	12.08	11.83
Ret on Equity%	16.36	16.33	14.88	15.86	13.48
Price/Earnings	8.12	5.99	3.10	3.81	2.83
Divid Cover	1.52	1.48	1.42	1.40	7.31
Divid Yield	8.10	11.25	22.73	18.75	4.83
Earning Yield%	12.31	16.68	32.21	26.27	35.33
NAV % Mrk Pr	76.16	91.56	220.15	26.00	37.36
Def Interval	0.06	-	-	-	-
Sus Grth Rate	14.21	14.06	12.78	0.35	0.32

SUBSIDIARY & ASSOCIATED COMPANIES

NUMA (PTY) LTD (34,67%)
PERSKORGROEP LTD (40,7%)

INVESTMENTS

O H FREWIN (EDMS) BEPERK (24 SH)
PERSKOR GROEP BPK (2423467SH)
THE PRESS CORPORATION OF SA LTD (45267 SH)

PERSKORGROEP BPK

ABBREVIATION : PERSKOR

JSE SHORT CODE : PRK

SECTOR : Industrial-Printing & Publishing

SHAREHOLDERS

Who Owns Whom's Assessment of the Identity of the Ultimate Controlling Shareholder: PERSBEL

SHAREHOLDER	PERCENTAGE 1992	1991
PERSKOR INV LTD	42.5	41.6
DAGBREEK TRUST BPK	10.2	13.7
CMB NOM P/L	6.8	---
STD BANK NOM TVL P/L	6.0	6.3
VOLKSKAS NOM P/L	5.0	5.9
SIMCHOWITZ M	4.0	4.5
STOCKSHARE NOM P/L	2.8	3.4
NEDBANK NOM LTD	1.6	3.0
MOMENTUM LIFE ASSURE LTD	1.6	---
YSKOR PENS FUND	1.2	---
PERSKORGROEP VOORSORGFONDS	1.1	---
MECHIEL DU TOIT NOM P/L	---	1.6
PERSKOR PENS FUND	---	1.1
TOTAL	82.6	81.1

DIRECTORS :
BUITENDAG JM (Executive Chairman),CROUSE CF PROF
DU PREEZ DJ ,HOWELL J DR
JOUBERT DM PROF (Vice Chairman),KORSTEN LP
MAREE HO PROF,MEYER H PROF,SLOET HA
VAN ASWEGEN MJ (Executive Director)
VAN DER MERWE DS (Managing Director)
VAN RENSBURG SJJ DR,VILJOEN JH ,WILKENS J

REGISTRATION NUMBER : 05/25989/06

REGISTERED OFFICE
28 Height Street, Doornfontein
Johannesburg
2001
TEL: 011-776 9111
FAX: 011-402 7648

TRANSFER SECRETARY
The Dagbreek Trust
P O Box 8161, Johannesburg

TEL: 011-776 9111

COMPANY SECRETARY
The Dagbreek Trust

NATURE OF BUSINESS
An investment company with subsidiaries mainly involved in printing and allied operations such as publishing, retail of books and distributing publications.The company holds 85,29% of Perskorporasie van SA Ltd.

BANKERS :
Volkskas Ltd

AUDITORS :
N/A

FAMILIAR BRAND NAMES
BLOEMNUUS,BONA,DIE NOORD-TRANSVALER
EXAKTA (BUSINESS FORMS),FARMERS WEEKLY
GARDEN & HOME,IMVO,KEUR,KLERKSDORP RECORD
LENTSWE,LIVING & LOVING,MIDDELBURG OBSERVER
NOORDELIKE STEM,ORKNEY RECORD,PERSONALITY
RAPPORT,ROOI ROSE,SCOPE,THANDI,THE CITIZEN

THE DALLER,THE TRANSVALER,VISTA
WESTERN TVL RECORD,YOUR FAMILY

CONTRIBUTION BY ACTIVITY
N/A

YEAR END : June

DIVIDEND :Ords 50c

Final	(Ldr)15/11/91	(Pay)30/01/92	Amt(c)28.5
Interim	(Ldr)16/04/92	(Pay)01/07/92	Amt(c)16
Final	(Ldr)27/11/92	(Pay)31/01/93	Amt(c)33

NUMBER OF EMPLOYEES : 5431

CAPITAL STRUCTURE

	AUTHORISED	ISSUED
Ords 50c	8000000	7866841
7% Red Cum Prefs R2	140000	0

FINANCIAL STATISTICS (AT FINANCIAL YEAR END)

(Amts in R'000)	1992 Jun	1991 Jun	1990 Jun	1989 Jun	1988 Jun
Ord S/H Int	185663	116188	88463	76555	67294
Long Trm Loans	42788	44346	45679	34207	23836
Iss Ord Share	7867	5952	5740	5740	5740
Total Liab	144175	148502	128132	100230	84497
Current Liab	101387	104156	82453	66023	60661
Total Assets	329738	264690	216595	176274	151791
Intang Assets	100	*	*	511	*
Current Assets	159877	162945	132061	102969	88166
Debtors	80163	77680	72400	55226	46349
Inventory	55637	63705	52020	44419	36913
Turnover	673329	599529	524069	445096	386122
Oper Profit	38296	29129	21612	19917	20044
Interest Paid	3653	2633	3799	2281	-
Tax Paid	18052	12208	9445	8391	7257
Prf af Int&Tax	23253	19442	14867	13733	12787
Prf att Ord Sh	25500	19610	13214	11752	9835
Btm Line Earn	26746	21065	13912	11245	10392
Dividend Paid	3855	2648	1894	1722	1378
Mkt Prce(c) YE	2650	2000	720	715	460
Depreciation	12534	10297	7861	6429	5210

PER SHARE STATISTICS (CENTS)

Net Asst Val	2358.75	1952.08	1541.17	1324.81	1172.37
Net Earnings	386.91	329.51	230.19	204.73	171.33
Dividends	49.00	44.50	33.00	30.00	24.00
Cash Flow	572.17	503.31	413.78	371.55	334.97

RATIOS AND OTHER INFORMATION

Mrk Cap(R000)	208476	119040	41328	41041	26404
Current Ratio	1.58	1.56	1.60	1.56	1.45
Quik/Acid Tst	1.03	0.95	0.97	0.89	0.84
A/C Rec T/ovr	8.40	7.72	7.24	8.06	8.33
Tot Ass T/ovr	2.04	2.27	2.42	2.53	2.54
Debt/Ass Rat	0.36	0.46	0.44	0.40	0.41
L T L Tot Ass	0.05	0.07	0.06	0.03	0.01
Debt to Eqity	0.64	1.05	1.07	0.93	0.92
Interest Cover	11.90	12.83	6.72	10.01	-
Oper Prof Mrg	5.69	4.86	4.12	4.47	5.19
Net Prof Marg%	3.79	3.27	2.52	2.64	2.55
Ret on Assets	14.79	13.64	13.45	14.21	13.46
Ret on Equity%	13.73	16.88	14.94	15.35	14.61
Price/Earnings	6.85	6.07	3.13	3.49	2.68
Divid Cover	7.90	7.40	6.98	6.82	7.14
Divid Yield	1.85	2.23	4.58	4.20	5.22
Earning Yield%	14.60	16.48	31.97	28.63	37.25
NAV % Mrk Pr	89.01	97.60	214.05	185.29	254.86
Effec Tax Rate	40.33	37.68	28.19	24.81	20.36
Def Interval	0.59	0.81	0.66	0.32	0.11
Sus Grth Rate	11.66	14.60	12.80	13.10	12.57

SUBSIDIARY & ASSOCIATED COMPANIES

ABPECTON MINI (EDMS) BPK
AURORA DRUKPERS (EDMS) BPK
DIE HOOFSTADPERS BPK
DIE MORESTER EN NOORD-TRANSVALER (EDMS)
DRAKENSBERGPERS BPK
EDUCUM NORTH LTD
EDUCUM UITGEWERS BPK
EJ KRUGER & KIE (EDMS) BPK
ESTIES PROPERTIES (PTY) LTD
EXAKTA BESIGHEIDSVORMS (EDMS) BPK
GALVIN & SALES (EDMS) BPK
GRIMSBY ROAD PROPERTIES (EDMS) BPK
IMPALA SKRYFBEHOEFTE-VERSPREIDERS (EDMS)
IMVO (EDMS) BPK
JOYNER ROAD PROPERTIES (EDMS) BPK
LUXEMBURG DRUKKERY (EDMS) BPK
MOTORGIDS (EDMS) BPK
N G KERK BOEKHANDEL (1981) (PTY) LTD (49.3%)
NATAL PICTORIAL (EDMS) BPK
NATAL PUBLICATIONS CO. (EDMS) BPK
OGGENDBLADPERS BPK
OH FREWIN (EDMS) BPK
PERSKOR (OVS) BPK
PERSKOR BOEKE (EDMS) BPK
PERSKOR BUITEFILIALE (EDMS) BPK
PERSKOR EIENDOMME (EDMS) BPK
PERSKOR INTERMEDIA (EDMS) BPK
PERSKOR INTERNE DIENSTE (EDMS) BPK
PERSKOR PUBLIKASIES (EDMS) BPK
PRELOW INVESTMENTS (EDMS) BPK
RAMA PUBLIKASIES (EDMS) BPK
REPUBLIKEINSE NUUSAGENTSKAP (PTY) LTD
REPUBLIKEINSE PERS (EDMS) BPK
SUPER COMIX (EDMS) BPK
TASMAN (EDMS) BPK
THANDAPERS (EDMS) BPK
THE CITIZEN (1978) (EDMS) BPK
THE CITIZEN BPK
THE KLERKSDORP RECORD (EDMS) BPK
THE PRESS CORPORATION OF SOUTH AFRICA LT
THE SOUTH AFRICAN FINANCIAL GAZETTE BPK
TRANSVAAL ENVELOPE MANUFACTURING CO. (ED
TW HAYNE BPK
UKHOZI PRESS BPK
ULYSSES BELEGGINGS (EDMS) BPK
VIVA UITGEWERS (EDMS) BPK
VOORTREKKERPERS BPK
WILHINT HOLDINGS (EDMS) BPK
WIZARD FEATURES (EDMS) BPK
WORTHWHILE INVESTMENTS (EDMS) BPK

INVESTMENTS

BOPHUTHATSWANA COMMERCIAL RADIO (PTY) LT (5%)
CAPITAL MEDIA (PTY) LTD (1 SH)
ELECTRONIC MEDIA NETWORK HOLDINGS (PTY) (15,14%)
MAISTER DIRECTORIES (1981) (PTY) LTD (500000 SH)
PARTNERSHIP IN PRINTING (PTY) LTD (3467 SH)

PETRA GRANITE LTD

ABBREVIATION : PETRA

JSE SHORT CODE : PET

SECTOR : Development Capital Market

SHAREHOLDERS

Who Owns Whom's Assessment of the Identity of the Ultimate Controlling Shareholder: ALPHA BANK

SHAREHOLDER	PERCENTAGE 1992	1991
BERLITAS INV NO 50 P/L	64.2	64.2
PETRA HOLDINGS P/L	34.2	34.2
TOTAL	98.4	98.4

DIRECTORS :
DU PLESSIS PJ ,NEL PJ (Chief Executive)
RAHN DR FJ (Chairman),VAN DER WALT CG

REGISTRATION NUMBER : 72/01062/06

REGISTERED OFFICE
4th Floor, AA Life Centre, 27 Diagonal Street
Johannesburg
2001
TEL: 018-94 277
FAX: 018-93 357

TRANSFER SECRETARY
Central Registrars Ltd
P O Box 4844, Johannesburg
2000
TEL: 011-331 0051

COMPANY SECRETARY
C G van der Walt

NATURE OF BUSINESS
The group owns mining rights to granite dimension stone reserves in the Duiwelskloof, Wolmaransstad and Potgietersrus areas of the Tvl, and conducts granite mining and beneficiation operations.

BANKERS :
Standard Bank of SA Ltd

AUDITORS :
Deloitte Pim Goldby

FAMILIAR BRAND NAMES
N/A

CONTRIBUTION BY ACTIVITY
N/A

YEAR END : September

NUMBER OF EMPLOYEES : 137

CAPITAL STRUCTURE

	AUTHORISED	ISSUED
Ords 25c	10000000	7014040

FINANCIAL STATISTICS (AT FINANCIAL YEAR END)

(Amts in R'000)	1991 Sep	1991 Feb	1989 Feb	1988 Feb	1987
Ord S/H Int	2387	1819	1940	1692	1092
Long Trm Loans	3192	-	264	344	1729
Iss Ord Share	7014	25351	25351	25351	23000
Total Liab	6166	-	3331	3070	2874
Current Liab	2974	-	3067	2726	1145
Total Assets	8553	1819	4345	3836	4738
Intang Assets	*	*	926	926	*
Current Assets	1262	1819	1219	1193	1917
Debtors	756	-	815	715	-
Inventory	447	-	384	276	1917
Turnover	5667	-	13844	11855	8517
Oper Profit	-5832	100	714	419	571
Interest Paid	170	22	254	77	1
Prf af Int&Tax	-6002	78	460	342	570
Prf att Ord Sh	-6002	78	460	594	570
Btm Line Earn	-2	-2130	248	-536	570
Dividend Paid	-	-	-	-	345
Mkt Prce(c) YE	160	10	14	21	37
Depreciation	311	-	430	227	-

PER SHARE STATISTICS (CENTS)

Net Asst Val	34.03	7.18	4.00	3.02	4.75
Net Earnings	-85.60	0.30	1.80	2.40	-
Cash Flow	-139.09	3.08	3.51	2.33	2.48

RATIOS AND OTHER INFORMATION

Mrk Cap(R000)	11222	2535	3549	5324	8510
Current Ratio	0.42	-	0.40	0.44	1.67
Quik/Acid Tst	0.27	-	0.27	0.34	-
A/C Rec T/ovr	12.85	-	16.99	16.58	-
Tot Ass T/ovr	1.14	-	3.19	3.09	1.80
Debt/Ass Rat	0.72	-	0.77	0.80	0.61
L T L Tot Ass	0.37	-	0.06	0.09	0.36
Debt to Eqity	2.58	-	1.72	1.81	2.63
Interest Cover	-34.31	4.55	2.81	5.44	571.00
Oper Prof Mrg	-102.91	-	5.16	3.53	6.70
Net Prof Marg%	-105.91	-	3.32	5.01	6.69
Ret on Assets	-116.89	5.50	16.43	10.92	12.05
Ret on Equity%	-431.05	4.29	23.71	35.11	52.20
Price/Earnings	-1.87	33.33	7.78	8.75	-
Earning Yield%	-53.50	3.00	12.86	11.43	-
NAV % Mrk Pr	21.27	71.75	28.57	14.39	12.83
Def Interval	-1.10	-	2.02	2.65	3.03
Sus Grth Rate	-251.45	4.29	23.71	35.11	20.60

SUBSIDIARY & ASSOCIATED COMPANIES

PETRA MINING, EXPLORATION AND GRANITE EX

INVESTMENTS

None

PICARDI APPLIANCES LTD

ABBREVIATION : PICAPLI

JSE SHORT CODE : PPL

SECTOR : Industrial-Furniture & Household

SHAREHOLDERS

Who Owns Whom's Assessment of the Identity of the Ultimate Controlling Shareholder: PICKARD FAMILY VIA PICBEL

SHAREHOLDER	PERCENTAGE 1992	1991
PICHOLD LTD	93.2	---
PICARDI HOLDINGS LTD	---	93.2
TOTAL	93.2	93.2

DIRECTORS :
BRAUDE PD ,PENZHORN EJV ,PICKARD JAJ (Chairman)
PICKARD JAJ (JNR) ,TEARE EP (Managing Director)
VERMOOTEN J D

REGISTRATION NUMBER : 05/27290/06

REGISTERED OFFICE
1372 Picbel Parkade, Strand Street
Cape Town
8001
TEL: 021-419 2220
FAX: 021-418 1411

TRANSFER SECRETARY
Picardi Investments Ltd
P O Box 1134, Cape Town
8000
TEL: 021-419 2220

COMPANY SECRETARY
Picardi Investments Ltd

NATURE OF BUSINESS
An investment holding company whose subsidiaries are involved in the distribution of household and electrical appliances.

BANKERS :
Nedperm Bank Ltd, Standard Bank of SA Ltd
Trust Bank of Africa Ltd, Volkskas Ltd

AUDITORS :
Coopers Theron Du Toit

FAMILIAR BRAND NAMES
N/A

CONTRIBUTION BY ACTIVITY
N/A

YEAR END : June

DIVIDEND : (Ldr)29/09/89 (Pay)13/10/89

NUMBER OF EMPLOYEES : 2922

CAPITAL STRUCTURE

	AUTHORISED	ISSUED
Ords 50c	27000000	25932721
10% Red Cum Prefs R1	820000	0
5,5% Cum Prefs R2	40000	40000
5,5% Red Cum Prefs R2	30000	0

FINANCIAL STATISTICS (AT FINANCIAL YEAR END)

(Amts in R'000)	1992 Jun	1991 Jun	1990 Jun	1989 Jun	1988 Jun
Ord S/H Int	54022	47293	33296	38737	21432
Long Trm Loans	28559	29036	11450	21721	31500
Iss Ord Share	25933	25933	25933	18455	10476
Total Liab	110295	111696	149855	216979	209754
Current Liab	81736	82660	138405	195258	178254
Total Assets	164317	158989	183151	255716	231186
Current Assets	143953	136456	158273	227487	211670
Debtors	68273	74951	86840	107137	93922
Inventory	69691	59432	67372	120344	116993
Oper Profit	24172	31598	14045	37235	34501
Interest Paid	13421	17154	27529	26678	11832
Tax Paid	2502	609	304	4853	9314
Prf af Int&Tax	8249	14007	-13472	5858	13355
Prf att Ord Sh	8245	14003	-13680	4812	11532
Btm Line Earn	6729	14003	-10176	6453	10801
Dividend Paid	-	-	-	1384	1571
Mkt Prce(c) YE	85	85	60	125	190
Depreciation	3430	3497	4195	4085	2350

PER SHARE STATISTICS (CENTS)

Net Asst Val	208.31	182.37	128.39	209.90	204.58
Net Earnings	31.80	54.00	-52.00	22.20	51.20
Dividends	25.40	32.00	-	7.50	15.00
Cash Flow	48.50	71.12	-36.58	36.38	60.78

RATIOS AND OTHER INFORMATION

Mrk Cap(R000)	22043	22043	15560	23069	19904
Current Ratio	1.76	1.65	1.14	1.17	1.19
Quik/Acid Tst	0.91	0.93	0.66	0.55	0.53
Debt/Ass Rat	0.66	0.69	0.82	0.81	0.84
L T L Tot Ass	0.16	0.17	0.06	0.05	0.07
Debt to Eqity	1.99	2.33	4.49	5.38	9.03
Interest Cover	1.80	1.84	0.51	1.40	2.92
Ret on Assets	14.71	19.98	7.84	14.62	14.92
Ret on Equity%	15.26	29.61	-41.09	12.42	53.81
Price/Earnings	2.67	1.57	-1.15	5.63	3.71
Divid Cover	1.25	1.69	-	2.96	3.41
Divid Yield	29.88	37.65	-	6.00	7.89
Earning Yield%	37.41	63.53	-86.67	17.76	26.95
NAV % Mrk Pr	245.07	214.55	213.99	167.92	107.67
Effec Tax Rate	9.97	0.09	-2.31	47.12	46.74
Def Interval	5.35	3.46	-11.62	17.28	8.30
Sus Grth Rate	15.26	29.61	-41.09	8.85	46.48

SUBSIDIARY & ASSOCIATED COMPANIES

CENTURY AIR CONDITIONING (PTY) LTD
FREEWAY PROPERTIES (PTY) LTD
HIGHVELD ELECTRIC (PTY) LTD
KIC (DURBAN) LTD
KIC (PE) (PTY) LTD
KIC LTD
KIC MANUFACTURING (PTY) LTD
MEGATRON CO OF SA (PTY) LTD

INVESTMENTS

None

PICARDI HOLDINGS LTD

ABBREVIATION : PICHOLD

JSE SHORT CODE : PHL

SECTOR : Industrial-Industrial Holding

SHAREHOLDERS

Who Owns Whom's Assessment of the Identity of the Ultimate Controlling Shareholder:
PICKARD FAMILY VIA PICBEL

SHAREHOLDER	PERCENTAGE 1992	1991
PICARDI INV LTD	68.7	68.7
PICFIN EMPLOYEES PROFIT SHARING FUND	4.5	4.8
MOMENTUM LIFE ASSURE LTD	2.5	2.5
TOTAL	75.8	76.0

DIRECTORS :
MULLER SL HON,PENZHORN EJV ,PICKARD JAJ (JNR)
PICKARD JAJ DR (Chairman)
VERMOOTEN J (Financial Director

REGISTRATION NUMBER : 05/15756/06

REGISTERED OFFICE
1372 Picbel Parkade, Strand Street
Cape Town
8001
TEL: 021-419 2220
FAX: 021-418 1411

TRANSFER SECRETARY
Picardi Investments Ltd
P O Box 1134, Cape Town
8000
TEL: 021-419 2220

COMPANY SECRETARY
Picardi Investments Ltd

NATURE OF BUSINESS
An investment holding company with controlling interests in quoted Picardi Appliances & Picardi Properties. Group activities include manufacture & distribution of domestic appliances and the manufacture of sport & leisure garments.

BANKERS :
Volkskas Ltd, Nedperm Bank Ltd
Standard Bank of SA Ltd

AUDITORS :
Coopers Theron Du Toit

FAMILIAR BRAND NAMES
ARENA,INDESIT,KIC,LE COQ SPORTIF,SAMSONITE
WHIRLPOOL

CONTRIBUTION BY ACTIVITY
Household appliances (% attr earnings) (80.4%)
Investments (14.5%)
Property (0.3%)
Sports & Leisure Garments (4.8%)

YEAR END : June

DIVIDEND : Ords 50c
Interim (Ldr)22/02/91 (Pay)08/03/91 Amt(c)100

NUMBER OF EMPLOYEES : 5127

CAPITAL STRUCTURE

	AUTHORISED	ISSUED
Ords 50c	10000000	6050000

FINANCIAL STATISTICS (AT FINANCIAL YEAR END)

(Amts in R'000)	1992 Jun	1991 Jun	1990 Jun	1989 Jun	1988 Jun
Ord S/H Int	76921	68655	84277	118858	93984
Long Trm Loans	12381	12949	19654	60180	53149
Iss Ord Share	6050	6050	6050	6050	6050
Total Liab	103455	104273	171280	319394	279060
Current Liab	91074	91324	151626	259214	225911
Total Assets	180376	172928	255557	430985	373044
Intang Assets	*	*	*	7267	*
Current Assets	155782	145929	206997	322532	283967
Debtors	75010	78846	93222	136398	121396
Inventory	73837	63657	73368	177001	158155
Turnover	-	-	526307	543955	488248
Oper Profit	24160	27408	19347	47924	45025
Interest Paid	10888	16980	40069	35588	17289
Tax Paid	3720	1061	960	5342	10012
Prf af Int&Tax	10123	11841	-15828	13010	17724
Prf att Ord Sh	9561	10906	-13407	10331	14220
Btm Line Earn	8267	-11313	-18668	10471	21579
Dividend Paid	-	6050	-	4175	4175
Mkt Prce(c) YE	410	360	450	700	800
Depreciation	3954	4042	8036	7147	5013

PER SHARE STATISTICS (CENTS)

Net Asst Val	1271.42	1134.79	1393.01	1844.48	1553.45
Net Earnings	158.00	180.20	-221.60	170.80	235.00
Dividends	-	100.00	-	69.00	69.00
Cash Flow	238.30	259.85	-107.60	297.75	318.35

RATIOS AND OTHER INFORMATION

Mrk Cap(R000)	24805	21780	27225	42350	48400
Current Ratio	1.71	1.60	1.37	1.24	1.26
Quik/Acid Tst	0.90	0.90	0.88	0.56	0.56
A/C Rec T/ovr	-	-	5.65	3.99	4.02
Tot Ass T/ovr	-	-	2.06	1.26	1.31
Debt/Ass Rat	0.54	0.58	0.65	0.66	0.68
L T L Tot Ass	0.03	0.05	0.05	0.06	0.08
Debt to Eqity	1.26	1.45	1.96	2.40	2.72
Interest Cover	2.26	1.62	0.60	1.50	2.60
Oper Prof Mrg	-	-	3.68	8.81	9.22
Net Prof Marg%	-	-	-2.55	1.90	2.91
Ret on Assets	13.71	17.28	10.10	12.52	12.07
Ret on Equity%	12.43	15.89	-15.91	8.69	15.13
Price/Earnings	2.59	2.00	-2.03	4.10	3.40
Divid Cover	-	1.80	-	2.48	3.41
Divid Yield	-	27.78	-	9.86	8.63
Earning Yield%	38.54	50.06	-49.24	24.40	29.38
NAV % Mrk Pr	310.10	315.22	309.56	263.50	194.18
Effec Tax Rate	17.04	4.91	-7.60	43.15	40.69
Def Interval	3.58	3.09	-18.36	11.82	8.69
Sus Grth Rate	12.43	7.07	-15.91	5.18	10.69

SUBSIDIARY & ASSOCIATED COMPANIES

BULL INVESTMENT NOMINEES LTD
KIC LIMITED
KIC MANUFACTURING (PTY) LTD
PHD OVERSEAS LTD
PICARDI APPLIANCES LTD
PICARDI PROPERTIES LTD
SECHIC (PTY) LTD
SOUTH AFRICAN & GENERAL INVESTMENT & TRU
TUSH (PTY) LTD

INVESTMENTS

DUKEL HOLDINGS LTD (118600 SH)
HURKEL INVESTMENTS (PTY) LTD (44 SH)
SMALL BUSINESS DEV CORP LTD (262000 SH)
TRADEHOLD LTD (735060 SH)
UNIDEV LTD (180000 SH)

PICARDI INVESTMENTS LTD

ABBREVIATION : PICBEL

JSE SHORT CODE : PBL

SECTOR : Industrial-Industrial Holding

SHAREHOLDERS

Who Owns Whom's Assessment of the Identity of the Ultimate Controlling Shareholder:
PICKARD FAMILY

SHAREHOLDER	PERCENTAGE 1992	1991
JAN INGRID P/L	26.3	26.3
JAN PICKARD ONDERNEMINGS BPK	21.0	21.0
MOMENTUM LIFE ASSURE LTD	9.5	9.5
TOP DOG NOM P/L	6.0	1.9
ROBROY BELANGE P/L	5.8	5.8
JAN PICKARD FAMILY TRUST	2.9	---
KELLY F	2.8	2.8
CMB NOM P/L	2.5	---
MARLED NOM P/L	1.5	---
STD BANK NOM TVL P/L	1.1	1.1
BONORUM INV P/L	---	1.6
HENWOODS P/L	---	3.7
SANLAM	---	2.5
THEO ROOD FAMILY TRUST	---	3.0
TOTAL	79.3	79.1

DIRECTORS :
KING ME ,MULLER SL HON,PENZHORN EJV
PICKARD JAJ (Chairman),PICKARD JAJ (JNR)
SIMS IJ ,STEYN IJ

REGISTRATION NUMBER : 05/29599/06

REGISTERED OFFICE
1372 Picbel Parkade, Strand Street
Cape Town
8001
TEL: 021-419 2220
FAX: 021-418 1411

TRANSFER SECRETARY
Picardi Investments Ltd
P O Box 1134, Cape Town
8000
TEL: 021-419 2220

COMPANY SECRETARY
J Vermooten

NATURE OF BUSINESS
An investment management company with a 68,7% shareholding in Pichold.

BANKERS :
Volkskas Ltd, Nedperm Bank Ltd
Standard Bank of SA Ltd
Trust Bank of Africa Ltd

AUDITORS :
Coopers Theron Du Toit

FAMILIAR BRAND NAMES
N/A

CONTRIBUTION BY ACTIVITY
Household appliances (% attr earnings) (73.4%)
Investments (22.1%)
Sport Goods (4.4%)
Property (0.1%)

YEAR END : June

DIVIDEND : Ords 50c
Interim (Ldr)22/02/91 (Pay)08/03/91 Amt(c)100

NUMBER OF EMPLOYEES : 5127

CAPITAL STRUCTURE

	AUTHORISED	ISSUED
Ords 50c	4500000	4444086
9% Red Cum Pref R1	4000000	0
5,5% Red Cum Pref R2	100000	0

FINANCIAL STATISTICS (AT FINANCIAL YEAR END)

(Amts in R'000)	1992 Jun	1991 Jun	1990 Jun	1989 Jun	1988 Jun
Ord S/H Int	61470	55073	65254	86533	66641
Long Trm Loans	36450	34452	46050	100522	89416
Iss Ord Share	4444	4444	4444	4444	4444
Total Liab	127892	126357	198637	359767	317099
Current Liab	91442	91905	152587	259245	227683
Total Assets	189362	181430	263891	446300	383740
Current Assets	164585	146647	207504	322710	284231
Debtors	75137	78840	93225	136399	121585
Inventory	73839	63657	73368	177001	158155
Turnover	-	-	526312	543956	488250
Oper Profit	23754	27197	19193	53726	45666
Interest Paid	10873	16923	40083	34945	17361
Tax Paid	3843	1097	967	5348	10008
Prf af Int&Tax	10750	12677	-14968	13433	18297
Prf att Ord Sh	7195	8327	-8259	6881	9105
Btm Line Earn	6381	-2081	-11861	10264	12175
Dividend Paid	-	4444	667	2222	1778
Mkt Prce(c) YE	410	400	400	530	690
Depreciation	3996	4086	8079	7183	5074

PER SHARE STATISTICS (CENTS)

Net Asst Val	1383.21	1239.27	1468.36	1947.19	1499.57
Net Earnings	161.90	187.40	-185.80	154.80	204.90
Dividends	-	100.00	15.00	50.00	40.00
Cash Flow	272.12	296.71	-25.34	328.53	319.67

RATIOS AND OTHER INFORMATION

Mrk Cap(R000)	18220	17776	17776	23553	30664
Current Ratio	1.80	1.60	1.36	1.24	1.25
Quik/Acid Tst	0.99	0.90	0.88	0.56	0.55
A/C Rec T/ovr	-	-	5.65	3.99	4.02
Tot Ass T/ovr	-	-	1.99	1.22	1.27
Debt/Ass Rat	0.52	0.55	0.63	0.64	0.67
L T L Tot Ass	0.03	0.05	0.05	0.06	0.08
Debt to Eqity	1.59	1.82	2.54	3.30	3.86
Interest Cover	2.31	1.68	0.62	1.54	2.63
Oper Prof Mrg	-	-	3.65	9.88	9.35
Net Prof Marg%	-	-	-1.57	1.26	1.86
Ret on Assets	13.45	16.92	10.04	12.04	11.90
Ret on Equity%	11.70	15.12	-12.66	7.95	13.66
Price/Earnings	2.53	2.13	-2.15	3.42	3.37
Divid Cover	-	1.87	-12.39	3.10	5.12
Divid Yield	-	25.00	3.75	9.43	5.80
Earning Yield%	39.49	46.85	-46.45	29.21	29.70
NAV % Mrk Pr	337.37	309.82	367.09	367.39	217.33

Effec Tax Rate	18.08	5.25	-7.57	29.50	39.88
Def Interval	4.26	3.67	-106.13	14.60	11.91
Sus Grth Rate	11.70	7.05	-13.68	5.38	10.99

SUBSIDIARY & ASSOCIATED COMPANIES

PICARDI HOLDINGS LTD
SAGIT PARK TOWNSHIPS (PTY) LTD

INVESTMENTS

None

PICK 'N PAY HOLDINGS LTD

ABBREVIATION : PIKWIK

JSE SHORT CODE : PWK

SECTOR : Industrial-Retailers & Wholesalers

SHAREHOLDERS

Who Owns Whom's Assessment of the Identity of the Ultimate Controlling Shareholder: RAYMOND ACKERMAN

SHAREHOLDER	PERCENTAGE 1992	1991
RAYMOND ACKERMAN P/L	50.2	50.2
SOUTHERN LIFE ASSOC LTD	6.9	6.9
CMB NOM P/L	6.1	---
PICK N PAY EMPLOYEE SHARE PURC SCHEME	4.6	4.4
LIBERTY LIFE ASSOC OF AFRICA LTD	3.5	2.9
COMMERCIAL UNION LIFE ASSURE CO SA LTD	1.7	---
EIGHTY ONE MAIN STREET NOM LTD	1.6	---
NEDBANK NOM LTD	1.3	1.3
STD BANK NOM TVL P/L	1.1	---
SASOL PENS FUND	1.0	---
COMMERCIAL UNION ASSURE CO SA LTD	---	1.9
ESCOM PENS & PROV FUND	---	2.2
SANLAM	---	6.0
TOTAL	77.9	75.7

DIRECTORS :
ACKERMAN GM ,ACKERMAN RD (Chairman)
ACKERMAN W MRS,DE WET RP ,FINE A ,GALOMBIK A
GORVY HA ,HERMAN HS
HURST CDG (Financial Director),ROSIN AJ

REGISTRATION NUMBER : 81/09610/06

REGISTERED OFFICE
5th Floor, Pick 'n Pay Centre
Cnr Main & Campground Rds, Claremont
7700
TEL: 021-658 1000
FAX: 021-683 2514

TRANSFER SECRETARY
Retail Share Registrars (Pty) Ltd
P O Box 23087, Claremont
7735
TEL: 021-683 2140

COMPANY SECRETARY
M Marsden

NATURE OF BUSINESS
The holding company of JSE-quoted Pick'n Pay Stores Ltd.

BANKERS :
Senbank

AUDITORS :
Arthur Andersen & Co

FAMILIAR BRAND NAMES
SEE PIKNPAY

CONTRIBUTION BY ACTIVITY
N/A

YEAR END : February

DIVIDEND : Ords 2,5c

Interim No 16	(Ldr)03/11/89	(Pay)16/11/89	Amt(c)5.19
Final No 17	(Ldr)27/04/90	(Pay)10/05/90	Amt(c)20.49
Interim No 18	(Ldr)02/11/90	(Pay)15/11/90	Amt(c)6.18
Final No 19	(Ldr)26/04/91	(Pay)08/05/91	Amt(c)22.23
Interim No 20	(Ldr)01/11/91	(Pay)14/11/91	Amt(c)6.18
Final No 21	(Ldr)24/04/92	(Pay)07/05/92	Amt(c)22.23
Interim No 22	(Ldr)30/10/92	(Pay)12/11/92	Amt(c)7.16

NUMBER OF EMPLOYEES : 28273

CAPITAL STRUCTURE

	AUTHORISED	ISSUED
Ords 1,25c	240000000	164467120

FINANCIAL STATISTICS (AT FINANCIAL YEAR END)

(Amts in R'000)	1992 Feb	1991 Feb	1990 Feb	1989 Feb	1988 Feb
Ord S/H Int	24900	24900	24900	24900	24900
Iss Ord Share	82234	82234	82234	82234	82234
Total Liab	18300	18300	16900	13500	10400
Current Liab	18300	18300	16900	13500	10400
Total Assets	43200	43200	41800	38400	35300
Current Assets	18500	18500	17100	13700	10600
Oper Profit	-	-	-	17100	13300
Tax Paid	-	-	-	-	100
Prf af Int&Tax	23300	23300	21100	17100	13200
Prf att Ord Sh	23300	23300	21100	17100	13200
Btm Line Earn	23300	23300	21100	17100	13200
Dividend Paid	23300	23300	21100	17100	13200
Mkt Prce(c) YE	1025	1275	690	610	390

PER SHARE STATISTICS (CENTS)

Net Asst Val	30.28	30.28	30.28	30.28	30.28
Net Earnings	28.40	28.40	25.69	20.74	16.05
Dividends	28.41	28.41	25.68	20.75	16.06
Cash Flow	28.33	28.33	25.66	20.79	16.05

RATIOS AND OTHER INFORMATION

Mrk Cap(R000)	842899	1048484	567415	501627	320713
Current Ratio	1.01	1.01	1.01	1.01	1.02
Quik/Acid Tst	1.01	1.01	1.01	1.01	1.02
Debt/Ass Rat	0.42	0.42	0.40	0.35	0.29
Debt to Eqity	0.73	0.73	0.68	0.54	0.42
Ret on Assets	53.94	53.94	50.48	44.53	37.68
Ret on Equity%	93.57	93.57	84.74	68.67	53.01
Price/Earnings	36.09	44.89	26.86	29.41	24.30
Divid Cover	1.00	1.00	1.00	1.00	1.00
Divid Yield	2.77	2.23	3.72	3.40	4.12

Earning Yield%	2.77	2.23	3.72	3.40	4.12
NAV % Mrk Pr	2.95	2.37	4.39	4.96	7.76
Effec Tax Rate	-	-	-	-	0.75
Sus Grth Rate	0.00	0.00	0.00	0.00	0.00

SUBSIDIARY & ASSOCIATED COMPANIES

PICK 'N PAY STORES LTD

INVESTMENTS

None

PICK 'N PAY STORES LTD

ABBREVIATION : PICKNPAY

JSE SHORT CODE : PIK

SECTOR : Industrial-Retailers & Wholesalers

SHAREHOLDERS

Who Owns Whom's Assessment of the Identity of the Ultimate Controlling Shareholder:
RAYMOND ACKERMAN VIA PIKWIK

SHAREHOLDER	PERCENTAGE 1992	1991
PICK 'N PAY HOLDINGS LTD	51.9	51.9
CMB NOM P/L	7.5	---
LIBERTY LIFE ASSOC OF AFRICA LTD	3.3	3.2
STD BANK NOM TVL P/L	3.0	2.2
ESCOM PENS & PROV FUND	2.5	2.6
SOUTHERN LIFE ASSOC LTD	2.2	2.2
FIRST NAT NOM P/L	2.0	2.2
PICK N PAY EMPLOYEE SHARE PURC SCHEME	1.9	2.1
COMMERCIAL UNION LIFE ASSURE CO SA LTD	1.1	---
MOMENTUM LIFE ASSURE LTD	---	1.3
COMMERCIAL UNION ASSURE CO SA LTD	---	1.4
SANLAM	---	7.5
TOTAL	75.4	76.4

DIRECTORS :
ACKERMAN GM ,ACKERMAN RD (Executive Chairman)
ACKERMAN W MRS (Personnel Director)
BLUMGART KM (Systems Director)
DE WET RP (Personnel Director),FINE A ,GORVY HA
HERMAN HS (Managing Director)
HURST CDG (Financial Director),JOUBERT IJ
ROSEN M (Sales Director),ROSIN AJ ,SUMMERS SR
ZELINSKY AE

REGISTRATION NUMBER : 68/08034/06

REGISTERED OFFICE
Pick 'n Pay Centre, Cnr Main & Campground Rds
Claremont
7700
TEL: 021-658 1000
FAX: 021-683 2514

TRANSFER SECRETARY
Retail Share Registrars (Pty) Ltd
P O Box 23087, Claremont
7735
TEL: 021-683 2140

COMPANY SECRETARY
M Marsden

NATURE OF BUSINESS
The group is a mass retailer of food and general merchandise, with core trading activity conducted from 14 hypermarkets & 106 supermarkets. Revenues are also derived from wholesaling, auto centres, & an upmarket household goods chain.

BANKERS :
Senbank

AUDITORS :
Arthur Andersen & Co

FAMILIAR BRAND NAMES
BOARDMANS,HYPERMARKET,NO NAME BRAND
PICK N PAY,PRICECLUB

CONTRIBUTION BY ACTIVITY
N/A

YEAR END : February

DIVIDEND : Ords 2,5c

Interim No 43	(Ldr)03/11/89	(Pay)16/11/89	Amt(c)10.5
Final No 44	(Ldr)27/04/90	(Pay)10/05/90	Amt(c)41.5
Interim No 45	(Ldr)02/11/90	(Pay)15/11/90	Amt(c)12.5
Final No 46	(Ldr)26/04/91	(Pay)08/05/91	Amt(c)45
Interim No 47	(Ldr)01/11/91	(Pay)14/11/91	Amt(c)12.5
Final No 48	(Ldr)24/04/92	(Pay)07/05/92	Amt(c)45
Interim No 49	(Ldr)30/10/92	(Pay)12/11/92	Amt(c)14.5

NUMBER OF EMPLOYEES : 28273

CAPITAL STRUCTURE

	AUTHORISED	ISSUED
10,75% Sec Red Debs 1000c	7000	7000
Ords 1,25c	178761680	156524888

FINANCIAL STATISTICS (AT FINANCIAL YEAR END)

(Amts in R'000)	1992 Feb	1991 Feb	1990 Feb	1989 Feb	1988 Feb
Ord S/H Int	340400	301000	267700	221400	185300
Long Trm Loans	6600	7700	8500	8100	8000
Iss Ord Share	78262	78262	78262	78262	78262
Total Liab	786300	648700	558200	500600	421400
Current Liab	779700	641000	549700	492500	413400
Total Assets	1126700	949700	824600	720700	606700
Intang Assets	*	*	1300	1300	*
Current Assets	617500	444300	421600	396100	338500
Debtors	10600	10100	10300	9700	11200
Inventory	416100	387700	352000	326700	247600
Turnover	5911100	5189200	4380900	3869100	3037600
Oper Profit	131200	136700	112900	106000	86100
Interest Paid	10200	5900	3800	5200	800
Tax Paid	54600	53000	48000	48200	38400
Prf af Int&Tax	84400	86600	83300	68100	52800
Prf att Ord Sh	84400	86600	82800	67700	52600
Btm Line Earn	84400	86600	87000	67700	52000
Dividend Paid	45000	45000	40700	32900	25700
Mkt Prce(c) YE	2075	2550	1525	1200	780
Depreciation	49300	33800	31800	27300	23900

PER SHARE STATISTICS (CENTS)

Net Asst Val	434 95	384 61	340 40	281 23	236 77
Net Earnings	107 90	110 60	105 90	86 40	67 17
Dividends	57 50	42 00	52 00	42 00	32 88
Cash Flow	170 84	153 84	146 43	121 39	97 75

RATIOS AND OTHER INFORMATION

Mrk Cap(R000)	1623937	1995681	1193496	939144	610444
Current Ratio	0 79	0 69	0 77	0 80	0 82
Quik/Acid Tst	0 26	0 09	0 13	0 14	0 22
A/C Rec T/ovr	557 65	513 78	425 33	398 88	271 21
Tot Ass T/ovr	5 25	5 46	5 31	5 37	5 01
Debt/Ass Rat	0 70	0 68	0 68	0 69	0 69
L T L Tot Ass	0 00	0 01	0 01	0 01	0 01
Debt to Eqity	2 31	2 15	2 08	2 26	2 27
Interest Cover	13 96	23 78	33 45	22 31	115 00
Oper Prof Mrg	2 22	2 63	2 58	2 74	2 83
Net Prof Marg%	1 43	1 67	1 89	1 75	1 73
Ret on Assets	13 24	15 32	16 38	16 86	15 16
Ret on Equity%	24 79	28 77	30 93	30 58	28 39
Price/Earnings	19 23	23 06	14 40	13 89	11 61
Divid Cover	1 88	2 63	2 04	2 06	2 04
Divid Yield	2 77	1 65	3 41	3 50	4 22
Earning Yield%	5 20	4 34	6 94	7 20	8 61
NAV % Mrk Pr	20 96	15 08	22 32	23 44	30 35
Effec Tax Rate	43 11	39 26	40 99	45 34	45 02
Def Interval	0 04	0 05	0 06	0 07	0 09
Sus Grth Rate	11 57	13 82	15 73	15 72	14 52

SUBSIDIARY & ASSOCIATED COMPANIES

ALSTAR (PTY) LTD
ASSOCIATED EXPORT COMPANY (PTY) LTD
BEDWORTH SENTRUM (PTY) LTD
BLUE RIBBON MEAT CORP (PTY) LTD (50%)
CARREFOUR (PTY) LTD
CHECKNET SYSTEMS (PTY) LTD
HYPERMARKETS (PTY) LTD
LANBAS INVESTMENTS (PTY) LTD
PEMBROTRADE (PTY) LTD
PICK 'N PAY (BELLVILLE) (PTY) LTD
PICK 'N PAY (BISHO) (PTY) LTD
PICK 'N PAY (BOPHUTHATSWANA) (PTY) LTD
PICK 'N PAY (CARLETONVILLE) (PTY) LTD
PICK 'N PAY (EAST LONDON) (PTY) LTD
PICK 'N PAY (GABRIEL ROAD) (PTY) LTD
PICK 'N PAY (KLERKSDORP) (PTY) LTD
PICK 'N PAY (MANGROVE PARK) (PTY) LTD
PICK 'N PAY (MITCHELLS PLAIN) LTD (50%)
PICK 'N PAY (NEWTON PARK) (PTY) LTD
PICK 'N PAY (OTTERY) (PTY) LTD
PICK 'N PAY (PTY) LTD
PICK 'N PAY (RANDPARK RIDGE) (PTY) LTD
PICK 'N PAY (STEELDALE) (PTY) LTD
PICK 'N PAY (STEELPARK) (PTY) LTD
PICK 'N PAY (VANDERBIJLPARK) (PTY) LTD
PICK 'N PAY (WALMER) (PTY) LTD
PICK 'N PAY (WESTONARIA) (PTY) LTD
PICK 'N PAY (WITBANK) (PTY) LTD
PICK 'N PAY RETAILERS (PTY) LTD
PICK 'N PAY WHOLESALERS (PTY) LTD
PICK 'N PAY WHOLESALERS (TRANSVAAL) (PTY
PICK 'N PAYNET (PTY) LTD
PRICECLUB CASH AND CARRY (PTY) LTD
RAYMOND ACKERMAN HOLDINGS LTD
RETAIL SHARE REGISTRARS (PTY) LTD
TOM BOARDMAN LTD

INVESTMENTS

BENACDEN (PTY) LTD (1 2%)
SMALL BUSINESS DEVELOPMENT CORP LTD (100000 SH)

PIONEER PROPERTY FUND

ABBREVIATION : PIONEER

JSE SHORT CODE : PNR

SECTOR : Financial-Property Trust

SHAREHOLDERS

Who Owns Whom's Assessment of the Identity of the Ultimate Controlling Shareholder:
SA MUTUAL

SHAREHOLDER	PERCENTAGE 1992	1991
SA MUTUAL	32 7	32 5
SAGE LIFE LTD	12 2	12 1
CMB NOM P/L	11 2	---
STD BANK NOM TVL P/L	4 6	3 4
CITY COUNCIL OF DURBAN	3 4	3 1
SIXTY SIX MARSHALL STREET NOM P/L	3 3	3 3
FIRST NAT NOM P/L	2 9	3 0
METAL IND GROUP PENS FUND	1 9	1 9
AECI PENS FUND	1 8	1 8
NEDBANK NOM LTD	1 8	1 6
EIGHTY ONE MAIN STREET NOM LTD	1 7	3 1
KAWALSKY C	1 7	1 7
ENGINEERING INDUSTRIES PENS FUND	1 5	1 5
SHARESTOCK NOM P/L	1 3	1 6
BARLOWS PENS FUND	1 3	---
SANLAM	---	9 4
UNILEVER SA PENS FUND	---	1 2
TOTAL	83 2	81 1

DIRECTORS :
BLAKE FG ,DE VILLIERS NA
MILLS ANB (Managing Director),NACKAN B
SHILL HL (Chairman

REGISTERED OFFICE
11th Floor, Sage Centre, 10 Fraser Street
Johannesburg
2001
TEL 011-491 0955
FAX 011-838 6129

TRANSFER SECRETARY
Fraser Street Registrars (Pty) Ltd
P O Box 61178, Marshalltown
2107
TEL 011-491 0911

COMPANY SECRETARY
C S Cant

NATURE OF BUSINESS
A property trust, holding a portfolio of mainly industrial properties, and land holdings on the Witwatersrand

BANKERS :
Nedperm Bank Ltd

AUDITORS :
Kessel Feinstein, KPMG Aiken & Peat

FAMILIAR BRAND NAMES
N/A

CONTRIBUTION BY ACTIVITY
Benrose (% Rental income by area) (35.5%)
Anderbolt/Boksburg East (11.8%)
City & Suburban (12.5%)
Park Central (7.0%)
Reuven (7.9%)
Eastgate (6.0%)
Wynberg (4.5%)
Alrode/Alrode South (2.4%)
Spartan/Isando/Sebenza (2.0%)
Wadeville (1.7%)
Jet Park (1.9%)
Other (4.0%)
Non-Industrial (2.8%)

YEAR END : March

DIVIDEND :Units

Interim No 23	(Ldr)24/08/90	(Pay)31/08/90	Amt(c)15.71
Final No 24	(Ldr)22/02/91	(Pay)28/02/91	Amt(c)17.38
Special No 25	(Ldr)24/05/91	(Pay)31/05/91	Amt(c)7.95
Final No 27	(Ldr)22/05/92	(Pay)29/05/92	Amt(c)17.40
Interim No 26	(Ldr)22/11/91	(Pay)29/11/91	Amt(c)17.06
Interim No 28	(Ldr)20/11/92	(Pay)30/11/92	Amt(c)17.10

NUMBER OF EMPLOYEES : 60

CAPITAL STRUCTURE

	AUTHORISED	ISSUED
Units	111396012	111396012

FINANCIAL STATISTICS (AT FINANCIAL YEAR END)

(Amts in R'000)	1992 Mar	1991 Mar	1989 Dec	1988	1987
Ord S/H Int	202396	202398	202397	153797	153797
Long Trm Loans	33820	33841	30102	12540	11417
Iss Ord Share	111396	111396	111396	92830	92830
Total Liab	54226	43688	45348	25080	22834
Current Liab	20406	9847	15246	12540	11417
Total Assets	256622	246086	247745	188180	193801
Current Assets	49054	44436	60226	21843	28587
Debtors	1605	2341	2563	-	-
Inventory	-	-	-	21843	28587
Oper Profit	5297	10515	2592	-	-
Tax Paid	. 5	-	-	-	-
Prf af Int&Tax	38385	45719	27535	23356	21230
Prf att Ord Sh	38385	45719	27535	23356	21230
Btm Line Earn	38385	45719	27535	23356	21230
Dividend Paid	38387	45717	27535	23356	21230
Mkt Prce(c) YE	360	375	320	250	300

PER SHARE STATISTICS (CENTS)

Net Asst Val	181.69	181.69	181.69	165.68	165.68
Net Earnings	34.46	41.04	28.85	-	-
Dividends	34.46	41.04	28.85	-	-
Cash Flow	34.46	32.83	24.72	25.16	22.87

RATIOS AND OTHER INFORMATION

Mrk Cap(R000)	401026	417735	356467	232075	278490
Current Ratio	2.40	4.51	3.95	1.74	2.50
Quik/Acid Tst	2.40	4.51	3.95	-	-
Debt/Ass Rat	0.21	0.18	0.18	0.13	0.12
L T L Tot Ass	0.13	0.14	0.12	0.07	0.06
Debt to Eqity	0.27	0.22	0.22	0.16	0.15
Ret on Assets	14.96	14.86	11.11	12.41	10.95
Ret on Equity%	18.97	18.07	13.60	15.19	13.80
Price/Earnings	10.45	9.14	11.09	-	-
Divid Cover	1.00	1.00	1.00	-	-
Divid Yield	9.57	10.94	9.02	-	-
Earning Yield%	9.57	10.94	9.02	-	-
NAV % Mrk Pr	50.47	48.45	56.78	66.27	55.23
Effec Tax Rate	0.09	-	-	-	-
Def Interval	0.91	0.61	1.11	0.54	0.54
Sus Grth Rate	0.00	0.00	0.00	0.00	0.00

SUBSIDIARY & ASSOCIATED COMPANIES

ALFKAY PROPERTIES (PTY) LTD
AUBRYL INVESTMENTS (PTY) LTD
AXIAL CRAIGHALL (PTY) LTD
BENROSE HOLDINGS (PTY) LTD
BENROSE SHOPPING CENTRE (PTY) LTD
BESIT PROPERTY (PTY) LTD
BHI SERVICES (PTY) LTD
BIRKENRUTH ESTATES (PTY) LTD
CHARCOAL INVESTMENTS (PTY) LTD
DANEZIO HOLDINGS 553 (PTY) LTD
DANJUL INVESTMENTS (PTY) LTD
DON SUPREME (PTY) LTD
EASTGATE STANDS (146 - 159) (PTY) LTD
EDITH CAVELL STREET INVESTMENTS (PTY) LT
ERF 36 BENROSE (PTY) LTD
ERF FOUR HUNDRED AND SIXTY WYNBERG (PTY)
FACTORY ENTERPRISES (PTY) LTD
FOXPHILIP PROPERTIES (PTY) LTD
FREEWAY FOUR FOUR ONE (PTY) LTD
FUCHS STREET PROPERTIES (PTY) LTD
GAG INVESTMENTS (PTY) LTD
GEORGE GOCH INVESTMENTS (PTY) LTD
GLOWBEN INVESTMENTS (PTY) LTD
GOLDMARK INVESTMENTS (PTY) LTD
GOY INVESTMENTS (PTY) LTD
GRAMSUN INVESTMENTS (PTY) LTD
HERON INVESTMENTS (PTY) LTD
HORKAY HOLDINGS (PTY) LTD
INDUSTRIAL REALTY TRUST (PTY) LTD
IVANSETH INVESTMENTS (PTY) LTD
JOHANNESBURG WEST PROPERTIES (PTY) LTD
JULBERT INVESTMENTS (PTY) LTD
JUPITER INDUSTRIAL SITES (PTY) LTD
LAMBRETTA HOUSE (PTY) LTD
LOG SQUARE (PTY) LTD
MAINFOX PROPERTIES (PTY) LTD
MIQUELON PROPERTIES (PTY) LTD
NEW MODDER TOWNSHIP (PTY) LTD
NEWOBOR PROPERTIES (PTY) LTD
NIMROD PROPERTIES (PTY) LTD
ORNI PROPERTIES (PTY) LTD
PARK CENTRAL TOWNSHIPS (PTY) LTD
PHILIPMAIN PROPERTIES (PTY) LTD
PIONEER ALRODE (PTY) LTD
PIONEER ANDERBOLT (PTY) LTD
PIONEER HOLDINGS & FINANCE CORP. (PTY) L
PIONEER JET PARK (PTY) LTD
PIONEER STRUCTURES (PTY) LTD
PREMIER WIRE PROPERTIES (PTY) LTD
RENFREW HOUSE (PTY) LTD
SAM JOFFEE PROPERTIES (PTY) LTD
SPAN DEVELOPMENTS (PTY) LTD
STRUCTURAL YARD (PTY) LTD
TWO TWO FOUR BENROSE (PTY) LTD
TYNE INVESTMENTS (PTY) LTD
UTAH INVESTMENTS (PTY) LTD
WENBER PROPERTIES (PTY) LTD
WHITWORTH ROAD PROPERTIES (PTY) LTD
WYNBERG STAND 164 (PTY) LTD
WYNBERG STAND 485 (PTY) LTS

INVESTMENTS

None

PLASTALL LTD

ABBREVIATION : PLASTAL

JSE SHORT CODE : PST

SECTOR : Industrial-Paper & Packaging

SHAREHOLDERS

Who Owns Whom's Assessment of the Identity of the Ultimate Controlling Shareholder: DANGLO

SHAREHOLDER	PERCENTAGE 1992	1991
PLASTALL INV P/L	85.3	85.3
PALLAS C J	2.0	1.4
ZBINDEN M	1.6	1.2
TOTAL	88.9	87.8

DIRECTORS :
BETTESWORTH RA (Financial Director)
HENDERSON JH ,PALLAS CJ ,RAMSAY GD ,REEVES RE
WENTELER WAR (Chairman),ZBINDEN M

REGISTRATION NUMBER : 05/15274/06

REGISTERED OFFICE
Linton Jones Street, Industries East
Germiston
1401
TEL: 011-51 9611
FAX: 011-51 5415

TRANSFER SECRETARY
Central Registrars Ltd
P O Box 4844, Johannesburg
2000
TEL: 011-331 0051

COMPANY SECRETARY
Danglo Ltd

NATURE OF BUSINESS
Plastal is a holding company, its subsidiaries manufacture and distribute:- a full range of printed and unprinted polyethylene bags and sheeting with a consumer base consisting of the industrial consumer market; a product range of conveyor idler rollers; and furniture components together with a comprehensive range of in-house designed furniture and contract seating.

BANKERS :
Central Merchant Bank Ltd

AUDITORS :
Deloitte Pim Goldby

FAMILIAR BRAND NAMES
GUNDLE,HI-PAK,HORIZON,SWAZI

CONTRIBUTION BY ACTIVITY
N/A

YEAR END : September

DIVIDEND : Ords no par value
Dividend (Ldr)03/01/92 (Pay)17/01/92 Amt(c)4.25

NUMBER OF EMPLOYEES : 180

CAPITAL STRUCTURE

	AUTHORISED	ISSUED
Ords no par value	83554926	14386962

FINANCIAL STATISTICS (AT FINANCIAL YEAR END)

(Amts in R'000)	1990 Sep	1989 Sep	1988 Sep	1987
Ord S/H Int	11621	11484	11081	8070
Long Trm Loans	1730	1362	1844	5473
Iss Ord Share	14387	14387	14387	-
Total Liab	19163	14082	16089	9622
Current Liab	17433	12720	14245	4149
Total Assets	30784	25566	24115	20022
Intang Assets	*	*	3055	*
Current Assets	17802	16146	14987	6479
Debtors	10496	8998	8001	-
Inventory	7046	6484	4646	6479
Turnover	64816	51611	45624	22743
Oper Profit	-31	4396	3221	1554
Interest Paid	1337	1055	1325	274
Tax Paid	27	210	18	339
Prf af Int&Tax	-1337	3167	1957	734
Prf att Ord Sh	-1337	3167	1957	734
Btm Line Earn	-1378	3458	487	734
Dividend Paid	-	-	-	224
Mkt Prce(c) YE	60	50	55	-
Depreciation	1472	1226	1317	-

PER SHARE STATISTICS (CENTS)

Net Asst Val	80.77	79.82	55.79	-
Net Earnings	-9.30	22.00	13.60	-
Cash Flow	1.22	30.58	23.03	-

RATIOS AND OTHER INFORMATION

Mrk Cap(R000)	8632	7194	7913	-
Current Ratio	1.02	1.27	1.05	1.56
Quik/Acid Tst	0.62	0.76	0.73	-
A/C Rec T/ovr	6.18	5.74	5.70	-
Tot Ass T/ovr	2.11	2.02	1.89	1.14
Debt/Ass Rat	0.62	0.55	0.67	0.48
L T L Tot Ass	0.05	0.05	0.07	0.27
Debt to Eqity	1.64	1.22	1.45	1.19
Interest Cover	-0.02	4.17	2.43	4.92
Oper Prof Mrg	-0.05	8.52	7.06	6.83
Net Prof Marg%	-2.06	6.14	4.29	3.23
Ret on Assets	0.09	17.34	13.68	6.73
Ret on Equity%	-11.51	27.58	17.66	9.10
Price/Earnings	-6.45	2.27	4.04	-
Earning Yield%	-15.50	44.00	24.73	-
NAV % Mrk Pr	134.62	159.64	101.43	-
Effec Tax Rate	1.07	6.04	0.15	26.48
Def Interval	44.76	0.61	1.56	7.46
Sus Grth Rate	-11.51	27.58	17.66	6.32

SUBSIDIARY & ASSOCIATED COMPANIES

CARBIDE TECHNOLOGY (PTY) LTD
EGA-GLO (PTY) LTD
ERF 884 SOUTH GERMISTON EXTENSION 2 (PTY
GERMISTON PACKAGING (PTY) LTD
GLOBAL PROJECTS (PTY) LTD
HORIZON ENGINEERING (PTY) LTD
HORIZON INTERSEAT (PTY) LTD
PLASTALL FLEXIBLE PACKAGING (PTY) LTD
PLASTICS AND PACKAGING CONVERTERS (PTY)
RECYCLED PACKAGING (PTY) LTD
STAND 141 DISTRICT PTA (PTY) LTD
SWAZI PLASTIC INDUSTRIES LTD

INVESTMENTS

None

PLATE GLASS & SHATTERPRUFE INDUSTRIES LTD

ABBREVIATION : PLATE-GL

JSE SHORT CODE : PGS

SECTOR : Industrial-Industrial Holding

SHAREHOLDERS

Who Owns Whom's Assessment of the Identity of the Ultimate Controlling Shareholder: ANGLO AMERICAN VIA SA BREWERIES

SHAREHOLDER	PERCENTAGE 1992	1991
PLATE GLASS CONSOLIDATED INV CO P/L	17.2	25.9
SA BREWERIES LTD	17.1	---
PLACOR HLDGS LTD	15.9	23.8
CMB NOM P/L	7.4	---
EIGHTY ONE MAIN STREET NOM LTD	3.9	2.8
LIBERTY LIFE ASSOC OF AFRICA LTD	3.5	3.4
SOUTHERN LIFE ASSOC LTD	2.5	3.0
ENGINEERING INDUSTRIES PENS FUND	2.5	1.8
STD BANK NOM TVL P/L	2.3	1.6
YSKOR PENS FUND	2.1	2.6
MOMENTUM LIFE ASSURE LTD	2.0	2.2
METAL IND GROUP PENS FUND	2.0	1.2
SA MUTUAL	1.7	---
GREENMARKET SQUARE NOM P/L	1.2	1.5
DE BEERS PENS FUND	1.1	1.1
MUTUAL & FEDERAL INSURANCE CO LTD	1.1	---
FIRST NAT NOM P/L	---	1.6
ESCOM PENS & PROV FUND	---	2.0
SANLAM	---	7.2
TOTAL	83.5	81.6

DIRECTORS :
BRODIE B ,COHEN LAH ,KAHN JM ,LEVY LN ,LUBNER B
LUBNER R (Chairman & Chief Exec.),MACFARLANE WS
MARKILES PS ,MILLARD DH
READ MWS (Financial Director),SCOTT MW
SHAKINOVSKY ML ,VAN DER WATT L ,WYMAN MI

REGISTRATION NUMBER : 05/24266/06

REGISTERED OFFICE
322 Main Street, Jeppestown
2094
TEL: 011-618 1640
FAX: 011-618 2128

TRANSFER SECRETARY
Mercantile Registrars Ltd
P O Box 1053, Johannesburg
2000
TEL: 011-333 8181

COMPANY SECRETARY
M W S Read

NATURE OF BUSINESS
The group is engaged in the following activities in SA: Manufacture, processing, distribution and installation of float and safety glass & related products; Manufacture and upgrading of particle-board and durable, decorative surfaces, and the distribution of board & allied products; Outside of SA: Manufacture & upgrading of particleboard & allied products & the distribution of glass, board timber and building materials; Distribution and installation of automotive glass.

BANKERS :
Standard Bank of SA Ltd
French Bank of SA Ltd
UAL Merchant Bank Ltd, Nedbank Ltd

AUDITORS :
Arthur Andersen & Co

FAMILIAR BRAND NAMES
AUTOGLASS,BELRON INTERNATIONAL,BISONBORD
CARGLASS,FORMICA,FREDERICK SAGE (ZIM)
GLASS SA,O'BRIEN GLASS,PG AUTOGLASS,PG BISON
PG GLASS,PG WOOD,PILKINGTON,TIMBER CITY
WINDSCREENS O'BRIEN,WINDSHIELD AMERICA

CONTRIBUTION BY ACTIVITY
Building Industry (% Sales Distribution) (17.3%)
Motor Industry (51.6%)
Furniture (12.1%)
Other (19.0%)

YEAR END : March

DIVIDEND :Ords 50c

Interim No 65	(Ldr)15/12/89	(Pay)10/01/90	Amt(c)65
Final No 66	(Ldr)06/07/90	(Pay)01/08/90	Amt(c)157
Interim No 67	(Ldr)14/12/90	(Pay)10/01/91	Amt(c)65
Final No 68	(Ldr)05/07/91	(Pay)31/07/91	Amt(c)157
Interim No 69	(Ldr)03/01/92	(Pay)13/01/92	Amt(c)65
Final No 70	(Ldr)13/03/92	(Pay)29/07/92	Amt(c)85
Interim No 71	(Ldr)18/12/92	(Pay)31/12/92	Amt(c)65

NUMBER OF EMPLOYEES : 19600

CAPITAL STRUCTURE

	AUTHORISED	ISSUED
6,5% Non-Red "B" Cum Prefs R1	500000	500000
6,5% Red Cum Prefs R2	518000	0
8,5% Red Cum Prefs R1	5000000	0
Var Rate Red Cum Prefs 1c	4000000	0
"B" Var Rate Red Cum Prefs 1c	6400000	333332
Ords 50c	34533104	24708578
"C" Var Rate Red Cum Prefs 1c	6000000	1500
"A" Auto Conv Cum Prefs 50c	20000000	12916667

FINANCIAL STATISTICS (AT FINANCIAL YEAR END)

(Amts in R'000)	1992 Mar	1991 Mar	1990 Mar	1989 Mar	1988 Mar
Ord S/H Int	193398	325688	335655	378856	358153
Long Trm Loans	169631	328029	482669	423059	323041
Iss Ord Share	16472	16472	16472	16472	16472
Total Liab	1070453	1151598	1415652	1116671	938918
Current Liab	900822	823569	932983	693612	615877
Total Assets	1263851	1477286	1751307	1495527	1297071
Current Assets	705695	877245	1123548	952335	786692
Debtors	435039	518448	682191	593007	467268
Inventory	257495	342204	431615	349876	308316
Turnover	1981341	2298877	3131273	2761633	2324393
Oper Profit	238108	294695	290346	283745	204194
Interest Paid	44371	52665	80969	71747	42155
Tax Paid	102551	136054	122528	108710	77208
Prf af Int&Tax	113905	134316	111198	123794	96749
Prf att Ord Sh	50839	67358	58438	79507	65987
Btm Line Earn	-25058	-8289	-11240	29585	60414
Dividend Paid	24708	36569	36569	36569	30474
Mkt Prce(c) YE	5400	5850	6375	4800	3750
Depreciation	62162	61844	75212	66926	55339

PER SHARE STATISTICS (CENTS)

Net Asst Val	1174.10	1977.22	2037.73	2300.00	2174.31
Net Earnings	308.60	408.90	354.80	482.70	400.60
Dividends	150.00	222.00	222.00	222.00	185.00
Cash Flow	691.23	780.92	765.74	847.94	610.49

RATIOS AND OTHER INFORMATION

Mrk Cap(R000)	889488	963612	1050090	790656	617700
Current Ratio	0.78	1.07	1.20	1.37	1.28
Quik/Acid Tst	0.50	0.65	0.74	0.87	0.78
A/C Rec T/ovr	4.55	4.43	4.59	4.66	4.97
Tot Ass T/ovr	1.57	1.56	1.79	1.85	1.79
Debt/Ass Rat	0.75	0.59	0.67	0.61	0.57
L T L Tot Ass	0.04	0.03	0.14	0.15	0.10
Debt to Eqity	4.91	2.69	3.52	2.41	2.08
Interest Cover	5.51	5.72	3.67	4.04	4.84
Oper Prof Mrg	12.02	12.82	9.27	10.27	8.78
Net Prof Marg%	2.57	2.93	1.87	2.88	2.84
Ret on Assets	21.33	21.98	18.35	21.28	17.34
Ret on Equity%	26.29	20.68	17.41	20.99	18.42
Price/Earnings	17.50	14.31	17.97	9.94	9.36
Divid Cover	2.06	1.84	1.60	2.17	2.17
Divid Yield	2.78	3.79	3.48	4.63	4.93
Earning Yield%	5.71	6.99	5.57	10.06	10.68
NAV % Mrk Pr	21.74	33.80	31.96	47.92	57.98
Effec Tax Rate	46.92	48.54	53.92	44.03	43.91
Def Interval	2.94	2.41	3.86	2.33	3.03
Sus Grth Rate	13.51	9.45	6.52	11.33	9.92

SUBSIDIARY & ASSOCIATED COMPANIES

FIFE STREET BUILDINGS (PVT) LTD
FREDERICK SAGE & CO. LTD
INTERNATIONAL GLASS HOLDINGS LTD
LIKE NU WINDSCREENS (PTY) LIMITED (48.4%)
O'BRIEN GLASS HOLDINGS (PTY) LTD (48,9%)
PG BISON LTD (47,8%)
PG INDUSTRIES MALAWI LIMITED
PG WOOD EXCO (PTY) LTD
PG WOOD INDUSTRIES LTD
PGSI MANAGEMENT SERVICES (PTY) LTD
PGWI INVESTMENTS (PTY) LTD (46%)
PILKINGTON GLASS (ZIMBABWE) (PVT) LTD (40%)
RAYMOND AMORETTI JOINERY (PTY) LTD (40%)
TANACROSS INVESTMENTS (PTY) LTD (50%)
UPINGTON GLASS WORKS (PTY) LTD (24,2%)

INVESTMENTS

COBROLE LTD (133056 SH)
SMALL BUSINESS DEV. CORP. LTD (172800 SH)
YORK TIMBER ORGANISATION LTD (800 SH)

POINTER FASHION INTERNATIONAL LTD

ABBREVIATION : POINTER

JSE SHORT CODE : PNT

SECTOR : Industrial-Clothing, Footwear & Textiles

SHAREHOLDERS

Who Owns Whom's Assessment of the Identity of the Ultimate Controlling Shareholder: DIRECTORS CONTROL 31,58% (JUNE 1991)

SHAREHOLDER	PERCENTAGE 1992	1991
WARRANT TRUSTEES LTD	44.7	44.7
STEIN J	15.3	19.7
TUROK L L	13.8	13.8
PATEL I M	2.5	2.5
TUROK S Y	1.7	1.5
SMALLE M	1.4	1.0
HEATH G G	1.3	---
TOTAL	80.7	83.3

DIRECTORS :
STEIN J (Managing Director),TUROK LL (Chairman

REGISTRATION NUMBER : 05/14601/06

REGISTERED OFFICE
5th Floor, Matrix House, 73 Strand Street
Cape Town
8001
TEL: 021-511 9180
FAX: 021-511 5693

TRANSFER SECRETARY
Rand Registrars Ltd
P O Box 82549, Southdale
2135
TEL: 011-835 1016

COMPANY SECRETARY
Park Mall Trust CC

NATURE OF BUSINESS
Manufacturers and distributors of leather fashion accessories and garments.

BANKERS :
First National Bank of SA Ltd

AUDITORS :
Cecil Kilpin & Co

FAMILIAR BRAND NAMES
LEISURE LEATHER,POINTER DOG

CONTRIBUTION BY ACTIVITY
N/A

YEAR END : June

DIVIDEND :Ords no par value
Final No 8 (Ldr)09/11/90 (Pay)30/11/90 Amt(c)2

NUMBER OF EMPLOYEES : 220

CAPITAL STRUCTURE

	AUTHORISED	ISSUED
Ords no par value	12000000	8030496

FINANCIAL STATISTICS (AT FINANCIAL YEAR END)

(Amts in R'000)	1991 Jun	1990 Jun	1989 Jun	1988 Jun	1987 Jun
Ord S/H Int	1911	2066	1753	1475	1292
Long Trm Loans	1213	1367	1264	1086	54
Iss Ord Share	8030	8030	8030	8000	8000
Total Liab	3675	7024	5708	3939	3072
Current Liab	2462	5657	4444	2853	3018
Total Assets	5586	9090	7461	5414	4364
Current Assets	4780	8342	6923	5014	4072
Debtors	1924	5659	4488	2733	2164
Inventory	2578	2675	2434	2279	1906
Turnover	14092	15825	13698	9140	7576
Oper Profit	528	1864	1457	1313	887
Interest Paid	629	508	523	274	174
Tax Paid	95	590	424	513	332
Prf af Int&Tax	-172	794	510	526	381
Prf att Ord Sh	-372	594	510	526	381
Btm Line Earn	-372	594	510	526	381
Dividend Paid	-	281	240	240	196
Mkt Prce(c) YE	15	20	38	30	-
Depreciation	88	105	59	55	42

PER SHARE STATISTICS (CENTS)

Net Asst Val	23.80	25.73	21.83	18.44	16.15
Net Earnings	-4.63	7.40	6.35	6.58	4.76
Dividends	-	3.50	3.00	3.00	2.45
Cash Flow	-0.62	11.15	7.09	7.26	5.29

RATIOS AND OTHER INFORMATION

Mrk Cap(R000)	1205	1606	3051	2400	-
Current Ratio	1.94	1.47	1.56	1.76	1.35
Quik/Acid Tst	0.89	1.00	1.01	0.96	0.72
A/C Rec T/ovr	7.32	2.80	3.05	3.34	3.50
Tot Ass T/ovr	2.52	1.74	1.84	1.69	1.74
Debt/Ass Rat	0.66	0.77	0.77	0.73	0.70
L T L Tot Ass	0.22	0.15	0.17	0.20	0.01
Debt to Eqity	1.92	3.40	3.26	2.67	2.38
Interest Cover	0.84	3.67	2.79	4.79	5.10
Oper Prof Mrg	3.75	11.78	10.64	14.37	11.71
Net Prof Marg%	-2.64	3.75	3.72	5.75	5.03
Ret on Assets	9.88	20.81	19.53	24.25	20.33
Ret on Equity%	-19.47	28.75	29.09	35.66	29.49
Price/Earnings	-3.24	2.70	5.98	4.56	-
Divid Cover	-	2.11	2.12	2.19	1.94
Divid Yield	-	17.50	7.89	10.00	-
Earning Yield%	-30.87	37.00	16.71	21.93	-
NAV % Mrk Pr	158.66	128.64	57.45	61.46	-
Effec Tax Rate	-	42.92	45.40	47.74	46.56
Def Interval	-4.42	2.69	3.63	2.60	3.89
Sus Grth Rate	-19.47	15.15	15.40	19.39	14.32

SUBSIDIARY & ASSOCIATED COMPANIES

CUSTOMCRAFT ORIGINALS (PTY) LTD
FASHION LEATHERCRAFT (PTY) LTD
FASHION WORLD ACCESSORIES (PTY) LTD
POINTER MANUFACTURERS (PTY) LTD

INVESTMENTS

None

PORTLAND HOLDINGS LTD

ABBREVIATION : PORTHLD

JSE SHORT CODE : POR

SECTOR : Industrial-Building & Construction

SHAREHOLDERS

Who Owns Whom's Assessment of the Identity of the Ultimate Controlling Shareholder:
ANGLO AMERICAN / MINORITIES

DIRECTORS :
BARRON RW ,LEWIS AJL ,MARGESSON MV
MCCLELLAND AH ,SHELTON DJ ,SLY JR (Chairman)
STIRLING A ,STOBBS JH (Managing Director)
TAYLOR JR

REGISTERED OFFICE
Portland House, Cnr Main Str & 13th Ave
Bulawayo, Zimbabwe

TEL: 09263-979241
FAX: 09263-979240

TRANSFER SECRETARY
KPMG Aiken & Peat
P O Box 7400, Johannesburg
2000
TEL: 011-332 7111

COMPANY SECRETARY
C E Rickwood

NATURE OF BUSINESS
The group operates in Zimbabwe. Activities include manufacture & supply of cement & concrete products

BANKERS :
N/A

AUDITORS :
Deloitte & Touche

FAMILIAR BRAND NAMES
N/A

CONTRIBUTION BY ACTIVITY
N/A

YEAR END : July

DIVIDEND :Ords 50c
Interim No 66 (Ldr)27/04/90 (Pay)24/05/90 Amt(c)2.25
Final No 67 (Ldr)02/11/90 (Pay)16/11/90 Amt(c)4.75
Interim No 68 (Ldr)26/04/91 (Pay)24/05/91 Amt(c)2.25
Final No 69 (Ldr)01/11/91 (Pay)22/11/91 Amt(c)5.25

Interim No 70	(Ldr)24/04/92	(Pay)09/06/92	Amt(c)7.0
Final No 71	(Ldr)20/11/92	(Pay)15/12/92	Amt(c)3

NUMBER OF EMPLOYEES : 1600

CAPITAL STRUCTURE

	AUTHORISED	ISSUED
Ords 50c	45000000	42998448
Cum Red Conv Prefs 50c (Not Liste	15000000	14332816

FINANCIAL STATISTICS (AT FINANCIAL YEAR END)

(Amts in Z$)	1992 Jul	1991 Jul	1990 Jul	1989 Aug	1988 Aug
Ord S/H Int	114629	85129	41291	37258	33269
Long Trm Loans	102945	48763	4465	1284	513
Iss Ord Share	42998	42998	28666	28666	14333
Total Liab	201407	91824	28674	20159	13108
Current Liab	98462	43061	24209	18875	12595
Total Assets	316036	176953	69965	57417	46377
Current Assets	70959	67438	37379	31514	23058
Debtors	31499	20014	14179	9602	7146
Inventory	37185	33922	20707	17013	13262
Turnover	254624	141094	93928	63219	47692
Oper Profit	51807	17169	9262	6553	5775
Interest Paid	6085	1155	499	-	170
Tax Paid	10593	5273	2706	1805	1230
Prf af Int&Tax	36291	13137	6347	4748	4375
Prf att Ord Sh	33800	11491	6040	4528	4199
Btm Line Earn	33800	11491	6040	5708	4199
Dividend Paid	4300	3225	2007	1720	1720
Mkt Prce(c) YE	37	50	40	70	65
Depreciation	4500	3544	2042	1727	1477

PER SHARE STATISTICS (CENTS)

Net Asst Val	266.59	197.98	144.04	129.97	232.11
Net Earnings	78.60	29.20	21.10	15.80	29.30
Dividends	10.00	7.50	7.00	6.00	12.00
Cash Flow	89.07	34.97	28.19	21.82	39.60

RATIOS AND OTHER INFORMATION

Mrk Cap(R000)	15909	21499	11466	20066	9316
Current Ratio	0.72	1.57	1.54	1.67	1.83
Quik/Acid Tst	0.34	0.78	0.69	0.77	0.78
A/C Rec T/ovr	8.08	7.05	6.62	6.58	6.67
Tot Ass T/ovr	0.81	0.80	1.34	1.10	1.03
Debt/Ass Rat	0.61	0.47	0.40	0.34	0.27
L T L Tot Ass	0.30	0.23	0.05	0.01	-
Debt to Eqity	1.68	0.98	0.67	0.52	0.38
Interest Cover	8.51	14.86	18.56	-	33.97
Oper Prof Mrg	20.35	12.17	9.86	10.37	12.11
Net Prof Marg%	13.27	8.14	6.43	7.16	8.80
Ret on Assets	16.76	11.06	13.65	11.41	12.45
Ret on Equity%	29.49	13.50	14.63	12.15	12.62
Price/Earnings	0.47	1.71	1.90	4.43	2.22
Divid Cover	7.86	3.89	3.01	2.63	2.44
Divid Yield	27.03	15.00	17.50	8.57	18.46
Earning Yield%	212.43	58.40	52.75	22.57	45.08
NAV % Mrk Pr	720.52	395.97	360.10	185.68	357.10
Effec Tax Rate	21.22	28.67	29.89	27.54	21.94
Def Interval	3.93	3.98	1.05	0.97	0.54
Sus Grth Rate	25.74	9.71	9.77	7.54	7.45

SUBSIDIARY & ASSOCIATED COMPANIES

ARLINGTON PROPERTIES (PVT) LTD
FORT CONCRETE HOLDINGS (PVT) LTD
MINERAL RESEARCH (PTY) LTD
PREMIER PORTLAND CEMENT CO. LTD
PREMIER READYMIX (PVT) LTD
UNITED PORTLAND CEMENT CO (PVT) LTD

INVESTMENTS

None

POTGIETERSRUST PLATINUMS LTD

ABBREVIATION : PP RUST

JSE SHORT CODE : PRS

SECTOR : Metals & Minerals-Platinum

SHAREHOLDERS

Who Owns Whom's Assessment of the Identity of the Ultimate Controlling Shareholder: ANGLO AMERICAN VIA JCI

SHAREHOLDER	PERCENTAGE 1992	1991
STD BANK NOM TVL P/L	34.0	---
LYDENBURG PLATINUM LTD	7.9	---
RESIDENT NOM LTD	6.7	---
DIDO NOM LTD	6.1	---
SA MUTUAL	4.6	---
CMB NOM P/L	3.9	---
FERMAIN NOM LTD	3.6	---
JOHANNESBURG CONSOLIDATED INV CO LTD	2.7	---
LEBOWA DEVELOPMENT CORP LTD	2.6	---
PINTAIL INV LTD	2.5	---
PETARD NOM LTD	2.5	---
FIRST NAT NOM P/L	1.7	---
SIXTY SIX MARSHALL STREET NOM P/L	1.6	---
AECI PENS FUND	1.4	---
LEBOWA MINERALS BUREAU	1.4	---
TAURUS NOM LTD	1.2	---
TOTAL	84.3	---

DIRECTORS :
BRAY VG ,BRUCE JT ,DAVISON BE (Chairman)
MACCONACHIE AW ,RETIEF PF ,SCOTT-RUSSELL H DR
SUTHERLAND RB

REGISTRATION NUMBER : 01/08353/06

REGISTERED OFFICE
Consolidated Building, Cnr Fox & Harrison Streets
Johannesburg
2001
TEL: 011-373 9111
FAX: 011-836 6130

TRANSFER SECRETARY
Consolidated Share Registrars Ltd
P O Box 61051, Marshalltown
2107
TEL: 011-492 1620

COMPANY SECRETARY
Johannesburg Consolidated Inv Co Ltd

NATURE OF BUSINESS
Activities include the acquisition & exploitation of mining title to precious metals & base minerals on farms on the Platreef. Mining operations are

conducted by open pit methods. Production includes platinum, palladium,gold, rhodium, nickel & copper

BANKERS :
Standard Bank of SA Ltd

AUDITORS :
Ernst & Young

FAMILIAR BRAND NAMES
N/A

CONTRIBUTION BY ACTIVITY
N/A

YEAR END : June

CAPITAL STRUCTURE

	AUTHORISED	ISSUED
Ords 2,5c	160000000	120264625

FINANCIAL STATISTICS (AT FINANCIAL YEAR END)

(Amts in R'000)	1991 Jun
Ord S/H Int	396159
Total Liab	774
Current Liab	774
Total Assets	396933
Current Assets	365361

PER SHARE STATISTICS (CENTS)

RATIOS AND OTHER INFORMATION

Current Ratio	472.04
Quik/Acid Tst	472.04
Debt/Ass Rat	0.00
Debt to Eqity	0.00

SUBSIDIARY & ASSOCIATED COMPANIES

None

INVESTMENTS

None

POWER TECHNOLOGIES LTD

ABBREVIATION : POWTECH

JSE SHORT CODE : POW

SECTOR : Industrial-Electronics, Electrical & Bat

SHAREHOLDERS

Who Owns Whom's Assessment of the Identity of the Ultimate Controlling Shareholder:
W VENTER VIA ALTRON

SHAREHOLDER	PERCENTAGE 1992	1991
ALLIED ELECTRONICS CORP LTD	40.6	41.3
BILVEN P/L	21.7	21.8
CMB NOM P/L	8.6	---
RESIDENT NOM LTD	5.9	5.9
EIGHTY ONE MAIN STREET NOM LTD	4.5	2.7
STD BANK NOM TVL P/L	3.8	3.6
FIRST NAT NOM P/L	2.2	2.4
SANLAM	---	6.7
TOTAL	87.3	84.5

DIRECTORS :
ALTY JAR (Executive Director),BELL FJ
BOUSTRED WG ,BROWN HM
COUTTS-TROTTER CM (Executive Director)
GARBERS CF DR,JACOBSON DH DR
MCCARROLL WS (Financial Director),STRIDE CA
VENTER WP DR,WATT PA (Executive Chairman

REGISTRATION NUMBER : 05/22346/06

REGISTERED OFFICE
Knightsbridge Manor, 33 Sloane Street
Bryanston
2152
TEL: 011-706 7184
FAX: 011-706 7890

TRANSFER SECRETARY
Central Registrars Ltd
P O Box 4844, Johannesburg
2000
TEL: 011-331 0051

COMPANY SECRETARY
Powertech Management Services (Pty) Ltd

NATURE OF BUSINESS
The group has four major segments of business: power generation, transmission and distribution; power and communication cables; energy management and control; lighting and electrical accessories. Products incl : Insulation materials, Automotive & industrial lead acid batteries, Power, control and industrial electrical equipment (capacitors,motors transformers,miniature substations), Earth leakage protection equipment, Process control instruments, Wiring accessories, Switches, Luminaires & chokes.

BANKERS :
Standard Bank of SA Ltd

AUDITORS :
KPMG Aiken & Peat

FAMILIAR BRAND NAMES
BROWN BOVERI,CRABTREE,DELTA CONTROLS
LASCON LIGHTING,LIGHTECH,LIGHTING STRUCTURES
LITEMASTER,MICRO-XL,NORPLEX OAK,SA MICA
WHITELEYS,WJ PARRY,YELLAND

CONTRIBUTION BY ACTIVITY
N/A

YEAR END : February

DIVIDEND : Ords no par value

Dividend No 13	(Ldr)25/05/90	(Pay)11/06/90	Amt(c)8.4
Dividend No 14	(Ldr)24/05/91	(Pay)10/06/91	Amt(c)9.3

Dividend No 15 (Ldr)29/05/92 (Pay)08/06/92 Amt(c)9.7

NUMBER OF EMPLOYEES : 6665

CAPITAL STRUCTURE

	AUTHORISED	ISSUED
Ords no par value	170534722	134861426

FINANCIAL STATISTICS (AT FINANCIAL YEAR END)

(Amts in R'000)	1992 Feb	1991 Feb	1990 Feb	1989 Feb	1988 Feb
Ord S/H Int	246343	216525	192084	165972	146056
Long Trm Loans	137924	132228	107708	83705	87395
Iss Ord Share	134861	134184	133718	133400	133400
Total Liab	385439	400755	383189	365333	229409
Current Liab	247515	268527	275481	281628	142014
Total Assets	631782	617280	570277	531305	375465
Intang Assets	*	*	4996	*	*
Current Assets	438756	451762	415491	391964	245597
Debtors	209855	207087	177193	186139	114682
Inventory	179639	185734	210195	198550	130543
Turnover	1151758	1204157	1157052	853652	599345
Oper Profit	112721	128825	114906	68875	47351
Interest Paid	3317	8219	23036	13724	6198
Tax Paid	52863	57119	38760	19294	15394
Prf af Int&Tax	69924	69728	62566	42030	25759
Prf att Ord Sh	43436	41208	37102	28559	18068
Btm Line Earn	43436	40076	37102	28559	18068
Dividend Paid	13095	12479	11232	8671	6136
Mkt Prce(c) YE	365	255	195	200	130
Depreciation	20084	18893	16490	14129	13228

PER SHARE STATISTICS (CENTS)

Net Asst Val	182.66	161.36	139.91	124.42	109.49
Net Earnings	32.30	30.80	27.80	21.40	13.50
Dividends	9.70	9.30	8.40	6.50	4.60
Cash Flow	41.50	47.89	39.03	27.12	23.15

RATIOS AND OTHER INFORMATION

Mrk Cap(R000)	492243	342169	260750	266800	173420
Current Ratio	1.77	1.68	1.51	1.39	1.73
Quik/Acid Tst	1.05	0.99	0.75	0.69	0.81
A/C Rec T/ovr	5.49	5.81	6.53	4.59	5.23
Tot Ass T/ovr	1.82	1.95	2.03	1.61	1.60
Debt/Ass Rat	0.41	0.45	0.50	0.55	0.40
L T L Tot Ass	0.02	0.02	0.02	0.02	0.02
Debt to Eqity	1.04	1.29	1.49	1.75	1.02
Interest Cover	35.55	15.97	5.07	5.11	7.64
Oper Prof Mrg	9.79	10.70	9.93	8.07	7.90
Net Prof Marg%	3.77	3.42	3.21	3.35	3.01
Ret on Assets	20.12	22.00	21.81	14.13	12.61
Ret on Equity%	17.63	19.03	19.32	17.21	12.37
Price/Earnings	11.30	8.28	7.01	9.35	9.63
Divid Cover	3.33	3.31	3.31	3.29	2.93
Divid Yield	2.66	3.65	4.31	3.25	3.54
Earning Yield%	8.85	12.08	14.26	10.70	10.38
NAV % Mrk Pr	50.05	63.28	71.75	62.21	84.22
Effec Tax Rate	50.74	40.86	41.05	41.61	38.24
Def Interval	0.24	0.20	0.91	1.56	0.52
Sus Grth Rate	12.32	13.27	13.47	11.98	8.17

SUBSIDIARY & ASSOCIATED COMPANIES

ABERDARE CABLES AFRICA LTD
ABERDARE MARKETING (PTY) LTD
BBT INDUSTRY (PTY) LTD (50%)
BROWN BOVERI PROPERTIES (PTY) LTD (50%)
INSTRUMENTATION & CONTROL TECHNOLOGIES (
LIGHTING STRUCTURES (PTY) LTD
LIGHTING TECHNOLOGIES (PTY) LTD
LIGHTS BY LIGHTS (PTY) LTD
POWERTECH INDUSTRIES (PTY) LTD
RICHARDS BAY CABLE DISTRIBUTORS (PTY) LT
STRIKE TECHNOLOGIES (PTY) LTD (37,5%)
TECHNOLOGIES (PTY) LTD
WILLARD BATTERIES (NAMIBIA) (PTY) LTD
YELLAND ENGINEERING (PTY) LTD (50%)
YELLAND POWER MANAGEMENT (PTY) LTD (37.5%)
YELLAND TECHNOLOGY HOLDINGS (PTY) LTD (50%)

INVESTMENTS

None

PREMIER GROUP LTD

ABBREVIATION : PREM-GRP

JSE SHORT CODE : PML

SECTOR : Industrial-Food

SHAREHOLDERS

Who Owns Whom's Assessment of the Identity of the Ultimate Controlling Shareholder: ANGLO AMERICAN / LIBERTY

SHAREHOLDER	PERCENTAGE 1992	1991
LIBERTY LIFE INV TRUST P/L	24.4	24.6
PREMSAB HOLDINGS LTD	23.5	23.7
STD BANK NOM TVL P/L	18.7	18.5
LIBERTY LIFE ASSOC OF AFRICA LTD	5.4	6.3
CMB NOM P/L	2.9	---
DE BEERS HOLDINGS P/L	2.6	2.6
FIRST NAT NOM P/L	2.0	1.9
SOUTHERN LIFE ASSOC LTD	1.9	1.9
METAL IND GROUP PENS FUND	1.6	1.5
ESCOM PENS & PROV FUND	1.4	1.6
GUARDIAN NOM P/L	1.4	---
ENGINEERING INDUSTRIES PENS FUND	1.3	1.1
EIGHTY ONE MAIN STREET NOM LTD	1.1	---
SANLAM	---	2.9
TOTAL	88.1	86.6

DIRECTORS :

BLOOM AH ,BRAY VG ,CESMAN WE ,DE KOK WJ
FOWLER NB ,GORDON D (Joint Deputy Chairman)
KOVARSKY DC ,MABUZA NEJ ,MATHABATHE LM
RETIEF PF (Joint Deputy Chairman),SHER FB
SUNTER CL ,UTIAN GM (Deputy Chief Executive)
WHARTON-HOOD PD
WRIGHTON PGA (Chairman & Chief Exec.

REGISTRATION NUMBER : 01/04313/06

REGISTERED OFFICE

Premier Group Centre, 1 Newtown Avenue
Killarney, Johannesburg
2193
TEL: 011-446 9111
FAX: 011-446 2239

TRANSFER SECRETARY
Mercantile Registrars Ltd
P O Box 1053, Johannesburg
2000
TEL: 011-333 8181

COMPANY SECRETARY
P M Gishen (Ms)

NATURE OF BUSINESS
Maize and wheat millers, manufacturers and distributors of food products, edible oils and fats, poultry, animal feed, pharmaceutical and industrial chemicals; bakers and confectioners; sugar & cotton farmers & processors. The company holds controlling interests in quoted CNA Gallo, Gresham, Twins, Score Supermarkets, Metro Cash & Carry, & Hiscore Holdings.

BANKERS :
First National Bank of SA Ltd
Standard Bank of SA Ltd, Nedcor Bank Ltd

AUDITORS :
KPMG Aiken & Peat

FAMILIAR BRAND NAMES
ANCHOR YEAST (50%),BIG JACK,BLOSSOM
BLUE RIBBON,CARDIN,CLARK COTTON,CNA
COUNTRY QUALITY,CROSS,DE LA RUE,DINKY PUFFS
DUMA,EPIC,EPIC OIL MILLS,FARM FARE,FIDO
GOLD FISH,GOLD STAR (50%),GOLDFISH
HOSPITALITY,IMPALA,INVICTA,IONA,IWISA,JABULA
JABULA FOODS,KRAFT,MAMA'S PIES,MAYPOLE
NATIONAL FOOD DISTRIB.,NICE 'N EASY
NUTTY WHEAT,NYALA,OLE,PAN,PECKS ANCHOVETTE
PENTAX,PLUS PROMOTIONS,PRET,REDRO,SANYO
SEA DIAMOND,SEE ALSO SUBSIDIARIES,SKUNA
SNOWFLAKE,SUNBLEST,TELERAD,YAMAHA
YUM YUM PEANUT BUTTER

CONTRIBUTION BY ACTIVITY
Food (% of Turnover) (30.4%)
Pharmaceuticals (10.4%)
Cash & Carry (39.2%)
Retail (16.0%)
Entertainment,Leisure & Business systems (4.0%)

YEAR END : April

DIVIDEND :Ords 50c

Interim No 153	(Ldr)04/08/89	(Pay)29/12/89	Amt(c)25
Final No 154	(Ldr)15/06/90	(Pay)29/06/90	Amt(c)35
Interim No 155	(Ldr)14/12/90	(Pay)28/12/90	Amt(c)28
Final No 156	(Ldr)14/06/91	(Pay)28/06/91	Amt(c)42
Interim No 157	(Ldr)27/12/91	(Pay)17/01/92	Amt(c)32
Dividend	(Ldr)27/12/91	(Pay)17/01/92	Amt(c)5
Final No 158	(Ldr)17/07/92	(Pay)31/07/92	Amt(c)49
Dividend	(Ldr)17/07/92	(Pay)31/07/92	Amt(c)2

NUMBER OF EMPLOYEES : 49926

CAPITAL STRUCTURE

	AUTHORISED	ISSUED
5,5% Cum Prefs R2	621100	621100
Prefs 50c	6000000	0
Ords 50c	110000000	79255395

FINANCIAL STATISTICS (AT FINANCIAL YEAR END)

(Amts in R'000)	1992 Apr	1991 Mar	1990 Mar	1989 Mar	1988 Mar
Ord S/H Int	1103510	1125738	982707	638206	1665787
Long Trm Loans	785848	688935	645517	673931	643556
Iss Ord Share	79255	73601	71931	63808	56940
Total Liab	2590820	1708144	1613536	1527984	1243362
Current Liab	1804972	1019209	968019	854053	599806
Total Assets	3448753	2660091	2431608	2020308	2762251
Intang Assets	245577	173791	164635	145882	146898
Current Assets	2180494	1390066	1296114	1034835	733697
Debtors	747062	693318	577218	491160	402441
Inventory	1197093	552807	509896	413862	318331
Turnover	10638242	5094095	4341864	4150294	3204021
Oper Profit	455060	374728	336233	286796	227220
Interest Paid	132947	131081	124523	109453	80669
Tax Paid	164520	124963	110278	81670	54986
Prf af Int&Tax	255149	191884	169464	138913	161346
Prf att Ord Sh	202017	149592	118034	86461	197865
Btm Line Earn	190454	159246	73359	99904	184206
Dividend Paid	69599	51520	41162	31163	89278
Mkt Prce(c) YE	4100	2600	1700	4350	3300
Depreciation	102775	78843	55635	51914	46598

PER SHARE STATISTICS (CENTS)

Net Asst Val	1082.50	1293.39	1137.30	771.57	2667.53
Net Earnings	244.00	210.00	180.00	145.00	317.00
Dividends	81.00	70.00	60.00	50.00	140.00
Cash Flow	370.27	306.08	324.40	272.00	287.48

RATIOS AND OTHER INFORMATION

Mrk Cap(R000)	3249455	1913626	1222827	2775648	1879020
Current Ratio	1.21	1.36	1.34	1.21	1.22
Quik/Acid Tst	0.54	0.82	0.81	0.73	0.69
A/C Rec T/ovr	13.14	7.35	7.52	8.45	7.96
Tot Ass T/ovr	2.85	1.92	1.79	2.05	1.16
Debt/Ass Rat	0.57	0.47	0.49	0.58	0.34
L T L Tot Ass	0.05	0.08	0.09	0.16	0.13
Debt to Eqity	1.78	1.10	1.21	1.84	0.57
Interest Cover	3.63	3.04	2.86	2.74	3.68
Oper Prof Mrg	4.28	7.36	7.74	6.91	7.09
Net Prof Marg%	1.90	2.94	2.72	2.08	6.18
Ret on Assets	15.27	17.88	17.21	16.84	13.65
Ret on Equity%	16.90	13.29	12.01	13.55	11.88
Price/Earnings	16.80	12.38	9.44	30.00	10.41
Divid Cover	3.01	3.00	3.00	2.90	2.26
Divid Yield	1.98	2.69	3.53	1.15	4.24
Earning Yield%	5.95	8.08	10.59	3.33	9.61
NAV % Mrk Pr	26.40	49.75	66.90	17.74	80.83
Effec Tax Rate	35.59	36.18	22.44	20.02	27.12
Def Interval	0.94	2.17	2.24	3.45	2.39
Sus Grth Rate	12.00	8.71	7.82	8.66	6.52

SUBSIDIARY & ASSOCIATED COMPANIES

ACORNHOEK WHOLESALERS (PTY) LTD (33%)
AFRICAN CEREALS (PTY) LTD
AMENDU PRODUCTS (PTY) LTD (49%)
ASSOCIATED S A BAKERIES (PTY) LTD
ATLANTIC FISHING ENTERPRISES (PTY) LTD
BAKROO PROPERTIES (PTY) LTD (50%)
BALFOUR BAKERY (PTY) LTD (45%)
CLARENCE PROPERTIES (PTY) LTD (35%)
CNA GALLO LTD (33%)
COLOUR PROCESSING LABORATORIES (PTY) LTD (50%)
CONSOLIDATED FRAGRANCES (PTY) LTD (25%)
CORPORATE MANAGEMENT SERVICES LTD (33,27%)
DEE BEE SUPERMARKETS TRADING (PTY) LTD
DISPERSA PHARMACEUTICALS (PTY) LTD (24,6%)
EATWELL BAKERY (PTY) LTD (22,4%)
EDENDALE BAKERY LTD (50%)
ELLERMAN COLD STORAGE (PTY) LTD (50%)
EPIC OIL MILLS (PTY) LTD
EPOL (PTY) LTD (50%)
ETOSHA FISHING CORPORATION (PTY) LTD
FERMENTATION INDUSTRIES (PTY) LTD (50%)

GILUNION PP RUST (PTY) LTD (50%)
GRESHAM INDUSTRIES LTD
HARVELD PRODUCTS (PTY) LTD
HI-SCORE HOLDINGS LTD
HILLREY PROPERTIES (PTY) LTD (50%)
J L CLARK COTTON CO (PTY) LTD
JABULA FOODS (TRANSKEI) (PTY) LTD
JOHN OVENSTONE LIMITED
JOHN OVENSTONE WALVIS BAY LIMITED
KESTELL BAKERIES (PTY) LTD (33,3%)
KWAZULU BREWERIES (PTY) LTD
MADADENI BAKERY LTD (50%)
MADAUS PHARMACEUTICALS (PTY) LTD (24,6%)
MENATE BAKERIES (PTY) LTD (50%)
METGROUPHOLD LTD
METRO CASH & CARRY LTD
MOUL-BIE (SA) (PTY) LTD
MULLER & PHIPPS AFRICA (PTY) LTD (50,1%)
MZIWONKE TRADING (PTY) LTD (49%)
NASIONALE VISSERYE (EDMS) BPK (21%)
NATAL BAKERY (PTY) LTD (22,4%)
NATIONAL FOOD DISTRIBUTORS (PTY) LTD
NORTHERN BAKERY CONSORTIUM (PTY) LTD (24%)
OMNI MEDIA (PTY) LTD (50%)
PREMIER CONTRACT CATERERS (PTY) LTD
PREMIER FOOD HOLDINGS LTD
PREMIER FOOD INDUSTRIES LTD
PREMIER INTERNATIONAL (PTY) LTD (50%)
PREMIER MILLING CO (PTY) LTD
PREMIER PHARMACEUTICAL CO LTD (48,1%)
PRETORIA WEST FLOUR MILLING CO (PTY) LTD
PRONA PHARMACEUTICALS (PTY) LTD (25,05%)
PROPAN PHARMACEUTICALS (PTY) LTD
RICHARDS BAY BAKERY (PTY) LTD (50%)
RYMCO (PTY) LTD (50%)
SCORE DISCOUNT FOOD HOLDINGS (PTY) LTD
SCORE-CLICKS HOLDINGS LTD (50,72%)
SHAPE INVESTMENTS (PTY) LTD
SOUTHERN SEA FISHING (PTY) LTD
SQUARE DEAL INVESTMENTS (PTY) LTD (48,99%)
STANOP HOLDINGS LIMITED
SUPERKOS (PTY) LTD
TANDA MILLING CO LIMITED TRANSKEI
TELTRON (PTY) LTD (50%)
THEAKROCK PHARMACEUTICALS (PTY) LTD
TWINS PHARMACEUTICAL HOLDINGS LTD
TWINS PROPAN HOLDINGS (PTY) LTD (50,1%)
USUTHU FOODS (PTY) LTD (49%)
WAVEEN INVESTMENTS (PTY) LTD (25%)
WESTERN CAPE BAKERIES (PTY) LTD (30,6%)
Y-TEX (PTY) LTD (25,5%)

INVESTMENTS

CTP HOLDINGS LTD
WALTONS CONSOLIDATED INV HOLDINGS LTD (8,38%)

PREMIER PHARMACEUTICAL CO LTD

ABBREVIATION : PREMPHARM

JSE SHORT CODE : PRP

SECTOR : Industrial-Pharmaceutical & Medical

SHAREHOLDERS

Who Owns Whom's Assessment of the Identity of the Ultimate Controlling Shareholder: PREMIER GROUP

SHAREHOLDER	PERCENTAGE 1992	1991
TWINS PROPAN HOLDINGS P/L	94.7	94.7
NEDBANK NOM LTD	2.7	2.8
TOTAL	97.4	97.5

DIRECTORS :
KROK A ,KROK M ,NEEDHAM WG (Operations Director)
NORTIER PS (Chief Executive)
SHAPIRO H (Chief Operations Officer),UTIAN GM
WRIGHTON PGA (Chairman

REGISTRATION NUMBER : 63/02331/06

REGISTERED OFFICE
Twin Towers, Cnr Purlin Str & Isando Rd
Isando
1600
TEL: 011-921 1511
FAX: 011-921 1567

TRANSFER SECRETARY
Consolidated Share Registrars Ltd
P O Box 61051, Marshalltown
2107
TEL: 011-492 1620

COMPANY SECRETARY
M Tsinonis (Mrs)

NATURE OF BUSINESS
The main activities of the company are the manufacturing, marketing & distribution of pharmaceutical, animal health, visioncare and consumer products.

BANKERS :
First National Bank of SA Ltd
Standard Bank of SA Ltd, Nedbank Ltd

AUDITORS :
Arthur Andersen & Co

FAMILIAR BRAND NAMES
AESCULAP,ALAMYCIN,ALOHA,AMERICAN OPTICAL
ANIMALAX,AQUAJECT,ARTLINE,ATRIO,AUSSIE TAGS
BACTOL,BB TABLETS,BEEFEE POWDER,BETAFLEX
BETAPYN,BLACK GLYCERINE,BLUE LIQUID,BOBES
BROMOSEPT,BURDIZZO,CARTON,CAZAL,CELES
CENTUAR,CENTUAR LABORATORIES,CEPACAINE
CEPACOL,CHIEF,CLOMID,COBURN OPTICAL
COMPROPEN,CONTRA SHAMPOO,CORENZA C,CRAWFORD
DA VINCI,DAIRY DRENCH,DESIL,DIASIDIP,DIETENE
DILINCT,DIPPITY DO,DITROPAN,DOCDOL
DOLLY VARDEN,DOMILENS,DOSPAN,DOXYMYCIN
DRY IDEA,DYNEXAN,ELIZABETH ANNE,EQUIGARD
ESSILOR,FINADYNE,FISHER VET,FLEEDIP N7,FLYGO
FRESHEN SALTS,GILLETTE,GLUCOPHAGE,GRASSETT
GRIPPON,HE MAN,HI-TET,HOLLYWOOD CURL
ICD GRANULES,INDO,INTERFLORA,IRIS,JADE EAST
JIFFY,LCC,LEMON LITE,LENTOGESIC,LION BRIDGE
LURSELLE,MEDI-KEEL A,MENRAD,METZLER
MICROPHYLLIN,MILBORROW,MORGAN,MOUSSON,NEITZ
NOBESE,NOVESIN,OCULOSEN,ONDERSTEPOORT RANGE
OPTIFASHION,OSTER CLIPPERS,OWP
PANDORA GOLD MEDAL,PAPERMATE,PECTROLYTE

PENSTREP,PHILLIPS DRENCHING EQUIPMENT
PILOT (PENS),PROPAIN,RIFADIN,RIFATER
RIGHT GUARD,SAFILO,SBISA,SHAMIR
SHAMPOOCH PLUS,SILKIENCE,SOLA,SONOMED
SPASMED,SPERSACET C,SPERSADEX COMP
SPERSADEXOLINE,SPERSALLERG,SPHERICAL OPTICAL
STANOP (VISION RATING)
STANWAY (OPTHALMIC CHAIR),STEREO OPTICAL
STERICLEN,SUMIPLUS,SUPAMEL,SUPER ROSE
SUPER SCOTTS,SUPONA,SUPREME SABLE,SYNDOL
SYNEMED,TAKUBOMATIC,TECFEN,TENUATE,TONI
TOPCON,TREMOR-BLEN,TRILUDAN,ULTRAVAC,UNILENS
VECTOR VISION,VELCOTE,VISION EASE,VISTECH
VITADEX,VITIN-A,VITROLYTE,WEBSTER LENS
WILLIAM & BROTHERS,ZYLOWARE

CONTRIBUTION BY ACTIVITY
N/A

YEAR END : April

DIVIDEND :Ords no par value

Interim	(Ldr)17/11/89	(Pay)04/12/89	Amt(c)7
Final	(Ldr)25/05/90	(Pay)13/06/90	Amt(c)9
Interim	(Ldr)16/11/90	(Pay)03/12/90	Amt(c)7
Final	(Ldr)17/05/91	(Pay)06/06/91	Amt(c)9
Interim	(Ldr)20/12/91	(Pay)10/01/92	Amt(c)12
Final	(Ldr)19/06/92	(Pay)09/07/92	Amt(c)15

NUMBER OF EMPLOYEES : 1840

CAPITAL STRUCTURE

	AUTHORISED	ISSUED
Ords no par value	150000000	98060857
"A" Var Rate Red Cum Prefs 1c	7000000	0
"B" Var Rate Red Cum Prefs 1c	8000000	0
"C" Var Rate Red Cum Prefs 1c	36999990	0

FINANCIAL STATISTICS (AT FINANCIAL YEAR END)

(Amts in R'000)	1992 Apr	1991 Mar	1990 Mar	1989 Mar	1988 Mar
Ord S/H Int	254119	215574	199062	153195	149262
Long Trm Loans	40979	95799	120562	95773	52000
Iss Ord Share	98061	98061	91000	91000	91000
Total Liab	139468	158031	206022	206700	130483
Current Liab	98489	62232	85460	110927	78483
Total Assets	285372	265390	301025	265929	279745
Intang Assets	108215	108215	104059	93966	*
Current Assets	208127	185206	208679	200876	85324
Debtors	96854	95501	102778	96661	43033
Inventory	76920	86155	102759	100169	39881
Turnover	476874	493399	491818	426099	134457
Oper Profit	115179	81700	82958	75638	29976
Interest Paid	5246	15888	17901	13417	4212
Tax Paid	46956	27160	24675	20373	6636
Prf af Int&Tax	62977	38652	40382	41848	19128
Prf att Ord Sh	62977	38408	37625	32861	18610
Btm Line Earn	59137	32201	37625	32861	18610
Dividend Paid	20592	15689	13650	12740	-
Mkt Prce(c) YE	625	220	200	230	290
Depreciation	6408	4993	3485	3076	899

PER SHARE STATISTICS (CENTS)

Net Asst Val	148.79	109.48	104.40	65.09	164.02
Net Earnings	64.20	39.20	41.30	36.10	30.70
Dividends	27.00	16.00	16.00	14.00	12.00
Cash Flow	66.26	49.00	54.97	43.82	28.55

RATIOS AND OTHER INFORMATION

Mrk Cap(R000)	612881	215734	182000	209300	263900
Current Ratio	2.11	2.98	2.44	1.81	1.09
Quik/Acid Tst	1.33	1.59	1.24	0.91	0.58
A/C Rec T/ovr	4.54	5.17	4.79	4.41	4.69
Tot Ass T/ovr	1.54	1.86	1.63	1.60	0.72
Debt/Ass Rat	0.41	0.51	0.60	0.48	0.28
L T L Tot Ass	0.06	0.28	0.32	0.07	-
Debt to Eqity	0.46	0.63	0.91	0.84	0.53
Interest Cover	21.96	5.14	4.63	5.64	7.12
Oper Prof Mrg	24.15	16.56	16.87	17.75	22.29
Net Prof Marg%	13.21	7.78	7.65	7.71	13.84
Ret on Assets	37.26	30.78	27.56	28.44	17.25
Ret on Equity%	22.88	17.82	18.90	21.45	18.70
Price/Earnings	9.74	5.61	4.84	6.37	9.45
Divid Cover	2.38	2.45	2.58	2.58	2.56
Divid Yield	4.32	7.27	8.00	6.09	4.14
Earning Yield%	10.27	17.82	20.65	15.70	10.59
NAV % Mrk Pr	23.81	49.76	52.20	28.30	56.56
Effec Tax Rate	42.03	35.34	24.23	4.63	7.14
Def Interval	0.23	1.53	2.04	3.11	7.56
Sus Grth Rate	16.68	10.54	12.04	13.13	12.47

SUBSIDIARY & ASSOCIATED COMPANIES

BARTISS LABORATORIES (PTY) LTD
BIBI SALONS (PTY) LTD
INTERNATIONAL COSMETICS (PTY) LTD
MAX FRANK (PTY) LTD
MER-NATIONAL (PTY) LTD
MULLER & PHIPPS (MFG) (PTY) LTD
PANDORA PRODUCTS (PTY) LTD
RESTAN LABORATORIES (PTY) LTD
SALTERS-FISHER MEDICAL HOLDINGS LTD
STANDARD-VISTA-WISEMAN (PTY) LTD
TWIN TOWERS (PTY) LTD

INVESTMENTS

None

PRESIDENT MEDICAL INVESTMENTS LTD

ABBREVIATION : PRESMED

JSE SHORT CODE : PSM

SECTOR : Industrial-Pharmaceutical & Medical

SHAREHOLDERS

Who Owns Whom's Assessment of the Identity of the Ultimate Controlling Shareholder: DIRECTORS

SHAREHOLDER	PERCENTAGE 1992	1991
PRESMED HOLDINGS P/L	62.5	62.5
NEDBANK NOM LTD	8.1	8.0
VERSPREIDE INV P/L	2.1	2.1
BREMER P H N	1.8	1.8
JAFFE FAMILY TRUST	1.7	---
LAVANREN NOM P/L	1.5	1.7
JOHANNESBURG MUNICIPAL PENS FUND	1.2	---

JAFFE P J	---	2.1
TOTAL	78.8	78.1

DIRECTORS :
BREMER PHN (Chairman),CHAPMAN DE
GREYVENSTEYN C
GRILLENBERGER CA (Managing Director),JAFFE PJ
JOSEPH TW ,KENYON B ,LABUSCHAGNE I DR,WAGENHEIM R

REGISTRATION NUMBER : 85/01313/06

REGISTERED OFFICE
301 Leopont Building, 451 Church Str East
Pretoria
0002
TEL: 011-643 8011
FAX: 011-484 3289

TRANSFER SECRETARY
Mercantile Registrars Ltd
P O Box 1053, Johannesburg
2000
TEL: 011-333 8181

COMPANY SECRETARY
T W Joseph

NATURE OF BUSINESS
The group owns five private hospitals and eight day clinics which are located in the Transvaal, Cape and OFS provinces.

BANKERS :
Nedperm Bank Ltd

AUDITORS :
Coopers Theron Du Toit

FAMILIAR BRAND NAMES
BEDFORD GARDENS CLINIC
BRACKENFELL DAY CLINIC,COSMOS HOSPITAL
HEILET CLINIC,JAN S MARAIS CLINIC
MEDGATE CLINIC,MEDICYN FORUM CASUALTY
MEDOVS THEATRES,PEGLERAE DAY CLINIC
PRETORIA N DAY CLINIC,ROSEPARK HOSPITAL
ZANDFONTEIN CLINIC

CONTRIBUTION BY ACTIVITY
N/A

YEAR END : February

DIVIDEND : Ords 25c

Final	(Ldr)26/05/89	(Pay)23/06/89	Amt(c)2.7
Final	(Ldr)18/05/90	(Pay)22/06/90	Amt(c)4
Final	(Ldr)22/02/91	(Pay)01/06/91	Amt(c)5
Final	(Ldr)22/05/92	(Pay)19/06/92	Amt(c)6.7

NUMBER OF EMPLOYEES : 600

CAPITAL STRUCTURE

	AUTHORISED	ISSUED
12,5% Unsec Comp Conv Sub Debs 80	3480000	3480000
12% Unsec Comp Conv Sub Debs 250c	3000000	3000000
Ords 15,625c	40000000	18432000

FINANCIAL STATISTICS (AT FINANCIAL YEAR END)

(Amts in R'000)	1992 Feb	1991 Feb	1990 Feb	1989 Feb	1988 Feb
Ord S/H Int	11138	8535	6584	5951	3165
Long Trm Loans	15294	7177	6867	7198	1975
Iss Ord Share	11520	11520	8700	8700	8700
Total Liab	31473	17462	16401	13616	3542
Current Liab	16179	10285	9534	6418	1567
Total Assets	37214	22069	18975	15046	4441
Intang Assets	5397	3928	4010	4521	2266
Current Assets	27214	13626	11352	7990	1786
Debtors	13151	9296	8769	5960	1506
Inventory	2369	1598	1444	1166	271
Turnover	74277	51313	38786	22102	5387
Oper Profit	10662	7387	5711	2401	1250
Interest Paid	1254	1334	1266	914	117
Tax Paid	5461	3442	2288	747	562
Prf af Int&Tax	4880	3221	2317	740	571
Prf att Ord Sh	3563	2570	1339	708	533
Btm Line Earn	3563	2527	981	677	533
Dividend Paid	772	576	348	235	183
Mkt Prce(c) YE	250	120	65	40	55
Depreciation	1395	1464	1358	615	138

PER SHARE STATISTICS (CENTS)

Net Asst Val	49.84	39.99	29.59	16.44	10.33
Net Earnings	30.90	22.30	15.40	8.10	6.10
Dividends	6.70	5.00	4.00	2.70	2.10
Cash Flow	43.09	35.29	33.72	17.30	9.94

RATIOS AND OTHER INFORMATION

Mrk Cap(R000)	28800	13824	5655	3480	4785
Current Ratio	1.68	1.32	1.19	1.24	1.14
Quik/Acid Tst	1.54	1.17	1.04	1.06	0.97
A/C Rec T/ovr	5.65	5.52	4.42	3.71	3.58
Tot Ass T/ovr	2.00	2.33	2.04	1.47	1.21
Debt/Ass Rat	0.80	0.75	0.85	0.87	0.74
L T L Tot Ass	0.36	0.29	0.35	0.44	0.39
Debt to Eqity	2.66	1.95	2.45	2.20	1.04
Interest Cover	8.50	5.54	4.51	2.63	10.68
Oper Prof Mrg	14.35	14.40	14.72	10.86	23.20
Net Prof Marg%	4.80	5.01	3.45	3.20	9.89
Ret on Assets	31.16	36.24	30.94	15.96	28.15
Ret on Equity%	31.99	30.11	20.34	11.90	16.84
Price/Earnings	8.09	5.38	4.22	4.94	9.02
Divid Cover	4.61	4.46	3.85	3.00	2.90
Divid Yield	2.68	4.17	6.15	6.75	3.82
Earning Yield%	12.36	18.58	23.69	20.25	11.09
NAV % Mrk Pr	19.93	33.33	45.52	41.09	18.79
Effec Tax Rate	52.75	51.19	57.57	38.00	32.48
Def Interval	0.75	0.89	1.54	3.28	2.23
Sus Grth Rate	25.06	23.36	15.05	7.95	11.06

SUBSIDIARY & ASSOCIATED COMPANIES

BEDFORD GARDENS PRIVATE HOSPITAL (PTY) L
CLINICAL DISTRIBUTORS (PTY) LTD
COSMOS HOSPITAL (PTY) LTD
HOSPITAL PROJECTS LTD (BRITISH VIRGIN IS
JAN S MARAIS CLINIC (PTY) LTD
MEDICYN FORUM CASUALTY SERVICES (PTY) LT
PRESMED SURGICENTRE (PTY) LTD
PRETORIA NOORD DAGKLINIEK (EDMS) BPK
ROSEPARK HOSPITAL (PTY) LTD
ZANDFONTEIN CLINIC (PTY) LTD

INVESTMENTS

DAY CLINIC SUPPLIES (TVL) (PTY) LTD (PRE (4 SH)

PRESTO TRANSPORT HOLDINGS LTD

ABBREVIATION : PRESTO

JSE SHORT CODE : PRT

SECTOR : Industrial-Transportation

SHAREHOLDERS

Who Owns Whom's Assessment of the Identity of the Ultimate Controlling Shareholder:
STRAUSS FAMILY

SHAREHOLDER	PERCENTAGE 1992	1991
STRAUSS FAMILY TRUST	48.5	---
STRAUSS J C	46.6	---
SMBL NOM P/L	---	97.1
TOTAL	95.1	97.1

DIRECTORS :
LOURENS MJ ,SCHOEMAN JH ,STRAUSS JC (Chairman)
VENTER E MR

REGISTRATION NUMBER : 78/02618/06

REGISTERED OFFICE
Cnr Jones & Webb Streets, Jet Park
Boksburg
1459
TEL: 011-397 2150
FAX: 011-397 1923

TRANSFER SECRETARY
Central Registrars Ltd
P O Box 4844, Johannesburg
2000
TEL: 011-331 0051

COMPANY SECRETARY
J C Strauss

NATURE OF BUSINESS
The activity of the company and its subsidiaries is that of inter-city container and freight transportation and distribution.

BANKERS :
Standard Bank of SA Ltd

AUDITORS :
Herbert & Trakman

FAMILIAR BRAND NAMES
N/A

CONTRIBUTION BY ACTIVITY
N/A

YEAR END : July

DIVIDEND : Ords 1c
Final (Ldr)25/11/88 (Pay)09/12/88 Amt(c)5.25

NUMBER OF EMPLOYEES : 300

CAPITAL STRUCTURE

	AUTHORISED	ISSUED
Ords 1c	15000000	15000000
"A" Var Rate Red Cum Prefs 0,001c	10000000	10000000
"B" Var Rate Red Cum Prefs 0,001c	90000000	

FINANCIAL STATISTICS (AT FINANCIAL YEAR END)

(Amts in R'000)	1991 Jul	1990 Jul	1989 Jul	1988 Jul	1987 Jul
Ord S/H Int	2921	-18583	8954	8133	3783
Long Trm Loans	3160	1001	5145	2639	936
Iss Ord Share	15000	15000	15000	15000	10125
Total Liab	8473	36850	17389	10840	9471
Current Liab	5313	35849	12244	8201	8535
Total Assets	11394	18267	26343	18973	13254
Current Assets	3654	8593	11825	8401	5820
Debtors	3611	7232	7634	6199	5260
Inventory	40	151	1498	558	401
Turnover	23225	46327	51552	37756	31097
Oper Profit	-1859	-26338	5091	3183	2970
Interest Paid	908	2498	790	319	1512
Tax Paid	-68	-1881	1845	1293	624
Prf af Int&Tax	-2699	-26955	2456	1571	834
Prf att Ord Sh	-2699	-26955	2456	1571	834
Btm Line Earn	-2898	-27537	2456	1571	834
Dividend Paid	-	-	1635	787	-
Mkt Prce(c) YE	50	50	80	105	-
Depreciation	795	2395	947	542	1017

PER SHARE STATISTICS (CENTS)

Net Asst Val	19.47	-123.89	59.69	54.22	37.36
Net Earnings	-17.90	-179.70	16.40	10.50	5.60
Dividends	-	-	-	5.25	-
Cash Flow	-13.15	-178.07	28.55	18.95	21.32

RATIOS AND OTHER INFORMATION

Mrk Cap(R000)	7500	7500	12000	15750	-
Current Ratio	0.69	0.24	0.97	1.02	0.68
Quik/Acid Tst	0.68	0.24	0.84	0.96	0.63
A/C Rec T/ovr	6.43	6.41	6.75	6.09	5.91
Tot Ass T/ovr	2.04	2.54	1.96	1.99	2.35
Debt/Ass Rat	0.74	2.01	0.57	0.50	0.67
L T L Tot Ass	0.28	0.05	0.11	0.07	0.02
Debt to Eqity	2.89	-1.98	1.69	1.17	2.34
Interest Cover	-2.05	-10.54	6.44	9.98	1.96
Oper Prof Mrg	-8.00	-56.85	9.88	8.43	9.55
Net Prof Marg%	-11.62	-58.18	4.76	4.16	2.68
Ret on Assets	-16.32	-144.18	19.33	16.78	22.41
Ret on Equity%	-92.40	145.05	27.43	19.32	22.05
Price/Earnings	-2.79	-0.28	4.88	10.00	-
Divid Cover	-	-	-	2.00	-
Divid Yield	-	-	-	5.00	-
Earning Yield%	-35.80	-359.40	20.50	10.00	-
NAV % Mrk Pr	38.95	-247.77	74.62	51.64	-
Effec Tax Rate	-	-	-0.81	21.33	21.67
Def Interval	-3.06	-0.57	1.07	0.69	1.39
Sus Grth Rate	-92.40	145.05	9.17	9.64	22.05

SUBSIDIARY & ASSOCIATED COMPANIES

FANCON (PTY) LTD
LANGHOFF MOTORS (PTY) LTD
PRESTO AIR NATAL (PTY) LTD
PRESTO PANELBEATERS (PTY) LTD
PRESTO PARCEL SERVICES CAPE (PTY) LTD
SOUTH NORTH HAULAGE (PTY) LTD

INVESTMENTS

None

PRETORIA PORTLAND CEMENT CO LTD

ABBREVIATION : PPC

JSE SHORT CODE : PPC

SECTOR : Industrial-Building & Construction

SHAREHOLDERS

Who Owns Whom's Assessment of the Identity of the Ultimate Controlling Shareholder: SA MUTUAL VIA BARLOWS

SHAREHOLDER	PERCENTAGE 1992	1991
BARLOWS CEMENT INV LTD	60.0	---
STD BANK NOM TVL P/L	7.9	6.8
LIBERTY LIFE ASSOC OF AFRICA LTD	3.4	3.9
SA MUTUAL	3.1	3.2
CMB NOM P/L	2.6	---
ESCOM PENS & PROV FUND	2.0	2.1
SIXTY SIX MARSHALL STREET NOM P/L	1.9	1.9
SOUTHERN LIFE ASSOC LTD	1.8	2.0
FIRST NAT NOM P/L	1.6	1.6
GEMEENSKAPLIKE MUNISIPALE TVL PENS FUND	1.3	---
ENGINEERING INDUSTRIES PENS FUND	1.1	1.1
METAL IND GROUP PENS FUND	1.0	---
SANLAM	---	2.6
BARLOW FINANCIAL INV LTD	---	60.2
TOTAL	87.7	85.4

DIRECTORS :
BORNMAN LJ ,BULTERMAN GH ,CLEWLOW WAM
DUNNINGHAM GW ,GOMERSALL JE (Managing Director)
HALL JC (Chairman),HODGKISS JE ,HOLLMANN CN
LUYT GR ,SCHOLTZ SR ,SCOTT DS ,SENEKAL JC
SHEPHARD JH ,THEODOSSIOU D ,WATERSON CH
WROGEMANN CJ

REGISTRATION NUMBER : 01/00667/06

REGISTERED OFFICE
11 Sherborne Road, Parktown
Johannesburg
2193
TEL: 011-482 1300
FAX: 011-726 3537

TRANSFER SECRETARY
Rand Registrars Ltd
P O Box 82549, Southdale
2135
TEL: 011-835 1016

COMPANY SECRETARY
R J Murray

NATURE OF BUSINESS
The group supplies the major portion of the country's cement and lime needs. The company has investments in the ready mixed concrete industry and in other companies connected with the supply of cementitious products. Group companies manufacture and distribute cement, lime and limestone products, paper sacks and other containers. They also mine and sell gypsum.

BANKERS :
First National Bank of SA Ltd
French Bank of SA Ltd

AUDITORS :
KPMG Aiken & Peat

FAMILIAR BRAND NAMES
PPC

CONTRIBUTION BY ACTIVITY
Cement (% of turnover) (59.0%)
Lime (19.0%)
Packaging (10.0%)
Investment and other (12.0%)

YEAR END : September

DIVIDEND : Ords R1

Interim No 165	(Ldr)08/06/90	(Pay)02/07/90	Amt(c)42
Final No 166	(Ldr)23/11/90	(Pay)04/01/91	Amt(c)108
Special No 167	(Ldr)23/11/90	(Pay)04/01/91	Amt(c)80
Interim No 168	(Ldr)07/06/91	(Pay)01/07/91	Amt(c)45
Final No 169	(Ldr)22/11/91	(Pay)03/01/92	Amt(c)127
Interim No 170	(Ldr)29/05/92	(Pay)01/07/92	Amt(c)50
Final No 171	(Ldr)20/11/92	(Pay)04/01/93	Amt(c)145

NUMBER OF EMPLOYEES : 3924

CAPITAL STRUCTURE

	AUTHORISED	ISSUED
Ords R1	60000000	40377380

FINANCIAL STATISTICS (AT FINANCIAL YEAR END)

(Amts in R'000)	1991 Sep	1990 Sep	1989 Sep	1988 Sep	1987 Sep
Ord S/H Int	560775	513072	494880	435418	395786
Long Trm Loans	214429	215938	188429	206975	226212
Iss Ord Share	40377	40128	39990	38959	38951
Total Liab	364597	372775	331677	334569	316978
Current Liab	150168	156837	143248	127594	90766
Total Assets	925372	885847	826557	769987	712764
Current Assets	231440	242093	245980	203451	139162
Debtors	138785	127089	111409	99638	71824
Inventory	76356	72982	59665	46244	46544
Turnover	818560	739961	689187	588848	470916
Oper Profit	184967	172552	165530	157730	111356
Interest Paid	8509	5290	4491	6286	8933
Tax Paid	78406	83100	85111	71162	48239
Prf af Int&Tax	118188	109128	102422	80282	54184
Prf att Ord Sh	114839	106731	100384	78674	52850
Btm Line Earn	110428	107282	101370	78529	53458
Dividend Paid	69762	92346	52032	38959	23370
Mkt Prce(c) YE	3900	1900	2250	1470	1800
Depreciation	38441	32619	29074	27401	24736

PER SHARE STATISTICS (CENTS)

Net Asst Val	1388.85	1278.59	1237.51	1117.63	1016.11
Net Earnings	284.80	266.20	252.60	202.00	130.50
Dividends	172.00	230.00	130.00	100.00	60.00
Cash Flow	372.67	344.95	317.19	253.15	208.06

RATIOS AND OTHER INFORMATION

Mrk Cap(R000)	1574703	762432	899775	572697	701118
Current Ratio	1.54	1.54	1.72	1.59	1.53
Quik/Acid Tst	1.03	1.08	1.30	1.23	1.02
A/C Rec T/ovr	5.90	5.82	6.19	5.91	6.56
Tot Ass T/ovr	0.88	0.84	0.83	0.76	0.66
Debt/Ass Rat	0.20	0.21	0.18	0.19	0.17
L T L Tot Ass	0.04	0.03	0.00	0.02	0.04
Debt to Eqity	0.33	0.36	0.29	0.33	0.30
Interest Cover	22.93	34.06	39.90	25.09	12.47
Oper Prof Mrg	22.60	23.32	24.02	26.79	23.65
Net Prof Marg%	14.03	14.42	14.57	13.36	11.22
Ret on Assets	22.16	22.30	23.23	20.48	15.62
Ret on Equity%	20.48	20.80	20.28	18.07	13.35
Price/Earnings	13.69	7.14	8.91	7.28	13.79
Divid Cover	1.66	1.16	1.94	2.02	2.18
Divid Yield	4.41	12.11	5.78	6.80	3.33
Earning Yield%	7.30	14.01	11.23	13.74	7.25
NAV % Mrk Pr	35.61	67.29	55.00	76.03	56.45
Effec Tax Rate	42.51	45.54	50.23	50.68	45.13
Def Interval	0.25	0.24	0.08	0.25	0.51
Sus Grth Rate	8.04	2.80	9.77	9.12	7.45

SUBSIDIARY & ASSOCIATED COMPANIES

ASH RESOURCES (PTY) LTD (25%)
BETRAM (PTY) LTD (49%)
CAPE PORTLAND CEMENT CO. LTD
CEMENT DISTRIBUTORS (S.A.) (PTY) LTD (33%)
COOPER & COOPER HOLDINGS (PTY) LTD
COOPER & DE BEER (PTY) LTD
EASTERN PROVINCE CEMENT CO LTD
GANSVLEY PROPERTIES LTD
KOHLER SACKS LTD
NAMIBIA PORTLAND CEMENT LTD (50%)
NATAL PORTLAND CEMENT CO. (PTY) LTD (33,3%)
PAREM ENTERPRISES (PTY) LTD (50%)
PPC CEMENT SALES (PTY) LTD
PPC LIME LTD
PREPORT MINING (PTY) LTD
PRESTRESSED PRECAST BETON (SA) (PTY) LTD (50%)
SLAGMENT (PTY) LTD (33,3%)
SOUTH WESTERN MINERALS (PTY) LTD
VARSRIVIER MARMER (EDMS) BPK
ZEPHCON (PTY) LTD

INVESTMENTS

CIMENTS DE BOURBON S.A. (REUNION) (7%)

PRIMA PROPERTY TRUST

ABBREVIATION : PRIMA

JSE SHORT CODE : PRM

SECTOR : Financial-Property Trust

SHAREHOLDERS

Who Owns Whom's Assessment of the Identity of the Ultimate Controlling Shareholder:
SA MUTUAL / INSTITUTIONS

SHAREHOLDER	PERCENTAGE 1992	1991
PARKDEV PROPERTY P/L	17.1	---
FIRST NAT NOM P/L	16.5	2.5
ENGINEERING INDUSTRIES PENS FUND	6.7	3.9
STD BANK NOM TVL P/L	6.3	3.2
EIGHTY ONE MAIN STREET NOM LTD	5.7	8.3
CMB NOM P/L	5.2	---
PRIMA BANK LTD	2.9	---
NEDBANK NOM LTD	2.8	4.3
METAL IND GROUP PENS FUND	2.6	---
SA MUTUAL	2.3	22.0
MINES 1970 PENS FUND	1.3	1.9
PRIMA PROPERTY TRUST MANAGERS LTD	1.3	1.9
SA SPECIAL RISKS INSURANCE ASSOC LTD	1.1	1.6
YSKOR PENS FUND	---	2.3
EPF OLD MUTUAL NOM P/L	---	2.2
SHARESTOCK NOM P/L	---	1.1
BOARD OF EXECUTORS NOM P/L	---	1.6
SANLAM	---	7.4
TOTAL	71.9	64.2

DIRECTORS :
FERREIRA C ,HAASBROEK NFJ (Managing Director)
MOUTON WL PROF,THERON LAG ,TIMM RD

REGISTERED OFFICE
21 Girton Road, Parktown
2193
TEL: 011-484 4225
FAX: 011-643 5213

TRANSFER SECRETARY
Fraser Street Registrars (Pty) Ltd
P O Box 61178, Marshalltown
2107
TEL: 011-491 0911

COMPANY SECRETARY
R C van Zweel

NATURE OF BUSINESS
A unit property trust.

BANKERS :
Volkskas Ltd

AUDITORS :
KPMG Aiken & Peat

FAMILIAR BRAND NAMES
N/A

CONTRIBUTION BY ACTIVITY
Retail (% by gross rental income) (53.0%)
Commercial (45.8%)
Residential (1.2%)

YEAR END : June

DIVIDEND : Units

Interim 43	(Ldr)19/10/90	(Pay)31/10/90	Amt(c)4.67
Final No 44	(Ldr)12/07/91	(Pay)31/07/91	Amt(c)7.04
Interim No 45	(Ldr)24/01/92	(Pay)14/02/92	Amt(c)5.25
Final No 46	(Ldr)29/05/92	(Pay)14/08/92	Amt(c)5

NUMBER OF EMPLOYEES : 4

PRIMROSE GOLD MINES LTD

ABBREVIATION : PRIM-G-M

JSE SHORT CODE : PRG

SECTOR : Gold-Rand & others

SHAREHOLDERS

Who Owns Whom's Assessment of the Identity of the Ultimate Controlling Shareholder:
INVESTEC MERCHANT BANK

SHAREHOLDER	PERCENTAGE 1992	1991
METOREX P/L	31.4	30.5
INVESTEC SHARE NOM P/L	18.1	18.1
COMMON FUND INV SOC LTD	15.0	15.0
HUMPHREYS & LITTLE FALLS INV LTD	7.0	7.0
HUMPHREYS INV LTD	3.4	3.4
INVESTEC NOM P/L	2.3	2.2
CHAPLIN J B	1.9	1.9
TAYLOR D	1.8	1.8
TOTAL	80.8	79.9

DIRECTORS :
KING JC (Managing Director)
MALONE AS (Chairman),PARKER RDM ,TROLLIP AEG
VAN RENSBURG PWJ

REGISTRATION NUMBER : 05/05891/06

REGISTERED OFFICE
11th Floor, Cape Towers, Maclaren Street
Marshalltown
2001
TEL: 011-482 1724
FAX: 011-726 7517

TRANSFER SECRETARY
Mercantile Registrars Ltd
P O Box 1053, Johannesburg
2000
TEL: 011-333 8181

COMPANY SECRETARY
Meyer Wilson and Marsh

NATURE OF BUSINESS
The business of the company is the mining for gold on a reclamation basis by means of re-establishing abandoned mining areas and extracting and treating gold-bearing ore. Group activities are confined to the near East Rand/Germiston areas.

BANKERS :
Volkskas Ltd

AUDITORS :
Deloitte Pim Goldby

FAMILIAR BRAND NAMES
N/A

CONTRIBUTION BY ACTIVITY
N/A

YEAR END : June

CAPITAL STRUCTURE

	AUTHORISED	ISSUED
Units	133110000	133110000

FINANCIAL STATISTICS (AT FINANCIAL YEAR END)

(Amts in R'000)	1992 Jun	1991 Jun	1990 Mar	1989 Mar	1988 Mar
Ord S/H Int	61985	60548	60553	62630	47182
Long Trm Loans	-	-	-	282	282
Iss Ord Share	88740	88740	88740	88740	61200
Total Liab	5399	7368	5287	6245	6193
Current Liab	5399	7368	5287	5963	5911
Total Assets	67384	67916	65840	119084	53375
Current Assets	10347	16475	9673	18666	16151
Debtors	742	70	45	34	216
Oper Profit	-289	-391	-327	6472	5416
Prf af Int&Tax	12674	10391	8297	6472	5416
Prf att Ord Sh	12674	10391	8297	7748	6664
Btm Line Earn	13326	10387	5937	7748	6664
Dividend Paid	9096	10391	8297	6472	5416
Mkt Prce(c) YE	63	70	75	59	78

PER SHARE STATISTICS (CENTS)

Net Asst Val	69.85	68.23	68.24	70.58	77.09
Net Earnings	10.25	11.71	9.35	8.50	8.85
Dividends	10.25	11.71	9.35	8.50	8.85
Cash Flow	14.28	9.37	9.35	7.29	8.85

RATIOS AND OTHER INFORMATION

Mrk Cap(R000)	55906	62118	66555	52357	47736
Current Ratio	1.92	2.24	1.83	3.13	2.73
Quik/Acid Tst	1.92	2.24	1.83	3.13	2.73
Debt/Ass Rat	0.08	0.11	0.08	0.05	0.11
Debt to Eqity	0.09	0.12	0.09	0.10	0.13
Ret on Assets	18.81	12.24	12.60	5.43	10.15
Ret on Equity%	20.45	13.73	13.70	12.37	14.12
Price/Earnings	6.15	5.98	8.02	6.94	8.81
Divid Cover	1.00	1.00	1.00	1.00	1.00
Divid Yield	16.27	16.73	12.47	14.41	11.35
Earning Yield%	16.27	16.73	12.47	14.41	11.35
NAV % Mrk Pr	110.87	97.47	90.98	119.62	98.84
Def Interval	-	-	-	-	0.54
Sus Grth Rate	5.77	0.00	0.00	2.04	2.65

SUBSIDIARY & ASSOCIATED COMPANIES

101 MARKET ST (PTY) LTD
18E GOLDMAN STREET (PTY) LTD
AMPINE CONSTRUCTION (PTY) LTD
BESTERBROWN (PTY) LTD
BURKEA (PTY) LTD
FARE INVESTMENTS (PTY) LTD
FORTY FOUR RICHARD ST (PTY) LTD
INTERTHIRD PROPERTIES (PTY) LTD
MEDICAL DEVELOPMENT CORP. (PTY) LTD
NEW SHOPPING CENTRE PROPERTIES (PTY) LTD
SAMMY INVESTMENTS (PTY) LTD
SOUNDPROPS 1011 INVESTMENTS (PTY) LTD

INVESTMENTS

None

DIVIDEND : (Ldr)22/09/89 (Pay)16/10/89

NUMBER OF EMPLOYEES : 1848

CAPITAL STRUCTURE

	AUTHORISED	ISSUED
Ords 2,5c	16600000	12004423
Var Rate Opt Conv Red Cum Prefs 2	10000000	5401990

FINANCIAL STATISTICS (AT FINANCIAL YEAR END)

(Amts in R'000)	1992 Jun	1991 Jun	1990 Jun	1989 Jun	1988 Jun
Ord S/H Int	20208	15848	17603	16905	14952
Long Trm Loans	2069	3408	3356	314	-
Iss Ord Share	12004	12004	12004	11621	11616
Total Liab	7072	11452	9321	3040	1546
Current Liab	5003	8044	5965	2726	1546
Total Assets	27280	27300	26924	19945	16498
Current Assets	2653	2788	2250	2083	2139
Debtors	1958	1505	1718	1433	1143
Inventory	440	472	511	487	417
Turnover	29418	23049	16240	15590	11971
Oper Profit	3724	-134	285	2583	1608
Interest Paid	1185	1633	471	-	-
Tax Paid	-27	10	-56	-10	103
Prf af Int&Tax	2682	-1756	-112	2543	1505
Prf att Ord Sh	2496	-1756	-112	2543	1505
Btm Line Earn	2496	-1756	664	2543	2409
Dividend Paid	-	-	-48	595	1045
Mkt Prce(c) YE	55	50	105	130	120

PER SHARE STATISTICS (CENTS)

Net Asst Val	168 34	132 02	146 64	145 47	128 72
Net Earnings	20 80	-14 60	-	21 80	20 70
Dividends	-	-	-	8 00	9 00
Cash Flow	20 79	-14 67	-0 93	21 88	12 96

RATIOS AND OTHER INFORMATION

Mrk Cap(R000)	6602	6002	12604	15107	13939
Current Ratio	0 53	0 35	0 38	0 76	1 38
Quik/Acid Tst	0 44	0 29	0 29	0 59	1 11
A/C Rec T/ovr	15 02	15 31	9 45	10 88	10 47
Tot Ass T/ovr	1 08	0 84	0 60	0 78	0 73
Debt/Ass Rat	0 25	0 42	0 35	0 15	0 09
L T L Tot Ass	0 07	0 12	0 12	0 02	-
Debt to Eqity	0 34	0 72	0 53	0 18	0 10
Interest Cover	3 14	-0 08	0 61	-	-
Oper Prof Mrg	12 66	-0 58	1 75	16 57	13 43
Net Prof Marg%	8 48	-7 62	-0 69	16 31	12 57
Ret on Assets	14 08	-0 41	1 13	12 95	9 75
Ret on Equity%	12 35	-11 08	-0 64	15 04	10 07
Price/Earnings	2 64	-3 42	-	5 96	5 80
Divid Cover	-	-	-	2 73	2 30
Divid Yield	-	-	-	6 15	7 50
Earning Yield%	37 82	-29 20	-	16 77	17 25
NAV % Mrk Pr	306 08	264 05	139 66	111 90	107 27
Effec Tax Rate	-	-0 86	-4 76	1 55	5 29
Def Interval	1 85	-4 85	-62 63	0 44	0 06
Sus Grth Rate	12 35	11 08	-0 36	11 52	3 08

SUBSIDIARY & ASSOCIATED COMPANIES

BALMORAL GOLD MINING CO LTD
GLENCAIRN GOLD MINE (PTY) LTD
STANHOPE GOLD MINING CO LTD
VILLA VALONIA (PTY) LTD

INVESTMENTS

None

PROGRESS INDUSTRIES LTD

ABBREVIATION : PROGRESS

JSE SHORT CODE : PGR

SECTOR : Industrial-Clothing, Footwear & Textiles

SHAREHOLDERS

Who Owns Whom's Assessment of the Identity of the Ultimate Controlling Shareholder: DIRECTORS

SHAREHOLDER	PERCENTAGE 1992	1991
VIZOMA P/L	24 7	24 7
ARONOVSKY DAVID & VIVIENNE TRUST	19 2	---
SCOTT W J D	9 1	---
STD BANK NOM TVL P/L	7 7	8 9
ARONOVSKY M	4 0	4 0
HARDING D C	2 9	2 8
JACOBSON Z	2 6	2 6
NUSSBAUM R A W	1 8	1 0
KALMEK M	1 7	1 7
JACOBSON P D	1 6	1 6
ZIEGELSTEIN B	1 3	---
LOISEL NOM P/L	1 2	1 2
GOLDBERG D	1 1	1 1
DARONOV INV P/L	---	19 2
GROUP FIVE MULTI BENEFIT RETIREMENT FUND	---	7 3
TOTAL	78 7	76 0

DIRECTORS :
ARONOVSKY D (Chairman),AROVONSKY M
EPSTEIN LM (Financial Director)
JACOBSON PD (Chief Executive)
KALMEK M (Technical Director

REGISTRATION NUMBER : 05/18923/06

REGISTERED OFFICE
1st Floor, Industries House, 1 Victoria Embankment
Durban
4001
TEL 031-32 9722
FAX 031-37 1875

TRANSFER SECRETARY
Mercantile Registrars Ltd
P O Box 1053, Johannesburg
2000
TEL 011-333 8181

COMPANY SECRETARY
B J Esterhuizen

NATURE OF BUSINESS
An investment holding company with subsidiaries engaged in the manufacture of knitwear, clothing & knitted fabric Certain subsidiaries own fixed property

BANKERS :
Nedperm Bank Ltd

AUDITORS :
Kessel Feinstein

FAMILIAR BRAND NAMES
BLANC BLEU,ESSEX,P.K.M.,ST GERAIN,STALLION
STREET TALK,ZIPPITY

CONTRIBUTION BY ACTIVITY
N/A

YEAR END : December

DIVIDEND : Ords 50c

Interim No 50	(Ldr)23/11/90	(Pay)31/12/90	Amt(c)18
Final No 51	(Ldr)07/06/91	(Pay)28/06/91	Amt(c)16

NUMBER OF EMPLOYEES : 1800

CAPITAL STRUCTURE

	AUTHORISED	ISSUED
Ords 50c	3700000	2804450
6% Cum Prefs R2	100000	80000

FINANCIAL STATISTICS (AT FINANCIAL YEAR END)

(Amts in R'000)	1991 Dec	1990 Dec	1989 Dec	1988 Dec	1987 Dec
Ord S/H Int	25377	26569	21719	17688	14434
Long Trm Loans	12574	14149	11364	13185	8542
Iss Ord Share	2804	2804	2804	2804	2804
Total Liab	27670	27952	26373	24009	15514
Current Liab	15096	13803	15009	10824	6972
Total Assets	53047	54521	48092	41697	29948
Current Assets	26096	27277	25873	21736	15265
Debtors	13660	14494	14734	11743	9262
Inventory	12430	12767	11135	9902	6001
Turnover	65105	61660	65274	50831	42467
Oper Profit	3162	6418	10853	8153	6476
Interest Paid	3523	3314	2617	1479	474
Tax Paid	594	368	2861	2239	2997
Prf af Int&Tax	-933	2766	5387	4442	3005
Prf att Ord Sh	-884	2869	5377	4442	3005
Btm Line Earn	-884	2869	5377	4442	3005
Dividend Paid	308	953	1346	1188	1020
Mkt Prce(c) YE	160	310	325	460	365
Depreciation	1341	1240	994	807	642

PER SHARE STATISTICS (CENTS)

Net Asst Val	905.03	947.54	774.57	630.81	514.76
Net Earnings	-31.50	102.30	191.70	158.00	106.80
Dividends	11.00	34.00	48.00	42.00	36.00
Cash Flow	14.19	142.51	227.21	187.20	156.24

RATIOS AND OTHER INFORMATION

Mrk Cap(R000)	4486	8692	9113	12898	10235
Current Ratio	1.73	1.98	1.72	2.01	2.19
Quik/Acid Tst	0.91	1.05	0.98	1.09	1.33
A/C Rec T/ovr	4.77	4.25	4.43	4.33	4.59
Tot Ass T/ovr	1.23	1.13	1.36	1.22	1.42
Debt/Ass Rat	0.46	0.45	0.48	0.50	0.41
L T L Tot Ass	0.17	0.20	0.17	0.24	0.18
Debt to Eqity	0.96	0.93	1.06	1.17	0.85
Interest Cover	0.90	1.94	4.15	5.51	13.66
Oper Prof Mrg	4.86	10.41	16.63	16.04	15.25
Net Prof Marg%	-1.36	4.65	8.24	8.74	7.08
Ret on Assets	6.11	12.03	22.59	19.57	21.62
Ret on Equity%	-3.48	10.80	24.76	25.11	20.82
Price/Earnings	-5.08	3.03	1.70	2.91	3.42
Divid Cover	-2.86	3.01	3.99	3.76	2.97
Divid Yield	6.88	10.97	14.77	9.13	9.86
Earning Yield%	-19.69	33.00	58.98	34.35	29.26
NAV % Mrk Pr	565.64	305.66	238.33	137.13	141.03
Effec Tax Rate	-	11.52	34.75	26.40	37.70
Def Interval	33.20	3.35	1.37	2.03	1.28
Sus Grth Rate	-4.70	7.21	18.56	18.40	13.75

SUBSIDIARY & ASSOCIATED COMPANIES

LE TIGRE SPORTSWEAR S.A. (PTY) LTD
PROGRESS ADMINISTRATION SERVICES (PTY) L
PROGRESS KNITTING & TEXTILES LTD
SWAZI KNITS (PTY) LTD (SWAZILAND)

INVESTMENTS

None

PROPERTY CORPORATION OF SA LTD

ABBREVIATION : PROPCOR

JSE SHORT CODE : PCR

SECTOR : Financial-Property

SHAREHOLDERS

Who Owns Whom's Assessment of the Identity of the Ultimate Controlling Shareholder:
ABBEY HOLDINGS

SHAREHOLDER	PERCENTAGE 1992	1991
ABBEY (PROPCOR) HOLDINGS LTD	74.0	92.1
QUARTET INV LTD	14.6	---
GREEK R N TRUSTEES DORFMAN CHILDREN	2.6	2.6
RABMAN TRADING P/L	2.4	---
NAT BRICK HOLDINGS P/L	2.1	---
TOTAL	95.5	94.6

DIRECTORS :
CHAPMAN DE ,CONRADIE DCU DR,EDELSTEIN WH
EGLIN CW ,PENNY C (Financial Director)
RABINOWITZ BP (Chairman & Chief Exec.)
SAREMBOCK ML ,SCHAFFER JE (Executive Director)
WALTON CL

REGISTRATION NUMBER : 05/21141/06

REGISTERED OFFICE
1002 NBS Waldorf, 80 St George's Mall
Cape Town
8001
TEL: 021-22 2424
FAX: 021-22 2626

TRANSFER SECRETARY
Mercantile Registrars Ltd
P O Box 1053, Johannesburg
2000
TEL: 011-333 8181

COMPANY SECRETARY
C Penny

NATURE OF BUSINESS
The property arm of the Abbey Group, active in developing, trading in & investment in property. The company has investments in quoted Faircape Homes & Bristol Industrial Corp.

BANKERS :
First National Bank of SA Ltd, Bankorp Ltd

AUDITORS :
Coopers Theron Du Toit

FAMILIAR BRAND NAMES
N/A

CONTRIBUTION BY ACTIVITY
N/A

YEAR END : December

DIVIDEND :Ords 50c

Interim No 38	(Ldr)22/09/89	(Pay)06/10/89	Amt(c)4
Final No 39	(Ldr)14/09/90	(Pay)28/09/90	Amt(c)3

NUMBER OF EMPLOYEES : 21

CAPITAL STRUCTURE

	AUTHORISED	ISSUED
Ords 50c	50000000	24000000

FINANCIAL STATISTICS (AT FINANCIAL YEAR END)

(Amts in R'000)	1991 Dec	1990 Jun	1989 Jun	1988 Jun	1987
Ord S/H Int	17198	16631	19241	12016	13092
Long Trm Loans	15701	7	1173	767	3347
Iss Ord Share	24000	23000	22692	22692	22692
Total Liab	38245	9727	9174	6740	5008
Current Liab	22544	9720	8001	5973	1661
Total Assets	55443	26358	24711	18756	19980
Intang Assets	*	*	3704	*	*
Current Assets	36302	20189	11354	11264	3541
Debtors	4795	6285	8386	9605	-
Inventory	-	-	2477	965	3541
Turnover	-	-	22491	24318	6206
Oper Profit	935	648	3138	3262	870
Interest Paid	4975	926	83	163	192
Tax Paid	-	239	1294	991	47
Prf af Int&Tax	-1081	1213	2298	2537	631
Prf att Ord Sh	-950	1416	2771	2528	1132
Btm Line Earn	-950	-1673	2771	2528	1132
Dividend Paid	-	690	908	737	-
Mkt Prce(c) YE	40	50	50	50	-
Depreciation	-	232	216	230	-

PER SHARE STATISTICS (CENTS)

Net Asst Val	71.66	72.31	68.47	52.95	57.69
Net Earnings	-4.10	6.20	12.21	9.78	-
Dividends	-	3.00	4.00	3.25	-
Cash Flow	-2.71	6.22	10.57	7.81	2.78

RATIOS AND OTHER INFORMATION

Mrk Cap(R000)	9600	11500	11346	11346	-
Current Ratio	1.61	2.08	1.42	1.89	2.13
Quik/Acid Tst	1.61	2.08	1.11	1.72	-
A/C Rec T/ovr	-	-	2.68	1.90	-
Tot Ass T/ovr	-	-	0.91	0.97	0.31
Debt/Ass Rat	0.56	0.37	0.32	0.32	0.25
L T L Tot Ass	0.15	-	-	0.00	0.17
Debt to Eqity	1.80	0.58	0.42	0.50	0.38
Interest Cover	0.20	1.98	44.28	22.64	4.53
Oper Prof Mrg	-	-	13.95	13.41	14.02
Net Prof Marg%	-	-	12.32	10.40	18.24
Ret on Assets	4.68	9.88	18.08	16.14	4.35
Ret on Equity%	-3.68	8.51	14.40	15.78	8.65
Price/Earnings	-9.76	8.06	4.10	5.11	-
Divid Cover	-	2.07	3.05	3.01	-
Divid Yield	-	6.00	8.00	6.50	-
Earning Yield%	-10.25	12.40	24.42	19.56	-
NAV % Mrk Pr	179.15	144.62	136.94	105.91	-
Effec Tax Rate	-	89.51	30.34	-	6.93
Def Interval	-19.10	4.21	0.59	0.06	5.30
Sus Grth Rate	-5.52	4.37	9.68	14.91	8.65

SUBSIDIARY & ASSOCIATED COMPANIES

ABBEY FIXED INVESTMENTS NO 3 LTD
ABBEY FIXED INVESTMENTS NO 4 LTD
ABBEY FIXED INVESTMENTS NO 5 LTD
ABBEY FIXED INVESTMENTS NO 6 LTD
ABBEY PROPERTIES LTD
BELLCANTO (328) NOMINEES LTD
BELLCANTO (CROYDEN) NOMINEES LTD
BELLCANTO (ELOFF STR) INVESTMENTS LTD
BELLCANTO (HERPROP) SHARE BLOCK (PTY) LT
BELLCANTO (PTY) LTD
BRUMMERIA VIEW INVESTMENTS (PTY) LTD (50%)
CINNABAR PROPERTY LTD
FAIRBELL HOUT BAY NOMINEES (PTY) LTD (50%)
FAIRCAPE HOMES LTD (22,8%)
HAZRA (20) PROPERTY INVESTMENTS (PTY) LT (50%)
HERPROP (PTY) LTD
MOWBRAY PARTNERSHIP (50%)
P.I.P. (CAVENDISH) SHARE BLOCK LTD (50%)
P.I.P. (LONGWHARF) SHARE BLOCK (PTY) LTD (50%)
P.I.P. FIXED HOLDINGS LTD (50%)
P.I.P. HOLDINGS LTD
P.I.P. INVESTMENTS HOLDINGS LTD (50%)
P.I.P. INVESTMENTS NO 2 LTD (50%)
P.I.P. MANAGEMENT SERVICES LTD (50%)
P.I.P. NOMINEES LTD (50%)
P.I.P. NOMINEES NO 3 LTD (50%)
P.I.P. NOMINEES NO 4 LTD (50%)
P.I.P. NOMINEES NO 5 LTD (50%)
PARTNERS IN PROPERTY LTD
PREMCON (PRESMED) HOLDINGS LTD
PROPCOR (BELLCANTO) HOLDINGS LTD
PROPCOR (BRISTOL) HOLDINGS LTD
PROPCOR (FAIRCAPE) HOLDINGS LTD
PROPCOR (MOWBRAY) HOLDINGS LTD
PROPCOR FIXED HOLDINGS LTD
PROPCOR MANAGEMENT SERVICES LTD
PROPCOR NOMINEES LTD
RETCO (MYBURGH) LTD (50%)
RIVTEX (PTY) LTD
RS HOLDINGS (PTY) LTD
SAMPROP CONSTRUCTION (PTY) LTD (50%)

INVESTMENTS

BRISTOL INDUSTRIAL CORPORATION LTD (19,27%)
FENIX INDUSTRIES LTD (327200 SH)
FINANCE WEEK HOLDINGS LTD (1500 SH)
PCSA HOLDINGS (PTY) LTD (12% PREFS) (2250000 SH)

PROTEA ASSURANCE CO LTD

ABBREVIATION : PROSURE

JSE SHORT CODE : PAS

SECTOR : Financial-Insurance

SHAREHOLDERS

Who Owns Whom's Assessment of the Identity of the Ultimate Controlling Shareholder:
SUN ALLIANCE GROUP PLC

SHAREHOLDER	PERCENTAGE 1992	1991
LONDON ASSURE	79.8	79.7
EIGHTY ONE MAIN STREET NOM LTD	5.1	---
UAL NOM P/L	5.0	5.0
PROTEA ASSURE CO PENS FUND	1.6	1.6
STD BANK NOM TVL P/L	---	4.2
MURRAY & ROBERTS STAFF PENS FUND	---	1.7
TOTAL	91.4	92.2

DIRECTORS :
BARRON AJ ,BRAYSON JW (Operations Director)
CRANK AR ,FLETCHER DT (Chairman),GARLICK J
HYATT AM ,MAYHEW P ,NEVILLE RAG ,PETTY R
TAINTON AL (Managing Director

REGISTRATION NUMBER : 64/04622/06

REGISTERED OFFICE
Protea Assurance Building, Greenmarket Square
Cape Town
8001
TEL: 021-488 7922
FAX: 021-488 7322

TRANSFER SECRETARY
Fraser Street Registrars (Pty) Ltd
P O Box 61178, Marshalltown
2107
TEL: 011-491 0911

COMPANY SECRETARY
R D Fuller

NATURE OF BUSINESS
The company transacts both short & long-term insurance business in SA & neighbouring states.

BANKERS :
N/A

AUDITORS :
Ernst & Young

FAMILIAR BRAND NAMES
N/A

CONTRIBUTION BY ACTIVITY
N/A

YEAR END : December

DIVIDEND : Ords 25c

Interim No 45	(Ldr)01/09/89	(Pay)22/09/89	Amt(c)20
Final No 46	(Ldr)23/03/90	(Pay)30/04/90	Amt(c)33
Interim No 47	(Ldr)31/08/90	(Pay)21/09/90	Amt(c)20
Final No 48	(Ldr)12/04/91	(Pay)02/05/91	Amt(c)33
Interim No 49	(Ldr)16/04/92	(Pay)08/05/92	Amt(c)53
Final No 50	(Ldr)04/09/92	(Pay)25/09/92	Amt(c)25

NUMBER OF EMPLOYEES : 688

CAPITAL STRUCTURE

	AUTHORISED	ISSUED
Ords 25c	10000000	7865400

FINANCIAL STATISTICS (AT FINANCIAL YEAR END)

(Amts in R'000)	1991 Dec	1990 Dec	1989 Dec	1988	1987
Ord S/H Int	259488	196022	208479	140867	110191
Long Trm Loans	197189	150951	117973	122668	105158
Iss Ord Share	7865	7865	7865	7865	7865
Total Liab	238402	188587	145727	122668	105158
Current Liab	41213	37636	27754	-	-
Total Assets	497890	384609	354206	263535	213266
Current Assets	1497[illegible]3	115355	42088	-	-
Debtors	74844	52516	-	-	-
Oper Profit	-5342	-17797	18347	17227	15943
Tax Paid	-4	-4653	4295	5172	581
Prf af Int&Tax	-5338	-13144	14052	12141	11181
Prf att Ord Sh	-5995	-13661	13563	11744	11002
Btm Line Earn	-5995	-13661	13563	11744	11002
Dividend Paid	4169	4169	4169	3618	2831
Mkt Prce(c) YE	1300	1100	1350	800	680

PER SHARE STATISTICS (CENTS)

Net Asst Val	3299.28	2492.33	2650.72	1791.06	1401.03
Net Earnings	-76.20	-174.00	172.00	-	-
Dividends	53.00	53.00	53.00	-	-
Cash Flow	-76.29	-233.81	170.87	154.37	142.16

RATIOS AND OTHER INFORMATION

Mrk Cap(R000)	102245	86515	106178	62920	53482
Current Ratio	3.63	3.07	1.52	-	-
Quik/Acid Tst	3.63	3.07	1.52	-	-
Debt/Ass Rat	0.08	0.10	0.08	0.47	0.49
L T L Tot Ass	-	-	-	0.47	0.49
Debt to Eqity	0.16	0.19	0.13	0.87	0.95
Ret on Assets	-1.07	-4.63	5.18	6.57	5.52
Ret on Equity%	-2.31	-6.97	6.51	8.34	9.98
Price/Earnings	-17.06	-6.32	7.85	-	-
Divid Cover	-1.44	-3.28	3.25	-	-
Divid Yield	4.08	4.82	3.93	-	-
Earning Yield%	-5.86	-15.82	12.74	-	-
NAV % Mrk Pr	253.79	226.58	196.35	223.88	206.03
Effec Tax Rate	-0.02	-0.39	24.09	30.02	3.64
Def Interval	-3.51	-0.99	2.07	10.10	9.41
Sus Grth Rate	-3.92	-9.10	4.51	5.77	7.42

SUBSIDIARY & ASSOCIATED COMPANIES

PHOENIX ASSURANCE OF SOUTH AFRICA LTD
PLAYFORD INVESTMENTS (PTY) LTD
PORTION 1 STAND 210 ROSEBANK (PTY) LTD
PROTEA ASSURANCE PROPERTIES (PTY) LTD
PROTEA GMS (PTY) LTD

INVESTMENTS

None

PROTEA FURNISHERS LTD

ABBREVIATION : PROFURN

JSE SHORT CODE : PON

SECTOR : Industrial-Furniture & Household

SHAREHOLDERS

Who Owns Whom's Assessment of the Identity of the Ultimate Controlling Shareholder: EA RONBECK VIA SUPREME INDUSTRIAL

SHAREHOLDER	PERCENTAGE 1992	1991
SCHAFFER J E	80.1	52.5
ENFML NOM P/L	6.6	8.9
TRANSIT SECURITIES INC	3.2	4.3
PROFURN SHARE INC SCHEME TRUST	1.9	1.1
CHALKTON NOM CO P/L	---	1.1
STD BANK NOM TVL P/L	---	20.7
TOTAL	91.8	88.5

DIRECTORS :
HAFNER RA MR,HARE HA ,KAPLAN J MR,MARANEY A RONBECK EA (Chairman),ROSENBERG BH

REGISTRATION NUMBER : 68/15363/06

REGISTERED OFFICE
26th Floor, Kine Centre, 141 Commissioner Street
Johannesburg
2001
TEL: 011-403 4092
FAX: 011-339 2536

TRANSFER SECRETARY
Mercantile Registrars Ltd
P O Box 1053, Johannesburg
2000
TEL: 011-333 8181

COMPANY SECRETARY
B H Rosenberg

NATURE OF BUSINESS
A holding company, with subsidiaries engaged in the retail distribution of home furniture and appliances throughout South Africa,Botswana, Lesotho,Bophuthatswana,Venda & Ciskei. The group operates through 76 retail outlets.

BANKERS :
First National Bank of SA Ltd
Standard Bank of SA Ltd

AUDITORS :
Kessel Feinstein

FAMILIAR BRAND NAMES
N/A

CONTRIBUTION BY ACTIVITY
N/A

YEAR END : December

DIVIDEND : Ords no par value
Dividend No 35 (Ldr)28/03/91 (Pay)30/05/91 Amt(c)4
Dividend No 36 (Ldr)15/05/92 (Pay)29/05/92 Amt(c)4

NUMBER OF EMPLOYEES : 1913

CAPITAL STRUCTURE

	AUTHORISED	ISSUED
Ords no par value	100000000	103240366

FINANCIAL STATISTICS (AT FINANCIAL YEAR END)

(Amts in R'000)	1991 Dec	1990 Dec	1989 Aug	1988 Aug	1987 Aug
Ord S/H Int	51340	31872	14957	39502	37062
Long Trm Loans	49577	71237	33789	24437	37406
Iss Ord Share	95540	70250	65750	15000	15000
Total Liab	82081	122974	60609	60123	78634
Current Liab	32504	51737	26820	35686	41228
Total Assets	133421	154846	75566	99625	115696
Current Assets	129888	147972	63231	85708	88755
Debtors	114082	122335	54452	75535	76224
Inventory	11824	24759	7595	9943	12469
Turnover	131610	193046	70942	100088	66959
Oper Profit	26671	31688	-20872	7966	5215
Interest Paid	12801	12475	6691	5636	3774
Tax Paid	41	80	-201	7	70
Prf af Int&Tax	13829	19133	-27362	2323	1371
Prf att Ord Sh	13565	18825	-27375	2310	1358
Btm Line Earn	13565	18825	-34455	1645	1358
Dividend Paid	3822	2810	-	300	562
Mkt Prce(c) YE	30	40	22	45	117
Depreciation	321	481	354	783	473

PER SHARE STATISTICS (CENTS)

	1991	1990	1989	1988	1987
Net Asst Val	53.74	45.37	22.75	263.35	247.08
Net Earnings	18.90	27.30	-129.60	15.40	10.30
Dividends	4.00	4.00	-	2.00	4.00
Cash Flow	19.38	20.69	-128.97	20.15	13.81

RATIOS AND OTHER INFORMATION

	1991	1990	1989	1988	1987
Mrk Cap(R000)	28662	28100	14465	6750	17550
Current Ratio	4.00	2.86	2.36	2.40	2.15
Quik/Acid Tst	3.63	2.38	2.07	2.12	1.85
A/C Rec T/ovr	1.15	1.18	1.30	1.33	0.88
Tot Ass T/ovr	0.99	0.94	0.94	1.00	0.58
Debt/Ass Rat	0.61	0.79	0.80	0.60	0.66
L T L Tot Ass	0.37	0.46	0.44	0.24	0.30
Debt to Eqity	1.59	3.84	4.04	1.51	2.06
Interest Cover	2.08	2.54	-3.12	1.41	1.38
Oper Prof Mrg	20.27	16.41	-29.42	7.96	7.79
Net Prof Marg%	10.31	9.75	-38.59	2.31	2.03
Ret on Assets	19.99	15.35	-27.62	8.00	4.51
Ret on Equity%	26.42	44.30	-183.02	5.85	3.66
Price/Earnings	1.59	1.47	-0.17	2.92	11.36
Divid Cover	4.73	6.83	-	7.70	2.58
Divid Yield	13.33	10.00	-	4.44	3.42
Earning Yield%	63.00	68.25	-589.09	34.22	8.80
NAV % Mrk Pr	179.12	113.42	103.40	585.21	211.18
Effec Tax Rate	0.30	0.42	-0.02	3.91	5.00
Def Interval	3.55	2.75	-1.26	12.62	24.25
Sus Grth Rate	18.98	50.25	-183.02	5.09	2.15

SUBSIDIARY & ASSOCIATED COMPANIES

PROTEA FURNISHERS (BOTSWANA) (PTY) LTD
PROTEA FURNISHERS (WEST) (PTY) LTD
PROTEA FURNISHERS BOPHUTHATSWANA (PTY) L
PROTEA FURNISHERS SA (PTY) LTD
STEBARN ELECTRICAL APPLIANCE CORP. (PTY)
SUPREME FURNISHERS (BOTSWANA) (PTY) LTD
SUPREME FURNISHERS (LESOTHO) (PTY) LTD
SUPREME FURNISHERS (PTY) LTD

SUPREME FURNISHERS (SWAZILAND) (PTY) LTD
SUPREME FURNISHERS (TRANSKEI) (PTY) LTD
TRANSVAAL PLATINUM CONSORTIUM (PTY) LTD

INVESTMENTS

BARNETTS GROUP LTD (5500 SH)

PUBLICO HOLDINGS LTD

ABBREVIATION : PUBHOLD

JSE SHORT CODE : PBH

SECTOR : Industrial-Printing & Publishing

SHAREHOLDERS

Who Owns Whom's Assessment of the Identity of the Ultimate Controlling Shareholder:
DIRECTORS

SHAREHOLDER	PERCENTAGE 1992	1991
SHAPIRO J	17.7	17.8
SHAPIRO R S	17.7	17.8
CMB NOM P/L	12.6	---
BERTHEIM NOM CC	7.8	6.6
SA MUTUAL	6.8	6.9
HARVEST SECURITIES LTD	6.5	6.3
SEFOR L	4.0	2.7
ELLERINE BROS P/L	2.4	2.4
FIRST NAT NOM P/L	2.3	---
MURPHY T	2.0	2.0
MURPHY F T J	2.0	---
EVANCAR SA P/L	1.8	1.4
FINKELSTEIN J A	1.5	1.5
SFSS NOM P/L	---	1.2
SANLAM	---	12.7
SEMUR INV P/L	---	4.1
STD BANK NOM TVL P/L	---	1.0
TOTAL	85.0	84.4

DIRECTORS :
LUBNER B DR,RABINOWITZ J ,SHAPIRO J DR (Chairman)
SHAPIRO RS (Managing Director)

REGISTRATION NUMBER : 86/00785/06

REGISTERED OFFICE
Publico House, 30 Andries Street
Wynberg, Sandton
2090
TEL: 011-887 6500
FAX: 011-887 6551

TRANSFER SECRETARY
Central Registrars Ltd
P O Box 4844, Johannesburg
2000
TEL: 011-331 0051

COMPANY SECRETARY
A Fehler

NATURE OF BUSINESS
An investment holding company with a controlling interest in quoted Publico Ltd.

BANKERS :
N/A

AUDITORS :
Goldberg Jaffe Joselowsky & Partners

FAMILIAR BRAND NAMES
SEE PUBLICO LTD.

CONTRIBUTION BY ACTIVITY
N/A

YEAR END : February

DIVIDEND : Ords 5c

Final	(Ldr)22/06/90	(Pay)20/07/90	Amt(c)5.6
Final	(Ldr)21/06/91	(Pay)02/08/91	Amt(c)5.6
Final	(Ldr)05/06/92	(Pay)17/07/92	Amt(c)6.15

CAPITAL STRUCTURE

	AUTHORISED	ISSUED
Ords 5c	10000000	7897644

FINANCIAL STATISTICS (AT FINANCIAL YEAR END)

(Amts in R'000)	1992 Feb	1991 Feb	1990 Feb	1989 Feb	1988
Ord S/H Int	5335	4498	3896	4402	3236
Long Trm Loans	3227	3972	4221	1897	1861
Iss Ord Share	7898	7898	7738	7667	7065
Total Liab	9187	8797	9140	4615	4420
Current Liab	5960	4825	4919	2718	2559
Total Assets	14522	13295	13036	9017	7656
Current Assets	8973	7421	6971	4582	3431
Debtors	5809	6429	5920	3330	2171
Inventory	134	274	374	168	55
Oper Profit	3611	2217	2127	2128	1774
Interest Paid	600	429	345	266	11
Tax Paid	1282	403	485	637	881
Prf af Int&Tax	1729	1512	1420	1225	882
Prf att Ord Sh	1429	1198	1287	1315	962
Btm Line Earn	1492	1174	388	1315	962
Dividend Paid	486	444	516	158	377
Mkt Prce(c) YE	130	40	95	90	100
Depreciation	342	377	283	189	25

PER SHARE STATISTICS (CENTS)

Net Asst Val	67.55	56.95	50.35	57.41	45.80
Net Earnings	18.10	15.30	16.80	18.30	14.00
Dividends	6.15	5.63	5.63	7.20	5.20
Cash Flow	20.71	17.80	17.34	20.07	16.63

RATIOS AND OTHER INFORMATION

Mrk Cap(R000)	10267	3159	7351	6900	7065
Current Ratio	1.51	1.54	1.42	1.69	1.34
Quik/Acid Tst	1.48	1.48	1.34	1.62	1.32
Debt/Ass Rat	0.46	0.46	0.51	0.48	0.54
L T L Tot Ass	0.05	0.10	0.14	0.18	0.21
Debt to Eqity	1.26	1.37	1.72	0.98	1.29
Interest Cover	6.02	5.17	6.17	8.00	161.27
Ret on Assets	26.22	18.56	19.78	24.69	24.32
Ret on Equity%	26.79	26.63	33.03	29.87	29.73
Price/Earnings	7.18	2.61	5.65	4.92	7.14
Divid Cover	2.94	2.72	2.98	2.54	2.69
Divid Yield	4.73	14.08	5.93	8.00	5.20
Earning Yield%	13.92	38.25	17.68	20.33	14.00
NAV % Mrk Pr	51.96	142.38	53.00	63.79	45.80

Effec Tax Rate	40.52	24.02	20.84	32.49	36.07
Def Interval	0.48	0.96	1.34	1.12	1.41
Sus Grth Rate	17.68	16.76	19.79	26.28	18.08

SUBSIDIARY & ASSOCIATED COMPANIES

PUBLICO LTD

INVESTMENTS

None

PUBLICO LTD

ABBREVIATION : PUBLICO

JSE SHORT CODE : PBC

SECTOR : Industrial-Printing & Publishing

SHAREHOLDERS

Who Owns Whom's Assessment of the Identity of the Ultimate Controlling Shareholder: PUBLICO HOLDINGS

SHAREHOLDER	PERCENTAGE 1992	1991
PUBLICO HOLDINGS LTD	73.3	---
SMBL NOM P/L	10.8	---
CMB NOM P/L	3.2	---
EVANCAR SA P/L	2.1	7.3
PUBHOLD LTD	1.5	5.7
SFSS NOM P/L	1.3	2.8
SEFOR L	1.0	---
NEDBANK NOM LTD	---	2.8
BERTHEIM NOM CC	---	4.5
BROWN N R O	---	2.4
ELLERINE BROS P/L	---	2.3
SANLAM	---	11.9
SEMUR INV P/L	---	3.8
SHAPIRO J	---	16.8
SHAPIRO R S	---	16.8
TOTAL	93.2	77.3

DIRECTORS :
LUBNER B DR,RABINOWITZ J ,SHAPIRO J DR (Chairman)
SHAPIRO RS (Managing Director

REGISTRATION NUMBER : 57/00036/06

REGISTERED OFFICE
30 Andries Street, Wynberg
Sandton
2090
TEL: 011-887 6500
FAX: 011-887 6551

TRANSFER SECRETARY
Central Registrars Ltd
P O Box 4844, Johannesburg
2000
TEL: 011-331 0051

COMPANY SECRETARY
A Fehler

NATURE OF BUSINESS
A holding company. Subsidiaries carry on the business of publishers, printers & distributors of national, local, & specialist newspapers, magazines & diaries.

BANKERS :
First National Bank of SA Ltd
Standard Bank of SA Ltd, Nedcor Bank Ltd

AUDITORS :
Goldberg Jaffe Joselowsky & Partners

FAMILIAR BRAND NAMES
ALLIED/TSPORT BOOK OF SA SPORT,BRIDGE
COMPUTER WEEK,COMRADES MARATHON UPDATE
CRICKET NEWS,DRIVE,ELECTRONIC NEWS
ENGINEERING WEEK,FINE CARS,FLYING SPRINGBOK
HERALD TIMES,JHB JEWISH VOICE,JIVE
MARKETING MIX,MEDICINE TODAY
NEDBANK SHOPS & SHOPPING,NSL NEWS
OPERATION HUNGER NEWS,PRIMETIME
PUNCH LINE PERSPECTIVE,SA BOWLING NEWS
SA RUNNER,SAA AIR PARTNER
SOFTWARE USERS HANDBOOK,THE FIRST DECADE
THE MOTORIST/DIE MOTORIS,TOP 40,TRI-CYCLING

CONTRIBUTION BY ACTIVITY
N/A

YEAR END : February

DIVIDEND : Ords 1c

Final	(Ldr)22/06/90	(Pay)20/07/90	Amt(c)7.5
Final	(Ldr)21/06/91	(Pay)02/08/91	Amt(c)7.5
Final	(Ldr)05/06/92	(Pay)17/07/92	Amt(c)8.2

CAPITAL STRUCTURE

	AUTHORISED	ISSUED
Ords 1c	10000000	7897644

FINANCIAL STATISTICS (AT FINANCIAL YEAR END)

(Amts in R'000)	1992 Feb	1991 Feb	1990 Feb
Ord S/H Int	7425	6253	5452
Long Trm Loans	1455	2507	2967
Iss Ord Share	7898	7898	7738
Total Liab	7091	7036	7578
Current Liab	5636	4529	4611
Total Assets	14516	13289	13030
Current Assets	8973	7421	6971
Debtors	5809	6429	5920
Inventory	134	274	374
Oper Profit	3611	2217	2128
Interest Paid	600	429	345
Tax Paid	1282	403	485
Prf af Int&Tax	1729	1512	1420
Prf att Ord Sh	1925	1589	1715
Btm Line Earn	1988	1565	1715
Dividend Paid	648	592	580
Mkt Prce(c) YE	120	45	95
Depreciation	342	377	283

PER SHARE STATISTICS (CENTS)

Net Asst Val	94.01	79.17	70.46
Net Earnings	24.30	20.30	22.40
Dividends	8.20	7.50	7.50
Cash Flow	26.99	22.79	22.92

RATIOS AND OTHER INFORMATION

Mrk Cap(R000)	9478	3554	7351
Current Ratio	1.59	1.64	1.51
Quik/Acid Tst	1.57	1.58	1.43
Debt/Ass Rat	0.46	0.46	0.51
L T L Tot Ass	0.08	0.12	0.16
Debt to Eqity	0.91	0.98	1.22
Interest Cover	6.02	5.17	6.17
Ret on Assets	26.23	18.57	19.79
Ret on Equity%	25.93	25.41	31.46
Price/Earnings	4.94	2.22	4.24
Divid Cover	2.96	2.71	2.99
Divid Yield	6.83	16.67	7.89
Earning Yield%	20.25	45.11	23.58
NAV % Mrk Pr	78.34	175.94	74.17
Effec Tax Rate	40.52	24.02	20.84
Def Interval	0.37	0.75	1.01
Sus Grth Rate	17.20	15.94	20.82

SUBSIDIARY & ASSOCIATED COMPANIES

ABBM PRINTING & PUBLISHING CO (PTY) LTD
DRIVE NEWSPAPERS (PTY) LTD
HENDLERS PRINTERS (PTY) LTD
MEDICAL TELEVISION NETWORK (PTY) LTD
PUBLISHING CONCEPTS (PTY) LTD
R AND J PUBLICATIONS (PTY) LTD
SA JEWISH TIMES (PTY) LTD
SPORTSCO PUBLISHING (PTY) LTD
WORLDCOR GROUP (PTY) LTD

INVESTMENTS

None

PUTCO LTD

ABBREVIATION : PUTCO

JSE SHORT CODE : PTC

SECTOR : Industrial-Transportation

SHAREHOLDERS

Who Owns Whom's Assessment of the Identity of the Ultimate Controlling Shareholder: CARLEO FAMILY

SHAREHOLDER	PERCENTAGE 1992	1991
CARLEO ENTERPRISES P/L	52.5	52.5
STD BANK NOM TVL P/L	11.5	12.0
EIGHTY ONE MAIN STREET NOM LTD	8.4	8.4
LEWTOP P/L	3.7	3.2
FIRST NAT NOM P/L	2.8	2.2
ABSA NOM P/L	1.4	---
SHARESTOCK NOM P/L	1.2	---
DU-PISANI L A	1.1	1.1
R-V INV NOM CC	1.1	1.1
VOLKSKAS NOM P/L	---	1.4
TOTAL	83.8	82.0

DIRECTORS :
BORZONI F DR,CARLEO A (Chairman & Chief Exec.)
CARLEO L ,COETZEE JL ,LAWRIE AH ,MAPONYA MN MRS
VISSER JA DR (Managing Director

REGISTRATION NUMBER : 05/18672/06

REGISTERED OFFICE
Mimosa Park, Stand 793, Mimosa Way
Gallo Manor, Sandton
2144
TEL: 011-802 4300
FAX: 011-804 3837

TRANSFER SECRETARY
Central Registrars Ltd
P O Box 4844, Johannesburg
2000
TEL: 011-331 0051

COMPANY SECRETARY
B T J Hovelmeier

NATURE OF BUSINESS
The company operates a bus passenger transport service in the Wiwatersrand, Pretoria & Durban areas. Weekend services between urban & rural areas, & contract & special hire services are also provided.

BANKERS :
Nedperm Bank Ltd, Trust Bank of Africa Ltd
Volkskas Ltd

AUDITORS :
Ernst & Young

FAMILIAR BRAND NAMES
N/A

CONTRIBUTION BY ACTIVITY
N/A

YEAR END : June

DIVIDEND : Ords 40c

Special	(Ldr)25/05/90	(Pay)08/06/90	Amt(c)310
Dividend No 51	(Ldr)09/11/90	(Pay)23/11/90	Amt(c)6
Dividend No 52	(Ldr)08/11/91	(Pay)22/11/91	Amt(c)30
Dividend No 53	(Ldr)16/04/92	(Pay)30/04/92	Amt(c)12
Dividend No 54	(Ldr)02/10/92	(Pay)16/10/92	Amt(c)18

NUMBER OF EMPLOYEES : 5592

CAPITAL STRUCTURE

	AUTHORISED	ISSUED
Ords 40c	53550000	26425000

FINANCIAL STATISTICS (AT FINANCIAL YEAR END)

(Amts in R'000)	1992 Jun	1991 Jun	1990 Jun	1989 Jun	1988 Jun
Ord S/H Int	125724	116440	134130	190323	171190
Long Trm Loans	20211	16835	20173	24367	35148
Iss Ord Share	26425	26425	26425	26425	26425
Total Liab	99296	81690	79537	96711	78470
Current Liab	79085	64855	59364	72344	43322
Total Assets	225018	195610	211146	283867	246496
Intang Assets	2	2520	2521	3167	3164
Current Assets	85791	72300	61645	101182	113072
Debtors	38927	30092	19052	31223	57953
Inventory	23505	26691	41014	35407	29750
Turnover	397934	359677	364738	346040	302316

Oper Profit	23224	-7598	-8543	-861	19159
Interest Paid	6	1267	23	146	13
Tax Paid	14952	-2332	2094	9534	16775
Prf af Int&Tax	14055	-3465	4725	930	2371
Prf att Ord Sh	14062	-3631	4774	917	2409
Btm Line Earn	11544	4374	3911	917	1024
Dividend Paid	7928	7928	84560	2114	6477
Mkt Prce(c) YE	250	270	85	120	270
Depreciation	3472	3963	4223	16533	28281

PER SHARE STATISTICS (CENTS)

Net Asst Val	475.77	431.11	498.05	708.25	635.86
Net Earnings	53.20	-13.70	18.10	3.50	32.50
Dividends	30.00	30.00	320.00	8.00	24.50
Cash Flow	79.10	-10.75	17.99	25.29	179.48

RATIOS AND OTHER INFORMATION

Mrk Cap(R000)	66063	71348	22461	31710	71348
Current Ratio	1.08	1.11	1.04	1.40	2.61
Quik/Acid Tst	0.79	0.70	0.35	0.91	1.92
A/C Rec T/ovr	10.22	11.95	19.14	11.08	5.22
Tot Ass T/ovr	1.77	1.84	1.73	1.22	1.23
Debt/Ass Rat	0.35	0.33	0.28	0.25	0.18
Debt to Eqity	0.63	0.56	0.44	0.38	0.25
Interest Cover	3876.67	-5.82	-368.61	-5.45	1473.77
Oper Prof Mrg	5.84	-2.11	-2.34	-0.25	6.34
Net Prof Marg%	3.53	-1.01	1.31	0.26	0.80
Ret on Assets	12.90	-2.40	3.26	3.73	7.79
Ret on Equity%	11.18	-3.12	3.56	0.48	1.41
Price/Earnings	4.70	-19.71	4.70	34.29	8.31
Divid Cover	1.77	-0.46	0.06	0.44	1.33
Divid Yield	12.00	11.11	376.47	6.67	9.07
Earning Yield%	21.28	-5.07	21.29	2.92	12.04
NAV % Mrk Pr	190.31	159.67	585.94	590.21	235.50
Effec Tax Rate	38.85	-15.15	93.10	184.10	-
Def Interval	-	-1.63	1.15	0.34	0.07
Sus Grth Rate	4.88	-9.93	-59.48	-0.63	-2.38

SUBSIDIARY & ASSOCIATED COMPANIES

AAA STORAGE (PTY) LTD
AFRICAN BUS SERVICE (PRETORIA) (PTY) LTD
CARLEO, HEAD & ASSOCIATES (PTY) LTD (47,5%)
COMUTA SERVICES (PTY) LTD
ELECTRONIC COMMODITIES (PTY) LTD
FERNDALE BUS SERVICE (PTY) LTD
HANSAL PROPERTIES (PTY) LTD
VOMPARTS (PTY) LTD
VOMS (PTY) LTD

INVESTMENTS

None

PUTCO PROPERTIES LTD

ABBREVIATION : PUTPROP

JSE SHORT CODE : PPR

SECTOR : Financial-Property

SHAREHOLDERS

Who Owns Whom's Assessment of the Identity of the Ultimate Controlling Shareholder:
CARLEO FAMILY

SHAREHOLDER	PERCENTAGE 1992	1991
CARLEO ENTERPRISES P/L	52.5	52.5
EIGHTY ONE MAIN STREET NOM LTD	11.0	11.0
FIRST NAT NOM P/L	7.6	7.8
STD BANK NOM TVL P/L	4.6	5.6
NEDBANK NOM LTD	2.9	3.2
LEWTOP P/L	2.1	2.1
SHARESTOCK NOM P/L	1.3	---
DU-PISANI L A	1.1	1.1
R-V INV NOM CC	1.1	1.1
TOTAL	84.3	84.5

DIRECTORS :
CARLEO A (Chairman & Chief Exec.),CARLEO L
DE LOOR JH DR,VISSER JA DR (Managing Director

REGISTRATION NUMBER : 88/01085/06

REGISTERED OFFICE
Stand 793, Mimosa Park, Mimosa Way
Gallo Manor, Sandton
2148
TEL: 011-802 4300
FAX: 011-804 3837

TRANSFER SECRETARY
Central Registrars Ltd
P O Box 4844, Johannesburg
2000
TEL: 011-331 0051

COMPANY SECRETARY
B T J Hovelmeier

NATURE OF BUSINESS
The company has investments in commercial and industrial properties.

BANKERS :
N/A

AUDITORS :
Ernst & Young

FAMILIAR BRAND NAMES
N/A

CONTRIBUTION BY ACTIVITY
N/A

YEAR END : June

DIVIDEND :Ords no par value

Final No 4	(Ldr)09/11/90	(Pay)23/11/90	Amt(c)2
Interim No 5	(Ldr)17/05/91	(Pay)24/05/91	Amt(c)1
Final No 6	(Ldr)08/11/91	(Pay)22/11/91	Amt(c)3
Interim No 7	(Ldr)16/04/92	(Pay)30/04/92	Amt(c)1
Final No 8	(Ldr)02/10/92	(Pay)16/10/92	Amt(c)7

NUMBER OF EMPLOYEES : 8

CAPITAL STRUCTURE

	AUTHORISED	ISSUED
Ords no par value	50000000	26425000

FINANCIAL STATISTICS (AT FINANCIAL YEAR END)

(Amts in R'000)	1992 Jun	1991 Jun	1990 Jun	1989 Jun	1988 Jun

Ord S/H Int	73441	54573	54114	53628	53193
Long Trm Loans	44974	46843	50393	80702	45864
Iss Ord Share	26425	26425	26425	26425	26425
Total Liab	50036	53254	51792	82343	48953
Current Liab	5062	6411	1399	1641	3089
Total Assets	123477	107827	105906	135971	102146
Current Assets	2131	4413	3739	34203	1187
Debtors	813	918	1201	1073	1187
Oper Profit	13317	12348	11270	10656	5315
Interest Paid	9100	9949	14882	7821	2968
Tax Paid	1503	1588	1174	1554	1171
Prf af Int&Tax	3044	1214	1279	1281	1176
Prf att Ord Sh	3044	1214	1279	1281	1176
Btm Line Earn	3044	1516	1279	1281	1176
Dividend Paid	2114	1057	793	846	793
Mkt Prce(c) YE	80	110	70	55	-
Depreciation	6	6	-	-	-

PER SHARE STATISTICS (CENTS)

Net Asst Val	277.92	206.52	204.78	202.94	201.30
Net Earnings	12.00	5.00	5.00	5.00	9.00
Dividends	8.00	4.00	3.00	3.20	3.00
Cash Flow	11.34	5.53	3.97	5.93	335.46

RATIOS AND OTHER INFORMATION

Mrk Cap(R000)	21140	29068	18498	14534	-
Current Ratio	0.42	0.69	2.67	20.84	0.38
Quik/Acid Tst	0.42	0.69	2.67	20.84	0.38
Debt/Ass Rat	0.39	0.48	0.48	0.59	0.48
L T L Tot Ass	0.35	0.42	0.46	0.58	0.45
Debt to Eqity	0.66	0.95	0.93	1.51	0.92
Interest Cover	1.46	1.24	0.76	1.36	1.79
Ret on Assets	11.05	11.83	16.37	7.84	15.61
Ret on Equity%	4.14	2.22	2.36	2.39	6.63
Price/Earnings	6.67	22.00	14.00	11.00	-
Divid Cover	1.50	1.25	1.67	1.56	3.00
Divid Yield	10.00	3.64	4.29	5.82	-
Earning Yield%	15.00	4.55	7.14	9.09	-
NAV % Mrk Pr	347.40	187.75	292.55	368.99	-
Effec Tax Rate	47.39	48.11	57.24	44.76	43.97
Def Interval	14.55	31.72	46.99	50.55	104.32
Sus Grth Rate	1.27	0.29	0.90	0.81	0.72

SUBSIDIARY & ASSOCIATED COMPANIES

AFRICA BODY AND COACH (PTY) LTD
BARAVILLE (PTY) LTD
CARMANZAN (PTY) LTD
CC BUS SERVICE (PTY) LTD
CROWN BODY & COACH (PTY) LTD
DUBIGEON BODY AND COACH (PTY) LTD
EDENVALE BUS SERVICE (PTY) LTD
EVATON PASSENGER SERVICE (PTY) LTD
GLEA PROPERTY FOUR (PTY) LTD
NAMASOTA INVESTMENTS (PTY) LTD
PUTCOVILLE (PTY) LTD
PUTFIELD (PTY) LTD
PUTSEL (PTY) LTD
RAND BUS LINES (PTY) LTD
TURDRAZCON (PTY) LTD
UMBRIA (PTY) LTD
VIC EDWARDS (PTY) LTD
WEMBLEY PROPERTIES (PTY) LTD

INVESTMENTS

None

Q DATA LTD

ABBREVIATION : Q-DATA

JSE SHORT CODE : QDT

SECTOR : Industrial-Electronics, Electrical & Bat

SHAREHOLDERS

Who Owns Whom's Assessment of the Identity of the Ultimate Controlling Shareholder:
DIRECTORS / SILTEK

SHAREHOLDER	PERCENTAGE 1992	1991
SILTEK LTD	34.1	33.1
CMB NOM P/L	16.2	---
SILTEK INV P/L	9.3	---
DEN BOER P	6.1	9.2
WARREN R C	5.7	5.7
SA MUTUAL	5.7	---
GERS D C	3.5	5.2
VAN DER BIJL L	1.8	2.7
BESTER C J	1.7	2.5
Q DATA TRUST	1.6	4.4
VAN DER MERWE P F	1.5	2.3
VILJOEN N J	1.4	2.1
EPF SANLAM NOM P/L	1.2	1.2
GODSELL P J	1.2	1.9
PARRY M C	1.2	1.8
BIEBUYCK P J	---	1.8
SANLAM	---	10.5
SANTAMGROEI NOM P/L	---	1.8
STD BANK NOM TVL P/L	---	3.4
TOTAL	92.2	89.5

DIRECTORS :
DEN BOER P (Chairman & Managing Dir.)
DEN BOER PAUL ,DU TOIT JW ,FURST MR
GROBBELAAR M ,PARRY MC ,VAN DER BIJL L
VAN DER MERWE PF ,WARREN RC

REGISTRATION NUMBER : 78/02427/06

REGISTERED OFFICE
15th Road, Halfway House
1685
TEL: 011-313 5111
FAX: 011-313 5122

TRANSFER SECRETARY
Central Registrars Ltd
P O Box 4844, Johannesburg
2000
TEL: 011-331 0051

COMPANY SECRETARY
Q Data Administration (Pty) Ltd

NATURE OF BUSINESS
An investment holding company. Subsidiaries are active in the development & maintenance of computer systems, and associated activities.

BANKERS :
Volkskas Ltd

AUDITORS :
N/A

FAMILIAR BRAND NAMES
BOOLE & BABBAGE,CASE,HURQLES,MAINVIEW
MILLENIUM,PAYTECH,PAYTECH PC,Q PAC,SOFTTOOL
TETRARCH,XI-PLUS

CONTRIBUTION BY ACTIVITY
N/A

YEAR END : June

DIVIDEND :Ords 1c

Interim No 7	(Ldr)02/03/90	(Pay)09/03/90	Amt(c)4.1
Final No 8	(Ldr)05/10/90	(Pay)19/10/90	Amt(c)10.1
Interim No 9	(Ldr)22/02/91	(Pay)28/02/91	Amt(c)5
Final No 10	(Ldr)04/10/91	(Pay)18/10/91	Amt(c)12
Interim No 11	(Ldr)21/02/92	(Pay)28/02/92	Amt(c)6
Final No 12	(Ldr)09/10/92	(Pay)23/10/92	Amt(c)14.4

NUMBER OF EMPLOYEES : 850

CAPITAL STRUCTURE

	AUTHORISED	ISSUED
Ords 1c	20000000	16294793

FINANCIAL STATISTICS (AT FINANCIAL YEAR END)

(Amts In R'000)	1992 Jun	1991 Jun	1990 Jun	1989 Jun	1988 Jun
Ord S/H Int	24146	18890	14410	10450	7260
Long Trm Loans	3136	1924	2955	890	498
Iss Ord Share	16295	16295	16295	16295	12347
Total Liab	47554	29987	29146	12931	6144
Current Liab	44418	28063	26191	12041	5646
Total Assets	67565	46785	41637	21643	13117
Intang Assets	4135	2092	1919	1738	287
Current Assets	58637	36150	31368	15630	9159
Debtors	48020	32175	29618	12953	5020
Inventory	660	482	252	77	39
Turnover	148403	125357	93757	52257	23629
Oper Profit	19313	15258	12582	8926	4979
Interest Paid	357	499	375	110	31
Tax Paid	9539	7133	6266	4092	2332
Prf af Int&Tax	10513	8471	6459	4986	2616
Prf att Ord Sh	10311	8266	6311	4912	2622
Btm Line Earn	8503	7813	6274	4768	2472
Dividend Paid	3324	2770	2314	1970	1301
Mkt Prce(c) YE	380	400	150	205	140
Depreciation	2110	1975	1237	668	180

PER SHARE STATISTICS (CENTS)

Net Asst Val	122.80	103.09	76.66	53.46	56.48
Net Earnings	63.30	50.70	38.70	30.90	21.30
Dividends	20.40	17.00	14.20	12.30	10.60
Cash Flow	79.42	64.38	46.76	37.97	22.78

RATIOS AND OTHER INFORMATION

Mrk Cap(R000)	61921	65180	24443	33405	17286
Current Ratio	1.32	1.29	1.20	1.30	1.62
Quik/Acid Tst	1.31	1.27	1.19	1.29	1.62
A/C Rec T/ovr	3.09	3.90	3.17	4.03	4.71
Tot Ass T/ovr	2.20	2.68	2.25	2.41	1.80
Debt/Ass Rat	0.67	0.62	0.67	0.56	0.44
L T L Tot Ass	0.02	0.02	0.05	0.01	0.01
Debt to Eqity	1.88	1.55	1.95	1.16	0.80
Interest Cover	54.10	30.58	33.55	81.56	160.61
Oper Prof Mrg	13.01	12.17	13.42	17.08	21.07
Net Prof Marg%	6.95	6.59	6.73	9.40	11.10
Ret on Assets	30.21	34.42	31.46	42.45	37.96
Ret on Equity%	42.70	43.76	43.80	47.00	36.12
Price/Earnings	6.00	7.89	3.88	6.63	6.57
Divid Cover	3.10	2.98	2.73	2.51	2.01
Divid Yield	5.37	4.25	9.47	6.00	7.57
Earning Yield%	16.66	12.68	25.80	15.07	15.21
NAV % Mrk Pr	32.32	25.77	51.10	26.08	40.34
Effec Tax Rate	45.06	45.37	47.81	36.89	47.19
Def Interval	0.20	0.16	0.33	0.12	0.64
Sus Grth Rate	28.94	29.09	27.74	28.15	18.20

SUBSIDIARY & ASSOCIATED COMPANIES

ASAB DATA (EDMS) BPK (50%)
AUTOMATED REASONING (PTY) LTD (50%)
COMCON (PTY) LTD
COMCON-CSG PTY LTD
CSG STELSELS-KONSULTANTE (PTY) LTD
HURQLES (PTY) LTD
KNOWLEDGE SYSTEMS INTERNATIONAL (PTY) LT
MILLSOFT (PTY) LTD
MOTA DATA (PTY) LTD
PAYROLL SOFTWARE HOLDINGS (PTY) LTD
PAYTECH (PTY) LTD
PAYTECH PC (PTY) LTD
PC TRUST (PTY) LTD
PROFILE HOLDINGS (PTY) LTD (50%)
PROGRAM TRUST (PTY) LTD
Q DATA ADMINISTRATION (PTY) LTD
Q DATA BOTSWANA (PTY) LTD
Q DATA CONSULTING (PTY) LTD
Q MAGIC (PTY) LTD
Q MANAGEMENT CONTROL SYSTEMS (PTY) LTD
Q NET (PTY) LTD
Q PAC FINANCIAL SOFTWARE (PTY) LTD
Q PACKAGED PROGRAMS (PTY) LTD
Q TECHNOLOGY INTEGRATERS (PTY) LTD
SOFTWARE ENTERPRISES LTD

INVESTMENTS

None

QUAGGA HOLDINGS LTD

ABBREVIATION : QUAGGA

JSE SHORT CODE : QUA

SECTOR : Metals & Minerals-Other

SHAREHOLDERS

Who Owns Whom's Assessment of the Identity of the Ultimate Controlling Shareholder: DIRECTORS

SHAREHOLDER	PERCENTAGE 1992	1991
BERLITAS INV NO 14 P/L	47.4	52.1
TREECO NOM P/L	6.2	---
DE BRUIN L J D	4.2	5.1
QUAGGA SHARE INCENTIVE TRUST	3.1	3.1
CMB NOM P/L	2.7	---
DE BRUIN J TRUST	2.4	2.4
PETRUSSTRAAT INV P/L	2.3	3.0

ELOFF F C	2.1	1.1
STAPELBERG F P	2.0	2.0
NOMINEES ONLY P/L	1.5	---
HUMAN J H	---	1.1
HERSELMAN D	---	1.0
NEDBANK NOM LTD	---	1.1
LYELL E H	---	1.2
ALTENA MEWS P/L	---	2.7
HUTCHINSON H T P	---	1.3
TOTAL	73.8	76.9

DIRECTORS :
DE BRUIN DE WET CR (Managing Director)
MEIRING EJ ,TWIST D ,WESSELS JW

REGISTRATION NUMBER : 89/02053/06

REGISTERED OFFICE
46 Petrus Street, Waterkloof
Agricultural Holdings, Pretoria
0157
TEL: 012-345 1001
FAX: 012-345 3484

TRANSFER SECRETARY
Central Registrars Ltd
P O Box 4844, Johannesburg
2000
TEL: 011-331 0051

COMPANY SECRETARY
M L Steyn

NATURE OF BUSINESS
The business of the company is that of granite exploration, with the objective of proving viable deposits, the mining thereof and the processing of some of the granite so extracted.

BANKERS :
Standard Bank of SA Ltd

AUDITORS :
Ernst & Young

FAMILIAR BRAND NAMES
N/A

CONTRIBUTION BY ACTIVITY
N/A

YEAR END : February

DIVIDEND :15/12/91 and 15/06/91

CAPITAL STRUCTURE

	AUTHORISED	ISSUED
Ords 0.1c	60000000	51000000

FINANCIAL STATISTICS (AT FINANCIAL YEAR END)

(Amts in R'000)	1991 Feb	1990 Feb
Ord S/H Int	4431	3481
Long Trm Loans	1546	878
Iss Ord Share	51000	41053
Total Liab	3694	1279
Current Liab	2148	401
Total Assets	8125	4760
Current Assets	1537	310
Debtors	629	106
Inventory	890	202
Turnover	2035	289
Oper Profit	-2306	-879
Interest Paid	423	120
Prf af Int&Tax	-2729	-999
Prf att Ord Sh	-2729	-999
Btm Line Earn	-5615	-999
Mkt Prce(c) YE	17	-
Depreciation	676	117

PER SHARE STATISTICS (CENTS)

Net Asst Val	8.69	8.48
Net Earnings	-5.60	-2.40
Cash Flow	-4.03	-2.15

RATIOS AND OTHER INFORMATION

Mrk Cap(R000)	8670	-
Current Ratio	0.72	0.77
Quik/Acid Tst	0.30	0.27
A/C Rec T/ovr	3.24	2.73
Tot Ass T/ovr	0.25	0.06
Debt/Ass Rat	0.45	0.27
L T L Tot Ass	0.19	0.18
Debt to Eqity	0.83	0.37
Interest Cover	-5.45	-7.33
Oper Prof Mrg	-113.32	-304.15
Net Prof Marg%	-134.10	-345.67
Ret on Assets	-28.38	-18.47
Ret on Equity%	-61.59	-28.70
Price/Earnings	-3.04	-
Earning Yield%	-32.94	-
NAV % Mrk Pr	51.11	-
Def Interval	-1.60	-1.35
Sus Grth Rate	-61.59	-28.70

SUBSIDIARY & ASSOCIATED COMPANIES

EUREKA GRANITE (PTY) LTD
HUURWIL (PTY) LTD
INTERNATIONAL GRANITE (PTY) LTD
QUAGGA (BOP) (PTY) LTD
QUAGGA GRANITE (PTY) LTD

INVESTMENTS

None

QUICK HOLDINGS LTD

ABBREVIATION : QUICKCO

JSE SHORT CODE : QCK

SECTOR : Development Capital Market

SHAREHOLDERS

Who Owns Whom's Assessment of the Identity of the Ultimate Controlling Shareholder:
YIN WO CO LTD (HONG KONG)

SHAREHOLDER	PERCENTAGE 1992	1991
YIN WO CO LTD	42.5	68.9

FITTA P/L	39.7	---
OAK BRIDGE INV LTD	3.5	4.1
VASSILOPOULOS A	1.3	1.5
MAYFAIR NOM P/L	---	3.2
RIVOCOR HOLDINGS LTD	---	3.9
SHAND A B	---	2.0
TOTAL	86.8	83.6

DIRECTORS :
DALTON AKC ,EVANS DJF
HAMILTON-BARNS JM (Chairman),LUCAS GM ,WHITE SS

REGISTRATION NUMBER : 87/01103/06

REGISTERED OFFICE
Corner Skietlood & Iatel Sts, Isando Ext 3
Isando
1600
TEL: 011-462 3310
FAX: 011-462 3309

TRANSFER SECRETARY
Mercantile Registrars Ltd
P O Box 1053, Johannesburg
2000
TEL: 011-333 8181

COMPANY SECRETARY
G M Lucas

NATURE OF BUSINESS
The group is engaged in property development, coal mining, domestic & international air & sea freight

BANKERS :
First National Bank of SA Ltd

AUDITORS :
BDO Spencer Steward

FAMILIAR BRAND NAMES
N/A

CONTRIBUTION BY ACTIVITY
Freight (% Turnover) (98.1%)
Property (1.6%)
Holding Co (0.3%)

YEAR END : August

CAPITAL STRUCTURE

	AUTHORISED	ISSUED
Ords no par value	400000000	118000000
8% Red Conv Non-Cum Prefs 1c	6000000	0
6% Red Conv Non-Cum Prefs R1	40000	0

FINANCIAL STATISTICS (AT FINANCIAL YEAR END)

(Amts in R'000)	1991 Aug	1990 Aug	1989 Aug
Ord S/H Int	3560	5715	9567
Long Trm Loans	830	1746	-
Iss Ord Share	118000	100000	100000
Total Liab	8879	14498	4830
Current Liab	8049	12752	4830
Total Assets	11672	19461	13536
Intang Assets	767	752	861
Current Assets	5992	12989	10755
Debtors	5946	12559	7314
Turnover	8349	25495	5802
Oper Profit	1141	-783	1016
Interest Paid	1011	1059	633
Tax Paid	18	8	158
Prf af Int&Tax	112	-1850	225
Prf att Ord Sh	112	-1850	225
Btm Line Earn	-3235	-3852	-527
Mkt Prce(c) YE	2	4	21
Depreciation	267	503	54

PER SHARE STATISTICS (CENTS)

Net Asst Val	2.37	4.96	8.71
Net Earnings	0.11	-1.85	0.62
Cash Flow	0.32	-1.35	0.28

RATIOS AND OTHER INFORMATION

Mrk Cap(R000)	2360	4000	21000
Current Ratio	0.74	1.02	2.23
Quik/Acid Tst	0.74	1.02	2.23
A/C Rec T/ovr	1.40	2.03	0.79
Tot Ass T/ovr	0.72	1.31	0.43
Debt/Ass Rat	0.76	0.74	0.36
L T L Tot Ass	0.07	0.09	-
Debt to Eqity	2.49	2.54	0.50
Interest Cover	1.13	-0.74	1.61
Oper Prof Mrg	13.67	-3.07	17.51
Net Prof Marg%	1.34	-7.26	3.88
Ret on Assets	9.78	-4.02	7.51
Ret on Equity%	3.15	-32.37	2.35
Price/Earnings	18.18	-2.16	33.87
Earning Yield%	5.50	-46.25	2.95
NAV % Mrk Pr	118.35	124.08	41.46
Effec Tax Rate	17.69	-0.60	41.25
Def Interval	6.47	-3.93	-
Sus Grth Rate	3.15	-32.37	2.35

SUBSIDIARY & ASSOCIATED COMPANIES

BELFAST COAL HOLDINGS (PTY) LTD
GROSSO HIRE (PTY) LTD
GROSSO IMPEX (PTY) LTD
GROSSO PIPELINE (PTY) LTD
MBR CONSTRUCTION (PTY) LTD
MIMMA INVESTMENTS (PTY) LTD
MOUMERROW (PTY) LTD
MR DUFF THE CAD (PTY) LTD
NTHABANGALA GAME FARMS (PTY) LTD (31%)
QUICK & LOUW AND MOORE (NAMIBIA) (PTY) L
QUICK REALTY (PTY) LTD
QUICKAIR (PTY) LTD
QUICKFREIGHT (PTY) LTD
SEWATER (PTY) LTD
STAND 73 ANDERBOLT PROPERTIES (PTY) LTD

INVESTMENTS

None

QUORUM HOLDINGS LTD

ABBREVIATION : QUORUM

JSE SHORT CODE : QRM

SECTOR : Financial-Banks & Financial Services

SHAREHOLDERS

Who Owns Whom's Assessment of the Identity of the Ultimate Controlling Shareholder:
DIRECTORS CONTROL 80,1% (FEB 1991)

SHAREHOLDER	PERCENTAGE 1992	1991
HARALAMBOUS H	---	13.8
HARALAMBOUS M	---	2.3
MAKHLOUF I	---	11.8
MINA A A	---	1.2
ONE ZERO ONE INV HOLDINGS P/L	---	52.5
SANLAM	---	8.5
FISHER M	---	1.9
PROFSURE HOLDINGS P/L	---	2.5
TOTAL	---	94.5

DIRECTORS :
HARALAMBOUS H (Executive Chairman)
HARALAMBOUS M ,MAKHLOUF MG (Managing Director)
MATSUKIS NC (Financial Director

REGISTRATION NUMBER : 86/03434/06

REGISTERED OFFICE
3rd Floor,NTC House, 23 Wellington Rd,Parktown
Johannesburg
2001
TEL: 011-484 7300
FAX: 011-643 6037

TRANSFER SECRETARY
Mercantile Registrars Ltd
P O Box 1053, Johannesburg
2000
TEL: 011-333 8181

COMPANY SECRETARY
N C Matsukis

NATURE OF BUSINESS
An investment holding company. Subsidiaries are active in : The provision of structured financial agreements for a range of office automation products; The provision of short-term insurance facilities; The provision of trade finance facilities.

BANKERS :
Standard Bank of SA Ltd

AUDITORS :
Kessel Feinstein

FAMILIAR BRAND NAMES
N/A

CONTRIBUTION BY ACTIVITY
N/A

YEAR END : February

DIVIDEND :Ords 10c
Final No 1 (Ldr)11/05/90 (Pay)28/05/90 Amt(c)4

NUMBER OF EMPLOYEES : 100

CAPITAL STRUCTURE

	AUTHORISED	ISSUED
Ords 10c	20000000	12486118

FINANCIAL STATISTICS (AT FINANCIAL YEAR END)

(Amts in R'000)	1991 Feb	1990 Feb	1989 Feb	1988 Feb
Ord S/H Int	7081	6759	6154	8076
Long Trm Loans	1127	3218	166	89
Iss Ord Share	12386	12386	12386	10000
Total Liab	6935	5789	1373	7565
Current Liab	5808	2571	1207	7476
Total Assets	8654	7196	2175	15641
Intang Assets	5362	5352	5352	*
Current Assets	7645	3952	1659	10738
Debtors	1882	259	429	4570
Inventory	-	-	-	5961
Oper Profit	770	966	1020	1121
Interest Paid	278	65	19	270
Tax Paid	529	650	489	415
Prf af Int&Tax	495	1094	512	436
Prf att Ord Sh	322	1014	503	436
Btm Line Earn	322	1014	-2470	436
Dividend Paid	-	409	-	200
Mkt Prce(c) YE	31	40	40	-
Depreciation	111	74	36	85

PER SHARE STATISTICS (CENTS)

Net Asst Val	13.88	11.36	6.48	80.76
Net Earnings	2.60	8.20	6.00	-
Dividends	-	3.30	-	-
Cash Flow	3.50	8.78	4.35	7.82

RATIOS AND OTHER INFORMATION

Mrk Cap(R000)	3840	4954	4954	-
Current Ratio	1.32	1.54	1.37	1.44
Quik/Acid Tst	1.32	1.54	1.37	0.64
Debt/Ass Rat	0.68	0.38	0.62	0.48
L T L Tot Ass	0.01	0.02	0.07	0.01
Debt to Eqity	0.83	0.40	0.22	0.94
Interest Cover	2.77	14.86	53.68	4.15
Ret on Assets	15.05	25.14	46.90	10.75
Ret on Equity%	4.55	15.00	8.17	8.10
Price/Earnings	11.92	4.88	6.67	-
Divid Cover	-	2.48	-	-
Divid Yield	-	8.25	-	-
Earning Yield%	8.39	20.50	15.00	-
NAV % Mrk Pr	44.77	28.40	16.19	-
Effec Tax Rate	51.66	37.27	48.85	48.77
Def Interval	3.35	0.28	0.47	0.26
Sus Grth Rate	4.55	8.95	8.17	2.92

SUBSIDIARY & ASSOCIATED COMPANIES

CANOFIN FINANCE (PTY) LTD (50%)
FACSFIN (PTY) LTD
MUROUQ BROKERS (PTY) LTD
QUORUM GROUP HOLDINGS (PTY) LTD
QUORUM LEASING SERVICES (CAPE) (PTY) LTD
QUORUM LEASING SERVICES (NATAL) (PTY) LT
QUORUM LEASING SERVICES (PRETORIA) (PTY)
QUORUM LEASING SERVICES (PTY) LTD
QUORUM MANAGED PORTFOLIOS (PTY) LTD
RENTAL FINANCE (PTY) LTD

INVESTMENTS

None

RABIE INVESTMENT HOLDINGS LTD

ABBREVIATION : RABIE

JSE SHORT CODE : RAB

SECTOR : Financial-Property

SHAREHOLDERS

Who Owns Whom's Assessment of the Identity of the Ultimate Controlling Shareholder: DIRECTORS

SHAREHOLDER	PERCENTAGE 1992	1991
RABIE J S	37.2	36.2
COHEN L H	14.5	14.5
CMB NOM P/L	10.3	---
INVESTEC NOM P/L	6.3	6.3
CAMPOBELLO HOLDINGS P/L	4.2	---
BM NOM CC	4.2	4.1
MURRAY & ROBERTS LTD	1.9	1.9
TOP DOG NOM P/L	1.8	---
CHARISMA HOLDINGS P/L	1.5	---
HILL D A H	1.3	1.9
INVESTEC BANK LTD	1.3	1.3
RABIE SHARE INCENTIVE TRUST	1.2	---
NICK HAYLE HOLDINGS LTD	1.1	1.1
GAINSBOROUGH HOLDINGS INC	---	1.9
CHARTERHOUSE NOM P/L	---	6.4
HARRIS D	---	1.6
SANLAM	---	10.3
TOTAL	86.6	87.4

DIRECTORS :
ABBOT DW ,COHEN LH (Managing Director)
GELBART C ,RABIE JS (Chairman

REGISTRATION NUMBER : 87/01326/06

REGISTERED OFFICE
4th Floor, Sanclare, Dreyer Street
Claremont, Cape Town
7945
TEL: 021-683 3760
FAX: 021-618 454

TRANSFER SECRETARY
Mercantile Registrars Ltd
P O Box 1053, Johannesburg
2000
TEL: 011-333 8181

COMPANY SECRETARY
K C Maggs

NATURE OF BUSINESS
Developer of residential and industrial land, manufacture , marketing, rental and sale of a range of portable accommodation and playground equipment.

BANKERS :
First National Bank of SA Ltd

AUDITORS :
Baker Musikanth

FAMILIAR BRAND NAMES
BOKKIE,KWIKJAK,KWIKSPACE,KWIKSPAN,NOMAD PARKHOMES,PLETTENBERG,PORTACAMP,ZOZO

CONTRIBUTION BY ACTIVITY
N/A

YEAR END : June

DIVIDEND : (Ldr)27/10/89 (Pay)28/11/89

CAPITAL STRUCTURE

	AUTHORISED	ISSUED
Ords 1c	25000000	19439912

FINANCIAL STATISTICS (AT FINANCIAL YEAR END)

(Amts in R'000)	1992 Jun	1991 Jun	1990 Jun	1989 Jun	1988
Ord S/H Int	12183	11665	19069	13384	3378
Long Trm Loans	2729	4317	1159	8429	9023
Iss Ord Share	19440	19440	19440	18398	16098
Total Liab	19410	22120	12244	29589	17802
Current Liab	16681	17803	11085	21160	8779
Total Assets	31593	33785	31313	41366	23517
Intang Assets	*	*	*	1607	*
Current Assets	17223	19661	15827	29014	11116
Debtors	16364	18599	11331	14903	-
Inventory	855	1058	3283	5749	11116
Turnover	-	-	-	-	15240
Oper Profit	2697	535	6667	9949	5481
Interest Paid	2323	1243	1216	618	152
Tax Paid	-144	-302	1723	3272	20
Prf af Int&Tax	518	-406	4042	6250	5309
Prf att Ord Sh	518	-406	4042	6250	5309
Btm Line Earn	518	-7405	5741	6250	5309
Dividend Paid	-	-	56	828	2093
Mkt Prce(c) YE	48	60	145	200	25
Depreciation	289	460	458	529	-

PER SHARE STATISTICS (CENTS)

	1992	1991	1990	1989	1988
Net Asst Val	62.67	60.01	98.09	64.01	20.98
Net Earnings	2.70	-2.10	20.80	-	-
Cash Flow	4.15	-1.28	26.35	39.16	32.96

RATIOS AND OTHER INFORMATION

	1992	1991	1990	1989	1988
Mrk Cap(R000)	9331	11664	28188	36796	4025
Current Ratio	1.03	1.10	1.43	1.37	1.27
Quik/Acid Tst	0.98	1.04	1.13	1.10	-
Tot Ass T/ovr	-	-	-	-	0.65
Debt/Ass Rat	0.60	0.64	0.36	0.71	0.76
L T L Tot Ass	0.07	0.11	0.01	0.20	0.38
Debt to Eqity	1.55	1.85	0.60	2.19	5.27
Interest Cover	1.16	0.43	5.48	16.10	36.06
Oper Prof Mrg	-	-	-	-	35.96
Net Prof Marg%	-	-	-	-	34.84
Ret on Assets	8.54	1.58	22.29	24.51	23.31
Ret on Equity%	4.25	-3.48	21.20	46.70	157.16
Price/Earnings	17.78	-28.57	6.97	-	-
Earning Yield%	5.63	-3.50	14.34	-	-
NAV % Mrk Pr	130.56	100.01	67.65	32.01	83.94
Effec Tax Rate	-	-	6.92	26.61	0.38
Def Interval	15.65	-66.92	0.19	1.25	1.70
Sus Grth Rate	4.25	-3.48	20.90	40.51	95.20

SUBSIDIARY & ASSOCIATED COMPANIES

BURAD (PTY) LTD
BURAD PACIFIC INC (USA)
BURAD PROJECT MANAGEMENT SERVICES (PTY)
BURAD SECURITIES LTD
BURAD SERVICES (PTY) LTD
HAZELDENE HALL (PTY) LTD
KWIKSPACE HOLDINGS (PTY) LTD (40%)
LIJAN PROPERTIES (PTY) LTD
LUFRI INVESTMENTS (PTY) LTD
MISTY MOUNTAINS (PTY) LTD
PARKTOWN VIEW (PTY) LTD (33.3%)
RABIE PROPERTY DEVELOPERS (CAPE) (PTY) L
RABIE PROPERTY DEVELOPERS (NATAL) (PTY)
RABIE PROPERTY DEVELOPERS (TVL) (PTY) LT
RABIE PROPERTY DEVELOPERS NO 1 (PTY) LTD
RABIE PROPERTY DEVELOPERS NO 2 (PTY) LTD
RABIE PROPERTY DEVELOPERS NO 4 (PTY) LTD
RABIE PROPERTY DEVELOPERS NO 5 (PTY) LTD
RABIE PROPERTY DEVELOPERS NO 6 (PTY) LTD
RABIE PROPERTY DEVELOPERS NO 7 (PTY) LTD
RABIE PROPERTY DEVELOPERS NO 8 (PTY) LTD
RABIE PROPERTY DEVELOPERS NO 9 (PTY) LTD
WOODGREEN HOLDINGS (PTY) LTD
WOODMEAD CENTRE (PTY) LTD
WOODMEAD HOUSE (PTY) LTD

INVESTMENTS

None

RACY GROUP HOLDINGS LTD

ABBREVIATION : RACY

JSE SHORT CODE : RCY

SECTOR : Industrial-Transportation

SHAREHOLDERS

Who Owns Whom's Assessment of the Identity of the Ultimate Controlling Shareholder: DIRECTORS

SHAREHOLDER	PERCENTAGE 1992	1991
FALCK & CIE BANQUIERS	23.4	---
LANDAU & COETZEE FINANCE P/L	11.4	33.6
STOCKSHARE NOM P/L	9.0	---
GERVIS S	5.9	5.9
ELLERINE BROS P/L	4.7	4.7
HENDLER C	4.1	4.0
CREDFIN P/L	3.4	3.4
HENDLER E	3.4	3.2
NEDBANK NOM LTD	3.2	1.1
HENDLER R	3.2	3.2
KAPITAN A G	2.1	2.1
HARVEST SECURITIES LTD	2.0	2.0
LEVY C L	1.8	1.8
JACOBSON A	1.6	2.0
HARRY JACOBSON FAMILY HOLDINGS P/L	1.3	1.3
KAYEMESS NOM P/L	1.1	---
FREEMAN I M	---	1.2
RACY GROUP SHARE INCENTIVE TRUST	---	1.6
FINANSBANK NOM P/L	---	8.2
TOTAL	81.4	79.0

DIRECTORS :
FREEMAN IM (Financial Director),HENDLER C
HENDLER E ,HENDLER R
JACOBSON AC (Managing Director)
JACOBSON IJ (Chairman),JACOBSON JH

REGISTRATION NUMBER : 87/00974/06

REGISTERED OFFICE
Cnr Houer & Bonsmara Rds, City Deep Extension 1
Johannesburg
2001
TEL: 011-613 2033
FAX: 011-623 1849

TRANSFER SECRETARY
Mercantile Registrars Ltd
P O Box 1053, Johannesburg
2000
TEL: 011-333 8181

COMPANY SECRETARY
I M Freeman

NATURE OF BUSINESS
A holding company with subsidiaries engaged in industrial transportation and in the rebuilding, repairing and installation of diesel engines, transmission and fuel systems and the distribution of mechanical & electrical parts.

BANKERS :
First National Bank of SA Ltd
Standard Bank of SA Ltd, Boland Bank Ltd
Nedcor Bank Ltd

AUDITORS :
KPMG Aiken & Peat, Tuffias Shapiro Braude

FAMILIAR BRAND NAMES
DIESEL CITY,HENDLERS

CONTRIBUTION BY ACTIVITY
Hendlers (% Operating Income) (98.0%)
Diesel City (2.0%)

YEAR END : March

DIVIDEND : Ords 1c

Interim No 5	(Ldr)08/12/89	(Pay)03/01/90	Amt(c)2
Final No 6	(Ldr)22/02/91	(Pay)22/04/91	Amt(c)1.5
Final No 7	(Ldr)12/07/91	(Pay)31/07/91	Amt(c)1
Final No 8	(Ldr)28/08/92	(Pay)09/09/92	Amt(c)2

NUMBER OF EMPLOYEES : 128

CAPITAL STRUCTURE

	AUTHORISED	ISSUED
Ords 1c	40000000	25680000

FINANCIAL STATISTICS (AT FINANCIAL YEAR END)

(Amts in R'000)	1992 Mar	1991 Mar	1990 Mar	1989 Mar	1988 Mar
Ord S/H Int	21424	19790	18353	16925	16539
Long Trm Loans	8078	8121	8737	6515	1289
Iss Ord Share	25680	25680	25680	25680	24720
Total Liab	23437	22046	24340	18444	7949

Current Liab	15359	13925	15603	11929	6660
Total Assets	44861	41836	42693	35369	22257
Intang Assets	*	*	*	*	2231
Current Assets	21089	18289	18440	15465	11050
Debtors	12788	10526	10055	8370	6249
Inventory	8175	7129	7217	6684	4801
Turnover	66385	64389	55892	46263	32222
Oper Profit	5794	7125	5374	6151	3758
Interest Paid	1710	2327	1512	602	151
Tax Paid	1936	2377	1927	1915	937
Prf af Int&Tax	2148	2421	1935	3634	2670
Prf att Ord Sh	2148	2421	1935	3634	2670
Btm Line Earn	2148	2079	1935	3634	2670
Dividend Paid	514	642	514	1669	1360
Mkt Prce(c) YE	45	42	40	80	53
Depreciation	2788	2772	1818	1144	715

PER SHARE STATISTICS (CENTS)

Net Asst Val	83.43	77.06	71.47	65.91	57.88
Net Earnings	8.40	9.40	7.50	14.50	11.50
Dividends	2.00	2.50	2.00	6.50	5.50
Cash Flow	23.89	25.29	19.80	21.83	14.54

RATIOS AND OTHER INFORMATION

Mrk Cap(R000)	11556	10786	10272	20544	13102
Current Ratio	1.37	1.31	1.18	1.30	1.66
Quik/Acid Tst	0.84	0.80	0.72	0.74	0.94
A/C Rec T/ovr	5.19	6.12	5.56	5.53	5.16
Tot Ass T/ovr	1.48	1.54	1.31	1.31	1.45
Debt/Ass Rat	0.41	0.44	0.51	0.48	0.33
L T L Tot Ass	0.07	0.10	0.15	0.15	0.03
Debt to Eqity	0.87	0.92	1.19	1.01	0.44
Interest Cover	3.39	3.06	3.55	10.22	24.89
Oper Prof Mrg	8.73	11.07	9.61	13.30	11.66
Net Prof Marg%	3.24	3.76	3.46	7.86	8.29
Ret on Assets	12.92	17.03	12.59	17.39	16.88
Ret on Equity%	10.03	12.23	10.54	21.47	16.14
Price/Earnings	5.36	4.47	5.33	5.52	4.61
Divid Cover	4.20	3.76	3.75	2.23	2.09
Divid Yield	4.44	5.95	5.00	8.13	10.38
Earning Yield%	18.67	22.38	18.75	18.13	21.70
NAV % Mrk Pr	185.39	183.49	178.67	82.38	109.21
Effec Tax Rate	21.47	23.24	18.69	22.06	25.98
Def Interval	1.31	1.42	2.61	1.81	0.51
Sus Grth Rate	7.63	8.99	7.74	11.61	7.92

SUBSIDIARY & ASSOCIATED COMPANIES

BAB CARTAGE & WAREHOUSE (TRANSVAAL) (PTY
BESSESENS TRANSPORT (PTY) LTD
DIESEL FUEL INJECTION CO (PTY) LTD
DINSA HOLDINGS (PTY) LTD
ESSAKOWS TRANSPORT (PTY) LTD
HIGH SPEED DIESEL ENGINEERING (PTY) LTD
MAGWILL CARRIERS (PTY) LTD
PK ENGELBRECHT (PTY) LTD
PREMIER DIESEL COMPANY (PTY) LTD
RACY ENTERPRISES (PTY) LTD

INVESTMENTS

None

RADAR HOLDINGS

ABBREVIATION : RADAR

SECTOR : Zimbabwe Stock Exchange

SHAREHOLDERS

Who Owns Whom's Assessment of the Identity of the Ultimate Controlling Shareholder: MONOMATAPA DEVELOPMENT CO (PVT) LTD

SHAREHOLDER	PERCENTAGE 1992	1991
MONOMATAPA DEVELOPMENT CO PVT LTD	14.5	---
OLD MUTUAL INV CORP (PVT) LTD	9.5	---
LTA TRADING PVT LTD	7.6	---
FIDELITY LIFE ASSURE OF ZIM PVT LTD	6.6	---
ALPHA OMEGA INV PVT LTD	5.6	---
RADAR EMPLOYEES TRUST PVT LTD	5.1	---
TRUST NOM (PVT) LTD	3.3	---
SYFRETS NOM (PVT) LTD	2.8	---
FIRST MUTUAL LIFE ASSURE SOC OF ZIM	2.6	---
MINING INDUSTRY PENS FUND	2.2	---
SENIM PVT LTD	2.0	---
NANGLE E J	2.0	---
BARD NOM (PVT) LTD	1.9	---
CATERING INDUSTRY PENS FUND	1.7	---
BARTELUS (PVT) LTD	1.5	---
TONLY INV PVT LTD	1.5	---
NAT RAILWAYS OF ZIM CONTR PENS FUND	1.4	---
ZIMNAT LIFE ASSURE CO LTD	1.3	---
ZIMNAT INSURANCE CO LTD	1.3	---
CHRISTIE E J	1.2	---
TOTAL	75.5	---

DIRECTORS :
BOTT JA (Managing Director)
CHIPUDHLA PWT (Deputy Chairman),MACKAY CNW
RUSIKE ETM ,RUSIKE ZL ,SCHOFIELD CJL (Chairman)
SLY JR

REGISTERED OFFICE
1st Floor, Parham House
89 Joseph Tongogara Street, Bulawayo

TRANSFER SECRETARY
First Transfer Secretaries (Pvt) Ltd
P O Box 437, Bulawayo
Zimbabwe

TEL: 092634 - 702905

COMPANY SECRETARY
A M Feather

NATURE OF BUSINESS
RADAR HOLDINGS,a Zimbabwean-registered and controlled company,is the parent of a group which operates throughout the country and is involved in manufacturing, engineering,foundry, retailing and property interests.

BANKERS :
ANZ Grindlays Bank Plc
Barclays Bank of Zimbabwe Ltd
First Merchant Bank of Zimbabwe Ltd
Standard Chartered Bank Zimbabwe Ltd
Zimbabwe Banking Corporation Ltd

AUDITORS :
Coopers & Lybrand

FAMILIAR BRAND NAMES
N/A

CONTRIBUTION BY ACTIVITY
N/A

YEAR END : June

DIVIDEND : Ords Z$0,50

Dividend	(Ldr)18/10/91	(Pay)18/11/91	Amt(c)30
Dividend	(Ldr)03/04/92	(Pay)24/04/92	Amt(c)25

CAPITAL STRUCTURE

	AUTHORISED	ISSUED
Ords Z$0,50	10000000	8873507

FINANCIAL STATISTICS (AT FINANCIAL YEAR END)

(Amts in Z$)	1992 Jun	1991 Jun
Ord S/H Int	84684	51838
Long Trm Loans	15465	12642
Iss Ord Share	8874	6656
Total Liab	54007	46454
Current Liab	38542	33812
Total Assets	138691	98292
Current Assets	66578	45618
Debtors	23223	19045
Inventory	37931	22744
Turnover	135343	95986
Oper Profit	28860	16934
Interest Paid	1993	1931
Tax Paid	11851	5460
Prf af Int&Tax	15016	9543
Prf att Ord Sh	15016	9543
Btm Line Earn	14814	9476
Dividend Paid	5058	2663
Depreciation	3808	2897

PER SHARE STATISTICS (CENTS)

Net Asst Val	954 29	778 82
Net Earnings	176 90	142 40
Dividends	57 00	40 00
Cash Flow	223 92	194 77

RATIOS AND OTHER INFORMATION

Current Ratio	1 73	1 35
Quik/Acid Tst	0 74	0 68
A/C Rec T/ovr	5 83	5 04
Tot Ass T/ovr	0 98	0 98
Debt/Ass Rat	0 35	0 42
L T L Tot Ass	0 07	0 08
Debt to Eqity	0 57	0 80
Interest Cover	14 48	8 77
Oper Prof Mrg	21 32	17 64
Net Prof Marg%	11 09	9 94
Ret on Assets	20 81	17 23
Ret on Equity%	17 73	18 41
Divid Cover	3 10	3 56
Effec Tax Rate	40 21	34 55
Def Interval	0 75	1 29
Sus Grth Rate	11 76	13 27

SUBSIDIARY & ASSOCIATED COMPANIES

MACDONALD BROTHERS (PVT) LTD
RADAR BUILDING SUPPLIES (PVT) LTD
RADAR ENGINEERING LIMITED
RADAR MANAGEMENT SERVICES (PVT) LTD

INVESTMENTS

None

RAINBOW CHICKEN LTD

ABBREVIATION : RAINBOW

JSE SHORT CODE : RBW

SECTOR : Industrial-Food

SHAREHOLDERS

Who Owns Whom's Assessment of the Identity of the Ultimate Controlling Shareholder:
METHVEN TRUST / REMBRANDT

SHAREHOLDER	PERCENTAGE 1992	1991
METHVEN S C HOLDINGS P/L	60 7	60 7
HUNT LEUCHARS & HEPBURN HOLDINGS TRUST	11 8	11 8
LASH ESTABLISHMENT	8 1	8 1
PFEIFFER S TRUST	7 2	7 2
CMB NOM P/L	3 7	---
SSP INV TRUST	1 1	1 1
SANLAM	---	2 1
TOTAL	92 7	91 1

DIRECTORS :
GEOGHEGAN JB (Managing Director),HUNDLEY BR
LOCH DAVIS DJ (Chairman),METHVEN L ,MORRIS NJ
PFEIFFER SA ,RUPERT JP ,WAUD P
WELLS CF (Financial Director

REGISTRATION NUMBER : 66/04972/06

REGISTERED OFFICE
Head Office, 1 Bellevue Road
Kloof, Natal
3610
TEL 031-764 4227
FAX 031-764 5581

TRANSFER SECRETARY
Central Registrars Ltd
P O Box 4844, Johannesburg
2000
TEL 011-331 0051

COMPANY SECRETARY
S B Heath

NATURE OF BUSINESS
Group operates as an integrated broiler chicken producer and an animal feed miller

BANKERS :
Absa Bank Ltd

AUDITORS :
Deloitte & Touche

FAMILIAR BRAND NAMES
BONNY BIRD,EPOL ANIMAL FEEDS (50%)
FARMER BROWN,LEMOENKLOOF,RAINBOW

CONTRIBUTION BY ACTIVITY
N/A

YEAR END : March

DIVIDEND : Ords no par value

Interim No 52	(Ldr)02/03/90	(Pay)05/03/90	Amt(c)4.8
Final No 53	(Ldr)14/09/90	(Pay)12/10/90	Amt(c)5.9
Interim No 54	(Ldr)15/03/91	(Pay)22/03/91	Amt(c)4.3
Final No 55	(Ldr)22/05/92	(Pay)05/06/92	Amt(c)4.4

NUMBER OF EMPLOYEES : 11925

CAPITAL STRUCTURE

	AUTHORISED	ISSUED
Ords no par value	450000000	368500000
12,5% Cum Prefs R1	500000	500000

FINANCIAL STATISTICS (AT FINANCIAL YEAR END)

(Amts in R'000)	1992 Mar	1991 Mar	1990 Jun	1989 Jun	1988 Jun
Ord S/H Int	844159	566036	593833	537269	425579
Long Trm Loans	83897	184353	500	500	500
Iss Ord Share	368500	275000	275000	275000	275000
Total Liab	534371	712735	143713	134771	92406
Current Liab	450474	528382	143213	134271	91906
Total Assets	1328697	1228271	737546	672040	517985
Intang Assets	49833	50500	*	*	*
Current Assets	362190	335650	183762	202832	101771
Debtors	183246	167070	53291	49820	35112
Inventory	178939	166488	71060	52487	39915
Turnover	1510923	522844	635330	554156	454101
Oper Profit	76310	30182	74927	81421	61507
Interest Paid	32801	703	6	-	-
Tax Paid	-	12	6205	20696	12414
Prf af Int&Tax	49114	35873	86071	67458	49093
Prf att Ord Sh	48500	35842	86009	67396	49030
Btm Line Earn	46449	35842	86009	60971	49030
Dividend Paid	16214	11825	29425	18750	22000
Mkt Prce(c) YE	460	315	275	285	-
Depreciation	38806	16170	16963	11838	9543

PER SHARE STATISTICS (CENTS)

Net Asst Val	215.56	187.47	215.94	195.37	154.76
Net Earnings	13.80	13.00	31.30	26.80	19.60
Dividends	4.40	4.30	10.70	7.50	8.80
Cash Flow	24.86	25.22	37.44	31.56	23.43

RATIOS AND OTHER INFORMATION

Mrk Cap(R000)	1695100	866250	756250	783750	-
Current Ratio	0.80	0.64	1.28	1.51	1.11
Quik/Acid Tst	0.41	0.32	0.79	1.12	0.67
A/C Rec T/ovr	8.25	4.17	11.92	11.12	12.93
Tot Ass T/ovr	1.14	0.57	0.86	0.82	0.88
Debt/Ass Rat	0.37	0.55	0.19	0.20	0.18
L T L Tot Ass	0.03	0.12	-	-	-
Debt to Eqity	0.59	1.19	0.24	0.25	0.22
Interest Cover	2.33	42.93	12487.83	-	-
Oper Prof Mrg	5.05	5.77	11.79	14.69	13.54
Net Prof Marg%	3.21	6.86	13.54	12.16	10.80
Ret on Assets	6.17	3.97	12.51	13.12	11.87
Ret on Equity%	5.75	8.44	14.48	12.54	11.52
Price/Earnings	33.33	24.23	8.79	10.63	-
Divid Cover	3.14	3.02	2.93	3.57	2.23
Divid Yield	0.96	1.37	3.89	2.63	-
Earning Yield%	3.00	4.13	11.38	9.40	-
NAV % Mrk Pr	46.86	59.51	78.52	68.55	-
Effec Tax Rate	-	0.03	6.72	23.48	20.21
Def Interval	2.92	11.82	0.00	0.01	0.01
Sus Grth Rate	3.82	4.24	9.53	9.05	6.35

SUBSIDIARY & ASSOCIATED COMPANIES

BONNY BIRD FARMS (PTY) LTD
BONNY BIRD FARMS CISKEI (PTY) LTD
EAST END COURT (PTY) LTD
EPOL (PTY) LTD (50%)
FARMTRUCK (PTY) LTD
HYFLITE BREEDERS (PTY) LTD
RAINBOW CHICKEN FARMS (PTY) LTD
RAINBOW FARMS (PTY) LTD
TWO PEARSON ROAD (PTY) LTD

INVESTMENTS

None

RALE HOLDINGS LTD

ABBREVIATION : RALE

JSE SHORT CODE : RLE

SECTOR : Industrial-Industrial Holding

SHAREHOLDERS

Who Owns Whom's Assessment of the Identity of the Ultimate Controlling Shareholder:
DIRECTORS CONTROL 47% (FEB 1991)

SHAREHOLDER	PERCENTAGE 1992	1991
ABSA NOM P/L	27.6	---
ROBGUARD P/L	18.8	---
CMB NOM P/L	7.6	---
SHARESTOCK NOM P/L	6.4	---
RETAN NOM P/L	3.1	---
UNION TRUST CO LTD	2.1	---
VAN ROOYEN D	1.9	2.0
FIRST NAT NOM P/L	1.6	1.4
SHERRELL R E	1.6	---
RICHARDSON F E	1.6	1.6
NEDBANK NOM LTD	1.2	---
DE KLERK A	1.0	---
SMK NOM P/L	---	4.9
COLLINGWOOD C J	---	1.0
FINANSBANK NOM P/L	---	2.6
MAINGARD L M J P, P & L M J R TRUSTEES	---	6.3
MAINGARD L M J R	---	4.0
MAINGARD L M J R TRUSTEES	---	1.1
MAINGARD R TRUSTEES	---	3.4
ROBERT MAINGARD FAMILY TRUST	---	2.0
SANLAM	---	7.5
STD BANK NOM TVL P/L	---	1.4
VOLKSKAS NOM P/L	---	26.4
TPF NOM P/L	---	3.2
LOUBSER H G INV P/L	---	4.2
TOTAL	74.5	72.9

DIRECTORS :
MAINGARD B ,MAINGARD LMJP
MAINGARD LMJR (Chairman),MAUJEAN JJM
MCELLIGOTT RB ,SHERRELL RE ,VAN ROOYEN D

REGISTRATION NUMBER : 05/23515/06

REGISTERED OFFICE
Old Mill Site, Canelands
Natal
4341
TEL: 0322-33 4061
FAX: 0322-33 6293

TRANSFER SECRETARY
Central Registrars Ltd
P O Box 4844, Johannesburg
2000
TEL: 011-331 0051

COMPANY SECRETARY
BCD de Groot

NATURE OF BUSINESS
A holding company which has a controlling interest in quoted Farm-Ag Ltd.

BANKERS :
First National Bank of SA Ltd
Trust Bank of Africa Ltd

AUDITORS :
KPMG Aiken & Peat

FAMILIAR BRAND NAMES
N/A

CONTRIBUTION BY ACTIVITY
N/A

YEAR END : February

DIVIDEND : (Ldr)07/07/89 (Pay)21/07/89

CAPITAL STRUCTURE

	AUTHORISED	ISSUED
6% Cum Prefs R2	50000	50000
Red Prefs 1c	1000000	0
Ords 20c	10000000	9646257

FINANCIAL STATISTICS (AT FINANCIAL YEAR END)

(Amts in R'000)	1991 Feb	1990 Feb	1989 Feb	1988 Feb	1987
Ord S/H Int	15325	18665	21549	17047	42593
Long Trm Loans	10804	18198	29471	34410	63489
Iss Ord Share	96462	96462	68902	68902	68902
Total Liab	81383	155092	122724	107023	111509
Current Liab	70579	136894	93253	72613	48020
Total Assets	96408	172689	142251	124070	160048
Intang Assets	300	1068	2022	*	*
Current Assets	43913	120941	93439	82155	53966
Debtors	27221	72619	51998	45675	-
Inventory	5899	13829	36589	34194	53966
Turnover	73127	205813	153589	128848	56313
Oper Profit	7063	9044	18268	17589	8285
Interest Paid	20770	25625	11576	4990	1904
Tax Paid	-	28	199	1396	222
Prf af Int&Tax	-6702	-12265	7198	11203	5968
Prf att Ord Sh	-684	-6564	6147	8525	4913
Btm Line Earn	-3180	-8212	6866	8525	4913
Dividend Paid	-	-	2756	3273	1378
Mkt Prce(c) YE	23	25	40	59	140
Depreciation	962	4709	3500	2273	-

PER SHARE STATISTICS (CENTS)

Net Asst Val	15.58	18.24	28.34	24.74	61.82
Net Earnings	-0.90	-8.10	8.90	12.40	-
Dividends	-	-	4.00	4.75	-
Cash Flow	-5.63	-6.68	9.78	12.01	8.66

RATIOS AND OTHER INFORMATION

Mrk Cap(R000)	22186	24116	27561	40652	96463
Current Ratio	0.62	0.88	1.00	1.13	1.12
Quik/Acid Tst	0.54	0.78	0.61	0.66	-
A/C Rec T/ovr	2.69	2.83	2.95	2.82	-
Tot Ass T/ovr	0.76	1.19	1.08	1.04	0.35
Debt/Ass Rat	0.74	0.80	0.73	0.70	0.70
L T L Tot Ass	0.01	0.01	0.07	0.12	0.40
Debt to Eqity	4.64	7.44	4.82	5.11	2.62
Interest Cover	0.34	0.35	1.58	3.52	4.25
Oper Prof Mrg	9.66	4.39	11.89	13.65	14.71
Net Prof Marg%	-0.94	-3.19	4.00	6.62	8.72
Ret on Assets	20.34	9.79	15.38	16.22	5.06
Ret on Equity%	-4.46	-35.17	28.53	50.01	11.53
Price/Earnings	-25.56	-3.09	4.49	4.76	-
Divid Cover	-	-	2.23	2.61	-
Divid Yield	-	-	10.00	8.05	-
Earning Yield%	-3.91	-32.40	22.25	21.02	-
NAV % Mrk Pr	67.72	72.97	70.85	41.93	44.15
Effec Tax Rate	-	-	2.28	10.94	3.48
Def Interval	-11.57	-19.09	11.04	7.34	10.64
Sus Grth Rate	-4.46	-35.17	15.74	30.81	8.30

SUBSIDIARY & ASSOCIATED COMPANIES

FARM-AG LTD
R H INVESTMENTS (PTY) LTD

INVESTMENTS

None

RAND LEASES (VOGELSTRUISFTN) GOLD MINING CO

ABBREVIATION : RD-LEASE

JSE SHORT CODE : RLS

SECTOR : Gold-Rand & others

SHAREHOLDERS

Who Owns Whom's Assessment of the Identity of the Ultimate Controlling Shareholder:
G LAING

SHAREHOLDER	PERCENTAGE 1992	1991
EDWIN W BALDERSON NOM P/L	50.8	---
STD BANK NOM TVL P/L	16.2	82.3
BLOCKBUSTER INV P/L	9.1	---
BLOCKBUSTER INV HOLDINGS P/L	8.4	---

RAYBOULD W H	2.2	2.0
INTERNATIONAL COAL MARKETING CORP	1.1	—
SMBL NOM P/L	—	1.8
VOLKSKAS NOM P/L	—	2.2
TOTAL	87.9	88.4

DIRECTORS :
CARROLL LM ,LAING GJS (Chairman & Managing Dir.)
NISBET GY ,SEVERIN FV MR

REGISTRATION NUMBER : 05/04827/06

REGISTERED OFFICE
Ground Floor, AMR Office Park, Phase 2, Concorde Rd East
Bedfordview
2008
TEL: 011-674 5123
FAX: 011-674 3307

TRANSFER SECRETARY
Mercantile Registrars Ltd
P O Box 1053, Johannesburg
2000
TEL: 011-333 8181

COMPANY SECRETARY
Revere Resources Management Services (Pty) Ltd

NATURE OF BUSINESS
Mining operations are conducted by a contractor (Constantia Mining Services P/L), at an annually negotiated fixed cost per ton rate. Mining is estimated to be increased to a rate of 15000 tons per month at a recovered grade of 6 grams per ton for 4 years commencing Jan 1992. Dump retreatment operations are also conducted.

BANKERS :
Standard Bank of SA Ltd

AUDITORS :
Arthur Andersen & Co

FAMILIAR BRAND NAMES
N/A

CONTRIBUTION BY ACTIVITY
N/A

YEAR END : June

DIVIDEND : Ords 2,5c
Dividend (Ldr)09/10/92 (Pay)23/10/92 Amt(c)0.383

NUMBER OF EMPLOYEES : 481

CAPITAL STRUCTURE

	AUTHORISED	ISSUED
Ords 2,5c	140000000	118505000

FINANCIAL STATISTICS (AT FINANCIAL YEAR END)

(Amts in R'000)	1991 Jun	1990 Jun	1989 Jun	1988 Jun	1987
Ord S/H Int	41901	15130	27967	24639	20789
Long Trm Loans	-	4	9478	7921	11590
Iss Ord Share	118505	11851	11851	11840	11730
Total Liab	7426	33193	21470	16128	16520
Current Liab	7426	33189	11992	8207	4930
Total Assets	49327	48323	49437	40767	34096
Current Assets	1894	1417	2546	2307	1717
Debtors	273	429	1465	875	-
Inventory	541	983	912	1284	1717
Turnover	14791	22344	38757	31101	-
Oper Profit	-2961	-9683	3367	3987	391
Interest Paid	1963	3003	-	-	39
Tax Paid	-	153	39	137	2
Prf af Int&Tax	-4896	-12837	3328	3850	350
Prf att Ord Sh	-4896	-12837	3328	3850	350
Btm Line Earn	-4896	-12837	1815	3346	350
Mkt Prce(c) YE	27	65	220	305	800

PER SHARE STATISTICS (CENTS)

Net Asst Val	35.36	127.67	235.99	208.10	177.23
Net Earnings	-5.50	-107.00	28.10	32.60	-
Cash Flow	-55.59	-108.32	27.64	32.64	2.98

RATIOS AND OTHER INFORMATION

Mrk Cap(R000)	31996	7703	26072	36112	93840
Current Ratio	0.26	0.04	0.21	0.28	0.35
Quik/Acid Tst	0.18	0.01	0.14	0.12	-
A/C Rec T/ovr	54.18	52.08	26.46	35.54	-
Tot Ass T/ovr	0.30	0.46	0.78	0.76	-
Debt/Ass Rat	0.15	0.69	0.43	0.40	0.48
L T L Tot Ass	-	0.00	0.19	0.19	0.34
Debt to Eqity	0.18	2.19	0.77	0.65	0.79
Interest Cover	-1.51	-3.22	-	-	10.03
Oper Prof Mrg	-20.02	-43.34	8.69	12.82	-
Net Prof Marg%	-33.10	-57.45	8.59	12.38	-
Ret on Assets	-5.95	-20.03	6.81	9.78	1.15
Ret on Equity%	-11.68	-84.84	11.90	15.63	1.68
Price/Earnings	-4.91	-0.61	7.83	9.36	-
Earning Yield%	-20.37	-164.62	12.77	10.69	-
NAV % Mrk Pr	130.96	196.41	107.27	68.23	22.15
Effec Tax Rate	-	-1.21	2.73	3.44	0.57
Def Interval	-	-0.73	3.03	2.08	33.11
Sus Grth Rate	-11.68	-84.84	11.90	15.63	1.68

SUBSIDIARY & ASSOCIATED COMPANIES

SEVCORP GOLD MINING CO (PTY) LTD

INVESTMENTS

None

RAND LEASES PROPERTIES LTD

ABBREVIATION : RLPROPS

JSE SHORT CODE : RPR

SECTOR : Financial-Property Loan Stock

SHAREHOLDERS

Who Owns Whom's Assessment of the Identity of the Ultimate Controlling Shareholder:
OSSORY LTD

DIRECTORS :
CARROLL LM (Financial Director),LAING GJS
SEVERIN FV ,SEVERIN S (Chairman & Managing Dir.

REGISTRATION NUMBER : 78/00870/06

REGISTERED OFFICE
Main Reef Road, Florida
Roodepoort
1709

TEL: 011-674 5123
FAX: 011-674 3307

TRANSFER SECRETARY
Mercantile Registrars Ltd
P O Box 1053, Johannesburg
2000
TEL: 011-333 8181

COMPANY SECRETARY
Severin Development Corporation

NATURE OF BUSINESS
RL Props holds the property previously held by Rand Leases, being Portion 161 and Portion 48 of the farm Vogelstruisfontein 231 IQ, measuring approximately 470 hectares, situated in the Roodepoort Area, West Rand.

BANKERS :
Standard Merchant Bank Ltd

AUDITORS :
Arthur Andersen & Co

FAMILIAR BRAND NAMES
N/A

CONTRIBUTION BY ACTIVITY
N/A

YEAR END : June

CAPITAL STRUCTURE

	AUTHORISED	ISSUED
Ords 2c	15000000	11850500
Unsec Sub Var Rate Debs 75c	15000000	11850500

FINANCIAL STATISTICS (AT FINANCIAL YEAR END)

(Amts in R'000)	1992 Jun	1991 Jun
Ord S/H Int	1268	1026
Long Trm Loans	8888	-
Iss Ord Share	11850	19890
Total Liab	10249	1388
Current Liab	1361	1388
Total Assets	11517	2414
Current Assets	2626	360
Debtors	781	232
Turnover	4803	612
Oper Profit	1530	189
Interest Paid	868	-
Prf af Int&Tax	881	189
Prf att Ord Sh	881	189
Btm Line Earn	881	189
Dividend Paid	5	-
Depreciation	37	-

PER SHARE STATISTICS (CENTS)

Net Asst Val	10.70	5.16
Net Earnings	7.80	-
Cash Flow	7.75	0.95

RATIOS AND OTHER INFORMATION

Current Ratio	1.93	0.26
Quik/Acid Tst	1.93	0.26
A/C Rec T/ovr	6.15	2.64
Tot Ass T/ovr	0.42	0.25
Debt/Ass Rat	0.89	0.57
L T L Tot Ass	0.77	-
Debt to Eqity	8.08	1.35
Interest Cover	1.76	-
Oper Prof Mrg	31.86	30.88
Net Prof Marg%	18.34	30.88
Ret on Assets	15.19	7.83
Ret on Equity%	69.48	18.42
Def Interval	9.68	-
Sus Grth Rate	69.09	18.42

SUBSIDIARY & ASSOCIATED COMPANIES

None

INVESTMENTS

None

RAND MINES LTD

ABBREVIATION : RANDMIN

JSE SHORT CODE : RDM

SECTOR : Mining Financial-Mining Houses

SHAREHOLDERS

Who Owns Whom's Assessment of the Identity of the Ultimate Controlling Shareholder:
SA MUTUAL VIA BARLOWS

SHAREHOLDER	PERCENTAGE 1992	1991
BARLOW RAND LTD	---	4.0
BARLOWS MINING HLDGS & ESTATES LTD	---	40.3
BAROB INV P/L	---	1.3
COR GROUP PLUTO INV LTD	---	7.3
EIGHTY ONE MAIN STREET NOM LTD	---	4.1
FIRST NAT NOM P/L	---	1.5
GUARDIAN NOM P/L	---	1.8
LIBERTY LIFE ASSOC OF AFRICA LTD	---	3.9
RAND MINES HOLDINGS LTD	---	21.5
SA MUTUAL	---	1.3
STD BANK NOM TVL P/L	---	5.3
UK BRANCH REGISTER CONTROL ACCOUNT	---	1.1
TOTAL	---	93.2

DIRECTORS :
BULTERMAN GH ,CLEWLOW WAM ,COOK AB ,COOPER DE
DAVIN FJ ,GROENEWEG EM ,HALL JC
MANSELL-JONES RM ,SEALEY AA (Deputy Chairman)
STEVENS IG (Financial Director),TURNER JPS
WATERSON CH ,WATT DT (Chairman & Managing Dir.

REGISTRATION NUMBER : 01/00656/06

REGISTERED OFFICE
15th Floor, The Corner House
63 Fox Street, Johannesburg
2001
TEL: 011-491 2911
FAX: 011-834 5936

TRANSFER SECRETARY
Rand Registrars Ltd
P O Box 82549, Southdale
2135
TEL: 011-835 1016

COMPANY SECRETARY
Rand Mines (Mining & Services) Ltd

NATURE OF BUSINESS
The company's operations and interests include: The mining of gold, chrome, coal, and platinum; Mineral exploration; Forestry & timber industries; Property development; Management and financial services. The company has controlling interests in quoted Rand Mines Properties, Randcoal Ltd, Vansa Vanadium, Barplats Investments, Barbrook Mines & East Rand Proprietary Mines.

BANKERS :
First National Bank of SA Ltd

AUDITORS :
Deloitte Pim Goldby

FAMILIAR BRAND NAMES
N/A

CONTRIBUTION BY ACTIVITY
N/A

YEAR END : September

DIVIDEND : Ords R1

Interim No 101	(Ldr)08/06/90	(Pay)03/07/90	Amt(c)120
Final No 102	(Ldr)23/11/90	(Pay)03/01/91	Amt(c)440
Interim No 103	(Ldr)07/06/91	(Pay)02/07/91	Amt(c)100
Final No 104	(Ldr)22/11/91	(Pay)06/01/91	Amt(c)200
Interim No 105	(Ldr)05/06/92	(Pay)03/07/92	Amt(c)100
Final No 106	(Ldr)27/11/92	(Pay)05/01/93	Amt(c)215

NUMBER OF EMPLOYEES : 52212

CAPITAL STRUCTURE

	AUTHORISED	ISSUED
Ords R1	20000000	14910305

FINANCIAL STATISTICS (AT FINANCIAL YEAR END)

(Amts in R'000)	1991 Sep	1990 Sep	1989 Sep	1988 Sep	1987
Ord S/H Int	718400	1230600	829600	754000	634600
Long Trm Loans	1530400	2015500	1587200	1203300	1205100
Iss Ord Share	14910	14910	11211	11211	11211
Total Liab	2025600	2490800	2168200	1659800	1497400
Current Liab	495200	475300	581000	456500	292300
Total Assets	2744000	3721400	2997800	2413800	2285100
Current Assets	553400	471200	427200	683500	445400
Debtors	390700	191000	203400	214400	-
Inventory	131000	197700	105000	69100	445400
Turnover	1775800	1693800	1367700	957300	759600
Oper Profit	337900	301400	299600	241900	241400
Interest Paid	74100	63100	46900	-	20000
Tax Paid	21500	42500	59200	49100	51800
Prf af Int&Tax	301200	280100	271100	192800	139500
Prf att Ord Sh	250300	223100	210500	164500	125200
Btm Line Earn	-484800	150100	132600	130200	125200
Dividend Paid	44700	83400	62800	50400	48800
Mkt Prce(c) YE	7000	9000	9800	7300	11700
Depreciation	547700	591300	80900	67900	-

PER SHARE STATISTICS (CENTS)

Net Asst Val	4818.24	8253.52	7399.88	6725.54	5660.51
Net Earnings	1679.00	1569.00	1929.00	1467.00	-
Dividends	300.00	560.00	560.00	450.00	-
Cash Flow	5298.46	5638.14	2697.35	2145.21	1244.31

RATIOS AND OTHER INFORMATION

Mrk Cap(R000)	1043700	1341900	1098678	818403	1311687
Current Ratio	1.12	0.99	0.74	1.50	1.52
Quik/Acid Tst	0.85	0.58	0.55	1.35	-
A/C Rec T/ovr	4.55	8.87	6.72	4.47	-
Tot Ass T/ovr	0.65	0.46	0.46	0.40	0.33
Debt/Ass Rat	0.49	0.38	0.42	0.40	0.66
L T L Tot Ass	0.31	0.25	0.23	0.21	0.53
Debt to Eqity	1.86	1.15	1.51	1.27	2.36
Interest Cover	4.63	4.95	6.81	-	10.57
Oper Prof Mrg	19.03	17.79	21.91	25.27	31.78
Net Prof Marg%	14.10	13.17	15.39	17.18	16.48
Ret on Assets	14.46	10.36	12.58	10.02	9.25
Ret on Equity%	34.84	18.13	25.37	21.82	19.73
Price/Earnings	4.17	5.74	5.08	4.98	-
Divid Cover	5.60	2.80	3.44	3.26	-
Divid Yield	4.29	6.22	5.71	6.16	-
Earning Yield%	23.99	17.43	19.68	20.10	-
NAV % Mrk Pr	68.83	91.71	75.51	92.13	48.38
Effec Tax Rate	9.29	17.67	15.53	16.95	23.40
Def Interval	1.01	1.16	2.68	2.46	8.64
Sus Grth Rate	28.62	11.35	17.80	15.13	12.04

SUBSIDIARY & ASSOCIATED COMPANIES

ALBION COLLIERIES LTD, THE
ARNOLD WILHELMI & CO. (PTY) LTD
B & K TOWNSHIP LIMITED
BARBROOK MINES LTD (40%)
BARLOW GENERAL INVESTMENTS LTD
BAROUL LANDGOED (EDMS) BPK
BARPLATS INVESTMENTS LTD (45%)
BAYEX (PTY) LTD
BENTONITE NOMINEES LTD
BLACK DIAMOND COLLIERY LTD, THE
BLOEMENDAL CONSOLIDATED ANTHRACITE MINES
CAMBA CONSOLIDATED (PTY) LTD
CONSOLIDATED AFRICAN MINES LTD
CONSOLIDATED MARSFIELD COLLIERIES LTD
CONWIT MINING CO. (PTY) LTD
CORGROUP (MERCURY) INVESTMENTS LTD
CORGROUP (NEPTUNE) INVESTMENTS LTD
CORNELIUS JOHANNES VAN DER MERWE (PTY) L
DOUGLAS LAND & MINERAL HOLDINGS (PTY) LT
DUHVA OPENCAST SERVICES (PTY) LTD
EAST RAND PROPRIETARY MINES LTD (30%)
ELDOR FARMS (PTY) LTD
FRANTZINASRUST BOSBOU (EDMS) BPK
GAMAGARA MINING CO. (PTY) LTD
GEOTEST (PTY) LTD
HUBERTUS ESTATE (PTY) LTD
INLOOP BOSBOU (EDMS) BPK
KHUTALA MINING SERVICES (PTY) LTD
KOUDELAGER CONSOLIDATED ANTHRACITE MINES
MAJUBA COLLIERY (PTY) LTD
MARICO FLUORSPAR (PTY) LTD
MARIOSCA LANDGOED (EDMS) BPK
MIDDELBURG MINE SERVICES (PTY) LTD
MIDDLEBURG MINE
MINCHARLES ESTATE (PTY) LTD
MINNAAR-WITBANK COLLIERY LTD
MOOIDRAAI MINING (PTY) LTD
MOSEGA FLUORSPAR WORKS (PTY) LTD
OMNIA MINING CO. (PTY) LTD
OSTRAL BELEGGINGS (EDMS) BPK
P & M DU TOIT TIMBERS (PTY) LTD
P.Q.R. SERVICES (PTY) LTD
PALM SPRINGS ESTATES (PTY) LTD

PAN AFRICAN EXPLORATION SYNDICATE (PTY)
PILGRIMS REST ESTATES LIMITED
RAND MINES (MINING & SERVICES) LTD
RAND MINES LANDS LIMITED
RAND MINES MILLING & MINING CO. LTD
RAND MINES PROPERTIES LTD
RAND MINES WINDHOEK EXPLORATION (PTY) LT
RANDCOAL LTD
RHOMBUS SANDS LTD
RHOSAND MINING SERVICES (PTY) LTD
RIETSPRUIT OPENCAST SERVICES (PTY) LTD
RMB ALLOYS (PTY) LTD
ROTTCHER & FUNKE (PTY) LTD
SPA CONSOLIDATED ANTHRACITE MINES (PTY)
SUNFORMGER (PTY) LTD
TRANSVAAL & DELGOA BAY INVESTMENT CO. LT
TRANSVAAL CONSOLIDATED LAND & EXPLORATIO
TRANSVAAL GOLD MINING ESTATES LTD
UMGALA COLLIERY LTD
UNION COLLIERIES INVESTMENTS LTD
UNION COLLIERIES LTD
UNION FREE STATE DEVELOPMENT CORPORATION
VANSA VANADIUM SA LTD (50%)
VIRGINIA-MERRIESPRUIT INVESTMENTS LTD
ZIANA ESTATES (PTY) LTD

INVESTMENTS

BLYVOORUITZICHT GOLD MINING CO. LTD (5%)
BONLEAU INVESTMENTS (PTY) LTD (150000000)
BRACKEN MINES LTD (500SH)
BRACKLANDS PROPERTIES (PTY) LTD (141750 SH)
CACTUS INVESTMENTS (PTY) LTD (PREFS) (1770000 SH)
CAPE INVESTMENT BANK HOLDINGS LTD (504900SH)
DOORNFONTEIN GOLD MINING CO. LTD (500SH)
DURBAN ROODEPOORT DEEP LTD (15%)
EAST RAND GOLD & URANIUM CO (80000 SH)
EAST RAND PROPRIETARY MINES LTD (PREFS) (350000 SH)
HARMONY GOLD MINING CO LTD (3736151 SH)
IMPALA PLATINUM HOLDINGS LTD (267800 SH)
KINROSS MINES LTD (500 SH)
LESLIE GOLD MINES LTD (500SH)
LIBANON GOLD MINING CO LTD (9600 SH)
NATAL ASSOCIATED COLLIERIES (PTY) LTD (12329 SH)
RICHARDS BAY COAL TERMINAL CO LTD (93794 SH)
RUSTENBURG PLATINUM HOLDINGS LTD (224800 SH)
ST. HELENA GOLD MINES LTD (500SH)
TRANSVAAL COAL OWNERS ASSOC. (1923) (PTY (01052 SH)
VAAL REEFS EXPLORATION & MINING CO LTD (500 SH)
WEST RAND CON. MINES LTD (1200SH)
WESTERN DEEP LEVELS LTD (500 SH)
WINKELHAAK MINES LTD (500SH)
ZANDPAN GOLD MIN. CO. LTD (1673700SH)

RAND MINES PROPERTIES LTD

ABBREVIATION : R-M-PROPS

JSE SHORT CODE : RMP

SECTOR : Mining Financial-Mining Holding

SHAREHOLDERS

Who Owns Whom's Assessment of the Identity of the Ultimate Controlling Shareholder:
SA MUTUAL VIA BARLOWS

SHAREHOLDER	PERCENTAGE 1992	1991
RAND MINES LTD	56.8	56.8
BARLOW GENERAL INV LTD	19.6	19.6
FIRST NAT NOM P/L	4.7	4.8
UK BRANCH REGISTER CONTROL ACCOUNT	1.8	1.5
MAX SEGAL HLDGS P/L	1.1	1.1
TOTAL	83.9	83.8

DIRECTORS :
BULTERMAN GH ,DUNNINGHAM GW ,DYER DW ,HALL AB
HALL JC ,JAFFE CA ,LAUTRE RE ,STEVENS IG
STEYN CG (Managing Director),TURNER JPS
WATT DT (Chairman

REGISTRATION NUMBER : 68/01239/06

REGISTERED OFFICE
15th Floor, The Corner House, 63 Fox Street
Johannesburg
2092
TEL: 011-491 2911
FAX: 011-834 5936

TRANSFER SECRETARY
Rand Registrars Ltd
P O Box 82549, Southdale
2135
TEL: 011-835 1016

COMPANY SECRETARY
Rand Mines (Mining & Services) Ltd

NATURE OF BUSINESS
The company controls subsidiaries engaged in township development & investment mainly on the central Witwatersrand, and in the treatment of mine residues primarily for the recovery of gold.

BANKERS :
First National Bank of SA Ltd

AUDITORS :
Coopers Theron Du Toit

FAMILIAR BRAND NAMES
N/A

CONTRIBUTION BY ACTIVITY
Property (% of turnover) (23.0%)
Gold Recovery (77.0%)

YEAR END : September

DIVIDEND : Ords R1

Interim No 28	(Ldr)18/05/90	(Pay)22/06/90	Amt(c)40
Final No 29	(Ldr)09/11/90	(Pay)02/01/91	Amt(c)100
Interim No 30	(Ldr)17/05/91	(Pay)21/06/91	Amt(c)40
Final No 31	(Ldr)08/11/91	(Pay)02/01/92	Amt(c)80
Special No 32	(Ldr)08/11/91	(Pay)02/01/92	Amt(c)100
Interim No 33	(Ldr)15/05/92	(Pay)19/06/92	Amt(c)30
Final No 34	(Ldr)13/11/92	(Pay)05/01/93	Amt(c)55

NUMBER OF EMPLOYEES : 178

CAPITAL STRUCTURE

	AUTHORISED	ISSUED
Ords R1	15000000	12403337

FINANCIAL STATISTICS (AT FINANCIAL YEAR END)

(Amts in R'000)	1991 Sep	1990 Sep	1989 Sep	1988 Sep	1987
Ord S/H Int	149841	158366	154803	147152	133020
Long Trm Loans	36009	38037	38511	44984	42954
Iss Ord Share	12403	12403	12403	12403	12403
Total Liab	94492	85940	86678	72892	70752
Current Liab	58483	47903	48167	27908	27798
Total Assets	244333	244306	241481	220044	188503
Current Assets	67426	71559	67214	44765	12529
Debtors	9480	4889	11317	25135	-
Inventory	4820	5049	4735	4640	12529
Turnover	180603	172168	165702	154150	104687
Oper Profit	19915	22179	34807	42272	27579
Interest Paid	135	256	677	-	88
Tax Paid	12432	13054	14351	13991	8162
Prf af Int&Tax	18825	21085	25739	28281	19329
Prf att Ord Sh	18762	20928	25455	27802	19329
Btm Line Earn	18762	20928	25016	29016	19329
Dividend Paid	27287	17365	17365	14884	9923
Mkt Prce(c) YE	1350	1350	2200	1850	3600
Depreciation	11672	11265	12179	10183	-

PER SHARE STATISTICS (CENTS)

Net Asst Val	1208.10	1276.84	1248.11	1186.42	1072.48
Net Earnings	151.00	169.00	205.00	224.10	-
Dividends	120.00	140.00	140.00	120.00	-
Cash Flow	234.06	266.09	345.21	404.85	155.84

RATIOS AND OTHER INFORMATION

Mrk Cap(R000)	167441	167441	272866	229456	446508
Current Ratio	1.15	1.49	1.40	1.60	0.45
Quik/Acid Tst	1.07	1.39	1.30	1.44	-
A/C Rec T/ovr	19.05	35.22	14.64	6.13	-
Tot Ass T/ovr	0.74	0.70	0.69	0.70	0.56
Debt/Ass Rat	0.26	0.22	0.23	0.16	0.38
L T L Tot Ass	0.02	0.03	0.03	0.04	0.23
Debt to Eqity	0.43	0.34	0.36	0.25	0.53
Interest Cover	147.52	86.64	51.41	-	313.40
Oper Prof Mrg	11.03	12.88	21.01	27.42	26.34
Net Prof Marg%	10.39	12.16	15.36	18.04	18.46
Ret on Assets	12.85	14.08	16.88	19.21	14.63
Ret on Equity%	12.52	13.21	16.44	18.89	14.53
Price/Earnings	8.94	7.99	10.73	8.26	-
Divid Cover	1.26	1.21	1.46	1.87	-
Divid Yield	8.89	10.37	6.36	6.49	-
Earning Yield%	11.19	12.52	9.32	12.11	-
NAV % Mrk Pr	89.49	94.58	56.73	64.13	29.79
Effec Tax Rate	44.03	35.87	22.87	3.54	29.69
Def Interval	0.25	0.22	0.18	0.16	2.22
Sus Grth Rate	-5.69	2.25	5.23	8.78	7.07

SUBSIDIARY & ASSOCIATED COMPANIES

AGATE INVESTMENTS (PTY) LTD
AMETHYST PROPERTIES (PTY) LTD
CENTRAL WAREHOUSING LTD
CITY DEEP, LTD
CONSOLIDATED MAIN REEF MINES & ESTATE, L
CROWN CRUSHERS ESTATES (PTY) LTD
CROWN MINES, LTD
D.I S.C.O. (PTY) LTD
DAVE PROPERTIES (PTY) LTD
DECENTRALIZED OFFICES LTD
ENCO (PTY) LTD
FERREIRA ESTATE & INVESTMENT CO. LTD
GELDENHUIS DEEP LTD
GREAT STORAGE LTD
GREEN SPACE LTD
INDUSTRIAL ZONE LTD
JACKMORE INVESTMENTS (PTY) LTD
MANAGED PROPERTY INVESTMENTS (PTY) LTD
NEW CANADA PROPERTIES (PTY) LTD
RAND MINES MILLING & MINING CO. LTD
RMP BROKERS LTD
RMP HOLDINGS LTD
RMP MANAGEMENT SERVICES LTD
SELBY EXTENSION FOUR LTD
STORMILL (PTY) LTD
TRANSVAAL GOLD MINING ESTATES LTD
TREU ROAD INDUSTRIAL PROPERTIES LTD
TRIPSWITCH PROPERTIES (PTY) LTD
WADEVILLE INVESTMENT CO. (PTY) LTD

INVESTMENTS

None

RANDCOAL LTD

ABBREVIATION : RANDCOL

JSE SHORT CODE : RNC

SECTOR : Mining-Coal

SHAREHOLDERS

Who Owns Whom's Assessment of the Identity of the Ultimate Controlling Shareholder:
SA MUTUAL VIA BARLOWS

SHAREHOLDER	PERCENTAGE 1992	1991
RAND MINES LTD	70.5	70.5
ANGLO-TRANSVAAL COLLIERIES LTD	10.5	10.5
SA MUTUAL	5.0	4.8
LIBERTY LIFE ASSOC OF AFRICA LTD	1.9	1.9
MOMENTUM LIFE ASSURE LTD	1.7	2.0
FOX STREET NOM P/L	1.2	1.0
STD BANK NOM TVL P/L	---	1.1
TOTAL	90.8	91.7

DIRECTORS :
BENFIELD IL ,BOSTOCK DSL
COOK AB (Dep. Chair. & Chief Exec.),CROWE DJ
DU TOIT RL ,HALL JC ,HAWARDEN MW ,MACLEOD FD
MOHRING RP ,PARK GH ,SEALEY AA (Chairman)
STEVENS IG ,TURNER RMIW ,WATT DT ,WILSON RAD
ZOLEZZI N (Managing Director

REGISTRATION NUMBER : 01/01358/06

REGISTERED OFFICE
Randcoal House, 21 Chaplin Road
Illovo
2196
TEL: 011-441 1611

TRANSFER SECRETARY
Rand Registrars Ltd
P O Box 82549, Southdale
2135
TEL: 011-835 1016

COMPANY SECRETARY
Rand Mines (Mining & Services) Ltd

NATURE OF BUSINESS
Wit Cols is a Rand Mines Company which operates coal mines in the Transvaal, Free State and Natal, these include:- Douglas Colliery, Khutala, Duvha, Wolvekrans, Van Dyks Drift, Zimbutu, Middelburg, Majuba, Klipspruit, Umgala, Utrecht, Welgedacht, and Rietspruit (50%)

BANKERS :
Standard Bank of SA Ltd
First National Bank of SA Ltd

AUDITORS :
Deloitte Pim Goldby

FAMILIAR BRAND NAMES
N/A

CONTRIBUTION BY ACTIVITY
Export (% Tons Sold) (33.8%)
Inland (23.4%)
Eskom (42.8%)

YEAR END : September

DIVIDEND :Ords R2

Interim No 167	(Ldr)04/05/90	(Pay)25/05/90	Amt(c)210
Final No 168	(Ldr)02/11/90	(Pay)23/11/90	Amt(c)390
Interim No 169	(Ldr)10/05/91	(Pay)30/05/91	Amt(c)210

DIVIDEND :Ords 20c

Final No 170	(Ldr)08/11/91	(Pay)29/11/91	Amt(c)39
Interim No 171	(Ldr)15/05/92	(Pay)04/06/92	Amt(c)23
Final No 172	(Ldr)06/11/92	(Pay)27/11/92	Amt(c)37

NUMBER OF EMPLOYEES : 11900

CAPITAL STRUCTURE

	AUTHORISED	ISSUED
Ords 20c	150000000	102414637

FINANCIAL STATISTICS (AT FINANCIAL YEAR END)

(Amts in R'000)	1992 Sep	1991 Sep	1990 Sep	1989 Sep	1988 Sep
Ord S/H Int	1138872	1027952	736400	831734	711326
Long Trm Loans	913496	796860	616563	384357	342896
Iss Ord Share	102415	102415	7825	7825	7825
Total Liab	1245217	1077610	762837	561298	509483
Current Liab	331721	280750	146274	176941	166587
Total Assets	2384089	2105562	1499237	1393032	1220809
Current Assets	343019	291780	167966	208218	204008
Debtors	200964	164328	78365	108893	92716
Inventory	103212	97244	83975	22815	7909
Turnover	1620863	1244360	1087100	795508	542847
Oper Profit	222720	198064	190807	174124	74365
Interest Paid	48841	51987	51603	18048	15632
Tax Paid	5383	2211	1474	4272	4126
Prf af Int&Tax	172383	145028	143968	163444	64376
Prf att Ord Sh	172369	145028	143968	163444	64376
Btm Line Earn	172369	135901	143968	163444	64376
Dividend Paid	61449	46949	46949	43036	29734
Mkt Prce(c) YE	875	1325	970	7200	5000

PER SHARE STATISTICS (CENTS)

Net Asst Val	1112.02	1003.71	9410.86	10629.19	9090.43
Net Earnings	168.00	185.00	184.00	2089.00	823.00
Dividends	60.00	60.00	60.00	550.00	380.00
Cash Flow	168.30	185.34	183.99	2088.74	822.70

RATIOS AND OTHER INFORMATION

Mrk Cap(R000)	896131	1356999	75903	563400	391250
Current Ratio	1.03	1.04	1.15	1.18	1.22
Quik/Acid Tst	0.72	0.69	0.57	1.05	1.18
A/C Rec T/ovr	8.07	7.57	13.87	7.31	5.85
Tot Ass T/ovr	0.68	0.59	0.73	0.57	0.44
Debt/Ass Rat	0.52	0.51	0.51	0.40	0.42
L T L Tot Ass	0.38	0.38	0.41	0.28	0.28
Debt to Eqity	1.09	1.05	1.04	0.67	0.72
Interest Cover	4.57	3.81	3.75	9.76	4.82
Oper Prof Mrg	13.74	15.92	17.55	21.89	13.70
Net Prof Marg%	10.63	11.65	13.24	20.55	11.86
Ret on Assets	9.50	9.46	13.14	13.34	6.89
Ret on Equity%	15.14	14.11	19.55	19.65	9.05
Price/Earnings	5.21	7.16	5.27	3.45	6.08
Divid Cover	2.80	3.08	3.07	3.80	2.17
Divid Yield	6.86	4.53	6.19	7.64	7.60
Earning Yield%	19.20	13.96	18.97	29.01	16.46
NAV % Mrk Pr	127.09	75.75	970.19	147.63	181.81
Effec Tax Rate	0.81	0.19	1.03	2.80	6.42
Def Interval	4.60	4.80	3.94	2.37	5.35
Sus Grth Rate	9.74	9.54	13.17	14.48	4.87

SUBSIDIARY & ASSOCIATED COMPANIES

ALBION COLLIERIES LTD
BLACK DIAMOND COLLIERY LTD
CONSOLIDATED MARSFIELD COLLIERIES LTD
CORGROUP (JUPITER) INVESTMENTS LTD
DOUGLAS COLLIERY LTD
DOUGLAS LAND AND MINERAL HOLDINGS (PTY)
DUVHA OPENCAST SERVICES (PTY) LTD
KHUTALA MINING SERVICES (PTY) LTD
MAJUBA COLLIERY (PTY) LTD
MANHATTAN SYNDICATE LTD
MINCHARLES ESTATE (PTY) LTD
MINNAAR-WITBANK COLLIERY LTD
PQR SERVICES (PTY) LTD
UNION COLLIERIES INVESTMENTS LTD
UNION COLLIERIES LTD
WELGEDACHT EXPLORATION CO LTD

INVESTMENTS

DURBAN COAL TERMINAL COMPANY LTD (210572 SH)
NATAL ASSOCIATED COLLIERIES (PTY) LTD (12329 SH)

RANDEX LTD

ABBREVIATION : RANDEX

JSE SHORT CODE : RDX

SECTOR : Mining-Exploration

SHAREHOLDERS

Who Owns Whom's Assessment of the Identity of the Ultimate Controlling Shareholder: SANLAM VIA GENBEL

SHAREHOLDER	PERCENTAGE 1992	1991
ABSA NOM P/L	63.1	---

CMB NOM P/L	10.3	---
SA MUTUAL	8.0	8.0
EAST DAGGAFONTEIN MINES LTD	5.6	5.6
INDO-CHINA NOM P/L	2.3	---
STD BANK NOM TVL P/L	1.2	1.2
INDO-CHINA NOM SA P/L	---	2.3
SANLAM	---	10.3
VOLKSKAS NOM P/L	---	62.2
TOTAL	90.5	89.6

DIRECTORS :
BOTHA AD (Deputy Chairman & M.D.)
DE BEER TL (Chairman),SANER MG
VON CHRISTIERSON CI ,WOOD CD

REGISTRATION NUMBER : 05/06778/06

REGISTERED OFFICE
General Mining Building, 6 Hollard Street
Johannesburg
2001
TEL: 011-376 2440
FAX: 011-834 7016

TRANSFER SECRETARY
Central Registrars Ltd
P O Box 4844, Johannesburg
2000
TEL: 011-331 0051

COMPANY SECRETARY
OG Connellan

NATURE OF BUSINESS
Randex participates in mineral rights ventures in Southern Africa.

BANKERS :
First National Bank of SA Ltd, Volkskas Ltd

AUDITORS :
Deloitte & Touche

FAMILIAR BRAND NAMES
N/A

CONTRIBUTION BY ACTIVITY
N/A

YEAR END : June

DIVIDEND :15/08/91 and 15/01/92

NUMBER OF EMPLOYEES : 1360

CAPITAL STRUCTURE

	AUTHORISED	ISSUED
Ords 25c	164500000	90134170

FINANCIAL STATISTICS (AT FINANCIAL YEAR END)

(Amts in R'000)	1992 Jun	1991 Jun	1990 Jun	1989 Jun	1987
Ord S/H Int	23546	31074	35252	92053	8156
Long Trm Loans	-	-	-	-	1982
Iss Ord Share	90134	90134	90134	85991	-
Total Liab	4636	7373	9172	14873	3964
Current Liab	4636	7373	9172	14873	1982
Total Assets	28182	38447	40730	106926	14265
Intang Assets	*	*	3694	*	*
Current Assets	23356	25244	32303	32081	4127
Debtors	1868	2914	2177	2488	-
Inventory	-	-	-	-	4127
Turnover	-	-	-	-	24253
Oper Profit	-643	-1239	1450	-7157	414
Tax Paid	-	-	-	-	118
Prf af Int&Tax	1514	2112	5007	-7157	296
Prf att Ord Sh	1514	2112	5007	-7157	296
Btm Line Earn	-6904	-3282	-9243	-7157	296
Mkt Prce(c) YE	50	125	290	230	580

PER SHARE STATISTICS (CENTS)

Net Asst Val	26.12	34.48	35.01	107.05	-
Net Earnings	0.02	0.02	5.70	-118.00	-
Cash Flow	1.68	2.34	5.70	-8.32	-

RATIOS AND OTHER INFORMATION

Mrk Cap(R000)	45067	112668	261389	197779	-
Current Ratio	5.04	3.42	3.52	2.16	2.08
Quik/Acid Tst	5.04	3.42	3.52	2.16	-
Tot Ass T/ovr	-	-	-	-	1.70
Debt/Ass Rat	0.16	0.19	0.23	0.14	0.28
L T L Tot Ass	-	-	-	-	0.14
Debt to Eqity	0.20	0.24	0.26	0.16	0.49
Oper Prof Mrg	-	-	-	-	1.71
Net Prof Marg%	-	-	-	-	1.22
Ret on Assets	5.37	5.49	12.29	-6.69	2.90
Ret on Equity%	6.43	6.80	14.20	-7.77	3.63
Price/Earnings	2500.00	6250.00	50.88	-1.95	-
Earning Yield%	0.04	0.02	1.97	-51.30	-
NAV % Mrk Pr	52.25	27.58	12.07	46.54	-
Effec Tax Rate	-	-	-	-	28.50
Def Interval	-	-	-	-	6.70
Sus Grth Rate	6.43	6.80	14.20	-7.77	3.63

SUBSIDIARY & ASSOCIATED COMPANIES

DULLAMID HOLDINGS (PTY) LTD
JUNO EXPLORATION (PTY) LTD
RAND EXTENSIONS & EXPLORATION LTD
RANDEX NAMIBIA (PTY) LTD
RANDEX PLATINUM HOLDINGS (PTY) LTD

INVESTMENTS

BENGUELA CONCESSIONS LTD (4%)
LUCAS BLOCK MINERALS LTD (132 SH)
LYDENBURG EXPLORATION LTD (2,8%)
MARANDA MINING CO (PTY) LTD (620 SH)
SOUTHERN PLATREEF MINING CO LTD (10,5%)
WELTEVREDEN MINES LTD (5,4%)

RANDFONTEIN ESTATES GOLD MINING CO WITS LTD

ABBREVIATION : RANDFONTN

JSE SHORT CODE : RFN

SECTOR : Gold-Rand & others

SHAREHOLDERS

Who Owns Whom's Assessment of the Identity of the Ultimate Controlling Shareholder:
ANGLO AMERICAN VIA JCI

SHAREHOLDER	PERCENTAGE 1992	1991
STD BANK NOM TVL P/L	38.0	36.2
LONDON REGISTER ACCOUNT	12.3	11.9
CMB NOM P/L	10.1	---
FIRST NAT NOM P/L	9.3	8.8
INDO-CHINA NOM P/L	4.4	5.0
EIGHTY ONE MAIN STREET NOM LTD	3.8	3.0
SA MUTUAL	2.6	3.4
DEPOSITARY NOM INC	1.6	---
MINU NOM LTD	1.5	1.5
SOUTHERN LIFE ASSOC LTD	1.1	3.8
FOX STREET NOM P/L	---	1.6
INDO-CHINA NOM SA P/L	---	5.0
SANLAM	---	9.3
TOTAL	84.8	89.5

DIRECTORS :
CONN WP (Financial Director),CROSS GMW
MAXWELL KW (Chairman)
NAIRN WA (Managing Director),SCOTT-RUSSELL H DR
SIBIYA G DR,WANBLAD GP

REGISTRATION NUMBER : 01/00251/06

REGISTERED OFFICE
Consolidated Building, Fox & Harrison Streets
Johannesburg
2001
TEL: 011-373 9111
FAX: 011-836 6130

TRANSFER SECRETARY
Consolidated Share Registrars Ltd
P O Box 61051, Marshalltown
2107
TEL: 011-492 1620

COMPANY SECRETARY
Johannesburg Consolidated Inv Co Ltd

NATURE OF BUSINESS
The company conducts gold mining operations in the districts of Randfontein, Westonaria & Roodepoort.

BANKERS :
Standard Bank of SA Ltd

AUDITORS :
Deloitte & Touche

FAMILIAR BRAND NAMES
N/A

CONTRIBUTION BY ACTIVITY
N/A

YEAR END : June

DIVIDEND : Ords 20c

Interim No 109	(Ldr)12/01/90	(Pay)06/02/90	Amt(c)40
Final No 110	(Ldr)13/07/90	(Pay)03/08/90	Amt(c)60
Interim No 111	(Ldr)11/01/91	(Pay)05/02/91	Amt(c)20
Final No 112	(Ldr)21/06/91	(Pay)19/07/91	Amt(c)40
Interim No 113	(Ldr)10/01/92	(Pay)04/02/92	Amt(c)25
Final No 114	(Ldr)17/07/92	(Pay)07/08/92	Amt(c)60

NUMBER OF EMPLOYEES : 13483

CAPITAL STRUCTURE

	AUTHORISED	ISSUED
Ords 20c	61135530	61135530

FINANCIAL STATISTICS (AT FINANCIAL YEAR END)

(Amts in R'000)	1992 Jun	1991 Jun	1990 Jun	1989 Jun	1988 Jun
Ord S/H Int	2119532	1974974	1872840	1797688	1675090
Long Trm Loans	72035	64014	73521	41729	30689
Iss Ord Share	61136	61136	61136	6114	6114
Total Liab	333355	272330	260064	238739	203791
Current Liab	261320	208316	186543	197010	173102
Total Assets	2452887	2247304	2132904	2036427	1878881
Current Assets	337312	247547	203448	210639	184576
Debtors	37999	30009	34548	20127	16138
Inventory	47348	63168	57548	26717	27398
Turnover	1037649	921700	906917	862618	772156
Oper Profit	226285	131412	144198	225791	288400
Interest Paid	2489	2395	1212	-	-
Tax Paid	35633	13134	14576	23717	21890
Prf af Int&Tax	196523	121910	153192	202074	266510
Prf att Ord Sh	196523	121910	153192	202074	266510
Btm Line Earn	196523	121910	153192	202074	266870
Dividend Paid	51965	36681	61135	79476	70306
Mkt Prce(c) YE	1510	1475	1825	20000	25750

PER SHARE STATISTICS (CENTS)

Net Asst Val	3466.91	3230.46	3063.40	29402.81	27397.61
Net Earnings	321.00	199.00	251.00	3305.00	4359.00
Dividends	85.00	60.00	100.00	1300.00	1150.00
Cash Flow	321.45	199.41	250.58	3305.10	4359.01

RATIOS AND OTHER INFORMATION

Mrk Cap(R000)	923154	901756	1115732	1222800	1574355
Current Ratio	1.29	1.19	1.09	1.07	1.07
Quik/Acid Tst	1.11	0.89	0.78	0.93	0.91
A/C Rec T/ovr	27.31	30.71	26.25	42.86	47.85
Tot Ass T/ovr	0.42	0.41	0.43	0.42	0.41
Debt/Ass Rat	0.14	0.12	0.11	0.12	0.11
L T L Tot Ass	0.03	0.03	0.03	0.02	0.02
Debt to Eqity	0.16	0.14	0.13	0.13	0.12
Interest Cover	94.27	57.39	121.91	-	-
Oper Prof Mrg	21.81	14.26	15.90	26.18	37.35
Net Prof Marg%	18.94	13.23	16.89	23.43	34.52
Ret on Assets	9.57	6.12	7.92	11.09	15.35
Ret on Equity%	9.27	6.17	8.18	11.24	15.91
Price/Earnings	4.70	7.41	7.27	6.05	5.91
Divid Cover	3.78	3.32	2.51	2.54	3.79
Divid Yield	5.63	4.07	5.48	6.50	4.47
Earning Yield%	21.26	13.49	13.75	16.53	16.93
NAV % Mrk Pr	229.60	219.01	167.86	147.01	106.40
Effec Tax Rate	15.79	10.88	7.13	10.50	7.59
Def Interval	0.02	0.04	0.03	0.24	0.16
Sus Grth Rate	6.82	4.32	4.92	6.82	11.71

SUBSIDIARY & ASSOCIATED COMPANIES

None

INVESTMENTS

VENTERSPOST GOLD MINING CO LTD (DEF ORDS (1272000 SH)

RAPTOR MOTOR HOLDINGS LTD

ABBREVIATION : RAPTOR

JSE SHORT CODE : RAP

SECTOR : Development Capital Market

SHAREHOLDERS

Who Owns Whom's Assessment of the Identity of the Ultimate Controlling Shareholder:
DA KHONAT VIA SOUTHERN MOTORS

SHAREHOLDER	PERCENTAGE 1992	1991
SOUTHERN MOTOR HOLDINGS LTD	64.2	---
ADRIGOLE INV P/L	14.8	---
DADA I N M	9.9	---
MOONDA E S	9.9	---
M&PD ELECTRONICS LTD	---	90.0
ADENDORFF G & OTHERS	---	6.6
TOTAL	98.8	96.6

DIRECTORS :
DADA AS ,DADA INM ,KHONAT DA (Chairman)
MOONDA ES (Sales Director)
VAN HEERDEN HHL (Managing Director

REGISTRATION NUMBER : 81/08223/06

REGISTERED OFFICE
49 Van Staden Street, Rustenburg
0300
TEL: 0142-21 026
FAX: 0142-21 026

TRANSFER SECRETARY
Central Registrars Ltd
P O Box 4844, Johannesburg
2000
TEL: 011-331 0051

COMPANY SECRETARY
E S Moonda

NATURE OF BUSINESS
The company conducts a motor garage, fitting and service station, and the sale of new & used motor vehicles, & holds the Rustenburg Toyota franchise.

BANKERS :
Standard Bank of SA Ltd

AUDITORS :
Price Waterhouse Meyernel

FAMILIAR BRAND NAMES
RUSTENBURG TOYOTA

CONTRIBUTION BY ACTIVITY
N/A

YEAR END : October

DIVIDEND : Ords no par value
Final (Ldr)28/02/92 (Pay)06/03/92 Amt(c)45

NUMBER OF EMPLOYEES : 49

CAPITAL STRUCTURE

	AUTHORISED	ISSUED
Ords no par value	16981404	3263208

FINANCIAL STATISTICS (AT FINANCIAL YEAR END)

(Amts in R'000)	1990 Jun	1989 Jun	1988 Feb	1987
Ord S/H Int	1699	25151	266	-
Long Trm Loans	-	922	270	-
Iss Ord Share	56888	53274	10000	-
Total Liab	-	21693	4505	-
Current Liab	-	20771	4235	-
Total Assets	1699	28677	4771	-
Intang Assets	*	18167	*	*
Current Assets	1699	27655	3621	-
Debtors	1699	9996	943	-
Inventory	-	17659	2678	-
Turnover	34124	69127	4414	-
Oper Profit	1177	3770	-1184	-
Interest Paid	2350	1996	-	-
Tax Paid	-	155	26	-
Prf af Int&Tax	-1173	1619	-1210	-
Prf att Ord Sh	-1258	1619	-1210	-
Btm Line Earn	-25258	1575	-2010	-
Mkt Prce(c) YE	8	75	35	-
Depreciation	149	310	153	-

PER SHARE STATISTICS (CENTS)

Net Asst Val	2.99	13.11	2.66	-
Net Earnings	-2.20	5.10	-12.10	-
Cash Flow	-1.95	6.04	-10.73	-

RATIOS AND OTHER INFORMATION

Mrk Cap(R000)	4551	39956	3500	-
Current Ratio	-	1.33	0.86	-
Quik/Acid Tst	-	0.48	0.22	-
A/C Rec T/ovr	20.08	6.92	4.68	-
Tot Ass T/ovr	20.08	2.41	0.93	-
Debt/Ass Rat	-	0.76	0.94	-
L T L Tot Ass	-	0.03	0.06	-
Debt to Eqity	-	0.86	16.94	-
Interest Cover	0.50	1.89	-	-
Oper Prof Mrg	3.45	5.45	-26.82	-
Net Prof Marg%	-3.69	2.34	-27.41	-
Ret on Assets	69.28	13.15	-24.82	-
Ret on Equity%	-74.04	6.44	-454.89	-
Price/Earnings	-3.64	14.71	-2.89	-
Earning Yield%	-27.50	6.80	-34.57	-
NAV % Mrk Pr	37.33	17.48	7.60	-
Effec Tax Rate	-	8.85	-3.55	-
Def Interval	-	4.17	-1.25	-
Sus Grth Rate	-74.04	6.44	-454.89	-

SUBSIDIARY & ASSOCIATED COMPANIES

CANADIAN & INTERFACE PRODUCTS (PTY) LTD
P D BLACKMAN ELECTRONICS (PTY) LTD

INVESTMENTS

None

REALESTATE DEVELOPMENT CO LTD

ABBREVIATION : RDC

SECTOR : Botswana Stock Exchange

SHAREHOLDERS

Who Owns Whom's Assessment of the Identity of the Ultimate Controlling Shareholder: GIACHETTI FAMILY

SHAREHOLDER	PERCENTAGE 1992	1991
REALESTATE FINANCIERE SA	46.7	---
CHOBE FINANCIAL CORPORATION LTD	23.3	---
MITS P/L	5.3	---
BOTSWANA MOTOR VEHICLE INSURANCE FUND	3.0	---
IGI BOTSWANA LIFE ASSURE LTD	3.0	---
PARK INV P/L	2.6	---
BARCLAYS BANK OF BOTSWANA STAFF PENS FUN	2.3	---
BANK OF BOTSWANA STAFF PENS FUND	1.5	---
BOTSWANA RAILWAYS STAFF PENS FUND	1.5	---
IGI BOTSWANA INSURANCE LTD	1.5	---
TOTAL	90.8	---

DIRECTORS :
GIACHETTI G ,GIACHETTI MA (Chairman),KHAMA DC MATENGE GW ,OSTANO V

REGISTRATION NUMBER : 92/10

REGISTERED OFFICE
1st Floor, Botsalano House
The Mall, Gabarone

TEL: 312641
FAX: 373441

TRANSFER SECRETARY
Coopers & Lybrand Services (Pty) Ltd
P O Box 702, Harare
Zimbabwe

TEL: 0926 34 702771

COMPANY SECRETARY
Coopers & Lybrand Services

NATURE OF BUSINESS
RDC is a holding company which,through its subsidi aries, acquires properties for development and investment purposes. The group acquires fully dev eloped and undeveloped commercial, industrial and residential properties, whether freehold or lease-hold, directly or through joint venture arrange-ments. RDC develops properties through outside contractors. Developed properties are usually retained for investment purposes under outside administration, but may also be sold.

BANKERS :
Barclays Bank of Botswana Ltd
Standard Chartered Bank

AUDITORS :
Deloitte Pim Goldby

FAMILIAR BRAND NAMES
N/A

CONTRIBUTION BY ACTIVITY
N/A

YEAR END : December

CAPITAL STRUCTURE

	AUTHORISED	ISSUED
Ords P1	50000000	18301784

FINANCIAL STATISTICS (AT FINANCIAL YEAR END)

(Amts in P)	1991 Dec
Ord S/H Int	25595
Long Trm Loans	2475
Iss Ord Share	18302
Total Liab	4860
Current Liab	2385
Total Assets	30455
Current Assets	887
Debtors	633
Turnover	2734
Oper Profit	2211
Interest Paid	138
Tax Paid	576
Prf af Int&Tax	1497
Prf att Ord Sh	1497
Btm Line Earn	1497
Dividend Paid	3225

PER SHARE STATISTICS (CENTS)

Net Asst Val	139.85
Net Earnings	8.20
Dividends	17.60
Cash Flow	8.18

RATIOS AND OTHER INFORMATION

Current Ratio	0.37
Quik/Acid Tst	0.37
A/C Rec T/ovr	4.32
Tot Ass T/ovr	0.09
Debt/Ass Rat	0.16
L T L Tot Ass	0.08
Debt to Eqity	0.19
Interest Cover	16.02
Oper Prof Mrg	80.87
Net Prof Marg%	54.75
Ret on Assets	7.26
Ret on Equity%	5.85
Divid Cover	0.47
Effec Tax Rate	27.79
Def Interval	0.60
Sus Grth Rate	-6.75

SUBSIDIARY & ASSOCIATED COMPANIES

914 KASANE (PTY) LTD (50%)
PLAZA (PTY) LTD
PLOTS 1124-1127, THE MALL (PTY) LTD
REALESTATE MANAGEMENT CO LTD
S.M.B (PTY) LTD

INVESTMENTS

None

REDGWOODS HOLDING LTD

ABBREVIATION : REGGIES

JSE SHORT CODE : REG

SECTOR : Industrial-Retailers & Wholesalers

SHAREHOLDERS

Who Owns Whom's Assessment of the Identity of the Ultimate Controlling Shareholder: WALTONS STATIONERY CO

SHAREHOLDER	PERCENTAGE 1992	1991
WALTONS STATIONERY CO LTD	59.9	60.0
REDGWOODS HLDGS LTD EMP CONTROL ACC	3.0	---
SHER C M	2.5	1.9
REDGWOODS HOLDINGS EXEC SHARE TRUST	2.0	2.1
CROUDACE A H	1.8	1.2
SA MUTUAL	1.8	1.8
YSKOR PENS FUND	1.8	1.8
CS TRUST	1.3	1.3
DALES R M	1.2	1.2
ANGLO AMERICAN CORP PENS FUND	---	1.6
DE BEERS PENS FUND	---	2.6
LUSTIG G	---	2.6
ROBARTS F E A	---	1.2
TOTAL	75.3	79.1

DIRECTORS :
BELL JA ,CHIMES LI
CROUDACE AH (Managing Director),MUIRHEAD AA
ROBARTS FEA (Chairman),SHER CM

REGISTRATION NUMBER : 87/01650/06

REGISTERED OFFICE
99 North Coast Road, Briardene
Durban
4051
TEL: 031-83 7051
FAX: 031-83 6059

TRANSFER SECRETARY
Mercantile Registrars Ltd
P O Box 1053, Johannesburg
2000
TEL: 011-333 8181

COMPANY SECRETARY
N J van der Merwe

NATURE OF BUSINESS
The group retails babyware, including toys, prams clothing and related goods via 83 retail outlets.

BANKERS :
First National Bank of SA Ltd

AUDITORS :
Ernst & Young

FAMILIAR BRAND NAMES
ELBE,MOTHERS WORLD,REDGWOODS TOY WORLD
REGGIES KIDS WORLD,SAFEWAY,TOYS-R-US

CONTRIBUTION BY ACTIVITY
N/A

YEAR END : February

DIVIDEND : Ords no par value

Dividend No 3	(Ldr)07/06/91	(Pay)28/06/91	Amt(c)1
Dividend No 4	(Ldr)05/06/92	(Pay)26/06/92	Amt(c)1.2

NUMBER OF EMPLOYEES : 535

CAPITAL STRUCTURE

	AUTHORISED	ISSUED
Ords no par value	100000000	62100000

FINANCIAL STATISTICS (AT FINANCIAL YEAR END)

(Amts in R'000)	1992 Feb	1991 Feb	1990 Feb	1989 Feb	1988 Feb
Ord S/H Int	20548	19749	18750	19887	13772
Long Trm Loans	1172	2274	9073	13134	10414
Iss Ord Share	62100	62100	61600	61600	61100
Total Liab	13661	13921	22343	26513	20220
Current Liab	12489	11647	13270	13379	9806
Total Assets	31464	30925	37715	41415	33992
Intang Assets	2745	2745	3378	4985	*
Current Assets	24173	23825	29548	33839	26686
Debtors	5177	8529	6451	5872	4829
Inventory	18947	15265	22710	27341	20939
Turnover	78865	74650	74969	67653	54685
Oper Profit	3935	5953	7542	7254	6824
Interest Paid	1428	3251	7035	2564	980
Tax Paid	1446	1198	303	1746	1901
Prf af Int&Tax	1587	1591	337	3096	3942
Prf att Ord Sh	1544	1517	262	3096	3736
Btm Line Earn	1344	1642	-1592	3096	3736
Dividend Paid	745	621	-	1232	1466
Mkt Prce(c) YE	15	25	26	55	65
Depreciation	926	1187	1641	1298	830

PER SHARE STATISTICS (CENTS)

Net Asst Val	28.67	27.38	24.95	24.19	22.54
Net Earnings	2.50	2.50	0.40	5.10	6.10
Dividends	1.20	1.00	-	2.00	2.40
Cash Flow	4.88	5.00	2.69	7.18	7.24

RATIOS AND OTHER INFORMATION

Mrk Cap(R000)	9315	15525	16016	33880	39715
Current Ratio	1.94	2.05	2.23	2.53	2.72
Quik/Acid Tst	0.42	0.73	0.52	0.49	0.59
A/C Rec T/ovr	15.23	8.75	11.62	11.52	11.32
Tot Ass T/ovr	2.51	2.41	1.99	1.63	1.61
Debt/Ass Rat	0.41	0.44	0.59	0.63	0.59
L T L Tot Ass	0.02	0.07	0.24	0.31	0.30
Debt to Eqity	0.63	0.70	1.19	1.32	1.45
Interest Cover	2.76	1.83	1.07	2.83	6.96
Oper Prof Mrg	4.99	7.97	10.06	10.72	12.48
Net Prof Marg%	1.96	2.03	0.35	4.58	6.83
Ret on Assets	14.04	19.29	20.15	17.88	20.07
Ret on Equity%	7.51	7.68	1.40	15.57	27.13
Price/Earnings	6.00	10.00	65.00	10.78	10.66
Divid Cover	2.08	2.50	-	2.55	2.54
Divid Yield	8.00	4.00	-	3.64	3.69
Earning Yield%	16.67	10.00	1.54	9.27	9.38

NAV % Mrk Pr	191.12	109.53	95.98	43.98	34.68
Effec Tax Rate	30.60	32.52	88.91	14.87	19.40
Def Interval	0.23	0.86	8.79	3.51	2.72
Sus Grth Rate	3.89	4.54	1.40	9.37	16.48

SUBSIDIARY & ASSOCIATED COMPANIES

AKAL TOYS (PTY) LTD
BABY AND COMPANY (PTY) LTD
D'NAR DISTRIBUTORS (PTY) LTD
FIVE HUNDRED STRONG (PTY) LTD (50%)
LITTLE PEOPLE (PTY) LTD
LUDUS TRADING (PTY) LTD
MOTHERSWORLD (PTY) LTD
REDGWOODS (PTY) LTD
TOYBOX (PTY) LTD
TREASURE ISLAND (PTY) LTD

INVESTMENTS

None

REMBRANDT CONTROLLING INVESTMENTS LTD

ABBREVIATION : REMB-BEH

JSE SHORT CODE : RMB

SECTOR : Industrial-Tobacco & Match

SHAREHOLDERS

Who Owns Whom's Assessment of the Identity of the Ultimate Controlling Shareholder: RUPERT & HERTZOG FAMILIES VIA TIB

SHAREHOLDER	PERCENTAGE 1992	1991
TEGNIESE INV KORPORASIE BPK	40.6	40.6
CMB NOM P/L	10.8	---
TEGNIESE & INDUSTRIELE INV BPK	9.6	9.6
SA MUTUAL	7.1	7.3
STD BANK NOM TVL P/L	2.9	2.4
SOUTHERN LIFE ASSOC LTD	1.9	1.9
EIGHTY ONE MAIN STREET NOM LTD	1.9	---
ESCOM PENS & PROV FUND	1.1	1.1
YSKOR PENS FUND	1.1	1.1
SANLAM	---	2.7
SANKERN E/B	---	7.5
TOTAL	77.0	74.2

DIRECTORS :
DE VILLIERS JN ,ERASMUS PJ ,FRASER CA
HERTZOG E DE LA H DR,KOTZEE FP ,LEVENSTEIN EB
MALHERBE WS ,MARLOW DJ ,ROUX MJ
RUPERT AE DR (Chairman)
RUPERT JA (Managing Director),RUPERT JP
STEGMANN JA DR,STEINMETZ G ,STEYN PG
VAN DER ROSS RE ,VAN ZYL FW D

REGISTRATION NUMBER : 52/00002/06

REGISTERED OFFICE
Coetzier Street, Stellenbosch
7600
TEL: 02231-71645
FAX: 02231-832331

TRANSFER SECRETARY
Central Registrars Ltd
P O Box 4844, Johannesburg
2000
TEL: 011-331 0051

COMPANY SECRETARY
J C Engelbrecht

NATURE OF BUSINESS
An investment holding company with a controlling interest in JSE-quoted Rembrandt Group Ltd. The group interests consist mainly of investments in banking, forestry, timber processing, printing & packaging, financial services, engineering, life assurance, adhesives, medical services, mining, petrochemical products, portfolio investments, tobacco products, food, wine & spirits.

BANKERS :
N/A

AUDITORS :
Coopers Theron Du Toit

FAMILIAR BRAND NAMES
N/A

CONTRIBUTION BY ACTIVITY
Trade Mark Group (% net income) (43.8%)
Mining Interests (24.1%)
Industrial Interests (13.0%)
Financial Interests (7.5%)
Corporate Finance & Other (11.6%)

YEAR END : March

DIVIDEND : Ords 1c

Interim No 72	(Ldr)22/09/89	(Pay)16/10/89	Amt(c)6.48
Final No 73	(Ldr)23/03/90	(Pay)17/04/90	Amt(c)12.03
Interim No 74	(Ldr)21/09/90	(Pay)15/10/90	Amt(c)7.78
Final No 75	(Ldr)22/02/91	(Pay)28/02/91	Amt(c)14.43
Interim No 76	(Ldr)20/09/91	(Pay)15/10/91	Amt(c)9.33
Final No 77	(Ldr)21/02/92	(Pay)28/02/92	Amt(c)14.81
Special	(Ldr)21/02/92	(Pay)28/02/92	Amt(c)22.21

CAPITAL STRUCTURE

	AUTHORISED	ISSUED
Ords 1c	360000000	360000000

FINANCIAL STATISTICS (AT FINANCIAL YEAR END)

(Amts in R'000)	1992 Mar	1991 Mar	1990 Mar	1989 Mar	1988 Mar
Ord S/H Int	2812900	2359500	2018400	1657300	2745100
Long Trm Loans	3923600	3287500	2854700	1952500	2866200
Iss Ord Share	360000	360000	360000	360000	360000
Total Liab	4768300	4043000	3737300	2486700	3363500
Current Liab	844700	755500	882600	534200	497300
Total Assets	7484600	6301000	5692500	4144000	6108600
Intang Assets	96600	101500	63200	*	*
Current Assets	1551000	1030100	872000	1041500	947900
Debtors	339200	284000	226300	170000	165800
Inventory	843700	712900	599800	514100	357900
Oper Profit	934900	798600	643600	510800	452100
Interest Paid	59900	107700	101500	30000	17100
Tax Paid	426000	344800	281400	248500	195600
Prf af Int&Tax	747800	615700	489100	413700	438300
Prf att Ord Sh	480700	442000	384100	307000	378300

Btm Line Earn	598000	429800	409000	305500	367000
Dividend Paid	166900	80000	66600	53300	45300
Mkt Prce(c) YE	2050	1280	1070	685	820
Depreciation	64700	46000	37100	26800	15300

PER SHARE STATISTICS (CENTS)

Net Asst Val	754.53	627.22	543.11	460.36	762.53
Net Earnings	133.50	122.80	106.70	85.30	105.08
Dividends	46.35	22.21	18.51	14.81	12.58
Cash Flow	77.50	46.33	29.81	29.75	65.81

RATIOS AND OTHER INFORMATION

Mrk Cap(R000)	7380000	4608000	3852000	2466000	2952000
Current Ratio	1.84	1.36	0.99	1.95	1.91
Quik/Acid Tst	0.84	0.42	0.31	0.99	1.19
Debt/Ass Rat	0.14	0.15	0.18	0.15	0.09
L T L Tot Ass	0.03	0.03	0.02	0.02	0.01
Debt to Eqity	0.37	0.40	0.50	0.38	0.20
Interest Cover	19.43	9.58	8.22	22.00	38.07
Ret on Assets	20.09	22.07	20.90	22.22	13.23
Ret on Equity%	17.09	18.73	19.03	18.52	13.78
Price/Earnings	15.36	10.42	10.03	8.03	7.80
Divid Cover	2.88	5.53	5.76	5.76	8.35
Divid Yield	2.26	1.74	1.73	2.16	1.53
Earning Yield%	6.51	9.59	9.97	12.45	12.81
NAV % Mrk Pr	36.81	49.00	50.76	67.21	92.99
Effec Tax Rate	44.81	47.70	47.86	48.03	44.92
Def Interval	0.68	1.57	3.79	0.78	0.33
Sus Grth Rate	11.16	15.34	15.73	15.31	12.13

SUBSIDIARY & ASSOCIATED COMPANIES

REMBRANDT GROUP LTD

INVESTMENTS

None

REMBRANDT GROUP LTD

ABBREVIATION : REMGRO

JSE SHORT CODE : RMT

SECTOR : Industrial-Tobacco & Match

SHAREHOLDERS

Who Owns Whom's Assessment of the Identity of the Ultimate Controlling Shareholder:
RUPERT & HERTZOG FAMILIES VIA REMB BEH

SHAREHOLDER	PERCENTAGE 1992	1991
REMBRANDT CONTROLLING INV LTD	51.1	51.1
SA MUTUAL	6.8	6.9
STD BANK NOM TVL P/L	6.0	5.0
CMB NOM P/L	4.3	---
LIBERTY LIFE ASSOC OF AFRICA LTD	3.5	3.5
SOUTHERN LIFE ASSOC LTD	2.3	2.3
EIGHTY ONE MAIN STREET NOM LTD	2.0	1.7
FIRST NAT NOM P/L	1.7	1.7
YSKOR PENS FUND	1.1	1.1
SANLAM	---	1.1
SANKERN E/B	---	2.6
TOTAL	78.8	76.9

DIRECTORS :
FALCK DM ,FLACK PH
HERTZOG E DE LA H DR (Executive Vice Chairman)
KILIAN PJ DU PRE ,KRUGER JM ,MARREN AJW
MORRIS NJ ,MOSTERT DB
RUPERT JP (Executive Chairman),STEYN PG
VAN AS AC ,VAN WYK T ,VERMEULEN WJC
VISSER MH (Managing Director)

REGISTRATION NUMBER : 05/31037/06

REGISTERED OFFICE
Coetzier Street, Stellenbosch
7600
TEL: 02231-832333
FAX: 02231-71645

TRANSFER SECRETARY
Central Registrars Ltd
P O Box 4844, Johannesburg
2000
TEL: 011-331 0051

COMPANY SECRETARY
J C Engelbrecht

NATURE OF BUSINESS
An investment holding company with significant investments in a number of JSE-quoted companies & unquoted co's. Group interests include: banking, forestry, timber processing, printing & packaging, financial services, engineering, adhesives, life assurance, medical services, mining, petrochemical products, portfolio investments, tobacco products, food, wine & spirits.

BANKERS :
N/A

AUDITORS :
Coopers Theron Du Toit

FAMILIAR BRAND NAMES
SEE SUBSIDIARIES

CONTRIBUTION BY ACTIVITY
Trade Mark Group (% net income) (43.8%)
Mining Interests (24.1%)
Industrial Interests (13.0%)
Financial Services (7.5%)
Corporate & Other (11.6%)

YEAR END : March

DIVIDEND : Ords 1c

Interim No 79	(Ldr)22/09/89	(Pay)16/10/89	Amt(c)8.75
Final No 80	(Ldr)23/03/90	(Pay)17/04/90	Amt(c)16.25
Interim No 81	(Ldr)21/09/90	(Pay)15/10/90	Amt(c)10.5
Final No 82	(Ldr)22/02/91	(Pay)28/02/91	Amt(c)19.5
Interim No 83	(Ldr)20/09/91	(Pay)15/10/91	Amt(c)12.6
Final No 84	(Ldr)21/02/92	(Pay)28/02/92	Amt(c)20
Special	(Ldr)21/02/92	(Pay)28/02/92	Amt(c)30

CAPITAL STRUCTURE

	AUTHORISED	ISSUED
Ords 1c	522000000	522000000
6% Red Prefs R2	100000	0

FINANCIAL STATISTICS (AT FINANCIAL YEAR END)

(Amts in R'000)	1992 Mar	1991 Mar	1990 Mar	1989 Mar	1988 Mar
Ord S/H Int	5507200	4619600	3952100	3245100	2618600
Long Trm Loans	1228900	1027100	920900	364700	132700
Iss Ord Share	522000	522000	522000	522000	522000
Total Liab	2072700	1781900	1803200	898700	556800
Current Liab	843800	754800	882300	534000	424100
Total Assets	7483300	6300000	5692100	4097200	3175400
Intang Assets	96600	101500	63200	46600	*
Current Assets	1549700	1029100	871600	1041300	695000
Debtors	339200	284000	226300	170000	116700
Inventory	843700	712900	599600	514100	357900
Oper Profit	934900	798500	681600	515300	498800
Interest Paid	60100	107800	101500	34600	16600
Tax Paid	425900	344700	281400	248500	173200
Prf af Int&Tax	747700	615600	489000	413600	309000
Prf att Ord Sh	941100	865300	751900	600900	453000
Btm Line Earn	1170800	841400	800800	598000	449600
Dividend Paid	326800	156600	130500	104400	88700
Mkt Prce(c) YE	2875	1800	1430	925	1115
Depreciation	64700	46000	37100	26800	15300

PER SHARE STATISTICS (CENTS)

Net Asst Val	1036.51	865.54	745.00	612.74	501.65
Net Earnings	180.30	165.80	144.00	115.10	141.90
Dividends	62.60	30.00	25.00	20.00	17.00
Cash Flow	141.65	113.05	91.02	76.82	61.19

RATIOS AND OTHER INFORMATION

Mrk Cap(R000)	15007500	9396000	7464600	4828500	5820300
Current Ratio	1.84	1.36	0.99	1.95	1.64
Quik/Acid Tst	0.84	0.42	0.31	0.99	0.79
Debt/Ass Rat	0.14	0.15	0.18	0.15	0.15
L T L Tot Ass	0.03	0.03	0.02	0.02	0.02
Debt to Eqity	0.19	0.20	0.26	0.19	0.18
Interest Cover	19.37	9.57	8.59	19.21	30.05
Ret on Assets	20.09	22.07	20.90	22.59	20.40
Ret on Equity%	17.09	18.73	19.03	18.52	17.30
Price/Earnings	15.95	10.86	9.93	8.04	7.86
Divid Cover	2.88	5.53	5.76	5.76	8.35
Divid Yield	2.18	1.67	1.75	2.16	1.52
Earning Yield%	6.27	9.21	10.07	12.44	12.73
NAV % Mrk Pr	36.05	48.09	52.10	66.24	44.99
Effec Tax Rate	44.81	47.70	47.87	48.04	35.90
Def Interval	0.26	0.44	0.86	0.21	0.25
Sus Grth Rate	11.15	15.34	15.72	15.30	13.91

SUBSIDIARY & ASSOCIATED COMPANIES

ENTEK INVESTMENTS LTD
FALCONAIR LTD
FINANCIAL SECURITIES LTD
FRALEX LTD (39,2%)
GENCOR BEHEREND BPK (25,2%)
GFSA HOLDINGS LTD (40%)
HENKEL SA (PTY) LTD (50%)
HISTORICAL HOMES OF SA LTD
HUNTCOR LTD
INDUSTRIAL PARTNERSHIP INVESTMENTS LTD
INTERCONTINENTAL TOBACCO CO (PTY) LTD
LENCO (PTY) LTD (50%)
MATINDUS LTD
MEDI-CLINIC CORPORATION LTD (50%)
METKOR LTD (49,9%)
MFI INVESTMENTS (PTY) LTD
PARTNERSHIP IN INDUSTRY & MINING SA LTD
PARTNERSHIP IN PRINTING (PTY) LTD
PERSKOR BELEGGINGS LTD (28,4%)
PERSTAN (PTY) LTD
REMBRANDT FINANCE CORP LTD
REMBRANDT GROUP FINANCE CORP LTD
REMBRANDT SA LTD
REMBRANDT-KWV INVESTMENTS LTD (50%)
RUPERT INTERNATIONAL (PTY) LTD
RUPERT PARTNERSHIP IN INDUSTRY LTD
SAGECOR (PTY) LTD (50%)
STELLENRYK TRUST LTD
TEGNIESE MYNBELEGGINGS BPK
TOTAL SA (PTY) LTD (34,4%)
TRANS-HEX GROUP LTD (50%)
TRANSATLANTIC TOBACCO CO (PTY) LTD
UNIVERSA (PTY) LTD (39,4%)
VAN RIJN BELEGGINGSKORPORASIE BPK
W & A GILBEY (SA) (PTY) LTD (49%)

INVESTMENTS

AMALGAMATED BANKS OF SA LTD (12%)
BOLAND BANK LTD (9,9%)
DORBYL LTD (10%)
GOLD FIELDS OF SA LTD (17.3%)
LENCO HOLDINGS LTD (13,9%)
PRINTPAK LTD (19,6%)
SAGE HOLDINGS LTD (10.2%)

RENTMEESTER BELEGGINGS LTD

ABBREVIATION : RENTBEL

JSE SHORT CODE : RNT

SECTOR : Industrial-Industrial Holding

SHAREHOLDERS

Who Owns Whom's Assessment of the Identity of the Ultimate Controlling Shareholder: DIRECTORS CONTROL 37,48%

SHAREHOLDER	PERCENTAGE 1992	1991
RENTEKOR P/L	37.2	37.2
VERSPREIDE INV P/L	12.3	12.3
DE MUELENAERE J J G G	7.1	7.1
GROBBELAAR E J INSURANCE CO P/L	6.1	6.1
NOMINEES ONLY P/L	4.0	---
MAIZECOR PENS FUND	1.9	---
ROODE INV P/L	1.9	3.8
SPAARWINS LTD	1.7	1.7
VERMOOTEN J J TRUSTEES	1.7	1.7
PHILIP GUTKIN HOLDINGS P/L	1.6	2.1
MEDDENT ADMINISTRATORS P/L	1.6	---
DRAKENSBERG BOTTELIER P/L	1.0	1.0
FINABEL LTD	---	3.3
TOTAL	78.3	76.4

DIRECTORS :

BOSHOFF WH ,BOTHA DH DR,BREMER PHN (Chairman)
DE MUELENAERE GPMC DR,DE MUELENAERE JJGG PROF
DE MUELENAERE LGAGR DR,LAURIE DE G H ,POOLE H
VERMOOTEN JOACHIM (Managing Director)
VERMOOTEN JOHANNES

REGISTRATION NUMBER : 05/23539/06

REGISTERED OFFICE
102 Rentmeester Park, 74 Watermeyer Street
Val de Grace
0184
TEL: 012-86 2000
FAX: 012-86 4436

TRANSFER SECRETARY
Central Registrars Ltd
P O Box 4844, Johannesburg
2000
TEL: 011-331 0051

COMPANY SECRETARY
J P G Booysen

NATURE OF BUSINESS
An investment company deriving its income from dividends, interest and management fees.

BANKERS :
Volkskas Ltd, Central Merchant Bank Ltd

AUDITORS :
Meintjies Vermooten & Partners

FAMILIAR BRAND NAMES
N/A

CONTRIBUTION BY ACTIVITY
N/A

YEAR END : June

DIVIDEND : Ords 50c

Interim	(Ldr)21/02/90	(Pay)18/05/90	Amt(c)4
Final	(Ldr)18/09/90	(Pay)23/11/90	Amt(c)4

CAPITAL STRUCTURE

	AUTHORISED	ISSUED
Ords 50c	4000000	3625000

FINANCIAL STATISTICS (AT FINANCIAL YEAR END)

(Amts in R'000)	1991 Jun	1990 Jun	1989 Jun	1988 Jun	1987 Jun
Ord S/H Int	42824	33234	29151	26005	14652
Long Trm Loans	141755	125689	124234	103636	92220
Iss Ord Share	3625	3625	3625	3625	3625
Total Liab	217001	185843	190175	161924	144560
Current Liab	75246	60154	65941	58288	52340
Total Assets	255739	209590	210048	177827	159212
Intang Assets	4086	9487	9278	10102	*
Current Assets	66936	72049	71496	59547	56691
Debtors	26239	16634	22570	24166	22804
Inventory	12073	17019	20584	16934	17011
Turnover	134991	170076	180207	148693	138129
Oper Profit	-13746	-5311	7496	5478	6379
Interest Paid	6634	7664	6996	4774	4533
Tax Paid	-821	998	1948	1986	1047
Prf af Int&Tax	-8720	-3044	569	-1282	799
Prf att Ord Sh	-2658	2427	4412	2005	1222
Btm Line Earn	103	2457	4484	2289	1299
Dividend Paid	-	290	544	399	199
Mkt Prce(c) YE	500	490	450	550	380
Depreciation	4468	5167	4664	4646	3015

PER SHARE STATISTICS (CENTS)

Net Asst Val	1068.63	655.09	548.22	438.70	404.19
Net Earnings	-73.30	66.90	134.80	55.30	34.00
Dividends	-	8.00	15.00	11.00	5.50
Cash Flow	-130.43	69.19	190.32	101.41	76.66

RATIOS AND OTHER INFORMATION

Mrk Cap(R000)	18125	17763	16313	19938	13775
Current Ratio	0.89	1.20	1.08	1.02	1.08
Quik/Acid Tst	0.73	0.91	0.77	0.73	0.76
A/C Rec T/ovr	5.14	10.22	7.98	6.15	6.06
Tot Ass T/ovr	0.53	0.81	0.86	0.84	0.87
Debt/Ass Rat	0.36	0.37	0.41	0.45	0.86
L T L Tot Ass	0.07	0.08	0.10	0.12	0.53
Debt to Eqity	2.16	2.31	2.96	3.09	9.32
Interest Cover	-1.72	-0.38	1.36	1.15	1.41
Oper Prof Mrg	-10.18	-3.12	4.16	3.68	4.62
Net Prof Marg%	-1.97	1.43	2.45	1.35	0.88
Ret on Assets	0.99	5.07	6.10	4.54	4.54
Ret on Equity%	-6.21	7.30	15.13	7.71	8.34
Price/Earnings	-6.82	7.32	3.34	9.95	11.18
Divid Cover	-	8.36	8.99	5.03	6.18
Divid Yield	-	1.63	3.33	2.00	1.45
Earning Yield%	-14.66	13.65	29.96	10.05	8.95
NAV % Mrk Pr	213.73	133.69	121.83	79.76	106.37
Effec Tax Rate	-2.02	-24.23	164.20	371.73	88.89
Def Interval	-11.47	18.24	7.43	13.02	14.91
Sus Grth Rate	-6.21	6.43	13.27	6.18	6.98

SUBSIDIARY & ASSOCIATED COMPANIES

ALNET (PTY) LTD
APELDOORN-LIGHTHOUSE NET & TWINE (PTY) L
BENCO PROPERTIES (PTY) LTD
BIG ROCK (PTY) LTD
CARAPAX SHADEPORTS (PTY) LTD
CYCLOP ENGINEERING (PTY) LTD
FM BELEGGINGS (PTY) LTD
JAMES SYDNEY PROPERTIES (PTY) LTD
JOUBERT HOEK (PTY) LTD
KREMETART BELEGGERS (PTY) LTD
LAPRORETA (PTY) LTD (45%)
LOUGARDIA (PTY) LTD
LUXAVIA (PTY) LTD (43,75%)
MARITIME SUPPLY CO. (PTY) LTD (50%)
PLASNET (PTY) LTD
PRESIDENT INSURANCE CO. LTD
RENTMEESTER INSURERS LTD
RENTMEESTERGEBOU (LOUIS TRICHARDT) (PTY) (43%)
S M HARE & SON (PTY) LTD
SENIOR MOTORS LTD (50%)
SHADE DEALS (PTY) LTD
SILLENA ONTWIKKELINGSMAATSKAPPY (PTY) LT
SPAARWINS LTD (22,8%)
TRANSMEESTER BELEGGINGS (PTY) LTD (32%)
TREBBOB (PTY) LTD
TREK AIRWAYS (PTY) LTD (43,75%)
TRIOMF ONDERNEMINGS BPK

INVESTMENTS

ADMINSENTRUM (PTY) LTD (19%)
FINABEL LTD (14,95%)

REUNERT LTD

ABBREVIATION : REUNERT

JSE SHORT CODE : RLO

SECTOR : Industrial-Electronics, Electrical & Bat

SHAREHOLDERS

Who Owns Whom's Assessment of the Identity of the Ultimate Controlling Shareholder:
SA MUTUAL VIA BARLOWS

SHAREHOLDER	PERCENTAGE 1992	1991
BARLOW RAND LTD	77.5	78.1
CMB NOM P/L	6.6	---
STD BANK NOM TVL P/L	3.5	3.3
SA MUTUAL	2.7	2.3
FIRST NAT NOM P/L	1.3	1.4
SAGE LIFE LTD	1.2	---
METAL IND GROUP PENS FUND	1.1	1.1
ENGINEERING INDUSTRIES PENS FUND	1.1	1.1
SANLAM	---	6.7
TOTAL	95.0	94.0

DIRECTORS :
CLEWLOW WAM ,COOPER DE ,DYER DW
ELLINGFORD AJ (Managing Director)
PARKER CC (Chairman),PRETORIUS G ,SCHABORT CC
VAUX CFH (Financial Director),WATT DT

REGISTRATION NUMBER : 01/04355/06

REGISTERED OFFICE
Barlow Park, Katherine Street
Sandton
2199
TEL: 011-801 9151
FAX: 011-444 3609

TRANSFER SECRETARY
Rand Registrars Ltd
P O Box 82549, Southdale
2135
TEL: 011-835 1016

COMPANY SECRETARY
E B Simpson

NATURE OF BUSINESS
Reunert is a leading Engineering company in the electronic, telecommunications and electrical engineering markets, its major interests are in Circuit Breaker Industries, GEC General Products, Reutech and B & D Education Systems.

BANKERS :
First National Bank of SA Ltd
Nedperm Bank Ltd, Standard Bank of SA Ltd

AUDITORS :
Deloitte Pim Goldby

FAMILIAR BRAND NAMES
FUCHS,GEC,HEINEMANN,MARNET,PABX,SATCHWELL

CONTRIBUTION BY ACTIVITY
N/A

YEAR END : September

DIVIDEND :Ords 50c

Interim No 128	(Ldr)25/05/90	(Pay)30/06/90	Amt(c)22
Final No 129	(Ldr)23/11/90	(Pay)03/01/91	Amt(c)59
Interim No 130	(Ldr)24/05/91	(Pay)29/06/91	Amt(c)22
Final No 131	(Ldr)22/11/91	(Pay)03/01/92	Amt(c)59
Interim No 132	(Ldr)29/05/92	(Pay)27/06/92	Amt(c)27
Final No 133	(Ldr)27/11/92	(Pay)04/01/93	Amt(c)73

NUMBER OF EMPLOYEES : 13925

CAPITAL STRUCTURE

	AUTHORISED	ISSUED
Ord 50c	35000000	31479229
5.5% Cum Pref R2	350000	350000

FINANCIAL STATISTICS (AT FINANCIAL YEAR END)

(Amts in R'000)	1991 Sep	1990 Sep	1989 Sep	1988 Sep	1987 Sep
Ord S/H Int	232182	205594	175181	132062	157633
Long Trm Loans	197076	165272	138184	90680	109205
Iss Ord Share	31479	31335	31279	31072	31058
Total Liab	767140	714838	565566	462658	470640
Current Liab	570064	549566	427382	371978	361435
Total Assets	999322	920432	740747	594720	628273
Current Assets	677861	638279	513670	389472	400878
Debtors	290141	345013	235657	186158	177726
Inventory	295722	277143	261102	197377	217469
Turnover	1609187	1414933	1132791	869354	1151516
Oper Profit	130084	129138	107460	76960	88317
Interest Paid	25260	29518	13951	11203	13212
Tax Paid	33958	21290	28943	18610	27548
Prf af Int&Tax	85199	88468	73917	47147	47557
Prf att Ord Sh	74560	73307	63198	40361	37367
Btm Line Earn	50697	55294	61787	76255	36936
Dividend Paid	25497	25390	21894	13983	12422
Mkt Prce(c) YE	1750	1350	2300	850	3750
Depreciation	45144	36526	28420	28212	26107

PER SHARE STATISTICS (CENTS)

Net Asst Val	737.58	656.12	560.06	425.02	507.54
Net Earnings	237.50	234.10	202.70	130.00	120.00
Dividends	81.00	81.00	70.00	45.00	40.00
Cash Flow	354.09	332.87	266.70	193.58	187.97

RATIOS AND OTHER INFORMATION

Mrk Cap(R000)	550883	423023	719417	264112	1164675
Current Ratio	1.19	1.16	1.20	1.05	1.11
Quik/Acid Tst	0.67	0.66	0.59	0.52	0.51
A/C Rec T/ovr	5.55	4.10	4.81	4.67	6.48
Tot Ass T/ovr	1.61	1.54	1.53	1.46	1.83
Debt/Ass Rat	0.57	0.63	0.62	0.63	0.58
L T L Tot Ass	0.00	0.03	0.04	0.01	0.01
Debt to Eqity	2.47	2.83	2.63	2.84	2.32
Interest Cover	5.18	4.52	8.12	6.87	6.68
Oper Prof Mrg	8.08	9.13	9.49	8.85	7.67
Net Prof Marg%	4.63	5.18	5.58	4.64	3.25
Ret on Assets	15.31	16.05	16.92	14.40	14.85
Ret on Equity%	32.11	35.66	36.08	30.56	23.71
Price/Earnings	7.37	5.77	11.35	6.54	31.25
Divid Cover	2.93	2.89	2.90	2.89	3.00
Divid Yield	4.63	6.00	3.04	5.29	1.07
Earning Yield%	13.57	17.34	8.81	15.29	3.20
NAV % Mrk Pr	42.15	48.60	24.35	50.00	13.53
Effec Tax Rate	28.69	17.53	28.52	31.58	40.39
Def Interval	0.36	0.88	1.45	1.33	1.12
Sus Grth Rate	21.13	23.31	23.58	19.97	15.82

SUBSIDIARY & ASSOCIATED COMPANIES

AFCAB HOLDINGS (PTY) LTD (50%)
AFRICAN CABLES LTD (33,5%)
ASERMA MANUFACTURING (PTY) LTD
ATC (PTY) LTD (28%)
B & D EDUCATION SYSTEMS (PTY) LTD
BARCOM ELECTRONICS (PTY) LTD

BARGENEL INVESTMENTS LTD
BARMARC HOLDINGS (PTY) LTD
CIRCUIT BREAKER INDUSTRIES LTD
ERMETEK (PTY) LTD
ESD (PTY) LTD
FUCHS ELECTRONICS (PTY) LTD
GARTH LIGHT (PTY) LTD
GEC ALSTHOM SOUTH AFRICA (PTY) LTD (50%)
GEC ALSTHOM SOUTH AFRICA HOLDINGS (PTY) (50%)
GEC ELECTRIC MOTOR MANUFACTURERS (PTY) L (50%)
GEC ELLIOTT AUTOMATION (PTY) LTD (50%)
GEC ENGINEERING (PTY) LTD (50%)
GEC EQUIPMENT (PTY) LTD
GEC GENERAL PRODUCTS (PTY) LTD (50%)
GEC LARGE MACHINES (PTY) LTD (50%)
GEC PROJECTS (PTY) LTD (50%)
GEC SOUTH AFRICA (PTY) LTD (50%)
GEC TURBINE GENERATORS (PTY) LTD (50%)
HEINEMANN HOLDINGS LTD
INTERLEARN (PTY) LTD
LEAR MARKETING (PTY) LTD (50%)
LOGISTICS AND SYSTEMS SUPPORT CO (PTY) L
OMC ASERMA (PTY) LTD
REUNERT ELECTRONIC HOLDINGS LTD
REUNERT FINANCE CO. LTD
SACO SYSTEMS (PTY) LTD
SANDOCK AUSTRAL LTD
TELEPHONE MANUFACTURERS OF SOUTH AFRICA
TELKOR (PTY) LTD
TELKOR BUSINESS SYSTEMS (PTY) LTD
TELKOR HOLDINGS (PTY) LTD
TELKOR SALES (PTY) LTD
TELKOR SIGNALLING COMPANY (PTY) LTD

INVESTMENTS

ELECTRIC PRODUCTS INTERNATIONAL (PTY) LT (20%)
S A MICRO ELECTRONIC SYSTEMS (PTY) LTD (8%)

REVERE RESOURCES SA LTD

ABBREVIATION : REVERE

JSE SHORT CODE : RVR

SECTOR : Mining Financial-Mining Holding

SHAREHOLDERS

Who Owns Whom's Assessment of the Identity of the Ultimate Controlling Shareholder: GJS LAING

SHAREHOLDER	PERCENTAGE 1992	1991
STD BANK NOM TVL P/L	43.0	---
LAING G J S	19.3	---
BISICHI MINING EXPLORATION LTD	16.9	40.0
STOCKSHARE NOM P/L	9.0	---
NEDBANK NOM LTD	6.2	---
FIRST NAT NOM P/L	---	2.4
SOUTHWITS LTD	---	49.5
TOTAL	94.3	91.9

DIRECTORS :
HELLER MA ,LAING GJS (Chairman & Managing Dir.)
MACKILLIGIN RG ,STEVENS MC ,VAN ZYL L

REGISTRATION NUMBER : 89/03426/06

REGISTERED OFFICE
Ground Floor, AMR Office Park, Building 2, Concorde Rd East
Bedfordview
2008
TEL: 011-455 6434
FAX: 011-455 6435

TRANSFER SECRETARY
Mercantile Registrars Ltd
P O Box 1053, Johannesburg
2000
TEL: 011-333 8181

COMPANY SECRETARY
Revere Resources Management Services (Pty) Ltd

NATURE OF BUSINESS
Exploration & gold mining in the Murchison Range in the N E Tvl. The company also conducts dump retreatment operations, & holds a portfolio of mining assets.

BANKERS :
First National Bank of SA Ltd

AUDITORS :
KPMG Aiken & Peat

FAMILIAR BRAND NAMES
N/A

CONTRIBUTION BY ACTIVITY
N/A

YEAR END : February

NUMBER OF EMPLOYEES : 90

CAPITAL STRUCTURE

	AUTHORISED	ISSUED
Ords 1c (1 Ord Linked to 2 Option	50000000	44556485

FINANCIAL STATISTICS (AT FINANCIAL YEAR END)

(Amts in R'000)	1991 Feb	1990 Feb
Ord S/H Int	829	1441
Long Trm Loans	1183	269
Iss Ord Share	14556	14556
Total Liab	1389	1763
Current Liab	206	1494
Total Assets	826	1937
Intang Assets	1392	1267
Current Assets	103	1165
Debtors	85	8
Inventory	18	-
Turnover	109	-
Oper Profit	-555	-28
Interest Paid	89	-
Tax Paid	-	22
Prf af Int&Tax	-613	18
Prf att Ord Sh	-613	18
Btm Line Earn	-613	18
Mkt Prce(c) YE	10	25

PER SHARE STATISTICS (CENTS)

Net Asst Val	-3.87	1.20
Net Earnings	-4.21	0.16
Cash Flow	-4.21	0.12

RATIOS AND OTHER INFORMATION

Mrk Cap(R000)	1456	3639
Current Ratio	0.50	0.78
Quik/Acid Tst	0.41	0.78
A/C Rec T/ovr	1.28	-
Tot Ass T/ovr	0.13	-
Debt/Ass Rat	1.68	0.91
L T L Tot Ass	1.43	0.14
Debt to Eqity	1.68	1.22
Interest Cover	-6.24	-
Oper Prof Mrg	-509.17	-
Net Prof Marg%	-562.39	-
Ret on Assets	-63.44	2.07
Ret on Equity%	-73.94	1.25
Price/Earnings	-2.38	156.25
Earning Yield%	-42.10	0.64
NAV % Mrk Pr	-38.68	4.78
Effec Tax Rate	-	55.00
Def Interval	-2.02	92.83
Sus Grth Rate	-73.94	1.25

SUBSIDIARY & ASSOCIATED COMPANIES

FOSTON LTD
GOODSMAN MINING (PTY) LTD
MODDER B GOLD HOLDINGS LTD (43,6%)
RAND LEASES (VOGELSTRUISFONTEIN) GOLD MI (26%)
SOUTH MURCHISON GOLD MINING CO (PTY) LTD

INVESTMENTS

CONSOLIDATED MINING CORPORATION LTD (2,8%)

REX TRUEFORM CLOTHING CO LTD

ABBREVIATION : REX-TRUE

JSE SHORT CODE : RTO

SECTOR : Industrial-Clothing, Footwear & Textiles

SHAREHOLDERS

Who Owns Whom's Assessment of the Identity of the Ultimate Controlling Shareholder: ARICAN & OVERSEAS ENTERPRISES

SHAREHOLDER	PERCENTAGE 1992	1991
AFRICAN & OVERSEAS ENTERPRISES LTD	72.8	72.8
SA MUTUAL	8.2	8.2
LIBERTY LIFE ASSOC OF AFRICA LTD	5.2	5.2
STD BANK NOM TVL P/L	3.6	3.6
CAMPOBELLO HOLDINGS P/L	2.2	---
NESTLE PENS FUND	2.1	---
TORINO INV P/L	1.5	1.5
FNP PENS FUND	---	1.5
PULP & PAPER ENGINEERING CO P/L	---	2.2
TOTAL	95.5	94.9

DIRECTORS :
AXELSON NC ,BURSTEIN L ,CLAYTON JJ ,DIBOWITZ PJ
GILLARD NC ,HODGKINSON AA ,KEET AH ,ROBERTSON TH
SHUB CM ,SHUB SC (Chairman),SINCLAIRE CJ
SYKES DR ,THOMAS GM

REGISTRATION NUMBER : 05/09839/06

REGISTERED OFFICE
Rex Buildings, 263 Victoria Road
Salt River
7925
TEL: 021-448 4660
FAX: 021-448 1552

TRANSFER SECRETARY
Mercantile Registrars Ltd
P O Box 1053, Johannesburg
2000
TEL: 011-333 8181

COMPANY SECRETARY
African & Overseas Enterprises Ltd

NATURE OF BUSINESS
Manufacturers and suppliers of clothing for the local & export markets.

BANKERS :
Standard Bank of SA Ltd
UAL Merchant Bank Ltd

AUDITORS :
Ernst & Young

FAMILIAR BRAND NAMES
CASSIDY,DAKS LONDON,HANG TEN,JOHN STEPHEN
LANVIN,MISS CASSIDY,REX TRUEFORM,WALL STREET

CONTRIBUTION BY ACTIVITY
N/A

YEAR END : June

DIVIDEND : Ords 50c

Final No 46	(Ldr)16/11/90	(Pay)30/11/90	Amt(c)90
Final No 47	(Ldr)15/11/91	(Pay)29/11/91	Amt(c)70
Final No 48	(Ldr)13/11/92	(Pay)27/11/92	Amt(c)60

NUMBER OF EMPLOYEES : 3000

CAPITAL STRUCTURE

	AUTHORISED	ISSUED
Ords 50c	3250000	2730000
"A" Ords 50c	1400000	1400000
6% Cum Prefs R2	140000	140000
Var Rate Cum Red Prefs R1	1200	0

FINANCIAL STATISTICS (AT FINANCIAL YEAR END)

(Amts in R'000)	1992 Jun	1991 Jun	1990 Jun	1989 Jun	1988 Jun
Ord S/H Int	87959	84222	79737	72256	58407
Long Trm Loans	2669	3786	10382	17139	18636
Iss Ord Share	2730	2730	2730	2730	2730
Total Liab	27363	26498	31372	33373	33099
Current Liab	24694	22712	20990	16234	14463
Total Assets	115322	110720	111109	105629	91506
Current Assets	100055	97135	98935	94782	82148
Debtors	30329	30737	36043	34149	32451
Inventory	66377	58577	46785	41394	34925
Oper Profit	5820	6321	15144	15741	13855
Interest Paid	2043	1579	618	783	875

Tax Paid	-232	1276	6806	22	23
Prf af Int&Tax	5855	7120	11591	17777	12957
Prf att Ord Sh	5891	7276	10966	17194	11845
Btm Line Earn	5891	7276	10966	17194	10802
Dividend Paid	2478	2891	3717	3717	3098
Mkt Prce(c) YE	775	1100	1150	1250	960
Depreciation	2368	2402	2112	1568	1440

PER SHARE STATISTICS (CENTS)

Net Asst Val	3221.94	3085.05	2920.77	2646.74	2139.45
Net Earnings	142.60	176.20	265.50	416.30	286.80
Dividends	60.00	70.00	90.00	90.00	75.00
Cash Flow	288.17	365.09	463.08	662.89	486.63

RATIOS AND OTHER INFORMATION

Mrk Cap(R000)	21158	30030	31395	34125	26208
Current Ratio	4.05	4.28	4.71	5.84	5.68
Quik/Acid Tst	1.36	1.70	2.48	3.29	3.27
Debt/Ass Rat	0.23	0.23	0.28	0.20	0.23
L T L Tot Ass	0.02	0.03	0.09	0.04	0.07
Debt to Eqity	0.31	0.31	0.39	0.29	0.35
Interest Cover	3.05	4.37	24.50	20.10	15.83
Ret on Assets	6.71	9.04	17.51	18.22	15.14
Ret on Equity%	6.70	8.64	13.75	23.80	20.28
Price/Earnings	5.43	6.24	4.33	3.00	3.35
Divid Cover	2.38	2.52	2.95	4.63	3.82
Divid Yield	7.74	6.36	7.83	7.20	7.81
Earning Yield%	18.40	16.02	23.09	33.30	29.88
NAV % Mrk Pr	415.73	280.46	253.98	211.74	222.86
Effec Tax Rate	0.50	11.73	37.00	0.12	0.07
Def Interval	1.58	1.04	0.86	1.03	1.51
Sus Grth Rate	3.88	5.21	9.09	18.65	14.98

SUBSIDIARY & ASSOCIATED COMPANIES

ANGLO AMERICAN EXPORT & IMPORT CO. LTD
CASSIDY'S MANUFACTURING CO. (PTY) LTD (L
CASSIDY'S MANUFACTURING CO. (PTY) LTD (S
EVEREST MARKETING CORP LTD (50%)
JOHN STEPHEN CLOTHING CO. (PTY) LTD (LES
JOHN STEPHEN CLOTHING CO. (PTY) LTD (SWA
JOHN STEPHEN OF LONDON (S.A.) (PTY) LTD
JOHN STEPHEN OF LONDON (ZIMBABWE) (PVT)
JUDGE CLOTHING MANUFACTURERS LTD
KAMBETS (PTY) LTD
L'UOMO ATLANTIS (PTY) LTD
NICHOLSON AND CO. OF ENGLAND (S.A.) LTD
REX TRUEFORM (MARKETING ORGANISATION) (P
REX TRUEFORM (NAMIBIA) (PTY) LTD
REX TRUEFORM (PVT) LTD (ZIMBABWE)
REX TRUEFORM CLOTHING CO. (PTY) LTD (LES
REX TRUEFORM CLOTHING CO. (PTY) LTD (SWA
ROBE-RITE CLOTHING CORP. (S.A.) LTD
SIRS CLOTHING COMPANY LTD
VELLA SPORTSWEAR LTD
WYNBAC PROPERTIES (PTY) LTD

INVESTMENTS

EVEREST MARKETING CORPORATION LTD (6000 SH)
SA FRANCHISING (PTY) LTD (2 SHARES)
SMALL BUSINESS DEVELOPMENT CORP LTD (104800 SH)
SOUTHERN LIFE ASSOCIATION (500 SH)

RHOMBUS EXPLORATION LTD

ABBREVIATION : RHOEX

JSE SHORT CODE : RHE

SECTOR : Mining-Exploration

SHAREHOLDERS

Who Owns Whom's Assessment of the Identity of the Ultimate Controlling Shareholder:
DIRECTORS CONTROL 49%

SHAREHOLDER	PERCENTAGE 1992	1991
RAND MERCHANT NOM P/L	48.6	48.6
ANGLO AFRICAN SHIPPING CO 1936 P/L	11.4	11.2
STD BANK NOM TVL P/L	3.6	3.5
SMK NOM P/L	1.3	---
FIRST NAT NOM P/L	1.1	1.3
JUSPOINT NOM P/L	---	1.1
TOTAL	66.0	65.7

DIRECTORS :
ESTERHUIZEN AG ,FLETCHER AG (Chairman)
HOLMES LG ,JAGOE SD ,KUIPER JL ,SIMPSON AJ
STILL RG (Chief Executive),VELDSMAN HG

REGISTRATION NUMBER : 87/01030/06

REGISTERED OFFICE
3rd Floor, 20 Skeen Boulevard
Bedfordview
2008
TEL: 011-455 3326
FAX: 011-455 2849

TRANSFER SECRETARY
Mercantile Registrars Ltd
P O Box 1053, Johannesburg
2000
TEL: 011-333 8181

COMPANY SECRETARY
M J Betts

NATURE OF BUSINESS
The company's business is to identify and secure suitable prospecting and exploration opportunities in precious,base & industrial minerals on its own account and on behalf of third parties who contract with the company to do so.

BANKERS :
Trust Bank of Africa Ltd

AUDITORS :
Ernst & Young

FAMILIAR BRAND NAMES
N/A

CONTRIBUTION BY ACTIVITY
N/A

YEAR END : September

NUMBER OF EMPLOYEES : 12

CAPITAL STRUCTURE

	AUTHORISED	ISSUED
Ords 1c	50000000	33559000

FINANCIAL STATISTICS (AT FINANCIAL YEAR END)

(Amts in R'000)	1991 Sep	1990 Jun	1989 Jun	1988 Jun	1987
Ord S/H Int	30306	28104	27545	29054	10143
Long Trm Loans	872	34	46	439	207
Iss Ord Share	33559	33559	33537	33500	25000
Total Liab	16167	6015	3797	1752	375
Current Liab	15295	5981	3751	1313	168
Total Assets	44503	33649	31342	30806	19749
Intang Assets	1970	470	*	*	*
Current Assets	35385	29524	4250	8213	9399
Debtors	82	219	-	3	-
Inventory	-	-	-	-	9399
Oper Profit	-2073	-3677	-4577	-4634	-307
Tax Paid	841	-	-439	439	-
Prf af Int&Tax	2702	537	-1551	-2049	-307
Prf att Ord Sh	2702	537	-1551	-2010	-306
Btm Line Earn	2202	537	-1551	-2010	-306
Mkt Prce(c) YE	65	75	140	320	-
Depreciation	175	63	18	1	-

PER SHARE STATISTICS (CENTS)

Net Asst Val	84.44	82.34	82.13	86.73	40.57
Net Earnings	8.05	1.60	-4.63	-6.20	-
Cash Flow	8.86	1.79	-5.88	-4.84	-4.91

RATIOS AND OTHER INFORMATION

Mrk Cap(R000)	21813	25169	46952	107200	-
Current Ratio	2.31	4.94	1.13	6.26	55.95
Quik/Acid Tst	2.31	4.94	1.13	6.26	-
Debt/Ass Rat	0.34	0.18	0.12	0.04	0.02
L T L Tot Ass	0.00	0.00	0.00	-	0.01
Debt to Eqity	0.51	0.21	0.14	0.05	0.04
Ret on Assets	6.37	1.60	-6.35	-5.23	-6.22
Ret on Equity%	7.13	1.91	-5.63	-6.92	-12.07
Price/Earnings	8.07	46.88	-30.24	-51.61	-
Earning Yield%	12.38	2.13	-3.31	-1.94	-
NAV % Mrk Pr	129.90	109.79	58.67	27.10	-
Def Interval	2.37	8.44	-1.21	-	-2.70
Sus Grth Rate	8.92	1.91	-5.63	-6.92	-3.02

SUBSIDIARY & ASSOCIATED COMPANIES

DENBEL INVESTMENT INCORPORATED
RHOMBUS VANADIUM HOLDINGS LTD
RHOSCO HOLDINGS (PTY) LTD
SOUTHERN FREE STATE EXPLORATION (PTY) LT
TAAIBOSCHSPRUIT COLLIERY (50%)
TWEEFONTEIN EXPLORATION COMPANY (PTY) LT
ZEBEDIELA PLATINUM MINING (PTY) LTD

INVESTMENTS

EAGLE GRANITE (PTY) LTD (10%)
RHOMBUS VANADIUM HOLDINGS LTD (CONV DEBS (22,4%)

RHOMBUS VANADIUM HOLDINGS LTD

ABBREVIATION : RHOVAN

JSE SHORT CODE : RHV

SECTOR : Metals & Minerals-Other

SHAREHOLDERS

Who Owns Whom's Assessment of the Identity of the Ultimate Controlling Shareholder: RHOMBUS EXPLORATION

SHAREHOLDER	PERCENTAGE 1992	1991
RHOSCO HOLDINGS P/L	72.0	72.0
CMB NOM P/L	6.5	---
LESLIE GORDON HOLMES FAMILY TRUST	2.9	2.9
EDWIN W BALDERSON NOM P/L	1.1	1.5
SANLAM	---	6.5
TOTAL	82.4	82.9

DIRECTORS :
FLETCHER AG ,KOTZEE FP (Chairman),ROUTLEDGE GQ
SIMPSON AJ ,STILL RG (Chief Executive)
VELDSMAN HG

REGISTRATION NUMBER : 89/01678/06

REGISTERED OFFICE
3rd Floor, 20 Skeen Boulevard
Bedfordview, Johannesburg
2008
TEL: 011-455 3326
FAX: 011-455 2849

TRANSFER SECRETARY
Mercantile Registrars Ltd
P O Box 1053, Johannesburg
2000
TEL: 011-333 8181

COMPANY SECRETARY
M J Betts

NATURE OF BUSINESS
The company's subsidiary operates a mine near Brits, Bophuthatswana. Vanadiferous titaniferous magnetite ore is mined in an opencast operation, & processed to produce a magnetite concentrate, which is sold to Usko in terms of a long-term supply agreement.

BANKERS :
Central Merchant Bank Ltd

AUDITORS :
Ernst & Young

FAMILIAR BRAND NAMES
N/A

CONTRIBUTION BY ACTIVITY
N/A

YEAR END : September

DIVIDEND :15/05/91 and 15/11/91

NUMBER OF EMPLOYEES : 150

CAPITAL STRUCTURE

	AUTHORISED	ISSUED
Ords 0,01c	150000000	52500100
12% Conv Debs	24000000	24000000

FINANCIAL STATISTICS (AT FINANCIAL YEAR END)

(Amts in R'000)	1991 Sep	1990 Sep	1989 Sep
Ord S/H Int	31747	9883	9883
Long Trm Loans	16857	15606	15606
Iss Ord Share	52500	18000	18000
Total Liab	30720	31058	17530
Current Liab	13863	15452	1924
Total Assets	62467	40941	27413
Current Assets	22052	1262	15945
Debtors	21149	1084	895
Inventory	903	178	58
Turnover	11270	-	-
Oper Profit	5970	2037	-
Interest Paid	1017	1181	-
Prf af Int&Tax	4953	856	-
Prf att Ord Sh	3812	-80	-
Btm Line Earn	21862	-80	-
Mkt Prce(c) YE	25	25	53

PER SHARE STATISTICS (CENTS)

Net Asst Val	60.47	54.91	54.91
Cash Flow	9.04	4.76	-

RATIOS AND OTHER INFORMATION

Mrk Cap(R000)	13125	4500	9540
Current Ratio	1.59	0.08	8.29
Quik/Acid Tst	1.53	0.07	8.26
A/C Rec T/ovr	0.53	-	-
Tot Ass T/ovr	0.18	-	-
Debt/Ass Rat	0.47	0.76	0.64
L T L Tot Ass	0.25	0.38	0.57
Debt to Eqity	0.93	3.14	1.77
Interest Cover	5.87	1.72	-
Oper Prof Mrg	52.97	-	-
Net Prof Marg%	33.82	-	-
Ret on Assets	9.56	4.98	-
Ret on Equity%	12.01	-0.81	-
NAV % Mrk Pr	241.88	219.62	103.60
Def Interval	1.70	13.20	-
Sus Grth Rate	12.01	-0.81	-

SUBSIDIARY & ASSOCIATED COMPANIES

RHOMBUS VANADIUM (PTY) LTD

INVESTMENTS

None

RICCIA PROPERTY HOLDINGS LTD

SECTOR : Financial-Property

SHAREHOLDERS

Who Owns Whom's Assessment of the Identity of the Ultimate Controlling Shareholder:
DIRECTORS

DIRECTORS :
ODENDAAL GCV (Managing Director),PAYNE AF
RANEY SG ,SMITH HA (Chairman

REGISTRATION NUMBER : 89/01668/06

REGISTERED OFFICE
64 Wierda Road East, Wierda Valley
Sandton
2196
TEL: 011-883 2773
FAX: 011-883 5196

TRANSFER SECRETARY
Central Registrars Ltd
P O Box 4844, Johannesburg
2000
TEL: 011-331 0051

COMPANY SECRETARY
L T Luck (Ms)

NATURE OF BUSINESS
A property holding company which owns through its subsidiaries a selected portfolio of commercial properties.

BANKERS :
Nedcor Bank Ltd

AUDITORS :
Arthur Andersen & Co

FAMILIAR BRAND NAMES
N/A

CONTRIBUTION BY ACTIVITY
Midrand (% of income) (65.0%)
Witbank (11.0%)
Nelspruit (10.0%)
Sandton (9.0%)
Brits (5.0%)

YEAR END : November

CAPITAL STRUCTURE

	AUTHORISED	ISSUED
Ords 10c	12000000	10000000
Unsec Sub Var Rate Debs 500c	24197479	24197479

SUBSIDIARY & ASSOCIATED COMPANIES

None

INVESTMENTS

None

RICHEMONT SECURITIES AG

ABBREVIATION : RICHEMONT

JSE SHORT CODE : RCH

SECTOR : Industrial-Industrial Holding

SHAREHOLDERS

Who Owns Whom's Assessment of the Identity of the Ultimate Controlling Shareholder:
RUPERT & HERTZOG FAMILIES

DIRECTORS :
AESCHIMANN JP (Chairman)
DU PLESSIS JP (Financial Director),RENGGLI A D

REGISTERED OFFICE
Weinbergstrasse 5, 6300, Zug
Switzerland

FAX: (4142) 217102

TRANSFER SECRETARY
Rand Merchant Bank Ltd
P O Box 786273, Sandton
2146
TEL: 011-883 3650

COMPANY SECRETARY
A Grieve

NATURE OF BUSINESS
The group has international investments in tobacco products; luxury goods incl watches, writing instruments, menswear, leather goods and fragrances; real estate and insurance; refining & marketing of petroleum products, exploration for & production of oil & gas, & the manufacture of powdered metal products.

BANKERS :
N/A

AUDITORS :
Price Waterhouse Meyernel

FAMILIAR BRAND NAMES
ALFRED DUNHILL,CARTIER,CHLOE (FRAGRANCES)
DUNHILL,MEISTERSTUCK (WRITING INSTR)
MONTBLANC,PETER STUYVESANT,PIAGET,ROTHMANS
SOLITAIRE

CONTRIBUTION BY ACTIVITY
N/A

YEAR END : March

DIVIDEND : (Ldr)01/09/89 (Pay)22/09/89

NUMBER OF EMPLOYEES : 5000

CAPITAL STRUCTURE

	AUTHORISED	ISSUED
"A" Units	522000000	522000000
"B" Units (not listed)	52200	52200

FINANCIAL STATISTICS (AT FINANCIAL YEAR END)

(Amts in PS)	1992 Mar	1991 Mar	1990 Mar	1989 Mar	1988 Mar
Ord S/H Int	1296900	1141000	977000	828500	730000
Long Trm Loans	2081600	1982500	1887900	54000	52200
Iss Ord Share	522000	522000	522000	522000	522000
Total Liab	3747700	3413500	3078700	66300	89900
Current Liab	1666100	1431000	1190800	12300	37700
Total Assets	4521200	4054400	3674700	894800	819900
Intang Assets	523400	500100	381000	*	*
Current Assets	3793900	3331100	3017900	302300	334800
Debtors	888200	841600	752300	18000	13700
Inventory	1071500	1030000	906300	-	-
Turnover	7006600	6448500	5905300	-	-
Oper Profit	556700	535500	533300	145300	90400
Interest Paid	122800	122300	70400	4800	4700
Tax Paid	220600	222900	209300	51200	41100
Prf af Int&Tax	372000	352300	371100	110100	77000
Prf att Ord Sh	197300	177300	146300	106500	77000
Btm Line Earn	231000	177300	146300	109800	77000
Mkt Prce(c) YE	3570	2380	2200	1335	-
Depreciation	87900	74900	67700	1600	1200

PER SHARE STATISTICS (CENTS)

Net Asst Val	148.18	122.78	114.18	158.72	139.85
Net Earnings	343.60	308.70	254.70	185.40	134.10
Dividends	56.25	50.63	41.25	33.75	-
Cash Flow	48.20	49.60	42.66	20.71	14.98

RATIOS AND OTHER INFORMATION

Mrk Cap(R000)	18635400	12423600	11484000	6968700	-
Current Ratio	2.28	2.33	2.53	24.58	8.88
Quik/Acid Tst	1.63	1.61	1.77	24.58	8.88
A/C Rec T/ovr	7.89	7.66	7.85	-	-
Tot Ass T/ovr	1.55	1.59	1.61	-	-
Debt/Ass Rat	0.61	0.62	0.63	0.06	0.10
L T L Tot Ass	0.24	0.27	0.30	0.05	0.05
Debt to Eqity	2.12	2.20	2.36	0.06	0.11
Interest Cover	4.53	4.38	7.58	31.81	24.34
Oper Prof Mrg	7.95	8.30	9.03	-	-
Net Prof Marg%	2.82	2.75	2.48	-	-
Ret on Assets	16.43	17.72	17.71	18.56	14.98
Ret on Equity%	15.21	15.54	14.97	12.85	10.55
Price/Earnings	10.39	7.71	8.64	7.20	-
Divid Cover	6.11	6.10	6.17	5.49	-
Divid Yield	1.58	2.13	1.88	2.53	-
Earning Yield%	9.62	12.97	11.58	13.89	-
NAV % Mrk Pr	4.15	5.16	5.19	11.89	-
Effec Tax Rate	36.99	32.68	33.10	33.27	43.68
Def Interval	4.95	4.10	4.32	0.38	0.55
Sus Grth Rate	15.21	15.54	14.97	12.85	10.55

SUBSIDIARY & ASSOCIATED COMPANIES

A. SULKA & CO LTD (U K)
A. SULKA & COMPANY LTD (USA)
A. SULKA SA (FRANCE)
AFLFRED DUNHILL LTD (UK) (36%)
BAUME & MERCIER SA (SWITZERLAND)
BUSINESS CONTROL SA (SWIZERLAND)
CARRERAS GROUP LTD (JAMAICA) (29,5%)
CARRIER SA (SWITZERLAND)
CARTIER GMBH
CARTIER INC (USA)
CARTIER INTERNATIONAL BV (NETHERLANDS)
CARTIER INTERNATIONAL SA (SWITZERLAND)
CARTIER JAPAN LTD (39,4%)
CARTIER LTD (UK)
CARTIER MONDE SA (LUXEMBOURG)
CARTIER SA (FRANCE)
CHLOE SA (CANADA) (36%)
DUNHILL HOLDINGS PLC (UK) (36%)
FILMNET SA (LUXEMBOURG) (50%)
JUBILE SA (BELGIUM)
L.M.C. INTERNATIONAL SPA (ITALY)
LANE LTD (USA)
LES MUST DE CARTIER FAR EAST LTD
LUXCO SA (LUXEMBOURG)
MARTIN BRINKMANN AG (GERMANY)
MONTBLANC-SIMPLO GMBH (36%)
NORTH AMERICAN RESOURCES LTD (BRITISH CI (50%)
PBM INTERNATIONAL HOLDINGS SA (SWITZERLA

PJ CARROLL & CO LTD (IRELAND)
PJ CARROLL HOLDINGS PLC (IRELAND)
RICHEMONT INTERNATIONAL LTD (UK)
RICHEMONT SA LUXEMBOURG
ROTHMANS (FAR EAST) LTD (UK)
ROTHMANS (UK) LIMITED (40,6%)
ROTHMANS CIGARETTEN GMBH
ROTHMANS EXPORTS LTD
ROTHMANS HOLDINGS LTD (AUSTRALIA) (31,2%)
ROTHMANS INC (CANADA) (44,5%)
ROTHMANS INDUSTRIES LTD (SINGAPORE) (31,2%)
ROTHMANS INTERNATIONAL (EUROPE) BV
ROTHMANS INTERNATIONAL INVESTMENTS LTD
ROTHMANS INTERNATIONAL PLC (UK)
ROTHMANS INTERNATIONAL TOBACCO (UK) LTD
ROTHMANS INTERNATIONAL TOBACCO LTD (UK)
ROTHMANS OF PALL MALL (AUSTRALIA) LTD (31,2%)
ROTHMANS OF PALL MALL (NEW ZEALAND) LTD (31,2%)
ROTHMANS OF PALL MALL LTD (SWITZERLAND)
ROTHMANS TOBACCO CO BV (NETHERLANDS)
ROTHMANS TOBACCO HOLDINGS LTD (JERSEY)
ROTHMANS, BENSON & HEDGES INC (26,7%)
SA ANCIENNE FABRIQUE (SWITZERLAND)
SCHIMMELPENNINCK SIGARENFABRIEKEN BV (NE
SULLANA AG (SWITZERLAND)
TABACOFINA-VANDER ELST NV (BELGIUM)
THEODORUS NIEMEYER BV (NETHERLANDS)
TOBACCO EXPORTS INTERNATIONAL (USA) LTD

INVESTMENTS

GROUPE YVES SAINT LAURENT SCA (6,1%)
NORTH AMERICAN RESOURCES LTD (CONV PREFS (100%)

RIO TINTO ZIMBABWE LTD

ABBREVIATION : RIO ZIM

SECTOR : Zimbabwe Stock Exchange

SHAREHOLDERS

Who Owns Whom's Assessment of the Identity of the Ultimate Controlling Shareholder:
RTZ P/L UK

SHAREHOLDER	PERCENTAGE 1992	1991
RIO ZIMBABWE HOLDINGS LTD	55.6	---
RIO TINTO FOUNDATION CO PVT LTD	8.9	---
OLD MUTUAL INV CORP (PVT) LTD	6.9	---
SECURITY NOM LTD	3.8	---
FIRST MUTUAL LIFE ASSURE SOC OF ZIM	2.6	---
FIDELITY LIFE ASSURE OF ZIM PVT LTD	1.1	---
E S C STAFF PENS FUND	1.0	---
TOTAL	80.0	---

DIRECTORS :
BACK JHP ,BAILEY DC ,CALDER RJG ,GIBSON CA
KAHARI ME ,NIXON JL (Chief Executive & M.D.)
SACHIKONYE JHK (Financial Director)
STEYN CH (Dir Mining),STOBART GL ,STRONG CJ
TAWENGWA SC (Chairman

REGISTERED OFFICE
1 Kenilworth Road, Highlands
Harare, Zimbabwe

TEL: 705571
FAX: 732445

TRANSFER SECRETARY
First Transfer Secretaries (Pvt) Ltd
P O Box 437, Bulawayo
Zimbabwe

TEL: 092634 - 702905

COMPANY SECRETARY
SE Magombedze

NATURE OF BUSINESS
RIO TINTO ZIMBABWE,together with its subsidiaries, is engaged in the mining of gold and emeralds,toll refining of nickel and copper matte, as also, the manufacture and distribution of transport,agri-cultural and irrigation equipment and the distri-bution of chemicals.Ultimate holding company is RTZ CORPORATION PLC based in the United Kingdom.

BANKERS :
Zimbabwe Banking Corporation Ltd

AUDITORS :
Coopers & Lybrand

FAMILIAR BRAND NAMES
N/A

CONTRIBUTION BY ACTIVITY
Gold (% of Turnover) (36.9%)
Emeralds (3.1%)
Industrial Goods & Services (60.0%)

YEAR END : December

DIVIDEND : Ords Z$0,40

Dividend	(Ldr)06/09/91	(Pay)27/09/91	Amt(c)17
Dividend	(Ldr)06/03/92	(Pay)15/04/92	Amt(c)53

CAPITAL STRUCTURE

	AUTHORISED	ISSUED
Ords Z$0,40	25000000	22460895

FINANCIAL STATISTICS (AT FINANCIAL YEAR END)

(Amts in Z$)	1991 Dec	1990 Dec
Ord S/H Int	113477	78698
Long Trm Loans	17030	18785
Iss Ord Share	22461	22461
Total Liab	118985	79334
Current Liab	101955	60549
Total Assets	232462	158032
Current Assets	111992	75626
Debtors	49171	32309
Inventory	60580	42166
Turnover	274478	181258
Oper Profit	54906	19393
Interest Paid	5167	3706
Tax Paid	13624	1092
Prf af Int&Tax	36500	15480
Prf att Ord Sh	36163	15244
Btm Line Earn	36163	17700
Dividend Paid	15722	6738
Depreciation	14141	11777

PER SHARE STATISTICS (CENTS)

Net Asst Val	505.22	350.38
Net Earnings	161.00	67.90
Dividends	70.00	30.00
Cash Flow	222.96	119.75

RATIOS AND OTHER INFORMATION

Current Ratio	1.10	1.25
Quik/Acid Tst	0.50	0.55
A/C Rec T/ovr	5.58	5.61
Tot Ass T/ovr	1.18	1.15
Debt/Ass Rat	0.51	0.50
L T L Tot Ass	0.07	0.12
Debt to Eqity	1.04	1.00
Interest Cover	10.70	5.47
Oper Prof Mrg	20.00	10.70
Net Prof Marg%	13.18	8.41
Ret on Assets	23.88	12.91
Ret on Equity%	31.87	19.37
Divid Cover	2.30	2.26
Effec Tax Rate	27.72	4.80
Def Interval	0.98	2.00
Sus Grth Rate	18.01	10.81

SUBSIDIARY & ASSOCIATED COMPANIES

BROMPTON MINES LIMITED
CAM HOUSING (PVT) LIMITED
EMPRESS NICKEL REFINERY LIMITED
RI TINTO MANAGEMENT SERVICES (CENTRAL AF
RIO MINES LIMTED
RIO TINTO PROPERTIES LIMITED
RIOZIM DEVELOPMENT LIMITED
SKILLED ENGINEERING CONTRACTORS (PVT) LT
TINTO DISCS (PVT) LTD (50%)
TINTO INDUSTRIES LTD

INVESTMENTS

BCG LIMITED (25 SH)
ZIMBABWE ALLOYS LTD (4235000S)

RMB HOLDINGS LTD

ABBREVIATION : RMBH

JSE SHORT CODE : RMH

SECTOR : Financial-Insurance

SHAREHOLDERS

Who Owns Whom's Assessment of the Identity of the Ultimate Controlling Shareholder: DIRECTORS & MANAGEMENT / SAGE GROUP

SHAREHOLDER	PERCENTAGE 1992	1991
RMB FINANCIAL HOLDINGS P/L	30.0	30.0
SAGE STRATEGIC INV P/L	11.5	---
DIPPENAAR L L	10.1	10.0
FERREIRA G T	10.0	10.0
RAND MERCHANT NOM P/L	5.9	---
AMALGAMATED BANKS OF SA LTD	4.4	13.0
PK HARRIS INV P/L	3.8	---
EIGHTY ONE MAIN STREET NOM LTD	3.7	---
MOMENTUM LIFE ASSURE LTD	3.3	3.3
SMK NOM P/L	1.3	---
MINE OFFICIALS PENS FUND	1.2	1.2
GOSSAKER INV P/L	1.1	1.1
KEVNIC P/L	1.1	---
RAND MERCHANT BANK NOM P/L	---	3.5
SANLAM	---	3.4
GOSS P M INV P/L	---	3.8
SAGE INV P/L	---	11.4
TOTAL	87.3	90.7

DIRECTORS :
ALBOROUGH NVR ,ALDWORTH ARM ,BOTTEGA A DR
CARINUS JG ,DIPPENAAR LL ,DREYER JW ,DU TOIT PR
FERREIRA GT (Deputy Chairman),FLACK PH ,GOSS PM
GOUWS RB ,GOUWS RP ,GREYLING E DE V ,HARRIS PK
HUTCHISON RJ ,KITSHOFF JJ ,KRIGE JD ,LANGHAM DA
LOUBSER RM ,MITROVICH AW ,RUPERT AE
RUPERT JP (Chairman),SHERRELL RE ,TEDDER RJ

REGISTRATION NUMBER : 87/05115/06

REGISTERED OFFICE
25 Fredman Drive, Sandton
2199
TEL: 011-883 3650
FAX: 011-783 8651

TRANSFER SECRETARY
Fraser Street Registrars (Pty) Ltd
P O Box 61178, Marshalltown
2107
TEL: 011-491 0911

COMPANY SECRETARY
P F de Beer

NATURE OF BUSINESS
A controlling company, registered in terms of the Deposit-taking Institutions Act, 1990, holding 100% of Rand Merchant Bank Ltd.
Group activities include project finance & special projects, corporate finance & investments, banking services (merchant), financial market dealing and risk management, property management & insurance.
Has a 76,8% holding in Momentum Life.

BANKERS :
Volkskas Ltd

AUDITORS :
Coopers Theron Du Toit

FAMILIAR BRAND NAMES
N/A

CONTRIBUTION BY ACTIVITY
N/A

YEAR END : June

DIVIDEND : Ords 10c

Dividend	(Ldr)30/09/91	(Pay)18/10/91	Amt(c)21
Dividend	(Ldr)09/10/92	(Pay)19/10/92	Amt(c)17.5

NUMBER OF EMPLOYEES : 250

CAPITAL STRUCTURE

	AUTHORISED	ISSUED
Ords 10c	100000000	55080000

FINANCIAL STATISTICS (AT FINANCIAL YEAR END)

(Amts in R'000)	1992 Jun	1991 Jun	1990 Jun
Ord S/H Int	146074	121354	99423
Long Trm Loans	121922	21272	20624
Iss Ord Share	55080	55080	55080
Total Liab	2815759	2636729	2393139
Current Liab	2693837	2615457	2372515
Total Assets	2961833	2758083	2492562
Current Assets	2884640	2668276	2381541
Debtors	2036865	1909521	1874892
Oper Profit	36359	29603	24549
Interest Paid	-	-	93
Prf af Int&Tax	37018	30269	24790
Prf att Ord Sh	37000	30250	25200
Btm Line Earn	37000	32130	25200
Dividend Paid	14321	11567	9639
Depreciation	94	89	20

PER SHARE STATISTICS (CENTS)

Net Asst Val	265.20	220.32	180.51
Dividends	26.00	21.00	17.50
Cash Flow	67.35	55.08	45.79

RATIOS AND OTHER INFORMATION

Current Ratio	1.07	1.02	1.00
Quik/Acid Tst	1.07	1.02	1.00
Debt/Ass Rat	0.95	0.96	0.96
L T L Tot Ass	0.04	0.01	0.01
Debt to Eqity	19.28	21.73	24.07
Interest Cover	-	-	267.56
Ret on Assets	1.25	1.10	1.00
Ret on Equity%	25.33	24.93	25.35
Def Interval	58.70	63.59	94.51
Sus Grth Rate	15.53	15.40	15.65

SUBSIDIARY & ASSOCIATED COMPANIES

ANGLO AFRICAN SHIPPING CO (1936) (PTY) L
JENWAY INVESTMENTS (PTY) LTD
LONDON & DOMINION TRUST LTD
MAGNUM NATIONAL LIFE ASSURANCE CO LTD
MOMENTUM LIFE ASSURERS LTD
RAND CONSOLIDATED PROPERTIES (PTY) LTD
RAND MERCHANT BANK LTD
RAND MERCHANT NOMINEES (PTY) LTD
RMB ASSET MANAGEMENT (PTY) LTD

INVESTMENTS

None

RMS PROPERTY HOLDINGS LTD

ABBREVIATION : RMSPROP

JSE SHORT CODE : RMR

SECTOR : Financial-Property Loan Stock

SHAREHOLDERS

Who Owns Whom's Assessment of the Identity of the Ultimate Controlling Shareholder:
SA MUTUAL

SHAREHOLDER	PERCENTAGE 1992	1991
SA MUTUAL	54.1	57.1
EIGHTY ONE MAIN STREET NOM LTD	8.5	9.0
METAL IND GROUP PENS FUND	6.2	6.0
BARLOWS PENS FUND	6.0	3.8
NAMPAK PENS FUND	3.7	3.7
ENGINEERING INDUSTRIES PENS FUND	3.1	2.2
CORNER HOUSE PENS FUND	2.0	1.5
I G NOM P/L	1.6	1.6
SHARESTOCK NOM P/L	1.5	1.6
WORKMENS COMPENS COMMISSIONER IN TRUST	1.4	---
YSKOR PENS FUND	1.1	1.3
PLEVANS PENS FUND	1.0	---
TOTAL	90.2	87.6

DIRECTORS :
BROWN MC ,FLANAGAN JPD ,FORSSMAN BO
GERARD PCM (Chairman),POLWARTH S

REGISTRATION NUMBER : 87/04808/06

REGISTERED OFFICE
RMS Syfrets House, 27 Eton Road
Parktown
2193
TEL: 031-301 3131
FAX: 031-305 5893

TRANSFER SECRETARY
Central Registrars Ltd
P O Box 4844, Johannesburg
2000
TEL: 011-331 0051

COMPANY SECRETARY
Russell Marshall & Stride (Pty) Ltd

NATURE OF BUSINESS
An investment holding company with a portfolio of income producing industrial properties located in Durban & Jhb.

BANKERS :
Nedperm Bank Ltd, UAL Merchant Bank Ltd

AUDITORS :
Deloitte Pim Goldby

FAMILIAR BRAND NAMES
N/A

CONTRIBUTION BY ACTIVITY
N/A

YEAR END : September

DIVIDEND : Units

Interim No 6	(Ldr)11/05/90	(Pay)25/05/90	Amt(c)26.613
Final No 7	(Ldr)09/11/90	(Pay)23/11/90	Amt(c)33.5836
Interim No 8	(Ldr)10/05/91	(Pay)24/05/91	Amt(c)33.6162
Final No 9	(Ldr)08/11/91	(Pay)22/11/91	Amt(c)32.5444
Interim No 10	(Ldr)08/05/92	(Pay)22/05/92	Amt(c)33.2074
Final No 11	(Ldr)06/11/92	(Pay)20/11/92	Amt(c)26.2225

NUMBER OF EMPLOYEES : 52

CAPITAL STRUCTURE

	AUTHORISED	ISSUED
Units 500c (1 Ord : 1 Deb)	50000000	39745713

FINANCIAL STATISTICS (AT FINANCIAL YEAR END)

(Amts in R'000)	1992 Sep	1991 Sep	1990 Sep	1989 Sep	1988 Sep
Ord S/H Int	3026	3026	3066	106750	784
Long Trm Loans	195043	195064	205504	18791	124378
Iss Ord Share	39746	39746	39746	21546	21545
Total Liab	206555	208856	221083	25230	131262
Current Liab	11512	13792	15579	6439	6884
Total Assets	209581	211882	224149	131980	132046
Current Assets	23018	25631	41004	10286	9445
Debtors	1746	2118	2294	2305	2045
Turnover	30407	32067	30397	17657	15479
Oper Profit	20617	22481	16738	14653	14355
Interest Paid	23412	27120	26079	3417	2150
Tax Paid	220	245	239	123	122
Prf af Int&Tax	239	266	239	12249	12083
Prf att Ord Sh	239	266	239	123	122
Btm Line Earn	239	266	239	516	122
Dividend Paid	239	266	239	123	122
Mkt Prce(c) YE	475	630	560	600	470
Depreciation	-	-	-	43	48

PER SHARE STATISTICS (CENTS)

Net Asst Val	7.61	7.61	7.71	495.45	3.64
Net Earnings	59.43	66.16	-	56.90	56.10
Dividends	59.43	66.16	-	56.90	56.10
Cash Flow	0.60	0.67	0.60	57.05	56.31

RATIOS AND OTHER INFORMATION

Mrk Cap(R000)	188794	250400	222578	129276	101262
Current Ratio	2.00	1.86	2.63	1.60	1.37
Quik/Acid Tst	2.00	1.86	2.63	1.60	1.37
A/C Rec T/ovr	17.42	15.14	13.25	7.66	7.57
Tot Ass T/ovr	0.15	0.15	0.14	0.13	0.12
Debt/Ass Rat	0.99	0.99	0.99	0.19	0.99
L T L Tot Ass	0.93	0.92	0.92	0.14	0.94
Debt to Eqity	68.26	69.02	72.11	0.24	167.43
Interest Cover	0.88	0.83	0.64	4.62	6.68
Oper Prof Mrg	67.80	70.11	55.06	82.99	92.74
Net Prof Marg%	0.79	0.83	0.79	0.70	0.79
Ret on Assets	11.39	13.04	11.85	11.96	10.87
Ret on Equity%	7.90	8.79	7.80	0.12	15.56
Price/Earnings	7.99	9.52	-	10.54	8.38
Divid Cover	1.00	1.00	-	1.00	1.00
Divid Yield	12.51	10.50	-	9.48	11.94
Earning Yield%	12.51	10.50	-	9.48	11.94
NAV % Mrk Pr	1.60	1.21	1.38	82.58	0.77
Effec Tax Rate	47.93	47.95	50.00	1.09	1.00
Def Interval	44.46	49.30	100.26	1.53	2.05
Sus Grth Rate	0.00	0.00	0.00	0.00	0.00

SUBSIDIARY & ASSOCIATED COMPANIES

BRAMFIN INVESTMENTS SHARE BLOCK (PTY) LT
BRAMLEY VIEW 362 SHARE BLOCK (PTY) LTD
CHURCHWAY INVESTMENTS SHARE BLOCK (PTY)
CONS STAND 136 NEW CENTRE SHARE BLOCK (P
DOVEHOUSE INVESTMENTS SHARE BLOCK (PTY)
ERF 13 CITY WEST SHARE BLOCK (PTY) LTD
ERF 26 HUGHES EXTENSION 2 SHARE BLOCK (P
ERF 320 ISANDO SHARE BLOCK (PTY) LTD
ERF 325 WYNBERG SHARE BLOCK (PTY) LTD
ERF 386 BRAMLEYVIEW EXTENSION 6 SHARE BL
ERF 463 WYNBERG EXT (PTY) LTD
ERF 480 ISANDO SHARE BLOCK (PTY) LTD
ERF 492 KEW SHARE BLOCK (PTY) LTD
ERF 494 KEW SHARE BLOCK (PTY) LTD
ERF 511 ISANDO SHARE BLOCK (PTY) LTD
ERF 522 KEW SHARE BLOCK (PTY) LTD
ERF 54 SEBENZA SHARE BLOCK (PTY) LTD
ERF 550 SELBY SHARE BLOCK (PTY) LTD
ERF 572, 573, 574 AND 833 KEW SHARE BLOC
ERF 60 ANDERBOLT EXTENSION 47 SHARE BLOC
ERF 679 AND 680 KEW SHARE BLOCK (PTY) LT
ERF 84 ROBERTVILLE EXTENSION 1 SHARE BLO
ERF 97 SPARTAN SHARE BLOCK (PTY) LTD
GILLWIN PROPERTIES SHARE BLOCK (PTY) LTD
HEKRO TRUST
LOT THREE FOUR WATERVAL PARK SHARE BLOCK
PEKRO SHARE BLOCK (PTY) LTD
PORTION 118 RIETFONTEIN SHARE BLOCK (PTY
RE OF PORTION 2 EXTENSION 47 PAARDEKRAAL
ROHEK TRUST
SANANGELO SHARE BLOCK (PTY) LTD
SARLAND PROPERTIES SHARE BLOCK (PTY) LTD
SELBY TRUST
STAND 135 WYNBERG SHARE BLOCK (PTY) LTD
STAND 203 EASTGATE EXTENSION 13 SHARE BL
STAND 506 WYNBERG SHARE BLOCK (PTY) LTD
STAND 524 SELBY EXTENSION 11 SHARE BLOCK
STAND 88 STORMHILL THREE SHARE BLOCK (PT
STAND 90 STORMHILL SHARE BLOCK (PTY) LTD
STAND 91 HALFWAY HOUSE SHARE BLOCK (PTY)
SUB 47 SPRINGFIELD SHARE BLOCK (PTY) LTD
WILLANE INVESTMENTS SHARE BLOCK (PTY) LT

INVESTMENTS

None

ROMANO FURNITURE LTD

ABBREVIATION : ROMANO

JSE SHORT CODE : RMA

SECTOR : Industrial-Furniture & Household

SHAREHOLDERS

Who Owns Whom's Assessment of the Identity of the Ultimate Controlling Shareholder:
DE CHAUD FAMILY

SHAREHOLDER	PERCENTAGE 1992	1991
MARAIS P J	29.4	—
MARIO DE CHAUD FAMILY TRUST	18.9	18.9
DE CHAUD MARIO	10.0	10.0
LEVY C L	5.7	1.2
KAYEMESS NOM P/L	5.2	5.6
DE CHAUD A	4.4	4.8
NEDBANK NOM LTD	1.6	1.6
PRETORIUS A	1.4	—
JEMMA INCORPORATED	1.3	1.3
BARCHAUD PRODUCTS P/L	1.2	1.2
BLUMBERG J A	—	4.6
KAPLAN & STEWART INC	—	1.2
ROETZ J F	—	29.4
TOTAL	79.1	79.7

DIRECTORS :
DE CHAUD A (Financial Director), DE CHAUD M
GOSLAR AE ,MARAIS PJ (Chairman & Managing Dir.

REGISTRATION NUMBER : 87/01361/06

REGISTERED OFFICE
1335 Spyker Crescent, Stormill Ext 2
Roodepoort
1724
TEL: 011-474 2658
FAX: 011-474 8407

TRANSFER SECRETARY
Central Registrars Ltd
P O Box 4844, Johannesburg
2000
TEL: 011-331 0051

COMPANY SECRETARY
Mrs Z Hassen

NATURE OF BUSINESS
The company is engaged in the manufacture of tubular brass, chrome & epoxy-coated furniture, lamps & light fittings for domestic use.

BANKERS :
Volkskas Ltd, Standard Bank of SA Ltd

AUDITORS :
Coopers Theron Du Toit

FAMILIAR BRAND NAMES
ROMANO

CONTRIBUTION BY ACTIVITY
N/A

YEAR END : June

DIVIDEND :15/10/91

NUMBER OF EMPLOYEES : 220

CAPITAL STRUCTURE

	AUTHORISED	ISSUED
Ords no par value	62000000	55663008
Var Rate Red no par value Prefs	10000000	6000000

FINANCIAL STATISTICS (AT FINANCIAL YEAR END)

(Amts in R'000)	1991 Jun	1990 Jun	1989 Jun	1988 Jun
Ord S/H Int	1256	2118	2987	3180
Long Trm Loans	-	232	657	1106
Iss Ord Share	13916	12251	12916	12251
Total Liab	4116	3776	4547	4799
Current Liab	4116	3544	3890	3693
Total Assets	5372	5894	7534	7979
Current Assets	3549	3848	4990	5112
Debtors	1903	1853	2089	2226
Inventory	1646	1995	2900	2867
Turnover	10625	11629	10519	10597
Oper Profit	-530	-273	-156	1378
Interest Paid	457	557	374	124
Tax Paid	-	-26	-246	625
Prf af Int&Tax	-987	-804	-284	629
Prf att Ord Sh	-987	-810	-297	616
Btm Line Earn	-987	-994	-229	616
Dividend Paid	-	-	-	196
Mkt Prce(c) YE	8	11	18	35
Depreciation	232	315	306	231

PER SHARE STATISTICS (CENTS)

Net Asst Val	9.03	17.29	23.13	25.96
Net Earnings	7.10	-6.00	-2.30	5.00
Dividends	-	-	-	2.50
Cash Flow	-5.43	-3.88	-1.91	7.37

RATIOS AND OTHER INFORMATION

Mrk Cap(R000)	1113	1348	2325	4288
Current Ratio	0.86	1.09	1.28	1.38
Quik/Acid Tst	0.46	0.52	0.54	0.61
A/C Rec T/ovr	5.58	6.28	5.04	3.81
Tot Ass T/ovr	1.98	1.97	1.40	1.06
Debt/Ass Rat	0.77	0.62	0.57	0.53
L T L Tot Ass	-	0.02	0.05	0.07
Debt to Eqity	3.28	1.72	1.43	1.34
Interest Cover	-1.16	-0.49	-0.42	11.11
Oper Prof Mrg	-4.99	-2.35	-1.48	13.00
Net Prof Marg%	-9.29	-6.97	-2.82	5.81
Ret on Assets	-9.87	-4.63	-2.07	13.82
Ret on Equity%	-78.58	-38.24	-9.94	15.50
Price/Earnings	1.13	-1.83	-7.83	7.00
Divid Cover	-	-	-	2.00
Divid Yield	-	-	-	7.14
Earning Yield%	88.75	-54.55	-12.78	14.29
NAV % Mrk Pr	112.82	157.17	128.48	74.16
Effec Tax Rate	-	-	-1.70	27.43
Def Interval	-2.91	-3.64	-11.00	1.42
Sus Grth Rate	-78.58	-38.24	-9.94	13.21

SUBSIDIARY & ASSOCIATED COMPANIES

None

INVESTMENTS

None

ROMATEX LTD

ABBREVIATION : ROMATEX

JSE SHORT CODE : ROM

SECTOR : Industrial-Clothing, Footwear & Textiles

SHAREHOLDERS

Who Owns Whom's Assessment of the Identity of the Ultimate Controlling Shareholder: SA MUTUAL VIA BARLOWS VIA CG SMITH

SHAREHOLDER	PERCENTAGE 1992	1991
C G SMITH LTD	55.8	55.8
ASSOCIATED FURNITURE CO LTD	13.2	13.2
SANTHOLD INV LTD	6.8	6.8
FURNCOL LTD	6.3	6.3
CMB NOM P/L	1.8	---
LIBERTY LIFE ASSOC OF AFRICA LTD	1.5	1.5
VOLKSKAS NOM P/L	1.5	1.5
EIGHTY ONE MAIN STREET NOM LTD	1.2	1.3

ENGINEERING INDUSTRIES PENS FUND	1.2	1.2
METAL IND GROUP PENS FUND	1.0	1.0
SANLAM	---	1.8
TOTAL	90.3	90.3

DIRECTORS :
BOURNE-LANGE R ,BOWDEN WRH ,BURY NA ,CLEWLOW WAM
CONNELLAN BP ,CRUTCHLEY AL (Executive Chairman)
GAZENDAM HD ,GRAHAM RW ,HANKINSON MJ
MCCARTHY BC ,ROGER-LUND CKD ,VAN DER WATT L
WARD JH ,WILLIAMS RA ,WILMOT NN

REGISTRATION NUMBER : 05/16831/06

REGISTERED OFFICE
32 Manchester Street, Jacobs
Durban
4052
TEL: 031-48 4343
FAX: 031-43 4174

TRANSFER SECRETARY
Rand Registrars Ltd
P O Box 82549, Southdale
2135
TEL: 011-835 1016

COMPANY SECRETARY
M Walsh

NATURE OF BUSINESS
The group manufactures & supplies textiles, yarns, carpets, underfelts, fabrics and quilted products. The group also manufactures speciality chemicals for the textile industry, and provides bulk liquid storage facilities at Durban & on the Reef.

BANKERS :
Standard Bank of SA Ltd

AUDITORS :
Deloitte Pim Goldby

FAMILIAR BRAND NAMES
CHENILLE,CONSTANTIA,CONSTANTIA CREATIONS
CREATIONS,CRENETTE,CROSSLEY,FELTEX
FIBREMAKERS,FLORTIME,HEXTEX,HEXWOVEN
HORROCKSES,ISLAND VIEW STORAGE,KELLER
MARINO MASTERPIECES,PARKER WOOL
PTA WHOLESALE CARPETS,RAM,ROMACOAT,ROMAFIL
ROMALUXE,ROMAYARNS,TWISTEX,VAN DYCK,VANTONA
VELDSPUN,WEAVERS WORLD

CONTRIBUTION BY ACTIVITY
Fabrics (% pre-interest earnings) (15.0%)
Floorcoverings (-8.0%)
Industrials (41.0%)
Island View (52.0%)

YEAR END : September

DIVIDEND :Ords R1

Interim No 92	(Ldr)11/05/90	(Pay)06/06/90	Amt(c)25
Final No 93	(Ldr)16/11/90	(Pay)12/12/90	Amt(c)30
Interim No 94	(Ldr)10/05/91	(Pay)05/06/91	Amt(c)10
Final No 95	(Ldr)15/11/91	(Pay)11/12/91	Amt(c)4
Interim No 96	(Ldr)08/05/92	(Pay)03/06/92	Amt(c)10
Final No 97	(Ldr)13/11/92	(Pay)09/12/92	Amt(c)10

NUMBER OF EMPLOYEES : 9341

CAPITAL STRUCTURE

	AUTHORISED	ISSUED
Ords R1	26500000	26500000
"A" Ords R1	1000000	21353

FINANCIAL STATISTICS (AT FINANCIAL YEAR END)

(Amts in R'000)	1992 Sep	1991 Sep	1990 Sep	1989 Sep	1988 Sep
Ord S/H Int	308200	297300	300700	281700	244300
Long Trm Loans	45600	68200	79600	46100	23000
Iss Ord Share	26521	26521	26451	26404	23800
Total Liab	204000	220300	227500	202500	179500
Current Liab	158400	152100	147900	156400	156500
Total Assets	512200	517600	528200	484200	423800
Current Assets	261000	258500	266100	282600	254700
Debtors	156800	146400	126500	146600	121500
Inventory	102500	111200	134200	135900	123500
Turnover	722400	740400	715700	746300	674400
Oper Profit	39300	39400	62800	84600	86400
Interest Paid	15800	19900	9800	8400	2400
Tax Paid	11700	11300	16400	24800	32900
Prf af Int&Tax	12500	8600	37100	51900	51100
Prf att Ord Sh	12500	8600	37400	52400	51700
Btm Line Earn	15900	-100	32300	54600	49500
Dividend Paid	4900	3500	13600	19200	17900
Mkt Prce(c) YE	450	770	620	1020	725
Depreciation	33000	31700	24300	21600	17800

PER SHARE STATISTICS (CENTS)

Net Asst Val	1162.10	1121.00	1136.82	1066.88	1026.47
Net Earnings	50.50	34.90	151.60	214.30	217.20
Dividends	20.00	14.00	55.00	78.00	75.00
Cash Flow	165.91	161.13	249.59	295.08	286.55

RATIOS AND OTHER INFORMATION

Mrk Cap(R000)	119345	204212	163996	269321	172550
Current Ratio	1.65	1.70	1.80	1.81	1.63
Quik/Acid Tst	1.00	0.97	0.89	0.94	0.84
A/C Rec T/ovr	4.61	5.06	5.66	5.09	5.55
Tot Ass T/ovr	1.41	1.43	1.35	1.54	1.59
Debt/Ass Rat	0.37	0.39	0.39	0.38	0.37
L T L Tot Ass	0.06	0.10	0.11	0.05	0.00
Debt to Eqity	0.61	0.68	0.69	0.65	0.65
Interest Cover	2.53	2.00	6.46	10.13	36.00
Oper Prof Mrg	5.44	5.32	8.77	11.34	12.81
Net Prof Marg%	1.73	1.16	5.23	7.02	7.67
Ret on Assets	7.81	7.69	12.04	17.68	20.53
Ret on Equity%	4.06	2.89	12.44	18.60	21.16
Price/Earnings	8.91	22.06	4.09	4.76	3.34
Divid Cover	2.53	2.49	2.76	2.75	2.90
Divid Yield	4.44	1.82	8.87	7.65	10.34
Earning Yield%	11.22	4.53	24.45	21.01	29.96
NAV % Mrk Pr	258.24	145.58	183.36	104.60	141.58
Effec Tax Rate	54.47	61.03	30.94	34.51	40.48
Def Interval	1.14	2.22	1.45	0.58	0.17
Sus Grth Rate	2.47	1.72	7.91	11.79	13.84

SUBSIDIARY & ASSOCIATED COMPANIES

AFRICAN ALLTEX (PTY) LTD
AFRICAN ALLTEX (TVL) (PTY) LTD
AFRICAN ALLTEX HOLDINGS (PTY) LTD
AMALGAMATED QUILTING (PTY) LTD
AMPAX ROPES AND TWINES (PTY) LTD
APOLLO CAR SEAT COVERS (PTY) LTD
ASSOCIATED CARPET ENTERPRISES (PTY) LTD
BELLA ROSA CARPETS (PTY) LTD
BERG RIVER TEXTILES (PTY) LTD
CARPET CONTRACTS (PTY) LTD
CHENILLE CORPORATION OF SA (PTY) LTD

CONSTANTIA CARPET MILLS (PTY) LTD
CONSTANTIA INDUSTRIAL CORP. (PTY) LTD
CONSTANTIA TEXTILE MILLS (PTY) LTD
CONSTANTIA TEXTILE MILLS (SALES) (PTY) L
CONSTANTIA TEXTILE PROPERTIES (PTY) LTD
CRENETTE (PTY) LTD
CRESTA CARPETS (PTY) LTD
CYRIL DARLOW (PTY) LTD
DONSTAN (PTY) LTD
DURBAN KNITTING MILLS (1959) (PTY) LTD
EXTRUDED FABRICS (SA) (PTY) LTD
EXTRUDED FABRICS SALES (PTY) LTD
FELROSS (PTY) LTD
FELROSS PROPERTIES (PTY) LTD
FELT INDUSTRIES (PTY) LTD
FELTEX AUTOMOTIVE PRODUCTS (PTY) LTD
FELTEX FINANCE (PTY) LTD
FELTEX FOAM & AUTOMOTIVE PRODUCTS (PTY)
FELTEX FOAM & FABRICS (PTY) LTD
FELTEX INDUSTRIALS (PTY) LTD
FELTEX LTD
FELTEX NON-WOVENS (PTY) LTD
FIBRE SPINNERS & WEAVERS (DURBAN) (PTY)
FIBRE SPINNERS & WEAVERS (PTY) LTD
FIBREMAKERS (PTY) LTD
FILTAFLO (PTY) LTD
FLORTIME (PTY) LTD
GOLD REEF (PTY) LTD
HEXTEX (PTY) LTD
HIGHVELD BAG REPAIRERS (PTY) LTD
HOCHFELD NATAL (PTY) LTD
HORROCKSES SA (PTY) LTD
ISLAND VIEW HOLDINGS LTD
ISLAND VIEW STORAGE (PTY) LTD
LLAMA (PTY) LTD
NATIONAL CARPETS LTD
NETTING AGENCIES (PTY) LTD
OUTDOOR WORLD (PTY) LTD
PARKER WOOL QUILTING CORPORATION (PTY) L
POLYFIBRE (PTY) LTD
PREMIER CARPET DISTRIBUTORS (NATAL) (PTY
PRETORIA WHOLESALE CARPET CO. (PTY) LTD
REGINA CARPETS (PTY) LTD
REGINA ENTERPRISES (PTY) LTD
RENTATENT (PTY) LTD
ROMAFIL (PTY) LTD
ROMATEX CARPETS (PTY) LTD
ROMATEX CARTAGE (PTY) LTD
ROMATEX FABRICS LTD
ROMATEX FLOORCOVERINGS LTD
ROMATEX HOME TEXTILES (PTY) LTD
ROMATEX INDUSTRIALS LTD
ROMATEX INTERFACE (PTY) LTD
ROMATEX MANAGEMENT SERVICES (PTY) LTD
ROMATEX MILLS LTD
ROMATEX NYLON SPINNERS (PTY) LTD
ROMATEX ROPES AND TWINES (PTY) LTD
ROMATEX TEXTILES (PTY) LTD
ROMATEX WHOLESALE (PTY) LTD
ROMAYARNS (PTY) LTD
ROPES AND MATTINGS (PTY) LTD
SANTHOLD INVESTMENTS LTD
SHORESAL (CAPE TOWN) (PTY) LTD
SHORESL EXTENSIONS (PTY) LTD
STAND ONE TWO ONE BUNSEN STREET (PTY) LT
TAPSA LTD
THE CARPET MANUFACTURING CO. (SA) LTD
TIERVLEI INDUSTRIAL PROPERTIES (PTY) LTD
TWISTEX (PTY) LTD
ULTRALITE (PTY) LTD
VAN DYCK CARPETS (PTY) LTD
VDC CARPETS (PTY) LTD
VELDSPUN (PTY) LTD

INVESTMENTS

None

ROMENS HOLDINGS LTD

ABBREVIATION : ROMENS

JSE SHORT CODE : RMS

SECTOR : Development Capital Market

SHAREHOLDERS

Who Owns Whom's Assessment of the Identity of the Ultimate Controlling Shareholder: DIRECTORS CONTROL 70,66%

SHAREHOLDER	PERCENTAGE 1992	1991
MARACAY INV P/L	52.3	52.3
TIBER INV HOLDINGS CC	8.7	---
STD BANK NOM TVL P/L	7.0	7.0
REMUS INV P/L	4.4	4.4
TIBER INV CC	4.2	4.2
COWLING B	3.3	3.3
KAHN D M	2.1	1.3
SELIGSON M	1.7	1.7
NAVY INV P/L	---	8.7
TOTAL	83.6	82.7

DIRECTORS :
BESTER N ,KAHN DM (Chairman)
MARKS DJ (Chairman & Managing Dir.),STUBBS SFW
TILBURY J ,WRANKMORE RD

REGISTRATION NUMBER : 56/02868/06

REGISTERED OFFICE
16 Bree Street, Cape Town
8000
8000
TEL: 021-25 4081
FAX: 021-254082

TRANSFER SECRETARY
Mercantile Registrars Ltd
P O Box 1053, Johannesburg
2000
TEL: 011-333 8181

COMPANY SECRETARY
City Property Administration (Pty) Ltd

NATURE OF BUSINESS
A property loan stock company.

BANKERS :
Trust Bank of Africa Ltd
Standard Bank of SA Ltd, Boland Bank Ltd

AUDITORS :
Price Waterhouse Meyernel
Deloitte Pim Goldby

FAMILIAR BRAND NAMES
N/A

CONTRIBUTION BY ACTIVITY
Industrial/Commercial (% Gross Income) (50.0%)
Retail (40.0%)
Offices (8.0%)
Residential (2.0%)

YEAR END : August

DIVIDEND :15/03/91 and 15/09/91

CAPITAL STRUCTURE

	AUTHORISED	ISSUED
Ords no par value	20000000	13375000
13% Comp Conv Cum Prefs no par va	8560000	8560000
Ords 1c (1 Ord : 1 Deb)	100000000	47734097

FINANCIAL STATISTICS (AT FINANCIAL YEAR END)

(Amts in R'000)	1991 Jun	1990 Jun	1989 Jun	1988 Jun	1987
Ord S/H Int	122	1891	2524	2915	70
Long Trm Loans	3602	736	-	-	3906
Iss Ord Share	13375	13375	13375	13375	7
Total Liab	9845	10898	8113	6033	6462
Current Liab	6243	10162	8113	6033	2556
Total Assets	8863	11685	9533	8948	6798
Intang Assets	1104	1104	1104	*	*
Current Assets	7146	10231	8817	7775	2822
Debtors	1717	3012	2250	1700	-
Inventory	5209	7137	6567	5994	2822
Turnover	14184	18048	13416	9982	5875
Oper Profit	-503	336	398	1400	592
Interest Paid	1250	1147	368	94	38
Tax Paid	132	-	38	496	226
Prf af Int&Tax	-1769	-633	48	810	328
Prf att Ord Sh	-1769	-633	48	810	328
Btm Line Earn	-1769	-633	48	810	328
Dividend Paid	-	-	-	401	-
Mkt Prce(c) YE	50	40	33	40	-
Depreciation	189	116	99	47	-

PER SHARE STATISTICS (CENTS)

Net Asst Val	-7.34	5.88	10.62	21.79	1000.00
Net Earnings	-113.22	-4.73	0.64	6.05	-
Dividends	-	-	-	3.00	-
Cash Flow	-11.81	-3.87	1.10	6.41	4685.71

RATIOS AND OTHER INFORMATION

Mrk Cap(R000)	6688	5350	4414	5350	-
Current Ratio	1.14	1.01	1.09	1.29	1.10
Quik/Acid Tst	0.31	0.30	0.28	0.30	-
A/C Rec T/ovr	8.26	5.99	5.96	5.87	-
Tot Ass T/ovr	1.60	1.54	1.41	1.12	0.86
Debt/Ass Rat	0.79	0.93	0.85	0.67	0.95
L T L Tot Ass	0.08	0.06	-	-	0.57
Debt to Eqity	57.07	5.76	3.21	2.07	92.31
Interest Cover	-0.40	0.29	1.08	14.89	15.58
Oper Prof Mrg	-3.55	1.86	2.97	14.03	10.08
Net Prof Marg%	-12.47	-3.51	0.36	8.11	5.58
Ret on Assets	-4.37	4.40	4.76	15.65	8.71
Ret on Equity%	-1450.00	-33.47	1.90	27.79	468.57
Price/Earnings	-0.44	-8.46	51.56	6.61	-
Divid Cover	-	-	-	2.02	-
Divid Yield	-	-	-	7.50	-
Earning Yield%	-226.44	-11.83	1.94	15.13	-
NAV % Mrk Pr	-14.68	14.71	32.17	54.40	-
Effec Tax Rate	-8.06	-	44.19	37.98	40.79
Def Interval	-2.20	-9.89	19.84	1.25	11.91
Sus Grth Rate	-1450.00	-33.47	1.90	14.03	468.57

SUBSIDIARY & ASSOCIATED COMPANIES

DE WET BROERS (EDMS) BPK
MIAB (PTY) LTD
ROMENS (NAMIBIA) (PTY) LTD
ROMENS MENSWEAR (PTY) LTD

INVESTMENTS

None

ROOIBERG TIN LTD

ABBREVIATION : ROOIBERG

JSE SHORT CODE : ROI

SECTOR : Metals & Minerals-Tin

SHAREHOLDERS

Who Owns Whom's Assessment of the Identity of the Ultimate Controlling Shareholder: GFSA

SHAREHOLDER	PERCENTAGE 1992	1991
MINU NOM LTD	48.2	48.2
EIGHTY ONE MAIN STREET NOM LTD	9.6	9.6
FIRST NAT NOM P/L	7.1	9.7
FERBROS NOM P/L	3.4	---
SHKUDSKY A	3.1	2.4
STD BANK NOM TVL P/L	2.5	2.7
STOCKSHARE NOM P/L	1.0	---
HERTZOG D W R	---	1.4
TOTAL	74.9	74.0

DIRECTORS :
DAY BA ,FERGUSON DSB ,HOPWOOD JG ,HOUGHTON AB
ROBINSON RL (Chairman & Managing Dir.

REGISTRATION NUMBER : 01/02946/06

REGISTERED OFFICE
75 Fox Street, Johannesburg
2001
TEL: 011-639 9111
FAX: 011-639 2101/2

TRANSFER SECRETARY
Gold Fields of SA Ltd
P O Box 1167, Johannesburg
2000
TEL: 011-639 9111

COMPANY SECRETARY
Gold Fields of SA Ltd

NATURE OF BUSINESS
The company is engaged in tin mining and smelting, and owns freehold land and mineral rights in the Warmbaths district of the Tvl.

BANKERS :
Standard Bank of SA Ltd

AUDITORS :
Ernst & Young

FAMILIAR BRAND NAMES
N/A

CONTRIBUTION BY ACTIVITY
N/A

YEAR END : December

DIVIDEND : Ords 25c
Interm No 109 (Ldr)30/06/89 (Pay)09/08/89 Amt(c)30

NUMBER OF EMPLOYEES : 744

CAPITAL STRUCTURE

	AUTHORISED	ISSUED
Ords 25c	2250000	2075000

FINANCIAL STATISTICS (AT FINANCIAL YEAR END)

(Amts in R'000)	1991 Dec	1990 Dec	1989 Dec	1988	1987
Ord S/H Int	56813	58799	62123	60311	59819
Long Trm Loans	-	-	-	3935	2850
Iss Ord Share	2075	2075	2075	2075	2075
Total Liab	3316	2478	3356	7870	5700
Current Liab	3316	2478	3356	3935	2850
Total Assets	60129	61277	65479	81198	78072
Current Assets	12653	13726	17495	16952	15403
Debtors	2614	3886	3448	-	-
Inventory	4546	4780	3388	16952	15403
Turnover	17390	19248	25414	21495	22718
Oper Profit	-3803	-4999	867	1477	25
Prf af Int&Tax	-1846	-3599	2370	1477	25
Prf att Ord Sh	-1846	-3599	2370	977	25
Btm Line Earn	-1846	-3599	2370	977	25
Dividend Paid	-	-	622	1037	25
Mkt Prce(c) YE	270	310	725	750	650

PER SHARE STATISTICS (CENTS)

Net Asst Val	2737.98	2833.69	2993.88	2906.55	2882.84
Net Earnings	-88.00	-173.00	114.00	-	-
Dividends	-	-	30.00	-	-
Cash Flow	-88.96	-173.45	114.22	71.18	1.20

RATIOS AND OTHER INFORMATION

Mrk Cap(R000)	5603	6433	15044	15563	13488
Current Ratio	3.82	5.54	5.21	4.31	5.40
Quik/Acid Tst	2.44	3.61	4.20	-	-
A/C Rec T/ovr	6.65	4.95	7.37	-	-
Tot Ass T/ovr	0.29	0.31	0.39	0.26	0.29
Debt/Ass Rat	0.06	0.04	0.05	0.10	0.07
L T L Tot Ass	-	-	-	0.05	0.04
Debt to Eqity	0.06	0.04	0.05	0.13	0.10
Oper Prof Mrg	-21.87	-25.97	3.41	6.87	0.11
Net Prof Marg%	-10.62	-18.70	9.33	4.55	0.11
Ret on Assets	-3.07	-5.87	3.62	1.82	0.03
Ret on Equity%	-3.25	-6.12	3.82	1.62	0.04
Price/Earnings	-3.07	-1.79	6.36	-	-
Divid Cover	-	-	3.80	-	-
Divid Yield	-	-	4.14	-	-
Earning Yield%	-32.59	-55.81	15.72	-	-
NAV % Mrk Pr	1014.07	914.09	412.95	387.54	443.51
Def Interval	-	-	-	2.66	114.00
Sus Grth Rate	-3.25	-6.12	2.81	-0.10	0.00

SUBSIDIARY & ASSOCIATED COMPANIES

None

INVESTMENTS

None

ROTHMANS OF PALL MALL (ZIMBABWE) LTD

ABBREVIATION : ROTH ZIM

SECTOR : Zimbabwe Stock Exchange

SHAREHOLDERS

Who Owns Whom's Assessment of the Identity of the Ultimate Controlling Shareholder:
LIKOBRAND SA

SHAREHOLDER	PERCENTAGE 1992	1991
LIKOBRAND SA	50.0	---
OLD MUTUAL INV CORP (PVT) LTD	19.3	---
LEVER GROUP RETIREMENT FUND ZIMBABWE	2.1	---
UNILEVER SA PENS FUND	1.9	---
FIRST MUTUAL LIFE ASSURE SOC OF ZIM	1.6	---
MINING INDUSTRY PENS FUND	1.6	---
R M INSURANCE CO PVT LTD	1.4	---
TOTAL	77.9	---

DIRECTORS :
BARNARD R ,CHIPUDLA PWT
DAY B (Chairman & Chief Exec.)
LYNTON-EDWARDS MA (Managing Director),PALMER GA
RUSHWAYA SV ,STEEL JAD

REGISTERED OFFICE
1 Manchester Road, Southerton
Harare

TEL: 63647
FAX: 61934

TRANSFER SECRETARY
First Transfer Secretaries (Pvt) Ltd
P O Box 437, Bulawayo
Zimbabwe

TEL: 092634 - 702905

COMPANY SECRETARY
J H Oosthuizen

NATURE OF BUSINESS
ROTHMANS OF PALL MALL, incorporated in Zimbabwe, is a manufacturer and distributor of tobacco products.It also propagates and markets flowers.Associated companies manufacture and distribute wines and spirits (AFDIS) and farm implements (ZIMPLOW).

BANKERS :
Barclays Bank of Zimbabwe Ltd

AUDITORS :
Coopers & Lybrand

FAMILIAR BRAND NAMES
N/A

CONTRIBUTION BY ACTIVITY
Tobacco Products (% of Turnover) (82.2%)
Agency (12.8%)
Floriculture & Aquaculture (0.5%)

YEAR END : March

DIVIDEND : Ords Z$1

Interim	(Ldr)15/11/91	(Pay) / /	Amt(c)3.5
Final	(Ldr)01/09/92	(Pay) / /	Amt(c)9

CAPITAL STRUCTURE

	AUTHORISED	ISSUED
Ords Z$1	15000000	14000000

FINANCIAL STATISTICS (AT FINANCIAL YEAR END)

(Amts in Z$)	1992 Mar	1991 Mar
Ord S/H Int	64497	36610
Long Trm Loans	17457	6062
Iss Ord Share	14000	14000
Total Liab	60598	28360
Current Liab	43141	22298
Total Assets	125095	64970
Current Assets	63936	34602
Debtors	5327	5275
Inventory	46042	27000
Turnover	124317	88534
Oper Profit	18909	7224
Interest Paid	4233	1033
Tax Paid	9852	3526
Prf af Int&Tax	5069	2823
Prf att Ord Sh	12457	5627
Btm Line Earn	12457	5627
Dividend Paid	1750	1400
Depreciation	3102	2503

PER SHARE STATISTICS (CENTS)

Net Asst Val	460.69	261.50
Net Earnings	88.98	40.19
Dividends	12.50	10.00
Cash Flow	65.57	40.31

RATIOS AND OTHER INFORMATION

Current Ratio	1.48	1.55
Quik/Acid Tst	0.41	0.34
A/C Rec T/ovr	23.34	16.78
Tot Ass T/ovr	0.99	1.36
Debt/Ass Rat	0.43	0.34
L T L Tot Ass	0.08	-
Debt to Eqity	0.83	0.61
Interest Cover	4.49	7.06
Oper Prof Mrg	15.21	8.16
Net Prof Marg%	10.02	6.36
Ret on Assets	21.22	15.68
Ret on Equity%	19.31	15.37
Divid Cover	7.12	4.02
Effec Tax Rate	59.68	51.85
Def Interval	2.02	1.56
Sus Grth Rate	16.60	11.55

SUBSIDIARY & ASSOCIATED COMPANIES

AFDIS HOLDINGS (PRIVATE) LIMITED (25%)
VALTOBAC LIMITED S.A. (LUXEMBOURG)
ZIMPLOW LIMITED (48,8%)

INVESTMENTS

None

ROYAL CORPORATION LTD

ABBREVIATION : ROYAL

JSE SHORT CODE : RYL

SECTOR : Industrial-Industrial Holding

SHAREHOLDERS

Who Owns Whom's Assessment of the Identity of the Ultimate Controlling Shareholder:
ROYAL HOLDINGS

SHAREHOLDER	PERCENTAGE 1992	1991
ROYAL GROUP HLDGS LTD	51.1	51.7
SA MUTUAL	13.7	16.4
CMB NOM P/L	8.1	---
STD BANK NOM TVL P/L	7.5	6.9
SAFEGRO NOM P/L	4.5	4.6
SAGE LIFE LTD	2.3	2.3
COMMERCIAL UNION LIFE ASSURE CO SA LTD	2.1	---
NEDBANK NOM LTD	2.0	---
EPF OLD MUTUAL NOM P/L	---	1.5
COMMERCIAL UNION ASSURE CO SA LTD	---	1.5
SANLAM	---	8.2
TOTAL	91.3	93.1

DIRECTORS :
FRAGIS J MR (Financial Director)
IMERMAN S MR (Vice Chairman)
IMERMAN VS MR (Executive Chairman)
JOHNSTON DHB MR (Managing Director),LEVIN HR MR
MOOR B ST C MR (Dir Human Resources

REGISTRATION NUMBER : 84/09968/06

REGISTERED OFFICE
Lovasz Park, 247 - 15th Road
Randjespark, Midrand
1685
TEL: 011-314 2370
FAX: 011-314 2001

TRANSFER SECRETARY
Central Registrars Ltd
P O Box 4844, Johannesburg
2000
TEL: 011-331 0051

COMPANY SECRETARY
G S Katzeff

NATURE OF BUSINESS
The holding company of subsidiaries engaged in Manufacture, marketing & distribution of food and confectionery products, and Distribution of speciality, pharmaceutical & industrial chemicals.

BANKERS :
Standard Bank of SA Ltd

AUDITORS :
M Lutrin & Co, Fisher Hoffman Stride

FAMILIAR BRAND NAMES
BUBBLE-YUM,LUSHUS JELLY,ROYAL DESSERTS
SWEET-AID,TRIMPAK

CONTRIBUTION BY ACTIVITY
Foods & Confectionery (% Income) (64.0%)
Chemicals & Pharmaceuticals (36.0%)

YEAR END : August

DIVIDEND : Ords 5c

Dividend No 2	(Ldr)09/06/89	(Pay)30/06/89	Amt(c)5
Dividend No 3	(Ldr)08/06/90	(Pay)29/06/90	Amt(c)6
Dividend No 4	(Ldr)28/02/91	(Pay)24/05/91	Amt(c)7
Dividend No 5	(Ldr)15/11/91	(Pay)06/12/91	Amt(c)6.9
Dividend No 6	(Ldr)16/04/92	(Pay)05/06/92	Amt(c)7.6
Dividend No 7	(Ldr)13/11/92	(Pay)04/12/92	Amt(c)10.2

NUMBER OF EMPLOYEES : 280

CAPITAL STRUCTURE

	AUTHORISED	ISSUED
Ords 5c	80000000	67827275

FINANCIAL STATISTICS (AT FINANCIAL YEAR END)

(Amts in R'000)	1991 Aug	1990 Feb	1989 Feb	1988	1987
Ord S/H Int	180663	101715	36068	13382	5475
Long Trm Loans	136458	14122	12113	17232	12108
Iss Ord Share	67827	67811	26731	26731	20000
Total Liab	265801	51509	34473	28327	20944
Current Liab	129343	37387	22360	11095	8836
Total Assets	340331	106418	54539	52225	28469
Intang Assets	106133	46806	16002	*	*
Current Assets	167716	51128	37201	21611	10886
Debtors	82756	24996	18021	-	-
Inventory	84399	26132	19180	21611	10886
Turnover	460777	170511	63412	44597	30814
Oper Profit	55274	19556	5700	3870	2880
Interest Paid	11190	4997	1423	804	1292
Tax Paid	4232	1669	136	161	119
Prf af Int&Tax	39852	12890	4141	2905	1469
Prf att Ord Sh	26977	12611	4049	2905	1469
Btm Line Earn	27653	12611	4049	2905	1469
Dividend Paid	9427	4069	1337	802	-
Mkt Prce(c) YE	420	130	205	85	-
Depreciation	5684	1902	393	-	-

PER SHARE STATISTICS (CENTS)

Net Asst Val	109.88	80.97	75.07	50.06	27.38
Net Earnings	39.80	18.60	13.50	-	-
Dividends	13.90	6.00	5.00	-	-
Cash Flow	36.22	23.54	16.52	10.87	7.35

RATIOS AND OTHER INFORMATION

Mrk Cap(R000)	284873	88154	54799	22721	-
Current Ratio	1.30	1.37	1.66	1.95	1.23
Quik/Acid Tst	0.64	0.67	0.81	-	-
A/C Rec T/ovr	3.71	6.82	3.52	-	-
Tot Ass T/ovr	0.90	1.60	1.16	0.85	1.08
Debt/Ass Rat	0.38	0.45	0.60	0.54	0.74
L T L Tot Ass	0.00	0.10	0.19	0.33	0.43
Debt to Eqity	0.72	0.47	0.90	2.12	3.83
Interest Cover	4.94	3.91	4.01	4.81	2.23
Oper Prof Mrg	12.00	11.47	8.99	8.68	9.35
Net Prof Marg%	5.85	7.40	6.39	6.51	4.77
Ret on Assets	10.83	18.38	10.50	7.41	10.12
Ret on Equity%	9.95	12.40	11.23	21.71	26.83
Price/Earnings	10.55	6.99	15.19	-	-
Divid Cover	2.86	3.10	2.70	-	-
Divid Yield	3.31	4.62	2.44	-	-
Earning Yield%	9.48	14.31	6.59	-	-
NAV % Mrk Pr	26.16	62.29	36.62	58.90	-
Effec Tax Rate	0.10	1.52	3.18	5.25	7.49
Def Interval	0.19	0.98	2.70	5.93	8.24
Sus Grth Rate	9.71	8.40	7.52	15.72	26.83

SUBSIDIARY & ASSOCIATED COMPANIES

LOVASZ CHEMICAL CORPORATION (PTY) LTD
ROYAL FOODS LTD
ROYCHEM LTD
SOUTH AFRICAN PRESERVING CO (PTY) LTD

INVESTMENTS

None

ROYAL FOODS LTD

ABBREVIATION : ROYFOOD

JSE SHORT CODE : RYF

SECTOR : Industrial-Food

SHAREHOLDERS

Who Owns Whom's Assessment of the Identity of the Ultimate Controlling Shareholder:
ROYAL HOLDINGS VIA ROYAL CORPORATION

SHAREHOLDER	PERCENTAGE 1992	1991
ROYAL CORP LTD	65.2	65.2
SA MUTUAL	12.5	13.0
STD BANK NOM TVL P/L	4.9	---
CMB NOM P/L	3.8	---
EIGHTY ONE MAIN STREET NOM LTD	3.3	1.0
METAL IND GROUP PENS FUND	1.5	1.5
ENGINEERING INDUSTRIES PENS FUND	1.5	1.5
FIRST NAT NOM P/L	1.3	1.3
COMMERCIAL UNION LIFE ASSURE CO SA LTD	1.1	---
BOARD OF EXECUTORS NOM P/L	---	4.7
FEDLIFE ASSURE LTD	---	2.3
SANLAM	---	3.8
TOTAL	95.1	94.4

DIRECTORS :
BEDFORD AW ,FRAGIS J (Financial Director)
FRIELICK ER ,IMERMAN S (Vice Chairman)
IMERMAN VS (Executive Chairman)
JOHNSTON DHB (Managing Director)
MOOR B ST CLAIR (Dir Human Resources),MULLER MA

REGISTRATION NUMBER : 89/00733/06

REGISTERED OFFICE
Lovasz Park, 247-15th Road
Randjespark, Midrand
1685
TEL: 011-314 2370
FAX: 011-314 2225

TRANSFER SECRETARY
Central Registrars Ltd
P O Box 4844, Johannesburg
2000
TEL: 011-331 0051

COMPANY SECRETARY
G S Katzeff

NATURE OF BUSINESS
The company houses the food interests of the Royal group. Operations include manufacture, marketing and distribution of confectionery and dry grocery products, & canning & export of deciduous fruits.

BANKERS :
Standard Bank of SA Ltd

AUDITORS :
Fisher Hoffman Stride

FAMILIAR BRAND NAMES
BELLS BISCUITS,BREATHSAVERS,BUBBLE YUM
CARE FREE,DEL MONTE,FRESH-UP,GOLDEN HARVEST
LECOL,LUSHUS,MANHATTANS CC,SUPER C,SWEETAID
TUC

CONTRIBUTION BY ACTIVITY
N/A

YEAR END : August

DIVIDEND :Ords 1c

Dividend	(Ldr)16/04/92	(Pay)05/06/92	Amt(c)5.5
Dividend	(Ldr)13/11/92	(Pay)04/12/92	Amt(c)6.6

CAPITAL STRUCTURE

	AUTHORISED	ISSUED
Ords 1c	150000000	97428985

FINANCIAL STATISTICS (AT FINANCIAL YEAR END)

(Amts in R'000)	1991 Feb	1990 Feb
Ord S/H Int	191909	185345
Long Trm Loans	31426	19130
Iss Ord Share	97400	97400
Total Liab	62288	53630
Current Liab	30862	34500
Total Assets	184850	169628
Intang Assets	69347	69347
Current Assets	80414	68816
Debtors	47876	39103
Inventory	32538	29713
Turnover	213551	184211
Oper Profit	33138	28681
Interest Paid	6509	1505
Tax Paid	2383	5823
Prf af Int&Tax	24246	21353
Prf att Ord Sh	24246	21353
Btm Line Earn	24246	21353

PER SHARE STATISTICS (CENTS)

Net Asst Val	125.83	119.09
Net Earnings	24.90	21.90
Cash Flow	24.89	21.92

RATIOS AND OTHER INFORMATION

Current Ratio	2.61	1.99
Quik/Acid Tst	1.55	1.13
A/C Rec T/ovr	4.46	4.71
Tot Ass T/ovr	1.16	1.09
Debt/Ass Rat	0.34	0.32
L T L Tot Ass	0.17	0.11
Debt to Eqity	0.32	0.29
Interest Cover	5.09	19.06
Oper Prof Mrg	15.52	15.57
Net Prof Marg%	11.35	11.59
Ret on Assets	17.93	16.91
Ret on Equity%	12.63	11.52
Effec Tax Rate	8.95	21.43
Def Interval	1.30	0.90
Sus Grth Rate	12.63	11.52

SUBSIDIARY & ASSOCIATED COMPANIES

ROOIHOOGTE SUID FARM (PTY) LTD
ROYAL BEECH-NUT (PTY) LTD
SOUTH AFRICAN MARKETERS & BROKERS (PTY)
SOUTH AFRICAN PRESERVING CO (PTY) LTD

INVESTMENTS

None

ROYAL GROUP HOLDINGS LTD

ABBREVIATION : ROYHOLD

JSE SHORT CODE : RYH

SECTOR : Industrial-Industrial Holding

SHAREHOLDERS

Who Owns Whom's Assessment of the Identity of the Ultimate Controlling Shareholder:
IMERMAN FAMILY / ANGLO AMERICAN

SHAREHOLDER	PERCENTAGE 1992	1991
IMERMAN V S	52.5	52.5
ABSA NOM P/L	12.6	—
SA MUTUAL	8.8	8.8
CMB NOM P/L	4.9	—
IMERMAN S	4.6	4.6
STD BANK NOM TVL P/L	4.4	4.1
STOCKSHARE NOM P/L	3.3	3.3
SAFEGRO NOM P/L	1.7	1.7
STEIN G H	1.6	1.6
KATZEFF G S	1.1	1.1
SANLAM	—	4.9
VOLKSKAS NOM P/L	—	12.6
TOTAL	95.6	95.2

DIRECTORS :
IMERMAN J MR,IMERMAN S MR (Vice Chairman)
IMERMAN VS MR (Executive Chairman),LEVIN HR M

REGISTRATION NUMBER : 88/05984/06

REGISTERED OFFICE
Lovasz Park, 247-15th Road
Randjespark, Midrand
1685
TEL: 011-314 2370
FAX: 011-314 2001

TRANSFER SECRETARY
Central Registrars Ltd
P O Box 4844, Johannesburg
2000
TEL: 011-331 0051

COMPANY SECRETARY
G S Katzeff

NATURE OF BUSINESS
An investment holding company with a controlling interest in JSE-quoted Royal Corporation.

BANKERS :
Standard Bank of SA Ltd

AUDITORS :
Fisher Hoffman Stride

FAMILIAR BRAND NAMES
BEECH-NUT ROLLS,BEECHIES,CARE-FREE
GEMINI DELIVERIES (PTY) LTD,KILTY'S
LAZER GUM,LIFESAVERS,REPLAY
ROYAL BAKING POWDER,ROYAL INSTANT PUDDING
SUPER-C

CONTRIBUTION BY ACTIVITY
Foods & Confectionery (% Income) (66.0%)
Chemicals & Pharmaceuticals (34.0%)

YEAR END : August

DIVIDEND :Ords 1c

Dividend No 1	(Ldr)08/06/90	(Pay)29/06/90	Amt(c)6
Dividend No 2	(Ldr)28/02/91	(Pay)24/05/91	Amt(c)7
Dividend No 3	(Ldr)16/04/92	(Pay)05/06/92	Amt(c)7.6
Dividend No 4	(Ldr)13/11/92	(Pay)04/12/92	Amt(c)10.2

NUMBER OF EMPLOYEES : 300

CAPITAL STRUCTURE

	AUTHORISED	ISSUED
Ords 1c	75000000	35028390

FINANCIAL STATISTICS (AT FINANCIAL YEAR END)

(Amts in R'000)	1991 Aug	1990 Feb
Ord S/H Int	93312	45428
Long Trm Loans	223809	56639
Iss Ord Share	35028	35028
Total Liab	353152	94026
Current Liab	129343	37387
Total Assets	340331	106418
Intang Assets	106133	33036
Current Assets	167716	51128
Debtors	82756	24996
Inventory	84399	26132
Turnover	460777	170511
Oper Profit	55274	19556
Interest Paid	11190	4997
Tax Paid	4232	1669
Prf af Int&Tax	39852	12890
Prf att Ord Sh	13934	6514
Btm Line Earn	14283	6514
Dividend Paid	4869	2102
Mkt Prce(c) YE	420	145
Depreciation	5684	1902

PER SHARE STATISTICS (CENTS)

Net Asst Val	-36.60	35.38
Net Earnings	39.80	18.60
Dividends	13.90	6.00
Cash Flow	67.96	28.16

RATIOS AND OTHER INFORMATION

Mrk Cap(R000)	147118	50791
Current Ratio	1.30	1.37
Quik/Acid Tst	0.64	0.67
A/C Rec T/ovr	5.57	6.82
Tot Ass T/ovr	1.35	1.60
Debt/Ass Rat	0.38	0.45
L T L Tot Ass	0.00	0.10
Debt to Eqity	1.40	1.06
Interest Cover	4.94	3.91
Oper Prof Mrg	12.00	11.47
Net Prof Marg%	3.02	3.82
Ret on Assets	16.24	18.38
Ret on Equity%	14.93	14.34
Price/Earnings	10.55	7.80
Divid Cover	2.86	3.10
Divid Yield	3.31	4.14
Earning Yield%	9.48	12.83
NAV % Mrk Pr	-8.71	24.40
Effec Tax Rate	0.10	1.52
Def Interval	0.44	1.58
Sus Grth Rate	9.71	9.71

SUBSIDIARY & ASSOCIATED COMPANIES

ACETICO BIOCHEMICALS (PTY) LTD (50%)
ROYAL CORPORATION LTD

INVESTMENTS

None

ROYCHEM LTD

ABBREVIATION : ROYCHEM

JSE SHORT CODE : RYC

SECTOR : Industrial-Chemicals & Oils

SHAREHOLDERS

Who Owns Whom's Assessment of the Identity of the Ultimate Controlling Shareholder:
ROYAL HOLDINGS VIA ROYAL CORPORATION

SHAREHOLDER	PERCENTAGE 1992	1991

ROYAL CORP LTD	57.8	57.8
SA MUTUAL	20.1	20.3
STD BANK NOM TVL P/L	8.2	7.9
CMB NOM P/L	4.6	---
NEDBANK NOM LTD	1.8	1.8
METAL IND GROUP PENS FUND	1.5	1.5
ENGINEERING INDUSTRIES PENS FUND	1.5	1.5
SAFEGRO NOM P/L	1.4	1.4
COMMERCIAL UNION ASSURE CO SA LTD	---	1.2
SANLAM	---	4.6
TOTAL	96.7	97.9

DIRECTORS :
ENRIEU CAG MR,ERASMUS WG MR
FRAGIS J MR (Financial Director)
IMERMAN S MR (Vice Chairman)
IMERMAN VS MR (Executive Chairman)
JOHNSTON DHB MR (Managing Director),KATZEFF GS MR
LLOYD FH MR,MCDONALD T MR
MOOR B ST C MR (Dir Human Resources

REGISTRATION NUMBER : 89/02108/06

REGISTERED OFFICE
Lovasz Park, 247-15th Road
Randjespark, Midrand
1685
TEL: 011-314 2370
FAX: 011-314 2225

TRANSFER SECRETARY
Central Registrars Ltd
P O Box 4844, Johannesburg
2000
TEL: 011-331 0051

COMPANY SECRETARY
G S Katzeff

NATURE OF BUSINESS
The company houses the chemical interests of the Royal group. Operations include the purchase and processing of raw chemicals into pharmaceutical & speciality chemical products, & the manufacture of speciality plastics, coatings, colours and speciality ceramics.

BANKERS :
Standard Bank of SA Ltd

AUDITORS :
Fisher Hoffman Stride, M Lutrin & Co

FAMILIAR BRAND NAMES
FERRO,HOLPRO,LOVASZ

CONTRIBUTION BY ACTIVITY
N/A

YEAR END : August

DIVIDEND : Ords 1c

Dividend (Ldr)16/04/92 (Pay)05/06/92 Amt(c)6

CAPITAL STRUCTURE

	AUTHORISED	ISSUED
Ords 1c	80000000	48206570

FINANCIAL STATISTICS (AT FINANCIAL YEAR END)

(Amts in R'000)	1990 Feb
Ord S/H Int	90806
Long Trm Loans	33756
Total Liab	62474
Current Liab	28718
Total Assets	126280
Intang Assets	27000
Current Assets	67659
Debtors	33716
Inventory	33943
Turnover	121337
Oper Profit	14533
Interest Paid	3398
Tax Paid	1802
Prf af Int&Tax	9333
Prf att Ord Sh	9333
Btm Line Earn	9333

PER SHARE STATISTICS (CENTS)

RATIOS AND OTHER INFORMATION

Current Ratio	2.36
Quik/Acid Tst	1.17
A/C Rec T/ovr	3.60
Tot Ass T/ovr	0.96
Debt/Ass Rat	0.49
L T L Tot Ass	0.27
Debt to Eqity	0.69
Interest Cover	4.28
Oper Prof Mrg	11.98
Net Prof Marg%	7.69
Ret on Assets	11.51
Ret on Equity%	10.28
Effec Tax Rate	16.18
Def Interval	3.62
Sus Grth Rate	10.28

SUBSIDIARY & ASSOCIATED COMPANIES

ANPHARM CHEMICALS (PTY) LTD
EVERYMAN CHEMICALS (PTY) LTD
HOLPRO ANALYTICS (PTY) LTD
HOLPRO INTERNATIONAL (PTY) LTD
HOLPRO MEDICAL (PTY) LTD
HOLPRO PROPERTIES (PTY) LTD
HOLPRO SHIPPING (PTY) LTD
IMCHEM PROPERTIES (PTY) LTD
K HOLZ HOLDINGS (PTY) LTD
LOVASZ CHEMICAL CORPORATION (PTY) LTD
PACKAGING & ALLIED INDUSTRIES (PTY) LTD
RAWCHEM (PTY) LTD

INVESTMENTS

None

RUBENSTEIN HOLDINGS LTD

ABBREVIATION : RUHOLD

JSE SHORT CODE : RUH

SECTOR : Industrial-Industrial Holding

SHAREHOLDERS

Who Owns Whom's Assessment of the Identity of the Ultimate Controlling Shareholder:
DIRECTORS

SHAREHOLDER	PERCENTAGE 1992	1991
FEDLIFE CAPITAL FUND	26.3	---
STD BANK NOM TVL P/L	17.5	29.5
TORQUAY SECURITIES P/L	11.7	16.0
FIRST NAT NOM P/L	8.0	11.3
RUBENSTEIN IND P/L	7.4	1.4
RUBENSTEIN J E	4.5	4.5
RUBENSTEIN T M	4.5	4.5
TONY ALVES FAMILY TRUST	3.4	---
BRANSKY S	3.0	3.0
RUBENSTEIN SHARE INC TRUST	1.9	1.9
MAXERIC NOM P/L	1.2	1.2
ALVES A C	---	1.2
ENFML NOM P/L	---	1.5
SIMCHOWITZ M	---	2.3
J & T INVESTMENTS	---	11.0
TOTAL	89.4	89.3

DIRECTORS :
ALVES AC (Managing Director),GILLIS L
PAMENSKY JL ,PESCIVOLO PRM (Executive Director)
RISKOWITZ PR (Financial Director)
RUBENSTEIN J (Chairman

REGISTRATION NUMBER : 85/05817/06

REGISTERED OFFICE
8th Floor, Twin Towers (West)
Sandton City, 5th Street
2199
TEL: 011-783 8972
FAX: 011-883 4168

TRANSFER SECRETARY
Central Registrars Ltd
P O Box 4844, Johannesburg
2000
TEL: 011-331 0051

COMPANY SECRETARY
Refer to Directorate

NATURE OF BUSINESS
An investment holding company; areas of operation include: the provision of financial services, including instalment sale, financial leasing, letter of credit establishment, confirming, bond & venture capital financing; manufacture & marketing of plastic carrier bags, sheeting & shrink wrap; the recycling of plastic waste.

BANKERS :
Standard Bank of SA Ltd
Trust Bank of Africa Ltd
SA Bank of Athens Ltd
Bank of Lisbon International Ltd
Boland Bank Ltd, Nedcor Bank Ltd
Societe Generale South Africa Ltd

AUDITORS :
Ernst & Young

FAMILIAR BRAND NAMES
N/A

CONTRIBUTION BY ACTIVITY
N/A

YEAR END : February

DIVIDEND : Ords 1c

Dividend No 3	(Ldr)08/06/90	(Pay)22/06/90	Amt(c)4
Dividend No 4	(Ldr)07/06/91	(Pay)26/06/91	Amt(c)6
Dividend No 5	(Ldr)29/05/92	(Pay)12/06/92	Amt(c)7
Dividend No 6	(Ldr)09/10/92	(Pay)19/10/92	Amt(c)40

NUMBER OF EMPLOYEES : 500

CAPITAL STRUCTURE

	AUTHORISED	ISSUED
Ords 1c	50000000	33150000

FINANCIAL STATISTICS (AT FINANCIAL YEAR END)

(Amts in R'000)	1992 Feb	1991 Feb	1990 Feb	1989 Jun	1988 Jun
Ord S/H Int	38651	35879	23325	15708	17177
Long Trm Loans	14090	16473	9852	24527	12371
Iss Ord Share	33150	33150	33150	33150	33150
Total Liab	48269	66968	42948	60630	43170
Current Liab	34179	50495	33096	36103	30799
Total Assets	86920	102847	66273	73714	57398
Intang Assets	*	*	*	2624	2949
Current Assets	39486	53026	65507	41784	34534
Debtors	34986	41435	65503	34468	30216
Inventory	4458	6052	-	7021	3949
Turnover	71300	40834	-	-	-
Oper Profit	6315	4588	3463	6503	5085
Interest Paid	-	-	366	46	-
Tax Paid	447	86	1462	3007	796
Prf af Int&Tax	5868	4502	1635	3450	4289
Prf att Ord Sh	5701	5136	1635	3290	4252
Btm Line Earn	6216	5136	12507	3011	4284
Dividend Paid	2320	1989	1326	1989	1658
Mkt Prce(c) YE	70	73	80	90	100
Depreciation	6513	3160	3667	4105	2318

PER SHARE STATISTICS (CENTS)

Net Asst Val	116.59	108.23	70.36	39.47	42.92
Net Earnings	17.20	15.30	4.90	9.90	13.60
Dividends	7.00	6.00	4.00	6.00	5.00
Cash Flow	38.67	23.37	20.38	30.64	23.32

RATIOS AND OTHER INFORMATION

Mrk Cap(R000)	23205	24200	26520	29835	33150
Current Ratio	1.16	1.05	1.98	1.16	1.12
Quik/Acid Tst	1.02	0.93	1.98	0.96	0.99
A/C Rec T/ovr	2.04	0.99	-	-	-
Tot Ass T/ovr	0.82	0.40	-	-	-
Debt/Ass Rat	0.48	0.59	0.55	0.74	0.73
L T L Tot Ass	0.08	0.10	0.05	0.25	0.20
Debt to Eqity	1.07	1.69	1.58	3.46	2.46
Interest Cover	-	-	9.46	141.37	-
Oper Prof Mrg	8.86	11.24	-	-	-
Net Prof Marg%	8.00	12.58	-	-	-
Ret on Assets	7.07	5.08	5.23	8.82	8.86
Ret on Equity%	14.75	13.72	6.06	16.53	20.90
Price/Earnings	4.07	4.77	16.33	9.09	7.35
Divid Cover	2.46	2.55	1.23	1.65	2.72
Divid Yield	10.00	8.22	5.00	6.67	5.00
Earning Yield%	24.57	20.96	6.13	11.00	13.60
NAV % Mrk Pr	166.56	148.26	87.95	43.85	42.92
Effec Tax Rate	0.16	0.04	0.26	3.81	1.91

Def Interval	0.92	4.47	4.77	4.49	4.75
Sus Grth Rate	8.75	8.77	1.32	8.28	15.10

SUBSIDIARY & ASSOCIATED COMPANIES

CARLTON SECURITIES (PTY) LTD
G R RECYCLING (PTY) LTD
HAZEMAR LEASING & FINANCE (PTY) LTD
PACKSURE (PIETERSBURG) (PTY) LTD
PLASTECH (PTY) LTD (50%)
RECYCO (PTY) LTD
RUBENSTEIN FINANCE COMPANY (PTY) LTD
RUBENSTEIN PLASTICS (PTY) LTD
TRANSPOLY (PTY) LTD
YSEBRAND (NATAL) (PTY) LTD

INVESTMENTS

None

RUSFURN GROUP LTD

ABBREVIATION : RUSFURN

JSE SHORT CODE : RSF

SECTOR : Industrial-Furniture & Household

SHAREHOLDERS

Who Owns Whom's Assessment of the Identity of the Ultimate Controlling Shareholder:
BANKORP VIA SENBANK

SHAREHOLDER	PERCENTAGE 1992	1991
GILLIS-MASON INV P/L	16.4	17.5
FURNHOLD LTD	12.7	6.7
CMB NOM P/L	11.9	---
RUSFURN EXECUTIVE PARTICIPATION P/L	9.5	13.2
SA MUTUAL	9.2	10.1
STD BANK NOM TVL P/L	6.9	8.4
UNIRUS P/L	5.5	5.9
RUSFURN SHARE INCENTIVE TRUST	4.6	1.2
EIGHTY ONE MAIN STREET NOM LTD	3.0	5.4
INDO-CHINA NOM P/L	2.8	---
ENGINEERING INDUSTRIES PENS FUND	2.6	2.8
SEFALANA EMP BENEFITS ORG (SEBO)	2.0	---
METAL IND GROUP PENS FUND	1.8	1.9
FIRST NAT NOM P/L	---	1.1
BOP GOVERNMENT SERV PENS FUND	---	1.0
NEDBANK NOM LTD	---	3.6
SANLAM	---	12.6
TOTAL	88.8	91.4

DIRECTORS :
ADAMS BH ,GERSZT MB ,JACOBSON PH
KORSTEN LP (Executive Chairman),LEVY IS
PIENAAR A ,STURROCK IL

REGISTRATION NUMBER : 86/01785/06

REGISTERED OFFICE
2nd Floor, Sanlma Arena Entr 3, 10 Cradock Avenue
Rosebank, Johannesburg
2196
TEL: 011-880 6760
FAX: 011-880 6621

TRANSFER SECRETARY
Central Registrars Ltd
P O Box 4844, Johannesburg
2000
TEL: 011-331 0051

COMPANY SECRETARY
M I Jaye

NATURE OF BUSINESS
The group is engaged in the retailing of furniture TV & VCR's, appliances, sound equipment, leisure products and home goods, and provides contract flooring & carpeting services.

BANKERS :
Trust Bank of Africa Ltd
First National Bank of SA Ltd
First National Corp & Investment Bank
Allied Bank Ltd, Nedperm Bank Ltd
Standard Bank of SA Ltd, Finansbank Ltd
Mercantile Bank Ltd, Senbank

AUDITORS :
Fisher Hoffman Stride

FAMILIAR BRAND NAMES
DASHAUS,DIONS,FURNITURE HYPER
GENERAL CARPETS,GIDDY'S,HARMONY
MATTRESS WORLD,MONTANA,REMUS,RUDICKS
RUSSELLS,SQUARE DEALS,STYLE & VALUE,WANDA

CONTRIBUTION BY ACTIVITY
Wanda-Frasers (% Operating Profit) (42.0%)
Russells (44.2%)
Rudicks (7.8%)
Arrow (19.5%)
Giddy's (7.2%)
Corporate & Other Divisions (-20.8%)

YEAR END : June

DIVIDEND : Ords 1c

Interim No 5	(Ldr)06/04/90	(Pay)27/04/90	Amt(c)5.5
Final No 6	(Ldr)05/10/90	(Pay)20/10/90	Amt(c)10.5
Interim No 7	(Ldr)05/04/91	(Pay)26/04/91	Amt(c)5.5

NUMBER OF EMPLOYEES : 11300

CAPITAL STRUCTURE

	AUTHORISED	ISSUED
Ords 10c	275000000	17409000
Var Rate Unsec Sub Comp Conv Debs	300000000	250689600

FINANCIAL STATISTICS (AT FINANCIAL YEAR END)

(Amts in R'000)	1991 Jun	1990 Jun	1989 Jun	1988 Jun	1987 Jun
Ord S/H Int	51927	140726	230109	191735	135246
Long Trm Loans	218793	269323	175739	126852	13415
Iss Ord Share	190670	190670	165800	165800	129200
Total Liab	937496	847021	462238	384753	265729
Current Liab	718703	577698	286499	257901	252314
Total Assets	989423	987747	692347	576488	400975
Current Assets	971300	964573	670315	555117	374006
Debtors	754087	772488	519848	441527	289867
Inventory	217213	192085	149002	109238	84011
Turnover	1409189	1287052	934052	729571	264364
Oper Profit	6922	184878	92889	59793	22838
Interest Paid	107182	65794	25282	14342	8985

Tax Paid	-42927	59521	777	-	-
Prf af Int&Tax	-57333	59563	66830	45451	13853
Prf att Ord Sh	-79224	35078	60129	43143	14327
Btm Line Earn	-79224	26989	60129	42009	14327
Dividend Paid	9575	26528	17409	12435	-
Mkt Prce(c) YE	110	125	80	72	105
Depreciation	4263	3100	2237	2629	1250

PER SHARE STATISTICS (CENTS)

Net Asst Val	27.23	73.81	138.79	115.64	104.68
Net Earnings	-45.50	21.20	36.30	26.00	12.90
Dividends	5.50	16.00	10.50	7.50	-
Cash Flow	-61.87	59.99	37.62	26.68	16.78

RATIOS AND OTHER INFORMATION

Mrk Cap(R000)	209737	238338	132640	119376	135660
Current Ratio	1.35	1.67	2.34	2.15	1.48
Quik/Acid Tst	1.05	1.34	1.82	1.73	1.15
A/C Rec T/ovr	1.87	1.67	1.80	1.65	1.37
Tot Ass T/ovr	1.42	1.30	1.35	1.27	0.99
Debt/Ass Rat	0.73	0.58	0.57	0.65	0.64
L T L Tot Ass	-	-	0.16	0.21	0.01
Debt to Eqity	13.84	4.11	1.72	1.97	1.89
Interest Cover	0.06	2.81	3.67	4.17	2.54
Oper Prof Mrg	0.49	14.36	9.94	8.20	8.64
Net Prof Marg%	-5.62	2.73	6.44	5.91	5.42
Ret on Assets	0.70	18.72	13.42	10.64	8.96
Ret on Equity%	-152.57	24.93	26.13	22.50	15.89
Price/Earnings	-2.42	5.90	2.20	2.77	8.14
Divid Cover	-8.27	1.33	3.46	3.47	-
Divid Yield	5.00	12.80	13.13	10.42	-
Earning Yield%	-41.36	16.96	45.38	36.11	12.29
NAV % Mrk Pr	24.76	59.04	173.48	160.61	99.69
Effec Tax Rate	-4.36	1.45	1.15	-	-
Def Interval	-1.23	1.50	1.74	2.88	11.67
Sus Grth Rate	-171.01	6.08	18.57	16.02	10.59

SUBSIDIARY & ASSOCIATED COMPANIES

ARROW FURNISHERS (TRADING) (PTY) LTD
CISKEI FURNISHERS LTD (50%)
DASHAUS (1985) (PTY) LTD
DASHAUS MANAGEMENT (PTY) LTD
FINRUS (PTY) LTD
FRASERS (BOPHUTHATSWANA) LTD (50%)
FRASERS (BOTSHABELO) LTD (50%)
FRASERS FURNISHERS (BOTSWANA) (PTY) LTD
FRASERS FURNISHERS (QWA QWA) LTD (50%)
FRASERS FURNISHERS (SWAZILAND) (PTY) LTD
FRASERS KWAZULU LTD
FURNGROUP HOLDINGS (PTY) LTD
FURNITURE FAIR GROUP HOLDINGS LTD
FURNITURE FINANCE CO (PTY) LTD
GAYNORS "THE ELECTRICIANS" (PTY) LTD
GENERAL CARPETS (PTY) LTD
HARMONY FURNISHERS MANAGEMENT (PTY) LTD
HDC (PTY) LTD
HYPER SALES (PTY) LTD
M & L FURNISHERS (PTY) LTD
MATTRESS HOUSE FURNISHERS (PTY) LTD
MICDAW (PTY) LTD
MONARCH RETAIL LTD (49%)
MONTANA FURNISHERS MANAGEMENT (PTY) LTD
RUDICKS (BOP) (PTY) LTD
RUDICKS (PTY) LTD
RUSFIN (PTY) LTD
RUSFURN BUSINESS SCHOOL (PTY) LTD
RUSFURN MANAGEMENT (PTY) LTD
RUSFURN MANAGEMENT NAMIBIA (PTY) LTD
RUSSELL FURNISHERS (TRANSKEI) (PTY) LTD
RUSSELL FURNISHERS LESOTHO (PTY) LTD
RUSSELLS (PTY) LTD
RUSSELLS MANAGEMENT (TRANSKEI) (PTY) LTD
WANDA FRASERS FURNISHERS (LESOTHO) LTD
WANDA FRASERS FURNISHERS (MALUTI) LTD (50%)
WANDA FURNISHERS (CISKEI) (PTY) LTD
WANDA FURNISHERS (LESOTHO) (PTY) LTD
WANDA FURNISHERS (QWAQWA) (PTY) LTD (50%)
WANDA-FRASERS (BOP) (PTY) LTD (50%)
WANDA-FRASERS FURNISHERS (TRANSKEI) (PTY
WANDA-FRASERS FURNISHERS LTD
WANDA-FRASERS INVESTMENTS (PTY) LTD
WANDA-FRASERS MANAGEMENT (TRANSKEI) (PTY

INVESTMENTS

None

RUSTENBURG PLATINUM HOLDINGS LTD

ABBREVIATION : RUSPLAT

JSE SHORT CODE : RPT

SECTOR : Metals & Minerals-Platinum

SHAREHOLDERS

Who Owns Whom's Assessment of the Identity of the Ultimate Controlling Shareholder:
ANGLO AMERICAN VIA JOHNIES

SHAREHOLDER	PERCENTAGE 1992	1991
STD BANK NOM TVL P/L	33.3	32.5
LYDENBURG PLATINUM LTD	8.4	8.4
DIDO NOM LTD	6.9	6.9
RESIDENT NOM LTD	4.6	4.6
PINTAIL INV LTD	4.1	4.1
FERMAIN NOM LTD	4.1	4.1
FIRST NAT NOM P/L	4.0	4.4
JOHANNESBURG CONSOLIDATED INV CO LTD	3.5	3.5
SA MUTUAL	2.9	3.0
CMB NOM P/L	2.9	---
PETARD NOM LTD	2.8	2.8
INDO-CHINA NOM P/L	2.4	2.7
SIXTY SIX MARSHALL STREET NOM P/L	1.6	1.1
EIGHTY ONE MAIN STREET NOM LTD	1.5	---
TAURUS NOM LTD	1.3	1.3
LONDON REGISTER ACCOUNT	1.2	1.5
INDO-CHINA NOM SA P/L	---	2.7
SANLAM	---	2.2
TOTAL	85.3	85.6

DIRECTORS :
BRAY VG ,BRUCE JT
DAVISON BE (Managing Director),EMMETT DTG
HOLFORD GM ,KING MW ,MACCONACHIE AW ,MAXWELL KW
MCKERRON AB ,RETIEF PF (Chairman)
SCOTT-RUSSELL H DR,SUTHERLAND RB

REGISTRATION NUMBER : 05/22452/06

REGISTERED OFFICE
Consolidated Building, Cnr Fox & Harrison Streets
Johannesburg

2001
TEL: 011-373 9111
FAX: 011-838 5537

TRANSFER SECRETARY
Consolidated Share Registrars Ltd
P O Box 61051, Marshalltown
2107
TEL: 011-492 1620

COMPANY SECRETARY
Johannesburg Consolidated Inv Co Ltd

NATURE OF BUSINESS
The company operates three major mines which exploit the platinum-bearing ores of the Bushveld Igneous Complex.The primary product of the group is platinum; other metals recovered are palladium, rhodium, iridium, ruthenium, osmium, gold, silver, copper, and nickel.Cobalt sulphate, sulphuric acid and sodium sulphate are also produced.

BANKERS :
Standard Bank of SA Ltd

AUDITORS :
Ernst & Young

FAMILIAR BRAND NAMES
N/A

CONTRIBUTION BY ACTIVITY
N/A

YEAR END : June

DIVIDEND : Ords 10c

Interim No 73	(Ldr)09/02/90	(Pay)09/03/90	Amt(c)125
Final No 74	(Ldr)17/08/90	(Pay)15/09/90	Amt(c)185
Interim No 75	(Ldr)08/02/91	(Pay)08/03/91	Amt(c)125
Final No 76	(Ldr)04/10/91	(Pay)22/10/91	Amt(c)225
Interim No 78	(Ldr)07/02/92	(Pay)06/03/92	Amt(c)87.5
Final No 79	(Ldr)21/08/92	(Pay)25/09/92	Amt(c)142.5

CAPITAL STRUCTURE

	AUTHORISED	ISSUED
Ords 10c	125329806	125320431

FINANCIAL STATISTICS (AT FINANCIAL YEAR END)

(Amts in R'000)	1992 Jun	1991 Jun	1990 Jun	1989 Jun	1988 Jun
Ord S/H Int	1745400	1843000	1586700	1483900	1131800
Long Trm Loans	91600	93000	100000	3800	3200
Iss Ord Share	125320	125320	125320	125320	125320
Total Liab	820900	967200	886000	896800	665100
Current Liab	729300	874200	786000	893000	661900
Total Assets	2566300	2810200	2472700	2380700	1796900
Current Assets	1345300	1698600	1540200	1521900	1111500
Debtors	351300	479600	457000	268200	273600
Inventory	321200	148400	194100	163800	139500
Turnover	2910100	3425500	2943500	2831500	2366900
Oper Profit	665600	1125600	1061200	1318000	979600
Tax Paid	349600	660800	669500	839900	590700
Prf af Int&Tax	407000	608400	555900	600600	388900
Prf att Ord Sh	402300	604000	551300	595600	385100
Btm Line Earn	402300	604000	551300	595600	385100
Dividend Paid	600000	438600	388500	376000	275700
Mkt Prce(c) YE	8625	7325	8825	6250	3800

PER SHARE STATISTICS (CENTS)

Net Asst Val	1392.75	1470.64	1266.12	1184.09	903.13
Net Earnings	321.00	482.00	440.00	475.40	306.90
Dividends	479.00	350.00	310.00	300.00	220.00
Cash Flow	321.02	481.97	439.91	475.34	306.81

RATIOS AND OTHER INFORMATION

Mrk Cap(R000)	10808850	9179690	11059490	7832500	4762160
Current Ratio	1.84	1.94	1.96	1.70	1.68
Quik/Acid Tst	1.40	1.77	1.71	1.52	1.47
A/C Rec T/ovr	8.28	7.14	6.44	10.93	8.65
Tot Ass T/ovr	1.13	1.22	1.19	1.23	1.32
Debt/Ass Rat	0.32	0.34	0.36	0.38	0.37
L T L Tot Ass	0.03	0.03	0.04	-	-
Debt to Eqity	0.47	0.52	0.56	0.60	0.58
Oper Prof Mrg	22.87	32.86	36.05	44.96	41.39
Net Prof Marg%	13.82	17.63	18.73	20.32	16.27
Ret on Assets	29.48	45.16	49.56	60.51	54.52
Ret on Equity%	23.05	32.77	34.75	40.14	34.03
Price/Earnings	26.87	15.20	20.06	13.15	12.38
Divid Cover	0.67	1.38	1.42	1.58	1.40
Divid Yield	5.55	4.78	3.51	4.80	5.79
Earning Yield%	3.72	6.58	4.99	7.61	8.08
NAV % Mrk Pr	16.15	20.08	14.35	18.95	23.77
Effec Tax Rate	35.39	47.22	54.30	15.01	37.08
Sus Grth Rate	-11.33	8.97	10.26	14.80	9.67

SUBSIDIARY & ASSOCIATED COMPANIES

BRAKSPRUIT PLATINUM (PTY) LTD
D LANG & CO (UMTATA) (PTY) LTD
DITHABA PLATINUM (PTY) LTD
DWAALKOP PROSPECTING CO (PTY) LTD
EL RAMSDEN BLESKOP (PTY) LTD
ELAND PLATINUM MINING CO. LTD
MATTHEY RUSTENBURG REFINERS (PTY) LTD
MATTHEY RUSTENBURG REFINERS (U.K.) LTD
MATTHEY RUSTENBURG REFINERS (WADEVILLE)
MESSINA NICKEL MINING & EXPLORATION CO.
NORBUSH PROPERTIES (PTY) LTD
PENULTIMATE HOLDINGS (PTY) LTD
PGM (BRAKSPRUIT) (PTY) LTD
PLATINUM PROSPECTING CO. (PTY) LTD
PRECIOUS METALS REFINERS (PTY) LTD
RUSTENBURG BASE METALS REFINERS (PTY) LT
RUSTENBURG PLATINUM MINES LTD
TEMSO (PTY) LTD (40%)
TRANSVAAL LAND DEVELOPMENT CO. (PTY) LTD

INVESTMENTS

None

SA BIAS HOLDINGS LTD

ABBREVIATION : S-A-BIAS

JSE SHORT CODE : SBI

SECTOR : Industrial-Industrial Holding

SHAREHOLDERS

Who Owns Whom's Assessment of the Identity of the Ultimate Controlling Shareholder: SEABROOKE FAMILY VIA SABVEST

SHAREHOLDER	PERCENTAGE 1992	1991
SABVEST LTD	50.4	50.4
CMB NOM P/L	13.8	---
AFRICAN OXYGEN LTD PENS FUND	3.6	2.3
SA MUTUAL	3.5	---
FIRST NAT NOM P/L	2.2	2.4
FOSKOR PENS FUND	2.1	2.1
SANTAMGROEI NOM P/L	1.9	2.0
STD BANK NOM TVL P/L	1.9	1.9
NATAL JOINT MUNICIPAL PENS FUND SUPERANN	1.8	1.8
LONRHO GROUP PENS FUND	1.7	1.4
CAPE CLOTHING INDUSTRY PROV FUND	1.6	1.6
ALTRON GROUP PENS FUND	1.5	---
ELLERINE BROS P/L	1.3	1.3
GEMEENSKAPLIKE MUNISIPALE OFS PENS FUND	1.2	---
STEINMULLER SA PENS FUND	1.0	---
ANGLO AMERICAN CORP PENS FUND	---	2.1
DE BEERS PENS FUND	---	2.7
NEDBANK NOM LTD	---	1.1
SANLAM	---	12.4
SANLAM PERSONEEL PENS FUND	---	1.1
TOTAL	89.5	86.4

DIRECTORS :
COUTTS-TROTTER P (Deputy Chairman),FERGUSON DCE
HUGHES NSH ,PENCHARZ P ,SEABROOKE CS (Chairman)
ZAROOZNY M

REGISTRATION NUMBER : 05/22620/06

REGISTERED OFFICE
72 Delvers Street, Corner Pritchard Street
Johannesburg
2001
TEL: 011-337 5340
FAX: 011-337 6773

TRANSFER SECRETARY
Central Registrars Ltd
P O Box 4844, Johannesburg
2000
TEL: 011-331 0051

COMPANY SECRETARY
R Pleaner

NATURE OF BUSINESS
An investment holding company with controlling interests in quoted SA Bias Industries Ltd, and Merhold Ltd. The main activities of the group are : manufacture and distribution of trimmings and accessories to the clothing and footwear industries, trade finance and factoring, export trading, banking and industrial investment.

BANKERS :
First National Bank of SA Ltd

AUDITORS :
Levitt Kirson

FAMILIAR BRAND NAMES
N/A

CONTRIBUTION BY ACTIVITY
Industrial (Sab Ind) (% Attrib Income) (61.5%)
Financial & Trading [Merhold] (38.5%)

YEAR END : December

DIVIDEND :Ords 5c

Interim No 56	(Ldr)01/09/89	(Pay)15/09/89	Amt(c)11
Final No 57	(Ldr)05/04/90	(Pay)20/04/90	Amt(c)19
Interim No 58	(Ldr)14/09/90	(Pay)28/09/90	Amt(c)11
Final No 59	(Ldr)05/04/91	(Pay)26/04/91	Amt(c)19
Interim No 60	(Ldr)30/08/91	(Pay)27/09/91	Amt(c)11
Final No 61	(Ldr)28/02/92	(Pay)10/04/92	Amt(c)19
Interim No 62	(Ldr)28/08/92	(Pay)25/09/92	Amt(c)8.5

NUMBER OF EMPLOYEES : 2220

CAPITAL STRUCTURE

	AUTHORISED	ISSUED
Ords 5c	24000000	19248500

FINANCIAL STATISTICS (AT FINANCIAL YEAR END)

(Amts in R'000)	1991 Dec	1990 Dec	1989 Dec	1988 Dec	1987 Dec
Ord S/H Int	95271	84486	75215	60822	48183
Long Trm Loans	18269	27450	19402	15874	8085
Iss Ord Share	19249	19249	19249	19234	19234
Total Liab	56230	65574	38695	33633	42223
Current Liab	37961	38124	19293	17759	34138
Total Assets	151501	150060	113910	94455	90406
Current Assets	63912	62507	47299	38193	51831
Debtors	39832	38814	26035	25753	28836
Inventory	23383	21661	14489	11529	22042
Oper Profit	32782	29563	27542	20921	14803
Interest Paid	4053	2943	1423	893	1228
Tax Paid	4267	4131	4069	2127	991
Prf af Int&Tax	24462	22489	22050	17901	12584
Prf att Ord Sh	19158	19053	18936	15001	11772
Btm Line Earn	17821	18156	17932	12624	8533
Dividend Paid	5775	5775	5775	4808	3919
Mkt Prce(c) YE	450	365	425	370	350
Depreciation	6908	6339	3750	2922	2224

PER SHARE STATISTICS (CENTS)

Net Asst Val	494.94	438.91	390.75	316.22	250.51
Net Earnings	99.50	99.00	98.40	78.00	65.20
Dividends	30.00	30.00	30.00	25.00	21.00
Cash Flow	127.79	123.42	118.46	95.31	79.29

RATIOS AND OTHER INFORMATION

Mrk Cap(R000)	86621	70259	81808	71166	67319
Current Ratio	1.68	1.64	2.45	2.15	1.52
Quik/Acid Tst	1.07	1.07	1.70	1.50	0.87
Debt/Ass Rat	0.31	0.38	0.28	0.31	0.43
L T L Tot Ass	0.06	0.13	0.11	0.12	0.05
Debt to Eqity	0.50	0.68	0.42	0.48	0.80
Interest Cover	8.09	10.05	19.35	23.43	12.05
Ret on Assets	22.32	20.62	25.35	22.15	16.37
Ret on Equity%	20.11	22.55	25.18	24.66	24.43
Price/Earnings	4.52	3.69	4.32	4.74	5.37
Divid Cover	3.32	3.30	3.28	3.12	3.10
Divid Yield	6.67	8.22	7.06	6.76	6.00
Earning Yield%	22.11	27.12	23.15	21.08	18.63
NAV % Mrk Pr	109.99	120.25	91.94	85.47	71.57
Effec Tax Rate	16.47	16.33	6.61	2.83	4.63
Def Interval	0.64	1.24	0.61	0.75	1.23
Sus Grth Rate	14.05	15.72	17.50	16.76	16.30

SUBSIDIARY & ASSOCIATED COMPANIES

BIAS INDUSTRIAL HOLDINGS (PTY) LTD
MERHOLD LTD
SA BIAS FINANCIAL SERVICES (PTY) LTD
SA BIAS INDUSTRIES LTD

INVESTMENTS

None

SA BIAS INDUSTRIES LTD

ABBREVIATION : SAB IND

JSE SHORT CODE : SAI

SECTOR : Industrial-Clothing, Footwear & Textiles

SHAREHOLDERS

Who Owns Whom's Assessment of the Identity of the Ultimate Controlling Shareholder: SEABROOKE FAMILY VIA SABVEST & S A BIAS

SHAREHOLDER	PERCENTAGE 1992	1991
SA BIAS HOLDINGS LTD	87.3	87.9
EPF OLD MUTUAL NOM P/L	2.6	---
NEDBANK NOM LTD	1.6	---
ALTRON GROUP PENS FUND	1.4	---
CMB NOM P/L	1.3	---
ANGLO AMERICAN CORP PENS FUND	---	1.6
DE BEERS PENS FUND	---	2.1
SANLAM	---	1.7
SPINAZZE R	---	1.3
TOTAL	94.2	94.5

DIRECTORS :
COUTTS-TROTTER P (Managing Director),DEW J
GREAVES PR ,HAGEL J
MARTINDALE NH (Dir Information Resources)
NUNES JP ,ROCHE PJ ,SEABROOKE CS (Chairman)
ZAROOZNY M (Sales Director

REGISTRATION NUMBER : 63/04346/06

REGISTERED OFFICE
SA Bias House, 72 Deivers Street
Johannesburg
2001
TEL: 011-337 5340
FAX: 011-337 6773

TRANSFER SECRETARY
Central Registrars Ltd
P O Box 4844, Johannesburg
2000
TEL: 011-331 0051

COMPANY SECRETARY
R C Moore

NATURE OF BUSINESS
The group manufactures & distributes accessories & trimmings to the clothing, footwear & allied industries, & manufactures & distributes curtain suspension products.

BANKERS :
First National Bank of SA Ltd

AUDITORS :
Baker Musikanth

FAMILIAR BRAND NAMES
ARROW,KIRSCH,MODERNFOLD,RUFFLETTE,STORMLINE

CONTRIBUTION BY ACTIVITY
N/A

YEAR END : December

DIVIDEND : Ords 10c

Interim No 5	(Ldr)14/09/90	(Pay)28/09/90	Amt(c)7
Final No 6	(Ldr)22/02/91	(Pay)26/04/91	Amt(c)11
Interim No 7	(Ldr)30/08/91	(Pay)20/09/91	Amt(c)7
Final No 8	(Ldr)28/02/92	(Pay)10/04/92	Amt(c)11
Interim No 9	(Ldr)28/08/92	(Pay)25/09/92	Amt(c)3.5

NUMBER OF EMPLOYEES : 2101

CAPITAL STRUCTURE

	AUTHORISED	ISSUED
Ords 10c	50000000	28647417

FINANCIAL STATISTICS (AT FINANCIAL YEAR END)

(Amts in R'000)	1991 Dec	1990 Dec	1989 Dec	1988 Dec	1987 Dec
Ord S/H Int	56031	48233	39763	30634	18228
Long Trm Loans	11136	12590	6987	4441	4311
Iss Ord Share	28647	28547	28190	28190	25198
Total Liab	48226	48671	23874	19333	16874
Current Liab	37090	36081	16887	14892	12563
Total Assets	101107	93354	63637	49967	35102
Intang Assets	3150	3550	*	*	*
Current Assets	61420	57673	41218	33243	23642
Debtors	37350	33986	23808	20191	14231
Inventory	23383	21661	14489	11529	8959
Oper Profit	21920	19166	18118	13484	9599
Interest Paid	3936	1890	961	648	1289
Tax Paid	4267	4107	4049	2094	872
Prf af Int&Tax	13717	13169	13108	10742	7438
Prf att Ord Sh	13502	13463	13107	10705	7435
Btm Line Earn	12749	13463	12457	10792	7190
Dividend Paid	5150	5138	5074	4285	2469
Mkt Prce(c) YE	300	250	260	180	-
Depreciation	6895	6220	3747	2920	2219

PER SHARE STATISTICS (CENTS)

Net Asst Val	184.60	156.52	141.05	108.67	72.34
Net Earnings	47.30	47.30	47.00	39.00	-
Dividends	18.00	18.00	18.00	15.20	-
Cash Flow	70.65	67.16	64.92	51.61	39.80

RATIOS AND OTHER INFORMATION

Mrk Cap(R000)	85941	71368	73294	50742	-
Current Ratio	1.66	1.60	2.44	2.23	1.88
Quik/Acid Tst	1.03	1.00	1.58	1.46	1.17
Debt/Ass Rat	0.46	0.50	0.34	0.36	0.46
L T L Tot Ass	0.09	0.11	0.07	0.07	0.10
Debt to Eqity	0.83	0.96	0.54	0.59	0.88
Interest Cover	5.57	10.14	18.85	20.81	7.45
Ret on Assets	21.47	20.85	28.47	26.99	27.35
Ret on Equity%	24.10	27.91	32.96	34.94	40.79
Price/Earnings	6.34	5.29	5.53	4.62	-
Divid Cover	2.63	2.63	2.61	2.57	-
Divid Yield	6.00	7.20	6.92	8.44	-
Earning Yield%	15.77	18.92	18.08	21.67	-

NAV % Mrk Pr	61.53	62.61	54.25	60.37	-
Effec Tax Rate	26.31	25.12	9.95	4.15	6.14
Def Interval	0.78	1.05	0.25	0.33	0.58
Sus Grth Rate	14.91	17.26	20.20	20.96	27.24

SUBSIDIARY & ASSOCIATED COMPANIES

ABLE INVESTMENTS INC
ARROW CURTAIN & CARPET ACCESSORIES (PTY)
B & E BUCKLES (PTY) LTD
BARBOUR PERIVALE THREADS (PTY) LTD (50%)
BITRIM (UK) LTD
BITRIM INTERNATIONAL INC
BITRIM MANUFACTURERS AND DISTRIBUTORS (P
BITRIM PROPERTIES (PTY) LTD
BULLDICK ENTERPRISES (PTY) LTD
DAL-BAC (PTY) LTD
DESIGNER FINANCE (PTY) LTD
DESIGNER LABELS (PTY) LTD
EMAIN (PTY) LTD
FASHION BUTTONS (PTY) LTD
FORMATEX (PTY) LTD
FORSYTH UDWIN INVESTMENT CO (PTY) LTD
HANGER RECYCLING (PTY) LTD
HELIOTEXTIL SA (PTY) LTD
HELTROY (PTY) LTD
INTERNATIONAL TEXTILES (PTY) LTD
INTERNATIONAL TRIMMINGS PLC (50%)
KELMORE (PTY) LTD
KIRTON (PTY) LTD
NARROWTEX (PTY) LTD
NATIONAL BRAIDING INDUSTRIES (PTY) LTD
NATIONAL INDUSTRIES (PTY) LTD
NKM INVESTMENTS (PTY) LTD
ORVAC S A (PTY) LTD
PERIVALE-GUTERMANN (PTY) LTD
PLASTI-MULTI (PTY) LTD
PLASTI-MULTI HANGERS (PTY) LTD
PRIVATE LINE SALES (PTY) LTD
QUINTEX WEBBING (PTY) LTD
RUSSPACK PRINTING (PTY) LTD
SA BIAS METAL FITTINGS (PTY) LTD
SA BIAS PRINTING & LABELS (PTY) LTD
SA BIAS TRIMMINGS (PTY) LTD
SABB (CAPE) (PTY) LTD
SABB (NATAL) (PTY) LTD
SABB (TVL) (PTY) LTD
TAPES & LACES (KWAZULU) (PTY) LTD
TEXCOR (PTY) LTD
TEXPRINT MANUFACTURERS (PTY) LTD
TEXTAPE (PTY) LTD
THOMAS FRENCH & SONS (SOUTH AFRICA) (PTY

INVESTMENTS

None

SAAMBOU HOLDINGS LTD

ABBREVIATION : SAAMBOU

JSE SHORT CODE : SBO

SECTOR : Financial-Banks & Financial Services

SHAREHOLDERS

Who Owns Whom's Assessment of the Identity of the Ultimate Controlling Shareholder: FEDSURE

SHAREHOLDER	PERCENTAGE 1992	1991
FEDLIFE ASSURE LTD	33.4	—
NEW SA PRINCIPLES INV P/L	6.9	6.8
VENDU FINANS P/L	6.1	6.1
STOPPRESS INV P/L	6.0	5.0
BB INV CO P/L	5.4	—
EIGHTY ONE MAIN STREET NOM LTD	4.5	9.6
METROPOLITAN LIFE LTD	2.8	2.8
COLEMAN PROPERTIES P/L	2.6	2.6
C C EXCHANGE P/L	2.6	2.8
FEDERATED LIFE ASSURE CO LTD	—	31.9
TOTAL	70.3	67.6

DIRECTORS :
BARROW JA ,BASSERABIE AI ,BOTHA DH ,BUITENDAG JM
CARINUS PJ ,CRAFFORD JA
HOWELL J DR (Deputy Chairman)
MYBURGH JP (Managing Director),SACKS MI
SLOET HA (Chairman),VAN DEN BERG JL ,VAN ZYL JJM

REGISTRATION NUMBER : 87/04170/06

REGISTERED OFFICE
Saambou Park, Alkantrant Road
Lynnwood Manor
0081
TEL: 012-421 5000
FAX: 012-421 5242

TRANSFER SECRETARY
Mercantile Registrars Ltd
P O Box 1053, Johannesburg
2000
TEL: 011-333 8181

COMPANY SECRETARY
H F Bosman

NATURE OF BUSINESS
A registered controlling company of deposit-taking subsidiaries. The group offers banking & financial services & products, & insurance, trust & property development services.

BANKERS :
N/A

AUDITORS :
Coopers Theron Du Toit

FAMILIAR BRAND NAMES
SAAMBOU,TOPSAVE

CONTRIBUTION BY ACTIVITY
N/A

YEAR END : March

DIVIDEND : (Ldr)02/06/89 (Pay)23/06/89

NUMBER OF EMPLOYEES : 1444

CAPITAL STRUCTURE

	AUTHORISED	ISSUED
Ords R1	150000000	125124245

FINANCIAL STATISTICS (AT FINANCIAL YEAR END)

(Amts in R'000)	1992 Mar	1991 Mar	1990 Mar	1989 Mar	1988 Mar
Ord S/H Int	176100	189600	199000	191800	183200
Long Trm Loans	62700	106800	3334000	2880000	2358800
Iss Ord Share	125124	85403	85253	85253	85253
Total Liab	4093500	4010900	3498200	2955000	2404300
Current Liab	4030800	3904100	164200	75000	45500
Total Assets	4269600	4200500	3697200	3146800	2587500
Current Assets	341100	550500	489400	463800	205200
Debtors	191700	207600	149100	64400	25800
Inventory	-	-	90900	63900	38700
Oper Profit	-66000	-24500	28000	24800	29800
Tax Paid	2300	2100	4300	6400	12800
Prf af Int&Tax	-68300	-26600	23700	18400	17000
Prf att Ord Sh	-69000	-28700	23700	18400	17000
Btm Line Earn	-69000	-28700	17000	18400	17000
Dividend Paid	-	9800	9800	9800	4700
Mkt Prce(c) YE	87	100	115	118	102
Depreciation	15600	15300	12800	9700	6786

PER SHARE STATISTICS (CENTS)

Net Asst Val	140.74	222.01	233.42	224.98	214.89
Net Earnings	-59.00	-26.40	27.80	21.60	20.00
Dividends	-	11.50	11.50	11.50	5.50
Cash Flow	-43.80	-15.81	44.57	35.54	28.60

RATIOS AND OTHER INFORMATION

Mrk Cap(R000)	108858	85403	98041	100599	86958
Current Ratio	0.08	0.14	2.98	6.18	4.51
Quik/Acid Tst	0.08	0.14	2.43	5.33	3.66
Debt/Ass Rat	0.95	0.95	0.04	0.02	0.02
L T L Tot Ass	0.00	0.02	-	-	-
Debt to Eqity	22.98	20.96	0.83	0.39	0.25
Ret on Assets	-1.55	-0.58	0.76	0.79	1.15
Ret on Equity%	-39.18	-15.14	11.91	9.59	9.28
Price/Earnings	-1.47	-3.79	4.14	5.46	5.10
Divid Cover	-	-2.30	2.42	1.88	3.64
Divid Yield	-	11.50	10.00	9.75	5.39
Earning Yield%	-67.82	-26.40	24.17	18.31	19.61
NAV % Mrk Pr	161.77	222.01	202.98	190.66	210.68
Effec Tax Rate	-	-8.98	10.00	16.94	40.94
Def Interval	-70.92	-277.29	-	-	-
Sus Grth Rate	-39.18	-20.31	6.98	4.48	6.71

SUBSIDIARY & ASSOCIATED COMPANIES

BORDER TYPEWRITER (PTY) LTD (25%)
FEDGROWTH MANAGEMENT CO LTD (25%)
FEDLIFE ASSURANCE LIMITED (33.4%)
NATIONAL INSURERS LTD
PLANET FINANCE CORP (PTY) LTD
SAAMBOU BANK LTD
SAAMBOU BOARD OF EXECUTORS LTD
SAAMBOU INSURANCE BROKERS (PTY) LTD
SAAMBOU LIFE ASSURERS LTD
SAAMBOU PROPERTIES LTD
SAAMBOU PROPERTIES SERVICES LTD
SAAMBOU WONINGS (PTY) LTD
SAAMSHOR (PTY) LTD (50%)
UITBOU TRUST (PTY) LTD (44%)
VERDEV (PTY) LTD (24%)
WEST SOUTH HOUSE (PTY) LTD (44%)

INVESTMENTS

None

SABLE HOLDINGS LTD

ABBREVIATION : SABLE

JSE SHORT CODE : SBL

SECTOR : Financial-Property

SHAREHOLDERS

Who Owns Whom's Assessment of the Identity of the Ultimate Controlling Shareholder: ISDALE HOLDINGS NETHERLANDS

SHAREHOLDER	PERCENTAGE 1992	1991
ISDALE HLDGS BV	68.1	67.6
INTERNAT INV CONSULTANTS P/L	9.7	9.7
ABSA NOM P/L	3.0	—
NEDBANK NOM LTD	2.9	2.2
NATVAAL PROPERTIES P/L	2.2	2.2
STD BANK NOM TVL P/L	1.2	1.8
VOLKSKAS NOM P/L	—	3.0
TOTAL	87.1	86.4

DIRECTORS :
BOLLEURS AA ,ELMES B ,NASH J (Chairman)
NASH PH (Managing Director

REGISTRATION NUMBER : 68/10636/06

REGISTERED OFFICE
1A Stan Road, Morningside Ext 6
Sandton
2057
TEL: 011-884 8787
FAX: 011-884 6826

TRANSFER SECRETARY
Mercantile Registrars Ltd
P O Box 1053, Johannesburg
2000
TEL: 011-333 8181

COMPANY SECRETARY
I R Kemp

NATURE OF BUSINESS
An investment holding company with subsidiaries engaged in property investment and trading.

BANKERS :
Standard Bank of SA Ltd

AUDITORS :
Fisher Hoffman Stride

FAMILIAR BRAND NAMES
RENT-A-TOWEL,TOWELMASTER

CONTRIBUTION BY ACTIVITY
N/A

YEAR END : June

DIVIDEND : Ords 50c

Dividend No 29	(Ldr)09/11/90	(Pay)19/11/90	Amt(c)35
Dividend No 30	(Ldr)29/11/91	(Pay)09/12/91	Amt(c)45
Dividend No 31	(Ldr)11/12/92	(Pay)21/12/92	Amt(c)600

NUMBER OF EMPLOYEES : 35

CAPITAL STRUCTURE

	AUTHORISED	ISSUED
Ords 50c	10000000	7487652

FINANCIAL STATISTICS (AT FINANCIAL YEAR END)

(Amts in R'000)	1992 Jun	1991 Jun	1990 Jun	1989 Jun	1988 Feb
Ord S/H Int	63861	93462	42991	33651	23243
Long Trm Loans	2059	27512	18286	15146	3991
Iss Ord Share	7488	7488	7488	7487	7487
Total Liab	66198	61517	50163	43771	9723
Current Liab	64139	34005	31877	28625	5732
Total Assets	130059	154979	93154	77422	32966
Current Assets	70279	127863	53412	37345	10274
Debtors	2531	8482	27848	16890	2476
Inventory	13450	25994	15273	12016	7460
Turnover	31454	122339	93414	84350	12877
Oper Profit	13012	23858	18872	20688	5507
Interest Paid	1756	5739	4352	5302	794
Tax Paid	7422	7019	5425	5025	1747
Prf af Int&Tax	12122	13385	10678	10361	2966
Prf att Ord Sh	14522	53840	11961	13403	2966
Btm Line Earn	14522	53840	11961	13403	2966
Dividend Paid	44926	3369	2621	2995	1498
Mkt Prce(c) YE	1150	1100	600	450	210
Depreciation	180	3747	4029	3317	197

PER SHARE STATISTICS (CENTS)

Net Asst Val	852.84	1248.16	574.13	449.46	310.44
Net Earnings	164.50	135.00	104.70	112.60	39.60
Dividends	600.00	45.00	35.00	40.00	20.00
Cash Flow	164.29	184.33	163.69	127.02	42.25

RATIOS AND OTHER INFORMATION

Mrk Cap(R000)	86112	82368	44928	33692	15723
Current Ratio	1.10	3.76	1.68	1.30	1.79
Quik/Acid Tst	0.89	3.00	1.20	0.88	0.49
A/C Rec T/ovr	12.43	14.42	3.35	3.75	5.20
Tot Ass T/ovr	0.24	0.79	1.00	0.82	0.39
Debt/Ass Rat	0.51	0.23	0.47	0.53	0.29
L T L Tot Ass	0.02	0.02	0.13	0.16	0.12
Debt to Eqity	1.04	0.39	1.03	1.22	0.42
Interest Cover	7.41	4.16	4.34	3.90	6.94
Oper Prof Mrg	41.37	19.50	20.20	24.53	42.77
Net Prof Marg%	46.17	44.01	12.80	15.89	23.03
Ret on Assets	16.52	16.87	21.96	20.04	16.71
Ret on Equity%	22.74	57.61	27.82	29.87	12.76
Price/Earnings	6.99	8.15	5.73	4.00	5.30
Divid Cover	0.27	3.00	2.99	2.82	1.98
Divid Yield	52.17	4.09	5.83	8.89	9.52
Earning Yield%	14.30	12.27	17.45	25.02	18.86
NAV % Mrk Pr	74.16	113.47	95.69	99.88	147.83
Effec Tax Rate	37.98	33.82	31.29	26.61	37.07
Def Interval	0.89	1.12	1.79	1.38	1.66
Sus Grth Rate	-47.61	54.00	21.73	30.93	6.32

SUBSIDIARY & ASSOCIATED COMPANIES

507 INDUSTRIAL (PTY) LTD
753 PARKWOOD LTD
755 PARKWOOD LTD
756 PARKWOOD LTD
758 PARKWOOD LTD
759 PARKWOOD LTD
761 PARKWOOD LTD
762 PARKWOOD LTD
ASTOR MANSIONS (PTY) LTD
BICSMIT INVESTMENTS (PTY) LTD
BRAAMDES INVESTMENTS (PTY) LTD
CASA MIA COURT (PTY) LTD
CROYDES INVESTMENTS (PTY) LTD
CURRACH INVESTMENTS (PTY) LTD
DESAB INVESTMENTS (PTY) LTD
DESBAR INVESTMENTS (PTY) LTD
FOURTEENTH STAGE INVESTMENTS (PTY) LTD
G & D SABLE (PTY) LTD
G&D SABLE (TVL) (PTY) LTD
HOLLAENDER DEVELOPMENTS (PTY) LTD
HOLLAENDER INVESTMENTS (PTY) LTD
HOWEC METALS (1964) (PTY) LTD
MONTROSE MANSIONS (PTY) LTD
NAVAS INVESTMENTS (PTY) LTD
PAREEN'S PROPERTIES (PTY) LTD
SOMADEL HOTEL (PTY) LTD
SOMADEL INVESTMENTS (PTY) LTD
SOPER CAR PARK (PTY) LTD
STAND 750 PARKWOOD (PTY) LTD
THIRTY FIRST INVESTMENTS (PTY) LTD

INVESTMENTS

None

SABVEST LTD

ABBREVIATION : SABVEST

JSE SHORT CODE : SBV

SECTOR : Industrial-Industrial Holding

SHAREHOLDERS

Who Owns Whom's Assessment of the Identity of the Ultimate Controlling Shareholder:
SEABROOKE FAMILY TRUST

SHAREHOLDER	PERCENTAGE 1992	1991
COMFIN INV P/L	51.6	43.8
CMB NOM P/L	16.3	---
STD BANK NOM TVL P/L	6.6	6.5
DE BEERS PENS FUND	5.3	5.4
NEDBANK NOM LTD	4.6	4.6
ANGLO AMERICAN CORP PENS FUND	4.1	4.1
SIXTY SIX MARSHALL STREET NOM P/L	3.1	3.1
EIGHTY ONE MAIN STREET NOM LTD	2.6	1.6
ELLERINE BROS P/L	2.6	2.6
COMFIN SECURITIES P/L	---	7.7
SANLAM	---	16.2
TOTAL	96.6	95.6

DIRECTORS :
COUTTS-TROTTER P (Deputy Chairman),FERGUSON DCE
HUGHES NSH ,PENCHARZ P
SEABROOKE CS (Executive Chairman),ZAROOZNY M

REGISTRATION NUMBER : 87/03753/06

REGISTERED OFFICE
72 Delvers Street, Corner Pritchard Street
Johannesburg
2001
TEL: 011-337 35340
FAX: 011-337 6773

TRANSFER SECRETARY
Central Registrars Ltd
P O Box 4844, Johannesburg
2000
TEL: 011-331 0051

COMPANY SECRETARY
R Pleaner

NATURE OF BUSINESS
An investment holding company with a controlling interest in quoted SA Bias Holdings, which in turn holds quoted SA Bias Industries, and Merhold Ltd.

BANKERS :
First National Bank of SA Ltd

AUDITORS :
Levitt Kirson

FAMILIAR BRAND NAMES
N/A

CONTRIBUTION BY ACTIVITY
Industrial (Sab Ind) (% Attrib Income) (61.5%)
Financial & Trading [Merhold] (38.5%)

YEAR END : December

DIVIDEND : Ords 5c

Interim No 4	(Ldr)01/09/89	(Pay)15/09/89	Amt(c)5.5
Final No 5	(Ldr)06/04/90	(Pay)20/04/90	Amt(c)9.4
Interim No 6	(Ldr)14/09/90	(Pay)28/09/90	Amt(c)5.5
Final No 7	(Ldr)05/04/91	(Pay)26/04/91	Amt(c)9.4
Interim No 8	(Ldr)30/08/91	(Pay)27/09/91	Amt(c)5.5
Final No 9	(Ldr)28/02/92	(Pay)10/04/92	Amt(c)9.4
Interim No 10	(Ldr)28/08/92	(Pay)25/09/92	Amt(c)4.25

NUMBER OF EMPLOYEES : 2220

CAPITAL STRUCTURE

	AUTHORISED	ISSUED
Ords 5c	24000000	19390000

FINANCIAL STATISTICS (AT FINANCIAL YEAR END)

(Amts in R'000)	1991 Dec	1990 Dec	1989 Dec	1988 Dec	1987 Dec
Ord S/H Int	57232	57212	57212	57210	57210
Iss Ord Share	19390	19390	19390	19390	19390
Total Liab	1823	1823	1823	1542	1349
Current Liab	1823	1823	1823	1542	1349
Total Assets	59055	59035	59035	58752	58559
Current Assets	1829	1829	1831	1542	1349
Oper Profit	2909	2889	2891	2409	1348
Prf af Int&Tax	2909	2889	2891	2409	1348
Prf att Ord Sh	2909	2889	2891	2409	1348
Btm Line Earn	2909	2889	2891	2409	1348
Dividend Paid	2889	2889	2889	2409	1346
Mkt Prce(c) YE	200	190	250	170	175

PER SHARE STATISTICS (CENTS)

Net Asst Val	295.16	295.06	295.06	295.05	295.05
Net Earnings	49.80	49.50	56.80	12.40	6.90
Dividends	14.90	14.90	16.40	12.40	6.90
Cash Flow	15.00	14.90	14.91	12.42	6.95

RATIOS AND OTHER INFORMATION

Mrk Cap(R000)	38780	36841	48475	32963	33933
Current Ratio	1.00	1.00	1.00	1.00	1.00
Quik/Acid Tst	1.00	1.00	1.00	1.00	1.00
Debt/Ass Rat	0.03	0.03	0.03	0.03	0.02
Debt to Eqity	0.03	0.03	0.03	0.03	0.02
Ret on Assets	4.93	4.89	4.90	4.10	2.30
Ret on Equity%	5.08	5.05	5.05	4.21	2.36
Price/Earnings	4.02	3.84	4.40	13.71	25.36
Divid Cover	3.34	3.32	3.46	1.00	1.00
Divid Yield	7.45	7.84	6.56	7.29	3.94
Earning Yield%	24.90	26.05	22.72	7.29	3.94
NAV % Mrk Pr	147.58	155.29	118.02	173.56	168.60
Sus Grth Rate	0.03	0.00	0.00	0.00	0.00

SUBSIDIARY & ASSOCIATED COMPANIES

SA BIAS HOLDINGS LTD (50,4%)

INVESTMENTS

None

SAFETY TECHNOLOGIES LTD

ABBREVIATION : SAFETEC

JSE SHORT CODE : SFT

SECTOR : Industrial-Engineering

SHAREHOLDERS

Who Owns Whom's Assessment of the Identity of the Ultimate Controlling Shareholder: DIRECTORS

SHAREHOLDER	PERCENTAGE 1992	1991
DIAGONAL NOM P/L	63.4	52.8
TECHNOLOGY FINANCE CORP P/L	33.7	---
HARWILL INV P/L	---	5.7
TITAN NOM P/L	---	5.0
HILGLEN INV P/L	---	17.7
KRUGER A D	---	1.8
NOMINEES ONLY P/L	---	3.5
SACKS R	---	3.5
TOTAL	97.2	90.1

DIRECTORS :
GREYVENSTEIN LCJ ,MOOLMAN IJ ,SACKS R
VAN DER SPUY S

REGISTRATION NUMBER : 87/01596/06

REGISTERED OFFICE
Block 2, Constantia Park, 239 Old Pretoria Rd
Midrand
1685
TEL: 011-315 1866
FAX: 011-315 2988

TRANSFER SECRETARY
Central Registrars Ltd
P O Box 4844, Johannesburg
2000
TEL: 011-331 0051

COMPANY SECRETARY
G Vermooten

NATURE OF BUSINESS
Group activities include : manufacture and supply of road signs, reflective material & related safety equipment; development, installation and supply of electronic perimeter security systems, including the design, development & manufacture of related hardware & software. The group also acts as maintenance contractors on established security installations.

BANKERS :
Bankorp Ltd

AUDITORS :
Coopers Theron Du Toit

FAMILIAR BRAND NAMES
N/A

CONTRIBUTION BY ACTIVITY
N/A

YEAR END : June

DIVIDEND : (Ldr)22/09/89 (Pay)06/10/89

NUMBER OF EMPLOYEES : 240

CAPITAL STRUCTURE

	AUTHORISED	ISSUED
Ords 25c	1200000	9764400

FINANCIAL STATISTICS (AT FINANCIAL YEAR END)

(Amts in R'000)	1991 Jun	1990 Jun	1989 Jun	1988 Jun
Ord S/H Int	111	5224	4893	3680
Long Trm Loans	59	2774	193	161
Iss Ord Share	16264	14110	14110	12060
Total Liab	6639	10581	5810	3846
Current Liab	6580	7807	5617	3685
Total Assets	5999	13519	10274	7526
Intang Assets	751	2286	429	*
Current Assets	5137	9841	7480	5153
Debtors	2421	5935	3993	2456
Inventory	2157	3821	3349	2669
Turnover	18562	29813	17155	13214
Oper Profit	-511	2858	3515	2878
Interest Paid	1114	1457	324	165
Tax Paid	213	370	1614	1350
Prf af Int&Tax	-1838	1031	1577	1363
Prf att Ord Sh	-1838	1031	1577	1363
Btm Line Earn	-6513	331	1427	1233
Dividend Paid	-	-	529	422
Mkt Prce(c) YE	40	45	70	65
Depreciation	211	442	166	105

PER SHARE STATISTICS (CENTS)

Net Asst Val	-3.94	20.82	31.64	30.51
Net Earnings	-11.30	7.31	11.20	11.30
Dividends	-	-	3.75	3.50
Cash Flow	-10.07	10.71	12.17	12.58

RATIOS AND OTHER INFORMATION

Mrk Cap(R000)	6506	6350	9877	7839
Current Ratio	0.78	1.26	1.33	1.40
Quik/Acid Tst	0.45	0.77	0.74	0.67
A/C Rec T/ovr	7.67	5.02	4.30	5.38
Tot Ass T/ovr	3.09	2.21	1.67	1.76
Debt/Ass Rat	1.10	0.78	0.56	0.50
L T L Tot Ass	-	0.20	0.02	0.01
Debt to Eqity	59.28	2.01	1.18	1.03
Interest Cover	-0.46	1.96	10.85	17.44
Oper Prof Mrg	-2.75	9.59	20.49	21.78
Net Prof Marg%	-9.90	3.46	9.19	10.31
Ret on Assets	-8.52	21.14	34.21	38.24
Ret on Equity%	-1655.86	19.74	32.23	37.04
Price/Earnings	-3.54	6.16	6.25	5.75
Divid Cover	-	-	2.99	3.23
Divid Yield	-	-	5.36	5.38
Earning Yield%	-28.25	16.24	16.00	17.38
NAV % Mrk Pr	-9.84	46.27	45.20	46.94
Effec Tax Rate	-13.72	23.70	51.39	47.95
Def Interval	-2.36	2.70	1.44	0.59
Sus Grth Rate	-1655.86	19.74	21.42	25.57

SUBSIDIARY & ASSOCIATED COMPANIES

BUFFALO SIGN CO LTD
TRAFFIC AIDS (PTY) LTD

INVESTMENTS

None

SAFICON INVESTMENTS LTD

ABBREVIATION : SAFICON

JSE SHORT CODE : SAF

SECTOR : Industrial-Industrial Holding

SHAREHOLDERS

Who Owns Whom's Assessment of the Identity of the Ultimate Controlling Shareholder: SAKERS FINANCE & INVESTMENT CORP

SHAREHOLDER	PERCENTAGE 1992	1991
SAKERS FINANCE & INV CORP LTD	48.4	49.2
STD BANK NOM TVL P/L	8.2	8.5
TEMPORA INV LTD	8.0	9.2
CMB NOM P/L	7.9	---
DE BEERS PENS FUND	3.9	4.5
METAL IND GROUP PENS FUND	3.3	3.4
ENGINEERING INDUSTRIES PENS FUND	3.2	3.4

SA MUTUAL	2.5	---
EIGHTY ONE MAIN STREET NOM LTD	2.3	3.1
SAFIC P/L	2.0	2.3
KREHER R K	1.1	1.3
HIPPER K J	1.0	1.2
SANLAM	---	5.4
TOTAL	91.7	91.2

DIRECTORS :
ALDWORTH ARM ,BORSOOK S (Chairman),BORSUK FF
BRITTAN ID ,GLENDINING PR ,GOSS RJ
HIPPER KJ (Chief Executive),KREHER RK
PHILLIPS N ,TREAGUS JRF

REGISTRATION NUMBER : 63/00929/06

REGISTERED OFFICE
Saficon Place, 10 Sherborne Road
Parktown
2193
TEL: 011-482 1942
FAX: 011-726 8630

TRANSFER SECRETARY
Central Registrars Ltd
P O Box 4844, Johannesburg
2000
TEL: 011-331 0051

COMPANY SECRETARY
Saficon Group Services (Pty) Ltd

NATURE OF BUSINESS
The group holds the Mercedes-Benz & Honda franchises for the Alberton, Benoni, Brakpan, Germiston, Johannesburg & Klerksdorp districts, & the Volkswagen/Audi franchise for Johannesburg, Witwatersrand, Bloemfontein, Welkom, Virginia & East London.It derives income from the sale of new & used vehicles.It manufactures motor components, holds the Toyota Forklift truck franchise, and imports Porsche & Jaguar cars. The group has 64 outlets, & has a controlling interest in Boumat.

BANKERS :
Standard Bank of SA Ltd

AUDITORS :
KPMG Aiken & Peat, Ernst & Young

FAMILIAR BRAND NAMES
BARNES MOTORS (EL),BOUGICORD (CABLES)
CARGO MOTORS,DAIMLER,JAGUAR,LECTROLITE
LINDSAY SAKER LTD,LSM DISTRIBUTORS
MERCEDES-BENZ,NGK (SPARK PLUGS)
PHOENIX MOTORS (BLOEM),PORSCHE
TOYOTA FORKLIFT

CONTRIBUTION BY ACTIVITY
New passenger cars (% turnover) (37.0%)
New commercial vehicles (15.0%)
Used vehicles (19.0%)
Parts, service & petrol (25.0%)
Manufactured components (2.0%)
Other (2.0%)

YEAR END : March

DIVIDEND :Ords 25c

Interim No 53	(Ldr)23/11/90	(Pay)09/01/91	Amt(c)7
Final No 54	(Ldr)14/06/91	(Pay)02/08/91	Amt(c)7
Interim No 55	(Ldr)22/11/91	(Pay)09/01/92	Amt(c)7
Final No 56	(Ldr)19/06/92	(Pay)07/08/92	Amt(c)6

NUMBER OF EMPLOYEES : 7137

CAPITAL STRUCTURE

	AUTHORISED	ISSUED
Ords 25c	36100000	31155047

FINANCIAL STATISTICS (AT FINANCIAL YEAR END)

(Amts in R'000)	1992 Mar	1991 Mar	1990 Mar	1989 Mar	1988 Mar
Ord S/H Int	182722	159373	138453	112113	85180
Long Trm Loans	20390	25821	43345	38658	41952
Iss Ord Share	31155	29423	25161	25119	25111
Total Liab	249242	245848	248328	211754	145584
Current Liab	228852	220027	204983	173096	103632
Total Assets	431964	405221	386781	323867	230764
Current Assets	267067	262847	247554	210593	144227
Debtors	80507	64572	56810	50219	52190
Inventory	181094	193827	188321	141395	83052
Turnover	1530996	1463499	1540690	1298428	878904
Oper Profit	44508	52382	81519	69042	41901
Interest Paid	21813	25344	17694	10368	-
Tax Paid	10709	15149	32705	28624	20546
Prf af Int&Tax	12316	14760	33839	32219	21355
Prf att Ord Sh	16182	13778	37393	36822	23193
Btm Line Earn	22063	11997	36831	37480	26027
Dividend Paid	4050	4120	10813	10547	6696
Mkt Prce(c) YE	550	600	740	520	400
Depreciation	15700	13282	10244	7862	3625

PER SHARE STATISTICS (CENTS)

Net Asst Val	586.49	541.66	550.27	446.33	339.21
Net Earnings	53.00	49.00	149.00	220.00	139.00
Dividends	13.00	14.00	43.00	63.00	40.00
Cash Flow	82.29	92.77	171.57	142.38	97.89

RATIOS AND OTHER INFORMATION

Mrk Cap(R000)	171353	176538	186191	130619	100444
Current Ratio	1.17	1.19	1.21	1.22	1.39
Quik/Acid Tst	0.38	0.31	0.29	0.40	0.59
A/C Rec T/ovr	19.02	22.66	27.12	25.86	16.84
Tot Ass T/ovr	3.54	3.61	3.98	4.01	3.81
Debt/Ass Rat	0.57	0.60	0.63	0.65	0.62
L T L Tot Ass	0.04	0.05	0.10	0.11	0.17
Debt to Eqity	1.35	1.52	1.77	1.87	1.69
Interest Cover	2.04	2.07	4.61	6.66	-
Oper Prof Mrg	2.91	3.58	5.29	5.32	4.77
Net Prof Marg%	1.06	0.94	2.43	2.84	2.64
Ret on Assets	11.38	13.82	23.51	24.46	20.34
Ret on Equity%	8.86	8.65	27.01	32.84	27.23
Price/Earnings	10.38	12.24	4.97	2.36	2.88
Divid Cover	4.08	3.50	3.47	3.49	3.48
Divid Yield	2.36	2.33	5.81	12.12	10.00
Earning Yield%	9.64	8.17	20.14	42.31	34.75
NAV % Mrk Pr	106.64	90.28	74.36	85.83	84.80
Effec Tax Rate	52.07	54.00	49.07	52.04	43.88
Def Interval	3.27	3.45	1.86	1.54	1.07
Sus Grth Rate	6.64	6.06	19.20	23.44	19.37

SUBSIDIARY & ASSOCIATED COMPANIES

BARNES MOTORS (PTY) LTD
BARNES PROPERTIES (EAST LONDON) (PTY) LT
BEDA PROPERTIES (PTY) LTD
BETA INVESTMENTS (PTY) LTD
BOUMAT LTD
BRAMLEY GARDENS MOTORS (PTY) LTD
CARGO MOTOR CORPORATION (BENONI) (PTY) L
CARGO MOTOR CORPORATION (WESTERN TRANSVA
CARGO MOTOR CORPORATION EAST (PTY) LTD

CARGO MOTOR CORPORATION LTD
CARGO MOTOR WEST PROPERTIES (PTY) LTD
CARGO PROPERTIES (AUCKLAND PARK) (PTY) L
CARGO PROPERTIES (EAST) (PTY) LTD
COMMERCIAL CENTRE (PTY) LTD (50%)
DANLU INVESTMENTS (PTY) LTD
DASAF PROPERTIES (PTY) LTD
DLK BUILDINGS (PTY) LTD
ERF 203 & 204 APEX (PTY) LTD
HIGHMECH HANDLING (PTY) LTD
HYPERCAR (PTY) LTD
INTER-RENT SAFARI (PTY) LTD
KAYSAF PROPERTIES (PTY) LTD
KRONLEY MOTORS (PTY) LTD
LECTROLITE (PTY) LTD
LECTROLITE DISTRIBUTORS (PTY) LTD
LECTROLITE PRODUCTS (IRELAND) LTD
LECTROLITE PRODUCTS (SWAZILAND) LTD
LINDSAY SAKER (EAST RAND) (PTY) LTD
LINDSAY SAKER (FAR EAST RAND) (PTY) LTD
LINDSAY SAKER (JOHANNESBURG NORTH) (PTY)
LINDSAY SAKER (JOHANNESBURG) LTD
LINDSAY SAKER (RANDBURG) (PTY) LTD
LINDSAY SAKER (WEST RAND) (PTY) LTD
LINDSAY SAKER LTD
LINDSAY SAKER MOTOR HOLDINGS LTD
LSM (CITY WEST) PROPERTIES (PTY) LTD
LSM (DROSTE PARK) PROPERTIES (PTY) LTD
LSM (HIGHLANDS NORTH) PROPERTIES (PTY) L
LSM (KAALFONTEIN) PROPERTIES (PTY) LTD
LSM (KRUGERSDORP) PROPERTIES (PTY) LTD
LSM (RANDBURG) PROPERTIES (PTY) LTD
LSM (WESTERN AREA) PROPERTIES (PTY) LTD
LSM DISTRIBUTORS (PTY) LTD
LSM PROPERTIES (CARLETONVILLE) (PTY) LTD
LYNETTE HOLDINGS (PTY) LTD
LYNFIELD PROPERTIES (PTY) LTD
MIKE KOPPINGS TRUCK CENTRE (PTY) LTD
NCNB (PTY) LTD
NEVALEX BUILDINGS (PTY) LTD
PAINT-A-CAR (PTY) LTD
PHOENIX BUILDINGS (BLOEMFONTEIN) (PTY) L
PHOENIX MOTOR PROPERTIES (PTY) LTD
PHOENIX MOTORS (WELKOM) (PTY) LTD
PHOENIX MOTORS LTD
PHOENIX PROPERTIES (BLOEMFONTEIN) (PTY)
REEF INDUSTRIAL (SECURITIES) (PTY) LTD
SAFICON GROUP SERVICES (PTY) LTD
SAFICON HP LEASING (PTY) LTD
SAFICON INDUSTRIAL EQUIPMENT (PTY) LTD
SAFICON INTER-RENT (PTY) LTD
SAFICON PLACE (PTY) LTD
SAFICON PROPERTY INVESTMENTS (PTY) LTD
SAKER'S INDUSTRIAL HOLDINGS LTD
SAKER'S INVESTMENTS (PTY) LTD
SERONA HOLDINGS (PTY) LTD
SIE (PTY) LTD
TAGS HOLDINGS (PTY) LTD
ZASTRON STREET MOTORS (PTY) LTD

INVESTMENTS

None

SAFMARINE AND RENNIES HOLDINGS LTD

ABBREVIATION : SAFREN

JSE SHORT CODE : SFR

SECTOR : Industrial-Industrial Holding

SHAREHOLDERS

Who Owns Whom's Assessment of the Identity of the Ultimate Controlling Shareholder:
SA MUTUAL

SHAREHOLDER	PERCENTAGE 1992	1991
SA MUTUAL	39.7	40.0
STD BANK NOM TVL P/L	11.2	11.0
CAPITAL SECURITIES LTD	10.8	10.8
CMB NOM P/L	7.2	---
SOUTHERN LIFE ASSOC LTD	4.8	4.7
EIGHTY ONE MAIN STREET NOM LTD	2.6	1.5
ENGINEERING INDUSTRIES PENS FUND	2.4	2.7
METAL IND GROUP PENS FUND	1.9	2.2
ASHTREE INV P/L	1.2	1.2
COMMON FUND INV SOC LTD	1.1	1.1
MUTUAL & FEDERAL INSURANCE CO LTD	1.0	1.0
SANLAM	---	2.1
SANKERN E/B	---	4.9
TOTAL	84.0	83.4

DIRECTORS :
ABRAHAMSE LG ,BECK DE LA H WF ,DAVIN FJ
DUNNINGHAM GW ,FARR AZ ,FINLAY MJ ,FORSTER NM
GOSS RJ ,HAWTON DA (Dep. Chair. & Chief Exec.)
LEVETT MJ ,MACMILLAN GA (Chairman),ROSEVEAR KA
STEYN PC ,TROLLIP AEG ,VAN DER HORST JG D

REGISTRATION NUMBER : 84/10205/06

REGISTERED OFFICE
1100 BP Centre, Thibault Square
Cape Town
8001
TEL: 021-408 6911
FAX: 021-21 7344

TRANSFER SECRETARY
Central Registrars Ltd
P O Box 4844, Johannesburg
2000
TEL: 011-331 0051

COMPANY SECRETARY
C D N Stevens

NATURE OF BUSINESS
An investment holding company, with a controlling interest in quoted Kersaf Investments. Activities of the group include : Ship owning & operating; Air transport; Ships agencies; Freight movement; Bulk & container handling, distribution & storage; Stevedoring; Warehousing; National & international hotel resort & casino operations; Restaurants; Transport & travel; Film & television production; Cinemas & related services; fast foods & beverages Sports goods retail & wholesale; Insurance broking

BANKERS :
First National Bank of SA Ltd

AUDITORS :
Deloitte Pim Goldby

FAMILIAR BRAND NAMES
CHANDLING INTERNAT,MANICA TRAVEL GROUP
PENTOW MARINE,RENFREIGHT,RENNIES TRAVEL
RENT-A-BAKKIE,SAFAIR LINES,SAFTAINER
SEE INTERLEISURE,SEE SUNBOP,SEE TRANSKEI SUN
TREK AIRWAYS,UNICORN LINES
WLLIS FABER ENTHOVEN,XPS SERVICES

CONTRIBUTION BY ACTIVITY
Safmarine (% Turnover) (33.5%)
Kersaf (43.6%)
Rennies (22.1%)
Other (0.8%)

YEAR END : June

DIVIDEND :Ords 50c

Interim No 11	(Ldr)30/03/90	(Pay)17/04/90	Amt(c)55
Final No 12	(Ldr)12/10/90	(Pay)26/10/90	Amt(c)155
Interim No 13	(Ldr)28/03/91	(Pay)12/04/91	Amt(c)60
Final No 14	(Ldr)11/10/91	(Pay)25/10/91	Amt(c)177.5
Interim No 15	(Ldr)13/03/92	(Pay)16/04/92	Amt(c)65
Final No 16	(Ldr)25/09/92	(Pay)30/10/92	Amt(c)190

NUMBER OF EMPLOYEES : 28059

CAPITAL STRUCTURE

	AUTHORISED	ISSUED
7,5% Red Cum PrefS R2	800000	753600
7% Second Red Cum Prefs R1	218511	218336
Ords 50c	70000000	55189249

FINANCIAL STATISTICS (AT FINANCIAL YEAR END)

(Amts in R'000)	1992 Jun	1991 Jun	1990 Jun	1989 Jun	1988 Jun
Ord S/H Int	1428600	1207900	1010800	826100	671800
Long Trm Loans	2810300	2061800	1807700	1531400	1408900
Iss Ord Share	54207	53675	53433	53058	52690
Total Liab	4494400	3565700	3233700	2714300	2468400
Current Liab	1684100	1503900	1426000	1182900	1059500
Total Assets	5853100	4707700	4164300	3452300	3082000
Intang Assets	69900	65900	80200	88100	58200
Current Assets	1498700	1460400	1611300	1132200	1113800
Debtors	900300	659900	783000	623200	639700
Inventory	180400	145700	117600	96000	72200
Turnover	4698300	4369300	4002200	3655000	2799900
Oper Profit	759500	674000	634500	602100	436900
Interest Paid	68000	89800	94800	94100	31000
Tax Paid	200700	196300	230700	199600	115422
Prf af Int&Tax	621300	556200	464900	351200	290478
Prf att Ord Sh	331500	302400	259100	216900	154278
Btm Line Earn	269300	310500	268800	224500	144578
Dividend Paid	138000	127400	112200	95400	71100
Mkt Prce(c) YE	9600	7000	4000	2900	1950
Depreciation	214848	243979	151000	159000	104000

PER SHARE STATISTICS (CENTS)

Net Asst Val	2506.50	2127.62	1741.62	1390.93	1164.55
Net Earnings	617.00	565.50	505.00	404.00	293.00
Dividends	255.00	237.50	210.00	180.00	135.00
Cash Flow	1068.14	988.22	816.38	665.61	517.94

RATIOS AND OTHER INFORMATION

Mrk Cap(R000)	5203872	3757250	2137320	1538682	1027455
Current Ratio	0.89	0.97	1.13	0.96	1.05
Quik/Acid Tst	0.78	0.87	1.05	0.88	0.98
A/C Rec T/ovr	5.22	6.62	5.11	5.86	4.38
Tot Ass T/ovr	0.80	0.93	0.96	1.06	0.91
Debt/Ass Rat	0.47	0.49	0.53	0.54	0.58
L T L Tot Ass	0.18	0.17	0.19	0.20	0.23
Debt to Eqity	1.93	1.93	2.19	2.27	2.64
Interest Cover	12.41	8.32	7.38	6.44	14.09
Oper Prof Mrg	16.17	15.43	15.85	16.47	15.60
Net Prof Marg%	7.06	6.92	6.47	5.93	5.51
Ret on Assets	15.66	18.69	19.84	20.51	14.18
Ret on Equity%	23.20	25.04	25.63	26.26	22.96
Price/Earnings	15.56	12.38	7.92	7.18	6.66
Divid Cover	2.42	2.38	2.40	2.24	2.17
Divid Yield	2.66	3.39	5.25	6.21	6.92
Earning Yield%	6.43	8.08	12.63	13.93	15.03
NAV % Mrk Pr	26.11	30.39	43.54	47.96	59.72
Effec Tax Rate	9.98	14.09	22.72	24.06	20.00
Def Interval	1.99	1.57	1.70	2.07	3.25
Sus Grth Rate	13.54	14.49	14.53	14.71	12.38

SUBSIDIARY & ASSOCIATED COMPANIES

ACF MERCHANDISE (PTY) LTD
AERO MARINE PROPERTIES LTD
AERO MARINE SUPPLIES (PTY) LTD
AEROMARITIME INTERNATIONAL MANAGEMENT SE (50%)
AFRICAN ENTERTAINMENTS (PTY) LTD
AIR CAPE (PTY) LTD
ATLANTIC AGENCIES (SA) (PTY) LTD
AVIATION TECHNICAL & TERMINAL SERVICES
AVRONS SOUTH AFRICA (PTY) LTD
BEATRIXSTRAAT BELEGGINGS (EDMS) BPK
BILJCOS INVESTMENT CORP. LTD
BODINS FREIGHT (PTY) LTD
BOXLAND (PTY) LTD
BRINKS ARMOURED CAR SERVICES (PTY) LTD
BUREN BELEGGINGS (EDMS) BPK
CHAMPNEY PROPERTIES (PTY) LTD
CHANDLING INTERNATIONAL LTD
CHEMIX PRODUCTS (PTY) LTD
CITILINER HOLDINGS LTD
CITY BOND & WAREHOUSES LTD
CONTAINER CARE CO (PTY) LTD
CONTAINERBASES (PTY) LTD
CONTROL & RISK FINANCE (PTY) LTD
CORY MANN GEORGE (LOURENCO MARQUES) (PTY
CYGNUS INVESTMENTS (PTY) LTD
DE REIJGER BELEGGINGS (PTY) LTD
DEAL PARTY ERF 61 (PTY) LTD
DEAL PARTY PROPERTY (PTY) LTD
DEAVIN'S SECURITY (PTY) LTD
DISASTER BACK-UP UNIT (PTY) LTD
DYCKX COURT (PTY) LTD
FREIGHT COMPRESSION PACKAGING INTERNATIO
FREIGHT SERVICES (BEIRA) (PTY) LTD
FREIGHT SERVICES (SWA) LTD
FREIGHT SERVICES CONTAINER LTD
FREIGHT SERVICES FORWARDING LTD
FREIGHTMARINE SHIPPING LTD
GENESYS (PTY) LTD
HARDY BALLINGTON TRAVEL (PTY LTD
HOLMDENE PROPERTIES (PTY) LTD
HUNTER STREET MANSIONS (PTY) LTD
INTERLEISURE LTD
INVESTCO (PTY) LTD (50%)
IRON CRAFTS (PTY) LTD
JD FOSMAN (PTY) LTD
JORDAN & CO LTD (50%)
KBD PROPERTIES (PTY) LTD
KERSAF INVESTMENTS LTD
KILFS (PTY) LTD
LADIVAVIRGEN (EDMS) BPK
LANZA BELEGGINGS (EDMS) BPK

LLB MEAT SUPPLIERS (PTY) LTD
MAIN & MARSHALL PROPERTIES (PTY) LTD
MAKRO (PTY) LTD (33%)
MALAN'S TRANSPORTS (PTY) LTD
MANAGEMENT COMPUTER SERVICES SA (PTY) LT
MANICA FREIGHT SERVICES HOLDINGS LTD
MARSHMAIN (PTY) LTD
MAXHAP PROPERTIES (PTY) LTD
MILNERTON CONTAINER PARKS (PTY) LTD
MUSGROVE & WATSON TRAVEL LTD
MVW BELEGGINGS (EDMS) BPK
OCEAN CITY (PTY) LTD
OCEANMARINE HOLDINGS (PTY) LTD
OCMEC PROPERTIES (PTY) LTD
OLIE & TENKSKIP ORGANISASIE (PTY) LTD
OLYMPIC SPORTS (PTY) LTD
ORYX AVIATION (PTY) LTD
OWENAIR (PTY) LTD
P & I ASSOCIATES (PTY) LTD
PENTOW MARINE (PTY) LTD (50%)
PERISHABLE CARGO AGENTS (PTY) LTD
PORT ELIZABETH STEVEDORING LABOUR SUPPLY
POSEIDON SHIPS' AGENCIES (PTY) LTD
RADIO & HOUSEHOLD APPLIANCES (PTY) LTD
RAND TRAVEL AGENCY (PTY) LTD
RAYZELLE INVESTMENTS (PTY) LTD
RCH FINANCE CO. (PTY) LTD
RCH NOMINEES LTD
REDBURY HOLDINGS LTD (50%)
RENFREIGHT SHIPS AGENCY MARKETING LTD
RENNIE MURRAY & CO. (PTY) LTD
RENNIES BULK TERMINALS (PTY) LTD
RENNIES EXPRESS DELIVERY (PTY) LTD
RENNIES FREIGHT SERVICES INSURANCE BROKE
RENNIES FREIGHT SERVICES INVESTMENTS (PT
RENNIES GROUP LTD
RENNIES MANAGEMENT SERVICES (PTY) LTD
RENNIES PROPERTY HOLDINGS (PTY) LTD
RENNIES SHIPPING PROPERTIES (PTY) LTD
RENNIES SHIPS AGENCY LTD
RENNIES SHIPS SERVICES LTD
RENNIES TRAVEL HOLDINGS (PTY) LTD
RENT-A-BAKKIE (LOWVELD) (PTY) LTD
RENT-A-BAKKIE HOLDINGS (PTY) LTD
RGCS PROPERTIES (ADDINGTON) (PTY) LTD
RICHARDS BAY INVESTMENTS (PTY) LTD
RICHARDS BAY STEAMSHIP & SHIPS AGENCY CO
RICHARDS BAY STEVEDORES LTD
RIVIERA INTERNATIONAL (PTY) LTD (50%)
RO-RO STEVEDORES (PTY) LTD
ROBERT ENTHOVEN & CO. (NATAL) (PTY) LTD
ROBERT ENTHOVEN & CO. (TRANSVAAL) (PTY)
ROBERT ENTHOVEN & CO.(EASTERN PROVINCE)
ROBERT ENTHOVEN & THE BOARD (PTY) LTD
ROBERT ENTHOVEN CONSULTANTS (PTY) LTD &
ROBERT ENTHOVEN EMPLOYEE BENEFIT CONSULT
ROBERT ENTHOVEN PERSONAL FINANCIAL PLANN
ROCSA (PTY) LTD
RONDEAU HOLDINGS AG (SWISS)
SA CONTAINER DEPOTS (PTY) LTD
SA DIVING SERVICES (PTY) LTD (50%)
SA FUEL ENTERPRISE (PTY) LTD
SA MARINE CORP LTD
SA SHIPPING ENTERPRISE (PTY) LTD
SA STEVEDORES LTD
SAFAIR FREIGHTERS (PTY) LTD
SAFAIR HOLDINGS (PTY) LTD
SAFAIR LINES (PTY) LTD
SAFBULK (PTY) LTD
SAFCOVER (PTY) LTD
SAFDAN (PTY) LTD
SAFHOLD (PTY) LTD
SAFMARINE (NAMIBIA) (PTY) LTD
SAFMARINE (SOUTH EAST ASIA) LTD
SAFMARINE COMPUTER SERVICES (PTY) LTD
SAFORE (PTY) LTD
SAFROCK HOLDING (PTY) LTD
SAFSEKER (EDMS) BPK
SANDTON COACH (PTY) LTD
SANSO PROPERTIES PARKVIEW (PTY) LTD
SEALINK (PTY) LTD (50%)
SECURITY ASSIGNMENTS (PTY) LTD
SISHEN SHIPPING (PTY) LTD (50%)
SOUTH AFRICAN LINES (LONDON) LTD
SOUTH AFRICAN LINES LTD
SOUTH AFRICAN MARINE CORP. (N.Y.)
SOUTH AFRICAN MARINE CORP. (UK) LTD
SOUTH AFRICAN SUGAR CARRIERS (PTY) LTD
SPRINGBOK LINE LTD
SPRINGBOK SHIPPING CO. LTD
STH MARKETING & TRADING (PTY) LTD
STL INVESTMENTS (PTY) LTD
SUN FINANCING (PTY) LTD
SUN INTERNATIONAL HOLDINGS (PTY) LTD
SUN INTERNATIONAL OF LESOTHO (PTY) LTD (47%)
SUPERIOR IMPORTS (PTY) LTD
THOMAS COOK (BOPHUTHATSWANA) (PTY) LTD
THOMAS COOK (CISKEI) (PTY) LTD
THOMAS COOK (NAMIBIA) (PTY) LTD
THOMAS COOK (VENDA) (PTY) LTD
THOMAS COOK RENNIES TRAVEL (CISKEI) (PTY
THOMAS COOK RENNIES TRAVEL HOLDINGS (PTY
TREK AIRWAYS (PTY) LTD (38%)
TRIDENT MARINE SERVICES (PTY) LTD
TYRE TREADS (PTY) LTD
UNICORN SHIPPING HOLDINGS (40%)
WALVIS BAY STEVEDORING CO. (PTY) LTD
WESTPOINT TRAVELS (PTY) LTD
WFSA HOLDINGS (PTY) LTD
WILLIS FABER (BOPHUTHATSWANA) (PTY) LTD
WILLIS FABER (EASTERN CAPE) (PTY) LTD
WILLIS FABER (NATAL) (PTY) LTD
WILLIS FABER (OFS) (PTY) LTD
WILLIS FABER (PTY) LTD
WILLIS FABER (SOUTH WEST AFRICA) (PTY) L
WILLIS FABER (TRANSVAAL) (PTY) LTD
WILLIS FABER (WESTERN CAPE) (PTY) LTD
WILLIS FABER EMPLOYEE BENEFITS (PTY) LTD
WILLIS FABER ENTHOVEN LTD
WILLIS FABER REINSURANCE BROKERS (PTY) L
WILLIS FABER RISK MANAGEMENT (PTY) LTD
WILLIS FABER SERVICES (PTY) LTD
WITIN HOLDINGS (PTY) LTD
WONDERBOOM BELEGGINGS (EDMS) BPK
WORLDS VIEW INVESTMENT (PTY) LTD
WORSLEY MAYTHAM (PTY) LTD
XPS COURIERS (PTY) LTD
XPS SERVICES (PTY) LTD
ZEDA TRUCK RENTAL (PTY) LTD

INVESTMENTS

None

SAFRICAN LIFE INVESTMENT HOLDINGS LTD

ABBREVIATION : SAFLIFE

JSE SHORT CODE : SFL

SECTOR : Financial-Insurance

SHAREHOLDERS

Who Owns Whom's Assessment of the Identity of the Ultimate Controlling Shareholder:
HOSKEN VIA IGI

SHAREHOLDER	PERCENTAGE 1992	1991
SAFEGRO NOM P/L	44.8	43.8
CRENDELL INV CORP LTD	24.1	24.1
HOSKEN CONSOLIDATED INV LTD	10.7	10.7
STD BANK NOM TVL P/L	4.1	---
SAFLIFE INV HLDGS SHARE INC CONTROL ACC	3.4	3.1
STOCK	---	1.1
TRUCK & CAR CO P/L	---	3.8
TOTAL	87.1	86.6

DIRECTORS :
CUSHWAY PM MR (Managing Director),HOSKEN JH MR
LEVIN HR MR,LEWIS IMA MR (Executive Chairman)
MACKINTOSH GL MR,NATHAN L MR,NESTADT G M

REGISTRATION NUMBER : 05/29841/06

REGISTERED OFFICE
IGI House, 162 Anderson Street
Johannesburg
2001
TEL: 011-335 1911
FAX: 011-334 5650

TRANSFER SECRETARY
Mercantile Registrars Ltd
P O Box 1053, Johannesburg
2000
TEL: 011-333 8181

COMPANY SECRETARY
W T Green

NATURE OF BUSINESS
An investment holding company whose subsidiaries carry on the business of life assurance and pension fund management whilst others are home service assurers, property owning companies, property developers and other related service companies.

BANKERS :
Standard Bank of SA Ltd, Nedperm Bank Ltd

AUDITORS :
BDO Spencer Steward

FAMILIAR BRAND NAMES
N/A

CONTRIBUTION BY ACTIVITY
Annual Premiums (% of income) (70.6%)
Single Premiums (10.3%)
Investments (19.1%)

YEAR END : March

DIVIDEND : Ords 50c

Interim No 11	(Ldr)01/12/89	(Pay)18/12/89	Amt(c)5
Final No 12	(Ldr)15/06/90	(Pay)06/07/90	Amt(c)15
Interim No 13	(Ldr)30/11/90	(Pay)17/12/90	Amt(c)12.5
Final No 14	(Ldr)21/06/91	(Pay)05/07/91	Amt(c)15
Final No 16	(Ldr)31/07/92	(Pay)21/08/92	Amt(c)17.5
Specie No 17	(Ldr)31/07/92	(Pay)21/08/92	Amt(c)8.1
Interim No 18	(Ldr)04/12/92	(Pay)14/12/92	Amt(c)17.5

NUMBER OF EMPLOYEES : 1106

CAPITAL STRUCTURE

	AUTHORISED	ISSUED
Ords 50c	30000000	29584090
5,5% Red Cum Prefs R2	100000	0

FINANCIAL STATISTICS (AT FINANCIAL YEAR END)

(Amts in R'000)	1992 Mar	1991 Mar	1990 Mar	1989 Mar	1988 Mar
Ord S/H Int	47054	40868	35839	26565	19083
Long Trm Loans	806418	683300	577801	373745	70627
Iss Ord Share	29584	29584	29584	29584	24931
Total Liab	839898	707078	672308	390303	76501
Current Liab	33480	23778	94507	16558	5874
Total Assets	881782	743092	703270	416868	95584
Intang Assets	5170	4854	4877	*	*
Current Assets	70817	62509	119558	36791	21537
Debtors	49342	47936	31037	25837	15203
Inventory	331	636	1555	5268	966
Turnover	-	-	-	-	427109
Oper Profit	18551	17615	11739	8787	4102
Interest Paid	-	-	-	-	682
Tax Paid	1377	2930	1974	2559	438
Prf af Int&Tax	17174	14685	9765	6228	2982
Prf att Ord Sh	16105	13718	9703	6009	2615
Btm Line Earn	16105	13718	9703	6009	2615
Dividend Paid	9615	8136	5917	3675	1745
Mkt Prce(c) YE	710	420	310	145	100
Depreciation	1821	1271	510	533	187

PER SHARE STATISTICS (CENTS)

Net Asst Val	141.58	121.73	104.66	89.80	76.54
Net Earnings	54.00	46.00	32.80	21.40	10.50
Dividends	32.50	27.50	20.00	12.50	7.00
Cash Flow	60.59	50.16	34.31	21.95	11.24

RATIOS AND OTHER INFORMATION

Mrk Cap(R000)	210046	124253	91710	42897	24931
Current Ratio	2.12	2.63	1.27	2.22	3.67
Quik/Acid Tst	2.11	2.60	1.25	1.90	3.50
A/C Rec T/ovr	-	-	-	-	28.09
Tot Ass T/ovr	-	-	-	-	4.47
Debt/Ass Rat	0.06	0.03	0.15	0.08	0.24
L T L Tot Ass	0.02	0.00	0.02	0.04	0.18
Debt to Eqity	1.04	0.60	2.95	1.23	1.19
Interest Cover	-	-	-	-	6.01
Oper Prof Mrg	-	-	-	-	0.96
Net Prof Marg%	-	-	-	-	0.61
Ret on Assets	2.10	2.39	1.68	2.12	4.29
Ret on Equity%	34.23	33.57	27.07	22.62	13.70
Price/Earnings	13.15	9.13	9.45	6.78	9.52
Divid Cover	1.66	1.67	1.64	1.71	1.50
Divid Yield	4.58	6.55	6.45	8.62	7.00
Earning Yield%	7.61	10.95	10.58	14.76	10.50
NAV % Mrk Pr	19.94	28.98	33.76	61.93	76.54
Effec Tax Rate	7.42	16.58	16.82	29.10	13.01
Def Interval	0.85	0.04	8.05	1.92	4.50
Sus Grth Rate	13.79	13.66	10.56	8.79	4.56

SUBSIDIARY & ASSOCIATED COMPANIES

101 ANDERSON STREET (PTY) LTD
56 ANDERBOLT (PTY) LTD
CIVCEN INVESTMENTS (PTY) LTD
CRYSTAL REEF (PTY) LTD
DRANNOCK HOLDINGS (PTY) LTD

EIGHTY-SIX CRANBOURNE AVE (PTY) LTD
ENSUCO HOUSE (PTY) LTD
FENTON ROAD PROPERTIES (PTY) LTD (50%)
GCG (PTY) LTD
IGI CENTRE WITBANK (PTY) LTD
IGI HOLDINGS SA LTD
IGI LIFE ASSURANCE CO LTD
IGI LIFE FUND MANAGERS LTD
IGI NAMIBIA LIFE ASSURANCE (PTY) LTD
JORRLOVE (PTY) LTD
KELVIN PARK OFFICE DEVELOPMENTS (PTY) LT
KORCULA (PTY) LTD
LIFE AND PENSIONS ASSURANCE CORPORATION
LOWCLIFFE HOUSE (PTY) LTD
MAINJET CENTRE (PTY) LTD
MOOI & ANDERSON STREET PROPERTIES (PTY) (50%)
PE PALMERSTON (PTY) LTD
PETER REID & ASSOCIATES (PTY) LTD
SAFEGRO EMPLOYMENT BENEFIT CONSULTANTS ((50%)
SAFEGRO HOLDINGS LTD
SAFEGRO INSTITUTIONAL FUND MANAGEMENT LT
SAFEGRO PERSONAL ASSET MANAGEMENT LTD
SAFEGRO PROPERTY MANAGEMENT LTD
SAFRICAN ASSOCIATION LTD
SIGMA INDUSTRIAL PROPERTIES (PTY) LTD
SOUTH AFRICAN TRADE UNION ASSURANCE SOCI
TRADUNA COUGAR (PTY) LTD
TRADUNA FINANCE & INVESTMENTS CO LTD
TRADUNA GERMISTON 13 (PTY) LTD
TRADUNA GERMISTON 27 (PTY) LTD
TRADUNA LADYONE (PTY) LTD
TRADUNA PROPERTY HOLDINGS (PTY) LTD
TRADUNA RANDBURG (PTY) LTD
VALLEY GROVE (PTY) LTD
WOODKING INVESTMENTS (PTY) LTD

INVESTMENTS

AMITY INTERNATIONALE SA (LUXEMBOURG) (9%)
HCI (UK) HOLDINGS LTD (9%)

SAGE GROUP LTD

ABBREVIATION : SAGEGRP

JSE SHORT CODE : SGG

SECTOR : Financial-Insurance

SHAREHOLDERS

Who Owns Whom's Assessment of the Identity of the Ultimate Controlling Shareholder:
REMBRANDT IS MAJOR SHAREHOLDER

SHAREHOLDER	PERCENTAGE 1992	1991
STD BANK NOM TVL P/L	26.9	1.1
SAGECOR P/L	21.1	---
AMALGAMATED BANKS OF SA LTD	17.9	---
FINANCIAL SECURITIES LTD	9.2	---
NEDBANK NOM LTD	8.5	1.1
FIRST NAT NOM P/L	2.7	1.3
SAGE LIFE LTD	1.7	---
BISHOPGATE NOM LTD	1.4	---
MONTRIQUE P/L	1.3	---
SAGE HOLDINGS LTD	---	95.8
TOTAL	90.7	99.3

DIRECTORS :
BADENHORST PJ ,BOTES AJ ,BROOMBERG EB PROF
CHRISTIE-TAYLOR DR ,CRONJE DC DR,DALY KC
DICKASON GB ,HEFER HV ,ILSLEY BM DR,LANGLANDS EM
MILLS ANB ,MITROVICH AW ,NACKAN B ,ROUX MJ
SHILL HL (Chairman & Managing Dir.),STEINMETZ G
VAN WYK T

REGISTRATION NUMBER : 70/10541/06

REGISTERED OFFICE
11th Floor, Sage Centre, 10 Fraser Street
Johannesburg
2001
TEL: 011-491 0911
FAX: 011-834 2107

TRANSFER SECRETARY
Fraser Street Registrars (Pty) Ltd
P O Box 61178, Marshalltown
2107
TEL: 011-491 0911

COMPANY SECRETARY
CS Cant

NATURE OF BUSINESS
The group operates in the financial services sector. Activities include : long-term insurance, personal financial planning services, management of equity unit trusts, trust management, security trading, investment management, corporate finance & related activities, & investment banking.

BANKERS :
Absa Bank Ltd, Nedcor Bank Ltd

AUDITORS :
KPMG Aiken & Peat, Kessel Feinstein

FAMILIAR BRAND NAMES
N/A

CONTRIBUTION BY ACTIVITY
N/A

YEAR END : March

DIVIDEND : Ords 1c

Final	(Ldr)28/06/91	(Pay)12/07/91	Amt(c)15
Interim	(Ldr)06/12/91	(Pay)20/12/91	Amt(c)12
Final	(Ldr)26/06/92	(Pay)17/07/92	Amt(c)8
Special	(Ldr)26/06/92	(Pay)17/07/92	Amt(c)5

CAPITAL STRUCTURE

	AUTHORISED	ISSUED
Ords 1c	121802875	79690237
Cum Conv Red Prefs 1c	22246040	22246040
Var Rate Comp Conv Debs	2939400	3774180
Cum Red "A" Prefs 1c	80951085	80951085

FINANCIAL STATISTICS (AT FINANCIAL YEAR END)

(Amts in R'000)	1992 Mar	1991 Mar	1991 Dec	1989 Dec
Ord S/H Int	244417	278282	278282	223367
Long Trm Loans	2463809	1886399	1850364	1540595
Iss Ord Share	79690	81557	81557	81557

Total Liab	2713098	1977746	1941711	1619069
Current Liab	249289	91347	91347	78474
Total Assets	2843161	2169846	2169846	1743262
Intang Assets	114354	86182	50147	99174
Current Assets	314778	121333	121333	132188
Debtors	157871	88760	82146	70333
Inventory	12360	1362	1362	-
Oper Profit	39917	40854	40854	31498
Interest Paid	1119	4833	4833	8106
Tax Paid	13627	17707	17707	14200
Prf af Int&Tax	39162	39711	39711	22572
Prf att Ord Sh	43446	42828	42828	29219
Btm Line Earn	41813	76120	76120	34260
Dividend Paid	21216	21205	21205	14627
Mkt Prce(c) YE	450	435	435	-
Depreciation	490	1021	1021	427

PER SHARE STATISTICS (CENTS)

Net Asst Val	163.21	235.54	279.72	152.28
Net Earnings	51.20	52.50	52.50	36.00
Dividends	25.00	26.00	26.00	18.00
Cash Flow	23.41	31.37	24.54	20.36

RATIOS AND OTHER INFORMATION

Mrk Cap(R000)	358605	354773	354773	-
Current Ratio	1.26	1.33	1.33	1.68
Quik/Acid Tst	1.21	1.31	1.31	1.68
Debt/Ass Rat	0.13	0.05	0.05	0.05
L T L Tot Ass	0.05	0.01	0.01	0.01
Debt to Eqity	1.56	0.37	0.37	0.40
Interest Cover	48.18	12.88	12.88	5.54
Ret on Assets	2.79	3.71	2.99	3.33
Ret on Equity%	17.78	15.39	12.31	13.08
Price/Earnings	8.79	8.29	8.29	-
Divid Cover	2.05	2.02	2.02	2.00
Divid Yield	5.56	5.98	5.98	-
Earning Yield%	11.38	12.07	12.07	-
NAV % Mrk Pr	36.27	54.15	64.30	-
Effec Tax Rate	35.12	49.16	49.16	60.70
Def Interval	13.47	0.05	0.04	0.67
Sus Grth Rate	9.10	7.77	7.77	6.53

SUBSIDIARY & ASSOCIATED COMPANIES

AMALGAMATED INSURANCE HOLDINGS (PTY) LTD
FPS (NORTHERN TRANSVAAL) (PTY) LTD
FPS CONSULTANTS LTD
FPS LTD
FPS MARKETING & MANAGEMENT SYSTEMS (PTY)
INVESTORS MUTUAL FUNDS LTD
LAKEVIEW MANAGEMENT PROPERTIES (PTY) LTD
NEDREP INVESTMENTS (PTY) LTD
NETHERLANDS PROPERTIES (PTY) LTD
NEW PROPERTY VENTURES (PTY) LTD
RAND NATAL INVESTMENTS (PTY) LTD
SAGE CAPITAL MANAGERS (PTY) LTD
SAGE COMMUNICATION TECHNOLOGIES (PTY) LT
SAGE COMPUTING (PTY) LTD
SAGE CORPORATE SERVICES (PTY) LTD
SAGE HOLDINGS LTD
SAGE INSURANCE HOLDINGS (PTY) LTD
SAGE INVESTMENT TRUST LTD
SAGE LAND HOLDINGS (PTY) LTD
SAGE LIFE LTD
SAGE PROPERTIES LIMITED
SAGE PROPERTY HOLDINGS LTD
SAGE PROPERTY MANAGEMENT SERVICES (PTY)
SAGE PROPERTY PORTFOLIO MANAGERS (PTY) L
SAGE PROPERTY TRUST MANAGERS (PTY) LTD (49.6%)
SAGE SCHACHAT LIMITED
SAGE SECURITIES LTD
SAGE SECURITY DEALING CO (PTY) LTD
SAGE STRATEGIC INVESTMENTS (PTY) LTD
SAGE TRUST COMPANY (NATAL) (PTY) LTD
SAGE TRUST COMPANY MORTGAGE NOMINEES (NA
SAGE TRUST COMPANY PROPERTIES (NATAL) (P
SAGE TRUST COMPANY PROPERTIES (PTY) LTD
SANDOWN DEVELOPMENT HOLDINGS (PTY) LTD
SANDOWN PROPERTIES (RIVONIA FOUR) (PTY)
SATCO NOMINEES (NATAL) (PTY) LTD
SATCO NOMINEES (PTY) LTD
SSI SECURITIES (PTY) LTD
STRANDBON (PTY) LTD

INVESTMENTS

HIGHRISE HOME HOLDINGS (PTY) LTD (50 SH)
IMPERIAL CAR RENTAL (PTY) LTD (566287 SH)
RMB HOLDINGS LTD (11%)
SAK HOLDINGS (PTY) LTD (PREFS) (2013300 SH)
UNIVERSA (PTY) LTD (4250 SH)

SAKERS FINANCE AND INVESTMENT CORP LTD

ABBREVIATION : SAKERS

JSE SHORT CODE : SKR

SECTOR : Industrial-Industrial Holding

SHAREHOLDERS

Who Owns Whom's Assessment of the Identity of the Ultimate Controlling Shareholder:
BORSOOK FAMILY

SHAREHOLDER	PERCENTAGE 1992	1991
HYPAR INV P/L	30.0	30.7
CARGO INV CORP REF A	9.4	10.7
CARGO INV CORP REF B	9.4	10.7
TEMPORA INV LTD	9.2	9.9
CMB NOM P/L	7.6	—
SAFICON-BOUMAT PENS FUND	6.8	7.1
STD BANK NOM TVL P/L	3.5	2.9
EIGHTY ONE MAIN STREET NOM LTD	3.3	5.7
SA MUTUAL	3.2	---
JACK MINCER HOLDINGS P/L	2.4	2.8
KREHER R K	2.3	2.6
DE BEERS PENS FUND	1.5	1.7
SHAPIRO D H E/L	1.1	---
INDAVI INV P/L	---	3.5
SHAPIRO D H	---	1.3
TOTAL	89.7	89.5

DIRECTORS :
BORSOOK S MRS,GLENDINING PR ,HIPPER KJ
KREHER RK ,MAISEL PM

REGISTRATION NUMBER : 05/07759/06

REGISTERED OFFICE
Saficon Place, 10 Sherborne Road
Parktown
2193
TEL: 011-482 1942

FAX: 011-726 8630

TRANSFER SECRETARY
Central Registrars Ltd
P O Box 4844, Johannesburg
2000
TEL: 011-331 0051

COMPANY SECRETARY
Saficon Group Services (Pty) Ltd

NATURE OF BUSINESS
An investment holding company with a controlling interest in JSE-quoted Saficon Investments.

BANKERS :
Standard Bank of SA Ltd

AUDITORS :
KPMG Aiken & Peat

FAMILIAR BRAND NAMES
SEE SAFICON

CONTRIBUTION BY ACTIVITY
N/A

YEAR END : March

DIVIDEND : Ords 25c

Interim No 66	(Ldr)23/11/90	(Pay)09/01/91	Amt(c)11
Final No 67	(Ldr)04/10/91	(Pay)18/10/91	Amt(c)11
Interim No 68	(Ldr)22/11/91	(Pay)09/01/92	Amt(c)11
Final No 69	(Ldr)02/10/92	(Pay)16/10/92	Amt(c)9

NUMBER OF EMPLOYEES : 7137

CAPITAL STRUCTURE

	AUTHORISED	ISSUED
Ords 25c	12000000	9574060
5,5% Cum Prefs R2	450000	450000

FINANCIAL STATISTICS (AT FINANCIAL YEAR END)

(Amts in R'000)	1992 Mar	1991 Mar	1990 Mar	1989 Mar	1988 Mar
Ord S/H Int	93518	86263	87622	70793	53470
Long Trm Loans	110954	100249	97279	82928	75442
Iss Ord Share	9574	9574	9574	9574	9574
Total Liab	338475	318970	299173	253087	177166
Current Liab	227521	218721	201894	170159	101724
Total Assets	431993	405233	386795	323880	230636
Current Assets	267096	262859	247568	210606	144099
Debtors	80507	64572	56810	50219	52054
Inventory	181094	193827	188321	141395	83052
Turnover	1530996	1463499	1540690	1298428	878904
Oper Profit	44296	52138	81352	69011	41908
Interest Paid	21559	25050	17488	10320	-
Tax Paid	10795	15270	32778	28671	20581
Prf af Int&Tax	12272	14690	33805	32189	21327
Prf att Ord Sh	8351	7383	23726	23414	14695
Btm Line Earn	9170	746	23435	23833	16466
Dividend Paid	1915	2106	6606	6510	4117
Mkt Prce(c) YE	800	820	1300	825	700
Depreciation	15700	13282	10244	7862	3541

PER SHARE STATISTICS (CENTS)

Net Asst Val	976.79	901.01	915.21	739.43	558.49
Net Earnings	87.00	77.00	248.00	245.00	153.00
Dividends	20.00	22.00	69.00	68.00	43.00
Cash Flow	182.24	207.98	307.26	233.52	255.59

RATIOS AND OTHER INFORMATION

Mrk Cap(R000)	76592	78507	124462	78986	67018
Current Ratio	1.17	1.20	1.23	1.24	1.42
Quik/Acid Tst	0.38	0.32	0.29	0.41	0.60
A/C Rec T/ovr	19.02	22.66	27.12	25.86	16.88
Tot Ass T/ovr	3.54	3.61	3.98	4.01	3.81
Debt/Ass Rat	0.57	0.59	0.63	0.64	0.62
L T L Tot Ass	0.04	0.05	0.10	0.11	0.17
Debt to Eqity	2.62	2.79	2.77	2.91	2.65
Interest Cover	2.05	2.08	4.65	6.69	-
Oper Prof Mrg	2.89	3.56	5.28	5.31	4.77
Net Prof Marg%	0.55	0.50	1.54	1.80	1.67
Ret on Assets	11.33	13.76	23.46	24.45	20.35
Ret on Equity%	8.93	8.56	27.08	33.07	27.48
Price/Earnings	9.20	10.65	5.24	3.37	4.58
Divid Cover	4.35	3.50	3.59	3.60	3.56
Divid Yield	2.50	2.68	5.31	8.24	6.14
Earning Yield%	10.88	9.39	19.08	29.70	21.86
NAV % Mrk Pr	122.10	109.88	70.40	89.63	79.78
Effec Tax Rate	52.35	54.32	49.15	52.10	43.97
Def Interval	4.76	4.57	2.75	2.50	1.12
Sus Grth Rate	6.88	6.12	19.54	23.88	19.78

SUBSIDIARY & ASSOCIATED COMPANIES

SAFIC (PTY) LTD
SAFICON INVESTMENTS LTD

INVESTMENTS

None

SAMANCOR LTD

ABBREVIATION : SAMANCO

JSE SHORT CODE : SMA

SECTOR : Metals & Minerals-Manganese

SHAREHOLDERS

Who Owns Whom's Assessment of the Identity of the Ultimate Controlling Shareholder: SANLAM VIA GENCOR

SHAREHOLDER	PERCENTAGE 1992	1991
AFRICAN METALS LTD	36.0	35.4
DELAUNAY LTD	16.8	18.9
CONSOLIDATED NOM P/L	14.6	16.5
RESIDENT NOM LTD	8.1	2.7
SA MUTUAL	3.6	3.1
ABSA NOM P/L	2.7	---
DELAUNAY TWO LTD	2.6	3.0
STD BANK NOM TVL P/L	2.2	2.3
CMB NOM P/L	1.6	---
COMMON FUND INV SOC LTD	---	1.1
SOUTHERN LIFE ASSOC LTD	---	1.2
SANLAM	---	1.6
VOLKSKAS NOM P/L	---	1.7
TOTAL	88.2	87.4

DIRECTORS :
BOSHOFF HF ,BOUSTRED WG ,BOYD L ,CLARKE FS
ELLIS SP ,GILBERTSON BP (Chairman),KOTZEE FP
MCKERRON AB ,RADEMEYER P DE V ,ROUX FJP DR
SMITH HJ (Managing Director

REGISTRATION NUMBER : 01/08883/06

REGISTERED OFFICE
Samancor House, 88 Marshall Street
Johannesburg
2001
TEL: 011-491 7911
FAX: 011-491 7368

TRANSFER SECRETARY
Central Registrars Ltd
P O Box 4844, Johannesburg
2000
TEL: 011-331 0051

COMPANY SECRETARY
Samancor Management Services (Pty) Ltd

NATURE OF BUSINESS
The group is a producer of manganese products, chrome ore, ferrochrome, and is an exporter of silicon and ferrosilicon.

BANKERS :
N/A

AUDITORS :
KPMG Aiken & Peat, Deloitte Pim Goldby

FAMILIAR BRAND NAMES
N/A

CONTRIBUTION BY ACTIVITY
N/A

YEAR END : June

DIVIDEND : Ords 4c

Interim No 97	(Ldr)09/03/90	(Pay)30/03/90	Amt(c)40
Special No 98	(Ldr)09/03/90	(Pay)30/03/90	Amt(c)30
Interim No 101	(Ldr)08/03/91	(Pay)28/03/91	Amt(c)40
Final No 102	(Ldr)06/09/91	(Pay)27/09/91	Amt(c)70
Interim No 103	(Ldr)13/03/92	(Pay)27/03/92	Amt(c)40
Final No 99	(Ldr)07/09/90	(Pay)28/09/90	Amt(c)60
Special No 100	(Ldr)07/09/90	(Pay)28/09/90	Amt(c)50
Final No 104	(Ldr)04/09/92	(Pay)25/09/92	Amt(c)50

NUMBER OF EMPLOYEES : 11674

CAPITAL STRUCTURE

	AUTHORISED	ISSUED
Ords 4c	195000000	188968718

FINANCIAL STATISTICS (AT FINANCIAL YEAR END)

(Amts in R'000)	1992 Jun	1991 Jun	1990 Jun	1989 Jun	1988 Jun
Ord S/H Int	2064643	1330201	1152870	813005	549067
Long Trm Loans	621864	406655	326929	294110	252538
Iss Ord Share	188969	167345	167345	149845	149845
Total Liab	1255712	935431	1269515	1137972	542607
Current Liab	633848	528776	942586	843862	290069
Total Assets	3320355	2265632	2422385	1950977	1091674
Current Assets	1800863	1601470	1794729	1466934	628509
Debtors	553827	399098	448515	551025	271982
Inventory	729912	539443	514541	346691	288311
Turnover	2063904	1806016	2006150	2128135	912840
Oper Profit	334514	465417	779806	792140	233954
Interest Paid	35807	29289	9212	5876	-
Tax Paid	112990	210809	388494	328567	41975
Prf af Int&Tax	274604	363630	527886	510970	191979
Prf att Ord Sh	277064	362211	538729	568547	187805
Btm Line Earn	275006	362211	538729	568547	187805
Dividend Paid	170071	184080	301222	299690	112384
Mkt Prce(c) YE	3700	2925	2900	2075	1400
Depreciation	89777	57205	47270	40606	28225

PER SHARE STATISTICS (CENTS)

Net Asst Val	1092.58	794.89	688.92	542.56	366.42
Net Earnings	151.00	216.00	322.00	378.44	125.45
Dividends	90.00	110.00	180.00	200.00	75.00
Cash Flow	191.30	288.77	356.73	269.32	135.60

RATIOS AND OTHER INFORMATION

Mrk Cap(R000)	6991853	4894841	4853005	3109284	2097830
Current Ratio	2.84	3.03	1.90	1.74	2.17
Quik/Acid Tst	1.69	2.01	1.36	1.33	1.17
A/C Rec T/ovr	3.73	4.53	4.47	3.09	3.36
Tot Ass T/ovr	0.62	0.80	0.83	0.87	0.84
Debt/Ass Rat	0.19	0.24	0.39	0.44	0.29
L T L Tot Ass	0.00	0.01	0.00	0.01	0.03
Debt to Eqity	0.31	0.41	0.83	1.05	0.58
Interest Cover	9.51	16.13	84.66	134.82	-
Oper Prof Mrg	16.21	25.77	38.87	37.22	25.63
Net Prof Marg%	13.42	20.06	26.85	26.72	20.57
Ret on Assets	13.26	26.60	38.66	37.59	23.48
Ret on Equity%	13.42	27.23	46.73	55.95	34.20
Price/Earnings	24.50	13.54	9.01	5.48	11.16
Divid Cover	1.68	1.96	1.79	1.89	1.67
Divid Yield	2.43	3.76	6.21	9.64	5.36
Earning Yield%	4.08	7.38	11.10	18.24	8.96
NAV % Mrk Pr	29.53	27.16	23.76	26.15	26.17
Effec Tax Rate	29.26	22.65	37.72	41.75	20.56
Def Interval	0.47	0.31	0.25	0.12	0.38
Sus Grth Rate	5.18	13.39	20.60	33.07	13.74

SUBSIDIARY & ASSOCIATED COMPANIES

BATLHAKO FERROCHROME (PTY) LTD
BATLHAKO MINING LTD
BATLHAKO MINING LTD
CARBOGRAPHITE LTD (50%)
COLUMBUS JOINT VENTURE (50%)
CROMETALS (PTY) LTD
ELECTROLYTIC METAL CORPORATION (PTY) LTD
EUROMINAS SARL (LISBON) (50%)
FERROMETALS LTD
FERROVELD (PTY) LTD (50%)
HENRY GOULD (PTY) LTD
MANGANESE METAL CO (PTY) LTD (46.9%)
METALLOYS LTD
MIDDELBURG STEEL & ALLOYS (PTY) LTD
MIDDELKUIL CHROME LTD
MIDDLEPLAATS MANGANESE LTD
POLYFOS (PTY) LTD (50%)
SAMANCOR BRONNE (PTY) LTD
SAMANCOR CHROME LTD
SAMANCOR CHROME LTD
SAMANCOR INTERNATIONAL LTD
SAMANCOR MANAGEMENT SERVICES (PTY) LTD
SILICON SMELTERS (PTY) LTD
SOUTH AFRICAN MANGANESE (PTY) LTD
SOUTH AFRICAN MANGANESE (PTY) LTD
TUBATSE FERROCHROME (PTY) LTD
TUBATSE MINING & QUARRYING (PTY) LTD
WINTERVELD CHROME MINES LTD

INVESTMENTS

None

SANLAND PROPERTY TRUST

ABBREVIATION : SANLAND

JSE SHORT CODE : SNL

SECTOR : Financial-Property

SHAREHOLDERS

Who Owns Whom's Assessment of the Identity of the Ultimate Controlling Shareholder: SANLAM

SHAREHOLDER	PERCENTAGE 1992	1991
CMB NOM P/L	83 3	---
METROPOLITAN LIFE LTD	13 7	13 7
EIGHTY ONE MAIN STREET NOM LTD	---	26 1
SANLAM	---	47 5
STD BANK NOM TVL P/L	---	3 5
VOLKSKAS NOM P/L	---	2 8
TOTAL	97 0	93 6

DIRECTORS :
BESTER HSC ,HOWELL JJ (Chairman),KRUGER PS
MASSON R ,PRETORIUS WS ,VOSLOO PC

REGISTRATION NUMBER : 69/14411/06

REGISTERED OFFICE
7th Floor, TrustBank Centre
Randburg
2194
TEL 011-889 8911
FAX 011-787 5606

TRANSFER SECRETARY
Central Registrars Ltd
P O Box 4844, Johannesburg
2000
TEL 011-331 0051

COMPANY SECRETARY
Bankorp Limited

NATURE OF BUSINESS
A closed-end property unit fund managed by Sanland Property Trust Managers Ltd

BANKERS :
Bankorp Ltd

AUDITORS :
Coopers Theron Du Toit

FAMILIAR BRAND NAMES
N/A

CONTRIBUTION BY ACTIVITY
N/A

YEAR END : September

DIVIDEND : Units

Interim No 45	(Ldr)08/02/91	(Pay)25/02/91	Amt(c)5 76
Interim No 47	(Ldr)14/02/92	(Pay)28/02/92	Amt(c)5 78
Final No 46	(Ldr)09/08/91	(Pay)26/08/91	Amt(c)5 86
Final No 48	(Ldr)22/05/92	(Pay)29/05/92	Amt(c)2 75
Interim No 49	(Ldr)20/11/92	(Pay)27/11/92	Amt(c)6 09

CAPITAL STRUCTURE

	AUTHORISED	ISSUED
Units	194400000	194400000

FINANCIAL STATISTICS (AT FINANCIAL YEAR END)

(Amts in R'000)	1992 Sep	1992 Mar	1991 Jun	1990 Jun	1989 Jun
Ord S/H Int	129587	129592	144757	136366	136043
Iss Ord Share	194400	194400	194400	194400	194400
Total Liab	12944	7350	14647	15122	11397
Current Liab	12944	7350	14647	15122	11397
Total Assets	142531	136942	159404	151488	147440
Current Assets	37618	32165	39384	30593	61261
Debtors	382	912	2710	2044	1069
Oper Profit	11838	16579	17162	16612	22513
Tax Paid	4	4	-	-	
Prf af Int&Tax	11834	16575	22592	22297	22513
Prf att Ord Sh	11834	16575	22592	22297	22513
Btm Line Earn	11834	16575	30980	22624	22513
Dividend Paid	11839	16582	22589	22298	16939
Mkt Prce(c) YE	92	70	90	85	76
Depreciation	-		129	174	137

PER SHARE STATISTICS (CENTS)

Net Asst Val	66 66	66 66	74 46	70 15	69 98
Net Earnings	6 09	8 53	11 62	11 47	10 88
Dividends	6 09	8 53	11 62	11 47	10 88
Cash Flow	12 17	11 37	11 69	11 56	11 65

RATIOS AND OTHER INFORMATION

Mrk Cap(R000)	178848	136080	174960	165240	147744
Current Ratio	2 91	4 38	2 69	2 02	5 38
Quik/Acid Tst	2 91	4 38	2 69	2 02	5 38
Debt/Ass Rat	0 09	0 05	0 09	0 10	0 08
Debt to Eqity	0 10	0 06	0 10	0 11	0 08
Ret on Assets	16 61	16 14	14 17	14 72	15 27
Ret on Equity%	18 26	17 05	15 61	16 35	16 55
Price/Earnings	15 11	8 21	7 75	7 41	6 99
Divid Cover	1 00	1 00	1 00	1 00	1 00
Divid Yield	6 62	12 19	12 91	13 49	14 32
Earning Yield%	6 62	12 19	12 91	13 49	14 32
NAV % Mrk Pr	72 46	95 23	82 74	82 53	92 08
Effec Tax Rate	0 03	0 02	-	-	
Sus Grth Rate	0 00	0 01	0 00	0 00	4 10

SUBSIDIARY & ASSOCIATED COMPANIES

SASOL CHEMICALS INDUSTRIES (PTY) LTD

INVESTMENTS

DIE TRUST SENTRUM (JOHANNESBURG) (EDMS) (15 68%)
EXECUTIVE PROPERTY INVESTMENTS (EDMS) BE (4 04%)
FAVOURITE INVESTMENTS (PTY) LTD (1 77%)
GILBOOYSEN-BELEGGINGS (PTY) LTD (0 11%)
HUGUENOT CHANCERY BUILDINGS (PTY) LTD (3 42%)
KAPEL-BELEGGINGS (PTY) LTD (4 53%)
KEM BIRCH (PTY) LTD (1 17%)

KEMPSTRAAT P.E. (PTY) LTD (1.47%)
LE PAS INVESTMENTS (PTY) LTD (5.66%)
PIGGY PAUL INVESTMENTS (PTY) LTD (19.97%)
PRASLIN INVESTMENTS (PTY) LTD (0.61%)
RANDCHECK (PTY) LTD (1.82%)
SANLAMGEBOU SPRINGS (PTY) LTD (1.98%)
SANTRUST NOORDRIFWEG (PTY) LTD (4.47%)
SANTRUST PRETORIA KERKSTRAAT-OOS (PTY) L (1.16%)
SANTRUST TZANEEN (PTY) LTD (0.16%)
SANTRUST UMBILO (PTY) LTD (0.63%)
STERNS CENTRAL ADMINISTRATION COMPANY (P (8.79%)
VEREENIGING GEBOU MARKLAAN (PTY) LTD (0.17%)
WITBANK DEVELOPMENT CORPORATION (PTY) LT (11.57%)

SANLIC HARDWARE HOLDINGS LTD

ABBREVIATION : SANLIC

JSE SHORT CODE : SNI

SECTOR : Industrial-Retailers & Wholesalers

SHAREHOLDERS

Who Owns Whom's Assessment of the Identity of the Ultimate Controlling Shareholder:
ELGRO VIA ELCENTRE

SHAREHOLDER	PERCENTAGE 1992	1991
ELCENTRE CORP LTD	36.5	42.0
MICHAEL HYMAN FAMILY TRUST	8.5	---
NUSSBAUM L	6.1	6.7
CATHRON INV P/L	5.4	6.1
NUSSBAUM M M	5.0	5.5
NUSSBAUM H H	4.8	5.2
NUSSBAUM R P	4.8	5.2
MAXERIC NOM P/L	2.3	2.5
DA CRUZ C F	2.0	2.2
KAPLAN L	2.0	2.2
KRUGER R	1.3	---
NEDBANK NOM LTD	1.3	1.5
SILVER C H	1.1	5.3
GEDDES C R	1.1	---
CHARISMA HOLDINGS P/L	1.1	---
TOTAL	83.0	84.2

DIRECTORS :
BERZACK MC (Joint Managing Director)
ILLMAN B (Chairman)
ILLMAN SH (Joint Managing Director), NUSSBAUM L

REGISTRATION NUMBER : 68/09981/06

REGISTERED OFFICE
Voltex House, 3 River Road
Bedfordview
2008
TEL: 011-434 1313
FAX: 011-616 6305

TRANSFER SECRETARY
Central Registrars Ltd
P O Box 4844, Johannesburg
2000
TEL: 011-331 0051

COMPANY SECRETARY
Elcentre Holdings (Pty) Ltd

NATURE OF BUSINESS
The group is involved in three areas of activity: Distribution of locksmith supplies and security products; Distribution of electrical accessories and products aimed at the DIY market; Distribution of tools and hardware products.

BANKERS :
First National Bank of SA Ltd

AUDITORS :
KPMG Aiken & Peat

FAMILIAR BRAND NAMES
AMD AGENCIES, FS CONSUMER, GREATREX COASTAL
GREATREX INLAND, KTC CHAIN STORES
PACE CONSUMER PRODUCTS, SANLIC, SILCA

CONTRIBUTION BY ACTIVITY
N/A

YEAR END : June

DIVIDEND : (Ldr)20/10/89 (Pay)10/11/89

NUMBER OF EMPLOYEES : 129

CAPITAL STRUCTURE

	AUTHORISED	ISSUED
Ords 4c	100000000	17700000
Comp Conv Debs 60c	42800000	42800000

FINANCIAL STATISTICS (AT FINANCIAL YEAR END)

(Amts in R'000)	1992 Jun	1991 Jun	1990 Jun	1989 Jun	1988 Jun
Ord S/H Int	-23056	-17790	828	6430	5880
Long Trm Loans	25680	25680	37187	3750	-
Iss Ord Share	17700	17700	17700	16200	15500
Total Liab	55444	61340	57042	10092	6403
Current Liab	29764	35660	19855	6342	6403
Total Assets	25687	36817	43658	16522	12283
Intang Assets	6701	6733	14212	*	*
Current Assets	23703	33275	38778	15403	11353
Debtors	9526	13262	17071	6025	4602
Inventory	13921	19695	21379	9352	6733
Turnover	48554	82351	87069	21480	16259
Oper Profit	2156	1000	-654	2216	2582
Interest Paid	3646	4040	2865	777	170
Tax Paid	-	-	-	851	1180
Prf af Int&Tax	-1490	-3040	-3519	588	1232
Prf att Ord Sh	-1490	-3040	-3519	588	1232
Btm Line Earn	-5266	-18618	-6502	411	1232
Dividend Paid	-	-	-	162	589
Mkt Prce(c) YE	12	25	45	50	41
Depreciation	463	953	642	61	41

PER SHARE STATISTICS (CENTS)

Net Asst Val	-168.12	-138.55	-75.62	39.69	37.94
Net Earnings	-2.50	-5.00	-5.80	3.60	8.50
Dividends	-	-	-	1.00	3.80
Cash Flow	-5.80	-11.79	-4.76	4.01	8.73

RATIOS AND OTHER INFORMATION

Mrk Cap(R000)	2124	4425	7965	8100	6355
Current Ratio	0.80	0.93	1.95	2.43	1.77
Quik/Acid Tst	0.33	0.38	0.88	0.95	0.72

A/C Rec T/ovr	5.10	6.21	5.10	3.57	3.53
Tot Ass T/ovr	1.89	2.24	1.99	1.30	1.32
Debt/Ass Rat	2.16	1.67	1.31	0.61	0.52
L T L Tot Ass	1.00	0.70	0.85	0.23	-
Debt to Eqity	-2.40	-3.45	68.89	1.57	1.09
Interest Cover	0.59	0.25	-0.23	2.85	15.19
Oper Prof Mrg	4.44	1.21	-0.75	10.32	15.88
Net Prof Marg%	-3.07	-3.69	-4.04	2.74	7.58
Ret on Assets	8.39	2.72	-1.50	13.41	21.02
Ret on Equity%	6.46	17.09	-425.00	9.14	20.95
Price/Earnings	-4.80	-5.00	-7.76	13.89	4.82
Divid Cover	-	-	-	3.60	2.24
Divid Yield	-	-	-	2.00	9.27
Earning Yield%	-20.83	-20.00	-12.89	7.20	20.73
NAV % Mrk Pr	-1400.99	-554.19	-168.04	79.38	92.53
Effec Tax Rate	-	-	-	52.19	49.00
Def Interval	-21.31	-13.95	-7.73	8.98	1.02
Sus Grth Rate	6.46	17.09	-425.00	6.63	10.94

SUBSIDIARY & ASSOCIATED COMPANIES

None

INVESTMENTS

None

SANTAM LTD

ABBREVIATION : SANTAM

JSE SHORT CODE : SNT

SECTOR : Financial-Insurance

SHAREHOLDERS

Who Owns Whom's Assessment of the Identity of the Ultimate Controlling Shareholder:
SANLAM

SHAREHOLDER	PERCENTAGE 1992	1991
CMB NOM P/L	60.3	---
STD BANK NOM TVL P/L	3.2	---
EIGHTY ONE MAIN STREET NOM LTD	2.9	2.8
BOLAND BANK PENS FUND	2.8	1.4
METROPOLITAN LIFE LTD	2.1	2.1
SA MUTUAL	1.5	1.4
LIBERTY LIFE ASSOC OF AFRICA LTD	1.4	---
SANTAM PENS FUND	1.3	1.3
BOLAND BANK BPK	---	1.4
SANKORP BPK	---	46.7
SANLAM	---	17.3
TOTAL	75.3	74.4

DIRECTORS :
DALING MH ,GELDENHUYS JJ (Managing Director)
JOUBERT DM DR,LOUBSER JGH DR,OOSTHUIZEN CJ
PICKARD JAJ ,STEYN P
VAN ASWEGEN CHJ DR (Chairman),WIESE CH AD

REGISTRATION NUMBER : 04/01680/06

REGISTERED OFFICE
Santam Building, Burg Street
Cape Town
8001
TEL: 021-24 2254
FAX: 021-24 4572

TRANSFER SECRETARY
Central Registrars Ltd
P O Box 4844, Johannesburg
2000
TEL: 011-331 0051

COMPANY SECRETARY
W A Pretorius

NATURE OF BUSINESS
Santam and its wholly owned subsidiary, Santam Namibia Ltd, transact all classes of short-term insurance.

BANKERS :
Trust Bank of Africa Ltd

AUDITORS :
Coopers Theron Du Toit

FAMILIAR BRAND NAMES
MULTIPLEX

CONTRIBUTION BY ACTIVITY
N/A

YEAR END : September

DIVIDEND : Ords no par value

Interim No 72	(Ldr)29/06/90	(Pay)25/07/90	Amt(c)12
Final No 73	(Ldr)28/12/90	(Pay)23/01/91	Amt(c)15
Interim No 74	(Ldr)28/06/91	(Pay)31/07/91	Amt(c)14
Final No 75	(Ldr)27/12/91	(Pay)31/01/92	Amt(c)19
Interim No 76	(Ldr)26/06/92	(Pay)31/07/92	Amt(c)17
Final No 77	(Ldr)24/12/92	(Pay)29/01/93	Amt(c)25

NUMBER OF EMPLOYEES : 2376

CAPITAL STRUCTURE

	AUTHORISED	ISSUED
Ords no par value	150000000	71331000

FINANCIAL STATISTICS (AT FINANCIAL YEAR END)

(Amts in R'000)	1991 Sep	1990 Sep	1989 Sep	1988	1987
Ord S/H Int	402629	269309	218592	154794	137836
Long Trm Loans	480426	399668	388612	359799	277944
Iss Ord Share	71331	71075	70000	70000	70000
Total Liab	529291	440175	448251	359799	277944
Current Liab	48865	40507	59639	-	-
Total Assets	931920	709484	666843	682936	562465
Current Assets	261556	215224	219322	168343	146685
Debtors	97668	87413	90214	-	-
Inventory	-	-	-	168343	146685
Turnover	-	-	-	668064	642616
Oper Profit	50775	42582	51250	-	-
Prf af Int&Tax	50775	42582	51250	38766	29009
Prf att Ord Sh	50775	42582	51250	38766	29009
Btm Line Earn	50775	42582	51250	38766	29009
Dividend Paid	23539	19190	16100	12600	10500
Mkt Prce(c) YE	410	230	245	175	220

PER SHARE STATISTICS (CENTS)

Net Asst Val	564.45	378.91	312.27	221.13	196.91
Net Earnings	71.30	60.00	73.30	-	-
Dividends	33.00	27.00	23.00	-	-

Cash Flow	71 18	59 91	73 21	55 38	41 44

RATIOS AND OTHER INFORMATION

Mrk Cap(R000)	292457	183473	171500	122500	154000
Current Ratio	5 35	5 31	3 68	-	-
Quik/Acid Tst	5 35	5 31	3 68	-	-
Tot Ass T/ovr	-	-	-	0 98	1 14
Debt/Ass Rat	0 05	0 06	0 09	0 53	0 49
L T L Tot Ass	-	-	-	0 53	0 49
Debt to Eqity	0 12	0 15	0 27	2 32	2 02
Net Prof Marg%	-	-	-	5 80	4 51
Ret on Assets	5 45	6 00	7 69	5 68	5 16
Ret on Equity%	12 61	15 81	23 45	25 04	21 05
Price/Earnings	5 75	3 83	3 34	-	-
Divid Cover	2 16	2 22	3 19	-	-
Divid Yield	8 05	11 74	9 39	-	-
Earning Yield%	17 39	26 09	29 92	-	-
NAV % Mrk Pr	137 67	164 74	127 46	126 36	89 50
Def Interval	-		-	9 28	9 58
Sus Grth Rate	6 76	8 69	16 08	16 90	13 43

SUBSIDIARY & ASSOCIATED COMPANIES

MULTIPLEX INVESTMENT HOLDING CO (PTY) LT
SANTAM NAMIBIA LTD
SENTINEL INSURANCE CORP LTD (BRANDWAG VE

INVESTMENTS

None

SAPPI LTD

ABBREVIATION : SAPPI

JSE SHORT CODE : SAP

SECTOR : Industrial-Paper & Packaging

SHAREHOLDERS

Who Owns Whom's Assessment of the Identity of the Ultimate Controlling Shareholder:
SANLAM VIA GENCOR

SHAREHOLDER	PERCENTAGE 1992	1991
CONSOLIDATED NOM P/L	46 1	49 9
CMB NOM P/L	7 9	---
ABSA NOM P/L	5 4	---
STD BANK NOM TVL P/L	4 7	3 4
SA MUTUAL	3 9	1 3
INDUSTRIAL SELECTIONS LTD	3 2	3 8
SENBANK INV P/L	3 0	3 5
EIGHTY ONE MAIN STREET NOM LTD	2 6	1 8
PUBLIC INV COMMISSIONERS	2 6	2 3
NAT SELECTIONS LTD	2 3	2 8
ENGINEERING INDUSTRIES PENS FUND	1 8	1 8
METAL IND GROUP PENS FUND	1 3	1 4
SANLAM	---	1 9
VOLKSKAS NOM P/L	--	5 3
SANKERN E/B	---	5 2
TOTAL	84 8	84 4

DIRECTORS :
DE BEER TL ,FORBES ID ,FOUCHE JH ,GILBERTSON BP
HERON IC (Chief Operations Officer)
HEWITT WE (Financial Director),HUNT-DAVIS DNA
JOKIPII KC ,LECHMERE-OERTEL KR ,SMITH BA
STOKER P ,STRATTEN PM
VAN AS E (Executive Chairman),VLOK AGJ

REGISTRATION NUMBER : 05/08963/06

REGISTERED OFFICE
48 Ameshoff Street, Braamfontein
Johannesburg
2001
TEL 011-407 8111
FAX 011-339 1846

TRANSFER SECRETARY
Central Registrars Ltd
P O Box 4844, Johannesburg
2000
TEL 011-331 0051

COMPANY SECRETARY
D J O'Connor

NATURE OF BUSINESS
Sappi is a vertically integrated forests products company, with core business being beneficiation of natural wood fibres into a variety of products, including unbleached and bleached pulp, dissolving pulp, newsprint, linerboard, cast coated papers, corrugating medium, stationery paper, carbonless copy paper, structural & mining timber, coated art label paper, sackkraft and other kraft packaging papers, fibreboard, particle and laminated board and chemical by-products

BANKERS :
Standard Bank of SA Ltd
First National Bank of SA Ltd
Nedperm Bank Ltd

AUDITORS :
Deloitte Pim Goldby

FAMILIAR BRAND NAMES
AUDITOR,CAMELOT,CASEPRIDE,CLAYPEX,DUKUZA
ECONOLINE,EL TORO BOARDS,FLEXKRAFT,GRIPTIGHT
HARVEST,HI YIELD,HYCAL,KOPYCHIEF,KRAFTGUARD
KRAFTPRIDE,LASERFORM,LORD ARISTON
MULTIFLEX CLUPAK,NOVOBORD,NOVOCLAD,NOVODEK
NOVOGRAIN,NOVOLAM,NOVOPLY,OYSTER OPAQUE
PLATINUM,PLEDGE SECURITY CHEQUE PAPER
PREFECT,PRESSPRIDE,SAVANNAH,SCALA LEDGER
SHAKA PREMIUM ART,STERIBAG,TOKAI BOARDS
TYPEK,UMVOTI,VALET

CONTRIBUTION BY ACTIVITY
Kraft Packaging Paper (% turnover) (30.1%)
Fine Paper (20 9%)
Pulp (28 3%)
Wood Products (10 8%)
Newsprint (6 1%)
Tissue (3 2%)
Other (0 6%)

YEAR END : February

DIVIDEND : Ords R1

Final No 63	(Ldr)20/04/90	(Pay)29/05/90	Amt(c)120
Interim No 64	(Ldr)05/10/90	(Pay)30/10/90	Amt(c)80
Final No 65	(Ldr)03/05/91	(Pay)24/06/91	Amt(c)120
Interim No 66	(Ldr)18/10/91	(Pay)08/11/91	Amt(c)80

Final No 67	(Ldr)30/04/92	(Pay)19/06/92	Amt(c)120
Interim No 68	(Ldr)23/10/92	(Pay)06/11/92	Amt(c)80

NUMBER OF EMPLOYEES : 19324

CAPITAL STRUCTURE

	AUTHORISED	ISSUED
Ords R1	175000000	148764200

FINANCIAL STATISTICS (AT FINANCIAL YEAR END)

(Amts in R'000)	1992 Feb	1991 Feb	1990 Feb	1989 Feb	1987 Dec
Ord S/H Int	4225300	3116500	2938700	2079600	1205500
Long Trm Loans	1580200	1694000	1477100	1822000	998900
Iss Ord Share	125785	93174	93174	86369	31841
Total Liab	2526600	2595100	2545100	2543100	1457400
Current Liab	946400	901100	1068000	721100	458500
Total Assets	6751900	5711600	5483800	4622700	2662900
Current Assets	1834100	872900	1111900	1066500	545000
Debtors	696000	563100	658200	579700	314100
Inventory	397700	309800	314000	259800	201900
Turnover	2843700	2669000	2726500	2468600	1312300
Oper Profit	515300	623300	843100	651300	298600
Interest Paid	262600	303300	228500	100200	33500
Tax Paid	3200	2100	13500	16300	300
Prf af Int&Tax	303100	345600	638600	567000	265600
Prf att Ord Sh	312800	374700	605000	496700	216100
Btm Line Earn	312800	374700	605000	496700	216100
Dividend Paid	225400	186300	186200	152700	85200
Mkt Prce(c) YE	3950	3425	3850	3675	1825
Depreciation	189000	169700	142400	146600	90600

PER SHARE STATISTICS (CENTS)

Net Asst Val	3359.14	3344.82	3153.99	2407.81	3786.00
Net Earnings	305.00	402.00	650.00	607.00	248.00
Dividends	200.00	200.00	200.00	190.00	130.00
Cash Flow	424.21	509.91	784.00	692.92	489.11

RATIOS AND OTHER INFORMATION

Mrk Cap(R000)	4968508	3191210	3587199	3174061	581098
Current Ratio	1.94	0.97	1.04	1.48	1.19
Quik/Acid Tst	1.52	0.62	0.75	1.12	0.75
A/C Rec T/ovr	4.09	4.74	4.14	3.65	4.18
Tot Ass T/ovr	0.42	0.47	0.50	0.46	0.49
Debt/Ass Rat	0.28	0.38	0.35	0.36	0.37
L T L Tot Ass	0.14	0.22	0.16	0.21	0.20
Debt to Eqity	0.45	0.69	0.66	0.81	0.81
Interest Cover	1.97	2.07	3.75	6.58	8.94
Oper Prof Mrg	18.12	23.35	30.92	26.38	22.75
Net Prof Marg%	11.00	14.04	22.19	20.12	16.47
Ret on Assets	9.41	12.61	16.38	12.67	11.24
Ret on Equity%	7.40	12.02	20.59	20.47	17.93
Price/Earnings	12.95	8.52	5.92	6.05	7.36
Divid Cover	1.53	2.01	3.25	3.19	1.91
Divid Yield	5.06	5.84	5.19	5.17	7.12
Earning Yield%	7.72	11.74	16.88	16.52	13.59
NAV % Mrk Pr	85.04	97.66	81.92	65.52	207.45
Effec Tax Rate	1.05	0.61	1.41	-	-
Def Interval	2.68	3.39	1.95	1.63	2.40
Sus Grth Rate	2.07	6.05	14.25	16.54	10.86

SUBSIDIARY & ASSOCIATED COMPANIES

AANGELAP (EDMS) BPK
AFRICAN PULP & PAPER TRADERS (PTY) LTD
ALPHEUS WILLIAMS & SONS (PTY) LTD
AMPERPLAAS (EDMS) BPK
ANNLOR PROPERTIES (PTY) LTD
ARBORCO PLANTATIONS (PTY) LTD
BARNEVELD PLAAS (EDMS) BPK
BEAU ESTATE & FINANCE CO. (PTY) LTD
BOXES & SHOOKS (SWAZILAND) (PTY) LTD
BOXES & SHOOKS (TVL) (PTY) LTD
BUFFELJAG PLANTASIES (CAROLINA) (PTY) LT
DAMMI ASSOCIATES (PTY) LTD (50%)
DUMISA HOLDINGS (PTY) LTD
DUNSTANBOROUGH ESTATES (PTY) LTD
DYSON TIMBERS (PTY) LTD
EUREKA TIMBER CO (PTY) LTD
FEATHER RIVER SAW MILLS (PTY) LTD
FIV-WAY SUGAR CO (PTY) LTD
G LEROY (PTY) LTD
GARDNER WILLIAMS DUNNOTTAR PLANTATIONS L
GENERAL PRODUCTS MANUFACTURING CORP. (PT
H L & H PENICUIK (PTY) LTD
HAMAWASHA INVESTMENTS (PTY) LTD
HARVEY & SONS (SA ESTATES) (PTY) LTD
HILLTHORN (PTY) LTD
HODGSON ESTATES (PTY) LTD
HOUTBOSLOOP SAAGMEULE (EDMS) BPK
LEROY-NOVOLAM LTD
LOSA BROTHERS (PTY) LTD (20%)
MOOIFONTEIN PLANTASIES (EDMS) BPK
NDENJA (PTY) LTD
NDUBAZI RANCH (PTY) LTD
NGODWANA MILL LTD
NINCFOR (PTY) LTD
NOVOBORD (PTY) LTD
NOVOBORD BUILDINGS LTD
PALTIMBER INDUSTRIES (PTY) LTD
PB FORESTRY LANDS (SA ESTATES) (PTY) LTD
PETRUSVLEI PLANTATION (PTY) LTD
PINETA SAWMILLS (PTY) LTD
PROVINCIAL INVESTMENTS (PTY) LTD
RECANI FORESTS (PTY) LTD
SAICCARB (PTY) LTD
SAICCOR HOUSING CO (PTY) LTD
SALIGNA FORESTRY (PTY) LTD
SAPPI (ZIMBABWE) LTD
SAPPI CAPE KRAFT (PTY) LTD
SAPPI CAPE PROPERTIES (PTY) LTD
SAPPI EXPORT SERVICES (PTY) LTD
SAPPI FINE PAPERS (PTY) LTD
SAPPI FORESTS (PTY) LTD
SAPPI KRAFT (PTY) LTD
SAPPI LOWVELD PROPERTIES (PTY) LTD
SAPPI MANAGEMENT SERVICES (PTY) LTD
SAPPI MANUFACTURING (PTY) LTD
SAPPI NOVOBORD (PTY) LTD
SAPPI PE PROPERTIES (PTY) LTD
SAPPI SAICCOR (PTY) LTD
SAPPI SALES LTD
SAPPI SAWMILLS (PTY) LTD (50%)
SAPPI TIMBER INDUSTRIES (PTY) LTD
SAPPI WASTE PAPER (PTY) LTD
SUNSET PLANTATIONS (PTY) LTD
TECHNIBOARD PRODUCTS (PTY) LTD
TIMBERBOARD (PTY) LTD
TOPTREE TIMBER FARMS (PTY) LTD
UITKYK SAWMILLS (PTY) LTD
UMFOLOZI PROPERTIES (PTY) LTD
UMKOMANZI MANSIONS (PTY) LTD
UMVOTI PROPERTIES (PTY) LTD
USUTU PULP COMPANY LTD (49%)
VENUS TIMBERS LTD
VISICK FORESTRY (PTY) LTD
VISICK TIMBERS (PTY) LTD
WATERTON TIMBER CO (PTY) LTD
WELTEVREDEN PLANTATIONS (PTY) LTD
WESTRA MYNBOU (EDMS) BPK
YONDER BASE MINERALS (PTY) LTD
ZULULAND CONSTRUCTION (PTY) LTD

INVESTMENTS

None

SASFIN HOLDINGS LTD

ABBREVIATION : SASFIN

JSE SHORT CODE : SFN

SECTOR : Financial-Banks & Financial Services

SHAREHOLDERS

Who Owns Whom's Assessment of the Identity of the Ultimate Controlling Shareholder: DIRECTORS

SHAREHOLDER	PERCENTAGE 1992	1991
FIRST NAT NOM P/L	67 3	67 4
MARSAS INV P/L	10 6	10 7
UNITAS ENTERPRISES LTD	6 5	6 6
SASFIN INV P/L	1 8	1 8
LOWENCO NOM P/L	1 6	1 6
GUERNSEY ADMIN SERVICES NOM LTD	1 5	1 5
SASSOON A L E	1 4	1 4
BOWMAN N	1 0	1 0
TOTAL	91 7	91 9

DIRECTORS :
GLATT MB (Chairman)
KROWITZ DA (Operations Director),RABINOWITZ J
SASSOON RDEB (Managing Director)
SASSOON SE (President

REGISTRATION NUMBER : 87/02097/06

REGISTERED OFFICE
2nd Floor, Ivylink, 124 Ivy Road
Norwood
2192
TEL 011-728 7310
FAX 011-728 2489

TRANSFER SECRETARY
Central Registrars Ltd
P O Box 4844, Johannesburg
2000
TEL 011-331 0051

COMPANY SECRETARY
D A Krowitz

NATURE OF BUSINESS
The group provides trade & equipment finance facilities Activities include Instalment finance, Confirming, Invoice discounting, Export shipping, Countertrade & international merchandise converting services

BANKERS :
Nedperm Bank Ltd, Standard Bank of SA Ltd
First National Bank of SA Ltd
Central Merchant Bank Ltd, Volkskas Ltd
Allied Bank Ltd

AUDITORS :
Fisher Hoffman Stride

FAMILIAR BRAND NAMES
N/A

CONTRIBUTION BY ACTIVITY
N/A

YEAR END : June

DIVIDEND : Ords 1c

Dividend	(Ldr)07/09/90	(Pay)21/09/90	Amt(c)7
Dividend	(Ldr)20/09/91	(Pay)04/10/91	Amt(c)8 5
Dividend	(Ldr)16/10/92	(Pay)06/11/92	Amt(c)8 5

NUMBER OF EMPLOYEES : 54

CAPITAL STRUCTURE

	AUTHORISED	ISSUED
Ords 1c	40000000	11306000

FINANCIAL STATISTICS (AT FINANCIAL YEAR END)

(Amts in R'000)	1992 Jun	1991 Jun	1990 Jun	1989 Jun	1988 Jun
Ord S/H Int	8895	7569	5795	4392	3546
Long Trm Loans	452	417	423	378	347
Iss Ord Share	11306	11306	11306	11256	11256
Total Liab	23958	17549	12769	12570	7772
Current Liab	23506	17132	12346	12192	7425
Total Assets	32853	25118	18564	16962	11318
Current Assets	31001	23588	17808	16302	10918
Debtors	27534	18867	17122	13992	9772
Oper Profit	6212	4485	3934	3057	1601
Interest Paid	3671	2006	1862	1408	453
Tax Paid	43	55	54	39	26
Prf af Int&Tax	2498	2424	2018	1610	1122
Prf att Ord Sh	2475	2403	1997	1589	1105
Btm Line Earn	2475	2403	2172	1414	1105
Dividend Paid	961	961	791	563	281
Mkt Prce(c) YE	120	80	45	60	46
Depreciation	127	103	139	79	30

PER SHARE STATISTICS (CENTS)

Net Asst Val	78 68	66 95	51 26	39 02	31 50
Net Earnings	21 90	21 30	17 70	14 10	11 10
Dividends	8 50	8 50	7 00	5 00	2 50
Cash Flow	23 01	22 17	18 89	14 82	10 08

RATIOS AND OTHER INFORMATION

Mrk Cap(R000)	13567	9045	5088	6754	5178
Current Ratio	1 32	1 38	1 44	1 34	1 47
Quik/Acid Tst	1 32	1 38	1 44	1 34	1 47
Debt/Ass Rat	0 72	0 68	0 67	0 72	0 66
Debt to Eqity	2 64	2 26	2 13	2 78	2 09
Interest Cover	1 69	2 24	2 11	2 17	3 53
Ret on Assets	18 91	17 86	21 19	18 02	14 15
Ret on Equity%	27 82	31 75	34 46	36 18	31 16
Price/Earnings	5 48	3 76	2 54	4 26	4 14
Divid Cover	2 58	2 51	2 53	2 82	4 44
Divid Yield	7 08	10 63	15 56	8 33	5 43
Earning Yield%	18 25	26 63	39 33	23 50	24 13
NAV % Mrk Pr	65 56	83 68	113 90	65 03	68 49
Effec Tax Rate	1 69	2 22	2 61	2 37	2 26
Def Interval	5 16	4 51	4 12	5 46	3 76
Sus Grth Rate	17 02	19 05	20 81	23 36	23 24

SUBSIDIARY & ASSOCIATED COMPANIES

ACTRONIC FINANCE (PTY) LTD
FASTFAX FINANCE (PTY) LTD
FIELD OFFICE FINANCE (PTY) LTD (50%)
ROSEAUG INVESTMENTS (PTY) LTD (50%)
SASFIN (CENTRAL AFRICA) LTD
SASFIN (PTY) LTD
SUNLYN INVESTMENTS (PTY) LTD

INVESTMENTS

None

SASOL LTD

ABBREVIATION : SASOL

JSE SHORT CODE : SOL

SECTOR : Industrial-Chemicals & Oils

SHAREHOLDERS

Who Owns Whom's Assessment of the Identity of the Ultimate Controlling Shareholder:
STATE/INSTITUTIONAL CONTROL

SHAREHOLDER	PERCENTAGE 1992	1991
KONOIL P/L	16.9	16.9
CMB NOM P/L	12.9	---
PUBLIC INV COMMISSIONERS	9.5	9.9
STD BANK NOM TVL P/L	8.3	7.4
CAPITAL SECURITIES LTD	5.3	5.3
SA MUTUAL	4.6	4.5
EIGHTY ONE MAIN STREET NOM LTD	4.0	3.3
LIBERTY LIFE ASSOC OF AFRICA LTD	3.5	3.4
IND DEVELOPMENT CORP SA LTD	3.4	3.4
MINU NOM LTD	2.6	2.6
FIRST NAT NOM P/L	2.1	2.2
YSKOR PENS FUND	2.1	2.2
SOUTHERN LIFE ASSOC LTD	2.0	2.7
MOMENTUM LIFE ASSURE LTD	---	1.0
SANLAM	---	3.5
SANKERN E/B	---	8.4
TOTAL	77.0	76.7

DIRECTORS :
ADCOCK CS ,CLEWLOW WAM ,DE WAAL MT ,DU TOIT AG
HEFER HV ,KRUGER P DU P (Deputy Chairman & M.D.)
LEVETT MJ ,MOSTERT DF ,STEGMANN JA DR (Chairman)
VAN ROOY PJ ,WIESE CH

REGISTRATION NUMBER : 79/03231/06

REGISTERED OFFICE
1 Sturdee Avenue, Rosebank
2196
TEL: 011-441 3111
FAX: 011-788 5092

TRANSFER SECRETARY
Central Registrars Ltd
P O Box 4844, Johannesburg
2000
TEL: 011-331 0051

COMPANY SECRETARY
R Hugo

NATURE OF BUSINESS
Producers and marketers of liquid fuels, pipeline gas, fertilizers, explosives, petrochemicals and polymers, derived from coal and crude oil.

BANKERS :
Volkskas Ltd

AUDITORS :
KPMG Aiken & Peat

FAMILIAR BRAND NAMES
EMEX,FEDMIS,PERMEX,PRILLAN,PRILLEX

CONTRIBUTION BY ACTIVITY
N/A

YEAR END : June

DIVIDEND : Ords no par value

Interim No 21	(Ldr)16/03/90	(Pay)17/04/90	Amt(c)27.5
Final No 22	(Ldr)21/09/90	(Pay)15/10/90	Amt(c)32
Interim No 23	(Ldr)15/03/91	(Pay)15/04/91	Amt(c)32.5
Final No 24	(Ldr)20/09/91	(Pay)14/10/91	Amt(c)39
Interim No 25	(Ldr)13/03/92	(Pay)15/04/92	Amt(c)36.5
Final No 26	(Ldr)18/09/92	(Pay)14/10/92	Amt(c)41.5

NUMBER OF EMPLOYEES : 32100

CAPITAL STRUCTURE

	AUTHORISED	ISSUED
Ords no par value	1175000000	565629000
8,5% Unsec Auto Conv Sub Debs	56382400	56382400

FINANCIAL STATISTICS (AT FINANCIAL YEAR END)

(Amts in R'000)	1992 Jun	1991 Jun	1990 Jun	1989 Jun	1988 Jun
Ord S/H Int	5541100	4827900	4295570	3563482	3271408
Long Trm Loans	4616100	3521600	1734236	1728652	1631385
Iss Ord Share	565629	563741	563623	563471	563387
Total Liab	6954700	5850600	2894125	3020744	2498749
Current Liab	2338600	2329000	1159889	1292092	867364
Total Assets	12495800	10678500	6782318	6176057	5363853
Intang Assets	*	*	407377	408169	406304
Current Assets	3536000	2418000	1807645	2011602	1365890
Debtors	1213600	1043300	823224	780853	518774
Inventory	924100	1008200	758664	672614	529583
Turnover	7853900	7561800	5032854	4093647	3614604
Oper Profit	1784100	1897100	1231314	1097736	822499
Interest Paid	363200	542300	46033	42680	-
Tax Paid	359700	470100	254934	490742	348184
Prf af Int&Tax	1171500	1054700	1076091	634474	474315
Prf att Ord Sh	1139700	1041300	746327	629404	473469
Btm Line Earn	1139700	1041300	746327	647504	473469
Dividend Paid	440600	403100	335364	295814	267410
Mkt Prce(c) YE	1930	1420	1250	1280	790
Depreciation	610900	617834	314006	255196	246713

PER SHARE STATISTICS (CENTS)

Net Asst Val	979.64	856.40	689.86	559.98	508.55
Net Earnings	202.00	184.70	189.20	111.70	84.20
Dividends	78.00	71.50	59.50	52.50	42.00

Cash Flow	311.81	294.61	245.03	182.80	148.15

RATIOS AND OTHER INFORMATION

Mrk Cap(R000)	10916640	8005122	7045288	7212429	4450757
Current Ratio	1.51	1.04	1.56	1.56	1.57
Quik/Acid Tst	1.12	0.61	0.90	1.04	0.96
A/C Rec T/ovr	6.47	7.25	6.11	5.24	6.97
Tot Ass T/ovr	0.63	0.71	0.74	0.66	0.67
Debt/Ass Rat	0.42	0.38	0.23	0.27	0.23
L T L Tot Ass	0.23	0.17	0.06	0.07	0.07
Debt to Eqity	0.94	0.85	0.36	0.48	0.39
Interest Cover	4.92	3.51	28.40	26.31	-
Oper Prof Mrg	22.72	25.09	24.47	26.82	22.75
Net Prof Marg%	14.51	13.77	14.83	15.38	13.10
Ret on Assets	15.16	19.36	20.30	18.91	15.33
Ret on Equity%	20.57	21.57	17.37	17.66	14.47
Price/Earnings	9.55	7.69	6.61	11.46	9.38
Divid Cover	2.59	2.58	3.18	2.13	2.00
Divid Yield	4.04	5.04	4.76	4.10	5.32
Earning Yield%	10.47	13.01	15.14	8.73	10.66
NAV % Mrk Pr	50.76	60.31	55.19	43.75	64.37
Effec Tax Rate	22.83	33.29	20.25	31.39	28.41
Def Interval	1.29	1.31	0.30	0.40	0.50
Sus Grth Rate	12.62	13.22	9.57	9.36	6.30

SUBSIDIARY & ASSOCIATED COMPANIES

CARL BECHEM (AFRICA) (PTY) LTD
ENSIGN-BICKFORD (SOUTH AFRICA) (PTY) LTD
FELBITEM (PTY) LTD
HWH BELEGGINGS (PTY) LTD
LESLIE COAL DEVELOPMENT CO. (PTY) LTD
NATIONAL PETROLEUM REFINERS OF S A (PTY)
OPTICHEM FERTILIZERS (PTY) LTD
PRICE'S CANDLES (NATAL) (PTY) LTD
PRICE'S CANDLES (SA) (PTY) LTD
SA GAS DISTRIBUTION CORP LTD (50%)
SASOL (TRANSVAAL) TOWNSHIPS LTD
SASOL CHEMICAL EUROPE LTD
SASOL CHEMICALS INDUSTRIES (PTY) LTD
SASOL INDUSTRIES (PTY) LTD
SASOL INDUSTRIES (PTYO LTD
SASOL MINING (PTY) LTD
SASOL OIL & FERTILIZERS (PTY) LTD
SASOL OPERATIONS (PTY) LTD
SASOL TECHNOLOGY (PTY) LTD
SASOL THREE (PTY) LTD
SASOL TOWNSHIPS LTD
TOSAS (PTY) LTD
TOSAS BOTSWANA (PTY) LTD
TOSAS HOLDINGS (PTY) LTD
TWENTE WOONSTELLE (PTY) LTD
WINDMILL PROPERTIES (PTY) LTD
ZULULAND FERTILIZERS (PTY) LTD

INVESTMENTS

SMALL BUSINESS DEVELOPMENT CORP LTD (608000 SH)

SCHARRIGHUISEN HOLDINGS LTD

ABBREVIATION : SCHARIG

JSE SHORT CODE : SCG

SECTOR : Industrial-Engineering

SHAREHOLDERS

Who Owns Whom's Assessment of the Identity of the Ultimate Controlling Shareholder: SCHARRIGHUISEN FAMILY

SHAREHOLDER	PERCENTAGE 1992	1991
HENDRIK FAMILY INV P/L	18.9	21.6
CASPER FAMILY INV P/L	18.7	21.8
TEUNIS FAMILY INV P/L	18.7	21.8
SA MUTUAL	11.0	---
CMB NOM P/L	10.2	---
T J C TRADING P/L	5.3	5.3
CHALKTON NOM CO P/L	2.6	3.1
STEINLIS INV P/L	2.0	4.3
SCHARRIGHUISEN HOLDINGS LTD SHARE TRUST	1.3	---
NEDBANK NOM LTD	1.1	1.1
INTEQU INV P/L	1.1	---
SCHARRIGHUISEN HOLDINGS LTD	---	3.1
FOURVAT P/L	---	9.7
TOTAL	90.8	91.7

DIRECTORS :
BAILEY GC ,CASTLE CJ
FISHER LC (Joint Managing Director)
SCHARRIGHUISEN C (Chairman & Joint MD)
SCHARRIGHUISEN HC (Operations Director)
SCHARRIGHUISEN T (Financial Director)

REGISTRATION NUMBER : 69/08588/06

REGISTERED OFFICE
8 Patrick Street, Jet Park
Boksburg
1450
TEL: 011-826 4388
FAX: 011-826 3148

TRANSFER SECRETARY
Central Registrars Ltd
P O Box 4844, Johannesburg
2000
TEL: 011-331 0051

COMPANY SECRETARY
T Scharrighuisen

NATURE OF BUSINESS
An investment holding company with subsidiaries engaged in opencast mining, construction, plant hire and earthworks.

BANKERS :
Nedperm Bank Ltd

AUDITORS :
GL Palmer & Co

FAMILIAR BRAND NAMES
N/A

CONTRIBUTION BY ACTIVITY
Mining & mining services (% Turnover) (95.0%)
Plant Hire (4.3%)
Construction (0.7%)

YEAR END : December

DIVIDEND : Ords 4c

Interim No 1	(Ldr)05/04/90	(Pay)26/04/90	Amt(c)5
Interim No 2	(Ldr)19/10/90	(Pay)09/11/90	Amt(c)5

Final No 3	(Ldr)03/05/91	(Pay)24/05/91	Amt(c)7.5
Interim No 4	(Ldr)13/09/91	(Pay)04/10/91	Amt(c)9
Special No 5	(Ldr)06/12/91	(Pay)27/12/91	Amt(c)5
Final No 6	(Ldr)28/02/92	(Pay)27/05/92	Amt(c)11
Interim No 7	(Ldr)02/10/92	(Pay)16/10/92	Amt(c)12
Final No 8	(Ldr)11/12/92	(Pay)04/01/93	Amt(c)6

NUMBER OF EMPLOYEES : 600

CAPITAL STRUCTURE

	AUTHORISED	ISSUED
Ords 4c	40000000	27320000

FINANCIAL STATISTICS (AT FINANCIAL YEAR END)

(Amts in R'000)	1991 Dec	1990 Dec	1989 Dec
Ord S/H Int	60016	39396	33186
Long Trm Loans	21113	10816	13269
Iss Ord Share	27320	22100	22100
Total Liab	47763	27180	27907
Current Liab	26650	16364	14638
Total Assets	100386	56329	50846
Intang Assets	7393	10247	10247
Current Assets	30381	13929	9932
Debtors	9615	5896	3937
Inventory	6050	4692	1531
Turnover	99534	66255	41559
Oper Profit	23418	17157	10559
Interest Paid	3775	5162	-
Tax Paid	2683	3869	3167
Prf af Int&Tax	18269	9221	7392
Prf att Ord Sh	18269	9221	7392
Btm Line Earn	18269	7753	5924
Dividend Paid	6830	2165	4883
Mkt Prce(c) YE	300	150	130
Depreciation	8736	11227	-

PER SHARE STATISTICS (CENTS)

Net Asst Val	192.62	131.90	103.80
Net Earnings	70.80	53.10	34.80
Dividends	25.00	17.50	11.50
Cash Flow	107.88	58.46	33.45

RATIOS AND OTHER INFORMATION

Mrk Cap(R000)	81960	33150	28730
Current Ratio	1.14	0.85	0.68
Quik/Acid Tst	0.91	0.56	0.57
A/C Rec T/ovr	10.35	7.49	10.56
Tot Ass T/ovr	0.99	0.78	0.82
Debt/Ass Rat	0.40	0.39	0.52
L T L Tot Ass	0.13	0.10	0.23
Debt to Eqity	0.66	0.55	0.79
Interest Cover	6.20	3.32	-
Oper Prof Mrg	23.53	25.90	25.41
Net Prof Marg%	18.35	13.92	17.79
Ret on Assets	24.63	21.60	20.77
Ret on Equity%	30.44	15.60	22.27
Price/Earnings	4.24	2.82	3.74
Divid Cover	2.83	3.03	3.03
Divid Yield	8.33	11.67	8.85
Earning Yield%	23.60	35.40	26.77
NAV % Mrk Pr	64.21	87.93	79.84
Effec Tax Rate	-	29.56	29.99
Def Interval	1.03	0.52	2.87
Sus Grth Rate	19.06	17.91	7.56

SUBSIDIARY & ASSOCIATED COMPANIES

FRIGATE (PTY) LTD
FRIGATE MINING (PTY) LTD
SCHARRIGHUISEN ADMINISTRATION (PTY) LTD
SCHARRIGHUISEN CONSTRUCTION (1989) (PTY)
SCHARRIGHUISEN OPEN CAST MINING (1989) (
SCHARRIGHUISEN PLANT HIRE (1989) (PTY) L

INVESTMENTS

None

SCHWEPPE (CENTRAL AFRICA) LTD

ABBREVIATION : SCHWEP CA

SECTOR : Zimbabwe Stock Exchange

SHAREHOLDERS

Who Owns Whom's Assessment of the Identity of the Ultimate Controlling Shareholder: CADBURY SCHWEPPES ZIMBABWE

SHAREHOLDER	PERCENTAGE 1992	1991
CADBURY SCHWEPPES ZIM (PVT) LTD	46.1	---
OLD MUTUAL INV CORP (PVT) LTD	20.8	---
FINANCIAL SERVICES (PVT) LTD	5.3	---
NORTHCHART INV LTD	5.0	---
NAT RAILWAYS OF ZIM CONTR PENS FUND	4.8	---
SECURITY NOM LTD	2.9	---
IRVINE W M	2.2	---
TOTAL	87.0	---

DIRECTORS :
BIRD J ,CHAVUNDUKA DM ,DORWARD PD (Chairman)
FRANKLIN WFJ (Managing Director),HIND PHB
LEWIS DJ ,MCMANMON J ,PSILLOS A MR

REGISTERED OFFICE
Woolwich Road, Willowvale
Harare, Zimbabwe

TEL: 62661/7

TRANSFER SECRETARY
First Transfer Secretaries (Pvt) Ltd
P O Box 437, Bulawayo
Zimbabwe

TEL: 092634 - 702905

COMPANY SECRETARY
W F J Franklin

NATURE OF BUSINESS
The company is engaged in the manufacture and sale of soft drinks supplied through wholesale and retail outlets to licenced catering and grocery trades throughout Zimbabwe.

BANKERS :
First Merchant Bank of Zimbabwe Ltd
Standard Chartered Bank Zimbabwe Ltd

AUDITORS :
Ernst & Young

FAMILIAR BRAND NAMES
CALYPSO, MAZOE

CONTRIBUTION BY ACTIVITY
N/A

YEAR END : December

DIVIDEND : Ords Z$0,50

Dividend	(Ldr)26/03/92	(Pay)10/04/92	Amt(c)18
Dividend	(Ldr)14/08/92	(Pay)28/08/92	Amt(c)9

CAPITAL STRUCTURE

	AUTHORISED	ISSUED
Ords Z$0,50	10000000	9501107
5% Cum Conv Red Prefs 50c	700000	17500

FINANCIAL STATISTICS (AT FINANCIAL YEAR END)

(Amts in Z$)	1991 Dec	1990 Dec
Ord S/H Int	26349	24110
Long Trm Loans	1040	758
Iss Ord Share	9519	9519
Total Liab	20839	12172
Current Liab	19799	11414
Total Assets	47188	36282
Current Assets	23543	16326
Debtors	9652	7612
Inventory	6309	5166
Turnover	48510	33792
Oper Profit	8007	5200
Interest Paid	27	-
Tax Paid	3467	2001
Prf af Int&Tax	4513	3204
Prf att Ord Sh	4513	3204
Btm Line Earn	4513	3204
Dividend Paid	2275	1520
Depreciation	2034	1696

PER SHARE STATISTICS (CENTS)

Net Asst Val	276.80	253.28
Net Earnings	47.50	33.70
Dividends	24.00	16.00
Cash Flow	68.78	51.48

RATIOS AND OTHER INFORMATION

Current Ratio	1.19	1.43
Quik/Acid Tst	0.87	0.98
A/C Rec T/ovr	5.03	4.44
Tot Ass T/ovr	1.03	0.93
Debt/Ass Rat	0.44	0.34
L T L Tot Ass	0.02	0.02
Debt to Eqity	0.79	0.50
Interest Cover	296.56	-
Oper Prof Mrg	16.51	15.39
Net Prof Marg%	9.30	9.48
Ret on Assets	16.97	14.35
Ret on Equity%	17.13	13.29
Divid Cover	1.98	2.11
Effec Tax Rate	43.45	38.44
Def Interval	0.04	-
Sus Grth Rate	8.49	6.98

SUBSIDIARY & ASSOCIATED COMPANIES

None

INVESTMENTS

None

SCORE SUPERMARKETS LTD

ABBREVIATION : SCORE

JSE SHORT CODE : SCO

SECTOR : Industrial-Retailers & Wholesalers

SHAREHOLDERS

Who Owns Whom's Assessment of the Identity of the Ultimate Controlling Shareholder:
PREMIER GROUP

SHAREHOLDER	PERCENTAGE 1992	1991
MAJSUN HOLDINGS P/L	56.5	---
SCORE-CLICKS HOLDINGS LTD	14.5	14.6
STD BANK NOM TVL P/L	5.5	4.1
EIGHTY ONE MAIN STREET NOM LTD	4.3	8.1
CMB NOM P/L	2.7	---
HI SCORE INV HOLDINGS P/L	2.7	---
FIRST NAT NOM P/L	1.9	---
LIBERTY LIFE ASSOC OF AFRICA LTD	1.6	1.6
SHAPE INV P/L	1.4	---
STOCKSHARE NOM P/L	1.0	---
DEMOCRAT NOM P/L	---	1.2
SANLAM	---	2.9
SUSPENCE ACCOUNT	---	59.9
TOTAL	92.1	92.4

DIRECTORS :
ADENDORFF JC MR (Operations Director), BRITS G MR
BUHAI R MR, BURGESS CJ MR (Managing Director)
COGILL KCJ MR (Operations Director)
DOS SANTOS CS MR, TAUROG RD MR
UTIAN GM MR (Chairman)
WARBURTON KDM MR (Financial Director)
WRIGHTON PGA M

REGISTRATION NUMBER : 91/00976/06

REGISTERED OFFICE
1st Floor, 13/39 Wright-Boag Street
Village Deep
2001
TEL: 011-493 4988
FAX: 011-493 6371

TRANSFER SECRETARY
Central Registrars Ltd
P O Box 4844, Johannesburg
2000
TEL: 011-331 0051

COMPANY SECRETARY
M A Currie

NATURE OF BUSINESS
The group operates a chain of 160 retail outlets in both the urban & rural areas, with the target market being the lower income consumer. Product

range includes foodstuffs, hardware, software and basic household products.

BANKERS :
Standard Bank of SA Ltd
First National Bank of SA Ltd
Absa Bank Ltd

AUDITORS :
Ernst & Young

FAMILIAR BRAND NAMES
DEEBEE,FAIRWAYS,FOUR SQUARE,FRASERS,HOTLINE LUCKY 7,SCORE

CONTRIBUTION BY ACTIVITY
N/A

YEAR END : April

DIVIDEND :Ords 1c
Dividend (Ldr)26/06/92 (Pay)17/07/92 Amt(c)0.5

NUMBER OF EMPLOYEES : 3325

CAPITAL STRUCTURE

	AUTHORISED	ISSUED
Ords 1c	150000000	75608993

FINANCIAL STATISTICS (AT FINANCIAL YEAR END)

(Amts in R'000)	1992 Apr	1991 Feb	1990 Feb	1989 Feb	1988 Feb
Ord S/H Int	32327	44089	64187	53067	39461
Long Trm Loans	11171	13607	25081	15243	16132
Iss Ord Share	75609	15420	15070	14720	14720
Total Liab	112053	199116	236758	150994	130289
Current Liab	100882	185509	211677	135751	114157
Total Assets	134380	234887	287969	196450	169750
Intang Assets	10000	8318	12976	7611	*
Current Assets	93848	195009	235433	159370	137385
Debtors	13924	45810	36708	25052	25951
Inventory	79924	125270	169601	134318	108564
Turnover	512394	1352301	1360276	1099270	923095
Oper Profit	11384	30183	42738	26343	29824
Interest Paid	9149	22742	18454	5063	2451
Tax Paid	1184	-45	10047	8578	11952
Prf af Int&Tax	1051	8465	15321	12702	15421
Prf att Ord Sh	877	7867	14656	11843	14724
Btm Line Earn	877	-17537	15688	11980	14724
Dividend Paid	378	2478	6418	5983	6007
Mkt Prce(c) YE	20	550	480	875	1600
Depreciation	3142	2952	5329	4072	3993

PER SHARE STATISTICS (CENTS)

Net Asst Val	29.53	231.98	339.82	308.80	268.08
Net Earnings	2.30	52.21	100.00	80.50	100.00
Dividends	0.50	13.00	40.00	37.00	37.00
Cash Flow	5.32	60.19	143.61	111.28	127.15

RATIOS AND OTHER INFORMATION

Mrk Cap(R000)	15122	84810	72336	128800	235520
Current Ratio	0.93	1.05	1.11	1.17	1.20
Quik/Acid Tst	0.14	0.38	0.31	0.18	0.25
A/C Rec T/ovr	36.80	29.52	37.06	43.88	35.57
Tot Ass T/ovr	3.81	5.76	4.72	5.60	5.44
Debt/Ass Rat	0.82	0.85	0.80	0.74	0.71
L T L Tot Ass	0.07	0.06	0.06	0.04	0.04
Debt to Eqity	3.40	4.51	3.57	2.72	3.07
Interest Cover	1.24	1.33	2.32	5.20	12.17
Oper Prof Mrg	2.22	2.23	3.14	2.40	3.23
Net Prof Marg%	0.17	0.58	1.08	1.08	1.60
Ret on Assets	8.47	13.29	15.25	13.41	17.57
Ret on Equity%	2.71	17.84	22.83	22.32	37.31
Price/Earnings	8.70	10.53	4.80	10.87	16.00
Divid Cover	4.60	4.02	2.50	2.18	2.70
Divid Yield	2.50	2.36	8.33	4.23	2.31
Earning Yield%	11.50	9.49	20.83	9.20	6.25
NAV % Mrk Pr	147.65	42.18	70.80	35.29	16.75
Effec Tax Rate	52.98	4.70	23.35	33.06	36.77
Def Interval	2.88	7.57	2.83	1.47	0.38
Sus Grth Rate	1.54	12.22	12.83	11.04	22.09

SUBSIDIARY & ASSOCIATED COMPANIES

BALLENGEICH TRADING CO (PTY) LTD
DEE BEE SUPERMARKETS (PTY) LTD
DEE BEE SUPERMARKETS (TRADING) (PTY) LTD
FAIRWAYS NQUTU (PTY) LTD
FAIRWAYS SUPERMARKET LTD
FAIRWAYS SUPERMARKETS (BOPHUTHATSWANA) L (50%)
FAIRWAYS SUPERMARKETS (BOTSHABELO) LTD (50%)
FAIRWAYS SUPERMARKETS (BOTSWANA) (PTY) L
FAIRWAYS SUPERMARKETS (GAZANKULU) LTD (50%)
FAIRWAYS SUPERMARKETS (MALUTI) LTD (48%)
FAIRWAYS SUPERMARKETS (QWA QWA) LTD (50%)
FAIRWAYS SUPERMARKETS (TRADING) (PTY) LT
FAIRWAYS SUPERMARKETS (TRANSKEI) (PTY) L
FAIRWAYS SUPERMARKETS (VENDA) LTD (50%)
FIG BROS (PTY) LTD = DORMANT
FRASERS (BOTSWANA) (PTY) LTD
FRASERS (SWAZILAND) LTD
FRASERS LESOTHO LTD
GRAND ARCADE (PTY) LTD
GRAND BAZAARS (PTY) LTD
J & C PRODUCTS (PTY) LTD
JAZZ STORES VENDA (PTY) LTD
JAZZ SUPERMARKETS (PTY) LTD
K NOLAN (LESOTHO) (PTY) LTD
KONGOLANA HOTEL & TRADING STORES (PTY) L
LESOTHO FOODS CORPORATION (PTY) LTD
LOEWENSTEIN & MOFFETT (PTY) LTD
METROPOLITAN WAREHOUSE (PTY) LTD
MINE STORES (NATAL) (PTY) LTD
SACK & MORRIS (PTY) LTD
SASA (PTY) LTD
SCORE DISCOUNT FOOD STORES (WAYSIDE) (PT (50%)
SCORE DISCOUNT FOODS (GAZANKULU) (PTY) L (50%)
SCORE FOODS (BOPHUTHATSWANA) (PTY) LTD (50%)
SCORE FOODS (BUSHBUCKRIDGE) (PTY) LTD (50%)
SCORE RETAIL HOLDINGS (PTY) LTD
SCORE SUPERMARKETS (1968) (PTY) LTD
SMITH & WEBSTER (PTY) LTD
THE PEOPLE'S SCORE (TEMBISA) LIMITED (50%)
WILLIAM WESTGATE (PTY) LTD

INVESTMENTS

WHOLESALE & RETAIL MARTINDALE HOLDINGS L (2570 SH)

SCORE-CLICKS HOLDINGS LTD

ABBREVIATION : SCOCLIK

JSE SHORT CODE : SCK

SECTOR : Industrial-Retailers & Wholesalers

SHAREHOLDERS

Who Owns Whom's Assessment of the Identity of the Ultimate Controlling Shareholder:
PREMIER GROUP VIA HI-SCORE

SHAREHOLDER	PERCENTAGE 1992	1991
HI-SCORE HLDGS LTD	65 9	65 9
SHAPE INV P/L	26 8	15 7
CMB NOM P/L	1 9	---
DE BEERS PENS FUND	1 2	1 2
STD BANK NOM TVL P/L	---	1 3
RETAN NOM P/L	--	3 5
SANLAM	---	1 9
STOCKSHARE NOM P/L	---	5 8
TOTAL	95 7	95 3

DIRECTORS :
BURGESS CJ ,DOS SANTOS CS ,HONNEYSETT TC
RUBIN VD ,TAUROG RD ,UTIAN GM (Chairman)
WRIGHTON PGA

REGISTRATION NUMBER : 83/09470/06

REGISTERED OFFICE
1 Newtown Avenue, Killarney
Johannesburg
2041
TEL 011-446 9111
FAX 011-446 2239

TRANSFER SECRETARY
Central Registrars Ltd
P O Box 4844, Johannesburg
2000
TEL 011-331 0051

COMPANY SECRETARY
S Gore

NATURE OF BUSINESS
An investment holding company with a controlling interest in quoted Clicks Stores Ltd The group is engaged in the wholesaling and retailing of groceries, gifts, cosmetics, toiletries, small appliances and related merchandise

BANKERS :
Standard Bank of SA Ltd
First National Bank of SA Ltd
Trust Bank of Africa Ltd

AUDITORS :
Ernst & Young

FAMILIAR BRAND NAMES
CLICKS,DISKOM,TRADOR

CONTRIBUTION BY ACTIVITY
N/A

YEAR END : April

DIVIDEND : Ords 8c
Final No 18 (Ldr)10/07/92 (Pay)30/07/92 Amt(c)6

NUMBER OF EMPLOYEES : 8867

CAPITAL STRUCTURE

	AUTHORISED	ISSUED
Ords 8c	80000000	64106764

FINANCIAL STATISTICS (AT FINANCIAL YEAR END)

(Amts in R'000)	1992 Feb	1991 Feb	1990 Feb	1989 Jun	1988 Jun
Ord S/H Int	201198	161627	168623	157913	6484
Long Trm Loans	78779	74199	87294	67950	
Iss Ord Share	64107	57238	57238	57238	20000
Total Liab	203872	346610	373980	257509	1662
Current Liab	125093	272411	286686	189559	1662
Total Assets	405070	508237	427494	305677	8146
Intang Assets	*	*	115109	109745	*
Current Assets	220260	315467	340911	239684	1700
Debtors	15019	56000	45045	32294	
Inventory	160151	259467	255622	207390	
Turnover	1232710	1904207	1786451	1345701	
Oper Profit	55202	62905	75550	53596	2662
Interest Paid	9447	15845	19634	14559	
Tax Paid	22929	20120	26077	18319	
Prf af Int&Tax	22826	29055	31718	22601	2662
Prf att Ord Sh	11749	14894	17077	12095	2662
Btm Line Earn	4343	-165	17686	10908	2618
Dividend Paid	5849	5438	6972	5409	2620
Mkt Prce(c) YE	430	300	190	225	350
Depreciation	7658	10907	8657	5942	

PER SHARE STATISTICS (CENTS)

Net Asst Val	313 85	282 38	93 49	84 15	32 42
Net Earnings	20 40	26 02	30 00	21 13	13 31
Dividends	9 50	9 50	12 18	9 45	313 10
Cash Flow	35 37	42 97	48 30	49 52	13 31

RATIOS AND OTHER INFORMATION

Mrk Cap(R000)	275660	171714	108752	128786	70000
Current Ratio	1 76	1 16	1 19	1 26	1 02
Quik/Acid Tst	0 48	0 21	0 30	0 17	1 02
A/C Rec T/ovr	82 08	34 00	39 66	62 51	
Tot Ass T/ovr	3 04	3 75	4 18	6 60	
Debt/Ass Rat	0 31	0 56	0 71	0 65	0 20
L T L Tot Ass	0 00	0 03	0 04	0 03	
Debt to Eqity	0 63	1 77	1 80	1 27	0 26
Interest Cover	5 84	3 97	3 85	3 71	
Oper Prof Mrg	4 48	3 30	4 23	3 98	
Net Prof Marg%	0 95	0 78	0 96	0 90	-
Ret on Assets	13 63	12 79	18 14	27 22	32 68
Ret on Equity%	5 84	9 22	10 13	11 49	41 05
Price/Earnings	21 08	11 53	6 33	10 65	26 30
Divid Cover	2 15	2 74	2 46	2 24	0 04
Divid Yield	2 21	3 17	6 41	4 20	89 46
Earning Yield%	4 74	8 67	15 79	9 39	3 80
NAV % Mrk Pr	72 99	94 13	49 21	37 40	9 26
Effec Tax Rate	47 91	40 62	36 68	40 43	-
Def Interval	-	1 64	2 16	2 07	
Sus Grth Rate	2 93	5 85	5 99	4 23	0 65

SUBSIDIARY & ASSOCIATED COMPANIES

CLICKS STORES LTD (50,01%)

INVESTMENTS

METRO CASH & CARRY LTD (15%)
SCORE SUPERMARKETS LTD (15%)

SEARDEL CONSOLIDATED HOLDINGS LTD

ABBREVIATION : SEARCON

JSE SHORT CODE : SRC

SECTOR : Industrial-Clothing, Footwear & Textiles

SHAREHOLDERS

Who Owns Whom's Assessment of the Identity of the Ultimate Controlling Shareholder:
AARON SEARLL

SHAREHOLDER	PERCENTAGE 1992	1991
AARON SEARLL INV & HOLDING P/L	42.2	42.2
CMB NOM P/L	12.4	1.9
TEMPORA INV LTD	6.9	6.9
FIRST NAT NOM P/L	5.9	5.9
SEARLL A	5.4	5.4
LIBERTY LIFE ASSOC OF AFRICA LTD	3.3	3.3
ENGINEERING INDUSTRIES PENS FUND	3.2	3.2
METAL IND GROUP PENS FUND	3.1	3.1
STD BANK NOM TVL P/L	2.9	2.9
SUNCRUSH PENS FUND	2.8	2.8
SA MUTUAL	1.7	1.4
EIGHTY ONE MAIN STREET NOM LTD	1.6	3.1
COHEN D L	1.5	1.5
GEMEENSKAPLIKE MUNISIPALE TVL PENS FUND	1.3	1.3
SANLAM	---	8.6
TOTAL	94.0	93.3

DIRECTORS :
GALOMBIK A ,MASSON R ,SEARLL A DR (Chairman)
SEARLL AMG MRS,WILSON JR

REGISTRATION NUMBER : 87/01124/06

REGISTERED OFFICE
Monterey, Klaassens Road
Bishopscourt, Cape Town
7700
TEL: 021-761 8000
FAX: 021-761 0852

TRANSFER SECRETARY
Central Registrars Ltd
P O Box 4844, Johannesburg
2000
TEL: 011-331 0051

COMPANY SECRETARY
A D Jacobson

NATURE OF BUSINESS
A pyramid holding company with its subsidiary engaged in the manufacture and distribution of mens, womens and childrens apparel, toys and consumer electronics. The company has a controlling interest in quoted Seardel Inv Corp.

BANKERS :
Trust Bank of Africa Ltd
First National Bank of SA Ltd
Standard Bank of SA Ltd, Nedcor Bank Ltd

AUDITORS :
Arthur Andersen & Co

FAMILIAR BRAND NAMES
SEE SEARDEL

CONTRIBUTION BY ACTIVITY
Apparel (% Operating Income) (61.0%)
Toys (9.0%)
Consumer & Business Electronics (23.0%)
Non-Woven Textiles (4.0%)
Property & Travel (3.0%)

YEAR END : June

DIVIDEND : Ords 1c

Interim	(Ldr)22/02/91	(Pay)28/02/91	Amt(c)8
Final	(Ldr)08/11/91	(Pay)22/11/91	Amt(c)15

NUMBER OF EMPLOYEES : 15400

CAPITAL STRUCTURE

	AUTHORISED	ISSUED
Ords 1c	12000000	11735054

FINANCIAL STATISTICS (AT FINANCIAL YEAR END)

(Amts in R'000)	1992 Jun	1991 Jun	1990 Jun	1989 Jun	1988 Jun
Ord S/H Int	39030	39030	39030	39016	39016
Long Trm Loans	-	-	-	14	15
Iss Ord Share	11735	11735	11735	10281	10281
Total Liab	-	-	-	14	15
Total Assets	39030	39030	39030	39030	39031
Current Assets	15	15	15	15	15
Prf af Int&Tax	1115	2699	2582	2465	2075
Prf att Ord Sh	1115	2699	2582	2465	2075
Btm Line Earn	1115	2699	2582	2465	2075
Dividend Paid	1115	2699	2582	2465	2074
Mkt Prce(c) YE	275	340	210	315	300

PER SHARE STATISTICS (CENTS)

Net Asst Val	332.59	332.59	332.59	379.50	379.50
Net Earnings	9.50	23.00	22.00	21.00	17.20
Dividends	9.50	23.00	22.00	21.00	17.20
Cash Flow	9.50	23.00	22.00	23.98	20.18

RATIOS AND OTHER INFORMATION

Mrk Cap(R000)	32271	39899	24644	32385	30843
Ret on Assets	2.86	6.92	6.62	6.32	5.32
Ret on Equity%	2.86	6.92	6.62	6.32	5.32
Price/Earnings	28.95	14.78	9.55	15.00	17.44
Divid Cover	1.00	1.00	1.00	1.00	1.00
Divid Yield	3.45	6.76	10.48	6.67	5.73
Earning Yield%	3.45	6.76	10.48	6.67	5.73
NAV % Mrk Pr	120.94	97.82	158.38	120.47	126.50
Sus Grth Rate	0.00	0.00	0.00	0.00	0.00

SUBSIDIARY & ASSOCIATED COMPANIES

SEARDEL INVESTMENT CORPORATION LTD (50,1%)

INVESTMENTS

None

SEARDEL INVESTMENT CORPORATION LTD

ABBREVIATION : SEARDEL

JSE SHORT CODE : SER

SECTOR : Industrial-Clothing, Footwear & Textiles

SHAREHOLDERS

Who Owns Whom's Assessment of the Identity of the Ultimate Controlling Shareholder:
SEARCON

SHAREHOLDER	PERCENTAGE 1992	1991
SEARDEL CONSOLIDATED HOLDINGS LTD	50.1	50.1
LIBERTY LIFE ASSOC OF AFRICA LTD	11.0	10.8
CMB NOM P/L	6.5	---
SA MUTUAL	3.6	1.6
SEARDEL EXEC SHARE PARTICIPATION	2.9	1.6
ENGINEERING INDUSTRIES PENS FUND	2.7	2.7
STD BANK NOM TVL P/L	2.5	3.4
METAL IND GROUP PENS FUND	2.5	2.5
TEMPORA INV LTD	1.4	1.3
GUARDIAN NAT INSURANCE CO LTD	1.3	1.3
SANLAM	---	6.4
NEDCOR LTD	---	1.2
TOTAL	84.4	83.0

DIRECTORS :
BLUMBERG KA ,DE BRUIN GC DR (Executive Director)
DIAMOND SH (Executive Director)
DUBIN A (Executive Director)
JACOBSON AD (Executive Director),KATZ MM PROF
RICHARDS BG DR (Executive Director)
SCHAFFER M (Executive Director)
SEARLL A DR (Executive Chairman)
STERNBERG MR (Executive Director)
WINER K (Executive Director

REGISTRATION NUMBER : 68/11249/06

REGISTERED OFFICE
Monterey, Klaassens Road
Bishopscourt, Cape Town
7700
TEL: 021-761 8000
FAX: 021-761 0852

TRANSFER SECRETARY
Central Registrars Ltd
P O Box 4844, Johannesburg
2000
TEL: 011-331 0051

COMPANY SECRETARY
A D Jacobson

NATURE OF BUSINESS
An investment holding company with interests in the manufacture and distribution of clothing,toys, consumer electrics,non-woven textiles, traval & property investments.

BANKERS :
Trust Bank of Africa Ltd
First National Bank of SA Ltd
Standard Bank of SA Ltd, Senbank
Nedcor Bank Ltd

AUDITORS :
Arthur Andersen & Co

FAMILIAR BRAND NAMES
ADIDAS BALLS,AFTER DARK,AIRLINE,ARK PLUSH
AVIS,BABY ANGEL DOLLS,BABY LOVE DOLLS
BARBARELLA,BEST SELLER,BOOM-A-RING,BRASS
BRITBOND,BRITCOVER,BRITFILL,BRITSPUN
BRITSTITCH,BROOKSFIELD & CO,CAMBRIDGE
CARIBBEAN,CHAPEAU KELLER,CHESTERFIELD
CHIC SHOCK,CHICKADEE,CINNAMON,CLOUD NINE
COMFORT ZONE,COMPLICE,CONNOISSEUR,CYGNET
DERMAR,DERMAR TOO,DESIREE,DIANA DAVENPORT
DIDO,DIWELD,DONNA,DOODLE BUG,DREAM BABY
DREAM BUILDERS,EARLY BIRD,EDUCATIONAL TOYS
ELLIE,EXTRAVERT,EXTREMELY CUMFY
FESTIVE BALLOONS,FIBRESKIN,FIBRETREND
FIRESISTA,FLAIR DOLLS,FLOATIES,FREEMAN
FRIDO BALLS,FRISBEE,FUN FRILLS,GEAR UP
GHOSTBUSTERS,GI JOE,GLORY,GOLDEN BOOK,GOTCHA
GRUNDIG,GYPSY PLUSH,HASBRO,HEADLINES,HIJACK
HOUSE OF YOUTH,ICE CREAM,INCA GOLD
JOE BLOGGS,JUST JOY,KENNER PARKER TONKA
KEY WEST,LADY DONNA,LADY FLORIDA,LE GIRL
LIGNE SPORT,LITTLE NUMBER,LITTLE PEOPLE
LIVE ACT,LOOK TWICE,LOOMTEX,MAN ABOUT TOWN
MASTERMIND,MATCHBOX CARS,MECCANO,MELIA
MICHAEL LAURENZ,MILTON BRADLEY GAMES,MISS M
MONVISO,MOON,MR BRIAN,MUSASHI,MY LITTLE PONY
NEW BORN BABY DOLLS,NEW NAME,OLIVE
OOPSIE DAISY,OTOKYO,PARALLEL,PENNYWISE
PERFECT FILLER,PHASE 5,PIERRE CARDIN
PINK PANTHER,PLAYSKOOL,PLAYTIME ELECTRICAL
POLYAIR,POSTCARD,PRET A PORTER,PRIMA
PRIMA INFLATABLES,Q'DOS,QUINTS,RIVIERA
SALLY BON,SALLYBON,SCATTERGORIES,SCRIPTO
SEGA HOME ARCADE GAMES,SHARP,SINDY DOLLS
SLEEP MATE,SNOOPY,SOF TOYS,SPEEDO,ST TROPEZ
STICKLE BRICKS,STITCHES,STREET BEAT
SURFPHOBIA,TALK BACK TRACY,TEDDY RUXPIN
TEENAGE MUTANT NINJA TURTLES
THE PLATINUM LABEL,TIGER ELECTRONICS
TOPLIN PLASTIC TOYS,TOTS & TEENS
TRIUMPH INTERNATIONAL,TWICE AS NICE
TYCO SUPER BLOCKS,TYCO SUPER DOUGH,ULTRABOND
UNICURL,UPDATE,VIEWMASTER,WESTERN PUBLISHING
WILD THING,WRANGLER,X-ISLE,YOUNG SENSATION
ZENITH,ZONE

CONTRIBUTION BY ACTIVITY
Apparel (% Operating Income) (61.0%)
Toys (9.0%)
Consumer & Business Electronics (23.0%)
Non-woven Textiles (4.0%)
Property & Travel (3.0%)

YEAR END : June

DIVIDEND : Ords 25c

Interim No 38	(Ldr)22/02/91	(Pay)28/02/91	Amt(c)8
Final No 39	(Ldr)08/11/91	(Pay)22/11/91	Amt(c)15

NUMBER OF EMPLOYEES : 15400

CAPITAL STRUCTURE

	AUTHORISED	ISSUED
Ords 25c	25000000	23423248

FINANCIAL STATISTICS (AT FINANCIAL YEAR END)

(Amts in R'000)	1992 Jun	1991 Jun	1990 Jun	1989 Jun	1988 Jun
Ord S/H Int	153474	147464	116620	87932	72661
Long Trm Loans	138162	105657	105847	115497	98526
Iss Ord Share	23423	23423	23423	16812	16812
Total Liab	357159	316473	272491	264429	206785
Current Liab	218997	210816	166644	148932	108259
Total Assets	510493	463623	389111	352361	279446
Intang Assets	140	314	*	*	*
Current Assets	407271	378037	327065	291945	222256
Debtors	173589	156035	149251	139012	109519
Inventory	220278	205915	166763	150788	111135
Turnover	1058679	992360	899776	740451	566443
Oper Profit	55195	76078	73197	61477	41849
Interest Paid	43360	32933	32941	22372	11800
Tax Paid	7022	17535	16311	17673	9873
Prf af Int&Tax	11216	29179	26691	24204	20176
Prf att Ord Sh	10125	25316	23660	21229	17667
Btm Line Earn	8369	25316	23660	21264	17504
Dividend Paid	2225	5387	5153	3530	2942
Mkt Prce(c) YE	270	330	230	330	320
Depreciation	12834	13082	13612	9793	7174

PER SHARE STATISTICS (CENTS)

Net Asst Val	654.63	628.23	497.89	523.03	432.20
Net Earnings	43.00	108.00	101.00	97.00	105.00
Dividends	9.50	23.00	22.00	21.00	17.50
Cash Flow	77.29	176.24	218.97	181.05	150.65

RATIOS AND OTHER INFORMATION

Mrk Cap(R000)	63242	77296	53873	55480	53798
Current Ratio	1.86	1.79	1.96	1.96	2.05
Quik/Acid Tst	0.85	0.82	0.96	0.95	1.03
A/C Rec T/ovr	6.10	6.36	6.03	5.33	5.17
Tot Ass T/ovr	2.07	2.14	2.31	2.10	2.03
Debt/Ass Rat	0.65	0.63	0.64	0.68	0.65
L T L Tot Ass	0.23	0.17	0.21	0.26	0.26
Debt to Eqity	2.18	1.98	2.12	2.74	2.49
Interest Cover	1.32	2.37	2.22	2.76	3.55
Oper Prof Mrg	5.21	7.67	8.14	8.30	7.39
Net Prof Marg%	0.96	2.55	2.63	2.87	3.12
Ret on Assets	12.17	16.73	19.15	18.17	15.14
Ret on Equity%	6.60	17.17	20.29	24.14	24.31
Price/Earnings	6.28	3.06	2.28	3.40	3.05
Divid Cover	4.53	4.70	4.59	4.62	6.00
Divid Yield	3.52	6.97	9.57	6.36	5.47
Earning Yield%	15.93	32.73	43.91	29.39	32.81
NAV % Mrk Pr	242.46	190.37	216.47	158.49	135.06
Effec Tax Rate	53.80	29.48	8.69	44.27	35.85
Def Interval	7.48	2.68	2.07	3.96	3.71
Sus Grth Rate	5.15	13.51	15.87	20.13	20.27

SUBSIDIARY & ASSOCIATED COMPANIES

AIRSPEED NP CHARTERS PARTNERSHIP (50%)
ALPHA COMPUTER SERVICES (PTY) LTD
ATBAR HOLDINGS (PTY) LTD (50%)
BIBETTE (PTY) LTD (50%)
BLUE BELL WRANGLER (PTY) LTD
COMPASS CHARTERS JOINT VENTURE (36%)
DUBIN INVESTMENTS LTD
FUN FRILLS (PTY) LTD (50%)
IVANO (PTY) LTD
MILLS DISTRIBUTORS SA (PTY) LTD
MONVISO KNITWEAR (PTY) LTD
MONVISO KNITWEAR (PTY) LTD (50%)
NEW NAME CLOTHING (PTY) LTD
NEW NAME INVESTMENT HOLDINGS (PTY) LTD
OCEANAIR (PTY) LTD
PAROW PERMANENT INVESTMENTS (PTY) LTD
SEARDEL GROUP PROPERTIES (TVL) (PTY) LTD (50%)
SEARDEL GROUP TRADING (PTY) LTD
SEARGREG INVESTMENTS (PTY) LTD (50%)
SEARTEC INDUSTRIES (PTY) LTD
SEARTEC LTD
SERNEF INVESTMENT HOLDINGS (PTY) LTD (50%)
SHARP ELECTRONICS (S.A.) (PTY) LTD
SHARP ELECTRONICS (S.A.) (PTY) LTD

INVESTMENTS

None

SECHABA INVESTMENT TRUST CO LTD

ABBREVIATION : SECHABA

SECTOR : Botswana Stock Exchange

SHAREHOLDERS

Who Owns Whom's Assessment of the Identity of the Ultimate Controlling Shareholder: INSTITUTIONS

SHAREHOLDER	PERCENTAGE 1992	1991
BOTSWANA MOTOR VEHICLE INSURANCE FUND	18.6	---
BOTSWANA LIFE INSURANCE LTD	15.5	---
DEBSWANA PENS FUND	15.3	---
BARCLAYS BANK OF BOTSWANA STAFF PENS FUN	15.2	---
BOTSWANA DEVELOPMENT CORPORATION	10.1	---
IGI BOTSWANA LIFE ASSURE LTD	5.6	---
STD CHARTERED BANK STAFF PENS FUND	2.1	---
LONGDEN T	1.6	---
MYNHARDT J T	1.1	---
TOTAL	85.0	---

DIRECTORS :
BALETLWA T ,DISELE BM ,KOMANYANE EW (Chairman)
MASENYA WN ,MCMURRAY AJ ,MOFFETT MJ ,PARTON JG
STONEHAM GJ

REGISTERED OFFICE
Madirelo House, Lot 6377
Mmanaka Road, Gabarone

TEL: 374248
FAX: 373539

TRANSFER SECRETARY
N/A

COMPANY SECRETARY
A J MCMURRAY

NATURE OF BUSINESS
Sechaba is an investment holding company aiming to give its shareholders an interest in a wide spread of shares, both quoted and unquoted, principally in companies operating in Botswana.

BANKERS :
Barclays Bank of Botswana Ltd

AUDITORS :
Deloitte & Touche

FAMILIAR BRAND NAMES
N/A

CONTRIBUTION BY ACTIVITY
N/A

YEAR END : June

CAPITAL STRUCTURE

	AUTHORISED	ISSUED
Ords P0,25	30000000	29963800

FINANCIAL STATISTICS (AT FINANCIAL YEAR END)

(Amts in P)	1992 Jun	1991 Jun
Ord S/H Int	20100	16525
Iss Ord Share	29964	29964
Total Liab	4224	4072
Current Liab	4224	4072
Total Assets	24324	20597
Current Assets	4989	5082
Debtors	15	7
Oper Profit	5634	4810
Prf af Int&Tax	5634	4810
Prf att Ord Sh	7770	6985
Btm Line Earn	7770	6985
Dividend Paid	4195	3895

PER SHARE STATISTICS (CENTS)

Net Asst Val	67.08	55.15
Net Earnings	25.90	23.30
Dividends	14.00	13.00
Cash Flow	18.80	16.05

RATIOS AND OTHER INFORMATION

Current Ratio	1.18	1.25
Quik/Acid Tst	1.18	1.25
Debt/Ass Rat	0.17	0.20
Debt to Eqity	0.21	0.25
Ret on Assets	31.94	33.91
Ret on Equity%	38.66	42.27
Divid Cover	1.85	1.79
Sus Grth Rate	17.79	18.70

SUBSIDIARY & ASSOCIATED COMPANIES

BROADHURST INDUSTRIAL ESTATE (PTY) LTD (24%)
CAR RENTALS HOLDINGS (PTY) LTD (21%)
FRASERS (BOTSWANA) (PTY) LTD (24%)
KGALAGADI BREWERIES (PTY) LTD (20%)
MINET (BOTSWANA) (PTY) LTD (24%)

INVESTMENTS

BARCLAYS BANK OF BOTSWANA LTD (170500SH)
BOTSWANA BREWERIES (PTY) LTD (15%)
BOTSWANA INSURANCE HOLDINGS LTD (1920000SH)
FINANCIAL SERVICES CO OF BOTSWANA LTD (120000SH)
FRASMET (PTY) LTD (10%)
IGI BOTSWANA INSURANCE LTD (116000SH)
INCO HOLDINGS LTD (60000SH)
PEP BOTSWANA HOLDINGS LTD (69500SH)
SEFALANA HOLDING CO LTD (845000SH)
STANDARD CHARTERED BANK BOTSWANA LTD (152500SH)
SUN INTERNATIONAL (BOTSWANA) (PTY) LTD (10%)

SECHOLD LTD

ABBREVIATION : SECHOLD

JSE SHORT CODE : SEH

SECTOR : Financial-Banks & Financial Services

SHAREHOLDERS

Who Owns Whom's Assessment of the Identity of the Ultimate Controlling Shareholder: MANAGEMENT / INSTITUTIONS

SHAREHOLDER	PERCENTAGE 1992	1991
UBS INSURANCE CO LTD	15.1	15.1
SA MUTUAL	10.3	10.5
RAND MERCHANT BANK LTD	10.0	---
CMB NOM P/L	8.3	---
YSKOR PENS FUND	7.3	6.9
EIGHTY ONE MAIN STREET NOM LTD	6.3	1.2
KELLY A	5.6	5.6
ABRAHAMS P S	5.1	5.1
STD BANK NOM TVL P/L	2.4	---
ROUX W	2.0	2.0
NEDBANK NOM LTD	1.5	1.4
KOTZE J C	1.3	1.3
THIES J M	1.2	1.2
HASKINS M G	1.1	1.1
GOUWS D B	1.1	1.1
WYCHE M ST J	1.0	1.0
KEARNEY J P	---	2.1
OTTO J L	---	1.1
SHARESTOCK NOM P/L	---	1.1
SANLAM	---	8.3
SWART M	---	4.5
RAND MERCHANT BANK HOLDINGS LTD	---	10.0
TOTAL	79.6	80.4

DIRECTORS :
ABRAHAMS PS ,EHRLICH LN ,GOUWS DB ,HASKINS MG
KELLY A (Managing Director),LIEBENBERG HS
NOETH AA ,SCOTCHER WVG ,SWART M
THOMAS GS (Chairman),WALKER EA MRS,WARD DG

REGISTRATION NUMBER : 85/00754/06

REGISTERED OFFICE
2nd Floor, Sechold House, 15 Loveday Street
Johannesburg
2001
TEL: 011-836 3361
FAX: 011-834 7895

TRANSFER SECRETARY
Central Registrars Ltd
P O Box 4844, Johannesburg
2000
TEL: 011-331 0051

COMPANY SECRETARY
RJ Stoddart

NATURE OF BUSINESS
Sechold Ltd,a holding company,is a registered deposit-taking institution controlling company with subsidiaries involved in the following activities:Banking,securities trading,portfolio management and related financial services.

BANKERS :
Standard Bank of SA Ltd, Volkskas Ltd
First National Bank of SA Ltd

AUDITORS :
BDO Spencer Steward

FAMILIAR BRAND NAMES
DISTRIKBANK

CONTRIBUTION BY ACTIVITY
N/A

YEAR END : June

DIVIDEND :Ords 10c

Interim	(Ldr)02/03/90	(Pay)16/03/90	Amt(c)10
Final	(Ldr)31/08/90	(Pay)21/09/90	Amt(c)11
Interim	(Ldr)15/02/91	(Pay)28/02/91	Amt(c)12
Final	(Ldr)30/08/91	(Pay)20/09/91	Amt(c)13.5
Interim	(Ldr)14/02/92	(Pay)27/02/92	Amt(c)14.5
Final	(Ldr)28/08/92	(Pay)18/09/92	Amt(c)15.5

NUMBER OF EMPLOYEES : 190

CAPITAL STRUCTURE

	AUTHORISED	ISSUED
Ords 10c	30000000	23525989
Red Cum Non-Partic Prefs 1c	20000000	4000

FINANCIAL STATISTICS (AT FINANCIAL YEAR END)

(Amts in R'000)	1992 Jun	1991 Jun	1990 Jun	1989 Jun	1988 Mar
Ord S/H Int	62482	50895	41081	31020	22612
Long Trm Loans	7789444	7335009	447844	425553	409693
Iss Ord Share	23526	23526	23526	23526	23000
Total Liab	7793091	7338185	470537	471871	475220
Current Liab	3647	3176	22693	46318	65527
Total Assets	7855573	7389080	511348	502891	497832
Intang Assets	*	*	270	*	*
Current Assets	4030283	4683560	12172	54952	9302
Debtors	4030283	4683560	12172	54952	9302
Oper Profit	18325	14370	11962	12472	8102
Prf af Int&Tax	18325	14370	11962	12472	8102
Prf att Ord Sh	17454	14370	11962	12472	8102
Btm Line Earn	18412	14370	11962	12472	8102
Dividend Paid	7058	5999	4940	4264	2392
Mkt Prce(c) YE	665	410	290	290	530

PER SHARE STATISTICS (CENTS)

Net Asst Val	265.59	216.34	173.47	131.85	98.31
Net Earnings	74.00	61.00	51.00	53.00	34.00
Dividends	30.00	25.50	21.00	21.00	18.00
Cash Flow	74.19	61.08	50.85	42.41	34.44

RATIOS AND OTHER INFORMATION

Mrk Cap(R000)	156448	96457	68225	68225	121900
Current Ratio	1105.10	1474.67	0.54	1.19	0.14
Quik/Acid Tst	1105.10	1474.67	0.54	1.19	0.14
Debt/Ass Rat	0.00	0.00	0.04	0.09	0.13
Debt to Eqity	0.06	0.06	0.55	1.49	2.90
Ret on Assets	0.23	0.19	2.34	1.98	1.63
Ret on Equity%	27.93	28.23	29.12	32.17	35.83
Price/Earnings	8.99	6.72	5.69	5.47	15.59
Divid Cover	2.47	2.39	2.43	2.52	1.89
Divid Yield	4.51	6.22	7.24	7.24	3.40
Earning Yield%	11.13	14.88	17.59	18.28	6.42
NAV % Mrk Pr	39.94	52.76	59.82	45.47	18.55
Def Interval	2.29	-	-	-	-
Sus Grth Rate	16.64	16.45	17.09	26.46	25.25

SUBSIDIARY & ASSOCIATED COMPANIES

CM INTERBANK LTD
DISTRICT SECURITIES BANK LTD
IB NOMINEES (PTY) LTD
INTERBANK HOLDINGS LTD
MANIFEST HOUSE SHAREBLOCK (PTY) LTD
MARSHALL PLACE MORTGAGES (PTY) LTD
NDH BANK LTD
PRIMA MORTGAGÉS SECURITIES (PTY) LTD
SECFIN BANK LIMITED
SECHOLD FINANCE SERVICES (PTY) LTD
SECURITES COMPUTER SERVICES (PTY) LTD
SECURITIES EQUITIES (PTY) LTD
SECURITIES INVESTMENT BANK LTD
SECURITIES MANAGEMENT SERVICES (PTY) LTD
SECURITIES PORTFOLIO MANAGERS (PTY) LTD
SECURITIES PROPERTIES (PTY) LTD
SOUTH AFRICA MORTGAGES SECURITIES NO 2 (
SOUTH AFRICA MORTGAGES SECURITIES NO1 (P

INVESTMENTS

None

SEFALANA HOLDING CO LTD

ABBREVIATION : SEFALANA

SECTOR : Botswana Stock Exchange

SHAREHOLDERS

Who Owns Whom's Assessment of the Identity of the Ultimate Controlling Shareholder: MINORITIES

SHAREHOLDER	PERCENTAGE 1992	1991
BOTSWANA DEVELOPMENT CORPORATION	13.8	---
BOTSWANA LIFE INSURANCE LTD	10.5	---
SECHABA INV TRUST	5.3	---
DEBSWANA PENS FUND	4.9	---
IGI BOTSWANA LIFE ASSURE LTD	4.0	---
VELDMAN H R M	3.7	---
COUNIHAN W J	3.6	---
BETE TRUST	3.0	---
IGI - SHORT TERM	3.0	---
TARR R D	2.9	---
TOTAL	54.8	---

DIRECTORS :
FINLAY DW (Chairman),LEKALAKE LD ,LETHBRIDGE DE MAINE MTL MRS,NGANUNU JM ,VAN DEN BERG AA VELDMAN ST

REGISTRATION NUMBER : 1025/86

REGISTERED OFFICE
Fourth Floor, Barclays House
Khama Crescent, Gabarone

TEL: 312700
FAX: 312202

TRANSFER SECRETARY
N/A

COMPANY SECRETARY
J J Weigens

NATURE OF BUSINESS
Sefalana is a Botswana owned company engaged in maize and sorghum milling, producing vitamin enriched maize meal, sorghum meal and balanced animal feeds, at mills in Lobatse and Pilane.

BANKERS :
Barclays Bank of Botswana Ltd
Standard Chartered Bank

AUDITORS :
Deloitte Pim Goldby

FAMILIAR BRAND NAMES
N/A

CONTRIBUTION BY ACTIVITY
N/A

YEAR END : October

DIVIDEND :Ords P0,01

Dividend	(Ldr)19/07/91	(Pay)05/08/91	Amt(c)14
Dividend	(Ldr)17/01/92	(Pay)08/02/92	Amt(c)16

CAPITAL STRUCTURE

	AUTHORISED	ISSUED
Ords P0,01	30000000	16000000

FINANCIAL STATISTICS (AT FINANCIAL YEAR END)

(Amts in P)	1991 Oct	1990 Oct
Ord S/H Int	41841	32822
Long Trm Loans	2049	1085
Iss Ord Share	16000	16000
Total Liab	62848	52126
Current Liab	60799	51041
Total Assets	104689	84948
Current Assets	68833	55826
Debtors	21150	16349
Inventory	43013	34210
Turnover	360047	279468
Oper Profit	19951	17170
Interest Paid	384	252
Tax Paid	6538	6582
Prf af Int&Tax	14076	11354
Prf att Ord Sh	14039	11248
Btm Line Earn	14039	11248
Dividend Paid	4800	4000
Depreciation	3371	2364

PER SHARE STATISTICS (CENTS)

Net Asst Val	261.51	205.14
Net Earnings	87.80	70.30
Dividends	30.00	25.00
Cash Flow	108.53	86.16

RATIOS AND OTHER INFORMATION

Current Ratio	1.13	1.09
Quik/Acid Tst	0.42	0.42
A/C Rec T/ovr	17.02	17.09
Tot Ass T/ovr	3.44	3.29
Debt/Ass Rat	0.58	0.60
L T L Tot Ass	-	0.00
Debt to Eqity	1.45	1.56
Interest Cover	52.02	68.22
Oper Prof Mrg	5.54	6.14
Net Prof Marg%	3.90	4.02
Ret on Assets	20.06	21.41
Ret on Equity%	33.55	34.27
Divid Cover	2.93	2.81
Effec Tax Rate	36.50	38.21
Def Interval	0.68	0.02
Sus Grth Rate	22.08	22.08

SUBSIDIARY & ASSOCIATED COMPANIES

ACK MILLING CO (PTY) LTD (BOTSWANA)
ALUMINIUM 2000 (PTY) LTD
BARCLAYS BANK OF BOTSWANA LTD
BOTSWANA BONEMEAL FACTORY (PTY) LTD
BOTSWANA GRAIN & MILLING (PTY) LTD
COMP-U-CORP (PTY) LTD
CORN PRODUCTS (PTY) LTD
DUMELA DEVELOPMENT (PTY) LTD (BOTSWANA)
FOOD PACKERS & PRODUCTIONS (PTY) LTD
FOODS BOTSWANA (PTY) LTD
IGI BOTSWANA HOLDINGS LTD
INDUSTRIAL & COMMERCIAL EQUIPMENT (PTY)
MEYBEERNICK INVESTMENTS (PTY) LTD
NGWATO INDUSTRIAL DISTRIBUTING CO (PTY)
RIVERVIEW HOLDINGS (PTY) LTD
SEFALANA HOUSING (PTY) LTD
SEFALANA MAUN (PTY) LTD
SEFALANA MILLS (PTY) LTD
SEFALANA RSA (PTY) LTD
SELEBI-PIKWE WHOLESALE (PTY) LTD
STANDARD CHARTERED BANK BOTSWANA LTD
VALHALLA PROPERTIES (PTY) LTD
YA RONA PACKING & DISTRIBUTING (PTY) LTD

INVESTMENTS

None

SENTRACHEM LTD

ABBREVIATION : SENTRCHEM

JSE SHORT CODE : SCM

SECTOR : Industrial-Chemicals & Oils

SHAREHOLDERS

Who Owns Whom's Assessment of the Identity of the Ultimate Controlling Shareholder:
SANLAM VIA CENTRAL CHEMICAL INVESTMENTS

SHAREHOLDER	PERCENTAGE 1992	1991
CENTRAL CHEMICAL INV P/L	50.0	50.0
IND DEVELOPMENT CORP SA LTD	12.7	12.7
SA MUTUAL	10.5	11.3
CMB NOM P/L	6.4	---
EIGHTY ONE MAIN STREET NOM LTD	4.2	3.4
SENBANK NOM P/L	3.9	3.9
METAL IND GROUP PENS FUND	1.7	1.8
ENGINEERING INDUSTRIES PENS FUND	1.7	1.9
STD BANK NOM TVL P/L	1.5	1.6
FIRST NAT NOM P/L	1.1	1.2
SANKORP BPK	---	3.7
SANLAM	---	2.7
TOTAL	93.7	94.2

DIRECTORS :
CARTER GG ,DU PLÉSSIS SJP
HUNT-DAVIS DNA (Chairman)
JOB JL DR (Managing Director),KATZ MM PROF
MORRIS FCR (Financial Director),MORSE GR
ORPEN CMW ,OXENHAM RL ,PITHEY ER ,SMITH BA
VAN DER WALT JH ,VORSTER DR

REGISTRATION NUMBER : 67/02258/06

REGISTERED OFFICE
5 Protea Place, Sandton
2146
TEL: 011-783 2121
FAX: 011-783 2180

TRANSFER SECRETARY
Central Registrars Ltd
P O Box 4844, Johannesburg
2000
TEL: 011-331 0051

COMPANY SECRETARY
J G Joubert

NATURE OF BUSINESS
A holding company whose main interests are in the chemical industry. Group activities include the production of agricultural chemicals and veterinary products, animal feeds, industrial chemicals, foodstuffs, plastics, rubbers and fertilizers.

BANKERS :
First National Bank of SA Ltd
Nedperm Bank Ltd, Standard Bank of SA Ltd
Trust Bank of Africa Ltd, Volkskas Ltd

AUDITORS :
KPMG Aiken & Peat
Price Waterhouse Meyernel

FAMILIAR BRAND NAMES
N/A

CONTRIBUTION BY ACTIVITY
Plastics (% of Profit before Tax) (35.0%)
Agriculture (12.0%)
Food Stuffs (8.0%)
Industrial Chemicals (35.0%)
Mining Chemicals (3.0%)
Rubber (7.0%)

YEAR END : August

DIVIDEND :Ords R1

Final No 42	(Ldr)16/11/90	(Pay)30/11/90	Amt(c)9
Interim No 43	(Ldr)30/05/91	(Pay)14/06/91	Amt(c)6
Final No 44	(Ldr)15/11/91	(Pay)29/11/91	Amt(c)12
Interim No 45	(Ldr)29/05/92	(Pay)12/06/92	Amt(c)6
Final No 46	(Ldr)13/11/92	(Pay)27/11/92	Amt(c)14

NUMBER OF EMPLOYEES : 8200

CAPITAL STRUCTURE

	AUTHORISED	ISSUED
Ords R1	125000000	115479824
Var Rate Red Cum Prefs 1c	50000000	50000000
"B" Var Rate Red Cum Prefs 1c	50000000	50000000

FINANCIAL STATISTICS (AT FINANCIAL YEAR END)

(Amts in R'000)	1992 Aug	1991 Aug	1990 Aug	1989 Mar	1988 Mar
Ord S/H Int	638665	605246	582474	620876	564779
Long Trm Loans	646799	706725	718215	521643	634498
Iss Ord Share	115480	115480	115480	89519	89519
Total Liab	1423345	1452072	1438825	1047031	1082692
Current Liab	776546	745347	720610	525388	448194
Total Assets	2021194	2016897	1987917	1647288	1646529
Intang Assets	40816	40421	33382	20619	942
Current Assets	1097877	1041614	1020981	736469	680471
Debtors	556188	452336	434738	274705	280681
Inventory	464162	479525	453534	311905	326598
Turnover	2433168	2275380	2991422	1445624	1254197
Oper Profit	253309	233000	339937	214285	152676
Interest Paid	110482	127157	147666	74383	55095
Tax Paid	48289	30241	78838	57030	37702
Prf af Int&Tax	97156	78374	117604	91756	66902
Prf att Ord Sh	71599	62123	109648	93664	69152
Btm Line Earn	56515	43559	-203	84967	67173
Dividend Paid	23096	20787	42149	28870	22058
Mkt Prce(c) YE	540	600	490	750	385
Depreciation	-	-	-	-	67531

PER SHARE STATISTICS (CENTS)

Net Asst Val	517.71	489.11	475.49	670.54	629.85
Net Earnings	62.00	53.80	94.90	81.10	64.70
Dividends	20.00	18.00	21.50	25.00	20.00
Cash Flow	90.47	78.02	104.83	122.67	159.45

RATIOS AND OTHER INFORMATION

Mrk Cap(R000)	623592	692880	565852	671393	344648
Current Ratio	1.41	1.40	1.42	1.40	1.52
Quik/Acid Tst	0.82	0.75	0.79	0.81	0.79
A/C Rec T/ovr	4.37	5.03	4.86	5.26	4.47
Tot Ass T/ovr	1.20	1.13	1.06	0.88	0.76
Debt/Ass Rat	0.57	0.60	0.61	0.53	0.52
L T L Tot Ass	0.18	0.24	0.25	0.22	0.25
Debt to Eqity	1.79	2.02	2.09	1.42	1.53
Interest Cover	2.30	1.84	2.31	2.88	2.77
Oper Prof Mrg	10.41	10.24	11.36	14.82	12.17
Net Prof Marg%	2.94	2.73	3.67	6.48	5.51
Ret on Assets	12.78	11.75	12.28	14.13	10.23
Ret on Equity%	11.21	10.26	13.29	15.09	12.24
Price/Earnings	8.71	11.15	5.16	9.25	5.95
Divid Cover	3.10	2.99	4.41	3.24	3.24
Divid Yield	3.70	3.00	4.39	3.33	5.19
Earning Yield%	11.48	8.97	19.37	10.81	16.81
NAV % Mrk Pr	95.87	81.52	97.04	89.40	163.60
Effec Tax Rate	10.12	5.51	7.77	5.73	5.37
Def Interval	4.48	6.76	2.68	3.60	3.59
Sus Grth Rate	7.59	6.83	11.59	10.44	8.34

SUBSIDIARY & ASSOCIATED COMPANIES

ACADEMY PLASTIC SPECIALISTS (PTY) LTD
ACADEMY PLASTICS (PTY) LTD
AGRIHOLD LTD
BERGCHEM (PTY) LTD
CENTRAL CHEMICAL INVESTMENTS (PTY) LTD (50%)
FEDERALE KUNSMIS BPK
KLIPFONTEIN ORGANIESE PRODUKTE-KORP BPK
MEGAHITEC (EAST LONDON) (PTY) LTD
MOLADI TECHNOLOGIES (PTY) LTD
MULTI CONTRUCTION (PTY) LTD
NATIONAL CHEMICAL PRODUCTS LTD
NCP MARKETING CORP (PTY) LTD
ORANJE SOUTWERKE (EDMS) BPK
ORCHEM (PTY) LTD
PALMENT (PTY) LTD
PEARLAFLEX (PTY) LTD
PGM CHEMICALS (PTY) LTD
PLASTOMARK (PTY) LTD (49%)
S A POLYMER INDUSTRIES (PTY) LTD (50%)
SAFFOLA SEEDS (PTY) LTD
SAFRIPOL (PTY) LTD (50%)
SALT & CHEMICALS (PTY) LTD (SWA)
SANACHEM (PTY) LTD (50%)
SINGER & HERSCH INDUSTRIAL DEVELOPMENT C
SPECIALITIES (PTY) LTD
SUID AFRIKAANSE SOUTWERKE (EDMS) BPK
THE SYNTHETIC LATEX CO (PTY) LTD
THE SYNTHETIC RUBBER CO (PTY) LTD
UPINGTON SUPER SALT (PTY) LTD
WALVIS BAY SALT REFINERS (PTY) LTD

INVESTMENTS

FARM CHEMICALS (PTY) LTD (19,6%)

SERVGRO INTERNATIONAL LTD

ABBREVIATION : SERVGRO

JSE SHORT CODE : SRG

SECTOR : Industrial-Beverages & Hotels

SHAREHOLDERS

Who Owns Whom's Assessment of the Identity of the Ultimate Controlling Shareholder: SANLAM VIA SANKORP

SHAREHOLDER	PERCENTAGE 1992	1991
FEDSERVICES LTD	74 6	- -
CMB NOM P/L	5 2	---
EIGHTY ONE MAIN STREET NOM LTD	5 2	---
CAPITAL NOM P/L	1 6	---
SA MUTUAL	1 4	---
SHARESTOCK NOM P/L	1 3	---
STD BANK NOM TVL P/L	1 3	---
TOTAL	90 6	- -

DIRECTORS :
BOHLMANN TRT ,CALENBORNE AR ,EGAN MP
HEINAMANN PL ,HUNT-DAVIS DNA ,RUTSTEIN TB
SKOSANA IB
VAN DER WALT PJJ (Executive Chairman)
VAN HEERDEN G ,WIGLEY DM

REGISTRATION NUMBER : 03/00478/06

REGISTERED OFFICE
6th Floor, North Wing, President Place
148 Jan Smuts Ave, Rosebank
2196
TEL· 011-442 6320
FAX 011-442 6335

TRANSFER SECRETARY
Central Registrars Ltd
P O Box 4844, Johannesburg
2000
TEL 011-331 0051

COMPANY SECRETARY
J A Swanepoel

NATURE OF BUSINESS
An investment holding company with investments in companies which provide a range of services and leisure activities throughout South Africa, neighbouring countries and the United Kingdom

BANKERS :
Trust Bank of Africa Ltd, Volkskas Ltd

AUDITORS :
Coopers Theron Du Toit

FAMILIAR BRAND NAMES
AVIS,PRICE FORBES

CONTRIBUTION BY ACTIVITY
N/A

YEAR END : March

DIVIDEND : Ords 8c
Interim (Ldr)18/12/92 (Pay)08/01/93 Amt(c)7 5

CAPITAL STRUCTURE

	AUTHORISED	ISSUED
Ords 8c	300000000	110425000

FINANCIAL STATISTICS (AT FINANCIAL YEAR END)

(Amts in R'000)	1992 Mar
Ord S/H Int	100043
Long Trm Loans	287525
Iss Ord Share	25911
Total Liab	586313
Current Liab	298788
Total Assets	645922
Intang Assets	40434
Current Assets	322465
Debtors	166197
Inventory	34389
Turnover	810931
Oper Profit	100206
Interest Paid	13298
Tax Paid	34171
Prf af Int&Tax	52737
Prf att Ord Sh	42306
Btm Line Earn	40050

PER SHARE STATISTICS (CENTS)

Net Asst Val	230 05

Net Earnings	41.30
Dividends	16.70
Cash Flow	116.95

RATIOS AND OTHER INFORMATION

Current Ratio	1.08
Quik/Acid Tst	0.96
A/C Rec T/ovr	4.88
Tot Ass T/ovr	1.26
Debt/Ass Rat	0.81
L T L Tot Ass	0.34
Debt to Eqity	5.20
Interest Cover	7.54
Oper Prof Mrg	12.36
Net Prof Marg%	5.22
Ret on Assets	17.37
Ret on Equity%	14.99
Divid Cover	2.47
Effec Tax Rate	39.32
Def Interval	7.31
Sus Grth Rate	42.29

SUBSIDIARY & ASSOCIATED COMPANIES

FEDERALE GROEP BELEGGINGS BEPERK
FEDICS GROUP (PTY) LTD (46%)
INTERLEISURE LTD (40,5%)
INTERPARK (PTY) LTD (42,75%)
NASIONALE PERS BPK (22%)
PRICE FORBES GROUP (PTY) LTD (47%)
SATBEL INVESTMENT HOLDINGS (PTY) LTD (50%)
TELJOY HOLDINGS LTD (48%)
ZEDA HOLDINGS (PTY) LTD

INVESTMENTS

None

SHO-CRAFT LTD

ABBREVIATION : SHOCRAF

JSE SHORT CODE : SCF

SECTOR : Development Capital Market

SHAREHOLDERS

Who Owns Whom's Assessment of the Identity of the Ultimate Controlling Shareholder: DIRECTORS

SHAREHOLDER	PERCENTAGE 1992	1991
JUDIN M	40.6	43.1
HAYMANN F V	36.0	41.1
STAR BOX AG	9.2	---
INDO-CHINA NOM P/L	8.7	---
SHOCRAFT SHARE TRUST	1.7	1.7
NEDBANK NOM LTD	---	1.3
INDO-CHINA NOM SA P/L	---	8.7
TOTAL	96.2	95.9

DIRECTORS :
DE STEFANIS IP (Production Director)
HAYMANN FV (Chairman & Managing Dir.),JUDIN M
WILHELM C

REGISTRATION NUMBER : 68/12195/06

REGISTERED OFFICE
18 Minerva Avenue, Lea Glen
Roodepoort
1709
TEL: 011-674 1144
FAX: 011-674 4096

TRANSFER SECRETARY
Central Registrars Ltd
P O Box 4844, Johannesburg
2000
TEL: 011-331 0051

COMPANY SECRETARY
P E Van Diggelen

NATURE OF BUSINESS
The company is involved in the design, manufacture and supply of shopfittings, point-of-sale, signage and corporate identity items, exhibition stands,jewellery displays and specialised packaging for the jewellery, cosmetic and ancillary industries.The company is the SA licensee for SYMA-SYSTEM (SWISS).

BANKERS :
Standard Bank of SA Ltd

AUDITORS :
Brener Hatzkilson & Koff

FAMILIAR BRAND NAMES
SHO-OFF,SYMA-SYSTEM

CONTRIBUTION BY ACTIVITY
N/A

YEAR END : February

DIVIDEND : Ords 1c
Dividend (Ldr)27/09/91 (Pay)18/10/91 Amt(c)1

NUMBER OF EMPLOYEES : 220

CAPITAL STRUCTURE

	AUTHORISED	ISSUED
Ords 1c	48000000	13000000

FINANCIAL STATISTICS (AT FINANCIAL YEAR END)

(Amts in R'000)	1992 Feb	1991 Feb	1989 Feb	1988 Feb	1987 Feb
Ord S/H Int	4476	3716	3388	3294	1428
Long Trm Loans	1249	727	325	1	895
Iss Ord Share	13000	13000	13000	13000	100
Total Liab	2633	2116	1126	563	1344
Current Liab	1384	1389	801	562	449
Total Assets	6156	5141	3823	3857	2772
Intang Assets	953	691	691	*	*
Current Assets	4132	3343	3058	2449	1731
Debtors	2027	1069	1538	1645	1221
Inventory	1418	2131	1181	804	453
Turnover	6717	6354	5251	3751	3675
Oper Profit	987	556	626	440	456
Interest Paid	45	82	20	-	23
Tax Paid	98	188	100	43	-

Prf af Int&Tax	890	286	549	397	433
Prf att Ord Sh	890	286	549	397	433
Btm Line Earn	890	286	549	397	433
Dividend Paid	130	130	260	-	-
Mkt Prce(c) YE	50	50	30	30	-
Depreciation	355	288	149	106	106

PER SHARE STATISTICS (CENTS)

Net Asst Val	27.10	23.27	20.75	25.34	1428.00
Net Earnings	6.85	2.20	4.22	3.05	-
Dividends	1.00	1.00	2.00	1.50	-
Cash Flow	10.25	5.31	5.37	3.87	539.00

RATIOS AND OTHER INFORMATION

Mrk Cap(R000)	6500	6500	3900	3900	-
Current Ratio	2.99	2.41	3.82	4.36	3.86
Quik/Acid Tst	1.96	0.87	2.34	2.93	2.85
A/C Rec T/ovr	3.31	5.94	3.41	2.28	3.01
Tot Ass T/ovr	1.09	1.24	1.37	0.97	1.33
Debt/Ass Rat	0.39	0.39	0.29	0.15	0.48
L T L Tot Ass	0.17	0.12	0.09	0.00	0.32
Debt to Eqity	0.54	0.54	0.33	0.17	0.94
Interest Cover	21.93	6.78	31.30	-	19.83
Oper Prof Mrg	14.69	8.75	11.92	11.73	12.41
Net Prof Marg%	13.25	4.50	10.46	10.58	11.78
Ret on Assets	16.78	10.82	17.50	11.41	16.45
Ret on Equity%	16.82	7.08	15.03	12.05	18.64
Price/Earnings	7.30	22.73	7.11	9.84	-
Divid Cover	6.85	2.20	2.11	2.03	-
Divid Yield	2.00	2.00	6.67	5.00	-
Earning Yield%	13.70	4.40	14.07	10.17	-
NAV % Mrk Pr	54.20	46.54	69.15	84.46	-
Effec Tax Rate	1.01	15.19	15.41	9.77	-
Def Interval	0.78	0.89	1.00	0.45	2.08
Sus Grth Rate	16.98	4.20	8.53	12.05	30.32

SUBSIDIARY & ASSOCIATED COMPANIES

DISPLAY PACK (PTY) LTD
FORM BOX (PTY) LTD
SHO-CRAFT LEASING AND FINANCE (PTY) LTD
SHO-CRAFT SHOPFITTERS (PTY) LTD

INVESTMENTS

None

SHOPRITE HOLDINGS LTD

ABBREVIATION : SHOPRIT

JSE SHORT CODE : SHR

SECTOR : Industrial-Retailers & Wholesalers

SHAREHOLDERS

Who Owns Whom's Assessment of the Identity of the Ultimate Controlling Shareholder:
PEPGRO VIA PEPKOR

SHAREHOLDER	PERCENTAGE 1992	1991
PEPKOR BPK	80.0	80.0
CMB NOM P/L	5.0	---
DEMELER INV P/L	1.3	1.3
BASSGRO P/L	1.2	1.2
SANLAM	---	4.0
TOTAL	87.5	86.5

DIRECTORS :
BALL T ,BASSON JW (Managing Director),LOUW JA
ROGUT B (Systems Director),VAN ROOYEN R
WEYERS BR ,WIESE CH ADV (Chairman

REGISTRATION NUMBER : 70/09054/06

REGISTERED OFFICE
Jan van Riebeeck Drive, Beaconvale
Parow
7500
TEL: 021-931 8250
FAX: 021-933 2262

TRANSFER SECRETARY
Central Registrars Ltd
P O Box 4844, Johannesburg
2000
TEL: 011-331 0051

COMPANY SECRETARY
A N van Zyl

NATURE OF BUSINESS
An investment holding company with subsidiaries engaged in supermarket retailing. The group has 75 outlets.

BANKERS :
Nedperm Bank Ltd, Trust Bank of Africa Ltd
First National Bank of SA Ltd

AUDITORS :
Coopers Theron Du Toit

FAMILIAR BRAND NAMES
N/A

CONTRIBUTION BY ACTIVITY
N/A

YEAR END : February

DIVIDEND : Ords 4c

Final	(Ldr)18/05/90	(Pay)01/06/90	Amt(c)8
Interim	(Ldr)16/11/90	(Pay)30/11/90	Amt(c)5
Interim	(Ldr)15/11/91	(Pay)29/11/91	Amt(c)5.5
Final	(Ldr)15/05/92	(Pay)29/05/92	Amt(c)10

NUMBER OF EMPLOYEES : 5328

CAPITAL STRUCTURE

	AUTHORISED	ISSUED
Ords 4c	62500000	29550000

FINANCIAL STATISTICS (AT FINANCIAL YEAR END)

(Amts in R'000)	1992 Feb	1991 Feb	1990 Feb	1989 Feb	1988 Feb
Ord S/H Int	26997	22029	20469	16978	13093
Long Trm Loans	1035	323	1100	-	-
Iss Ord Share	29550	29550	29550	29550	29550
Total Liab	211794	159404	92706	66673	46008
Current Liab	210759	159081	91606	66673	46008
Total Assets	238791	181433	113175	83651	59101

Current Assets	201524	149777	100537	73498	50804
Debtors	22303	16762	10651	7063	6308
Inventory	150227	124982	85784	61721	41486
Turnover	1129072	732106	471414	350768	246363
Oper Profit	28640	16297	15232	10187	7857
Interest Paid	8990	5545	3309	231	-
Tax Paid	7718	3864	4827	3530	2746
Prf af Int&Tax	12170	7765	7974	6712	5111
Prf att Ord Sh	12153	8050	8136	6841	5126
Btm Line Earn	9548	5550	8136	6841	5126
Dividend Paid	4580	3989	3546	2955	2364
Mkt Prce(c) YE	540	305	245	270	235
Depreciation	6023	3494	1953	1119	992

PER SHARE STATISTICS (CENTS)

Net Asst Val	91.36	74.55	69.27	57.46	44.31
Net Earnings	41.10	27.20	27.50	23.20	17.30
Dividends	15.50	13.50	12.00	10.00	8.00
Cash Flow	63.98	38.10	33.59	26.50	20.65

RATIOS AND OTHER INFORMATION

Mrk Cap(R000)	159570	90128	72398	79785	69443
Current Ratio	0.96	0.94	1.10	1.10	1.10
Quik/Acid Tst	0.24	0.16	0.16	0.18	0.20
A/C Rec T/ovr	50.62	43.68	44.26	49.66	39.06
Tot Ass T/ovr	4.73	4.04	4.17	4.19	4.17
Debt/Ass Rat	0.88	0.88	0.81	0.80	0.78
Debt to Eqity	7.81	7.22	4.48	3.93	3.51
Interest Cover	3.19	2.94	4.60	44.10	-
Oper Prof Mrg	2.54	2.23	3.23	2.90	3.19
Net Prof Marg%	1.08	1.10	1.73	1.95	2.08
Ret on Assets	12.09	9.62	14.38	12.67	13.32
Ret on Equity%	45.02	36.54	39.75	40.29	39.15
Price/Earnings	13.14	11.21	8.91	11.64	13.58
Divid Cover	2.65	2.01	2.29	2.32	2.16
Divid Yield	2.87	4.43	4.90	3.70	3.40
Earning Yield%	7.61	8.92	11.22	8.59	7.36
NAV % Mrk Pr	16.92	24.44	28.27	21.28	18.85
Effec Tax Rate	35.22	32.94	38.25	29.61	6.19
Def Interval	-	0.95	0.15	0.04	0.05
Sus Grth Rate	28.05	18.43	22.42	22.89	21.10

SUBSIDIARY & ASSOCIATED COMPANIES

ROGEL INVESTMENTS (PTY) LTD
ROGEL WHOLESALERS (PTY) LTD
SHOPRITE (NAMIBIA) (PTY) LTD
SHOPRITE (VENDA) (PTY) LTD
SHOPRITE BELLVILLE (PTY) LTD
SHOPRITE CAPE (PTY) LTD
SHOPRITE MANAGEMENT (PTY) LTD
SHOPRITE MEAT MARKETS (PTY) LTD
SHOPRITE OFS AND NORTHERN CAPE (PTY) LTD
SHOPRITE PENINSULA (PTY) LTD
SHOPRITE TRANSVAAL (PTY) LTD
SHOPRITE WYNBERG (PTY) LTD

INVESTMENTS

None

SHOREDITS HOLDINGS LTD

ABBREVIATION : SHOREDITS

JSE SHORT CODE : SHO

SECTOR : Industrial-Building & Construction

SHAREHOLDERS

Who Owns Whom's Assessment of the Identity of the Ultimate Controlling Shareholder:
A K R SHOREDITS

SHAREHOLDER	PERCENTAGE 1992	1991
SHOREDITS A K R	49.6	49.6
TESAR F	15.5	15.5
STD BANK NOM TVL P/L	11.5	6.5
ADAMNON NOM P/L	4.3	4.3
RAATH M J	2.9	2.9
MACFAM P/L	1.9	1.9
FINANSBANK LTD	1.7	1.7
SAAMBOU PENS FUND	1.4	1.4
CMB NOM P/L	1.3	---
PRETORIA PERMANENT NOM P/L	1.2	1.2
GUARESCHI I G	1.0	---
SANLAM	---	1.3
STATS MISA PENS FUND	---	2.2
STATS MOTOR INDUSTRY PENS FUND	---	2.8
TOTAL	92.2	91.1

DIRECTORS :
BENDER L ,CRONJE PJP (Financial Director)
FALLER JEN ,MAHON TM ,MCINTOSH ARD ,RAATH MJ
SHOREDITS AKR (Chairman),STUTTERHEIM N DR
TESAR F (Vice Chairman

REGISTRATION NUMBER : 04/00039/06

REGISTERED OFFICE
14 Bloubokkie Street, Koedoespoort Industrial Sites
Pretoria
0186
TEL: 012-73 3005
FAX: 012-73 4380

TRANSFER SECRETARY
Mercantile Registrars Ltd
P O Box 1053, Johannesburg
2000
TEL: 011-333 8181

COMPANY SECRETARY
P J P Cronje

NATURE OF BUSINESS
Group activities comprise trading companies active in building & construction, property development & related fields. This includes civil contracting & earthworks, building restoration, air-conditioning design, manufacture, installation and maintenance, project development & management, precast concrete design and manufacture, the design and manufacture of switchboards, property management & development electronic control systems for buildings, forklift sales, hire & refurbishment, & indus refrigeration

BANKERS :
Standard Bank of SA Ltd
First National Bank of SA Ltd

AUDITORS :
BDO Spencer Steward

FAMILIAR BRAND NAMES
AKASIA ASPHALT,BOU RAATH,COOLCHEM
HRS PRECAST,LINDE,NORTHERN AIR,RENTAGENT
SAEC,STAEFA

CONTRIBUTION BY ACTIVITY
N/A

YEAR END : December

DIVIDEND :Ords no par value

Interim	(Ldr)16/11/90	(Pay)07/12/90	Amt(c)4
Final	(Ldr)19/04/91	(Pay)03/05/91	Amt(c)4
Interim	(Ldr)25/10/91	(Pay)15/11/91	Amt(c)4
Final	(Ldr)24/04/92	(Pay)22/05/92	Amt(c)4
Interim	(Ldr)27/11/92	(Pay)11/12/92	Amt(c)4

NUMBER OF EMPLOYEES : 1519

CAPITAL STRUCTURE

	AUTHORISED	ISSUED
Ords no par value	13000000	10771000

FINANCIAL STATISTICS (AT FINANCIAL YEAR END)

(Amts in R'000)	1991 Dec	1990 Dec	1989 Jun	1988 Jun	1987 Jun
Ord S/H Int	24836	22635	17436	16027	12950
Long Trm Loans	24783	19879	17867	12284	7296
Iss Ord Share	10771	10771	8976	8976	8646
Total Liab	91076	75198	79160	42364	27980
Current Liab	66293	55319	61293	30080	20684
Total Assets	105295	88321	89041	51017	40930
Intang Assets	10617	9512	7555	7374	*
Current Assets	57350	51515	53891	27908	19994
Debtors	23511	25497	22756	10745	3124
Inventory	31431	23610	31135	17163	433
Turnover	231927	328833	189797	66095	47789
Oper Profit	12113	12602	8790	5237	4096
Interest Paid	7572	6995	4074	1695	316
Tax Paid	1891	3381	1206	1012	1413
Prf af Int&Tax	3101	2717	3686	3076	2367
Prf att Ord Sh	3063	2659	3946	3023	2339
Btm Line Earn	3063	3362	2127	3023	3206
Dividend Paid	862	1364	718	746	864
Mkt Prce(c) YE	115	110	195	175	245
Depreciation	5900	7120	4602	988	619

PER SHARE STATISTICS (CENTS)

Net Asst Val	132.01	121.84	110.08	96.40	149.78
Net Earnings	28.40	25.90	30.40	24.30	21.30
Dividends	8.00	12.00	8.00	8.00	10.00
Cash Flow	97.75	75.20	106.63	54.92	49.95

RATIOS AND OTHER INFORMATION

Mrk Cap(R000)	12387	11848	17503	15708	21183
Current Ratio	0.87	0.93	0.88	0.93	0.97
Quik/Acid Tst	0.39	0.50	0.37	0.36	0.95
A/C Rec T/ovr	9.86	8.60	8.34	6.15	15.30
Tot Ass T/ovr	2.20	2.48	2.13	1.30	1.17
Debt/Ass Rat	0.74	0.73	0.79	0.68	0.53
L T L Tot Ass	0.11	0.10	0.10	0.09	0.02
Debt to Eqity	3.16	2.83	4.03	2.17	1.67
Interest Cover	1.60	1.80	2.16	3.20	12.96
Oper Prof Mrg	5.22	3.83	4.63	7.92	8.57
Net Prof Marg%	1.32	0.81	2.08	4.57	4.89
Ret on Assets	11.93	9.88	10.07	11.34	10.01
Ret on Equity%	12.33	7.83	22.63	18.86	18.06
Price/Earnings	4.05	4.25	6.41	7.20	11.50
Divid Cover	3.55	2.16	3.80	3.04	2.13
Divid Yield	6.96	10.91	4.10	4.57	4.08
Earning Yield%	24.70	23.55	15.59	13.89	8.69
NAV % Mrk Pr	114.79	110.76	56.45	55.09	61.13
Effec Tax Rate	3.97	16.57	3.74	2.38	1.38
Def Interval	3.52	1.25	2.92	3.61	1.47
Sus Grth Rate	8.86	5.72	18.51	14.21	11.39

SUBSIDIARY & ASSOCIATED COMPANIES

AKASIA ASPHALT (PTY) LTD
AKASIA ASPHALT BOPHUTHATSWANA (PTY) LTD
BAUHAUS HOUSING (PTY) LTD
BERGHOUT & ROUVOET (PTY) LTD
BERGHOUT & ROUVOET CONSTRUCTION (PTY) LT
BOU RAATH CIVIL CONTRACTORS (PTY) LTD
BOU RAATH CIVIL CONTRACTORS BOPHUTHATSWA
BOU RAATH PLANT HIRE (PTY) LTD
CLAYVILLE PROPERTY OF EIGHTY THREE (PTY)
COOLCHEM (PTY) LTD
DE HILVERSDAM INVESTMENTS (PTY) LTD
ERF 490 WONDERBOOM SOUTH (PTY) LTD
FTR HANDLING (PTY) LTD (50%)
GREAT GEAR (PTY) LTD
HRS FENCING NATAL (PTY) LTD
HRS PRECAST (PTY) LTD
KENIAN CONSTRUCTION (PTY) LTD
METROPROP (CAPE) (PTY) LTD
METROPROP (PTY) LTD
METROPROP (RAND) (PTY) LTD
METROPROP (TVL) (PTY) LTD
NORAIR AIR-CONDITIONING (PTY) LTD (BOTSW
NORAIR AIR-CONDITIONING SALES (PTY) LTD
NORTHERN AIR (PTY) LTD
NORTHERN AIR BOPHUTHATSWANA (PTY) LTD
NORTHERN AIR CISKEI (PTY) LTD
NORTHERN AIR INDUSTRIAL (PTY) LTD
NORTHERN AIR LESOTHO (PTY) LTD
PANDA PROPERTY (PTY) LTD
PRETORIA EXCAVATING CONTRACTORS (PTY) LT
PRORENT INVESTMENTS (PTY) LTD
RENTAGENT (PTY) LTD
RHOLEM BELEGGINGS (EDMS) BPK
SAEC ELECTRICAL (BOPHUTHATSWANA) (PTY) L
SAEC ELECTRICAL (PTY) LTD
SHORCOR (PTY) LTD
SHORDITS CIVIL CONTRACTORS (PTY) LTD
SHOREDITS CONSTRUCTION (PTY) LTD
SHOREDITS CONSTRUCTION BOPHUTHATSWANA (P
SHOREDITS RESTORATIONS (PTY) LTD
SHORSTEEL (PTY) LTD
STAEFA CONTROL SYSTEMS (PTY) LTD

INVESTMENTS

FEDSURE HOLDINGS LTD (17600S)
STRUBENGLEN HOLDINGS (PTY) LTD (345058S)

SILTEK LTD

ABBREVIATION : SILTEK

JSE SHORT CODE : STK

SECTOR : Industrial-Electronics, Electrical & Bat

SHAREHOLDERS

Who Owns Whom's Assessment of the Identity of the Ultimate Controlling Shareholder:
ANGLOVAAL VIA GRINTEK

SHAREHOLDER	PERCENTAGE 1992	1991
GRINAKER ELECTRONICS HLDGS LTD	60.5	62.8
SA MUTUAL	6.1	6.7
STD BANK NOM TVL P/L	5.5	5.6
SHARESTOCK NOM P/L	4.0	6.3
GRINAKER HOLDINGS LTD	3.3	3.5
EIGHTY ONE MAIN STREET NOM LTD	2.7	---
FIRST NAT NOM P/L	2.1	1.9
CMB NOM P/L	1.5	---
LIBERTY LIFE ASSOC OF AFRICA LTD	1.3	---
KOMBOU P/L	---	2.0
SANLAM	---	1.6
TOTAL	86.8	90.2

DIRECTORS :
BRUINETTE KE DR,DE BEER DD ,DIPPENAAR LL
FURST MR ,GROBBELAAR M ,LUDIN HET
MCGRATH MJ (Managing Director),MITCHELL AM
ROBBERTZE JC ,SAULEZ AN (Chairman

REGISTRATION NUMBER : 05/15386/06

REGISTERED OFFICE
Siltek 1, 275 Kent Avenue
Ferndale, Randburg
2194
TEL: 011-886 2410
FAX: 011-886 1976

TRANSFER SECRETARY
Anglovaal Ltd
P O Box 62379, Marshalltown
2107
TEL: 011-634 9111

COMPANY SECRETARY
M GROBBELAAR

NATURE OF BUSINESS
Designs, manufactures, distributes and services computer hardware and software.

BANKERS :
Standard Bank of SA Ltd
First National Bank of SA Ltd
Trust Bank of Africa Ltd, Nedperm Bank Ltd
Volkskas Ltd

AUDITORS :
Coopers Theron Du Toit

FAMILIAR BRAND NAMES
AMDAHL,ASSETS,AST RESEARCH,BONDWELL,BORLAND
CENTRAL POINT SOFTWARE,CIPHER
COMP CORP OF AMERICA,DALLAS,DATA TECH
DIAMOND FLOWER,EASY ACCESS,EPSON
FLEET MANAGEMENT,FOX SOFTWARE,FUJITSU
GENICOM,GOAL SYSTEMS,HEWLETT PACKARD
HIPERFORMANCE SYSTEMS,IRWIN,ISDX,LOTUS CORP
MCDONNELL DOUGLAS,MEDIS,MIAD,MICROSOFT
MICROTEK,MITEL,NETLAN,NETMANAGER,NOVELL
OKI MICROLINE,ORACLE,OUTPUT TECH,PRIME
QUALSTAR,QUME,REPAIR SHOP,ROLAND,SEAGATE
SELECT ACCOUNTING,SELECT PAYROLL,SELPOINT
SMC,TAX PARTNER,THE MANUFACTURER,TIMEOUT
TOSHIBA,WANGTEK,WESTERN DIGITAL,XENIX,ZYTRON

CONTRIBUTION BY ACTIVITY
N/A

YEAR END : June

DIVIDEND : Ords 30c

Interim No 71	(Ldr)09/03/90	(Pay)05/04/90	Amt(c)11
Final No 72	(Ldr)14/09/90	(Pay)12/10/90	Amt(c)15
Interim No 73	(Ldr)22/02/91	(Pay)12/04/91	Amt(c)10
Final No 74	(Ldr)27/09/91	(Pay)18/10/91	Amt(c)10
Interim No 75	(Ldr)28/02/92	(Pay)18/04/92	Amt(c)10
Final No 76	(Ldr)11/09/92	(Pay)09/10/92	Amt(c)13

NUMBER OF EMPLOYEES : 1633

CAPITAL STRUCTURE

	AUTHORISED	ISSUED
Ords 30c	60000000	48543793
"A" Red Prefs 30c	300000	0
"B" Red Prefs 30c	50000	0
"C" Red Prefs 30c	20000	0

FINANCIAL STATISTICS (AT FINANCIAL YEAR END)

(Amts in R'000)	1992 Jun	1991 Jun	1990 Jun	1989 Jun	1988 Jun
Ord S/H Int	147653	136597	249958	97624	64745
Long Trm Loans	16684	16873	31141	2418	2614
Iss Ord Share	48544	46472	45573	32509	29808
Total Liab	225186	193212	186558	49595	46317
Current Liab	208502	176339	155417	47177	43703
Total Assets	372839	329809	330952	147219	111062
Intang Assets	*	*	105564	*	*
Current Assets	311479	281006	285880	68641	99529
Debtors	178590	151250	129603	26145	32464
Inventory	121556	98934	137614	31659	26205
Turnover	978956	822459	737590	-	-
Oper Profit	68824	57665	70921	31355	27279
Interest Paid	7180	7250	12140	139	83
Tax Paid	33596	30775	20813	17223	14538
Prf af Int&Tax	38121	29661	41034	19884	15882
Prf att Ord Sh	36454	27940	40410	23395	14887
Btm Line Earn	20508	78	35007	21608	18065
Dividend Paid	11171	9294	11545	6691	4471
Mkt Prce(c) YE	700	700	900	1000	600
Depreciation	8012	8404	6503	2622	4065

PER SHARE STATISTICS (CENTS)

Net Asst Val	304.16	293.93	316.84	300.30	217.21
Net Earnings	75.10	60.10	91.40	74.80	50.30
Dividends	23.00	20.00	26.00	21.25	15.00
Cash Flow	86.78	70.26	98.52	65.92	64.64

RATIOS AND OTHER INFORMATION

Mrk Cap(R000)	339808	325304	410157	325090	178848
Current Ratio	1.49	1.59	1.84	1.45	2.28
Quik/Acid Tst	0.91	1.03	0.95	0.78	1.68
A/C Rec T/ovr	5.48	5.44	5.69	-	-
Tot Ass T/ovr	2.63	2.49	2.23	-	-
Debt/Ass Rat	0.58	0.57	0.55	0.32	0.39
L T L Tot Ass	0.02	0.03	0.08	-	-
Debt to Eqity	1.46	1.37	0.73	0.48	0.68
Interest Cover	9.64	7.99	5.86	247.40	367.51
Oper Prof Mrg	7.03	7.01	9.62	-	-
Net Prof Marg%	3.72	3.40	5.48	-	-
Ret on Assets	22.08	21.17	22.83	28.57	27.46
Ret on Equity%	24.69	20.45	16.17	23.96	22.99
Price/Earnings	9.32	11.65	9.85	13.37	11.93
Divid Cover	3.27	3.01	3.52	3.52	3.35
Divid Yield	3.29	2.86	2.89	2.13	2.50
Earning Yield%	10.73	8.59	10.16	7.48	8.38

NAV % Mrk Pr	43.45	41.99	35.20	30.03	36.20
Effec Tax Rate	44.92	54.82	36.66	52.07	52.77
Def Interval	0.27	0.58	0.71	0.00	-
Sus Grth Rate	17.12	13.65	11.55	17.11	16.09

SUBSIDIARY & ASSOCIATED COMPANIES

ARCHITECTURED NETWORK SYSTEMS (PTY) LTD
ASSOCIATED COMPUTER SOLUTIONS (PTY) LTD
CMC COMPUTER MACHINERY (PTY) LTD
COMPUCARE (PTY) LTD
COMPUTER CONFIGURATIONS HOLDINGS (PTY) L (37.5%)
DATA DEVICES (PTY) LTD
ELECTRONIC BACK-UP SERVICES (PTY) LTD
GENERAL DATA SYSTEMS (PTY) LTD (48%)
GRINAKER DATA SYSTEMS (PTY) LTD
GRINAKER NETWORK SYSTEMS (PTY) LTD
HIPERFORMANCE SYSTEMS (PTY) LTD (DISTR.
HIPERFORMANCE SYSTEMS (PTY) LTD (DISTR.
INFORMATION SYSTEMS SOLUTIONS (PTY) LTD (31%)
INTEGRATED DEVELOPMENT INTERNATIONAL (PT
LARGE SCALE SYSTEMS (PTY) LTD
LASERNET (PTY) LTD
LONOX (PTY) LTD
MATRIX COMPUTING SERVICES (PTY) LTD
MEDIS (PTY) LTD
MICROSCIENCES (PTY) LTD
MICROSCIENCES CABLING (PTY) LTD
OPENPRO (PTY) LTD
PASTEL SOFTWARE (PTY) LTD (42.5%)
PRIMARY COMPUTER SYSTEMS (PTY) LTD
PRIMARY COVER (PTY) LTD
Q DATA LTD (43.5%)
QUALICOM (PTY) LTD
RADIOKOM (PTY) LTD
SELECT SOFTWARE (PTY) LTD (42.5%)
SELECT SOFTWARE (PTY) LTD (47,29%)
SELECT SOFTWARE COPYRIGHT (PTY) LTD (42.5%)
SELECT SOFTWARE DEVELOPERS (PTY) LTD (42.5%)
SILTEK HOLDINGS (PTY) LTD
SILTEK INVESTMENTS (PTY) LTD
SMART TECHNOLOGIES (PTY) LTD (50%)
SOFTSOURCE (PTY) LTD
SOFTSOURCE (PTY) LTD
SPARC COMPUTER SERVICES (PTY) LTD
SX SYSTEMS SOLUTION (PTY) LTD
TECNETICS (PTY) LTD
TELEBOSS HOLDINGS (PTY) LTD
TELEBOSS SA (PTY) LTD
TELECO BUSINESS SYSTEMS (PTY) LTD (45.6%)
TRAN SYSTEMS (PTY) LTD

INVESTMENTS

None

SILVEROAK INDUSTRIES LTD

ABBREVIATION : SILOAK

JSE SHORT CODE : SLK

SECTOR : Industrial-Clothing, Footwear & Textiles

SHAREHOLDERS

Who Owns Whom's Assessment of the Identity of the Ultimate Controlling Shareholder:
O R TOWNSLEY

SHAREHOLDER	PERCENTAGE 1992	1991
UAL NOM P/L	48.5	49.7
AFRICAN HIDE HOLDINGS P/L	14.2	14.2
SILVEROAK IND LTD EMP SHARE PURCHASE TRU	5.4	5.4
FERBROS NOM P/L	4.7	2.8
MOMENTUM LIFE ASSURE LTD	4.4	5.5
NEDBANK NOM LTD	3.8	3.8
UNITED FINANCE CORP OF SA LTD	3.7	3.7
SAGE LIFE LTD	2.6	2.6
EHINGER E O	2.2	2.2
ALGEMENE HANDELS & BELEGGINGS CO N V	1.2	1.2
TOWNSLEY O R	1.1	1.1
STAPLES D C	---	1.6
TOTAL	91.8	93.8

DIRECTORS :
BAGE AM ,DEMUTH WG
GIBSON RF (Financial Director),GLUCKMAN GN
KATZ SJ (Vice Chairman),KAUFMANN PG (Chairman)
MOSSOP AR ,TOWNSLEY OR (Managing Director)
VAN DER MERWE-VANCE A

REGISTRATION NUMBER : 01/04071/06

REGISTERED OFFICE
1 Bagshaw Street, North End
Port Elizabeth
6001
TEL: 041-547 505
FAX: 041 544 905

TRANSFER SECRETARY
Central Registrars Ltd
P O Box 4844, Johannesburg
2000
TEL: 011-331 0051

COMPANY SECRETARY
J W Seaman

NATURE OF BUSINESS
The group is in the business of tanning bovine hides for export and sale as finished leather in the local market.

BANKERS :
Nedperm Bank Ltd, Standard Bank of SA Ltd
First National Bank of SA Ltd

AUDITORS :
Ernst & Young

FAMILIAR BRAND NAMES
AFBRO,AHT,EXOTAN,LADYSMITH LEATHERS,MOSSOP

CONTRIBUTION BY ACTIVITY
N/A

YEAR END : June

DIVIDEND : Ords 10c

Final	(Ldr)06/12/91	(Pay)13/12/91	Amt(c)8.11
Interim	(Ldr)10/04/92	(Pay)24/04/92.	Amt(c)16.2
Special	(Ldr)10/04/92	(Pay)24/04/92	Amt(c)5.4
Final	(Ldr)16/10/92	(Pay)30/10/92	Amt(c)10.8

NUMBER OF EMPLOYEES : 1192

CAPITAL STRUCTURE

	AUTHORISED	ISSUED
Ords 10c	21000000	18493500
Var Rate Red Prefs 1c	10000000	10000000

FINANCIAL STATISTICS (AT FINANCIAL YEAR END)

(Amts in R'000)	1992 Jun	1991 Jun	1990 Jun	1989 Jun	1988 Jun
Ord S/H Int	45628	42258	40662	44613	39169
Long Trm Loans	32021	21681	18106	11500	1500
Iss Ord Share	18494	18494	18494	18494	17612
Total Liab	72544	70359	74872	73533	51400
Current Liab	40523	48678	56766	62033	49900
Total Assets	116358	111087	113494	115596	90569
Intang Assets	1814	1530	2040	2550	*
Current Assets	81577	74774	79463	90180	69417
Debtors	45411	41612	45481	45139	32179
Inventory	36166	33162	33982	45041	37149
Turnover	178840	174971	200402	202903	178340
Oper Profit	17276	14599	9862	13836	8321
Interest Paid	5665	8049	8134	5394	1201
Tax Paid	-58	8	53	38	-
Prf af Int&Tax	11669	6542	1675	8404	7120
Prf att Ord Sh	10072	4868	21	7454	6808
Btm Line Earn	9364	2946	-2493	7186	6326
Dividend Paid	5995	1500	-	3606	2972
Mkt Prce(c) YE	150	180	270	260	200
Depreciation	6409	5770	2643	1927	1524

PER SHARE STATISTICS (CENTS)

Net Asst Val	236.91	220.22	208.84	227.44	222.40
Net Earnings	54.50	26.00	-	41.00	41.00
Dividends	32.40	15.00	-	19.00	16.88
Cash Flow	89.12	57.52	14.40	51.63	50.71

RATIOS AND OTHER INFORMATION

Mrk Cap(R000)	27741	33289	49934	48084	35224
Current Ratio	2.01	1.54	1.40	1.45	1.39
Quik/Acid Tst	1.12	0.85	0.80	0.73	0.65
A/C Rec T/ovr	3.94	4.20	4.41	4.50	5.54
Tot Ass T/ovr	1.54	1.58	1.77	1.76	1.97
Debt/Ass Rat	0.44	0.53	0.56	0.54	0.55
L T L Tot Ass	0.09	0.09	0.06	-	-
Debt to Eqity	1.12	1.39	1.56	1.39	1.27
Interest Cover	3.05	1.81	1.21	2.57	6.93
Oper Prof Mrg	9.66	8.34	4.92	6.82	4.67
Net Prof Marg%	5.63	2.78	0.01	3.67	3.82
Ret on Assets	14.85	13.14	8.69	11.97	9.19
Ret on Equity%	22.07	11.52	0.05	16.71	17.38
Price/Earnings	2.75	6.92	-	6.34	4.88
Divid Cover	1.68	1.73	-	2.16	2.43
Divid Yield	21.60	8.33	-	7.31	8.44
Earning Yield%	36.33	14.44	-	15.77	20.50
NAV % Mrk Pr	157.94	122.35	77.35	87.48	111.20
Effec Tax Rate	-0.50	0.12	3.07	0.45	-
Def Interval	2.13	4.11	19.74	5.51	4.01
Sus Grth Rate	8.94	7.97	0.05	8.63	9.79

SUBSIDIARY & ASSOCIATED COMPANIES

AFBRAN PROPERTIES (PTY) LTD
AFBREG MAINTENANCE CO (PTY) LTD
AFBRO PRODUCE BUYERS (PTY) LTD
AFBRO PRODUKTE KOPERS (TVL) (EDMS) BPK
AFRICAN GOAT & SHEEPSKIN (PTY) LTD
AFRICAN HIDE & SKIN BROKERS (PTY) LTD
AFRICAN HIDE (E P) (PTY) LTD
AFRICAN HIDE TRADING CORPORATION (PTY) L
AHT PROPERTIES (PTY) LTD
BORDER EXPORT CO (PTY) LTD
BOROLO (PTY) LTD
BREGIN & CO (CAPE) (PTY) LTD
CAPE PRODUCE EXPORT CO (PTY) LTD
EXOFELL (PTY) LTD
EXOTAN (PTY) LTD
H MENCK & CO (PTY) LTD
HISIN PROPERTIES (PTY) LTD
INDUSTRIAL RELATIONS ADVISORY SERVICES (
LADYSMITH LEATHERS (PTY) LTD
MARYLAND WOOLE (PTY) LTD
MAYTHAM, JOHNSON & HENRY (PTY) LTD
MIGTORIA PROPERTIES (PTY) LTD
MOSSOP & SON (PTY) LTD
MOUNTAIN VIEW TANNERY (PTY) LTD
NORTH STREET DEVELOPMENTS (PTY) LTD
NUVEL HUIDE & VELLE (EDMS) BPK
OSB EXPORTS (PTY) LTD
OSB PROPERTIES (PTY) LTD
OSB TRADING (PTY) LTD
POSTMASBURG PROPERTIES (PTY) LTD
S-TVL & N-NATAL HUIDE & VELLE (EDMS) BPK
SA BROKERS & AUCTIONEERS (PTY) LTD
SILOAK
SILVEROAK HIDE PRODUCE BUYERS (PTY) LTD
SILVEROAK TANNERS (PTY) LTD
SILVERTON TANNERY PROPERTIES (PTY) LTD
SWD HUIDE & VELLE (EDMS) BPK
VALSBAAI (PTY) LTD
W LANE & CO (PTY) LTD
WI VISSER (EDMS) BPK
WI VISSER BELEGGINGS (EDMS) BPK
WI VISSER KEIMOES (EDMS) BPK

INVESTMENTS

None

SIMMER AND JACK MINES LTD

ABBREVIATION : SIMMERS

JSE SHORT CODE : SIM

SECTOR : Gold-Rand & others

SHAREHOLDERS

Who Owns Whom's Assessment of the Identity of the Ultimate Controlling Shareholder: DIRECTORS

SHAREHOLDER	PERCENTAGE 1992	1991
SOLID G NOM P/L	41.4	51.5
TRANSATLANTIC MINING INV LTD	22.4	---
UK CONTROL ACCOUNT	7.3	14.2
DURRANT INV LTD	6.6	8.9
ABSA NOM P/L	1.7	---
THOR RESOURCES P/L	1.3	---
STD BANK NOM TVL P/L	1.2	1.7
CHALKTON NOM CO P/L	1.0	1.4
HAPPY ACRES P/L	1.0	1.4
SHARLAND J N	---	2.2
NEDBANK NOM LTD	---	1.2
BYSEL MANUFACTURING P/L	---	1.2

VOLKSKAS NOM P/L	---	1.5
CLIFFCOR CC	---	1.0
TOTAL	83.9	86.1

DIRECTORS :
IMRIE WNB ,MCCHESNEY M ,MCNEIL HA
MUMBY CC (Chairman),RAUNER W

REGISTRATION NUMBER : 01/07778/06

REGISTERED OFFICE
5th Floor, Southern Life Gardens
3 Gwen Lane, Sandton
2146
TEL: 011-883 6646
FAX: 011-884 5552

TRANSFER SECRETARY
Mercantile Registrars Ltd
P O Box 1053, Johannesburg
2000
TEL: 011-333 8181

COMPANY SECRETARY
Process & Mining Consultants (Pty) Ltd

NATURE OF BUSINESS
The company holds mining rights in the Germiston, Barberton, Nelspruit, Pilgrims Rest & Sabie areas. The company also owns income-producing properties.

BANKERS :
First National Bank of SA Ltd

AUDITORS :
Kessel Feinstein

FAMILIAR BRAND NAMES
N/A

CONTRIBUTION BY ACTIVITY
N/A

YEAR END : June

DIVIDEND :15/03/91

NUMBER OF EMPLOYEES : 1026

CAPITAL STRUCTURE

	AUTHORISED	ISSUED
Ords 2c	100000000	27064056

FINANCIAL STATISTICS (AT FINANCIAL YEAR END)

(Amts in R'000)	1991 Jun	1990	1989 Dec	1988 Dec	1987 Dec
Ord S/H Int	99480	18573	18573	16080	15664
Long Trm Loans	414	13678	9000	9000	10171
Iss Ord Share	27064	6750	6814	6750	6750
Total Liab	13897	18356	13231	9997	13173
Current Liab	13483	4678	4231	997	3002
Total Assets	113377	46052	31804	26077	28837
Current Assets	17758	13801	13354	8275	10661
Debtors	5313	-	1626	139	1247
Inventory	494	13801	-	-	-
Turnover	9158	7112	6141	-	10041
Oper Profit	-4693	5025	4054	1044	5798
Interest Paid	-	1948	977	1399	882
Tax Paid	453	488	488	-827	2300
Prf af Int&Tax	-3480	2589	2589	472	2616
Prf att Ord Sh	-3480	2589	2589	472	2616
Btm Line Earn	-43198	2589	2948	472	3410
Mkt Prce(c) YE	200	165	165	120	350
Depreciation	-	-	-	-	80

PER SHARE STATISTICS (CENTS)

Net Asst Val	367.57	275.16	272.57	238.22	232.06
Net Earnings	-35.76	-	37.99	6.99	38.70
Cash Flow	-8.57	38.36	38.00	-10.36	42.41

RATIOS AND OTHER INFORMATION

Mrk Cap(R000)	54128	11138	11243	8100	23625
Current Ratio	1.32	2.95	3.16	8.30	3.55
Quik/Acid Tst	1.28	-	3.16	8.30	3.55
A/C Rec T/ovr	1.15	-	3.78	-	8.05
Tot Ass T/ovr	0.05	0.15	0.19	-	0.35
Debt/Ass Rat	0.12	0.40	0.42	0.38	0.42
L T L Tot Ass	0.00	0.30	0.28	0.35	0.31
Debt to Eqity	0.14	0.99	0.71	0.62	0.77
Interest Cover	-	2.58	4.15	0.75	6.57
Oper Prof Mrg	-51.24	70.66	66.02	-	57.74
Net Prof Marg%	-38.00	36.40	42.16	-	26.05
Ret on Assets	-1.78	10.91	12.75	4.00	20.11
Ret on Equity%	-2.33	13.94	13.94	2.94	16.70
Price/Earnings	-5.59	-	4.34	17.17	9.04
Earning Yield%	-17.88	-	23.02	5.83	11.06
NAV % Mrk Pr	183.79	166.76	165.19	198.52	66.30
Effec Tax Rate	-0.07	15.86	15.86	-96.90	43.39
Def Interval	-1.93	5.28	4.23	-12.88	3.14
Sus Grth Rate	-3.50	13.94	13.94	2.94	16.70

SUBSIDIARY & ASSOCIATED COMPANIES

BOBSAT INVESTMENTS (PTY) LTD
CALEDONIAN MINING & EXPLORATION CO (PTY)
CENTURION GOLD MINING CO (PTY) LTD
MAKONJWAAN IMPERIAL MINING COMPANY (PTY)
OMARURU MINERALS (PTY) LTD
PERTINENT INVESTMENTS (PTY) LTD
SIMMER AND JACK INVESTMENTS (PTY) LTD
SIMMER AND JACK LAND DEVELOPMENT CO. LTD
SIMMER EXTENSIONS LTD
SOUTH AFRICAN SILICA BRICKS (PTY) LTD
SYNDICATE EIGHTEEN (PTY) LTD

INVESTMENTS

WEST WITWATERSRAND GOLD HOLDINGS LTD (750000 SH)

SM GOLDSTEIN LTD

ABBREVIATION : GOLDSTEIN

JSE SHORT CODE : GDS

SECTOR : Industrial-Building & Construction

SHAREHOLDERS

Who Owns Whom's Assessment of the Identity of the Ultimate Controlling Shareholder: GROUP FIVE LTD & MANAGEMENT CONSORTIUM

SHAREHOLDER	PERCENTAGE 1992	1991

GROUP FIVE LTD	45.0	45.0
MIV CONSTRUCTION HOLDINGS CO P/L	25.9	23.8
GRAYSTON NOM P/L	2.5	2.5
CLOGG P K	2.1	2.1
ENTHOVEN R	1.4	1.4
KELLY T P	1.2	1.2
JACKSON T N	1.1	1.1
STOCKSHARE NOM P/L	---	1.1
KOTZEE T J	---	1.0
TOTAL	79.1	79.0

DIRECTORS :
CLOGG PK (Chief Executive),CUNNINGHAM RWW
GOLDSTEIN SM (Chairman),HESEDING GB ,JACKSON TN
KOTZEE TJ ,WILSON EF

REGISTRATION NUMBER : 05/29557/06

REGISTERED OFFICE
371 Rivonia Boulevard, Rivonia
Sandton
2199
TEL: 011-803 1155
FAX: 011-803 5829

TRANSFER SECRETARY
Mercantile Registrars Ltd
P O Box 1053, Johannesburg
2000
TEL: 011-333 8181

COMPANY SECRETARY
D Zuccolotto

NATURE OF BUSINESS
The company is an investment holding company with a controlling interest in JSE-quoted Group Five Holdings, which in turn controls Group Five Ltd.

BANKERS :
First National Bank of SA Ltd

AUDITORS :
Coopers Theron Du Toit

FAMILIAR BRAND NAMES
N/A

CONTRIBUTION BY ACTIVITY
N/A

YEAR END : June

DIVIDEND : Ords 50c

Interim No 47	(Ldr)12/04/90	(Pay)27/04/90	Amt(c)33
Final No 48	(Ldr)14/09/90	(Pay)29/09/90	Amt(c)14
Interim No 49	(Ldr)22/02/91	(Pay)15/03/91	Amt(c)10
Final No 50	(Ldr)20/09/91	(Pay)04/10/91	Amt(c)16
Interim No 51	(Ldr)28/02/92	(Pay)20/03/92	Amt(c)10
Final No 52	(Ldr)16/10/92	(Pay)06/11/92	Amt(c)3

NUMBER OF EMPLOYEES : 15515

CAPITAL STRUCTURE

	AUTHORISED	ISSUED
Ords 50c	15000000	9995000

FINANCIAL STATISTICS (AT FINANCIAL YEAR END)

(Amts in R'000)	1992 Jun	1991 Jun	1990 Jun	1989 Jun	1988 Jun
Ord S/H Int	29190	28078	23053	22576	29875
Long Trm Loans	-	-	-	3149	40889
Iss Ord Share	9995	9995	9995	9995	9995
Total Liab	442	1734	1582	31512	159906
Current Liab	442	1734	1582	28363	119017
Total Assets	29632	29812	24635	54088	189781
Current Assets	437	1737	1637	33812	131075
Debtors	371	1678	1575	15013	93966
Inventory	-	-	-	18704	32162
Turnover	-	-	-	266123	457223
Oper Profit	-1381	-2637	-3299	-6908	2185
Interest Paid	-	-	-	6898	5098
Tax Paid	-	-	-	-791	-2153
Prf af Int&Tax	-45	-45	-51	-11237	-760
Prf att Ord Sh	4004	7869	6789	-3020	2048
Btm Line Earn	3723	8392	7834	-5947	1717
Dividend Paid	1299	2599	5597	1000	-
Mkt Prce(c) YE	250	225	140	135	135
Depreciation	-	-	-	2609	3824

PER SHARE STATISTICS (CENTS)

Net Asst Val	292.05	280.92	230.65	225.87	298.90
Net Earnings	40.00	78.70	67.90	-30.20	20.50
Dividends	13.00	26.00	56.00	10.00	-
Cash Flow	-0.45	-0.45	-0.51	-65.94	1.22

RATIOS AND OTHER INFORMATION

Mrk Cap(R000)	24988	22489	13993	13493	13493
Current Ratio	0.99	1.00	1.03	1.19	1.10
Quik/Acid Tst	0.99	1.00	1.03	0.53	0.83
A/C Rec T/ovr	-	-	-	17.73	4.87
Tot Ass T/ovr	-	-	-	4.92	2.41
Debt/Ass Rat	0.01	0.06	0.06	0.53	0.78
L T L Tot Ass	-	-	-	0.01	0.15
Debt to Eqity	0.02	0.06	0.07	1.28	4.93
Interest Cover	-	-	-	-0.74	0.43
Oper Prof Mrg	-	-	-	-2.60	0.48
Net Prof Marg%	-	-	-	-1.13	0.45
Ret on Assets	13.51	26.40	27.56	0.26	3.04
Ret on Equity%	13.72	28.03	29.45	-13.38	6.86
Price/Earnings	6.25	2.86	2.06	-4.47	6.59
Divid Cover	3.08	3.03	1.21	-3.02	-
Divid Yield	5.20	11.56	40.00	7.41	-
Earning Yield%	16.00	34.98	48.50	-22.37	15.19
NAV % Mrk Pr	116.82	124.85	164.75	167.31	221.41
Effec Tax Rate	-	-	-	-0.84	-0.69
Def Interval	-	-	-	-1.61	331.52
Sus Grth Rate	9.27	18.77	5.17	-17.81	6.86

SUBSIDIARY & ASSOCIATED COMPANIES

GOLDSTEIN MANAGEMENT SERVICES (PTY) LTD
GROUP FIVE HOLDINGS LTD (45%)

INVESTMENTS

None

SMALDEEL COAL LTD

ABBREVIATION : SMALDEL

JSE SHORT CODE : SML

SECTOR : Mining-Coal

SHAREHOLDERS

Who Owns Whom's Assessment of the Identity of the Ultimate Controlling Shareholder:
EW YOUNG

SHAREHOLDER	PERCENTAGE 1992	1991
SAFCOAL P/L	68.1	---
SCHAUM H H	8.5	---
STRYDOM J E DE L	7.3	---
NEW ERA INSURANCE CO LTD	5.1	---
MANBOS NOM P/L	4.9	---
MITROSPARAS M J	1.3	---
TOTAL	95.2	---

DIRECTORS :
DU PLOOY CJ (Managing Director)
SCHAUM HH (Executive Director)
STRYDOM JEDL (Executive Director)
VAN ROOYEN VP (Executive Director)
YOUNG EW (Executive Chairman

REGISTRATION NUMBER : 91/03572/06

REGISTERED OFFICE
Randpark Building, 20 Dover Street
Randburg
2194
TEL: 011-880 2469
FAX: 011-786 8186

TRANSFER SECRETARY
Rand Registrars Ltd
P O Box 82549, Southdale
2135
TEL: 011-835 1016

COMPANY SECRETARY
RHL White

NATURE OF BUSINESS
The company mines and process coal from deposits in the Ogies area of the Eastern Transvaal. Coal will be processed at the mine premises at Bankfontein from a coal crushing, screening and washing plant.

BANKERS :
Standard Bank of SA Ltd

AUDITORS :
N/A

FAMILIAR BRAND NAMES
N/A

CONTRIBUTION BY ACTIVITY
N/A

YEAR END : July

CAPITAL STRUCTURE

	AUTHORISED	ISSUED
Ords no par value	250000000	44000000

FINANCIAL STATISTICS (AT FINANCIAL YEAR END)

(Amts in R'000)	1992 Jul	1991 Dec
Ord S/H Int	-	34241
Long Trm Loans	-	10200
Iss Ord Share	44000	34000
Total Liab	-	11659
Current Liab	-	1459
Total Assets	-	45900
Current Assets	-	8000
Turnover	18436	-
Oper Profit	5650	-
Interest Paid	3428	-
Tax Paid	1131	-
Prf af Int&Tax	1091	-
Prf att Ord Sh	1091	-
Btm Line Earn	1091	-

PER SHARE STATISTICS (CENTS)

Net Asst Val	-	100.71
Net Earnings	3.71	-
Cash Flow	2.48	-

RATIOS AND OTHER INFORMATION

Current Ratio	-	5.48
Quik/Acid Tst	-	5.48
Debt/Ass Rat	-	0.25
L T L Tot Ass	-	0.22
Debt to Eqity	-	0.34
Interest Cover	1.65	-
Oper Prof Mrg	30.65	-
Net Prof Marg%	5.92	-
Effec Tax Rate	50.90	-

SUBSIDIARY & ASSOCIATED COMPANIES

SMADEEL COLLIERIES (PTY) LTD

INVESTMENTS

None

SMART CENTRE HOLDINGS LTD

ABBREVIATION : SMART

JSE SHORT CODE : SRT

SECTOR : Industrial-Retailers & Wholesalers

SHAREHOLDERS

Who Owns Whom's Assessment of the Identity of the Ultimate Controlling Shareholder:
PEPGRO VIA PEPKOR

SHAREHOLDER	PERCENTAGE 1992	1991
SMART-HOLD BPK	60.8	---
EIGHTY ONE MAIN STREET NOM LTD	10.8	15.5
FIRST NAT NOM P/L	8.5	6.9
STD BANK NOM TVL P/L	5.6	4.9
SMART CENTRE HLDGS LTD EMPL SHARE SCHEME	5.1	5.3
ABSA NOM P/L	3.4	---
VOLKSKAS NOM P/L	3.1	3.0
TRADEGRO ADMIN P/L	---	59.5
TOTAL	97.3	95.1

DIRECTORS :
FOX CW (Managing Director),KORSMAN AC ,LOUW JA
NDLOVU L ,REID AS (Financial Director)
STASSEN C ,WELMAN BE (Dir Human Resources)
WIESE CH (Chairman

REGISTRATION NUMBER : 69/01469/06

REGISTERED OFFICE
Cnr Hyser & Whitworth Str, Heriotdale
2195
TEL: 011-626 3220
FAX: 011-626 2309

TRANSFER SECRETARY
Fraser Street Registrars (Pty) Ltd
P O Box 61178, Marshalltown
2107
TEL: 011-491 0911

COMPANY SECRETARY
A S Reid

NATURE OF BUSINESS
The group retails clothing, footwear, textiles & accessories, which include luggage. The target market of the group is the middle to upper income black consumer market. The group has 136 outlets.

BANKERS :
Standard Bank of SA Ltd

AUDITORS :
Coopers Theron Du Toit

FAMILIAR BRAND NAMES
NEWLANS,PATRICK DANIELS,SMART CENTRE
TOP CENTRE

CONTRIBUTION BY ACTIVITY
N/A

YEAR END : February

DIVIDEND : Ords 1c

Final No 1	(Ldr)14/09/90	(Pay)26/09/90	Amt(c)8.5
Interim No 2	(Ldr)01/03/91	(Pay)30/03/91	Amt(c)3
Final No 3	(Ldr)27/09/91	(Pay)01/11/91	Amt(c)7
Interim No 4	(Ldr)22/05/92	(Pay)24/06/92	Amt(c)7

NUMBER OF EMPLOYEES : 1000

CAPITAL STRUCTURE

	AUTHORISED	ISSUED
Ords 1c	50000000	35692190

FINANCIAL STATISTICS (AT FINANCIAL YEAR END)

(Amts in R'000)	1992 Feb	1991 Jun	1990 Jun	1989 Jun
Ord S/H Int	60563	55175	47964	13970
Long Trm Loans	8598	6093	3737	14010
Iss Ord Share	34949	34522	33697	-
Total Liab	63851	57350	30499	43497
Current Liab	55253	51257	26762	29487
Total Assets	124414	112525	78463	57467
Current Assets	104800	95432	66280	48969
Debtors	70561	65216	50209	33861
Inventory	34213	30181	15838	14803
Turnover	118309	181983	128888	104852
Oper Profit	20363	26340	20585	14248
Interest Paid	2525	4231	4913	2396
Tax Paid	9340	10760	6975	5294
Prf af Int&Tax	8498	11349	8697	6558
Prf att Ord Sh	7688	10287	7847	6052
Btm Line Earn	5388	7901	8147	6052
Dividend Paid	-	1721	2864	880
Mkt Prce(c) YE	395	275	135	-
Depreciation	1614	1918	996	689

PER SHARE STATISTICS (CENTS)

Net Asst Val	173.29	159.83	142.34	-
Net Earnings	22.00	30.00	23.20	-
Dividends	7.00	10.00	8.50	-
Cash Flow	41.58	36.89	28.14	-

RATIOS AND OTHER INFORMATION

Mrk Cap(R000)	138049	94936	45491	-
Current Ratio	1.90	1.86	2.48	1.66
Quik/Acid Tst	1.28	1.27	1.88	1.16
A/C Rec T/ovr	2.52	2.79	2.57	3.10
Tot Ass T/ovr	1.43	1.62	1.64	1.82
Debt/Ass Rat	0.48	0.48	0.37	0.76
L T L Tot Ass	0.04	0.03	0.03	0.24
Debt to Eqity	0.99	0.98	0.60	3.11
Interest Cover	8.06	6.23	4.19	5.95
Oper Prof Mrg	17.21	14.47	15.97	13.59
Net Prof Marg%	6.50	5.65	6.09	5.77
Ret on Assets	24.55	23.41	26.24	24.79
Ret on Equity%	19.04	18.64	16.36	43.32
Price/Earnings	17.95	9.17	5.82	-
Divid Cover	3.14	3.00	2.73	-
Divid Yield	1.77	3.64	6.30	-
Earning Yield%	5.57	10.91	17.19	-
NAV % Mrk Pr	43.87	58.12	105.44	-
Effec Tax Rate	44.88	45.09	39.36	35.06
Def Interval	4.07	2.08	0.53	3.81
Sus Grth Rate	12.69	15.53	10.39	37.02

SUBSIDIARY & ASSOCIATED COMPANIES

SMART CENTRE (BOPHUTHATSWANA) (1988) (PT (50%)
SMART CENTRE (BOTSHABELO) LTD (50%)
SMART CENTRE (BOTSWANA) (PTY) LTD
SMART CENTRE (GAZANKULU) LTD (50%)
SMART CENTRE (KWA ZULU) LTD
SMART CENTRE (LESOTHO) (1988) LTD
SMART CENTRE (MALUTI) (1988) LTD (50%)
SMART CENTRE (NCEDISIZWE) LTD
SMART CENTRE (PTY) LTD
SMART CENTRE (QWA QWA) LTD (50%)
SMART CENTRE (SWAZILAND) (PTY) LTD
SMART CENTRE (TRANSKEI) (PTY) LTD
SMART CENTRE (VENDA) (1988) LTD (50%)
TOP CENTRE (BOPHUTHATSWANA) (PTY) LTD
TOP CENTRE (LESOTHO) (PTY) LTD
TOP CENTRE (VENDA) (PTY) LTD
UNQUOTED LOANS & EQUITIES (PTY) LTD

INVESTMENTS

None

SOLCHEM INVESTMENT HOLDINGS LTD

ABBREVIATION : SOLCHEM

JSE SHORT CODE : SLC

SECTOR : Industrial-Printing & Publishing

SHAREHOLDERS

Who Owns Whom's Assessment of the Identity of the Ultimate Controlling Shareholder:
ANGLO VIA CTP

SHAREHOLDER	PERCENTAGE 1992	1991
CTP LTD	79.7	78.9
ARGUS PENS FUND	7.5	7.5
HORTORS GROUP PENS FUND	3.7	3.7
ARGUS HOLDINGS LTD	2.9	2.9
TOTAL	93.8	93.0

DIRECTORS :
AARONS S (Managing Director),COBURN NM
CRABB KM ,FEATHERSTONE JG
JANKELOWITZ EM (Chairman),LUCK GP ,MOOLMAN TD
SHORT MDW ,SMUTS JHL

REGISTRATION NUMBER : 83/05300/06

REGISTERED OFFICE
Caxton Building, Cor Commando & Blumberg Sts
Industria West, Johannesburg
2092
TEL: 011-402 3990
FAX: 011-402 0119

TRANSFER SECRETARY
Mercantile Registrars Ltd
P O Box 1053, Johannesburg
2000
TEL: 011-333 8181

COMPANY SECRETARY
K M Crabb

NATURE OF BUSINESS
The group's principal activity is the manufacture of printing inks.

BANKERS :
First National Bank of SA Ltd
Standard Bank of SA Ltd

AUDITORS :
KPMG Aiken & Peat

FAMILIAR BRAND NAMES
N/A

CONTRIBUTION BY ACTIVITY
N/A

YEAR END : March

DIVIDEND : Ords 10c

Dividend	(Ldr)21/06/91	(Pay)12/07/91	Amt(c)1
Dividend	(Ldr)03/07/92	(Pay)24/07/92	Amt(c)2

NUMBER OF EMPLOYEES : 279

CAPITAL STRUCTURE

	AUTHORISED	ISSUED
Ords 10c	60000000	40200000

FINANCIAL STATISTICS (AT FINANCIAL YEAR END)

(Amts in R'000)	1992 Mar	1991 Mar	1990 Mar	1989 Mar	1988 Mar
Ord S/H Int	15259	13782	12256	10443	9665
Long Trm Loans	339	603	745	640	136
Iss Ord Share	40200	40200	40200	40200	40200
Total Liab	18614	19358	13640	17775	15284
Current Liab	18275	18755	12895	17135	15148
Total Assets	33873	33140	25896	28218	24949
Current Assets	24743	24232	19441	21020	19234
Debtors	10572	10747	8354	8493	7691
Inventory	13541	13448	11076	12094	10539
Turnover	53763	49202	47658	41951	44724
Oper Profit	5908	5121	5128	2791	5323
Interest Paid	1224	1422	1627	953	530
Tax Paid	2216	1845	1478	613	2214
Prf af Int&Tax	2482	1927	2056	1259	2609
Prf att Ord Sh	2482	1927	2056	1259	2609
Btm Line Earn	2440	1927	2215	1180	1191
Dividend Paid	804	402	402	402	804
Mkt Prce(c) YE	25	35	28	35	60
Depreciation	810	496	454	421	437

PER SHARE STATISTICS (CENTS)

Net Asst Val	37.96	34.28	30.49	25.98	24.04
Net Earnings	6.17	4.79	5.12	3.13	7.55
Dividends	2.00	1.00	1.00	1.00	2.00
Cash Flow	7.95	5.99	6.79	4.18	5.69

RATIOS AND OTHER INFORMATION

Mrk Cap(R000)	10050	14070	11256	14070	24120
Current Ratio	1.35	1.29	1.51	1.23	1.27
Quik/Acid Tst	0.61	0.57	0.65	0.52	0.57
A/C Rec T/ovr	5.09	4.58	5.70	4.94	3.88
Tot Ass T/ovr	1.59	1.48	1.84	1.49	1.20
Debt/Ass Rat	0.55	0.58	0.52	0.63	0.61
L T L Tot Ass	0.01	0.01	0.02	0.02	0.01
Debt to Eqity	1.21	1.39	1.10	1.70	1.58
Interest Cover	4.83	3.60	3.15	2.93	10.05
Oper Prof Mrg	10.99	10.41	10.76	6.65	11.90
Net Prof Marg%	4.62	3.92	4.31	3.00	5.83
Ret on Assets	17.48	15.67	19.93	10.01	14.30
Ret on Equity%	16.27	13.98	16.78	12.06	17.99
Price/Earnings	4.05	7.31	5.47	11.18	7.95
Divid Cover	3.09	4.79	5.12	3.13	3.78
Divid Yield	8.00	2.86	3.57	2.86	3.33
Earning Yield%	24.68	13.69	18.29	8.94	12.58
NAV % Mrk Pr	151.83	97.95	108.88	74.22	40.07
Effec Tax Rate	48.89	48.67	40.27	35.36	47.92
Def Interval	2.73	4.84	2.63	6.84	0.99
Sus Grth Rate	11.00	11.07	13.50	8.21	18.67

SUBSIDIARY & ASSOCIATED COMPANIES

HENGI INVESTMENTS (PTY) LTD
HR TARR & SONS (PTY) LTD
SOLCHEM (PTY) LTD
SOLCHEM CAPE (PTY) LTD
SOLCHEM NATAL (PTY) LTD
SOLCHEM PROPERTIES (PTY) LTD
SOLCHEM TVL (PTY) LTD
SUNCHEM PROPERTIES (PTY) LTD

INVESTMENTS

None

SONDOR INDUSTRIES LTD

ABBREVIATION : SONDOR

JSE SHORT CODE : SNR

SECTOR : Industrial-Engineering

SHAREHOLDERS

Who Owns Whom's Assessment of the Identity of the Ultimate Controlling Shareholder: DIRECTORS

SHAREHOLDER	PERCENTAGE 1992	1991
KILGETTY NOM P/L	---	54.0
ZIMCO HOLDINGS P/L	---	37.3
TOTAL	---	91.2

DIRECTORS :
ASQUITH BK ,BUCHANAN DA
COPELAND GH (Financial Director)
GOLDMAN SL (Chairman),HAUGHLAND N ,HINDE MHD
JORDAAN L ,MARX RMS (Joint Managing Director)
MCCOY S ,TILNEY BD (Joint Managing Director)
WEIR PJ

REGISTRATION NUMBER : 87/03475/06

REGISTERED OFFICE
901 Monte Carlo Building, Foreshore
Cape town
8001
TEL: 021-419 3800
FAX: 021-25 1590

TRANSFER SECRETARY
Kilgetty Trust (Pty) Ltd
P O Box 4033, Cape Town
8000
TEL: 021-21 1860

COMPANY SECRETARY
Kilgetty Secretarial Services (Pty) Ltd

NATURE OF BUSINESS
The company manufactures expanded polyethylenes and vinyl acetates, and converts open and closed cell expanded rubbers and plastics. Products incl plastic foam sheeting, foam strip and foam cord, insulation laminations, foam packaging inserts, sound absorption polyurethane foam, foam tubing, adhesive foam tapes, vacuum formed foam sheets, and heat mouldings (shin guards, helmet liners).

BANKERS :
First National Bank of SA Ltd

AUDITORS :
BDO Spencer Steward

FAMILIAR BRAND NAMES
ACRYBAND,FORMAJOINT,GLAZEX,GROUTEX,JOINTEX
LAPSEAL,POLYCLOSURES,POLYCORD,SONDORBAND
SOUNDSEAL

CONTRIBUTION BY ACTIVITY
N/A

YEAR END : March

DIVIDEND : Ords no par value

Interim	(Ldr)16/11/90	(Pay)14/12/90	Amt(c)2.5
Final	(Ldr)28/06/91	(Pay)19/07/91	Amt(c)3

NUMBER OF EMPLOYEES : 243

CAPITAL STRUCTURE

	AUTHORISED	ISSUED
Ords no par value	80003000	24000000
Red Unsec Sub Debs 35c (Linked to	24000000	24000000

FINANCIAL STATISTICS (AT FINANCIAL YEAR END)

(Amts in R'000)	1992 Mar	1991 Mar	1990 Mar	1989 Jun	1988 Jun
Ord S/H Int	4476	10417	7330	4046	1789
Long Trm Loans	11873	5077	3392	4262	3748
Iss Ord Share	24000	24000	24000	24000	24000
Total Liab	15547	7512	5495	6802	5504
Current Liab	3674	2435	2103	2540	1756
Total Assets	19702	17929	12825	10848	7293
Intang Assets	321	*	*	*	*
Current Assets	11171	9736	9131	7965	6143
Debtors	5684	3284	3693	5016	2901
Inventory	5328	3182	1932	2758	1957
Turnover	25569	19230	14151	17720	12772
Oper Profit	5184	5267	4388	5568	3769
Interest Paid	173	118	-	-	-
Tax Paid	2445	2062	1104	1576	1531
Prf af Int&Tax	2566	3087	3284	3992	2238
Prf att Ord Sh	-5834	3087	3284	3992	2238
Btm Line Earn	-5941	3087	3284	3992	2238
Dividend Paid	-	-	-	1734	4590
Mkt Prce(c) YE	70	70	80	95	45
Depreciation	983	416	241	295	194

PER SHARE STATISTICS (CENTS)

Net Asst Val	17.31	43.40	30.54	16.86	7.45
Net Earnings	10.69	12.86	13.68	16.63	7.70
Dividends	-	-	-	5.50	3.85
Cash Flow	16.69	19.26	19.75	18.28	10.48

RATIOS AND OTHER INFORMATION

Mrk Cap(R000)	16800	16800	19200	22800	10800
Current Ratio	3.04	4.00	4.34	3.14	3.50
Quik/Acid Tst	1.59	2.69	3.42	2.05	2.38
A/C Rec T/ovr	4.50	5.86	5.11	3.53	4.40
Tot Ass T/ovr	1.30	1.07	1.47	1.63	1.75
Debt/Ass Rat	0.70	0.34	0.41	0.61	0.74
L T L Tot Ass	0.51	0.21	0.25	0.38	0.50
Debt to Eqity	3.07	0.59	0.72	1.64	3.03
Interest Cover	29.97	44.64	-	-	-
Oper Prof Mrg	20.27	27.39	31.01	31.42	29.51
Net Prof Marg%	-22.82	16.05	23.21	22.53	17.52
Ret on Assets	26.31	29.38	45.62	51.33	51.68
Ret on Equity%	-130.34	29.63	59.74	98.67	125.10
Price/Earnings	6.55	5.44	5.85	5.71	5.84
Divid Cover	-	-	-	3.02	2.00

Divid Yield	-	-	-	5.79	8.56
Earning Yield%	15.27	18.37	17.10	17.51	17.11
NAV % Mrk Pr	24.73	62.01	38.18	17.75	16.56
Effec Tax Rate	39.67	0.97	-	1.99	11.25
Def Interval	0.50	0.56	0.11	0.20	0.00
Sus Grth Rate	-130.34	29.63	44.80	55.81	-131.47

SUBSIDIARY & ASSOCIATED COMPANIES

SONDOR CONVERTERS (PTY) LTD
SONDOR TAPE CONVERTERS (PTY) LTD

INVESTMENTS

None

SOUTH AFRICAN BREWERIES LTD

ABBREVIATION : SA-BREWS

JSE SHORT CODE : SAB

SECTOR : Industrial-Beverages & Hotels

SHAREHOLDERS

Who Owns Whom's Assessment of the Identity of the Ultimate Controlling Shareholder: ANGLO AMERICAN / LIBERTY VIA BEVCON

SHAREHOLDER	PERCENTAGE 1992	1991
GEMLIB INV P/L	34.3	34.9
SA MUTUAL	13.4	13.5
STD BANK NOM TVL P/L	9.4	8.9
CMB NOM P/L	8.7	---
LIBERTY LIFE ASSOC OF AFRICA LTD	4.7	4.7
FIRST NAT NOM P/L	1.6	1.6
EIGHTY ONE MAIN STREET NOM LTD	1.5	1.0
SOUTHERN LIFE ASSOC LTD	1.2	---
LONDON REGISTER ACCOUNT	---	1.0
SANLAM	---	3.0
SANKERN E/B	---	4.7
TOTAL	74.7	73.3

DIRECTORS :
BECK DE LA H WF ,BRAY VG ,COX NG ,DE VILLIERS HP
GORDON D ,HOOD GW ,KAHN JM (Executive Chairman)
LEVETT MJ ,LLOYD RL
MACFARLANE WS (Financial Director),MACKAY EAG
MAXWELL KW ,RETIEF PF ,ROSHOLT AM ,SUNTER CL
VAN DER WATT L ,WILLIAMS KR ,WYMAN MI

REGISTRATION NUMBER : 69/16025/06

REGISTERED OFFICE
2 Jan Smuts Avenue, Johannesburg
2001
TEL: 011-339 4711
FAX: 011-339 1830

TRANSFER SECRETARY
Consolidated Share Registrars Ltd
P O Box 61051, Marshalltown
2107
TEL: 011-492 1620

COMPANY SECRETARY
A O C Tonkinson

NATURE OF BUSINESS
An investment holding company with significant interests in the Hotel, Beverage, Retailing, Furniture, Footwear, Beer & Consumer Goods sectors of the SA economy. The company has a controlling interest in a number of listed companies.

BANKERS :
Standard Bank of SA Ltd
First National Bank of SA Ltd

AUDITORS :
N/A

FAMILIAR BRAND NAMES
ABC SHOES,ALPINE (FURNITURE),AMSTEL BEER
AQUARIUS (APPLIANCES),BERDA (APPLIANCES)
BLAIKIES,CARLING BLACK LABEL,CASTLE BEER
CASTLE MILK STOUT,CELROSE,CHIBUKU
COTTAGE LOOK (TEXTILES),CRICKET (LIGHTERS)
CUTHBERTS,DAYDREAM (TEXTILES),EARLY BIRD TV
ECKO (APPLIANCES),EDBLO (BEDDING)
EDENROSE (TEXTILES),EDGARS,EXPRESS,FAIRDEAL
FASCO (TEXTILES),FIREFLY (LIGHTERS)
FRYSTARK (FURNITURE),FUJICA (APPLIANCES)
FURNITURE CITY,GEEN & RICHARDS
GRAFTON EVEREST (FURNITURE),GRAPETISER
GREAVES & THOMAS (FURNITURE),HANSA BEER,HAZ
HEINEKEN,HERITAGE,HIGHPOINT (FURNITURE)
HOLIDAY INN,IMPULSE (FURNITURE),INTERPAK
JATEX (TEXTILES),JET,JUST JUICE,KING COBBLER
LASER (LIGHTERS),LION BEER,LION MATCHES
LONDON BRIDGE,LOVING TOUCH (SHAVERS),LUBNERS
MADISON (FURNITURE),MAMKHULU,MANDELLES
MATTEX (TEXTILES),MCNAMEES,MELODYS
MULTIPRINT,MULTISERV,OHLSSONS BEER
PARKER KNOLL (FURNITURE)
PEACH & HATTON (FURNITURE),PINE NUT
PINEWARE (APPLIANCES),POWERCRAFT (FURNITURE)
PREMIER SPRINGS,PRONTAPRINT
RELIABLE (FURNITURE),ROWENTA (APPLIANCES)
RUF (BEDDING),SALES HOUSE
SALTON (APPLIANCES),SARMA (FURNITURE),SCOTTS
SEALY (BEDDING),SELECT-A-SHOE
SLUMBERLAND (BEDDING),SOFTEX (BEDDING)
STAR (FURNITURE),STEELCRAFT (APPLIANCES)
STEELFURN (FURNITURE),SUN HOTELS
SURELITE MATCHES,THER-A-PEDIC (BEDDING)
TIP TOP,TIVLI (APPLIANCES),TRIANGLE
UNITA (FURNITURE),VITAFOAM,WILKINSON SWORD

CONTRIBUTION BY ACTIVITY
Beverages (% Turnover) (35.0%)
Retail (49.0%)
Manufacturing (7.8%)
Hotels (3.2%)
Other (5.0%)

YEAR END : March

DIVIDEND : Ords 20c

Interim	(Ldr)24/11/89	(Pay)29/12/89	Amt(c)25
Final	(Ldr)01/06/90	(Pay)02/07/90	Amt(c)76
Interim	(Ldr)23/11/90	(Pay)31/12/90	Amt(c)30
Final	(Ldr)30/05/91	(Pay)01/07/91	Amt(c)88
Interim	(Ldr)29/11/91	(Pay)31/12/91	Amt(c)33
Final	(Ldr)29/05/92	(Pay)02/07/92	Amt(c)97
Interim	(Ldr)27/11/92	(Pay)31/12/92	Amt(c)35

NUMBER OF EMPLOYEES : 89500

CAPITAL STRUCTURE

	AUTHORISED	ISSUED
7% Red Cum Prefs R1	44000000	42630618
7% Cum Prefs R1	2475000	2475000
Ords 20c	330000000	272690899
Auto Conv Cum Prefs 20c	36000000	8897477
6,2% Cum Prefs R2	1000000	1000000
14% Unsec Corporate Bonds	2000	2000

FINANCIAL STATISTICS (AT FINANCIAL YEAR END)

(Amts in R'000)	1992 Mar	1991 Mar	1990 Mar	1989 Mar	1988 Mar
Ord S/H Int	3677100	3130900	2706300	2278000	1948800
Long Trm Loans	3628400	3156700	2603400	2521900	1639700
Iss Ord Share	268135	268135	268100	268000	268000
Total Liab	8160200	7179300	5670300	4722000	3277600
Current Liab	4531800	4022600	3066900	2200100	1637900
Total Assets	11837300	10310200	8376600	6999000	5226400
Intang Assets	*	*	*	1000	*
Current Assets	4716700	4323600	3709300	2774400	2194900
Debtors	2296000	2041700	1706400	1270300	1023900
Inventory	2231000	1973600	1680300	1272300	1116600
Turnover	17698600	16121900	13250500	10596800	8682500
Oper Profit	1822300	1732400	1316400	981400	746100
Interest Paid	449200	373400	328600	179000	109720
Tax Paid	559800	607900	445200	332800	228137
Prf af Int&Tax	1009900	932500	716400	562000	408243
Prf att Ord Sh	778800	710600	603700	501800	388943
Btm Line Earn	768100	700700	611500	499100	383543
Dividend Paid	348600	316400	270800	225100	176900
Mkt Prce(c) YE	5650	4725	3400	2300	1775
Depreciation	566928	504378	338645	231607	170302

PER SHARE STATISTICS (CENTS)

Net Asst Val	1371.36	1167.66	1009.44	849.63	727.16
Net Earnings	290.40	265.00	225.20	187.20	146.50
Dividends	130.00	118.00	101.00	84.00	66.00
Cash Flow	507.96	458.20	358.88	267.84	204.39

RATIOS AND OTHER INFORMATION

Mrk Cap(R000)	15149628	12669379	9115400	6164000	4757000
Current Ratio	1.04	1.07	1.21	1.26	1.34
Quik/Acid Tst	0.55	0.58	0.66	0.68	0.66
A/C Rec T/ovr	7.71	7.90	7.77	8.34	8.48
Tot Ass T/ovr	1.50	1.56	1.58	1.51	1.66
Debt/Ass Rat	0.53	0.55	0.52	0.50	0.46
L T L Tot Ass	0.15	0.16	0.15	0.18	0.15
Debt to Eqity	1.71	1.81	1.61	1.53	1.23
Interest Cover	4.22	4.82	4.21	5.77	6.80
Oper Prof Mrg	10.30	10.75	9.93	9.26	8.59
Net Prof Marg%	4.40	4.41	4.56	4.74	4.48
Ret on Assets	17.36	18.96	18.96	16.61	16.27
Ret on Equity%	21.18	22.70	22.31	22.03	19.96
Price/Earnings	19.46	17.83	15.10	12.29	12.12
Divid Cover	2.23	2.25	2.23	2.23	2.22
Divid Yield	2.30	2.50	2.97	3.65	3.72
Earning Yield%	5.14	5.61	6.62	8.14	8.25
NAV % Mrk Pr	24.27	24.71	29.69	36.94	40.97
Effec Tax Rate	38.51	41.02	36.14	35.78	25.83
Def Interval	2.17	1.95	2.12	2.38	1.81
Sus Grth Rate	11.70	12.59	12.30	12.15	10.88

SUBSIDIARY & ASSOCIATED COMPANIES

AMALGAMATED BEVERAGE CANNERS (PTY) LTD (24%)
AMALGAMATED BEVERAGE INDUSTRIES LTD
AMALGAMATED RETAIL LTD
APPLETISER PURE FRUIT JUICES (PTY) LTD
ASSOCIATED FURNITURE COMPANIES LTD
BOYMANS LTD (36%)
CANTERBURY OVERSEAS INC
CAPE DISPLAY (PTY) LTD
CERES FRUIT JUICES (PTY) LTD (49%)
CONSHU HOLDINGS LTD (33%)
DA GAMA TEXTILE CO LTD
DISTILLERS CORPORATION (SA) LTD (30%)
EDGARS STORES LTD
KALLENBACH-HENDLER (PTY) LTD (50%)
LION MATCH CO LTD
OHLSSON'S BREWERY TRANSKEI (PTY) LTD
OHLSSON'S CAPE BREWERIES LTD
OHLSSON'S CAPE BREWERIES LTD
OK BAZAARS (1929) LTD
OKFIN (PTY) LTD (50%)
RESINKEM (PTY) LTD (50%)
ROMATEX LIMITED (21%)
SAB HOP FARMS (PTY) LTD
SABFIN (PTY) LTD
SABRE FINANCE LTD
SEYCHELLES BREWERIES LTD (20%)
SOUTHERN SUN HOTEL HOLDINGS LTD
SPANKOR LTD (50%)
STELLENBOSCH FARMERS WINERY GROUP LTD (30%)
SUN INTERNATIONAL INC (20%)
UNITED BREWERIES (PTY) LTD
WESTERN PROVINCE PRESERVING CO (PTY) LTD
WESTERN PROVINCE PRESERVING CO. (PTY) LT

INVESTMENTS

DELTA CORPORATION LTD (17%)
SUN INTERNATIONAL (BOPHUTHATSWANA) LTD (2%)
TRANSKEI SUN INTERNATIONAL LTD (2%)

SOUTH AFRICAN DRUGGISTS LTD

ABBREVIATION : SA-DRUG

JSE SHORT CODE : SDG

SECTOR : Industrial-Pharmaceutical & Medical

SHAREHOLDERS

Who Owns Whom's Assessment of the Identity of the Ultimate Controlling Shareholder:
SANLAM VIA SANKORP VIA MALBAK

SHAREHOLDER	PERCENTAGE 1992	1991
MALBAK INV (SAD) P/L	84.0	---
CMB NOM P/L	11.7	---
METROPOLITAN LIFE LTD	1.3	2.3
YSKOR PENS FUND	---	1.0
FEDERALE SELEKSIES BPK	---	68.0
SANLAM	---	21.1
TOTAL	97.0	92.4

DIRECTORS :
BARBAROVICH FJM (Financial Director)
BENINGFIELD PJJ (Chief Executive),EDMOND RT
HOMANN NC (Dir Human Resources),MICHAEL GGF
MORRIS LR ,NEL JL ,O'DONNELL BT ,RETIEF FP PROF
STANTON CL ,THOMAS GS (Chairman),VAN DER WALT PJJ

REGISTRATION NUMBER : 05/07450/06

REGISTERED OFFICE
7 Sturdee Avenue, Rosebank
Johannesburg
2196
TEL: 011-788 2060
FAX: 011-788 2069

TRANSFER SECRETARY
Central Registrars Ltd
P O Box 4844, Johannesburg
2000
TEL: 011-331 0051

COMPANY SECRETARY
J M C Visser

NATURE OF BUSINESS
The group is engaged in the manufacture, marketing and distribution of pharmaceutical products & the distribution of medical, dental, veterinary and sundry products.

BANKERS :
Standard Bank of SA Ltd, Nedperm Bank Ltd
Trust Bank of Africa Ltd

AUDITORS :
KPMG Aiken & Peat
Price Waterhouse Meyernel

FAMILIAR BRAND NAMES
APEX BUDDIES,BRUT,COMOPHARM,DURACELL,DUREX EXCEL,FABERGE,LABETHICA,LADY AFRICA,LENNON LENSTRIP,LINK,PANVET,REGULETTES,SAFYR BLEU SERAVAC,ULSANIC,WOODS PEPPERMINT CURE

CONTRIBUTION BY ACTIVITY
Pharmaceutical (% income before tax) (60.1%)
Distribution (32.2%)
Chemical & Medical Equipment (15.4%)
Corporate (-7.7%)

YEAR END : August

DIVIDEND :Ords 30c

Interim No 83	(Ldr)01/12/89	(Pay)05/01/90	Amt(c)4.75
Final No 84	(Ldr)01/06/90	(Pay)04/07/90	Amt(c)5.25
Interim No 85	(Ldr)07/12/90	(Pay)04/01/91	Amt(c)4.75
Final No 86	(Ldr)30/05/91	(Pay)05/07/91	Amt(c)5.25
Interim No 87	(Ldr)06/12/91	(Pay)03/01/92	Amt(c)23.75
Final No 88	(Ldr)20/11/92	(Pay)04/12/92	Amt(c)26.25

NUMBER OF EMPLOYEES : 3934

CAPITAL STRUCTURE

	AUTHORISED	ISSUED
Ords 30c	150000000	50838449

FINANCIAL STATISTICS (AT FINANCIAL YEAR END)

(Amts in R'000)	1992 Aug	1991 Mar	1990 Mar	1989 Mar	1988 Mar
Ord S/H Int	369357	202938	191704	167170	139319
Long Trm Loans	37824	39150	18952	10430	16235
Iss Ord Share	50838	28230	28230	28230	28230
Total Liab	521103	313877	203745	154007	117940
Current Liab	483279	274727	184793	143577	101705
Total Assets	890460	516815	395434	321150	257259
Intang Assets	*	*	15	27	*
Current Assets	593200	360966	312656	247649	194637
Debtors	326754	184177	161126	132191	98606
Inventory	264791	172064	148786	113269	94775
Turnover	1508627	1061880	948016	790602	675036
Oper Profit	101600	84001	97729	92803	66050
Interest Paid	40823	24030	23805	19789	5067
Tax Paid	26664	28829	33760	37093	28677
Prf af Int&Tax	35975	33302	41773	42584	32306
Prf att Ord Sh	35404	33095	40581	41041	32004
Btm Line Earn	-26247	32370	38491	41992	34079
Dividend Paid	20050	14115	14115	14115	11364
Mkt Prce(c) YE	1425	1000	1500	1400	1100
Depreciation	24529	14866	5420	4485	3756

PER SHARE STATISTICS (CENTS)

Net Asst Val	726.54	718.87	679.03	592.08	493.51
Net Earnings	94.00	117.20	140.60	144.30	113.40
Dividends	50.00	50.00	50.00	50.00	40.00
Cash Flow	108.31	170.56	168.28	165.71	122.47

RATIOS AND OTHER INFORMATION

Mrk Cap(R000)	724442	282300	423450	395220	310530
Current Ratio	1.23	1.31	1.69	1.72	1.91
Quik/Acid Tst	0.68	0.69	0.89	0.94	0.98
A/C Rec T/ovr	3.26	5.77	5.88	5.98	6.85
Tot Ass T/ovr	1.20	2.05	2.40	2.46	2.62
Debt/Ass Rat	0.58	0.60	0.51	0.47	0.45
L T L Tot Ass	0.04	0.07	0.04	0.02	0.05
Debt to Eqity	1.40	1.53	1.05	0.90	0.83
Interest Cover	2.49	3.50	4.11	4.69	13.04
Oper Prof Mrg	6.73	7.91	10.31	11.74	9.78
Net Prof Marg%	2.35	3.12	4.28	5.19	4.74
Ret on Assets	8.20	16.67	25.12	30.97	25.74
Ret on Equity%	6.77	16.31	21.17	24.55	22.97
Price/Earnings	15.16	8.53	10.67	9.70	9.70
Divid Cover	1.88	2.34	2.81	2.89	2.84
Divid Yield	3.51	5.00	3.33	3.57	3.64
Earning Yield%	6.60	11.72	9.37	10.31	10.31
NAV % Mrk Pr	50.99	71.89	45.27	42.29	44.86
Effec Tax Rate	46.31	46.09	44.12	45.74	49.06
Def Interval	1.75	2.86	1.12	0.49	0.54
Sus Grth Rate	4.16	9.35	13.81	16.11	14.81

SUBSIDIARY & ASSOCIATED COMPANIES

CONTINENTAL ETHICALS (PTY) LTD
EI ROGOFF CHEMICALS (PTY) LTD
FINE CHEMICALS CORPORATION (PTY) LTD
FINE CHEMICALS CORPORATION (PTY) LTD
HEYNES MATHEW LIMITED
HEYNES MATTHEW LTD
LABETHICA (PTY) LTD
LENNON DIAGNOSTICS (PTY) LTD
LENNON LIMITED
LENNON LTD
MANEL DISTRIBUTORS (PTY) LTD
PROTEA MEDICAL & LABORATORY LTD
SUPERWEAVE (PTY) LTD
SURGICARE (PTY) LTD

INVESTMENTS

ETKINDS MANAGEMENT SERVICES (PTY) LTD (50 SH)
MEGAMED (PTY) LTD (200 SH)
NORISTAN HOLDINGS LTD (2754 SH)

SOUTH AFRICAN EAGLE INSURANCE CO LTD

ABBREVIATION : S-A-EAGLE

JSE SHORT CODE : SAE

SECTOR : Financial-Insurance

SHAREHOLDERS

Who Owns Whom's Assessment of the Identity of the Ultimate Controlling Shareholder:
BAT INDUSTRIES PLC

SHAREHOLDER	PERCENTAGE 1992	1991
FIRST NAT NOM P/L	56.6	---
INSTITUTIONAL INV LTD	24.1	24.1
UAL NOM P/L	2.6	2.4
SA MUTUAL	2.4	---
SA FIRE HOUSE LTD	1.8	1.8
EIGHTY ONE MAIN STREET NOM LTD	1.4	1.4
RESIDENT NOM LTD	1.3	1.3
BARCLAYS NAT NOM P/L	---	58.1
TOTAL	90.1	89.0

DIRECTORS :
BISHOP DB ,BRAGG WFE ,CHARTRAND P
DE RAUVILLE JPG ,DOWLING JP ,EDMUNDS DB
HASLETT FN (Chairman),KING MW ,LOCKWOOD GH
MARTIN PT (Managing Director),MULLER SL HON
PAMENSKY JL
WILKINSON BC (Deputy Managing Director

REGISTRATION NUMBER : 65/06764/06

REGISTERED OFFICE
5th Floor, Eagle House, 70 Fox Str
Johannesburg
2001
TEL: 011-370 9111
FAX: 011-836 5541

TRANSFER SECRETARY
Mercantile Registrars Ltd
P O Box 1053, Johannesburg
2000
TEL: 011-333 8181

COMPANY SECRETARY
H J van den Brink

NATURE OF BUSINESS
S A Eagle conducts all classes of short term insurance business in SA and neighbouring territories.

BANKERS :
N/A

AUDITORS :
N/A

FAMILIAR BRAND NAMES
N/A

CONTRIBUTION BY ACTIVITY
N/A

YEAR END : December

DIVIDEND : Ords 25c

Interim No 36	(Ldr)24/08/90	(Pay)17/09/90	Amt(c)60
Final No 37	(Ldr)22/02/91	(Pay)22/03/91	Amt(c)90
Interim No 38	(Ldr)23/08/91	(Pay)17/09/91	Amt(c)60
Final No 39	(Ldr)21/02/92	(Pay)20/03/92	Amt(c)105
Interim No 40	(Ldr)21/08/92	(Pay)15/09/92	Amt(c)75

NUMBER OF EMPLOYEES : 1999

CAPITAL STRUCTURE

	AUTHORISED	ISSUED
Ords 25c	13207360	12257360

FINANCIAL STATISTICS (AT FINANCIAL YEAR END)

(Amts in R'000)	1991 Dec	1990 Dec	1989 Dec	1988	1987
Ord S/H Int	652722	486458	158983	118369	93318
Long Trm Loans	209721	175065	180202	414729	371790
Iss Ord Share	12163	12158	12257	12257	12257
Total Liab	514944	461585	463155	414729	371790
Current Liab	305223	286520	282953	-	-
Total Assets	1167666	948043	622138	648835	572268
Current Assets	205708	162188	145532	115737	116851
Debtors	20153	16921	18796	-	-
Inventory	-	-	-	115737	116851
Turnover	724573	589271	506080	-	-
Oper Profit	-7003	-41270	17321	73712	37462
Tax Paid	12811	-12826	22785	37781	8950
Prf af Int&Tax	34935	23974	47026	46665	25414
Prf att Ord Sh	34935	23974	45753	46665	25414
Btm Line Earn	34935	23974	45753	46665	25414
Dividend Paid	20070	18238	22795	21595	14997
Mkt Prce(c) YE	2400	2050	2100	1725	1075
Depreciation	9416	6721	5426	-	-

PER SHARE STATISTICS (CENTS)

Net Asst Val	5366.46	4001.14	1297.08	965.73	761.34
Net Earnings	287.50	198.50	392.00	-	-
Dividends	165.00	150.00	190.00	-	-
Cash Flow	435.54	133.36	463.40	380.72	207.34

RATIOS AND OTHER INFORMATION

Mrk Cap(R000)	291912	249239	257397	211433	131763
Current Ratio	0.67	0.57	0.51	-	-
Quik/Acid Tst	0.67	0.57	0.51	-	-
A/C Rec T/ovr	35.95	34.82	26.92	-	-
Tot Ass T/ovr	0.62	0.62	0.81	-	-
Debt/Ass Rat	0.26	0.30	0.46	0.64	0.65
L T L Tot Ass	0.00	0.00	0.00	0.64	0.65
Debt to Eqity	0.47	0.59	1.79	3.50	3.98
Oper Prof Mrg	-0.97	-7.00	3.42	-	-
Net Prof Marg%	4.82	4.07	9.04	-	-
Ret on Assets	4.09	1.18	11.22	13.02	6.00
Ret on Equity%	5.35	4.93	28.78	39.42	27.23
Price/Earnings	8.35	10.33	5.36	-	-
Divid Cover	1.74	1.32	2.06	-	-
Divid Yield	6.88	7.32	9.05	-	-
Earning Yield%	11.98	9.68	18.67	-	-
NAV % Mrk Pr	223.60	195.18	61.77	55.98	70.82
Effec Tax Rate	-54.71	-4.01	78.62	51.25	23.89
Def Interval	0.24	0.58	0.62	8.89	14.63
Sus Grth Rate	2.28	1.18	14.44	21.18	11.16

SUBSIDIARY & ASSOCIATED COMPANIES

AFRICAN GUARANTEE & INDEMNITY CO. LTD
BOTSWANA EAGLE INSURANCE CO. LTD
BRITISH AFRICAN PROPERTIES LTD
EAGLE INSURANCE COMPANY LTD (ZIMBABWE)
EAGLE PROPERTIES (BENONI) (PTY) LTD
EAGLE PROPERTIES (BLOEMFONTEIN) (PTY) LT
EAGLE PROPERTIES (EAST LONDON) (PTY) LTD
EAGLE PROPERTIES (KRUGERSDORP) (PTY) LTD
EAGLE PROPERTIES (NELSPRUIT) (PTY) LTD
EAGLE STAR CO OF SA LTD
EAGLE STAR HOUSE (JOHANNESBURG) LTD
SURREY VIEW (PTY) LTD
TARAZED (PTY) LTD
THE SOUTH AFRICAN FIRE & ACCIDENT CO LTD
THREADNEEDLE PROPERTIES (SA) LTD
WAVERLEY PROPERTIES (PTY) LTD

INVESTMENTS

None

SOUTH AFRICAN FREIGHT CORP LTD

ABBREVIATION : SAFCOR

JSE SHORT CODE : SFC

SECTOR : Industrial-Industrial Holding

SHAREHOLDERS

Who Owns Whom's Assessment of the Identity of the Ultimate Controlling Shareholder:
CURRIE FINANCE CORP

SHAREHOLDER	PERCENTAGE 1992	1991
CURRIE FINANCE CORP LTD	50.0	50.0
COMBINE CARGO INV LTD	10.4	10.4
AVI DIVERSIFIED HOLDINGS LTD	9.2	9.2
STD BANK NOM TVL P/L	8.8	6.0
CMB NOM P/L	2.4	---
SFSS NOM P/L	2.3	2.2
JOHANNESBURG MUNICIPAL PENS FUND	1.4	1.2
NEDBANK NOM LTD	1.4	---
OCEAN MANDARIN LTD	---	1.8
DESILLA J P	---	2.2
SANLAM	---	1.7
VOLKSKAS NOM P/L	---	1.2
TOTAL	85.9	85.9

DIRECTORS :
BRODIE MH (Executive Chairman)
CAWOOD EL (Operations Director)
COX C (Operations Director)
DESILLA JP (Managing Director),ROBBERTZE JC
ROYSTON D ,THOMPSON NB (Financial Director)
VISSER HD (Operations Director)
WOMERSLEY PD (Operations Director

REGISTRATION NUMBER : 69/14720/06

REGISTERED OFFICE
46 Webber Street, Selby
Johannesburg
2001
TEL: 011-493 4900
FAX: 011-493 2734

TRANSFER SECRETARY
Mercantile Registrars Ltd
P O Box 1053, Johannesburg
2000
TEL: 011-333 8181

COMPANY SECRETARY
N B Thompson

NATURE OF BUSINESS
The group is engaged in air and sea freight, forwarding and clearing operations, road transport, domestic freight distribution and warehousing.

BANKERS :
First National Bank of SA Ltd

AUDITORS :
Ernst & Young

FAMILIAR BRAND NAMES
SAFCOR

CONTRIBUTION BY ACTIVITY
N/A

YEAR END : June

DIVIDEND : Ords 1c

Interim No 6	(Ldr)02/03/90	(Pay)16/03/90	Amt(c)12
Final No 7	(Ldr)31/08/90	(Pay)14/09/90	Amt(c)18
Interim No 8	(Ldr)01/03/91	(Pay)15/03/91	Amt(c)13
Final No 9	(Ldr)30/08/91	(Pay)20/09/91	Amt(c)24
Interim No 10	(Ldr)28/02/92	(Pay)13/03/92	Amt(c)18
Final No 11	(Ldr)11/09/92	(Pay)25/09/92	Amt(c)29

NUMBER OF EMPLOYEES : 1118

CAPITAL STRUCTURE

	AUTHORISED	ISSUED
Ords 1c	25000000	22523333

FINANCIAL STATISTICS (AT FINANCIAL YEAR END)

(Amts in R'000)	1992 Jun	1991 Jun	1990 Jun	1989 Jun	1988 Jun
Ord S/H Int	57397	47631	37811	30912	25304
Long Trm Loans	-	493	3532	3974	2436
Iss Ord Share	22523	22523	22073	21857	21840
Total Liab	69828	80564	89166	89362	59301
Current Liab	69828	80071	85634	85388	56865
Total Assets	127225	128195	126977	120033	84605
Intang Assets	*	*	*	241	*
Current Assets	108136	111962	105363	100064	69598
Debtors	89537	66343	66501	75600	55481
Inventory	-	-	644	796	465
Turnover	1201618	918185	961261	824019	583272
Oper Profit	34026	30418	27058	23193	14539
Interest Paid	35	74	675	700	314
Tax Paid	15901	14333	13322	12040	7328
Prf af Int&Tax	18718	16446	13329	10903	6897
Prf att Ord Sh	18797	16478	13546	10768	7311
Btm Line Earn	20796	17672	14201	10768	6489

Dividend Paid	10586	8334	6622	5464	3494
Mkt Prce(c) YE	750	550	280	220	190
Depreciation	4740	5241	5565	3794	2876

PER SHARE STATISTICS (CENTS)

Net Asst Val	254.84	211.48	171.30	140.33	115.86
Net Earnings	83.50	73.50	61.70	49.30	33.90
Dividends	47.00	37.00	30.00	25.00	16.00
Cash Flow	104.15	95.34	84.83	66.38	46.35

RATIOS AND OTHER INFORMATION

Mrk Cap(R000)	168923	123877	61804	48085	41496
Current Ratio	1.55	1.40	1.23	1.17	1.22
Quik/Acid Tst	1.55	1.40	1.22	1.16	1.22
A/C Rec T/ovr	13.42	13.84	14.45	10.90	10.51
Tot Ass T/ovr	9.44	7.16	7.57	6.86	6.89
Debt/Ass Rat	0.55	0.62	0.69	0.73	0.69
L T L Tot Ass	-	-	0.02	0.02	0.01
Debt to Eqity	1.22	1.68	2.32	2.84	2.29
Interest Cover	974.43	415.11	40.25	33.78	46.30
Oper Prof Mrg	2.83	3.31	2.81	2.81	2.49
Net Prof Marg%	1.56	1.79	1.41	1.31	1.25
Ret on Assets	27.30	24.10	21.83	19.88	17.70
Ret on Equity%	32.75	34.60	35.83	34.83	28.89
Price/Earnings	8.98	7.48	4.54	4.46	5.60
Divid Cover	1.78	1.99	2.06	1.97	2.12
Divid Yield	6.27	6.73	10.71	11.36	8.42
Earning Yield%	11.13	13.36	22.04	22.41	17.84
NAV % Mrk Pr	33.98	38.45	61.18	63.78	60.98
Effec Tax Rate	47.52	47.93	50.51	52.91	49.42
Def Interval	-	-	0.11	0.18	0.11
Sus Grth Rate	14.31	17.10	18.31	17.16	15.08

SUBSIDIARY & ASSOCIATED COMPANIES

ALEX CARTAGE (PTY) LTD
COGO FREIGHT LTD (HONG KONG)
COMBINE CARGO LTD
CRANDOR AGENCIES (PTY) LTD
HUTTON ENTERPRISES (PTY) LTD
INTERCITY EXPRESS (PTY) LTD
MARITZBURG FINANCE COMPANY (PTY) LTD
O AND A LOUW TRANSPORT (PTY) LTD
OCEANAIR FREIGHT (PTY) LTD
RSA CARGO (CAPE) (PTY) LTD
SAFCOR (NATAL) (PTY) LTD
SAFCOR AIRCARGO (PTY) LTD
SAFCOR EXPORT PROMOTIONS (PTY) LTD
SAFCOR FORWARDING (JOHANNESBURG) (PTY) L
SAFCOR FORWARDING (PTY) LTD
SAFCOR FREIGHT (PTY) LTD
SAFCOR FREIGHT PROJECTS (PTY) LTD
SAFCOR HOUSE (PTY) LTD
SAFCOR HUTTON FORWARDING (PTY) LTD
SAFCOR ISANDO PROPERTY (PTY) LTD
SAFCOR TRANSVAAL (PTY) LTD
SOUTH AFRICAN DOMESTIC FREIGHT CONSOLIDA
SOUTH AFRICAN FREIGHT CONSOLIDATORS (PTY
SOUTH AFRICAN SHIPS AGENCY (PTY) LTD
SOUTH AFRICAN SHIPS AGENCY MARKETING (PT
SWAZI FREIGHT CORPORATION (PTY) LTD
TRUST (ASIA) LTD

INVESTMENTS

None

SOUTH AFRICAN LAND & EXPLORATION CO LTD

ABBREVIATION : SALLIES

JSE SHORT CODE : SAL

SECTOR : Gold-Rand & others

SHAREHOLDERS

Who Owns Whom's Assessment of the Identity of the Ultimate Controlling Shareholder: ANGLO AMERICAN

SHAREHOLDER	PERCENTAGE 1992	1991
ANGLO AMERICAN CORP OF SA LTD	---	4.6
FERMAIN NOM LTD	---	1.8
FIRST NAT NOM P/L	---	3.2
HIPPO QUARRIES LTD	---	2.2
INDO-CHINA NOM SA P/L	---	6.1
LEWISOHN R B	---	4.5
LONDON CONTROL ACCOUNT	---	15.1
NEDBANK NOM LTD	---	1.1
PETARD NOM LTD	---	18.6
RESIDENT NOM LTD	---	19.7
STD BANK NOM TVL P/L	---	4.2
TOTAL	---	81.0

DIRECTORS :
DOYLE MM ,EUSTACE PJ ,HOLFORD GM ,HOSKING KM
KEWITT L (Chairman & Managing Dir.),MOSTERT PJ
OPPENHEIMER NF ,SUNTER CL ,VAN DER COLF SW

REGISTRATION NUMBER : 01/01879/06

REGISTERED OFFICE
44 Main Street, Johannesburg
2001
TEL: 011-638 9111
FAX: 011-638 5281

TRANSFER SECRETARY
Consolidated Share Registrars Ltd
P O Box 61051, Marshalltown
2107
TEL: 011-492 1620

COMPANY SECRETARY
Anglo American Corp. of SA Ltd

NATURE OF BUSINESS
Since underground operations within the company's mining lease ceased at the end of 1976, the company has treated material from outside sources in its gold plant.

BANKERS :
First National Bank of SA Ltd

AUDITORS :
Ernst & Young

FAMILIAR BRAND NAMES
N/A

CONTRIBUTION BY ACTIVITY
N/A

YEAR END : December

DIVIDEND : Ords 35c

Interim No 98	(Ldr)03/08/90	(Pay)14/09/90	Amt(c)20
Final No 99	(Ldr)08/02/91	(Pay)15/03/91	Amt(c)22
Interim No 100	(Ldr)09/08/91	(Pay)13/09/91	Amt(c)10
Final No 101	(Ldr)07/02/92	(Pay)13/03/92	Amt(c)18

NUMBER OF EMPLOYEES : 309

CAPITAL STRUCTURE

	AUTHORISED	ISSUED
Ords 35c	9500000	9314132

FINANCIAL STATISTICS (AT FINANCIAL YEAR END)

(Amts in R'000)	1991 Dec	1990 Dec	1989 Dec	1988	1987
Ord S/H Int	40273	40654	40671	40525	40480
Long Trm Loans	-	-	-	7751	8891
Iss Ord Share	9314	9183	9183	9207	9183
Total Liab	5877	6564	6666	15502	17782
Current Liab	5877	6564	6666	7751	8891
Total Assets	46150	47218	47337	59987	62478
Current Assets	9561	10304	10359	11711	13107
Debtors	4829	4753	2765	-	-
Inventory	2312	2175	1986	11711	13107
Turnover	51058	51819	46001	45849	48597
Oper Profit	2213	4224	5512	8297	10596
Tax Paid	505	1507	2391	3742	4716
Prf af Int&Tax	2227	3653	4180	4555	5880
Prf att Ord Sh	2227	3653	4180	4348	5637
Btm Line Earn	2605	3918	4214	4348	5637
Dividend Paid	2608	3924	4172	4604	5510
Mkt Prce(c) YE	130	190	390	350	675

PER SHARE STATISTICS (CENTS)

Net Asst Val	432.39	442.71	442.89	440.15	440.81
Net Earnings	28.00	42.00	46.00	-	-
Dividends	28.00	42.00	45.00	-	-
Cash Flow	23.91	39.78	45.52	49.47	64.03

RATIOS AND OTHER INFORMATION

Mrk Cap(R000)	12108	17448	35814	32225	61985
Current Ratio	1.63	1.57	1.55	1.51	1.47
Quik/Acid Tst	1.23	1.24	1.26	-	-
A/C Rec T/ovr	10.57	10.90	16.64	-	-
Tot Ass T/ovr	1.11	1.10	0.97	0.76	0.78
Debt/Ass Rat	0.13	0.14	0.14	0.26	0.28
L T L Tot Ass	-	-	-	0.13	0.14
Debt to Eqity	0.15	0.16	0.16	0.38	0.44
Oper Prof Mrg	4.33	8.15	11.98	18.10	21.80
Net Prof Marg%	4.36	7.05	9.09	9.48	11.60
Ret on Assets	5.92	10.93	13.88	13.83	16.96
Ret on Equity%	5.53	8.99	10.28	10.73	13.93
Price/Earnings	4.64	4.52	8.48	-	-
Divid Cover	1.00	1.00	1.02	-	-
Divid Yield	21.54	22.11	11.54	-	-
Earning Yield%	21.54	22.11	11.79	-	-
NAV % Mrk Pr	332.61	233.00	113.56	125.76	65.31
Effec Tax Rate	18.54	29.28	-	45.10	44.51
Def Interval	-	-	-	1.70	1.51
Sus Grth Rate	-0.95	-0.67	0.02	-0.63	0.31

SUBSIDIARY & ASSOCIATED COMPANIES

None

INVESTMENTS

None

SOUTH AFRICAN RESERVE BANK LTD

ABBREVIATION : SA-RES-BK

JSE SHORT CODE : SRB

SECTOR : Financial-Banks & Financial Services

SHAREHOLDERS

Who Owns Whom's Assessment of the Identity of the Ultimate Controlling Shareholder: STATE

DIRECTORS :
BROWNE GWG DR,DE LA HARPE BECK WF
DE SWARDT CJ DR (Deputy Governor),DE WAAL MT DR
JOOSTE JA ,KONAR D DR (Deputy Governor)
MEIJER JH DR (Deputy Governor),MOOLMAN IJ
NXUMALO OEHM PROF,VAN DER HORST JG DR,WIESE C

REGISTERED OFFICE
370 Church Street, Pretoria
0002
TEL: 012-313 3911
FAX: 012-313 3197

TRANSFER SECRETARY
SARB
P O Box 427, Pretoria
0001
TEL: 012-313 3911

COMPANY SECRETARY
Dr C J Swanepoel

NATURE OF BUSINESS
Central bank of the Republic of South Africa

BANKERS :
N/A

AUDITORS :
Deloitte Pim Goldby, Coopers Theron Du Toit

FAMILIAR BRAND NAMES
N/A

CONTRIBUTION BY ACTIVITY
N/A

YEAR END : March

DIVIDEND : South African Reserv

Final	(Ldr)24/04/92	(Pay)15/05/92	Amt(c)5

CAPITAL STRUCTURE

	AUTHORISED	ISSUED
South African Reserve Bank Stock	2000000	2000000

FINANCIAL STATISTICS (AT FINANCIAL YEAR END)

(Amts in R'000)	1991 Mar	1990 Mar	1989 Mar

Ord S/H Int	79832	71957	7694404
Long Trm Loans	17823523	20952434	12111077
Total Liab	25723175	29325594	12111077
Current Liab	7899652	8373160	-
Total Assets	25803007	29397551	18349962
Intang Assets	*	*	1455519
Current Assets	14851076	17193785	-
Oper Profit	78951	163642	54265
Prf af Int&Tax	78951	163642	54265
Prf att Ord Sh	78951	163642	54265
Btm Line Earn	78951	163642	54265
Dividend Paid	200	200	200
Mkt Prce(c) YE	85	75	68

PER SHARE STATISTICS (CENTS)

Dividends	10.00	5.00	5.00

RATIOS AND OTHER INFORMATION

Current Ratio	1.88	2.05	-
Quik/Acid Tst	1.88	2.05	-
Debt/Ass Rat	0.61	0.70	0.66
L T L Tot Ass	0.30	0.42	0.66
Debt to Eqity	195.68	287.72	1.57
Ret on Assets	0.31	0.56	0.30
Ret on Equity%	98.90	227.42	0.71
Divid Yield	11.76	6.67	7.35
Def Interval	97.80	75.35	120.44
Sus Grth Rate	98.65	227.14	0.70

SUBSIDIARY & ASSOCIATED COMPANIES

None

INVESTMENTS

None

SOUTH DEEP EXPLORATION CO LTD

ABBREVIATION : SOUDEX

JSE SHORT CODE : SDE

SECTOR : Mining-Exploration

SHAREHOLDERS

Who Owns Whom's Assessment of the Identity of the Ultimate Controlling Shareholder: ANGLO AMERICAN

SHAREHOLDER	PERCENTAGE 1992	1991
STD BANK NOM TVL P/L	44.1	43.6
RESIDENT NOM LTD	32.4	32.4
MINU NOM LTD	9.5	9.5
CONSOLIDATED NOM P/L	3.3	4.6
EIGHTY ONE MAIN STREET NOM LTD	2.6	2.6
FOX STREET NOM P/L	2.4	2.4
FERMAIN NOM LTD	2.3	2.3
GOUDSTAD NOM P/L	1.5	---
TOTAL	98.0	97.3

DIRECTORS :
BROWNRIGG JF ,CONN WP ,CROSS GMW ,HOSKING KM
JANISCH PR ,MAXWELL KW (Chairman)
NAIRN WA (Managing Director),SCOTT-RUSSELL H DR
WANBLAD GP ,YATES CWP

REGISTRATION NUMBER : 88/03931/06

REGISTERED OFFICE
Consolidated Building, Cnr Fox & Harrison Str
Johannesburg
2001
TEL: 011-373 9111
FAX: 011-834 5064

TRANSFER SECRETARY
Consolidated Share Registrars Ltd
P O Box 61051, Marshalltown
2107
TEL: 011-492 1620

COMPANY SECRETARY
Johannesburg Consolidated Inv Co Ltd

NATURE OF BUSINESS
An exploration & mining company which holds mineral rights over 1236 ha in the West Wits area.

BANKERS :
Standard Bank of SA Ltd

AUDITORS :
KPMG Aiken & Peat

FAMILIAR BRAND NAMES
N/A

CONTRIBUTION BY ACTIVITY
N/A

YEAR END : June

CAPITAL STRUCTURE

	AUTHORISED	ISSUED
Ords 1c	400000000	39416000

FINANCIAL STATISTICS (AT FINANCIAL YEAR END)

(Amts in R'000)	1991 Jun
Ord S/H Int	300560
Iss Ord Share	39416
Total Liab	8661
Current Liab	8661
Total Assets	309221
Current Assets	176956
Oper Profit	-91
Tax Paid	1731
Prf af Int&Tax	11871
Prf att Ord Sh	11871
Btm Line Earn	11871
Mkt Prce(c) YE	650

PER SHARE STATISTICS (CENTS)

Net Asst Val	762.53
Net Earnings	46.80
Cash Flow	30.12

RATIOS AND OTHER INFORMATION

Mrk Cap(R000)	256204
Current Ratio	20.43
Quik/Acid Tst	20.43
Debt/Ass Rat	0.03
Debt to Eqity	0.03
Ret on Assets	4.40
Ret on Equity%	3.95
Price/Earnings	13.89
Earning Yield%	7.20
NAV % Mrk Pr	117.31
Effec Tax Rate	48.51
Sus Grth Rate	3.95

SUBSIDIARY & ASSOCIATED COMPANIES

None

INVESTMENTS

None

SOUTH EAST RAND GOLD HOLDINGS LTD

ABBREVIATION : SOUTHGO

JSE SHORT CODE : STG

SECTOR : Gold-Rand & others

SHAREHOLDERS

Who Owns Whom's Assessment of the Identity of the Ultimate Controlling Shareholder: CONSOLIDATED MINING CORP VIA EGOLI

SHAREHOLDER	PERCENTAGE 1992	1991
EGOLI CONSOLIDATED MINES LTD	76.3	76.3
STD BANK NOM TVL P/L	3.2	5.1
LOWENCO NOM P/L	2.4	---
JAN SILVIS NOM P/L	1.7	---
SOUTH EAST RAND GOLD HLDGS SHR INC TRUST	1.2	1.4
BOARD OF EXECUTORS NOM P/L	---	2.3
EIGHTY ONE MAIN STREET NOM LTD	---	2.0
VOLKSKAS NOM P/L	---	1.1
TOTAL	84.7	88.0

DIRECTORS :

BUITENDAG HC ,FLOWERDAY RA ,LOWENTHAL ND
LOWENTHAL RY ,RUBENSTEIN GB (Chairman)
SCHECHTER M ,SUDDENS BD ,THOMPSON MW ,TURNER CF

REGISTRATION NUMBER : 83/11384/06

REGISTERED OFFICE

39th Floor, Carlton Centre
Commissioner Street, Johannesburg
2001
TEL: 011-331 9181
FAX: 011-331 6189

TRANSFER SECRETARY

Mercantile Registrars Ltd
P O Box 1053, Johannesburg
2000
TEL: 011-333 8181

COMPANY SECRETARY

Consolidated Mining Management Services Ltd

NATURE OF BUSINESS

A mining holding company holding controlling interests in JSE-quoted Nigel, West Wits & Wits Nigel. The group conducts gold mining & dump retreatment operations & owns fixed property.

BANKERS :

Nedcor Bank Ltd
First National Bank of SA Ltd

AUDITORS :

Charles Orbach & Co

FAMILIAR BRAND NAMES

N/A

CONTRIBUTION BY ACTIVITY

N/A

YEAR END : March

DIVIDEND : Ords 1c

Final No 2	(Ldr)27/07/90	(Pay)24/08/90	Amt(c)2
Final No 3	(Ldr)12/06/92	(Pay)03/07/92	Amt(c)2.25

CAPITAL STRUCTURE

	AUTHORISED	ISSUED
Ords 1c	250000000	132318000

FINANCIAL STATISTICS (AT FINANCIAL YEAR END)

(Amts in R'000)	1992 Mar	1991 Mar	1990 Mar	1988	1987
Ord S/H Int	92843	143716	139936	58737	34060
Long Trm Loans	65946	97886	92861	26078	10387
Iss Ord Share	132318	132318	132318	61517	46575
Total Liab	98621	157127	125966	46103	14760
Current Liab	32675	59241	33105	20025	4373
Total Assets	191464	300843	265902	88215	50217
Current Assets	16289	12826	31682	2306	5770
Debtors	6055	9453	8925	-	-
Inventory	1889	2661	2039	2306	5770
Turnover	129685	127304	144043	19715	6637
Oper Profit	17923	10200	21763	2750	1697
Interest Paid	1848	4344	4528	1235	286
Tax Paid	468	730	73	-	48
Prf af Int&Tax	15958	7402	18913	1515	1363
Prf att Ord Sh	9490	4524	9265	-501	9
Btm Line Earn	-38678	3780	12583	-501	9
Dividend Paid	2977	-	2646	-	-
Mkt Prce(c) YE	15	40	155	98	450

PER SHARE STATISTICS (CENTS)

Net Asst Val	70.17	108.61	105.76	95.48	73.13
Net Earnings	7.20	3.40	7.90	-	-
Dividends	2.25	-	2.00	-	-
Cash Flow	7.17	3.42	6.41	2.46	2.93

RATIOS AND OTHER INFORMATION

Mrk Cap(R000)	19848	52927	205093	60287	209588
Current Ratio	0.50	0.22	0.96	0.12	1.32
Quik/Acid Tst	0.44	0.17	0.90	-	-

A/C Rec T/ovr	21.42	13.47	12.91	-	-
Tot Ass T/ovr	0.68	0.42	0.43	0.22	0.13
Debt/Ass Rat	0.18	0.22	0.14	0.52	0.29
L T L Tot Ass	0.00	0.02	0.02	0.30	0.21
Debt to Eqity	0.36	0.45	0.27	0.78	0.43
Interest Cover	9.70	2.57	5.02	2.23	5.93
Oper Prof Mrg	13.82	8.01	15.11	13.95	25.57
Net Prof Marg%	7.32	3.55	6.43	-2.54	0.14
Ret on Assets	9.54	4.15	7.05	3.12	3.38
Ret on Equity%	10.22	3.06	5.14	-0.85	0.03
Price/Earnings	2.08	11.76	19.62	-	-
Divid Cover	3.20	-	3.95	-	-
Divid Yield	15.00	-	1.29	-	-
Earning Yield%	48.00	8.50	5.10	-	-
NAV % Mrk Pr	467.78	271.54	68.23	97.43	16.25
Effec Tax Rate	3.78	10.20	0.52	-	3.40
Def Interval	0.85	7.63	1.24	17.21	7.62
Sus Grth Rate	7.02	3.15	4.73	-0.85	0.03

SUBSIDIARY & ASSOCIATED COMPANIES

BENONI GOLD HOLDINGS LTD
BENONI GOLD MINE (PTY) LTD
NIGEL GOLD MINING HOLDINGS LTD
WEST WITWATERSRAND GOLD HOLDINGS LTD
WEST WITWATERSRAND GOLD MINES LTD
WITWATERSRAND NIGEL LTD

INVESTMENTS

None

SOUTH ROODEPOORT MAIN REEF AREAS LTD

ABBREVIATION : STH-RODPT

JSE SHORT CODE : SRO

SECTOR : Gold-Rand & others

SHAREHOLDERS

Who Owns Whom's Assessment of the Identity of the Ultimate Controlling Shareholder: DIRECTORS CONTROL 36% (JUNE 1991)

SHAREHOLDER	PERCENTAGE 1992	1991
SALENE MINING P/L	33.2	33.2
INDO-CHINA NOM P/L	18.5	---
OBRUM INV P/L	2.7	2.7
POUROULIS L C	2.6	2.6
ABSA NOM P/L	2.0	---
FIRST NAT NOM P/L GATR DEPOT	1.8	1.2
POUROULIS A	1.6	1.6
STD BANK NOM TVL P/L	1.1	1.7
INDO-CHINA NOM SA P/L	---	19.0
VOLKSKAS NOM P/L	---	2.0
TOTAL	63.5	64.0

DIRECTORS :
COOMBES ED ,CROSS TA ,DANIEL RJ
GIBBS TL (Chairman)
POUROULIS LC (Managing Director

REGISTRATION NUMBER : 05/05814/06

REGISTERED OFFICE
4th Floor, Burlington House, 22 Rissik Street
Johannesburg
2000
TEL: 011-765 1062
FAX: 011-765 1611

TRANSFER SECRETARY
Gold Equity Registrars (Pty) Ltd
P O Box 62185, Marshalltown
2107
TEL: 011-834 5623

COMPANY SECRETARY
Gold Equity Registrars (Pty) Ltd

NATURE OF BUSINESS
The company conducts gold mining operations in the Roodepoort and Langlaagte areas, Tvl.

BANKERS :
Volkskas Ltd

AUDITORS :
Coopers Theron Du Toit

FAMILIAR BRAND NAMES
N/A

CONTRIBUTION BY ACTIVITY
N/A

YEAR END : June

DIVIDEND :15/02/91 and 15/08/91

NUMBER OF EMPLOYEES : 377

CAPITAL STRUCTURE

	AUTHORISED	ISSUED
Ords 56c	25000000	17455405

FINANCIAL STATISTICS (AT FINANCIAL YEAR END)

(Amts in R'000)	1991 Jun	1990 Jun	1989 Jun	1988 Jun	1987
Ord S/H Int	74054	76679	75731	77383	70167
Long Trm Loans	-	-	206	372	5864
Iss Ord Share	17456	17455	17455	17455	10001
Total Liab	11827	11438	11465	10101	11728
Current Liab	11827	11438	11259	9729	5864
Total Assets	85881	88117	87196	87484	83146
Current Assets	913	2796	2227	4847	7115
Debtors	562	1782	907	3116	-
Inventory	343	956	1280	1627	7115
Turnover	24368	38759	32750	43567	30378
Oper Profit	-1838	1633	-1028	8893	8434
Interest Paid	765	681	598	184	140
Tax Paid	23	6	26	-56	432
Prf af Int&Tax	-2625	948	-1652	8898	7901
Prf att Ord Sh	-2625	948	-1652	8898	7901
Btm Line Earn	-2625	948	-1652	9834	7901
Dividend Paid	-	-	-	2618	4600
Mkt Prce(c) YE	40	80	55	200	370

PER SHARE STATISTICS (CENTS)

Net Asst Val	424.23	439.30	433.86	443.33	701.60
Net Earnings	-15.00	5.40	-9.50	51.00	-
Dividends	-	-	-	15.00	-

Cash Flow	-15.04	5.43	-9.46	50.98	79.00

RATIOS AND OTHER INFORMATION

Mrk Cap(R000)	6982	13964	9600	34910	37004
Current Ratio	0.08	0.24	0.20	0.50	1.21
Quik/Acid Tst	0.05	0.16	0.08	0.33	-
A/C Rec T/ovr	43.36	21.75	36.11	13.98	-
Tot Ass T/ovr	0.28	0.44	0.38	0.50	0.37
Debt/Ass Rat	0.14	0.13	0.13	0.12	0.14
L T L Tot Ass	-	-	0.00	0.00	0.07
Debt to Eqity	0.16	0.15	0.15	0.13	0.17
Interest Cover	-2.40	2.40	-1.72	49.05	60.52
Oper Prof Mrg	-7.54	4.21	-3.14	20.41	27.76
Net Prof Marg%	-10.77	2.45	-5.04	20.42	26.01
Ret on Assets	-2.14	1.86	-1.18	10.32	10.19
Ret on Equity%	-3.54	1.24	-2.18	11.50	11.26
Price/Earnings	-2.67	14.81	-5.79	3.92	-
Divid Cover	-	-	-	3.40	-
Divid Yield	-	-	-	7.50	-
Earning Yield%	-37.50	6.75	-17.27	25.50	-
NAV % Mrk Pr	1060.58	549.12	788.84	221.66	189.62
Effec Tax Rate	-0.88	0.63	-1.60	0.65	5.21
Def Interval	-0.69	0.95	-0.66	0.20	0.74
Sus Grth Rate	-3.54	1.24	-2.18	8.12	4.70

SUBSIDIARY & ASSOCIATED COMPANIES

LANGLAAGTE MINES (PTY) LTD

INVESTMENTS

None

SOUTHERN LIFE ASSOCIATION LTD

ABBREVIATION : SOTHERN

JSE SHORT CODE : SON

SECTOR : Financial-Insurance

SHAREHOLDERS

Who Owns Whom's Assessment of the Identity of the Ultimate Controlling Shareholder: ANGLO AMERICAN

SHAREHOLDER	PERCENTAGE 1992	1991
ANGLO AMERICAN INSURANCE HOLDINGS LTD	32.3	32.3
FIRST NAT BANK OF SA LTD	29.2	29.2
SERPOLLET HOLDINGS LTD	8.3	8.3
FIRST NAT NOM P/L	5.4	5.4
KING M W, DAVIS D J L & SWART B J	4.4	4.4
LIBERTY LIFE ASSOC OF AFRICA LTD	2.3	2.4
SIXTY SIX MARSHALL STREET NOM P/L	1.5	1.7
CMB NOM P/L	1.3	---
ENGINEERING INDUSTRIES PENS FUND	1.0	---
SANLAM	---	1.2
TOTAL	85.6	84.8

DIRECTORS :
ALBERTYN HGL ,ARDINGTON AJ
ARNOTT AH (Executive Director),BARTLETT VW
CALITZ JR (Managing Director)
CHAPMAN TN (Chairman),KING MW (Deputy Chairman)
LIDDLE CC (Executive Director)
LOCH DAVIS DJ (Deputy Chairman),MAHANYELE M
MCDONALD SA ,MOTLANA NH ,NICHOLSON DG
OGILVIE THOMPSON J
PATHER S (Executive Director),RELLY GWH
SWART BJ ,VAN DER ROSS BJ
VAN DER ZWAN AJJ (Executive Director),WILLIAMS DW

REGISTRATION NUMBER : 01/02186/06

REGISTERED OFFICE
Great Westerford, Main Road
Rondebosch
7700
TEL: 021-658 0911
FAX: 021-689 1323

TRANSFER SECRETARY
Consolidated Share Registrars Ltd
P O Box 61051, Marshalltown
2107
TEL: 011-492 1620

COMPANY SECRETARY
A von Geusau

NATURE OF BUSINESS
Principal group activities is the transaction of life assurance, pension & provident fund business, and the management & investment of funds derived.

BANKERS :
First National Bank of SA Ltd

AUDITORS :
Ernst & Young

FAMILIAR BRAND NAMES
N/A

CONTRIBUTION BY ACTIVITY
Net Premium (% total income) (65.0%)
Net Investment (35.0%)

YEAR END : March

DIVIDEND : Ords 5c

Interim No 42	(Ldr)08/12/89	(Pay)08/01/90	Amt(c)18.5
Final No 43	(Ldr)08/06/90	(Pay)02/07/90	Amt(c)27
Interim No 44	(Ldr)07/12/90	(Pay)07/01/91	Amt(c)22.5
Final No 45	(Ldr)14/06/91	(Pay)12/07/91	Amt(c)32
Interim No 46	(Ldr)06/12/91	(Pay)06/01/92	Amt(c)27
Final No 47	(Ldr)12/06/92	(Pay)10/07/92	Amt(c)38
Interim No 48	(Ldr)04/12/92	(Pay)08/01/93	Amt(c)32

NUMBER OF EMPLOYEES : 3948

CAPITAL STRUCTURE

	AUTHORISED	ISSUED
Special class "A" share of 5c	1	1
Ords 5c	180000000	168736241

FINANCIAL STATISTICS (AT FINANCIAL YEAR END)

(Amts in R'000)	1992 Mar	1991 Mar	1990 Mar
Ord S/H Int	617880	563040	516810
Long Trm Loans	16672740	13930720	13191510

Iss Ord Share	168736	168736	164632
Total Liab	17057810	14295310	13535490
Current Liab	385070	364590	343980
Total Assets	17675690	14858350	14052300
Current Assets	428790	365520	269350
Debtors	285830	326520	259260
Oper Profit	2642870	2436990	2174950
Tax Paid	48480	25020	61510
Prf af Int&Tax	2594390	2411970	2113440
Prf att Ord Sh	730150	1207300	980200
Btm Line Earn	730150	1207300	980200
Dividend Paid	109680	91960	76770
Mkt Prce(c) YE	2025	1530	1160

PER SHARE STATISTICS (CENTS)

Net Asst Val	366.18	333.68	313.92
Net Earnings	97.50	81.90	68.30
Dividends	65.00	54.50	45.50
Cash Flow	1537.38	1429.33	1252.51

RATIOS AND OTHER INFORMATION

Mrk Cap(R000)	3416904	2581661	1909731
Current Ratio	1.11	1.00	0.78
Quik/Acid Tst	1.11	1.00	0.78
Debt/Ass Rat	0.05	0.06	0.06
L T L Tot Ass	0.03	0.04	0.03
Debt to Eqity	1.39	1.58	1.59
Ret on Assets	14.95	16.40	15.48
Ret on Equity%	118.17	214.43	189.66
Price/Earnings	20.77	18.68	16.98
Divid Cover	1.50	1.50	1.50
Divid Yield	3.21	3.56	3.92
Earning Yield%	4.81	5.35	5.89
NAV % Mrk Pr	18.08	21.81	27.06
Effec Tax Rate	1.60	1.53	2.83
Def Interval	0.18	0.22	0.23
Sus Grth Rate	100.42	198.09	174.81

SUBSIDIARY & ASSOCIATED COMPANIES

AFRICAN LIFE ASSURANCE CO LTD
FIRST CONSOLIDATED HOLDINGS (PTY) LTD
SOUTHAMPTON ASSURANCE CO. OF ZIMBABWE LT
SOUTHERN LIFE PROPERTY HOLDINGS LTD
SOUTHERN LIFE SPECIAL INVESTMENTS (PTY)

INVESTMENTS

ANGLO AMERICAN CORPORATION OF SOUTH AFRI (6,8%)
BARLOW RAND LTD (3,9%)
BOTSWANA INSURANCE HOLDINGS (10.1%)
FOSCHINI LTD (2,7%)
GENCOR LTD (5,3%)
ISCOR LTD (3,3%)
REMBRANDT GROUP (5,3%)
RICHEMONT SECURITIES (6,3%)
WOOLTRU LTD (3,7%)

SOUTHERN PLATREEF MINING CO LTD

ABBREVIATION : SOPLATS

JSE SHORT CODE : SLT

SECTOR : Mining-Exploration

SHAREHOLDERS

Who Owns Whom's Assessment of the Identity of the Ultimate Controlling Shareholder: SOUTHERN WITWATERSRAND EXPLORATION CO

SHAREHOLDER	PERCENTAGE 1992	1991
SFSS NOM P/L	47.8	47.8
SOUTH WITS INV HOLDINGS P/L	33.8	33.8
RANDEX LTD	10.5	10.5
ANGLO AFRICAN SHIPPING CO 1936 P/L	2.2	2.2
BISICHI MINING PLC	1.6	1.6
STD BANK NOM TVL P/L	1.3	—
AA LIFE ASSURE ASSOC LTD	—	1.4
TOTAL	97.1	97.3

DIRECTORS :
DE VILLIERS JR (Financial Director)
STAVRAKIS N (Chairman & Managing Dir.)
TAYLOR CJB ,WELTHAGEN M

REGISTRATION NUMBER : 88/00763/06

REGISTERED OFFICE
13 Frensch Hoek Rd, Northcliff Ext 19
Roodepoort
1709

TRANSFER SECRETARY
Mercantile Registrars Ltd
P O Box 1053, Johannesburg
2000
TEL: 011-333 8181

COMPANY SECRETARY
SA Meyer & Co

NATURE OF BUSINESS
A mining & exploration company which holds a prospecting and option contract over the Potgietersrus Venture Area.

BANKERS :
First National Bank of SA Ltd

AUDITORS :
KPMG Aiken & Peat

FAMILIAR BRAND NAMES
N/A

CONTRIBUTION BY ACTIVITY
N/A

YEAR END : February

CAPITAL STRUCTURE

	AUTHORISED	ISSUED
Ords 1c	100000000	10663840

FINANCIAL STATISTICS (AT FINANCIAL YEAR END)

(Amts in R'000)	1991 Feb	1990 Jul	1990 Feb
Ord S/H Int	1535	4116	-207
Long Trm Loans	2	95	224
Iss Ord Share	10664	10664	9000

Total Liab	67	522	225
Current Liab	65	427	1
Total Assets	1577	4638	1
Intang Assets	25	*	17
Current Assets	1361	4526	1
Debtors	13	-	-
Oper Profit	-3026	-219	-
Interest Paid	11	-	-
Prf af Int&Tax	-2727	-219	-
Prf att Ord Sh	-2727	-219	-
Btm Line Earn	-2727	-219	-
Mkt Prce(c) YE	150	-	-
Depreciation	16	-	-

PER SHARE STATISTICS (CENTS)

Net Asst Val	14.16	38.60	-2.49
Net Earnings	-26.97	-	-2.06
Cash Flow	-25.42	-4.11	-

RATIOS AND OTHER INFORMATION

Mrk Cap(R000)	15996	-	-
Current Ratio	20.94	10.60	1.00
Quik/Acid Tst	20.94	10.60	1.00
Debt/Ass Rat	0.04	0.11	225.00
L T L Tot Ass	0.00	0.02	224.00
Debt to Eqity	0.04	0.13	-1.09
Interest Cover	-275.09	-	-
Ret on Assets	-172.23	-9.44	-
Ret on Equity%	-177.65	-10.64	-
Price/Earnings	-5.56	-	-
Earning Yield%	-17.98	-	-
NAV % Mrk Pr	9.44	-	-
Def Interval	0.00	-2.93	-
Sus Grth Rate	-177.65	-5.32	-

SUBSIDIARY & ASSOCIATED COMPANIES

None

INVESTMENTS

None

SOUTHERN WITWATERSRAND EXPLORATION CO LTD

ABBREVIATION : SOWITS

JSE SHORT CODE : SWT

SECTOR : Mining-Exploration

SHAREHOLDERS

Who Owns Whom's Assessment of the Identity of the Ultimate Controlling Shareholder: DIRECTORS

SHAREHOLDER	PERCENTAGE 1992	1991
FIRST NAT NOM P/L	48.4	64.0
SOUTHERN WITWATERSRAND EXPL CO LTD	15.3	---
HERBEST NOM P/L	3.0	2.0
DORFAN J G	2.1	---
STOCKSHARE NOM P/L	1.2	---
NEDBANK NOM LTD	---	2.0
EIGHTY ONE MAIN STREET NOM LTD	---	3.1
SA MUTUAL	---	4.0
TOTAL	70.0	75.1

DIRECTORS :
DE VILLIERS JR (Financial Director), HAYWARD GA
STAVRAKIS N (Chairman & Managing Dir.)
WELTHAGEN M

REGISTRATION NUMBER : 87/03452/06

REGISTERED OFFICE
13 Frensch Hoek Road, Northcliff Ext 19
Roodepoort
1709
TEL: 011-802 5002
FAX: 011-804 4819

TRANSFER SECRETARY
Mercantile Registrars Ltd
P O Box 1053, Johannesburg
2000
TEL: 011-333 8181

COMPANY SECRETARY
S A Meyer & Co

NATURE OF BUSINESS
The main business of the company is mining & exploration for precious stones & metals, base minerals, ferrous & non-ferrous metals, coal & allied minerals and turning to account of its mineral interests. In terms of area, approx 50% of the company's prospects are gold based, 30% have coal and base mineral potential, and the remaining 20% are orientated towards diamonds and platinum group metals.

BANKERS :
Nedperm Bank Ltd
First National Bank of SA Ltd

AUDITORS :
KPMG Aiken & Peat

FAMILIAR BRAND NAMES
N/A

CONTRIBUTION BY ACTIVITY
N/A

YEAR END : February

NUMBER OF EMPLOYEES : 10

CAPITAL STRUCTURE

	AUTHORISED	ISSUED
Ords 1c	50000000	32765816

FINANCIAL STATISTICS (AT FINANCIAL YEAR END)

(Amts in R'000)	1992 Feb	1991 Feb	1990 Feb	1989 Feb	1988
Ord S/H Int	5296	5780	3225	3716	786
Long Trm Loans	356	1946	1371	23	121
Iss Ord Share	32766	32766	30216	29816	27105
Total Liab	906	2668	1881	172	208

Current Liab	550	722	510	149	87
Total Assets	5706	6198	5104	3283	1582
Intang Assets	496	2250	2	605	*
Current Assets	3341	2279	2496	3154	675
Debtors	2030	288	8	34	-
Inventory	55	84	-	-	675
Turnover	802	1404	-	-	-
Oper Profit	-1247	-5632	-985	-1756	-480
Interest Paid	57	130	5	-	-
Tax Paid	-	-	23	-	-
Prf af Int&Tax	-1046	-5180	-647	-1426	-480
Prf att Ord Sh	-484	-4082	-652	-1426	-480
Btm Line Earn	-484	-135	-652	-1426	-480
Mkt Prce(c) YE	10	20	140	90	-
Depreciation	640	891	22	16	-

PER SHARE STATISTICS (CENTS)

Net Asst Val	14.65	10.77	10.67	10.43	2.90
Net Earnings	-1.48	-12.55	-2.17	-4.96	-
Cash Flow	0.48	-9.81	-2.09	-4.90	-1.77

RATIOS AND OTHER INFORMATION

Mrk Cap(R000)	3277	6553	42302	26834	-
Current Ratio	6.07	3.16	4.89	21.17	7.76
Quik/Acid Tst	5.97	3.04	4.89	21.17	-
A/C Rec T/ovr	0.40	4.88	-	-	-
Tot Ass T/ovr	0.14	0.23	-	-	-
Debt/Ass Rat	0.12	0.13	0.10	0.05	0.13
L T L Tot Ass	0.02	0.02	0.00	0.01	0.08
Debt to Eqity	0.13	0.14	0.16	0.05	0.26
Interest Cover	-21.88	-43.32	-194.40	-	-
Oper Prof Mrg	-155.49	-401.14	-	-	-
Net Prof Marg%	-60.35	-290.74	-	-	-
Ret on Assets	-17.33	-81.48	-12.13	-43.44	-30.34
Ret on Equity%	-9.14	-70.62	-20.22	-38.37	-61.07
Price/Earnings	-6.76	-1.59	-64.52	-18.15	-
Earning Yield%	-14.80	-62.75	-1.55	-5.51	-
NAV % Mrk Pr	146.49	53.87	7.62	11.59	-
Effec Tax Rate	-	-	-3.61	-	-
Def Interval	0.87	-0.09	-0.02	-0.02	-0.25
Sus Grth Rate	-9.14	-70.62	-20.22	-38.37	-61.07

SUBSIDIARY & ASSOCIATED COMPANIES

DEEP RIVER DIAMOND MINE (PTY) LTD
NEW UITKYK COLLIERY (PTY) LTD
SOUTHERN PLATREEF MINING CO LTD
SOUTHWITS INVESTMENT HOLDINGS (PTY) LTD

INVESTMENTS

REVERE RESOURCES SA LTD (9201000SH)

SOUTHVAAL HOLDINGS LTD

ABBREVIATION : SOUTHVAAL

JSE SHORT CODE : SVL

SECTOR : Gold-Klerksdorp

SHAREHOLDERS

Who Owns Whom's Assessment of the Identity of the Ultimate Controlling Shareholder:
ANGLO AMERICAN

SHAREHOLDER	PERCENTAGE 1992	1991
VAAL REEFS EXPLORAT & MINING CO LTD	25.0	25.0
RESIDENT NOM LTD	9.0	9.7
TAURUS NOM LTD	7.4	7.4
INDO-CHINA NOM P/L	7.3	9.0
STD BANK NOM TVL P/L	5.8	4.4
CMB NOM P/L	5.6	—
PETARD NOM LTD	5.4	5.4
OVERSEAS NOM CO INC	4.5	4.5
FREE STATE CONS GOLD MINES (OPS) LTD	3.1	3.1
SA MUTUAL	2.5	2.6
FIRST NAT NOM P/L	2.0	2.5
ABSA NOM P/L	2.0	—
EIGHTY ONE MAIN STREET NOM LTD	1.8	—
LONDON CONTROL ACCOUNT	1.0	1.0
CITIBANK NOM P/L	1.0	1.0
SOUTHERN LIFE ASSOC LTD	—	2.7
INDO-CHINA NOM SA P/L	—	9.0
SANLAM	—	5.5
TOTAL	83.4	92.9

DIRECTORS :
HEWITT L ,HOLFORD GM
HOSKING KM (Managing Director),KING MW
MAXWELL KW ,SUNTER CL (Chairman),WOODWARD GW

REGISTRATION NUMBER : 66/11806/06

REGISTERED OFFICE
44 Main Street, Johannesburg
2001
TEL: 011-638 9111
FAX: 011-638 5281

TRANSFER SECRETARY
Consolidated Share Registrars Ltd
P O Box 61051, Marshalltown
2107
TEL: 011-492 1620

COMPANY SECRETARY
Anglo American Corp of SA Ltd

NATURE OF BUSINESS
SOUTH VAAL HOLDINGS is a finance company whose income is derived from a royalty receivable in respect of the mining of the South Lease Area of VAAL REEFS.

BANKERS :
First National Bank of SA Ltd

AUDITORS :
Ernst & Young

FAMILIAR BRAND NAMES
N/A

CONTRIBUTION BY ACTIVITY
Royalty (% pre-tax profit) (99.0%)
Interest (1.0%)

YEAR END : December

DIVIDEND : Ords 50c

Interim No 27	(Ldr)03/08/90	(Pay)14/09/90	Amt(c)180
Final No 28	(Ldr)08/02/91	(Pay)15/03/91	Amt(c)145
Interim No 29	(Ldr)09/08/91	(Pay)13/09/91	Amt(c)90
Final No 30	(Ldr)07/02/92	(Pay)13/03/92	Amt(c)250

NUMBER OF EMPLOYEES : 1

CAPITAL STRUCTURE

	AUTHORISED	ISSUED
Ords 50c	26000000	26000000

FINANCIAL STATISTICS (AT FINANCIAL YEAR END)

(Amts in R'000)	1991 Dec	1990 Dec	1989 Dec	1988	1987
Ord S/H Int	16867	16159	16010	16758	16971
Long Trm Loans	-	-	-	114433	167029
Iss Ord Share	26000	26000	26000	26000	26000
Total Liab	54287	45000	102177	228866	334058
Current Liab	54287	45000	102177	114433	167029
Total Assets	68154	58159	115187	254748	359774
Intang Assets	3000	3000	3000	*	*
Current Assets	49210	38477	94819	123557	175774
Debtors	9464	1456	30347	-	-
Inventory	-	-	-	123557	175774
Oper Profit	121209	161381	274929	368757	348780
Tax Paid	59746	83085	141651	184370	174378
Prf af Int&Tax	65708	84649	142252	184387	174402
Prf att Ord Sh	65708	84649	142252	184387	174402
Btm Line Earn	65708	84649	142252	184387	174402
Dividend Paid	65000	84500	143000	184600	174200
Mkt Prce(c) YE	6325	8700	16600	11000	15600

PER SHARE STATISTICS (CENTS)

Net Asst Val	53.33	50.61	50.04	64.45	65.27
Net Earnings	253.00	326.00	547.00	-	-
Dividends	250.00	325.00	550.00	-	-
Cash Flow	252.72	325.57	547.12	709.18	670.78

RATIOS AND OTHER INFORMATION

Mrk Cap(R000)	1644500	2262000	4316000	2860000	4056000
Current Ratio	0.91	0.86	0.93	1.08	1.05
Quik/Acid Tst	0.91	0.86	0.93	-	-
Debt/Ass Rat	0.80	0.77	0.89	0.90	0.93
L T L Tot Ass	-	-	-	0.45	0.46
Debt to Eqity	3.22	2.78	6.38	13.66	19.68
Ret on Assets	184.07	288.41	246.47	144.75	96.94
Ret on Equity%	389.57	523.85	888.52	1100.29	1027.65
Price/Earnings	25.00	26.69	30.35	-	-
Divid Cover	1.01	1.00	0.99	-	-
Divid Yield	3.95	3.74	3.31	-	-
Earning Yield%	4.00	3.75	3.30	-	-
NAV % Mrk Pr	0.84	0.58	0.30	0.59	0.42
Effec Tax Rate	48.48	50.23	75.79	50.00	50.00
Def Interval	-	-	-	0.62	0.96
Sus Grth Rate	4.20	0.92	-4.67	-1.27	1.19

SUBSIDIARY & ASSOCIATED COMPANIES

None

INVESTMENTS

CACTUS INVESTMENTS (PTY) LTD (16372 SH)

SPECIALTY STORES LTD

ABBREVIATION : SPECLTY

JSE SHORT CODE : SPY

SECTOR : Industrial-Retailers & Wholesalers

SHAREHOLDERS

Who Owns Whom's Assessment of the Identity of the Ultimate Controlling Shareholder: STORECO

SHAREHOLDER	PERCENTAGE 1992	1991
STORECO LTD	63.2	63.2
EIGHTY ONE MAIN STREET NOM LTD	10.9	1.5
SHARESTOCK NOM P/L	7.2	7.3
SA MUTUAL	4.2	7.6
MENTEITH INV LTD	3.6	3.6
SA SPECIAL RISKS INSURANCE ASSOC LTD	3.4	---
STD BANK NOM TVL P/L	1.5	---
SPECIALTY STAFF SHARE TRUST	1.1	---
BOARD OF EXECUTORS NOM P/L	---	1.3
SYFRETS NOM LTD	---	7.9
UNIVERSITY OF OFS	---	1.0
TOTAL	95.1	93.4

DIRECTORS :

BLACKMAN TO
CHIAPPINI LJ (Joint Managing Director)
COHEN SB (Joint Managing Director),GAMBLE KR
HAINE JP ,HUME GM ,LABUSCHAGNE NA DR (Chairman)
MCADAM WJ (Deputy Chairman),RUBENSTEIN SM
YUILL CS (Financial Director

REGISTRATION NUMBER : 05/04418/06

REGISTERED OFFICE

16th Floor, Southern Life Building
88 Field Street, Durban
4001
TEL: 031-301 2252
FAX: 031-304 5820

TRANSFER SECRETARY

Mercantile Registrars Ltd
P O Box 1053, Johannesburg
2000
TEL: 011-333 8181

COMPANY SECRETARY

C S Yuill

NATURE OF BUSINESS

The main business of the group is the retail of fashion clothing and shoes via a network of 171 specialty stores. Investments are also held in retailing, shopfitting and computers service co's.

BANKERS :

Standard Bank of SA Ltd

AUDITORS :

Ernst & Young

FAMILIAR BRAND NAMES

COLLECTIF

CONTRIBUTION BY ACTIVITY

Retailing (% of Profit before Tax) (96.9%)
Shopfitting,computer services & other (3.1%)

YEAR END : February

DIVIDEND :Ords 12,5c

Interim No 3	(Ldr)02/11/90	(Pay)03/12/90	Amt(c)9.5
Final No 4	(Ldr)10/05/91	(Pay)01/07/91	Amt(c)18
Interim No 5	(Ldr)01/11/91	(Pay)06/12/91	Amt(c)10
Final No 6	(Ldr)08/05/92	(Pay)01/07/92	Amt(c)20
Interim No 7	(Ldr)30/10/92	(Pay)04/12/92	Amt(c)10

NUMBER OF EMPLOYEES : 1985

CAPITAL STRUCTURE

	AUTHORISED	ISSUED
Ords 12,5c	22600000	16500000
5,5% Cum Prefs R2	150000	150000

FINANCIAL STATISTICS (AT FINANCIAL YEAR END)

(Amts in R'000)	1992 Feb	1991 Feb	1990 Feb
Ord S/H Int	75179	68606	60882
Long Trm Loans	2509	1355	3624
Iss Ord Share	16500	16500	16500
Total Liab	107898	75663	64490
Current Liab	105389	74308	60866
Total Assets	182480	143457	124333
Intang Assets	597	812	1039
Current Assets	159992	121719	110659
Debtors	100797	81038	72783
Inventory	56274	40187	36656
Turnover	293595	245893	185425
Oper Profit	33958	28978	23485
Interest Paid	8519	6566	3755
Tax Paid	11639	10003	9290
Prf af Int&Tax	13800	12409	10440
Prf att Ord Sh	13784	12393	10424
Btm Line Earn	11392	12393	10424
Dividend Paid	4950	4538	4125
Mkt Prce(c) YE	560	500	400
Depreciation	4821	3796	2610

PER SHARE STATISTICS (CENTS)

Net Asst Val	452.01	410.87	362.68
Net Earnings	83.50	75.10	70.30
Dividends	30.00	27.50	25.00
Cash Flow	119.67	84.32	94.86

RATIOS AND OTHER INFORMATION

Mrk Cap(R000)	92400	82500	66000
Current Ratio	1.52	1.64	1.82
Quik/Acid Tst	0.98	1.10	1.22
A/C Rec T/ovr	2.91	3.03	2.55
Tot Ass T/ovr	1.61	1.71	1.49
Debt/Ass Rat	0.58	0.52	0.50
L T L Tot Ass	0.00	0.00	0.01
Debt to Eqity	1.41	1.09	1.01
Interest Cover	3.99	4.41	6.25
Oper Prof Mrg	11.57	11.78	12.67
Net Prof Marg%	4.69	5.04	5.62
Ret on Assets	18.61	20.20	18.89
Ret on Equity%	18.33	18.06	17.12
Price/Earnings	6.71	6.66	5.69
Divid Cover	2.78	2.73	2.81
Divid Yield	5.36	5.50	6.25
Earning Yield%	14.91	15.02	17.58
NAV % Mrk Pr	80.72	82.17	90.67
Effec Tax Rate	0.08	0.33	0.84
Def Interval	2.15	2.19	1.59
Sus Grth Rate	11.75	11.45	10.35

SUBSIDIARY & ASSOCIATED COMPANIES

AVFIN COSMETICS (PTY) LTD
FASHION HOUSE HOLDINGS AND ADMINISTRATOR
FASHION RETAILERS (PTY) LTD
FOOTGEAR (PTY) LTD
GKL TRADING (PTY) LTD
JOHN ORR (NATAL) LTD
JOHN ORR (ZIMBABWE) (PVT) LTD
MADAME LORRAINE FASHION HOLDINGS (PTY) L
MILADY'S (PTY) LTD
MILADY'S FINANCIAL SERVICES LIMITED (50%)
ORR-CO PROPERTIES LTD
ORRCO MANAGEMENT SERVICES (PTY) LTD
ORRCO RETAIL LTD
PEERS INVESTMENTS LTD
RETAIL SHOPFITTING SERVICES (PTY) LTD
RITA EASTON (PTY) LTD
STORECO MANAGEMENT SERVICES (PTY) LTD
WEILS FASHIONS (PTY) LTD

INVESTMENTS

None

SPESCOM ELECTRONICS LTD

ABBREVIATION : SPESCOM

JSE SHORT CODE : SPS

SECTOR : Industrial-Electronics, Electrical & Bat

SHAREHOLDERS

Who Owns Whom's Assessment of the Identity of the Ultimate Controlling Shareholder: DIRECTORS

SHAREHOLDER	PERCENTAGE 1992	1991
FARAH A	27.4	28.7
CMB NOM P/L	14.7	---
SMBL NOM P/L	5.7	5.7
ANTHONY FARAH FAMILY TRUST	5.1	5.1
TAYLOR R	4.9	---
STEYN J P	3.3	3.3
LEITNER J R	2.8	2.3
ABSA NOM P/L	2.6	---
MODRY J	2.5	2.8
SPESCOM ELECTRONICS LTD SHARE TRUST	2.5	2.5
MPM NOM LTD	1.5	1.5
STD BANK NOM TVL P/L	1.5	1.4
CROOKES D V	1.3	1.3
FLEISCHER H H	1.1	---
KALLMEYER L A	1.0	---
ISAACMAN H	1.0	---
KEL TRUST	---	4.9
SANLAM	---	14.7
SPESCOM ELECTRONICS HOLDINGS P/L	---	2.0
VOLKSKAS NOM P/L	---	2.6
TOTAL	78.8	78.7

DIRECTORS :
BAKER K ,FARAH A (Executive Chairman)
KALLMEYER LA ,LEITNER JR DR
STEYN JP (Managing Director),TAYLOR EL

REGISTRATION NUMBER : 87/01083/06

REGISTERED OFFICE
Spescom Park, Cnr Alexandra Rd & 2nd St
Halfway House, Midrand
1685
TEL: 011-315 0757
FAX: 011-805 1192

TRANSFER SECRETARY
Central Registrars Ltd
P O Box 4844, Johannesburg
2000
TEL: 011-331 0051

COMPANY SECRETARY
PCS Merry

NATURE OF BUSINESS
An investment holding company. Group activities include : Supply of computer graphics hardware & associated peripheral equipment; Design, development , manufacture & distribution of high technology, & electronic products; Marketing of electronic products,computer-based instrumentation and allied products.

BANKERS :
First National Bank of SA Ltd

AUDITORS :
Ernst & Young

FAMILIAR BRAND NAMES
N/A

CONTRIBUTION BY ACTIVITY
Electricity,Transport (% of Turnover) (39.0%)
Security,Instrumentation & other (33.0%)
New Technology (28.0%)

YEAR END : April

DIVIDEND : Ords 1c

Final No 4	(Ldr)03/07/92	(Pay)10/07/92	Amt(c)3
Interim No 5	(Ldr)11/12/92	(Pay)22/12/92	Amt(c)2

NUMBER OF EMPLOYEES : 216

CAPITAL STRUCTURE

	AUTHORISED	ISSUED
Ords 1c	25000000	19798300

FINANCIAL STATISTICS (AT FINANCIAL YEAR END)

(Amts in R'000)	1992 Apr	1991 Apr	1990 Apr	1989 Feb	1988 Feb
Ord S/H Int	15853	14999	21540	22677	19711
Long Trm Loans	2932	2040	639	467	236
Iss Ord Share	19798	19798	19798	19798	19500
Total Liab	23740	17842	12364	16489	7860
Current Liab	20808	15802	11725	16022	7624
Total Assets	38816	31740	26842	31254	19920
Intang Assets	777	1101	7062	7912	7651
Current Assets	22828	16666	15917	23439	12276
Debtors	11515	6813	7774	15028	6767
Inventory	8939	7415	6010	6293	2366
Turnover	45944	32899	33243	33728	28025
Oper Profit	3391	2440	2181	-18688	2821
Interest Paid	1788	2177	1113	314	107
Tax Paid	-218	-6	7	523	893
Prf af Int&Tax	1836	521	1215	-19276	2484
Prf att Ord Sh	1836	521	1213	3523	2484
Btm Line Earn	1448	521	-1137	3523	2484
Dividend Paid	594	-	-	990	633
Mkt Prce(c) YE	45	42	30	135	130
Depreciation	846	703	475	380	269

PER SHARE STATISTICS (CENTS)

Net Asst Val	76.15	70.20	73.13	74.58	61.85
Net Earnings	9.30	2.60	6.10	17.80	13.60
Dividends	3.00	-	-	5.00	3.25
Cash Flow	12.42	6.18	7.32	-93.89	15.19

RATIOS AND OTHER INFORMATION

Mrk Cap(R000)	8909	8315	5939	26727	25350
Current Ratio	1.10	1.05	1.36	1.46	1.61
Quik/Acid Tst	0.67	0.59	0.84	1.07	1.30
A/C Rec T/ovr	3.99	4.83	3.67	2.24	4.14
Tot Ass T/ovr	1.18	1.04	1.06	1.08	1.41
Debt/Ass Rat	0.57	0.52	0.45	0.52	0.39
L T L Tot Ass	0.03	0.02	0.01	0.00	0.01
Debt to Eqity	1.39	1.10	0.56	0.71	0.40
Interest Cover	1.90	1.12	1.96	-59.22	32.56
Oper Prof Mrg	7.38	7.42	6.56	-55.41	10.07
Net Prof Marg%	4.00	1.58	3.65	10.45	8.86
Ret on Assets	8.77	8.48	7.45	13.95	17.49
Ret on Equity%	11.58	3.47	4.83	15.54	12.60
Price/Earnings	4.84	16.15	4.92	7.58	9.56
Divid Cover	3.10	-	-	3.56	4.18
Divid Yield	6.67	-	-	3.70	2.50
Earning Yield%	20.67	6.19	20.33	13.19	10.46
NAV % Mrk Pr	169.22	167.14	243.76	55.24	47.57
Effec Tax Rate	0.37	-	0.57	-1.15	31.80
Def Interval	4.20	7.24	3.80	-0.33	0.41
Sus Grth Rate	7.83	3.47	5.63	11.17	9.39

SUBSIDIARY & ASSOCIATED COMPANIES

ADEPT TECHNOLOGIES (PTY) LTD
ALPHADATA (PTY) LTD
ALPHADATA COMPUTERS (PTY) LTD
ALPHADATA PERIPHERALS (PTY) LTD
GENERAL PRECISION MECHANICS (PTY) LTD (40%)
SPESCOM (PTY) LTD
SPESCOM EDGE TECHNOLOGIES (PTY) LTD
SPESCOM TMS (PTY) LTD

INVESTMENTS

None

SPICER-MITCHELL HOLDINGS LTD

ABBREVIATION : SPICER

JSE SHORT CODE : SPI

SECTOR : Development Capital Market

SHAREHOLDERS

Who Owns Whom's Assessment of the Identity of the Ultimate Controlling Shareholder:
DIRECTORS

SHAREHOLDER	PERCENTAGE 1992	1991
FIRST NAT NOM P/L	78.8	78.7
EDWIN W BALDERSON NOM P/L	2.6	2.1
PRINCE S	1.4	1.4
NEDBANK NOM LTD	1.0	1.3
TOTAL	83.8	83.5

DIRECTORS :
MULLER K ,PRINCE RS (Chairman & Managing Dir.)
WHEELER PB (Financial Director

REGISTRATION NUMBER : 84/05392/06

REGISTERED OFFICE
9 Flamink Road, Alrode Ext 7
Alrode
1451
TEL: 011-908 5580
FAX: 011-864 7313

TRANSFER SECRETARY
Union Provident Trust SA Ltd
P O Box 2322, Johannesburg
2000
TEL: 011-833 6700

COMPANY SECRETARY
P B Wheeler

NATURE OF BUSINESS
An industrial holding company. Subsidiaries are involved in the following activities: Specialist chemical & high pressure water cleaning services; Erection & maintenance of air pollution control systems; Design & manufacture of metal finishing & effluent treatment plants & their ancillary systems; Manufacture of specialty chemical compositions.

BANKERS :
First National Bank of SA Ltd

AUDITORS :
Ernst & Young

FAMILIAR BRAND NAMES
N/A

CONTRIBUTION BY ACTIVITY
N/A

YEAR END : February

DIVIDEND : Ords 1c
Interim (Ldr)22/02/91 (Pay)28/02/91 Amt(c)3

NUMBER OF EMPLOYEES : 73

CAPITAL STRUCTURE

	AUTHORISED	ISSUED
Ords 1c	20000000	10000000

FINANCIAL STATISTICS (AT FINANCIAL YEAR END)

(Amts in R'000)	1992 Feb	1991 Feb	1990 Feb	1989 Feb	1988 Feb
Ord S/H Int	1300	1668	1069	2589	2269
Long Trm Loans	666	898	1009	696	759
Iss Ord Share	10000	10000	10000	10000	10000
Total Liab	4924	5663	5938	2784	1968
Current Liab	4258	4765	4929	2088	1209
Total Assets	6224	7331	7007	5373	4237
Current Assets	3771	4808	4343	3764	2678
Debtors	2722	3152	3354	2606	2232
Inventory	908	1397	840	543	446
Turnover	13762	16096	15548	9510	8143
Oper Profit	70	1301	-1074	1059	947
Interest Paid	842	371	415	-	45
Tax Paid	-152	357	31	539	505
Prf af Int&Tax	-620	573	-1520	520	397
Prf att Ord Sh	-657	486	-1520	520	397
Btm Line Earn	-657	899	-1520	520	397
Dividend Paid	-	300	-	200	100
Mkt Prce(c) YE	10	27	19	22	30
Depreciation	1038	636	691	505	418

PER SHARE STATISTICS (CENTS)

Net Asst Val	13.00	16.68	10.69	25.89	22.69
Net Earnings	-6.60	4.90	-15.20	5.20	4.60
Dividends	-	3.00	-	2.00	1.00
Cash Flow	1.56	13.17	-9.62	8.70	10.73

RATIOS AND OTHER INFORMATION

Mrk Cap(R000)	1000	2700	1900	2200	3000
Current Ratio	0.89	1.01	0.88	1.80	2.22
Quik/Acid Tst	0.67	0.72	0.71	1.54	1.85
A/C Rec T/ovr	5.06	5.11	4.64	3.65	3.65
Tot Ass T/ovr	2.21	2.20	2.22	1.77	1.92
Debt/Ass Rat	0.75	0.71	0.81	0.44	0.33
L T L Tot Ass	0.07	0.06	0.10	0.05	0.04
Debt to Eqity	3.59	3.10	5.29	0.91	0.61
Interest Cover	0.08	3.51	-2.59	-	21.04
Oper Prof Mrg	0.51	8.08	-6.91	11.14	11.63
Net Prof Marg%	-4.77	3.02	-9.78	5.47	4.88
Ret on Assets	1.12	17.75	-15.33	19.71	22.35
Ret on Equity%	-50.54	29.14	-142.19	20.08	17.50
Price/Earnings	-1.52	5.51	-1.25	4.23	6.52
Divid Cover	-	1.63	-	2.60	4.60
Divid Yield	-	11.11	-	9.09	3.33
Earning Yield%	-66.00	18.15	-80.00	23.64	15.33
NAV % Mrk Pr	130.00	61.78	56.26	117.68	75.63
Effec Tax Rate	-9.07	19.14	-11.69	65.53	38.14
Def Interval	17.40	2.33	-3.13	0.69	0.42
Sus Grth Rate	-50.54	11.15	-142.19	12.36	13.09

SUBSIDIARY & ASSOCIATED COMPANIES

CRANE & RIGGING SERVICES (PTY) LTD
CRANE HIRE SERVICES (TVL) (PTY) LTD
EDENTEC INDUSTRIAL (PTY) LTD
PRECIPITATOR SERVICES (PTY) LTD
ROHR REIN CHEMIE (PTY) LTD
SPICER-MITCHELL CONSTRUCTION (PTY) LTD
SPICER-MITCHELL PROJECTS (PTY) LTD
SSS ENGINEERING (PTY) LTD

INVESTMENTS

None

SPL LTD

ABBREVIATION : SPL

JSE SHORT CODE : SPL

SECTOR : Industrial-Electronics, Electrical & Bat

SHAREHOLDERS

Who Owns Whom's Assessment of the Identity of the Ultimate Controlling Shareholder:
DIRECTORS / SANLAM

SHAREHOLDER	PERCENTAGE 1992	1991
CMB NOM P/L	42.3	---
COMPUTER MANAGEMENT INC	19.0	17.6
NEDBANK NOM LTD	8.3	4.8
FOLB L J	2.8	2.8
STEYN H S	1.5	1.5
FOLB L	1.4	1.4
HEYNS M A	1.4	1.4
STD BANK NOM TVL P/L	1.3	4.0
SPL EXECUTIVE SHARE SCHEME	1.3	1.5
ALTRON GROUP RETIREMENT FUND	1.2	---
JOHANNESBURG MUNICIPAL PENS FUND	1.2	---
SFSS NOM P/L	1.2	---
ALTENA MEWS P/L	---	2.3
EVANS G J H	---	5.6
GARDNER J A	---	1.3
SANKORP BPK	---	25.1
SANLAM	---	11.0
TOTAL	82.9	80.2

DIRECTORS :
DU PLESSIS AS ,EVANS GJH
FOLB LJ (Managing Director),HEYNS MA
ISRAELSTAM LS (Chairman),WIESNER HS M

REGISTRATION NUMBER : 70/00054/07

REGISTERED OFFICE
Willow Grove, 196 Louis Botha Avenue
Houghton Estate
2198
TEL: 011-803 7200
FAX: 011-803 7232

TRANSFER SECRETARY
Fraser Street Registrars (Pty) Ltd
P O Box 61178, Marshalltown
2107
TEL: 011-491 0911

COMPANY SECRETARY
B W Kalil

NATURE OF BUSINESS
An investment holding company. Subsidiaries are active in the following operations: Marketing & support of software packages, & system software products; Development of computer-based systems; Provision of training courses to product users; Personnel service, offering computer specialists for permanent placement.

BANKERS :
Nedperm Bank Ltd

AUDITORS :
Freedman Scher

FAMILIAR BRAND NAMES
ALM (ASSET/LIABILITY),AUTO-MATE
CFS (CURRENCY FORECASTING),COMMANDER EIS
CON-TROL,HEALTHNET/2,IFS (FORECASTING SYS)
MENTOR 3,ON/2 (FINANCIAL TRANS),STORENET/2
SYSTEM W,WALKER (FINANCIAL SYSTEMS)

CONTRIBUTION BY ACTIVITY
Software Products (% operating profit) (69.0%)
Software Development (19.0%)
Personnel Services (12.0%)

YEAR END : February

DIVIDEND : Ords 10c

Final No 9	(Ldr)11/05/90	(Pay)13/06/90	Amt(c)8
Interim No 10	(Ldr)09/11/90	(Pay)03/12/90	Amt(c)3
Final No 11	(Ldr)10/05/91	(Pay)03/06/91	Amt(c)8
Interim No 12	(Ldr)01/11/91	(Pay)29/11/91	Amt(c)5
Final No 13	(Ldr)15/05/92	(Pay)01/06/92	Amt(c)10
Interim No 14	(Ldr)13/11/92	(Pay)27/11/92	Amt(c)6

NUMBER OF EMPLOYEES : 407

CAPITAL STRUCTURE

	AUTHORISED	ISSUED
Ords 10c	20000000	16130000

FINANCIAL STATISTICS (AT FINANCIAL YEAR END)

(Amts in R'000)	1992 Feb	1991 Feb	1990 Feb	1989 Feb	1988 Feb
Ord S/H Int	21261	17816	16418	10549	8071
Long Trm Loans	3552	4127	4504	2920	1486
Iss Ord Share	16130	16130	16130	15300	15300
Total Liab	23357	21055	18726	21540	10254
Current Liab	19805	16928	14222	18620	8768
Total Assets	44556	38838	35144	32089	18325
Intang Assets	62	33	*	*	*
Current Assets	31586	24874	20235	23169	13575
Debtors	26922	23496	18412	23039	11981
Turnover	91930	70750	62512	49205	35383
Oper Profit	11100	6642	9362	9017	6319
Interest Paid	699	1683	1457	473	284
Tax Paid	5389	2105	3196	4058	2933
Prf af Int&Tax	5865	3372	4709	4486	3102
Prf att Ord Sh	5865	3372	4672	4390	3064
Btm Line Earn	5865	3172	4344	4390	2957
Dividend Paid	2420	1774	2131	1912	1362
Mkt Prce(c) YE	165	90	185	245	145
Depreciation	3218	3526	2659	1643	742

PER SHARE STATISTICS (CENTS)

Net Asst Val	131.43	110.25	101.79	68.95	52.75
Net Earnings	36.40	20.90	30.10	28.70	20.00
Dividends	15.00	11.00	13.50	12.50	8.90
Cash Flow	57.90	44.54	52.45	39.70	27.10

RATIOS AND OTHER INFORMATION

Mrk Cap(R000)	26615	14517	29841	37485	22185
Current Ratio	1.59	1.47	1.42	1.24	1.55
Quik/Acid Tst	1.59	1.47	1.42	1.24	1.55
A/C Rec T/ovr	3.41	3.01	3.40	2.14	2.95
Tot Ass T/ovr	2.06	1.82	1.78	1.53	1.93
Debt/Ass Rat	0.47	0.49	0.49	0.65	0.53
L T L Tot Ass	0.03	0.05	0.09	0.07	0.06
Debt to Eqity	0.99	1.06	1.05	1.98	1.21
Interest Cover	15.88	3.95	6.43	19.06	22.25
Oper Prof Mrg	12.07	9.39	14.98	18.33	17.86
Net Prof Marg%	6.38	4.77	7.47	8.92	8.66
Ret on Assets	26.83	18.44	26.64	28.10	34.48

Ret on Equity%	27.59	18.93	28.46	41.62	37.96
Price/Earnings	4.53	4.31	6.15	8.54	7.25
Divid Cover	2.43	1.90	2.23	2.30	2.25
Divid Yield	9.09	12.22	7.30	5.10	6.14
Earning Yield%	22.06	23.22	16.27	11.71	13.79
NAV % Mrk Pr	79.65	122.50	55.02	28.14	36.38
Effec Tax Rate	45.89	32.54	29.45	47.02	43.26
Def Interval	0.29	0.90	1.06	1.22	0.49
Sus Grth Rate	16.20	8.97	15.48	23.49	21.09

SUBSIDIARY & ASSOCIATED COMPANIES

COMPUTER PERSONNEL (PTY) LTD
COMPUTERISED PERSONNEL SYSTEMS (PTY) LTD
CPL COMPUTER PERSONNEL (PTY) LTD
CPL CONTRACT SERVICES (PTY) LTD
CPL RECRUITMENT & CONSULTING SERVISES (P
SPL (NAMIBIA) (PTY) LTD
SPL BUSINESS SYSTEMS (PTY) LTD
SYSTEMS PROGRAMMING (PTY) LTD

INVESTMENTS

None

SPUR HOLDINGS LTD

ABBREVIATION : SPURHLD

JSE SHORT CODE : SPH

SECTOR : Industrial-Beverages & Hotels

SHAREHOLDERS

Who Owns Whom's Assessment of the Identity of the Ultimate Controlling Shareholder: DIRECTORS

SHAREHOLDER	PERCENTAGE 1992	1991
AMTOP INV P/L	50.7	44.7
STD BANK NOM TVL P/L	15.3	---
CMB NOM P/L	9.0	---
SA SPECIAL RISKS INSURANCE ASSOC LTD	6.5	---
SFSS NOM P/L	4.8	---
AMBOR A J	2.6	25.5
JOFFE P R	1.1	---
COMYN R	---	1.2
SANLAM	---	11.4
WEAL INV & LICENCING LTD	---	4.4
TOTAL	90.0	87.1

DIRECTORS :
AMBOR AJ (Chairman),GETZ K
JOFFE PR (Financial Director)
TOPAT G (Managing Director

REGISTRATION NUMBER : 85/03350/06

REGISTERED OFFICE
5th Floor, Matrix House, 73 Strand Street
Cape Town
8001
TEL: 021-462 1186
FAX: 021-461 6857

TRANSFER SECRETARY
Mercantile Registrars Ltd
P O Box 1053, Johannesburg
2000
TEL: 011-333 8181

COMPANY SECRETARY
P R Joffe

NATURE OF BUSINESS
An investment holding company with interests in the manufacture & export of catering equipment, franchised steakhouse & fast food outlets and the provision of management & training services. The company has a controlling interest in JSE-quoted Spur Steak Ranches.

BANKERS :
Nedbank Ltd

AUDITORS :
Cecil Kilpin & Co

FAMILIAR BRAND NAMES
N/A

CONTRIBUTION BY ACTIVITY
N/A

YEAR END : February

DIVIDEND :Ords 1c

Interim No 5	(Ldr)03/11/89	(Pay)24/11/89	Amt(c)4
Final No 6	(Ldr)18/05/90	(Pay)15/06/90	Amt(c)6.75
Interim No 7	(Ldr)02/11/90	(Pay)23/11/90	Amt(c)5
Final No 8	(Ldr)03/05/91	(Pay)24/05/91	Amt(c)9
Interim No 9	(Ldr)08/11/91	(Pay)29/11/91	Amt(c)6.5
Final No 10	(Ldr)22/05/92	(Pay)12/06/92	Amt(c)11.5
Interim No 11	(Ldr)23/10/92	(Pay)20/11/92	Amt(c)8.5

NUMBER OF EMPLOYEES : 60

CAPITAL STRUCTURE

	AUTHORISED	ISSUED
Ords 1c	20000000	12553000
Red Prefs 1c	100	0

FINANCIAL STATISTICS (AT FINANCIAL YEAR END)

(Amts in R'000)	1992 Feb	1991 Feb	1990 Feb	1989 Feb	1988 Feb
Ord S/H Int	9528	6514	5966	7233	6401
Long Trm Loans	11748	7226	2697	2197	2120
Iss Ord Share	14770	12553	12531	12500	12500
Total Liab	17416	12643	4326	3820	3297
Current Liab	5668	5417	1629	1623	1177
Total Assets	9798	9360	7135	6523	9698
Intang Assets	17146	9797	3157	4530	*
Current Assets	7663	7217	3228	3190	1995
Debtors	5709	4163	1355	1442	250
Inventory	631	480	56	88	-
Turnover	29608	23554	6023	7528	7011
Oper Profit	10386	7829	1014	2139	1615
Interest Paid	561	563	17	178	159
Tax Paid	4539	3628	197	622	625
Prf af Int&Tax	6248	4175	1238	1520	937
Prf att Ord Sh	3950	2290	2025	2211	1480
Btm Line Earn	3950	2290	2025	2211	1480
Dividend Paid	2520	1757	1347	1250	1250
Mkt Prce(c) YE	280	150	90	120	88
Depreciation	366	353	170	121	137

PER SHARE STATISTICS (CENTS)

Net Asst Val	-51.58	-26.15	22.42	21.62	51.21
Net Earnings	23.00	18.20	12.88	12.00	12.00
Dividends	18.00	14.00	10.75	10.00	10.00
Cash Flow	30.21	22.46	11.24	13.13	8.42

RATIOS AND OTHER INFORMATION

Mrk Cap(R000)	41356	18830	11278	15000	11000
Current Ratio	1.35	1.33	1.98	1.97	1.69
Quik/Acid Tst	1.24	1.24	1.95	1.91	1.69
A/C Rec T/ovr	5.19	5.66	4.45	5.22	28.04
Tot Ass T/ovr	3.02	2.52	0.84	1.15	0.72
Debt/Ass Rat	1.45	0.98	0.61	0.59	0.34
L T L Tot Ass	0.88	0.40	0.38	0.34	0.22
Debt to Eqity	1.49	1.41	0.73	0.53	0.52
Interest Cover	18.51	13.91	61.18	12.02	10.16
Oper Prof Mrg	35.08	33.24	16.84	28.41	23.04
Net Prof Marg%	13.34	9.72	33.62	29.37	21.11
Ret on Assets	115.82	89.38	34.42	46.16	23.57
Ret on Equity%	41.46	28.33	31.32	30.57	23.12
Price/Earnings	12.17	8.24	6.99	10.00	7.33
Divid Cover	1.28	1.30	1.20	1.20	1.20
Divid Yield	6.43	9.33	11.94	8.33	11.36
Earning Yield%	8.21	12.13	14.31	10.00	13.64
NAV % Mrk Pr	-18.42	-17.44	24.91	18.02	58.19
Effec Tax Rate	42.08	46.49	13.98	29.04	40.01
Def Interval	1.78	0.65	0.49	1.40	2.02
Sus Grth Rate	15.01	8.18	11.36	13.29	3.59

SUBSIDIARY & ASSOCIATED COMPANIES

AD WORKSHOP (PTY) LTD
AMTOP HOLDINGS (PTY) LTD
COMANCHE SPUR STEAK RANCH (PTY) LTD (50%)
GOLDEN STEER STEAKHOUSE (PTY) LTD
HARD ROCK CAFE (PTY) LTD
ILLINOIS SPUR STEAK RANCH (PTY) LTD (50%)
PAROW FAST FOODS (PTY) LTD
RED HAWK RESTAURANT (PTY) LTD
SEVEN SPUR (PTY) LTD (50%)
SEVEN SPUR STEAK RANCH (PTY) LTD
SOMERSET WEST FAST FOODS (PTY) LTD
SPUR COOL CORPORATION (PTY) LTD
SPUR STEAK RANCHES LIMITED
STEFAT (PTY) LTD (50%)

INVESTMENTS

None

SPUR STEAK RANCHES LTD

ABBREVIATION : SPUR

JSE SHORT CODE : SPU

SECTOR : Industrial-Beverages & Hotels

SHAREHOLDERS

Who Owns Whom's Assessment of the Identity of the Ultimate Controlling Shareholder:
SPUR HOLDINGS

SHAREHOLDER	PERCENTAGE 1992	1991
SPUR HOLDINGS LTD	54.6	54.5
AMTOP HOLDINGS P/L	10.0	10.0
CMB NOM P/L	9.5	—
WEAL INV & LICENCING LTD	6.4	2.6
BOYES D J G	1.3	1.3
SFSS NOM P/L	1.1	—
AMBOR A J	—	3.8
SANLAM	—	9.5
TOTAL	82.8	81.6

DIRECTORS :
AMBOR AJ (Chairman),GETZ K
JOFFE PR (Financial Director)
TOPAT G (Managing Director)

REGISTRATION NUMBER : 86/00818/07

REGISTERED OFFICE
5th Floor, Matrix House, 73 Strand Street
Cape Town
8001
TEL: 021-462 1186
FAX: 021-461 6857

TRANSFER SECRETARY
Mercantile Registrars Ltd
P O Box 1053, Johannesburg
2000
TEL: 011-333 8181

COMPANY SECRETARY
P R Joffe

NATURE OF BUSINESS
A holding company of a group involved primarily in the establishment, marketing and control of a chain of franchise restuarants & also the manufacturing and selling of restuarent supplies.

BANKERS :
Nedcor Bank Ltd

AUDITORS :
Cecil Kilpin & Co

FAMILIAR BRAND NAMES
HARD ROCK CAFE,SPUR

CONTRIBUTION BY ACTIVITY
N/A

YEAR END : February

DIVIDEND : Ords 1c

Interim No 8	(Ldr)03/11/89	(Pay)24/11/89	Amt(c)5
Final No 9	(Ldr)18/05/90	(Pay)15/06/90	Amt(c)7.75
Interim No 10	(Ldr)02/11/90	(Pay)23/11/90	Amt(c)6.5
Final No 11	(Ldr)03/05/91	(Pay)24/05/91	Amt(c)10.5
Interim No 12	(Ldr)08/11/91	(Pay)29/11/91	Amt(c)8.5
Final No 13	(Ldr)22/05/92	(Pay)12/06/92	Amt(c)14.5
Interim No 14	(Ldr)23/10/92	(Pay)20/11/92	Amt(c)11.5

NUMBER OF EMPLOYEES : 60

CAPITAL STRUCTURE

	AUTHORISED	ISSUED
Ords 1c	20000000	15846000
5% Conv Red Cum Prefs 1c	2375000	0

FINANCIAL STATISTICS (AT FINANCIAL YEAR END)

(Amts in R'000)	1992 Feb	1991 Feb	1990 Feb	1989 Feb	1988 Feb
Ord S/H Int	8935	7534	6724	6384	5416
Long Trm Loans	1881	797	721	1160	1137
Iss Ord Share	15846	15846	15797	15749	13333
Total Liab	8650	5020	3632	3197	2368
Current Liab	6769	4223	2911	2037	1231
Total Assets	17002	11971	9773	9581	7784
Intang Assets	583	583	583	*	*
Current Assets	7281	5257	3376	2945	1391
Debtors	2280	1442	1669	1787	604
Inventory	631	400	389	349	210
Turnover	26600	17728	13357	8836	5658
Oper Profit	8827	6799	4565	3198	2294
Interest Paid	21	95	199	-	-
Tax Paid	4466	3418	2161	1547	1047
Prf af Int&Tax	4910	3484	2335	1651	1247
Prf att Ord Sh	4910	3484	2335	1630	1199
Btm Line Earn	4910	3484	2335	1630	1199
Dividend Paid	3645	2694	2014	1629	1199
Mkt Prce(c) YE	340	160	100	102	95
Depreciation	282	175	113	55	52

PER SHARE STATISTICS (CENTS)

Net Asst Val	52.71	43.87	38.87	40.54	40.62
Net Earnings	30.98	22.00	15.00	11.03	9.00
Dividends	23.00	17.00	12.75	11.00	9.00
Cash Flow	32.77	23.09	15.50	10.70	9.38

RATIOS AND OTHER INFORMATION

Mrk Cap(R000)	53876	25354	15797	16064	12666
Current Ratio	1.08	1.24	1.16	1.45	1.13
Quik/Acid Tst	0.98	1.15	1.03	1.27	0.96
A/C Rec T/ovr	11.67	12.29	8.00	4.94	9.37
Tot Ass T/ovr	1.56	1.48	1.37	0.92	0.73
Debt/Ass Rat	0.51	0.42	0.37	0.33	0.18
L T L Tot Ass	0.11	0.07	0.07	0.12	0.02
Debt to Eqity	0.97	0.67	0.54	0.50	0.26
Interest Cover	420.33	71.57	22.94	-	-
Oper Prof Mrg	33.18	38.35	34.18	36.19	40.54
Net Prof Marg%	18.46	19.65	17.48	18.45	21.19
Ret on Assets	55.27	58.45	48.04	33.38	29.47
Ret on Equity%	54.95	46.24	34.73	25.53	22.14
Price/Earnings	10.97	7.27	6.67	9.25	10.56
Divid Cover	1.35	1.29	1.18	1.00	1.00
Divid Yield	6.76	10.63	12.75	10.78	9.47
Earning Yield%	9.11	13.75	15.00	10.81	9.47
NAV % Mrk Pr	15.50	27.42	38.87	39.74	42.76
Effec Tax Rate	47.63	49.52	48.06	48.37	45.64
Def Interval	0.38	0.28	0.53	0.79	0.92
Sus Grth Rate	14.16	10.49	4.77	0.02	0.00

SUBSIDIARY & ASSOCIATED COMPANIES

AVBERG INVESTMENTS (PTY) LTD
CHAMPION SNACK BAR (PTY) LTD
HARD ROCK ADVERTISING (PTY) LTD
PANAROTTIS ADVERTISING (PTY) LTD
PANAROTTIS PIZZA PASTA FRANCHISE (PTY) L
PSS INVESTMENTS (PTY) LTD
RANCH ADVERTISING (PTY) LTD
SPUR ADVERTISING (PTY) LTD
SPUR FAST FOODS (PTY) LTD
SPUR STEAK RANCHES FRANCHISE (PTY) LTD

INVESTMENTS

None

ST HELENA GOLD MINES LTD

ABBREVIATION : ST-HELENA

JSE SHORT CODE : STH

SECTOR : Gold-OFS

SHAREHOLDERS

Who Owns Whom's Assessment of the Identity of the Ultimate Controlling Shareholder: INSTITUTIONAL / MANAGED BY GENMIN

SHAREHOLDER	PERCENTAGE 1992	1991
CONSOLIDATED NOM P/L	24.5	24.5
LONDON CONTROL ACCOUNT	13.4	13.3
ORANGE FREE STATE INV TRUST LTD	13.0	13.0
INDO-CHINA NOM P/L	10.1	---
SOCIETE INTERPROF POUR LA COMPENSATION	7.0	6.4
FERMAIN NOM LTD	5.5	5.5
DEPOSITARY NOM INC	4.1	1.9
CITIBANK NOM P/L	3.4	3.4
FREE STATE CONS GOLD MINES (OPS) LTD	3.3	3.3
SEPON LTD J ACCOUNT	3.2	3.0
STD BANK NOM TVL P/L	2.7	1.8
FIRST NAT NOM P/L	2.5	2.4
FIRST NAT NOM P/L GATR DEPOT	1.6	---
ABSA NOM P/L	1.4	---
CMB NOM P/L	1.2	---
BANK OF NEW YORK NOM LTD	---	2.2
INDO-CHINA NOM SA P/L	---	12.9
SANLAM	---	1.2
VOLKSKAS NOM P/L	---	1.2
TOTAL	96.8	96.0

DIRECTORS :
ELLIS SP ,EUSTACE PJ ,HOSKING KM
MAUDE G (Chairman),OLIVIER JE ,ROBINSON PDK
ROUX FJP DR,SUNTER CL ,VOS P

REGISTRATION NUMBER : 05/20743/06

REGISTERED OFFICE
General Mining Building, 6 Hollard Street
Johannesburg
2001
TEL: 011-376 9111
FAX: 011-836 8708

TRANSFER SECRETARY
Central Registrars Ltd
P O Box 4844, Johannesburg
2000
TEL: 011-331 0051

COMPANY SECRETARY
General Mining Metals & Minerals Ltd

NATURE OF BUSINESS

The company operates the St Helena gold mine, in the Welkom area, and the Oryx gold mine in the Theunissen area of the OFS. Silver is recovered at both operations as a by-product. The company also mills and treats ores mined by Unisel Gold Mines.

BANKERS :

First National Bank of SA Ltd
Trust Bank of Africa Ltd

AUDITORS :

Deloitte Pim Goldby

FAMILIAR BRAND NAMES

N/A

CONTRIBUTION BY ACTIVITY

N/A

YEAR END : December

DIVIDEND : Ords R1

Interim No 70	(Ldr)03/08/90	(Pay)14/09/90	Amt(c)165
Final No 71	(Ldr)02/02/91	(Pay)14/03/91	Amt(c)115
Interim No 72	(Ldr)02/08/91	(Pay)13/09/91	Amt(c)50
Final No 73	(Ldr)31/01/92	(Pay)13/03/92	Amt(c)150

NUMBER OF EMPLOYEES : 6923

CAPITAL STRUCTURE

	AUTHORISED	ISSUED
Ords R1	10000000	9625000
"A" Cum Prefs R1	7000000	3825035
"B" Cum Prefs R1	5000000	3825035
"C" Cum Prefs R1	3000000	2465000

FINANCIAL STATISTICS (AT FINANCIAL YEAR END)

(Amts in R'000)	1991 Dec	1990 Dec	1989 Dec	1988 Dec	1987
Ord S/H Int	480290	467751	450808	412577	321246
Long Trm Loans	988996	639849	376782	176705	98906
Iss Ord Share	9625	9625	9625	9625	9625
Total Liab	1076770	725371	494220	278833	159665
Current Liab	87774	85522	117438	102128	60759
Total Assets	1557060	1193122	945028	691410	475423
Current Assets	81108	76556	104940	99956	55271
Debtors	14671	9046	19660	22152	-
Inventory	12381	11478	10530	8648	55271
Turnover	282489	339125	350356	324676	260880
Oper Profit	131997	104203	84175	74414	63630
Interest Paid	94562	55724	16399	-	892
Tax Paid	5725	6534	3828	7010	444
Prf af Int&Tax	31818	42525	63948	67404	52739
Prf att Ord Sh	31818	42525	63948	67404	10129
Btm Line Earn	31818	42525	63948	130802	10129
Dividend Paid	19250	26950	29356	29356	15881
Mkt Prce(c) YE	2300	2600	4400	2525	3600

PER SHARE STATISTICS (CENTS)

Net Asst Val	4990.03	4859.75	4683.72	4286.51	3337.62
Net Earnings	216.00	285.00	284.00	316.00	-
Dividends	200.00	280.00	305.00	305.00	-
Cash Flow	330.58	410.65	664.39	700.30	547.94

RATIOS AND OTHER INFORMATION

Mrk Cap(R000)	221375	250250	423500	243031	346500
Current Ratio	0.92	0.90	0.89	0.98	0.91
Quik/Acid Tst	0.78	0.76	0.80	0.89	-
A/C Rec T/ovr	19.25	37.49	17.82	14.66	-
Tot Ass T/ovr	0.18	0.28	0.37	0.47	0.55
Debt/Ass Rat	0.69	0.60	0.51	0.38	0.34
L T L Tot Ass	0.63	0.53	0.38	0.24	0.21
Debt to Eqity	2.22	1.53	1.07	0.64	0.50
Interest Cover	1.40	1.88	5.13	-	60.62
Oper Prof Mrg	46.73	30.73	24.03	22.92	24.39
Net Prof Marg%	11.26	12.54	18.25	20.76	3.88
Ret on Assets	8.48	8.78	8.91	10.76	11.37
Ret on Equity%	6.62	9.09	14.19	16.34	3.15
Price/Earnings	10.65	9.12	15.49	7.99	-
Divid Cover	1.08	1.02	0.93	1.04	-
Divid Yield	8.70	10.77	6.93	12.08	-
Earning Yield%	9.39	10.96	6.45	12.51	-
NAV % Mrk Pr	216.96	186.91	106.45	169.76	92.71
Effec Tax Rate	15.29	19.66	5.65	9.42	0.71
Def Interval	31.15	16.19	6.39	2.90	1.88
Sus Grth Rate	2.62	3.33	7.67	9.22	-1.79

SUBSIDIARY & ASSOCIATED COMPANIES

None

INVESTMENTS

None

STANDARD BANK INVESTMENT CORP LTD

ABBREVIATION : SBIC

JSE SHORT CODE : SBC

SECTOR : Financial-Banks & Financial Services

SHAREHOLDERS

Who Owns Whom's Assessment of the Identity of the Ultimate Controlling Shareholder: LIBERTY LIFE 40% / SA MUTUAL 21%

SHAREHOLDER	PERCENTAGE 1992	1991
STALIT P/L	24.4	23.2
LIBERTY LIFE ASSOC OF AFRICA LTD	13.5	13.5
SA MUTUAL	12.8	12.8
MINU NOM LTD	9.8	9.8
CAPITAL SECURITIES LTD	7.2	7.2
STD BANK NOM TVL P/L	5.8	5.8
ASHTREE INV P/L	2.3	1.9
EIGHTY ONE MAIN STREET NOM LTD	1.7	1.7
MINE OFFICIALS PENS FUND	1.5	1.5
SANLAM	1.5	1.5
LRS INV TRUST P/L	1.2	2.4
SOUTHERN LIFE ASSOC LTD	1.1	---
DE BEERS HOLDINGS P/L	1.1	---
RESIDENT NOM LTD	---	1.5
TOTAL	83.5	82.7

DIRECTORS :

BRADLEY E LE R MS
CLEWLOW WAM (Joint Deputy Chairman)
DE LOOR JH DR,DHLOMO OD DR,GEACH CH ,GEELING KLG
GORDON D (Joint Deputy Chairman),KAHN JM
MABUZA EJ ,MCALPINE JR ,PLUMBRIDGE RA ,RELLY GWH

RETIEF PF ,SAUNDERS CJ ,STRAUSS CB DR (Chairman)
THERON EP (Managing Director)
VOSLOO MH (Executive Director)

REGISTRATION NUMBER : 69/17128/06

REGISTERED OFFICE
Standard Bank Centre, 5 Simmonds Street
Johannesburg
2001
TEL: 011-636 9112
FAX: 011-636 4975

TRANSFER SECRETARY
Rand Registrars Ltd
P O Box 82549, Southdale
2135
TEL: 011-835 1016

COMPANY SECRETARY
C W Bjerre

NATURE OF BUSINESS
The holding company of deposit-taking subsidiaries engaged in the provision of banking and financial services, insurance broking and trust services.

BANKERS :
N/A

AUDITORS :
KPMG Aiken & Peat

FAMILIAR BRAND NAMES
N/A

CONTRIBUTION BY ACTIVITY
Standard Bank (% net income after tax) (59.1%)
Stannic & Stancor (14.5%)
Standard Merchant Bank (6.8%)
Standard Bank of Bophuthatswana (5.0%)
Standard Bank Namibia (1.9%)
Investment/Finance/Other Service Co's (10.2%)
Associates (2.5%)

YEAR END : December

DIVIDEND :Ords R1

Interim No 40	(Ldr)18/08/89	(Pay)08/09/89	Amt(c)32
Final No 41	(Ldr)02/03/90	(Pay)23/03/90	Amt(c)80
Interim No 42	(Ldr)24/08/90	(Pay)07/09/90	Amt(c)37
Final No 43	(Ldr)22/02/91	(Pay)11/04/91	Amt(c)96
Interim No 44	(Ldr)23/08/91	(Pay)09/10/91	Amt(c)44
Final No 45	(Ldr)28/02/92	(Pay)16/04/92	Amt(c)116
Interim No 46	(Ldr)21/08/92	(Pay)07/10/92	Amt(c)53

NUMBER OF EMPLOYEES : 28611

CAPITAL STRUCTURE

	AUTHORISED	ISSUED
6,5% First Cum Prefs R1	8000000	8000000
Ords R1	126141138	118767176

FINANCIAL STATISTICS (AT FINANCIAL YEAR END)

(Amts in R'000)	1991 Dec	1990 Dec	1989 Dec	1988	1987
Ord S/H Int	2662500	2194200	1886000	1572300	1411400
Long Trm Loans	2362900	3683600	2512600	28098000	20654800
Iss Ord Share	102373	98023	74025	74000	74000
Total Liab	47734100	43317200	37962100	56170800	41286600
Current Liab	45371200	39633600	35449500	28072800	20631800
Total Assets	50396600	45511400	39848100	29670300	22066200
Current Assets	46762000	41723900	35438800	-	-
Debtors	43600500	39454300	31183700	-	-
Oper Profit	794200	615900	-726200	2572800	1710600
Interest Paid	-	-	3916900	2166600	1381200
Tax Paid	317400	245200	216500	91100	99900
Prf af Int&Tax	476800	370700	328500	268600	229500
Prf att Ord Sh	510700	413200	333200	264200	220100
Btm Line Earn	491000	431600	342000	264200	220100
Dividend Paid	163400	130400	109700	96100	257300
Mkt Prce(c) YE	5225	5300	3000	1925	1700
Depreciation	156900	130100	101700	-	-

PER SHARE STATISTICS (CENTS)

Net Asst Val	2600.78	2238.45	2547.79	2124.73	1907.30
Net Earnings	507.00	422.00	340.00	-	-
Dividends	160.00	133.00	112.00	-	-
Cash Flow	651.92	567.24	510.14	362.97	310.14

RATIOS AND OTHER INFORMATION

Mrk Cap(R000)	5348989	5195219	2220750	1424500	1258000
Current Ratio	1.03	1.05	1.00	-	-
Quik/Acid Tst	1.03	1.05	1.00	-	-
Debt/Ass Rat	0.91	0.88	0.89	1.89	1.87
L T L Tot Ass	0.01	0.01	-	0.95	0.94
Debt to Eqity	17.15	18.20	18.80	35.73	29.25
Interest Cover	-	-	-0.16	1.17	1.24
Ret on Assets	1.67	1.47	11.23	8.51	7.75
Ret on Equity%	19.18	18.83	17.67	16.80	15.59
Price/Earnings	10.31	12.56	8.82	-	-
Divid Cover	3.17	3.17	3.04	-	-
Divid Yield	3.06	2.51	3.73	-	-
Earning Yield%	9.70	7.96	11.33	-	-
NAV % Mrk Pr	49.78	42.23	84.93	110.38	112.19
Effec Tax Rate	29.59	24.89	25.89	22.43	30.33
Def Interval	66.73	69.22	63.46	104.61	90.00
Sus Grth Rate	13.04	12.89	11.85	10.69	-2.64

SUBSIDIARY & ASSOCIATED COMPANIES

A BROWN & SHEPHERD (PTY) LTD
AGRICULTURAL & INDUS. MECH. PROP.(BRONKS
AILERON INVESTMENTS (PTY) LTD
AIMANER INVESTMENTS (PTY) LTD
ALGOA TRANSPORT CO. (PTY) LTD
ALISIER INVESTMENTS (PTY) LTD
AMALER & CO. (PTY) LTD
ANDREWS CARTAGE (PTY) LTD
AP YOUNG PROPERTY HOLDINGS (PTY) LTD
BALFOUR CENTRE (PTY) LTD
BANK SCAN (PTY) LTD
BANNER NOMINEES (PTY) LTD
BEAU-GESTE INVESTMENTS (PTY) LTD
BERG NOMINEES (PTY) LTD
BERGSTOCK LTD (50%)
BILLHAWK INVESTMENTS (PTY) LTD (50%)
BKF PROJECTS (PTY) LTD
BOUMAT PROPERTIES (PTY) LTD (20%)
BRICKTREE INVESTMENTS (PTY) LTD
CHURCHILL DRIVE INVESTMENTS (PTY) LTD
CIGARETTE VENDING MACHINES (PTY) LTD
CITIRAND TRUST (PTY) LTD
CITY CREDIT (TRANSVAAL) (PTY) LTD
COMDATA (PTY) LTD
CRANBOURNE PROPERTIES (PTY) LTD
DAMDAL BELEGGINGS (PTY) LTD
DAVID MANN (PTY) LTD
DE CANHA BROS. (PTY) LTD
DEKOCK'S TRANSPORT (CAPE) (PTY) LTD
DERIAN COURT (PTY) LTD
DIAMOND JUBILEE (PTY) LTD
DINERS CLUB SA (PTY) LTD
DUAL EQUITY LTD

DURBAN PROPERTY HOLDINGS LTD
EASTERN HOUSE (PTY) LTD
EJ RORICH (PTY) LTD
ELDEE (PTY) LTD
ELOF HOLDINGS (PTY) LTD
ERF 14 WELKOM (PTY) LTD
ERF THREE SIX SPARTAN (PTY) LTD
EXPORT SERVICES (PTY) LTD
FELDMAN INVESTMENTS (PTY) LTD
FINCH INVESTMENTS (PTY) LTD
FINCOR LTD (49.0%)
FINLAW PROPERTIES (PTY) LTD
FLEET LEASE (PTY) LTD
FRASERS INTERNATIONAL (BOTSWANA) (PTY) L
FRASERS INTERNATIONAL (PTY) LTD
FRASERS INTERNATIONAL AIRCARGO (PTY) LTD
FRASERS INTERNATIONAL FREIGHT FORWARDERS
FRASERS INTERNATIONAL SERVICES (PTY) LTD
GC SHEPPARD & ASSOCIATES (PTY) LTD
GILLIS-MASON INVESTMENTS (PTY) LTD
GILMET INVESTMENTS (PTY) LTD
GOLDEN BEACH INVESTMENTS (PTY) LTD
GOLDIE & CO. (PTY) LTD
GOLDSTEINS CORNER LTD
GOSHAWK FINANCE (PTY) LTD
GOURMET FOODS (PTY) LTD
GROENEWOUDS TRANSPORT (PTY) LTD
GROSVENOR ROSEBANK POPERTY LTD
GULF EXPORT (PTY) LTD (47.5%)
GULF PROPERTIES (PTY) LTD (47.5%)
GULF STEEL (PTY) LTD (47.5%)
HESINCA (PTY) LTD
HESPERUS HOLDINGS LTD
HESPERUS MANAGEMENT SERVICES (PTY) LTD
HESPERUS SECURITIES (PTY) LTD
HILBER (PTY) LTD
HUMAN RESOURCE DEVELOPMENT (PTY) LTD
JACK WELLSTED (PTY) LTD
JACOWOL INVESTMENTS (PTY) LTD
JD SALES (PTY) LTD (27,5%)
JET PARK PROPERTIES (PTY) LTD
JOHAN NEL (PTY) LTD
KINGSWOOD PARK (PTY) LTD
L. SUZMAN (AGENCIES) (PTY) LTD
L. SUZMAN (BENONI) (PTY) LTD
L. SUZMAN (BORDER) (PTY) LTD
L. SUZMAN (MANAGEMENT SERVICES) (PTY) LT
L. SUZMAN (MIDLANDS) (PTY) LTD
L. SUZMAN (NATAL) (PTY) LTD
L. SUZMAN (PROPERTIES) (PTY) LTD
L. SUZMAN (RAND) (PTY) LTD
L. SUZMAN (U.K.) LTD
L. SUZMAN (VEREENIGING) (PTY) LTD
L. SUZMAN (WESTERN TRANSVAAL) (PTY) LTD
L. SUZMAN DISTRIBUTORS (PTY) LTD
L. SUZMAN LTD
L.S. FINANCE (PTY) LTD
LASER TRANSPORT HOLDINGS LTD
LIBERTAS NOMINEES (PTY) LTD
LIBIC INVESTMENT HOLDINGS LTD
LIBLIFE CONTROLLING CORPORATION (PTY) LT (50%)
LUDGATE HOLDINGS LTD (40%)
LUXOT LTD
M & L DISTRIBUTORS (PTY) LTD
M & L WHOLESALERS (PTY) LTD
M.I.C. INVESTMENTS LTD
M.I.C. REAL ESTATE HOLDINGS (PTY) LTD
MACJOLUM INVESTMENTS (PTY) LTD
MACKAYS (PTY) LTD
MANASTONE (PTY) LTD
MARBLE FACTORS (PTY) LTD
MARKETING DEVELOPMENT CO. SA (PTY) LTD
MATADOR BUILDING (PTY) LTD
MAXIM PACKERS (PTY) LTD
MCCALL ASSOCIATES (PTY) LTD
MECHANICAL HNDLING CONSULTANTS
MERRIMAN SQUARE LTD
METEQUITY LTD
METROPOLITAN BOARD BOND PARTICIPATION NO
METROPOLITAN BOARD NOMINEES LTD
MIDLAND PROPERTIES (PTY) LTD
MINING SERVICES LTD
MORKELS FURNITURE REMOVALS (NATAL) (PTY)
MORKELS TRANSPORT (CAPE) (PTY) LTD
MORKELS TRANSPORT (PTY) LTD
MOTOR & TRANSPORT INVESTMENT CORP. (PTY)
MOUNTAIN HOMES (PTY) LTD
MULTI PROJECTS LTD
MURCHISON PLAINS BLACK WATTLE CO (PTY) L
NATAL MORTGAGES (PTY) LTD
NATIONAL CIGARETTE WHOLESALERS (PTY) LTD
NEWSTOCK (PTY) LTD (50%)
NICFIELD PROPERTIES (PTY) LTD
NORDEL PROPERTY INVESTMENTS (PTY) LTD
NORTHFORD PROPERTY (PTY) LTD
ODEON INVESTMENT CO. (PTY) LTD
P-E COMPUTER & TELECOMMUNICATIONS (PTY)
P-E CONSULTING GROUP SA (PTY) LTD
P-E CORPORATE SERVICES (PTY) LTD
P.L. PALM TRANSPORT (PTY) LTD
P.L.P. PROPERTY HOLDINGS (PTY) LTD (UK)
PAIZES HOLDINGS (PTY) LTD
PAIZES PROPERTIES (PTY) LTD
PICKFORDS PROPERTIES GEORGE (PTY) LTD
PICKFORDS REMOVALS (S.A.) (PTY) LTD
PIETERBERG EXECUTIVE APARTMENTS (PTY) LT
PLOVER SECURITIES LTD
PRET-HILL INVESTMENTS (PTY) LTD
PRETORIA TOBACCO CO. (PTY) LTD
PRODUCTION ENGINEERING (CENTRAL AFRICA)
PRODUCTION ENGINEERING HOLDINGS (SA) (PT
PROFESSIONAL CONSULTING GROUP (PTY) LTD
PROJAT (PTY) LTD
PROJEK ADMINISTRASIE TEGNIEK (EDMS) BPK
RALPH PARROTT ASSOCIATES (PTY) LTD
RALPH PARROTT CONSULTING SERVICES (PTY)
RETIEFBURG PROPERTIES (PTY) LTD
RONTIVIA (PTY) LTD
ROSEN & WASHKANSKY (PTY) LTD
RUM & MAPLE TOBACCO CORP. (SA) (PTY) LTD
S.C.B. (PTY) LTD
S.C.L. INVESTMENTS (PTY) LTD
SANDBRATH (PTY) LTD
SANDTON SALES (PTY) LTD
SBIC MANAGEMENT SERVICES (PTY) LTD
SBSA PROPERTY DE DOORNS (PTY) LTD
SECURITY EXECUTOR & TRUST CO. LTD
SECURITY TRUST BOND NOMINEES CO. (PTY) L
SECURITY TRUST NOMINEES (PTY) LTD
SHERIM INVESTMENTS (PTY) LTD
SIMMONDS STREET OLDINGS (PTY) LTD
SIX CRADOCK AVENUE (PTY) LTD
SLAWAL NOMINEES (PTY) LTD
STAND THIRTY EIGHT SPARTAN (PTY) LTD
STANDARD BANK ARENA ELLIS PARK (PTY) LTD
STANDARD BANK ASSURANCE BROKERS (PTY) LT
STANDARD BANK BOND INVESTMENT LTD
STANDARD BANK CENTRE (PTY) LTD
STANDARD BANK CORPORATE FINANCE LTD
STANDARD BANK DEVELOPMENT FINANCE (PTY)
STANDARD BANK FACTORS LTD
STANDARD BANK FINANCIAL SERVICES HOLDING
STANDARD BANK FUND MANAGERS LTD
STANDARD BANK IMPORT AND EXPORT FINANCE
STANDARD BANK INSURANCE BROKERS (PTY) LT
STANDARD BANK NAMIBIA LTD
STANDARD BANK OF BOPHUTHATSWANA LTD
STANDARD BANK OF SA LTD

STANDARD BANK PROPERTIES (ADDERLEY STREE
STANDARD BANK PROPERTIES (BELLVILLE) LTD
STANDARD BANK PROPERTIES (BERRY'S CORNER
STANDARD BANK PROPERTIES (BOKSBURG) LTD
STANDARD BANK PROPERTIES (CAPE TOWN ABC)
STANDARD BANK PROPERTIES (CLAREMONT) LTD
STANDARD BANK PROPERTIES (COMMISSIONER S
STANDARD BANK PROPERTIES (ELOFF STREET)
STANDARD BANK PROPERTIES (FERREIRASTOWN)
STANDARD BANK PROPERTIES (FORDSBURG) LTD
STANDARD BANK PROPERTIES (HEIDELBERG) LT
STANDARD BANK PROPERTIES (LADYSMITH) LTD
STANDARD BANK PROPERTIES (LIBRARY GARDEN
STANDARD BANK PROPERTIES (LONG STREET) L
STANDARD BANK PROPERTIES (MARSHALLS) LTD
STANDARD BANK PROPERTIES (NELSPRUIT) LTD
STANDARD BANK PROPERTIES (NORTH END) LTD
STANDARD BANK PROPERTIES (ORKNEY) LTD
STANDARD BANK PROPERTIES (OXFORD ROAD) L
STANDARD BANK PROPERTIES (PIETERSBURG) L
STANDARD BANK PROPERTIES (PLUMSTEAD) LTD
STANDARD BANK PROPERTIES (PORT ELIZABETH
STANDARD BANK PROPERTIES (PORT ELIZABETH
STANDARD BANK PROPERTIES (PRETORIA) LTD
STANDARD BANK PROPERTIES (RONDEBOSCH) LT
STANDARD BANK PROPERTIES (ROSEBANK) LTD
STANDARD BANK PROPERTIES (SEA POINT) LTD
STANDARD BANK PROPERTIES (SMAL STREET) L
STANDARD BANK PROPERTIES (SMALL STREET)
STANDARD BANK PROPERTIES (STANDARD HOUSE
STANDARD BANK PROPERTIES (STANGER) LTD
STANDARD BANK PROPERTIES (UMTATA) LTD
STANDARD BANK PROPERTIES (WEST END) LTD
STANDARD BANK PROPERTIES (WYNBERG) LTD
STANDARD BANK PROPERTIES LTD
STANDARD BANK PROPERTIES WOODBROOK (PTY)
STANDARD BANK PROPERTY FUND (39%)
STANDARD BANK PROPERTY FUND MANAGERS LTD
STANDARD BANK TRAINING COMPANY LTD
STANDARD CREDIT CORPORATION LTD
STANDARD MERCHANT BANK LTD
STANDARD MERCHANT SECURITIES (PTY) LTD
STANDARD TRUST LTD
STANSURE (PTY) LTD
STANVEST (PTY) LTD
STEVELLA INVESTMENTS (PTY) LTD
STONECRAFT (PTY) LTD
STRUCTURAL HOLLOW FLOOR CO. (PTY) LTD (24.9%)
STUTTAFORDS VAN LINES (PTY) LTD
SUITABLE INVESTMENT NOMINEES (PTY) LTD
T. JOCHELSON (PTY) LYD
TAVERN INVESTMENTS (PTY) LTD
THIRTY THREE BOLTON ROAD (PTY) LTD
TOBACCO & GENERAL SUPPLIES LTD
TOLUX SA LTD
TRUCKERS (PTY) LTD
UNIONBANK OF SWAZILAND LTD (49%)
UNISEC GROUP LTD
UNISEC HIGH INCOME PORTFOLIO (PTY) LTD
UNISEC INDUSTRIAL GROUP (PTY) LTD
UNISEC ISSUING AND UNDERWRITING (PTY) LT
UNISEC MANAGEMENT SERVICES (PTY) LTD
UNISEC SECURITES LTD
UNISECURE INVESTMENTS (PTY) LTD
UNISECURE NOMINEES (PTY) LTD
UNISECURE PROPERTIES (PTY) LTD
UNIT SECURITIES & TRUST CO. OF S.A. LTD
VAAL TOBACCO CO. (1979) (PTY) LTD
VAALEAST INVESTMENTS (PTY) LTD
VOKER INVESTMENTS PTY LTD
VOORHOUT STREET PROPERTIES (PTY) LTD
WARPET (PTY) LTD
WELLPICK PROPERTIES (PTY) LTD
WEYBRIDGE INVESTMENTS (PTY) LTD

ZATTO INC. (50%)

INVESTMENTS

AFRICAN BANK OF SA LTD (4,6%)
BANCO STANDARD TOTTA DE ANGOLA SARL (5%)
BANCO STANDARD TOTTA DE MOZAMBIQUE (5%)
FIRST INTERNATIONAL TRUST LTD (4%)
HISTORIC GRAHAMSTOWN (PTY) LTD (3,1%)
HISTORICAL HOMES OF S.A. LTD (4%)
TRANSATLANTIC HOLDINGS LTD (600000 SH)

STANDARD BANK PROPERTY FUND

ABBREVIATION : STANPRO

JSE SHORT CODE : SPR

SECTOR : Financial-Property Trust

SHAREHOLDERS

Who Owns Whom's Assessment of the Identity of the Ultimate Controlling Shareholder: STANDARD BANK / SA MUTUAL

SHAREHOLDER	PERCENTAGE 1992	1991
UNISEC HIGH INCOME PORTFOLIO P/L	33.4	33.4
SA MUTUAL	28.6	30.4
LIBERTY LIFE ASSOC OF AFRICA LTD	5.4	5.4
EIGHTY ONE MAIN STREET NOM LTD	4.5	4.4
STD BANK NOM TVL P/L	3.2	2.8
SLAWAL NOM P/L	2.6	2.6
BARLOWS PENS FUND	2.1	1.2
ENGINEERING INDUSTRIES PENS FUND	2.0	1.4
METAL IND GROUP PENS FUND	1.7	1.6
CMB NOM P/L	1.5	---
NESTLE PENS FUND	1.4	---
BP THIBAULT NOM P/L	1.3	1.3
FNP PENS FUND	---	1.0
SANLAM	---	1.3
TOTAL	87.7	86.8

DIRECTORS :
BELL GC ,BRADLEY E LE R MRS,CESMAN WE ,FOX DM
KIRCHMANN WM ,MOKOATLE BN
SHAW-TAYLOR S (Managing Director),STRAUSS CB DR
THERON EP (Chairman

REGISTERED OFFICE
10th Floor, 78 Fox St
Johannesburg
2001
TEL: 011-636 9111
FAX: 011-492 1022

TRANSFER SECRETARY
Central Registrars Ltd
P O Box 4844, Johannesburg
2000
TEL: 011-331 0051

COMPANY SECRETARY
FS Lombard

NATURE OF BUSINESS
Stanpro is a closed-end property unit trust with interests in commercial, residential & industrial properties.

BANKERS :
Standard Bank of SA Ltd

AUDITORS :
KPMG Aiken & Peat

FAMILIAR BRAND NAMES
N/A

CONTRIBUTION BY ACTIVITY
Residential (% Net Rental Income) (23.8%)
Retail & Offices (42.8%)
Industrial (19.6%)
Specialised (13.8%)

YEAR END : December

DIVIDEND :Units

Final No 13	(Ldr)09/02/90	(Pay)21/02/90	Amt(c)8.05
Interim No 14	(Ldr)06/07/90	(Pay)31/08/90	Amt(c)9.7
Final No 15	(Ldr)08/02/91	(Pay)28/02/91	Amt(c)7.45
Interim No 16	(Ldr)16/08/91	(Pay)31/08/91	Amt(c)9.25
Final No 17	(Ldr)14/02/92	(Pay)21/02/92	Amt(c)10

CAPITAL STRUCTURE

	AUTHORISED	ISSUED
Units	280140000	280140000

FINANCIAL STATISTICS (AT FINANCIAL YEAR END)

(Amts in R'000)	1991 Dec	1990 Dec	1989 Dec	1988	1987
Ord S/H Int	304940	305082	255194	247408	243572
Long Trm Loans	-	-	-	16507	13564
Iss Ord Share	280140	280140	243600	243600	243600
Total Liab	28747	21708	20333	33014	27128
Current Liab	28747	21708	20333	16507	13564
Total Assets	333687	326790	275527	293374	289548
Current Assets	33440	75735	49565	29459	32412
Debtors	1340	3703	8811	-	-
Inventory	-	-	-	29459	32412
Oper Profit	-2028	-1726	-1376	29966	26552
Prf af Int&Tax	53933	44500	36546	29966	26552
Prf att Ord Sh	53933	44500	36546	29966	26552
Btm Line Earn	53785	49463	44326	29966	26552
Dividend Paid	53927	44500	36540	29963	26552
Mkt Prce(c) YE	150	125	140	95	112

PER SHARE STATISTICS (CENTS)

Net Asst Val	108.85	108.90	104.76	101.56	99.99
Net Earnings	19.25	17.15	15.00	-	-
Dividends	19.25	17.15	15.00	-	-
Cash Flow	19.25	15.88	15.00	12.30	10.90

RATIOS AND OTHER INFORMATION

Mrk Cap(R000)	420210	350175	341040	231420	272832
Current Ratio	1.16	3.49	2.44	1.78	2.39
Quik/Acid Tst	1.16	3.49	2.44	-	-
Debt/Ass Rat	0.09	0.07	0.07	0.11	0.09
L T L Tot Ass	-	-	-	0.06	0.05
Debt to Eqity	0.09	0.07	0.08	0.13	0.11
Ret on Assets	16.16	13.62	13.26	10.21	9.17
Ret on Equity%	17.69	14.59	14.32	12.11	10.90
Price/Earnings	7.79	7.29	9.33	-	-
Divid Cover	1.00	1.00	1.00	-	-
Divid Yield	12.83	13.72	10.71	-	-
Earning Yield%	12.83	13.72	10.71	-	-
NAV % Mrk Pr	72.57	87.12	74.83	106.91	89.28
Def Interval	0.01	0.02	0.02	0.55	0.51
Sus Grth Rate	0.00	0.00	0.00	0.00	0.00

SUBSIDIARY & ASSOCIATED COMPANIES

APARTMENT INVESTMENTS (PTY) LTD
BANKET INVESTMENTS (PTY) LTD
BEDFORD GARDENS (PTY) LTD
BEINSONS (PTY) LTD
CITYLAB PROPERTIES (PTY) LTD
COAST LAND & INVESTMENT CO LTD
CROUSLEY BUILDINGS (PTY) LTD
DELMAT HOUSE (PTY) LTD
FIELD STREET INVESTMENTS (PTY) LTD
FOUR EIGHT FOUR PARKTOWN NORTH (PTY) LTD
GILLMA INVESTMENTS (PTY) LTD
GREEN HANSOM INVESTMENTS (PTY) LTD
GREENMARKET INVESTMENTS (PTY) LTD
HJK INVESTMENTS (PTY) LTD
JDB BELEGGINGS (EDMS) BPK
JJ & E (PTY) LTD
KLEIN & KOTZE STREET PROPERTIES (PTY) LT
LILABE INVESTMENTS (PTY) LTD
LORRAINE INVESTMENTS (PTY) LTD
MANNBANK INVESTMENTS (PTY) LTD
MANRICH HOLDINGS (PTY) LTD
MAXISAT INVESTMENTS (PTY) LTD
MICHAELCHRIS INVESTMENTS (PTY) LTD
MODERN FLATS (PTY) LTD
NADA (PTY) LTD
NAMONT INVESTMENTS (PTY) LTD
NORBANK (PTY) LTD
NSJ (PTY) LTD
NUFIELD PROPERTIES (PTY) LTD
OATORIAN PROPERTY HOLDINGS (PTY) LTD
OSHBRO INVESTMENTS 5 (PTY) LTD
PAIZES HOLDINGS (PTY) LTD
PETERKLEIN INVESTMENTS (PTY) LTD
RESERVOIR INVESTMENTS (PTY) LTD
RISSID PROPERTIES (PTY) LTD
RONTIVIA (PTY) LTD
S X PROPS (PTY) LTD
SEVENTY JORISSEN STREET (PTY) LTD
SPRINGSITE (PTY) LTD
STRYDOMPARK EXT 25 (PTY) LTD
TBR PROPERTIES LTD
TEXTILE CENTRE (PTY) LTD
VANGUARD ESTATES (PTY) LTD
VIA-JOEL INVESTMENTS (PTY) LTD

INVESTMENTS

None

STANDARD CHARTERED BANK BOTSWANA LTD

ABBREVIATION : STANBOT

SECTOR : Botswana Stock Exchange

SHAREHOLDERS

Who Owns Whom's Assessment of the Identity of the Ultimate Controlling Shareholder:
STANDARD CHARTERED BANK AFRICA PLC

SHAREHOLDER	PERCENTAGE 1992	1991
STD CHARTERED BANK AFRICA PLC	75.0	---
BOTSWANA LIFE INSURANCE LTD	7.0	---
DEBSWANA PENS FUND	4.3	---
BOTSWANA MOTOR VEHICLE INSURANCE FUND	2.0	---
TOTAL	88.2	---

DIRECTORS :
CALEY SJ ,FREEMAN HC ,GRANT DG ,HEATON JR
LEKALAKE PMS ,MALLARD CJ (Managing Director)
MPOTOKWANE LM ,MPUCHANE SA
STEENKAMP PMS (Chairman

REGISTERED OFFICE
5th Floor Standard House, The Mall
Gabarone, Botswana

TEL: 353111
FAX: 372933

TRANSFER SECRETARY
N/A

COMPANY SECRETARY
N M M Kgabi

NATURE OF BUSINESS
The company is engaged in the business of commercial banking and provides a wide range of financial services.

BANKERS :
N/A

AUDITORS :
Price Waterhouse Meyernel

FAMILIAR BRAND NAMES
N/A

CONTRIBUTION BY ACTIVITY
N/A

YEAR END : December

NUMBER OF EMPLOYEES : 782

CAPITAL STRUCTURE

	AUTHORISED	ISSUED
Ords P1	40000000	28806257

FINANCIAL STATISTICS (AT FINANCIAL YEAR END)

(Amts in P)	1991 Dec	1990 Dec
Ord S/H Int	64594	46515
Long Trm Loans	784	1813
Iss Ord Share	28806	12803
Total Liab	682526	408085
Current Liab	681742	406272
Total Assets	747120	454600
Current Assets	209061	100202
Oper Profit	21276	16349
Tax Paid	7585	6077
Prf af Int&Tax	13691	10272
Prf att Ord Sh	13691	10272
Btm Line Earn	13691	10272
Dividend Paid	6313	5122
Depreciation	1454	1040

PER SHARE STATISTICS (CENTS)

Net Asst Val	224.24	363.31
Net Earnings	51.30	40.10
Dividends	38.00	40.00
Cash Flow	49.00	89.91

RATIOS AND OTHER INFORMATION

Current Ratio	0.31	0.25
Quik/Acid Tst	0.31	0.25
Debt/Ass Rat	0.91	0.89
Debt to Eqity	10.55	8.73
Ret on Assets	2.85	3.60
Ret on Equity%	21.20	22.08
Divid Cover	1.35	1.00
Effec Tax Rate	40.49	36.91
Sus Grth Rate	11.42	11.07

SUBSIDIARY & ASSOCIATED COMPANIES

None

INVESTMENTS

None

STANDARD ENGINEERING LTD

ABBREVIATION : STANDRD

JSE SHORT CODE : SDR

SECTOR : Industrial-Engineering

SHAREHOLDERS

Who Owns Whom's Assessment of the Identity of the Ultimate Controlling Shareholder: SANLAM VIA MALBAK & MURRAY & ROBERTS

SHAREHOLDER	PERCENTAGE 1992	1991
MALBAK INV (STANDARD ENGINEERING) LTD	38.0	72.8
M & R CORPORATE INV P/L	38.0	---
EIGHTY ONE MAIN STREET NOM LTD	16.0	5.8
STD BANK NOM TVL P/L	5.3	7.0
CMB NOM P/L	1.2	---
RAND MERCHANT NOM P/L	---	1.4
BARLOW RAND LTD	---	1.3
SANLAM	---	5.6
VOLKSKAS NOM P/L	---	1.3
MALBAK GROUP PENS FUND	---	2.9
TOTAL	98.5	98.1

DIRECTORS :
BINGHAM R ,BIRD LB ,BRINK DC
BROWN HF (Chairman),CAMPBELL DN ,COLEPEPER IG
DAVIDSON RT (Managing Director),DONE BM
HOBBS RN ,LEE L

REGISTRATION NUMBER : 01/04912/06

REGISTERED OFFICE
Malbak House, 1 Protea Place
Off Fredman Drive, Sandown
2196
TEL: 011-783 4480
FAX: 011-783 0408

TRANSFER SECRETARY
Central Registrars Ltd
P O Box 4844, Johannesburg
2000
TEL: 011-331 0051

COMPANY SECRETARY
Malbak Group Management Co (Pty) Ltd

NATURE OF BUSINESS
The group is involved in the following areas of activity: Manufacture & distribution of gearboxes, axles & brake components for trailers and heavy commercial vehicles; Spring manufacturing, metal pressing & roofing products; Manufacture and distribution of pumps, fluid management and pump systems, drill steels, pressure vessels, steel pipe; Manufacture of electric & diesel locomotives passenger coaches, electric multiple trainsets and wagons for rail transportation organisations.

BANKERS :
First National Bank of SA Ltd

AUDITORS :
Ernst & Young

FAMILIAR BRAND NAMES
ABERTECH,ALLIS CHALMERS,AMASTEEL,ASTAS
HALL LONGMORE,HARVEYTILE
UNION CARRIAGE & WAGON

CONTRIBUTION BY ACTIVITY
Automotive Division (% of Turnover) (27.8%)
Fluid Handling Division (26.2%)
Metal Pressing Division (12.8%)
Pipe Division (22.5%)
Rolling Stock Division (10.7%)

YEAR END : August

DIVIDEND :Ords 50c

Interim	(Ldr)11/05/90	(Pay)18/05/90	Amt(c)14
Final	(Ldr)21/09/90	(Pay)07/12/90	Amt(c)18

DIVIDEND :Ords no par value

Interim	(Ldr)03/05/91	(Pay)17/05/91	Amt(c)14
Final	(Ldr)22/11/91	(Pay)06/12/91	Amt(c)26
Interim	(Ldr)01/05/92	(Pay)15/05/92	Amt(c)14
Final	(Ldr)20/11/92	(Pay)04/12/92	Amt(c)28

NUMBER OF EMPLOYEES : 3653

CAPITAL STRUCTURE

	AUTHORISED	ISSUED
5,5% Cum Prefs R2	150000	75000
Ords no par value	100000000	35421724

FINANCIAL STATISTICS (AT FINANCIAL YEAR END)

(Amts in R'000)	1992 Aug	1991 Aug	1990 Aug	1989 Aug	1988 Aug
Ord S/H Int	208610	189326	167146	104286	18900
Long Trm Loans	54618	61663	66162	40591	1304
Iss Ord Share	35422	34268	34268	22778	3150
Total Liab	242475	265349	260676	162549	19370
Current Liab	187857	203686	194514	121958	18066
Total Assets	451085	454675	427822	266835	38270
Current Assets	289221	306380	301227	195852	22021
Debtors	141595	122440	107757	84917	10332
Inventory	146014	181852	188587	107204	11667
Turnover	688433	639077	690541	408855	56909
Oper Profit	67519	70361	74891	40811	-3839
Interest Paid	15583	18120	18631	7393	791
Tax Paid	7200	5781	21364	9695	-
Prf af Int&Tax	48097	49687	40175	26347	-4630
Prf att Ord Sh	43040	41415	25665	20509	-4638
Btm Line Earn	23459	35882	10280	12935	-4638
Dividend Paid	14878	13708	8630	6460	-
Mkt Prce(c) YE	725	875	600	410	280
Depreciation	19525	17858	18212	7760	2703

PER SHARE STATISTICS (CENTS)

Net Asst Val	588.93	552.49	487.76	457.84	600.00
Net Earnings	122.00	120.90	95.20	92.10	-147.20
Dividends	42.00	40.00	32.00	29.00	-
Cash Flow	182.89	174.26	167.61	126.73	-61.43

RATIOS AND OTHER INFORMATION

Mrk Cap(R000)	256810	299845	205608	93390	8820
Current Ratio	1.54	1.50	1.55	1.61	1.22
Quik/Acid Tst	0.76	0.61	0.58	0.73	0.57
A/C Rec T/ovr	4.86	5.22	6.41	4.81	5.51
Tot Ass T/ovr	1.53	1.41	1.61	1.53	1.49
Debt/Ass Rat	0.42	0.46	0.48	0.47	0.50
L T L Tot Ass	0.00	0.01	0.02	0.02	0.03
Debt to Eqity	0.90	1.11	1.22	1.21	1.02
Interest Cover	4.33	3.88	4.02	5.52	-4.85
Oper Prof Mrg	9.81	11.01	10.85	9.98	-6.75
Net Prof Marg%	6.25	6.48	3.72	5.02	-8.15
Ret on Assets	15.71	16.18	18.74	16.28	-10.03
Ret on Equity%	20.63	21.87	15.35	19.67	-24.54
Price/Earnings	5.94	7.24	6.30	4.45	-1.90
Divid Cover	2.90	3.02	2.98	3.18	-
Divid Yield	5.79	4.57	5.33	7.07	-
Earning Yield%	16.83	13.82	15.87	22.46	-52.57
NAV % Mrk Pr	81.23	63.14	81.29	111.67	214.29
Effec Tax Rate	12.15	12.59	32.56	27.00	-
Def Interval	0.96	1.39	1.47	1.41	-4.00
Sus Grth Rate	13.50	14.63	10.19	13.47	-24.54

SUBSIDIARY & ASSOCIATED COMPANIES

A S TRANSMISSIONS & STEERINGS (PTY) LTD
ABERTECH INDUSTRIES (PTY) LTD
ABERTECH MANAGEMENT & OFFSHORE SERVICES
AFH DEVERS (PTY) LTD
APHEX COMMUNICATIONS (PTY) LTD
ASTAS AUTOMOTIVE (PTY) LTD
ASTAS HOLDINGS (PTY) LTD
ASTAS INVESTMENTS LTD
AUTOFLUG SOUTH AFRICA (PTY) LTD
DBM SYSTEMS (PTY) LTD
DRILL STEELS (PTY) LTD
FILJO PUMPS (PTY) LTD
FLUID HOLDINGS LTD
FORDSBURG PROPERTIES (PTY) LTD
HALL LONGMORE & CO (PTY) LTD
HALL LONGMORE CONTRACTORS (PTY) LTD
HALL LONGMORE INVESTMENTS LTD
HALL LONGMORE PROPERTIES (PTY) LTD
HARVEYTILE (PTY) LTD
MABCON INDUSTRIES LTD
MAISEY MATRIX (PTY) LTD
MALLEABLE PROPERTIES (PTY) LTD
MALLEABLE PROPERTIES (PTY) LTD
MONO PUMPS ESTATES (NEWCASTLE) (PTY) LTD

MONO PUMPS PROPERTIES (PTY) LTD
MONO PUMPS PROPERTIES (ZULULAND) (PTY) L
NAMIBIA PIPE (PTY) LTD
OCTOQUAT INVESTMENTS (PTY) LTD
OILCHEM (PTY) LTD
PACKARD INSTRUMENTS (PTY) LTD
PELICAN PIPELINES (PTY) LTD
PELICAN PROJECTS (PTY) LTD
PLASTELECT SERVICES (PTY) LTD
PROTEA DATA SYSTEMS (PTY) LTD
PROTEA TECHNOLOGY LTD
SA AXLES (PTY) LTD
TAMBIT MINING SERVICES (PTY) LTD
TUFFTILE LTD
UNION CARRIAGE & WAGON COMPANY (PTY) LTD
UNION CARRIAGE INVESTMENTS LTD
VIBERFREE (PTY) LTD
WEBROY (TVL) (PTY) LTD

INVESTMENTS

None

STELLENBOSCH FARMERS WINERY GROUP LTD

ABBREVIATION : SFW

JSE SHORT CODE : SFW

SECTOR : Industrial-Beverages & Hotels

SHAREHOLDERS

Who Owns Whom's Assessment of the Identity of the Ultimate Controlling Shareholder:
REMBRANDT GROUP/KWV

SHAREHOLDER	PERCENTAGE 1992	1991
REMBRANDT-KWV INV LTD	60.0	60.0
SA BREWERIES LTD	30.0	30.0
LIBERTY LIFE ASSOC OF AFRICA LTD	3.7	3.7
NEDBANK NOM LTD	2.0	1.2
MOMENTUM LIFE ASSURE LTD	---	1.1
TOTAL	95.6	96.0

DIRECTORS :
ADCOCK CS ,BAYLY FC ,DAVIN FJ (Chairman)
DE LA BAT RS ,JONKER LN ,MALHERBE JF ,NOLTE BL
STROEBEL FH (Managing Director),WEBB RC
WINSHAW WJ ,WYMAN MI

REGISTRATION NUMBER : 04/02134/06

REGISTERED OFFICE
Oude Libertas, Adam Tas Road
Stellenbosch
7600
TEL: 02231-73400
FAX: 02231-71355

TRANSFER SECRETARY
Central Registrars Ltd
P O Box 4844, Johannesburg
2000
TEL: 011-331 0051

COMPANY SECRETARY
J A Starke

NATURE OF BUSINESS
Group activities include production & wholesale distribution of wines & spirits and, to a lesser extent, of non-alcoholic beverages. The group also has an investment in retail marketing of liquor.

BANKERS :
N/A

AUDITORS :
Coopers Theron Du Toit

FAMILIAR BRAND NAMES
CHATEAU LIBERTAS,LA GRATITUDE,LANZERAC,MONIS
NEDERBURG,TASHEIMER,WESTERN PROV CELLARS
ZONNEBLOEM

CONTRIBUTION BY ACTIVITY
N/A

YEAR END : June

DIVIDEND : Ords no par value

Interim No 3	(Ldr)16/03/90	(Pay)12/04/90	Amt(c)4
Final No 4	(Ldr)14/09/90	(Pay)15/10/90	Amt(c)7.5
Interim No 5	(Ldr)21/02/92	(Pay)28/02/92	Amt(c)4
Interim No 5	(Ldr)22/02/91	(Pay)28/02/91	Amt(c)4
Final No 6	(Ldr)13/09/91	(Pay)16/10/91	Amt(c)7.5
Interim No 7	(Ldr)21/02/92	(Pay)28/02/92	Amt(c)4
Final No 8	(Ldr)18/09/92	(Pay)14/10/92	Amt(c)8.5

NUMBER OF EMPLOYEES : 4000

CAPITAL STRUCTURE

	AUTHORISED	ISSUED
Ords no par value	160000000	140000000

FINANCIAL STATISTICS (AT FINANCIAL YEAR END)

(Amts in R'000)	1992 Jun	1991 Jun	1990 Jun	1989 Jun	1988 Jun
Ord S/H Int	597535	538973	491980	457234	382944
Long Trm Loans	67133	64139	65870	45630	45701
Iss Ord Share	140000	140000	140000	140000	140000
Total Liab	197834	199066	202056	178920	155939
Current Liab	130701	134927	136186	133290	110238
Total Assets	795369	738039	694036	636154	538883
Current Assets	414494	381064	350759	322357	268469
Debtors	94391	91634	90211	85783	69883
Inventory	319961	289179	256070	232205	193723
Oper Profit	108458	105615	109778	106276	89746
Interest Paid	8523	12121	7259	6948	6338
Tax Paid	46343	44726	50880	49203	40054
Prf af Int&Tax	58392	54651	53554	51071	43354
Prf att Ord Sh	43438	39165	42789	43470	38325
Btm Line Earn	41852	34611	42789	43470	38325
Dividend Paid	17500	16100	16100	14700	-
Mkt Prce(c) YE	185	175	125	130	300
Depreciation	16868	18572	16228	14184	12732

PER SHARE STATISTICS (CENTS)

Net Asst Val	426.81	384.98	351.41	326.60	273.53
Net Earnings	31.00	28.00	40.40	39.02	32.80

Dividends	12.50	11.50	11.50	10.50	-
Cash Flow	55.21	52.05	48.12	46.84	39.87

RATIOS AND OTHER INFORMATION

Mrk Cap(R000)	259000	245000	175000	182000	420000
Current Ratio	3.17	2.82	2.58	2.42	2.44
Quik/Acid Tst	0.72	0.68	0.70	0.68	0.68
Debt/Ass Rat	0.23	0.26	0.28	0.26	0.27
L T L Tot Ass	0.07	0.07	0.08	0.05	0.07
Debt to Eqity	0.31	0.35	0.39	0.37	0.38
Interest Cover	12.90	8.99	15.15	15.32	14.16
Ret on Assets	14.33	15.18	16.57	17.48	17.20
Ret on Equity%	7.27	7.27	8.70	9.51	10.01
Price/Earnings	5.97	6.25	3.09	3.33	9.15
Divid Cover	2.48	2.43	3.51	3.72	-
Divid Yield	6.76	6.57	9.20	8.08	-
Earning Yield%	16.76	16.00	32.32	30.02	10.93
NAV % Mrk Pr	230.71	219.99	281.13	251.23	91.18
Effec Tax Rate	42.56	46.58	50.80	48.44	47.89
Def Interval	0.68	0.80	1.09	0.94	1.19
Sus Grth Rate	4.34	4.28	5.42	6.29	10.01

SUBSIDIARY & ASSOCIATED COMPANIES

BOFOR PROPERTIES (PTY) LTD (50%)
DEVON ROAD PROPERTY (PTY) LTD
EXPO LIQUOR LTD (40%)
HENRY TAYLER & RIES LTD (25%)
NAMIBIA WINES & SPIRITS LTD
NEDERBURG WINE FARMS LTD
NEDERBURG WINES (PTY) LTD
SFW HOLDINGS LTD
STELLENBOCH FARMERS' WINERY (TRANSKEI) L
STELLENBOCH FARMERS' WINERY LTD
SWAZILAND LIQUOR DISTRIBUTORS LTD (33,3%)
UD IMPORTS (PTY) LTD (25%)
WESTERN PROVINCE CELLARS LTD (50%)

INVESTMENTS

None

STERLING CLOTHING LTD

ABBREVIATION : STERLING

JSE SHORT CODE : STL

SECTOR : Industrial-Clothing, Footwear & Textiles

SHAREHOLDERS

Who Owns Whom's Assessment of the Identity of the Ultimate Controlling Shareholder:
DIRECTORATE / BERMAN FAMILY

SHAREHOLDER	PERCENTAGE 1992	1991
EIGHTY ONE MAIN STREET NOM LTD	22.1	20.5
ABRAM BERMAN FAMILY SORREL TRUST	10.5	10.5
ABRAM BERMAN FAMILY LUELLA TRUST	10.5	10.5
BARBIERI M FAMILY TRUST	7.5	7.5
DESMET B J	4.5	4.5
HOTZ S	3.9	3.9
SILPERT A L	3.5	3.5
BERMAN S E/L	3.1	3.1
KOTON L	3.1	3.1
CROSLEY B D	2.5	2.5
COPPOLA N	2.2	2.2
ESTERHUIZEN A M	2.2	2.2
FIRST NAT NOM P/L	2.0	2.0
BARBIERI M A	1.9	1.9
LIBERTY LIFE ASSOC OF AFRICA LTD	1.0	1.0
BERMAN A	1.0	2.6
BERMAN ARCHIE	---	1.0
STD BANK NOM TVL P/L	---	1.3
TOTAL	81.3	83.7

DIRECTORS :
BARBIERI M MR,DESMET BJ MR
HASLETT FN MR (Chairman),LEVENBERG M M

REGISTRATION NUMBER : 53/02077/06

REGISTERED OFFICE
Sterling House, 131 Pritchard Street
Johannesburg
2001
TEL: 011-333 9101
FAX: 011-29 9484

TRANSFER SECRETARY
Fraser Street Registrars (Pty) Ltd
P O Box 61178, Marshalltown
2107
TEL: 011-491 0911

COMPANY SECRETARY
S Hotz

NATURE OF BUSINESS
An investment holding company and through its subsidiaries carries on business as manufacturer and distributor of men's clothing.

BANKERS :
Standard Bank of SA Ltd, Nedperm Bank Ltd

AUDITORS :
LA Resnick & Co

FAMILIAR BRAND NAMES
DAKOTA,MOUSTACHE,NICO ARNALDI,RIDING HIGH STERLING

CONTRIBUTION BY ACTIVITY
N/A

YEAR END : December

DIVIDEND : Ords 7c

Dividend No 42	(Ldr)05/04/91	(Pay)29/04/91	Amt(c)4
Dividend No 43	(Ldr)10/04/92	(Pay)04/05/92	Amt(c)2.5

NUMBER OF EMPLOYEES : 1000

CAPITAL STRUCTURE

	AUTHORISED	ISSUED
Ords 7c	25000000	19389000

FINANCIAL STATISTICS (AT FINANCIAL YEAR END)

(Amts in R'000)	1990 Dec	1989 Dec	1988 Dec	1987 Dec
Ord S/H Int	10190	9133	7599	3912
Long Trm Loans	1670	1390	425	1210

Iss Ord Share	19389	19389	19389	30100
Total Liab	13093	13807	9559	8540
Current Liab	11423	12417	9134	7330
Total Assets	23283	22940	17158	12452
Current Assets	20182	20295	15715	11573
Debtors	10784	10300	8666	7090
Inventory	9397	9989	7047	4481
Turnover	38655	34893	30082	25232
Oper Profit	5152	6216	5076	3560
Interest Paid	1736	873	579	352
Tax Paid	1782	2596	2170	1653
Prf af Int&Tax	1824	2815	2383	1555
Prf att Ord Sh	1824	2815	2383	1555
Btm Line Earn	1824	2815	2033	1305
Dividend Paid	775	1280	1077	575
Mkt Prce(c) YE	40	62	60	-
Depreciation	520	386	226	246

PER SHARE STATISTICS (CENTS)

Net Asst Val	52.56	47.10	39.19	13.00
Net Earnings	9.40	14.50	14.20	10.30
Dividends	4.00	6.60	6.00	3.80
Cash Flow	12.41	16.77	12.81	11.40

RATIOS AND OTHER INFORMATION

Mrk Cap(R000)	7756	12021	11633	-
Current Ratio	1.77	1.63	1.72	1.58
Quik/Acid Tst	0.94	0.83	0.95	0.97
A/C Rec T/ovr	3.58	3.39	3.47	3.56
Tot Ass T/ovr	1.66	1.52	1.75	2.03
Debt/Ass Rat	0.55	0.60	0.55	0.64
L T L Tot Ass	0.06	0.05	0.02	0.05
Debt to Eqity	1.27	1.50	1.25	2.05
Interest Cover	2.97	7.12	8.77	10.11
Oper Prof Mrg	13.33	17.81	16.87	14.11
Net Prof Marg%	4.72	8.07	7.92	6.16
Ret on Assets	22.94	27.39	29.91	28.59
Ret on Equity%	17.90	30.82	31.36	39.75
Price/Earnings	4.26	4.28	4.23	-
Divid Cover	2.35	2.20	2.37	2.71
Divid Yield	10.00	10.65	10.00	-
Earning Yield%	23.50	23.39	23.67	-
NAV % Mrk Pr	131.39	75.97	65.32	-
Effec Tax Rate	47.70	47.03	57.65	54.18
Def Interval	2.96	1.77	1.00	2.12
Sus Grth Rate	10.29	16.81	17.19	25.05

SUBSIDIARY & ASSOCIATED COMPANIES

CASUAL CLOTHING (PTY) LTD
COBLO (PTY) LTD
GRAND CLOTHING MANUFACTURERS (PTY) LTD
NORMAN TRADING & MANUFACTURING COMPANY (
STERLING CLOTHING MANUFACTURERS (PTY) LT

INVESTMENTS

None

STILFONTEIN GOLD MINING CO LTD

ABBREVIATION : STILFTN

JSE SHORT CODE : STI

SECTOR : Gold-Klerksdorp

SHAREHOLDERS

Who Owns Whom's Assessment of the Identity of the Ultimate Controlling Shareholder:
GENCOR (MANAGED BY)

SHAREHOLDER	PERCENTAGE 1992	1991
STD BANK NOM TVL P/L	67.0	65.6
CONSOLIDATED NOM P/L	10.0	9.2
LONDON CONTROL ACCOUNT	7.2	8.4
INDO-CHINA NOM P/L	6.1	---
SOCIETE INTERPROF POUR LA COMPENSATION	2.2	1.9
SEPON LTD J ACCOUNT	1.7	1.4
FIRST NAT NOM P/L	1.2	1.5
DEPOSITARY NOM INC	1.2	---
INDO-CHINA NOM SA P/L	---	7.3
TOTAL	96.7	95.2

DIRECTORS :
BURKE JHJ ,FIELD AJ ,KRAFFT GC
MAUDE G (Chairman),WILSON RAD

REGISTRATION NUMBER : 05/33412/06

REGISTERED OFFICE
General Mining Building, 6 Hollard Street
Johannesburg
2001
TEL: 011-376 9111

TRANSFER SECRETARY
Central Registrars Ltd
P O Box 4844, Johannesburg
2000
TEL: 011-331 0051

COMPANY SECRETARY
General Mining Metals & Minerals Ltd

NATURE OF BUSINESS
The company operates a gold mine in the Klerksdorp area, Tvl. Silver is recovered as a by-product.

BANKERS :
First National Bank of SA Ltd

AUDITORS :
KPMG Aiken & Peat

FAMILIAR BRAND NAMES
N/A

CONTRIBUTION BY ACTIVITY
N/A

YEAR END : December

DIVIDEND : Ords 50c

Interim No 70	(Ldr)04/08/89	(Pay)15/09/89	Amt(c)200
Final No 71	(Ldr)22/02/90	(Pay)16/03/90	Amt(c)130
Interim No 72	(Ldr)03/08/90	(Pay)14/09/90	Amt(c)10
Final No 73	(Ldr)01/02/91	(Pay)15/03/91	Amt(c)60

NUMBER OF EMPLOYEES : 1087

STOCKS AND STOCKS HOLDINGS LTD

ABBREVIATION : STOCKS

JSE SHORT CODE : SKS

SECTOR : Industrial-Building & Construction

SHAREHOLDERS

Who Owns Whom's Assessment of the Identity of the Ultimate Controlling Shareholder: DIRECTORS 43% / STAFF 29% (APRIL 1991)

SHAREHOLDER	PERCENTAGE 1992	1991
DORRESTEIN A H	14.3	14.3
STD BANK NOM TVL P/L	8.0	---
STOCK GROUP EMPLOYEES TRUST	6.3	2.3
SEFALANA EMP BENEFITS ORG (SEBO)	4.8	---
FARENHEM D M	4.6	4.6
EDWARDS R A	4.5	4.5
YSKOR PENS FUND	3.6	3.6
MARGOT EDWARDS TRUST	3.3	3.3
EDWARDS COLIN TRUST	3.3	3.3
EDWARDS CRAIG TRUST	3.3	3.3
FULLARD M P	3.2	1.3
SA MUTUAL	2.8	2.8
KRUGER W F K	2.6	2.6
JANSEN VAN VUUREN J M	2.6	2.6
RICHE FAMILY TRUST	2.4	2.4
LIBERTY LIFE ASSOC OF AFRICA LTD	1.9	1.9
KNIGHT A M	1.8	1.8
NEDBANK NOM LTD	1.7	---
VAN ZIJL A M	1.4	1.4
MUNDELL G W	1.4	2.6
NAMPAK PENS FUND	1.3	1.3
GLANVILL FAMILY TRUST	---	1.3
GLANVILL R T	---	1.3
MAESTRO SECURITIES P/L	---	2.8
NIXON R J	---	1.3
SFSS NOM P/L	---	1.9
SOUTHERN LIFE ASSOC LTD	---	5.7
STIER G H W	---	2.5
TOTAL	78.9	76.6

DIRECTORS :
DORRESTEIN AH (Executive Deputy Chairman)
EDWARDS RA (Executive Chairman), FARENHEM DM
JANSEN VAN VUUREN JM

REGISTRATION NUMBER : 76/03313/06

REGISTERED OFFICE
Stocks House, 23a 10th Avenue
Rivonia
2128
TEL: 011-806 4000
FAX: 011-806 4008

TRANSFER SECRETARY
Central Registrars Ltd
P O Box 4844, Johannesburg
2000
TEL: 011-331 0051

CAPITAL STRUCTURE

	AUTHORISED	ISSUED
Ords 50c	14000000	13062920

FINANCIAL STATISTICS (AT FINANCIAL YEAR END)

(Amts in R'000)	1991 Dec	1990 Dec	1989 Dec	1988	1987
Ord S/H Int	175017	250346	270154	299627	259712
Long Trm Loans	1842	2212	8241	69203	90576
Iss Ord Share	13063	13063	13063	13063	13063
Total Liab	22800	39648	67399	123586	169934
Current Liab	20958	37436	59158	54383	79358
Total Assets	194268	286445	337553	508765	470698
Intang Assets	3549	3549	*	*	*
Current Assets	38789	64407	114870	139935	120410
Debtors	10618	8577	12910	-	-
Inventory	8680	13526	17136	139935	120410
Turnover	112620	140878	158303	141165	220641
Oper Profit	-13807	-1506	29085	42312	59518
Interest Paid	21	102	-	-	-
Tax Paid	527	3246	11358	23110	28732
Prf af Int&Tax	-14311	-4615	18340	19202	30786
Prf att Ord Sh	-14311	-5048	17224	18673	22416
Btm Line Earn	-7913	-7757	17224	18673	22416
Dividend Paid	-	9144	43107	15022	19594
Mkt Prce(c) YE	315	725	1575	1200	1800

PER SHARE STATISTICS (CENTS)

Net Asst Val	1312.62	1889.28	2068.09	2293.71	1988.15
Net Earnings	-	-59.00	132.00	-	-
Dividends	-	70.00	330.00	-	-
Cash Flow	-109.55	-39.07	131.05	147.00	235.67

RATIOS AND OTHER INFORMATION

Mrk Cap(R000)	41148	94707	205742	156756	235134
Current Ratio	1.85	1.72	1.94	2.57	1.52
Quik/Acid Tst	1.44	1.36	1.65	-	-
A/C Rec T/ovr	10.61	16.43	12.26	-	-
Tot Ass T/ovr	0.58	0.49	0.47	0.28	0.47
Debt/Ass Rat	0.11	0.13	0.18	0.24	0.36
L T L Tot Ass	0.00	0.00	-	0.14	0.19
Debt to Eqity	0.12	0.15	0.22	0.41	0.65
Interest Cover	-655.38	-12.42	-	-	-
Oper Prof Mrg	-12.26	-1.07	18.37	29.97	26.98
Net Prof Marg%	-12.71	-3.58	10.88	13.23	10.16
Ret on Assets	-7.08	-0.44	8.80	8.32	12.64
Ret on Equity%	-8.18	-2.02	6.38	6.23	8.63
Price/Earnings	-	-12.29	11.93	-	-
Divid Cover	-	-0.84	0.40	-	-
Divid Yield	-	9.66	20.95	-	-
Earning Yield%	-	-8.14	8.38	-	-
NAV % Mrk Pr	416.71	260.59	131.31	191.14	110.45
Effec Tax Rate	-3.81	-190.92	34.01	54.62	48.27
Def Interval	-0.01	-0.04	-	3.60	2.94
Sus Grth Rate	-8.18	-5.67	-9.58	1.22	1.09

SUBSIDIARY & ASSOCIATED COMPANIES

CHEMWES LTD

INVESTMENTS

None

COMPANY SECRETARY
D L Roberts

NATURE OF BUSINESS
The group is engaged in building and civil contracting, related service industries, property development, hotels & leisure, health care, timeshare, manufacturing, information technology products sales & services, home building & marketing, and township development.

BANKERS :
First National Bank of SA Ltd

AUDITORS :
Ernst & Young

FAMILIAR BRAND NAMES
SIGNON SYSTEMS,STOCKS & STOCKS

CONTRIBUTION BY ACTIVITY
N/A

YEAR END : April

DIVIDEND : Ords no par value

Interim No 3	(Ldr)09/02/90	(Pay)23/02/90	Amt(c)4
Final No 4	(Ldr)17/08/90	(Pay)31/08/90	Amt(c)6
Interim No 5	(Ldr)08/02/91	(Pay)01/03/91	Amt(c)4
Final No 7	(Ldr)17/08/91	(Pay)31/08/91	Amt(c)6
Interim No 8	(Ldr)14/02/92	(Pay)28/02/92	Amt(c)5
Final No 9	(Ldr)14/08/92	(Pay)28/08/92	Amt(c)6

NUMBER OF EMPLOYEES : 10800

CAPITAL STRUCTURE

	AUTHORISED	ISSUED
Ords no par value	65000000	52300000

FINANCIAL STATISTICS (AT FINANCIAL YEAR END)

(Amts in R'000)	1991 Apr	1990 Apr	1989 Apr	1988 Apr
Ord S/H Int	151773	121944	110663	93896
Long Trm Loans	53456	52451	42982	54809
Iss Ord Share	52300	48800	48800	48800
Total Liab	457371	372728	321636	266826
Current Liab	403915	320277	278654	212017
Total Assets	609144	494672	432299	360722
Current Assets	490220	393369	350702	283648
Debtors	102636	84480	68996	46341
Inventory	343415	289146	211089	154867
Turnover	1356502	1103555	1074236	756898
Oper Profit	44568	42540	33351	22789
Interest Paid	17050	16678	10891	7060
Tax Paid	3259	4328	2623	1153
Prf af Int&Tax	24309	21563	19870	14576
Prf att Ord Sh	23364	21610	19455	13791
Btm Line Earn	23168	20452	19455	13791
Dividend Paid	4880	4880	4880	1440
Mkt Prce(c) YE	125	120	150	-
Depreciation	14339	13048	9384	7645

PER SHARE STATISTICS (CENTS)

Net Asst Val	290.20	249.89	226.77	192.41
Net Earnings	47.00	44.00	40.00	-
Dividends	10.00	10.00	10.00	-
Cash Flow	82.96	78.95	62.29	44.15

RATIOS AND OTHER INFORMATION

Mrk Cap(R000)	65375	58560	73200	
Current Ratio	1.21	1.23	1.26	1.34
Quik/Acid Tst	0.36	0.33	0.50	0.61
A/C Rec T/ovr	13.22	13.06	15.57	16.33
Tot Ass T/ovr	2.23	2.23	2.48	2.10
Debt/Ass Rat	0.72	0.72	0.72	0.72
L T L Tot Ass	0.06	0.08	0.08	0.13
Debt to Eqity	2.89	2.94	2.82	2.75
Interest Cover	2.62	2.55	3.07	3.23
Oper Prof Mrg	3.29	3.85	3.10	3.01
Net Prof Marg%	1.72	1.96	1.81	1.82
Ret on Assets	7.33	8.62	7.73	6.33
Ret on Equity%	14.68	16.80	17.58	14.69
Price/Earnings	2.66	2.73	3.75	-
Divid Cover	4.70	4.40	4.00	-
Divid Yield	8.00	8.33	6.67	-
Earning Yield%	37.60	36.67	26.67	-
NAV % Mrk Pr	232.16	208.24	151.18	-
Effec Tax Rate	0.13	1.55	4.62	6.42
Def Interval	1.77	2.21	1.45	3.30
Sus Grth Rate	12.18	13.72	13.17	13.15

SUBSIDIARY & ASSOCIATED COMPANIES

215 NORTH RIDGE ROAD (PTY) LTD
295 FLORIDA ROAD (PTY) LTD
35 WALE STREET (PTY) LTD (24%)
ABKINS S&S STEEL & PIPE MERCHANTS (PTY) (50%)
AC SHOPFITTERS (DOORS) (PTY) LTD (50%)
ACCENT LIGHTING (PTY) LTD
ALKANTRANT INVESTMENTS (PTY) LTD
ALKANTRANT PROPERTIES (PTY) LTD
ALLSTO FINANCE (PTY) LTD (50%)
ANIRENT (PTY) LTD
ARTHUR PERRIOR & SONS (BOPHUTHATSWANA) (
BRACKLENT VILLAGE (PTY) LTD
BREAKERS INVESTMENTS (PTY) LTD
CENTURION LAKE INVESTMENTS (PTY) LTD (50%)
CITIMAKERS (PTY) LTD
CLINI-MANAGEMENT SERVICES (PTY) LTD
CLINISERV HEALTH CARE (PTY) LTD (50%)
CONTINUOUS PROCESSING SYSTEMS (PTY) LTD
DELENE HOMES (PTY) LTD
DOORNKLOOF CENTRE (PTY) LTD
DOORNKLOOF PROPERTIES (PTY) LTD
EDP ENGINEERS (PTY) LTD
ELLISRAS PROPERTIES (PTY) LTD
ERF 159 & 160 ROGGEBAAI (PTY) LTD
ERF 18663 BELLVILLE (PTY) LTD
ERF 19944 UNIVERSITAS (PTY) LTD
ERF 2403 INVESTMENTS (PTY) LTD (50%)
ERF 4818 NEWCASTLE (PTY) LTD
ERF 571 SANDOWN EXT 52 (PTY) LTD
ERF SIXTY NINE EDENBURG (PTY) LTD
GROSVENOR STREET PROPERTIES (PTY) LTD
HABITECH (CAPE) (PTY) LTD
HABITECH (FAERIE GLEN) (PTY) LTD
HABITECH (PRETORIA) (PTY) LTD
HABITECH CAPE (DALJ) (PTY) LTD (50%)
HABITECH CAPE (LAP) (PTY) LTD (50%)
HABITECH CAPE (LUYOLOVILLE) (PTY) LTD (50%)
HABITECH EEN TWEE VIER NUL (PTY) LTD
HABITECH FINANSIERING (PTY) LTD (50%)
HABITECH HOMES (PTY) LTD
HABITECH SPROKIELAAN (PTY) LTD
HABITECH SUNNYSIDE (PTY) LTD
HABITECH VOORSTEDE (PTY) LTD
HAWAAN VIEW (PTY) LTD
HL PAINE JOINERY (PTY) LTD
IDEAL PLUMBING SUPPLIES (PTY) LTD
LA COTE D'AZUR (PTY) LTD (25%)
LOT 26 OF PORTION 6 PARKTOWN (PTY) LTD
MASERU REINFORCING (PTY) LTD
MDC CONTRACTORS (PTY) LTD
MILLSTREET INVESTMENTS (PTY) LTD (50%)

MM PROPERTY CO (PTY) LTD
MULTI DISCIPLINE CONTRACTORS (PTY) LTD
NU-AGE HOMES (PTY) LTD
PILANSBERG RESORTS (PTY) LTD
PORT 2 OF LOT 8 SANDOWN (PTY) LTD
PORTION 1 OF DOORNKLOOF 391 (PTY) LTD
POSTEN (PTY) LTD
PRESTOCRETE (PTY) LTD
PROFESSIONAL LIGHTING INDUSTRIES (PTY) L
PROJECT PLANNING SYSTEMS (PTY) LTD
SIGNON (PTY) LTD
SIGNON APPLICATIONS (PTY) LTD
SIGNON CIM (PTY) LTD
SIGNON MICRO (PTY) LTD
SIGNON SYSTEMS (PTY) LTD
SPATIAL INFORMATION TECHNOLOGIES (PTY) L
STAND 452 KINGSWOOD CRESCENT (PTY) LTD
STENSON INVESTMENTS (PTY) LTD (50%)
STOBAR REINFORCING (PTY) LTD
STOCKAIR (PTY) LTD
STOCKMEAD (PTY) LTD (50%)
STOCKRAY INVESTMENTS (PTY) LTD
STOCKS & STOCKS (BOTSWANA) (PTY) LTD
STOCKS & STOCKS (CAPE) (PTY) LTD
STOCKS & STOCKS (CISKEI) (PTY) LTD
STOCKS & STOCKS (E CAPE) (PTY) LTD
STOCKS & STOCKS (KWAZULU) (PTY) LTD
STOCKS & STOCKS (LESOTHO) (PTY) LTD
STOCKS & STOCKS (NAMIBIA) (PTY) LTD
STOCKS & STOCKS (NATAL) (PTY) LTD
STOCKS & STOCKS (OFS) (PTY) LTD
STOCKS & STOCKS (PTY) LTD
STOCKS & STOCKS (TRANSKEI) (PTY) LTD
STOCKS & STOCKS (TVL) (PTY) LTD
STOCKS & STOCKS (VENDA) (PTY) LTD
STOCKS & STOCKS CIVILS HOLDINGS (PTY) LT
STOCKS & STOCKS CONSTRUCTION HOLDINGS (P
STOCKS & STOCKS INDUSTRIAL HOLDINGS (PTY
STOCKS & STOCKS MARKETING (PTY) LTD
STOCKS & STOCKS NEWCASTLE PROPERTIES (PT
STOCKS & STOCKS NO 10
STOCKS & STOCKS NO 11 (PTY) LTD
STOCKS & STOCKS NO 2 (PTY) LTD
STOCKS & STOCKS NO 9 (PTY) LTD
STOCKS & STOCKS PROPERTIES (PTY) LTD
STOCKS & STOCKS PROPERTY HOLDINGS (PTY)
STOCKS AMANZIMTOTI PROPERTIES (PTY) LTD
STOCKS BARNARD AND HAUPTFLEISCH (PTY) LT
STOCKS BOPHUTHATSWANA PROPERTIES (PTY) L
STOCKS CIVILS (PTY) LTD
STOCKS CIVILS (PTY) LTD
STOCKS CIVILS (SWAZILAND) (PTY) LTD
STOCKS CLEANING SERVICES (PTY) LTD
STOCKS CONSTRUCTION (BOPHUTHATSWANA) (PT
STOCKS CONSTRUCTION (MMABATHO) (PTY) LTD
STOCKS CONSTRUCTION (RAND) (PTY) LTD
STOCKS CONSTRUCTION (TRANSKEI) (PTY) LTD
STOCKS ELECTRICAL (PTY) LTD
STOCKS HOTEL MANAGEMENT SERVICES (PTY) L
STOCKS HOUSING (CAPE) (PTY) LTD
STOCKS HOUSING (PTY) LTD
STOCKS LEISURE DEVELOPMENTS (PTY) LTD
STOCKS NATAL CONSTRUCTION (PTY) LTD
STOCKS NATAL HOUSING (PTY) LTD
STOCKS NATAL PLUMBING (PTY) LTD
STOCKS NATIONAL PROPERTIES (PTY) LTD
STOCKS PLUMBING (BOPHUTHATSWANA) (PTY) L
STOCKS PLUMBING (PTY) LTD
STOCKS PRECAST (PTY) LTD
STOCKS RAND INVESTMENTS (PTY) LTD
STOCKS RAND PROPERTIES (PTY) LTD
STOCKS RUSTENBURG PROPERTIES (PTY) LTD
STOCKS SECURITY SERVICES (PTY) LTD
STOCKS STAND FINANCE (PTY) LTD (50%)
STOCKS STEEL WAREHOUSING (PTY) LTD (50%)
STOCKS STRUCTURES (PTY) LTD
STOCKS SYSTEMS TECHNOLOGY (PTY) LTD
STOCKSBO (PTY) LTD (50%)
STOCON REINFORCING (PTY) LTD
STOCOR FINANCE (PTY) LTD
STONIB (PTY) LTD
STORMHAVEN TRUST (PTY) LTD (50%)
STOTOOLS (PTY) LTD
STOTRUST FINANCE (PTY) LTD (50%)
SUNHILLS PROPERTIES (PTY) LTD
SUNRAY HOMES (PTY) LTD
SYNERGY CONSULTING (PTY) LTD
TILLCOR (PTY) LTD
UNISTO (PTY) LTD (50%)
VAVIN INVESTMENTS (PTY) LTD (25%)
VMB STOCKS FINANCE (PTY) LTD (50%)
W OOSTHUIZEN PLUMBERS (PTY) LTD
WILD ALMOND RIDGE (PTY) LTD

INVESTMENTS

CONQUEROR INVESTMENTS (PTY) LTD (11%)
DE JAGER ST PROPERTIES (PTY) LTD (15%)
FEDSURE HOLDINGS LTD

STORECO LTD

ABBREVIATION : STORECO

JSE SHORT CODE : STC

SECTOR : Industrial-Retailers & Wholesalers

SHAREHOLDERS

Who Owns Whom's Assessment of the Identity of the Ultimate Controlling Shareholder:
SB COHEN & LJ CHIAPPINI

SHAREHOLDER	PERCENTAGE 1992	1991
STORECO CONTROLLING CO P/L	50.0	---
MENTEITH INV LTD	11.5	11.5
STD BANK NOM TVL P/L	9.9	---
SHARESTOCK NOM P/L	3.6	3.3
ARTHUR YOUNG NOM NATAL P/L	3.6	3.6
MANEEZ INV P/L	3.1	3.6
EIGHTY ONE MAIN STREET NOM LTD	3.0	3.7
SA SPECIAL RISKS INSURANCE ASSOC LTD	2.4	---
BOARD OF EXECUTORS NOM P/L	---	4.1
CCMB INV HOLDINGS LTD	---	50.0
SA MUTUAL	---	2.4
STORECO PENS FUND	---	1.7
TOTAL	87.1	83.9

DIRECTORS :
CHIAPPINI LJ (Joint Managing Director)
COHEN SB (Joint Managing Director)
LABUSCHAGNE NA DR (Chairman)
MCADAM WJ (Deputy Chairman),YUILL CS

REGISTRATION NUMBER : 05/04348/06

REGISTERED OFFICE
Southern Life Building, 88 Field Street

Durban
4001
TEL: 031-301 2252
FAX: 031-304 5820

TRANSFER SECRETARY
Mercantile Registrars Ltd
P O Box 1053, Johannesburg
2000
TEL: 011-333 8181

COMPANY SECRETARY
C S Yuill

NATURE OF BUSINESS
An investment holding company with a controlling interest in JSE-quoted retailer Specialty Stores.

BANKERS :
Standard Bank of SA Ltd

AUDITORS :
Ernst & Young

FAMILIAR BRAND NAMES
FOOTGEAR,MILADY'S,MR PRICE'S,SHOES UNLIMITED
THE HUB

CONTRIBUTION BY ACTIVITY
Retailing (% of Profit before Tax) (96.9%)
Shopfitting,Computer Services & Other (3.1%)

YEAR END : February

DIVIDEND : Ords 10c

Interim No 93	(Ldr)02/11/90	(Pay)03/12/90	Amt(c)19
Final No 94	(Ldr)10/05/91	(Pay)01/07/91	Amt(c)36
Interim No 95	(Ldr)01/11/91	(Pay)06/12/91	Amt(c)20
Final No 96	(Ldr)08/05/92	(Pay)01/07/92	Amt(c)40
Interim No 97	(Ldr)30/10/92	(Pay)04/12/92	Amt(c)20

NUMBER OF EMPLOYEES : 1985

CAPITAL STRUCTURE

	AUTHORISED	ISSUED
Ords 10c	20000000	5217772

FINANCIAL STATISTICS (AT FINANCIAL YEAR END)

(Amts in R'000)	1992 Feb	1991 Feb	1990 Feb	1989 Feb	1988 Feb
Ord S/H Int	19915	19906	19897	19590	30951
Long Trm Loans	-	-	-	791	2127
Iss Ord Share	5218	5218	5218	5218	5218
Total Liab	2089	1880	1724	20464	38375
Current Liab	2089	1880	1724	19673	36248
Total Assets	22004	21786	21621	40054	69326
Current Assets	2091	1878	1722	22123	54057
Debtors	-	-	-	285	34415
Inventory	-	-	-	-	19206
Turnover	-	-	-	136940	117796
Oper Profit	-	-	-	552	10887
Interest Paid	-	-	-	2442	1817
Tax Paid	-	-	-	7027	4695
Prf af Int&Tax	3139	2879	2617	-4484	4375
Prf att Ord Sh	3139	2879	2605	-4540	4704
Btm Line Earn	3139	2879	2916	-3740	7863
Dividend Paid	3130	2870	2609	2505	1826
Mkt Prce(c) YE	800	1050	750	825	560
Depreciation	-	-	-	2215	1589

PER SHARE STATISTICS (CENTS)

Net Asst Val	381.66	381.49	381.31	375.43	593.16
Net Earnings	60.20	55.20	49.90	48.40	90.20
Dividends	60.00	55.00	50.00	48.00	35.00
Cash Flow	60.16	55.17	49.92	-37.01	102.64

RATIOS AND OTHER INFORMATION

Mrk Cap(R000)	41744	54789	39135	43049	29221
Current Ratio	1.00	1.00	1.00	1.12	1.49
Quik/Acid Tst	1.00	1.00	1.00	1.12	0.96
A/C Rec T/ovr	-	-	-	480.49	3.42
Tot Ass T/ovr	-	-	-	3.42	1.70
Debt/Ass Rat	0.09	0.09	0.08	0.49	0.52
Debt to Eqity	0.10	0.09	0.09	1.00	1.17
Interest Cover	-	-	-	2.04	5.99
Oper Prof Mrg	-	-	-	0.40	9.24
Net Prof Marg%	-	-	-	-3.32	3.99
Ret on Assets	14.27	13.21	12.10	12.45	15.70
Ret on Equity%	15.76	14.46	13.09	-23.18	15.20
Price/Earnings	13.29	19.02	15.03	17.05	6.21
Divid Cover	1.00	1.00	1.00	1.01	2.58
Divid Yield	7.50	5.24	6.67	5.82	6.25
Earning Yield%	7.52	5.26	6.65	5.87	16.11
NAV % Mrk Pr	47.71	36.33	50.84	45.51	105.92
Effec Tax Rate	-	-	-	-31.27	16.76
Def Interval	-	-	-	-8.95	3.28
Sus Grth Rate	0.05	0.05	-0.02	-35.96	9.30

SUBSIDIARY & ASSOCIATED COMPANIES

SPECIALTY STORES LTD

INVESTMENTS

SPECIALTY STORES LTD (5,5% CUM PREFS R2) (53%)

STREBEL GROUP LTD

ABBREVIATION : STREBEL

JSE SHORT CODE : SBE

SECTOR : Industrial-Clothing, Footwear & Textiles

SHAREHOLDERS

Who Owns Whom's Assessment of the Identity of the Ultimate Controlling Shareholder:
STREBEL FAMILY

SHAREHOLDER	PERCENTAGE 1992	1991
J STREBEL INV P/L	50.7	50.7
SA MUTUAL	11.5	11.5
STREBEL FOUNDATION TRUST	8.1	8.1
STREBEL Y	4.5	4.5
STREBEL P	3.5	3.5
CMB NOM P/L	3.3	---
QUARTO NOM P/L	2.3	2.3
BALL R W	1.5	1.5
EIGHTY ONE MAIN STREET NOM LTD	1.3	1.3
ARGOVIA INV C C	1.3	---
LANCELLAS N W	1.1	1.1
SANLAM	---	3.3
TOTAL	89.3	88.0

DIRECTORS :
DAVISON A ,DURWARD R (Executive Director)
LANCELLAS NW (Financial Director)
MARGARITIS D (Executive Director)
MUELLER A (Executive Director)
STREBEL FP (Chairman & Managing Dir.),STREBEL J

REGISTRATION NUMBER : 86/00334/06

REGISTERED OFFICE
9 Calcutta Street, Paarden Eiland
Cape Town
7405
TEL: 021-551 2360
FAX: 021-551 2863

TRANSFER SECRETARY
Mercantile Registrars Ltd
P O Box 1053, Johannesburg
2000
TEL: 011-333 8181

COMPANY SECRETARY
N W Lancellas

NATURE OF BUSINESS
Strebel is a manufacturer and distributor of trimmings, fasteners and accessories, and is a producer of knitted and non-woven fabric and embroidered products, supplying the clothing, retail and home textile industries.

BANKERS :
First National Bank of SA Ltd
Nedcor Bank Ltd

AUDITORS :
Gross Hendler & Frank

FAMILIAR BRAND NAMES
ATLANTIS,EMBROITEX,GENERAL DYERS
HEREFORD INDUSTRIES,MM REINHARDT,PERL TAPE
PERL-OPTI,SA BUTTON,SIDLEY,SIDLEYTEX,STRESA

CONTRIBUTION BY ACTIVITY
N/A

YEAR END : June

DIVIDEND : Ords 1c

Interim No 4	(Ldr)30/03/90	(Pay)20/04/90	Amt(c)5
Final No 5	(Ldr)28/09/90	(Pay)15/10/90	Amt(c)8
Interim No 6	(Ldr)28/03/91	(Pay)26/04/91	Amt(c)3.5
Final No 7	(Ldr)04/10/91	(Pay)21/10/91	Amt(c)4

NUMBER OF EMPLOYEES : 1550

CAPITAL STRUCTURE

	AUTHORISED	ISSUED
Ords 1c	20000000	15000000

FINANCIAL STATISTICS (AT FINANCIAL YEAR END)

(Amts in R'000)	1992 Jun	1991 Jun	1990 Jun	1989 Jun	1988 Jun
Ord S/H Int	25245	25734	39590	35785	31677
Long Trm Loans	5322	5345	6289	5801	3559
Iss Ord Share	15000	15000	15000	15000	15000
Total Liab	24892	23913	23749	20099	14227
Current Liab	19570	18568	17460	14298	10668
Total Assets	50137	49647	47408	39953	30835
Intang Assets	*	*	15931	15931	15069
Current Assets	36814	35513	33603	28006	21713
Debtors	22288	21732	19666	17135	11846
Inventory	13655	13255	12648	9919	6815
Oper Profit	341	6333	11220	10531	7642
Interest Paid	1792	1317	1133	788	472
Tax Paid	-756	1857	4521	3980	2131
Prf af Int&Tax	-635	3200	5696	5969	5039
Prf att Ord Sh	-635	3200	5694	5965	5035
Btm Line Earn	-489	3200	5756	6058	5147
Dividend Paid	-	1125	1950	1950	1125
Mkt Prce(c) YE	100	180	220	190	140
Depreciation	2194	2313	2208	1668	987

PER SHARE STATISTICS (CENTS)

Net Asst Val	168.30	171.56	157.73	132.36	110.72
Net Earnings	-3.50	21.30	38.00	39.80	35.30
Dividends	-	7.50	13.00	13.00	7.50
Cash Flow	5.24	38.44	57.66	57.14	42.96

RATIOS AND OTHER INFORMATION

Mrk Cap(R000)	15000	27000	33000	28500	21000
Current Ratio	1.88	1.91	1.92	1.96	2.04
Quik/Acid Tst	1.18	1.20	1.20	1.27	1.40
Debt/Ass Rat	0.45	0.42	0.44	0.45	0.43
L T L Tot Ass	0.06	0.05	0.07	0.09	0.08
Debt to Eqity	0.90	0.81	0.53	0.50	0.42
Interest Cover	0.19	4.81	9.91	13.40	16.19
Ret on Assets	0.80	12.84	23.94	26.87	24.78
Ret on Equity%	-2.52	12.43	14.38	16.67	15.89
Price/Earnings	-28.57	8.45	5.79	4.77	3.97
Divid Cover	-	2.84	2.92	3.06	4.71
Divid Yield	-	4.17	5.91	6.84	5.36
Earning Yield%	-3.50	11.83	17.27	20.95	25.21
NAV % Mrk Pr	168.30	95.31	71.69	69.66	79.09
Effec Tax Rate	-1.94	31.72	36.95	30.67	28.33
Def Interval	14.53	1.75	1.05	0.76	0.75
Sus Grth Rate	-2.52	8.06	9.46	11.22	12.34

SUBSIDIARY & ASSOCIATED COMPANIES

CAPE EMBROIDERY WORKS (PTY) LTD
HEREFORD INDUSTRIES (PTY) LTD
JOHN STREBEL (PTY) LTD
PERL-OPTI (PTY) LTD
S A BADGE & EMBROIDERY WORKS (PTY) LTD
SIDLEY MANUFACTURING (PTY) LTD
SIDLEYTEX (PTY) LTD
STREBEL TRADING (PTY) LTD

INVESTMENTS

None

SUB NIGEL GOLD MINING CO LTD

ABBREVIATION : SUB-N

JSE SHORT CODE : SBN

SECTOR : Gold-Rand & others

SHAREHOLDERS

Who Owns Whom's Assessment of the Identity of the Ultimate Controlling Shareholder:
HOLMES FAMILY

SHAREHOLDER	PERCENTAGE 1992	1991
LESLIE GORDON HOLMES FAMILY TRUST	35.4	35.4
FIRST NAT NOM P/L	6.1	10.3
GOUDSTAD NOM P/L	5.1	—
ASTRUP R C	1.9	—
CORNISH FAMILY HLDGS P/L	1.5	1.5
STD BANK NOM TVL P/L	1.5	1.3
INDO-CHINA NOM P/L	1.4	—
SRL INV CC	1.4	1.4
SWEETWATERS DEVELOPMENT CO P/L	1.4	1.4
BARCLAYS NAT NOM P/L	—	1.9
TOTAL	55.7	53.2

DIRECTORS :
HOLMES B MRS,HOLMES LG (Chairman),JAFFE CA
PRESTON IMW

REGISTRATION NUMBER : 84/06179/06

REGISTERED OFFICE
Dunnottar Road, Nigel
1490
TEL: 011-739 6709

TRANSFER SECRETARY
Mercantile Registrars Ltd
P O Box 1053, Johannesburg
2000
TEL: 011-333 8181

COMPANY SECRETARY
S C Scanlon

NATURE OF BUSINESS
The company operates a gold mine in the Nigel Municipal area of the Transvaal.

BANKERS :
Trust Bank of Africa Ltd, Nedperm Bank Ltd

AUDITORS :
Ernst & Young

FAMILIAR BRAND NAMES
N/A

CONTRIBUTION BY ACTIVITY
N/A

YEAR END : June

DIVIDEND :15/01/92 and 15/07/91

NUMBER OF EMPLOYEES : 659

CAPITAL STRUCTURE

	AUTHORISED	ISSUED
Ords no par value	30000000	26494000

FINANCIAL STATISTICS (AT FINANCIAL YEAR END)

(Amts in R'000)	1991 Jun	1990 Jun	1989 Jun	1988 Jun	1987
Ord S/H Int	20126	20993	21876	20363	16136
Long Trm Loans	8927	842	14	-	6015
Iss Ord Share	26494	26494	26440	26440	22492
Total Liab	9343	9263	8966	9377	12027
Current Liab	416	8421	8952	9377	6012
Total Assets	29469	30256	30842	29740	24236
Current Assets	247	533	2112	2399	2085
Debtors	140	533	957	1808	-
Inventory	-	-	948	582	2085
Turnover	3099	20339	21483	20446	9070
Oper Profit	-309	354	2316	4155	3970
Interest Paid	558	1273	1214	-	848
Tax Paid	-	-	-	-	240
Prf af Int&Tax	-867	-919	1381	4155	3361
Prf att Ord Sh	-867	-919	1381	4155	3361
Btm Line Earn	-867	-919	1381	4155	3361
Dividend Paid	-	-	-	-	2249
Mkt Prce(c) YE	18	68	80	280	830

PER SHARE STATISTICS (CENTS)

Net Asst Val	75.96	79.24	82.74	77.02	71.74
Net Earnings	-3.27	-3.47	5.22	16.06	-
Cash Flow	-3.27	-3.47	5.22	16.05	14.94

RATIOS AND OTHER INFORMATION

Mrk Cap(R000)	4769	18016	21152	74032	186684
Current Ratio	0.59	0.06	0.24	0.26	0.35
Quik/Acid Tst	0.59	0.06	0.13	0.19	-
A/C Rec T/ovr	22.14	38.16	22.45	11.31	-
Tot Ass T/ovr	0.11	0.67	0.70	0.69	0.37
Debt/Ass Rat	0.32	0.31	0.29	0.32	0.50
L T L Tot Ass	0.30	0.03	0.00	-	0.25
Debt to Eqity	0.46	0.44	0.41	0.46	0.75
Interest Cover	-0.55	0.28	2.14	-	5.25
Oper Prof Mrg	-9.97	1.74	10.78	20.32	43.77
Net Prof Marg%	-27.98	-4.52	6.43	20.32	37.06
Ret on Assets	-1.05	1.17	8.41	13.97	18.36
Ret on Equity%	-4.31	-4.38	6.31	20.40	20.83
Price/Earnings	-5.50	-19.60	15.33	17.43	-
Earning Yield%	-18.17	-5.10	6.53	5.74	-
NAV % Mrk Pr	422.02	116.52	103.42	27.51	8.64
Effec Tax Rate	-	-	-	-	7.69
Def Interval	-10.30	-9.17	4.14	1.29	1.79
Sus Grth Rate	-4.31	-4.38	6.31	20.40	6.89

SUBSIDIARY & ASSOCIATED COMPANIES

None

INVESTMENTS

None

SUN INTERNATIONAL (BOPHUTHATSWANA) LTD

ABBREVIATION : SUN-BOP

JSE SHORT CODE : SUB

SECTOR : Industrial-Beverages & Hotels

SHAREHOLDERS

Who Owns Whom's Assessment of the Identity of the Ultimate Controlling Shareholder:
SA MUTUAL VIA SAFREN

SHAREHOLDER	PERCENTAGE 1992	1991
SUN INTERNAT BOPHUTHATSWANA HLDGS P/L	73.5	78.7
BOP NAT DEVELOPMENT CORPORATION	3.3	1.0
SUN INTERNATIONAL INC	2.6	---
SA MUTUAL	2.3	2.1
EIGHTY ONE MAIN STREET NOM LTD	2.1	1.7
CMB NOM P/L	2.1	---
SEFALANA EMP BENEFITS ORG (SEBO)	2.1	2.0
STD BANK NOM TVL P/L	1.7	1.1
SHARESTOCK NOM P/L	1.3	1.3
AECI PENS FUND	---	1.1
FIRST NAT NOM P/L	---	1.1
SANLAM	---	2.1
TOTAL	91.1	92.1

DIRECTORS :
ALLISON JR ,GOULD ID ,HAWTON DA ,KEIKELAME BE
KERZNER S (Chairman),MACMILLAN GA ,MAREE JAJ
ROSEVEAR KA (Deputy Chairman),VAN BILJON AF
WAGNER PH (Managing Director),YOUNG LG

REGISTRATION NUMBER : 85/04741/10

REGISTERED OFFICE
Mmabatho Sun Hotel, Lobatsi Road
Mmabatho, Bophuthatswana

TEL: 011-780 7444
FAX: 011-780 7702

TRANSFER SECRETARY
Fraser Street Registrars (Pty) Ltd
P O Box 61178, Marshalltown
2107
TEL: 011-491 0911

COMPANY SECRETARY
S A Bailes

NATURE OF BUSINESS
The company holds exclusive casino rights for Bophuthatswana and presently operates resort hotels in Bophuthatswana.

BANKERS :
Standard Bank of Bophuthatswana Ltd

AUDITORS :
N/A

FAMILIAR BRAND NAMES
MMABATHO SUN,MOLOPO SUN,MORULA SUN
NALEDI SUN,SUN CITY,TAUNG SUN,THABA'NCHU SUN
TLHABANE SUN

CONTRIBUTION BY ACTIVITY
N/A

YEAR END : June

DIVIDEND :Ords 15c

Interim	(Ldr)09/03/90	(Pay)29/03/90	Amt(c)45
Final	(Ldr)31/08/90	(Pay)25/09/90	Amt(c)63
Interim	(Ldr)08/03/91	(Pay)28/03/91	Amt(c)55
Final	(Ldr)23/08/91	(Pay)27/09/91	Amt(c)77
Interim	(Ldr)28/08/92	(Pay)28/09/92	Amt(c)68
Interim	(Ldr)27/01/92	(Pay)28/02/92	Amt(c)64
Final	(Ldr)28/08/92	(Pay)28/09/92	Amt(c)68

NUMBER OF EMPLOYEES : 7514

CAPITAL STRUCTURE

	AUTHORISED	ISSUED
Ords 15c	150000000	119302501

FINANCIAL STATISTICS (AT FINANCIAL YEAR END)

(Amts in R'000)	1992 Jun	1991 Jun	1990 Jun	1989 Jun	1988 Jun
Ord S/H Int	1095465	571380	425014	343098	276669
Long Trm Loans	184893	88762	57000	71011	76787
Iss Ord Share	119302	108410	108410	108410	108410
Total Liab	575655	453928	361788	335684	239265
Current Liab	390762	365166	304788	264673	162478
Total Assets	1671120	1025308	786802	678782	515934
Current Assets	66721	108022	250391	227643	133695
Debtors	39457	21645	24660	23640	26937
Inventory	3386	2734	2734	1961	1503
Turnover	1000397	772486	626505	499163	348050
Oper Profit	265897	226249	198684	179703	101980
Interest Paid	163	683	15317	25251	3208
Tax Paid	54005	63938	67333	59144	34031
Prf af Int&Tax	216022	191806	155972	114409	68658
Prf att Ord Sh	216022	191806	157399	114456	68658
Btm Line Earn	216022	191806	157399	114456	68658
Dividend Paid	152501	143101	117083	85102	50953
Mkt Prce(c) YE	3950	2825	1650	1200	595
Depreciation	44587	29785	18645	13345	8254

PER SHARE STATISTICS (CENTS)

Net Asst Val	918.23	527.05	392.04	316.48	255.21
Net Earnings	191.00	176.90	145.20	105.60	63.30
Dividends	132.00	132.00	108.00	78.50	47.00
Cash Flow	228.35	208.09	161.07	117.84	68.25

RATIOS AND OTHER INFORMATION

Mrk Cap(R000)	4712429	3062583	1788765	1300920	645040
Current Ratio	0.17	0.30	0.82	0.86	0.82
Quik/Acid Tst	0.16	0.29	0.81	0.85	0.81
A/C Rec T/ovr	25.35	35.69	25.41	21.12	12.92
Tot Ass T/ovr	0.60	0.75	0.80	0.74	0.67
Debt/Ass Rat	0.33	0.41	0.43	0.45	0.41
L T L Tot Ass	0.09	0.06	0.04	0.06	0.10
Debt to Eqity	0.50	0.74	0.79	0.90	0.77
Interest Cover	1651.30	336.04	13.12	7.16	31.79
Oper Prof Mrg	26.58	29.29	31.71	36.00	29.30
Net Prof Marg%	21.59	24.83	25.12	22.93	19.73
Ret on Assets	16.17	25.01	30.51	29.30	20.53
Ret on Equity%	19.72	33.57	37.03	33.36	24.82
Price/Earnings	20.68	15.97	11.36	11.36	9.40
Divid Cover	1.45	1.34	1.34	1.35	1.35
Divid Yield	3.34	4.67	6.55	6.54	7.90
Earning Yield%	4.84	6.26	8.80	8.80	10.64
NAV % Mrk Pr	23.25	18.66	23.76	26.37	42.89
Effec Tax Rate	1.45	1.84	30.47	34.28	35.98
Def Interval	0.62	0.30	0.17	0.41	0.78
Sus Grth Rate	5.80	8.52	9.49	8.56	6.40

SUBSIDIARY & ASSOCIATED COMPANIES

MOLOPO SUN (PTY) LTD
SUN FINANCING BOPHUTHATSWANA (PTY) LTD

INVESTMENTS

None

SUN INTERNATIONAL (CISKEI) LTD

ABBREVIATION : SUNCISK

JSE SHORT CODE : SNS

SECTOR : Industrial-Beverages & Hotels

SHAREHOLDERS

Who Owns Whom's Assessment of the Identity of the Ultimate Controlling Shareholder:
CISKEIAN GOVT / SA MUTUAL VIA KERSAF

SHAREHOLDER	PERCENTAGE 1992	1991
SUN INTERNAT (CISKEI) HLDGS P/L	66.7	66.7
CMB NOM P/L	13.4	---
RAKE INV P/L	8.0	---
CORVEST (CISKEI) P/L	2.7	---
NEDBANK NOM LTD	1.4	---
STD BANK NOM TVL P/L	1.2	1.2
FERBROS NOM P/L	---	1.1
BROWNLEE A A TRUST	---	1.7
ANGLO AFRICAN SHIPPING CO 1936 P/L	---	8.0
EDIMED P/L	---	1.1
SANLAM	---	12.2
KANUKA TRANSPORT LINES P/L	---	2.7
TOTAL	93.3	94.5

DIRECTORS :
ALLISON JR ,COLLINS G ,MACILDOWIE PM
MEISENHOLL FS ,ROSEVEAR KA (Chairman)
SERRURIER GN ,SONDIYAZI MJ (Deputy Chairman)
VAN BILJON AF

REGISTRATION NUMBER : 91/01336/10

REGISTERED OFFICE
Amatola Sun Hotel, Erf1, Komga Road
Bisho, Republic of Ciskei

TEL: 011-780 7763
FAX: 011-783 7446

TRANSFER SECRETARY
Fraser Street Registrars (Pty) Ltd
P O Box 61178, Marshalltown
2107
TEL: 011-491 0911

COMPANY SECRETARY
S A Bailes

NATURE OF BUSINESS
Operation of casino and hotel resorts in Ciskei.

BANKERS :
First National Bank of SA Ltd

AUDITORS :
N/A

FAMILIAR BRAND NAMES
AMATOLA SUN,FISH RIVER SUN,MDANTSANE HOTEL
MPEKWENI SUN MARINE RESORT

CONTRIBUTION BY ACTIVITY
N/A

YEAR END : June

DIVIDEND : Ords 5c

Final	(Ldr)30/08/91	(Pay)27/09/91	Amt(c)6.7
Interim	(Ldr)06/03/92	(Pay)27/03/92	Amt(c)15
Final	(Ldr)04/09/92	(Pay)28/09/92	Amt(c)12

NUMBER OF EMPLOYEES : 1247

CAPITAL STRUCTURE

	AUTHORISED	ISSUED
Ords 5c	80000000	75000000

FINANCIAL STATISTICS (AT FINANCIAL YEAR END)

(Amts in R'000)	1991 Jun	1990 Jun
Ord S/H Int	51436	33292
Long Trm Loans	30928	40393
Iss Ord Share	75000	50000
Total Liab	61654	65400
Current Liab	30726	25007
Total Assets	113090	98692
Current Assets	18480	5772
Debtors	2282	4106
Inventory	542	405
Turnover	103126	82058
Oper Profit	32779	27026
Interest Paid	4386	7636
Tax Paid	-64	475
Prf af Int&Tax	28557	18915
Prf att Ord Sh	28557	18915
Btm Line Earn	27788	18915
Dividend Paid	34643	13200
Mkt Prce(c) YE	250	-
Depreciation	4228	4164

PER SHARE STATISTICS (CENTS)

Net Asst Val	68.58	66.58
Net Earnings	41.50	37.80
Dividends	31.40	26.40
Cash Flow	47.69	46.16

RATIOS AND OTHER INFORMATION

Mrk Cap(R000)	187500	-
Current Ratio	0.60	0.23
Quik/Acid Tst	0.58	0.21
A/C Rec T/ovr	45.19	19.98
Tot Ass T/ovr	0.91	0.83
Debt/Ass Rat	0.55	0.66
L T L Tot Ass	0.27	0.41
Debt to Eqity	1.20	1.96
Interest Cover	7.47	3.54
Oper Prof Mrg	31.79	32.94
Net Prof Marg%	27.69	23.05
Ret on Assets	29.07	27.38
Ret on Equity%	55.52	56.82
Price/Earnings	6.02	-
Divid Cover	1.32	1.43
Divid Yield	12.56	-
Earning Yield%	16.60	-
NAV % Mrk Pr	27.43	-
Def Interval	0.97	1.85
Sus Grth Rate	-11.83	17.17

SUBSIDIARY & ASSOCIATED COMPANIES

LENTON INVESTMENTS (CISKEI) (PTY) LTD

INVESTMENTS

None

SUNCRUSH LTD

ABBREVIATION : SUNCRUSH

JSE SHORT CODE : SUN

SECTOR : Industrial-Beverages & Hotels

SHAREHOLDERS

Who Owns Whom's Assessment of the Identity of the Ultimate Controlling Shareholder: DALYS LTD

SHAREHOLDER	PERCENTAGE 1992	1991
DALYS LTD	50.2	50.2
SA MUTUAL	12.9	12.9
CMB NOM P/L	10.4	---
STD BANK NOM TVL P/L	3.3	---
ESCOM PENS & PROV FUND	2.9	2.9
VOLKSKAS OPEN TRUST INV P/L	1.5	1.5
SANLAMTRUST NOM P/L	1.4	1.4
SHARESTOCK NOM P/L	---	1.0
ALTENA MEWS P/L	---	2.2
BANNER NOM P/L	---	2.3
SA NAT MEDICAL FUND LTD	---	1.1
SANLAM	---	6.7
TOTAL	82.6	82.1

DIRECTORS :
ALLISON BS ,COOK DB (Deputy Managing Director)
EVANS IJS ,HAMILTON JW
HAMILTON RD (Chairman & Managing Dir.)
HOWELL HJ ,SMIT DJ

REGISTRATION NUMBER : 05/05097/06

REGISTERED OFFICE
491 Ridge Road, Durban
4001
TEL: 031-29 4371
FAX: 031-29 9125

TRANSFER SECRETARY
Dalys Ltd
P O Box 1177, Durban
4000
TEL: 031-29 4371

COMPANY SECRETARY
J Reekie

NATURE OF BUSINESS
An investment holding company with a controlling interest in quoted Tempora Investments. The group manufactures and markets soft drinks, and are authorised bottlers of Coca-Cola, Schweppes, Tab, Fanta, Sprite, Krest, Lemon Twist, Sparletta, Stoney and Appletiser.

BANKERS :
Standard Bank of SA Ltd

AUDITORS :
Deloitte Pim Goldby

FAMILIAR BRAND NAMES
APPLETISER,COCA-COLA,FANTA,KREST,LEMON TWIST SCHWEPPES,SPARLETTA,SPRITE,STONEY,TAB

CONTRIBUTION BY ACTIVITY
N/A

YEAR END : June

DIVIDEND : Ords 50c

Interim No 83	(Ldr)16/03/90	(Pay)30/03/90	Amt(c)96
Final No 84	(Ldr)12/10/90	(Pay)02/11/90	Amt(c)254
Interim No 85	(Ldr)15/03/91	(Pay)26/03/91	Amt(c)125
Final No 86	(Ldr)11/10/91	(Pay)01/11/91	Amt(c)335
Interim No 87	(Ldr)13/03/92	(Pay)27/03/92	Amt(c)150
Final No 88	(Ldr)09/10/92	(Pay)30/10/92	Amt(c)390

NUMBER OF EMPLOYEES : 2183

CAPITAL STRUCTURE

	AUTHORISED	ISSUED
Ords 50c	5000000	2712576
7% Red Pref R1	500000	0

FINANCIAL STATISTICS (AT FINANCIAL YEAR END)

(Amts in R'000)	1992 Jun	1991 Jun	1990 Jun	1989 Jun	1988 Jun
Ord S/H Int	195775	157203	133914	110078	90290
Long Trm Loans	56579	62041	55759	37669	37693
Iss Ord Share	2713	2713	2713	2713	2713
Total Liab	166130	143392	124873	87591	84918
Current Liab	109551	81351	69114	49922	47225
Total Assets	361905	300595	258298	197669	175208
Intang Assets	*	*	489	*	*
Current Assets	90307	114226	90508	57091	49831
Debtors	27866	27497	22972	17506	13441
Inventory	38250	34583	25749	19459	21801
Turnover	534824	444942	356349	277051	228755
Oper Profit	85153	70729	56412	43740	39567
Interest Paid	6254	5528	2775	4039	2868
Tax Paid	39993	33984	29653	21995	17845
Prf af Int&Tax	48333	43799	33035	23105	18854
Prf att Ord Sh	48430	43401	32209	22370	18486
Btm Line Earn	55190	36255	32841	22370	18814
Dividend Paid	14648	12477	9494	6781	5560
Mkt Prce(c) YE	44000	38000	16000	10000	5800
Depreciation	11174	9600	6333	5560	4154

PER SHARE STATISTICS (CENTS)

Net Asst Val	7216.18	5794.43	4917.99	4057.43	3328.05
Net Earnings	1785.00	1600.00	1187.00	828.00	681.00
Dividends	540.00	460.00	350.00	250.00	205.00
Cash Flow	2220.16	1991.08	1516.29	1051.79	955.22

RATIOS AND OTHER INFORMATION

Mrk Cap(R000)	1193720	1030940	434080	271300	157354
Current Ratio	0.82	1.40	1.31	1.14	1.06
Quik/Acid Tst	0.48	0.98	0.94	0.75	0.59
A/C Rec T/ovr	19.19	16.18	15.51	15.83	17.02
Tot Ass T/ovr	1.48	1.48	1.38	1.40	1.31
Debt/Ass Rat	0.42	0.39	0.39	0.33	0.37

L T L Tot Ass	0.11	0.12	0.12	0.08	0.10
Debt to Eqity	0.77	0.74	0.75	0.60	0.72
Interest Cover	14.36	13.77	22.21	12.00	13.80
Oper Prof Mrg	15.92	15.90	15.83	15.79	17.30
Net Prof Marg%	9.06	9.75	9.04	8.07	8.08
Ret on Assets	26.17	28.02	25.54	25.09	22.75
Ret on Equity%	24.74	27.61	24.05	20.32	20.47
Price/Earnings	24.65	23.75	13.48	12.08	8.52
Divid Cover	3.31	3.48	3.39	3.31	3.32
Divid Yield	1.23	1.21	2.19	2.50	3.53
Earning Yield%	4.06	4.21	7.42	8.28	11.74
NAV % Mrk Pr	16.40	15.25	30.74	40.57	57.38
Effec Tax Rate	43.45	42.32	43.50	51.42	38.89
Def Interval	1.04	0.72	0.82	0.60	0.83
Sus Grth Rate	17.26	19.67	16.96	14.16	14.32

SUBSIDIARY & ASSOCIATED COMPANIES

INTERTRUCK HOLDINGS (PTY) LTD
MMABATHO MINERAL WATERS (PTY) LTD
QUEENSTOWN BOTTLERS (PTY) LTD
WELKOM BOTTLING CO. (PTY) LTD

INVESTMENTS

None

SUPALEK HOLDINGS LTD

ABBREVIATION : SUPALEK

JSE SHORT CODE : SUP

SECTOR : Industrial-Electronics, Electrical & Bat

SHAREHOLDERS

Who Owns Whom's Assessment of the Identity of the Ultimate Controlling Shareholder:
ANBEECO INVESTMENT HOLDINGS

SHAREHOLDER	PERCENTAGE 1992	1991
ANBEECO INV HOLDINGS LTD	52.5	52.5
MENBLACK NOM P/L	14.1	13.2
CMB NOM P/L	11.9	---
MANUFACTURERS INV CO P/L	10.1	10.1
SANTAMGROEI NOM P/L	3.6	---
CYRIL COHEN FAMILY HOLDINGS CC	---	3.6
IVAN COHEN FAMILY TRUST	---	3.6
SANLAM	---	5.0
TOTAL	92.1	87.8

DIRECTORS :
BROOKSTONE AN (Chairman)
COHEN C (Joint Managing Director)
COHEN II (Joint Managing Director),JACOBSON SI
JANKELOW W ,MITCHELL J MRS (Financial Director)
SHATENSTEIN SI

REGISTRATION NUMBER : 87/04570/06

REGISTERED OFFICE
cnr Southern Klipriversberg Rd, and Outspan Rd
South Hills, Johannesburg
2197
TEL: 011-613 1611
FAX: 011-613 1897

TRANSFER SECRETARY
Central Registrars Ltd
P O Box 4844, Johannesburg
2000
TEL: 011-331 0051

COMPANY SECRETARY
J Mitchell (Mrs)

NATURE OF BUSINESS
The holding company of a subsidiary which has the sole rights of distribution to and carries on the business of importing, distributing, marketing and servicing the Kenwood & Cortina ranges of audio equipment,Samsung tv's and other allied products.

BANKERS :
First National Corp & Investment Bank

AUDITORS :
Kessel Feinstein

FAMILIAR BRAND NAMES
CORTINA,KENWOOD,SAMSUNG

CONTRIBUTION BY ACTIVITY
N/A

YEAR END : April

DIVIDEND :Ords 1c

Interim No 4	(Ldr)06/10/89	(Pay)20/10/89	Amt(c)1
Final No 5	(Ldr)16/03/90	(Pay)20/04/90	Amt(c)3
Interim No 6	(Ldr)01/02/91	(Pay)15/02/91	Amt(c)4
Final No 7	(Ldr)19/07/91	(Pay)16/08/91	Amt(c)4
Interim No 8	(Ldr)07/02/92	(Pay)21/02/92	Amt(c)4
Final No 9	(Ldr)17/07/92	(Pay)14/08/92	Amt(c)2

NUMBER OF EMPLOYEES : 160

CAPITAL STRUCTURE

	AUTHORISED	ISSUED
Ords 1c	50000000	32250000

FINANCIAL STATISTICS (AT FINANCIAL YEAR END)

(Amts in R'000)	1992 Apr	1991 Apr	1990 Apr	1988 Dec	1987 Dec
Ord S/H Int	10988	10525	17436	6331	4662
Long Trm Loans	430	717	301	234	111
Iss Ord Share	32250	32250	32250	32250	32250
Total Liab	9807	20336	9138	7680	7973
Current Liab	9377	19619	8837	7446	7862
Total Assets	20438	30504	16554	14011	12635
Intang Assets	357	357	10020	*	*
Current Assets	19015	28797	15862	13188	11853
Debtors	11094	12359	9518	5785	9592
Inventory	5637	9435	3519	3701	2257
Turnover	58887	73147	49033	36349	20124
Oper Profit	5294	10603	5932	5857	3545
Interest Paid	1150	1017	736	254	25
Tax Paid	2038	4517	2959	2743	1715
Prf af Int&Tax	2398	5331	2733	2860	1805
Prf att Ord Sh	2398	5331	2733	2860	1805
Btm Line Earn	2398	5331	2733	2860	1805
Dividend Paid	1935	2580	1290	1129	484
Mkt Prce(c) YE	50	55	21	26	55
Depreciation	303	255	129	114	45

PER SHARE STATISTICS (CENTS)

Net Asst Val	32.96	31.53	23.00	19.63	14.46
Net Earnings	7.40	16.50	8.50	8.87	7.29
Dividends	6.00	8.00	4.00	3.50	1.50
Cash Flow	8.38	17.32	8.87	9.22	11.47

RATIOS AND OTHER INFORMATION

Mrk Cap(R000)	16125	17738	6773	8385	17738
Current Ratio	2.03	1.47	1.79	1.77	1.51
Quik/Acid Tst	1.43	0.99	1.40	1.27	1.22
A/C Rec T/ovr	5.31	5.92	5.15	6.28	4.20
Tot Ass T/ovr	2.88	2.40	2.96	2.59	3.19
Debt/Ass Rat	0.48	0.67	0.55	0.55	0.63
L T L Tot Ass	0.02	0.02	0.02	0.02	0.01
Debt to Eqity	0.89	1.93	0.52	1.21	1.71
Interest Cover	4.60	10.43	8.06	23.06	141.80
Oper Prof Mrg	8.99	14.50	12.10	16.11	17.62
Net Prof Marg%	4.07	7.29	5.57	7.87	8.97
Ret on Assets	27.33	35.62	38.83	41.80	56.11
Ret on Equity%	21.82	50.65	15.67	45.17	77.43
Price/Earnings	6.76	3.33	2.47	2.93	7.54
Divid Cover	1.23	2.06	2.13	2.53	4.86
Divid Yield	12.00	14.55	19.05	13.46	2.73
Earning Yield%	14.80	30.00	40.48	34.12	13.25
NAV % Mrk Pr	65.93	57.32	109.50	75.50	26.28
Effec Tax Rate	45.94	45.87	51.99	48.96	48.72
Def Interval	0.67	0.16	0.08	0.05	1.26
Sus Grth Rate	4.21	26.14	8.28	27.34	28.34

SUBSIDIARY & ASSOCIATED COMPANIES

SUPALEK (PTY) LTD

INVESTMENTS

None

SUPREME INDUSTRIAL HOLDINGS LTD

ABBREVIATION : SUPREME

JSE SHORT CODE : SPM

SECTOR : Industrial-Building & Construction

SHAREHOLDERS

Who Owns Whom's Assessment of the Identity of the Ultimate Controlling Shareholder:
EA RONBECK VIA SUPREME BOND TRUST

SHAREHOLDER	PERCENTAGE 1992	1991
SUPREME HOLDINGS LTD	86.8	1.9
PAULS TRUST INVESTMENTS	1.6	---
SUPREME INV HOLDINGS P/L	1.2	---
HOMESTEAD INV P/L	---	2.5
SUPREME BOND TRUST LTD	---	87.4
TOTAL	89.6	91.8

DIRECTORS :
ESTERHUISEN P (Financial Director),HAFNER RA
HIGGS DW ,HODGSON AJ (Managing Director)
RONBECK EA (Chairman),RUBENSTEIN GB

REGISTRATION NUMBER : 87/03373/06

REGISTERED OFFICE
26th Floor, Kine Centre, 141 Commissioner Street
Johannesburg
2001
TEL: 011-331 6532
FAX: 011-331 8760

TRANSFER SECRETARY
Central Registrars Ltd
P O Box 4844, Johannesburg
2000
TEL: 011-331 0051

COMPANY SECRETARY
R A Hafner

NATURE OF BUSINESS
The holding company of furniture manufacturers, stainless steel fabricators, cold and freezer room and refrigeration unit manufacturers, as well as a furniture retailing group.

BANKERS :
First National Bank of SA Ltd

AUDITORS :
Charles Orbach & Co

FAMILIAR BRAND NAMES
PROTEA FURNISHERS,SUPREME FURNISHERS

CONTRIBUTION BY ACTIVITY
N/A

YEAR END : December

DIVIDEND : Ords 1c

Final No 3	(Ldr)12/04/90	(Pay)27/04/90	Amt(c)7
Final No 5	(Ldr)28/03/91	(Pay)30/05/91	Amt(c)10
Final No 6	(Ldr)15/05/92	(Pay)29/05/92	Amt(c)12

NUMBER OF EMPLOYEES : 3195

CAPITAL STRUCTURE

	AUTHORISED	ISSUED
Ords 1c	40000000	33802682

FINANCIAL STATISTICS (AT FINANCIAL YEAR END)

(Amts in R'000)	1991 Dec	1990 Dec	1989 Dec	1988 Feb	1988 Dec
Ord S/H Int	66001	35067	31383	6632	7430
Long Trm Loans	80575	116231	62933	106	103
Iss Ord Share	32104	19224	19224	11300	11300
Total Liab	131659	188042	114561	3060	2246
Current Liab	51084	71811	51628	2954	2143
Total Assets	197660	223109	145944	9692	9676
Current Assets	169747	189809	114332	7644	7602
Debtors	131942	144989	84614	2805	3361
Inventory	25012	43290	27559	4485	4216
Turnover	203117	216129	75654	12539	11994
Oper Profit	28942	33336	8675	2571	2172
Interest Paid	16058	20330	2595	18	26
Tax Paid	-567	-268	1124	1232	1076
Prf af Int&Tax	13451	13274	4956	1321	1070
Prf att Ord Sh	8612	5760	3304	1321	1070

Btm Line Earn	8507	5683	3304	1321	1070
Dividend Paid	506	1922	1346	339	565
Mkt Prce(c) YE	140	95	130	65	85
Depreciation	3142	3282	1859	119	143

PER SHARE STATISTICS (CENTS)

Net Asst Val	205.58	182.41	163.25	58.69	65.75
Net Earnings	32.20	30.00	18.60	9.40	-
Dividends	12.00	10.00	7.00	5.00	-
Cash Flow	41.68	45.07	30.57	13.69	12.85

RATIOS AND OTHER INFORMATION

Mrk Cap(R000)	44946	18263	24991	7345	9605
Current Ratio	3.32	2.64	2.21	2.59	3.55
Quik/Acid Tst	2.83	2.04	1.68	1.07	1.58
A/C Rec T/ovr	1.54	1.49	0.89	4.47	4.28
Tot Ass T/ovr	1.03	0.97	0.52	1.29	1.49
Debt/Ass Rat	0.60	0.77	0.69	0.30	0.22
L T L Tot Ass	0.34	0.45	0.34	-	-
Debt to Eqity	1.80	4.88	3.21	0.45	0.29
Interest Cover	1.80	1.64	3.34	142.83	83.54
Oper Prof Mrg	14.25	15.42	11.47	20.50	18.11
Net Prof Marg%	4.24	2.67	4.37	10.54	8.92
Ret on Assets	14.64	14.94	5.94	26.53	26.94
Ret on Equity%	13.05	16.43	10.53	19.92	17.28
Price/Earnings	4.35	3.17	6.99	6.91	-
Divid Cover	2.68	3.00	2.66	1.88	-
Divid Yield	8.57	10.53	5.38	7.69	-
Earning Yield%	23.00	31.58	14.31	14.46	-
NAV % Mrk Pr	146.85	192.01	125.58	90.29	77.36
Effec Tax Rate	0.33	0.85	14.29	46.10	50.28
Def Interval	6.82	12.36	10.25	0.05	0.28
Sus Grth Rate	12.28	10.94	6.24	14.81	6.80

SUBSIDIARY & ASSOCIATED COMPANIES

ANDAIR REFRIGERATION (PTY) LTD
BEAU BELEGGINGS (PTY) LTD
HERJANE INVESTMENTS (PTY) LTD - PROPERTY
HOME NEEDS (PTY) LTD - DORMANT
INSULATED STRUCTURES (1989) (PTY) LTD
MARKS ENGINEERING WORKS (PTY) LTD - DORM
MEWA (TRANSVAAL) (PTY) LTD - DORMANT
MEWA MANUFACTURING CO (PTY) LTD
MEWA MANUFACTURING CO (PTY) LTD
PROTEA FURNISHERS (BOTSWANA) (PTY) LTD
PROTEA FURNISHERS (WEST) (PTY) LTD
PROTEA FURNISHERS BOPHUTHATSWANA (PTY) L
PROTEA FURNISHERS LTD
PROTEA FURNISHERS SA (PTY) LTD
STEBARN ELECTRICAL APPLIANCE CORP (PTY)
STEEL AND BARNETT LTD
STEELEBORD (PTY) LTD
STEIN CRAFT FURNITURE MANUFACTURERS (PTY
SUPERTRAP HOLDINGS & INVESTMENTS (PTY) L
SUPREME FURNISHERS (BOTSWANA) (PTY) LTD
SUPREME FURNISHERS (LESOTHO) (PTY) LTD
SUPREME FURNISHERS (PTY) LTD
SUPREME FURNISHERS (SWAZILAND) (PTY) LTD
SUPREME MANUFACTURING HOLDINGS LTD
TOTEM (PTY) LTD
TOTEM KITCHENS (PTY) LTD
TRANSVAAL PLATINUM CONSORTIUM (PTY) LTD
TV LIFE (PTY) LTD
VICTORIA LEWIS BEDDING MANUFACTURERS (PT
VICTORIA LEWIS MARKETING (PTY) LTD

INVESTMENTS

None

SUPREME MANUFACTURING HOLDINGS LTD

ABBREVIATION : SUPRMAN

JSE SHORT CODE : SRN

SECTOR : Industrial-Furniture & Household

SHAREHOLDERS

Who Owns Whom's Assessment of the Identity of the Ultimate Controlling Shareholder:
E A RONBECK VIA SUPREME INDUSTRIAL

SHAREHOLDER	PERCENTAGE 1992	1991
SUPREME IND HOLDINGS LTD	97.8	97.1
TOTAL	97.8	97.1

DIRECTORS :
HAFNER R ,HIGGS D
HODGSON AJ (Managing Director)
RONBECK E (Chairman),RUBENSTEIN GB

REGISTRATION NUMBER : 87/00962/06

REGISTERED OFFICE
26th Floor, Kine Centre, Commissioner Str
Johannesburg
2001
TEL: 011-462 4720

TRANSFER SECRETARY
Mercantile Registrars Ltd
P O Box 1053, Johannesburg
2000
TEL: 011-333 8181

COMPANY SECRETARY
R Haffner

NATURE OF BUSINESS
The company holds subsidiaries active in furniture manufacturing, stainless steel fabrication, cold/freezer room and refrigeration unit manufacture.

BANKERS :
Nedperm Bank Ltd
First National Bank of SA Ltd

AUDITORS :
Charles Orbach & Co

FAMILIAR BRAND NAMES
MEWA

CONTRIBUTION BY ACTIVITY
N/A

YEAR END : December

DIVIDEND :15/12/91 and 15/06/91

NUMBER OF EMPLOYEES : 950

CAPITAL STRUCTURE

	AUTHORISED	ISSUED
Ords 1c	150000000	98700000

FINANCIAL STATISTICS (AT FINANCIAL YEAR END)

(Amts in R'000)	1991 Dec	1990 Dec	1989 Dec	1988 Feb	1987 Feb
Ord S/H Int	38516	38370	36657	8087	5468
Long Trm Loans	3618	10603	18337	3288	1289
Iss Ord Share	98700	98700	98700	17500	-
Total Liab	25456	29649	35996	8111	3734
Current Liab	21838	19046	17659	4823	2445
Total Assets	63972	68019	72653	16198	9202
Current Assets	39598	41599	42694	7366	6009
Debtors	17622	22584	24957	4092	3426
Inventory	13188	18531	17311	3136	1814
Turnover	71507	63828	38529	-	-
Oper Profit	533	6095	3659	2366	1532
Interest Paid	2546	4588	3067	321	143
Tax Paid	-608	-348	-420	842	588
Prf af Int&Tax	196	2005	1012	1203	801
Prf att Ord Sh	254	1963	994	1203	801
Btm Line Earn	146	1936	994	1011	801
Dividend Paid	-	-	-	613	-
Mkt Prce(c) YE	10	13	30	30	-
Depreciation	2821	2801	1574	417	386

PER SHARE STATISTICS (CENTS)

Net Asst Val	39.02	38.88	37.14	46.21	-
Net Earnings	0.26	2.00	6.20	6.90	-
Dividends	-	-	-	3.50	-
Cash Flow	2.50	4.44	2.89	10.36	-

RATIOS AND OTHER INFORMATION

Mrk Cap(R000)	9870	12831	29610	5250	-
Current Ratio	1.81	2.18	2.42	1.53	2.46
Quik/Acid Tst	1.21	1.21	1.44	0.88	1.72
A/C Rec T/ovr	4.06	2.83	2.06	-	-
Tot Ass T/ovr	1.12	0.94	0.71	-	-
Debt/Ass Rat	0.40	0.43	0.48	0.47	0.38
L T L Tot Ass	0.06	0.15	0.24	0.18	0.11
Debt to Eqity	0.66	0.76	0.95	0.95	0.64
Interest Cover	0.21	1.33	1.19	7.37	10.71
Oper Prof Mrg	0.75	9.55	9.50	-	-
Net Prof Marg%	0.36	3.08	2.58	-	-
Ret on Assets	3.34	9.18	6.72	14.61	16.65
Ret on Equity%	0.66	5.12	3.62	14.88	14.65
Price/Earnings	38.46	6.50	4.84	4.35	-
Divid Cover	-	-	-	1.97	-
Divid Yield	-	-	-	11.67	-
Earning Yield%	2.60	15.38	20.67	23.00	-
NAV % Mrk Pr	390.23	299.04	123.80	154.04	-
Effec Tax Rate	-0.24	1.75	1.35	31.74	-
Def Interval	4.72	4.00	8.53	2.43	0.81
Sus Grth Rate	0.66	5.12	2.71	7.30	14.65

SUBSIDIARY & ASSOCIATED COMPANIES

ANDAIR REFRIGERATION (PTY) LTD
BEAU BELEGGINGS (PTY) LTD
HERJANE INVESTMENTS (PTY) LTD
INSULATED STRUCTURES (1989) (PTY) LTD
MEWA MANUFACTURING CO (PTY) LTD
STEELEBORD (PTY) LTD
STEIN-CRAFT FURNITURE MANUFACTURERS (PTY
VICTORIA LEWIS BEDDING MANUFACTURERS (PT
VICTORIA LEWIS FURNITURE MANUFACTURERS (
VICTORIA LEWIS MARKETING (PTY) LTD

INVESTMENTS

None

SYFRETS & COMMERCIAL UNION PROPERTY FUND

ABBREVIATION : SYCOM

JSE SHORT CODE : SYC

SECTOR : Financial-Property Trust

SHAREHOLDERS

Who Owns Whom's Assessment of the Identity of the Ultimate Controlling Shareholder: INSTITUTIONS

SHAREHOLDER	PERCENTAGE 1992	1991
CMB NOM P/L	18.8	—
SA MUTUAL	13.2	14.4
COMMERCIAL UNION LIFE ASSURE CO SA LTD	9.2	—
SIXTY SIX MARSHALL STREET NOM P/L	8.0	7.6
EIGHTY ONE MAIN STREET NOM LTD	7.2	6.9
NATAL JOINT MUNICIPAL PENS FUND SUPERANN	3.6	3.6
ANGLO AMERICAN CORP PENS FUND	2.6	1.2
DE BEERS PENS FUND	2.6	1.1
METROPOLITAN LIFE LTD	2.4	2.4
AECI PENS FUND	2.0	2.0
PROFESSIONAL PROV SOC OF SA	1.7	1.7
ENGINEERING INDUSTRIES PENS FUND	1.6	1.4
METAL IND GROUP PENS FUND	1.5	1.3
CITY COUNCIL OF DURBAN	1.5	1.5
UAL NOM P/L	1.4	1.9
FIRST LAND DEVELOPMENTS LTD	1.2	1.2
SYFRETS NOM LTD	—	1.6
COMMERCIAL UNION ASSURE CO SA LTD	—	11.0
SANLAM	—	15.4
UNILEVER SA PENS FUND	—	1.1
TOTAL	78.6	77.3

DIRECTORS :
CRAGG JC ,KINVIG JA (Chairman),MEYEROWITZ LA
PETERS JK (Managing Director),POLWARTH S
TURNER CJF ,WANLESS RRM

REGISTERED OFFICE
2nd Floor, 100 Main Street
Johannesburg
2001
TEL: 011-630 6111
FAX: 011-630 6338

TRANSFER SECRETARY
Central Registrars Ltd
P O Box 4844, Johannesburg
2000
TEL: 011-331 0051

COMPANY SECRETARY
Russell Marshall & Stride (Tvl) (Pty) Ltd

NATURE OF BUSINESS
A property trust fund managed by UAL Property Fund Managers.

BANKERS :
Nedperm Bank Ltd

AUDITORS :
Deloitte Pim Goldby

FAMILIAR BRAND NAMES
N/A

CONTRIBUTION BY ACTIVITY
Retail (% Gross Income) (48.9%)
Offices (46.4%)
Residential (1.6%)
Parking (3.2%)

YEAR END : September

DIVIDEND :Units

Interim No 8	(Ldr)11/05/90	(Pay)25/05/90	Amt(c)38.5
Final No 9	(Ldr)09/11/90	(Pay)23/11/90	Amt(c)39.2
Interim No 10	(Ldr)10/05/91	(Pay)24/05/91	Amt(c)38.2
Special No 11	(Ldr)12/07/91	(Pay)29/11/91	Amt(c)25.85
Final No 12	(Ldr)15/11/91	(Pay)29/11/91	Amt(c)11.13
Interim No 13	(Ldr)15/05/92	(Pay)29/05/92	Amt(c)38.45
Final No 14	(Ldr)13/11/92	(Pay)27/11/92	Amt(c)39.35

NUMBER OF EMPLOYEES : 70

CAPITAL STRUCTURE

	AUTHORISED	ISSUED
Units	64853664	64853664

FINANCIAL STATISTICS (AT FINANCIAL YEAR END)

(Amts in R'000)	1991 Sep	1990 Sep	1989 Sep	1988 Sep	1987
Ord S/H Int	366996	292014	183788	149134	149093
Long Trm Loans	-	-	-	-	8812
Iss Ord Share	64854	54045	36169	30141	30141
Total Liab	21490	20998	13803	9814	17624
Current Liab	21490	20998	13803	9814	8812
Total Assets	388486	313012	197591	158948	171187
Current Assets	71633	47564	32643	9793	13282
Debtors	757	1495	592	15	-
Inventory	-	-	-	-	13282
Oper Profit	-2106	-2174	25846	18190	15536
Prf af Int&Tax	41818	41243	25846	18190	15536
Prf att Ord Sh	41818	41243	25846	18190	15536
Btm Line Earn	42578	42041	26501	18190	15536
Dividend Paid	41834	41248	25873	18175	15522
Mkt Prce(c) YE	775	715	820	575	925

PER SHARE STATISTICS (CENTS)

Net Asst Val	565.88	540.32	508.14	494.79	494.65
Net Earnings	75.18	76.32	72.60	60.30	-
Dividends	75.18	76.32	72.60	60.30	-
Cash Flow	64.48	76.31	71.46	60.35	51.54

RATIOS AND OTHER INFORMATION

Mrk Cap(R000)	502619	386422	296586	173311	278804
Current Ratio	3.33	2.27	2.36	1.00	1.51
Quik/Acid Tst	3.33	2.27	2.36	1.00	-
Debt/Ass Rat	0.06	0.07	0.07	0.06	0.10
L T L Tot Ass	-	-	-	-	0.05
Debt to Eqity	0.06	0.07	0.08	0.07	0.12
Ret on Assets	10.76	13.18	13.08	11.44	9.08
Ret on Equity%	11.39	14.12	14.06	12.20	10.42
Price/Earnings	10.31	9.37	11.29	9.54	-
Divid Cover	1.00	1.00	1.00	1.00	-
Divid Yield	9.70	10.67	8.85	10.49	-
Earning Yield%	9.70	10.67	8.85	10.49	-
NAV % Mrk Pr	73.02	75.57	61.97	86.05	53.48
Def Interval	-	-	-	-	0.57
Sus Grth Rate	0.00	0.00	-0.01	0.01	0.01

SUBSIDIARY & ASSOCIATED COMPANIES

BATHGATE (PTY) LTD
CARLON FALCO DEVELOPMENT CO (PTY) LTD
CENTEX OFFICE PARK (PTY) LTD
CENTRE SOUTH PROPERTIES (PTY) LTD
EGIDE (PTY) LTD
FOLDAL PROPERTIES (PTY) LTD
HURLINGHAM PROPERTY INVESTMENTS (PTY) LT
INTALEX SOUTH AFRICA (PTY) LTD
KASLE PROPERTIES (PTY) LTD
LOT 549 PARKTOWN (PTY) LTD
MORNING GLEN SHOPPING CENTRE (PTY) LTD
N1 CITY FOUR (PTY) LTD
NBSA CENTRE LTD
PORTION 2 OF LOT 3 SANDOWN (PTY) LTD
PORTION 224 ZANDFONTEIN (PTY) LTD
PORTION 5 HURLINGHAM EXT 5 (PTY) LTD
PORTION 6 HURLINGHAM EXT 5 (PTY) LTD
SANDTON FIVE FORTY (PTY) LTD
SOUTHDALE SHOPPING CENTRE (PTY) LTD
STAND 646 NEW REDRUTH (PTY) LTD
STEAD PROPERTY INVESTMENTS (PTY) LTD
SUNNY DEVENISH PLACE (PTY) LTD
UPPARK (PTY) LTD
VETENG PROPERTIES (PTY) LTD
WENDYWOOD SHOPPING CENTRE (PTY) LTD

INVESTMENTS

SOUTHGATE SHOPPING MALL (12,95%)

T&N HOLDINGS LTD

ABBREVIATION : T-&-N

JSE SHORT CODE : TUN

SECTOR : Industrial-Industrial Holding

SHAREHOLDERS

Who Owns Whom's Assessment of the Identity of the Ultimate Controlling Shareholder:
TURNER & NEWALL PLC

SHAREHOLDER	PERCENTAGE 1992	1991
T & N INTERNATIONAL LTD	47.2	47.2
EIGHTY ONE MAIN STREET NOM LTD	7.7	9.4
SA SPECIAL RISKS INSURANCE ASSOC LTD	6.5	6.5
AECI PENS FUND	5.0	5.0
T & N EMPLOYEES SHARE TRUST	4.9	4.9
DUBLIN CONSOLIDATED ASBESTOS MINE P/L	3.9	3.9
FIRST NAT NOM P/L	2.9	3.9
DORBYL PENS FUND	2.6	2.6
AFRICAN OXYGEN LTD PENS FUND	1.7	1.7

WORKMENS COMPENS COMMISSIONER IN TRUST	1 7	---
STD BANK NOM TVL P/L	1 5	2 0
FERBROS NOM P/L	1 3	---
NATAL JOINT MUNICIPAL PENS FUND SUPERANN	1 2	1 2
SIXTY SIX MARSHALL STREET NOM P/L	1 0	1 7
METAL IND GROUP PENS FUND	1 0	1 0
TOTAL	90 1	91 0

DIRECTORS :
COOPER WW (Chief Executive),DE LOOR J DR
GOOD CB ,HOPE CFN (Chairman),LUTTIG J ,MEYER JA
MUCH IFR ,PARRY EM
PRETORIUS MC (Deputy Chairman)
VAN DER MERWE-VANCE A

REGISTRATION NUMBER : 71/12146/06

REGISTERED OFFICE
4th Floor, Unilever House, 2 Aliwal Street
Durban
4001
TEL 031-32 2679
FAX 031-37 7141

TRANSFER SECRETARY
Central Registrars Ltd
P O Box 4844, Johannesburg
2000
TEL 011-331 0051

COMPANY SECRETARY
C J W Hilt

NATURE OF BUSINESS
Group operations include developing, manufacturing marketing and trading products in the following industries Chemicals & Plastics - food additives, synthetic resins, urea and melamine formaldehyde moulding powders, paper resins, defoamers and synthetic sizes & acidulents, Industrial Products pump & valve gland packing, industrial gaskets, sheet jointing,link sealing & machining & bearings Automotive - gaskets, pistons, repair of radiators friction materials, gudgeon pins, valves & bushes

BANKERS :
Nedperm Bank Ltd, Rand Merchant Bank Ltd
UAL Merchant Bank Ltd
Standard Bank of SA Ltd

AUDITORS :
KPMG Aiken & Peat

FAMILIAR BRAND NAMES
AE,ALFIN,BELACO-BERAL (28%),BIP CHEMICALS
CMJ,DANBRAKE,DURATORQUE,FERODO,FHE
FLEXITALLIC,HARPO,HYPAJET
METALINE (BRAKE PADS),MOTOBRAKE,PAYEN
SILVERTON,STAG,TBA,TUMALL,VELTOL PARKO

CONTRIBUTION BY ACTIVITY
N/A

YEAR END : December

DIVIDEND :Ords 20c

Interim	(Ldr)07/09/90	(Pay)31/10/90	Amt(c)3 8
Final	(Ldr)15/03/91	(Pay)30/04/91	Amt(c)10
Interim	(Ldr)13/09/91	(Pay)31/10/91	Amt(c)7 5
Final	(Ldr)20/03/92	(Pay)30/04/92	Amt(c)16 5
Interim	(Ldr)18/09/92	(Pay)31/10/92	Amt(c)11

NUMBER OF EMPLOYEES : 3683

CAPITAL STRUCTURE

	AUTHORISED	ISSUED
Ords 20c	25000000	23099798

FINANCIAL STATISTICS (AT FINANCIAL YEAR END)

(Amts in R'000)	19OV	1991 Dec	1990 Dec	1989 Dec	1988 Dec
Ord S/H Int	100000	122904	113211	108820	99974
Long Trm Loans	75700	51353	50782	53423	19785
Iss Ord Share	23100	23100	23100	23100	23100
Total Liab	134800	198422	198382	173477	91399
Current Liab	59100	147069	147600	120054	71614
Total Assets	259100	321326	292566	263270	191373
Intang Assets	*	*	19027	19027	*
Current Assets	75800	179150	169806	154903	83805
Debtors	-	42000	44101	49840	32099
Inventory	75800	85695	88863	85461	43115
Turnover	234700	425727	413429	391439	234665
Oper Profit	26300	36412	32728	39533	26243
Interest Paid	5800	21473	21122	15949	5832
Tax Paid	6200	594	1517	4919	6238
Prf af Int&Tax	14300	18250	10089	18665	14173
Prf att Ord Sh	20300	16160	8079	16001	20251
Btm Line Earn	20300	16002	7579	16001	4768
Dividend Paid	-	5543	3188	7161	10165
Mkt Prce(c) YE	800	290	260	550	800
Depreciation	-	12618	10966	8985	4476

PER SHARE STATISTICS (CENTS)

Net Asst Val	432 90	532 05	407 72	388 71	432 79
Net Earnings	-	70 00	35 00	69 30	87 70
Dividends	-	24 00	13 80	31 00	44 00
Cash Flow	61 90	126 29	84 19	108 16	79 55

RATIOS AND OTHER INFORMATION

Mrk Cap(R000)	184800	66990	60060	127050	184800
Current Ratio	1 28	1 22	1 15	1 29	1 17
Quik/Acid Tst	-	0 64	0 55	0 58	0 57
A/C Rec T/ovr	-	10 14	9 37	7 85	7 31
Tot Ass T/ovr	0 91	1 32	1 41	1 49	1 23
Debt/Ass Rat	0 52	0 60	0 61	0 59	0 46
L T L Tot Ass	0 29	0 14	0 11	0 13	0 08
Debt to Eqty	1 35	1 57	1 58	1 42	0 88
Interest Cover	4 53	1 85	1 55	2 48	4 50
Oper Prof Mrg	11 21	8 55	7 92	10 10	11 18
Net Prof Marg%	8 65	3 80	1 95	4 09	8 63
Ret on Assets	10 15	12 42	11 05	15 02	17 03
Ret on Equity%	20 30	13 15	7 14	14 70	20 26
Price/Earnings	-	4 14	7 43	7 94	9 12
Divid Cover		2 92	2 54	2 24	1 99
Divid Yield	-	8 28	5 31	5 64	5 50
Earning Yield%		24 14	13 46	12 60	10 96
NAV % Mrk Pr	54 11	183 47	156 82	70 68	54 10
Effec Tax Rate	30 24	3 80	13 07	20 05	28 89
Def Interval	5 29	3 25	5 38	3 82	0 94
Sus Grth Rate	20 30	8 64	4 32	8 12	10 09

SUBSIDIARY & ASSOCIATED COMPANIES

ASBESTOS AND COTTON PACKING (PTY) LTD
ASSENG LTD
BEETLE PRODUCTS CO (SA) (PTY) LTD
BELACO (PTY) LTD
BELACO BERAL (PTY) LTD
BERAL SWAZILAND (PTY) LTD
BIP PROPERTIES (PTY) LTD (50%)
BRITISH INDUSTRIAL PLASTICS (SA) (PTY) L
BUTAKEM (PTY) LTD

CORK HOLDINGS (PTY) LTD
DANCOR LTD (35,7%)
FEROBRAKE (PTY) LTD
FERODO (PTY) LTD
FERODO HEAT EXCHANGERS (PTY) LTD
FHE AUTOMOTIVE TECHNOLOGIES (PTY) LTD
FLEXITALLIC GASKETS AFRICA LTD
HARPO GASKETS (PTY) LTD
IMPACT PACKINGS (PTY) LTD
INDUSTRIAL GASKETS (PTY) LTD
LONGWALL MINING EQUIPMENT (PTY) LTD
MARIX (PTY) LTD
MOTOR REPLACEMENTS (PTY) LTD
PAYEN COMPONENTS SA LTD
SA PACKING & JOINTING MANUFACTURERS (PTY
SIBEX ENGINEERING SERVICES (PTY) LTD
SILVERTON ENGINEERING (PTY) LTD
SILVERTON ENGINEERING HOLDINGS (PTY) LTD
SILVERTON ENGINEERING PROPERTIES (PORT E
SILVERTON ENGINEERING PROPERTIES (PRETOR
SILVERTON SERVICES LTD
STAG PACKINGS (PTY) LTD
T & N INDUSTRIAL PRODUCTS (PTY) LTD
TBA INDUSTRIAL PRODUCTS (PTY) LTD
TURNER & NEWALL INDUSTRIAL PRODUCTS (PTY
TURNERS ENGINEERING PRODUCTS (TVL) (PTY)
TURNRITE CHEMICALS (PTY) LTD

INVESTMENTS

None

T.A. HOLDINGS LTD

ABBREVIATION : TA HOLD

SECTOR : Zimbabwe Stock Exchange

SHAREHOLDERS

Who Owns Whom's Assessment of the Identity of the Ultimate Controlling Shareholder:
OLD MUTUTAL INVESTMENT CORP

DIRECTORS :
CHAMBATI AM (Chairman & Chief Exec.)
CHIPUDHLA PWT ,CHIWESHE ET ,DORWARD PD
MAPONDERA HE ,SHLOM B ,SNELL JWM ,TURPIN WH
VINCENT DJM

REGISTERED OFFICE
Cooksey House, 2 Simon Mazorodze Road
Harare, Zimbabwe

TEL: 702905
FAX: 794361

TRANSFER SECRETARY
T A Trading Corporation (Pvt) Ltd
P O Box 3546, Harare
Zimbabwe

TEL: 702905

COMPANY SECRETARY
J W M Snell

NATURE OF BUSINESS
Is today one of the largest wholly owned Zimbabwean public companies, having diversified to result in a group of companies in the retail, communications, leisure, industrial, packaging, motor, road transport, clearing and forwarding, insurance, removals and storage, chemicals, investment and property sectors. Operates a group of companies in Botswana involved in business equipment, bakeries, property, cosmetics, hotels, packaging and storage and transport.

BANKERS :
N/A

AUDITORS :
Price Waterhouse Meyernel

FAMILIAR BRAND NAMES
N/A

CONTRIBUTION BY ACTIVITY
N/A

YEAR END : May

DIVIDEND : Ords Z$0,50

Dividend	(Ldr)14/02/92	(Pay)06/03/92	Amt(c)10
Dividend	(Ldr)11/09/92	(Pay)25/09/92	Amt(c)13

CAPITAL STRUCTURE

	AUTHORISED	ISSUED
Ords Z$0,50	153000000	72138000
Def Ords Z$0,50	7000000	5000000
Cum Conv Red Prefs Z$100	200000	200000

FINANCIAL STATISTICS (AT FINANCIAL YEAR END)

(Amts in Z$)	1992 May	1991 May
Ord S/H Int	382430	257462
Long Trm Loans	378609	191693
Iss Ord Share	82138	61594
Total Liab	674248	398834
Current Liab	295639	207141
Total Assets	1056678	656296
Current Assets	384251	243656
Debtors	168778	118593
Inventory	184235	120941
Turnover	1171735	801418
Oper Profit	95936	59909
Interest Paid	32388	13988
Tax Paid	22887	18892
Prf af Int&Tax	40661	27029
Prf att Ord Sh	39446	33082
Btm Line Earn	39446	33082
Dividend Paid	17742	14570
Depreciation	23412	13376

PER SHARE STATISTICS (CENTS)

Net Asst Val	465.59	418.00
Net Earnings	53.60	50.40
Dividends	23.00	22.00
Cash Flow	71.86	65.53

RATIOS AND OTHER INFORMATION

Current Ratio	1.30	1.18
Quik/Acid Tst	0.68	0.59
A/C Rec T/ovr	6.94	6.76
Tot Ass T/ovr	1.11	1.22
Debt/Ass Rat	0.44	0.40

L T L Tot Ass	0.16	0.09
Debt to Eqity	1.21	1.03
Interest Cover	2.96	4.28
Oper Prof Mrg	8.19	7.48
Net Prof Marg%	3.37	4.13
Ret on Assets	10.06	10.64
Ret on Equity%	10.31	12.85
Divid Cover	2.33	2.29
Effec Tax Rate	27.46	33.17
Def Interval	4.48	2.96
Sus Grth Rate	5.68	7.19

SUBSIDIARY & ASSOCIATED COMPANIES

AFCO ENTERPRISES (PVT) LTD
AGRIFOODS (PVT) LTD (40%)
AMALGAMATED MOTOR CORPORATION (PVT) LTD
AMCAR (PVT) LTD
AROMA BAKERIES (PVT) LTD
BERNSTEIN MANUFACTURING CO (1961) (PVT)
BLUE RIBBON FOODS LTD
BLUE RIBBON INDUSTRIES LTD
BMS (PTY) LTD (BOTSWANA)
BON BON BAKERY (PVT) LTD (49,9%)
BUSINESS COMPUTERS BOTSWANA (PTY) LTD
CHAESHIRE PROPERTIES (PTY) LTD (BOTSWANA
COMBINE CARGO INVESTMENTS LTD (SOUTH AFR (48,2%)
CRESTA MARAKANELO HOTELS (PTY) LTD
CUMMINS ZIMBABWE (PVT) LTD (49,4%)
DOWNINGS BAKERY (BOTSWANA) (PTY) LTD
ECONOMIC CYCLES (PVT) LTD
EMQUIP (PVT) LTD
GILCHRIST & COOKSEY (PVT) LTD (39%)
GLENS (PTY) LTD (GABORONE)
GLENS PROPERTIES (PVT) LTD
INDIGO PROPERTY & INVESTMENTS CO (PTY) L
J L ROBINSON AGENCIES (PVT) LTD
JOCK SMITH'S SPRAYPAINTS (PVT) LTD (30,9%)
LONDON SHIRTS CO (PVT) LTD
M K ELECTRIC (ZIMBABWE) (PVT) LTD
MAKULU INVESTMENTS (PTY) LTD (BOTSWANA)
MINET INSURANCE BROKERS (ZIMBABWE) (PVT) (30,3%)
NATIONAL WHOLESALERS (PVT) LTD
PRESTIGE BUILDERS BOTSWANA (PTY) LTD
PROPAK (PVT) LTD (HARARE) (37%)
SABATA HOLDINGS LTD
SABLE CHEMICAL INDUSTRIES LTD (50,9%)
SMITH & BENNETT (PVT) LTD
STUTTAFORDS (PVT) LTD (26%)
T A BOTSWANA (PTY) LTD - BOTSWANA
T A ELECTRIC (PVT) LTD
T A MINING COMPANY LIMITED
T A PROPERTIES (PVT) LTD
T A REAL ESTATE LIMITED
T A TRADING CORPORATION (PVT) LTD
TRANS INDUSTRIES (PTY) LTD (BOTSWANA)
UNITED REFINERIES LTD
VARAPI CENTRE (PVT) LTD
Z F C LIMITED (22,5%)
ZIMBABWE CYCLE INDUSTRIES LTD (BULAWAYO)
ZIMBABWE MOTOR INVESTMENTS (PVT) LTD (33,3%)
ZIMNAT INSURANCE CO LTD
ZIMNAT LIFE ASSURANCE CO LTD

INVESTMENTS

None

TABEX HOLDINGS LTD

ABBREVIATION : TABEX

SECTOR : Zimbabwe Stock Exchange

SHAREHOLDERS

Who Owns Whom's Assessment of the Identity of the Ultimate Controlling Shareholder:
BLAIR HOLDINGS

SHAREHOLDER	PERCENTAGE 1992	1991
BLAIR HOLDING PVT LTD	60.7	---
ZIMBABWE REINSURANCE CORP LTD	4.8	---
SYFRETS NOM (PVT) LTD	2.9	---
CONSTRUCTION INDUSTRY PENS FUND	2.3	---
FIDELITY LIFE ASSURE OF ZIM PVT LTD	2.1	---
KILLARNEY PROPERTIES PVT LTD	1.2	---
TOTAL	73.8	---

DIRECTORS :
DURRAD BW ,GALLOWAY CD ,MADZIVIRE BW
PICHANICK ALA
TABERER ACB (Chairman & Managing Dir.)
TABERER CMB ,THOMPSON AC

REGISTERED OFFICE
Cnr Salford & Simon Mazorodze, Harare
Zimbabwe

TEL: 68377
FAX: 61881

TRANSFER SECRETARY
Zimbabwe Banking Corporation Ltd
P O Box 3198, Harare
Zimbabwe

TEL: 092634-735011

COMPANY SECRETARY
K Carroll

NATURE OF BUSINESS
Incorporated in Zimbabwe, the main operatons of TABEX HOLDINGS are agricultural services,commodity broking,flower and seed cultivation,freight services and gold mining.It also has interests in the insurance,transport, travel, steel and information technology sectors.

BANKERS :
Zimbabwe Banking Corporation Ltd

AUDITORS :
Ernst & Young

FAMILIAR BRAND NAMES
N/A

CONTRIBUTION BY ACTIVITY
N/A

YEAR END : March

DIVIDEND :Ords Z$0,25

Dividend	(Ldr)15/11/91	(Pay)27/11/91	Amt(c)1.25
Dividend	(Ldr)12/06/92	(Pay)30/06/92	Amt(c)3.80

CAPITAL STRUCTURE

	AUTHORISED	ISSUED
Ords Z$0,25	200000000	190227000

FINANCIAL STATISTICS (AT FINANCIAL YEAR END)

(Amts in Z$)	1992 Mar	1991 Mar
Ord S/H Int	150538	81394
Long Trm Loans	36809	27465
Iss Ord Share	190227	189264
Total Liab	544144	202486
Current Liab	507335	175021
Total Assets	694682	283880
Current Assets	515595	190492
Debtors	346008	112655
Inventory	129388	74817
Turnover	562201	230629
Oper Profit	40329	28924
Interest Paid	23711	18578
Tax Paid	760	-
Prf af Int&Tax	19665	11887
Prf att Ord Sh	22568	12828
Btm Line Earn	22568	12828
Dividend Paid	9594	5574
Depreciation	5209	3707

PER SHARE STATISTICS (CENTS)

Net Asst Val	79.14	43.01
Net Earnings	11.90	6.78
Dividends	5.05	2.95
Cash Flow	12.95	8.11

RATIOS AND OTHER INFORMATION

Current Ratio	1.02	1.09
Quik/Acid Tst	0.76	0.66
A/C Rec T/ovr	1.62	2.05
Tot Ass T/ovr	0.81	0.81
Debt/Ass Rat	0.77	0.69
L T L Tot Ass	0.04	0.08
Debt to Eqity	3.57	2.41
Interest Cover	1.83	1.61
Oper Prof Mrg	7.17	12.54
Net Prof Marg%	4.01	5.56
Ret on Assets	6.81	11.15
Ret on Equity%	14.99	15.76
Divid Cover	2.36	2.30
Effec Tax Rate	4.40	-
Def Interval	20.04	11.34
Sus Grth Rate	8.62	8.91

SUBSIDIARY & ASSOCIATED COMPANIES

AGMIN (PVT) LTD
AIR TABEX (PVT) LTD
BULK FREIGHT SERVICES (PVT) LTD
CONQUEST INTERTRADE (PVT) LTD
FL'AIR (PVT) LTD (T/A) TABEX FLOWERS
FREXPO TRADING (PVT) LTD (40%)
GENERAL HOLDINGS (PVT) LTD
INTERNATIONAL COMPUTER SERVICES (PVT) LT
OLDHAM SEEDS (PVT) LTD
RIVERLEA MINES (PVT) LTD
T H I (PVT) LTD (50%)
TABEX (PVT) LIMITED
TABEX BURLEY UNIT (PVT) LTD
TABEX MINING (PVT) LTD
TABEX STEEL (PVT) LTD
TABEX-DIBRELL PROCESSORS (PVT) LTD (50%)
TRYST (PVT) LTD (29,2%)
ZIMBABWE & OVERSEAS TOBACCO CO (PVT) LTD

INVESTMENTS

None

TAFELBERG FURNITURE STORES LTD

ABBREVIATION : TAFLBRG

JSE SHORT CODE : TFB

SECTOR : Industrial-Furniture & Household

SHAREHOLDERS

Who Owns Whom's Assessment of the Identity of the Ultimate Controlling Shareholder: DIRECTORS

SHAREHOLDER	PERCENTAGE 1992	1991
TAFELBERG FURNITURE P/L	36.7	43.2
HEIL H	8.4	5.0
GERBER H E/L	8.3	—
LOUW A H P	6.0	2.7
THERON E J	4.0	4.0
FOURIE H J	4.0	4.0
RINRIC NOM P/L	2.3	2.7
ROMER A P	1.8	1.8
THERON A F M	1.3	1.3
VOIGT GROUP P/L	1.2	1.2
GERBER H	—	8.3
TOMLINSON K I	—	1.1
TOTAL	74.0	75.4

DIRECTORS :
HEIL HG (Financial Director),LOUW AHP
STEINMANN P ,THERON EJ (Chairman),THERON GR

REGISTRATION NUMBER : 87/01012/06

REGISTERED OFFICE
128 Durban Road, Bellville
7530
TEL: 021-946 3330
FAX: 021-94 4507

TRANSFER SECRETARY
Rand Registrars Ltd
P O Box 82549, Southdale
2135
TEL: 011-835 1016

COMPANY SECRETARY
HG Heil

NATURE OF BUSINESS
A company active in the retail of household furniture and electrical applicances, as well as sophisticated sound and television equipment.

BANKERS :
First National Bank of SA Ltd

AUDITORS :
JP Coetzee & Co

FAMILIAR BRAND NAMES
TAFELBERG FURNISHERS

CONTRIBUTION BY ACTIVITY
N/A

YEAR END : February

DIVIDEND : Ords 10c

Interim No 7	(Ldr)12/10/90	(Pay)16/11/90	Amt(c)1.5
Final No 8	(Ldr)17/05/91	(Pay)17/06/91	Amt(c)2
Interim No 9	(Ldr)18/10/91	(Pay)15/11/91	Amt(c)1.5
Final No 10	(Ldr)15/05/92	(Pay)19/06/92	Amt(c)2
Interim No 11	(Ldr)16/10/92	(Pay)13/11/92	Amt(c)1

NUMBER OF EMPLOYEES : 93

CAPITAL STRUCTURE

	AUTHORISED	ISSUED
Ords 10c	15000000	12377272

FINANCIAL STATISTICS (AT FINANCIAL YEAR END)

(Amts in R'000)	1992 Feb	1991 Feb	1990 Feb	1989 Feb	1988
Ord S/H Int	4585	4226	3730	3423	2937
Long Trm Loans	1474	1401	1420	80	81
Iss Ord Share	12377	12377	12377	12377	12377
Total Liab	10641	9106	7976	5558	5001
Current Liab	9167	7705	6556	5478	4920
Total Assets	15226	13332	11706	8853	7797
Intang Assets	*	*	*	128	141
Current Assets	13063	10484	8677	7358	6423
Debtors	2315	2724	1923	1743	1499
Inventory	10443	7627	6634	5611	4919
Turnover	45727	41522	31149	29490	19312
Oper Profit	1439	1757	1820	1784	1198
Interest Paid	475	491	348	136	30
Tax Paid	685	824	857	822	584
Prf af Int&Tax	865	932	868	826	584
Prf att Ord Sh	865	932	868	826	584
Btm Line Earn	793	932	868	826	584
Dividend Paid	433	433	433	433	313
Mkt Prce(c) YE	20	28	23	26	32
Depreciation	136	205	224	158	60

PER SHARE STATISTICS (CENTS)

Net Asst Val	37.04	34.14	30.14	26.62	22.59
Net Earnings	6.99	7.53	7.00	7.40	5.40
Dividends	3.50	3.50	3.50	3.50	2.60
Cash Flow	8.09	9.19	8.82	7.95	6.49

RATIOS AND OTHER INFORMATION

Mrk Cap(R000)	2475	3466	2847	3218	3961
Current Ratio	1.43	1.36	1.32	1.34	1.31
Quik/Acid Tst	0.29	0.37	0.31	0.32	0.31
A/C Rec T/ovr	19.75	15.24	16.20	16.92	15.46
Tot Ass T/ovr	3.00	3.11	2.66	3.33	2.97
Debt/Ass Rat	0.69	0.67	0.68	0.63	0.64
L T L Tot Ass	0.08	0.10	0.12	0.01	0.01
Debt to Eqity	2.28	2.12	2.13	1.62	1.70
Interest Cover	3.03	3.58	5.23	13.12	39.93
Oper Prof Mrg	3.15	4.23	5.84	6.05	6.20
Net Prof Marg%	1.89	2.24	2.79	2.80	3.02
Ret on Assets	13.30	16.85	17.71	20.15	18.44
Ret on Equity%	18.87	22.05	23.27	24.13	23.86
Price/Earnings	2.86	3.72	3.29	3.51	5.93
Divid Cover	2.00	2.15	2.00	2.11	2.08
Divid Yield	17.50	12.50	15.22	13.46	8.13
Earning Yield%	34.95	26.89	30.43	28.46	16.88
NAV % Mrk Pr	185.22	121.94	131.03	102.39	70.59
Effec Tax Rate	44.52	46.81	49.68	49.88	50.00
Def Interval	2.67	2.22	1.91	1.79	0.90
Sus Grth Rate	9.42	11.81	11.66	11.48	9.23

SUBSIDIARY & ASSOCIATED COMPANIES

AUDIO FEVER (PTY) LTD
MAILMARK (PTY) LTD
TAFPROP (BELLVILLE) (PTY) LTD
TELEMARK (PTY) LTD

INVESTMENTS

None

TAMBOTI PROPERTY FUND

ABBREVIATION : TAMBOTI

JSE SHORT CODE : TAM

SECTOR : Financial-Property Trust

SHAREHOLDERS

Who Owns Whom's Assessment of the Identity of the Ultimate Controlling Shareholder: INSTITUTIONAL INVESTORS

SHAREHOLDER	PERCENTAGE 1992	1991
CMB NOM P/L	16.7	---
FIRST NAT NOM P/L	11.0	10.9
CITY COUNCIL OF DURBAN	7.3	7.3
EIGHTY ONE MAIN STREET NOM LTD	6.4	8.6
ANGLO AMERICAN GROUP PENS FUND	6.0	2.9
STD BANK NOM TVL P/L	5.5	1.4
METAL IND GROUP PENS FUND	4.3	4.3
ENGINEERING INDUSTRIES PENS FUND	4.2	4.2
BARLOWS PENS FUND	3.6	2.1
SA MUTUAL	3.6	5.0
ABSA NOM P/L	1.6	---
DURBAN CORP SUPERANNUATION FUND	1.6	1.6
AFRICAN OXYGEN LTD PENS FUND	1.4	1.2
SIXTY SIX MARSHALL STREET NOM P/L	1.2	1.2
WORKMENS COMPENS COMMISSIONER IN TRUST	1.2	---
CORNER HOUSE PENS FUND	1.2	---
PROTEA ASSURE CO LTD	1.0	---
SHARESTOCK NOM P/L	---	1.2
SMBL NOM P/L	---	1.1
BOARD OF EXECUTORS NOM P/L	---	2.7
SANLAM	---	16.4
TOTAL	78.0	72.1

DIRECTORS :
CHAPMAN HG ,DICKSON AJL ,FARRER M ,NOYCE MJ
SMALE JR ,SMITHYMAN MV ,TAYLOR G

REGISTRATION NUMBER : 83/08365/06

REGISTERED OFFICE
Protea Assurance Building, 321 Smith Street
Durban
4001
TEL: 031-304 2731
FAX: 031-305 1521

TRANSFER SECRETARY
Mercantile Registrars Ltd
P O Box 1053, Johannesburg
2000
TEL: 011-333 8181

COMPANY SECRETARY
Russell Marriot & Boyd Trust (Pty) Ltd

NATURE OF BUSINESS
A unit trust scheme in property shares.

BANKERS :
First National Bank of SA Ltd

AUDITORS :
David Strachan & Tayler
Deloitte Pim Goldby

FAMILIAR BRAND NAMES
N/A

CONTRIBUTION BY ACTIVITY
Industrial (Portfolio by Sector) (47.0%)
Office Blocks (33.0%)
Shops & Offices (20.0%)

YEAR END : September

DIVIDEND : Units R2

Interim No 8	(Ldr)11/05/90	(Pay)28/05/90	Amt(c)13.6
Final No 9	(Ldr)19/11/90	(Pay)30/11/90	Amt(c)14.7
Interim No 10	(Ldr)10/05/91	(Pay)27/05/91	Amt(c)14.8
Final No 13	(Ldr)15/05/92	(Pay)29/05/92	Amt(c)16
Final No 14	(Ldr)13/11/92	(Pay)27/11/92	Amt(c)16.5

CAPITAL STRUCTURE

	AUTHORISED	ISSUED
Units R2	78400000	78400000

FINANCIAL STATISTICS (AT FINANCIAL YEAR END)

(Amts in R'000)	1992 Sep	1991 Sep	1989 Sep	1988 Sep	1987
Ord S/H Int	171044	171044	109854	109653	109653
Long Trm Loans	-	-	-	-	6830
Iss Ord Share	78400	78400	56000	56000	56000
Total Liab	13609	6986	3968	7236	13660
Current Liab	13609	6986	3968	7236	6830
Total Assets	184653	178030	113822	116889	135255
Current Assets	51875	59475	6919	9001	18772
Debtors	2813	1691	43	27	-
Inventory	-	-	-	-	18772
Turnover	-	-	11540	14138	13691
Oper Profit	25480	19325	11019	13440	12839
Prf af Int&Tax	25480	19325	11019	13440	12839
Prf att Ord Sh	25480	19325	11019	13440	12839
Btm Line Earn	25480	19704	11222	13440	12839
Dividend Paid	25480	19320	11021	13440	12840
Mkt Prce(c) YE	290	245	270	210	270

PER SHARE STATISTICS (CENTS)

Net Asst Val	218.17	218.17	196.17	195.81	195.31
Net Earnings	32.50	28.30	19.68	24.00	-
Dividends	32.50	28.30	19.68	24.00	-
Cash Flow	32.50	24.65	26.24	24.00	22.93

RATIOS AND OTHER INFORMATION

Mrk Cap(R000)	227360	192080	151200	117600	151200
Current Ratio	3.81	8.51	1.74	1.24	2.75
Quik/Acid Tst	3.81	8.51	1.74	1.24	-
A/C Rec T/ovr	-	-	357.83	523.63	-
Tot Ass T/ovr	-	-	0.14	0.12	0.10
Debt/Ass Rat	0.07	0.04	0.03	0.06	0.10
L T L Tot Ass	-	-	-	-	0.05
Debt to Eqity	0.08	0.04	0.04	0.07	0.12
Oper Prof Mrg	-	-	95.49	95.06	93.78
Net Prof Marg%	-	-	95.49	95.06	93.78
Ret on Assets	13.80	10.85	12.91	11.50	9.49
Ret on Equity%	14.90	11.30	13.37	12.26	11.71
Price/Earnings	8.92	8.66	13.72	8.75	-
Divid Cover	1.00	1.00	1.00	1.00	-
Divid Yield	11.21	11.55	7.29	11.43	-
Earning Yield%	11.21	11.55	7.29	11.43	-
NAV % Mrk Pr	75.23	89.05	72.65	93.24	72.52
Def Interval	-	-	-	-	0.53
Sus Grth Rate	0.00	0.00	0.00	0.00	0.00

SUBSIDIARY & ASSOCIATED COMPANIES

425 WEST STREET (PTY) LTD
ALUPROPS (PTY) LTD
ASP PROPERTIES (PTY) LTD
BENTOP (PTY) LTD
BO HOLDINGS (PTY) LTD
BROADBILL INVESTMENTS (PTY) LTD
CAMAJE (PTY) LTD
DEVELOPMENT FOUR ONE FIVE (PTY) LTD
FINCHPROP INVESTMENTS (PTY) LTD
FRISES (PTY) LTD
GUILLEMOT INVESTMENTS (PTY) LTD
GULLPROP INVESTMENTS (PTY) LTD
HALVERT INVESTMENTS (PTY) LTD
HARLING INVESTMENTS (PTY) LTD
HILKEW INVESTMENTS (PTY) LTD
KITEPROPS (PTY) LTD
LOT 802 SPRINGFIELD (PTY) LTD
PELMA PROPERTIES (PTY) LTD
RAMI'S INVESTMENTS (PTY) LTD
REDUAL (PTY) LTD
SANDGROUSE (PTY) LTD
SPARROWHAWK (PTY) LTD
STAND 180 THE WOLDS (PTY) LTD
STONDELL INVESTMENTS (PTY) LTD
STORK INVESTMENTS (PTY) LTD
TAMCO INVESTMENTS (PTY) LTD
VALGRACE INVESTMENTS (PTY) LTD
ZERUS PROPERTIES (PTY) LTD

INVESTMENTS

None

TANGANDA TEA COMPANY LTD

ABBREVIATION : TANGANDA

SECTOR : Zimbabwe Stock Exchange

SHAREHOLDERS

Who Owns Whom's Assessment of the Identity of the Ultimate Controlling Shareholder: VESTOR HOLDINGS (PVT) LTD

DIRECTORS :
CAMERON MV ,FENNELL RJ
HAGGIE AS (Managing Director)
MOXTON JRT (Chairman),SAGONDA DMK ,STEPHENS DE
WARD JM

REGISTERED OFFICE
3rd Floor, Travel Centre
Jason Moyo Avenue, Harare

TEL: 703786

TRANSFER SECRETARY
N/A

COMPANY SECRETARY
Thomas Meikle Trust & Investment Co

NATURE OF BUSINESS
The company is the largest producer, packer and distributor of tea products in Zimbabwe. It is divided into two main operating divisions - Agricultural and Beverage.

BANKERS :
Barclays Bank of Zimbabwe Ltd
Merchant Bank of Central Africa

AUDITORS :
Price Waterhouse Meyernel

FAMILIAR BRAND NAMES
N/A

CONTRIBUTION BY ACTIVITY
N/A

YEAR END : August

DIVIDEND :Ords Z$1

Dividend	(Ldr)03/01/92	(Pay)10/01/92	Amt(c)8

CAPITAL STRUCTURE

	AUTHORISED	ISSUED
Ords Z$1	60000000	153121000

FINANCIAL STATISTICS (AT FINANCIAL YEAR END)

(Amts in Z$)	1991 Aug	1990 Aug
Ord S/H Int	86562	63300
Long Trm Loans	6	13
Iss Ord Share	153121	5165
Total Liab	16576	15107
Current Liab	16570	15094
Total Assets	102953	78222
Intang Assets	185	185
Current Assets	32068	26508
Debtors	9493	8631
Inventory	22183	14622
Turnover	43325	41858
Oper Profit	10722	11941
Interest Paid	444	140
Tax Paid	2047	3799
Prf af Int&Tax	8292	8088
Prf att Ord Sh	8292	8088
Btm Line Earn	8292	8088
Dividend Paid	4250	4028
Depreciation	1892	1791

PER SHARE STATISTICS (CENTS)

Net Asst Val	56.41	1221.97
Net Earnings	16.84	17.40
Dividends	8.00	8.67
Cash Flow	6.65	191.27

RATIOS AND OTHER INFORMATION

Current Ratio	1.94	1.76
Quik/Acid Tst	0.60	0.79
A/C Rec T/ovr	4.56	4.85
Tot Ass T/ovr	0.42	0.54
Debt/Ass Rat	0.16	0.19
L T L Tot Ass	0.00	0.00
Debt to Eqity	0.19	0.24
Interest Cover	24.15	85.29
Oper Prof Mrg	24.75	28.53
Net Prof Marg%	19.14	19.32
Ret on Assets	10.47	15.38
Ret on Equity%	9.58	12.78
Divid Cover	2.11	2.01
Effec Tax Rate	19.81	32.46
Def Interval	0.37	-
Sus Grth Rate	4.67	6.41

SUBSIDIARY & ASSOCIATED COMPANIES

DHJ INDUSTRIES (SA) (PTY) LTD

INVESTMENTS

None

TARGET EXPLORATION COMPANY LTD

ABBREVIATION : TARGET

JSE SHORT CODE : TAG

SECTOR : Mining-Exploration

SHAREHOLDERS

Who Owns Whom's Assessment of the Identity of the Ultimate Controlling Shareholder: ANGLOVAAL VIA LORAINE

SHAREHOLDER	PERCENTAGE 1992	1991
FOX STREET NOM P/L	56.0	56.0
LORAINE GOLD MINES LTD	25.1	25.1
RESIDENT NOM LTD	8.4	8.4
PETARD NOM LTD	5.5	5.5
FERMAIN NOM LTD	2.4	2.4
TOTAL	97.4	97.4

DIRECTORS :
EUSTACE PJ ,GELDENHUYS JJ (Chairman),HERSOV BE
LAWRENSON BJ ,MAUDE G ,MENELL CS ,OLIVIER JE
ROBBERTZE GJ ,WILSON RAD ,YATES CWP

REGISTRATION NUMBER : 90/07025/06

REGISTERED OFFICE
Anglovaal House, 56 Main Street
Johannesburg
2001
TEL: 011-634 9111
FAX: 011-634 0038

TRANSFER SECRETARY
Anglovaal Ltd
P O Box 62379, Marshalltown
2107
TEL: 011-634 9111

COMPANY SECRETARY
Anglovaal Ltd

NATURE OF BUSINESS
An exploration and mining company with mineral interests in the Odendaalsrus area of the OFS.

BANKERS :
First National Bank of SA Ltd

AUDITORS :
Deloitte & Touche

FAMILIAR BRAND NAMES
N/A

CONTRIBUTION BY ACTIVITY
N/A

YEAR END : June

CAPITAL STRUCTURE

	AUTHORISED	ISSUED
Ords 1c	25000000	21851786

FINANCIAL STATISTICS (AT FINANCIAL YEAR END)

(Amts in R'000)	1992 Jun	1991 Jun
Ord'S/H Int	11739	29153
Iss Ord Share	21852	21852
Total Liab	671	3780
Current Liab	671	3780
Total Assets	11704	32227
Intang Assets	706	706
Current Assets	11704	32227
Debtors	266	544
Oper Profit	-20409	-16904
Interest Paid	-	12
Prf af Int&Tax	-17252	-14430
Prf att Ord Sh	-17252	-14430
Btm Line Earn	-17252	-14430
Mkt Prce(c) YE	310	275

PER SHARE STATISTICS (CENTS)

Net Asst Val	50.49	130.18
Cash Flow	-78.95	-66.04

RATIOS AND OTHER INFORMATION

Mrk Cap(R000)	67741	60093
Current Ratio	17.44	8.53
Quik/Acid Tst	17.44	8.53
Debt/Ass Rat	0.06	0.12
Debt to Eqity	0.06	0.13
Interest Cover	-	-1408.67
Ret on Assets	-147.40	-44.74
Ret on Equity%	-146.96	-49.50
NAV % Mrk Pr	16.29	47.34
Sus Grth Rate	-146.96	-49.50

SUBSIDIARY & ASSOCIATED COMPANIES

None

INVESTMENTS

None

TECFIN INVESTMENTS LTD

ABBREVIATION : TECFIN

JSE SHORT CODE : TCF

SECTOR : Venture Capital Market

SHAREHOLDERS

Who Owns Whom's Assessment of the Identity of the Ultimate Controlling Shareholder:
DIRECTORS

SHAREHOLDER	PERCENTAGE 1992	1991
ICICLE ENGINEERING P/L	40.5	41.8
SMITH B P	14.7	14.3
CANDY T M P	14.7	14.3
RHODES INV LTD	4.8	2.2
NEDBANK NOM LTD	4.1	4.1
MANG C D M	3.2	3.2
BIRD P N E E S I S	2.9	2.9
BIRD FAMILY TRUST	2.1	3.9
KOPPING M	1.4	1.4
LAURIE B	1.4	---
TOTAL	89.9	88.0

DIRECTORS :
BIRD PN (Chairman & Managing Dir.),CANDY TMP
FABRY FC ,MOODIE DR ,MSIBI GL D

REGISTRATION NUMBER : 87/06380/06

REGISTERED OFFICE
317 Chamberlain Road, Jacobs, Durban
4001

TRANSFER SECRETARY
Mercantile Registrars Ltd
P O Box 1053, Johannesburg
2000
TEL: 011-333 8181

COMPANY SECRETARY
F C Fabry

NATURE OF BUSINESS
Manufacture and distribution of specialised fasteners such as expanding anchors, wedge anchors and drop in anchors used in the construction, building & allied fields; The manufacture and distribution of a range of consumer products such

as picture hooks, cuphooks, tie-downs, stick-on-hooks, nails, plastic plugs, screws, expanding anchors and drills for the DIY market; The manufacture of a range of peripheral capital equipment such as centrifuges.

BANKERS :
First National Bank of SA Ltd
Trust Bank of Africa Ltd, Nedbank Ltd

AUDITORS :
RJ Kidd Stott & Co
Michael Rogers & Maingard

FAMILIAR BRAND NAMES
ADRENALIN,KLING,KLINGBOLT

CONTRIBUTION BY ACTIVITY
N/A

YEAR END : February

NUMBER OF EMPLOYEES : 65

CAPITAL STRUCTURE

	AUTHORISED	ISSUED
Ords 1c	50000000	24516500

FINANCIAL STATISTICS (AT FINANCIAL YEAR END)

(Amts in R'000)	1992 Feb	1991 Feb	1990 Feb
Ord S/H Int	7369	7324	6490
Long Trm Loans	3192	3058	3264
Iss Ord Share	24517	24517	23436
Total Liab	6034	5795	5446
Current Liab	2842	2737	2182
Total Assets	13015	12560	11600
Intang Assets	388	559	336
Current Assets	5974	5584	4870
Debtors	867	694	1265
Inventory	5107	4890	3605
Turnover	10861	9969	4749
Oper Profit	1043	1203	661
Interest Paid	557	669	111
Prf af Int&Tax	486	534	554
Prf att Ord Sh	486	534	554
Btm Line Earn	45	534	396
Mkt Prce(c) YE	30	28	25
Depreciation	289	359	229

PER SHARE STATISTICS (CENTS)

Net Asst Val	28.47	27.59	26.26
Net Earnings	2.00	2.20	3.10
Cash Flow	3.16	3.64	4.40

RATIOS AND OTHER INFORMATION

Mrk Cap(R000)	7355	6865	5859
Current Ratio	2.10	2.04	2.23
Quik/Acid Tst	0.31	0.25	0.58
A/C Rec T/ovr	12.53	14.36	3.75
Tot Ass T/ovr	0.83	0.79	0.41
Debt/Ass Rat	0.46	0.46	0.47
L T L Tot Ass	0.25	0.24	0.28
Debt to Eqity	0.82	0.79	0.84
Interest Cover	1.87	1.80	5.95
Oper Prof Mrg	9.60	12.07	13.92
Net Prof Marg%	4.47	5.36	11.67
Ret on Assets	8.01	9.58	5.73
Ret on Equity%	5.30	5.44	6.07
Price/Earnings	15.00	12.73	8.06
Earning Yield%	6.67	7.86	12.40
NAV % Mrk Pr	94.91	98.55	105.03
Def Interval	6.14	4.94	5.96
Sus Grth Rate	6.60	7.29	8.54

SUBSIDIARY & ASSOCIATED COMPANIES

FASTENING SYSTEMS (PTY) LTD
TAKE HOME PRODUCTS (PTY) LTD

INVESTMENTS

None

TECHNICAL & INDUSTRIAL INVESTMENTS LTD

ABBREVIATION : TIB

JSE SHORT CODE : TIB

SECTOR : Industrial-Tobacco & Match

SHAREHOLDERS

Who Owns Whom's Assessment of the Identity of the Ultimate Controlling Shareholder:
RUPERT & HERTZOG FAMILIES

SHAREHOLDER	PERCENTAGE 1992	1991
REMBRANDT TRUST P/L	44.5	44.5
SA MUTUAL	14.7	14.7
CMB NOM P/L	7.9	---
SOUTHERN LIFE ASSOC LTD	3.7	3.6
RUPERT A TRUST	3.2	3.2
ABSA NOM P/L	2.8	---
YSKOR PENS FUND	2.0	2.0
EIGHTY ONE MAIN STREET NOM LTD	2.0	1.3
STD BANK NOM TVL P/L	1.0	---
SANLAM	---	2.6
VOLKSKAS NOM P/L	---	2.9
SANKERN E/B	---	5.3
TOTAL	81.7	80.0

DIRECTORS :
HERTZOG E DE LA H DR,ROUX MJ
RUPERT AE DR (Chairman),RUPERT JA ,RUPERT JP

REGISTRATION NUMBER : 05/15859/06

REGISTERED OFFICE
Coetzier Street, Stellenbosch
7600
TEL: 02231-832331
FAX: 02231-71645

TRANSFER SECRETARY
Central Registrars Ltd
P O Box 4844, Johannesburg
2000
TEL: 011-331 0051

COMPANY SECRETARY
G S Otto

NATURE OF BUSINESS
An investment holding company with a controlling interest in quoted Technical Inv Corp, which in turn controls quoted Rembrandt Controlling Inv, which in turn controls quoted Rembrandt Group Ltd. The company also has a minority interest of 9,6% in Rembrandt Controlling Investments Ltd.

BANKERS :
N/A

AUDITORS :
Coopers Theron Du Toit

FAMILIAR BRAND NAMES
N/A

CONTRIBUTION BY ACTIVITY
Trade Mark Group (% net income) (43.7%)
Mining Interests (24.1%)
Industrial Interests (13.0%)
Financial Services (7.5%)
Corporate Finance & Other (11.7%)

YEAR END : March

DIVIDEND : Ords 1c

Interim No 65	(Ldr)22/09/89	(Pay)16/10/89	Amt(c)6.02
Final No 66	(Ldr)23/03/90	(Pay)17/04/90	Amt(c)11.2
Interim No 67	(Ldr)21/09/90	(Pay)15/10/90	Amt(c)7.23
Final No 68	(Ldr)22/02/91	(Pay)28/02/91	Amt(c)13.43
Interim no 69	(Ldr)20/09/91	(Pay)15/10/91	Amt(c)8.67
Final No 70	(Ldr)21/02/92	(Pay)28/02/92	Amt(c)13.78
Special	(Ldr)21/02/92	(Pay)28/02/92	Amt(c)20.66

CAPITAL STRUCTURE

	AUTHORISED	ISSUED
Ords 1c	132000000	132000000

FINANCIAL STATISTICS (AT FINANCIAL YEAR END)

(Amts in R'000)	1992 Mar	1991 Mar	1990 Mar	1989 Mar	1988 Mar
Ord S/H Int	959000	804500	688200	565200	456100
Long Trm Loans	5777700	4842700	4185000	3044800	2295200
Iss Ord Share	132000	132000	132000	132000	132000
Total Liab	6622600	5598300	5067800	3578800	2719500
Current Liab	844900	755600	882800	534000	424300
Total Assets	7485000	6301300	5692800	4144000	3175600
Intang Assets	96600	101500	63200	*	*
Current Assets	1551400	1030400	872300	1041500	695200
Debtors	339200	283900	226300	170000	116900
Inventory	843700	712900	599600	514100	357900
Oper Profit	934900	798600	643700	510900	498800
Interest Paid	59800	107600	101500	30000	16600
Tax Paid	426000	344900	281400	248500	173200
Prf af Int&Tax	747900	615700	489200	413800	309000
Prf att Ord Sh	163900	150700	131100	104700	78900
Btm Line Earn	203900	146500	139500	104200	78300
Dividend Paid	56900	27300	22700	18200	15500
Mkt Prce(c) YE	1850	1170	990	620	720
Depreciation	64700	46000	37100	26800	15300

PER SHARE STATISTICS (CENTS)

Net Asst Val	653.33	532.58	473.48	428.18	345.53
Net Earnings	124.17	114.20	99.30	79.30	59.80
Dividends	43.11	20.66	17.22	13.78	11.70
Cash Flow	-28.64	-94.32	-110.38	-72.12	51.74

RATIOS AND OTHER INFORMATION

Mrk Cap(R000)	2442000	1544400	1306800	818400	950400
Current Ratio	1.84	1.36	0.99	1.95	1.64
Quik/Acid Tst	0.84	0.42	0.31	0.99	0.79
Debt/Ass Rat	0.14	0.15	0.18	0.15	0.15
L T L Tot Ass	0.03	0.03	0.02	0.02	0.02
Debt to Eqity	1.09	1.17	1.48	1.11	1.05
Interest Cover	19.47	9.59	8.22	22.00	30.05
Ret on Assets	20.09	22.07	20.90	22.23	16.53
Ret on Equity%	17.09	18.73	19.05	18.52	17.30
Price/Earnings	14.90	10.25	9.97	7.82	12.04
Divid Cover	2.88	5.53	5.77	5.75	5.11
Divid Yield	2.33	1.77	1.74	2.22	1.63
Earning Yield%	6.71	9.76	10.03	12.79	8.31
NAV % Mrk Pr	35.32	45.52	47.83	69.06	47.99
Effec Tax Rate	44.81	47.70	47.85	48.02	35.90
Def Interval	-4.99	-2.10	-2.79	-0.87	1.15
Sus Grth Rate	11.16	15.34	15.75	15.30	13.90

SUBSIDIARY & ASSOCIATED COMPANIES

TECHNICAL INVESTMENT CORP. LTD

INVESTMENTS

REMBRANDT CONTROLLING INVESTMENTS LTD (9,6%)

TECHNICAL INVESTMENT CORP LTD

ABBREVIATION : TEGKOR

JSE SHORT CODE : TEG

SECTOR : Industrial-Tobacco & Match

SHAREHOLDERS

Who Owns Whom's Assessment of the Identity of the Ultimate Controlling Shareholder:
RUPERT & HERTZOG FAMILIES VIA TIB

SHAREHOLDER	PERCENTAGE 1992	1991
TEGNIESE & INDUSTRIELE INV BPK	60.4	60.4
CMB NOM P/L	9.1	---
SA MUTUAL	7.9	7.9
STD BANK NOM TVL P/L	3.7	3.7
SOUTHERN LIFE ASSOC LTD	2.7	2.7
EIGHTY ONE MAIN STREET NOM LTD	1.4	---
FIRST NAT NOM P/L	1.3	1.3
SANLAM	---	3.2
SANKERN E/B	---	5.2
TOTAL	86.5	84.4

DIRECTORS :
HERTZOG E DE LA H ,ROUX MJ
RUPERT AE DR (Chairman),RUPERT JA ,RUPERT JOHANN P

REGISTRATION NUMBER : 05/20656/06

REGISTERED OFFICE
Coetzier Street, Stellenbosch
7600

TEL: 02231-2333

TRANSFER SECRETARY
Central Registrars Ltd
P O Box 4844, Johannesburg
2000
TEL: 011-331 0051

COMPANY SECRETARY
G S Otto

NATURE OF BUSINESS
An investment holding company with a controlling interest of 40,6% in quoted Rembrandt Controlling Investments Ltd, which in turn has a controlling interest in quoted Rembrandt Group Ltd. The group has significant investments in banking, forestry, printing & packaging, financial services, medical services, engineering, adhesives, life assurance, mining, petrochemical products, tobacco products, food, wine and spirits, and portfolio investments.

BANKERS :
N/A

AUDITORS :
Coopers Theron Du Toit

FAMILIAR BRAND NAMES
N/A

CONTRIBUTION BY ACTIVITY
Trade Mark Group (% net income) (43.8%)
Mining interests (24.1%)
Industrial interests (13.0%)
Financial Services (7.5%)
Corporate Finance & Other (11.6%)

YEAR END : March

DIVIDEND :Ords 1c

Interim No 62	(Ldr)22/09/89	(Pay)16/10/89	Amt(c)5.68
Final No 63	(Ldr)23/03/90	(Pay)17/04/90	Amt(c)10.56
Interim No 64	(Ldr)21/09/90	(Pay)15/10/90	Amt(c)6.82
Final No 65	(Ldr)22/02/91	(Pay)28/02/91	Amt(c)12.67
Interim No 66	(Ldr)20/09/91	(Pay)15/10/91	Amt(c)8.18
Final No 67	(Ldr)21/02/92	(Pay)28/02/92	Amt(c)13
Special	(Ldr)21/02/92	(Pay)28/02/92	Amt(c)19.49

CAPITAL STRUCTURE

	AUTHORISED	ISSUED
Ords 1c	166441200	166441200

FINANCIAL STATISTICS (AT FINANCIAL YEAR END)

(Amts in R'000)	1992 Mar	1991 Mar	1990 Mar	1989 Mar	1988 Mar
Ord S/H Int	1141300	957300	819000	672600	542700
Long Trm Loans	5595400	4689800	4054200	2937400	2208600
Iss Ord Share	166441	166441	166441	166441	166441
Total Liab	6440200	5445400	4936900	3471400	2632800
Current Liab	844800	755600	882700	534000	424200
Total Assets	7484900	6301200	5692700	4144000	3175500
Intang Assets	96600	101500	63200	*	*
Current Assets	1551300	1030300	872200	1041500	695100
Debtors	339200	284000	226300	170000	116800
Inventory	843700	712900	599600	514100	357900
Oper Profit	934900	798600	681700	510800	498800
Interest Paid	59900	107600	101500	30000	16600
Tax Paid	426000	344900	281400	248500	173200
Prf af Int&Tax	747800	615700	489100	413700	309000
Prf att Ord Sh	195000	179300	155900	124500	93900
Btm Line Earn	242600	174300	165900	123900	93200
Dividend Paid	67700	32400	27000	21600	18400
Mkt Prce(c) YE	1750	1125	895	585	675
Depreciation	64700	46000	37100	26800	15300

PER SHARE STATISTICS (CENTS)

Net Asst Val	627.67	514.18	454.09	404.11	326.06
Net Earnings	117.16	107.73	93.67	74.80	92.16
Dividends	40.67	19.49	16.24	13.00	11.04
Cash Flow	-4.03	-57.92	-72.64	-45.30	47.10

RATIOS AND OTHER INFORMATION

Mrk Cap(R000)	2912718	1872461	1489647	973680	1123477
Current Ratio	1.84	1.36	0.99	1.95	1.64
Quik/Acid Tst	0.84	0.42	0.31	0.99	0.79
Debt/Ass Rat	0.14	0.15	0.18	0.15	0.15
L T L Tot Ass	0.03	0.03	0.02	0.02	0.02
Debt to Eqity	0.91	0.99	1.24	0.93	0.88
Interest Cover	19.43	9.59	8.59	22.00	30.05
Ret on Assets	20.09	22.07	20.90	22.22	16.68
Ret on Equity%	17.09	18.73	19.04	18.51	17.30
Price/Earnings	14.94	10.44	9.55	7.82	7.32
Divid Cover	2.88	5.53	5.77	5.75	8.35
Divid Yield	2.32	1.73	1.81	2.22	1.64
Earning Yield%	6.69	9.58	10.47	12.79	13.65
NAV % Mrk Pr	35.87	45.70	50.74	69.08	48.31
Effec Tax Rate	44.81	47.70	47.86	48.03	35.90
Def Interval	-28.18	-2.71	-3.36	-1.10	1.01
Sus Grth Rate	11.15	15.35	15.74	15.30	13.91

SUBSIDIARY & ASSOCIATED COMPANIES

REMBRANDT CONTROLLING INVESTMENTS LTD (40,6%)

INVESTMENTS

None

TECHNIHIRE LTD

ABBREVIATION : TECHIRE

JSE SHORT CODE : TCH

SECTOR : Industrial-Industrial Holding

SHAREHOLDERS

Who Owns Whom's Assessment of the Identity of the Ultimate Controlling Shareholder:
ECCO SA (FRANCE)

SHAREHOLDER	PERCENTAGE 1992	1991
NOORD BRABANTSE INSTALLATIE CO BV	60.0	—
JACK ELIASOV HOLDINGS P/L	8.4	1.3
JACK ELIASOV FAMILY TRUST	8.1	47.4
WESTERMAN S M	1.6	3.1
FROST L	1.2	3.0
NEDBANK NOM LTD	—	22.1
KAPLAN & STEWART INC	—	1.1
TOTAL	79.3	78.0

DIRECTORS :
ELIASOV J (Chief Executive)
FORIEL-DESTEZET P (Chairman)
LIPS H (Vice Chairman),NALDJIAN T
RAYNAUD CR MRS,SLOAN AH ,WALKER RR

REGISTRATION NUMBER : 87/03252/06

REGISTERED OFFICE
6th Floor, Nedbank Place, Cnr Market & Sauer Streets
Johannesburg
2001
TEL: 011-836 8041
FAX: 011-836 4601

TRANSFER SECRETARY
Mercantile Registrars Ltd
P O Box 1053, Johannesburg
2000
TEL: 011-333 8181

COMPANY SECRETARY
Coopers Theron Du Toit Services (Jhb) (Pty) Ltd

NATURE OF BUSINESS
The group offers the following services:
Hiring out of draughtsmen, engineers & tracers, artisans, technicians, comptometer operators, administrative personnel; Professional placement services; Collection & administration of debts; Computer isographs of constructual plans.

BANKERS :
Nedperm Bank Ltd

AUDITORS :
HP Berman & Associates

FAMILIAR BRAND NAMES
ACCOUNTING ASSIGNMENTS,STANLEY WESTERMAN ASOC

CONTRIBUTION BY ACTIVITY
N/A

YEAR END : December

DIVIDEND : Ords 1c
Dividend No 2 (Ldr)22/02/91 (Pay)15/03/91 Amt(c)3.5

NUMBER OF EMPLOYEES : 325

CAPITAL STRUCTURE

	AUTHORISED	ISSUED
Ords 1c	20000000	12667600

FINANCIAL STATISTICS (AT FINANCIAL YEAR END)

(Amts in R'000)	1991 Mar	1991 Dec	1990 Mar
Ord S/H Int	3294	3258	2677
Long Trm Loans	-	50	-
Iss Ord Share	12668	12668	12668
Total Liab	2524	2130	2746
Current Liab	2524	2080	2746
Total Assets	5301	4497	4969
Intang Assets	517	891	454
Current Assets	4462	3772	4227
Debtors	4414	3411	4224
Turnover	6632	5046	6850
Oper Profit	1956	924	2607
Interest Paid	86	110	216
Tax Paid	1047	537	1264
Prf af Int&Tax	961	378	1279
Prf att Ord Sh	1060	363	1357
Btm Line Earn	1060	-35	907
Dividend Paid	443	-	380
Mkt Prce(c) YE	28	40	30
Depreciation	77	92	60

PER SHARE STATISTICS (CENTS)

Net Asst Val	21.92	18.68	17.55
Net Earnings	8.40	2.86	11.00
Dividends	3.50	-	3.00
Cash Flow	8.19	3.71	10.84

RATIOS AND OTHER INFORMATION

Mrk Cap(R000)	3547	5067	3800
Current Ratio	1.77	1.81	1.54
Quik/Acid Tst	1.77	1.81	1.54
A/C Rec T/ovr	1.50	1.48	1.62
Tot Ass T/ovr	1.25	1.12	1.38
Debt/Ass Rat	0.48	0.47	0.55
L T L Tot Ass	-	0.01	-
Debt to Eqity	0.77	0.65	1.03
Interest Cover	23.23	8.40	12.25
Oper Prof Mrg	29.49	18.31	38.06
Net Prof Marg%	15.98	7.19	19.81
Ret on Assets	41.37	22.46	57.09
Ret on Equity%	32.18	11.14	50.69
Price/Earnings	3.33	13.99	2.73
Divid Cover	2.40	-	3.67
Divid Yield	12.50	-	10.00
Earning Yield%	30.00	7.15	36.67
NAV % Mrk Pr	78.29	46.71	58.49
Effec Tax Rate	53.26	58.69	50.50
Def Interval	1.24	0.65	1.09
Sus Grth Rate	18.73	11.14	36.50

SUBSIDIARY & ASSOCIATED COMPANIES

ADVANCED CREDIT BUREAU LTD
SA DRAFTING (PTY) LTD (50%)
STANLEY WESTERMAN ASSOCIATES (PTY) LTD
TRADEHIRE NAMIBIA (PTY) LTD

INVESTMENTS

BLOCKTECH LTD (232500 SH)

TEDCO LTD

ABBREVIATION : TEDCO

SECTOR : Zimbabwe Stock Exchange

SHAREHOLDERS

Who Owns Whom's Assessment of the Identity of the Ultimate Controlling Shareholder:
SCMBZ

SHAREHOLDER	PERCENTAGE 1992	1991
STD CHART MERCHANT BANK ZIM NOM PVT LTD	48.7	—
SECURITY NOM LTD	4.7	—
NAT RAILWAYS OF ZIM CONTR PENS FUND	4.0	—

GOULDSBURY ENTERPRISES PVT LTD	3.2	---
FIRST NOM (PVT) LTD	2.6	---
NORTHCHART INV LTD	2.6	---
JASPER INV P/L	2.4	---
TANVEST PVT LTD	2.2	---
OLD MUTUAL INV CORP (PVT) LTD	2.0	---
CARSAN INV CO (PVT) LTD	1.2	---
CU FIRE MARINE & GEN INSURANCE CO LTD	1.1	---
TRUST NOM (PVT) LTD	1.0	---
TOTAL	75.7	---

DIRECTORS :
CHIPUDLHA PWT ,CLARKE WR (Managing Director)
DORWARD AI ,DORWARD GA ,DORWARD PD (Chairman)
KERSWELL RG

REGISTERED OFFICE
Second Floor, 54 Jason Moyo Avenue
Harare, Zimbabwe

TEL: 704111

TRANSFER SECRETARY
First Transfer Secretaries (Pvt) Ltd
P O Box 437, Bulawayo
Zimbabwe

TEL: 092634 - 702905

COMPANY SECRETARY
Tedco Management Services, R Ellis.

NATURE OF BUSINESS
Main activity is the retail sale of clothing, furniture and soft furnishings. The group is also involved in the manufacture and wholesale distribution of furniture through Zimbabwe Furnishers, C W, Benatars, Blooms Manufacturers, Luxaire Bedding, Springmaster and Grillbro.

BANKERS :
ANZ Grindlays Bank Plc
Merchant Bank of Central Africa
First Merchant Bank of Zimbabwe Ltd
Standard Chartered Bank Zimbabwe Ltd
Zimbabwe Banking Corporation Ltd

AUDITORS :
Ernst & Young

FAMILIAR BRAND NAMES
N/A

CONTRIBUTION BY ACTIVITY
N/A

YEAR END : September

DIVIDEND : Ords Z$0,40

Dividend	(Ldr)07/02/92	(Pay)28/02/92	Amt(c)5.65
Dividend	(Ldr)26/06/92	(Pay)31/07/92	Amt(c)2.50

CAPITAL STRUCTURE

	AUTHORISED	ISSUED
Ords Z$0,40	60000000	56349000

FINANCIAL STATISTICS (AT FINANCIAL YEAR END)

(Amts in Z$)	1991 Sep	1990 Sep
Ord S/H Int	49466	30265
Long Trm Loans	4078	8924
Iss Ord Share	56349	24737
Total Liab	54028	53724
Current Liab	49950	44800
Total Assets	100449	80926
Intang Assets	3045	3063
Current Assets	74931	65458
Debtors	40603	30463
Inventory	33460	34330
Turnover	114702	81005
Oper Profit	15749	11791
Interest Paid	3698	2339
Tax Paid	6056	5145
Prf af Int&Tax	9584	6950
Prf att Ord Sh	9584	6950
Btm Line Earn	9584	6950
Dividend Paid	4508	3092
Depreciation	2880	1809

PER SHARE STATISTICS (CENTS)

Net Asst Val	82.38	109.96
Net Earnings	18.30	14.00
Dividends	8.00	12.50
Cash Flow	22.44	40.70

RATIOS AND OTHER INFORMATION

Current Ratio	1.50	1.46
Quik/Acid Tst	0.83	0.69
A/C Rec T/ovr	2.82	2.66
Tot Ass T/ovr	1.14	1.00
Debt/Ass Rat	0.50	0.62
L T L Tot Ass	0.00	0.06
Debt to Eqity	1.01	1.65
Interest Cover	4.26	5.04
Oper Prof Mrg	13.73	14.56
Net Prof Marg%	8.36	8.58
Ret on Assets	19.25	17.84
Ret on Equity%	19.37	22.96
Divid Cover	2.29	1.12
Effec Tax Rate	37.53	31.71
Def Interval	1.97	2.19
Sus Grth Rate	10.26	12.75

SUBSIDIARY & ASSOCIATED COMPANIES

SAVOY INVESTMENTS (PTY) LTD

INVESTMENTS

None

TEDELEX LTD

ABBREVIATION : TEDELEX

JSE SHORT CODE : TDX

SECTOR : Industrial-Electronics, Electrical & Bat

SHAREHOLDERS

Who Owns Whom's Assessment of the Identity of the Ultimate Controlling Shareholder:
SANLAM VIA MALBAK

SHAREHOLDER	PERCENTAGE 1992	1991
MALBAK INV (TEDELEX) LTD	96.7	96.7
TOTAL	96.7	96.7

DIRECTORS :
BERNHARDT SG (Manufacturing Director)
COHEN J (Managing Director)
COHEN SPN (Administration Director)
DEETLEFS JH (Dir Human Resources)
JACOBS DJ (Chairman),KATZ MM PROF,KILIAN C
MCGLASHAN DS ,REYNOLDS RJ
SIFRIS J (Financial Director),SOLOMON WJ
VAN DYK J

REGISTRATION NUMBER : 68/14639/06

REGISTERED OFFICE
11th Floor, Penmor Towers, 1 Rissik Street
Johannesburg
2001
TEL: 011-683 5800
FAX: 011-683 2803

TRANSFER SECRETARY
Central Registrars Ltd
P O Box 4844, Johannesburg
2000
TEL: 011-331 0051

COMPANY SECRETARY
S P N Cohen

NATURE OF BUSINESS
An investment holding company with subsidiaries engaged in the manufacture and distribution of audio & video consumer products, domestic appliances,house & kitchenware,other consumer products,business machines, electronic & communication equipment,commercial & industrial products, sewing and knitting machines.The group also operates a chain of TV & video rental outlets.

BANKERS :
N/A

AUDITORS :
Deloitte Pim Goldby

FAMILIAR BRAND NAMES
BLAUPUNKT,CANDY,CARLTON,CASIO,COMMODORE
DOMINEC,EMPISAL,HAZ,HITECH,LITTON
PROCTOR SILEX,SONY,TECH,TEDELEX,TOMY
VIDEO TECHNOLOGY,WESTPOINT

CONTRIBUTION BY ACTIVITY
N/A

YEAR END : August

DIVIDEND :Ords 25c

Interim	(Ldr)27/04/90	(Pay)11/05/90	Amt(c)5
Final	(Ldr)09/11/90	(Pay)14/12/90	Amt(c)5
Interim	(Ldr)26/04/91	(Pay)10/05/91	Amt(c)7
Final	(Ldr)08/11/91	(Pay)12/12/91	Amt(c)7

NUMBER OF EMPLOYEES : 4156

CAPITAL STRUCTURE

	AUTHORISED	ISSUED
12,5% Conv Red Cum Prefs R1	2537167	0
Ords 25c	100000000	61020696

FINANCIAL STATISTICS (AT FINANCIAL YEAR END)

(Amts in R'000)	1991 Aug	1990 Aug	1989 Aug	1988 Aug	1987 Aug
Ord S/H Int	220783	202657	189943	164630	138688
Long Trm Loans	67086	57931	53037	67263	70777
Iss Ord Share	61021	61021	61021	61021	60478
Total Liab	140146	129208	131288	137311	123615
Current Liab	73060	71277	78251	70048	52838
Total Assets	360929	331865	321231	301941	262303
Current Assets	292962	266092	262334	261158	226879
Debtors	133048	136793	110556	126601	94789
Inventory	159914	129091	151446	133877	130512
Turnover	511876	429796	405682	392033	327164
Oper Profit	39836	32630	42272	39732	25932
Interest Paid	14641	15312	11752	8079	11185
Tax Paid	168	-505	-188	804	5306
Prf af Int&Tax	25966	18462	31118	30849	9441
Prf att Ord Sh	26668	18816	30510	30339	7216
Btm Line Earn	26668	18816	30457	31225	22163
Dividend Paid	8542	6102	10373	6102	1209
Mkt Prce(c) YE	245	160	210	175	400
Depreciation	8553	6264	4294	2318	3861

PER SHARE STATISTICS (CENTS)

Net Asst Val	361.81	332.11	311.27	269.79	229.32
Net Earnings	44.00	31.00	50.00	50.00	12.00
Dividends	14.00	10.00	17.00	10.00	2.00
Cash Flow	57.72	40.41	55.75	53.77	27.47

RATIOS AND OTHER INFORMATION

Mrk Cap(R000)	149501	97634	128144	106787	241912
Current Ratio	4.01	3.73	3.35	3.73	4.29
Quik/Acid Tst	1.82	1.92	1.42	1.82	1.82
A/C Rec T/ovr	3.85	3.14	3.67	3.10	5.18
Tot Ass T/ovr	1.42	1.30	1.26	1.30	1.87
Debt/Ass Rat	0.39	0.39	0.40	0.45	0.47
L T L Tot Ass	0.18	0.17	0.16	0.22	0.27
Debt to Eqity	0.63	0.63	0.68	0.82	0.88
Interest Cover	2.72	2.13	3.60	4.92	2.32
Oper Prof Mrg	7.78	7.59	10.42	10.13	7.93
Net Prof Marg%	5.21	4.38	7.52	7.74	2.21
Ret on Assets	11.30	10.02	13.29	13.16	14.83
Ret on Equity%	12.08	9.28	16.06	18.43	7.80
Price/Earnings	5.57	5.16	4.20	3.50	33.33
Divid Cover	3.14	3.10	2.94	5.00	6.00
Divid Yield	5.71	6.25	8.10	5.71	0.50
Earning Yield%	17.96	19.38	23.81	28.57	3.00
NAV % Mrk Pr	147.68	207.57	148.23	154.17	57.33
Effec Tax Rate	0.64	0.54	1.93	2.54	35.98
Def Interval	2.10	2.79	1.81	2.32	10.31
Sus Grth Rate	8.21	6.27	10.60	14.72	4.33

SUBSIDIARY & ASSOCIATED COMPANIES

APPLIANCE SALES CORPORATION (PTY) LTD
CAPE CABINETS (PTY) LTD
CARLTON LIGHTING (C.T.) (PTY) LTD
CARLTON LIGHTING (DISCOUNT BOKSBURG) (PT
CARLTON LIGHTING (DURBAN) (PTY) LTD
CARLTON LIGHTING (PTY) LTD
CARLTON LIGHTING HOLDINGS (PTY) LTD
CONSEW MACHINES (PTY) LTD
CONSUMER SALES CORPORATION (PTY) LTD
DISCOUNT FINANCE & CREDIT CORP. (PTY) LT
EMPISAL (PTY) LTD

EMPISAL SEWING MACHINE MANUFACTURING CO.
ENZIO DE VILLIERS & CO. (PTY) LTD
ETERNAL HOLDINGS (PTY) LTD
EURO ENTERPRISES (PTY) LTD
GOLDLINE SEWING & KNITTING CO. (PTY) LTD
HAZ APPLIANCES (PTY) LTD
HAZ PRODUCTS (PTY) LTD
HERO INVESTMENTS (PTY) LTD
ITALEX IMPORT (PTY) LTD
JOHNSONS DOWNTOWN FURNISHERS (PTY) LTD
JONES SEWING MACHINE DISTRIBUTORS (PTY)
METAL FASTENERS MANUFACTURING IND. (PTY)
METALWARE MANUFACTURING (PTY) LTD
POROCELL PLASTICS (PTY) LTD
R & H METAL PRODUCTS (PTY) LTD
SA LIGHTING (EP) (PTY) LTD
SA LIGHTING (PTY) LTD
SA LIGHTING (TVL) (PTY) LTD
SABRE PROPERTIES (PTY) LTD
SARLOME INVESTMENTS (PTY) LTD
TEDELEX (NAMIBIA) (PTY) LTD
TEDELEX LIGHTING (PTY) LTD
TEDELEX MAMIF (PTY) LTD
TEDELEX PROPERTIES (ANDREA ROAD) (PTY) L
TEDELEX PROPERTIES (ATLANTIS) (PTY) LTD
TEDELEX PROPERTIES (PTY) LTD
TEDELEX SOUND & VISION (PTY) LTD
TEDELEX TIME (PTY) LTD
TELEVIEW (PTY) LTD (50%)
TELEVISION & ELECTRICAL (PTY) LTD
TELEVISION & ELECTRICAL DISTRIBUTORS (PT
UITENHAGE WOOL & TEXTILES (PTY) LTD

INVESTMENTS

SMALL BUSINESS DEVELOPMENT CORP LTD (130000)

TELEMETRIX PLC

ABBREVIATION : TMX

JSE SHORT CODE : TMX

SECTOR : Industrial-Electronics, Electrical & Bat

SHAREHOLDERS

Who Owns Whom's Assessment of the Identity of the Ultimate Controlling Shareholder:
WP VENTER

SHAREHOLDER	PERCENTAGE 1992	1991
LONDON CONTROL ACCOUNT	81.0	---
SA MUTUAL	6.7	---
CMB NOM P/L	3.1	---
STD BANK NOM TVL P/L	2.0	---
FIRST NAT NOM P/L	1.5	---
MOULTRIE I A	1.2	---
TOTAL	95.3	---

DIRECTORS :
COTTERILL R ,CURTIS TM (Chief Executive)
DELACAVE JTL ,GARDENER WK
RATTRAY BD (Financial Director),SNEDDEN DC
STRIDE CA ,WALSH AS (Chairman

REGISTRATION NUMBER : 1378777 (UK)

REGISTERED OFFICE
Knaves Beach Estate, Loudwater, High Wycombe, Buckinghamsh
HP10 9QZ, England

TEL: 011-899 6959
FAX: 011-914 3984

TRANSFER SECRETARY
Central Registrars Ltd
P O Box 4844, Johannesburg
2000
TEL: 011-331 0051

COMPANY SECRETARY
M E Sefton

NATURE OF BUSINESS
The Telemetrix group is engaged in the manufacture & sale of specialised electronic products in the UK, Europe, USA, Africa & the Far East. Operations include: Manufacture of miniaturised magnetics-based signal processing components for LAN's, Semiconductor manufacture; Sourcing of electronic components; Manufacture and supply of computer graphics, data communications, image processing & secure communications products. The group has no operations currently active in SA.

BANKERS :
First National Corp & Investment Bank

AUDITORS :
KPMG Aiken & Peat

FAMILIAR BRAND NAMES
CONSOLIDATED LIGHTING,ESCO,RASTEREX,STC
TREND,VALOR,ZETEX

CONTRIBUTION BY ACTIVITY
N/A

YEAR END : December

DIVIDEND : Ords 5p

Final	(Ldr)16/04/92	(Pay)21/04/92	Amt(c)0.6

CAPITAL STRUCTURE

	AUTHORISED	ISSUED
Ords 5p	110000000	87174106

FINANCIAL STATISTICS (AT FINANCIAL YEAR END)

(Amts in PS)	1991 Dec	1990 Dec
Ord S/H Int	13451	11953
Long Trm Loans	10426	10032
Iss Ord Share	86155	84377
Total Liab	28648	29903
Current Liab	18222	19871
Total Assets	42099	41856
Current Assets	30852	30847
Debtors	14716	14700
Inventory	12714	13783
Turnover	83721	72493
Oper Profit	5291	4237
Interest Paid	1023	688
Tax Paid	1365	1223
Prf af Int&Tax	3114	2470
Prf att Ord Sh	1802	1672
Btm Line Earn	1802	1672

Dividend Paid	517	506
Mkt Prce(c) YE	175	-
Depreciation	2194	2488

PER SHARE STATISTICS (CENTS)

Net Asst Val	15.61	14.17
Net Earnings	2.10	2.00
Dividends	0.60	0.60
Cash Flow	4.81	5.29

RATIOS AND OTHER INFORMATION

Mrk Cap(R000)	150771	-
Current Ratio	1.69	1.55
Quik/Acid Tst	1.00	0.86
A/C Rec T/ovr	5.69	4.93
Tot Ass T/ovr	1.99	1.73
Debt/Ass Rat	0.58	0.65
L T L Tot Ass	0.15	0.17
Debt to Eqity	1.82	2.26
Interest Cover	5.17	6.16
Oper Prof Mrg	6.32	5.84
Net Prof Marg%	2.15	2.31
Ret on Assets	13.07	10.47
Ret on Equity%	13.40	13.99
Price/Earnings	83.33	-
Divid Cover	3.50	3.33
Divid Yield	0.34	-
Earning Yield%	1.20	-
NAV % Mrk Pr	8.92	-
Effec Tax Rate	34.90	23.80
Def Interval	1.51	1.60
Sus Grth Rate	9.55	9.75

SUBSIDIARY & ASSOCIATED COMPANIES

CARHENA FINANCE LTD (UK)
COMPONENT TRADING LTD (UK)
CONSOLIDATED LIGHTING (PVT) LTD
ELECTRONIC SUPPLY CORPORATION (USA)
GTI CORPORATION (USA)
GTI-IRELAND LTD
RASTEREX (INTERNATIONAL) AS (NORWAY)
RASTEREX INTERNATIONAL LTD (UK)
STANDARD TELEPHONE & CABLES (ZIMBABWE) (
TREND COMMUNICATIONS LTD (UK)
TREND GROUP LTD (UK)
VALOR ELECTRONICS INC (USA)
WESTWARD TECHNOLOGIE GMBH
WESTWARD TECHNOLOGY LTD (UK)
ZETEX ASIA LTD (HONG KONG)
ZETEX GMBH
ZETEX INC (USA)
ZETEX PLC (UK)

INVESTMENTS

None

TELJOY HOLDINGS LTD

ABBREVIATION : TELJOY

JSE SHORT CODE : TLJ

SECTOR : Industrial-Retailers & Wholesalers

SHAREHOLDERS

Who Owns Whom's Assessment of the Identity of the Ultimate Controlling Shareholder:
SANLAM VIA SANKORP

SHAREHOLDER	PERCENTAGE 1992	1991
FEDSERVICES LTD	40.0	---
STD BANK NOM TVL P/L	11.3	5.3
SA MUTUAL	8.4	---
SERVGRO INTERNATIONAL BPK	7.6	---
METROPOLITAN LIFE LTD	6.9	6.9
THEO RUSTEIN HOLDINGS P/L	6.0	8.6
CMB NOM P/L	5.8	---
EIGHTY ONE MAIN STREET NOM LTD	2.9	---
TELJOY HOLDINGS SHARE TRUST	1.7	1.4
SHARESTOCK NOM P/L	1.0	---
FEDERALE TELECTRA LTD	---	37.2
SANKORP BPK	---	32.0
SANLAM	---	1.2
TOTAL	91.7	92.6

DIRECTORS :
ANDREWES EWE ,BOHLMANN TRT ,FORWORD JD
HUNT-DAVIS DNA ,KENNEDY DC (Financial Director)
ORGAN NJ ,POTGIETER HJ
RUTSTEIN TB (Chairman & Chief Exec.),TAFFS BE
VAN DER WALT PJJ

REGISTRATION NUMBER : 87/01394/06

REGISTERED OFFICE
Television City, 12 Claim Street
Johannesburg
2001
TEL: 011-29 2241
FAX: 011-333 1412

TRANSFER SECRETARY
Central Registrars Ltd
P O Box 4844, Johannesburg
2000
TEL: 011-331 0051

COMPANY SECRETARY
M Young

NATURE OF BUSINESS
An investment holding company whose subsidiaries and divisions are engaged in TV and VCR rental, M-Net decoder distribution, the servicing & repair of appliances, and the manufacture, distribution & installation of audio and audio-visual products for commercial & industrial purposes.

BANKERS :
Trust Bank of Africa Ltd, Nedperm Bank Ltd

AUDITORS :
Coopers Theron Du Toit
Price Waterhouse Meyernel

FAMILIAR BRAND NAMES
EMPISAL,MASTERCARE,MATV,RENT-A-COLOR
RENT-A-VISION,TELEVISTA,TELJOY,VISIONHIRE

CONTRIBUTION BY ACTIVITY
N/A

YEAR END : March

DIVIDEND :Ords 1c

Interim No 7	(Ldr)14/12/90	(Pay)04/01/91	Amt(c)4 5
Final No 8	(Ldr)10/06/91	(Pay)15/07/91	Amt(c)9
Interim No 9	(Ldr)13/12/91	(Pay)03/01/92	Amt(c)4 5
Final No 10	(Ldr)26/06/92	(Pay)15/07/92	Amt(c)9
Interim No 11	(Ldr)11/12/92	(Pay)04/01/92	Amt(c)4 5

NUMBER OF EMPLOYEES : 929

CAPITAL STRUCTURE

	AUTHORISED	ISSUED
Ords 1c	100000000	57992000

FINANCIAL STATISTICS (AT FINANCIAL YEAR END)

(Amts in R'000)	1992 Mar	1991 Mar	1990 Mar	1989 Mar	1988 Mar
Ord S/H Int	67959	58078	46787	38624	27920
Long Trm Loans	62283	61132	27619	27298	17535
Iss Ord Share	57992	57992	57992	57157	56300
Total Liab	107715	109752	74442	63546	39566
Current Liab	45432	48620	46823	36248	22031
Total Assets	170364	163877	120023	100888	67486
Intang Assets	5310	3953	1206	1149	*
Current Assets	26962	26681	17804	15890	7258
Debtors	18681	18084	12180	9557	4527
Inventory	8225	8067	5579	6112	2509
Turnover	173656	146767	119916	93138	68323
Oper Profit	36797	33764	28246	26706	21933
Interest Paid	18773	15683	9039	3412	2220
Tax Paid	4010	3086	3735	6102	5830
Prf af Int&Tax	17710	18623	15823	17192	13883
Prf att Ord Sh	17710	18623	15823	17192	13883
Btm Line Earn	17710	19120	15992	16822	13883
Dividend Paid	7829	7829	7829	7829	6287
Mkt Prce(c) YE	280	220	260	240	195
Depreciation	31169	29868	25150	19753	16441

PER SHARE STATISTICS (CENTS)

Net Asst Val	108 03	93 33	78 60	65 57	49 59
Net Earnings	30 50	32 10	27 30	30 00	25 00
Dividends	13 50	13 50	13 50	13 50	11 00
Cash Flow	84 29	78 27	66 59	63 18	56 12

RATIOS AND OTHER INFORMATION

Mrk Cap(R000)	162378	127582	150779	137177	109785
Current Ratio	0 59	0 55	0 38	0 44	0 33
Quik/Acid Tst	0 41	0 38	0 26	0 27	0 22
A/C Rec T/ovr	9 30	8 12	9 85	9 75	15 09
Tot Ass T/ovr	1 02	0 90	1 00	0 92	1 01
Debt/Ass Rat	0 63	0 67	0 59	0 58	0 50
L T L Tot Ass	0 37	0 37	0 20	0 22	0 18
Debt to Eqity	1 58	1 89	1 52	1 51	1 22
Interest Cover	1 96	2 15	3 12	7 83	9 88
Oper Prof Mrg	21 19	23 01	23 55	28 67	32 10
Net Prof Marg%	10 20	12 69	13 20	18 46	20 32
Ret on Assets	23 77	22 82	23 83	26 47	32 50
Ret on Equity%	26 06	32 07	33 82	44 51	49 72
Price/Earnings	9 18	6 85	9 52	8 00	7 80
Divid Cover	2 26	2 38	2 02	2 22	2 27
Divid Yield	4 82	6 14	5 19	5 63	5 64
Earning Yield%	10 89	14 59	10 50	12 50	12 82
NAV % Mrk Pr	38 58	42 42	30 23	27 32	25 43
Effec Tax Rate	8 31	23 78	15 59	14 26	25 35
Def Interval	1 74	1 88	1 28	0 82	0 49
Sus Grth Rate	14 54	18 59	17 09	24 24	27 21

SUBSIDIARY & ASSOCIATED COMPANIES

AVBAR RENTALS (PTY) LTD
CLINICVISION (PTY) LTD
COLORENT (PTY) LTD
FILM FUN HOLDINGS (PTY) LTD
OAKTREE INVESTMENTS (PTY) LTD
OKAVANGO ELECTRONICS (PTY) LTD
REDITRON (PTY) LTD
TELEVISION TUBE REBUILDERS (PTY) LTD
TELGELUK (EDMS) BPK
TELJOY (PTY) LTD
TELJOY (PTY) LTD (SWAZILAND)
TELJOY BUSINESS SERVICES (BOPHUTHATSWANA
TELJOY BUSINESS SERVICES (PTY) LTD
TELJOY BUSINESS SERVICES CISKEI (PTY) LT
TELJOY REDIFUSION (PTY) LTD
VISIONHIRE (PTY) LTD

INVESTMENTS

BM RENTALS (PTY) LTD (45 SH)
MP TELEVISION (PTY) LTD (490 SH)

TEMPORA INVESTMENTS LTD

ABBREVIATION : TEMPORA

JSE SHORT CODE : TEM

SECTOR : Financial-Investment Trusts

SHAREHOLDERS

Who Owns Whom's Assessment of the Identity of the Ultimate Controlling Shareholder:
DALYS VIA SUNCRUSH

SHAREHOLDER	PERCENTAGE 1992	1991
SUNCRUSH LTD	43 4	43 2
CMB NOM P/L	16 2	---
EIGHTY ONE MAIN STREET NOM LTD	7 6	7 5
STD BANK NOM TVL P/L	4 1	4 0
COMMERCIAL UNION LIFE ASSURE CO SA LTD	3 9	---
HAMILTON R D	3 3	3 6
YSKOR PENS FUND	2 6	2 6
SEFALANA EMP BENEFITS ORG (SEBO)	2 6	2 6
NEDBANK NOM LTD	1 9	1 8
HAMILTON J W	1 4	1 6
R D TRUST	1 2	1 2
SANLAMTRUST NOM P/L	1 1	1 1
FERBROS NOM P/L	1 0	1 3
J W TRUST	---	1 2
COMMERCIAL UNION ASSURE CO SA LTD	---	3 9
SANLAM	---	15 1
TOTAL	90 4	90 7

DIRECTORS :
COOK DB MR,EVANS IJS MR,HAMILTON JW MR
HAMILTON RD MR (Chairman

REGISTRATION NUMBER : 71/04777/06

REGISTERED OFFICE
491 Ridge Road, Durban
4001
TEL 031-29 4371

TRANSFER SECRETARY
Dalys Ltd
P O Box 1177, Durban
4000
TEL: 031-29 4371

COMPANY SECRETARY
J Reekie

NATURE OF BUSINESS
The company's principal activity is that of investment.

BANKERS :
Standard Bank of SA Ltd

AUDITORS :
Deloitte Pim Goldby

FAMILIAR BRAND NAMES
N/A

CONTRIBUTION BY ACTIVITY
N/A

YEAR END : June

DIVIDEND : Ords 1c

Final	(Ldr)11/08/89	(Pay)18/08/89	Amt(c)28
Final	(Ldr)10/08/90	(Pay)17/08/90	Amt(c)32
Final	(Ldr)22/05/92	(Pay)16/06/92	Amt(c)32

CAPITAL STRUCTURE

	AUTHORISED	ISSUED
Ords 1c	50000000	27309532

FINANCIAL STATISTICS (AT FINANCIAL YEAR END)

(Amts in R'000)	1992 Jun	1991 Jun	1990 Jun	1989 Jun	1988 Jun
Ord S/H Int	298378	31027	30860	29827	29773
Iss Ord Share	27310	10820	10820	10820	10820
Total Liab	6006	3575	3987	3871	2110
Current Liab	6006	3575	3987	3871	2110
Total Assets	304384	34602	34847	33698	31883
Current Assets	77890	4154	7057	7117	11238
Debtors	421	265	723	557	158
Oper Profit	-118	-69	-58	4001	2065
Tax Paid	879	321	719	917	413
Prf af Int&Tax	7305	3373	3477	3084	1652
Prf att Ord Sh	7305	3373	3477	3084	1652
Btm Line Earn	7394	3629	4494	3084	1652
Dividend Paid	6991	3462	3462	3030	1623
Mkt Prce(c) YE	1700	2450	990	690	500

PER SHARE STATISTICS (CENTS)

Net Asst Val	1092.56	286.76	285.21	275.67	275.17
Net Earnings	36.40	31.20	32.10	28.50	20.40
Dividends	32.00	32.00	32.00	28.00	15.00
Cash Flow	26.75	31.17	32.13	28.50	20.42

RATIOS AND OTHER INFORMATION

Mrk Cap(R000)	464270	265090	107118	74658	54100
Current Ratio	12.97	1.16	1.77	1.84	5.33
Quik/Acid Tst	12.97	1.16	1.77	1.84	5.33
Debt/Ass Rat	0.02	0.10	0.11	0.11	0.07
Debt to Eqity	0.02	0.12	0.13	0.13	0.07
Ret on Assets	2.69	10.68	12.04	11.87	6.48
Ret on Equity%	2.45	10.87	11.27	10.34	5.55
Price/Earnings	46.70	78.53	30.84	24.21	24.51
Divid Cover	1.14	0.98	1.00	1.02	1.36
Divid Yield	1.88	1.31	3.23	4.06	3.00
Earning Yield%	2.14	1.27	3.24	4.13	4.08
NAV % Mrk Pr	64.27	11.70	28.81	39.95	55.03
Effec Tax Rate	50.58	52.54	51.39	22.92	20.00
Sus Grth Rate	0.11	-0.29	0.05	0.18	0.10

SUBSIDIARY & ASSOCIATED COMPANIES

CADBURY SCHWEPPES SA LTD (21,7%)
DALYS LTD (20,6%)

INVESTMENTS

AMALGAMATED BEVERAGE INDUSTRIES LTD (150000 SH)
CADBURY SCHWEPPES (SA) LTD (7622000SH)
DALYS LTD (2888200SH)
SAFICON INVESTMENTS LTD (28555448SH)
SAKERS FINANCE & INVESTMENT CORPORATION (971981 SH)
SEARCON LTD (804140 SH)
SEARDEL INVESTMENT CORPORATION LTD (321500 SH)
SOUTH AFRICAN BREWERIES LTD (232059 SH)

TEXTILE MILLS (1947) HOLDINGS LTD

ABBREVIATION : TEX-MILLS

JSE SHORT CODE : TML

SECTOR : Industrial-Clothing, Footwear & Textiles

SHAREHOLDERS

Who Owns Whom's Assessment of the Identity of the Ultimate Controlling Shareholder: DIRECTORS

SHAREHOLDER	PERCENTAGE 1992	1991
J T R INV P/L	---	4.3
MACDONIC HLDGS P/L	---	1.1
SECURITY MILLS	---	91.5
TOTAL	---	96.8

DIRECTORS :
BEIGEL J MRS,HAMMETT MJ (Managing Director)
LANE RJ ,ZLATTNER RS (Chairman

REGISTERED OFFICE
Cnr Josiah Chinamano, & Bellevue Roads
Light Industrial Sites, Bulawayo, Zimbabwe

TEL: 09263-9 69381

TRANSFER SECRETARY
Tuffias Shapiro Braude
P O Box 87009, Houghton
2041
TEL: 011-486 1460

COMPANY SECRETARY
C W Armstrong

NATURE OF BUSINESS
The company and its subsidiary and associated company operate in the textile industry. The main activities are the manufacturing, marketing and distribution of fabric and knitted garments.

BANKERS :
Zimbabwe Banking Corporation Ltd

AUDITORS :
Coopers Theron Du Toit

FAMILIAR BRAND NAMES
N/A

CONTRIBUTION BY ACTIVITY
N/A

YEAR END : September

DIVIDEND :Ords 50c

Dividend No 31	(Ldr)17/08/90	(Pay)31/08/90	Amt(c)10
Dividend No 32	(Ldr)28/03/91	(Pay)05/05/91	Amt(c)10
Dividend No 33	(Ldr)20/03/92	(Pay)31/03/92	Amt(c)10

NUMBER OF EMPLOYEES : 701

CAPITAL STRUCTURE

	AUTHORISED	ISSUED
Ords 50c	2000000	1990840
6% Cum Prefs Zim$2	100000	50000

FINANCIAL STATISTICS (AT FINANCIAL YEAR END)

(Amts in Zim$)	1991 Sep	1990 Dec	1989 Dec	1988 Dec	1987 Dec
Ord S/H Int	7710	4300	3655	3340	2937
Long Trm Loans	808	788	893	750	822
Iss Ord Share	1991	1991	1991	1991	1991
Total Liab	6979	5666	4926	3930	4112
Current Liab	6171	4878	4033	3180	3290
Total Assets	14689	9966	8581	7270	7049
Current Assets	9386	8027	6650	5363	5091
Debtors	2386	2011	1708	1483	1391
Inventory	6525	5839	4779	3842	2928
Turnover	16157	9991	11834	10015	9435
Oper Profit	1742	1491	1633	1427	1243
Interest Paid	444	237	242	196	82
Tax Paid	585	594	723	663	653
Prf af Int&Tax	721	669	681	620	600
Prf att Ord Sh	645	631	615	588	582
Btm Line Earn	645	631	615	588	582
Dividend Paid	199	199	199	186	325
Mkt Prce(c) YE	90	82	80	90	150
Depreciation	172	126	180	201	173

PER SHARE STATISTICS (CENTS)

Net Asst Val	387.24	215.97	183.58	167.75	147.51
Net Earnings	32.38	31.71	30.87	29.20	28.85
Dividends	10.00	10.00	10.00	9.00	16.00
Cash Flow	43.60	34.46	40.93	38.12	35.66

RATIOS AND OTHER INFORMATION

Mrk Cap(R000)	1792	1633	1593	1792	2987
Current Ratio	1.52	1.65	1.65	1.69	1.55
Quik/Acid Tst	0.46	0.45	0.46	0.48	0.66
A/C Rec T/ovr	6.77	4.97	6.93	6.75	6.78
Tot Ass T/ovr	1.10	1.00	1.38	1.38	1.34
Debt/Ass Rat	0.42	0.49	0.47	0.44	0.47
Debt to Eqity	0.80	1.13	1.10	0.95	1.12
Interest Cover	3.92	6.29	6.78	7.39	15.21
Oper Prof Mrg	10.78	14.92	13.80	14.25	13.17
Net Prof Marg%	3.99	6.32	5.20	5.87	6.17
Ret on Assets	11.91	15.05	19.18	20.34	18.94
Ret on Equity%	8.37	14.67	16.83	17.60	19.82
Price/Earnings	2.78	2.59	2.59	3.08	5.20
Divid Cover	3.24	3.17	3.09	3.24	1.80
Divid Yield	11.11	12.20	12.50	10.00	10.67
Earning Yield%	35.98	38.67	38.59	32.44	19.23
NAV % Mrk Pr	430.27	263.38	229.47	186.39	98.34
Effec Tax Rate	40.89	52.65	50.32	54.91	54.36
Def Interval	3.83	. 3.48	2.48	1.52	1.74
Sus Grth Rate	5.78	10.05	11.38	12.04	8.75

SUBSIDIARY & ASSOCIATED COMPANIES

TEXPRINT (PVT) LTD
ZIMBABWE BLEACHERS & DYERS (PVT) LTD

INVESTMENTS

None

TIGER OATS LTD

ABBREVIATION : TIGR-OATS

JSE SHORT CODE : TIG

SECTOR : Industrial-Food

SHAREHOLDERS

Who Owns Whom's Assessment of the Identity of the Ultimate Controlling Shareholder: SA MUTUAL VIA BARLOWS & CG SMITH

SHAREHOLDER	PERCENTAGE 1992	1991
C G SMITH FOODS LTD	52.7	52.8
STD BANK NOM TVL P/L	9.9	9.6
CMB NOM P/L	5.2	---
LIBERTY LIFE ASSOC OF AFRICA LTD	2.8	2.8
SOUTHERN LIFE ASSOC LTD	1.7	1.6
EIGHTY ONE MAIN STREET NOM LTD	1.3	1.5
ESCOM PENS & PROV FUND	1.3	1.7
FIRST NAT NOM P/L	1.2	1.3
COMMERCIAL UNION LIFE ASSURE CO SA LTD	1.0	---
COMMERCIAL UNION ASSURE CO SA LTD	---	1.2
SANLAM	---	1.3
SANKERN E/B	---	3.0
TOTAL	77.2	76.7

DIRECTORS :
ADAMS BH ,APSEY CA ,BROWN D ,DENNIS N
FRANKEL JA ,FRANKLIN MH (Financial Director)
HALL CA ,LEWIS WA ,MCBAIN JH ,MILLAR TW
SMITH HA ,STEELE BP ,VAN DEN BERG JL

REGISTRATION NUMBER : 05/17881/06

REGISTERED OFFICE
85 Bute Lane, Sandown
Sandton
2196
TEL: 011-884 4500
FAX: 011-884 2029

TRANSFER SECRETARY
Rand Registrars Ltd
P O Box 82549, Southdale
2135
TEL: 011-835 1016

COMPANY SECRETARY
H Yudelowitz

NATURE OF BUSINESS
An investment holding company with operations in milling, baking, confectionery, food processing & production, pharmaceutical & healthcare products & fishing. The company holds controlling interests in quoted Adcock-Ingram & Oceana Fishing.

BANKERS :
Nedcor Bank Ltd

AUDITORS :
Arthur Andersen & Co

FAMILIAR BRAND NAMES
ACE,ALDOMET,ALL GOLD,AMBER LINK
AMERICAN CREAMIA,AUNT CAROLINE,BABY BEST
BEACON SWEETS,BESENOL,BIOPLUS,BLACK CAT
BROWNS CASH & CARRY,CATMOR,COLDCAPS,COLMANS
COMPRAL,CORDON BLEU,COUNTY FAIR,COW AND GATE
CROWN,CUPPA CREAMS,DOGMOR,DREWS LIVER SALTS
EDIB,FAMILY CIRCLE PHARMACY,FARMERS TABLE
FATTI'S & MONI'S,FIESTA SHAMPOO
FINESSE SHAMPOO,FRUIT CHEWS,GILL SHAMPOO
GLENRYCK,GOLDEN CLOUD,GOLDEN LAY
GOLDEN SPREAD,GOOD MORNING,HELDERBERG,HUGOS
INDUNA,INGRAMS CAMPHOR,INSIDE STORY
JE T'AIME,JEYES,JUNGLE OATS,KING KORN
KINGS BREW,KOO,KWIKSPAR,LUCKY PET,LUCKY STAR
MABELA,MABELLA CORN RICE,MALTEX,MEADOW
MORVITE,NATURLITE,NOW BAR,NUT PUFFS,OAT BRAN
OATSO EASY,OLD CAPE,OLD MILL STREAM
OMNIPAQUE,PANADO,PASTABARONE
PHIPPS MILK OF MAGNESIA,PLANTERS,PRIZE PET
RECORD,RENITEK,RONEL,SALDHANA,SAVEMORE
SAVOURY CLASSICS,SILVER LEAF,SLIM SLICE
SOMOL,SPAR,STAR,STEARNS,STOPAYNE,SUGUS
SUNNY DAY SOFT,SUNSHINE D,SUPA-WHEAT
SUPERIEUR,SURPRISE RICE,TASTIC,TAYSTEE WHEAT
TIGER OATS,TINKIES,TV BAR,WAGTER
WEIRS CASH & CARRY,WET WIPES,WOODEN SPOON
ZOCOR

CONTRIBUTION BY ACTIVITY
Milling & Baking (% Turnover) (25.1%)
Animal Feeds & Agri-Business (22.0%)
Edible Oils & Derivatives (10.8%)
Trading & Distribution (Food) (27.0%)
Pharmaceuticals (11.2%)
Fishing (4.0%)

YEAR END : September

DIVIDEND :Ords 10c

Interim No 91	(Ldr)08/06/90	(Pay)11/07/90	Amt(c)22
Final No 92	(Ldr)30/11/90	(Pay)07/01/91	Amt(c)41
Interim No 93	(Ldr)07/06/91	(Pay)12/07/91	Amt(c)25
Final No 94	(Ldr)29/11/91	(Pay)13/01/92	Amt(c)46
Interim No 95	(Ldr)05/06/92	(Pay)13/07/92	Amt(c)28

NUMBER OF EMPLOYEES : 36353

CAPITAL STRUCTURE

	AUTHORISED	ISSUED
5,5% Cum Prefs R2	555000	555000
Ords 10c	183500000	150066388

FINANCIAL STATISTICS (AT FINANCIAL YEAR END)

(Amts in R'000)	1991 Sep	1990 Sep	1989 Sep	1988 Sep	1987 Sep
Ord S/H Int	1249600	1073400	916400	778729	718543
Long Trm Loans	457100	413900	321500	342201	205169
Iss Ord Share	139389	139055	138818	138550	138550
Total Liab	2205400	1987200	1642100	1494169	1013524
Current Liab	1748300	1573300	1320600	1151968	808355
Total Assets	3455000	3060600	2558500	2272898	1732067
Current Assets	2122400	1895700	1606000	1482341	1143532
Debtors	1035800	933700	798100	646856	453689
Inventory	987100	862300	722700	641225	406550
Turnover	7980500	6779900	5743400	4394826	3535114
Oper Profit	600000	496200	434300	352564	253592
Interest Paid	132000	96500	71300	16002	14424
Tax Paid	173100	155800	142400	131060	86239
Prf af Int&Tax	343000	283300	264700	205502	152929
Prf att Ord Sh	288600	255100	219000	175404	135898
Btm Line Earn	265900	239800	205600	107069	103975
Dividend Paid	99000	87600	75600	60268	46685
Mkt Prce(c) YE	3425	2275	2200	11800	12650
Depreciation	149900	132500	94200	69898	60441

PER SHARE STATISTICS (CENTS)

Net Asst Val	896.48	771.92	660.14	562.06	518.62
Net Earnings	207.00	184.00	158.10	127.00	98.00
Dividends	71.00	63.00	54.50	44.00	34.00
Cash Flow	313.33	279.53	227.79	176.34	133.73

RATIOS AND OTHER INFORMATION

Mrk Cap(R000)	4774073	3163501	3053996	16348900	17526575
Current Ratio	1.21	1.20	1.22	1.29	1.41
Quik/Acid Tst	0.65	0.66	0.67	0.73	0.91
A/C Rec T/ovr	7.70	7.26	7.20	6.79	7.79
Tot Ass T/ovr	2.31	2.22	2.24	1.93	2.04
Debt/Ass Rat	0.55	0.56	0.55	0.55	0.50
L T L Tot Ass	0.04	0.04	0.04	0.05	0.03
Debt to Eqity	1.52	1.59	1.55	1.61	1.21
Interest Cover	4.60	5.24	6.34	22.03	17.58
Oper Prof Mrg	7.52	7.32	7.56	8.02	7.17
Net Prof Marg%	3.62	3.76	3.81	3.99	3.84
Ret on Assets	18.91	17.54	18.67	15.50	14.94
Ret on Equity%	23.10	23.77	23.90	22.52	18.91
Price/Earnings	16.55	12.36	13.92	92.91	129.08
Divid Cover	2.92	2.92	2.90	2.89	2.88
Divid Yield	2.07	2.77	2.48	0.37	0.27
Earning Yield%	6.04	8.09	7.19	1.08	0.77
NAV % Mrk Pr	26.17	33.93	30.01	4.76	4.10
Effec Tax Rate	34.40	35.36	36.43	39.38	37.74
Def Interval	1.55	1.57	1.48	2.03	1.56
Sus Grth Rate	15.17	15.60	15.65	14.79	12.42

SUBSIDIARY & ASSOCIATED COMPANIES

ADCOCK INGRAM INVESTMENTS LTD
ADCOCK INGRAM LTD
ADELAIDE BAKERY (PTY) LTD
AFRICAN FEATHER WORKS (PTY) LTD
ALBANY BAKERIES (EASTERN CAPE) (PTY) LTD
ALBANY BAKERIES (NATAL) (PTY) LTD
ALBANY BAKERIES (WESTERN CAPE) (PTY) LTD
ALBANY BAKERIES LTD
ALBANY BAKERS AND CONFECTIONERS (PTY) LT
ALBANY BAKERY (JOHANNESBURG) (PTY) LTD
AMALGAMATED WAREHOUSING (PTY) LTD

AMBER-LINK CHICK SALES (NATAL) (PTY) LTD
AMBER-LINK CHICK SALES (PTY) LTD
ASTRA BAKERY (PTY) LTD
B & W PROPERTIES (PTY) LTD
BAKOVEN (P.E.) (PTY) LTD
BARKLY WEST BAKERY (PTY) LTD
BENONI MINERAL WATER WORKS (PTY) LTD
BESSBREN (PTY) LTD
BETHULIE PROPERTIES (PTY) LTD
BIZANA BAKERY (PTY) LTD
BLUMSTEIN INVESTMENTS (PTY) LTD
BOBREN (PTY) LTD
BOET SMIT EGG SALES (PTY) LTD
BOLAND BROILERS (PTY) LTD (50%)
BONAIR (PTY) LTD
BOSCHRAND MELKPRODUKTE BPK
BRANDVLEI EIERPRODUSEERDERS (EDMS) BPK
BREMER MILLS (PTY) LTD
BREMER THREE FEATHERS (PTY) LTD
BREMTIG PROPERTY HOLDINGS (PTY) LTD
BRENNERS TRUST CO. (PTY) LTD
BROMVLEI BROILERS (PTY) LTD (50%)
BROWN GROUP (PTY) LTD
BS & R BEARE (PTY) LTD
BUCKWHEAT HOLDINGS (PTY) LTD
BUTTERWORTH BAKERY (PTY) LTD
CAKE ARTISTS (PTY) LTD
CAPE MARINE OIL HOLDINGS (PTY) LTD
CAPE OIL PRODUCTS LTD
CF RADUE AND CO (PTY) LTD
CLIDELL GRAIN STORE (PTY) LTD
COCKSCOMB POULTRY FARMS (PTY) LTD
COCO OIL (PTY) LTD
COLIGNY PROPERTIES LTD
COLLEN'S BAKERY (PTY) LTD
COUNTY FAIR FOODS (PTY) LTD
COURTIG PROPERTIES (PTY) LTD
CRATIG PROPERTIES (PTY) LTD
CROWN INTERNATIONAL (PTY) LTD
CROWN OIL MILLS (PTY) LTD
CURSUL INVESTMENTS (PTY) LTD
D LUND FARMS (PTY) LTD (42%)
DE WILDT MILLING CO. (PTY) LTD
DEEPWATER FARMS (PTY) LTD (50%)
DELBURG PROPERTIES (PTY) LTD
DELHOE PROPERTIES LTD
DELLET PROPERTIES LTD
DELMAS DISTRIBUTORS (BOPHUTATSWANA) (PTY
DELMAS MILLING DISTRIBUTORS (PTY) LTD
DELTIG PROPERTIES LTD
DIAMOND HENKEL (PTY) LTD (50%)
DIAMOND PROCESS CHEMICALS (PTY) LTD
DIE EIERBEURS (EDMS) BPK
DONWELL (PTY) LTD (49%)
DOORTIG PROPERTIES (PTY) LTD
DRUMDEL PROPERTIES (PTY) LTD
DURBAN BULK SHIPPING CO. (PTY) LTD
DURBAN CONFECTIONERY WORKS (PTY) LTD (50,01%)
EDIBLE PRODUCTS (AFRICA) (PTY) LTD
EGG POWER (PTY) LTD
EGGLAND (PTY) LTD
ENGCOBO BAKERY (PTY) LTD (49%)
ERMTIG PROPERTIES (PTY) LTD
FAIRTIG PROPERTIES (PTY) LTD
FARMERS TABLE (PTY) LTD (50%)
FATTIS & MONIS LTD
FATTIS MANSIONS (PTY) LTD
FAUCIGLIETTI BAKERY (PTY) LTD
FORTIG PROPERTIES (PTY) LTD
FRANTIG INVESTMENTS LTD
GALOVO (PTY) LTD
GLENMOR PRODUCTS LTD
GOLDEN PRIDE EGG RANCHES (PTY) LTD
GONUBIE BAKERY (PTY) LTD
GOODHOPE BAKERY (PTY) LTD
GOTURA WHOLESALERS (PTY) LTD
GRASKOP BAKERY (PTY) LTD
GRATIG PROPERTIES (PTY) LTD
HARJUMAT INVESTMENTS (PTY) LTD
HENSNEST (PTY) LTD
HUSTEDS WHOLESALE (PTY) LTD (50%)
HYPRO CONSTRUCTION (PTY) LTD (50%)
IMEX INTERNATIONAL (PTY) LTD
INDEPENDENT BAKERY (PTY) LTD
INDEPENDENT PROPERTIES (PTY) LTD
INDEPENDENT REARERS (JHB) (PTY) LTD
INDEPENDENT REARERS (PTY) LTD
INDEPENDENT REARERS (TVL) (PTY) LTD
JAMES W WEIR & CO (PTY) LTD
JAMES W WEIR (TRANSKEI) (PTY) LTD
JANVIC PROPERTIES (PTY) LTD
JUSTNORM PROPERTIES (PTY) LTD
KHULANI BROWN (PTY) LTD (50%)
KING PROPERTIES (PTY) LTD
KOSTER BAKERY (PTY) LTD
KOTIG PROPERTIES (PTY) LTD
KSM MILLING CO (NATAL) LTD
KSM MILLING CO LTD
KWAMBONAMBI BAKERY (PTY) LTD
LADY FRERE BAKERY (PTY) LTD
LANGEBERG HOLDINGS LTD
LEKNARF INVESTMENTS (PTY) LTD
LESELBARY INVESTMENTS (PTY) LTD (25%)
LICHTENBURG MILLS LTD
LOUBREN MALT (PTY) LTD
LOUIS TRICHARDT BAKERY (PTY) LTD
LOUTIG PROPERTIES (PTY) LTD
LUSIKISIKI BAKERY (PTY) LTD
MA WAGNER (NATAL) (PTY) LTD
MA WAGNER (PTY) LTD
MACLEAR BAKERY (PTY) LTD
MAFEKING MELKPRODUKTE (EDMS) BPK
MAKANDA ESTATES LTD
MALESI PRODUCTS (PTY) LTD
MANDLO BAKERY (PTY) LTD
MANNA BAKERY (PTY) LTD
MANNA BAKERY PROPERTIES (PTY) LTD
MARINE OIL REFINERS OF AFRICA LTD
MARTIG PROPERTIES (PTY) LTD
MARVEL BOTTLERS (PRETORIA) (PTY) LTD
MARVEL BOTTLERS (PTY) LTD
MEADOW FEED MILLS (CAPE) LTD
MIDDE VRYSTAAT BAKKERYE (PTY) LTD
MILLING & TRADING (E.L.) LTD
MILLING & TRADING (P.E.) LTD
MONI BROS. (PTY) LTD
MONIS AND FATTIS INDUSTRIES (PTY) LTD
MOOI RIVER BAKERY & TEA ROOM (PTY) LTD
MPUMALANGA BAKERY (PTY) LTD
NATIONAL NUT AND PRESERVES (PTY) LTD
NFH INVESTMENTS LTD
NONGOMA PROPERTIES (PTY) LTD
NORTHERN CAPE BAKERIES (PTY) LTD
OCEANA FISHING GROUP LTD
ODENDAALRUS BAKERY (PTY) LTD (50%)
OGIES BAKERY (PTY) LTD
ORIGINAL CHICKEN GRILL (PTY) LTD (50%)
P G SELBY (PTY) LTD
PAULINE PROPERTIES (PTY) LTD
PCP PRODUCTS (1964) (PTY) LTD
PENDALE FARM (PTY) LTD
PHALABORWA BAKKERY (PTY) LTD
PICOR INVESTMENTS (PTY) LTD
PIET RETIEF BAKERIES (PTY) LTD
PIETERSBURG MILLING COMPANY (PTY) LTD
PIETIG PROPERTIES (PTY) LTD
PINETOP ESTATE (PTY) LTD (50%)
POTCHEFSTROOM MALT & PRODUCE (PTY) LTD

PRODKOR (PTY) LTD
PROTEA SWISS BAKERY (PTY) LTD
QUEENTIG PROPERTIES (PTY) LTD
RADUE WEIR (CISKEI) (PTY) LTD (38,1%)
RADUE WEIR MANAGEMENT SERVICES (PTY) LTD
RADUE WEIR PROPERTIES (PTY) LTD (38.1%)
RADUE WEIR S.A. (PTY) LTD (38,1%)
RADUE WEIR SUPERMARKETS (PTY) LTD (38,1%)
RADUE-WEIR HOLDINGS (PTY) LTD
RADUES ROLLER MILLS (PTY) LTD
RAMSBOOY INVESTMENTS (PTY) LTD
RAMSWEP INVESTMENTS (PTY) LTD
RANTIG PROPERTIES (PTY) LTD
REGINA CONFECTIONERY (PTY) LTD
RICHARDS BAY MILLING CO. (PTY) LTD
RICHTIG PROPERTIES (PTY) LTD
RLL MACHINERY CO (PTY) LTD
ROTOCRAFT SA (PTY) LTD
RUSDEL PROPERTIES (PTY) LTD
RYWAL PROPERTIES (PTY) LTD
SA FOOD PRODUCTS (PTY) LTD
SA MARGARINE (PTY) LTD
SASOLBURG BAKERY (PTY) LTD
SASTIG PROPERTIES (PTY) LTD
SAVOY INVESTMENTS (PTY) LTD
SEKONDERE FINANSIERING (PTY) LTD
SILPROP (PTY) LTD
SILVERLEAF BAKERY (PTY) LTD
SIMRIV INVESTMENTS (PTY) LTD
SOMTIG PROPERTIES (PTY) LTD
SOVA FARMS (PTY) LTD
SPRINGBOK CEREAL INDUSTRIES (PTY) LTD
SPRINGKLIP (EDMS) BPK (50%)
STAR FOODS (PTY) LTD
STEIN BROS. (HOLDINGS) (PTY) LTD
STEIN BROS. (HOLDINGS) LTD
STEINBRO FARM EGGS (PTY) LTD
STEINBRO TRADING LTD
SULLICUR INVESTMENTS (PTY) LTD
SUNNYSIDE MANSIONS (PTY) LTD
SWADEP LTD
SWARTHEN (EDMS) BPK (50%)
TAPIOCA DEVELOPMENT CO. (PTY) LTD
TARLTON POULTRY FARM (PTY) LTD
TASTIC RICE CORP LTD
THADDEUS (PTY) LTD
THREE BEARS CEREALS LTD
TIGDAL PROPERTIES (PTY) LTD
TIGER BAKERIES LTD
TIGER COUNTY FAIR (PTY) LTD
TIGER FOODS (KIMBERLEY) (PTY) LTD
TIGER FOODS (NATAL) LTD
TIGER MANAGEMENT SERVICES LTD
TIGER MILLING & FEEDS LTD
TIGER OATS ESTATES LTD
TIGER PROTEIN INDUSTRIES (PTY) LTD
TIGHAR PROPERTIES (PTY) LTD
TIGIX PROPERTIES (PTY) LTD
TIGREEN PROPERTIES (PTY) LTD
TOP PINE ESTATE (PTY) LTD (50%)
TORLEDO (PTY) LTD (50%)
TRANS AFRICAN INDUSTRIAL CORP (PTY) LTD
TRANSKEI BAKERIES (PTY) LTD (50%)
TROXLER INVESTMENTS (PTY) LTD
TSHIFHERE BAKERY (PTY) LTD (49%)
ULTRA BAKERY & RESTAURANT (PTY) LTD
ULUNDI BAKERY (PTY) LTD (25%)
UMTIG PROPERTIES (PTY) LTD
UNITED OCEANA HOLDINGS LTD
UNIVERSAL GRAIN LTD
UNIVERSAL GROUP LTD
UNIVERSAL STARCH INDUSTRIES (PTY) LTD
VAALTIG PROPERTIES (PTY) LTD
VENETRAN (PTY) LTD
VIRTIG PROPERTIES (PTY) LTD
VRYTIG PROPERTIES (PTY) LTD
W ANDERSONS CAKE SHOP (PTY) LTD
WECO DISTRIBUTORS (PTY) LTD
WELKOM MILLING CO. LTD
WG BROWN INVESTMENTS LTD
WHITELODGE POULTRY FARM (PTY) LTD
WIENER BAKERY (PTY) LTD
WRENSCHTOWN BAKERY (PTY) LD

INVESTMENTS

AFRICAN FEATHER WORKS (PTY) LTD (16988 SH)
BALFOUR BAKERY (PTY) LTD (2486)
CONCORDE PIG PRODUCERS (PTY) LTD (10)
DRAKENSBERG KO-OP BPK (278 SH)
FEDERAL MARINE LTD (600 SH)
NORISTAN HOLDINGS LIMITED (12750 SH)
ORANJERIVIER VISSERYE BPK (3200 SH)
SA FROZEN ROCK LOBSTER PACKERS (PTY) LTD (18 SH)
SMART CENTRE HOLDINGS LTD (1129523 SH)
SOUTH WEST AFRICA FISHING INDUSTRIES LTD (832000SH)
SWA FROZEN ROCK LOBSTER PACKERS (PTY) LT (3 SH)
TONGAAT-HULETT GROUP LTD (151200 SH)
UNITED FISHING ENTERPRISES (PTY) LTD (1000SH)

TIGER WHEELS HOLDINGS LTD

ABBREVIATION : TIWHEEL

JSE SHORT CODE : TWL

SECTOR : Industrial-Motor

SHAREHOLDERS

Who Owns Whom's Assessment of the Identity of the Ultimate Controlling Shareholder: DIRECTORS

SHAREHOLDER	PERCENTAGE 1992	1991
EDDIE KEIZAN FAMILY HOLDINGS P/L	24.4	24.2
REPUBLIC NOM P/L	21.1	21.0
MARWHEEL INV P/L	19.3	18.7
KEIZAN E I	8.5	8.4
TIGMAR INV P/L	6.1	6.1
COUZYN E N	4.2	4.7
RIVERS K W	2.9	3.0
GJJ NOM P/L	1.5	1.8
MOMENTUM LIFE ASSURE LTD	1.1	1.1
STD BANK NOM TVL P/L	1.0	---
TOTAL	90.1	89.1

DIRECTORS :
COUZYN EN ,GARDNER MRH
GLATT MB (Joint Chairman)
KEIZAN EI (Chairman & Chief Exec.),RIVERS KW
VENTER PJ

REGISTRATION NUMBER : 67/10435/06

REGISTERED OFFICE
26 Western Boulevard, City West
Johannesburg
2092

TEL: 011-833 7260
FAX: 011-836 6891

TRANSFER SECRETARY
Consolidated Share Registrars Ltd
P O Box 61051, Marshalltown
2107
TEL: 011-492 1620

COMPANY SECRETARY
M Gardner

NATURE OF BUSINESS
The group is involved in the following activities: Manufacturing of aluminium road wheels and the application of finishing processes to steel wheels Wholesaling of motor car & motorcycle tyres, steel & aluminium wheels, accessories & motor vehicle body parts; Retailing of motor car wheels, tyres and accessories.

BANKERS :
First National Bank of SA Ltd
Trust Bank of Africa Ltd

AUDITORS :
Fisher Hoffman Stride

FAMILIAR BRAND NAMES
BBS,DOTZ TYRES,METZELER,MICHELIN,PIRELLI
SCOTT,SWALLOW,TIGER WHEEL & TYRE,YOKOHAMA

CONTRIBUTION BY ACTIVITY
N/A

YEAR END : June

DIVIDEND :Ords 1c

Dividend No 3	(Ldr)02/11/90	(Pay)26/11/90	Amt(c)4.5
Dividend No 4	(Ldr)01/11/91	(Pay)29/11/91	Amt(c)3
Dividend No 5	(Ldr)02/10/92	(Pay)30/10/92	Amt(c)5

NUMBER OF EMPLOYEES : 445

CAPITAL STRUCTURE

	AUTHORISED	ISSUED
Ords 1c	40000000	31014700

FINANCIAL STATISTICS (AT FINANCIAL YEAR END)

(Amts in R'000)	1992 Jun	1991 Jun	1990 Jun	1989 Jun	1988 Jun
Ord S/H Int	19179	13691	11790	8742	6138
Long Trm Loans	7403	7789	6445	2076	1180
Iss Ord Share	31015	29523	28147	25970	25000
Total Liab	22808	20724	16341	10774	8902
Current Liab	15405	12935	9896	8698	7722
Total Assets	41922	34350	28066	19471	15040
Intang Assets	65	65	65	45	*
Current Assets	29043	23335	19083	13329	10512
Debtors	11490	9336	10262	6410	4539
Inventory	16961	13412	8491	6034	5387
Turnover	87458	64400	51739	41167	27621
Oper Profit	6400	3988	5647	4966	3554
Interest Paid	1963	1700	679	435	294
Tax Paid	745	385	1647	1526	1241
Prf af Int&Tax	3807	1979	3441	3014	2019
Prf att Ord Sh	3788	1843	3421	2923	1004
Btm Line Earn	5541	1770	3157	2923	979
Dividend Paid	173	-118	564	319	273
Mkt Prce(c) YE	80	50	60	65	50
Depreciation	1819	1510	1032	734	571

PER SHARE STATISTICS (CENTS)

Net Asst Val	61.63	46.15	41.66	33.49	24.55
Net Earnings	12.50	6.30	12.20	11.30	8.60
Dividends	5.00	3.00	4.50	4.50	2.50
Cash Flow	20.61	12.96	18.07	15.20	7.13

RATIOS AND OTHER INFORMATION

Mrk Cap(R000)	24812	14762	16888	16881	12500
Current Ratio	1.89	1.80	1.93	1.53	1.36
Quik/Acid Tst	0.78	0.77	1.07	0.84	0.66
A/C Rec T/ovr	7.61	6.90	5.04	6.42	6.09
Tot Ass T/ovr	2.09	1.87	1.84	2.11	1.84
Debt/Ass Rat	0.50	0.57	0.55	0.53	0.57
L T L Tot Ass	0.13	0.19	0.19	0.08	0.06
Debt to Eqity	1.09	1.42	1.30	1.18	1.41
Interest Cover	3.26	2.35	8.32	11.42	12.09
Oper Prof Mrg	7.32	6.19	10.91	12.06	12.87
Net Prof Marg%	4.33	2.86	6.61	7.10	3.63
Ret on Assets	15.50	11.44	20.48	25.08	23.63
Ret on Equity%	19.75	13.46	29.02	33.44	16.36
Price/Earnings	6.40	7.94	4.92	5.75	5.81
Divid Cover	2.50	2.10	2.71	2.51	3.44
Divid Yield	6.25	6.00	7.50	6.92	5.00
Earning Yield%	15.63	12.60	20.33	17.38	17.20
NAV % Mrk Pr	77.04	92.31	69.43	51.52	49.10
Effec Tax Rate	2.35	4.61	20.89	25.51	35.34
Def Interval	1.02	1.98	1.17	0.44	0.78
Sus Grth Rate	18.85	14.32	24.23	29.79	11.91

SUBSIDIARY & ASSOCIATED COMPANIES

APROPOS (PTY) LTD
BURGERS MAIN REEF PROPERTIES (PTY) LTD
MUSCLE PRODUCTS (PTY) LTD
PLUMLINE (PTY) LTD
TIGER PPC ALLOY WHEELS (PTY) LTD
TIGER WHEELS (CAPE) (PTY) LTD
TIGER WHEELS (PTY) LTD
TIGER WHEELS BABELEGI (PTY) LTD
TIGER WHEELS NATAL (PTY) LTD
TIGER WHEELS PUMPHOUSE (PTY) LTD

INVESTMENTS

None

TIME HOLDINGS LTD

ABBREVIATION : TIME

JSE SHORT CODE : TIM

SECTOR : Financial-Banks & Financial Services

SHAREHOLDERS

Who Owns Whom's Assessment of the Identity of the Ultimate Controlling Shareholder: DIRECTORS / CONCOR

SHAREHOLDER	PERCENTAGE 1992	1991
HIBBERT C T	38.3	40.8

RAND MERCHANT BANK LTD	10.6	11.3
CORBANK NOM P/L	9.4	10.0
SAFEGRO NOM P/L	8.3	4.0
TIME HOLDINGS SHARE TRUST	5.4	---
STD BANK NOM TVL P/L	4.9	---
MACKAY B M	3.1	3.3
ILSE F G INV P/L	2.9	1.4
SHARESTOCK NOM P/L	2.4	2.5
CMB NOM P/L	2.0	---
ANDEX NOM P/L	1.8	2.0
FIRST NAT NOM P/L	1.3	1.5
AA LIFE ASSURE ASSOC LTD	---	4.8
SANLAM	---	2.2
TOTAL	90.4	83.8

DIRECTORS :
FERREIRA GT ,HASLAM WJ
HIBBERT CT (Executive Chairman),IRISH MC
MACKAY BM ,MULLER JT ,RAGGETT MH ,ROOD TB D

REGISTRATION NUMBER : 84/02541/06

REGISTERED OFFICE
FHS House, 15 Girton Road
Parktown
2193
TEL: 011-883 9180
FAX: 011-883 9008

TRANSFER SECRETARY
Mercantile Registrars Ltd
P O Box 1053, Johannesburg
2000
TEL: 011-333 8181

COMPANY SECRETARY
R Da Costa

NATURE OF BUSINESS
The company is an investment holding company and provides administrative services. Subsidiaries are active in the business of project management, property development, construction & operate as a life insurance company. The group also operates a unit trust fund.

BANKERS :
Standard Bank of SA Ltd
First National Bank of SA Ltd
FirstCorp Merchant Bank Ltd

AUDITORS :
Fisher Hoffman Stride

FAMILIAR BRAND NAMES
N/A

CONTRIBUTION BY ACTIVITY
N/A

YEAR END : December

DIVIDEND :Ords no par value

Dividend No 3	(Ldr)23/03/90	(Pay)20/04/90	Amt(c)10
Dividend No 4	(Ldr)05/04/91	(Pay)02/05/91	Amt(c)5

NUMBER OF EMPLOYEES : 120

CAPITAL STRUCTURE

	AUTHORISED	ISSUED
Ords no par value	60000000	38033786
6% Conv Red Prefs R1	5000000	3333333
14% Cum Red Conv Prefs R1	10000000	9872662

FINANCIAL STATISTICS (AT FINANCIAL YEAR END)

(Amts in R'000)	1991 Dec	1990 Dec	1989 Dec	1988 Dec	1987 Dec
Ord S/H Int	14704	24408	30580	24862	8554
Long Trm Loans	57666	32138	19032	7245	6078
Iss Ord Share	40559	35681	37822	36300	26216
Total Liab	150108	91960	66557	43211	42190
Current Liab	92442	59822	47525	35966	36112
Total Assets	156101	104037	83906	61097	50744
Intang Assets	8711	12331	13231	6976	*
Current Assets	96438	66452	64207	51213	49104
Debtors	47901	36233	36470	20379	3861
Inventory	35023	25979	25538	30505	26735
Turnover	281267	275595	231304	182569	105940
Oper Profit	1435	4347	10926	12263	6444
Interest Paid	8743	1888	2730	689	232
Tax Paid	1555	-1606	-783	3510	2097
Prf af Int&Tax	-7467	4358	9112	8064	4115
Prf att Ord Sh	-9585	2593	8957	8032	3464
Btm Line Earn	-13086	-2958	7467	6542	3464
Dividend Paid	-	1784	3778	3637	1179
Mkt Prce(c) YE	60	80	72	120	110
Depreciation	1507	1539	1102	527	126

PER SHARE STATISTICS (CENTS)

Net Asst Val	14.78	33.85	45.87	49.27	32.63
Net Earnings	-25.80	7.30	25.00	26.00	14.00
Dividends	-	5.00	10.00	10.00	6.00
Cash Flow	-18.46	7.03	22.63	34.50	21.28

RATIOS AND OTHER INFORMATION

Mrk Cap(R000)	24335	28545	27232	43560	28838
Current Ratio	1.04	1.11	1.35	1.42	1.36
Quik/Acid Tst	0.66	0.68	0.81	0.58	0.62
A/C Rec T/ovr	5.87	7.61	6.34	8.96	27.44
Tot Ass T/ovr	1.80	2.65	2.76	2.99	2.09
Debt/Ass Rat	0.67	0.59	0.59	0.62	0.76
L T L Tot Ass	0.08	0.02	0.02	0.03	0.05
Debt to Eqity	7.08	2.53	1.61	1.52	4.53
Interest Cover	0.26	2.46	4.05	17.80	27.78
Oper Prof Mrg	0.51	1.58	4.72	6.72	6.08
Net Prof Marg%	-3.41	0.94	3.87	4.40	3.27
Ret on Assets	1.81	4.46	13.18	20.07	12.70
Ret on Equity%	-65.19	10.62	29.29	32.31	40.50
Price/Earnings	-2.33	10.96	2.88	4.62	7.86
Divid Cover	-	1.46	2.50	2.60	2.33
Divid Yield	-	6.25	13.89	8.33	5.45
Earning Yield%	-43.00	9.13	34.72	21.67	12.73
NAV % Mrk Pr	24.63	42.31	63.71	41.06	29.66
Effec Tax Rate	-12.94	0.24	8.72	12.32	6.50
Def Interval	-5.19	6.69	1.64	0.93	0.59
Sus Grth Rate	-65.19	3.31	16.94	17.68	26.71

SUBSIDIARY & ASSOCIATED COMPANIES

ASSURED ADVANCES (PTY) LTD
BURGUNDY INVESTMENTS (PTY) LTD
FERNABA (PTY) LTD
FOREST GLEN SHARE BLOCK (PTY) LTD
GOLDEN CITY HOUSING (PTY) LTD
ICM CONSTRUCTION (PTY) LTD
ICM SPACE FRAME (PTY) LTD
JS CONSTRUCTION CO (PTY) LTD
MARGINAL INVESTMENTS (PTY) LTD
NEXUS PTN 5/6 SANDTON SQUARE (PTY) LTD
NORTH RIDING DEVELOPMENT CO (PTY) LTD
R MCARTHY (PTY) LTD
REGISTERED INVESTMENTS (PTY) LTD
SECURITIES PORTFOLIO MANAGERS (PTY) LTD

TIME BRIDGING FINANCE (PTY) LTD
TIME COMMERCIAL PROPERTY HOLDINGS (PTY)
TIME DEVELOPMENTS (PTY) LTD
TIME DEVELOPMENTS CISKEI (PTY) LTD
TIME GROUP FINANCE (PTY) LTD (50%)
TIME HOLDINGS (PTY) LTD
TIME HOME SALES (PTY) LTD
TIME HOUSING (CAPE) (PTY) LTD
TIME HOUSING (CENTRAL) (PTY) LTD
TIME HOUSING (CISKEI) (PTY) LTD
TIME HOUSING (NATAL) (PTY) LTD
TIME HOUSING (NORTH EAST) (PTY) LTD
TIME HOUSING (PTY) LTD
TIME HOUSING (TRANSKEI) (PTY) LTD
TIME HOUSING (WEST DIVISION) (PTY) LTD
TIME HOUSING (WESTERN CAPE) (PTY) LTD
TIME HOUSING PROPERTIES (EMPANGENI) (PTY
TIME LAND (PTY) LTD
TIME LIFE INSURANCE LTD
TIME LIFE PROPERTIES INVESTMENTS (PTY) L
TIME LIFE UNIT TRUST MANAGEMENT CO LTD
TIME MANAGEMENT & CORPORATE SERVICES (PT
TIME MINING & INDUSTRIAL SERVICES (PTY)
TIME PROJECTS (BOTSWANA) (PTY) LTD
TIME PROJECTS (NATAL) (PTY) LTD
TIME PROJECTS (PTY) LTD
TPB (PTY) LTD
TRI-TIME HOUSING (PTY) LTD
UNDERCROFT INVESTMENTS (PTY) LTD
ZWALUW (PTY) LTD

INVESTMENTS

None

TIMES MEDIA LTD

ABBREVIATION : T-M-L

JSE SHORT CODE : TME

SECTOR : Industrial-Printing & Publishing

SHAREHOLDERS

Who Owns Whom's Assessment of the Identity of the Ultimate Controlling Shareholder: ANGLO AMERICAN VIA ARGUS

SHAREHOLDER	PERCENTAGE 1992	1991
ARGUS HOLDINGS LTD	36 5	37.1
STD BANK NOM TVL P/L	28.4	29.3
FIRST NAT NOM P/L	18 5	18 3
TIMES MEDIA LTD PENS FUND	2 4	2 9
SAGE LIFE LTD	2 2	2 2
CMB NOM P/L	2.1	---
EIGHTY ONE MAIN STREET NOM LTD	2 0	---
TOTAL	92 1	89 7

DIRECTORS :
CILLIERS C ,CLARK LR (Financial Director)
GRINDROD WM ,KOVARSKY DC (Managing Director)
MABUZA NEJ
PAULSON RH (Deputy Managing Director)
RETIEF PF (Chairman),WATERSON CH

REGISTRATION NUMBER : 05/12393/06

REGISTERED OFFICE
10th Floor, 11 Diagonal Street
Johannesburg
2001
TEL: 011-497 2711
FAX. 011-836 4665

TRANSFER SECRETARY
Central Registrars Ltd
P O Box 4844, Johannesburg
2000
TEL: 011-331 0051

COMPANY SECRETARY
B D Harris

NATURE OF BUSINESS
Principal group activity is the dissemination of information, via published and electronic media. Core business is newspaper & magazine publishing The company has interests in television, radio & information businesses, & substantial investments in publishing companies.

BANKERS :
Standard Bank of SA Ltd

AUDITORS :
Deloitte & Touche

FAMILIAR BRAND NAMES
ALGOA SUN,BUILDING PRODUCT NEWS,BUSINESS DAY
CALLNET,CAPE TIMES,CHEMICAL EQUIPMENT NEWS
COMMERCIAL EXCHANGE BULLETIN
COMMERCIAL TRANSPORT,COMPUTAFORM
COMPUTING SA,DAILY DISPATCH
DAILY TENDER BULLETIN,DENTEKSA,DRIVE ON
E P HERALD,ENTRAC (ELECTRONIC TENDERING)
EVENING POST,EXECUTIVE,FINANCIAL MAIL
FOOD INDUSTRIES,HELDERBERG REVIEW
HOLIDAY MAKER,I-NET (50%),INFORM
IVS (VETERINARY HANDBOOK),KONTAK
LA FEMME FAIR,LEADERSHIP,MERKELS
MIMS DESK REFERENCE
MIMS MEDICAL SPECIALITIES,MINING
NATAL IND TRADE SHOW,NEW EQUIPMENT NEWS
PEOPLE,PRETORIA NEWS (45%),PROMAT NEWS
RETAILING NEWS,SA COMPUTER FAIRE
SA JOURNAL OF EPEDIOMOLOGY,SA OPTOMETRIST
SECRETARY'S HANDBOOK,SITE & ROAD,STORE OWNER
SUNDAY TIMES,TAXI TALK,TENDERSCAN
TIRANDATA (TENDER INFO),TM,TRADE-NET
TRANSPORT MANAGEMENT,TRAVELLERS FRIEND
UNIX TIMES,WEEKEND POST,WIEL

CONTRIBUTION BY ACTIVITY
N/A

YEAR END : March

DIVIDEND : Ords 5c

Interim No 65	(Ldr)24/11/89	(Pay)15/12/89	Amt(c)18
Final No 66	(Ldr)22/06/90	(Pay)13/07/90	Amt(c)36
Interim No 67	(Ldr)30/11/90	(Pay)21/12/90	Amt(c)20
Final No 68	(Ldr)14/06/91	(Pay)05/07/91	Amt(c)40
Interim No 69	(Ldr)06/12/91	(Pay)20/12/91	Amt(c)22
Final No 70	(Ldr)03/07/92	(Pay)17/07/32	Amt(c)47
Interim No 71	(Ldr)20/11/92	(Pay)04/12/92	Amt(c)24

NUMBER OF EMPLOYEES : 1125

CAPITAL STRUCTURE

	AUTHORISED	ISSUED
Ords 5c	50000000	22217250

FINANCIAL STATISTICS (AT FINANCIAL YEAR END)

(Amts In R'000)	1992 Mar	1991 Mar	1990 Mar	1989 Mar	1988 Mar
Ord S/H Int	121007	93614	74978	59447	43395
Long Trm Loans	2617	4092	6350	-	-
Iss Ord Share	22097	21901	21501	20156	20106
Total Liab	86299	81942	83219	41938	21166
Current Liab	83682	77850	76869	41938	21166
Total Assets	194927	161245	143668	99863	64561
Intang Assets	12379	14311	14529	1522	*
Current Assets	66430	96990	90896	66172	42451
Debtors	48553	37461	31426	23040	20757
Inventory	1261	1455	1608	417	611
Turnover	319978	266054	237916	181014	154323
Oper Profit	53500	39570	40505	33138	23737
Interest Paid	2132	1774	2085	1179	886
Tax Paid	29711	25532	24388	12735	-
Prf af Int&Tax	39468	25393	25379	25074	26835
Prf att Ord Sh	41665	31643	25429	25074	26835
Btm Line Earn	42402	24756	25508	25074	26936
Dividend Paid	15246	13138	11611	9067	6032
Mkt Prce(c) YE	2150	1050	690	630	380
Depreciation	5072	4392	3908	2015	1497

PER SHARE STATISTICS (CENTS)

Net Asst Val	491.60	362.10	281.15	287.38	215.83
Net Earnings	189.00	145.00	119.00	45.00	30.00
Dividends	69.00	60.00	54.00	125.00	134.00
Cash Flow	180.04	118.77	137.70	130.53	141.09

RATIOS AND OTHER INFORMATION

Mrk Cap(R000)	475086	229961	148357	126983	76403
Current Ratio	0.79	1.25	1.18	1.58	2.01
Quik/Acid Tst	0.78	1.23	1.16	1.57	1.98
A/C Rec T/ovr	6.59	7.10	7.57	7.86	7.43
Tot Ass T/ovr	1.64	1.65	1.66	1.81	2.39
Debt/Ass Rat	0.44	0.51	0.58	0.42	0.33
L T L Tot Ass	0.01	0.03	0.04	-	-
Debt to Eqity	0.71	0.88	1.11	0.71	0.49
Interest Cover	28.75	23.38	20.58	29.70	30.07
Oper Prof Mrg	16.72	14.87	17.02	18.31	15.38
Net Prof Marg%	13.02	11.89	10.69	13.85	17.39
Ret on Assets	38.07	36.56	36.13	39.04	42.94
Ret on Equity%	34.43	33.80	33.92	42.18	61.84
Price/Earnings	11.38	7.24	5.80	14.00	12.67
Divid Cover	2.74	2.42	2.20	0.36	0.22
Divid Yield	3.21	5.71	7.83	19.84	35.26
Earning Yield%	8.79	13.81	17.25	7.14	7.89
NAV % Mrk Pr	22.86	34.49	40.75	45.62	56.80
Effec Tax Rate	55.18	60.00	51.38	37.70	-
Def Interval	0.07	0.09	0.08	-	-
Sus Grth Rate	21.83	19.77	18.43	26.93	47.94

SUBSIDIARY & ASSOCIATED COMPANIES

ALLIED MEDIA DISTRIBUTORS (PTY) LTD (30%)
ALLIED PUBLISHING (PTY) LTD (29%)
BRAMCO HOUSE (PTY) LTD
BREMLIV BUILDINGS (PTY) LTD
BURG STREET PROPERTIES (PTY) LTD
CALLNET (PTY) LTD
CAPE TIMES LTD
CORRY & GRANGER (COMMUNICATIONS) (PTY) L
DISPATCH MEDIA LTD (29%)
EASTERN PROVINCE NEWSPAPERS LTD
ELECTRONIC MEDIA NETWORK HOLDINGS (PTY) (23%)
ERNII (PTY) LTD (33,33%)
FINANCIAL MAIL (PTY) LTD
INTELLIGENT NETWORK (PTY) LTD (50%)
LEADERSHIP PUBLICATIONS (PTY) LTD
LIBRARY NETWORK (PTY) LTD
NATAL NEWSPAPERS (PTY) LTD (30%)
PRETORIA NEWS (PTY) LTD (45%)
RACING NETWORK (PTY) LTD (50%)
RAND DAILY MAILS LTD
SUNDAY TIMES SYNDICATE (PTY) LTD
TRADE INFORMATION SERVICES (PTY) LTD (33,33%)

INVESTMENTS

BOPHUTHATSWANA COMMERCIAL RADIO (PTY) LT (5%)
ELECTRONIC MEDIA NETWORK LTD (4%)

TITACO CONSOLIDATED INVESTMENTS LTD

ABBREVIATION : TITACO

JSE SHORT CODE : TTC

SECTOR : Industrial-Engineering

SHAREHOLDERS

Who Owns Whom's Assessment of the Identity of the Ultimate Controlling Shareholder: DIRECTORS

SHAREHOLDER	PERCENTAGE 1992	1991
TITACO ADMIN HOLDINGS CC	48.6	45.6
SA EAGLE INSURANCE CO LTD	9.9	9.9
EIGHTY ONE MAIN STREET NOM LTD	6.3	6.3
BRIDSON G B F	4.4	4.4
BASIL GERALD SMIDT FAMILY TRUST	2.5	2.5
PATRICK JOHN DAVIES FAMILY TRUST	2.5	2.5
REINER POSTHUMUS MEYJES FAMILY	2.5	2.5
LINTON S P	1.7	1.1
WILSON W G	1.6	1.6
VAN NIEKERK G	1.3	1.3
WANT B C	1.2	1.2
RUBIN V D	---	1.2
TOMES C O	---	1.3
TOTAL	82.4	81.3

DIRECTORS :
BORTZ JM ,DAVIES PJ ,GREENHALGH MP ,HASLETT FN
MEYJES RP (Chairman & Chief Exec.),RUBIN VD
SMIDT BG (Managing Director),WILSON WG

REGISTRATION NUMBER : 82/03648/06

REGISTERED OFFICE
6th Floor, Titaco House
63 Juta Street, Braamfontein
2001
TEL: 011-403 5941
FAX: 011-403 1783

TRANSFER SECRETARY
Mercantile Registrars Ltd
P O Box 1053, Johannesburg
2000
TEL: 011-333 8181

COMPANY SECRETARY
G B K Jarvis

NATURE OF BUSINESS
The holding company of an engineering group, operating in industrial, chemical, electrical and mining fixed capital investment projects.

BANKERS :
Standard Bank of SA Ltd

AUDITORS :
Ernst & Young

FAMILIAR BRAND NAMES
N/A

CONTRIBUTION BY ACTIVITY
N/A

YEAR END : February

DIVIDEND : Ords 10c
Dividend No 5 (Ldr)28/06/91 (Pay)26/07/91 Amt(c)4.5

NUMBER OF EMPLOYEES : 170

CAPITAL STRUCTURE

	AUTHORISED	ISSUED
Ords 10c	20000000	6042000

FINANCIAL STATISTICS (AT FINANCIAL YEAR END)

(Amts in R'000)	1992 Feb	1991 Feb	1990 Feb	1989 Feb	1988 Feb
Ord S/H Int	7780	6876	5641	4967	3920
Long Trm Loans	1024	2549	2550	2242	1568
Iss Ord Share	6042	6042	6042	6042	6000
Total Liab	12867	17535	32027	28725	13222
Current Liab	11843	14986	29477	26483	11654
Total Assets	18969	24282	37539	33563	17142
Intang Assets	1678	129	129	129	*
Current Assets	16532	21061	33234	30384	15004
Debtors	9405	15698	23437	20683	8604
Inventory	6287	5044	9222	8900	6352
Turnover	38968	73244	88815	53790	45372
Oper Profit	-399	2093	1847	2476	1724
Interest Paid	702	1741	1003	962	199
Tax Paid	-1264	268	208	504	599
Prf af Int&Tax	183	1807	639	1227	926
Prf att Ord Sh	183	1807	639	1226	926
Btm Line Earn	904	1507	639	1226	907
Dividend Paid	-	272	-	362	300
Mkt Prce(c) YE	55	60	90	115	130
Depreciation	827	943	869	534	457

PER SHARE STATISTICS (CENTS)

Net Asst Val	100.99	111.67	91.23	80.07	65.33
Net Earnings	3.00	29.90	10.60	20.40	15.40
Dividends	-	4.50	-	6.00	5.00
Cash Flow	-4.20	48.08	24.96	36.08	33.03

RATIOS AND OTHER INFORMATION

Mrk Cap(R000)	3323	3625	5438	6948	7800
Current Ratio	1.40	1.41	1.13	1.15	1.29
Quik/Acid Tst	0.87	1.07	0.81	0.81	0.74
A/C Rec T/ovr	4.14	4.67	3.79	2.60	5.27
Tot Ass T/ovr	2.05	3.02	2.37	1.60	2.65
Debt/Ass Rat	0.64	0.64	0.81	0.79	0.69
L T L Tot Ass	0.02	0.03	0.02	0.00	0.01
Debt to Eqity	1.57	2.27	5.36	5.36	3.02
Interest Cover	-0.54	2.19	1.84	2.58	8.66
Oper Prof Mrg	-1.02	2.86	2.08	4.60	3.80
Net Prof Marg%	0.47	2.47	0.72	2.28	2.04
Ret on Assets	-2.00	15.72	4.93	8.02	10.06
Ret on Equity%	2.35	26.28	11.33	24.68	23.62
Price/Earnings	18.33	2.01	8.49	5.64	8.44
Divid Cover	-	6.64	-	3.40	3.08
Divid Yield	-	7.50	-	5.22	3.85
Earning Yield%	5.45	49.83	11.78	17.74	11.85
NAV % Mrk Pr	183.62	186.11	101.36	69.63	50.26
Effec Tax Rate	-	32.10	24.64	5.21	-
Def Interval	-15.19	1.73	1.17	2.56	1.28
Sus Grth Rate	2.35	22.32	11.33	17.39	15.97

SUBSIDIARY & ASSOCIATED COMPANIES

DAGENTI (PTY) LTD
ELECTRICAL DESIGN & CONSTRUCTION (PTY) L
ERENCO POWER (PTY) LTD
ERENCO SOUTH AFRICA (PTY) LTD
FIVES-CAIL TITACO (PTY) LTD
TITACO CONTRACTING (PTY) LTD
TITACO DAVY JOINT VENTURE
TITACO FIRE AND SECURITY (PTY) LTD
TITACO LTD (ISRAEL)
TITACO MINING (PTY) LTD
TITACO PROJECTS (PTY) LTD

INVESTMENTS

None

TOCO HOLDINGS LTD

ABBREVIATION : TOCO

JSE SHORT CODE : TOC

SECTOR : Industrial-Industrial Holding

SHAREHOLDERS

Who Owns Whom's Assessment of the Identity of the Ultimate Controlling Shareholder: MANAGEMENT

SHAREHOLDER	PERCENTAGE 1992	1991
FIRST NAT NOM P/L	20.2	24.8
STD BANK NOM TVL P/L	13.8	11.4
SA MUTUAL	11.4	6.9
CMB NOM P/L	7.4	---
CRAIGENDORAN NOM P/L	7.4	7.3
METROPOLITAN BOARD NOM LTD	4.4	---
RETAN NOM P/L	3.8	10.8
AFRICAN OXYGEN LTD PENS FUND	3.5	4.7
ALTRON GROUP PENS FUND	2.3	---
KF INV HOLDINGS P/L	2.0	2.0
INVESTEC GROUP PENS FUND	1.8	---

ACME DIAMOND NOM P/L	1.6	1.6
KAMINER L	1.3	1.4
BARCLAYS NAT NOM P/L	---	1.1
POLOVIN T P	---	4.4
SANLAM	---	4.5
TOTAL	80.9	80.8

DIRECTORS :
BLUEN RM (Financial Director)
GOODMAN AL (Managing Director),HOBBS CAC
LURIE R ,MAYER E ,TODD MM ,TODD PM (Chairman)
WESEK R

REGISTRATION NUMBER : 87/01894/06

REGISTERED OFFICE
6th Floor, Himont House, 80 Jorissen St
Braamfontein
2001
TEL: 011-873 3690
FAX: 011-873 2925

TRANSFER SECRETARY
Mercantile Registrars Ltd
P O Box 1053, Johannesburg
2000
TEL: 011-333 8181

COMPANY SECRETARY
R M Bluen

NATURE OF BUSINESS
The group is engaged in the following operations: Assembling, marketing & servicing of lifting equip goods hoists & domestic lifts; Manufacture of steel wire rope & slings; Marketing of special steels; Specialised heat treatment & hardening of steels; Furnace brazing; Manufacture & marketing of gaskets, washers & industrial components; Manufacture of vitreous enamel steel panels and automotive refinishing products.

BANKERS :
Standard Bank of SA Ltd

AUDITORS :
Glass-Arenson

FAMILIAR BRAND NAMES
PREMIER CAR CARE,RELIABLE PRESSINGS
VERSATILE GASKETS,VITRALUX

CONTRIBUTION BY ACTIVITY
Lifting Equipment (% Bottomline Earn'gs) (18.0%)
Steel Operations (20.0%)
Gaskets (17.0%)
Building Products (19.0%)
Automotive Refinishing (26.0%)

YEAR END : March

DIVIDEND :Ords 1c

Final	(Ldr)08/06/90	(Pay)29/06/90	Amt(c)6
Interim	(Ldr)30/11/90	(Pay)18/12/90	Amt(c)2.5
Final	(Ldr)22/02/91	(Pay)28/06/91	Amt(c)5
Interim	(Ldr)20/12/91	(Pay)31/01/92	Amt(c)2.75
Final	(Ldr)07/08/92	(Pay)11/09/92	Amt(c)5

NUMBER OF EMPLOYEES : 600

CAPITAL STRUCTURE

	AUTHORISED	ISSUED
Ords 1c	100000000	76184169

FINANCIAL STATISTICS (AT FINANCIAL YEAR END)

(Amts in R'000)	1992 Mar	1991 Mar	1990 Mar	1989 Mar	1988 Mar
Ord S/H Int	69429	58659	47276	37766	32941
Long Trm Loans	17943	18928	6445	2567	1185
Iss Ord Share	74720	72548	65886	62206	62206
Total Liab	55589	52854	31192	20951	12309
Current Liab	37646	33926	24747	18384	11124
Total Assets	98871	86750	54821	39996	29072
Intang Assets	26147	24763	23647	18721	16178
Current Assets	67802	56515	38730	29666	21323
Debtors	26716	24943	14830	11535	8375
Inventory	40976	31475	23842	16566	10266
Turnover	153584	131291	101658	69274	26081
Oper Profit	20855	17571	13414	10723	6027
Interest Paid	2844	3361	1974	989	232
Tax Paid	2207	2596	2060	2116	1561
Prf af Int&Tax	15804	11614	9380	7797	4437
Prf att Ord Sh	14383	12590	10188	7935	4390
Btm Line Earn	14383	12590	10188	7935	4390
Dividend Paid	5791	5275	3953	3110	1680
Mkt Prce(c) YE	110	115	90	48	65
Depreciation	1731	1365	640	1134	508

PER SHARE STATISTICS (CENTS)

Net Asst Val	57.93	46.72	35.86	30.62	26.95
Net Earnings	19.30	18.80	16.00	12.80	11.70
Dividends	7.75	7.50	6.00	5.00	2.70
Cash Flow	22.72	19.07	15.70	13.95	13.91

RATIOS AND OTHER INFORMATION

Mrk Cap(R000)	82192	83430	59297	29859	40434
Current Ratio	1.80	1.67	1.57	1.61	1.92
Quik/Acid Tst	0.71	0.74	0.60	0.71	0.99
A/C Rec T/ovr	5.75	5.26	6.85	6.01	3.11
Tot Ass T/ovr	1.55	1.51	1.85	1.73	0.90
Debt/Ass Rat	0.44	0.48	0.57	0.52	0.41
L T L Tot Ass	0.06	0.09	0.11	0.06	0.03
Debt to Eqity	0.63	0.72	0.66	0.55	0.36
Interest Cover	7.33	5.23	6.80	10.84	26.85
Oper Prof Mrg	13.58	13.38	13.20	15.48	23.11
Net Prof Marg%	9.36	9.59	10.02	11.45	16.83
Ret on Assets	21.09	22.01	25.94	27.60	21.43
Ret on Equity%	20.72	21.46	21.55	21.01	13.33
Price/Earnings	5.70	6.12	5.63	3.75	5.56
Divid Cover	2.49	2.51	2.67	2.56	4.33
Divid Yield	7.05	6.52	6.67	10.42	4.15
Earning Yield%	17.55	16.35	17.78	26.67	18.00
NAV % Mrk Pr	52.66	40.63	39.85	63.78	41.46
Effec Tax Rate	7.86	15.82	17.19	23.88	21.28
Def Interval	1.59	1.92	1.16	0.97	0.87
Sus Grth Rate	12.38	12.47	13.19	12.78	8.23

SUBSIDIARY & ASSOCIATED COMPANIES

A.F.C.O. VALVES (PTY) LTD
ADRO TRADING (PTY) LTD
ALZAC HOLDINGS (PTY) LTD
ALZAC MANAGEMENT & FINANCE CO (PTY) LTD
ALZAC MANAGEMENT (PTY) LTD
BITCON INDUSTRIES (PTY) LTD
BORDA TRADING (PTY) LTD
BRANDT HOLDINGS LTD
BRANDT TRADING (PTY) LTD
DYMET DIMENSIONS (PTY) LTD
EAST RAND CHEMICAL HOLDINGS (PTY) LTD

EDEN GEAR (PTY) LTD
HARBULK INVESTMENT HOLDINGS (PTY) LTD
MICRO GRIND (PTY) LTD
NATIONAL HARDWARE WHOLESALERS (PTY) LTD
PARK PLUS (SA) (PTY) LTD
PETROL ENGINE MANUFACTURERS SA (PTY) LTD
PH HEAT TREATMENT (1987) (PTY) LTD
PH HEAT TREATMENT HOLDINGS (PTY) LTD
POLO-STEEL (1986) (PTY) LTD
PREMIER CHEMICAL INDUSTRIES (PTY) LTD
RELIABLE PRESSINGS (PTY) LTD
RG TWADDLE & PARTNERS (PTY) LTD
ROGER GOURLEY (PTY) LTD
S A INDUSTRIAL SUPPLIES (PTY) LTD
SHORTS LIFTS (PTY) LTD
SPECTRUM INDUSTRIAL LTD
TOCO (RAND) (PTY) LTD
TOCO CAPE (PTY) LTD
TOCO INDUSTRIAL (PTY) LTD
TOCO INDUSTRIAL HOLDINGS (PTY) LTD
TOCO MACHINE TOOLS (PTY) LTD
TOCO MANUFACTURING COMPANY (PTY) LTD
TOCO NATAL (PTY) LTD
TOCO PRINT (PTY) LTD
TRACS ROPE & CHAIN (PTY) LTD
TRICOT EXCLUSIVE (1992) (PTY) LTD
TRICOT EXCLUSIVE (PTY) LTD
VERSATILE GASKET COMPANY (PTY) LTD
VITREX (PTY) LTD
VITREX ARCHITECTURAL SYSTEMS (PTY) LTD
VITREX BOPHUTHATSWANA (PTY) LTD
VITREX CAPE (PTY) LTD
VITREX NATAL (PTY) LTD
VITREX SYSTEMS SWAZILAND (PTY) LTD
WILAN PROJECTS (PTY) LTD

INVESTMENTS

None

TOLLGATE HOLDINGS LTD

ABBREVIATION : TGH

JSE SHORT CODE : TGH

SECTOR : Industrial-Industrial Holding

SHAREHOLDERS

Who Owns Whom's Assessment of the Identity of the Ultimate Controlling Shareholder: INSTITUTIONS

SHAREHOLDER	PERCENTAGE 1992	1991
LONDON CONTROL ACCOUNT	27.4	21.9
STD BANK NOM TVL P/L	19.9	7.4
SAFEGRO NOM P/L	18.6	26.8
SA MUTUAL	7.4	10.7
VOLKSKAS BANK BPK	6.4	9.2
CMB NOM P/L	5.1	6.8
FIRST NAT NOM P/L	1.9	3.1
EDWARDSTONE P/L	1.7	2.4
METROPOLITAN LIFE LTD	1.2	---
MERCANTILE & GEN REINSURANCE CO SA LTD	1.1	---
DUROS SHARE TRUST	---	1.2
TOTAL	90.7	89.4

DIRECTORS :
ASKIN JMC (Chairman), LEWIS IMA , MACKINTOSH GL
MCADAM WJ , TOSE NL

REGISTRATION NUMBER : 05/26633/06

REGISTERED OFFICE
29th Floor, Trust Bank Centre, Adderley Street
Cape Town
8001
TEL: 021-419 0404
FAX: 021-418 1813

TRANSFER SECRETARY
Central Registrars Ltd
P O Box 4844, Johannesburg
2000
TEL: 011-331 0051

COMPANY SECRETARY
N Blackshaw

NATURE OF BUSINESS
The group is involved in the food, distribution, textile, transportation, travel & leisure sectors. Offshore (UK) operations include the distribution of industrial fasteners & wire mesh products.

BANKERS :
Senbank

AUDITORS :
Kessel Feinstein

FAMILIAR BRAND NAMES
BUDGET AUTOLEASE, MOTORVIA, ORYX TOURS
SPRINGBOK ATLAS

CONTRIBUTION BY ACTIVITY
Transportation (% Operating Profit) (32.0%)
Distribution (21.0%)
Food (19.0%)
Textiles (14.0%)
Tourism, Sport & Leisure (7.0%)
Property, Finance & Administration (7.0%)

YEAR END : December

DIVIDEND : Ords 50c

Interim	(Ldr)17/03/89	(Pay)31/03/89	Amt(c)10
Interim	(Ldr)15/09/89	(Pay)30/09/89	Amt(c)15
Interim	(Ldr)20/09/91	(Pay)15/11/91	Amt(c)3
Final	(Ldr)26/04/91	(Pay)05/07/91	Amt(c)10
Final	(Ldr)19/06/92	(Pay)31/07/92	Amt(c)10

NUMBER OF EMPLOYEES : 2500

CAPITAL STRUCTURE

	AUTHORISED	ISSUED
Ords 50c	100000000	40535455
14% Unsec Sub Comp Conv Debs 50c	6388684	6388684
14% "A" Unsec Sub Comp Conv Debs	3987732	3987732

FINANCIAL STATISTICS (AT FINANCIAL YEAR END)

(Amts in R'000)	1991 Dec	1990 Dec	1989 Dec	1988 Jun	1987 Jun
Ord S/H Int	94632	87724	65372	43877	3451

Long Trm Loans	121329	130214	279798	959	3994
Iss Ord Share	40535	28071	18260	13907	1425
Total Liab	526032	476960	750381	25519	5380
Current Liab	404703	346746	470583	24560	1386
Total Assets	473485	455693	720678	69396	8831
Intang Assets	147179	108991	95075	*	*
Current Assets	197812	143709	405110	9226	1711
Debtors	98538	80441	163238	6795	693
Inventory	32833	50371	181811	2431	1018
Turnover	551494	598515	1138474	204217	2858
Oper Profit	43700	13012	70746	17089	116
Interest Paid	35794	47867	63765	2611	310
Tax Paid	1323	3734	10945	7598	164
Prf af Int&Tax	13877	-31425	3470	7630	-358
Prf att Ord Sh	3642	-25308	-1297	7630	-366
Btm Line Earn	-42808	-82927	-11875	37897	-933
Dividend Paid	4896	2807	7327	4902	-
Mkt Prce(c) YE	240	240	900	650	1050
Depreciation	12434	18626	34720	131	51

PER SHARE STATISTICS (CENTS)

Net Asst Val	-129.63	-75.76	-162.67	315.50	242.18
Net Earnings	13.00	-138.60	-8.00	31.70	-25.70
Dividends	13.00	10.00	25.00	20.00	-
Cash Flow	74.30	-11.04	186.32	97.54	-21.96

RATIOS AND OTHER INFORMATION

Mrk Cap(R000)	97284	67370	164340	90396	14963
Current Ratio	0.49	0.41	0.86	0.38	1.23
Quik/Acid Tst	0.41	0.27	0.47	0.28	0.50
A/C Rec T/ovr	5.60	7.44	6.97	30.05	4.12
Tot Ass T/ovr	1.16	1.31	1.58	2.94	0.32
Debt/Ass Rat	1.06	0.96	0.81	0.36	0.59
L T L Tot Ass	0.20	0.20	0.16	0.01	0.44
Debt to Eqity	5.30	5.01	8.94	0.58	1.52
Interest Cover	1.40	0.32	1.22	6.55	0.37
Oper Prof Mrg	7.92	2.17	6.21	8.37	4.06
Net Prof Marg%	0.66	-4.23	-0.11	3.74	-12.81
Ret on Assets	11.17	4.78	10.94	25.71	1.31
Ret on Equity%	3.85	-28.85	-1.98	17.39	-10.61
Price/Earnings	18.46	-1.73	-112.50	20.50	-40.86
Divid Cover	1.00	-13.86	-0.32	1.59	-
Divid Yield	5.42	4.17	2.78	3.08	-
Earning Yield%	5.42	-57.75	-0.89	4.88	-2.45
NAV % Mrk Pr	-54.01	-31.57	-18.07	48.54	23.06
Effec Tax Rate	47.76	-4.14	167.09	19.40	-74.23
Def Interval	14.78	-110.26	13.49	1.98	-3.25
Sus Grth Rate	-1.33	-32.05	-13.19	6.22	-10.61

SUBSIDIARY & ASSOCIATED COMPANIES

ARROWGATE PROPERTY CORP LTD
AUTOVIA (PTY) LTD
BAAKENS HOLDINGS LTD
BARON INSURANCE LTD
BOLAND PASSENGER TRANSPORT LTD
BUROGRO INVESTMENTS (PTY) LTD
CITY TRAMWAYS LTD
DUROS INVESTMENTS LTD
DUROS PROPERTY HOLDINGS (PTY) LTD
EARLGO (PTY) LTD
ENTERCOR HOLDINGS LTD
ENTERCOR LTD
FETLAR FOODS (PTY) LTD
FETLAR HOLDINGS LIMITED
GANTS FOODS (TRANSKEI) (PTY) LTD
GANTS FOODS (VENDA) (PTY) LTD
GOLDEN RIDGE PINEAPPLES (PTY) LTD
GREYHOUND COACH LINES (PTY) LTD
HELDERBERG PASSENGER TRANSPORT FINANCE ((50%)
HORIZON TOURS & SAFARIS (PTY) LTD
HOSKEN CONSOLIDATED INVESTMENTS LTD (25%)
JATON HOLDINGS LTD (UK)
KWAZULU CANNING CO (PTY) LTD
MARINE AUTO & RAIL INSURERS LIMITED
MEERENSTEYN (PTY) LTD
MORLICH LIMITED
MOTORVIA (PTY) LTD
MOTORVIA HOLDINGS LTD
MULTISUPPLIERS (PTY) LTD
ORYX TOURS OF NAMIBIA (PTY) LTD
PEATY MILLS & CO (PTY) LTD (26%)
REINSURANCE CONSULTANTS & INTERMEDIARIES
SECONTA (PTY) LTD
SIX STREET STUDIOS (PTY) LTD
SOUTHERN CAPE PASSENGER TRANSPORT LTD
SPRINGBOK ATLAS SAFARIS (PTY) LTD
SUNMARK GRAIN & SEED (PTY) LTD (50%)
TRAMWAY HOLDINGS LTD
TRAVELCOR (CAPE) (PTY) LTD
ZFP (PTY) LTD

INVESTMENTS

None

TOLUX SA (LUXEMBOURG)

ABBREVIATION : TOLUX

JSE SHORT CODE : TLX

SECTOR : Financial-Investment Trusts

SHAREHOLDERS

Who Owns Whom's Assessment of the Identity of the Ultimate Controlling Shareholder:
ZATTO GROUP (LUXEMBOURG)

SHAREHOLDER	PERCENTAGE 1992	1991
LUXEMBOURG SUSPENSE ACCOUNT	80.5	80.5
SMBL NOM P/L	5.3	5.3
STD BANK NOM TVL P/L	4.1	4.3
SLAWAL NOM P/L	3.6	3.6
SMT LTD	2.1	2.1
TOTAL	95.7	95.9

DIRECTORS :
BODONI J ,BUCKLAND QAF ,HEITER F ,JAVETT MB
KOCH UE DR,SMITH R

REGISTERED OFFICE
2 Boulevard Royal, Luxembourg, L-2953

TRANSFER SECRETARY
Central Registrars Ltd
P O Box 4844, Johannesburg
2000
TEL: 011-331 0051

COMPANY SECRETARY
N/A

NATURE OF BUSINESS
TOLUX SA is an investment holding company which was incorporated on 5 May 1976 in the grand Duchy of Luxembourg and operates as an internationally diversified investment company

BANKERS :
Banque Internationale A Luxembourg SA

AUDITORS :
KPMG Peat Marwick (Luxembourg)

FAMILIAR BRAND NAMES
N/A

CONTRIBUTION BY ACTIVITY
N/A

YEAR END : September

DIVIDEND : (Ldr)23/02/90 (Pay)12/03/90

CAPITAL STRUCTURE

	AUTHORISED	ISSUED
Ords npv (Auth'd incl 62500 Pref	8067728	1817728
Repurchaseable Con Cum Non Part V	62500	12500
Preferred ords (repurchased by co		50000

FINANCIAL STATISTICS (AT FINANCIAL YEAR END)

(Amts in US$)	1991 Sep	1990 Sep	1989 Sep	1988 Sep	1987 Sep
Ord S/H Int	17199	15213	14575	13551	55831
Long Trm Loans	94	19	19	-	-
Iss Ord Share	1818	1818	1818	1818	1818
Total Liab	4341	1239	1353	696	18608
Current Liab	4247	1220	1334	696	18608
Total Assets	21540	16452	15928	14247	74439
Current Assets	21479	16408	15928	14247	66786
Debtors	11891	209	150	1172	2299
Oper Profit	-197	-151	754	1699	2726
Interest Paid	-	-	1	806	1119
Tax Paid	61	59	51	55	105
Prf af Int&Tax	1417	1576	2095	-19713	1835
Prf att Ord Sh	1434	1576	1570	-20238	1835
Btm Line Earn	3222	1690	1570	-20238	1835
Dividend Paid	1161	1052	527	-	1969
Mkt Prce(c) YE	1825	1950	2150	1400	2000

PER SHARE STATISTICS (CENTS)

Net Asst Val	946 04	836 80	801 71	745 38	3071 01
Net Earnings	1 05	55 00	68 00	-2 51	-0 07
Dividends	35 00	29 00	29 00	-	-
Cash Flow	77 94	86 69	86 36	-1113 20	134 58

RATIOS AND OTHER INFORMATION

Mrk Cap(R000)	33179	35451	39087	25452	36360
Current Ratio	5 06	13 45	11 94	20 47	3 59
Quik/Acid Tst	5 06	13 45	11 94	20 47	3 59
Debt/Ass Rat	0 20	0 07	0 08	0 05	0 25
Debt to Eqity	0 25	0 08	0 09	0 05	0 33
Interest Cover	-	-	799 00	-23 39	2 73
Ret on Assets	6 94	9 94	13 48	-132 32	5 48
Ret on Equity%	8 34	10 36	10 77	-149 35	4 38
Price/Earnings	1738 10	35 45	31 62	-557 77	-28571 43
Divid Cover	0 03	1 90	2 34	-	-
Divid Yield	1 92	1 49	1 35	-	-
Earning Yield%	0 06	2 82	3 16	-0 18	0 00
NAV % Mrk Pr	51 84	42 91	37 29	53 24	153 55
Effec Tax Rate	-	-	2 43	6 16	6 53
Def Interval	-	-	-	-	11 20
Sus Grth Rate	1 59	3 44	7 16	-149 35	-0 24

SUBSIDIARY & ASSOCIATED COMPANIES

FINRAND FUND ADVISORY SERVICES SA (50%)
TOLUX BV (NETHERLANDS)
TOLUX INC (PANAMA)
TOLUX NV (NETHERLANDS ANTILLES)

INVESTMENTS

None

TOMKOR LTD

ABBREVIATION : TOMKOR

JSE SHORT CODE : TMK

SECTOR : Financial-Property

SHAREHOLDERS

Who Owns Whom's Assessment of the Identity of the Ultimate Controlling Shareholder:
DIRECTORS

SHAREHOLDER	PERCENTAGE 1992	1991
ACCORD HOLDINGS P/L	---	3 6
ALPIET INV P/L	---	11 6
CHAI SYNDICATE P/L	---	2 0
CITY PROPERTY ADMIN P/L	---	1 2
GALHAR HLDGS	---	2 6
HEVANS HOLDINGS P/L	---	2 8
HEYNS J A J	---	4 0
HUGHOF INV P/L	---	1 1
KEURBOOM INV P/L	---	1 4
KOLLENBERG FAMILY TRUST	---	1 0
LEFKOPAUL P/L	---	5 9
NEDBANK NOM LTD	---	3 1
NEDPERM BANK LTD	---	7 6
POLLACK J	---	1 5
SANLAM	---	1 8
STD BANK NOM TVL P/L	---	1 5
THEMY HOLDINGS P/L	---	2 6
ZETISKY B	---	1 2
ZETISKY L	---	1 7
JEPNICK HOLDINGS P/L	---	1 1
SHARICK HOLDINGS P/L	---	1 1
KOPPING D INV HLDGS CO P/L	---	1 7
LIWESA HOLDINGS P/L	---	1 1
TOTAL	---	63 1

DIRECTORS :
HOLMES MJ ,POLLACK J (Financial Director)
VAN AARDT SM ,VAN DER MERWE-VANCE A
VAN DER WESTHUIZEN AL
WAPNICK A (Chairman & Managing Dir

REGISTRATION NUMBER : 69/02462/06

REGISTERED OFFICE
Downies Building, 373 Proes Street
Pretoria
0001

TEL: 012-26 8811
FAX: 012-325 2209

TRANSFER SECRETARY
Investment Registrars (Pty) Ltd
P O Box 9167, Johannesburg
2000
TEL: 011-725 6004

COMPANY SECRETARY
City Property Administration (Pty) Ltd

NATURE OF BUSINESS
An investment holding company deriving income from dividends, ineterest & management fees generated by its subsidiaries which own commercial, business & industrial properties, situated mainly in PTA.

BANKERS :
Nedcor Bank Ltd

AUDITORS :
Deloitte Pim Goldby

FAMILIAR BRAND NAMES
N/A

CONTRIBUTION BY ACTIVITY
N/A

YEAR END : February

DIVIDEND :Ords 50c

Interim No 27	(Ldr)03/11/89	(Pay)07/12/89	Amt(c)8
Final No 28	(Ldr)01/06/90	(Pay)26/06/90	Amt(c)10
Interim No 29	(Ldr)16/11/90	(Pay)14/12/90	Amt(c)7
Final No 30	(Ldr)10/05/91	(Pay)07/06/91	Amt(c)7
Interim No 31	(Ldr)01/11/91	(Pay)10/12/91	Amt(c)7
Final No 32	(Ldr)16/04/92	(Pay)01/06/92	Amt(c)12
Interim No 33	(Ldr)30/10/92	(Pay)07/12/92	Amt(c)10

NUMBER OF EMPLOYEES : 70

CAPITAL STRUCTURE

	AUTHORISED	ISSUED
Ords 50c	12000000	10607577

FINANCIAL STATISTICS (AT FINANCIAL YEAR END)

(Amts in R'000)	1992 Feb	1991 Feb	1990 Feb	1989 Feb	1988 Feb
Ord S/H Int	95555	55359	111191	81876	81098
Long Trm Loans	58239	55432	116618	83728	60778
Iss Ord Share	10608	10608	10608	8945	8926
Total Liab	67555	59052	125509	100686	68871
Current Liab	9316	3620	8891	16958	8093
Total Assets	163110	114411	236700	182562	149969
Current Assets	1498	1174	4023	3185	3310
Debtors	1358	1072	3327	3015	2448
Turnover	18208	24889	27448	20422	16883
Oper Profit	14060	18924	21686	17202	13484
Interest Paid	11746	17438	18099	10567	7426
Tax Paid	912	637	1870	3273	2995
Prf af Int&Tax	2108	1506	1901	3485	3160
Prf att Ord Sh	2108	1506	1901	3486	3160
Btm Line Earn	2212	13376	2661	3745	3329
Dividend Paid	2016	69208	1909	3041	2856
Mkt Prce(c) YE	285	205	370	380	380
Depreciation	99	119	64	27	29

PER SHARE STATISTICS (CENTS)

Net Asst Val	900.78	521.86	1048.18	915.33	908.56
Net Earnings	19.90	14.20	18.40	39.00	35.40
Dividends	19.00	14.00	18.00	34.00	32.00
Cash Flow	21.29	14.28	17.22	40.17	34.82

RATIOS AND OTHER INFORMATION

Mrk Cap(R000)	30233	21746	39250	33991	33919
Current Ratio	0.16	0.32	0.45	0.19	0.41
Quik/Acid Tst	0.16	0.32	0.45	0.19	0.41
A/C Rec T/ovr	13.41	23.22	8.25	6.77	6.90
Tot Ass T/ovr	0.11	0.22	0.12	0.11	0.11
Debt/Ass Rat	0.41	0.51	0.53	0.55	0.46
L T L Tot Ass	0.36	0.48	0.49	0.46	0.40
Debt to Eqity	0.70	1.06	1.13	1.22	0.85
Interest Cover	1.20	1.09	1.20	1.63	1.82
Oper Prof Mrg	77.22	76.03	79.01	84.23	79.87
Net Prof Marg%	11.58	6.05	6.93	17.07	18.72
Ret on Assets	9.05	17.11	9.24	9.49	9.06
Ret on Equity%	2.21	2.72	1.71	4.26	3.90
Price/Earnings	14.32	14.44	20.11	9.74	10.73
Divid Cover	1.05	1.01	1.02	1.15	1.11
Divid Yield	6.67	6.83	4.86	8.95	8.42
Earning Yield%	6.98	6.93	4.97	10.26	9.32
NAV % Mrk Pr	316.06	254.57	283.29	240.88	239.09
Effec Tax Rate	28.75	34.63	49.15	47.31	50.05
Def Interval	25.21	35.56	63.45	23.51	17.66
Sus Grth Rate	0.10	-122.30	-0.01	0.54	0.37

SUBSIDIARY & ASSOCIATED COMPANIES

BARTLUCIA INVESTMENTS SHAREBLOCK (PTY) L
BREEPLEIN PROPERTIES (PTY) LTD
BROOKLYN MALL PROPERTIES (PTY) LTD
CARINE PROPERTIES SHARE BLOCK (PTY) LTD
DU PROES SHARE BLOCK (PTY) LTD
DUSKU INVESTMENTS SHAREBLOCK (PTY) LTD
ELARDUSPARK SHOPPING CENTRE SHARE BLOCK
ELLENBY EIENDOMME (PTY) LTD
ERF ONE ONE EIGHT BELLEVUE (PTY) LTD
ETM BELEGGINGS (PTY) LTD
FILKEM HOUSE SHARE BLOCK (PTY) LTD
GRAMIK (PTY) LTD
HACKLU ENTERPRISES SHARE BLOCK (PTY) LTD
HERACLE SHARE BLOCK (PTY) LTD
LANDKIRK PROPERTIES (PTY) LTD
LENTICULAR (PTY) LTD
LPA BELEGGINGS SHARE BLOCK (PTY) LTD
LYNNDEALE'S PROPERTIES (PTY) LTD
MIDDEL STREET SHARE BLOCK (PTY) LTD
OORSKOT BELEGGINGS (PTY) LTD
PODAR SHARE BLOCK (PTY) LTD
POTPOES (PTY) LTD
PRESMOOI (PTY) LTD
PRETPOT (PTY) LTD
PRINSMAN PROPERTIES SHARE BLOCK (PTY) LT
PRIZE INVESTMENTS SHARE BLOCK (PTY) LTD
REGRAM INVESTMENTS (PTY) LTD
REZMEP INVESTMENTS SHARE BLOCK (PTY) LTD
RICHWAY INVESTMENTS SHARE BLOCK (PTY) LT
ROVON INVESTMENTS SHARE BLOCK (PTY) LTD
RUMPRO INVESTMENTS SHAREBLOCK (PTY) LTD
SINEL INVESTMENTS (PTY) LTD
TOMROSS PROPERTIES (PTY) LTD
TOMSYNDICATIONS (PTY) LTD
TOMZEIL SHARE BLOCK (PTY) LTD
WILBROWN INVESTMENTS (PTY) LTD

INVESTMENTS

HOLTA HOLDINGS (PTY) LTD (2 SH)
KERLIN (PTY) LTD (1 SH)
PAREDZ INVESTMENTS (PTY) LTD (170 SH)
PINSLUB PROPERTIES (PTY) LTD (50 SH)
TOMSUNDER (PTY) LTD (500 SH)

TONGAAT-HULETT GROUP LTD

ABBREVIATION : TONGAAT

JSE SHORT CODE : TNT

SECTOR : Industrial-Sugar

SHAREHOLDERS

Who Owns Whom's Assessment of the Identity of the Ultimate Controlling Shareholder:
ANGLO AMERICAN VIA AMIC

SHAREHOLDER	PERCENTAGE 1992	1991
RESIDENT NOM LTD	26.0	5.6
CMB NOM P/L	13.5	---
LODESTONE HLDGS LTD	11.0	11.0
EIGHTY ONE MAIN STREET NOM LTD	5.2	3.9
STD BANK NOM TVL P/L	4.7	3.5
SA MUTUAL	3.8	2.4
TAURUS NOM LTD	2.7	2.7
METAL IND GROUP PENS FUND	2.7	3.0
ENGINEERING INDUSTRIES PENS FUND	2.7	3.0
DIDO NOM LTD	1.9	1.9
TONGAAT-HULETT EMPLOYEES SHARE TRUST	1.8	2.5
FERMAIN NOM LTD	1.7	1.7
TONGAAT-HULETT PENS FUND	1.2	1.2
ESCOM PENS & PROV FUND	---	1.3
MENTEITH INV LTD	---	1.4
ANGLO AMERICAN IND CORP LTD	---	20.3
SANLAM	---	10.9
TOTAL	78.9	76.2

DIRECTORS :
ARMSTRONG RSR ,BOYD L ,BRADLEY E LE R MRS
BULETT BE ,CLEASBY TG DR,DOUGHERTY SM ,DUNCAN NE
GARNER ESC (Financial Director),HANKINSON AD
KING MW ,MANN TG (Personnel Director)
RIDGWAY RK ,SAUNDERS CJ (Chairman),SAUNDERS SJ
SAVAGE CML (Managing Director),STEVENS RHJ
STRACHAN DW ,TRAHAR AJ ,VANDER POL C D

REGISTRATION NUMBER : 02/00610/06

REGISTERED OFFICE
Amanzimnyama Hill, Tongaat
Natal
4400
TEL: 0322-2 1000
FAX: 0322-21 094

TRANSFER SECRETARY
Consolidated Share Registrars Ltd
P O Box 61051, Marshalltown
2107
TEL: 011-492 1620

COMPANY SECRETARY
R B A Cruikshank

NATURE OF BUSINESS
The activities of the group are as follows:
Sugar milling, refining & farming; Production of clay face, paving & plaster bricks & blocks, tiles & concrete bricks; Food processing, producing mushrooms, edible oils, animal feeds, maize meal, dehydrated foodstuffs & eggs, cotton ginning, industrial & commercial catering; Manufacture of aluminium products; Textile mills which produce knitting & weaving yarns & fabrics; Production of speciality starches & syrups & maizegerm.

BANKERS :
Standard Bank of SA Ltd
First National Bank of SA Ltd
Nedperm Bank Ltd

AUDITORS :
Deloitte Pim Goldby

FAMILIAR BRAND NAMES
BLUEBIRD,BRICK 'N TILE,CASHMART,COMET
COROBRIK,COROKROMA,COROWALL
COTONA (COOKING OIL),DE NIM
DENNY (MUSHROOMS),EROS (COOKING OIL)
FARM SUNRISE,FUNA,GABLE,HELIOS (COOKING OIL)
HULETT FOIL,HULETTS,INKANYEZI,INYONI
LILYWHITE,MARIGOLD,MAXI BRIK
MOONLIGHT (MUSHROOMS),SILVERSTREAM,TODAY
TONGAATI,VICTRINE GHEE,VOERMOL,WHITEHEADS
WINELANDS

CONTRIBUTION BY ACTIVITY
Foods (% sales) (26.9%)
Sugar (27.6%)
Aluminium (19.4%)
Building materials (10.3%)
Textiles (7.4%)
Starch & sweeteners (8.4%)

YEAR END : March

DIVIDEND : Ords R1

Interim No 125	(Ldr)12/01/90	(Pay)12/02/90	Amt(c)26
Final No 126	(Ldr)20/07/90	(Pay)13/08/90	Amt(c)53
Interim No 127	(Ldr)11/01/91	(Pay)11/02/91	Amt(c)23
Final No 128	(Ldr)19/07/91	(Pay)12/08/91	Amt(c)50
Interim No 129	(Ldr)10/01/92	(Pay)10/02/92	Amt(c)23
Final No 130	(Ldr)17/07/92	(Pay)10/08/92	Amt(c)50
Interim No 131	(Ldr)15/01/93	(Pay)15/02/93	Amt(c)23

NUMBER OF EMPLOYEES : 31881

CAPITAL STRUCTURE

	AUTHORISED	ISSUED
Ords R1	80000000	74843979
Var Rate Red Cum Prefs R2	7000000	0
6,5% Red Cum Prefs R1	5500000	0

FINANCIAL STATISTICS (AT FINANCIAL YEAR END)

(Amts in R'000)	1992 Mar	1991 Mar	1990 Mar	1989 Mar	1988 Mar
Ord S/H Int	1730495	1691830	1674210	1452253	873362
Long Trm Loans	455494	534085	454010	368239	367857
Iss Ord Share	74844	74844	74844	73462	73463
Total Liab	1118342	1164503	1045087	893162	808670
Current Liab	662848	630418	591077	524923	440813
Total Assets	2848837	2856333	2641758	2345415	1682032
Intang Assets	*	*	77539	*	*
Current Assets	1118795	1084486	990751	827285	683794
Debtors	602680	557583	494322	396726	355651
Inventory	488164	521284	493395	421371	319802

Turnover	3968297	3798415	3708809	3157703	2622133
Oper Profit	284124	321228	377438	322183	240887
Interest Paid	112533	115517	98971	69455	51371
Tax Paid	26327	68697	102967	94683	64686
Prf af Int&Tax	151239	143739	181022	164126	124830
Prf att Ord Sh	150231	142681	177050	141845	119193
Btm Line Earn	96334	149795	183671	144051	120066
Dividend Paid	54636	54636	59127	52158	39670
Mkt Prce(c) YE	2450	1575	1790	1600	1010
Depreciation	76812	67320	61586	58572	54045

PER SHARE STATISTICS (CENTS)

Net Asst Val	2312.14	2260.48	2133.33	1976.88	1188.85
Net Earnings	200.70	190.60	236.60	214.30	162.30
Dividends	73.00	73.00	79.00	71.00	54.00
Cash Flow	312.48	337.47	414.96	349.85	275.77

RATIOS AND OTHER INFORMATION

Mrk Cap(R000)	1833678	1178793	1339708	1175392	741976
Current Ratio	1.69	1.72	1.68	1.58	1.55
Quik/Acid Tst	0.95	0.89	0.84	0.77	0.83
A/C Rec T/ovr	6.58	6.81	7.50	7.96	7.37
Tot Ass T/ovr	1.39	1.33	1.40	1.35	1.56
Debt/Ass Rat	0.30	0.32	0.31	0.31	0.41
L T L Tot Ass	0.07	0.10	0.09	0.08	0.14
Debt to Eqity	0.50	0.53	0.50	0.50	0.78
Interest Cover	2.58	2.84	3.87	4.73	4.69
Oper Prof Mrg	7.16	8.46	10.18	10.20	9.19
Net Prof Marg%	3.79	3.76	4.77	4.49	4.55
Ret on Assets	10.18	11.48	14.50	14.00	14.32
Ret on Equity%	8.68	8.43	10.58	9.77	13.65
Price/Earnings	12.21	8.26	7.57	7.47	6.22
Divid Cover	2.75	2.61	2.99	3.02	3.01
Divid Yield	2.98	4.63	4.41	4.44	5.35
Earning Yield%	8.19	12.10	13.22	13.39	16.07
NAV % Mrk Pr	94.37	143.52	119.18	123.55	117.71
Effec Tax Rate	26.22	11.77	11.82	21.37	18.76
Def Interval	1.11	1.49	1.05	0.99	1.50
Sus Grth Rate	5.52	5.20	7.04	6.18	9.11

SUBSIDIARY & ASSOCIATED COMPANIES

AFRICAN PRODUCTS (PTY) LTD
ALUMINIUM CITY (PTY) LTD
AMPLIFORM SA (PTY) LTD
BDU VENTURES (PTY) LTD
BRICKOR PRECAST (EASTERN TVL) (PTY) LTD
BRICKOR PRECAST (PTY) LTD (50,5%)
BROCKLEY QUARRIES LTD
CANE CARRIERS (PTY) LTD
CHIRON PROPERTIES (PTY) LTD
COROBRICK (PTY) LTD
COROBRIK DISTRIBUTION (PTY) LTD
COROBRIK FREE STATE (PTY) LTD
COROBRIK NATAL (PTY) LTD
COROBRIK TRANSVAAL (PTY) LTD
COROBRIK WESTERN CAPE (PTY) LTD
COROCRETE (PTY) LTD
DAVID WHITEHEAD & SONS (SA) (PTY) LTD
FARMER GILES (PTY) LTD
HEBOX TEXTILES (PTY) LTD - DORMANT S
HULETT ALUMINIUM (PTY) LTD
HULETT ALUMINIUM METALS (PTY) LTD
HULETT ALUMINIUM PROFILES (PTY) LTD
HULETT ALUMINIUM ROLLED PRODUCTS (PTY) L
HULETT ALUMINIUM TRANSPORT SERVICES (PTY
HULETT REFINERIES LTD
HULSAKANE LTD
JOHN J KIRKNESS (PTY) LTD
KHULANI CATTERING SERVICES (PTY) LTD
KUMLUCKY FARM (PTY) LTD
KWA ZULU EIER PRODUSENTE (PTY) LTD
MECHANISED TRUCK LOADING (PTY) LTD
MORELAND ESTATES LTD
MORELAND TOWNSHIPS (PTY) LTD
NATIONAL BASE METALS (PTY) LTD
NOVA MILLS (PTY) LTD
OK BAZAARS (CISKEI) LTD
OK BAZAARS (LESOTHO) (PTY) LTD
OK BAZAARS (MITCHELLS PLAIN) LTD
OK BAZAARS (VENDA) LTD
OK KWAZULU LTD
OK ORLANDO (PTY) LTD
PRILLA MILLS (PTY) LTD
ROODEPOORT BRICK WORKS (PTY) LTD
SCOTTS PROPERTIES LTD
SELLAIR (PTY) LTD
SUKUMANI DEVELOPMENT CO (PTY) LTD
SUKUMANI VEHICLES (PTY) LTD
SUPERVISION FOOD SERVICES (BOPHUTHATSWAN
SUPERVISION FOOD SERVICES (CISKEI) (PTY)
SUPERVISION FOOD SERVICES (GAZANKULU) (P
SUPERVISION FOOD SERVICES (LEBOWA) (PTY)
SUPERVISION FOOD SERVICES (QWA QWA) (PTY
SUPERVISION FOOD SERVICES (SWA) (PTY) LT
SUPERVISION FOOD SERVICES (TRANSKEI) (PT
SUPERVISION FOOD SERVICES KANGWANE (PTY)
SWAZILAND COTONA COTTON GINNING CO LTD
T-H SECURITY (PTY) LTD
TEXSTYLE INTERNATIONAL LTD
THE NATAL ESTATES LTD
TM INSURANCE BROKERS (PTY) LTD
TONGAAT EMPLOYEES TRADING COMPANY LTD
TONGAAT FOODS (PTY) LTD
TONGAAT FOODS MARKETING CO LTD
TONGAAT GROUP LTD (THE)
TONGAAT OIL & FOOD PRODUCTS (NATAL) LTD
TONGAAT PROPERTIES (PTY) LTD
TONGAAT TEXTILES (PTY) LTD
TONGAAT-HULETT MANAGEMENT SERVICES (PTY)
TONGAAT-HULETT PROPERTIES LTD
TONGAAT-HULETT SUGAR LTD
TONGAAT-HULETT SUGAR MILLS & ESTATES (PT
WATERFORD SPAWN LABORATORY (PTY) LTD
ZIMBALI DEVELOPMENT CO (PTY) LTD (50%)

INVESTMENTS

ALUSAF (PTY) LTD
SA SUGAR DISTRIBUTORS (PTY) LTD (648 SH)
SMALL BUSINESS DEVELOPMENT CORP LTD (1300 SH)

TOWLES, EDGAR JACOBS LTD

ABBREVIATION : T-E-J

JSE SHORT CODE : TEJ

SECTOR : Industrial-Clothing, Footwear & Textiles

SHAREHOLDERS

Who Owns Whom's Assessment of the Identity of the Ultimate Controlling Shareholder:
DIRECTORS CONTROL 31,48% (JUNE 1991)

SHAREHOLDER	PERCENTAGE 1992	1991

JACOBS R M	15.9	15.9
WHITECROFT INV P/L	14.4	14.4
BOLLAND M U	8.3	8.3
MONDI TEXTIL GMBH	7.5	7.5
BARNETT-HARRIS R C A	7.5	7.5
T E J SHARE PURCHASE TRUST	4.2	15.0
OWEN B A	3.8	---
MED INV P/L	3.0	2.7
ANDERSON I C	2.0	---
JACOBS K H M	2.0	2.0
SUSMAN D R	1.9	1.9
ORTON E W	1.7	---
GUSH R P	1.4	1.1
ANNEMORE INV P/L	1.1	1.1
HENKEL A W	1.0	---
TOTAL	75.8	77.4

DIRECTORS :
ANDERSON IC (Deputy Chairman),BALL AC
JACOBS KHM ,JACOBS RM (Chairman),ORTON EW
OWEN BA (Managing Director),WALTON CL

REGISTRATION NUMBER : 51/04039/06

REGISTERED OFFICE
327 Main Road, Steenberg
Cape Town
7945
TEL: 021-72 1132
FAX: 021-701 1210

TRANSFER SECRETARY
Mercantile Registrars Ltd
P O Box 1053, Johannesburg
2000
TEL: 011-333 8181

COMPANY SECRETARY
E W Orton

NATURE OF BUSINESS
The group manufactures and markets knitwear and other outerwear under the trade names, TEJ,Tejmen, Copperfield, Mondi, Pate and Portfolio.It also markets clothing and accessories from the imported ranges of Bruestle, Mondi, Patrizia and Slendor and manufactures for two European houses and Woolworths and other retail groups under their brand names.

BANKERS :
First National Bank of SA Ltd
Trust Bank of Africa Ltd
Standard Bank of SA Ltd

AUDITORS :
Deloitte Pim Goldby

FAMILIAR BRAND NAMES
BRAEMAR,BRUESTLE,COPPERFIELD
LAKESIDE KNITWEAR,MONDI,PATE,PATRIZIA
PORTARA,PORTFOLIO,PRINGLE,SLENDOR,TEJ
TEJ BOUTIQUE,TEJMEN

CONTRIBUTION BY ACTIVITY
N/A

YEAR END : June

NUMBER OF EMPLOYEES : 784

CAPITAL STRUCTURE

	AUTHORISED	ISSUED
Ords 50c	5600000	2951060
Var Rate Comp Conv Prefs 50c	2000000	1930600

FINANCIAL STATISTICS (AT FINANCIAL YEAR END)

(Amts in R'000)	1991 Jun	1990 Jun	1989 Jun	1988 Jun	1987 Jun
Ord S/H Int	7759	7625	6275	6627	6019
Long Trm Loans	6998	7797	3124	2537	1541
Iss Ord Share	2951	2758	2758	2758	2508
Total Liab	15163	18384	19399	12618	7545
Current Liab	8165	10587	16275	10081	6004
Total Assets	22596	25637	25255	19245	13564
Intang Assets	326	372	419	*	*
Current Assets	14447	17129	18234	12880	8631
Debtors	7931	9304	9460	5764	2976
Inventory	6419	7601	8758	7092	5454
Turnover	35925	38138	32301	22992	17633
Oper Profit	3647	2401	1103	1428	1986
Interest Paid	2259	2864	2082	941	554
Tax Paid	-	-	-167	167	1
Prf af Int&Tax	1388	-463	-801	320	1431
Prf att Ord Sh	1148	-550	-801	320	1431
Btm Line Earn	60	-550	161	320	1261
Dividend Paid	-	-	-	-	125
Mkt Prce(c) YE	50	60	70	115	170
Depreciation	819	797	628	400	185

PER SHARE STATISTICS (CENTS)

Net Asst Val	251.88	262.98	212.33	240.28	239.99
Net Earnings	38.90	-19.90	-29.00	11.60	57.10
Dividends	-	-	-	-	5.00
Cash Flow	66.66	8.96	-12.33	32.16	64.43

RATIOS AND OTHER INFORMATION

Mrk Cap(R000)	1476	1655	1931	3172	4264
Current Ratio	1.77	1.62	1.12	1.28	1.44
Quik/Acid Tst	0.98	0.90	0.58	0.57	0.53
A/C Rec T/ovr	4.53	4.10	3.41	3.99	5.93
Tot Ass T/ovr	1.59	1.49	1.28	1.19	1.30
Debt/Ass Rat	0.59	0.65	0.77	0.65	0.56
L T L Tot Ass	0.23	0.23	0.12	0.12	0.11
Debt to Eqity	1.72	2.17	3.09	1.88	1.25
Interest Cover	1.61	0.84	0.53	1.52	3.58
Oper Prof Mrg	10.15	6.30	3.41	6.21	11.26
Net Prof Marg%	3.20	-1.44	-2.48	1.39	8.12
Ret on Assets	16.14	9.37	4.41	7.42	14.64
Ret on Equity%	14.80	-7.21	-12.76	4.83	23.77
Price/Earnings	1.29	-3.02	-2.41	9.91	2.98
Divid Cover	-	-	-	-	11.42
Divid Yield	-	-	-	-	2.94
Earning Yield%	77.80	-33.17	-41.43	10.09	33.59
NAV % Mrk Pr	503.76	438.30	303.33	208.94	141.17
Effec Tax Rate	-	-	-	-	0.07
Def Interval	3.71	45.88	-34.01	7.99	2.53
Sus Grth Rate	14.80	-7.21	-12.76	4.83	21.70

SUBSIDIARY & ASSOCIATED COMPANIES

MONDI KNITWEAR (PTY) LTD
TEJ MANUFACTURING LTD
TEJ SALES (SA) LTD

INVESTMENTS

None

TOYOTA SA LTD

ABBREVIATION : TOYOTA

JSE SHORT CODE : TOY

SECTOR : Industrial-Motor

SHAREHOLDERS

Who Owns Whom's Assessment of the Identity of the Ultimate Controlling Shareholder:
WESCO INVESTMENTS

SHAREHOLDER	PERCENTAGE 1992	1991
WESCO INV LTD	50 0	50 0
STD BANK NOM TVL P/L	20 2	27 8
EIGHTY ONE MAIN STREET NOM LTD	7 5	7 5
FIRST NAT NOM P/L	1 9	2 8
ABSA NOM P/L	1 0	-
NEDBANK NOM LTD		2 5
TOTAL	89 6	90 5

DIRECTORS :
ADCOCK CS ,BRADLEY E LE R MS (Vice Chairman)
BROADLEY RS ,NKABINDE AC PROF,PRETORIUS SG
RETIEF PF ,ROBINSON PR (Financial Director)
WESSELS AJJ (Executive Chairman

REGISTRATION NUMBER : 05/20429/06

REGISTERED OFFICE
Toyota Building, Stand One, Wesco Park
Sandton
2199
TEL 011-809 9111

TRANSFER SECRETARY
Central Registrars Ltd
P O Box 4844, Johannesburg
2000
TEL 011-331 0051

COMPANY SECRETARY
C P Marais

NATURE OF BUSINESS
Toyota SA holds the franchise for the importation, assembly, manufacture & distribution of Toyota & Hino motor vehicles in SA.

BANKERS :
Standard Bank of SA Ltd, Volkskas Ltd
Nedperm Bank Ltd
First National Bank of SA Ltd, Bankorp Ltd

AUDITORS :
N/A

FAMILIAR BRAND NAMES
COROLLA,CRESSIDA,DYNA,HI-ACE,HILUX,STOUT,TUV

CONTRIBUTION BY ACTIVITY
Light Commercial Vehicles (% market) (34 2%)
Heavy Commercial Vehicles (% market) (23 7%)
Passenger Cars (% market) (26 1%)

YEAR END · December

DIVIDEND :Ords 1,67c

Interim	(Ldr)11/10/91	(Pay)25/10/91	Amt(c)19
Final	(Ldr)20/03/92	(Pay)30/04/92	Amt(c)28 5

NUMBER OF EMPLOYEES : 7148

CAPITAL STRUCTURE

	AUTHORISED	ISSUED
Ords 1,67c	68664000	40668000

FINANCIAL STATISTICS (AT FINANCIAL YEAR END)

(Amts in R'000)	1991 Dec	1990 Dec	1989 Dec	1988 Dec	1987 Dec
Ord S/H Int	918379	818633	610443	534515	421118
Long Trm Loans	278475	145538	105645	118010	79870
Iss Ord Share	40668	40668	40668	40668	40668
Total Liab	737019	530567	523223	364389	254571
Current Liab	458544	385029	417578	246379	174701
Total Assets	1655398	1349200	1133666	898904	675689
Current Assets	839643	655449	587662	460943	318545
Debtors	367595	275509	277534	198849	151609
Inventory	467350	377580	308407	258395	163095
Turnover	3466947	3117937	2920180	2511747	1915082
Oper Profit	243827	246246	201398	200401	163192
Interest Paid	57596	95936	46276	89980	57510
Tax Paid	138895	138796	89563	64838	22733
Prf af Int&Tax	123502	113555	86570	88234	82949
Prf att Ord Sh	120888	112386	87375	89171	83627
Btm Line Earn	120888	112386	87375	89171	83627
Dividend Paid	19317	19317	16674	14640	12200
Mkt Prce(c) YE	2400	1100	850	750	900
Depreciation	105688	98032	91629	66962	61440

PER SHARE STATISTICS (CENTS)

Net Asst Val	2258 23	2012 97	1501 04	1314 34	1035 50
Net Earnings	297 30	276 40	214 90	165 80	209 80
Dividends	47 50	47 50	41 00	36 00	30 00
Cash Flow	559 31	552 67	458 09	394 04	334 97

RATIOS AND OTHER INFORMATION

Mrk Cap(R000)	976032	447348	345678	305010	366012
Current Ratio	1 83	1 70	1 41	1 87	1 82
Quik/Acid Tst	0 81	0 72	0 67	0 82	0 89
A/C Rec T/ovr	9 43	11 32	10 52	12 63	12 63
Tot Ass T/ovr	2 09	2 3'	2 58	2 79	2 83
Debt/Ass Rat	0 40	0 32	0 40	0 40	0 37
L T L Tot Ass	0 12	0 04	0 03	0 12	0 11
Debt to Eqity	0 72	0 53	0 74	0 66	0 59
Interest Cover	4 24	2 64	4 45	2 30	2 84
Oper Prof Mrg	7 03	7 90	6 90	7 98	8 52
Net Prof Marg%	3 49	3 60	2 99	3 55	4 37
Ret on Assets	19 34	25 83	19 69	27 14	24 25
Ret on Equity%	13 16	13 73	14 31	16 68	19 86
Price/Earnings	8 07	3 98	3 96	4 52	4 29
Divid Cover	6 26	5 82	5 24	4 61	6 99
Divid Yield	1 98	4 32	4 82	4 80	3 33
Earning Yield%	12 39	25 13	25 28	22 11	23 31
NAV % Mrk Pr	94 09	183 00	176 59	175 25	115 06
Effec Tax Rate	52 86	49 09	47 47	7 12	1 89
Def Interval	1 05	0 35	0 74	0 83	0 60
Sus Grth Rate	11 06	11 37	11 58	13 94	16 96

SUBSIDIARY & ASSOCIATED COMPANIES

AMSA PARTS AND ACCESSORIES (PTY) LTD
AUTO CREDIT AID INVESTMENTS (PTY) LTD
AUTOMOBILE DISTRIBUTION & MANUFACTURING (40%)
BETA INVESTMENTS (PTY) LTD (BOTSWANA)
COMPASS MOTOR INDUSTRIES (PTY) LTD
GAMMA MOTORS LTD

JATI INVESTMENTS (PTY) LTD
LIPRON INDUSTRIAL (PTY) LTD
MACWES PROPERTIES (PTY) LTD
MOTOR ASSEMBLIES PROPERTIES (PTY) LTD
PROSPECTON HIRE (PTY) LTD
ROWEN PROPERTIES (S.A.) (PTY) LTD
TOYOTA PROPERTIES LTD
TOYOTA S.A. MANUFACTURING LTD
TOYOTA SA MOTORS (PTY) LTD
TSA INVESTMENT COMPANY LTD (ISLAND OF GU
TSA MANAGEMENT CO LIMITED
TSA PROCUREMENT LTD
TSM STAMPING DIVISION LTD
TWO TWO EIGHT EIGHT PROSPECTON INDUSTRIA

INVESTMENTS

None

TPN INVESTMENTS LTD

ABBREVIATION : TPN

JSE SHORT CODE : TPN

SECTOR : Industrial-Engineering

SHAREHOLDERS

Who Owns Whom's Assessment of the Identity of the Ultimate Controlling Shareholder: CERRAI FAMILY

SHAREHOLDER	PERCENTAGE 1992	1991
FIRST NAT NOM P/L	34.5	34.5
CERRAI L TRUST	17.0	17.0
CERRAI E TRUST	16.3	16.3
CLARPAT P/L	10.8	10.8
CERRAI E	9.1	2.0
CERRAI I	2.0	2.0
CERRAI L	2.0	2.0
CERRAI S	2.0	2.0
MERCABANK BPK	1.8	1.8
STOCKSHARE NOM P/L	1.3	1.3
CERRAI P	---	7.1
TOTAL	96.9	96.9

DIRECTORS :
CERRAI E ,CERRAI I ,CERRAI L (Chairman)
CERRAI P ,CERRAI S

REGISTRATION NUMBER : 05/23536/06

REGISTERED OFFICE
1st Floor, 108 Fox Street
Johannesburg
2001
TEL: 011-868 1231
FAX: 011-900 1532

TRANSFER SECRETARY
Gold Equity Registrars (Pty) Ltd
P O Box 62185, Marshalltown
2107
TEL: 011-834 5623

COMPANY SECRETARY
P Ambrosini

NATURE OF BUSINESS
Holding company whose subsidiaries manufacture and distribute industrial fasteners.

BANKERS :
Nedcor Bank Ltd

AUDITORS :
Clarke & Patterson

FAMILIAR BRAND NAMES
N/A

CONTRIBUTION BY ACTIVITY
N/A

YEAR END : June

DIVIDEND : Ords no par value

Final No 36	(Ldr)05/10/90	(Pay)15/10/90	Amt(c)2
Final No 37	(Ldr)18/10/91	(Pay)28/10/91	Amt(c)2
Final No 38	(Ldr)16/10/92	(Pay)26/10/92	Amt(c)4

NUMBER OF EMPLOYEES : 273

CAPITAL STRUCTURE

	AUTHORISED	ISSUED
Ords no par value	100000000	50000000
15% Red Cum Prefs R1	27000	27000

FINANCIAL STATISTICS (AT FINANCIAL YEAR END)

(Amts in R'000)	1992 Jun	1991 Jun	1990 Jun	1989 Jun	1988 Jun
Ord S/H Int	22074	21960	19617	17668	15019
Long Trm Loans	5399	6224	6716	5467	2957
Iss Ord Share	50000	50000	50000	50000	50000
Total Liab	10345	10911	11578	14127	9203
Current Liab	4946	4687	4862	8660	6246
Total Assets	32419	32871	31195	31795	24222
Current Assets	21265	20577	19238	19569	14164
Debtors	7332	11376	9262	7616	4573
Inventory	7895	8328	8315	11945	8192
Oper Profit	2703	4279	6375	7125	5261
Interest Paid	354	407	196	111	13
Tax Paid	783	863	2732	3088	2682
Prf af Int&Tax	2114	3345	3703	4154	2835
Prf att Ord Sh	2114	3343	3699	4150	2831
Btm Line Earn	2114	3343	3699	4150	2831
Dividend Paid	2000	1000	1750	1500	1250
Mkt Prce(c) YE	18	35	40	45	50
Depreciation	2207	2274	2030	1751	1366

PER SHARE STATISTICS (CENTS)

Net Asst Val	44.15	43.92	39.23	35.34	30.04
Net Earnings	4.20	6.70	7.40	8.30	5.70
Dividends	4.00	2.00	3.50	3.00	2.50
Cash Flow	8.08	10.95	11.69	13.02	10.23

RATIOS AND OTHER INFORMATION

Mrk Cap(R000)	9000	17500	20000	22500	25000
Current Ratio	4.30	4.39	3.96	2.26	2.27
Quik/Acid Tst	2.70	2.61	2.25	0.88	0.96
Debt/Ass Rat	0.22	0.23	0.25	0.33	0.26
L T L Tot Ass	0.07	0.08	0.10	0.06	-
Debt to Eqity	0.32	0.34	0.40	0.60	0.42
Interest Cover	7.64	10.51	32.53	64.19	404.69

Ret on Assets	10.03	14.04	21.26	23.13	22.83
Ret on Equity%	9.58	15.22	18.86	23.49	18.85
Price/Earnings	4.29	5.22	5.41	5.42	8.77
Divid Cover	1.05	3.35	2.11	2.77	2.28
Divid Yield	22.22	5.71	8.75	6.67	5.00
Earning Yield%	23.33	19.14	18.50	18.44	11.40
NAV % Mrk Pr	245.27	125.49	98.08	78.52	60.08
Effec Tax Rate	36.73	23.91	38.20	34.26	30.38
Def Interval	0.54	0.50	0.52	0.56	0.35
Sus Grth Rate	0.52	10.67	9.94	15.00	10.53

SUBSIDIARY & ASSOCIATED COMPANIES

TPN HOLDINGS (PTY) LTD
TRANSVAAL PRESSED NUTS, BOLTS AND RIVETS

INVESTMENTS

None

TRADEGRO LTD

ABBREVIATION : TRADGRO

JSE SHORT CODE : TGR

SECTOR : Industrial-Retailers & Wholesalers

SHAREHOLDERS

Who Owns Whom's Assessment of the Identity of the Ultimate Controlling Shareholder:
PEPGRO VIA TRADEHOLD

SHAREHOLDER	PERCENTAGE 1992	1991
SUNDEX P/L	53.3	1.4
CMB NOM P/L	8.6	---
SEPDU INV P/L	8.3	55.6
INTERHOLD LTD	8.1	---
SA MUTUAL	7.3	11.9
TRADEHOLD LTD	5.3	---
METROPOLITAN LIFE LTD	1.5	---
YSKOR PENS FUND	1.3	---
STD BANK NOM TVL P/L	---	4.5
TRADEGRO TRUST	---	1.8
EIGHTY ONE MAIN STREET NOM LTD	---	1.8
SANKORP BPK	---	2.5
SANLAM	---	3.3
TOTAL	93.5	82.8

DIRECTORS :
BASSON JW ,FOUCHE JJ ,LOUW JA ,MOORE E
STASSEN C ,WIESE CH (Chairman

REGISTRATION NUMBER : 05/07721/06

REGISTERED OFFICE
36 Stellenberg Road, Parow Industria
7500
TEL: 021-932 9911
FAX: 021-931 0848

TRANSFER SECRETARY
Central Registrars Ltd
P O Box 4844, Johannesburg
2000
TEL: 011-331 0051

COMPANY SECRETARY
Pepkor Ltd

NATURE OF BUSINESS
An investment holding company. The group retails food and consumer durables through supermarkets and department stores.

BANKERS :
Standard Bank of SA Ltd, Senbank

AUDITORS :
Fisher Hoffman Stride

FAMILIAR BRAND NAMES
CHECKERS,COREPROP,GREATERMANS,SHOPRITE
STUTTAFORDS

CONTRIBUTION BY ACTIVITY
N/A

YEAR END : February

DIVIDEND : Ords 50c

Interim No 89	(Ldr)23/03/90	(Pay)02/05/90	Amt(c)5
Final No 90	(Ldr)12/10/90	(Pay)01/11/90	Amt(c)6
Interim No 91	(Ldr)22/03/91	(Pay)02/05/91	Amt(c)5
Final No 92	(Ldr)11/10/91	(Pay)21/10/91	Amt(c)21

NUMBER OF EMPLOYEES : 17515

CAPITAL STRUCTURE

	AUTHORISED	ISSUED
Ords no par value	99437673	25717819
6% Non-Conv Cum Prefs R2	175000	175000
5% Non-Conv Cum Prefs R2	325000	325000
Second 5% Non-Conv Cum Prefs R2	225000	225000
Third 5% Non-Conv Cum Prefs R2	1000000	500000

FINANCIAL STATISTICS (AT FINANCIAL YEAR END)

(Amts in R'000)	1992 Feb	1991 Jun	1990 Jun	1989 Jun	1988 Jun
Ord S/H Int	173564	196529	297857	278577	234646
Long Trm Loans	19438	23936	487681	786083	721429
Iss Ord Share	257178	185020	68689	57290	57226
Total Liab	625447	665472	1804488	2267526	1953299
Current Liab	606009	641536	1316807	1481443	1231870
Total Assets	799011	862001	1954861	2451717	2097251
Intang Assets	*	*	147484	94386	90694
Current Assets	612812	666750	1602348	1863118	1568611
Debtors	98653	102490	370603	391521	300096
Inventory	325170	313565	929387	868047	742210
Turnover	2215169	7772883	7232674	7202425	6115736
Oper Profit	-28129	52301	165156	260713	166148
Interest Paid	18115	86578	50886	82005	34943
Tax Paid	719	25664	36415	38544	30038
Prf af Int&Tax	-44097	-59434	79343	140596	101167
Prf att Ord Sh	-44749	-37216	13041	45704	26972
Btm Line Earn	-90204	-66734	-6502	49038	41922
Dividend Paid	-	17849	6988	5729	2861
Mkt Prce(c) YE	70	160	155	165	103
Depreciation	26893	55612	53579	48698	47880

PER SHARE STATISTICS (CENTS)

Net Asst Val	67.49	106.22	218.92	321.51	251.55

Net Earnings	-19.40	-7.90	22.00	78.60	46.40
Dividends	-	26.00	11.00	10.00	5.00
Cash Flow	-11.61	24.53	151.25	211.50	171.20

RATIOS AND OTHER INFORMATION

Mrk Cap(R000)	180025	296032	106468	94529	58943
Current Ratio	1.01	1.04	1.22	1.26	1.27
Quik/Acid Tst	0.47	0.55	0.51	0.67	0.67
A/C Rec T/ovr	33.68	75.84	19.52	18.40	20.38
Tot Ass T/ovr	4.16	9.02	3.70	2.94	2.92
Debt/Ass Rat	0.77	0.76	0.77	0.73	0.75
L T L Tot Ass	0.01	0.02	0.10	0.13	0.16
Debt to Eqity	3.55	3.35	5.08	6.43	6.66
Interest Cover	-1.39	0.61	3.27	3.18	4.75
Oper Prof Mrg	-1.27	0.67	2.28	3.62	2.72
Net Prof Marg%	-2.02	-0.48	0.18	0.63	0.44
Ret on Assets	-4.78	6.31	8.52	10.63	7.96
Ret on Equity%	-38.67	-18.94	4.38	16.41	11.49
Price/Earnings	-3.61	-20.25	7.05	2.10	2.22
Divid Cover	-	-0.30	2.00	7.86	9.28
Divid Yield	-	16.25	7.10	6.06	4.85
Earning Yield%	-27.71	-4.94	14.19	47.64	45.05
NAV % Mrk Pr	96.41	66.39	141.24	194.85	244.22
Effec Tax Rate	-1.14	-74.83	31.68	21.10	23.96
Def Interval	-5.96	3.71	1.35	2.60	3.29
Sus Grth Rate	-25.78	-28.02	2.03	14.35	10.28

SUBSIDIARY & ASSOCIATED COMPANIES

ABELSOHNS (PTY) LTD
ABMONT HOLDINGS (PTY) LTD
ACE IMPORTS (PTY) LTD
AFRIMET LTD
AK NYMAN (PTY) LTD
ALBERPROP (PTY) LTD
ALBERTON DEVELOP DEPARTMENT PROPERTIES
ALEXIN (PTY) LTD
ALMA E. PALACHE (PTY) LTD
AMALINDA DEVELOPMENT PROPERTIES (PTY) LT
ANDRON BELEGGINGS BPK
ARMIST WHOLESALERS (PTY) LTD
BEBIDAS PROPERTIES (PTY) LTD
BELFAST WAREHOUSE LTD
BENONI PLANNING PROPERTIES (PTY) LTD
BETHAL WHOLESALERS (PTY) LTD
BIG D DISCOUNT HYPER LTD
BOPHUTHATSWANA CHAIN STORES LTD (50%)
CARFETS (PTY) LTD
CARLETONVILLE DEVELOPMENT PROPERTIES (PT
CASH-HOLD LTD
CH. ABELSOHN (PTY) LTD
CHECKAPROP LTD
CHECKERS PHOENIX LTD (49%)
CHECKERS PROPERTIES BENONI (PTY) LTD
CHECKERS PROPERTIES LTD
CHECKERS PROPERTIES MAYFAIR (PTY) LTD
CHECKERS PROPERTIES SPRINGS (PTY) LTD
CHECKERS PROPERTIES VANDERBIJLPARK (PTY)
CHECKERS SOUTH AFRICA LTD
CHECKERS SUPERMARKETS (PORT SHEPSTONE) (
CHECKERS SUPERMARKETS (PTY) LTD
CHECKOR AIR (PTY) LTD
CHECKOR BUTCHERIES (N. TVL) (PTY) LTD (49.9%)
CHECKOR BUTCHERIES (NATAL) (PTY) LTD (49.9%)
CHECKOR BUTCHERIES (TVL) (PTY) LTD (49.9%)
CHECKOR BUTCHERIES GROUP LTD (49.9%)
CISKEI CHAIN STORES LTD (50%)
CITADEL OUTFITTERS (PTY) LTD
CONVENIENCE STORES (PTY) LTD
COREPROP INVESTMENTS (PTY) LTD
COREPROP LTD
COUNTRY GIRL BUTCHERIES (BLOEMFONTEIN) ((49.9%)
COUNTRY GIRL BUTCHERIES (BOLAND) (PTY) L (49.9%)
COUNTRY GIRL BUTCHERIES (E. CAPE) (PTY) (49.9%)
COUNTRY GIRL BUTCHERIES (E. TVL) (PTY) L (49.9%)
COUNTRY GIRL BUTCHERIES (JEPPE ST) (PTY) (49.9%)
COUNTRY GIRL BUTCHERIES (NATAL) (PTY) LT (49.9%)
COUNTRY GIRL BUTCHERIES (NOORDKAAP) (PTY (49.9%)
COUNTRY GIRL BUTCHERIES (O.F.S.) (PTY) L (49.9%)
COUNTRY GIRL BUTCHERIES (PRETORIA) (PTY) (49.9%)
COUNTRY GIRL BUTCHERIES (VALSBAD) (PTY) (49.9%)
COUNTRY GIRL BUTCHERIES (W. CAPE) (PTY) (49.9%)
COUNTRY GIRL BUTCHERIES (W. COAST) (PTY) (49.9%)
COUNTRY GIRL BUTCHERIES (WITS) (PTY) LTD (49.9%)
CT DE MENDONCA (PTY) LTD
CURDY CORNER PROPERTIES (PTY) LTD
DECWED (PTY) LTD
DEE BEE SUPERMARKET (PTY) LTD (50%)
DELTA DISTRIBUTORS (PTY) LTD (50%)
DOUBLE EIGHT INVESTMENTS (PTY) LTD
DOYDAL HOLDINGS (PTY) LTD
EMHALL LTD
EMON (PTY) LTD
EMQUAT LTD
EMSES LTD
F & S WHOLESALERS (PTY) LTD
FAR SALES (BETHAL) (PTY) LTD
FELAN (PTY) LTD
FORTCO (PTY) LTD
FRED MADDISON (DURBAN) (PTY) LTD
FRESHMARK (PTY) LTD (40%)
FROSTMORE PROPERTIES (PTY) LTD
FURNITURE & BEDDING (KEMPTON PARK) (PTY)
FURNITURE & BEDDING CENTRE (KEMPTON PARK
GEM DISCOUNT (PTY) LTD
GENTLEMEN'S CORNER (PTY) LTD
GOLDREEF ENTERPRISES (PTY) LTD
GOOD HUMOUR ICE CREAM CO. (PTY) LTD (50%)
GRANT DISTRIBUTION CORPORATION (PTY) LTD
GREATERMANS ASSOCIATES LTD
GREATERMANS DEPARTMENT STORES LTD
GREATERMANS FINANCE CO. (PTY) LTD
GREATERMANS HOLDINGS LTD
GREATERMANS MANAGEMENT SERVICES LTD
GREATERMANS NATAL AND FREE STATE HOLDING
GREATWAY (PTY) LTD
GRETSHAM INVESTMENTS LTD
GROOTRIVIER VERSPREIDERS (EDMS) BPK
GROUPS INVESTMENT IN UNION WINE LTD
GUS REICHMAN (PTY) LTD
H & A PAYNE LTD
H HURWITZ & SONS (PTY) LTD
HARVEY GREENACRE & CO. LTD
HILLCREST NOMINEES (PTY) LTD
HPH INVESTMENTS (PTY) LTD
INERFINANCE CORPORATION (PTY) LTD
ISSIEJAY (PTY) LTD
J KATZ & SONS (PTY) LTD
JANDU INVESTMENTS (PTY) LTD
JEDWOOD BROS (PTY) LTD
JETRO INTERNATIONAL NV
JOSIM INVESTMENTS (PTY) LTD
KINGWILLIAMSTOWN NOMINEES (PTY) LTD
LAMBTON PLANNING PROPERTIES (PTY) LTD
LANS CARPETS (PTY) LTD
LARE PROPERTIES (PTY) LTD (50%)
LENTICULAR (PTY) LTD
LILBER (PTY) LTD
LILROY PREPAK (PTY) LTD
LONGCORP (BERMUDA) LTD
LOVEDAY BROKERS (PTY) LTD
LYNN & SILBERT (PTY) LTD
MA ENGINEERING INVESTMENTS
MACKAYS FURNISHERS GLENCOE (PTY) LTD
MACKAYS FURNISHERS LADYSMITH (PTY) LTD
MACKAYS FURNISHERS MARITZBURG (PTY) LTD
MACKAYS FURNISHERS PINETOWN (PTY) LTD

MALUTI MARKETING CO (PTY) LTD
MANBOYS HOLDINGS (PTY) LTD
MARGATE NOMINEES (PTY) LTD
MATUS & CO. (KLERKSDORP) (PTY) LTD
MATUS & CO. (LICHTENBURG) (PTY) LTD
MATUS & CO. (RUSTENBURG) (PTY) LTD
MAX GREENSTEIN INVESTMENTS (PTY) LTD
METCASH LTD
METCASH N.V (NETHERLANDS ANTILLES)
METCASH PROPERTIES (PTY) LTD
METCORP (BERMUDA) LTD
METCORP (HONG KONG) LTD
METGROUPHOLD LTD
METHOLD (PTY) LTD
METRO (BOTSHABELO) (PTY) LTD (50%)
METRO (KANGWANE) (PTY) LTD (50%)
METRO (KWANDEBELE) (PTY) LTD (50%)
METRO (LEBOWA) (PTY) LTD (50%)
METRO (NOLIZWE) (PTY) LTD (50%)
METRO (QWA QWA) (PTY) LTD (50%)
METRO (SWAZILAND) (PTY) LTD (50%)
METRO (TRADEMARKET) (PTY) LTD
METRO (U.P.T.I.) (PTY) LTD
METRO (VENDA) (PTY) LTD (50%)
METRO BOTSWANA LTD
METRO CASH & CARRY (BOPHUTHATSWANA) (PTY (50%)
METRO CASH & CARRY (PTY) LTD
METRO CASH & CARRY HOMELAND GROUP (50%)
METRO GROUP LTD (47%)
METRO LESOTHO (PTY) LTD (50%)
MICROS
MONDU INVESTMENTS (PTY) LTD (50%)
MYER ROSEN INVESTMENTS (PTY) LTD
NOSTALGIA LTD
PARYS DEVELOPMENT PROPERTIES (PTY) LTD
PAYNE BROS. (CAPE) LTD
PAYNE BROS. (PE.) LTD
PE CASH & CARRY WHOLESALERS (PTY) LTD
PHALABORWA NOMINEES (PTY) LTD
PHALABORWA PLANNING PROPERTIES (PTY) LTD
PHIL SAFFER (PTY) LTD
PINE PROPS (PTY) LTD
PLANNING PROPERTIES LENASIA (PTY) LTD
PLANNING PROPERTIES NIGEL (PTY) LTD
PLANNING PROPERTIES WORCESTER (PTY) LTD
PODAR (PTY) LTD
POLYPLAS (PTY) LTD (50%)
PORTHIGH PROPERTIES (PTY) LTD
PRICEFIGHTER (PTY) LTD
PRUDENTIAL SHIPPERS S.A. LTD
RAGLAN BUILDINGS (PTY) LTD
RAVE PROPS (PTY) LTD
REYJALYN (PTY) LTD
ROSELYN AGENCIES (PTY) LTD
RUSCON (PTY) LTD (50%)
RUSPROP (BLOEMFONTEIN) (PTY) LTD
RUSPROP (CITY DEEP) (PTY) LTD
RUSPROP (DURBAN) (PTY) LTD
RUSPROP (NEWCASTLE) (PTY) LTD
RUSPROP (PIETERSBURG) (PTY) LTD
RUSPROP (WESTONARIA) (PTY) LTD
RUSPROP (WORCESTER) (PTY) LTD
RUSPROP WAREHOUSE (PTY) LTD
RUSSELL KATZ & CO. (PTY) LTD
RUSSELL KATZ (CAPE) (PTY) LTD
RUSSELL KATZ (CARLETONVILLE) (PTY) LTD
RUSSELL KATZ (EAST RAND) (PTY) LTD
RUSSELL KATZ (KLERKSDORP) (PTY) LTD
RUSSELL KATZ (KLERKSDORP) (PTY) LTD (MAF
RUSSELL KATZ (NATAL) (PTY) LTD
RUSSELL KATZ (VEREENIGING) (PTY) LTD
RUSSELL MACKAY HOLDINGS (PTY) LTD
RUSSOP (PTY) LTD
S.W. UNITED AGENCIES (PTY) LTD (50%)
SATSEPT (PTY) LTD
SCOTTSVILLE SHOPPING CENTRE (PTY) LTD
SKYCIL PROPERTIES (PTY) LTD (50%)
SODEV (PTY) LTD
STAND 321 WADEVILLE 3 (PTY) LTD
STEINBROMAT (PTY) LTD
SUNQUAD (PTY) LTD
SUNTER INVESTMENTS (PTY) LTD
SUPERAMA LTD (44.5%)
SW UNITED AGENCIES (PTY) LTD (50%)
THABAZIMBI DEVELOPMENT PROPERTIES (PTY)
TONY RAHME (PTY) LTD
TONY RAHME PROPERTIES (PTY) LTD
TOY MAIL (PTY) LTD
TRADE PROPERTIES (MAFEKING) (PTY) LTD
TRADEGRO ADMIN LTD
TRADEGRO INVESTMENTS LTD
TRADEGRO MANAGEMENT SERVICES (BOP) (PTY)
TRADEGRO MANAGEMENT SERVICES (CISKEI) (P
TRADEGRO MANAGEMENT SERVICES (PTY) LTD
TRADEGRO MANAGEMENT SERVICES (SWAZILAND)
U PAY & TAKE IT (BETHLEHEM) (PTY) LTD
U PAY & TAKE IT (BLOEMFONTEIN (PTY) LTD
U PAY & TAKE IT (WORCESTER) (PTY) LTD
UNLANG INVESTMENTS (PTY) LTD (50%)
VICTOR ROBINSON INVESTMENTS (PTY) LTD
VICUNOR INVESTMENTS (PTY) LTD
VONAMURR (PTY) LTD
W MACKAY & CO (PTY) LTD
WANDA FURNISHERS HOMELAND GROUP (50%)
WESEPT (PTY) LTD
ZENGO INVESTMENTS (PTY) LTD
ZULULAND WHOLESALERS (PTY) LTD

INVESTMENTS

None

TRADEHOLD LTD

ABBREVIATION : TRADHLD

JSE SHORT CODE : TRH

SECTOR : Industrial-Retailers & Wholesalers

SHAREHOLDERS

Who Owns Whom's Assessment of the Identity of the Ultimate Controlling Shareholder:
PEPGRO VIA PEPKOR

SHAREHOLDER	PERCENTAGE 1992	1991
GROCEHOLD P/L	75.9	---
CMB NOM P/L	12.9	---
STD BANK NOM TVL P/L	1.4	6.2
SANKORP BPK	---	17.1
SANLAM	---	13.1
STATUS INV P/L	---	56.3
TOTAL	90.1	92.7

DIRECTORS :
BASSON JW ,FOUCHE JJ ,LOUW JA ,MOORE C
STASSEN C ,WIESE CH (Chairman

REGISTRATION NUMBER : 77/02046/06

REGISTERED OFFICE
36 Stellenberg Road, Parow Industria
7500
TEL: 021-932 9911
FAX: 021-931 0848

TRANSFER SECRETARY
Central Registrars Ltd
P O Box 4844, Johannesburg
2000
TEL: 011-331 0051

COMPANY SECRETARY
Pepkor Ltd

NATURE OF BUSINESS
An investment holding company with a controlling interest in quoted Tradegro Ltd. The Group is involved in the retail & wholesale industries.

BANKERS :
Standard Bank of SA Ltd, Senbank

AUDITORS :
Fisher Hoffman Stride

FAMILIAR BRAND NAMES
N/A

CONTRIBUTION BY ACTIVITY
N/A

YEAR END : February

DIVIDEND : Ords no par value

Interim	(Ldr)23/03/90	(Pay)02/05/90	Amt(c)2
Final	(Ldr)12/10/90	(Pay)01/11/90	Amt(c)3
Interim	(Ldr)22/03/91	(Pay)02/05/91	Amt(c)2

NUMBER OF EMPLOYEES : 34800

CAPITAL STRUCTURE

	AUTHORISED	ISSUED
Ords no par value	69234684	9513964
Var Rate Red Cum Prefs 1c	9000000	0
Sec Var Rate Red Cum Prefs 1c	50000000	

FINANCIAL STATISTICS (AT FINANCIAL YEAR END)

(Amts in R'000)	1992 Feb	1991 Jun	1990 Jun	1989 Jun	1988 Jun
Ord S/H Int	70919	84692	80629	36610	29823
Long Trm Loans	125371	152640	634707	941287	39765
Iss Ord Share	190279	128567	40807	23989	23989
Total Liab	734205	816560	1961736	2442198	42506
Current Liab	608834	663920	1327029	1500911	2741
Total Assets	805124	901252	1967263	2476763	72329
Intang Assets	*	*	75102	2045	*
Current Assets	612894	687301	1613149	1881448	11221
Debtors	98735	123041	380650	409518	10275
Inventory	325170	313565	929390	868047	-
Turnover	2215169	7772883	7232674	7202426	-
Oper Profit	-27964	52251	164912	261986	815
Interest Paid	21909	91882	50909	82601	-
Tax Paid	719	25603	36398	39168	189
Prf af Int&Tax	-47418	-64727	79093	140649	626
Prf att Ord Sh	-27741	-25631	2505	7850	4178
Btm Line Earn	-47543	-12534	-2258	8541	7314
Dividend Paid	-	24787	1703	1079	480
Mkt Prce(c) YE	50	90	60	75	55
Depreciation	26893	55612	53579	48698	-

PER SHARE STATISTICS (CENTS)

Net Asst Val	37.27	65.87	13.54	144.09	124.32
Net Earnings	-16.60	-10.10	7.70	32.70	17.40
Dividends	-	60.70	5.00	4.50	2.00
Cash Flow	-0.72	69.68	199.75	258.07	-0.61

RATIOS AND OTHER INFORMATION

Mrk Cap(R000)	95140	115710	24484	17992	13194
Current Ratio	1.01	1.04	1.22	1.25	4.09
Quik/Acid Tst	0.47	0.56	0.52	0.68	4.09
A/C Rec T/ovr	33.65	63.17	19.00	17.59	-
Tot Ass T/ovr	4.13	8.62	3.68	2.91	-
Debt/Ass Rat	0.77	0.75	0.74	0.67	0.46
L T L Tot Ass	0.01	0.02	0.06	0.07	0.42
Debt to Eqity	8.72	8.03	17.96	45.50	1.12
Interest Cover	-1.13	0.57	3.27	3.18	-
Oper Prof Mrg	-1.26	0.67	2.28	3.64	-
Net Prof Marg%	-1.25	-0.33	0.03	0.11	-
Ret on Assets	-4.66	6.03	8.45	10.57	12.63
Ret on Equity%	-58.67	-30.26	3.11	21.44	14.01
Price/Earnings	-3.01	-8.91	7.79	2.29	3.16
Divid Cover	-	-0.17	1.54	7.27	8.70
Divid Yield	-	67.44	8.33	6.00	3.64
Earning Yield%	-33.20	-11.22	12.83	43.60	31.64
NAV % Mrk Pr	74.54	73.19	22.57	192.12	226.04
Effec Tax Rate	-1.06	-64.57	31.74	21.36	23.19
Def Interval	-182.48	3.59	2.00	5.20	-61.47
Sus Grth Rate	-39.12	-59.53	0.99	18.49	12.40

SUBSIDIARY & ASSOCIATED COMPANIES

CYLIL INVESTMENTS (PTY) LTD
INTERHOLD LTD
ISLEV INVESTMENTS (PTY) LTD
KIMET REAL ESTATE LTD
LEON TRAUB INVESTMENTS (PTY) LTD
LIMIN INVESTMENTS (PTY) LTD
S & P FAMILY HOLDINGS (PTY) LTD
SUNDEC (PTY) LTD
TRADEGRO LTD

INVESTMENTS

TRADEGRO LTD (925000 SH)

TRANS HEX GROUP LTD

ABBREVIATION : TRNSHEX

JSE SHORT CODE : TSX

SECTOR : Mining-Diamonds

SHAREHOLDERS

Who Owns Whom's Assessment of the Identity of the Ultimate Controlling Shareholder: REMBRANDT

SHAREHOLDER	PERCENTAGE 1992	1991
TEGNIESE MYNBELEGGINGS BPK	50.0	50.0

CMB NOM P/L	14.2	---
STD BANK NOM TVL P/L	4.0	3.3
SA MUTUAL	2.3	2.3
TBA NOM P/L	1.5	2.4
LA GRANGE P L	1.5	1.5
YSKOR PENS FUND	1.1	---
BURG NOM P/L	1.1	1.1
SANLAM	---	7.5
SANLAMTRUST NOM P/L	---	2.1
TOTAL	75.5	70.2

DIRECTORS :
CARINUS PJ ,COETZEE JP ,FLACK PH
HERTZOG E DE LA H DR,HOFFMAN F (Chairman)
HOOGENHOUT DM (Financial Director),MALAN WC
MOSTERT FA ,PIENAAR PJ (Dir Industrial Minerals)
SWIEGERS GJ ,VAN WYK SS

REGISTRATION NUMBER : 63/07579/06

REGISTERED OFFICE
405 Voortrekker Road, Parow
7500
TEL: 021-92 1105
FAX: 021-92 0711

TRANSFER SECRETARY
Central Registrars Ltd
P O Box 4844, Johannesburg
2000
TEL: 011-331 0051

COMPANY SECRETARY
F W Knoetze

NATURE OF BUSINESS
An investment holding company with interests in diamond mining, and in mining, processing and marketing of base minerals.

BANKERS :
Volkskas Ltd

AUDITORS :
Coopers Theron Du Toit

FAMILIAR BRAND NAMES
CLC,GLUTONE,GLUWASH,PREMIER COTE,SKIMCRETE
TYLON,VERDE FONTAIN

CONTRIBUTION BY ACTIVITY
Diamonds (% of Net income) (90.6%)
Industrial minerals (12.4%)
Exploration & Development (-3.0%)

YEAR END : March

DIVIDEND : Ords no par value

Interim No 18	(Ldr)22/12/89	(Pay)12/01/90	Amt(c)20
Final No 19	(Ldr)22/06/90	(Pay)27/07/90	Amt(c)26
Interim No 20	(Ldr)28/12/90	(Pay)18/01/91	Amt(c)23
Final No 21	(Ldr)22/02/91	(Pay)28/02/91	Amt(c)28
Interim No 22	(Ldr)20/12/91	(Pay)17/01/92	Amt(c)25
Final No 23	(Ldr)12/06/92	(Pay)30/06/92	Amt(c)34
Interim No 24	(Ldr)16/10/92	(Pay)30/10/92	Amt(c)27

NUMBER OF EMPLOYEES : 1334

CAPITAL STRUCTURE

	AUTHORISED	ISSUED
Ords no par value	30000000	15067500

FINANCIAL STATISTICS (AT FINANCIAL YEAR END)

(Amts in R'000)	1992 Mar	1991 Mar	1990 Mar	1989 Mar	1988 Mar
Ord S/H Int	115463	93936	74680	56448	44311
Long Trm Loans	14934	10026	17654	9123	7628
Iss Ord Share	15068	15068	15068	15068	15068
Total Liab	62233	65191	74913	38524	23746
Current Liab	47299	55165	57259	29401	16118
Total Assets	137896	121426	148938	94972	68057
Intang Assets	39800	37701	655	*	*
Current Assets	60704	58193	64372	44882	34724
Debtors	17857	11593	12987	11094	7443
Inventory	38733	38614	41434	28094	19283
Oper Profit	61609	58192	47288	34821	18895
Interest Paid	442	278	233	266	138
Tax Paid	32536	34811	26783	20223	8171
Prf af Int&Tax	28735	24481	20877	14432	10659
Prf att Ord Sh	28336	23921	22446	16948	12017
Btm Line Earn	28336	23921	22446	16948	11590
Dividend Paid	8890	7684	6931	5424	4068
Mkt Prce(c) YE	2225	2150	2700	1325	470
Depreciation	10434	10925	10458	8691	8126

PER SHARE STATISTICS (CENTS)

Net Asst Val	502.14	373.21	491.27	374.62	294.07
Net Earnings	186.30	157.80	147.90	105.80	77.80
Dividends	59.00	51.00	46.00	36.00	27.00
Cash Flow	296.87	252.09	214.71	181.67	148.10

RATIOS AND OTHER INFORMATION

Mrk Cap(R000)	335263	323962	406836	199651	70820
Current Ratio	1.28	1.05	1.12	1.53	2.15
Quik/Acid Tst	0.46	0.35	0.40	0.57	0.96
Debt/Ass Rat	0.34	0.45	0.45	0.31	0.24
L T L Tot Ass	-	-	0.07	-	0.00
Debt to Eqity	0.41	0.59	0.90	0.52	0.37
Interest Cover	139.62	214.28	205.55	131.28	137.45
Ret on Assets	44.27	48.48	33.10	38.36	29.43
Ret on Equity%	24.54	25.47	30.06	30.02	27.12
Price/Earnings	11.94	13.62	18.26	12.52	6.04
Divid Cover	3.16	3.09	3.22	2.94	2.88
Divid Yield	2.65	2.37	1.70	2.72	5.74
Earning Yield%	8.37	7.34	5.48	7.98	16.55
NAV % Mrk Pr	22.57	17.36	18.20	28.27	62.57
Effec Tax Rate	43.02	50.76	50.43	34.62	20.17
Def Interval	-	-	-	0.00	0.05
Sus Grth Rate	16.84	17.29	20.78	20.42	17.94

SUBSIDIARY & ASSOCIATED COMPANIES

BELLSBANK MINING NUMBER ONE (PTY) LTD
BITTERFONTEIN GRANITE WORKS (PTY) LTD
BONTEBOK LIME WORKS (PTY) LTD (50%)
BOSHDIAM HOLDINGS (PTY) LTD
BRAZIL DIAMANTE LTD
BUFFELSBANK DIAMANTE LTD
CAPE FELDSPAR (PTY) LTD
CAPE LIME (NATAL) (PTY) LTD
CAPE LIME (TVL) LTD
CAPE LIME (W.P.) LTD
CAPE LIME CO. LTD
CAPE LIME HOLDINGS LTD
CAPE LIME LTD
CAPE PROVINCE RESOURCES (PTY) LTD
DE BRUYNS BELLSBANK MINE (PTY) LTD
DOKOLWAYO DIAMOND MINES (PTY) LTD (SWAZI (50%)
EILAND DIAMANTE LTD
ELAND EXPLORATION (PTY) LTD
KEIR & CAWDER (SWAZILAND) (PTY) LTD
KWALINI (PTY) LTD (SWAZILAND)
MOLOPO MYNBOU LTD

NAMEX (PTY) LTD
NEW ELANDS DIAMANTPROSPEKTEERDERS (EDMS)
OCTHA MANAGEMENT SERVICES (PTY) LTD
OCTHA MINING HOLDINGS (PTY) LTD
ORANJE-KUNENE DIAMANTE BPK
POMPEY MINERALE (EDMS) BPK
PREMIER LIME CO. (PTY) LTD
REDMO (SPRINGBOK) LTD
SEELAND MYNBOU (EDMS) BPK
STELLENRYN BPK
STONEHAVEN INVESTMENTS (PTY) LTD
TERRA MARINA MYNBOUMAATSKAPPY LTD
TRANS HEX (SWAZILAND) (PTY) LTD
TRANS HEX BELGIE NV (BELGIUM)
TRANS HEX BEMARKING BEPERK
TRANS HEX DIAMANTE LTD
TRANS HEX DIAMOND TRADING (PTY) LTD
TRANS HEX DIENSTE BEPERK
TRANS HEX EKSPLORASIE (EDMS) BPK
TRANS HEX FINANSIERING BEPERK
TRANS HEX INGENIEURSDIENSTE LTD
TRANS HEX MINERALE BEPERK
TRANS HEX MYNBOU BPK
TRANS HEX ONDERNEMINGS LTD
TRANS TROPIC TRADING INC (BRITISH VIRGIN
VOORTREKKERWEG 405 BEPERK
VREDENDAL GRANITE (PTY) LTD
WESKUS MYNBOU LTD
WESMIN (EDMS) BPK (50%)

INVESTMENTS

None

TRANS NATAL COAL CORP LTD

ABBREVIATION : TRANS-NTL

JSE SHORT CODE : TNC

SECTOR : Mining-Coal

SHAREHOLDERS

Who Owns Whom's Assessment of the Identity of the Ultimate Controlling Shareholder:
SANLAM VIA GENCOR

SHAREHOLDER	PERCENTAGE 1992	1991
CONSOLIDATED NOM P/L	46.0	46.0
ABSA NOM P/L	10.1	---
EIGHTY ONE MAIN STREET NOM LTD	9.5	7.8
CMB NOM P/L	7.5	---
STD BANK NOM TVL P/L	4.3	4.3
FIRST NAT NOM P/L	3.3	3.8
LIBERTY LIFE ASSOC OF AFRICA LTD	2.7	1.9
SA MUTUAL	2.4	3.6
LIBSASRIA NOM P/L	1.0	---
VOLKSKAS NOM P/L	---	10.9
BANNER NOM P/L	---	1.3
SANLAM	---	6.2
TOTAL	86.8	85.7

DIRECTORS :
DU PLESSIS SJP ,ELLIS SP
GILBERTSON BP (Chairman),HENDERSON PG
JELINEK M ,JELINK M DR,JURD RG ,OSTERLOH GP
RADEMEYER P DE V ,SALAMON M (Managing Director)
SCURR T ,SMIT CL

REGISTRATION NUMBER : 63/01000/06

REGISTERED OFFICE
80 Marshall Street, Johannesburg
2001
TEL: 011-376 9111
FAX: 011-376 2433

TRANSFER SECRETARY
Central Registrars Ltd
P O Box 4844, Johannesburg
2000
TEL: 011-331 0051

COMPANY SECRETARY
General Mining Metals & Minerals Ltd

NATURE OF BUSINESS
An investment holding company with subsidiaries engaged in prospecting, acquisition & exploitation of coal reserves, the financing of coal mining projects, and coal marketing.

BANKERS :
First National Bank of SA Ltd
Nedperm Bank Ltd, Trust Bank of Africa Ltd
Volkskas Ltd

AUDITORS :
Coopers Theron Du Toit

FAMILIAR BRAND NAMES
N/A

CONTRIBUTION BY ACTIVITY
Export (% of Sales) (64.0%)
Eskom (19.0%)
Inland (17.0%)

YEAR END : June

DIVIDEND : Ords 50c

Interim No 52	(Ldr)23/02/90	(Pay)15/03/90	Amt(c)20
Final No 53	(Ldr)24/08/90	(Pay)14/09/90	Amt(c)40
Interim No 54	(Ldr)22/02/91	(Pay)15/03/91	Amt(c)22
Final No 55	(Ldr)23/08/91	(Pay)13/09/91	Amt(c)53
Interim No 56	(Ldr)21/02/92	(Pay)13/03/92	Amt(c)23
Final No 57	(Ldr)28/08/92	(Pay)18/09/92	Amt(c)57

NUMBER OF EMPLOYEES : 11872

CAPITAL STRUCTURE

	AUTHORISED	ISSUED
Ords 50c	80000000	79668997

FINANCIAL STATISTICS (AT FINANCIAL YEAR END)

(Amts in R'000)	1992 Jun	1991 Jun	1990 Jun	1989 Jun	1988 Jun
Ord S/H Int	679000	521000	445700	360400	307000
Long Trm Loans	499000	576500	629500	547300	545800
Iss Ord Share	79669	70482	70482	69697	69697
Total Liab	858100	905000	891600	744200	734500
Current Liab	359100	328500	262100	196900	188700
Total Assets	1537100	1426000	1337300	1104600	1041500
Current Assets	404000	479800	468900	300800	208700

Debtors	129800	129700	119200	143700	149600
Inventory	78300	43100	66900	66500	37700
Turnover	1564100	1427000	1386400	1071900	874100
Oper Profit	170500	126600	197800	86700	17900
Interest Paid	17200	30000	29900	27800	16600
Tax Paid	56100	24900	89700	11100	4600
Prf af Int&Tax	147000	137700	131400	60300	-3300
Prf att Ord Sh	143600	127200	121500	50400	-13200
Btm Line Earn	143600	128200	121500	74300	-37800
Dividend Paid	63700	52900	42300	20900	-
Mkt Prce(c) YE	1075	1410	910	750	410
Depreciation	4700	4100	700	500	800

PER SHARE STATISTICS (CENTS)

Net Asst Val	852.28	739.20	632.36	517.10	440.48
Net Earnings	180.20	172.00	173.00	76.40	-4.20
Dividends	80.00	75.00	60.00	30.00	-
Cash Flow	196.24	192.91	289.17	86.80	-14.40

RATIOS AND OTHER INFORMATION

Mrk Cap(R000)	856442	993796	641386	522728	285758
Current Ratio	1.13	1.46	1.79	1.53	1.11
Quik/Acid Tst	0.91	1.33	1.53	1.19	0.91
A/C Rec T/ovr	12.05	11.00	11.63	7.46	5.84
Tot Ass T/ovr	1.02	1.00	1.04	0.97	0.84
Debt/Ass Rat	0.37	0.44	0.45	0.47	0.49
L T L Tot Ass	0.14	0.21	0.25	0.29	0.30
Debt to Eqity	0.85	1.20	1.34	1.44	1.65
Interest Cover	9.94	4.25	6.63	3.13	1.08
Oper Prof Mrg	10.90	8.87	14.27	8.09	2.05
Net Prof Marg%	9.18	8.91	8.76	4.70	-1.51
Ret on Assets	14.11	13.48	18.77	8.98	1.72
Ret on Equity%	21.15	24.41	27.26	13.98	-4.30
Price/Earnings	5.97	8.20	5.26	9.82	-97.62
Divid Cover	2.25	2.29	2.88	2.55	-
Divid Yield	7.44	5.32	6.59	4.00	-
Earning Yield%	16.76	12.20	19.01	10.19	-1.02
NAV % Mrk Pr	79.28	52.43	69.49	68.95	107.43
Effec Tax Rate	29.06	22.71	8.52	16.06	930.77
Def Interval	0.61	0.96	0.70	2.45	-14.84
Sus Grth Rate	11.77	14.26	17.77	8.19	-4.30

SUBSIDIARY & ASSOCIATED COMPANIES

ALPHA CONSOLIDATED WITBANK COLLIERIES LT
AMERSFOORT COAL (PTY) LTD
D & H COAL LTD
EIKEBOOM COLLIERY (PTY) LTD
EMASWATI HOLDING COMPANY (PTY) LTD
ERMELO MINES SERVICES (PTY) LTD
FEDERALE PROSPEKTEERDERS LTD
FREE STATE FARMERS MUTUAL EXP. & MIN. CO
GOEDGEMEEND COAL LTD
KANGWANE ANTHRACITE (PTY) LTD
MATLA COAL LTD (50%)
MCALPINE MINERALS CORP (PTY) LTD
MCALPINE SA LTD
MORETELE COAL CO. (PTY) LTD
NAUDVEN BOERDERY BELEGGINGS (PTY) LTD
PIENAARSRIVIER MYNBOUMAATSKAPPY BPK
REMHO STEENKOOLMYNE (PTY) LTD
RICHARDS BAY COAL TERMINAL CO LTD (21.1%)
ROEDTAN MINING CO. LTD
SAVAGE & LOVEMORE MINING (PTY) LTD
SETTLERS MYNBOUMAATSKAPPY BPK
T-PROJECT HOLDINGS (PTY) LTD (39.2%)
THE TRANSVAAL NAVIGATION COLLIERS & ESTA
THEUNISSEN COAL (PTY) LTD
TIM BRADBURY ASSOCIATES (PTY) LTD
TRANS-NATAL COLLIERIES LTD
TRANS-NATAL MARKETING SERVICES (NATAL) (
TRANS-NATAL MARKETING SERVICES (TVL) (PT
TRANS-NATAL SYNFUEL (PTY) LTD
UNITED CARBON PRODUCERS (1990) (PTY) LTD (34%)
WARMBAD COAL CO. LTD

INVESTMENTS

DURBAN COAL TERMINAL CO LTD (19.2%)

TRANSKEI SUN INTERNATIONAL LTD

ABBREVIATION : TRANSUN

JSE SHORT CODE : TSN

SECTOR : Industrial-Beverages & Hotels

SHAREHOLDERS

Who Owns Whom's Assessment of the Identity of the Ultimate Controlling Shareholder:
SA MUTUAL VIA KERSAF & SAFREN

SHAREHOLDER	PERCENTAGE 1992	1991
SUN HOTELS INTERNATIONAL LTD	53.2	53.2
TRANSKEI DEV CORP LTD	28.6	28.6
SA MUTUAL	9.4	9.2
CMB NOM P/L	2.4	---
ETABLISSEMENT SPORTS ET LOISIRS	1.2	1.2
SANLAM	---	2.4
TOTAL	94.7	94.5

DIRECTORS :
ALLISON JR ,CHIARANDA A (Managing Director)
GOSS PM ,HAWTON DA ,MATEBESE SHL ,MDLELENI KN
ROSEVEAR KA (Chairman),SWANA MMM ,VAN BILJON AF

REGISTRATION NUMBER : 87/00036/10

REGISTERED OFFICE
Wild Coast Sun Hotel, Main Bizana Road
Mzamba Beach, Transkei

TEL: 011-780 7763
FAX: 011-783 7446

TRANSFER SECRETARY
Fraser Street Registrars (Pty) Ltd
P O Box 61178, Marshalltown
2107
TEL: 011-491 0911

COMPANY SECRETARY
S A Bailes

NATURE OF BUSINESS
The group owns & operates the Wild Coast Sun casino resort, & three electronic gaming machine outlets in the Transkei.

BANKERS :
Standard Bank of SA Ltd

AUDITORS :
Deloitte Pim Goldby

FAMILIAR BRAND NAMES
WILD COAST SUN

CONTRIBUTION BY ACTIVITY
N/A

YEAR END : June

DIVIDEND :Ords 10c

Interim	(Ldr)09/03/90	(Pay)29/03/90	Amt(c)13
Final	(Ldr)31/08/90	(Pay)25/09/90	Amt(c)12.5
Interim	(Ldr)08/03/91	(Pay)28/03/91	Amt(c)13.75
Final	(Ldr)23/08/91	(Pay)27/09/91	Amt(c)13.25
Interim	(Ldr)06/03/92	(Pay)27/03/92	Amt(c)14
Final	(Ldr)28/08/92	(Pay)28/09/92	Amt(c)13.25

NUMBER OF EMPLOYEES : 2308

CAPITAL STRUCTURE

	AUTHORISED	ISSUED
Ords 10c	200000000	144946032

FINANCIAL STATISTICS (AT FINANCIAL YEAR END)

(Amts in R'000)	1992 Jun	1991 Jun	1990 Jun	1989 Jun	1988 Jun
Ord S/H Int	166497	148045	129049	103797	89501
Long Trm Loans	38926	38899	39859	40294	40047
Iss Ord Share	144946	144946	144946	144946	144946
Total Liab	128232	136350	121805	109563	94091
Current Liab	89306	97451	81946	69269	54044
Total Assets	294729	284395	246951	207926	178158
Intang Assets	*	*	3903	5434	5434
Current Assets	46202	98825	82939	62769	38434
Debtors	7382	5389	4879	3935	4078
Inventory	551	613	542	381	349
Turnover	209159	192623	163126	145157	116661
Oper Profit	66264	67925	64192	62473	50426
Interest Paid	125	106	362	1050	1358
Tax Paid	19290	21717	19729	17917	11159
Prf af Int&Tax	53625	53457	49429	45090	37909
Prf att Ord Sh	53625	53457	49429	45090	37909
Btm Line Earn	52324	52156	47898	42240	37909
Dividend Paid	39497	39135	36961	34062	28989
Mkt Prce(c) YE	255	270	270	212	260
Depreciation	10515	7798	7059	5848	5387

PER SHARE STATISTICS (CENTS)

Net Asst Val	114.87	102.14	86.34	67.86	58.00
Net Earnings	37.00	36.90	34.10	31.10	26.20
Dividends	27.25	27.00	25.50	23.50	20.00
Cash Flow	44.27	41.60	38.67	35.05	31.38

RATIOS AND OTHER INFORMATION

Mrk Cap(R000)	369612	391354	391354	307286	376860
Current Ratio	0.52	1.01	1.01	0.91	0.71
Quik/Acid Tst	0.51	1.01	1.01	0.90	0.70
A/C Rec T/ovr	28.33	35.74	33.43	36.89	28.61
Tot Ass T/ovr	0.71	0.68	0.66	0.70	0.65
Debt/Ass Rat	0.43	0.48	0.49	0.52	0.52
L T L Tot Ass	0.13	0.13	0.16	0.18	0.21
Debt to Eqity	0.77	0.92	0.93	1.04	1.03
Interest Cover	530.11	640.80	177.33	59.50	37.13
Oper Prof Mrg	31.68	35.26	39.35	43.04	43.22
Net Prof Marg%	25.64	27.75	30.30	31.06	32.50
Ret on Assets	24.78	26.47	28.15	30.81	28.30
Ret on Equity%	32.21	36.11	38.30	43.44	42.36
Price/Earnings	6.89	7.32	7.92	6.82	9.92
Divid Cover	1.36	1.37	1.34	1.32	1.31
Divid Yield	10.69	10.00	9.44	11.08	7.69
Earning Yield%	14.51	13.67	12.63	14.67	10.08
NAV % Mrk Pr	45.05	37.83	31.98	32.01	22.31
Effec Tax Rate	26.42	29.96	29.16	28.64	19.57
Def Interval	0.60	0.64	0.68	0.76	0.88
Sus Grth Rate	8.49	9.67	9.66	10.62	9.97

SUBSIDIARY & ASSOCIATED COMPANIES

SUN INTERNATIONAL (WILD COAST) (PTY) LTD
TRANSGAMES (PTY) LTD
TRANSKEI SPORTING & TATTERSALL CO (PTY)

INVESTMENTS

None

TRANSPACO LTD

ABBREVIATION : TRNPACO

JSE SHORT CODE : TPC

SECTOR : Industrial-Paper & Packaging

SHAREHOLDERS

Who Owns Whom's Assessment of the Identity of the Ultimate Controlling Shareholder: DIRECTORS

SHAREHOLDER	PERCENTAGE 1992	1991
SAMUEL ABELHEIM HLDGS P/L	29.9	29.9
MANUFACTURERS INV CO P/L	20.4	20.4
ABELHEIM P N	8.7	9.8
ABELHEIM M B	8.6	8.6
DRUION S A	3.7	3.7
CMB NOM P/L	3.5	---
NEDBANK NOM LTD	2.7	2.0
COLOUR TIME P/L	2.7	---
ELLERINE BROS P/L	2.3	2.3
NUSSBAUM R S A W	1.6	---
STONEHAGE NOM INC	1.4	1.4
GORHAM R E	1.3	1.3
BOUZAGLOU M	1.2	1.2
FOBB S	---	1.5
SANLAM	---	4.9
TOTAL	88.0	86.9

DIRECTORS :
AARON AJ ,ABELHEIM MB (Joint Managing Director)
ABELHEIM PN (Joint Managing Director)
ABELHEIM S (Chairman)
BOUZAGLOU C (Executive Director)
DRUION SA (Executive Director),JACOBSON SI

REGISTRATION NUMBER : 51/00799/06

REGISTERED OFFICE
9 Booysens Station Road, Stafford Township
Johannesburg
2197
TEL: 011-493 5220
FAX: 011-493 5229

TRANSFER SECRETARY
Investment Registrars (Pty) Ltd
P O Box 9167, Johannesburg
2000
TEL: 011-725 6004

COMPANY SECRETARY
N/A

NATURE OF BUSINESS
The group carries on the business of general wholesaling of paper, plastics & other packaging related products. The Group is also involved in the manufacture of customised plastic carrier bags plastic packaging products & tubular cores.

BANKERS :
Nedcor Bank Ltd

AUDITORS :
Kessel Feinstein

FAMILIAR BRAND NAMES
POLYBUILD,TRANSPACO

CONTRIBUTION BY ACTIVITY
N/A

YEAR END : March

DIVIDEND :Ords 1c

Dividend	(Ldr)08/09/89	(Pay)20/09/89	Amt(c)1.8
Dividend	(Ldr)21/06/91	(Pay)05/07/91	Amt(c)4
Dividend	(Ldr)29/11/91	(Pay)13/12/91	Amt(c)1
Dividend	(Ldr)03/07/92	(Pay)24/07/92	Amt(c)1.5

CAPITAL STRUCTURE

	AUTHORISED	ISSUED
Ords 1c	20000000	11000000

FINANCIAL STATISTICS (AT FINANCIAL YEAR END)

(Amts in R'000)	1992 Mar	1991 Mar	1990 Mar	1988 Dec	1987 Dec
Ord S/H Int	6946	6530	4751	4751	4676
Long Trm Loans	2294	3085	4033	2745	1390
Iss Ord Share	11000	11000	11000	11000	11000
Total Liab	16192	14567	18602	12846	6052
Current Liab	13898	11482	14569	10101	4662
Total Assets	23125	21086	23351	17597	10728
Intang Assets	13	11	2	*	*
Current Assets	17486	15684	16750	13100	8219
Debtors	11714	9928	10418	8414	5098
Inventory	4801	5520	6246	4622	3049
Turnover	50448	51398	56317	35089	22091
Oper Profit	1876	3259	2169	2661	1661
Interest Paid	878	1507	1581	542	317
Tax Paid	575	762	306	1046	670
Prf af Int&Tax	580	1007	282	1073	674
Prf att Ord Sh	580	1047	198	1091	665
Btm Line Earn	480	1047	198	982	665
Dividend Paid	275	440	198	440	132
Mkt Prce(c) YE	40	35	35	40	42
Depreciation	1047	1167	1252	720	303

PER SHARE STATISTICS (CENTS)

Net Asst Val	63.03	59.26	43.17	43.19	42.51
Net Earnings	5.27	9.52	1.80	9.92	7.60
Dividends	2.50	4.00	1.80	4.00	1.00
Cash Flow	13.78	21.58	12.26	20.86	10.65

RATIOS AND OTHER INFORMATION

Mrk Cap(R000)	4400	3850	3850	4400	4620
Current Ratio	1.26	1.37	1.15	1.30	1.76
Quik/Acid Tst	0.91	0.89	0.72	0.84	1.11
A/C Rec T/ovr	4.31	5.18	5.41	4.17	4.33
Tot Ass T/ovr	2.18	2.44	2.41	1.99	2.06
Debt/Ass Rat	0.67	0.64	0.76	0.68	0.52
L T L Tot Ass	0.07	0.10	0.14	0.10	0.09
Debt to Eqity	2.22	2.07	3.73	2.51	1.20
Interest Cover	2.14	2.16	1.37	4.91	5.24
Oper Prof Mrg	3.72	6.34	3.85	7.58	7.52
Net Prof Marg%	1.15	2.04	0.35	3.11	3.01
Ret on Assets	8.79	15.54	9.29	15.12	15.48
Ret on Equity%	8.35	16.03	4.17	22.96	14.22
Price/Earnings	7.59	3.68	19.44	4.03	5.53
Divid Cover	2.11	2.38	1.00	2.48	7.60
Divid Yield	6.25	11.43	5.14	10.00	2.38
Earning Yield%	13.18	27.20	5.14	24.80	18.10
NAV % Mrk Pr	157.57	169.32	123.35	107.98	101.21
Effec Tax Rate	59.39	30.53	69.22	26.52	34.67
Def Interval	3.47	2.37	5.86	2.52	2.19
Sus Grth Rate	4.39	9.30	0.00	13.70	11.40

SUBSIDIARY & ASSOCIATED COMPANIES

CONSUMER PLASTICS (PTY) LTD
FRAMEN PAPER PRODUCTS (1988) (PTY) LTD
PLASTAFRICA (PTY) LTD
TRANSPACO (NATAL) (PTY) LTD
TRANSPACO INDUSTRIES (PTY) LTD
TRANSVAAL PAPER & PACKAGING INDUSTRIES (

INVESTMENTS

None

TRANSVAAL DISTILLERS HOLDINGS LTD

ABBREVIATION : TDL

JSE SHORT CODE : TDL

SECTOR : Development Capital Market

SHAREHOLDERS

Who Owns Whom's Assessment of the Identity of the Ultimate Controlling Shareholder:
JANSE VAN RENSBURG FAMILY

SHAREHOLDER	PERCENTAGE 1992	1991
J W C INV P/L	---	25.4
M B M NOMINEES	---	2.9
STIEFEL H J	---	1.1
VAN RENSBURG C W J	---	7.9
VAN RENSBURG G F J	---	7.9
VAN RENSBURG P J	---	9.3
VAN RENSBURG R R J TRUSTEES	---	7.7
TOTAL	---	62.2

DIRECTORS :
BOTHA HJT ,DU TOIT PA (Sales Director)
JANSE VAN RENSBURG RR (Chairman & Chief Exec.)
SHEAHAN RA ,STIEFEL HJ

REGISTRATION NUMBER : 87/01810/06

REGISTERED OFFICE
2nd Floor, Boland Bank Building
18 Lower Burg Street, Cape Town
8001
TEL: 02211-633495

TRANSFER SECRETARY
Finpak Registrars (Pty) Ltd
2100 Cartwrights Corner House, Adderley Street
Cape Town
8000
TEL: 021-418 5040

COMPANY SECRETARY
H Hamman

NATURE OF BUSINESS
The main business of the company is that of a holding company in the field of liquor distillers, brewers, producers & distributors.

BANKERS :
First National Bank of SA Ltd

AUDITORS :
Cameron Prentice & Rodger
Fenwick Faris Allison & Alberts

FAMILIAR BRAND NAMES
N/A

CONTRIBUTION BY ACTIVITY
N/A

YEAR END : February

CAPITAL STRUCTURE

	AUTHORISED	ISSUED
Ords 1c	200000000	122595224
Conv Red Partic Prefs 1c	5000000	0

FINANCIAL STATISTICS (AT FINANCIAL YEAR END)

(Amts in R'000)	1989 Feb	1988 Feb
Ord S/H Int	11330	5470
Long Trm Loans	3615	3651
Iss Ord Share	9799	9799
Total Liab	8495	5004
Current Liab	4880	1353
Total Assets	14229	8025
Intang Assets	5596	2449
Current Assets	5090	2252
Debtors	1605	791
Inventory	2125	1160
Turnover	8082	1557
Oper Profit	857	-677
Tax Paid	4	-
Prf af Int&Tax	853	-677
Prf att Ord Sh	852	-702
Btm Line Earn	852	-702

PER SHARE STATISTICS (CENTS)

Net Asst Val	58.52	30.83
Cash Flow	8.69	-7.16

RATIOS AND OTHER INFORMATION

Current Ratio	1.04	1.66
Quik/Acid Tst	0.61	0.81
A/C Rec T/ovr	5.04	1.97
Tot Ass T/ovr	0.57	0.19
Debt/Ass Rat	0.48	0.62
L T L Tot Ass	0.13	0.45
Debt to Eqity	0.60	0.91
Oper Prof Mrg	10.60	-43.48
Net Prof Marg%	10.54	-45.09
Ret on Assets	6.02	-8.44
Ret on Equity%	7.07	-9.27
Effec Tax Rate	0.47	-
Def Interval	4.18	-5.58
Sus Grth Rate	7.52	-12.83

SUBSIDIARY & ASSOCIATED COMPANIES

LIQUOR INTERNATIONAL WHOLESALERS (PTY) L
PRESTIGE CELLARS (PTY) LTD
RICO BREWERIES LTD (45%)
TZANEEN DISTILLERS (PTY) LTD

INVESTMENTS

None

TRENCOR LTD

ABBREVIATION : TRENCOR

JSE SHORT CODE : TRE

SECTOR : Industrial-Transportation

SHAREHOLDERS

Who Owns Whom's Assessment of the Identity of the Ultimate Controlling Shareholder:
MOBILE INDUSTRIES

SHAREHOLDER	PERCENTAGE 1992	1991
MOBILE INDUSTRIES LTD	47.3	48.0
SA MUTUAL	14.1	14.9
STD BANK NOM TVL P/L	9.4	9.6
EIGHTY ONE MAIN STREET NOM LTD	6.3	1.6
PROFESSIONAL PROV SOC OF SA	3.4	3.4
CMB NOM P/L	2.0	---
SOUTHERN LIFE ASSOC LTD	1.4	---
PRINTING INDUSTRY PENS FUND	1.3	---
YSKOR RETIREMENT FUND	---	1.1
JOWELL D I	---	1.2
SYFRETS NOM LTD	---	2.6
NAT IND COUNCIL PRINTING & NEWSPAPER SA	---	1.4
YSKOR PENS FUND	---	1.1
TOTAL	85.1	84.8

DIRECTORS :
GALOMBIK A ,GORVY HA ,HASSON RRH ,JOWELL C
JOWELL NI (Chairman),SIMS IJ

REGISTRATION NUMBER : 55/02869/06

REGISTERED OFFICE
1313 Main Tower, Standard Bank Centre
Heerengracht, Cape Town
8001
TEL 021-21 7310
FAX 021-419 3692

TRANSFER SECRETARY
Consolidated Share Registrars Ltd
P O Box 61051, Marshalltown
2107
TEL 011-492 1620

COMPANY SECRETARY
G W Norval

NATURE OF BUSINESS
A holding company with subsidiaries engaged in the following operations the manufacture of truck trailers, road tankers and cargo and tank containers, road haulage in the Cape Province, Tvl and SWA, and an express goods service in these areas, tyre retreading and the marketing of new tyres, commodity exports to the East and vehicle franchises & motor spares outlets in the NW Cape

BANKERS :
First National Bank of SA Ltd
Standard Bank of SA Ltd

AUDITORS :
Arthur Andersen & Co

FAMILIAR BRAND NAMES
GOODYEAR,HENRED FREUEHAUF,JOWELLS,KELLY MASTERTREADS,MIDAS MOTOR SPARES NAMAKWALAND BUSDIENS,NAMAKWALAND LUGDIENS RENTCO TRAILERS,STUARTS TRANSPORT,TRENTYRE

CONTRIBUTION BY ACTIVITY
Manufacturing (% income before taxation) (17 2%)
Transport (6 5%)
Trading & Other (59 1%)
Motor Trade & Tyres (17 2%)

YEAR END June

DIVIDEND .Ords 5c

Interim No 58	(Ldr)27/04/90	(Pay)18/05/90	Amt(c)30
Final No 59	(Ldr)26/10/90	(Pay)16/11/90	Amt(c)100
Interim No 60	(Ldr)22/02/91	(Pay)28/02/91	Amt(c)35
Final No 61	(Ldr)25/10/91	(Pay)15/11/91	Amt(c)125
Interim No 62	(Ldr)24/04/92	(Pay)15/05/92	Amt(c)42
Final No 63	(Ldr)11/09/92	(Pay)23/09/92	Amt(c)153

NUMBER OF EMPLOYEES 3395

CAPITAL STRUCTURE

	AUTHORISED	ISSUED
Ords 5c	20000000	14529482
6% Unsec Auto Conv Sub Debs 9100c	2862680	2862680

FINANCIAL STATISTICS (AT FINANCIAL YEAR END)

(Amts in R'000)	1992 Jun	1991 Jun	1990 Jun	1989 Jun	1988 Jun
Ord S/H Int	443365	310734	230651	168845	122045
Long Trm Loans	343968	66201	66329	69744	46696
Iss Ord Share	14529	14313	14313	14313	14310
Total Liab	548068	287128	232803	195395	144282
Current Liab	204100	220927	166474	125651	97586
Total Assets	991433	597862	463454	364240	266327
Current Assets	585212	318415	235276	176338	132642
Debtors	333400	255605	175850	111946	83700
Inventory	74306	51125	50691	39384	31853
Turnover	997737	829153	784614	689703	514099
Oper Profit	175092	147262	118240	82091	63607
Interest Paid	22660	16296	11847	9339	3667
Tax Paid	35155	22367	24355	23792	20062
Prf af Int&Tax	134994	109625	87685	53924	39878
Prf att Ord Sh	130019	105175	81826	48352	36299
Btm Line Earn	131299	104095	81103	50091	37349
Dividend Pa d	28332	22901	18607	9591	7155
Mkt Prce(c) YE	14500	8000	3800	2700	1200
Depreciation	20805	16548	16592	12816	9141

PER SHARE STATISTICS (CENTS)

Net Asst Val	3051 59	2170 99	1611 48	1179 66	852 87
Net Earnings	905 00	734 80	572 00	338 00	253 70
Dividends	195 00	160 00	130 00	67 00	50 00
Cash Flow	1048 30	856 63	730 75	494 44	341 84

RATIOS AND OTHER INFORMATION

Mrk Cap(R000)	2106705	1145040	543894	386451	171720
Current Ratio	2 87	1 44	1 41	1 40	1 36
Quik/Acid Tst	2 50	1 21	1 11	1 09	1 03
A/C Rec T/ovr	2 99	3 24	4 46	6 16	6 14
Tot Ass T/ovr	1 01	1 39	1 69	1 89	1 93
Debt/Ass Rat	0 47	0 38	0 38	0 41	0 44
L T L Tot Ass	0 27	0 01	0 02	0 07	0 07
Debt to Eqity	1 06	0 72	0 76	0 89	0 95
Interest Cover	7 73	9 04	9 98	8 79	17 35
Oper Prof Mrg	17 55	17 76	15 07	11 90	12 37
Net Prof Marg%	13 03	12 68	10 43	7 01	7 06
Ret on Assets	19 45	24 80	26 73	23 90	23 88
Ret on Equity%	29 33	33 85	35 48	28 64	29 74
Price/Earnings	16 02	10 89	6 64	7 99	4 73
Divid Cover	4 64	4 59	4 40	5 04	5 07
Divid Yield	1 34	2 00	3 42	2 48	4 17
Earning Yield%	6 24	9 19	15 05	12 52	21 14
NAV % Mrk Pr	21 05	27 14	42 41	43 69	71 07
Effec Tax Rate	1 12	7 55	8 30	11 83	28 35
Def Interval	0 28	0 70	0 75	1 13	0 95
Sus Grth Rate	22 94	26 48	27 41	22 96	23 88

SUBSIDIARY & ASSOCIATED COMPANIES

BRAKE & AXLE COMPONENTS (PTY) LTD
FRUEHAUF LTD
FRUEHAUF TRAILERS (SWAZILAND) (PTY) LTD
HENRED FRUEHAUF (PTY) LTD
HENRED FRUEHAUF PROPERTIES (CAPE) LTD
HENRED FRUEHAUF PROPERTIES (MG) (PTY) LT
HENRED-FRUEHAUF PROPERTIES (NATAL) (PTY)
HENRED FRUEHAUF PROPERTIES (OFS) (PTY) L
HENRED-FRUEHAUF PROPERTIES (PTY) LTD
HENRED FRUEHAUF PROPERTIES (WADEVILLE) (
HENRED-FRUEHAUF TRAILERS (PTY) LTD
HENRED FRUEHAUF TRAILERS HOLDINGS (PTY)
HENRED FRUEHAUF TRAILERS NAMIBIA (PTY) L
INDIAN OCEAN EXPORT COMPANY (PTY) LTD (50%)
JOWELLS CAPE TRANSPORT (PTY) LTD
JOWELLS EXPRESS (PTY) LTD
JOWELLS GARAGE & TRANSPORT (PTY) LTD
JOWELLS TRANSPORT (NORTHERN CAPE) (PTY)
JOWELLS TRANSPORT NAMAQUALAND (PTY) LTD
JOWELLS TRANSPORT NAMIBIA (PTY) LTD
KUMIREN PROPERTIES (PTY) LTD
MINTO MIDAS (PTY) LTD
NAMAKWALAND BUSDIENS (EDMS) BPK (50%)
O OKIEP MOTORS (PTY) LTD
POFADDER TRANSPORT (EDMS) BPK
RENTCO TRAILERS (PTY) LTD

STUARTS TRANSPORT (PTY) LTD
STUARTS TRANSPORT NAMIBIA (PTY) LTD
TRAILCON HOLDINGS LTD
TRANS COACH (PTY) LTD
TRANS-AFRICA PARTS NAMIBIA (PTY) LTD
TRENCOR MARKETING (PTY) LTD
TRENCOR PROPERTIES NO 1 (PTY) LTD
TRENCOR PROPERTIES NO 2 (PTY) LTD
TRENCOR PROPERTIES NO 3 (PTY) LTD
TRENCOR PROPERTIES NO 4 (PTY) LTD
TRENCOR PROPERTIES NO 5 (PTY) LTD
TRENCOR PROPERTIES NO 6 (PTY) LTD
TRENCOR PROPERTIES NO 7 (PTY) LTD
TRENCOR PROPERTIES NO 8 (PTY) LTD
TRENCOR PROPERTIES NO 9 (PTY) LTD
TRENCOR PROPERTIES NO 10 (PTY) LTD
TRENCOR PROPERTIES NO 11 (PTY) LTD
TRENCOR PROPERTIES NO 12 (PTY) LTD
TRENCOR PROPERTIES NO 13 (PTY) LTD
TRENCOR SERVICES (PTY) LTD
TRENTRADE (PTY) LTD
TRIOFIN ACCEPTANCES (PTY) LTD
TYCON (PTY) LTD (21%)
VEHICLE & CONTAINER AID SA (PTY) LTD
VITAWARE (PTY) LTD
VITAWARE INVESTORS CO. (PTY) LTD
WADEVILLE INDUSTRIAL NO. 2 (PTY) LTD

INVESTMENTS

BRYCOL ENGINEERING (PTY) LTD (3400 SH)
BUDGET TAINER SERVICES (PTY) LTD (100 SH)
CONTRED (PTY) LTD (7683 SH)
INDIAN OCEAN EXPORT TRADING (PTY) LTD (50 SH)
IOE HOLDINGS (PTY) LTD (50 SH)
NAMAKWALAND BUSDIENS (EDMS) BPK (15000 SH)
TECHNICAL TRANSPORT SERVICES (PTY) LTD (20 SH)
TRANS-AFRICA PARTS (PTY) LTD (1 SH)
TREDCOR MANAGEMENT SERVICES (PTY) LTD (1108 SH)
TRENCOR LTD (1989/1998 DEBS) (1388 DB)

TRIMTEX HOLDINGS LTD

ABBREVIATION : TRIMTEX

JSE SHORT CODE : TRX

SECTOR : Industrial-Clothing, Footwear & Textiles

SHAREHOLDERS

Who Owns Whom's Assessment of the Identity of the Ultimate Controlling Shareholder: DIRECTORS CONTROL 62% (MARCH 1991)

SHAREHOLDER	PERCENTAGE 1992	1991
FOURNES HOLDINGS CORP	40.5	40.5
SAFEGRO NOM P/L	10.8	10.8
STD BANK NOM TVL P/L	9.6	9.6
DS TEPERSON INV P/L	7.7	7.7
LINSA SA P/L	7.7	7.7
SACKS W E	3.3	3.3
ATTON J	2.0	1.8
TEPERSON D S	1.8	1.5
SHARESTOCK NOM P/L	1.2	1.2
DA FONSECA G	1.1	---
TOTAL	85.7	84.2

DIRECTORS :
HURLIMANN CH ,SACHS WE ,STEEL B
TEPERSON DS (Executive Chairman

REGISTRATION NUMBER : 73/15122/06

REGISTERED OFFICE
49 Halifax Road, Pinetown
3600
TEL: 031 701 4536
FAX: 031-728 721

TRANSFER SECRETARY
Central Registrars Ltd
P O Box 4844, Johannesburg
2000
TEL: 011-331 0051

COMPANY SECRETARY
H J Greenbaum

NATURE OF BUSINESS
An investment holding company with a controlling interest in quoted Trimtex Trading.

BANKERS :
First National Bank of SA Ltd

AUDITORS :
Kessel Feinstein

FAMILIAR BRAND NAMES
BABY DAY,HELSA,QUICKDRY

CONTRIBUTION BY ACTIVITY
N/A

YEAR END : March

DIVIDEND : Ords 1c
Final No 3 (Ldr)20/07/90 (Pay)03/08/90 Amt(c)3

NUMBER OF EMPLOYEES : 525

CAPITAL STRUCTURE

	AUTHORISED	ISSUED
Ords 1c	50000000	17366132

FINANCIAL STATISTICS (AT FINANCIAL YEAR END)

(Amts in R'000)	1991 Mar	1990 Mar	1989 Mar	1988 Mar	1987
Ord S/H Int	5700	11013	14975	12270	2460
Long Trm Loans	3937	5907	2530	2217	5549
Iss Ord Share	17366	17366	17336	16550	8300
Total Liab	17485	19670	13029	9045	10609
Current Liab	13548	13763	10499	6828	5060
Total Assets	23110	26182	22462	15766	14799
Intang Assets	75	4501	5542	5549	*
Current Assets	17770	20815	18342	12320	6790
Debtors	10056	10751	9999	7087	-
Inventory	7417	9706	8229	5220	6790
Turnover	37507	40219	34975	26557	15236
Oper Profit	536	4937	4893	3698	1383
Interest Paid	2534	2307	962	400	337
Tax Paid	-99	793	960	1134	412
Prf af Int&Tax	-1899	1837	2971	2164	634
Prf att Ord Sh	-1424	1377	2971	2164	634

Btm Line Earn	-5313	1377	2971	2277	634
Dividend Paid	-	1563	266	828	300
Mkt Prce(c) YE	17	45	100	75	-
Depreciation	1129	1049	802	597	-

PER SHARE STATISTICS (CENTS)

Net Asst Val	32.39	37.50	54.41	40.61	29.64
Net Earnings	-10.90	10.60	17.10	14.00	-
Dividends	-	3.00	6.00	5.00	-
Cash Flow	-3.24	13.77	21.54	17.95	7.64

RATIOS AND OTHER INFORMATION

Mrk Cap(R000)	2952	7815	17336	12413	-
Current Ratio	1.31	1.51	1.75	1.80	1.34
Quik/Acid Tst	0.76	0.81	0.96	1.04	-
A/C Rec T/ovr	3.73	3.74	3.50	3.75	-
Tot Ass T/ovr	1.62	1.54	1.56	1.68	1.03
Debt/Ass Rat	0.68	0.64	0.57	0.55	0.72
L T L Tot Ass	0.10	0.11	0.10	0.12	0.37
Debt to Eqity	2.76	1.51	0.85	0.71	4.31
Interest Cover	0.21	2.14	5.09	9.24	4.10
Oper Prof Mrg	1.43	12.28	13.99	13.92	9.08
Net Prof Marg%	-3.80	3.42	8.49	8.15	4.16
Ret on Assets	2.32	18.86	21.78	23.46	9.35
Ret on Equity%	-24.98	12.50	19.84	17.64	25.77
Price/Earnings	-1.56	4.25	5.85	5.36	-
Divid Cover	-	3.53	2.85	2.80	-
Divid Yield	-	6.67	6.00	6.67	-
Earning Yield%	-64.12	23.56	17.10	18.67	-
NAV % Mrk Pr	190.53	83.33	54.41	54.15	-
Effec Tax Rate	-	1.03	-	28.05	39.39
Def Interval	-18.89	4.46	2.15	1.46	8.75
Sus Grth Rate	-24.98	-1.69	18.06	10.89	13.58

SUBSIDIARY & ASSOCIATED COMPANIES

TRIMTEX TRADING LTD

INVESTMENTS

None

TRIMTEX TRADING LTD

ABBREVIATION : TRIMTRD

JSE SHORT CODE : TMT

SECTOR : Industrial-Clothing, Footwear & Textiles

SHAREHOLDERS

Who Owns Whom's Assessment of the Identity of the Ultimate Controlling Shareholder: TRIMTEX HOLDINGS

SHAREHOLDER	PERCENTAGE 1992	1991
SA MUTUAL	40.7	43.0
STD BANK NOM TVL P/L	10.4	9.9
FOURNES HOLDINGS CORP	8.5	8.5
SAFEGRO NOM P/L	8.3	10.3
ATTON J	7.5	7.5
SFSS NOM P/L	2.3	---
DS TEPERSON INV P/L	1.5	1.5
LINSA SA P/L	1.5	1.5
ARBUTHNOT J	1.4	---
NUSSBAUM R A W	1.4	1.0
TOTAL	83.6	83.2

DIRECTORS :
GAGNON WN ,GREENBAUM HJ (Managing Director)
HURLIMANN CH ,SACHS WE
SPAIN HS (Deputy Chairman),STEEL B
TEPERSON DS (Executive Chairman

REGISTRATION NUMBER : 89/07256/06

REGISTERED OFFICE
49 Halifax Road, Pinetown
3600
TEL: 031-701 4536
FAX: 031-25 2850

TRANSFER SECRETARY
Central Registrars Ltd
P O Box 4844, Johannesburg
2000
TEL: 011-331 0051

COMPANY SECRETARY
H J Greenbaum

NATURE OF BUSINESS
An investment holding company with subsidiaries engaged in the manufacture & distribution of garment interlinings, shirt & clothing components & shoulder pads, surgical & hospital non-woven fabrics & elastic products.

BANKERS :
First National Bank of SA Ltd

AUDITORS :
Kessel Feinstein

FAMILIAR BRAND NAMES
ECONOPADS,HOOK & LOOP,PROCARE,TRICOT

CONTRIBUTION BY ACTIVITY
N/A

YEAR END : March

DIVIDEND : Ords 1c
Dividend No 1 (Ldr)20/07/90 (Pay)03/08/90 Amt(c)4

NUMBER OF EMPLOYEES : 525

CAPITAL STRUCTURE

	AUTHORISED	ISSUED
Ords 1c	50000000	17366132

FINANCIAL STATISTICS (AT FINANCIAL YEAR END)

(Amts in R'000)	1991 Mar	1990 Mar
Ord S/H Int	7460	10978
Long Trm Loans	2205	3163
Iss Ord Share	17366	17366
Total Liab	15753	16928
Current Liab	13548	13763
Total Assets	23138	26211
Intang Assets	75	1693
Current Assets	17770	20815

Debtors	10056	10751
Inventory	7417	9706
Turnover	37507	40219
Oper Profit	536	4937
Interest Paid	2534	2307
Tax Paid	-99	793
Prf af Int&Tax	-1899	1837
Prf att Ord Sh	-1899	1837
Btm Line Earn	-4047	1837
Dividend Paid	-	695
Mkt Prce(c) YE	17	48
Depreciation	1129	1049

PER SHARE STATISTICS (CENTS)

Net Asst Val	42.53	53.47
Net Earnings	-10.90	10.60
Dividends	-	4.00
Cash Flow	-5.97	16.42

RATIOS AND OTHER INFORMATION

Mrk Cap(R000)	2952	8336
Current Ratio	1.31	1.51
Quik/Acid Tst	0.76	0.81
A/C Rec T/ovr	3.73	3.74
Tot Ass T/ovr	1.62	1.53
Debt/Ass Rat	0.68	0.64
L T L Tot Ass	0.10	0.11
Debt to Eqity	2.11	1.52
Interest Cover	0.21	2.14
Oper Prof Mrg	1.43	12.28
Net Prof Marg%	-5.06	4.57
Ret on Assets	2.32	18.84
Ret on Equity%	-25.46	16.73
Price/Earnings	-1.56	4.53
Divid Cover	-	2.65
Divid Yield	-	8.33
Earning Yield%	-64.12	22.08
NAV % Mrk Pr	250.15	111.39
Effec Tax Rate	-	1.03
Def Interval	-10.24	3.74
Sus Grth Rate	-25.46	10.40

SUBSIDIARY & ASSOCIATED COMPANIES

DHJ INDUSTRIES (SA) (PTY) LTD
HELSATEX AFRICA (PTY) LTD
LININGS (NATAL) (PTY) LTD
PROCARE (PTY) LTD
TRICOT FASTENERS (PTY) LTD

INVESTMENTS

None

TRUWORTHS LTD ZIMBABWE

ABBREVIATION : TRUZIM

SECTOR : Zimbabwe Stock Exchange

SHAREHOLDERS

Who Owns Whom's Assessment of the Identity of the Ultimate Controlling Shareholder:
SONOMA LTD / OLD MUTUAL INV CORP

SHAREHOLDER	PERCENTAGE 1992	1991
SONOMA LTD	33.3	---
OLD MUTUAL INV CORP (PVT) LTD	22.4	---
SOUTHERN LIFE ASSOC ZIM LTD	4.8	---
FIDELITY LIFE ASSURE OF ZIM PVT LTD	3.7	---
BARTELUS (PVT) LTD	2.7	---
TRUWORTHS ZIM LTD SHARE PURCH SCHEME TRU	2.6	---
ENFIELD HOLDINGS LTD	1.6	---
MINING INDUSTRY PENS FUND	1.1	---
LOCAL AUTHORITIES PENS FUND	1.1	---
TOTAL	73.4	---

DIRECTORS :
BLANCHFIELD JC (Managing Director)
CHAVUNDUKA DM
FAIRLAMB WE (Deputy Managing Director)
FLEMING G ,HALL CA ,LEWIS DJ (Chairman)
MUDZVOVA BL (Financial Director),MUZARIRI PW
PARFETT AE

REGISTERED OFFICE
Kelvin Road North, Harare
Zimbabwe

TEL: 702951
FAX: 702890

TRANSFER SECRETARY
First Transfer Secretaries (Pvt) Ltd
P O Box 437, Bulawayo
Zimbabwe

TEL: 092634 - 702905

COMPANY SECRETARY
B L Mudzvova

NATURE OF BUSINESS
Incorporated in Zimbabwe, TRUWORTHS is engaged in the manufacture, retailing and export of ladies fashion wear, children's wear and the retailing of men's wear throughout the country.

BANKERS :
First Merchant Bank of Zimbabwe Ltd
Standard Chartered Bank Zimbabwe Ltd
Zimbabwe Banking Corporation Ltd

AUDITORS :
Ernst & Young

FAMILIAR BRAND NAMES
N/A

CONTRIBUTION BY ACTIVITY
N/A

YEAR END : June

DIVIDEND : Ords Z$0,50

Dividend	(Ldr)24/09/91	(Pay)25/10/91	Amt(c)7.8
Dividend	(Ldr)10/04/92	(Pay)23/04/92	Amt(c)6.3

CAPITAL STRUCTURE

	AUTHORISED	ISSUED
Ords Z$0,50	40000000	31250000

FINANCIAL STATISTICS (AT FINANCIAL YEAR END)

(Amts in Z$)	1992 Jun	1991 Jun
Ord S/H Int	42559	22441
Long Trm Loans	3742	1381
Iss Ord Share	31250	5000
Total Liab	26923	30167
Current Liab	23181	28786
Total Assets	69482	52608
Current Assets	48366	44479
Debtors	28734	26046
Inventory	19227	18191
Turnover	90665	72134
Oper Profit	13066	15314
Interest Paid	3493	1308
Tax Paid	4382	3400
Prf af Int&Tax	5191	10606
Prf att Ord Sh	5191	10606
Btm Line Earn	5191	10606
Dividend Paid	1969	3300
Depreciation	3069	1929

PER SHARE STATISTICS (CENTS)

Net Asst Val	136.19	448.82
Net Earnings	17.80	42.10
Dividends	6.30	13.20
Cash Flow	26.43	250.70

RATIOS AND OTHER INFORMATION

Current Ratio	2.09	1.55
Quik/Acid Tst	1.26	0.91
A/C Rec T/ovr	3.16	2.77
Tot Ass T/ovr	1.30	1.37
Debt/Ass Rat	0.39	0.57
L T L Tot Ass	0.05	0.03
Debt to Eqity	0.63	1.34
Interest Cover	3.74	11.71
Oper Prof Mrg	14.41	21.23
Net Prof Marg%	5.73	14.70
Ret on Assets	18.80	29.11
Ret on Equity%	12.20	47.26
Divid Cover	2.83	3.19
Effec Tax Rate	42.96	24.17
Def Interval	1.72	0.94
Sus Grth Rate	7.57	32.56

SUBSIDIARY & ASSOCIATED COMPANIES

BRAVETTE MANUFACTURING CO (PVT) LTD
EFFECTIVE DEBT COLLECTION (PVT) LTD
MAJOR MERCHANDISING (PVT) LTD
NUMBER 1 STORES (1987) (PVT) LTD
TOP CENTRE (PVT) LTD
TOPIC STORES (PVT) LTD
TRUWORTHS MANAGEMENT SERVICES (PVT) LTD

INVESTMENTS

None

TSL LTD

ABBREVIATION : TSL

SECTOR : Zimbabwe Stock Exchange

SHAREHOLDERS

Who Owns Whom's Assessment of the Identity of the Ultimate Controlling Shareholder:
CORNER PROPERTIES (PVT) LTD

SHAREHOLDER	PERCENTAGE 1992	1991
CORNER PROPERTIES PVT LTD	70.5	---
OLD MUTUAL INV CORP (PVT) LTD	18.5	---
TOTAL	89.1	---

DIRECTORS :
ALCOCK IB ,BROWN JS ,BUTLER ME ,JOUSSE CP
LEWIS DJ ,MACKENZIE KM
MULLEN BH (Financial Director)
NICHOLSON JS (Managing Director),RICHARDS PW
TAWENGWA SC ,TRACEY CG (Chairman

REGISTERED OFFICE
28 Simon Mazorodze Road, Kopje
Harare, Zimbabwe

TEL: 68685
FAX: 68698

TRANSFER SECRETARY
Zimbabwe Banking Corporation Ltd
P O Box 3198, Harare
Zimbabwe

TEL: 092634-735011

COMPANY SECRETARY
Tobacco Sales Administration Services

NATURE OF BUSINESS
Holding company operating in the tobacco and timber sector, trading and storage services, property investments, touring and travel services, printing, airfreight and airport services and fork-lift services.

BANKERS :
N/A

AUDITORS :
Ernst & Young

FAMILIAR BRAND NAMES
N/A

CONTRIBUTION BY ACTIVITY
N/A

YEAR END : October

DIVIDEND : Ords Z$0,25

Dividend	(Ldr)17/04/92	(Pay)04/05/92	Amt(c)6.5
Dividend	(Ldr)03/07/92	(Pay)17/07/92	Amt(c)2.0

NUMBER OF EMPLOYEES : 243

CAPITAL STRUCTURE

	AUTHORISED	ISSUED
Ords Z$0,25	300000000	264612931

FINANCIAL STATISTICS (AT FINANCIAL YEAR END)

(Amts in Z$)	1991 Oct	1990 Oct

Ord S/H Int	228905	127465
Long Trm Loans	3751	30040
Iss Ord Share	264613	15874
Total Liab	91481	79776
Current Liab	87730	49736
Total Assets	317892	204524
Intang Assets	2494	2717
Current Assets	156947	62153
Debtors	71128	20148
Inventory	34283	16528
Turnover	205794	124199
Oper Profit	58477	27384
Interest Paid	4078	3818
Tax Paid	26967	11626
Prf af Int&Tax	29796	13176
Prf att Ord Sh	38008	19107
Btm Line Earn	42882	20497
Dividend Paid	17835	4921
Depreciation	6796	4360

PER SHARE STATISTICS (CENTS)

Net Asst Val	85.56	785.86
Net Earnings	18.40	9.26
Dividends	6.74	2.38
Cash Flow	13.75	114.51

RATIOS AND OTHER INFORMATION

Current Ratio	1.79	1.25
Quik/Acid Tst	1.40	0.92
A/C Rec T/ovr	2.89	6.16
Tot Ass T/ovr	0.65	0.61
Debt/Ass Rat	0.28	0.38
L T L Tot Ass	-	0.13
Debt to Eqity	0.38	0.60
Interest Cover	14.34	7.17
Oper Prof Mrg	28.42	22.05
Net Prof Marg%	18.47	15.38
Ret on Assets	21.87	17.04
Ret on Equity%	16.60	14.99
Divid Cover	2.73	3.89
Effec Tax Rate	47.68	48.21
Def Interval	0.34	2.26
Sus Grth Rate	8.81	11.13

SUBSIDIARY & ASSOCIATED COMPANIES

AGRICOR LTD (ZIMBABWE) (36%)
AGRICULTURAL BUYING SERVICES (PVT) LTD
AGRICURA (PVT) LTD (36%)
BAK STORAGE (PVT) LTD
CAR RENTAL SERVICES (PVT) LTD
CARIBONUM (CENTRAL AFRICA) (PVT) LTD
FORK-LIFT SERVICES (SUCCESORS) (PVT) LTD
GLIEMAN SATELLITE SERVICES (PVT) LTD
JET TOURS (PVT) LTD (40%)
LITHO SERVICES (PVT) LTD
MODRO MANUFACTURERS (1988) (PVT) LTD
NATIONAL AIRFREIGHT & AIRPORT SERVICES (
OLDOWAN TRADING COMPANY (PVT) LTD
PREMIER MILLING CO (PVT) LTD (36%)
PRINT HOLDINGS (PVT) LTD
PROPAK (PVT) LTD (HARARE) (26%)
RUMEVITE (PVT) LTD (36%)
SYSTEGRAM ZIMBABWE (PVT) LTD
T.S. TIMBER (PVT) LTD
T.S.L. MANAGEMENT SERVICES (PVT) LTD
THOMAS COOK NATIONAL (PVT) LTD (40%)
TOBACCO SALES ADMINISTRATION SERVICES (P
TOBACCO SALES COMPUTER SERVICES (PVT) LT
TOBACCO SALES FLOOR LIMITED
TOBACCO SALES SERVICES (PVT) LTD
TOBACCO SALES WAREHOUSE (PVT) LTD
TOBACCO WAREHOUSE & EXPORT CO (1946) LTD
VANGUARD INVESTMENTS (PVT) LTD
WOOD SALES (PVT) LTD

INVESTMENTS

AGRICAIR (PVT) LTD (17%)
WILLIS CORROON HOLDINGS (PVT) LTD (12%)

TWEEFONTEIN UNITED COLLERIES LTD

ABBREVIATION : TWEEFONTN

JSE SHORT CODE : TWE

SECTOR : Mining Financial-Mining Holding

SHAREHOLDERS

Who Owns Whom's Assessment of the Identity of the Ultimate Controlling Shareholder:
LONRHO PLC

SHAREHOLDER	PERCENTAGE 1992	1991
WPH INV LTD	56.0	56.0
STD BANK NOM TVL P/L	19.0	19.6
EIGHTY ONE MAIN STREET NOM LTD	8.3	8.3
NAT PARKS BRD CURATORS STAFF PENS FUND	2.6	2.6
NORTHCHART INV LTD	2.3	2.3
FIRST NAT NOM P/L	2.1	---
BARCLAYS NAT NOM P/L	---	2.1
TOTAL	90.2	90.9

DIRECTORS :
LEE RA ,NEL MM ,WILKINSON KP
WILKINSON TA (Chairman & Managing Dir.

REGISTRATION NUMBER : 01/05279/06

REGISTERED OFFICE
1st Floor, 19 Girton Road
Parktown
2193
TEL: 011-642 7691
FAX: 011-642 9717

TRANSFER SECRETARY
Mercantile Registrars Ltd
P O Box 1053, Johannesburg
2000
TEL: 011-333 8181

COMPANY SECRETARY
Lonrho Management Services (Pty) Ltd

NATURE OF BUSINESS
An investment holding company with interests in quoted Duiker Exploration.

BANKERS :
First National Bank of SA Ltd

AUDITORS :
KPMG Aiken & Peat

FAMILIAR BRAND NAMES
N/A

CONTRIBUTION BY ACTIVITY
N/A

YEAR END : September

DIVIDEND : Ords 50c

Interim No 122	(Ldr)30/03/90	(Pay)25/04/90	Amt(c)57
Final No 123	(Ldr)28/09/90	(Pay)24/10/90	Amt(c)30
Interim No 124	(Ldr)28/03/91	(Pay)24/04/91	Amt(c)55
Final No 125	(Ldr)27/09/91	(Pay)23/10/91	Amt(c)38
Interim No 126	(Ldr)27/03/92	(Pay)23/04/92	Amt(c)40
Final No 127	(Ldr)25/09/92	(Pay)21/10/92	Amt(c)62

NUMBER OF EMPLOYEES : 1567

CAPITAL STRUCTURE

	AUTHORISED	ISSUED
Ords 50c	2000000	1735000
Red Prefs 50c	2000	0

FINANCIAL STATISTICS (AT FINANCIAL YEAR END)

(Amts in R'000)	1992 Sep	1991 Sep	1990 Sep	1989 Sep	1988 Sep
Ord S/H Int	4284	6024	6231	6210	6141
Long Trm Loans	-	-	1211	1202	1174
Iss Ord Share	1735	1735	1735	1735	1735
Total Liab	5025	705	1939	2078	2210
Current Liab	5025	705	728	876	1036
Total Assets	9309	6729	8170	8288	8351
Current Assets	5157	797	859	977	1292
Debtors	1134	714	582	618	587
Oper Profit	-109	-97	595	1988	1595
Tax Paid	8	6	8	-134	60
Prf af Int&Tax	1797	1626	1925	2122	1535
Prf att Ord Sh	1797	1626	1531	1596	1114
Btm Line Earn	3899	1626	1531	1596	1162
Dividend Paid	5639	1614	1510	1527	2099
Mkt Prce(c) YE	1150	1100	1600	1975	2000

PER SHARE STATISTICS (CENTS)

Net Asst Val	246.92	347.20	359.14	357.93	353.95
Net Earnings	103.60	93.90	88.20	92.00	64.20
Dividends	102.00	93.00	87.00	88.00	121.00
Cash Flow	103.57	93.72	88.24	91.99	64.21

RATIOS AND OTHER INFORMATION

Mrk Cap(R000)	19953	19085	27760	34266	34700
Current Ratio	1.03	1.13	1.18	1.12	1.25
Quik/Acid Tst	1.03	1.13	1.18	1.12	1.25
Debt/Ass Rat	0.54	0.10	0.09	0.11	0.12
Debt to Eqity	1.17	0.12	0.12	0.14	0.17
Ret on Assets	19.39	24.25	23.66	23.99	19.10
Ret on Equity%	41.95	26.99	24.57	25.70	18.14
Price/Earnings	11.10	11.71	18.14	21.47	31.15
Divid Cover	1.02	1.01	1.01	1.05	0.53
Divid Yield	8.87	8.45	5.44	4.46	6.05
Earning Yield%	9.01	8.54	5.51	4.66	3.21
NAV % Mrk Pr	21.47	31.56	22.45	18.12	17.70
Effec Tax Rate	-8.79	-7.14	1.08	0.25	3.76
Sus Grth Rate	-89.68	0.20	0.34	1.11	-16.04

SUBSIDIARY & ASSOCIATED COMPANIES

CORONATION SYNDICATE LTD
DUIKER EXPLORATION LTD (22,2%)

INVESTMENTS

None

U-CONTROL LTD

ABBREVIATION : U-CON

JSE SHORT CODE : UCN

SECTOR : Industrial-Engineering

SHAREHOLDERS

Who Owns Whom's Assessment of the Identity of the Ultimate Controlling Shareholder: DIRECTORS

SHAREHOLDER	PERCENTAGE 1992	1991
UNIHOLD INV P/L	33.5	38.2
SOUTHERN LIFE ASSOC LTD	22.8	23.2
HASLAM A L	7.9	8.0
MCLEAN I	6.1	5.6
BURHAM FOUNDATION	5.1	5.2
BUTLER J W	4.4	3.9
LOCH-DAVIS D J & PFEIFFER S A	3.8	3.5
HASLAM EDUCATIONAL TRUST	3.4	1.4
NEDBANK NOM LTD	3.0	2.3
STOCKSHARE NOM P/L	1.2	---
SFSS NOM P/L	1.0	---
TOTAL	92.0	91.1

DIRECTORS :
BRADFORD DG ,BUTLER JW (Managing Director)
CRIMP GE ,HASLAM JC (Chairman),HASLAM WJ
LOCH DAVIS DJ

REGISTRATION NUMBER : 67/10361/06

REGISTERED OFFICE
2nd Floor, Lakeside Place, Queen Street
Bruma, Johannesburg
2198
TEL: 011-615 7017
FAX: 011-615 8149

TRANSFER SECRETARY
Mercantile Registrars Ltd
P O Box 1053, Johannesburg
2000
TEL: 011-333 8181

COMPANY SECRETARY
B T MacDonald

NATURE OF BUSINESS
An investment holding company with a controlling interest in JSE-quoted Unihold Ltd.

BANKERS :
First National Bank of SA Ltd

AUDITORS :
Deloitte Pim Goldby

FAMILIAR BRAND NAMES
N/A

CONTRIBUTION BY ACTIVITY
N/A

YEAR END : December

DIVIDEND : Ords no par value

Special No 1	(Ldr)12/04/90	(Pay)20/04/91	Amt(c)3
Interim No 2	(Ldr)14/09/90	(Pay)09/10/90	Amt(c)2 25
Final No 3	(Ldr)15/03/91	(Pay)28/03/91	Amt(c)4 5
Interim No 4	(Ldr)06/09/91	(Pay)09/10/91	Amt(c)2 25
Final No 5	(Ldr)13/03/92	(Pay)15/04/92	Amt(c)4 5

NUMBER OF EMPLOYEES : 2050

CAPITAL STRUCTURE

	AUTHORISED	ISSUED
Ords no par value	65000000	63766438
15% Conv Debs 45c	14561296	14561296

FINANCIAL STATISTICS (AT FINANCIAL YEAR END)

(Amts in R'000)	1991 Dec	1990 Dec	1989 Dec
Ord S/H Int	30727	22871	8238
Long Trm Loans	-	6553	-
Iss Ord Share	63434	46692	200
Total Liab	2908	8692	-
Current Liab	2908	2139	-
Total Assets	33635	31563	8238
Current Assets	2892	2140	-
Debtors	2855	2093	-
Oper Profit	3	952	-174
Interest Paid	4	7	59
Prf af Int&Tax	4266	5899	217
Prf att Ord Sh	4266	5062	217
Btm Line Earn	4266	4503	1013
Dividend Paid	4265	4500	1749
Mkt Prce(c) YE	85	70	-

PER SHARE STATISTICS (CENTS)

Net Asst Val	48 44	48 98	4119 00
Net Earnings	6 70	9 60	-
Dividends	9 75	9 75	4 50
Cash Flow	6 73	12 63	108 50

RATIOS AND OTHER INFORMATION

Mrk Cap(R000)	53919	32684	-
Current Ratio	0 99	1 00	-
Quik/Acid Tst	0 99	1 00	-
Debt/Ass Rat	0 09	0 28	-
L T L Tot Ass	-	0 21	-
Debt to Eqity	0 09	0 38	-
Interest Cover	1065 25	842 00	4 68
Ret on Assets	12 70	18 71	3 35
Ret on Equity%	13 88	22 13	2 63
Price/Earnings	12 69	7 29	
Divid Cover	0 69	0 98	-
Divid Yield	11 47	13 93	-
Earning Yield%	7 88	13 71	-
NAV % Mrk Pr	56 99	69 98	-
Sus Grth Rate	0 00	2 46	-18 60

SUBSIDIARY & ASSOCIATED COMPANIES

UNIHOLD LTD

INVESTMENTS

None

UDC LTD

ABBREVIATION : UDC

SECTOR : Zimbabwe Stock Exchange

SHAREHOLDERS

Who Owns Whom's Assessment of the Identity of the Ultimate Controlling Shareholder: EDESA HOLDINGS / OLD MUTUAL INV CORP

SHAREHOLDER	PERCENTAGE 1992	1991
EDESA HOLDINGS LTD	30 0	---
OLD MUTUAL INV CORP (PVT) LTD	12 5	---
MINING INDUSTRY PENS FUND	11 2	---
INTERNATIONAL FINANCE CORP LTD	9 1	---
UDC STAFF SHARE PURCHASE TRUST	5 0	---
SOUTHAMPTON ASSURE CO ZIM LTD	3 7	---
LOCAL AUTHORITIES PENS FUND	3 5	---
TOTAL	75 2	---

DIRECTORS :
ANDERSON BJ (Executive Director),BLOHM HR
DICK JW (Executive Director)
GERBER RW (Chairman)
GRINT RP (Executive Director),MAKONI JT DR
MALABA G ,NKOMO SS ,READ FRG

REGISTERED OFFICE
Twelth Floor, udc Centre
Union Ave/First Street, Harare

TEL 702181
FAX 263-4-736042

TRANSFER SECRETARY
Zimbabwe Banking Corporation Ltd
P O Box 3198, Harare
Zimbabwe

TEL 092634-735011

COMPANY SECRETARY
D J Joe

NATURE OF BUSINESS
udc is the largest finance house in Zimbabe Apart from the head office situated in Harare,there are branch offices in Bulawayo, Chinhoyi,Gweru,Masvingo and Mutare As a deposit receiving institu_ tion,the activities of the companies are the pro_ vision of hire purchase and leasing,loans and fac toring services to both private and public com_ panies Hire purchase finance is also available to individuals In addition,the company provides business loan finance to companies and individuals

BANKERS :
N/A

AUDITORS :
Price Waterhouse Meyernel

FAMILIAR BRAND NAMES
N/A

CONTRIBUTION BY ACTIVITY
N/A

YEAR END : December

DIVIDEND : Ords Z$1
Dividend (Ldr)13/03/92 (Pay)23/03/92 Amt(c)6.5

CAPITAL STRUCTURE

	AUTHORISED	ISSUED
Ords Z$1	30000000	26800000

FINANCIAL STATISTICS (AT FINANCIAL YEAR END)

(Amts in Z$)	1991 Dec	1990 Dec
Ord S/H Int	46917	19052
Iss Ord Share	26800	7000
Total Liab	573972	346779
Current Liab	573972	346779
Total Assets	620889	365831
Current Assets	555457	327478
Debtors	505998	309478
Oper Profit	5869	3953
Prf af Int&Tax	5869	3953
Prf att Ord Sh	5869	3953
Btm Line Earn	5869	3953
Dividend Paid	2967	1960
Depreciation	3042	5152

PER SHARE STATISTICS (CENTS)

Net Asst Val	175.06	272.17
Net Earnings	28.49	22.59
Dividends	13.50	28.00
Cash Flow	43.26	130.07

RATIOS AND OTHER INFORMATION

Current Ratio	0.97	0.94
Quik/Acid Tst	0.97	0.94
Debt/Ass Rat	0.92	0.95
Debt to Eqity	12.23	18.20
Ret on Assets	0.95	1.08
Ret on Equity%	12.51	20.75
Divid Cover	2.11	0.81
Def Interval	64.41	38.09
Sus Grth Rate	6.19	10.46

SUBSIDIARY & ASSOCIATED COMPANIES

None

INVESTMENTS

None

UMDONI PROPERTY FUND

ABBREVIATION : UMDONI

JSE SHORT CODE : UMN

SECTOR : Financial-Property Trust

SHAREHOLDERS

Who Owns Whom's Assessment of the Identity of the Ultimate Controlling Shareholder: VARIOUS INSTITUTIONAL INVESTORS

SHAREHOLDER	PERCENTAGE 1992	1991
CMB NOM P/L	13.6	---
FIRST NAT NOM P/L	12.1	4.1
EIGHTY ONE MAIN STREET NOM LTD	8.7	7.8
STD BANK NOM TVL P/L	8.2	4.8
SA MUTUAL	7.6	11.2
BARLOWS PENS FUND	3.1	1.2
PROFESSIONAL PROV SOC OF SA	2.4	2.4
SHARESTOCK NOM P/L	2.3	2.7
ENGINEERING INDUSTRIES PENS FUND	1.9	1.9
METAL IND GROUP PENS FUND	1.5	1.5
SMBL NOM P/L	1.3	1.3
GEMEENSKAPLIKE MUNISIPALE TVL PENS FUND	1.2	---
SIXTY SIX MARSHALL STREET NOM P/L	1.2	1.4
CORNER HOUSE PENS FUND	1.0	---
NAT PARKS BRD CURATORS STAFF PENS FUND	1.0	---
MERCANTILE & GEN REINSURANCE CO SA LTD	---	1.1
ANGLOVAAL PENS FUND	---	1.2
BARCLAYS NAT NOM P/L	---	6.2
SANAFCO PENS FUND	---	1.1
SANLAM	---	13.0
TOTAL	67.2	62.8

DIRECTORS :
CHAPMAN HG MR,DICKSON AJL MR,FARRER M MR
NOYCE MJ MR (Chairman),SMALE JR MR
SMITHYMAN MV MR,TAYLOR G M

REGISTRATION NUMBER : 83/08365/06

REGISTERED OFFICE
Protea Assurance Building, 321 Smith Street
Durban
4001
TEL: 031-304 2731
FAX: 031-304 2377

TRANSFER SECRETARY
Mercantile Registrars Ltd
P O Box 1053, Johannesburg
2000
TEL: 011-333 8181

COMPANY SECRETARY
Russell Marriott & Boyd Trust (Pty) Ltd

NATURE OF BUSINESS
Umdoni has a portfolio of industrial, commercial and retail property in the Durban and Johannesburg metropolitan areas which it leases and maintains. The fund is managed by Yellowwood Property Fund Managers Ltd.

BANKERS :
First National Bank of SA Ltd

AUDITORS :
David Strachan & Tayler
Deloitte Pim Goldby

FAMILIAR BRAND NAMES
N/A

CONTRIBUTION BY ACTIVITY
Industrial (% Fund by Property Sector) (54.0%)
Shops & Offices (24.0%)
Office Blocks (14.0%)
Parking (7.0%)
Residential (1.0%)

YEAR END : September

DIVIDEND : Units

Final No 26	(Ldr)11/05/90	(Pay)28/05/90	Amt(c)4
Interim No 27	(Ldr)17/08/90	(Pay)31/08/90	Amt(c)3.9
Final No 28	(Ldr)16/11/90	(Pay)30/11/90	Amt(c)4.05
Interim No 29	(Ldr)08/02/91	(Pay)25/02/91	Amt(c)4.1
Final No 30	(Ldr)10/05/91	(Pay)27/05/91	Amt(c)4.2
Interim No 31	(Ldr)16/08/91	(Pay)30/08/91	Amt(c)4.3
Final No 32	(Ldr)15/11/91	(Pay)29/11/91	Amt(c)4.4
Interim No 33	(Ldr)14/02/92	(Pay)28/02/92	Amt(c)4.45
Final No 34	(Ldr)15/05/92	(Pay)29/05/92	Amt(c)4.6
Interim No 35	(Ldr)14/08/92	(Pay)28/08/92	Amt(c)4.65
Final No 36	(Ldr)13/11/92	(Pay)27/11/92	Amt(c)4.75

CAPITAL STRUCTURE

	AUTHORISED	ISSUED
Units	97500000	97500000

FINANCIAL STATISTICS (AT FINANCIAL YEAR END)

(Amts in R'000)	1992 Sep	1991 Sep	1990 Sep	1989 Sep	1988 Sep
Ord S/H Int	106111	104294	100172	99422	98727
Iss Ord Share	97500	97500	97500	97500	97500
Total Liab	5120	4482	4203	3703	3405
Current Liab	5120	4482	4203	3703	3405
Total Assets	111231	108776	104375	103125	102132
Current Assets	10938	8794	4576	7765	10219
Debtors	179	75	25	127	185
Oper Profit	17989	16579	15110	10384	12677
Prf af Int&Tax	17989	16579	15110	10384	12677
Prf att Ord Sh	17989	16579	15110	10384	12677
Btm Line Earn	17989	16579	15110	10384	12677
Dividend Paid	17989	16575	15113	10384	12675
Mkt Prce(c) YE	160	160	130	145	110

PER SHARE STATISTICS (CENTS)

Net Asst Val	108.83	106.97	102.74	101.97	101.26
Net Earnings	18.45	17.00	15.50	10.65	13.00
Dividends	18.45	17.00	15.50	10.65	13.00
Cash Flow	18.45	17.00	15.50	10.65	13.00

RATIOS AND OTHER INFORMATION

Mrk Cap(R000)	156000	156000	126750	141375	107250
Current Ratio	2.14	1.96	1.09	2.10	3.00
Quik/Acid Tst	2.14	1.96	1.09	2.10	3.00
Debt/Ass Rat	0.05	0.04	0.04	0.04	0.03
Debt to Eqity	0.05	0.04	0.04	0.04	0.03
Ret on Assets	16.17	15.24	14.48	10.07	12.41
Ret on Equity%	16.95	15.90	15.08	10.44	12.84
Price/Earnings	8.67	9.41	8.39	13.62	8.46
Divid Cover	1.00	1.00	1.00	1.00	1.00
Divid Yield	11.53	10.63	11.92	7.34	11.82
Earning Yield%	11.53	10.63	11.92	7.34	11.82
NAV % Mrk Pr	68.02	68.86	79.03	70.33	92.05
Sus Grth Rate	0.00	0.00	0.00	0.00	0.00

SUBSIDIARY & ASSOCIATED COMPANIES

206 CHURCH STREET (PMB) (PTY) LTD
ABC BAKERY (PTY) LTD, THE
AVOCET INVESTMENTS (PTY) LTD
BENPORATH INVESTMENTS (PTY) LTD
BERG PARK (PTY) LTD
BONDFIELD (PTY) LTD
BREIGHTMET PROPERTIES (PTY) LTD
BRICK RIDGE PROPERTIES (PTY) LTD
BUTCHER BROTHERS (PTY) LTD
CALANDRA INVESTMENTS (PTY) LTD
CUSTODIAN PROPERTIES (PTY) LTD
DELPHI INVESTMENTS (PTY) LTD
DJ KAISER PROPERTIES (PTY) LTD
EIGHTEEN BUREAU CRESCENT (PTY) LTD
ERF TWO SEVENTY SPARTAN (PTY) LTD
FENLOR (PTY) LTD
FRED W DUKES (PTY) LTD
FRETPROPS INVESTMENTS (PTY) LTD
GRINDROD PROPERTIES (CITY DEEP) (PTY) LT
HADEDAH INVESTMENTS (PTY) LTD
HILLPROPS (PTY) LTD
IRELAND & COMPANY (PTY) LTD
LOT FOURTEEN LA LUCIA (PTY) LTD
MORTON ROAD PROPERTY INVESTMENTS (PTY) L
NODUMI (PTY) LTD
ORIOLE PROPERTIES (PTY) LTD
PHOENIX KHULANI (PTY) LTD
QUAILPROP INVESTMENTS (PTY) LTD
RADNATAL INVESTMENTS (PTY) LTD
SAN FELICE (PTY) LTD
SARASOTA PROPERTY HOLDINGS (PTY) LTD
SIXTEEN PASCOE ROAD (PTY) LTD
STAND 436 WADEVILLE EXT NO 6 (PTY) LTD
STAND 624 ALRODE (PTY) LTD
SWIFTPROPS (PTY) LTD
THATCHERPROPS (PTY) LTD
UNITED FACTORS (PTY) LTD
VILLAGE CENTRE (PTY) LTD
WATERPROPS (PTY) LTD
XASPROPS (PTY) LTD

INVESTMENTS

None

UNIDEV CONSOLIDATED HOLDINGS LTD

ABBREVIATION : UNICON

JSE SHORT CODE : UNC

SECTOR : Industrial-Industrial Holding

SHAREHOLDERS

Who Owns Whom's Assessment of the Identity of the Ultimate Controlling Shareholder:
JK BRETT & AH CHONOWITZ

SHAREHOLDER	PERCENTAGE 1992	1991
TOP-HI INV P/L	96.6	78.9
CMB NOM P/L	1.1	---
GRYLLS G P	---	4.6
ANGLO AMERICAN CORP PENS FUND	---	2.0
DE BEERS PENS FUND	---	2.0
HIRSCHSON I	---	1.3
ANGLO AMERICAN GROUP PENS FUND	---	1.0
PHELPS L S	---	2.0
WILLMORE L H	---	2.8
TOTAL	97.7	94.5

DIRECTORS :
BRETT JK (Joint Managing Director)
CHONOWITZ AH (Joint Managing Director)
DU TOIT PE (Financial Director),HARRIS GS

REGISTRATION NUMBER : 82/09823/06

REGISTERED OFFICE
3rd Floor, Entrance 2 or 5, 156 Fifth Street
Sandown
2196
TEL: 011-883 9320
FAX: 011-883 9043

TRANSFER SECRETARY
Central Registrars Ltd
P O Box 4844, Johannesburg
2000
TEL: 011-331 0051

COMPANY SECRETARY
G S Harris

NATURE OF BUSINESS
An investment holding company with a controlling interest in JSE-quoted Unidev Ltd.

BANKERS :
Senbank

AUDITORS :
Kessel Feinstein

FAMILIAR BRAND NAMES
N/A

CONTRIBUTION BY ACTIVITY
N/A

YEAR END : December

DIVIDEND :15/05/91

CAPITAL STRUCTURE

	AUTHORISED	ISSUED
Ords 3,5c	132857144	127016009

FINANCIAL STATISTICS (AT FINANCIAL YEAR END)

(Amts in R'000)	1991 Dec	1990 Dec	1989 Dec	1988 Dec
Ord S/H Int	24477	2158	27834	7147
Long Trm Loans	-	614	-	-
Iss Ord Share	127016	20088	20088	5609
Total Liab	651	1282	7907	175
Current Liab	651	668	7907	175
Total Assets	25128	3440	35741	7322
Current Assets	-	4	3543	20
Debtors	-	4	1393	-
Oper Profit	-	-25735	1791	316
Interest Paid	-	16	115	10
Tax Paid	-	-	661	3
Prf af Int&Tax	-	-25676	3872	323
Prf att Ord Sh	-	-25676	3872	323
Btm Line Earn	-	-25676	21565	323
Dividend Paid	-	-	6629	323
Mkt Prce(c) YE	60	165	230	120

PER SHARE STATISTICS (CENTS)

Net Asst Val	19.27	10.74	138.56	127.42
Net Earnings	-	-127.80	23.10	2.00
Dividends	-	-	33.00	2.00
Cash Flow	-	-127.82	23.08	2.02

RATIOS AND OTHER INFORMATION

Mrk Cap(R000)	76210	33145	46202	6731
Current Ratio	-	0.01	0.45	0.11
Quik/Acid Tst	-	0.01	0.45	0.11
Debt/Ass Rat	0.03	0.37	0.22	0.02
L T L Tot Ass	-	0.18	-	-
Debt to Eqity	0.03	0.59	0.28	0.02
Interest Cover	-	-1608.44	27.68	31.60
Ret on Assets	-	-745.93	13.00	4.59
Ret on Equity%	-	-1189.81	13.91	4.52
Price/Earnings	-	-1.29	9.96	60.00
Divid Cover	-	-	0.70	1.00
Divid Yield	-	-	14.35	1.67
Earning Yield%	-	-77.45	10.04	1.67
NAV % Mrk Pr	32.12	6.51	60.24	106.18
Effec Tax Rate	-	-	21.04	0.92
Def Interval	-	-	0.16	0.52
Sus Grth Rate	-	-1189.81	-9.91	0.00

SUBSIDIARY & ASSOCIATED COMPANIES

UNIDEV LTD

INVESTMENTS

None

UNIDEV LTD

ABBREVIATION : UNIDEV

JSE SHORT CODE : UDV

SECTOR : Industrial-Industrial Holding

SHAREHOLDERS

Who Owns Whom's Assessment of the Identity of the Ultimate Controlling Shareholder:
UNICON

SHAREHOLDER	PERCENTAGE 1992	1991
UNIDEV CONSOLIDATED HOLDINGS LTD	82.2	46.7
UNIDEV CONSOLIDATED LTD	2.2	9.0

NEDBANK NOM LTD	1.4	1.1
SOUTHERN LIFE ASSOC LTD	1.2	8.6
STD BANK NOM TVL P/L	1.0	1.8
UNIDEV SHARE OPTION SCHEME	---	2.4
FIRST NAT NOM P/L	---	4.2
AA MUTUAL LIFE ASSURE ASSOC LTD	---	3.0
ELLERINE BROS P/L	---	1.1
MEYER D	---	1.6
SANLAM	---	4.8
TOTAL	88.0	84.3

DIRECTORS :
BRETT JK (Joint Managing Director)
CHONOWITZ AH (Joint Managing Director)
DU TOIT PE ,HARRIS GS (Financial Director

REGISTRATION NUMBER : 68/02187/06

REGISTERED OFFICE
3rd Floor, Entrance 2 or 5, 156 Fifth Street
Sandown
2196
TEL: 011-883 9320
FAX: 011-883 9043

TRANSFER SECRETARY
Central Registrars Ltd
P O Box 4844, Johannesburg
2000
TEL: 011-331 0051

COMPANY SECRETARY
G S Harris

NATURE OF BUSINESS
An investment holding company. Operations include manufacture, marketing and distribution of general housewares, kitchen utensils, galvanised products and domestic & industrial bakeware; An investment in Medicor, which is involved in health-care.

BANKERS :
Bankorp Ltd

AUDITORS :
Kessel Feinstein

FAMILIAR BRAND NAMES
BABY CLUB,COOKPRIDE,EWBANK,KROST,MARATHON MASTERBAKER,OVENPRIDE,PRESTIGE,SEE HYPERETTE

CONTRIBUTION BY ACTIVITY
N/A

YEAR END : December

DIVIDEND : Ords 25c

Interim No 33	(Ldr)01/09/89	(Pay)25/09/89	Amt(c)6
Final No 34	(Ldr)27/04/90	(Pay)11/05/90	Amt(c)8

CAPITAL STRUCTURE

	AUTHORISED	ISSUED
Ords 25c	170000000	129831691

FINANCIAL STATISTICS (AT FINANCIAL YEAR END)

(Amts in R'000)	1991 Dec	1990 Dec	1989 Dec	1988 Dec	1987 Dec
Ord S/H Int	34155	2097	87675	60081	53252
Long Trm Loans	39104	59083	71624	28278	21537
Iss Ord Share	129832	31048	30669	17039	85193
Total Liab	64645	151744	211082	109382	50989
Current Liab	25541	92661	139458	81104	29452
Total Assets	98800	153841	276026	154931	103642
Intang Assets	*	*	22731	14532	599
Current Assets	24376	30188	114740	85297	44946
Debtors	11793	12312	52625	39874	30338
Inventory	12583	17876	54302	40004	13701
Oper Profit	3483	-80229	18521	11415	10372
Interest Paid	4834	12036	15296	6370	539
Tax Paid	-	-	246	-364	-43
Prf af Int&Tax	1015	-90485	5208	9233	9876
Prf att Ord Sh	2040	-86793	11635	8874	9543
Btm Line Earn	-19896	-86793	11635	8874	9543
Dividend Paid	-	-	3476	2045	3557
Mkt Prce(c) YE	25	40	150	220	85
Depreciation	1327	1408	3324	2513	868

PER SHARE STATISTICS (CENTS)

Net Asst Val	26.31	6.75	211.76	267.32	61.80
Net Earnings	2.00	-280.40	55.80	52.10	61.00
Dividends	-	-	14.00	12.00	22.50
Cash Flow	1.85	-307.74	39.44	60.20	62.20

RATIOS AND OTHER INFORMATION

Mrk Cap(R000)	32458	12419	46004	37486	72414
Current Ratio	0.95	0.33	0.82	1.05	1.53
Quik/Acid Tst	0.46	0.13	0.43	0.56	1.06
Debt/Ass Rat	0.60	0.64	0.52	0.60	0.39
L T L Tot Ass	0.35	0.04	0.02	0.08	0.10
Debt to Eqity	1.75	46.82	1.65	1.56	0.75
Interest Cover	0.72	-6.67	1.24	1.89	19.24
Ret on Assets	7.39	-44.58	9.94	10.30	10.62
Ret on Equity%	5.97	-4138.91	13.27	14.77	17.92
Price/Earnings	12.50	-0.14	2.69	4.22	1.39
Divid Cover	-	-	3.99	4.34	2.71
Divid Yield	-	-	9.33	5.45	26.47
Earning Yield%	8.00	-701.00	37.20	23.68	71.76
NAV % Mrk Pr	105.23	16.89	141.17	121.51	72.71
Effec Tax Rate	-	-	6.92	0.57	0.76
Def Interval	28.30	-1.44	15.74	4.98	2.44
Sus Grth Rate	5.97	-4138.91	9.31	11.37	11.24

SUBSIDIARY & ASSOCIATED COMPANIES

ABACUS SECURITIES (PTY) LTD
AQUANAUT INVESTMENTS (PTY) LTD
BEAU-GESTE INVESTMENTS (PTY) LTD
BEST SALES (PTY) LTD
BONSAI TRADING CO (PTY) LTD
COMPUTER INSTALLATION GROUP LTD (20%)
COMPUTER SYSTEMS SA (PTY) LTD
CORPORATE DATA CONTROL LTD
CORTECH ELECTRONICS LTD
DAVOS COFFEE BAR (PTY) LTD
DRAAIKLOOF PROPERTIES (PTY) LTD
DURBAN PROPERTY HOLDINGS LTD
EFI (PTY) LTD
ENGINEERING DATA SYSTEMS (SOUTH AFRICA)
FURNITURE FAIR GROUP HOLDINGS LTD (29%)
GILLIS-MASON (PTY) LTD
HARD DECISIONS DISTRIBUTORS (PTY) LTD (49%)
HERALD INVESTMENTS (PTY) LTD (50%)
HYPERETTE
HYPERETTE STORES LTD (33%)
JAYSAT INVESTMENTS (PTY) LTD (50%)
KENILWORTH CLINIC PROPERTIES (PTY) LTD
KIRKNEY EXTENSION 15 (PTY) LTD (50%)
KROST BROTHERS (PTY) LTD
KROST HOUSEWARES (PTY) LTD
KWIKSHOP HOLDINGS (PTY) LTD (50%)
MEDICOR LTD (50%)
MERCANTILE BANK HOLDINGS LTD (28%)
MERCANTILE SECURITIES LTD (37%)

NATIONAL COMPUTER CO (PTY) LTD (25%)
NATIONAL PROPERTIES LTD
NEWFIN ENTERTAINMENT CO (PTY) LTD (43%)
NEWFIN PRODUCTIONS (PTY) LTD (30%)
NICFIELD PROPERTIES (PTY) LTD
OCEAN DIAMOND MINING HOLDINGS LTD (23%)
PEDAL INVESTMENTS (PTY) LTD
PIETERSBURG EXECUTIVE APARTMENTS (PTY) L
PLASTIC PACKAGING INVESTMENTS LTD
PRESTIGE GROUP LTD
PRESTIGE GROUP MANAGEMENT SERVICES (PTY)
PRESTIGE HOUSEWARES (PTY) LTD
PRESTIGE PROPERTIES (PTY) LTD
PRET-HILL INVESTMENTS (PTY) LTD
Q FARM HOLDINGS (PTY) LTD (50%)
Q FINANCE (PTY) LTD (49%)
QUAESTOR IV LTD (50%)
QUANTUM FINANCE (PTY) LTD (49%)
SANDBRATH (PTY) LTD
SCB (PTY) LTD
SECOND USER SYSTEMS (PTY) LTD
SEETEK (PTY) LTD
SHERIM INVESTMENTS (PTY) LTD
SK COMPUTER SYSTEMS (PTY) LTD
SK GROUP
SKYLINE PRODUCTS (PTY) LTD
STATION ROAD MANSIONS PROPERTY INVESTMEN
STELPLAN (PTY) LTD
STEVELA INVESTMENTS (PTY) LTD
TELSTAR ESTATES (PTY) LTD (50%)
TRUROLL (PTY) LTD
UNIDEV FINANCIAL SERVICES LTD
UNIDEV HOSPITAL INVESTMENTS LTD
UNIDEV INVESTMENT HOLDINGS LTD
UNIDEV MANAGEMENT SERVICES LTD
UNIDEV PROJECT INVESTMENTS LTD
UNIDEV RETAIL HOLDINGS LTD
UNIDEV STRATEGIC INVESTMENT HOLDINGS NO
UNIDEV STRATEGIC INVESTMENT HOLDINGS NO
UNIDEV STRATEGIC INVESTMENT HOLDINGS NO
UNIDEV STRATEGIC INVESTMENT HOLDINGS NO
UNIDEV STRATEGIC INVESTMENT HOLDINGS NO
UNIDEV STRATEGIC INVESTMENT HOLDINGS NO
UNIDEV STRATEGIC INVESTMENT HOLDINGS NO
UNIDEV STRATEGIC INVESTMENT HOLDINGS NO
UNIDEV STRATEGIC INVESTMENT HOLDINGS NO1
UNIDEV TEXTILE INVESTMENTS LTD
UNIDEV VENTURE INVESTMENTS LTD
UNIRUS INVESTMENTS (PTY) LTD
VAN RIEBEECKSTAD DEVELOPMENT CO LTD
VOORHOUT STREET PROPERTIES (PTY) LTD
VULCAN STEEL PROPERTY INVESTMENT HOLDING
WILD RICE INVESTMENTS (PTY) LTD

INVESTMENTS

ABS HOLDINGS LTD (1,44%)
BESTER INVESTMENTS LTD (4825 SH)
DEBONAIR GROUP LTD (4%)
MACADAMS BAKERY SUPPLIES LTD (3,24%)
MACMED HEALTH CARE LTD (250000 SH)
RUSFURN GROUP LTD (16,43%)

UNIHOLD LTD

ABBREVIATION : UNIHOLD

JSE SHORT CODE : UHS

SECTOR : Industrial-Engineering

SHAREHOLDERS

Who Owns Whom's Assessment of the Identity of the Ultimate Controlling Shareholder:
U-CONTROL LTD

SHAREHOLDER	PERCENTAGE 1992	1991
U-CONTROL LTD	54.2	77.5
SOUTHERN LIFE ASSOC LTD	17.5	2.9
NEDBANK NOM LTD	9.7	---
ZUMTOBEL LICHT GMBH	2.0	---
ZUMTOBEL HOLDING AG	1.4	---
HARVEST SECURITIES LTD	1.1	1.5
SFSS NOM P/L	1.1	1.2
BANK OF LISBON STAFF PENS FUND	1.0	---
EIGHTY ONE MAIN STREET NOM LTD	---	1.5
MACVEN NOM P/L	---	1.0
TOTAL	88.0	85.5

DIRECTORS :
ARTHUR R (BOB) MR (Chairman)
BUTLER JW MR (Managing Director),COHEN NJ MR
CRIMP GE MR,DU PLESSIS R MR (Chief Executive)
HASLAM JC MR,LOCH DAVIS DJ MR (Deputy Chairman)
MCLEAN I MR,POOLE JGW M

REGISTRATION NUMBER : 68/00216/06

REGISTERED OFFICE
2nd Floor, Lakeside Place, Queens Street
Bruma, Johannesburg
2001
TEL: 011-615 7017
FAX: 011-615 8149

TRANSFER SECRETARY
Mercantile Registrars Ltd
P O Box 1053, Johannesburg
2000
TEL: 011-333 8181

COMPANY SECRETARY
B T MacDonald

NATURE OF BUSINESS
The group manufactures and supplies industrial products to the mining, lighting, automotive and general engineering industries. Operations are conducted through electrical, engineering and foundry divisions. Group products include pumps, process equipment, high pressure pipe fittings, stainless steel wedgewire, hydraulic mine props, reflective & non-reflective number plates & safety signs, silkscreen products, signage & manganese steel wearparts.

BANKERS :
Standard Bank of SA Ltd
First National Bank of SA Ltd
Nedcor Bank Ltd

AUDITORS :
Deloitte Pim Goldby

FAMILIAR BRAND NAMES
BOKSBURG FOUNDRY,CHESTERTON PUMPS,DECALIGHT
DENVER,DENVER ORION,RELY,SHEARLOCK,THORN
UNIQUE ENGINEERING,WALRO AUTOMOTIVE
WALRO FLEX,WILCO,WILFLO,ZUMTOBEL

CONTRIBUTION BY ACTIVITY
Engineering (29.4%)
Electrical (34.4%)
Foundry (% of Turnover) (36.2%)

YEAR END : December

DIVIDEND : Ords 50c

Interim No 26	(Ldr)14/09/90	(Pay)09/10/90	Amt(c)4.5
Final No 27	(Ldr)15/03/91	(Pay)28/03/91	Amt(c)9
Interim No 28	(Ldr)06/09/91	(Pay)09/10/91	Amt(c)4.5
Final No 29	(Ldr)13/03/92	(Pay)15/04/92	Amt(c)9

NUMBER OF EMPLOYEES : 2396

CAPITAL STRUCTURE

	AUTHORISED	ISSUED
Ords 50c	100000000	58005000
9,5% Red Cum Conv Prefs R1	1750000	0
5,5% Red Cum Pref R1	200000	200000

FINANCIAL STATISTICS (AT FINANCIAL YEAR END)

(Amts in R'000)	1991 Dec	1990 Dec	1989 Dec	1988 Dec	1987 Dec
Ord S/H Int	66506	39558	34830	25755	15947
Long Trm Loans	31021	34765	25629	23512	19628
Iss Ord Share	40912	30156	28493	26076	24804
Total Liab	88640	73615	64162	45543	38651
Current Liab	57619	38850	38533	22031	19023
Total Assets	155146	113173	98992	71298	54598
Current Assets	76444	64548	57068	40037	30026
Debtors	36094	27874	24426	19905	14711
Inventory	39866	36674	32622	20047	15217
Turnover	216091	196854	158976	116661	84145
Oper Profit	19505	23184	22102	13039	8797
Interest Paid	7364	6597	5633	3555	2422
Tax Paid	3229	6260	4928	-18	-37
Prf af Int&Tax	8912	10327	11541	9502	6412
Prf att Ord Sh	8795	8395	10671	9388	6502
Btm Line Earn	8795	8395	10625	9388	6569
Dividend Paid	5441	4049	3406	3129	2463
Mkt Prce(c) YE	175	145	140	120	75
Depreciation	8329	6377	4743	3025	2425

PER SHARE STATISTICS (CENTS)

Net Asst Val	162.56	131.18	122.24	98.77	64.29
Net Earnings	22.40	23.60	30.20	36.90	27.30
Dividends	13.50	13.50	12.00	12.00	10.00
Cash Flow	44.47	58.31	60.21	48.40	37.12

RATIOS AND OTHER INFORMATION

Mrk Cap(R000)	71596	43726	39890	31291	18603
Current Ratio	1.33	1.66	1.48	1.82	1.58
Quik/Acid Tst	0.63	0.72	0.63	0.91	0.78
A/C Rec T/ovr	5.99	7.06	6.51	5.86	5.72
Tot Ass T/ovr	1.39	1.74	1.61	1.64	1.54
Debt/Ass Rat	0.48	0.54	0.56	0.55	0.60
L T L Tot Ass	0.11	0.20	0.17	0.25	0.25
Debt to Eqity	1.13	1.55	1.59	1.53	2.06
Interest Cover	2.65	3.51	3.92	3.67	3.63
Oper Prof Mrg	9.03	11.78	13.90	11.18	10.45
Net Prof Marg%	4.07	4.26	6.71	8.05	7.73
Ret on Assets	12.57	20.49	22.33	18.29	16.11
Ret on Equity%	13.22	21.22	30.64	36.45	40.77
Price/Earnings	7.81	6.14	4.64	3.25	2.75
Divid Cover	1.66	1.75	2.52	3.08	2.73
Divid Yield	7.71	9.31	8.57	10.00	13.33
Earning Yield%	12.80	16.28	21.57	30.75	36.40
NAV % Mrk Pr	92.89	90.47	87.31	82.31	85.72
Effec Tax Rate	22.68	28.45	20.61	0.95	-
Def Interval	2.95	1.74	1.59	1.43	0.59
Sus Grth Rate	5.04	10.99	20.86	24.30	25.33

SUBSIDIARY & ASSOCIATED COMPANIES

DIMBAZA FOUNDRIES (PTY) LTD
LEON HELFET MANUFACTURING CO (PTY) LTD (
U-LITE HOLDINGS (PTY) LTD (50%)
UGL MANAGEMENT SERVICES (PTY) LTD
ZUMTOBEL MANAGEMENT SERVICES (PTY) LTD (50%)

INVESTMENTS

None

UNION COLD STORAGE OF SA LTD

ABBREVIATION : UNI-COLD

JSE SHORT CODE : UCS

SECTOR : Industrial-Pharmaceutical & Medical

SHAREHOLDERS

Who Owns Whom's Assessment of the Identity of the Ultimate Controlling Shareholder: FINGER FAMILY

SHAREHOLDER	PERCENTAGE 1992	1991
REPUBLIC NOM P/L	29.7	29.7
UNITED FINANCE CORP OF SA LTD	28.4	28.0
M H FINGER INV P/L	23.3	23.3
SIMSID INV LTD	8.1	8.1
FINGER M H	5.0	5.0
SILVERSANDS ESTATES LTD	2.7	2.7
TOTAL	97.1	96.7

DIRECTORS :
FINGER MD ,FINGER MH (Chairman),GORDON ALKIN
GORDON ARNOLD ,HOFFMAN RC

REGISTRATION NUMBER : 02/01318/06

REGISTERED OFFICE
2nd Floor FHS House, 15 Girton Road
Parktown
2193
TEL: 011-643 7361
FAX: 011-643 2229

TRANSFER SECRETARY
Central Registrars Ltd
P O Box 4844, Johannesburg
2000
TEL: 011-331 0051

COMPANY SECRETARY
FHS Secretarial Services CC

NATURE OF BUSINESS
The company carries on the business of investment and financier.Its subsidiaries are engaged in property and land development and finance.

BANKERS :
First National Bank of SA Ltd

AUDITORS :
Deloitte & Touche

FAMILIAR BRAND NAMES
N/A

CONTRIBUTION BY ACTIVITY
N/A

YEAR END : June

DIVIDEND :Ords 3c

Dividend No 42	(Ldr)02/11/90	(Pay)22/11/90	Amt(c)70
Dividend No 43	(Ldr)01/11/91	(Pay)27/11/91	Amt(c)80
Dividend No 44	(Ldr)23/10/92	(Pay)06/11/92	Amt(c)100
Dividend No 45	(Ldr)23/10/92	(Pay)06/11/92	Amt(c)200

CAPITAL STRUCTURE

	AUTHORISED	ISSUED
Ords 3c	12959616	1300450

FINANCIAL STATISTICS (AT FINANCIAL YEAR END)

(Amts in R'000)	1992 Jun	1991 Jun	1990 Jun	1989 Jun	1988 Jun
Ord S/H Int	13251	16635	16170	15292	15313
Iss Ord Share	1300	1300	1300	1300	1300
Total Liab	4056	2002	1675	1469	1442
Current Liab	4056	2002	1675	1469	1442
Total Assets	17307	18637	17845	16761	16755
Current Assets	12161	12653	12001	5752	4491
Debtors	164	213	211	152	79
Oper Profit	-161	-146	-156	2784	1346
Interest Paid	-	-	-	1270	-
Tax Paid	1153	1202	831	575	715
Prf af Int&Tax	1373	1602	1034	939	631
Prf att Ord Sh	1374	1573	1199	1075	762
Btm Line Earn	517	1662	1787	889	793
Dividend Paid	3901	1040	910	910	910
Mkt Prce(c) YE	1700	1700	2000	1725	1200
Depreciation	32	32	32	7	5

PER SHARE STATISTICS (CENTS)

Net Asst Val	1019.31	1279.62	1243.85	1176.31	1177.92
Net Earnings	105.70	120.90	92.30	82.70	78.10
Dividends	300.00	80.00	70.00	70.00	70.00
Cash Flow	108.08	125.69	82.00	72.77	48.92

RATIOS AND OTHER INFORMATION

Mrk Cap(R000)	22100	22100	26000	22425	15600
Current Ratio	3.00	6.32	7.16	3.92	3.11
Quik/Acid Tst	3.00	6.32	7.16	3.92	3.11
Debt/Ass Rat	0.23	0.11	0.09	0.09	0.09
Debt to Eqity	0.31	0.12	0.10	0.10	0.09
Interest Cover	-	-	-	2.19	-
Ret on Assets	14.60	14.89	11.38	17.42	8.82
Ret on Equity%	10.37	9.46	7.41	7.03	4.98
Price/Earnings	16.08	14.06	21.67	20.86	15.36
Divid Cover	0.35	1.51	1.32	1.18	1.12
Divid Yield	17.65	4.71	3.50	4.06	5.83
Earning Yield%	6.22	7.11	4.61	4.79	6.51
NAV % Mrk Pr	59.96	75.27	62.19	68.19	98.16
Effec Tax Rate	48.55	48.47	51.11	37.98	39.45
Def Interval	-	-	-	0.22	0.35
Sus Grth Rate	-19.07	3.20	1.79	1.08	-0.97

SUBSIDIARY & ASSOCIATED COMPANIES

BOTHA GARDENS INVESTMENTS (PTY) LTD
CENTRAL MATTRESS CO. LTD
MARFRICK INVESTMENTS (PTY) LTD (50%)
MAYDAY ESTATES (PTY) LTD
WELTEVREDEN ENTERPRISES (PTY) LTD (35%)

INVESTMENTS

DE BEERS / CENTENARY LINKED UNITS (15000 SH)
DEELKRAAL GOLD MINING CO LTD (5000 SH)
DISTILLERS CORPORATION (NAMIBIA) LTD (1200 SH)
ESCOM (14% LOAN STOCK) 1992
ISCOR LTD (1400 SH)
MATABELELAND FARMERS CO-OP LTD (56 SH)
MIDDLE WITS (WESTERN AREAS) LTD (27500 SH)
PREMIER PHARMACEUTICAL CO LTD (3002 SH)
RAND MINES PROPERTIES LTD (4000 SH)
REP OF SA 15% LOAN STOCK 2007
RUSFURN GROUP LTD (2500 SH)
SA BREWERIES LTD (20374 SH)
SA DRUGGISTS LTD LENNON D (1250 SH)
SASOL LTD (22500 SH)
STELLENBOSCH FARMERS WINERY LTD (1200 SH)
TRADEGRO LTD (700 SH)
TRANS-NATAL COAL CORPORATION LTD (5750 SH)
UNITED FINANCE CORP OF SA LTD (25400 SH)
WESTERN AREAS GOLD MINING CO LTD (5000 SH)

UNION MINES LTD

ABBREVIATION : UNION

JSE SHORT CODE : UNN

SECTOR : Metals & Minerals-Tin

SHAREHOLDERS

Who Owns Whom's Assessment of the Identity of the Ultimate Controlling Shareholder:
DIRECTORS CONTROL 41%

SHAREHOLDER	PERCENTAGE 1992	1991
ILSE F G INV P/L	21.3	13.5
NORBERTON LTD	12.3	12.3
NEW CHAKARI MINES P/L	5.0	12.5
FLOODTIDE SYNDICATE P/L	4.6	4.6
ASHMEAD HOLDINGS P/L	4.2	4.2
KATZ J H	3.1	3.1
LARSEN B K	2.6	2.6
KEYSER J DE LA H	2.0	2.0
FRANKE R R	1.9	---
DU PLESSIS P	1.6	1.6
HARDING D C	1.5	1.5
VAN DER BERGH J	1.4	---
THOMPSON F R L	1.4	1.4

COMBINED SAND CC	1.4	1.4
STD BANK NOM TVL P/L	1.3	1.3
ANDROMEDA P/L	1.3	1.3
HURWORTH N M	1.2	1.2
ASHMEAD G L	1.0	1.0
FIRST NAT NOM P/L	---	1.9
NEDBANK NOM LTD	---	1.8
TOTAL	68.9	68.9

DIRECTORS :
ASHMEAD GL ,ILSE FG ,VAN DER BURGH EJ

REGISTRATION NUMBER : 05/32935/08

REGISTERED OFFICE
122 Bree Street, Cape Town
8001
TEL: 021-23 4174
FAX: 021-22 1980

TRANSFER SECRETARY
Central Registrars Ltd
P O Box 4844, Johannesburg
2000
TEL: 011-331 0051

COMPANY SECRETARY
N/A

NATURE OF BUSINESS
The company ceased underground tin mining operations and dump retreatment in 1986. The plant has been placed on care and maintenance.

BANKERS :
Standard Bank of SA Ltd

AUDITORS :
Friedberg Miller Gruft & Co

FAMILIAR BRAND NAMES
N/A

CONTRIBUTION BY ACTIVITY
N/A

YEAR END : December

DIVIDEND :15/00/91

CAPITAL STRUCTURE

	AUTHORISED	ISSUED
Ords 25c	2600000	2400000

FINANCIAL STATISTICS (AT FINANCIAL YEAR END)

(Amts in R'000)	1991 Dec	1990 Dec	1989 Dec	1988 Dec	1987
Ord S/H Int	4878	5365	5838	1942	5284
Long Trm Loans	-	-	-	-	65
Iss Ord Share	2400	2400	2400	2400	2400
Total Liab	1342	907	453	62	130
Current Liab	1342	907	453	62	65
Total Assets	4463	4515	4534	2004	6352
Intang Assets	1757	1757	1757	*	*
Current Assets	5	48	61	661	1003
Debtors	2	36	21	69	-
Inventory	2	11	40	41	1003
Oper Profit	-276	-353	-491	-14	-245
Interest Paid	210	121	6	-	-
Prf af Int&Tax	-486	-474	-458	46	-73
Prf att Ord Sh	-486	-474	-458	46	-73
Btm Line Earn	-486	-474	-458	46	-73
Mkt Prce(c) YE	2	70	135	175	110

PER SHARE STATISTICS (CENTS)

Net Asst Val	130.04	150.33	170.04	80.92	220.17
Net Earnings	-20.30	-19.70	-19.00	2.00	-
Cash Flow	-20.25	-19.75	-19.08	1.92	-3.04

RATIOS AND OTHER INFORMATION

Mrk Cap(R000)	48	1680	3240	4200	2640
Current Ratio	0.00	0.05	0.13	10.66	15.43
Quik/Acid Tst	0.00	0.04	0.05	10.00	-
Debt/Ass Rat	0.30	0.20	0.10	0.03	0.02
L T L Tot Ass	-	-	-	-	0.01
Debt to Eqity	0.28	0.17	0.08	0.03	0.02
Interest Cover	-1.31	-2.92	-81.83	-	-
Ret on Assets	-6.18	-7.82	-9.97	2.30	-1.15
Ret on Equity%	-9.96	-8.84	-7.85	2.37	-1.38
Price/Earnings	-0.10	-3.55	-7.11	87.50	-
Earning Yield%	-1015.00	-28.14	-14.07	1.14	-
NAV % Mrk Pr	6502.08	214.76	125.96	46.24	200.15
Def Interval	-2.59	-1.71	-0.74	-	-0.89
Sus Grth Rate	-9.96	-8.84	-7.85	2.37	-1.38

SUBSIDIARY & ASSOCIATED COMPANIES

None

INVESTMENTS

None

UNISEL GOLD MINES LTD

ABBREVIATION : UNISEL

JSE SHORT CODE : UNL

SECTOR : Gold-OFS

SHAREHOLDERS

Who Owns Whom's Assessment of the Identity of the Ultimate Controlling Shareholder:
SANLAM VIA GENCOR

SHAREHOLDER	PERCENTAGE 1992	1991
CONSOLIDATED NOM P/L	40.0	43.2
RESIDENT NOM LTD	18.4	18.4
ABSA NOM P/L	14.2	---
STD BANK NOM TVL P/L	7.4	7.8
INDO-CHINA NOM P/L	4.2	4.4
FIRST NAT NOM P/L GATR DEPOT	2.0	---
CMB NOM P/L	1.7	---
FIRST NAT NOM P/L	---	1.1
INDO-CHINA NOM SA P/L	---	4.4
SANLAM	---	1.6
VOLKSKAS NOM P/L	---	10.4
TOTAL	87.9	91.2

DIRECTORS :
BOTHA AD ,DE VILLIERS JS DR,ELLIS SP ,EUSTACE PJ
MAUDE G (Chairman),OLIVIER JE ,ROBINSON PDK

REGISTRATION NUMBER : 72/10604/06

REGISTERED OFFICE
General Mining Building, 6 Hollard Street
Johannesburg
2001
TEL: 011-376 9111

TRANSFER SECRETARY
Central Registrars Ltd
P O Box 4844, Johannesburg
2000
TEL: 011-331 0051

COMPANY SECRETARY
General Mining Metals & Minerals Ltd

NATURE OF BUSINESS
The company operates a gold mine in the Welkom AREA, OFS. Silver and pyrite are recovered as by-products of the gold mining process.

BANKERS :
Trust Bank of Africa Ltd

AUDITORS :
Deloitte & Touche

FAMILIAR BRAND NAMES
N/A

CONTRIBUTION BY ACTIVITY
Gold (% of Turnover) (99.9%)
Silver (0.1%)

YEAR END : September

DIVIDEND : Ords no par value

Interim No 21	(Ldr)04/05/90	(Pay)15/06/90	Amt(c)50
Final No 22	(Ldr)02/11/90	(Pay)14/12/90	Amt(c)26
Interim No 23	(Ldr)03/05/91	(Pay)14/06/91	Amt(c)10

NUMBER OF EMPLOYEES : 3385

CAPITAL STRUCTURE

	AUTHORISED	ISSUED
Ords no par value	28000000	28000000

FINANCIAL STATISTICS (AT FINANCIAL YEAR END)

(Amts in R'000)	1991 Sep	1990 Sep	1989 Sep	1988	1987
Ord S/H Int	182570	169134	150213	129959	120709
Long Trm Loans	186	244	-	49137	75505
Iss Ord Share	28000	28000	28000	28000	28000
Total Liab	14618	29860	54898	98178	150810
Current Liab	14432	29616	54898	49041	75305
Total Assets	197188	198994	205111	230988	281667
Current Assets	16634	35304	60149	54745	85453
Debtors	3295	3721	892	-	-
Inventory	3858	4349	4238	54745	85453
Turnover	153115	181356	201741	196902	235654
Oper Profit	16753	58526	86054	86076	136783
Interest Paid	23	54	-	-	-
Tax Paid	1950	17939	36258	44662	82401
Prf af Int&Tax	14896	40701	49849	41414	54222
Prf att Ord Sh	14896	40701	49849	30677	44229
Btm Line Earn	14896	40701	49849	30677	44229
Dividend Paid	2800	21280	29400	32200	44800

Mkt Prce(c) YE	975	2250	1950	1125	3300

PER SHARE STATISTICS (CENTS)

Net Asst Val	652.04	604.05	536.48	464.14	431.10
Net Earnings	-7.00	76.00	105.00	-	-
Dividends	10.00	79.00	106.00	-	-
Cash Flow	53.20	145.36	178.03	147.91	193.65

RATIOS AND OTHER INFORMATION

Mrk Cap(R000)	273000	630000	546000	315000	924000
Current Ratio	1.15	1.19	1.10	1.12	1.13
Quik/Acid Tst	0.89	1.05	1.02	-	-
A/C Rec T/ovr	46.47	48.74	226.17	-	-
Tot Ass T/ovr	0.78	0.91	0.98	0.85	0.84
Debt/Ass Rat	0.07	0.15	0.27	0.43	0.54
L T L Tot Ass	0.00	0.00	-	0.21	0.27
Debt to Eqity	0.08	0.18	0.37	0.76	1.25
Interest Cover	733.30	1086.85	-	-	-
Oper Prof Mrg	10.94	32.27	42.66	43.72	58.04
Net Prof Marg%	9.73	22.44	24.71	15.58	18.77
Ret on Assets	8.55	29.50	41.98	37.26	48.51
Ret on Equity%	8.16	24.06	33.19	23.61	36.64
Price/Earnings	-139.29	29.61	18.57	-	-
Divid Cover	-0.70	0.96	0.99	-	-
Divid Yield	1.03	3.51	5.44	-	-
Earning Yield%	-0.72	3.38	5.38	-	-
NAV % Mrk Pr	66.88	26.85	27.51	41.26	13.06
Effec Tax Rate	11.65	30.68	42.13	51.89	60.24
Def Interval	0.01	0.01	-	1.19	1.39
Sus Grth Rate	6.63	11.48	13.61	-1.17	-0.47

SUBSIDIARY & ASSOCIATED COMPANIES

None

INVESTMENTS

None

UNISPIN HOLDINGS LTD

ABBREVIATION : UNISPIN

JSE SHORT CODE : UNS

SECTOR : Industrial-Clothing, Footwear & Textiles

SHAREHOLDERS

Who Owns Whom's Assessment of the Identity of the Ultimate Controlling Shareholder:
DIRECTORS CONTROL 74%

SHAREHOLDER	PERCENTAGE 1992	1991
CONSOLIDATED FRAME TEXTILES LTD	46.2	---
FINANCIAL ADMINISTRATORS NOM P/L	38.8	72.0
STD BANK NOM TVL P/L	2.5	---
SOCIETE BANCAIRE JULIUS BAER SA	1.5	2.9
UNISPIN SHARE INCENTIVE TRUST	---	1.4
CHE INV P/L	---	1.0
AA LIFE ASSURE ASSOC LTD	---	4.2
BARTEL H O	---	1.4
TOTAL	89.0	83.0

DIRECTORS :
DAVIS SJM ,ELLERINE E ,ELLERINE S ,GAMSU SS
KROK A ,KROK S ,SNIJMAN CJA (Managing Director)
WASCHBERGER R (Chairman

REGISTRATION NUMBER : 87/00336/06

REGISTERED OFFICE
Bedford Street, Neave Industrial Township
Port Elizabeth
6001
TEL: 041-43 1888
FAX: 041-43 5977

TRANSFER SECRETARY
Central Registrars Ltd
P O Box 4844, Johannesburg
2000
TEL: 011-331 0051

COMPANY SECRETARY
J N Erasmus

NATURE OF BUSINESS
The company is the investment holding company of a group of subsidiaries engaging in the manufacture and supply of hand knitting and industrial yarns and a producer of spun cotton cotton yarns.

BANKERS :
Nedperm Bank Ltd
First National Bank of SA Ltd, Senbank

AUDITORS :
Deloitte Pim Goldby

FAMILIAR BRAND NAMES
BEEHIVE,CHICK,COTTON SPINNING,DESIGN STUDIO
ELLE,FIESTA,FROLIC,INDUSTRIALS,JAEGER
KNITTERS CLUB,MIRAGE,PATONS
PATONS & BALDWINS,SHEPHERD
SHORT STAPLE SPINNING,SHORT STAPLE YARNS
SIRDAR,YARNS & WOOLS

CONTRIBUTION BY ACTIVITY
N/A

YEAR END : September

DIVIDEND : Ords 1c
Interim (Ldr)18/05/90 (Pay)08/06/90 Amt(c)2.5

NUMBER OF EMPLOYEES : 1858

CAPITAL STRUCTURE

	AUTHORISED	ISSUED
Ords 1c	50000000	35000000
Cum Red Prefs 1c	10000000	10000000
Cum Red Conv Prefs 1c (Not Listed	30000000	30000000

FINANCIAL STATISTICS (AT FINANCIAL YEAR END)

(Amts in R'000)	1991 Sep	1990 Sep	1989 Sep	1988 Jun	1987 Jun
Ord S/H Int	53323	58223	61512	51139	5910
Long Trm Loans	82660	63018	35917	23656	23591
Iss Ord Share	35000	35000	35000	35000	22800
Total Liab	165726	135118	83287	47345	64478
Current Liab	83066	72100	47370	23689	40887
Total Assets	206235	185067	136111	98484	70388
Intang Assets	12814	8274	8688	*	*
Current Assets	96786	87025	68699	63433	38594
Debtors	42732	38491	27940	23575	16515
Inventory	53489	47789	40625	25765	22057
Turnover	131674	123931	118558	76653	19355
Oper Profit	18486	11224	22172	14949	3668
Interest Paid	21776	12347	4512	944	530
Prf af Int&Tax	-3290	-1123	17660	14005	3138
Prf att Ord Sh	-4914	-2414	16274	13716	3138
Btm Line Earn	-4914	-2414	15274	13716	3138
Dividend Paid	-	875	4900	4900	-
Mkt Prce(c) YE	50	85	185	150	-
Depreciation	9220	6182	3445	2107	696

PER SHARE STATISTICS (CENTS)

Net Asst Val	115.74	142.71	150.93	146.11	25.92
Net Earnings	-14.00	-6.90	46.50	39.20	-
Dividends	-	2.50	14.00	14.00	-
Cash Flow	12.30	10.77	45.07	45.21	67.26

RATIOS AND OTHER INFORMATION

Mrk Cap(R000)	17500	29750	64750	52500	-
Current Ratio	1.17	1.21	1.45	2.68	0.94
Quik/Acid Tst	0.52	0.54	0.59	1.59	0.40
A/C Rec T/ovr	3.08	3.22	3.39	3.25	4.69
Tot Ass T/ovr	0.64	0.67	0.70	0.78	1.10
Debt/Ass Rat	0.66	0.68	0.54	0.38	0.92
L T L Tot Ass	0.26	0.29	0.19	0.14	0.34
Debt to Eqity	2.55	2.15	1.19	0.73	10.91
Interest Cover	0.85	0.91	4.91	15.84	6.92
Oper Prof Mrg	14.04	9.06	18.70	19.50	18.95
Net Prof Marg%	-3.73	-1.95	13.73	17.89	16.21
Ret on Assets	8.96	6.06	13.03	15.18	20.84
Ret on Equity%	-9.22	-4.15	21.17	26.82	212.39
Price/Earnings	-3.57	-12.32	3.98	3.83	-
Divid Cover	-	-2.76	3.32	2.80	-
Divid Yield	-	2.94	7.57	9.33	-
Earning Yield%	-28.00	-8.12	25.14	26.13	-
NAV % Mrk Pr	231.48	167.90	81.58	97.41	-
Def Interval	32.44	29.34	1.92	1.56	31.00
Sus Grth Rate	-9.22	-5.65	18.49	17.24	53.10

SUBSIDIARY & ASSOCIATED COMPANIES

BERNEVE (PTY) LTD
PATONS & BALDWINS SOUTH AFRICA (PTY) LTD
SIRDAR FABRICS (SA) (PTY) LTD
SIRDAR WOOLS (PTY) LTD
STAPLE PROPERTIES (PTY) LTD
UNIFABRIC (PTY) LTD
UNION SPINNING MILLS (PTY) LTD
UNIWEAVE (PTY) LTD
YARNS & WOOLS (PTY) LTD

INVESTMENTS

None

UNITED SERVICE TECHNOLOGIES LTD

ABBREVIATION : UNISERV

JSE SHORT CODE : USV

SECTOR : Industrial-Industrial Holding

SHAREHOLDERS

Who Owns Whom's Assessment of the Identity of the Ultimate Controlling Shareholder: ANUBIS TRUST (BRITISH VIRGIN ISLANDS)

SHAREHOLDER	PERCENTAGE 1992	1991
PTR HOLDINGS INC	58.4	57.1
SA MUTUAL	9.3	2.7
YSKOR PENS FUND	4.3	4.0
FIRST NAT NOM P/L	4.1	3.0
SHARESTOCK NOM P/L	4.0	5.2
DORBYL PENS FUND	3.8	---
LIBERTY LIFE ASSOC OF AFRICA LTD	3.6	3.8
AFRICAN OXYGEN LTD PENS FUND	2.3	1.1
STD BANK NOM TVL P/L	---	1.6
NEDBANK NOM LTD	---	1.3
GUNDELFINGER A A	---	1.5
SA SPECIAL RISKS INSURANCE ASSOC LTD	---	4.3
SIXTY SIX MARSHALL STREET NOM P/L	---	1.7
WRAGGE K A	---	1.3
TOTAL	89.8	88.5

DIRECTORS :
GUNDELFINGER AA ,KERR RC ,MORRIS DR
ROSENZWEIG AM ,SAXTON BM (Deputy Chairman)
SOUTHEY EM ,WESSELS MJ (Chairman

REGISTERED OFFICE
First Floor, Bank of Nova Scotia Building
Road Town, Tortola, British Virgin Islands

TEL: 011-456 2215
FAX: 011-456 2104

TRANSFER SECRETARY
Mercantile Registrars Ltd
P O Box 1053, Johannesburg
2000
TEL: 011-333 8181

COMPANY SECRETARY
L R Samuels

NATURE OF BUSINESS
An investment holding company incorporated in the British Virgin Isle. Subsidiaries provide freight, courier and travel services, on an international and domestic basis.

BANKERS :
Nedperm Bank Ltd

AUDITORS :
Deloitte Pim Goldby

FAMILIAR BRAND NAMES
BURLINGTON/WTC,MOUNTIES,OVERNITE EXPRESS
SUN COURIERS

CONTRIBUTION BY ACTIVITY
Africa (% Operating profit) (72.0%)
Europe (28.0%)

YEAR END : February

DIVIDEND : Ords no par value

Dividend No 3	(Ldr)11/05/90	(Pay)08/06/90	Amt(c)8
Dividend No 4	(Ldr)10/05/91	(Pay)24/05/91	Amt(c)8

NUMBER OF EMPLOYEES : 350

CAPITAL STRUCTURE

	AUTHORISED	ISSUED
Ords no par value	60000000	[illegible],8389126
"A" Var Rate Cum Conv Prefs 50c (	1500000	1500000
"B" Var Rate Cum Conv Prefs npv	8000000	5333333

FINANCIAL STATISTICS (AT FINANCIAL YEAR END)

(Amts in R'000)	1992 Feb	1991 Feb	1990 Feb	1989 Feb	1988
Ord S/H Int	58817	58006	49925	19464	5854
Long Trm Loans	18646	20285	18613	4649	442
Iss Ord Share	46080	45280	45278	35266	21304
Total Liab	111443	83705	92313	63873	5186
Current Liab	92797	63420	73700	59224	4744
Total Assets	136617	109327	110812	83337	11040
Intang Assets	33643	32384	31426	*	*
Current Assets	104064	82327	89715	69853	7353
Debtors	95218	63788	79324	69179	4014
Turnover	-	-	-	-	17181
Oper Profit	5822	18373	18977	11356	3328
Interest Paid	5480	5233	6549	4123	385
Tax Paid	832	1421	1271	1152	1273
Prf af Int&Tax	2192	13658	13421	7911	1670
Prf att Ord Sh	764	12230	12001	7143	1612
Btm Line Earn	764	10731	13181	7143	1612
Dividend Paid	-	3622	3622	2465	277
Mkt Prce(c) YE	90	130	120	140	135
Depreciation	8820	6407	4965	3430	478

PER SHARE STATISTICS (CENTS)

	1992	1991	1990	1989	1988
Net Asst Val	54.63	56.59	40.86	55.19	27.48
Net Earnings	1.70	27.00	26.50	20.30	10.50
Dividends	-	8.00	8.00	6.00	1.30
Cash Flow	20.77	41.58	39.06	29.98	9.81

RATIOS AND OTHER INFORMATION

	1992	1991	1990	1989	1988
Mrk Cap(R000)	41472	58864	54334	49372	28760
Current Ratio	1.12	1.30	1.22	1.18	1.55
Quik/Acid Tst	1.12	1.30	1.22	1.18	1.55
A/C Rec T/ovr	-	-	-	-	4.28
Tot Ass T/ovr	-	-	-	-	1.56
Debt/Ass Rat	0.72	0.64	0.71	0.77	0.47
L T L Tot Ass	0.05	0.06	0.05	0.06	0.04
Debt to Eqity	1.68	1.21	1.58	3.28	0.89
Interest Cover	1.06	3.51	2.90	2.75	8.64
Oper Prof Mrg	-	-	-	-	19.37
Net Prof Marg%	-	-	-	-	9.38
Ret on Assets	6.22	18.58	19.17	15.82	30.14
Ret on Equity%	1.30	21.08	24.04	36.70	27.54
Price/Earnings	52.94	4.81	4.53	6.90	12.86
Divid Cover	-	3.38	3.31	3.38	8.08
Divid Yield	-	6.15	6.67	4.29	0.96
Earning Yield%	1.89	20.77	22.08	14.50	7.78
NAV % Mrk Pr	60.70	43.53	34.05	39.42	20.35
Effec Tax Rate	32.90	8.16	3.76	12.71	43.26
Def Interval	2.15	0.93	1.26	1.46	0.56
Sus Grth Rate	1.30	14.84	16.78	24.03	22.80

SUBSIDIARY & ASSOCIATED COMPANIES

DELDEVCO PROPERTIES (PTY) LTD
GODDARD LIMITED
GRANAT PROPERTY INVESTMENTS (PTY) LTD
KARIBE INVESTMENTS LTD
MARINE LINK (PTY) LTD
OVERNITE EXPRESS (PTY) LTD
PYRAMID FREIGHT (PTY) LTD

PYRAMID FREIGHT INVESTMENTS (PTY) LTD
SPEEDWHEEL DELIVERIES (PTY) LTD
SUN COURIERS (PTY) LTD
THOMAS INTERNATIONAL FREIGHT AUDITORS LI
UNITED SERVICE TECHNOLOGIES SOCIETE ANON

INVESTMENTS

None

UNITRANS LTD

ABBREVIATION : UNITRAN

JSE SHORT CODE : UTR

SECTOR : Industrial-Transportation

SHAREHOLDERS

Who Owns Whom's Assessment of the Identity of the Ultimate Controlling Shareholder: SANLAM VIA SANKORP & MURRAY & ROBERTS

SHAREHOLDER	PERCENTAGE 1992	1991
UNITED GENERAL INV P/L	77.9	80.0
CMB NOM P/L	5.9	---
EIGHTY ONE MAIN STREET NOM LTD	4.3	2.2
METAL IND GROUP PENS FUND	1.6	1.6
ENGINEERING INDUSTRIES PENS FUND	1.4	1.4
STD BANK NOM TVL P/L	1.3	1.9
SANLAM	---	5.2
TOTAL	92.4	92.3

DIRECTORS :
GUTIERREZ-GARCIA E (Chief Executive),HEFER HV
LE ROUX EJ ,MCMANUS JR (Financial Director)
STEYN P ,VAN DER COLFE AM (Chairman

REGISTRATION NUMBER : 67/03403/06

REGISTERED OFFICE
Unitrans House, 291 Kent Avenue
Ferndale, Randburg
2194
TEL: 011-787 9400
FAX: 011-787 0009

TRANSFER SECRETARY
Central Registrars Ltd
P O Box 4844, Johannesburg
2000
TEL: 011-331 0051

COMPANY SECRETARY
D A King

NATURE OF BUSINESS
The group provides road transportation & related services which include warehousing, distribution, forestry harvesting, container services, logistics management and fuel terminal management services.

BANKERS :
Standard Bank of SA Ltd

AUDITORS :
KPMG Aiken & Peat

FAMILIAR BRAND NAMES
N/A

CONTRIBUTION BY ACTIVITY
N/A

YEAR END : June

DIVIDEND : Ords 10c

Interim No 4	(Ldr)17/11/89	(Pay)15/12/89	Amt(c)7.5
Final No 5	(Ldr)22/06/90	(Pay)09/07/90	Amt(c)12
Interim No 6	(Ldr)30/11/90	(Pay)14/12/90	Amt(c)9.5
FinaL No 7	(Ldr)21/06/91	(Pay)08/07/91	Amt(c)14
Interim No 8	(Ldr)29/11/91	(Pay)13/12/91	Amt(c)10
Final No 9	(Ldr)28/02/92	(Pay)11/03/92	Amt(c)5
Interim No 10	(Ldr)18/09/92	(Pay)02/10/92	Amt(c)17

NUMBER OF EMPLOYEES : 3270

CAPITAL STRUCTURE

	AUTHORISED	ISSUED
Ords 10c	60000000	37368000
16% Unsec Comp Conv Debs	15009000	15009000

FINANCIAL STATISTICS (AT FINANCIAL YEAR END)

(Amts in R'000)	1992 Jun	1991 Mar	1990 Mar	1989 Mar	1988 Mar
Ord S/H Int	163017	113201	96391	74604	58183
Long Trm Loans	86360	83724	78241	27165	9377
Iss Ord Share	37368	36400	36400	36400	36400
Total Liab	173411	141805	119033	68327	46041
Current Liab	87051	58081	40792	41162	36664
Total Assets	336428	255006	215188	142931	104224
Intang Assets	*	*	236	*	*
Current Assets	125438	72457	63191	40846	34424
Debtors	61942	44795	35309	31213	17674
Inventory	7102	4738	3735	4070	2742
Turnover	409143	257124	216182	185343	115093
Oper Profit	66223	41790	42328	32401	19175
Interest Paid	18747	14196	8683	2694	137
Tax Paid	15168	1502	5482	9991	7845
Prf af Int&Tax	41825	27316	29093	20100	11193
Prf att Ord Sh	40529	26408	28393	19818	10109
Btm Line Earn	40529	26408	28393	19818	10109
Dividend Paid	11814	8554	7098	5096	3414
Mkt Prce(c) YE	800	550	415	270	170
Depreciation	45972	30750	24616	17316	9664

PER SHARE STATISTICS (CENTS)

Net Asst Val	436.25	310.99	264.16	204.96	159.84
Net Earnings	111.10	72.50	78.00	54.40	24.10
Dividends	32.00	23.50	19.50	14.00	9.40
Cash Flow	185.19	156.49	145.63	102.02	54.32

RATIOS AND OTHER INFORMATION

Mrk Cap(R000)	298944	200200	151060	98280	61880
Current Ratio	1.44	1.25	1.55	0.99	0.94
Quik/Acid Tst	1.36	1.17	1.46	0.89	0.86
A/C Rec T/ovr	5.28	5.74	6.12	5.94	6.51
Tot Ass T/ovr	0.97	1.01	1.00	1.30	1.10
Debt/Ass Rat	0.49	0.53	0.52	0.44	0.36
L T L Tot Ass	0.23	0.30	0.33	0.15	0.01
Debt to Eqity	1.01	1.19	1.16	0.84	0.65
Interest Cover	3.53	2.94	4.87	12.03	139.96

Oper Prof Mrg	16.19	16.25	19.58	17.48	16.66
Net Prof Marg%	9.91	10.27	13.13	10.69	8.78
Ret on Assets	18.01	16.87	20.10	22.94	18.40
Ret on Equity%	19.89	23.33	29.46	26.56	17.37
Price/Earnings	7.20	7.59	5.32	4.96	7.05
Divid Cover	3.47	3.09	4.00	3.89	2.56
Divid Yield	4.00	4.27	4.70	5.19	5.53
Earning Yield%	13.89	13.18	18.80	20.15	14.18
NAV % Mrk Pr	54.53	56.54	63.65	75.91	94.03
Effec Tax Rate	26.21	4.44	15.33	33.30	41.55
Def Interval	0.23	0.51	0.30	0.69	0.23
Sus Grth Rate	17.61	15.77	22.09	19.73	11.51

SUBSIDIARY & ASSOCIATED COMPANIES

BULWARK TRANSPORT MALAWI LTD
TANKFREIGHT (PTY) LTD
UNITRANS BOTSWANA (PTY) LTD
UNITRANS BULK (PTY) LTD
UNITRANS CAPE (PTY) LTD
UNITRANS EXPLOSIVES (PTY) LTD
UNITRANS FORESTRY (PTY) LTD
UNITRANS INTERNATIONAL (PTY) LTD
UNITRANS LESOTHO (PTY) LTD
UNITRANS LOWVELD (PTY) LTD
UNITRANS MALAWI (PTY) LTD
UNITRANS NATAL (PTY) LTD
UNITRANS PROPERTIES (PTY) LTD
UNITRANS REEF (PTY) LTD
UNITRANS SUGAR (PTY) LTD
UNITRANS SWAZI HOLDINGS (PTY) LTD
UNITRANS SWAZILAND LTD
UNITRANS ZULULAND (PTY) LTD
WARDES TRANSPORT (PTY) LTD

INVESTMENTS

None

URQUHART MOTOR GROUP LTD

ABBREVIATION : URQHART

JSE SHORT CODE : URQ

SECTOR : Industrial-Motor

SHAREHOLDERS

Who Owns Whom's Assessment of the Identity of the Ultimate Controlling Shareholder: URQUHART AND KOCH FAMILIES

SHAREHOLDER	PERCENTAGE 1992	1991
I C H INV CO P/L	95.1	95.1
SFSS NOM P/L	2.4	---
TOTAL	97.5	95.1

DIRECTORS :
BADER J ,BROOME MR
LENNOX BGG (Managing Director)
URQUHART GA (Executive Chairman),WHYTE VJ M

REGISTRATION NUMBER : 05/23787/06

REGISTERED OFFICE
5 Hillside Road, Parktown
2193
TEL: 011-484 1965
FAX: 011-484 9242

TRANSFER SECRETARY
Central Registrars Ltd
P O Box 4844, Johannesburg
2000
TEL: 011-331 0051

COMPANY SECRETARY
A E Roy

NATURE OF BUSINESS
An investment holding company. Subsidiaries are engaged in the business of motor retailing, and the ownership of motor dealership properties. Franchises held by the group are for Audi, Ford, Honda, Mercedes-Benz, Nissan, Toyota and VW motor cars and commercial vehicles.

BANKERS :
Standard Bank of SA Ltd
First National Bank of SA Ltd

AUDITORS :
Ernst & Young

FAMILIAR BRAND NAMES
AUDI,FORD,HONDA,HORNBY MOTORS
KILLARNEY TOYOTA,MERCEDES BENZ,NISSAN
PERRY FORD,RONNIES MOTORS,SUPERSKIMMER
VOLKSWAGEN,WEMBLEY USED CARS,WESTERN FORD

CONTRIBUTION BY ACTIVITY
New passenger vehicles (44.7%)
New heavy vehicles (11.0%)
Used vehicles (17.3%)
Parts (15.2%)
Service (5.8%)
Driveway (6.0%)

YEAR END : June

DIVIDEND :Ords 35c
Special (Ldr)06/09/91 (Pay)27/09/91 Amt(c)93.5
DIVIDEND :Ords 70c
Final (Ldr)09/10/92 (Pay)21/10/92 Amt(c)6

NUMBER OF EMPLOYEES : 650

CAPITAL STRUCTURE

	AUTHORISED	ISSUED
Ords 70c	15000000	12882836
Pref Ords 70c	15000000	6183761
Cum Red Prefs R1	2000000	0

FINANCIAL STATISTICS (AT FINANCIAL YEAR END)

(Amts in R'000)	1991 Jun	1990 Jun	1989 Jun	1988 Jun	1987 Jun
Ord S/H Int	39886	28686	12829	15742	9939
Long Trm Loans	-	-	984	1105	1187
Iss Ord Share	25766	25766	12455	9226	8080
Total Liab	24078	32093	17373	18554	11951
Current Liab	24078	32093	16389	17449	10764
Total Assets	63964	60779	25877	23045	21890
Intang Assets	*	*	4325	11251	*
Current Assets	60680	51537	16554	14039	13924

Debtors	11425	16780	8895	7445	10090
Inventory	27001	32231	4351	5942	3308
Turnover	234795	305540	25330	23999	23222
Oper Profit	6273	3345	-1961	-3311	3385
Interest Paid	66	2027	1992	-	377
Tax Paid	-	221	639	-39	-116
Prf af Int&Tax	6207	1097	-4592	-3272	3124
Prf att Ord Sh	6207	1724	-2975	-2121	4032
Btm Line Earn	11200	-7414	-10125	-1244	6897
Dividend Paid	-	-	-	-	1293
Mkt Prce(c) YE	120	160	120	160	335
Depreciation	728	1204	1115	1092	714

PER SHARE STATISTICS (CENTS)

Net Asst Val	154.80	111.33	68.28	48.68	123.01
Net Earnings	24.10	6.70	-30.90	-18.10	50.40
Dividends	-	-	-	-	16.00
Cash Flow	26.92	8.93	-36.11	-23.63	44.67

RATIOS AND OTHER INFORMATION

Mrk Cap(R000)	30919	41226	14946	14762	27068
Current Ratio	2.52	1.61	1.01	0.80	1.29
Quik/Acid Tst	1.40	0.60	0.74	0.46	0.99
A/C Rec T/ovr	20.55	18.21	2.85	3.22	2.30
Tot Ass T/ovr	3.67	5.03	0.98	1.04	1.06
Debt/Ass Rat	0.38	0.53	0.67	0.81	0.55
L T L Tot Ass	-	-	0.04	0.05	0.05
Debt to Eqity	0.60	1.12	1.35	1.18	1.20
Interest Cover	95.05	1.65	-0.98	-	8.98
Oper Prof Mrg	2.67	1.09	-7.74	-13.80	14.58
Net Prof Marg%	2.64	0.56	-11.74	-8.84	17.36
Ret on Assets	9.81	6.54	-1.33	-9.37	19.61
Ret on Equity%	15.56	6.01	-23.19	-13.47	40.57
Price/Earnings	4.98	23.88	-3.88	-8.84	6.65
Divid Cover	-	-	-	-	3.15
Divid Yield	-	-	-	-	4.78
Earning Yield%	20.08	4.19	-25.75	-11.31	15.04
NAV % Mrk Pr	129.00	69.58	56.90	30.42	36.72
Effec Tax Rate	-	-	-	1.18	4.85
Def Interval	-	3.09	-2.99	-5.99	1.67
Sus Grth Rate	15.56	6.01	-23.19	-13.47	27.56

SUBSIDIARY & ASSOCIATED COMPANIES

ANCHOR LEASING (PTY) LTD
BAILEYS SPRAY PAINTING & PANEL BEATING (
CHEMALY'S GARAGE (PTY) LTD
DAFFODIL PLASTICS (PTY) LTD
DEKJAN (PTY) LTD
DICKRON INVESTMENTS (PTY) LTD
DONNELLAN & PERRY LTD
FALDO PROPERTIES (PTY) LTD
FILTRASEP (PTY) LTD
HORNBY HOLDING CO (PTY) LTD
ICH MOTOR GROUP LTD
ICH PROPERTIES LTD
MACDONALD, FORMAN & CO LTD
MAXPAR INVESTMENTS (PTY) LTD
MIKE APPEL MOTOR COMPANY LTD
NT PROPERTIES (PTY) LTD - PROPERTY
PLASMOULD INJECTA (PTY) LTD
PLASTRIM FABRICATIONS (PTY) LTD
PREMIUM ACCEPTANCES (PTY) LTD
RAYDOR INVESTMENTS (PTY) LTD
RONNIES MOTORS (PTY) LTD
ROYCE MOTORS (PTY) LTD
S HORNBY MOTORS (PTY) LTD
SINCLAIR INDUSTRIES (PTY) LTD
SINCLAIR LICENSING (PTY) LTD
SINCLAIR MANAGEMENT (PTY) LTD
SINCLAIR PROPERTIES (PTY) LTD
STAND 70 AMALGAM (PTY) LTD
WESTERN GARAGE OFS LTD
WESTERN ICH INVESTMENTS LTD
WESTLIKE TRANSVAAL MOTORS EN TREKKERS (E
WESTRIDGE (PTY) LTD
YELLOW CABS (1938) LTD

INVESTMENTS

INVENTION FACTORY (PTY) LTD (5%)
NEW INNOVATIVE INVESTMENT (PTY) LTD (10%)

USKO LTD

ABBREVIATION : USKO

JSE SHORT CODE : USK

SECTOR : Industrial-Electronics, Electrical & Bat

SHAREHOLDERS

Who Owns Whom's Assessment of the Identity of the Ultimate Controlling Shareholder: ISCOR / REMBRANDT VIA METKOR

SHAREHOLDER	PERCENTAGE 1992	1991
ISCOR LTD	27.1	28.0
METKOR GROUP LTD	27.1	27.1
STD BANK NOM TVL P/L	11.6	12.4
SA MUTUAL	8.6	8.6
EIGHTY ONE MAIN STREET NOM LTD	2.9	2.9
AFRICAN TUBES & PIPES P/L	2.2	2.2
SA IRON & STEEL INDUSTRIAL CORP LTD	1.6	1.6
DIAGONAL NOM P/L	1.3	1.3
KATZ J	1.1	---
LONDON REGISTER ACCOUNT	---	1.3
TOTAL	83.4	85.3

DIRECTORS :
DE VILLIERS PC ,JENKINS KN ,KOTZEE FP (Chairman)
OLIVIER PA ,ROUX MJ ,VAN DER MERWE GF
VAN NIEKERK LL ,VAN WYK T

REGISTRATION NUMBER : 01/03874/06

REGISTERED OFFICE
273 General Hertzog Road, Peacehaven
Vereeniging
1939
TEL: 016-45122
FAX: 016-43476

TRANSFER SECRETARY
Central Registrars Ltd
P O Box 4844, Johannesburg
2000
TEL: 011-331 0051

COMPANY SECRETARY
P E Brink

NATURE OF BUSINESS
The company specialise in the manufacture and sale of copper wire, electrical cable, aluminium conductor as well as stainless steel wire.

BANKERS :
First National Bank of SA Ltd, Volkskas Ltd

AUDITORS :
Deloitte Pim Goldby

FAMILIAR BRAND NAMES
N/A

CONTRIBUTION BY ACTIVITY
Steel Sales (% Turnover) (48.6%)
Non-Ferrous Sales (47.8%)
Vanadium Pentoxide (3.6%)

YEAR END : September

DIVIDEND : Ords 50c
Final (Ldr)21/12/90 (Pay)31/01/91 Amt(c)7

NUMBER OF EMPLOYEES : 3132

CAPITAL STRUCTURE

	AUTHORISED	ISSUED
Ords no par value	769415912	30927513
"C" Comp Conv Cum Prefs 50c	20307000	20307000
"B" Var Rate Comp Conv Cum Prefs	199814600	199814600
"A" Var Rate Red/Part Conv Prefs	1351	1051

FINANCIAL STATISTICS (AT FINANCIAL YEAR END)

(Amts in R'000)	1991 Sep	1990 Sep	1989 Sep	1988 Sep	1987 Sep
Ord S/H Int	-111290	129337	135501	118971	95939
Long Trm Loans	26834	169483	106472	88973	103482
Iss Ord Share	30928	30928	29792	29010	29010
Total Liab	267640	255270	254791	166489	167933
Current Liab	240806	85787	148319	77516	64451
Total Assets	156350	384607	390292	285460	263872
Current Assets	131882	222415	253518	165432	137934
Debtors	43566	93673	85470	70680	65348
Inventory	29122	123458	133708	81996	70830
Turnover	554007	612601	543759	434906	378094
Oper Profit	-44804	26433	38233	37215	21805
Interest Paid	21478	27837	16600	7831	11268
Prf af Int&Tax	-58427	4056	27496	32460	10537
Prf att Ord Sh	-58427	1213	21766	26850	4815
Btm Line Earn	-238796	-9572	19925	26850	19264
Dividend Paid	-	-	3873	3771	-
Mkt Prce(c) YE	70	165	460	170	82
Depreciation	9444	11442	9954	10011	7046

PER SHARE STATISTICS (CENTS)

Net Asst Val	-359.84	418.19	454.82	410.10	330.71
Net Earnings	-198.11	4.01	73.06	90.55	16.25
Dividends	-	-	13.00	13.00	-
Cash Flow	-158.38	41.81	116.02	136.87	50.69

RATIOS AND OTHER INFORMATION

Mrk Cap(R000)	21650	51031	137043	49317	23788
Current Ratio	0.55	2.59	1.71	2.13	2.14
Quik/Acid Tst	0.43	1.15	0.81	1.08	1.04
A/C Rec T/ovr	12.72	6.54	6.36	6.15	5.79
Tot Ass T/ovr	3.54	1.59	1.39	1.52	1.43
Debt/Ass Rat	1.58	0.61	0.60	0.41	0.44
L T L Tot Ass	0.04	0.39	0.22	0.13	0.20
Debt to Eqity	-2.22	1.82	1.73	0.97	1.22
Interest Cover	-1.88	1.09	2.55	5.15	1.94
Oper Prof Mrg	-8.09	4.31	7.03	8.56	5.77
Net Prof Marg%	-10.55	0.20	4.00	6.17	1.27
Ret on Assets	-23.63	8.29	11.30	14.11	8.26
Ret on Equity%	52.50	0.94	16.06	22.57	5.02
Price/Earnings	-0.35	41.15	6.30	1.88	5.05
Divid Cover	-	-	5.62	6.97	-
Divid Yield	-	-	2.83	7.65	-
Earning Yield%	-283.01	2.43	15.88	53.26	19.82
NAV % Mrk Pr	-514.05	253.45	98.87	241.24	403.30
Def Interval	-3.95	12.64	4.64	2.16	7.15
Sus Grth Rate	52.50	0.94	13.21	19.40	5.02

SUBSIDIARY & ASSOCIATED COMPANIES

ALUSTANG (PTY) LTD (42,5%)
AVON WIRE (PTY) LTD
CITY NON-FERROUS METALS (PTY) LTD (50%)
LAMBDA CABLES (PTY) LTD (50%)
THAMES WIRE & CABLE (PTY) LTD (50%)
TINTO DISCS (PVT) LTD (50%)
TRANSVAAL COPPER ROD CO LTD (50%)
UNIE STAALKORPORASIE VAN SA (PTY) LTD
USCO ALUMINIUM CORP (PTY) LTD
USCO ALUMINIUM SYSTEMS (PTY) LTD
USCO KABELMAATSKAPPY (PTY) LTD
VELDMASTER (PTY) LTD
VELDMASTER INC (USA)

INVESTMENTS

EPI (PTY) LTD (20%)

UTICO HOLDINGS LTD

ABBREVIATION : UTICO

JSE SHORT CODE : UTI

SECTOR : Industrial-Tobacco & Match

SHAREHOLDERS

Who Owns Whom's Assessment of the Identity of the Ultimate Controlling Shareholder:
BAT INDUSTRIES PLC

SHAREHOLDER	PERCENTAGE 1992	1991
BRITISH-AMERICAN TOBACCO CO LTD	63.6	63.6
SA MUTUAL	18.1	18.1
FAIRHEADS NOM P/L	1.6	1.4
FIRST NAT NOM P/L	1.4	---
NAMPAK PENS FUND	1.3	1.3
STD BANK NOM TVL P/L	---	1.7
BARCLAYS NAT NOM P/L	---	1.3
TOTAL	85.9	87.3

DIRECTORS :
BENN MG ,CHONIN SL (Financial Director)
EDMUNDS DB (Managing Director),GREEN JL
HARTLEY RS (Deputy Chairman)
HASLETT FN (Chairman),STEVENS JB ,SUTHERLAND SM
WOODCOCK J

REGISTRATION NUMBER : 04/02230/06

REGISTERED OFFICE
Cnr Main Reef Road & Kelvin, Street Extension
Industria, Johannesburg

2093
TEL: 011-474 1668
FAX: 011-474 3442

TRANSFER SECRETARY
Mercantile Registrars Ltd
P O Box 1053, Johannesburg
2000
TEL: 011-333 8181

COMPANY SECRETARY
H P Thomson

NATURE OF BUSINESS
Utico manufactures and markets a wide range of well-known branded cigarette, tobacco, snack food and fruit juice products.

BANKERS :
Standard Bank of SA Ltd

AUDITORS :
Deloitte Pim Goldby

FAMILIAR BRAND NAMES
A 1 SPECIAL,ALBANY,BB,BELMONT
BENSON & HEDGES,BIG KORN BITES,CHA CHA'S
CHEASNAKS,CHEESE CURLS,CHIC'N NAKS
CIGARO GEMS,CLUB,CRINKLE CUT,CURRY NAKS
FIVE STAR,FLAIR,FLANAGANS,FLINGS
FRESH-UP 100,GOLD DOLLAR,HORSESHOE
JOHN PLAYER SPECIAL,KENT,KIM,LADUMA,LIFE
LUCKY STRIKE,MANHATTANS STRAIGHT CUTS
MARQUIS,MONSTER MUNCH,PARTY PALS,PROGRESS
SENIOR SERVICE,SPRINGBOK,STATE EXPRESS
STIMOROL,TANGO'S,TEXAN,VICEROY,WEST 85
WILLARDS,WILSON (TOP MILL),WINSTON

CONTRIBUTION BY ACTIVITY
N/A

YEAR END : December

DIVIDEND : Ords R1

Interim	(Ldr)07/09/90	(Pay)28/09/90	Amt(c)75
Final	(Ldr)12/04/91	(Pay)22/05/91	Amt(c)130
Interim	(Ldr)06/09/91	(Pay)30/09/91	Amt(c)105
Final	(Ldr)04/09/92	(Pay)30/09/92	Amt(c)117

NUMBER OF EMPLOYEES : 3000

CAPITAL STRUCTURE

	AUTHORISED	ISSUED
Ords R1	14600000	6075000

FINANCIAL STATISTICS (AT FINANCIAL YEAR END)

(Amts in R'000)	1991 Dec	1990 Dec	1989 Dec	1988 Dec	1987 Dec
Ord S/H Int	116641	103463	93562	84183	75059
Long Trm Loans	34820	29214	23175	16313	15599
Iss Ord Share	6075	6075	6075	6075	6075
Total Liab	147738	121699	100821	85780	71365
Current Liab	112918	92485	77646	69467	55766
Total Assets	264379	225162	194383	169963	146424
Current Assets	172582	155163	129722	114566	99007
Debtors	48000	43850	35482	32483	22823
Inventory	124582	111313	94240	79428	72110
Turnover	517472	440467	360999	310660	269336
Oper Profit	56496	45684	37608	31587	26980
Interest Paid	3582	2745	1622	191	1013
Tax Paid	24594	20596	17325	15589	12749
Prf af Int&Tax	28320	22355	18674	15807	13218
Prf att Ord Sh	28320	22355	18674	15807	13218
Btm Line Earn	28320	22355	18674	15807	13218
Dividend Paid	17010	12454	9295	6683	5285
Mkt Prce(c) YE	5600	2400	1550	1425	900
Depreciation	10128	8880	7539	5906	5184

PER SHARE STATISTICS (CENTS)

Net Asst Val	1920.02	1703.09	1540.12	1385.73	1235.54
Net Earnings	466.00	368.00	307.00	260.20	218.00
Dividends	280.00	205.00	153.00	110.00	87.00
Cash Flow	705.23	514.16	478.60	384.89	334.21

RATIOS AND OTHER INFORMATION

Mrk Cap(R000)	340200	145800	94163	86569	54675
Current Ratio	1.53	1.68	1.67	1.65	1.78
Quik/Acid Tst	0.43	0.47	0.46	0.51	0.48
A/C Rec T/ovr	10.78	10.04	10.17	9.56	11.80
Tot Ass T/ovr	1.96	1.96	1.86	1.83	1.84
Debt/Ass Rat	0.46	0.45	0.42	0.41	0.39
L T L Tot Ass	0.04	0.03	0.02	0.00	0.01
Debt to Eqity	1.05	0.97	0.88	0.83	0.77
Interest Cover	15.77	16.65	23.19	165.38	26.63
Oper Prof Mrg	10.92	10.37	10.42	10.17	10.02
Net Prof Marg%	5.47	5.08	5.17	5.09	4.91
Ret on Assets	21.37	20.29	19.35	18.58	18.43
Ret on Equity%	24.28	21.61	19.96	18.78	17.61
Price/Earnings	12.02	6.52	5.05	5.48	4.13
Divid Cover	1.66	1.80	2.01	2.37	2.51
Divid Yield	5.00	8.54	9.87	7.72	9.67
Earning Yield%	8.32	15.33	19.81	18.26	24.22
NAV % Mrk Pr	34.29	70.96	99.36	97.24	137.28
Effec Tax Rate	39.79	47.97	40.49	44.43	42.53
Def Interval	0.37	0.50	0.38	0.09	0.15
Sus Grth Rate	9.70	9.57	10.02	10.84	10.57

SUBSIDIARY & ASSOCIATED COMPANIES

BENSON & HEDGES (PTY) LTD
BROWN & WILLIAMSON TOBACCO CORP. (PTY) L
CARLTON CIGARETTE CO LTD (ZIMBABWE)
CARLTON CIGARETTE CO. (PTY) LTD
COMMANDO (PTY) LTD
DAMASCUS CONFECTIONERS (PTY) LTD
DISTINCTIVE MARKETING (PTY) LTD
FRESHUP (PTY) LTD
HARARE TOBACCO CO. (PVT) LTD
INTERNATIONAL TOBACCO CO. LTD
JOHN PLAYER & SONS (PTY) LTD
LAMBERT & BUTLER LTD
LAUTREC ET CIE S.A. (PTY) LTD
MUNDEL & HERZFELD (PTY) LTD
PRECISION ENGINEERING CO. (1946) (PTY) L
UTICO DISTRIBUTORS (PTY) LTD
UTICO EXPORTS (PTY) LTD
UTICO MANAGEMENT SERVICES (PTY) LTD
UTICO PROPERTIES ROODEPOORT (PTY) LTD
WD & HO WILLS (PTY) LTD
WESTMINSTER TOBACCO CO. (CAPE & LONDON)
WILLARDS FOODS (PTY) LTD
WILSON (TOP MILL) (PTY) LTD

INVESTMENTS

None

VAAL REEFS EXPLORATION & MINING CO LTD

ABBREVIATION : VAAL-REEF

JSE SHORT CODE : VAR

SECTOR : Gold-Klerksdorp

SHAREHOLDERS

Who Owns Whom's Assessment of the Identity of the Ultimate Controlling Shareholder:
ANGLO AMERICAN

SHAREHOLDER	PERCENTAGE 1992	1991
STD BANK NOM TVL P/L	13.8	10.2
INDO-CHINA NOM P/L	10.7	---
FERMAIN NOM LTD	7.9	7.9
PETARD NOM LTD	7.6	7.6
LONDON CONTROL ACCOUNT	6.1	5.7
TAURUS NOM LTD	4.2	4.2
FIRST NAT NOM P/L	3.9	4.4
SA MUTUAL	3.8	3.6
RESIDENT NOM LTD	3.7	4.8
CMB NOM P/L	3.6	---
FIRST NAT NOM P/L GATR DEPOT	2.5	2.4
EIGHTY ONE MAIN STREET NOM LTD	2.4	1.8
NAT CITY NOM LTD	2.0	2.0
SOUTHERN LIFE ASSOC LTD	1.9	3.6
OVERSEAS NOM CO INC	1.8	1.8
ANGLO AMERICAN GOLD INV CO LTD	1.7	1.7
FIRST NAT CITY TRUST CO	1.4	1.4
ANGLO AMERICAN CORP OF SA LTD	1.0	---
INDO-CHINA NOM SA P/L	---	11.5
SANLAM	---	3.4
TOTAL	79.8	77.9

DIRECTORS :
GODSELL RM ,HEWITT L (Managing Director)
HOSKING KM ,KING MW ,MAYER N ,OPPENHEIMER NF
PRETORIUS TL ,QUINN AM ,SCHMID E
SUNTER CL (Chairman),VAN DER COLF SW
WILLIAMS KH ,WOODWARD GW

REGISTRATION NUMBER : 05/17354/06

REGISTERED OFFICE
44 Main Street, Johannesburg
2001
TEL: 011-638 9111
FAX: 011-638 5281

TRANSFER SECRETARY
Consolidated Share Registrars Ltd
P O Box 61051, Marshalltown
2107
TEL: 011-492 1620

COMPANY SECRETARY
Anglo American Corporation of SA Ltd

NATURE OF BUSINESS
The company conducts gold mining operations in the Klerksdorp district, Transvaal and the Viljoenskroon district, OFS. The company also produces uranium oxide and sulphuric acid.

BANKERS :
First National Bank of SA Ltd

AUDITORS :
Ernst & Young

FAMILIAR BRAND NAMES
N/A

CONTRIBUTION BY ACTIVITY
Gold, Silver & Osmiridium (% profit) (88.0%)
Uranium & Sulphuric Acid (3.0%)
Other (incl investment income) (6.0%)
Trubuting agreements (1.0%)
Dividends from Southvaal (2.0%)

YEAR END : December

DIVIDEND : Ords 50c

Interim No 68	(Ldr)03/08/90	(Pay)14/09/90	Amt(c)485
Final No 69	(Ldr)08/02/91	(Pay)15/03/91	Amt(c)550
Interim No 70	(Ldr)09/08/91	(Pay)13/09/91	Amt(c)435
Final No 71	(Ldr)07/02/92	(Pay)13/03/92	Amt(c)600

NUMBER OF EMPLOYEES : 51993

CAPITAL STRUCTURE

	AUTHORISED	ISSUED
Ords 50c	20000000	19114643

FINANCIAL STATISTICS (AT FINANCIAL YEAR END)

(Amts in R'000)	1991 Dec	1990 Dec	1989 Dec	1988	1987
Ord S/H Int	3169900	2845900	2482800	2174300	1862400
Long Trm Loans	7100	4800	13300	730400	670300
Iss Ord Share	19115	19000	19000	19000	19000
Total Liab	427400	394500	493600	1449200	1325700
Current Liab	420300	389700	480300	718800	655400
Total Assets	3597300	3240400	2976400	3651800	3211100
Current Assets	425000	371700	448700	747100	678400
Debtors	169000	172300	137000	-	-
Inventory	-	-	-	747100	678400
Turnover	2577300	2495900	2577500	2713700	2532700
Oper Profit	528900	519400	706400	1104000	1313300
Interest Paid	1500	1600	1400	-	900
Tax Paid	79000	54500	217900	436500	492400
Prf af Int&Tax	520300	540900	603500	667500	601200
Prf att Ord Sh	520300	540900	603500	364500	361300
Btm Line Earn	197100	197600	296300	364500	361300
Dividend Paid	197800	198100	305300	361500	361000
Mkt Prce(c) YE	19050	20000	40000	26200	36000

PER SHARE STATISTICS (CENTS)

Net Asst Val	16583.31	14978.42	13067.37	11443.68	9802.11
Net Earnings	1031.00	1034.00	1554.00	-	-
Dividends	1035.00	1035.00	1600.00	-	-
Cash Flow	2721.95	2846.84	3176.32	3513.16	3164.21

RATIOS AND OTHER INFORMATION

Mrk Cap(R000)	3641408	3800000	7600000	4978000	6840000
Current Ratio	1.01	0.95	0.93	1.04	1.04
Quik/Acid Tst	1.01	0.95	0.93	-	-
A/C Rec T/ovr	15.25	14.49	18.81	-	-
Tot Ass T/ovr	0.72	0.77	0.87	0.74	0.79
Debt/Ass Rat	0.12	0.12	0.17	0.40	0.41
L T L Tot Ass	0.00	0.00	0.00	0.20	0.21
Debt to Eqity	0.13	0.14	0.20	0.67	0.71
Interest Cover	367.53	343.19	531.57	-	1216.11
Oper Prof Mrg	20.52	20.81	27.41	40.68	51.85
Net Prof Marg%	20.19	21.67	23.41	13.43	14.27

Ret on Assets	16.70	18.42	27.64	30.23	34.08
Ret on Equity%	16.41	19.01	24.31	16.76	19.40
Price/Earnings	18.48	19.34	25.74	-	-
Divid Cover	1.00	1.00	0.97	-	-
Divid Yield	5.43	5.18	4.00	-	-
Earning Yield%	5.41	5.17	3.89	-	-
NAV % Mrk Pr	87.05	74.89	32.67	43.68	27.23
Effec Tax Rate	9.98	5.09	19.79	39.54	37.52
Def Interval	0.03	0.02	0.03	1.09	1.11
Sus Grth Rate	10.17	12.05	12.01	0.14	0.02

SUBSIDIARY & ASSOCIATED COMPANIES

SOUTHVAAL HOLDINGS LTD (25%)
VAAL REEFS STARS (PTY) LTD
WESTERN REEFS EXPLORATION & DEVELOPMENT

INVESTMENTS

ADVANCED MINING SOFTWARE LTD (9400 SH)
CACTUS INVESTMENTS (PTY) LTD (25526 SH)
CHAMBER OF MINES BUILDING CO LTD, THE (133188 SH)
DEPFIN INVESTMENTS (PTY) LTD (15000000)
EMPLOYMENT BUREAU OF AFRICA LTD, THE (179521 SH)
GOLDCO LTD (1 SH)
INTER-MINE SERVICES OFS (PTY) LTD (560 SH)
INTERNATIONAL GOLD CORPORATION LTD (4995 SH)
LANSAN INVESTMENT HOLDINGS LTD (3438 SH)
MINE LABOUR ORGANISATIONS (N.R.C.) LTD (27565 SH)
NUCLEAR FUELS CORPORATION OF SA (PTY) LT (801300 SH)
RAND MUTUAL ASSURANCE CO LTD, THE (2108 SH)
RAND REFINERY LTD (56847 SH)
STONE & ALLIED INDUSTRIES (OFS) LTD (100000 SH)
WELTEVREDEN MINES LTD (400000 SH)

VAALAUTO LTD

ABBREVIATION : VALAUTO

JSE SHORT CODE : VLT

SECTOR : Industrial-Motor

SHAREHOLDERS

Who Owns Whom's Assessment of the Identity of the Ultimate Controlling Shareholder: VAALTRUCAR

SHAREHOLDER	PERCENTAGE 1992	1991
VAALTRUCAR LTD	81.1	81.1
FBCF NOM P/L	10.3	10.3
TRONSHOLD INV P/L	2.4	2.4
MARLED NOM P/L	1.3	---
TOTAL	95.1	93.8

DIRECTORS :
ESTERHUIZEN CJ (Financial Director)
GERMISHUIZEN GAJ
GERMISHUIZEN SF (Chairman & Chief Exec.)
GOLDSTUCK OI ,LANGE DGB

REGISTRATION NUMBER : 83/13044/06

REGISTERED OFFICE
11 Church St, Middelburg
1050
TEL: 0132-25211
FAX: 0132-25211

TRANSFER SECRETARY
Rand Registrars Ltd
P O Box 82549, Southdale
2135
TEL: 011-835 1016

COMPANY SECRETARY
C J Esterhuizen

NATURE OF BUSINESS
The company, via subsidiaries, is involved in the retail motor trade, including new & used vehicles, parts, service & petrol. The company also has a 38% interest in a timber farm in Spiegelsrivier.

BANKERS :
First National Bank of SA Ltd
Standard Bank of SA Ltd
Trust Bank of Africa Ltd, Volkskas Ltd

AUDITORS :
Jordaan Botha & Partners

FAMILIAR BRAND NAMES
N/A

CONTRIBUTION BY ACTIVITY
New Vehicles (% Turnover) (44.0%)
Used Vehicles (24.0%)
Parts (16.0%)
Petrol & Service (16.0%)

YEAR END : February

DIVIDEND : Ords 4c
Dividend No 1 (Ldr)24/05/91 (Pay)03/06/91 Amt(c)4

NUMBER OF EMPLOYEES : 308

CAPITAL STRUCTURE

	AUTHORISED	ISSUED
Ords 4c	25000000	16500000

FINANCIAL STATISTICS (AT FINANCIAL YEAR END)

(Amts in R'000)	1992 Feb	1991 Feb
Ord S/H Int	9017	12422
Long Trm Loans	1334	1452
Iss Ord Share	16500	16500
Total Liab	22631	22008
Current Liab	21297	20556
Total Assets	31648	34430
Current Assets	18692	22564
Debtors	5372	7022
Inventory	13228	14811
Turnover	120957	138278
Oper Profit	-625	3814
Interest Paid	2501	2623
Tax Paid	821	334
Prf af Int&Tax	-3445	1204
Prf att Ord Sh	-3460	1204
Btm Line Earn	-3460	1827
Dividend Paid	-	892
Mkt Prce(c) YE	60	70

Depreciation	424	390

PER SHARE STATISTICS (CENTS)

Net Asst Val	54.65	75.28
Net Earnings	-21.00	7.30
Dividends	-	4.00
Cash Flow	-19.67	138.95

RATIOS AND OTHER INFORMATION

Mrk Cap(R000)	9900	11550
Current Ratio	0.88	1.10
Quik/Acid Tst	0.26	0.38
A/C Rec T/ovr	22.52	19.69
Tot Ass T/ovr	3.82	4.02
Debt/Ass Rat	0.71	0.63
L T L Tot Ass	0.04	0.04
Debt to Eqity	2.51	1.76
Interest Cover	-0.25	1.45
Oper Prof Mrg	-0.52	2.76
Net Prof Marg%	-2.86	0.87
Ret on Assets	-0.39	12.09
Ret on Equity%	-38.37	9.69
Price/Earnings	-2.86	9.59
Divid Cover	-	1.83
Divid Yield	-	5.71
Earning Yield%	-35.00	10.43
NAV % Mrk Pr	91.08	107.55
Effec Tax Rate	-1.10	16.58
Def Interval	-1.99	2.04
Sus Grth Rate	-38.37	2.51

SUBSIDIARY & ASSOCIATED COMPANIES

AUTOENORM (PTY) LTD
EASTVAAL MOTORS (PTY) LTD
EASTVAAL PROPERTIES (ERMELO) (PTY) LTD
EASTVAAL PROPERTIES (SECUNDA) (PTY) LTD
EASTVAAL PROPERTIES (WITBANK) (PTY) LTD
MARIJA (PTY) LTD
VAALTRU FINANCE (PTY) LTD
VAALTRUCAR PROPERTIES (SPIEGELSRIVIER) (

INVESTMENTS

None

VAALTRUCAR LTD

ABBREVIATION : VALCAR

JSE SHORT CODE : VCR

SECTOR : Industrial-Motor

SHAREHOLDERS

Who Owns Whom's Assessment of the Identity of the Ultimate Controlling Shareholder: DIRECTORS

SHAREHOLDER	PERCENTAGE 1992	1991
MACSTEEL COMMERCIAL HLDGS P/L	25.5	1.2
GERMISHUIZEN S F	20.8	27.4
GERMISHUIZEN G TRUST	19.3	19.3
SAFEGRO NOM P/L	12.3	12.3
GERMISHUIZEN S F INV P/L	6.7	---
ELLERINE BROS P/L	3.0	3.0
VAALTRUCAR EMPL SHARE INC TRUST	3.0	---
SEFALANA EMP BENEFITS ORG (SEBO)	3.0	---
EIGHTY ONE MAIN STREET NOM LTD	---	3.0
RINRIC NOM P/L	---	3.0
TRONSHOLD INV P/L	---	24.2
TOTAL	93.5	93.5

DIRECTORS :
ESTERHUIZEN CJ ,GERMISHUIZEN GAJ
GERMISHUIZEN SF (Chairman),GOLDSTUCK OI

REGISTRATION NUMBER : 87/00988/06

REGISTERED OFFICE
11 Church St, Middelburg
1050
TEL: 0132-25211
FAX: 0132-25211

TRANSFER SECRETARY
Rand Registrars Ltd
P O Box 82549, Southdale
2135
TEL: 011-835 1016

COMPANY SECRETARY
C J Esterhuizen

NATURE OF BUSINESS
An investment holding company with a controlling interest in quoted Vaalauto Ltd.

BANKERS :
First National Bank of SA Ltd, Volkskas Ltd
Trust Bank of Africa Ltd
Standard Bank of SA Ltd

AUDITORS :
Jordaan Botha & Partners

FAMILIAR BRAND NAMES
DELTA (DEALER),EDDIES,FORD (DEALER)
ISUZU (DEALER),OPEL (DEALER),SPARECO

CONTRIBUTION BY ACTIVITY
New Vehicles (% Turnover) (44.0%)
Used Vehicles (24.0%)
Parts (16.0%)
Petrol & Service (16.0%)

YEAR END : February

DIVIDEND : Ords 10c
Dividend No 7 (Ldr)24/05/91 (Pay)03/06/91 Amt(c)3.2

NUMBER OF EMPLOYEES : 308

CAPITAL STRUCTURE

	AUTHORISED	ISSUED
Ords 10c	20000000	16500000

FINANCIAL STATISTICS (AT FINANCIAL YEAR END)

(Amts in R'000)	1992 Feb	1991 Feb	1990 Feb	1989 Feb	1988 Feb
Ord S/H Int	7072	9833	15326	8707	6177
Long Trm Loans	3044	3805	1146	115	130

Iss Ord Share	16500	16500	16500	16500	16500
Total Liab	24341	24355	14394	11918	7700
Current Liab	21297	20550	13248	11803	7570
Total Assets	31413	34188	25576	20625	13877
Intang Assets	*	*	4144	*	*
Current Assets	18692	22564	17291	15922	13043
Debtors	5372	7022	4012	4034	3409
Inventory	13228	14811	12870	11735	8492
Turnover	120957	138278	102100	91253	54129
Oper Profit	-625	3814	4029	4556	2341
Interest Paid	2501	2623	1511	830	529
Tax Paid	821	334	184	1429	222
Prf af Int&Tax	-3445	1204	2596	2317	1590
Prf att Ord Sh	-2806	932	2596	2317	1590
Btm Line Earn	-2806	1508	2569	2317	1490
Dividend Paid	-	3854	825	743	510
Mkt Prce(c) YE	60	70	57	60	60
Depreciation	444	390	224	241	116

PER SHARE STATISTICS (CENTS)

Net Asst Val	42.86	59.59	67.77	52.77	37.44
Net Earnings	-17.00	5.70	15.70	14.10	12.00
Dividends	-	3.20	5.00	4.50	3.80
Cash Flow	-15.58	8.49	17.75	15.50	12.88

RATIOS AND OTHER INFORMATION

Mrk Cap(R000)	9900	11550	9405	9900	9900
Current Ratio	0.88	1.10	1.31	1.35	1.72
Quik/Acid Tst	0.26	0.38	0.33	0.35	0.60
A/C Rec T/ovr	22.52	19.69	25.45	22.62	15.88
Tot Ass T/ovr	3.85	4.04	3.99	4.42	3.90
Debt/Ass Rat	0.72	0.64	0.56	0.58	0.55
L T L Tot Ass	0.04	0.04	0.04	0.01	0.01
Debt to Eqity	3.20	2.22	0.93	1.37	1.25
Interest Cover	-0.25	1.45	2.67	5.49	4.43
Oper Prof Mrg	-0.52	2.76	3.95	4.99	4.32
Net Prof Marg%	-2.32	0.67	2.54	2.54	2.94
Ret on Assets	-0.39	12.17	16.78	22.19	16.87
Ret on Equity%	-39.68	9.48	16.94	26.61	25.74
Price/Earnings	-3.53	12.28	3.63	4.26	5.00
Divid Cover	-	1.78	3.14	3.13	3.16
Divid Yield	-	4.57	8.77	7.50	6.33
Earning Yield%	-28.33	8.14	27.54	23.50	20.00
NAV % Mrk Pr	71.43	85.13	118.89	87.95	62.39
Effec Tax Rate	-1.10	16.58	1.76	38.15	12.25
Def Interval	-2.51	2.44	0.82	0.25	0.05
Sus Grth Rate	-39.68	-29.72	11.56	18.08	17.48

SUBSIDIARY & ASSOCIATED COMPANIES

VAALAUTO LTD

INVESTMENTS

None

VEKTRA CORPORATION PLC

ABBREVIATION : VEKTRA

JSE SHORT CODE : VKT

SECTOR : Industrial-Motor

SHAREHOLDERS

Who Owns Whom's Assessment of the Identity of the Ultimate Controlling Shareholder:
FSI GROUP VIA TEAMCOR

SHAREHOLDER	PERCENTAGE 1992	1991
TEAMCOR LTD	80.5	---
STD BANK NOM TVL P/L	2.6	2.3
LIBERTY LIFE ASSOC OF AFRICA LTD	2.4	2.4
ERIC ELLERINE TRUST P/L	1.7	1.7
NEDBANK NOM LTD	1.7	1.8
SIDNEY ELLERINE TRUST P/L	1.2	1.2
CMB NOM P/L	1.1	---
AUSMAY TRUST P/L	---	1.3
FSI CORP PENS FUND	---	1.1
HUNTS LTD	---	78.0
TOTAL	91.2	89.6

DIRECTORS :
CROCKETT RJ (Joint Managing Director)
HILEWITZ DR ,ISMAIL MV ,PIETERSMA RJ ,ROLFE TW
SCHLESINGER AM (Chairman & Joint MD)
STEELE MJ (Financial Director)

REGISTRATION NUMBER : 10/00012/10

REGISTERED OFFICE
St Paul's House, Warwick Lane
London, ECP4P 4BN

TEL: 011-402 3200
FAX: 011-402 7508

TRANSFER SECRETARY
Mercantile Registrars Ltd
P O Box 1053, Johannesburg
2000
TEL: 011-333 8181

COMPANY SECRETARY
B E Liebesman

NATURE OF BUSINESS
Vehicle sales & service, distribution of franchise spares & wholesale distribution of automotive replacement parts, & petrol sales.

BANKERS :
First National Bank of SA Ltd
Standard Bank of SA Ltd

AUDITORS :
KPMG Aiken & Peat

FAMILIAR BRAND NAMES
ALLEN,BOWER/BCA (BEARINGS)
FELX AUTOMOTIVE COMP,FEMO AUTO PARTS,HUNTER
ISUZU,LOMBARDINI DIESEL ENG,MAKITA,MONZA
NATAL ENGINE SPARES,NATIONAL (OIL SEALS)
NEWBYS,OPEL,P & H U-JOINT CENTRE
P&H SPARES CENTRE,PRETORIA ENG COMPONENT
REMA TIP TOP,RIDGID,ROCKWELL,STIHL,SUZUKI
WILLARD BATTERIES,WILLIAMS HUNT DELTA

CONTRIBUTION BY ACTIVITY
N/A

YEAR END : December

DIVIDEND : Ords 5p

Interim	(Ldr)15/09/89	(Pay)06/10/89	Amt(c)15
Final	(Ldr)23/03/90	(Pay)13/04/90	Amt(c)20
Interim	(Ldr)05/10/90	(Pay)26/10/90	Amt(c)10
Final	(Ldr)12/04/91	(Pay)03/05/91	Amt(c)6
Interim	(Ldr)11/10/91	(Pay)01/11/91	Amt(c)6
Final	(Ldr)16/04/92	(Pay)08/05/92	Amt(c)7
Interim	(Ldr)02/10/92	(Pay)23/10/92	Amt(c)6

NUMBER OF EMPLOYEES : 1279

CAPITAL STRUCTURE

	AUTHORISED	ISSUED
Ords 5p	25000000	11885000
6% Cum Prefs 1 Pound	150000	150000
Var Rate Cum Red Prefs 1p	50000000	0
Var Rate Unsec Sub Comp Conv Debs	5700000	5700000

FINANCIAL STATISTICS (AT FINANCIAL YEAR END)

(Amts In R'000)	19OV Dec	1991 Dec	1989 Dec	1988 Dec	1987
Ord S/H Int	34541	39296	52465	34841	29521
Long Trm Loans	41691	67968	63817	5816	2292
Iss Ord Share	11541	11885	11885	11594	11488
Total Liab	77266	116851	109849	41392	21010
Current Liab	35575	48883	46032	35576	18718
Total Assets	146828	137838	131556	76233	50531
Intang Assets	*	18309	30758	*	*
Current Assets	70596	95601	85780	70597	43840
Debtors	-	42260	36094	23044	16029
Inventory	70596	52756	42620	47223	27610
Turnover	284911	493526	466904	284912	204654
Oper Profit	14277	25502	34231	15296	9504
Interest Paid	1416	20171	13927	1416	936
Tax Paid	3333	1188	10078	3333	497
Prf af Int&Tax	10547	4364	12999	10547	8071
Prf att Ord Sh	10508	4466	12734	10508	8038
Btm Line Earn	10508	4466	21364	8599	7936
Dividend Paid	3478	1545	4160	3478	2642
Mkt Prce(c) YE	425	220	525	425	400
Depreciation	-	1697	740	603	650

PER SHARE STATISTICS (CENTS)

Net Asst Val	299.29	176.58	182.64	300.51	256.97
Net Earnings	-	38.00	108.50	91.00	-
Dividends	-	13.00	35.00	30.00	-
Cash Flow	91.39	40.35	151.44	96.27	76.61

RATIOS AND OTHER INFORMATION

Mrk Cap(R000)	49049	26147	62396	49275	45952
Current Ratio	1.98	1.96	1.86	1.98	2.34
Quik/Acid Tst	-	0.88	0.94	0.66	0.87
A/C Rec T/ovr	-	11.68	12.94	12.36	12.77
Tot Ass T/ovr	1.94	3.58	3.55	3.74	4.05
Debt/Ass Rat	0.53	0.85	0.77	0.54	0.42
L T L Tot Ass	0.28	0.49	0.42	0.08	0.05
Debt to Eqity	2.24	2.97	1.94	1.19	0.71
Interest Cover	10.80	1.26	2.46	10.80	10.15
Oper Prof Mrg	5.01	5.17	7.33	5.37	4.64
Net Prof Marg%	3.69	0.90	2.73	3.69	3.93
Ret on Assets	10.42	18.66	28.13	20.06	18.81
Ret on Equity%	30.42	11.37	24.27	30.16	27.23
Price/Earnings	-	5.79	4.84	4.67	-
Divid Cover	-	2.92	3.10	3.03	-
Divid Yield	-	5.91	6.67	7.06	-
Earning Yield%	-	17.27	20.67	21.41	-
NAV % Mrk Pr	70.42	80.27	34.79	70.71	64.24
Effec Tax Rate	25.92	45.68	25.80	24.01	5.80
Def Interval	3.95	7.18	0.91	1.11	0.94
Sus Grth Rate	20.35	7.43	16.34	20.18	18.28

SUBSIDIARY & ASSOCIATED COMPANIES

DELTAPART (PTY) LTD
FEMO AUTO PARTS (PTY) LTD
MODERN LEASING SERVICES (PTY) LTD
MOTOR & GENERAL SUPPLIES (BOTSWANA) (PTY
MUKWA PROPERTIES (PVT) LTD
PARTS CENTRE HOLDINGS (PTY) LTD
V&R HOLDINGS (PTY) LTD
WILLIAMS HUNT (PTY) LTD
WILLIAMS HUNT INDUSTRIAL DISTRIBUTORS (P
WV GRIMWOOD & CO (PTY) LTD

INVESTMENTS

None

VENTER LEISURE & COMMERCIAL TRAILERS

ABBREVIATION : VENTEL

JSE SHORT CODE : VTL

SECTOR : Industrial-Transportation

SHAREHOLDERS

Who Owns Whom's Assessment of the Identity of the Ultimate Controlling Shareholder: DIRECTORS

SHAREHOLDER	PERCENTAGE 1992	1991
LEISURE & COMMERCIAL TRAILERS HLDGS LTD	44.8	---
JENAPR INV P/L	19.2	---
EIGHTY ONE MAIN STREET NOM LTD	8.2	---
MOMENTUM LIFE ASSURE LTD	4.5	---
VENTER J M	4.2	---
METROPOLITAN LIFE LTD	3.8	---
MERCANTILE NOM P/L	3.0	---
SAFEGRO NOM P/L	1.5	---
DU PLESSIS GERT VAN EDEN	1.1	---
STD BANK NOM TVL P/L	1.0	---
TOTAL	91.4	---

DIRECTORS :
DU PLESSIS G VAN E (Chairman)
FOURIE JF (Manufacturing Director)
KATCS MW (Deputy Chairman),MERLO DGA ,MILLS J
NIEUWOUDT TW ,PINSHOW L ,STEWART R
VAN STADEN WJ (Operations Director),VENTER JM

REGISTRATION NUMBER : 92/00186/10

REGISTERED OFFICE
3rd Floor, 88 Grayston Drive
Sandton
2199
TEL: 011-486 2280
FAX: 011-486 2282

TRANSFER SECRETARY
Mercantile Registrars Ltd
P O Box 1053, Johannesburg
2000
TEL: 011-333 8181

COMPANY SECRETARY
W Boshoff

NATURE OF BUSINESS
The holding company of three operating subsidiaries which are engaged in the manufacture and sale of trailers for the use in the domestic leisure and commercial markets. Two of the subsidiaries are located in Babelegi and the third is located in Naboomspruit.

BANKERS :
Standard Bank of SA Ltd
First National Bank of SA Ltd
Trust Bank of Africa Ltd
Mercantile Bank Ltd

AUDITORS :
Price Waterhouse Meyernel

FAMILIAR BRAND NAMES
N/A

CONTRIBUTION BY ACTIVITY
N/A

YEAR END : December

NUMBER OF EMPLOYEES : 380

CAPITAL STRUCTURE

	AUTHORISED	ISSUED
Ords 1c	100000000	50000000

FINANCIAL STATISTICS (AT FINANCIAL YEAR END)

(Amts in R'000)	1991 Sep	1991 Dec
Iss Ord Share	29661	50000
Oper Profit	9068	12386
Tax Paid	3142	4297
Prf af Int&Tax	6473	8854
Prf att Ord Sh	6473	8854
Btm Line Earn	6473	8854

PER SHARE STATISTICS (CENTS)

Cash Flow	21.82	17.71

RATIOS AND OTHER INFORMATION

Effec Tax Rate	32.68	32.67

SUBSIDIARY & ASSOCIATED COMPANIES

RUBAX (PTY) LTD
VENTER MANUFACTURING (PTY) LTD
VENTER MARKETING (PTY) LTD

INVESTMENTS

None

VENTERSPOST GOLD MINING CO LTD

ABBREVIATION : VENTERS

JSE SHORT CODE : VEN

SECTOR : Gold-West Witwatersrand

SHAREHOLDERS

Who Owns Whom's Assessment of the Identity of the Ultimate Controlling Shareholder:
GFSA

SHAREHOLDER	PERCENTAGE 1992	1991
MINU NOM LTD	41.7	31.0
INDO-CHINA NOM P/L	11.2	---
STD BANK NOM TVL P/L	10.0	2.7
FIRST NAT NOM P/L	4.8	6.2
RANDFONTEIN ESTATES GOLD MIN CO WITS LTD	2.5	---
FIRST NAT MERCHANT BANK LTD	1.3	---
DEPOSITARY NOM INC	---	1.9
FIRST NAT NOM P/L GATR DEPOT	---	1.1
INDO-CHINA NOM SA P/L	---	25.9
VOLKSKAS NOM P/L	---	1.3
TOTAL	71.5	70.0

DIRECTORS :
ADAN MJ ,ALVEY GP ,DAY BA ,DYKES DC ,FENTON CT HOUGHTON AB ,KAHLE H ,MOOLMAN A ,MUNRO AH TAGG MJ (Chairman & Managing Dir.

REGISTRATION NUMBER : 05/05632/06

REGISTERED OFFICE
75 Fox Street, Johannesburg
2001
TEL: 011-639 9111
FAX: 011-639 2101

TRANSFER SECRETARY
Gold Fields of SA Ltd
P O Box 1167, Johannesburg
2000
TEL: 011-639 9111

COMPANY SECRETARY
Gold Fields of SA Ltd

NATURE OF BUSINESS
The company conducts gold mining operations in the West Witwatersrand area.

BANKERS :
Standard Bank of SA Ltd

AUDITORS :
Ernst & Young

FAMILIAR BRAND NAMES
N/A

CONTRIBUTION BY ACTIVITY
N/A

YEAR END : June

DIVIDEND : Ords 25c

Interim No 97	(Ldr)30/12/88	(Pay)08/02/89	Amt(c)25
Final No 98	(Ldr)30/06/89	(Pay)09/08/89	Amt(c)35

NUMBER OF EMPLOYEES : 6816

CAPITAL STRUCTURE

	AUTHORISED	ISSUED
Ords 25c	50000000	50000000

FINANCIAL STATISTICS (AT FINANCIAL YEAR END)

(Amts in R'000)	1991 Jun	1990 Jun	1989 Jun	1988 Jun	1987
Ord S/H Int	300375	305669	141954	118799	110944
Long Trm Loans	-	-	-	-	30999
Iss Ord Share	20200	20200	20200	20200	5050
Total Liab	20908	30870	33499	29137	61998
Current Liab	20908	30870	33499	29137	30999
Total Assets	321283	336539	175453	147936	197336
Current Assets	80209	150053	33471	54069	55393
Debtors	5606	5690	1810	1937	-
Inventory	5088	5221	5851	4949	55393
Turnover	165009	196218	-	186937	183476
Oper Profit	-23876	-4133	16323	25193	45566
Tax Paid	-	3364	2852	1433	16541
Prf af Int&Tax	-6110	4433	13471	23760	29025
Prf att Ord Sh	-6110	4433	13471	23760	16025
Btm Line Earn	-6110	4433	13471	23760	16025
Dividend Paid	-	-	12120	16160	15655
Mkt Prce(c) YE	285	485	535	700	4250

PER SHARE STATISTICS (CENTS)

Net Asst Val	1487.00	1513.21	702.74	588.11	2196.91
Net Earnings	-30.00	22.00	62.00	78.00	-
Dividends	-	-	60.00	80.00	-
Cash Flow	-30.25	21.95	66.69	117.62	574.75

RATIOS AND OTHER INFORMATION

Mrk Cap(R000)	57570	97970	108070	141400	214625
Current Ratio	3.84	4.86	1.00	1.86	1.79
Quik/Acid Tst	3.59	4.69	0.82	1.69	-
A/C Rec T/ovr	29.43	34.48	-	96.51	-
Tot Ass T/ovr	0.51	0.58	-	1.26	0.93
Debt/Ass Rat	0.07	0.09	0.19	0.20	0.31
L T L Tot Ass	-	-	-	-	0.16
Debt to Eqity	0.07	0.10	0.24	0.25	0.56
Oper Prof Mrg	-14.47	-2.11	-	13.48	24.83
Net Prof Marg%	-3.70	2.26	-	12.71	8.73
Ret on Assets	-1.90	2.32	9.30	17.03	23.09
Ret on Equity%	-2.03	1.45	9.49	20.00	14.44
Price/Earnings	-9.50	22.05	8.63	8.97	-
Divid Cover	-	-	1.03	0.98	-
Divid Yield	-	-	11.21	11.43	-
Earning Yield%	-10.53	4.54	11.59	11.14	-
NAV % Mrk Pr	521.76	312.00	131.35	84.02	51.69
Effec Tax Rate	-	43.14	17.47	5.69	36.30
Def Interval	-	-	-	-	1.07
Sus Grth Rate	-2.03	1.45	0.95	6.40	0.33

SUBSIDIARY & ASSOCIATED COMPANIES

None

INVESTMENTS

None

VENTRON CORPORATION LTD

ABBREVIATION : VENTRON

JSE SHORT CODE : VNT

SECTOR : Industrial-Electronics, Electrical & Bat

SHAREHOLDERS

Who Owns Whom's Assessment of the Identity of the Ultimate Controlling Shareholder:
W VENTER

SHAREHOLDER	PERCENTAGE 1992	1991
BILTRON P/L	41.2	41.2
VENTER W P	19.9	27.3
RESIDENT NOM LTD	19.2	19.2
ANGLO AMERICAN IND CORP LTD	9.6	2.2
SA MUTUAL	3.9	3.9
LIBERTY LIFE ASSOC OF AFRICA LTD	1.3	1.2
FIRST NAT NOM P/L	1.2	1.1
TOTAL	96.3	96.1

DIRECTORS :
BOUSTRED WG ,BOYD L
SEREBRO HA DR (Executive Director)
STRIDE CA (Deputy Chairman),VENTER CG
VENTER RE ,VENTER WP DR (Executive Chairman

REGISTRATION NUMBER : 51/03937/06

REGISTERED OFFICE
Altron Corporate Offices, Cnr Brakpan & Van Dyk Roads
Boksburg East
1459
TEL: 011-899 6111
FAX: 011-914 3984

TRANSFER SECRETARY
Central Registrars Ltd
P O Box 4844, Johannesburg
2000
TEL: 011-331 0051

COMPANY SECRETARY
Altron Management Serv.(Pty)Ltd - PA Armstrong

NATURE OF BUSINESS
An investment holding company controlling 53,8% of JSE-quoted Allied Electronics Corp.

BANKERS :
Standard Bank of SA Ltd
First National Bank of SA Ltd
Absa Bank Ltd, Nedcor Bank Ltd

AUDITORS :
KPMG Aiken & Peat, Fisher Hoffman Stride

FAMILIAR BRAND NAMES
N/A

CONTRIBUTION BY ACTIVITY
N/A

YEAR END : February

DIVIDEND : Ords 500c

Dividend No 52	(Ldr)25/05/90	(Pay)11/06/90	Amt(c)46
Dividend No 53	(Ldr)24/05/91	(Pay)10/06/91	Amt(c)53
Dividend No 54	(Ldr)29/05/92	(Pay)08/06/92	Amt(c)59

NUMBER OF EMPLOYEES : 3442

CAPITAL STRUCTURE

	AUTHORISED	ISSUED
Ords 500c	31700000	26951747

FINANCIAL STATISTICS (AT FINANCIAL YEAR END)

(Amts In R'000)	1992 Feb	1991 Feb	1990 Feb	1989 Feb	1988 Feb
Ord S/H Int	369706	337660	312945	298876	126945
Long Trm Loans	749742	679831	534244	476681	400142
Iss Ord Share	26952	26952	26952	26364	26364
Total Liab	1420964	1321981	1290067	1189508	881524
Current Liab	671222	642150	755823	712827	481382
Total Assets	1607935	1478836	1421182	1338106	1008469
Intang Assets	182735	180805	181830	150278	*
Current Assets	1186762	1025718	1002623	994200	717185
Debtors	431335	425592	432128	464769	359412
Inventory	446183	413718	482641	472321	293413
Turnover	2645461	2655030	2630696	2153776	1565469
Oper Profit	274933	286102	251649	231333	211385
Interest Paid	7024	66991	66449	42687	17994
Tax Paid	119260	116244	81431	83298	75240
Prf af Int&Tax	192849	173008	139759	146821	118151
Prf att Ord Sh	49799	41715	30043	40347	32265
Btm Line Earn	46562	40183	14757	39674	32265
Dividend Paid	15902	14284	12398	12127	9755
Mkt Prce(c) YE	1800	2150	1150	2000	1475
Depreciation	61567	55464	55641	39439	35039

PER SHARE STATISTICS (CENTS)

Net Asst Val	693.72	581.98	486.48	563.64	481.51
Net Earnings	184.80	154.80	112.70	153.00	122.40
Dividends	59.00	53.00	46.00	46.00	37.00
Cash Flow	364.42	351.61	322.09	293.50	262.60

RATIOS AND OTHER INFORMATION

Mrk Cap(R000)	485136	579468	309948	527280	388869
Current Ratio	1.77	1.60	1.33	1.39	1.49
Quik/Acid Tst	1.10	0.95	0.69	0.73	0.88
A/C Rec T/ovr	6.13	6.24	6.09	4.63	4.36
Tot Ass T/ovr	1.65	1.80	1.85	1.61	1.55
Debt/Ass Rat	0.43	0.45	0.54	0.54	0.49
L T L Tot Ass	0.02	0.02	0.01	0.01	0.01
Debt to Eqity	1.89	1.99	2.46	2.43	3.90
Interest Cover	41.95	4.48	3.83	5.70	11.75
Oper Prof Mrg	10.39	10.78	9.57	10.74	13.50
Net Prof Marg%	1.88	1.57	1.14	1.87	2.06
Ret on Assets	19.94	24.17	20.32	20.47	20.96
Ret on Equity%	13.47	12.35	9.60	13.50	25.42
Price/Earnings	9.74	13.89	10.20	13.07	12.05
Divid Cover	3.13	2.92	2.45	3.33	3.31
Divid Yield	3.28	2.47	4.00	2.30	2.51
Earning Yield%	10.27	7.20	9.80	7.65	8.30
NAV % Mrk Pr	38.54	27.07	42.30	28.18	32.64
Effec Tax Rate	43.45	39.55	41.56	39.20	37.66
Def Interval	0.30	0.37	1.80	1.80	0.66
Sus Grth Rate	9 17	8.12	5.84	9.44	17.73

SUBSIDIARY & ASSOCIATED COMPANIES

ALLIED ELECTRONICS CORP. LTD
VENTECH (PTY) LTD

INVESTMENTS

None

VESTACOR LTD

ABBREVIATION : VESTCOR

JSE SHORT CODE : VTR

SECTOR : Financial-Investment Trusts

SHAREHOLDERS

Who Owns Whom's Assessment of the Identity of the Ultimate Controlling Shareholder: RINGO FAMILY

SHAREHOLDER	PERCENTAGE 1992	1991
RINGO FAMILY INV P/L	41.9	41.9
SA MUTUAL	9.1	9.1
FIRST NAT NOM P/L	9.1	12.1
ITI INVESTMENTS CC	7.7	---
ELLERINE BROS P/L	5.1	5.1
STOCKSHARE NOM P/L	4.8	2.7
STD BANK NOM TVL P/L	3.1	3.1
FERBROS NOM P/L	2.3	2.3
MENBLACK NOM P/L	2.2	4.2
DATNOW L S	1.6	1.6
MACSTEEL COMMERCIAL HLDGS P/L	1.3	1.3
NIKA TRADING CC	---	2.3
NIKA CC	---	1.3
NICA CC	---	1.6
TOTAL	88.1	88.7

DIRECTORS :
ANDREWS GS PROF,COLQUHOUN AM ,DATNOW CS
DAVIES NO ,DE LA H BECK J (Managing Director)
GANT HM ,HELYAR DWH ,RINGO AL (Chairman)
TRAHAR PJ

REGISTRATION NUMBER : 60/02468/06

REGISTERED OFFICE
25 Bath Avenue, Rosebank, Johannesburg
2196
TEL: 011-880 8080
FAX: 011-880 5858

TRANSFER SECRETARY
Central Registrars Ltd
P O Box 4844, Johannesburg
2000
TEL: 011-331 0051

COMPANY SECRETARY
Mathieson & Ashley Management Services (Pty) Ltd

NATURE OF BUSINESS
An investment holding company controlling 74,4% of Mathieson & Ashley.

BANKERS :
First National Bank of SA Ltd
Nedperm Bank Ltd, Standard Bank of SA Ltd
Central Merchant Bank Ltd

AUDITORS :
Ernst & Young

FAMILIAR BRAND NAMES
SEE MATHIESON & ASHLEY

CONTRIBUTION BY ACTIVITY
Office Furniture Operations (100.0%)

YEAR END : June

DIVIDEND :Ords 5c

Interim No 47	(Ldr)12/04/90	(Pay)27/04/90	Amt(c)8.5
Final No 48	(Ldr)26/10/90	(Pay)09/11/90	Amt(c)13.5

NUMBER OF EMPLOYEES : 1600

CAPITAL STRUCTURE

	AUTHORISED	ISSUED
Ords 5c	10000000	7819120

FINANCIAL STATISTICS (AT FINANCIAL YEAR END)

(Amts in R'000)	1992 Jun	1991 Jun	1990 Jun	1989 Jun	1988 Jun
Ord S/H Int	15265	16562	18064	16471	13410
Long Trm Loans	33095	39157	40653	28056	19526
Iss Ord Share	7819	7819	7819	1955	1955
Total Liab	65181	63057	64955	50325	38223
Current Liab	32086	23900	24302	22269	18697
Total Assets	80446	79619	83019	66796	51633
Current Assets	52041	50292	58210	53794	46179
Debtors	26006	23960	26927	24486	17730
Inventory	25861	24977	25137	18993	15328
Turnover	145681	125024	134822	99395	39019
Oper Profit	664	2307	11015	14600	7827
Interest Paid	5769	3939	3122	2192	216
Tax Paid	40	-330	391	210	3872
Prf af Int&Tax	-3225	-467	9146	12198	3739
Prf att Ord Sh	-944	-111	4126	5831	2713
Btm Line Earn	-1907	-1502	3313	4761	8560
Dividend Paid	-	-	1720	1700	1016
Mkt Prce(c) YE	200	290	1975	1400	1450
Depreciation	5050	3745	3945	1729	667

PER SHARE STATISTICS (CENTS)

Net Asst Val	195.23	211.82	231.03	842.51	685.93
Net Earnings	-12.10	-1.40	52.80	74.50	138.80
Dividends	-	-	22.00	21.80	52.00
Cash Flow	52.67	39.92	105.32	96.89	169.62

RATIOS AND OTHER INFORMATION

Mrk Cap(R000)	15638	22675	154425	27370	28348
Current Ratio	1.62	2.10	2.40	2.42	2.47
Quik/Acid Tst	0.82	1.06	1.36	1.56	1.65
A/C Rec T/ovr	5.60	5.22	5.01	4.06	2.20
Tot Ass T/ovr	1.81	1.57	1.62	1.49	0.76
Debt/Ass Rat	0.54	0.49	0.46	0.46	0.43
L T L Tot Ass	0.14	0.19	0.16	0.13	0.06
Debt to Eqity	2.84	2.35	2.10	1.88	1.64
Interest Cover	0.12	0.59	3.53	6.66	36.24
Oper Prof Mrg	0.46	1.85	8.17	14.69	20.06
Net Prof Marg%	-0.65	-0.09	3.06	5.87	6.95
Ret on Assets	3.21	3.95	15.25	21.86	15.16
Ret on Equity%	-6.18	-0.67	22.84	35.40	20.23
Price/Earnings	-16.53	-207.14	37.41	18.79	10.45
Divid Cover	-	-	2.40	3.42	2.67
Divid Yield	-	-	1.11	1.56	3.59
Earning Yield%	-6.05	-0.48	2.67	5.32	9.57
NAV % Mrk Pr	97.61	73.04	11.70	60.18	47.31
Effec Tax Rate	-	-	2.38	0.75	51.98
Def Interval	3.99	4.93	1.66	1.16	1.01
Sus Grth Rate	-6.18	-0.67	13.32	25.08	12.65

SUBSIDIARY & ASSOCIATED COMPANIES

MATHIESON & ASHLEY HOLDINGS LTD
SEDOW HOLDINGS (PTY) LTD

INVESTMENTS

None

VIERFONTEIN COLLIERY LTD

ABBREVIATION : VIERFONTN

JSE SHORT CODE : VFN

SECTOR : Mining-Coal

SHAREHOLDERS

Who Owns Whom's Assessment of the Identity of the Ultimate Controlling Shareholder: GFSA

SHAREHOLDER	PERCENTAGE 1992	1991
CONSOLIDATED GOLD FIELDS PLC	13.2	13.2
AFRICAN & EUROPEAN INV CO LTD	6.4	6.4
SA EQUITIES LTD	5.3	6.4
PROGENY INV P/L	3.4	3.4
ARNOTT J A	3.3	3.3
HILLEL COHEN CC	2.7	2.5
KIOILOS L	2.0	2.0
JUSPOINT NOM P/L	2.0	2.1
SABLIER H	1.6	---
STD BANK NOM TVL P/L	1.6	1.7
NEDBANK NOM LTD	1.6	2.0
DUIGAN K G	1.5	1.2
YOOSOOF A K	1.5	1.5
GRAMOCO CC	1.4	1.4
NORTHWEST ESTATE AGENTS RENTS P/L	1.3	1.3
BLOMOCO INV CC	1.2	1.1
LEWTOP P/L	1.2	1.2
TOTAL	50.9	50.4

DIRECTORS :
HOPWOOD JG ,LESLIE JS ,RANKIN D (Chairman)
ST JOHN BA ,STACEY HB

REGISTRATION NUMBER : 05/37061/06

REGISTERED OFFICE
44 Main Street, Johannesburg
2001
TEL: 011-638 9111
FAX: 011-638 4044

TRANSFER SECRETARY
Consolidated Share Registrars Ltd
P O Box 61051, Marshalltown
2107
TEL: 011-492 1620

COMPANY SECRETARY
Anglo American Corporation of SA Ltd

NATURE OF BUSINESS
The company's colliery situated in the Viljoenskroon district of the Northern Orange Free State, produced bituminous coal under contract for ESKOM's Vierfontein power station. However, production has ceased.

BANKERS :
N/A

AUDITORS :
Deloitte Pim Goldby

FAMILIAR BRAND NAMES
N/A

CONTRIBUTION BY ACTIVITY
N/A

YEAR END : March

DIVIDEND : Ords 50c

Interim No 71	(Ldr)01/12/89	(Pay)05/01/90	Amt(c)2
Final No 72	(Ldr)22/06/90	(Pay)27/07/90	Amt(c)2

CAPITAL STRUCTURE

	AUTHORISED	ISSUED
Ords 50c	4000000	4000000

FINANCIAL STATISTICS (AT FINANCIAL YEAR END)

(Amts in R'000)	1992 Mar	1991 Mar	1990 Mar	1989 Mar	1988 Mar
Ord S/H Int	2477	2457	2449	2712	3219
Iss Ord Share	4000	4000	4000	4000	4000
Total Liab	51	66	207	481	1642
Current Liab	51	66	207	481	1642
Total Assets	2528	2523	2656	3193	4861
Current Assets	467	454	576	943	2181
Debtors	17	42	25	32	810
Inventory	-	-	3	-	-
Turnover	-	-	-	-	9456
Oper Profit	-35	-53	-56	71	399
Tax Paid	25	20	100	338	318
Prf af Int&Tax	20	8	-50	-267	81
Prf att Ord Sh	20	8	-50	-267	81
Btm Line Earn	28	19	99	163	83
Dividend Paid	-	-	160	240	120
Mkt Prce(c) YE	10	20	45	55	40

PER SHARE STATISTICS (CENTS)

Net Asst Val	61.93	61.43	61.22	67.80	80.47
Net Earnings	0.70	0.50	2.50	4.10	2.00
Dividends	-	-	4.00	6.00	3.00
Cash Flow	0.50	0.20	-1.25	-6.68	2.03

RATIOS AND OTHER INFORMATION

Mrk Cap(R000)	400	800	1800	2200	1600
Current Ratio	9.16	6.88	2.78	1.96	1.33
Quik/Acid Tst	9.16	6.88	2.77	1.96	1.33
A/C Rec T/ovr	-	-	-	-	11.67
Tot Ass T/ovr	-	-	-	-	1.95
Debt/Ass Rat	0.02	0.03	0.08	0.15	0.34
Debt to Eqity	0.02	0.03	0.08	0.18	0.51
Oper Prof Mrg	-	-	-	-	4.22
Net Prof Marg%	-	-	-	-	0.86
Ret on Assets	1.78	1.11	1.88	2.22	8.21
Ret on Equity%	0.81	0.33	-2.04	-9.85	2.52
Price/Earnings	14.29	40.00	18.00	13.41	20.00
Divid Cover	-	-	0.63	0.68	0.67
Divid Yield	-	-	8.89	10.91	7.50
Earning Yield%	7.00	2.50	5.56	7.45	5.00
NAV % Mrk Pr	619.25	307.13	136.06	123.27	201.19
Effec Tax Rate	57.78	78.57	200.00	476.06	79.70
Def Interval	-	0.25	-0.42	-	0.94
Sus Grth Rate	0.81	0.33	-8.57	-18.69	-1.21

SUBSIDIARY & ASSOCIATED COMPANIES

None

INVESTMENTS

None

VILLAGE MAIN REEF GOLD MINING CO (1934) LTD

ABBREVIATION : VILLAGE

JSE SHORT CODE : VIL

SECTOR : Gold-Rand & others

SHAREHOLDERS

Who Owns Whom's Assessment of the Identity of the Ultimate Controlling Shareholder: ANGLOVAAL

SHAREHOLDER	PERCENTAGE 1992	1991
FOX STREET NOM P/L	38.1	38.1
LEWISOHN R B	5.3	5.3
CISKEI ELEC CONTRACTORS P/L	3.1	3.1
HARVEST SECURITIES LTD	2.6	1.5
STD BANK NOM TVL P/L	2.5	2.0
STOCKSHARE NOM P/L	1.5	2.7
FIRST NAT NOM P/L	1.2	1.2
ARNOTT J A	1.2	---
NEDBANK NOM LTD	1.1	1.3
MENBLACK NOM P/L	---	1.8
TOTAL	56.6	56.9

DIRECTORS :
FUNSTON BJ ,GELDENHUYS JJ ,SPINDLER TV ,TAGG MJ
WILSON RAD (Chairman

REGISTRATION NUMBER : 05/05703/06

REGISTERED OFFICE
Anglovaal House, 56 Main Street
Johannesburg
2001
TEL: 011-634 9111
FAX: 011-634 0038

TRANSFER SECRETARY
Anglovaal Ltd
P O Box 62379, Marshalltown
2107
TEL: 011-634 9111

COMPANY SECRETARY
Anglovaal Ltd

NATURE OF BUSINESS
The company conducts, as its main business, the operation of a plant in the Johannesburg district for the recovery of gold from sand dumps.

BANKERS :
First National Bank of SA Ltd

AUDITORS :
Coopers Theron Du Toit

FAMILIAR BRAND NAMES
N/A

CONTRIBUTION BY ACTIVITY
N/A

YEAR END : June

DIVIDEND :Ords 12,5c

Interim No 54	(Ldr)21/12/90	(Pay)25/01/91	Amt(c)13
Final No 55	(Ldr)21/06/91	(Pay)26/07/91	Amt(c)16
Final No 57	(Ldr)19/06/92	(Pay)24/07/92	Amt(c)10
Interim No 56	(Ldr)20/12/91	(Pay)24/04/92	Amt(c)10
Interim No 58	(Ldr)11/12/92	(Pay)15/01/93	Amt(c)10

NUMBER OF EMPLOYEES : 170

CAPITAL STRUCTURE

	AUTHORISED	ISSUED
Ords 12,5c	8000000	6068446

FINANCIAL STATISTICS (AT FINANCIAL YEAR END)

(Amts in R'000)	1992 Jun	1991 Jun	1990 Jun	1989 Jun	1988 Jun
Ord S/H Int	19765	19958	19376	17630	14594
Long Trm Loans	903	1001	1087	1126	1200
Iss Ord Share	6068	6068	6068	6068	6068
Total Liab	3895	4326	6507	4049	3758
Current Liab	2992	3325	5420	2923	2558
Total Assets	23660	24284	25883	21679	18352
Current Assets	4538	4991	6881	4384	4078
Debtors	1700	932	1073	755	1112
Inventory	698	654	350	276	262
Turnover	23503	24262	25189	19304	17351
Oper Profit	1029	2652	5191	5295	5690
Interest Paid	215	242	275	-	-
Tax Paid	283	839	2218	408	1266
Prf af Int&Tax	1021	2342	3991	4887	4424
Prf att Ord Sh	1021	2342	3991	4887	4424
Btm Line Earn	1021	2342	3991	4887	4424
Dividend Paid	1214	1760	2245	1851	1517
Mkt Prce(c) YE	95	220	250	210	250

PER SHARE STATISTICS (CENTS)

Net Asst Val	325.73	328.91	319.31	290.54	240.51
Net Earnings	20.00	34.00	39.00	31.00	28.00
Dividends	20.00	29.00	37.00	31.00	25.00
Cash Flow	16.83	38.60	65.77	80.54	72.91

RATIOS AND OTHER INFORMATION

Mrk Cap(R000)	5765	13350	15170	12743	15170
Current Ratio	1.52	1.50	1.27	1.50	1.59
Quik/Acid Tst	1.28	1.30	1.20	1.41	1.49
A/C Rec T/ovr	13.83	26.03	23.48	25.57	15.60
Tot Ass T/ovr	0.99	1.00	0.97	0.89	0.95
Debt/Ass Rat	0.16	0.18	0.25	0.19	0.20
L T L Tot Ass	0.04	0.04	0.04	0.05	0.07
Debt to Eqity	0.20	0.22	0.34	0.23	0.26
Interest Cover	4.79	10.96	18.88	-	-
Oper Prof Mrg	4.38	10.93	20.61	27.43	32.79
Net Prof Marg%	4.34	9.65	15.84	25.32	25.50
Ret on Assets	6.42	14.10	25.05	24.42	31.00
Ret on Equity%	5.17	11.73	20.60	27.72	30.31
Price/Earnings	4.75	6.47	6.41	6.77	8.93
Divid Cover	1.00	1.17	1.05	1.00	1.12
Divid Yield	21.05	13.18	14.80	14.76	10.00
Earning Yield%	21.05	15.45	15.60	14.76	11.20
NAV % Mrk Pr	342.87	149.50	127.73	138.35	96.20
Effec Tax Rate	21.70	26.38	35.72	7.71	22.25
Def Interval	0.88	0.43	0.27	0.23	0.27
Sus Grth Rate	-0.98	2.92	9.01	17.22	19.92

SUBSIDIARY & ASSOCIATED COMPANIES

MINVEST (PTY) LTD

INVESTMENTS

None

VLAKFONTEIN GOLD MINING CO LTD

ABBREVIATION : VLAKS

JSE SHORT CODE : VLA

SECTOR : Gold-Curtailed Operations

SHAREHOLDERS

Who Owns Whom's Assessment of the Identity of the Ultimate Controlling Shareholder:
GFSA

SHAREHOLDER	PERCENTAGE 1992	1991
MINU NOM LTD	38.2	26.5
STD BANK NOM TVL P/L	4.2	4.8
INDO-CHINA NOM P/L	4.0	—
FIRST NAT NOM P/L	3.4	2.0
MOON M W W	3.4	—
SA EQUITIES LTD	2.2	1.0
LOWENCO NOM P/L	2.1	1.6
JUSPOINT NOM P/L	2.0	2.8
RINRIC NOM P/L	1.4	—
NAT CITY NOM LTD	1.2	1.2
FINNEGAND NOM LTD	1.2	1.2
EDWIN W BALDERSON NOM P/L	1.0	1.5
NEDBANK NOM LTD	1.0	—
JR NOM P/L	1.0	1.2
INDO-CHINA NOM SA P/L	—	3.2
TOTAL	66.4	46.9

DIRECTORS :
ADAN MJ ,ALVEY GP ,DAY BA
FULLER-GOOD MR (Chairman & Managing Dir.)
MOOLMAN A ,WRIGHT AJ

REGISTRATION NUMBER : 05/06155/06

REGISTERED OFFICE
75 Fox Street, Johannesburg
2001
TEL: 011-639 9111
FAX: 011-639 2101/2

TRANSFER SECRETARY
Gold Fields of SA Ltd
P O Box 1167, Johannesburg
2000
TEL: 011-639 9111

COMPANY SECRETARY
Gold Fields of SA Ltd

NATURE OF BUSINESS
The company has disposed of its mining title to the Droogebult section of the May Reef to Nigel Gold Mining Holdings in return for a 21% interest in that company. Activities currently include milling & treatment of remaining surface gold tonnage around the Vlakfontein plant. Closure procedures are underway.

BANKERS :
Standard Bank of SA Ltd

AUDITORS :
Ernst & Young

FAMILIAR BRAND NAMES
N/A

CONTRIBUTION BY ACTIVITY
N/A

YEAR END : June

DIVIDEND :15/12/91 and 15/06/91

NUMBER OF EMPLOYEES : 273

CAPITAL STRUCTURE

	AUTHORISED	ISSUED
Ords 20c	10000000	6800000

FINANCIAL STATISTICS (AT FINANCIAL YEAR END)

(Amts in R'000)	1992 Jun	1991 Jun	1990 Jun	1989 Jun	1988 Jun
Ord S/H Int	-5652	651	14976	16379	14573
Iss Ord Share	6800	6800	6800	6800	6800
Total Liab	6097	7702	6444	7938	8200
Current Liab	6097	7702	6444	7938	8200
Total Assets	445	8353	21420	24317	22773
Current Assets	148	2404	1937	2510	2211
Debtors	148	2353	558	432	254
Inventory	-	-	963	1399	1208
Turnover	12	3339	28093	-	28286
Oper Profit	-2138	-1040	731	1822	2609
Interest Paid	1076	1049	-	-	-
Tax Paid	-	56	58	96	-53
Prf af Int&Tax	-2463	-1697	1448	1726	2662
Prf att Ord Sh	-2463	-1697	1448	1726	2662
Btm Line Earn	-6303	-14097	-1529	1726	2662
Dividend Paid	-	-	-	-	2040
Mkt Prce(c) YE	30	115	340	275	350

PER SHARE STATISTICS (CENTS)

Net Asst Val	-83.12	9.57	220.24	240.87	214.31
Net Earnings	-36.00	-25.00	21.00	-	30.00
Dividends	-	-	-	-	30.00
Cash Flow	-36.22	-24.96	21.29	25.38	39.15

RATIOS AND OTHER INFORMATION

Mrk Cap(R000)	2040	7820	23120	18700	23800
Current Ratio	0.02	0.31	0.30	0.32	0.27
Quik/Acid Tst	0.02	0.31	0.15	0.14	0.12
A/C Rec T/ovr	0.08	1.42	50.35	-	111.36
Tot Ass T/ovr	0.03	0.40	1.31	-	1.24
Debt/Ass Rat	13.70	0.92	0.30	0.33	0.36
Debt to Eqity	-1.08	11.83	0.43	0.48	0.56
Interest Cover	-1.99	-0.99	-	-	-
Oper Prof Mrg	-17816.67	-31.15	2.60	-	9.22
Net Prof Marg%	-20525.00	-50.82	5.15	-	9.41
Ret on Assets	-311.69	-7.09	7.03	7.49	11.46
Ret on Equity%	43.58	-260.68	9.67	10.54	18.27
Price/Earnings	-0.83	-4.60	16.19	-	11.67
Divid Cover	-	-	-	-	1.00
Divid Yield	-	-	-	-	8.57
Earning Yield%	-120.00	-21.74	6.18	-	8.57
NAV % Mrk Pr	-277.06	8.32	64.78	87.59	61.23
Effec Tax Rate	-	-3.41	3.85	3.95	-2.03
Def Interval	-2.27	-3.93	3.15	2.25	1.12
Sus Grth Rate	43.58	-260.68	9.67	10.54	4.27

SUBSIDIARY & ASSOCIATED COMPANIES

NIGEL GOLD MINING HOLDINGS LTD (21,6%)

INVESTMENTS

EAST DAGGAFONTEIN MINES LTD (87822 SH)

VOGELSTRUISBULT METAL HOLDINGS LTD

ABBREVIATION : VOGELS

JSE SHORT CODE : VOG

SECTOR : Mining Financial-Mining Holding

SHAREHOLDERS

Who Owns Whom's Assessment of the Identity of the Ultimate Controlling Shareholder:
GFSA

SHAREHOLDER	PERCENTAGE 1992	1991
MINU NOM LTD	69.5	69.5
STD BANK NOM TVL P/L	6.2	6.2
NEDBANK NOM LTD	1.9	1.7
NAT PARKS BRD PERS PENS FUND	1.6	—
CMB NOM P/L	1.1	—
FIRST NAT NOM P/L	1.1	1.2
NAT PARKS BRD CURATORS STAFF PENS FUND	—	1.6
TOTAL	81.5	80.3

DIRECTORS :
ALVEY GP ,DAY BA
FULLER-GOOD MR (Managing Director),HOPWOOD JG
KAHLE H ,ROBINSON RL ,WRIGHT AJ (Chairman

REGISTRATION NUMBER : 05/04346/06

REGISTERED OFFICE
75 Fox Street, Johannesburg
2001
TEL: 011-639 9111
FAX: 011-639 2101/2

TRANSFER SECRETARY
Gold Fields of SA Ltd
P O Box 1167, Johannesburg
2000
TEL: 011-639 9111

COMPANY SECRETARY
Gold Fields of SA Ltd

NATURE OF BUSINESS
Vogels is an investment and share dealing company.

BANKERS :
Standard Bank of SA Ltd

AUDITORS :
Deloitte Pim Goldby

FAMILIAR BRAND NAMES
N/A

CONTRIBUTION BY ACTIVITY
Base Minerals (% profit before tax) (75.6%)
Energy (23.1%)
Industrial & Commercial (-0.7%)
Mining Finance (2.0%)

YEAR END : December

DIVIDEND :Ords 2,5c

Final No 86	(Ldr)26/01/90	(Pay)28/02/90	Amt(c)35
Interim No 87	(Ldr)31/08/90	(Pay)26/09/90	Amt(c)25
Final No 88	(Ldr)25/01/91	(Pay)26/02/91	Amt(c)35
Interim No 89	(Ldr)30/08/91	(Pay)25/09/91	Amt(c)25
Final No 90	(Ldr)31/01/92	(Pay)26/02/92	Amt(c)35
Interim No 91	(Ldr)28/08/92	(Pay)23/09/92	Amt(c)15

NUMBER OF EMPLOYEES : 1

CAPITAL STRUCTURE

	AUTHORISED	ISSUED
Ords 2,5c	20000000	18393600

FINANCIAL STATISTICS (AT FINANCIAL YEAR END)

(Amts in R'000)	1991 Dec	1990 Dec	1989 Dec	1988	1987
Ord S/H Int	53677	52850	48269	38382	33572
Long Trm Loans	-	-	-	5430	3952
Iss Ord Share	18394	18394	18394	18394	18394
Total Liab	6616	6583	6862	10860	7904
Current Liab	6616	6583	6862	5430	3952
Total Assets	60293	59433	55131	51687	43669
Current Assets	8794	13884	19482	7875	6145
Debtors	6895	9564	11684	-	-
Inventory	-	-	-	7875	6145
Oper Profit	-664	-627	367	9567	6900
Tax Paid	15	445	431	31	265
Prf af Int&Tax	11863	15617	20923	9536	6635
Prf att Ord Sh	11863	15617	20923	9536	6635
Btm Line Earn	11863	15617	20923	9536	6635
Dividend Paid	11036	11036	11036	7357	5518
Mkt Prce(c) YE	425	430	555	600	340

PER SHARE STATISTICS (CENTS)

Net Asst Val	291.82	287.32	262.42	208.67	182.52
Net Earnings	65.00	85.00	114.00	-	-
Dividends	60.00	60.00	60.00	-	-
Cash Flow	64.49	84.90	113.75	51.84	36.07

RATIOS AND OTHER INFORMATION

Mrk Cap(R000)	78175	79094	102087	110364	62540
Current Ratio	1.33	2.11	2.84	1.45	1.55
Quik/Acid Tst	1.33	2.11	2.84	-	-
Debt/Ass Rat	0.11	0.11	0.12	0.21	0.18
L T L Tot Ass	-	-	-	0.11	0.09
Debt to Eqity	0.12	0.12	0.14	0.28	0.24
Ret on Assets	19.70	27.03	38.73	18.51	15.80
Ret on Equity%	22.10	29.55	43.35	24.84	19.76
Price/Earnings	6.54	5.06	4.87	-	-
Divid Cover	1.08	1.42	1.90	-	-
Divid Yield	14.12	13.95	10.81	-	-
Earning Yield%	15.29	19.77	20.54	-	-
NAV % Mrk Pr	68.66	66.82	47.28	34.78	53.68
Effec Tax Rate	-9.68	51.21	32.48	0.32	3.84
Def Interval	-	-	-	0.57	0.60
Sus Grth Rate	1.54	8.67	20.48	5.68	3.33

SUBSIDIARY & ASSOCIATED COMPANIES

O'OKIEP COPPER CO LTD (30%)
ROOIBERG TIN LTD (30%)
STRUISBULT INVESTMENTS LTD
ZINC CORPORATION OF S.A. LTD (38%)

INVESTMENTS

BLACK MOUNTAIN MINERAL DEVELOPMENT CO (P (1%)
GOLD FIELDS COAL LTD (14%)
MINU NOMINEES LTD (1 SH)
NEW WITS LTD (670000 SH)
NORTHAM PLATINUM LTD (2%)
SASOL LTD (570000 SH)

VOLTEX HOLDINGS LTD

ABBREVIATION : VOLTEX

JSE SHORT CODE : VLX

SECTOR : Industrial-Electronics, Electrical & Bat

SHAREHOLDERS

Who Owns Whom's Assessment of the Identity of the Ultimate Controlling Shareholder:
ELCENTRE

SHAREHOLDER	PERCENTAGE 1992	1991
ELCENTRE CORP LTD	38.1	42.8
EIGHTY ONE MAIN STREET NOM LTD	18.1	3.3

BERZACK BROS HOLDINGS LTD	11.7	42.7
FIRST NAT NOM P/L	6.7	1.1
STD BANK NOM TVL P/L	6.2	1.3
CMB NOM P/L	5.1	---
NEDBANK NOM LTD	2.9	---
FEDLIFE ASSURE LTD	2.1	---
AECI PENS FUND	1.7	---
ANDERSON J	1.7	---
BOARD OF EXECUTORS NOM P/L	---	1.3
ELCENTRE GROUP HOLDINGS LTD	---	3.9
TOTAL	94.2	96.5

DIRECTORS :
AGINSKY PC ,BERZACK A ,BERZACK MC
ILLMAN B (Chairman),ILLMAN SH ,MOWSZOWKSI NP

REGISTRATION NUMBER : 81/06220/06

REGISTERED OFFICE
Voltex House, 3 River Road
Bedfordview
2008
TEL: 011-622 4910
FAX: 011-616 4967

TRANSFER SECRETARY
Central Registrars Ltd
P O Box 4844, Johannesburg
2000
TEL: 011-331 0051

COMPANY SECRETARY
Voltex Management Services (Pty) Ltd

NATURE OF BUSINESS
The principal activities of the group are the manufacture of electric cable & electrical wire, injection mouldings, rigid & soft extrusions, and the distribution of cable, wire, industrial and commercial electrical, electronic & lighting requisites.

BANKERS :
First National Bank of SA Ltd
International Bank of Johannesburg Ltd
Nedperm Bank Ltd, Standard Bank of SA Ltd
Trust Bank of Africa Ltd
Standard Merchant Bank Ltd

AUDITORS :
Charles Orbach & Co, KPMG Aiken & Peat

FAMILIAR BRAND NAMES
N/A

CONTRIBUTION BY ACTIVITY
N/A

YEAR END : June

DIVIDEND :Ords 1c

Interim No 1	(Ldr)15/06/90	(Pay)02/07/90	Amt(c)9
Final No 2	(Ldr)19/10/90	(Pay)31/10/90	Amt(c)2
Final No 3	(Ldr)18/10/91	(Pay)31/10/91	Amt(c)4.75
Interim No 4	(Ldr)08/05/92	(Pay)22/05/92	Amt(c)2.75
Final No 5	(Ldr)30/10/92	(Pay)16/11/92	Amt(c)4

NUMBER OF EMPLOYEES : 3900

CAPITAL STRUCTURE

	AUTHORISED	ISSUED
Ords 1c	800000000	300000000
Comp Conv Debs 60c	120170973	120170973

FINANCIAL STATISTICS (AT FINANCIAL YEAR END)

(Amts in R'000)	1992 Jun	1991 Jun	1990 Jun
Ord S/H Int	535753	577826	558107
Long Trm Loans	321418	349156	206694
Iss Ord Share	300000	300000	300000
Total Liab	652663	648789	390308
Current Liab	331245	299633	183614
Total Assets	817958	802193	594971
Intang Assets	370458	424422	353444
Current Assets	465601	436099	316684
Debtors	248882	231291	142972
Inventory	188787	190307	133759
Turnover	1226571	1257591	1075020
Oper Profit	91083	126951	140832
Interest Paid	32953	43376	14151
Tax Paid	-1105	480	257
Prf af Int&Tax	59985	83886	126424
Prf att Ord Sh	50722	60578	99987
Btm Line Earn	-21823	44469	75433
Dividend Paid	20250	24750	33000
Mkt Prce(c) YE	105	160	170
Depreciation	31395	29037	21178

PER SHARE STATISTICS (CENTS)

Net Asst Val	55.10	51.13	68.22
Net Earnings	15.80	19.00	25.30
Dividends	6.75	8.25	8.25
Cash Flow	32.11	35.83	39.45

RATIOS AND OTHER INFORMATION

Mrk Cap(R000)	315000	480000	510000
Current Ratio	1.41	1.46	1.72
Quik/Acid Tst	0.84	0.82	1.00
A/C Rec T/ovr	4.93	5.44	7.52
Tot Ass T/ovr	1.50	1.57	1.81
Debt/Ass Rat	0.77	0.80	0.66
L T L Tot Ass	0.37	0.42	0.35
Debt to Eqity	1.18	1.10	0.70
Interest Cover	2.79	2.94	9.95
Oper Prof Mrg	7.43	10.09	13.10
Net Prof Marg%	4.14	4.82	9.30
Ret on Assets	11.40	16.07	23.67
Ret on Equity%	9.47	10.48	17.92
Price/Earnings	6.65	8.42	6.72
Divid Cover	2.34	2.30	3.07
Divid Yield	6.43	5.16	4.85
Earning Yield%	15.05	11.88	14.88
NAV % Mrk Pr	52.47	31.96	40.13
Effec Tax Rate	1.35	-	-
Def Interval	2.28	1.91	-
Sus Grth Rate	5.69	6.20	12.00

SUBSIDIARY & ASSOCIATED COMPANIES

AIB INVESTMENTS (PTY) LTD (50%)
AMALGAMATED PLASTIC INDUSTRIES (PTY) LTD (35%)
BENNETT & FOUNTAIN GROUP PLC
ELECTRIC PRODUCTS INTERNATIONAL (PTY) LT (20%)
FORWARD PLASTICS MANUFACTURING (PTY) LTD (40%)
VOLTEX (PTY) LTD
VOLTEX DISTRIBUTORS (PTY) LTD
VOLTEX MANUFACTURERS (PTY) LTD
VOLTEX PROPERTIES (PTY) LTD

INVESTMENTS

EPI (PTY) LTD (20%)

W & A INVESTMENT CORP LTD

ABBREVIATION : W-&-A

JSE SHORT CODE : WAA

SECTOR : Industrial-Industrial Holding

SHAREHOLDERS

Who Owns Whom's Assessment of the Identity of the Ultimate Controlling Shareholder:
FS GROUP VIA WAICOR

SHAREHOLDER	PERCENTAGE 1992	1991
WAICOR LTD	56.4	50.1
CMB NOM P/L	10.8	1.2
WAICOR SHARE INV P/L	7.5	7.6
STD BANK NOM TVL P/L	4.4	3.9
ENVOY INV P/L	1.4	1.4
VMB NOM P/L	1.4	1.3
LIBERTY LIFE ASSOC OF AFRICA LTD	1.3	1.3
HALL G W	1.3	1.3
AECI PENS FUND	1.0	1.0
FSI CORP LTD	---	7.5
DE BEERS PENS FUND	---	1.5
SANLAM	---	8.4
TOTAL	85.4	86.5

DIRECTORS :
AARON AJ ,COHEN N (Financial Director),GUTKIN M
LIEBESMAN BE
LIEBESMAN JM (Chairman & Chief Exec.)
NICHOLSON RG ,ROLFE TW (Joint Deputy Chairman)
SLOM S ,TUTTON CW
VAN DER MERWE HR (Joint Deputy Chairman)
WEINTROUB S

REGISTRATION NUMBER : 52/01223/06

REGISTERED OFFICE
6th Floor, FSI Centre, 35 Siemert Road
Doornfontein
2094
TEL: 011-402 3200
FAX: 011-402 7508

TRANSFER SECRETARY
Central Registrars Ltd
P O Box 4844, Johannesburg
2000
TEL: 011-331 0051

COMPANY SECRETARY
B E Liebesman

NATURE OF BUSINESS
An investment holding company with interests in the manufacture of footwear,tyres and rubber products, toys, medical equipment, builtin cupboards, modular buildings, automotive wheels power cables, scaffolding, fasteners, automotive components & healthcare products; Distribution of toys, medical equipment, textiles, coal, vehicles automotive parts & refinishing products, garage equipment, hand tools & electrical goods; Retail of footwear, furniture & consumer electronics.

BANKERS :
Nedperm Bank Ltd, Standard Bank of SA Ltd
First National Bank of SA Ltd
Central Merchant Bank Ltd

AUDITORS :
Kessel Feinstein

FAMILIAR BRAND NAMES
ACTIV,AEROTECH,ALLOY WHEELS INTERNATIONAL
ARWA,AUTORITE,AVDEL,BADGER,BERKSHIRE,BOSS
BRADLOWS,BRIGGS & STRATTON,BURHOSE,CAMEO
CHRISTIAN DIOR,CONTINENTAL,COUNTRY CLASSICS
DELTA (DEALERS),DODO'S,DUCO,EAGLE TOYS
EDWORKS,ESCORT,FEDERAL MOGUL,FELIX,FEMO
FEMO AUTO,FITRITE,FIXSCAFF,FORM-SCAFF
GALTUCCI LINEN,GDS MINING,GENERAL BELTING
GENERAL TYRES,GILL & RAMSDEN,GLO-MAIL
GOLDEN GIRL (HOSIERY),GOLDIES MOTOR SUPPLIES
GUD,HARMONY,HI-TENSILE HYDRAULICS,HITACHI
HOMEWISE,HOUSEWARES,HOUSEWARES EXCLUSIVE
HUCK,HYGIENIA,IMPERIAL TABLEWARE,JOHN CRAIG
JOSHUA DOORE,KITCHEN TRENDS,KOKO
LOCKBOLT FASTENING,LOMBARDINI,LORDS,MACPHAIL
MARCELLO,MATOOL (WHOLESALE)
MATUS (WHOLESALE),METROTOY,MILANO ORIGINALS
MOBILBAU,MONOPOLY & OTHER BOARD GAMES
MULTI-PINE,MURATTI,NATIONAL BOLTS
O F S JAMES,OHANA,OMEGA COAL,PARAGON RUBBER
PARTS CENTRE,PEDIGREE TOYS,PICK A PAIR
PLAYFUL TOYS,PREMIER CONSTRUCTION
PRICE N PRIDE,PRIMET (RAINWEAR),REVOLUTION
ROWE-INNOTEX,ROYAL TABLEWARE,SASCO
SCORE FURNISHERS,SEAGULL TOYS
SELWYN NEIMAN/LEE,SEMBEL-IT,SEMBIL-IT,SGB
SKYHOOKS,SOUTHERN COAL TRADERS,STAHLWILLE
STIHL TOOLS,SWANKS,SWEET DREAMS,TARGET
TARRY'S,THE FABRIC LIBRARY,TRIANG,UNIROYAL
UNIT-SPANBUILDING SYSTEMS,UNIVERSAL CLIPS
V&R ENGINE SPARES,VANELI,VOLTAN,WEMBLEY TOYS
WHID (WHOLESALE),WILFRACE,WILLIAMS HUNT
YOKOTA

CONTRIBUTION BY ACTIVITY
Tyres/Rubber Products (% attrib profit) (32.0%)
Hosiery (16.0%)
Coal Distribution (4.0%)
Automotive Distribution (2.0%)
Retail Furniture (13.0%)
Consumer Distribution (13.0%)
Toys & Outdoor Products (-1.0%)
Scaffolding,Shoring & Formwork (33.0%)
System Building/Automotive Wheels (9.0%)
Fasteners,Tools & Equipment (12.0%)
Corporate Services & Financing (-33.8%)
Healthcare (0.5%)
Consumer Electronics (0.2%)
Automotive Refinishing Supplies (0.1%)

YEAR END : December

DIVIDEND : Ords 5c

Interim No 60	(Ldr)29/09/89	(Pay)20/10/89	Amt(c)120
Final No 61	(Ldr)05/04/90	(Pay)27/04/90	Amt(c)300
Interim No 62	(Ldr)19/10/90	(Pay)09/11/90	Amt(c)15.5
Final No 63	(Ldr)26/04/91	(Pay)26/06/91	Amt(c)26.5
Interim No 64	(Ldr)04/10/91	(Pay)15/11/91	Amt(c)15.5
Final No 65	(Ldr)24/04/92	(Pay)13/05/92	Amt(c)26.5
Interim No 66	(Ldr)25/09/92	(Pay)06/11/92	Amt(c)11

NUMBER OF EMPLOYEES : 22860

CAPITAL STRUCTURE

	AUTHORISED	ISSUED
Ords 5c	180000000	112317549
Pref Ords 5c	20000000	18847872
6% Red Cum Prefs R2	149900	149900
6,75c Div Var Rate Red Cum Prefs	4000000	0
7,2c Div Var Rate Red Cum Prefs 1	4000000	0
Var Rate Red Cum Pref 1c	282189850	0
"A" Var Rate Unsec Sub Comp Conv	26470588	26470588
"B" Var Rate Unsec Sub Comp Conv	6241506	6241506
12% "C" Unsec Sub Comp Conv Debs	21875000	21875000

FINANCIAL STATISTICS (AT FINANCIAL YEAR END)

(Amts in R'000)	1991 Dec	1990 Dec	1989 Dec	1988 Dec	1987 Dec
Ord S/H Int	717040	760162	397251	331778	210019
Long Trm Loans	1474765	1521867	1078506	599850	211719
Iss Ord Share	131165	131165	75038	75038	51571
Total Liab	2362278	2331081	1595830	850852	319288
Current Liab	887513	809214	517324	251002	107569
Total Assets	2676376	2708587	1707789	1109335	529307
Intang Assets	402942	382656	285292	73295	*
Current Assets	1397082	1646028	1218276	652316	210579
Debtors	765707	961332	661846	257513	105457
Inventory	556031	571276	436718	262338	95928
Turnover	3227630	3036537	2333030	1450180	829589
Oper Profit	354532	327772	303250	178152	93223
Interest Paid	232708	183721	122433	35765	11607
Tax Paid	3603	20614	64299	42062	20466
Prf af Int&Tax	180093	178154	163298	101871	61150
Prf att Ord Sh	89969	96974	86075	52487	37528
Btm Line Earn	80628	66913	97995	52606	126193
Dividend Paid	62202	48422	31516	19070	13924
Mkt Prce(c) YE	480	550	810	400	500
Depreciation	57599	38909	28357	17360	12436

PER SHARE STATISTICS (CENTS)

Net Asst Val	239.47	287.81	149.20	344.47	407.24
Net Earnings	69.00	94.00	114.70	953.00	731.00
Dividends	42.00	42.00	42.00	350.00	270.00
Cash Flow	113.89	114.60	1416.95	1264.50	973.39

RATIOS AND OTHER INFORMATION

Mrk Cap(R000)	629592	721408	607808	300152	257855
Current Ratio	1.57	2.03	2.35	2.60	1.96
Quik/Acid Tst	0.95	1.33	1.51	1.55	1.07
A/C Rec T/ovr	4.22	3.16	3.53	5.63	7.87
Tot Ass T/ovr	1.21	1.12	1.37	1.31	1.57
Debt/Ass Rat	0.74	0.73	0.55	0.45	0.30
L T L Tot Ass	0.40	0.43	0.25	0.23	0.09
Debt to Eqity	2.75	2.59	2.36	1.52	0.75
Interest Cover	1.53	1.84	2.52	5.02	8.03
Oper Prof Mrg	10.98	10.79	13.00	12.28	11.24
Net Prof Marg%	2.79	3.19	3.69	3.62	4.52
Ret on Assets	15.60	14.47	21.19	16.20	17.61
Ret on Equity%	12.55	12.76	21.67	15.82	17.87
Price/Earnings	6.96	5.85	7.06	0.42	0.68
Divid Cover	1.64	2.24	2.73	2.72	2.71
Divid Yield	8.75	7.64	5.19	87.50	54.00
Earning Yield%	14.38	17.09	14.16	238.25	146.20
NAV % Mrk Pr	49.89	52.33	18.42	86.12	81.45
Effec Tax Rate	5.27	12.05	26.63	29.54	25.08
Def Interval	5.69	7.52	4.25	3.91	1.15
Sus Grth Rate	3.87	6.39	13.73	10.07	11.24

SUBSIDIARY & ASSOCIATED COMPANIES

AAF FINANCE CO. LTD
ATHOL JOINT VENTURE
CENTURION JOINT VENTURE (PARTNERSHIP)
CURNOW M&G LTD (36%)
FS TEAM DISTRIBUTORS LTD
GENTYRE INDUSTRIES LTD
GLEN ANIL INVESTMENTS (PTY) LTD
HOMEMAKERS GROUP LTD
HOMEMAKERS HOLDINGS LTD
HOUSEWARES LTD
HUNTS LTD
HUNTS PROPERTIES LTD
JD GROUP LTD (50%)
MACPHAIL HOLDINGS LTD
METROTOY (PTY) LTD
MILSTAN HOLDINGS LTD (31%)
NORISTAN HOLDINGS LTD (21%)
PENINSULA JOINT VENTURE (PARTNERSHIP)
PUTCOTON JOINT VENTURE (50%)
ROOIKRUIN BELEGGINGS BPK (46%)
SCORE SUPERMARKETS LTD
TEAMCOR LTD
USM HOLDINGS (PTY) LTD
V&J SYNDICATE (PARTNERSHIP) (50%)
V&R ENGINE SPARES CENTRE JHB (PARTNERSHI
VEKTRA CORPORATION PLC
W & A MANUFACTURING (PTY) LTD
W & A MANUFACTURING HOLDINGS LTD

INVESTMENTS

FRIGATE GROUP LTD (500000 SH)
SA EAGLE INSURANCE CO LTD (100 SH)
SMALL BUSINESS DEVELOPMENT CORP LTD (28840 SH)
UNISPIN HOLDINGS LTD (10000 SH)

WAICOR LTD

ABBREVIATION : WAICOR

JSE SHORT CODE : WAC

SECTOR : Industrial-Industrial Holding

SHAREHOLDERS

Who Owns Whom's Assessment of the Identity of the Ultimate Controlling Shareholder: FS GROUP VIA FSI CORP

SHAREHOLDER	PERCENTAGE 1992	1991
FSI CORP LTD	60.8	60.9
CMB NOM P/L	8.8	3.8
SA MUTUAL	5.2	5.2
STD BANK NOM TVL P/L	5.0	4.3
AECI PENS FUND	3.3	3.3
BUILMA NOM P/L	3.0	---
DE BEERS PENS FUND	2.2	2.5
NEDBANK NOM LTD	1.5	1.4
ANGLO AMERICAN GROUP PENS FUND	1.3	1.3
SEFALANA EMP BENEFITS ORG (SEBO)	1.3	1.3
BOARD OF EXECUTORS NOM P/L	---	1.3

FSI CORP PENS FUND	---	2.0
SANLAM	---	5.0
TOTAL	92.2	92.3

DIRECTORS :
COHEN N (Financial Director),KAMINER B
LIEBESMAN JM (Chairman),ROLFE TW
SCHLESINGER AM ,SLOM S ,VAN DER MERWE HR

REGISTRATION NUMBER : 67/04493/06

REGISTERED OFFICE
6th Floor, FSI Centre, 35 Siemert Road
Doornfontein
2001
TEL: 011-402 3200
FAX: 011-402 7508

TRANSFER SECRETARY
Central Registrars Ltd
P O Box 4844, Johannesburg
2000
TEL: 011-331 0051

COMPANY SECRETARY
B E Liebesman

NATURE OF BUSINESS
An investment holding company with a controlling interest in quoted W & A Investment Corporation.

BANKERS :
Nedperm Bank Ltd

AUDITORS :
Kessel Feinstein

FAMILIAR BRAND NAMES
N/A

CONTRIBUTION BY ACTIVITY
N/A

YEAR END : December

DIVIDEND : Ords 5c

Interim No 37	(Ldr)29/09/89	(Pay)20/10/89	Amt(c)49
Final No 38	(Ldr)05/04/90	(Pay)27/04/90	Amt(c)119
Interim No 39	(Ldr)19/10/90	(Pay)09/11/90	Amt(c)6
Final No 40	(Ldr)26/04/91	(Pay)26/06/91	Amt(c)10.5
Interim No 41	(Ldr)04/10/91	(Pay)15/11/91	Amt(c)6
Final No 42	(Ldr)24/04/92	(Pay)13/05/92	Amt(c)10.5
Interim No 43	(Ldr)06/11/92	(Pay)25/09/92	Amt(c)4.5

CAPITAL STRUCTURE

	AUTHORISED	ISSUED
Ords 5c	300000000	176507056
Pref Ords 5c	50000000	46742436
Var Rate Red Cum Prefs 1c	7480000	0
Var Rate Unsec Sub Comp Conv Debs	65693430	65693430

FINANCIAL STATISTICS (AT FINANCIAL YEAR END)

(Amts in R'000)	1991 Dec	1990 Dec	1989 Dec	1988 Dec	1987 Dec
Ord S/H Int	381644	382160	50849	50836	15748
Long Trm Loans	180000	180000	-	-	-
Iss Ord Share	223249	223249	6392	6392	6393
Total Liab	245183	228082	22700	22287	5099
Current Liab	65183	48082	22700	22287	5099
Total Assets	626827	610242	73549	73123	20847
Current Assets	66192	49607	10764	10338	5114
Oper Profit	-25	-78	-70	-	-
Interest Paid	1265	-	954	528	12
Prf af Int&Tax	42154	31497	15048	9753	6783
Prf att Ord Sh	42154	31497	15048	6578	6783
Btm Line Earn	42154	31437	15048	6578	6783
Dividend Paid	42670	30688	10739	6904	6712
Mkt Prce(c) YE	170	3300	3600	1800	3450

PER SHARE STATISTICS (CENTS)

Net Asst Val	170.95	171.18	795.51	795.31	246.33
Net Earnings	28.10	38.80	47.90	383.00	239.00
Dividends	16.50	16.50	16.80	147.00	105.00
Cash Flow	18.88	20.14	168.15	143.45	106.12

RATIOS AND OTHER INFORMATION

Mrk Cap(R000)	379523	7367217	230112	115056	220559
Current Ratio	1.02	1.03	0.47	0.46	1.00
Quik/Acid Tst	1.02	1.03	0.47	0.46	1.00
Debt/Ass Rat	0.39	0.37	0.31	0.30	0.24
L T L Tot Ass	0.29	0.29	-	-	-
Debt to Eqity	0.64	0.60	0.45	0.44	0.32
Interest Cover	34.32	-	16.77	19.47	566.25
Ret on Assets	6.93	5.16	21.76	14.06	32.59
Ret on Equity%	11.05	8.24	29.59	12.94	43.07
Price/Earnings	6.05	85.05	75.16	4.70	14.44
Divid Cover	1.70	2.35	2.85	2.61	2.28
Divid Yield	9.71	0.50	0.47	8.17	3.04
Earning Yield%	16.53	1.18	1.33	21.28	6.93
NAV % Mrk Pr	100.56	5.19	22.10	44.18	7.14
Def Interval	1.09	0.72	0.86	1.25	-
Sus Grth Rate	-0.14	0.21	8.47	-0.64	0.45

SUBSIDIARY & ASSOCIATED COMPANIES

W & A INVESTMENT CORP LTD
WAICOR SHARE INVESTMENTS (PTY) LTD

INVESTMENTS

None

WALTONS CONSOLIDATED INVESTMENT HOLDINGS LTD

ABBREVIATION : WALHOLD

JSE SHORT CODE : WLH

SECTOR : Industrial-Retailers & Wholesalers

SHAREHOLDERS

Who Owns Whom's Assessment of the Identity of the Ultimate Controlling Shareholder:
DIRECTORS / CNA GALLO

SHAREHOLDER	PERCENTAGE 1992	1991
CNA GALLO LTD	15.7	15.1
SYMMETRICAL INV P/L	10.4	10.4
CMB NOM P/L	10.0	---
WALTON N H	8.9	9.1

DE BEERS PENS FUND	6.4	6.4
STD BANK NOM TVL P/L	6.0	5.4
ROBARTS F E A	4.2	4.2
ANGLO AMERICAN CORP PENS FUND	3.8	3.8
VAN RENSBURG J P	3.3	3.3
MEINTJES D E	2.2	2.2
SHARESTOCK NOM P/L	1.7	2.4
FIRST NAT NOM P/L	1.6	1.4
EIGHTY ONE MAIN STREET NOM LTD	1.6	---
MUIRHEAD AA &DUANE K &ASHERSON D TRUST	1.4	1.4
SA SPECIAL RISKS INSURANCE ASSOC LTD	1.4	---
SMITH J C & L C & SCHLOSBERG B	1.3	1.5
NEDBANK NOM LTD	1.1	---
SA MUTUAL	1.1	1.1
CHIMES L I	---	1.3
SANLAM	---	10.0
TOTAL	81.9	79.0

DIRECTORS :
CHIMES LI ,CUZEN ADL ,DAVIS MH ,GOUGH CS
MUIRHEAD AA ,PHELPS LS
ROBARTS FEA (Chairman & Managing Dir.)
VAN RENSBURG JP ,WALTON NH (Deputy Chairman)
WILSON R

REGISTRATION NUMBER : 83/13542/06

REGISTERED OFFICE
71 Dock Road, Cape Town
8001
TEL: 021-21 4920
FAX: 021-418 2377

TRANSFER SECRETARY
Mercantile Registrars Ltd
P O Box 1053, Johannesburg
2000
TEL: 011-333 8181

COMPANY SECRETARY
D J Pewsey

NATURE OF BUSINESS
An investment holding company with a controlling interest in JSE-quoted Waltons Stationery Co Ltd. The group supplies commercial stationery through a network of branches in SA.

BANKERS :
Standard Bank of SA Ltd
First National Bank of SA Ltd
Nedperm Bank Ltd, Trust Bank of Africa Ltd
Volkskas Ltd

AUDITORS :
Coopers Theron Du Toit

FAMILIAR BRAND NAMES
N/A

CONTRIBUTION BY ACTIVITY
N/A

YEAR END : February

DIVIDEND : Ords no par value

Interim	(Ldr)18/11/89	(Pay)01/12/89	Amt(c)7
Final	(Ldr)01/06/90	(Pay)22/06/90	Amt(c)14
Interim	(Ldr)16/11/90	(Pay)30/11/90	Amt(c)7
Special	(Ldr)22/02/91	(Pay)17/05/91	Amt(c)12
Final	(Ldr)28/02/92	(Pay)15/05/92	Amt(c)12
Interim	(Ldr)15/11/91	(Pay)29/11/91	Amt(c)7
Interim	(Ldr)20/11/92	(Pay)27/11/92	Amt(c)5

NUMBER OF EMPLOYEES : 6250

CAPITAL STRUCTURE

	AUTHORISED	ISSUED
Ords no par value	55000000	35650500

FINANCIAL STATISTICS (AT FINANCIAL YEAR END)

(Amts in R'000)	1992 Feb	1991 Feb	1990 Feb	1989 Feb	1988 Feb
Ord S/H Int	33721	33721	33721	24721	22294
Long Trm Loans	-	-	365	-	-
Iss Ord Share	35651	35651	35651	34151	33425
Total Liab	4278	4715	5431	4149	3188
Current Liab	4278	4715	5066	4149	3188
Total Assets	37999	38436	39152	28870	25482
Current Assets	4820	4683	6197	4441	3275
Oper Profit	522	543	601	6397	4535
Tax Paid	251	272	300	257	178
Prf af Int&Tax	6773	6773	7487	6140	4357
Prf att Ord Sh	6773	6773	7487	6140	4357
Btm Line Earn	6773	6773	7487	6140	4357
Dividend Paid	6773	6773	7487	6140	4357
Mkt Prce(c) YE	425	585	450	560	370

PER SHARE STATISTICS (CENTS)

Net Asst Val	94.59	94.59	94.59	72.39	66.70
Net Earnings	19.00	19.00	21.00	18.00	13.00
Dividends	19.00	19.00	21.00	18.00	13.00
Cash Flow	19.00	19.00	21.00	18.03	13.00

RATIOS AND OTHER INFORMATION

Mrk Cap(R000)	151517	208558	160430	191246	123673
Current Ratio	1.13	0.99	1.22	1.07	1.03
Quik/Acid Tst	1.13	0.99	1.22	1.07	1.03
Debt/Ass Rat	0.11	0.12	0.14	0.14	0.13
L T L Tot Ass	-	-	0.01	-	-
Debt to Eqity	0.13	0.14	0.16	0.17	0.14
Ret on Assets	18.48	18.33	19.89	22.16	17.80
Ret on Equity%	20.09	20.09	22.20	24.84	19.54
Price/Earnings	22.37	30.79	21.43	31.11	28.46
Divid Cover	1.00	1.00	1.00	1.00	1.00
Divid Yield	4.47	3.25	4.67	3.21	3.51
Earning Yield%	4.47	3.25	4.67	3.21	3.51
NAV % Mrk Pr	22.26	16.17	21.02	12.93	18.03
Effec Tax Rate	48.08	50.09	49.92	4.02	3.93
Def Interval	-	0.06	-	0.00	0.00
Sus Grth Rate	0.00	0.00	0.00	0.00	0.00

SUBSIDIARY & ASSOCIATED COMPANIES

WALTONS STATIONERY CO. LTD (50,1%)

INVESTMENTS

None

WALTONS STATIONERY CO LTD

ABBREVIATION : WALTONS

JSE SHORT CODE : WAL

SECTOR : Industrial-Retailers & Wholesalers

SHAREHOLDERS

Who Owns Whom's Assessment of the Identity of the Ultimate Controlling Shareholder:
WALTONS CONSOLIDATED INVESTMENT HOLDINGS

SHAREHOLDER	PERCENTAGE 1992	1991
WALTONS CONSOLIDATED INV HOLDINGS LTD	50.1	50.1
STD BANK NOM TVL P/L	12.1	11.7
CMB NOM P/L	6.2	---
DE BEERS PENS FUND	4.1	4.1
EIGHTY ONE MAIN STREET NOM LTD	3.6	1.3
ANGLO AMERICAN CORP PENS FUND	2.3	2.3
NEDBANK NOM LTD	1.8	1.5
HORTORS GROUP PENS FUND	1.3	1.3
CNA GALLO LTD	1.3	1.2
SHARESTOCK NOM P/L	1.3	1.6
SAGE LIFE LTD	1.0	1.0
WALTONS STATIONERY EXEC SH PURC TRUST	---	1.9
SANLAM	---	6.1
SYFRETS NOM LTD	---	1.2
TOTAL	85.1	85.5

DIRECTORS :
CHIMES LI ,DAVIS MH ,GOUGH CS ,MUIRHEAD AA
ROBARTS FEA (Chairman & Managing Dir.)
VAN RENSBURG JP ,WALTON NH (Deputy Chairman)
WILSON R

REGISTRATION NUMBER : 78/01319/06

REGISTERED OFFICE
71 Dock Road, Cape Town
8001
TEL: 021-21 4920
FAX: 021-418 2377

TRANSFER SECRETARY
Mercantile Registrars Ltd
P O Box 1053, Johannesburg
2000
TEL: 011-333 8181

COMPANY SECRETARY
D J Pewsey

NATURE OF BUSINESS
Group operations include: Stationery manufacture, wholesale & distribution; Distribution of price marking & labelling machines, & the manufacture of labels; Manufacture & distribution of typewriter & computer ribbons; Distribution of drawing office & plan printing equipment, computer stationery, CAD systems & office equipemnt; Retailing of babyware, toys, & prams; Maintenance & distribution of photo copy & facsimile machines. The group controls JSE quoted Redgewoods, & has 29% of Lithosaver Systems

BANKERS :
First National Bank of SA Ltd
Standard Bank of SA Ltd
Trust Bank of Africa Ltd, Nedperm Bank Ltd

AUDITORS :
Coopers Theron Du Toit

FAMILIAR BRAND NAMES
KING-PAC,REPLICA

CONTRIBUTION BY ACTIVITY
N/A

YEAR END : February

DIVIDEND :Ords no par value

Interim	(Ldr)18/11/89	(Pay)01/12/89	Amt(c)7
Final	(Ldr)01/06/90	(Pay)22/06/90	Amt(c)14
Interim	(Ldr)16/11/90	(Pay)30/11/90	Amt(c)7
Final	(Ldr)22/02/91	(Pay)17/05/91	Amt(c)12
Final	(Ldr)28/02/92	(Pay)15/05/92	Amt(c)12
Interim	(Ldr)15/11/91	(Pay)29/11/91	Amt(c)7
Interim	(Ldr)20/11/92	(Pay)27/11/92	Amt(c)5

NUMBER OF EMPLOYEES : 5604

CAPITAL STRUCTURE

	AUTHORISED	ISSUED
Ords no par value	110000000	68250000

FINANCIAL STATISTICS (AT FINANCIAL YEAR END)

(Amts in R'000)	1992 Feb	1991 Feb	1990 Feb	1989 Feb	1988 Feb
Ord S/H Int	161920	150544	127942	88874	61688
Long Trm Loans	114051	78407	121669	145569	52962
Iss Ord Share	68250	68250	68250	65250	64200
Total Liab	256995	237453	255500	269665	135443
Current Liab	142944	159046	133831	124096	82481
Total Assets	401577	363398	360237	333665	197131
Intang Assets	17338	24599	23205	24874	*
Current Assets	305146	274785	277350	254653	148820
Debtors	137289	118011	114966	100646	65458
Inventory	159435	147661	151874	147993	78653
Turnover	748163	685310	648086	547931	329648
Oper Profit	99274	106022	109015	85574	57265
Interest Paid	19833	20824	29015	19021	3823
Tax Paid	41553	42047	31211	9753	22288
Prf af Int&Tax	40039	44304	49905	57977	31154
Prf att Ord Sh	32490	35894	42427	35811	24437
Btm Line Earn	24231	35583	35228	36698	22119
Dividend Paid	12968	12968	14333	11730	8334
Mkt Prce(c) YE	425	585	435	560	370
Depreciation	18470	15549	13353	12598	5802

PER SHARE STATISTICS (CENTS)

Net Asst Val	211.84	184.53	153.46	98.08	96.09
Net Earnings	47.60	52.60	63.60	55.00	39.00
Dividends	19.00	19.00	21.00	18.00	13.00
Cash Flow	79.06	76.82	83.61	97.03	47.19

RATIOS AND OTHER INFORMATION

Mrk Cap(R000)	290063	399263	296888	365400	237540
Current Ratio	2.13	1.73	2.07	2.05	1.80
Quik/Acid Tst	1.02	0.80	0.94	0.86	0.85
A/C Rec T/ovr	5.45	5.81	5.64	5.44	5.04
Tot Ass T/ovr	1.86	1.89	1.80	1.64	1.67
Debt/Ass Rat	0.52	0.55	0.63	0.73	0.59
L T L Tot Ass	0.16	0.12	0.26	0.36	0.18
Debt to Eqity	1.29	1.34	1.77	2.74	1.90
Interest Cover	5.01	5.09	3.76	4.50	14.98
Oper Prof Mrg	13.27	15.47	16.82	15.62	17.37
Net Prof Marg%	4.34	5.24	6.55	6.54	7.41
Ret on Assets	25.53	29.52	30.56	26.16	29.26
Ret on Equity%	20.07	23.84	33.16	40.29	39.61
Price/Earnings	8.93	11.12	6.84	10.18	9.49
Divid Cover	2.51	2.77	3.03	3.06	3.00
Divid Yield	4.47	3.25	4.83	3.21	3.51

Earning Yield%	11.20	8.99	14.62	9.82	10.54
NAV % Mrk Pr	49.85	31.54	35.28	17.52	25.97
Effec Tax Rate	45.07	44.11	21.78	13.20	33.34
Def Interval	1.73	1.86	2.37	2.50	1.54
Sus Grth Rate	12.06	15.23	21.96	27.10	26.10

SUBSIDIARY & ASSOCIATED COMPANIES

ATOMIC HOLDINGS (PTY) LTD
CENTON PROPERTIES (PTY) LTD (50%)
GALA STATIONERY (EASTERN PROVINCE) (PTY)
GALA STATIONERY (EASTERN TVL) (PTY) LTD
GALA STATIONERY (NATAL) (PTY) LTD
GALA STATIONERY (WESTERN PROVINCE) (PTY)
HI-MAUR SYSTEMS (PTY) LTD
KING-PAC (PTY) LTD
MULTIPRO HOLDINGS (PTY) LTD
OZALID (SA) (PTY) LTD
PIRIE APPLETON & CO. AFRICA (PTY) LTD (50%)
R L ESSON (PTY) LTD
REDGWOODS HOLDINGS LTD
ROBIN CONSOLIDATED INDUSTRIES LTD
ROLL-A-PAK CONVERTERS (PTY) LTD
SILVERAY PROPERTIES (PTY) LTD (50%)
SILVERAY STATIONERY (TRANSVAAL) (PTY) LT (50%)
WALTONS STATIONERY CO (BOPHUTHATSWANA) (
WALTONS STATIONERY CO (NAMIBIA) (PTY) LT

INVESTMENTS

None

WANKIE COLLIERY CO LTD (ZIMBABWE)

ABBREVIATION : WANKIE

JSE SHORT CODE : WAN

SECTOR : Mining-Coal

SHAREHOLDERS

Who Owns Whom's Assessment of the Identity of the Ultimate Controlling Shareholder:
ZIMBABWEAN GOVT

SHAREHOLDER	PERCENTAGE 1992	1991
LONDON REGISTER ACCOUNT	21.0	---
ANGLO AMERICAN CORP ZIMBABWE LTD	13.7	---
ZIMBABWE REINSURANCE CORP LTD	3.7	---
NORTHCHART INV LTD	3.0	---
NRI LTD	2.8	---
SECURITY NOM LTD	2.7	---
JOHANNESBURG REGISTER ACCOUNT	2.3	---
TURNER R	2.2	---
FIRST MUTUAL LIFE ASSURE SOC OF ZIM	1.8	---
ANGLO AMERICAN CORP ZIM PENS FUND	1.7	---
NAT RAILWAYS OF ZIM CONTR PENS FUND	1.7	---
GILES A F	1.3	---
BARCLAYS ZIMBABWE NOM (PVT) LTD	1.2	---
LOGAN J	1.2	---
LIVINGSTONE INV CO LTD	1.1	---
OLD MUTUAL INV CORP (PVT) LTD	1.1	---
MINING INDUSTRY PENS FUND	1.1	---
TRUST NOM (PVT) LTD	1.0	---
FIRST NAT NOM P/L	---	1.5
GORDON-GRAY J L	---	8.5
LASKER INV P/L	---	3.4
MESSINA INV LTD	---	8.8
NEDBANK NOM LTD	---	5.9
SEPON SA P/L	---	1.0
VOLKSKAS NOM P/L	---	1.3
WILSON K R	---	9.9
BENT R A R	---	1.0
BURNS L A	---	1.0
DE ROME C	---	1.7
FOREST HOLDINGS P/L	---	1.2
RUBIN R	---	1.5
TIPPING R H	---	5.5
VAN DORT A	---	1.4
TOTAL	64.5	53.6

DIRECTORS :
BWERINOFA OK (Managing Director),FRY DJ
KUDENGA N (Chairman),MUNEZVENYU P DR
MURANGARI DEH ,RAVENSCROFT AFB ,VOSS JG PRO

REGISTRATION NUMBER : 53/00010/10

REGISTERED OFFICE
67-69 Union Avenue, Harare
Zimbabwe

TEL: 703 946

TRANSFER SECRETARY
Mercantile Registrars Ltd
P O Box 1053, Johannesburg
2000
TEL: 011-333 8181

COMPANY SECRETARY
E P Monteiro

NATURE OF BUSINESS
The company is involved in coal mining at Hwange in Zimbabwe.

BANKERS :
Eximbank (USA), Barclays Bank Plc
RAL Merchant Bank Ltd

AUDITORS :
Coopers Theron Du Toit

FAMILIAR BRAND NAMES
N/A

CONTRIBUTION BY ACTIVITY
N/A

YEAR END : February

DIVIDEND : Ords Z$1
Final No 124 (Ldr)17/05/91 (Pay)07/06/91 Amt(c)10

NUMBER OF EMPLOYEES : 4997

CAPITAL STRUCTURE

	AUTHORISED	ISSUED
Ords Z$1	43000000	25333488
"A" Ords Z$1 (Incl in Auth'd Ords		16889392

FINANCIAL STATISTICS (AT FINANCIAL YEAR END)

(Amts in Zim$)	1992 Feb	1991 Feb	1990 Feb	1989 Feb	1988 Feb
Ord S/H Int	438538	170066	141485	130821	112174
Long Trm Loans	31811	41819	46260	58101	73232
Iss Ord Share	42223	42223	42223	42223	42223
Total Liab	151100	104370	98535	98985	109404
Current Liab	119289	62551	52275	40884	36172
Total Assets	589638	274436	240020	229806	221578
Current Assets	138529	101102	71953	49266	47614
Debtors	59009	53328	33969	19596	16722
Inventory	64823	36704	26629	5417	7099
Turnover	210252	185348	144208	126813	108264
Oper Profit	31306	40169	29819	29551	28095
Interest Paid	12922	8619	9679	10904	10603
Prf af Int&Tax	22427	35759	20140	18647	17492
Prf att Ord Sh	22427	35759	20140	18647	17492
Btm Line Earn	22427	35759	10664	18647	17492
Dividend Paid	-	7178	-	-	5982
Mkt Prce(c) YE	110	90	85	130	110
Depreciation	15088	13443	12866	11847	9083

PER SHARE STATISTICS (CENTS)

Net Asst Val	1038.62	402.78	335.09	309.83	265.67
Net Earnings	47.00	75.00	42.00	39.00	36.60
Dividends	-	15.00	-	-	12.50
Cash Flow	78.40	102.82	68.97	63.73	55.53

RATIOS AND OTHER INFORMATION

Mrk Cap(R000)	46445	38001	35890	54890	46445
Current Ratio	1.16	1.62	1.38	1.21	1.32
Quik/Acid Tst	0.62	1.03	0.87	1.07	1.12
A/C Rec T/ovr	3.56	3.48	4.25	6.47	6.47
Tot Ass T/ovr	0.36	0.68	0.60	0.55	0.49
Debt/Ass Rat	0.26	0.38	0.41	0.43	0.49
L T L Tot Ass	0.05	0.15	0.19	0.25	0.33
Debt to Eqity	0.34	0.61	0.70	0.76	0.98
Interest Cover	2.42	4.66	3.08	2.71	2.65
Oper Prof Mrg	14.89	21.67	20.68	23.30	25.95
Net Prof Marg%	10.67	19.29	13.97	14.70	16.16
Ret on Assets	6.00	16.17	12.42	12.86	12.68
Ret on Equity%	5.11	21.03	14.23	14.25	15.59
Price/Earnings	2.34	1.20	2.02	3.33	3.01
Divid Cover	-	5.00	-	-	2.93
Divid Yield	-	16.67	-	-	11.36
Earning Yield%	42.73	83.33	49.41	30.00	33.27
NAV % Mrk Pr	944.20	447.53	394.22	238.33	241.52
Def Interval	1.93	1.47	2.35	2.80	3.32
Sus Grth Rate	5.11	16.81	14.23	14.25	10.26

SUBSIDIARY & ASSOCIATED COMPANIES

None

INVESTMENTS

None

WAYNE MANUFACTURING LTD

ABBREVIATION : WAYNE

JSE SHORT CODE : WYN

SECTOR : Industrial-Chemicals & Oils

SHAREHOLDERS

Who Owns Whom's Assessment of the Identity of the Ultimate Controlling Shareholder:
SA BREWERIES / SANLAM VIA CONSHU

SHAREHOLDER	PERCENTAGE 1992	1991
CONSHU HOLDINGS LTD	88.2	84.9
DANIEL BUSINESS TRUST	3.3	---
HARRINGTON FAMILY TRUST	2.3	2.3
LIBERTY LIFE ASSOC OF AFRICA LTD	1.4	1.4
DANIEL L T	---	3.3
SCHUTZ H TRUST	---	3.3
TOTAL	95.1	95.2

DIRECTORS :
DANIEL LT ,FEINBLUM RM (Chairman),HARRINGTON TN RADFORD RD ,RAPP CEL ,SMIT FJ

REGISTRATION NUMBER : 81/05338/06

REGISTERED OFFICE
4th Floor, Hyde Park Corner, Jan Smuts Avenue
Sandton
2196
TEL: 011-788 7250
FAX: 011-880 2395

TRANSFER SECRETARY
Central Registrars Ltd
P O Box 4844, Johannesburg
2000
TEL: 011-331 0051

COMPANY SECRETARY
J H Granger

NATURE OF BUSINESS
The group is a manufacturer of rubber and PVC moulded and extruded products for the building, agricultural, footwear, mining & motor industries.

BANKERS :
Trust Bank of Africa Ltd

AUDITORS :
Deloitte Pim Goldby

FAMILIAR BRAND NAMES
N/A

CONTRIBUTION BY ACTIVITY
N/A

YEAR END : June

DIVIDEND : Ords 1c

Interim No 5	(Ldr)09/03/90	(Pay)30/03/90	Amt(c)1.5
Final No 6	(Ldr)07/09/90	(Pay)28/09/90	Amt(c)3.7
Interim No 7	(Ldr)08/03/91	(Pay)29/03/91	Amt(c)1.75
Final No 8	(Ldr)06/09/91	(Pay)27/09/91	Amt(c)4.25
Interim No 9	(Ldr)06/03/92	(Pay)27/03/92	Amt(c)1.75
Final No 10	(Ldr)04/09/92	(Pay)25/09/92	Amt(c)3.45

NUMBER OF EMPLOYEES : 350

CAPITAL STRUCTURE

	AUTHORISED	ISSUED
Ords 1c	100000000	60732294

FINANCIAL STATISTICS (AT FINANCIAL YEAR END)

WB HOLDINGS LTD

(Amts in R'000)	1992 Jun	1991 Jun	1990 Jun	1989 Jun	1988 Jun
Ord S/H Int	68953	65913	60325	4743	3870
Long Trm Loans	9566	8605	4582	2321	1661
Iss Ord Share	60732	60732	60732	10698	10420
Total Liab	32994	29409	23797	6035	4820
Current Liab	23428	20804	19215	3714	3159
Total Assets	101947	95322	84122	10778	8690
Current Assets	48981	36945	34381	5740	4847
Debtors	25837	22756	21186	3600	2280
Inventory	20771	14115	12978	1858	1713
Turnover	129438	129779	110634	21490	16035
Oper Profit	10999	14439	12966	2993	1967
Interest Paid	3974	3914	2444	454	-
Tax Paid	3666	4243	2673	1393	1015
Prf af Int&Tax	6198	9232	7895	1205	952
Prf att Ord Sh	6198	9232	7895	1236	952
Btm Line Earn	6198	9232	7895	1236	952
Dividend Paid	3158	3644	3158	492	386
Mkt Prce(c) YE	80	80	60	90	60
Depreciation	6061	4718	4284	695	549

PER SHARE STATISTICS (CENTS)

Net Asst Val	113.54	108.53	99.33	44.34	37.14
Net Earnings	10.20	15.20	13.00	11.60	-
Dividends	5.20	6.00	5.20	4.60	-
Cash Flow	22.83	29.01	24.41	21.10	16.94

RATIOS AND OTHER INFORMATION

Mrk Cap(R000)	48586	48586	36439	9628	6252
Current Ratio	2.09	1.78	1.79	1.55	1.53
Quik/Acid Tst	1.20	1.10	1.11	1.05	0.99
A/C Rec T/ovr	5.01	5.70	5.22	5.97	7.03
Tot Ass T/ovr	1.27	1.36	1.32	1.99	1.85
Debt/Ass Rat	0.23	0.23	0.24	0.44	0.44
L T L Tot Ass	0.00	0.01	0.01	0.10	0.08
Debt to Eqity	0.35	0.33	0.33	1.01	0.99
Interest Cover	2.77	3.69	5.31	6.59	-
Oper Prof Mrg	8.50	11.13	11.72	13.93	12.27
Net Prof Marg%	4.79	7.11	7.14	5.75	5.94
Ret on Assets	13.57	18.24	15.47	28.32	22.64
Ret on Equity%	8.99	14.01	13.09	26.06	24.60
Price/Earnings	7.84	5.26	4.62	7.76	-
Divid Cover	1.96	2.53	2.50	2.52	-
Divid Yield	6.50	7.50	8.67	5.11	-
Earning Yield%	12.75	19.00	21.67	12.89	-
NAV % Mrk Pr	141.92	135.66	165.55	49.26	61.90
Effec Tax Rate	20.97	5.42	0.27	41.53	38.18
Def Interval	0.09	0.20	0.16	0.69	0.66
Sus Grth Rate	4.41	8.48	7.85	15.69	14.63

SUBSIDIARY & ASSOCIATED COMPANIES

H.W. INJECTION MOULDERS LTD
PHOENIX RUBBER (PTY) LTD
WAYNE MANAGEMENT (PTY) LTD
WAYNE PLASTICS (PTY) LTD
WAYNE RESIN (PTY) LTD
WAYNE RUBBER CO (PTY) LTD
WAYNE RUBBER WESTERN CAPE (PTY) LTD

INVESTMENTS

None

ABBREVIATION : WBHOLD

JSE SHORT CODE : WBH

SECTOR : Industrial-Food

SHAREHOLDERS

Who Owns Whom's Assessment of the Identity of the Ultimate Controlling Shareholder:
SILVERMAN FAMILY

SHAREHOLDER	PERCENTAGE 1992	1991
SGM INV P/L	53.7	41.2
NEDBANK NOM LTD	6.1	5.1
HARVEST SECURITIES LTD	4.3	4.3
SFSS NOM P/L	2.9	2.0
MACVEN NOM P/L	2.8	3.5
FIRST NAT NOM P/L	1.5	1.2
ELLERINE BROS P/L	1.3	1.3
SWAVIC P/L	1.1	1.1
STIER L A	1.1	—
FLOWERS W B	—	1.1
RITOS A G	—	1.1
SALDANHA BAY CANNING CO P/L	—	1.4
WEST POINT FISHING CORP P/L	—	10.9
ATLANTIC & CONTINENT ASSURE CO SA LTD	—	1.6
TOTAL	74.6	75.7

DIRECTORS :
PECK B ,RICKETTS BG ,ROOD TB DR,SACKS B
SILVERMAN A (Managing Director),SILVERMAN K
SILVERMAN R (Chairman),WILCK L

REGISTRATION NUMBER : 88/00570/06

REGISTERED OFFICE
2101 Nasionale Pers Sentrum, Heerengracht
Cape Town
8001
TEL: 021-21 4413
FAX: 021-419 4351

TRANSFER SECRETARY
Kilgetty Trust (Pty) Ltd
P O Box 4033, Cape Town
8000
TEL: 021-21 1860

COMPANY SECRETARY
C B J Upton

NATURE OF BUSINESS
The company has investments in deciduous fruit farming in the Villiersdorp & Grabouw areas in the Cape.

BANKERS :
Standard Bank of SA Ltd

AUDITORS :
BDO Spencer Steward

FAMILIAR BRAND NAMES
N/A

CONTRIBUTION BY ACTIVITY
N/A

YEAR END : December

DIVIDEND :Ords 1c

Final	(Ldr)20/04/90	(Pay)28/05/90	Amt(c)11
Interim	(Ldr)05/10/90	(Pay)26/11/90	Amt(c)7
Final	(Ldr)19/04/91	(Pay)27/05/91	Amt(c)14
Interim	(Ldr)04/10/91	(Pay)25/11/91	Amt(c)7
Final	(Ldr)16/04/92	(Pay)25/05/92	Amt(c)18
Interim	(Ldr)09/10/92	(Pay)27/11/92	Amt(c)7

NUMBER OF EMPLOYEES : 740

CAPITAL STRUCTURE

	AUTHORISED	ISSUED
Ords 1c	20000000	9400000

FINANCIAL STATISTICS (AT FINANCIAL YEAR END)

(Amts in R'000)	1991 Dec	1990 Dec	1989 Dec	1988 Dec	1987
Ord S/H Int	32035	28940	21332	15359	11205
Long Trm Loans	345	-	530	526	2763
Iss Ord Share	9400	9400	9400	9400	9400
Total Liab	3977	2835	3761	1560	5011
Current Liab	3632	2835	3231	1034	2248
Total Assets	36012	31775	25093	16919	24478
Current Assets	2965	10928	3403	13463	10510
Debtors	237	297	2484	2632	-
Inventory	383	1278	776	-	10510
Turnover	15364	11805	7149	6842	4266
Oper Profit	5927	4101	2562	2727	3889
Interest Paid	21	73	117	30	59
Tax Paid	487	237	1772	1324	1013
Prf af Int&Tax	5445	4254	3420	4999	2856
Prf att Ord Sh	5445	4254	3420	4999	2857
Btm Line Earn	5445	4453	3897	4999	2857
Dividend Paid	2350	1974	3384	846	2068
Mkt Prce(c) YE	350	220	180	205	120
Depreciation	657	296	125	2	-

PER SHARE STATISTICS (CENTS)

Net Asst Val	340.80	307.87	226.94	163.39	119.20
Net Earnings	57.92	45.26	36.38	53.18	-
Dividends	25.00	21.00	36.00	25.00	-
Cash Flow	68.59	48.40	37.71	53.33	30.38

RATIOS AND OTHER INFORMATION

Mrk Cap(R000)	32900	20680	16920	19270	11280
Current Ratio	0.82	3.85	1.05	13.02	4.68
Quik/Acid Tst	0.71	3.40	0.81	13.02	-
A/C Rec T/ovr	64.83	39.75	2.88	2.60	-
Tot Ass T/ovr	0.43	0.37	0.28	0.40	0.17
Debt/Ass Rat	0.10	0.09	0.13	0.06	0.20
L T L Tot Ass	-	-	-	-	0.11
Debt to Eqity	0.11	0.10	0.15	0.07	0.45
Interest Cover	283.48	62.52	45.38	211.77	66.58
Oper Prof Mrg	38.58	34.74	35.84	39.86	91.16
Net Prof Marg%	35.44	36.04	47.84	73.06	66.97
Ret on Assets	16.53	14.36	21.16	37.55	16.05
Ret on Equity%	17.00	14.70	16.03	32.55	25.50
Price/Earnings	6.04	4.86	4.95	3.85	-
Divid Cover	2.32	2.16	1.01	2.13	-
Divid Yield	7.14	9.55	20.00	12.20	-
Earning Yield%	16.55	20.57	20.21	25.94	-
NAV % Mrk Pr	97.37	139.94	126.08	79.70	99.34
Effec Tax Rate	2.01	5.29	72.47	44.38	26.45
Def Interval	0.03	0.05	0.05	0.16	0.97
Sus Grth Rate	9.66	7.88	0.17	27.04	7.04

SUBSIDIARY & ASSOCIATED COMPANIES

BOSKLOOF FRUIT & TIMBER INDUSTRIES (PTY)
DORADO FISH PRODUCTS LTD
GLASER FARMS HOLDINGS (PTY) LTD
SARUBAR (PTY) LTD
THEEWATERSKLOOF HOLDINGS (PTY) LTD
WILBARZ INVESTMENTS (PTY) LTD
WUNDERBAR INVESTMENTS (PTY) LTD

INVESTMENTS

CALEDON RIVIERSONDEREND CO-OPERATIVE LTD (500 SH)
ELGIN CO-OPERATIVE FRUIT GROWERS LTD (21074 SH)
ELGIN IRRIGATION SERVICES (PTY) LTD (20SH)
KROMRIVIER APPLE CO-OPERATIVE LTD (155190 SH)
SA DRIED FRUIT CO-OPERATIVE LTD (240 SH)
UNIVERSAL FRUITRADE CO-OPERATIVE LTD (2 SH)
VILLIERSDORP CO-OPERATIVE LTD (1849 SH)
WESTERN PROVINCE KO-OPERATIEWE BPK (41SH)

WELKOM GOLD HOLDINGS LTD

ABBREVIATION : WELKOM

JSE SHORT CODE : WEL

SECTOR : Gold-OFS

SHAREHOLDERS

Who Owns Whom's Assessment of the Identity of the Ultimate Controlling Shareholder:
ANGLO AMERICAN

SHAREHOLDER	PERCENTAGE 1992	1991
FREE STATE CONS GOLD MINES (OPS) LTD	19.9	19.9
STD BANK NOM TVL P/L	13.7	10.6
PETARD NOM LTD	10.1	10.1
ORANGE FREE STATE INV TRUST LTD	9.3	9.3
FERMAIN NOM LTD	9.3	9.3
TAURUS NOM LTD	6.6	6.6
AFRICAN & EUROPEAN INV CO LTD	6.0	6.0
FIRST NAT NOM P/L	3.7	3.6
INDO-CHINA NOM P/L	3.7	---
LONDON CONTROL ACCOUNT	2.7	2.3
FIRST NAT NOM P/L GATR DEPOT	2.4	2.5
RESIDENT NOM LTD	2.3	5.7
SA MUTUAL	1.4	1.7
EIGHTY ONE MAIN STREET NOM LTD	1.3	---
SA TOWNSHIPS MINING & FINANCE CORP LTD	1.3	1.3
INDO-CHINA NOM SA P/L	---	3.6
TOTAL	93.6	92.4

DIRECTORS :
FRASER CA ,HEWITT L (Chairman & Managing Dir.)
HOLFORD GM ,HOSKING KM ,KING MW ,SUNTER CL
VAN DER COLF SW

REGISTRATION NUMBER : 05/24464/06

REGISTERED OFFICE
44 Main Street, Johannesburg
2001

TEL: 011-638 9111
FAX: 011-638 5281

TRANSFER SECRETARY
Consolidated Share Registrars Ltd
P O Box 61051, Marshalltown
2107
TEL: 011-492 1620

COMPANY SECRETARY
Anglo American Corporation of SA Ltd

NATURE OF BUSINESS
Welkom Gold Holdings is an investment holding company which holds 30,37% in Orange Free State Investments and 5,22% in Free State Consolidated Gold Mines. Ofsils major asset is its 49,96% holding in Freegold.

BANKERS :
N/A

AUDITORS :
Deloitte Pim Goldby

FAMILIAR BRAND NAMES
N/A

CONTRIBUTION BY ACTIVITY
N/A

YEAR END : March

DIVIDEND :Ords 50c

Interim No 69	(Ldr)08/11/91	(Pay)13/12/91	Amt(c)70
Final No 70	(Ldr)08/05/92	(Pay)12/06/92	Amt(c)88
Interim No 71	(Ldr)13/11/92	(Pay)18/12/92	Amt(c)70

CAPITAL STRUCTURE

	AUTHORISED	ISSUED
Ords 50c	66000000	35350937

FINANCIAL STATISTICS (AT FINANCIAL YEAR END)

(Amts in R'000)	1992 Mar	1991 Mar	1990 Mar	1989 Mar	1987 Sep
Ord S/H Int	205900	205928	205844	205644	205568
Iss Ord Share	35351	35351	35351	35351	35351
Total Liab	31523	20580	34996	38495	38842
Current Liab	31523	20580	34996	38495	38842
Total Assets	237423	226508	240840	244139	244410
Current Assets	31870	20955	35287	38586	38857
Debtors	31273	20390	34845	38338	37461
Oper Profit	55772	32906	70153	104734	73818
Tax Paid	32	22	10	19	31
Prf af Int&Tax	55826	32960	70195	104715	73787
Prf att Ord Sh	55826	32960	70195	104715	73787
Btm Line Earn	55826	32960	70195	104715	73787
Dividend Paid	55854	32876	69995	104639	73884
Mkt Prce(c) YE	1725	1250	3100	2300	3700

PER SHARE STATISTICS (CENTS)

Net Asst Val	582.44	582.52	582.29	581.72	581.51
Net Earnings	158.00	93.00	199.00	296.00	209.00
Dividends	158.00	93.00	198.00	296.00	209.00
Cash Flow	157.92	93.24	198.57	197.48	208.73

RATIOS AND OTHER INFORMATION

Mrk Cap(R000)	609805	441888	1095881	813073	1307987
Current Ratio	1.01	1.02	1.01	1.00	1.00
Quik/Acid Tst	1.01	1.02	1.01	1.00	1.00
Debt/Ass Rat	0.13	0.09	0.15	0.16	0.16
Debt to Eqity	0.15	0.10	0.17	0.19	0.19
Ret on Assets	23.53	14.56	29.15	28.60	30.20
Ret on Equity%	27.11	16.01	34.10	33.95	35.89
Price/Earnings	10.92	13.44	15.58	7.77	17.70
Divid Cover	1.00	1.00	1.01	1.00	1.00
Divid Yield	9.16	7.44	6.39	12.87	5.65
Earning Yield%	9.16	7.44	6.42	12.87	5.65
NAV % Mrk Pr	33.76	46.60	18.78	25.29	15.72
Effec Tax Rate	0.06	0.07	0.01	0.02	0.04
Sus Grth Rate	-0.01	0.04	0.10	0.04	-0.05

SUBSIDIARY & ASSOCIATED COMPANIES

ORANGE FREE STATE INVESTMENTS LTD (30,37%)

INVESTMENTS

FREE STATE CONSOLIDATED GOLD MINES LTD (5.29%)

WESCO INVESTMENTS LTD

ABBREVIATION : WESCO

JSE SHORT CODE : WES

SECTOR : Industrial-Motor

SHAREHOLDERS

Who Owns Whom's Assessment of the Identity of the Ultimate Controlling Shareholder: DIRECTORS

SHAREHOLDER	PERCENTAGE 1992	1991
SA TRUST & FINANCE CO LTD	31.8	30.6
CONTAX INV P/L	12.1	12.1
STD BANK NOM TVL P/L	11.2	5.9
ALPHA INSTITUUT P/L	10.5	10.5
SA MUTUAL	8.8	8.8
BP THIBAULT NOM P/L	4.9	4.9
EIGHTY ONE MAIN STREET NOM LTD	4.0	4.3
ALBERT W TRUST	3.8	5.0
FIRST NAT NOM P/L	3.7	3.8
MOMENTUM LIFE ASSURE LTD	2.8	3.1
WESPEC P/L	1.1	1.1
NEDBANK NOM LTD	---	6.0
TOTAL	94.7	96.3

DIRECTORS :
ADCOCK CS
BRADLEY E LE R MRS (Executive Chairman)
DU PREEZ DJ ,RAPP AR (Managing Director)
WESSELS AJJ

REGISTRATION NUMBER : 68/05871/06

REGISTERED OFFICE
3rd Floor, Albert Wessels Building
19 Girton Road, Parktown
2193
TEL: 011-643 4801
FAX: 011-484 3025

TRANSFER SECRETARY
Central Registrars Ltd
P O Box 4844, Johannesburg
2000
TEL: 011-331 0051

COMPANY SECRETARY
A V Stewart

NATURE OF BUSINESS
Major investments are held in the motor manufacturing industry, motor component industry, furniture manufacturing industry and shipping container industry.

BANKERS :
N/A

AUDITORS :
N/A

FAMILIAR BRAND NAMES
HINO,TOYOTA

CONTRIBUTION BY ACTIVITY
N/A

YEAR END : December

DIVIDEND : Ords R1

Dividend No 21	(Ldr)02/05/90	(Pay)30/05/90	Amt(c)60
Dividend No 22	(Ldr)07/06/91	(Pay)28/06/91	Amt(c)72
Dividend No 23	(Ldr)10/04/92	(Pay)04/05/92	Amt(c)86

NUMBER OF EMPLOYEES : 15

CAPITAL STRUCTURE

	AUTHORISED	ISSUED
"A" Cum Red Prefs 1c	2000000	0
Ords R1	9980000	8401800

FINANCIAL STATISTICS (AT FINANCIAL YEAR END)

(Amts in R'000)	1991 Dec	1990 Dec	1989 Dec	1988 Dec	1987 Dec
Ord S/H Int	527934	468743	358014	312539	239823
Long Trm Loans	745248	562213	417723	391708	322211
Iss Ord Share	8402	8402	8402	8402	8402
Total Liab	1200090	942996	830329	633795	468861
Current Liab	454842	380783	412606	242087	146650
Total Assets	1728024	1411739	1188343	946334	708684
Current Assets	841848	667432	606621	473585	327949
Debtors	368350	276200	278069	199413	154511
Inventory	467350	377580	308407	258395	163095
Turnover	3466947	3117937	2920180	2511747	1915082
Oper Profit	241217	246170	203031	199884	163621
Interest Paid	58013	96046	47970	89309	57559
Tax Paid	138895	140564	89563	64838	22728
Prf af Int&Tax	123767	116495	88743	89397	83334
Prf att Ord Sh	59971	60875	49723	49795	45686
Btm Line Earn	59859	59873	49553	49813	47548
Dividend Paid	7226	6073	5113	4201	3361
Mkt Prce(c) YE	5800	2800	2050	1600	2500
Depreciation	105724	98036	91639	66968	61447

PER SHARE STATISTICS (CENTS)

Net Asst Val	6283.43	5578.95	4261.06	3719.82	2854.36
Net Earnings	714.00	724.00	589.00	593.00	544.00
Dividends	86.00	72.00	60.00	50.00	40.00
Cash Flow	1996.60	2044.82	1729.89	1084.92	1443.10

RATIOS AND OTHER INFORMATION

Mrk Cap(R000)	487316	235256	172241	134432	210050
Current Ratio	1.85	1.75	1.47	1.96	2.24
Quik/Acid Tst	0.82	0.76	0.72	0.89	1.12
A/C Rec T/ovr	9.41	11.29	10.50	12.60	12.39
Tot Ass T/ovr	2.01	2.21	2.46	2.65	2.70
Debt/Ass Rat	0.38	0.30	0.37	0.37	0.31
L T L Tot Ass	0.12	0.04	0.03	0.11	0.11
Debt to Eqity	1.25	0.92	1.24	1.12	0.93
Interest Cover	4.21	2.64	4.32	2.31	2.84
Oper Prof Mrg	6.96	7.90	6.95	7.96	8.54
Net Prof Marg%	1.73	1.95	1.70	1.98	2.39
Ret on Assets	18.50	25.13	19.39	26.21	23.64
Ret on Equity%	11.36	12.99	13.89	15.93	19.05
Price/Earnings	8.12	3.87	3.48	2.70	4.60
Divid Cover	8.30	10.06	9.82	11.86	13.60
Divid Yield	1.48	2.57	2.93	3.13	1.60
Earning Yield%	12.31	25.86	28.73	37.06	21.76
NAV % Mrk Pr	108.34	199.25	207.86	232.49	114.17
Effec Tax Rate	49.10	47.07	43.80	41.47	4.47
Def Interval	1.43	0.46	1.02	1.68	0.76
Sus Grth Rate	9.99	11.69	12.46	14.59	17.65

SUBSIDIARY & ASSOCIATED COMPANIES

AE WESLEY INVESTMENTS (PTY) LTD
CAMARGUE TRANSPORT SYSTEMS (PTY) LTD
GOMMAGOMMA HOLDINGS (PTY) LTD (43%)
JATI INVESTMENTS (PTY) LTD
TOYOTA S.A. LTD (50%)
WESCO BESTUURSMAATSKAPPY (PTY) LTD

INVESTMENTS

ANGLO AMERICAN CORP. S.A. LTD (1244 SH)
ELECTRA INVESTMENTS (SA) LTD (PREF SHARE (15000000 S)
METAIR INVESTMENTS LTD (5665000SH)

WEST RAND CONSOLIDATED MINES LTD

ABBREVIATION : W-R-CONS

JSE SHORT CODE : WRC

SECTOR : Gold-Rand & others

SHAREHOLDERS

Who Owns Whom's Assessment of the Identity of the Ultimate Controlling Shareholder: GENCOR (MANAGED BY)

SHAREHOLDER	PERCENTAGE 1992	1991
SOCIETE INTERPROF POUR LA COMPENSATION	21.4	18.1
LONDON CONTROL ACCOUNT	21.3	18.3
CONSOLIDATED NOM P/L	12.6	3.0
INDO-CHINA NOM P/L	8.3	---
STD BANK NOM TVL P/L	7.2	6.1
DEPOSITARY NOM INC	3.4	---
FIRST NAT NOM P/L	2.7	4.3
EPF OLD MUTUAL NOM P/L	2.1	4.5
YSKOR UITTREDINGSFONDS	1.9	---

SEPON LTD	1.5	1.4
BANK OF NEW YORK NOM LTD	---	2.4
GENERAL MINING UNION CORP	---	9.6
INDO-CHINA NOM SA P/L	---	8.0
VOLKSKAS NOM P/L	---	1.6
YSKOR PENS FUND	---	4.5
TOTAL	82.4	81.6

DIRECTORS :
BURKE JHJ ,COOK PJ ,DU PLESSIS AJ ,FIELD AJ
KRAFFT GC ,MAUDE G (Chairman & Managing Dir.

REGISTRATION NUMBER : 01/01978/06

REGISTERED OFFICE
General Mining Building, 6 Hollard Street
Johannesburg
2001
TEL: 011-376 9111
FAX: 011-836 8708

TRANSFER SECRETARY
Central Registrars Ltd
P O Box 4844, Johannesburg
2000
TEL: 011-331 0051

COMPANY SECRETARY
General Mining Metals & Minerals Ltd

NATURE OF BUSINESS
The company operates a gold mine in the Krugersdorp area, Tvl. Silver is recovered as a by-product.

BANKERS :
Trust Bank of Africa Ltd

AUDITORS :
Coopers Theron Du Toit

FAMILIAR BRAND NAMES
N/A

CONTRIBUTION BY ACTIVITY
Gold (% Turnover) (99.9%)
Silver (0.1%)

YEAR END : December

DIVIDEND : Ords R1

Final No 113	(Ldr)02/02/90	(Pay)16/03/90	Amt(c)40
Interim No 114	(Ldr)03/08/90	(Pay)14/09/90	Amt(c)20
Final No 115	(Ldr)01/02/91	(Pay)15/03/91	Amt(c)50
Interim No 116	(Ldr)02/08/91	(Pay)13/09/91	Amt(c)35
Final No 117	(Ldr)31/01/92	(Pay)13/03/92	Amt(c)20

NUMBER OF EMPLOYEES : 1832

CAPITAL STRUCTURE

	AUTHORISED	ISSUED
Def Shares R2	25000	25000
Ords R1	4250000	4250000

FINANCIAL STATISTICS (AT FINANCIAL YEAR END)

(Amts in R'000)	1991 Dec	1990 Dec	1989 Dec	1988 Dec	1987
Ord S/H Int	52378	58045	58611	59713	61857
Long Trm Loans	3132	3132	3132	3132	20775
Iss Ord Share	4275	4275	4275	4275	4250
Total Liab	18295	17808	14972	18399	38306
Current Liab	15163	14676	11840	15267	17531
Total Assets	70673	75853	73583	78112	118858
Current Assets	29292	33042	27560	31528	36216
Debtors	3949	1367	1899	5732	-
Inventory	1922	2603	2381	3024	36216
Turnover	67628	70396	71262	117562	117927
Oper Profit	-2566	5631	1284	-1603	5044
Interest Paid	-	-	3	15	117
Tax Paid	4	2304	366	495	1273
Prf af Int&Tax	-2550	3400	1166	-1820	3654
Prf att Ord Sh	-1120	6612	1903	-2091	3654
Btm Line Earn	-1120	6612	1903	-2091	3654
Dividend Paid	3117	3966	2267	-	2267
Mkt Prce(c) YE	460	850	940	475	775

PER SHARE STATISTICS (CENTS)

Net Asst Val	1225.22	1357.78	1371.02	1396.80	1455.46
Net Earnings	-	116.00	33.00	-49.00	-
Dividends	55.00	70.00	40.00	-	-
Cash Flow	-59.65	79.53	27.27	-42.57	85.98

RATIOS AND OTHER INFORMATION

Mrk Cap(R000)	19665	36338	40185	20306	32938
Current Ratio	1.93	2.25	2.33	2.07	2.07
Quik/Acid Tst	1.81	2.07	2.13	1.87	-
A/C Rec T/ovr	17.13	51.50	37.53	20.51	-
Tot Ass T/ovr	0.96	0.93	0.97	1.51	0.99
Debt/Ass Rat	0.26	0.23	0.20	0.24	0.32
L T L Tot Ass	0.04	0.04	0.04	0.04	0.17
Debt to Eqity	0.35	0.31	0.26	0.31	0.62
Interest Cover	-	-	511.67	-87.33	43.11
Oper Prof Mrg	-3.79	8.00	1.80	-1.36	4.28
Net Prof Marg%	-1.66	9.39	2.67	-1.78	3.10
Ret on Assets	-3.60	7.52	2.09	-1.68	4.24
Ret on Equity%	-2.14	11.39	3.25	-3.50	5.91
Price/Earnings	-	7.33	28.48	-9.69	-
Divid Cover	-	1.66	0.83	-	-
Divid Yield	11.96	8.24	4.26	-	-
Earning Yield%	-	13.65	3.51	-10.32	-
NAV % Mrk Pr	266.35	159.74	145.85	294.06	187.80
Effec Tax Rate	-0.16	40.92	28.57	-30.59	25.84
Def Interval	-	-	-	-	5.69
Sus Grth Rate	-8.09	4.56	-0.62	-3.50	2.24

SUBSIDIARY & ASSOCIATED COMPANIES

None

INVESTMENTS

None

WEST WITWATERSRAND GOLD HOLDINGS LTD

ABBREVIATION : WESWITS

JSE SHORT CODE : WSW

SECTOR : Gold-West Witwatersrand

SHAREHOLDERS

Who Owns Whom's Assessment of the Identity of the Ultimate Controlling Shareholder: CONSOLIDATED MINING VIA SOUTHGO

SHAREHOLDER	PERCENTAGE 1992	1991
SOUTH EAST RAND GOLD HLDGS LTD	59.0	59.4
JIMBERLANA MINERALS NL	22.1	22.2
STD BANK NOM TVL P/L	1.2	1.3
TOTAL	82.3	83.0

DIRECTORS :
BUITENDAG HC ,DONALD JC ,FLOWERDAY RA
LEE RA (Chairman),LOWENTHAL ND ,LOWENTHAL RY
RUBENSTEIN GB ,SCHECHTER M ,SUDDENS BD
THOMPSON MW ,TURNER CF

REGISTRATION NUMBER : 71/05928/06

REGISTERED OFFICE
39th Floor, Carlton Centre, Commissioner Str
Johannesburg
2001
TEL: 011-331 9181
FAX: 011-331 6189

TRANSFER SECRETARY
Mercantile Registrars Ltd
P O Box 1053, Johannesburg
2000
TEL: 011-333 8181

COMPANY SECRETARY
Consolidated Mining Management Services Ltd

NATURE OF BUSINESS
The company is engaged in the production of gold from underground mining, opencast operations, the retreatment of dump material & the process of heap leaching.

BANKERS :
First National Bank of SA Ltd
Bank of Lisbon International Ltd

AUDITORS :
Charles Orbach & Co

FAMILIAR BRAND NAMES
N/A

CONTRIBUTION BY ACTIVITY
N/A

YEAR END : March

DIVIDEND : Ords no par value

Final No 1	(Ldr)11/05/90	(Pay)15/06/90	Amt(c)5
Interim No 2	(Ldr)09/11/90	(Pay)07/12/90	Amt(c)2
Final No 3	(Ldr)22/05/92	(Pay)29/05/92	Amt(c)4
Interim No 4	(Ldr)13/11/92	(Pay)27/11/92	Amt(c)2

NUMBER OF EMPLOYEES : 685

CAPITAL STRUCTURE

	AUTHORISED	ISSUED
Ords no par value	100000000	91500000
Conv Red Cum Prefs 66,66c	12000000	0

FINANCIAL STATISTICS (AT FINANCIAL YEAR END)

(Amts in R'000)	1992 Mar	1991 Mar	1990 Mar	1989 Mar	1987
Ord S/H Int	98030	91996	87983	81832	61368
Long Trm Loans	-	4300	4300	4300	27489
Iss Ord Share	91500	90860	90860	90000	75000
Total Liab	19205	17567	16974	17723	45674
Current Liab	19205	13267	12674	13423	18185
Total Assets	117235	109563	104957	99555	92907
Current Assets	11976	5649	10104	10426	4051
Debtors	3839	3767	5134	4332	-
Inventory	1258	1381	1467	1647	4051
Turnover	85567	68202	67098	62607	33281
Oper Profit	10151	6250	10578	3446	6704
Interest Paid	771	861	683	887	817
Tax Paid	166	8	70	50	27
Prf af Int&Tax	9434	5830	10352	3202	5833
Prf att Ord Sh	9434	5830	10352	3202	4774
Btm Line Earn	9434	5830	10352	3202	4774
Dividend Paid	3660	1817	4543	-	-
Mkt Prce(c) YE	43	50	165	50	161

PER SHARE STATISTICS (CENTS)

Net Asst Val	107.14	101.25	96.83	90.92	81.82
Net Earnings	10.40	6.40	11.50	3.60	-
Dividends	4.00	2.00	5.00	-	-
Cash Flow	10.38	6.42	11.46	3.56	7.78

RATIOS AND OTHER INFORMATION

Mrk Cap(R000)	39345	45430	149919	45000	120750
Current Ratio	0.62	0.43	0.80	0.78	0.22
Quik/Acid Tst	0.56	0.32	0.68	0.65	-
A/C Rec T/ovr	22.29	18.11	13.07	14.45	-
Tot Ass T/ovr	0.73	0.62	0.64	0.63	0.36
Debt/Ass Rat	0.16	0.16	0.16	0.18	0.49
L T L Tot Ass	-	0.04	0.04	0.04	0.30
Debt to Eqity	0.20	0.19	0.19	0.22	0.74
Interest Cover	13.17	7.26	15.49	3.89	8.17
Oper Prof Mrg	11.86	9.16	15.77	5.50	20.14
Net Prof Marg%	11.03	8.55	15.43	5.11	14.34
Ret on Assets	8.85	6.11	10.58	4.16	7.19
Ret on Equity%	9.62	6.34	11.77	3.91	7.78
Price/Earnings	4.13	7.81	14.35	13.89	-
Divid Cover	2.60	3.20	2.30	-	-
Divid Yield	9.30	4.00	3.03	-	-
Earning Yield%	24.19	12.80	6.97	7.20	-
NAV % Mrk Pr	249.15	202.50	58.69	181.85	50.82
Effec Tax Rate	0.36	0.14	0.67	1.54	0.46
Def Interval	0.48	1.60	0.42	2.22	4.71
Sus Grth Rate	5.89	4.36	6.60	3.91	7.78

SUBSIDIARY & ASSOCIATED COMPANIES

KRUGERSDORP STONE CRUSHERS (PTY) LTD
WEST WITWATERSRAND GOLD MINES LTD
WEST WITWATERSRAND MINERAL & MIN. CORP.

INVESTMENTS

None

WESTERN AREAS GOLD MINING CO LTD

ABBREVIATION : WES-AREAS

JSE SHORT CODE : WAR

SECTOR : Gold-West Witwatersrand

SHAREHOLDERS

Who Owns Whom's Assessment of the Identity of the Ultimate Controlling Shareholder:
ANGLO AMERICAN VIA JCI

SHAREHOLDER	PERCENTAGE 1992	1991
STD BANK NOM TVL P/L	25.9	11.0
INDO-CHINA NOM P/L	9.8	---
FIRST NAT NOM P/L	8.8	5.6
NAT CITY NOM LTD	4.6	3.9
LONDON REGISTER ACCOUNT	4.5	4.2
ELSBURG GOLD MINING CO LTD	4.4	48.7
FERMAIN NOM LTD	4.4	3.4
EIGHTY ONE MAIN STREET NOM LTD	3.6	---
RESIDENT NOM LTD	1.5	---
AECI PENS FUND	1.4	1.5
DEPOSITARY NOM INC	1.2	---
FIRST NAT NOM P/L GATR DEPOT	---	3.8
INDO-CHINA NOM SA P/L	---	6.2
TOTAL	70.0	88.4

DIRECTORS :
BRAY VG ,CONN WP ,EUSTACE PJ ,KOVARSKY DC
MAXWELL KW (Chairman)
NAIRN WA (Managing Director),RETIEF PF
SCOTT-RUSSELL H D

REGISTRATION NUMBER : 59/03209/06

REGISTERED OFFICE
Consolidated Building, Fox & Harrison Streets
Johannesburg
2001
TEL: 011-373 9111
FAX: 011-836 6130

TRANSFER SECRETARY
Consolidated Share Registrars Ltd
P O Box 61051, Marshalltown
2107
TEL: 011-492 1620

COMPANY SECRETARY
Johannesburg Consolidated Inv Co Ltd

NATURE OF BUSINESS
The company conducts gold & uranium mining operations in the Westonaria district, Tvl.

BANKERS :
N/A

AUDITORS :
KPMG Aiken & Peat

FAMILIAR BRAND NAMES
N/A

CONTRIBUTION BY ACTIVITY
N/A

YEAR END : June

DIVIDEND :15/01/92

NUMBER OF EMPLOYEES : 7780

CAPITAL STRUCTURE

	AUTHORISED	ISSUED
Ords R1	41000000	40306950
Prefs 0,01c	100000000	0

FINANCIAL STATISTICS (AT FINANCIAL YEAR END)

(Amts in R'000)	1992 Jun	1991 Jun	1990 Jun	1989 Jun	1988 Jun
Ord S/H Int	769436	747881	602191	624897	628681
Long Trm Loans	27152	6750	9250	11550	13750
Iss Ord Share	40307	40307	40307	40307	40307
Total Liab	101336	88656	180507	144194	78935
Current Liab	74184	81906	171257	132644	65185
Total Assets	870772	836537	782698	769091	707616
Current Assets	94517	94929	61837	53701	32830
Debtors	13267	14264	32713	19360	9063
Inventory	30639	32314	25995	30238	21554
Turnover	388473	399091	479258	422951	372354
Oper Profit	25357	27407	-4261	758	-3376
Interest Paid	4473	13981	22295	-	-
Prf af Int&Tax	21161	13605	-22708	758	-3376
Prf att Ord Sh	21161	13605	-22708	758	-3376
Btm Line Earn	22035	146361	-22708	758	-3376
Mkt Prce(c) YE	280	685	480	440	660

PER SHARE STATISTICS (CENTS)

Net Asst Val	1908.94	1855.46	1494.01	1550.34	1559.73
Net Earnings	52.50	33.80	-56.30	-98.90	-97.80
Cash Flow	52.50	33.75	-56.33	1.88	-8.38

RATIOS AND OTHER INFORMATION

Mrk Cap(R000)	112860	276103	193474	177351	266026
Current Ratio	1.27	1.16	0.36	0.40	0.50
Quik/Acid Tst	0.86	0.76	0.21	0.18	0.17
A/C Rec T/ovr	29.28	27.98	14.65	21.85	41.09
Tot Ass T/ovr	0.45	0.48	0.61	0.55	0.53
Debt/Ass Rat	0.12	0.11	0.23	0.19	0.11
L T L Tot Ass	0.03	0.01	0.01	0.02	0.02
Debt to Eqity	0.13	0.12	0.30	0.23	0.13
Interest Cover	5.73	1.97	-0.19	-	-
Oper Prof Mrg	6.53	6.87	-0.89	0.18	-0.91
Net Prof Marg%	5.45	3.41	-4.74	0.18	-0.91
Ret on Assets	2.94	3.30	-0.05	0.10	-0.48
Ret on Equity%	2.75	1.82	-3.77	0.12	-0.54
Price/Earnings	5.33	20.27	-8.53	-4.45	-6.75
Earning Yield%	18.75	4.93	-11.73	-22.48	-14.82
NAV % Mrk Pr	681.76	270.87	311.25	352.35	236.32
Def Interval	1.27	0.55	-0.42	78.82	-
Sus Grth Rate	2.75	1.82	-3.77	0.12	-0.54

SUBSIDIARY & ASSOCIATED COMPANIES

None

INVESTMENTS

None

WESTERN DEEP LEVELS LTD

ABBREVIATION : WSTN-DEEP

JSE SHORT CODE : WDL

SECTOR : Gold-West Witwatersrand

SHAREHOLDERS

Who Owns Whom's Assessment of the Identity of the Ultimate Controlling Shareholder:
ANGLO AMERICAN

SHAREHOLDER	PERCENTAGE 1992	1991
RESIDENT NOM LTD	9.4	9.4
TAURUS NOM LTD	9.2	9.2
PETARD NOM LTD	9.0	9.0
FERMAIN NOM LTD	8.9	8.9
INDO-CHINA NOM P/L	8.0	7.9
STD BANK NOM TVL P/L	5.2	4.3
DIDO NOM LTD	4.9	4.9
MINU NOM LTD	4.4	4.4
FIRST NAT NOM P/L	4.4	4.5
LONDON CONTROL ACCOUNT	4.1	3.9
SA MUTUAL	3.8	3.9
DEPOSITARY NOM INC	3.0	2.5
CMB NOM P/L	2.9	---
FIRST NAT NOM P/L GATR DEPOT	2.5	2.5
GALATES INV HLDGS LTD	2.3	2.3
LIBERTY LIFE ASSOC OF AFRICA LTD	1.4	1.7
SOUTHERN LIFE ASSOC LTD	1.4	2.0
WESTERN ULTRA DEEP LEVELS LTD	1.2	1.2
INDO-CHINA NOM SA P/L	---	7.9
SANLAM	---	2.4
TOTAL	85.7	92.6

DIRECTORS :
AMERY HJ HON,GODSELL RM
HEWITT L (Managing Director),HOSKING KM
LANGTON G ,MCLUSKIE J ,MUNRO AH
OGILVIE THOMPSON J ,SUNTER CL (Chairman)
WRIGHT AJ

REGISTRATION NUMBER : 57/02349/06

REGISTERED OFFICE
44 Main Street, Johannesburg
2001
TEL: 011-638 9111
FAX: 011-638 5281

TRANSFER SECRETARY
Consolidated Share Registrars Ltd
P O Box 61051, Marshalltown
2107
TEL: 011-492 1620

COMPANY SECRETARY
Anglo American Corporation of SA Ltd

NATURE OF BUSINESS
The company was incorporated in 1957 and conducts gold-mining operations in the Oberholzer and Potchefstroom districts, Transvaal.

BANKERS :
First National Bank of SA Ltd

AUDITORS :
KPMG Aiken & Peat

FAMILIAR BRAND NAMES
N/A

CONTRIBUTION BY ACTIVITY
Gold, Silver & Osmiridium (% profit) (94.3%)
Other (incl investment income) (6.7%)

YEAR END : December

DIVIDEND : Ords R2

Interim No 57	(Ldr)03/08/90	(Pay)14/09/90	Amt(c)160
Final No 58	(Ldr)08/02/91	(Pay)15/03/91	Amt(c)150
Interim No 59	(Ldr)09/08/91	(Pay)13/09/91	Amt(c)180
Final No 60	(Ldr)07/02/92	(Pay)13/03/92	Amt(c)210

NUMBER OF EMPLOYEES : 26726

CAPITAL STRUCTURE

	AUTHORISED	ISSUED
Ords R2	28000000	27713044

FINANCIAL STATISTICS (AT FINANCIAL YEAR END)

(Amts in R'000)	1991 Dec	1990 Dec	1989 Dec	1988	1987
Ord S/H Int	2923300	2653600	2367800	2070700	1805600
Long Trm Loans	7400	8700	15900	310700	213100
Iss Ord Share	27713	27194	27194	27194	27194
Total Liab	228200	159500	229000	602800	400200
Current Liab	220800	150800	213100	292100	187100
Total Assets	3151500	2813100	2596800	2683700	2220400
Current Assets	235200	152300	195700	302300	201700
Debtors	70200	91800	61900	-	-
Inventory	-	-	-	302300	201700
Turnover	1366600	1238100	1307800	1260600	1089200
Oper Profit	404800	335700	483700	594800	497800
Interest Paid	1100	2100	2900	3600	2800
Tax Paid	54100	9100	89200	182300	153200
Prf af Int&Tax	377300	345400	421300	408900	341800
Prf att Ord Sh	377300	345400	421300	150700	135100
Btm Line Earn	108200	86500	131300	150700	135100
Dividend Paid	108100	86000	131600	150400	136300
Mkt Prce(c) YE	11250	10100	18350	10225	13900

PER SHARE STATISTICS (CENTS)

Net Asst Val	10548.48	9758.03	8707.07	7614.55	6639.70
Net Earnings	390.00	312.00	479.00	-	-
Dividends	390.00	310.00	480.00	-	-
Cash Flow	1361.45	1270.13	1549.24	1503.64	1256.89

RATIOS AND OTHER INFORMATION

Mrk Cap(R000)	3117713	2746594	4990099	2780587	3779966
Current Ratio	1.07	1.01	0.92	1.03	1.08
Quik/Acid Tst	1.07	1.01	0.92	-	-
A/C Rec T/ovr	19.47	13.49	21.13	-	-
Tot Ass T/ovr	0.43	0.44	0.50	0.47	0.49
Debt/Ass Rat	0.07	0.06	0.09	0.22	0.18
L T L Tot Ass	0.00	0.00	0.01	0.12	0.10
Debt to Eqity	0.08	0.06	0.10	0.29	0.22
Interest Cover	372.73	162.33	168.31	165.22	177.79
Oper Prof Mrg	29.62	27.11	36.99	47.18	45.70
Net Prof Marg%	27.61	27.90	32.21	11.95	12.40
Ret on Assets	13.72	12.68	19.77	22.16	22.42
Ret on Equity%	12.91	13.02	17.79	7.28	7.48
Price/Earnings	28.85	32.37	38.31	-	-
Divid Cover	1.00	1.01	1.00	-	-
Divid Yield	3.47	3.07	2.62	-	-
Earning Yield%	3.47	3.09	2.61	-	-
NAV % Mrk Pr	93.76	96.61	47.45	74.47	47.77
Effec Tax Rate	11.00	2.61	14.86	30.84	30.95
Def Interval	0.02	0.02	0.00	0.76	0.62
Sus Grth Rate	9.21	9.78	12.23	0.01	-0.07

SUBSIDIARY & ASSOCIATED COMPANIES

None

INVESTMENTS

ELANDSRAND GOLD MINING CO. LTD (2788992 SH)

WILLSGROVE BRICK AND POTTERIES LTD

ABBREVIATION : WSGROVE

SECTOR : Zimbabwe Stock Exchange

SHAREHOLDERS

Who Owns Whom's Assessment of the Identity of the Ultimate Controlling Shareholder: CONSOLIDATED AFEX CORP CONTROLS 34,5%

SHAREHOLDER	PERCENTAGE 1992	1991
ZIMCOR LTD	27.6	---
RADIO HOLDING LTD	10.0	---
ROCKIES (BULAWAYO) PVT LTD	10.0	---
MASHONALAND HOLDINGS LTD	9.8	---
LATILLA-CAMPBELL P	8.6	---
ANGLO AMERICAN CORP ZIMBABWE LTD	8.4	---
EDWARDS NOM PVT LTD	7.9	---
OLD MUTUAL INV CORP (PVT) LTD	7.3	---
HENRY ALTY ZIMBABWE (PVT) LTD	2.3	---
HOLLARD NOM PVT LTD	1.2	---
CATERING INDUSTRY PENS FUND	1.0	---
TOTAL	94.2	---

DIRECTORS :
JOUSSE CP ,MARSHALL DC ,PALMGREN AM
STEPHENS RG (Chairman),WIGLEY FL

REGISTERED OFFICE
Halyet House, 9th Avenue
Bulawayo, Zimbabwe

TEL: 092639-70741
FAX: 092639-64017

TRANSFER SECRETARY
KPMG Peat Marwick
P O Box 702, Harare
Zimbabwe

TEL: 09263 962831

COMPANY SECRETARY
Buluwayo Board of Executors and Trust Co Ltd

NATURE OF BUSINESS
The main activities of the group companies are the manufacture of bricks, a full range of hotel and household crockery, the renting of property and the provision of transport services.

BANKERS :
N/A

AUDITORS :
Deloitte & Touche

FAMILIAR BRAND NAMES
N/A

CONTRIBUTION BY ACTIVITY
Bricks (% of turnover) (37.8%)
Ceramics (61.4%)
Transport Services (0.8%)

YEAR END : June

CAPITAL STRUCTURE

	AUTHORISED	ISSUED
Ords 50c	2000000	1638056

FINANCIAL STATISTICS (AT FINANCIAL YEAR END)

(Amts in Zim$)	1991 Jun	1990 Jun	1989 Jun	1988 Jun	1987
Ord S/H Int	24694	11566	5548	4365	4029
Long Trm Loans	72	771	109	90	1762
Iss Ord Share	1638	1638	1638	1638	1638
Total Liab	4460	3818	1398	1422	3445
Current Liab	4388	3047	1289	1332	1683
Total Assets	29154	15265	6946	5787	9767
Intang Assets	*	119	*	*	*
Current Assets	8208	3913	3048	3541	3976
Debtors	7030	2756	1655	2135	-
Inventory	1149	1067	1342	1092	3976
Turnover	16103	10358	4772	4544	5765
Oper Profit	355	1350	1564	795	1028
Interest Paid	135	17	-	-	52
Tax Paid	-30	92	53	141	570
Prf af Int&Tax	883	1264	1511	654	444
Prf att Ord Sh	5085	1264	1511	654	444
Btm Line Earn	5085	1264	1511	664	444
Dividend Paid	655	328	328	328	246
Depreciation	153	336	208	165	-

PER SHARE STATISTICS (CENTS)

Net Asst Val	1507.57	698.84	338.71	266.48	245.97
Net Earnings	95.10	77.20	92.30	39.90	-
Dividends	40.00	-	20.00	20.00	-
Cash Flow	58.30	98.17	105.19	50.00	27.11

RATIOS AND OTHER INFORMATION

Current Ratio	1.87	1.28	2.36	2.66	2.36
Quik/Acid Tst	1.61	0.93	1.32	1.84	-
A/C Rec T/ovr	2.29	3.76	2.88	2.13	-
Tot Ass T/ovr	0.55	0.68	0.69	0.79	0.59
Debt/Ass Rat	0.15	0.21	0.19	0.23	0.35
L T L Tot Ass	0.00	0.01	-	-	0.18
Debt to Eqity	0.18	0.27	0.23	0.31	0.86
Interest Cover	2.63	79.41	-	-	20.50
Oper Prof Mrg	2.20	13.03	32.77	17.50	17.83
Net Prof Marg%	31.58	12.20	31.66	14.39	7.70
Ret on Assets	5.70	8.99	22.52	13.74	10.91
Ret on Equity%	20.59	10.93	27.24	14.98	11.02
Divid Cover	2.38	-	4.62	2.00	-
Effec Tax Rate	5.98	6.12	1.92	16.35	58.40
Def Interval	0.80	0.74	-	-	3.97
Sus Grth Rate	17.94	8.09	21.32	7.47	4.91

SUBSIDIARY & ASSOCIATED COMPANIES

MOWELD FENCING AND WIRE PRODUCTS (PRIVAT
WILLDALE (PRIVATE) LTD (30%)
WILLSGROVE TRANSPORT SERVICES (PRIVATE)

INVESTMENTS

None

WINBEL LTD

ABBREVIATION : WINBEL

JSE SHORT CODE : WNB

SECTOR : Industrial-Engineering

SHAREHOLDERS

Who Owns Whom's Assessment of the Identity of the Ultimate Controlling Shareholder: WAR WENTELER & CONSORTIUM CONTROL 49,9%

SHAREHOLDER	PERCENTAGE 1992	1991
JAN SILVIS NOM P/L	27.5	27.9
WENTELER W A R	25.0	25.0
SA MUTUAL	21.6	21.6
CMB NOM P/L	5.1	---
BOTHMA D W	1.7	---
FERBROS NOM P/L	1.7	1.7
UAL NOM P/L	1.6	1.0
UAL MERCHANT BANK LTD	1.0	1.0
MOOSA A S	1.0	---
SANLAM	---	5.1
STD BANK NOM TVL P/L	---	1.7
TOTAL	86.3	85.0

DIRECTORS :
BETTESWORTH RA ,HENDERSON JH
RABINOWITZ J (Chairman)
WENTELER WAR (Managing Director

REGISTRATION NUMBER : 69/09225/06

REGISTERED OFFICE
Linton Jones Street, Industries East
Germiston
1401
TEL: 011-873 3655
FAX: 011-873 4094

TRANSFER SECRETARY
Mercantile Registrars Ltd
P O Box 1053, Johannesburg
2000
TEL: 011-333 8181

COMPANY SECRETARY
Winhold Ltd

NATURE OF BUSINESS
An investment holding company with a controlling investment in quoted Winhold Ltd.Winhold Ltd in turn has a controlling interest in quoted Inmins Ltd and Plastall Ltd.

BANKERS :
Standard Bank of SA Ltd

AUDITORS :
Deloitte Pim Goldby

FAMILIAR BRAND NAMES
N/A

CONTRIBUTION BY ACTIVITY
Inmins Ltd (% Operating Profit) (59.0%)
Plastall Ltd (40.0%)
Unlisted Operations (1.0%)

YEAR END : September

DIVIDEND :15/07/91 and 15/01/92

NUMBER OF EMPLOYEES : 2000

CAPITAL STRUCTURE

	AUTHORISED	ISSUED
Ords no par value	65000000	52110746
Unsec Auto Conv Debs 170c	6015873	6015873

FINANCIAL STATISTICS (AT FINANCIAL YEAR END)

(Amts in R'000)	1991 Sep	1990 Sep	1989 Sep	1987	1986
Ord S/H Int	484	316	6559	19946	14156
Long Trm Loans	20088	20755	32758	62653	24651
Iss Ord Share	52110	52110	52110	25391	23495
Total Liab	89268	98987	95144	88496	37833
Current Liab	69180	78232	62386	25843	13182
Total Assets	89752	99303	101703	135872	59277
Current Assets	66172	70624	74112	53273	20470
Debtors	36757	41629	32054	-	-
Inventory	26902	28730	-	53273	20470
Turnover	230530	255087	273320	150580	49249
Oper Profit	10364	145	14643	6289	2257
Interest Paid	11217	13376	9533	1559	296
Tax Paid	145	30	376	462	20
Prf af Int&Tax	-325	-10649	6191	4268	2233
Prf att Ord Sh	-330	-6385	2068	2116	1358
Btm Line Earn	158	-7041	903	2116	1358
Dividend Paid	-	-	-	1087	916
Mkt Prce(c) YE	4	7	20	135	-
Depreciation	2673	3173	2975	-	-

PER SHARE STATISTICS (CENTS)

	1991 Sep	1990 Sep	1989 Sep	1987	1986
Net Asst Val	0.93	0.61	12.59	78.56	60.25
Net Earnings	-0.60	-12.30	3.90	-	-
Cash Flow	4.49	-6.09	9.29	16.81	9.50

RATIOS AND OTHER INFORMATION

	1991 Sep	1990 Sep	1989 Sep	1987	1986
Mrk Cap(R000)	2084	3648	10422	34278	-
Current Ratio	0.96	0.90	1.19	2.06	1.55
Quik/Acid Tst	0.57	0.54	1.19	-	-
A/C Rec T/ovr	6.27	6.13	8.53	-	-
Tot Ass T/ovr	2.57	2.57	2.69	1.11	0.83
Debt/Ass Rat	0.94	0.95	0.81	0.65	0.64
L T L Tot Ass	0.17	0.16	0.20	0.46	0.42
Debt to Eqity	174.56	299.12	12.61	4.44	2.67
Interest Cover	0.92	0.01	1.54	4.03	8.61
Oper Prof Mrg	4.50	0.06	5.36	4.18	4.58
Net Prof Marg%	-0.14	-2.50	0.76	1.41	2.76
Ret on Assets	12.30	2.78	15.83	4.63	4.30
Ret on Equity%	-68.18	-2020.57	31.53	10.61	9.59
Price/Earnings	-6.67	-0.57	5.13	-	-

Earning Yield%	-15.00	-175.71	19.50	-	-
NAV % Mrk Pr	23.22	8.66	62.93	58.19	-
Effec Tax Rate	-83.33	0.10	8.83	9.77	1.02
Def Interval	14.84	-12.07	5.83	14.68	11.04
Sus Grth Rate	-68.18	-2020.57	31.53	5.16	3.12

SUBSIDIARY & ASSOCIATED COMPANIES

WINHOLD INV (PTY) LTD
WINHOLD LTD

INVESTMENTS

None

WINHOLD LTD

ABBREVIATION : WINHOLD

JSE SHORT CODE : WNH

SECTOR : Industrial-Engineering

SHAREHOLDERS

Who Owns Whom's Assessment of the Identity of the Ultimate Controlling Shareholder:
WINBEL LTD

SHAREHOLDER	PERCENTAGE 1992	1991
WINHOLD INV P/L	61.1	61.1
SA MUTUAL	18.0	18.0
CMB NOM P/L	5.5	---
FERBROS NOM P/L	1.0	1.0
SANLAM	---	5.1
TOTAL	85.6	85.2

DIRECTORS :
BETTESWORTH RA ,HENDERSON JH
RABINOWITZ J (Chairman)
WENTELER WAR (Managing Director

REGISTRATION NUMBER : 05/19679/06

REGISTERED OFFICE
Linton Jones Street, Industries East
Germiston
1401
TEL: 011-873 3655
FAX: 011-873 4094

TRANSFER SECRETARY
Mercantile Registrars Ltd
P O Box 1053, Johannesburg
2000
TEL: 011-333 8181

COMPANY SECRETARY
R A Bettesworth

NATURE OF BUSINESS
An investment holding company with controlling interests in quoted Inmins Ltd, & Plastall Ltd.
The group is engaged in the following activities: Manufacture & supply of engineering equipment & allied services to the mining industry; Supply of capital equipment & consumables to the electrical, mining and general industries; Manufacture and distribution of polyethylene sheeting and bags, furniture and components, and material handling equipment to the mining industry.

BANKERS :
Nedperm Bank Ltd

AUDITORS :
Deloitte Pim Goldby

FAMILIAR BRAND NAMES
N/A

CONTRIBUTION BY ACTIVITY
Inmins Ltd (% Operating Profit) (60.0%)
Plastall Ltd (41.0%)
Unlisted Operations (-1.0%)

YEAR END : September

DIVIDEND :15/05/91 and 15/11/91

NUMBER OF EMPLOYEES : 9

CAPITAL STRUCTURE

	AUTHORISED	ISSUED
Ords 50c	75000000	64488130
5% Red Cum Prefs R2	75000	0
Var Rate Red Cum Prefs 1c	5000000	0
9% Auto Conv Cum Prefs 1c (auth'd		888889
Unsec Auto Conv Debs 170c	6015873	6015873

FINANCIAL STATISTICS (AT FINANCIAL YEAR END)

(Amts in R'000)	1991 Sep	1990 Sep	1989 Sep	1988 Sep	1987 Sep
Ord S/H Int	2289	1994	12149	18231	37936
Long Trm Loans	19197	19979	28028	31487	7839
Iss Ord Share	64488	64488	64488	64488	42624
Total Liab	87214	97309	89551	146498	60838
Current Liab	68017	77330	61523	115011	52999
Total Assets	89503	99303	101700	157157	98774
Intang Assets	*	*	*	7572	*
Current Assets	65923	70624	74109	110414	63743
Debtors	36758	41629	41388	53733	23803
Inventory	26902	28730	32064	53444	34450
Turnover	230530	255087	273320	326392	84025
Oper Profit	10222	-42	16057	11966	6016
Interest Paid	11063	13148	11039	10969	1751
Tax Paid	145	30	376	2140	369
Prf af Int&Tax	-313	-10608	6198	1311	3896
Prf att Ord Sh	-503	-10386	3398	1178	3462
Btm Line Earn	295	-11462	2220	-30772	1625
Dividend Paid	-	-	-	-	1445
Mkt Prce(c) YE	4	8	18	25	155
Depreciation	2673	3173	2975	4686	2003

PER SHARE STATISTICS (CENTS)

Net Asst Val	3.55	3.09	18.84	16.53	89.00
Net Earnings	-0.80	-16.10	5.20	-9.60	15.00
Dividends	-	-	-	-	4.50
Cash Flow	3.36	-11.12	9.57	9.14	22.83

RATIOS AND OTHER INFORMATION

Mrk Cap(R000)	2580	5159	11608	16122	66067
Current Ratio	0.97	0.91	1.20	0.96	1.20
Quik/Acid Tst	0.57	0.54	0.68	0.50	0.55
A/C Rec T/ovr	6.27	6.13	6.60	6.07	3.53

Tot Ass T/ovr	2.58	2.57	2.69	2.08	0.85
Debt/Ass Rat	0.93	0.94	0.81	0.87	0.58
L T L Tot Ass	0.17	0.16	0.20	0.14	0.04
Debt to Eqity	36.40	46.95	6.74	7.53	1.50
Interest Cover	0.92	0.00	1.45	1.09	3.44
Oper Prof Mrg	4.43	-0.02	5.87	3.67	7.16
Net Prof Marg%	-0.22	-4.07	1.24	0.36	4.12
Ret on Assets	12.17	2.59	17.32	9.18	6.09
Ret on Equity%	-21.97	-520.86	27.97	6.46	9.13
Price/Earnings	-5.00	-0.50	3.46	-2.60	10.33
Divid Cover	-	-	-	-	3.33
Divid Yield	-	-	-	-	2.90
Earning Yield%	-20.00	-201.25	28.89	-38.40	9.68
NAV % Mrk Pr	88.74	38.65	104.66	66.11	57.42
Effec Tax Rate	-89.29	0.10	8.82	62.59	13.36
Def Interval	16.45	-5.46	4.73	10.11	4.78
Sus Grth Rate	-21.97	-520.86	27.97	6.46	5.32

SUBSIDIARY & ASSOCIATED COMPANIES

COLUMBIA ENGINEERING (PTY) LTD
CONCOAL (PTY) LTD
GLOBAL GROUND CONTROL (PTY) LTD
GMIC MANAGEMENT (PTY) LTD
HI-PAK PLASTICS (PTY) LTD
IDLER ENGINEERING (PTY) LTD
INMINS INVESTMENTS LTD
INMINS LTD
KROONSTAD BEARING WORKS (PTY) LTD
NFS MOTORS FINANCE COMPANY (PTY) LTD
NORTHERN FREE STATE MOTORS PROPERTIES LT
PLASTALL INVESTMENTS (PTY) LTD
PLASTALL LTD
REGEN PLASTICS (PTY) LTD
SUPERSTRUT (PTY) LTD
TRUCKING AND ENGINEERING (PTY) LTD
TURNCLIFF ENGINEERING (PTY) LTD
TURNCLIFF HEAVY ENGINEERING (PTY) LTD
TURNCLIFF HOLDINGS (PTY) LTD
TURNCLIFF MINING & ENGINEERING SERVICES
TWB INVESTMENTS (PTY) LTD
URSUS ENGINEERING (PTY) LTD
VIBEPROP (PTY) LTD
VORI (PTY) LTD

INVESTMENTS

None

WINKELHAAK MINES LTD

ABBREVIATION : WINKELS

JSE SHORT CODE : WIN

SECTOR : Gold-Evander

SHAREHOLDERS

Who Owns Whom's Assessment of the Identity of the Ultimate Controlling Shareholder:
SANLAM VIA GENCOR

SHAREHOLDER	PERCENTAGE 1992	1991
ABSA NOM P/L	20.6	—
CONSOLIDATED NOM P/L	20.0	20.0
NEDBANK NOM LTD	7.4	7.3
INDO-CHINA NOM P/L	6.7	—
OVERSEAS NOM CO INC	6.7	6.7
CMB NOM P/L	5.2	—
SA MUTUAL	4.4	4.5
FIRST NAT CITY TRUST CO	3.3	3.3
FIRST NAT NOM P/L GATR DEPOT	2.8	1.5
GUARDIAN NOM P/L	2.8	2.8
FIRST NAT NOM P/L	2.5	3.2
STD BANK NOM TVL P/L	2.4	4.0
DEPOSITARY NOM INC	1.9	1.9
MINU NOM LTD	1.8	1.8
LONDON CONTROL ACCOUNT	1.5	1.4
SEPON LTD	1.5	1.5
EIGHTY ONE MAIN STREET NOM LTD	1.4	—
GREENMARKET SQUARE NOM P/L	1.2	1.2
INDO-CHINA NOM SA P/L	—	12.7
SANDTON NOM LTD	—	1.2
SANLAM	—	5.2
VOLKSKAS NOM P/L	—	12.7
TOTAL	94.0	92.8

DIRECTORS :
BOTHA AD ,ELLIS SP ,EUSTACE PJ ,FORBES JR
GILBERTSON BP (Chairman),MAUDE G ,MUNRO AH
OLIVIER JE ,STEENKAMP TI ,VOS P

REGISTRATION NUMBER : 55/03606/06

REGISTERED OFFICE
General Mining Building, 6 Hollard Street
Johannesburg
2001
TEL: 011-376 9111

TRANSFER SECRETARY
Central Registrars Ltd
P O Box 4844, Johannesburg
2000
TEL: 011-331 0051

COMPANY SECRETARY
General Mining Metals & Minerals Ltd

NATURE OF BUSINESS
The company operates a gold mine in the Evander area, Eastern Transvaal. Silver and osmiridium are recovered as by-products of gold.

BANKERS :
First National Bank of SA Ltd

AUDITORS :
Deloitte & Touche

FAMILIAR BRAND NAMES
N/A

CONTRIBUTION BY ACTIVITY
Gold (% of Turnover) (99.5%)
Silver (0.1%)
Osmiridium (0.4%)

YEAR END : September

DIVIDEND : Ords R1

Interim No 60	(Ldr)04/05/90	(Pay)15/06/90	Amt(c)165
Final No 61	(Ldr)02/11/90	(Pay)14/12/90	Amt(c)150
Interim No 62	(Ldr)03/05/91	(Pay)14/06/91	Amt(c)100

NUMBER OF EMPLOYEES : 8937

CAPITAL STRUCTURE

	AUTHORISED	ISSUED
Ords R1	12180000	12180000

FINANCIAL STATISTICS (AT FINANCIAL YEAR END)

(Amts in R'000)	1991 Sep	1990 Sep	1989 Sep	1988 Sep	1987
Ord S/H Int	559516	478819	388204	324361	242647
Long Trm Loans	1185	445	-	-	76894
Iss Ord Share	12180	12180	12180	12180	12180
Total Liab	101091	81756	74331	77824	153707
Current Liab	99906	81311	74331	77824	76813
Total Assets	660607	560575	462535	402185	409143
Current Assets	114053	94547	85244	91839	89602
Debtors	5072	2786	3398	3029	-
Inventory	6131	7575	8011	6565	89602
Turnover	367893	416247	367182	382910	360190
Oper Profit	98341	167337	141702	169250	198203
Tax Paid	6243	39463	40897	49189	62862
Prf af Int&Tax	92877	129446	102769	120819	135458
Prf att Ord Sh	92877	128982	102210	120081	39364
Btm Line Earn	92877	128982	102210	120081	39364
Dividend Paid	12180	38367	38367	38367	43239
Mkt Prce(c) YE	3900	7500	7650	5150	9800

PER SHARE STATISTICS (CENTS)

Net Asst Val	4593.73	3931.19	3187.22	2663.06	1992.18
Net Earnings	107.00	334.00	316.00	326.00	-
Dividends	100.00	315.00	315.00	315.00	-
Cash Flow	762.54	1062.76	843.75	991.28	1112.13

RATIOS AND OTHER INFORMATION

Mrk Cap(R000)	475020	913500	931770	627270	1193640
Current Ratio	1.14	1.16	1.15	1.18	1.17
Quik/Acid Tst	1.08	1.07	1.04	1.10	-
A/C Rec T/ovr	72.53	149.41	108.06	126.41	-
Tot Ass T/ovr	0.56	0.74	0.79	0.95	0.88
Debt/Ass Rat	0.15	0.15	0.16	0.19	0.38
L T L Tot Ass	0.00	0.00	-	-	0.19
Debt to Eqity	0.18	0.17	0.19	0.24	0.63
Oper Prof Mrg	26.73	40.20	38.59	44.20	55.03
Net Prof Marg%	25.25	30.99	27.84	31.36	10.93
Ret on Assets	15.00	30.13	31.06	42.27	48.47
Ret on Equity%	16.60	26.94	26.33	37.02	16.22
Price/Earnings	36.45	22.46	24.21	15.80	-
Divid Cover	1.07	1.06	1.00	1.03	-
Divid Yield	2.56	4.20	4.12	6.12	-
Earning Yield%	2.74	4.45	4.13	6.33	-
NAV % Mrk Pr	117.79	52.42	41.66	51.71	20.33
Effec Tax Rate	6.35	23.58	28.86	29.11	31.72
Def Interval	0.57	0.00	-	-	0.57
Sus Grth Rate	14.42	18.92	16.45	25.19	-1.60

SUBSIDIARY & ASSOCIATED COMPANIES

None

INVESTMENTS

None

WITWATERSRAND GOLD MINING CO LTD

ABBREVIATION : WIT-G-M

JSE SHORT CODE : WKN

SECTOR : Gold-Curtailed Operations

SHAREHOLDERS

Who Owns Whom's Assessment of the Identity of the Ultimate Controlling Shareholder:
ISLAMIC INSTITUTE

SHAREHOLDER	PERCENTAGE 1992	1991
INDO-CHINA NOM SA P/L	31.4	31.4
FIRST NAT NOM P/L	22.8	10.2
UK CONTROL ACCOUNT	3.1	3.1
MIA Y I M	2.9	2.9
MIA A R A	2.8	2.8
MIA AHMED MAHOMED	2.8	2.8
MIA IBRAHIM MAHOMED	2.8	2.8
MIA ISMAIL MAHOMED	2.8	2.8
MIA K M	2.8	2.8
MIA M A M	2.8	2.8
MIA A A	1.5	1.5
GIANT REEFS GOLD MINING CO LTD	1.5	1.0
MIA A F M	1.4	1.4
MIA AABEDA AHMED	1.4	1.4
MIA AAMENA MAHOMED	1.4	1.4
MIA AASIYA AHMED	1.4	1.4
MIA AAYESHA RASHEDA MAHOMED	1.4	1.4
MIA ATIYYA AHMED	1.4	1.4
MIA M M	1.4	1.4
SAPEIKA M L	1.1	1.1
BARCLAYS NAT NOM P/L	---	12.9
TOTAL	90.5	90.3

DIRECTORS :
KATZENELLENBOGEN RF ,MAISELS KDH ,MIA AM ,MIA YI
WASSUNG DCL

REGISTRATION NUMBER : 01/00032/06

REGISTERED OFFICE
5 Bezuidenhout Street, Ferreirasdorp
Johannesburg
2001
TEL: 011-836 0178

TRANSFER SECRETARY
Mercantile Registrars Ltd
P O Box 1053, Johannesburg
2000
TEL: 011-333 8181

COMPANY SECRETARY
Oriental Trust Co. Ltd

NATURE OF BUSINESS
Income sources include: Royalties & site rentals in terms of an agreement with Knights Gold Mining Co; Tributing revenue in terms of the tributing agreement with Balmoral Gold Mining Co iro portion of Wit GM's mining title; Rentals from letting of mine property & buildings.

BANKERS :
First National Bank of SA Ltd

AUDITORS :
Kessel Feinstein

FAMILIAR BRAND NAMES
N/A

CONTRIBUTION BY ACTIVITY
N/A

YEAR END : June

DIVIDEND : Ords no par value

Final No 123	(Ldr)16/11/90	(Pay)30/11/90	Amt(c)2
Interim No 124	(Ldr)26/04/91	(Pay)17/05/91	Amt(c)1
Final No 125	(Ldr)08/11/91	(Pay)22/11/91	Amt(c)2
Interim No 126	(Ldr)24/04/92	(Pay)15/05/92	Amt(c)1
Final No 127	(Ldr)04/12/92	(Pay)18/12/92	Amt(c)2

CAPITAL STRUCTURE

	AUTHORISED	ISSUED
Ords no par value	30000000	9392500

FINANCIAL STATISTICS (AT FINANCIAL YEAR END)

(Amts in R'000)	1992 Jun	1991 Jun	1990 Jun	1989 Jun	1988 Jun
Ord S/H Int	6325	5440	3546	2046	1673
Iss Ord Share	9393	9393	9393	9393	9392
Total Liab	602	789	1124	745	626
Current Liab	602	789	1124	745	626
Total Assets	6927	6229	4670	2791	2299
Current Assets	1591	3385	2645	879	420
Debtors	1040	998	431	432	55
Turnover	3193	2677	3153	1598	-
Oper Profit	1805	1198	1907	882	354
Interest Paid	-	-	-	3	7
Tax Paid	994	751	1021	455	175
Prf af Int&Tax	1074	1113	1306	424	172
Prf att Ord Sh	1074	1113	1306	424	172
Btm Line Earn	1167	2176	1782	505	523
Dividend Paid	282	282	282	131	56
Mkt Prce(c) YE	150	150	150	120	180
Depreciation	16	19	20	13	12

PER SHARE STATISTICS (CENTS)

Net Asst Val	67.34	57.92	37.75	21.78	17.81
Net Earnings	11.43	11.85	13.90	4.51	1.83
Dividends	3.00	3.00	3.00	1.40	0.60
Cash Flow	11.60	12.05	14.12	4.65	1.96

RATIOS AND OTHER INFORMATION

Mrk Cap(R000)	14090	14090	14090	11272	16906
Current Ratio	2.64	4.29	2.35	1.18	0.67
Quik/Acid Tst	2.64	4.29	2.35	1.18	0.67
A/C Rec T/ovr	3.07	2.68	7.32	3.70	-
Tot Ass T/ovr	0.46	0.43	0.68	0.57	-
Debt/Ass Rat	0.09	0.13	0.24	0.27	0.27
Debt to Eqity	0.10	0.15	0.32	0.36	0.37
Interest Cover	-	-	-	294.00	50.57
Oper Prof Mrg	56.53	44.75	60.48	55.19	-
Net Prof Marg%	33.64	41.58	41.42	26.53	-
Ret on Assets	29.85	29.92	49.83	31.60	15.40
Ret on Equity%	16.98	20.46	36.83	20.72	10.28
Price/Earnings	13.12	12.66	10.79	26.61	98.36
Divid Cover	3.81	3.95	4.63	3.22	3.05
Divid Yield	2.00	2.00	2.00	1.17	0.33
Earning Yield%	7.62	7.90	9.27	3.76	1.02
NAV % Mrk Pr	44.89	38.61	25.17	18.15	9.90
Effec Tax Rate	48.49	48.17	50.37	51.76	50.43
Sus Grth Rate	12.52	15.28	28.88	14.32	6.93

SUBSIDIARY & ASSOCIATED COMPANIES

NATIONAL SOIL GROUP PROPERTY CO. (PTY) L

INVESTMENTS

BLAJOHN MIDDELBURG PROPERTIES (PTY) LTD (15000 SH)
CARWOOD & WILLIAMS (PTY) LTD (200 SH)
DE BEERS CONSOLIDATED MINES LTD (1000 SH)
GENCOR LTD (1000 SH)
ISCOR LTD (5000 SH)
KNIGHTS GOLD MINING COMPANY LTD (5000000 SH)
LANGEBERG HOLDINGS LTD (1000 SH)
RAND MINES PROPERTIES LTD (4300 SH)
SIMMER & JACK MINES LTD (2000 SH)
SUNPIE FOODS (PTY) LTD (200 SH)
YORK TIMBERS LTD (16100 SH)

WITWATERSRAND NIGEL LTD

ABBREVIATION : WIT-NIGEL

JSE SHORT CODE : WNI

SECTOR : Gold-Rand & others

SHAREHOLDERS

Who Owns Whom's Assessment of the Identity of the Ultimate Controlling Shareholder: CONSOLIDATED MINING VIA SOUTHGO

SHAREHOLDER	PERCENTAGE 1992	1991
SOUTH EAST RAND GOLD HLDGS LTD	68.7	68.7
LOWENCO NOM P/L	8.2	1.5
UK CONTROL ACCOUNT	5.3	5.3
DOLPHIN A I	3.0	3.0
INDO-CHINA NOM P/L	2.3	—
FIRST NAT NOM P/L	2.0	—
INDO-CHINA NOM SA P/L	1.5	10.2
BARCLAYS NAT NOM P/L	—	1.3
TOTAL	91.0	89.9

DIRECTORS :
BUITENDAG HC ,DONALD JC ,FLOWERDAY RA
LEE RA (Chairman),LOWENTHAL ND ,LOWENTHAL RY
RUBENSTEIN GB ,SCHECHTER M ,SUDDENS BD
THOMPSON MW ,TURNER CF

REGISTRATION NUMBER : 05/04523/06

REGISTERED OFFICE
39th Floor, Carlton Centre, Commissioner Str
Johannesburg
2001
TEL: 011-331 9181
FAX: 011-331 6189

TRANSFER SECRETARY
Mercantile Registrars Ltd
P O Box 1053, Johannesburg
2000
TEL: 011-333 8181

COMPANY SECRETARY
Consolidated Mining Management Services Ltd

NATURE OF BUSINESS
The company conducts gold mining operations in the districts of Heidelberg and Nigel, Transvaal.

BANKERS :
Bank of Lisbon International Ltd
Volkskas Ltd

AUDITORS :
Charles Orbach & Co

FAMILIAR BRAND NAMES
N/A

CONTRIBUTION BY ACTIVITY
N/A

YEAR END : March

DIVIDEND :15/00/91

NUMBER OF EMPLOYEES : 1

CAPITAL STRUCTURE

	AUTHORISED	ISSUED
Ords 25c	50000000	29366407

FINANCIAL STATISTICS (AT FINANCIAL YEAR END)

(Amts in R'000)	1992 Mar	1991 Mar	1990 Mar	1988 Dec	1987 Dec
Ord S/H Int	25577	31906	32511	25015	34164
Long Trm Loans	-	-	49	49	180
Iss Ord Share	29366	29366	29366	15366	15337
Total Liab	8020	7686	7526	12402	11903
Current Liab	8020	7686	7477	12353	11723
Total Assets	33597	39592	40037	37417	46067
Current Assets	268	413	888	2912	9145
Debtors	233	413	207	954	6695
Inventory	-	-	246	1934	2385
Turnover	386	1110	6180	31016	32065
Oper Profit	-167	721	1514	-4764	-858
Interest Paid	1480	1326	1382	954	356
Tax Paid	8	-	-70	70	-
Prf af Int&Tax	-1655	-605	202	-5788	-1214
P:f att Ord Sh	-1655	-605	202	-5788	-1214
Btm Line Earn	-6329	-605	-883	-9153	-1214
Mkt Prce(c) YE	16	150	100	70	190

PER SHARE STATISTICS (CENTS)

Net Asst Val	87.10	108.65	110.71	162.79	222.76
Net Earnings	-5.60	-2.10	0.80	-59.60	-8.90
Cash Flow	-5.64	-2.06	0.62	-37.68	-7.92

RATIOS AND OTHER INFORMATION

Mrk Cap(R000)	4699	44049	29366	10756	29140
Current Ratio	0.03	0.05	0.12	0.24	0.78
Quik/Acid Tst	0.03	0.05	0.09	0.08	0.58
A/C Rec T/ovr	1.66	2.69	23.88	32.51	4.79
Tot Ass T/ovr	0.01	0.03	0.12	0.83	0.70
Debt/Ass Rat	0.24	0.19	0.19	0.33	0.25
Debt to Eqity	0.31	0.24	0.23	0.49	0.34
Interest Cover	-0.11	0.54	1.10	-4.99	-2.41
Oper Prof Mrg	-43.26	64.95	24.50	-15.36	-2.68
Net Prof Marg%	-428.76	-54.50	3.27	-18.66	-3.79
Ret on Assets	-0.50	1.82	3.03	-12.73	-1.86
Ret on Equity%	-6.47	-1.90	0.50	-23.14	-3.55
Price/Earnings	-2.86	-71.43	125.00	-1.17	-21.35
Earning Yield%	-35.00	-1.40	0.80	-85.14	-4.68
NAV % Mrk Pr	544.36	72.43	110.71	232.56	117.24
Effec Tax Rate	-	-	-	-1.22	-
Def Interval	-4.39	-11.78	23.05	-1.28	-1.52
Sus Grth Rate	-6.47	-1.90	0.62	-23.14	-3.55

SUBSIDIARY & ASSOCIATED COMPANIES

None

INVESTMENTS

NIGEL GOLD MINING HOLDINGS LTD (6,3%)

WOODROW HOLDINGS LTD

ABBREVIATION : WOODROW

JSE SHORT CODE : WDR

SECTOR : Industrial-Engineering

SHAREHOLDERS

Who Owns Whom's Assessment of the Identity of the Ultimate Controlling Shareholder: DIRECTORS

SHAREHOLDER	PERCENTAGE 1992	1991
GENQUIP P/L	28.6	28.6
MERHOLD INV P/L	20.7	20.6
WOODROW INC	15.6	15.6
NEDBANK NOM LTD	9.8	6.9
SOLID G NOM P/L	3.2	—
FIRST NAT NOM P/L	2.9	3.0
VAN DEN BERG G	2.7	2.7
WEAVER M G	2.4	2.4
EIGHTY ONE MAIN STREET NOM LTD	2.1	2.1
BENREN NOM P/L	—	1.4
SAXON INV P/L	—	3.7
VENTER M C	—	2.2
TOTAL	87.9	89.2

DIRECTORS :
BOLD BEL ,NEL GE (Chief Executive & M.D.)
RODRIGUES NN (Financial Director)
SACKS HW (Executive Chairman),SEABROOKE CS
TRAUB P ,VAN HEERDEN TJ

REGISTRATION NUMBER : 88/04781/06

REGISTERED OFFICE
7 Patton Street, Vereeniging
1930
TEL: 011-880 6430
FAX: 011-609 2405

TRANSFER SECRETARY
Central Registrars Ltd
P O Box 4844, Johannesburg
2000
TEL: 011-331 0051

COMPANY SECRETARY
N N Rodrigues

NATURE OF BUSINESS
An industrial holding engaged in the manufacture & supply of fluid-handling equipment, consumables, spares & service back-up to the petrochemical, mining & general industries. The group is focused in fluid-handling with interest in: measurement & control, valves, hydraulics & combustion.

BANKERS :
Standard Bank of SA Ltd

AUDITORS :
JC Mouton & Partners

FAMILIAR BRAND NAMES
ASCOREG,ASCOREG,BOWMAN,ENRAF-NONIUS
FILL-RITE,HYDRAULIC STEEL TUBE,METER SYSTEMS
THE COMBUSTION GROUP,TOKICO

CONTRIBUTION BY ACTIVITY
N/A

YEAR END : February

DIVIDEND :Ords 1c

Dividend No 2	(Ldr)01/06/90	(Pay)15/06/90	Amt(c)5
Dividend No 3	(Ldr)22/02/91	(Pay)05/04/91	Amt(c)6
Dividend No 4	(Ldr)15/11/91	(Pay)29/11/91	Amt(c)2
Dividend No 5	(Ldr)28/02/92	(Pay)10/04/92	Amt(c)4.3
Dividend No 6	(Ldr)13/11/92	(Pay)27/11/92	Amt(c)2.5

NUMBER OF EMPLOYEES : 150

CAPITAL STRUCTURE

	AUTHORISED	ISSUED
Ords 1c	25000000	14651707
Var Rate Comp Conv Debs 85c	3871368	3871368

FINANCIAL STATISTICS (AT FINANCIAL YEAR END)

(Amts in R'000)	1992 Feb	1991 Feb	1990 Feb	1989 Feb	1988
Ord S/H Int	9131	9229	7464	3715	2650
Long Trm Loans	3935	4079	3607	633	2568
Iss Ord Share	14652	14652	14652	7000	7000
Total Liab	16108	16739	20277	3352	4523
Current Liab	12173	12660	16670	2719	1955
Total Assets	21783	22206	24596	6265	8291
Intang Assets	3456	3762	3145	802	*
Current Assets	19844	20891	23044	4255	3073
Debtors	11580	8614	11614	1673	-
Inventory	8129	10884	10710	2581	3073
Turnover	38173	40506	33257	5067	5899
Oper Profit	4403	5346	3600	589	934
Interest Paid	1161	1793	1038	136	79
Tax Paid	527	889	672	235	445
Prf af Int&Tax	2715	2664	1890	280	410
Prf att Ord Sh	2649	2644	1883	443	421
Btm Line Earn	825	2644	1883	443	421
Dividend Paid	923	879	733	140	-
Mkt Prce(c) YE	80	60	90	50	-
Depreciation	178	241	205	47	-

PER SHARE STATISTICS (CENTS)

Net Asst Val	38.73	37.31	29.48	41.61	37.86
Net Earnings	18.10	18.00	16.10	6.30	-
Dividends	6.30	6.00	5.00	2.00	-
Cash Flow	19.30	22.78	17.85	5.16	8.79

RATIOS AND OTHER INFORMATION

Mrk Cap(R000)	11722	8791	13187	3500	-
Current Ratio	1.63	1.65	1.38	1.56	1.57
Quik/Acid Tst	0.96	0.79	0.74	0.62	-
A/C Rec T/ovr	3.30	4.70	2.86	4.54	-
Tot Ass T/ovr	1.75	1.82	1.35	1.21	1.07
Debt/Ass Rat	0.71	0.72	0.82	0.48	0.55
L T L Tot Ass	0.16	0.15	0.15	0.04	0.31
Debt to Eqity	1.71	1.74	2.72	0.80	1.71
Interest Cover	3.79	2.98	3.47	4.79	11.82
Oper Prof Mrg	11.53	13.20	10.82	11.62	15.83
Net Prof Marg%	6.94	6.53	5.66	8.74	7.14
Ret on Assets	20.21	24.07	14.64	21.55	16.90
Ret on Equity%	29.01	28.65	24.98	17.12	23.83
Price/Earnings	4.42	3.33	5.59	7.94	-
Divid Cover	2.87	3.00	3.22	3.15	-
Divid Yield	7.88	10.00	5.56	4.00	-
Earning Yield%	22.63	30.00	17.89	12.60	-
NAV % Mrk Pr	48.41	62.19	32.75	83.23	-
Effec Tax Rate	16.22	12.27	26.23	51.88	52.05
Def Interval	1.62	1.45	2.29	5.12	9.40
Sus Grth Rate	18.90	19.12	15.41	8.16	15.89

SUBSIDIARY & ASSOCIATED COMPANIES

COMBUSTION HOLDINGS LTD
FADOS ENGINEERING (PTY) LTD
KASAI TRADING (PTY) LTD
METER SYSTEMS TRADING (PTY) LTD
NEUMAX SA (PTY) LTD
RIOCO (PTY) LTD

INVESTMENTS

None

WOOLTRU LTD

ABBREVIATION : WOOLTRU

JSE SHORT CODE : WLO

SECTOR : Industrial-Retailers & Wholesalers

SHAREHOLDERS

Who Owns Whom's Assessment of the Identity of the Ultimate Controlling Shareholder: SA MUTUAL

SHAREHOLDER	PERCENTAGE 1992	1991
SA MUTUAL	26.8	26.9
LIBERTY LIFE ASSOC OF AFRICA LTD	10.0	9.7
SOUTHERN LIFE ASSOC LTD	9.1	9.5
CMB NOM P/L	6.9	---
STD BANK NOM TVL P/L	6.4	5.7
WOOLTRU LTD TRUST	3.8	3.9

FIRST NAT NOM P/L	3.4	3.6
ENGINEERING INDUSTRIES PENS FUND	2.2	2.0
METAL IND GROUP PENS FUND	2.2	2.0
MOMENTUM LIFE ASSURE LTD	1.4	—
SUSMAN D R	1.4	1.4
WOOLTRU 1982 SHARE PURCHASE TRUST	1.1	1.1
SYFRETS NOM LTD	—	1.1
SANLAM	—	6.6
TOTAL	74.8	73.4

DIRECTORS :

HALL CA (Dep. Chair. & Chief Exec.),KUIPER HC
LAMBERTI MJ (Executive Director)
LAVIES PJ (Executive Director),LOEBENBERG EJ
MULLER SA (Executive Director)
PARFETT AE (Executive Director)
RABB JB (Executive Director),SIMS IJ
SUSMAN DR (Chairman

REGISTRATION NUMBER : 05/08278/06

REGISTERED OFFICE

Wooltru House, 93 Longmarket Street
Cape Town
8001
TEL: 021-407 9114
FAX: 021-462 2400

TRANSFER SECRETARY

Mercantile Registrars Ltd
P O Box 1053, Johannesburg
2000
TEL: 011-333 8181

COMPANY SECRETARY

R B Dyamond

NATURE OF BUSINESS

An investment holding company with subsidiaries engaged in the retailing & wholesaling of food, clothing & other merchandise.

BANKERS :

Standard Bank of SA Ltd

AUDITORS :

Ernst & Young

FAMILIAR BRAND NAMES

DANIEL HECHTER,ESPRIT,FINNEGANS,MAKRO
PRINCESS,TOPICS,TRUWORTHS,WOOLWORTHS

CONTRIBUTION BY ACTIVITY

N/A

YEAR END : June

DIVIDEND : Ords 50c

Interim No 107	(Ldr)16/03/90	(Pay)05/04/90	Amt(c)64
Final No 108	(Ldr)21/09/90	(Pay)12/10/90	Amt(c)86
Interim No 109	(Ldr)22/03/91	(Pay)12/04/91	Amt(c)77
Final No 110	(Ldr)20/09/91	(Pay)11/10/91	Amt(c)93
Interim No 111	(Ldr)20/03/92	(Pay)10/04/92	Amt(c)77
Final No 112	(Ldr)18/09/92	(Pay)09/10/92	Amt(c)93

NUMBER OF EMPLOYEES : 13000

CAPITAL STRUCTURE

	AUTHORISED	ISSUED
6,75% Cum Prefs R2	500000	500000
Ords 50c	15795740	14832250
6% Cum Prefs R2	230000	230000
"A" Ords 50c	20134800	20084100

FINANCIAL STATISTICS (AT FINANCIAL YEAR END)

(Amts in R'000)	1992 Jun	1991 Jun	1990 Jun	1989 Jun	1988 Jun
Ord S/H Int	774500	696400	569200	346200	301300
Long Trm Loans	249600	304300	165200	77700	85000
Iss Ord Share	34916	34810	34800	34773	34285
Total Liab	796200	814100	592400	478500	336000
Current Liab	546600	509800	427200	400800	251000
Total Assets	1570700	1510500	1161600	824700	637300
Current Assets	678400	655000	487000	436000	309500
Debtors	303600	274500	195900	177500	135000
Inventory	334900	346800	260000	219500	174500
Turnover	3804400	3303200	2707700	2095700	1667600
Oper Profit	198200	290100	266700	198700	140900
Interest Paid	67500	44500	32800	24600	19200
Tax Paid	72300	118800	118100	83500	59100
Prf af Int&Tax	92400	149700	130700	96300	62600
Prf att Ord Sh	91900	146900	130600	96200	61300
Btm Line Earn	143400	160100	138400	97000	68000
Dividend Paid	59300	59200	52200	39000	27400
Mkt Prce(c) YE	5950	7800	4400	2450	1500
Depreciation	71900	51900	40600	30300	24800

PER SHARE STATISTICS (CENTS)

Net Asst Val	2218.18	2000.57	1635.63	995.60	878.81
Net Earnings	263.30	422.00	375.00	269.00	179.00
Dividends	170.00	170.00	150.00	112.00	80.00
Cash Flow	497.42	593.68	493.10	362.77	259.76

RATIOS AND OTHER INFORMATION

Mrk Cap(R000)	2077502	2715180	1531200	851939	514275
Current Ratio	1.24	1.28	1.14	1.09	1.23
Quik/Acid Tst	0.63	0.60	0.53	0.54	0.54
A/C Rec T/ovr	12.53	12.03	13.82	11.81	12.35
Tot Ass T/ovr	2.42	2.19	2.33	2.54	2.62
Debt/Ass Rat	0.48	0.52	0.50	0.57	0.52
L T L Tot Ass	0.14	0.18	0.13	0.08	0.12
Debt to Eqity	0.98	1.13	1.02	1.35	1.10
Interest Cover	3.09	6.74	8.36	8.31	7.34
Oper Prof Mrg	5.21	8.78	9.85	9.48	8.45
Net Prof Marg%	2.42	4.45	4.82	4.59	3.68
Ret on Assets	14.78	20.72	24.24	24.78	22.11
Ret on Equity%	11.87	21.09	22.94	27.79	20.35
Price/Earnings	22.60	18.48	11.73	9.11	8.38
Divid Cover	1.55	2.48	2.50	2.40	2.24
Divid Yield	2.86	2.18	3.41	4.57	5.33
Earning Yield%	4.43	5.41	8.52	10.98	11.93
NAV % Mrk Pr	37.28	25.65	37.17	40.64	58.59
Effec Tax Rate	7.90	13.37	34.02	32.51	37.80
Def Interval	1.51	1.39	0.97	0.59	1.04
Sus Grth Rate	4.21	12.59	13.77	16.52	11.25

SUBSIDIARY & ASSOCIATED COMPANIES

AATB WOOLTRU TRAVEL (PTY) LTD (50%)
DROP INN GROUP HOLDINGS LTD
MAKRO SA (PTY) LTD
MASSMART HOLDINGS (PTY) LTD
SPECIALITY RETAIL GROUP LIMITED
TOPIC STORES (PTY) LTD
TRUWORTHS LTD
TRUWORTHS LTD
WOOLTRU FINANCE (PTY) LTD
WOOLTRU INSURANCE BROKERS (PTY) LTD
WOOLTRU PROPERTIES (PTY) LTD
WOOLTRU PROPERTIES (PTY) LTD
WOOLWORTHS (PTY) LTD
WOOLWORTHS (WARWICK SQUARE) PROPERTIES S (50%)
WOOLWORTHS BUTCHERIES (PTY) LTD (45%)

INVESTMENTS

ELECTRA BELEGGINGS (PTY) LTD (15%)
REICHMANS LTD (15%)
RUSFURN INVESTMENTS (PTY) LTD (10%)
URD BELEGGINGS (PTY) LTD (RED CUM PREFS) (30%)

YABENG INVESTMENT HOLDING CO LTD

ABBREVIATION : YABENG

JSE SHORT CODE : YBG

SECTOR : Financial-Investment Trusts

SHAREHOLDERS

Who Owns Whom's Assessment of the Identity of the Ultimate Controlling Shareholder: BOPHUTATSWANA NAT DEVELOPMENT CORP

SHAREHOLDER	PERCENTAGE 1992	1991
BOP NAT DEVELOPMENT CORPORATION	43.6	45.0
CMB NOM P/L	15.8	—
SEFALANA EMP BENEFITS ORG (SEBO)	10.4	—
EIGHTY ONE MAIN STREET NOM LTD	4.9	2.6
METROPOLITAN LIFE INV BOP P/L	3.7	3.7
SA MUTUAL	2.6	4.0
STD BANK NOM TVL P/L	2.4	1.5
VOLKSKAS OPEN TRUST INV P/L	1.6	1.4
ALTENA MEWS P/L	—	1.7
BOP GOVERNMENT SERV PENS FUND	—	4.9
BOP UNEMPLOYMENT INSURANCE FUND	—	1.5
BOPHUTHATSWANA NAT PROV FUND	—	2.2
SANLAM	—	13.1
TOTAL	85.0	81.4

DIRECTORS :
CLARK PT ,GOULD ID (Managing Director)
KEIKELAME BE ,MAREE JAJ (Chairman),MOJA MAF MS
SEHUME KCAV

REGISTRATION NUMBER : 83/0126 (BOP

REGISTERED OFFICE
1st Floor, Development House
Mmabatho, Bophuthatswana
8681
TEL: 0140-842 466
FAX: 0140-842 484

TRANSFER SECRETARY
Fraser Street Registrars (Pty) Ltd
P O Box 61178, Marshalltown
2107
TEL: 011-491 0911

COMPANY SECRETARY
Bophuthatswana National Development Corp Ltd

NATURE OF BUSINESS
An investment holding company with investments in the equity and loan capital of companies operating primarily in Bophuthatswana.

BANKERS :
Standard Bank of Bophuthatswana Ltd

AUDITORS :
N/A

FAMILIAR BRAND NAMES
N/A

CONTRIBUTION BY ACTIVITY
N/A

YEAR END : March

DIVIDEND : Ords 25c

Dividend No 7	(Ldr)01/06/90	(Pay)18/06/90	Amt(c)16
Dividend No 8	(Ldr)30/05/91	(Pay)17/06/91	Amt(c)21
Dividend No 9	(Ldr)06/07/92	(Pay)07/08/92	Amt(c)24
Dividend No 9	(Ldr)10/07/92	(Pay)14/08/92	Amt(c)24

NUMBER OF EMPLOYEES : 12

CAPITAL STRUCTURE

	AUTHORISED	ISSUED
Ords 25c	80000000	54240395

FINANCIAL STATISTICS (AT FINANCIAL YEAR END)

(Amts in R'000)	1992 Mar	1991 Mar	1990 Mar	1989 Mar	1988
Ord S/H Int	82773	78082	74131	62782	5335
Long Trm Loans	-	-	-	-	2301
Iss Ord Share	51884	51884	51884	48844	14652
Total Liab	13156	11877	9243	5906	4602
Current Liab	13156	11877	9243	5906	2301
Total Assets	95929	89959	83374	68688	9972
Current Assets	3956	12968	10595	7053	2336
Debtors	1411	900	375	282	-
Inventory	-	-	-	-	2336
Oper Profit	-1099	-854	-568	7346	1712
Tax Paid	1208	1105	611	173	80
Prf af Int&Tax	17143	14847	10798	7173	1632
Prf att Ord Sh	17143	14847	10798	7173	1632
Btm Line Earn	17143	14847	10798	7173	1632
Dividend Paid	12452	10896	8301	5617	1099
Mkt Prce(c) YE	510	380	285	150	-
Depreciation	79	104	87	-	-

PER SHARE STATISTICS (CENTS)

Net Asst Val	159.53	150.49	142.88	128.54	36.41
Net Earnings	33.00	28.60	20.80	14.70	-
Dividends	24.00	21.00	16.00	11.50	-
Cash Flow	33.19	28.82	21.00	14.69	11.14

RATIOS AND OTHER INFORMATION

Mrk Cap(R000)	264608	197159	147869	73266	-
Current Ratio	0.30	1.09	1.15	1.19	1.02
Quik/Acid Tst	0.30	1.09	1.15	1.19	-
Debt/Ass Rat	0.14	0.13	0.11	0.09	0.46
L T L Tot Ass	-	-	-	-	0.23
Debt to Eqity	0.16	0.15	0.12	0.09	0.86
Ret on Assets	19.13	17.73	13.68	10.69	17.17
Ret on Equity%	20.71	19.01	14.57	11.43	30.59
Price/Earnings	15.45	13.29	13.70	10.20	-
Divid Cover	1.38	1.36	1.30	1.28	-
Divid Yield	4.71	5.53	5.61	7.67	-

Earning Yield%	6.47	7.53	7.30	9.80	-
NAV % Mrk Pr	31.28	39.60	50.13	85.69	-
Effec Tax Rate	51.89	48.83	52.31	2.36	4.67
Def Interval	-	-	0.00	-	1.41
Sus Grth Rate	5.67	5.06	3.37	2.48	9.99

SUBSIDIARY & ASSOCIATED COMPANIES

AMALGAMATED FURNISHERS (BOP) (PTY) LTD (50%)
BOPHUTHATSWANA BAKERIES (PTY) LTD (50%)
BOPHUTHATSWANA BREWERIES (PTY) LTD (50%)
BOPHUTHATSWANA CHAIN STORES LTD (50%)
CASHBUILD (BOPHUTHATSWANA) (PTY) LTD (46,5%)
CUTHBERTS (BOP) (1990) (PTY) LTD (50%)
DAMMI ASSOCIATES (PTY) LTD (25%)
EDWORKS BOPHUTHATSWANA (PTY) LTD (50%)
ELLE BOPHUTHATSWANA (PTY) LTD (50%)
FAIRWAYS SUPERMARKETS (BOPHUTHATSWANA) L (50%)
FRASERS (BOP) LTD (50%)
FRASERS-TIRISANO (PTY) LTD (50%)
GA FURNITURE BOPHUTHATSWANA (PTY) LTD (45%)
METRO CASH & CARRY (BOPHUTHATSWANA) LTD (45%)
MOGALE MMABATHO BUTCHERIES (PTY) LTD (50%)
MULTISERV (BOP) (PTY) LTD (50%)
SCOTTS RETAIL (BOP) (PTY) LTD (50%)
SHOECORP SHOE STORES (BOPHUTHATSWANA) (P (50%)
SMART CENTRE (BOP) (1988) (PTY) LTD (50%)
UNITED BREWERIES (PTY) LTD (30%)
WANDA-FRASERS (BOP) (PTY) LTD (49,9%)

INVESTMENTS

BOPHUTHATSWANA COMMERCIAL RADIO (PTY) LT (19,5%)
SEFALANA HOLDINGS LIMITED (8.19%)
SUN INTERNATIONAL (BOPHUTHATSWANA) HOLDI (5%)
SUN INTERNATIONAL (BOPHUTHATSWANA) LTD (0.85%)

YORK TIMBER ORGANISATION LTD

ABBREVIATION : YORKCOR

JSE SHORT CODE : YRK

SECTOR : Industrial-Building & Construction

SHAREHOLDERS

Who Owns Whom's Assessment of the Identity of the Ultimate Controlling Shareholder: TUCKER FAMILY

SHAREHOLDER	PERCENTAGE 1992	1991
MAX TUCKER & SON P/L	43.4	45.2
STONEMAX INV P/L	21.7	22.7
NINETEEN SYNDICATE P/L	10.2	10.5
TUCKER E	3.8	4.2
FIRST NAT NOM P/L	2.4	2.7
TUCKER I S D	1.5	1.7
FOUNTAINS VALLEY INV CC	1.2	---
TUCKER S	1.1	1.3
MERCABANK NOM P/L	---	1.2
TOTAL	85.4	89.4

DIRECTORS :
ACKERMAN DP ,MAHANYELE M
TUCKER ISD (Managing Director)
TUCKER S (Chairman & Chief Exec.)
VAN VUUREN MJC DR,WILKINSON RS ,WILSON JR

REGISTRATION NUMBER : 01/04890/06

REGISTERED OFFICE
5th Floor, Yorkcor Park, 86 Watermeyer Str
Val de Grace, Pretoria
0184
TEL: 012-86 9730
FAX: 012-86 9781

TRANSFER SECRETARY
Consolidated Share Registrars Ltd
P O Box 61051, Marshalltown
2107
TEL: 011-492 1620

COMPANY SECRETARY
J G Buhrs

NATURE OF BUSINESS
The holding company of a group with interests in timber, furniture manufacture and realty. The core business of the group is sawmilling. Activities include the manufacture and export of DIY pine furniture, the supply of sawn wood products to general industry, and the marketing of forest products produced outside the group. The group has interests in revenue-producing realty.

BANKERS :
First National Bank of SA Ltd
Standard Bank of SA Ltd

AUDITORS :
KPMG Aiken & Peat

FAMILIAR BRAND NAMES
AGENTIMBER,NEW YORK PINE,NICHOLSON & MULLIN
VELDMAN & TOM

CONTRIBUTION BY ACTIVITY
Sawmilling & Timber Marketing(% Profits) (118.0%)
Furniture Manufacture (-27.0%)
Realty (4.7%)
Warehousing & others (4.3%)

YEAR END : December

DIVIDEND : Ords 5c

Interim No 23	(Ldr)11/08/89	(Pay)01/09/89	Amt(c)5
Final No 24	(Ldr)23/02/90	(Pay)16/03/90	Amt(c)8
Interim No 25	(Ldr)17/08/90	(Pay)12/09/90	Amt(c)6
Final No 26	(Ldr)22/02/91	(Pay)15/03/91	Amt(c)8
Final No 27	(Ldr)21/02/92	(Pay)24/02/92	Amt(c)14

NUMBER OF EMPLOYEES : 1273

CAPITAL STRUCTURE

	AUTHORISED	ISSUED
Ords 5c	10000000	10527856

FINANCIAL STATISTICS (AT FINANCIAL YEAR END)

(Amts in R'000)	1991 Dec	1990 Dec	1989 Dec	1988 Dec	1987 Dec
Ord S/H Int	24849	22387	21868	20016	13673
Long Trm Loans	7000	8362	9333	5082	9812
Iss Ord Share	9976	9439	8960	8960	8960

Total Liab	17146	17522	20087	14313	15727
Current Liab	10146	9160	10754	9231	5915
Total Assets	41064	37392	39438	31812	26883
Intang Assets	931	2517	2517	2517	2517
Current Assets	13197	12035	13540	11539	11547
Debtors	6997	7562	5223	5560	6500
Inventory	5866	4363	3727	2907	1951
Turnover	39792	36913	35999	33760	28474
Oper Profit	2532	2779	5833	5361	1319
Interest Paid	2266	1751	803	775	911
Tax Paid	29	-1129	1249	1794	30
Prf af Int&Tax	237	2157	3781	2792	378
Prf att Ord Sh	237	2157	3770	2774	360
Btm Line Earn	237	749	2865	2801	324
Dividend Paid	265	790	1165	896	90
Mkt Prce(c) YE	170	230	230	850	700
Depreciation	1618	1592	1479	968	960

PER SHARE STATISTICS (CENTS)

Net Asst Val	239.76	210.51	215.97	195.30	124.51
Net Earnings	2.40	22.90	42.10	31.00	4.00
Dividends	14.00	14.00	13.00	10.00	1.00
Cash Flow	18.59	27.16	66.98	46.60	14.73

RATIOS AND OTHER INFORMATION

Mrk Cap(R000)	16959	21710	20608	76160	62720
Current Ratio	1.30	1.31	1.26	1.25	1.95
Quik/Acid Tst	0.72	0.83	0.91	0.94	1.62
A/C Rec T/ovr	5.69	4.88	6.89	6.07	4.38
Tot Ass T/ovr	0.97	0.99	0.91	1.06	1.06
Debt/Ass Rat	0.42	0.47	0.48	0.43	0.58
L T L Tot Ass	0.17	0.22	0.21	0.14	0.36
Debt to Eqity	0.69	0.78	0.86	0.68	1.13
Interest Cover	1.12	1.59	7.26	6.92	1.45
Oper Prof Mrg	6.36	7.53	16.20	15.88	4.63
Net Prof Marg%	0.60	5.84	10.47	8.22	1.26
Ret on Assets	6.17	7.43	14.79	16.85	4.91
Ret on Equity%	0.95	9.64	17.24	13.86	2.63
Price/Earnings	70.83	10.04	5.46	27.42	175.00
Divid Cover	0.17	1.64	3.24	3.10	4.00
Divid Yield	8.24	6.09	5.65	1.18	0.14
Earning Yield%	1.41	9.96	18.30	3.65	0.57
NAV % Mrk Pr	141.03	91.53	93.90	22.98	17.79
Effec Tax Rate	10.90	5.45	9.88	29.68	7.35
Def Interval	4.78	3.96	1.65	1.31	7.61
Sus Grth Rate	-0.11	6.11	11.91	9.38	1.97

SUBSIDIARY & ASSOCIATED COMPANIES

AGENTIMBER (PTY) LTD
BETH WAREHOUSE (PTY) LTD
INLAND REALTY LTD
KATZENELLENBOGEN (PTY) LTD
LONGBOGEN (PTY) LTD
MOUNT BOGEN VIEW (PTY) LTD
PHOENIX DOORS (PTY) LTD
POWER TUNE GARAGE (PTY) LTD
PRETORIA AMALGAMATED TRANSPORT LTD
SILVERBOGEN (PTY) LTD
SONRACH PROPERTIES (PTY) LTD
YORK TIMBERS LTD

INVESTMENTS

FIRST NATIONAL BANK HOLDINGS LTD (1100 SH)

ZAMBIA COPPER INVESTMENTS LTD

ABBREVIATION : Z-C-I

JSE SHORT CODE : ZCI

SECTOR : Metals & Minerals-Copper

SHAREHOLDERS

Who Owns Whom's Assessment of the Identity of the Ultimate Controlling Shareholder:
ANGLO AMERICAN VIA MINORCO

SHAREHOLDER	PERCENTAGE 1992	1991
LONDON CONTROL ACCOUNT	---	96.3
LUXEMBOURG GLOBAL ACCOUNT	---	1.7
TOTAL	---	98.0

DIRECTORS :
FISHER DE ,FRASER HR ,LEA AW ,MUTCH F
OGILVIE THOMPSON J ,PHILLIMORE JRB
RELLY GWH (Chairman

REGISTRATION NUMBER : 70 00023 10

REGISTERED OFFICE
Clarendon House, 2 Church Street
Hamilton, Bermuda

TEL: 09352-4041101
FAX: 09352-40411020

TRANSFER SECRETARY
Consolidated Share Registrars Ltd
P O Box 61051, Marshalltown
2107
TEL: 011-492 1620

COMPANY SECRETARY
N Jordan

NATURE OF BUSINESS
The company has a 27,3% investment in Zambia Consolidated Copper Mines Ltd, a company engaged in base metal mining, especially copper & cobalt, in Zambia. The group also has an investment in Botswana RST Ltd.

BANKERS :
N/A

AUDITORS :
Deloitte & Touche

FAMILIAR BRAND NAMES
N/A

CONTRIBUTION BY ACTIVITY
N/A

YEAR END : June

DIVIDEND :15/00/91

CAPITAL STRUCTURE

	AUTHORISED	ISSUED
Ord BD$0.24 ZCI	130000000	122559866
Deferred BD$0.24	50000	50000

FINANCIAL STATISTICS (AT FINANCIAL YEAR END)

(Amts in $)	1992 Jun	1991 Jun	1990 Jun	1989 Jun	1988 Jun
Ord S/H Int	132451	131735	129693	127238	126134
Long Trm Loans	1668	839	1204	635	1098
Iss Ord Share	122560	122560	122560	122560	122560
Total Liab	3504	2136	2555	1679	2240
Current Liab	1836	1297	1351	1044	1142
Total Assets	135955	133871	132248	128917	128374
Current Assets	28767	27443	25304	22545	20956
Debtors	352	417	295	95	213
Oper Profit	771	1291	1313	-867	1164
Tax Paid	55	73	85	32	36
Prf af Int&Tax	716	2042	2455	1104	1128
Prf att Ord Sh	716	2042	2455	1104	1128
Btm Line Earn	716	2042	2455	1104	1128
Mkt Prce(c) YE	230	335	125	200	130

PER SHARE STATISTICS (CENTS)

Net Asst Val	108.07	107.49	105.82	103.82	102.92
Net Earnings	0.58	1.67	2.00	0.90	0.92
Cash Flow	0.58	1.67	2.00	0.90	0.92

RATIOS AND OTHER INFORMATION

Mrk Cap(R000)	281888	410576	153200	245120	159328
Current Ratio	15.67	21.16	18.73	21.59	18.35
Quik/Acid Tst	15.67	21.16	18.73	21.59	18.35
Debt/Ass Rat	0.01	0.01	0.01	0.01	0.01
Debt to Eqity	0.01	0.01	0.01	0.01	0.01
Ret on Assets	0.57	1.58	1.92	0.88	0.91
Ret on Equity%	0.54	1.55	1.89	0.87	0.89
Price/Earnings	396.55	200.60	62.50	222.22	141.30
Earning Yield%	0.25	0.50	1.60	0.45	0.71
NAV % Mrk Pr	46.99	32.09	84.66	51.91	79.17
Effec Tax Rate	7.13	5.65	6.47	2.82	3.09
Sus Grth Rate	0.54	1.55	1.89	0.87	0.89

SUBSIDIARY & ASSOCIATED COMPANIES

ZAMBIA CONSOLIDATED COPPER MINES LTD (27,3%)

INVESTMENTS

BOTSWANA RST LTD (11.8%)

ZANDPAN GOLD MINING CO LTD

ABBREVIATION : ZANDPAN

JSE SHORT CODE : ZAN

SECTOR : Gold-Klerksdorp

SHAREHOLDERS

Who Owns Whom's Assessment of the Identity of the Ultimate Controlling Shareholder: ANGLOVAAL

SHAREHOLDER	PERCENTAGE 1992	1991
STD BANK NOM TVL P/L	23.0	15.0
FOX STREET NOM P/L	20.4	20.2
ANGLO AMERICAN GOLD INV CO LTD	12.8	12.8
OVERSEAS NOM CO INC	7.6	7.6
FERMAIN NOM LTD	6.3	6.3
FIRST NAT NOM P/L	4.4	2.6
CMB NOM P/L	2.8	—
INDO-CHINA NOM P/L	1.8	—
SA MUTUAL	1.7	3.9
AMOSITE NOM LTD	—	1.3
RESIDENT NOM LTD	—	3.2
SANDTON NOM LTD	—	1.2
SANLAM	—	2.4
TOTAL	80.7	76.4

DIRECTORS :
BARBER DD ,EUSTACE PJ ,FUNSTON BJ ,HERSOV BE LAWRENSON BJ ,MENELL CS ,WILLIAMS KH WILSON RAD (Chairman

REGISTRATION NUMBER : 55/02414/06

REGISTERED OFFICE
Anglovaal House, 56 Main Street
Johannesburg
2001
TEL: 011-634 9111
FAX: 011-634 0038

TRANSFER SECRETARY
Anglovaal Ltd
P O Box 62379, Marshalltown
2107
TEL: 011-634 9111

COMPANY SECRETARY
Anglovaal Ltd/K G Williams

NATURE OF BUSINESS
An investment company whose main investment is in the Hartebeesfontein Gold Mining Co. Ltd

BANKERS :
First National Bank of SA Ltd

AUDITORS :
Ernst & Young

FAMILIAR BRAND NAMES
N/A

CONTRIBUTION BY ACTIVITY
N/A

YEAR END : June

DIVIDEND : Ords 10c

Interim No 37	(Ldr)21/12/90	(Pay)25/01/91	Amt(c)8.25
Final No 38	(Ldr)21/06/91	(Pay)26/07/91	Amt(c)8.25
Interim No 39	(Ldr)20/12/91	(Pay)24/01/92	Amt(c)8.25
Final No 40	(Ldr)19/06/92	(Pay)24/07/92	Amt(c)7
Interim No 41	(Ldr)11/12/92	(Pay)15/01/93	Amt(c)4.75

CAPITAL STRUCTURE

	AUTHORISED	ISSUED
Ords 10c	150000000	130202850

FINANCIAL STATISTICS (AT FINANCIAL YEAR END)

(Amts in R'000)	1992 Jun	1991 Jun	1990 Jun	1989 Jun	1988 Jun
Ord S/H Int	22086	21719	21731	21822	21844
Iss Ord Share	130203	130203	130203	130203	130203
Total Liab	9900	11433	15691	22725	20015
Current Liab	9900	11433	15691	22725	20015
Total Assets	31986	33152	37422	44547	41859
Current Assets	11086	12252	16522	23647	20959
Debtors	194	28	17	11	5
Turnover	21102	22260	29345	40140	34126
Oper Profit	-763	-708	-555	-506	33545
Prf af Int&Tax	20223	21471	28553	39429	33545
Prf att Ord Sh	20223	21471	28553	39429	33545
Btm Line Earn	20223	21471	28553	39429	33545
Dividend Paid	19856	21483	28644	39451	33331
Mkt Prce(c) YE	243	335	405	480	365

PER SHARE STATISTICS (CENTS)

Net Asst Val	16.96	16.68	16.69	16.76	16.78
Net Earnings	15.50	16.50	21.90	30.30	25.80
Dividends	15.25	16.50	22.00	30.30	25.60
Cash Flow	15.53	16.49	21.93	30.28	25.76

RATIOS AND OTHER INFORMATION

Mrk Cap(R000)	316393	436180	527322	624974	475241
Current Ratio	1.12	1.07	1.05	1.04	1.05
Quik/Acid Tst	1.12	1.07	1.05	1.04	1.05
A/C Rec T/ovr	108.77	795.00	1726.18	3649.09	6825.20
Tot Ass T/ovr	0.66	0.67	0.78	0.90	0.82
Debt/Ass Rat	0.31	0.34	0.42	0.51	0.48
Debt to Eqity	0.45	0.53	0.72	1.04	0.92
Oper Prof Mrg	-3.62	-3.18	-1.89	-1.26	98.30
Net Prof Marg%	95.83	96.46	97.30	98.23	98.30
Ret on Assets	63.22	64.77	76.30	88.51	80.14
Ret on Equity%	91.56	98.86	131.39	180.68	153.57
Price/Earnings	15.68	20.30	18.49	15.84	14.15
Divid Cover	1.02	1.00	1.00	1.00	1.01
Divid Yield	6.28	4.93	5.43	6.31	7.01
Earning Yield%	6.38	4.93	5.41	6.31	7.07
NAV % Mrk Pr	6.98	4.98	4.12	3.49	4.60
Sus Grth Rate	1.66	-0.06	-0.42	-0.10	0.98

SUBSIDIARY & ASSOCIATED COMPANIES

None

INVESTMENTS

ANGLO AMERICAN CORP. OF S.A. LTD (1800 SH)
DOORNFONTEIN GOLD MINING CO. LTD (5500 SH)
EASTERN TRANSVAAL CONSOLIDATED MINES LTD (224000SH)
FREE STATE CONSOLIDATED MINES LTD (1900 SH)
HARTEBEESTFONTEIN GOLD MINING CO LTD (19,6%)
LORAINE GOLD MINES LTD (2500 SH)
MIDDLE WITWATERSRAND (WESTERN AREAS) LTD (245000 SH)
SOUTHVAAL HOLDINGS LTD (1800 SH)
TARGET EXPLORATION COMPANY LTD (2500 SH)
VAAL REEFS EXPLORATION & MINING CO LTD (1000 SH)
VILLAGE MAIN REEF GOLD MINING CO (1934) (10000 SH)

ZECO LTD

ABBREVIATION : ZECO

SECTOR : Zimbabwe Stock Exchange

SHAREHOLDERS

Who Owns Whom's Assessment of the Identity of the Ultimate Controlling Shareholder:
MEIKLES CONSOLIDATED / JOHNSON & FLETCHE

DIRECTORS :
BUXTON RC ,CAMERON MC ,MOXON JRT (Chairman)
STEPHENS DE ,VENABLES EL

REGISTERED OFFICE
Josiah Chinamano Road, Bulawayo
Zimbabwe

TEL: 78931
FAX: 72259

TRANSFER SECRETARY
N/A

COMPANY SECRETARY
M A J Da Silva

NATURE OF BUSINESS
Incorporated in Zimbabwe, ZECO's main business con sists of the manufacture for local and export mar kets of railway rolling stock, structural engin-eering,erection contracting,steam,diesel and all electric locomotive rehabilitation and assembly.

BANKERS :
Barclays Bank of Zimbabwe Ltd

AUDITORS :
Deloitte & Touche

FAMILIAR BRAND NAMES
N/A

CONTRIBUTION BY ACTIVITY
N/A

YEAR END : February

DIVIDEND : Ords Z$0,50
Dividend (Ldr)20/05/92 (Pay)10/06/92 Amt(c)5.6

CAPITAL STRUCTURE

	AUTHORISED	ISSUED
Ords Z$0,50	70000000	59847408

FINANCIAL STATISTICS (AT FINANCIAL YEAR END)

(Amts in Z$)	1992 Feb	1991 Feb
Ord S/H Int	64096	54908
Iss Ord Share	59847	59847
Total Liab	62014	32163
Current Liab	62014	32163
Total Assets	126110	87071
Current Assets	85159	53664
Debtors	54293	41374
Inventory	30432	11708
Turnover	61447	74623
Oper Profit	8234	4443
Interest Paid	1562	612
Prf af Int&Tax	6698	3887
Prf att Ord Sh	6698	3887
Btm Line Earn	6698	3887
Dividend Paid	3351	1915
Depreciation	1499	767

PER SHARE STATISTICS (CENTS)

Net Asst Val	107.10	91.75
Net Earnings	11.20	9.50
Dividends	5.60	3.20
Cash Flow	13.70	7.78

RATIOS AND OTHER INFORMATION

Current Ratio	1.37	1.67
Quik/Acid Tst	0.88	1.30
A/C Rec T/ovr	1.13	1.80
Tot Ass T/ovr	0.49	0.86
Debt/Ass Rat	0.49	0.37
Debt to Eqity	0.97	0.59
Interest Cover	5.27	7.26
Oper Prof Mrg	13.40	5.95
Net Prof Marg%	10.90	5.21
Ret on Assets	6.55	5.17
Ret on Equity%	10.45	7.08
Divid Cover	2.00	2.97
Def Interval	2.74	1.48
Sus Grth Rate	5.22	3.59

SUBSIDIARY & ASSOCIATED COMPANIES

None

INVESTMENTS

None

ZIMBABWE ALLOYS LTD

ABBREVIATION : ZIMALLOYS

SECTOR : Zimbabwe Stock Exchange

SHAREHOLDERS

Who Owns Whom's Assessment of the Identity of the Ultimate Controlling Shareholder: ANGLO AMERICAN / INSTITUTIONS

SHAREHOLDER	PERCENTAGE 1992	1991
SECURITY NOM LTD	53.1	---
J B AFRICAN INV LTD	13.2	---
OLD MUTUAL INV CORP (PVT) LTD	5.3	---
MONOMATAPA DEVELOPMENT CO PVT LTD	3.2	---
PECHINEY	2.3	---
RIO TINTO ZIMBABWE LTD	2.1	---
FIRST NOM PVT LTD	1.6	---
ZIMBABWE ALLOYS LTD EMPL SHARE PART TRUS	1.4	---
FIDELITY LIFE ASSURE OF ZIM PVT LTD	1.3	---
TOTAL	83.3	---

DIRECTORS :
CALVER AH ,LANDER RP (Chairman),MASUNDA MA
NGUGAMA EG (Financial Director),PARKE CCW
PIENAAR SP ,RAMSAY AG ,SCHOFIELD CJL
SMART WK (Managing Director),TAYLOR JR
WISHART AB

REGISTERED OFFICE
70 Samora Machel Avenue, Harare C4
Zimbabwe

TEL: 704461
FAX: TELEX:703734

TRANSFER SECRETARY
First Transfer Secretaries (Pvt) Ltd
P O Box 437, Bulawayo
Zimbabwe

TEL: 092634 - 702905

COMPANY SECRETARY
Anglo American Corporation Sevices

NATURE OF BUSINESS
ZIMBABWE ALLOYS,which is incorporated in Zimbabwe, has as its main business the mining,refining and export of chrome ores, and the production and export of ferro-alloys.

BANKERS :
N/A

AUDITORS :
Deloitte & Touche

FAMILIAR BRAND NAMES
N/A

CONTRIBUTION BY ACTIVITY
N/A

YEAR END : March

DIVIDEND :Ords Z$1

Dividend	(Ldr)22/11/91	(Pay)16/12/91	Amt(c)15
Dividend	(Ldr)22/06/92	(Pay)20/07/92	Amt(c)11

CAPITAL STRUCTURE

	AUTHORISED	ISSUED
Ords Z$1	63000000	60968180

FINANCIAL STATISTICS (AT FINANCIAL YEAR END)

(Amts in Z$)	1992 Mar	1991 Mar
Ord S/H Int	367452	224086
Long Trm Loans	5795	26545
Iss Ord Share	60968	43394
Total Liab	117149	105711
Current Liab	111354	79166
Total Assets	484601	329797
Current Assets	250464	165786
Debtors	74776	45012
Inventory	175552	119065
Turnover	316735	199857
Oper Profit	95366	50164
Interest Paid	9037	4753
Tax Paid	27273	15711
Prf af Int&Tax	59056	29700
Prf att Ord Sh	59056	29700
Btm Line Earn	49056	19700
Dividend Paid	15819	10388
Depreciation	3875	1686

PER SHARE STATISTICS (CENTS)

Net Asst Val	602.70	516.40
Net Earnings	96.80	68.10
Dividends	25.95	23.94

Cash Flow	103.22	72.33

RATIOS AND OTHER INFORMATION

Current Ratio	2.25	2.09
Quik/Acid Tst	0.67	0.59
A/C Rec T/ovr	4.24	4.44
Tot Ass T/ovr	0.65	0.61
Debt/Ass Rat	0.24	0.32
L T L Tot Ass	0.01	0.08
Debt to Eqity	0.32	0.47
Interest Cover	10.55	10.55
Oper Prof Mrg	30.11	25.10
Net Prof Marg%	18.65	14.86
Ret on Assets	19.68	15.21
Ret on Equity%	16.07	13.25
Divid Cover	3.73	2.84
Effec Tax Rate	31.59	34.65
Def Interval	0.53	1.73
Sus Grth Rate	11.77	8.62

SUBSIDIARY & ASSOCIATED COMPANIES

ZIMBABWE ALLOYS MINES LIMITED

INVESTMENTS

None

ZIMBABWE BANKING CORPORATION LTD

ABBREVIATION : ZIMBANK

SECTOR : Zimbabwe Stock Exchange

SHAREHOLDERS

Who Owns Whom's Assessment of the Identity of the Ultimate Controlling Shareholder:
GOVERNMENT OF ZIMBABWE

SHAREHOLDER	PERCENTAGE 1992	1991
GOVERNMENT OF ZIMBABWE	58.8	---
OLD MUTUAL INV CORP (PVT) LTD	14.5	---
ZIMBANK GROUP STAFF TRUST	3.8	---
FIRST MUTUAL LIFE ASSURE SOC OF ZIM	2.6	---
NAT RAILWAYS OF ZIM CONTR PENS FUND	2.3	---
FIDELITY LIFE ASSURE OF ZIM PVT LTD	2.1	---
TOTAL	84.1	---

DIRECTORS :
BUTLER ME ,HYWOOD RH ,MUNJANGANJA LEV DR
MUPAWAENDA AC MRS,NDUDZO M ,NHAU AF
PARKE RE (Chairman),PICHANICK ALA ,SAGONDA DMK
SIBANDA SKM
TSUMBA LL DR (Chief Executive & M.D.),]ESAT EH

REGISTERED OFFICE
Zimbank House, 46 Speke Avenue
Harare, Zimbabwe

TEL: 735011
FAX: 735600

TRANSFER SECRETARY
Zimbabwe Banking Corporation Ltd
P O Box 3198, Harare
Zimbabwe

TEL: 092634-735011

COMPANY SECRETARY
I G Cormack

NATURE OF BUSINESS
Incorporated in Zimbabwe,ZIMBABWE BANKING CORPORATION,with some 58% of its shares held by government,offers a full range of banking services, including merchant banking through its subsidiary, SYFRETS MERCHANT BANK.Other subsidiary companies include WILLIS CORROON, FREIGHT INTERNATIONAL and TRAVEL INTERNATIONAL.

BANKERS :
N/A

AUDITORS :
Deloitte & Touche

FAMILIAR BRAND NAMES
N/A

CONTRIBUTION BY ACTIVITY
N/A

YEAR END : December

DIVIDEND : Ords Z$1

Dividend	(Ldr)27/12/91	(Pay)07/01/92	Amt(c)31.5
Dividend	(Ldr)08/05/92	(Pay)19/05/92	Amt(c)14.5

CAPITAL STRUCTURE

	AUTHORISED	ISSUED
Ords Z$1	10000000	6000000

FINANCIAL STATISTICS (AT FINANCIAL YEAR END)

(Amts in Z$)	1991 Sep	1990 Sep
Ord S/H Int	109974	87464
Iss Ord Share	16361	16361
Total Liab	3609823	2120832
Current Liab	3609823	2120832
Total Assets	3719797	2208296
Current Assets	3664071	2171409
Debtors	3216616	1802083
Oper Profit	26416	19502
Prf af Int&Tax	26416	19502
Prf att Ord Sh	26416	19502
Btm Line Earn	26416	19502
Dividend Paid	7444	5972

PER SHARE STATISTICS (CENTS)

Net Asst Val	672.17	534.59
Net Earnings	149.91	111.18
Dividends	45.50	36.50
Cash Flow	161.46	119.20

RATIOS AND OTHER INFORMATION

Current Ratio	1.02	1.02
Quik/Acid Tst	1.02	1.02
Debt/Ass Rat	0.97	0.96
Debt to Eqity	32.82	24.25
Ret on Assets	0.71	0.88

Ret on Equity%	24.02	22.30
Divid Cover	3.29	3.05
Def Interval	43.68	34.79
Sus Grth Rate	17.25	15.47

SUBSIDIARY & ASSOCIATED COMPANIES

DATA CENTRE (PVT) LTD
SCOTFIN LIMITED
SYFRETS MERCHANT BANK LIMITED
SYFRETS TRUST & EXECUTORS LIMITED
ZIMBANK BOTSWANA LIMITED

INVESTMENTS

None

ZIMBABWE NEWSPAPERS (1980) LTD

ABBREVIATION : ZIM NEWS

SECTOR : Zimbabwe Stock Exchange

SHAREHOLDERS

Who Owns Whom's Assessment of the Identity of the Ultimate Controlling Shareholder: ZIMBABWE MASS MEDIA TRUST

DIRECTORS :
CAPEL PS ,KACHINGWE S MRS,MCNAUGHT GW
MIDZI DT (Managing Director)
MKUSHI HP (Vice Chairman),MUTAMBIRWA R
MUVUTI D ,RAE DA ,SADZA DM DR (Chairman),TODD J
ZAMCHIYA DM

REGISTERED OFFICE
6th Floor, Herald House
George Silunkika Avenue, Harare

TEL: 795771
FAX: 791311

TRANSFER SECRETARY
N/A

COMPANY SECRETARY
L Charidza

NATURE OF BUSINESS
Incorporated in Zimbabwe, ZIMBABWE NEWSPAPERS pro duces and range of dailies, Sunday and Weekly news papers and also publishes books,magazines,trade directories,dairies,calenders and the Zimbabwe telephone and telex dictionaries.

BANKERS :
Standard Chartered Bank Zimbabwe Ltd

AUDITORS :
Deloitte & Touche

FAMILIAR BRAND NAMES
N/A

CONTRIBUTION BY ACTIVITY
N/A

YEAR END : December

DIVIDEND : Ords Z$1

Dividend	(Ldr)24/10/91	(Pay)29/11/91	Amt(c)3.33
Dividend	(Ldr)22/05/92	(Pay)29/06/92	Amt(c)4

CAPITAL STRUCTURE

	AUTHORISED	ISSUED
Ords Z$1	14400000	4800000

FINANCIAL STATISTICS (AT FINANCIAL YEAR END)

(Amts in Z$)	1991 Dec	1990 Dec
Ord S/H Int	29774	25551
Long Trm Loans	33226	18228
Iss Ord Share	4800	4800
Total Liab	69446	51135
Current Liab	36220	32907
Total Assets	99220	76686
Current Assets	45067	33755
Debtors	26758	21086
Inventory	16629	10112
Turnover	138445	103581
Oper Profit	11835	12905
Interest Paid	3146	1351
Tax Paid	3871	5734
Prf af Int&Tax	4818	5820
Prf att Ord Sh	4894	5924
Btm Line Earn	4894	5924
Dividend Paid	1056	1440
Depreciation	4653	3244

PER SHARE STATISTICS (CENTS)

Net Asst Val	620.29	532.31
Net Earnings	102.00	131.00
Dividends	44.00	60.00
Cash Flow	257.27	237.08

RATIOS AND OTHER INFORMATION

Current Ratio	1.24	1.03
Quik/Acid Tst	0.79	0.72
A/C Rec T/ovr	5.17	4.91
Tot Ass T/ovr	1.40	1.35
Debt/Ass Rat	0.56	0.52
L T L Tot Ass	0.20	0.10
Debt to Eqity	1.87	1.57
Interest Cover	3.76	9.55
Oper Prof Mrg	8.55	12.46
Net Prof Marg%	3.53	5.72
Ret on Assets	12.00	16.96
Ret on Equity%	16.44	23.19
Divid Cover	2.32	2.18
Effec Tax Rate	10.91	29.01
Def Interval	2.84	1.80
Sus Grth Rate	12.89	17.55

SUBSIDIARY & ASSOCIATED COMPANIES

COLORSCAN (PVT) LTD (40%)
RICHARD STRATHMORE (PVT) LTD

INVESTMENTS

None

ZIMBABWE SPINNERS AND WEAVERS LTD

ABBREVIATION : ZIMSPIN

SECTOR : Zimbabwe Stock Exchange

SHAREHOLDERS

Who Owns Whom's Assessment of the Identity of the Ultimate Controlling Shareholder: INSTITUTIONS

SHAREHOLDER	PERCENTAGE 1992	1991
STD CHART MERCHANT BANK ZIM NOM PVT LTD	84.3	---
GOULDSBURY ENTERPRISES PVT LTD	4.6	---
KNIGHT S M G	1.5	---
KNIGHT E R P	1.4	---
OLD MUTUAL INV CORP (PVT) LTD	1.2	---
TOTAL	92.9	---

DIRECTORS :
BADAT FI ,DORWARD PD (Chairman),KNIGHT SMG
MABODOKO NJ ,TSINGO KS

REGISTERED OFFICE
Gordon Buildings, 23,George Silundika Avenue
Harare, Zimbabwe

TEL: 723998
FAX: 791699

TRANSFER SECRETARY
First Transfer Secretaries (Pvt) Ltd
P O Box 437, Bulawayo
Zimbabwe

TEL: 092634 - 702905

COMPANY SECRETARY
K S Tsingo

NATURE OF BUSINESS
ZIMBABWE SPINNERS,Incorporated in Zimbabwe,has as its main activities:spinning,weaving,bleaching, finishing,the shrinking and printing of cotton, cotton/polyester piece goods and the manufacture of mosquito netting, bed sheeting and interlinings

BANKERS :
Standard Chartered Bank Zimbabwe Ltd
First Merchant Bank of Zimbabwe Ltd
Zimbabwe Banking Corporation Ltd

AUDITORS :
Price Waterhouse Meyernel

FAMILIAR BRAND NAMES
N/A

CONTRIBUTION BY ACTIVITY
N/A

YEAR END : December

DIVIDEND : Ords Z$0,50

Dividend	(Ldr)06/03/92	(Pay)20/03/92	Amt(c)8.5
Dividend	(Ldr)21/08/92	(Pay)11/09/92	Amt(c)3.5

CAPITAL STRUCTURE

	AUTHORISED	ISSUED
Ords Z$0,50	76000000	67580414
"A" Ords Z$0,10	20000000	17042720
"A" Red Cum Prefs Z$0,10	1000000	150000
"B" Red Cum Prefs 10c	5000000	2000000
Conv Red Cum Prefs 10c	11000000	10674700

FINANCIAL STATISTICS (AT FINANCIAL YEAR END)

(Amts in Z$)	1991 Dec	1990 Dec
Ord S/H Int	118583	86135
Long Trm Loans	32702	23984
Iss Ord Share	84623	42312
Total Liab	62070	56445
Current Liab	29368	32461
Total Assets	180653	142580
Current Assets	56845	41324
Debtors	37038	29599
Inventory	19807	10700
Turnover	96033	68056
Oper Profit	39871	23048
Interest Paid	5272	2775
Prf af Int&Tax	34599	20273
Prf att Ord Sh	34240	20015
Btm Line Earn	34240	20015
Dividend Paid	10155	6446
Depreciation	10737	6426

PER SHARE STATISTICS (CENTS)

Net Asst Val	140.13	203.57
Net Earnings	40.50	23.70
Dividends	12.00	8.00
Cash Flow	53.15	31.25

RATIOS AND OTHER INFORMATION

Current Ratio	1.94	1.27
Quik/Acid Tst	1.26	0.94
A/C Rec T/ovr	2.59	2.30
Tot Ass T/ovr	0.53	0.48
Debt/Ass Rat	0.34	0.39
L T L Tot Ass	0.17	0.17
Debt to Eqity	0.51	0.65
Interest Cover	7.56	8.31
Oper Prof Mrg	41.52	33.87
Net Prof Marg%	35.65	29.41
Ret on Assets	22.07	16.16
Ret on Equity%	28.87	23.24
Divid Cover	3.38	2.96
Def Interval	0.91	0.98
Sus Grth Rate	20.31	15.75

SUBSIDIARY & ASSOCIATED COMPANIES

AGVEST TIMBER HOLDINGS (PVT) LTD
BLUEBERRY PRINTS (PVT) LTD
COULON (PTY) LTD
GLENDALE SPINNERS MANAGEMENT (PVT) LTD
KADOMA NON-WOVEN (PVT) LTD
KADOMA TEXTILES MANAGEMENT (PVT) LTD
MARTIN FIELD SPINNERS (PVT) LTD
PROTEX CLOTHING (PVT) LTD
QUALITY PROPERTIES (PVT) LTD
RICHARD STRATHMORE (PVT) LTD
Z.S.W. ADMINISTRATION (PVT) LTD

INVESTMENTS

None

ZIMBABWE SUGAR REFINERS LTD

ABBREVIATION : ZSR

SECTOR : Zimbabwe Stock Exchange

SHAREHOLDERS

Who Owns Whom's Assessment of the Identity of the Ultimate Controlling Shareholder:
TATE AND LYLE HOLDINGS LTD (UK)

SHAREHOLDER	PERCENTAGE 1992	1991
TATE & LYLE HOLDINGS LTD	50.1	---
SECURITY NOM LTD	4.9	---
TANVEST PVT LTD	3.4	---
LEKATERA ESTATES PVT LTD	3.4	---
ABRY INV PVT LTD	3.0	---
TURNER R	2.9	---
DIANCANA FINANCE CORP PVT LTD	2.7	---
ZIMNAT LIFE ASSURE CO LTD	2.6	---
NAT RAILWAYS OF ZIM CONTR PENS FUND	2.4	---
E S C STAFF PENS FUND	2.3	---
ZIMBABWE ASSETS INV CO LTD	1.3	---
SAMUEL RABINOWITZ TRUST & INV CO PVT LTD	1.3	---
TOTAL	80.1	---

DIRECTORS :
FRYER CWB (Chairman),GIFFORD S ,HINDE GHD
MIRSKY PJ
MUSESENGWA SH (Chief Executive & M.D.),VAMBE LC
WHALEY WR

REGISTERED OFFICE
Cnr Nuffield & Charing Cross, Roads
Workington, Harare

TEL: 66701
FAX: 68906

TRANSFER SECRETARY
First Transfer Secretaries (Pvt) Ltd
P O Box 437, Bulawayo
Zimbabwe

TEL: 092634 - 702905

COMPANY SECRETARY
G W Hooper

NATURE OF BUSINESS
Sugar refining, packaging and distribution, and the production of speciality sugars such as liquid sugar and caramel.The company is also engaged in the recycling of waste plastic, the production of bone charcoal and wholesale trading.

BANKERS :
Zimbabwe Banking Corporation Ltd
Merchant Bank of Central Africa

AUDITORS :
Coopers & Lybrand

FAMILIAR BRAND NAMES
GOLD STAR

CONTRIBUTION BY ACTIVITY
N/A

YEAR END : March

DIVIDEND :15/07/91 and 15/12/91

NUMBER OF EMPLOYEES : 1650

CAPITAL STRUCTURE

	AUTHORISED	ISSUED
Ords 50c	28000000	21150000

FINANCIAL STATISTICS (AT FINANCIAL YEAR END)

(Amts in Zim$)	1992 Mar	1991 Mar	1990 Mar	1989 Mar	1988 Mar
Ord S/H Int	55286	47119	38926	19717	19641
Long Trm Loans	833	575	295	206	94
Iss Ord Share	21150	21150	3525	3525	3525
Total Liab	76707	39409	33922	19096	15101
Current Liab	75874	38834	33627	18890	15007
Total Assets	131993	86528	72848	38813	34742
Current Assets	77798	35399	27730	16241	13941
Debtors	21164	11478	7093	3610	3545
Inventory	38270	21743	17690	11464	9361
Turnover	371103	288879	184677	140059	129730
Oper Profit	22635	14907	1821	147	1950
Interest Paid	1188	2320	2106	-	-
Tax Paid	10600	3284	37	-	1002
Prf af Int&Tax	11657	9434	-228	147	948
Prf att Ord Sh	11657	9434	-228	147	948
Btm Line Earn	11657	9434	-228	147	948
Dividend Paid	3490	3067	212	71	458
Mkt Prce(c) YE	-	115	125	115	200
Depreciation	4721	3869	4400	2263	2592

PER SHARE STATISTICS (CENTS)

Net Asst Val	261.40	222.78	1104.28	559.35	557.19
Net Earnings	55.10	44.60	-1.10	4.00	26.90
Dividends	16.50	14.50	1.00	2.00	13.00
Cash Flow	77.44	62.90	118.35	68.37	101.02

RATIOS AND OTHER INFORMATION

Mrk Cap(R000)	-	24323	4406	4054	7050
Current Ratio	1.03	0.91	0.82	0.86	0.93
Quik/Acid Tst	0.52	0.35	0.30	0.25	0.31
A/C Rec T/ovr	17.53	25.17	26.04	38.80	36.60
Tot Ass T/ovr	2.81	3.34	2.54	3.61	3.73
Debt/Ass Rat	0.58	0.46	0.47	0.49	0.43
L T L Tot Ass	0.01	0.01	0.00	0.01	0.00
Debt to Eqity	1.39	0.84	0.87	0.97	0.77
Interest Cover	19.05	6.43	0.86	-	-
Oper Prof Mrg	6.10	5.16	0.99	0.10	1.50
Net Prof Marg%	3.14	3.27	-0.12	0.10	0.73
Ret on Assets	17.76	17.38	2.63	0.38	5.61
Ret on Equity%	21.08	20.02	-0.59	0.75	4.83
Price/Earnings	-	2.58	-113.64	28.75	7.43
Divid Cover	3.34	3.08	-1.10	2.00	2.07
Divid Yield	-	12.61	0.80	1.74	6.50
Earning Yield%	-	38.78	-0.88	3.48	13.45
NAV % Mrk Pr	-	193.73	883.43	486.39	278.60
Effec Tax Rate	47.63	25.82	-19.37	-	50.31
Def Interval	0.60	0.42	4.81	3.30	0.95
Sus Grth Rate	14.77	13.51	-1.13	0.39	2.49

SUBSIDIARY & ASSOCIATED COMPANIES

GILLETI (PVT) LTD
GRANT CHEMICALS (PVT) LTD
POLYFILM (PVT) LTD
QUALITY FURNITURE WORKS (PVT) LTD
QUALITY PROPERTIES (PVT) LTD
SUGAR DISTRIBUTORS (PVT) LTD

INVESTMENTS

None

ZIMBABWE SUN LTD

ABBREVIATION : ZIM SUN

SECTOR : Zimbabwe Stock Exchange

SHAREHOLDERS

Who Owns Whom's Assessment of the Identity of the Ultimate Controlling Shareholder:
DELTA CORPORATION LTD

SHAREHOLDER	PERCENTAGE 1992	1991
DELTA CORP LTD	64.0	---
OLD MUTUAL INV CORP (PVT) LTD	13.1	---
FIRST MUTUAL LIFE ASSURE SOC OF ZIM	2.7	---
ZIM SUN EMPL SHARE PART CO PVT LTD	1.5	---
SOUTHAMPTON ASSURE CO ZIM LTD	1.2	---
TOTAL	82.5	---

DIRECTORS :
BLOCH EW ,CHIURA ED (Chairman),MASUNDA MA
MUPAWOSE RM ,ROONEY JP (Deputy Chairman)
WRIGHT AT (Managing Director

REGISTERED OFFICE
Sable House, Northridge Close
Harare, Zimbabwe

TEL: 737944
FAX: 734739

TRANSFER SECRETARY
First Transfer Secretaries (Pvt) Ltd
P O Box 437, Bulawayo
Zimbabwe

TEL: 092634 - 702905

COMPANY SECRETARY
H D Gaitskell

NATURE OF BUSINESS
ZIMBABWE SUN, a subsidiary of DELTA CORPORATION,is the largest hotel and leisure orientated company in the country,owning and controlling a number of hotels, casinos,safari camps and tourist-related operations.

BANKERS :
N/A

AUDITORS :
Price Waterhouse Meyernel

FAMILIAR BRAND NAMES
N/A

CONTRIBUTION BY ACTIVITY
N/A

YEAR END : March

DIVIDEND : Ords Z$1
Dividend (Ldr)22/11/91 (Pay)20/12/91 Amt(c)6.5
Dividend (Ldr)22/05/92 (Pay)12/06/92 Amt(c)8.01

CAPITAL STRUCTURE

	AUTHORISED	ISSUED
Ords Z$1	250000000	203000000

FINANCIAL STATISTICS (AT FINANCIAL YEAR END)

(Amts in Z$)	1992 Mar	1991 Mar
Ord S/H Int	264405	240277
Long Trm Loans	133419	27149
Iss Ord Share	203000	203000
Total Liab	183691	134094
Current Liab	50272	106945
Total Assets	448096	374371
Current Assets	60648	128913
Debtors	38929	15451
Inventory	12000	5847
Turnover	197349	130405
Oper Profit	45524	26303
Interest Paid	9694	3039
Tax Paid	980	-
Prf af Int&Tax	53996	32166
Prf att Ord Sh	53583	31842
Btm Line Earn	53583	31842
Dividend Paid	29455	17499
Depreciation	8196	5052

PER SHARE STATISTICS (CENTS)

Net Asst Val	130.25	118.36
Net Earnings	26.40	17.72
Dividends	14.51	8.62
Cash Flow	30.43	18.17

RATIOS AND OTHER INFORMATION

Current Ratio	1.21	1.21
Quik/Acid Tst	0.97	1.15
A/C Rec T/ovr	5.07	8.44
Tot Ass T/ovr	0.44	0.35
Debt/Ass Rat	0.40	0.35
L T L Tot Ass	0.29	0.06
Debt to Eqity	0.68	0.54
Interest Cover	4.70	8.66
Oper Prof Mrg	23.07	20.17
Net Prof Marg%	27.15	24.42
Ret on Assets	14.43	9.40
Ret on Equity%	20.27	13.25
Divid Cover	1.82	2.06
Effec Tax Rate	1.78	-
Def Interval	2.20	2.54
Sus Grth Rate	9.13	5.97

SUBSIDIARY & ASSOCIATED COMPANIES

MAKASA SUN (PRIVATE) LTD
TOUCH THE WILD (PRIVATE) LTD (50%)

INVESTMENTS

None

ZIMPLOW LTD

ABBREVIATION : ZIMPLOW

SECTOR : Zimbabwe Stock Exchange

SHAREHOLDERS

Who Owns Whom's Assessment of the Identity of the Ultimate Controlling Shareholder: ROTHMANS OF PALL MALL (ZIMB) LTD

DIRECTORS :
COLE RH ,DAY B (Chairman),LYNTON-EDWARDS MA
MAPONDERA HE ,THOMPSON AC

REGISTERED OFFICE
Steelworks Road, Heavy Industrial Sites
Bulawayo

TEL: 71363

TRANSFER SECRETARY
N/A

COMPANY SECRETARY
A J Crosly

BANKERS :
Barclays Bank of Zimbabwe Ltd

AUDITORS :
KPMG Peat Marwick

FAMILIAR BRAND NAMES
N/A

CONTRIBUTION BY ACTIVITY
N/A

YEAR END : March

DIVIDEND :Ords Z$0,50

Dividend	(Ldr)22/11/91	(Pay)10/12/91	Amt(c)2
Dividend	(Ldr)17/07/92	(Pay)31/07/92	Amt(c)3

CAPITAL STRUCTURE

	AUTHORISED	ISSUED
Ords Z$0,50	12000000	11550000

FINANCIAL STATISTICS (AT FINANCIAL YEAR END)

(Amts in Z$)	1992 Mar	1991 Mar
Ord S/H Int	12042	9897
Long Trm Loans	1235	1309
Iss Ord Share	11550	2310
Total Liab	5281	5055
Current Liab	4046	3746
Total Assets	17323	14952
Current Assets	9825	7688
Debtors	2331	1831
Inventory	7494	5857
Turnover	15060	10612
Oper Profit	4986	2380
Interest Paid	230	142
Tax Paid	2033	1072
Prf af Int&Tax	2723	1166
Prf att Ord Sh	2723	1166
Btm Line Earn	2723	1166
Dividend Paid	578	346
Depreciation	759	679

PER SHARE STATISTICS (CENTS)

Net Asst Val	104.26	428.44
Net Earnings	23.60	10.10
Dividends	5.00	3.00
Cash Flow	30.13	82.99

RATIOS AND OTHER INFORMATION

Current Ratio	2.43	2.05
Quik/Acid Tst	0.58	0.49
A/C Rec T/ovr	6.46	5.80
Tot Ass T/ovr	0.87	0.71
Debt/Ass Rat	0.23	0.25
Debt to Eqity	0.34	0.38
Interest Cover	21.68	16.76
Oper Prof Mrg	33.11	22.43
Net Prof Marg%	18.08	10.99
Ret on Assets	28.78	15.92
Ret on Equity%	22.61	11.78
Divid Cover	4.72	3.37
Effec Tax Rate	44.30	48.08
Def Interval	0.25	0.59
Sus Grth Rate	17.81	8.29

SUBSIDIARY & ASSOCIATED COMPANIES

POLYFILM (PVT) LTD

INVESTMENTS

None

PART TWO

M c G R E G O R ' S

WHO OWNS WHOM

INDEXES

INDEX OF SHAREHOLDERS OF LISTED COMPANIES

KINDLY REFER TO SCHEDULE OF COMPANY ABBREVIATIONS FOR IDENTIFICATION OF ABBREVIATIONS

THE NAMES PRINTED IN FULL HAVE 1% OR MORE OF THE ISSUED ORDINARY SHARE CAPITAL OF THE COMPANY ABBREVIATED

A

A BEAUMONT INV P/L	DISPTCH	16.4
A JAFFE COMMERCIAL HOLDINGS P/L	CURFIN	4.3
A JAFFE INDUSTRIAL HOLDINGS P/L	CURFIN	7.1
A W & J I INV (PVT) LTD	FSI ZIM	3.0
A Y INV 280 P/L	JASCO	3.1
AARON SEARLL INV & HOLDING P/L	SEARCON	42.2
ABACUS INDUSTRIAL HOLDINGS LTD	CERAMIC	59.5
ABBEY (FNX) HOLDINGS LTD	FENIX	12.2
ABBEY (PROPCOR) HOLDINGS LTD	PROPCOR	74.0
ABBEY CONTROLLING INTEREST P/L	ABBEY	33.1
ABBEY HOLDINGS LTD	FENIX	66.7
ABBEY TRADING LTD	DEBNAIR	65.9
ABBEY TRADING LTD	FENIX	4.2
ABBOTT A D	MESTORE	6.3
ABBOTT D W	BIVEC	2.1
ABELHEIM M B	TRNPACO	8.6
ABELHEIM P N	TRNPACO	8.7
ABERDARE INV P/L	ABERDARE	34.3
ABRAHAMS P S	SECHOLD	5.1
ABRAHAMSON A E	GEN-OPTIC	2.1
ABRAM BERMAN FAMILY LUELLA TRUST	STERLING	10.5
ABRAM BERMAN FAMILY SORREL TRUST	STERLING	10.5
ABRAMOWITZ M	HYPERET	4.3
ABRY INV PVT LTD	J & F	2.7
ABRY INV PVT LTD	ZSR	3.0
ABS COMPUTER (NATAL) CC	ABS	2.1
ABS MANAGEMENT P/L	ABS	41.6
ABSA NOM P/L	ABACUS	5.9
ABSA NOM P/L	ABSA	1.3
ABSA NOM P/L	AMREL	1.8
ABSA NOM P/L	ANG-ALPHA	2.5
ABSA NOM P/L	BARNEX	16.3
ABSA NOM P/L	BASREAD	6.5
ABSA NOM P/L	BEARMAN	1.6
ABSA NOM P/L	BEATRIX	5.1
ABSA NOM P/L	BIVEC	1.7
ABSA NOM P/L	BRACKEN	1.4
ABSA NOM P/L	BUFFELS	1.3
ABSA NOM P/L	CAFCA	6.9
ABSA NOM P/L	CHUBB	1.9
ABSA NOM P/L	CURFIN	1.4
ABSA NOM P/L	DE BEERS	1.1
ABSA NOM P/L	EGOLI	2.2
ABSA NOM P/L	ENGEN	6.4
ABSA NOM P/L	FARM-AG	6.1
ABSA NOM P/L	FOODCRP	1.7
ABSA NOM P/L	G5HOLD	5.3
ABSA NOM P/L	GENBEHEER	4.2
ABSA NOM P/L	GROOTVLEI	2.7
ABSA NOM P/L	HARMONY	1.2
ABSA NOM P/L	HARTIES	1.1
ABSA NOM P/L	HARWILL	15.8
ABSA NOM P/L	IMPLATS	11.4
ABSA NOM P/L	KINROSS	12.3
ABSA NOM P/L	KLOOF	1.0
ABSA NOM P/L	KNIGHTS	1.2
ABSA NOM P/L	KNJ	1.4
ABSA NOM P/L	LENVEST	1.5
ABSA NOM P/L	LESLIE	1.5
ABSA NOM P/L	MALHOLD	5.6
ABSA NOM P/L	MCCARTHY	1.1
ABSA NOM P/L	MCPHAIL	1.8
ABSA NOM P/L	MCRTAIL	4.7
ABSA NOM P/L	MEDHOLD	15.6
ABSA NOM P/L	MESSINA	1.9
ABSA NOM P/L	MICOR	1.5
ABSA NOM P/L	MOMENTUM	1.9
ABSA NOM P/L	MSAULI	1.4
ABSA NOM P/L	NATRUST	16.3
ABSA NOM P/L	ORYX	14.5
ABSA NOM P/L	PEPGRO	9.8
ABSA NOM P/L	PEPKOR	1.4
ABSA NOM P/L	PUTCO	1.4
ABSA NOM P/L	RALE	27.6
ABSA NOM P/L	RANDEX	63.1
ABSA NOM P/L	ROYHOLD	12.6
ABSA NOM P/L	SABLE	3.0
ABSA NOM P/L	SAMANCO	2.7
ABSA NOM P/L	SAPPI	5.4
ABSA NOM P/L	SIMMERS	1.7
ABSA NOM P/L	SMART	3.4
ABSA NOM P/L	SOUTHVAAL	2.0
ABSA NOM P/L	SPESCOM	2.6
ABSA NOM P/L	ST-HELENA	1.4
ABSA NOM P/L	STH-RODPT	2.0
ABSA NOM P/L	TAMBOTI	1.6
ABSA NOM P/L	TIB	2.8
ABSA NOM P/L	TOYOTA	1.0
ABSA NOM P/L	TRANS-NTL	10.1
ABSA NOM P/L	UNISEL	14.2
ABSA NOM P/L	WINKELS	20.6
ACCORD HOLDINGS P/L	OCTODEC	3.6
ACCORD HOLDINGS P/L	TOMKOR	3.6
ACME DIAMOND NOM P/L	TOCO	1.6
ADAMNON NOM P/L	SHOREDITS	4.3
ADCORP SHARE TRUST	ADCORP	4.4
ADONIS KNITWEAR SHARE TRUST	ADONIS	5.6
ADRIANOPLE COLLIERY P/L	FOSTON	7.1
ADRIGOLE INV P/L	RAPTOR	14.8
AECI LTD	CHEMSERVE	64.6
AECI LTD	CURNOW	35.8
AECI PENS FUND	AFR-LEASE	1.5
AECI PENS FUND	AFROX	1.2
AECI PENS FUND	AMAPROP	1.9
AECI PENS FUND	CAPITAL	4.2
AECI PENS FUND	CBD-FUND	1.6
AECI PENS FUND	CENPROP	5.4
AECI PENS FUND	CLICKS	2.0
AECI PENS FUND	DOORNS	3.7
AECI PENS FUND	EVERITE	3.9
AECI PENS FUND	HUDACO	1.7
AECI PENS FUND	I-&-J	1.4
AECI PENS FUND	KH PROPS	3.7
AECI PENS FUND	LYD-PLAT	2.3

AECI PENS FUND	OCEANA	4.9
AECI PENS FUND	PIONEER	1.8
AECI PENS FUND	PP RUST	1.4
AECI PENS FUND	SYCOM	2.0
AECI PENS FUND	T-&-N	5.0
AECI PENS FUND	VOLTEX	1.7
AECI PENS FUND	W-&-A	1.0
AECI PENS FUND	WAICOR	3.3
AECI PENS FUND	WES-AREAS	1.4
AFC GROUP PENS FUND	N-KLEINS	3.7
AFC INV LTD	CONTROL	1.3
AFC INV LTD	N-KLEINS	61.3
AFCAB HOLDINGS P/L	AF-CABLE	79.7
AFCOL SHARE TRUST	AFCOL	1.3
AFDIS HOLDINGS PVT LTD	AFDISTIL	58.4
AFEX HOLDINGS P/L	AECI	24.3
AFMED P/L	CAXTON	74.5
AFMIN HOLDINGS LTD	MINGRAN	15.5
AFRICAN & EUROPEAN INV CO LTD	AMCOAL	19.5
AFRICAN & EUROPEAN INV CO LTD	AMIC	2.0
AFRICAN & EUROPEAN INV CO LTD	ELANDS	3.1
AFRICAN & EUROPEAN INV CO LTD	ERGO	4.7
AFRICAN & EUROPEAN INV CO LTD	FREGOLD	1.7
AFRICAN & EUROPEAN INV CO LTD	NEW-CENT	4.6
AFRICAN & EUROPEAN INV CO LTD	OFSIL	1.7
AFRICAN & EUROPEAN INV CO LTD	VIERFONTN	6.4
AFRICAN & EUROPEAN INV CO LTD	WELKOM	6.0
AFRICAN & OVERSEAS ENTERPRISES LTD	REX-TRUE	72.8
AFRICAN EXPLORATION CO LTD	MINGRAN	16.2
AFRICAN HIDE HOLDINGS P/L	SILOAK	14.2
AFRICAN LIFE ASSURE CO LTD	MAINPRO	1.1
AFRICAN LIFE ASSURE CO LTD	MASHOLD	4.3
AFRICAN LIFE PENS FUND	AFLIFE	2.4
AFRICAN METALS LTD	SAMANCO	36.0
AFRICAN OXYGEN LTD PENS FUND	CHEMSERVE	1.1
AFRICAN OXYGEN LTD PENS FUND	HIGATE	1.4
AFRICAN OXYGEN LTD PENS FUND	MASONITE	3.6
AFRICAN OXYGEN LTD PENS FUND	S-A-BIAS	3.6
AFRICAN OXYGEN LTD PENS FUND	T-&-N	1.7
AFRICAN OXYGEN LTD PENS FUND	TAMBOTI	1.4
AFRICAN OXYGEN LTD PENS FUND	TOCO	3.5
AFRICAN OXYGEN LTD PENS FUND	UNISERV	2.3
AFRICAN OXYGEN UNIT TRUST	AFROX	7.6
AFRICAN TUBES & PIPES P/L	DORBYL	1.6
AFRICAN TUBES & PIPES P/L	USKO	2.2
AFRIKAANSE PERS FONDS	PERSBEL	7.5
AIB NOM LTD	BIVEC	1.4
AIDA FAMILY TRUST	AIDA	51.1
AIM TRUST CHIDRAWI	AIMARK	1.6
ALBERT P	DARMAG	3.4
ALBERT W TRUST	WESCO	3.8
ALGEMENE HANDELS & BELEGGINGS CO	SILOAK	1.2
ALLEN R N	BENCO	1.3
ALLIED ELECTRONICS CORP LTD	ALTECH	14.8
ALLIED ELECTRONICS CORP LTD	FINTECH	75.0
ALLIED ELECTRONICS CORP LTD	POWTECH	40.6
ALLIED TECHNOLOGIES LTD	AUTOPGE	70.8
ALLSOP M J	DIALMOV	1.9
ALLSOP M J	INMINS	2.3
ALLWEAR GROUP LTD	ALLWEAR	59.0
ALMONTE INV P/L	DISA	39.3
ALPHA INSTITUUT P/L	WESCO	10.5
ALPHA OMEGA INV PVT LTD	RADAR	5.6
ALPIET INV P/L	TOMKOR	11.6
ALTER B M & OTHERS	DUKEL	21.8
ALTINI T	ITLTILE	1.8
ALTINI T G	ITLTILE	7.8
ALTRON GROUP PENS FUND	ALTECH	1.3
ALTRON GROUP PENS FUND	BOUMAT	1.9
ALTRON GROUP PENS FUND	HYPROP	1.7
ALTRON GROUP PENS FUND	OCTODEC	2.1
ALTRON GROUP PENS FUND	S-A-BIAS	1.5
ALTRON GROUP PENS FUND	SAB IND	1.4
ALTRON GROUP PENS FUND	TOCO	2.3
ALTRON GROUP RETIREMENT FUND	SPL	1.2
ALTRON INV HOLDINGS P/L	ALTECH	1.7
ALTRON INV HOLDINGS P/L	FINTECH	1.3
ALTUR INV LTD	ANG-ALPHA	54.8
AMALGAMATED BANKS OF SA LTD	BOLAND	9.7
AMALGAMATED BANKS OF SA LTD	CUSAF	30.0
AMALGAMATED BANKS OF SA LTD	RMBH	4.4
AMALGAMATED BANKS OF SA LTD	SAGEGRP	17.9
AMALGAMATED RETAIL LTD	BOYMANS	75.6
AMBOR A J	SPURHLD	2.6
AMEC OVERSEAS INV LTD	GULLIVER	35.1
AMOSITE NOM LTD	E-R-P-M	1.2
AMTOP HOLDINGS P/L	SPUR	10.0
AMTOP INV P/L	SPURHLD	50.7
ANAGNOSTAPOULOS J	CHOICE	1.2
ANB HOLDINGS P/L	ANBEECO	27.9
ANBEECO INV HOLDINGS LTD	SUPALEK	52.5
ANDERGAL NOM P/L	GEN-OPTIC	9.9
ANDERSON B N	ADCORP	3.1
ANDERSON I C	T-E-J	2.0
ANDERSON J	VOLTEX	1.7
ANDEX NOM P/L	FREDDEV	2.4
ANDEX NOM P/L	IBJOFFE	3.2
ANDEX NOM P/L	ICH	7.1
ANDEX NOM P/L	LESLIE	1.2
ANDEX NOM P/L	NEW-CENT	2.3
ANDEX NOM P/L	TIME	1.8
ANDROMEDA P/L	UNION	1.3
ANGLO AFRICAN SHIPPING CO 1936 P/L	HICORL	1.1
ANGLO AFRICAN SHIPPING CO 1936 P/L	RHOEX	11.4
ANGLO AFRICAN SHIPPING CO 1936 P/L	SOPLATS	2.2
ANGLO ALPHA LTD	OMNIA	26.1
ANGLO AMERICAN ASSURE CO PENS FUND	PORTHLD	6.5
ANGLO AMERICAN CORP OF SA LTD	ALTRON	4.2
ANGLO AMERICAN CORP OF SA LTD	AMCOAL	2.4
ANGLO AMERICAN CORP OF SA LTD	AMGOLD	13.3
ANGLO AMERICAN CORP OF SA LTD	AMIC	3.4
ANGLO AMERICAN CORP OF SA LTD	ANAMINT	32.8
ANGLO AMERICAN CORP OF SA LTD	ELANDS	19.0
ANGLO AMERICAN CORP OF SA LTD	ERGO	3.2
ANGLO AMERICAN CORP OF SA LTD	FREGOLD	1.4
ANGLO AMERICAN CORP OF SA LTD	JOHNNIES	5.1
ANGLO AMERICAN CORP OF SA LTD	L-T-A	4.3
ANGLO AMERICAN CORP OF SA LTD	SALLIES	4.6
ANGLO AMERICAN CORP OF SA LTD	VAAL-REEF	1.0
ANGLO AMERICAN CORP PENS FUND	AF-CABLE	1.2
ANGLO AMERICAN CORP PENS FUND	APEX	5.5
ANGLO AMERICAN CORP PENS FUND	ARGUS	3.5
ANGLO AMERICAN CORP PENS FUND	CASHBIL	1.1
ANGLO AMERICAN CORP PENS FUND	CLICKS	1.5
ANGLO AMERICAN CORP PENS FUND	CTP	1.9
ANGLO AMERICAN CORP PENS FUND	CULLINAN	1.5
ANGLO AMERICAN CORP PENS FUND	EDGARS	2.2
ANGLO AMERICAN CORP PENS FUND	FOSCHINI	1.2
ANGLO AMERICAN CORP PENS FUND	MAINPRO	6.0
ANGLO AMERICAN CORP PENS FUND	MIDAS	2.8
ANGLO AMERICAN CORP PENS FUND	SABVEST	4.1
ANGLO AMERICAN CORP PENS FUND	SYCOM	2.6
ANGLO AMERICAN CORP PENS FUND	WALHOLD	3.8
ANGLO AMERICAN CORP PENS FUND	WALTONS	2.3
ANGLO AMERICAN CORP ZIM PENS FUND	WANKIE	1.7
ANGLO AMERICAN CORP ZIMBABWE LTD	WANKIE	13.7
ANGLO AMERICAN CORP ZIMBABWE LTD	WSGROVE	8.4
ANGLO AMERICAN GOLD INV CO LTD	BLYVOOR	6.6
ANGLO AMERICAN GOLD INV CO LTD	DOORNS	4.4
ANGLO AMERICAN GOLD INV CO LTD	DRIES	5.1
ANGLO AMERICAN GOLD INV CO LTD	ELANDS	19.6
ANGLO AMERICAN GOLD INV CO LTD	ERGO	5.0
ANGLO AMERICAN GOLD INV CO LTD	GFSA	7.1
ANGLO AMERICAN GOLD INV CO LTD	HARTIES	15.2
ANGLO AMERICAN GOLD INV CO LTD	VAAL-REEF	1.7
ANGLO AMERICAN GOLD INV CO LTD	ZANDPAN	12.8

ANGLO AMERICAN GROUP PENS FUND	APEX	3.4
ANGLO AMERICAN GROUP PENS FUND	ARGUS	1.7
ANGLO AMERICAN GROUP PENS FUND	BERGERS	7.2
ANGLO AMERICAN GROUP PENS FUND	BOUMAT	2.3
ANGLO AMERICAN GROUP PENS FUND	CTP	1.3
ANGLO AMERICAN GROUP PENS FUND	FOCUS	1.6
ANGLO AMERICAN GROUP PENS FUND	HIGATE	6.2
ANGLO AMERICAN GROUP PENS FUND	INTELES	3.7
ANGLO AMERICAN GROUP PENS FUND	KEELEY	2.3
ANGLO AMERICAN GROUP PENS FUND	KELGRAN	1.1
ANGLO AMERICAN GROUP PENS FUND	MAINPRO	4.7
ANGLO AMERICAN GROUP PENS FUND	MASCON	9.6
ANGLO AMERICAN GROUP PENS FUND	MASHOLD	1.2
ANGLO AMERICAN GROUP PENS FUND	MERHLD	4.6
ANGLO AMERICAN GROUP PENS FUND	MIDAS	2.1
ANGLO AMERICAN GROUP PENS FUND	MOBILE	2.0
ANGLO AMERICAN GROUP PENS FUND	TAMBOTI	6.0
ANGLO AMERICAN GROUP PENS FUND	WAICOR	1.3
ANGLO AMERICAN IND CORP LTD	AECI	11.8
ANGLO AMERICAN IND CORP LTD	ALTRON	3.6
ANGLO AMERICAN IND CORP LTD	HIVELD	44.8
ANGLO AMERICAN IND CORP LTD	VENTRON	9.6
ANGLO AMERICAN INSURANCE HOLDINGS	SOTHERN	32.3
ANGLO AMERICAN INV TRUST LTD	DE BEERS	23.7
ANGLO AMERICAN PROPERTIES LTD	APEX	13.2
ANGLO AMERICAN PROPERTIES LTD	COMPASS	50.0
ANGLO AMERICAN PROPERTIES LTD	MAINPRO	2.8
ANGLO RAND INV HOLDINGS P/L	EQUIKOR	5.8
ANGLO RAND INV P/L	EQUIKOR	25.2
ANGLO-TRANSVAAL COLLIERIES LTD	RANDCOL	10.5
ANGLOVAAL HOLDINGS LTD	ANGLOVAAL	49.4
ANGLOVAAL IND LTD	CONSOL	55.8
ANGLOVAAL IND LTD	CONTROL	26.2
ANGLOVAAL IND LTD	GRINAKER	51.0
ANGLOVAAL IND LTD	I-&-J	68.2
ANGLOVAAL INSURANCE HOLDINGS LTD	CRULIFE	60.0
ANGLOVAAL LTD	A-V-I	6.3
ANGLOVAAL LTD	ASS-MANG	5.1
ANGLOVAAL LTD	AVF GRP	57.5
ANGLOVAAL LTD	MID-WITS	31.1
ANNEMORE INV P/L	T-E-J	1.1
ANTHONY BUCHAN TRUST	MINVEST	39.2
ANTHONY FARAH FAMILY TRUST	SPESCOM	5.1
APEX CORP OF ZIMBABWE LTD	MWEAR	40.0
ARBUTHNOT J	TRIMTRD	1.4
ARC SECURITIES BVI LTD	PANPROP	2.8
ARGOVIA INV C C	STREBEL	1.3
ARGUS HOLDINGS LTD	CAXTON	13.8
ARGUS HOLDINGS LTD	CTP	19.9
ARGUS HOLDINGS LTD	HORTORS	7.6
ARGUS HOLDINGS LTD	M-NET	4.1
ARGUS HOLDINGS LTD	SOLCHEM	2.9
ARGUS HOLDINGS LTD	T-M-L	36.5
ARGUS PENS FUND	ARGUS	9.9
ARGUS PENS FUND	SOLCHEM	7.5
ARNOTT J A	VIERFONTN	3.3
ARNOTT J A	VILLAGE	1.2
AROMA WINE & BRANDY CO P/L	AROMA	34.1
ARONOVSKY DAVID & VIVIENNE TRUST	PROGRESS	19.2
ARONOVSKY M	PROGRESS	4.0
ARONSOHN M	DELSWA	1.1
ARONSTAM B S	FORIM	8.0
ART CORP LTD	KADOMA	50.6
ART GROUP EMPLYEES TRUST PVT LTD	ART	11.8
ARTHUR KAPLAN JEWELLERS SHARE INC	AKJ	1.4
ARTHUR YOUNG NOM NATAL P/L	STORECO	3.6
ARUN HOLDINGS LTD	NAMSEA	1.3
ASHMEAD G L	UNION	1.0
ASHMEAD HOLDINGS P/L	UNION	4.2
ASHTREE INV P/L	BARLOWS	1.9
ASHTREE INV P/L	GFSA	6.0
ASHTREE INV P/L	SAFREN	1.2
ASHTREE INV P/L	SBIC	2.3
ASSOCIATED ELECTRICAL IND LTD	AF-CABLE	9.6
ASSOCIATED FURNITURE CO LTD	ROMATEX	13.2
ASSOCIATED INTERNATIONAL CEMENT LTD	CIRCLE	76.4
ASSOCIATED ORE & METAL CORP LTD	ASS-MANG	43.0
ASTRA FOODS PVT LTD	CAIRNS	55.3
ASTRA FOODS PVT LTD	NATFOOD	17.0
ASTRUP R C	SUB-N	1.8
ATAG ASSET MANAGEMENT LTD	CONCOR	4.6
ATKINSON & JOSCELYNE P/L	MORKELS	4.3
ATTON J	TRIMTEX	2.0
ATTON J	TRIMTRD	7.5
AUBREN HOLDINGS P/L	KAROS	1.8
AUDIODEK SHARE INCENTIVE TRUST	AUTODEK	1.7
AUERBACH FAMILY TRUST	ADVTECH	4.3
AUERBACH N W	ADVTECH	20.2
AURORA CACEY SA	AFMIN	6.7
AUSTEN D C	KLIPTON	1.3
AUSTEN N J	KLIPTON	1.5
AVENG P/L	BEARMAN	51.0
AVF GROUP LTD	AVINS	86.7
AVF GROUP LTD	BOE	39.8
AVI DIVERSIFIED HOLDINGS LTD	SAFCOR	9.2

B

B J BALLADON & SONS P/L	GLODINA	69.9
B M JOFFE HOLDINGS P/L	IBJOFFE	78.0
B M KASS PVT LTD	MWEAR	1.0
B P S E INV P/L	BUFFCOR	36.8
BACON P N	NATRAWL	2.3
BADENHORST L J	DIGOCO	1.2
BAILEY A G	BSG	1.1
BAILEYS NOM P/L	ARGUS	1.1
BAILEYS NOM P/L	BARPROP	2.2
BAKER V C	ADCORP	1.1
BALL R W	STREBEL	1.4
BALL T	HARWILL	1.9
BALLY CASTLE INV P/L	KUDU	18.2
BALTSTEIN I	CON-MURCH	1.2
BANK OF BOTSWANA STAFF PENS FUND	RDC	1.5
BANK OF LISBON STAFF PENS FUND	UNIHOLD	1.0
BANK OF NEW YORK NOM LTD	BLYVOOR	1.0
BANK OF NEW YORK NOM LTD	DOORNS	1.1
BANK OF NEW YORK NOM LTD	E-DAGGA	1.2
BARBIERI M A	STERLING	1.9
BARBIERI M FAMILY TRUST	STERLING	7.5
BARCHAUD PRODUCTS P/L	ROMANO	1.2
BARCLAYS BANK OF BOTSWANA STAFF PENS	FSC	1.7
BARCLAYS BANK OF BOTSWANA STAFF PENS	INCO	1.0
BARCLAYS BANK OF BOTSWANA STAFF PENS	RDC	2.3
BARCLAYS BANK OF BOTSWANA STAFF PENS	SECHABA	15.2
BARCLAYS BANK PLC	BB BOT	74.9
BARCLAYS NAT NOM P/L GATR DEPOT	E-DAGGA	1.1
BARCLAYS ZIMBABWE NOM (PVT) LTD	WANKIE	1.2
BARCLAYS ZIMBABWE NOM P/L	PORTHLD	2.2
BARD NOM (PVT) LTD	FMB	1.5
BARD NOM (PVT) LTD	GULLIVER	2.5
BARD NOM (PVT) LTD	KADOMA	1.0
BARD NOM (PVT) LTD	MWEAR	1.2
BARD NOM (PVT) LTD	RADAR	1.9
BARD NOM P/L	PORTHLD	1.4
BARLOW A W	CENMAG	18.3
BARLOW GENERAL INV LTD	R-M-PROPS	19.6
BARLOW RAND LTD	BARPROP	62.2
BARLOW RAND LTD	CGSMITH	38.2
BARLOW RAND LTD	RANDMIN	4.0
BARLOW RAND LTD	REUNERT	77.5
BARLOWS CEMENT INV LTD	PPC	60.0
BARLOWS MINING HLDGS & ESTATES LTD	RANDMIN	40.3
BARLOWS PENS FUND	CBD-FUND	1.6
BARLOWS PENS FUND	CENPROP	1.1
BARLOWS PENS FUND	GROPROP	7.9

BARLOWS PENS FUND	HIGATE	1.8
BARLOWS PENS FUND	HISTONE	4.9
BARLOWS PENS FUND	LEFIC	1.4
BARLOWS PENS FUND	PIONEER	1.3
BARLOWS PENS FUND	RMSPROP	6.0
BARLOWS PENS FUND	STANPRO	2.1
BARLOWS PENS FUND	TAMBOTI	3.6
BARLOWS PENS FUND	UMDONI	3.1
BARNARD P A	CITYHLD	16.0
BARNARD W	AIDA	1.3
BARNATO HLDGS LTD	CMI	3.1
BARNETSON A U	OVBEL	2.8
BARNETT-HARRIS R C A	OVBEL	1.9
BARNETT-HARRIS R C A	T-E-J	7.5
BARNEY FORMAN HOLDINGS P/L	FORIM	18.2
BARNEY FORMAN WILL TRUST	FORIM	4.3
BAROB INV P/L	BARPROP	15.9
BAROB INV P/L	NBSHOLD	19.1
BAROB INV P/L	RANDMIN	1.3
BARPLATS HOLDINGS P/L	BARPLAT	59.8
BARPLATS INV LTD	BARMINE	66.0
BARRADAS FAMILY TRUST	CHOICE	5.2
BARRADAS J	MICOR	1.1
BARRY J K P	ADCORP	46.1
BARTEL H O	ENSIGN	2.2
BARTEL H O	GLODINA	1.2
BARTEL H O E/L	CAFCA	6.3
BARTELUS (PVT) LTD	RADAR	1.5
BARTELUS (PVT) LTD	TRUZIM	2.7
BASIL GERALD SMIDT FAMILY TRUST	TITACO	2.5
BASIL READ HOLDINGS SHARE TRUST	BASREAD	6.1
BASIL STARKE FAMILY HOLDINGS P/L	BSI	56.6
BASIL STARKE INV LTD	BSG	86.8
BASIL STARKE STAFF SHARE TRUST	BSI	1.7
BASSERABIE A I	FEDSURE	1.3
BASSGRO P/L	SHOPRIT	1.2
BASSON J A	BESTER	4.2
BATEMAN C L	ED-L-BATE	5.9
BATEMAN W G L & CLARKE D R	ED-L-BATE	6.8
BATTISS J L	CENMAG	1.0
BAXTER A J	CMS	27.3
BB INV CO P/L	SAAMBOU	5.4
BB SHARE PURCHASE SCHEME	BOLAND	1.6
BEACOM L E	DISPTCH	1.9
BEARE HOLDINGS P/L	GROWALK	2.1
BEARE J H	CONTRAV	3.2
BECK G J	CONTROL	3.5
BECKER J P FAMILY HLDGS P/L	OZZ	4.2
BECKER M	OZZ	4.5
BECKER P	ENBOT	1.6
BEEVERS M J	MICOR	1.5
BEHRMANN P J	HYPROP	1.5
BENCEN J	ADONIS	24.4
BENCEN K	ADONIS	45.5
BENNETT J D	COATES	5.2
BERCO TRUST	CLINICS	27.0
BERGER M	LITHO	1.2
BERGER S M	CLINICS	1.1
BERGERS GROUP LTD	BERTRAD	93.3
BERGERS HOLDINGS LTD	BERGERS	44.1
BERLIN C A	GDM	3.1
BERLITAS INV NO 14 P/L	QUAGGA	47.4
BERLITAS INV NO 50 P/L	PETRA	64.2
BERMAN A	STERLING	1.0
BERMAN A TRUST	BIDCORP	1.4
BERMAN C	*BURLINGTN*	*4.4*
BERMAN M TRUST	BIDCORP	1.4
BERMAN S E/L	STERLING	3.0
BERNMOND P/L	AF-&-OVER	51.8
BERTHEIM NOM CC	PUBHOLD	7.8
BERZACK A	BERZACK	1.2
BERZACK A	BIVEC	7.8
BERZACK BROS HOLDINGS LTD	VOLTEX	11.7

BERZACK E	BIVEC	1.1
BERZACK H	BIVEC	1.4
BERZACK L	BIVEC	1.3
BERZACK L TRUST	BIVEC	1.1
BERZACK M	BIVEC	3.7
BERZACK M C	BERZACK	1.2
BERZACK M C	BIVEC	5.6
BERZACK R M	BERZACK	1.1
BERZACK R M	BIVEC	5.0
BERZACK-ILLMAN INV CORP LTD	BERZACK	50.3
BESTER C J	Q-DATA	1.7
BESTER J J	BESTER	2.6
BESTER T	BESTER	20.0
BETA GLOBAL EMERGING MARKETS TRUST	PEP BOT	1.4
BETE TRUST	SEFALANA	3.0
BETTY & DICKSON CC	MEDHOLD	1.4
BETTY D R	GAZGOLD	2.1
BEVLIT INV HOLDINGS LTD	BEVCON	27.3
BID CORP LTD	BIDVEST	77.5
BIDVEST GROUP LTD	AFRICOM	6.8
BIDVEST GROUP LTD	CROWN	71.2
BIDVEST LTD	AFRICOM	80.0
BIGGS C R M	CROOKES	1.2
BILL LYNCH FAMILY HOLDINGS P/L	IMPERIAL	4.9
BILTRON P/L	ALTRON	1.3
BILTRON P/L	VENTRON	41.2
BILVEN P/L	ALTECH	36.6
BILVEN P/L	POWTECH	21.7
BIRCH D	LITHO	1.6
BIRD C D	MAST	1.3
BIRD FAMILY TRUST	TECFIN	2.1
BIRD P N E E S I S	TECFIN	2.9
BISHOPGATE NOM LTD	SAGEGRP	1.4
BISICHI MINING EXPLORATION LTD	REVERE	16.9
BISICHI MINING PLC	SOPLATS	1.6
BISSET E/L J J	CAFCA	1.2
BLAF INV CC	CENMAG	4.4
BLAIR HOLDING PVT LTD	TABEX	60.7
BLEWETT B R	INCO	21.0
BLOCH HOLDINGS CHANNEL ISLANDS LTD	BLOCHS	25.0
BLOCH HOLDINGS P/L	BLOCHS	10.0
BLOCH SUPERMARKETS PENS FUND	BLOCHS	3.6
BLOCKBUSTER INV HOLDINGS P/L	RD-LEASE	8.4
BLOCKBUSTER INV P/L	RD-LEASE	9.1
BLOMOCO INV CC	VIERFONTN	1.2
BLUE CHIP INV P/L	INHOLD	1.4
BLUE CIRCLE LTD	GYPSUM	32.4
BLUE CIRCLE PENS FUND	M-&-F	2.1
BLUE STAR HLDGS P/L	OCFISH	3.9
BM NOM CC	DECOVO	6.8
BM NOM CC	HICORL	1.8
BM NOM CC	RABIE	4.2
BOARD OF EXECUTORS NOM P/L	BOE	6.3
BOARD OF EXECUTORS NOM P/L	CFC	1.9
BOARD OF EXECUTORS NOM P/L	OVBEL	17.3
BOARD OF EXECUTORS NOM P/L	OVCON	3.5
BOART INTERNATIONAL LTD	L-T-A	22.8
BOC HOLDINGS	AFROX	57.7
BOE NOM P/L	AUTOPGE	1.7
BOE SELECTIONS LTD	FIDBANK	33.1
BOESCH A & P A & OTHERS FOR FAMILY	MACADAM	3.2
BOILER TUBES AFRICA P/L	LITHO	1.1
BOLAND BANK BPK	ILCO	1.9
BOLAND BANK PENS FUND	BOLAND	4.8
BOLAND BANK PENS FUND	GARDIAN	2.0
BOLAND BANK PENS FUND	*ILCO*	*1.0*
BOLAND BANK PENS FUND	SANTAM	2.8
BOLLAND M U	T-E-J	8.2
BOLTON FOOTWEAR INC TRUST	BOLWEAR	2.7
BOLTONS INDUSTRIAL HOLDINGS LTD	BOLWEAR	74.1
BONKEM INC	AGRICOR	32.5
BOP NAT DEVELOPMENT CORPORATION	SUN-BOP	3.3
BOP NAT DEVELOPMENT CORPORATION	YABENG	43.6

C

CATERING INDUSRTY PENS FUND	PORTHLD	1.1
CATERING INDUSTRY PENS FUND	FMB	1.1
CATERING INDUSTRY PENS FUND	INTERNAT	1.2
CATERING INDUSTRY PENS FUND	RADAR	1.7
CATERING INDUSTRY PENS FUND	WSGROVE	1.0
CATHRON INV P/L	SANLIC	5.4
CATTON E A	PAG	4.6
CAVENDISH SECURITIES LTD	AIMARK	3.1
CAVERSHAM TRUSTEES LTD	EUREKA	11.0
CAVERSHAM TRUSTEES LTD	MACADAM	1.0
CAXTON LTD	CTP	52.7
CAYANIS J	FRALEX	1.7
CCGG INV HOLDINGS LTD	MEDHOLD	10.5
CELESTIAL P/L	MARCONS	1.6
CEMENTATION CO PROVIDENT FUND	CEMENCO	1.5
CENMAG SHARE INC SCHEME	CENMAG	2.1
CENTAUR MANAGERS P/L	MICOR	30.2
CENTRAL CHEMICAL INV P/L	SENTRCHEM	50.0
CENTRAL HOLDINGS LTD	OMNIA	2.1
CERRAI E	TPN	9.1
CERRAI E TRUST	TPN	16.3
CERRAI I	TPN	2.0
CERRAI L	TPN	2.0
CERRAI L TRUST	TPN	17.0
CERRAI S	TPN	2.0
CFC PROPERTY HOLDINGS LTD	CONFED	70.5
CHAFKIN M	LEPPIN	2.3
CHAGAN N P	BUFFCOR	1.6
CHAI SYNDICATE P/L	TOMKOR	2.0
CHALKTON NOM CO P/L	AFLIFE	2.4
CHALKTON NOM CO P/L	BIDCORP	5.1
CHALKTON NOM CO P/L	CONTROL	1.0
CHALKTON NOM CO P/L	FORIM	12.8
CHALKTON NOM CO P/L	KNIGHTS	1.9
CHALKTON NOM CO P/L	N-KLEINS	1.2
CHALKTON NOM CO P/L	SCHARIG	2.6
CHALKTON NOM CO P/L	SIMMERS	1.0
CHAMPEL INC LTD	MICOR	2.3
CHANCE E K	CROOKES	2.7
CHANCELESS INV PVT LTD	FP HOLD	8.1
CHANEL KEELEY TRUST	KEELEY	7.2
CHANEL KEELEY TRUST	KELGRAN	3.4
CHAPLIN J B	PRIM-G-M	1.9
CHAPPEL M H	ANBEECO	1.5
CHARISMA HOLDINGS P/L	FAIRCAP	5.6
CHARISMA HOLDINGS P/L	RABIE	1.5
CHARISMA HOLDINGS P/L	SANLIC	1.1
CHARLES G FAMILY TRUST	DECHOLD	3.7
CHARLES TRUSTEES	OVCON	10.0
CHASKELSON J	DINETTE	4.7
CHENG TSIN KI	HICORL	1.4
CHERAND INV C C	JASCO	1.7
CHIPKIN M, B R, I A & SHIRES H &	BIDCORP	10.9
CHOBE FINANCIAL CORPORATION LTD	RDC	23.3
CHOICEHOLD LTD	GAZGOLD	10.2
CHRISTIE E J	RADAR	1.1
CHUBB EXECUTIVE EMPLOYEE TRUST	CHUBB	2.4
CHUBB INTERNATIONAL LTD	CHUBB	67.8
CINOA HOLDINGS LTD	HCI	1.4
CINOA HOLDINGS LTD	PENROSE	8.3
CISKEI ELEC CONTRACTORS P/L	VILLAGE	3.1
CITIBANK NOM P/L	LIBANON	3.9
CITIBANK NOM P/L	LORAINE	2.5
CITIBANK NOM P/L	SOUTHVAAL	1.0
CITIBANK NOM P/L	ST-HELENA	3.4
CITY COUNCIL OF DURBAN	CAPITAL	4.0
CITY COUNCIL OF DURBAN	CBD-FUND	3.9
CITY COUNCIL OF DURBAN	HIGATE	2.6
CITY COUNCIL OF DURBAN	HISTONE	12.3
CITY COUNCIL OF DURBAN	MAINPRO	1.1
CITY COUNCIL OF DURBAN	PIONEER	3.4
CITY COUNCIL OF DURBAN	SYCOM	1.5
CITY COUNCIL OF DURBAN	TAMBOTI	7.3
CITY DENTAL LABORATORIES P/L	NAMFISH	8.6
CITY PROPERTY ADMIN P/L	TOMKOR	1.1
CLANOR PROPERTY & INV CO P/L	MALHOLD	1.1
CLARENCE B G	PANPROP	1.1
CLARK J R S	OVBEL	2.1
CLARPAT P/L	TPN	10.8
CLAYTONS AGENCIES PVT LTD	FP HOLD	6.0
CLEGG W	CLEGG	15.7
CLINTON NOM P/L	MACADAM	1.1
CLOGG P K	GOLDSTEIN	2.1
CLOGG PETER INV P/L	G5HOLD	2.2
CLUFF MINERAL EXPLORATION LTD	CLUFF ZIM	82.4
CLUFF RESOURCES ZIMBABWE EMPL TRUST	CLUFF ZIM	3.1
CMB NOM P/L	A-V-I	3.6
CMB NOM P/L	ABERDARE	1.5
CMB NOM P/L	ABI	1.3
CMB NOM P/L	ABS	3.1
CMB NOM P/L	ABSA	24.1
CMB NOM P/L	ACREM	3.9
CMB NOM P/L	ADCOCK	2.9
CMB NOM P/L	AECI	1.8
CMB NOM P/L	AFCOL	5.8
CMB NOM P/L	AFROX	1.5
CMB NOM P/L	ALEXNDR	2.3
CMB NOM P/L	ALTECH	10.7
CMB NOM P/L	ALTRON	6.3
CMB NOM P/L	AMCOAL	2.7
CMB NOM P/L	AMGOLD	1.3
CMB NOM P/L	AMIC	1.6
CMB NOM P/L	AMREL	12.4
CMB NOM P/L	AMSHOE	5.9
CMB NOM P/L	ANAMINT	2.9
CMB NOM P/L	ANBEECO	10.9
CMB NOM P/L	ANG-ALPHA	2.1
CMB NOM P/L	ANGLO-S	4.1
CMB NOM P/L	ANGLOVAAL	1.7
CMB NOM P/L	APEX	3.4
CMB NOM P/L	BARLOWS	8.3
CMB NOM P/L	BARMINE	5.6
CMB NOM P/L	BARNEX	3.4
CMB NOM P/L	BEATRIX	9.0
CMB NOM P/L	BEVCON	2.3
CMB NOM P/L	BIDCORP	10.8
CMB NOM P/L	BIDVEST	5.6
CMB NOM P/L	BLOCHS	6.3
CMB NOM P/L	BOUMAT	3.2
CMB NOM P/L	BRENMIL	5.1
CMB NOM P/L	CADSWEP	3.0
CMB NOM P/L	CAPITAL	6.4
CMB NOM P/L	CARLCOR	8.2
CMB NOM P/L	CASHBIL	1.5
CMB NOM P/L	CBD-FUND	1.5
CMB NOM P/L	CENPROP	21.0
CMB NOM P/L	CG SUGAR	7.5
CMB NOM P/L	CGS-FOOD	2.8
CMB NOM P/L	CGSMITH	4.7
CMB NOM P/L	CHARTER	5.0
CMB NOM P/L	CLICKS	11.4
CMB NOM P/L	CMH	3.8
CMB NOM P/L	CONSHU	36.7
CMB NOM P/L	CONSOL	2.1
CMB NOM P/L	CURFIN	3.9
CMB NOM P/L	CURNOW	1.8
CMB NOM P/L	DA-GAMA	4.4
CMB NOM P/L	DALYS	6.6
CMB NOM P/L	DARMAG	2.2
CMB NOM P/L	DATAKOR	2.7
CMB NOM P/L	DE BEERS	6.2
CMB NOM P/L	DIDATA	1.0
CMB NOM P/L	DISA	10.0
CMB NOM P/L	DISTIL	1.6
CMB NOM P/L	DORBYL	8.3
CMB NOM P/L	DRIES	4.7

CMB NOM P/L	E-DAGGA	10.4
CMB NOM P/L	E-T-CONS	1.8
CMB NOM P/L	ED-L-BATE	1.2
CMB NOM P/L	EDGARS	1.9
CMB NOM P/L	EERSLNG	3.7
CMB NOM P/L	ELLERINE	9.9
CMB NOM P/L	ENGEN	4.8
CMB NOM P/L	EQUIKOR	17.4
CMB NOM P/L	ERGO	2.0
CMB NOM P/L	EVERITE	2.3
CMB NOM P/L	F-S-GROUP	17.8
CMB NOM P/L	F-S-I	10.2
CMB NOM P/L	FARM-AG	6.9
CMB NOM P/L	FINTECH	2.0
CMB NOM P/L	FIRSTBK	3.1
CMB NOM P/L	FOODCRP	7.5
CMB NOM P/L	FOSCHINI	2.8
CMB NOM P/L	FRAME	1.5
CMB NOM P/L	FREDDEV	5.4
CMB NOM P/L	G5HOLD	2.8
CMB NOM P/L	GENBEHEER	54.0
CMB NOM P/L	GENBEL	9.8
CMB NOM P/L	GENCOR	3.4
CMB NOM P/L	GRINAKER	10.8
CMB NOM P/L	GRINCOR	2.4
CMB NOM P/L	GRINTEK	12.4
CMB NOM P/L	GROUP-5	6.1
CMB NOM P/L	GROWPNT	8.5
CMB NOM P/L	HARTIES	6.4
CMB NOM P/L	HIGATE	9.9
CMB NOM P/L	HISCORE	7.1
CMB NOM P/L	HISTONE	16.4
CMB NOM P/L	HLH	6.9
CMB NOM P/L	HOLDAIN	9.8
CMB NOM P/L	HUDACO	7.1
CMB NOM P/L	HUNTCOR	6.6
CMB NOM P/L	HYPROP	7.6
CMB NOM P/L	I-&-J	3.4
CMB NOM P/L	IBJOFFE	4.5
CMB NOM P/L	IMPERIAL	2.2
CMB NOM P/L	IMPHOLD	2.1
CMB NOM P/L	IMPLATS	7.6
CMB NOM P/L	IND-SELE	7.4
CMB NOM P/L	INMINS	7.0
CMB NOM P/L	INTELES	3.3
CMB NOM P/L	INVICTA	3.1
CMB NOM P/L	INVSTEC	5.8
CMB NOM P/L	ISCOR	9.8
CMB NOM P/L	ISG	1.8
CMB NOM P/L	JASCO	2.4
CMB NOM P/L	JDGROUP	3.9
CMB NOM P/L	JOEL	8.0
CMB NOM P/L	JOHNNIES	1.7
CMB NOM P/L	KAROS	5.2
CMB NOM P/L	KEELEY	4.5
CMB NOM P/L	KELGRAN	2.2
CMB NOM P/L	KERSAF	3.6
CMB NOM P/L	KINROSS	7.5
CMB NOM P/L	KLOOF	7.9
CMB NOM P/L	KNIGHTS	8.3
CMB NOM P/L	KOPP	8.7
CMB NOM P/L	KWV-BEL	1.2
CMB NOM P/L	LEFIC	2.1
CMB NOM P/L	LENCO	6.9
CMB NOM P/L	LENVEST	12.8
CMB NOM P/L	LEPLAT	2.0
CMB NOM P/L	LIB HOLD	1.9
CMB NOM P/L	LIBERTY	2.8
CMB NOM P/L	LONRHO	1.9
CMB NOM P/L	LYD-PLAT	3.6
CMB NOM P/L	LYDEX	3.6
CMB NOM P/L	M&R-HLD	32.0
CMB NOM P/L	M&R-INV	60.7
CMB NOM P/L	M-NET	1.9
CMB NOM P/L	MAINPRO	2.2
CMB NOM P/L	MALBAK	21.1
CMB NOM P/L	MALHOLD	20.8
CMB NOM P/L	MARLIN	4.0
CMB NOM P/L	MASCON	8.9
CMB NOM P/L	MASHOLD	6.0
CMB NOM P/L	MATH-ASH	4.1
CMB NOM P/L	MCCARTHY	7.7
CMB NOM P/L	MCRTAIL	3.1
CMB NOM P/L	MERHLD	3.1
CMB NOM P/L	MERITEX	6.1
CMB NOM P/L	MESSINA	17.3
CMB NOM P/L	METCASH	2.7
CMB NOM P/L	METKOR	1.6
CMB NOM P/L	METPOL	55.1
CMB NOM P/L	MID-WITS	9.0
CMB NOM P/L	MIDAS	11.7
CMB NOM P/L	MINORCO	2.6
CMB NOM P/L	MORKELS	4.1
CMB NOM P/L	NAMPAK	3.8
CMB NOM P/L	NAMSEA	2.9
CMB NOM P/L	NATRAWL	22.6
CMB NOM P/L	NATRUST	26.6
CMB NOM P/L	NATSEL	10.9
CMB NOM P/L	NEW-CENT	1.3
CMB NOM P/L	NEW-WITS	4.7
CMB NOM P/L	NORTHAM	5.2
CMB NOM P/L	O-K	2.5
CMB NOM P/L	OAKFLDS	3.2
CMB NOM P/L	OCEANA	8.2
CMB NOM P/L	OCFISH	3.0
CMB NOM P/L	OFSIL	1.5
CMB NOM P/L	ORYX	17.0
CMB NOM P/L	OZZ	19.7
CMB NOM P/L	PANPROP	3.8
CMB NOM P/L	PEP	1.2
CMB NOM P/L	PEPGRO	19.2
CMB NOM P/L	PEPKOR	18.8
CMB NOM P/L	PERSBEL	5.0
CMB NOM P/L	PERSKOR	6.8
CMB NOM P/L	PERSTEC	1.7
CMB NOM P/L	PICBEL	2.5
CMB NOM P/L	PICKNPAY	7.5
CMB NOM P/L	PIKWIK	6.1
CMB NOM P/L	PIONEER	11.2
CMB NOM P/L	PLATE-GL	7.4
CMB NOM P/L	POWTECH	8.6
CMB NOM P/L	PP RUST	3.9
CMB NOM P/L	PPC	2.6
CMB NOM P/L	PREM-GRP	2.9
CMB NOM P/L	PUBHOLD	12.6
CMB NOM P/L	PUBLICO	3.2
CMB NOM P/L	Q-DATA	16.2
CMB NOM P/L	QUAGGA	2.6
CMB NOM P/L	RABIE	10.3
CMB NOM P/L	RAINBOW	3.7
CMB NOM P/L	RALE	7.6
CMB NOM P/L	RANDEX	10.3
CMB NOM P/L	RANDFONTN	10.1
CMB NOM P/L	REMB-BEH	10.8
CMB NOM P/L	REMGRO	4.3
CMB NOM P/L	REUNERT	6.6
CMB NOM P/L	RHOVAN	6.5
CMB NOM P/L	ROMATEX	1.8
CMB NOM P/L	ROYAL	8.1
CMB NOM P/L	ROYCHEM	4.5
CMB NOM P/L	ROYFOOD	3.8
CMB NOM P/L	ROYHOLD	4.9
CMB NOM P/L	RUSFURN	11.9
CMB NOM P/L	RUSPLAT	2.9
CMB NOM P/L	S-A-BIAS	13.8
CMB NOM P/L	SA-BREWS	8.7

D

DE BEERS PENS FUND	CLICKS	5.2
DE BEERS PENS FUND	CTP	1.9
DE BEERS PENS FUND	EDGARS	1.9
DE BEERS PENS FUND	FOSCHINI	1.9
DE BEERS PENS FUND	FRAME	1.3
DE BEERS PENS FUND	LEFIC	2.0
DE BEERS PENS FUND	MAINPRO	6.4
DE BEERS PENS FUND	PLATE-GL	1.1
DE BEERS PENS FUND	SABVEST	5.3
DE BEERS PENS FUND	SAFICON	3.9
DE BEERS PENS FUND	SAKERS	1.5
DE BEERS PENS FUND	SCOCLIK	1.2
DE BEERS PENS FUND	SYCOM	2.6
DE BEERS PENS FUND	WAICOR	2.2
DE BEERS PENS FUND	WALHOLD	6.4
DE BEERS PENS FUND	WALTONS	4.1
DE BRUIN J TRUST	QUAGGA	2.4
DE BRUIN L J D	QUAGGA	4.2
DE BRUYN D A	LANCHEM	4.2
DE CHAUD A	ROMANO	4.4
DE CHAUD MARIO	ROMANO	10.0
DE GRANDIS G	ITLTILE	3.9
DE KLERK A	RALE	1.0
DE KOCK J B R	LOGTEK	1.2
DE KOCK M J	PENROSE	1.9
DE MUELENAERE J J G G	RENTBEL	7.1
DE RAUVILLE J P G TRUST	MARCONS	1.5
DE VILLIERS J V	MACADAM	1.5
DE VOS C D	CAFCA	1.1
DEACON R	PENROSE	1.2
DEBONAIR GROUP SHARE INC SCHEME	DEBNAIR	1.9
DEBSWANA DIAMOND CO P/L	DE BEERS	5.3
DEBSWANA PENS FUND	BB BOT	3.2
DEBSWANA PENS FUND	BOTINS	1.3
DEBSWANA PENS FUND	ENBOT	6.2
DEBSWANA PENS FUND	FSC	10.1
DEBSWANA PENS FUND	IGI BOT	1.9
DEBSWANA PENS FUND	INCO	4.5
DEBSWANA PENS FUND	PEP BOT	4.8
DEBSWANA PENS FUND	SECHABA	15.3
DEBSWANA PENS FUND	SEFALANA	4.9
DEBSWANA PENS FUND	STANBOT	4.3
DECOR SHARE INCENTIVE TRUST	DECHOLD	2.7
DELAUNAY LTD	SAMANCO	16.8
DELAUNAY TWO LTD	SAMANCO	2.6
DELMAT INV P/L	DPF-INV	67.9
DELSWA LTD SHARE PARTICIPATION FUND	DELSWA	1.9
DELTA CORP LTD	ZIM SUN	64.0
DELTA ELECTRICAL INDUSTRIES LTD	JASCO	20.7
DELTA EMPL PART TRUST CO PVT LTD	DELTA ZIM	2.9
DELTA SA P/L	DELTA	49.6
DEMELER INV P/L	PEPGRO	2.8
DEMELER INV P/L	SHOPRIT	1.3
DEMESNE INV P/L	FREDDEV	2.1
DEN BOER P	Q-DATA	6.1
DENBI STATIONERY PVT LTD	ART	1.7
DENIS KAYE FAMILY TRUST	LASER	10.5
DEPOSITARY NOM INC	AMGOLD	1.3
DEPOSITARY NOM INC	BLYVOOR	1.5
DEPOSITARY NOM INC	BRACKEN	2.5
DEPOSITARY NOM INC	BUFFELS	5.8
DEPOSITARY NOM INC	DOORNS	5.9
DEPOSITARY NOM INC	E-DAGGA	1.4
DEPOSITARY NOM INC	ERGO	1.4
DEPOSITARY NOM INC	HARMONY	1.6
DEPOSITARY NOM INC	IMPLATS	1.1
DEPOSITARY NOM INC	KINROSS	1.8
DEPOSITARY NOM INC	LESLIE	1.7
DEPOSITARY NOM INC	LIBANON	1.1
DEPOSITARY NOM INC	OFSIL	3.0
DEPOSITARY NOM INC	RANDFONTN	1.6
DEPOSITARY NOM INC	ST-HELENA	4.1
DEPOSITARY NOM INC	STILFTN	1.2

DEPOSITARY NOM INC	W-R-CONS	3.4
DEPOSITARY NOM INC	WES-AREAS	1.2
DEPOSITARY NOM INC	WINKELS	1.9
DEPOSITARY NOM INC	WSTN-DEEP	3.0
DERMAN A J	BERGERS	1.5
DERSLEY R M	DARMAG	6.2
DESAI P	ENBOT	1.6
DESBAR INV P/L	ABCON	1.2
DESMET B J	STERLING	4.5
DETENTE NOM LTD	PALS	17.0
DETTMANN I J	MAXMECH	57.8
DEUTSCHER AKV	HIVELD	2.9
DEVITT R	BERGERS	10.7
DG MURRAY TRUST	M&R-INV	4.7
DIAGONAL NOM P/L	FAIRCAP	1.4
DIAGONAL NOM P/L	NICTUS	3.8
DIAGONAL NOM P/L	SAFETEC	63.4
DIAGONAL NOM P/L	USKO	1.3
DIAL-A-MOVIE MENLYN P/L	DIALMOV	11.3
DIAMOND CORP P/L	ANGLO-S	3.2
DIANCANA FINANCE CORP PVT LTD	ZSR	2.7
DICKS D W	MINVEST	2.8
DIDO NOM LTD	AFR-LEASE	2.2
DIDO NOM LTD	AMAPROP	4.7
DIDO NOM LTD	AMCOAL	6.1
DIDO NOM LTD	AMIC	7.3
DIDO NOM LTD	ANGLO-S	2.9
DIDO NOM LTD	BEATRIX	1.3
DIDO NOM LTD	CMI	3.0
DIDO NOM LTD	LEPLAT	5.4
DIDO NOM LTD	MCCARTHY	8.6
DIDO NOM LTD	NEW-CENT	2.8
DIDO NOM LTD	PP RUST	6.1
DIDO NOM LTD	RUSPLAT	6.9
DIDO NOM LTD	TONGAAT	1.9
DIDO NOM LTD	WSTN-DEEP	4.9
DIENST C W	OMNIA	1.2
DIENSVENNOTE CC	CITYHLD	13.8
DIENSVENNOTE P/L	CITYHLD	50.2
DIMENSION DATA INV P/L	DIDATA	20.3
DIPPENAAR L L	RMBH	10.1
DOCWIL TRUST NO 1	CLYDE	38.8
DOLPHIN A I	WIT-NIGEL	3.0
DOMINION IND TRUST P/L	BRISTOL-I	1.6
DOMINO LTD	BOTREST	11.8
DOMIRO P/L	BURLINGTN	16.7
DONIAN PROPERTIES PVT LTD	J & F	44.4
DORBYL PENS FUND	EERSLNG	1.1
DORBYL PENS FUND	GF-PROPS	3.2
DORBYL PENS FUND	T-&-N	2.6
DORBYL PENS FUND	UNISERV	3.8
DOREG INV P/L	COM-FUND	13.4
DORFAN J G	SOWITS	2.1
DORFMAN D	ABBEY	4.2
DORITOS HOLDINGS LTD	ALEXWYT	6.2
DORRESTEIN A H	STOCKS	14.3
DOWNARD C R	NICTUS	2.1
DOWNARD C R	VIERFONTN	1.0
DPF INV LTD	GROWALK	11.2
DRAKENSBERG BOTTELIER P/L	RENTBEL	1.0
DRUION S A	TRNPACO	3.7
DRURY A M	CUSAF	2.7
DRUSINSKY A	LIB HOLD	1.0
DRYSDALE D M	NINIAN	2.9
DS TEPERSON INV P/L	TRIMTEX	7.7
DS TEPERSON INV P/L	TRIMTRD	1.5
DU PLESSIS E INV CO P/L	JASCO	3.1
DU PLESSIS GERT VAN EDEN	VENTEL	1.1
DU PLESSIS J H	CITYHLD	1.0
DU PLESSIS P	UNION	1.6
DU PREEZ F J	FOSTON	2.1
DU PREEZ K	CITYHLD	1.3
DU TOIT P J TRUST	KUDU	45.1

DU-PISANI L A	PUTCO	1.1
DU-PISANI L A	PUTPROP	1.1
DUBLIN CONSOLIDATED ASBESTOS MINE	T-&-N	3.8
DUIGAN K G	VIERFONTN	1.5
DUIKER EXPL LTD SHR INC SCHEME TRUST	DUIKERS	1.7
DUMARESQ D W	BSI	3.1
DUNCAN VAN DER POEL INV P/L	DUKEL	7.3
DUNDEE CAPITAL CORP P/L	KNIGHTS	24.0
DUNLOP NOM SA P/L	BTRDUN	37.9
DURBAN CORP SUPERANNUATION FUND	BOEPROP	1.6
DURBAN CORP SUPERANNUATION FUND	CAPITAL	1.2
DURBAN CORP SUPERANNUATION FUND	GROPROP	13.6
DURBAN CORP SUPERANNUATION FUND	HIGATE	2.5
DURBAN CORP SUPERANNUATION FUND	HISTONE	4.1
DURBAN CORP SUPERANNUATION FUND	TAMBOTI	1.6
DURBAN DEEP	CHOICE	14.9
DURBAN MUNICIPAL PENS FUND	BOEPROP	4.1
DURBAN MUNICIPAL PENS FUND	CAPITAL	1.4
DURBAN MUNICIPAL PENS FUND	GROPROP	5.4
DURBAN MUNICIPAL PENS FUND	HIGATE	1.1
DUROS LTD	GAZGOLD	3.3
DURRANT INV LTD	SIMMERS	6.6

E

E KAHN TEXTILES P/L	CLEGG	2.6
E S C STAFF PENS FUND	CAPS	1.7
E S C STAFF PENS FUND	INTERNAT	1.1
E S C STAFF PENS FUND	RIO ZIM	1.0
E S C STAFF PENS FUND	ZSR	2.3
E T & M INV & FARMING PVT LTD	FP HOLD	7.5
EAST DAGGAFONTEIN MINES LTD	LYDEX	12.4
EAST DAGGAFONTEIN MINES LTD	RANDEX	5.6
EBURY HOLDINGS LTD	OZZ	1.1
ED L BATE STAFF HOLDINGS P/L	ED-L-BATE	24.8
EDDIE KEIZAN FAMILY HOLDINGS P/L	TIWHEEL	24.4
EDEL P R	CUTRITE	5.7
EDESA HOLDINGS LTD	UDC	30.0
EDGARS CONSOLIDATED INV LTD	EDGARS	51.3
EDGCUMBE A A	CROOKES	1.5
EDSPARE INV HOLDINGS LTD	EDDIES	65.2
EDWARD L BATEMAN EXEC SHARE INC TRUST	ED-L-BATE	3.5
EDWARDS COLIN TRUST	STOCKS	3.3
EDWARDS CRAIG TRUST	STOCKS	3.3
EDWARDS NOM P/L	PORTHLD	1.9
EDWARDS NOM PVT LTD	WSGROVE	7.9
EDWARDS R	OZZ	1.9
EDWARDS R A	STOCKS	4.5
EDWARDSTONE P/L	TGH	1.7
EDWIN W BALDERSON NOM P/L	AFR-LEASE	1.4
EDWIN W BALDERSON NOM P/L	FAIRCAP	3.3
EDWIN W BALDERSON NOM P/L	FOSTON	75.5
EDWIN W BALDERSON NOM P/L	RD-LEASE	50.8
EDWIN W BALDERSON NOM P/L	RHOVAN	1.1
EDWIN W BALDERSON NOM P/L	SPICER	2.6
EDWIN W BALDERSON NOM P/L	VLAKS	1.0
EEN MARGARET	CONAFEX	1.0
EGGER G A	CLEGG	16.7
EGOLI CONSOLIDATED MINES LTD	CARRIGS	76.6
EGOLI CONSOLIDATED MINES LTD	SOUTHGO	76.3
EHINGER E O	SILOAK	2.2
EIGHTY ONE MAIN STREET NOM LTD	A-V-I	2.3
EIGHTY ONE MAIN STREET NOM LTD	ABCON	22.8
EIGHTY ONE MAIN STREET NOM LTD	ABSA	5.1
EIGHTY ONE MAIN STREET NOM LTD	AFCOL	1.7
EIGHTY ONE MAIN STREET NOM LTD	ALEXNDR	13.6
EIGHTY ONE MAIN STREET NOM LTD	ALTECH	2.7
EIGHTY ONE MAIN STREET NOM LTD	ALTRON	1.3
EIGHTY ONE MAIN STREET NOM LTD	AMAPROP	2.3
EIGHTY ONE MAIN STREET NOM LTD	AMCOAL	1.7
EIGHTY ONE MAIN STREET NOM LTD	AMGOLD	1.6
EIGHTY ONE MAIN STREET NOM LTD	AMIC	1.7

EIGHTY ONE MAIN STREET NOM LTD	AMREL	1.2
EIGHTY ONE MAIN STREET NOM LTD	ANG-ALPHA	1.3
EIGHTY ONE MAIN STREET NOM LTD	ANGLO-S	2.5
EIGHTY ONE MAIN STREET NOM LTD	ARGUS	7.0
EIGHTY ONE MAIN STREET NOM LTD	ASSORE	2.3
EIGHTY ONE MAIN STREET NOM LTD	AVF GRP	1.5
EIGHTY ONE MAIN STREET NOM LTD	BARLOWS	3.1
EIGHTY ONE MAIN STREET NOM LTD	BENONI	10.6
EIGHTY ONE MAIN STREET NOM LTD	BERZACK	17.9
EIGHTY ONE MAIN STREET NOM LTD	BEVCON	1.4
EIGHTY ONE MAIN STREET NOM LTD	BIDCORP	1.7
EIGHTY ONE MAIN STREET NOM LTD	BOEPROP	39.7
EIGHTY ONE MAIN STREET NOM LTD	BOLAND	1.2
EIGHTY ONE MAIN STREET NOM LTD	BTRDUN	6.8
EIGHTY ONE MAIN STREET NOM LTD	CARGO	2.0
EIGHTY ONE MAIN STREET NOM LTD	CBD-FUND	4.0
EIGHTY ONE MAIN STREET NOM LTD	CENPROP	3.8
EIGHTY ONE MAIN STREET NOM LTD	CG SUGAR	5.6
EIGHTY ONE MAIN STREET NOM LTD	CHEMSERVE	3.0
EIGHTY ONE MAIN STREET NOM LTD	CHUBB	3.9
EIGHTY ONE MAIN STREET NOM LTD	CLINICS	5.6
EIGHTY ONE MAIN STREET NOM LTD	CNAGALO	2.3
EIGHTY ONE MAIN STREET NOM LTD	CONFRAM	4.2
EIGHTY ONE MAIN STREET NOM LTD	CONSHU	3.4
EIGHTY ONE MAIN STREET NOM LTD	COPI	2.2
EIGHTY ONE MAIN STREET NOM LTD	CROOKES	2.7
EIGHTY ONE MAIN STREET NOM LTD	CTP	4.2
EIGHTY ONE MAIN STREET NOM LTD	CURFIN	11.4
EIGHTY ONE MAIN STREET NOM LTD	DA-GAMA	8.7
EIGHTY ONE MAIN STREET NOM LTD	DALYS	1.6
EIGHTY ONE MAIN STREET NOM LTD	DE BEERS	2.8
EIGHTY ONE MAIN STREET NOM LTD	DELTA	9.6
EIGHTY ONE MAIN STREET NOM LTD	DORBYL	4.1
EIGHTY ONE MAIN STREET NOM LTD	DUIKERS	3.9
EIGHTY ONE MAIN STREET NOM LTD	E-DAGGA	2.3
EIGHTY ONE MAIN STREET NOM LTD	ED-L-BATE	6.2
EIGHTY ONE MAIN STREET NOM LTD	ENGEN	1.8
EIGHTY ONE MAIN STREET NOM LTD	ERGO	1.7
EIGHTY ONE MAIN STREET NOM LTD	EVERITE	3.6
EIGHTY ONE MAIN STREET NOM LTD	FIRSTBK	2.2
EIGHTY ONE MAIN STREET NOM LTD	FIT	2.8
EIGHTY ONE MAIN STREET NOM LTD	FOODCRP	3.5
EIGHTY ONE MAIN STREET NOM LTD	FOSCHINI	2.6
EIGHTY ONE MAIN STREET NOM LTD	FRAME	11.4
EIGHTY ONE MAIN STREET NOM LTD	FREGOLD	1.2
EIGHTY ONE MAIN STREET NOM LTD	GENBEHEER	1.2
EIGHTY ONE MAIN STREET NOM LTD	GENCOR	1.8
EIGHTY ONE MAIN STREET NOM LTD	GF-PROPS	4.4
EIGHTY ONE MAIN STREET NOM LTD	GFNAMIB	13.5
EIGHTY ONE MAIN STREET NOM LTD	GFSA	1.0
EIGHTY ONE MAIN STREET NOM LTD	GRESHAM	3.6
EIGHTY ONE MAIN STREET NOM LTD	GRINAKER	1.8
EIGHTY ONE MAIN STREET NOM LTD	GROPROP	7.7
EIGHTY ONE MAIN STREET NOM LTD	GROWPNT	3.4
EIGHTY ONE MAIN STREET NOM LTD	HIGATE	4.0
EIGHTY ONE MAIN STREET NOM LTD	HISTONE	1.3
EIGHTY ONE MAIN STREET NOM LTD	HIVELD	5.4
EIGHTY ONE MAIN STREET NOM LTD	HUDACO	15.7
EIGHTY ONE MAIN STREET NOM LTD	HUNTCOR	2.6
EIGHTY ONE MAIN STREET NOM LTD	HYPROP	15.1
EIGHTY ONE MAIN STREET NOM LTD	I-&-J	1.7
EIGHTY ONE MAIN STREET NOM LTD	I-C-S	4.9
EIGHTY ONE MAIN STREET NOM LTD	ICH	9.7
EIGHTY ONE MAIN STREET NOM LTD	IMPERIAL	1.9
EIGHTY ONE MAIN STREET NOM LTD	IMPHOLD	4.1
EIGHTY ONE MAIN STREET NOM LTD	IND-SELE	1.2
EIGHTY ONE MAIN STREET NOM LTD	INTELES	2.8
EIGHTY ONE MAIN STREET NOM LTD	INVSTEC	2.4
EIGHTY ONE MAIN STREET NOM LTD	ISCOR	6.4
EIGHTY ONE MAIN STREET NOM LTD	ISG	1.1
EIGHTY ONE MAIN STREET NOM LTD	JOHNNIES	1.5
EIGHTY ONE MAIN STREET NOM LTD	KEELEY	3.4
EIGHTY ONE MAIN STREET NOM LTD	KELGRAN	1.8

EIGHTY ONE MAIN STREET NOM LTD	KERSAF	1.9
EIGHTY ONE MAIN STREET NOM LTD	KH PROPS	6.7
EIGHTY ONE MAIN STREET NOM LTD	KLIPTON	12.8
EIGHTY ONE MAIN STREET NOM LTD	KUDU	9.2
EIGHTY ONE MAIN STREET NOM LTD	L-T-A	5.7
EIGHTY ONE MAIN STREET NOM LTD	LEFIC	1.8
EIGHTY ONE MAIN STREET NOM LTD	LENCO	11.0
EIGHTY ONE MAIN STREET NOM LTD	LENVEST	5.0
EIGHTY ONE MAIN STREET NOM LTD	LEPLAT	1.2
EIGHTY ONE MAIN STREET NOM LTD	LIB HOLD	2.3
EIGHTY ONE MAIN STREET NOM LTD	LIBERTY	1.8
EIGHTY ONE MAIN STREET NOM LTD	LONRHO	2.7
EIGHTY ONE MAIN STREET NOM LTD	LYD-PLAT	1.4
EIGHTY ONE MAIN STREET NOM LTD	M&R-HLD	3.9
EIGHTY ONE MAIN STREET NOM LTD	M&R-INV	7.0
EIGHTY ONE MAIN STREET NOM LTD	M-&-F	3.9
EIGHTY ONE MAIN STREET NOM LTD	MAINPRO	1.7
EIGHTY ONE MAIN STREET NOM LTD	MALBAK	2.5
EIGHTY ONE MAIN STREET NOM LTD	MALHOLD	1.1
EIGHTY ONE MAIN STREET NOM LTD	MCCARTHY	2.5
EIGHTY ONE MAIN STREET NOM LTD	MCRTAIL	2.6
EIGHTY ONE MAIN STREET NOM LTD	MERITEX	1.6
EIGHTY ONE MAIN STREET NOM LTD	METAIR	1.0
EIGHTY ONE MAIN STREET NOM LTD	METCASH	6.4
EIGHTY ONE MAIN STREET NOM LTD	METKOR	6.2
EIGHTY ONE MAIN STREET NOM LTD	METPOL	4.7
EIGHTY ONE MAIN STREET NOM LTD	METPROP	2.5
EIGHTY ONE MAIN STREET NOM LTD	MICOR	3.6
EIGHTY ONE MAIN STREET NOM LTD	MID-WITS	3.1
EIGHTY ONE MAIN STREET NOM LTD	MINORCO	2.1
EIGHTY ONE MAIN STREET NOM LTD	MLNHOLD	3.3
EIGHTY ONE MAIN STREET NOM LTD	MOBILE	2.4
EIGHTY ONE MAIN STREET NOM LTD	NAMPAK	1.1
EIGHTY ONE MAIN STREET NOM LTD	NATSEL	2.6
EIGHTY ONE MAIN STREET NOM LTD	NEDCOR	3.6
EIGHTY ONE MAIN STREET NOM LTD	NEW-CENT	1.7
EIGHTY ONE MAIN STREET NOM LTD	NORTHAM	9.2
EIGHTY ONE MAIN STREET NOM LTD	O-K	2.1
EIGHTY ONE MAIN STREET NOM LTD	OCTODEC	5.6
EIGHTY ONE MAIN STREET NOM LTD	OFSIL	1.5
EIGHTY ONE MAIN STREET NOM LTD	PALAMIN	2.0
EIGHTY ONE MAIN STREET NOM LTD	PANPROP	14.1
EIGHTY ONE MAIN STREET NOM LTD	PERSTEC	1.0
EIGHTY ONE MAIN STREET NOM LTD	PIKWIK	1.6
EIGHTY ONE MAIN STREET NOM LTD	PIONEER	1.7
EIGHTY ONE MAIN STREET NOM LTD	PLATE-GL	3.9
EIGHTY ONE MAIN STREET NOM LTD	PORT	1.1
EIGHTY ONE MAIN STREET NOM LTD	POWTECH	4.5
EIGHTY ONE MAIN STREET NOM LTD	PREM-GRP	1.1
EIGHTY ONE MAIN STREET NOM LTD	PROSURE	5.0
EIGHTY ONE MAIN STREET NOM LTD	PUTCO	8.4
EIGHTY ONE MAIN STREET NOM LTD	PUTPROP	11.0
EIGHTY ONE MAIN STREET NOM LTD	RANDFONTN	3.8
EIGHTY ONE MAIN STREET NOM LTD	RANDMIN	4.1
EIGHTY ONE MAIN STREET NOM LTD	REMB-BEH	1.9
EIGHTY ONE MAIN STREET NOM LTD	REMGRO	2.0
EIGHTY ONE MAIN STREET NOM LTD	RMBH	3.7
EIGHTY ONE MAIN STREET NOM LTD	RMSPROP	8.5
EIGHTY ONE MAIN STREET NOM LTD	ROMATEX	1.2
EIGHTY ONE MAIN STREET NOM LTD	ROOIBERG	9.6
EIGHTY ONE MAIN STREET NOM LTD	ROYFOOD	3.3
EIGHTY ONE MAIN STREET NOM LTD	RUSFURN	3.0
EIGHTY ONE MAIN STREET NOM LTD	RUSPLAT	1.4
EIGHTY ONE MAIN STREET NOM LTD	S-A-EAGLE	1.4
EIGHTY ONE MAIN STREET NOM LTD	SA-BREWS	1.5
EIGHTY ONE MAIN STREET NOM LTD	SAAMBOU	4.5
EIGHTY ONE MAIN STREET NOM LTD	SABVEST	2.6
EIGHTY ONE MAIN STREET NOM LTD	SAFICON	2.2
EIGHTY ONE MAIN STREET NOM LTD	SAFREN	2.6
EIGHTY ONE MAIN STREET NOM LTD	SAKERS	3.3
EIGHTY ONE MAIN STREET NOM LTD	SANTAM	2.9
EIGHTY ONE MAIN STREET NOM LTD	SAPPI	2.6
EIGHTY ONE MAIN STREET NOM LTD	SASOL	3.9
EIGHTY ONE MAIN STREET NOM LTD	SBIC	1.7
EIGHTY ONE MAIN STREET NOM LTD	SCORE	4.3
EIGHTY ONE MAIN STREET NOM LTD	SEARCON	1.6
EIGHTY ONE MAIN STREET NOM LTD	SECHOLD	6.3
EIGHTY ONE MAIN STREET NOM LTD	SENTRCHEM	4.2
EIGHTY ONE MAIN STREET NOM LTD	SERVGRO	5.2
EIGHTY ONE MAIN STREET NOM LTD	SILTEK	2.7
EIGHTY ONE MAIN STREET NOM LTD	SMART	10.8
EIGHTY ONE MAIN STREET NOM LTD	SOUDEX	2.6
EIGHTY ONE MAIN STREET NOM LTD	SOUTHVAAL	1.8
EIGHTY ONE MAIN STREET NOM LTD	SPECLTY	10.9
EIGHTY ONE MAIN STREET NOM LTD	STANDRD	16.0
EIGHTY ONE MAIN STREET NOM LTD	STANPRO	4.5
EIGHTY ONE MAIN STREET NOM LTD	STERLING	22.1
EIGHTY ONE MAIN STREET NOM LTD	STORECO	3.0
EIGHTY ONE MAIN STREET NOM LTD	STREBEL	1.3
EIGHTY ONE MAIN STREET NOM LTD	SUN-BOP	2.1
EIGHTY ONE MAIN STREET NOM LTD	SYCOM	7.2
EIGHTY ONE MAIN STREET NOM LTD	T-&-N	7.7
EIGHTY ONE MAIN STREET NOM LTD	T-M-L	2.0
EIGHTY ONE MAIN STREET NOM LTD	TAMBOTI	6.4
EIGHTY ONE MAIN STREET NOM LTD	TEGKOR	1.4
EIGHTY ONE MAIN STREET NOM LTD	TELJOY	2.9
EIGHTY ONE MAIN STREET NOM LTD	TEMPORA	7.6
EIGHTY ONE MAIN STREET NOM LTD	TIB	2.0
EIGHTY ONE MAIN STREET NOM LTD	TIGR-OATS	1.3
EIGHTY ONE MAIN STREET NOM LTD	TITACO	6.3
EIGHTY ONE MAIN STREET NOM LTD	TONGAAT	5.2
EIGHTY ONE MAIN STREET NOM LTD	TOYOTA	7.5
EIGHTY ONE MAIN STREET NOM LTD	TRANS-NTL	9.5
EIGHTY ONE MAIN STREET NOM LTD	TRENCOR	6.3
EIGHTY ONE MAIN STREET NOM LTD	TWEEFONTN	8.3
EIGHTY ONE MAIN STREET NOM LTD	UMDONI	8.7
EIGHTY ONE MAIN STREET NOM LTD	UNITRAN	4.3
EIGHTY ONE MAIN STREET NOM LTD	USKO	2.9
EIGHTY ONE MAIN STREET NOM LTD	VAAL-REEF	2.4
EIGHTY ONE MAIN STREET NOM LTD	VENTEL	8.2
EIGHTY ONE MAIN STREET NOM LTD	VETRUST	5.7
EIGHTY ONE MAIN STREET NOM LTD	VOLTEX	18.1
EIGHTY ONE MAIN STREET NOM LTD	WALHOLD	1.6
EIGHTY ONE MAIN STREET NOM LTD	WALTONS	3.6
EIGHTY ONE MAIN STREET NOM LTD	WELKOM	1.3
EIGHTY ONE MAIN STREET NOM LTD	WES-AREAS	3.6
EIGHTY ONE MAIN STREET NOM LTD	WESCO	4.0
EIGHTY ONE MAIN STREET NOM LTD	WINKELS	1.4
EIGHTY ONE MAIN STREET NOM LTD	WOODROW	2.0
EIGHTY ONE MAIN STREET NOM LTD	YABENG	4.9
ELCENTRE CORP LTD	SANLIC	36.5
ELCENTRE CORP LTD	VOLTEX	38.1
ELCENTRE GROUP HOLDINGS LTD	ELCENTR	54.1
ELECTRICAL SYSTEMS PVT LTD	MASHONA	4.4
ELECTRONIC INV P/L	MULTI	4.6
ELECTRONIC MEDIA NETWORK HOLDINGS	M-NET	60.9
ELEMENT INV HOLDINGS P/L	MEDHOLD	3.6
ELFIN UNDIES P/L	NINIAN	9.7
ELHAR TRUST PVT LTD	MWEAR	2.0
ELIJEAN INV P/L	CROOKES	1.2
ELLEN D M	MINVEST	2.4
ELLENMARY NOM P/L	INVICTA	8.6
ELLERBY BV	INTERNAT	71.5
ELLERINE BROS P/L	ABS	2.5
ELLERINE BROS P/L	BIDCORP	6.1
ELLERINE BROS P/L	BOYMANS	5.7
ELLERINE BROS P/L	CHUBB	1.8
ELLERINE BROS P/L	CROWN	1.6
ELLERINE BROS P/L	DINETTE	3.3
ELLERINE BROS P/L	ELLERINE	3.2
ELLERINE BROS P/L	EUREKA	1.7
ELLERINE BROS P/L	F-S-GROUP	1.2
ELLERINE BROS P/L	FARM-AG	1.7
ELLERINE BROS P/L	G5HOLD	1.4
ELLERINE BROS P/L	GROUP-5	3.0
ELLERINE BROS P/L	JDGROUP	1.9

ELLERINE BROS P/L	MCPHAIL	3.4
ELLERINE BROS P/L	MCRTAIL	1.0
ELLERINE BROS P/L	MERHLD	1.9
ELLERINE BROS P/L	MILSTAN	4.1
ELLERINE BROS P/L	PUBHOLD	2.4
ELLERINE BROS P/L	RACY	4.7
ELLERINE BROS P/L	S-A-BIAS	1.3
ELLERINE BROS P/L	SABVEST	2.6
ELLERINE BROS P/L	TRNPACO	2.3
ELLERINE BROS P/L	VALCAR	3.0
ELLERINE BROS P/L	VESTCOR	5.1
ELLERINE BROS P/L	WBHOLD	1.3
ELLERINE D T	ELLERINE	1.1
ELLERINE E	F-S-GROUP	1.1
ELLERINE E	MILSTAN	2.2
ELLERINE N P	ELLERINE	1.1
ELLERINE S	MILSTAN	1.5
ELLINGHAM ESTATE P/L	CROOKES	7.0
ELLIOTTONA INV P/L	G-I-C	61.9
ELLIS I	GRINAKER	2.3
ELMES B	BIDVEST	2.4
ELOFF F	CITYHLD	3.6
ELOFF F C	QUAGGA	2.1
ELOFF STREET NOM P/L	DIDATA	5.4
ELS M H O	LONGRAIL	2.7
ELSBURG GOLD MINING CO LTD	WES-AREAS	4.4
EMARJAY NOM P/L	LYDEX	1.9
EMDON A L	AKJ	7.7
EMOYENI MANAGEMENT & INV CO P/L	GRINCOR	3.3
EMZED CC	CMH	1.3
ENFIELD HOLDINGS LTD	TRUZIM	1.6
ENFML NOM P/L	PROFURN	6.6
ENGELBRECHT I Z	LANCHEM	2.1
ENGELBRECHT P	NISWA	1.2
ENGINEERING INDUSTRIES PENS FUND	ABCON	2.0
ENGINEERING INDUSTRIES PENS FUND	ABSA	1.1
ENGINEERING INDUSTRIES PENS FUND	AECI	1.3
ENGINEERING INDUSTRIES PENS FUND	ALTECH	1.3
ENGINEERING INDUSTRIES PENS FUND	AMCOAL	1.1
ENGINEERING INDUSTRIES PENS FUND	ANG-ALPHA	2.5
ENGINEERING INDUSTRIES PENS FUND	BARLOWS	1.9
ENGINEERING INDUSTRIES PENS FUND	BOEPROP	2.9
ENGINEERING INDUSTRIES PENS FUND	BOUMAT	2.1
ENGINEERING INDUSTRIES PENS FUND	BTRDUN	5.2
ENGINEERING INDUSTRIES PENS FUND	CAPITAL	2.5
ENGINEERING INDUSTRIES PENS FUND	CARGO	2.3
ENGINEERING INDUSTRIES PENS FUND	CBD-FUND	1.4
ENGINEERING INDUSTRIES PENS FUND	CENPROP	1.5
ENGINEERING INDUSTRIES PENS FUND	CGSMITH	2.7
ENGINEERING INDUSTRIES PENS FUND	CLICKS	1.1
ENGINEERING INDUSTRIES PENS FUND	CROWN	1.3
ENGINEERING INDUSTRIES PENS FUND	CULLINAN	5.4
ENGINEERING INDUSTRIES PENS FUND	DORBYL	2.5
ENGINEERING INDUSTRIES PENS FUND	ELLERINE	1.4
ENGINEERING INDUSTRIES PENS FUND	FENNER	3.7
ENGINEERING INDUSTRIES PENS FUND	FINTECH	2.3
ENGINEERING INDUSTRIES PENS FUND	FIRSTBK	2.8
ENGINEERING INDUSTRIES PENS FUND	GENBEL	1.9
ENGINEERING INDUSTRIES PENS FUND	GENCOR	1.0
ENGINEERING INDUSTRIES PENS FUND	GRINCOR	1.6
ENGINEERING INDUSTRIES PENS FUND	GROPROP	1.5
ENGINEERING INDUSTRIES PENS FUND	HIGATE	2.2
ENGINEERING INDUSTRIES PENS FUND	HISCORE	1.3
ENGINEERING INDUSTRIES PENS FUND	HISTONE	3.3
ENGINEERING INDUSTRIES PENS FUND	HIVELD	3.1
ENGINEERING INDUSTRIES PENS FUND	HOLDAIN	2.3
ENGINEERING INDUSTRIES PENS FUND	HUDACO	2.6
ENGINEERING INDUSTRIES PENS FUND	HYPROP	1.2
ENGINEERING INDUSTRIES PENS FUND	IMPHOLD	3.6
ENGINEERING INDUSTRIES PENS FUND	INVSTEC	2.2
ENGINEERING INDUSTRIES PENS FUND	ISCOR	2.2
ENGINEERING INDUSTRIES PENS FUND	ISG	1.8
ENGINEERING INDUSTRIES PENS FUND	KH PROPS	2.9
ENGINEERING INDUSTRIES PENS FUND	KWV-BEL	7.1
ENGINEERING INDUSTRIES PENS FUND	LIONMATCH	4.1
ENGINEERING INDUSTRIES PENS FUND	MAINPRO	4.9
ENGINEERING INDUSTRIES PENS FUND	MALHOLD	1.8
ENGINEERING INDUSTRIES PENS FUND	MCCARTHY	5.0
ENGINEERING INDUSTRIES PENS FUND	METPROP	3.9
ENGINEERING INDUSTRIES PENS FUND	MIDAS	1.6
ENGINEERING INDUSTRIES PENS FUND	MOMENTUM	4.0
ENGINEERING INDUSTRIES PENS FUND	NAMPAK	1.5
ENGINEERING INDUSTRIES PENS FUND	NBSHOLD	2.6
ENGINEERING INDUSTRIES PENS FUND	NEDCOR	2.0
ENGINEERING INDUSTRIES PENS FUND	NEI-AFR	2.7
ENGINEERING INDUSTRIES PENS FUND	NEIHOLD	3.6
ENGINEERING INDUSTRIES PENS FUND	PERSTEC	1.8
ENGINEERING INDUSTRIES PENS FUND	PIONEER	1.5
ENGINEERING INDUSTRIES PENS FUND	PLATE-GL	2.5
ENGINEERING INDUSTRIES PENS FUND	PPC	1.1
ENGINEERING INDUSTRIES PENS FUND	PREM-GRP	1.2
ENGINEERING INDUSTRIES PENS FUND	REUNERT	1.1
ENGINEERING INDUSTRIES PENS FUND	RMSPROP	3.1
ENGINEERING INDUSTRIES PENS FUND	ROMATEX	1.2
ENGINEERING INDUSTRIES PENS FUND	ROYCHEM	1.5
ENGINEERING INDUSTRIES PENS FUND	ROYFOOD	1.5
ENGINEERING INDUSTRIES PENS FUND	RUSFURN	2.6
ENGINEERING INDUSTRIES PENS FUND	SAFICON	3.2
ENGINEERING INDUSTRIES PENS FUND	SAFREN	2.4
ENGINEERING INDUSTRIES PENS FUND	SAPPI	1.8
ENGINEERING INDUSTRIES PENS FUND	SEARCON	3.1
ENGINEERING INDUSTRIES PENS FUND	SEARDEL	2.7
ENGINEERING INDUSTRIES PENS FUND	SENTRCHEM	1.7
ENGINEERING INDUSTRIES PENS FUND	SOTHERN	1.0
ENGINEERING INDUSTRIES PENS FUND	STANPRO	2.0
ENGINEERING INDUSTRIES PENS FUND	SYCOM	1.6
ENGINEERING INDUSTRIES PENS FUND	TAMBOTI	4.2
ENGINEERING INDUSTRIES PENS FUND	TONGAAT	2.7
ENGINEERING INDUSTRIES PENS FUND	UMDONI	1.9
ENGINEERING INDUSTRIES PENS FUND	UNITRAN	1.4
ENGINEERING INDUSTRIES PENS FUND	VETRUST	6.7
ENGINEERING INDUSTRIES PENS FUND	WOOLTRU	2.2
ENGLAND A R	HARWILL	2.8
ENTHOVEN R	GOLDSTEIN	1.4
ENVIRONMENTAL RESOURCES SA	ENROL	2.8
ENVOY INV P/L	W-&-A	1.4
EPF LIBAM NOM P/L	IMPHOLD	1.4
EPF OLD MUTUAL NOM P/L	AFR-LEASE	3.0
EPF OLD MUTUAL NOM P/L	FMCOTEC	2.0
EPF OLD MUTUAL NOM P/L	LENCO	1.3
EPF OLD MUTUAL NOM P/L	METPROP	1.3
EPF OLD MUTUAL NOM P/L	SAB IND	2.6
EPF OLD MUTUAL NOM P/L	W-R-CONS	2.1
EPF SANLAM NOM P/L	Q-DATA	1.2
EPF SMB NOM P/L	LENCO	1.3
EPF UAL NOM P/L	HIGATE	1.2
EPF UAL NOM P/L	KH PROPS	1.5
EPSIDON TECHNOLOGY P/L	CLEGG	3.5
ERIC ELLERINE TRUST P/L	ELLERINE	3.9
ERIC ELLERINE TRUST P/L	VEKTRA	1.7
ERIC KOHLER TRUST	ARIES	31.8
ESCOM PENS & PROV FUND	ALTRON	1.6
ESCOM PENS & PROV FUND	ANGLOVAAL	2.6
ESCOM PENS & PROV FUND	BARLOWS	1.1
ESCOM PENS & PROV FUND	CADSWEP	2.3
ESCOM PENS & PROV FUND	CGSMITH	1.0
ESCOM PENS & PROV FUND	LIBERTY	1.8
ESCOM PENS & PROV FUND	METPOL	1.5
ESCOM PENS & PROV FUND	PEPKOR	1.1
ESCOM PENS & PROV FUND	PICKNPAY	2.5
ESCOM PENS & PROV FUND	PPC	2.0
ESCOM PENS & PROV FUND	PREM-GRP	1.4
ESCOM PENS & PROV FUND	REMB-BEH	1.1
ESCOM PENS & PROV FUND	SUNCRUSH	2.9
ESCOM PENS & PROV FUND	TIGR-OATS	1.3
ESTERHUIZEN A M	STERLING	2.2

FIRST CORP NOM P/L	GROOTVLEI	1.4
FIRST CORP NOM P/L	HARTIES	1.5
FIRST CORP NOM P/L	KINROSS	2.5
FIRST CORP NOM P/L	LESLIE	1.1
FIRST CORP NOM P/L	O-K	1.8
FIRST LAND DEVELOPMENTS LTD	SYCOM	1.2
FIRST MUTUAL LIFE ASSURE SOC OF ZIM	BORDER	1.1
FIRST MUTUAL LIFE ASSURE SOC OF ZIM	CAIRNS	1.4
FIRST MUTUAL LIFE ASSURE SOC OF ZIM	CAPS	2.6
FIRST MUTUAL LIFE ASSURE SOC OF ZIM	DELTA ZIM	2.1
FIRST MUTUAL LIFE ASSURE SOC OF ZIM	FMB	3.4
FIRST MUTUAL LIFE ASSURE SOC OF ZIM	GULLIVER	1.8
FIRST MUTUAL LIFE ASSURE SOC OF ZIM	J & F	2.9
FIRST MUTUAL LIFE ASSURE SOC OF ZIM	KADOMA	2.3
FIRST MUTUAL LIFE ASSURE SOC OF ZIM	MASHONA	4.0
FIRST MUTUAL LIFE ASSURE SOC OF ZIM	NATFOOD	1.3
FIRST MUTUAL LIFE ASSURE SOC OF ZIM	PGI	3.0
FIRST MUTUAL LIFE ASSURE SOC OF ZIM	RADAR	2.6
FIRST MUTUAL LIFE ASSURE SOC OF ZIM	RIO ZIM	2.6
FIRST MUTUAL LIFE ASSURE SOC OF ZIM	ROTH ZIM	1.6
FIRST MUTUAL LIFE ASSURE SOC OF ZIM	WANKIE	1.8
FIRST MUTUAL LIFE ASSURE SOC OF ZIM	ZIM SUN	2.7
FIRST MUTUAL LIFE ASSURE SOC OF ZIM	ZIMBANK	2.6
FIRST NAT BANK LTD	CASHBIL	3.1
FIRST NAT BANK OF SA LTD	SOTHERN	29.2
FIRST NAT CITY TRUST CO	VAAL-REEF	1.4
FIRST NAT CITY TRUST CO	WINKELS	3.3
FIRST NAT MERCHANT BANK LTD	CONTROL	6.0
FIRST NAT MERCHANT BANK LTD	OZZ	1.4
FIRST NAT MERCHANT BANK LTD	VENTERS	1.3
FIRST NAT NOM P/L	A-V-I	2.3
FIRST NAT NOM P/L	ABSA	1.4
FIRST NAT NOM P/L	ADONIS	2.9
FIRST NAT NOM P/L	AFMIN	9.8
FIRST NAT NOM P/L	AFR-LEASE	1.1
FIRST NAT NOM P/L	AFROX	1.1
FIRST NAT NOM P/L	AKJ	3.3
FIRST NAT NOM P/L	AMGOLD	2.4
FIRST NAT NOM P/L	ANAMINT	1.2
FIRST NAT NOM P/L	ANGLO-S	1.4
FIRST NAT NOM P/L	ARGUS	2.5
FIRST NAT NOM P/L	ASS-MANG	1.7
FIRST NAT NOM P/L	AUTODEK	73.2
FIRST NAT NOM P/L	BARLOWS	2.0
FIRST NAT NOM P/L	BARPLAT	1.1
FIRST NAT NOM P/L	BASREAD	1.0
FIRST NAT NOM P/L	BEATRIX	1.8
FIRST NAT NOM P/L	BERZACK	1.3
FIRST NAT NOM P/L	BEVCON	1.4
FIRST NAT NOM P/L	BLOCHS	16.0
FIRST NAT NOM P/L	BOEPROP	4.3
FIRST NAT NOM P/L	BOUMAT	3.4
FIRST NAT NOM P/L	BOYMANS	1.2
FIRST NAT NOM P/L	BRACKEN	4.3
FIRST NAT NOM P/L	BTRDUN	2.4
FIRST NAT NOM P/L	BUFFELS	5.1
FIRST NAT NOM P/L	CAFCA	4.9
FIRST NAT NOM P/L	CASHBIL	4.3
FIRST NAT NOM P/L	CEMENCO	1.5
FIRST NAT NOM P/L	CENPROP	1.4
FIRST NAT NOM P/L	CHEMSERVE	2.5
FIRST NAT NOM P/L	CLINICS	2.8
FIRST NAT NOM P/L	CMH	4.8
FIRST NAT NOM P/L	CMS	11.0
FIRST NAT NOM P/L	CNAGALO	1.4
FIRST NAT NOM P/L	COMPASS	10.6
FIRST NAT NOM P/L	CON-MURCH	5.4
FIRST NAT NOM P/L	CONSOL	1.1
FIRST NAT NOM P/L	CONTRAV	6.1
FIRST NAT NOM P/L	COPI	1.7
FIRST NAT NOM P/L	COR-SYND	1.7
FIRST NAT NOM P/L	CORWIL	11.2
FIRST NAT NOM P/L	CROOKES	6.5
FIRST NAT NOM P/L	CULLINAN	1.7
FIRST NAT NOM P/L	DA-GAMA	1.3
FIRST NAT NOM P/L	DABI	2.4
FIRST NAT NOM P/L	DATAKOR	2.1
FIRST NAT NOM P/L	DBN-DEEP	13.8
FIRST NAT NOM P/L	DE BEERS	1.6
FIRST NAT NOM P/L	DEBNAIR	1.1
FIRST NAT NOM P/L	DECHOLD	8.4
FIRST NAT NOM P/L	DEELKRL	1.8
FIRST NAT NOM P/L	DELTA	3.2
FIRST NAT NOM P/L	DIDATA	4.5
FIRST NAT NOM P/L	DOORNS	4.1
FIRST NAT NOM P/L	DORBYL	2.5
FIRST NAT NOM P/L	DRIES	1.2
FIRST NAT NOM P/L	E-DAGGA	5.1
FIRST NAT NOM P/L	E-T-CONS	5.9
FIRST NAT NOM P/L	ED-L-BATE	1.8
FIRST NAT NOM P/L	EDGARS	1.7
FIRST NAT NOM P/L	ELANDS	1.5
FIRST NAT NOM P/L	EQUIKOR	4.0
FIRST NAT NOM P/L	ERGO	2.6
FIRST NAT NOM P/L	F-S-I	2.2
FIRST NAT NOM P/L	FARM-AG	2.5
FIRST NAT NOM P/L	FEDSURE	4.8
FIRST NAT NOM P/L	FINTECH	2.1
FIRST NAT NOM P/L	FIRSTBK	7.9
FIRST NAT NOM P/L	FOCUS	1.8
FIRST NAT NOM P/L	FREDDEV	1.7
FIRST NAT NOM P/L	FREGOLD	2.8
FIRST NAT NOM P/L	GAZGOLD	1.5
FIRST NAT NOM P/L	GEN-OPTIC	2.4
FIRST NAT NOM P/L	GENBEL	3.3
FIRST NAT NOM P/L	GENTYRE-A	7.3
FIRST NAT NOM P/L	GF-PROPS	1.3
FIRST NAT NOM P/L	GLODINA	1.3
FIRST NAT NOM P/L	GRINCOR	1.7
FIRST NAT NOM P/L	GRINTEK	1.1
FIRST NAT NOM P/L	GROOTVLEI	3.7
FIRST NAT NOM P/L	GROWALK	15.1
FIRST NAT NOM P/L	GUBINGS	1.7
FIRST NAT NOM P/L	GYPSUM	1.0
FIRST NAT NOM P/L	HAGGIE	3.3
FIRST NAT NOM P/L	HARMONY	1.3
FIRST NAT NOM P/L	HARTIES	2.8
FIRST NAT NOM P/L	HARWILL	45.0
FIRST NAT NOM P/L	HICORL	1.2
FIRST NAT NOM P/L	HIGATE	13.6
FIRST NAT NOM P/L	HISTONE	18.0
FIRST NAT NOM P/L	HIVELD	1.4
FIRST NAT NOM P/L	HLH	1.2
FIRST NAT NOM P/L	HUDACO	5.0
FIRST NAT NOM P/L	I-C-S	1.8
FIRST NAT NOM P/L	IMPHOLD	1.9
FIRST NAT NOM P/L	IMPLATS	1.8
FIRST NAT NOM P/L	IND-SELE	2.1
FIRST NAT NOM P/L	INHOLD	6.2
FIRST NAT NOM P/L	INVICTA	65.8
FIRST NAT NOM P/L	JDGROUP	10.2
FIRST NAT NOM P/L	JOEL	3.1
FIRST NAT NOM P/L	JOHNNIES	1.4
FIRST NAT NOM P/L	KEELEY	2.3
FIRST NAT NOM P/L	KELGRAN	1.1
FIRST NAT NOM P/L	KINROSS	1.2
FIRST NAT NOM P/L	KLOOF	2.5
FIRST NAT NOM P/L	KNIGHTS	1.2
FIRST NAT NOM P/L	LANCHEM	2.2
FIRST NAT NOM P/L	LESLIE	5.4
FIRST NAT NOM P/L	LIB HOLD	1.7
FIRST NAT NOM P/L	LIBANON	4.2
FIRST NAT NOM P/L	LIBVEST	2.4
FIRST NAT NOM P/L	LIONMATCH	9.2
FIRST NAT NOM P/L	LORAINE	5.0
FIRST NAT NOM P/L	M-&-F	1.1

FIRST NAT NOM P/L	MAINPRO	1.3
FIRST NAT NOM P/L	MALHOLD	1.7
FIRST NAT NOM P/L	MASHOLD	2.0
FIRST NAT NOM P/L	MCCARTHY	1.1
FIRST NAT NOM P/L	MCRTAIL	10.5
FIRST NAT NOM P/L	METKOR	1.7
FIRST NAT NOM P/L	METPOL	1.6
FIRST NAT NOM P/L	MICOR	6.6
FIRST NAT NOM P/L	MID-WITS	4.4
FIRST NAT NOM P/L	MIDAS	1.1
FIRST NAT NOM P/L	MINGRAN	5.7
FIRST NAT NOM P/L	MLNHOLD	2.0
FIRST NAT NOM P/L	MODDER	8.5
FIRST NAT NOM P/L	MOLYSLP	2.4
FIRST NAT NOM P/L	MSAULI	15.5
FIRST NAT NOM P/L	NAMFISH	1.1
FIRST NAT NOM P/L	NAMPAK	1.7
FIRST NAT NOM P/L	NAMSEA	1.0
FIRST NAT NOM P/L	NATSEL	1.3
FIRST NAT NOM P/L	NBSHOLD	9.6
FIRST NAT NOM P/L	NEDCOR	1.5
FIRST NAT NOM P/L	NEI-AFR	2.0
FIRST NAT NOM P/L	NEIHOLD	3.2
FIRST NAT NOM P/L	NEW-WITS	6.4
FIRST NAT NOM P/L	NINIAN	1.1
FIRST NAT NOM P/L	NORTHAM	1.5
FIRST NAT NOM P/L	O-K	1.7
FIRST NAT NOM P/L	OCTODEC	1.2
FIRST NAT NOM P/L	OFSIL	1.4
FIRST NAT NOM P/L	OMNIA	2.2
FIRST NAT NOM P/L	OTIS	1.6
FIRST NAT NOM P/L	OZZ	26.3
FIRST NAT NOM P/L	PANPROP	1.8
FIRST NAT NOM P/L	PERSBEL	1.5
FIRST NAT NOM P/L	PICKNPAY	2.0
FIRST NAT NOM P/L	PIONEER	2.9
FIRST NAT NOM P/L	POWTECH	2.2
FIRST NAT NOM P/L	PP RUST	1.7
FIRST NAT NOM P/L	PPC	1.5
FIRST NAT NOM P/L	PREM-GRP	2.0
FIRST NAT NOM P/L	PUBHOLD	2.3
FIRST NAT NOM P/L	PUTCO	2.8
FIRST NAT NOM P/L	PUTPROP	7.6
FIRST NAT NOM P/L	R-M-PROPS	4.6
FIRST NAT NOM P/L	RALE	1.6
FIRST NAT NOM P/L	RANDFONTN	9.3
FIRST NAT NOM P/L	RANDMIN	1.5
FIRST NAT NOM P/L	REMGRO	1.7
FIRST NAT NOM P/L	REUNERT	1.3
FIRST NAT NOM P/L	RHOEX	1.1
FIRST NAT NOM P/L	ROOIBERG	7.1
FIRST NAT NOM P/L	ROYFOOD	1.3
FIRST NAT NOM P/L	RUHOLD	8.0
FIRST NAT NOM P/L	RUSPLAT	4.0
FIRST NAT NOM P/L	S-A-BIAS	2.2
FIRST NAT NOM P/L	S-A-EAGLE	56.6
FIRST NAT NOM P/L	SA-BREWS	1.6
FIRST NAT NOM P/L	SAGEGRP	2.7
FIRST NAT NOM P/L	SALLIES	3.2
FIRST NAT NOM P/L	SASFIN	67.3
FIRST NAT NOM P/L	SASOL	2.1
FIRST NAT NOM P/L	SCORE	1.9
FIRST NAT NOM P/L	SEARCON	5.9
FIRST NAT NOM P/L	SENTRCHEM	1.1
FIRST NAT NOM P/L	SILTEK	2.1
FIRST NAT NOM P/L	SMART	8.5
FIRST NAT NOM P/L	SOTHERN	5.4
FIRST NAT NOM P/L	SOUTHVAAL	2.0
FIRST NAT NOM P/L	SOWITS	48.3
FIRST NAT NOM P/L	SPICER	78.8
FIRST NAT NOM P/L	ST-HELENA	2.5
FIRST NAT NOM P/L	STERLING	1.9
FIRST NAT NOM P/L	STILFTN	1.2
FIRST NAT NOM P/L	SUB-N	6.1
FIRST NAT NOM P/L	T-&-N	2.9
FIRST NAT NOM P/L	T-M-L	18.5
FIRST NAT NOM P/L	TAMBOTI	11.0
FIRST NAT NOM P/L	TEGKOR	1.3
FIRST NAT NOM P/L	TGH	1.9
FIRST NAT NOM P/L	TIGR-OATS	1.2
FIRST NAT NOM P/L	TIME	1.3
FIRST NAT NOM P/L	TMX	1.5
FIRST NAT NOM P/L	TOCO	20.2
FIRST NAT NOM P/L	TOYOTA	1.9
FIRST NAT NOM P/L	TPN	34.5
FIRST NAT NOM P/L	TRANS-NTL	3.3
FIRST NAT NOM P/L	TWEEFONTN	2.1
FIRST NAT NOM P/L	UMDONI	12.1
FIRST NAT NOM P/L	UNISERV	4.1
FIRST NAT NOM P/L	UTICO	1.4
FIRST NAT NOM P/L	VAAL-REEF	3.9
FIRST NAT NOM P/L	VENTERS	4.8
FIRST NAT NOM P/L	VENTRON	1.2
FIRST NAT NOM P/L	VESTCOR	9.1
FIRST NAT NOM P/L	VETRUST	16.5
FIRST NAT NOM P/L	VILLAGE	1.2
FIRST NAT NOM P/L	VLAKS	3.4
FIRST NAT NOM P/L	VOGELS	1.1
FIRST NAT NOM P/L	VOLTEX	6.7
FIRST NAT NOM P/L	W-R-CONS	2.7
FIRST NAT NOM P/L	WALHOLD	1.6
FIRST NAT NOM P/L	WBHOLD	1.5
FIRST NAT NOM P/L	WELKOM	3.7
FIRST NAT NOM P/L	WES-AREAS	8.8
FIRST NAT NOM P/L	WESCO	3.7
FIRST NAT NOM P/L	WINKELS	2.5
FIRST NAT NOM P/L	WIT-G-M	22.8
FIRST NAT NOM P/L	WIT-NIGEL	2.0
FIRST NAT NOM P/L	WOODROW	2.9
FIRST NAT NOM P/L	WOOLTRU	3.4
FIRST NAT NOM P/L	WSTN-DEEP	4.4
FIRST NAT NOM P/L	YORKCOR	2.4
FIRST NAT NOM P/L	ZANDPAN	4.4
FIRST NAT NOM P/L GATR DEPOT	BLYVOOR	6.5
FIRST NAT NOM P/L GATR DEPOT	BRACKEN	6.7
FIRST NAT NOM P/L GATR DEPOT	BUFFELS	1.4
FIRST NAT NOM P/L GATR DEPOT	DBN-DEEP	3.1
FIRST NAT NOM P/L GATR DEPOT	DE BEERS	1.6
FIRST NAT NOM P/L GATR DEPOT	DOORNS	1.1
FIRST NAT NOM P/L GATR DEPOT	DRIES	4.4
FIRST NAT NOM P/L GATR DEPOT	E-DAGGA	3.3
FIRST NAT NOM P/L GATR DEPOT	FREDDEV	1.6
FIRST NAT NOM P/L GATR DEPOT	FREGOLD	1.8
FIRST NAT NOM P/L GATR DEPOT	GFSA	1.4
FIRST NAT NOM P/L GATR DEPOT	GROOTVLEI	5.7
FIRST NAT NOM P/L GATR DEPOT	HARTIES	5.6
FIRST NAT NOM P/L GATR DEPOT	IMPLATS	1.4
FIRST NAT NOM P/L GATR DEPOT	KINROSS	2.4
FIRST NAT NOM P/L GATR DEPOT	KLOOF	5.1
FIRST NAT NOM P/L GATR DEPOT	LIBANON	1.5
FIRST NAT NOM P/L GATR DEPOT	LORAINE	6.6
FIRST NAT NOM P/L GATR DEPOT	MODDER	2.3
FIRST NAT NOM P/L GATR DEPOT	OFSIL	2.2
FIRST NAT NOM P/L GATR DEPOT	ST-HELENA	1.6
FIRST NAT NOM P/L GATR DEPOT	STH-RODPT	1.8
FIRST NAT NOM P/L GATR DEPOT	UNISEL	1.9
FIRST NAT NOM P/L GATR DEPOT	VAAL-REEF	2.5
FIRST NAT NOM P/L GATR DEPOT	WELKOM	2.4
FIRST NAT NOM P/L GATR DEPOT	WINKELS	2.8
FIRST NAT NOM P/L GATR DEPOT	WSTN-DEEP	2.5
FIRST NOM (PVT) LTD	TEDCO	2.6
FIRST NOM P/L	PORTHLD	1.7
FIRST NOM PVT LTD	AFDISTIL	3.9
FIRST NOM PVT LTD	BINDURA	1.3
FIRST NOM PVT LTD	CIH	9.5
FIRST NOM PVT LTD	CIRCLE	1.4

FIRST NOM PVT LTD	HIPPO	3.5
FIRST NOM PVT LTD	MASHONA	19.2
FIRST NOM PVT LTD	NATFOOD	1.5
FIRST NOM PVT LTD	ZIMALLOYS	1.5
FIRST SHELF CO PVT LTD	FMB	2.4
FIRST TEAM TRUST	DINETTE	1.0
FISHER M	QUORUM	1.9
FISONS INV HOLDINGS (ZIMBABWE)	GULLIVER	1.3
FITTA P/L	QUICKCO	39.7
FLACK P H	FRALEX	1.6
FLASHSPORTS P/L	AMSHOE	34.9
FLEISCHER H H	SPESCOM	1.1
FLOODTIDE SYNDICATE P/L	UNION	4.6
FMB HOLDINGS EMPL SHARE TRUST	FMB	2.5
FNX NOM LTD	FAIRCAP	27.1
FOLB L	SPL	1.4
FOLB L J	SPL	2.8
FOLIO INV CO P/L	BOE	1.1
FOORD & MEINTJES GROUP PROV FUND	COMPASS	1.1
FORBES J A	DIDATA	1.0
FORD V	PROPFIN	2.2
FORM SCAFF TRUST SHARE INC	F-S-I	3.9
FORM-SCAFF INV P/L	F-S-GROUP	18.1
FORMAN G	FORIM	2.3
FORMAN J	FORIM	8.5
FORMAN J E	FORIM	4.3
FORMAN JOSEPH HOLDINGS P/L	FORIM	18.2
FORMAN S	FORIM	1.1
FOSCHINI LTD	LEFIC	10.0
FOSCHINI LTD	OCEANA	41.8
FOSKOR PENS FUND	BOLTONS	1.2
FOSKOR PENS FUND	S-A-BIAS	2.1
FOSTER I & SCHWINGES C INV P/L	DEBNAIR	12.8
FOUNTAINS VALLEY INV CC	YORKCOR	1.2
FOURIE H J	TAFLBRG	4.0
FOURNES HOLDINGS CORP	TRIMTEX	40.5
FOURNES HOLDINGS CORP	TRIMTRD	8.5
FOWLER A S	MCPHAIL	1.2
FOWLER J M	CFC	1.3
FOX STREET NOM P/L	A-T-COLL	25.7
FOX STREET NOM P/L	A-V-HOLD	51.0
FOX STREET NOM P/L	A-V-I	52.7
FOX STREET NOM P/L	ANG-ALPHA	1.2
FOX STREET NOM P/L	ANGLOVAAL	4.8
FOX STREET NOM P/L	ASS-MANG	41.6
FOX STREET NOM P/L	ASSORE	12.4
FOX STREET NOM P/L	AVF GRP	1.9
FOX STREET NOM P/L	BOE	1.9
FOX STREET NOM P/L	CON-MURCH	7.3
FOX STREET NOM P/L	CONSOL	3.9
FOX STREET NOM P/L	CONTROL	1.4
FOX STREET NOM P/L	DOORNS	2.0
FOX STREET NOM P/L	E-T-CONS	51.6
FOX STREET NOM P/L	HARTIES	7.8
FOX STREET NOM P/L	LORAINE	7.6
FOX STREET NOM P/L	MID-WITS	22.7
FOX STREET NOM P/L	RANDCOL	1.2
FOX STREET NOM P/L	SOUDEX	2.4
FOX STREET NOM P/L	TARGET	56.0
FOX STREET NOM P/L	VILLAGE	38.1
FOX STREET NOM P/L	ZANDPAN	20.4
FOXCLAUDE P/L	A-V-HOLD	2.3
FOXGLEN INV LTD	CMI	4.9
FOXVALLEY INV P/L	CMI	6.5
FRADAV TRUST	BSI	3.3
FRALEX LTD	ALEXNDR	57.8
FRALEX SHARE TRUST	FRALEX	4.6
FRAME GROUP HOLDINGS LTD	CONFRAM	67.3
FRAME POLYPROPYLENE MILLS P/L	CONFRAM	2.6
FRAN BRENNER INV P/L	BRENMIL	1.8
FRANCIS MINELECT PROPERTIES PVT LTD	CIH	1.5
FRANKE R R	UNION	1.9
FRANKLE P M	MAXMECH	10.6
FRASER ALEXANDER PROV FUND	FRALEX	1.7
FRASER ALEXANDER SHARE TRUST	ALEXNDR	3.9
FRATER K J M	ARIES	1.8
FREDERICK EMARY INV TRUST CO P/L	JASCO	9.7
FREE STATE CONS GOLD MINES (OPS)	SOUTHVAAL	3.1
FREE STATE CONS GOLD MINES (OPS)	ST-HELENA	3.3
FREE STATE CONS GOLD MINES (OPS)	WELKOM	19.9
FRITIN P/L	CONCOR	1.3
FROST L	TECHIRE	1.2
FS DISTRIBUTORS LTD	ELCENTR	5.5
FS GROUP LTD	F-S-I	64.5
FSI CORP LTD	WAICOR	60.8
FSI CORP PENS FUND	ELCENTR	10.1
FSI INV (PVT) LTD	FSI ZIM	42.1
FULIT P/L	FIT	19.2
FULLARD M P	STOCKS	3.2
FULMEN TELECOMMUNICATIONS P/L	ALTECH	5.9
FURNCOL LTD	AFCOL	14.8
FURNCOL LTD	ROMATEX	6.3
FURNHOLD LTD	RUSFURN	12.6
FYNBOS TRUST	MCCARTHY	5.9
FYNBOS TRUST	MCRTAIL	25.7

G

G A WARE & ASSOCIATES PVT LTD	MWEAR	1.1
G A WARE HOLDINGS P/L	MWEAR	17.2
G C & M NOM NATAL P/L	CFC	1.7
G J COATES INV P/L	COATES	1.0
G R E NOM LTD	LIB HOLD	2.9
G VAN E DU PLESSIS INV P/L	NUWORLD	10.8
GABI BRENNER INV P/L	BRENMIL	4.5
GAGGINS C	CAFCA	3.6
GALATES INV HLDGS LTD	JOHNNIES	7.5
GALATES INV HLDGS LTD	WSTN-DEEP	2.3
GALAXY INV LTD	NATRAWL	13.5
GALHAR HLDGS	TOMKOR	2.6
GALLO AFRICA LTD	CTP	2.2
GALLO AFRICA LTD	MAST	30.9
GALLO INV HOLDINGS LTD	MAST	5.0
GAMBIE R	OVCON	2.0
GANTRY HOLDINGS P/L	ADCORP	17.2
GARDINER FAMILY HOLDINGS P/L	OAKFLDS	5.7
GARSFONTEIN PARK NOM CC	GROWPNT	1.2
GAUSS W	BLOCHS	1.3
GAYLE BRENNER INV P/L	BRENMIL	3.0
GEDDES C R	SANLIC	1.1
GEEKIE J K	CFC	1.5
GEFFEN A	AIDA	12.4
GELBART W F	FORIM	4.3
GELDKOR P/L	BESTER	4.6
GEMEENSKAPLIKE MUNISIPALE OFS PENS	BOLTONS	1.5
GEMEENSKAPLIKE MUNISIPALE OFS PENS	LENCO	1.1
GEMEENSKAPLIKE MUNISIPALE OFS PENS	S-A-BIAS	1.2
GEMEENSKAPLIKE MUNISIPALE TVL PENS	FOSCHINI	1.3
GEMEENSKAPLIKE MUNISIPALE TVL PENS	IND-SELE	1.5
GEMEENSKAPLIKE MUNISIPALE TVL PENS	METKOR	1.2
GEMEENSKAPLIKE MUNISIPALE TVL PENS	PPC	1.3
GEMEENSKAPLIKE MUNISIPALE TVL PENS	SEARCON	1.3
GEMEENSKAPLIKE MUNISIPALE TVL PENS	UMDONI	1.2
GEMEENSKAPLIKE MUNISIPALE TVL PENS	VOLTEX	1.0
GEMLIB INV P/L	SA-BREWS	34.3
GENCOR BEHEREND LTD	GENCOR	10.9
GENERAL TYRE SHARE INCENTIVE TRUST	GENTYRE-A	1.6
GENESIS EMERGING MARKETS FUND	PEP BOT	1.9
GENQUIP P/L	WOODROW	28.6
GENTYRE INDUSTRIES SHARE INC TRUST	GENTYRE-A	1.3
GERBER H E/L	TAFLBRG	8.3
GERBRI FINANCE INV HOLDINGS CC	AKJ	4.7
GERMISHUIZEN G TRUST	VALCAR	19.3
GERMISHUIZEN S F	VALCAR	20.8
GERMISHUIZEN S F INV P/L	VALCAR	6.7

H

HARVEST SECURITIES LTD	AUTOPGE	2.1
HARVEST SECURITIES LTD	COR-SYND	4.3
HARVEST SECURITIES LTD	CURFIN	1.4
HARVEST SECURITIES LTD	MILSTAN	1.4
HARVEST SECURITIES LTD	N-KLEINS	5.0
HARVEST SECURITIES LTD	OTIS	1.5
HARVEST SECURITIES LTD	PUBHOLD	6.5
HARVEST SECURITIES LTD	RACY	1.9
HARVEST SECURITIES LTD	UNIHOLD	1.1
HARVEST SECURITIES LTD	VILLAGE	2.6
HARVEST SECURITIES LTD	WBHOLD	4.3
HASHAY NOM P/L	CONCOR	1.2
HASHAY NOM P/L	KUDU	2.0
HASHAY NOM P/L	PROPFIN	8.9
HASKINS M G	SECHOLD	1.1
HASLAM A L	U-CON	7.9
HASLAM EDUCATIONAL TRUST	U-CON	3.4
HASSON D	OHIO	3.8
HASSON R R H	MOBILE	2.9
HAWKINS C A TRUST	AIMARK	1.3
HAYLEY BRENNER INV P/L	BRENMIL	4.5
HAYMANN F V	SHOCRAF	36.0
HAYREES P/L	COM-FUND	20.9
HAYWARD G E	ALEXWYT	1.5
HEATH G G	POINTER	1.2
HEAVEN INV P/L	DPF-INV	3.1
HEIL H	TAFLBRG	8.3
HELYAR D W H	MATH-ASH	2.0
HENDLER C	RACY	4.1
HENDLER E	RACY	3.4
HENDLER R	RACY	3.2
HENDRIK FAMILY INV P/L	SCHARIG	18.9
HENKEL A W	T-E-J	1.0
HENRY ALTY ZIMBABWE (PVT) LTD	WSGROVE	2.3
HERBERT & TRAKMAN NOM P/L	ACREM	7.6
HERBEST NOM P/L	GEFCO	3.4
HERBEST NOM P/L	SOWITS	3.0
HERMANN MELCHER & CO P/L	CFC	1.4
HERON R J	PALS	2.3
HERSOV B	CONTROL	3.0
HERTA ERNST INV P/L	METJE-&-Z	52.6
HEVANS HOLDINGS P/L	OCTODEC	2.8
HEVANS HOLDINGS P/L	TOMKOR	2.8
HEYNS J A J	OCTODEC	1.8
HEYNS J A J	TOMKOR	4.0
HEYNS M A	SPL	1.4
HG & S NOM P/L	ISG	1.8
HG & S NOM P/L	PERSTEC	5.0
HI SCORE INV HOLDINGS P/L	METCASH	1.8
HI SCORE INV HOLDINGS P/L	SCORE	2.6
HI-SCORE HLDGS LTD	SCOCLIK	65.9
HIBBERD G	OHIO	1.6
HIBBERT C T	TIME	38.3
HICOR P/L	ALLGRP	88.6
HICOR P/L	ALLWEAR	24.7
HIGHVELD STAFF PENS FUND	HIGATE	1.4
HIGHWICK PROPERTY P/L	ENSIGN	41.5
HILL A R C	ENBOT	1.6
HILL D A H	RABIE	1.3
HILL P N	ENBOT	1.6
HILL R S	BROADACRE	1.1
HILLEL COHEN CC	VIERFONTN	2.6
HILLFAM INV P/L	ARGUS	2.7
HINDS G	OHIO	1.6
HIPPER K J	SAFICON	1.0
HIPPO QUARRIES LTD	SALLIES	2.2
HIRSCHSON I T	EQUIKOR	1.1
HOFFMAN S V	KAROS	2.7
HOFFMANN J TRUST	KAROS	3.7
HOGG G B	BOYMANS	1.5
HOLDAINS INV (CARLCOR) P/L	CARLCOR	8.2
HOLDEM P/L	ILCO	93.8
HOLLARD INSURANCE CO LTD	OVBEL	1.5

HOLLARD NOM PVT LTD	WSGROVE	1.2
HOLLARDSTRAAT SES INV BPK	GENCOR	5.0
HOLMWOOD INV LTD	HARWILL	4.5
HOMEMAKERS GROUP LTD	JDGROUP	50.1
HORNE F	PROPFIN	1.0
HORTORS GROUP PENS FUND	DABI	1.1
HORTORS GROUP PENS FUND	G5HOLD	2.2
HORTORS GROUP PENS FUND	HYPROP	1.1
HORTORS GROUP PENS FUND	NEW-CENT	4.3
HORTORS GROUP PENS FUND	SOLCHEM	3.7
HORTORS GROUP PENS FUND	WALTONS	1.3
HORTORS LTD	CLEGG	28.2
HOSKEN CONS INV SHARE INC TRUST	HCI	3.2
HOSKEN CONSOLIDATED INV LTD	CRENDEL	73.1
HOSKEN CONSOLIDATED INV LTD	I-G-I	55.5
HOSKEN CONSOLIDATED INV LTD	SAFLIFE	10.6
HOSKEN F W	HCI	1.3
HOSKEN HUBERT WILL TRUST	HCI	3.6
HOSKEN STAFF SHARE INC CONTROL ACC	HCI	2.4
HOSKEN W TRUST	HCI	7.5
HOTEL ADMINISTRATORS NATAL P/L	KAROS	3.7
HOTZ S	STERLING	3.8
HOUSE OF INV LTD	LANCHEM	8.6
HUGHES I W	CAFCA	1.3
HUGHOF INV P/L	TOMKOR	1.1
HUGOHOF INV P/L	GROWPNT	1.6
HUMPHREYS & LITTLE FALLS INV LTD	PRIM-G-M	7.0
HUMPHREYS INV LTD	PRIM-G-M	3.4
HUNT LEUCHARS & HEPBURN HOLDINGS	RAINBOW	11.8
HUNTCOR LTD	HLH	76.6
HUNTS MANUFACTURING CO P/L	GENTYRE-A	78.4
HUNYANI WORKERS TRUST	HUNYANI	11.9
HURRY R G FAMILY HOLDINGS P/L	KH PROPS	2.0
HURWITZ B	CLINICS	23.4
HURWITZ J L	CLINICS	2.4
HURWITZ SELWIN FAMILY TRUST	KAROS	7.5
HURWORTH N M	UNION	1.2
HYLTON V E	ICH	2.3
HYLTON V TRUST	ICH	2.6
HYMAN A J	CUTRITE	12.6
HYPAR INV P/L	SAKERS	30.0
HYPERETTE STORES SHARE INC SCHEME	HYPERET	5.9

I

I & J EMPLOYEE SHARE PURC TRUST LTD	I-&-J	2.4
I & J PENS FUND	APEX	1.3
I & J PENS FUND	MCCARTHY	1.0
I B JOFFE SHARE TRUST	IBJOFFE	1.4
I C H INV CO P/L	URQHART	95.1
I G NOM P/L	RMSPROP	1.6
ICI SA LTD	AECI	20.4
ICI THETA BV	AECI	5.8
ICICLE ENGINEERING P/L	TECFIN	40.5
IGI - SHORT TERM	SEFALANA	3.0
IGI BOTSWANA INSURANCE LTD	RDC	1.5
IGI BOTSWANA LIFE ASSURE LTD	BB BOT	1.3
IGI BOTSWANA LIFE ASSURE LTD	BOTINS	1.7
IGI BOTSWANA LIFE ASSURE LTD	FSC	6.1
IGI BOTSWANA LIFE ASSURE LTD	PEP BOT	2.6
IGI BOTSWANA LIFE ASSURE LTD	RDC	3.0
IGI BOTSWANA LIFE ASSURE LTD	SECHABA	5.6
IGI BOTSWANA LIFE ASSURE LTD	SEFALANA	4.0
IGI BOTSWANA LTD	INCO	1.2
IGI INSURANCE CO LTD CONTROL ACC	I-G-I	9.9
IGI INSURANCE HOLDINGS LTD	IGI BOT	74.3
IGI SHARE INCENTIVE TRUST	I-G-I	1.6
ILLMAN B	BIVEC	4.6
ILLMAN B	GEN-OPTIC	10.6
ILLMAN S H	BIVEC	17.6
ILSE F G INV P/L	BASREAD	3.8
ILSE F G INV P/L	CONCOR	3.8

ILSE F G INV P/L	TIME	2.9
ILSE F G INV P/L	UNION	21.3
IMERMAN I L	ELLERINE	1.1
IMERMAN S	ROYHOLD	4.6
IMERMAN V S	ROYHOLD	52.5
IMPERIAL GROUP LTD	IMPHOLD	60.4
INBARR J G	JADE	2.6
IND DEVELOPMENT CORP OF ZIM LTD	HUNYANI	23.9
IND DEVELOPMENT CORP SA LTD	IND-SELE	52.1
IND DEVELOPMENT CORP SA LTD	ISCOR	16.1
IND DEVELOPMENT CORP SA LTD	NATSEL	50.8
IND DEVELOPMENT CORP SA LTD	SASOL	3.4
IND DEVELOPMENT CORP SA LTD	SENTRCHEM	12.7
IND PARTNERSHIP INV LTD	DORBYL	9.9
IND PARTNERSHIP INV LTD	HUNTCOR	65.9
IND PARTNERSHIP INV LTD	METKOR	50.0
INDO-CHINA NOM P/L	AFMIN	6.0
INDO-CHINA NOM P/L	AFR-LEASE	16.0
INDO-CHINA NOM P/L	AMGOLD	3.3
INDO-CHINA NOM P/L	BEATRIX	1.7
INDO-CHINA NOM P/L	BLYVOOR	17.2
INDO-CHINA NOM P/L	BRACKEN	24.7
INDO-CHINA NOM P/L	BUFFELS	22.2
INDO-CHINA NOM P/L	CLEGG	18.4
INDO-CHINA NOM P/L	CON-MURCH	1.7
INDO-CHINA NOM P/L	DABI	3.5
INDO-CHINA NOM P/L	DBN-DEEP	26.2
INDO-CHINA NOM P/L	DE BEERS	1.8
INDO-CHINA NOM P/L	DRIES	6.3
INDO-CHINA NOM P/L	E-DAGGA	14.2
INDO-CHINA NOM P/L	E-R-P-M	2.6
INDO-CHINA NOM P/L	E-T-CONS	6.7
INDO-CHINA NOM P/L	ELANDS	5.5
INDO-CHINA NOM P/L	ERGO	6.0
INDO-CHINA NOM P/L	FREDDEV	4.3
INDO-CHINA NOM P/L	FREGOLD	8.2
INDO-CHINA NOM P/L	GROOTVLEI	25.3
INDO-CHINA NOM P/L	HARMONY	9.1
INDO-CHINA NOM P/L	HARTIES	11.9
INDO-CHINA NOM P/L	HARWILL	8.6
INDO-CHINA NOM P/L	HICORL	4.6
INDO-CHINA NOM P/L	IMPLATS	5.5
INDO-CHINA NOM P/L	INVSTEC	2.0
INDO-CHINA NOM P/L	KINROSS	11.0
INDO-CHINA NOM P/L	KLOOF	12.5
INDO-CHINA NOM P/L	KNIGHTS	1.8
INDO-CHINA NOM P/L	LESLIE	14.0
INDO-CHINA NOM P/L	LIBANON	24.5
INDO-CHINA NOM P/L	LORAINE	12.6
INDO-CHINA NOM P/L	LYD-PLAT	1.3
INDO-CHINA NOM P/L	MEDHOLD	27.1
INDO-CHINA NOM P/L	MINGRAN	2.7
INDO-CHINA NOM P/L	MODDER	24.9
INDO-CHINA NOM P/L	NEIHOLD	4.8
INDO-CHINA NOM P/L	NIGEL	2.2
INDO-CHINA NOM P/L	OFSIL	8.3
INDO-CHINA NOM P/L	PEPGRO	1.1
INDO-CHINA NOM P/L	RANDEX	2.3
INDO-CHINA NOM P/L	RANDFONTN	4.4
INDO-CHINA NOM P/L	RUSFURN	2.8
INDO-CHINA NOM P/L	RUSPLAT	2.4
INDO-CHINA NOM P/L	SHOCRAF	8.7
INDO-CHINA NOM P/L	SOUTHVAAL	7.3
INDO-CHINA NOM P/L	ST-HELENA	10.1
INDO-CHINA NOM P/L	STH-RODPT	18.5
INDO-CHINA NOM P/L	STILFTN	6.1
INDO-CHINA NOM P/L	SUB-N	1.4
INDO-CHINA NOM P/L	UNISEL	4.2
INDO-CHINA NOM P/L	VAAL-REEF	10.7
INDO-CHINA NOM P/L	VENTERS	11.2
INDO-CHINA NOM P/L	VLAKS	4.0
INDO-CHINA NOM P/L	W-R-CONS	8.3
INDO-CHINA NOM P/L	WELKOM	3.7
INDO-CHINA NOM P/L	WES-AREAS	9.8
INDO-CHINA NOM P/L	WINKELS	6.7
INDO-CHINA NOM P/L	WIT-NIGEL	2.3
INDO-CHINA NOM P/L	WSTN-DEEP	8.0
INDO-CHINA NOM P/L	ZANDPAN	1.8
INDO-CHINA NOM SA P/L	DEELKRL	7.3
INDO-CHINA NOM SA P/L	DOORNS	18.7
INDO-CHINA NOM SA P/L	GF-PROPS	2.1
INDO-CHINA NOM SA P/L	SALLIES	6.1
INDO-CHINA NOM SA P/L	WIT-G-M	31.4
INDO-CHINA NOM SA P/L	WIT-NIGEL	1.5
INDUSTRIAL FINANCE CORP OF SA LTD	CGSMITH	1.7
INDUSTRIAL SELECTIONS LTD	CGSMITH	4.1
INDUSTRIAL SELECTIONS LTD	GUBINGS	17.5
INDUSTRIAL SELECTIONS LTD	IMPLATS	4.7
INDUSTRIAL SELECTIONS LTD	PALAMIN	1.1
INDUSTRIAL SELECTIONS LTD	SAPPI	3.2
INMINS INV LTD	INMINS	73.4
INNISFALLEN INV P/L	MCCARTHY	9.8
INSTITUTIONAL INV LTD	S-A-EAGLE	24.1
INTEQU INV P/L	SCHARIG	1.1
INTERBOARD HOLDINGS BV	CERAMIC	1.5
INTERHOLD LTD	TRADGRO	8.1
INTERNAT INV CONSULTANTS P/L	SABLE	9.7
INTERNAT PIPE & STEEL INV SA P/L	DORBYL	52.0
INTERNATIONAL BUSINESS CORP LTD	MJM	15.9
INTERNATIONAL COAL MARKETING CORP	RD-LEASE	1.1
INTERNATIONAL DIAMONDS P/L	NAMSEA	1.6
INTERNATIONAL FINANCE CORP LTD	FMB	10.0
INTERNATIONAL FINANCE CORP LTD	UDC	9.1
INVERSIONES MALDIVAS SA	LANCHEM	6.6
INVESTEC BANK LTD	RABIE	1.3
INVESTEC GROUP PENS FUND	TOCO	1.8
INVESTEC HOLDINGS LTD	INVSTEC	48.0
INVESTEC HOLDINGS POOL ACCOUNT	INHOLD	1.1
INVESTEC HOLDINGS-DES S3 FIVE CONTR	INHOLD	1.1
INVESTEC INV LTD	INTRUST	47.8
INVESTEC INV TRUST LTD	BERZACK	1.3
INVESTEC INV TRUST LTD	BIDVEST	4.6
INVESTEC INV TRUST LTD	FEDSURE	2.3
INVESTEC INV TRUST LTD	FENNER	28.4
INVESTEC MERCHANT BANK LTD	BARNETS	10.5
INVESTEC NOM P/L	BIDCORP	20.4
INVESTEC NOM P/L	FEDSURE	26.1
INVESTEC NOM P/L	GRINCOR	5.6
INVESTEC NOM P/L	GROWPNT	2.6
INVESTEC NOM P/L	INHOLD	8.8
INVESTEC NOM P/L	INVSTEC	1.7
INVESTEC NOM P/L	MCRTAIL	13.3
INVESTEC NOM P/L	PRIM-G-M	2.3
INVESTEC NOM P/L	RABIE	6.3
INVESTEC SHARE NOM P/L	BARNETS	17.6
INVESTEC SHARE NOM P/L	PRIM-G-M	18.1
IPCORN LTD	ART	2.9
IPCORN LTD	CAPS	3.7
IPCORN LTD	HIPPO	1.2
IPCORN LTD	HUNYANI	3.8
IPCORN SERVICES (PVT) LTD	FSI ZIM	1.0
IRVIN & JOHNSON LTD	NATRAWL	8.9
IRVINE W M	SCHWEP CA	2.2
IRVROB INV P/L	ANBEECO	10.7
ISAACMAN H	SPESCOM	1.0
ISAACS B	FORIM	1.0
ISCOR LTD	USKO	27.1
ISDALE HLDGS BV	SABLE	68.1
ISG HOLDINGS P/L	ISG	60.4
ISIDOR BALTSTEIN TRUST NOM P/L	CON-MURCH	1.3
ISIDOR BALTSTEIN TRUST NOM P/L	GEFCO	1.1
ISIDOR BALTSTEIN TRUST NOM P/L	MSAULI	7.7
ISM TRUST	ISG	3.0
ISM TRUST	PERSTEC	2.9
ISSADEEN A K	INCO	10.5
ITI INVESTMENTS CC	VESTCOR	7.7

IVAN COHEN FAMILY TRUST	AIMARK	8.8
IVELL D	LANCHEM	1.6

J

J B AFRICAN INV LTD	ZIMALLOYS	13.1
J STREBEL INV P/L	STREBEL	50.7
J T R INV P/L	TEX-MILLS	4.3
J W C INV P/L	TDL	25.4
JACK BECKER P/L	OZZ	2.2
JACK ELIASOV FAMILY TRUST	TECHIRE	8.1
JACK ELIASOV HOLDINGS P/L	TECHIRE	8.4
JACK MINCER HOLDINGS P/L	SAKERS	2.4
JACK W A	AFLIFE	1.6
JACKSON T N	G5HOLD	1.1
JACKSON T N	GOLDSTEIN	1.1
JACOB I	NISWA	1.2
JACOBS K H M	T-E-J	2.0
JACOBS M F	CURFIN	1.0
JACOBS R M	T-E-J	15.9
JACOBSON A	RACY	1.6
JACOBSON MERVYN	BERGERS	1.6
JACOBSON P D	PROGRESS	1.6
JACOBSON Z	PROGRESS	2.6
JAFF DELSWA INV LTD	DELSWA	46.6
JAFF P	JADE	9.3
JAFF P H	DELSWA	1.4
JAFF S H	JADE	2.6
JAFF S L	DELSWA	3.9
JAFF S L	JADE	5.6
JAFFE FAMILY TRUST	AUTOQIP	1.0
JAFFE FAMILY TRUST	PRESMED	1.6
JAGINI TRUST	LASER	8.9
JAMIESON D B	KNJ	6.5
JAMMINE APH, SACKS MI & VAN STADEN	FEDSURE	2.6
JAMSEN INV P/L	JASCO	9.6
JAN INGRID P/L	PICBEL	26.3
JAN PICKARD FAMILY TRUST	PICBEL	2.9
JAN PICKARD ONDERNEMINGS BPK	PICBEL	21.0
JAN SILVIS NOM P/L	CITYHLD	7.0
JAN SILVIS NOM P/L	MINGRAN	3.4
JAN SILVIS NOM P/L	SOUTHGO	1.7
JAN SILVIS NOM P/L	WINBEL	27.5
JANILL INV P/L	NINIAN	1.2
JANKELOWITZ I	DINETTE	3.3
JANSEN VAN VUUREN J M	STOCKS	2.6
JANSZ A L	DIALMOV	4.9
JARDINE E E	BASREAD	1.5
JARRARD C J	MULTI	6.4
JARVIS C C	BASREAD	1.9
JASPER INV P/L	TEDCO	2.4
JATI INV P/L	METAIR	28.0
JAYFAM MINERALS P/L	MINVEST	2.0
JEBB MCINTOSH INV HLDGS CO P/L	CMH	17.3
JEMMA INCORPORATED	ROMANO	1.3
JENAPR INV P/L	BUFFCOR	12.5
JENAPR INV P/L	VENTEL	19.2
JENKINGS F J	OVBEL	1.1
JENKINS K N	KNJ	55.9
JENKINS P L	BOWCALF	2.2
JENNIRO INV P/L	CROOKES	1.1
JEPNICK HOLDINGS P/L	TOMKOR	1.1
JESDENE LTD	AVINS	1.0
JF KING LTD	HIGATE	1.3
JIMBERLANA MINERALS NL	WESWITS	22.1
JNG FAMILY TRUST	HCI	1.6
JOAN ST LEDGER LINDBURGH NOM CO P/L	CNAGALO	6.0
JOFAMILY INV P/L	CLAW	4.6
JOFFE B	BIDCORP	17.1
JOFFE C	ADONIS	2.0
JOFFE P R	SPURHLD	1.1
JOHANNESBURG CONSOLIDATED INV CO	CMI	35.4
JOHANNESBURG CONSOLIDATED INV CO	JOEL	1.4
JOHANNESBURG CONSOLIDATED INV CO	LEPLAT	4.1
JOHANNESBURG CONSOLIDATED INV CO	PP RUST	2.7
JOHANNESBURG CONSOLIDATED INV CO	RUSPLAT	3.5
JOHANNESBURG MUNICIPAL PENS FUND	ABS	2.5
JOHANNESBURG MUNICIPAL PENS FUND	CURFIN	1.6
JOHANNESBURG MUNICIPAL PENS FUND	GROPROP	11.7
JOHANNESBURG MUNICIPAL PENS FUND	PRESMED	1.2
JOHANNESBURG MUNICIPAL PENS FUND	SAFCOR	1.4
JOHANNESBURG MUNICIPAL PENS FUND	SPL	1.2
JOHANNESBURG REGISTER ACCOUNT	M-C-M	6.3
JOHANNESBURG REGISTER ACCOUNT	WANKIE	2.3
JOHANSSON B E G	BASREAD	1.6
JOHN ASBURY FAMILY HLDGS P/L	HCI	1.2
JOHNSON P M P	KAROS	2.8
JOJILL (PVT) LTD	FSI ZIM	1.5
JONEL INV P/L	FEDSURE	9.8
JONES R J	FRALEX	1.4
JONKER M TRUST	MJM	47.8
JOPAIR P/L	CAFCA	1.2
JOSEPH JOWELLS HLDGS P/L	MOBILE	39.8
JOSS BRENNER INV P/L	BRENMIL	1.8
JOSSEL B	MCPHAIL	1.0
JOUBERT G L	PENROSE	3.6
JOUBERT L T	AKJ	5.2
JR NOM P/L	AUTOPGE	2.3
JR NOM P/L	BROADACRE	2.3
JR NOM P/L	CUTRITE	1.3
JR NOM P/L	HYPROP	2.2
JR NOM P/L	ICH	1.3
JR NOM P/L	OHIO	1.3
JR NOM P/L	VLAKS	1.0
JUBILEE PROSPECTORS LTD	JOEL	1.4
JUDIN M	SHOCRAF	40.6
JURVEST HOLDINGS PVT LTD	BINDURA	1.2
JUSCO NOM P/L	COASTAL	1.3
JUSPOINT NOM P/L	MINGRAN	1.7
JUSPOINT NOM P/L	VIERFONTN	2.0
JUSPOINT NOM P/L	VLAKS	2.0

K

K E THOMSON PVT LTD	CAPS	1.7
K E THOMSON PVT LTD	CIRCLE	3.2
KAGAN G S TRUST	PALS	7.1
KAGAN H A TRUST	PALS	7.1
KAGAN J E	PALS	2.1
KAGAN S R	PALS	6.4
KAGAN SECURITIES P/L	PALS	32.5
KAHN D M	ROMENS	2.1
KAIYA INTERNATIONAL LTD	NATRAWL	1.1
KALLMEYER L A	SPESCOM	1.0
KALMEK M	PROGRESS	1.7
KAMACON P/L	CONCOR	2.1
KAMINER L	OZZ	3.8
KAMINER L	TOCO	1.3
KAMINSKI J W S	OVCON	7.6
KANE P J	ALEXWYT	8.9
KANE R	ALEXWYT	7.0
KANE S A	ALEXWYT	7.0
KANE T P	ALEXWYT	11.9
KANTOR B INV HOLDINGS P/L	INHOLD	4.2
KAPITAN A G	RACY	2.1
KAPLAN A N	AKJ	1.7
KAPLAN A N INV CC	AKJ	69.3
KAPLAN C B	MICOR	3.2
KAPLAN L	SANLIC	2.0
KAPLAN M J	MICOR	1.8
KAPLAN P	IMPERIAL	2.4
KARAX INV P/L	METJE-&-Z	2.1
KARDOL B INV HOLDINGS P/L	INHOLD	1.6
KATZ ADA	MARCONS	1.1

KATZ J	ENSIGN	2.1
KATZ J	MARCONS	3.5
KATZ J	MARSHAL	3.4
KATZ J	METJE-&-Z	1.5
KATZ J	USKO	1.1
KATZ J H	UNION	3.1
KATZEFF G S	ROYHOLD	1.1
KAWALSKY C	PIONEER	1.7
KAWITZKY P	BURLINGTN	3.6
KAY K	ALEXWYT	7.2
KAY P D	ALEXWYT	10.5
KAYE D	LASER	1.4
KAYE D H	LASER	25.8
KAYEMESS NOM P/L	BRACKEN	1.0
KAYEMESS NOM P/L	ELCENTR	1.2
KAYEMESS NOM P/L	FAIRCAP	2.6
KAYEMESS NOM P/L	RACY	1.1
KAYEMESS NOM P/L	ROMANO	5.2
KCSA HOLDINGS P/L	CARLCOR	52.0
KEBBLE R B	FOSTON	1.4
KEELEY GROUP HOLDINGS LTD	KELGRAN	50.0
KEEVY B	LONGRAIL	6.5
KEIZAN E I	TIWHEEL	8.5
KELLY A	SECHOLD	5.6
KELLY F	PICBEL	2.8
KELLY F H INV P/L	DUKEL	30.2
KELLY T P	GOLDSTEIN	1.2
KERIAN INV CC	DUKEL	2.7
KEURBOOM INV P/L	TOMKOR	1.4
KEVNIC P/L	RMBH	1.1
KEYSER J DE LA H	UNION	2.0
KF INV HOLDINGS P/L	F-S-GROUP	8.4
KF INV HOLDINGS P/L	F-S-I	2.1
KF INV HOLDINGS P/L	TOCO	2.0
KHAN R	DIGOCO	1.2
KILGETTY NOM P/L	SONDOR	54.0
KILLARNEY PROPERTIES PVT LTD	TABEX	1.2
KIMBERLEY-CLARK CORP	CARLCOR	12.7
KINALE TRUST	LASER	10.5
KING M W, DAVIS D J L & SWART B J	SOTHERN	4.4
KIOILOS L	VIERFONTN	2.0
KIRCHMANN P F	KH PROPS	1.2
KIRCHMANN P FAMILY HOLDINGS P/L	KH PROPS	2.8
KIRKNESS INV P/L	DIGOCO	7.0
KIRSTEN D G	MINVEST	12.0
KLEIN M S	AIMARK	30.0
KLEIN W J	AIMARK	1.9
KNIGHT A M	STOCKS	1.8
KNIGHT E R P	ZIMSPIN	1.4
KNIGHT M D D	OVCON	1.1
KNIGHT S M G	ZIMSPIN	1.5
KNJ INDUSTRIAL HOLDINGS P/L	MIDMAC	88.0
KNOESEN H	ABCON	3.3
KOCH N R	JASCO	2.6
KOCH S TRUST	ICH	4.6
KOEGELENBERG J H D	CONFED	1.0
KOEKEMOER V	NICTUS	9.4
KOLLENBERG FAMILY TRUST	TOMKOR	1.0
KOMMETJE ESTATES LTD	COM-FUND	3.9
KONG D	KOPP	2.0
KONOIL P/L	SASOL	16.9
KOPP ELECTRONICS SHARE TRUST	KOPP	3.0
KOPP INV CC	KOPP	52.6
KOPP J	KOPP	3.8
KOPPING D INV HLDGS CO P/L	TOMKOR	1.7
KOPPING M	TECFIN	1.4
KOSEFF S INV HOLDINGS P/L	INHOLD	2.5
KOTON L	STERLING	3.0
KOTZE J C	SECHOLD	1.3
KOVENSKY FAMILY TRUST	AROMA	25.8
KOVENSKY M L	AROMA	25.3
KRAINHOFNER W	KOPP	3.4
KRAMER SHARON FAMILY TRUST	OCTODEC	6.3
KREHER R K	SAFICON	1.1
KREHER R K	SAKERS	2.3
KRIEL H	NISWA	1.4
KROK R	LOGTEK	1.0
KROOK R D	ABCON	1.1
KROOK S B	ABCON	1.1
KRUGER AJ &SHARP A ADMIN E/LC DUT	CLINICS	1.6
KRUGER R	SANLIC	1.3
KRUGER W F K	STOCKS	2.6
KUDU GRANITE HOLDINGS LTD	KUDU	5.4
KUHN W J	NICTUS	2.5
KUPER R	GDM	1.3

L

L M TRUST	BEARMAN	12.0
LA GRANGE P L	TRNSHEX	1.5
LACIS INV P/L	PEPGRO	1.5
LAGAN INV HLDGS LTD	FIRSTBK	13.7
LAING G J S	REVERE	19.3
LANCELLAS N W	STREBEL	1.1
LANDAU & COETZEE FINANCE P/L	RACY	11.4
LANDCO P/L	GEN-OPTIC	3.6
LANDSDOWN SECURITIES LTD	DECHOLD	7.6
LANDSWYN INV BPK	NICTUS	29.7
LANE C J E	CENMAG	3.0
LANE FAMILY INV P/L	CENMAG	10.3
LANGEBERG CO-OPARATIVE LTD	LANGBRG	30.0
LARRY EARL BRENNER INV P/L	BRENMIL	1.8
LARSEN B K	UNION	2.6
LASER TRANSPORT HOLDINGS LTD	LASER	1.4
LASER TRANSPORT HOLDINGS PENS FUND	LASER	1.7
LASH ESTABLISHMENT	RAINBOW	8.1
LATEULERE SALES P/L	PANPROP	1.7
LATILLA-CAMPBELL P	WSGROVE	8.6
LAURENS R C	LONGRAIL	1.2
LAURIE B	TECFIN	1.4
LAVANREN NOM P/L	ADONIS	1.5
LAVANREN NOM P/L	NICTUS	3.9
LAVANREN NOM P/L	PRESMED	1.5
LAW PETER FAMILY TRUST	MINVEST	2.4
LE GRANGE J P	ABS	3.2
LEBAKA EMPL SHARE INC TRUST	LEBAKA	4.0
LEBOWA DEVELOPMENT CORP LTD	LEPLAT	8.4
LEBOWA DEVELOPMENT CORP LTD	PP RUST	2.6
LEBOWA MINERALS BUREAU	PP RUST	1.4
LEFKOPAUL P/L	TOMKOR	5.9
LEISURE & COMMERCIAL TRAILERS HLDGS	VENTEL	44.8
LEITH S J S	OVBEL	1.7
LEITNER J R	SPESCOM	2.8
LEKATERA ESTATES PVT LTD	ZSR	3.4
LENCO HOLDINGS LTD	AMSHOE	54.9
LENCO HOLDINGS LTD SHARE TRUST	LENCO	1.5
LENCO INV HOLDINGS P/L	LENCO	50.3
LENCO P/L	LENVEST	39.8
LENCO SHARE TRUST	LENCO	1.8
LENCRES PROPERTIES P/L	GROWALK	3.7
LENWIL FAMILY HOLDINGS P/L	IMPERIAL	3.6
LEON DU PLESSIS INV P/L	DUKEL	30.2
LEON TRUSTEES P/L	A-V-HOLD	1.3
LEON TRUSTEES P/L	ANGLOVAAL	1.1
LEONMED INV P/L	BIDCORP	4.2
LEPPIN FAMILY HLD P/L	LEPPIN	75.6
LESLIE GORDON HOLMES FAMILY TRUST	RHOVAN	2.9
LESLIE GORDON HOLMES FAMILY TRUST	SUB-N	35.4
LEVENSTEIN E B	ABS	1.9
LEVER GROUP RETIREMENT FUND ZIMBABWE	ROTH ZIM	2.1
LEVIN H	EQUIKOR	2.4
LEVIN H R	OAKFLDS	2.1
LEVIN J	BENCO	1.1
LEVY C L	BROADACRE	4.9
LEVY C L	MCPHAIL	1.5

LEVY C L	MODDER	1.0
LEVY C L	RACY	1.8
LEVY C L	ROMANO	5.7
LEWIS FOSCHINI INV P/L	FOSCHINI	50.0
LEWIS I M A	HCI	11.2
LEWIS I M A	IGI BOT	1.2
LEWIS M W A	OVCON	1.0
LEWIS S	LEFIC	8.0
LEWISOHN R B	SALLIES	4.5
LEWISOHN R B	VILLAGE	5.3
LEWTOP P/L	BOLPRO	1.7
LEWTOP P/L	PUTCO	3.7
LEWTOP P/L	PUTPROP	2.1
LEWTOP P/L	VIERFONTN	1.2
LIBERTAS ADMIN & MANAGEMENT P/L	NATRAWL	26.8
LIBERTY ASSET MANAGEMENT LTD	BOE	11.7
LIBERTY HOLDINGS LTD	GARDIAN	45.4
LIBERTY HOLDINGS LTD	LIBERTY	52.5
LIBERTY LIFE ASSOC OF AFRICA LTD	A-V-I	1.0
LIBERTY LIFE ASSOC OF AFRICA LTD	ADCOCK	8.3
LIBERTY LIFE ASSOC OF AFRICA LTD	AFCOL	3.7
LIBERTY LIFE ASSOC OF AFRICA LTD	AFRICOM	3.8
LIBERTY LIFE ASSOC OF AFRICA LTD	ALEXNDR	1.6
LIBERTY LIFE ASSOC OF AFRICA LTD	ALTRON	2.2
LIBERTY LIFE ASSOC OF AFRICA LTD	AMCOAL	4.6
LIBERTY LIFE ASSOC OF AFRICA LTD	ANAMINT	1.4
LIBERTY LIFE ASSOC OF AFRICA LTD	ANG-ALPHA	2.6
LIBERTY LIFE ASSOC OF AFRICA LTD	ANGLO-S	2.2
LIBERTY LIFE ASSOC OF AFRICA LTD	ANGLOVAAL	2.9
LIBERTY LIFE ASSOC OF AFRICA LTD	BARLOWS	2.4
LIBERTY LIFE ASSOC OF AFRICA LTD	BERGERS	2.5
LIBERTY LIFE ASSOC OF AFRICA LTD	BEVCON	6.8
LIBERTY LIFE ASSOC OF AFRICA LTD	BTRDUN	3.8
LIBERTY LIFE ASSOC OF AFRICA LTD	CGSMITH	2.2
LIBERTY LIFE ASSOC OF AFRICA LTD	CHARTER	1.5
LIBERTY LIFE ASSOC OF AFRICA LTD	CHEMSERVE	3.0
LIBERTY LIFE ASSOC OF AFRICA LTD	CONSHU	3.5
LIBERTY LIFE ASSOC OF AFRICA LTD	CONSOL	4.6
LIBERTY LIFE ASSOC OF AFRICA LTD	DE BEERS	1.3
LIBERTY LIFE ASSOC OF AFRICA LTD	DISTIL	3.7
LIBERTY LIFE ASSOC OF AFRICA LTD	EDGARS	8.1
LIBERTY LIFE ASSOC OF AFRICA LTD	EVERITE	1.4
LIBERTY LIFE ASSOC OF AFRICA LTD	FIRSTBK	2.9
LIBERTY LIFE ASSOC OF AFRICA LTD	FIT	25.2
LIBERTY LIFE ASSOC OF AFRICA LTD	FRAME	6.8
LIBERTY LIFE ASSOC OF AFRICA LTD	GENCOR	2.3
LIBERTY LIFE ASSOC OF AFRICA LTD	GENTYRE-A	5.4
LIBERTY LIFE ASSOC OF AFRICA LTD	HAGGIE	5.9
LIBERTY LIFE ASSOC OF AFRICA LTD	HUDACO	6.2
LIBERTY LIFE ASSOC OF AFRICA LTD	HYPROP	3.6
LIBERTY LIFE ASSOC OF AFRICA LTD	I-C-S	4.2
LIBERTY LIFE ASSOC OF AFRICA LTD	ISG	1.9
LIBERTY LIFE ASSOC OF AFRICA LTD	JOHNNIES	2.6
LIBERTY LIFE ASSOC OF AFRICA LTD	KINROSS	1.4
LIBERTY LIFE ASSOC OF AFRICA LTD	KLIPTON	5.3
LIBERTY LIFE ASSOC OF AFRICA LTD	KWV-BEL	8.5
LIBERTY LIFE ASSOC OF AFRICA LTD	LIBVEST	9.6
LIBERTY LIFE ASSOC OF AFRICA LTD	LINDUM	4.4
LIBERTY LIFE ASSOC OF AFRICA LTD	M-&-F	1.1
LIBERTY LIFE ASSOC OF AFRICA LTD	METCASH	1.6
LIBERTY LIFE ASSOC OF AFRICA LTD	NAMPAK	6.9
LIBERTY LIFE ASSOC OF AFRICA LTD	NATSEL	1.2
LIBERTY LIFE ASSOC OF AFRICA LTD	NEDCOR	1.3
LIBERTY LIFE ASSOC OF AFRICA LTD	NORTHAM	4.6
LIBERTY LIFE ASSOC OF AFRICA LTD	OCTODEC	9.9
LIBERTY LIFE ASSOC OF AFRICA LTD	PERSTEC	5.0
LIBERTY LIFE ASSOC OF AFRICA LTD	PICKNPAY	3.3
LIBERTY LIFE ASSOC OF AFRICA LTD	PIKWIK	3.5
LIBERTY LIFE ASSOC OF AFRICA LTD	PLATE-GL	3.5
LIBERTY LIFE ASSOC OF AFRICA LTD	PPC	3.4
LIBERTY LIFE ASSOC OF AFRICA LTD	PREM-GRP	5.4
LIBERTY LIFE ASSOC OF AFRICA LTD	RANDCOL	1.9
LIBERTY LIFE ASSOC OF AFRICA LTD	RANDMIN	3.9
LIBERTY LIFE ASSOC OF AFRICA LTD	REMGRO	3.5
LIBERTY LIFE ASSOC OF AFRICA LTD	REX-TRUE	5.2
LIBERTY LIFE ASSOC OF AFRICA LTD	ROMATEX	1.5
LIBERTY LIFE ASSOC OF AFRICA LTD	SA-BREWS	4.7
LIBERTY LIFE ASSOC OF AFRICA LTD	SANTAM	1.4
LIBERTY LIFE ASSOC OF AFRICA LTD	SASOL	3.4
LIBERTY LIFE ASSOC OF AFRICA LTD	SBIC	13.5
LIBERTY LIFE ASSOC OF AFRICA LTD	SCORE	1.6
LIBERTY LIFE ASSOC OF AFRICA LTD	SEARCON	3.3
LIBERTY LIFE ASSOC OF AFRICA LTD	SEARDEL	11.0
LIBERTY LIFE ASSOC OF AFRICA LTD	SFW	3.7
LIBERTY LIFE ASSOC OF AFRICA LTD	SILTEK	1.2
LIBERTY LIFE ASSOC OF AFRICA LTD	SOTHERN	2.3
LIBERTY LIFE ASSOC OF AFRICA LTD	STANPRO	5.4
LIBERTY LIFE ASSOC OF AFRICA LTD	STERLING	1.0
LIBERTY LIFE ASSOC OF AFRICA LTD	STOCKS	1.9
LIBERTY LIFE ASSOC OF AFRICA LTD	TIGR-OATS	2.8
LIBERTY LIFE ASSOC OF AFRICA LTD	TRANS-NTL	2.7
LIBERTY LIFE ASSOC OF AFRICA LTD	UNISERV	3.6
LIBERTY LIFE ASSOC OF AFRICA LTD	VEKTRA	2.4
LIBERTY LIFE ASSOC OF AFRICA LTD	VENTRON	1.3
LIBERTY LIFE ASSOC OF AFRICA LTD	W-&-A	1.3
LIBERTY LIFE ASSOC OF AFRICA LTD	WAYNE	1.4
LIBERTY LIFE ASSOC OF AFRICA LTD	WOOLTRU	10.0
LIBERTY LIFE ASSOC OF AFRICA LTD	WSTN-DEEP	1.4
LIBERTY LIFE INV TRUST P/L	PREM-GRP	24.4
LIBERTY PENS FUND	HUDACO	1.2
LIBIC INV HOLDINGS P/L	FIT	6.1
LIBLIFE CONTROLLING CORP P/L	LIB HOLD	52.0
LIBRARY CHAMBERS NOM P/L	GEN-OPTIC	8.6
LIBSASRIA NOM P/L	F-S-GROUP	1.1
LIBSASRIA NOM P/L	TRANS-NTL	1.0
LIFETIME INV PVT LTD	FP HOLD	6.0
LIKOBRAND SA	ROTH ZIM	50.0
LILLINGSTON M C	GEFCO	1.6
LILLINGSTON M C	MSAULI	1.4
LILLINGSTON M C	PORTHLD	1.6
LIMBEROPOULOS I	CHOICE	49.3
LIMBEROPOULOS P	CHOICE	5.0
LINBEROPLOS J	CHOICE	2.7
LINKSFIELD INV P/L	MINGRAN	7.8
LINSA SA P/L	TRIMTEX	7.7
LINSA SA P/L	TRIMTRD	1.5
LINTON S P	TITACO	1.7
LION MATCH GROUP PENS FUND	HISTONE	1.6
LIPSCHITZ G	DINETTE	1.5
LIVINGSTONE INV CO LTD	WANKIE	1.1
LIWESA HOLDINGS P/L	TOMKOR	1.1
LLP INV P/L	ABS	1.9
LLP INV P/L	C-MATIC	2.0
LLP INV P/L	EUREKA	5.8
LLP INV P/L	MACADAM	3.1
LOBBAN J H H	FEDSURE	1.3
LOCAL AUTHORITIES PENS FUND	TRUZIM	1.1
LOCAL AUTHORITIES PENS FUND	UDC	3.5
LOCARNO EXPLORATION CO P/L	CON-MURCH	1.5
LOCH-DAVIS D J & PFEIFFER S A	U-CON	3.8
LODESTONE HLDGS LTD	AMIC	1.1
LODESTONE HLDGS LTD	ERGO	2.3
LODESTONE HLDGS LTD	NEW-CENT	5.6
LODESTONE HLDGS LTD	TONGAAT	11.0
LOGAN J	GULLIVER	1.7
LOGAN J	WANKIE	1.2
LOI G	MAXMECH	1.3
LOISEL NOM P/L	PROGRESS	1.2
LONDON ACCOUNTS	LONFIN	66.1
LONDON ASSURE	PROSURE	79.7
LONDON CONTROL & AMALGAMATED	GROOTVLEI	3.8
LONDON CONTROL ACCOUNT	AFEX SA	95.0
LONDON CONTROL ACCOUNT	AMGOLD	2.0
LONDON CONTROL ACCOUNT	ANGLO-S	2.4
LONDON CONTROL ACCOUNT	BOTREST	55.4
LONDON CONTROL ACCOUNT	BRACKEN	10.5

LONDON CONTROL ACCOUNT	BUFFELS	16.6
LONDON CONTROL ACCOUNT	CHARTER	85.5
LONDON CONTROL ACCOUNT	CON-MURCH	22.8
LONDON CONTROL ACCOUNT	CONAFEX	61.5
LONDON CONTROL ACCOUNT	DE BEERS	7.3
LONDON CONTROL ACCOUNT	ERGO	1.3
LONDON CONTROL ACCOUNT	FALCON	46.7
LONDON CONTROL ACCOUNT	FREGOLD	5.3
LONDON CONTROL ACCOUNT	GENBEL	1.3
LONDON CONTROL ACCOUNT	GENCOR	1.4
LONDON CONTROL ACCOUNT	JOHNNIES	2.6
LONDON CONTROL ACCOUNT	LESLIE	9.7
LONDON CONTROL ACCOUNT	LINDUM	2.8
LONDON CONTROL ACCOUNT	LYD-PLAT	1.4
LONDON CONTROL ACCOUNT	MINORCO	56.4
LONDON CONTROL ACCOUNT	N-KLEINS	14.3
LONDON CONTROL ACCOUNT	NEW-CENT	4.0
LONDON CONTROL ACCOUNT	OFSIL	5.7
LONDON CONTROL ACCOUNT	SALLIES	15.1
LONDON CONTROL ACCOUNT	SOUTHVAAL	1.0
LONDON CONTROL ACCOUNT	ST-HELENA	13.4
LONDON CONTROL ACCOUNT	STILFTN	7.2
LONDON CONTROL ACCOUNT	TGH	27.4
LONDON CONTROL ACCOUNT	TMX	81.0
LONDON CONTROL ACCOUNT	VAAL-REEF	6.1
LONDON CONTROL ACCOUNT	W-R-CONS	21.3
LONDON CONTROL ACCOUNT	WELKOM	2.7
LONDON CONTROL ACCOUNT	WINKELS	1.5
LONDON CONTROL ACCOUNT	WSTN-DEEP	4.1
LONDON CONTROL ACCOUNT	Z-C-I	96.3
LONDON REGISTER ACCOUNT	BARNEX	1.8
LONDON REGISTER ACCOUNT	DABI	1.6
LONDON REGISTER ACCOUNT	FREDDEV	3.5
LONDON REGISTER ACCOUNT	JOEL	1.1
LONDON REGISTER ACCOUNT	LIBERTY	2.8
LONDON REGISTER ACCOUNT	M-C-M	6.1
LONDON REGISTER ACCOUNT	RANDFONTN	12.3
LONDON REGISTER ACCOUNT	RUSPLAT	1.2
LONDON REGISTER ACCOUNT	WANKIE	21.0
LONDON REGISTER ACCOUNT	WES-AREAS	4.5
LONDURBAN P/L	LONFIN	27.9
LONFIN INV P/L	BARPLAT	4.0
LONGDEN T	SECHABA	1.6
LONRHO GROUP PENS FUND	BOLTONS	1.9
LONRHO GROUP PENS FUND	DUIKERS	2.2
LONRHO GROUP PENS FUND	ED-L-BATE	1.1
LONRHO GROUP PENS FUND	LENCO	1.1
LONRHO GROUP PENS FUND	S-A-BIAS	1.7
LONRHO INTERNATIONAL LTD	LONSUGR	99.7
LONSDALE P N	MARCONS	1.4
LORAINE GOLD MINES LTD	TARGET	25.1
LORD HENDRY TRUST	DARMAG	22.1
LORNWOOD P/L	CROOKES	2.1
LOUIS C M & S L TRUSTEES	LEFIC	1.9
LOUW A H P	TAFLBRG	6.0
LOVELL A	OVCON	1.0
LOW AH KAI	OHIO	2.9
LOWENCO NOM P/L	AUTODEK	1.4
LOWENCO NOM P/L	BARPLAT	3.7
LOWENCO NOM P/L	BUFFCOR	18.8
LOWENCO NOM P/L	CARRIGS	7.1
LOWENCO NOM P/L	EGOLI	1.4
LOWENCO NOM P/L	G-I-C	9.7
LOWENCO NOM P/L	MESSINA	1.0
LOWENCO NOM P/L	NIGEL	2.2
LOWENCO NOM P/L	SASFIN	1.6
LOWENCO NOM P/L	SOUTHGO	2.4
LOWENCO NOM P/L	VLAKS	2.1
LOWENCO NOM P/L	WIT-NIGEL	8.2
LRS INV TRUST P/L	SBIC	1.2
LSP INV N04 P/L	ABS	3.6
LTA TRADING PVT LTD	RADAR	7.6
LUBNER D M	DINETTE	9.6

LUBNER J	DINETTE	5.5
LUCK A	ABBEY	1.8
LUTHER A	LONGRAIL	6.5
LUXDURBAN INV HOLDINGS P/L	CONAFEX	25.6
LUXEMBOURG GLOBAL ACCOUNT	MINORCO	24.5
LUXEMBOURG GLOBAL ACCOUNT	Z-C-I	1.7
LUXEMBOURG SUSPENSE ACCOUNT	TOLUX	80.5
LYDENBURG EXPLORATION LTD	BENCO	3.3
LYDENBURG PLATINUM LTD	BENCO	5.6
LYDENBURG PLATINUM LTD	LEPLAT	7.3
LYDENBURG PLATINUM LTD	LYDEX	20.9
LYDENBURG PLATINUM LTD	PP RUST	7.8
LYDENBURG PLATINUM LTD	RUSPLAT	8.4
LYNARA HOLDINGS LTD	INVICTA	1.1

M

M & R CORPORATE INV P/L	STANDRD	38.0
M & R INV LTD	M&R-HLD	25.1
M B M NOMINEES	TDL	2.9
M H FINGER INV P/L	UNI-COLD	23.3
M INV P/L	ABS	1.9
M INV P/L	C-MATIC	2.0
M INV P/L	EUREKA	5.8
M INV P/L	MACADAM	3.1
M-C NOM P/L	CONTROL	1.8
MACDONIC HLDGS P/L	TEX-MILLS	1.1
MACE D W	OVCON	5.2
MACFAM P/L	SHOREDITS	1.9
MACKAY B M	TIME	3.1
MACMED SHARE TRUST	MACMED	9.2
MACMED TRUST	MACMED	58.3
MACNAIR A D	KNJ	3.3
MACOSA AGENCIES P/L	CLEGG	5.7
MACPHAIL EXECUTIVE SHARE PURCHASE	MCPHAIL	1.5
MACSTEEL COMMERCIAL HLDGS P/L	VALCAR	25.5
MACSTEEL COMMERCIAL HLDGS P/L	VESTCOR	1.3
MACVEN NOM P/L	DIALMOV	1.1
MACVEN NOM P/L	N-KLEINS	1.5
MACVEN NOM P/L	WBHOLD	2.8
MADA TRUST P/L (BOUSFIELD S J)	ENBOT	2.0
MAESTRO SECURITIES P/L	ITLTILE	3.1
MAESTRO SECURITIES P/L	LINDUM	1.0
MAGID M	BIVEC	1.9
MAHOMMEDY H	CAFCA	1.5
MAIZECOR PENS FUND	RENTBEL	1.9
MAJORBEE INV P/L	MCCARTHY	2.7
MAJORBEE INV P/L	MCRTAIL	12.0
MAJSUN HOLDINGS P/L	SCORE	56.5
MAKHLOUF I	QUORUM	11.8
MALBAK INV (CARLCOR) P/L	CARLCOR	15.8
MALBAK INV (ELLERINES) LTD	ELLERINE	59.7
MALBAK INV (FEDFOOD) P/L	FOODCRP	71.2
MALBAK INV (HAGGIE) LTD	HAGGIE	10.0
MALBAK INV (HOLDAINS) LTD	HOLDAIN	67.4
MALBAK INV (SAD) P/L	SA-DRUG	84.0
MALBAK INV (STANDARD ENGINEERING)	STANDRD	38.0
MALBAK INV (TEDELEX) LTD	TEDELEX	96.7
MALCOLM KEELEY TRUST	KEELEY	7.2
MALCOLM KEELEY TRUST	KELGRAN	3.4
MALDWYN ZIMMERMAN INV HLDGS CO P/L	CMH	38.7
MALGAS P/L	A-T-COLL	1.3
MALHOLD LTD	MALBAK	37.5
MANAGEMENT SERVICES CORP LTD	OSPREY	15.6
MANBOS NOM P/L	SMALDEL	4.9
MANEEZ INV P/L	STORECO	3.1
MANG C D M	TECFIN	3.2
MANKOWITZ L	DINETTE	1.7
MANN E/L MAX	CORWIL	23.1
MANN E/L MAX	DUIKERS	1.6
MANN J, LEFTIN P M, KING D G T, MANN	GUBINGS	2.1
MANRO HOLDINGS P/L	MANRO	66.1

MANTRAK NOM P/L	CONTROL	1.2
MANUFACTURERS INV CO P/L	ANBEECO	21.8
MANUFACTURERS INV CO P/L	SUPALEK	10.1
MANUFACTURERS INV CO P/L	TRNPACO	20.4
MARACAY INV P/L	ROMENS	52.3
MARAIS INV TRUST P/L	PORT	5.9
MARAIS P J	ROMANO	29.4
MARAIS W T	OMNIA	2.3
MARAIS W T TRUST P/L	OMNIA	12.2
MARCH NOM SOC ANONYME	AFMIN	1.5
MARCH NOM SOC ANONYME	MINGRAN	19.7
MARCO VAN EMBDEN TRUST	MASCON	24.4
MARGILLA P/L	BIVEC	2.0
MARGOT EDWARDS TRUST	STOCKS	3.3
MARIO DE CHAUD FAMILY TRUST	ROMANO	18.9
MARIUS ELS INV P/L	LONGRAIL	58.7
MARJORAM HOLDINGS LTD	AMIC	2.0
MARJORAM HOLDINGS LTD	ERGO	4.7
MARLED NOM P/L	CHOICE	2.2
MARLED NOM P/L	PICBEL	1.5
MARLED NOM P/L	VALAUTO	1.3
MARLIN HOLDINGS LTD	MARLIN	69.2
MAROCK D	HYPERET	4.3
MAROT J E M	GROWALK	1.9
MARSAS INV P/L	SASFIN	10.6
MARSH N	BSI	1.8
MARSHALL D C	MARCONS	1.4
MARSHALL D C	MARSHAL	1.2
MARSHALLS CONTROLLING INV P/L	MARSHAL	69.2
MARSHALLS HOLDINGS CO P/L	MARCONS	55.1
MARSHALLS HOLDINGS CO P/L	MARSHAL	9.8
MARTIN JONKER TRUST (BEHEREND)	MJM	5.8
MARVOL HOLDINGS SA	CONTRAV	51.0
MARWHEEL INV P/L	TIWHEEL	19.3
MASEGRE P/L	CONCOR	1.5
MASHOLD CONSOLIDATED INV HOLDINGS	MASHOLD	57.9
MASHONALAND HOLDINGS LTD	WSGROVE	9.8
MASON C H	KH PROPS	2.0
MASON LTD	MIDMAC	2.2
MASON P J	PENROSE	5.5
MASONITE CORP	MASONITE	66.7
MATELECT NOM P/L	CONTROL	29.6
MATHIESON & ASHLEY HLDGS SHARE TRUST	MATH-ASH	2.5
MATTHEWS I N	KLIPTON	3.0
MATTHEWS R J L	KLIPTON	6.4
MAUDSLEY HOLDINGS LTD	AMIC	1.1
MAUERBERGER H	BERGERS	3.6
MAURO INV P/L	BRISTOL-I	1.2
MAX SEGAL HLDGS P/L	R-M-PROPS	1.1
MAX TUCKER & SON P/L	YORKCOR	43.4
MAXERIC NOM P/L	A-V-HOLD	2.1
MAXERIC NOM P/L	JDGROUP	3.7
MAXERIC NOM P/L	OSPREY	7.0
MAXERIC NOM P/L	RUHOLD	1.2
MAXERIC NOM P/L	SANLIC	2.3
MAYFAIR SPECULATORS P/L	DECOVO	53.6
MBCA NOM (PVT) LTD	J & F	5.6
MBCA NOM (PVT) LTD	MWEAR	8.3
MBS FINANCE P/L	AIMARK	1.3
MCCARTHY GROUP LTD	MIDAS	36.3
MCELLIGOTT M R A & SCHRODER D V	NINIAN	5.4
MCELLIGOTT M R A & SCHRODER J H	NINIAN	5.2
MCEVEDY B F	BIDVEST	1.2
MCEVOY K J, C E & OTHER MCEVOY FAMILY	MACADAM	9.5
MCGRATH M J	NORVIC	83.1
MCINNES B G	HUDACO	1.8
MCINTOSH D W	FRALEX	1.2
MCINTOSH J	CMH	3.1
MCLEAN I	U-CON	6.1
MCMILLAN A N	BASREAD	2.2
MECHIEL DU TOIT NOM P/L	FMCOTEC	57.3
MED INV P/L	T-E-J	3.0
MEDDENT ADMINISTRATORS P/L	RENTBEL	1.6
MEDICAL SERVICES (EUROPE) LTD	GAZGOLD	1.0
MEGAFID INTERNATIONAL AG	GAZGOLD	1.3
MEINERT J	BIVEC	1.1
MEINTJES D E	WALHOLD	2.2
MEKLER J	PENROSE	7.4
MENASHE I	BUFFCOR	11.0
MENBLACK NOM P/L	ABS	2.1
MENBLACK NOM P/L	ANBEECO	13.7
MENBLACK NOM P/L	E-T-CONS	1.2
MENBLACK NOM P/L	EDDIES	4.9
MENBLACK NOM P/L	GAZGOLD	1.6
MENBLACK NOM P/L	SUPALEK	14.1
MENBLACK NOM P/L	VESTCOR	2.2
MENTEITH INV LTD	BOE	1.5
MENTEITH INV LTD	ICH	2.4
MENTEITH INV LTD	OVBEL	8.0
MENTEITH INV LTD	OVCON	1.3
MENTEITH INV LTD	SPECLTY	3.6
MENTEITH INV LTD	STORECO	11.5
MERCABANK BPK	BUFFCOR	1.5
MERCABANK BPK	TPN	1.8
MERCANTILE & GEN REINSURANCE CO SA	HISTONE	1.2
MERCANTILE & GEN REINSURANCE CO SA	INTERNAT	1.0
MERCANTILE & GEN REINSURANCE CO SA	MARLIN	1.4
MERCANTILE & GEN REINSURANCE CO SA	TGH	1.1
MERCANTILE NOM P/L	VENTEL	3.0
MERCEDES INFORMATION TECHNOLOGIES	DATAKOR	82.5
MERCEDES INFORMATION TECHNOLOGIES	DIDATA	23.5
MERHOLD GROUP SHARE TRUST	MERHLD	3.9
MERHOLD INV P/L	WOODROW	20.7
MERHOLD SECURITIES P/L	AUTOQIP	20.3
MERHOLD SECURITIES P/L	LOGTEK	16.2
MERITEX HOLDINGS LTD SIS ACC	MERITEX	3.7
MERWOOL P/L	GUBINGS	50.4
MESSINA INV LTD	CORWIL	11.3
METAL IND GROUP PENS FUND	ABCON	2.9
METAL IND GROUP PENS FUND	ABSA	1.1
METAL IND GROUP PENS FUND	AECI	1.1
METAL IND GROUP PENS FUND	ALTECH	1.5
METAL IND GROUP PENS FUND	AMIC	1.0
METAL IND GROUP PENS FUND	ANG-ALPHA	2.7
METAL IND GROUP PENS FUND	BARLOWS	1.7
METAL IND GROUP PENS FUND	BOEPROP	3.6
METAL IND GROUP PENS FUND	BOUMAT	2.2
METAL IND GROUP PENS FUND	BTRDUN	5.2
METAL IND GROUP PENS FUND	CAPITAL	4.3
METAL IND GROUP PENS FUND	CARGO	2.3
METAL IND GROUP PENS FUND	CBD-FUND	1.3
METAL IND GROUP PENS FUND	CENPROP	1.6
METAL IND GROUP PENS FUND	CGSMITH	2.7
METAL IND GROUP PENS FUND	CLICKS	1.2
METAL IND GROUP PENS FUND	CROWN	1.7
METAL IND GROUP PENS FUND	CULLINAN	5.7
METAL IND GROUP PENS FUND	DORBYL	2.2
METAL IND GROUP PENS FUND	ELLERINE	2.0
METAL IND GROUP PENS FUND	FENNER	3.2
METAL IND GROUP PENS FUND	FINTECH	2.4
METAL IND GROUP PENS FUND	FIRSTBK	2.5
METAL IND GROUP PENS FUND	GENBEL	1.4
METAL IND GROUP PENS FUND	GRINCOR	1.6
METAL IND GROUP PENS FUND	GROPROP	1.9
METAL IND GROUP PENS FUND	HIGATE	2.2
METAL IND GROUP PENS FUND	HISCORE	1.3
METAL IND GROUP PENS FUND	HIVELD	3.3
METAL IND GROUP PENS FUND	HOLDAIN	2.4
METAL IND GROUP PENS FUND	HUDACO	2.6
METAL IND GROUP PENS FUND	HYPROP	1.5
METAL IND GROUP PENS FUND	IMPHOLD	3.6
METAL IND GROUP PENS FUND	ISCOR	3.0
METAL IND GROUP PENS FUND	ISG	2.2
METAL IND GROUP PENS FUND	LIONMATCH	4.8
METAL IND GROUP PENS FUND	MAINPRO	1.1
METAL IND GROUP PENS FUND	MALHOLD	2.0

METAL IND GROUP PENS FUND	MCCARTHY	4.1
METAL IND GROUP PENS FUND	METPROP	4.1
METAL IND GROUP PENS FUND	MIDAS	1.6
METAL IND GROUP PENS FUND	MOMENTUM	3.6
METAL IND GROUP PENS FUND	NAMPAK	1.7
METAL IND GROUP PENS FUND	NBSHOLD	2.8
METAL IND GROUP PENS FUND	NEDCOR	1.9
METAL IND GROUP PENS FUND	NEI-AFR	2.7
METAL IND GROUP PENS FUND	NEIHOLD	3.6
METAL IND GROUP PENS FUND	PANPROP	1.7
METAL IND GROUP PENS FUND	PERSTEC	2.1
METAL IND GROUP PENS FUND	PIONEER	1.9
METAL IND GROUP PENS FUND	PLATE-GL	2.0
METAL IND GROUP PENS FUND	PPC	1.0
METAL IND GROUP PENS FUND	PREM-GRP	1.6
METAL IND GROUP PENS FUND	REUNERT	1.1
METAL IND GROUP PENS FUND	RMSPROP	6.2
METAL IND GROUP PENS FUND	ROMATEX	1.0
METAL IND GROUP PENS FUND	ROYCHEM	1.5
METAL IND GROUP PENS FUND	ROYFOOD	1.5
METAL IND GROUP PENS FUND	RUSFURN	1.8
METAL IND GROUP PENS FUND	SAFICON	3.3
METAL IND GROUP PENS FUND	SAFREN	1.9
METAL IND GROUP PENS FUND	SAPPI	1.3
METAL IND GROUP PENS FUND	SEARCON	3.1
METAL IND GROUP PENS FUND	SEARDEL	2.5
METAL IND GROUP PENS FUND	SENTRCHEM	1.7
METAL IND GROUP PENS FUND	STANPRO	1.7
METAL IND GROUP PENS FUND	SYCOM	1.5
METAL IND GROUP PENS FUND	T-&-N	1.0
METAL IND GROUP PENS FUND	TAMBOTI	4.3
METAL IND GROUP PENS FUND	TONGAAT	2.7
METAL IND GROUP PENS FUND	UMDONI	1.5
METAL IND GROUP PENS FUND	UNITRAN	1.6
METAL IND GROUP PENS FUND	VETRUST	2.6
METAL IND GROUP PENS FUND	WOOLTRU	2.2
METAL RECOUP INC	ENROL	1.4
METALLIC INV P/L	GEFCO	2.8
METALMIL P/L	ENROL	3.4
METBOARD PROP FUND MANAGERS LTD	METPROP	1.9
METGROUPHOLD LTD	METCASH	29.2
METHVEN S C HOLDINGS P/L	RAINBOW	60.7
METJE I M	METJE-&-Z	1.0
METKOR GROUP LTD	DORBYL	3.0
METKOR GROUP LTD	USKO	27.1
METOREX P/L	PRIM-G-M	31.4
METROPOLITAN BOARD NOM LTD	TOCO	4.4
METROPOLITAN LIFE INV BOP P/L	YABENG	3.7
METROPOLITAN LIFE LTD	ALEXNDR	1.6
METROPOLITAN LIFE LTD	BENCO	4.8
METROPOLITAN LIFE LTD	BERGERS	5.2
METROPOLITAN LIFE LTD	BERTRAD	1.5
METROPOLITAN LIFE LTD	BOLAND	1.0
METROPOLITAN LIFE LTD	CASHBIL	3.5
METROPOLITAN LIFE LTD	CONSHU	3.7
METROPOLITAN LIFE LTD	DIDATA	4.2
METROPOLITAN LIFE LTD	FMCOTEC	1.6
METROPOLITAN LIFE LTD	FOODCRP	1.1
METROPOLITAN LIFE LTD	FOSCHINI	1.7
METROPOLITAN LIFE LTD	GENBEL	1.3
METROPOLITAN LIFE LTD	GROPROP	14.2
METROPOLITAN LIFE LTD	IMPERIAL	6.2
METROPOLITAN LIFE LTD	MALHOLD	1.2
METROPOLITAN LIFE LTD	MARLIN	3.1
METROPOLITAN LIFE LTD	MASHOLD	2.1
METROPOLITAN LIFE LTD	METCASH	1.2
METROPOLITAN LIFE LTD	MLNHOLD	1.9
METROPOLITAN LIFE LTD	OVBEL	2.4
METROPOLITAN LIFE LTD	PEPGRO	1.7
METROPOLITAN LIFE LTD	SA-DRUG	1.3
METROPOLITAN LIFE LTD	SAAMBOU	2.8
METROPOLITAN LIFE LTD	SANLAND	13.7
METROPOLITAN LIFE LTD	SANTAM	2.1

METROPOLITAN LIFE LTD	SYCOM	2.4
METROPOLITAN LIFE LTD	TELJOY	6.9
METROPOLITAN LIFE LTD	TGH	1.2
METROPOLITAN LIFE LTD	TRADGRO	1.5
METROPOLITAN LIFE LTD	VENTEL	3.8
MEYERSOHN WILFRED & CO P/L	PEP	5.4
MEZ HLDGS P/L	MIDMAC	2.0
MIA A A	WIT-G-M	1.5
MIA A F M	WIT-G-M	1.4
MIA A R A	WIT-G-M	2.8
MIA AABEDA AHMED	WIT-G-M	1.4
MIA AAMENA MAHOMED	WIT-G-M	1.4
MIA AASIYA AHMED	WIT-G-M	1.4
MIA AAYESHA RASHEDA MAHOMED	WIT-G-M	1.4
MIA AHMED MAHOMED	WIT-G-M	2.8
MIA ATIYYA AHMED	WIT-G-M	1.4
MIA IBRAHIM MAHOMED	WIT-G-M	2.8
MIA ISMAIL MAHOMED	WIT-G-M	2.8
MIA K M	WIT-G-M	2.8
MIA M A M	WIT-G-M	2.8
MIA M M	WIT-G-M	1.4
MIA Y I M	WIT-G-M	2.9
MICHAEL DELPORT INV P/L	DECOVO	34.9
MICHAEL HYMAN FAMILY TRUST	SANLIC	8.5
MICHAEL JORDAAN ENTERPRISES CC	MJM	15.9
MICOR HOLDINGS LTD	MICIND	91.5
MILJAPP TRUST	MILSTAN	11.5
MINA A A	QUORUM	1.2
MINE EMPLOYEES PENS FUND	ABSA	2.0
MINE EMPLOYEES PENS FUND	BOLAND	1.4
MINE EMPLOYEES PENS FUND	FIRSTBK	1.1
MINE OFFICIALS PENS FUND	ABSA	2.4
MINE OFFICIALS PENS FUND	BOLAND	2.6
MINE OFFICIALS PENS FUND	FIRSTBK	1.9
MINE OFFICIALS PENS FUND	NEDCOR	1.0
MINE OFFICIALS PENS FUND	RMBH	1.2
MINE OFFICIALS PENS FUND	SBIC	1.4
MINERALE DIENSTE BELEGGINGS E/B	BENCO	3.9
MINES 1970 PENS FUND	HYPROP	1.5
MINES 1970 PENS FUND	VETRUST	1.3
MINING INDUSTRY PENS FUND	CIH	2.5
MINING INDUSTRY PENS FUND	FALGOLD	1.1
MINING INDUSTRY PENS FUND	FMB	1.0
MINING INDUSTRY PENS FUND	INTERNAT	1.3
MINING INDUSTRY PENS FUND	MASHONA	2.7
MINING INDUSTRY PENS FUND	PGI	1.1
MINING INDUSTRY PENS FUND	RADAR	2.2
MINING INDUSTRY PENS FUND	ROTH ZIM	1.6
MINING INDUSTRY PENS FUND	TRUZIM	1.1
MINING INDUSTRY PENS FUND	UDC	11.2
MINING INDUSTRY PENS FUND	WANKIE	1.1
MINU NOM LTD	CEMENCO	24.0
MINU NOM LTD	CUSAF	24.1
MINU NOM LTD	DEELKRL	49.2
MINU NOM LTD	DOORNS	35.5
MINU NOM LTD	DRIES	35.0
MINU NOM LTD	E-DAGGA	5.0
MINU NOM LTD	ELANDS	5.0
MINU NOM LTD	ERGO	2.1
MINU NOM LTD	G-F-COAL	79.2
MINU NOM LTD	GF-PROPS	51.6
MINU NOM LTD	GFNAMIB	8.0
MINU NOM LTD	GFSA	43.7
MINU NOM LTD	KLOOF	34.3
MINU NOM LTD	LIBANON	32.9
MINU NOM LTD	LIBERTY	2.0
MINU NOM LTD	NEW-WITS	55.8
MINU NOM LTD	NIGEL	23.1
MINU NOM LTD	NORTHAM	65.1
MINU NOM LTD	RANDFONTN	1.5
MINU NOM LTD	ROOIBERG	48.2
MINU NOM LTD	SASOL	2.6
MINU NOM LTD	SBIC	9.8

MINU NOM LTD	SOUDEX	9.5
MINU NOM LTD	VENTERS	41.7
MINU NOM LTD	VLAKS	38.2
MINU NOM LTD	VOGELS	69.5
MINU NOM LTD	WINKELS	1.8
MINU NOM LTD	WSTN-DEEP	4.4
MISYB TRUST	CROOKES	7.7
MITCHELL B C	FEDSURE	1.3
MITCHELL D H	FEDSURE	1.1
MITCHELL J I	DIALMOV	4.9
MITROSPARAS M J	SMALDEL	1.3
MITS P/L	RDC	5.3
MIV CONSTRUCTION HOLDINGS CO P/L	G5HOLD	5.7
MIV CONSTRUCTION HOLDINGS CO P/L	GOLDSTEIN	25.9
MJBC INV P/L	BARNETS	52.4
MOBICAST C C	NISWA	1.6
MOBILE INDUSTRIES LTD	TRENCOR	47.3
MODRY J	SPESCOM	2.5
MODUS CORP P/L	ODMHOLD	1.5
MOFFAT A A	OVCON	1.1
MOGWAI INV HOLDINGS P/L	INHOLD	1.8
MOMENTUM LIFE ASSURE LTD	ABCON	27.0
MOMENTUM LIFE ASSURE LTD	ABSA	1.8
MOMENTUM LIFE ASSURE LTD	ADCOCK	2.2
MOMENTUM LIFE ASSURE LTD	ALTECH	1.6
MOMENTUM LIFE ASSURE LTD	BARLOWS	1.9
MOMENTUM LIFE ASSURE LTD	BOLAND	9.3
MOMENTUM LIFE ASSURE LTD	CARGO	2.7
MOMENTUM LIFE ASSURE LTD	E-DAGGA	3.8
MOMENTUM LIFE ASSURE LTD	EVHOLD	9.9
MOMENTUM LIFE ASSURE LTD	FMCOTEC	3.4
MOMENTUM LIFE ASSURE LTD	G5HOLD	4.3
MOMENTUM LIFE ASSURE LTD	GRINAKER	1.5
MOMENTUM LIFE ASSURE LTD	GRINTEK	1.4
MOMENTUM LIFE ASSURE LTD	GROUP-5	8.8
MOMENTUM LIFE ASSURE LTD	HUDACO	2.1
MOMENTUM LIFE ASSURE LTD	HUNTCOR	16.2
MOMENTUM LIFE ASSURE LTD	HYPROP	33.3
MOMENTUM LIFE ASSURE LTD	INTELES	1.7
MOMENTUM LIFE ASSURE LTD	JDGROUP	4.0
MOMENTUM LIFE ASSURE LTD	JOHNNIES	1.6
MOMENTUM LIFE ASSURE LTD	KAROS	26.1
MOMENTUM LIFE ASSURE LTD	KLIPTON	9.5
MOMENTUM LIFE ASSURE LTD	KNJ	2.6
MOMENTUM LIFE ASSURE LTD	LENVEST	12.7
MOMENTUM LIFE ASSURE LTD	LORAINE	3.5
MOMENTUM LIFE ASSURE LTD	MERITEX	12.0
MOMENTUM LIFE ASSURE LTD	METAIR	18.8
MOMENTUM LIFE ASSURE LTD	METKOR	1.5
MOMENTUM LIFE ASSURE LTD	NEIHOLD	3.7
MOMENTUM LIFE ASSURE LTD	PEPKOR	3.7
MOMENTUM LIFE ASSURE LTD	PERSBEL	4.5
MOMENTUM LIFE ASSURE LTD	PERSKOR	1.6
MOMENTUM LIFE ASSURE LTD	PICBEL	9.5
MOMENTUM LIFE ASSURE LTD	PICHOLD	2.5
MOMENTUM LIFE ASSURE LTD	PLATE-GL	2.0
MOMENTUM LIFE ASSURE LTD	RANDCOL	1.7
MOMENTUM LIFE ASSURE LTD	RMBH	3.3
MOMENTUM LIFE ASSURE LTD	SILOAK	4.4
MOMENTUM LIFE ASSURE LTD	TIWHEEL	1.1
MOMENTUM LIFE ASSURE LTD	VENTEL	4.5
MOMENTUM LIFE ASSURE LTD	WESCO	2.8
MOMENTUM LIFE ASSURE LTD	WOOLTRU	1.4
MON CHOIX P/L	HIPPO	1.8
MONDI TEXTIL GMBH	T-E-J	7.5
MONEX INTERNATIONAL P/L	PEPGRO	9.1
MONEX INV P/L	PEPGRO	1.3
MONEX SECURITIES P/L	PEPGRO	7.4
MONITOR INV P/L	DELSWA	11.1
MONITOR INV P/L	JADE	56.0
MONOMATAPA DEVELOPMENT CO PVT LTD	RADAR	14.5
MONOMATAPA DEVELOPMENT CO PVT LTD	ZIMALLOYS	3.1
MONTREAL CONTROL A/C CANADA	COPI	79.3
MONTRIQUE P/L	SAGEGRP	1.3
MOOLMAN T D	CAXTON	4.3
MOOLMAN T D & COBURN N M	CTP	1.2
MOON M W W	GF-PROPS	2.3
MOON M W W	VLAKS	3.4
MOONDA E S	RAPTOR	9.9
MOORE P H	AF-&-OVER	2.2
MOORE P H	GLODINA	1.5
MOORE P H	GRINCOR	1.4
MOORE P H	MASONITE	3.1
MOOSA A S	WINBEL	1.0
MORENA J	LEBAKA	4.0
MORFORD R A	COASTAL	17.1
MOROSS H	KH PROPS	2.5
MOSER J E	FAIRCAP	3.3
MOSS J	LOGTEK	2.0
MOSS M S	LOGTEK	8.4
MOTOR & GENERAL SUPPLIES P/L	CURNOW	1.5
MOULTRIE I A	CROOKES	1.0
MOULTRIE I A	TMX	1.2
MOWSZOWSKI R	VOLTEX	1.7
MPM NOM LTD	SPESCOM	1.5
MPOTOKWANE L M	INCO	17.5
MUIRHEAD AA &DUANE K &ASHERSON D	WALHOLD	1.4
MUKUNDE B	OHIO	4.3
MULTITECH P/L	CONCOR	2.9
MUNDELL G W	STOCKS	1.4
MUNRO T L R	EERSLNG	1.6
MURPHY F T J	PUBHOLD	2.0
MURPHY T	PUBHOLD	2.0
MURRAY & ROBERTS LTD	RABIE	1.9
MURRAY & ROBERTS STAFF PENS FUND	CRULIFE	1.1
MURRAY & ROBERTS TRUST	M&R-HLD	3.9
MUTUAL & FEDERAL INSURANCE CO LTD	A-V-I	1.2
MUTUAL & FEDERAL INSURANCE CO LTD	BARPROP	11.2
MUTUAL & FEDERAL INSURANCE CO LTD	COM-FUND	6.9
MUTUAL & FEDERAL INSURANCE CO LTD	FOSCHINI	1.7
MUTUAL & FEDERAL INSURANCE CO LTD	NATSEL	2.0
MUTUAL & FEDERAL INSURANCE CO LTD	PLATE-GL	1.1
MUTUAL & FEDERAL INSURANCE CO LTD	SAFREN	1.0
MUTUAL & FEDERAL INV LTD	M-&-F	79.1
MYNHARDT J T	IGI BOT	1.1
MYNHARDT J T	INCO	1.5
MYNHARDT J T	SECHABA	1.1

N

NAIAD INV LTD	GROWALK	2.7
NAIAD INV LTD	MARCONS	5.3
NAMIB CONSOLIDATED INV P/L	NISWA	46.0
NAMIBIAN SEA PRODUCTS LTD	NAMFISH	26.4
NAMNOR SA	NAMSEA	22.4
NAMPAK PENS FUND	BOEPROP	1.4
NAMPAK PENS FUND	GROPROP	3.8
NAMPAK PENS FUND	GROWPNT	2.6
NAMPAK PENS FUND	RMSPROP	3.7
NAMPAK PENS FUND	STOCKS	1.3
NAMPAK PENS FUND	UTICO	1.3
NANGLE E J	GULLIVER	1.0
NANGLE E J	RADAR	2.0
NANSEN INV LTD	MULTI	27.4
NAPIER HOLDINGS INC	DINETTE	17.0
NAT BRICK HOLDINGS P/L	ABBEY	20.0
NAT BRICK HOLDINGS P/L	DEBNAIR	5.3
NAT BRICK HOLDINGS P/L	FAIRCAP	24.9
NAT BRICK HOLDINGS P/L	PROPCOR	2.1
NAT CITY NOM LTD	BLYVOOR	4.4
NAT CITY NOM LTD	BRACKEN	2.9
NAT CITY NOM LTD	DBN-DEEP	5.0
NAT CITY NOM LTD	DRIES	1.6
NAT CITY NOM LTD	GROOTVLEI	1.5
NAT CITY NOM LTD	HARTIES	1.3

NAT CITY NOM LTD	LIBANON	3.0
NAT CITY NOM LTD	LORAINE	11.6
NAT CITY NOM LTD	VAAL-REEF	2.0
NAT CITY NOM LTD	VLAKS	1.2
NAT CITY NOM LTD	WES-AREAS	4.6
NAT DEVELOPMENT BANK	FSC	29.2
NAT FOODS WORKERS TRUST PVT LTD	NATFOOD	10.0
NAT INSURANCE CO OF ZIM PVT LTD	HUNYANI	1.0
NAT PARKS BRD CURATORS STAFF PENS	FRAME	1.9
NAT PARKS BRD CURATORS STAFF PENS	TWEEFONTN	2.6
NAT PARKS BRD CURATORS STAFF PENS	UMDONI	1.0
NAT PARKS BRD PERS PENS FUND	VOGELS	1.6
NAT PERS BPK	M-NET	6.3
NAT PERS BPK	PENROSE	29.1
NAT PERS BPK	PERSBEL	25.1
NAT RAILWAYS OF ZIM CONTR PENS FUND	ART	1.6
NAT RAILWAYS OF ZIM CONTR PENS FUND	BORDER	2.0
NAT RAILWAYS OF ZIM CONTR PENS FUND	CAPS	2.9
NAT RAILWAYS OF ZIM CONTR PENS FUND	DELTA ZIM	1.7
NAT RAILWAYS OF ZIM CONTR PENS FUND	FALGOLD	1.6
NAT RAILWAYS OF ZIM CONTR PENS FUND	FMB	2.3
NAT RAILWAYS OF ZIM CONTR PENS FUND	FSI ZIM	5.2
NAT RAILWAYS OF ZIM CONTR PENS FUND	GULLIVER	5.2
NAT RAILWAYS OF ZIM CONTR PENS FUND	HUNYANI	1.0
NAT RAILWAYS OF ZIM CONTR PENS FUND	MASHONA	4.2
NAT RAILWAYS OF ZIM CONTR PENS FUND	MWEAR	1.0
NAT RAILWAYS OF ZIM CONTR PENS FUND	PGI	2.4
NAT RAILWAYS OF ZIM CONTR PENS FUND	RADAR	1.4
NAT RAILWAYS OF ZIM CONTR PENS FUND	SCHWEP CA	4.8
NAT RAILWAYS OF ZIM CONTR PENS FUND	TEDCO	4.0
NAT RAILWAYS OF ZIM CONTR PENS FUND	WANKIE	1.7
NAT RAILWAYS OF ZIM CONTR PENS FUND	ZIMBANK	2.3
NAT RAILWAYS OF ZIM CONTR PENS FUND	ZSR	2.4
NAT SELECTIONS LTD	CGSMITH	2.6
NAT SELECTIONS LTD	IMPLATS	4.7
NAT SELECTIONS LTD	PALAMIN	2.8
NAT SELECTIONS LTD	SAPPI	2.3
NAT TURF INV LTD	OAKFLDS	1.7
NATAL IND SUPPLIERS P/L	CONFRAM	3.1
NATAL JOINT MUNICIPAL PENS FUND	S-A-BIAS	1.8
NATAL JOINT MUNICIPAL PENS FUND	SYCOM	3.6
NATAL JOINT MUNICIPAL PENS FUND	T-&-N	1.2
NATAL MASTER BUILDERS & ALLIED IND	FEDSURE	1.1
NATAL VENTURE P/L	CFC	3.6
NATURAL SILK CO LTD	FARM-AG	5.6
NATVAAL PROPERTIES P/L	SABLE	2.2
NEALE-MAY G	COASTAL	32.3
NEARCO TRUSTEE CO JERSEY LTD	MACMED	19.6
NECKEL D	ARIES	19.7
NEDBANK NOM LTD	ABSA	1.1
NEDBANK NOM LTD	AFR-LEASE	7.5
NEDBANK NOM LTD	AFROX	1.1
NEDBANK NOM LTD	AIMARK	1.8
NEDBANK NOM LTD	AMAPROP	1.7
NEDBANK NOM LTD	APEX	1.3
NEDBANK NOM LTD	AUTOQIP	26.5
NEDBANK NOM LTD	BASREAD	25.9
NEDBANK NOM LTD	BEATRIX	1.6
NEDBANK NOM LTD	BOEPROP	4.9
NEDBANK NOM LTD	BUFFELS	4.0
NEDBANK NOM LTD	CBD-FUND	6.6
NEDBANK NOM LTD	CNAGALO	1.2
NEDBANK NOM LTD	CRULIFE	3.1
NEDBANK NOM LTD	CUTRITE	22.6
NEDBANK NOM LTD	DIDATA	8.1
NEDBANK NOM LTD	EERSLNG	3.5
NEDBANK NOM LTD	FOSCHINI	1.1
NEDBANK NOM LTD	G5HOLD	1.7
NEDBANK NOM LTD	GEN-OPTIC	21.0
NEDBANK NOM LTD	GFSA	5.2
NEDBANK NOM LTD	GRINAKER	4.8
NEDBANK NOM LTD	GYPSUM	1.5
NEDBANK NOM LTD	HARMONY	2.5
NEDBANK NOM LTD	HCI	18.1
NEDBANK NOM LTD	HISCORE	1.8
NEDBANK NOM LTD	HLH	1.1
NEDBANK NOM LTD	HOLDAIN	1.3
NEDBANK NOM LTD	HORTORS	2.9
NEDBANK NOM LTD	ICH	4.3
NEDBANK NOM LTD	INMINS	1.3
NEDBANK NOM LTD	INTELES	1.1
NEDBANK NOM LTD	KEELEY	1.4
NEDBANK NOM LTD	KINROSS	2.5
NEDBANK NOM LTD	KLIPTON	1.3
NEDBANK NOM LTD	KNIGHTS	5.8
NEDBANK NOM LTD	KUDU	4.2
NEDBANK NOM LTD	L-T-A	3.6
NEDBANK NOM LTD	LESLIE	1.7
NEDBANK NOM LTD	LYD-PLAT	2.6
NEDBANK NOM LTD	M&R-HLD	1.3
NEDBANK NOM LTD	MACADAM	8.1
NEDBANK NOM LTD	MANRO	18.0
NEDBANK NOM LTD	MCRTAIL	2.4
NEDBANK NOM LTD	METAIR	2.5
NEDBANK NOM LTD	METJE-&-Z	1.3
NEDBANK NOM LTD	MICOR	1.5
NEDBANK NOM LTD	MILSTAN	30.8
NEDBANK NOM LTD	MINGRAN	2.1
NEDBANK NOM LTD	MORKELS	75.3
NEDBANK NOM LTD	NEDCOR	2.7
NEDBANK NOM LTD	NICTUS	3.7
NEDBANK NOM LTD	OCTODEC	1.1
NEDBANK NOM LTD	OMNIA	4.1
NEDBANK NOM LTD	OSPREY	16.0
NEDBANK NOM LTD	PANPROP	5.4
NEDBANK NOM LTD	PERSBEL	1.2
NEDBANK NOM LTD	PERSKOR	1.6
NEDBANK NOM LTD	PIKWIK	1.3
NEDBANK NOM LTD	PIONEER	1.8
NEDBANK NOM LTD	PORT	2.0
NEDBANK NOM LTD	PREMPHARM	2.7
NEDBANK NOM LTD	PRESMED	8.1
NEDBANK NOM LTD	PUTPROP	2.9
NEDBANK NOM LTD	RACY	3.2
NEDBANK NOM LTD	RALE	1.2
NEDBANK NOM LTD	REVERE	6.2
NEDBANK NOM LTD	ROMANO	1.6
NEDBANK NOM LTD	ROYAL	2.0
NEDBANK NOM LTD	ROYCHEM	1.8
NEDBANK NOM LTD	SAB IND	1.6
NEDBANK NOM LTD	SABLE	2.9
NEDBANK NOM LTD	SABVEST	4.6
NEDBANK NOM LTD	SAFCOR	1.4
NEDBANK NOM LTD	SAGEGRP	8.5
NEDBANK NOM LTD	SALLIES	1.1
NEDBANK NOM LTD	SANLIC	1.3
NEDBANK NOM LTD	SCHARIG	1.1
NEDBANK NOM LTD	SECHOLD	1.5
NEDBANK NOM LTD	SFW	2.0
NEDBANK NOM LTD	SILOAK	3.8
NEDBANK NOM LTD	SPICER	1.0
NEDBANK NOM LTD	SPL	8.3
NEDBANK NOM LTD	STOCKS	1.7
NEDBANK NOM LTD	SUNCISK	1.4
NEDBANK NOM LTD	TECFIN	4.1
NEDBANK NOM LTD	TEMPORA	1.9
NEDBANK NOM LTD	TOMKOR	3.1
NEDBANK NOM LTD	TRNPACO	2.7
NEDBANK NOM LTD	U-CON	3.0
NEDBANK NOM LTD	UNIDEV	1.4
NEDBANK NOM LTD	UNIHOLD	9.7
NEDBANK NOM LTD	VEKTRA	1.7
NEDBANK NOM LTD	VETRUST	2.8
NEDBANK NOM LTD	VIERFONTN	1.5
NEDBANK NOM LTD	VILLAGE	1.1
NEDBANK NOM LTD	VLAKS	1.0

NEDBANK NOM LTD	VOGELS	1.9
NEDBANK NOM LTD	VOLTEX	2.9
NEDBANK NOM LTD	WAICOR	1.4
NEDBANK NOM LTD	WALHOLD	1.1
NEDBANK NOM LTD	WALTONS	1.8
NEDBANK NOM LTD	WBHOLD	6.1
NEDBANK NOM LTD	WINKELS	7.4
NEDBANK NOM LTD	WOODROW	9.8
NEDLAW INV & TRUST CORP LTD	ART	46.0
NEDPERM BANK LTD	BARNETS	7.1
NEDPERM BANK LTD	OCTODEC	8.5
NEDPERM BANK LTD	TOMKOR	7.6
NEI AFRICA HLDGS P/L	NEI-AFR	53.3
NEI OVERSEAS HOLDINGS LTD	NEI-AFR	3.0
NEI OVERSEAS HOLDINGS LTD	NEIHOLD	56.7
NEL J D FAMILY TRUST	HICORL	1.9
NERINA KEELEY TRUST	KEELEY	7.2
NERINA KEELEY TRUST	KELGRAN	3.4
NESER M S B	ABCON	1.8
NESER MSB, JM, LC & LEONARD M	ABCON	1.5
NESTADT G	HCI	1.9
NESTLE PENS FUND	CBD-FUND	2.2
NESTLE PENS FUND	CONSOL	1.6
NESTLE PENS FUND	REX-TRUE	2.1
NESTLE PENS FUND	STANPRO	1.4
NEW CHAKARI MINES P/L	UNION	5.0
NEW ERA CONSOLIDATED LTD	ANAMINT	2.0
NEW ERA INSURANCE CO LTD	SMALDEL	5.1
NEW SA PRINCIPLES INV P/L	SAAMBOU	6.9
NEWMAN A E	GAZGOLD	1.1
NEWMAN F H	GAZGOLD	4.1
NEWMAN F H & A E TRUST	GAZGOLD	2.1
NFH INV LTD	NATFOOD	11.6
NGK SINODALE TVL PENS FUND	BOUMAT	1.5
NICK HAYLE HOLDINGS LTD	RABIE	1.1
NICTUS EKSEKUTEURSKAMER P/L	NICTUS	1.7
NIGEL GOLD MIN HLDGS SHARE INC TRUST	NIGEL	1.8
NILVOLARD P/L	HYPERET	41.8
NINETEEN SYNDICATE P/L	YORKCOR	10.2
NOLENE KEELEY TRUST	KEELEY	7.2
NOLENE KEELEY TRUST	KELGRAN	3.5
NOM INV & TRUST CO P/L	ICH	21.3
NOMINEES ONLY P/L	BOLTONS	1.5
NOMINEES ONLY P/L	LANCHEM	5.0
NOMINEES ONLY P/L	QUAGGA	1.5
NOMINEES ONLY P/L	RENTBEL	4.0
NOOIENSFONTEIN INV P/L	BOLAND	3.7
NOORD BRABANTSE INSTALLATIE CO BV	TECHIRE	60.0
NORBERTON LTD	UNION	12.3
NORTH & OSBORNE P/L	ARIES	1.5
NORTH PENS FUND	INVICTA	1.1
NORTHCHART INV LTD	COR-SYND	1.0
NORTHCHART INV LTD	MASHONA	1.9
NORTHCHART INV LTD	SCHWEP CA	4.9
NORTHCHART INV LTD	TEDCO	2.6
NORTHCHART INV LTD	TWEEFONTN	2.3
NORTHCHART INV LTD	WANKIE	3.0
NORTHERN ENG IND AFRICA EMPL S/P	NEI-AFR	1.9
NORTHWEST ESTATE AGENTS RENTS P/L	VIERFONTN	1.3
NORWICH LIFE SA LTD	NBSHOLD	25.4
NORWITZ R	MIDAS	1.0
NOYCE A G	NATRAWL	1.2
NPL NOM P/L	CMS	3.4
NRI LTD	WANKIE	2.8
NRZ CONTRIBUTORY PENS FUND	CIH	25.6
NRZ CONTRIBUTORY PENS FUND	J & F	1.3
NUMITOR INV HLDGS	DE BEERS	2.4
NUPEN G R B	MAST	1.3
NUSSBAUM H H	SANLIC	4.8
NUSSBAUM L	SANLIC	6.1
NUSSBAUM M M	SANLIC	5.0
NUSSBAUM R A W	ADONIS	1.0
NUSSBAUM R A W	CURNOW	1.2
NUSSBAUM R A W	KOPP	2.9
NUSSBAUM R A W	PROGRESS	1.8
NUSSBAUM R A W	TRIMTRD	1.4
NUSSBAUM R P	SANLIC	4.8
NUSSBAUM R S A W	BURLINGTN	2.0
NUSSBAUM R S A W	CLYDE	1.4
NUSSBAUM R S A W	ENSIGN	1.4
NUSSBAUM R S A W	TRNPACO	1.6

O

O'CONNOR J J	LANCHEM	2.0
O'DONNELL R	GAZGOLD	1.2
OAK BRIDGE INV LTD	QUICKCO	3.4
OBRUM INV P/L	STH-RODPT	2.7
OCTOGROWTH CC	OCTODEC	1.1
OCTOGROWTH TWO CC	OCTODEC	1.1
ODDES B S	FORIM	1.4
OHIO SHARE INCENTIVE TRUST	OHIO	1.1
OK BAZAARS EXEC SHARE INC SCHEME	O-K	3.9
OLAPEG INV P/L	GRINAKER	2.6
OLD MUTUAL INV CORP (PVT) LTD	AFDISTIL	2.9
OLD MUTUAL INV CORP (PVT) LTD	AGRICOR	16.5
OLD MUTUAL INV CORP (PVT) LTD	ART	21.2
OLD MUTUAL INV CORP (PVT) LTD	CAIRNS	10.5
OLD MUTUAL INV CORP (PVT) LTD	CAPS	11.5
OLD MUTUAL INV CORP (PVT) LTD	CIH	4.0
OLD MUTUAL INV CORP (PVT) LTD	DELTA ZIM	16.6
OLD MUTUAL INV CORP (PVT) LTD	FMB	14.4
OLD MUTUAL INV CORP (PVT) LTD	HIPPO	15.4
OLD MUTUAL INV CORP (PVT) LTD	HUNYANI	12.5
OLD MUTUAL INV CORP (PVT) LTD	J & F	3.1
OLD MUTUAL INV CORP (PVT) LTD	KADOMA	16.1
OLD MUTUAL INV CORP (PVT) LTD	M-C-M	6.3
OLD MUTUAL INV CORP (PVT) LTD	MASHONA	20.9
OLD MUTUAL INV CORP (PVT) LTD	NATFOOD	15.2
OLD MUTUAL INV CORP (PVT) LTD	PGI	32.2
OLD MUTUAL INV CORP (PVT) LTD	RADAR	9.5
OLD MUTUAL INV CORP (PVT) LTD	RIO ZIM	6.9
OLD MUTUAL INV CORP (PVT) LTD	ROTH ZIM	19.3
OLD MUTUAL INV CORP (PVT) LTD	SCHWEP CA	20.8
OLD MUTUAL INV CORP (PVT) LTD	TEDCO	2.0
OLD MUTUAL INV CORP (PVT) LTD	TRUZIM	22.4
OLD MUTUAL INV CORP (PVT) LTD	TSL	18.5
OLD MUTUAL INV CORP (PVT) LTD	UDC	12.5
OLD MUTUAL INV CORP (PVT) LTD	WANKIE	1.1
OLD MUTUAL INV CORP (PVT) LTD	WSGROVE	7.3
OLD MUTUAL INV CORP (PVT) LTD	ZIM SUN	13.1
OLD MUTUAL INV CORP (PVT) LTD	ZIMALLOYS	5.2
OLD MUTUAL INV CORP (PVT) LTD	ZIMBANK	14.5
OLD MUTUAL INV CORP (PVT) LTD	ZIMSPIN	1.2
OLD MUTUAL INV CORP P/L	PORTHLD	1.4
OLD MUTUAL ZIMBABWE	FSI ZIM	21.9
OLESEN H	MAST	1.9
OLIVIER C J	DIALMOV	4.9
OMNI MEDIA P/L	CNAGALO	65.2
OMNIA EXEC SHARE PARTICIPATION SCHEME	OMNIA	1.9
OMNIA SHARE INCENTIVE SCHEME	OMNIA	2.3
ONE ZERO ONE INV HOLDINGS P/L	QUORUM	52.5
OOSTHUIZEN A J H	ALLWEAR	1.3
ORANGE FREE STATE INV LTD	FREGOLD	49.9
ORANGE FREE STATE INV TRUST LTD	FREGOLD	2.0
ORANGE FREE STATE INV TRUST LTD	LORAINE	1.2
ORANGE FREE STATE INV TRUST LTD	OFSIL	5.1
ORANGE FREE STATE INV TRUST LTD	ST-HELENA	13.0
ORANGE FREE STATE INV TRUST LTD	WELKOM	9.3
ORESTEEL INV P/L	ASSORE	52.0
ORIOLE INV LTD	ERGO	1.5
ORTON E W	T-E-J	1.7
OSBORN W G	CAIRNS	1.2
OSCHINSKY P	BUFFCOR	1.6
OSPREY SHARE INCETIVE	OSPREY	1.7

OSTROWIAK D M FAMILY TRUST	ALEXWYT	5.4
OSTROWIAK T J	ALEXWYT	7.0
OTIS ELEVATOR CO	OTIS	42.5
OTTE K E	DUKEL	4.0
OUDOU P/L	BESTER	3.4
OVBEL HOLDINGS LTD	OVCON	20.0
OVBEL R TRUST	OVBEL	9.5
OVBEL R TRUST	OVCON	1.6
OVENSTONE A D P	OVBEL	3.9
OVERSEAS NOM CO INC	AMCOAL	1.3
OVERSEAS NOM CO INC	DRIES	3.1
OVERSEAS NOM CO INC	HARTIES	2.2
OVERSEAS NOM CO INC	KLOOF	4.0
OVERSEAS NOM CO INC	SOUTHVAAL	4.5
OVERSEAS NOM CO INC	VAAL-REEF	1.7
OVERSEAS NOM CO INC	WINKELS	6.7
OVERSEAS NOM CO INC	ZANDPAN	7.6
OWEN B A	T-E-J	3.8
OWENS-ILLINOIS INC	CONSOL	19.3
OZZ LTD SHARE TRUST	OZZ	1.0
OZZ LTD SHARE TRUST CONTROL ACC	OZZ	6.1

P

P B INV & HOLDINGS P/L	ENBOT	3.9
PAG HOLDINGS P/L	PAG	49.6
PAG INCENTIVE TRUST	PAG	3.0
PAG NOM P/L	PAG	2.0
PAG PERSONNEL LTD	PAG	24.3
PALABORA HLDGS LTD	PALAMIN	61.4
PALLAS C J	PLASTAL	1.9
PARK INV P/L	RDC	2.6
PARKDEV PROPERTY P/L	VETRUST	17.1
PARKER G C	HAIB	4.1
PARKER W B	MINVEST	6.0
PARRY M C	Q-DATA	1.2
PARSONAGE S C	PALS	2.2
PATEL I M	POINTER	2.5
PATERNOSTER NOM P/L	BSI	1.8
PATRICK JOHN DAVIES FAMILY TRUST	TITACO	2.5
PATRIVIA INV P/L	BURLINGTN	2.4
PAUL I G	OVCON	2.1
PAULS TRUST INVESTMENTS	SUPREME	1.6
PECHINEY	ZIMALLOYS	2.3
PECKETT R	OVCON	1.6
PEDLAR D S	DIALMOV	4.9
PEDRETTI M	MLNHOLD	2.3
PEER A C	DPF-INV	1.9
PELICAN LTD	NINIAN	8.2
PENNYSHINE FOUNDATION	BERTRAD	1.0
PEPGRO LTD	PEPKOR	53.1
PEPGRO LTD SHARE INC SCHEME	PEPGRO	3.7
PEPKOR BPK	PEP	78.5
PEPKOR BPK	SHOPRIT	80.0
PEPKOR LTD SHR PURCHASE SCHEME -	PEPKOR	1.5
PEPPER J D	LITHO	15.8
PEPPER SEAN MICHAEL	LITHO	1.9
PEPPER SHIRLEY MARGUARITE	LITHO	1.6
PERLOV M	NINIAN	1.4
PERSETECH HOLDINGS P/L	PERSTEC	58.0
PERSKOR INV LTD	PERSKOR	42.5
PERSKORGROEP VOORSORGFONDS	PERSKOR	1.1
PERSKORPORASIE VAN SA BPK	M-NET	2.8
PETARD NOM LTD	AECI	1.1
PETARD NOM LTD	AFR-LEASE	9.7
PETARD NOM LTD	AMAPROP	5.9
PETARD NOM LTD	AMCOAL	5.4
PETARD NOM LTD	AMGOLD	4.9
PETARD NOM LTD	ANGLO-S	5.6
PETARD NOM LTD	BUFFELS	8.8
PETARD NOM LTD	CMI	3.0
PETARD NOM LTD	CULLINAN	7.6
PETARD NOM LTD	DEELKRL	3.4
PETARD NOM LTD	DRIES	3.0
PETARD NOM LTD	ELANDS	6.4
PETARD NOM LTD	HARTIES	1.5
PETARD NOM LTD	LEPLAT	2.2
PETARD NOM LTD	LORAINE	7.3
PETARD NOM LTD	MCCARTHY	3.2
PETARD NOM LTD	OFSIL	1.4
PETARD NOM LTD	PP RUST	2.5
PETARD NOM LTD	RUSPLAT	2.8
PETARD NOM LTD	SALLIES	18.6
PETARD NOM LTD	SOUTHVAAL	5.4
PETARD NOM LTD	TARGET	5.5
PETARD NOM LTD	VAAL-REEF	7.5
PETARD NOM LTD	WELKOM	10.1
PETARD NOM LTD	WSTN-DEEP	9.0
PETER A	PROPFIN	1.7
PETERBRIDGE TRUST	LASER	1.1
PETRA HOLDINGS P/L	PETRA	34.2
PETROLEUM INV HOLDING CO LTD	ENBOT	70.0
PETRUSSTRAAT INV P/L	QUAGGA	2.3
PFEIFFER S TRUST	RAINBOW	7.2
PFI GROUP PENS FUND	CLUFF ZIM	1.0
PG GLASS PENS FUND	HYPROP	1.3
PG WOOD & PG BISON PENS FUND	HYPROP	1.2
PHARO G H	NATRAWL	1.2
PHELPS L S	EQUIKOR	1.1
PHEZULU INV CC	BOLPRO	3.5
PHILIP GUTKIN HOLDINGS P/L	RENTBEL	1.6
PHIMAX P/L	CONFRAM	5.8
PHOENIX ASSURE SA LTD	NATRAWL	1.2
PHR SECURITIES P/L	BURLINGTN	15.2
PICARDI INV LTD	PICHOLD	68.7
PICFIN EMPLOYEES PROFIT SHARING FUND	PICHOLD	4.5
PICHOLD LTD	PICAPLI	93.2
PICK 'N PAY HOLDINGS LTD	PICKNPAY	51.9
PICK N PAY EMPLOYEE SHARE PURC SCHEME	PICKNPAY	1.9
PICK N PAY EMPLOYEE SHARE PURC SCHEME	PIKWIK	4.6
PILKINGTON GROUP PENS FUND	GROWPNT	1.2
PILKINGTON GROUP PENS FUND	HYPROP	1.2
PILLAY B	BARNETS	1.6
PINTAIL INV LTD	PP RUST	2.5
PINTAIL INV LTD	RUSPLAT	4.1
PIONEER NOM LTD	NEW-CENT	3.5
PK HARRIS INV P/L	RMBH	3.8
PLACOR HLDGS LTD	PLATE-GL	15.9
PLASTALL INV P/L	PLASTAL	85.3
PLATE GLASS CONSOLIDATED INV CO P/L	PLATE-GL	17.2
PLEVANS PENS FUND	GROPROP	1.3
PLEVANS PENS FUND	RMSPROP	1.0
POLLACK J	TOMKOR	1.5
POLLACK JOSEPH INV CC	OCTODEC	2.4
POLLACK MYRON INV CC	OCTODEC	1.0
PONSFORD F	CAFCA	2.6
PORTER A M	PORT	1.4
PORTER B J L	PORT	22.2
PORTHOLD TRUST P/L	PORTHLD	3.2
POTCHEFSTROOM GOLD AREAS LTD	LYDEX	2.8
POULIART R J	MACADAM	25.3
POUROULIS A	STH-RODPT	1.6
POUROULIS L C	MODDER	2.7
POUROULIS L C	STH-RODPT	2.6
POWELL O	CURNOW	1.3
POWERTECH INV HOLDINGS P/L	ABERDARE	12.8
POWERTECH PROPERTIES & INV LTD	ABERDARE	7.4
PREMIER GROUP HLDGS LTD	CMS	33.3
PREMIER GROUP PENS FUND	E-DAGGA	2.3
PREMIER GROUP PENS FUND	GRESHAM	1.2
PREMIER GROUP PENS FUND	METCASH	1.6
PREMSAB HOLDINGS LTD	BEVCON	26.3
PREMSAB HOLDINGS LTD	PREM-GRP	23.5
PRESMED HOLDINGS P/L	PRESMED	62.5
PRESS H	COPI	1.1

PRESS H	MOBILE	1.3
PRESTIGE INV PVT LTD	PGI	45.4
PRETORIA PERMANENT NOM P/L	SHOREDITS	1.2
PRETORIA WHOLESALE DRUGGISTS	GRESHAM	86.0
PRETORIUS A	ROMANO	1.4
PRETORIUS A F	LONGRAIL	3.8
PRICE L	EUREKA	3.2
PRICE M R	EUREKA	3.2
PRICE RONALD SYDNEY	EUREKA	34.5
PRICE RYAN SEAN	EUREKA	3.2
PRIMA BANK LTD	DPF-INV	13.3
PRIMA BANK LTD	VETRUST	2.9
PRIMA PROPERTY TRUST MANAGERS LTD	VETRUST	1.3
PRIMSEC P/L	NINIAN	7.0
PRINCE S	SPICER	1.4
PRINTING INDUSTRY PENS FUND	MOBILE	1.5
PRINTING INDUSTRY PENS FUND	TRENCOR	1.3
PROFESSIONAL PROV SOC OF SA	CENPROP	2.6
PROFESSIONAL PROV SOC OF SA	I-&-J	1.2
PROFESSIONAL PROV SOC OF SA	SYCOM	1.7
PROFESSIONAL PROV SOC OF SA	TRENCOR	3.4
PROFESSIONAL PROV SOC OF SA	UMDONI	2.4
PROFSURE HOLDINGS P/L	QUORUM	2.5
PROFURN SHARE INC SCHEME TRUST	PROFURN	1.9
PROGENY INV P/L	VIERFONTN	3.4
PROPCOR (BRISTOL) HOLDINGS LTD	BRISTOL-I	21.4
PROSPECTS OF ZIMBABWE PVT LTD	BINDURA	8.7
PROTEA ASSURE CO LTD	LEFIC	2.2
PROTEA ASSURE CO LTD	NAMFISH	1.6
PROTEA ASSURE CO LTD	NEW-CENT	1.1
PROTEA ASSURE CO LTD	OCEANA	1.3
PROTEA ASSURE CO LTD	TAMBOTI	1.0
PROTEA ASSURE CO PENS FUND	CRULIFE	1.5
PROTEA ASSURE CO PENS FUND	HISTONE	2.0
PROTEA ASSURE CO PENS FUND	INVICTA	1.5
PROTEA ASSURE CO PENS FUND	NEW-CENT	1.3
PROTEA ASSURE CO PENS FUND	PROSURE	1.6
PRYCE-WILLIAMS K	CMS	7.0
PT INV CO P/L	INHOLD	7.0
PTR HOLDINGS INC	UNISERV	58.4
PUBHOLD LTD	PUBLICO	1.5
PUBLIC INV COMMISSIONERS	GENBEHEER	1.2
PUBLIC INV COMMISSIONERS	PEPKOR	3.1
PUBLIC INV COMMISSIONERS	SAPPI	2.6
PUBLIC INV COMMISSIONERS	SASOL	9.5
PUBLICITY CONSULTANTS INC	ADCORP	1.2
PUBLICO HOLDINGS LTD	PUBLICO	73.3
PUTTER INV P/L	OMNIA	1.0

Q

Q DATA TRUST	Q-DATA	1.6
QUAGGA SHARE INCENTIVE TRUST	QUAGGA	3.1
QUARTET INV LTD	ABBEY	16.9
QUARTET INV LTD	FENIX	7.9
QUARTET INV LTD	PROPCOR	14.6
QUARTO NOM P/L	FREDDEV	1.4
QUARTO NOM P/L	LEEGALL	43.3
QUARTO NOM P/L	LYDEX	2.0
QUARTO NOM P/L	STREBEL	2.3
QUIBOY LTD	GAZGOLD	4.6

R

R D TRUST	TEMPORA	1.2
R H TRUST	CONCOR	7.3
R M INSURANCE CO PVT LTD	CAPS	1.1
R M INSURANCE CO PVT LTD	ROTH ZIM	1.4
R M NOM P/L	HAIB	3.9
R-V INV NOM CC	DELSWA	3.6
R-V INV NOM CC	PUTCO	1.1
R-V INV NOM CC	PUTPROP	1.1
RAATH M J	SHOREDITS	2.9
RABFAM SECURITIES P/L	ABBEY	6.3
RABIE J S	RABIE	37.2
RABIE SHARE INCENTIVE TRUST	RABIE	1.2
RABINOWITZ B (NOMINEE)	BLOCHS	10.6
RABINOWITZ D (NOMINEE)	BLOCHS	10.6
RABMAN TRADING P/L	PROPCOR	2.4
RADAR EMPLOYEES TRUST PVT LTD	RADAR	5.1
RADIO HOLDING LTD	WSGROVE	10.0
RAE G F	FRALEX	1.2
RAHAVANNIG INV P/L	IMPERIAL	16.2
RAINIER INC	DELTA ZIM	14.5
RAKE INV P/L	ITLTILE	5.0
RAKE INV P/L	SUNCISK	8.0
RALE HOLDINGS LTD	FARM-AG	65.1
RALLEN P/L	ITLTILE	57.6
RAMNIT P/L	ADCORP	7.2
RAND AMERICAN INV P/L	ERGO	2.3
RAND EXTENSIONS & EXPLORATION LTD	LYDEX	2.8
RAND MERCHANT BANK HOLDINGS LTD	MOMENTUM	43.2
RAND MERCHANT BANK LTD	LENCO	2.4
RAND MERCHANT BANK LTD	LENVEST	17.3
RAND MERCHANT BANK LTD	SECHOLD	10.0
RAND MERCHANT BANK LTD	TIME	10.6
RAND MERCHANT NOM P/L	RHOEX	48.6
RAND MERCHANT NOM P/L	RMBH	5.9
RAND MINES HOLDINGS LTD	RANDMIN	21.5
RAND MINES LTD	BARPLAT	12.2
RAND MINES LTD	BLYVOOR	4.9
RAND MINES LTD	DBN-DEEP	15.0
RAND MINES LTD	E-R-P-M	28.3
RAND MINES LTD	HARMONY	12.3
RAND MINES LTD	R-M-PROPS	56.8
RAND MINES LTD	RANDCOL	70.5
RAND SELECTION CORP LTD	AMGOLD	7.4
RAND SELECTION CORP LTD	ANAMINT	7.5
RAND SELECTION CORP LTD	BUFFELS	1.0
RAND SELECTION CORP LTD	ELANDS	2.8
RAND SELECTION CORP LTD	ERGO	2.4
RAND SELECTION CORP LTD	L-T-A	2.9
RANDEX LTD	SOPLATS	10.5
RANDFONTEIN ESTATES GOLD MIN CO WITS	VENTERS	2.5
RANDSEL INV LTD	ERGO	2.3
RAWLINS G K	ABS	2.0
RAYBOULD W H	RD-LEASE	2.2
RAYMOND ACKERMAN P/L	PIKWIK	50.2
RAYOCT P/L	BERGERS	3.7
RE-INVEST INV HOLDINGS P/L	KH PROPS	2.2
REA BROTHERS	MINGRAN	11.6
REALESTATE FINANCIERE SA	RDC	46.7
REALLY NOBLE INV LTD	BOE	8.6
REDGWOODS HLDGS LTD EMP CONTROL ACC	REGGIES	2.9
REDGWOODS HOLDINGS EXEC SHARE TRUST	REGGIES	2.0
REDMAN P G	KNJ	4.8
REED B S	MAXMECH	1.2
REED W G	MAXMECH	1.1
REGENBAUM H	BOYMANS	2.4
REICHMANS IND INV P/L	IBJOFFE	8.4
REID D F M	BSI	4.5
REINER POSTHUMUS MEYJES FAMILY	TITACO	2.5
RELAG AG	GUBINGS	1.4
REMBRANDT CONTROLLING INV LTD	REMGRO	51.1
REMBRANDT TRUST P/L	TIB	44.5
REMBRANDT-KWV INV LTD	DISTIL	60.0
REMBRANDT-KWV INV LTD	SFW	60.0
REMUS INV P/L	ROMENS	4.3
RENIER BEHERENDE E/B	HARWILL	2.0
RENTEKOR P/L	RENTBEL	37.2
REPUBLIC NOM P/L	LIBVEST	7.3
REPUBLIC NOM P/L	TIWHEEL	21.1
REPUBLIC NOM P/L	UNI-COLD	29.7
REPUBLIC SHUTTERING P/L	F-S-GROUP	2.3

RESIDENT NOM LTD	AECI	1.1
RESIDENT NOM LTD	AFR-LEASE	23.5
RESIDENT NOM LTD	ALTECH	2.5
RESIDENT NOM LTD	ALTRON	4.2
RESIDENT NOM LTD	AMAPROP	56.8
RESIDENT NOM LTD	AMCOAL	6.2
RESIDENT NOM LTD	AMGOLD	7.8
RESIDENT NOM LTD	AMIC	22.7
RESIDENT NOM LTD	ANAMINT	6.1
RESIDENT NOM LTD	ANGLO-S	11.7
RESIDENT NOM LTD	ARGUS	9.3
RESIDENT NOM LTD	BEATRIX	1.5
RESIDENT NOM LTD	BOTREST	4.5
RESIDENT NOM LTD	BUFFELS	3.9
RESIDENT NOM LTD	CMI	13.6
RESIDENT NOM LTD	CNAGALO	1.2
RESIDENT NOM LTD	DE BEERS	2.9
RESIDENT NOM LTD	DOORNS	1.6
RESIDENT NOM LTD	ELANDS	3.9
RESIDENT NOM LTD	ERGO	11.1
RESIDENT NOM LTD	GFSA	3.8
RESIDENT NOM LTD	HAGGIE	33.4
RESIDENT NOM LTD	HIVELD	9.9
RESIDENT NOM LTD	ISCOR	3.1
RESIDENT NOM LTD	JOEL	8.4
RESIDENT NOM LTD	JOHNNIES	32.5
RESIDENT NOM LTD	KLOOF	7.9
RESIDENT NOM LTD	L-T-A	41.6
RESIDENT NOM LTD	LEPLAT	7.3
RESIDENT NOM LTD	MCCARTHY	8.0
RESIDENT NOM LTD	NEW-CENT	34.5
RESIDENT NOM LTD	OFSIL	2.3
RESIDENT NOM LTD	ORYX	3.0
RESIDENT NOM LTD	PALAMIN	2.7
RESIDENT NOM LTD	POWTECH	5.9
RESIDENT NOM LTD	PP RUST	6.7
RESIDENT NOM LTD	RUSPLAT	4.6
RESIDENT NOM LTD	S-A-EAGLE	1.3
RESIDENT NOM LTD	SALLIES	19.7
RESIDENT NOM LTD	SAMANCO	8.1
RESIDENT NOM LTD	SOUDEX	32.4
RESIDENT NOM LTD	SOUTHVAAL	8.9
RESIDENT NOM LTD	TARGET	8.4
RESIDENT NOM LTD	TONGAAT	26.0
RESIDENT NOM LTD	UNISEL	18.4
RESIDENT NOM LTD	VAAL-REEF	3.7
RESIDENT NOM LTD	VENTRON	19.2
RESIDENT NOM LTD	WELKOM	2.3
RESIDENT NOM LTD	WES-AREAS	1.5
RESIDENT NOM LTD	WSTN-DEEP	9.4
RESNICK L	BURLINGTN	4.4
RETAN NOM P/L	PROPFIN	1.7
RETAN NOM P/L	RALE	3.1
RETAN NOM P/L	TOCO	3.8
RETIEF J F	MACMED	1.5
RETIEF M J TRUST	HICORL	1.5
REVERE RESOURCES SA LTD	HAIB	79.9
REX J B	LOGTEK	1.6
REXHILL TRUST	MACADAM	6.0
REYNOLDS R E	DIGOCO	1.0
RHODES FAMILY TRUST	ADCORP	5.2
RHODES INV LTD	TECFIN	4.8
RHOSCO HOLDINGS P/L	RHOVAN	72.0
RICE K M	OHIO	1.6
RICHARDSON F E	RALE	1.6
RICHE FAMILY TRUST	STOCKS	2.4
RIDGE NOM P/L	BOLPRO	1.7
RIDGE NOM P/L	BOLTONS	1.7
RIDGE NOM P/L	BOLWEAR	1.9
RIDGE NOM P/L	CARGO	2.2
RILEY D B	MIDAS	1.2
RINGO FAMILY INV P/L	VESTCOR	41.9
RINRIC NOM P/L	DBN-DEEP	1.0
RINRIC NOM P/L	FREDDEV	1.6
RINRIC NOM P/L	MSAULI	3.1
RINRIC NOM P/L	TAFLBRG	2.3
RINRIC NOM P/L	VLAKS	1.4
RIO TINTO FOUNDATION CO PVT LTD	RIO ZIM	8.9
RIO TINTO SA LTD	PALAMIN	3.5
RIO TINTO ZIMBABWE LTD	ZIMALLOYS	2.1
RIO ZIMBABWE HOLDINGS LTD	RIO ZIM	55.6
RISTONE FINANCIAL HOLDINGS P/L	LANCHEM	21.2
RITOS AKTIENGESELLSCHAFT	BOLPRO	1.2
RITOS AKTIENGESELLSCHAFT	BOLTONS	1.2
RIVERBANK LTD	ADVTECH	3.6
RIVERS K W	TIWHEEL	2.9
RIWER NOM P/L	HICORL	43.1
RMB FINANCIAL HOLDINGS P/L	RMBH	30.0
ROBARTS F E A	WALHOLD	4.2
ROBERTSON B M	CFC	1.2
ROBERTSON J B ROBERTSON R M & SWAIN	CFC	1.0
ROBERTSON R M	CFC	1.2
ROBGUARD P/L	RALE	18.8
ROBRIAN INV P/L	BENCO	2.0
ROBROY BELANGE P/L	PICBEL	5.8
ROCAP INV P/L	PEPGRO	7.9
ROCCON HLDGS A G	CONCOR	10.8
ROCK PENS FUND	EVHOLD	4.2
ROCKIES (BULAWAYO) PVT LTD	WSGROVE	10.0
ROELOF LE ROUX VAN DER MERWE TRUST	M&R-INV	2.3
ROGOFF A	CONTRAV	14.4
ROHIRRIM INV P/L	LIB HOLD	1.1
ROLFE T W	F-S-I	1.4
ROMER A P	TAFLBRG	1.8
RONHAM INV P/L	DALYS	25.8
RONOEL PROPERTIES P/L	CAFCA	1.7
ROODE INV P/L	RENTBEL	1.9
ROODENRAND MAIN REEF MINES LTD	FREDDEV	2.1
ROODERAND MAIN REEF MINES LTD	DABI	2.6
ROSENBERG T	MCCARTHY	1.4
ROSENBERG T	MCRTAIL	6.0
ROSENSTEIN M	LEPPIN	7.0
ROTHSEY INV CO P/L	AVINS	2.9
ROTHSEY INV CO P/L	CRULIFE	3.8
ROTRUST P/L	PEPGRO	4.3
ROUSSOUW S A	JASCO	2.1
ROUX W	SECHOLD	2.0
ROY D	ENSIGN	6.4
ROY L E	ENSIGN	1.8
ROY R	ENSIGN	4.9
ROYAL CORP LTD	ROYCHEM	57.8
ROYAL CORP LTD	ROYFOOD	65.2
ROYAL GROUP HLDGS LTD	ROYAL	51.1
ROYTOWSKI R	ENSIGN	1.6
RSP INV P/L	ABS	1.9
RSP INV P/L	C-MATIC	2.0
RSP INV P/L	EUREKA	5.8
RSP INV P/L	MACADAM	3.1
RUBENSTEIN IND P/L	RUHOLD	7.4
RUBENSTEIN J E	RUHOLD	4.5
RUBENSTEIN L	COMPASS	2.8
RUBENSTEIN SHARE INC TRUST	RUHOLD	1.9
RUBENSTEIN T M	RUHOLD	4.5
RUDOLF J A	GYPSUM	2.0
RUNCORN HLDGS LTD	AMAPROP	3.0
RUNCORN HLDGS LTD	FIRSTBK	2.3
RUNCORN HLDGS LTD	JOHNNIES	1.1
RUPERT A TRUST	TIB	3.2
RUSFURN EXECUTIVE PARTICIPATION P/L	RUSFURN	9.5
RUSFURN SHARE INCENTIVE TRUST	RUSFURN	4.6
RUSH P J	JASCO	2.8
RUSSELL GROUP P/L	OVBEL	1.1
RUTHVAN P/L	A-T-COLL	1.1

S

S M GOLDSTEIN LTD	G5HOLD	45.4
S M HARRIS PVT LTD	NATFOOD	6.7
SA BIAS HOLDINGS LTD	MERHLD	79.8
SA BIAS HOLDINGS LTD	SAB IND	87.3
SA BOTTLING CO P/L	ABI	1.9
SA BREWERIES LTD	ABI	67.6
SA BREWERIES LTD	AFCOL	55.9
SA BREWERIES LTD	AMREL	68.7
SA BREWERIES LTD	CONSHU	33.1
SA BREWERIES LTD	DA-GAMA	11.7
SA BREWERIES LTD	DISTIL	30.0
SA BREWERIES LTD	EDGARS	11.2
SA BREWERIES LTD	LIONMATCH	70.6
SA BREWERIES LTD	O-K	69.0
SA BREWERIES LTD	PLATE-GL	17.1
SA BREWERIES LTD	SFW	30.0
SA EAGLE INSURANCE CO LTD	TITACO	9.9
SA EQUITIES LTD	ENSIGN	24.1
SA EQUITIES LTD	VIERFONTN	5.3
SA EQUITIES LTD	VLAKS	2.2
SA FIRE HOUSE LTD	S-A-EAGLE	1.8
SA IRON & STEEL INDUSTRIAL CORP LTD	METKOR	25.7
SA IRON & STEEL INDUSTRIAL CORP LTD	USKO	1.6
SA MINES SELECTION LTD	ERGO	4.7
SA MUTUAL	A-T-COLL	56.8
SA MUTUAL	A-V-HOLD	3.1
SA MUTUAL	A-V-I	10.1
SA MUTUAL	ABSA	4.6
SA MUTUAL	AECI	6.0
SA MUTUAL	AF-&-OVER	24.9
SA MUTUAL	AFCOL	6.8
SA MUTUAL	AFRICOM	1.5
SA MUTUAL	AFROX	6.0
SA MUTUAL	ALTECH	8.4
SA MUTUAL	ALTRON	10.7
SA MUTUAL	AMCOAL	12.8
SA MUTUAL	AMGOLD	2.3
SA MUTUAL	AMIC	5.8
SA MUTUAL	AMREL	6.5
SA MUTUAL	ANAMINT	13.1
SA MUTUAL	ANG-ALPHA	5.3
SA MUTUAL	ANGLO-S	7.6
SA MUTUAL	ANGLOVAAL	10.8
SA MUTUAL	ARGUS	5.9
SA MUTUAL	ASSORE	14.7
SA MUTUAL	AVF GRP	1.8
SA MUTUAL	BARLOWS	22.2
SA MUTUAL	BARMINE	12.5
SA MUTUAL	BARNEX	30.4
SA MUTUAL	BEATRIX	1.4
SA MUTUAL	BENCO	39.1
SA MUTUAL	BOEPROP	1.3
SA MUTUAL	BOLTONS	8.7
SA MUTUAL	BOLWEAR	7.3
SA MUTUAL	BOUMAT	2.1
SA MUTUAL	CAPITAL	51.4
SA MUTUAL	CASHBIL	7.3
SA MUTUAL	CBD-FUND	42.9
SA MUTUAL	CEMENCO	27.2
SA MUTUAL	CENPROP	6.7
SA MUTUAL	CG SUGAR	2.9
SA MUTUAL	CGS-FOOD	2.2
SA MUTUAL	CHEMSERVE	1.4
SA MUTUAL	CHUBB	2.7
SA MUTUAL	CMH	3.6
SA MUTUAL	CMI	3.8
SA MUTUAL	COATES	11.4
SA MUTUAL	COM-FUND	34.8
SA MUTUAL	CONSHU	1.1
SA MUTUAL	CROWN	4.1
SA MUTUAL	CULLINAN	43.1
SA MUTUAL	DA-GAMA	7.0
SA MUTUAL	DATAKOR	1.9
SA MUTUAL	DE BEERS	12.0
SA MUTUAL	DEELKRL	14.8
SA MUTUAL	DELTA	10.3
SA MUTUAL	DRIES	3.6
SA MUTUAL	E-DAGGA	13.3
SA MUTUAL	EERSLNG	4.1
SA MUTUAL	ELANDS	2.6
SA MUTUAL	ENGEN	2.1
SA MUTUAL	ERGO	8.1
SA MUTUAL	EVERITE	25.7
SA MUTUAL	EVHOLD	15.8
SA MUTUAL	FENNER	5.7
SA MUTUAL	FIRSTBK	2.4
SA MUTUAL	FIT	4.2
SA MUTUAL	FMCOTEC	17.2
SA MUTUAL	FOSCHINI	5.3
SA MUTUAL	G5HOLD	5.5
SA MUTUAL	GDM	11.2
SA MUTUAL	GEFCO	14.6
SA MUTUAL	GENBEHEER	3.5
SA MUTUAL	GENBEL	3.2
SA MUTUAL	GENCOR	7.5
SA MUTUAL	GFSA	3.4
SA MUTUAL	GRINAKER	8.7
SA MUTUAL	GRINTEK	13.5
SA MUTUAL	GROPROP	12.0
SA MUTUAL	GROUP-5	19.7
SA MUTUAL	GROWPNT	68.2
SA MUTUAL	HAGGIE	4.4
SA MUTUAL	HARTIES	1.8
SA MUTUAL	HIGATE	17.0
SA MUTUAL	HIVELD	5.4
SA MUTUAL	HUDACO	14.0
SA MUTUAL	HYPROP	3.7
SA MUTUAL	I-C-S	3.2
SA MUTUAL	ICH	3.6
SA MUTUAL	IMPERIAL	15.6
SA MUTUAL	IMPHOLD	4.0
SA MUTUAL	IMPLATS	3.6
SA MUTUAL	IND-SELE	18.5
SA MUTUAL	INHOLD	3.0
SA MUTUAL	ISCOR	10.1
SA MUTUAL	ISG	7.9
SA MUTUAL	JASCO	3.1
SA MUTUAL	JDGROUP	11.3
SA MUTUAL	JOHNNIES	10.7
SA MUTUAL	KEELEY	4.5
SA MUTUAL	KELGRAN	2.2
SA MUTUAL	KERSAF	4.5
SA MUTUAL	KH PROPS	21.9
SA MUTUAL	KINROSS	1.1
SA MUTUAL	KNIGHTS	2.4
SA MUTUAL	KWV-BEL	8.6
SA MUTUAL	L-T-A	4.0
SA MUTUAL	LANGBRG	1.0
SA MUTUAL	LEFIC	10.6
SA MUTUAL	LENCO	1.5
SA MUTUAL	LEPLAT	3.6
SA MUTUAL	LIBERTY	1.8
SA MUTUAL	LOGTEK	9.0
SA MUTUAL	LONRHO	2.8
SA MUTUAL	LYD-PLAT	67.8
SA MUTUAL	LYDEX	34 5
SA MUTUAL	M&R-HLD	2.2
SA MUTUAL	M&R-INV	5.3
SA MUTUAL	M-&-F	3.2
SA MUTUAL	MAINPRO	1.1
SA MUTUAL	MALBAK	3.6
SA MUTUAL	MASCON	1.4
SA MUTUAL	MASHOLD	7.8
SA MUTUAL	MCCARTHY	3.1
SA MUTUAL	METAIR	15.9

SA MUTUAL	METJE-&-Z	5.9
SA MUTUAL	METPROP	51.0
SA MUTUAL	MID-WITS	7.0
SA MUTUAL	MIDAS	11.7
SA MUTUAL	MINORCO	1.4
SA MUTUAL	MLNHOLD	11.1
SA MUTUAL	MOBILE	20.3
SA MUTUAL	MORKELS	8.5
SA MUTUAL	NAMFISH	8.6
SA MUTUAL	NAMPAK	1.2
SA MUTUAL	NAMSEA	8.2
SA MUTUAL	NATSEL	11.3
SA MUTUAL	NEDCOR	51.1
SA MUTUAL	NEI-AFR	26.3
SA MUTUAL	NEIHOLD	21.0
SA MUTUAL	NEW-WITS	2.7
SA MUTUAL	OCEANA	19.8
SA MUTUAL	OFSIL	2.7
SA MUTUAL	OMNIA	4.5
SA MUTUAL	OTIS	23.3
SA MUTUAL	PALAMIN	7.5
SA MUTUAL	PANPROP	35.0
SA MUTUAL	PEP	3.8
SA MUTUAL	PIONEER	32.6
SA MUTUAL	PLATE-GL	1.7
SA MUTUAL	PP RUST	4.5
SA MUTUAL	PPC	3.1
SA MUTUAL	PUBHOLD	6.8
SA MUTUAL	Q-DATA	5.7
SA MUTUAL	RANDCOL	5.0
SA MUTUAL	RANDEX	8.0
SA MUTUAL	RANDFONTN	2.6
SA MUTUAL	RANDMIN	1.3
SA MUTUAL	REGGIES	1.8
SA MUTUAL	REMB-BEH	7.1
SA MUTUAL	REMGRO	6.8
SA MUTUAL	REUNERT	2.7
SA MUTUAL	REX-TRUE	8.2
SA MUTUAL	RMSPROP	54.1
SA MUTUAL	ROYAL	13.7
SA MUTUAL	ROYCHEM	20.1
SA MUTUAL	ROYFOOD	12.5
SA MUTUAL	ROYHOLD	8.8
SA MUTUAL	RUSFURN	9.2
SA MUTUAL	RUSPLAT	2.9
SA MUTUAL	S-A-BIAS	3.5
SA MUTUAL	S-A-EAGLE	2.4
SA MUTUAL	SA-BREWS	13.4
SA MUTUAL	SAFICON	2.5
SA MUTUAL	SAFREN	39.7
SA MUTUAL	SAKERS	3.2
SA MUTUAL	SAMANCO	3.6
SA MUTUAL	SANTAM	1.5
SA MUTUAL	SAPPI	3.9
SA MUTUAL	SASOL	4.6
SA MUTUAL	SBIC	12.8
SA MUTUAL	SCHARIG	11.0
SA MUTUAL	SEARCON	1.7
SA MUTUAL	SEARDEL	3.6
SA MUTUAL	SECHOLD	10.3
SA MUTUAL	SENTRCHEM	10.5
SA MUTUAL	SERVGRO	1.4
SA MUTUAL	SILTEK	6.1
SA MUTUAL	SOUTHVAAL	2.5
SA MUTUAL	SPECLTY	4.2
SA MUTUAL	STANPRO	28.6
SA MUTUAL	STOCKS	2.8
SA MUTUAL	STREBEL	11.5
SA MUTUAL	SUN-BOP	2.3
SA MUTUAL	SUNCRUSH	12.9
SA MUTUAL	SYCOM	13.2
SA MUTUAL	TAMBOTI	3.6
SA MUTUAL	TEGKOR	7.9

SA MUTUAL	TELJOY	8.4
SA MUTUAL	TGH	7.4
SA MUTUAL	TIB	14.7
SA MUTUAL	TMX	6.7
SA MUTUAL	TOCO	11.4
SA MUTUAL	TONGAAT	3.8
SA MUTUAL	TRADGRO	7.3
SA MUTUAL	TRANS-NTL	2.4
SA MUTUAL	TRANSUN	9.4
SA MUTUAL	TRENCOR	14.1
SA MUTUAL	TRIMTRD	40.7
SA MUTUAL	TRNSHEX	2.3
SA MUTUAL	UMDONI	7.6
SA MUTUAL	UNISERV	9.3
SA MUTUAL	USKO	8.5
SA MUTUAL	UTICO	18.0
SA MUTUAL	VAAL-REEF	3.8
SA MUTUAL	VENTRON	3.9
SA MUTUAL	VESTCOR	9.1
SA MUTUAL	VETRUST	2.3
SA MUTUAL	WAICOR	5.2
SA MUTUAL	WALHOLD	1.0
SA MUTUAL	WELKOM	1.4
SA MUTUAL	WESCO	8.8
SA MUTUAL	WINBEL	21.6
SA MUTUAL	WINHOLD	18.0
SA MUTUAL	WINKELS	4.3
SA MUTUAL	WOOLTRU	26.8
SA MUTUAL	WSTN-DEEP	3.8
SA MUTUAL	YABENG	2.6
SA MUTUAL	ZANDPAN	1.7
SA MUTUAL PENS FUND	LEFIC	1.4
SA PROPERTY INV P/L	ABCON	3.3
SA SPECIAL RISKS INSURANCE ASSOC	BOLPRO	8.5
SA SPECIAL RISKS INSURANCE ASSOC	DABI	5.1
SA SPECIAL RISKS INSURANCE ASSOC	INTELES	1.2
SA SPECIAL RISKS INSURANCE ASSOC	NATSEL	1.1
SA SPECIAL RISKS INSURANCE ASSOC	NEW-WITS	1.3
SA SPECIAL RISKS INSURANCE ASSOC	PANPROP	1.2
SA SPECIAL RISKS INSURANCE ASSOC	PERSTEC	1.2
SA SPECIAL RISKS INSURANCE ASSOC	SPECLTY	3.4
SA SPECIAL RISKS INSURANCE ASSOC	SPURHLD	6.5
SA SPECIAL RISKS INSURANCE ASSOC	STORECO	2.4
SA SPECIAL RISKS INSURANCE ASSOC	T-&-N	6.5
SA SPECIAL RISKS INSURANCE ASSOC	VETRUST	1.1
SA SPECIAL RISKS INSURANCE ASSOC	WALHOLD	1.4
SA TOWNSHIPS MINING & FINANCE CORP	AMGOLD	7.6
SA TOWNSHIPS MINING & FINANCE CORP	ELANDS	2.7
SA TOWNSHIPS MINING & FINANCE CORP	ERGO	2.4
SA TOWNSHIPS MINING & FINANCE CORP	WELKOM	1.3
SA TRUST & FINANCE CO LTD	METAIR	4.7
SA TRUST & FINANCE CO LTD	WESCO	31.8
SAAD P A	GROWALK	1.7
SAAMBOU BANK LTD	IMPERIAL	1.7
SAAMBOU PENS FUND	PERSBEL	1.8
SAAMBOU PENS FUND	SHOREDITS	1.4
SABLIER H	VIERFONTN	1.6
SABVEST LTD	S-A-BIAS	50.4
SACHSE E U H	GAZGOLD	1.4
SACKS W E	TRIMTEX	3.3
SAFCOAL P/L	SMALDEL	68.1
SAFEGRO NOM P/L	ABACUS	80.0
SAFEGRO NOM P/L	BIDCORP	1.0
SAFEGRO NOM P/L	BOEPROP	1.5
SAFEGRO NOM P/L	CERAMIC	36.9
SAFEGRO NOM P/L	CRENDEL	26.4
SAFEGRO NOM P/L	EQUIKOR	20.1
SAFEGRO NOM P/L	GROWPNT	1.4
SAFEGRO NOM P/L	HCI	1.7
SAFEGRO NOM P/L	I-G-I	5.5
SAFEGRO NOM P/L	INVSTEC	4.4
SAFEGRO NOM P/L	ITLTILE	4.5
SAFEGRO NOM P/L	PENROSE	20.1

SAFEGRO NOM P/L	ROYAL	4.5
SAFEGRO NOM P/L	ROYCHEM	1.4
SAFEGRO NOM P/L	ROYHOLD	1.7
SAFEGRO NOM P/L	SAFLIFE	44.8
SAFEGRO NOM P/L	TGH	18.6
SAFEGRO NOM P/L	TIME	8.3
SAFEGRO NOM P/L	TRIMTEX	10.8
SAFEGRO NOM P/L	TRIMTRD	8.3
SAFEGRO NOM P/L	VALCAR	12.3
SAFEGRO NOM P/L	VENTEL	1.5
SAFIC P/L	SAFICON	2.0
SAFICON-BOUMAT PENS FUND	BOUMAT	2.2
SAFICON-BOUMAT PENS FUND	O-K	1.0
SAFICON-BOUMAT PENS FUND	SAKERS	6.8
SAFLIFE INV HLDGS SHARE INC CONTROL	SAFLIFE	3.4
SAFMARINE & RENNIES HLDGS LTD	KERSAF	75.8
SAGE LIFE LTD	BOUMAT	1.3
SAGE LIFE LTD	CBD-FUND	16.1
SAGE LIFE LTD	CHUBB	7.0
SAGE LIFE LTD	CNAGALO	1.8
SAGE LIFE LTD	COPI	1.1
SAGE LIFE LTD	CUTRITE	18.5
SAGE LIFE LTD	E-DAGGA	1.3
SAGE LIFE LTD	EVHOLD	1.7
SAGE LIFE LTD	HUDACO	1.8
SAGE LIFE LTD	LIONMATCH	1.1
SAGE LIFE LTD	PENROSE	2.7
SAGE LIFE LTD	PIONEER	12.1
SAGE LIFE LTD	REUNERT	1.2
SAGE LIFE LTD	ROYAL	2.3
SAGE LIFE LTD	SAGEGRP	1.7
SAGE LIFE LTD	SILOAK	2.6
SAGE LIFE LTD	T-M-L	2.2
SAGE LIFE LTD	WALTONS	1.0
SAGE STRATEGIC INV P/L	RMBH	11.5
SAGECOR P/L	SAGEGRP	21.1
SAGIT INV LTD	PORTHLD	4.7
SAKERS FINANCE & INV CORP LTD	SAFICON	48.4
SAKERS IND HOLDINGS LTD	BOUMAT	51.0
SALDSMAN B D	MILSTAN	1.0
SALDSMAN L B D	MILSTAN	1.0
SALENE MINING P/L	MODDER	20.9
SALENE MINING P/L	STH-RODPT	33.2
SALLY ANN BRENNER INV P/L	BRENMIL	3.0
SALZWEDEL H B	BASREAD	1.8
SAMBREN P/L	BRENMIL	43.3
SAMUEL ABELHEIM HLDGS P/L	TRNPACO	29.8
SAMUEL RABINOWITZ TRUST & INV CO	ZSR	1.2
SANDTON NOM LTD	BARNEX	2.7
SANDVELT INV P/L	CMI	2.4
SANLAM	BOLAND	11.3
SANLAM	BOUMAT	3.6
SANLAM	DOORNS	1.8
SANLAM	LASER	10.5
SANLAM	NEDCOR	2.2
SANLAM	QUORUM	8.5
SANLAM	SBIC	1.4
SANLAM	TOMKOR	1.8
SANLAMTRUST NOM P/L	KEELEY	2.1
SANLAMTRUST NOM P/L	KELGRAN	1.0
SANLAMTRUST NOM P/L	METPOL	2.8
SANLAMTRUST NOM P/L	SUNCRUSH	1.4
SANLAMTRUST NOM P/L	TEMPORA	1.1
SANTAM BPK	BOLAND	1.1
SANTAM PENS FUND	SANTAM	1.3
SANTAMGROEI NOM P/L	ANBEECO	2.1
SANTAMGROEI NOM P/L	S-A-BIAS	1.9
SANTAMGROEI NOM P/L	SUPALEK	3.6
SANTHOLD INV LTD	ROMATEX	6.8
SAPEIKA M L	WIT-G-M	1.1
SAPHIC HOLDINGS PVT LTD	J & F	4.3
SAREMBOCK L A	AFEX SA	1.5
SARUSAS DEVELOPMENT CORP P/L	NAMFISH	11.8

SASFIN INV P/L	SASFIN	1.8
SASKO BEHEREND E/B	LEBAKA	74.2
SASOL PENS FUND	PIKWIK	1.0
SASS H W	BOWCALF	2.0
SASSOON A L E	SASFIN	1.4
SATBEL INV HOLDINGS P/L	INTELES	74.9
SAUDI INV SA P/L	GAZGOLD	31.2
SAUNDERS P B	MICOR	2.2
SAVATKO INV CC	COMPASS	10.3
SBG HOLDINGS P/L	KAROS	9.3
SCAC-DELMAS V	GRINCOR	6.9
SCAW METALS PENS FUND	HIGATE	1.4
SCHAFFER J E	PROFURN	80.1
SCHARRIGHUISEN HOLDINGS LTD SHARE	SCHARIG	1.3
SCHAUM H H	SMALDEL	8.5
SCHEBEN L H D	NAMFISH	1.6
SCHILBACH K G D	CONCOR	1.1
SCHMET K	LANCHEM	1.9
SCHOEMAN W D O F	MINVEST	2.4
SCHOEPAUL P/L	OCTODEC	8.8
SCHRODER D V	NINIAN	8.7
SCHRODER D V & MCELLIGOTT M R A	NINIAN	2.7
SCHRODER J H	NINIAN	4.2
SCHRODER J H & MCELLIGOTT M R A	NINIAN	2.9
SCORE DISCOUNT FOOD HOLDINGS P/L	HISCORE	59.1
SCORE-CLICKS HOLDINGS LTD	CLICKS	50.1
SCORE-CLICKS HOLDINGS LTD	METCASH	14.6
SCORE-CLICKS HOLDINGS LTD	SCORE	14.5
SCOTT W J D	AF-&-OVER	5.2
SCOTT W J D	PROGRESS	9.1
SCOTT W J D I	NINIAN	2.2
SCRIP NOM P/L	IMPHOLD	2.7
SEARDEL CONSOLIDATED HOLDINGS LTD	SEARDEL	50.1
SEARDEL EXEC SHARE PARTICIPATION	SEARDEL	2.9
SEARGREG INV P/L	FRAME	32.2
SEARLL A	SEARCON	5.4
SECHABA INV TRUST	SEFALANA	5.3
SECHABA INV TRUST CO LTD	BOTINS	16.2
SECHABA INV TRUST CO LTD	FSC	1.0
SECHABA INV TRUST CO LTD	IGI BOT	1.1
SECURITIES EQUITIES P/L	BOLAND	1.1
SECURITIES EQUITIES P/L	BOLTONS	1.2
SECURITIES EQUITIES P/L	MICOR	6.3
SECURITY MILLS	TEX-MILLS	91.5
SECURITY NOM LTD	AFDISTIL	4.3
SECURITY NOM LTD	ART	1.3
SECURITY NOM LTD	BINDURA	64.5
SECURITY NOM LTD	BORDER	54.2
SECURITY NOM LTD	BOTREST	12.0
SECURITY NOM LTD	CAPS	9.2
SECURITY NOM LTD	FALGOLD	6.2
SECURITY NOM LTD	FMB	43.1
SECURITY NOM LTD	HIPPO	43.4
SECURITY NOM LTD	INTERNAT	5.1
SECURITY NOM LTD	MASHONA	5.1
SECURITY NOM LTD	NATFOOD	25.1
SECURITY NOM LTD	PORTHLD	19.1
SECURITY NOM LTD	RIO ZIM	3.8
SECURITY NOM LTD	SCHWEP CA	2.9
SECURITY NOM LTD	TEDCO	4.7
SECURITY NOM LTD	WANKIE	2.7
SECURITY NOM LTD	ZIMALLOYS	53.1
SECURITY NOM LTD	ZSR	4.9
SECURITY TECHNOLOGY HOLDINGS LTD	CIH	30.7
SEDGWICK E W & CO P/L	OVBEL	6.0
SEDOW HOLDINGS P/L	MATH-ASH	1.6
SEEMAN E H J	OVCON	1.5
SEFALANA EMP BENEFITS ORG (SEBO)	MLNHOLD	1.6
SEFALANA EMP BENEFITS ORG (SEBO)	RUSFURN	2.0
SEFALANA EMP BENEFITS ORG (SEBO)	STOCKS	4.8
SEFALANA EMP BENEFITS ORG (SEBO)	SUN-BOP	2.1
SEFALANA EMP BENEFITS ORG (SEBO)	TEMPORA	2.6
SEFALANA EMP BENEFITS ORG (SEBO)	VALCAR	3.0

SEFALANA EMP BENEFITS ORG (SEBO)	WAICOR	1.3
SEFALANA EMP BENEFITS ORG (SEBO)	YABENG	10.4
SEFOR L	PUBHOLD	4.0
SEFOR L	PUBLICO	1.0
SEIDLE BARNEY HOLDINGS P/L	MINGRAN	1.9
SELIGSON M	ROMENS	1.7
SELTEAM P/L	OVBEL	1.2
SENBANK INV P/L	SAPPI	3.0
SENBANK NOM P/L	SENTRCHEM	3.9
SENDER B M	OVBEL	1.0
SENIM PVT LTD	RADAR	2.0
SENTRALE AKSEPBANK BPK	NATRUST	26.0
SEPDU INV P/L	TRADGRO	8.3
SEPON LTD	BRACKEN	9.8
SEPON LTD	LESLIE	13.3
SEPON LTD	W-R-CONS	1.5
SEPON LTD	WINKELS	1.5
SEPON LTD J ACCOUNT	BUFFELS	2.0
SEPON LTD J ACCOUNT	GROOTVLEI	10.5
SEPON LTD J ACCOUNT	KINROSS	1.4
SEPON LTD J ACCOUNT	ST-HELENA	3.2
SEPON LTD J ACCOUNT	STILFTN	1.7
SERENVEST P/L	CONCOR	1.5
SERPOLLET HOLDINGS LTD	SOTHERN	8.3
SERVGRO INTERNATIONAL BPK	INTELES	2.6
SERVGRO INTERNATIONAL BPK	TELJOY	7.6
SESBES P/L	BESTER	5.0
SEVEN SIXTY TWO PARKWOOD LTD	ABCON	1.8
SEVERIN F V	EERSLNG	2.6
SFSS NOM P/L	ABS	1.4
SFSS NOM P/L	ADCORP	2.2
SFSS NOM P/L	ARIES	3.1
SFSS NOM P/L	BOE	1.1
SFSS NOM P/L	BOLTONS	1.4
SFSS NOM P/L	CRULIFE	1.4
SFSS NOM P/L	CURFIN	1.6
SFSS NOM P/L	DIALMOV	7.3
SFSS NOM P/L	LOGTEK	25.3
SFSS NOM P/L	MASHOLD	1.4
SFSS NOM P/L	MOLYSLP	2.7
SFSS NOM P/L	MULTI	6.5
SFSS NOM P/L	N-KLEINS	1.8
SFSS NOM P/L	OTIS	1.4
SFSS NOM P/L	PUBLICO	1.3
SFSS NOM P/L	SAFCOR	2.3
SFSS NOM P/L	SOPLATS	47.7
SFSS NOM P/L	SPL	1.1
SFSS NOM P/L	SPUR	1.1
SFSS NOM P/L	SPURHLD	4.8
SFSS NOM P/L	TRIMTRD	2.3
SFSS NOM P/L	U-CON	1.0
SFSS NOM P/L	UNIHOLD	1.1
SFSS NOM P/L	URQHART	2.4
SFSS NOM P/L	WBHOLD	2.8
SGM INV P/L	WBHOLD	53.7
SHAPE INV P/L	HISCORE	20.7
SHAPE INV P/L	METCASH	1.4
SHAPE INV P/L	SCOCLIK	26.8
SHAPE INV P/L	SCORE	1.4
SHAPIRO C S	BSG	1.3
SHAPIRO D H E/L	SAKERS	1.1
SHAPIRO J	PUBHOLD	17.7
SHAPIRO R S	PUBHOLD	17.7
SHARESTOCK NOM P/L	ABS	1.3
SHARESTOCK NOM P/L	AFLIFE	1.6
SHARESTOCK NOM P/L	AUTOQIP	1.5
SHARESTOCK NOM P/L	BASREAD	2.2
SHARESTOCK NOM P/L	CHEMSERVE	2.5
SHARESTOCK NOM P/L	CNAGALO	1.3
SHARESTOCK NOM P/L	CONFED	1.2
SHARESTOCK NOM P/L	CRULIFE	1.5
SHARESTOCK NOM P/L	CURFIN	4.3
SHARESTOCK NOM P/L	DELSWA	1.9

SHARESTOCK NOM P/L	DIDATA	1.2
SHARESTOCK NOM P/L	DINETTE	7.3
SHARESTOCK NOM P/L	FEDSURE	1.2
SHARESTOCK NOM P/L	GAZGOLD	2.8
SHARESTOCK NOM P/L	GDM	2.8
SHARESTOCK NOM P/L	GEFCO	1.6
SHARESTOCK NOM P/L	GROPROP	1.4
SHARESTOCK NOM P/L	I-&-J	1.1
SHARESTOCK NOM P/L	JASCO	1.1
SHARESTOCK NOM P/L	KNJ	1.5
SHARESTOCK NOM P/L	KOPP	3.4
SHARESTOCK NOM P/L	MACADAM	3.8
SHARESTOCK NOM P/L	METPOL	1.8
SHARESTOCK NOM P/L	MINVEST	3.9
SHARESTOCK NOM P/L	MSAULI	1.8
SHARESTOCK NOM P/L	NAMSEA	1.7
SHARESTOCK NOM P/L	NORVIC	11.4
SHARESTOCK NOM P/L	PIONEER	1.3
SHARESTOCK NOM P/L	PUTCO	1.2
SHARESTOCK NOM P/L	PUTPROP	1.3
SHARESTOCK NOM P/L	RALE	6.4
SHARESTOCK NOM P/L	RMSPROP	1.5
SHARESTOCK NOM P/L	SERVGRO	1.3
SHARESTOCK NOM P/L	SILTEK	4.0
SHARESTOCK NOM P/L	SPECLTY	7.2
SHARESTOCK NOM P/L	STORECO	3.6
SHARESTOCK NOM P/L	SUN-BOP	1.3
SHARESTOCK NOM P/L	TELJOY	1.0
SHARESTOCK NOM P/L	TIME	2.4
SHARESTOCK NOM P/L	TRIMTEX	1.2
SHARESTOCK NOM P/L	UMDONI	2.3
SHARESTOCK NOM P/L	UNISERV	4.0
SHARESTOCK NOM P/L	WALHOLD	1.7
SHARESTOCK NOM P/L	WALTONS	1.2
SHARICK HOLDINGS P/L	TOMKOR	1.1
SHARLAND J N	EGOLI	1.6
SHARLAND J N	NATRAWL	3.0
SHARP A	CLINICS	1.2
SHEIDAN INV P/L	METPROP	1.0
SHELFORD P/L	LEEGALL	15.7
SHELLEY BRENNER INV P/L	BRENMIL	1.8
SHER C M	REGGIES	2.5
SHER S	LEPPIN	4.1
SHERRELL R E	BEARMAN	8.1
SHERRELL R E	RALE	1.6
SHERRY J A	JASCO	20.4
SHEVITZ C	BOYMANS	1.4
SHKUDSKY A	MERITEX	1.0
SHKUDSKY A	ROOIBERG	3.1
SHOCRAFT SHARE TRUST	SHOCRAF	1.7
SHOREDITS A K R	SHOREDITS	49.6
SHUI LUNG INVESTMENT CO LTD	BROADACRE	70.6
SIBUL H	MCRTAIL	1.8
SIDNEY ELLERINE TRUST P/L	ELLERINE	2.6
SIDNEY ELLERINE TRUST P/L	VEKTRA	1.2
SIERRA HOLDINGS LTD	CHOICE	1.2
SILPERT A L	STERLING	3.5
SILTEK INV P/L	Q-DATA	9.3
SILTEK LTD	Q-DATA	34.1
SILVER C H	SANLIC	1.1
SILVEROAK IND LTD EMP SHARE PURCHASE	SILOAK	5.4
SILVERSANDS ESTATES LTD	UNI-COLD	2.7
SIMCHOWITZ M	DINETTE	13.3
SIMCHOWITZ M	PERSKOR	4.0
SIMMONSCO NOM P/L	OAKFLDS	1.0
SIMSID INV LTD	UNI-COLD	8.1
SINGER E M	CLINICS	1.0
SIVE I B FAMILY HOLDINGS P/L	KAROS	9.4
SIXTY SIX MARSHALL STREET NOM P/L	ABCON	7.4
SIXTY SIX MARSHALL STREET NOM P/L	AMREL	1.0
SIXTY SIX MARSHALL STREET NOM P/L	ANAMINT	1.0
SIXTY SIX MARSHALL STREET NOM P/L	ANGLOVAAL	1.5
SIXTY SIX MARSHALL STREET NOM P/L	APEX	18.4

SIXTY SIX MARSHALL STREET NOM P/L	BARLOWS	1.1
SIXTY SIX MARSHALL STREET NOM P/L	CAPITAL	1.3
SIXTY SIX MARSHALL STREET NOM P/L	CENPROP	6.9
SIXTY SIX MARSHALL STREET NOM P/L	DIDATA	1.2
SIXTY SIX MARSHALL STREET NOM P/L	EVHOLD	2.3
SIXTY SIX MARSHALL STREET NOM P/L	FIRSTBK	2.2
SIXTY SIX MARSHALL STREET NOM P/L	HIGATE	1.7
SIXTY SIX MARSHALL STREET NOM P/L	I-&-J	2.1
SIXTY SIX MARSHALL STREET NOM P/L	ISCOR	1.6
SIXTY SIX MARSHALL STREET NOM P/L	KH PROPS	11.5
SIXTY SIX MARSHALL STREET NOM P/L	M&R-HLD	1.1
SIXTY SIX MARSHALL STREET NOM P/L	M-&-F	1.6
SIXTY SIX MARSHALL STREET NOM P/L	MCCARTHY	1.4
SIXTY SIX MARSHALL STREET NOM P/L	METPOL	2.5
SIXTY SIX MARSHALL STREET NOM P/L	METPROP	6.6
SIXTY SIX MARSHALL STREET NOM P/L	MOBILE	3.2
SIXTY SIX MARSHALL STREET NOM P/L	NEDCOR	2.7
SIXTY SIX MARSHALL STREET NOM P/L	PALAMIN	2.5
SIXTY SIX MARSHALL STREET NOM P/L	PIONEER	3.3
SIXTY SIX MARSHALL STREET NOM P/L	PP RUST	1.6
SIXTY SIX MARSHALL STREET NOM P/L	PPC	1.9
SIXTY SIX MARSHALL STREET NOM P/L	RUSPLAT	1.6
SIXTY SIX MARSHALL STREET NOM P/L	SABVEST	3.1
SIXTY SIX MARSHALL STREET NOM P/L	SOTHERN	1.5
SIXTY SIX MARSHALL STREET NOM P/L	SYCOM	8.0
SIXTY SIX MARSHALL STREET NOM P/L	T-&-N	1.0
SIXTY SIX MARSHALL STREET NOM P/L	TAMBOTI	1.2
SIXTY SIX MARSHALL STREET NOM P/L	UMDONI	1.2
SKJ FAMILY HOLDINGS P/L	CMH	3.4
SLABBER J	CITYHLD	2.5
SLAM NOM P/L	HUDACO	3.8
SLAM NOM P/L	MOBILE	2.4
SLAM NOM P/L	OCEANA	2.6
SLAWAL NOM P/L	STANPRO	2.6
SLAWAL NOM P/L	TOLUX	3.6
SLUSHERS & FABRICATION INC (SWISS)	KNJ	1.5
SMALL BUSNESS DEVELOPMENT CORP LTD	FOODCRP	1.4
SMALL BUSNESS DEVELOPMENT CORP LTD	NAMFISH	11.1
SMALL BUSNESS DEVELOPMENT CORP LTD	OCFISH	7.8
SMALLE M	POINTER	1.4
SMART CENTRE HLDGS LTD EMPL SHARE	SMART	5.1
SMART-HOLD BPK	SMART	60.8
SMBL NOM P/L	BOEPROP	3.1
SMBL NOM P/L	BOLWEAR	2.7
SMBL NOM P/L	CARGO	1.9
SMBL NOM P/L	CROWN	8.9
SMBL NOM P/L	EERSLNG	27.6
SMBL NOM P/L	FEDSURE	1.6
SMBL NOM P/L	INVSTEC	5.1
SMBL NOM P/L	KH PROPS	4.0
SMBL NOM P/L	KLIPTON	11.0
SMBL NOM P/L	MAST	25.7
SMBL NOM P/L	MEDHOLD	3.4
SMBL NOM P/L	PUBLICO	10.8
SMBL NOM P/L	SPESCOM	5.7
SMBL NOM P/L	TOLUX	5.3
SMBL NOM P/L	UMDONI	1.3
SMEDLEY V	CAFCA	1.7
SMG RESOURCES P/L	KEELEY	1.1
SMILG J H	CLINICS	2.9
SMILG J H & CO INV P/L	CLINICS	5.1
SMIT H S TRUSTEES	KUDU	1.1
SMIT J	AROMA	1.0
SMIT M E	DIGOCO	1.9
SMITH A M	ABS	1.4
SMITH B P	TECFIN	14.7
SMITH J C & L C & SCHLOSBERG B	WALHOLD	1.3
SMITH R J	OVCON	1.0
SMITH T I	AUTOQIP	2.0
SMITH W P M	OHIO	5.9
SMK NOM P/L	BEARMAN	20.0
SMK NOM P/L	FARM-AG	1.8
SMK NOM P/L	HICORL	1.5
SMK NOM P/L	ITLTILE	2.3
SMK NOM P/L	LENVEST	5.2
SMK NOM P/L	MESTORE	13.3
SMK NOM P/L	NUWORLD	3.0
SMK NOM P/L	RHOEX	1.3
SMK NOM P/L	RMBH	1.3
SMT LTD	TOLUX	2.1
SMYTHE JM & MFJ, & EP NICALAIDES	FEDSURE	1.2
SOCIETE BANCAIRE JULIUS BAER SA	UNISPIN	1.5
SOCIETE DE BANQUE SUISSE	AMGOLD	5.6
SOCIETE INTERPROF POUR LA COMPENSATION	BUFFELS	4.3
SOCIETE INTERPROF POUR LA COMPENSATION	ST-HELENA	7.0
SOCIETE INTERPROF POUR LA COMPENSATION	STILFTN	2.2
SOCIETE INTERPROF POUR LA COMPENSATION	W-R-CONS	21.3
SOCIETE SUISSE DE CIMENT PORTLAND	ANG-ALPHA	2.3
SOFMORE CONSTRUCTION P/L	ED-L-BATE	2.0
SOGES FIDUCEM SOC ANONYME	BOTREST	8.0
SOGES FIDUCEM SOC ANONYME	MINORCO	1.0
SOLID G NOM P/L	KNIGHTS	17.7
SOLID G NOM P/L	LEEGALL	30.4
SOLID G NOM P/L	OMNIA	6.3
SOLID G NOM P/L	SIMMERS	41.4
SOLID G NOM P/L	WOODROW	3.2
SOLOMON P (W HERRICK TRUST)	CULLINAN	1.1
SOLPHIL INV P/L	BRISTOL-I	2.7
SONOMA LTD	TRUZIM	33.3
SONRIC P/L	GEN-OPTIC	3.0
SOUTH EAST RAND GOLD HLDGS LTD	BENONI	63.2
SOUTH EAST RAND GOLD HLDGS LTD	NIGEL	57.6
SOUTH EAST RAND GOLD HLDGS LTD	WESWITS	59.0
SOUTH EAST RAND GOLD HLDGS LTD	WIT-NIGEL	68.7
SOUTH EAST RAND GOLD HLDGS SHR INC	SOUTHGO	1.2
SOUTH WITS INV HOLDINGS P/L	SOPLATS	33.8
SOUTHAMPTON ASSURE CO ZIM LTD	ART	1.1
SOUTHAMPTON ASSURE CO ZIM LTD	FP HOLD	3.5
SOUTHAMPTON ASSURE CO ZIM LTD	GULLIVER	6.6
SOUTHAMPTON ASSURE CO ZIM LTD	KADOMA	3.8
SOUTHAMPTON ASSURE CO ZIM LTD	MASHONA	1.2
SOUTHAMPTON ASSURE CO ZIM LTD	UDC	3.7
SOUTHAMPTON ASSURE CO ZIM LTD	ZIM SUN	1.2
SOUTHERN LIFE ASSOC LTD	A-V-I	2.5
SOUTHERN LIFE ASSOC LTD	AFLIFE	75.7
SOUTHERN LIFE ASSOC LTD	AGRICOR	4.2
SOUTHERN LIFE ASSOC LTD	AMCOAL	1.6
SOUTHERN LIFE ASSOC LTD	AMGOLD	2.2
SOUTHERN LIFE ASSOC LTD	AMIC	2.1
SOUTHERN LIFE ASSOC LTD	ANGLO-S	2.2
SOUTHERN LIFE ASSOC LTD	APEX	25.1
SOUTHERN LIFE ASSOC LTD	BARLOWS	3.6
SOUTHERN LIFE ASSOC LTD	BEVCON	2.2
SOUTHERN LIFE ASSOC LTD	BOEPROP	4.8
SOUTHERN LIFE ASSOC LTD	BOTINS	10.0
SOUTHERN LIFE ASSOC LTD	CAPITAL	8.0
SOUTHERN LIFE ASSOC LTD	CENPROP	27.5
SOUTHERN LIFE ASSOC LTD	CG SUGAR	2.0
SOUTHERN LIFE ASSOC LTD	CGS-FOOD	1.0
SOUTHERN LIFE ASSOC LTD	CLINICS	3.7
SOUTHERN LIFE ASSOC LTD	CONFRAM	3.6
SOUTHERN LIFE ASSOC LTD	DA-GAMA	5.0
SOUTHERN LIFE ASSOC LTD	DE BEERS	2.2
SOUTHERN LIFE ASSOC LTD	DIDATA	3.9
SOUTHERN LIFE ASSOC LTD	DOORNS	1.5
SOUTHERN LIFE ASSOC LTD	FIRSTBK	8.5
SOUTHERN LIFE ASSOC LTD	FOSCHINI	8.2
SOUTHERN LIFE ASSOC LTD	FRAME	2.7
SOUTHERN LIFE ASSOC LTD	GENCOR	2.6
SOUTHERN LIFE ASSOC LTD	GFNAMIB	4.9
SOUTHERN LIFE ASSOC LTD	IMPLATS	1.4
SOUTHERN LIFE ASSOC LTD	IND-SELE	1.2
SOUTHERN LIFE ASSOC LTD	ISCOR	5.8
SOUTHERN LIFE ASSOC LTD	JOHNNIES	2.0
SOUTHERN LIFE ASSOC LTD	KELGRAN	1.4
SOUTHERN LIFE ASSOC LTD	KERSAF	2.0

SOUTHERN LIFE ASSOC LTD	LEFIC	15.6
SOUTHERN LIFE ASSOC LTD	LIBERTY	1.4
SOUTHERN LIFE ASSOC LTD	M&R-HLD	4.1
SOUTHERN LIFE ASSOC LTD	MAINPRO	28.8
SOUTHERN LIFE ASSOC LTD	MALBAK	1.5
SOUTHERN LIFE ASSOC LTD	MALHOLD	4.7
SOUTHERN LIFE ASSOC LTD	MOBILE	8.9
SOUTHERN LIFE ASSOC LTD	NAMPAK	2.7
SOUTHERN LIFE ASSOC LTD	NATSEL	1.4
SOUTHERN LIFE ASSOC LTD	NEDCOR	2.1
SOUTHERN LIFE ASSOC LTD	OCEANA	7.6
SOUTHERN LIFE ASSOC LTD	OFSIL	4.5
SOUTHERN LIFE ASSOC LTD	OVCON	7.0
SOUTHERN LIFE ASSOC LTD	PANPROP	11.9
SOUTHERN LIFE ASSOC LTD	PICKNPAY	2.2
SOUTHERN LIFE ASSOC LTD	PIKWIK	6.9
SOUTHERN LIFE ASSOC LTD	PLATE-GL	2.5
SOUTHERN LIFE ASSOC LTD	PPC	1.8
SOUTHERN LIFE ASSOC LTD	PREM-GRP	1.9
SOUTHERN LIFE ASSOC LTD	RANDFONTN	1.1
SOUTHERN LIFE ASSOC LTD	REMB-BEH	1.9
SOUTHERN LIFE ASSOC LTD	REMGRO	2.3
SOUTHERN LIFE ASSOC LTD	SA-BREWS	1.2
SOUTHERN LIFE ASSOC LTD	SAFREN	4.8
SOUTHERN LIFE ASSOC LTD	SASOL	2.0
SOUTHERN LIFE ASSOC LTD	SBIC	1.1
SOUTHERN LIFE ASSOC LTD	TEGKOR	2.7
SOUTHERN LIFE ASSOC LTD	TIB	3.7
SOUTHERN LIFE ASSOC LTD	TIGR-OATS	1.7
SOUTHERN LIFE ASSOC LTD	TRENCOR	1.4
SOUTHERN LIFE ASSOC LTD	U-CON	22.8
SOUTHERN LIFE ASSOC LTD	UNIDEV	1.2
SOUTHERN LIFE ASSOC LTD	UNIHOLD	17.5
SOUTHERN LIFE ASSOC LTD	VAAL-REEF	1.9
SOUTHERN LIFE ASSOC LTD	WOOLTRU	9.1
SOUTHERN LIFE ASSOC LTD	WSTN-DEEP	1.4
SOUTHERN LIFE ASSOC ZIM LTD	KADOMA	1.1
SOUTHERN LIFE ASSOC ZIM LTD	TRUZIM	4.8
SOUTHERN LIFE SPECIAL INV P/L	FIRSTBK	17.2
SOUTHERN MOTOR HOLDINGS LTD	RAPTOR	64.2
SOUTHERN TUNA CO LTD	NAMSEA	7.8
SOUTHERN WITWATERSRAND EXPL CO LTD	SOWITS	15.3
SOUTHWIND INV PVT LTD	FP HOLD	26.3
SPAARWINS LTD	RENTBEL	1.7
SPANJAARD D	MOLYSLP	4.4
SPANJAARD R J W	MOLYSLP	7.3
SPARKS N D	CUTRITE	1.5
SPECIALTY STAFF SHARE TRUST	SPECLTY	1.1
SPENCER BARLOW TRUST	CENMAG	3.3
SPERIAM SECURITIES INC	CDC	98.4
SPESCOM ELECTRONICS LTD SHARE TRUST	SPESCOM	2.5
SPICER R W	SPICER	1.0
SPIKE INV NOM P/L	EDGARS	2.4
SPL EXECUTIVE SHARE SCHEME	SPL	1.3
SPUR HOLDINGS LTD	SPUR	54.5
SPURR R T	ADVTECH	1.8
SRL INV CC	SUB-N	1.4
SSP INV TRUST	RAINBOW	1.1
ST ANTONIO INV INC	PROPFIN	3.6
ST PAUL (UK) LTD	BOTINS	30.9
STALIT P/L	SBIC	24.4
STANLEY & ZEA LEWIS HOLDINGS LTD	LEFIC	20.3
STANLEY & ZEA LEWIS HOLDINGS LTD	OCEANA	2.8
STAPELBERG F P	QUAGGA	2.0
STAR BOX AG	SHOCRAF	9.1
STARKE B E	BSI	1.9
STARKE R L	BSG	1.1
STATE (ISCOR) SHARE TRUST	ISCOR	1.5
STD BANK NOM TVL P/L	A-V-HOLD	3.8
STD BANK NOM TVL P/L	A-V-I	5.2
STD BANK NOM TVL P/L	ABCON	4.1
STD BANK NOM TVL P/L	ABERDARE	1.2
STD BANK NOM TVL P/L	ABS	1.2

STD BANK NOM TVL P/L	ABSA	2.5
STD BANK NOM TVL P/L	ADVTECH	2.1
STD BANK NOM TVL P/L	AECI	1.5
STD BANK NOM TVL P/L	AF-&-OVER	5.7
STD BANK NOM TVL P/L	AF-CABLE	7.5
STD BANK NOM TVL P/L	AFCOL	5.6
STD BANK NOM TVL P/L	AFMIN	6.6
STD BANK NOM TVL P/L	AFRICOM	1.3
STD BANK NOM TVL P/L	AFROX	3.0
STD BANK NOM TVL P/L	AIDA	2.2
STD BANK NOM TVL P/L	AIMARK	1.7
STD BANK NOM TVL P/L	ALEXNDR	6.5
STD BANK NOM TVL P/L	ALTECH	4.1
STD BANK NOM TVL P/L	AMAPROP	3.3
STD BANK NOM TVL P/L	AMCOAL	6.4
STD BANK NOM TVL P/L	AMGOLD	4.3
STD BANK NOM TVL P/L	AMIC	3.1
STD BANK NOM TVL P/L	ANAMINT	4.2
STD BANK NOM TVL P/L	ANG-ALPHA	4.1
STD BANK NOM TVL P/L	ANGLO-S	4.7
STD BANK NOM TVL P/L	ANGLOVAAL	5.9
STD BANK NOM TVL P/L	ARGUS	37.0
STD BANK NOM TVL P/L	ARIES	10.9
STD BANK NOM TVL P/L	ASS-MANG	4.2
STD BANK NOM TVL P/L	ASSORE	8.2
STD BANK NOM TVL P/L	AUTOPGE	16.5
STD BANK NOM TVL P/L	AVF GRP	4.8
STD BANK NOM TVL P/L	AVINS	1.6
STD BANK NOM TVL P/L	BARLOWS	8.3
STD BANK NOM TVL P/L	BARMINE	1.9
STD BANK NOM TVL P/L	BARNEX	38.4
STD BANK NOM TVL P/L	BARPLAT	2.2
STD BANK NOM TVL P/L	BARPROP	1.0
STD BANK NOM TVL P/L	BEATRIX	4.4
STD BANK NOM TVL P/L	BENCO	4.3
STD BANK NOM TVL P/L	BERGERS	2.5
STD BANK NOM TVL P/L	BERZACK	10.7
STD BANK NOM TVL P/L	BEVCON	20.1
STD BANK NOM TVL P/L	BIDCORP	2.6
STD BANK NOM TVL P/L	BIDVEST	3.5
STD BANK NOM TVL P/L	BIVEC	6.7
STD BANK NOM TVL P/L	BLYVOOR	49.9
STD BANK NOM TVL P/L	BOEPROP	15.9
STD BANK NOM TVL P/L	BOTREST	2.8
STD BANK NOM TVL P/L	BOUMAT	7.4
STD BANK NOM TVL P/L	BOYMANS	2.2
STD BANK NOM TVL P/L	BRACKEN	3.8
STD BANK NOM TVL P/L	BRISTOL-I	4.2
STD BANK NOM TVL P/L	BTRDUN	7.9
STD BANK NOM TVL P/L	BUFFCOR	2.9
STD BANK NOM TVL P/L	BUFFELS	1.8
STD BANK NOM TVL P/L	CADSWEP	4.8
STD BANK NOM TVL P/L	CASHBIL	4.7
STD BANK NOM TVL P/L	CBD-FUND	1.7
STD BANK NOM TVL P/L	CFC	1.1
STD BANK NOM TVL P/L	CGS-FOOD	2.4
STD BANK NOM TVL P/L	CGSMITH	2.0
STD BANK NOM TVL P/L	CHEMSERVE	2.8
STD BANK NOM TVL P/L	CHOICE	12.7
STD BANK NOM TVL P/L	CLICKS	12.8
STD BANK NOM TVL P/L	CLINICS	6.8
STD BANK NOM TVL P/L	CMH	1.9
STD BANK NOM TVL P/L	CMI	10.8
STD BANK NOM TVL P/L	CMS	5.3
STD BANK NOM TVL P/L	CNAGALO	4.4
STD BANK NOM TVL P/L	COM-FUND	1.7
STD BANK NOM TVL P/L	COMPASS	8.3
STD BANK NOM TVL P/L	CON-MURCH	33.8
STD BANK NOM TVL P/L	CONAFEX	3.2
STD BANK NOM TVL P/L	CONCOR	11.0
STD BANK NOM TVL P/L	CONFRAM	1.2
STD BANK NOM TVL P/L	CONSHU	10.9
STD BANK NOM TVL P/L	COPI	8.9

STD BANK NOM TVL P/L	COR-SYND	1.5
STD BANK NOM TVL P/L	CORWIL	34.3
STD BANK NOM TVL P/L	CROOKES	5.1
STD BANK NOM TVL P/L	CRULIFE	1.2
STD BANK NOM TVL P/L	CTP	4.1
STD BANK NOM TVL P/L	CULLINAN	3.3
STD BANK NOM TVL P/L	CURFIN	6.1
STD BANK NOM TVL P/L	CUTRITE	1.3
STD BANK NOM TVL P/L	DA-GAMA	1.6
STD BANK NOM TVL P/L	DABI	59.3
STD BANK NOM TVL P/L	DALYS	3.6
STD BANK NOM TVL P/L	DBN-DEEP	4.6
STD BANK NOM TVL P/L	DE BEERS	5.0
STD BANK NOM TVL P/L	DEELKRL	2.0
STD BANK NOM TVL P/L	DELSWA	3.0
STD BANK NOM TVL P/L	DELTA	13.9
STD BANK NOM TVL P/L	DIDATA	5.3
STD BANK NOM TVL P/L	DOORNS	3.5
STD BANK NOM TVL P/L	DORBYL	6.7
STD BANK NOM TVL P/L	DRIES	4.0
STD BANK NOM TVL P/L	DUIKERS	2.8
STD BANK NOM TVL P/L	E-DAGGA	18.9
STD BANK NOM TVL P/L	E-R-P-M	1.0
STD BANK NOM TVL P/L	E-T-CONS	2.0
STD BANK NOM TVL P/L	ED-L-BATE	1.4
STD BANK NOM TVL P/L	EDGARS	6.3
STD BANK NOM TVL P/L	EERSLNG	9.4
STD BANK NOM TVL P/L	ELANDS	2.1
STD BANK NOM TVL P/L	ELCENTR	12.0
STD BANK NOM TVL P/L	ENGEN	8.8
STD BANK NOM TVL P/L	ERGO	9.1
STD BANK NOM TVL P/L	EVHOLD	30.0
STD BANK NOM TVL P/L	F-S-GROUP	4.5
STD BANK NOM TVL P/L	F-S-I	1.7
STD BANK NOM TVL P/L	FIRSTBK	4.9
STD BANK NOM TVL P/L	FIT	8.5
STD BANK NOM TVL P/L	FMCOTEC	3.9
STD BANK NOM TVL P/L	FOCUS	16.2
STD BANK NOM TVL P/L	FOODCRP	1.4
STD BANK NOM TVL P/L	FOSCHINI	3.9
STD BANK NOM TVL P/L	FRAME	13.0
STD BANK NOM TVL P/L	FREDDEV	44.9
STD BANK NOM TVL P/L	FREGOLD	10.3
STD BANK NOM TVL P/L	G-F-COAL	5.8
STD BANK NOM TVL P/L	G-I-C	6.5
STD BANK NOM TVL P/L	G5HOLD	2.0
STD BANK NOM TVL P/L	GDM	4.1
STD BANK NOM TVL P/L	GEN-OPTIC	7.8
STD BANK NOM TVL P/L	GENBEHEER	1.2
STD BANK NOM TVL P/L	GENBEL	8.6
STD BANK NOM TVL P/L	GENCOR	6.1
STD BANK NOM TVL P/L	GENTYRE-A	1.1
STD BANK NOM TVL P/L	GF-PROPS	5.9
STD BANK NOM TVL P/L	GFNAMIB	3.2
STD BANK NOM TVL P/L	GFSA	3.8
STD BANK NOM TVL P/L	GLODINA	3.7
STD BANK NOM TVL P/L	GRINAKER	2.4
STD BANK NOM TVL P/L	GRINCOR	2.8
STD BANK NOM TVL P/L	GROOTVLEI	3.6
STD BANK NOM TVL P/L	GROUP-5	1.6
STD BANK NOM TVL P/L	HAGGIE	3.2
STD BANK NOM TVL P/L	HARMONY	36.0
STD BANK NOM TVL P/L	HARTIES	4.8
STD BANK NOM TVL P/L	HCI	14.4
STD BANK NOM TVL P/L	HIGATE	2.7
STD BANK NOM TVL P/L	HISTONE	23.0
STD BANK NOM TVL P/L	HIVELD	4.3
STD BANK NOM TVL P/L	HLH	5.5
STD BANK NOM TVL P/L	HOLDAIN	1.3
STD BANK NOM TVL P/L	HUDACO	11.3
STD BANK NOM TVL P/L	I-&-J	5.6
STD BANK NOM TVL P/L	I-C-S	7.2
STD BANK NOM TVL P/L	I-G-I	8.5
STD BANK NOM TVL P/L	ICH	11.4
STD BANK NOM TVL P/L	IMPERIAL	8.5
STD BANK NOM TVL P/L	IMPHOLD	2.5
STD BANK NOM TVL P/L	IMPLATS	2.7
STD BANK NOM TVL P/L	IND-SELE	2.7
STD BANK NOM TVL P/L	INTRUST	46.5
STD BANK NOM TVL P/L	INVICTA	1.9
STD BANK NOM TVL P/L	INVSTEC	2.4
STD BANK NOM TVL P/L	ISCOR	12.8
STD BANK NOM TVL P/L	JADE	2.2
STD BANK NOM TVL P/L	JOEL	54.8
STD BANK NOM TVL P/L	JOHNNIES	8.1
STD BANK NOM TVL P/L	KAROS	5.8
STD BANK NOM TVL P/L	KEELEY	5.7
STD BANK NOM TVL P/L	KELGRAN	4.0
STD BANK NOM TVL P/L	KERSAF	3.4
STD BANK NOM TVL P/L	KH PROPS	17.6
STD BANK NOM TVL P/L	KINROSS	7.7
STD BANK NOM TVL P/L	KLIPTON	26.7
STD BANK NOM TVL P/L	KLOOF	3.3
STD BANK NOM TVL P/L	KNIGHTS	6.1
STD BANK NOM TVL P/L	KWV-BEL	2.3
STD BANK NOM TVL P/L	LANCHEM	3.7
STD BANK NOM TVL P/L	LASER	2.5
STD BANK NOM TVL P/L	LEEGALL	5.8
STD BANK NOM TVL P/L	LEFIC	3.3
STD BANK NOM TVL P/L	LENCO	12.0
STD BANK NOM TVL P/L	LENVEST	5.0
STD BANK NOM TVL P/L	LEPLAT	35.8
STD BANK NOM TVL P/L	LESLIE	5.2
STD BANK NOM TVL P/L	LIB HOLD	6.3
STD BANK NOM TVL P/L	LIBANON	3.3
STD BANK NOM TVL P/L	LIBERTY	9.5
STD BANK NOM TVL P/L	LINDUM	77.0
STD BANK NOM TVL P/L	LOGTEK	4.7
STD BANK NOM TVL P/L	LONRHO	1.1
STD BANK NOM TVL P/L	LORAINE	2.8
STD BANK NOM TVL P/L	LYD-PLAT	3.1
STD BANK NOM TVL P/L	LYDEX	8.1
STD BANK NOM TVL P/L	M&R-HLD	5.1
STD BANK NOM TVL P/L	M&R-INV	2.6
STD BANK NOM TVL P/L	MAINPRO	30.9
STD BANK NOM TVL P/L	MALBAK	1.8
STD BANK NOM TVL P/L	MARLIN	6.8
STD BANK NOM TVL P/L	MASCON	3.3
STD BANK NOM TVL P/L	MASHOLD	5.6
STD BANK NOM TVL P/L	MASONITE	7.2
STD BANK NOM TVL P/L	MAST	15.2
STD BANK NOM TVL P/L	MATH-ASH	2.8
STD BANK NOM TVL P/L	MCCARTHY	2.7
STD BANK NOM TVL P/L	MCRTAIL	5.4
STD BANK NOM TVL P/L	MEDCLIN	2.0
STD BANK NOM TVL P/L	MERITEX	60.3
STD BANK NOM TVL P/L	MESSINA	11.9
STD BANK NOM TVL P/L	METAIR	6.8
STD BANK NOM TVL P/L	METCASH	3.7
STD BANK NOM TVL P/L	METKOR	2.1
STD BANK NOM TVL P/L	METPOL	2.7
STD BANK NOM TVL P/L	METPROP	2.0
STD BANK NOM TVL P/L	MICOR	6.7
STD BANK NOM TVL P/L	MID-WITS	6.7
STD BANK NOM TVL P/L	MIDAS	8.8
STD BANK NOM TVL P/L	MINGRAN	5.9
STD BANK NOM TVL P/L	MINORCO	3.4
STD BANK NOM TVL P/L	MINVEST	22.2
STD BANK NOM TVL P/L	MLNHOLD	7.7
STD BANK NOM TVL P/L	MOBILE	1.1
STD BANK NOM TVL P/L	MODDER	4.8
STD BANK NOM TVL P/L	MSAULI	1.3
STD BANK NOM TVL P/L	NAMFISH	1.6
STD BANK NOM TVL P/L	NAMPAK	2.7
STD BANK NOM TVL P/L	NATRAWL	1.2
STD BANK NOM TVL P/L	NATSEL	4.2

STD BANK NOM TVL P/L	NEDCOR	2.1
STD BANK NOM TVL P/L	NEW-CENT	1.4
STD BANK NOM TVL P/L	NEW-WITS	6.9
STD BANK NOM TVL P/L	NIGEL	3.7
STD BANK NOM TVL P/L	NORTHAM	5.7
STD BANK NOM TVL P/L	O-K	5.7
STD BANK NOM TVL P/L	OCTODEC	5.6
STD BANK NOM TVL P/L	OFSIL	11.7
STD BANK NOM TVL P/L	OMNIA	2.7
STD BANK NOM TVL P/L	ORYX	1.3
STD BANK NOM TVL P/L	OSPREY	5.1
STD BANK NOM TVL P/L	OVBEL	1.8
STD BANK NOM TVL P/L	OZZ	12.1
STD BANK NOM TVL P/L	PALAMIN	4.2
STD BANK NOM TVL P/L	PANPROP	3.9
STD BANK NOM TVL P/L	PEP	4.4
STD BANK NOM TVL P/L	PERSBEL	2.1
STD BANK NOM TVL P/L	PERSKOR	6.0
STD BANK NOM TVL P/L	PERSTEC	5.8
STD BANK NOM TVL P/L	PICBEL	1.1
STD BANK NOM TVL P/L	PICKNPAY	3.0
STD BANK NOM TVL P/L	PIKWIK	1.1
STD BANK NOM TVL P/L	PIONEER	4.6
STD BANK NOM TVL P/L	PLATE-GL	2.3
STD BANK NOM TVL P/L	POWTECH	3.8
STD BANK NOM TVL P/L	PP RUST	34.0
STD BANK NOM TVL P/L	PPC	7.9
STD BANK NOM TVL P/L	PREM-GRP	18.7
STD BANK NOM TVL P/L	PROGRESS	7.7
STD BANK NOM TVL P/L	PUTCO	11.5
STD BANK NOM TVL P/L	PUTPROP	4.6
STD BANK NOM TVL P/L	RANDEX	1.2
STD BANK NOM TVL P/L	RANDFONTN	38.0
STD BANK NOM TVL P/L	RANDMIN	5.3
STD BANK NOM TVL P/L	RD-LEASE	16.2
STD BANK NOM TVL P/L	REMB-BEH	2.9
STD BANK NOM TVL P/L	REMGRO	6.0
STD BANK NOM TVL P/L	REUNERT	3.5
STD BANK NOM TVL P/L	REVERE	43.0
STD BANK NOM TVL P/L	REX-TRUE	3.6
STD BANK NOM TVL P/L	RHOEX	3.6
STD BANK NOM TVL P/L	ROMENS	7.0
STD BANK NOM TVL P/L	ROOIBERG	2.5
STD BANK NOM TVL P/L	ROYAL	7.5
STD BANK NOM TVL P/L	ROYCHEM	8.2
STD BANK NOM TVL P/L	ROYFOOD	4.9
STD BANK NOM TVL P/L	ROYHOLD	4.3
STD BANK NOM TVL P/L	RUHOLD	17.5
STD BANK NOM TVL P/L	RUSFURN	6.8
STD BANK NOM TVL P/L	RUSPLAT	33.3
STD BANK NOM TVL P/L	S-A-BIAS	1.9
STD BANK NOM TVL P/L	SA-BREWS	9.4
STD BANK NOM TVL P/L	SABLE	1.2
STD BANK NOM TVL P/L	SABVEST	6.6
STD BANK NOM TVL P/L	SAFCOR	8.8
STD BANK NOM TVL P/L	SAFICON	8.2
STD BANK NOM TVL P/L	SAFLIFE	4.1
STD BANK NOM TVL P/L	SAFREN	11.2
STD BANK NOM TVL P/L	SAGEGRP	26.9
STD BANK NOM TVL P/L	SAKERS	3.5
STD BANK NOM TVL P/L	SALLIES	4.2
STD BANK NOM TVL P/L	SAMANCO	2.2
STD BANK NOM TVL P/L	SANTAM	3.2
STD BANK NOM TVL P/L	SAPPI	4.7
STD BANK NOM TVL P/L	SASOL	8.3
STD BANK NOM TVL P/L	SBIC	5.8
STD BANK NOM TVL P/L	SCORE	5.5
STD BANK NOM TVL P/L	SEARCON	2.9
STD BANK NOM TVL P/L	SEARDEL	2.5
STD BANK NOM TVL P/L	SECHOLD	2.4
STD BANK NOM TVL P/L	SENTRCHEM	1.5
STD BANK NOM TVL P/L	SERVGRO	1.3
STD BANK NOM TVL P/L	SHOREDITS	11.5
STD BANK NOM TVL P/L	SILTEK	5.5
STD BANK NOM TVL P/L	SIMMERS	1.2
STD BANK NOM TVL P/L	SMART	5.6
STD BANK NOM TVL P/L	SOPLATS	1.3
STD BANK NOM TVL P/L	SOUDEX	44.1
STD BANK NOM TVL P/L	SOUTHGO	3.2
STD BANK NOM TVL P/L	SOUTHVAAL	5.7
STD BANK NOM TVL P/L	SPECLTY	1.5
STD BANK NOM TVL P/L	SPESCOM	1.5
STD BANK NOM TVL P/L	SPL	1.3
STD BANK NOM TVL P/L	SPURHLD	15.3
STD BANK NOM TVL P/L	ST-HELENA	2.7
STD BANK NOM TVL P/L	STANDRD	5.3
STD BANK NOM TVL P/L	STANPRO	3.2
STD BANK NOM TVL P/L	STH-RODPT	1.1
STD BANK NOM TVL P/L	STILFTN	67.0
STD BANK NOM TVL P/L	STOCKS	8.0
STD BANK NOM TVL P/L	STORECO	9.9
STD BANK NOM TVL P/L	SUB-N	1.5
STD BANK NOM TVL P/L	SUN-BOP	1.7
STD BANK NOM TVL P/L	SUNCISK	1.2
STD BANK NOM TVL P/L	SUNCRUSH	3.3
STD BANK NOM TVL P/L	T-&-N	1.5
STD BANK NOM TVL P/L	T-M-L	28.4
STD BANK NOM TVL P/L	TAMBOTI	5.5
STD BANK NOM TVL P/L	TEGKOR	3.7
STD BANK NOM TVL P/L	TELJOY	11.3
STD BANK NOM TVL P/L	TEMPORA	4.1
STD BANK NOM TVL P/L	TGH	19.9
STD BANK NOM TVL P/L	TIB	1.0
STD BANK NOM TVL P/L	TIGR-OATS	9.9
STD BANK NOM TVL P/L	TIME	4.9
STD BANK NOM TVL P/L	TIWHEEL	1.0
STD BANK NOM TVL P/L	TMX	1.9
STD BANK NOM TVL P/L	TOCO	13.8
STD BANK NOM TVL P/L	TOLUX	4.1
STD BANK NOM TVL P/L	TOMKOR	1.5
STD BANK NOM TVL P/L	TONGAAT	4.7
STD BANK NOM TVL P/L	TOYOTA	29.2
STD BANK NOM TVL P/L	TRADHLD	1.4
STD BANK NOM TVL P/L	TRANS-NTL	4.3
STD BANK NOM TVL P/L	TRENCOR	9.4
STD BANK NOM TVL P/L	TRIMTEX	9.6
STD BANK NOM TVL P/L	TRIMTRD	10.4
STD BANK NOM TVL P/L	TRNSHEX	4.0
STD BANK NOM TVL P/L	TWEEFONTN	19.0
STD BANK NOM TVL P/L	UMDONI	8.2
STD BANK NOM TVL P/L	UNIDEV	1.0
STD BANK NOM TVL P/L	UNION	1.3
STD BANK NOM TVL P/L	UNISEL	7.4
STD BANK NOM TVL P/L	UNISPIN	2.5
STD BANK NOM TVL P/L	UNITRAN	1.3
STD BANK NOM TVL P/L	USKO	11.6
STD BANK NOM TVL P/L	VAAL-REEF	13.8
STD BANK NOM TVL P/L	VEKTRA	2.6
STD BANK NOM TVL P/L	VENTEL	1.0
STD BANK NOM TVL P/L	VENTERS	10.0
STD BANK NOM TVL P/L	VESTCOR	3.1
STD BANK NOM TVL P/L	VETRUST	6.3
STD BANK NOM TVL P/L	VIERFONTN	1.6
STD BANK NOM TVL P/L	VILLAGE	2.5
STD BANK NOM TVL P/L	VLAKS	4.2
STD BANK NOM TVL P/L	VOGELS	6.2
STD BANK NOM TVL P/L	VOLTEX	6.2
STD BANK NOM TVL P/L	W-&-A	4.4
STD BANK NOM TVL P/L	W-R-CONS	7.2
STD BANK NOM TVL P/L	WAICOR	5.0
STD BANK NOM TVL P/L	WALHOLD	6.0
STD BANK NOM TVL P/L	WALTONS	12.1
STD BANK NOM TVL P/L	WELKOM	13.7
STD BANK NOM TVL P/L	WES-AREAS	25.9
STD BANK NOM TVL P/L	WESCO	11.2
STD BANK NOM TVL P/L	WESWITS	1.2

T

TANVEST PVT LTD	TEDCO	2.2
TANVEST PVT LTD	ZSR	3.4
TARR R D	SEFALANA	2.9
TARRY ANN	PROPFIN	7.8
TARRY F J	PROPFIN	42.8
TARRY GROUP P/L	CURNOW	35.8
TARRY J	PROPFIN	1.4
TARRY M A	PROPFIN	12.6
TARRY V	PROPFIN	7.8
TATE & LYLE HOLDINGS LTD	HIPPO	8.3
TATE & LYLE HOLDINGS LTD	ZSR	50.1
TAURUS NOM LTD	AFR-LEASE	9.7
TAURUS NOM LTD	AMAPROP	4.5
TAURUS NOM LTD	AMCOAL	3.6
TAURUS NOM LTD	AMGOLD	2.9
TAURUS NOM LTD	AMIC	5.2
TAURUS NOM LTD	ANGLO-S	3.4
TAURUS NOM LTD	CMI	3.0
TAURUS NOM LTD	DEELKRL	2.0
TAURUS NOM LTD	DRIES	2.8
TAURUS NOM LTD	ELANDS	9.5
TAURUS NOM LTD	HARTIES	1.7
TAURUS NOM LTD	HIVELD	7.8
TAURUS NOM LTD	LEPLAT	1.1
TAURUS NOM LTD	MCCARTHY	6.6
TAURUS NOM LTD	OFSIL	2.4
TAURUS NOM LTD	PP RUST	1.2
TAURUS NOM LTD	RUSPLAT	1.3
TAURUS NOM LTD	SOUTHVAAL	7.4
TAURUS NOM LTD	TONGAAT	2.7
TAURUS NOM LTD	VAAL-REEF	4.2
TAURUS NOM LTD	WELKOM	6.6
TAURUS NOM LTD	WSTN-DEEP	9.2
TAVADAC P/L	MULTI	7.1
TAYLOR D	PRIM-G-M	1.8
TAYLOR R	SPESCOM	4.9
TBA NOM P/L	BENCO	2.1
TBA NOM P/L	TRNSHEX	1.5
TEAL RECORD CO LTD	MAST	7.0
TEAMCOR LTD	VEKTRA	80.5
TECHNOLOGY FINANCE CORP P/L	SAFETEC	33.7
TECHNOTEST P/L	TITACO	4.4
TEGNIESE & INDUSTRIELE INV BPK	REMB-BEH	9.6
TEGNIESE & INDUSTRIELE INV BPK	TEGKOR	60.4
TEGNIESE INV KORPORASIE BPK	REMB-BEH	40.6
TEGNIESE MYNBELEGGINGS BPK	FRALEX	39.2
TEGNIESE MYNBELEGGINGS BPK	GENBEHEER	25.2
TEGNIESE MYNBELEGGINGS BPK	TRNSHEX	50.0
TELGAR HOLDINGS P/L	MICOR	1.0
TELJOY HOLDINGS SHARE TRUST	TELJOY	1.7
TEMPORA INV LTD	CADSWEP	21.5
TEMPORA INV LTD	DALYS	20.6
TEMPORA INV LTD	SAFICON	8.0
TEMPORA INV LTD	SAKERS	9.2
TEMPORA INV LTD	SEARCON	6.9
TEMPORA INV LTD	SEARDEL	1.4
TENDRIL LTD	PEP BOT	70.0
TEPERSON D S	TRIMTEX	1.8
TESAR F	SHOREDITS	15.5
TEUNIS FAMILY INV P/L	SCHARIG	18.7
TEXTILE & GENERAL HOLDINGS LTD	BRISTOL-I	55.9
TEXTURED YARNS PVT LTD	AFDISTIL	1.8
TEXTURED YARNS PVT LTD	BINDURA	1.3
TEXTURED YARNS PVT LTD	KADOMA	1.3
THATON LTD	ERGO	3.7
THEMY HOLDINGS P/L	TOMKOR	2.5
THEO RUSTEIN HOLDINGS P/L	TELJOY	6.0
THERON A F M	TAFLBRG	1.3
THERON E J	TAFLBRG	4.0
THIART S J J	HARWILL	1.3
THIES J M	SECHOLD	1.2
THOMAS F	CFC	1.7
THOMAS F	CONFED	1.2
THOMAS J M	OVCON	7.5
THOMAS P R S	INHOLD	1.4
THOMPSON F R L	UNION	1.4
THOMSON K E P/L	PORTHLD	1.9
THOR RESOURCES P/L	SIMMERS	1.3
TIBER INV CC	ROMENS	4.2
TIBER INV HOLDINGS CC	ROMENS	8.7
TIGATEL BV	DELTA ZIM	8.2
TIGER OATS LTD	ADCOCK	74.1
TIGER OATS LTD	LANGBRG	57.4
TIGER OATS LTD	OCFISH	69.4
TIGMAR INV P/L	TWHEEL	6.1
TILL G	BEARMAN	1.5
TIME HOLDINGS SHARE TRUST	TIME	5.4
TIMES MEDIA LTD	DISPTCH	28.7
TIMES MEDIA LTD	M-NET	4.1
TIMES MEDIA LTD PENS FUND	T-M-L	2.4
TINEYI INV PVT LTD	FP HOLD	7.5
TIRAS P/L	NAMSEA	1.1
TITACO ADMIN HOLDINGS CC	TITACO	48.6
TITAN INSURANCE CO LTD	FINTECH	1.6
TITAN NOM P/L	BOLAND	5.2
TITAN NOM P/L	COMPASS	4.7
TITAN NOM P/L	HARWILL	2.8
TITAN NOM P/L	INVICTA	9.4
TITAN NOM P/L	PEPGRO	15.9
TOBACCO HAIL INSURANCE PVT LTD	CAPS	1.1
TONGAAT-HULETT EMPLOYEES SHARE TRUST	TONGAAT	1.8
TONGAAT-HULETT PENS FUND	CROOKES	2.7
TONGAAT-HULETT PENS FUND	TONGAAT	1.2
TONLY INV PVT LTD	CIRCLE	1.5
TONLY INV PVT LTD	RADAR	1.5
TONY ALVES FAMILY TRUST	RUHOLD	3.4
TOP CORP P/L	DIALMOV	31.8
TOP DOG NOM P/L	OAKFLDS	2.9
TOP DOG NOM P/L	PICBEL	6.0
TOP DOG NOM P/L	RABIE	1.8
TOP-HI INV P/L	UNICON	96.6
TORF R	DINETTE	3.3
TORINO INV P/L	PERSBEL	1.4
TORINO INV P/L	REX-TRUE	1.5
TORQUAY SECURITIES P/L	RUHOLD	11.7
TOWNSLEY O R	SILOAK	1.1
TOWY TRUST P/L	CONFED	6.3
TOZER K G	OHIO	4.7
TPH HOLDINGS P/L	MULTI	41.5
TRACY BRENNER INV P/L	BRENMIL	1.8
TRADEHOLD LTD	TRADGRO	5.3
TRAFALGAR HSE O/SEAS CONSTR HLDGS	CEMENCO	37.3
TRANSATLANTIC MINING INV LTD	SIMMERS	22.4
TRANSIT SECURITIES INC	PROFURN	3.2
TRANSKEI DEV CORP LTD	TRANSUN	28.6
TREECO NOM P/L	QUAGGA	6.2
TRIDENT NOM LTD	HICORL	13.3
TROCOR P/L	NICTUS	9.0
TROGON P/L	CFC	1.9
TROGON P/L	OVBEL	1.8
TRONSHOLD INV P/L	VALAUTO	2.4
TROY NOM P/L	OCEANA	2.0
TRUST BANK NOM P/L	LANCHEM	3.6
TRUST NOM (PVT) LTD	BINDURA	1.3
TRUST NOM (PVT) LTD	CAPS	1.0
TRUST NOM (PVT) LTD	FMB	1.3
TRUST NOM (PVT) LTD	MASHONA	1.9
TRUST NOM (PVT) LTD	RADAR	3.3
TRUST NOM (PVT) LTD	TEDCO	1.0
TRUST NOM (PVT) LTD	WANKIE	1.0
TRUST NOM P/L	PORTHLD	2.0
TRUWORTHS ZIM LTD SHARE PURCH SCHEME	TRUZIM	2.6
TSL LTD	AGRICOR	35.9
TUCKER E	YORKCOR	3.8
TUCKER I S D	YORKCOR	1.5
TUCKER S	YORKCOR	1.1

TULELE SUGAR ESTATES P/L	MARCONS	1.4
TURNER R	AFDISTIL	1.0
TURNER R	WANKIE	2.2
TURNER R	ZSR	2.9
TUROK L L	POINTER	13.8
TUROK S Y	POINTER	1.7
TVL EMERALD MINING CO P/L	FEDSURE	1.2
TWEEFONTEIN UNITED COLLIERIES LTD	COR-SYND	62.2
TWEEFONTEIN UNITED COLLIERIES LTD	DUIKERS	22.2
TWENTY SIXTH STAGE INV P/L	MICOR	3.6
TWINING INV P/L	OMNIA	1.1
TWINS PROPAN HOLDINGS P/L	PREMPHARM	94.7
TYCOMET P/L	MOLYSLP	70.2

U

U-CONTROL LTD	UNIHOLD	54.2
UAL MERCHANT BANK LTD	CLYDE	3.7
UAL MERCHANT BANK LTD	EVERITE	2.3
UAL MERCHANT BANK LTD	GDM	12.5
UAL MERCHANT BANK LTD	HUDACO	1.4
UAL MERCHANT BANK LTD	OAKFLDS	12.0
UAL MERCHANT BANK LTD	PENROSE	3.2
UAL MERCHANT BANK LTD	WINBEL	1.0
UAL NOM P/L	APEX	2.2
UAL NOM P/L	ASS-MANG	1.4
UAL NOM P/L	AVF GRP	5.5
UAL NOM P/L	CRULIFE	4.3
UAL NOM P/L	GRINCOR	6.0
UAL NOM P/L	INMINS	1.1
UAL NOM P/L	OAKFLDS	11.1
UAL NOM P/L	OCEANA	1.0
UAL NOM P/L	PROSURE	5.0
UAL NOM P/L	S-A-EAGLE	2.6
UAL NOM P/L	SILOAK	48.5
UAL NOM P/L	SYCOM	1.4
UAL NOM P/L	WINBEL	1.6
UBS HOLDINGS LTD	AIDA	25.3
UBS INSURANCE CO LTD	AVF GRP	5.2
UBS INSURANCE CO LTD	NATRUST	6.0
UBS INSURANCE CO LTD	SECHOLD	15.1
UDC STAFF SHARE PURCHASE TRUST	UDC	5.0
UK BRANCH REGISTER CONTROL ACCOUNT	BARLOWS	1.2
UK BRANCH REGISTER CONTROL ACCOUNT	BLYVOOR	5.1
UK BRANCH REGISTER CONTROL ACCOUNT	DBN-DEEP	17.9
UK BRANCH REGISTER CONTROL ACCOUNT	E-R-P-M	62.6
UK BRANCH REGISTER CONTROL ACCOUNT	HARMONY	30.7
UK BRANCH REGISTER CONTROL ACCOUNT	R-M-PROPS	1.8
UK BRANCH REGISTER CONTROL ACCOUNT	RANDMIN	1.1
UK CONTROL ACCOUNT	COR-SYND	20.5
UK CONTROL ACCOUNT	E-DAGGA	2.8
UK CONTROL ACCOUNT	O-K	3.2
UK CONTROL ACCOUNT	SIMMERS	7.3
UK CONTROL ACCOUNT	WIT-G-M	3.1
UK CONTROL ACCOUNT	WIT-NIGEL	5.3
UNICEM PENS FUND	PORTHLD	3.5
UNIDEV CONSOLIDATED HOLDINGS LTD	UNIDEV	82.2
UNIDEV CONSOLIDATED LTD	UNIDEV	2.2
UNIDEV ELECTRONIC HOLDINGS LTD	ODMHOLD	23.5
UNIDEV LTD	EQUIKOR	5.2
UNIDEV RETAIL HOLDINGS LTD	HYPERET	5.5
UNIDEV STRATEGIC INV HOLDINGS P/L	HYPERET	25.8
UNIHOLD INV P/L	U-CON	33.4
UNILEVER SA PENS FUND	PORTHLD	2.2
UNILEVER SA PENS FUND	ROTH ZIM	1.9
UNION BANK OF SWITZERLAND	AMGOLD	7.7
UNION TRUST CO LTD	RALE	2.1
UNIRUS P/L	RUSFURN	5.5
UNISEC HIGH INCOME PORTFOLIO P/L	STANPRO	33.4
UNITAS ENTERPRISES LTD	SASFIN	6.5
UNITED FACTORS PVT LTD	FALGOLD	2.0
UNITED FINANCE CORP OF SA LTD	SILOAK	3.7
UNITED FINANCE CORP OF SA LTD	UNI-COLD	28.4
UNITED GENERAL INV P/L	UNITRAN	77.9
UNITED TECHNOLOGIES HOLDINGS PLC	OTIS	9.0
UNIVERSA P/L	ABSA	16.0
USAT NOM P/L	MARLIN	3.2
USAT NOM P/L	MLNHOLD	61.0
USKO PENS FUND NOM P/L	HYPROP	1.1
UTAS INV P/L	GLODINA	5.1

V

VAAL REEFS EXPLORAT & MINING CO LTD	SOUTHVAAL	25.0
VAALTRUCAR EMPL SHARE INC TRUST	VALCAR	3.0
VAALTRUCAR LTD	VALAUTO	81.1
VAN ALPHEN G T	OVCON	1.1
VAN DEN BERG G	WOODROW	2.7
VAN DEN HEEVER P J	AFMIN	1.4
VAN DER BERGH J	UNION	1.4
VAN DER BIJL L	Q-DATA	1.8
VAN DER HORST J G	COM-FUND	1.6
VAN DER MERWE P F	Q-DATA	1.5
VAN DER POEL A D	DUKEL	1.3
VAN DOORN C	METJE-&-Z	27.8
VAN DRIEL A	NISWA	2.5
VAN DYK G	BOLPRO	1.6
VAN EMBDEN A TRUST	MASCON	24.2
VAN EMBDEN S	MASCON	22.9
VAN FLYMEN B	DINETTE	1.7
VAN LANDSBERG J P H E/L	DIGOCO	1.7
VAN NIEKERK G	TITACO	1.3
VAN NIEKERK J J	DINETTE	10.0
VAN REIGERSBERG VERSLUYS M L H	GAZGOLD	3.6
VAN RENSBURG C W J	TDL	7.9
VAN RENSBURG G F J	TDL	7.9
VAN RENSBURG J P	WALHOLD	3.3
VAN RENSBURG P J	TDL	9.3
VAN RENSBURG R R J TRUSTEES	TDL	7.7
VAN RIJN INV CORP LTD	MEDCLIN	92.9
VAN RIJN INV CORP LTD	PERSBEL	28.3
VAN ROOYEN D	RALE	1.9
VAN ROOYEN G J	HICORL	1.1
VAN ZIJL A M	STOCKS	1.4
VASSILOPOULOS A	QUICKCO	1.3
VATKO P/L	COMPASS	5.0
VEEDEN M J	OVCON	1.4
VELDMAN H R M	SEFALANA	3.7
VENDU FINANS P/L	SAAMBOU	6.1
VENTAL HOLDINGS SA	ENROL	88.0
VENTECH P/L	ALTRON	40.5
VENTER J M	VENTEL	4.1
VENTER L TRUST	ALTRON	1.2
VENTER W P	VENTRON	19.9
VENTRON CORP LTD	ALTRON	13.0
VERITAS EKSEKUTEURSKAMER E/B	NICTUS	11.1
VERMOOTEN J J TRUSTEES	RENTBEL	1.7
VERSPREIDE INV P/L	I-G-I	1.3
VERSPREIDE INV P/L	PRESMED	2.1
VERSPREIDE INV P/L	RENTBEL	12.3
VESTACOR LTD	MATH-ASH	74.4
VICTORY ENTERPRISES P/L	LIBVEST	2.9
VIETRI M J	FAIRCAP	11.2
VILJOEN N J	Q-DATA	1.4
VILJOEN P DU T	OVBEL	3.0
VIRGINIA MERRIESPRUIT INV LTD	HARMONY	1.4
VIRROXSAM INV P/L	ED-L-BATE	9.9
VIZOMA P/L	PROGRESS	24.7
VKP NOM P/L	M-NET	1.8
VMB NOM P/L	AVF GRP	14.0
VMB NOM P/L	F-S-I	3.6
VMB NOM P/L	KNJ	3.6
VMB NOM P/L	MANRO	9.9
VMB NOM P/L	W-&-A	1.4

W

X

Y

Z

INDEX OF DIRECTORS

KINDLY REFER TO SCHEDULE OF COMPANY ABBREVIATIONS FOR IDENTIFICATION OF ABBREVIATIONS

A

AAB FAW	CONCOR
AARON AJ	EDGARS
	ICH
	TRNPACO
	W-&-A
AARONS S	SOLCHEM
ABBOT DW	RABIE
ABELHEIM MB	TRNPACO
ABELHEIM PN	TRNPACO
ABELHEIM S	TRNPACO
ABELKOP P	IMPERIAL
	IMPHOLD
ABELKOP SD	IMPERIAL
	IMPHOLD
ABRAHAMS PS	SECHOLD
ABRAHAMSE LG	M-&-F
	NEIHOLD
	SAFREN
ABRAHAMSE LG DR	NEDCOR
ABRAHAMSON AE THE HON	GEN-OPTIC
ABRAHAMSON LP	GEN-OPTIC
ACKERMAN DE	CHUBB
ACKERMAN DP	YORKCOR
ACKERMAN GM	PICKNPAY
	PIKWIK
ACKERMAN RD	PICKNPAY
	PIKWIK
ACKERMAN W MRS	PICKNPAY
	PIKWIK
ACKHURST MJ	CADSWEP
ADAM BH	ADCOCK
ADAMS BH	MOMENTUM
	RUSFURN
	TIGR-OATS
ADAMS T	COR-SYND
ADAMSON RG	CLUFF ZIM
ADAN MJ	DEELKRL
	G-F-COAL
	GF-PROPS
	LIBANON
	VENTERS
	VLAKS
ADCOCK CS	CADSWEP
	CULLINAN
	NEDCOR
	NEI-AFR
	NEIHOLD
	SASOL
	SFW
	TOYOTA
	WESCO
ADCOCK RJ	MIDMAC
ADENDORFF JC MR	SCORE
AESCHIMANN JP	RICHEMONT
AGINSKY PC	ELCENTR
	VOLTEX
AITCHISON RA MR	COATES
AITKEN BR MR	PALAMIN
AITKEN DG	TONGAAT
AKAL WC	MIDAS
AKWENYE OS	NAMSEA
ALBERT P	DARMAG
ALBERTI JP	DATAKOR
ALBERTS L DR	ED-L-BATE
ALBERTS LJ	MEDCLIN
ALBERTS LM	BOUMAT
ALBERTYN HGL	SOTHERN
ALBOROUGH NVR	RMBH
ALCOCK IB	TSL
ALDERTON AJ	LIONMATCH
ALDWORTH ARM	ABSA
	RMBH
	SAFICON
ALISON AW	MIDAS
ALLISON BS	SUNCRUSH
ALLISON JR	SUN-BOP
	SUNCISK
	TRANSUN
ALLNATT MI	MANRO
ALLSOP RJ	AFDISTIL
ALTBEKER L MRS	CONTRAV
ALTINI T	ITLTILE
ALTY JAR	POWTECH
ALVES AC	RUHOLD
ALVEY GP	GF-PROPS
	VENTERS
	VLAKS
	VOGELS
AMBOR AJ	SPUR
	SPURHLD
AMERY HJ HON	WSTN-DEEP
ANDERSON BJ	UDC
ANDERSON DH	PEPKOR
ANDERSON IC	T-E-J
ANDERSON L MS	AFLIFE
ANDERSON GR	CLINICS
ANDREWES EWE	TELJOY
ANDREWS GS	AIDA
ANDREWS GS DR	MATH-ASH
ANDREWS GS PROF	VESTCOR
ANDREWS JD	DUN ZIM
ANDREWS RC	HCI
	I-G-I
	IGI BOT
ANGEL RJ	ENGEN
ANGREWS GS DR	CARGO
ANTONCICH M MR	FIDBANK
APPELBAUM HI	LIBVEST
APPELO M	SAFLIFE
APSEY CA	LANGBRG
	TIGR-OATS
APTEKER D	DUKEL
ARDINGTON AJ	HIGATE
	HISTONE
	SOTHERN
ARMSTRONG RH	CLUFF ZIM
ARMSTRONG RSR	TONGAAT
ARNOLD DB	DISPTCH
ARNOTT AH	AFLIFE
	SOTHERN
ARNOTT PJ	BARPROP
ARONOVSKY D	PROGRESS
AROVONSKY M	PROGRESS
ARTHUR DR	EUREKA
ARTHUR PRN	GAZGOLD
ARTHUR R (BOB) MR	UNIHOLD
ARTHUR RA	FENNER
ASHERSON JD	MACADAM
ASHLEY MJ	CLUFF ZIM
ASHMEAD GL	UNION

D

DALING MH	GENCOR
	M&R-HLD
	M&R-INV
	MALHOLD
	SANTAM
DALLAMORE SWB	MAST
DALTON AKC	QUICKCO
DALY KC	SAGEGRP
DALY PF	FRALEX
DALY SB	ALEXNDR
	FRALEX
DAMBE CS	PEP BOT
DANIEL LT	WAYNE
DANIEL RJ	MODDER
	STH-RODPT
DANNHEISSER MO	LITHO
DANNHEISSER PS	LITHO
DANZIGER DJ	CLICKS
DATNOW CS	MATH-ASH
	VESTCOR
DAUBENEY PEG	AECI
DAUGHERTY DE	CFC
	CONFED
DAUN DE	MORKELS
DAVIDSON KM	ABACUS
	CERAMIC
DAVIDSON P	DUN ZIM
DAVIDSON RT	STANDRD
DAVIDSON TJ	DEB CENT
DAVIDSON KM	GDM
DAVIES AJ	CMS
DAVIES BT	ALEXWYT
DAVIES CJ	DUIKERS
DAVIES CP	NBSHOLD
DAVIES DC	DELTA
DAVIES GSJ	DECHOLD
DAVIES HK	AMIC
	HIVELD
	L-T-A
DAVIES MG	JASCO
DAVIES NO	MATH-ASH
	VESTCOR
DAVIES PJ	TITACO
DAVIES RSP	OCEANA
DAVIGNON E VISCOUN	MINORCO
DAVIN FJ	BSG
	BSI
	M-&-F
	NEDCOR
	RANDMIN
	SAFREN
	SFW
DAVIN GH	INHOLD
	INVSTEC
DAVIS LA	PALAMIN
DAVIS MH	WALHOLD
	WALTONS
DAVIS SJM	UNISPIN
DAVISON A	STREBEL
DAVISON BE	CMI
	JOHNNIES
	LEPLAT
	PP RUST
	RUSPLAT
DAY B	INTERNAT
	ROTH ZIM
	ZIMPLOW
DAY BA	DOORNS
	GF-PROPS
	NEW-WITS
	ROOIBERG
	VENTERS
	VLAKS
DAY BA	VOGELS
DAY D	SASOL
DAYARAM K	CLICKS
DE BEER DD	AVF GRP
	AVINS
	CRULIFE
	SILTEK
DE BEER JW	HICORL
DE BEER TL	ENGEN
	FOODCRP
	GENBEL
	GENCOR
	ISCOR
	MALHOLD
	RANDEX
	SAPPI
DE BLANCHE EM	ABSA
	CUSAF
DE BRUIN GC DR	SEARDEL
DE BRUIN DE WET CR	QUAGGA
DE BRUYN P	SAPPI
DE CHAUD A	ROMANO
DE CHAUD M	ROMANO
DE CLERK PB	MEDCLIN
DE HAAS P	MOLYSLP
DE JAGER GD	AMSHOE
	LENCO
	LENVEST
DE JAGER GJ	LENCO
	LENVEST
DE JONG P	MICIND
DE KATZ G	FOCUS
DE KLERK AM	CLYDE
DE KLERK BH	HLH
DE KLERK H	AFCOL
DE KLERK HJP	FOSTON
DE KLERK IH	NICTUS
DE KOCK MJ	PENROSE
DE KOK WJ	PREM-GRP
DE LA BAT RS	KWV-BEL
	SFW
DE LA H BECK J	MATH-ASH
	VESTCOR
DE LA H BECK WF	KERSAF
DE LA HARPE BECK WF	M&R-INV
	SA-RES-BK
DE LA HARPE BECK WF MR	COATES
DE LA RUE A	CLUFF ZIM
DE LOOR J DR	T-&-N
DE LOOR JH	EVHOLD
DE LOOR JH DR	PUTPROP
	SBIC
DE LOOR DR JH	CLINICS
DE MUELENAERE GPMC DR	RENTBEL
DE MUELENAERE JJGG PROF	RENTBEL
DE MUELENAERE LGAGR DR	RENTBEL
DE RAUVILLE JPG	GROWALK
	S-A-EAGLE
DE REUCK F	BOLAND
DE RIDDER C	SOTHERN
DE ROTHSCHILD BARON E	DE BEERS
	DEB CENT
DE ROTHSCHILD E SIR	DE BEERS
	DEB CENT
DE STEFANIS IP	SHOCRAF
DE V GRAAFF J DR	NEDCOR
DE VILLIERS HP	AFROX
	BEVCON
	CONFRAM
	FRAME
	GARDIAN
	GFSA
	ISG

DE VILLIERS HP	LIBERTY
	LIBVEST
	SA-BREWS
DE VILLIERS HP MR	FIT
DE VILLIERS JN	MEDCLIN
	REMB-BEH
DE VILLIERS JR	SOPLATS
	SOWITS
DE VILLIERS JS DR	BARNEX
	FREDDEV
	UNISEL
DE VILLIERS JTM DR	COR-SYND
	DUIKERS
DE VILLIERS LM	DATAKOR
DE VILLIERS NA	CBD-FUND
	PIONEER
DE VILLIERS PC	USKO
DE VILLIERS R	SAPPI
DE VILLIERS HP	LIB HOLD
DE VOS SJ	MIDAS
DE VRIES AJM PROF	BOLAND
DE VRIES MJ PROF	BOLAND
DE WAAL MT	SASOL
DE WAAL MT DR	ISCOR
	SA-RES-BK
DE WET CPC THE HON	CUSAF
DE WET RP	PICKNPAY
	PIKWIK
DE WIT C	ABERDARE
DEAN T	BEARMAN
DEDNAM E	BTRDUN
DEETLEFS JH	TEDELEX
DEKKER LW	MJM
DELACAVE JTL	TMX
DELAHUNT MJ	MICOR
DELAHUNT SMOLENIEC PB	PENROSE
DELANEY PP	DPF-INV
DELPORT MM MR	DECOVO
DEMETRIADES G	CROWN
DEMETRIADES G MR	AFRICOM
	BIDCORP
	BIDVEST
DEMMERS AC	ILCO
DEMUTH WG	SILOAK
DEN BOER P	Q-DATA
DEN BOER PAUL	Q-DATA
DEN HAAN J	CUSAF
DENNETT DE	BORDER
	FMB
	HIPPO
DENNIS N	CGS-FOOD
	I-C-S
	TIGR-OATS
DENNISS PS	CRENDEL
	HCI
	I-G-I
	IGI BOT
DERCKSEN W	VENTEL
DERSLEY RM	DARMAG
DESAI PV	ENBOT
DESILLA JP	CURFIN
	SAFCOR
DESMET BJ MR	STERLING
DESMIDT JMP	AMGOLD
DETTMANN IJ	MAXMECH
DEUDNEY NA	ENGEN
DEVITT RB	BERGERS
	BERTRAD
DEW J	SAB IND
DEYZEL JG MR	PALAMIN
DHLOMO OD DR	ANGLOVAAL
	HLH
	HUNTCOR

DHLOMO OD DR	SBIC
DIAMOND SH	SEARDEL
DIBOWITZ PJ	AF-&-OVER
	REX-TRUE
DICK B	SAPPI
DICK JW	UDC
DICKASON GB	ABSA
	CITYLDG
	MAINPRO
	SAGEGRP
DICKERSON RI	CHUBB
DICKIE AC	ART
DICKMAN AB	AMGOLD
DICKS JK	N-KLEINS
DICKS KV	FREGOLD
DICKSON AJL	BOE
	BOEPROP
	TAMBOTI
DICKSON AJL MR	UMDONI
DICKSON WM	CITYLDG
DIKE CW	AFCOL
DIPPENAAR JJA MR	FIDBANK
DIPPENAAR L	MOMENTUM
DIPPENAAR LL	FRALEX
	KOPP
	RMBH
	SILTEK
DISELE BM	SECHABA
DISON L	BASREAD
DIXON JR	ANGLOVAAL
DONALD JC	BENONI
	NIGEL
	WESWITS
	WIT-NIGEL
DONE BM	STANDRD
DONEHOWER JW	CARLCOR
DORAN W	LASER
DORRESTEIN AH	STOCKS
DORRINGTON I	STREBEL
DORWARD AI	TEDCO
DORWARD GA	TEDCO
DORWARD PD	SCHWEP CA
	TA HOLD
	TEDCO
	ZIMSPIN
DOS SANTOS CS	CLICKS
	HISCORE
	METCASH
	SCOCLIK
DOS SANTOS CS MR	SCORE
DOS SANTOS M	MILSTAN
DOUGHERTY SM	TONGAAT
DOUGLAS AAB	CEMENCO
DOWER JMR	BLOCHS
DOWLING JP	S-A-EAGLE
DOYLE BW	BOWCALF
DOYLE MM	ANG-ALPHA
	SALLIES
DRAUDSING AJE	DABI
DREW NE	DARMAG
DREYER JW	RMBH
DRITZ J	ELLERINE
DRUCKMAN DS	MICIND
DRUION SA	TRNPACO
DRYDEN G	LANCHEM
DRYSDALE DM	NINIAN
DU PLESSIS AJ	GROOTVLEI
	W-R-CONS
DU PLESSIS AS	ABSA
	CONSHU
	M&R-HLD
	M&R-INV
	METPOL

E

ELLIS SP	WINKELS
ELLMAN-BROWN DA	AGRICOR
ELLWOOD RR	HIVELD
ELMES B	SABLE
ELMS RA	M-&-F
ELOFF FC PROF	CITYHLD
ELS MHO	LONGRAIL
ELS PS	ILCO
EMARY FE	JASCO
EMDON AL	AKJ
EMMETT DTG	RUSPLAT
ENDERLE HR	CITYLDG
ENGELAGE E	MOMENTUM
ENGELBERG S	GRESHAM
ENGELBRECHT S	CHEMSERVE
ENGELBRECHT P	CLAW
ENGELS J	HARTIES
ENGLISH G	ASSORE
ENRIEU CAG MR	ROYCHEM
ENTHOVEN R	G5HOLD
	GROUP-5
EPSTEIN LM	PROGRESS
ERASMUS DH	PERSTEC
ERASMUS PJ	REMB-BEH
ERASMUS WG MR	ROYCHEM
ESCOTT RAG	BBZIM
ESTERHUISEN P	SUPREME
ESTERHUIZEN AG	RHOEX
ESTERHUIZEN CJ	VALAUTO
	VALCAR
ESTERHUYSE WP	M&R-HLD
ESTERHUYSE WP PROF	M&R-INV
	METPOL
ETHERIDGE DW	ED ZIM
	EDGARS
ETKIND LT	MILSTAN
ETKIND MB	MILSTAN
ETKIND R	MILSTAN
ETKIND SI	MILSTAN
ETTER M	MAXMECH
EUSTACE PJ	AFR-LEASE
	BEATRIX
	BLYVOOR
	BUFFELS
	DOORNS
	ERGO
	HARMONY
	LORAINE
	SALLIES
	ST-HELENA
	TARGET
	UNISEL
	WES-AREAS
	WINKELS
	ZANDPAN
EVANS BD	NAT TYRE
EVANS D	AFCOL
EVANS DJF	QUICKCO
EVANS GJH	SPL
EVANS IJS	DALYS
	SUNCRUSH
EVANS IJS MR	TEMPORA
EVANS J	BTRDUN
EVANS KRM	PERSTEC
EVANS M	PROGRESS
EVANS T	NAMPAK
EVENWEL JK	BESTER
EVERED RHH	BOUMAT

F

FABRY FC	TECFIN
FAIRBAIRN DA	GYPSUM
FAIRLAMB WE	TRUZIM
FALCK DM	LENCO
	LENVEST
	REMGRO
FALLER JEN	SHOREDITS
FALLS RER	ED-L-BATE
FALOWITZ F	LEEGALL
FALOWITZ L	LEEGALL
FARACI JV	MASONITE
FARAH A	SPESCOM
FARENHEM DM	STOCKS
FARKAS V	CENMAG
FARR AZ	SAFREN
FARRELL KM	HARTIES
FARRER M	NBSHOLD
	TAMBOTI
FARRER M MR	UMDONI
FARRUGIA JC	OAKFLDS
FAUCONNIER CJ DR	CON-MURCH
FEARFIELD MA	OMNIA
FEATHERSTONE JG	ARGUS
	CTP
	HORTORS
	SOLCHEM
FEHLER A	PUBLICO
FEINBERG H	CUTRITE
FEINBLUM RM	CONSHU
	WAYNE
FEINBLUM SG	CLINICS
FELDTMANN CS	USKO
FELTOE R	FMB
FENNELL RJ	TANGANDA
FENTON CT	DEELKRL
	DOORNS
	DRIES
	G-F-COAL
	GFNAMIB
	GFSA
	ISCOR
	KLOOF
	LIBANON
	NORTHAM
	VENTERS
FENWICK F MR	PALAMIN
FERGUSON DB	DISA
FERGUSON DCE	S-A-BIAS
	SABVEST
FERGUSON DSB	ROOIBERG
FERGUSON HD	ED ZIM
FERGUSON PRA	CONCOR
	E-DAGGA
FERGUSSON AJF	LIBERTY
FERREIRA C	VETRUST
FERREIRA CG DR	BUFFCOR
FERREIRA EMAF DR	ANGLO-S
FERREIRA GT	LENCO
	LENVEST
	MOMENTUM
	RMBH
	TIME
FERREIRA M	BOLWEAR
FERREIRA P	ANG-ALPHA
	E-T-CONS
FERREIRA DR CG	LANCHEM
FERRIMAN EA	PERSTEC
FERROW P	PAG
FEWELL PT	BUFFELS
	GROOTVLEI
	LESLIE
FICHARDT EA	NICTUS
FIELD AJ	BUFFELS
	STILFTN

K

KELLY JAW	AGRICOR
KEMBLE JR	ERGO
KEMP AR	CONFED
KEMP GP	BTRDUN
KEMP S	BOLAND
KENNEALY DP	ELLERINE
	MALBAK
KENNEDY DC	TELJOY
KENNEDY R	SASOL
KENNELLY ND	ENGEN
KENT BH	FMCOTEC
	KUDU
	MANRO
KENYON B	PRESMED
KERR RC	AFEX SA
	CONAFEX
	UNISERV
KERSWELL RG	TEDCO
KERZNER S	SUN-BOP
KESWICK JCL	CHARTER
KETS ND	MCPHAIL
KEWITT L	SALLIES
KEYS NJ	BOTREST
KEYS NJ MR	PALAMIN
KEYSER M	ITLTILE
KHAMA DC	RDC
KHONAT DA	RAPTOR
KHOZA RJ	ISG
KIDD J MR	KAROS
KIDSON J	ABERDARE
KILIAN C	FOODCRP
	TEDELEX
KILIAN PJ DU PRE	REMGRO
KIMMEL HM	PANPROP
KING DF MR	COATES
KING JC	PRIM-G-M
KING JW	GARDIAN
KING ME	AVF GRP
	AVINS
	CONFRAM
	FIRSTBK
	FRAME
	PICBEL
KING MW	AMAPROP
	AMCOAL
	AMGOLD
	AMIC
	ANAMINT
	ANGLO-S
	BOTREST
	CMI
	COMPASS
	DORBYL
	ERGO
	FIRSTBK
	HIVELD
	JOHNNIES
	LEPLAT
	NEW-CENT
	OFSIL
	RUSPLAT
	S-A-EAGLE
	SOTHERN
	SOUTHVAAL
	TONGAAT
	VAAL-REEF
	WELKOM
KING PMB	ELANDS
	WSTN-DEEP
KING RD	CIH
KINMONT GA	AFCOL
KINNEAR BH	DARMAG
KINVIG JA	CUSAF

KINVIG JA	SYCOM
KIRCHMANN WM	STANPRO
KIRCHMANN PF	KH PROPS
KIRCHMANN WM	KH PROPS
KIRKMAN KD	BBZIM
KIRKPATRICK CWM	PGI
KIRSCH D	AMREL
KIRSH W	LOGTEK
KIRSTEN DG	MINVEST
KISJES RJ	GULLIVER
KITSHOFF JJ	LENCO
	LENVEST
	RMBH
KLASS J MR	PDC
KLEBE EHK	CLAW
KLEIN A	BOUMAT
KLEIN MS	AIMARK
KLEIN RM	AIMARK
KLINTWORTH RI	JOEL
KLOPPERS HB	ILCO
KLUGMAN KM MR	MERHLD
KNEEN JR	CLAW
KNIGHT AH	CAIRNS
KNIGHT SMG	ZIMSPIN
KNOBBS C	KNIGHTS
KNOETZE FW	ODMHOLD
KNOLL LB DR	CEMENCO
KNOX FW	GEFCO
	MSAULI
KOCH EL	F-S-I
KOCH JRR	ICH
KOCH UE DR	TOLUX
KOCK AD	SA-RES-BK
KOHLBERG KAH	L-T-A
KOHLER GE	ARIES
KOHLER PH	BBZIM
KOHN GM MR	PDC
KOK TFL	GROOTVLEI
	KINROSS
	STILFTN
	W-R-CONS
KOLBE AL	BOUMAT
KOMANYANE EW	SECHABA
KONG D	KOPP
KOPMAN A	JDGROUP
KOPP A	KOPP
KORSMAN AC	SMART
KORSTEN LP	PERSBEL
	PERSKOR
	RUSFURN
KOSEFF S	FEDSURE
	GROWPNT
	INHOLD
	INTRUST
	INVSTEC
	METPROP
KOSEFF S MR	BIDCORP
KOTZE JM	BOLAND
KOTZEE FP	DORBYL
	METKOR
	REMB-BEH
	RHOVAN
	SAMANCO
	USKO
KOTZEE TJ	EVERITE
	EVHOLD
	G5HOLD
	GOLDSTEIN
	GROUP-5
KOVARSKY D	M-NET
KOVARSKY DC	DABI
	GRESHAM
	PREM-GRP

L

M

MENELL CS	LORAINE
	MID-WITS
	TARGET
	ZANDPAN
MENELL MV MS	IMPLATS
MENELL RP	A-V-HOLD
	ANGLOVAAL
MENNELL MV MS	BARMINE
	BARPLAT
	MESSINA
MERLO DGA	VENTEL
MERRIFIELD PW	DIALMOV
MESTRINER J	SUN-BOP
METHVEN L	RAINBOW
MEYER H PROF	PERSBEL
	PERSKOR
MEYER HP	MOMENTUM
MEYER JA	T-&-N
MEYER SE	GROWALK
MEYEROWITZ LA	SYCOM
MEYJES RP	TITACO
MHLANGA L DR	ART
MIA AM	WIT-G-M
MIA YI	WIT-G-M
MICHAEKS EJ	DISA
MICHAEL GGF	SA-DRUG
MICHAEL MH	CARLCOR
MIDDLEMOST DE	PGI
MIDZI DT	HUNYANI
	ZIM NEWS
MIELKE KD	GUBINGS
MILBURN JM	HAGGIE
MILLAR JR	OVBEL
	OVCON
MILLAR TW	TIGR-OATS
MILLARD DH	PLATE-GL
MILLER LN	BERGERS
MILLER SD	SUN-BOP
MILLER LH	CLINICS
MILLING JW	ASS-MANG
	ASSORE
MILLS ANB	CBD-FUND
	PIONEER
	SAGEGRP
MILLS J	VENTEL
MILNE IF	J & F
MILWID GF	MWEAR
MINIE C	SAAMBOU
MINNIE ND	HOLDAIN
MIRSKY PJ	ZSR
MISSELHORN HJ	TONGAAT
MITCHELL AM	GRINAKER
	GRINTEK
	SILTEK
MITCHELL DH	FEDSURE
	INHOLD
MITCHELL J MRS	SUPALEK
MITCHELL JI	DIALMOV
MITCHELL T	SUPALEK
MITROVICH AW	RMBH
	SAGEGRP
MKUSHI HP	CAFCA
	ZIM NEWS
MKUSHI JP	ED ZIM
MOATSHE F	SUN-BOP
MOFFETT MJ	ENBOT
	FSC
	PEP BOT
	SECHABA
MOFFETT PJ	DATAKOR
MOHRING RP	RANDCOL
MOJA MAF MS	YABENG
MOKGETHI DN	BOTREST
MOKHOBO DNM MS	METPOL
MOKOATLE BN	STANPRO
MOLE EW	MULTI
MOLEFANE MO	BOTINS
MOLL JN	CROOKES
MOLLER CF	ELANDS
	WSTN-DEEP
MONK FJW	INTERNAT
MONTHE RW	G-I-C
MOODIE DR	TECFIN
MOOLMAN A	DOORNS
	GF-PROPS
	VENTERS
	VLAKS
MOOLMAN IJ	SA-RES-BK
	SAFETEC
MOOLMAN MN	LOGTEK
MOOLMAN TD	ARGUS
	CAXTON
	CTP
	SOLCHEM
MOON WNL	AUTOPGE
MOONDA ES	RAPTOR
MOONEY MB	FSC
MOOR B ST C MR	ROYAL
	ROYCHEM
MOOR B ST CLAIR	ROYFOOD
MOORE C	PEPKOR
	TRADHLD
MOORE E	TRADGRO
MOORE RG	ANGLOVAAL
MORALEE G	BTRDUN
MORGAN DLL	CAPRI
MORKEL CT DR	BOLAND
MORLEY JW	CAPRI
	CIRCLE
	PGI
MORLEY WM	GULLIVER
MOROSS H	KH PROPS
MORRIS DR	UNISERV
MORRIS FCR	SENTRCHEM
MORRIS JRP DR	MERITEX
MORRIS K	GRESHAM
MORRIS K MR	PDC
MORRIS LR	SA-DRUG
MORRIS NJ	HLH
	HUNTCOR
	RAINBOW
	REMGRO
MORRISON A	GRINCOR
MORRISON JT	I-&-J
MORROW JK	CUSAF
MORSE GR	SENTRCHEM
MORUM GP	ISCOR
MOSELEY BL	BEARMAN
MOSER JE	FAIRCAP
MOSES EPM	BARPROP
MOSKOVITZ I	AIDA
MOSS RM	HYPERET
MOSSOP AR	SILOAK
MOSTERT DB	DORBYL
	METKOR
	REMGRO
MOSTERT DF	SASOL
MOSTERT FA	TRNSHEX
MOSTERT IB	LYD-PLAT
MOSTERT JS	ANGLOVAAL
MOSTERT PJ	ERGO
	SALLIES
MOTLANA NH	SOTHERN
MOTLANA NH DR	ADCOCK
MOTSUENYANE SM DR	BARLOWS
	FIRSTBK

N

O

P

PETERS JK	SYCOM
PETERSEN DH	MOLYSLP
PETTY R	PROSURE
PETYT PJ	ARIES
PETZSCH HJ	BOLAND
PFEDERKAEMPER WE	AF-CABLE
PFEIFFER SA	RAINBOW
PHARO AJ	BENCO
	NATRAWL
PHARO GH	NATRAWL
PHASHA MJ	LEBAKA
PHEAR SC	AGRICOR
PHELPS LS	ABS
	EQUIKOR
	WALHOLD
PHILIP RFD MR	FIDBANK
PHILLIMORE JRB	MINORCO
	Z-C-I
PHILLIPS BR	ANBEECO
PHILLIPS FD	DIDATA
PHILLIPS M	BSG
	BSI
PHILLIPS N	SAFICON
PHILLIPS RDI	TONGAAT
PHIMISTER JG	M-C-M
PHUMAPHI MP	FSC
PICCININI F DR	CONCOR
PICHANICK ALA	FSI ZIM
	TABEX
	ZIMBANK
PICK S	OCFISH
PICKARD JAJ	METPOL
	PICAPLI
	PICBEL
	SANTAM
PICKARD JAJ DR	PICHOLD
PICKARD JAJ (JNR)	PICAPLI
	PICBEL
	PICHOLD
PIENAAR A	RUSFURN
PIENAAR AJ DR	HIVELD
PIENAAR AV	SBIC
PIENAAR PJ	TRNSHEX
PIENAAR SP	BINDURA
	ZIMALLOYS
PIENAAR WD PROF	INVSTEC
PIETERSMA NJ	DA-GAMA
PIETERSMA RJ	VEKTRA
PIKE EJ	SA-RES-BK
PILLAY B	BARNETS
PINSHOW L	VENTEL
PITCHFORD RA	CLUFF ZIM
PITHEY ER	SENTRCHEM
PLANTING DS	CHEMSERVE
PLATTS-MILLS JL	LONRHO
PLIT RD	ADVTECH
PLUMBRIDGE RA	DRIES
	GFSA
	KLOOF
	NORTHAM
	SBIC
PLUMMER AD	METAIR
POETSCHKE F	FENNER
POGIR R MR	PDC
POKROY EL	BRISTOL-I
POLLACK J	OCTODEC
	TOMKOR
POLOVIN GA	ACREM
POLWARTH S	RMSPROP
	SYCOM
POMMEREL W	ABERDARE
POOLE H	RENTBEL
POOLE JGW MR	UNIHOLD
POOLE PM	HUDACO
PORTER AM	PORT
PORTER D	AIDA
PORTER LA DR	NEDCOR
POSTMUS JH	SA-RES-BK
POTGIETER HJ	TELJOY
POTGIETER MG	OCFISH
POTTAS JJ	NICTUS
POULIART RJ	MACADAM
POUROULIS LC	MODDER
	STH-RODPT
PRATT M	LASER
PRESTON IMW	SUB-N
PRETORIUS AF	LONGRAIL
PRETORIUS EF	PEPGRO
	PEPKOR
PRETORIUS G	REUNERT
PRETORIUS JG	ANG-ALPHA
	OMNIA
PRETORIUS JH DR	LEPLAT
PRETORIUS MC	T-&-N
PRETORIUS Q	SOTHERN
PRETORIUS SG	TOYOTA
PRETORIUS TL	AMCOAL
	AMGOLD
	ANGLO-S
	JOHNNIES
	L-T-A
	NEW-CENT
	VAAL-REEF
PRETORIUS TL MR	PALAMIN
PRETORIUS VTK	GENTYRE-A
PRETORIUS WS	GENBEHEER
	METPOL
	SANLAND
PRICE DNJ	CARLCOR
	HOLDAIN
PRICE PD	CAPITAL
	CENPROP
PRICE RS	C-MATIC
	EUREKA
PRICE SA	NORVIC
PRINCE RS	SPICER
PRINSEP IRM	ODMHOLD
PRINSLOO LJ	CRULIFE
PRINSLOO PW	PERSKOR
PRYCE-WILLIAMS K	CMS
PRYOR E	SOTHERN
PSILLOS A MRS	SCHWEP CA
PUCCINI E	LASER
PUCHERT BF	BOLPRO
PUDNEY JP	DE BEERS
PUGH-JONES A	NBSHOLD

Q

QUIGLEY PK	GULLIVER
QUINN AM	VAAL-REEF
QUINN DG	GROWALK
QUINTON P	METPROP

R

RAATH MJ	SHOREDITS
RABB JB	WOOLTRU
RABIE JS	RABIE
RABIE J	FAIRCAP
RABIN D	ITLTILE
RABIN J	ABBEY
RABINOWITZ B	BLOCHS
RABINOWITZ BP	ABBEY

RABINOWITZ BP	DEBNAIR
	FENIX
	PROPCOR
RABINOWITZ D	BLOCHS
RABINOWITZ J	GROWPNT
	PUBHOLD
	PUBLICO
	SASFIN
	WINBEL
	WINHOLD
RABINOWITZ BP	DEBNAIR
RACTLIFFE GWJ	M&R-HLD
RADEMEYER FH	KOPP
RADEMEYER JG	HARWILL
	HICORL
RADEMEYER P DE V	BEATRIX
	BRACKEN
	BUFFELS
	KEELEY
	KELGRAN
	LESLIE
	SAMANCO
	TRANS-NTL
RADFORD RD	CONSHU
	WAYNE
RAE DA	ZIM NEWS
RAE GF	ALEXNDR
	FRALEX
RAGGETT MH	TIME
RAHMER GW	NINIAN
RAHN FJ DR	GAZGOLD
RAHN DR FJ	PETRA
RALFE GM	DE BEERS
	DEB CENT
RALLS JL	BOTREST
RALPHS L	BIDVEST
RALPHS L MR	AFRICOM
RALPHS LP	CURNOW
RALSTON NC	FP HOLD
RAMPHELE MA DR	ANGLO-S
RAMSAY AG	BINDURA
	ZIMALLOYS
RAMSAY GD	INMINS
	PLASTAL
RAMSBOTTOM R	PORT
RANKIN D	AMCOAL
	ANGLO-S
	VIERFONTN
RAPP AR	METAIR
	WESCO
RAPP CEL	CONSHU
	WAYNE
RAPP M	LIBERTY
	LIBVEST
RAPP M MR	FIT
RAPP M	LIB HOLD
RATHBONE CJL	L-T-A
RATTRAY BD	TMX
RATTRAY JS	CUSAF
RAUBENHEIMER FJ	MASONITE
RAUNER W	SIMMERS
RAUTENBACH GJ	BARNETS
RAVAZZOTTI GAM	ITLTILE
RAVENSCROFT AFB	WANKIE
RAVNO AB	CG SUGAR
RAYNAUD CR MRS	TECHIRE
RAYNER GG	MANRO
RAYNOR KA	SUNCRUSH
READ FRG	UDC
READ KL	BEARMAN
READ MWS	PLATE-GL
READ NB	RENTBEL
REDMAN PG	KNJ

REDSHAW PD	ALTRON
	FINTECH
REECE WM	DIDATA
REELER CG	ENSIGN
REES SC	LIBERTY
REES TL	MACMED
REEVES DC	DUIKERS
REEVES RE	PLASTAL
REGENBAUM H	BOYMANS
REID AS	SMART
REID DFM	BSG
REID HA	ABI
REID HR	AMCOAL
REINECKE PT	SUN-BOP
RELLY GWH	AECI
	AMIC
	ANAMINT
	ANGLO-S
	CHARTER
	DE BEERS
	DEB CENT
	SBIC
	SOTHERN
	Z-C-I
RENAULT S	GRINCOR
RENGGLI A DR	RICHEMONT
RETIEF FP PROF	SA-DRUG
RETIEF PF	ANGLO-S
	BEVCON
	JOHNNIES
	LEPLAT
	PP RUST
	PREM-GRP
	RUSPLAT
	SA-BREWS
	SBIC
	T-M-L
	TOYOTA
	WES-AREAS
REUNERT JM	CRULIFE
REYNOLDS JC	COASTAL
REYNOLDS RJ	TEDELEX
RHODES K	ADCORP
RICE KM	OHIO
RICH JA	MIDAS
RICHARDS BG DR	SEARDEL
RICHARDS PW	TSL
RICHARDS RF	MINORCO
RICHARDSON G	NEDCOR
RICHARDSON GA	NORCHART
RICHARDSON GVC	ANGLOVAAL
RICHARDSON JG	OFSIL
RICHARDSON NH	ANGLOVAAL
RICHARDSON RS	MESTORE
RICHTER J MS	AIDA
RICKETTS BG	WBHOLD
RIDDLE DM	KADOMA
RIDGWAY RK	TONGAAT
RIDLEY MT	EVHOLD
RIDSDALE FJ	ANG-ALPHA
RIECKHOFF ACJ	IMPHOLD
RIEKERT MN	KEELEY
	KELGRAN
RILEY DB	AFROX
	HOLDAIN
	MALHOLD
	MCCARTHY
	MIDAS
RILEY S	SUPRMAN
RINGO AL	MATH-ASH
	VESTCOR
RISKOWITZ PR	RUHOLD
RITCHIE CE	MINORCO

S

SPANJAARD RJW	MOLYSLP
SPENGLER RP	CLICKS
SPERBER G	MORKELS
SPERRIN J	STREBEL
SPICER PGB	LONRHO
SPINAZZE LC	FMCOTEC
SPINDLER DCB	CONSOL
SPINDLER TV	ANGLOVAAL
	E-T-CONS
	VILLAGE
SPINKS J	SOTHERN
SPRAGUE WI	CAIRNS
SPRINGETT PA	OMNIA
SPROULE GN	FSI ZIM
	GENTYRE-A
SPRUYT WF	PERSTEC
SQUIRE-HOWE RC	HIGATE
	HISTONE
ST JOHN BA	AMCOAL
	VIERFONTN
STACEY HB	AMCOAL
	VIERFONTN
STAFFELBACH UJ MR	OTIS
STAFFORD AH	AFLIFE
STAGG-MACEY I	ED-L-BATE
STANDER MCB	NORTHAM
STANFORD DMH	DISA
STANTON CL	SA-DRUG
STAPLETON K	SUNCISK
STARKE BE	BSG
	BSI
STASSEN C	CASHBIL
	PEPKOR
	SMART
	TRADGRO
	TRADHLD
STAVRAKIS N	SOPLATS
	SOWITS
STEAD R DR	ADVTECH
STEEL B	TRIMTEX
	TRIMTRD
STEEL JAD	ROTH ZIM
STEELE BP	CGS-FOOD
	CGSMITH
	LANGBRG
	TIGR-OATS
STEELE MJ	VEKTRA
STEENKAMP PMS	STANBOT
STEENKAMP TI	BRACKEN
	BUFFELS
	ENGEN
	GENCOR
	LESLIE
	WINKELS
STEGMANN JA	ABSA
STEGMANN JA DR	ALTRON
	GFSA
	REMB-BEH
	SASOL
STEIN CM	JDGROUP
STEIN GH	BOLPRO
	BOLTONS
	BOLWEAR
	CARGO
	CONFRAM
	FEDSURE
	FRAME
STEIN J	POINTER
STEIN R	MASCON
	MASHOLD
STEINGOLD NJ MR	CONTRAV
STEINMANN P	TAFLBRG
STEINMETZ G	GENBEHEER
STEINMETZ G	REMB-BEH
	SAGEGRP
STEPHENS DE	J & F
	TANGANDA
	ZECO
STEPHENS RG	FALCON
	FALGOLD
	WSGROVE
STERGIANOS T	DISA
STERLING SL	AMIC
STERN IH	OZZ
STERNBERG F	BERTRAD
STERNBERG MR	SEARDEL
STERNSLOW J	STREBEL
STEVENS BS	MESTORE
STEVENS IG	BARMINE
	BARPLAT
	BLYVOOR
	DBN-DEEP
	E-R-P-M
	HARMONY
	R-M-PROPS
	RANDCOL
	RANDMIN
STEVENS JB	UTICO
STEVENS MC	REVERE
STEVENS RHJ	TONGAAT
STEVENS WEC	MESTORE
STEVENSON BB	COPI
STEWART BV	BOTREST
STEWART DC	METAIR
STEWART J	TRANSUN
STEWART MG	MAINPRO
STEWART R	VENTEL
STEWART RW	CULLINAN
STEYGER R MR	DECOVO
STEYN CG	R-M-PROPS
STEYN CH	RIO ZIM
STEYN CJ	PEP
STEYN E	CULLINAN
STEYN IJ	PICBEL
STEYN JC THE HON	METPOL
STEYN JH	FIRSTBK
STEYN JH HON	BARLOWS
STEYN JH THE HON	ANGLO-S
STEYN JL DR	ALTECH
STEYN JP	SPESCOM
STEYN P	ABSA
	SANTAM
	UNITRAN
STEYN PC	SAFREN
STEYN PG	REMB-BEH
	REMGRO
STEYN SJ	ENGEN
STEYN W	FENNER
STEYTLER WB	ABS
STIEFEL HJ	TDL
STILL RG	RHOEX
	RHOVAN
STIRLING A	PORTHLD
STIRLING W	CARGO
STOBART GL	RIO ZIM
STOBBS JH	PORTHLD
STOHR RV	EVERITE
STOKER P	SAPPI
STOKES FJ	ALEXNDR
	FRALEX
STOLOFF W	MCPHAIL
STONEHAM GJ	DE BEERS
	DEB CENT
	ENBOT
	SECHABA
STONESTREET SJ	DA-GAMA

T

VAN DER MERWE-VANCE A	T-&-N
	TOMKOR
VAN DER PAS T	ENGEN
VAN DER POL C DR	CFC
VAN DER POST WZ	ELANDS
VAN DER ROSS BJ	SOTHERN
VAN DER ROSS RE	REMB-BEH
VAN DER SPUY MT	BOLAND
VAN DER SPUY S	SAFETEC
VAN DER VEEN WHP	R-M-PROPS
VAN DER VYVER D MS	LASER
VAN DER WALT JH	SENTRCHEM
VAN DER WALT PJJ	CHUBB
	INTELES
	SA-DRUG
	SERVGRO
	TELJOY
VAN DER WALT TJ	FOODCRP
VAN DER WALT Z	CMI
VAN DER WALT CG	PETRA
VAN DER WATT L	AFCOL
	CONSHU
	DA-GAMA
	LIONMATCH
	PLATE-GL
	ROMATEX
	SA-BREWS
VAN DER WESTHUIZEN AE	CLICKS
VAN DER WESTHUIZEN AL	OCTODEC
	TOMKOR
VAN DER WESTHUIZEN JN MR	METPOL
VAN DER WESTHUIZEN PD	KUDU
VAN DER ZWAN AJJ	BOTINS
	SOTHERN
VAN DEVENTER J	MJM
VAN DOORN CS MRS	METJE-&-Z
VAN DYK J	TEDELEX
VAN EMBDEN H	MASCON
	MASHOLD
VAN EMBDEN M	MASCON
	MASHOLD
VAN GRAAN WJJ	METKOR
VAN HEERDEN G	SERVGRO
VAN HEERDEN JJ	BAT
VAN HEERDEN TJ	WOODROW
VAN HEERDEN HHL	RAPTOR
VAN HEESCH AJA	FENIX
VAN JAARSVELD RJ	CMI
VAN JAARSVELDT C	BTRDUN
VAN KATZ A	FOCUS
VAN LEEUWEN JP	AECI
VAN LOGGERENBERG GD	PERSKOR
VAN NIEKERK GS	LYD-PLAT
VAN NIEKERK J	DISTIL
VAN NIEKERK JE	ANGLOVAAL
	BUFFELS
	E-T-CONS
	FREDDEV
	MID-WITS
VAN NIEKERK LL	METKOR
	USKO
VAN NIEKERK MD	CURNOW
VAN NIEKERK WP	GROWPNT
VAN NIEKERK JJ	DINETTE
VAN RENSBURG A	OCFISH
VAN RENSBURG JJJ	GROPROP
VAN RENSBURG JJJ MR	METPOL
VAN RENSBURG JP	WALHOLD
	WALTONS
VAN RENSBURG LJ	MOMENTUM
VAN RENSBURG PWJ	LINDUM
	PRIM-G-M
VAN RENSBURG SJJ DR	PERSBEL
VAN RENSBURG SJJ DR	PERSKOR
VAN ROOY PJ	IMPLATS
	IND-SELE
	NATSEL
	SASOL
VAN ROOYEN AC	FEDSURE
VAN ROOYEN BR	DRIES
	GFNAMIB
	GFSA
	KLOOF
VAN ROOYEN D	FARM-AG
	RALE
VAN ROOYEN J	HARWILL
VAN ROOYEN R	ALLGRP
	ALLWEAR
	HARWILL
	HICORL
	PEPGRO
	PEPKOR
	SHOPRIT
VAN ROOYEN R (JNR)	HARWILL
VAN ROOYEN R (SNR)	HICORL
VAN ROOYEN VP	SMALDEL
VAN RYNEVELD AJ	M-&-F
VAN RYSSEN JLC MR	AFRICOM
VAN STADEN EW	FEDSURE
VAN STADEN WJ	VENTEL
VAN TICHELEN AH	A-T-COLL
VAN TONDER DJ	BOLAND
VAN VEIJEREN CG	LANGBRG
VAN VUGHT LC	CHEMSERVE
VAN VUUREN MJC DR	YORKCOR
VAN WYK AH PROF	BOLAND
	DISTIL
VAN WYK AJ	GENBEHEER
VAN WYK AL	MEDCLIN
VAN WYK CJ DR	IND-SELE
	ISCOR
	NATSEL
VAN WYK J	SAPPI
VAN WYK SS	TRNSHEX
VAN WYK T	ABSA
	DORBYL
	FRALEX
	HLH
	HUNTCOR
	METKOR
	REMGRO
	SAGEGRP
	USKO
VAN WYK T ADV	GFSA
VAN WYK W	DORBYL
	ISCOR
	METKOR
VAN ZYL D	BARNETS
VAN ZYL EW	DELTA
VAN ZYL FW DR	REMB-BEH
VAN ZYL JJM	DISTIL
	SAAMBOU
VAN ZYL L	HAIB
	REVERE
VAN ZYL LS	FIRSTBK
VAN ZYL NL	FMCOTEC
VAN ZYL PA	GEFCO
	MSAULI
VANDER POL C DR	TONGAAT
VASS GS	SUNCISK
VAUX CFH	AF-CABLE
	REUNERT
VEALE HT	GROPROP
VEARY T	SPL
VELDMAN ST	SEFALANA
VELDSMAN HG	RHOEX

W

INDEX OF SUBSIDIARY AND ASSOCIATE COMPANIES

KINDLY REFER TO SCHEDULE OF COMPANY ABBREVIATIONS FOR IDENTIFICATION OF ABBREVIATIONS. THE ABBREVIATED NAMES ARE THE PARENTS OF THE COMPANIES PRINTED IN FULL

A

INDEX OF SUBSIDIARY AND ASSOCIATE COMPANIES

B

C

D

E

G

I

J

K

L

LASER PROPERTIES (KIMBERLEY) (PTY)	LASER
LASER PROPERTIES (KNYSNA) (PTY) LTD	LASER
LASER PROPERTIES (MARKMAN) (PTY)	LASER
LASER PROPERTIES (MIDRAND) (PTY)	LASER
LASER PROPERTIES (MONTAGUE GARDEN)	LASER
LASER PROPERTIES (PHILIPPI) (PTY)	LASER
LASER PROPERTIES (PORT ELIZABETH)	LASER
LASER PROPERTIES (PROSPECTON) (PTY)	LASER
LASER PROPERTIES (PTY) LTD	LASER
LASER PROPERTIES (SILVERTON) (PTY)	LASER
LASER PROPERTIES (SOUTHERN CAPE)	LASER
LASER PROPERTIES (STORMILL) (PTY)	LASER
LASER PROPERTIES (WINDHOEK) (PTY)	LASER
LASER REMOVALS (PTY) LTD	LASER
LASER TRANSPLANT SERVICES (PTY) LTD	LASER
LASERNET (PTY) LTD	SILTEK
LASERTRANS (PTY) LTD	LASER
LASM INVESTMENTS (PTY) LTD	CTP
LASMITCH SHAREBLOCK (PTY) LTD	OCTODEC
LATTICE TECHNOLOGIES (CAPE) (PTY)	DIDATA
LATTICE TECHNOLOGIES (PTY) LTD	DIDATA
LATTICE TECHNOLOGIES (TVL) (PTY)	DIDATA
LAUMAN INVESTMENTS (PTY) LTD	GROWALK
LAURSEN BROTHERS (PTY) LTD	BTRDUN
LAURSEN BROTHERS PROPERTY (PTY) LTD	BTRDUN
LAUSITZER GRAUWACKE GMBH INC.	MINORCO
LAUTREC ET CIE S.A. (PTY) LTD	UTICO
LAVINO (PTY) LTD	ANGLOVAAL
LAZFIN FINANCE (PTY) LTD	ADVTECH
LE BONHEUR WYNLANDGOED (EDMS) BPK	DISTIL
LE TIGRE SPORTSWEAR S.A. (PTY) LTD	PROGRESS
LEA BUILDINGS (PTY) LTD	AMAPROP
LEACH & BROWN HOLDINGS (PTY) LTD	ANG-ALPHA
LEADERSHIP PUBLICATIONS (PTY) LTD	T-M-L
LEAR MARKETING (PTY) LTD	REUNERT
LEARNTRON (PTY) LTD	ADVTECH
LEASECOR AFRICA (PTY) LTD	CMH
LEBOWA CANVAS WORKS (PTY) LTD	IBJOFFE
LEBOWA GRANITE (PTY) LTD	KELGRAN
LEBOWA LEATHERWORKS (PTY) LTD	IBJOFFE
LEBOWA PLATINUM MINES LTD	JOHNNIES
LEBOWA SADDLETREE (PTY) LTD	IBJOFFE
LECTROLITE (PTY) LTD	SAFICON
LECTROLITE DISTRIBUTORS (PTY) LTD	SAFICON
LECTROLITE PRODUCTS (IRELAND) LTD	SAFICON
LECTROLITE PRODUCTS (SWAZILAND) LTD	SAFICON
LEEUWENDAL NURSING HOME (PTY) LTD	MEDCLIN
LEEUWFONTEIN MYNE (EDMS) BPK	M&R-HLD
LEGAN INTERNATIONAL (PTY) LTD	PEP
LEISURE LAZE (BOPHUTHATSWANA) (PTY)	IBJOFFE
LEKNARF INVESTMENTS (PTY) LTD	TIGR-OATS
LENCA FERROUS PROCESSORS (PTY) LTD	AMIC
LENCHEN PROPERTY DEVELOPMENTS (PTY)	ABCON
LENCO (PTY) LTD	REMGRO
LENCO HOLDINGS LTD	LENVEST
LENCO PROPERTIES ATLANTIS (PTY) LTD	LENCO
LENGALE (PTY) LTD	ABI
LENNINGS LTD	JOHNNIES
LENNINGS MANGANESE LTD	JOHNNIES
LENNINGS RAIL SERVICES	L-T-A
LENNON DIAGNOSTICS (PTY) LTD	SA-DRUG
LENNON LIMITED	SA-DRUG
LENTICULAR (PTY) LTD	TOMKOR
LENTICULAR (PTY) LTD	TRADGRO
LENTON INVESTMENTS (CISKEI) (PTY)	SUNCISK
LEO DISTRIBUTIONS LTD	NEW-WITS
LEO OFFICE FURNITURE (PTY) LTD	CTP
LEON DEACON MOTORS (PTY) LTD	PORT
LEON HELFET MANUFACTURING CO (PTY)	UNIHOLD
LEON SWARTZBERG & CO. (PTY) LTD	BOUMAT
LEON TRAUB INVESTMENTS (PTY) LTD	TRADHLD
LEONARD BRUSHWARE PROPERTIES (PTY)	CAPITAL
LEPPIN PRODUCTS (PTY) LTD	LEPPIN
LERAMEL COMPANY (PTY) LTD	ELCENTR
LEROY-NOVOLAM LTD	SAPPI
LES MUST DE CARTIER FAR EAST LTD	RICHEMONT
LESEC LIFT SYSTEMS (PTY) LTD	OTIS
LESELBARY INVESTMENTS (PTY) LTD	TIGR-OATS
LESLIE COAL DEVELOPMENT CO. (PTY)	SASOL
LESLIE D. FRENKEL (PTY) LTD	CARLCOR
LESOTHO BROADCASTING (PTY) LTD	M-NET
LESOTHO COMPONENT PRODUCTS (PTY)	AMSHOE
LESOTHO DEVELOPMENT CONTRACTORS (PTY)	BASREAD
LESOTHO DOORS AND JOINERY (PTY) LTD	CERAMIC
LESOTHO FOODS CORPORATION (PTY) LTD	SCORE
LESOTHO MILLING COMPANY (PTY) LTD	CGS-FOOD
LESOTHO REINFORCING (PTY) LTD	L-T-A
LESOTHO SHOES (PTY) LTD	AMSHOE
LESOTHO STEEL (PTY) LTD	L-T-A
LESOTHO SUN (PTY) LTD	KERSAF
LETABA COPPER & ZINC CORPORATION	MID-WITS
LEVISONS STORES (PTY) LTD	BOYMANS
LEWIS & EVERITT (PTY) LTD	ANG-ALPHA
LEWIS FOSCHINI INVESTMENTS (PTY)	LEFIC
LEXPRESS DATA (PTY) LTD	MAST
LEYVAN (PTY) LTD	I-G-I
LIBANON TRANSPORT (PTY) LTD	ANG-ALPHA
LIBERTAS STEENKOOLVERSPREIDERS (PTY)	MCPHAIL
LIBERTY LIFE ASSOCIATION OF AFRICA	LIB HOLD
LIBERTY LIFE INVESTMENT TRUST LTD	LIBERTY
LIBERTY LIFE PROPERTIES (PTY) LTD	LIB HOLD
LIBHOF PROPERTY SHARE BLOCK (PTY)	PANPROP
LIBIC INVESTMENT HOLDINGS LTD	SBIC
LIBLIFE CONTROLLING CORP. (PTY) LTD	LIBVEST
LIBLIFE CONTROLLING CORPORATION (PTY)	SBIC
LIBPAC INVESTMENT HOLDINGS LTD	LIBERTY
LIBRA ASSAY LABORATORY (PTY) LTD	CONSMNG
LIBRAGEM HOLDINGS (PTY) LTD	BENCO
LIBRAGEM MINING (PTY) LTD	BENCO
LIBRARY NETWORK (PTY) LTD	T-M-L
LICHTENBURG MILLS LTD	TIGR-OATS
LIFE AND PENSIONS ASSURANCE CORPORATION	SAFLIFE
LIFEFIN SHARE BLOCK (PTY) LTD	HYPROP
LIGHTING STRUCTURES (PTY) LTD	POWTECH
LIGHTING TECHNOLOGIES (PTY) LTD	POWTECH
LIGHTS BY LIGHTS (PTY) LTD	POWTECH
LIKE NU WINDSCREENS (PTY) LIMITED	PLATE-GL
LILABE INVESTMENTS (PTY) LTD	STANPRO
LILBER (PTY) LTD	TRADGRO
LILROY PREPAK (PTY) LTD	TRADGRO
LIMIN INVESTMENTS (PTY) LTD	TRADHLD
LINDSAY SAKER (EAST RAND) (PTY) LTD	SAFICON
LINDSAY SAKER (FAR EAST RAND) (PTY)	SAFICON
LINDSAY SAKER (JOHANNESBURG NORTH)	SAFICON
LINDSAY SAKER (JOHANNESBURG) LTD	SAFICON
LINDSAY SAKER (RANDBURG) (PTY) LTD	SAFICON
LINDSAY SAKER (WEST RAND) (PTY) LTD	SAFICON
LINDSAY SAKER LTD	SAFICON
LINDSAY SAKER MOTOR HOLDINGS LTD	SAFICON
LINDUM REEFS GOLD MINING CO LTD	JOHNNIES
LININGS (NATAL) (PTY) LTD	TRIMTRD
LION APPLIANCE ENTERPRISES (PTY)	LIONMATCH
LION MATCH CO LTD	SA-BREWS
LIONS MOTORS (PTY) LTD	METJE-&-Z
LIPRON INDUSTRIAL (PTY) LTD	TOYOTA
LISHEEN ESTATES (PTY) LTD	AMAPROP
LISKEY (PTY) LTD	GYPSUM
LITERARY GROUP (PTY) LTD, THE	CNAGALO
LITET LTD	ANGLO-S
LITHO SERVICES (PVT) LTD	TSL
LITHOCORP (PTY) LTD	CTP
LITHOCRAFT (1974) (PTY) LTD	ALEXWYT
LITHOSAVER WEST RAND (PTY) LTD	LITHO
LITTLE BEAR INVESTMENTS (PTY) LTD	MORKELS
LITTLE PEOPLE (PTY) LTD	REGGIES
LIVINGSTONE FURNISHERS LIMITED	MORKELS

M

N

O

P

Q

R

S

T

U

V

W

INDEX OF SUBSIDIARY AND ASSOCIATE COMPANIES

WELLBILT PRODUCTS (PTY) LTD	INMINS
WELRO PROPERTIES (PTY) LTD	CAPITAL
WELSTATE WHOLESALE CHEMISTS (PTY)	ADCOCK
WELTEVREDEN ENTERPRISES (PTY) LTD	UNI-COLD
WELTEVREDEN PLANTATIONS (PTY) LTD	SAPPI
WEMBLEY PROPERTIES (PTY) LTD	PUTPROP
WENBER PROPERTIES (PTY) LTD	PIONEER
WENDYWOOD SHOPPING CENTRE (PTY) LTD	SYCOM
WERDA WESKUSONTWIKKELING (PTY) LTD	NICTUS
WESCARE (PTY) LTD	FIRSTBK
WESCO BESTUURSMAATSKAPPY (PTY) LTD	WESCO
WESCULES (EDMS) BPK	BESTER
WESECHOR UITGEWERS (PTY) LTD	CTP
WESEPT (PTY) LTD	TRADGRO
WESKUS MYNBOU LTD	TRNSHEX
WESMIN (EDMS) BPK	TRNSHEX
WEST CRUSHERS (PTY) LTD	ANG-ALPHA
WEST DRIEFONTEIN GOLD MINING CO.	DRIES
WEST GARDINER DEVELOPMENT (PTY) LTD	FIRSTBK
WEST RAND ENGINEERING WORKS (PTY)	OZZ
WEST SOUTH HOUSE (PTY) LTD	SAAMBOU
WEST SPAARWATER LTD	EGOLI
WEST WITWATERSRAND AREAS LTD	GF-PROPS
WEST WITWATERSRAND GOLD HOLDINGS	CONSMNG
WEST WITWATERSRAND GOLD HOLDINGS	EGOLI
WEST WITWATERSRAND GOLD HOLDINGS	SOUTHGO
WEST WITWATERSRAND GOLD MINES LTD	CONSMNG
WEST WITWATERSRAND GOLD MINES LTD	EGOLI
WEST WITWATERSRAND GOLD MINES LTD	SOUTHGO
WEST WITWATERSRAND GOLD MINES LTD	WESWITS
WEST WITWATERSRAND MINERAL & MIN.	WESWITS
WESTBRIDGE INVESTMENTS (PTY) LTD	DORBYL
WESTCHESTER TRUST (BVI)	MATH-ASH
WESTDALE GARDENS (PTY) LTD	DPF-INV
WESTERN CAPE AUCTIONEERS (PTY) LTD	BOLAND
WESTERN CAPE BAKERIES (PTY) LTD	PREM-GRP
WESTERN CHEMICALS CORP LTD	*ED-L-BATE*
WESTERN DEEP LEVELS LTD	ANGLO-S
WESTERN GARAGE OFS LTD	URQHART
WESTERN GOLD EXPLORATION & MINING	MINORCO
WESTERN ICH INVESTMENTS LTD	URQHART
WESTERN MACHINERY AND EQUIPMENT CO	LONRHO
WESTERN PLATINUM LTD (SA)	IMPLATS
WESTERN PLATINUM LTD (SA)	LONRHO
WESTERN PLATINUM LTD KAREE MINE DIVISIO	IMPLATS
WESTERN PLATINUM LTD KAREE MINE DIVISIO	LONRHO
WESTERN PLATINUM REFINERY LTD (SA)	LONRHO
WESTERN PROVINCE BEARINGS (PTY) LTD	HUDACO
WESTERN PROVINCE CELLARS LTD	SFW
WESTERN PROVINCE MILK PRODUCTS (PTY)	I-C-S
WESTERN PROVINCE PRESERVING CO. (PTY)	SA-BREWS
WESTERN REEFS EXPLORATION & DEVELOPMENT	VAAL-REEF
WESTERN SELECTION PLC	LONFIN
WESTERN ULTRA DEEP LEVELS LTD	AMGOLD
WESTERN ULTRA DEEP LEVELS LTD	ANGLO-S
WESTINGHOUSE BRAKE & EQUIPMENT (PTY)	M&R-HLD
WESTLIKE TRANSVAAL MOTORS EN TREKKERS	URQHART
WESTMINSTER TOBACCO CO. (CAPE & LONDON)	UTICO
WESTONARIA PHARMACY (PTY) LTD	ADCOCK
WESTRA MYNBOU (EDMS) BPK	SAPPI
WESTRIDGE (PTY) LTD	URQHART
WESTWARD TECHNOLOGIE GMBH	TMX
WESTWARD TECHNOLOGY LTD (UK)	TMX
WEUSTHOFF (SOUTH AFRICA) LTD	LENCO
WF JOHNSTONE & CO LTD	BARLOWS
WG BROWN INVESTMENTS LTD	*TIGR-OATS*
WH PRESS HOUSE LTD	I-G-I
WHEEL SHOPPING CENTRE (PTY) LTD,	MOMENTUM
WHEELS OF MAN (PTY) LTD	MIDAS
WHIMBREL INVESTMENTS (PTY) LTD	HIGATE
WHITE EYE INVESTMENTS (PTY) LTD	HIGATE
WHITE INVESTMENTS (PTY) LTD	ALEXWYT
WHITEHALL COURT (PTY) LTD	MAINPRO
WHITEHOUSE MOTORS (PTY) LTD	CMH
WHITEHOUSE PROPERTIES (GLENLEA) (PTY)	ALEXWYT
WHITEHOUSE PROPERTIES (NATAL) (PTY)	ALEXWYT
WHITEHOUSE PROPERTIES (NELSPRUIT)	ALEXWYT
WHITEHOUSE PROPERTIES (PAARL) (PTY)	ALEXWYT
WHITELODGE POULTRY FARM (PTY) LTD	TIGR-OATS
WHITWORTH ROAD PROPERTIES (PTY) LTD	PIONEER
WI VISSER (EDMS) BPK	SILOAK
WI VISSER BELEGGINGS (EDMS) BPK	SILOAK
WI VISSER KEIMOES (EDMS) BPK	SILOAK
WICKMAN MACHINE TOOLS (PTY) LTD	KNJ
WIDAH BIRD INVESTMENTS (PTY) LTD	HIGATE
WIDNEY (ZIMBABWE) (PVT) LTD	METKOR
WIELE KORPORASIE (PTY) LTD	DORBYL
WIENER BAKERY (PTY) LTD	TIGR-OATS
WIERDA ROAD SHARE BLOCK (PTY) LTD	BOEPROP
WIERDA VALLEY PLACE (PTY) LTD	ABCON
WIGANDIA (PTY) LTD	PORT
WILAN PROJECTS (PTY) LTD	TOCO
WILBARZ INVESTMENTS (PTY) LTD	WBHOLD
WILBROWN INVESTMENTS (PTY) LTD	TOMKOR
WILD ALMOND RIDGE (PTY) LTD	STOCKS
WILD RICE INVESTMENTS (PTY) LTD	UNIDEV
WILFRED MEYERSOHN & CO (PTY) LTD	PEPKOR
WILFRED MEYERSOHN TWEE (PTY) LTD	PEPKOR
WILHINT HOLDINGS (EDMS) BPK	PERSKOR
WILLANE INVESTMENTS SHARE BLOCK (PTY)	RMSPROP
WILLARD BATTERIES (NAMIBIA) (PTY)	POWTECH
WILLARDS FOODS (PTY) LTD	UTICO
WILLDALE (PRIVATE) LTD	MASHONA
WILLDALE (PRIVATE) LTD	WSGROVE
WILLIAM BAIN & CO (SA) (PTY) LTD	CEMENCO
WILLIAM HOSKEN & CO (PTY) LTD	HCI
WILLIAM WESTGATE (PTY) LTD	SCORE
WILLIAMS HUNT (PTY) LTD	VEKTRA
WILLIAMS HUNT INDUSTRIAL DISTRIBUTORS	VEKTRA
WILLIS FABER ENTHOVEN LTD	*SAFREN*
WILLOUGHBY'S CONSOLIDATED PLC (UK)	LONRHO
WILLOWS FOUR (PTY) LTD	DORBYL
WILLOWVALE ENGINEERING (PVT) LTD	MWEAR
WILLSBOROUGH PROPERTIES LTD	GROWALK
WILLSGROVE BRICK & POTTERIES LTD	CONAFEX
WILLSGROVE BRICK AND POTTERIES LTD	AFEX SA
WILLSGROVE TRANSPORT SERVICES (PRIVATE)	WSGROVE
WILSON (TOP MILL) (PTY) LTD	UTICO
WILSON COLLINS & CO (PTY) LTD	MICIND
WILSON COLLINS TRAVEL (PTY) LTD	MICIND
WINBEL MANAGEMENT SERVICES (PTY)	INMINS
WINDMILL PROPERTIES (PTY) LTD	SASOL
WINDMILL QUARRIES (PTY) LTD	ANG-ALPHA
WINDRIFTER SHARE BLOCK (PTY) LTD	KH PROPS
WINGATE HOLDINGS LTD	LOGTEK
WINHOLD INV (PTY) LTD	WINBEL
WINHOLD LTD	WINBEL
WINKELHAAK MINES LTD	GENCOR
WINTERVELD CHROME MINES LTD	SAMANCO
WINTERVELD CHROME MINES LTD	BARLOWS
WIRE ELECTRIC (TVL) (PTY) LTD	DELTA
WISPECO (PTY) LTD	METKOR
WISPECO DU VENHAGE (PTY) LTD	METKOR
WISPECO HOLDINGS (PTY) LTD	METKOR
WISPECO LTD	METKOR
WITBANK COAL HOLDINGS LTD	AMCOAL
WITBANK COLLIERY LTD	BARLOWS
WITWATERSRAND DEEP INVESTMENTS LTD	GFSA
WITWATERSRAND DEEP LIMITED	*GFSA*
WITWATERSRAND DEEP LTD	NEW-WITS
WITWATERSRAND LTD	JOHNNIES
WITWATERSRAND NIGEL LTD	CONSMNG
WITWATERSRAND NIGEL LTD	EGOLI
WITWATERSRAND NIGEL LTD	SOUTHGO
WIZARD DEVELOPMENTS (PTY) LTD	PORT
WIZARD FEATURES (EDMS) BPK	PERSKOR

X

Y

Z

INDEX OF INVESTMENTS

KINDLY REFER TO SCHEDULE OF COMPANY ABBREVIATIONS FOR IDENTIFICATION OF ABBREVIATIONS. THE ABBREVIATED NAMES HAVE INVESTMENTS IN THE COMPANIES PRINTED IN FULL

A

9,5% VEREENIGING MUNICIPAL STOCKS	AMCOAL
ABRASIVE GRIT SALES LTD	ANGLO-S
ABRASIVE GRIT SALES LTD (A SHARES)	ANAMINT
ABRASIVE GRIT SALES LTD (A SHARES)	DE BEERS
ABRASIVE GRIT SALES LTD - "A"	JOHNNIES
ABS HOLDINGS LTD	UNIDEV
ADCOCK INGRAM LTD	BARLOWS
ADCOCK INGRAM PHARMACEUTICALS LTD	BARLOWS
ADCOCK-INGRAM	COM-FUND
ADMINSENTRUM (PTY) LTD	RENTBEL
ADVANCED FOOD RESEARCH (PTY) LTD	IND-SELE
ADVANCED FOOD RESEARCH (PTY) LTD	NATSEL
ADVANCED MINING SOFTWARE LTD	FREGOLD
ADVANCED MINING SOFTWARE LTD	VAAL-REEF
AECI	COM-FUND
AECI LTD	ANGLO-S
AECI LTD	DE BEERS
AEGIS INSURANCE CO LTD	ABSA
AFCOM GROUP LTD	MICIND
AFRICAN BANK LTD	FIRSTBK
AFRICAN BANK OF SA LTD	SBIC
AFRICAN DISTILLERS LTD	DELTA ZIM
AFRICAN FEATHER WORKS (PTY) LTD	TIGR-OATS
AFRICAN GRANITE (PTY) LTD	ASSORE
AFRICAN OXYGEN LTD	HCI
AFRIKANDER LEASE LTD, THE	AMGOLD
AGRICAIR (PVT) LTD	TSL
AIB INVESTMENTS (PTY) LTD	ALTRON
ALGORAX (PTY) LTD	IND-SELE
ALGORAX (PTY) LTD	NATSEL
ALLIED BANK LTD	HCI
ALLIED ELECTRONICS CORP. LTD	ANGLO-S
ALLIED LYONS PLC	BARLOWS
ALLIED LYONS PLC	CGS-FOOD
ALLIED TECHNOLOGIES LTD	ANGLO-S
ALTERNATIVE STRATEGIES LTD	FOSTON
ALUMINIUM & TIMBER SECURITIES LTD	LONFIN
ALUSAF (PTY) LTD	IND-SELE
ALUSAF (PTY) LTD	TONGAAT
ALUSTANG (PTY) LTD	ABERDARE
ALUSTANG (PTY) LTD	ALTRON
AMALGAMATED BANK OF SA LIMITED	BRISTOL-I
AMALGAMATED BANK OF SA LIMITED	COM-FUND
AMALGAMATED BANKS OF SA LTD	HCI
AMALGAMATED BANKS OF SA LTD	REMGRO
AMALGAMATED BEEF INDUSTRIES LTD	NISWA
AMALGAMATED BEVERAGE INDUSTRIES LTD	CADSWEP
AMALGAMATED BEVERAGE INDUSTRIES LTD	TEMPORA
AMERICAN BRANDS INC.	CONAFEX
AMITY INTERNATIONALE SA (LUXEMBOURG)	SAFLIFE
ANCHUSA HOLDINGS LTD	M&R-HLD
ANDPROES (PTY) LTD	CURFIN
ANGLO ALPHA LTD	ANGLOVAAL
ANGLO ALPHA LTD	HCI
ANGLO ALPHA LTD	NATRUST
ANGLO AMERICAN (OFS) HOUSING CO.	ANGLO-S
ANGLO AMERICAN COAL CORP. LTD	COM-FUND
ANGLO AMERICAN COAL CORP. LTD	DE BEERS
ANGLO AMERICAN COAL CORP. LTD	MID-WITS
ANGLO AMERICAN COAL CORP. LTD	NEW-CENT
ANGLO AMERICAN CORP OF S.A. LTD	HCI
ANGLO AMERICAN CORP OF SA	COM-FUND
ANGLO AMERICAN CORP OF SA LTD	CONFED
ANGLO AMERICAN CORP OF SA LTD	NATRUST
ANGLO AMERICAN CORP OF SA LTD	DE BEERS
ANGLO AMERICAN CORP. OF S.A. LTD	NEW-CENT
ANGLO AMERICAN CORP. OF S.A. LTD	ZANDPAN
ANGLO AMERICAN CORP. S.A. LTD	WESCO
ANGLO AMERICAN CORP. ZIMBABWE LTD	DE BEERS
ANGLO AMERICAN CORPORATION OF SA	CFC
ANGLO AMERICAN CORPORATION OF SOUTH	AMIC
ANGLO AMERICAN CORPORATION OF SOUTH	SOTHERN
ANGLO AMERICAN CORPORATION ZIMBABWE	BASREAD
ANGLO AMERICAN FARMS LTD	OFSIL
ANGLO AMERICAN GOLD INVESTMENT	COM-FUND
ANGLO AMERICAN GOLD INVESTMENT CO.	ANGLOVAAL
ANGLO AMERICAN GOLD INVESTMENT CO.	DE BEERS
ANGLO AMERICAN GOLD INVESTMENT CO.	NEW-CENT
ANGLO AMERICAN INDUSTRIAL CORP LTD	HCI
ANGLO AMERICAN INDUSTRIAL CORP. LTD	COM-FUND
ANGLO AMERICAN INDUSTRIAL CORP. LTD	NEW-CENT
ANGLO AMERICAN INDUSTRIAL CORPORATION	DE BEERS
ANGLO AMERICAN INVESTMENT TRUST LTD	CFC
ANGLO AMERICAN INVESTMENT TRUST LTD	COM-FUND
ANGLO AMERICAN INVESTMENT TRUST LTD	CONFED
ANGLO AMERICAN INVESTMENT TRUST LTD	DE BEERS
ANGLO AMERICAN INVESTMENT TRUST LTD	HCI
ANGLO AMERICAN INVESTMENT TRUST LTD	NEW-WITS
ANGLO AMERICAN PROPERTIES LTD	DE BEERS
ANGLO PACIFIC RESOURCES PLC	MID-WITS
ANGLO-ALPHA	COM-FUND
ANGLOVAAL INDUSTRIES LTD	MID-WITS
ANGLOVAAL LTD	ASSORE
ANGLOVAAL LTD	DE BEERS
ANGLOVAAL LTD	MID-WITS
ANGLOVAAL LTD 'A'	HCI
ANGLOVAAL LTD ("N" SHARES)	NATRUST
ANGLOVAAL LTD (N ORDS)	MID-WITS
ANGLOVAAL LTD (N)	HCI
ANTWERPSE DIAMANTBANK N.V.	DEB CENT
APEX PROPERTY FUND	AMAPROP
APEX PROPERTY FUND	ANGLO-S
ARGUS HOLDINGS LTD	ANGLO-S
ASFA SERVICES (PTY) LTD	ALEXNDR
ASFA SERVICES (PTY) LTD	ALEXNDR
ASH RESOURCES (PTY) LTD	BARLOWS
ASSOCIATED MANGANESE MINES OF SA	MID-WITS
ASSOCIATED ORE & METAL CORP LTD	MID-WITS
ASSOCIATED ORE & METAL CORP. LTD	ANGLOVAAL
ATLANTIC CANNED FISH SALES (PTY)	FOODCRP
ATLANTIC CANNED FISH SALES (PTY)	NAMFISH
ATLANTIC CANNED FISH SALES (PTY)	NAMSEA
AUDIT BUREAU OF CIRCULATIONS OF SA	ARGUS
AUTOMOTIVE OVERSEAS INV (PTY) LTD	IND-SELE
AUTOMOTIVE OVERSEAS INVESTMENTS (PTY)	NATSEL

B

BALFOUR BAKERY (PTY) LTD	FOODCRP
BALFOUR BAKERY (PTY) LTD	TIGR-OATS
BANCO STANDARD TOTTA DE ANGOLA SARL	SBIC
BANCO STANDARD TOTTA DE MOZAMBIQUE	SBIC
BANK LEU FS 100 (BONS DE PART.)	CONAFEX
BANK WINDHOEK BEHEREND LTD	NICTUS
BANK WINDHOEK LTD	ABSA
BANKORP HOLDINGS LTD	IND-SELE
BARBROOK MINES LTD	AMCOAL

BARBROOK MINES LTD	AMGOLD
BARBROOK MINES LTD	BARLOWS
BARBROOK MINES LTD	DE BEERS
BARCLAYS BANK OF BOTSWANA LTD	SECHABA
BARLOW RAND	COM-FUND
BARLOW RAND LIMITED	DE BEERS
BARLOW RAND LTD	AMCOAL
BARLOW RAND LTD	ANGLO-S
BARLOW RAND LTD	BRISTOL-I
BARLOW RAND LTD	CFC
BARLOW RAND LTD	CONFED
BARLOW RAND LTD	HCI
BARLOW RAND LTD	NATRUST
BARLOW RAND LTD	NEW-CENT
BARLOW RAND LTD	SOTHERN
BARLOW RAND PROPERTIES	COM-FUND
BARNETTS GROUP LTD	PROFURN
BARPLATS INVESTMENTS LTD	LONFIN
BARPLATS MINES LTD	BARLOWS
BARPLATS MINES LTD CON DEBS	BARLOWS
BCG LIMITED	RIO ZIM
BCL LIMITED PREF	DE BEERS
BEACON ISLAND SHARE BLOCK	GRESHAM
BEATRIX MINES LTD	AMGOLD
BEATRIX MINES LTD	ANGLO-S
BEIRA CORRIDOR GROUP LTD	CIRCLE
BEISA MINES LTD	ANGLO-S
BEISA ORYX (PTY) LTD	ANGLO-S
BENACDEN (PTY) LTD	PICKNPAY
BENGUELA CONCESSIONS LTD	LYD-PLAT
BENGUELA CONCESSIONS LTD	LYDEX
BENGUELA CONCESSIONS LTD	RANDEX
BENGUELA CONCESSIONS LTD (OPTIONS)	LYD-PLAT
BENGUELA CONCESSIONS LTD (OPTIONS)	LYDEX
BENONI MILLING CO (PTY) LTD	FOODCRP
BENVOORT PROPERTIES (PTY) LTD	CURFIN
BERCON COMPONENTS CC = HEAVY DIESEL	HCI
BERZACK BROTHERS HOLDINGS LTD	INTRUST
BESTER INVESTMENTS LTD	UNIDEV
BETRAM (PTY) LTD	BARLOWS
BEVERAGE & CONSUMER INDUSTRY HOLDINGS	ANGLO-S
BEVERAGE & CONSUMER INDUSTRY HOLDINGS	DE BEERS
BID CORP LTD	HCI
BLACK MOUNTAIN MINERAL DEVELOPMENT	VOGELS
BLAJOHN MIDDELBURG PROPERTIES (PTY)	WIT-G-M
BLOCKTECH LTD	TECHIRE
BLUE CIRCLE	COM-FUND
BLUE CIRCLE LTD	HCI
BLUE CONTINENT PRODUCTS (PTY) LTD	BARLOWS
BLYVOORUITZICHT GOLD MINING CO LTD	BARLOWS
BLYVOORUITZICHT GOLD MINING CO. LTD	AMGOLD
BLYVOORUITZICHT GOLD MINING CO. LTD	RANDMIN
BM RENTALS (PTY) LTD	TELJOY
BOARD OF EXECUTORS	CFC
BOARD OF EXECUTORS LTD	LIB HOLD
BOARD PROPERTIES LINK UNITS	HCI
BOE GROWTH FUND COMMERCIAL FINANCE	BOE
BOEING CO. INC.	CONAFEX
BOLAND BANK LTD	ABSA
BOLAND BANK LTD	REMGRO
BONLEAU INVESTMENTS (PTY) LTD	RANDMIN
BOPHUTHATSWANA COMMERCIAL RADIO (PTY)	KERSAF
BOPHUTHATSWANA COMMERCIAL RADIO (PTY)	PERSKOR
BOPHUTHATSWANA COMMERCIAL RADIO (PTY)	T-M-L
BOPHUTHATSWANA COMMERCIAL RADIO (PTY)	YABENG
BOTSWANA BREWERIES (PTY) LTD	SECHABA
BOTSWANA DEVELOPMENT CORPORATION	BOTINS
BOTSWANA INSURANCE HOLDINGS	SOTHERN
BOTSWANA INSURANCE HOLDINGS LTD	SECHABA
BOTSWANA RST LTD	ANGLO-S
BOTSWANA RST LTD	CHARTER
BOTSWANA RST LTD	DE BEERS
BOTSWANA RST LTD	Z-C-I
BOUMAT LTD	NATRUST
BRACKEN MINES LTD	ANGLO-S
BRACKEN MINES LTD	GENCOR
BRACKEN MINES LTD	RANDMIN
BRACKLANDS PROPERTIES (PTY) LTD	RANDMIN
BRANDT HOLDINGS LTD RED CUM PREF	ENGEN
BRISTOL INDUSTRIAL CORPORATION LTD	PROPCOR
BROWN DAVIS & MCCORQUODALE (PTY)	BARLOWS
BROWN DAVIS & MCCORQUODALE SECURIT	BARLOWS
BRYCOL ENGINEERING (PTY) LTD	TRENCOR
BTR DUNLOP LTD	CFC
BUDGET TAINER SERVICES (PTY) LTD	TRENCOR
BUFFELSBED SHARE BLOCK LTD	ALEXNDR
BUFFELSFONTEIN GOLD MINING CO LTD	BEATRIX
BUFFELSFONTEIN GOLD MINING CO. LTD	ANGLO-S
BUFFELSFONTEIN GOLD MINING CO. LTD	GENCOR
BURLINGTON GROUP PLC	LONFIN
C	
C G SMITH FOODS LTD	IND-SELE
C G SMITH LTD	CROOKES
C G SMITH LTD	IND-SELE
C G SMITH LTD (50% ATTRIBUTABLE VIA	NATSEL
C G SMITH LTD (HELD BY IND FIN CORP	IND-SELE
C G SMITH SUGAR LTD	COM-FUND
C.G. SMITH SUGAR LTD	BRISTOL-I
CACTUS (PTY) LTD (PREFS)	BARLOWS
CACTUS INVESTMENTS (PTY) LTD	DE BEERS
CACTUS INVESTMENTS (PTY) LTD	DISTIL
CACTUS INVESTMENTS (PTY) LTD	SOUTHVAAL
CACTUS INVESTMENTS (PTY) LTD	VAAL-REEF
CACTUS INVESTMENTS (PTY) LTD (PREFS)	DE BEERS
CACTUS INVESTMENTS (PTY) LTD (PREFS)	RANDMIN
CACTUS INVESTMENTS (PTY) LTD (RED	ERGO
CACTUS INVESTMENTS (PTY) LTD (RED	FREGOLD
CACTUS INVESTMENTS (PTY) LTD (RED	PALAMIN
CACTUS INVESTMENTS (PTY) LTD RED	ENGEN
CADBURY SCHWEPPES (SA) LTD	TEMPORA
CADBURY SCHWEPPES SA LTD	HCI
CALEDON RIVIERSONDEREND CO-OPERATIVE	WBHOLD
CALGENE INC	BARLOWS
CALLIOPE HOLDINGS LTD	AMCOAL
CAPE INVESTMENT BANK HOLDINGS LTD	RANDMIN
CAPE INVESTMENT BANK LTD	BARLOWS
CAPE VERDE (PTY) LTD	AMGOLD
CAPITAL MEDIA (PTY) LTD	PERSKOR
CAPITAL SECURITIES LTD (PREFS)	BOE
CARAT INVESTMENTS LIMITED	DE BEERS
CARLTON CENTRE LTD	DE BEERS
CARWOOD & WILLIAMS (PTY) LTD	WIT-G-M
CCJ DEVELOPMENTS (PTY) LTD (VAR RATE	PEP
CEMENTATION CO (AFRICA) LTD	NEW-WITS
CENTRAL RESERVES (PTY) LTD	DE BEERS
CERAMIC INDUSTRIES LTD	I-G-I
CG SMITH FOODS	COM-FUND
CG SMITH FOODS LTD	BRISTOL-I
CG SMITH FOODS LTD	CFC
CG SMITH FOODS LTD	NATSEL
CG SMITH LTD	CFC
CG SMITH LTD	HCI
CG SMITH LTD	NATSEL
CHAMBER OF MINES BUILDING CO LTD,	VAAL-REEF
CHAMBER OF MINES OF SOUTH AFRICA	FREGOLD
CHAMBER OF MINES OF SOUTH AFRICA	FREGOLD
CHARTER CONSOLIDATED PLC	BRISTOL-I
CIMENTS DE BOURBON S.A	ANG-ALPHA
CIMENTS DE BOURBON S.A. (REUNION)	PPC
CMB NOMINEES (EDMS) BPK	E-DAGGA
CNA GALLO LTD	ANGLO-S
COASTAL CLOTHING MANUFACTURERS LTD	ACREM
COATES BROTHERS (SA)	CFC

D

E

F

G

H

I

ISCOR LTD	WIT-G-M
ITALTILE LTD	HCI
ITALTILE LTD	I-G-I

J

JD SALES (PTY) LTD (VAR RATE RED	JDGROUP
JEANETTE GOLD MINES LTD	FREGOLD
JEANNETTE GOLD MINES LTD	OFSIL
JOHANNESBURG CONSOLIDATED INVESTMENT	DE BEERS
JOHANNESBURG CONSOLIDATED INVESTMENT	HCI
JOHANNESBURG CONSOLIDATED INVESTMENT	NEW-CENT
JOHANNESBURG CONSOLIDATED INVESTMENT	CFC
JOHANNESBURG CONSOLIDATED INVESTMENT	DABI
JOHANNESBURG CONSOLIDATED INVESTMENT	M-&-F
JOHANNESBURG CONSOLIDATED INVESTMENT	NEW-CENT
JOHNSON MATTHEY	MINORCO
JUBILEE PROSPECTORS LTD	JOHNNIES

K

KANSAS CITY SOUTHERN INDUSTRIES INC.	CONAFEX
KAPEL-BELEGGINGS (PTY) LTD	SANLAND
KEELEY GROUP HOLDINGS LTD	HCI
KELGRAN LTD	GENCOR
KELGRAN LTD	HCI
KEM-BIRCH (PTY) LTD	SANLAND
KEMPSTRAAT P.E. (PTY) LTD	SANLAND
KERLIN (PTY) LTD	TOMKOR
KERSAF INVESTMENTS	COM-FUND
KHAYELIHLE HOMEMAKERS (PTY) LTD	CASHBIL
KINROSS GOLD MINING CO LTD	BARLOWS
KINROSS MINES LTD	AMGOLD
KINROSS MINES LTD	ANGLO-S
KINROSS MINES LTD	CFC
KINROSS MINES LTD	HCI
KINROSS MINES LTD	NEW-CENT
KINROSS MINES LTD	NEW-WITS
KINROSS MINES LTD	RANDMIN
KLOOF GOLD MINING CO LTD	ANGLOVAAL
KLOOF GOLD MINING CO LTD	GFSA
KLOOF GOLD MINING CO LTD (UNSECURED	GF-PROPS
KLOOF GOLD MINING CO. LTD	HCI
KLOOF GOLD MINING CO. LTD	MID-WITS
KLOOF GOLD MINING CO. LTD	AMGOLD
KLOOF GOLD MINING COMPANY LTD	BRISTOL-I
KLOOF GOLD MINING COMPANY LTD (FINANCIA	AMGOLD
KLOOF GOLD MINING COMPANY LTD (FINANCIA	CFC
KLOOF GOLD MINING COMPANY LTD (FINANCIA	GF-PROPS
KLOOF GOLD MINING COMPANY LTD (FINANCIA	HCI
KLOOF GOLD MINING COMPANY LTD (FINANCIA	MID-WITS
KLOOF GOLD MINING COMPANY LTD (FINANCIA	NEW-WITS
KNIGHTS GOLD MINING COMPANY LTD	WIT-G-M
KNJ GROUP LTD	ABSA
KROMRIVIER APPLE CO-OPERATIVE LTD	WBHOLD
KWA NOBUHLE ELECTRICITY SUPPLY CO.	GUBINGS
KWAZULU FINANCE & INVESTMENTS CORP	ENGEN

L

L & C STEINMULLER (AFRICA) (PTY)	IND-SELE
L & C STEINMULLER (AFRICA) (PTY)	NATSEL
LA RIVIERA (PTY) LTD	FREGOLD
LA RIVIERA (PTY) LTD	OFSIL
LAEVELD COOPERATIVE SOCIETY	GROWALK
LAMPREY INVESTMENT HOLDINGS LIMITED	FREGOLD
LANGEBERG HOLDINGS LTD	BARLOWS
LANGEBERG HOLDINGS LTD	WIT-G-M
LANSAN INVESTMENT HOLDINGS LTD	AMCOAL
LANSAN INVESTMENT HOLDINGS LTD	ERGO
LANSAN INVESTMENT HOLDINGS LTD	FREGOLD
LANSAN INVESTMENT HOLDINGS LTD	HIVELD
LANSAN INVESTMENT HOLDINGS LTD	OFSIL
LANSAN INVESTMENT HOLDINGS LTD	VAAL-REEF
LASPROP (PTY) LTD	LASER
LE PAS INVESTMENTS (PTY) LTD	SANLAND
LEAGUE PROPERTIES (SHARE BLOCK) (PTY)	M&R-HLD
LEAR SIEGLER INC.	CONAFEX
LEBOWA PLATINUM MINES	COM-FUND
LEBOWA PLATINUM MINES	HCI
LEBOWA PLATINUM MINES LTD	ANGLO-S
LEBOWA PLATINUM MINES LTD	DABI
LEBOWA PLATINUM MINES LTD	LYD-PLAT
LEBOWA PLATINUM MINES LTD	NEW-CENT
LENCO HOLDINGS LTD	HOLDAIN
LENCO HOLDINGS LTD	REMGRO
LESEDI CLINIC (PTY) LTD	AFROX
LESLIE GOLD MINES LTD	GENCOR
LESLIE GOLD MINES LTD	RANDMIN
LEXAN TRADING INC.	DEB CENT
LIBANON G.M. CO. LTD	DABI
LIBANON GOLD MINING CO LTD	GFSA
LIBANON GOLD MINING CO LTD	NEW-WITS
LIBANON GOLD MINING CO LTD	RANDMIN
LIBERTAS CONSOLIDATED HOLDINGS (PTY)	BASREAD
LIBERTY HOLDINGS LTD	BRISTOL-I
LIBERTY LIFE ASSOCIATION OF AFRICA	ANGLO-S
LIBERTY LIFE ASSOCIATION OF AFRICA	GFSA
LILLY (ELI) & COMPANY	CONAFEX
LIQUID AIR (PTY) LTD	MALBAK
LLG GROUP INVESTMENT (PTY) LTD	ARGUS
LOG-TEK HOLDINGS LTD	MERHLD
LONGMILE	COM-FUND
LORAINE GOLD MINES LTD	AMGOLD
LORAINE GOLD MINES LTD	ANGLOVAAL
LORAINE GOLD MINES LTD	MID-WITS
LORAINE GOLD MINES LTD	ZANDPAN
LUCAS BLOCK MINERALS LTD	RANDEX
LYDENBURG EXPLORATION LTD	FREDDEV
LYDENBURG EXPLORATION LTD	LYD-PLAT
LYDENBURG EXPLORATION LTD	RANDEX
LYDENBURG EXPLORATION LTD (OPTIONS)	FREDDEV
LYDENBURG EXPLORATION LTD (OPTIONS)	LYD-PLAT
LYDENBURG PLATINUM LTD	ANGLO-S

M

MABULA TIME SHARING SHARE BLOCK LTD	MICIND
MABULA TIMESHARING SHARE BLOCK LTD	CASHBIL
MACADAMS BAKERY SUPPLIES LTD	UNIDEV
MACMED HEALTH CARE LTD	UNIDEV
MACY (R.H.) & CO. INC.	CONAFEX
MAGALIESBURGSE GRAANKOOPERASIE BPK	IMPLATS
MAIN PLACE HOLDINGS LTD	DE BEERS
MAIN STREET PROPERTY FUND	AMAPROP
MAIN STREET PROPERTY FUND MANAGERS	FIRSTBK
MAISTER DIRECTORIES (1981) (PTY)	PERSKOR
MALBAK LTD	HCI
MALBAK LTD	NATRUST
MAPLETON TRUST	GROWALK
MAR LIMPIO LTD	FOODCRP
MARANDA MINING CO (PTY) LTD	RANDEX
MAS HOLDINGS LTD	HCI
MATABELELAND FARMERS CO-OP LTD	UNI-COLD
MAY DEPT. STORES INC.	CONAFEX
MCCARTHY GROUP LTD	ANGLO-S
MCCARTHY GROUP LTD	CFC
MCCARTHY GROUP LTD	HCI
MCCARTHY MAIN HOLDINGS LTD	ANGLO-S
MCCARTHY RETAIL LTD	BRISTOL-I
MEDICAL INVESTMENTS LIMITED	CIRCLE
MEGAMED (PTY) LTD	SA-DRUG

N

O

P

T

U

V

W

Y

Z

PART THREE

M c G R E G O R ' S

WHO OWNS WHOM

SCHEDULES

ABBREVIATIONS OF LISTED COMPANIES

ABBREV	COMPANY
A-T-COLL	ANGLO-TRANSVAAL COLLIERIES LTD
A-V-HOLD	ANGLOVAAL HOLDINGS LTD
A-V-I	ANGLOVAAL INDUSTRIES LTD
ABACUS	ABACUS INDUSTRIAL HOLDINGS LTD
ABBEY	ABBEY HOLDINGS LTD
ABCON	ABCON PROPERTIES LTD
ABERDARE	ABERDARE CABLES AFRICA LTD
ABI	AMALGAMATED BEVERAGE INDUSTRIES LTD
ABS	ABS HOLDINGS LTD
ABSA	AMALGAMATED BANKS OF SA LTD
ACREM	ACREM HOLDINGS LTD
ADCOCK	ADCOCK INGRAM LTD
ADCORP	ADCORP HOLDINGS LTD
ADONIS	ADONIS KNITWEAR HOLDINGS LTD
ADVTECH	ADVANCED TECHNICAL SYSTEMS LTD
AECI	AECI LTD
AF-&-OVER	AFRICAN & OVERSEAS ENTERPRISES LTD
AF-CABLE	AFRICAN CABLES LTD
AFCOL	ASSOCIATED FURNITURE COMPANIES LTD
AFDISTIL	AFRICAN DISTILLERS LTD
AFEX SA	AFEX CORPORATION SOCIETE ANONYME
AFLIFE	AFRICAN LIFE ASSURANCE CO LTD
AFMIN	AFMIN HOLDINGS LTD
AFR-LEASE	AFRIKANDER LEASE LTD
AFRICOM	AFCOM GROUP LTD
AFROX	AFRICAN OXYGEN LTD
AGRICOR	AGRICOR LTD
AIDA	AIDA HOLDINGS LTD
AIMARK	AIMARK HOLDINGS LTD
AKJ	ARTHUR KAPLAN JEWELLERY HOLDINGS LTD
ALEXNDR	FRASER ALEXANDER LTD
ALEXWYT	ALEX WHITE HOLDINGS LTD
ALLGRP	ALLWEAR GROUP LTD
ALLWEAR	ALLWEAR LTD
ALTECH	ALLIED TECHNOLOGIES LTD
ALTRON	ALLIED ELECTRONICS CORP. LTD
AMAPROP	ANGLO AMERICAN PROPERTIES LTD
AMCOAL	ANGLO AMERICAN COAL CORP LTD
AMGOLD	ANGLO AMERICAN GOLD INVEST CO LTD
AMIC	ANGLO AMERICAN INDUSTRIAL CORP LTD
AMREL	AMALGAMATED RETAIL LTD
AMSHOE	AMALGAMATED SHOES LTD
ANAMINT	ANGLO AMERICAN INVESTMENT TRUST LTD
ANBEECO	ANBEECO INVESTMENT HOLDINGS LTD
ANG-ALPHA	ANGLO ALPHA LTD
ANGLO-S	ANGLO AMERICAN CORPORATION OF SA LTD
ANGLOVAAL	ANGLOVAAL LTD
APEX	APEX PROPERTY FUND
ARGUS	ARGUS HOLDINGS LTD
ARIES	ARIES PACKAGING LTD
AROMA	AROMA LIQUOR HOLDINGS LTD
ART	ART CORPORATION LTD
ASS-MANG	ASSOCIATED MANGANESE MINES OF SA LTD
ASSORE	ASSOCIATED ORE AND METAL CORP LTD
AUTODEK	AUDIODEK HOLDINGS LTD
AUTOPGE	AUTOPAGE HOLDINGS LTD
AUTOQIP	AUTOQUIP GROUP LTD
AVF GRP	AVF GROUP LTD
AVINS	ANGLOVAAL INSURANCE HOLDINGS LTD
BARLOWS	BARLOW RAND LTD
BARMINE	BARPLATS MINES LTD
BARNETS	BARNETTS GROUP LTD
BARNEX	BARNATO EXPLORATION LTD
BARPLAT	BARPLATS INVESTMENTS LTD
BARPROP	BARLOW RAND PROPERTIES LTD
BASREAD	BASIL READ HOLDINGS LTD
BAT	B.A.T. ZIMBABWE LTD
BB BOT	BARCLAYS BANK OF BOTSWANA LTD

ABBREV	COMPANY
BBZIM	BARCLAYS BANK OF ZIMBABWE LTD
BEARMAN	BEARING MAN LTD
BEATRIX	BEATRIX MINES LTD
BENCO	BENGUELA CONCESSIONS LTD
BENONI	BENONI GOLD HOLDINGS LTD
BERGERS	BERGERS GROUP LTD
BERTRAD	BERGERS TRADING HOLDINGS LTD
BERZACK	BERZACK BROTHERS (HOLDINGS) LTD
BESTER	BESTER INVESTMENTS LTD
BEVCON	BEVERAGE & CONSUMER INDUSTRY HOLDINGS LT
BIDCORP	BID CORPORATION LTD
BIDVEST	BIDVEST GROUP LTD
BINDURA	BINDURA NICKEL CORPORATION LTD
BIVEC	BERZACK-ILLMAN INVESTMENT CORPORATION LT
BLOCHS	BLOCH LTD
BLYVOOR	BLYVOORUITZICHT GOLD MINING CO LTD
BOE	BOARD OF EXECUTORS LTD
BOEPROP	BOARDPROP LTD
BOLAND	BOLAND BANK LTD
BOLPRO	BOLTON PROPERTIES LTD
BOLTONS	BOLTON INDUSTRIAL HOLDINGS LTD
BOLWEAR	BOLTON FOOTWEAR LTD
BORDER	BORDER TIMBERS LTD
BOTINS	BOTSWANA INSURANCE HOLDINGS LTD
BOTREST	BOTSWANA RST LTD
BOUMAT	BOUMAT LTD
BOWCALF	BOWLER METCALF LTD
BOYMANS	BOYMANS LTD
BRACKEN	BRACKEN MINES LTD
BRENMIL	BRENNER MILLS LTD
BRISTOL-I	BRISTOL INDUSTRIAL CORP LTD
BROADACRE	BROADACRES INVESTMENTS LTD
BSG	BASIL STARKE GROUP LTD
BSI	BASIL STARKE INVESTMENTS LTD
BTRDUN	BTR DUNLOP LTD
BUFFCOR	BUFFALO CORPORATION LTD
BUFFELS	BUFFELSFONTEIN GOLD MINING CO LTD
BURLINGTN	BURLINGTON INDUSTRIES LTD
C-MATIC	COMPUTERMATIC HOLDINGS LTD
CADSWEP	CADBURY SCHWEPPES SA LTD
CAFCA	CENTRAL AFRICAN CABLES LTD
CAIRNS	CAIRNS HOLDINGS LTD
CAPITAL	CAPITAL PROPERTY FUND
CAPRI	CAPRI GROUP LTD
CAPS	CAPS HOLDINGS LTD
CARGO	CARGO CARRIERS LTD
CARLCOR	CARLTON PAPER CORP LTD
CARRIGS	CARRIG DIAMONDS LTD
CASHBIL	CASHBUILD LTD
CAXTON	CAXTON LTD
CBD-FUND	CBD PROPERTY FUND
CDC	CONSOLIDATED DIAMOND CORPORATION LTD
CEMENCO	CEMENTATION CO (AFRICA) LTD
CENMAG	CENMAG HOLDINGS LTD
CENPROP	CENTRECITY PROPERTY FUND
CERAMIC	CERAMIC INDUSTRIES LTD
CFC	COMMERCIAL FINANCE CO LTD
CG SUGAR	CG SMITH SUGAR LTD
CGS-FOOD	CG SMITH FOODS LTD
CGSMITH	CG SMITH LTD
CHARTER	CHARTER CONSOLIDATED PLC
CHEMSERVE	CHEMICAL SERVICES LTD
CHOICE	CHOICE HOLDINGS LTD
CHUBB	CHUBB HOLDINGS LTD
CIH	COMMERCIAL & INDUSTRIAL HOLDINGS LTD (ZI
CIRCLE	CIRCLE CEMENT LTD
CITYHLD	CITY INVESTMENT HOLDINGS LTD
CITYLDG	CITY LODGE HOTELS LTD

ABBREV	COMPANY
CLAW	CLAW INVESTMENT HOLDINGS LTD
CLEGG	CLEGG HOLDINGS LTD
CLICKS	CLICKS STORES LTD
CLINICS	CLINIC HOLDINGS LTD
CLUFF ZIM	CLUFF RESOURCES ZIMBABWE LTD
CLYDE	CLYDE INDUSTRIAL CORPORATION LTD
CMH	COMBINED MOTOR HOLDINGS LTD
CMI	CONSOLIDATED METALLURGICAL INDUSTRIES LT
CMS	CORPORATE MANAGEMENT SERVICES LTD
CNAGALO	CNA GALLO LTD
COASTAL	COASTAL CLOTHING MANUFACTURERS LTD
COATES	COATES BROTHERS SA LTD
COM-FUND	COMMON FUND INVESTMENT SOCIETY LTD
COMPASS	COMPASS PROPERTY HOLDINGS LTD
CON-MURCH	CONSOLIDATED MURCHISON LTD
CONAFEX	CONSOLIDATED AFEX CORPORATION SA
CONCOR	CONCOR LTD
CONFED	CONGELLA FEDERATION LTD
CONFRAM	CONSOLIDATED FRAME TEXTILES LTD
CONSHU	CONSHU HOLDINGS LTD
CONSMNG	CONSOLIDATED MINING CORPORATION LTD
CONSOL	CONSOL LTD
CONTRAV	CONCORDE TRAVEL HOLDINGS LTD
CONTROL	CONTROL INSTRUMENTS GROUP LTD
COPI	CANADIAN OVERSEAS PACKAGING INDUSTRIES L
COR-SYND	CORONATION SYNDICATE LTD
CORWIL	CORWIL INVESTMENTS LTD
CRENDEL	CRENDELL INVESTMENT CORPORATION LTD
CROOKES	CROOKES BROTHERS LTD
CROWN	CROWN FOOD HOLDINGS LTD
CRULIFE	CRUSADER LIFE ASSURANCE CORP LTD
CTP	CTP HOLDINGS LTD
CULLINAN	CULLINAN HOLDINGS LTD
CURFIN	CURRIE FINANCE CORP LTD
CURNOW	CURNOW M&G LTD
CUSAF	COMMERCIAL UNION OF SA LTD
CUTRITE	CUTRITE INVESTMENTS LTD
DA-GAMA	DA GAMA TEXTILE CO LTD
DABI	DAB INVESTMENTS LTD
DALYS	DALYS LTD
DARMAG	DARMAG LTD
DATAKOR	DATAKOR LTD
DBN-DEEP	DURBAN ROODEPOORT DEEP LTD
DE BEERS	DE BEERS CONSOLIDATED MINES LTD
DEB CENT	DE BEERS CENTENARY AG
DEBNAIR	DEBONAIR GROUP LTD
DECHOLD	DECOR INVESTMENT HOLDINGS LTD
DECOVO	DECOVO INVESTMENTS LTD
DEELKRL	DEELKRAAL GOLD MINING CO LTD
DELSWA	DELSWA LTD
DELTA	DELTA ELECTRICAL INDUSTRIES LTD
DELTA ZIM	DELTA CORPORATION LTD (ZIMBABWE)
DIALMOV	DIAL-A-MOVIE LTD
DIDATA	DIMENSION DATA HOLDINGS LTD
DIGOCO	DIGOCO MINING LTD
DINETTE	DINETTE INDUSTRIES LTD
DISA	DISA DEVELOPMENT CORPORATION LTD
DISPTCH	DISPATCH MEDIA LTD
DISTIL	DISTILLERS CORPORATION (SA) LTD
DOORNS	DOORNFONTEIN GOLD MINING CO LTD
DORBYL	DORBYL LTD
DPF-INV	DPF INVESTMENTS LTD
DRIES	DRIEFONTEIN CONSOLIDATED LTD
DUIKERS	DUIKER EXPLORATION LTD
DUKEL	LEISURE RESOURCES CORPORATION LTD
DUN ZIM	DUNLOP ZIMBABWE LTD
DW TEX	DAVID WHITEHEAD TEXTILES LTD (ZIMBABWE)
E-DAGGA	EAST DAGGAFONTEIN MINES LTD
E-R-P-M	EAST RAND PROPRIETARY MINES LTD
E-T-CONS	EASTERN TRANSVAAL CONSOLIDATED MINES LTD
ED ZIM	EDGARS STORES ZIMBABWE LTD

ABBREV	COMPANY
ED-L-BATE	EDWARD L BATEMAN LTD
EDDIES	EDDIES STORES LTD
EDGARS	EDGARS STORES LTD
EERSLNG	EERSTELING GOLD MINING CO LTD
EGOLI	EGOLI CONSOLIDATED MINES LTD
ELANDS	ELANDSRAND GOLD MINING CO LTD
ELCENTR	ELCENTRE CORPORATION LTD
ELLERINE	ELLERINE HOLDINGS LTD
ENBOT	ENGEN BOTSWANA LTD
ENGEN	ENGEN LTD
ENROL	ENVIRONMENTAL RESOURCES LTD
ENSIGN	ENSIGN CLOTHING LTD
EQUIKOR	EQUIKOR HOLDINGS LTD
ERGO	EAST RAND GOLD AND URANIUM CO LTD
EUREKA	EUREKA INDUSTRIAL LTD
EVERITE	EVERITE GROUP LTD
EVHOLD	EVERITE HOLDINGS LTD
F-S-GROUP	FS GROUP LTD
F-S-I	FSI CORPORATION LTD
FAIRCAP	FAIRCAPE HOMES LTD
FALCON	FALCON MINES PLC
FALGOLD	FALCON GOLD ZIMBABWE LTD
FARM-AG	FARM-AG LTD
FEDSURE	FEDSURE HOLDINGS LTD
FENIX	FENIX INDUSTRIES LTD
FENNER	FENNER GROUP SA LTD
FIDBANK	FIDELITY BANK LTD
FINTECH	FINTECH LTD
FIRSTBK	FIRST NATIONAL BANK HOLDINGS LTD
FIT	FIRST INTERNATIONAL TRUST LTD
FMB	FMB HOLDINGS LTD
FMCOTEC	FEMCO TECHNOLOGY HOLDINGS LTD
FOCUS	FOCUS HOLDINGS LTD
FOODCRP	FOODCORP LTD
FORIM	FORIM HOLDINGS LTD
FOSCHINI	FOSCHINI LTD
FOSTON	FOSTON LTD
FP HOLD	FP HOLDINGS LTD
FRALEX	FRALEX LTD
FRAME	FRAME GROUP HOLDINGS LTD
FREDDEV	FREE STATE DEVELOPMENT & INVESTMENT CORP
FREGOLD	FREE STATE CONSOLIDATED GOLD MINES LTD
FSC	FINANCIAL SERVICES CO OF BOTSWANA LTD
FSI ZIM	FSI HOLDINGS LTD (ZIMBABWE)
G-F-COAL	GOLD FIELDS COAL LTD
G-I-C	GOLDFIELDS INDUSTRIAL CORPORATION LTD
G5HOLD	GROUP FIVE HOLDINGS LTD
GARDIAN	GUARDIAN NATIONAL INSURANCE CO LTD
GAZGOLD	GAZANKULU GOLD HOLDINGS LTD
GDM	GDM FINANCE LTD
GEFCO	GRIQUALAND EXPLORATION & FINANCE CO LTD
GEN-OPTIC	GENERAL OPTICAL CO LTD
GENBEHEER	GENCOR BEHEREND BPK
GENBEL	GENBEL INVESTMENTS LTD
GENCOR	GENCOR LTD
GENTYRE-A	GENTYRE INDUSTRIES LTD
GF-PROPS	GOLD FIELDS PROPERTY CO LTD
GFNAMIB	GOLD FIELDS NAMIBIA LTD
GFSA	GOLD FIELDS OF SA LTD
GLODINA	GLODINA HOLDINGS LTD
GOLDSTEIN	SM GOLDSTEIN LTD
GRESHAM	GRESHAM INDUSTRIES LTD
GRINAKER	GRINAKER HOLDINGS LTD
GRINCOR	GRINDROD UNICORN GROUP LTD
GRINTEK	GRINTEK LTD
GROOTVLEI	GROOTVLEI PROPRIETARY MINES LTD
GROPROP	GROVE PROPERTY FUND
GROUP-5	GROUP FIVE LTD
GROWALK	GROVEWALK HOLDINGS LTD
GROWPNT	GROWTHPOINT PROPERTIES LTD
GUBINGS	GUBB AND INGGS LTD

ABBREV	COMPANY
GULLIVER	GULLIVER CONSOLIDATED LTD
GYPSUM	GYPSUM INDUSTRIES LTD
H & S	HADDON & SLY LTD
HAGGIE	HAGGIE LTD
HAIB	HAIB COPPER MINING & EXPLORATION INVESTM
HARMONY	HARMONY GOLD MINING CO LTD
HARTIES	HARTEBEESTFONTEIN GOLD MINING CO LTD
HARWILL	HARWILL INVESTMENTS LTD
HCI	HOSKEN CONSOLIDATED INVESTMENTS LTD
HICORL	HICOR LTD
HIGATE	HIGATE PROPERTY FUND
HIPPO	HIPPO VALLEY ESTATES LTD
HISCORE	HI-SCORE HOLDINGS LTD
HISTONE	HIGHSTONE PROPERTY FUND
HIVELD	HIGHVELD STEEL & VANADIUM CORP LTD
HLH	HUNT LEUCHARS & HEPBURN HOLDINGS LTD
HOLDAIN	HOLDAINS LTD
HORTORS	HORTORS LTD
HUDACO	HUDACO INDUSTRIES LTD
HUNTCOR	HUNTCOR LTD
HUNYANI	HUNYANI HOLDINGS LTD
HYPERET	HYPERETTE STORES LTD
HYPROP	HYPROP INVESTMENTS LTD
I-&-J	IRVIN & JOHNSON LTD
I-C-S	ICS HOLDINGS LTD
I-G-I	IGI INSURANCE CO LTD
IBJOFFE	IB JOFFE LTD
ICH	INDUSTRIAL & COMMERCIAL HOLDINGS GROUP L
IGI BOT	IGI BOTSWANA HOLDINGS LTD
ILCO	ILCO HOMES LTD
IMPERIAL	IMPERIAL GROUP LTD
IMPHOLD	IMPHOLD LTD
IMPLATS	IMPALA PLATINUM HOLDINGS LTD
INCO	INCO HOLDINGS LTD
IND-SELE	INDUSTRIAL SELECTIONS LTD
INHOLD	INVESTEC HOLDINGS LTD
INMINS	INMINS LTD
INTELES	INTERLEISURE LTD
INTERNAT	INTERNATIONAL HOLDINGS LTD
INTRUST	INVESTEC INVESTMENT TRUST LTD
INVICTA	INVICTA HOLDINGS LTD
INVSTEC	INVESTEC BANK LTD
ISCOR	ISCOR LTD
ISG	INFORMATION SERVICES GROUP LTD
ITLTILE	ITALTILE LTD
J & F	JOHNSON & FLETCHER LTD
JADE	JAFF-DELSWA INVESTMENTS LTD
JASCO	JASCO ELECTRONICS HOLDINGS LTD
JDGROUP	JD GROUP LTD
JOEL	HJ JOEL GOLD MINING CO LTD
JOHNNIES	JOHANNESBURG CONSOLIDATED INVESTMENT CO
KADOMA	KADOMA CONSOLIDATED INDUSTRIES LTD
KAROS	KAROS HOTELS LTD
KEELEY	KEELEY GROUP HOLDINGS LTD
KELGRAN	KELGRAN LTD
KERSAF	KERSAF INVESTMENTS LTD
KH PROPS	KIRCHMANN-HURRY PROPERTIES LTD
KINROSS	KINROSS MINES LTD
KLIPTON	KLIPTON LTD
KLOOF	KLOOF GOLD MINING CO LTD
KNIGHTS	KNIGHTS GOLD MINING COMPANY LTD
KNJ	KNJ GROUP LTD
KOPP	KOPP ELECTRONICS LTD
KUDU	KUDU GRANITE HOLDINGS LTD
KWV-BEL	KWV INVESTMENTS LTD
L-T-A	LTA LTD
LANCHEM	LANCHEM LTD
LANGBRG	LANGEBERG HOLDINGS LIMITED
LASER	LASER TRANSPORT HOLDINGS LTD
LEBAKA	LEBOWA BAKERIES LTD
LEEGALL	LEEGALL CLOTHING CO LTD

ABBREV	COMPANY
LEFIC	LEWIS FOSCHINI INVESTMENT CO LTD
LENCO	LENCO HOLDINGS LTD
LENVEST	LENCO INVESTMENT HOLDINGS LIMITED
LEPLAT	LEBOWA PLATINUM MINES LTD
LEPPIN	LEPPIN HOLDINGS LTD
LESLIE	LESLIE GOLD MINES LTD
LIB HOLD	LIBERTY HOLDINGS LTD
LIBANON	LIBANON GOLD MINING CO LTD
LIBERTY	LIBERTY LIFE ASSOCIATION OF AFRICA LTD
LIBVEST	LIBERTY INVESTORS LTD
LINDUM	LINDUM REEFS GOLD MINING CO LTD
LIONMATCH	LION MATCH CO LTD
LITHO	LITHOSAVER SYSTEMS LTD
LOGTEK	LOG-TEK HOLDINGS LTD
LONFIN	LONDON FINANCE AND INVESTMENT GROUP PLC
LONGRAIL	LONGRAIL LTD
LONRHO	LONRHO PLC
LONSUGR	LONRHO SUGAR CORPORATION LTD
LORAINE	LORAINE GOLD MINES LTD
LYD-PLAT	LYDENBURG PLATINUM LTD
LYDEX	LYDENBERG EXPLORATION LTD
M&R-HLD	MURRAY & ROBERTS HOLDINGS LTD
M&R-INV	MURRAY & ROBERTS INVESTMENTS LTD
M-&-F	MUTUAL & FEDERAL INSURANCE CO LTD
M-C-M	MHANGURA COPPER MINES LTD
M-NET	ELECTRONIC MEDIA NETWORK LTD
MACADAM	MACADAMS BAKERY SUPPLIES HOLDINGS LTD
MACMED	MACMED HEALTH CARE LTD
MAINPRO	MAIN STREET PROPERTY FUND
MALBAK	MALBAK LTD
MALHOLD	MALHOLD LTD
MANRO	MANRO CHEMICAL HOLDINGS LTD
MARCONS	MARSHALLS CONTROLLING INVESTMENTS LTD
MARLIN	MARLIN CORPORATION LTD
MARSHAL	MARSHALLS LTD
MASCON	MASHOLD CONSOLIDATED INV HOLDINGS LTD
MASHOLD	MAS HOLDINGS LTD
MASHONA	MASHONALAND HOLDINGS LTD
MASONITE	MASONITE (AFRICA) LTD
MAST	MAST HOLDINGS LTD
MATH-ASH	MATHIESON & ASHLEY HOLDINGS LTD
MAXMECH	MAXMECH MECHANICAL SEALS LTD
MCCARTHY	MCCARTHY GROUP LTD
MCPHAIL	MACPHAIL HOLDINGS LTD
MCRTAIL	MCCARTHY RETAIL LTD
MEDCLIN	MEDI-CLINIC CORPORATION LTD
MEDHOLD	MEDHOLD LTD
MERHLD	MERHOLD LTD
MERITEX	MERITEX HOLDINGS LTD
MERLIN	MERLIN LTD
MESSINA	MESSINA LTD
MESTORE	ME STORES HOLDINGS LTD
METAIR	METAIR INVESTMENTS LTD
METCASH	METRO CASH & CARRY LTD
METJE-&-Z	METJE AND ZIEGLER LTD
METKOR	METKOR GROUP LTD
METPOL	METROPOLITAN LIFE LTD
METPROP	METBOARD PROPERTY FUND
MICIND	MICOR INDUSTRIAL CORPORATION LTD
MICOR	MICOR HOLDINGS LTD
MID-WITS	MIDDLE WITWATERSRAND (WESTERN AREAS) LTD
MIDAS	MIDAS LTD
MIDMAC	MIDMACOR INDUSTRIES LTD
MILSTAN	MILSTAN HOLDINGS LTD
MINGRAN	MINACO GRANITE & MARBLE LTD
MINORCO	MINORCO SOCIETE ANONYME
MINVEST	MESSINA INVESTMENTS LTD
MJM	MARTIN JONKER HOLDINGS LTD
MLNHOLD	MARLIN HOLDINGS LTD
MOBILE	MOBILE INDUSTRIES LTD
MODDER	CONSOLIDATED MODDERFONTEIN MINES LTD

ABBREV	COMPANY
MOLYSLP	MOLYSLIP LTD
MOMENTUM	MOMENTUM LIFE ASSURERS LTD
MORKELS	MORKELS LTD
MSAULI	MSAULI ASBES BPK
MULTI	MULTISOURCE HOLDINGS LTD
MWEAR	MORE WEAR INDUSTRIAL HOLDINGS LTD
N-KLEINS	NK PROPERTIES LTD
NAMFISH	NAMIBIAN FISHING INDUSTRIES LTD
NAMPAK	NAMPAK LTD
NAMSEA	NAMIBIAN SEA PRODUCTS LTD
NAT TYRE	NATIONAL TYRE SERVICES LTD
NATFOOD	NATIONAL FOODS HOLDINGS LTD
NATRAWL	NATAL OCEAN TRAWLING LTD
NATRUST	NATRUST LTD
NATSEL	NATIONAL SELECTIONS LTD
NBSHOLD	NBS HOLDINGS LTD
NEDCOR	NEDCOR LTD
NEI-AFR	NORTHERN ENGINEERING INDUSTRIES AFRICA L
NEIHOLD	NEI AFRICA HOLDINGS LTD
NEW-CENT	NEW CENTRAL WITWATERSRAND AREAS LTD
NEW-WITS	NEW WITS LTD
NICTUS	NICTUS FINANSIELE INSTELLING BPK
NIGEL	NIGEL GOLD MINING HOLDINGS LTD
NINIAN	NINIAN & LESTER HOLDINGS LTD
NISWA	NISWA LTD
NORCHART	NORTHCHART INVESTMENTS LTD
NORTHAM	NORTHAM PLATINUM LTD
NORVIC	NORVIC MANUFACTURING COMPANY LTD
NUWORLD	NU-WORLD HOLDINGS LTD
O-K	OK BAZAARS (1929) LTD
OAKFLDS	OAKFIELDS THOROUGHBREDS LTD
OCEANA	OCEANA INVESTMENT CORPORATION PLC
OCFISH	OCEANA FISHING GROUP LTD
OCTODEC	OCTODEC INVESTMENTS LTD
ODMHOLD	OCEAN DIAMOND MINING HOLDINGS LTD
OFSIL	ORANGE FREE STATE INVESTMENTS LTD
OHIO	OHIO GROUP LTD
OMNIA	OMNIA HOLDINGS LTD
ORYX	ORYX GOLD HOLDINGS LTD
OSPREY	OSPREY GOLD MINE LTD
OTIS	OTIS ELEVATOR CO LTD
OVBEL	OVBEL HOLDINGS LTD
OVCON	OVCON LTD
OZZ	OZZ LTD
PAG	PAG LTD
PALAMIN	PALABORA MINING CO LTD
PALS	PALS HOLDINGS LTD
PANPROP	PANGBOURNE PROPERTIES LTD
PDC	PDC HOLDINGS LTD
PENROSE	PENROSE HOLDINGS LTD
PEP	PEP LTD
PEP BOT	PEP BOTSWANA HOLDINGS LTD
PEPGRO	PEPGRO LTD
PEPKOR	PEPKOR LTD
PERSBEL	PERSKOR BELEGGINGS BPK
PERSKOR	PERSKORGROEP BPK
PERSTEC	PERSETECH LTD
PETRA	PETRA GRANITE LTD
PGI	P G INDUSTRIES (ZIMBABWE) LTD
PICAPLI	PICARDI APPLIANCES LTD
PICBEL	PICARDI INVESTMENTS LTD
PICHOLD	PICARDI HOLDINGS LTD
PICKNPAY	PICK 'N PAY STORES LTD
PIKWIK	PICK 'N PAY HOLDINGS LTD
PIONEER	PIONEER PROPERTY FUND
PLASTAL	PLASTALL LTD
PLATE-GL	PLATE GLASS & SHATTERPRUFE INDUSTRIES LT
POINTER	POINTER FASHION INTERNATIONAL LTD
PORT	BRIAN PORTER HOLDINGS LTD
PORTHLD	PORTLAND HOLDINGS LTD
POWTECH	POWER TECHNOLOGIES LTD

ABBREV	COMPANY
PP RUST	POTGIETERSRUST PLATINUMS LTD
PPC	PRETORIA PORTLAND CEMENT CO LTD
PREM-GRP	PREMIER GROUP LTD
PREMPHARM	PREMIER PHARMACEUTICAL CO LTD
PRESMED	PRESIDENT MEDICAL INVESTMENTS LTD
PRESTO	PRESTO TRANSPORT HOLDINGS LTD
PRIM-G-M	PRIMROSE GOLD MINES LTD
PROFURN	PROTEA FURNISHERS LTD
PROGRESS	PROGRESS INDUSTRIES LTD
PROPCOR	PROPERTY CORPORATION OF SA LTD
PROPFIN	CONSOLIDATED PROPERTY & FINANCE LTD
PROSURE	PROTEA ASSURANCE CO LTD
PUBHOLD	PUBLICO HOLDINGS LTD
PUBLICO	PUBLICO LTD
PUTCO	PUTCO LTD
PUTPROP	PUTCO PROPERTIES LTD
Q-DATA	Q DATA LTD
QUAGGA	QUAGGA HOLDINGS LTD
QUICKCO	QUICK HOLDINGS LTD
QUORUM	QUORUM HOLDINGS LTD
R-M-PROPS	RAND MINES PROPERTIES LTD
RABIE	RABIE INVESTMENT HOLDINGS LTD
RACY	RACY GROUP HOLDINGS LTD
RADAR	RADAR HOLDINGS
RAINBOW	RAINBOW CHICKEN LTD
RALE	RALE HOLDINGS LTD
RANDCOL	RANDCOAL LTD
RANDEX	RANDEX LTD
RANDFONTN	RANDFONTEIN ESTATES GOLD MINING CO WITS
RANDMIN	RAND MINES LTD
RAPTOR	RAPTOR MOTOR HOLDINGS LTD
RD-LEASE	RAND LEASES (VOGELSTRUISFTN) GOLD MINING
RDC	REALESTATE DEVELOPMENT CO LTD
REGGIES	REDGWOODS HOLDING LTD
REMB-BEH	REMBRANDT CONTROLLING INVESTMENTS LTD
REMGRO	REMBRANDT GROUP LTD
RENTBEL	RENTMEESTER BELEGGINGS LTD
REUNERT	REUNERT LTD
REVERE	REVERE RESOURCES SA LTD
REX-TRUE	REX TRUEFORM CLOTHING CO LTD
RHOEX	RHOMBUS EXPLORATION LTD
RHOVAN	RHOMBUS VANADIUM HOLDINGS LTD
RICHEMONT	RICHEMONT SECURITIES AG
RIO ZIM	RIO TINTO ZIMBABWE LTD
RLPROPS	RAND LEASES PROPERTIES LTD
RMBH	RMB HOLDINGS LTD
RMSPROP	RMS PROPERTY HOLDINGS LTD
ROMANO	ROMANO FURNITURE LTD
ROMATEX	ROMATEX LTD
ROMENS	ROMENS HOLDINGS LTD
ROOIBERG	ROOIBERG TIN LTD
ROTH ZIM	ROTHMANS OF PALL MALL (ZIMBABWE) LTD
ROYAL	ROYAL CORPORATION LTD
ROYCHEM	ROYCHEM LTD
ROYFOOD	ROYAL FOODS LTD
ROYHOLD	ROYAL GROUP HOLDINGS LTD
RUHOLD	RUBENSTEIN HOLDINGS LTD
RUSFURN	RUSFURN GROUP LTD
RUSPLAT	RUSTENBURG PLATINUM HOLDINGS LTD
S-A-BIAS	SA BIAS HOLDINGS LTD
S-A-EAGLE	SOUTH AFRICAN EAGLE INSURANCE CO LTD
SA-BREWS	SOUTH AFRICAN BREWERIES LTD
SA-DRUG	SOUTH AFRICAN DRUGGISTS LTD
SA-RES-BK	SOUTH AFRICAN RESERVE BANK LTD
SAAMBOU	SAAMBOU HOLDINGS LTD
SAB IND	SA BIAS INDUSTRIES LTD
SABLE	SABLE HOLDINGS LTD
SABVEST	SABVEST LTD
SAFCOR	SOUTH AFRICAN FREIGHT CORP LTD
SAFETEC	SAFETY TECHNOLOGIES LTD
SAFICON	SAFICON INVESTMENTS LTD

ABBREV	COMPANY
SAFLIFE	SAFRICAN LIFE INVESTMENT HOLDINGS LTD
SAFREN	SAFMARINE AND RENNIES HOLDINGS LTD
SAGEGRP	SAGE GROUP LTD
SAKERS	SAKERS FINANCE AND INVESTMENT CORP LTD
SALLIES	SOUTH AFRICAN LAND & EXPLORATION CO LTD
SAMANCO	SAMANCOR LTD
SANLAND	SANLAND PROPERTY TRUST
SANLIC	SANLIC HARDWARE HOLDINGS LTD
SANTAM	SANTAM LTD
SAPPI	SAPPI LTD
SASFIN	SASFIN HOLDINGS LTD
SASOL	SASOL LTD
SBIC	STANDARD BANK INVESTMENT CORP LTD
SCHARIG	SCHARRIGHUISEN HOLDINGS LTD
SCHWEP CA	SCHWEPPE (CENTRAL AFRICA) LTD
SCOCLIK	SCORE-CLICKS HOLDINGS LTD
SCORE	SCORE SUPERMARKETS LTD
SEARCON	SEARDEL CONSOLIDATED HOLDINGS LTD
SEARDEL	SEARDEL INVESTMENT CORPORATION LTD
SECHABA	SECHABA INVESTMENT TRUST CO LTD
SECHOLD	SECHOLD LTD
SEFALANA	SEFALANA HOLDING CO LTD
SENTRCHEM	SENTRACHEM LTD
SERVGRO	SERVGRO INTERNATIONAL LTD
SFW	STELLENBOSCH FARMERS WINERY GROUP LTD
SHOCRAF	SHO-CRAFT LTD
SHOPRIT	SHOPRITE HOLDINGS LTD
SHOREDITS	SHOREDITS HOLDINGS LTD
SILOAK	SILVEROAK INDUSTRIES LTD
SILTEK	SILTEK LTD
SIMMERS	SIMMER AND JACK MINES LTD
SMALDEL	SMALDEEL COAL LTD
SMART	SMART CENTRE HOLDINGS LTD
SOLCHEM	SOLCHEM INVESTMENT HOLDINGS LTD
SONDOR	SONDOR INDUSTRIES LTD
SOPLATS	SOUTHERN PLATREEF MINING CO LTD
SOTHERN	SOUTHERN LIFE ASSOCIATION LTD
SOUDEX	SOUTH DEEP EXPLORATION CO LTD
SOUTHGO	SOUTH EAST RAND GOLD HOLDINGS LTD
SOUTHVAAL	SOUTHVAAL HOLDINGS LTD
SOWITS	SOUTHERN WITWATERSRAND EXPLORATION CO LT
SPECLTY	SPECIALTY STORES LTD
SPESCOM	SPESCOM ELECTRONICS LTD
SPICER	SPICER-MITCHELL HOLDINGS LTD
SPL	SPL LTD
SPUR	SPUR STEAK RANCHES LTD
SPURHLD	SPUR HOLDINGS LTD
ST-HELENA	ST HELENA GOLD MINES LTD
STANBOT	STANDARD CHARTERED BANK BOTSWANA LTD
STANDRD	STANDARD ENGINEERING LTD
STANPRO	STANDARD BANK PROPERTY FUND
STERLING	STERLING CLOTHING LTD
STH-RODPT	SOUTH ROODEPOORT MAIN REEF AREAS LTD
STILFTN	STILFONTEIN GOLD MINING CO LTD
STOCKS	STOCKS AND STOCKS HOLDINGS LTD
STORECO	STORECO LTD
STREBEL	STREBEL GROUP LTD
SUB-N	SUB NIGEL GOLD MINING CO LTD
SUN-BOP	SUN INTERNATIONAL (BOPHUTHATSWANA) LTD
SUNCISK	SUN INTERNATIONAL (CISKEI) LTD
SUNCRUSH	SUNCRUSH LTD
SUPALEK	SUPALEK HOLDINGS LTD
SUPREME	SUPREME INDUSTRIAL HOLDINGS LTD
SUPRMAN	SUPREME MANUFACTURING HOLDINGS LTD
SYCOM	SYFRETS & COMMERCIAL UNION PROPERTY FUND
T-&-N	T&N HOLDINGS LTD
T-E-J	TOWLES, EDGAR JACOBS LTD
T-M-L	TIMES MEDIA LTD
TA HOLD	T.A. HOLDINGS LTD
TABEX	TABEX HOLDINGS LTD
TAFLBRG	TAFELBERG FURNITURE STORES LTD
TAMBOTI	TAMBOTI PROPERTY FUND
TANGANDA	TANGANDA TEA COMPANY LTD
TARGET	TARGET EXPLORATION COMPANY LTD
TDL	TRANSVAAL DISTILLERS HOLDINGS LTD
TECFIN	TECFIN INVESTMENTS LTD
TECHIRE	TECHNIHIRE LTD
TEDCO	TEDCO LTD
TEDELEX	TEDELEX LTD
TEGKOR	TECHNICAL INVESTMENT CORP LTD
TELJOY	TELJOY HOLDINGS LTD
TEMPORA	TEMPORA INVESTMENTS LTD
TEX-MILLS	TEXTILE MILLS (1947) HOLDINGS LTD
TGH	TOLLGATE HOLDINGS LTD
TIB	TECHNICAL & INDUSTRIAL INVESTMENTS LTD
TIGR-OATS	TIGER OATS LTD
TIME	TIME HOLDINGS LTD
TITACO	TITACO CONSOLIDATED INVESTMENTS LTD
TIWHEEL	TIGER WHEELS HOLDINGS LTD
TMX	TELEMETRIX PLC
TOCO	TOCO HOLDINGS LTD
TOLUX	TOLUX SA (LUXEMBOURG)
TOMKOR	TOMKOR LTD
TONGAAT	TONGAAT-HULETT GROUP LTD
TOYOTA	TOYOTA SA LTD
TPN	TPN INVESTMENTS LTD
TRADGRO	TRADEGRO LTD
TRADHLD	TRADEHOLD LTD
TRANS-NTL	TRANS NATAL COAL CORP LTD
TRANSUN	TRANSKEI SUN INTERNATIONAL LTD
TRENCOR	TRENCOR LTD
TRIMTEX	TRIMTEX HOLDINGS LTD
TRIMTRD	TRIMTEX TRADING LTD
TRNPACO	TRANSPACO LTD
TRNSHEX	TRANS HEX GROUP LTD
TRUZIM	TRUWORTHS LTD ZIMBABWE
TSL	TSL LTD
TWEEFONTN	TWEEFONTEIN UNITED COLLERIES LTD
U-CON	U-CONTROL LTD
UDC	UDC LTD
UMDONI	UMDONI PROPERTY FUND
UNI-COLD	UNION COLD STORAGE OF SA LTD
UNICON	UNIDEV CONSOLIDATED HOLDINGS LTD
UNIDEV	UNIDEV LTD
UNIHOLD	UNIHOLD LTD
UNION	UNION MINES LTD
UNISEL	UNISEL GOLD MINES LTD
UNISERV	UNITED SERVICE TECHNOLOGIES LTD
UNISPIN	UNISPIN HOLDINGS LTD
UNITRAN	UNITRANS LTD
URQHART	URQUHART MOTOR GROUP LTD
USKO	USKO LTD
UTICO	UTICO HOLDINGS LTD
VAAL-REEF	VAAL REEFS EXPLORATION & MINING CO LTD
VALAUTO	VAALAUTO LTD
VALCAR	VAALTRUCAR LTD
VEKTRA	VEKTRA CORPORATION PLC
VENTEL	VENTER LEISURE & COMMERCIAL TRAILERS
VENTERS	VENTERSPOST GOLD MINING CO LTD
VENTRON	VENTRON CORPORATION LTD
VESTCOR	VESTACOR LTD
VETRUST	PRIMA PROPERTY TRUST
VIERFONTN	VIERFONTEIN COLLIERY LTD
VILLAGE	VILLAGE MAIN REEF GOLD MINING CO (1934)
VLAKS	VLAKFONTEIN GOLD MINING CO LTD
VOGELS	VOGELSTRUISBULT METAL HOLDINGS LTD
VOLTEX	VOLTEX HOLDINGS LTD
W-&-A	W & A INVESTMENT CORP LTD
W-R-CONS	WEST RAND CONSOLIDATED MINES LTD
WAICOR	WAICOR LTD
WALHOLD	WALTONS CONSOLIDATED INVESTMENT HOLDINGS
WALTONS	WALTONS STATIONERY CO LTD

ABBREV	COMPANY
WANKIE	WANKIE COLLIERY CO LTD (ZIMBABWE)
WAYNE	WAYNE MANUFACTURING LTD
WBHOLD	WB HOLDINGS LTD
WELKOM	WELKOM GOLD HOLDINGS LTD
WES-AREAS	WESTERN AREAS GOLD MINING CO LTD
WESCO	WESCO INVESTMENTS LTD
WESWITS	WEST WITWATERSRAND GOLD HOLDINGS LTD
WINBEL	WINBEL LTD
WINHOLD	WINHOLD LTD
WINKELS	WINKELHAAK MINES LTD
WIT-G-M	WITWATERSRAND GOLD MINING CO LTD
WIT-NIGEL	WITWATERSRAND NIGEL LTD
WOODROW	WOODROW HOLDINGS LTD
WOOLTRU	WOOLTRU LTD
WSGROVE	WILLSGROVE BRICK AND POTTERIES LTD
WSTN-DEEP	WESTERN DEEP LEVELS LTD
YABENG	YABENG INVESTMENT HOLDING CO LTD
YORKCOR	YORK TIMBER ORGANISATION LTD
Z-C-I	ZAMBIA COPPER INVESTMENTS LTD
ZANDPAN	ZANDPAN GOLD MINING CO LTD
ZECO	ZECO LTD
ZIM NEWS	ZIMBABWE NEWSPAPERS (1980) LTD
ZIM SUN	ZIMBABWE SUN LTD
ZIMALLOYS	ZIMBABWE ALLOYS LTD
ZIMBANK	ZIMBABWE BANKING CORPORATION LTD
ZIMPLOW	ZIMPLOW LTD
ZIMSPIN	ZIMBABWE SPINNERS AND WEAVERS LTD
ZSR	ZIMBABWE SUGAR REFINERS LTD

COMPANIES CATEGORISED BY SECTOR

Mining-Coal
ANGLO AMERICAN COAL CORP LTD
ANGLO-TRANSVAAL COLLIERIES LTD
GOLD FIELDS COAL LTD
RANDCOAL LTD
SMALDEEL COAL LTD
TRANS NATAL COAL CORP LTD
VIERFONTEIN COLLIERY LTD
WANKIE COLLIERY CO LTD (ZIMBABWE)

Mining-Diamonds
ANGLO AMERICAN INVESTMENT TRUST LTD
BROADACRES INVESTMENTS LTD
CARRIG DIAMONDS LTD
CONSOLIDATED DIAMOND CORPORATION LTD
DE BEERS CENTENARY AG
DE BEERS CONSOLIDATED MINES LTD
INDUSTRIAL & COMMERCIAL HOLDINGS GROUP LTD
TRANS HEX GROUP LTD

Gold-Rand & others
BENONI GOLD HOLDINGS LTD
CONSOLIDATED MODDERFONTEIN MINES LTD
DURBAN ROODEPOORT DEEP LTD
EAST RAND GOLD AND URANIUM CO LTD
EAST RAND PROPRIETARY MINES LTD
EASTERN TRANSVAAL CONSOLIDATED MINES LTD
EERSTELING GOLD MINING CO LTD
FALCON MINES PLC
GAZANKULU GOLD HOLDINGS LTD
GROOTVLEI PROPRIETARY MINES LTD
KNIGHTS GOLD MINING COMPANY LTD
LINDUM REEFS GOLD MINING CO LTD
NIGEL GOLD MINING HOLDINGS LTD
OSPREY GOLD MINE LTD
PRIMROSE GOLD MINES LTD
RAND LEASES (VOGELSTRUISFTN) GOLD MINING CO LTD
RANDFONTEIN ESTATES GOLD MINING CO WITS LTD
SIMMER AND JACK MINES LTD
SOUTH AFRICAN LAND & EXPLORATION CO LTD
SOUTH EAST RAND GOLD HOLDINGS LTD
SOUTH ROODEPOORT MAIN REEF AREAS LTD
SUB NIGEL GOLD MINING CO LTD
VILLAGE MAIN REEF GOLD MINING CO (1934) LTD
WEST RAND CONSOLIDATED MINES LTD
WITWATERSRAND NIGEL LTD

Gold-Evander
BRACKEN MINES LTD
KINROSS MINES LTD
LESLIE GOLD MINES LTD
WINKELHAAK MINES LTD

Gold-Klerksdorp
AFRIKANDER LEASE LTD
BUFFELSFONTEIN GOLD MINING CO LTD
HARTEBEESTFONTEIN GOLD MINING CO LTD
SOUTHVAAL HOLDINGS LTD
STILFONTEIN GOLD MINING CO LTD
VAAL REEFS EXPLORATION & MINING CO LTD
ZANDPAN GOLD MINING CO LTD

Gold-OFS
BEATRIX MINES LTD
FREE STATE CONSOLIDATED GOLD MINES LTD
HARMONY GOLD MINING CO LTD
HJ JOEL GOLD MINING CO LTD
LORAINE GOLD MINES LTD
ORANGE FREE STATE INVESTMENTS LTD
ORYX GOLD HOLDINGS LTD
ST HELENA GOLD MINES LTD
UNISEL GOLD MINES LTD
WELKOM GOLD HOLDINGS LTD

Gold-West Witwatersrand
BLYVOORUITZICHT GOLD MINING CO LTD
DEELKRAAL GOLD MINING CO LTD
DOORNFONTEIN GOLD MINING CO LTD
DRIEFONTEIN CONSOLIDATED LTD
ELANDSRAND GOLD MINING CO LTD
KLOOF GOLD MINING CO LTD
LIBANON GOLD MINING CO LTD
VENTERSPOST GOLD MINING CO LTD
WEST WITWATERSRAND GOLD HOLDINGS LTD
WESTERN AREAS GOLD MINING CO LTD
WESTERN DEEP LEVELS LTD

Gold-Curtailed Operations
VLAKFONTEIN GOLD MINING CO LTD
WITWATERSRAND GOLD MINING CO LTD

Metals & Minerals-Copper
BOTSWANA RST LTD
MHANGURA COPPER MINES LTD
PALABORA MINING CO LTD
ZAMBIA COPPER INVESTMENTS LTD

Metals & Minerals-Manganese
ASSOCIATED MANGANESE MINES OF SA LTD
SAMANCOR LTD

Metals & Minerals-Platinum
BARPLATS INVESTMENTS LTD
BARPLATS MINES LTD
IMPALA PLATINUM HOLDINGS LTD
LEBOWA PLATINUM MINES LTD
LYDENBURG PLATINUM LTD
MESSINA LTD
NORTHAM PLATINUM LTD
POTGIETERSRUST PLATINUMS LTD
RUSTENBURG PLATINUM HOLDINGS LTD

Metals & Minerals-Tin
ROOIBERG TIN LTD
UNION MINES LTD

Metals & Minerals-Other
CONSOLIDATED MURCHISON LTD
GRIQUALAND EXPLORATION & FINANCE CO LTD
KEELEY GROUP HOLDINGS LTD
KELGRAN LTD
KUDU GRANITE HOLDINGS LTD
MARLIN CORPORATION LTD
MARLIN HOLDINGS LTD
MINACO GRANITE & MARBLE LTD
MSAULI ASBES BPK
QUAGGA HOLDINGS LTD
RHOMBUS VANADIUM HOLDINGS LTD

Mining Financial-Mining Houses

ANGLO AMERICAN CORPORATION OF SA LTD
ANGLOVAAL HOLDINGS LTD
ANGLOVAAL LTD
CHARTER CONSOLIDATED PLC
CONSOLIDATED MINING CORPORATION LTD
GENCOR BEHEREND BPK
GENCOR LTD
GOLD FIELDS OF SA LTD
JOHANNESBURG CONSOLIDATED INVESTMENT CO LTD
RAND MINES LTD

Mining Financial-Mining Holding

AFMIN HOLDINGS LTD
ANGLO AMERICAN GOLD INVEST CO LTD
ASSOCIATED ORE AND METAL CORP LTD
CORONATION SYNDICATE LTD
DAB INVESTMENTS LTD
DUIKER EXPLORATION LTD
EAST DAGGAFONTEIN MINES LTD
EGOLI CONSOLIDATED MINES LTD
GENBEL INVESTMENTS LTD
GOLD FIELDS NAMIBIA LTD
LONDON FINANCE AND INVESTMENT GROUP PLC
MESSINA INVESTMENTS LTD
MIDDLE WITWATERSRAND (WESTERN AREAS) LTD
MINORCO SOCIETE ANONYME
NEW CENTRAL WITWATERSRAND AREAS LTD
NEW WITS LTD
RAND MINES PROPERTIES LTD
REVERE RESOURCES SA LTD
TWEEFONTEIN UNITED COLLERIES LTD
VOGELSTRUISBULT METAL HOLDINGS LTD

Mining-Exploration

BARNATO EXPLORATION LTD
BENGUELA CONCESSIONS LTD
DIGOCO MINING LTD
FOSTON LTD
FREE STATE DEVELOPMENT & INVESTMENT CORP LTD
HAIB COPPER MINING & EXPLORATION INVESTMENT CO.
LYDENBERG EXPLORATION LTD
OCEAN DIAMOND MINING HOLDINGS LTD
RANDEX LTD
RHOMBUS EXPLORATION LTD
SOUTH DEEP EXPLORATION CO LTD
SOUTHERN PLATREEF MINING CO LTD
SOUTHERN WITWATERSRAND EXPLORATION CO LTD
TARGET EXPLORATION COMPANY LTD

Financial-Banks & Financial Services

ADCORP HOLDINGS LTD
AMALGAMATED BANKS OF SA LTD
BOARD OF EXECUTORS LTD
BOLAND BANK LTD
FIDELITY BANK LTD
FIRST NATIONAL BANK HOLDINGS LTD
GDM FINANCE LTD
INVESTEC BANK LTD
INVESTEC HOLDINGS LTD
MAST HOLDINGS LTD
MERHOLD LTD
NBS HOLDINGS LTD
NEDCOR LTD
PAG LTD
QUORUM HOLDINGS LTD
SAAMBOU HOLDINGS LTD
SASFIN HOLDINGS LTD
SECHOLD LTD
SOUTH AFRICAN RESERVE BANK LTD
STANDARD BANK INVESTMENT CORP LTD
TIME HOLDINGS LTD

Financial-Insurance

AFRICAN LIFE ASSURANCE CO LTD
ANGLOVAAL INSURANCE HOLDINGS LTD
AVF GROUP LTD
COMMERCIAL UNION OF SA LTD
CRUSADER LIFE ASSURANCE CORP LTD
FEDSURE HOLDINGS LTD
GUARDIAN NATIONAL INSURANCE CO LTD
HOSKEN CONSOLIDATED INVESTMENTS LTD
IGI INSURANCE CO LTD
LIBERTY HOLDINGS LTD
LIBERTY INVESTORS LTD
LIBERTY LIFE ASSOCIATION OF AFRICA LTD
METROPOLITAN LIFE LTD
MOMENTUM LIFE ASSURERS LTD
MUTUAL & FEDERAL INSURANCE CO LTD
PROTEA ASSURANCE CO LTD
RMB HOLDINGS LTD
SAFRICAN LIFE INVESTMENT HOLDINGS LTD
SAGE GROUP LTD
SANTAM LTD
SOUTH AFRICAN EAGLE INSURANCE CO LTD
SOUTHERN LIFE ASSOCIATION LTD

Financial-Investment Trusts

COMMON FUND INVESTMENT SOCIETY LTD
CORWIL INVESTMENTS LTD
CRENDELL INVESTMENT CORPORATION LTD
FIRST INTERNATIONAL TRUST LTD
INDUSTRIAL SELECTIONS LTD
INVESTEC INVESTMENT TRUST LTD
NATIONAL SELECTIONS LTD
NATRUST LTD
TEMPORA INVESTMENTS LTD
TOLUX SA (LUXEMBOURG)
VESTACOR LTD
YABENG INVESTMENT HOLDING CO LTD

Financial-Property

ABBEY HOLDINGS LTD
BESTER INVESTMENTS LTD
BOLTON PROPERTIES LTD
BRISTOL INDUSTRIAL CORP LTD
CONGELLA FEDERATION LTD
CONSOLIDATED PROPERTY & FINANCE LTD
DISA DEVELOPMENT CORPORATION LTD
DPF INVESTMENTS LTD
EQUIKOR HOLDINGS LTD
FAIRCAPE HOMES LTD
FORIM HOLDINGS LTD
GOLD FIELDS PROPERTY CO LTD
GROVEWALK HOLDINGS LTD
MARSHALLS CONTROLLING INVESTMENTS LTD
MARSHALLS LTD
OVBEL HOLDINGS LTD
PROPERTY CORPORATION OF SA LTD
PUTCO PROPERTIES LTD
RABIE INVESTMENT HOLDINGS LTD
RICCIA PROPERTY HOLDINGS LTD
SABLE HOLDINGS LTD
SANLAND PROPERTY TRUST

TOMKOR LTD

Financial-Property Loan Stock

ABCON PROPERTIES LTD
ANGLO AMERICAN PROPERTIES LTD
BARLOW RAND PROPERTIES LTD
BOARDPROP LTD
COMPASS PROPERTY HOLDINGS LTD
GROWTHPOINT PROPERTIES LTD
HYPROP INVESTMENTS LTD
KIRCHMANN-HURRY PROPERTIES LTD
NK PROPERTIES LTD
OCTODEC INVESTMENTS LTD
PANGBOURNE PROPERTIES LTD
RAND LEASES PROPERTIES LTD
RMS PROPERTY HOLDINGS LTD

Financial-Property Trust

APEX PROPERTY FUND
CAPITAL PROPERTY FUND
CBD PROPERTY FUND
CENTRECITY PROPERTY FUND
GROVE PROPERTY FUND
HIGATE PROPERTY FUND
HIGHSTONE PROPERTY FUND
MAIN STREET PROPERTY FUND
METBOARD PROPERTY FUND
PIONEER PROPERTY FUND
PRIMA PROPERTY TRUST
STANDARD BANK PROPERTY FUND
SYFRETS & COMMERCIAL UNION PROPERTY FUND
TAMBOTI PROPERTY FUND
UMDONI PROPERTY FUND

Industrial-Industrial Holding

AFEX CORPORATION SOCIETE ANONYME
ANGLO AMERICAN INDUSTRIAL CORP LTD
ANGLOVAAL INDUSTRIES LTD
BARLOW RAND LTD
BID CORPORATION LTD
BIDVEST GROUP LTD
BOLTON INDUSTRIAL HOLDINGS LTD
BTR DUNLOP LTD
CG SMITH LTD
CONSOLIDATED AFEX CORPORATION SA
CULLINAN HOLDINGS LTD
CURRIE FINANCE CORP LTD
EUREKA INDUSTRIAL LTD
FARM-AG LTD
FS GROUP LTD
FSI CORPORATION LTD
GRINDROD UNICORN GROUP LTD
HUNT LEUCHARS & HEPBURN HOLDINGS LTD
HUNTCOR LTD
IMPERIAL GROUP LTD
IMPHOLD LTD
KLIPTON LTD
KNJ GROUP LTD
LONRHO PLC
MACPHAIL HOLDINGS LTD
MALBAK LTD
MALHOLD LTD
METJE AND ZIEGLER LTD
MICOR HOLDINGS LTD
MICOR INDUSTRIAL CORPORATION LTD
MURRAY & ROBERTS HOLDINGS LTD
MURRAY & ROBERTS INVESTMENTS LTD
NICTUS FINANSIELE INSTELLING BPK
OZZ LTD
PICARDI HOLDINGS LTD
PICARDI INVESTMENTS LTD
PLATE GLASS & SHATTERPRUFE INDUSTRIES LTD
RALE HOLDINGS LTD
RENTMEESTER BELEGGINGS LTD
RICHEMONT SECURITIES AG
ROYAL CORPORATION LTD
ROYAL GROUP HOLDINGS LTD
RUBENSTEIN HOLDINGS LTD
SA BIAS HOLDINGS LTD
SABVEST LTD
SAFICON INVESTMENTS LTD
SAFMARINE AND RENNIES HOLDINGS LTD
SAKERS FINANCE AND INVESTMENT CORP LTD
SOUTH AFRICAN FREIGHT CORP LTD
T&N HOLDINGS LTD
TECHNIHIRE LTD
TOCO HOLDINGS LTD
TOLLGATE HOLDINGS LTD
UNIDEV CONSOLIDATED HOLDINGS LTD
UNIDEV LTD
UNITED SERVICE TECHNOLOGIES LTD
W & A INVESTMENT CORP LTD
WAICOR LTD

Industrial-Beverages & Hotels

AMALGAMATED BEVERAGE INDUSTRIES LTD
BEVERAGE & CONSUMER INDUSTRY HOLDINGS LTD
CITY LODGE HOTELS LTD
DALYS LTD
DISTILLERS CORPORATION (SA) LTD
ELECTRONIC MEDIA NETWORK LTD
INTERLEISURE LTD
KAROS HOTELS LTD
KERSAF INVESTMENTS LTD
KWV INVESTMENTS LTD
OAKFIELDS THOROUGHBREDS LTD
SERVGRO INTERNATIONAL LTD
SOUTH AFRICAN BREWERIES LTD
SPUR HOLDINGS LTD
SPUR STEAK RANCHES LTD
STELLENBOSCH FARMERS WINERY GROUP LTD
SUN INTERNATIONAL (BOPHUTHATSWANA) LTD
SUN INTERNATIONAL (CISKEI) LTD
SUNCRUSH LTD
TRANSKEI SUN INTERNATIONAL LTD

Industrial-Building & Construction

ANGLO ALPHA LTD
BASIL READ HOLDINGS LTD
BASIL STARKE GROUP LTD
BASIL STARKE INVESTMENTS LTD
BOUMAT LTD
CERAMIC INDUSTRIES LTD
CONCOR LTD
EVERITE GROUP LTD
EVERITE HOLDINGS LTD
GRINAKER HOLDINGS LTD
GROUP FIVE HOLDINGS LTD
GROUP FIVE LTD
GYPSUM INDUSTRIES LTD
ILCO HOMES LTD
ITALTILE LTD
LTA LTD
MASONITE (AFRICA) LTD
OTIS ELEVATOR CO LTD
OVCON LTD
PORTLAND HOLDINGS LTD

PRETORIA PORTLAND CEMENT CO LTD
SHOREDITS HOLDINGS LTD
SM GOLDSTEIN LTD
STOCKS AND STOCKS HOLDINGS LTD
SUPREME INDUSTRIAL HOLDINGS LTD
YORK TIMBER ORGANISATION LTD

Industrial-Chemicals & Oils

AECI LTD
CHEMICAL SERVICES LTD
ENGEN LTD
MANRO CHEMICAL HOLDINGS LTD
OMNIA HOLDINGS LTD
ROYCHEM LTD
SASOL LTD
SENTRACHEM LTD
WAYNE MANUFACTURING LTD

Industrial-Clothing, Footwear & Textiles

ADONIS KNITWEAR HOLDINGS LTD
AFRICAN & OVERSEAS ENTERPRISES LTD
ALLWEAR GROUP LTD
ALLWEAR LTD
AMALGAMATED SHOES LTD
BOLTON FOOTWEAR LTD
BURLINGTON INDUSTRIES LTD
COASTAL CLOTHING MANUFACTURERS LTD
CONSHU HOLDINGS LTD
CONSOLIDATED FRAME TEXTILES LTD
CUTRITE INVESTMENTS LTD
DA GAMA TEXTILE CO LTD
DEBONAIR GROUP LTD
DELSWA LTD
ENSIGN CLOTHING LTD
FENIX INDUSTRIES LTD
FRAME GROUP HOLDINGS LTD
GLODINA HOLDINGS LTD
GUBB AND INGGS LTD
JAFF-DELSWA INVESTMENTS LTD
LEEGALL CLOTHING CO LTD
LENCO HOLDINGS LTD
LENCO INVESTMENT HOLDINGS LIMITED
MERITEX HOLDINGS LTD
NINIAN & LESTER HOLDINGS LTD
PALS HOLDINGS LTD
POINTER FASHION INTERNATIONAL LTD
PROGRESS INDUSTRIES LTD
REX TRUEFORM CLOTHING CO LTD
ROMATEX LTD
SA BIAS INDUSTRIES LTD
SEARDEL CONSOLIDATED HOLDINGS LTD
SEARDEL INVESTMENT CORPORATION LTD
SILVEROAK INDUSTRIES LTD
STERLING CLOTHING LTD
STREBEL GROUP LTD
TEXTILE MILLS (1947) HOLDINGS LTD
TOWLES, EDGAR JACOBS LTD
TRIMTEX HOLDINGS LTD
TRIMTEX TRADING LTD
UNISPIN HOLDINGS LTD

Industrial-Electronics, Electrical & Bat

ABACUS INDUSTRIAL HOLDINGS LTD
ABERDARE CABLES AFRICA LTD
ABS HOLDINGS LTD
ADVANCED TECHNICAL SYSTEMS LTD
AFRICAN CABLES LTD
ALLIED ELECTRONICS CORP. LTD
ALLIED TECHNOLOGIES LTD
ANBEECO INVESTMENT HOLDINGS LTD
AUDIODEK HOLDINGS LTD
AUTOPAGE HOLDINGS LTD
CENTRAL AFRICAN CABLES LTD
COMPUTERMATIC HOLDINGS LTD
CONTROL INSTRUMENTS GROUP LTD
CORPORATE MANAGEMENT SERVICES LTD
DARMAG LTD
DATAKOR LTD
DELTA ELECTRICAL INDUSTRIES LTD
DIMENSION DATA HOLDINGS LTD
ELCENTRE CORPORATION LTD
FEMCO TECHNOLOGY HOLDINGS LTD
FINTECH LTD
GRINTEK LTD
INFORMATION SERVICES GROUP LTD
JASCO ELECTRONICS HOLDINGS LTD
KOPP ELECTRONICS LTD
LOG-TEK HOLDINGS LTD
MULTISOURCE HOLDINGS LTD
NU-WORLD HOLDINGS LTD
OHIO GROUP LTD
PERSETECH LTD
POWER TECHNOLOGIES LTD
Q DATA LTD
REUNERT LTD
SILTEK LTD
SPESCOM ELECTRONICS LTD
SPL LTD
SUPALEK HOLDINGS LTD
TEDELEX LTD
TELEMETRIX PLC
USKO LTD
VENTRON CORPORATION LTD
VOLTEX HOLDINGS LTD

Industrial-Engineering

AFRICAN OXYGEN LTD
BERZACK BROTHERS (HOLDINGS) LTD
BERZACK-ILLMAN INVESTMENT CORPORATION LTD
BUFFALO CORPORATION LTD
CEMENTATION CO (AFRICA) LTD
CHUBB HOLDINGS LTD
CLYDE INDUSTRIAL CORPORATION LTD
DORBYL LTD
EDWARD L BATEMAN LTD
FENNER GROUP SA LTD
FRALEX LTD
FRASER ALEXANDER LTD
GOLDFIELDS INDUSTRIAL CORPORATION LTD
HAGGIE LTD
HUDACO INDUSTRIES LTD
INMINS LTD
METKOR GROUP LTD
NEI AFRICA HOLDINGS LTD
NORTHERN ENGINEERING INDUSTRIES AFRICA LTD
SAFETY TECHNOLOGIES LTD
SCHARRIGHUISEN HOLDINGS LTD
SONDOR INDUSTRIES LTD
STANDARD ENGINEERING LTD
TITACO CONSOLIDATED INVESTMENTS LTD
TPN INVESTMENTS LTD
U-CONTROL LTD
UNIHOLD LTD
WINBEL LTD
WINHOLD LTD
WOODROW HOLDINGS LTD

Industrial-Fishing

NAMIBIAN FISHING INDUSTRIES LTD
NAMIBIAN SEA PRODUCTS LTD
NATAL OCEAN TRAWLING LTD
OCEANA FISHING GROUP LTD

Industrial-Food
BRENNER MILLS LTD
CADBURY SCHWEPPES SA LTD
CG SMITH FOODS LTD
CROWN FOOD HOLDINGS LTD
FOODCORP LTD
ICS HOLDINGS LTD
IRVIN & JOHNSON LTD
LANGEBERG HOLDINGS LIMITED
LEBOWA BAKERIES LTD
MACADAMS BAKERY SUPPLIES HOLDINGS LTD
PREMIER GROUP LTD
RAINBOW CHICKEN LTD
ROYAL FOODS LTD
TIGER OATS LTD
WB HOLDINGS LTD

Industrial-Furniture & Household
AMALGAMATED RETAIL LTD
ASSOCIATED FURNITURE COMPANIES LTD
BARNETTS GROUP LTD
DECOVO INVESTMENTS LTD
ELLERINE HOLDINGS LTD
JD GROUP LTD
MATHIESON & ASHLEY HOLDINGS LTD
PICARDI APPLIANCES LTD
PROTEA FURNISHERS LTD
ROMANO FURNITURE LTD
RUSFURN GROUP LTD
SUPREME MANUFACTURING HOLDINGS LTD
TAFELBERG FURNITURE STORES LTD

Industrial-Motor
BRIAN PORTER HOLDINGS LTD
COMBINED MOTOR HOLDINGS LTD
GENTYRE INDUSTRIES LTD
LEISURE RESOURCES CORPORATION LTD
MARTIN JONKER HOLDINGS LTD
METAIR INVESTMENTS LTD
MIDMACOR INDUSTRIES LTD
TIGER WHEELS HOLDINGS LTD
TOYOTA SA LTD
URQUHART MOTOR GROUP LTD
VAALAUTO LTD
VAALTRUCAR LTD
VEKTRA CORPORATION PLC
WESCO INVESTMENTS LTD

Industrial-Paper & Packaging
AFCOM GROUP LTD
ALEX WHITE HOLDINGS LTD
ARIES PACKAGING LTD
BOWLER METCALF LTD
CANADIAN OVERSEAS PACKAGING INDUSTRIES LTD
CARLTON PAPER CORP LTD
CLEGG HOLDINGS LTD
COATES BROTHERS SA LTD
CONSOL LTD
CTP HOLDINGS LTD
HARWILL INVESTMENTS LTD
HOLDAINS LTD
HORTORS LTD
NAMPAK LTD
PLASTALL LTD
SAPPI LTD
TRANSPACO LTD

Industrial-Pharmaceutical & Medical
ADCOCK INGRAM LTD
CLINIC HOLDINGS LTD
GENERAL OPTICAL CO LTD
MACMED HEALTH CARE LTD
MEDHOLD LTD
MEDI-CLINIC CORPORATION LTD
PDC HOLDINGS LTD
PREMIER PHARMACEUTICAL CO LTD
PRESIDENT MEDICAL INVESTMENTS LTD
SOUTH AFRICAN DRUGGISTS LTD
UNION COLD STORAGE OF SA LTD

Industrial-Printing & Publishing
ARGUS HOLDINGS LTD
CAXTON LTD
DISPATCH MEDIA LTD
LITHOSAVER SYSTEMS LTD
PENROSE HOLDINGS LTD
PERSKOR BELEGGINGS BPK
PERSKORGROEP BPK
PUBLICO HOLDINGS LTD
PUBLICO LTD
SOLCHEM INVESTMENT HOLDINGS LTD
TIMES MEDIA LTD

Industrial-Retailers & Wholesalers
ACREM HOLDINGS LTD
AROMA LIQUOR HOLDINGS LTD
ARTHUR KAPLAN JEWELLERY HOLDINGS LTD
AUTOQUIP GROUP LTD
BEARING MAN LTD
BERGERS GROUP LTD
BERGERS TRADING HOLDINGS LTD
BOYMANS LTD
CASHBUILD LTD
CLAW INVESTMENT HOLDINGS LTD
CLICKS STORES LTD
CNA GALLO LTD
CONCORDE TRAVEL HOLDINGS LTD
CURNOW M&G LTD
DECOR INVESTMENT HOLDINGS LTD
DIAL-A-MOVIE LTD
EDDIES STORES LTD
EDGARS STORES LTD
FOCUS HOLDINGS LTD
FOSCHINI LTD
GRESHAM INDUSTRIES LTD
HI-SCORE HOLDINGS LTD
HICOR LTD
IB JOFFE LTD
LEWIS FOSCHINI INVESTMENT CO LTD
MAS HOLDINGS LTD
MASHOLD CONSOLIDATED INV HOLDINGS LTD
MCCARTHY GROUP LTD
MCCARTHY RETAIL LTD
METRO CASH & CARRY LTD
MIDAS LTD
MILSTAN HOLDINGS LTD
MORKELS LTD
OCEANA INVESTMENT CORPORATION PLC
OK BAZAARS (1929) LTD
PEP LTD

PEPGRO LTD
PEPKOR LTD
PICK 'N PAY HOLDINGS LTD
PICK 'N PAY STORES LTD
REDGWOODS HOLDING LTD
SANLIC HARDWARE HOLDINGS LTD
SCORE SUPERMARKETS LTD
SCORE-CLICKS HOLDINGS LTD
SHOPRITE HOLDINGS LTD
SMART CENTRE HOLDINGS LTD
SPECIALTY STORES LTD
STORECO LTD
TELJOY HOLDINGS LTD
TRADEGRO LTD
TRADEHOLD LTD
WALTONS CONSOLIDATED INVESTMENT HOLDINGS LTD
WALTONS STATIONERY CO LTD
WOOLTRU LTD

Industrial-Steel & Allied

CONSOLIDATED METALLURGICAL INDUSTRIES LTD
HIGHVELD STEEL & VANADIUM CORP LTD
ISCOR LTD

Industrial-Sugar

CG SMITH SUGAR LTD
CROOKES BROTHERS LTD
LONRHO SUGAR CORPORATION LTD
TONGAAT-HULETT GROUP LTD

Industrial-Tobacco & Match

LION MATCH CO LTD
REMBRANDT CONTROLLING INVESTMENTS LTD
REMBRANDT GROUP LTD
TECHNICAL & INDUSTRIAL INVESTMENTS LTD
TECHNICAL INVESTMENT CORP LTD
UTICO HOLDINGS LTD

Industrial-Transportation

CARGO CARRIERS LTD
LASER TRANSPORT HOLDINGS LTD
LONGRAIL LTD
MOBILE INDUSTRIES LTD
PRESTO TRANSPORT HOLDINGS LTD
PUTCO LTD
RACY GROUP HOLDINGS LTD
TRENCOR LTD
UNITRANS LTD
VENTER LEISURE & COMMERCIAL TRAILERS

Development Capital Market

AIDA HOLDINGS LTD
AIMARK HOLDINGS LTD
BLOCH LTD
CENMAG HOLDINGS LTD
CHOICE HOLDINGS LTD
CITY INVESTMENT HOLDINGS LTD
COMMERCIAL FINANCE CO LTD
ENVIRONMENTAL RESOURCES LTD
HYPERETTE STORES LTD
INVICTA HOLDINGS LTD
LANCHEM LTD
LEPPIN HOLDINGS LTD
MAXMECH MECHANICAL SEALS LTD
ME STORES HOLDINGS LTD
MOLYSLIP LTD
NISWA LTD
NORVIC MANUFACTURING COMPANY LTD
PETRA GRANITE LTD
QUICK HOLDINGS LTD
RAPTOR MOTOR HOLDINGS LTD
ROMENS HOLDINGS LTD
SHO-CRAFT LTD
SPICER-MITCHELL HOLDINGS LTD
TRANSVAAL DISTILLERS HOLDINGS LTD

Venture Capital Market

DINETTE INDUSTRIES LTD
TECFIN INVESTMENTS LTD

Botswana Stock Exchange

BARCLAYS BANK OF BOTSWANA LTD
BOTSWANA INSURANCE HOLDINGS LTD
ENGEN BOTSWANA LTD
FINANCIAL SERVICES CO OF BOTSWANA LTD
IGI BOTSWANA HOLDINGS LTD
INCO HOLDINGS LTD
PEP BOTSWANA HOLDINGS LTD
REALESTATE DEVELOPMENT CO LTD
SECHABA INVESTMENT TRUST CO LTD
SEFALANA HOLDING CO LTD
STANDARD CHARTERED BANK BOTSWANA LTD

Namibian Stock Exchange

NAMIBIAN FISHING INDUSTRIES LTD
NAMIBIAN SEA PRODUCTS LTD
NICTUS FINANSIELE INSTELLING BPK
STANDARD BANK INVESTMENT CORP LTD

Zimbabwe Stock Exchange

AFRICAN DISTILLERS LTD
AGRICOR LTD
APEX CORPORATION OF ZIMBABWE LTD
ART CORPORATION LTD
B.A.T. ZIMBABWE LTD
BARCLAYS BANK OF ZIMBABWE LTD
BINDURA NICKEL CORPORATION LTD
BORDER TIMBERS LTD
CAIRNS HOLDINGS LTD
CAPRI GROUP LTD
CAPS HOLDINGS LTD
CENTRAL AFRICAN CABLES LTD
CIRCLE CEMENT LTD
CLUFF RESOURCES ZIMBABWE LTD
COMMERCIAL & INDUSTRIAL HOLDINGS LTD (ZIMBABWE)
DAVID WHITEHEAD TEXTILES LTD (ZIMBABWE)
DELTA CORPORATION LTD (ZIMBABWE)
DUNLOP ZIMBABWE LTD
EDGARS STORES ZIMBABWE LTD
FALCON GOLD ZIMBABWE LTD
FALCON MINES PLC
FMB HOLDINGS LTD
FP HOLDINGS LTD
FSI HOLDINGS LTD (ZIMBABWE)
GULLIVER CONSOLIDATED LTD
HADDON & SLY LTD
HIPPO VALLEY ESTATES LTD
HUNYANI HOLDINGS LTD
INTERNATIONAL HOLDINGS LTD
JOHNSON & FLETCHER LTD
KADOMA CONSOLIDATED INDUSTRIES LTD
MASHONALAND HOLDINGS LTD
MERLIN LTD
MHANGURA COPPER MINES LTD
MORE WEAR INDUSTRIAL HOLDINGS LTD
NATIONAL FOODS HOLDINGS LTD

NATIONAL TYRE SERVICES LTD
NORTHCHART INVESTMENTS LTD
P G INDUSTRIES (ZIMBABWE) LTD
PORTLAND HOLDINGS LTD
RADAR HOLDINGS
RIO TINTO ZIMBABWE LTD
ROTHMANS OF PALL MALL (ZIMBABWE) LTD
SCHWEPPE (CENTRAL AFRICA) LTD
T.A. HOLDINGS LTD
TABEX HOLDINGS LTD
TANGANDA TEA COMPANY LTD
TEDCO LTD
TRUWORTHS LTD ZIMBABWE
TSL LTD
UDC LTD
WANKIE COLLIERY CO LTD (ZIMBABWE)
WILLSGROVE BRICK AND POTTERIES LTD
ZECO LTD
ZIMBABWE ALLOYS LTD
ZIMBABWE BANKING CORPORATION LTD
ZIMBABWE NEWSPAPERS (1980) LTD
ZIMBABWE SPINNERS AND WEAVERS LTD
ZIMBABWE SUGAR REFINERS LTD
ZIMBABWE SUN LTD
ZIMPLOW LTD

COMPANIES LISTED BY FINANCIAL YEAR END

January
MERITEX

February
ABCON
ADVTECH
AIDA
AKJ
ALLGRP
ALLWEAR
ALTECH
ALTRON
AMSHOE
AROMA
AUTOPGE
BESTER
BOLPRO
BOLTONS
BOLWEAR
BOYMANS
BRENMIL
BRISTOL-I
C-MATIC
CARGO
CENMAG
CERAMIC
CHOICE
CLAW
CLYDE
CMH
COASTAL
CUTRITE
DIGOCO
EDDIES
EUREKA
FINTECH
FORIM
GROPROP
H & S
HICORL
JASCO
KEELEY
KELGRAN
LENCO
LENVEST
LIBVEST
LITHO
LONGRAIL
MACADAM
MASCON
MASHOLD
MAST
MAXMECH
MIDAS
MILSTAN
MJM
MOLYSLP
MULTI
NISWA
OHIO
PAG
PEP
PEP BOT
PEPGRO
PEPKOR
PICKNPAY
PIKWIK
POWTECH
PRESMED
PROPFIN
PUBHOLD
PUBLICO
QUAGGA
QUORUM
RALE
REGGIES
REVERE
RUHOLD
SAPPI
SHOCRAF
SHOPRIT
SMART
SOPLATS
SOWITS
SPECLTY
SPICER
SPL
SPUR
SPURHLD
STORECO
TAFLBRG
TDL
TECFIN
TITACO
TOMKOR
TRADGRO
TRADHLD
UNISERV
VALAUTO.
VALCAR
VENTRON
WALHOLD
WALTONS
WANKIE
WOODROW
ZECO

March
ABACUS
ABI
ABSA
ACREM
AFCOL
AFDISTIL
AFLIFE
AMAPROP
AMCOAL
AMGOLD
AMREL
ANAMINT
ANGLO-S
APEX
ARGUS
BENONI
BEVCON
BOLAND
BOUMAT
CAPS
CARRIGS
CAXTON
CBD-FUND
CHARTER
CHUBB
CNAGALO
COM-FUND
COMPASS
CONSMNG
CONTRAV
CORWIL
CRENDEL
CROOKES
CTP
DA-GAMA
DARMAG
DATAKOR
DELTA ZIM
E-DAGGA
EDGARS
EGOLI
ERGO
FALCON
FALGOLD
FOSCHINI
FREGOLD
G-I-C
GAZGOLD
GULLIVER
HCI
HIPPO
HLH
HORTORS
HUNTCOR
I-G-I
IGI BOT
INHOLD
INTRUST
INVSTEC
J & F
KAROS
L-T-A
LEEGALL
LEFIC
LIONMATCH
LONSUGR
M-NET
MAINPRO
MASHONA
MEDCLIN
METPROP
MOMENTUM
MORKELS
NATFOOD
NBSHOLD
NEW-CENT
NIGEL
O-K
OCEANA
ODMHOLD
OFSIL
OVBEL
OVCON
OZZ
PGI
PIONEER
PLATE-GL
RACY
RAINBOW
REMB-BEH
REMGRO

RICHEMONT
ROTH ZIM
SA-BREWS
SA-RES-BK
SAAMBOU
SAFICON
SAFLIFE
SAGEGRP
SAKERS
SERVGRO
SOLCHEM
SONDOR
SOTHERN
SOUTHGO
T-M-L
TABEX
TEGKOR
TELJOY
TIB
TOCO
TONGAAT
TRIMTEX
TRIMTRD
TRNPACO
TRNSHEX
VIERFONTN
WELKOM
WESWITS
WIT-NIGEL
YABENG
ZIM SUN
ZIMALLOYS
ZIMPLOW
ZSR

April

ANBEECO
CLICKS
CMS
DELSWA
FMCOTEC
GDM
GRESHAM
HIGATE
HISCORE
HISTONE
JADE
LOGTEK
MESTORE
METCASH
PDC
PREM-GRP
PREMPHARM
SCOCLIK
SCORE
SPESCOM
STOCKS
SUPALEK

May

TA HOLD

June

A-V-HOLD
A-V-I
AF-&-OVER
AFRICOM
AGRICOR
ALEXNDR
ALEXWYT
ANGLOVAAL
ASSORE
AUTOQIP
AVF GRP
AVINS
BARMINE
BARNETS
BARNEX
BARPLAT
BASREAD
BEARMAN
BENCO
BERZACK
BIDCORP
BIDVEST
BIVEC
BLOCHS
BLYVOOR
BROADACRE
BUFFCOR
BUFFELS
CAPRI
CASHBIL
CDC
CLEGG
CMI
CON-MURCH
CONCOR
CONFRAM
CONSHU
CONSOL
CONTROL
COPI
CROWN
CRULIFE
CULLINAN
CURFIN
DABI
DALYS
DEBNAIR
DECHOLD
DEELKRL
DIALMOV
DINETTE
DISPTCH
DISTIL
DOORNS
DPF-INV
DRIES
DUKEL
E-T-CONS
ED-L-BATE
EERSLNG
ELCENTR
EVERITE
EVHOLD
FAIRCAP
FOSTON
FRALEX
FRAME
FREDDEV
FSC
G5HOLD
GEN-OPTIC
GENBEL
GFSA
GOLDSTEIN
GRINAKER
GRINTEK
GROUP-5
GROWALK
GUBINGS
GYPSUM
HARMONY
HARTIES
HARWILL
HYPERET
I-&-J
ICH
ILCO
IMPERIAL
IMPHOLD
IMPLATS
IND-SELE
INTELES
INTERNAT
ISCOR
ITLTILE
JOEL
JOHNNIES
KERSAF
KLIPTON
KLOOF
KNIGHTS
KNJ
KOPP
KUDU
KWV-BEL
LANCHEM
LEPLAT
LIBANON
LINDUM
M&R-HLD
M&R-INV
M-&-F
M-C-M
MATH-ASH
MCCARTHY
MCRTAIL
MEDHOLD
MESSINA
METJE-&-Z
MICIND
MICOR
MID-WITS
MIDMAC
MINORCO
MINVEST
MLNHOLD
MOBILE
MODDER
MWEAR
N-KLEINS
NAT TYRE
NATSEL
NEW-WITS
NICTUS
NORTHAM
NORVIC
OSPREY
PALS
PANPROP
PENROSE
PERSBEL
PERSKOR
PICAPLI
PICBEL
PICHOLD
POINTER
PORT
PP RUST
PRIM-G-M
PUTCO
PUTPROP
Q-DATA
RABIE

RADAR
RANDEX
RANDFONTN
RD-LEASE
RENTBEL
REX-TRUE
RLPROPS
RMBH
ROMANO
RUSFURN
RUSPLAT
SABLE
SAFCOR
SAFETEC
SAFREN
SAMANCO
SANLIC
SASFIN
SASOL
SEARCON
SEARDEL
SECHABA
SECHOLD
SFW
SILOAK
SILTEK
SIMMERS
SOUDEX
STH-RODPT
STREBEL
SUB-N
SUN-BOP
SUNCISK
SUNCRUSH
T-E-J
TARGET
TEMPORA
TIWHEEL
TPN
TRANS-NTL
TRANSUN
TRENCOR
TRUZIM
UNI-COLD
UNITRAN
URQHART
VENTERS
VESTCOR
VETRUST
VILLAGE
VLAKS
VOLTEX
WAYNE
WES-AREAS
WIT-G-M
WOOLTRU
WSGROVE
Z-C-I
ZANDPAN

July

CITYLDG
ED ZIM
FOCUS
LEPPIN
OAKFLDS
PORTHLD
PRESTO
SMALDEL

August

BEATRIX
CAIRNS
CARLCOR
DISA
ELLERINE
ENBOT
ENGEN
FARM-AG
FENNER
FOODCRP
FP HOLD
GENBEHEER
GENCOR
HOLDAIN
MALBAK
MALHOLD
NUWORLD
OCTODEC
ORYX
QUICKCO
ROMENS
ROYAL
ROYCHEM
ROYFOOD
ROYHOLD
SA-DRUG
SENTRCHEM
STANDRD
TANGANDA
TEDELEX

September

A-T-COLL
ABS
ADCOCK
ADONIS
AF-CABLE
AFEX SA
AFROX
BARLOWS
BARPROP
BOE
BOEPROP
BORDER
BRACKEN
CEMENCO
CG SUGAR
CGS-FOOD
CGSMITH
CITYHLD
CLINICS
CONAFEX
COR-SYND
DORBYL
DUIKERS
DW TEX
FIDBANK
FIRSTBK
HUNYANI
I-C-S
INMINS
ISG
KINROSS
LANGBRG
LASER
LEBAKA
LESLIE
LONRHO
LORAINE
LYDEX
METKOR
METPOL
NAMPAK
NEDCOR
NORCHART
OCFISH
PERSTEC
PETRA
PLASTAL
PPC
R-M-PROPS
RANDCOL
RANDMIN
REUNERT
RHOEX
RHOVAN
RMSPROP
ROMATEX
SANLAND
SANTAM
SYCOM
TAMBOTI
TEDCO
TEX-MILLS
TIGR-OATS
TOLUX
TWEEFONTN
UMDONI
UNISEL
UNISPIN
USKO
WINBEL
WINHOLD
WINKELS

October

ENROL
GROWPNT
INCO
LYD-PLAT
RAPTOR
SEFALANA
TSL

November

CIRCLE
HUDACO
OTIS

December

ABBEY
ABERDARE
ADCORP
AECI
AFMIN
AFR-LEASE
AIMARK
AMIC
ANG-ALPHA
ARIES
ART
ASS-MANG
AUTODEK
BAT
BB BOT
BBZIM
BERGERS
BERTRAD
BINDURA
BOTINS
BOTREST
BOWCALF

BSG
BSI
BTRDUN
BURLINGTN
CADSWEP
CAFCA
CAPITAL
CENPROP
CFC
CHEMSERVE
CIH
CLUFF ZIM
COATES
CONFED
CURNOW
CUSAF
DBN-DEEP
DE BEERS
DECOVO
DELTA
DIDATA
DUN ZIM
E-R-P-M
ELANDS
ENSIGN
EQUIKOR
F-S-GROUP
F-S-I
FEDSURE
FENIX
FIT
FMB
FSI ZIM
G-F-COAL
GARDIAN
GEFCO
GENTYRE-A
GF-PROPS
GFNAMIB
GLODINA
GRINCOR
GROOTVLEI
HAGGIE
HAIB
HIVELD
HYPROP
IBJOFFE
INVICTA
JDGROUP
KADOMA
KH PROPS
LIB HOLD
LIBERTY
LONFIN
MACMED
MANRO
MARCONS
MARLIN
MARSHAL
MASONITE
MCPHAIL
MERHLD
MERLIN
METAIR
MINGRAN
MSAULI
NAMFISH
NAMSEA
NATRAWL
NATRUST
NEI-AFR
NEIHOLD
NINIAN
OMNIA
PALAMIN
PROFURN
PROGRESS
PROPCOR
PROSURE
RDC
RIO ZIM
ROOIBERG
S-A-BIAS
S-A-EAGLE
SAB IND
SABVEST
SALLIES
SBIC
SCHARIG
SCHWEP CA
SHOREDITS
SOUTHVAAL
ST-HELENA
STANBOT
STANPRO
STERLING
STILFTN
SUPREME
SUPRMAN
T-&-N
TECHIRE
TGH
TIME
TMX
TOYOTA
U-CON
UDC
UNICON
UNIDEV
UNIHOLD
UNION
UTICO
VAAL-REEF
VEKTRA
VENTEL
VOGELS
W-&-A
W-R-CONS
WAICOR
WBHOLD
WESCO
WSTN-DEEP
YORKCOR
ZIM NEWS
ZIMBANK
ZIMSPIN

COMPANIES CATEGORISED BY TRANSFER SECRETARY

Anglovaal Ltd
A-T-COLL
A-V-HOLD
A-V-I
ANG-ALPHA
ANGLOVAAL
ASS-MANG
AVF GRP
AVINS
CONSOL
CRULIFE
E-T-CONS
GRINAKER
GRINTEK
HARTIES
I-&-J
LORAINE
MID-WITS
SILTEK
TARGET
VILLAGE
ZANDPAN

Argus Holdings Ltd
ARGUS

CIH Trading & Finance (Pvt) Ltd
CIH

Capri Group Ltd
CAPRI

Cementation Co (Africa) Ltd
CEMENCO

Central Registrars Ltd
ABSA
ADCORP
ADONIS
AFEX SA
AFMIN
AIDA
AIMARK
AKJ
ALEXWYT
ALTECH
ALTRON
AMSHOE
ANBEECO
AROMA
AUTODEK
BARMINE
BARPLAT
BASREAD
BEARMAN
BEATRIX
BERGERS
BERTRAD
BESTER
BLOCHS
BOLAND
BOUMAT
BOYMANS
BRACKEN
BRENMIL
BROADACRE
BUFFCOR
BUFFELS
C-MATIC
CAPITAL
CARLCOR
CASHBIL
CAXTON
CENMAG
CENPROP
CHEMSERVE
CHOICE
CITYHLD
CITYLDG
CLAW
CLEGG
CLICKS
CLYDE
CMH
COASTAL
CONAFEX
CONSHU
CROWN
CULLINAN
DARMAG
DECHOLD
DECOVO
DELTA
DIDATA
DISA
DISPTCH
DISTIL
DUKEL
ED-L-BATE
EDGARS
ELLERINE
ENGEN
EUREKA
FAIRCAP
FALCON
FARM-AG
FINTECH
FIT
FMCOTEC
FOODCRP
FORIM
FOSTON
G-I-C
GARDIAN
GDM
GEFCO
GEN-OPTIC
GENBEHEER
GENBEL
GENCOR
GRINCOR
GROOTVLEI
GROPROP
HAIB
HARWILL
HISCORE
HOLDAIN
IBJOFFE
IMPLATS
ISCOR
JASCO
JDGROUP
KEELEY
KELGRAN
KINROSS
KNJ
KUDU
KWV-BEL
LENCO
LENVEST
LESLIE
LIB HOLD
LIBERTY
LIBVEST
LONFIN
LYD-PLAT
M&R-HLD
M&R-INV
M-&-F
M-C-M
M-NET
MANRO
MARCONS
MARSHAL
MASONITE
MATH-ASH
MEDCLIN
MEDHOLD
MERHLD
MESSINA
MESTORE
METAIR
METCASH
METKOR
METPOL
MIDAS
MIDMAC
MILSTAN
MINGRAN
MINVEST
MJM
MOLYSLP
MOMENTUM
MORKELS
MSAULI
N-KLEINS
NATRAWL
NATRUST
NATSEL
NISWA
NUWORLD
OHIO
OMNIA
ORYX
PALS
PANPROP
PENROSE
PEP
PEPGRO
PEPKOR
PETRA
PLASTAL
POWTECH
PRESTO

PUBHOLD
PUBLICO
PUTCO
PUTPROP
Q-DATA
QUAGGA
RAINBOW
RALE
RANDEX
RAPTOR
REMB-BEH
REMGRO
RENTBEL
RMSPROP
ROMANO
ROYAL
ROYCHEM
ROYFOOD
ROYHOLD
RUHOLD
RUSFURN
S-A-BIAS
SA-DRUG
SAB IND
SABVEST
SAFETEC
SAFICON
SAFREN
SAKERS
SAMANCO
SANLAND
SANLIC
SANTAM
SAPPI
SASFIN
SASOL
SCHARIG
SCOCLIK
SCORE
SEARCON
SEARDEL
SECHOLD
SENTRCHEM
SERVGRO
SFW
SHOCRAF
SHOPRIT
SILOAK
SPESCOM
ST-HELENA
STANDRD
STANPRO
STILFTN
STOCKS
SUPALEK
SUPREME
SYCOM
T-&-N
T-M-L
TEDELEX
TEGKOR
TELJOY
TGH
TIB
TMX
TOLUX
TOYOTA
TRADGRO
TRADHLD
TRANS-NTL
TRIMTEX
TRIMTRD
TRNSHEX
UNI-COLD
UNICON
UNIDEV
UNION
UNISEL
UNISPIN
UNITRAN
URQHART
USKO
VENTRON
VESTCOR
VOLTEX
W-&-A
W-R-CONS
WAICOR
WAYNE
WESCO
WINKELS
WOODROW

Consolidated Share Registrars Ltd

ABCON
AECI
AF-CABLE
AFCOL
AFLIFE
AFR-LEASE
AMAPROP
AMCOAL
AMGOLD
AMIC
AMREL
ANAMINT
ANGLO-S
APEX
BARNEX
BEVCON
BOTREST
CHARTER
CMI
COMPASS
CON-MURCH
COPI
DABI
DATAKOR
DE BEERS
DEB CENT
DIALMOV
DIGOCO
DINETTE
DORBYL
ELANDS
ERGO
FIRSTBK
FREDDEV
FREGOLD
GLODINA
GUBINGS
HIVELD
HUDACO
ILCO
IND-SELE
JOEL
JOHNNIES
KLIPTON
LASER
LEEGALL
LEPLAT
LINDUM
LOGTEK
MAINPRO
MINORCO
MOBILE
MULTI
NEW-CENT
OFSIL
PP RUST
PREMPHARM
PROPFIN
RANDFONTN
RUSPLAT
SA-BREWS
SALLIES
SOTHERN
SOUDEX
SOUTHVAAL
TIWHEEL
TONGAAT
TRENCOR
VAAL-REEF
VIERFONTN
WELKOM
WES-AREAS
WSTN-DEEP
YORKCOR
Z-C-I

Coopers & Lybrand Services (Pty) Ltd

BOTINS
FSC
RDC

Dalys Ltd

DALYS
SUNCRUSH
TEMPORA

Ernst & Young

METJE-&-Z
NAMFISH

Finpak Registrars (Pty) Ltd

ENSIGN
TDL

First Transfer Secretaries (Pvt) Ltd

AGRICOR
ART
CAIRNS
DELTA ZIM
FMB
GULLIVER
HIPPO
INTERNAT
MASHONA
MWEAR
NATFOOD
PGI
RADAR
RIO ZIM
ROTH ZIM
SCHWEP CA
TEDCO
TRUZIM
ZIM SUN
ZIMALLOYS

ZIMSPIN
ZSR

Fraser Street Registrars (Pty) Ltd

ADVTECH
AUTOQIP
BOLPRO
BOLTONS
BOLWEAR
BSG
BSI
CARGO
CBD-FUND
CNAGALO
COATES
COM-FUND
CUTRITE
HLH
HUNTCOR
INTELES
INVICTA
KERSAF
LANCHEM
LITHO
MICIND
MICOR
NICTUS
NINIAN
PIONEER
PORT
PROSURE
RMBH
SAGEGRP
SMART
SPL
STERLING
SUN-BOP
SUNCISK
TRANSUN
VETRUST
YABENG

Gold Equity Registrars (Pty) Ltd

BOWCALF
MODDER
NORVIC
STH-RODPT
TPN

Gold Fields of SA Ltd

CUSAF
DEELKRL
DOORNS
DRIES
G-F-COAL
GF-PROPS
GFNAMIB
GFSA
KLOOF
LIBANON
NEW-WITS
NORTHAM
ROOIBERG
VENTERS
VLAKS
VOGELS

Investment Registrars (Pty) Ltd

OCTODEC
OSPREY
PAG
TOMKOR
TRNPACO

KPMG Aiken & Peat

LIONMATCH
PORTHLD

KPMG Peat Marwick

DUN ZIM
ED ZIM
MERLIN
WSGROVE

Kilgetty Trust (Pty) Ltd

SONDOR
WBHOLD

Lonrho Zimbabwe Management Serv (Pvt)Ltd

DW TEX
NORCHART

Mercantile Registrars Ltd

ABACUS
ABBEY
ABERDARE
ABI
ACREM
AF-&-OVER
AFRICOM
AFROX
ALEXNDR
ALLGRP
ALLWEAR
ARIES
AUTOPGE
BARNETS
BENCO
BENONI
BERZACK
BIDCORP
BIDVEST
BIVEC
BOE
BOEPROP
BTRDUN
CADSWEP
CAFCA
CARRIGS
CDC
CERAMIC
CHUBB
CMS
CONCOR
CONFRAM
CONSMNG
CONTRAV
COR-SYND
CORWIL
CRENDEL
CTP
CURFIN
CURNOW
DA-GAMA
DEBNAIR
DELSWA
DPF-INV
DUIKERS
E-DAGGA
EDDIES
EERSLNG
EGOLI
ELCENTR
ENROL
EQUIKOR
EVERITE
EVHOLD
F-S-GROUP
F-S-I
FEDSURE
FENIX
FENNER
FIDBANK
FOCUS
FOSCHINI
FRALEX
FRAME
G5HOLD
GENTYRE-A
GOLDSTEIN
GRESHAM
GROUP-5
GROWPNT
GYPSUM
HAGGIE
HCI
HICORL
HIGATE
HISTONE
HORTORS
HYPERET
I-G-I
IMPERIAL
IMPHOLD
INHOLD
INMINS
INTRUST
INVSTEC
ITLTILE
JADE
KNIGHTS
LEBAKA
LEFIC
LEPPIN
LONGRAIL
LONRHO
LONSUGR
LYDEX
MACADAM
MACMED
MALBAK
MALHOLD
MARLIN
MASCON
MASHOLD
MCCARTHY
MCPHAIL
MCRTAIL
MERITEX
METPROP
MLNHOLD
NEI-AFR
NEIHOLD

NIGEL
O-K
OCEANA
ODMHOLD
OTIS
OZZ
PDC
PLATE-GL
PREM-GRP
PRESMED
PRIM-G-M
PROFURN
PROGRESS
PROPCOR
QUICKCO
QUORUM
RABIE
RACY
RD-LEASE
REGGIES
REVERE
REX-TRUE
RHOEX
RHOVAN
RLPROPS
ROMENS
S-A-EAGLE
SAAMBOU
SABLE
SAFCOR
SAFLIFE
SHOREDITS
SIMMERS
SOLCHEM
SOPLATS
SOUTHGO
SOWITS
SPECLTY
SPUR
SPURHLD
STORECO
STREBEL
SUB-N
SUPRMAN
T-E-J
TAMBOTI
TECFIN
TECHIRE
TIME
TITACO
TOCO
TWEEFONTN
U-CON
UMDONI
UNIHOLD
UNISERV
UTICO
VEKTRA
VENTEL
WALHOLD
WALTONS
WANKIE
WESWITS
WINBEL
WINHOLD
WIT-G-M
WIT-NIGEL
WOOLTRU

Natal Registrars (Pty) Ltd

CFC
CONFED

Natal Securities Trust (Pty) Ltd

CROOKES

National Tyre Services Ltd

NAT TYRE

PW Business Services (Pty) Ltd

IGI BOT

Picardi Investments Ltd

PICAPLI
PICBEL
PICHOLD

Piyushkant Virendrakumar Desai

ENBOT

R D Hugo

BURLINGTN

Rand Merchant Bank Ltd

RICHEMONT

Rand Registrars Ltd

ADCOCK
BARLOWS
BARPROP
BLYVOOR
CG SUGAR
CGS-FOOD
CGSMITH
DBN-DEEP
E-R-P-M
HARMONY
HYPROP
I-C-S
ISG
KH PROPS
LANGBRG
MAST
MAXMECH
NAMPAK
NAMSEA
NBSHOLD
NEDCOR
OCFISH
PERSTEC
POINTER
PPC
R-M-PROPS
RANDCOL
RANDMIN
REUNERT
ROMATEX
SBIC
SMALDEL
TAFLBRG
TIGR-OATS
VALAUTO
VALCAR

Retail Share Registrars (Pty) Ltd

PICKNPAY
PIKWIK

SARB

SA-RES-BK

Sagit Transfer Secretaries (Pvt) ltd

AFDISTIL

Stability Services (Pty) Ltd

ABS
BRISTOL-I
CLINICS
KAROS

T A Trading Corporation (Pvt) Ltd

TA HOLD

The Dagbreek Trust

PERSBEL
PERSKOR

Tuffias Shapiro Braude

TEX-MILLS

Union Provident Trust (Botswana) Ltd

PEP BOT

Union Provident Trust SA Ltd

ASSORE
CONTROL
GAZGOLD
GROWALK
ICH
KOPP
L-T-A
OAKFLDS
PALAMIN
SPICER

Zimbabwe Banking Corporation Ltd

CLUFF ZIM
FALGOLD
FP HOLD
FSI ZIM
KADOMA
TABEX
TSL
UDC
ZIMBANK

NEWLY LISTED COMPANIES

COMPANY NAME	DATE OF LIST
ABCON PROPERTIES	DEC 2 1991
CG SMITH SUGAR LIMITED	FEB 13 1992
CITY LODGE HOTELS LTD	NOV 18 1992
LANGEBERG HOLDINGS LIMITED	JUNE 1 1992
LENCO INVESTMENT HOLDINGS LIMITED	JULY 29 1992
NISWA LIMITED	MAY 18 1992
PERSETECH LIMITED	MAR 2 1992
POTGIETRSRUST PLATINUMS	OCT 31 1991
RAND LEASES PROPERTIES LIMITED	FEB 24 1992
SCORE SUPERMARKETS	OCT 14 1991
SERVGRO INTERNATIONAL LIMITED	AUG 7 1992
SMALDEEL COAL	DEC 31 1991
TELEMETRIX PLC	NOV 28 1991
VENTER LEISURE AND COMMERCIAL TRAIL	MAR 4 1992

COMPANIES RECENTLY DELISTED

COMPANY	REASON FOR DELISTING
ADPROM HOLDINGS	FININFO BUY-OUT OF MINORITIES
ANCOM JET AVIATION	TERMINATED BY JSE COMMITTEE
ASSENG	ORDS CONVERTED INTO PREFS AND REDEEMED AT 140c
BANKORP HOLDINGS	ASSIMILATED INTO ABSA
BARBROOK MINES LIMITED	LISTING TERMINATED DUE TO LIQUIDATION
BIOPOLYMERS	LISTING TERMINATED-OFFER TO MINORITIES
BLOCKTECH	LISTING WITHDRAWN BY DIRECTORS
BLUE CIRCLE	DUE TO OFFER TO MINORITIES BY MURRAY & ROBERTS
BUFFALO CORPORATION	OFFER TO MINORITIES BY PEPKOR
CLAUDE NEON	TERMINATED BY JSE COMMITTEE
COLFIN INVESTMENTS	ASSIMILATED TO COLFIN HOLDINGS
COMPUTERMATIC HOLDINGS	CASH SHELL
CONSOLIDATED MODDERFONTEIN MINES	LISTING WITHDRAWN BY DIRECTORS
DALSIG MINING	TERMINATED BY JSE COMMITTEE
DARLING & HODGSON	OFFER TO MINORITIES BY MURRAY & ROBERTS
DPF INVESTMENTS	PROVISIONAL LIQUIDATION
DROP-INN GROUP HOLDINGS	FOLLOWING AN OFFER BY MASSMART
ELCENTRE GROUP	TERMINATED DUE TO OFFER TO MINORITIES
ELSBURG GOLD	VOLUNTARY WINDING-UP
EUREVEST	UNSATISFACTORY SHAREHOLDER SPREAD
EUROPA ACCEPTANCES	FINAL WINDING-UP ORDER
FILATI HOLDINGS	FINANCIAL POSITION
FINTECH INFORMATICS	LISTING WITHDRAWN BY DIRECTORS
FRIGATE GROUP HOLDINGS	LISTING TERMINATED AT DIRECTOR'S REQUEST
GOLDFIELDS INDUSTRIAL CORPORATION	ORDS CONVERTED INTO PREFS AND REDEEMED AT 644c
GRANT ANDREWS HOLDINGS	ORDS CONVERTED INTO PREFS AND REDEEMED AT 25c
HAIB COPPER MINING AND EXPLORATION	FINANCIAL POSITION
KANHYM INVESTMENTS	TERMINATED DUE TO MERGER WITH FEDFOOD
KEMTRADE HOLDINGS	FINANCIAL POSITION AND RESTRUCTURE PROPOSALS
LANCHEM	ORDS CONVERTED INTO RED PREF SHARES AND DELISTED
LEEGALL CLOTHING COMPANY	PROVISIONAL LIQUIDATION
LIBANON GOLD MINING COMPANY	DUE TO SCHEME OF ARRANGEMENT
LONGMILE LIMITED	ORDS CONVERTED INTO PREFS AND REDEEMED AT 260c
LYNTEX TRANSPORT	FINAL WINDING UP ORDER
MANAGEMENT SERVICES CORPORATION	TERMINATED BY JSE COMMITTEE
MARKET MOTOR GROUP	ASSIMILATED INTO MALBAK INDUSTRIAL HOLDINGS
MASTERBORE	FINAL WINDING UP ORDER
METER SYSTEMS	TERMINATED BY JSE COMMITTEE
MODDER B GOLD HOLDINGS	FINAL WINDING UP ORDER
MONEY AND MANAGEMENT HOLDINGS	FINANCIAL POSITION
MUSICA (AFRICA) HOLDINGS	TERMINATED DUE TO OFFER BY CLICKS STORES
N T C	OFFER TO MINORITIES
NATIONAL TRADING HOLDINGS	TERMINATED DUE TO OFFER TO MINORITY SHAREHOLDERS
NEW COMPANY INVESTMENTS	FINANCIAL POSITION
NIGEL GOLD MINING	FINAL WINDING-UP ORDER
PENNYPINCHERS BOARDS	ASSIMILATED INTO PENNYPINCHERS HOLDINGS
PENNYPINCHERS HOLDINGS	OFFER TO MINORITIES
PLACOR HOLDINGS	TERMINATED DUE TO SCHEME OF ARRANGEMENTS
PLEASURE FOODS	ORDS CONVERTED INTO PREFS AND REDEEMED AT 125c
PRESTIGE GROUP	LISTING WITHDRAWN BY DIRECTORS
RAND LONDON CORPORATION	FINANCIAL POSITION
RICO BREWERIES	FINAL WINDING-UP ORDER
S.A. DRUGGISTS	ASSIMILATED INTO FEDVOLKS
SAGE HOLDINGS	TERMINATED DUE TO SCHEME OF ARRANGEMENT
SAGE PROPERTY HOLDINGS	TERMINATED DUE TO SCHEME OF ARRANGEMENT
SCORE FOOD HOLDINGS	ASSIMILATED INTO METCASH
SHOPRITE HOLDINGS	CASH SHELL
SOUTH ROODEPOORT MAIN REEF AREAS	LISTING WITHDRAWN BY DIRECTORS
SPRINGTEX	ASSIMILATED INTO MASCON
SUN PACKAGING HOLDINGS	TERMINATED DUE TO SCHEME OF ARRANGEMENT
SUN PACKAGING INVESTMENTS	TERMINATED DUE TO SCHEME OF ARRANGEMENT
SURE GROUP HOLDINGS	TERMINATED BY JSE COMMITTEE
TR SERVICES HOLDINGS	LISTING WITHDRAWN BY DIRECTORS
TRABILD GROUP HOLDINGS	LISTING WITHDRAWN BY DIRECTORS
TRANSVAAL DISTILLERS HOLDINGS	FINAL LIQUIDATION ORDER
TRIMTEX HOLDINGS	PROVISIONAL LIQUIDATION
TRIMTEX TRADING	PROVISIONAL LIQUIDATION
VADEK PAINTS	FINAL LIQUIDATION ORDER

COMPANY	REASON FOR DELISTING
VALARD	TERMINATED DUE TO SCHEME OF ARRANGEMENT
VALHOLD	TERMINATED DUE TO SCHEME OF ARRANGEMENT
VANSA VANADIUM SA	COMPANY NO LONGER MEETS WITH THE LISTING REQS
VENTERSPOST GOLD MINING	TERMINATED DUE TO SCHEME OF ARRANGEMENT
WAVERLEY GOLD MINES	TERMINATED DUE TO SCHEME OF ARRANGEMENT

COMPANY NAME CHANGES

FORMER NAME	NEW NAME
AUDIOBUILD HOLDINGS	CERAMIC INDUSTRIES
COLFIN HOLDINGS LTD	LOG-TEK HOLDINGS LTD
COMMERCIAL UNION ASSURANCE CO OF SA	COMMERCIAL UNION OF SOUTH AFRICA
CRB HOLDINGS	OCEAN DIAMOND MINING HOLDINGS
FEDFOOD LIMITED	FOODCORP LIMITED
IMPERIAL COLD STORAGE AND SUPPLY CO	ICS HOLDINGS
MERVEST	HAIB COPPER MINING AND EXPLORATION
PREFCOR HOLDINGS LTD	MCCARTHY RETAIL LTD
SAGE FINANCIAL SERVICES	SAGE GROUP
TECHNOLOGY SYSTEMS INTERNATIONAL	INFORMATION SERVICES GROUP
TWINS PHARMACEUTICALS	PREMIER PHARMACEUTICAL COMPANY
UNION TIN MINES	UNION MINES
WITBANK COLLIERY	RANDCOAL

Hugo Lambrechts
Graduate School of Management
University of Pretoria
Pretoria 0002
Tel (012) 420-3382
Fax (012) 437-223

UNIT TRUSTS SURVEY

Table 1 UNIT TRUST PERFORMANCES TO JUNE 1992*
Lump Sum Investment

UNIT TRUSTS & INDICES	**Quarter (%)	1 YEAR (repurchase to repurchase) (%)	1 YEAR (selling to repurchase) (%)	3 YEARS (%)	5 YEARS (%)	7 YEARS (%)	10 YEARS (%)	15 YEARS (%)
GENERAL EQUITY FUNDS								
All-Share Index	**3,78**	**14,13**	**14,13**	**15,68**	**13,74**	**23,15**	**29,03**	**28,62**
ABSA (Volkskas)	4,65	20,76	12,97	—	—	—	—	—
BOE Growth	4,96	20,28	12,38	—	—	—	—	—
Community Growth Fund	—	—	—	—	—	—	—	—
CU Growth	2,10	18,73	10,86	—	—	—	—	—
Fedgro	5,16	18,85	11,08	—	—	—	—	—
Guardbank Growth	4,43	16,51	9,12	18,74	17,77	24,04	28,78	29,57
IGI Unit Trust (Safegro)	1,44	15,81	8,37	—	—	—	—	—
Metfund	4,99	19,86	11,73	15,37	—	—	—	—
Metlife	2,73	—	—	—	—	—	—	—
Momentum	3,90	12,58	5,32	19,88	—	—	—	—
NBS Hallmark	4,34	14,01	6,48	15,41	—	—	—	—
Norwich	7,63	14,18	6,64	12,08	—	—	—	—
Old Mutual Investors' Fund	2,70	18,84	10,83	17,80	16,48	26,45	29,20	29,13
Sage Fund	2,18	17,84	10,05	19,95	16,69	23,29	26,87	27,34
Sanlam Index Trust	2,39	12,94	5,60	16,51	15,86	23,28	26,55	26,86
Sanlam Dividend Trust	1,88	17,11	9,23	17,68	13,31	20,15	21,13	23,17
Sanlam Trust	2,91	15,18	7,60	19,28	14,86	20,99	24,83	25,54
Senbank General Trust	2,44	19,89	12,50	—	—	—	—	—
Southern Equity	4,35	23,82	15,84	17,00	—	—	—	—
Standard Bank Mutual	4,52	18,50	11,40	19,75	17,58	23,38	26,09	26,24
Syfrets Growth Fund	2,41	23,18	15,35	25,34	21,43	—	—	—
Syfrets Trustees	3,52	—	—	—	—	—	—	—
UAL Unit Trust	3,56	20,21	12,68	18,08	15,78	21,58	26,80	26,84
SPECIALIST EQUITY FUNDS								
Mining and Resources Funds								
Mining Producers' Index	[illegible]	[illegible]	[illegible]	[illegible]	[illegible]	**18,20**	**26,05**	**25,76**
Mining Financial Index	[illegible]	[illegible]	[illegible]	[illegible]	**8,09**	**21,11**	**29,35**	**29,66**
Guardbank Resources	3,33	4,89	(1,75)	7,67	10,75	—	—	—
Old Mutual Mining Fund	2,56	(3,43)	(9,94)	0,89	3,95	—	—	—
Sage Resources	3,51	6,04	(0,76)	6,05	—	—	—	—
Sanlam Mining Trust	4,40	1,23	(5,48)	5,90	5,53	15,57	19,75	21,31
Southern Mining	3,48	4,06	(2,68)	3,71	—	—	—	—
UAL Mining and Resources	6,52	11,30	4,31	8,67	9,32	18,38	22,79	24,48
Gold Funds								
All-Gold Index	[illegible]	[illegible]	[illegible]	[illegible]	[illegible]	**6,67**	**18,50**	**21,85**
Old Mutual Gold Fund	(3,75)	(20,70)	(26,08)	—	—	—	—	—
Standard Bank Gold Fund	(0,99)	(13,47)	(18,84)	(5,12)	(4,82)	8,40	—	—
Industrial Funds								
Industrial Index	**1,40**	**21,49**	**21,49**	**23,82**	**22,73**	**28,80**	**30,34**	**30,05**
Guardbank Industrial	—	—	—	—	—	—	—	—
Old Mutual Industrial Fund	3,41	22,83	14,42	—	—	—	—	—
Sanlam Industrial Trust	2,17	19,82	12,05	24,34	18,25	24,11	26,99	27,60
Senbank Industrial Trust	1,99	24,53	17,22	—	—	—	—	—
Standard Bank Industrial	—	—	—	—	—	—	—	—
Other Specialist Equity Funds								
Old Mutual Top Companies Fund	3,26	—	—	—	—	—	—	—
Southern Pure	—	—	—	—	—	—	—	—
Standard Bank International	—	—	—	—	—	—	—	—
UAL Selected Opportunities	2,97	16,12	8,52	17,99	12,82	—	—	—
HIGH INCOME FUNDS								
CPI (Estimated for June 1992)	**3,10**	**15,10**	**15,10**	**14,60**	**14,40**	**15,10**	**14,60**	**14,30**
Guardbank Income	6,71	21,45	18,96	20,25	16,87	—	—	—
Metboard Income Fund (Corbank)	6,65	21,44	20,16	18,88	15,18	—	—	—
Old Mutual Income Fund	5,40	18,27	16,98	17,52	—	—	—	—
Standard Bank Extra Income	4,43	17,00	15,72	18,71	16,54	16,28	15,87	—
Syfrets Income	5,93	19,00	17,80	17,46	—	—	—	—
GILT FUNDS								
All-Bond Index	**8,12**	**23,39**	**23,39**	**20,64**	**16,64**	—	—	—
Syfrets Gilt	—	—	—	—	—	—	—	—
UAL Gilt Unit Trust	7,16	21,40	20,19	19,24	17,40	—	—	—

* Performances (including those of indices) include capital appreciation / depreciation plus dividend income.
* Assumption: Dividends are reinvested on the date of payment at the selling price.
** It can be dangerous to take long term investment decisions based on short term performance figures.

Hugo Lambrechts
Graduate School of Management
University of Pretoria
Pretoria 0002
Tel (012) 420-3382
Fax (012) 437-223

UNIT TRUSTS SURVEY

Table 2 UNIT TRUST PERFORMANCES TO JUNE 1992 *
Level Monthly Investment

UNIT TRUSTS & INDICES	1 YEAR (repurchase to repurchase) (%)	1 YEAR (selling to repurchase) (%)	3 YEARS (%)	5 YEARS (%)	7 YEARS (%)	10 YEARS (%)	15 YEARS (%)
GENERAL EQUITY FUNDS							
All -Share Index	**11,48**	**11,48**	**14,36**	**17,31**	**17,06**	**19,28**	**21,54**
ABSA (Volkskas)	17,54	4,12	—	—	—	—	—
BOE Growth	18,06	4,36	—	—	—	—	—
Community Growth Fund	—	—	—	—	—	—	—
CU Growth	13,02	(0,33)	—	—	—	—	—
Fedgro	15,42	1,88	—	—	—	—	—
Guardbank Growth	15,23	1,97	15,80	21,22	22,02	24,16	26,92
IGI Unit Trust (Safegro)	11,15	(1,68)	—	—	—	—	—
Metfund	17,53	2,98	15,29	—	—	—	—
Metlife	—	—	—	—	—	—	—
Momentum	12,55	(0,38)	16,56	—	—	—	—
NBS Hallmark	14,40	0,97	13,68	—	—	—	—
Norwich	17,06	3,36	11,73	—	—	—	—
Old Mutual Investors' Fund	12,59	(0,92)	15,22	20,41	22,26	24,85	26,85
Sage Fund	13,33	(0,10)	16,79	20,77	20,96	22,60	24,85
Sanlam Index Trust	14,98	1,57	15,24	20,62	21,44	23,16	24,51
Sanlam Dividend Trust	11,23	(1,88)	18,71	18,82	19,06	19,37	20,74
Sanlam Trust	11,37	(1,70)	16,23	19,60	19,82	20,86	22,86
Southern Equity	20,83	7,19	17,23	—	—	—	—
Standard Bank Mutual	16,95	4,47	16,97	20,80	21,58	22,98	24,03
Syfrets Growth Fund	18,45	7,18	22,82	26,25	—	—	—
Syfrets Trustees	—	—	—	—	—	—	—
UAL Unit Trust	17,17	4,09	16,05	21,04	20,06	21,99	24,29
SPECIALIST EQUITY FUNDS							
Mining and Resources Funds							
Mining Producers' Index	**5,98**	**5,98**	**2,60**	**6,79**	**7,67**	**12,03**	**15,95**
Mining Financial Index	**6,38**	**6,38**	**4,90**	**9,67**	**10,97**	**15,60**	**19,53**
Guardbank Resources	6,92	(5,22)	5,09	11,50	—	—	—
Old Mutual Mining Fund	(2,89)	(14,86)	(4,59)	2,74	—	—	—
Sage Resources	6,18	(6,36)	2,70	—	—	—	—
Sanlam Mining Trust	2,76	(9,54)	1,78	8,42	10,18	14,43	17,82
Southern Mining	5,87	(6,38)	0,37	—	—	—	—
UAL Mining and Resources	11,53	(1,21)	6,71	11,99	13,55	17,63	21,04
Gold Funds							
All-Gold Index	**(10,70)**	**(10,70)**	**(13,77)**	**(9,66)**	**(6,99)**	**(0,55)**	**7,71**
Old Mutual Gold Fund	(16,04)	(26,70)	—	—	—	—	—
Standard Bank Gold Fund	(9,50)	(19,95)	(11,91)	(4,96)	(0,51)	—	—
Industrial Funds							
Industrial Index	**14,41**	**14,41**	**24,77**	**26,59**	**25,78**	**24,75**	**24,87**
Guardbank Industrial	—	—	—	—	—	—	—
Old Mutual Industrial Fund	26,40	4,54	—	—	—	—	—
Sanlam Industrial Trust	15,31	1,95	23,32	23,93	23,37	23,67	25,09
Senbank Industrial Trust	19,27	5,52	—	—	—	—	—
Standard Bank Industrial	—	—	—	—	—	—	—
Other Specialist Equity Funds							
Old Mutual Top Companies Fund	—	—	—	—	—	—	—
Southern Pure	—	—	—	—	—	—	—
Standard Bank International	—	—	—	—	—	—	—
UAL Selected Opportunities	11,32	(1,62)	17,82	18,11	—	—	—
HIGH INCOME FUNDS							
CPI (Estimated for June 1992)	**13,98**	**13,98**	**14,73**	**14,59**	**14,66**	**14,81**	**14,56**
Guardbank Income	24,16	19,63	19,43	18,38	—	—	—
Metboard Income Fund (Corbank)	24,25	21,92	18,35	17,25	—	—	—
Old Mutual Income Fund	19,82	17,32	16,54	—	—	—	—
Standard Bank Extra Income	17,42	15,15	17,72	17,42	17,30	16,34	—
Syfrets Income	21,55	19,37	17,11	—	—	—	—
GILT FUNDS							
All-Bond Index	**28,87**	**28,87**	**20,59**	**18,75**	—	—	—
Syfrets Prima	—	—	—	—	—	—	—
UAL Gilt Unit Trust	24,92	22,70	18,63	18,15	—	—	—

* Performances (including those of indices) include capital appreciation / depreciation plus dividend income.
* Assumption: Dividends are reinvested on the date of payment at the selling price.

Hugo Lambrechts
Graduate School of Management
University of Pretoria
Pretoria 0002
Tel (012) 420-3382
Fax (012) 437-223

UNIT TRUSTS SURVEY

Table 3 TOP PERFORMERS TO JUNE 1992 (based on a lump sum investment)

One Year (Repurchase to Repurchase)	(%)
*Senbank Industrial Trust (S)	24,53
*Southern Equity (G)	23,82
*Old Mutual Industrial Fund (S)	22,83
Guardbank Income Fund (I)	21,45
Rate of inflation (Estimated for June 1992)	15,10

One Year (Selling to Repurchase)	(%)
UAL Gilt Unit Trust (I)	20,19
Metboard Income Fund (I)	20,16
Guardbank Income Fund (I)	18,96
Syfrets Income (I)	17,80
Rate of inflation (Estimated for June 1992)	15,10

Three Years	(%)
*Syfrets Growth Fund (G)	25,34
Guardbank Income Fund (I)	20,25
*Sage Fund (G)	19,95
*Momentum Unit Trust (G)	19,88
Rate of inflation	14,60

Five Years	(%)
*Syfrets Growth Fund (G)	21,43
Sanlam Industrial Trust (S)	18,25
*Guardbank Growth Fund (G)	17,77
*Standard Bank Mutual Fund(G)	17,58
Rate of inflation	14,40

Seven Years	(%)
*Old Mutual Investors' Fund (G)	26,45
Sanlam Industrial Trust (S)	24,11
*Guardbank Growth Fund (G)	24,04
*Standard Bank Mutual Fund (G)	23,38
Rate of inflation	15,10

Ten Years	(%)
*Old Mutual Investors' Fund (G)	29,20
*Guardbank Growth Fund (G)	28,78
Sanlam Industrial Trust (S)	26,99
Sage Fund (G)	26,87
Rate of inflation	14,60

Fifteen Years	(%)
*Guardbank Growth Fund (G)	29,57
*Old Mutual Investors' Fund (G)	29,13
Sanlam Industrial Trust (S)	27,60
Sage Fund (G)	27,34
Rate of inflation	14,30

Category:
G – General equity fund
S – Specialist equity fund
I – Income fund
* – indicates that a particular fund has beaten the index (Income funds are not compared against an index).

Table 4 LIQUIDITY LEVEL OF GENERAL EQUITY FUNDS SINCE DECEMBER 1990

GENERAL EQUITY FUNDS	DEC 90 %	MAR 91 %	JUNE 91 %	SEPT 91 %	DEC 91 %	MAR 92 %	JUNE 92 %
ABSA (Volkskas)	–	–	8	24	16	18	37
BOE Growth	31	20	14	15	10	7	16
CU Growth	27	32	19	17	18	13	14
Fedgro	–	54	29	15	22	12	12
Guardbank	23	22	19	23	18	13	12
Metfund	16	12	18	14	12	13	12
Metlife	–	–	–	–	31	21	10
Momentum	29	10	9	13	12	9	13
NBS Hallmark	34	24	24	22	22	8	20
Norwich	36	49	8	10	7	9	17
Old Mutual Investors'	18	18	14	12	10	9	9
IGI (Safegro)	32	19	16	16	13	8	13
Sage	27	23	20	20	18	15	17
Sanlam Dividend	–	–	–	15	17	12	21
Sanlam Index	28	16	13	9	10	8	12
Sanlam Trust	30	20	9	11	8	8	12
Senbank General Trust	–	–	46	19	14	21	16
Southern Equity	29	8	12	18	15	15	17
Standard Bank	44	43	41	39	40	40	39
Syfrets Trustees	–	–	–	–	21	21	18
Syfrets Growth Fund	33	9	5	4	3	15	10
UAL Unit Trust	26	34	24	22	21	18	26
TOTAL						14 (R1 349,0m)	14 (R1 478,3m)

Table 5 LIQUIDITY LEVEL OF SPECIALIST EQUITY FUNDS SINCE DECEMBER 1990

SPECIALIST EQUITY FUNDS	DEC 90 %	MAR 91 %	JUNE 91 %	SEPT 91 %	DEC 91 %	MAR 92 %	JUNE 92 %
Guardbank Industrial	–	–	–	–	–	–	29
Guardbank Resources	28	18	20	24	18	14	22
Old Mutual Gold	15	11	10	9	9	10	11
Old Mutual Industrial	10	15	9	12	9	7	10
Old Mutual Mining	22	18	8	8	8	6	7
Old Mutual Top Companies	–	–	–	–	34	26	24
Sage Resources	37	31	27	22	14	17	15
Sanlam Mining	28	12	9	7	11	9	9
Sanlam Industrial	26	16	15	16	15	15	14
Senbank Industrial Trust	–	–	61	26	23	53	24
Southern Mining	21	22	10	13	8	12	16
Standard Bank Gold	30	33	28	25	25	22	23
Standard Bank International	–	–	–	–	–	–	25
Standard Bank Industrial	–	–	–	–	–	–	61
UAL Mining and Resources	25	27	23	17	15	9	14
UAL Selected Opportunities	13	17	14	12	17	18	15
TOTAL						14 (R182,7m)	16 (R227,8m)

Hugo Lambrechts
Graduate School of Management
University of Pretoria
Pretoria 0002
Tel (012) 420-3382
Fax (012) 437-223

UNIT TRUSTS SURVEY

ADDENDUM

PORTFOLIO STRUCTURES OF UNIT TRUSTS (% of market value)

As at 30 June for each of the years indicated below.

GENERAL EQUITY FUNDS	Mkt Value (R m)	Gold				Min Fin				Other Min				Tot Min				Fin & Ind				Liq Ass				Other			
		92	91	90	89	92	91	90	89	92	91	90	89	92	91	90	89	92	91	90	89	92	91	90	89	92	91	90	89
ABSA (VOLKSKAS)	47,9	6	15	—	—	9	8	—	—	3	3	—	—	18	26	—	—	43	44	—	—	37	8	—	—	2	22	—	—
BOE GROWTH	69,0	2	0	0	—	11	13	12	—	10	12	14	—	23	25	26	—	57	60	22	—	16	14	52	—	4	1	0	—
CU GROWTH	27,4	5	3	11	—	13	12	19	—	10	10	10	—	28	25	40	—	58	56	50	—	14	19	10	—	0	0	0	—
FEDGRO	34,2	2	5	—	—	20	16	—	—	7	2	—	—	29	23	—	—	49	48	—	—	12	29	—	—	10	0	—	—
GUARDBANK	1516,5	3	5	3	3	14	14	16	16	8	10	10	6	25	29	29	25	56	52	54	59	12	19	17	11	7	0	0	5
IGI UNIT TRUST	45,3	2	7	3	—	8	13	11	—	2	11	13	—	12	31	27	—	75	53	31	—	13	16	38	—	0	0	4	—
METFUND	30,6	2	2	5	11	13	13	20	18	10	13	12	4	25	28	37	33	62	54	40	55	13	18	23	12	0	0	0	0
METLIFE	18,6	5	—	—	—	20	—	—	—	6	—	—	—	31	—	—	—	46	—	—	—	10	—	—	—	13	—	—	—
MOMENTUM	57,0	11	19	0	10	12	18	5	14	2	3	14	12	25	30	19	36	62	57	64	55	13	9	17	6	0	4	0	3
NBS HALLMARK	42,2	4	3	7	0	13	14	20	20	7	6	9	13	24	23	36	33	56	49	34	40	20	24	25	27	0	4	6	0
NORWICH	23,4	3	8	8	3	22	21	15	10	19	14	15	20	44	43	38	33	39	41	30	53	17	8	25	14	0	8	7	0
OLD MUTUAL INVESTORS'	3383,6	3	4	5	7	20	18	19	16	12	13	17	16	35	25	41	39	56	51	42	43	9	14	17	18	0	0	0	0
SAGE	995,6	3	2	4	5	12	11	13	14	8	7	8	8	23	20	25	27	58	57	49	52	17	20	22	18	2	3	4	3
SANLAM DIVIDEND	85,6	4	7	5	5	13	10	19	11	8	18	22	26	25	35	46	42	54	59	39	37	21	6	15	21	0	0	0	0
SANLAM INDEX TRUST	935,2	8	9	5	8	17	17	18	18	14	18	19	20	39	44	42	46	49	43	42	45	12	13	16	9	0	0	0	0
SANLAM TRUST	615,2	6	10	4	6	16	18	17	18	12	14	17	13	34	42	38	37	54	49	42	42	12	9	20	21	0	0	0	0
SENBANK GENERAL TRUST	7,4	3	—	—	—	19	—	—	—	6	—	—	—	28	—	—	—	56	—	—	—	16	—	—	—	0	—	—	—
SOUTHERN EQUITY	129,4	1	5	8	7	18	14	23	22	10	10	16	17	29	29	47	46	53	47	36	34	17	12	17	20	1	12	0	0
STANDARD BANK	595,7	2	3	4	6	12	11	15	17	4	4	6	5	18	18	25	28	43	41	39	40	39	41	36	25	0	0	0	7
SYFRETS TRUSTEE	362,2	0	—	—	—	15	—	—	—	10	—	—	—	25	—	—	—	57	—	—	—	18	—	—	—	0	—	—	—
SYFRETS GROWTH FUND	626,9	4	0	0	5	12	13	18	17	9	9	13	15	25	22	31	37	59	58	41	52	10	15	28	11	6	15	0	0
UAL	657,0	0	0	0	3	16	15	15	16	14	15	25	22	30	30	40	41	44	46	37	44	26	24	23	15	0	0	0	0

TOTAL MARKET VALUE R10305,4m (+ 4,37%)

PORTFOLIO STRUCTURES As at 30 June

SPECIALIST EQUITY FUNDS	Mkt Value (R m)	Gold				Min Fin				Other Min				Tot Min				Fin & Ind				Liq Ass				Other			
		92	91	90	89	92	91	90	89	92	91	90	89	92	91	90	89	92	91	90	89	92	91	90	89	92	91	90	89
GUARDBANK RESOURCES	50,9	11	20	12	17	21	24	25	24	22	24	33	34	54	68	70	75	16	12	13	7	22	20	17	14	8	0	0	4
GUARDBANK INDUSTRIAL	6,0	0	—	—	—	0	—	—	—	0	—	—	—	0	—	—	—	71	—	—	—	29	—	—	—	0	—	—	—
OLD MUTUAL GOLD	46,6	70	72	59	—	19	17	25	—	0	1	4	—	89	90	88	—	0	0	0	—	11	10	12	—	0	0	0	—
OLD MUTUAL INDUSTRIAL	108,7	0	0	0	—	0	0	0	—	0	0	0	—	0	0	0	—	90	91	85	—	10	9	15	—	0	0	0	—
OLD MUTUAL MINING	110,7	13	16	17	18	41	37	26	26	34	30	34	30	88	83	77	74	5	9	8	9	7	8	15	17	0	0	0	0
OLD MUTUAL TOP CO.	137,8	0	—	—	—	12	—	—	—	12	—	—	—	24	—	—	—	52	—	—	—	24	—	—	—	0	—	—	—
SAGE RESOURCES	59,8	19	9	15	15	28	24	24	26	21	21	24	21	68	54	63	62	17	19	12	24	15	27	25	14	0	0	0	0
SANLAM INDUSTRIAL	220,5	0	0	0	0	3	4	4	5	0	0	0	0	3	4	4	5	83	81	76	75	14	15	20	20	0	0	0	0
SANLAM MINING	96,8	21	20	9	12	31	28	26	29	36	40	41	24	88	88	76	65	3	3	9	11	9	9	15	24	0	0	0	0
SENBANK IND. TRUST	2,9	0	0	—	—	0	0	—	—	4	0	—	—	4	0	—	—	72	39	—	—	24	61	—	—	0	0	—	—
SOUTHERN MINING	24,2	13	22	23	19	37	36	33	40	30	24	21	25	80	82	77	84	4	3	6	0	16	10	17	16	0	5	0	0
STANDARD BANK INDUSTRIAL	6,2	0	—	—	—	0	—	—	—	0	—	—	—	0	—	—	—	39	—	—	—	61	—	—	—	0	—	—	—
STANDARD BANK GOLD	199,1	48	50	54	59	29	22	21	21	0	0	1	2	77	72	76	82	0	0	0	0	23	28	20	14	0	0	4	4
STANDARD BANK INTER	19,8	0	—	—	—	18	—	—	—	14	—	—	—	32	—	—	—	43	—	—	—	25	—	—	—	0	—	—	—
UAL MINING+RESOURCES	227,8	7	7	9	16	39	30	30	30	37	38	44	33	83	75	83	79	3	2	2	7	14	23	15	14	0	0	0	0
UAL SEL OPP	120,9	2	0	4	2	3	3	0	5	5	7	16	5	10	10	20	12	75	76	69	80	15	14	11	8	0	0	0	0

TOTAL MARKET VALUE R1438,7m (+ 7,08%)

PORTFOLIO STRUCTURES As at 30 June

INCOME/GILT FUNDS	Mkt Value (R m)	Liquid Assets				Approved Assets			
		92	91	90	89	92	91	90	89
GUARDBANK INCOME	63,9	21	56	70	50	79	44	30	50
METBOARD INCOME	17,6	24	—	—	—	76	—	—	—
OLD MUTUAL INCOME	75,7	27	56	72	90	73	44	28	10
STD EXTRA INCOME	254,6	89	82	70	31	11	18	30	69
SYFRETS INCOME	369,9	32	23	22	46	68	77	78	54
SYFRETS PRIMA	27,0	5	—	—	—	95	—	—	—
UAL GILT	305,1	22	35	42	66	78	65	58	34

TOTAL MARKET VALUE R1 113,7m (+ 21,53%)

TOTAL MARKET VALUE OF ALL 45 SOUTH AFRICAN UNIT TRUSTS = R12 857,6 million (+ 5,96%)

TOTAL MARKET VALUE OF THE UNITED KINGDOM'S 1 414 UNIT TRUSTS (END MAY 1992) = £60,3bn (154 MANAGEMENT COMPANIES AND 4,4m ACCOUNTS)

TOTAL MARKET VALUE OF USA UNIT TRUSTS (END MAY 1992) AMOUNTS TO $1 473,4bn

TOTAL MARKET VALUE OF AUSTRALIA'S 549 UNIT TRUSTS (END MARCH 1992) = A$41,6bn (44 MANAGEMENT COMPANIES AND 1,797m ACCOUNTS)

MINES WORKING RESULTS (Jan to June 92)

NAME OF MINE	OPERATOR OF MINE	GRADE OF ORE gms/metric ton	WORKING COST Rand/metric ton	WORKING COST Rand/gm gold
DRIEFONTEIN (WEST)	GOLDFIELDS	11 47	190 16	16 58
HARTEBEESTFONTEIN (LOW GRD)	ANGLOVAAL	1 36	23 15	17 06
DRIEFONTEIN (EAST)	GOLDFIELDS	9 16	166 38	18 17
BEATRIX	GENCOR	6 00	134 59	22 44
ELANDSRAND	ANGLO AMERICAN	8 10	191 95	23 71
DEELKRAAL	GOLDFIELDS	6 11	145 26	23 78
KINROSS	GENCOR	6 45	155 56	24 12
VAAL REEFS	ANGLO AMERICAN	6 54	160 56	24 56
HARTEBEESTFONTEIN (HIGH GRD)	ANGLOVAAL	8 84	225 82	25 54
BRACKEN	GENCOR	9 99	257 37	25 76
RANDFONTEIN	ANGLO VIA JCI	3 63	96 06	26 44
MARIEVALE	GENCOR	4 02	106 59	26 54
WESTERN DEEP LEVELS	ANGLO AMERICAN	5 69	152 66	26 84
WINKELHAAK	GENCOR	6 34	171 20	27 00
UNISEL	GENCOR	6 38	177 50	27 81
H J JOEL	ANGLO VIA JCI	6 21	176 33	28 38
FREE STATE CONS (SOUTH)	ANGLO AMERICAN	3 88	110 17	28 39
FREE STATE CONS (NORTH)	ANGLO AMERICAN	4 91	140 81	28 67
GROOTVLEI	GENCOR	5 30	152 80	28 84
ERPM	BARLOW RAND	2 82	83 30	29 52
LESLIE	GENCOR	5 38	160 94	29 93
BUFFELSFONTEIN	GENCOR	6 02	181 58	30 19
ST HELENA	GENCOR	7 41	190 29	30 66
BARBERTON	GENCOR	7 85	245 30	31 25
DURBAN DEEP	BARLOW RAND	2 49	78 43	31 48
LIBANON	GOLDFIELDS	5 17	163 94	31 73
BLYVOORUITZICHT	BARLOW RAND	3 74	121 70	32 56
WESTERN AREAS	ANGLO VIA JCI	5 58	192 36	34 50
LORAINE	ANGLOVAAL	4 77	170 21	35 67
DOORNFONTEIN	GOLDFIELDS	3 95	145 12	36 72
VENTERSPOST	GOLDFIELDS	3 72	140 13	37 68
STILFONTEIN	GENCOR	0 96	37 44	38 81
WEST RAND CONSOLIDATED	GENCOR	3 11	141 68	45 50
HARMONY	BARLOW RAND	4 92	148 53	53 16
KLOOF	GOLDFIELDS	20 66	488 09	53 40

FINANCIAL AND RATIO DEFINITIONS

FINANCIAL DEFINITIONS

Ordinary Shareholders' Interest :
The sum of Ordinary Share Capital, Share Premium, Non-Distributable Reserves and Distributable Reserves.

Long Term Liabilities :
The sum of Convertible Debentures, Directors/Shareholders loans Non Interest Bearing and Interest Bearing Liabilities.

Current Assets :
The sum of Inventory, Debtors, Cash & Near Cash, Dividends, Tax and Other.

Current Liabilities :
The sum of Trade Creditors, Dividends, Tax, Interest Bearing and Non Interest Bearing Liabilities.

Total Assets :
The sum of Fixed Assets/Mining Assets, Non Current Assets, Investments & Loans and Current Assets.

Total Liabilities :
The sum of Preference Shares, Outside Shareholders Interest, Deferred Tax, Other, Long Term Liabilities and Current Liabilities.

Operating Profit:
Profit before Investment Income, Interest Received, Interest & Finance Charges and Tax paid.

Bottom Line Earnings :
Profit Attributable to Ordinary Shareholders after Extra Ordinary Items.

RATIO DEFINITIONS

INCOME STATEMENT

A : Profit after Interest and Tax
B : Profit attributable to Ordinary Shareholders
C : Deferred Tax
D : Depreciation
E : Preference Dividends
F : Minority Shareholders' Interest

BALANCE SHEET

G : Ordinary Shareholders' Interest
H : Intangible Assets
I : Interest Bearing Long Term Liabilities
J : Interest Bearing Current Liabilities
K : Irredeemable Preference Shares
L : Convertible Preference Shares
M : Convertible Debentures

RATIO	METHOD OF CALCULATION FORMULA
Price/Earnings	$\frac{\text{Share price at Y/E (cents)}}{\text{Earnings per share (cents)}}$
Earnings Yield %	$\frac{\text{(Earnings per share (cents))} \times 100}{\text{Share price at Y/E}}$
Current Effective Tax Rate %	$\frac{\text{(Current tax)} \times 100}{\text{Profit before tax (excluding Investment Income)}}$
Dividend Yield %	$\frac{\text{(Dividends per share) (cents)} \times 100}{\text{Share price at Y/E (cents)}}$
Dividend Cover	$\frac{\text{Earnings per share}}{\text{Dividends per share}}$
Return on Equity %	$\frac{B \times 100}{G} \times \frac{12}{\text{No of months}}$
Return on Assets %	$\frac{\text{(Investment Income + Operating Profit + Interest Received + Income from Associated Companies)} \times 100}{\text{total assets}} \times \frac{12}{\text{No of months}}$
Current Ratio	$\frac{\text{current assets}}{\text{current liabilities}}$
Quick Ratio	$\frac{\text{current assets-inventory}}{\text{current liabilities}}$
Earnings per share	$\frac{B}{\text{No of shares in issue at Y/E}} \times \frac{12}{\text{No of months}}$
Cash Flow Per Share (cents)	$\frac{(A + C + D - E - F) \times 100}{\text{No of shares in issue at Y/E}} \times \frac{12}{\text{No of months}}$
Net Tangible Asset Value Per Share (cents)	$\frac{(G - H) \times 100}{\text{No of shares in issue at Y/E}}$
Net Asset Value Per Share	$\frac{(G + K + L + M - H)}{\text{No of shares in issue at Y/E}}$
Net Asset Value% Market Price	$\frac{(G - H) \times 100}{\text{((Market price} \times \text{No of shares)/100)}}$
Sustainable Growth Rate %	$\frac{B \times 100}{G} \times \frac{\text{Ordinary dividends paid}}{B}$
Operating Profit Margin %	$\frac{\text{(Operating profit)} \times 100}{\text{Turnover}}$
Net Profit Margin %	$\frac{B \times 100}{\text{Turnover}}$
Total Asset Turnover	$\frac{\text{Turnover}}{\text{Total Assets}} \times \frac{12}{\text{No of months}}$
Debit/Asset Ratio	$\frac{\text{Long term liabilities + Current liabilities}}{\text{Total Assets}}$
Debit/Equity Ratio	$\frac{\text{Long term liabilities + Current liabilities}}{G}$
Interest Cover	$\frac{\text{Investment Income + Operating Profit}}{\text{Interest \& Finance Charges paid}}$
Defensive Interval	$\frac{\text{Red Pref Shares + Dir/Shlds Loans} + I + J}{A + C + D - E - F} \times \frac{12}{\text{No of months}}$
Market Capitalisation	Share Price at Y/E × No of Shares in Issue at Y/E
Accounts Receivable to Turnover	$\frac{\text{Turnover}}{\text{Debtors}} \times \frac{12}{\text{No of months}}$

THE PURCHASING POWER OF THE RAND: 1910 – 1992

(ALL ITEMS: APRIL, 1970 = 100)

YEAR	INDEX	CHANGE	VALUE	YEAR	INDEX	CHANGE	VALUE
		%				%	
1910	25 3	0 0	3 95	1951	58 0	7 2	1 72
1911	26 7	5 5	3 75	1952	65 3	12 6	1 53
1912	27 6	3 4	3 62	1953	65 3	0 0	1 53
1913	27 6	1 1	3 58	1954	66 5	1 8	1 50
1914	27 6	1 1	3 62	1955	68 6	3 2	1 46
1915	27 1	1 8	3 69	1956	69 9	1 9	1 43
1916	30 9	14 0	3 24	1957	72 0	3 0	1 39
1917	33 8	9 4	2 96	1958	74 5	3 5	1 34
1918	36 1	6 8	2 77	1959	75 4	1 2	1 33
1919	39 9	10 5	2 51	1960	76 5	1 5	1 31
1920	49 5	24 1	2 02	1961	77 9	1 8	1 28
1921	44 8	−9 5	2 23	1962	79 1	1 5	1 26
1922	37 4	−16 5	2 67	1963	80 0	1 1	1 25
1923	36 3	−2 9	2 75	1964	82 0	2 5	1 22
1924	36 8	1 4	2 72	1965	85 0	3 7	1 18
1925	36 6	−0 5	2 73	1966	88 1	3 6	1 14
1926	36 1	−1 4	2 77	1967	91 0	3 3	1 10
1927	36 3	0 6	2 75	1968	92 6	1 8	1 08
1928	36 3	0 0	2 75	1969	95 3	2 9	1 05
1929	36 2	−0 3	2 76	1970	100 0	4 2	1 00
1930	35 4	−2 2	2 82	1971	105 6	5 6	0 95
1931	34 0	−4 0	2 94	1972	112 5	6 5	0 89
1932	32 5	−4 4	3 08	1973	123 1	9 4	0 81
1933	31 7	−2 5	3 15	1974	137 4	11 7	0 73
1934	32 1	1 3	3 12	1975	156 0	13 5	0 64
1935	31 9	−0 6	3 13	1976	173 5	11 2	0 58
1936	32 1	0 6	3 12	1977	192 8	11 2	0 52
1937	32 7	1 9	3 06	1978	212 5	10 2	0 47
1938	33 9	3 7	2 95	1979	240 2	13 1	0 42
1939	33 9	0 0	2 95	1980	273 5	13 8	0 37
1940	35 1	3 5	2 85	1981	315 0	15 2	0 32
1941	35 7	4 7	2 80	1982	361 3	14 7	0 28
1942	39 9	11 8	2 51	1983	405 8	12 3	0 25
1943	42 3	6 0	2 36	1984	453 0	11 6	0 22
1944	43 8	3 5	2 28	1985	526 5	16 2	0 19
1945	44 9	2 5	2 23	1986	624 5	18 6	0 16
1946	45 6	1 6	2 19	1987	725 7	16 1	0 14
1947	47 4	3 9	2 11	1988	819 3	12 9	0 12
1948	50 2	5 9	1 99	1989	939 7	14 7	0 11
1949	52 0	3 6	1 92	1990	1074 5	14 4	0 09
1950	54 1	4 0	1 85	1991	1238 9	15 3	0 08
				1992	1413 6	14 1	0 07

NOTES

The INDEX column is based on the consumer index calculated by Central Statistical Services The values relate to the base value in 1970 set at R100 For example if an article cost R100 in 1970 the same article would cost R624 50 in 1986

The CHANGE represents the percentage change from the previous year s index value

The VALUE column relates to the base value in 1970 set at R1 For example if the Rand was worth 100 cents in 1970 it would be worth 37 cents in 1980

www.ingramcontent.com/pod-product-compliance
Lightning Source LLC
Chambersburg PA
CBHW080037290525
27262CB00020B/380
* 9 7 8 1 8 5 3 3 3 9 0 8 0 *